# TEXAS ALMANAC

## 2004–2005

Published by

### The Dallas Morning News

Elizabeth Cruce Alvarez, Editor
Robert Plocheck, Associate Editor
Sharron Schumann, Account Executive
Anna Palmer, Art Director

---

**Cover image is an oil painting of Fort Davis National Historic Site in Jeff Davis County by Bart Forbes.**

Bart Forbes has established himself as one of the nation's foremost illustrators. His work has appeared in many publications, including *Sports Illustrated* and *Time*. He has designed more than 20 postage stamps; among them are the Lou Gehrig and Jesse Owens stamps, as well as the "America the Beautiful" series. His work is included in many private collections, including those of Presidents Carter and Bush, and in the Ronald Reagan Presidential Library. Forbes' studio is in his Texas home, where he lives with his wife, Mary Jo. They have a daughter, Sarah, and a son, Ted, who are following in their father's creative footsteps as graphic designers.

---

ISBN (hardcover) 0-914511-34-3    ISBN (softcover) 0-914511-35-1

Library of Congress Control Number: 2003094976

Copyright © 2004, The Dallas Morning News, L.P.
A subsidiary of Belo Corp.
P. O. Box 655237  Dallas, TX 75265-5237

www.texasalmanac.com

Distributed by Texas A&M University Press Consortium
4354 TAMUS, College Station, Texas 77843-4354

To order online, log on to texasalmanac.com • To order by telephone, call 1-800-826-8911

The *Texas Almanac* also publishes the *Texas Almanac Teacher's Guide,* a 100-plus page supplement containing lessons, activities, maps and puzzles that make use of the factually dense *Texas Almanac.* The Teacher's Guide was developed by a team of veteran social-studies teachers and curriculum writers, and each lesson is coded to indicate how it helps fulfill TEKS requirements and TAKS objectives.

Printed in the United States of America

THE SOURCE FOR ALL THINGS TEXAN SINCE 1857

# TABLE OF CONTENTS

STATE PROFILE . . . . . . . . . . . . . . . . . . . . . 10

STATE FLAGS AND SYMBOLS . . . . . . . . . 12

HISTORY . . . . . . . . . . . . . . . . . . . . . . . . . 16
The Frontier Forts of Texas . . . . . . . . . . 16
Women at the Frontier Forts . . . . . . . . 22
Camp Cooper, Fort Belknap and the
    Indian Reservations . . . . . . . . . . . . . . 26
Fort Anahuac and the Texas
    Revolution . . . . . . . . . . . . . . . . . . . . . 27
A Brief Sketch of Texas History . . . . . . . 31

ENVIRONMENT . . . . . . . . . . . . . . . . . . . . 57
The Physical State of Texas . . . . . . . . . . 57
    Physical Regions . . . . . . . . . . . . . . . 58
    Geology of Texas . . . . . . . . . . . . . . 61
    Soils of Texas . . . . . . . . . . . . . . . . . 63
Water Resources . . . . . . . . . . . . . . . . . 66
    Texas' Major Aquifers . . . . . . . . . . . 67
    Texas' Major Rivers . . . . . . . . . . . . . 68
    Lakes and Reservoirs . . . . . . . . . . . 73
Texas Plant Life . . . . . . . . . . . . . . . . . . . 78
    Texas Forest Resources . . . . . . . . . . 80
    National Forests and
        Grasslands in Texas . . . . . . . . . . 83
    Texas State Forests . . . . . . . . . . . . . 84
National Natural Landmarks
    in Texas . . . . . . . . . . . . . . . . . . . . . . 85
Threatened and Endangered Species
    in Texas . . . . . . . . . . . . . . . . . . . . . . 85
Texas Wildlife . . . . . . . . . . . . . . . . . . . . 86
    National Wildlife Refuges
        in Texas . . . . . . . . . . . . . . . . . . . 89
    Texas Wildlife Management
        Areas . . . . . . . . . . . . . . . . . . . . . 91

WEATHER . . . . . . . . . . . . . . . . . . . . . . . . 92
Weather Highlights 2001 . . . . . . . . . . . 92
Weather Highlights 2002 . . . . . . . . . . . 95
Destructive Weather . . . . . . . . . . . . . . . 97
Heat and Chill Index . . . . . . . . . . . . . . 103
Weather Records by County . . . . . . . 104

ASTRONOMICAL CALENDAR FOR
2004 AND 2005 . . . . . . . . . . . . . . . . . . . 110
Calendar for 2004 . . . . . . . . . . . . . . . 112
Calendar for 2005 . . . . . . . . . . . . . . . 115
201-Year Calendar . . . . . . . . . . . . . . . 118

RECREATION . . . . . . . . . . . . . . . . . . . . . 119
Texas State Parks . . . . . . . . . . . . . . . . 119
Birding in Texas . . . . . . . . . . . . . . . . . 130
National Parks, Historical Sites and
    Recreation Areas . . . . . . . . . . . . . . 131
Freshwater and Saltwater Fish
    and Fishing . . . . . . . . . . . . . . . . . . . 134
    Sea Center Texas . . . . . . . . . . . . . 135
    Hunting and Fishing Licenses . . . . . 135
Fairs, Festivals and Special Events . . . . 136

COUNTIES OF TEXAS . . . . . . . . . . . . . . 138
254 Maps and County Profiles . . . . . . . 138

TEXAS POPULATION . . . . . . . . . . . . . . . 296
Cities and Towns . . . . . . . . . . . . . . . . 300
City Population History, 1850–2000 . . . . 378
County Population History, 1850–2000 . . . 389

POLITICS AND ELECTIONS . . . . . . . . . . . 395
Legislature 2003 . . . . . . . . . . . . . . . . . 398
General Election, 2002 . . . . . . . . . . . . . 399
Texas Primary Elections, 2002 . . . . . . . . 407
Historical Elections . . . . . . . . . . . . . . . 411

HISTORICAL DOCUMENTS . . . . . . . . . . . 422
Declaration of Independence of the
    Republic of Texas . . . . . . . . . . . . . . 422
Constitution of Texas, Amendments
    2001 and 2003 . . . . . . . . . . . . . . . . 425
Joint Resolution for Annexing Texas
    to the United States . . . . . . . . . . . . 426

TEXAS' GOVERNMENT OFFICIALS . . . . . 427
Spanish Royal Governors,
    1691–1821 . . . . . . . . . . . . . . . . . . . 427
Governors Under Mexican Rule,
    1822–1835 . . . . . . . . . . . . . . . . . . . 427

Republic of Texas and State Officials,
1836–2003 . . . . . . . . . . . . . . . . . . . . . . 427

**STATE GOVERNMENT** . . . . . . . . . . . . . . . . . **433**
Texas Legislature . . . . . . . . . . . . . . . . . 433
Texas State Judiciary . . . . . . . . . . . . . . . 435
Texas' Courts by County . . . . . . . . . 437
District Judges in Texas . . . . . . . . 439
State Agencies . . . . . . . . . . . . . . . . . 441
Boards and Commissions . . . . . . . 445
Government Income and
Expenses . . . . . . . . . . . . . . . . . . 458

**LOCAL GOVERNMENTS** . . . . . . . . . . . . . **460**
Mayors and City Managers of
Texas Cities . . . . . . . . . . . . . . . . . . 460
Galveston and Amarillo Were Municipal
Government Pioneers . . . . . . . . . . . . 468
Regional Councils of
Government . . . . . . . . . . . . . . . . . . 470
County Tax Appraisers . . . . . . . . . . . . 471
Wet-Dry Counties . . . . . . . . . . . . . . . 472
County Courts . . . . . . . . . . . . . . . . . 473
Texas County and District Officials . . . . . 474

**FEDERAL GOVERNMENT** . . . . . . . . . . . . . **486**
Texans in Congress . . . . . . . . . . . . . . . 486
Federal Courts in Texas . . . . . . . . . . . . 488
Major Military Installations . . . . . . . . . . 490
Federal Funds to Texas
by County, 2002 . . . . . . . . . . . . . . 492
U.S. Tax Collections in Texas . . . . . . . . 494
Medal of Freedom . . . . . . . . . . . . . . . 495

**CULTURE AND THE ARTS** . . . . . . . . . . . . **496**
Film and Television Work in Texas . . . . . 496
Fine Arts Organizations
Across the State . . . . . . . . . . . . . . . 497
Texas Museums . . . . . . . . . . . . . . . . . 498
Arts and Humanities Awards . . . . . . . . 501
Public Libraries of Texas . . . . . . . . . . . . 504
Polish-Texans . . . . . . . . . . . . . . . . . . 512
Holidays, Anniversaries and Festivals
2004–2005 . . . . . . . . . . . . . . . . . . . . 516

**RELIGION** . . . . . . . . . . . . . . . . . . . . . . . . **517**
Franciscan Missionaries in Texas
before 1690 . . . . . . . . . . . . . . . . . . 517
Spanish Nun Part of Religious History
of Texas . . . . . . . . . . . . . . . . . . . . . 522
Timeline of Events: 1500s–1600s . . . . . . 523
Religious Groups in Texas, 2000 . . . . . . 525

**HEALTH AND SCIENCE** . . . . . . . . . . . . . . **531**
Death and Birth Rates . . . . . . . . . . . . . 531
Health Services . . . . . . . . . . . . . . . . . . 536
Texans in the National Academy of
Sciences . . . . . . . . . . . . . . . . . . . . . 538

**CRIME IN TEXAS, 2002** . . . . . . . . . . . . . . **539**

**EDUCATION** . . . . . . . . . . . . . . . . . . . . . . **544**
Texas Public Schools . . . . . . . . . . . . . . 544
Higher Education in Texas . . . . . . . . . . 547
Universities and Colleges . . . . . . . . 549

**MEDIA** . . . . . . . . . . . . . . . . . . . . . . . . . . **555**
Belo Corp. . . . . . . . . . . . . . . . . . . . . . 555
History of the Texas Almanac . . . . . . . . 559
Texas Newspapers, Radio and Television
Stations . . . . . . . . . . . . . . . . . . . . . 560

**BUSINESS AND TRANSPORTATION** . . . . . **566**
Economy . . . . . . . . . . . . . . . . . . . . . . 566
Employment . . . . . . . . . . . . . . . . . 576
Banking . . . . . . . . . . . . . . . . . . . . 577
Insurance . . . . . . . . . . . . . . . . . . . 584
Construction . . . . . . . . . . . . . . . . . 585
Foreign Trade Zones in Texas . . . . . 586
Foreign Consulates in Texas . . . . . . 587
Texas Ports . . . . . . . . . . . . . . . . . . 589
Texas Transportation System . . . . . 590
Fuel Minerals . . . . . . . . . . . . . . . . . . . 599
Nonpetroleum Minerals . . . . . . . . . . . 610
Utilities . . . . . . . . . . . . . . . . . . . . . . . 617

**AGRICULTURE IN TEXAS** . . . . . . . . . . . . . **620**
Principal Crops . . . . . . . . . . . . . . . . . 623
Vegetable "Truck" Crops . . . . . . . . . . . 627
Fruits and Nuts . . . . . . . . . . . . . . . . . 628
Livestock and Their Products . . . . . . . . 630

**TEXAS PRONUNCIATION GUIDE** . . . . . . . **633**

**OBITUARIES, JULY 2001–JULY 2003** . . . . . **638**

**ADVERTISERS INDEX** . . . . . . . . . . . . . . . . **642**

**GENERAL INDEX** . . . . . . . . . . . . . . . . . . . **642**

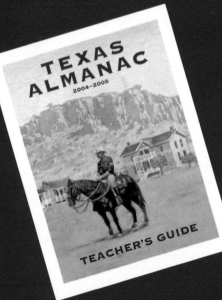

# Texas

## The Lone Star State

On this and the following page we present a demographic and geographic profile of the second-largest, second-most-populous state in the United States. Look in the index to find more-detailed information on each subject.

### The Government

**Capital:** Austin
**Government:** Bicameral Legislature
**28th State to enter the Union:** Dec. 29, 1845
**Present Constitution adopted:** 1876

**State motto:** Friendship (1930)
**State symbols:**
    **Flower:** Bluebonnet (1901)
    **Bird:** Mockingbird (1927)
    **Tree:** Pecan (1919)
    **Song:** "Texas, Our Texas" (1929)

**Origin of name:** Texas, or Tejas, was the Spanish pronunciation of a Caddo Indian word meaning "friends" or "allies."

**Nickname:** Texas is called the Lone Star State because of the design of the state flag: a broad vertical blue stripe at left centered by a single white star, and at right, horizontal bars of white (top) and red.

### The People

**Population (Jan. 2002 State Data**
    **Center estimate)** .................. 21,518,555
**Population (July 2002 U.S. Bureau**
    **of the Census estimate)** ............ 21,779,893
**Population, 2000 U.S. Census count** ..... 20,851,820
**Population, 1990 U.S. Census count** ..... 16,986,510
**Population increase, 1990-2000** ............ **22.8%**

**Ethnicity** (2000) (for explanation of categories, see page 138):

| | Number | Percent |
|---|---|---|
| Anglo | 11,074,716 | 53.11% |
| Hispanic | 6,669,666 | 31.99% |
| Black | 2,421,653 | 11.61% |
| Other | 685,785 | 3.29% |

**Population density (2000)** ......... **79.6 per sq. mi.**

**Voting-age population (2002)** .......... **15,514,289**

*(2000 Statistical Abstract of the United States, Census Bureau)*

---

#### On an Average Day in Texas in 2001:

There were **1,000** resident live births.
There were **417** resident deaths.
There were **583** more births than deaths.
There were **526** marriages.
There were **229** divorces.
*(2001 Texas Vital Statistics, Texas Dept. of Health)*

---

**Ten largest cities:**
Houston (Harris Co.) ................. 1,980,950
Dallas (Dallas Co.) .................. 1,201,759
San Antonio (Bexar Co.). ............. 1,182,840
Austin (Travis Co.) ...................... 678,198
El Paso (El Paso Co.) .................... 573,787
Fort Worth (Tarrant Co.) ................. 555,110
Arlington (Tarrant Co.) ................... 344,751
Corpus Christi (Nueces Co.) .............. 279,241
Plano (Collin Co.) ....................... 237,495
Garland (Dallas Co.) ..................... 219,010
*(January 2002 State Data Center estimate)*

**Number of counties** ......................... 254
**Number of incorporated cities** .............. 1,201
**Number of cities of 100,000 pop. or more** ........ 24
**Number of cities of 50,000 pop. or more** ......... 51
**Number of cities of 10,000 pop. or more** ........ 209

### The Natural Environment

| | |
|---|---|
| **Area (total)** ............... 268,581 sq. miles | |
| (171,891,840 acres) | |
| **Land area** ............... 261,797 sq. miles | |
| (167,550,080 acres) | |
| **Water area** ................. 6,784 sq. miles | |
| (4,341,760 acres) | |

**Geographic center:** About 15 miles northeast of Brady in northern McCulloch County.
**Highest point:** Guadalupe Peak (8,749 ft.) in Culberson County in far West Texas.
**Lowest point:** Gulf of Mexico (sea level).

**Normal average annual precipitation range:**
  From 58.3 inches at Orange, on the Gulf Coast, to 8.8 inches at El Paso, in West Texas.
**Record highest temperature:**
  Seymour, August 12, 1936 ............... 120°F
  Monahans, June 28, 1994 ................ 120°F
**Record lowest temperature:**
  Tulia, Feb. 12, 1899 ..................... -23°F
  Seminole, Feb. 8, 1933 .................. -23°F

### Business

**Gross State Product** (2002). ........... $807.4 billion
**Per Capita Personal Income** (2001) ........ $28,472
**Civilian Labor Force** (March 2003) ....... 10,885,333
*(GSP: Texas Comptroller of Public Accounts; Per capita income and civilian labor force: 2002 Statistical Abstract of the United States, U.S. Census Bureau)*

**Principal products:**

    **Manufactures:** Chemicals and allied products, petroleum and coal products, food and kindred products, transportation equipment.

    **Farm products:** Cattle, cotton, nursery and greenhouse, dairy products.

    **Minerals:** Petroleum, natural gas, natural gas liquids.

**Finance** (as of 12/31/2002):
  Number of banks ........................ 669
  Total deposits. ................ $128,898,604,000
  Number of savings and loan associations ........ 24
  Total assets .................. $43,940,058,000
  Number of savings banks .................... 24
  Total assets .................. $15,445,211,000
*(Banks: Federal Reserve Bank of Dallas; savings and loans and savings banks: Texas Savings and Loan Dept.)*

**Agriculture:**
  Total farm marketings, 1998 ........ $13,206 million
  Number of farms, 1999 .................. 227,000
  Land in farms (acres, 1999). ........... 131 million
  Cropland (acres, 1997) .............. 26,762,000
  Pastureland (acres, 1997) ............. 15,807,000
  Rangeland (acres, 1997) .............. 95,323,000
*(2000 Statistical Abstract of the United States)*

# Texas' Rank Among the United States

Texas' rank among the United States in selected categories are given below. Others categories are covered in other chapters in the book; i.e., Agriculture, Business and Transportation, Science and Health.
Source (unless otherwise noted): Statistical Abstract of the United States, 2002, U.S. Census. Bureau: www.census.gov/statab/www/

## Ten Most Populous States, 2000

| Rank | Population 2000 | %Change 1990-2000 |
|---|---|---|
| 1. | California . . . . . . 33,871,648 | 13.8 |
| 2. | **Texas . . . . . . . . . 20,851,820** | **22.8** |
| 3. | New York . . . . . . . 18,976,457 | 5.5 |
| 4. | Florida . . . . . . 15,982,378 | 23.5 |
| 5. | Illinois . . . . . . . . . 12,419,293 | 8.6 |
| 6. | Pennsylvania . . . . 12,281,054 | 3.4 |
| 7. | Ohio . . . . . . . . . . 11,353,140 | 4.7 |
| 8. | Michigan . . . . . . . . 9,938,444 | 6.9 |
| 9. | New Jersey . . . . . . 8,414,350 | 8.9 |
| 10. | Georgia . . . . . . . . 8,186,453 | 26.4 |

(United States . . . . . . . 281,421,906 . . . . . . . . . 13.2)

## Ten Fastest Growing States, 2000

| Rank | State | Population Change 1990–2000 |
|---|---|---|
| 1. | Nevada . . . . . . . . . . . . . . . . . . . . . . . | 66.3 % |
| 2. | Arizona . . . . . . . . . . . . . . . . . . . . . . . | 40.0 % |
| 3. | Colorado . . . . . . . . . . . . . . . . . . . . . | 30.6 % |
| 4. | Utah . . . . . . . . . . . . . . . . . . . . . . . . . | 29.6 % |
| 5. | Idaho . . . . . . . . . . . . . . . . . . . . . . . . | 28.5 % |
| 6. | Georgia . . . . . . . . . . . . . . . . . . . . . . | 26.4 % |
| 7. | Florida . . . . . . . . . . . . . . . . . . . . . . . | 23.5 % |
| 8. | **Texas** . . . . . . . . . . . . . . . . . . . . . . | **22.8 %** |
| 9. | North Carolina . . . . . . . . . . . . . . . . . | 21.4 % |
| 10. | Washington . . . . . . . . . . . . . . . . . . . . | 21.1 % |

## States with Highest Birth Rates, 2001

| Rank | State | Births per 1,000 Pop. |
|---|---|---|
| 1. | Utah . . . . . . . . . . . . . . . . . . . . . . . . | 21.7 |
| 2. | **Texas . . . . . . . . . . . . . . . . . . . . . . . . . . . .** | **17.2** |
| 3. | Georgia . . . . . . . . . . . . . . . . . . . . . . | 16.3 |
| 4. | California . . . . . . . . . . . . . . . . . . . . . | 15.6 |
| 5. | New Mexico . . . . . . . . . . . . . . . . . . . | 15.6 |

(United States . . . . . . . . . . . . . . . . . . . . . . . . . 14.6)

## States with Highest Immigration, 2000

| Rank | State | Immigrants |
|---|---|---|
| 1. | California . . . . . . . . . . . . . . . . . | 217,753 |
| 2. | New York . . . . . . . . . . . . . . . . . | 106,061 |
| 3. | Florida . . . . . . . . . . . . . . . . . . . | 98,391 |
| 4. | **Texas . . . . . . . . . . . . . . . . . . . . . . .** | **63,840** |
| 5. | New Jersey . . . . . . . . . . . . . . . . . | 40,013 |

(United States . . . . . . . . . . . . . . . . . . . . . . . 849,807)

## Selected Economic Data by State, 2000

The chart includes the top 10 states in numbers of employed (non-farm) and the states bordering Texas. The information on union members and the percent of workers who are union members includes agricultural as well as non-agricultural workers. The union figures compare the years 1983 and 2000.

| State | Employment (Non-farm) | Businesses | Total Payroll ($1,000) | Per employee | Union members 1983 | Union members 2000 | Percent of workers 1983 | Percent of workers 2000 |
|---|---|---|---|---|---|---|---|---|
| **United States** | 114,064,976 | 7,070,048 | $ 3,879,430,052 | $ 34,011 | 17,717,400 | 16,258,200 | 20.1 | 13.5 |
| California | 12,884,692 | 799,863 | 514,360,478 | 39,920 | 2,118,900 | 2,295,100 | 21.9 | 16.0 |
| **Texas** | 8,026,438 | 471,509 | 269,917,800 | 33,629 | 583,700 | 505,400 | 9.7 | 5.8 |
| New York | 7,353,209 | 492,073 | 330,586,554 | 44,958 | 2,155,600 | 1,958,000 | 32.5 | 25.5 |
| Florida | 6,217,386 | 428,438 | 177,378,971 | 28,530 | 393,700 | 433,600 | 10.2 | 6.8 |
| Illinois | 5,501,036 | 308,067 | 201,319,268 | 36,597 | 1,063,800 | 1,046,300 | 24.2 | 18.6 |
| Pennsylvania | 5,087,237 | 294,741 | 165,108,376 | 32,455 | 1,195,700 | 869,600 | 27.5 | 16.9 |
| Ohio | 5,001,980 | 270,509 | 155,035,151 | 30,995 | 1,011,000 | 879,000 | 25.1 | 17.3 |
| Michigan | 4,072,786 | 236,912 | 145,482,490 | 35,721 | 1,005,400 | 938,300 | 30.4 | 20.8 |
| New Jersey | 3,548,429 | 233,559 | 147,082,234 | 41,450 | 882,100 | 762,000 | 26.9 | 20.8 |
| Georgia | 3,483,500 | 200,442 | 112,899,269 | 32,410 | 267,000 | 228,100 | 11.9 | 6.3 |
| Louisiana | 1,592,357 | 101,016 | 42,975,159 | 26,988 | 204,200 | 121,900 | 13.8 | 7.1 |
| Oklahoma | 1,201,606 | 85,094 | 31,700,630 | 26,382 | 131,500 | 93,800 | 11.5 | 6.8 |
| Arkansas | 990,830 | 63,185 | 24,663,335 | 24,892 | 82,200 | 61,500 | 11.0 | 5.8 |
| New Mexico | 549,352 | 42,782 | 14,303,193 | 26,036 | 52,600 | 56,200 | 11.8 | 8.1 |

Source: U.S. Bureau of the Census, Department of Commerce.

## States with Most Farms, 1999

| Rank | State | No. of Farms |
|---|---|---|
| 1. | **Texas . . . . . . . . . . . . . . . . . . . . . . . . . .** | **227,000** |
| 2. | Missouri . . . . . . . . . . . . . . . . . . . . . . . . | 110,000 |
| 3. | Iowa . . . . . . . . . . . . . . . . . . . . . . . . . | 96,000 |
| 4. | Kentucky . . . . . . . . . . . . . . . . . . . . . | 91,000 |
| (tie) | Tennessee . . . . . . . . . . . . . . . . . . . . | 91,000 |

## States with Most Land in Farms, 1999

| Rank | State | Farm Acreage |
|---|---|---|
| 1. | **Texas . . . . . . . . . . . . . . . . . . . . . . . .** | **131,000,000** |
| 2. | Montana . . . . . . . . . . . . . . . . . . . . . . | 57,000,000 |
| 3. | Kansas . . . . . . . . . . . . . . . . . . . . . . . | 48,000,000 |
| 4. | Nebraska . . . . . . . . . . . . . . . . . . . . . | 46,000,000 |
| 5. | New Mexico . . . . . . . . . . . . . . . . . . . | 45,000,000 |

# State Flags and Symbols

*Our thanks to Charles A. Spain, Jr., of Houston for his advice in updating this section of the Texas Almanac.*

United States, 1845–1861; 1865–Present

Republic, 1836–1845; State, 1845–Present

Spain
1519–1685
1690–1821

Mexico
1821–1836

France
1685–1690

Confederate
States of
America
1861–1865

Texas often is called the **Lone Star State** because of its state flag with a single star. The state flag was also the **flag of the Republic of Texas**. The following information about historic Texas flags, the current flag and other Texas symbols may be supplemented by information available from the **Texas State Library** in Austin. (On the Web: **www.texasalmanac.com/flags.htm** and **www.tsl.state.tx.us/ref/abouttx/index.html#flags**)

## Six Flags of Texas

Six different flags have flown over Texas during eight changes of sovereignty. The accepted sequence of these flags follows:

Spanish — 1519–1685
French — 1685–1690
Spanish — 1690–1821
Mexican — 1821–1836
Republic of Texas — 1836–1845
United States — 1845–1861
Confederate States of America — 1861–1865
United States — 1865 to the present.

## Evolution of the Lone Star Flag

The Convention at Washington-on-the-Brazos in March 1836 allegedly adopted a flag for the Republic that was designed by Lorenzo de Zavala. The design of de Zavala's flag is unknown, but the convention journals state that a "Rainbow and star of five points above the western horizon; and a star of six points sinking below" was added to de Zavala's flag.

There was a suggestion that the letters "T E X A S"

be placed around the star in the flag, but there is no evidence that the Convention ever approved a final flag design. Probably because of the hasty dispersion of the Convention and loss of part of the Convention notes, nothing further was done with the Convention's proposals for a national flag. A **so-called "Zavala flag"** is sometimes flown in Texas today that consists of a blue field with a white five-pointed star in the center and letters "T E X A S" between the star points, but there is no historical evidence to support this flag's design.

The **first official flag of the Republic,** known as the **National Standard of Texas** or **David G. Burnet's flag,** was adopted by the Texas Congress and approved by President Sam Houston on Dec. 10, 1836. The design "shall be an azure ground with a large golden star central."

## The Lone Star Flag

On Jan. 25, 1839, President Mirabeau B. Lamar approved the adoption by Congress of a new national flag. This flag consisted of "a blue perpendicular stripe of the width of one third of the whole length of the flag, with a white star of five points in the centre thereof, and two horizontal stripes of equal breadth, the upper stripe white, the lower red, of the length of two thirds of the length of the whole flag." This is the **Lone Star Flag,** which later became the state flag.

Although Senator William H. Wharton proposed the adoption of the Lone Star Flag in 1838, no one knows who actually designed the flag. The legislature in 1879 inadvertently repealed the law establishing the state flag, but the legislature adopted a new law in 1933 that

legally re-established the flag's design.

The red, white and blue of the state flag stand, respectively, for bravery, purity and loyalty. The proper finial for use with the state flag is either a star or a spearhead. Texas is one of only two states that has a flag that formerly served as the flag of an independent nation. The other is Hawaii.

### Rules for Display of the State Flag

The Texas Flag Code was first adopted in 1933 and completely revised in 1993. Laws governing display of the state flag are found in sections 3100.051 through 3100.072 of the Texas Government Code. (On the Web: **www.tsl.state.tx.us/ref/abouttx/flagcode.html**). A summary of those rules follows:

The Texas flag should be displayed on state and national holidays and on special occasions of historical significance, and it should be displayed at every school on regular school days. **When flown out-of-doors,** the Texas flag should not be flown earlier than sunrise nor later than sunset unless properly illuminated. It should not be left out in inclement weather unless a weatherproof flag is used. It should be flown with the white stripe uppermost except in case of distress.

No flag other than the **United States flag** should be placed above or, if on the same level, to the state flag's right (observer's left). The state flag should be underneath the national flag when the two are flown from the same halyard. **When flown from adjacent flagpoles,** the national flag and the state flag should be of approximately the same size and on flagpoles of equal height; the national flag should be on the flag's own right (observer's left).

**If the state flag is displayed with the flag of another U.S. state, a nation other than the U.S., or an international organization,** the state flag should be, from an observer's perspective, to the left of the other flag on a separate flagpole or flagstaff, and the state flag should not be above the other flag on the same flagpole or flagstaff or on a taller flagpole or flagstaff. If the state flag and the U.S. flag are displayed from crossed flagstaffs, the state flag should be, from an observer's perspective, to the right of the U.S. flag and the state flag's flagstaff should be behind the U.S. flag's flagstaff.

**When the flag is displayed horizontally,** the white stripe should be above the red stripe and, from an observer's perspective, to the right of the blue stripe. **When the flag is displayed vertically,** the blue stripe should be uppermost and the white stripe should be to the state flag's right (observer's left).

If the state and national flags are both **carried in a procession,** the national flag should be on the marching right and state flag should be on the national flag's left (observer's right).

**On Memorial Day,** the state flag should be displayed at half-staff until noon and at that time raised to the peak of the flagpole. **On Peace Officers Memorial Day** (May 15), the state flag should be displayed at half-staff all day, unless that day is also Armed Forces Day.

The state flag should not touch anything beneath it or be dipped to any person or things except the U.S. flag. Advertising should not be fastened to a flagpole, flagstaff or halyard on which the state flag is displayed. If a state flag is no longer used or useful as an emblem for display, it should be destroyed, preferably by burning. A

flag retirement ceremony is set out in the Texas Government Code at the Texas State Library Web site mentioned above.

### Pledge to the Texas Flag

A pledge to the Texas flag was adopted by the 43rd Legislature. It contained a phrase, "Flag of 1836," which inadvertently referred to the David G. Burnet flag instead of the Lone Star Flag adopted in 1839. In 1965, the 59th Legislature changed the pledge to its current form:

> "Honor the Texas flag;
> I pledge allegiance to thee,
> Texas, one and indivisible."

A person reciting the pledge to the state flag should face the flag, place the right hand over the heart and remove any easily removable hat.

The pledge to the Texas flag may be recited at all public and private meetings at which the pledge of allegiance to the national flag is recited and at state historical events and celebrations. The pledge to the Texas flag should be recited after the pledge of allegiance to the United States flag if both are recited.

### State Song

The state song of Texas is **"Texas, Our Texas."** The music was written by the late William J. Marsh (who died Feb. 1, 1971, in Fort Worth at age 90), and the words by Marsh and Gladys Yoakum Wright, also of Fort Worth. It was the winner of a state song contest sponsored by the legislature and was adopted in 1929. The wording has been changed once: Shortly after Alaska became a state in Jan. 1959, the word "Largest" in the third line was changed by Mr. Marsh to "Boldest." The text follows:

### Texas, Our Texas

Texas, our Texas! All hail the mighty State!
Texas, our Texas! So wonderful, so great!
Boldest and grandest, Withstanding ev'ry test;
O Empire wide and glorious, You stand supremely blest.

**Chorus**
God bless you Texas!
And keep you brave and strong,
That you may grow in power and worth,
Thro'out the ages long.

**Refrain**
Texas, O Texas! Your freeborn single star,
Sends out its radiance to nations near and far.
Emblem of freedom! It sets our hearts aglow,
With thoughts of San Jacinto and glorious Alamo.

Texas, dear Texas! From tyrant grip now free,
Shines forth in splendor your star of destiny!
Mother of heroes! We come your children true,
Proclaiming our allegiance, our faith, our love for you.

### State Motto

The state motto is **"Friendship."** The word Texas, or Tejas, was the Spanish pronunciation of a Caddo Indian word meaning "friends" or "allies." (41st Legislature in 1930.)

### State Citizenship Designation

The people of Texas usually call themselves **Texans.** However, **Texian** was generally used in the early period of the state's history.

## State Seal

The design of the **obverse (front)** of the State Seal consists of "a star of five points encircled by olive and live oak branches, and the words, 'The State of Texas'." (State Constitution, Art. IV, Sec. 19.) This design is a slight modification of the Great Seal of the Republic of Texas, adopted by the Congress of the Republic, Dec. 10, 1836, and readopted with modifications in 1839.

An official design for the **reverse (back)** of the seal was adopted by the 57th Legislature in 1961, but there were discrepancies between the written description and the artistic rendering that was adopted at the same time. To resolve the problems, the 72nd Legislature in 1991 adopted an official design.

The 73rd Legislature in 1993 finally adopted the reverse by law. The current description is in the Texas Government Code, section 3101.001:

"(b) The reverse side of the state seal contains a shield displaying a depiction of: (1) the Alamo; (2) the cannon of the Battle of Gonzales; and (3) Vince's Bridge. (c) The shield on the reverse side of the state seal is encircled by: (1) live oak and olive branches; and (2) the unfurled flags of: (A) the Kingdom of France; (B) the Kingdom of Spain; (C) the United Mexican States: (D) the Republic of Texas; (E) the Confederate States of America; and (F) the United States of America. (d) Above the shield is emblazoned the motto, "REMEMBER THE ALAMO," and beneath the shield are the words, "TEXAS ONE AND INDIVISIBLE." (e) A white five-pointed star hangs over the shield, centered between the flags."

## State Symbols

**State Bird** — The **mockingbird** (*Mimus polyglottos*) is the state bird of Texas, adopted by the 40th Legislature of 1927 at the request of the Texas Federation of Women's Clubs.

**State Flower** — The state flower of Texas is the **bluebonnet,** also called **buffalo clover, wolf flower** and *el conejo* (the rabbit). The bluebonnet was adopted as the state flower, on request of the Society of Colonial Dames in Texas, by the 27th Legislature in 1901. The original resolution designated *Lupinus subcarnosus* as the state flower, but a resolution by the 62nd Legislature in 1971 provided legal status as the state flower of Texas for "*Lupinus Texensis* and any other variety of bluebonnet."

**State Tree** — The **pecan** is the state tree of Texas. The sentiment that led to its official adoption probably grew out of the request of Gov. James Stephen Hogg that a pecan tree be planted at his grave. The 36th Legislature in 1919 adopted the pecan tree.

## Other Symbols

*(In 2001, the legislature placed restrictions on the adoption of future symbols by requiring that a joint resolution to designate a symbol must specify the item's historical or cultural significance to the state.)*

**State Air Force** — The **Confederate Air Force**, based in Midland at the Midland International Airport, was proclaimed the state air force of Texas by the 71st Legislature in 1989.

**State Dinosaur** — The **Brachiosaur Sauropod, Pleurocoelus,** was designated the state dinosaur by the 75th Legislature in 1997.

**State Dish** — **Chili** was proclaimed the Texas state dish by the 65th Legislature in 1977.

**State Fiber and Fabric** — **Cotton** was designated the state fiber and fabric by the 75th Legislature in 1997.

**State Fish** — The **Guadalupe bass,** a member of the genus *Micropterus* within the sunfish family, was named the state fish of Texas by the 71st Legislature in 1989. It is one of

## State Seal of Texas

a group of fish collectively known as black bass.

**State Folk Dance** — The **square dance** was designated the state folk dance by the 72nd Legislature in 1991.

**State Fruit** — The **Texas red grapefruit** was designated the state fruit by the 73rd Legislature in 1993.

**State Gem** — **Texas blue topaz,** the state gem of Texas, is found in the Llano uplift area, especially west to northwest of Mason. It was designated by the 61st Legislature in 1969.

**State Grass** — **Sideoats grama** (*Bouteloua curtipendula*), a native grass found on many different soils, was designated by the 62nd Legislature as the state grass of Texas in 1971.

**State Insect** — The **Monarch butterfly** (*Danaus plexippus*) was designated the state insect by the 74th Legislature in 1995.

**State Mammals** — The **armadillo** was designated the state **small mammal**; the **longhorn** was designated the state **large mammal**; and the **Mexican free-tailed bat** was designated the **flying mammal** by the 74th Legislature in 1995.

**State Musical Instrument** — The **guitar** was named the state musical instrument of Texas by the 75th Legislature in 1997.

**State Native Pepper** — The **chiltepin** was named the state native pepper of Texas by the 75th Legislature in 1997.

**State Pepper** — The **jalapeño pepper** was designated the state pepper by the 74th Legislature in 1995.

**State Plant** — The **prickly pear cactus** was designated the state plant by the 74th Legislature in 1995.

**State Reptile** — The **Texas horned lizard** was named the state reptile by the 73rd Legislature in 1993.

**State Seashell** — The **lightning whelk** (*Busycon perversum pulleyi*) was named as the official state seashell by the 70th Legislature in 1987. One of the few shells that open on the left side, the lightning whelk is named for its colored stripes. It is found only on the Gulf Coast.

**State Ship** — The battleship **Texas** was designated the state ship by the 74th Legislature in 1995.

**State Shrub** — The **crape myrtle** (*Lagerstroemia indica*) was designated the official state shrub by the 75th Legislature in 1997.

**State Sport** — **Rodeo** was named the state sport of Texas by the 75th Legislature in 1997.

**State Stone** — **Petrified palmwood**, found in Texas principally in counties near the Texas Gulf Coast, was designated the state stone by the 61st Legislature in 1969.

**State Tartan** — The **Texas Bluebonnet Tartan** was named the official state tartan by the 71st Texas Legislature in 1989.

**State Vegetable** — The **Texas sweet onion** was designated the state vegetable by the 75th Legislature in 1997. ☆

# The Frontier Forts of Texas
## By Bryan Woolley

After the Republic of Texas was annexed to the United States in late 1845, Texans had high hopes that the federal government would do what the impoverished Republic had been unable to do: subdue the aggressive Indian tribes on the new state's western frontier and open the vast emptiness of West Texas to safe Anglo settlement. Instead, the annexation of Texas soon precipitated the Mexican War, which kept the United States Army preoccupied with events south of the Rio Grande until 1849.

The commanding officer's quarters at Fort McKavett were built in 1856. When Brevet Lt. Col. William Grigsby Freeman arrived at McKavett in 1853 during his forts inspection, he discovered himself finally in real Indian country. File photo.

The Treaty of Guadalupe Hidalgo, which ended the war in 1848 and transferred ownership of the present American Southwest and California from Mexico to the United States, also placed an obligation upon the U.S. government to protect Mexico from raids across the new international border by the Indian tribes of the North. The Comanches and Kiowas, ferocious South Plains horsemen who had wreaked havoc on Texas frontier settlements for 20 years, had from time immemorial considered northern Mexican towns and haciendas their personal raiding ground and commissary.

As the history of the next quarter-century would prove, this promise to Mexico was one the American government couldn't keep. Nor could it effectively protect its own settlers on the wild western edge of Texas settlement. But in October 1849, it set about trying. Brevet Maj. Gen. George M. Brooke, commanding the 8th Military Department at San Antonio, ordered the establishment of a line of forts along the Rio Grande from Brownsville to Eagle Pass, and northward from there to the Red River.

## Westward Expansion

When Gen. Brooke issued his order, the California gold rush was under way. The southern route to the gold fields crossed the Texas wilderness from San Antonio to the Pass of the North (present-day El Paso) and on to the West Coast. The hopeful pilgrims traveling that cruel road across the Chihuahuan and Sonoran deserts had to be protected, too.

As Anglo settlement quickly pressed beyond the first forts, some of which were still under construction, the U.S. Army in 1851–52 began establishing a second line of posts about 200 miles west of the first. While the new forts were being erected, many of the older ones were abandoned or consolidated with the newer ones. For example, Fort Gates, established in October 1849 near

present-day Gatesville in Coryell County, and Fort Lincoln, built in July 1849 a mile north of present-day D'Hanis in Medina County, were evacuated in 1852 because the frontier already had passed them by.

By 1853, about one-third of the U.S. Army was stationed in Texas, many of the troops serving in primitive, under-manned outposts along the border and the western frontier. Brevet Lt. Col. William Grigsby Freeman set out in June of that year on the first inspection tour of those new forts and later wrote a detailed report to the assistant adjutant general in Washington. His report paints a vivid picture of the earliest U.S. Army installations on Texas soil and the kind of life the soldiers endured in them.

## A Thorough Inspection

The first post Freeman inspected was Fort Ewell, "situated on the right, or south, bank of the Nueces River at the point where it is crossed by the road leading from San Antonio to Laredo." The fort, he found, was on slightly elevated ground, but it was surrounded by a salt marsh. It lacked timber and stone for building and grazing for the animals. The soldiers had been unable even to get a kitchen garden to grow. "Indeed a less inviting spot for occupation by troops cannot well be conceived," he wrote. When he was about to depart Ewell, a rainstorm flooded the marsh around the post and held him prisoner for five days, "and even then I was compelled to swim my animals to get away."

He recommended that Fort Ewell be moved to a better spot 40 miles away, but the army soon decided to abandon it instead.

The damp colonel made a quick trip to Fort Merrill, about 60 miles northwest of Corpus Christi, then on to Fort Brown, situated just below Brownsville on the Rio Grande. The site of Fort Brown had been thought to be a healthful one, he wrote, but in the last two years "it has been visited by four epidemics — yellow fever, cholera and the dengue twice." During the last quarter of 1852 alone, 189 of the post's 459 men came down with dengue fever.

Ringgold Barracks, upriver from Brownsville, seemed in a more healthful location. It stood on a high bank of the Rio Grande within half a mile of a village of 300 souls called Rio Grande City, "a place of some notoriety in the late frontier disturbances." Freeman was pleased to find a reading room at Ringgold, "with a

number of well selected books and newspapers for the use of the enlisted men — such a provision for their instruction and amusement is worthy of general introduction."

Freeman then traveled 120 miles farther upstream to Fort McIntosh, just outside Laredo, an old Mexican village of about 800 people "of which not more than 40 are Americans." Across the river, he noticed another village had sprung up since the peace with Mexico. It was called "New Laredo." Fort McIntosh had been without a medical officer for more than a month. Freeman discovered a number of sick men in the post hospital, "but no citizen physician could be obtained in the neighborhood."

The most distant of the line of Rio Grande posts, Fort Duncan, stood across a deep ravine from Eagle Pass, a village comprising "eight or 10 tolerably good buildings and the same number of mud hovels occupied by the lower order of Mexicans." There also were "three or four stores for sale of goods principally adapted to the Mexican market." The illnesses suffered by Fort Duncan's soldiers, Freeman found, were "those occasioned by intemperance and, during the winter months, by the sudden changes of temperature caused by northers."

## A Fort of Primary Importance

Fort Duncan completed Freeman's inspection of the Rio Grande forts. He turned northward to inspect Fort Clark and Fort Inge on the San Antonio–El Paso road. On Aug. 1, 1853, he arrived at Fort Clark, near the present-day town of Brackettville, where troops were constructing comfortable quarters for themselves on land the government leased from Samuel A. Maverick of San Antonio.

The colonel liked what he saw: "I regard Fort Clark as a point of primary importance, being the limit of arable land in the direction of El Paso, and from its salient position looking both to the Rio Grande and Indian frontiers. It ought to have a strong garrison of horse and foot, and it is well fitted for a Cavalry station, timber for building stables being convenient, and an abundance of excellent grazing in the immediate vicinity."

Freeman had a good eye. Fort Clark would be an important post throughout the Indian wars and beyond. After the Civil War, it would be home for the intrepid Seminole-Negro Indian Scouts, or Black Seminole Scouts, descendants of slaves who had escaped into the Florida Everglades many years earlier and had been adopted into the Seminole tribe. When the government removed the Seminoles to a reservation in Oklahoma, their black tribesmen went with them. They won renown as trackers and would prove invaluable to the U.S. Army throughout West Texas during the wars against the Plains tribes and the Apaches. Four Black Seminoles won the Medal of Honor during their service at Fort Clark.

Fort Clark remained a major post until 1944, when it was deactivated. It was one of the last horse cavalry posts to go.

Freeman was less impressed with nearby Fort Inge

on the Frio River. "The men," he wrote, "occupy two buildings constructed of upright poles, chinked up, with thatched roofs. These, besides being insufficient, are in a wretched state of dilapidation. Part of the troops also live in tents." The regimental band, he noted, "was very small and not mounted."

## Freeman Heads North

From Inge, Freeman returned to San Antonio to refit before beginning his tour of the northern Texas posts. He began at Fort Martin Scott, a tiny post near Fredericksburg that served mainly as a forage depot for wagon trains supplying the upper posts, and then in mid-August he continued to Fort Mason, 23 miles from San Saba. "Fort Mason was the first post in Texas at which I met Indians," Freeman wrote. "They were the Tonkaway tribe, some 30 in number, and had come in to beg, and a more squalid, half-starved looking race I have never seen." He found Mason to be a well-built post manned by well-trained soldiers. But by November 1853, the army had decided to abandon it.

At Fort McKavett, two miles from the source of the San Saba River, he discovered himself finally in real Indian country. Three Comanche bands led by Yellow Wolf, Ketunseh and San-a-co were living on the Concho River and at the headwaters of the Colorado, within 60 to 100 miles of the post.

The men at McKavett were "variously armed and clothed, which besides the inconvenience attending its instruction, greatly detracts from its appearance on parade occasions." The post was "wretchedly equipped, being deficient in many essential articles and without the means of keeping in order those on hand." It had only 30 serviceable horses. The nearest post office was at San Antonio, 164 miles away.

"During the whole summer," Freeman wrote, "the men were engaged in building the post; they were exposed during the day to the heat of the sun, and at

The names of soldiers are carved in the ruins at Fort Chadbourne in Bronte, Coke County. File photo.

The old powder magazine still stands at Fort Phantom Hill, north of Abilene. File photo.

night they slept either upon the ground or in tents, and alcoholic liquors were used in excess."

Fort Terrett, on the North Fork of the Llano River, was under construction, too. The fort's barracks were "mere shelters" without doors, floors or windows. The best thing Freeman found at Fort Terrett was the band, which "though small, is quite good, and does much to relieve the monotony of garrison life at an isolated, frontier station."

## Rustic Conditions

Freeman returned to Fort McKavett, then departed for Fort Chadbourne, 95 miles to the northwest on Oak Creek, a small tributary of the Colorado. It was a four-day journey. Except for the officers, who lived in "two or three rude, jacal huts," the troops there were still living in tents.

"The Comanches are the only Indians who have visited the post since its establishment," he wrote. "I could obtain only a vague estimate of their numbers. They have no permanent camps, but for the last year the band of San-a-co, one of the principal chiefs, has lived within 50 or 60 miles of the post."

At Fort Phantom Hill, between the Elm and Clear Forks of the Brazos River near present-day Abilene, the soldier's life was no better than at McKavett. "The aspect of the place is uninviting," Freeman wrote. "No post visited, except Fort Ewell, presented so few attractions."

He couldn't even review the troops because nearly all of them were raw, untrained recruits who hadn't yet learned how to march, and 50 of them didn't yet even have weapons. To complete the dismal scene: "The officers and soldiers are living in pole huts built in the early part of last year. They are now in a dilapidated condition. The company quarters will, in all probability, fall down during the prevalence of the severe northers of the coming winter."

At Fort Belknap, on the Clear Fork of the Brazos northeast of Phantom Hill, the prospect was brighter. There was plenty of good stone and brick clay for construction; the post stood over a field of bituminous coal that could be dug for fuel, and excellent springs were only a few hundred yards away.

The post had been visited recently by small bands of Caddos, Anadarkos, Ionies, Wacos, Keechies and Tawakonis, as well as 300 Comanches under the ubiquitous Buffalo Hump and San-a-co. "Their camps are move-

able," Freeman wrote, "but during the winter they live within 40 miles, on the Clear Fork."

From Belknap, Freeman swung eastward to a small collection of log buildings called Fort Worth, at the mouth of the Clear Fork of the Trinity River. "The nearest towns or villages are Dallas, with 350 inhabitants, 38 miles east, and Birdville and Alton, with a population of 50 each, distant 9 and 35 miles respectively."

Fort Worth had been established in 1849. When Freeman arrived there in September 1853, its commander had gotten orders to abandon the post and move his troops to Fort Belknap.

"I was gratified to find — it was the solitary exception throughout my tour — the Guard House, that saddest of all places in a garrison, without a single prisoner. Bvt. Maj. Merrill informs me that most of his men belong to the temperance society, and that he has rarely occasion to confine any one of them."

The last two forts on Freeman's tour — Fort Graham, 56 miles southwest of Fort Worth, and Fort Croghan, in the center of Texas 50 miles northwest of Austin — also were in the process of shutting down. With a few exceptions, most of the other posts he visited would follow them into oblivion within a few years. Settlers already were pushing the frontier miles beyond their usefulness.

They hadn't been a deterrent against Indians raids anyway. They never had enough troops or the right equipment to perform their mission. Most of their troops were infantry. To expect them to chase down on foot the greatest horsemen in the world was sheer governmental folly. The Comanches and Kiowas who visited the forts and took a look around must have had a good laugh when they returned to their camps.

Why did the army keep its mounted troops at its eastern forts, far from the frontier, while sending its infantry to the western posts, where the Indian horsemen roamed? Brevet Gen. Persifor Smith, commander of the Department of Texas, had decided to quarter his horses where the forage was best. And there was more grass in the east.

## The Trans-Pecos Posts

In late 1848, the War Department also had authorized the establishment of a post at the western tip of Texas, across the Rio Grande from the Mexican village of El Paso del Norte (present-day Ciudad Juarez, Chihuahua). Its mission would be to defend the border and

# List of the Frontier Forts of Texas

*The list below is in order of the forts' establishment. The names in parentheses are other names by which the post was known. The name following the comma is the present-day county where the fort was located. In cases in which the exact dates of establishment and deactivation were different in the various sources used to compile this list, we have used the dates that appeared most likely to be correct.*

*Most of the forts that were still in operation at the outbreak of the Civil War were surrendered to the control of the army of the Confederate States of America. In this list, we include only the dates of first establishment and final deactivation of each post, except in the few cases in which a post was not occupied at all for a number of years. In those cases, we include the dates of reactivation and final deactivation.*

**Fort Brown** (Fort Texas), Cameron
March 28, 1846 — 1944

**Fort Bliss** (Post El Paso; Camp Concordia), El Paso
Sept. 8, 1848 — still in operation.

**Ringgold Barracks** (Post at Davis' Landing; Camp Ringgold; Fort Ringgold), Starr
Oct. 26, 1848 — 1944

**Fort Martin Scott** (Camp Houston), Gillespie
Dec. 5, 1848 — Dec. 1866

**Fort McIntosh** (Camp Crawford), Webb
March 3, 1849 — May 31,1946

**Fort Inge** (Camp Leona), Uvalde
March 13, 1849 — March 1869

**Fort Croghan** (McCulloch's Station; Camp Croghan; Camp Hamilton), Burnet
March 18, 1849 — Dec. 1853 (or 1855)

**Fort Graham,** Hill
March 24, 1849 — Nov. 9, 1853.

**Fort Duncan** (Camp Eagle Pass), Maverick
March 27, 1849 — 1922

**Fort Worth** (Camp Worth), Tarrant
June 6, 1849 — Sept. 17, 1853

**Fort Lincoln,** Medina
July 7, 1849 — July 20, 1852

**Fort Gates** (Camp Gates), Coryell
October 26, 1849 — March 1852

**Fort Merrill,** Live Oak
Feb. 26, 1850 — Dec. 1, 1855

**Fort Belknap,** Young
June 24, 1851 — Sept. 1867

**Fort Mason,** Mason
July 6, 1851 — March 23, 1869

**Fort Phantom Hill** (Post on the Clear Fork of the Brazos), Jones
Nov. 14, 1851 — April 6, 1854

**Fort Terrett** (Camp Terrett), Sutton
Feb. 2, 1852 — Feb. 26, 1854

**Fort McKavett** (Camp San Saba), Menard
March 14, 1852 — March 22, 1859
April 1, 1868 — June 30, 1883.

**Fort Ewell,** La Salle
May 18, 1852 — Oct. 1854

**Fort Clark** (Fort Riley), Kinney
June 20, 1852 — Feb. 9, 1946.

**Fort Chadbourne,** Coke
Oct. 28, 1852 — 1867

**Fort Davis,** Jeff Davis
Oct. 7, 1854 — 1891

**Fort Lancaster** (Camp Lancaster), Crockett
Aug. 20, 1855 — March 19, 1861
*(Texas Rangers and militia used site sporadically during the Indian campaigns of the 1870s.)*

**Fort Quitman,** Hudspeth
Sept. 28, 1858 — Jan. 5, 1877
1880 – April 1882.

**Fort Stockton,** Pecos
March 23, 1859 — late June 30, 1886

**Fort Griffin** (Camp Wilson), Shackelford
July 31, 1867 — May 31, 1881

**Fort Concho** (Camp Hatch, Camp Kelly), Tom Green
Nov. or Dec. 1867 — June 20, 1889

**Fort Richardson,** Jack
Nov. 1867 — May 23, 1878

**Fort Hancock** (Camp Rice), Hudspeth
April 15, 1881 — Dec. 6, 1895 ☆

protect California-bound travelers and the few local settlers from Indian attack. Brevet Maj. Jefferson Van Horne and 257 soldiers arrived there in September 1849. The troops occupied several sites along the river, but in 1851 they were ordered to withdraw to Fort Fillmore, 40 miles to the north in New Mexico. In January 1854 the border post was re-established and named Fort Bliss.

Later that year, Secretary of War Jefferson Davis ordered the establishment of a second post in the Trans-Pecos to defend the San Antonio–El Paso road. The road intersected several war trails traveled by the Comanches and Apaches on their raids into and out of Mexico.

In October 1854, Gen. Smith personally selected — for its "pure water and salubrious climate" — the site of Fort Davis (named for the secretary of war) near Limpia Creek at the southern base of the Davis Mountains (also named for the secretary). Six companies of infantry under Lt. Col. Washington Seawell constructed a primitive post of mud and wood in a box canyon near the creek.

In August 1855, Capt. Stephen Carpenter and two infantry companies established Fort Lancaster on Live Oak Creek above its confluence with the Pecos River near the present-day town of Sheffield. In September 1858, Capt. Arthur T. Lee and his infantry command established Fort Quitman on a barren plain of the Rio Grande, 80 miles downstream from Fort Bliss. And in March 1859 Fort Stockton was established at Comanche Springs, a favorite watering spot on that tribe's war trail into Mexico.

The duties of the soldiers at all these posts were to escort freight wagon trains and the mail, patrol their segments of the road to keep track of the Indians' whereabouts, and pursue and punish the raiders — still an impractical, if not impossible, mission for infantry in such harsh country against such skillful horsemen.

*Sleeping Lion Mountain creates a natural fortress behind Officer's Row at Fort Davis. The fort in Jeff Davis County is now a National Historical Site. File photo.*

*Fort Richardson, one of the post–Civil War forts, was built in 1868 and was the U.S. Army's northernmost fort in Texas. File photo.*

## The Civil War Years

Before the soldiers at the Trans-Pecos forts could build permanent, comfortable quarters for themselves and their animals, Texas seceded from the Union in 1861 and joined the Confederacy. Brig. Gen. David E. Twiggs, commander of the 8th U.S. Military District, ordered the federal garrisons to evacuate all the posts and surrender them to Confederate authorities. Elements of the 2nd Regiment of the Texas Mounted Rifles occupied most of the West Texas forts, some for a few months, some for a year or more.

During the year that Col. John R. Baylor and Confederate troops manned Fort Davis, a detachment of cavalry gave chase to an Apache raiding party. Thinking he had overtaken the raiders somewhere in the Big Bend, Lt. Reuben Mays and his 13 men rode into an ambush. The Apaches wiped out the soldiers, and only a Mexican guide escaped.

In 1862, the soldiers from the Trans-Pecos posts marched on to Fort Bliss and were part of the army led by Brig. Gen. Henry Hopkins Sibley that attempted to conquer New Mexico for the Confederacy. After the disastrous Battle of Glorieta Pass, the Confederates abandoned the Trans-Pecos and retreated to San Antonio. The deserted forts fell into ruin. Apaches looted and burned much of Fort Davis.

Except for Fort Bliss, which Union troops reoccupied after Glorieta, the war left the frontier settlements and travelers as naked to Indian attack as they had been before Texas joined the Union. Many families abandoned their homes and pulled back to more populous areas. Others "forted up" together and depended on a few companies of Texas Rangers and minuteman volunteers to protect them.

## U.S. Army Returns to Texas

When the Civil War ended, the U.S. Army returned to Texas, this time to stay until the frontier was tamed. In 1867 and 1868, federal troops reoccupied Fort Davis, Fort Stockton, Fort Lancaster and Fort Quitman, this time building permanent housing and facilities of stone and adobe to replace the uncomfortable and unsanitary pre-war *jacales*.

In addition, the army built a trio of new forts to contend with the Comanche threat east of the Pecos. On "a flat, treeless, dreary prairie" beside the Concho River at present-day San Angelo, it established Fort Concho to replace old Fort Chadbourne. On the Clear Fork of the Brazos River near present-day Albany, it established Fort Griffin, and the older posts of Belknap, Phantom Hill and Chadbourne were reduced in status to subposts of Griffin. On Lost Creek, a tributary of the Trinity near Jacksboro, it built Fort Richardson, the northernmost army post in Texas. Much later, Camp Rice, later to be renamed Fort Hancock, was built on the Rio Grande downstream from El Paso as a subpost of Fort Davis to defend against Indians and Mexican bandits.

From these posts and a few of the older ones such as Fort Clark, the army over the next 15 years or so would eventually eliminate the Indian resistance to Anglo settlement of West Texas. The names of some of the officers who commanded the forts would be writ large in the broader history of the American West. And events that happened at some of the forts would become important chapters in the history of the army and in frontier folklore.

## The West Texas Wars

In early 1871, Col. Ranald Slidell Mackenzie, who at various times commanded Fort Brown, Fort McKavett, Fort Clark, Fort Concho and Fort Richardson, began a series of expeditions from Concho into the Panhandle and the Llano Estacado in pursuit of renegade Comanches, Kiowas and other Indians who continued to cross the Red River and raid into Texas from their reservations near Fort Sill, Indian Territory. Two years later, operating from Fort Clark with cavalry and Black Seminole trackers, Mackenzie made an illegal raid into Mexico in pursuit of Indian cattle thieves. He burned a Kickapoo village in Coahuila and brought 40 white captives back to Texas. His victory put an end to the border cattle raids.

In July 1874, Mackenzie's was one of five army commands ordered to close in on Indian hideouts in the canyons along the eastern edge of the Llano Estacado. The troops engaged the Indians in several battles and skirmishes, and in November 1874, Mackenzie's command destroyed five Comanche, Kiowa, Cheyenne and Arapaho villages in Palo Duro Canyon and captured 1,500 horses. Mackenzie ordered the horses slaughtered, thus destroying both the buffalo-centered economy of the Southern Plains tribes and their ability to continue raiding. This conflict, which became known as the Red River War, ended on June 2, 1875, when Comanche Chief Quanah Parker arrived at Fort Sill with 407 fol-

lowers and finally accepted reservation life.

During the five years after Mackenzie's victory, white hunters converged upon the Plains and systematically slaughtered the great southern buffalo herd for the animals' hides and for sport. Fort Griffin and the nearby raucous village called "The Flat" became the center of the odoriferous hide commerce and attracted hordes of gamblers, prostitutes, gunmen and thieves bent on relieving the hunters of their money. By 1881, both the Comanche presence and the buffalo were gone, so the army closed Fort Griffin.

## The Victorio Campaign

But in the Trans-Pecos the army was still fighting, mostly against Apaches who were raiding across the Rio Grande from strongholds in the mountains of Chihuahua and Coahuila. In September 1879, a large band of Mescalero and Warm Springs Apaches, under the leadership of Victorio, began a series of attacks in the mountain-and-desert country west of Fort Davis. Col. Benjamin H. Grierson, a Union hero during the Civil War, led troops from forts Davis, Concho and Stockton in a campaign against the raiders. Instead of chasing the Apaches across the rugged landscape, Grierson stationed his troops around the region's few watering places and deprived the warriors of the one commodity without which even Apaches couldn't survive. After several hard-fought battles, Victorio crossed back into Mexico. Mexican troops killed him and many of his followers in the Battle of Tres Castillos in October 1880.

Victorio led Mescalero and Warm Springs Apaches in a series of attacks west of Fort Davis. Photo courtesy of Fort Davis National Historical Site.

Col. Benjamin H. Grierson led troops from forts Davis, Concho and Stockton against Victorio's warriors. Photo courtesy of Fort Davis National Historical Site.

The Victorio campaign was the last major conflict between Indians and the U.S. Army on Texas soil.

Much of the fighting in both the Panhandle and the Trans-Pecos wars was done by black troops to whom the Plains tribes had affixed the nickname "Buffalo Soldiers" because of their curly hair. Since former slaves had served in the Union Army with distinction, Congress authorized the establishment of six regiments of black troops to serve on the post–Civil War frontier: the 9th and 10th Cavalry and the 38th, 39th, 40th and 41st Infantry. In 1869, the four infantry regiments were consolidated into the 24th and 25th Infantry.

## Prejudice on the Frontier

Not even the black soldier's valor could win them respect from many of the white citizens whose lives they protected. A number of white officers, including George Armstrong Custer, refused to serve as their commanders. But other white officers, Grierson most notable among them, treated the black soldiers well and achieved victory and honor in their company. They proved to be brave, reliable soldiers. Fourteen enlisted men from the black regiments and four Seminole-Negro Indian Scouts earned the Medal of Honor during the Indian wars.

Second Lt. Henry Ossian Flipper believed racial prejudice caused his dismissal from the service. He was pardoned in 1999. File photo.

The most notorious case of racial prejudice in the frontier army was the ordeal of 2nd Lt. Henry Ossian Flipper, the first black graduate of West Point, who was dismissed from the service in June 1882 after he was found guilty of "conduct unbecoming an officer and a gentleman" in a court-martial trial at Fort Davis.

Flipper was born into slavery in Georgia in 1856, graduated from the Military Academy in 1877 and was assigned to the 10th Cavalry. He served at forts Sill, Elliott, Concho and Quitman before coming to Fort Davis. He distinguished himself as an engineer, helped move Quanah Parker's Comanches from Palo Duro to Fort Sill, and fought in two battles during the Victorio campaign.

When Col. William Rufus "Pecos Bill" Shafter became commanding officer of Fort Davis in 1881, Flipper was both post quartermaster and in charge of the commissary. Shafter immediately relieved him of his quartermaster duties, giving that job to the regiment's quartermaster, and later filed embezzlement charges against Flipper when commissary funds were missing. The lieutenant claimed that the charges against him were motivated by race. A divided court-martial acquitted him of embezzlement but ruled him guilty of "conduct unbecoming an officer and a gentleman." Although dismissal was the army's punishment for such a conviction, many soldiers got lighter sentences. In Flipper's case, however, he was dismissed from the U.S. Army while with his company at Fort Quitman.

Flipper moved on to a long and distinguished career as a mining engineer in the Southwest and Mexico and even became an assistant to the U.S. secretary of the interior. He maintained his innocence of the Fort Davis charges and tried unsuccessfully on several occasions to clear his name. Almost a century after his discharge, the army "corrected" Flipper's records to show that he was "separated" from the army by "honorable" discharge,

and on Feb. 19, 1999, President Bill Clinton posthumously pardoned him.

## The End of an Era

With the migration of Anglo farmers, ranchers and other settlers westward behind the army, the frontier era was rushing toward its close. Fort Lancaster was abandoned in 1873 and Fort Richardson in 1878. After the removal of the South Plains tribes and the Apaches from Texas, the remaining West Texas forts settled into quiet garrison routine. Eventually, one by one, the army shut them down: Fort Quitman in 1882, Fort Stockton in 1886, Fort Concho in 1889, Fort Davis in 1891, Fort Hancock in 1895. Fort Duncan on the Rio Grande lasted until 1922. Four other border posts survived into the World War II era: Ringgold and Brown until 1944, and Clark and McIntosh until 1946. Today only Fort Bliss remains as an important 21st-century missile base.

Some of the old posts have won new life in recent years as historical treasures. Fort Davis, the largest and best preserved of them, is now a national historical site; Fort Concho is a national historical landmark; Fort Griffin, Fort Richardson, Fort McKavett and Fort Lancaster are state historical parks, and others like Fort Stockton, Fort Phantom Hill and Fort Chadbourne are cared for by local government and historical groups. ☆

*Bryan Woolley is a senior writer for The Dallas Morning News and a novelist.*

### For Further Reading:

*Along the Texas Forts Trail* by B. W. Aston and Donathan Taylor; University of North Texas Press, Denton, 1997.

*Black Frontiersman: The Memoirs of Henry O. Flipper,* compiled and edited by Theodore D. Harris; Texas Christian University Press, Fort Worth, 1997.

*The Buffalo Soldiers: A Narrative of the Negro Cavalry in the West* by William H. Leckie with Shirley A. Leckie; University of Oklahoma Press, Norman, 2003.

*Fort Concho and the Texas Frontier* by J. Evetts Haley; San Angelo Standard Times, San Angelo, 1952.

*Fort Davis: Outpost on the Texas Frontier* by Robert Wooster; Texas State Historical Association, Austin, 1994.

*Fort Griffin on the Texas Frontier* by Carl Coke Rister; University of Oklahoma Press, Norman, 1956.

*Fort Lancaster: Texas Frontier Sentinel* by Lawrence John Francell; Texas State Historical Association, Austin, 1999.

*Freeman's Report on the Eighth Military Department,* edited by M. L. Crimmins; The Southwestern Historical Quarterly, Austin, July 1947–April 1950.

*Frontier Forts of Texas,* edited by Harold B. Simpson; Texian Press, Waco, 1966.

*If These Walls Could Speak: Historic Forts of Texas,* text by Robert M. Utley, paintings by J. U. Salvant; University of Texas Press, Austin, 1985.

*The Most Promising Young Officer: A Life of Ranald Slidell Mackenzie* by Michael D. Pierce; University of Oklahoma Press, Norman, 1993.

*Musket, Saber and Missile: A History of Fort Bliss* by Leon C. Metz; Mangan, El Paso, 1962.

*The New Handbook of Texas,* Ron Tyler, editor in chief; Texas State Historical Association, Austin, 1996.

*The Old Army in Texas: A Research Guide to the U.S. Army in Nineteenth-Century Texas* by Thomas T. Smith; Texas State Historical Association, Austin, 2000.

Old Fort Davis by Barry Scobee; San Antonio, Naylor, 1947.

*Soldiers, Sutlers, and Settlers: Garrison Life on the Texas Frontier* by Robert Wooster; Texas A&M University Press, College Station, 1987.

*Standing in the Gap: Subposts, Minor Posts, and Picket Stations on the Texas Frontier, 1866–1886* by Lloyd M. Uglow; Texas Christian University Press, Fort Worth, 2001.

*Texas' Last Frontier: Fort Stockton and the Trans-Pecos, 1861–1895* by Clayton W. Williams; Texas A&M University Press, College Station, 1982.

*The U. S. Army and the Texas Frontier Economy, 1845–1900* by Thomas T. Smith; Texas A&M University Press, College Station, 1999.

# Women at the Frontier Forts
## By Mary G. Ramos

*F*rontier forts, despite their primitive environments and military purposes, were not exclusively male enclaves. A surprising number of women and children shared forts with the U.S. Army's troops.

Some women were wives of officers or enlisted men. The officers' households often included female servants: governesses, housekeepers, maids and cooks. The military also employed laundresses, and a few post hospitals hired female nurses when male stewards were in short supply. This is a glimpse of these women's lives on the Texas frontier.

Some army officers who were posted to Texas, believing that frontier life would be intolerable to their gently bred Eastern wives, left their families behind. But some army wives with a strong sense of duty — or those who were ignorant of what awaited them — packed up households, children, servants and pets and headed southwest, following their husbands from post to post, determined to create as comfortable a home for their families as possible.

Before railroads arrived in the southwest, getting to her husband's post was the army wife's first challenge. From the late 1840s to the Civil War, the best route to Texas from the East was by ship to New Orleans and by wagon or coach from there to the fort. Stagecoaches were uncomfortable and were tempting targets for bandits. One of the most popular conveyances was called an ambulance: a two-wheeled light carriage pulled by two or four mules. One soldier's wife had her rocking chair fastened to the floor of the ambulance, traveling to her husband's post sitting in the back of the wagon amid her belongings. Others preferred to travel in a heavier, roomier four-wheeled Studebaker wagon, about 10 feet long and three-and-a-half feet wide.

Those traveling across Texas in summer were often roused from sleep to start their day's journey by 2 a.m. so they could avoid the heat of the day. At night, travelers were often forced to sleep in tents on the bare ground. When rains came, wagons bogged down in the mud and travelers risked flash floods.

## The Environment

The environment that awaited army families varied greatly. In letters to her family, Helen Chapman, wife of the first quartermaster of Fort Brown, described houses in Brownsville and neighboring Matamoros as being shaded by pomegranates, lemons, oranges, figs and oleanders, with mesquite, acacia and ebony trees growing wild. She assured her mother, "You must remember there are other posts far worse and that he might have been ordered to Santa Fe, Oregon or California."

*Alice K. Grierson (left) lived at both Fort Concho (1875–1882) and Fort Davis (1882–1885) with her husband, Col. Benjamin H. Grierson of the 10th U.S. Cavalry. Alice followed her husband from one western frontier post to another, in Texas and New Mexico, for more than 20 years. Helen Fuller Davis (right) was Grierson's niece and the wife of 1st Lt. William Davis, Jr. She and her husband called Fort Davis home from fall 1884 to spring 1885. Photos courtesy of Fort Davis National Historical Site.*

Forts Croghan (Burnet), Martin Scott (Fredericksburg), Graham (west of Hillsboro) and Bliss (El Paso) won praise from army wives for their pleasantness and beauty. Winters at forts Duncan (Eagle Pass) and McIntosh (Laredo) were mild, but summers were blistering, with the temperature sometimes hitting 107 degrees in the shade. Ringgold Barracks (Rio Grande City) was also miserably hot, while Fort Davis was mild and pleasant in summer. At Fort Concho in 1868, hail beat down every tent, stampeded the horses and left two inches of ice covering the parade ground.

The post surgeon at Fort McKavett (near Menard) reported that the area's animal life included gray wolves, coyotes, bears, deer, jackrabbits and wild horses, along with rattlesnakes, cottonmouths, tarantulas and centipedes. Frontier families learned to shake out bedding before "hitting the sack." Fleas often caused more distress than snakes, however, for which fort residents used the old frontier remedy of putting a tin of water under each leg of the bed before retiring.

## Housing

At the forts, families found a great diversity of housing. At times they were greeted with tents, in which they lived until other housing was built.

Picket houses were often used as a transition between tents and permanent structures. Picket construction involved digging a rectangular ditch one to two feet deep along the perimeter of the building. A large post was upended in the trench at each corner of the house. Smaller wooden posts were set upright between them, with their lower ends in the trench (rather than horizontal, as in a traditional log house). Wood salvaged from packing crates was fashioned into window and door frames, and spaces between the logs were chinked with wood chips, mud and lime. Roofs of canvas and straw were anchored to wooden frames laid across the tops of the walls.

Since the picket houses were intended only as temporary housing, they were rarely maintained. However, they were commonly used well past the time when they should have been replaced. As the green logs dried, they shrank and the chinking fell out, allowing rain and snow to pour through the cracks.

At Fort Richardson in 1871, housing was so scarce that officer Robert G. Carter fitted together a complex of tents at the east end of officer's row for himself and his bride. A norther arrived in November 1872 while his wife was giving birth to their first child; soldiers had to hold down the guy ropes and picket pins to keep the tent from blowing away.

After the Civil War, forts Richardson, Lancaster, McKavett, and probably Fort Griffin used Turnley Portable Cottages while awaiting permanent buildings. Invented by Quartermaster Parmenas Taylor Turnley, this early day manufactured housing could be transported on army wagons and erected in about four hours by three men. The structures came in two sizes: small, which could house two officers, and large, for use as barracks, hospital or storehouse; both had canvas roofs and came complete with locks, keys, sashes and blinds.

Commanding officers' quarters had up to six rooms, porches front and back, and a kitchen, which was often separate from the house because of the threat of fire. Other officers' families commonly were allowed two rooms plus a kitchen; single officers had one room each.

Forts were usually laid out with a central parade ground, with officers' quarters along one side and enlisted men's barracks on the other. Married enlisted men's and laundresses' tents, jacales, or picket houses were usually stuck away in the least desirable area of the fort, commonly called "Suds Row" or "Sudsville," and other structures, such as the commissary, hospital, bakery, powder magazine, carpenter's shed, smithy and stables were scattered around the post.

## Food

Foods available to men and their families were as variable as the housing. Alice Grierson, whose husband, Col. Benjamin H. Grierson, was the commanding officer at Fort Concho and Fort Davis, lamented the lack of fresh eggs, milk and vegetables, while Helen Chapman at Fort Brown spoke glowingly of her varied diet of "game, beef, vegetables, tea, butter and good bread." In mid-winter one year, she bought radishes, cabbages, carrots, lettuce and green peas from local farmers. Up river at Ringgold Barracks, supply boats couldn't operate on the Rio Grande when the river was low, so military families had to make do with the commissary's moldy flour

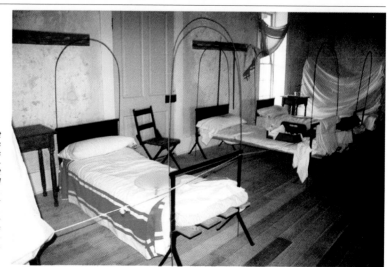

A few hospitals at the frontier forts hired female nurses when male stewards were in short supply. The hospital at Fort Richardson, southwest of Jacksboro in Jack County, has been authentically restored and is part of the Fort Richardson State Historical Park. File photo.

and rancid pork. The most isolated posts subsisted on beef, bacon, bread, coffee, dried potatoes and beans. The bread was often made from only flour, salt and water. At posts with settlers living nearby, army wives could sometimes buy eggs, fresh milk and chickens.

Gardening was tried at some posts. It failed miserably at forts Duncan and Clark. At Fort McKavett in the 1870s, troops laid out a garden, irrigated it from the San Saba River, and produced onions, beets, cabbage, radishes, corn, lettuce, squash, parsley, turnips, okra, cucumbers, string beans, peas, tomatoes, melons and pumpkins. Gardening efforts at Fort Davis yielded similar bounty.

## Health

Post hospitals served the families of the troops and often were the only medical service available to civilians in surrounding settlements and on neighboring ranches. At various times, the forts were subject to epidemics of diarrhea, constipation, dysentery and cholera. Typhoid fever killed Alice Grierson's 13-year-old daughter Edith while the family lived at Fort Concho. At Fort Brown, Helen Chapman reported cases of yellow fever and cholera in 1849 and dengue fever in 1850. Regimental surgeons commonly treated cases of snakebite, scurvy, common cold, bronchitis, pleurisy, pneumonia and tuberculosis — and the ever-present venereal diseases.

## The Women's Daily Lives

### Officers' Wives

The commanding officer's wife functioned as post hostess, as moral standard-bearer, and often as a "den mother" and sympathetic ear for the younger officers and sometimes enlisted men, as well. They and other officers' wives led efforts to set up schools and church services, organized dances and planned entertainments. In a letter home, Helen Chapman expressed her awareness of the value of feminine presence at the frontier forts: "Ladies with all their faults, do certainly exercise a most favorable influence over men in softening their natures, preserving their gentlemanly habits and checking their excesses." However, Alice Grierson grew tired

of the responsibility of housing, feeding and entertaining visitors and newly arrived officers' families while coping with frequent pregnancies and caring for her growing family.

### Servants

Household help was scarce and unreliable. Female servants brought from the East often returned home after getting a taste of the isolation and boredom of frontier life. Others found husbands among the troops and quit domestic service. Helen Chapman for a time employed a 12-year-old Irish orphan, who worked a full day around the house and sewed in her spare time.

### Nurses

Because of a shortage of male stewards for the hospitals, some medical officers hired women nurses for the forts' hospitals. In the 1840s and '50s, female nurses could not live among a garrison of men at frontier forts without being considered morally loose, but women nurses gained acceptance during the Civil War. The forts' nurses helped doctors with the patients, cleaned the facilities and washed the hospital's linen.

### Laundresses

The army hired three or four laundresses per company to do laundry on a piece-work basis. The army furnished lodging and food; each soldier paid the laundress for her services. Typical of army laundresses were those at Fort Duncan between 1850 and 1860: All were foreign-born, hailing from Ireland, Germany, France, Switzerland and Mexico. Many were wives of enlisted men. The black units — the Buffalo Soldiers — generally had black laundresses. Despite a shortage of soap, they apparently did a good job of cleaning garments on rocks or scrubboards in rivers or creeks. A hardworking laundress could earn between $30 to $40 per month (compared to $16 per month paid to an enlisted man). Some laundresses worked as prostitutes to earn extra money, which prompted the assistant surgeon at Ringgold Barracks to suggest that troops wash their own clothes, since half the patients in his hospital were there because of venereal diseases transmitted by the laundresses.

## Schools

If a teacher was not available in the fort, mothers often taught their own children. Sometimes subscription schools were set up, with each family paying part of the teacher's salary, or the chaplain might teach school in addition to his pastoral duties. Classes were not limited to children: Some teachers also held classes for soldiers, many of whom were illiterate. At Fort Concho in 1879, Chaplain Dunbar was holding one class for white children, one for black children (37 children in all), and a third for 55 soldiers. At Fort Griffin, children from neighboring ranches attended classes at the post with the army children. Some officers sent their children away to boarding schools when they were old enough.

## Nearby Settlements

Shortly after the establishment of nearly every fort, a civilian settlement sprang up beside it. At the larger posts, this town sometimes included legitimate businesses that served not only the fort's residents, but also the surrounding civilian population: hardware stores, general stores, and the like. But many businesses, drawn to army posts like leeches to blood, were there simply to part the soldiers from their pay: saloons, gambling dens, seedy dance halls and brothels. Particularly large and rough was "The Flat," the town that developed between Fort Griffin and the Clear Fork of the Brazos. Its customer base was broader than at other forts because it included not only the fort's residents, but also, in the 1870s and '80s, bison hunters and cowboys coming through with cattle drives. Although a town's general store often could supply wares that army wives could not find at the post sutler's store, most women would not venture into town without a male escort.

## Entertainment

Any excuse was used for a diversion: holidays, birthdays or no reason at all. Many forts had post bands that played daily mini-concerts and for weekly or semi-weekly post dances. Dances were also held to celebrate weddings and to welcome newly arrived officers. Fort Richardson had a glee club as well as a post band, the Jolly Blues, that played for post dances and for civilian events in Jacksboro.

Men and their wives, with children in tow, went on hunting or fishing excursions, which were often overnight or two-day trips in wagons packed with picnic hampers, tents, and other equipment and driven by servants or enlisted men. Picnics and, in Central Texas, pecan-gathering trips were popular one-day expeditions.

Many posts had libraries, but they varied greatly in quality and quantity of reading material. The library at Fort Richardson contained 500 books in 1869; when the post closed nine years later, it boasted more than 1,800 volumes. The Fort Griffin library, by contrast, was started in 1869 with a few volumes donated by the post surgeon: texts on medicine, science, physics, chemistry, pharmacology, and such titles as "Treatise on Diseases of the Ear." Fort Concho had 720 books in 1875, built around classics by such writers as Charles Dickens and Sir Walter Scott. By 1879, it also had subscriptions to daily newspapers from Chicago, Cincinnati, St. Louis, Louisville and New York, as well as to 27 magazines, such as *Harper's Weekly, Illustrated London News, Scientific American* and *Atlantic Monthly.*

Army families kept a wide assortment of pets, ranging from the usual dogs, cats and ponies to mockingbirds, orioles, a parrot, doves, chickens, prairie dogs, a fawn, a squirrel and a bison calf.

Mail was always welcome. Scheduled to arrive once or twice a week, it was often delayed. Along with letters from family members and friends, officers and their wives sometimes received magazines and catalogs. Alice Grierson made her stay at Fort Concho more tolerable by ordering merchandise from the Altman's and Doyle catalogs.

Some posts had their own newspapers, ranging from the hand-written "Little Joker" at Fort Belknap, which was passed from person to person, to Fort Richardson's 1869 "The Flea," which included advertisements for Jacksboro merchants: J.L. Oldham's store advertised dry goods, groceries, boots, hats, hardware, cutlery, woodware, tinware, "Yankee notions," hosiery, gloves, and "a General Assortment of Goods suited to the necessities of Frontier Life."

Life on the primitive frontier was a rude shock for army wives who had been accustomed to relative comfort. But for the most part they faced their trials with fortitude and good will, attempting to create a happy, safe home for their families. As she departed Ringgold Barracks in the 1850s after coping with hot wind, dust storms, red ants, muddy drinking water and spoiled meat, Teresa Viélé wrote that her stay ended "with as much pain as pleasure. I left behind me warm hearts, and brought with me sweet memories, and new and enlarged views of life as it really is." ☆

*Mary G. Ramos* is editor emerita of the Texas Almanac.

### For Further Reading:

*The Colonel's Lady on the Western Frontier: The Correspondence of Alice Kirk Grierson,* edited by Shirley A. Leckie; University of Nebraska Press, Lincoln, 1989.

*The Dancing Was Lively: Fort Concho, Texas: A Social History, 1867-1882* by Bill Green; Fort Concho Sketches Publishing Co., San Angelo, 1974.

*Fort McKavett: A Texas Frontier Post* by Jerry M. Sullivan; West Texas Museum Association, Texas Tech University, Lubbock, 1981.

*Fort Phantom Hill: Outpost on the Clear Fork* by H. Allen Anderson; Museum Journal, Vol. XVI, 1976, West Texas Museum Association, Texas Tech University, Lubbock.

*If These Walls Could Speak: Historic Forts of Texas* by Robert M. Utley, paintings by J.U. Salvant; University of Texas Press, Austin, 1985.

*The News from Brownsville: Helen Chapman's Letters from the Texas Military Frontier, 1848-1852* edited by Caleb Coker; published for Barker Texas History Center by the Texas State Historical Association, Austin, 1992.

*Sentinel of the Southern Plains: Fort Richardson and the Northwest Texas Frontier, 1866-1878* by Allen Lee Hamilton; Texas Christian University Press, Fort Worth, 1988.

*Soldiers, Sutlers, and Settlers: Garrison Life on the Texas Frontier* by Robert Wooster; Texas A&M University Press, College Station, 1987.

*A Texas Frontier: The Clear Fork Country and Fort Griffin, 1849-1887* by Ty Cashion; University of Oklahoma Press, Norman, 1996.

# Camp Cooper, Fort Belknap and the Indian Reservations
## By Mary G. Ramos

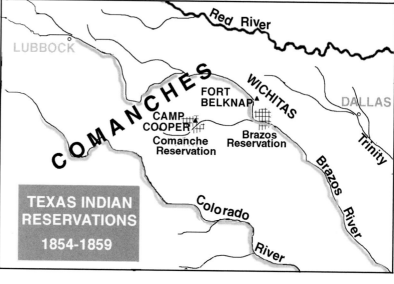

Conflict was inevitable as land-hungry settlers, lured by the state's promises of cheap land, began pushing onto the Texas plains shortly after Texas was annexed to the United States in 1845. The push became a tidal wave of "nesters" after the end of the Mexican War in 1848.

But the plains on which the new-comers intended to live were not empty. They were occupied by ear-lier immigrants from the north: Comanches, Wichitas, Tawakonis, Ana-darkos, Caddos and others. Most Plains Indians were nomadic; free access to the land was basic to their cul-ture. They had no understanding of the concept of indi-vidual ownership of land, which was the very dream that had drawn the white newcomers to the area.

In the early 1850s, the meager number of U.S. Army troops assigned to Texas could not adequately defend the state's 1,200-mile-long frontier against Indian raids and aggression. And the Treaty of Guadalupe Hidalgo that marked the end of the Mexican War greatly increased those troops' responsibilities by providing that the U.S. Army also defend northern Mexico from marauding bands of Plains Indians.

Attempting to defuse the culture clash between set-tlers and Indians, the federal government negotiated treaties with various Plains Indian tribes. It also appointed Indian agents to handle problems between Indians and settlers and to dole out regular consign-ments of beef, blankets and other goods to their charges. Despite these efforts, relations between the Indians and whites continued to be punctuated by violence.

## The Reservation Experiment

On Feb. 6, 1854, the Texas Legislature authorized the establishment of two Indian reservations, each four square leagues of land (18,576 acres) in size, in west-central Texas. The Comanche Indian Reservation was established on the Clear Fork of the Brazos in Throck-morton County about 25 miles north of present-day Albany. The Brazos Indian Reservation, for the Caddos, Wacos and other, more sedentary, tribes, was located 12 miles south of Fort Belknap, also on the Brazos River.

Indian agents persuaded about 2,000 Indians to move onto the Brazos Reservation, to be monitored by troops from Fort Belknap. Nearly 450 Comanches warily moved onto the Comanche Reservation.

To keep watch on the Comanches, Camp Cooper was established in January 1856 by Lt. Col. Albert Sid-ney Johnston. Cooper became the headquarters for four companies of the famed 2nd U.S. Cavalry under the command of Lt. Col. Robert E. Lee. Lee served at Camp Cooper for about 19 months, though he was often absent, serving in courts-martial at other posts.

Camp Cooper was beset by severe weather, wolves, rattlesnakes, irregular supply trains and plagues of grasshoppers.

## Doomed to Fail

The reservation experiment limped along for several years, but it was doomed to fail. The reservation dwell-ers attempted to farm, but because of the arid conditions, they were unable to raise enough crops to feed them-selves.

Indians living off the reservations continued to raid white settlements. Many settlers blamed all Indian raids on reservation Indians and retaliated accordingly.

Fearing for the Indians' lives, Maj. Robert S. Neigh-bors, Indian agent for the Comanches, finally, and with great sadness, recommended abandoning the two reser-vations and moving the Indians to Indian Territory (now Oklahoma). On Sept. 1, 1859, Major Neighbors deliv-ered the former residents of both reservations to the Wichita Indian agency in the Washita Valley.

Camp Cooper's usefulness came to an end by the start of the Civil War, and the post was officially aban-doned on Feb. 21, 1861. Union forces also left Belknap in early 1861, and during the Civil War, it was occupied occasionally by the Frontier regiment. Briefly reoccu-pied by the 6th U.S. Cavalry in April 1867, Belknap was shut down five months later. ☆

*Mary G. Ramos is editor emerita of the Texas Almanac.*

# Fort Anahuac and the Texas Revolution

## By Bryan Woolley

*I*n November 1830, Colonel Juan Davis Bradburn, a Kentuckian serving in the army of Mexico, chose a bluff overlooking the mouth of the Trinity River as the site of a new town and a fort. The place was to be called Anahuac, after the ancient home of the Aztecs. It was one of six outposts that the Mexican government planned to build at strategic entries into Texas. The site that Bradburn chose was just across Galveston Bay from the plain where the Battle of San Jacinto would be fought in April 1836.

The six forts and their garrisons were designed to enforce the Law of April 6, 1830 — passed only seven months before Colonel Bradburn arrived on his bluff — which was as repugnant to some of the Anglo colonists of Texas as England's Stamp Act had been to their forebears on the eve of the American Revolution. And it would have much the same effect.

In 1832, Texian* anger at Colonel Bradburn's efforts to enforce the law would boil into an armed conflict that many consider the opening skirmishes of the Texas Revolution. One of the principal instigators of the conflict was a young lawyer recently arrived from Alabama named William Barret Travis, who four years later would die as Texian commander of the Alamo.

## Unearthing the Ruins

Until recently, the remains of Fort Anahuac, where much of this Texian version of the Boston Tea Party occurred, had been almost lost to history. Some residents of Chambers County knew approximately where the fort had been, but nearly all vestiges of it had disappeared. During the past few years, however, systematic archaeological work by the Texas Historical Commission and a private firm hired by Chambers County has uncovered the foundations and other remains of the old post. The county now has ambitious hopes to preserve the things that have been found and to develop a

*Texian was used in pre-Republic days and during the Republic of Texas. After annexation, Texan became more common. The Texas Almanac referred to Texians as late as 1868.

Fort Anahuac in Chambers County was built in 1830 by the Mexican government when Texas was considered part of Mexico. During the last few years, the old fort's walls and many artifacts have been uncovered. Photo courtesy of Hicks & Company.

museum and historical park around them. This would allow tiny Anahuac to join the Alamo, Goliad and Gonzales among the shrines of Texas independence.

Among the intents of the Law of April 6, 1830, which Colonel Bradburn had come to the Texas coast to enforce — and they were several — were to increase the Mexican military presence in Texas, prohibit the further importation of slaves into Texas, collect duties on imports into the Anglo colonies, void colonization contracts that had not yet been fulfilled, and (most onerous of all from the Texian point of view) curtail the flow of immigrants into Texas from the United States, many of whom were coming illegally. Fearing the presence of so many rambunctious Americans within its national borders, the Mexican government hoped to populate its vast, nearly empty northern territory with Mexicans and Europeans instead.

Bradburn also was ordered to inspect land titles (the illegals among the Texian settlers had none) and issue licenses to lawyers (which an amazing number of the Texians claimed to be).

Upon his arrival, the colonel and his soldiers built a temporary wooden fort near the site of the present Chambers County courthouse. It comprised a barracks, a guardhouse and quarters for Bradburn. Heavy rains prevented immediate construction of the permanent fort, so Bradburn's soldiers spent their time digging clay for the future manufacture of bricks. Construction of the permanent post finally began in March 1831.

## Bradburn's Poor Start

From the beginning, the colonel and the Texians didn't get along. For the past decade, the larger Mexican nation had been preoccupied with its own revolution, political turmoil and civil war and had ignored the Anglo settlers on its far-off northern frontier. The Americans had become accustomed to the absence of Mexican governmental authority and enjoyed their freedom from it. Now, suddenly, it seemed that the government had come to apply a despotic boot to the Texians' necks.

The Texians were quick to take umbrage at any number of real, imagined and fictitious offenses committed by Bradburn and his soldiers.

Although Bradburn apparently was trying only to fulfill the duties his government required of him, his public-relations skills were disastrous. Almost immediately after his arrival, he questioned the right of the land commissioner, who had been appointed by the state, to issue titles to some settlers who the colonel believed to be mere squatters.

Ship captains objected to Bradburn's insistence that all ships about to enter Galveston Bay had to make their way to Anahuac first for customs inspection. Anahuac was out of the way of the main shipping lanes, and the waters that had to be navigated to reach it were treacherous. Coastal merchants resented the very existence of the tariffs, which they had never had to pay before. Also, Bradburn demanded to see the licenses of all lawyers, since there were so many men in Texas who claimed to be lawyers who really were not.

## Arrests and a Mysterious Man

But the spark that ignited the settlers' discontent into armed rebellion was Bradburn's arrest and imprisonment of Patrick Jack, William Travis' law partner.

Jack, a firebrand much like Travis, helped organize a local vigilante group and was elected its captain. Ostensibly, the purpose of this irregular force was to defend the settlement against Indians, but its real purpose, its members acknowledged privately, was to oppose the Mexicans. Since under the law only Bradburn had the authority to organize a militia, he arrested Jack, whose imprisonment inspired such fury among the settlers that Bradburn eventually had to release him. Jack's supporters welcomed him back with a public ceremony that ridiculed Bradburn.

*William Barret Travis was one of the instigators of the revolt against the Law of April 6, 1830, after his law partner, Patrick Jack, was arrested. Texas State Archives photo.*

Travis launched a campaign to further undermine the colonel's authority. When a few escaped slaves from Louisiana showed up in Anahuac, Bradburn declared them free men and enlisted them as soldiers in his garrison. This infuriated local slave owners. (Slavery was illegal in Mexico, but under Stephen Austin's agreement with an earlier government, Americans had been permitted to bring their slaves into Texas as "indentured servants.") About the same time, eight American mutineers from a New Orleans ship were captured by Mexican soldiers and imprisoned at Anahuac. Travis wrote inflammatory letters to the New Orleans newspapers protesting both these actions.

One night a mysterious, tall man, his face hidden in a cloak, slipped a letter to one of Bradburn's soldiers, warning the colonel that 100 Louisianans were marching toward Anahuac to retrieve the escaped slaves. Bradburn sent out his cavalry to scour the countryside for them, but the soldiers found no one. When the colonel realized the letter was a hoax, he suspected Travis to be the man in the cloak. He arrested and imprisoned him. When Patrick Jack protested his friend's arrest, Bradburn imprisoned him, too.

## Texian Opposition Grows

The conflict between Bradburn and the Texians began to resemble an Errol Flynn movie, full of alarms and excursions: mobs marched, Texians from other communities headed to Anahuac to join the fray, Bradburn made more arrests, women and children fled. Eventually the Fort Anahuac guardhouse held 15 prisoners.

Meanwhile, the Texians ambushed the 19 cavalrymen that Bradburn had sent out to find them and made prisoners of them all. In negotiation, the Texians and Bradburn agreed that the soldiers would be released in exchange for Bradburn's prisoners. The Texians kept their end of the bargain; Bradburn did not.

A crowd of outraged settlers gathered on Turtle Bayou, not far from Fort Anahuac, to form an army to rescue their imprisoned friends. The rebels also drew up a set of resolutions, detailing their grievances against Bradburn and aligning themselves with Antonio Lopez de Santa Anna's Federalist faction in its struggle against the despotic Centralist government of Mexican President Bustamante, thus giving their actions a larger-than-local political focus. (Bradburn, of course, was an officer of the Centralist government.)

While the Texians were writing their resolutions, Bradburn strengthened his fort and sent a messenger to his commanding officer, Colonel Jose de las Piedras, at Nacogdoches to ask for help. When Piedras came riding to the rescue, a large rebel force intercepted him and his men. Fearing that he did not have a force strong enough to defeat the Texians, he capitulated to their demand and agreed to release Bradburn's prisoners and remove the colonel from his command.

On July 1, 1832, Bradburn turned over his troops to his second-in-command, Lt. Juan Cortina, and, fearing for his life, fled into the woods, hiding in creek bottoms and corncribs until he reached New Orleans. Americans who had sided with him during the disturbances — called "Tories" by the rebels — also were driven out of Anahuac, some of them tarred and feathered. By July 23, all Mexican troops had evacuated, and Fort Anahuac was vacant. Soon afterward, someone set fire to it and destroyed its wooden parts.

Three years later, in June 1835, the Mexican government (now run by Santa Anna) again sent troops to Anahuac to attempt to rebuild the fort and collect tariffs. But a Texian force led by Travis attacked from the sea and on June 30, 1835, before any fighting had begun in earnest, the Mexican force surrendered. The Mexican government demanded that the Texians give up Travis for a military trial, but they, of course, refused.

By the end of the year, the Texas Revolution was in full flame. After Texas won its independence in 1836, local residents hauled away most of the bricks from the Fort Anahuac ruins and put them to other purposes. Eventually, even the fort's foundations were buried and forgotten.

## The Excavation

In 1968, several years after the site had become part of a Chambers County park, a group of amateur archaeologists did a haphazard excavation at the site, but no serious archaeology was attempted until 2001, when the county government asked the Texas Historical Commission to survey the park with a magnetometer to try to ascertain the fort's exact location. The magnetometer found the foundations of about half the fort — enough to determine that it had been diamond-shaped — and one of its bastions.

Texas Historical Commission archaeologist James Bruseth recommended to the Chambers County commissioners court that it conduct archaeological testing to determine how much of the fort could be found and preserved. He also recommended the construction of an interpretive museum and, perhaps, a replica of the original fort. The county engaged Hicks & Company, an Austin environmental consulting firm, to test the site.

"Our test excavation confirmed what everybody suspected the configuration of the fort was," says Rachel Feit, the Hicks archaeologist who directed the work. "We found a number of construction techniques."

"One wall in the plaza was constructed of brick rubble. We don't know what it was, whether it was a corral or a hospital. We found a series of brick-lined aqueducts or drains that would have been built below the surface of the plaza. Recent excavations have revealed that these features were designed to drain water away from the fort, rather than catch water within it."

Since souvenir hunters had picked over the site for so many years, the archaeologists initially found few artifacts to offer clues to the functions of the fort's various structures. However, the most recent excavations did reveal a well-preserved outbuilding feature with an intact floor surface.

Artifacts picked up from this surface included a large number of cut nails, ceramics, a gun flint and a Mexican uniform button. The building is thought to have had wood-frame walls and featured a front porch facing the water. Archeologists believe that it might be a customs house or the jail.

Beanie Rowland, chair of the Chambers County Historical Commission, says the county is trying to raise grant money for further archaeology and to draw up architectural plans for the proposed museum.

"Anahuac was important to Texas history," she says. "We want to show schoolchildren where the first shot of the Texas Revolution was fired. We want them to be able to imagine, looking out over the bluff, that first customs house on the Trinity River. We want to let them relive our history." ☆

*Bryan Woolley is a senior writer for The Dallas Morning News and a novelist.*

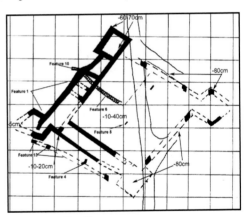

*A series of brick-lined aqueducts or drains have been uncovered at Fort Anahuac (above). They would have been built below the surface of the plaza and were designed to drain water away from the fort. Below is a plan map of the fort's walls, which has evolved during excavation. Photos courtesy of Hicks & Company.*

### For Further Reading:

*"Fort Anahuac: Birthplace of the Texas Revolution"* by Carroll A. Lewis Jr.; Texana, Vol. VI, No. 1, Texian Press, Waco, 1968.

*The New Handbook of Texas,* Ron Tyler, editor in chief; Texas State Historical Association, Austin, 1996.

*Juan Davis Bradburn: A Reappraisal of the Mexican Commander of Anahuac* by Margaret Swett Henson; Texas A&M University Press, College Station, 1982.

*The Texas Almanac 1857–1873: A Compendium of Texas History* compiled by James M. Day; Texian Press, Waco, 1967.

*Fort Anahuac: Archeological Testing at a Mexican Era Fort in Chambers County Texas* by Rachel Feit and John W. Clark; Hicks & Company, Austin, 2003.

# A Brief Sketch of Texas History

*This brief, two-part sketch of Texas' past, from prehistoric times to 1980, is based on "A Concise History of Texas" by former Texas Almanac editor Mike Kingston. Mr. Kingston's history was published in the 1986–87 sesquicentennial edition of the Texas Almanac. Robert Plocheck, associate editor of the Texas Almanac, edited and expanded Mr. Kingston's history.*

## Prehistory to Annexation

### Prehistoric Texas

Early Texans are believed to have been descendants of Asian groups that migrated across the Bering Strait during the Ice Ages of the past 50,000 years.

At intermittent periods, enough water accumulated in massive glaciers worldwide to lower the sea level several hundred feet. During these periods, the Bering Strait became a 1,300-mile-wide land bridge between North America and Asia.

These early adventurers worked their way southward for thousands of years, eventually getting as far as Tierra del Fuego in South America about 10,000 years ago.

Biologically they were completely modern homo sapiens. No evidence has been found to indicate that any evolutionary change occurred in the New World.

Four basic stages reflecting cultural advancement of early inhabitants are used by archaeologists in classifying evidence. These stages are the Paleo-Indian (20,000 to 7,000 years ago), Archaic (7,000 years ago to about the time of Christ), Woodland (time of Christ to 800–1,000 years ago), and Neo-American or Late Prehistoric (800–1,000 years ago until European contact).

Not all early people advanced through all these stages in Texas. Much cultural change occurred in adaptation to changes in climate. The Caddo tribes of East Texas, for example, reached the Neo-American stage before the Spanish and French explorers made contact in the 1500s and 1600s.

Others, such as the Karankawas of the Gulf Coast, advanced no further than the Archaic stage of civilization at the same time. Still others advanced and then regressed in the face of a changing climate.

The earliest confirmed evidence indicates that humans were in Texas between 10,000 and 13,000 years ago.

**Paleo-Indians** were successful big-game hunters. Artifacts from this period are found across the state but not in great number, indicating that they were a small, nomadic population.

As Texas' climate changed at the end of the Ice Age about 7,000 years ago, inhabitants adapted. Apparently the state experienced an extended period of warming and drying, and the population during the **Archaic** period increased.

These Texans began to harvest fruits and nuts and, to exploit rivers for food, as indicated by the fresh-water mussel shells in ancient garbage heaps.

The **Woodland** stage is distinguished by the development of settled societies, with crops and local wild plants providing much of their diet. The bow and arrow came into use, and the first pottery is associated with this period.

Pre-Caddoan tribes in East Texas had formed villages and were building distinctive mounds for burials

*An ancient pictograph named Speaking Rock is engraved in the rocks at Hueco Tanks State Park near El Paso. File photo.*

and for ritual.

The **Neo-American** period is best exemplified by the highly civilized Caddoes, who had a complex culture with well-defined social stratification. They were fully agricultural and participated in trade over a wide area of North America.

### The Spanish Explorations

Spain's exploration of North America was one of the first acts of a vigorous nation that was emerging from centuries of campaigns to oust the Islamic Moors from the Iberian Peninsula.

In early **1492**, the Spanish forces retook the province of Granada, completing the *reconquista* or reconquest. Later in the year, the Catholic royals of the united country, Ferdinand and Isabella, took a major stride toward shaping world history by commissioning Christopher Columbus for the voyage that was to bring Europeans to America.

As early as **1519, Capt. Alonso Alvarez de Pineda**, in the service of the governor of Jamaica, mapped the coast of Texas.

The **first recorded exploration of today's Texas** was made in the 1530s by **Alvar Núñez Cabeza de Vaca**, along with two other Spaniards and a Moorish slave named Estevanico. They were members of an expedition commanded by Panfilo de Narváez that left Cuba in 1528 to explore what is now the southeastern United States. Ill-fated from the beginning, many members of the expedition lost their lives, and others, including Cabeza de Vaca, were shipwrecked on the Texas coast. Eventually the band wandered into Mexico in 1536.

*Horse armor and stirrups offer a glimpse of the Spanish explorers in Texas. These artifacts reside at the Bob Bullock Texas State History Museum in Austin. File photo.*

In **1540**, Francisco Vázquez de Coronado was commissioned to lead an exploration of the American Southwest. The quest took him to the land of the Pueblo Indians in what is now New Mexico. Native Americans, who had learned it was best to keep Europeans away from their homes, would suggest vast riches could be found in other areas. So Coronado pursued a fruitless search for gold and silver across the **High Plains of Texas**, Oklahoma and Kansas.

While Coronado was investigating Texas from the west, Luis de Moscoso Alvarado approached from the east. He assumed leadership of Hernando de Soto's expedition when the commander died on the banks of the Mississippi River. In **1542,** Moscoso's group ventured as far west as **Central Texas** before returning to the Mississippi.

Forty years passed after the Coronado and Moscoso expeditions before Fray Agustín Rodríguez, a Franciscan missionary, and Francisco Sánchez Chamuscado, a soldier, led an expedition into Texas and New Mexico.

Following the Río Conchos in Mexico to its confluence with the Rio Grande near present-day **Presidio** and then turning northwestward up the great river's valley, the explorers passed through the El Paso area in **1581.**

Juan de Oñate was granted the right to develop this area populated by Pueblo Indians in 1598. He blazed a trail across the desert from Santa Barbara, Chihuahua, to intersect the Rio Grande at the Pass of the North. For the next 200 years, this was the supply route from the interior of Mexico that served the northern colonies.

Texas was attractive to the Spanish in the 1600s. Small expeditions found trade possibilities, and missionaries ventured into the territory. Frays Juan de Salas and Diego López responded to a request by the Jumano Indians for religious instruction in **1629**, and for a brief

time priests lived with the Indians near present-day **San Angelo**.

The first permanent settlement in Texas was established in **1681–82** after New Mexico's Indians rebelled and drove Spanish settlers southward. The colonists retreated to the **El Paso** area, where the missions of Corpus Christi de la Isleta and Nuestra Señora del Socorro — each named for a community in New Mexico — were established. Ysleta pueblo originally was located on the south side of the Rio Grande, but as the river changed course, it ended up on the north bank. Now part of El Paso, the community is considered the oldest European settlement in Texas.

## French Exploration

In 1682, **René Robert Cavelier, Sieur de La Salle**, explored the Mississippi River to its mouth at the Gulf of Mexico. La Salle claimed the vast territory drained by the river for France.

Two years later, La Salle returned to the New World with four ships and enough colonists to establish his country's claim. Guided by erroneous maps, this second expedition overshot the mouth of the Mississippi by 400 miles and ended up on the Texas coast. Though short of supplies because of the loss of two of the ships, the French colonists established Fort Saint Louis on Garcitas Creek several miles inland from Lavaca Bay.

In 1687, La Salle and a group of soldiers began an overland trip to find French outposts on the Mississippi. Somewhere west of the Trinity River, the explorer was murdered by some of his men. His grave has never been found. (A more detailed account of La Salle's expedition can be found in the *Texas Almanac 1998–1999* and on the Texas Almanac Web site.)

In 1689, Spanish authorities sent **Capt. Alonso de León**, governor of Coahuila (which at various times included Texas in its jurisdiction), into Texas to confront the French. He headed eastward from present-day **Eagle Pass** and found the tattered remnants of Fort Saint Louis.

Indians had destroyed the settlement and killed many colonists. León continued tracking survivors of the ill-fated colony into East Texas.

## Spanish Rule

Father **Damián Massanet** accompanied León on this journey. The priest was fascinated with tales about the "Tejas" Indians of the region.

**Tejas** meant *friendly,* but at the time the term was considered a tribal name. Actually these Indians were members of the Caddo Confederacy that controlled parts of four present states: Texas, Louisiana, Arkansas and Oklahoma.

The Caddo religion acknowledged one supreme god, and when a Tejas chief asked Father Massanet to stay

and instruct his people in his faith, the Spaniards promised to return and establish a mission.

The pledge was redeemed in **1690** when the mission San Francisco de los Tejas was founded near present-day Weches in Houston County.

Twin disasters struck this missionary effort. Spanish government officials quickly lost interest when the French threat at colonization diminished. And as was the case with many New World Indians who had no resistance to European diseases, the Tejas soon were felled by an epidemic. The Indians blamed the new religion and resisted conversion. The mission languished, and it was hard to supply from other Spanish outposts in northern Mexico. In 1693, the Spanish officials closed the mission effort in **East Texas**. *(See page 517 for an account of early Spanish missionaries in Texas.)*

Although Spain had not made a determined effort to settle Texas, great changes were coming to the territory. Spain introduced horses into the Southwest. By the late 1600s, Comanches were using the horses to expand their range southward across the plains, displacing the Apaches.

In the **1720s**, the **Apaches** moved onto the lower Texas Plains, usurping the traditional hunting grounds of the Jumanos and others. The nomadic Coahuiltecan bands were particularly hard hit.

In 1709, Fray Antonio de San Buenaventura y Olivares had made an initial request to establish a mission at San Pedro Springs (today's San Antonio) to minister to the Coahuiltecans. The request was denied. However, new fears of French movement into East Texas changed that.

Another Franciscan, **Father Francisco Hidalgo**, who had earlier served at the missions in East Texas, returned to them when he and **Father Antonio Margil de Jesús** accompanied **Capt. Diego Ramón** on an expedition to the area in 1716. In that year, the mission of San Francisco de los Neches was established near the site of the old San Francisco de los Tejas mission. Nuestra Señora de Guadalupe was located at the present-day site of Nacogdoches, and Nuestra Señora de los Dolores was placed near present-day San Augustine.

The East Texas missions did little better on the second try, and supplying the frontier missions remained difficult. It became apparent that a way station between northern Mexico and East Texas was needed.

In **1718,** Spanish officials consented to Fray Olivares' request to found a mission at San Pedro Springs. That mission, called **San Antonio de Valero**, was later to be known as the **Alamo**. Because the Indians of the region often did not get along with each other, other missions were established to serve each group.

These missions flourished and each became an early ranching center. But the large herds of cattle and horses attracted trouble. The San Antonio missions began to face the wrath of the Apaches. The mission system, which attempted to convert the Indians to Christianity and to "civilize" them, was partially successful in subduing minor tribes but not larger tribes like the Apaches.

The Spanish realized that more stable colonization efforts must be made. Indians from Mexico, such as the Tlascalans who fought with Cortés against the Aztecs, were brought into Texas to serve as examples of "good" Indians for the wayward natives.

In **1731**, Spanish colonists from the **Canary Islands** were brought to Texas and founded the **Villa of San Fernando de Béxar**, the first civil jurisdiction in the province and today's **San Antonio.**

In the late 1730s, Spanish officials became concerned over the vulnerability of the large area between the Sierra Madre Oriental and the Gulf Coast in northern Mexico. The area was unsettled, a haven for runaway Indian slaves and marauders, and it was a wide-open pathway for the English or French from the Gulf to the rich silver mines in Durango.

For seven years the search for the right colonizer went on before **José de Escandón** was selected in 1746. A professional military man and successful administrator, Escandón earned a high reputation by subduing Indians in central Mexico. On receiving the assignment, he launched a broad land survey of the area running from the mountains to the Gulf and from the Río Pánuco in Tamaulipas, Mexico, to the Nueces River in Texas.

In 1747, he began placing colonists in settlements throughout the area. **Tomás Sánchez** received a land grant on the Rio Grande in **1755** from which **Laredo** developed. And other small Texas communities along the river sprang up as a result of Escandón's well-executed plan. Many old Hispanic families in Texas hold title of their land based on grants in this period.

In the following decades, a few other Spanish colonists settled around the old missions and frontier forts. **Antonio Gil Ybarbo** led one group that settled **Nacogdoches** in the **1760s and 1770s.**

## The Demise of Spain

Spain's final 60 years of control of the province of Texas were marked with a few successes and a multitude of failures, all of which could be attributed to a breakdown in the administrative system.

Charles III, the fourth of the Bourbon line of kings, took the Spanish throne in 1759. He launched a series of reforms in the New World. The king's choice of administrators was excellent. In 1765, José de Gálvez was dispatched to New Spain (an area that then included all of modern Mexico and much of today's American West) with instructions to improve both the economy and the defense.

Gálvez initially toured parts of the vast region, gaining first-hand insight into the practical problems of the colony. There were many that could be traced to Spain's basic concepts of colonial government. Texas, in particular, suffered from the mercantilist economic system that attempted to funnel all colonial trade through ports in Mexico.

But administrative reforms by Gálvez and his nephew, Bernardo Gálvez, namesake of Galveston, were to be followed by ill-advised policies by successors.

Problems with the Comanches, Apaches and "Norteños," as the Spanish called some tribes, continued to plague the province, too.

About the same time, Spain undertook the administration of Louisiana Territory. One of the terms of the cession by France was that the region would enjoy certain trading privileges denied to other Spanish dependencies. So although Texas and Louisiana were neighbors, trade between the two provinces was banned.

The crown further complicated matters by placing the administration of Louisiana under authorities in Cuba, while Texas remained under the authorities in

Mexico City.

The death of Charles III in 1788 and the beginning of the French Revolution a year later weakened Spain's hold on the New World dominions. Charles IV was not as good a sovereign as his predecessor, and his choice of ministers was poor. The quality of frontier administrators declined, and relations with Indians soured further.

Charles IV's major blunder, however, was to side with French royalty during the revolution, earning Spain the enmity of Napoleon Bonaparte. Spain also allied with England in an effort to thwart Napoleon, and in this losing cause, the Spanish were forced to cede Louisiana back to France.

In 1803, Napoleon broke a promise to retain the territory and sold it to the United States. Spain's problems in the New World thereby took on an altogether different dimension. Now, Anglo-Americans cast longing eyes on the vast undeveloped territory of Texas.

With certain exceptions for royalists who left the American colonies during the revolution, Spain had maintained a strict prohibition against Anglo or other non-Spanish settlers in their New World territories. But they were unprepared to police the eastern border of Texas after removing the presidios in the 1760s. What had been a provincial line became virtually overnight an international boundary, and an ill-defined one at that.

## American Immigrants

Around 1800, Anglo-Americans began to probe the Spanish frontier. Some settled in East Texas and others crossed the Red River and were tolerated by authorities.

Others, however, were thought to have nefarious designs. Philip Nolan was the first of the American filibusters to test Spanish resolve. Several times he entered Texas to capture wild horses to sell in the United States.

But in 1801, the Spanish perceived an attempted insurrection by Nolan and his followers. He was killed in a battle near present-day Waco, and his company was taken captive to work in the mines in northern Mexico.

Spanish officials were beginning to realize that the economic potential of Texas must be developed if the Anglo-Americans were to be neutralized. But Spain's centuries-long role in the history of Texas was almost over.

Resistance to Spanish rule had developed in the New World colonies. Liberal ideas from the American and French revolutions had grown popular, despite the crown's attempts to prevent their dissemination.

In Spain, three sovereigns — Charles IV, Napoleon's brother Joseph Bonaparte, and Ferdinand VII — claimed the throne, often issuing different edicts simultaneously. Since the time of Philip II, Spain had been a tightly centralized monarchy with the crown making most decisions. Now, chaos reigned in the colonies.

As Spain's grip on the New World slipped between 1790 and 1820, Texas was almost forgotten, an internal province of little importance. Colonization was ignored; the Spanish government had larger problems in Europe and in Mexico.

Spain's mercantile economic policy penalized colonists in the area, charging them high prices for trade goods and paying low prices for products sent to markets in the interior of New Spain. As a result, settlers from central Mexico had no incentives to come to Texas.

Indeed, men of ambition in the province often prospered by turning to illegal trade with Louisiana or to smuggling. On the positive side, however, Indians of the province had been mollified through annual gifts and by developing a dependence on Spain for trade goods.

Ranching flourished. In 1795, a census found 69 families living on 45 ranches in the San Antonio area. A census in 1803 indicated that there were 100,000 head of cattle in Texas. But aside from a few additional families in Nacogdoches and La Bahía (near present-day Goliad), the province was thinly populated.

The largest group of early immigrants from the United States was not Anglo, but Indian.

As early as 1818, Cherokees of the southeastern United States came to Texas, settling north of Nacogdoches on lands between the Trinity and Sabine rivers. The Cherokees had been among the first U.S. Indians to accept the federal government's offers of resettlement. As American pioneers entered the newly acquired lands of Georgia, Alabama and other areas of the Southeast, the Indians were systematically removed, through legal means or otherwise.

Some of the displaced groups settled on land provided in Arkansas Territory, but others, such as the Cherokees, came to Texas. These Cherokees were among the "Five Civilized Tribes" that had adopted agriculture and many Anglo customs in an unsuccessful attempt to get along with their new neighbors. Alabama and Coushatta tribes had exercised squatters' rights in present Sabine County in the early 1800s, and soon after the Cherokees arrived, groups of Shawnee, Delaware and Kickapoo Indians came from the United States.

A second wave of Anglo immigrants began to arrive in Texas, larger than the first and of a different character. These Anglos were not so interested in agricultural opportunities as in other schemes to quickly recoup their fortunes.

Spain recognized the danger represented by the unregulated colonization by Americans. The Spanish Cortes' colonization law of 1813 attempted to build a buffer between the eastern frontier and northern Mexico. Special permission was required for Americans to settle within 52 miles of the international boundary, although this prohibition often was ignored.

As initially envisioned, Americans would be allowed to settle the interior of Texas. Colonists from Europe and Mexico would be placed along the eastern frontier to limit contact between the Americans and the United States. Spanish officials felt that the Americans already in Texas illegally would be stable if given a stake in the province through land ownership.

Moses Austin, a former Spanish subject in the vast Louisiana Territory, applied for the first empresario grant from the Spanish government. With the intercession of Baron de Bastrop, a friend of Austin's from Missouri Territory, the request was approved in January 1821.

Austin agreed to settle 300 families on land bounded by the Brazos and Colorado rivers on the east and west, by El Camino Real (the old military road running from San Antonio to Nacogdoches) on the north and by the Gulf Coast.

But Austin died in June 1821, leaving the work to his son, Stephen F. Austin. Problems began as soon as the first authorized colonists arrived in Texas the follow-

ing December when it was learned that Mexico had gained independence from Spain.

## Mexico, 1821–1836

Mexico's war for independence, 1810–1821, was savage and bloody in the interior provinces, and Texas suffered as well.

In early 1812, Mexican revolutionary José Bernardo Gutiérrez de Lara traveled to Natchitoches, La., where, with the help of U.S. agents, an expedition was organized. **Augustus W. Magee**, a West Point graduate, commanded the troop, which entered Texas in August 1812. This "Republican Army of the North" easily took Nacogdoches, where it gathered recruits.

After withstanding a siege at La Bahía, the army took San Antonio and proclaimed the First Republic of Texas in April 1813. A few months later, the republican forces were bloodily subdued at the Battle of Medina River.

Royalist Gen. Joaquín de Arredondo executed a staggering number of more than 300 republicans, including some Americans, at San Antonio, and a young lieutenant, **Antonio López de Santa Anna**, was recognized for valor under fire.

When the war finally ended in Mexico in 1821, little more had been achieved than separation from Spain.

Sensing that liberal reforms in Spain would reduce the authority of royalists in the New World, Mexican conservatives had led the revolt against the mother country. They also achieved early victories in the debate over the form of government the newly independent Mexico should adopt.

An independent Mexico was torn between advocates of centralist and federalist forms of government.

The former royalists won the opening debates, settling Emperor Agustín de Iturbide on the new Mexican throne. But he was overthrown and the Constitution of 1824, a federalist document, was adopted.

The Mexican election of 1828 was a turning point in the history of the country when the legally elected administration of Manuel Gómez Pedraza was overthrown by supporters of Vicente Guerrero, who in turn was ousted by his own vice president Anastasio Bustamante. Mexico's most chaotic political period followed. Between 1833 and 1855, the Mexican presidency changed hands 36 times.

## Texas, 1821–1833

Mexico's **land policy**, like Spain's, differed from the U.S. approach. Whereas the United States sold land directly to settlers or to speculators who dealt with the pioneers, the Mexicans retained tight control of the property transfer until predetermined agreements for development were fulfilled.

But a 4,428-acre *sitio* — a square league — and a 177-acre *labor* could be obtained for only surveying costs and administrative fees as low as $50. The empresario was rewarded with grants of large tracts of land, but only when he fulfilled his quota of families to be brought to the colonies.

Considering the prices the U.S. government charged, Texas' land was indeed a bargain and a major attraction to those Americans looking for a new start.

More than 25 empresarios were commissioned to settle colonists. Empresarios included **Green DeWitt**

and **Martín de León**, who in 1824 founded the city of Guadalupe Victoria (present-day Victoria).

By 1830, Texas boasted an estimated population of 15,000, with Anglo-Americans outnumbering Hispanics by a margin of four to one.

Stephen F. Austin was easily the most successful empresario. After his initial success, Austin was authorized in 1825 to bring 900 more families to Texas, and in

1831, he and his partner, **Samuel Williams**, received another concession to bring 800 Mexican and European families.

Through Austin's efforts, 1,540 land titles were issued to settlers.

In the early years of colonization, the settlers busied themselves clearing land, planting crops, building homes and fending off Indian attacks. Many were successful

*Stephen F. Austin was responsible for much of the early immigration to Texas. File photo.*

in establishing a subsistence economy.

One weakness of the Mexican colonial policy was that it did not provide the factors for a market economy. Although towns were established, credit, banks and good roads were not provided by the government.

Ports were established at Galveston and Matagorda bays after Mexican independence, but the colonists felt they needed more, particularly one at the mouth of the Brazos. And foreign ships were barred from coastwise trade, which posed a particular hardship since Mexico had few merchant ships.

To settle in Texas, pioneers had to become Mexican citizens and to embrace Roman Catholicism. Most of the Americans were Protestants, if they adhered to any religion, and they were fiercely defensive of the right to **religious freedom** enjoyed in the United States.

Although no more than one-fourth of the Americans ever swore allegiance to the Catholic Church, the requirement was a long-standing irritation.

**Slavery**, too, was a point of contention. Mexico prohibited the introduction of slavery after December 1827. Nevertheless, several efforts were made to evade the government policy. Austin got the state Legislature to recognize labor contracts under which slaves were technically free but bound themselves to their masters for life. Often entire families were covered by a single contract. While many early Anglo colonists were not slaveholders, they were Southerners, and the ownership of slaves was a cultural institution that they supported. The problem was never settled during the colonial period despite the tensions it generated.

Most of the early Anglo-American colonists in Texas intended to fulfill their pledge to become good Mexican citizens. But the political turmoil following the 1828 presidential election raised doubts in the Americans' minds about the ability of Mexico to make representative government function properly.

On a tour of Texas in 1827 and 1828, Gen. Manuel

Mier y Terán noted that the Texans "carried their constitutions in their pockets." And he feared the Americans' desire for more rights and liberties than the government was prepared to offer would lead to rebellion.

Unrest increased in Texas when Gen. Mier y Terán began reinforcing existing garrisons and establishing new ones.

But a major factor in the discontent of Americans came with the **decree of April 6, 1830**, when the Mexican government in essence banned further American immigration into Texas and tried to control slavery. *(For a related account on how Texans opposed this decree at Fort Anahuac, see page 27.)*

Austin protested that the prohibition against American immigration would not stop the flow of Anglos into Texas; it would stop only the stable, prosperous Americans from coming.

Austin's predictions were fulfilled. Illegal immigrants continued to come. By 1836, the estimated number of people in Texas had reached 35,000.

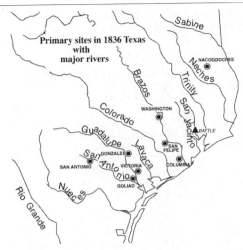

## Prelude to Revolution

In the midst of all the turmoil, Texas was prospering. By 1834, some 7,000 bales of cotton with a value of $315,000 were shipped to New Orleans. In the middle of the decade, Texas exports, including cotton and beaver, otter and deer skins, amounted to $500,000.

Trade ratios were out of balance, however, because $630,000 in manufactured goods were imported. And, there was little currency in Texas. Ninety percent of the business transactions were conducted in barter or credit.

In 1833 and 1834, the **Coahuila y Texas** legislature was diligently trying to respond to the complaints of the Texas colonists. The English language was recognized for official purposes. Religious toleration was approved. The court system was revised, providing Texas with an appellate court and trial by jury.

In Mexico City, however, a different scenario was developing. **Santa Anna** assumed supreme authority in April 1834 and began dismantling the federalist government. Among the most offensive changes dictated by Santa Anna was the reduction of the state militias to one man per each 500 population. The intent was to eliminate possible armed opposition to the emerging centralist government.

But liberals in the state of Zacatecas in central Mexico rebelled. Santa Anna's response was particularly brutal, as he tried to make an example of the rebels. Troops were allowed to sack the state capital after the victory over the insurgents.

Trouble also was brewing closer to the Texans.

In March 1833, the Coahuila y Texas legislature moved the state capital from Saltillo to Monclova. The Monclova legislature in 1834 gave the governor authority to sell 400 sitios — or 1.77 million acres of land — to finance the government and to provide for protection. A year later the lawmakers criticized Santa Anna's reputation on federalism. Seeing a chance to regain lost prestige, Saltillo declared for Santa Anna and set up an opposition government. In the spring of 1835, Santa Anna sent his brother-in-law, Martín Perfecto de Cos, to break up the state government at Monclova.

Texans were appalled by the breakdown in state government, coming on the heels of so many assurances that the political situation was to improve.

Texas politics were polarizing. A "war party" advocated breaking away from Mexico altogether, while a "peace party" urged calm and riding out the political storm. Most of the settlers, however, aligned with neither group.

In January 1835, Santa Anna sent a detachment of soldiers to Anahuac to reinforce the customs office, but duties were being charged irregularly at various ports on the coast. William B. Travis, in an act not supported by all colonists, led a contingent of armed colonists against the Mexican soldiers, who withdrew without a fight.

Although some members of the peace party wrote Mexican Gen. **Martín Perfecto de Cos**, stationed at Matamoros, apologizing for the action, he was not compromising. Cos demanded that the group be arrested and turned over to him. The Texans refused.

The committees of correspondence, organized at the Convention of 1832 (which had asked that Texas be separated from Coahuila), began organizing another meeting. Because the term "convention" aroused visions of revolution in the eyes of Mexican officials, the gathering at Washington-on-the-Brazos in October 1835 was called a "consultation." But with the breakdown of state government and with Santa Anna's repeal of the Constitution of 1824, the American settlers felt well within their rights to provide a new framework with which to govern Texas.

Fresh from brutally putting down the rebellion in Zacatecas, Santa Anna turned his attention to Texas. Gen. Cos was determined to regarrison the state, and the settlers were equally determined to keep soldiers out.

Col. **Domingo de Ugartechea**, headquartered at San Antonio, became concerned about armed rebellion when he heard of the incident at Anahuac. He recalled a six-pound cannon that had been given DeWitt colonists to fight Indians.

Ugartechea ordered Cpl. Casimira de León with five men to Gonzales to retrieve the weapon. No problems were expected, but officials at Gonzales refused to surrender the weapon. When the Mexicans reinforced Cpl. León's men, a call was sent out for volunteers to help the Gonzales officials. Dozens responded.

Oct. 2, 1835, the Texans challenged the Mexicans

with a **"come-and-take-it" flag** over the cannon. After a brief skirmish, the Mexicans withdrew, but the first rounds in the Texas Revolution had been fired.

## Winning Independence

As 1836 opened, Texans felt in control of their destiny and secure in their land and their liberties. The Mexican army had been driven from their soil.

But tragedy loomed. Easy victories over government forces at Anahuac, Nacogdoches, Goliad, Gonzales and San Antonio in the fall of 1835 had given them a false sense of security. That independent mood was their undoing, for no government worthy of the name coordinated the defense of Texas. Consequently, as the Mexican counterattack developed, no one was in charge. Sam Houston was titular commander-in-chief of the Texas forces, but he had little authority.

Some even thought the Mexicans would not try to re-enter Texas. Few Texans counted on the energy and determination of Santa Anna, the dictator of Mexico.

The status of the strongholds along the San Antonio River was of concern to Houston. In mid-January, Houston sent **James Bowie** to San Antonio to determine if the Alamo was defensible. If not, Bowie had orders to destroy it and withdraw the men and artillery to Gonzales and Copano.

On Feb. 8, David Crockett of Tennessee, bringing 12 men with him, arrived to aid the revolutionaries.

On Feb. 12, 1836, Santa Anna's main force crossed the Rio Grande headed for San Antonio. The Mexican battle plan had been debated. But Mexico's national pride was bruised by the series of defeats the nation's army had suffered in 1835, capped by Gen. Cos's ouster from San Antonio in December.

On Feb. 11, the Consultation's "governor of the government" **Henry Smith**, sent **William B. Travis** to San Antonio. Immediately a split in command at the **Alamo** garrison arose. Most were American volunteers who looked to the Houston-appointed Bowie as their leader. Travis had only a handful of Texas army regulars. Bowie and Travis agreed to share the command of 150 men.

Arriving at the Alamo on Feb. 23, Santa Anna left no doubt regarding his attitude toward the defenders. He hoisted a blood-red flag, the traditional Mexican symbol of no quarter, no surrender, no mercy. Travis and Bowie defiantly answered the display with a cannon shot.

Immediately the Mexicans began surrounding the Alamo and bombarding it. Throughout the first night and nights to come, Santa Anna kept up a continual din to destroy the defenders' morale.

On Feb. 24, Bowie became ill and relinquished his share of command to Travis. Although the Mexican bombardment of the Alamo continued, none of the defenders was killed. In fact, they conducted several successful forays outside the fortress to burn buildings that were providing cover for the Mexican gunners and to gather firewood.

Messengers also successfully moved through the Mexican lines at will, and 32 reinforcements from Gonzales made it into the Alamo without a loss on March 1.

Historians disagree over which flag flew over the defenders of the Alamo.

Mexican sources have said that Santa Anna was outraged when he saw flying over the fortress a Mexican tricolor, identical to the ones carried by his troops except with the numbers "1 8 2 4" emblazoned upon it. Some Texas historians have accepted this version because the defenders of the Alamo could not have known that Texas' independence had been declared on March 2. To the knowledge of the Alamo's defenders, the last official position taken by Texas was in support of the Constitution of 1824, which the flag symbolized. But the only flag found after the battle, according to historian Walter Lord, was one flown by the **New Orleans Greys**.

By March 5, Santa Anna had 4,000 men in camp, a force he felt sufficient to subdue the Alamo.

Historians disagree on the date, but the story goes that on March 3 or 5, Travis called his command together and explained the bleak outlook. He then asked those willing to die for freedom to stay and fight; those not willing could try to get through enemy lines to safety. Even the sick Jim Bowie vowed to stay. Only Louis (Moses) Rose, a veteran of Napoleon's retreat from Moscow slipped out of the Alamo that night.

At dawn March 6, Santa Anna's forces attacked. When the fighting stopped between 8:30 and 9 a.m., all the defenders were dead. Only a few women, children and black slaves survived the assault. **Davy Crockett**'s fate is still debated. Mexican officer Enrique de la Peña held that Crockett was captured with a few other defenders and was executed by Santa Anna.

Santa Anna's victory came at the cost of almost one-third his forces killed or wounded. Their deaths in such number set back Santa Anna's timetable. The fall of the Alamo also brutally shook Texans out of their lethargy.

Sam Houston, finally given command of the entire Texas army, left the convention at **Washington-on-the-Brazos** on the day of the fall of the Alamo.

On March 11, he arrived at Gonzales to begin organizing the troops. Two days later, **Susanna Dickinson**, the wife of one of the victims of the Alamo, and two slaves arrived at Houston's position at Gonzales with news of the fall of the San Antonio fortress.

Houston then ordered **James Fannin** to abandon the old presidio **La Bahía** at Goliad and to retreat to Victoria. Fannin had arrived at the fort in late January with more than 400 men. As a former West Pointer, he had a background in military planning, but Fannin had refused Travis' pleas for help, and after receiving Houston's orders, Fannin waited for scouting parties to return.

Finally, on March 19, he left, but too late. Forward elements of Gen. José de Urrea's troops caught Fannin's command on an open prairie. After a brief skirmish Fannin surrendered.

Santa Anna was furious when Gen. Urrea appealed for clemency for the captives. The Mexican leader issued orders for their execution. On March 27, a Palm Sunday, most of the prisoners were divided into groups and marched out of Goliad, thinking they were being transferred to other facilities. When the executions began, many escaped. But about 350 were killed.

On March 17, Houston reached the Colorado near the present city of La Grange and began receiving reinforcements. Within a week, the small force of several hundred had become almost respectable, with 1,200-1,400 men in camp.

At the time Houston reached the Colorado, the convention at Washington-on-the-Brazos was completing

work. **David Burnet**, a New Jersey native, was named interim president of the new Texas government, and **Lorenzo de Zavala**, a Yucatán native, was named vice president.

On March 27, Houston moved his men to San Felipe on the Brazos. The Texas army was impatient for a fight, and there was talk in the ranks that, if action did not develop soon, a new commander should be elected.

As the army marched farther back toward the San Jacinto River, two Mexican couriers were captured and gave Houston the information he had hoped for. Santa Anna in his haste had led the small Mexican force in front of Houston. Now the Texans had an opportunity to win the war.

*A replica of the first capitol of the Republic of Texas stands in West Columbia in Brazoria County. In 1836, when it was the capital, the town was called simply Columbia. File photo.*

Throughout the revolt, Houston's intelligence system had operated efficiently. Scouts, commanded by **Erastus "Deaf" Smith**, kept the Texans informed of Mexican troop movements. **Hendrick Arnold**, a free black, was a valuable spy, posing as a runaway slave to enter Mexican camps to gain information.

Early on April 21, Gen. Cos reinforced Santa Anna's troops with more than 500 men. The new arrivals, who had marched all night, disrupted the camp's routine for a time, but soon all the soldiers and officers settled down for a midday rest.

About 3 p.m., Houston ordered his men to parade and the battle was launched at 4:30 p.m.

A company of Mexican-Texans, commanded by **Juan Seguín**, had served as the rear guard for Houston's army through much of the retreat across Texas and had fought many skirmishes with the Mexican army in the process.

Perhaps fearing the Mexican-Texans would be mistaken for Santa Anna's soldiers, Houston had assigned the company to guard duty as the battle approached. But after the men protested, they fought in the battle of San Jacinto.

Historians disagree widely on the number of troops on each side. Houston probably had about 900 while Santa Anna had between 1,100 and 1,300.

But the Texans had the decided psychological advantage. Two thirds of the fledging Republic's army were "old Texans" who had family and land to defend. They had an investment of years of toil in building their homes. And they were eager to avenge the massacre of men at the Alamo and Goliad.

In less than 20 minutes they set the Mexican army to rout. More than 600 Mexicans were killed and hundreds more wounded or captured. Only nine of the Texans died in the fight.

It was not until the following day that Santa Anna was captured. One Texan noticed that a grubby soldier his patrol found in the high grass had a silk shirt under his filthy jacket. Although denying he was an officer, he was taken back to camp, where he was acknowledged with cries of "El Presidente" by other prisoners.

Santa Anna introduced himself when taken to the wounded Houston.

President Burnet took charge of Santa Anna, and on May 14 the dictator signed **two treaties at Velasco**, a public document and a secret one. The public agreement declared that hostilities would cease, that the Mexican army would withdraw to south of the Rio Grande, that prisoners would be released and that Santa Anna would be shipped to Veracruz as soon as possible.

In the secret treaty, Santa Anna agreed to recognize Texas' independence, to give diplomatic recognition, to negotiate a commercial treaty and to set the **Rio Grande** as the new Republic's boundary.

## Republic of Texas, 1836–1845

**Sam Houston** was easily the most dominant figure through the nearly 10-year history of the Republic of Texas. While he was roundly criticized for the retreat across Texas during the revolution, the victory at San Jacinto endeared him to most of the new nation's inhabitants.

Houston handily defeated Henry Smith and Stephen F. Austin in the election called in September 1836 by the interim government, and he was inaugurated as president on Oct. 22.

In the same September election, voters overwhelmingly approved a proposal to request annexation to the United States.

The first cabinet appointed by the new president represented an attempt to heal old political wounds. Austin was named secretary of state and Smith was secretary of the treasury. But Texas suffered a major tragedy in late December 1836 when Austin, the acknowledged **"Father of Texas,"** died of pneumonia.

A host of problems faced the new government. Santa Anna was still in custody, and public opinion favored his execution. Texas' leadership wisely kept Santa Anna alive, first to keep from giving the Mexicans an emotional rallying point for launching another invasion. Second, the Texas leaders hoped that the dictator would keep his promise to work for recognition of Texas.

Sam Houston was the first elected president of the Republic of Texas and its most dominant figure during its 10-year history. File photo.

Mirabeau B. Lamar was the Republic's second president. Lamar and Houston differed greatly in their spending and Indian policies. File photo.

Early in 1839, Lamar gained recognition as the "**Father of Education**" in Texas when the Congress granted each of the existing 23 counties three leagues of land to be used for education. Fifty leagues of land were set aside for a university.

Despite the lip service paid to education, the government did not have the money for several years to set up a school system. Most education during the Republic was provided by private schools and churches.

**Lamar's Indian policies** differed greatly from those under Houston. Houston had lived with Cherokees as a youth, was adopted as a member of a tribe and advocated Indian rights long before coming to Texas. Lamar reflected more the frontier attitude toward American Indians. His first experience in public life was as secretary to Gov. George Troup of Georgia, who successfully opposed the federal government's policy of assimilation of Indians at the time. Indians were simply removed from Georgia.

Texans first tried to negotiate the Cherokees' removal from the region, but in July 1839, the Indians were forcibly ejected from Texas at the **Battle of the Neches River** in Van Zandt County. Houston's close friend, the aging Cherokee chief **Philip Bowles**, was killed in the battle while Houston was visiting former President Jackson in Tennessee. The Cherokees moved on to Arkansas and Indian Territory.

Houston was returned to the presidency of the Republic in 1841. His second administration was even more frugal than his first; soon income almost matched expenditures.

Houston re-entered negotiations with the Indians in Central Texas in an attempt to quell the raids on settlements. A number of trading posts were opened along the frontier to pacify the Indians.

War fever reached a high pitch in Texas in 1842, and Houston grew increasingly unpopular because he would not launch an offensive war against Mexico.

In March 1842, Gen. **Rafael Vásquez** staged guerrilla raids on San Antonio, Victoria and Goliad, but quickly left the Republic.

A force of 3,500 Texas volunteers gathered at San Antonio demanding that Mexico be punished. Houston urged calm, but the clamor increased when Mexican **Gen. Adrian Woll** captured San Antonio in September. He raised the Mexican flag and declared the reconquest of Texas.

Ranger Capt. **Jack Hays** was camped nearby. Within days 600 volunteers had joined him, eager to drive the Mexican invaders from Texas soil. Gen. Woll withdrew after the **Battle of Salado**.

**Alexander Somervell** was ordered by Houston to follow with 700 troops and harass the Mexican army. He reached Laredo in December and found no Mexican troops. Somervell crossed the Rio Grande to find military targets. A few days later, the commander returned home, but 300 soldiers decided to continue the raid under the command of William S. Fisher. On Christmas

Santa Anna was released in November 1836 and made his way to Washington, D.C. Houston hoped the dictator could persuade U.S. President **Andrew Jackson** to recognize Texas. Jackson refused to see Santa Anna, who returned to Mexico, where he had fallen from power.

Another major challenge was the Texas army. The new commander, Felix Huston, favored an invasion of Mexico, and the troops, made up now mostly of American volunteers who came to Texas after the battle of San Jacinto, were rebellious and ready to fight.

President Houston tried to replace Felix Huston with **Albert Sidney Johnston**, but Huston seriously wounded Johnston in a duel. In May 1837, Huston was asked to the capital in Columbia to discuss the invasion. While Huston was away from the troops, Houston sent **Thomas J. Rusk**, the secretary of war, to furlough the army without pay — but with generous land grants. Only 600 men were retained in the army.

The Republic's other problems were less tractable. The economy needed attention, Indians still were a threat, Mexico remained warlike, foreign relations had to be developed, and relations with the United States had to be solidified.

The greatest disappointment in Houston's first term was the failure to have the Republic annexed to the United States. Henry Morfit, President Jackson's agent, toured the new Republic in the summer of 1836. Although impressed, Morfit reported that Texas' best chance at continued independence lay in the "stupidity of the rulers of Mexico and the financial embarrassment of the Mexican government." He recommended that annexation be delayed.

Houston's foreign policy achieved initial success when **J. Pinckney Henderson** negotiated a trade treaty with Great Britain. Although the agreement was short of outright diplomatic recognition, it was progress. In the next few years, France, Belgium, The Netherlands and some German states recognized the new Republic.

Under the constitution, Houston's first term lasted only two years, and he could not succeed himself. His successor, **Mirabeau B. Lamar**, had grand visions and was a spendthrift. Houston's first term cost Texas only about $500,000, while President Lamar and the Congress spent $5 million in the next three years.

day, this group attacked the village of **Mier**, only to be defeated by a Mexican force that outnumbered them 10-to-1.

After attempting mass escape, the survivors of the Mier expedition were marched to Mexico City where Santa Anna, again in political power, ordered their execution. When officers refused to carry out the order, it was amended to require execution of one of every 10 Texans. The prisoners drew beans to determine who would be shot; bearers of **black beans** were executed. Texans again were outraged by the treatment of prisoners, but the war fever soon subsided.

As Houston completed his second term, the United States was becoming more interested in annexation. Texas had seriously flirted with Great Britain and France, and the Americans did not want a rival republic with close foreign ties on the North American continent.

Houston orchestrated the early stages of the final steps toward annexation. It was left to his successor, **Anson Jones**, to complete the process.

The Republic of Texas' main claim to fame is simply endurance. Its settlers, unlike other Americans who had military help, had cleared a large region of Indians by themselves, had established farms and communities and had persevered through extreme economic hardship.

Adroit political leadership gained the Republic recognition from many foreign countries. Although dreams of empire may have dimmed, Texans had established an identity on a major portion of the North American continent. The frontier had been pushed to a line running from Corpus Christi through San Antonio and Austin to the Red River.

The U.S. presidential campaign of 1844 was to make Texas a part of the Union. ☆

# Annexation to 1978

## Annexation

Annexation to the United States was far from automatic for Texas once independence from Mexico was gained in 1836. Sam Houston noted that Texas "was more coy than forward" as negotiations reached a climax in 1845.

**William H. Wharton** was Texas' first representative in Washington. His instructions were to gain diplomatic recognition of the new Republic's independence.

After some squabbles, the U.S. Congress appropriated funds for a minister to Texas, and President Andrew Jackson recognized the new country in one of his last acts in office in March 1837.

Texas President **Mirabeau B. Lamar** (1838–41) opposed annexation. He held visions of empire in which Texas would rival the United States for supremacy on the North American continent.

During his administration, Great Britain began a close relationship with Texas and made strenuous efforts to get Mexico to recognize the Republic. This relationship between Great Britain and Texas raised fears in the United States that Britain might attempt to make Texas part of its empire.

Southerners feared for the future of slavery in Texas, which had renounced the importation of slaves as a concession to get a trade treaty with Great Britain, and American newspapers noted that trade with Texas had suffered after the Republic received recognition from European countries.

In Houston's second term in the Texas presidency, he instructed **Isaac Van Zandt**, his minister in Washington, to renew the annexation negotiations. Although U.S. President **John Tyler** and his cabinet were eager to annex Texas, they were worried about ratification in the U.S. Senate. The annexation question was put off.

In January 1844, Houston again gave Van Zandt instructions to propose annexation talks. This time the United States agreed to Houston's standing stipulation that, for serious negotiations to take place, the United States must provide military protection to Texas. U.S. naval forces were ordered to the Gulf of Mexico and U.S. troops were positioned on the southwest border close to Texas.

On April 11, 1844, Texas and the United States signed a treaty for annexation. Texas would enter the Union as a territory, not a state, under terms of the treaty. The United States would assume Texas' debt up to $10 million and would negotiate Texas' southwestern boundary with Mexico.

On June 8, 1844, the U.S. Senate rejected the treaty with a vote of 35-16, with much of the opposition coming from the slavery abolition wing of the Whig Party.

But **westward expansion** became a major issue in the U.S. presidential election that year. James K. Polk, the Democratic nominee, was a supporter of expansion, and the party's platform called for adding Oregon and Texas to the Union.

After Polk won the election in November, President Tyler declared that the people had spoken on the issue of annexation, and he resubmitted the matter to Congress.

Several bills were introduced in the U.S. House of Representatives containing various proposals.

In **February 1845**, the U.S. Congress approved a resolution that would bring Texas into the Union as a state. Texas would cede its public property, such as forts and custom houses, to the United States, but it could keep its public lands and must retain its public debt. The region could be divided into four new states in addition to the original Texas. And the United States would negotiate the Rio Grande boundary claim.

British officials asked the Texas government to delay consideration of the U.S. offer for 90 days to attempt to get Mexico to recognize the Republic. The delay did no good: Texans' minds were made up.

President Anson Jones, who succeeded Houston in 1844, called a convention to write a **state constitution** in Austin on July 4, 1845.

Mexico finally recognized Texas' independence, but the recognition was rejected. **Texas voters overwhelmingly accepted the U.S. proposal** and approved the new constitution in a referendum.

On **Dec. 29, 1845**, the U.S. Congress accepted the state constitution, and Texas became the 28th state in the Union. The first meeting of the Texas Legislature took place on Feb. 16, 1846.

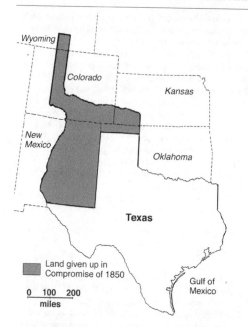

Land claimed by Texas when it entered the Union in 1845 included more than half of present-day New Mexico, about a third of Colorado, a corner of Kansas, the Oklahoma Panhandle and a small portion of Wyoming. In the Compromise of 1850, the state gave up its claim to the shadded area in exchange for the United States' assumption of the state's $10 million debt. Texas kept its public lands in the deal.

## 1845–1860

The entry of Texas into the Union touched off the **War with Mexico**, a war that some historians now think was planned by President James K. Polk to obtain the vast American Southwest.

Gen. **Zachary Taylor** was sent to Corpus Christi, just above the Nueces River, in July 1845. In February 1846, right after Texas formally entered the Union, the general was ordered to move troops into the disputed area south of the Nueces to the mouth of the Rio Grande. Mexican officials protested the move, claiming the status of the territory was under negotiation.

After Gen. Taylor refused to leave, Mexican President **Mariano Paredes** declared the opening of a defensive war against the United States on April 24, 1846.

After initial encounters at **Palo Alto** and **Resaca de la Palma**, both a few miles north of today's **Brownsville**, the war was fought south of the Rio Grande.

President Polk devised a plan to raise 50,000 volunteers from every section of the United States to fight the war. About 5,000 Texans saw action in Mexico.

Steamboats provided an important supply link for U.S. forces along the Rio Grande. Historical figures such as **Richard King**, founder of the legendary King Ranch, and **Mifflin Kenedy**, another rancher and businessman, first came to the **Lower Rio Grande Valley** as steamboat operators during the war.

Much farther up the Rio Grande, the war was hardly noticed. U.S. forces moved south from Santa Fe, which

had been secured in December 1846. After a minor skirmish with Mexican forces north of El Paso, the U.S. military established American jurisdiction in this part of Texas.

Gen. **Winfield Scott** brought the war to a close in March 1847 with the capture of Mexico City.

When the **Treaty of Guadalupe Hidalgo** was signed on Feb. 2, 1848, the United States had acquired the American Southwest for development. And in Texas, the Rio Grande became an international boundary.

Europeans, of whom the vast majority were **German**, rather than Anglos, were the first whites to push the Texas frontier into west Central Texas after annexation. **John O. Meusebach** became leader of the German immigration movement in Texas, and he led a wagon train of some 120 settlers to the site of **Fredericksburg** in May 1846.

Germans also migrated to the major cities, such as San Antonio and Galveston, and by 1850 there were more people of German birth or parentage in Texas than there were Mexican-Texans.

The estimated population of 150,000 at annexation grew to 212,592, including 58,161 slaves, in the first U.S. census count in Texas in 1850.

As the state's population grew, the regions developed distinct population characteristics. The southeast and eastern sections attracted immigrants from the Lower South, the principal slaveholding states. Major plantations developed in these areas.

North Texas got more Upper Southerners and Midwesterners. These immigrants were mostly small farmers and few owned slaves.

Mexican-Texans had difficulty with Anglo immigrants. The **"cart war"** broke out in 1857. Mexican teamsters controlled the transportation of goods from the Gulf coast to San Antonio and could charge lower rates than their competition.

A campaign of terror was launched by Anglo haulers, especially around Goliad, in an attempt to drive the Mexican-Texans out of business. Intervention by the U.S. and Mexican governments finally brought the situation under control, but it stands as an example of the attitudes held by Anglo-Texans toward Mexican-Texans.

**Cotton** was by far the state's largest money crop, but corn, sweet potatoes, wheat and sugar also were produced. **Saw milling** and grain milling became the major industries, employing 40 percent of the manufacturing workers.

Land disputes and the public-debt issue were settled with the **Compromise of 1850**. Texas gave up claims to territory extending to Santa Fe and beyond in exchange for $10 million from the federal government. That sum was used to pay off the debt of the Republic.

Personalities, especially Sam Houston, dominated elections during early statehood, but, for most Texans, politics were unimportant. Voter turnouts were low in the 1850s until the movement toward secession gained strength.

## Secession

Texas' population almost tripled in the decade between 1850 and 1860, when 604,215 people were counted, including 182,921 slaves.

Many of these new settlers came from the Lower South, a region familiar with slavery. Although three-

quarters of the Texas population and two-thirds of the farmers did not own slaves, slaveowners controlled 60 to 70 percent of the wealth of the state and dominated the politics.

In 1850, 41 percent of the state's officeholders were from the slaveholding class; a decade later, more than 50 percent of the officeholders had slaves.

In addition to the political power of the slaveholders, they also provided role models for new immigrants to the state. After these newcomers got their first land, they saw slave ownership as another step up the economic ladder, whether they owned slaves or not. Slave ownership was an economic goal.

This attitude prevailed even in areas of Texas where slaveholding was not widespread or even practical.

These factors were the wind that fanned the flames of the secessionist movement throughout the late 1850s.

The appearance of the **Know-Nothing Party**, which based its platform on a pro-American, anti-immigrant foundation, began to move Texas toward party politics. Because of the large number of foreign-born settlers, the party attracted many Anglo voters.

In 1854, the Know-Nothings elected candidates to city offices in San Antonio, and a year later, the mayor of Galveston was elected with the party's backing. Also in 1855, the Know-Nothings elected 20 representatives and five senators to the Legislature.

The successes spurred the **Democrats** to serious party organization for the first time. In 1857, **Hardin Runnels** was nominated for governor at the Democratic convention held in Waco.

**Sam Houston** sought the governorship as an independent, but he also got Know-Nothing backing. Democrats were organized, however, and Houston was dealt the only election defeat in his political career.

Runnels was a strong states'-rights Democrat who irritated many Texans during his administration by advocating reopening the slave trade. His popularity on the frontier also dropped when Indian raids became more severe.

Most Texans still were ambivalent about secession. The Union was seen as a protector of physical and economic stability. No threats to person or property were perceived in remaining attached to the United States.

In 1859, Houston again challenged Runnels, basing his campaign on Unionism. Combined with Houston's personal popularity, his position on the secession issue apparently satisfied most voters, for they gave him a solid victory over the more radical Runnels. In addition, Unionists **A.J. Hamilton** and **John H. Reagan** won the state's two congressional seats. Texans gave the states'-rights Democrats a sound whipping at the polls.

Within a few months, however, events were to change radically the political atmosphere of the state. On the frontier, the army could not control Indian raids, and with the later refusal of a Republican-controlled Congress to provide essential aid in fighting Indians, the federal government fell into disrepute.

**Secessionists** played on the growing distrust. Then in the summer of 1860, a series of fires in the cities around the state aroused fears that an abolitionist plot was afoot and that a slave uprising might be at hand — a traditional concern in a slaveholding society.

Vigilantes lynched blacks and Northerners across Texas, and a siege mentality developed.

When **Abraham Lincoln** was elected president (he was not on the ballot in Texas), secessionists went to work in earnest.

Pleas were made to Gov. Houston to call the Legislature into session to consider secession. Houston refused, hoping the passions would cool. They did not. Finally, **Oran M. Roberts** and other secessionist leaders issued a call to the counties to hold elections and send delegates to a convention in Austin. Ninety-two of 122 counties responded, and on Jan. 28, 1861, the meeting convened.

Only eight delegates voted against secession, while 166 supported it. An election was called for Feb. 23, 1861, and the ensuing campaign was marked by intolerance and violence. Opponents of secession were often intimidated — except the governor, who courageously stumped the state opposing withdrawal from the Union. Houston also argued that if Texas did secede it should revert to its status as an independent republic and not join the Confederacy.

Only one-fourth of the state's population had been in Texas during the days of independence, and the argument carried no weight. On election day, 76 percent of 61,000 voters favored secession.

President Lincoln, who took office within a couple of weeks, reportedly sent the Texas governor a letter offering 50,000 federal troops to keep Texas in the Union. But after a meeting with other Unionists, Houston declined the offer. "I love Texas too well to bring strife and bloodshed upon her," the governor declared.

On March 16, Houston refused to take an oath of loyalty to the Confederacy and was replaced in office by Lt. Gov. **Edward Clark**.

## Civil War

Texas did not suffer the devastation of its Southern colleagues in the Civil War. On but a few occasions did Union troops occupy territory in Texas, except in the El Paso area.

The state's cotton was important to the Confederate war effort because it could be transported from Gulf ports when other Southern shipping lanes were blockaded.

Some goods became difficult to buy, but unlike other states of the Confederacy, Texas still received consumer goods because of the trade that was carried on through Mexico during the war.

Although accurate figures are not available, historians estimate that between 70,000 and 90,000 Texans fought for the South, and between 2,000 and 3,000, including some former slaves, saw service in the Union army.

Texans became disenchanted with the Confederate government early in the war. State taxes were levied for the first time since the Compromise of 1850, and by war's end, the Confederacy had collected more than $37 million from the state.

But most of the complaints about the government centered on Brig. Gen. **Paul O. Hebert**, the Confederate commander of the Department of Texas.

In April 1862, Gen. Hebert declared martial law without notifying state officials. Opposition to the South's new conscription law, which exempted persons owning more than 15 slaves among other categories of exemptions, prompted the action.

In November 1862, the commander prohibited the export of cotton except under government control, and this proved a disastrous policy.

The final blow came when Gen. Hebert failed to defend **Galveston** and it fell into Union hands in the fall of 1862.

Maj. Gen. **John B. Magruder**, who replaced Hebert, was much more popular. The new commander's first actions were to combat the Union offensive against Texas ports. Sabine Pass had been closed in September 1862 by the Union blockade, and Galveston was in Northern hands.

On Jan. 1, 1863, Magruder retook Galveston with the help of two steamboats lined with cotton bales. Sharpshooters aboard proved devastating in battles against the Union fleet. Three weeks later, Magruder used two other cotton-clad steamboats to break the Union blockade of Sabine Pass, and two of the state's major ports were reopened.

Late in 1863, the Union launched a major offensive against the Texas coast that was partly successful. On Sept. 8, however, Lt. **Dick Dowling** and 42 men fought off a 1,500-man Union invasion force at **Sabine Pass**. In a brief battle, Dowling's command sank two Union gunboats and put the other invasion ships to flight.

Federal forces were more successful at the mouth of the Rio Grande. On Nov. 1, 1863, 7,000 Union troops landed at **Brazos Santiago**, and five days later, Union forces entered Brownsville.

Texas Unionists led by **E.J. Davis** were active in the Valley, moving as far upriver as Rio Grande City. Confederate Col. **John S. "Rip" Ford**, commanding state troops, finally pushed the Union soldiers out of

*E.J. Davis lead Union soldiers in the Valley in 1863. But Confederates pushed them out again in 1864. File photo.*

Brownsville in July 1864, reopening the important port for the Confederacy.

Most Texans never saw a Union soldier during the war. The only ones they might have seen were in the **prisoner-of-war camps**. The largest, **Camp Ford**, near Tyler, housed 5,000 prisoners. Others operated in Kerr County and at Hempstead.

As the war dragged on, the mood of Texans changed. Those on the homefront began to feel they were sacrificing loved ones and suffering hardship so cotton speculators could profit.

Public order broke down as refugees flocked to Texas. And slaves from other states were sent to Texas for safekeeping. When the war ended, there were an estimated 400,000 slaves in Texas, more than double the number counted in the 1860 census.

Morale was low in Texas in early 1865. Soldiers at Galveston and Houston began to mutiny. At Austin, Confederate soldiers raided the state treasury in March and found only $5,000 in specie. Units began breaking up, and the army was beginning to dissolve before Gen.

**Robert E. Lee** surrendered at **Appomattox** in April 1865. He surrendered the Army of Northern Virginia, and while this assured Union victory, the surrender of other Confederate units was to follow until the last unit gave up in Oklahoma at the end of June.

The last land battle of the Civil War was fought at **Palmito Ranch** near Brownsville on May 13, 1865. After the Confederate's victory, they learned the governors of the Western Rebel states had authorized the disbanding of armies, and, a few days later, they accepted a truce with the Union forces.

## Reconstruction

On June 19, 1865, **Gen. Gordon Granger**, under the command of Gen. Philip M. Sheridan, arrived in Galveston with 1,800 federal troops to begin the Union occupation of Texas. Gen. Granger proclaimed the emancipation of the slaves.

**A.J. Hamilton**, a Unionist and former congressman from Texas, was named provisional governor by President Andrew Johnson.

Texas was in turmoil. Thousands of the state's men had died in the conflict. Indian raids had caused as much damage as the skirmishes with the Union army, causing the frontier to recede up to 100 miles eastward in some areas.

Even worse, confusion reigned. No one knew what to expect from the conquering forces.

Gen. Granger dispatched troops to the population centers of the state to restore civil authority. But only a handful of the 50,000 federal troops that came to Texas was stationed in the interior. Most were sent to the Rio Grande as a show of force against the French forces in Mexico, and clandestine aid was supplied to Mexican President Benito Juarez in his fight against the French and Mexican royalists.

The **frontier forts**, most of which were built during the early 1850s by the federal government to protect western settlements, had been abandoned by the U.S. Army after secession. These were not remanned, and a prohibition against a militia denied settlers a means of self-defense against Indian raids. *(For an overview of the frontier forts, see the main feature story on page 16.)*

Thousands of freed black slaves migrated to the cities, where they felt the federal soldiers would provide protection. Still others traveled the countryside, seeking family members and loved ones from whom they had been separated during the war.

The **Freedman's Bureau**, authorized by Congress in March 1865, began operation in September 1865 under Gen. E.M. Gregory. It had the responsibility to provide education, relief aid, labor supervision and judicial protection for the newly freed slaves.

The bureau was most successful in opening schools for blacks. Education was a priority because 95 percent of the freed slaves were illiterate.

The agency also was partially successful in getting blacks back to work on plantations under reasonable labor contracts.

Some plantation owners harbored hopes that they would be paid for their property loss when the slaves were freed. In some cases, the slaves were not released from plantations for up to a year.

To add to the confusion, some former slaves had the false notion that the federal government was going to

parcel out the plantation lands to them. These blacks simply bided their time, waiting for the division of land.

Under pressure from President Johnson, Gov. Hamilton called for an election of delegates to a **constitutional convention** in January 1866. Hamilton told the gathering what was expected: Former slaves were to be given civil rights; the secession ordinance had to be repealed; Civil War debt had to be repudiated; and slavery was to be abolished with ratification of the Thirteenth Amendment.

Many delegates to the convention were former secessionists, and there was little support for compromise.

**J.W. Throckmorton**, a Unionist and one of eight men who had opposed secession in the convention of 1861, was elected chairman of the convention. But a coalition of conservative Unionists and Democrats controlled the meeting. As a consequence, Texas took limited steps toward appeasing the victorious North.

Slavery was abolished, and blacks were given some civil rights. But they still could not vote and were barred from testifying in trials against whites.

No action was taken on the Thirteenth Amendment because, the argument went, the amendment already had been ratified.

Otherwise, the constitution that was written followed closely the constitution of 1845. President Johnson in August 1866 accepted the new constitution and declared insurrection over in Texas, the last of the states of the Confederacy so accepted under **Presidential Reconstruction**.

Throckmorton was elected governor in June, along with other state and local officials. However, Texans had not learned a lesson from the war.

When the Legislature met, a series of laws limiting the rights of blacks were passed. In labor disputes, for example, the employers were to be the final arbitrators. The codes also bound an entire family's labor, not just the head of the household, to an employer.

Funding for black education would be limited to what could be provided by black taxpayers. Since few blacks owned land or had jobs, that provision effectively denied education to black children. However, the thrust of the laws and the attitude of the legislators was clear: Blacks simply were not to be considered full citizens.

Many of the laws later were overturned by the Freedman's Bureau or military authorities when, in March 1867, Congress began a **Reconstruction plan** of its own. The Southern states were declared to have no legal government and the former Confederacy was divided into districts to be administered by the military until satisfactory Reconstruction was effected. Texas and Louisiana made up the Fifth Military District under the command of Gen. Philip H. Sheridan.

Gov. Throckmorton clashed often with Gen. Sheridan. The governor thought the state had gone far enough in establishing rights for the newly freed slaves and other matters. Finally in August 1867, Throckmorton and other state officials were removed from office by Sheridan because they were considered an "impediment to the reconstruction." **E.M. Pease**, the former two-term governor and a Unionist, was named provisional governor by the military authorities.

A **new constitutional convention** was called by Gen. Winfield S. Hancock, who replaced Sheridan in November 1867. For the first time, blacks were allowed to participate in the elections that selected delegates. A total of 59,633 whites and 49,497 blacks registered. The elected delegates met on June 1, 1868. Deliberations got bogged down on partisan political matters, however, and the convention spent $200,000, an astronomical sum for the time.

This constitution of 1869, as it came to be known, granted full rights of citizenship to blacks, created a system of education, delegated broad powers to the governor and generally reflected the views of the state's Unionists.

Gov. Pease, disgusted with the convention and with military authorities, resigned in September 1869. Texas had no chief executive until January 1870, when the newly elected **E.J. Davis** took office.

Meeting in February 1870, the Legislature created a **state militia** under the governor's control; created a **state police force**, also controlled by the governor; postponed the 1870 general election to 1872; enabled the governor to appoint more than 8,500 local officeholders; and granted subsidized **bonds for railroad construction** at a rate of $10,000 a mile.

For the first time, a **system of public education** was created. The law required compulsory attendance at school for four months a year, set aside one-quarter of the state's annual revenue for education and levied a poll tax to support education. Schools also were to be integrated, which enraged many white Texans.

The Davis administration was the most unpopular in Texas' history. In fairness, historians have noted that Davis did not feel that whites could be trusted to assure the rights of the newly freed blacks.

Violence was rampant in Texas. One study found that between the close of the Civil War and mid-1868, 1,035 people were murdered in Texas, including 486 blacks, mostly victims of white violence.

Gov. Davis argued that he needed broad police powers to restore order. Despite their unpopularity, the state police and militia — blacks made up 40 percent of the police and a majority of the militia — brought the lawlessness under control in many areas.

Democrats, aided by moderate Republicans, regained control of the Legislature in the 1872 elections, and, in 1873, the lawmakers set about stripping the governor of many of his powers.

The political turmoil ended with the gubernatorial election of 1873, when **Richard Coke** easily defeated Davis. Davis tried to get federal authorities to keep him in office, but President Grant refused to intervene.

In January of 1874, Democrats were in control of state government again. The end of Reconstruction concluded the turbulent Civil War era, although the attitudes that developed during the period lasted well into the 20th century.

## Capital and Labor

A **constitutional convention** was called in 1875 to rewrite the 1869 constitution, a hated vestige of Radical Republican rule.

Every avenue to cutting spending at any level of government was explored. Salaries of public officials were slashed. The number of offices was reduced. Judgeships, along with most other offices, were made elective rather than appointive.

The state road program was curtailed, and the immigration bureau was eliminated.

Perhaps the worst change was the destruction of the statewide school system. The new charter created a "community system" without a power of taxation, and schools were segregated by race.

Despite the basic reactionary character, the new constitution also was visionary. Following the lead of several other states, the Democrats declared railroads to be common carriers and subject to regulation.

To meet the dual challenge of lawlessness and Indian insurrection, Gov. Coke in 1874 re-established the **Texas Rangers**.

While cowboys and cattle drives are romantic subjects for movies on the Texas of this period, the fact is that the simple cotton farmer was the backbone of the state's economy.

But neither the farmer nor the cattleman prospered throughout the last quarter of the 19th century. At the root of their problems was federal monetary policy and the lingering effects of the Civil War.

Although the issuance of paper money had brought about a business boom in the Union during the war, inflation also increased. Silver was demonetized in 1873. Congress passed the Specie Resumption Act in 1875 that returned the nation to the gold standard in 1879.

Almost immediately a contraction in currency began. Between 1873 and 1891, the amount of national bank notes in circulation declined from $339 million to $168 million.

The reduction in the money supply was devastating in the defeated South. Land values plummeted. In 1870, Texas land was valued at an average of $2.62 an acre, compared with the national average of $18.26 an acre.

With the money supply declining and the national economy growing, farm prices dropped. In 1870, a bushel of wheat brought $1. In the 1890s, wheat was 60 cents a bushel. Except for a brief spurt in the early 1880s, cattle prices followed those of crops.

Between 1880 and 1890, the number of farms in Texas doubled, but the number of tenants tripled. By 1900, almost half the state's farmers were tenants.

The much-criticized crop-lien system was developed following the war to meet credit needs of the small farmers. Merchants would extend credit to farmers through the year in exchange for liens on their crops. But the result of the crop-lien system, particularly when small farmers did not have enough acreage to operate efficiently, was a state of continual debt and despair.

The work ethic held that a man would benefit from his toil. When this apparently failed, farmers looked to the monetary system and the railroads as the causes. Their discontent hence became the source of the agrarian revolt that developed in the 1880s and 1890s.

The entry of the Texas & Pacific and the Missouri-Kansas-Texas **railroads** from the northeast changed trade patterns in the state.

Since the days of the Republic, trade generally had flowed to Gulf ports, primarily Galveston. Jefferson in Northeast Texas served as a gateway to the Mississippi River, but it never carried the volume of trade that was common at Galveston.

The earliest railroad systems in the state also were centered around Houston and Galveston, again directing trade southward. With the T&P and Katy lines, North Texas had direct access to markets in St. Louis and the East.

Problems developed with the railroads, however. In 1882, Jay Gould and Collis P. Huntington, owner of the Southern Pacific, entered into a secret agreement that amounted to creation of a monopoly of rail service in Texas. They agreed to stop competitive track extensions; to divide under a pooling arrangement freight moving from New Orleans and El Paso; to purchase all competing railroads in Texas; and to share the track between Sierra Blanca and El Paso.

The Legislature made weak attempts to regulate railroads, as provided by the state constitution. Gould thwarted an attempt to create a commission to regulate the railroads in 1881 with a visit to the state during the Legislature's debate.

The railroad tycoon subdued the lawmakers' interest with thinly disguised threats that capital would abandon Texas if the state interfered with railroad business.

As the 19th century closed, Texas remained an agricultural state. But the industrial base was growing. Between 1870 and 1900, the per capita value of manufactured goods in the United States rose from $109 to $171. In Texas, these per capita values increased from $14 to $39, but manufacturing values in Texas industry still were only one-half of annual agricultural values.

James Stephen Hogg

In 1886, a new breed of Texas politician appeared. **James Stephen Hogg** was not a Confederate veteran, and he was not tied to party policies of the past.

As a reform-minded attorney general, Hogg had actively enforced the state's few railroad regulatory laws. With farmers' support, Hogg was elected governor in 1890, and at the same time, a debate on the constitutionality of a **railroad commission** was settled when voters amended the constitution to provide for one.

The reform mood of the state was evident. Voters returned only 22 of the 106 members of the Texas House in 1890.

Despite his reputation as a reformer, Hogg accepted the growing use of **Jim Crow laws** to limit blacks' access to public services. In 1891, the Legislature responded to public demands and required railroads to provide separate accommodations for blacks and whites.

The stage was being set for one of the major political campaigns in Texas history, however. Farmers did not think that Hogg had gone far enough in his reform program, and they were distressed that Hogg had not appointed a farmer to the railroad commission. Many began to look elsewhere for the solutions to their problems. The **People's Party** in Texas was formed in August 1891.

The 1892 general election was one of the most spirited in the state's history. Gov. Hogg's supporters shut conservative Democrats out of the convention in Houston, so the conservatives bolted and nominated railroad attorney George Clark for governor.

The People's Party, or **Populists**, for the first time

had a presidential candidate, James Weaver, and a gubernatorial candidate, T.L. Nugent.

Texas Republicans also broke ranks. The party's strength centered in the black vote. After the death of former Gov. E.J. Davis in 1883, **Norris Wright Cuney**, a black, was party leader. Cuney was considered one of the most astute politicians of the period, and he controlled federal patronage.

*Norris Wright Cuney was a leader among black Republicans. File photo.*

White Republicans revolted against the black leadership, and these "Lilywhites" nominated **Andrew Jackson Houston**, son of Sam Houston, for governor.

Black Republicans recognized that alone their strength was limited, and throughout the latter part of the 19th century, they practiced fusion politics, backing candidates of third parties when they deemed it appropriate. Cuney led the Republicans into a coalition with the conservative Democrats in 1892, backing George Clark.

The election also marked the first time major Democratic candidates courted the black vote. Gov. Hogg's supporters organized black voter clubs, and the governor got about half of the black vote.

Black farmers were in a quandary. Their financial problems were the same as those small farmers who backed the Populists.

White Populists varied in their sympathy with the racial concerns of blacks. On the local level, some whites showed sympathy with black concerns about education, voting and law enforcement. Black farmers also were reluctant to abandon the Republican Party because it was their only political base in Texas.

Hogg was re-elected in 1892 with a 43 percent plurality in a field of five candidates.

Populists continued to run well in state races until 1898. Historians have placed the beginning of the party's demise in the 1896 presidential election in which national Populists fused with the Democrats and supported **William Jennings Bryan**.

Although the Populist philosophy lived on, the party declined in importance after 1898. Farmers remained active in politics, but most returned to the Democratic Party, which usurped many of the Populists' issues.

## Oil

Seldom can a people's history be profoundly changed by a single event on a single day. But Texas' entrance into the industrial age can be linked directly to the discovery of oil at **Spindletop**, three miles from **Beaumont**, on Jan. 10, 1901.

From that day, Texas' progress from a rural, agricultural state to a modern industrial giant was steady.

### 1900–1920

One of the greatest natural disasters ever to strike the state occurred on Sept. 8, 1900, when a **hurricane dev-**

*The Santa Rita #1 was the first oil well to blow in on University of Texas lands on May 18, 1923. File photo.*

astated Galveston, killing 6,000 people. (For a more detailed account, see "After the Great Storm" in the 1998-1999 *Texas Almanac*). In rebuilding from that disaster, Galveston's civic leaders fashioned the **commission form of municipal government**.

Amarillo later refined the system into the **council-manager organization** that is widely used today.

The great Galveston storm also reinforced arguments by Houston's leadership that an inland port should be built for protection against such tragedies and disruptions of trade. The **Houston Ship Channel** was soon a reality.

The reform spirit in government was not dead after the departure of Jim Hogg. In 1901, the Legislature prohibited the issuing of railroad passes to public officials. More than 270,000 passes were issued to officials that year, and farmers claimed that the free rides increased their freight rates and influenced public policy as well.

In 1903, state Sen. **A.W. Terrell** got a major **election-reform law** approved, a measure that was further modified two years later. A **primary system** was established to replace a hodgepodge of practices for nominating candidates that had led to charges of irregularities after each election.

Also in the reform spirit, the Legislature in 1903 prohibited abuse of **child labor** and set minimum ages at which children could work in certain industries. The action preceded federal child-labor laws by 13 years.

However, the state, for the first time, imposed the **poll tax** as a requirement for voting. Historians differ on whether the levy was designed to keep blacks or poor whites — or both — from voting. Certainly the poll tax cut election turnouts. Black voter participation dropped from about 100,000 in the 1890s to an estimated 5,000 in 1906.

The Democratic State Executive Committee also recommended that county committees limit participa-

tion in primaries to whites only, and most accepted the suggestion.

The election of **Thomas M. Campbell** as governor in 1906 marked the start of a progressive period in Texas politics. Interest revived in controlling corporate influence.

Under Campbell, the state's **antitrust laws** were strengthened and a **pure food and drug bill** was passed. Life insurance companies were required to invest in Texas 75 percent of their reserves on policies in the state. Less than one percent of the reserves had been invested prior to the law.

Some companies left Texas. But the law was beneficial in the capital-starved economy. In 1904, voters amended the constitution to allow the state to charter **banks** for the first time, and this eased some of the farmers' credit problems. In 1909, the Legislature approved a bank-deposit insurance plan that predated the federal program.

With corporate influence under acceptable control, attention turned to the issue of prohibition of alcohol. Progressives and prohibitionists joined forces against the conservative establishment to exert a major influence in state government for the next two decades.

**Prohibitionists** had long been active in Texas. They had the **local-option clause** written into the Constitution of 1876, which allowed counties or their subdivisions to be voted dry. But in 1887, a prohibition amendment to the state constitution had been defeated by a two-to-one margin, and public attention had turned to other problems.

In the early 20th century, the prohibition movement gathered strength. Most of Texas already was dry because of local option. When voters rejected a prohibition amendment by a slim margin in 1911, the state had 167 dry counties and 82 wet or partially wet counties. The heavily populated counties, however, were wet. Prohibition continued to be a major issue.

Problems along the U.S.-Mexico border escalated in 1911 as the decade-long **Mexican Revolution** broke out. Soon the revolutionaries controlled some northern Mexican states, including Chihuahua. Juarez and El Paso were major contact points. El Paso residents could stand on rooftops to observe the fighting between revolutionaries and government troops. Some Americans were killed.

After pleas to the federal government got no action, Gov. Oscar Colquitt sent state militia and Texas Rangers into the Valley in 1913 to protect Texans after Matamoros fell to the rebels. Unfortunately, the Rangers killed many innocent Mexican-Texans during the operation. In addition to problems caused by the fighting and raids, thousands of Mexican refugees flooded Texas border towns to escape the violence of the revolution.

In 1914, **James E. Ferguson** entered Texas politics and for the next three decades, "Farmer Jim" was one of the most dominating and colorful figures on the political stage. Ferguson, a banker from Temple, skirted the prohibition issue by pledging to veto any legislation pertaining to alcoholic beverages.

His strength was among farmers, however. Sixty-two percent of Texas' farmers were tenants, and Ferguson pledged to back legislation to limit tenant rents. Ferguson also was a dynamic orator. He easily won the

*James E. Ferguson was known as "Farmer Jim" in Texas politics. File photo.*

primary and beat out three opponents in the general election.

Ferguson's first administration was successful. The Legislature passed the law limiting tenants' rents, although it was poorly enforced, and aid to rural schools was improved.

In 1915, the border problems heated up. A Mexican national was arrested in the Lower Rio Grande Valley carrying a document outlining plans for Mexican-Americans, Indians, Japanese and blacks in Texas and the Southwest to eliminate all Anglo males over age 16 and create a new republic. The document, whose author was never determined, started a bloodbath in the Valley. Mexican soldiers participated in raids across the Rio Grande, and Gov. Ferguson sent in the Texas Rangers.

Historians differ on the number of people who were killed, but a safe assessment would be hundreds. Gov. Ferguson and Mexican President Venustiano Carranza met at Nuevo Laredo in November 1915 in an attempt to improve relations. The raids continued.

**Pancho Villa** raided Columbus, N.M., in early 1916; two small Texas villages in the Big Bend, Glenn Springs and Boquillas, also were attacked. In July, President **Woodrow Wilson** determined that the hostilities were critical and activated the National Guard.

Soon 100,000 U.S. troops were stationed along the border. **Fort Bliss** in El Paso housed 60,000 men, and **Fort Duncan** near Eagle Pass was home to 16,000 more.

With the exception of Gen. John J. Pershing's pursuit of Villa into Northern Mexico, few U.S. troops crossed into Mexico. But the service along the border gave soldiers basic training that was put to use when the United States entered World War I in 1917.

Ferguson was easily re-elected in 1916, and he worked well with the Legislature the following year. But after the Legislature adjourned, the governor got into a dispute with the board of regents of the **University of Texas**. The disagreement culminated in the governor's vetoing all appropriations for the school.

As the controversy swirled, the Travis County grand jury indicted Ferguson for misappropriation of funds and for embezzlement. In July 1917, Speaker of the Texas House F.O. Fuller called a special session of the Legislature to consider **impeachment** of the governor.

The Texas House voted 21 articles of impeachment, and the Senate in August 1917 convicted Ferguson on 10 of the charges. The Senate's judgment not only removed Ferguson from office, but also barred him from seeking office again. Ferguson resigned the day before the Senate rendered the decision in an attempt to avoid the prohibition against seeking further office.

Texas participated actively in **World War I**. Almost 200,000 young Texans, including 31,000 blacks, volun-

Ranching has been a longtime part of Texas life and its economy. Cowhands gather at the chuckwagon during a roundup on the JA Ranch near Palo Duro Canyon in 1898. Famed cattleman Charles Goodnight is credited for inventing the chuckwagon. File photo.

teered for military service, and 450 Texas women served in the nurses' corps. Five thousand lost their lives overseas, either fighting or in the **influenza pandemic** that swept the globe.

Texas also was a major training ground during the conflict, with 250,000 soldiers getting basic training in the state.

On the negative side, the war frenzy opened a period of intolerance and nativism in the state. German-Texans were suspect because of their ancestry. A law was passed to prohibit speaking against the war effort. Persons who failed to participate in patriotic activities often were punished. Gov. William P. Hobby even vetoed the appropriation for the German department at the University of Texas.

Ferguson's removal from office was a devastating blow to the anti-prohibitionists. Word that the former governor had received a $156,000 loan from members of the brewers' association while in office provided ammunition for the progressives.

In February 1918, a special session of the Legislature prohibited saloons within a 10-mile radius of military posts and ratified the national prohibition amendment, which had been introduced in Congress by Texas Sen. **Morris Sheppard**.

**Women** also were given the **right to vote in state primaries** at the same session.

Although national prohibition was to become effective in early 1920, the Legislature presented a prohibition amendment to voters in May 1919, and it was approved, bringing prohibition to Texas earlier than to the rest of the nation. At the same time, a woman suffrage amendment, which would have granted women the right to vote in all elections, was defeated.

Although World War I ended in November 1918, it brought many changes to Texas. Rising prices during the war had increased the militancy of labor unions.

Blacks also became more militant after the war. Discrimination against black soldiers led in 1917 to a riot in Houston in which several people were killed.

With the election of Mexican President Alvaro Obregón in 1920, the fighting along the border subsided.

In 1919, state Rep. J.T. Canales of Brownsville initi-

ated an investigation of the **Texas Rangers'** role in the border problems. As a result of the study, the Rangers' manpower was reduced from 1,000 members to 76, and stringent limitations were placed on the agency's activities. Standards for members of the force also were upgraded.

By 1920, although still a rural state, the face of Texas was changing. Nearly one-third of the population was in the cities.

**Pat M. Neff** won the gubernatorial election of 1920, beating Sen. Joseph W. Bailey in the primary. As a former prosecuting attorney in McLennan County, Neff made law and order the major thrust of his administration. During his tenure the state took full responsibility for developing a **highway system**, a **gasoline tax** was imposed, and a state **park board** was established.

In 1921, a group of West Texans threatened to form a new state because Neff vetoed the creation of a new college in their area. Two years later, **Texas Technological College** (now Texas Tech University) was authorized in Lubbock and opened its doors in 1925.

Although still predominantly a rural state, Texas cities were growing. In 1900, only 17 percent of the population lived in urban areas; by 1920, that figure had almost doubled to 32 percent. A discontent developed with the growth of the cities. Rural Texans had long seen cities as hotbeds of vice and immorality. Simple rural values were cherished, and it seemed that those values were threatened in a changing world. After World War I, this transition accelerated.

### KKK and Minorities

In addition, "foreigners" in the state became suspect; nativism reasserted itself. German-Texans were associated with the enemy in the war, and Mexican-Texans were mostly Roman Catholics and likened to the troublemakers along the border. Texas was a fertile ground for the new **Ku Klux Klan** that entered the state in late 1920. The Klan's philosophy was a mixture of patriotism, law-and-order, nativism, white supremacy and Victorian morals. Its influence spread quickly across the state, and reports of Klan violence and murder were rampant.

**Prohibition** had brought a widespread disrespect for

*The covered wagon or "prairie schooner" played an important part in the settlement of Texas. This photo was taken in Hale County north of Lubbock around 1920. File photo.*

law. Peace officers and other officials often ignored speakeasies and gambling. The Klan seemed to many Texans to be an appropriate instrument for restoring law and order and for maintaining morality in towns and cities. By 1922, many of the state's large communities were under direct Klan influence, and a Klan-backed candidate, Earle Mayfield, was elected to the U.S. Senate, giving Texas the reputation as the most powerful Klan bastion in the Union. Hiram Wesley Evans of Dallas also was elected imperial wizard of the national Klan in that year.

The Klan became more directly involved in politics and planned to elect the next governor in 1924. Judge Felix Robertson of Dallas got the organization's backing in the Democratic primary. Former governor Jim Ferguson filed to run for the office, but the Texas Supreme Court ruled that he could not because of his impeachment conviction. So Ferguson placed his wife, **Miriam A. Ferguson**, on the ballot. Several other prominent Democrats also entered the race.

The Fergusons made no secret that Jim would have a big influence on his wife's administration. One campaign slogan was, "Two governors for the price of one." Mrs. Ferguson easily won the runoff against Robertson when many Texans decided that "Fergusonism" was preferable to the Klan in the governor's office.

Minorities began organizing in Texas to seek their civil rights. The National Association for the Advancement of Colored People (**NAACP**) opened a Texas chapter in 1912, and by 1919, there were chapters in 31 Texas communities. Similarly, Mexican-Texans formed Orden Hijos de America in 1921, and in 1929, the **League of United Latin American Citizens** (LULAC) was organized in Corpus Christi.

The Klan dominated the Legislature in 1923, passing a law barring blacks from participation in the Democratic primary. Although blacks had in fact been barred from voting in primaries for years, this law gave **Dr. Lawrence A. Nixon**, a black dentist from El Paso, the opportunity to go to court to fight the all-white primary.

In 1927, the U.S. Supreme Court overturned the statute, but that was only the beginning of several court battles, which were not resolved until 1944.

Disgruntled Democrats and Klansmen tried to beat Mrs. Ferguson in the general election in 1924, but she was too strong. Voters also sent 91 new members to the Texas House, purging it of many of the Klan-backed representatives. After that election, the Klan's power ebbed rapidly in Texas.

Mrs. Ferguson named Emma Grigsby Meharg as Texas' first woman secretary of state in 1925. The governors Ferguson administration was stormy. Jim was accused of cronyism in awarding highway contracts and in other matters. And "Ma" returned to her husband's practice of liberal clemency for prisoners. In two years, Mrs. Ferguson extended clemency to 3,595 inmates.

Although Jim Ferguson was at his bombastic best in the 1926 Democratic primary, young Attorney General **Dan Moody** had little trouble winning the nomination and the general election.

At age 33, Moody was the youngest person ever to become governor of Texas. Like many governors during this period, he was more progressive than the Legislature, and much of his program did not pass. Moody was successful in some government reorganization. He also cleaned up the highway department, which had been criticized under the Fergusons, and abandoned the liberal clemency policy for prisoners. And Moody worked at changing Texas' image as an anti-business state. "The day of the political trust-buster is gone," he told one Eastern journalist.

Progressives and prohibitionists still had a major influence on the Democratic Party, and 1928 was a watershed year for them. Moody easily won renomination and re-election. But the state party was drifting away from the direction of national Democrats. When **Al Smith**, a wet and a Roman Catholic, won the presidential nomination at the national Democratic convention in Houston, Texans were hard-pressed to remain faithful to the "party of the fathers." Moody, who had

been considered a potential national figure, ruined his political career trying to straddle the fence, angering both wets and drys, Catholics and Protestants. Former governor O.B. Colquitt led an exodus of so-called "**Hoovercrats**" from the state Democratic convention in 1928, and for the first time in its history, Texas gave its electoral votes to a Republican, Herbert Hoover, in the general election.

Through the 1920s, oil continued to increase in importance in Texas' economy. New discóveries were made at Mexia in 1920, Luling in 1922, Big Lake in Reagan Conty in 1923, in the Wortham Field in 1924 and in Borger in 1926. But oil still did not dominate the state's economic life.

As late as **1929**, meat packing, cottonseed processing and various milling operations exceeded the added value of petroleum refining. And as the 1920s ended, lumbering and food processing shared major economic roles with the petroleum industry. During the decade, Texas grew between 35 and 42 percent of U.S. cotton and 20-30 percent of the world crop. Irrigation and mechanization opened the South Plains to cotton growing. Eight years later, more than 1.1 million bales were grown in the region, mostly around Lubbock.

But Texas, with the rest of the nation, was on the threshhold of a major economic disaster that would have irreversible consequences. The **Great Depression** was at hand.

### Depression Years

Historians have noted that the state's economic collapse was not as severe as that which struck the industrialized states. Texas' economy had sputtered through the decade of the 1920s, primarily because of the fluctuation of the price of cotton and other agricultural products. But agricultural prices were improving toward the end of the decade.

The Fergusons attempted a political comeback in the gubernatorial election of 1930. But Texans elected **Ross S. Sterling**, the founder of Humble Oil Co. Early in the Depression, Texans remained optimistic that the economic problems were temporary, another of the cyclical downturns the nation experienced periodically. Indeed, some Texans even felt that the hardships would be beneficial, ridding the economy of speculators and poor businessmen. Those attitudes gave way to increasing concern as the poor business conditions dragged on.

A piece of good luck turned into a near economic disaster for the state in late 1930. **C.M. "Dad" Joiner** struck oil near Kilgore, and soon the **East Texas oil boom** was in full swing. Millions of barrrels of new oil flooded the market, making producers and small landowners wealthy. Soon the glut of new oil drove market prices down from $1.10 a barrel in 1930 to 10 cents in 1931. Many wells had to be shut in around the state because they could not produce oil profitably at the low prices.

The Texas Railroad Commission attempted in the spring of 1931 to control production through proration, which assigned production quotas to each well (called the allowable). The first proration order limited each well to about 1,000 barrels a day of production. **Proration** had two goals: to protect reserves through conservation and to maintain prices by limiting production. But, on July 28, a federal court ruled that proration was

an illegal attempt to fix prices.

In August 1931, Gov. Sterling placed four counties of the East Texas field under martial law and briefly shut down oil production there altogether. A federal court later ruled the governor's actions illegal. Gov. Sterling was roundly criticized for sending troops. Opponents said the action was taken to aid the major oil companies to the disadvantage of independent producers.

In 1932, Gov. Sterling appointed **Ernest O. Thompson** to a vacancy on the railroad commission. Thompson, who had led a coalition in favor of output regulation, is credited with fashioning a compromise between independents and major oil companies. In April 1933, the railroad commission prorated production on the basis, in part, of bottom-hole pressure in each well, and the courts upheld this approach. But enforcement remained a problem.

Finally in 1935, Texas' Sen. **Tom Connally** authored the Hot Oil Act, which involved the federal government in regulation by prohibiting oil produced in violation of state law from being sold in interstate commerce. Thereafter, Texas' producers accepted the concept of proration. Since Texas was the nation's largest oil producer, the railroad commission could set the national price of oil through proration for several decades thereafter.

Despite these problems, the oil boom helped East Texas weather the Depression better than other parts of the state. Farmers were hit particularly hard in 1931. Bumper crops had produced the familiar reduction in prices. Cotton dropped from 18 cents per pound in 1928 to six cents in 1931. That year Louisiana Gov. **Huey Long** proposed a ban on growing cotton in 1932 to eliminate the surplus. The Louisiana legislature enacted the ban, but Texas was the key state to the plan since it led the nation in cotton production. Gov. Sterling was cool to the idea, but responded to public support of it by calling a special session of the Legislature. The lawmakers passed a **cotton acreage limitation** bill in 1931, but the law was declared unconstitutional the following year.

One feature of the Depression had become the number of transients drifting from city to city looking for work. Local governments and private agencies tried to provide relief for the unemployed, but the effort was soon overwhelmed by the number of persons needing help. In Houston, blacks and Mexican-Texans were warned not to apply for relief because there was not enough money to take care of whites, and many Mexicans returned to Mexico voluntarily and otherwise.

To relieve the local governments, Gov. Sterling proposed a bond program to repay counties for highways they had built and to start a public-works program. Texans' long-held faith in self-reliance and rugged individualism was put to a severe test.

By **1932**, many were looking to the federal government to provide relief from the effects of the Depression.

U.S. Speaker of the House **John Nance Garner** of Texas was a presidential candidate when the Democrats held their national convention. To avoid a deadlocked convention, Garner maneuvered the Texans to change strategy. On the fourth ballot, the Texas delegation voted for the eventual nominee, New York Gov. **Franklin D. Roosevelt**. Garner got the second place on the ticket that

swept into office in the general election.

In Texas, **Miriam Ferguson** was successful in unseating Gov. Sterling in the Democratic primary, winning by about 4,000 votes. Her second administration was less turbulent than the first. State government costs were reduced, and voters approved $20 million in so-called "bread bonds" to help provide relief. In 1933, **horse racing** came to the state, authorized through a rider on an appropriations bill legalizing pari-mutuel betting. The law was repealed in 1937. Prohibition also was repealed in 1933, although much of Texas remained dry under the **local-option** laws and the prohibition against open saloons.

State government faced a series of financial problems during Mrs. Ferguson's second term. The annual deficit climbed to $14 million, and the state had to default on the interest payments on some bonds. Voters aggravated the situation by approving a $3,000 **homestead exemption**. Many property owners were losing their homes because they could not pay taxes. And while the exemption saved their homesteads, it worsened the state's financial problems.

Many Texas banks failed during the Depression, as did banks nationally. One of Roosevelt's first actions was to declare a national bank holiday in 1933. Gov. Ferguson closed state banks at the same time, although she had to "assume" authority that was not in the law.

### The New Deal

In Washington, Texans played an important role in shaping Roosevelt's **New Deal**. As vice president, Garner presided over the Senate and maneuvered legislation through the upper house. **Texans** also chaired major committees in the House: **Sam Rayburn**, Interstate and Foreign Commerce; **Hatton W. Sumners**, Judiciary; **Fritz G. Lanham**, Public Buildings and Grounds; **J.J. Mansfield**, Rivers and Harbors; and **James P. Buchanan**, Appropriations. With this influence, the Texas delegation supported the president's early social programs. In addition, **Jesse Jones** of Houston served as director of the Reconstruction Finance Corporation, the Federal Loan Administration and as Secretary of Commerce. Jones was one of the most influential men in Washington and second only to Roosevelt in wielding financial power to effect recovery.

Poor conservation practices had left many of the state's farmlands open to erosion. During the **Dust Bowl** days of the early and mid-1930s, for example, the weather bureau in Amarillo reported 192 dust storms within a three-year period. Cooperation between state and federal agencies helped improve farmers' conservation efforts and reduced the erosion problem by the end of the decade.

Mrs. Ferguson did not seek re-election in 1934, and Attorney General **James V. Allred** was elected. Under his administration, several social-welfare programs were initiated, including old-age pensions, teachers' retirement and worker's compensation. Allred was re-elected in 1936.

Some of the New Deal's luster dimmed when the nation was struck by another recession in 1937.

Although Texas' economic condition improved toward the end of the decade, a full recovery was not realized until the beginning of World War II — when the state went through another industrial revolution.

Tragedy struck the small East Texas town of **New London** in Rusk County on March 18, 1937. At 3:05 p.m., natural gas, which had seeped undetected into an enclosed area beneath a school building from a faulty pipe connection, exploded when a shop teacher turned on a sander. Approximately 298 of the 540 students and teachers in the school died, and all but 130 of the survivors were injured. The disaster prompted the Legislature to pass a law requiring that a malodorant be added to gas so leaks could be detected by smell.

In 1938, voters elected one of the most colorful figures in the state's political history to the governor's office. **W. Lee "Pappy" O'Daniel**, a flour salesman and leader of a radio hillbilly band, came from nowhere to defeat a field of much better known candidates in the Democratic primary and to easily win the general election. When re-elected two years later, O'Daniel became the first candidate to poll more than one million votes in a Texas election.

But O'Daniel's skills of state did not equal his campaigning ability, and throughout his administration, the governor and the Legislature were in conflict. In early **1941**, long-time U.S. Senator Morris Sheppard died, and O'Daniel wanted the office. He appointed Andrew Jackson Houston, Sam Houston's aged son, to fill the vacancy. Houston died after only 24 days in office. O'Daniel won the special election for the post in a close race with a young congressman, **Lyndon B. Johnson**.

Lt. Gov. **Coke R. Stevenson** succeeded O'Daniel as governor and brought a broad knowledge of government to the office. Stevenson was elected to two full terms. Thanks to frugal management and greatly increasing revenues during the war years, he left the state treasury with a surplus in 1947. Voters also solved the continuing deficit problem by approving a pay-as-you-go amendment to the constitution in 1942. It requires the state comptroller to certify that tax revenues will be available to support appropriations. Otherwise the money cannot be spent.

### World War II

As in every war after Texas entered the Union, young Texans flocked to military service when the United States entered World War II. More than 750,000 served, including 12,000 women in the auxiliary services. In December 1942, U.S. Secretary of the Navy Frank Knox said Texas contributed the largest percentage of its male population to the armed forces of any state. Thirty Texans won Congressional Medals of Honor in the fighting. **Audie Murphy**, a young farm boy from Farmersville, became one of the most decorated soldiers of the war. Dallas-born **Sam Dealey** was the most-decorated Navy man.

Important contributions also were made at home. Texas was the site of 15 training posts, at which more than one and a quarter million men were trained, and of several prisoner-of-war camps.

World War II irrevocably changed the face of Texas. During the decade of the 1940s, the state's population switched from predominantly rural to 60 percent **urban**. The number of **manufacturing** workers almost doubled. And as had been the dream of Texas leaders for more than a century, the state began to attract new industries.

### Conservatives vs. Liberals

The state's politics became increasingly controlled by conservative Democrats after Gov. Allred left office.

In 1946, **Beauford H. Jester**, a member of the railroad commission, gained the governorship. Under Jester in 1947, the Legislature passed the state's **right-to-work** law, prohibiting mandatory union membership, and reorganized public education with passage of the **Gilmer-Aikin Act**.

During the Jester administration several major constitutional amendments were adopted. Also, one of Texas' greatest tragedies occurred on April 16, 1947, when the French ship *SS Grandcamp*, carrying a load of ammonium nitrate, exploded at **Texas City**. More than 500 died and 4,000 sustained injuries. Property damage exceeded $200 million.

In **1948**, Sen. W. Lee O'Daniel did not seek re-election. Congressman Lyndon Johnson and former Gov. Coke Stevenson vied for the Democratic nomination. In the runoff, Johnson won by a mere **87 votes** in the closest — and most hotly disputed — statewide election in Texas' history. Johnson quickly rose to a leadership position in the U.S. Senate, and, with House Speaker Sam Rayburn, gave Texas substantial influence in national political affairs.

Although re-elected in 1948, Jester died in July 1949, the only Texas governor to die in office, and Lt. Gov. **Allan Shivers** succeeded him. During Shivers' administration, state spending more than doubled, reaching $805.7 million in 1956, as the governor increased appropriations for public-health institutions, school salaries, retirement benefits, highways and old-age pensions.

Shivers broke with tradition, successfully winning three full terms as governor after completing Jester's unexpired term. Shivers also led a revolt by Texas Democrats against the national party in **1952**. The governor, who gained both the Democratic and Republican nominations for the office under the law that allowed cross-filing that year, supported Republican Dwight Eisenhower for the presidency. Many Texas Democrats broke with the national party over the so-called "**Tidelands** issue.**" Texas claimed land 12 miles out into the Gulf as state lands. The issue was important because revenue from oil and natural gas production from the area supported public education in the state.

Major oil companies also backed Texas' position because state royalties on minerals produced from the land were much lower than federal royalties. President Harry S. Truman vetoed legislation that would have given Texas title to the land. Democratic presidential nominee Adlai Stevenson was no more sympathetic to the issue, and Texas gave its electoral votes to Republican Dwight Eisenhower in an election that attracted a two million-vote turnout for the first time in Texas. President Eisenhower signed a measure into law guaranteeing Texas' tidelands.

Scandal struck state government in 1954 when irregularities were discovered in the handling of funds in the veterans' land program in the General Land Office. Land Commissioner Bascom Giles was convicted of several charges and sent to prison. Several insurance companies also went bankrupt in the mid-1950s, prompting a reorganization of the State Board of Insurance in 1957.

In 1954, the U.S. Supreme Court ruled unconstitutional the segregation of schools, and for the next quarter-century, **school integration** became a major political issue. By the late 1960s, most institutions were integrated, but the state's major cities continued to wage court battles against forced busing of students to attain racial balance. Blacks and Mexican-Texans also made gains in voting rights during the 1950s.

Shivers had easily defeated **Ralph W. Yarborough** in the Democratic primary in 1952, but the divisions between the party's loyalists and those who bolted ranks to join Republicans in presidential races were growing. Shivers barely led the first 1954 primary over Yarborough and won the nomination with 53 percent of the vote in the runoff. Yarborough ran an equally close race against **Price Daniel**, a U.S. Senator who sought the governorship in 1956. Upon election as governor, Daniel left the Senate, and Yarborough won a special election to fill the vacancy in 1957. Yarborough won re-election in 1964 before losing to **Lloyd Bentsen** in 1970 in the Democratic primary. Although a liberal, Yarborough proved to be unusually durable in Texas' conservative political climate.

The state budget topped $1 billion for the first time in 1958. The Legislature met for 205 days in regular and special sessions in 1961–62 and levied, over Gov. Daniel's opposition, the state's first broad-based **sales tax in 1962**.

### Technological Growth

Through the 1950s and 1960s, Texas' industrial base had expanded and diversified. Petroleum production and refining remained the cornerstones, but other industries grew. Attracted by cheap electricity, the aluminum industry came to Texas. Starting from the base developed during World War II, defense industries and associated high-tech firms, specializing in electronics and computers, centered on the Dallas–Fort Worth area and Houston. One of the most important scientific breakthroughs of the century came in 1958 in Dallas. **Jack Kilby**, an engineer at **Texas Instruments**, developed and patented the integrated circuit that became the central part of computers.

Sen. Lyndon Johnson unsuccessfully sought the Democratic presidential nomination in 1960, and **John F. Kennedy** subsequently selected the Texan as his running mate. Johnson is credited with keeping several Southern states, including Texas, in the Democratic column in the close election. Kennedy was a Roman Catholic and a liberal, a combination normally rejected by the Southern states. When Johnson left the Senate to assume his new office in 1961, **John Tower** won a special election that attracted more than 70 candidates. Tower became the first Republican since Reconstruction to serve as a Texas senator.

During the early 1960s, Harris County was chosen as the site for the National Aeronautics and Space Administration's manned spacecraft center. The acquisition of **NASA** further diversified Texas' industrial base.

In 1962, **John B. Connally**, a former aide to LBJ and Secretary of the Navy under Kennedy, returned to Texas to seek the governorship. Gov. Daniel sought an unprecedented fourth term and was defeated in the Democratic primary. Connally won a close Democratic runoff over liberal **Don Yarborough** and was elected easily. As governor, Connally concentrated on improving **public education, state services** and **water development**. He was re-elected in 1964 and 1966.

*President John F. Kennedy (at left) was assassinated in Dallas on Nov. 22, 1963. Lee Harvey Oswald was arrested for the murder of the president that afternoon, but Oswald was killed by Dallas nightclub operator Jack Ruby (at right) two days later.*

## The Assassination

One of the major tragedies in the nation's history occurred in Dallas on **Nov. 22, 1963**, when President Kennedy was assassinated while riding in a motorcade. Gov. Connally also was seriously wounded. Lyndon Johnson was administered the oath of the presidency by Federal Judge Sarah T. Hughes of Dallas aboard Air Force One at Love Field. Lee Harvey Oswald was arrested for the murder of the president on the afternoon of the assassination, but Oswald was killed by Dallas nightclub operator Jack Ruby two days later.

An extensive investigation into the assassination of President Kennedy was conducted by the Warren Commission. The panel concluded that Oswald was the killer and that he acted alone. Ruby, who was convicted of killing Oswald, died of cancer in the Dallas County

*President Lyndon B. Johnson won a landslide election in 1964. File photo.*

jail in 1967 while the case was being appealed.

The assassination damaged the Republican Party in Texas, however. Building strength in Texas' conservative political atmosphere in 1962, eight Republicans, the most in decades, had been elected to the Texas House. And two Republicans — Ed Foreman of Odessa and Bruce Alger of Dallas — served in Congress. All were defeated in the 1964 general election.

In the emotional aftermath of the tragedy, Johnson, who won the presidency outright in a **landslide election in 1964**, persuaded the Congress to pass a series of civil-rights and social-welfare programs that changed the face of the nation. Texas was particularly affected by the civil-rights legislation and a series of lawsuits challeng-

ing election practices. During the 1960s, the state constitutional limitation of urban representation in the Legislature was overturned. The poll tax was declared unconstitutional, and the practice of electing officials from at-large districts fell to the so-called "one-man, one-vote" ruling. As a result, more Republican, minority and liberal officials were elected, particularly from urban areas. In 1966, **Curtis Graves** and **Barbara Jordan** of Houston and **Joe Lockridge** of Dallas became the first blacks to serve in the Texas Legislature since 1898.

Lyndon Johnson did not seek re-election in 1968. The nation had become involved in an unpopular war in Vietnam, and Johnson bowed out of the race in the interest of national unity.

## Sharpstown Scandal

Democrats, however, stayed firmly in control of state government. **Preston Smith** was elected governor, and **Ben Barnes** gained the lieutenant governorship. Both also were re-elected in 1970. Although state spending continued to increase, particularly on education, the Legislature otherwise was quiet. A minimum-wage law was approved, and public kindergartens were authorized in 1969.

At a special session, the **Sharpstown scandal**, one of the state's major scandals developed. Gov. Smith allowed the lawmakers to consider special banking legislation supported by Houston banker Frank Sharp. Several public officials were implicated in receiving favors from the banker for seeing that the legislation passed. Texas House Speaker Gus Mutscher and Rep. Tommy Shannon were convicted of conspiracy to accept bribes in a trial held in Abilene.

Voters in **1972** demanded a new leadership in the state capital. Smith and Barnes were defeated in the Democratic primary, and **Dolph Briscoe** was elected governor. In the fall, Texans gave presidential candidate Richard Nixon the state's electoral votes. Nixon carried 246 counties over Democrat George McGovern and received more than 65 percent of the popular vote.

The Legislature in 1973 was dominated by a reform atmosphere in the wake of the Sharpstown scandal. Price Daniel Jr., son of the former governor, was

selected speaker of the House, and several laws concerning ethics and disclosure of campaign donations and spending were passed. Open meetings and open records statutes also were approved.

By 1970, Texas had become an even more urban state. The census found almost 11.2 million people in the state, ranking it sixth nationally. Three Texas cities, Houston, Dallas and San Antonio, were among the 10 largest in the nation.

Through the first half of the 1970s, several major changes were made in state policy. **Liquor-by-the-drink** became legal and the **age of majority** was lowered from 20 to 18, giving young people the right to vote. Also, the state's first **Public Utilities Commission** was created, hearing its initial case in September 1976.

### Prosperity

Texas entered a period of unparalleled prosperity in 1973 when the Organization of Petroleum Exporting Countries (OPEC) boycotted the U.S. market. Severe energy shortages resulted, and the price of oil and natural gas skyrocketed. The federal government had allowed foreign oil to be imported through the 1960s, severely reducing the incentives to find and produce domestic oil. Consequently, domestic producers could not compensate for the loss in foreign oil as a result of the boycott. The Texas Railroad Commission had long complained about the importation of foreign oil, and in 1972, the panel had removed proration controls from wells in the state, allowing 100 percent production. For the rest of the decade, domestic producers mounted a major exploration effort, drilling thousands of wells. Nevertheless, **Texas' oil and gas production peaked in 1970** and has been declining since. Newly discovered oil and gas have not replaced the declining reserves. While Texans suffered from the inflation that followed, the state prospered. Tax revenues at all levels of government increased, and state revenues, basically derived from oil and gas taxes, spiraled, as did the state budget.

With the new revenue from inflation and petroleum taxes, state spending rose from $2.95 billion in 1970 to $8.6 billion in 1979, and education led the advance, moving from 42 percent of the budget to 51.5 percent. But there was no increase in state tax rates.

It was no surprise that **education** was one of the major beneficiaries of increased state spending. After World War II, more emphasis was placed on education across the state. **Community colleges** sprang up in many cities, and a total of 109 colleges were established between the end of the war and 1980. Quantity did not assure quality, however, and Texas' public and higher education seldom were ranked among national leaders.

In 1972, voters approved an amendment authorizing the Legislature to sit as a **constitutional convention** to rewrite the 1876 charter. The lawmakers met for several months and spent $5 million, but they failed to propose anything to be considered by voters. The public was outraged, and in 1975, the Legislature presented the work of the convention to voters in the form of eight constitutional amendments. All were defeated in a special election in November 1975.

Texas voters participated in their **first presidential primary in 1976**. Jimmy Carter of Georgia won the Democratic primary, and eventually the presidency. Ronald Reagan carried the state's Republicans, but lost the party's nomination to President Gerald Ford.

The state proved politically volatile in **1978**. First, Attorney General **John Hill** defeated Gov. Dolph Briscoe in the Democratic primary. A political newcomer, Dallas businessman **William P. Clements**, upset Hill in the general election, giving Texas its first Republican governor since Reconstruction. Also for the first time since Reconstruction, state officials were elected to **four-year terms**. ☆

# TEXAS A&M

College Station, Texas
800-826-8911
Fax: 888-617-2421
www.tamu.edu/upress

## UNIVERSITY PRESS

**TEXAS FLAGS**
Robert Maberry, Jr.
$50.00

**TREES OF TEXAS**
*An Easy Guide to Leaf Identification*
Carmine Stahl and Ria McElvaney
$29.95

**BIRDS OF NORTHEAST TEXAS**
Matt White
$34.95 cloth; $19.95 paper

**SPRINGS OF TEXAS**
Gunnar Brune
With a new introduction by Helen C. Besse
$75.00

**BIG BEND LANDSCAPES**
Paintings and drawings by Dennis Blagg
Introduction by Ron Tyler
$40.00

**THE ROOTS OF TEXAS MUSIC**
Edited by Lawrence S. Clayton and
Joe W. Specht
$29.95

**MARIA VON BLÜCHER'S CORPUS CHRISTI**
*Letters from the South Texas Frontier,
1849–1879*
Edited by Bruce S. Cheeseman
$29.95

**DINING AT THE GOVERNOR'S MANSION**
Carl R. McQueary
$24.95

**SAN ANTONIO ON PARADE**
*Six Historic Festivals*
Judith Berg Sobré
$29.95

**THE TEXAS POST OFFICE MURALS**
*Art for the People*
Philip Parisi
$45.00

**ROCK BENEATH THE SAND**
*Country Churches in Texas*
Photographs by Clark Baker
Text by Lois E. Myers and
Rebecca Sharpless
$35.00

**CHASING BIRDS ACROSS TEXAS**
*A Birding Big Year*
Mark T. Adams
$40.00 cloth; $18.95 paper

**INSECTS OF THE TEXAS LOST PINES**
Stephen Welton Taber and Scott B. Fleenor
$50.00 cloth; $24.95 paper

**THE NEW TEXAS CHALLENGE**
*Population Change and the Future of Texas*
Steve H. Murdock, et al.
$19.95 paper

*Distributed by Texas A&M Press*
**TEXAS ALMANAC 2004–2005**
62nd Edition
$19.95 cloth; $13.95 paper
$9.95 teacher's guide

# Environment

Extending from sea level at the Gulf of Mexico to over 8,000 feet in the Guadalupe Mountains of far West Texas and from the semitropical Lower Rio Grande Valley to the High Plains of the Panhandle, Texas has a natural environment of remarkable variety. This section discusses the physical features, geology, soils, water, vegetation, and wildlife that are found in the Lone Star State.

## The Physical State of Texas

### Area of Texas

Texas occupies about 7 percent of the total water and land area of the United States. **Second in size** among the states, Texas has a land and water area of 268,580 square miles as compared with Alaska's 663,267 square miles, according to the United States Bureau of the Census. California, the third largest state, has 163,696 square miles. Texas is as large as all of New England, New York, Pennsylvania, Ohio and North Carolina combined.

The **state's area** consists of 261,797 square miles of land and 6,783 square miles of water.

### Length and Breadth

The **longest straight-line distance** in a general north-south direction is 801 miles from the northwest corner of the Panhandle to the extreme southern tip of Texas on the Rio Grande below Brownsville. The greatest east-west distance is 773 miles from the extreme eastward bend in the Sabine River in Newton County to the extreme western bulge of the Rio Grande just above El Paso.

The **geographic center** of Texas is southwest of Mercury in northern McCulloch County at approximately 99° 20' west longitude and 31° 08'north latitude.

### Texas' Boundary Lines

The boundary of Texas by segments, including only larger river bends and only the great arc of the coastline, is as follows:

| Boundary | Miles |
|---|---|
| Rio Grande | 889.0 |
| Coastline | 367.0 |
| Sabine River, Lake and Pass | 180.0 |
| *Sabine River to Red River | 106.5 |
| † Red River | 480.0 |
| *East Panhandle line | 133.6 |
| *North Panhandle line | 167.0 |
| *West Panhandle line | 310.2 |
| *Along 32nd parallel | 209.0 |
| **Total** | **2,842.3** |

Following the smaller meanderings of the rivers and the tidewater coastline, the following are the boundary measurements:

| | |
|---|---|
| Rio Grande | 1,254 |
| Coastline (tidewater) | 624 |
| Sabine River, Lake and Pass | 292 |
| † Red River | 726 |
| *The five unchanged line segments above | 926 |
| **Total** (including segments marked *) | **3,822** |

† A history of the **Red River boundary dispute** between Texas and Oklahoma can be found in the 2002–2003 Texas Almanac.

### Latitude and Longitude

The extremes of latitude and longitude are as follows: From 25° 50' north latitude at the extreme southern turn of the Rio Grande on the south line of Cameron County to 36° 30' north latitude along the north line of the Panhandle, and from 93° 31' west. longitude at the extreme eastern point on the Sabine River on the east line of Newton County to 106° 38' west longitude on the extreme westward point on the Rio Grande above El Paso.

### Texas' Highs and Lows

The highest point in the state is **Guadalupe Peak** at **8,749 feet** above sea level. Its twin, **El Capitan**, stands at **8,085** feet and also is located in Culberson County near the New Mexico state line. Both are in the Guadalupe Mountains National Park, which includes scenic McKittrick Canyon. These elevations and the others in this article have been determined by the U.S. Geological Survey, unless otherwise noted.

The named peaks above 8,000 feet and the counties in which they are located are listed below. These elevations may differ from those in earlier editions of the Almanac because of the more accurate measuring methods currently being used by the USGS.

### Named Peaks in Texas Above 8,000 Feet

| Name, County | Elevation |
|---|---|
| Guadalupe Peak, Culberson | 8,749 |
| Bush Mountain, Culberson | 8,631 |
| Shumard Peak, Culberson | 8,615 |
| Bartlett Peak, Culberson | 8,508 |
| Mount Livermore (Baldy Peak), Jeff Davis | 8,378 |
| Hunter Peak (Pine Top Mtn.), Culberson | 8,368 |
| El Capitan, Culberson | 8,085 |

**Fort Davis** in Jeff Davis County is the **highest town** of any size in Texas at 5,050 feet, and the county has the **highest average elevation**. The **highest state highway point** also is in the county at **McDonald Observatory** at the end of a tap from State Highway 118 on **Mount Locke**. The observatory stands at 6,781 feet, as determined by the Texas Department of Transportation.

The **highest railway point** is Paisano Pass, 14 miles east of Marfa in Presidio County.

Sea level is the **lowest elevation** determined in Texas, and it can be found in all the coastal counties. No point in the state has been found by the geological survey to be below sea level. ☆

# Physical Regions

This section was reviewed by Dr. William M. Holmes, former chairman of the Department of Geography at the University of North Texas in Denton.

The principal physical regions of Texas are usually listed as follows (see also **Vegetational Areas** and **Soils**):

## The Gulf Coastal Plains

Texas' Gulf Coastal Plains are the western extension of the coastal plain extending from the Atlantic to beyond the Rio Grande. Its characteristic rolling to hilly surface covered with a heavy growth of pine and hardwoods extends into East Texas. In the increasingly arid west, however, its forests become secondary in nature, consisting largely of post oaks and, farther west, prairies and brushlands.

The interior limit of the Gulf Coastal Plains in Texas is the line of the **Balcones Fault and Escarpment.** This geologic fault or shearing of underground strata extends eastward from a point on the Rio Grande near Del Rio. It extends to the northwestern part of Bexar County where it turns northeastward and extends through Comal, Hays and Travis counties, intersecting the Colorado River immediately above Austin. The fault line is a single, definite geologic feature, accompanied by a line of southward- and eastward-facing hills.

The resemblance of the hills to balconies when viewed from the plain below accounts for the Spanish name for this area: *balcones*.

North of Waco, features of the fault zone are sufficiently inconspicuous that the interior boundary of the Coastal Plain follows the traditional geologic contact between upper and lower Cretaceous rocks. This contact is along the western edge of the **Eastern Cross Timbers.**

This fault line is usually accepted as the boundary between lowland and upland Texas. Below the fault line the surface is characteristically coastal plains. Above the Balcones Fault the surface is characteristically interior rolling plains.

### Pine Belt or "Piney Woods"

The Pine Belt, called the "Piney Woods," extends into Texas from the east 75 to 125 miles. From north to south it extends from the Red River to within about 25 miles of the Gulf Coast. Interspersed among the pines are some hardwood timbers, usually in valleys of rivers and creeks. This area is the source of practically all of Texas' commercial timber production (see "Forests" in index). It was settled early in Texas' history and is an older farming area of the state.

This area's soils and climate are adaptable to production of a variety of fruit and vegetable crops. Cattle raising is widespread, accompanied by the development of pastures planted to improved grasses. Lumber production is the principal industry. There is a large iron-and-steel industry near Daingerfield in Morris County based on nearby iron deposits. Iron deposits are also worked in Rusk and one or two other counties.

A great oil field discovered in Gregg, Rusk and Smith counties in 1931 has done more than anything else to contribute to the economic growth of the area. This area has a variety of clays, lignite and other minerals as potentials for development.

### Post Oak Belt

The main Post Oak Belt of Texas is wedged between the Pine Belt on the east, Blacklands on the west, and the Coastal Prairies on the south, covering a considerable area in East Central Texas. The principal industry is diversified farming and livestock raising. Throughout, it is spotty in character, with some insular areas of blackland soil and some that closely resemble those of the Pine Belt. There is a small isolated area of pines in Bastrop County known as the **"Lost Pines."** The Post Oak Belt has lignite, commercial clays and some other minerals.

### Blackland Belt

The Blackland Belt stretches from the Rio Grande to the Red River, lying just below the line of the **Balcones Fault,** and varying in width from 15 to 70 miles. It is narrowest below the segment of the Balcones Fault from the Rio Grande to Bexar County and gradually widens as it runs northeast to the Red River. Its rolling prairie, easily turned by the plow, developed rapidly as a farming area until the 1930s and was the principal cotton-producing area of Texas. Now, however, other Texas irrigated, mechanized areas lead in farming. Because of the early growth, the Blackland Belt is still the most thickly populated area in the state and contains within it and along its border more of the state's large and middle-sized cities than any other area. Primarily because of this concentration of population, this belt has the most diversified manufacturing industry of the state.

### Coastal Prairies

The Texas Coastal Prairies extend westward along the coast from the Sabine River, reaching inland 30 to 60 miles. Between the Sabine and Galveston Bay, the line of demarcation between the prairies and the Pine Belt forests to the north is very distinct. The Coastal Prairie extends along the Gulf from the Sabine to the Lower Rio Grande Valley. The eastern half is covered with a heavy growth of grass; the western half, which is more arid, is covered with short grass and, in some places, with small timber and brush. The soil is heavy clay. Grass supports the densest cattle population in Texas, and cattle ranching is the principal agricultural industry. Rice is a major crop, grown under irrigation from wells and rivers. Cotton, grain sorghum and truck crops are grown.

Coastal Prairie areas have seen the greatest industrial development in Texas history since World War II. Chief concentration has been from Orange and Beaumont to Houston, and much of the development has been in petrochemicals.

Corpus Christi, in the Coastal Bend, and Brownsville, in the Lower Rio Grande Valley, have seaports and agricultural and industrial sections. Cotton, grain, vegetables and citrus fruits are the principal crops. Cattle production is significant, with the famed King Ranch and other large ranches located here.

### Lower Rio Grande Valley

The deep alluvial soils and distinctive economy cause the Lower Rio Grande Valley to be classified as a subregion of the Gulf Coastal Plain. The Lower Valley, as it is called locally, is Texas' greatest citrus-winter vegetable area because of the normal absence of freezing weather and the rich delta soils of the Rio Grande. Despite occasional damaging freezes, as in 1951 and 1961, the Lower Valley ranks high among the nation's fruit-and-truck regions. Much of the acreage is irrigated, although dryland farming also is practiced.

### Rio Grande Plain

This may be roughly defined as lying south of San Antonio between the Rio Grande and the Gulf Coast. The Rio Grande Plain shows characteristics of both the Texas Gulf Coastal Plain and the North Mexico Plains because there is similarity of topography, climate and plant life all the way from the Balcones Escarpment in Texas to the Sierra Madre Oriental in Mexico, which runs past Monterrey about 160 miles south of Laredo.

The Rio Grande Plain is partly prairie, but much of it is covered with a dense growth of **prickly pear, cactus, mesquite, dwarf oak, catclaw, guajillo, huisache, blackbrush, cenizo** and other wild shrubs. This country is devoted primarily to raising cattle, sheep and goats. The

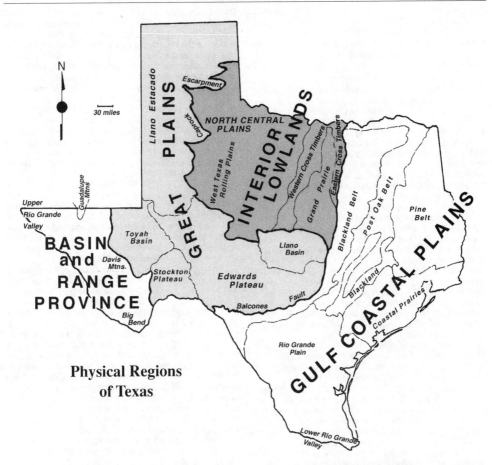

**Physical Regions
of Texas**

Texas Angora goat and mohair industry centers in this area and on the **Edwards Plateau,** which borders it on the north. San Antonio and Laredo are its chief commercial centers, with San Antonio dominating trade.

There is some farming, and the **Winter Garden,** centering in Dimmit and Zavala counties north of Laredo, is irrigated from wells and streams to produce vegetables in late winter and early spring. Primarily, however, the central and western part of the Rio Grande Plain is devoted to livestock raising. The rainfall is less than 25 inches annually and the hot summers bring heavy evaporation, so that cultivation without irrigation is limited. Over a large area in the central and western parts of the Rio Grande Plain, the growth of **small oaks, mesquite, prickly pear (Opuntia) cactus** and a variety of wild shrubs is very dense and it is often called the **Brush Country.** It is also referred to as the **chaparral** and the **monte.** (Monte is a Spanish word, one meaning of which is dense brush.)

### Interior Lowlands
#### North Central Plains

The North Central Plains of Texas are a southwestern extension into Texas of the interior lowlands that extend northward to the Canadian border, paralleling the Great Plains to the West. The North Central Plains of Texas extend from the Blackland Belt on the east to the Caprock Escarpment on the west. From north to south they extend from the Red River to the Colorado.

#### West Texas Rolling Plains

The West Texas Rolling Plains, approximately the western two-thirds of the North Central Plains in Texas,

rise from east to west in altitude from about 750 feet to 2,000 feet at the base of the **Caprock Escarpment**. Annual rainfall ranges from about 30 inches on the east to 20 on the west. Temperature varies rather widely between summer's heat and winter's cold.

This area still has a large cattle-raising industry with many of the state's largest ranches. However, there is much level, cultivable land.

#### Grand Prairie

Near the eastern edge of the North Central Plains is the Grand Prairie, extending south from the Red River in an irregular band through Cooke, Montague, Wise, Denton, Tarrant, Parker, Hood, Johnson, Bosque, Coryell and some adjacent counties. It is a limestone-based area, usually treeless except along the numerous streams, and adapted primarily to livestock raising and staple-crop growing. Sometimes called the Fort Worth Prairie, it has an agricultural economy and largely rural population, with no large cities except Fort Worth on its eastern boundary.

#### Eastern and Western Cross Timbers

Hanging over the top of the Grand Prairie and dropping down on each side are the Eastern and Western Cross Timbers. The two southward-extending bands are connected by a narrow strip along the Red River. The Eastern Cross Timbers extend southward from the Red River through eastern Denton County and along the Dallas-Tarrant County boundary, then through Johnson County to the Brazos River and into Hill County. The much larger Western Cross Timbers extend from the Red River south through Clay, Montague, Jack, Wise, Parker, Palo

Pinto, Hood, Erath, Eastland, Comanche, Brown and Mills counties to the Colorado River, where they meet the Edwards Plateau. Their soils are adapted to fruit and vegetable crops, which reach considerable commercial production in some areas in Parker, Erath, Eastland and Comanche counties.

## Great Plains

The Great Plains which lie to the east of the base of the Rocky Mountains extend into Northwest Texas. This area, which is a vast, flat, high plain covered with thick layers of alluvial material, is known as the **Staked Plains** or the Spanish equivalent, **Llano Estacado**.

Historians differ as to the origin of this name. Some think that it came from the fact that the Coronado expedition, crossing the trackless sea of grass, staked its route so that it would be guided on its return trip. Others think that the "estacado" refers to the palisaded appearance of the Caprock in many places, especially the west-facing escarpment in New Mexico.

The **Caprock Escarpment** is the dividing line between the High Plains and the Lower Rolling Plains of West Texas. Like the Balcones Escarpment, the Caprock Escarpment is a striking physical feature, rising abruptly 200, 500 and in some places almost 1,000 feet above the plains. Unlike the **Balcones Escarpment**, the Caprock was caused by surface erosion. Where rivers issue from the eastern face of the Caprock, there frequently are notable canyons, such as the **Palo Duro Canyon** on the **Prairie Dog Town Fork (main channel) of the Red River** and the breaks along the Canadian as it crosses the Panhandle north of Amarillo.

Along the eastern edge of the Panhandle there is a gradual descent of the earth's surface from high to low plains, but at the Red River the Caprock Escarpment becomes a striking surface feature. It continues as an east-facing wall south through Briscoe, Floyd, Motley, Dickens, Crosby, Garza and Borden counties, gradually decreasing in elevation. South of Borden County the escarpment is less obvious, and the boundary between the High Plains and the Edwards Plateau occurs where the alluvial cover of the High Plains disappears.

Stretching over the largest level plain of its kind in the United States, the **High Plains** rise gradually from about 2,700 feet on the east to more than 4,000 in spots along the New Mexico border.

Chiefly because of climate and the resultant agriculture, subdivisions are called the North Plains and South Plains. The North Plains, from Hale County north, has primarily wheat and grain sorghum farming, but with significant ranching and petroleum developments. Amarillo is the largest city, with Plainview on the south and Borger on the north as important commercial centers. The South Plains, also a leading grain sorghum region, leads Texas in cotton production. Lubbock is the principal city, and Lubbock County is one of the state's largest cotton producers. Irrigation from underground reservoirs, centered around Lubbock and Plainview, waters much of the crop acreage.

### Edwards Plateau

Geographers usually consider that the Great Plains at the foot of the Rocky Mountains actually continue southward from the High Plains of Northwest Texas to the Rio Grande and the Balcones Escarpment. This southern and lower extension of the Great Plains in Texas is known as the Edwards Plateau.

It lies between the Rio Grande and the Colorado River. Its southeastern border is the **Balcones Escarpment** from the Rio Grande at Del Rio eastward to San Antonio and thence to Austin on the Colorado. Its upper boundary is the Pecos River, though the **Stockton Plateau** is geologically and topographically classed with the Edwards Plateau. The Edwards Plateau varies from about 750 feet high at its southern and eastern borders to about 2,700 feet in places. Almost the entire surface is a thin, lime-

stone-based soil covered with a medium to thick growth of **cedar, small oak** and **mesquite** with a varying growth of **prickly pear.** Grass for cattle, weeds for sheep and tree foliage for the browsing goats support three industries — cattle, goat and sheep raising — upon which the area's economy depends. It is the **nation's leading Angora goat and mohair producing region** and one of the nation's leading sheep and wool areas. A few crops are grown.

### Toyah Basin

To the northwest of the Edwards and Stockton plateaus is the Toyah Basin, a broad, flat remnant of an old sea floor that occupied the region as recently as Quaternary time. Located in the Pecos River Valley, this region, in relatively recent time, has become important for many agricultural products as a result of irrigation. Additional economic activity is afforded by local oil fields.

### The Hill Country

The Hill Country is a popular name for an area of hills and spring-fed streams along the edge of the **Balcones Escarpment**. Notable large springs include **Barton Springs** at Austin, **San Marcos Springs** at San Marcos, **Comal Springs** at New Braunfels, several springs at San Antonio, and a number of others.

### The Llano Basin

The Llano Basin lies at the junction of the Colorado and Llano rivers in Burnet and Llano counties. Earlier this was known as the **"Central Mineral Region,"** because of the evidence there of a large number of minerals.

On the Colorado River in this area, a succession of dams impounds two large and five small reservoirs. Uppermost is **Lake Buchanan,** one of the large reservoirs, between Burnet and Llano counties. Below it in the western part of Travis County is **Lake Travis.** Between these two large reservoirs are three smaller ones, **Inks, L. B. Johnson** (formerly Granite Shoals) and **Marble Falls** reservoirs, used primarily for maintaining heads to produce electric power from the overflow from Lake Buchanan. **Lake Austin** is just above the city of Austin. Still another small lake, **Town Lake,** is formed by a low-water dam in Austin. The recreational area around these lakes is called the **Highland Lakes Country**. This is an interesting area with Precambrian and Paleozoic rocks found on the surface.

## Basin and Range Province

The Basin and Range province, with its center in Nevada, surrounds the Colorado Plateau on the west and south and enters far West Texas from southern New Mexico. It consists of broad interior drainage, basins interspersed with scattered fault-block mountain ranges. Although this is the only part of Texas regarded as mountainous, these should not be confused with the Rockies. Of all the independent ranges in West Texas, only the Davis Mountains resemble the Rockies and there is much debate about this.

Texas west of the Edwards Plateau, bounded on the north by New Mexico and on the south by the Rio Grande, is distinctive in its physical and economic conditions. Traversed from north to south by an eastern range of the Rockies, it contains all of **Texas' true mountains** and also is very interesting geologically.

Highest of the Trans-Pecos Mountains is the **Guadalupe Range,** which enters the state from New Mexico. It comes to an abrupt end about 20 miles south of the boundary line, where **Guadalupe Peak**, (8,749 feet, highest in Texas) and **El Capitan** (8,085 feet) are situated. El Capitan, because of perspective, appears to the observer on the plain below to be higher than Guadalupe. Lying just west of the Guadalupe range and extending to the **Hueco Mountains** a short distance east of El Paso is the **Diablo Plateau** or basin. It has no drainage outlet to the sea. The runoff from the scant rain that falls on its surface drains into a series of salt lakes that lie just west of the Guadalupe Mountains. These lakes are dry during periods of low

rainfall, exposing bottoms of solid salt, and for years they were a source of **commercial salt**.

### Davis Mountains

The Davis Mountains are principally in Jeff Davis County. The highest peak, **Mount Livermore**, (8,378 feet) is **one of the highest in Texas;** there are several others more than 7,000 feet high. These mountains intercept the moisture-bearing winds and receive more precipitation than elsewhere in the Trans-Pecos, so they have more vegetation than the other Trans-Pecos mountains. Noteworthy are the **San Solomon Springs** at the northern base of these mountains.

### Big Bend

South of the Davis Mountains lies the Big Bend country, so called because it is encompassed on three sides by a great southward swing of the Rio Grande. It is a mountainous country of scant rainfall and sparse population. Its principal mountains, the **Chisos**, rise to 7,825 feet in **Mount Emory**. Along the Rio Grande are the **Santa Elena, Mariscal** and **Boquillas canyons** with rim eleva-

tions of 3,500 to 3,775 feet. They are among the noteworthy canyons of the North American continent. Because of its remarkable topography and plant and animal life, the southern part of this region along the Rio Grande is home to the **Big Bend National Park**, with headquarters in a deep valley in the Chisos Mountains. It is a favorite recreation area.

### Upper Rio Grande Valley

The Upper Rio Grande (El Paso) Valley is a narrow strip of irrigated land running down the river from El Paso for a distance of 75 miles or more. In this area are the historic towns and missions of **Ysleta, Socorro and San Elizario, oldest in Texas**. Cotton is the chief product of the valley, much of it the long-staple variety. This limited area has a dense urban and rural population, in marked contrast to the territory surrounding it. ☆

*For Further Reading:*
*"Texas: A Geography," by Terry G. Jordan with John L. Bean Jr. and William M. Holmes; Westview Press, Boulder and London, 1984.*

# Geology of Texas

Source: Bureau of Economic Geology, The University of Texas at Austin; www.beg.utexas.edu/

## History in the Rocks

Mountains, seas, coastal plains, rocky plateaus, high plains, forests — all this physiographic variety in Texas is controlled by the varied rocks and structures that underlie and crop out across the state. The fascinating geologic history of Texas is recorded in the rocks — both those exposed at the surface and those penetrated by holes drilled in search of oil and natural gas. The rocks reveal a dynamic, ever-changing earth — ancient mountains, seas, volcanoes, earthquake belts, rivers, hurricanes and winds. Today, the volcanoes and great earthquake belts are no longer active, but rivers and streams, wind and rain, and the slow, inexorable alterations of rocks at or near the surface continue to change the face of Texas. The geologic history of Texas, as documented by the rocks, began more than a billion years ago. Its legacy is the mineral wealth and varied land forms of modern Texas.

## Geologic Time Travel

The story preserved in rocks requires an understanding of the origin of strata and how they have been deformed. **Stratigraphy** is the study of the composition, sequence and origin of rocks: what rocks are made of, how they were formed and the order in which the layers were formed. Structural geology reveals the architecture of rocks: the locations of the mountains, volcanoes, sedimentary basins and earthquake belts. The map on the following page shows where rocks of various geologic ages are visible on the surface of Texas today. History concerns events through time, but geologic time is such a grandiose concept, most find it difficult to comprehend. So, geologists have named the various chapters of earth history.

## Precambrian Eon

**Precambrian** rocks, more than 600 million years old, are exposed at the surface in the **Llano Uplift** of Central Texas and in scattered outcrops in **West Texas**, around and north of Van Horn and near El Paso. These rocks, some more than a billion years old, include complexly deformed rocks that were originally formed by cooling from a liquid state as well as rocks that were altered from pre-existing rocks.

Precambrian rocks, often called the "basement complex," are thought to form the foundation of continental masses. They underlie all of Texas. The outcrop in Central Texas is only the exposed part of the **Texas Craton**, which is primarily buried by younger rocks. (A craton is a stable, almost immovable portion of the earth's crust that forms the nuclear mass of a continent.)

## Paleozoic Era

During the early part of the Paleozoic Era (approximately 600 million to 350 million years ago), broad, relatively shallow seas repeatedly inundated the Texas Craton and much of

*Rock climbing is a favorite activity at Lake Mineral Wells State Park in Parker County. The area has outcroppings of Cretaceous, Pennsylvanian and Mississippian rock. File photo.*

North and West Texas. The evidence for these events is found exposed around the Llano Uplift and in far West Texas near Van Horn and El Paso, and also in the subsurface throughout most of West and North Texas. The evidence includes early Paleozoic rocks — sandstones, shales and limestones, similar to sediments that form in seas today — and the fossils of animals, similar to modern crustaceans — the brachiopods, clams, snails and related organisms that live in modern marine environments.

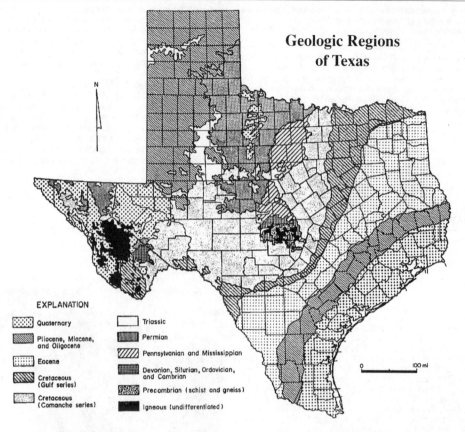

## Geologic Regions of Texas

N

EXPLANATION

- Quaternary
- Pliocene, Miocene, and Oligocene
- Eocene
- Cretaceous (Gulf series)
- Cretaceous (Comanche series)
- Triassic
- Permian
- Pennsylvanian and Mississippian
- Devonian, Silurian, Ordovician, and Cambrian
- Precambrian (schist and gneiss)
- Igneous (undifferentiated)

0        100 mi

By **late Paleozoic** (approximately 350 million to 240 million years ago), the Texas Craton was bordered on the east and south by a long, deep marine basin called the **Ouachita Trough.** Sediments slowly accumulated in this trough until late in the Paleozoic Era. Plate-tectonic theory postulates that the collision of the North American Plate (upon which the Texas Craton is located) with the European and African–South American plates uplifted the thick sediments that had accumulated in the trough to form the Ouachita Mountains. At that time, the Ouachitas extended across Texas. Today, the Texas portion of the old mountain range is entirely buried by younger rocks, and all that remains at the surface of the once-majestic Ouachita Mountain chain is exposed only in southeastern Oklahoma and southwestern Arkansas.

During the **Pennsylvanian Period**, however, the Ouachita Mountains bordered the eastern margin of shallow inland seas that covered most of West Texas. Rivers flowed westward from the mountains to the seas bringing sediment to form deltas along an ever-changing coastline. The sediments were then reworked by the waves and currents of the inland sea. Today, these fluvial, delta and shallow marine deposits compose the late Paleozoic rocks that crop out and underlie the surface of North-Central Texas.

Broad marine shelves divided the West Texas seas into several sub-basins, or deeper areas, that received more sediments than accumulated on the limestone shelves. Limestone reefs rimmed the deeper basins. Today, these reef limestones are important **oil reservoirs in West Texas**. These seas gradually withdrew from Texas, and by the late **Permian Period,** all that was left in West Texas were shallow basins and wide tidal flats in which salt, gypsum and red muds accumulated in a hot, arid land. Strata deposited during the Permian Period are exposed today along the edge of the Panhandle, as far east as Wichita Falls and south to Concho County, and in the Trans-Pecos.

## Mesozoic Era

Approximately 240 million years ago, the major geologic events in Texas shifted from West Texas to East and Southeast Texas. The European and African–South American plates, which had collided with the North American plate to form the Ouachita Mountains, began to separate from North America. A series of faulted basins, or rifts, extending from Mexico to Nova Scotia were formed. These rifted basins received sediments from adjacent uplifts. As Europe and the southern continents continued to drift away from North America, the Texas basins were eventually buried beneath thick deposits of marine salt within the newly formed East Texas and Gulf Coast basins.

**Jurassic** and **Cretaceous** rocks in East and Southeast Texas document a sequence of broad limestone shelves at the edge of the developing Gulf of Mexico. From time to time, the shelves were buried beneath deltaic sandstones and shales, which built the northwestern margin of the widening Gulf of Mexico to the south and southeast. As the underlying salt was buried more deeply by dense sediments, the salt became unstable and moved toward areas of least pressure. As the salt moved, it arched or pierced overlying sediments forming, in some cases, columns known as **"salt domes."** In some cases, these salt domes moved to the surface; others remain beneath a sedimentary overburden. This mobile salt formed numerous structures that would later serve to trap oil and natural gas.

By the early **Cretaceous** (approximately 140 million years ago), the shallow **Mesozoic seas** covered a large part of Texas, eventually extending west to the Trans-Pecos area and north almost to present-day state boundaries. Today, the limestone deposited in those seas are exposed in the walls of the magnificent **canyons of the Rio Grande** in the Big Bend National Park area and in the canyons and headwaters of streams that drain the Edwards Plateau, as well as in Central Texas from San Antonio to Dallas.

Animals of many types lived in the shallow Mesozoic seas,

tidal pools and coastal swamps. Today these lower Cretaceous rocks are some of the most fossiliferous in the state. Tracks of **dinosaurs** occur in several localities, and remains of **terrestrial, aquatic** and **flying reptiles** have been collected from Cretaceous rocks in many parts of Texas.

During most of the late Cretaceous, much of Texas lay beneath **marine waters** that were deeper than those of the early Cretaceous seas, except where rivers, deltas and shallow marine shelves existed. River delta and strandline sandstones are the reservoir rocks for the most prolific oil field in Texas. When discovered in 1930, this East Texas oil field contained recoverable reserves estimated at 5.6 billion barrels. The chalky rock that we now call the **"Austin Chalk"** was deposited when the Texas seas became deeper. Today, the chalk (and other Upper Cretaceous rocks) crops out in a wide band that extends from near Eagle Pass on the Rio Grande, east to San Antonio, north to Dallas and east to the Texarkana area. The Austin Chalk and other upper Cretaceous rocks dip southeastward beneath the East Texas and Gulf Coast basins. The late Cretaceous was the time of the last major seaway across Texas, because mountains were forming in the western United States that influenced areas as far away as Texas.

A **chain of volcanoes** formed beneath the late Cretaceous seas in an area roughly parallel to and south and east of the old, buried Ouachita Mountains. The eruptions of these volcanoes were primarily on the sea floor and great clouds of steam and ash likely accompanied them. Between eruptions, invertebrate marine animals built reefs on the shallow volcanic cones. **Pilot Knob**, located southeast of Austin, is one of these old volcanoes that is now exposed at the surface.

### Cenozoic Era

At the dawn of the Cenozoic Era, approximately 65 million years ago, deltas fed by rivers were in the northern and northwestern margins of the East Texas Basin. These streams flowed eastward, draining areas to the north and west. Although there were minor incursions of the seas, the Cenozoic rocks principally document extensive seaward building by broad deltas, marshy lagoons, sandy barrier islands and embayments. Thick vegetation covered the levees and areas between the streams. Coastal plains were taking shape under the same processes still at work today.

The Mesozoic marine salt became buried by thick sediments in the coastal plain area. The salt began to form ridges and domes in the Houston and Rio Grande areas. The heavy load of sand, silt and mud deposited by the deltas eventually caused some areas of the coast to subside and form large fault systems, essentially parallel to the coast. Many of these coastal faults moved slowly and probably generated little earthquake activity. However, movement along the Balcones and Luling-Mexia-Talco zones, a **complex system of faults** along the western and northern edge of the basins, likely generated large earthquakes millions of years ago.

Predecessors of modern animals roamed the Texas Cenozoic coastal plains and woodlands. Bones and teeth of **horses, camels, sloths, giant armadillos, mammoths, mastodons, bats, rats, large cats** and other modern or extinct mammals have been excavated from coastal plain deposits. Vegetation in the area included varieties of plants and trees both similar and dissimilar to modern ones. **Fossil palmwood**, the Texas **"state stone,"** is found in sediments of early Cenozoic age.

The Cenozoic Era in Trans-Pecos Texas was entirely different. There, **extensive volcanic eruptions** formed great calderas and produced copious lava flows. These eruptions ejected great clouds of volcanic ash and rock particles into the air — many times the amount of material ejected by the 1980 eruption of Mount St. Helens. Ash from the eruptions drifted eastward and is found in many of the sand-and-siltstones of the Gulf Coastal Plains. **Lava** flowed over older Paleozoic and Mesozoic rocks, and igneous intrusions melted their way upward into crustal rocks. These volcanic and intrusive igneous rocks are well exposed in arid areas of the Trans-Pecos today.

In the Texas Panhandle, streams originating in the recently elevated southern Rocky Mountains brought floods of gravel and sand into Texas. As the braided streams crisscrossed the area, they formed great **alluvial fans**. These fans, which were deposited on the older **Paleozoic** and **Mesozoic** rocks, occur from northwestern Texas into Nebraska. Between 1 million and 2 million years ago, the streams of the Texas Panhandle were isolated from their Rocky Mountain source, and the eastern edge of this sheet of alluvial material began to retreat westward, forming the **Caprock** of the modern High Plains of Texas.

Late in the Cenozoic Era, a great **Ice Age** descended on the northern North American continent. For more than 2 million years, there were successive advances and retreats of the thick sheets of glacial ice. Four periods of extensive glaciation were separated by warmer interglacial periods. Although the glaciers never reached as far south as Texas, the state's climate and sea level underwent major changes with each period of glacial advance and retreat. Sea level during times of glacial advance was 300 to 450 feet lower than during the warmer interglacial periods because so much sea water was captured in the ice sheets. The climate was both more humid and cooler than today, and the major Texas rivers carried more water and more sand and gravel to the sea. These deposits underlie the outer 50 miles or more of the Gulf Coastal Plain.

Approximately 3,000 years ago, sea level reached its modern position. The rivers, deltas, lagoons, beaches and barrier islands that we know as coastal Texas today have formed since that time. ☆

*Oil and natural gas, as well as nonfuel minerals, are important to the Texas economy. For a more detailed discussion, look for "Minerals" in the index.*

# Soils of Texas

*Source: Natural Resources Conservation Service, U. S. Department of Agriculture, Temple, Texas; www.tx.nrcs.usda.gov/*

Soil is one of Texas' most important natural resources. The soils of Texas are complex because of the wide diversity of climate, vegetation, geology and landscape. **More than 1,200 different kinds of soil** are recognized in Texas. Each has a specific set of properties that affect its use.

The location of each soil and information about use are in soil survey reports available for most counties. Contact the **Natural Resources Conservation Service** for more information: 101 S. Main St., Temple 76501-7602; phone: 254-742-9850. On the Web: **www.tx.nrcs.usda.gov**; click on "Information About: Soils."

The vast expanse of Texas soils encouraged wasteful use of soil and water throughout much of the state's history. About 21 percent of all land area in Texas has been classified as "prime farmland."

Settlers, attracted by these rich soils and the abundant water of the eastern half of the region, used them to build an agriculture and agribusiness of vast proportions, and then found their abuse had created critical problems.

## Soil Conservation

In the 1930s, interest in soil and water conservation began to mount. In 1935, the Soil Conservation Service, now called the **Natural Resources Conservation Service,** was created in the U.S. Department of Agriculture. In 1939, the **Texas Soil Conservation Law** made it possible for landowners to organize local soil and water conservation districts.

As of July 2003, Texas had **216 conservation districts,** which manage conservation functions within the district. A subdivision of state government, each district is governed by a board of five elected landowners. Technical assistance in planning and applying conservation work is provided through the USDA, Natural Resources Conservation Service. State funds for districts are administered through the **Texas State Soil and Water Conservation Board.**

The 1997 National Resources Inventory showed that **land use** in Texas consisted of about 57 percent rangeland, 16 percent cropland, 9 percent pastureland, 6 percent forestland, 5

percent developed land, 2 percent federal land, 2 percent land in the conservation reserve program (CRP), 1 percent miscellaneous land and 2 percent water.

## Soil Subdivisions

Texas can be divided into major subdivisions, called **Major Land Resource Areas,** that have similar or related soils, vegetation, topography, climate and land uses. Brief descriptions of these subdivisions follow.

### 1. Trans-Pecos Soils

The 18.7 million acres of the Trans-Pecos, mostly west of the Pecos River, are diverse plains and valleys intermixed with mountains. Surface drainage is slow to rapid. This arid region is used mainly as rangeland. A small amount of irrigated cropland is on the more fertile soils along the Rio Grande and the Pecos River. Vineyards are a more recent use of these soils, as is the disposal of large volumes of municipal wastes.

Upland soils are mostly well-drained, light reddish- brown to brown clay loams, clays and sands (some have a large amount of gypsum or other salts). Many areas have shallow soils and rock outcrops, and sizable areas have deep sands. Bottomland soils are deep, well-drained, dark grayish-brown to reddish-brown silt loams, loams, clay loams and clays. Lack of soil moisture and wind erosion are the major soil-management problems. Only irrigated crops can be grown on these soils, and most areas lack an adequate source of good water.

### 2. Upper Pecos, Canadian Valleys and Plains Soils

The Upper Pecos and Canadian Valleys and Plains area occupies a little over a half-million acres and is in the northwest part of Texas near the Texas-New Mexico border. It is characterized by broad rolling plains and tablelands broken by drainageways and tributaries of the Canadian River. It includes the Canadian Breaks, which are rough, steep lands below the adjacent High Plains. The average annual precipitation is about 15 inches, but it fluctuates widely from year to year. Surface drainage is slow to rapid.

The soils are well drained and alkaline. The mostly reddish-brown clay loams and sandy loams were formed mostly in material weathered from sandstone and shale. Depths range from shallow to very deep.

The area is used mainly as rangeland and wildlife habitat. Native vegetation is mid- to short-grass prairie species, such as hairy grama, sideoats grama, little bluestem, alkali sacaton, vine-mesquite, and galleta in the plains and tablelands. Juniper and mesquite grow on the relatively higher breaks. Soil management problems include low soil moisture and brush control.

### 3. High Plains Soils

The High Plains area comprises a vast high plateau of more than 19.4 million acres in northwestern Texas. It lies in the southern part of the Great Plains province that includes large similar areas in Oklahoma and New Mexico. The flat, nearly level treeless plain has few streams to cause local relief. However, several major rivers originate in the High Plains or cross the area. The largest is the Canadian River, which has cut a deep valley across the Panhandle section.

Playas, small intermittent lakes scattered through the area, lie up to 20 feet below the surrounding plains. A 1965 survey counted more than 19,000 playas in 44 counties occupying some 340,000 acres. Most runoff from rainfall is collected in the playas, but only 10 to 40 percent of this water percolates back to the Ogallala Aquifer. The aquifer is virtually the exclusive water source in this area.

Upland soils are mostly well-drained, deep, neutral to alkaline clay loams and sandy loams in shades of brown or red. Sandy soils are in the southern part. Many soils have large amounts of lime at various depths and some are shallow over caliche. Soils of bottomlands are minor in extent.

The area is used mostly for cropland, but significant areas of rangeland are in the southwestern and extreme northern parts. Millions of cattle populate the many large feedlots in the area. The soils are moderately productive, and the flat surface encourages irrigation and mechanization. Limited soil moisture, constant danger of wind erosion and irrigation water management are the major soil-management problems, but the region is Texas' leading producer of three important crops: cotton, grain sorghums and wheat.

### 4. Rolling Plains Soils

The Rolling Plains include 21.7 million acres east of the High Plains in northwestern Texas. The area lies west of the North Central Prairies and extends from the edge of the Edwards Plateau in Tom Green County northward into Oklahoma. The landscape is nearly level to strongly rolling, and surface drainage is moderate to rapid. Outcrops of red beds geologic materials and associated reddish soils led to use of the name **"Red Plains"** by some. Limestone underlies the soils in the southeastern part. The eastern part contains large areas of badlands.

Upland soils are mostly deep, pale-brown through reddish-brown to dark grayish-brown, neutral to alkaline sandy loams, clay loams and clays; some are deep sands. Many soils have a large amount of lime in the lower part, and a few others are saline; some are shallow and stony. Bottomland soils are mostly reddish-brown and sandy to clayey; some are saline.

This area is used mostly for rangeland, but cotton, grain sorghums and wheat are important crops. The major soil-management problems are brush control, wind erosion, low fertility and lack of soil mosture. Salt spots are a concern in some areas.

### 5. North Central Prairie Soils

The North Central Prairie occupies about 7 million acres in North Central Texas. Adjacent to this area on the north is the rather small (less than 1 million acres) Rolling Red Prairies area, which extends into Oklahoma and is included here because the soils and land use are similar. This area lies between the Western Cross Timbers and the Rolling Plains. It is dominantly grassland intermixed with small wooded areas. The landscape is undulating with slow to rapid surface drainage.

Upland soils are mostly deep, well-drained, brown or reddish-brown, slightly acid loams over neutral to alkaline, clayey subsoils. Some soils are shallow or moderately deep to shale. Bottomland soils are mostly well-drained, dark-brown or gray loams and clays.

This area is used mostly as rangeland, but wheat, grain sorghums and other crops are grown on the better soils. Brush control, wind and water erosion and limited soil moisture are the major soil-management concerns.

### 6. Edwards Plateau Soils

The 22.7 million acres of the Edwards Plateau are in southwest Texas east of the Trans-Pecos and west of the Blackland Prairie. Uplands are nearly level to undulating except near large stream valleys where the landscape is hilly with deep canyons and steep slopes. Surface drainage is rapid.

Upland soils are mostly shallow, stony or gravelly, dark alkaline clays and clay loams underlain by limestone. Lighter-colored soils are on steep sideslopes and deep, less-stony soils are in the valleys. Bottomland soils are mostly deep, dark-gray or brown, alkaline loams and clays.

Raising beef cattle is the main enterprise in this region, but it is also the center of Texas' and the nation's mohair and wool production. The area is a major deer habitat; hunting leases produce income. Cropland is mostly in the valleys on the deeper soils and is used mainly for growing forage crops and hay. The major soil-management concerns are brush control, large stones, low fertility, excess lime and limited soil moisture.

### 7. Central Basin Soils

The Central Basin, also known as the **Llano Basin,** occupies a relatively small area in Central Texas. It includes parts of all of Llano, Mason, Gillespie and adjoining counties. The total area is about 1.6 million acres of undulating to hilly landscape.

Upland soils are mostly shallow, reddish-brown to brown, mostly gravelly and stony, neutral to slightly acid sandy loams over granite, limestone, gneiss and schist bedrock. Large boulders are on the soil surface in some areas. Deeper, less stony sandy-loam soils are in the valleys. Bottomland soils are minor areas of deep, dark-gray or brown loams and clays.

Ranching is the main enterprise, with some farms producing peaches, grain sorghum and wheat. The area provides excellent deer habitat, and hunting leases are a major source of income. Brush control, large stones and limited soil moisture are soil-management concerns.

## 8. Northern Rio Grande Plain Soils

The Northern Rio Grande Plain comprises about 6.3 million acres in Southern Texas extending from Uvalde to Beeville. The landscape is nearly level to rolling, mostly brush-covered plains with slow to rapid surface drainage.

The major upland soils are deep, reddish-brown or dark grayish-brown, neutral to alkaline loams and clays. Bottomland soils are mostly dark-colored loams.

The area is mostly rangeland with significant areas of cropland. Grain sorghums, cotton, corn and small grains are the major crops. Crops are irrigated in the western part, especially in the Winter Garden area, where vegetables such as spinach, carrots and cabbage are grown. Much of the area is good deer and dove habitat; hunting leases are a major source of income. Brush control, soil fertility, and irrigation-water management are the major soil-management concerns.

## 9. Western Rio Grande Plain Soils

The Western Rio Grande Plain comprises about 5.3 million acres in an area of southwestern Texas from Del Rio to Rio Grande City. The landscape is nearly level to undulating except near the Rio Grande where it is hilly. Surface drainage is slow to rapid.

The major soils are mostly deep, brown or gray alkaline clays and loams. Some are saline.

Most of the soils are used for rangeland. Irrigated grain sorghums and vegetables are grown along the Rio Grande. Hunting leases are a major source of income. Brush control and limited soil moisture are the major soil-management problems.

## 10. Central Rio Grande Plain Soils

The Central Rio Grande Plain comprises about 5.9 million acres in an area of Southern Texas from Live Oak County to Hidalgo County. It Includes the South Texas Sand Sheet, an area of deep, sandy soils and active sand dunes. The landscape is nearly level to gently undulating. Surface drainage is slow to rapid.

Upland soils are mostly deep, light-colored, neutral to alkaline sands and loams. Many are saline or sodic. Bottomland soils are of minor extent.

Most of the area is used for raising beef cattle. A few areas, mostly in the northeast part, are used for growing grain sorghums, cotton and small grains. Hunting leases are a major source of income. Brush control is the major soil-management problem on rangeland; wind erosion and limited soil moisture are major concerns on cropland.

## 11. Lower Rio Grande Valley Soils

The Lower Rio Grande Valley comprises about 2.1 million acres in extreme southern Texas. The landscape is level to gently sloping with slow surface drainage.

Upland soils are mostly deep, grayish-brown, neutral to alkaline loams; coastal areas are mostly gray, silty clay loam and silty clay; some are saline. Bottomland soils are minor in extent.

Most of the soils are used for growing irrigated vegetables and citrus, along with cotton, grain sorghums and sugar cane. Some areas are used for growing beef cattle. Irrigation water management and wind erosion are the major soil-management problems on cropland; brush control is the major problem on rangeland.

## 12. Western Cross Timbers Soils

The Western Cross Timbers area comprises about 2.6 million acres. It includes the wooded section west of the Grand Prairie and extends from the Red River southward to the north edge of Brown County. The landscape is undulating and is dissected by many drainageways including the Brazos and Red rivers. Surface drainage is rapid.

Upland soils are mostly deep, grayish-brown, slightly acid loams with loamy and clayey subsoils. Bottomland soils along the major rivers are deep, reddish-brown, neutral to alkaline silt loams and clays.

The area is used mostly for grazing beef and dairy cattle on native range and improved pastures. Crops are peanuts, grain sorghums, small grains, peaches, pecans and vegetables. The major soil-management problem on grazing lands is brush control. Waste management on dairy farms is a more recent concern. Wind and water erosion are the major problems on cropland.

## 13. Eastern Cross Timbers Soils

The Eastern Cross Timbers area comprises about 1 million acres in a long narrow strip of wooded land that separates the northern parts of the Blackland Prairie and Grand Prairie and extends from the Red River southward to the Hill County. The landscape is gently undulating to rolling and is dissected by many streams, including the Red and Trinity rivers. Sandstone-capped hills are prominent in some areas. Surface runoff is moderate to rapid.

The upland soils are mostly deep, light-colored, slightly acid sandy loams and loamy sands with reddish loamy or clayey subsoils. Bottomland soils are reddish-brown to dark gray, slightly acid to alkaline loams or gray clays.

Grassland consisting of native range and improved pastures is the major land use. Peanuts, grain sorghums, small grains, peaches, pecans and vegetables are grown in some areas. Brush control, water erosion and low fertility are the major concerns in soil management.

## 14. Grand Prairie Soils

The Grand Prairie comprises about 6.3 million acres in North Central Texas. It extends from the Red River to about the Colorado River. It lies between the Eastern and Western Cross Timbers in the northern part and just west of the Blackland Prairie in the southern part. The landscape is undulating to hilly and is dissected by many streams including the Red, Trinity and Brazos rivers. Surface drainage is rapid.

Upland soils are mostly dark-gray, alkaline clays; some are shallow over limestone and some are stony. Some areas have light-colored loamy soils over chalky limestone. Bottomland soils along the Red and Brazos rivers are reddish silt loams and clays. Other bottomlands have dark-gray loams and clays.

Land use is a mixture of rangeland, pastureland and cropland. The area is mainly used for growing beef cattle. Some small grain, grain sorghums, corn and hay are grown. Brush control and water erosion are the major management concerns.

## 15. Blackland Prairie Soils

The Blackland Prairies consist of about 12.6 million acres of east-central Texas extending southwesterly from the Red River to Bexar County. There are smaller areas to the southeast. The landscape is undulating with few scattered wooded areas that are mostly in the bottomlands. Surface drainage is moderate to rapid.

Both upland and bottomland soils are deep, dark-gray to black alkaline clays. Some soils in the western part are shallow to moderately deep over chalk. Some soils on the eastern edge are neutral to slightly acid, grayish clays and loams over mottled clay subsoils (sometimes called graylands). Blackland soils are known as "cracking clays" because of the large, deep cracks that form in dry weather. This high shrink-swell property can cause serious damage to foundations, highways and other structures and is a safety hazard in pits and trenches.

Land use is divided about equally between cropland and grassland. Cotton, grain sorghums, corn, wheat, oats and hay are grown. Grassland is mostly improved pastures, with native range on the shallower and steeper soils. Water erosion, cotton root rot, soil tilth and brush control are the major management problems.

## 16. Claypan Area Soils

The Claypan Area consists of about 6.1 million acres in east-central Texas just east of the Blackland Prairie. The landscape is a gently undulating to rolling, moderately dissected woodland also known as the **Post Oak Belt** or **Post Oak Savannah.** Surface drainage is moderate.

Upland soils commonly have a thin, light-colored, acid sandy loam surface layer over dense, mottled red, yellow and gray claypan subsoils. Some deep, sandy soils with less clayey subsoils exist. Bottomlands are deep, highly fertile, reddish-brown to dark-gray loamy to clayey soils.

Land use is mainly rangeland. Some areas are in improved pastures. Most cropland is in bottomlands that are protected from flooding. Major crops are cotton, grain sorghums, corn, hay and forage crops, most of which are irrigated. Brush control on rangeland and irrigation water management on cropland are the major management problems. Water erosion is a serious problem on the highly erosive claypan soils, especially where they are overgrazed.

### 17. East Texas Timberland Soils

The East Texas Timberlands area comprises about 16.1 million acres of the forested eastern part of the state. The landscape is gently undulating to hilly and well dissected by many streams. Surface drainage is moderate to rapid.

This area has many kinds of upland soils but most are deep, light-colored, acid sands and loams over loamy and clayey subsoils. Deep sands are in scattered areas and red clays are in areas of "redlands." Bottomland soils are mostly brown to dark-gray, acid loams and some clays.

The land is used mostly for growing commercial pine timber and for woodland grazing. Improved pastures are scattered throughout and are used for grazing beef and dairy cattle and for hay production. Some commercial hardwoods are in the bottomlands. Woodland management problems include seedling survival, invasion of hardwoods in pine stands, effects of logging on water quality and control of the southern pine beetle. Lime and fertilizers are necessary for productive cropland and pastures.

### 18. Coast Prairie Soils

The Coast Prairie includes about 8.7 million acres near the Gulf Coast in southeast Texas. It ranges from 30 miles to 80 miles in width and parallels the coast from the Sabine River in Orange County to Baffin Bay in Kleberg County. The landscape is level to gently undulating with slow surface drainage.

Upland soils are mostly deep, dark-gray, neutral to slightly acid clay loams and clays. Lighter-colored and more-sandy soils are in a strip on the northwestern edge; some soils in the southern part are alkaline; some are saline and sodic. Bottomland soils are mostly deep, dark-colored clays and loams along small streams but are greatly varied along the rivers.

Land use is mainly grazing lands and cropland. Some hardwood timber is in the bottomlands. Many areas are also managed for wetland wildlife habitat. The nearly level topography and productive soils encourage farming. Rice, grain sorghums, cotton, corn and hay are the main crops. Brush management on grasslands and removal of excess water on cropland are the major management concerns.

### 19. Coast Saline Prairies Soils

The Coast Saline Prairies area includes about 3.2 million acres along a narrow strip of wet lowlands adjacent to the coast; it includes the barrier islands that extend from Mexico to Louisiana. The surface is at or only a few feet above sea level with many areas of salt-water marsh. Surface drainage is very slow. The soils are mostly deep, dark-colored clays and loams; many are saline and sodic. Light-colored sandy soils are on the barrier islands. The water table is at or near the surface of most soils.

Cattle grazing is the chief economic use of the various salt-tolerant cordgrasses and sedges. Many areas are managed for wetland wildlife. Recreation is popular on the barrier islands. Providing fresh water and access to grazing areas are the major management concerns.

### 20. Gulf Coast Marsh Soils

This 150,000-acre area lies in the extreme southeastern corner of Texas. The area can be subdivided into four parts: freshwater, intermediate, brackish, and saline (saltwater) marsh. The degree of salinity of this system grades landward from saltwater marshes along the coast to freshwater marshes inland. Surface drainage is very slow.

This area contains many lakes, bayous, tidal channels, and man-made canals. About one-half of the marsh is fresh, and one-half is salty. Most of the area is susceptible to flooding either by fresh water drained from lands adjacent to the marsh or by saltwater from the Gulf of Mexico.

Most of the soils are very poorly drained, continuously saturated, soft and can carry little weight. In general, the organic soils have a thick layer of dark gray, relatively undecomposed organic material over a gray, clayey subsoil. The mineral soils have a surface of dark gray, highly decomposed organic material over a gray, clayey subsoil.

Most of the almost treeless and uninhabited area is in marsh vegetation, such as grasses, sedges and rushes. It is used mainly for wildlife habitat. Part of the fertile and productive estuarine complex that supports marine life of the Gulf of Mexico, it provides wintering ground for waterfowl and habitat for many fur-bearing animals and alligators.

A significant acreage is firm enough to support livestock and is used for winter grazing of cattle. The major management problems are providing fresh water and access to grazing areas.

### 21. Flatwoods Soils

The Flatwoods area includes about 2.5 million acres of woodland in humid southeast Texas just north of the Coast Prairie and extending into Louisiana. The landscape is level to gently undulating. Surface drainage is slow.

Upland soils are mostly deep, light-colored, acid loams with gray, loamy or clayey subsoils. Bottomland soils are deep, dark-colored, acid clays and loams. The water table is near the surface at least part of the year.

The land is mainly used for forest, although cattle are grazed in some areas. Woodland management problems include seedling survival, invasion of hardwoods in pine stands, effects of logging on water quality and control of the southern pine beetle. ☆

# Water Resources

Source: Texas Water Development Board; www.twdb.state.tx.us

## Surface Water and Ground Water

In Texas, **water law has been historically different for surface water** and **ground water.** Surface water belongs to the state and, except for limited amounts of water for household and on-farm livestock use, requires permits for use.

In general, ground water is considered the property of the surface landowner by "right of capture," meaning the landowner may pump as much water from beneath his land as he can for any beneficial use. This right may be limited only through the creation of ground-water conservation districts, which may make rules to protect and conserve ground-water supplies within their boundaries.

The **Texas Commission on Environmental Quality** is responsible for permitting and adjudicating surface-water rights and uses. It is the primary regulator of surface water and polices contamination and pollution of both surface and ground water.

The **Texas Water Development Board** collects data on occurrence, availability and quality of water within the state; plans for future supply and use; and administers the state's funds for grants and loans to finance future water development and supply.

In January 2002, the Texas Water Development Board developed a comprehensive **statewide water plan,** which the 75th Texas Legislature in 1997 had required the board to do. The TWDB divided the state into 16 regional water-planning areas, and each area's Regional Water Planning Group is required to adopt a water plan that addresses conservation of water supplies, how to meet future water needs and how to respond to future droughts.

### Ground-water Supplies and Use

Texas has historically relied on its wealth of fresh to slightly saline water that underlies more than 81 percent of the state. About 60 percent of the approximately 16 million acre-feet of water used yearly in Texas is derived from underground formations that make up 9 major and 21 minor aquifers.

Nearly 80 percent of the ground water produced in 2000 was used for irrigating crops, especially in the Panhandle region. Ground water also supplies about 36 percent of the state's municipal needs.

# MAJOR AQUIFERS OF TEXAS

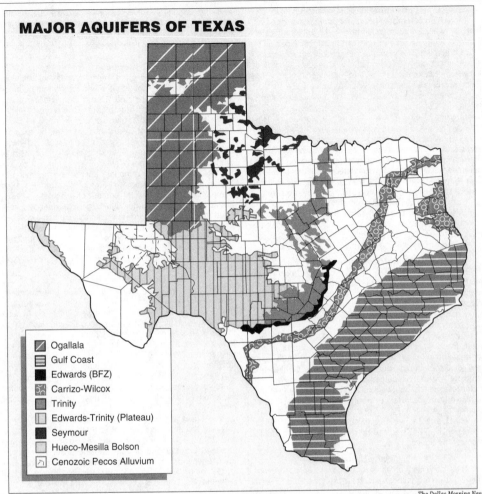

Ogallala

Gulf Coast

Edwards (BFZ)

Carrizo-Wilcox

Trinity

Edwards-Trinity (Plateau)

Seymour

Hueco-Mesilla Bolson

Cenozoic Pecos Alluvium

*The Dallas Morning News*

## Texas' Major Aquifers

### Ogallala

The Ogallala aquifer extends under 46 counties of the Texas Panhandle and is the southernmost extension of the largest aquifer (High Plains aquifer) in North America. The Ogallala Formation of late Miocene to early Pliocene age consists of heterogeneous sequences of coarse-grained sand and gravel in the lower part, grading upward into clay, silt and fine sand. In Texas, the Panhandle is the most extensive region irrigated with ground water. About 96 percent of the water pumped from the Ogallala is used for irrigation.

Water-level declines are occurring in part of the region because of extensive pumping that far exceeds recharge. Water-conservation measures by agricultural and municipal users are being promoted. Computer models of the northern and southern portions of the Ogallala aquifer were completed by the TWDB and its contractor. Several agencies are investigating playa recharge and agricultural re-use projects over the aquifer.

### Gulf Coast Aquifer

The Gulf Coast aquifer forms an irregularly shaped belt that parallels the Texas coastline and extends through 54 counties from the Rio Grande northeastward to the

Louisiana border. The **aquifer system** is composed of the water-bearing units of the Catahoula, Oakville, Fleming, Goliad, Willis, Lissie, Bentley, Montgomery and Beaumont formations.

This system has been divided into three major water-producing components referred to as the **Chicot, Evangeline,** and **Jasper** aquifers. Municipal uses account for about 53 percent and irrigation accounts for about 35 percent of the total pumpage from the aquifer. Water quality is generally good northeast of the San Antonio River basin, but deteriorates to the southwest. Years of heavy pumpage have caused significant water-level declines in portions of the aquifer. Some of these declines have resulted in significant **land-surface subsidence,** particularly in the Houston-Galveston area. TWDB is developing computer models of the northern, central and southern portions of the aquifer.

### Edwards (Balcones Fault Zone)

The Edwards (BFZ) aquifer forms a narrow belt extending through nine counties from a ground-water divide in Kinney County through the San Antonio area northeastward to the Leon River in Bell County. A poorly defined ground-water divide in Hays County hydrologically separates the aquifer into the San Antonio and Austin regions. Water in the aquifer occurs in fractures, honeycomb zones and solution channels in the Edwards and

associated limestone formations of Cretaceous age.

More than 50 percent of aquifer pumpage is for municipal use, while irrigation is the principal use in the western segment. San Antonio is one of the largest cities in the world that relies solely on a single ground-water source for its municipal supply. The aquifer also feeds several well-known recreational springs and underlies some of the most environmentally sensitive areas in the state.

In 1993, the Edwards Aquifer Authority was created by the legislature to regulate aquifer pumpage to benefit all users from Uvalde County through a portion of Hays County. Barton Springs-Edwards Aquifer Conservation District provides aquifer management for the rest of Hays and southern Travis counties. The EAA has an active program to educate the public on water conservation and also operates several active groundwater recharge sites. The San Antonio River Authority also has a number of flood-control structures that effectively recharge the aquifer.

Conservation districts are promoting more-efficient irrigation techniques, and market-based, voluntary transfers of unused agricultural water rights to municipal uses are more common. The EAA is developing a computer model of the San Antonio segment of the Edwards aquifer.

### Carrizo-Wilcox

Extending from the Rio Grande in South Texas northeastward into Arkansas and Louisiana, the Carrizo-Wilcox aquifer provides water to all or parts of 60 counties. The Wilcox Group and overlying Carrizo Sand form a hydrologically connected system of sand locally interbedded with clay, silt, lignite and gravel.

Throughout most of its extent in Texas, the aquifer yields fresh to slightly saline water, which is used primarily for irrigation in the **Winter Garden District** of South Texas and for public supply and industrial use in Central and Northeast Texas. Because of excessive pumping, the water level in the aquifer has been significantly lowered, particularly in the artesian portion of the Winter Garden District of Atascosa, Frio and Zavala counties and in municipal and industrial areas in Angelina and Smith counties. The TWDB has completed a computer model for much of the aquifer.

### Trinity Group

The Trinity aquifer consists of basal Cretaceous-age Trinity Group formations extending from the Red River in North Texas to the Hill Country of Central Texas. Formations comprising the aquifer include the **Twin Mountains, Glen Rose** and **Paluxy.** Where the Glen Rose thins or is absent, the Twin Mountains and Paluxy formations coalesce to form the **Antlers Formation.** In the south, the Trinity includes the Glen Rose and underlying **Travis Peak** formations. Water from the Antlers portion is used mainly for irrigation in the outcrop area of North and Central Texas.

Elsewhere, water from the Trinity is used primarily for municipal and domestic supply. Extensive development of the Trinity aquifer in the Dallas-Fort Worth and Waco areas has historically resulted in water-level declines of several hundred feet. In 2000, TWBD completed a computer model of the Hill Country area and is working on a model of the northern portion of the aquifer.

### Edwards-Trinity (Plateau)

This aquifer underlies the **Edwards Plateau**, extending from the Hill Country of Central Texas westward to the Trans-Pecos region. It consists of sandstone and limestone formations of the Trinity Group formations, and limestones and dolomites of the Edwards and associated limestone formations. Ground-water movement is generally toward the southeast.

Near the plateau's edge, flow is toward the main streams, where the water issues from springs. Irrigation, mainly in the northwestern portion of the region, accounted for about 70 percent of total aquifer use in 2000

and has resulted in significant water-level declines in Glasscock and Reagan counties. Elsewhere, the aquifer supplies fresh but hard water for municipal, domestic and livestock use. The TWDB is developing a computer model of this aquifer.

### Seymour

This aquifer consists of isolated areas of alluvium found in parts of 22 north-central and Panhandle counties in the upper Red River and Brazos River basins. Eastward-flowing streams during the Quaternary Period deposited discontinuous beds of poorly sorted gravel, sand, silt and clay that were later dissected by erosion, resulting in the isolated remnants of the formation. Individual accumulations vary greatly in thickness, but most of the Seymour is less than 100 feet.

The lower, more permeable part of the aquifer produces the greatest amount of ground water. Irrigation pumpage accounted for 93 percent of the total use from the aquifer in 1994. Water quality generally ranges from fresh to slightly saline. However, the salinity has increased in many heavily pumped areas to the point where the water has become unsuitable for domestic and municipal use. Natural salt pollution in the upper reaches of the Red and Brazos River basins precludes the full utilization of these water resources.

### Hueco-Mesilla Bolson

These aquifers are located in El Paso and Hudspeth counties in far western Texas and occur in Quaternary basin-fill deposits that extend northward into New Mexico and westward into Mexico. The Hueco Bolson, located on the eastern side of the Franklin Mountains, consists of up to 9,000 feet of clay, silt, sand and gravel and is the principal source of drinking water for both El Paso and Juarez. Located west of the Franklin Mountains, the Mesilla Bolson reaches up to 2,000 feet in thickness and contains three separate water-producing zones. Ground-water depletion of the Hueco Bolson has become a serious problem.

Historical large-scale ground-water withdrawals, especially for the municipal uses of El Paso and Juarez, have caused major water-level declines and significantly changed the direction of flow, causing a deterioration of the chemical quality of the ground water in the aquifer. The USGS, along with El Paso Water Utilities, is developing a computer model of this aquifer.

### Cenozoic Pecos Alluvium

Located in the upper Pecos River Valley of West Texas, this aquifer is the principal source of water for irrigation in Reeves and northwestern Pecos counties and for industrial uses, power supply and municipal use elsewhere. Consisting of up to 1,500 feet of alluvial fill, the aquifer occupies two hydrologically separate basins: the Pecos Trough in the west and the Monument Draw Trough in the east.

Water from the aquifer is generally hard and contains dissolved-solids concentrations ranging from less than 300 to more than 5,000 parts per million. Water-level declines in excess of 200 feet have historically occurred in Reeves and Pecos counties, but have moderated since the mid-1970s with the decrease in irrigation pumpage. TWDB is developing a computer model of the aquifer.

# Texas' Major Rivers

Some **11,247 named Texas streams** are identified in the **U.S. Geological Survey Geographic Names Information System.** Their combined length is about 80,000 miles, and they drain 263,513 square miles within Texas. **Thirteen major rivers** are described below, starting with the southernmost and moving northward:

### Rio Grande

The Pueblo Indians called this river **P'osoge,** which means the "river of great water." In 1582, **Antonio de**

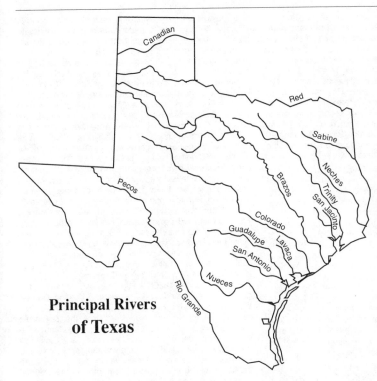

## Principal Rivers of Texas

**Espejo** of Nueva Vizcaya, Mexico, followed the course of the **Río Conchos** to its confluence with a great river, which Espejo named **Río del Norte (River of the North).** The name **Rio Grande** was first given the stream apparently by the explorer **Juan de Oñate,** who arrived on its banks near present-day El Paso in 1598.

Thereafter the names were often consolidated, as **Río Grande del Norte.** It was shown also on early Spanish maps as **Río San Buenaventura** and **Río Ganapetuan.** In its lower course it early acquired the name **Río Bravo,** which is its name on most Mexican maps. At times it has also been known as **Río Turbio,** probably because of its muddy appearance during its frequent rises. Some people erroneously call this watercourse the **Rio Grande River.** From source to mouth, the Rio Grande drops 12,000 feet to sea level as a snow-fed mountain torrent, desert stream and meandering coastal river. Along its banks and in its valley Indian civilizations developed, and Europeans established some of their first North American settlements.

This river rises in Colorado, flows the north-south length of New Mexico and **forms the boundary of Texas and international U.S.-Mexican boundary for 889 to 1,254 river miles,** depending upon method of measurement. (See **Texas Boundary Line.**) The length of the Rio Grande, as of other rivers, depends on method of measurement and varies yearly as its course changes. The latest **International Boundary and Water Commission** figure is 1,896 miles, which is considerably below the 2,200-mile figure often used. Depending upon methods of measurement, the Rio Grande is the fourth- or fifth-longest North American river, exceeded only by the Missouri-Mississippi, McKenzie-Peace, St. Lawrence and possibly Yukon. Since all of these except the Missouri-Mississippi are partly in Canada, the Rio Grande is the **second-longest river entirely within or bordering the United States.** It is **Texas' longest river.**

The snow-fed flow of the Rio Grande is used for **irriga-**

**tion** in Colorado below the San Juan Mountains, where the river rises at the Continental Divide. Turning south, it flows through a canyon in northern New Mexico and again irrigates a broad valley of central New Mexico. This is the oldest irrigated area of the United States, where Spanish missionaries encouraged Indian irrigation in the 1600s. Southern New Mexico impounds Rio Grande waters in Elephant Butte Reservoir for irrigation of 150 miles of valley above and below El Paso. Here is the **oldest irrigated area in Texas** and one of the oldest in the United States. Extensive irrigation practically exhausts the water supply. In this valley are situated the **three oldest towns in Texas — Ysleta, Socorro** and **San Elizario.** At the lower end of the El Paso irrigated valley, the upper Rio Grande virtually ends except in seasons of above-normal flow.

It starts as a perennially flowing stream again where the Río Conchos of Mexico flows into it at Presidio-Ojinaga. Through the **Big Bend** the Rio Grande flows through three successive **canyons,** the **Santa Elena,** the **Mariscal** and the **Boquillas.** The Santa Elena has a river bed elevation of 2,145 feet and a canyon-rim elevation of 3,661. Corresponding figures for Mariscal are 1,925 and 3,625, and for Boquillas, 1,850 and 3,490. The river here flows around the base of the **Chisos Mountains.** For about 100 miles the river is the southern boundary of **Big Bend National Park.** Below the Big Bend, the Rio Grande gradually emerges from mountains onto the Coastal Plains. A 191.2-mile strip on the American shore from Big Bend National Park downstream to the Terrell-Val Verde County line, has federal designation as the **Rio Grande Wild and Scenic River.**

At the confluence of the Rio Grande and the Devils River, the United States and Mexico have built **Amistad Dam,** to impound 3,505,400 acre-feet of water, of which Texas' share is 56.2 percent. **Falcon Reservoir,** also an international project, impounds 2,767,400 acre-feet of water, of which Texas' share in Zapata and Starr counties is 58.6 percent. The Rio Grande, where it joins the Gulf of Mexico, has created a fertile delta called the **Lower Rio Grande Valley,** a major vegetable- and fruit-growing area. The Rio Grande drains 48,259 square miles of Texas. Principal tributaries flowing from the Texas side of the Rio Grande are the **Pecos** and **Devils** rivers. On the Mexican side are **Río Conchos, Río Salado** and **Río San Juan.** About three-fourths of the water running into the Rio Grande below El Paso comes from the Mexican side.

### Nueces River

The Nueces River rises in Edwards County and flows 315 miles to Nueces Bay on the Gulf near Corpus Christi. Draining 16,950 square miles, it is a beautiful, **spring-fed stream** flowing through **canyons** until it issues from the **Balcones Escarpment** onto the Coastal Plain in northern Uvalde County. **Alonso de León,** in 1689, gave it its name. (Nueces, plural of nuez, means nuts in Spanish.) Much earlier, Cabeza de Vaca had referred to a **Río de las**

**Nueces** in this region, probably the same stream. Its original Indian name seems to have been **Chotilapacquen.** Crossing Texas in 1691, Terán de los Rios named the river **San Diego.** The Nueces was the boundary line between the Spanish provinces of Texas and Nuevo Santander.

After the Revolution of 1836, both Texas and Mexico claimed the territory between the Nueces and the Rio Grande, a dispute which was settled by the **Treaty of Guadalupe Hidalgo** in 1848, which fixed the international boundary at the Rio Grande. Nueces runoff is about 620,000 acre-feet a year in its lower course. Principal water conservation projects are **Lake Corpus Christi** and **Choke Canyon Reservoir.** Principal tributaries of the Nueces are the **Frio** and the **Atascosa.**

### San Antonio River

The San Antonio River has its source in **large springs** within and near the city limits of San Antonio. It flows 180 miles across the Coastal Plain to a junction with the **Guadalupe** near the Gulf Coast. Its channel through San Antonio has been developed into a parkway known as the River Walk. Its principal tributaries are the **Medina River** and **Cibolo Creek,** both spring-fed streams and this, with its spring origin, gives it a remarkably steady flow of clear water. This stream was first named the **León** by Alonso de León in 1689. León was not naming the stream for himself, but called it "lion" because its channel was filled with a rampaging flood.

Because of its limited and arid drainage area (4,180 square miles) the average runoff of the San Antonio River is relatively small, about 350,000 acre-feet annually near its mouth, but its flow, because of its springs, is one of the steadiest of Texas rivers.

### Guadalupe River

The Guadalupe rises in its north and south prongs in the west-central part of Kerr County. A **spring-fed stream,** it flows eastward through the **Hill Country** until it issues from the **Balcones Escarpment** near New Braunfels. It then crosses the Coastal Plain to San Antonio Bay. Its total length is about 250 miles, and its drainage area is about 6,700 square miles. Its principal tributaries are the **San Marcos,** another spring-fed stream, which joins it in Gonzales County; the San Antonio, which joins it just above its mouth on San Antonio Bay; and the Comal, which joins it at New Braunfels.

The **Comal River** has its source in large springs within the city limits of New Braunfels and flows only about 2.5 miles to the Guadalupe. It is the **shortest river in Texas** and also the **shortest river in the United States** carrying an equivalent amount of water.

There has been power development on the Guadalupe near Gonzales and Cuero for many years, and there is also power generation at **Canyon Lake.** Because of its springs, and its considerable drainage area, the Guadalupe has an annual runoff of more than 1 million acre-feet in its lower course. The name Guadalupe is derived from **Nuestra Señora de Guadalupe,** the name given the stream by Alonso de León.

### Lavaca River

The Lavaca is considered a primary stream in the Texas Basin because it flows directly into the Gulf through Lavaca Bay. Without a spring-water source and with only a small watershed, including that of its principal tributary, the **Navidad,** its flow is intermittent. The Spanish called it the Lavaca (cow) River because of the numerous bison they found near it. It is the principal stream running to the Gulf between the Guadalupe and the Colorado, and drains 2,309 square miles. The principal lake on the **Navidad** is **Lake Texana.** Runoff averages about 600,000 acre-feet yearly into the Gulf.

### Colorado River

Measured by length and drainage area, the Colorado is the **largest river wholly in Texas.** (The drainage basin

of the Brazos River extends into New Mexico.) Rising in Dawson County, the Colorado flows about 600 miles to Matagorda Bay on the Gulf. Its drainage area is 39,893 square miles. Its runoff reaches a volume of more than 2 million acre-feet near the Gulf. Its name is a Spanish word meaning **"reddish."** There is evidence that Spanish explorers originally named the muddy Brazos "Colorado," but Spanish mapmakers later transposed the two names.

The river flows through a rolling, mostly prairie terrain to the vicinity of San Saba County, where it enters the rugged **Hill Country** and **Burnet-Llano Basin.** It passes through a picturesque series of **canyons** until it issues from the **Balcones Escarpment** at Austin and flows across the Coastal Plain to the Gulf. In this area **the most remarkable series of reservoirs in Texas** has been built. The largest of these are **Lake Buchanan** in Burnet and Llano counties and **Lake Travis** in Travis County. Between the two in Burnet County are three smaller reservoirs: **Inks, Johnson** (formerly **Granite Shoals**) and **Marble Falls,** built to aid power production from water running over the Buchanan Lake spillway. Below Lake Travis is the older **Lake Austin,** largely filled with silt, whose dam is used to produce power from waters flowing down from the lakes above. **Town Lake** is in the city of Austin. This area is known as the **Highland Lakes Country.**

As early as the 1820s, Anglo-Americans settled on the banks of the lower Colorado, and in 1839 the **Capital Commission of the Republic of Texas** chose the picturesque area where the river flows from the **Balcones Escarpment** as the site of a new capital of the Republic — now **Austin,** capital of the state. The early colonists encouraged navigation along the lower channel with some success, and boats occasionally ventured as far upstream as Austin. However, a **natural log "raft"** in the channel near the Gulf blocked river traffic. Conservation and utilization of the waters of the Colorado are under jurisdiction of three agencies created by the state Legislature, the **Lower, Central** and **Upper Colorado River Authorities.**

The principal tributaries of the Colorado River are the several prongs of the **Concho River** on its upper course, **Pecan Bayou (farthest west "bayou"** in the United States) and the **Llano, San Saba** and **Pedernales** rivers. All except Pecan Bayou flow into the Colorado from the **Edwards Plateau** and are spring-fed, perennially flowing. In the numerous mussels found along these streams, **pearls** occasionally have been found. On early Spanish maps, the Middle Concho was called **Río de las Perlas.**

### Brazos River

The Brazos is the largest river between the Rio Grande and the Red River and is **third in size** of all rivers in Texas. It rises in three upper forks, the **Double Mountain, Salt** and **Clear forks** of the Brazos. The Brazos River proper is considered as beginning where the Double Mountain and Salt Forks flow together in Stonewall County. The Clear Fork joins this main stream in Young County, just above **Possum Kingdom Lake.** The Brazos crosses most of the main physiographic regions of Texas — High Plains, West Texas Lower Rolling Plains, Western Cross Timbers, Grand Prairie and Gulf Coastal Plain.

The total length from the source of its longest upper prong, the Double Mountain Fork, to the mouth of the main stream at the Gulf, was reported to be 923.2 miles in a 1970 study by the Army Corps of Engineers. The drainage area is about 43,000 square miles. It flows directly into the Gulf near Freeport. Its annual runoff at places along its lower channel exceeds 5 million acre-feet.

The original name of this river was **Brazos de Dios,** meaning "Arms of God." There are several legends as to why. One is that the Coronado expedition, wandering on the trackless **Llano Estacado,** exhausted its water and was threatened with death from thirst. Arriving at the bank of the river, they gave it the name "Brazos de Dios" in thankfulness. Another is that a ship exhausted its water

supply and its crew was saved when they found the mouth of the Brazos. Still another story is that miners on the San Saba were forced by drought to seek water near present-day Waco and in gratitude called it Brazos de Dios.

Much early Anglo-American colonization of Texas took place in the Brazos Valley. Along its channel were **San Felipe de Austin,** capital of Austin's colony; **Washington-on-the-Brazos,** where Texans declared independence; and other historic settlements.

*Gentle rapids form on a stretch of the Sabine River in East Texas. Sabine comes from the Spanish word for cypress. This river has the largest water discharge at its mouth of any Texas river — 6.8 million acre-feet annually. File photo.*

There was some **navigation of the lower channel** of the Brazos in this period. Near its mouth it intersects the **Gulf Intracoastal Waterway,** which provides connection with the commerce on the Mississippi.

Most of the Brazos Valley lies within the boundaries of the **Brazos River Authority,** which conducts a multipurpose program for development. A large reservoir on the Brazos is **Whitney Lake** (627,000 acre-feet capacity) on the main channel, where it is the boundary line between Hill and Bosque counties. Another large reservoir is **Possum Kingdom Lake** in Palo Pinto, Stephens, Young and Jack counties. **Waco Lake** on the Bosque and **Belton Lake** on the Leon are among the principal reservoirs on its tributaries. In addition to its three upper forks, other chief tributaries are the **Paluxy, Little** and **Navasota** rivers.

### San Jacinto River

A short river with a drainage basin of 2,800 square miles and nearly 2 million acre-feet runoff, the San Jacinto runs directly to the Gulf through Galveston Bay. It is formed by the junction of its East and West forks in the northeastern part of Harris County. Its total length, including the East Fork, is about 85 miles.

**Lake Conroe** is on the **West Fork,** and **Lake Houston** is located at the junction of the West Fork and the **East Fork.** The **Houston Ship Channel** runs through the lower course of the San Jacinto and its tributary, **Buffalo Bayou,** connecting the Port of Houston with the Gulf.

There are two stories of the origin of its name. One is that when early explorers discovered it, its channel was choked with hyacinth ("**jacinto**" is the Spanish word for hyacinth). The other is that it was discovered on Aug. 17, St. Hyacinth's Day.

The **Battle of San Jacinto** was fought on the shore of this river on April 21, 1836, when Texas won its independence from Mexico. **San Jacinto State Park and monument** commemorate the battle.

### Trinity River

The Trinity rises in its East Fork, Elm Fork, West Fork and Clear Fork in Grayson, Montague, Archer and Parker counties, respectively. The main stream begins with the junction of the Elm and West forks at Dallas. Its length is 550 river miles, and its drainage area is 17,969 square miles. Because of moderate to heavy rainfall over its drainage area, it has a flow of 5.8 million acre-feet near its mouth on the Gulf, exceeded only by the Neches, Red and Sabine river basins.

The Trinity derives its name from the Spanish "**Trinidad.**" Alonso de León named it **La Santísima Trinidad** (the Most Holy Trinity).

**Navigation** was developed along its lower course with several riverport towns, such as **Sebastopol** in Trinity County. For many years there has been a basin-wide movement for navigation, conservation and utilization of its water. The **Trinity River Authority** is a state agency and the **Trinity Improvement Association** is a publicly supported nonprofit organization advocating its development.

The Trinity has in its valley **more large cities, greater population and more industrial development** than any other river basin in Texas. On the Lower Coastal Plain there is large use of its waters for **rice irrigation.** Largest reservoir on the Elm Fork is **Lewisville Lake** (formerly **Garza-Little Elm** and **Lake Dallas**). There are four reservoirs above Fort Worth — **Lake Worth, Eagle Mountain** and **Bridgeport** on the West Fork and **Benbrook Lake** on the Clear Fork.

**Lavon Lake** in southeast Collin County and **Lake Ray Hubbard** in Collin, Dallas, Kaufman and Rockwall counties are on the East Fork. **Livingston Lake** is in Polk, San Jacinto, Trinity and Walker counties. The three major reservoirs below the Dallas-Fort Worth area are **Cedar Creek Reservoir** and **Richland-Chambers Reservoir**.

### Neches River

The Neches is in East Texas, with total length of about 416 miles and drainage area of 10,011 square miles. Abundant rainfall over its entire basin gives it a flow near the Gulf of about 6 million acre-feet a year. The river takes its name from the **Neches Indians** that the early Spanish explorers found living along its banks. Principal tributary of the Neches, and comparable with the Neches in length and flow above their confluence, is the **Angelina River,** so named from **Angelina (Little Angel),** a Hainai Indian girl who converted to Christianity and played an important role in the early development of this region.

Both the Neches and the Angelina run most of their courses in the **Piney Woods** and there was much settlement along them as early as the 1820s. **Sam Rayburn (McGee Bend) Reservoir,** near Jasper on the Angelina River, was completed and dedicated in 1965.

Reservoirs located on the Neches River include **Lake Palestine** in the upper portion of the basin and **B. A. Steinhagen Lake** located at the junction of the Neches and the Angelina rivers.

### Sabine River

The Sabine River is formed by three forks rising in Collin and Hunt counties. From its sources to its mouth on **Sabine Lake,** it flows approximately 360 miles and drains 7,426 square miles. Sabine comes from the **Spanish word for cypress,** as does the name of the **Sabinal River,** which flows into the Frio in Southwest Texas. The Sabine has the **largest water discharge at its mouth of any Texas river** (6.8 million acre-feet).

Throughout most of Texas history the lower Sabine has been the **eastern Texas boundary line,** though for a while there was doubt as to whether the Sabine or the Arroyo Hondo, east of the Sabine in Louisiana, was the boundary. For a number of years the outlaw-infested **neutral ground** lay between them. There was also a **boundary dispute** in which it was alleged that the Neches was

*The Canadian River Wagon Bridge crosses the river in Hemphill County in the Panhandle. The bridge was built in 1916 and is now used as an exercise trail. File photo.*

really the Sabine and, therefore, the boundary.

Travelers over the part of the **Camino Real** known as the **Old San Antonio Road,** crossed the Sabine at the **Gaines Ferry,** and there were crossings for the **Atascosito Road** and other travel and trade routes of that day. Two of Texas' largest man-made reservoirs have been created by dams on the Sabine River. The first of these is **Lake Tawakoni,** in Hunt, Rains and Van Zandt counties, with a capacity of 927,440 acre-feet. **Toledo Bend Reservoir** impounds 4,477,000 acre-feet of water on the Sabine in Newton, Panola, Sabine and Shelby counties. This is a joint project of Texas and Louisiana, through the **Sabine River Authority**.

### Red River

The Red River (1,360 miles) is **exceeded in length only by the Rio Grande** among rivers associated with Texas. Its original source is water in Curry County, New Mexico, near the Texas boundary, forming a definite channel as it crosses Deaf Smith County, Texas, in tributaries that flow into **Prairie Dog Town Fork of the Red River.** These waters carve the spectacular **Palo Duro Canyon** of the High Plains before the Red River leaves the **Caprock Escarpment,** flowing eastward.

Where the Red River crosses the 100th meridian, the river becomes the **Texas-Oklahoma boundary** and is soon joined by the Salt Fork to form the main channel. Its length across the Panhandle is about 200 miles and, from the Panhandle east, it is the Texas-Oklahoma boundary line for 440 miles and thereafter the **Texas-Arkansas boundary** for 40 miles before it flows into Arkansas, where it swings south to flow through Louisiana.

The Red River, which drains 24,463 square miles, is a part of the **Mississippi drainage basin,** and at one time it emptied all of its water into the Mississippi. In recent years, however, part of its water, especially at flood stage, has flowed to the Gulf via the **Atchafalaya**.

The Red River takes its name from the red color of the current. This caused every explorer who came to its banks to call it "red" regardless of the language he spoke — **Río Rojo** or **Río Roxo** in Spanish, **Riviere Rouge** in French and **Red River** in English. The Spanish and French names were often found on maps until the mid-19th century when English came to be generally accepted. At an early date, the river became the axis for French advance from Louisiana northwestward as far as present-day Montague

County. There was consistent **early navigation** of the river from its mouth on the Mississippi to Shreveport, above which navigation was blocked by a **natural log raft**.

A number of important gateways into Texas from the North were established along the stream such as **Pecan Point** and **Jonesborough** in Red River County, **Colbert's Ferry** and **Preston** in Grayson County and, later, **Doan's Store Crossing** in Wilbarger County.

The river was a menace to the early traveler because of both its variable current and its **quicksands,** which brought disaster to many a trail-herd cow as well as ox team and covered wagon.

The largest water conservation project on the Red River is **Texoma Lake,** which is the **largest lake** lying wholly or partly in Texas and the **tenth-largest reservoir (in capacity) in the United States.** Its capacity is 5,382,000 acre feet. Texas' share is 2,643,300.

Red River water's high content of salt and other minerals limits its usefulness along its upper reaches. Ten **salt springs** and tributaries in Texas and Oklahoma contribute most of these minerals.

The uppermost tributary of the Red River in Texas is **Tierra Blanca Creek,** which rises in Curry County, N.M., and flows easterly across Deaf Smith and Randall counties to become the **Prairie Dog Town Fork** a few miles east of Canyon. Other principal tributaries in Texas are the **Pease** and the **Wichita** in North Central Texas and the **Sulphur** in Northeast Texas, which flows into the Red River after it has crossed the boundary line into Arkansas.

The last major tributary in Northeast Texas is **Cypress Creek,** which flows into Louisiana before joining with the Red River. Major reservoirs on the Northeast Texas tributaries are **Wright Patman Lake, Lake O' the Pines** and **Caddo Lake**. From Oklahoma the principal tributary is the **Washita**. The **Ouachita,** a river with the same pronunciation of its name, though spelled differently, is the principal tributary to its lower course.

The Red River boundary dispute, a long-standing feud between Oklahoma and Texas, was finally settled in 2000.

### Canadian River

The Canadian River heads near **Raton Pass** in northern New Mexico near the Colorado boundary line and flows into Texas on the west line of Oldham County. It crosses the Texas Panhandle into Oklahoma and there flows into the Arkansas. It drains 12,700 square miles, and most of its course across the Panhandle is in a deep gorge. A tributary dips into Texas' northern Panhandle and then flows to a confluence with the main channel in Oklahoma. One of several theories as to how the Canadian got its name is that some early explorers thought it flowed into Canada. **Lake Meredith,** formed by **Sanford Dam** on the Canadian, provides water for 11 Panhandle cities.

Because of the **deep gorge** and the **quicksand** at many places, the Canadian has been a particularly difficult stream to bridge. It is known especially in its lower course in Oklahoma as outstanding among the streams of the country for the great amount of quicksand in its channel. ☆

# Lakes and Reservoirs

The large increase in the number of reservoirs in Texas during the past half-century has greatly improved water conservation and supplies. As late as 1913, Texas had only eight major reservoirs with a total storage capacity of 376,000 acre-feet. Most of this capacity was in Medina Lake in southwest Texas, with 254,000 acre-feet capacity, created by a dam completed in May 1913. (An acre-foot is the amount of water necessary to cover an acre of surface area with water one foot deep.)

Kayakers glide across Joe Pool Reservoir at Cedar Hill State Park. The reservoir is in Dallas, Tarrant and Ellis counties. File photo.

the listed reservoirs are those that were completed by Jan. 1, 2003, and in use.

Conservation storage capacity is used in the table below; the surface area used is that area at conservation elevation only. (Different methods of computing capacity area are used, and detailed information may be obtained from the **Texas Water Development Board,** Austin, from the **U.S. Army Corps of Engineers,** or from local sources.) Also, it should be noted that boundary reservoir capacities include water designated for

By 1920, Texas had 11 major reservoirs with combined storage capacity of 449,710 acre-feet. The state water agency reported 32 reservoirs and 1,284,520 acre-feet capacity in 1930. By 1950, this number had increased to 66 with 9,623,870 acre-feet capacity and to 168 with total capacity of 36,290,059 acre-feet in 1980. By January 2003, Texas had 204 major reservoirs (those with a normal capacity of 5,000 acre-feet or larger) existing or under construction, with a total conservation surface area of 1,678,708 acres and a conservation storage capacity of 40,947,816 acre-feet.

According to the U.S. Statistical Abstract of 2001, Texas has **4,959 square miles of inland water,** ranking it first in the 48 contiguous states, followed by Minnesota, with 4,780 sq. mi.; Florida, 4,683; and Louisiana, 4,153. There are about **6,736 reservoirs** in Texas with a normal storage capacity of 10 acre-feet or larger.

The following table lists reservoirs in Texas having **more than 4,000 acre-feet capacity.** With few exceptions,

Texas use and non-Texas water, as well.

In the list below, information is given in the following order: (1) Name of lake or reservoir; (2) county or counties in which located; (3) river or creek on which located; (4) location with respect to some city or town; (5) purpose of reservoir; (6) owner of reservoir. Some of these items, when not listed, are not available. For the larger lakes and reservoirs, the dam impounding water to form the lake bears the same name, unless otherwise indicated. Abbreviations in the list below are as follows: L., lake; R., river; Co., county; Cr., creek; (C) conservation; (FC) flood control; (R) recreation; (P) power; (M) municipal; (D) domestic; (Ir.) irrigation; (In.) industry; (Mi.) mining, including oil production; (FH) fish hatchery; USAE, United States Army Corps of Engineers; WC&ID, Water Control and Improvement District; WID, Water Improvement District; USBR, United States Bureau of Reclamation; Auth., Authority; LCRA, Lower Colorado River Authority; USDA, United States Department of Agriculture; Imp., impounded. ☆

| Lakes and Reservoirs | Conservation Surface Area (Acres) | Conservation Storage Capacity (Acre-Ft.) |
|---|---|---|
| **Abilene, L.** — Taylor Co.; Elm Cr.; 6 mi. NW Tuscola; (M-In.-R); City of Abilene | 595 | 7,900 |
| **Alan Henry Reservoir** — Garza Co.; Double Mountain Fork Brazos River; 10 mi. E Justiceburg; (M-In.-Ir.); City of Lubbock | 3,504 | 115,937 |
| **Addicks Reservoir** — Harris Co.; South Mayde Cr.; 1 mi. E of Addicks | 16,423 | 200,800 |
| **Alcoa L.** — Milam Co.; Sandy Cr.; 7 mi. SW Rockdale; (In.-R); Aluminum Co. of America (also called **Sandow L.**) | 880 | 14,750 |
| **Amistad Reservoir, International** — Val Verde Co.; Rio Grande; an international project of the U.S. and Mexico; 12 mi. NW Del Rio; (C-R-Ir.-P-FC); International Boundary and Water Com. (Texas' share of conservation capacity is 56.2 percent.) (Formerly **Diablo R.**) | 64,900 | 3,505,400 |
| **Amon G. Carter, L.** — Montague Co.; Big Sandy Cr.; 6 mi. S Bowie; (M-In.); City of Bowie | 1,848 | 28,589 |
| **Anahuac, L.** — Chambers Co.; Turtle Bayou; near Anahuac; (Ir.-In.-Mi.); Chambers-Liberty Counties Navigation District; (also called **Turtle Bayou Reservoir**) | 5,300 | 35,300 |
| **Anzalduas Channel Dam** — Hidalgo Co.; Rio Grande; 11 mi. upstream from Hidalgo; (Ir.-FC); United States and Mexico | — | 8,400 |
| **Aquilla L.** — Hill Co.; Aquilla Cr.; 10.2 mi. W of Hillsboro; (FC-M-Ir.-In.-R); USAE-Brazos R. Auth | 3,280 | 52,400 |
| **Arlington, L.** — Tarrant Co.; Village Cr.; 7 mi. W Arlington; (M-In.); City of Arlington | 2,275 | 45,710 |
| **Arrowhead, L.** — Clay Co.; Little Wichita R.; 13 mi. SE Wichita Falls; (M); City of Wichita Falls | 16,200 | 262,100 |
| **Athens, L.** — Henderson Co.; 8 mi. E Athens; (M-FC-R); Athens Mun. Water Authority (formerly **Flat Creek Reservoir**) | 1,520 | 32,790 |
| **Austin, L.** — Travis Co.; Colorado R.; W Austin city limits; (M-In.-P); City of Austin, leased to LCRA (Imp. by **Tom Miller Dam**) | 1,830 | 21,000 |
| **Ballinger, L.** — Runnels Co.; Valley Creek; 5 mi. W Ballinger; (M); City of Ballinger (also known as **Lake Moonen**) | — | 6,850 |
| **Balmorhea, L.** — Reeves Co.; Sandia Cr.; 3 mi. SE Balmorhea; (Ir.); Reeves Co. WID No. 1 | 573 | 6,350 |
| **Bardwell, L.** — Ellis Co.; Waxahachie Cr.; 3 mi. SE Bardwell; (FC-C-R); USAE | 3,570 | 54,900 |
| **Barker Reservoir** — Harris Co.; above Buffalo Bayou | 16,739 | 209,000 |
| **Barney M. Davis Cooling Reservoir** — Nueces Co.; off-channel storage reservoir of Laguna Madre arm of Gulf; 14 mi. SE Corpus Christi; (In.); Central Power & Light Co. | 1,100 | 6,600 |

| Name / Description | Surface Acres | Capacity |
|---|---|---|
| **Bastrop, L.** — Bastrop Co.; Spicer Cr.; 3 mi. NE Bastrop; (In.); LCRA | 906 | 16,590 |
| **Baylor Creek L.** — Childress Co.; 10 mi. NW Childress; (M-R); City of Childress | 610 | 9,220 |
| **Belton L.** — Bell-Coryell counties; Leon R.; 3 mi. N. Belton; (M-FC-In.-Ir.); USAE-Brazos R. Auth. | 12,300 | 457,600 |
| **Benbrook L.** — Tarrant Co.; Clear Fk. Trinity R.; 10 mi. SW Fort Worth; (FC-R); USAE | 3,770 | 88,250 |
| **Big Creek Reservoir** — Delta Co; Big Creek; 1 mi. N Cooper; (M); City of Cooper | — | 4,890 |
| **Bivins L.** — Randall Co.; Palo Duro Cr.; 8 mi. NW Canyon; (M); Amarillo; City of Amarillo (also called **Amarillo City Lake**) | 379 | 5,120 |
| **Bob Sandlin, L.** — Titus-Wood-Camp-Franklin counties; Big Cypress Cr.; 5 mi. SW Mount Pleasant; (In.-M-R); Titus Co. FWSD No. 1 (Imp. by **Fort Sherman Dam**) | 9,460 | 213,350 |
| **Bonham, L.** — Fannin Co.; Timber Cr.; 5 mi. NE Bonham; (M); Bonham Mun. Water Auth. | 1,020 | 12,000 |
| **Brady Creek Reservoir** — McCulloch Co.; Brady Cr.; 3 mi. W Brady; (M-In.); City of Brady | 2,020 | 30,430 |
| **Brandy Branch Reservoir** — Harrison Co.; Brandy Br.; 10 mi. SW Marshall; (In.); Southwestern Electric Power Co. | 1,242 | 29,513 |
| **Brazoria Reservoir** — Brazoria Co.; off-channel reservoir; 1 mi. NE Brazoria; (In.); Dow Chemical Co. | 1,865 | 21,970 |
| **Bridgeport, L.** — Wise-Jack counties; W. Fk. of Trinity R.; 4 mi. W Bridgeport; (M-In.-FC-R); Tarrant Co. WC&ID Dist. No. 1 | 13,000 | 386,420 |
| **Brownwood, L.** — Brown Co.; Pecan Bayou; 8 mi. N Brownwood; (M-In.-Ir.); Brown Co. WC&ID No. 1 | 7,300 | 143,400 |
| **Bryan Utilities L.** — Brazos Co.; unnamed stream; 6 mi. NW Bryan; (R-In.); City of Bryan | 829 | 15,227 |
| **Buchanan, L.** — Burnet-Llano-San Saba counties; Colorado R.; 13 mi. W Burnet; (M-Ir.-Mi-P); LCRA | 23,100 | 922,000 |
| **Buffalo Lake** — Randall Co.; Tierra Blanca Cr.; 2 mi. S. Umbarger; (R); U.S. Fish and Wildlife Service; (Imp. by **Umbarger Dam**) | 1,900 | 18,150 |
| **Buffalo Springs L.** — Lubbock Co.; Double Mtn.Fk. Brazos R.; 9 mi. SE Lubbock; (M-In.-R); Lubbock Co. WC & ID No. 1; Imp. by **W. G. McMillan Sr. Dam**) | 200 | 4,200 |
| **Caddo L.** — Harrison-Marion counties, Texas and Caddo Parish, La. An original natural lake, whose surface and capacity were increased by construction of dam on Cypress Creek near Mooringsport, La. | 26,800 | 129,000 |
| **Calaveras L.** — Bexar Co.; Calaveras Cr.; 15 mi. SE San Antonio; (In.); Pub. Svc. Bd. of San Antonio | 3,624 | 63,200 |
| **Camp Creek L.** — Robertson Co.; 13 mi. E Franklin; (R); Camp Creek Water Co. | 750 | 8,550 |
| **Canyon L.** — Comal Co.; Guadalupe R.; 12 mi. NW New Braunfels; (M-In.-P-FC); Guadalupe-Blanco R. Authority & USAE. | 8,240 | 386,200 |
| **Casa Blanca L.** — Webb Co.; Chacon Cr.; 3 mi. NE Laredo; (R); Webb Co.; (Imp. by **Country Club Dam**) | 1,656 | 20,000 |
| **Cedar Bayou Cooling Reservoir** — Chambers Co.; Cedar Bayou; 15 mi. SW Anahuac; (In.); Houston Lighting & Power Co. | 2,750 | 19,250 |
| **Cedar Creek Reservoir** — Henderson-Kaufman counties; Cedar Cr.; 3 mi. NE Trinidad; (also called **Joe B. Hogsett, L.**); (M-R); Tarrant Co. WC&ID No. 1. | 33,750 | 679,200 |
| **Cedar Creek Reservoir** — Fayette Co.; Cedar Cr.; 8.5 mi. E. La Grange; (In.); LCRA | 2,420 | 74,080 |
| **Champion Creek Reservoir** — Mitchell Co.; 7 mi. S. Colorado City; (M-In.); Texas Electric Service Co. | 1,560 | 42,500 |
| **Cherokee, L.** — Gregg-Rusk counties; Cherokee Bayou; 12 mi. SE Longview; (M-In.-R); Cherokee Water Co. | 3,987 | 46,700 |
| **Choke Canyon Reservoir** — Live Oak-McMullen counties; Frio R.; 4 mi. W Three Rivers; (M-In.-R-FC); City of Corpus Christi-USBR | 25,733 | 689,314 |
| **Cisco, L.** — Eastland Co.; Sandy Cr.; 4 mi. N. Cisco; (M); City of Cisco (Imp. by **Williamson Dam**) | 445 | 8,800 |
| **Cleburne, L. Pat** — Johnson Co.; Nolan R.; 4 mi. S. Cleburne; (M); City of Cleburne | 1,550 | 25,560 |
| **Clyde, L.** — Callahan Co.; N. Prong Pecan Bayou; 6 mi. S. Clyde; (M); City of Clyde and USDA Soil Conservation Service. | 449 | 5,748 |
| **Coffee Mill L.** — Fannin Co.; Coffee Mill Cr.; 12 mi. NW Honey Grove; (R); U.S. Forest Service | 650 | 8,000 |
| **Coleman, L.** — Coleman Co.; Jim Ned Cr.; 14 mi. N. Coleman; (M-In.); City of Coleman | 2,000 | 40,000 |
| **Coleto Creek Reservoir** — Goliad-Victoria counties; Coleto Cr.; 12 mi. SW Victoria; (In); Guadalupe-Blanco River Auth. | 3,100 | 31,040 |
| **Colorado City, L.** — Mitchell Co.; Morgan Cr.; 4 mi. SW Colorado City; (M-In.-P); Texas Elec. Service Co. | 1,612 | 31,805 |
| **Conroe, L.** — Montgomery-Walker counties; W. Fk. San Jacinto R.; 7 mi. NW Conroe; (M-In.-Mi.); San Jacinto River Authority, City of Houston and Texas Water Dev. Bd. | 20,985 | 430,260 |
| **Cooper, L.** — Archer Co.; Mesquite Crk; 8 mi. E Megargel; (W-R); City of Olney; (also called **L. Olney**) | — | 6,650 |
| **Cooper L.** — Delta-Hopkins counties (see **Jim Chapman Lake**) | | |
| **Corpus Christi, L.** — Live Oak-San Patricio-Jim Wells counties; Nueces R.; 4 mi. SW Mathis; (P-M-In.-Ir.-R.); Lower Nueces River WSD (Imp. by **Wesley E. Seale Dam**) | 19,251 | 237,473 |
| **Cox Creek Reservoir** — Calhoun Co.; Cox Creek; (In); Aluminum Co. of America; (Also called **Raw Water Lake** and **Recycle Lake**) | 541 | 5,034 |
| **Crook, L.** — Lamar Co.; Pine Cr.; 5 Mi. N. Paris; (M); City of Paris | 1,226 | 9,664 |
| **Cypress Springs, L.** — Franklin Co.; Big Cypress Cr.; 8 mi. SE Mount Vernon; (In-M); Franklin Co. WD and Texas Water Development Board (formerly **Franklin Co. L.**); (Imp. by **Franklin Co. Dam**) | 3,400 | 72,800 |
| **Daniel, L.** — Stephens Co.; Gunsolus Cr.; 7 mi. S Breckenridge; (M-In.); City of Breckenridge; (Imp. by **Gunsolus Creek Dam**) | 924 | 9,515 |
| **Davis, L.** — Knox Co.; Double Dutchman Cr.; 5 mi. SE Benjamin; (Ir); League Ranch | 585 | 5,454 |
| **Delta Lake Res. Units 1 and 2** — Hidalgo Co.; Rio Grande (off channel); 4 mi. N. Monte Alto; (Ir.); Hidalgo-Willacy counties WC&ID No. 1 (formerly **Monte Alto Reservoir**) | 2,451 | 22,068 |
| **Diversion, L.** — Archer-Baylor counties; Wichita R.; 14 mi. W Holliday; (M-In.); City of Wichita Falls and Wichita Co. WID No. 2 | 3,419 | 40,000 |
| **Dunlap, L.** — Guadalupe Co.; Guadalupe R.; 9 mi. NW Seguin; (P); Guadalupe-Blanco R. Auth.; (Imp. by **TP-1 Dam**) | 410 | 5,900 |
| **Eagle L.** — Colorado Co.; Colorado R. (off channel); in Eagle Lake; (Ir.); Lakeside Irrigation Co. | 1,200 | 9,600 |
| **Eagle Mountain Lake** — Tarrant-Wise counties; W. Fk. Trinity R.; 14 mi. NW Fort Worth; (M-In.-Ir.); Tarrant Co. WC&ID No. 1 | 9,200 | 190,460 |
| **Eagle Nest Lake** — Brazoria Co.; off-channel Brazos R.; 12 mi. WNW Angleton; (Ir.); T.M. Smith, et al. (also called **Manor Lake**). | — | 18,000 |
| **Eastman Lakes** — 8 lakes; Harrison Co.; Sabine R. basin; NW of Longview; Texas Eastman Co. | — | 8,135 |
| **Electra, L.** — Wilbarger Co.; Camp Cr. and Beaver Cr.; 7 mi. SW Electra; (In.-M); City of Electra | 600 | 8,050 |
| **Ellison Creek Reservoir** — Morris Co.; Ellison Cr.; 8 mi. S. Daingerfield; (P-In.); Lone Star Steel | 1,516 | 24,700 |
| **E.V. Spence Reservoir** (see **Spence Reservoir, E.V.**) | | |
| **Fairfield L.** — Freestone Co.; Big Brown Cr.; 11 mi. NE Fairfield; (In.); TP&L, Texas Elec. Service Co., DP&L and Industrial Generating Co. (formerly **Big Brown Creek Reservoir**) | 2,350 | 50,600 |

| | | |
|---|---|---|
| **Falcon Reservoir, International** — Starr-Zapata counties; Rio Grande; (International—U.S.-Mexico); 3 mi. W Falcon Heights; (M-In.-Ir.-FC-P-R); International Boundary and Water Com.; (Texas' share of total conservation capacity is 58.6 per cent) | 87,210 | 2,767,400 |
| **Farmers Creek Reservoir** — Montague Co.; 8 mi. NE Nocona; (M-In.-Mi.); No. Montague County Water Supply District (also known as **Lake Nocona**) | 1,470 | 25,400 |
| **Forest Grove Reservoir** — Henderson Co.; Caney Cr.; 7 mi. NW Athens; (In.); Texas Utilities Services, Inc., Agent . . . . . . . . . | 1,502 | 20,038 |
| **Fort Phantom Hill, Lake** — Jones Co.; Elm Cr.; 5 mi. S. Nugent; (M-R); City of Abilene | 4,246 | 74,310 |
| **Galveston County Industrial Water Reservoir** — Galveston Co.; off-channel storage Dickinson Bayou; 16 mi. S La Porte; (In.-M.); Galveston Co. Water Auth. . . . . . . . . . | 812 | 7,308 |
| **Georgetown, L.** — Williamson Co.; N. Fk. San Gabriel R.; 3.5 mi. W Georgetown; (FC-M-In.); USAE | 1,310 | 37,100 |
| **Gibbons Creek Reservoir** — Grimes Co.; Gibbons Cr.; 9.5 mi NW Anderson; (In.); Texas Mun. Power Agency . . . . . . . . . | 2,490 | 26,824 |
| **Gilmer Reservoir** — Upshur Co.; Kelsey Creek; 15 mi. N of Longview; 4 mi. W of Gilmer | 1,010 | 12,720 |
| **Gladewater, L.** — Upshur Co.; Glade Cr.; in Gladewater; (M-R); City of Gladewater . . . . . . . . . | 800 | 6,950 |
| **Gonzales, Lake** — Gonzales Co.; Guadalupe R.; 4.5 mi. SE Belmont; (P); Guadalupe-Blanco R. Auth. (also called **H-4 Reservoir**) . . . . . . . . . | 696 | 6,500 |
| **Graham, L.** — Young Co.; Flint and Salt Creeks; 2 mi. NW Graham; (M-In.); City of Graham . . . . . . . . . | 2,550 | 52,386 |
| **Granbury, L.** — Hood-Parker counties; Brazos R.; 8 mi. SE Granbury; (M-In.-Ir.-P); Brazos River Authority (Imp. by **DeCordova Bend Dam**) . . . . . . . . . | 8,700 | 153,500 |
| **Granger L.** — Williamson Co.; San Gabriel R.; 10 mi. NE Taylor; (FC-M-In.); USAE (formerly **Laneport L.**). . . . . . . . . . | 4,400 | 82,000 |
| **Grapevine L.** — Tarrant-Denton counties; Denton Cr.; 2 mi. NE Grapevine; (M-FC-In.-R.); USAE | 7,380 | 188,550 |
| **Greenbelt L.** — Donley Co.; Salt Fk. Red R.; 5 mi. N Clarendon; (M-In.); Greenbelt M&I Water Auth. . . . . | 2,025 | 60,400 |
| **Greenville City Lakes** — 6 lakes; Hunt Co.; Conleech Fork, Sabine R.; 2 mi. Greenville; (M-Other); City of Greenville. . . . . . | — | 6,864 |
| **H-4 Reservoir** (see **Gonzales, Lake**) | | |
| **Halbert, L.** — Navarro Co.; Elm Cr.; 4 mi. SE Corsicana; (M-In-R); City of Corsicana . . . . . . . . . | 650 | 7,420 |
| **Harris Reservoir, William** — Brazoria Co.; off-channel between Brazos R. and Oyster Cr.; 8 mi. NW Angleton; (In.); Dow Chemical Co. . . . . . . . . . | 1,663 | 12,000 |
| **Hawkins, L.** — Wood Co.; Little Sandy Cr.; 3 mi. NW Hawkins; (FC-R); Wood County; (Imp. by **Wood Co. Dam No. 3**). . . . . . . . . . | 776 | 11,890 |
| **Holbrook, L.** — Wood Co.; Keys Cr.; 4 mi. NW Mineola; (FC-R); Wood County; (Imp. by **Wood Co. Dam No. 2**). . . . . . . . . . | 653 | 7,990 |
| **Hords Creek L.** — Coleman Co.; Hords Cr.; 5 mi. NW Valera; (M-FC); City of Coleman and USAE . . . . . | 510 | 8,640 |
| **Houston, L.** — Harris Co.; San Jacinto R.; 4 mi. N Sheldon; (M-In.-Ir.-Mi.-R); City of Houston . . . . . . . . . | 12,240 | 146,700 |
| **Houston County L.** — Houston Co.; Little Elkhart Cr.; 10 mi. NW Crockett; (M-In.); Houston Co. WC&ID No. 1. . . . . . . . . . | 1,282 | 19,500 |
| **Hubbard Creek Reservoir** — Stephens Co.; 6 mi. NW Breckenridge; (M-In.-Mi.); West Central Texas Mun. Water Authority | 15,250 | 317,750 |
| **Imperial Reservoir** — Reeves-Pecos counties; Pecos R.; 35 mi. N Fort Stockton; (Ir.); Pecos County WC&ID No. 2 . . . . . . . . . | 1,530 | 6,000 |
| **Inks L.** — Burnet-Llano counties; Colorado R.; 12 mi. W Burnet; (M-Ir.-Mi.-P); LCRA | 803 | 17,500 |
| **Jacksonville, L.** — Cherokee Co.; Gum Cr.; 5 mi. SW Jacksonville; (M-R); City of Jacksonville; (Imp. by **Buckner Dam**). . . . . . . . . . | 1,320 | 30,500 |
| **J. B. Thomas, L.** — Scurry-Borden counties; Colorado R.; 16 mi. SW Snyder; (M- In.-R); Colorado River Mun. Water Dist.; (Imp. by **Colorado R. Dam**). . . . . . . . . . | 7,820 | 203,600 |
| **J. D. Murphree Wildlife Management Area Impoundments** — Jefferson Co.; off-channel reservoirs between Big Hill and Taylor bayous; at Port Acres; (FH-R); TP&WD (formerly **Big Hill Reservoir**) . . . . | 6,881 | 13,500 |
| **Jim Chapman Lake**— (formerly **Cooper Lake**) Delta-Hopkins counties; Sulphur R.; 3 mi.SE Cooper; (FC-M-R); USAE . . . . . . . . . | 19,280 | 310,000 |
| **Joe Pool Reservoir** — Dallas- Tarrant-Ellis counties; Mountain Cr.; 14 mi. SW Dallas; (FC-M-R); USAE-Trinity River Auth. (formerly **Lakeview Lake**) | 7,470 | 181,200 |
| **Johnson Creek Reservoir** — Marion Co.; 13 mi. NW Jefferson; (In.); Southwestern Electric Co. | 650 | 10,100 |
| **Kemp, L.** — Baylor Co.; Wichita R.; 6 mi. N Mabelle; (M-P-Ir.); City of Wichita Falls; Wichita Co. WID 2 | 15,590 | 268,000 |
| **Kickapoo, L.** — Archer Co.; N. Fk. Little Wichita R.; 10 mi. NW Archer City; (M); City of Wichita Falls . . . | 6,200 | 106,000 |
| **Kiowa, L.** — Cooke Co.; Indian Cr.; 8 mi. SE Gainesville; (R); Lake Kiowa, Inc. . . . . . . . . . | 560 | 7,000 |
| **Kirby, L.** — Taylor Co.; Cedar Cr.; 5 mi. S. Abilene; (M); City of Abilene | 740 | 7,620 |
| **Kurth, L.** — Angelina Co.; off-channel reservoir; 8 mi. N Lufkin; (In.); Southland Paper Mills, Inc. . . . . . . | 770 | 16,200 |
| **Lake Creek L.** — McLennan Co.; Manos Cr.; 4 mi. SW Riesel; (In.); Texas P&L Co. | 550 | 8,400 |
| **Lake Fork Reservoir** — Wood-Rains counties; Lake Fork Cr.; 5 mi. W Quitman; (M-In.); SRA | 27,690 | 675,819 |
| **Lake O' the Pines** — Marion-Upshur-Harrison-Morris-Camp counties; Cypress Cr.; 9 mi. W Jefferson; (FC-C-R-In.-M); USAE (Imp. by **Ferrell's Bridge Dam**) | 19,780 | 254,900 |
| **Lavon L.** (Enlargement) — Collin Co.; East Fk. Trinity R.; 2 mi. W Lavon; (M-FC-In.); USAE | 21,400 | 456,500 |
| **Leon, Lake** — Eastland Co.; Leon R.; 7 mi. S Ranger; (M-In.); Eastland Co. Water Supply Dist. . . . . . . . | 1,590 | 27,290 |
| **Lewis Creek Reservoir** — Montgomery Co.; Lewis Cr.; 10 mi. NW Conroe; (In.); Gulf States Util. Co. . . . | 1,010 | 16,400 |
| **Lewisville L.** — Denton Co.; Elm Fk. Trinity R.; 2 mi. NE Lewisville; (M-FC-In.-R); USAE; (also called **Lake Dallas** and **Garza-Little Elm**). . . . . . . . . . | 29,592 | 640,986 |
| **Limestone, L.** — Leon-Limestone-Robertson cos.; Navasota R.; 7 mi. NW Marquez; (M-In.-Ir.); BRA | 14,200 | 217,494 |
| **Livingston, L.** — Polk-San Jacinto-Trinity-Walker counties; Trinity R.; 6 mi. SW Livingston; (M-In.-Ir.); City of Houston and Trinity River Authority . . . . . . . . . | 82,600 | 1,750,000 |
| **Loma Alta Lake** — Cameron Co.; off-channel Rio Grande; 8 mi. NE Brownsville; (M-In.); Brownsville Navigation Dist. . . . . . . . . . | 2,490 | 26,500 |
| **Lost Creek Reservoir** — Jack Co.; Lost Cr.; 4 mi. NE Jacksboro; (M); City of Jacksboro . . . . . . . . . . . | 368 | 11,961 |
| **Lynchburg Reservoir** — Harris Co., off-channel Trinity R. (San Jacinto R. basin); on Houston Ship Channel near Baytown; (M-In.); Coastal Water Authority . . . . . . . . . | 200 | 4,700 |
| **Lyndon B. Johnson, L.** — Burnet-Llano counties; Colorado R.; 5 mi. SW Marble Falls; (P); LCRA; (Imp. by **Alvin Wirtz Dam**); (formerly **Granite Shoals L.**) . . . . . . . . . | 6,380 | 138,000 |
| **Mackenzie Reservoir** — Briscoe Co.; Tule Cr.; 9 mi. NW Silverton; (M); Mackenzie Mun. Water Auth. . . . | 896 | 46,450 |
| **Manor Lake** — (see **Eagle Nest Lake**) | | |
| **Marble Falls, L.** — Burnet Co.; Colorado R.; (Imp. by **Max Starcke Dam**); 1.25 mi. SE Marble Falls; (P); LCRA . . . . . . . . . | 780 | 8,760 |
| **Martin L.** — Rusk-Panola counties; Martin Cr.; 17 mi. NE Henderson; (P); Texas Util. Service Co., Inc. | 5,020 | 77,619 |

| | | |
|---|---:|---:|
| **McQueeney, L.** — Guadalupe Co.; Guadalupe R.; 5 mi. W Seguin; (P); Guadalupe-Blanco R. Authority; (Imp. by **Abbott Dam**) | 396 | 5,000 |
| **Medina L.** — Medina-Bandera counties; Medina R.; 8 mi. W Rio Medina; (Ir.); Bexar- Medina-Atascosa Co. WID No. 1 | 5,575 | 254,000 |
| **Meredith, L.** — Moore-Potter-Hutchinson counties; Canadian R.; 10 mi. NW Borger; (M-In.- FC-R); cooperative project for municipal water supply to Amarillo, Lubbock and other High Plains cities. Canadian R. Municipal Water Authority-USBR; (Imp. by **Sanford Dam**) | 17,320 | 920,300 |
| **Mexia, L.** — Limestone Co.; Navasota R.; 7 mi. SW Mexia; (M-In); Bistone Mun. Water Dist.; (impounded by **Bistone Dam**) | 1,200 | 10,000 |
| **Millers Creek Reservoir** — Baylor Co.; Millers Cr.; 9 mi. SE Goree; (M); North Central Texas Mun. Water Auth. and Texas Water Development Board | 1,900 | 25,520 |
| **Mineral Wells, L.** — Parker Co.; Rock Cr.; 4 mi. E Mineral Wells; (M); Palo Pinto Co. Mun. WD No. 1 | 646 | 6,760 |
| **Mitchell County Reservoir** — Mitchell Co.; Beals Creek; (Mi.-In.); Colorado River MWD | 1,463 | 27,266 |
| **Monticello Reservoir** — Titus Co.; Blundell Cr.; 2.5 mi. E. Monticello; (In.); Industrial Generating Co. | 2,000 | 40,100 |
| **Moss L., Hubert H.** — Cooke Co.; Fish Cr.; 10 mi. NW Gainesville; (M-In.); City of Gainesville | 1,125 | 23,210 |
| **Mountain Creek L.** — Dallas Co.; Mountain Cr.; 4 mi. SE Grand Prairie; (In.); Dallas P&L Co. | 3,050 | 25,720 |
| **Murphree, J. D. Area Impoundments** — (see **J. D. Murphree**) | | |
| **Murvaul L.** — Panola Co.; Murvaul Bayou; 10 mi. W Carthage; (M-In.-R); Panola Co. Fresh Water Supply Dist. No. 1 | 3,800 | 44,650 |
| **Mustang Lake East** & **Mustang Lake West** — Brazoria Co.; Mustang Bayou; 6 mi. S Alvin; (Ir.-In.-R); Chocolate Bayou Land & Water Co. | — | 6,451 |
| **Nacogdoches, L.** — Nacogdoches Co.; Bayo Loco Cr.; 10 mi. W Nacogdoches; (M); City of Nacogdoches | 2,210 | 41,140 |
| **Nasworthy, L.** — Tom Green Co.; S Concho R.; 6 mi. SW San Angelo; (M-In.-Ir); City of San Angelo | 1,596 | 12,390 |
| **Natural Dam L.** — Howard Co.; Sulphur Springs Draw; 8 mi. W Big Spring; (FC); Wilkinson Ranch & Colorado River MWD | — | 28,000 |
| **Navarro Mills L.** — Navarro-Hill counties; Richland Cr.; 16 mi. SW Corsicana; (M-FC); USAE | 5,070 | 63,300 |
| **North Fk. Buffalo Creek Reservoir** — Wichita Co.; 5 mi. NW Iowa Park; (M); Wichita Co. WC&ID No.3 | 1,500 | 15,400 |
| **North L.** — Dallas Co.; S. Fork Grapevine Cr.; 2 mi. SE Coppell; (In.); Dallas P&L Co. | 800 | 17,000 |
| **Oak Creek Reservoir** — Coke Co.; 5 mi. SE Blackwell; (M-In.); City of Sweetwater | 2,375 | 39,360 |
| **O. C. Fisher L.** — Tom Green Co.; N. Concho R.; 3 mi. NW San Angelo; (M-FC-C- Ir.-R-In.-Mi); USAE —Upper Colo. River Auth. (formerly **San Angelo L.**) | 5,440 | 119,200 |
| **O. H. Ivie Reservoir** — Coleman-Concho-Runnels counties; 24 mi. SE Ballinger; (M-In.), Colorado R. Mun. Water Dist. (formerly **Stacy Reservoir**) | 19,149 | 554,339 |
| **Olney, Lake** (see **Cooper, Lake**) | | |
| **Palestine, L.** — Anderson-Cherokee-Henderson-Smith counties; Neches R.; 4 mi. E Frankston; (M-In.-R); Upper Neches R. MWA (Imp. by **Blackburn Crossing Dam**) | 25,560 | 411,840 |
| **Palo Duro Reservoir** — Hansford Co.; Palo Duro Cr.; 12 mi. N Spearman; (M-R); Palo Duro River Auth. | 2,413 | 60,897 |
| **Palo Pinto, L.** — Palo Pinto Co.; 15 mi. SW Mineral Wells; (M-In.); Palo Pinto Co. Muni. Water Dist. 1 | 2,498 | 27,650 |
| **Pat Mayse L.** — Lamar Co.; Sanders Cr.; 2 mi. SW Arthur City; (M-In.-FC); USAE | 5,993 | 124,500 |
| **Pauline, L.** — Hardeman Co.; Wanderers Creek, 10 mi. W Chillicothe; (In-R);West Texas Utilities Co. | — | 4,136 |
| **Pinkston Reservoir** — Shelby Co.; Sandy Cr.; 12.5 mi. SW Center; (M); City of Center; (formerly **Sandy Creek Reservoir**) | 523 | 7,380 |
| **Possum Kingdom L.** — Palo Pinto-Young-Stephens-Jack counties; Brazos R.; 11 mi. SW Graford; (M-In.-Ir.-Mi.-P-R); Brazos R. Authority; (Imp. by **Morris Sheppard Dam**) | 14,440 | 504,100 |
| **Proctor L.** — Comanche Co.; Leon R.; 9 mi. NE Comanche; (M-In.-Ir.-FC); USAE- Brazos River Auth. | 4,610 | 59,400 |
| **Quitman, L.** — Wood Co.; Dry Cr.; 4 mi. N Quitman; (FC-R); Wood County (Imp. by **Wood Co. Dam No.1**) | 814 | 7,440 |
| **Randell L.** — Grayson Co.; Shawnee Cr.; 4 mi. NW Denison; (M); City of Denison | 280 | 5,400 |
| **Raw Water Lake** — Calhoun Co. (See **Cox Lake**) | | |
| **Ray Hubbard, L.** — Collin-Dallas-Kaufman-Rockwall counties; (formerly **Forney Reservoir**); E. Fk. Trinity R.; 15 mi. E Dallas; (M); City of Dallas | 22,745 | 490,000 |
| **Ray Roberts, L.** — Denton-Cooke-Grayson counties; Elm Fk. Trinity R.; 11 mi. NE Denton; (FC-M-D); City of Denton, Dallas, USAE; (also known as **Aubrey Reservoir**) | 29,350 | 799,600 |
| **Recycle Lake** — Calhoun Co. (see **Cox Lake**) | | |
| **Red Bluff Reservoir** — Loving-Reeves counties, Texas; and Eddy Co.; N.M.; Pecos R.; 5 mi. N Orla; (Ir.-P); Red Bluff Water Power Control District | 11,700 | 310,000 |
| **Red Draw L.** — Howard Co.; Red Draw; 5 mi. E Bi Spring; (Mi.-In.); Colorado River MWD | 374 | 8,538 |
| **Resacas** — Cameron-Hidalgo-Willacy counties; Rio Grande; these reservoirs are primarily for storage of water during periods of normal or above-normal flow in the river for use when the river's water volume is low. Some of these are old loops and bends in the river that have been isolated by the river's changing its channel. They are known by the Spanish name of resacas. Also a number of reservoirs have been constructed for irrigation water storage and connected with the main channel of the river by ditches through which the reservoirs are filled either by gravity flow or by pumping. | — | — |
| **Retamal Channel Dam** — Hidalgo Co.; Rio Grande; 16 mi. SE McAllen; (Ir.-FC); United States/Mexico | — | 4,900 |
| **Retama Reservoir** — Hidalgo Co.; Off-Channel Rio Grande; 5 mi. N Edinburg; (Ir. ); Santa Cruz ID #15; (also known as **Edinburg Lake**) | — | 5,000 |
| **Richland-Chambers Reservoir** — Freestone-Navarro counties; Richland Cr.; 20 mi. SE Corsicana; (M); Tarrant Co. WCID No. 1 | 44,752 | 1,181,866 |
| **Rita Blanca, L.** — Hartley Co.; Rita Blanca Cr.; 2 mi. S Dalhart; (R) City of Dalhart | 524 | 12,100 |
| **River Crest L.** — Red River Co.; off-channel reservoir; 7 mi. SE Bogata; (In.); Texas P&L | 555 | 7,000 |
| **Sam Rayburn Reservoir** — Jasper-Angelina-Sabine-Nacogdoches-San Augustine counties; Angelina R.; (formerly **McGee Bend Reservoir**); (FC-P-M-In.-Ir.-R); USAE | 114,500 | 2,898,500 |
| **San Bernard Reservoirs #1, #2, #3** — Brazoria Co.; Off-Channel San Bernard R.; 3 mi. N Sweeney; (In.); Phillips 66 Co. | — | 8,610 |
| **Santa Rosa L.** — Wilbarger Co.; Beaver Cr.; 15 mi. S Vernon; (Mi.); W. T. Waggoner Estate | 1,625 | 9,556 |
| **Sheldon Reservoir** — Harris Co.; Carpenters Bayou; 2 mi. SW Sheldon; (R-FH); TP&WD | 1,700 | 5,420 |
| **Smithers L.** — Fort Bend Co.; Dry Creek; 10 mi. SE Richmond; (In.); Houston Lighting & Power Co. | 2,430 | 16,300 |
| **Somerville L.** — Burleson-Washington counties; Yegua Cr.; 2 mi. S Somerville; (M-In.-Ir.- FC); USAE-Brazos River Authority | 11,460 | 160,100 |

| | | |
|---|---|---|
| **South Texas Project Reservoir** — Matagorda Co.; off-channel Colorado R.; 16 mi. S Bay City; (In.); Houston Lighting & Power | 7,000 | 202,600 |
| **Spence Reservoir, E. V.** — Coke Co.; Colorado R.; 2 mi. W. Robert Lee; (M-In.-Mi); Colorado R. Mun. Water Dist.; (Imp. by **Robert Lee Dam**) | 14,950 | 488,760 |
| **Squaw Creek Reservoir** — Somervell-Hood counties; Squaw Cr.; 4.5 mi. N Glen Rose; (In.); Texas Utilities Services, Inc. | 3,228 | 151,047 |
| **Stamford, L.** — Haskell Co.; Paint Cr.; 10 mi. SE Haskell; (M-In.); City of Stamford | 4,690 | 53,930 |
| **Steinhagen L., B. A.** — (Also called **Town Bluff Reservoir** and **Dam B. Reservoir**); Tyler-Jasper counties; Neches R.; 1/2 mi. N Town Bluff; (FC-R-C); (Imp. by **Town Bluff Dam**) | 13,700 | 94,200 |
| **Stillhouse Hollow L.** — Bell Co.; Lampasas R.; 5 mi. SW Belton; (M-In.-Ir.-FC); USAE-BRA; (also called **Lampasas Reservoir**) | 6,430 | 235,700 |
| **Striker Creek Reservoir** — Rusk-Cherokee counties; Striker Cr.; 18 mi. SW Henderson; (M -In.); Angelina-Nacogdoches WC&ID No. 1 | 1,920 | 16,930 |
| **Sulphur Springs, L.** — Hopkins Co.; White Oak Cr.; 2 mi. N Sulphur Springs; (M); Sulphur Springs WD; formerly called **White Oak Creek Reservoir**) | 1,557 | 14,370 |
| **Sweetwater, L.** — Nolan Co.; Bitter Creek; 6 mi. SE Sweetwater (M-R); City of Sweetwater | 630 | 11,900 |
| **Tawakoni, L.** — Rains-Van Zandt-Hunt counties; Sabine R.; 9 mi. NE Wills Point; (M-In.-Ir-R); Sabine River Authority; (Imp. by **Iron Bridge Dam**) | 36,153 | 927,440 |
| **Terrell City L., New** — Kaufman Co.; Muddy Cedar Cr.; 6 mi. E Terrell; (M-R); City of Terrell | 830 | 8,712 |
| **Texana, L.** — Jackson Co.; Navidad R. and Sandy Cr.; 6.8 mi. SE Edna; (M-Ir); USBR, Lavaca-Navidad R. Auth., Texas Water Dev. Bd.; (formerly **Palmetto Bend Reservoir**) | 10,134 | 163,506 |
| **Texoma, L.** — Grayson-Cooke cos., Texas; Bryan-Marshall-Love cos., Okla.; (Imp. by **Denison Dam** on Red R. short distance below confluence of Red and Washita Rivers; (P-FC-C-R); USAE; Texas' share. | 88,000 | 2,643,300 |
| **Toledo Bend Reservoir** — Newton-Panola-Sabine-Shelby counties; Sabine R.; 14 mi. NE Burkeville; (M-In.-Ir.-PR); Sabine River Authority (Texas' share of capacity is half amount shown) | 181,600 | 4,477,000 |
| **Town Lake** — Travis Co.; Colorado R.; within Austin city limits; (R); City of Austin | 469 | 6,248 |
| **Tradinghouse Creek Reservoir** — McLennan Co.; Tradinghouse Cr.; 9 mi. E Waco; (In.); Texas P&L | 2,010 | 37,814 |
| **Travis, L.** — Travis-Burnet counties; Colorado R.; 13 mi. NW Austin; (M-In.-Ir.- Mi.-P-FC-R); LCRA: (Imp. by **Mansfield Dam**) | 18,930 | 1,172,600 |
| **Trinidad L.** — Henderson Co.; off-channel reservoir Trinity R.; 2 mi. S. Trinidad; (P); Texas P&L Co. | 740 | 7,450 |
| **Truscott Brine L.** — Knox Co.; Bluff Cr.; 26 mi. NNW Knox City; (Chlorine Control); Red River Auth. | 5,750 | 156,000 |
| **Twin Buttes Reservoir** — Tom Green Co.; Concho R.; 8 mi. SW San Angelo; (M-In. -FC-Ir.-R.); City of San Angelo-USBR-Tom Green Co. WC&ID No. 1 | 9,080 | 186,200 |
| **Twin Oaks Reservoir** — Robertson Co.; Duck Cr.; 12 mi. N. Franklin; (In); Texas P&L | 2,330 | 30,319 |
| **Tyler, L. /Lake Tyler East** — Smith Co.; Prairie and Mud Creeks.; 12 mi. SE Tyler; (M-In); City of Tyler; (Imp. by **Whitehouse** and **Mud Creek** dams) | 4,880 | 80,900 |
| **Upper Nueces L.** — Zavala Co.; Nueces R.; 6 mi. N Crystal City; (Ir.); Zavala-Dimmit Co. WID No. 1 | 316 | 7,590 |
| **Valley Acres Reservoir** — Hidalgo Co.; off-channel Rio Grande; 7 mi. N Mercedes; (Ir-M-FC); Valley Acres Water Dist. | 906 | 7,840 |
| **Valley L.** — Fannin-Grayson counties; 2.5 mi. N Savoy; (P); TP&L; (formerly **Brushy Creek Reservoir**) | 1,080 | 16,400 |
| **Victor Braunig L.** — Bexar Co.; Arroyo Seco; 15 mi. SE San Antonio; (In.); Pub. Svc. Bd./San Antonio | 1,350 | 26,500 |
| **Waco, L.** — McLennan Co.; Bosque R.; 2 mi. W Waco; (M-FC-C-R); City of Waco- USAE-BRA | 7,270 | 152,500 |
| **Walter E. Long, L.** — Travis Co.; Decker Cr.; 9 mi. E Austin; (M-In.-R); City of Austin; (formerly **Decker Lake**) | 1,269 | 33,940 |
| **Waxahachie, L.** — Ellis Co.; S Prong Waxahachie Cr.; 4 mi. SE Waxahachie; (M-In); Ellis County WC&ID No. 1; (Imp. by **S. Prong Dam**) | 690 | 13,500 |
| **Weatherford, L.** — Parker Co.; Clear Fork Trinity River; 7 mi. E Weatherford; (M-In.); City of Weatherford | 1,210 | 19,470 |
| **Welsh Reservoir** — Titus Co.; Swauano Cr.; 11 mi. SE Mount Pleasant; (R-In.); Southwestern Electric Power Co.; (formerly **Swauano Creek Reservoir**) | 1,365 | 23,590 |
| **White River L.** — Crosby Co.; 16 mi. SE Crosbyton; (M-In.-Mi.); White River Municipal Water Dist. | 1,808 | 38,600 |
| **White Rock L.** — Dallas Co.; White Rock Cr.; within NE Dallas city limits; (R); City of Dallas | 1,119 | 10,740 |
| **Whitney, L.** — Hill-Bosque-Johnson counties; Brazos R.; 5.5 mi. SW Whitney; (FC-P); USAE | 23,560 | 627,100 |
| **Wichita, L.** — Wichita Co.; Holliday Cr.; 6 mi. SW Wichita Falls; (M-P-R); City of Wichita Falls | 2,200 | 14,000 |
| **Winnsboro, L.** — Wood Co.; Big Sandy Cr.; 6 mi. SW Winnsboro; (FC-R); Wood County; (Imp. by **Wood Co. Dam No. 4**) | 806 | 8,100 |
| **Winters, L./New Lake Winters** — Runnels Co.; Elm Cr.; 4.5 mi. E Winters; (M); City of Winters | 643 | 8,374 |
| **Wood, L.** — Gonzales, Guadalupe, Guadalupe R.; 3 mi. Gonzales; (P-R); Guadalupe-Blanco River Authority | 345 | 4,000 |
| **Worth, L.** — Tarrant Co.; W. Fk. Trinity R.; in NW Fort Worth; (M); City of Fort Worth | 3,560 | 38,130 |
| **Wright Patman L.** — Bowie-Cass-Morris-Titus-Red River counties; Sulphur R.; 8 mi. SW Texarkana; (FC-M); USAE; (formerly **Texarkana Lake**) | 33,750 | 145,300 |

*Sun lovers swim at Ray Roberts Lake State Park. The park and lake system in Denton, Cooke and Grayson counties attract 2.3 million visitors each year. File photo.*

*Giant tree trunks are reflected in the muddy water of Caddo Lake, a natural lake in Harrison and Marion counties on the Texas and Louisiana border. File photo.*

# Texas Plant Life

*This article was updated for The Texas Almanac by Stephan L. Hatch, Director, S.M. Tracy Herbarium and Professor, Dept. of Rangeland Ecology and Management, Texas A&M University.*

## Vegetational Diversity

Variations in amount and frequency of rainfall, in soils and in frost-free days, gives Texas a great variety of vegetation. From the forests of East Texas to the deserts of West Texas, from the grassy plains of North Texas to the semi-arid brushlands of South Texas, plant species change continuously.

More than 100 million acres of Texas are devoted to providing grazing for domestic and wild animals. This is the **largest single use for land in the state.** More than 80 percent of the acreage is devoted to range in the Edwards Plateau, Cross Timbers and Prairies, South Texas Plains and Trans-Pecos Mountains and Basins.

**Sideoats grama**, which occurs on more different soils in Texas than any other native grass, was officially designated as the **state grass of Texas** by the Texas Legislature in 1971.

The **10 principal plant life areas** of Texas, starting in the east, are:

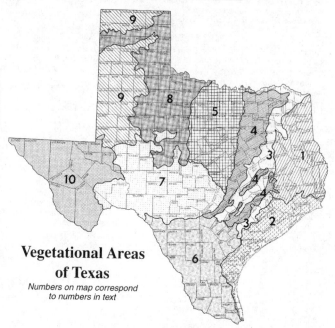

## Vegetational Areas of Texas

*Numbers on map correspond to numbers in text*

### 1. Pineywoods

Most of this area of some 16 million acres ranges from about 50 to 700 feet above sea level and receives 40 to 56 inches of rain yearly. Many rivers, creeks and bayous drain the region. Nearly all of Texas' commercial timber comes from this area. There are three native species of pine, the principal timber: longleaf, shortleaf and loblolly. An introduced species, the **slash pine**, also is widely grown. Hardwoods include **oaks, elm, hickory, magnolia, sweet and black gum, tupelo** and others.

The area is interspersed with **native and improved grasslands.** Cattle are the primary grazing animals. **Deer** and **quail** are abundant in properly managed localities. Primary forage plants, under proper grazing management, include species of the **bluestems, rossettegrass, panicums, paspalums, blackseed needlegrass, Canada and Virginia wildryes, purpletop, broadleaf and spike woodoats, switchcane, lovegrasses, indiangrass** and numerous **legume** species.

Highly disturbed areas have understory and overstory of undesirable woody plants that suppress growth of pine and desirable grasses. The primary forage grasses have been reduced and the grasslands have been invaded by **threeawns, annual grasses, weeds, broomsedge bluestem, red lovegrass** and shrubby woody species.

### 2. Gulf Prairies and Marshes

The Gulf Prairies and Marshes cover approximately 10 million acres. There are two subunits: (a) The marsh and salt grasses immediately at tidewater, and (b) a little farther inland, a strip of bluestems and tall grasses, with some gramas in the western part. Many of these grasses make excellent grazing.

**Oaks, elm** and other hardwoods grow to some extent, especially along streams, and the area has some **post oak** and brushy extensions along its borders. Much of the Gulf Prairies is fertile farmland. The area is well suited for cattle.

Principal grasses of the Gulf Prairies are **tall bunchgrasses,** including **big bluestem, little bluestem, seacoast bluestem, indiangrass, eastern gamagrass, Texas wintergrass, switchgrass** and **gulf cordgrass. Coastal saltgrass** occurs on moist saline sites.

Heavy grazing has changed the native vegetation in many cases so the predominant grasses are the less desirable **broomsedge bluestem, smutgrass, threeawns, tumblegrass** and many other inferior grasses. Other plants that have invaded the productive grasslands include **oak**

underbrush, **Macartney rose, huisache, mesquite, prickly pear, ragweed, bitter sneezeweed, broomweed** and others.

Vegetation of the Gulf Marshes consists primarily of **sedges, bullrush, flat-sedges, beakrush** and other rushes, **smooth cordgrass, marshhay cordgrass, marsh millet** and **maidencane.** The marshes are grazed best during winter.

### 3. Post Oak Savannah

This secondary forest region, also called the **Post Oak Belt,** covers some 7 million acres. It is immediately west of the primary forest region, with less annual rainfall and a little higher elevation. Principal trees are **post oak, blackjack oak** and **elm. Pecans, walnuts** and other kinds of water-demanding trees grow along streams. The southwestern extension of this belt is often poorly defined, with large areas of prairie.

The upland soils are **sandy and sandy loam,** while the bottomlands are **sandy loams and clays.**

The original vegetation consisted mainly of **little bluestem, big bluestem, indiangrass, switchgrass, purpletop, silver bluestem, Texas wintergrass, spike woodoats, longleaf woodoats, post oak** and **blackjack oak.** The area is still largely native or improved grasslands, with small farms located throughout. Intensive grazing has contributed to dense stands of a woody understory of **yaupon, greenbriar** and **oak** brush.

**Mesquite** has become a serious problem. Good forage plants have been replaced by such plants as **splitbeard bluestem, red lovegrass, broomsedge bluestem, broomweed, bullnettle** and **western ragweed.**

### 4. Blackland Prairies

This area of about 12 million acres, while called a "prairie," has much timber along the streams, including a variety of **oaks, pecan, elm, horse-apple (bois d'arc)** and **mesquite.** In its native state it was largely a grassy plain — the first native grassland in the westward extension of the Southern Forest Region.

Most of this fertile area has been cultivated, and only small acreages of meadowland remain in original vegetation. In heavily grazed pastures, the tall bunchgrass has been replaced by **buffalograss, Texas grama** and other less productive grasses. **Mesquite, lotebush** and other woody plants have invaded the grasslands.

The original grass vegetation includes **big** and **little**

bluestem, indiangrass, switchgrass, sideoats grama, hairy grama, tall dropseed, Texas wintergrass and buffalograss. Non-grass vegetation is largely legumes and composites.

## 5. Cross Timbers and Prairies

Approximately 15 million acres of alternating woodlands, often called the Western Cross Timbers, and prairies constitute this region. Sharp changes in the vegetational cover are associated with different soils and topography, but the grass composition is rather uniform.

The prairie-type grasses are big bluestem, little bluestem, indiangrass, switchgrass, Canada wildrye, sideoats grama, hairy grama, tall grama, tall dropseed, Texas wintergrass, blue grama and buffalograss.

On the Cross Timbers soils, the grasses are composed of big bluestem, little bluestem, hooded windmillgrass, sand lovegrass, indiangrass, switchgrass and many species of legumes. The woody vegetation includes shinnery, blackjack, post and live oaks.

The entire area has been invaded heavily by woody brush plants of oaks, mesquite, juniper and other unpalatable plants that furnish little forage for livestock.

## 6. South Texas Plains

South of San Antonio, between the coast and the Rio Grande, are some 21 million acres of subtropical dryland vegetation, consisting of small trees, shrubs, cactus, weeds and grasses. The area is noteworthy for extensive brushlands, known as the brush country, or the Spanish equivalents of chaparral or monte. Principal plants are mesquite, small live oak, post oak, prickly pear (Opuntia) cactus, catclaw, blackbrush, whitebrush, guajillo, huisache, cenizo and others which often grow very densely.

The original vegetation was mainly perennial warm-season bunchgrasses in post oak, live oak and mesquite savannahs. Other brush species form dense thickets on the ridges and along streams. Long-continued grazing has contributed to the dense cover of brush. Most of the desirable grasses have persisted under the protection of brush and cacti.

There are distinct differences in the original plant communities on various soils. Dominant grasses on the sandy loam soils are seacoast bluestem, bristlegrass, paspalum, windmillgrass, silver bluestem, big sandbur and tanglehead. Dominant grasses on the clay and clay loams are silver bluestem, Arizona cottontop, buffalograss, common curlymesquite, bristlegrass, pappusgrass, gramas, plains lovegrass, Texas cupgrass, vinemesquite, other panicums and Texas wintergrass.

Low saline areas are characterized by gulf cordgrass, coastal saltgrass, alkali sacaton and switchgrass. In the post oak and live oak savannahs, the grasses are mainly seacoast bluestem, indiangrass, switchgrass, crinkleawn, paspalums and panicums. Today much of the area has been reseeded to buffelgrass.

## 7. Edwards Plateau

These 25 million acres are rolling to mountainous, with woodlands in the eastern part and grassy prairies in the west. There is a good deal of brushy growth in the central and eastern parts. The combination of grasses, weeds and small trees is ideal for cattle, sheep, goats, deer and wild turkey.

This limestone-based area is characterized by the large number of springfed, perennially flowing streams which originate in its interior and flow across the Balcones Escarpment, which bounds it on the south and east. The soils are shallow, ranging from sands to clays and are calcareous in reaction. This area is predominantly rangeland, with cultivation confined to the deeper soils.

In the east-central portion is the well-marked Central Basin centering in Mason, Llano and Burnet counties, with a mixture of granitic and sandy soils. The western portion of the area comprises the semi-arid Stockton Plateau.

Noteworthy is the growth of cypress along the perennially flowing streams. Separated by many miles from cypress growth of the moist Southern Forest Belt, they constitute one of Texas' several "islands" of vegetation. These trees, which grow to stately proportions, were commercialized in the past.

The principal grasses of the clay soils are cane bluestem, silver bluestem, little bluestem, sideoats grama, hairy grama, indiangrass, common curlymesquite, buffalograss, fall witchgrass, plains lovegrass, wildryes and Texas wintergrass.

The rocky areas support tall or mid-grasses with an overstory of live oak, shinnery oak, juniper and mesquite. The heavy clay soils have a mixture of tobosagrass, buffalograss, sideoats grama and mesquite.

Throughout the Edwards Plateau, live oak, shinnery oak, mesquite and juniper dominate the woody vegetation. Woody plants have invaded to the degree that they should be controlled before range forage plants can re-establish.

## 8. Rolling Plains

This is a region of approximately 24 million acres of alternating woodlands and prairies. The area is half mesquite woodland and half prairie. Mesquite trees have steadily invaded and increased in the grasslands for many years, despite constant control efforts.

Soils range from coarse sands along outwash terraces adjacent to streams to tight or compact clays on redbed clays and shales. Rough broken lands on steep slopes are found in the western portion. About two-thirds of the area is rangeland, but cultivation is important in certain localities.

The original vegetation includes big, little, sand and silver bluestems, Texas wintergrass, indiangrass, switchgrass, sideoats and blue gramas, wildryes, tobosagrass and buffalograss on the clay soils.

The sandy soils support tall bunchgrasses, mainly sand bluestem. Sand shinnery oak, sand sagebrush and mesquite are the dominant woody plants.

Continued heavy grazing contributes to the increase in woody plants, low-value grasses such as red grama, red lovegrass, tumblegrass, gummy lovegrass, Texas grama, sand dropseed, sandbur, western ragweed, croton and many other weeds. Yucca is a problem plant on certain rangelands.

## 9. High Plains

The High Plains, some 19 million treeless acres, are an extension of the Great Plains to the north. The level nature and porous soils prevent drainage over wide areas. The relatively light rainfall flows into the numerous shallow "playa" lakes or sinks into the ground to feed the great underground aquifer that is the source of water for the countless wells that irrigate the surface of the plains. A large part of this area is under irrigated farming, but native grassland remains in about one-half of the High Plains.

Blue grama and buffalograss comprise the principal vegetation on the clay and clay loam "hardland" soils. Important grasses on the sandy loam "sandy land" soils are little bluestem, western wheatgrass, indiangrass, switchgrass and sand reedgrass. Sand shinnery oak, sand sagebrush, mesquite and yucca are conspicuous invading brushy plants.

## 10. Trans-Pecos, Mountains and Basins

With as little as eight inches of annual rainfall, long hot summers and usually cloudless skies to encourage evaporation, this 18-million-acre area produces only drought-resistant vegetation without irrigation. Grass is usually short and sparse.

The principal vegetation consists of lechuguilla, ocotillo, yucca, cenizo and other arid land plants. In the more arid areas, gyp and chino grama and tobosagrass prevail. There is some mesquite. The vegetation includes creosote-tarbush, desert shrub, grama grassland, yucca and juniper savannahs, pine oak forest and saline flats.

The mountains are 3,000 to 8,751 feet in elevation and support piñon pine, juniper and some ponderosa pine and other forest vegetation on a few of the higher slopes.

The grass vegetation, especially on the high mountain slopes, includes many southwestern and Rocky Mountain species not present elsewhere in Texas. On the desert flats, black grama, burrograss and fluffgrass are frequent.

More productive sites have numerous species of grama, muhly, Arizona cottontop, dropseed and perennial threeawn grasses. At the higher elevations, plains bristlegrass, little bluestem, Texas bluestem, sideoats grama, chino grama, blue grama, piñon ricegrass, wolftail and several species of needlegrass are frequent.

The common invaders on all depleted ranges are woody plants, burrograss, fluffgrass, hairy erioneuron, ear muhly, sand muhly, red grama, broom snakeweed, croton, cacti and several poisonous plants. ☆

### For Further Reading

Hatch, S. L., K. N. Gandhi and L. E. Brown, Checklist of the Vascular Plants of Texas; MP1655, Texas Agricultural Experiment Station, College Station, 1990.

# Texas Forest Resources

Source: Texas Forest Service, The Texas A&M University System, Tarrow Drive, Suite 364, College Station, TX 77840; http://txforestservice.tamu.edu/

Texas' forest resources are abundant and diverse. Trees cover roughly 13 percent of the state's land area. The 22 million acres of forests and woodlands in Texas is an area larger than the states of Massachusetts, Connecticut, New Hampshire, Rhode Island and Vermont combined. The principal forest and woodlands regions are: the East Texas pine-hardwood region, often called the Piney Woods; the Post Oak Belt, which lies immediately west of the pine-hardwood forest; the Eastern and Western Cross Timbers areas of North Central Texas; the Cedar Brakes of Central Texas; the mountain forests of West Texas; and the coastal forests of the southern Gulf Coast.

The forest-products industry in Texas produces lumber, plywood, oriented-strand board, poles, railroad crossties, wood furniture, pulp, paper and paperboard. File photo.

## East Texas Piney Woods

Although Texas' forests and woodlands are extensive, detailed forest resource data is available for only the 43-county East Texas timber region. The Piney Woods, which form the western edge of the southern pine region, extending from Bowie and Red River counties in Northeast Texas to Jefferson, Harris and Waller counties in southeast Texas, contain 11.9 million acres of forest and produce nearly all of the state's commercial timber. Following is a summary of the findings of the most recent Forest Survey of East Texas, conducted in 1992 by the USDA Forest Service Southern Forest Experiment Station.

### Timberland Acreage and Ownership

Nearly all (11.8 of 11.9 million acres) of the East Texas forest is classified as "timberland," which is suitable for production of timber products and not reserved as parks or wilderness areas. In contrast to the trends in several other Southern states, Texas timberland acreage increased by 2 percent between 1986 and 1992. Seventy-four percent of the new timberland acres came from agricultural lands, such as idle farmland and pasture, which was either intentionally planted with trees or naturally reverted to forest.

Sixty-one percent of East Texas timberland is owned by approximately 150,000 farmers, private individuals, families, partnerships and non-wood-using corporations. Thirty-two percent is owned by forest-products companies, and 7 percent is owned by the government. The following table shows acreage of timberland by ownership:

| Ownership Class | Thous. Acres |
|---|---|
| Non-industrial Private: | |
| Farmer | 1,161.8 |
| Corporate | 954.3 |
| Individual | 5,106.9 |
| Forest Industry | 3,767.4 |
| Public: | |
| National Forest | 576.7 |
| Misc. Federal | 91.8 |
| State | 68.1 |
| County & Municipal | 46.8 |
| Total | 11,773.8 |

There are distinct regional differences in ownership patterns. Most forest-industry land is found south of Nacogdoches County, and timberland in some counties, such as Polk and Hardin, is as much as 75 percent owned by the forest-products industry. North of Nacogdoches, the nonindustrial private landowner predominates, and industry owns a much smaller percent of the timberland.

### Forest Types

Six major forest types are found in the East Texas Piney Woods. Two pine-forest types are most common. The loblolly-shortleaf and longleaf-slash forest types are dominated by the four species of southern yellow pine. In these forests, pine trees make up at least 50 percent of trees.

Oak-hickory is the second most common forest type. These are upland hardwood forests in which oaks and hickories make up at least 50 percent of trees, and pine species are less than 25 percent. Oak-pine is a mixed-forest type in which more than 50 percent of the trees are hardwoods, but pines make up 25 to 49 percent of the trees.

Two forest types, oak-gum-cypress and elm-ash-cottonwood, are bottomland types that are commonly found along creeks, river bottoms, swamps and other wet areas. The oak-gum-cypress forests are typically made up of many species including blackgum, sweetgum, oaks and southern cypress. The elm-ash-cottonwood bottomland forests are dominated by those trees but also contain many other species, such as willows, sycamore and maple. The following table shows the breakdown in acreage by forest type:

| Forest Type Group | Thous. Acres |
|---|---|
| Southern Pine: | |
| Loblolly-shortleaf | 4,063.7 |
| Longleaf-slash | 232.9 |
| Oak-pine | 2,503.8 |
| Oak-hickory | 3,146.9 |
| Bottomland Hardwood: | |
| Oak-gum-cypress | 1,755.8 |
| Elm-ash-cottonwood | 71.0 |
| Total | 11,773.8 |

Southern pine plantations, established by tree planting and usually managed intensively to maximize timber production, are an increasingly important source of wood fiber. Texas forests include 1.8 million acres of pine plantations, 72 percent of which are on forest-industry-owned land, 22 percent on nonindustrial private and 6 percent on public land. Plantation acreage increased 48 percent between 1986 and 1992. Genetically superior tree seedlings, produced at industry and Texas Forest Service nurseries, are usually planted to improve survival and growth.

### Timber Volume and Number of Trees

Texas timberland contains 12.9 billion cubic feet of timber "growing-stock" volume. This is enough wood fiber to produce 200 billion copies of National Geographic. The inventory of softwood remained steady at 7.9 billion cubic feet, while the hardwood inventory increased nearly 12 percent to 5.1 billion cubic feet between 1986 and 1992.

There are an estimated 6.9 billion live trees in East Texas, according to the 1992 survey. This includes 2 billion softwoods, 4.1 billion hardwoods and 0.7 billion trees of noncommercial species. The predominant species are loblolly and shortleaf pine; 1.9 billion trees of these two

species are found in East Texas.

### Timber Growth and Removals

Between 1986 and 1992, an annual average of 691.6 million cubic feet of timber was removed from the inventory either through harvest or land-use changes. Meanwhile, 728.6 million cubic feet were added to the inventory through growth each year, resulting in a net increase in timber inventory in East Texas.

For pine, however, slightly more is being cut than is being grown. An average 530.5 million cubic feet were removed during those years, while 522.9 million feet were added by growth. For hardwoods, 161.1 million feet were removed, while 205.7 million cubic feet were added by growth.

## Other Tree Regions

Compared to commercially important East Texas, relatively little data are available for the other tree regions of Texas. However, these areas are environmentally important with benefits of wildlife habitat, improved water quality, recreation and aesthetics. A brief description of these areas can be found in the descriptions of Texas' vegetation regions preceding this article.

## Economic Impact of Timber in Texas

Timber is a major contributor to the state's economy. The forest-products industry in Texas produces lumber, plywood, oriented-strand board (OSB), poles, railroad crossties, wood furniture, pulp, paper and paperboard, and a host of other products from the timber grown in Texas forests. Consider these Texas forest-industry facts:

• Texas is one of the top producers of forest products in the nation. In 1999, it was the source of 3.5 percent of softwood lumber, 11 percent of structural panels, and 3 percent of paper and paperboard produced in the United States.

• In 1999, timber ranked first in East Texas and fifth statewide in the value of agricultural production after beef, cotton, poultry and milk. The delivered value of the timber harvest was $1.06 billion.

• In 1999, the forest-products industry in Texas produced and sold goods valued at $9.2 billion, 50 percent of which came from the paper sector.

• In 2000, the forest industry directly employed 99,300 people: 49,500 in lumber and wood-products industries, 21,000 in the furniture industry and 29,000 in the paper industry.

## The 2001 Timber Harvest

### Total Removals

Total removals in East Texas in 2001, including both pine and hardwood, continued its descent. The total volume removed from the 43-county region was 674.2 million cubic feet in 2001, compared to 728.5 million in 2000, a 7.5 percent decline. Included in total removal is timber harvested for industrial use and an estimate of logging residue and other timber removals.

By species group, removals comprised 536.1 million cubic feet of pine and 138.1 million cubic feet of hardwood. Pine removal was down 4 percent, while hardwood removal slipped 18.9 percent from 2000.

Eighty-nine percent of timber removal in East Texas, including 91.1 percent of pine trees and 81 percent of hardwoods, was used in the manufacture of wood products. This portion of total removal, called the "industrial roundwood harvest," totaled 488.5 and 111.4 million cubic feet for pine and hardwood, respectively. The pine industrial roundwood harvest was down 4 percent, and the hardwood roundwood harvest was off by 17.5 percent from 2000. The combined harvest was down 6.8 percent to 599.9 million cubic feet. Top producing counties included Tyler, Jasper, Angelina, Polk, Newton, Cass and Hardin counties. Angelina, Tyler, Jasper, Chambers and Gregg counties experienced the greatest number of cubic feet per acre of timber harvested during 2001.

### Total Harvest Value

**Stumpage value** of the timber harvest decreased 15.4 percent in 2001 from its 2000 level, to $455.8 million,

and the delivered value was down 9.3 percent to $849.2 million. Pine timber accounted for 92.4 percent of the total stumpage value and 91 percent of the total delivered value.

The harvest of **sawlogs** for production of lumber was down 2.5 percent to 1,486.5 million board feet and comprised 40.4 percent of the total 2001 timber harvest. The pine sawlog cut totaled 1,259.6 million board feet, down 5.5 percent, while the hardwood sawlog harvest rose 17.7 percent to 226.9 million board feet. Cass, Jasper, Angelina, Newton and Tyler counties were the top producers of sawlogs. See next page for table of sawlog harvest by county.

Timber cut for the production of **structural panels, including plywood, OSB and harwood** veneer, totaled 177.8 million cubic feet and represented 29.6 percent of the timber harvest in 2001. This was a 10.2 percent decrease from the 2000 harvest, primarily because of plywood mill closures and the curtailment of OSB mill production in East Texas. Pine timber represented 99.2 percent of volume in this product category. Polk, Tyler, Jasper, Newton and Harrison were the top producers of veneer and panel roundwood.

Harvest of timber for manufacture of **pulp and paper products** continued to slide in 2001 after a sharp drop in 2000 and was down 10.2 percent from 2000 to 2.2 million cords. The roundwood pulpwood harvest constituted 30 percent of the timber harvest in 2001. Pine pulpwood made up 59.1 percent of the total pulpwood production in 2001. Jasper, Hardin, Angelina, Cass and Newton counties were the top producers of pulpwood.

**Other roundwood** harvested, including posts, poles and pilings, totaled 2.7 million cubic feet in 2001.

### Import-Export Trends

Texas was a net importer of timber products to surrounding states in 2001. Net import of roundwood was 10.3 million cubic feet, or about 1.7 percent of industrial wood production in Texas. Exports of roundwood from Texas were 75.2 million cubic feet, while imports totaled 85.5 million cubic feet. About 87.5 percent of the timber harvested in the state was consumed by Texas mills in 2001. The remainder was processed mainly in Arkansas, Louisiana and Oklahoma.

### Production of Forest Products

**Lumber:** Texas sawmills produced 1,507.6 million board feet of lumber in 2001, a decrease of 5.5 percent over 2000. Production of pine lumber dropped 8.3 percent to 1,293.8 million board feet in 2001. Hardwood lumber production decreased by 16.1 percent to 213.8 million board feet in 2001. The following tables present the 10-year trend in lumber production.

### Texas Lumber Production, 1992–2001

| Year | *Lumber Production | |
| | Pine | Hardwood |
| | (thousand board feet) | |
| 1992 | 1,092,738 | 138,874 |
| 1993 | 1,244,373 | 171,976 |
| 1994 | 1,340,882 | 195,693 |
| 1995 | 1,139,462 | 159,831 |
| 1996 | 1,248,627 | 175,570 |
| 1997 | 1,316,762 | 160,553 |
| 1998 | 1,293,432 | 191,165 |
| 1999 | 1,279,487 | 225,570 |
| 2000 | 1,410,999 | 184,172 |
| 2001 | 1,293,823 | 213,795 |

*Includes tie volumes.

**Primary Mill Residue:** Total mill residue, including chips, sawdust, shavings and bark in primary mills such as sawmills, panel mills and chip mills in 2001 was 8.5 million short tons, a substantial increase from 2000, partly due to adjustments of residue production ratio in 2001 for estimating the quantity of chips and bark. Fifty-six percent of residue was from pine species and 44 percent was from hardwood species. Mill residue included 52.5 percent barks, 34 percent chips, 10.4 percent sawdust and 3.3 percent shavings.

**Treated Wood:** The volume of wood processed by Texas wood treaters decreased by 15 percent in 2001. The total volume treated was 47.3 million cubic feet.

Among major treated products, lumber accounted for 68 percent of total volume. Crossties accounted for 12 percent of total volume, while utility poles and switch ties accounted for 7 percent and 9 percent, respectively.

**Structural Panel Products:** The production of structural panels, including plywood and OSB, was down 16.3 percent to 2,732.9 million square feet (3/8-inch basis) in 2001.

### Texas Structural Panel Production, 1992–2001

| Year | Pine (Thd. sq. ft.*) | Year | Pine (Thd. sq. ft.*) |
|---|---|---|---|
| 1992 . . . . . . | 2,557,103 | 1997 . . . . . | 3,200,317 |
| 1993 . . . . . . | 2,754,949 | 1998 . . . . . | 3,169,713 |
| 1994 . . . . . . | 2,632,833 | 1999 . . . . . | 3,260,055 |
| 1995 . . . . . . | 2,721,487 | 2000 | 3,265,644 |
| 1996 . . . . . . | 3,042,736 | 2001 | 2,732,940 |

*3/8-inch basis

### Texas Pulp, Paper and Paperboard Production, 1992–2001

| Year | Paper | Paper-board* | Total Paper Products | Market Pulp |
|---|---|---|---|---|
| | (short tons) | | | |
| 1992 | 1,528,274 | 1,695,569 | 3,223,843 | 332,483 |
| 1993 | 1,566,076 | 1,619,561 | 3,185,637 | 367,648 |
| 1994 | 1,522,661 | 1,817,192 | 3,339,853 | 351,687 |
| 1995 | 1,542,927 | 1,854,376 | 3,397,303 | 359,277 |
| 1996 | 1,454,265 | 1,881,257 | 3,335,522 | 321,071 |
| 1997 | 1,499,268 | 1,540,303 | 3,039,571 | 323,357 |
| 1998 | 1,509,898 | 1,415,958 | 2,925,856 | 302,099 |
| 1999 | 1,462,647 | 1,458,124 | 2,920,771 | 303,426 |
| 2000 | 995,117 | 2,037,148 | 2,992,265 | 48,413 |
| 2001 | 599,902 | 2,083,326 | 2,683,228 | 0 |

*Includes fiberboard and miscellaneous products.

**Paper Products:** Paper and paperboard production totaled 2.68 million tons in 2001, down 10.3 percent from 2000. Paper production dropped 37.2 percent to 0.6 million tons, while output of paperboard was up 2.3 percent to 2.08 million tons. There was no market pulp production in Texas in 2001.

## Total Timber Production and Value by County in Texas, 2001

| County | Pine | Hardwood | Total | Stumpage Value | Delivered Value |
|---|---|---|---|---|---|
| | Cubic feet | | | Thousand dollars | |
| Anderson | 6,354,656 | 4,183,506 | 10,538,162 | $ 6,364 | $ 12,855 |
| Angelina | 27,186,347 | 6,300,665 | 33,487,012 | 24,670 | 46,239 |
| Bowie | 10,945,461 | 3,230,406 | 14,175,867 | 13,239 | 23,078 |
| Camp | 685,710 | 598,347 | 1,284,057 | 783 | 1,530 |
| Cass | 24,558,250 | 7,765,279 | 32,323,529 | 25,142 | 46,015 |
| Chambers | 503,552 | 585,520 | 1,089,072 | 718 | 1,269 |
| Cherokee | 15,854,653 | 7,423,949 | 23,278,602 | 17,810 | 33,237 |
| Franklin | 152,541 | 680,797 | 833,338 | 441 | 891 |
| Gregg | 1,932,029 | 3,865,418 | 5,797,447 | 3,329 | 6,631 |
| Grimes | 2,025,075 | 68,422 | 2,093,497 | 2,266 | 3,847 |
| Hardin | 27,008,506 | 4,860,409 | 31,868,915 | 16,271 | 34,986 |
| Harris | 3,739,320 | 1,209,840 | 4,949,160 | 4,491 | 7,707 |
| Harrison | 17,100,732 | 3,766,528 | 20,867,260 | 14,018 | 27,216 |
| Henderson | 272,902 | 20,560 | 293,462 | 290 | 503 |
| Houston | 10,039,764 | 1,152,833 | 11,192,597 | 10,389 | 18,510 |
| Jasper | 40,847,991 | 2,838,889 | 43,686,880 | 31,599 | 61,061 |
| Jefferson | 912,974 | 903,895 | 1,816,869 | 748 | 1,651 |
| Leon | 535,746 | 232,937 | 768,683 | 733 | 1,294 |
| Liberty | 16,779,469 | 7,005,034 | 23,784,503 | 14,903 | 28,711 |
| Madison | 2,847 | 0 | 2,847 | 4 | 6 |
| Marion | 9,429,800 | 2,823,247 | 12,253,047 | 8,331 | 16,105 |
| Montgomery | 13,498,890 | 4,884,218 | 18,383,108 | 16,229 | 28,344 |
| Morris | 2,281,664 | 689,491 | 2,971,155 | 2,841 | 4,910 |
| Nacogdoches | 22,332,916 | 5,318,989 | 27,651,905 | 22,781 | 41,526 |
| Newton | 31,064,800 | 2,111,293 | 33,176,093 | 25,365 | 48,265 |
| Orange | 1,712,720 | 750,594 | 2,463,314 | 1,703 | 3,205 |
| Panola | 19,969,226 | 4,684,662 | 24,653,888 | 16,732 | 32,450 |
| Polk | 29,375,051 | 3,984,378 | 33,359,429 | 26,810 | 48,896 |
| Red River | 2,753,984 | 1,695,966 | 4,449,950 | 3,817 | 6,739 |
| Rusk | 13,823,284 | 3,635,604 | 17,458,888 | 15,541 | 27,655 |
| Sabine | 10,194,897 | 1,772,912 | 11,967,809 | 10,334 | 18,486 |
| San Augustine | 17,500,504 | 2,495,929 | 19,996,433 | 18,340 | 32,471 |
| San Jacinto | 9,494,795 | 228,727 | 9,723,522 | 10,105 | 17,331 |
| Shelby | 16,563,076 | 2,972,535 | 19,535,611 | 15,155 | 27,974 |
| Smith | 4,753,350 | 3,915,131 | 8,668,481 | 5,469 | 10,640 |
| Titus | 472,435 | 1,655,809 | 2,128,244 | 880 | 1,825 |
| Trinity | 11,468,184 | 862,402 | 12,330,586 | 10,981 | 19,665 |
| Tyler | 41,331,470 | 4,077,451 | 45,408,921 | 29,962 | 59,271 |
| Upshur | 4,652,137 | 3,336,537 | 7,988,674 | 5,598 | 10,338 |
| Van Zandt | 270,897 | 81,840 | 352,737 | 245 | 460 |
| Walker | 12,133,628 | 246,310 | 12,379,938 | 13,018 | 22,403 |
| Waller | 15,148 | 0 | 15,148 | 17 | 28 |
| Wood | 1,836,958 | 1,233,740 | 3,070,698 | 2,180 | 4,018 |
| Other Counties | 4,087,500 | 1,262,462 | 5,349,962 | 5,181 | 9,005 |
| **Totals** | **488,455,839** | **111,413,461** | **599,869,300** | **$455,821** | **$849,248** |

### Growth and Removal

The annual removal has steadily declined since 1999. The estimated growth, in contrast, has steadily risen since 1999. The pine removal was 536.1 million cubic feet, 14 percent below the estimated growth of 621.6 million cubic feet in 2001. Hardwood removal totaled 138.1 million cubic feet, compared to 237.4 million cubic feet of estimated growth, indicating that only 58 percent of growth was removed during the year. The estimated hardwood growth, however, included growth that occurred in environmentally sensitive areas that may not be accessible for harvest.

### Reforestation

A total of 156,875 acres was planted during the winter 2000/spring 2001 planting season, down 4.6 percent from the previous year. Industrial landowners planted 108,254 acres, a 10.2 percent drop from the previous year. The non-industrial private forest (NIPF) landowners planted 48,438 acres, up 12.2 percent. Public landowners only planted 183 acres in 2001. The NIPF landowners received $917,730 in cost share assistance for reforestation through federal and industrial cost share programs. Federal programs provided $602,700 in cost share funds. The Texas Reforestation Foundation provided $315,030 cost-share funding in 2001 and 348,272 in 2002. The foundation, sponsored by the Texas Forestry Association, distributed funds in 29 East Texas counties.

### Forest Fires

Texas experienced relatively low wildfire activity in 2002, thanks to more plentiful rainfall than in previous years. Texas Forest Service fire crews battled 955 wildfires that consumed a total of 23,713 acres of grass, brush and forest. Fire reports received from a small portion of the fire departments across the state indicated local firefighters battled 1,256 fires that burned 3,764 acres before being controlled.

Texas mobilized thousands of firefighters from across the country early in 2003, not to fight wildfires but to assist with efforts to recover debris from the Columbia space shuttle disaster. Heavy accumulations of vegetation promoted by rains in 2002 increased the potential severity of wildfires in 2003.

### Forest Pests

The Texas Forest Service Forest Pest Management office headquartered in Lufkin has trained forest health specialists (four entomologists and one pathologist) on staff to assist the citizens of Texas with tree pest problems.

The southern pine beetle is the most destructive insect pest in the 12 million acres of commercial forests in East Texas. Typically, this bark beetle kills more timber annually than forest fires. Fortunately, this destructive insect has been at very low levels in East Texas for the past several years.

The Texas Forest Service coordinates all beetle control activity on state and private forest lands in Texas. These activities include detecting infestations from the air, checking infestations on the ground to evaluate the need for control, and notifying landowners and providing technical assistance when control is warranted. Even though southern pine beetle populations currently are at low levels, other forest and tree pests are always present.

Extensive mortality of live oaks in Central Texas (generally some 60 counties between Dallas and San Antonio) is causing considerable public concern. A vascular wilt disease, called oak wilt, is the major cause of live oak mortality in Central Texas. A suppression project, administered by the Texas Forest Service, provides technical assistance and education for affected landowners.

Forest Health Management personnel also administer the Western Gulf Forest Pest Management Cooperative. Through this coop, applied research and technical assistance are provided to members for a variety of forest pests including cone and seed insects, regeneration insects, and Texas leaf-cutting ants.

### Urban Forests

Texas is an urban state with three of the nation's 10 largest cities. In fact, just six counties hold about one-half or 10 million of our population. In addition, Texas added over three million new residents between 1990 and 2000 — almost all to our cities. Because an estimated 86 percent of Texans now live in urban areas, urban trees and forests play an even more important role in the lives of Texans. Trees reduce the urban heat island effect by shading and evaporative cooling.

They also purify the air by absorbing pollutants, slowing the chemical reactions that produce harmful ozone, and filtering dust. Urban forests reduce storm water runoff and soil erosion and buffer against noise, glare and strong winds, while providing habitat for urban wildlife. Environmental benefits from a single tree may be worth more than $275 each year. The value to real estate and the emotional and psychological benefits of urban trees raise the value of our urban trees even higher. ☆

# National Forests and Grasslands in Texas

*Source: National Forest Service, Lufkin and Albuquerque, NM; www.r8web.com/texas/*

There are four national forests and all or part of five national grasslands in Texas. These federally owned lands are administered by the U.S. Department of Agriculture Forest Service and by district rangers. The national forests cover 637,472 acres in parts of 12 Texas counties. The national grasslands cover a total of 117,394 acres in six Texas counties. Two of these grasslands extend into Oklahoma, as well.

Supervision of the **East Texas forests** and **North Texas grasslands** is by the Forest Supervisor of the division known as the National Forests and Grasslands in Texas (701 N. 1st St., Lufkin 75901; 936-639-8501).

The three **West Texas grasslands** (Black Kettle, McClellan Creek and Rita Blanca) are administered by the Forest Supervisor in Albuquerque, NM, as units of the Cibola National Forest. The following list gives the name of the forest or grassland, the administrative district(s) for each, the acreage in each county and the total acreage:

## National Forests in Texas

**Angelina National Forest** — Angelina Ranger District (Zavalla); Angelina County, 58,539 acres; Jasper, 21,013; Nacogdoches, 9,238; San Augustine, 64,389. Total, 153,179.

**Davy Crockett National Forest** — Davy Crockett District (Ratcliff); Houston County, 93,324 acres; Trinity, 67,323. Total, 160,647.

**Sabine National Forest** — Sabine District (Hemphill); Jasper County, 64 acres; Newton, 1,781; Sabine, 95,546; San Augustine, 4,287; Shelby, 59,218. Total, 160,806.

**Sam Houston National Forest** — Sam Houston District (New Waverly); Montgomery County, 47,801 acres; San Jacinto, 60,639; Walker, 54,597. Total, 163,037.

## National Grasslands in Texas

**Black Kettle National Grassland** — Lake Marvin District Ranger in Cheyenne, Okla.; Hemphill County, 576 acres; Roger Mills County, Okla., 30,724 acres. Total, 31,300.

**Lyndon B. Johnson** and **Caddo National Grasslands** — District Ranger at Decatur; Fannin County, 17,873 acres; Montague, 61 acres; Wise, 20,252. Total, 38,186.

**McClellan Creek National Grassland** — District Ranger at Cheyenne, Okla.; Gray County, 1,449 acres. Total, 1,449.

**Rita Blanca National Grassland** — District Ranger at Clayton, NM; Dallam County, 77,463 acres; Cimarron County, Okla., 15,860 acres. Total, 93,323. ☆

*A U.S. Forest Service wildlife biologist surveys part of the Sabine National Forest. The 160,806-acre forest is in Jasper, Newton, Sabine, San Augustine and Shelby counties. File photo.*

## Establishment of National Forests and Grasslands

**National Forests** in Texas were established by invitation of the Texas Legislature by an Act of 1933, authorizing the purchase of lands in Texas for the establishment of national forests. President Franklin D. Roosevelt proclaimed these purchases on Oct. 15, 1936.

The **National Grasslands** were originally submarginal Dust Bowl project lands, purchased by the federal government primarily under the Bankhead-Jones Farm Tenant Act (1937). Today they are well covered with grasses and native shrubs.

### Uses of National Forests and Grasslands

The forests are managed for multiple uses, including production and sales of timber and minerals and programs involving recreation, fish and wildlife, soil and water. The grasslands are administered for uses including range, watershed, recreation and wildlife.

### Timber Production

About 486,000 acres of the National Forests in Texas are suitable for timber production. Sales of sawtimber, pulpwood and other forest products are planned to implement forest plans and objectives. The estimated net growth is over 200 million board feet per year and is valued at $50 million. A portion of this growth is normally removed by cutting. The balance is left to increase standing volume.

### Cattle Grazing

Permits to graze cattle on national forests and national grasslands are granted to the public for an annual fee. Approximately 750 head of cattle are grazed on the Caddo-Lyndon B. Johnson National Grasslands annually. On the Rita Blanca NG, 5,425 are grazed each year, most of them in Texas.

### Hunting and Fishing

State hunting and fishing laws and regulations apply to all national-forest land. Game-law enforcement is carried out by the Texas Parks and Wildlife. The Angelina, Sabine, Neches and San Jacinto rivers, Sam Rayburn and Toledo Bend reservoirs, Lake Conroe and many small streams provide a wide variety of fishing opportunities. Hunting is not permitted on the McClellan Creek N.G. nor the Lake Marvin Unit of the Black Kettle N.G.

### Recreation Facilities

An estimated 3 million people visit the recreational areas in the National Forests and Grasslands in Texas each year, primarily for picnicking, swimming, fishing, camping, boating and nature enjoyment. These areas are listed in the chapter on Recreation and Sports. ☆

# Texas State Forests

Texas has five state forests, all of which are used primarily for demonstration and research. Recreational opportunities, such as camping, hiking, bird-watching, and picnicking, are available in all but the Masterson forest.

The **I.D. Fairchild State Forest,** Texas' largest, is located west of Rusk in Cherokee County. This forest was transferred from the state prison system in 1925. Additional land was obtained in 1963 from the Texas State Hospitals and Special Schools, for a total acreage of 2,740.

The **W. Goodrich Jones State Forest**, south of Conroe in Montgomery County, containing 1,733 acres, was purchased in 1926 and named for the founder of the Texas Forestry Association.

The 600-acre **John Henry Kirby State Forest** in Tyler County was donated by the late lumberman, John Henry Kirby, in 1929, and later donors. Revenue from this forest is given to the Association of Former Students of Texas A&M University for student-loan purposes.

The 519-acre **Paul N. Masterson Memorial Forest** in Jasper County was donated in the fall of 1984 by Mrs. Leonora O'Neal Masterson of Beaumont in honor of her husband, an active member of the Texas Forestry Association and a tree farmer.

The first state forest, now known as the **E.O. Siecke State Forest** in Newton County, was purchased by the state in 1924. It contains 1,722 acres of pine land. An additional 100 acres was obtained by a 99-year lease in 1946. ☆

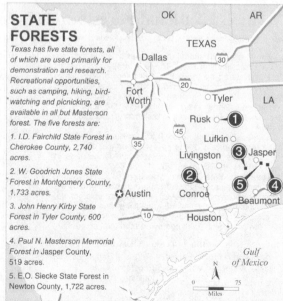

**STATE FORESTS**

*Texas has five state forests, all of which are used primarily for demonstration and research. Recreational opportunities, such as camping, hiking, bird-watching and picnicking, are available in all but Masterson forest. The five forests are:*

*1. I.D. Fairchild State Forest in Cherokee County, 2,740 acres.*

*2. W. Goodrich Jones State Forest in Montgomery County, 1,733 acres.*

*3. John Henry Kirby State Forest in Tyler County, 600 acres.*

*4. Paul N. Masterson Memorial Forest in Jasper County, 519 acres.*

*5. E.O. Siecke State Forest in Newton County, 1,722 acres.*

# National Natural Landmarks in Texas

Nineteen Texas natural areas have been listed on the **National Registry of Natural Landmarks**. The registry was established by the Secretary of the Interior in 1962 to identify and encourage the preservation of geological and ecological features that represent nationally significant examples of the nation's natural heritage.

The registry currently lists a total of 587 national natural landmarks. Texas areas on the list, as of August 2001, and their characteristics, are these (dates of listing in parentheses):

**Attwater Prairie Chicken Preserve**, Colorado County, 55 miles west of Houston in the national wildlife refuge, is rejuvenated Gulf Coastal Prairie, which is habitat for Attwater's prairie chickens. (April 1968)

**Bayside Resaca Area**, Cameron County, Laguna Atascosa National Wildlife Refuge, 28 miles north of Brownsville. Excellent example of a resaca, supporting coastal salt-marsh vegetation and rare birds. (Aug. 1980)

**Catfish Creek**, Anderson County, 20 miles northwest of Palestine, is undisturbed riparian habitat. (June 1983)

**Caverns of Sonora**, Sutton County, 16 miles southwest of Sonora, has unusual geological formations. (Oct. 1965)

*Huge geological formations stand in the Castle of the White Giants room in the Natural Bridge Caverns National Natural Landmark in Comal County west of New Braunfels. File photo.*

**Devil's Sink Hole**, Edwards County, 9 miles northeast of Rocksprings, is a deep, bell-shaped, collapsed limestone sink with cave passages extending below the regional water table. (Oct. 1972)

**Dinosaur Valley**, Somervell County, in Dinosaur Valley State Park, four miles west of Glen Rose, contains fossil footprints exposed in bed of Paluxy River. (Oct. 1968)

**Enchanted Rock**, Gillespie and Llano counties, 12 miles southwest of Oxford, is a classic batholith, composed of coarse-grained pink granite. (Oct. 1971)

**Ezell's Cave**, Hays County, within the city limits of San Marcos, houses at least 36 species of cave creatures. (Oct. 1971)

**Fort Worth Nature Center and Refuge**, Tarrant County, within the city limits of Fort Worth, contains remnants of the Fort Worth Prairie and a portion of the Cross Timbers, with limestone ledges and marshes. (Nov. 1980)

**Greenwood Canyon**, Montague County, along a tributary of Braden Branch, is a rich source of Cretaceous fossils. (May 1975)

**High Plains Natural Area**, Randall County, Buffalo Lake National Wildlife Refuge, 26 miles southwest of Amarillo, is a grama-buffalo shortgrass area. (Aug. 1980)

**Little Blanco River Bluff**, Blanco County, comprises an Edwards Plateau limestone-bluff plant community. (May 1981)

**Longhorn Cavern**, Burnet County, 11 miles southwest of Burnet. Formed at least 450 million years ago, cave contains several unusual geologic features. (Oct. 1971)

**Lost Maples State Natural Area**, Bandera and Real counties, 61 miles northwest of San Antonio, contains Edwards Plateau fauna and flora, including unusual bigtooth maple. Largest known nesting population of golden-cheeked warbler. (Feb. 1980)

**Muleshoe National Wildlife Refuge**, Bailey County, 59 miles northwest of Lubbock, contains playa lakes and typical High Plains shortgrass grama grasslands. (Aug. 1980)

**Natural Bridge Caverns**, Comal County, 16 miles west of new Braunfels, is a multilevel cavern system, with beautiful and unusual geological formations. (Oct. 1971)

**Odessa Meteor Crater**, Ector County, 10 miles southwest of Odessa, is one of only two known meteor sites in the country. (April 1965)

**Palo Duro Canyon State Park**, Armstrong and Randall counties, 22 miles south-southwest of Amarillo. Cut by waters of the Red River, it contains cross-sectional views of sedimentary rocks representing four geological periods. (May 1976)

**Santa Ana National Wildlife Refuge**, Hidalgo County, 7 miles south of Alamo, is a lowland forested area with jungle-like vegetation. It is habitat for more than 300 species of birds and some rare mammals. (Oct. 1966) ☆

# Texas' Threatened and Endangered Species

Endangered species are those which the Texas Parks and Wildlife Department (TPW) has named as being at risk of statewide extinction. Threatened species are those which are likely to become endangered in the future. The following species of Texas flora and fauna are either endangered or threatened as of July 15, 2003, according to the TPW. This list varies slightly from the federal list. Any questions about protected species should be directed to the Endangered Resources Branch, Texas Parks and Wildlife, 4200 Smith School Road, Austin 78744; 1-800-792-1112; www.tpwd.state.tx.us/nature/endang/endang.htm

## Endangered Species

**Mammals:** Greater long-nosed bat; black-footed ferret; jaguar; jaguarundi; West Indian manatee; ocelot; black right, blue, humpback, finback and sperm whales; gray, Mexican and red wolves.

**Birds:** Whooping crane; Eskimo curlew; peregrine, American peregrine and northern aplomado falcons; southwestern willow flycatcher; eastern brown pelican; Attwater's greater prairie chicken; interior least tern; black-capped vireo; ivory-billed and red-cockaded woodpecker; Bachman's and golden-cheeked warblers.

**Reptiles:** Atlantic hawksbill, leatherback and Kemp's ridley sea turtles.

**Amphibians:** Barton Springs and Texas blind salamanders; Houston toad.

**Fishes:** Fountain darter; Big Bend, Clear Creek, Pecos and San Marcos gambusias; Rio Grande silvery minnow; Comanche Springs and Leon Springs pupfishes.

**Crustaceans:** Peck's cave amphipod

**Mollusks:** Ouachita rock pocketbook.

**Vascular Plants:** Black lace, Lloyd's hedgehog, Nellie Cory, Sneed pincushion, star and Tobusch fishhook cactus; Davis' green pitaya; little aguja pondweed; Texas wildrice; Navasota ladies'-tresses; Texas ayenia; Johnston's frankenia; Walker's manioc; Texas snowbells; South Texas ambrosia; Zapata and white bladderpod; Terlingua Creek cat's-eye; ashy dogweed; Texas trailing phlox; Texas poppy-mallow; Texas prairie dawn; slender rush-pea; large-fruited sand verbena.

## Threatened Species

**Mammals:** Rafinesque's big-eared, southern yellow and spotted bats; black and Louisiana black bears; white-nosed coati; Atlantic spotted and rough-toothed dolphins; margay; Palo Duro mouse; Coues' rice and Texas kangaroo rats; dwarf sperm, false killer, Gervais' beaked, goose-beaked, killer, pygmy killer, pygmy sperm and short-finned pilot whales.

The red-cockaded woodpecker is endangered but can be found in the forests of East Texas. File photo.

The Pecos Puzzle sunflower is a threatened species and occurs naturally in only three areas of West Texas and New Mexico. File photo.

The Houston toad has been on the endangered species list since 1970. It can be found mainly in the Lost Pines ecosystem of Bastrop County, including Bastrop State Park. File photo.

**Birds:** Rose-throated becard; bald eagle; reddish egret; Arctic peregrine falcon; common black, gray, white-tailed and zone-tailed hawks; white-faced ibis; swallow-tailed kite; Mexican spotted owl; cactus ferruginous pygmy-owl; tropical parula; piping plover; Bachman's, Texas Botteri's and Arizona Botteri's sparrows; wood stork; sooty tern; northern beardless tyrannulet.

**Reptiles:** Speckled racer; Big Bend blackhead, black-striped, Brazos water, Concho water, indigo, Louisiana pine, northern cat-eyed, smooth green, scarlet and Texas lyre snakes and timber (canebrake) rattlesnake; Texas tortoise; alligator snapping and Chihuahuan mud turtles; loggerhead and green sea turtles; American alligator; reticulated gecko; mountain short-horned, reticulate collared and Texas horned lizards.

**Amphibians:** Black-spotted newt; Blanco blind, Cascade Caverns, Comal blind and San Marcos salamanders; South Texas siren (large form); Mexican burrowing toad; Mexican treefrog; white-lipped and sheep frogs.

**Fishes:** Toothless and widemouth blindcats; Rio Grande chub; creek chubsucker; blackside and Rio Grande darters; blotched gambusia; river and blackfin gobies; Devil's River minnow; paddlefish; opossum pipefish; Conchos and Pecos pupfishes; bluehead, bluntnose, Arkansas, Chihuahua and proserpine shiners; Mexican stoneroller; shovelnose sturgeon; blue sucker.

**Vascular Plants:** Bunched cory, Chisos Mountains hedgehog and Lloyd's mariposa cactus; Hinckley's oak; McKittrick pennyroyal; Pecos Puzzle sunflower. ☆

# Texas Wildlife

Source: Texas Parks and Wildlife, Austin

Texas has many native animals and birds, as well as introduced species. More than **540 species of birds** — about three fourths of all different species found in the United States — have been identified in Texas.

Some **142 species of animals,** including some that today are extremely rare, are found in Texas. A list of plant and animal species designated as threatened or endangered by state wildlife officials is found elsewhere in this chapter.

A few of the leading land mammals of Texas are described here. Those marked by an asterisk (*) are non-native species. Information was provided by the **Nongame and Urban Program,** Texas Parks and Wildlife, and updated using the online version of *The Mammals of Texas* by William B. Davis and David J. Schmidly: **www.nsrl.ttu.edu/tmot1/contents.htm**; the print version was published by Texas Parks and Wildlife Press, Austin, 1994. For additional wildlife information on the Web: **www.tpwd.state.tx.us/nature/wild/wild.htm**.

The nine-banded armadillo can be found throughout most of Texas. File photo.

## Mammals

**Armadillo** — The **nine-banded armadillo** *(Dasypus novemcinctus)* is one of Texas' most interesting mammals. It is found in most of the state except the western Trans-Pecos. It is now common as far north and east as Oklahoma and Mississippi.

**Badger** — The **badger** *(Taxidea taxus)* is found throughout the state, except the extreme eastern parts. It is a fierce fighter, and it is valuable in helping control rodent population.

**Bat** — Thirty-two species of these winged mammals have been found in Texas, more than in any other state in the United States. Of these, 27 species are known residents, though they are seldom seen by the casual observer. The **Mexican,** or **Brazilian, free-tailed bat** *(Tadarida brasiliensis)* and the **cave myotis** *(Myotis velifer)* constitute most of the cave-dwelling bats of Southwest and West Texas. They have some economic value for their deposits of nitrogen-rich **guano.** Some commercial guano has been produced from **James River Bat Cave,** Mason

County; **Beaver Creek Cavern**, Burnet County; and from large deposits in other caves including **Devil's Sinkhole** in Edwards County, **Blowout Cave** in Blanco County and **Bandera Bat Cave**, Bandera County. The largest concentration of bats in the world is found at **Bracken Cave** in Comal County, thought to hold between 20 and 40 million bats. The **big brown bat** *(Eptesicus fuscus)*, the **red bat** *(Lasiurus borealis)* and the **evening bat** *(Nycticeius humeralis)* are found in East and Southeast Texas. The evening and big brown bats are forest and woodland dwelling mammals.

Most of the rarer species of Texas bats have been found along the Rio Grande and in the Trans-Pecos. Bats can be observed at dusk near a water source, and many species may also be found foraging on insects attracted to street lights. Everywhere bats occur, they are the main predators of night-flying insects, including mosquitoes and many crop pests. On the Web: **www.batcon.org/**

**Bear** — The **black bear** *(Ursus americanus)*, formerly common throughout most of the state, is now surviving in remnant populations in portions of the Trans-Pecos.

**Beaver** — The **American beaver** *(Castor canadensis)* is found over most of the state except for the Llano Estacado and parts of the Trans-Pecos.

**Bighorn** — (See **Sheep**.)

**Bison** — The largest of native terrestrial wild mammals of North America, the **American bison** *(Bos bison)*, commonly called **buffalo**, was formerly found in the western two-thirds of the state. Today it is extirpated or confined on ranches. Deliberate slaughter of this majestic animal for hides and to eliminate the Plains Indians' main food source reached a peak about 1877-78, and the bison was almost eradicated by 1885. Estimates of the number of buffalo killed vary, but as many as 200,000 hides were sold in Fort Worth at a single two-day sale. Except for the interest of the late **Col. Charles Goodnight** and a few other foresighted men, the bison might be extinct.

**Cat** — The **jaguar** *(Felis onca)* is probably now extinct in Texas and, along with the **ocelot, jaguarundi** and **margay**, is listed as rare and endangered by both federal and state wildlife agencies. The **mountain lion** *(Felis concolor)*, also known as **cougar** and **puma**, was once found statewide. It is now found in the mountainous areas of the trans-Pecos and the dense Rio Grande Plain brushland. The **ocelot** *(Felis pardalis)*, also known as the **leopard cat,** is found usually along the border. The **red-and-gray cat**, or **jaguarundi** *(Felis yagouaroundi Geoffroy)* is found, rarely, in extreme South Texas. The **margay** *(Felis wiedii)* was reported in the 1850s near Eagle Pass. The **bobcat** *(Lynx rufus)* is found over the state in large numbers.

**Chipmunk** — The **gray-footed chipmunk** *(Tamias canipes)* is found at high altitudes in the Guadalupe and Sierra Diablo ranges of the Trans-Pecos (see also **Ground Squirrel**, with which it is often confused in public reference).

**Coati** — The **white-nosed coati** *(Nasua narica)*, a relative of the raccoon, is occasionally found in southern Texas from Brownsville to the Big Bend. It inhabits woodland areas and feeds both on the ground and in trees. The coati, which is on the list of threatened species, is also found occasionally in Big Bend National Park.

**Coyote** — The **coyote** *(Canis latrans)*, great in number, is the most destructive Texas predator of livestock. On the other hand, it is probably the most valuable predator in the balance of nature. It is a protection to crops and range lands by its control of rodents and rabbits. It is found throughout the state, but is most numerous in the brush country of southwest Texas. It is the second-most important fur-bearing animal in the state.

**Deer** — The **white-tailed deer** *(Odocoileus virginianus)*, found throughout the state in brushy or wooded areas, is the most important Texas game animal. Its numbers in Texas are estimated at more than 3 million. The **mule deer** *(Odocoileus heminous)* is found principally in

*Bobcats are found all over Texas in large numbers, but urban growth is pushing them out of their natural habitat. File photo.*

the Trans-Pecos and Panhandle areas. It has increased in number in recent years. The little **Del Carmen deer** (white-tailed subspecies) is found in limited numbers in the high valleys of the Chisos Mountains in the Big Bend. The only native **elk** in Texas *(Cervus merriami)*, found in the southern Guadalupe Mountains, became extinct about the turn of the 20th century. The **wapiti** or **elk** *(Cervus elaphus)*, was introduced into the same area about 1928. There are currently several herds totalling several hundred individuals.

A number of exotic deer species have been introduced, mostly for hunting purposes. The **axis deer\*** *(Cervus axix)* is the most numerous of the exotics. Native to India, It is found mostly in central and southern Texas, both free-ranging and confined on ranches. **Blackbuck\*** *(Antilope cervicapra)*, also native to India, is the second-most numerous exotic deer in the state and is found on ranches in 86 counties. **Fallow deer\*** *(Cervus dama)*, native to the Mediterranean, has been introduced to 93 counties, while the **nilgai\*** *(Boselaphus tragocamelus)*, native of India and Pakistan, is found mostly on ranches in Kenedy and Willacy counties. The **sika deer\*** *(Cervus nippon)*, native of southern Siberia, Japan and China, has been introduced in 77 counties in central and southern Texas.

**Ferret** — The **black-footed ferret** *(Mustela nigripes)* was formerly found widely ranging through the West Texas country of the prairie dog on which it preyed. It is now considered extinct in Texas. It is of the same genus as the weasel and the mink.

**Fox** — The **common gray fox** *(Urocyon cinereoargenteus)* is found throughout most of the state, primarily in the woods of East Texas, in broken parts of the Edwards Plateau, and in the rough country at the foot of the Staked Plains. The **kit** or **Swift fox** *(Vulpes velox)* is found in the western one-third of the state. A second species of **kit fox** *(Vulpes macrotis)* is found in the Trans-Pecos and is fairly numerous in some localities. The **red fox\*** *(Vulpes vulpes)*, which ranges across Central Texas, was introduced for sport.

**Gopher** — Nine species of pocket gopher occur in Texas. The **Botta's pocket gopher** *(Thomomys bottae)* is found from the Trans-Pecos eastward across the Edwards Plateau. The **plains pocket gopher** *(Geomys bursarius)*

is found from Midland and Tom Green counties east and north to McLennan, Dallas and Grayson counties. The **desert pocket gopher** *(Geomys arenarius)* is found only in the Trans-Pecos, while the **yellow-faced pocket gopher** *(Cratogeomys castanops)* is found in the western one-third of the state, with occasional sightings along the Rio Grande in Maverick and Cameron counties. The **Texas pocket gopher** *(Geomys personatus)* is found in South Texas from San Patricio County to Val Verde County. **Attwater's pocket gopher** *(Geomys attwateri)* and **Baird's pocket gopher** *(Geomys breviceps)* are both found generally in East Texas from the Brazos River to the San Antonio River and south to Matagorda and San Patricio counties. **Jones' pocket gopher** *(Geomys knoxjonesi)* is found only in far West Texas, while the **Llano pocket gopher** *(Geomys texensis)* is found only in two isolated areas of the Hill Country.

*Signs of wildlife are evident on the shores of Lake Whitney State Park. File photo.*

**Ground Squirrel** — Five or more species of ground squirrel live in Texas, mostly in the western part of the state. The **rock squirrel** *(Spermophilus variegatus)* is found throughout the Edwards Plateau and Trans-Pecos. The **Mexican ground squirrel** *(Spermophilus mexicanus)* is found in southern and western Texas. The **spotted ground squirrel** *(Spermophilus spilosoma)* is found generally in the western half of the state. The **thirteen-lined ground squirrel** *(Spermophilus tridecemlineatus)* is found in a narrow strip from Dallas and Tarrant counties to the Gulf. The **Texas antelope squirrel** *(Ammospermophilus interpres)* is found along the Rio Grande from El Paso to Val Verde County.

**Hog, Feral** — (see Pig, Feral)

**Javelina** — The **javelina** or **collared peccary** *(Tayassu tajacu)* is found in brushy semidesert where prickly pear, a favorite food, is found. The javelina was hunted commercially for its hide until 1939. They are harmless to livestock and to people, though they can defend themselves ferociously when attacked by hunting dogs.

**Mink** — The **mink** *(Mustela vison)* is found in the eastern half of the state, always near streams, lakes or other water sources. Although it is an economically important fur-bearing animal in the eastern United States, it ranked only 13th in numbers and 9th in economic value to trappers in Texas in 1988-89, according to a Texas Parks and Wildlife Department survey.

**Mole** — The **eastern mole** *(Scalopus aquaticus)* is found in the eastern two-thirds of the state.

**Muskrat** — The **common muskrat** *(Ondatra zibethica)*, occurs in aquatic habitats in the northern, southeastern and southwestern parts of the state. Although the muskrat was once economically valuable for its fur, its numbers have declined, mostly because of the loss of habitat.

**Nutria*** — This introduced species *(Myocastor coypus)*, native to South America, is found in the eastern two-thirds of the state. The fur is not highly valued and, since nutria are in competition with muskrats, their spread is discouraged. They have been used widely in Texas as a cure-all for ponds choked with vegetation, with spotty results.

**Opossum** — A marsupial, the **Virginia opossum** *(Didelphis virginiana)* is found in nearly all parts of the state. The opossum has economic value for its pelt, and its meat is considered a delicacy by some. It is one of the chief contributors to the Texas fur crop.

**Otter** — A few **river otter** *(Lutra canadensis)* are found in the eastern quarter of the state. It has probably been extirpated from the Panhandle, north-central and southern Texas.

**Pig, Feral** — Feral pigs, found in areas of the Rio Grande and coastal plains as well as the woods of East Texas, are descendants of escaped domestic hogs or of European wild hogs that were imported for sport.

**Porcupine** — The **yellow-haired porcupine** *(Erethizon dorsatum)* is found from the western half of the state east to Bosque County.

**Prairie Dog** — Until recent years probably no sight was so universal in West Texas as the **black-tailed prairie dog** *(Cynomys ludovicianus)*. Naturalists estimated its population in the hundreds of millions, and prairie-dog towns often covered many acres with thickly spaced burrows. Its destruction of range grasses and cultivated crops has caused farmers and ranchers to destroy many of them, and it is extirpated from much of its former range. It is being propagated in several public zoos, notably in the **prairie dog town in Mackenzie Park** at Lubbock. It has been honored in Texas by the naming of the **Prairie Dog Town Fork** of the Red River, along one segment of which is located the beautiful **Palo Duro Canyon**.

**Pronghorn** — The **Pronghorn** *(Antilocapra americana)* formerly was found in the western two-thirds of the state. It is currently found only in limited areas from the Panhandle to the Trans-Pecos. Despite management efforts, its numbers have been decreasing in recent years.

**Rabbit** — The **black-tailed jack rabbit** *(Lepus californicus)* is found throughout Texas except in the Big Thicket area of East Texas. It breeds rapidly, and its long hind legs make it one of the world's faster-running animals. The **Eastern cottontail** *(Sylvilagus floridanus)* is found mostly in the eastern three-quarters of the state. The **desert cottontail** *(Sylvilagus auduboni)* is found in the western half of the state, usually on the open range. The **swamp rabbit** *(Sylvilagus aquaticus)* is found in East Texas and the coastal area.

**Raccoon** — The **raccoon** *(Procyon lotor)* is found throughout Texas, especially along streams and in urban settings. It is the most important fur-bearing animal in the state.

**Rats and Mice** — There are 40 to 50 species of rats and mice in Texas of varying characteristics, habitats and economic destructiveness. The **Norway rat*** *(Rattus norvegicus)* and the **roof rat*** *(Rattus rattus)*, both non-native species, are probably the most common and the most destructive. They also are instrumental in the transmission of several dread diseases, including bubonic plague and typhus. The **common house mouse*** *(Mus musculis)* is estimated in the hundreds of millions annually. The **Mexican vole** *(Microtus mexicanus guadalupensis)*, also called the **Guadalupe Mountain vole,** is found only in the higher elevations of the Guadalupe Mountains National Park and just over the border into New Mexico.

**Ringtail** — The **ringtail** *(Bassariscus astutus)* is found statewide but is rare in the Lower Valley and the Coastal

Plains.

**Sheep** — The mountain sheep (*Ovis canadensis*), also called **desert bighorn**, formerly was found in isolated areas of the mountainous Trans-Pecos, but the last native sheep were seen in 1959. They have been recently introduced into the same areas. The **barbary sheep\*** (*Ammotragus lervia*), or **aoudad**, first introduced to the Palo Duro Canyon area in 1957-58, has become firmly established. Private introductions have brought it into the Edwards Plateau, Trans-Pecos, South Texas, Rolling Plains and Post Oak Savannah regions.

**Shrew** — Four species are found in Texas: the **southern short-tailed shrew** (*Blarina Carolinensis*), found in the eastern one-fourth of the state; the **least shrew** (*Cryptotis parva*), in the eastern and central parts of the state; the **Elliot's short-tailed shrew** (*Blarina hylophaga*), known only in Aransas, Montague and Bastrop counties); and the **desert shrew** (*Notiosorex crawfordi*), found in the western two-thirds of the state.

**Skunk** — There are six species of skunk in Texas. The **Eastern spotted skunk** (*Spilogale putorius*) is found in the eastern half of the state and across north-central Texas to the Panhandle. A small skunk, it is often erroneously called civet cat. This skunk also is found in East Texas and the Gulf area. The **Western spotted skunk** (*Spilogale gracilis*) is found in the southwestern part of the state north to Garza and Howard counties and east to Bexar and Duval counties. The **striped skunk** (*Mephitis mephitis*) is found statewide, mostly in brush or wooded areas. The **hooded skunk** (*Mephitis macroura*) is found in limited numbers in the Big Bend and adjacent parts of the Trans-Pecos. The **eastern hog-nosed skunk** (*Conepatus leuconotus*), found in the Gulf coastal plains, ranges southward into Mexico. The **common hog-nosed skunk** (*Conepatus mesoleucus*) is found in southwestern, central and southern Texas, north to Collin and Lubbock counties.

**Squirrel** — The **eastern fox squirrel** (*Sciurus niger*) is found in the eastern two-thirds of the state. The **eastern gray squirrel** (*Sciurus carolinensis*) is found generally in the eastern third of the state. The **flying squirrel** (*Glaucomys volans*) is found in wooded areas of East Texas.

**Weasel** — The **long-tailed weasel** (*Mustela frenata*), akin to the mink, is found statewide, but is scarce in West Texas.

**Wolf** — The **red wolf** (*Canis rufus*) was once found throughout the eastern half of the state. It has now been extirpated from the wild, with the only known remnants of the population now in captive propagation. The **gray wolf** (*Canis lupus*) once had a wide range over the western two-thirds of the state. It is now considered extinct in Texas. The **red wolf** and **gray wolf** are on the federal and state rare and endangered species lists.

## Reptiles and Arachnids

Most of the more than **100 species and subspecies of snakes** found in Texas are beneficial, as also are other reptiles. There are **16 poisonous species and subspecies**.

**Poisonous reptiles** include **three species of copperheads** (southern, broad-banded and Trans-Pecos); one kind of **cottonmouth** (western)**; 11 kinds of rattlesnakes** (canebrake, western massasauga, desert massasauga, western pigmy, western diamondback, timber, banded rock, mottled rock, northern blacktailed, Mcjave and prairie); and the **Texas coral snake**.

Also noteworthy are the **horned lizard**, also called **horned toad**, which is on the list of **threatened species**; the **vinegarone**, a type of whip scorpion; **tarantula**, a hairy spider; and **alligator**. ✩

# National Wildlife Refuges

*Source: U.S. Fish and Wildlife Service, U.S. Department of the Interior.*

Texas has more than 470,000 acres in **17 national wildlife refuges**. Their descriptions, with date of acquisition in parentheses, follow. Included in this acreage are two conservation easement refuges, which may be visited at different times of the year for bird watching and wildlife viewing, as well as hunting and fishing. Write or call before visiting to check on facilities and days and hours of operation. On the Web: **http://southwest.fws.gov/refuges/index.html**.

**Anahuac (1963):** The more than 34,000 acres of this refuge are located along the upper Gulf Coast in Chambers County. **Fresh and saltwater marshes** and miles of beautiful, sweeping **coastal prairie** provide wintering habitat for large flocks of waterfowl, including **geese, 27 species of ducks and six species of rails. Roseate spoonbills and white ibis** are among the other birds frequenting the refuge. Other species include **alligator, muskrat** and **bobcat**. Fishing, bird watching, auto tours and hunting are available. Office: Box 278, Anahuac 77514; 409-267-3337.

**Aransas (1937):** This refuge comprises 70,504 acres on Blackjack Peninsula and three satellite units in Aransas and Refugio counties. The three mainland units consist of **oak woodlands, fresh and saltwater marshes** and **coastal grasslands**. Besides providing wintering grounds for the endangered **whooping crane**, the refuge is home to many species of waterfowl and other migratory birds — more than 390 different bird species in all. Refuge is open daily, sunrise to sunset. Interpretive center is open daily, 8:30 a.m.-4:30 p.m. Other facilities include a 40-foot observation tower, paved auto-tour loop and walking trails. Office: Box 100, Austwell 77950; 361-286-3559.

**Attwater Prairie Chicken (1972):** Established in 1972 in Colorado County to preserve habitat for the endangered Attwater's prairie chicken, the refuge comprises more than 10,000 acres of **native tallgrass prairie,** potholes, sandy knolls and some wooded areas. An auto-tour route is available year-round, and 350 acres of marsh are accessible for watching the more than 250 species of birds that visit the refuge. Refuge open sunrise to sunset. Office: Box 519, Eagle Lake 77434; 979-234-3021.

**Balcones Canyonlands (1992):** This 25,000-acre refuge was dedicated in 1992. Located in Burnet, Travis and Williamson counties northwest of Austin, it was established to protect the nesting habitat of two endangered birds: **black-capped vireo** and **golden-cheeked warbler.** Eventually, the refuge will encompass 30,500 acres of **oak-juniper woodlands** and other habitats. An observation deck can be used for birdwatching. Hunting available. Office: 10711 Burnet Rd., #201, Austin 78758; 512-339-9432.

**Big Boggy (1983):** This refuge occupies 4,526 acres of **coastal prairie** and **salt marsh** along East Matagorda Bay for the benefit of wintering **waterfowl. The refuge is generally closed,** and visitors are encouraged to visit nearby **San Bernard or Brazoria refuges.** Waterfowl hunting is permitted in season. Office: 1212 N. Velasco, #200, Angleton 77515; 409-964-3639.

**Brazoria (1966):** The 43,388 acres of this refuge, located along the Gulf Coast in Brazoria County, serve as haven for wintering waterfowl and a wide variety of other migratory birds. The refuge also supports many **marsh** and **water birds**, from **roseate spoonbills** and **great blue herons** to **white ibis** and **sandhill cranes**. Brazoria Refuge is within the **Freeport Christmas Bird Count** circle, which frequently achieves the highest number of species seen in a 24-hour period. Open daily 8 a.m.-4 p.m., Sept.–May, when visitors can drive through the refuge to observe

coastal wildlife. From June 1 through Aug. 31, refuge is open the first full weekend each month and intermittently throughout the week. Hunting and fishing also available. Call for details. Office: 1212 N. Velasco, #200, Angleton 77515; 979-849-7771.

**Buffalo Lake (1958):** Comprising 7,664 acres in the **Central Flyway** in Randall County in the Panhandle, this refuge contains some of the best remaining **shortgrass prairie** in the United States. Buffalo Lake is now dry; a **marsh area** is artificially maintained for the numerous birds, reptiles and mammals. Available activities include picnicking, auto tour, birding, photography and hiking. Office: Box 179, Umbarger 79091; 806-499-3382.

**Hagerman (1946):** Hagerman National Wildlife Refuge lies on the Big Mineral arm of Texoma Lake in Grayson County. The 3,000 acres of **marsh** and water and 8,000 acres of **upland and farmland** provide a feeding and resting

*Hamilton Pool Preserve is a natural swimming hole in the Balcones Canyonlands National Wildlife Refuge. The refuge, northwest of Austin, is located in Burnet, Travis and Williamson counties. File photo.*

place for migrating **waterfowl.** Bird watching, fishing and hunting are available. Office: 6465 Refuge Road, Sherman 75092-5817; 903-786-2826.

**Laguna Atascosa:** Established in 1946 as southernmost waterfowl refuge in the **Central Flyway,** this refuge contains more than 45,000 acres fronting on the **Laguna Madre** in the Lower Rio Grande Valley in Cameron and Willacy counties. Open **lagoons, coastal prairies, salt flats and brushlands** support a wide diversity of wildlife. The United States' largest concentration of **redhead ducks** winters here, along with many other species of **waterfowl** and **shorebirds. White-tailed deer, javelina and armadillo** can be found, along with endangered **ocelot.** Bird watching and nature study are popular; auto-tour roads and nature trails are available. Camping and fishing are permitted within Adolph Thomae Jr. County Park. Hunting also available. Office: Box 450, Rio Hondo 78583; 956-748-3607.

**Lower Rio Grande Valley (1979):** The U.S. Fish and Wildlife Service has acquired approximately half the planned acreage in the Lower Rio Grande Valley for this refuge, which will eventually include 132,500 acres within Cameron, Hidalgo, Starr and Willacy counties. The refuge will include 11 different habitat types, including **sabal palm forest, tidal flats, coastal brushland, mid-delta thorn forest, woodland potholes and basins, upland thorn scrub, flood forest, barretal, riparian woodland** and **Chihuahuan thorn forest.** More than 400 species of birds and over 300 butterfly species have been found there, as well as four of the five cats that occur within the United States: **jaguarundi, ocelot, bobcat** and **mountain lion.** Office: Santa Ana/Lower Rio Grande Valley National Wildlife Refuges, Rt. 2, Box 202A, Alamo 78516; 956-787-3079.

**Matagorda Island:** Matagorda Island is **jointly owned and managed by the U.S. Fish and Wildlife Service and the State of Texas** under an agreement reached in 1983. Please check table of **Texas Wildlife Management Areas** on next page for facilities.

**McFaddin (1980):** Purchased in 1980, this refuge's 55,000 acres, in Jefferson and Chambers counties, are of great importance to wintering populations of **migratory waterfowl.** One of the densest populations of **alligators** in Texas is found here. Activities on the refuge include wildlife observation, hunting, fishing and crabbing. Access best by boat; limited roadways. Office: Box 609, Sabine Pass 77655; 409-971-2909.

**Muleshoe (1935):** Oldest of national refuges in Texas, Muleshoe provides winter habitat for **waterfowl** and the continent's largest wintering population of **sandhill cranes.** Comprising 5,809 acres in the High Plains of Bailey County, the refuge contains three **playa lakes, marsh areas, caliche outcroppings** and **native grasslands.** A nature trail, campground and picnic area are available. Office: Box 549, Muleshoe 79347; 806-946-3341.

**San Bernard (1968):** Located in Brazoria and Matagorda counties on the Gulf Coast near Freeport, this refuge's 27,414 acres attract **migrating waterfowl,** including thousands of **white-fronted and Canada geese and several duck species,** which spend the winter on the refuge. Habitats, consisting of **coastal prairies, salt/mud flats** and saltwater and freshwater ponds and potholes, also attract **yellow rails, roseate spoonbills, reddish egrets** and **American bitterns.** Visitors enjoy auto and hiking trails, photography, bird watching, fishing, and waterfowl hunting in season. Office: Rt. 1, Box 1335, Brazoria 77422; 979-964-3639.

**Santa Ana (1943):** Santa Ana is located on the north bank of the Rio Grande in Hidalgo County. Santa Ana's 2,088 acres of **subtropical forest** and **native brushland** are at an **ecological crossroads** of **subtropical, Gulf Coast, Great Plains** and **Chihuahuan desert habitats.** Santa Ana attracts birders from across the United States who can view many species of **Mexican birds** as they reach the northern edge of their ranges in South Texas. Also found at Santa Ana are **ocelot** and **jaguarundi,** endangered members of the cat family. Visitors enjoy a tram or auto drive, bicycling and hiking trails. Office: Rt. 2, Box 202A, Alamo 78516; 956-784-7500.

**Texas Point (1980):** Texas Point's 8,900 acres are located in Jefferson County on the Upper Gulf Coast, 12 miles east of McFaddin NWR, where they serve a large wintering population of **waterfowl** as well as migratory birds. The endangered **southern bald eagle** and **peregrine falcon** may occasionally be seen during peak fall and spring migrations. **Alligators** are commonly observed during the spring, summer and fall months. Activities include wildlife observation, hunting, fishing and crabbing. Access to the refuge is by boat and on foot only. Office: Box 609, Sabine Pass 77655; 409-971-2909.

**Trinity River (1994):** Established to protect remnant **bottomland hardwood forests** and associated **wetlands,** this refuge, located in northern Liberty County off State Highway 787 approximately 15 miles east of Cleveland, provides habitat for **wintering, migrating and breeding waterfowl** and a variety of other wetland-dependent wildlife. Approximately 4,547 acres of the proposed 20,000-acre refuge have been purchased. Office: Box 10015, Liberty 77575; 936-336-9786. ☆

# Texas Wildlife Management Areas

Source: Texas Parks and Wildlife Department

Texas Parks and Wildlife (TPW) is currently responsible for managing 51 wildlife management areas (WMAs) totaling approximately three quarters of a million acres. Of these, 32 WMAs are owned in fee title, while 19 are managed under license agreements with other agencies.

Wildlife management areas are used principally for hunting, but many are also used for research, fishing, wildlife viewing, hiking, camping, bicycling and horseback riding, when those activities are compatible with the primary goals for which the WMA was established.

Access to WMAs at times designated for public use is provided by various permits, depending on the activity performed. Hunting permits include Special ($50 or $100),

Regular daily ($10), or Annual ($40). A Limited Public Use Permit ($10) allows access for such activities as birdwatching, hiking, camping or picnicking and on some WMAs under the Texas Conservation Passport (Gold $50, Silver $25). The Gold Passport also allows entry to state parks.

For further information, write to Texas Parks and Wildlife Department, 4200 Smith School Rd., Austin 78744; 1-800-792-1112, menu #5, selection #1. On the Web: www.tpwd.state.tx.us/wma/index.htm. A brief description of the WMAs is given below. On most WMAs, restrooms and drinking water are not provided; check with the TPW at the contacts above before you go.

| WMA (Acreage) | COUNTY | Day Use Only | Hunting | Fishing | Camping | Wildlife Viewing | Hiking | Interpretive Trail | Auto Tour | Bicycling | Horseback Riding | Comments |
|---|---|---|---|---|---|---|---|---|---|---|---|---|
| Candy Abshier (207) | CHAMBERS | ★ | | | | ★ | | | | | | Excellent birding spring and fall |
| Alabama Creek (14,561) | TRINITY | | ★ | ★ | ★ | ★ | ★ | | ★ | ★ | ★ | In Davy Crockett National Forest |
| Alazan Bayou (1,973) | NACOGDOCHES | ★ | ★ | ★ | | ★ | | | | ★ | | |
| Angelina-Neches/Dam B (16,360) | JASPER/TYLER | | ★ | ★ | ★ | ★ | ★ | | ★ | ★ | | |
| Aquilla (9,700) | HILL | ★ | ★ | ★ | | ★ | ★ | | | | | |
| Atkinson Island (150) | HARRIS | ★ | | | | ★ | | | | | | Boat access only |
| Bannister (25,695) | SAN AUGUSTINE | | ★ | ★ | ★ | ★ | ★ | | ★ | ★ | ★ | In San Augustine National Forest |
| Big Lake Bottom (3,176) | ANDERSON | ★ | ★ | ★ | | ★ | ★ | | | | | 900 acres available to public |
| Black Gap (105,708) | BREWSTER | | ★ | ★ | ★ | ★ | ★ | | ★ | ★ | ★ | East of Big Bend National Park |
| Walter Buck (2,155) | KIMBLE | ★ | ★ | | | ★ | ★ | | ★ | ★ | | Camping at adjacent state park |
| Caddo Lake State Park & WMA (6,929) | MARION/HARRISON | | ★ | ★ | ★ | ★ | ★ | | ★ | ★ | ★ | |
| Caddo National Grasslands (16,150) | FANNIN | | ★ | ★ | ★ | ★ | ★ | | | | ★ | |
| Cedar Creek Islands (160) | HENDERSON | ★ | | ★ | | ★ | | | | | | Access by boat only |
| Chaparral (15,200) | LA SALLE/DIMMIT | | ★ | | ★ | ★ | ★ | | ★ | | | |
| Cooper (14,480) | DELTA/HOPKINS | ★ | ★ | ★ | | ★ | ★ | | | | | Camping at nearby state park |
| James E. Daughtrey (4,000) | LIVE OAK/MCMULLEN | ★ | ★ | | ★ | ★ | | | | | | Primitive camping for hunters |
| Elephant Mountain (23,147) | BREWSTER | | ★ | | ★ | ★ | ★ | ★ | ★ | | | Primitive camping only |
| Gus Engling (10,958) | ANDERSON | | ★ | ★ | ★ | ★ | ★ | | ★ | | | |
| Granger (11,116) | WILLIAMSON | | ★ | ★ | ★ | ★ | ★ | | ★ | ★ | | Primitive camping only |
| Guadalupe Delta (6,000) | REFUGIO | ★ | ★ | ★ | | ★ | ★ | | ★ | ★ | | Freshwater marsh |
| Tony Houseman (3,313) | ORANGE | | ★ | ★ | ★ | ★ | ★ | | | | | |
| Sam Houston Natl Forest (161,154) | SAN JACINTO/WALKER/ | | ★ | ★ | ★ | ★ | ★ | | ★ | ★ | ★ | Also Montgomery County |
| Gene Howe (5,821) | HEMPHILL | | ★ | ★ | ★ | ★ | ★ | ★ | ★ | ★ | ★ | Riding March - August only |
| Keechi Creek (1,500) | LEON | | ★ | | | | | | | | | |
| Kerr (6,493) | KERR | | ★ | | | ★ | | | ★ | ★ | | |
| **Las Palomas:** | | | | | | | | | | | | |
|   Lower Rio Grande Valley Units (5,886) | CAMERON/HIDALGO | ★ | ★ | | | ★ | ★ | | | | | Also Starr & Willacy counties |
|   Ocotillo Unit (2,082) | PRESIDIO | | ★ | ★ | ★ | ★ | ★ | | ★ | ★ | | |
| Lower Neches (7,998) | ORANGE | ★ | ★ | ★ | | ★ | ★ | | | | | Coastal marsh |
| Mad Island (7,281) | MATAGORDA | ★ | ★ | | | ★ | | | | | | Coastal wetlands |
| Mason Mountain (5,301) | MASON | ★ | ★ | | | | | | | | | Restricted access |
| Matador (28,183) | COTTLE | | ★ | ★ | ★ | ★ | ★ | | ★ | ★ | ★ | Primitive camping |
| Matagorda Island (43,900) | CALHOUN | | ★ | ★ | ★ | ★ | ★ | | | | | Access by boat only |
| Pat Mayse (8,925) | LAMAR | ★ | ★ | ★ | ★ | ★ | ★ | | ★ | ★ | | |
| Moore Plantation (27,547) | SABINE/JASPER | | ★ | ★ | ★ | ★ | ★ | | ★ | ★ | ★ | In Sabine National Forest |
| J.D. Murphree (24,366) | JEFFERSON | ★ | ★ | ★ | | ★ | | | | | | Access by boat only |
| W.A. Pat Murphy (889) | LIPSCOMB | ★ | ★ | ★ | | ★ | ★ | | | | | |
| The Nature Center (85) | SMITH | ★ | | | | ★ | | ★ | | | | Primarily for public-school groups |
| M.O. Neasloney (100) | GONZALES | ★ | | | | ★ | ★ | ★ | | | | Primarily for public-school groups |
| North Toldeo Bend (3,650) | SHELBY | | ★ | ★ | ★ | ★ | ★ | | | | ★ | Limited use of horses |
| Old Sabine Bottom (5,158) | SMITH | ★ | ★ | ★ | | ★ | ★ | | ★ | ★ | ★ | Canoeing |
| Old Tunnel (11) | KENDALL | ★ | | | | ★ | | ★ | | | | Bat-viewing June-October |
| Peach Point (10,311) | BRAZORIA | | ★ | | | ★ | ★ | ★ | | | | On Texas Coastal Birding Trail |
| Playa Lakes (1,096 in 3 units) | CASTRO/DONLEY | ★ | ★ | | | ★ | ★ | | | | | Hunting only on Donley Co. unit |
| Redhead Pond (37) | NUECES | ★ | | | | ★ | | | | | | Freshwater wetland |
| Richland Creek (13,796) | FREESTONE/NAVARRO | | ★ | ★ | ★ | ★ | ★ | | ★ | ★ | ★ | Primitive camping only |
| Ray Roberts (41,220) | COOKE/DENTON | ★ | ★ | ★ | | ★ | ★ | | | | | Also Grayson Co. |
| Sierra Diablo (11,625) | CULBERSON | | ★ | | | | | | | | | Restricted access |
| Somerville (3,180) | BURLESON/LEE | ★ | ★ | ★ | | ★ | ★ | | ★ | ★ | | |
| Tawakoni (1,562) | HUNT/VAN ZANDT | | ★ | ★ | ★ | ★ | ★ | | | | ★ | |
| Welder Flats (1,480) | CALHOUN | ★ | ★ | | | | | | | | | Boat access only |
| White Oak Creek (25,700) | BOWIE/CASS/MORRIS | ★ | ★ | | | ★ | ★ | | | | ★ | Also Titus Co. |
| D.R. Wintermann (246) | WHARTON | | ★ | | | ★ | | | | | | Restricted access; bird refuge |

# Weather

*Source: Unless otherwise noted, this information is provided by John W. Nielsen-Gammon, Texas State Climatologist; graduate assistant Andrew Odins; and undergraduate assistants Kelsey Curtiss and Brent Maddox, Texas A&M University, College Station*

## Weather Highlights 2001

**January 1–31: Drought** plagued numerous counties in Deep South Texas during January. Counties affected included Brooks, Cameron, Hidalgo, Jim Hogg, Kenedy, Starr, Willacy and Zapata. The counties of Zapata and Starr also were declared drought stricken in August 2000. Damage was estimated at $25 million across Cameron, Hidalgo, Starr and Willacy counties.

**April 10:** In the Upper Trans-Pecos region, a strong gradient produced by a **cold front** resulted in a **71-mph wind** that killed one, injured three and caused nearly $1.5 million in damage. Blowing dust caused visibility to drop to nearly zero resulting in an accident involving nine cars.

**April 16: Hail** up to 1-3/4 inches fell in Harris County causing damage to cars, windows and trees. Accumulations were several inches deep in some areas and lingered on the ground for up to 24 hours. The storm caused $20.0 million in damage.

**May 6:** A **thunderstorm** formed over the San Antonio area that developed into one of the most devastating combinations of **hail and wind** in the history of Bexar County. Hail up to 4 inches in diameter pummeled the area combined with winds reaching 60 mph. Cost estimations included $120 million in property damage and $30 million in crop damage.

**June 5-10: Tropical Storm Allison** made landfall on the western end of Galveston Island on the 6th. Allison produced record rainfall across a large portion of Southeast Texas that lead to devastating floods. Rainfall rates up to 4 inches or more per hour were observed at times. In and around the Houston area, precipitation totaled more than 30 inches. This tropical system caused 24 deaths and damage to over 48,000 homes, 70,000 automobiles and about 2,000 businesses. Damage was estimated at $5.2 billion.

**July–August:** Very hot temperatures and dry conditions led to **excessive heat** across the Upper Coastal region of Texas. Harris County reported 17 heat-related deaths during this period.

**October 12:** A stationary front and associated low-pressure system caused the development of **thunderstorms** and showers. Some of these thunderstorms became severe, and a few developed tornadoes. In Medina County, an **F2 tornado** formed resulting damage to 150 homes in Hondo, 50 homes outside the city and 100 mobile homes within the county being damaged. The Hondo Airport suffered severe damage from this storm. Estimated costs were at $20 million. In addition, a **100-mph straight-line downburst wind** in Hondo caused another $2 million in damage.

**November:** There were 8 deaths and 190 injuries as a result of **flash flooding** during the month.

**December 1–31:** The drought affects of 2001 became apparent as the year-end agricultural reports were completed by the Texas Agricultural Extension Service at Texas A&M University. The total **crop damage due to the 2001 drought** across the South Plains of Texas totaled $420 million. Dry land crops such as cotton, wheat, grain sorghum and corn suffered extensive losses.

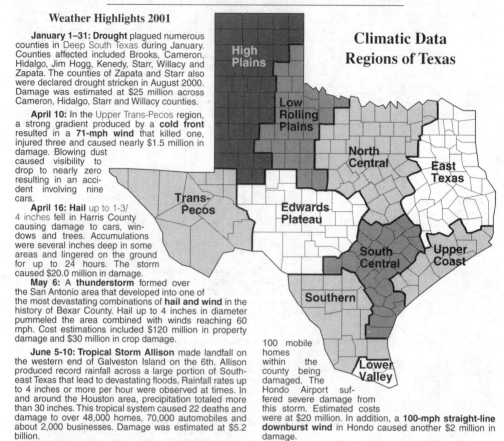

## Climatic Data Regions of Texas

## Average Temperatures 2001

| | High Plains | Low Plains | North Central | East Texas | Trans-Pecos | Edwards Plateau | South Central | Upper Coast | South Texas | Lower Valley |
|---|---|---|---|---|---|---|---|---|---|---|
| Jan. | 35.4 | 39.6 | 42.3 | 42.9 | 43.6 | 44.4 | 49.9 | 50.1 | 52.6 | 57.9 |
| Feb. | 41.8 | 45.1 | 49.6 | 52.4 | 52.7 | 52.4 | 58.7 | 60.1 | 61.6 | 66.2 |
| Mar. | 45.9 | 48.8 | 51.3 | 52.6 | 55.6 | 52.9 | 57.0 | 58.2 | 60.4 | 66.0 |
| April | 61.5 | 64.7 | 66.8 | 68.4 | 67.7 | 67.6 | 71.5 | 72.1 | 75.3 | 77.3 |
| May | 67.9 | 72.1 | 73.8 | 74.1 | 75.6 | 74.8 | 76.8 | 76.6 | 80.4 | 80.1 |
| June | 77.8 | 81.1 | 80.0 | 78.1 | 82.8 | 82.2 | 82.0 | 81.0 | 86.6 | 85.4 |
| July | 83.6 | 87.8 | 86.3 | 83.8 | 84.1 | 85.4 | 85.1 | 84.0 | 88.2 | 86.2 |
| Aug. | 79.0 | 82.9 | 84.7 | 83.1 | 81.5 | 83.6 | 85.0 | 83.8 | 87.6 | 86.2 |
| Sep. | 71.0 | 73.5 | 74.4 | 74.6 | 75.9 | 75.2 | 77.6 | 78.0 | 80.2 | 81.6 |
| Oct. | 60.3 | 63.2 | 64.2 | 63.8 | 67.3 | 65.8 | 69.0 | 69.0 | 72.6 | 76.0 |
| Nov. | 51.2 | 55.8 | 58.7 | 60.1 | 56.8 | 59.7 | 64.1 | 64.7 | 66.8 | 70.4 |
| Dec. | 41.3 | 45.5 | 49.1 | 51.2 | 46.3 | 49.4 | 55.3 | 57.2 | 56.2 | 63.3 |
| Ann. | 59.7 | 63.3 | 65.1 | 65.4 | 65.8 | 66.1 | 69.3 | 69.6 | 72.4 | 74.7 |

## Precipitation 2001

**(Inches)**

| | High Plains | Low Plains | North Central | East Texas | Trans-Pecos | Edwards Plateau | South Central | Upper Coast | South Texas | Lower Valley |
|---|---|---|---|---|---|---|---|---|---|---|
| Jan. | 1.20 | 1.56 | 3.20 | 5.31 | 0.56 | 2.06 | 2.98 | 5.00 | 1.69 | 0.87 |
| Feb. | 0.89 | 1.89 | 4.88 | 5.79 | 0.46 | 1.16 | 0.93 | 0.72 | 0.58 | 1.31 |
| Mar. | 2.28 | 2.29 | 4.62 | 7.87 | 0.39 | 2.09 | 3.87 | 5.68 | 2.00 | 0.62 |
| April | 0.37 | 0.41 | 1.30 | 1.13 | 0.25 | 0.92 | 0.99 | 0.90 | 0.81 | 1.14 |
| May | 3.91 | 4.07 | 3.91 | 4.53 | 0.59 | 2.64 | 3.11 | 3.82 | 1.44 | 0.45 |
| June | 0.93 | 0.66 | 2.00 | 8.52 | 0.48 | 0.61 | 2.47 | 11.57 | 0.85 | 3.14 |
| July | 0.57 | 0.22 | 0.95 | 1.39 | 1.17 | 0.65 | 1.00 | 2.90 | 0.74 | 1.31 |
| Aug. | 2.44 | 2.95 | 3.98 | 4.16 | 1.48 | 3.44 | 7.55 | 8.58 | 3.37 | 2.86 |
| Sep. | 1.45 | 2.18 | 3.60 | 6.61 | 0.62 | 2.75 | 4.71 | 7.03 | 3.35 | 4.67 |
| Oct. | 0.14 | 0.72 | 2.54 | 4.70 | 0.15 | 1.41 | 2.84 | 5.41 | 0.27 | 0.51 |
| Nov. | 2.02 | 3.79 | 2.92 | 4.61 | 1.02 | 4.53 | 5.07 | 5.33 | 3.64 | 2.30 |
| Dec. | 0.24 | 0.55 | 3.61 | 6.97 | 0.14 | 0.94 | 3.78 | 4.86 | 1.97 | 1.00 |
| Ann. | 16.44 | 21.29 | 37.51 | 61.59 | 7.31 | 23.20 | 39.30 | 61.80 | 20.71 | 20.18 |

## 2001 Weather Extremes

**Lowest Temp.:** Libscomb, Lipscomb Co., Feb. 10 . . . . . . 1° F
**Highest Temp.:** Heath Canyon, Brewster Co., May 29  116° F
**24-hour Precip.:** Houston-Port, Harris Co., June 9 . . . . 18.40"
**Monthly Precip.:** Houston-Port, Harris Co., June . . . . 41.42"
**Least Annual Precip.:** Boquillas Ranger Station,
          Brewster Co. . . . . . . . . . . . . . . . . . . . 3.37"
**Greatest Annual Precip.:** Anahuac, Chambers Co. . . . 91.72"

## Monthly Summaries 2001

**January** was cool and wet, with only three of Texas' 19 first-order weather stations reporting below precipitation. A mid-month winter storm brought cold conditions to the state's northern portions.

**February** was a contrast temperature-wise as the cool weather pattern that had been in place for the past few months ended. All of the first-order weather stations reported above-normal temperatures, and more than half reported below normal precipitation.

**March** was a return to January weather, and temperatures were dramatically cooler than in February. Temperatures were below normal for all but one first-order station, and precipitation was abundant; only two stations experienced below-normal precipitation.

**April** weather was dramatically different from March. Temperatures were back to above normal for all but two first-order stations, and precipitation was below normal for all stations. The month ended with warm conditions after a rebound from a cold front in the last week of the month.

**May** was much like April regarding precipitation and temperature. Much of the state reported below-normal precipitation and above -normal temperatures. However, a strong Canadian air mass caused record low temperatures in the second to last week of the month. May ended with very warm weather and record high temperatures.

**June** will always be remembered for the incredible amounts of precipitation that fell across the Upper Coast and East regions of Texas. Tropical Storm Allison made landfall at the beginning of the month dumping vast amounts of precipitation, causing flooding and major damage, especially in the Houston area. Ironically, while this major precipitation event was taking place, almost all of the weather stations around the state received less than normal precipitation. Temperatures were above normal for the most part.

Hot and dry best describe **July.** All of the first-order stations reported above-normal temperatures. Because of the lack of precipitation during the past few months, the Trans-Pecos and Lower Valley regions were rated Severe Drought by the Palmer Drought Severity Index. Also, the remainder of the state, with the exception of the East, South Central and Upper Coast, were rated Moderate Drought. Record high temperatures were reported across the state. A blocking pattern that prevented the development of showers and thunderstorms was in place until the end of the month. Unstable conditions returned to the state when the pattern finally shifted west. More precipitation was experienced at month's end.

Some rainfall relief was received in **August,** although only 4 of the 19 first-order stations experienced above-normal precipitation. Unfortunately this plentiful rain did not change the drought conditions much. The Trans-Pecos was still rated Severe Drought, and the High Plains was rated Moderate Drought. Although precipitation was plentiful in August, the heat was still in place, as well, with 18 of 19 stations reporting above-normal temperatures. August concluded with more rain.

In **September,** dry conditions continued across the state through with half of the weather stations reporting precipitation below normal. However temperatures were mild compared to August, with almost all stations at or below normal. Precipitation was abundant in some areas and sparse in others. According to the Palmer Index, the East and South-Central regions were rated as Unusual Moist Spell, as opposed to the Trans-Pecos, which was rated Severe Drought. The end of September was more fall-like and dominated by a cold Canadian air mass.

**October** continued the trend of mild-weather that was set in September. Drier conditions resumed with every station in Texas reporting below-normal precipitation. Temperatures were primarily below normal across the state. Drought conditions intensified in West Texas with the Trans-Pecos region rated Extreme Drought, according to the Palmer Index. The High Plains and Low Rolling Plains were rated Moderate Drought. The last precipitation of October fell in the middle of the month. The end of the month was quiet and mild.

**November** was characterized by warm and wet conditions. All but one station recorded above-normal temperatures, and all but four stations reported above-normal precipitation. Record precipitation, record high temperatures, as well as record wet months were experienced in some areas. The end of the month brought cold Canadian air as well as winter-like precipitation, including record snowfall to several areas.

**December** brought considerable variation in the weather, from near-record warmth to near-record cold, from very dry to unusually wet. Most regions experienced a mix of conditions. All but one weather station reported above-normal temperatures. Precipitation was mixed throughout the state with western and extreme southern areas receiving less than normal precipitation. Winter weather was reported toward month's end, including ice and snowfall.

## 2001 Weather In-depth

**January** began 2001 with **cool temperatures and sufficient rainfall.** Only three stations reported below-normal precipitation (Brownsville, College Station and El Paso). Lubbock reported an impressive 374 percent of the normal precipitation expected for January. The first few days of the month were dominated by cooler weather and even some winter weather in the northern portions of the state. In the middle of the month, an intense low-pressure system brought snow and rain to the state.

The cool weather trend experienced the past few months ended in **February** as every first-order station in Texas recorded **above-normal temperatures** for the month. Above normal temperatures ranged from +0.1 degrees F in Wichita Falls to +5.4 degrees F in Houston. February was also quite a dry month in Texas as 11 of 19 stations recorded below-normal precipitation.

**March** was **dramatically cooler and wetter** than February; every station reported below-normal temperatures with the exception of El Paso. Temperatures ranged from -1.9 degrees F below normal in Galveston and Brownsville, to an impressive -8.6 degrees F below normal in Austin. Every first-order station in Texas received 100 percent of normal precipitation for the month, with the exception of Brownsville and Wichita Falls. Amarillo reported an amazing 413 percent of normal rainfall for March with 3.96 inches.

**April,** on the other hand, returned to the **warmer pattern** of February with only two stations reporting below-normal temperatures. Temperatures ranged from -1.3 degrees F below normal in Abilene, to +4.2 degrees F above normal in Amarillo. This month also was extremely dry across Texas,

## Average Temperatures 2002

| | High Plains | Low Plains | North Central | East Texas | Trans-Pecos | Edwards Plateau | South Central | Upper Coast | South Texas | Lower Valley |
|---|---|---|---|---|---|---|---|---|---|---|
| Jan. | 40.2 | 44.5 | 47.2 | 48.8 | 47.9 | 48.8 | 54.4 | 55.8 | 57.6 | 62.3 |
| Feb. | 40.2 | 43.9 | 45.8 | 46.8 | 46.3 | 47.3 | 52.0 | 52.6 | 55.2 | 59.4 |
| Mar. | 46.1 | 50.2 | 53.1 | 55.0 | 55.7 | 56.6 | 60.5 | 62.0 | 64.5 | 68.5 |
| April | 60.7 | 64.1 | 68.2 | 69.0 | 70.5 | 71.0 | 74.0 | 73.1 | 78.1 | 78.5 |
| May | 67.8 | 70.7 | 72.5 | 73.2 | 76.3 | 76.3 | 77.5 | 76.8 | 81.6 | 81.8 |
| June | 78.0 | 79.0 | 79.1 | 79.1 | 83.0 | 81.6 | 82.2 | 81.1 | 85.8 | 84.5 |
| July | 78.7 | 80.3 | 81.5 | 82.5 | 80.4 | 80.3 | 82.1 | 83.2 | 83.7 | 85.3 |
| Aug. | 79.5 | 83.4 | 83.7 | 83.0 | 82.7 | 83.6 | 84.1 | 83.5 | 86.5 | 87.0 |
| Sep. | 71.2 | 75.1 | 77.6 | 78.2 | 75.4 | 76.2 | 78.6 | 79.4 | 79.6 | 82.2 |
| Oct. | 56.3 | 59.7 | 63.9 | 66.1 | 65.4 | 66.3 | 70.9 | 72.4 | 74.3 | 78.3 |
| Nov. | 45.5 | 49.6 | 52.7 | 53.4 | 52.3 | 52.7 | 58.0 | 59.6 | 59.8 | 64.7 |
| Dec. | 41.3 | 45.5 | 49.1 | 51.2 | 46.3 | 49.4 | 55.3 | 57.2 | 56.2 | 63.3 |
| Ann. | 58.8 | 62.2 | 64.5 | 65.5 | 65.2 | 65.8 | 69.1 | 69.7 | 71.9 | 74.7 |

## Precipitation 2002

(Inches)

| | High Plains | Low Plains | North Central | East Texas | Trans-Pecos | Edwards Plateau | South Central | Upper Coast | South Texas | Lower Valley |
|---|---|---|---|---|---|---|---|---|---|---|
| Jan. | 0.86 | 0.80 | 1.99 | 2.20 | 0.12 | 0.36 | 0.81 | 1.70 | 0.07 | 0.16 |
| Feb. | 0.47 | 0.98 | 1.58 | 2.61 | 0.77 | 0.76 | 0.69 | 0.91 | 0.22 | 0.48 |
| Mar. | 1.55 | 2.46 | 4.37 | 5.34 | 0.22 | 1.16 | 0.88 | 1.70 | 0.28 | 0.21 |
| April | 1.08 | 2.13 | 3.03 | 3.12 | 0.42 | 1.13 | 1.99 | 3.73 | 1.12 | 0.54 |
| May | 0.93 | 1.65 | 4.31 | 3.68 | 0.49 | 1.45 | 1.53 | 2.28 | 1.67 | 1.41 |
| June | 1.55 | 2.55 | 2.87 | 3.29 | 0.82 | 2.22 | 3.77 | 5.53 | 1.51 | 1.79 |
| July | 1.82 | 5.01 | 4.35 | 4.25 | 2.61 | 6.88 | 7.31 | 5.74 | 9.86 | 1.47 |
| Aug. | 2.65 | 1.22 | 1.21 | 2.34 | 1.23 | 0.59 | 1.84 | 6.92 | 0.87 | 0.64 |
| Sep. | 1.32 | 1.64 | 2.05 | 2.77 | 0.58 | 2.26 | 6.50 | 8.81 | 8.13 | 7.38 |
| Oct. | 4.41 | 5.44 | 6.96 | 7.53 | 2.96 | 7.06 | 9.52 | 12.53 | 4.81 | 6.90 |
| Nov. | 0.42 | 0.72 | 1.12 | 4.13 | 0.28 | 0.96 | 4.19 | 4.81 | 2.04 | 5.05 |
| Dec. | 0.24 | 0.55 | 3.61 | 6.97 | 0.14 | 0.94 | 3.78 | 4.86 | 1.97 | 1.00 |
| Ann. | 17.30 | 25.15 | 37.45 | 48.23 | 10.64 | 25.77 | 42.81 | 59.52 | 32.55 | 27.03 |

and every station received less than normal precipitation. The closest to the 100 percent of normal rainfall was San Antonio with 2.29 inches, which was 92 percent of normal. Midland and El Paso received no rain during the April.

The above-normal temperatures of April persisted through **May** in most areas. Many **record high temperatures** were reported. On the 17th, temperatures of 101 degrees F tied records in Del Rio and San Angelo and broke a record in Midland. Midland also broke an additional record on the 27th, with 102 degrees F. Thirteen of 19 weather stations experienced below-normal precipitation. Victoria received the most rainfall at 6.01 inches — 134 percent of normal monthly precipitation. Warm temperatures were recorded in May, as 17 of 19 first-order stations reported above-normal departures. However, a **cold front from Canada** roared through the state on the 21st bringing relatively cold air and some light rain to some areas. This contributed to six **record low temperatures** or tied record lows around the state between the 22nd and 23rd.

**June** was a month to remember as **Tropical Storm Allison** left her mark on the Upper Coastal region of Texas. However, most of the state reported below-normal precipitation, with the exception of the areas affected by this intense storm. College Station, Corpus Christi, Galveston, Houston and Port Arthur received above-normal precipitation, with an impressive 387 percent of normal precipitation reported in Houston. Temperatures were above normal for the most part, with the exception of Austin, Dallas–Fort Worth, Port Arthur and Waco. Tropical Storm Allison hovered over the eastern part of the state for almost six days and dumped up to **40 inches of rain in some areas.** At the Houston Bush Intercontinental Airport, 16.49 inches of rain was reported. This storm caused dangerous flooding and extreme damage, with a total of $2.0 billion in damage reported. There were a few temperature records in June. On the 12th, Lubbock broke a **record high temperature** with 105 degrees F. The irony of June was that both record heat and record cold were experienced. A cold front passed through toward month's end, and Waco reported a record low temperature of 62 degrees F.

Hot and dry best sum up **July.** Only 2 of 19 stations reported above-normal precipitation. Dallas–Fort Worth and Galveston received 167 percent and 132 percent of normal precipitation, respectively. All 19 first-order stations experienced above-normal temperatures. Mean temperatures ranged from +0.1 degrees F in Austin and Port Arthur, to +5.3 degrees F in Amarillo and Lubbock. A variety of records from precipitation to high temperatures were set, as well. On the 16th in Lubbock, a record high temperature of 105 degrees F was reported. Corpus Christi set a 24-hour precipitation record of 1.30 inches on the second. According to the Palmer Drought Severity Index, areas of concern were the Trans-Pecos and Lower Valley regions, which were rated **Severe Drought** in July. The remainder of the state, with the exception of the East, South Central and Upper Coast, were rated Moderate Drought.

**August** was a relief for Texas. Only four weather stations (Amarillo, Brownsville, Del Rio and Lubbock) recorded below-average rainfall. Port Arthur recorded an amazing 13.81 inches of rain, which was 259 percent of normal rainfall. The Trans-Pecos and High Plains were still rated **Severe Drought and Moderate Drought**, respectively. Temperatures across the state were higher than average, with 16 stations reporting above-normal temperatures. Toward month's end, a strong southerly flow brought abundant moisture from the south and was coupled with a low-pressure trough. This combination brought a wet end to August. Port Arthur reported 12.85 inches of rain from the 25th to the 31st, with 5.27 inches on the 30th and 4.44 inches on the 31st. Austin (4.95 inches), College Station (3.45 inches), Corpus Christi (5.61 inches), Galveston (9.06 inches), Houston (4.29 inches), San Antonio (7.66 inches), Victoria (7.13 inches) and Waco (4.49 inches) recorded the majority of their monthly totals during this seven-

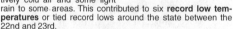
*A seagull finds calm weather at sunrise over the Gulf of Mexico. File photo.*

day period.

**September** was not quite as warm as August, with 15 of 19 stations reporting below-normal mean temperatures. Compared to September 2000, when several stations recorded **all-time maximum high temperatures,** only three stations (Del Rio, Midland and Wichita Falls) broke the century mark. Monthly mean temperatures ranged from -4.8 degrees F in Austin, to +2.4 degrees F in El Paso. The Eastern region received the most rain. Both College Station and Houston received 180 percent of their average precipitation (8.77 and 8.82 inches, respectively), while in the Low Rolling Plains region, Wichita Falls only recorded 13 percent of its normal precipitation. As a result of the abundant precipitation in the east, the East and South-Central regions were rated **Unusual Moist Spell**, while the Trans-Pecos was rated **Severe Drought**. The month of September 2001 ended with a typical fall weather pattern of mild days and chilly nights.

**October** continued the **mild temperature** trend set in September. Thirteen of 19 stations recorded below-normal mean temperatures, which spanned from -5.6 degrees F in Austin, to +3.6 degrees F in El Paso. The month was dry, indeed, as all stations received below-normal precipitation. Because of the lack of rainfall this month, the **drought intensified around the state.** According to the Palmer Drought Severity Index, the Trans-Pecos region was rated Extreme Drought, and the High Plains and Low Rolling Plains were classified as experiencing Moderate Drought conditions.

**November** was a contrast to October's cool temperatures, and all but one first-order station reported above-normal temperatures. Amarillo and Wichita Falls had the most impressive departures from normal for the month with +4.8 degrees F and +5.2 degrees F, respectively. Temperature records were broken in Wichita Falls on Nov. 1 with 87 degrees F, and records were tied in Midland on the 1st with 87 degrees F, in Lubbock on the 2nd with 83 degrees F, and in College Station on the 3rd with 86 degrees F.

**Precipitation was in abundance in November;** only 4 of 19 stations reported below-normal monthly rainfall. Corpus Christi recorded an impressive 7.44 inches of rain, which was 468 percent of normal. San Angelo also received 3.46 inches, which was 320 percent of normal. In Austin, 10.51 inches were reported for November, which was 443 percent of normal monthly rainfall. Record precipitation was recorded on the 15th and 16th, and Austin received 8.68 inches on the 15th. San Angelo reported 2.46 inches on the 15th, and San Antonio received 1.89 inches, as well.

McAllen received 4.08 inches on the 16th, and **a new 24-hour record was set** in Corpus Christi, with 4.55 inches. Victoria also set records on both the 15th and 16th, with 1.83 inches and 0.90 inches, respectively. Lubbock had the wettest November on record, with 3.45 inches, while Abilene had the sixth wettest and ninth warmest November on record. The end of November delivered **cold Canadian air** as well as rain, freezing rain and record snowfall in places. A record low of 37 degrees F was experienced in Waco on the 28th, while record snows of 7.3 inches and 8 inches fell in Wichita Falls and Midland, respectively.

**December** saw **variations in weather** from near record warmth to near record cold temperatures, and very dry to unusually wet. Eighteen of 19 stations reported above-normal temperatures. Rain was abundant in some areas but not in others; 11 stations reported below-normal precipitation. The state experienced divergent conditions, with the central to eastern portions reaping the benefits of precipitation, while the western half was dry. The month began warm, but quickly changed as **extremely cold temperatures** fell upon the state as well as **snowfall and ice.** Lubbock received 1 inch of snow and Amarillo acquired 2 inches on the 30th, and Waco saw a trace of snow. Most of the monthly precipitation fell early due to the passage of numerous cold fronts. Month's end brought another cold front, which in its wake dropped temperatures as much as 20 degrees in some southern communities.

## Weather Highlights 2002

**March 19:** A **supercell thunderstorm** that moved from San Angelo northeast to Ballinger produced **three tornadoes.** These tornadoes caused minor damage. The largest amount of damage occurred from 1.75-inches hail produced by this storm. **Hail up to golf-ball size** fell for an extended time causing drifts several feet deep in places. About 3,500 homes suffered light to moderate damage, as well as damage to 4,000 automobiles. The hail was so deep in places that it remained on the ground for up to 8 hours. The total damage was estimated at $16.0 million.

**July: Severe flooding** describes this month perfectly. Of the two major occurrences, the less severe occurred in Brown County from July 6–8 causing $42 million in damage. Showers and thunderstorms formed on the night of July 6 and remained stationary throughout the night dumping nearly 12–14 inches of rain on this North-Central county. Damage of minor and major caliber was reported in Coleman, Brown, Callahan and Taylor counties. Damage amounting to $15.0 million occurred in Taylor County. On June 30–July 7, a tropical wave wreaked havoc across the South Central and Edwards Plateau regions. Seven deaths were reported as a result of this storm. The damage to this area amounted to $250 million. San Antonio felt the brunt of this system as **rivers rose well above flood stage.** Some areas reported rainfall up to 30 inches. President Bush declared 29 counties federal disaster areas. The damage from the entire event was estimated at more than $2 billion.

**September 5–7:** Tropical Storm Fay made landfall on the 7th near Palacios in Matagorda County. Fay quickly weakened to a **tropical depression** and caused **five tornadoes** along a northwest path defined from Freeport in Brazoria County to Wharton County near Hungerford. Three injuries occurred when a tornado damaged a mobile home. The worst damage from Fay occurred from severe rainwater flooding. Nearly 10–20 inches of rain fell in an area from Freeport north-northwest to Boling in Wharton County. In Brazoria County, the hardest hit area was Sweeny. Total damage from flooding was $4.5 million.

**October 24:** A stationary frontal system triggered numerous showers and thunderstorms across the South Central region. An **F2 tornado** was produced by one of these storms and tore through the Del Mar College campus in Corpus Christi, causing one fatality and 20 injuries. The campus sustained the most damage, which totaled $75 million.

### 2002 Weather Extremes

**Lowest Temp.:** Dalhart, Dallam Co, Dec .26 . . . . . . . -6° F
**Highest Temp.:** Heath Canyon, Brewster Co., Aug. 28 . . . 116°F
**24-hour Precip:** Fowlerton, La Salle Co., Sept. 9 . . 12.80"
**Monthly Precip.:** Camp Verde, Kerr Co., July . . . . . 33.67"
**Least Annual Precip.:** Fort Hancock, Hudspeth Co. . 5.47"
**Greatest Annual Precip.:** Port Arthur City, Jefferson Co. . . . . . . . . . . . . . . . . . . . . . . . . . . 90.76"

## Monthly Summaries 2002

During **January**, temperatures were above normal for the entire state and precipitation was below normal with the exception of four weather stations.

Cool and dry weather characterized **February.** All 19 of Texas' first-order weather stations experienced below normal temperatures, and all but Abilene, El Paso and Midland received below normal precipitation. Also, numerous minimum temperature records were reported around the state.

**March** brought record cold temperatures to Texas and little precipitation. The Lower Valley and Trans-Pecos regions were considered to be in moderate drought conditions.

**April** was a dry and very warm month for the majority of the state, with all 19 weather stations reporting above normal temperatures. Six out of 19 stations received above normal precipitation.

**May** brought a continuation of slightly above normal temperatures and almost all stations had below normal precipitation. Because the month was drier than normal, drought conditions worsened.

This trend continued in **June**, as well, and in response, 29 counties instated burn bans. Severe weather caused a

# Meteorological Data

*Source: Updated as of July 2003 by the National Climatic Data Center. Additional data for these locations are listed by county in the table of Texas temperature, freeze, growing season and precipitation records.*

| City | Temperature | | | | | | Precipitation | | | | | Relative Humidity | | Wind | | | Sun |
|---|---|---|---|---|---|---|---|---|---|---|---|---|---|---|---|---|---|
| | Record High | Month & Year | Record Low | Month & Year | No. Days Max. 90° and Above | No. Days Min. 32° and Below | Maximum in 24 Hours | Month & Year | Snowfall (Mean Annual) | Max. Snowfall in 24 Hours | Month & Year | 6:00 a.m., CST | Noon, CST | Speed, MPH (Mean Annual) | Highest MPH | Month & Year | Percent Possible Sunshine |
| Abilene | 110 | 7/1978 | -9 | 1/1947 | 96 | 50 | 6.70 | 9/1961 | 4.6 | 9.3 | 4/1996 | 74 | 52 | 11.9 | 55 | 4/1998 | 70 |
| Amarillo | 108 | 6/1990 | -14 | 2/1951 | 64 | 111 | 6.75 | 5/1951 | 16.2 | 20.6 | 3/1934 | 73 | 48 | 13.5 | 60 | 6/1994 | 74 |
| Austin | 112 | 9/2000 | -2 | 1/1949 | 108 | 19 | 15.00 | 9/1921 | 0.9 | 9.7 | 11/1937 | 83 | 59 | 9.0 | 52 | 9/1987 | 60 |
| Brownsville | 106 | 3/1984 | 16 | 12/1989 | 121 | 2 | 12.19 | 9/1967 | ** | 0.0 | | 89 | 63 | 11.3 | 51 | 9/1996 | 59 |
| Corpus Christi | 109 | 9/2000 | 13 | 12/1989 | 106 | 5 | 8.92 | 8/1980 | ** | 1.1 | 2/1973 | 89 | 65 | 12.0 | 56 | 5/1999 | 60 |
| Dallas-Fort Worth | 113 | 6/1980 | -1 | 12/1989 | 97 | 37 | 5.91 | 10/1959 | 3.2 | 12.1 | 1/1964 | 81 | 58 | 10.7 | 73 | 8/1959 | 61 |
| Del Rio | 112 | 6/1988 | 10 | 12/1989 | 129 | 16 | 11.87 | 8/1998 | 0.9 | 8.6 | 1/1985 | 77 | 58 | 9.7 | 60 | 8/1970 | 84 |
| El Paso | 114 | 7/1994 | -8 | 1/1962 | 108 | 60 | 2.63 | 7/1968 | 5.4 | 22.4 | 12/1987 | 56 | 28 | 8.8 | 64 | 1/1996 | 84 |
| Galveston | 104 | 9/2000 | 8 | 2/1999 | 12 | 3 | 14.35 | 7/2000 | 0.2 | 15.4 | 2/1895 | 83 | 72 | 11.0 | *100 | 9/1900 | 59 |
| †Houston | 109 | 9/2000 | 7 | 12/1989 | 99 | 18 | 11.02 | 6/2001 | 0.4 | 2.0 | 1/1973 | 90 | 63 | 7.7 | 51 | 8/1983 | 72 |
| Lubbock | 114 | 6/1994 | -16 | 1/1963 | 81 | 92 | 5.82 | 10/1983 | 10.1 | 16.3 | 1/1983 | 73 | 48 | 12.4 | 70 | 3/1952 | 72 |
| Midland-Odessa | 116 | 6/1994 | -11 | 2/1985 | 100 | 63 | 5.99 | 7/1961 | 4.5 | 9.8 | 12/1998 | 73 | 45 | 11.1 | 67 | 2/1960 | 74 |
| Prt. Arthur-Beaumont | 108 | 8/2000 | 12 | 12/1989 | 83 | 14 | 17.76 | 7/1943 | 0.3 | 4.4 | 2/1960 | 91 | 66 | 9.6 | 55 | 6/1986 | 60 |
| San Angelo | 111 | ‡7/1960 | -4 | 12/1989 | 109 | 52 | 6.25 | 9/1980 | 3.1 | 7.4 | 1/1978 | 77 | 52 | 10.3 | 75 | 4/1969 | 70 |
| San Antonio | 111 | 9/2000 | 0 | 1/1949 | 113 | 21 | 13.35 | 10/1998 | 0.7 | 13.2 | 1/1985 | 83 | 57 | 9.1 | 48 | 7/1979 | 60 |
| Victoria | 111 | 9/2000 | 9 | 12/1989 | 106 | 10 | 9.87 | 4/1991 | 0.1 | 2.1 | 1/1985 | 90 | 63 | 9.9 | 99 | 7/1963 | 49 |
| Waco | 112 | 8/1969 | -5 | 1/1949 | 109 | 33 | 7.98 | 12/1997 | 1.4 | 7.0 | 1/1949 | 84 | 59 | 11.1 | 69 | 6/1961 | 59 |
| Wichita Falls | 117 | 6/1980 | -8 | 2/1985 | 104 | 64 | 6.19 | 12/1980 | 5.8 | 9.8 | 1/1925 | 81 | 53 | 11.6 | 62 | 6/1954 | 60 |
| §Shreveport, LA | 109 | ‡8/2000 | 3 | 1/1962 | 90 | 35 | 12.44 | 7/1933 | 1.5 | 11 | 12/1929 | 87 | 61 | 8.3 | 63 | 5/2000 | 64 |

*100 mph recorded at 6:15 p.m. Sept. 8 just before the anemometer blew away. Maximum velocity was estimated to be 120 mph from the northeast between 7:30 p.m. and 8:30 p.m.

†The official Houston station was moved from near downtown to Intercontinental Airport, located 12 miles north of the old station.

‡ Also recorded on earlier dates, months or years.

§Shreveport is included because it is near the boundary line and its data can be considered representative of the eastern border of Texas.

**Trace, an amount too small to measure.

swath of wind damage from Amarillo to Houston and from Lubbock to Tyler. The heat persisted with little precipitation as well.

The phrase "tropical insurgence of moisture" describes **July.** The Edwards Plateau, South Central, Southern and East Texas regions were bombarded with incredible amounts of moisture that trekked across the state. San Antonio and surrounding counties felt the brunt of this system. This increase in precipitation caused drought conditions to ebb and most burn bans were lifted. This system caused more than 2 billion dollars in damage.

**August** fell back into a dry and warm pattern similar to April, May and June. Eighteen of 19 first-order weather stations had above normal monthly temperatures and 15 had below normal precipitation.

A cold front in **September** caused temperatures to drop 20 degrees in some areas. But ironically the average temperatures for the month were above normal for 14 stations. Drier conditions prevailed at only six stations reporting above normal precipitation.

Much cooler temperatures were experienced in **October** with 11 stations having below normal temperatures. All first-order stations in Texas received above normal precipitation, with many daily and monthly precipitation records reported.

**November** was much drier than October as 13 stations reported below normal precipitation. Temperatures were below normal for all stations.

Precipitation was abundant in **December** and all but one station reported above normal precipitation for the month. This month saw fluctuations in weather with some stations reporting both record high and minimum temperatures. Twelve stations had above normal temperatures. The year concluded with close to normal temperature readings.

## 2002 Weather In-depth

**January's** temperatures were well above normal, but ironically by month's end, a **strong cold front** moved across the state and brought winter weather to the High Plains and Low Rolling Plains regions. Lubbock reported 0.8 inches of snow on the 24th. Highest maximum temperatures reached the 80s for a majority of the stations.

**February** was much cooler than January with average temperatures ranging from -0.9°F in Amarillo to -5.6°F in College Station. Numerous **low temperature records** were set around the state from Feb. 26–28, including College Station, Dallas-Fort Worth, Corpus Christi, Victoria, Waco and Wichita Falls. Low temperatures dipped into the teens in some regions.

**March** brought **severe weather** to several locations, with reports of tornadoes and hail that caused considerable damage around mid-month. The majority of the 19 first-order weather stations were below normal, with Austin having the most extreme below normal average at -4.7°F. Brownsville, Corpus Christi and Del Rio experienced temperatures slightly above normal. Precipitation was most notable in the High Plains, Low Rolling Plains and North Central regions. Abilene had 4.01 inches for the month, which was 284 percent of the normal amount expected. Dallas had an impressive 7.39 inches.

In **April**, all stations had above normal temperatures, which ranged from +2.0°F in Wichita Falls to +6.4°F in Del Rio. April was dry, as well, with only six first-order stations reaching 100 percent of average precipitation. Amarillo, Dallas-Fort Worth, Houston, San Antonio, Victoria and Wichita Falls experienced above normal precipitation. Toward month's end, the approaching dry line caused many **supercells** to develop in the Fort Worth area. These storms produced **numerous tornadoes** and caused serious damage around Arlington and surrounding areas.

**May** temperatures were a roller coaster ride, with extremes on both sides of the scale. The passage of frequent cold fronts led to many records being set. The lowest minimum temperature was 39°F in Amarillo and Lubbock, and the highest maximum temperature was 105°F in Del Rio. Severe weather events were also numerous. The beginning of the month saw many **hail and tornado reports** caused by frontal or dry line boundaries. May is thought to be one of the wettest months of the year in Texas, however this month was an exception. Precipitation was well below normal for the majority of the state, except in Abilene and Dallas-Fort Worth, with above normal measurements of 3.24 inches and 5.40 inches, respectively. **Drought conditions worsened** all across the southern and western portions of the state. As a result of the extremely dry conditions, many burn bans were issued across the state.

**June** did not change the drought-like conditions that were prevalent for several months. There was no relief from the lack of precipitation across the state, with only the North Central region and the northern part of the East region relatively unaffected by the drought. At least 29 counties instituted **burn bans** for at least a portion of the month. Severe weather was prevalent in the first half of the month. A swath of severe weather events occurred resulting in **hail and wind damage**. In the Wichita Falls area there was a report of a clocked wind of 92 mph. Uprooted trees, downed power lines across roadways and damaged roofs were some of the 80 reports to the Storm Prediction Center. There were six stations that experienced above normal precipitation including: Austin, Del Rio, Galveston, Lubbock, Victoria and Wichita Falls.

**July** was a bit of a different story precipitation-wise. Some stations in Texas received more rain in the first few days of July than they should have for the year-to-date total. This month will be remembered for the incredible amounts of rain that fell across the South Central, Edwards Plateau, Southern and Eastern regions of Texas. Twelve of 19 stations reported above normal precipitation for the month. Some of the impressive totals include: Abilene, 8.04 inches; Austin, 5.32 inches; College Station, 5.66 inches; and Houston, 7.10 inches. In and around the San Antonio areas, rivers crested at or above flood stage causing amazing amounts of damage, according to the National Weather Service and National Climatic Data Center.

Some monthly totals from in and around the San Antonio area are: Camp Verde, 34.17 inches; Comfort, 31.59 inches; and Sisterdale, 30.75 inches. San Antonio received 16.16 inches for the month and 9.52 inches July 1 alone. There were seven deaths reported and $250 million in damage. The huge amount of rain brought the extreme drought to an end across much of the south, east and central portions of Texas. Rain-cooled air kept temperatures slightly below normal for most stations. All told, there was $2 billion in damage in July.

**August** was a contrast to July. Below normal precipitation and warmer temperatures were experienced by most of the state. However, **tropical moisture** resulted in impressive rainfall totals on the Aug. 15 in Galveston and Port Arthur with 11.46 inches and 5.79 inches, respectively, a new 24-hour rainfall record for Galveston. Wink reported a national high of 113°F on Aug. 15.

**September** began much like August until a cold front moved across the state toward month's end. Despite the cold front, temperatures during September were above normal. Precipitation was also sparse with only 6 of 19 first-order stations reporting above normal rainfall. Of the stations that did receive more than ample precipitation, Corpus Christi reported a rainfall record on Sept. 15, probably as a result of the landfall of Tropical Storm Fay.

**October** was **cooler,** and because of numerous frontal passages, there were 24-hour precipitation records broken on the 19th. Most stations in Texas experienced below normal temperatures, but all were above normal precipitation-wise. Very impressive precipitation totals for the month include: Austin, 9.11 inches; Brownsville, 8.31 inches; College Station, 9.79 inches; Corpus Christi, 9.50 inches; Galveston, 11.81 inches; Houston, 14.65 inches; Port Arthur, 14.05 inches; and Waco, 9 inches. Three fatalities were reported due to numerous severe weather events, particularly tornadoes.

**November's** precipitation was a contrast to October's. A stationary front parked along the Rio Grande Valley, triggering numerous **showers and thunderstorms** that resulted in many impressive 24-hour precipitation totals. College Station reported 4.56 inches on the 4th, which also broke the 24-hour record from 1914 of 3.61 inches. Record highs also were reported this month as high temperatures soared into the 80s on the 10th. The month concluded with much cooler temperatures as a **large Arctic air mass** made its way into the state on the 28th. High temperatures ranged from the 30s in the Panhandle to the 50s in South Texas.

**December** saw **considerable fluctuations** in weather, as some stations reported record maximum and minimum temperatures, as well as record amounts of precipitation in some cases. In the Panhandle, snow fell on the 3rd and 4th due to a strong **Arctic frontal passage** that caused temperatures to drop as much as 20 degrees below normal. Ample precipitation was received across most of the state, with the exception of Del Rio, which received only 41 percent of its average precipitation. The end of the month brought severe weather as a result of the strong clash of cold Canadian air and the muggy sub-tropical jet-triggered storms. ✩

# Destructive Weather

*Source: This list of exceptionally destructive weather in Texas since 1766 was compiled from ESSA-Weather Bureau information.*

**Sept. 4, 1766: Hurricane. Galveston Bay.** A Spanish mission destroyed.

**Sept. 12, 1818: Hurricane. Galveston Island.** Salt water flowed four feet deep. Only six buildings remained habitable. Of the six vessels and two barges in the harbor, even the two not seriously damaged were reduced to dismasted hulks. **Pirate Jean Lafitte** moved to one hulk so his **Red House** might serve as a hospital.

**Aug. 6, 1844: Hurricane. Mouth of Rio Grande.** All houses destroyed at the mouth of the river and at **Brazos Santiago,** eight miles north; 70 lives lost.

**Sept. 19, 1854: Hurricane.** After striking near **Matagorda,** the hurricane moved inland northwestward over **Columbus.** The main impact fell in **Matagorda and Lavaca bays.** Almost all buildings in Matagorda were destroyed. Four lives were lost in the town; more lives were lost on the peninsula.

**Oct. 3, 1867: Hurricane.** This hurricane moved inland **south of Galveston,** but raked the entire Texas coast **from the Rio Grande to the Sabine. Bagdad and Clarksville,** towns at the mouth of the Rio Grande, were destroyed. Much of Galveston was flooded and property damage there was estimated at $1 million.

**Sept. 16, 1875: Hurricane.** Struck **Indianola,** Calhoun County. Three-fourths of town swept away; 176 lives lost. Flooding from the bay caused nearly all destruction.

**Aug. 13, 1880: Hurricane.** Center struck **Matamoros, Mexico; lower Texas coast** affected.

**Oct. 12-13, 1880: Hurricane. Brownsville.** City nearly destroyed, many lives lost.

**Aug. 23-24, 1882: Torrential rains** caused **flooding** on the **North and South Concho and Bosque rivers** (South Concho reported 45 feet above normal level), destroying **Benficklen,** then county seat of Tom Green County, leaving only the courthouse and jail. More than 50 persons drowned in **Tom Green and Erath counties,** with property damage at $200,000 and 10,000 to 15,000 head of livestock lost.

**Aug. 19-21, 1886: Hurricane. Indianola.** Every house destroyed or damaged. Indianola was never rebuilt.

**Oct. 12, 1886: Hurricane. Sabine,** Jefferson County. Hurricane passed over Sabine. The inundation extended 20 miles inland and nearly every house in the vicinity was moved from its foundation; 150 persons were drowned.

**April 28, 1893: Tornado. Cisco,** Eastland County; 23 killed, 93 injured; damage $400,000.

**May 15, 1896: Tornadoes, Sherman,** Grayson County; **Justin,** Denton County; **Gribble Springs,** Cooke County; 76 killed; damage $225,000.

**Sept. 12, 1897: Hurricane.** Many houses in **Port Arthur** were demolished; 13 killed, damage $150,000.

**May 1, 1898: Tornado. Mobeetie,** Wheeler County. Four killed, several injured; damage $35,000.

**June 27-July 1, 1899: Rainstorm.** A storm, centered over the **Brazos River watershed,** precipitated an average of 17 inches over an area of 7,000 square miles. At **Hearne** the gage overflowed at 24 inches, and there was an estimated total rainfall of 30 inches. At **Turnersville,** Coryell County, 33 inches were recorded in three days. This rain caused the **worst Brazos River flood on record.** Between 30 and 35 lives were lost. Property damage was estimated at $9 million.

# Texas Is Tornado Capital

An average of 132 tornadoes touch Texas soil each year. The annual total varies considerably, and certain areas are struck more often than others. Tornadoes occur with greatest frequency in the Red River Valley.

Tornadoes may occur in any month and at any hour of the day, but they occur with greatest frequency during the late spring and early summer months, and between the hours of 4 p.m. and 8 p.m. Between 1959 and 2002, nearly 63 percent of all Texas tornadoes occurred within the three-month period of April, May and June, with almost one-third of the total tornadoes occurring in May.

More tornadoes have been recorded in Texas than in any other state, which is partly due to the state's size. Between 1959 and 2002, 6,461 funnel clouds reached the ground, thus becoming tornadoes. Texas ranks 11th among the 50 states in the density of tornadoes, with an average of 5.7 tornadoes per 10,000 square miles per year during this period.

The greatest outbreak of tornadoes on record in Texas was associated with Hurricane Beulah in September 1967. Within a five-day period, Sept. 19–23, 115 known tornadoes, all in Texas, were spawned by this great hurricane. There were 67 on Sept. 20, a Texas record for a single day.

In addition to Hurricane Beulah's 115 tornadoes, there were another 9 tornadoes in September for a total of 124, a Texas record for a single month. The greatest number in Texas in a single year was 232, also in 1967. The second-highest number in a single year was in 1995, when 223 tornadoes occurred in Texas. In 1982, 123 tornadoes occurred in May, making it the worst outbreak of spring tornadoes in Texas.

The accompanying table compiled by the National Climatic Data Center, Environmental Data Service and the National Oceanic and Atmospheric Administration lists tornado occurrences in Texas by months for the period 1951–2002.

## Number of Tornadoes In Texas, 1959–2002

*Source: Office of State Climatologist*

| Year | Jan. | Feb. | March | April | May | June | July | Aug. | Sept. | Oct. | Nov. | Dec. | Annual |
|------|------|------|-------|-------|-----|------|------|------|-------|------|------|------|--------|
| 1959 | 0 | 0 | 8 | 4 | 32 | 14 | 10 | 3 | 4 | 5 | 6 | 0 | 86 |
| 1960 | 4 | 1 | 0 | 8 | 29 | 14 | 3 | 4 | 2 | 11 | 1 | 0 | 77 |
| 1961 | 0 | 1 | 21 | 15 | 24 | 30 | 9 | 2 | 12 | 0 | 10 | 0 | 124 |
| 1962 | 0 | 4 | 12 | 9 | 25 | 56 | 12 | 15 | 7 | 2 | 0 | 1 | 143 |
| 1963 | 0 | 0 | 3 | 9 | 19 | 24 | 8 | 4 | 6 | 4 | 5 | 0 | 82 |
| 1964 | 0 | 1 | 6 | 22 | 15 | 11 | 9 | 7 | 3 | 1 | 3 | 0 | 78 |
| 1965 | 2 | 5 | 3 | 7 | 43 | 24 | 2 | 9 | 4 | 6 | 0 | 3 | 108 |
| 1966 | 0 | 4 | 1 | 21 | 22 | 15 | 3 | 8 | 3 | 0 | 0 | 0 | 77 |
| 1967 | 0 | 2 | 11 | 17 | 34 | 22 | 10 | 5 | 124 | 2 | 0 | 5 | 232 |
| 1968 | 2 | 1 | 3 | 13 | 47 | 21 | 4 | 8 | 5 | 8 | 11 | 16 | 139 |
| 1969 | 0 | 1 | 1 | 16 | 65 | 16 | 6 | 7 | 6 | 8 | 1 | 0 | 127 |
| 1970 | 1 | 3 | 5 | 23 | 23 | 9 | 5 | 20 | 9 | 20 | 0 | 3 | 121 |
| 1971 | 0 | 20 | 10 | 24 | 27 | 33 | 7 | 20 | 7 | 16 | 4 | 23 | 191 |
| 1972 | 1 | 0 | 19 | 13 | 43 | 12 | 19 | 13 | 8 | 9 | 7 | 0 | 144 |
| 1973 | 14 | 1 | 29 | 25 | 21 | 24 | 4 | 8 | 5 | 3 | 9 | 4 | 147 |
| 1974 | 2 | 1 | 8 | 19 | 18 | 26 | 3 | 9 | 6 | 22 | 2 | 0 | 116 |
| 1975 | 5 | 2 | 9 | 12 | 50 | 18 | 10 | 3 | 3 | 3 | 1 | 1 | 117 |
| 1976 | 1 | 1 | 8 | 53 | 63 | 11 | 16 | 6 | 13 | 4 | 0 | 0 | 176 |
| 1977 | 0 | 0 | 3 | 34 | 50 | 4 | 5 | 5 | 12 | 0 | 6 | 4 | 123 |
| 1978 | 0 | 0 | 0 | 34 | 65 | 10 | 13 | 6 | 6 | 1 | 2 | 0 | 137 |
| 1979 | 1 | 2 | 24 | 33 | 39 | 14 | 12 | 10 | 4 | 15 | 3 | 0 | 157 |
| 1980 | 0 | 2 | 7 | 26 | 44 | 21 | 2 | 34 | 10 | 5 | 0 | 2 | 153 |
| 1981 | 0 | 7 | 7 | 9 | 71 | 26 | 5 | 20 | 5 | 23 | 3 | 0 | 176 |
| 1982 | 0 | 0 | 6 | 27 | 123 | 36 | 4 | 0 | 3 | 0 | 3 | 1 | 203 |
| 1983 | 5 | 7 | 24 | 1 | 62 | 35 | 4 | 22 | 5 | 0 | 7 | 14 | 186 |
| 1984 | 0 | 13 | 9 | 18 | 19 | 19 | 0 | 4 | 1 | 5 | 2 | 5 | 95 |
| 1985 | 0 | 0 | 5 | 41 | 28 | 5 | 3 | 1 | 1 | 3 | 1 | 2 | 90 |
| 1986 | 0 | 1 | 4 | 21 | 50 | 24 | 3 | 5 | 4 | 7 | 1 | 0 | 131 |
| 1987 | 1 | 1 | 7 | 0 | 54 | 19 | 11 | 3 | 8 | 0 | 16 | 4 | 124 |
| 1988 | 0 | 0 | 0 | 11 | 7 | 7 | 6 | 2 | 42 | 4 | 10 | 0 | 89 |
| 1989 | 3 | 0 | 5 | 3 | 70 | 63 | 0 | 6 | 3 | 6 | 1 | 0 | 160 |
| 1990 | 3 | 3 | 4 | 56 | 62 | 20 | 5 | 2 | 3 | 0 | 0 | 0 | 158 |
| 1991 | 20 | 5 | 2 | 39 | 72 | 36 | 1 | 2 | 3 | 8 | 4 | 0 | 192 |
| 1992 | 0 | 5 | 13 | 22 | 43 | 66 | 4 | 4 | 4 | 7 | 21 | 0 | 189 |
| 1993 | 1 | 4 | 5 | 17 | 39 | 4 | 4 | 0 | 12 | 23 | 8 | 0 | 117 |
| 1994 | 0 | 1 | 1 | 48 | 88 | 2 | 1 | 4 | 3 | 9 | 8 | 0 | 165 |
| 1995 | 6 | 0 | 13 | 36 | 66 | 75 | 11 | 3 | 2 | 1 | 0 | 10 | 223 |
| 1996 | 7 | 1 | 2 | 21 | 33 | 9 | 3 | 8 | 33 | 8 | 4 | 1 | 130 |
| 1997 | 0 | 6 | 7 | 31 | 59 | 50 | 2 | 2 | 1 | 16 | 3 | 0 | 177 |
| 1998 | 0 | 2 | 5 | 4 | 9 | 11 | 6 | 3 | 5 | 3 | 28 | 1 | 109 |
| 1999 | 22 | 0 | 22 | 23 | 70 | 26 | 3 | 8 | 0 | 0 | 0 | 4 | 178 |
| 2000 | 0 | 7 | 49 | 33 | 23 | 8 | 3 | 0 | 0 | 10 | 20 | 1 | 154 |
| 2001 | 0 | 0 | 4 | 12 | 36 | 12 | 0 | 7 | 15 | 24 | 27 | 5 | 142 |
| 2002 | 0 | 0 | 44 | 25 | 61 | 5 | 1 | 4 | 13 | 8 | 0 | 22 | 183 |
| Total | 127 | 149 | 475 | 1070 | 2086 | 1061 | 275 | 344 | 433 | 357 | 227 | 138 | 6742 |

# Texas Droughts, 1892–2002

The following tables show the **duration and extent of Texas droughts by climatic division, 1892-2000.** For this purpose, droughts are arbitrarily defined as when the division has less than 75 percent of the 1931-1960 average precipitation. The 1931-1960 average precipitation in inches is shown at the bottom of the table for each division. The short table at bottom right shows the frequency of droughts in each area and the total years of droughts in the area.

| Year | High Plains | Low Rolling Plains | North Central | East Texas | Trans-Pecos | Edwards Plateau | South Central | Upper Coast | Southern | Lower Valley |
|---|---|---|---|---|---|---|---|---|---|---|
| 1892 | | | | | 68 | | | 73 | | |
| 1893 | | | 67 | 70 | | 49 | 56 | 64 | 53 | 59 |
| 1894 | | | | | 68 | | | | | |
| 1897 | | | | | | 73 | | 72 | | |
| 1898 | | | | | | | | | 69 | 51 |
| 1901 | | 71 | 70 | | | 60 | 62 | 70 | 44 | |
| 1902 | | | | | | | | 65 | 73 | |
| 1907 | | | | | | | | | | 65 |
| 1909 | | | 72 | 68 | 67 | 74 | 70 | | | |
| 1910 | 59 | 59 | 64 | 69 | 43 | 65 | 69 | 74 | 59 | |
| 1911 | | | | | | | | | | 70 |
| 1916 | | 73 | | 74 | 70 | | 73 | 69 | | |
| 1917 | 58 | 50 | 63 | 59 | 44 | 46 | 42 | 50 | 32 | 48 |
| 1920 | | | | | | | | | | 71 |
| 1921 | | | | | 72 | | | | | 73 |
| 1922 | | | | | 68 | | | | | |
| 1924 | | | 73 | 73 | | 71 | | 72 | | |
| 1925 | | | 72 | | | | 72 | | | |
| 1927 | | | | | | | | 74 | | 74 |
| 1933 | 72 | | | | 62 | 68 | | | | |
| 1934 | 66 | | | | 46 | 69 | | | | |
| 1937 | | | | | | | | | 72 | |
| 1939 | | | | | | | 69 | | | 72 |
| 1943 | | | 72 | | | | | | | |
| 1948 | | | 73 | 74 | 62 | | 71 | 67 | | |
| 1950 | | | | | | | 68 | | 74 | 64 |
| 1951 | | | | | 61 | 53 | | | | |
| 1952 | 68 | 66 | | | 73 | | | | 56 | 70 |
| 1953 | 69 | | | | 49 | 73 | | | | |
| 1954 | 70 | 71 | 68 | 73 | | 50 | 50 | 57 | 71 | |
| 1956 | 51 | 57 | 61 | 68 | 44 | 43 | 55 | 62 | 53 | 53 |
| 1962 | | | | | | 68 | | | 67 | 65 |
| 1963 | | | 63 | 68 | | 65 | 61 | 73 | | |
| 1964 | 74 | | | | 69 | | | | | 63 |
| 1970 | 65 | 63 | | | | 72 | | | | |
| 1988 | | | | | | 67 | 62 | 67 | 68 | |
| 1989 | | | | | | 72 | | | 66 | 64 |
| 1990 | | | | | | | | | | 73 |
| 1994 | | | | | 68 | | | | | |
| 1996 | | | | | | | 71 | | 60 | 70 |
| 1998 | | 69 | | | 71 | | | | | |
| 1999 | | | 73 | | | 67 | 69 | 69 | | |
| 2000 | | | | | 74 | | | | | 67 |
| 2001 | | | | | 56 | | | | | |
| 2002 | | | | | | | | | | |

### Normal Annual Rainfall by Region

Listed below is the normal annual rainfall in inches for four 30-year periods in each geographical division. The normals for each division are given in the same order as the divisions which appear in the table above.

| Period | Normal Rainfall in Inches | | | | | | | | | |
|---|---|---|---|---|---|---|---|---|---|---|
| 1931-1960 | 18.51 | 22.99 | 32.93 | 45.96 | 12.03 | 25.91 | 33.24 | 46.19 | 22.33 | 24.27 |
| 1941-1970 | 18.59 | 23.18 | 32.94 | 45.37 | 11.57 | 23.94 | 33.03 | 46.43 | 21.95 | 23.44 |
| 1951-1980 | 17.73 | 22.80 | 32.14 | 44.65 | 11.65 | 23.52 | 34.03 | 45.93 | 22.91 | 24.73 |
| 1961-1990 | 18.88 | 23.77 | 33.99 | 45.67 | 13.01 | 24.00 | 34.49 | 47.63 | 23.47 | 25.31 |

**April 5-8, 1900: Rainstorm.** This storm began in two centers, over **Val Verde County** on the Rio Grande, and over **Swisher County** on the High Plains, and converged in the vicinity of **Travis County**, causing disastrous floods in the **Colorado, Brazos and Guadalupe rivers.** McDonald Dam on the Colorado River at Austin crumbled suddenly. A wall of water swept through the city taking at least 23 lives. Damage was estimated at $1,250,000.

**Sept. 8-9, 1900: Hurricane. Galveston.** The Great Galveston Storm was the **worst natural disaster in U.S. history** in terms of human life. Loss of life at Galveston has been estimated at 6,000 to 8,000, but the exact number has never been exactly determined. The island was completely inundated; not a single structure escaped damage. Most of the loss of life was due to drowning by storm tides that reached 15 feet or more. The anemometer blew away when the wind reached 100 miles per hour at 6:15 p.m. on the 8th. Wind reached an estimated maximum velocity of 120 miles per hour between 7:30 and 8:30 p.m. Property damage has been estimated at $30 to $40 million.

**May 18, 1902: Tornado. Goliad.** This tornado cut a 250-yard-wide path through town, turning 150 buildings into rubble. Several churches were destroyed, one of which was holding services; all 40 worshippers were either killed or injured. This tornado killed 114, injured 230, and caused an estimated $200,000 in damages.

**April 26, 1906: Tornado. Bellevue,** Clay County, demolished; considerable damage done at **Stoneburg,** seven miles east; 17 killed, 20 injured; damage $300,000.

**May 6, 1907: Tornado. North of Sulphur Springs,** Hopkins County; five killed, 19 injured.

**May 13, 1908: Tornado. Linden,** Cass County. Four killed, seven injured; damage $75,000.

**May 22-25, 1908: Rainstorm;** unique because it originated on the Pacific Coast. It moved first into **North Texas** and southern Oklahoma and thence to **Central Texas,** precipitating as much as 10 inches. Heaviest floods were in the upper Trinity basin, but flooding was general as far south as the Nueces. Property damage exceeded $5 million and 11 lives were lost in the Dallas vicinity.

**March 23, 1909: Tornado. Slidell,** Wise County; 11 killed, 10 injured; damage $30,000.

**May 30, 1909: Tornado. Zephyr,** Brown County; 28 killed, many injured; damage $90,000.

**July 21, 1909: Hurricane. Velasco,** Brazoria County. One-half of town destroyed, 41 lives lost; damage $2,000,000.

**Dec. 1-5, 1913: Rainstorm.** This caused the **second major Brazos River flood,** and caused more deaths than the storm of 1899. It formed over **Central Texas** and spread both southwest and northeast with precipitation of 15 inches at **San Marcos** and 11 inches at **Kaufman.** Floods caused loss of 177 lives and $8,541,000 damage.

**April 20-26, 1915: Rainstorm.** Originated over Central Texas and spread into North and East Texas with precipitation up to 17 inches, causing floods in **Trinity, Brazos, Colorado, and Guadalupe rivers.** More than 40 lives lost and $2,330,000 damage.

**Aug. 16-19, 1915: Hurricane. Galveston.** Peak wind gusts of 120 miles recorded at Galveston; tide ranged 9.5 to 14.3 feet above mean sea level in the city, and up to 16.1 feet near the causeway. Business section flooded with 5 to 6 feet of water. At least 275 lives lost, damage $56 million. A new seawall prevented a repetition of the 1900 disaster.

**Aug. 18, 1916: Hurricane. Corpus Christi.** Maximum wind speed 100 miles per hour. 20 Lives lost; damage $1,600,000.

### Drought Frequency

This table shows the number of years of drought and the number of separate droughts. For example, the **High Plains** has had 10 drought years, consisting of five 1-year droughts, one 2-year drought and one 3-year drought, a total of 7 droughts.

| Years | High Plains | Low Rolling Plains | North Central | East Texas | Trans-Pecos | Edwards Plateau | South Central | Upper Coast | Southern | Lower Valley |
|---|---|---|---|---|---|---|---|---|---|---|
| 1 | 5 | 8 | 9 | 6 | 8 | 8 | 13 | 10 | 10 | 14 |
| 2 | 1 | 1 | 2 | 2 | 4 | 5 | 2 | 2 | 3 | 2 |
| 3 | 1 | | | | 1 | | | | | |
| Total Droughts | 7 | 9 | 11 | 8 | 13 | 13 | 15 | 12 | 13 | 16 |
| Drght Yrs. | 10 | 10 | 13 | 10 | 20 | 18 | 17 | 14 | 16 | 18 |

**Jan. 10-12, 1918: Blizzard.** This was the most severe since that of February, 1899; it was accompanied by zero degree temperature in **North Texas** and temperatures from 7° to 12° below freezing along the **lower coast**.

**April 9, 1919: Tornado. Leonard, Ector and Ravenna** in Fannin County; 20 killed, 45 injured; damage $125,000.

**April 9, 1919: Tornado. Henderson, Van Zandt, Wood, Camp, and Red River counties,** 42 killed, 150 injured; damage $450,000.

**May 7, 1919: Windstorms. Starr, Hidalgo, Willacy and Cameron counties.** Violent thunderstorms with high winds, hail and rain occurred between **Rio Grande City** and the coast, killing 10 persons. Damage to property and crops was $500,000. Seven were killed at **Mission**.

**Sept. 14, 1919: Hurricane.** Near **Corpus Christi**. Center moved inland south of Corpus Christi; tides 16 feet above normal in that area and 8.8 feet above normal at **Galveston**. Extreme wind at Corpus Christi measured at 110 miles per hour; 284 lives lost; damage $20,272,000.

**April 13, 1921: Tornado. Melissa,** Collin County, and **Petty,** Lamar County. Melissa was practically destroyed; 12 killed, 80 injured; damage $500,000.

**April 15, 1921: Tornado. Wood, Cass and Bowie counties;** 10 killed, 50 injured; damage $85,000.

**Sept. 8-10, 1921: Rainstorm.** Probably the **greatest rainstorm in Texas history,** it entered Mexico as a hurricane from the Gulf. Torrential rains fell as the storm moved northeasterly across Texas. **Record floods** occurred in **Bexar, Travis, Williamson, Bell** and **Milam counties,** killing 215 persons, with property losses over $19 million. Five to nine feet of water stood in downtown **San Antonio**. A total of 23.98 inches was measured at the U.S. Weather Bureau station at **Taylor** during a period of 35 hours, with a 24-hour maximum of 23.11 on September 9-10. The **greatest rainfall recorded in United States history during 18 consecutive hours** (measured at an unofficial weather-monitoring site) **fell at Thrall,** Williamson County, 36.40 inches fell on Sept. 9.

**April 8, 1922: Tornado. Rowena,** Runnels County. Seven killed, 52 injured; damage $55,000.

**April 8, 1922: Tornado. Oplin,** Callahan County. Five killed, 30 injured; damage $15,000.

**April 23-28, 1922: Rainstorm.** An exceptional storm entered Texas from the west and moved from the **Panhandle** to **North Central** and **East Texas**. Rains up to 12.6 inches over Parker, Tarrant and Dallas counties caused severe floods in the Upper Trinity at **Fort Worth;** 11 lives were lost; damage was estimated at $1 million.

**May 4, 1922: Tornado. Austin,** Travis County; 12 killed, 50 injured; damage $500,000.

**May 14, 1923: Tornado. Howard and Mitchell counties;** 23 killed, 100 injured; damage $50,000.

**April 12, 1927: Tornado. Edwards, Real and Uvalde counties;** 74 killed, 205 injured; damage $1,230,000. Most of damage

was in **Rocksprings** where 72 deaths occurred and town was practically destroyed.

**May 9, 1927: Tornado. Garland;** eleven killed; damage $100,000.

**May 9, 1927: Tornado. Nevada,** Collin County; **Wolfe City,** Hunt County; and **Tigertown,** Lamar County; 28 killed, over 200 injured; damage $900,000.

**Jan. 4, 1929: Tornado.** Near **Bay City**, Matagorda County. Five killed, 14 injured.

**April 24, 1929: Tornado. Slocum,** Anderson County; seven killed, 20 injured; damage $200,000.

**May 24-31, 1929: Rainstorm.** Beginning over **Caldwell County,** a storm spread over much of **Central and Coastal Texas** with maximum rainfall of 12.9 inches, causing **floods in Colorado, Guadalupe, Brazos, Trinity, Neches and Sabine rivers.** Much damage at **Houston** from overflow of bayous. Damage estimated at $6 million.

**May 6, 1930: Tornado. Bynum, Irene and Mertens** in Hill County; **Ennis,** Ellis County; and **Frost,** Navarro County; 41 killed; damage $2,100,000.

**May 6, 1930: Tornado. Kenedy and Runge** in Karnes County; **Nordheim,** DeWitt County; 36 killed, 34 injured; damage $127,000.

**June 30-July 2, 1932: Rainstorm.** Torrential rains fell over the upper watersheds of the **Nueces and Guadalupe rivers,** causing destructive floods. Seven persons drowned; property losses exceeded $500,000.

**Aug. 13, 1932: Hurricane.** Near **Freeport,** Brazoria County. Wind speed at **East Columbia** estimated at 100 miles per hour; 40 lives lost, 200 injured; damage $7,500,000.

**March 30, 1933: Tornado. Angelina, Nacogdoches and San Augustine counties;** 10 killed, 56 injured; damage $200,000.

**April 26, 1933: Tornado. Bowie County** near Texarkana. Five killed, 38 injured; damage $14,000.

**July 22-25, 1933: Tropical Storm.** One of the greatest U.S. storms in area and general rainfall. The storm reached the vicinity of **Freeport** late on July 22 and moved very slowly overland across eastern Texas, July 22-25. The storm center moved into northern Louisiana on the 25th. Rainfall averaged 12.50 inches over an area of about 25,000 square miles. Twenty inches or more fell in a small area of eastern Texas and western Louisiana surrounding Logansport, La. The 4-day total at Logansport was 22.30 inches. Property damage was estimated at $1,114,790.

**July 30, 1933: Tornado. Oak Cliff section of Dallas,** Dallas County. Five killed, 30 injured; damage $500,000.

**Sept. 4-5, 1933: Hurricane.** Near **Brownsville.** Center passed inland a short distance north of Brownsville, where an extreme wind of 106 miles per hour was measured before the anemometer blew away. Peak wind gusts were estimated at 120 to 125 miles per hour. 40 known dead, 500 injured; damage $16,903,100. About 90 percent of the citrus crop in the **Lower Rio Grande Valley**

# Extreme Weather Records in Texas

NOAA Environmental Data Service lists the following recorded extremes of weather in Texas:

## Temperature

| | |
|---|---|
| Lowest - Tulia, February 12, 1899 | -23°F |
| Seminole, February 8, 1933 | -23°F |
| Highest - Seymour, August 12, 1936 | 120°F |
| Monahans, June 28, 1994 | 120°F |
| Coldest Winter | 1898-1899 |

## Snowfall

| | |
|---|---|
| Greatest seasonal - Romero, 1923-1924 | 65.0 in. |
| Greatest monthly - Hale Center, Feb. 1956 | 36.0 in. |
| Greatest single storm - Hale Center, Feb. 2-5, 1956 | 33.0 in. |
| Greatest in 24 Hours - Plainview, Feb. 3-4, 1956 | 24.0 in. |
| Maximum depth on ground - Hale Center, Feb. 5, 1956 | 33.0 in. |

## Rainfall

| | | |
|---|---|---|
| Wettest year - entire state | 1941 | 42.62 in. |
| Driest year - entire state | 1917 | 14.30 in. |
| Greatest annual - Clarksville | 1873 | 109.38 in. |
| Least annual - Wink | 1956 | 1.76 in. |
| †Greatest in 24 hours - Alvin, July 25-26, 1979 | | 43.00 in. |

*†This is an unofficial estimate of rainfall that occurred during Tropical Storm Claudette. The greatest 24-hour rainfall ever recorded in Texas at an official observing site occurred at Albany, Shackelford County, on Aug. 4, 1978: 29.05 inches.*

## Wind Velocity

| | |
|---|---|
| Highest sustained wind (fastest mile) | |
| *Matagorda - Sept. 11, 1961 | SE, 145 mph |
| *Port Lavaca - Sept. 11, 1961 | NE, 145 mph |
| Highest peak gust (instantaneous velocity) | |
| *Aransas Pass - Aug. 3, 1970 | SW, 180 mph |
| *Robstown - Aug. 3, 1970 (est.) | WSW, 180 mph |

*These velocities occurred during hurricanes. Theoretically, much higher velocities are possible within the vortex of a tor-* nado, but no measurement with an anemometer has ever been made. The U.S. Weather Bureau's experimental Doppler radar equipment, a device which permits direct measurement of the high speeds in a spinning tornado funnel, received its first big test in the Wichita Falls tornado of April 2, 1958. This was the first tornado tracked by the Doppler radar, and for the first time in history, rotating winds up to 280 mph were clocked.

was destroyed.

**July 25, 1934: Hurricane.** Near **Seadrift**, Calhoun County, 19 lives lost, many minor injuries; damage $4.5 million. About 85 percent of damage was in crops.

**Sept. 15-18, 1936: Rainstorm.** Excessive rains over the **North Concho and Middle Concho rivers** caused a sharp rise in the Concho River, which overflowed **San Angelo**. Much of the business district and 500 homes were flooded. Four persons drowned and property losses estimated at $5 million. Four-day storm rainfall at San Angelo measured 25.19 inches, of which 11.75 inches fell on the 15th.

**June 10, 1938: Tornado.** Clyde, Callahan County; 14 killed, 9 injured; damage $85,000.

**Sept. 23, 1941: Hurricane.** Near **Matagorda**. Center moved inland near Matagorda, and passed over **Houston** about midnight. Extremely high tides along coast in the **Matagorda to Galveston** area. Heaviest property and crop losses were in counties from Matagorda County to the Sabine River. Four lives lost. Damage was $6,503,300.

**April 28, 1942: Tornado. Crowell,** Foard County; 11 killed, 250 injured; damage $1,500,000.

**Aug. 30, 1942: Hurricane. Matagorda Bay.** Highest wind estimated 115 miles per hour at **Seadrift**. Tide at **Matagorda,**14.7 feet. Storm moved west-north-westward and finally diminished over the **Edwards Plateau;** eight lives lost, property damage estimated at $11.5 million, and crop damage estimated at $15 million.

**May 10, 1943: Tornado. Laird Hill,** Rusk County, and **Kilgore,** Gregg County. Four killed, 25 injured; damage $1 million.

**July 27, 1943: Hurricane.** Near **Galveston**. Center moved inland across **Bolivar Peninsula and Trinity Bay**. A wind gust of 104 miles per hour was recorded at **Texas City**; 19 lives lost; damage estimated at $16,550,000.

**Aug. 26-27, 1945: Hurricane. Aransas-San Antonio Bay** area. At **Port O'Connor**, the wind reached 105 miles per hour when the cups were torn from the anemometer. Peak gusts of 135 miles per hour were estimated at **Seadrift, Port O'Connor and Port Lavaca;** three killed, 25 injured; damage $20,133,000.

**Jan. 4, 1946: Tornado.** Near **Lufkin**, Angelina County and **Nacogdoches**, Nacogdoches County; 13 killed, 250 injured; damage $2,050,000.

**Jan. 4, 1946: Tornado.** Near **Palestine**, Anderson County; 15 killed, 60 injured; damage $500,000.

**May 18, 1946: Tornado. Clay, Montague and Denton counties.** Four killed, damage $112,000.

**April 9, 1947: Tornado. White Deer,** Carson County; **Glazier,** Hemphill County; and **Higgins,** Lipscomb County; 68 killed, 201 injured; damage $1,550,000. Glazier completely destroyed. **One of the largest tornadoes on record.** Width of path, 1 miles at Higgins; length of path, 221 miles across portions of Texas, Oklahoma and Kansas. This tornado also struck Woodward, Okla.

**May 3, 1948: Tornado. McKinney,** Collin County; three killed, 43 injured; $2 million damage.

**May 15, 1949: Tornado. Amarillo** and vicinity; six killed, 83 injured. Total damage from tornado, wind and hail, $5,310,000. Total destruction over one-block by three-block area in southern part of city; airport and 45 airplanes damaged; 28 railroad boxcars blown off track.

**Sept. 8-10, 1952: Rainstorm.** Heavy rains over the **Colorado and Guadalupe River watersheds** in southwestern Texas caused major flooding. From 23 to 26 inches fell between **Kerrville, Blanco and Boerne**. Highest stages ever known occurred in the **Pedernales River;** five lives lost, three injured; 17 homes destroyed, 454 damaged. Property loss several million dollars.

**March 13, 1953: Tornado. Jud and O'Brien,** Haskell County; and **Knox City,** Knox County; 17 killed, 25 injured; damage $600,000.

**May 11, 1953: Tornado.** Near **San Angelo,** Tom Green County; eleven killed, 159 injured; damage $3,239,000.

**May 11, 1953: Tornado. Waco,** McLennan County; 114 killed, 597 injured; damage $41,150,000. **One of two most disastrous tornadoes;** 150 homes destroyed, 900 homes damaged; 185 other buildings destroyed; 500 other buildings damaged.

**April 2, 1957: Tornado. Dallas,** Dallas County; 10 killed, 200 injured; damage $4 million. Moving through Oak Cliff and West Dallas, it damaged 574 buildings, largely homes.

**April-May, 1957: Torrential Rains.** Excessive flooding occurred throughout the area **east of the Pecos River to the Sabine River** during the last 10 days of April; 17 lives were lost, and several hundred homes were destroyed. During May, more than 4,000 persons were evacuated from unprotected lowlands on the **West Fork of the Trinity above Fort Worth** and along creeks in Fort Worth.

Twenty-nine houses at **Christoval** were damaged or destroyed and 83 houses and furnishings at **San Angelo** were damaged. Five persons were drowned in floods in **South Central Texas.**

**May 15, 1957: Tornado. Silverton,** Briscoe County; 21 killed, 80 injured; damage $500,000.

**June 27, 1957: Hurricane Audrey.** Center crossed the Gulf coast near the Texas-Louisiana line. **Orange** was in the western portion of the eye between 9 and 10 a.m. In Texas, nine lives were lost, 450 persons injured; property damage was $8 million. Damage was extensive in **Jefferson and Orange counties,** with less in **Chambers and Galveston counties.** Maximum wind reported in Texas, 85 m.p.h. at **Sabine Pass,** with gusts to 100 m.p.h.

**Oct. 28, 1960: Rainstorm.** Rains of 7-10 inches fell in **South Central Texas;** 11 died from drowning in flash floods. In **Austin** about 300 families were driven from their homes. Damage in Austin was estimated at $2.5 million.

**Sept. 8-14, 1961: Hurricane Carla. Port O'Connor;** maximum wind gust at **Port Lavaca** estimated at 175 miles per hour. Highest tide was 18.5 feet at Port Lavaca. Most damage was to **coastal counties between Corpus Christi and Port Arthur** and inland **Jackson, Harris and Wharton counties.** In Texas, 34 persons died; seven in a **tornado** that swept across **Galveston Island;** 465 persons were injured. Property and crop damage conservatively estimated at $300 million. The evacuation of an estimated 250,000 persons kept loss of life low. **Hurricane Carla was the largest hurricane of record.**

**Sept. 7, 1962: Rainstorm. Fort Worth.** Rains fell over the Big Fossil and Denton Creek watersheds ranging up to 11 inches of fall in three hours. Extensive damage from flash flooding occurred in **Richland Hills and Haltom City.**

**Sept. 16-20, 1963: Hurricane Cindy.** Rains of 15 to 23.5 inches fell in portions of **Jefferson, Newton and Orange counties** when Hurricane Cindy became stationary west of **Port Arthur.** Flooding from the excessive rainfall resulted in total property damage of $11,600,000 and agricultural losses of $500,000.

**April 3, 1964: Tornado. Wichita Falls.** Seven killed, 111 injured; damage $15 million; 225 homes destroyed, 50 with major damage, and 200 with minor damage. Sixteen other buildings received major damage.

**Sept. 21-23, 1964: Rainstorm. Collin, Dallas and Tarrant counties.** Rains of more than 12 inches fell during the first eight hours of the 21st. Flash flooding of tributaries of the Trinity River and smaller creeks and streams resulted in two drownings and an estimated $3 million property damage. Flooding of homes occurred in all sections of **McKinney.** In **Fort Worth,** there was considerable damage to residences along Big Fossil and White Rock creeks. Expensive homes in **North Dallas** were heavily damaged.

**Jan. 25, 1965: Dust Storm. West Texas.** The worst dust storm since February 1956 developed on the **southern High Plains.** Winds, gusting up to 75 miles per hour at **Lubbock,** sent dust billowing to 31,000 feet in the area **from the Texas-New Mexico border eastward to a line from Tulia to Abilene.** Ground visibility was reduced to about 100 yards in many sections. The worst hit was the **Muleshoe, Seminole, Plains, Morton** area on the South Plains. The rain gage at Reese Air Force Base, Lubbock, contained 3 inches of fine sand.

**June 2, 1965: Tornado. Hale Center,** Hale County. Four killed, 76 injured; damage $8 million.

**June 11, 1965: Rainstorm. Sanderson,** Terrell County. Torrential rains of up to eight inches in two hours near Sanderson caused a major flash flood that swept through the town. As a result, 26 persons drowned and property losses were estimated at $2,715,000.

**April 22-29, 1966: Flooding. Northeast Texas.** Twenty to 26 inches of rain fell in portions of Wood, Smith, Morris, Upshur, Gregg, Marion and Harrison counties. Nineteen persons drowned in the rampaging rivers and creeks that swept away bridges, roads and dams, and caused an estimated $12 million damage.

**April 28, 1966: Flash flooding. Dallas County.** Flash flooding from torrential rains in Dallas County resulted in 14 persons drowned and property losses estimated at $15 million.

**Sept. 18-23, 1967: Hurricane Beulah.** Near **Brownsville.** The **third largest hurricane of record,** Hurricane Beulah moved inland near the mouth of the Rio Grande on the 20th. Wind gusts of 136 miles per hour were reported during Beulah's passage. Rains 10 to 20 inches over much of the area **south of San Antonio** resulted in record-breaking floods. An unofficial gaging station at **Falfurrias** registered the highest accumulated rainfall, 36 inches. The resultant stream overflow and surface runoff inundated 1.4 million acres. Beulah spawned 115 tornadoes, all in Texas, the **greatest number of tornadoes on record for any hurricane.** Hurricane Beulah caused 13 deaths and 37 injuries, of which five deaths and

34 injuries were attributed to tornadoes. Property losses were estimated at $100 million and crop losses at $50 million.

**April 18, 1970: Tornado.** Near **Clarendon**, Donley County. Seventeen killed, 42 injured; damage $2,100,000. Fourteen persons were killed at a resort community at Green Belt Reservoir, 7 miles north of Clarendon.

**May 11, 1970: Tornado. Lubbock**, Lubbock County. Twenty-six killed, 500 injured; damage $135 million. Fifteen square miles, almost one-quarter of the city of Lubbock, suffered damage.

**Aug. 3-5, 1970: Hurricane Celia. Corpus Christi.** Hurricane Celia was a unique but severe storm. Measured in dollars, it was **the costliest in the state's history to that time.** Sustained wind speeds reached 130 miles per hour, but it was great bursts of kinetic energy of short duration that appeared to cause the severe damage. Wind gusts of 161 miles per hour were measured at the **Corpus Christi** National Weather Service Office. At **Aransas Pass**, peak wind gusts were estimated as high as 180 miles per hour, after the wind equipment had been blown away. Celia caused 11 deaths in Texas, at least 466 injuries, and total property and crop damage in Texas estimated at $453,773,000. Hurricane Celia crossed the Texas coastline midway between Corpus Christi and Aransas Pass about 3:30 p.m. CST on Aug. 3. Hardest hit was the metropolitan area of **Corpus Christi**, including **Robstown, Aransas Pass, Port Aransas** and small towns on the north side of Corpus Christi Bay.

**Feb. 20-22, 1971: Blizzard. Panhandle.** Paralyzing blizzard, worst since March 22-25, 1957, storm transformed Panhandle into one vast snowfield as six to 26 inches of snow were whipped by 40 to 60 miles per hour winds into drifts up to 12 feet high. At **Follett**, three-day snowfall was 26 inches. Three persons killed; property and livestock losses were $3.1 million.

**Sept. 9-13, 1971: Hurricane Fern. Coastal Bend.** Ten to 26 inches of rain resulted in some of worst flooding since Hurricane Beulah in 1967. Two persons killed; losses were $30,231,000.

**May 11-12, 1972: Rainstorm. South Central Texas.** Seventeen drowned at **New Braunfels**, one at **McQueeney.** New Braunfels and **Seguin** hardest hit. Property damage $17.5 million.

**June 12-13, 1973: Rainstorm. Southeastern Texas.** Ten drowned. Over $50 million in property and crop damage. From 10-15 inches of rain recorded.

**Nov. 23-24, 1974: Flash Flooding. Central Texas.** Over $1 million in property damage. Thirteen people killed, ten in **Travis County.**

**Jan. 31-Feb. 1, 1975: Flooding. Nacogdoches County.** Widespread heavy rain caused flash flooding here, resulting in three deaths; damage over $5.5 million.

**May 23, 1975: Rainstorm. Austin** area. Heavy rains, high winds and hail resulted in over $5 million property damage; 40 people injured. Four deaths were caused by drowning.

**June 15, 1976: Rainstorm. Harris County.** Rains in excess of 13 inches caused damage estimated at near $25 million. Eight deaths were storm-related, including three drownings.

**Aug. 1-4, 1978: Heavy Rains, Flooding. Edwards Plateau, Low Rolling Plains.** Remnants of **Tropical Storm Amelia** caused some of the worst flooding of this century. As much as 30 inches of rain fell near **Albany** in Shackelford County, where six drownings were reported. Bandera, Kerr, Kendall and Gillespie counties were hit hard, as 27 people drowned and the damage total was at least $50 million.

**Dec. 30-31, 1978: Ice Storm. North Central Texas.** Possibly the **worst ice storm in 30 years** hit Dallas County particularly hard. Damage estimates reached $14 million, and six deaths were storm-related.

**April 10, 1979: The worst single tornado in Texas' history** hit **Wichita Falls.** Earlier on the same day, **several tornadoes** hit farther west. The destruction in Wichita Falls resulted in 42 dead, 1,740 injured, over 3,000 homes destroyed and damage of approximately $400 million. An estimated 20,000 persons were left homeless by this storm. In all, the tornadoes on April 10 killed 53 people, injured 1,812 and caused over $500 million damages.

**May 3, 1979: Thunderstorms. Dallas County** was hit by a wave of the most destructive thunderstorms in many years; 37 injuries and $5 million in damages resulted.

**July 25-26, 1979: Tropical storm Claudette** caused over $750 million in property and crop damages, but fortunately only few injuries. Near **Alvin**, an estimated 43 inches of rain fell, a new state record for 24 hours.

**Aug. 24, 1979:** One of the worst **hailstorms** in West Texas in the past 100 years; $200 million in crops, mostly cotton, destroyed.

**Sept. 18-20, 1979: Coastal flooding** from heavy rain, 18 inches in 24 hours at **Aransas Pass**, and 13 inches at **Rockport**.

**Aug. 9-11, 1980: Hurricane Allen** hit **South Texas** and left three dead, causing $650 million-$750 million in property and crop damages. Over 250,000 coastal residents had to be evacuated. The worst damage occurred along **Padre Island** and in **Corpus Christi**. Over 20 inches of rain fell in **extreme South Texas**, and 29 tornadoes occurred; one of the worst hurricane-related outbreaks.

**Summer 1980: One of the hottest summers** in rhe history of the Lone Star State.

**Sept. 5-8, 1980: Hurricane Danielle** brought **rain and flooding** to both **Southeast and Central Texas**. Seventeen inches of rain fell at **Port Arthur**, and 25 inches near **Junction**.

**May 24-25, 1981: Severe flooding** in **Austin** claimed 13 lives, injured about 100 and caused $40 million in damages. Up to 5.5 inches of rain fell in one hour just west of the city.

**Oct. 11-14, 1981: Record rains** in North Central Texas caused by the remains of **Pacific Hurricane Norma.** Over 20 inches fell in some locations.

**April 2, 1982: A tornado outbreak in Northeast Texas.** The most severe tornado struck **Paris**; 10 people were killed, 170 injured and 1,000 left homeless. Over $50 million in damages resulted. A total of 7 tornadoes that day left 11 dead and 174 injured.

**May, 1982:** Texas recorded **123 tornadoes**, the most ever in May, and one less than the most recorded in any single month in the state. One death and 23 injuries occurred.

**Dec. 1982: Heavy snow.** El Paso recorded 18.2 inches of snow, the most in any month there.

**Aug. 15-21, 1983: Hurricane Alicia** was the first hurricane to make landfall in the continental U.S. in three years (Aug. 18), and **one of the costliest in Texas history** ($3 billion). Alicia caused widespread damage to a large section of **Southeast Texas**, including coastal areas near **Galveston** and the entire **Houston** area. Alicia spawned 22 tornadoes, and highest winds were estimated near 130 mph. In all, 18 people in South Texas were killed and 1,800 injured as a result of the tropical storm.

**Jan. 12-13, 1985: A record-breaking snowstorm** struck **West and South Central Texas** with up to 15 inches of snow that fell at many locations **between San Antonio and the Rio Grande**. San Antonio recorded 13.2 inches of snow for Jan. 12 (the greatest in a day) and 13.5 inches for the two-day total. **Eagle Pass** reported 14.5 inches of snow.

**June 26, 1986: Hurricane Bonnie** made landfall between **High Island and Sabine Pass** around 3:45 a.m. The highest wind measured in the area was a gust to 97 m.p.h., which was recorded at the **Sea Rim State Park.** As much as 13 inches of rain fell in **Ace** in southern Polk County. There were several reports of funnel clouds, but no confirmed tornadoes. While the storm caused no major structural damage, there was widespread minor damage. Numerous injuries were reported.

**May 22, 1987:** A strong, **multiple-vortex tornado** struck the town of **Saragosa**, Reeves Co.), essentially wiping it off the map. Of the town's 183 inhabitants, 30 were killed and 121 were injured. Eight-five percent of the town's structures were completely destroyed, while total damage topped $1.3 million.

**October 15-19, 1994: Extreme amounts of rainfall**, up to 28.90 inches over a 4-day period, fell throughout southeastern part of the state. Seventeen lives were lost, most of them victims of flash flooding. Many rivers reached record flood levels. **Houston** was cut off from many other parts of the state, as numerous roads, including Interstate 10, were under water. Damage was estimated to be near $700 million; 26 counties were declared disaster areas.

**May 5, 1995:** A thunderstorm moved across the **Dallas/Fort Worth** area with 70 mph wind gusts and rainfall rates of almost three inches in 30 minutes (five inches in one hour). Twenty people lost their lives as a result of this storm, 109 people were injured by large hail and, with more than $2 billion in damage, the National Oceanic and Atmospheric Administration dubbed it the **"costliest thunderstorm event in history."**

**May 28, 1995:** A supercell thunderstorm produced extreme winds and giant hail in **San Angelo**, injuring at least 80 people and causing about $120 million in damage. Sixty-one homes were destroyed, and more than 9,000 were slightly damaged. In some areas, hail was six inches deep, with drifts to two feet.

**February 21, 1996:** Anomalously **high temperatures** were reported over the **entire state**, breaking records in nearly every region of the state. Temperatures near 100°F shattered previous records by as many as 10°F as Texans experienced heat more characteristic of mid-summer than winter.

**May 10, 1996:** Hail up to five inches in diameter fell in **Howard County**, causing injuries to 48 people and $30 million worth of property damage.

**May 27, 1997:** A half-mile-wide **F5 tornado** struck **Jarrell**, Williamson Co., leveling the Double Creek subdivision, claiming 27 lives, injuring 12 others, and causing more than $40 million in dam-

age.

**March-May, 1998:** According to the Climate Prediction Center, this three-month period ranks as the **seventh driest** for a region including Texas, Oklahoma, Arkansas, Louisiana and Mississippi. May 1998 has been ranked as both the **warmest and the driest May** that this region has ever seen.

**August 22-25, 1998: Tropical Storm Charley** brought torrential rains and flash floods to the **Hill Country**. Thirteen people lost their lives and more than 200 were injured.

**October 17-19, 1998: A massive and devastating flood** set all-time records for rainfall and river levels, resulted in the deaths of 25 people, injured more than 2,000 others, and caused more than $500 million damage from the **Hill Country to the counties surrounding San Antonio to the south and east.**

**January 22, 1999:** Golf ball- and softball-sized **hail** fell in the **Bryan/College Station** area, resulting in $10 million in damage to cars, homes and offices.

**May 1999:** Numerous severe weather outbreaks caused **damaging winds, large hail, dangerous lightning, and numerous tornadoes.** An F3 tornado moved through **De Kalb's** downtown area and high

*Floodwaters wash out a road in Concan in Uvalde County after excessive rains inundated the area in late June and early July 2002. File photo.*

school on the 4th, injuring 22 people and causing $125 million to the community. On the same day, **two F2 tornadoes** roared through **Kilgore** simultaneously. On the 11th, an **F4 tornado** moved through parts of **Loyal Valley**, taking the life of one and injuring six. The 25th saw storms produce **2.5-inch hail** in **Levelland** and **Amarillo.** The total cost of damages caused by May storms was more than $157 million.

**August 1999:** Excessive heat throughout the month resulted in 16 fatalities in the **Dallas/Fort Worth** area. The airport reported 26 consecutive days of 100°F or greater temperatures.

**January-October 2000:** A severe drought plagued **most of Texas.** Some regions experienced little to no rain for several months during the summer. Abilene saw no rain for 72 consecutive days, while **Dallas** had **no rain for 84 consecutive days** during the summer. During July, aquifers hit all-time lows, and lakes and streams fell to critical levels. Most regions had to cut back or stop agricultural activities because of the drought, which resulted in $515 million in agricultural loss, according to USDA figures.

**March 28, 2000:** A supercell over **Fort Worth** produced an F3 tornado, which injured 80 people and caused significant damage. Flooding claimed the lives of two people.

**May 20, 2000:** A flash flood in the **Liberty** and **Dayton** area was caused by 18.3 inches of rain's falling in five hours. Up to 80 people had to be rescued from the flood waters; property damage totalled an estimated $10 million.

**July 2000:** Excessive heat resulted from a high-pressure ridge, particularly from the 12th to the 21st. **Dallas/Fort Worth** airport reported a **10-day average of 103.3°F. College Station** had **12 consecutive days of 100°F or greater** temperatures. The heat caused 34 deaths in North and Southeast Texas, primarily among the elderly.

**August 2, 2000: Lightning** struck a tree at Astroworld in **Houston** injuring 17 teens.

**September 5, 2000: Excessive heat** resulted in at least eight **all-time high temperature records** around the state, one of which was **Possum Kingdom Lake,** which reached 114°F. This day is being regarded as the **hottest day ever in Texas, considering the state as a whole.**.

**December 13 and 24-25, 2000:** Two major winter storms blanketed **Northeast Texas** with up to six inches of ice from each storm. Eight inches of snow fell in the **Panhandle,** while areas in North Texas received 12 inches. Thousands of motorists were stranded on Interstate 20 and had to be rescued by the National Guard; 235,000 people lost electric service from the first storm alone. Roads were treacherous, driving was halted in several counties, and the total cost of damages from both storms reached more than $156 million.

**January 1–31, 2001:** The U.S. Department of Agriculture Farm Service Agency received a **Presidential Disaster Declaration** in December 2000 because of **persistent drought** conditions in **deep Southern Texas;** $125 million in damage was reported in the region.

**May 2001:** May is typically a month of extreme weather, and May 2001 was not exception, with numerous storms causing excessive damage. **Four-inch hail** caused nearly $150 million in damages in **San Antonio** on the 6th. On the 30th, supercell **thunderstorms** in the **High Plains** region produced winds over 100 mph and golf-ball- sized hail caused more than $186 million in damage. All told, storms caused 36 injuries and more than $358 million in damage to property and agriculture.

**June–December 2001: Significant drought-like conditions** occurred in Texas from early summer through December. After the yearly drought report was filed, it was determined that the total crop damage across the South Plains region was about $420 million. Consequential losses occurred to crops such as cotton, wheat, grain sorghum and corn.

**June 5–10, 2001: Tropical Storm Allison** hit the **Houston** area, which dumped large amounts of rain on the city. The storm made landfall on the western end of **Galveston Island** and over the next five days produced record rainfall. These amazing amounts of precipitation led to devastating flooding across southeastern Texas. Some weather stations in the Houston area reported more than 40 inches of rain total and more than 18 inches in a 24-hour period. Twenty-two deaths and $5.2 billion in damage resulted.

**July–August 2001: Excessive heat** plagued Texas during July and August, which resulted in 17 deaths in the Houston area.

**October 12, 2001: An F2 tornado** in **Hondo** caused $20 million in damage. The tornado injured 25 people and damaged the Hondo Airport and the National Guard Armory. A large hangar and nearly two dozen aircraft were destroyed at the airport. The armory's roofs and concrete walls were damaged. Nearly 150 homes in Hondo and 50 on its outskirts were damaged, and nearly 100 mobile homes were damaged.

**November 15, 2001:** Storms caused **flash flooding** and some weak **tornadoes** in the Edwards Plateau, South Central and southern portions of North Central regions. Flash flooding caused 8 deaths and 198 injuries.

**March 2002:** Several **violent storms** occurred, which produced hail, tornadoes and strong winds. Hail 1-3/4 inches in diameter caused $16 million in damage to **San Angelo** on the 19th, while 30 people where injured on the same day by an **F2 tornado** in **Somerset** that also caused $2 million in damage. For the month, there were three fatalities, 64 injuries and more than $37.5 million in damage.

**June 30–July 7, 2002: Excessive rainfall** occurred in the **South Central** and **Edwards Plateau** regions, with some areas reporting more than 30 inches of rain. In the South Central region alone nearly $250 million dollars worth of damage was reported from this significant weather event. In central Texas, 29 counties were devastated by the flooding and declared federal disaster areas by President George W. Bush. The total event damage was estimated at more than $2 billion.

**September 5–7, 2002: Tropical Storm Fay** made landfall along the southeast Texas coast on the 6th. This system produced extremely heavy rainfall, strong damaging wind gusts and tornadoes. Ten to 20 inches of rain fell in eastern **Wharton County. Brazoria County** was hit the hardest from this system with about 1,500 homes flooded. Tropical Storm Fay produced five tornadoes, flooded many areas and caused significant wind damage. Damage of $4.5 million was reported.

**October 24, 2002:** Severe **thunderstorms** in south Texas and produced heavy rain, causing flooding and two tornadoes in **Corpus Christi.** The most extensive damage occurred across **Del Mar College.** The storm caused one death, 26 injuries and Total storm damages exceeded more then $85 million in damage. ☆

# How Hot Does It Feel?

In the 40-year period from 1936 to 1975, nearly 20,000 people were killed in the United States by the effects of excessive heat. The overall effect of excessive heat on the body is known as heat stress. Major factors contributing to heat stress are air temperature; humidity; air movement; radiant heat from solar radiation, bright lights, stove or other source; atmospheric pressure; physiological factors which vary among people; physical activity; and clothing.

Of the above factors, temperature and humidity can be controlled by air conditioning. Air movement may be controlled by fans; even a slight breeze is usually effective in reducing heat stress in hot, muggy weather.

However, at very high temperatures (above normal body temperature of about 98.6 °F.), winds above 10 miles per hour can increase heat stress in a shaded area by adding more heat to the body, whereas when the body is exposed to direct sunlight the effect of wind is nearly always to reduce heat stress. Radiant heating can be mitigated by shielding or by moving away from the source (for example, seeking shade). Atmospheric pressure is not usually a significant factor. However, at very high elevations, decreased pressure (and therefore decreased air supply) can contribute to heat exhaustion.

## General Heat Stress Index

| Danger Category | Apparent Temperature (°F) | Heat Syndrome |
|---|---|---|
| 1. Caution | 80°-90° | Fatigue possible with prolonged exposure and physical activity. |
| 2. Extreme Caution | 90°-105° | Sunstroke, heat cramps and heat; exhaustion possible with prolonged exposure and physical activity. |
| 3. Danger | 105°-130° | Sunstroke, heat cramps or heat exhaustion likely. Heatstroke possible with prolonged exposure and physical activity. |
| 4. Extreme Danger | Greater than 130° | Heatstroke or sunstroke imminent. |

Note: Degree of heat stress may vary with age, health and body characteristics.

## Heat Discomfort Chart

| Actual Thermometer Reading (°F) | Relative Humidity (%) | | | | | | | | | | |
|---|---|---|---|---|---|---|---|---|---|---|---|
| | 0 | 10 | 20 | 30 | 40 | 50 | 60 | 70 | 80 | 90 | 100 |
| | Apparent Temperature (°F) | | | | | | | | | | |
| 70 | 64.8 | 65.6 | 66.4 | 67.3 | 68.1 | 68.8 | 69.6 | 70.4 | 71.1 | 71.8 | 72.5 |
| 75 | 70.1 | 71.2 | 72.1 | 73.0 | 73.7 | 74.6 | 75.3 | 76.1 | 77.1 | 78.2 | 79.2 |
| 80 | 75.6 | 76.6 | 77.5 | 78.4 | 79.4 | 80.5 | 81.7 | 83.0 | 84.7 | 86.4 | 88.3 |
| 85 | 79.9 | 81.0 | 82.2 | 83.6 | 85.0 | 86.7 | 88.7 | 91.0 | 93.7 | 96.8 | 100.6 |
| 90 | 84.0 | 85.5 | 87.1 | 89.0 | 91.2 | 94.1 | 97.0 | 101.0 | 105.4 | 110.8 | |
| 95 | 88.0 | 90.0 | 92.4 | 95.3 | 98.4 | 102.6 | 107.4 | 113.9 | | | |
| 100 | 91.8 | 94.6 | 97.8 | 101.7 | 106.6 | 112.7 | 120.4 | | | | |

| | Relative Humidity (%) | | | | | | | | | | |
|---|---|---|---|---|---|---|---|---|---|---|---|
| | 0 | 5 | 10 | 15 | 20 | 25 | 30 | 35 | 40 | 45 | 50 |
| 105 | 95.8 | 97.5 | 99.4 | 101.5 | 103.8 | 106.4 | 109.3 | 112.4 | 116.5 | 121.1 | 126.0 |
| 110 | 99.7 | 101.9 | 104.2 | 107.0 | 110.3 | 113.8 | 118.0 | 121.8 | 128.6 | | |
| 115 | 103.6 | 106.4 | 109.6 | 113.3 | 117.6 | 122.6 | 128.4 | | | | |
| 120 | 107.4 | 111.1 | 115.2 | 120.1 | 125.7 | 132.2 | | | | | |

The table above was devised by Dr. Robert G. Steadman, Texas Tech University, and was furnished to the Texas Almanac by NOAA.

# How Cold Does It Feel?

## Calculating Wind Chill

Many factors enter into the feeling of coolness or extreme cold, the temperature and wind speed being most important.

The table at right was revised by the National Weather Service's Office of Climate, Water and Weather Services in November 2001.

Thermometer readings are listed in boldface type across the top of the chart; the wind speeds are shown in boldface type down the left side. To determine how chilly it really feels, find the proper column for each.

Note the figure where they cross. For example, if the temperature is 20 and the wind speed is 15 miles per hour, the perceived temperature is 6° above zero.

### Wind Chill Chart

| Wind (mph) | Actual Temperature Reading (°F) | | | | | | | | | | | | |
|---|---|---|---|---|---|---|---|---|---|---|---|---|---|
| Calm | 40 | 35 | 30 | 25 | 20 | 15 | 10 | 5 | 0 | -5 | -10 | -15 | -20 |
| 5 | 36 | 31 | 25 | 19 | 13 | 7 | 1 | -5 | -11 | -16 | -22 | -28 | -34 |
| 10 | 34 | 27 | 21 | 15 | 9 | 3 | -4 | -10 | -16 | -22 | -28 | -35 | -41 |
| 15 | 32 | 25 | 19 | 13 | 6 | 0 | -7 | -13 | -19 | -26 | -32 | -39 | -45 |
| 20 | 30 | 24 | 17 | 11 | 4 | -2 | -9 | -15 | -22 | -29 | -35 | -42 | -48 |
| 25 | 29 | 23 | 16 | 9 | 3 | -4 | -11 | -17 | -24 | -31 | -37 | -44 | -51 |
| 30 | 28 | 22 | 15 | 8 | 1 | -5 | -12 | -19 | -26 | -33 | -39 | -46 | -53 |
| 35 | 28 | 21 | 14 | 7 | 0 | -7 | -14 | -21 | -27 | -34 | -41 | -48 | -55 |
| 40 | 27 | 20 | 13 | 6 | -1 | -8 | -15 | -22 | -29 | -36 | -43 | -50 | -57 |
| 45 | 26 | 19 | 12 | 5 | -2 | -9 | -16 | -23 | -30 | -37 | -44 | -51 | -58 |
| 50 | 26 | 19 | 12 | 4 | -3 | -10 | -17 | -24 | -31 | -38 | -45 | -52 | -60 |
| 55 | 25 | 18 | 11 | 4 | -3 | -11 | -18 | -25 | -32 | -39 | -46 | -54 | -61 |
| 60 | 25 | 17 | 10 | 3 | -4 | -11 | -19 | -26 | -33 | -40 | -48 | -55 | -62 |

# Texas Temperature, Freeze, Growing Season and Precipitation Records by Counties

Data in the table below are from the office of the State Climatologist for Texas, College Station. Because of the small change in averages, data are revised only at intervals of 10 years. Data below are the latest compilations, as of Jan. 1, 1993. Table shows temperature, freeze, growing season and precipitation for each county in Texas. Data for counties where a National Weather Service Station has not been maintained long enough to establish a reliable mean are interpolated from isoline charts prepared from mean values from stations with long-established records. Mean maximum temperature for July is computed from the sum of the daily maxima. Mean minimum January is computed from the sum of the daily minima. For stations where precipitation "Length of Record" are designated with an "N", data are based on the 30-year normal period 1961-90. Stations which have a specified precipitation "Length of Record" are based on data mainly from the period 1931-1993.

| County and Station | Temp. Length of Record (Yr.) | Mean Max. July (F.) | Mean Min. January (F.) | Record Highest (F.) | Record Lowest (F.) | Last in Spring | First in Fall | Growing Season Days | Length of Record (Yr.) | Jan. (In.) | Feb. (In.) | Mar. (In.) | Apr. (In.) | May (In.) | June (In.) | July (In.) | Aug. (In.) | Sept. (In.) | Oct. (In.) | Nov. (In.) | Dec. (In.) | Annual (In.) |
|---|---|---|---|---|---|---|---|---|---|---|---|---|---|---|---|---|---|---|---|---|---|---|
| Anderson, Palestine | N | 94 | 36 | 114 | -6 | Mar. 8 | Nov. 27 | 264 | 29 | 3.1 | 3.2 | 3.9 | 3.9 | 4.8 | 4.5 | 2.3 | 2.3 | 3.6 | 4.4 | 3.9 | 3.6 | 43.3 |
| Andrews, Andrews | 29 | 94 | 29 | 113 | 0 | Apr. 6 | Nov. 5 | 213 | 29 | 0.4 | 0.5 | 0.6 | 0.9 | 1.6 | 2.0 | 2.5 | 1.9 | 2.5 | 1.5 | 0.6 | 0.4 | 15.4 |
| Angelina, Lufkin | N | 93 | 37 | 108 | 5 | Mar. 14 | Nov. 13 | 244 | N | 3.7 | 2.8 | 3.2 | 3.3 | 4.9 | 4.2 | 2.6 | 2.4 | 4.0 | 3.5 | 3.1 | 2.3 | 38.9 |
| Aransas, Rockport | N | 91 | 44 | 103 | 9 | Feb. 7 | Dec. 16 | 312 | N | 2.0 | 2.4 | 2.0 | 2.1 | 4.2 | 4.7 | 3.2 | 3.1 | 6.2 | 4.0 | 2.1 | 2.7 | 36.9 |
| Archer, Archer City | 27 | 98 | 29 | 114 | -10 | Mar. 31 | Nov. 6 | 220 | N | 1.0 | 1.7 | 2.0 | 2.6 | 4.3 | 3.0 | 1.7 | 2.5 | 4.3 | 2.9 | 1.8 | 1.3 | 29.3 |
| Armstrong, Claude | 28 | 92 | 20 | 108 | -7 | Apr. 6 | Nov. 5 | 213 | N | 0.4 | 0.6 | 1.1 | 1.1 | 3.0 | 3.7 | 2.9 | 3.1 | 2.4 | 1.7 | 0.8 | 0.4 | 21.2 |
| Atascosa, Poteet | N | 96 | 38 | 110 | -1 | Feb. 25 | Dec. 2 | 282 | N | 1.4 | 1.7 | 1.2 | 2.5 | 4.0 | 3.2 | 1.8 | 3.2 | 3.6 | 3.9 | 1.8 | 1.4 | 28.0 |
| Austin, Sealy | N | 94 | 39 | 110 | -1 | Feb. 27 | Dec. 2 | 282 | N | 3.0 | 2.9 | 2.6 | 2.7 | 4.8 | 4.4 | 2.3 | 3.2 | 4.6 | 3.9 | 3.6 | 1.4 | 40.4 |
| Bailey, Muleshoe | 15 | 92 | 19 | 112 | -21 | Apr. 22 | Oct. 20 | 181 | N | 0.4 | 0.5 | 0.6 | 0.9 | 1.9 | 2.6 | 2.8 | 2.6 | 1.4 | 1.4 | 0.8 | 0.5 | 16.8 |
| Bandera, Medina | N | 94 | 31 | 109 | 5 | Mar. 26 | Nov. 16 | 235 | N | 1.7 | 1.8 | 2.2 | 3.3 | 4.5 | 2.9 | 2.1 | 2.9 | 3.7 | 3.7 | 2.3 | 3.0 | 35.1 |
| Bastrop, Smithville | N | 95 | 35 | 111 | -14 | Mar. 7 | Nov. 30 | 268 | N | 1.8 | 2.5 | 2.2 | 2.9 | 5.1 | 3.9 | 2.1 | 4.7 | 4.5 | 4.0 | 3.7 | 0.5 | 38.3 |
| Baylor, Seymour | N | 97 | 26 | 116 | 9 | Apr. 22 | Nov. 3 | 214 | 15 | 0.9 | 1.6 | 1.6 | 2.2 | 4.0 | 3.4 | 2.1 | 2.3 | 4.7 | 2.7 | 2.3 | 1.2 | 27.3 |
| Bee, Beeville | N | 94 | 41 | 109 | -4 | Feb. 2 | Dec. 4 | 285 | N | 2.0 | 1.9 | 2.2 | 2.3 | 3.6 | 3.8 | 2.8 | 2.4 | 4.7 | 4.1 | 3.2 | 2.6 | 32.1 |
| Bell, Temple | N | 95 | 35 | 112 | 0 | Mar. 9 | Nov. 24 | 260 | N | 1.9 | 2.7 | 2.5 | 2.9 | 4.6 | 3.6 | 2.0 | 2.3 | 4.1 | 2.7 | 1.3 | 1.2 | 34.9 |
| Bexar, San Antonio | N | 95 | 38 | 108 | -6 | Mar. 6 | Nov. 26 | 265 | N | 1.7 | 1.8 | 1.5 | 2.5 | 4.2 | 3.8 | 2.2 | 2.5 | 4.8 | 3.3 | 2.0 | 1.6 | 31.0 |
| Blanco, Blanco | N | 94 | 31 | 109 | -1 | Mar. 26 | Nov. 15 | 234 | N | 1.9 | 2.4 | 2.2 | 2.8 | 4.5 | 3.8 | 2.3 | 2.3 | 3.8 | 3.2 | 2.9 | 2.3 | 34.2 |
| Borden, Gail | 27 | 94 | 31 | 113 | -3 | Apr. 23 | Nov. 6 | 214 | N | 0.5 | 0.6 | 1.5 | 0.5 | 1.2 | 2.2 | 2.7 | 3.0 | 3.3 | 1.5 | 1.5 | 0.5 | 16.9 |
| Bosque, Lake Whitney | 18 | 97 | 33 | 111 | -6 | Mar. 21 | Nov. 21 | 243 | 18 | 1.9 | 2.3 | 2.2 | 2.9 | 4.4 | 3.5 | 1.6 | 2.7 | 3.9 | 2.7 | 2.9 | 2.0 | 31.6 |
| Bowie, Texarkana | N | 93 | 35 | 101 | -3 | Mar. 5 | Nov. 11 | 235 | N | 3.6 | 3.3 | 4.2 | 5.1 | 4.4 | 3.9 | 3.5 | 3.2 | 3.3 | 2.8 | 3.9 | 3.9 | 45.3 |
| Brazoria, Angleton | N | 92 | 41 | 105 | -3 | Mar. 1 | Nov. 28 | 268 | N | 4.5 | 3.6 | 3.3 | 3.2 | 5.2 | 6.3 | 5.2 | 5.1 | 7.3 | 4.0 | 3.9 | 4.1 | 56.4 |
| Brazos, College Station | N | 94 | 39 | 110 | -9 | Mar. 1 | Nov. 30 | 274 | N | 2.7 | 2.6 | 2.6 | 3.4 | 4.8 | 3.7 | 2.7 | 2.6 | 3.3 | 3.8 | 4.7 | 2.8 | 39.1 |
| Brewster, Alpine | N | 89 | 30 | 106 | -6 | Apr. 8 | Nov. 8 | 223 | N | 0.6 | 0.6 | 0.4 | 0.6 | 1.2 | 2.3 | 2.2 | 3.0 | 2.7 | 1.5 | 0.6 | 0.5 | 16.9 |
| Brewster, Chisos Basin | N | 85 | 35 | 103 | 3 | Mar. 31 | Nov. 9 | 223 | N | 0.4 | 0.5 | 0.4 | 0.6 | 2.8 | 4.2 | 2.2 | 2.5 | 4.9 | 1.9 | 0.6 | 0.6 | 19.2 |
| Briscoe, Silverton | N | 91 | 20 | 109 | -4 | Apr. 10 | Nov. 5 | 214 | N | 0.5 | 0.7 | 1.1 | 1.3 | 3.2 | 3.2 | 3.1 | 2.1 | 3.3 | 1.6 | 0.9 | 0.5 | 21.4 |
| Brooks, Falfurrias | 29 | 97 | 43 | 111 | -3 | Feb. 22 | Dec. 10 | 303 | 29 | 1.3 | 1.6 | 0.7 | 1.3 | 3.6 | 3.4 | 2.2 | 2.4 | 4.9 | 2.7 | 1.2 | 1.1 | 25.9 |
| Brown, Brownwood | N | 97 | 33 | 111 | 11 | Mar. 1 | Nov. 19 | 242 | N | 1.3 | 1.7 | 1.9 | 2.6 | 5.1 | 3.6 | 1.7 | 2.0 | 3.5 | 2.9 | 1.6 | 1.4 | 27.3 |
| Burleson, Somerville | N | 93 | 37 | 105 | -8 | Mar. 27 | Nov. 14 | 275 | 16 | 2.7 | 2.0 | 2.4 | 3.9 | 4.8 | 4.4 | 2.2 | 3.3 | 4.9 | 3.4 | 3.1 | 2.8 | 39.1 |
| Burnet, Burnet | 16 | 93 | 32 | 108 | -4 | Mar. 19 | Nov. 29 | 230 | N | 1.7 | 2.2 | 2.1 | 2.7 | 4.8 | 3.5 | 2.2 | 2.1 | 4.9 | 3.5 | 2.1 | 1.5 | 31.2 |
| Caldwell, Luling | N | 96 | 36 | 110 | -3 | Feb. 28 | Dec. 16 | 275 | N | 2.2 | 2.2 | 1.9 | 3.0 | 4.8 | 4.4 | 1.7 | 3.3 | 6.1 | 3.5 | 3.1 | 1.9 | 35.3 |
| Calhoun, Port O'Connor | N | 90 | 46 | 107 | 11 | Mar. 4 | Nov. 12 | 300 | 16 | 3.1 | 2.7 | 1.6 | 1.7 | 4.0 | 3.7 | 3.7 | 2.1 | 3.1 | 3.5 | 2.7 | 2.4 | 39.4 |
| Callahan, Putnam | 27 | 96 | 32 | 110 | -8 | Mar. 21 | Nov. 14 | 228 | N | 1.4 | 1.4 | 1.7 | 2.0 | 3.0 | 2.7 | 1.8 | 2.8 | 6.0 | 2.9 | 1.7 | 1.1 | 25.2 |
| Cameron, Brownsville | N | 93 | 50 | 106 | 16 | Feb. 17 | Dec. 12 | 341 | 27 | 1.6 | 1.1 | 0.5 | 1.6 | 2.9 | 3.4 | 1.9 | 2.2 | 4.0 | 2.8 | 1.5 | 1.3 | 26.6 |
| Camp, Pittsburg | N | 93 | 33 | 106 | -10 | Mar. 14 | Nov. 14 | 238 | N | 2.9 | 3.3 | 3.8 | 5.4 | 4.8 | 3.7 | 2.7 | 3.1 | 2.3 | 3.2 | 4.0 | 3.5 | 43.3 |
| Carson, Panhandle | 29 | 93 | 22 | 109 | -8 | Apr. 17 | Oct. 25 | 191 | N | 0.5 | 0.8 | 1.1 | 1.3 | 2.6 | 3.7 | 2.9 | 2.2 | 1.7 | 1.7 | 0.9 | 0.5 | 20.8 |
| Cass, Linden | 29 | 93 | 31 | 103 | -10 | Mar. 19 | Nov. 11 | 237 | N | 3.3 | 3.9 | 4.9 | 5.0 | 4.5 | 4.8 | 2.9 | 3.1 | 3.2 | 3.6 | 4.9 | 4.5 | 48.3 |
| Castro, Dimmitt | N | 91 | 19 | 107 | -8 | Apr. 17 | Oct. 25 | 193 | N | 0.4 | 0.6 | 0.8 | 0.8 | 2.3 | 3.0 | 2.3 | 2.8 | 2.4 | 1.5 | 0.7 | 0.5 | 18.0 |
| Chambers, Anahuac | N | 92 | 41 | 110 | 8 | Mar. 6 | Nov. 20 | 261 | 22 | 4.0 | 2.9 | 3.0 | 3.6 | 4.8 | 5.8 | 4.5 | 4.5 | 6.2 | 3.8 | 4.4 | 4.2 | 51.7 |

| County and Station | Length of Record (Yr.) | July Mean Max. (F.) | January Mean Min. (F.) | Record Highest (F.) | Record Lowest (F.) | Last in Spring Mo. | Last in Spring Day | First in Fall Mo. | First in Fall Day | Growing Season (Days) | Length of Record (Yr.) | January (In.) | February (In.) | March (In.) | April (In.) | May (In.) | June (In.) | July (In.) | August (In.) | September (In.) | October (In.) | November (In.) | December (In.) | Annual (In.) |
|---|---|---|---|---|---|---|---|---|---|---|---|---|---|---|---|---|---|---|---|---|---|---|---|---|
| Cherokee, Rusk | N | 93 | 35 | 107 |  | Mar. | 8 | Nov. | 21 | 258 | N | 3.7 | 3.5 | 3.6 | 4.1 | 4.0 | 5.1 | 4.0 | 2.9 | 2.2 | 4.2 | 4.2 | 4.2 | 46.1 |
| Childress, Childress | N | 96 | 26 | 117 | -7 | Mar. | 3 | Nov. | 6 | 217 | N | 0.5 | 0.9 | 1.2 | 1.5 | 3.0 | 3.0 | 1.9 | 2.1 | 2.8 | 2.0 | 1.0 | 0.7 | 20.7 |
| Clay, Henrietta | N | 97 | 26 | 116 | -8 | Mar. | 27 | Nov. | 14 | 232 | N | 1.3 | 2.0 | 2.5 | 3.0 | 4.3 | 3.9 | 1.8 | 3.3 | 4.2 | 3.1 | 3.1 | 1.6 | 31.9 |
| Cochran, Morton | 27 | 91 | 22 | 110 | -12 | Apr. | 18 | Oct. | 24 | 189 | N | 0.4 | 0.6 | 0.6 | 0.9 | 1.8 | 2.7 | 2.4 | 3.3 | 4.2 | 1.7 | 0.7 | 0.5 | 18.6 |
| Coke, Robert Lee | 28 | 96 | 28 | 111 |  | Mar. | 31 | Nov. | 12 | 226 | N | 0.8 | 1.2 | 1.1 | 1.8 | 3.3 | 2.8 | 1.6 | 2.0 | 3.7 | 2.8 | 1.2 | 0.9 | 23.2 |
| Coleman, Coleman | N | 96 | 32 | 114 | -4 | Mar. | 26 | Nov. | 16 | 235 | N | 1.2 | 1.5 | 1.3 | 1.8 | 4.1 | 3.3 | 2.0 | 2.4 | 4.6 | 3.4 | 1.6 | 1.2 | 28.0 |
| Collin, McKinney | Z | 95 | 32 | 118 | -7 | Apr. | 5 | Nov. | 3 | 230 | N | 2.0 | 2.8 | 3.5 | 3.9 | 5.8 | 4.0 | 2.4 | 2.9 | 3.6 | 3.0 | 3.1 | 2.3 | 40.0 |
| Collingsworth, Wellington | N | 97 | 26 | 113 | -6 | Mar. | 1 | Dec. | 6 | 212 | N | 0.5 | 0.8 | 1.3 | 1.7 | 3.4 | 3.2 | 2.0 | 2.9 | 5.0 | 2.0 | 1.0 | 0.6 | 21.5 |
| Colorado, Columbus | 28 | 95 | 37 | 108 |  | Mar. | 12 | Nov. | 25 | 280 | N | 3.3 | 2.2 | 3.2 | 2.6 | 5.5 | 4.1 | 2.0 | 2.9 | 4.1 | 3.5 | 3.6 | 2.9 | 41.8 |
| Comal, New Braunfels | N | 95 | 37 | 110 | 2 | Mar. | 27 | Nov. | 20 | 261 | N | 1.9 | 2.2 | 1.8 | 3.1 | 5.0 | 3.4 | 2.0 | 2.5 | 4.0 | 3.5 | 2.8 | 2.0 | 34.3 |
| Comanche, Proctor Reservoir | 27 | 95 | 30 | 108 | -8 | Mar. | 29 | Nov. | 12 | 238 | N | 1.6 | 1.9 | 2.1 | 3.1 | 4.6 | 2.9 | 1.9 | 2.1 | 4.0 | 2.6 | 2.0 | 1.3 | 24.8 |
| Concho, Paint Rock | N | 98 | 31 | 111 | -1 | Mar. | 27 | Nov. | 8 | 228 | N | 1.0 | 1.3 | 1.4 | 3.2 | 3.4 | 3.5 | 2.0 | 2.4 | 4.5 | 2.4 | 1.1 | 1.1 | 20.4 |
| Cooke, Gainesville | N | 95 | 27 | 111 | -1 | Mar. | 25 | Nov. | 21 | 226 | N | 1.7 | 2.3 | 3.3 | 3.2 | 4.7 | 3.9 | 2.0 | 2.5 | 3.7 | 4.0 | 2.4 | 1.8 | 35.8 |
| Coryell, Gatesville | N | 96 | 33 | 112 |  | Apr. | 2 | Nov. | 7 | 241 | N | 1.8 | 2.0 | 2.4 | 3.1 | 4.3 | 3.9 | 2.1 | 2.2 | 3.7 | 3.1 | 3.0 | 1.8 | 32.9 |
| Cottle, Paducah | N | 96 | 25 | 112 | -6 | Mar. | 31 | Nov. | 11 | 219 | N | 0.7 | 1.0 | 2.0 | 3.1 | 3.2 | 3.4 | 1.8 | 2.5 | 3.1 | 3.1 | 1.3 | 0.8 | 22.3 |
| Crane, Crane | 28 | 97 | 31 | 118 | -7 | Apr. | 26 | Nov. | 14 | 225 | 28 | 0.4 | 0.6 | 0.4 | 0.9 | 1.7 | 2.0 | 1.6 | 1.9 | 3.0 | 1.6 | 0.7 | 0.5 | 14.8 |
| Crockett, Ozona | N | 94 | 30 | 115 | 3 | Apr. | 10 | Nov. | 2 | 233 | N | 0.5 | 0.9 | 1.2 | 1.3 | 2.3 | 3.0 | 1.6 | 3.1 | 3.3 | 2.1 | 1.0 | 0.7 | 19.2 |
| Crosby, Crosbyton | N | 93 | 23 | 109 | 4 | Apr. | 23 | Nov. | 10 | 206 | N | 0.3 | 0.9 | 0.2 | 0.3 | 2.9 | 1.4 | 2.1 | 3.1 | 3.6 | 1.3 | 0.7 | 0.7 | 22.6 |
| Culberson, Van Horn | N | 94 | 28 | 113 | -6 | Mar. | 23 | Nov. | 18 | 224 | N | 0.4 | 0.3 | 0.2 | 1.1 | 0.6 | 2.4 | 3.1 | 2.3 | 3.6 | 3.9 | 2.4 | 0.6 | 13.1 |
| Dallam, Dalhart | N | 92 | 19 | 112 | -7 | Apr. | 8 | Oct. | 13 | 178 | N | 1.8 | 0.5 | 3.2 | 1.0 | 2.6 | 2.4 | 3.1 | 2.3 | 1.8 | 1.8 | 0.7 | 0.4 | 17.9 |
| Dallas, Dallas | N | 96 | 35 | 107 | -2 | Mar. | 16 | Nov. | 13 | 235 | N | 1.8 | 2.3 | 3.2 | 3.3 | 5.0 | 3.5 | 2.4 | 1.9 | 4.1 | 3.2 | 3.2 | 1.9 | 36.1 |
| Dawson, Lamesa | N | 95 | 25 | 113 | 1 | Mar. | 25 | Oct. | 29 | 210 | N | 0.4 | 0.6 | 0.8 | 1.0 | 2.3 | 2.8 | 2.9 | 3.0 | 3.2 | 1.4 | 0.7 | 0.5 | 16.2 |
| De Witt, Yoakum | N | 95 | 39 | 114 | -12 | Feb. | 27 | Nov. | 28 | 270 | N | 2.4 | 3.1 | 2.0 | 3.3 | 4.3 | 4.5 | 1.9 | 3.1 | 2.1 | 1.4 | 3.0 | 3.0 | 37.0 |
| Deaf Smith, Hereford | N | 90 | 20 | 110 | -12 | Apr. | 4 | Oct. | 13 | 195 | N | 0.4 | 0.6 | 0.8 | 1.0 | 0.8 | 3.0 | 1.9 | 3.1 | 3.6 | 1.8 | 0.8 | 0.4 | 17.2 |
| Delta, Cooper | 15 | 94 | 30 | 108 | -17 | Mar. | 19 | Nov. | 8 | 233 | N | 2.7 | 2.9 | 3.6 | 4.8 | 5.0 | 3.9 | 2.8 | 2.2 | 4.5 | 4.0 | 3.3 | 3.4 | 42.7 |
| Denton, Denton | N | 94 | 30 | 110 | -1 | Apr. | 9 | Nov. | 7 | 226 | N | 1.3 | 2.3 | 3.0 | 3.7 | 5.3 | 3.3 | 2.0 | 3.3 | 4.5 | 4.0 | 2.6 | 2.1 | 37.3 |
| Dickens, Dickens | N | 94 | 26 | 113 | -1 | Mar. | 16 | Nov. | 11 | 217 | N | 0.5 | 0.8 | 0.8 | 1.8 | 3.2 | 2.6 | 1.3 | 3.3 | 2.9 | 1.7 | 0.7 | 0.4 | 20.7 |
| Dimmit, Carrizo Springs | 28 | 94 | 41 | 110 | -3 | Feb. | 19 | Dec. | 6 | 290 | N | 1.5 | 0.6 | 1.0 | 1.7 | 3.1 | 2.0 | 1.3 | 3.3 | 4.1 | 3.5 | 1.4 | 0.6 | 21.7 |
| Donley, Clarendon | N | 96 | 41 | 114 | 0 | Apr. | 9 | Nov. | 1 | 217 | N | 0.3 | 1.2 | 0.9 | 2.0 | 3.5 | 3.0 | 2.0 | 2.7 | 2.5 | 2.5 | 0.9 | 0.9 | 22.0 |
| Duval, Freer | N | 96 | 41 | 109 | 10 | Mar. | 6 | Nov. | 11 | 298 | N | 0.7 | 1.3 | 1.1 | 0.8 | 4.2 | 2.7 | 1.3 | 2.3 | 3.0 | 2.8 | 1.2 | 1.3 | 24.8 |
| Eastland, Rising Star | 27 | 99 | 29 | 109 | -8 | Mar. | 21 | Nov. | 11 | 299 | N | 1.5 | 1.7 | 2.1 | 2.7 | 4.2 | 3.8 | 2.1 | 2.3 | 2.5 | 3.1 | 1.3 | 1.3 | 29.7 |
| Ector, Penwell | 27 | 95 | 28 | 110 | 0 | Apr. | 12 | Nov. | 6 | 217 | 27 | 0.3 | 0.6 | 0.5 | 0.3 | 1.9 | 1.6 | 1.3 | 1.3 | 3.0 | 1.2 | 0.7 | 0.7 | 13.1 |
| Edwards, Carta Valley | N | 96 | 34 | 114 | -8 | Mar. | 20 | Nov. | 12 | 250 | N | 0.7 | 1.2 | 0.9 | 2.0 | 2.9 | 2.5 | 2.5 | 1.3 | 2.4 | 2.4 | 1.1 | 0.7 | 22.0 |
| El Paso, El Paso | N | 96 | 29 | 109 | -8 | Apr. | 13 | Nov. | 21 | 248 | N | 0.4 | 0.4 | 0.3 | 0.3 | 0.3 | 0.7 | 1.5 | 1.6 | 1.7 | 0.8 | 0.4 | 0.4 | 8.8 |
| Ellis, Waxahachie | N | 96 | 34 | 114 | -4 | Apr. | 20 | Nov. | 20 | 246 | N | 1.9 | 2.8 | 3.1 | 3.8 | 5.1 | 3.4 | 2.2 | 2.0 | 3.9 | 3.8 | 2.7 | 2.4 | 36.8 |
| Erath, Dublin | N | 96 | 36 | 112 | -7 | Apr. | 25 | Nov. | 18 | 238 | N | 1.7 | 2.1 | 2.3 | 3.2 | 4.7 | 3.5 | 2.2 | 2.8 | 3.6 | 3.3 | 2.1 | 1.6 | 32.9 |
| Falls, Marlin | N | 94 | 40 | 112 | -4 | Mar. | 10 | Nov. | 25 | 257 | N | 2.1 | 2.4 | 2.7 | 3.3 | 5.2 | 4.5 | 2.5 | 2.3 | 4.1 | 3.8 | 3.4 | 2.5 | 36.8 |
| Fannin, Bonham | N | 95 | 30 | 114 | -7 | Mar. | 2 | Nov. | 10 | 228 | N | 2.1 | 3.1 | 3.9 | 3.0 | 6.1 | 2.7 | 3.1 | 2.5 | 4.9 | 4.1 | 2.9 | 2.7 | 44.0 |
| Fayette, Flatonia | N | 96 | 22 | 110 | 2 | Apr. | 7 | Dec. | 4 | 277 | N | 2.5 | 2.5 | 2.5 | 3.3 | 4.8 | 4.5 | 3.1 | 2.5 | 5.0 | 3.2 | 3.2 | 2.0 | 37.1 |
| Fisher, Rotan | 28 | 92 | 24 | 116 | -3 | Apr. | 2 | Nov. | 6 | 218 | N | 0.7 | 1.1 | 1.0 | 2.0 | 3.0 | 2.8 | 1.9 | 2.6 | 3.8 | 2.4 | 1.2 | 1.3 | 24.3 |
| Floyd, Floydada | N | 93 | 24 | 111 | -9 | Mar. | 14 | Nov. | 7 | 213 | N | 1.1 | 0.7 | 1.0 | 1.2 | 2.8 | 2.5 | 2.2 | 2.6 | 3.0 | 1.7 | 0.9 | 0.5 | 20.5 |
| Foard, Crowell | N | 93 | 41 | 114 | -7 | Feb. | 23 | Nov. | 2 | 219 | N | 0.9 | 1.1 | 1.0 | 2.0 | 4.1 | 2.4 | 3.7 | 4.1 | 3.5 | 2.7 | 1.2 | 3.3 | 23.9 |
| Fort Bend, Sugar Land | 18 | 93 | 33 | 106 | 6 | Mar. | 11 | Dec. | 14 | 296 | 18 | 3.3 | 3.3 | 2.8 | 2.8 | 4.6 | 4.6 | 3.4 | 4.1 | 5.6 | 3.5 | 4.0 | 4.8 | 45.3 |
| Franklin, Mount Vernon | N | 95 | 36 | 109 | -1 | Mar. | 11 | Nov. | 12 | 234 | N | 2.8 | 3.3 | 4.3 | 4.4 | 4.7 | 4.1 | 3.7 | 2.5 | 4.9 | 3.9 | 3.7 | 4.8 | 46.8 |
| Freestone, Fairfield | 29 | 95 | 36 | 109 | -2 | Mar. | 11 | Nov. | 11 | 263 | 29 | 2.5 | 3.1 | 3.0 | 3.7 | 4.9 | 3.5 | 2.0 | 2.3 | 4.0 | 4.1 | 3.6 | 3.0 | 39.8 |
| Frio, Pearsall | N | 97 | 38 | 111 | 9 | Feb. | 23 | Dec. | 2 | 291 | N | 1.2 | 1.3 | 1.0 | 2.2 | 3.6 | 3.3 | 1.6 | 2.5 | 3.0 | 3.1 | 3.1 | 1.1 | 25.4 |

| County and Station | Temp. Length of Record (Yr.) | July Mean Max. (F.) | January Mean Min. (F.) | Record Highest (F.) | Record Lowest (F.) | Last in Spring Mo. | Last in Spring Day | First in Fall Mo. | First in Fall Day | Growing Season (Days) | Precip. Length of Record (Yr.) | Jan. (In.) | Feb. (In.) | Mar. (In.) | Apr. (In.) | May (In.) | June (In.) | July (In.) | Aug. (In.) | Sept. (In.) | Oct. (In.) | Nov. (In.) | Dec. (In.) | Annual (In.) |
|---|---|---|---|---|---|---|---|---|---|---|---|---|---|---|---|---|---|---|---|---|---|---|---|---|
| Gaines, Seminole | N | 94 | 25 | 114 | -9 | Apr. | 8 | Nov. | 4 | 210 | N | 0.5 | 0.7 | 0.7 | 0.9 | 2.0 | 2.6 | 2.5 | 2.3 | 2.5 | 1.4 | 0.8 | 0.6 | 17.5 |
| Galveston, Galveston | N | 87 | 47 | 101 | 8 | Jan. | 24 | Dec. | 25 | 335 | N | 3.3 | 2.3 | 2.2 | 2.4 | 3.6 | 4.4 | 4.0 | 4.5 | 5.9 | 2.0 | 3.4 | 3.5 | 42.3 |
| Garza, Post | 28 | 94 | 27 | 115 | -1 | Apr. | 5 | Nov. | 7 | 216 | N | 0.6 | 0.8 | 0.9 | 1.2 | 2.8 | 3.1 | 2.1 | 2.8 | 2.9 | 2.0 | 0.7 | 0.7 | 20.9 |
| Gillespie, Fredericksburg | N | 93 | 35 | 109 | -5 | Apr. | 1 | Nov. | 6 | 219 | N | 1.3 | 1.8 | 1.4 | 2.5 | 4.2 | 3.6 | 2.2 | 2.7 | 3.6 | 3.0 | 1.9 | 1.3 | 30.0 |
| Glasscock, Garden City | 26 | 94 | 25 | 114 | 0 | Apr. | 2 | Nov. | 10 | 222 | N | 0.6 | 0.7 | 0.7 | 1.2 | 2.1 | 2.0 | 2.2 | 2.0 | 3.3 | 1.8 | 0.8 | 0.6 | 18.0 |
| Goliad, Goliad | N | 95 | 43 | 112 | 7 | Feb. | 24 | Dec. | 6 | 285 | N | 2.1 | 2.1 | 1.4 | 2.8 | 4.1 | 3.5 | 1.9 | 3.4 | 5.0 | 3.6 | 2.3 | 2.0 | 36.5 |
| Gonzales, Nixon | N | 95 | 40 | 113 | 3 | Feb. | 28 | Dec. | 1 | 276 | N | 2.2 | 2.1 | 1.6 | 2.9 | 4.0 | 3.6 | 2.4 | 2.6 | 4.6 | 3.2 | 2.4 | 1.7 | 32.4 |
| Gray, Pampa | N | 92 | 21 | 111 | -12 | Apr. | 15 | Oct. | 27 | 195 | N | 0.5 | 0.9 | 1.4 | 1.3 | 2.9 | 3.6 | 2.9 | 2.1 | 2.4 | 1.5 | 1.0 | 0.5 | 21.0 |
| Grayson, Sherman | N | 95 | 30 | 110 | -2 | Mar. | 27 | Nov. | 9 | 227 | N | 1.9 | 2.7 | 3.4 | 3.9 | 5.8 | 4.2 | 1.9 | 2.1 | 5.1 | 4.2 | 3.1 | 2.0 | 40.4 |
| Gregg, Longview | N | 93 | 33 | 110 | -7 | Mar. | 16 | Nov. | 15 | 247 | N | 3.5 | 3.6 | 4.1 | 4.3 | 5.1 | 4.4 | 2.9 | 2.8 | 3.9 | 4.3 | 4.3 | 4.3 | 47.0 |
| Grimes, Anderson | 9 | 96 | 40 | 108 | 4 | Mar. | 1 | Dec. | 4 | 278 | N | 3.1 | 3.3 | 4.1 | 3.3 | 5.1 | 3.4 | 2.4 | 2.8 | 4.1 | 3.4 | 4.3 | 4.3 | 40.4 |
| Guadalupe, Seguin | N | 96 | 40 | 110 | 0 | Mar. | 10 | Nov. | 28 | 267 | N | 1.8 | 2.5 | 1.8 | 3.3 | 3.4 | 2.9 | 1.8 | 2.1 | 4.1 | 3.4 | 2.1 | 1.7 | 31.4 |
| Hale, Plainview | N | 96 | 24 | 110 | -7 | Apr. | 6 | Nov. | 4 | 211 | N | 0.5 | 0.7 | 0.8 | 1.7 | 3.0 | 3.5 | 2.4 | 2.5 | 2.5 | 1.7 | 0.8 | 0.6 | 19.8 |
| Hall, Memphis | N | 96 | 32 | 117 | -11 | Apr. | 10 | Nov. | 6 | 213 | N | 0.5 | 0.7 | 1.3 | 1.7 | 3.5 | 3.1 | 1.7 | 2.5 | 2.4 | 2.1 | 0.9 | 0.6 | 20.5 |
| Hamilton, Hico | N | 96 | 32 | 111 | -22 | Apr. | 4 | Nov. | 21 | 239 | N | 1.9 | 2.0 | 2.4 | 3.0 | 4.6 | 3.2 | 1.7 | 2.2 | 3.4 | 3.3 | 2.2 | 1.5 | 31.8 |
| Hansford, Spearman | N | 95 | 21 | 109 | -15 | Apr. | 27 | Oct. | 25 | 186 | N | 0.4 | 0.7 | 1.1 | 1.7 | 2.9 | 3.0 | 2.9 | 2.5 | 1.9 | 1.6 | 1.0 | 0.9 | 24.5 |
| Hardeman, Quanah | N | 97 | 23 | 119 | 12 | Mar. | 31 | Nov. | 7 | 221 | N | 0.8 | 1.0 | 1.5 | 1.7 | 3.5 | 3.2 | 2.4 | 2.5 | 3.6 | 2.3 | 1.2 | 0.9 | 24.5 |
| Hardin, Evadale | 22 | 93 | 37 | 102 | 7 | Mar. | 31 | Dec. | 11 | 246 | 22 | 4.8 | 3.9 | 4.0 | 3.8 | 5.4 | 5.8 | 4.7 | 4.0 | 5.3 | 4.0 | 4.9 | 5.1 | 55.7 |
| Harris, Houston | N | 92 | 43 | 107 | 2 | Feb. | 14 | Dec. | 11 | 300 | N | 3.3 | 3.2 | 3.2 | 3.2 | 5.2 | 5.0 | 3.6 | 3.5 | 4.9 | 3.9 | 3.8 | 3.5 | 46.1 |
| Harrison, Marshall | N | 93 | 32 | 110 | -9 | Mar. | 16 | Nov. | 17 | 245 | N | 3.8 | 4.0 | 4.0 | 4.4 | 4.9 | 4.4 | 3.0 | 2.5 | 3.8 | 4.3 | 4.3 | 4.5 | 47.7 |
| Hartley, Channing | 13 | 92 | 21 | 112 | -6 | Apr. | 22 | Oct. | 19 | 180 | 13 | 0.4 | 0.5 | 0.7 | 1.2 | 2.2 | 2.9 | 2.1 | 2.3 | 1.9 | 1.2 | 0.7 | 0.2 | 16.1 |
| Haskell, Haskell | N | 96 | 27 | 115 | -2 | Mar. | 28 | Nov. | 16 | 232 | N | 0.9 | 1.4 | 1.4 | 2.8 | 3.6 | 3.0 | 2.1 | 2.9 | 3.7 | 2.6 | 1.3 | 1.1 | 26.1 |
| Hays, San Marcos | N | 95 | 36 | 110 | -14 | Mar. | 14 | Nov. | 23 | 254 | N | 2.0 | 2.3 | 1.8 | 2.8 | 5.0 | 4.2 | 2.1 | 2.3 | 3.7 | 3.1 | 1.9 | 2.1 | 34.6 |
| Hemphill, Canadian | N | 96 | 22 | 112 | -2 | Apr. | 9 | Oct. | 30 | 204 | N | 0.3 | 0.8 | 1.4 | 1.4 | 3.4 | 3.1 | 1.9 | 2.6 | 2.6 | 1.4 | 0.9 | 0.5 | 20.1 |
| Henderson, Athens | N | 95 | 35 | 110 | 17 | Mar. | 11 | Nov. | 26 | 260 | N | 2.5 | 3.1 | 3.6 | 4.3 | 5.2 | 3.6 | 2.6 | 1.8 | 2.6 | 4.0 | 3.7 | 3.3 | 39.7 |
| Hidalgo, McAllen | 27 | 96 | 49 | 106 | -1 | Feb. | 7 | Dec. | 8 | 327 | 39 | 1.4 | 1.3 | 0.6 | 1.7 | 2.8 | 2.7 | 1.7 | 2.4 | 4.4 | 3.1 | 1.5 | 1.1 | 23.4 |
| Hill, Hillsboro | N | 92 | 34 | 113 | -16 | Mar. | 13 | Nov. | 18 | 250 | N | 1.9 | 2.6 | 2.6 | 3.0 | 4.8 | 3.9 | 2.2 | 3.1 | 3.4 | 3.7 | 2.5 | 2.3 | 35.1 |
| Hockley, Levelland | N | 97 | 22 | 115 | -6 | Apr. | 15 | Oct. | 28 | 196 | N | 0.4 | 0.7 | 0.6 | 0.9 | 2.0 | 2.6 | 2.5 | 3.1 | 3.3 | 1.7 | 0.7 | 0.6 | 19.3 |
| Hood, Granbury | 28 | 94 | 33 | 110 | 0 | Mar. | 26 | Nov. | 13 | 232 | 28 | 1.9 | 2.0 | 4.1 | 3.9 | 4.9 | 3.4 | 1.8 | 2.9 | 2.9 | 3.2 | 4.0 | 1.5 | 30.9 |
| Hopkins, Sulphur Springs | N | 94 | 30 | 110 | -13 | Mar. | 23 | Nov. | 16 | 238 | N | 3.5 | 3.3 | 4.1 | 4.7 | 5.5 | 4.1 | 3.0 | 2.2 | 3.8 | 4.6 | 3.8 | 3.5 | 46.0 |
| Houston, Crockett | N | 93 | 34 | 110 | -3 | Mar. | 6 | Nov. | 26 | 265 | N | 3.5 | 2.9 | 4.1 | 4.1 | 4.4 | 3.7 | 3.0 | 2.2 | 4.4 | 3.9 | 3.8 | 3.5 | 46.0 |
| Howard, Big Spring | N | 95 | 28 | 114 | -12 | Apr. | 4 | Nov. | 11 | 217 | N | 0.4 | 0.3 | 0.2 | 1.3 | 2.8 | 2.3 | 1.7 | 2.0 | 3.9 | 1.6 | 0.8 | 0.6 | 19.2 |
| Hudspeth, Cornudas Ser. | N | 94 | 25 | 108 | -7 | — | — | — | — | — | N | 2.2 | 3.0 | 3.8 | 4.2 | 0.5 | 1.1 | 1.5 | 2.0 | 1.9 | 0.9 | 0.4 | 0.4 | 10.0 |
| Hunt, Greenville | N | 94 | 29 | 108 | 4 | Mar. | 21 | Nov. | 13 | 237 | N | 2.2 | 0.9 | 1.3 | 4.1 | 5.7 | 3.4 | 2.7 | 2.2 | 4.5 | 4.1 | 3.3 | 2.6 | 41.6 |
| Hutchinson, Borger | N | 93 | 23 | 113 | -7 | Apr. | 20 | Oct. | 24 | 187 | N | 0.5 | 1.1 | 1.0 | 1.3 | 2.8 | 3.7 | 2.7 | 2.2 | 2.0 | 0.9 | 0.8 | 0.4 | 20.3 |
| Irion, Mertzon | N | 95 | 32 | 104 | 17 | Mar. | 27 | Nov. | 14 | 232 | N | 0.7 | 1.6 | 2.1 | 1.6 | 2.8 | 3.4 | 1.5 | 2.2 | 3.1 | 1.3 | 0.8 | 0.5 | 21.1 |
| Jack, Jacksboro | N | 95 | 29 | 107 | -10 | Apr. | 1 | Nov. | 5 | 218 | N | 1.3 | 2.8 | 1.7 | 2.8 | 3.1 | 2.3 | 1.5 | 2.5 | 3.1 | 2.0 | 1.2 | 0.9 | 30.7 |
| Jackson, Edna | 8 | 94 | 42 | 105 | 12 | Feb. | 19 | Nov. | 6 | 290 | N | 2.2 | 1.6 | 4.4 | 2.8 | 4.7 | 4.6 | 2.2 | 2.2 | 3.8 | 3.9 | 2.0 | 1.5 | 21.1 |
| Jasper, Jasper | 22 | 93 | 36 | 106 | 12 | Mar. | 18 | Nov. | 13 | 230 | N | 4.4 | 4.4 | 0.4 | 2.8 | 5.1 | 5.3 | 3.8 | 3.4 | 5.7 | 3.6 | 2.8 | 2.5 | 40.9 |
| Jeff Davis, Mount Locke | N | 82 | 30 | 104 | -5 | Mar. | 11 | Nov. | 16 | 250 | 26 | 0.5 | 0.5 | 3.2 | 0.5 | 1.5 | 2.6 | 3.9 | 4.3 | 3.5 | 1.9 | 4.6 | 5.3 | 52.7 |
| Jefferson, Port Arthur | N | 92 | 42 | 107 | -12 | Feb. | 15 | Dec. | 15 | 303 | N | 4.8 | 3.4 | 0.7 | 3.5 | 5.7 | 5.6 | 5.4 | 5.3 | 6.3 | 3.6 | 0.7 | 0.6 | 20.8 |
| Jim Hogg, Hebbronville | N | 97 | 42 | 109 | 7 | Feb. | 18 | Dec. | 15 | 289 | N | 1.1 | 3.2 | 0.7 | 1.7 | 3.4 | 2.9 | 3.9 | 2.0 | 5.1 | 4.3 | 4.9 | 4.8 | 57.2 |
| Jim Wells, Alice | N | 96 | 43 | 111 | — | Mar. | 11 | Dec. | 18 | 233 | N | 1.3 | 1.6 | 2.9 | 1.6 | 3.2 | 3.5 | 1.5 | 2.7 | 4.1 | 1.9 | 1.6 | 0.9 | 22.7 |
| Johnson, Cleburne | N | 97 | 33 | 111 | -5 | Mar. | 25 | Nov. | 14 | 233 | N | 1.9 | 1.6 | 2.9 | 3.6 | 5.4 | 3.5 | 2.0 | 2.2 | 2.7 | 3.3 | 2.1 | 1.1 | 27.8 |
| Jones, Anson | N | 96 | 31 | 114 | -12 | Mar. | 31 | Nov. | 9 | 223 | N | 1.0 | 1.4 | 1.3 | 2.2 | 3.4 | 2.9 | 2.0 | 2.6 | 4.3 | 3.3 | 1.8 | 1.1 | 34.0 |
| Karnes, Kenedy | 18 | 97 | 41 | 112 | 7 | Feb. | 24 | Dec. | 2 | 281 | 18 | 2.3 | 2.4 | 1.3 | 2.2 | 4.0 | 4.2 | 1.2 | 3.0 | 5.3 | 3.6 | 2.0 | 1.8 | 33.2 |

| County and Station | Temperature | | | | | Average Freeze Dates | | | | Growing Season | Normal Total Precipitation | | | | | | | | | | | | | |
|---|---|---|---|---|---|---|---|---|---|---|---|---|---|---|---|---|---|---|---|---|---|---|---|---|
| | Length of Record (Yr.) | July Mean Max. (F.) | January Mean Min. (F.) | Record Highest (F.) | Record Lowest (F.) | Last in Spring (Mo. / Day) | | First in Fall (Mo. / Day) | | (Days) | Length of Record (Yr.) | January (In.) | February (In.) | March (In.) | April (In.) | May (In.) | June (In.) | July (In.) | August (In.) | September (In.) | October (In.) | November (In.) | December (In.) | Annual (In.) |
|---|---|---|---|---|---|---|---|---|---|---|---|---|---|---|---|---|---|---|---|---|---|---|---|---|
| Kaufman, Kaufman | N | 95 | 32 | 112 | -3 | Mar. 18 | | Nov. 21 | | 248 | N | 2.4 | 3.0 | 3.2 | 3.8 | 5.0 | 3.1 | 3.1 | 2.6 | 3.8 | 3.9 | 3.3 | 3.0 | 38.9 |
| Kendall, Boerne | N | 93 | 33 | 107 | 3 | Mar. 25 | | Nov. 11 | | 236 | N | 1.7 | 2.1 | 2.1 | 3.1 | 4.1 | 3.8 | 3.8 | 2.2 | 4.2 | 3.6 | 2.7 | 1.8 | 34.2 |
| Kenedy, Armstrong | 14 | 95 | 45 | 110 | 14 | Feb. 2 | | Dec. 18 | | 319 | 14 | 1.2 | 1.7 | 0.5 | 1.3 | 4.4 | 3.4 | 3.4 | 2.1 | 6.4 | 2.9 | 1.3 | 1.3 | 29.7 |
| Kent, Jayton | 18 | 96 | 25 | 116 | -4 | Apr. 4 | | Nov. 6 | | 216 | 18 | 0.7 | 0.7 | 2.0 | 1.6 | 3.0 | 2.9 | 1.8 | 2.7 | 3.2 | 2.1 | 0.9 | 0.8 | 21.8 |
| Kerr, Kerrville | N | 94 | 32 | 110 | -5 | Apr. 6 | | Nov. 6 | | 216 | N | 1.6 | 2.2 | 2.0 | 3.1 | 3.8 | 2.6 | 1.7 | 2.5 | 4.0 | 3.6 | 1.6 | 1.6 | 29.8 |
| Kimble, Junction | N | 96 | 31 | 110 | -7 | Apr. 3 | | Nov. 8 | | 213 | N | 1.0 | 1.1 | 1.1 | 1.6 | 3.6 | 2.8 | 1.9 | 2.7 | 3.7 | 2.4 | 1.2 | 1.1 | 23.8 |
| King, Guthrie | 27 | 98 | 24 | 119 | -11 | Apr. 8 | | Nov. 3 | | 219 | 27 | 0.9 | 1.1 | 0.9 | 2.3 | 2.6 | 3.1 | 1.9 | 2.9 | 2.4 | 2.4 | 1.2 | 0.7 | 23.8 |
| Kinney, Brackettville | 23 | 95 | 36 | 109 | -10 | Mar. 1 | | Nov. 26 | | 270 | 23 | 0.8 | 1.3 | 1.6 | 1.6 | 3.4 | 4.0 | 2.2 | 2.9 | 4.3 | 2.7 | 1.4 | 0.8 | 21.7 |
| Kleberg, Kingsville | N | 95 | 45 | 108 | 4 | Feb. 5 | | Dec. 16 | | 314 | N | 1.5 | 1.4 | 1.8 | 2.1 | 3.7 | 3.0 | 2.0 | 2.6 | 4.9 | 3.8 | 1.3 | 1.0 | 27.6 |
| Knox, Munday | N | 98 | 28 | 117 | -9 | Apr. 9 | | Nov. 6 | | 217 | N | 0.9 | 1.4 | 1.6 | 1.8 | 3.2 | 2.2 | 2.0 | 1.5 | 3.3 | 3.0 | 1.3 | 1.0 | 26.2 |
| La Salle, Fowlerton | N | 99 | 38 | 111 | 7 | Feb. 20 | | Dec. 6 | | 288 | N | 1.1 | 1.4 | 1.8 | 2.1 | 3.2 | 3.0 | 2.0 | 2.4 | 3.3 | 3.0 | 1.2 | 1.0 | 22.5 |
| Lamar, Paris | N | 94 | 30 | 112 | -7 | Mar. 25 | | Nov. 14 | | 235 | N | 2.2 | 3.2 | 4.2 | 4.0 | 5.9 | 3.9 | 3.6 | 2.7 | 3.3 | 4.6 | 3.9 | 3.3 | 46.1 |
| Lamb, Littlefield | N | 91 | 22 | 112 | -14 | Apr. 16 | | Oct. 27 | | 194 | N | 0.4 | 0.6 | 0.6 | 1.0 | 2.3 | 3.3 | 2.4 | 2.8 | 2.5 | 1.6 | 0.7 | 0.5 | 18.7 |
| Lampasas, Lampasas | N | 95 | 30 | 111 | -12 | Apr. 1 | | Nov. 10 | | 223 | N | 1.5 | 2.0 | 2.1 | 2.7 | 4.1 | 2.9 | 2.5 | 2.7 | 3.1 | 3.3 | 1.7 | 1.7 | 29.6 |
| Lavaca, Hallettsville | N | 95 | 41 | 111 | 5 | Mar. 1 | | Dec. 6 | | 280 | N | 2.8 | 2.5 | 2.4 | 3.0 | 5.3 | 4.4 | 2.5 | 2.9 | 5.1 | 3.8 | 3.3 | 2.4 | 39.1 |
| Lee, Lexington | 28 | 94 | 36 | 104 | 11 | Mar. 1 | | Dec. 1 | | 273 | 28 | 2.2 | 3.6 | 3.1 | 3.9 | 4.8 | 3.8 | 1.7 | 2.4 | 4.2 | 3.8 | 3.0 | 3.1 | 35.6 |
| Leon, Centerville | N | 95 | 34 | 111 | -3 | Mar. 6 | | Dec. 1 | | 270 | N | 3.1 | 3.1 | 3.1 | 3.5 | 4.4 | 3.5 | 2.5 | 4.0 | 5.7 | 4.5 | 5.2 | 3.1 | 40.5 |
| Liberty, Liberty | N | 93 | 39 | 107 | 7 | Mar. 3 | | Dec. 1 | | 261 | N | 3.8 | 3.1 | 3.4 | 3.6 | 4.9 | 3.4 | 4.5 | 4.0 | 4.7 | 4.1 | 3.4 | 4.8 | 54.1 |
| Limestone, Mexia | N | 95 | 33 | 110 | -5 | Mar. 15 | | Nov. 19 | | 255 | N | 2.5 | 3.1 | 3.4 | 3.6 | 4.9 | 3.5 | 1.9 | 2.3 | 4.1 | 4.1 | 3.4 | 3.2 | 40.3 |
| Lipscomb, Follett | N | 93 | 20 | 110 | -12 | Apr. 26 | | Oct. 10 | | 202 | N | 0.5 | 1.0 | 1.9 | 1.7 | 3.5 | 3.4 | 2.3 | 3.1 | 2.1 | 1.4 | 0.7 | 0.7 | 22.8 |
| Live Oak, George West | N | 95 | 41 | 109 | -12 | Feb. 20 | | Dec. 6 | | 289 | N | 1.7 | 1.8 | 1.6 | 2.5 | 3.3 | 2.8 | 1.5 | 2.9 | 4.7 | 3.1 | 1.9 | 1.4 | 27.6 |
| Llano, Llano | N | 96 | 31 | 113 | -6 | Mar. 29 | | Nov. 13 | | 229 | N | 1.2 | 1.8 | 1.8 | 2.5 | 3.8 | 2.8 | 1.8 | 2.4 | 3.0 | 3.0 | 1.8 | 1.2 | 26.4 |
| Loving, Mentone | N | 96 | 28 | 114 | -14 | Apr. 8 | | Nov. 3 | | 222 | N | 0.3 | 0.3 | 0.3 | 1.0 | 1.1 | 0.9 | 1.8 | 1.4 | 2.6 | 1.0 | 0.5 | 0.3 | 9.1 |
| Lubbock, Lubbock | N | 92 | 25 | 114 | -16 | Apr. 9 | | Nov. 9 | | 208 | N | 0.4 | 0.7 | 0.9 | 1.0 | 2.4 | 2.8 | 2.4 | 2.5 | 2.6 | 1.9 | 0.8 | 0.5 | 18.7 |
| Lynn, Tahoka | N | 92 | 24 | 111 | -5 | Apr. 5 | | Nov. 6 | | 217 | N | 0.5 | 0.7 | 0.9 | 1.4 | 2.7 | 2.8 | 2.2 | 2.2 | 2.6 | 1.8 | 0.8 | 0.7 | 19.7 |
| Madison, Madisonville | N | 96 | 38 | 110 | -2 | Mar. 18 | | Dec. 2 | | 272 | N | 3.0 | 2.8 | 2.8 | 2.9 | 5.0 | 3.9 | 3.0 | 2.5 | 2.6 | 2.0 | 3.8 | 3.0 | 41.6 |
| Marion, Jefferson | N | 94 | 32 | 110 | -5 | Mar. 9 | | Nov. 9 | | 236 | N | 3.9 | 3.5 | 3.9 | 5.3 | 4.6 | 3.4 | 3.1 | 2.6 | 3.6 | 3.1 | 4.1 | 4.1 | 44.7 |
| Martin, Lenorah | N | 95 | 30 | 109 | -8 | Apr. 18 | | Nov. 5 | | 215 | N | 0.6 | 0.6 | 0.8 | 1.2 | 2.3 | 3.1 | 1.9 | 2.4 | 2.7 | 1.6 | 0.6 | 0.6 | 17.2 |
| Mason, Mason | N | 95 | 31 | 109 | -5 | Apr. 5 | | Nov. 6 | | 217 | N | 1.1 | 1.6 | 1.9 | 1.5 | 3.7 | 3.3 | 1.6 | 2.6 | 3.2 | 3.1 | 1.6 | 1.1 | 26.8 |
| Matagorda, Matagorda | 28 | 91 | 45 | 102 | 9 | Feb. 17 | | Dec. 10 | | 296 | 28 | 3.6 | 2.6 | 2.6 | 2.6 | 4.5 | 4.0 | 4.0 | 3.3 | 6.9 | 3.9 | 3.9 | 2.7 | 44.7 |
| Maverick, Eagle Pass | N | 98 | 38 | 115 | 10 | Feb. 21 | | Dec. 3 | | 285 | N | 0.7 | 0.7 | 0.8 | 1.9 | 3.4 | 3.0 | 1.8 | 1.8 | 2.8 | 2.4 | 2.4 | 0.7 | 21.5 |
| McCulloch, Brady | N | 95 | 30 | 110 | -7 | Mar. 31 | | Nov. 12 | | 218 | N | 1.1 | 1.6 | 1.9 | 1.4 | 3.6 | 2.9 | 2.3 | 2.3 | 3.6 | 2.4 | 1.5 | 1.1 | 26.1 |
| McLennan, Waco | N | 97 | 34 | 112 | -5 | Mar. 16 | | Nov. 24 | | 256 | N | 2.2 | 2.1 | 2.3 | 3.2 | 4.6 | 3.3 | 2.0 | 2.0 | 3.5 | 3.4 | 2.4 | 1.9 | 32.0 |
| McMullen, Tilden | N | 98 | 40 | 112 | -8 | Feb. 19 | | Dec. 7 | | 291 | N | 1.3 | 1.7 | 1.4 | 1.8 | 3.0 | 3.0 | 1.7 | 1.7 | 3.5 | 3.4 | 1.4 | 1.0 | 23.4 |
| Medina, Hondo | N | 94 | 37 | 115 | 4 | Feb. 6 | | Nov. 24 | | 263 | N | 1.4 | 1.5 | 1.4 | 3.2 | 3.8 | 2.9 | 1.7 | 2.7 | 3.1 | 3.2 | 1.5 | 1.4 | 27.3 |
| Menard, Menard | N | 95 | 30 | 107 | -2 | Mar. 31 | | Nov. 6 | | 220 | N | 1.0 | 0.6 | 1.9 | 1.8 | 2.8 | 3.0 | 2.4 | 2.6 | 2.5 | 2.4 | 1.2 | 0.9 | 24.3 |
| Midland, Midland | N | 95 | 29 | 116 | -11 | Apr. 3 | | Nov. 6 | | 218 | N | 0.5 | 0.6 | 0.5 | 0.7 | 2.8 | 2.1 | 1.4 | 1.6 | 1.9 | 1.4 | 0.7 | 0.7 | 15.2 |
| Milam, Cameron | N | 95 | 38 | 109 | 2 | Mar. 13 | | Nov. 24 | | 256 | N | 2.2 | 2.6 | 2.2 | 3.2 | 4.7 | 2.9 | 1.9 | 2.5 | 3.6 | 3.0 | 2.3 | 2.3 | 34.2 |
| Mills, Goldthwaite | N | 95 | 34 | 110 | -7 | Mar. 31 | | Nov. 16 | | 230 | N | 1.3 | 1.9 | 1.9 | 2.4 | 3.7 | 3.2 | 1.6 | 2.1 | 3.4 | 3.1 | 2.4 | 1.4 | 27.6 |
| Mitchell, Colorado City | 24 | 97 | 30 | 112 | -7 | Apr. 4 | | Nov. 5 | | 217 | 24 | 0.6 | 0.7 | 0.7 | 1.4 | 2.9 | 3.2 | 1.7 | 2.3 | 3.1 | 2.1 | 1.0 | 0.7 | 19.8 |
| Montague, Bowie | N | 96 | 31 | 115 | -11 | Mar. 27 | | Nov. 11 | | 229 | N | 1.4 | 2.0 | 2.6 | 2.9 | 4.8 | 3.4 | 2.0 | 2.3 | 4.1 | 3.7 | 2.3 | 1.6 | 32.9 |
| Montgomery, Conroe | N | 94 | 38 | 107 | 3 | Mar. 1 | | Nov. 26 | | 270 | N | 3.6 | 3.6 | 2.9 | 3.8 | 5.4 | 3.6 | 4.5 | 3.5 | 5.0 | 3.7 | 4.2 | 4.0 | 47.3 |
| Moore, Dumas | N | 92 | 20 | 109 | -18 | Apr. 30 | | Oct. 12 | | 185 | N | 0.4 | 0.7 | 0.7 | 0.8 | 2.7 | 2.8 | 2.4 | 2.8 | 1.9 | 1.1 | 0.9 | 0.4 | 17.4 |
| Morris, Daingerfield | N | 95 | 35 | 109 | 4 | Mar. 21 | | Nov. 21 | | 236 | N | 2.9 | 3.5 | 4.4 | 4.8 | 4.7 | 3.6 | 2.8 | 2.8 | 3.2 | 3.9 | 4.5 | 4.1 | 44.6 |
| Motley, Matador | N | 95 | 26 | 116 | -5 | Apr. 3 | | Nov. 7 | | 218 | N | 0.6 | 0.8 | 0.8 | 1.3 | 2.8 | 3.4 | 2.1 | 2.1 | 2.4 | 2.0 | 1.0 | 0.7 | 21.2 |
| Nacogdoches, Nacogdoches | N | 94 | 36 | 110 | 0 | Mar. 16 | | Nov. 12 | | 243 | N | 4.2 | 3.9 | 3.7 | 4.8 | 5.5 | 3.9 | 2.0 | 2.5 | 3.8 | 3.3 | 3.8 | 4.7 | 47.5 |

| County and Station | Temperature Length of Record (Yr.) | July Mean Max. (F.) | January Mean Min. (F.) | Record Highest (F.) | Record Lowest (F.) | Last in Spring Mo. | Last in Spring Day | First in Fall Mo. | First in Fall Day | Growing Season Days | Precip. Length of Record (Yr.) | January (In.) | February (In.) | March (In.) | April (In.) | May (In.) | June (In.) | July (In.) | August (In.) | September (In.) | October (In.) | November (In.) | December (In.) | Annual (In.) |
|---|---|---|---|---|---|---|---|---|---|---|---|---|---|---|---|---|---|---|---|---|---|---|---|---|
| Navarro, Corsicana | N | 94 | 33 | 113 | -5 | Mar. | 10 | Nov. | 19 | 253 | N | 2.2 | 2.8 | 3.1 | 3.6 | 5.8 | 3.1 | 2.1 | 1.9 | 3.4 | 4.2 | 2.9 | 2.9 | 37.9 |
| Newton, Kirbyville Forest Service | 27 | 93 | 40 | 107 | 7 | Mar. | 24 | Nov. | 9 | 228 | 27 | 4.8 | 4.3 | 3.7 | 4.6 | 5.3 | 4.6 | 5.3 | 3.7 | 4.3 | 3.8 | 4.7 | 6.0 | 56.0 |
| Nolan, Roscoe | N | 94 | 30 | 113 | -11 | Apr. | 9 | Nov. | 9 | 221 | N | 1.0 | 1.2 | 1.3 | 1.7 | 3.3 | 2.9 | 2.0 | 2.4 | 4.3 | 3.0 | 1.6 | 0.9 | 24.4 |
| Nueces, Corpus Christi | 26 | 93 | 45 | 104 | 13 | Feb. | 9 | Dec. | 15 | 309 | N | 1.7 | 2.0 | 0.9 | 1.7 | 3.3 | 3.4 | 2.4 | 3.3 | 5.5 | 3.0 | 1.6 | 1.3 | 30.1 |
| Ochiltree, Perryton | 26 | 94 | 17 | 110 | -8 | Apr. | 18 | Oct. | 26 | 191 | 26 | 0.4 | 0.7 | 0.9 | 1.1 | 2.4 | 3.3 | 2.4 | 2.4 | 1.8 | 1.1 | 1.1 | 0.5 | 19.5 |
| Oldham, Vega | 27 | 91 | 19 | 108 | -17 | Apr. | 19 | Oct. | 21 | 186 | N | 0.5 | 0.6 | 0.8 | 1.1 | 2.4 | 2.8 | 2.8 | 2.5 | 1.6 | 1.2 | 0.7 | 0.5 | 17.4 |
| Orange, Orange | 27 | 91 | 39 | 104 | 10 | Mar. | 16 | Nov. | 11 | 240 | 27 | 5.2 | 3.9 | 3.5 | 3.4 | 5.4 | 5.6 | 5.6 | 4.7 | 6.2 | 4.3 | 4.7 | 5.5 | 58.3 |
| Palo Pinto, Mineral Wells | N | 96 | 30 | 114 | 3 | Mar. | 31 | Nov. | 7 | 221 | N | 1.6 | 2.0 | 2.6 | 3.4 | 4.5 | 3.5 | 2.2 | 2.4 | 3.4 | 3.5 | 1.9 | 1.4 | 32.2 |
| Panola, Carthage | N | 94 | 33 | 108 | 1 | Mar. | 16 | Nov. | 11 | 240 | N | 4.0 | 3.7 | 3.8 | 4.0 | 4.9 | 4.4 | 3.2 | 2.7 | 4.1 | 3.9 | 4.7 | 4.6 | 48.0 |
| Parker, Weatherford | N | 96 | 28 | 119 | -10 | Mar. | 29 | Nov. | 9 | 225 | N | 1.6 | 2.2 | 2.7 | 3.3 | 4.5 | 3.6 | 2.3 | 2.4 | 3.5 | 3.3 | 2.0 | 1.6 | 32.9 |
| Parmer, Friona | 28 | 90 | 21 | 108 | -15 | Apr. | 20 | Oct. | 20 | 183 | 28 | 0.5 | 0.6 | 0.7 | 0.7 | 1.9 | 2.8 | 2.3 | 2.7 | 2.2 | 1.3 | 0.7 | 0.5 | 16.8 |
| Pecos, Fort Stockton | N | 95 | 30 | 117 | 1 | Mar. | 31 | Nov. | 10 | 224 | N | 0.5 | 0.5 | 0.4 | 0.7 | 1.5 | 1.6 | 1.3 | 1.8 | 2.8 | 1.3 | 0.8 | 0.6 | 13.9 |
| Polk, Livingston | N | 94 | 35 | 111 | 3 | Mar. | 17 | Nov. | 16 | 250 | N | 4.0 | 3.4 | 3.8 | 3.6 | 5.5 | 4.7 | 3.6 | 3.1 | 4.5 | 3.5 | 4.3 | 4.7 | 48.7 |
| Potter, Amarillo | N | 92 | 21 | 108 | -14 | Apr. | 17 | Oct. | 24 | 190 | N | 0.5 | 0.6 | 1.0 | 1.0 | 2.5 | 3.2 | 2.6 | 3.2 | 1.4 | 1.6 | 0.7 | 0.4 | 19.6 |
| Presidio, Marfa | N | 90 | 26 | 106 | -2 | Mar. | 20 | Nov. | 13 | 238 | 22 | 0.4 | 0.4 | 0.3 | 0.6 | 1.2 | 2.1 | 1.7 | 2.9 | 2.0 | 1.6 | 0.6 | 0.5 | 15.9 |
| Presidio, Presidio | N | 102 | 34 | 117 | 4 | Mar. | 20 | Nov. | 13 | 238 | 22 | 0.3 | 0.4 | 0.2 | 0.6 | 0.6 | 1.7 | 1.7 | 1.9 | 2.0 | 1.6 | 0.6 | 0.5 | 10.8 |
| Rains, Emory | 29 | 94 | 31 | 110 | -5 | Mar. | 21 | Nov. | 18 | 242 | N | 2.6 | 3.4 | 3.7 | 4.1 | 5.7 | 3.9 | 2.5 | 2.1 | 3.7 | 4.2 | 3.6 | 3.3 | 42.9 |
| Randall, Canyon | 27 | 92 | 23 | 107 | -14 | Apr. | 15 | Oct. | 27 | 195 | N | 0.4 | 0.6 | 0.9 | 0.9 | 2.4 | 3.5 | 2.2 | 3.1 | 2.0 | 1.6 | 0.8 | 0.4 | 18.9 |
| Reagan, Big Lake | 27 | 94 | 28 | 109 | -1 | Mar. | 28 | Nov. | 12 | 229 | N | 0.6 | 0.9 | 0.9 | 1.5 | 2.4 | 1.8 | 2.0 | 1.9 | 3.1 | 2.2 | 1.0 | 0.8 | 19.2 |
| Real, Prade Ranch | 19 | 92 | 29 | 107 | 0 | Mar. | 26 | Nov. | 17 | 236 | 19 | 1.2 | 1.5 | 1.4 | 2.3 | 3.3 | 3.0 | 2.6 | 3.1 | 3.1 | 2.5 | 1.1 | 1.1 | 25.7 |
| Red River, Clarksville | N | 96 | 29 | 112 | -5 | Mar. | 23 | Nov. | 12 | 234 | N | 2.3 | 3.2 | 4.0 | 4.3 | 5.5 | 3.9 | 2.9 | 3.1 | 3.9 | 4.5 | 4.2 | 3.7 | 44.9 |
| Reeves, Balmorhea | N | 96 | 29 | 112 | -9 | Apr. | 2 | Nov. | 11 | 226 | N | 0.5 | 0.5 | 0.4 | 0.6 | 1.4 | 1.3 | 1.8 | 2.4 | 3.0 | 1.3 | 0.7 | 0.5 | 14.3 |
| Reeves, Pecos | 29 | 99 | 27 | 118 | -9 | Apr. | 1 | Nov. | 12 | 226 | N | 0.4 | 0.5 | 0.4 | 0.4 | 1.0 | 1.2 | 1.2 | 1.7 | 2.1 | 1.1 | 0.7 | 0.5 | 11.0 |
| Refugio, Refugio | N | 94 | 43 | 106 | 8 | Feb. | 14 | Dec. | 15 | 304 | N | 2.0 | 2.3 | 1.3 | 2.3 | 4.1 | 4.4 | 3.6 | 3.5 | 6.7 | 3.9 | 2.1 | 1.7 | 38.0 |
| Roberts, Miami | 26 | 95 | 20 | 111 | -15 | Apr. | 16 | Oct. | 25 | 192 | 26 | 0.5 | 0.7 | 1.3 | 1.6 | 3.3 | 4.4 | 3.6 | 2.4 | 2.4 | 1.6 | 1.1 | 0.5 | 21.6 |
| Robertson, Franklin | N | 95 | 37 | 110 | -7 | Mar. | 6 | Nov. | 29 | 268 | N | 2.7 | 2.8 | 2.7 | 3.6 | 4.5 | 2.9 | 2.0 | 2.4 | 4.3 | 4.0 | 2.8 | 2.8 | 37.5 |
| Rockwall, Rockwall | N | 96 | 33 | 118 | -1 | Mar. | 23 | Nov. | 14 | 236 | N | 2.1 | 2.4 | 3.1 | 3.6 | 5.2 | 3.1 | 2.4 | 2.0 | 3.8 | 3.3 | 2.5 | 2.4 | 36.9 |
| Runnels, Ballinger | N | 95 | 30 | 114 | -9 | Mar. | 30 | Nov. | 13 | 228 | N | 1.0 | 1.3 | 1.2 | 1.9 | 3.4 | 2.6 | 1.5 | 2.5 | 3.5 | 2.8 | 1.3 | 1.0 | 23.3 |
| Rusk, Henderson | 6 | 93 | 33 | 108 | -1 | Mar. | 11 | Nov. | 16 | 250 | N | 3.6 | 3.6 | 3.8 | 4.0 | 5.1 | 4.3 | 2.8 | 2.5 | 3.6 | 4.0 | 4.3 | 3.9 | 45.6 |
| Sabine, Hemphill | 24 | 93 | 36 | 104 | 9 | Mar. | 21 | Nov. | 12 | 238 | N | 4.5 | 3.9 | 5.7 | 4.8 | 5.1 | 4.5 | 4.0 | 2.9 | 4.3 | 4.5 | 4.0 | 4.5 | 52.5 |
| San Augustine, Broaddus | 24 | 93 | 35 | 106 | 9 | Mar. | 19 | Nov. | 12 | 238 | 24 | 4.5 | 3.2 | 3.9 | 3.8 | 4.8 | 4.6 | 3.4 | 2.9 | 4.3 | 4.5 | 4.3 | 5.0 | 48.6 |
| San Jacinto, Coldspring | N | 93 | 36 | 105 | 8 | Mar. | 5 | Nov. | 21 | 261 | N | 3.7 | 3.3 | 3.5 | 3.4 | 5.5 | 5.5 | 3.1 | 3.1 | 5.7 | 3.8 | 4.1 | 4.7 | 48.3 |
| San Patricio, Sinton | N | 94 | 43 | 107 | 11 | Feb. | 14 | Dec. | 14 | 303 | N | 1.1 | 1.7 | 1.8 | 2.1 | 4.1 | 3.5 | 3.4 | 3.1 | 6.1 | 3.8 | 1.8 | 1.4 | 35.0 |
| Schleicher, Eldorado | 27 | 92 | 32 | 112 | -10 | Apr. | 1 | Nov. | 14 | 227 | N | 0.7 | 0.9 | 0.7 | 1.7 | 2.5 | 2.8 | 1.6 | 2.4 | 2.8 | 2.3 | 2.0 | 1.2 | 26.3 |
| Scurry, Snyder | 15 | 93 | 28 | 107 | -8 | Mar. | 28 | Nov. | 12 | 229 | 15 | 0.6 | 0.8 | 0.8 | 1.7 | 3.2 | 1.9 | 1.6 | 2.1 | 3.1 | 2.1 | 1.0 | 0.6 | 19.0 |
| Shackelford, Albany | N | 97 | 25 | 115 | -10 | Apr. | 4 | Nov. | 9 | 214 | N | 1.2 | 1.6 | 1.7 | 2.6 | 4.0 | 3.0 | 2.0 | 3.0 | 3.9 | 2.8 | 0.9 | 0.8 | 22.2 |
| Shelby, Center | N | 94 | 31 | 115 | -8 | Mar. | 30 | Nov. | 9 | 224 | N | 4.3 | 4.0 | 4.1 | 4.0 | 5.3 | 4.4 | 3.3 | 3.5 | 4.5 | 3.9 | 4.2 | 4.7 | 50.2 |
| Sherman, Stratford | N | 92 | 18 | 110 | -19 | Mar. | 22 | Oct. | 21 | 182 | N | 0.5 | 0.5 | 0.9 | 1.2 | 2.7 | 3.0 | 2.7 | 2.5 | 1.9 | 0.9 | 0.7 | 0.4 | 17.2 |
| Smith, Tyler | N | 94 | 33 | 108 | -11 | Mar. | 7 | Nov. | 21 | 259 | N | 3.0 | 3.3 | 3.5 | 4.9 | 4.9 | 3.3 | 2.8 | 2.5 | 4.1 | 3.4 | 3.8 | 3.7 | 43.1 |
| Somervell, Glen Rose | 27 | 98 | 29 | 110 | -15 | Apr. | 23 | Nov. | 16 | 236 | 27 | 1.7 | 2.1 | 2.7 | 3.2 | 5.3 | 3.7 | 2.2 | 1.8 | 3.5 | 3.4 | 2.0 | 1.8 | 33.3 |
| Starr, Rio Grande City | N | 99 | 43 | 115 | 10 | Feb. | 16 | Dec. | 7 | 314 | N | 1.1 | 1.1 | 0.5 | 1.5 | 2.8 | 2.5 | 1.4 | 1.8 | 5.2 | 2.1 | 1.0 | 1.0 | 22.3 |
| Stephens, Breckenridge | N | 97 | 28 | 111 | -7 | Apr. | 1 | Nov. | 7 | 222 | 27 | 1.4 | 1.5 | 1.8 | 2.6 | 3.6 | 3.0 | 2.0 | 1.9 | 3.8 | 3.1 | 1.7 | 1.3 | 27.6 |
| Sterling, Sterling City | N | 96 | 27 | 112 | -2 | Mar. | 31 | Nov. | 10 | 220 | 27 | 0.8 | 0.9 | 0.9 | 1.4 | 2.9 | 2.4 | 1.6 | 2.1 | 3.8 | 1.7 | 1.1 | 0.8 | 20.3 |
| Stonewall, Aspermont | 29 | 97 | 27 | 117 | -7 | Mar. | 31 | Nov. | 10 | 220 | N | 1.1 | 1.3 | 1.3 | 1.9 | 3.2 | 3.0 | 1.7 | 2.3 | 3.6 | 2.4 | 1.3 | 0.8 | 23.3 |
| Sutton, Sonora | N | 96 | 30 | 109 | -8 | Mar. | 26 | Nov. | 16 | 235 | N | 0.8 | 1.2 | 1.0 | 1.9 | 2.6 | 2.2 | 2.1 | 2.7 | 3.4 | 2.7 | 1.2 | 0.7 | 22.4 |

| County and Station | Temperature Length of Record (Yr.) | July Mean Max. (°F) | January Mean Min. (°F) | Record Highest (°F) | Record Lowest (°F) | Last in Spring Mo. | Last in Spring Day | First in Fall Mo. | First in Fall Day | Growing Season (Days) | Precip. Length of Record (Yr.) | January (In.) | February (In.) | March (In.) | April (In.) | May (In.) | June (In.) | July (In.) | August (In.) | September (In.) | October (In.) | November (In.) | December (In.) | Annual (In.) |
|---|---|---|---|---|---|---|---|---|---|---|---|---|---|---|---|---|---|---|---|---|---|---|---|---|
| Swisher, Tulia | N | 91 | 22 | 110 | -10 | Apr. | 10 | Nov. | 1 | 205 | N | 0.5 | 0.7 | 0.9 | 1.0 | 2.4 | 3.9 | 2.0 | 2.6 | 2.5 | 1.5 | 0.8 | 0.6 | 19.4 |
| Tarrant, Fort Worth | N | 96 | 35 | 108 | 4 | Mar. | 26 | Nov. | 11 | 230 | 29 | 2.0 | 2.2 | 2.5 | 3.6 | 4.6 | 3.0 | 1.8 | 1.7 | 2.5 | 2.6 | 2.4 | 2.4 | 31.3 |
| Taylor, Abilene | 28 | 95 | 31 | 110 | -9 | Mar. | 31 | Nov. | 11 | 225 | N | 1.0 | 1.4 | 1.9 | 1.9 | 3.0 | 2.9 | 2.1 | 2.1 | 3.2 | 2.8 | 1.5 | 1.0 | 24.4 |
| Terrell, Sanderson | N | 92 | 29 | 110 | 0 | Mar. | 21 | Nov. | 13 | 237 | N | 0.3 | 0.6 | 0.4 | 1.0 | 1.6 | 1.8 | 1.3 | 1.8 | 2.7 | 1.8 | 0.7 | 0.5 | 14.3 |
| Terry, Brownfield | N | 93 | 24 | 111 | -8 | Apr. | 10 | Nov. | 2 | 206 | N | 0.5 | 0.7 | 0.6 | 0.9 | 2.7 | 3.0 | 2.4 | 2.4 | 2.6 | 1.7 | 0.6 | 0.6 | 19.0 |
| Throckmorton, Throckmorton | N | 96 | 27 | 114 | -11 | Mar. | 31 | Nov. | 6 | 220 | N | 1.0 | 1.5 | 1.6 | 2.5 | 3.5 | 3.1 | 2.0 | 2.6 | 4.2 | 2.6 | 1.4 | 1.3 | 27.1 |
| Titus, Mount Pleasant | N | 94 | 29 | 111 | -12 | Mar. | 23 | Nov. | 12 | 233 | N | 2.8 | 3.7 | 4.4 | 4.3 | 5.1 | 4.3 | 3.4 | 2.4 | 3.9 | 4.2 | 4.5 | 3.9 | 46.8 |
| Tom Green, San Angelo | N | 96 | 31 | 111 | -4 | Mar. | 25 | Nov. | 15 | 235 | N | 0.8 | 1.1 | 0.9 | 1.7 | 3.0 | 2.3 | 1.1 | 1.9 | 3.4 | 2.4 | 1.1 | 0.8 | 20.5 |
| Travis, Austin | N | 95 | 39 | 109 | -2 | Mar. | 3 | Nov. | 28 | 270 | N | 1.7 | 2.2 | 1.9 | 2.6 | 4.8 | 3.7 | 2.0 | 2.1 | 3.3 | 3.4 | 2.4 | 1.9 | 31.9 |
| Trinity, Groveton | 23 | 94 | 36 | 108 | 1 | Mar. | 6 | Nov. | 21 | 260 | 23 | 3.6 | 3.2 | 3.6 | 3.4 | 4.8 | 4.5 | 3.3 | 3.1 | 4.1 | 3.4 | 3.9 | 4.1 | 44.9 |
| Tyler, Warren | N | 93 | 38 | 106 | 6 | Mar. | 17 | Nov. | 11 | 241 | N | 4.5 | 4.0 | 3.9 | 3.4 | 6.0 | 5.8 | 3.8 | 3.4 | 4.5 | 3.4 | 4.8 | 5.8 | 54.3 |
| Upshur, Gilmer | N | 93 | 30 | 109 | -4 | Mar. | 16 | Nov. | 16 | 245 | N | 2.9 | 3.7 | 4.3 | 4.8 | 4.6 | 3.6 | 2.8 | 2.3 | 4.0 | 3.8 | 4.4 | 4.0 | 45.2 |
| Upton, McCamey | N | 95 | 31 | 113 | -2 | Mar. | 26 | Nov. | 12 | 232 | N | 0.4 | 0.6 | 0.4 | 0.9 | 1.7 | 1.5 | 1.0 | 2.7 | 2.2 | 2.2 | 0.7 | 0.6 | 14.3 |
| Uvalde, Uvalde | N | 96 | 36 | 111 | 6 | Mar. | 10 | Nov. | 21 | 255 | N | 1.1 | 1.4 | 1.1 | 2.3 | 3.3 | 2.8 | 1.9 | 2.7 | 2.8 | 3.0 | 1.3 | 1.1 | 24.8 |
| Val Verde, Del Rio | N | 96 | 39 | 112 | 10 | Feb. | 12 | Dec. | 9 | 300 | N | 0.6 | 1.0 | 0.7 | 1.7 | 2.0 | 2.1 | 1.9 | 1.5 | 2.8 | 2.2 | 0.9 | 0.6 | 18.2 |
| Van Zandt, Wills Point | N | 95 | 32 | 113 | -2 | Mar. | 16 | Nov. | 21 | 250 | N | 2.7 | 3.2 | 3.6 | 4.7 | 5.4 | 4.2 | 2.2 | 3.0 | 3.9 | 3.5 | 3.6 | 3.3 | 43.0 |
| Victoria, Victoria | N | 94 | 43 | 107 | 9 | Feb. | 19 | Dec. | 6 | 290 | N | 2.2 | 3.1 | 1.6 | 2.4 | 4.5 | 4.9 | 3.3 | 2.5 | 5.6 | 3.5 | 2.0 | 2.0 | 37.4 |
| Walker, Huntsville | 15 | 94 | 38 | 107 | 2 | Feb. | 16 | Dec. | 19 | 265 | N | 2.8 | 3.1 | 3.1 | 3.5 | 5.2 | 4.2 | 2.4 | 3.3 | 5.0 | 3.6 | 3.9 | 3.8 | 45.0 |
| Waller, Hempstead | N | 94 | 38 | 107 | 13 | Feb. | 28 | Nov. | 7 | 283 | N | 2.8 | 2.9 | 2.1 | 3.9 | 4.7 | 3.6 | 2.0 | 1.4 | 4.6 | 4.0 | 1.1 | 3.0 | 38.2 |
| Ward, Monahans | N | 96 | 27 | 120 | -9 | Apr. | 3 | Dec. | 4 | 223 | N | 0.4 | 0.6 | 0.4 | 0.7 | 1.8 | 1.4 | 1.4 | 1.4 | 2.4 | 1.4 | 1.0 | 0.5 | 12.7 |
| Washington, Brenham | N | 96 | 41 | 110 | 1 | Feb. | 5 | Dec. | 10 | 277 | N | 3.1 | 3.0 | 2.8 | 3.3 | 5.2 | 4.3 | 2.0 | 2.5 | 4.8 | 3.6 | 3.1 | 3.2 | 41.4 |
| Webb, Laredo | 27 | 99 | 43 | 110 | 13 | Feb. | 7 | Dec. | 26 | 322 | 27 | 0.9 | 1.0 | 0.8 | 1.8 | 2.7 | 3.1 | 1.4 | 3.6 | 5.9 | 2.5 | 1.5 | 0.9 | 21.4 |
| Wharton, Danevang | N | 92 | 41 | 108 | 7 | Mar. | 5 | Nov. | 5 | 266 | N | 3.4 | 2.6 | 1.5 | 3.0 | 4.9 | 4.7 | 3.6 | 2.5 | 2.8 | 3.9 | 1.4 | 2.7 | 42.3 |
| Wheeler, Shamrock | N | 95 | 22 | 113 | -8 | Apr. | 7 | Nov. | 1 | 208 | 27 | 0.6 | 0.8 | 1.8 | 2.3 | 3.5 | 3.4 | 2.0 | 2.5 | 3.6 | 1.8 | 1.3 | 0.5 | 22.1 |
| Wichita, Wichita Falls | N | 97 | 28 | 117 | -8 | Mar. | 27 | Nov. | 7 | 229 | N | 1.0 | 1.2 | 1.8 | 2.3 | 4.1 | 3.5 | 2.0 | 2.3 | 5.8 | 2.7 | 2.0 | 1.3 | 28.9 |
| Wilbarger, Vernon | N | 97 | 25 | 119 | -9 | Mar. | 31 | Nov. | 7 | 221 | N | 0.9 | 1.2 | 0.8 | 1.5 | 3.8 | 2.9 | 2.0 | 3.1 | 4.2 | 2.6 | 0.6 | 0.8 | 25.7 |
| Willacy, Raymondville | N | 96 | 46 | 107 | 14 | Feb. | 6 | Dec. | 11 | 331 | N | 1.3 | 1.6 | 1.2 | 2.9 | 3.1 | 3.3 | 1.7 | 2.3 | 3.6 | 2.2 | 0.6 | 1.2 | 27.6 |
| Williamson, Taylor | N | 96 | 34 | 112 | -5 | Mar. | 11 | Nov. | 24 | 258 | 28 | 2.0 | 2.5 | 1.2 | 2.9 | 4.7 | 3.6 | 2.0 | 2.0 | 3.6 | 3.6 | 2.0 | 2.1 | 34.4 |
| Wilson, Floresville | N | 96 | 36 | 108 | 7 | Feb. | 24 | Dec. | 1 | 280 | N | 1.5 | 1.9 | 1.2 | 2.9 | 3.4 | 2.9 | 1.7 | 2.3 | 3.6 | 2.7 | 0.6 | 1.6 | 29.4 |
| Winkler, Wink | N | 97 | 28 | 117 | -14 | Apr. | 3 | Nov. | 8 | 219 | N | 0.3 | 0.4 | 0.4 | 0.7 | 1.0 | 1.9 | 2.3 | 2.0 | 1.4 | 1.5 | 0.6 | 0.5 | 12.6 |
| Wise, Bridgeport | N | 99 | 30 | 115 | -8 | Mar. | 31 | Nov. | 6 | 220 | N | 1.5 | 1.9 | 2.6 | 4.7 | 5.3 | 3.5 | 3.0 | 2.5 | 3.3 | 3.3 | 0.6 | 3.6 | 32.6 |
| Wood, Mineola | 14 | 94 | 31 | 107 | 2 | Mar. | 17 | Nov. | 18 | 246 | 14 | 1.3 | 3.0 | 4.0 | 1.0 | 3.1 | 3.4 | 2.1 | 2.3 | 3.6 | 4.3 | 3.7 | 3.6 | 45.0 |
| Yoakum, Plains | N | 91 | 22 | 111 | -12 | Apr. | 15 | Oct. | 31 | 199 | N | 0.4 | 0.7 | 0.6 | 1.4 | 2.1 | 2.4 | 1.6 | 2.0 | 4.2 | 2.6 | 0.7 | 1.4 | 17.7 |
| Young, Graham | N | 96 | 26 | 112 | -8 | Apr. | 2 | Nov. | 4 | 216 | N | 1.3 | 1.6 | 1.9 | 1.8 | 4.5 | 3.4 | 2.1 | 2.3 | 4.3 | 3.1 | 1.9 | 0.9 | 30.6 |
| Zapata, Zapata | 27 | 99 | 43 | 112 | 16 | Feb. | 14 | Dec. | 15 | 304 | 12 | 0.8 | 1.1 | 0.6 | 1.4 | 2.5 | 2.5 | 1.6 | 1.7 | 4.3 | 1.6 | 1.0 | 0.9 | 19.7 |
| Zavala, Crystal City | N | 97 | 42 | 109 | 11 | Feb. | 24 | Dec. | 1 | 280 | N | 0.9 | 1.2 | 0.8 | 1.8 | 2.9 | 2.8 | 1.6 | 1.9 | 2.7 | 2.5 | 1.1 | 0.8 | 21.0 |

# Astronomical Calendar for 2004 and 2005

The subsequent calendars were calculated principally from data on the **U.S. Naval Observatory's Web site** (http://aa.usno.navy.mil/data/), and from its publication, **Astronomical Phenomena** for **2004** and **2005**.

Times listed here are **Central Standard Time**, except for the period from 2:00 a.m. on the first Sunday in April until 2:00 a.m. on the last Sunday in October, when **Daylight Saving Time,** which is one hour later than Central Standard Time, is in effect.

All of Texas is in the Central Time Zone, except El Paso and Hudspeth counties and the northwest corner of Culberson County, which observe **Mountain Time** (see accompanying map). Mountain Time is one hour earlier than Central Time.

**All times are calculated for the intersection of 99° 20' west longitude and 31° 08' north latitude,** which is about 15 miles northeast of Brady, McCulloch County. This point is the **approximate geographical center of the state.**

**To get the time of sunrise or sunset, moonrise or moonset for any point in Texas**, apply the following rule: Add four minutes to the time given in this calendar for each degree of longitude that the place lies west of the 99th meridian; subtract four minutes for each degree of longitude the place lies east of the 99th meridian.

At times there will be considerable variation for distances north and south of the line of 31° 08' north latitude, but the rule for calculating it is complicated. The formula given above will get sufficiently close results. An accompanying map shows the intersection for which all times given here are calculated, with some major Texas cities and their longitudes. These make it convenient to calculate time at any given point.

The Naval Observatory's Web site will allow you to determine more exactly the rise and set times of the Sun and the Moon at your location on a given date or for an entire year.

### Planetary Configurations and Phenomena

The phenomena and planetary configurations of heavens for 2004 and 2005 are given in the center column of the calendar on pages 112–117. Below is an explanation of the symbols used in those tables:

| | | |
|---|---|---|
| ☉ The Sun | ● The Earth | ♅ Uranus |
| ☾ The Moon | ♂ Mars | ♆ Neptune |
| ☿ Mercury | ♃ Jupiter | ♇ Pluto |
| ♀ Venus | ♄ Saturn | |

### Aspects

☌ This symbol appearing between the symbols for heavenly bodies means they are "in conjunction," that is, having the same longitude as applies to the sky and appearing near each other.

☍ This symbol means that the two heavenly bodies are in "opposition," or differ by 180 degrees of longitude.

### Common Astronomical Terms

★ **Aphelion** — Point at which a planet's orbit is farthest from the sun.

★ **Perihelion** — Point at which a planet's orbit is nearest the sun.

★ **Apogee** — That point of the moon's orbit farthest from the earth.

★ **Perigee** — That point of the moon's orbit nearest the earth.

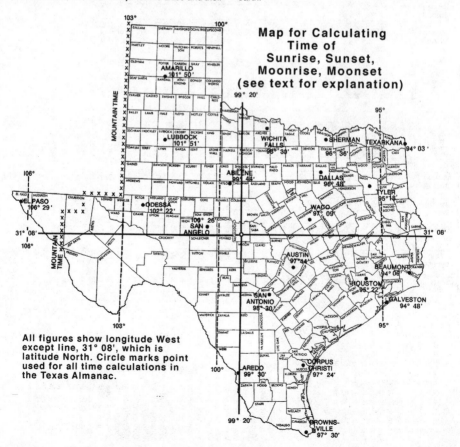

**Map for Calculating Time of Sunrise, Sunset, Moonrise, Moonset (see text for explanation)**

All figures show longitude West except line, 31° 08', which is latitude North. Circle marks point used for all time calculations in the Texas Almanac.

# The Seasons, 2004 and 2005

### 2004

The seasons of 2004 begin as follows: **Spring**, March 20, 12:49 a.m. (CST); **Summer**, June 20, 7:57 p.m. (CDT); **Fall**, Sept. 22, 11:30 a.m. (CDT); **Winter**, Dec. 21, 6:42 a.m. (CST).

### 2005

The seasons of 2005 begin as follows: **Spring**, March 20, 6:33 a.m. (CST); **Summer**, June 21, 1:46 a.m. (CDT); **Fall**, Sept. 22, 5:23 p.m. (CDT); **Winter**, Dec. 21, 12:35 p.m. (CST).

## Morning and Evening Stars, 2004 and 2005

### Morning Stars, 2004

Jupiter — Jan. 1– March 4; Oct. 5–Dec. 31
Saturn — July 27–Dec. 31
Mars — Oct. 30–Dec. 31
Venus — June 15–Dec. 31

### Evening Stars, 2004

Saturn — Jan. 1–June 20
Mars — Jan. 1–July 31
Jupiter — March 4–Sept. 8
Venus — Jan. 1–June 2

### Morning Stars, 2005

Jupiter — Jan. 1–April 3; Nov. 5–Dec. 31
Venus — Jan. 1–Feb. 19
Mars — Jan. 1–Nov. 7
Saturn — Jan. 1–Jan. 13; Aug. 11–Dec. 31

### Evening Stars, 2005

Saturn —Jan. 1–July 5
Jupiter — April 3–Oct. 9
Mars — Nov. 7–Dec. 31
Venus — May 9–Dec. 31

## Eclipses, 2004 and 2005

### Eclipses, 2004

There will be four eclipses during 2004, two of the Sun and two of the Moon, as follows:

**April 19 — Partial eclipse of the sun**, visible in Antarctica, southeast Atlantic Ocean, southern half of Africa and Madagascar.

**May 4 — Total eclipse of the moon,** visible in Antarctica, Australia except New Zealand, Asia except northeast region, southern Japan, Africa, Indian Ocean, Europe and eastern portion of South America.

**Oct. 14 — Partial eclipse of the sun**, visible in northeast Asia, Japan, western Pacific Ocean, Hawaii and western portion of Alaska.

**Oct. 28 — Total eclipse of the moon**, visible in Arctic regions, western Russia, Arabia, Africa, parts of Antarctica, Europe, Greenland, North America, Central America, South America, eastern Pacific Ocean and eastern tip of Siberia.

### Eclipses, 2005

There will be four eclipses in 2005, two of the Sun and two of the Moon, as follows:

**April 8 —Annular-total eclipse of the sun**, visible in New Zealand, part of Antarctica, southern United States, Central America, the Caribbean, South America except eastern and southern portions.

**April 24 — Prenumbral eclipse of the moon,** visible in North America, Central America, South America, New Zealand, eastern Australia, eastern Indonesia, most of Antarctica, North Pacific Ocean except extreme western portion, South Pacific Ocean, Bering Sea, western Atlantic Ocean and most of Mexico.

**Oct. 3 — Annular eclipse of the sun, visible in** eastern Greenland, Iceland, Europe, British Isles, Africa except southern tip, western Asia including India.

**Oct. 17 — Partial eclipse of the moon**, visible in parts of Antarctica, Australia, central and eastern Asia, North America except eastern portion, Central America.

## Major Meteor Showers

Note: These are approximate dates. Listen to local news and weather broadcasts several days before the listed dates to determine peak observation days and hours. Generally, viewing will be better after 2:00 a.m.

*(Meteor shower dates provided by Peter Brown, University of Western Ontario, Department of Physics and Astronomy, London, Ontario, Canada.)*

| Meteor Shower | Peak 2004 | Peak 2005 |
|---|---|---|
| Quadrantid | Jan. 4 | Jan. 3 |
| Perseid | Aug. 12 | Aug. 12 |
| Orionid | Oct. 20 | Oct. 21 |
| Leonid | Nov. 17 | Nov. 17 |
| Geminid | Dec. 13 | Dec. 13 |

## Chronological Eras and Cycles, 2004 and 2005

### Chronological Eras, 2004

The year 2004 of the **Christian** era comprises the latter part of the 228th and the beginning of the 229th year of the independence of the United States of America, and corresponds to the year 6717 of the Julian period. All dates in the list below are given in terms of the Gregorian calendar, in which Jan. 14, 2004, corresponds to Jan. 1, 2004, Julian calendar.

| Era | Year | Begins |
|---|---|---|
| Byzantine | 7513 | Sept. 14 |
| Jewish (A.M.)* | 5765 | Sept. 15 |
| Chinese (Jai-shen) | 4641 | Jan. 22 |
| Roman (A.U.C.) | 2757 | Jan. 14 |
| Nabonassar | 2753 | April 22 |
| Japanese | 2664 | Jan. 1 |
| Grecian (Seleucidae) | 2316 | Sept. 14 or Oct. 14 |
| Indian (Saka) | 1926 | March 21 |
| Diocletian | 1721 | Sept. 11 |
| Islamic (Hegira)* | 1425 | Feb. 21 |

*Year begins at sunset.

### Chronological Cycles, 2004

| | | | |
|---|---|---|---|
| Dominical Letter | DC | Julian Period | 6717 |
| Epact | 8 | Roman Indiction | 12 |
| Golden Number or Lunar Cycle | X | Solar Cycle | 25 |

### Chronological Eras, 2005

The year 2005 of the **Christian** era comprises the latter part of the 229th and the beginning of the 230th year of the independence of the United States of America, and corresponds to the year 6718 of the Julian period. All dates in the list below are given in terms of the Gregorian calendar, in which Jan. 14, 2005, corresponds to Jan. 1, 2005, of the Julian calendar:

| Era | Year | Begins |
|---|---|---|
| Byzantine | 7514 | Sept. 14 |
| Jewish (A.M.)* | 5766 | Oct. 3 |
| Chinese (Yi-you) | 4642 | Feb. 9 |
| Roman (A.U.C.) | 2758 | Jan. 14 |
| Nabonassar | 2754 | April 22 |
| Japanese | 2665 | Jan. 1 |
| Grecian (Seleucidae) | 2317 | Sept. 14 or Oct. 14 |
| Indian (Saka) | 1927 | March 22 |
| Diocletian | 1722 | Sept. 11 |
| Islamic (Hegira)* | 1426 | Feb. 9 |

*Year begins at sunset.

### Chronological Cycles, 2005

| | | | |
|---|---|---|---|
| Dominical Letter | B | Julian Period | 6718 |
| Epact | 19 | Roman Indiction | 13 |
| Golden Number or Lunar Cycle | XI | Solar Cycle | 26 |

# Calendar for 2004

Times are **Central Standard Time**, except from April 4 to Oct. 31, during which **Daylight Saving Time** is observed. **Boldface times for moonrise and moonset** indicate p.m. Times are figured for the point **99° 10' West and 31° 23' North,** the approximate geographical center of the state. **See page 110 for explanation of how to get the approximate time at any other Texas point. (On the Web: http://aa.usno.navy.mil/data/)** Please note: Not all **eclipses** are visible in United States. For visibility, see listing on p. 111.

## 1st Month — January 2004 — 31 Days

**Moon's Phases** — Full, Jan. 7, 9:40 a.m.; Last Qtr., Jan. 14, 10:46 p.m.; New, Jan. 21, 3:05 p.m.; First Qtr., Jan. 29, 12:03 a.m.

| Day of | | | Planetary Configurations and Phenomena | *Hour of | | | |
|---|---|---|---|---|---|---|---|
| Year | Month | Week | | Sunrise | Sunset | Moon-rise | Moon-set |
| 1 | 1 | Th. | | 7:36 | 5:46 | **1:44** | 2:22 |
| 2 | 2 | Fr. | | 7:36 | 5:47 | **2:14** | 3:17 |
| 3 | 3 | Sa. | ☾ at apogee | 7:36 | 5:47 | **2:48** | 4:13 |
| 4 | 4 | Su. | ♃ stationary; ● at perihelion | 7:36 | 5:48 | **3:26** | 5:09 |
| 5 | 5 | Mo. | | 7:37 | 5:49 | **4:10** | 6:06 |
| 6 | 6 | Tu. | ☿ stationary; ♄ ☌ ☾ | 7:37 | 5:50 | **4:59** | 7:01 |
| 7 | 7 | We. | | 7:37 | 5:50 | **5:54** | 7:52 |
| 8 | 8 | Th. | | 7:37 | 5:51 | **6:53** | 8:39 |
| 9 | 9 | Fr. | | 7:37 | 5:52 | **7:53** | 9:21 |
| 10 | 10 | Sa. | | 7:37 | 5:53 | **8:54** | 9:58 |
| 11 | 11 | Su. | | 7:37 | 5:54 | **9:55** | 10:31 |
| 12 | 12 | Mo. | ♃ ☌ ☾ | 7:37 | 5:55 | **10:55** | 11:02 |
| 13 | 13 | Tu. | | 7:37 | 5:55 | **11:56** | 11:32 |
| 14 | 14 | We. | ♀ ☌ ♅ | 7:37 | 5:56 | ... | **12:02** |
| 15 | 15 | Th. | | 7:36 | 5:57 | 12:59 | **12:34** |
| 16 | 16 | Fr. | | 7:36 | 5:58 | 2:05 | **1:10** |
| 17 | 17 | Sa. | ☿ greatest elongation W | 7:36 | 5:59 | 3:14 | **1:51** |
| 18 | 18 | Su. | | 7:36 | 6:00 | 4:25 | **2:41** |
| 19 | 19 | Mo. | ☾ at perigee; ☿ ☌ ☾ | 7:36 | 6:01 | 5:37 | **3:39** |
| 20 | 20 | Tu. | | 7:35 | 6:02 | 6:44 | **4:46** |
| 21 | 21 | We. | | 7:35 | 6:02 | 7:43 | **5:56** |
| 22 | 22 | Th. | | 7:35 | 6:03 | 8:32 | **7:07** |
| 23 | 23 | Fr. | ♅ ☌ ☾ | 7:34 | 6:04 | 9:14 | **8:14** |
| 24 | 24 | Sa. | ♀ ☌ ☾ | 7:34 | 6:05 | 9:49 | **9:18** |
| 25 | 25 | Su. | | 7:33 | 6:06 | 10:20 | **10:18** |
| 26 | 26 | Mo. | | 7:33 | 6:07 | 10:49 | **11:16** |
| 27 | 27 | Tu. | ♂ ☌ ☾ | 7:33 | 6:08 | 11:16 | ... |
| 28 | 28 | We. | | 7:32 | 6:09 | 11:44 | 12:12 |
| 29 | 29 | Th. | | 7:32 | 6:10 | **12:13** | 1:08 |
| 30 | 30 | Fr. | | 7:31 | 6:11 | **12:46** | 2:04 |
| 31 | 31 | Sa. | ☾ at apogee | 7:30 | 6:11 | **1:22** | 3:01 |

## 2nd Month — February 2004 — 29 Days

**Moon's Phases** — Full, Feb. 6, 2:47 a.m.; Last Qtr., Feb. 13, 7:40 a.m.; New, Feb. 20, 3:18 a.m.; First Qtr., Feb. 27, 9:24 p.m.

| Day of | | | Planetary Configurations and Phenomena | *Hour of | | | |
|---|---|---|---|---|---|---|---|
| Year | Month | Week | | Sunrise | Sunset | Moon-rise | Moon-set |
| 32 | 1 | Su. | | 7:30 | 6:12 | **2:04** | 3:57 |
| 33 | 2 | Mo. | ♆ ☌ ☉; ♄ ☌ ☾ | 7:29 | 6:13 | **2:52** | 4:53 |
| 34 | 3 | Tu. | | 7:28 | 6:14 | **3:45** | 5:46 |
| 35 | 4 | We. | | 7:28 | 6:15 | **4:43** | 6:34 |
| 36 | 5 | Th. | | 7:27 | 6:16 | **5:44** | 7:18 |
| 37 | 6 | Fr. | | 7:26 | 6:17 | **6:46** | 7:57 |
| 38 | 7 | Sa. | | 7:26 | 6:18 | **7:47** | 8:32 |
| 39 | 8 | Su. | ♃ ☌ ☾ | 7:25 | 6:18 | **8:49** | 9:04 |
| 40 | 9 | Mo. | | 7:24 | 6:19 | **9:51** | 9:34 |
| 41 | 10 | Tu. | | 7:23 | 6:20 | **10:53** | 10:04 |
| 42 | 11 | We. | | 7:22 | 6:21 | **11:58** | 10:36 |
| 43 | 12 | Th. | | 7:22 | 6:22 | ... | 11:10 |
| 44 | 13 | Fr. | | 7:21 | 6:23 | 1:05 | 11:48 |
| 45 | 14 | Sa. | | 7:20 | 6:24 | 2:14 | **12:34** |
| 46 | 15 | Su. | ☿ ☌ ♆ | 7:19 | 6:24 | 3:23 | **1:27** |
| 47 | 16 | Mo. | ☾ at perigee | 7:18 | 6:25 | 4:30 | **2:28** |
| 48 | 17 | Tu. | | 7:17 | 6:26 | 5:30 | **3:36** |
| 49 | 18 | We. | ♆ ☌ ☾ | 7:16 | 6:27 | 6:22 | **4:45** |
| 50 | 19 | Th. | | 7:15 | 6:28 | 7:06 | **5:54** |
| 51 | 20 | Fr. | | 7:14 | 6:28 | 7:44 | **6:59** |
| 52 | 21 | Sa. | ♅ ☌ ☉ | 7:13 | 6:29 | 8:17 | **8:02** |
| 53 | 22 | Su. | | 7:12 | 6:30 | 8:46 | **9:01** |
| 54 | 23 | Mo. | ♀ ☌ ☾ | 7:11 | 6:31 | 9:15 | **9:59** |
| 55 | 24 | Tu. | | 7:10 | 6:32 | 9:43 | **10:56** |
| 56 | 25 | We. | ♂ ☌ ☾ | 7:09 | 6:32 | 10:12 | **11:53** |
| 57 | 26 | Th. | | 7:08 | 6:33 | 10:43 | ... |
| 58 | 27 | Fr. | | 7:07 | 6:34 | 11:18 | 12:50 |
| 59 | 28 | Sa. | ☾ at apogee | 7:06 | 6:35 | 11:58 | 1:47 |
| 60 | 29 | Su. | | 7:05 | 6:35 | **12:43** | 2:43 |

*See text before January calendar for explanation.

## 3rd Month — March 2004 — 31 Days

**Moon's Phases** — Full, March 6, 5:14 p.m.; Last Qtr., March 13, 3:01 p.m.; New, March 20, 4:41 p.m.; First Qtr., March 28, 5:48 p.m.

| Day of | | | Planetary Configurations and Phenomena | *Hour of | | | |
|---|---|---|---|---|---|---|---|
| Year | Month | Week | | Sunrise | Sunset | Moon-rise | Moon-set |
| 61 | 1 | Mo. | ♄ ☌ ☾ | 7:03 | 6:36 | **1:34** | 3:37 |
| 62 | 2 | Tu. | | 7:02 | 6:37 | **2:30** | 4:27 |
| 63 | 3 | We. | ☿ superior; ♃ ☍ | 7:01 | 6:38 | **3:29** | 5:13 |
| 64 | 4 | Th. | | 7:00 | 6:38 | **4:31** | 5:54 |
| 65 | 5 | Fr. | | 6:59 | 6:39 | **5:34** | 6:30 |
| 66 | 6 | Sa. | ♃ ☌ ☾ | 6:58 | 6:40 | **6:37** | 7:03 |
| 67 | 7 | Su. | ♄ sationary | 6:57 | 6:40 | **7:40** | 7:35 |
| 68 | 8 | Mo. | | 6:55 | 6:41 | **8:44** | 8:05 |
| 69 | 9 | Tu. | | 6:54 | 6:42 | **9:49** | 8:37 |
| 70 | 10 | We. | | 6:53 | 6:42 | **10:57** | 9:10 |
| 71 | 11 | Th. | ☾ at perigee | 6:52 | 6:43 | ... | 9:48 |
| 72 | 12 | Fr. | | 6:50 | 6:44 | 12:06 | 10:31 |
| 73 | 13 | Sa. | | 6:49 | 6:44 | 1:16 | 11:22 |
| 74 | 14 | Su. | | 6:48 | 6:45 | 2:23 | **12:20** |
| 75 | 15 | Mo. | | 6:47 | 6:46 | 3:24 | **1:25** |
| 76 | 16 | Tu. | | 6:46 | 6:47 | 4:18 | **2:32** |
| 77 | 17 | We. | ♆ ☌ ☾ | 6:44 | 6:47 | 5:03 | **3:40** |
| 78 | 18 | Th. | ♅ ☌ ☾ | 6:43 | 6:48 | 5:42 | **4:45** |
| 79 | 19 | Fr. | | 6:42 | 6:48 | 6:16 | **5:47** |
| 80 | 20 | Sa. | **Spring equinox** | 6:41 | 6:49 | 6:46 | **6:48** |
| 81 | 21 | Su. | ☿ ☌ ☾ | 6:39 | 6:50 | 7:14 | **7:46** |
| 82 | 22 | Mo. | | 6:38 | 6:50 | 7:42 | **8:43** |
| 83 | 23 | Tu. | | 6:37 | 6:51 | 8:10 | **9:41** |
| 84 | 24 | We. | ♀ ☌ ☾; ♇ stationary | 6:36 | 6:52 | 8:41 | **10:38** |
| 85 | 25 | Th. | ♂ ☌ ☾ | 6:34 | 6:52 | 9:14 | **11:36** |
| 86 | 26 | Fr. | | 6:33 | 6:53 | 9:52 | ... |
| 87 | 27 | Sa. | ☾ at apogee | 6:32 | 6:54 | 10:35 | 12:33 |
| 88 | 28 | Su. | ♄ ☌ ☾ | 6:31 | 6:54 | 11:23 | 1:28 |
| 89 | 29 | Mo. | ☿,♀ greatest elongation E | 6:29 | 6:55 | **12:17** | 2:19 |
| 90 | 30 | Tu. | | 6:28 | 6:56 | **1:14** | 3:06 |
| 91 | 31 | We. | | 6:27 | 6:56 | **2:15** | 3:49 |

## 4th Month — April 2004 — 30 Days

**Moon's Phases** — Full, April 5, 6:03 a.m.; Last Qtr., April 11, 10:46 p.m.; New, April 19, 8:21 a.m.; First Qtr., April 27, 12:32 p.m.

| Day of | | | Planetary Configurations and Phenomena | *Hour of | | | |
|---|---|---|---|---|---|---|---|
| Year | Month | Week | | Sunrise | Sunset | Moon-rise | Moon-set |
| 92 | 1 | Th. | | 6:26 | 6:57 | **3:17** | 4:26 |
| 93 | 2 | Fr. | ♃ ☌ ☾ | 6:24 | 6:58 | **4:19** | 5:00 |
| 94 | 3 | Sa. | | 6:23 | 6:58 | **5:22** | 5:32 |
| 95 | † 4 | Su. | | 7:22 | 7:59 | **7:27** | 7:03 |
| 96 | 5 | Mo. | | 7:21 | 8:00 | **8:33** | 7:34 |
| 97 | 6 | Tu. | ☿ stationary | 7:19 | 8:00 | **9:42** | 8:08 |
| 98 | 7 | We. | ☾ at perigee | 7:18 | 8:01 | **10:53** | 8:44 |
| 99 | 8 | Th. | | 7:17 | 8:01 | ... | 9:27 |
| 100 | 9 | Fr. | | 7:16 | 8:02 | 12:05 | 10:16 |
| 101 | 10 | Sa. | | 7:15 | 8:03 | 1:15 | 11:13 |
| 102 | 11 | Su. | | 7:13 | 8:03 | 2:20 | **12:17** |
| 103 | 12 | Mo. | | 7:12 | 8:04 | 3:16 | **1:24** |
| 104 | 13 | Tu. | ♆ ☌ ☾ | 7:11 | 8:05 | 4:04 | **2:31** |
| 105 | 14 | We. | ♅ ☌ ☾ | 7:10 | 8:05 | 4:43 | **3:37** |
| 106 | 15 | Th. | | 7:09 | 8:06 | 5:18 | **4:39** |
| 107 | 16 | Fr. | ☿ inferior | 7:08 | 8:07 | 5:48 | **5:39** |
| 108 | 17 | Sa. | | 7:07 | 8:07 | 6:16 | **6:37** |
| 109 | 18 | Su. | | 7:06 | 8:08 | 6:44 | **7:34** |
| 110 | 19 | Mo. | Eclipse ☉ | 7:04 | 8:09 | 7:11 | **8:31** |
| 111 | 20 | Tu. | | 7:03 | 8:09 | 7:41 | **9:28** |
| 112 | 21 | We. | | 7:02 | 8:10 | 8:13 | **10:26** |
| 113 | 22 | Th. | | 7:01 | 8:11 | 8:49 | **11:24** |
| 114 | 23 | Fr. | ♀ ☌ ☾; ♂ ☌ ☾; ☾ at apogee | 7:00 | 8:11 | 9:30 | ... |
| 115 | 24 | Sa. | | 6:59 | 8:12 | 10:16 | 12:19 |
| 116 | 25 | Su. | ♄ ☌ ☾ | 6:58 | 8:13 | 11:07 | 1:12 |
| 117 | 26 | Mo. | | 6:57 | 8:13 | **12:02** | 2:01 |
| 118 | 27 | Tu. | | 6:56 | 8:14 | **1:01** | 2:44 |
| 119 | 28 | We. | | 6:55 | 8:15 | **2:01** | 3:23 |
| 120 | 29 | Th. | ☿ stationary; ♃ ☌ ☾ | 6:54 | 8:15 | **3:02** | 3:58 |
| 121 | 30 | Fr. | | 6:53 | 8:16 | **4:03** | 4:30 |

† Daylight Saving Time begins at 2:00 a.m.

# Calendar for 2004 (Cont'd.)

## 5th Month — May 2004 — 31 Days

**Moon's Phases** — Full, May 4, 3:33 p.m.; Last Qtr., May 11, 6:04 a.m.; New, May 18, 11:52 p.m.; First Qtr., May 27, 2:57 a.m.

| Day of Year | Day of Month | Day of Week | Planetary Configurations and Phenomena | *Hour of Sunrise | *Hour of Sunset | *Hour of Moon-rise | *Hour of Moon-set |
|---|---|---|---|---|---|---|---|
| 122 | 1 | Sa. | | 6:52 | 8:17 | **5:06** | 5:00 |
| 123 | 2 | Su. | ♀ greatest brilliancy | 6:51 | 8:17 | **6:11** | 5:30 |
| 124 | 3 | Mo. | | 6:51 | 8:18 | **7:19** | 6:02 |
| 125 | 4 | Tu. | Eclipse ☾ | 6:50 | 8:19 | **8:30** | 6:38 |
| 126 | 5 | We. | ♃ stationary; ☾ at perigee | 6:49 | 8:19 | **9:44** | 7:18 |
| 127 | 6 | Th. | | 6:48 | 8:20 | **10:58** | 8:05 |
| 128 | 7 | Fr. | | 6:47 | 8:21 | . . . | 9:01 |
| 129 | 8 | Sa. | | 6:46 | 8:22 | 12:08 | 10:05 |
| 130 | 9 | Su. | | 6:46 | 8:22 | 1:10 | 11:14 |
| 131 | 10 | Mo. | ♆ ☌ ☾ | 6:45 | 8:23 | 2:02 | **12:23** |
| 132 | 11 | Tu. | | 6:44 | 8:24 | 2:45 | **1:30** |
| 133 | 12 | We. | ⛢ ☌ ☾ | 6:43 | 8:24 | 3:21 | **2:33** |
| 134 | 13 | Th. | | 6:43 | 8:25 | 3:52 | **3:33** |
| 135 | 14 | Fr. | ☿ greatest elongation W | 6:42 | 8:26 | 4:20 | **4:31** |
| 136 | 15 | Sa. | | 6:41 | 8:26 | 4:48 | **5:28** |
| 137 | 16 | Su. | ☿ ☌ ☾ | 6:41 | 8:27 | 5:15 | **6:24** |
| 138 | 17 | Mo. | ♆ stationary; ♀ stationary | 6:40 | 8:28 | 5:43 | **7:21** |
| 139 | 18 | Tu. | | 6:40 | 8:28 | 6:14 | **8:18** |
| 140 | 19 | We. | | 6:39 | 8:29 | 6:48 | **9:16** |
| 141 | 20 | Th. | | 6:39 | 8:30 | 7:27 | **10:12** |
| 142 | 21 | Fr. | ☾ at apogee; ♀ ☌ ☾ | 6:38 | 8:30 | 8:11 | **11:06** |
| 143 | 22 | Sa. | ♂ ☌ ☾; ♄ ☌ ☾ | 6:38 | 8:31 | 9:01 | **11:56** |
| 144 | 23 | Su. | | 6:37 | 8:31 | 9:55 | . . . |
| 145 | 24 | Mo. | ♂ [illegible] ♄ | 6:37 | 8:32 | 10:52 | 12:41 |
| 146 | 25 | Tu. | | 6:36 | 8:33 | 11:50 | 1:21 |
| 147 | 26 | We. | | 6:36 | 8:33 | **12:50** | 1:56 |
| 148 | 27 | Th. | ♃ ☌ ☾ | 6:35 | 8:34 | **1:49** | 2:29 |
| 149 | 28 | Fr. | | 6:35 | 8:34 | **2:49** | 2:59 |
| 150 | 29 | Sa. | | 6:35 | 8:35 | **3:51** | 3:28 |
| 151 | 30 | Su. | | 6:35 | 8:36 | **4:56** | 3:58 |
| 152 | 31 | Mo. | | 6:34 | 8:36 | **6:04** | 4:31 |

## 6th Month — June 2004 — 30 Days

**Moon's Phases** — Full, June 2, 11:20 p.m.; Last Qtr., June 9, 3:02 p.m.; New, June 17, 3:27 p.m.; First Qtr., June 25, 2:08 p.m.

| Day of Year | Day of Month | Day of Week | Planetary Configurations and Phenomena | *Hour of Sunrise | *Hour of Sunset | *Hour of Moon-rise | *Hour of Moon-set |
|---|---|---|---|---|---|---|---|
| 153 | 1 | Tu. | | 6:34 | 8:37 | **7:17** | 5:08 |
| 154 | 2 | We. | | 6:34 | 8:37 | **8:32** | 5:51 |
| 155 | 3 | Th. | ☾ at perigee | 6:34 | 8:38 | **9:46** | 6:44 |
| 156 | 4 | Fr. | | 6:33 | 8:38 | **10:54** | 7:46 |
| 157 | 5 | Sa. | | 6:33 | 8:39 | **11:53** | 8:55 |
| 158 | 6 | Su. | | 6:33 | 8:39 | . . . | 10:07 |
| 159 | 7 | Mo. | ♆ ☌ ☾ | 6:33 | 8:40 | 12:41 | 11:17 |
| 160 | 8 | Tu. | ♀ inferior; ⛢ ☌ ☾ | 6:33 | 8:40 | 1:20 | **12:24** |
| 161 | 9 | We. | | 6:33 | 8:41 | 1:54 | **1:26** |
| 162 | 10 | Th. | ⛢ stationary | 6:33 | 8:41 | 2:24 | **2:26** |
| 163 | 11 | Fr. | ♇ ☍ | 6:33 | 8:41 | 2:51 | **3:23** |
| 164 | 12 | Sa. | | 6:33 | 8:42 | 3:19 | **4:19** |
| 165 | 13 | Su. | | 6:33 | 8:42 | 3:46 | **5:16** |
| 166 | 14 | Mo. | | 6:33 | 8:42 | 4:16 | **6:12** |
| 167 | 15 | Tu. | | 6:33 | 8:43 | 4:49 | **7:10** |
| 168 | 16 | We. | | 6:33 | 8:43 | 5:26 | **8:07** |
| 169 | 17 | Th. | ☾ at apogee | 6:33 | 8:43 | 6:09 | **9:02** |
| 170 | 18 | Fr. | ☿ superior | 6:33 | 8:44 | 6:57 | **9:53** |
| 171 | 19 | Sa. | ♄ ☌ ☾ | 6:34 | 8:44 | 7:50 | **10:40** |
| 172 | 20 | Su. | ♂ ☌ ☾; **summer solstice** | 6:34 | 8:44 | 8:46 | **11:21** |
| 173 | 21 | Mo. | | 6:34 | 8:44 | 9:44 | **11:57** |
| 174 | 22 | Tu. | | 6:34 | 8:45 | 10:43 | . . . |
| 175 | 23 | We. | ♃ ☌ ☾ | 6:35 | 8:45 | 11:41 | 12:30 |
| 176 | 24 | Th. | | 6:35 | 8:45 | **12:40** | 1:00 |
| 177 | 25 | Fr. | | 6:35 | 8:45 | **1:39** | 1:28 |
| 178 | 26 | Sa. | | 6:35 | 8:45 | **2:40** | 1:57 |
| 179 | 27 | Su. | | 6:36 | 8:45 | **3:45** | 2:27 |
| 180 | 28 | Mo. | | 6:36 | 8:45 | **4:53** | 3:01 |
| 181 | 29 | Tu. | ♀ stationary | 6:36 | 8:45 | **6:05** | 3:40 |
| 182 | 30 | We. | | 6:37 | 8:45 | **7:20** | 4:27 |

*See text before January calendar for explanation.

## 7th Month — July 2004 — 31 Days

**Moon's Phases** — Full, July 2, 6:09 a.m.; Last Qtr., July 9, 2:34 a.m.; New, July 17, 6:24 a.m.; First Qtr., July 24, 10:37 p.m.; Full, July 31, 1:05 p.m.

| Day of Year | Day of Month | Day of Week | Planetary Configurations and Phenomena | *Hour of Sunrise | *Hour of Sunset | *Hour of Moon-rise | *Hour of Moon-set |
|---|---|---|---|---|---|---|---|
| 183 | 1 | Th. | ☾ at perigee | 6:37 | 8:45 | **8:31** | 5:24 |
| 184 | 2 | Fr. | | 6:38 | 8:45 | **9:36** | 6:30 |
| 185 | 3 | Sa. | | 6:38 | 8:45 | **10:30** | 7:42 |
| 186 | 4 | Su. | ♆ ☌ ☾ | 6:39 | 8:45 | **11:14** | 8:56 |
| 187 | 5 | Mo. | ● at aphelion; ⛢ ☌ ☾ | 6:39 | 8:45 | **11:52** | 10:07 |
| 188 | 6 | Tu. | | 6:39 | 8:45 | . . . | 11:13 |
| 189 | 7 | We. | | 6:40 | 8:45 | 12:24 | **12:16** |
| 190 | 8 | Th. | ♄ ☌ ☉ | 6:40 | 8:44 | 12:53 | **1:15** |
| 191 | 9 | Fr. | | 6:41 | 8:44 | 1:21 | **2:13** |
| 192 | 10 | Sa. | ☿ ☌ ♂ | 6:41 | 8:44 | 1:49 | **3:10** |
| 193 | 11 | Su. | | 6:42 | 8:44 | 2:18 | **4:07** |
| 194 | 12 | Mo. | | 6:43 | 8:43 | 2:50 | **5:04** |
| 195 | 13 | Tu. | ♀ ☌ ☾ | 6:43 | 8:43 | 3:26 | **6:01** |
| 196 | 14 | We. | ☾ at apogee; ♀ gr. brilliancy | 6:44 | 8:43 | 4:07 | **6:57** |
| 197 | 15 | Th. | | 6:44 | 8:42 | 4:53 | **7:49** |
| 198 | 16 | Fr. | | 6:45 | 8:42 | 5:45 | **8:38** |
| 199 | 17 | Sa. | | 6:45 | 8:41 | 6:40 | **9:20** |
| 200 | 18 | Su. | ♂ ☌ ☾ | 6:46 | 8:41 | 7:38 | **9:58** |
| 201 | 19 | Mo. | ☿ ☌ ☾ | 6:47 | 8:40 | 8:37 | **10:32** |
| 202 | 20 | Tu. | | 6:47 | 8:40 | 9:36 | **11:03** |
| 203 | 21 | We. | ♃ ☌ ☾ | 6:48 | 8:39 | 10:34 | **11:31** |
| 204 | 22 | Th. | | 6:48 | 8:39 | 11:33 | **11:59** |
| 205 | 23 | Fr. | | 6:49 | 8:38 | **12:32** | . . . |
| 206 | 24 | Sa. | | 6:50 | 8:38 | **1:34** | 12:28 |
| 207 | 25 | Su. | | 6:50 | 8:37 | **2:38** | 1:00 |
| 208 | 26 | Mo. | ☿ greatest elongation E | 6:51 | 8:37 | **3:47** | 1:35 |
| 209 | 27 | Tu. | | 6:51 | 8:36 | **4:58** | 2:17 |
| 210 | 28 | We. | | 6:52 | 8:35 | **6:10** | 3:08 |
| 211 | 29 | Th. | | 6:53 | 8:34 | **7:16** | 4:08 |
| 212 | 30 | Fr. | ☾ at perigee | 6:53 | 8:34 | **8:15** | 5:17 |
| 213 | 31 | Sa. | ♆ ☌ ☾ | 6:54 | 8:33 | **9:04** | 6:30 |

## 8th Month — August 2004 — 31 Days

**Moon's Phases** — Last Qtr., Aug. 7, 5:01 p.m.; New, Aug. 15, 8:24 p.m.; First Qtr., Aug. 23, 5:12 a.m.; Full, Aug. 29, 9:22 p.m.;

| Day of Year | Day of Month | Day of Week | Planetary Configurations and Phenomena | *Hour of Sunrise | *Hour of Sunset | *Hour of Moon-rise | *Hour of Moon-set |
|---|---|---|---|---|---|---|---|
| 214 | 1 | Su. | | 6:55 | 8:32 | **9:45** | 7:43 |
| 215 | 2 | Mo. | ⛢ ☌ ☾ | 6:55 | 8:31 | **10:20** | 8:53 |
| 216 | 3 | Tu. | | 6:56 | 8:31 | **10:51** | 9:59 |
| 217 | 4 | We. | | 6:56 | 8:30 | **11:20** | 11:02 |
| 218 | 5 | Th. | ♆ ☍ | 6:57 | 8:29 | **11:49** | **12:02** |
| 219 | 6 | Fr. | | 6:58 | 8:28 | . . . | **1:00** |
| 220 | 7 | Sa. | | 6:58 | 8:27 | 12:18 | **1:58** |
| 221 | 8 | Su. | | 6:59 | 8:26 | 12:49 | **2:56** |
| 222 | 9 | Mo. | ☿ stationary | 7:00 | 8:25 | 1:24 | **3:54** |
| 223 | 10 | Tu. | | 7:00 | 8:24 | 2:03 | **4:50** |
| 224 | 11 | We. | ☾ at apogee; ♀ ☌ ☾ | 7:01 | 8:23 | 2:48 | **5:44** |
| 225 | 12 | Th. | | 7:02 | 8:22 | 3:38 | **6:34** |
| 226 | 13 | Fr. | ♄ ☌ ☾ | 7:02 | 8:21 | 4:33 | **7:19** |
| 227 | 14 | Sa. | | 7:03 | 8:20 | 5:31 | **7:58** |
| 228 | 15 | Su. | | 7:03 | 8:19 | 6:30 | **8:34** |
| 229 | 16 | Mo. | ☿ ☌ ♂ | 7:04 | 8:18 | 7:29 | **9:05** |
| 230 | 17 | Tu. | ♃ ☌ ☾ | 7:05 | 8:17 | 8:29 | **9:35** |
| 231 | 18 | We. | | 7:05 | 8:16 | 9:27 | **10:03** |
| 232 | 19 | Th. | | 7:06 | 8:15 | 10:27 | **10:31** |
| 233 | 20 | Fr. | | 7:06 | 8:14 | 11:28 | **11:01** |
| 234 | 21 | Sa. | | 7:07 | 8:13 | **12:31** | **11:35** |
| 235 | 22 | Su. | | 7:08 | 8:12 | **1:37** | . . . |
| 236 | 23 | Mo. | ☿ inferior | 7:08 | 8:11 | **2:46** | 12:14 |
| 237 | 24 | Tu. | | 7:09 | 8:10 | **3:56** | 1:00 |
| 238 | 25 | We. | | 7:10 | 8:08 | **5:02** | 1:55 |
| 239 | 26 | Th. | | 7:10 | 8:07 | **6:03** | 2:58 |
| 240 | 27 | Fr. | ☾ at perigee; ⛢ ☍ | 7:11 | 8:06 | **6:54** | 4:08 |
| 241 | 28 | Sa. | ♆ ☌ ☾ | 7:11 | 8:05 | **7:38** | 5:21 |
| 242 | 29 | Su. | | 7:12 | 8:04 | **8:15** | 6:32 |
| 243 | 30 | Mo. | | 7:12 | 8:02 | **8:48** | 7:39 |
| 244 | 31 | Tu. | ♇ stationary | 7:13 | 8:01 | **9:18** | 8:44 |

# Calendar for 2004 (Cont'd.)

## September 2004

9th Month — 30 Days

**Moon's Phases** — Last Qtr., Sept. 6, 10:11 a.m.; New, Sept. 14, 9:29 a.m.; First Qtr., Sept. 21, 10:54 a.m.; Full, Sept. 28, 8:09 a.m.

| Day of | | | Planetary Configurations and Phenomena | *Hour of | | | |
|---|---|---|---|---|---|---|---|
| Year | Month | Week | | Sunrise | Sunset | Moon-rise | Moon-set |
| 245 | 1 | We. | | 7:14 | 8:00 | **9:47** | 9:46 |
| 246 | 2 | Th. | | 7:14 | 7:59 | **10:16** | 10:46 |
| 247 | 3 | Fr. | | 7:15 | 7:58 | **10:47** | 11:46 |
| 248 | 4 | Sa. | | 7:15 | 7:56 | **11:21** | **12:45** |
| 249 | 5 | Su. | | 7:16 | 7:55 | **11:59** | **1:44** |
| 250 | 6 | Mo. | | 7:17 | 7:54 | . . . | **2:41** |
| 251 | 7 | Tu. | ☾ at apogee | 7:17 | 7:53 | 12:42 | **3:37** |
| 252 | 8 | We. | | 7:18 | 7:51 | 1:30 | **4:28** |
| 253 | 9 | Th. | ☿ greatest elongation W | 7:18 | 7:50 | 2:23 | **5:15** |
| 254 | 10 | Fr. | ♀ ☌ ☾ | 7:19 | 7:49 | 3:20 | **5:56** |
| 255 | 11 | Sa. | | 7:19 | 7:47 | 4:19 | **6:33** |
| 256 | 12 | Su. | ☿ ☌ ☾ | 7:20 | 7:46 | 5:19 | **7:06** |
| 257 | 13 | Mo. | | 7:21 | 7:45 | 6:18 | **7:36** |
| 258 | 14 | Tu. | | 7:21 | 7:44 | 7:18 | **8:05** |
| 259 | 15 | We. | ♂ ☌ ☉ | 7:22 | 7:42 | 8:19 | **8:34** |
| 260 | 16 | Th. | | 7:22 | 7:41 | 9:20 | **9:04** |
| 261 | 17 | Fr. | | 7:23 | 7:40 | 10:24 | **9:36** |
| 262 | 18 | Sa. | | 7:24 | 7:38 | 11:30 | **10:13** |
| 263 | 19 | Su. | | 7:24 | 7:37 | **12:38** | **10:57** |
| 264 | 20 | Mo. | | 7:25 | 7:36 | **1:48** | **11:49** |
| 265 | 21 | Tu. | ♃ ☌ ☉ | 7:25 | 7:35 | **2:55** | . . . |
| 266 | 22 | We. | **Fall equinox;** ☾ at perigee | 7:26 | 7:33 | **3:56** | 12:49 |
| 267 | 23 | Th. | | 7:26 | 7:32 | **4:49** | 1:55 |
| 268 | 24 | Fr. | ♆ ☌ ☾ | 7:27 | 7:31 | **5:34** | 3:05 |
| 269 | 25 | Sa. | ⛢ ☌ ☾ | 7:28 | 7:29 | **6:13** | 4:15 |
| 270 | 26 | Su. | | 7:28 | 7:28 | **6:46** | 5:22 |
| 271 | 27 | Mo. | | 7:29 | 7:27 | **7:16** | 6:27 |
| 272 | 28 | Tu. | | 7:29 | 7:26 | **7:45** | 7:30 |
| 273 | 29 | We. | | 7:30 | 7:24 | **8:14** | 8:31 |
| 274 | 30 | Th. | | 7:31 | 7:23 | **8:45** | 9:31 |

## October 2004

10th Month — 31 Days

**Moon's Phases** — Last Qtr., Oct. 6, 5:12 a.m; New, Oct. 13, 9:48 p.m.; First Qtr., Oct. 20, 4:59 p.m.; Full, Oct. 27, 10:07 p.m.

| Day of | | | Planetary Configurations and Phenomena | *Hour of | | | |
|---|---|---|---|---|---|---|---|
| Year | Month | Week | | Sunrise | Sunset | Moon-rise | Moon-set |
| 275 | 1 | Fr. | | 7:31 | 7:22 | **9:17** | 10:31 |
| 276 | 2 | Sa. | | 7:32 | 7:21 | **9:54** | 11:31 |
| 277 | 3 | Su. | | 7:33 | 7:19 | **10:35** | **12:30** |
| 278 | 4 | Mo. | | 7:33 | 7:18 | **11:21** | **1:27** |
| 279 | 5 | Tu. | ☿ superior; ☾ at apogee | 7:34 | 7:17 | . . . | **2:20** |
| 280 | 6 | We. | | 7:34 | 7:16 | 12:12 | **3:09** |
| 281 | 7 | Th. | ♄ ☌ ☾ | 7:35 | 7:14 | 1:08 | **3:52** |
| 282 | 8 | Fr. | | 7:36 | 7:13 | 2:05 | **4:30** |
| 283 | 9 | Sa. | | 7:36 | 7:12 | 3:05 | **5:04** |
| 284 | 10 | Su. | ♀ ☌ ☾ | 7:37 | 7:11 | 4:04 | **5:35** |
| 285 | 11 | Mo. | | 7:38 | 7:10 | 5:04 | **6:05** |
| 286 | 12 | Tu. | ♃ ☌ ☾ | 7:38 | 7:08 | 6:04 | **6:33** |
| 287 | 13 | We. | Eclipse ☉ | 7:39 | 7:07 | 7:06 | **7:03** |
| 288 | 14 | Th. | | 7:40 | 7:06 | 8:10 | **7:35** |
| 289 | 15 | Fr. | | 7:40 | 7:05 | 9:17 | **8:11** |
| 290 | 16 | Sa. | | 7:41 | 7:04 | 10:27 | **8:54** |
| 291 | 17 | Su. | ☾ at perigee | 7:42 | 7:03 | 11:38 | **9:44** |
| 292 | 18 | Mo. | | 7:43 | 7:02 | **12:48** | **10:42** |
| 293 | 19 | Tu. | | 7:43 | 7:01 | **1:52** | **11:47** |
| 294 | 20 | We. | | 7:44 | 7:00 | **2:47** | . . . |
| 295 | 21 | Th. | ♆ ☌ ☾ | 7:45 | 6:59 | **3:34** | 12:56 |
| 296 | 22 | Fr. | | 7:45 | 6:58 | **4:13** | 2:05 |
| 297 | 23 | Sa. | ⛢ ☌ ☾ | 7:46 | 6:57 | **4:47** | 3:12 |
| 298 | 24 | Su. | ♆ stationary | 7:47 | 6:56 | **5:18** | 4:16 |
| 299 | 25 | Mo. | | 7:48 | 6:55 | **5:46** | 5:18 |
| 300 | 26 | Tu. | | 7:48 | 6:54 | **6:15** | 6:18 |
| 301 | 27 | We. | | 7:49 | 6:53 | **6:44** | 7:18 |
| 302 | 28 | Th. | Eclipse ☾ | 7:50 | 6:52 | **7:15** | 8:18 |
| 303 | 29 | Fr. | | 7:51 | 6:51 | **7:50** | 9:18 |
| 304 | 30 | Sa. | | 7:52 | 6:50 | **8:29** | 10:18 |
| 305 | †31 | Su. | | 6:52 | 5:49 | **8:14** | 10:16 |

*See text before January calendar for explanation.
† Daylight Saving Time ends at 2:00 a.m.

## November 2004

11th Month — 30 Days

**Moon's Phases** — Last Qtr., Nov. 4, 11:53 p.m.; New, Nov. 12, 8:27 a.m.; First Qtr., Nov. 18, 11:50 p.m.; Full, Nov. 26, 2:07 p.m.

| Day of | | | Planetary Configurations and Phenomena | *Hour of | | | |
|---|---|---|---|---|---|---|---|
| Year | Month | Week | | Sunrise | Sunset | Moon-rise | Moon-set |
| 306 | 1 | Mo. | | 6:53 | 5:48 | **9:03** | 11:11 |
| 307 | 2 | Tu. | ☾ at apogee | 6:54 | 5:47 | **9:57** | **12:02** |
| 308 | 3 | We. | ♄ ☌ ☾ | 6:55 | 5:47 | **10:53** | **12:47** |
| 309 | 4 | Th. | ♀ ☌ ♃ | 6:56 | 5:46 | **11:51** | **1:27** |
| 310 | 5 | Fr. | | 6:56 | 5:45 | . . . | **2:02** |
| 311 | 6 | Sa. | | 6:57 | 5:44 | 12:50 | **2:34** |
| 312 | 7 | Su. | | 6:58 | 5:44 | 1:48 | **3:03** |
| 313 | 8 | Mo. | ♄ stationary | 6:59 | 5:43 | 2:47 | **3:31** |
| 314 | 9 | Tu. | ♃ ☌ ☾; ♀ ☌ ☾ | 7:00 | 5:42 | 3:48 | **4:00** |
| 315 | 10 | We. | ♂ ☌ ☾ | 7:01 | 5:42 | 4:50 | **4:31** |
| 316 | 11 | Th. | ⛢ stationary | 7:01 | 5:41 | 5:56 | **5:05** |
| 317 | 12 | Fr. | | 7:02 | 5:41 | 7:06 | **5:45** |
| 318 | 13 | Sa. | ☿ ☌ ☾ | 7:03 | 5:40 | 8:19 | **6:33** |
| 319 | 14 | Su. | ☾ at perigee | 7:04 | 5:39 | 9:32 | **7:31** |
| 320 | 15 | Mo. | | 7:05 | 5:39 | 10:41 | **8:36** |
| 321 | 16 | Tu. | | 7:06 | 5:38 | 11:42 | **9:46** |
| 322 | 17 | We. | ♆ ☌ ☾ | 7:07 | 5:38 | **12:32** | **10:57** |
| 323 | 18 | Th. | | 7:07 | 5:38 | **1:14** | . . . |
| 324 | 19 | Fr. | ⛢ ☌ ☾ | 7:08 | 5:37 | **1:50** | 12:05 |
| 325 | 20 | Sa. | ☿ greatest elongation E | 7:09 | 5:37 | **2:21** | 1:10 |
| 326 | 21 | Su. | | 7:10 | 5:36 | **2:50** | 2:12 |
| 327 | 22 | Mo. | | 7:11 | 5:36 | **3:18** | 3:11 |
| 328 | 23 | Tu. | | 7:12 | 5:36 | **3:46** | 4:10 |
| 329 | 24 | We. | | 7:13 | 5:36 | **4:16** | 5:09 |
| 330 | 25 | Th. | | 7:13 | 5:35 | **4:49** | 6:08 |
| 331 | 26 | Fr. | | 7:14 | 5:35 | **5:26** | 7:08 |
| 332 | 27 | Sa. | | 7:15 | 5:35 | **6:09** | 8:07 |
| 333 | 28 | Su. | | 7:16 | 5:35 | **6:56** | 9:03 |
| 334 | 29 | Mo. | | 7:17 | 5:35 | **7:49** | 9:56 |
| 335 | 30 | Tu. | ☾ at apogee; ☿ stationary | 7:18 | 5:35 | **8:44** | 10:43 |

## December 2004

12th Month — 31 Days

**Moon's Phases** — Last Qtr., Dec. 4, 6:53 p.m.; New, Dec. 11, 7:29 p.m.; First Qtr., Dec. 18, 10:40 a.m.; Full, Dec. 26, 9:06 a.m.

| Day of | | | Planetary Configurations and Phenomena | *Hour of | | | |
|---|---|---|---|---|---|---|---|
| Year | Month | Week | | Sunrise | Sunset | Moon-rise | Moon-set |
| 336 | 1 | We. | | 7:18 | 5:35 | **9:42** | 11:24 |
| 337 | 2 | Th. | | 7:19 | 5:35 | **10:39** | **12:01** |
| 338 | 3 | Fr. | | 7:20 | 5:35 | **11:36** | **12:33** |
| 339 | 4 | Sa. | | 7:21 | 5:35 | . . . | **1:02** |
| 340 | 5 | Su. | ♀ ☌ ♂ | 7:22 | 5:35 | 12:34 | **1:30** |
| 341 | 6 | Mo. | | 7:22 | 5:35 | 1:31 | **1:58** |
| 342 | 7 | Tu. | ♃ ☌ ☾ | 7:23 | 5:35 | 2:31 | **2:27** |
| 343 | 8 | We. | | 7:24 | 5:35 | 3:34 | **2:58** |
| 344 | 9 | Th. | ♂ ☌ ☾; ♀ ☌ ☾ | 7:25 | 5:35 | 4:40 | **3:35** |
| 345 | 10 | Fr. | ☿ inferior | 7:25 | 5:35 | 5:52 | **4:19** |
| 346 | 11 | Sa. | | 7:26 | 5:36 | 7:06 | **5:12** |
| 347 | 12 | Su. | ☾ at perigee | 7:27 | 5:36 | 8:19 | **6:15** |
| 348 | 13 | Mo. | ♇ ☌ ☉ | 7:27 | 5:36 | 9:26 | **7:26** |
| 349 | 14 | Tu. | | 7:28 | 5:37 | 10:23 | **8:40** |
| 350 | 15 | We. | ♆ ☌ ☾ | 7:29 | 5:37 | 11:11 | **9:53** |
| 351 | 16 | Th. | ⛢ ☌ ☾ | 7:29 | 5:37 | 11:50 | **11:01** |
| 352 | 17 | Fr. | | 7:30 | 5:38 | **12:23** | . . . |
| 353 | 18 | Sa. | | 7:30 | 5:38 | **12:53** | 12:05 |
| 354 | 19 | Su. | | 7:31 | 5:39 | **1:21** | 1:06 |
| 355 | 20 | Mo. | ☿ stationary | 7:31 | 5:39 | **1:49** | 2:05 |
| 356 | 21 | Tu. | **Winter solstice** | 7:32 | 5:40 | **2:18** | 3:03 |
| 357 | 22 | We. | | 7:32 | 5:40 | **2:50** | 4:02 |
| 358 | 23 | Th. | | 7:33 | 5:41 | **3:26** | 5:01 |
| 359 | 24 | Fr. | | 7:33 | 5:41 | **4:06** | 5:59 |
| 360 | 25 | Sa. | | 7:34 | 5:42 | **4:52** | 6:57 |
| 361 | 26 | Su. | | 7:34 | 5:42 | **5:43** | 7:50 |
| 362 | 27 | Mo. | ☾ at apogee; ♄ ☌ ☾ | 7:35 | 5:43 | **6:38** | 8:39 |
| 363 | 28 | Tu. | ☿ ☌ ♀ | 7:35 | 5:44 | **7:35** | 9:23 |
| 364 | 29 | We. | ☿ greatest elongation W | 7:35 | 5:44 | **8:32** | 10:01 |
| 365 | 30 | Th. | | 7:35 | 5:45 | **9:29** | 10:34 |
| 366 | 31 | Fr. | | 7:36 | 5:46 | **10:26** | 11:04 |

# Calendar for 2005

Times are **Central Standard Time**, except from April 3 to Oct. 30, during which **Daylight Saving Time** is observed. **Boldface times for moonrise and moonset** indicate p.m. Times are figured for the point **99° 10' West and 31° 23' North**, the approximate geographical center of the state. **See page 110 for explanation of how to get the approximate time at any other Texas point. (On the Web: http://aa.usno.navy.mil/data/)** Please note: Not all **eclipses** are visible in United States. For visibility, see listing on p. 111.

**1st Month** — **January 2005** — **31 Days**

Moon's Phases — Last Qtr., Jan. 3, 11:46 a.m.; New, Jan. 10, 6:03 a.m.; First Qtr., Jan. 17, 12:57 a.m.; Full, Jan. 25, 4:32 a.m.

| Year | Month | Week | Planetary Configurations and Phenomena | Sunrise | Sunset | Moon-rise | Moon-set |
|---|---|---|---|---|---|---|---|
| 1 | 1 | Sa. | ● at perihelion | 7:36 | 5:45 | **11:22** | 11:32 |
| 2 | 2 | Su. | | 7:36 | 5:46 | ... | 11:58 |
| 3 | 3 | Mo. | ♃ ☌ ☾ | 7:36 | 5:46 | 12:19 | **12:25** |
| 4 | 4 | Tu. | | 7:36 | 5:47 | 1:18 | **12:55** |
| 5 | 5 | We. | | 7:37 | 5:48 | 2:20 | **1:27** |
| 6 | 6 | Th. | | 7:37 | 5:49 | 3:27 | **2:06** |
| 7 | 7 | Fr. | ♂ ☌ ☾ | 7:37 | 5:49 | 4:38 | **2:53** |
| 8 | 8 | Sa. | ☿ ☌ ☾; ♀ ☌ ☾ | 7:37 | 5:50 | 5:51 | **3:51** |
| 9 | 9 | Su. | | 7:37 | 5:51 | 7:02 | **4:58** |
| 10 | 10 | Mo. | ☾ at perigee | 7:37 | 5:52 | 8:05 | **6:13** |
| 11 | 11 | Tu. | ♆ ☌ ☾ | 7:37 | 5:53 | 8:59 | **7:28** |
| 12 | 12 | We. | | 7:37 | 5:54 | 9:43 | **8:41** |
| 13 | 13 | Th. | ♅ ☌ ☾; ♄ ☍; ☿ ☌ ♀ | 7:37 | 5:54 | 10:20 | **9:50** |
| 14 | 14 | Fr. | | 7:36 | 5:55 | 10:52 | **10:55** |
| 15 | 15 | Sa. | | 7:36 | 5:56 | 11:22 | **11:56** |
| 16 | 16 | Su. | | 7:36 | 5:57 | 11:51 | ... |
| 17 | 17 | Mo. | | 7:36 | 5:58 | **12:20** | 12:56 |
| 18 | 18 | Tu. | | 7:36 | 5:59 | **12:51** | 1:56 |
| 19 | 19 | We. | | 7:35 | 6:00 | **1:26** | 2:55 |
| 20 | 20 | Th. | | 7:35 | 6:01 | **2:05** | 3:54 |
| 21 | 21 | Fr. | | 7:35 | 6:02 | **2:49** | 4:51 |
| 22 | 22 | Sa. | | 7:34 | 6:02 | **3:38** | 5:46 |
| 23 | 23 | Su. | ☾ at apogee | 7:34 | 6:03 | **4:32** | 6:37 |
| 24 | 24 | Mo. | ♄ ☌ ☾ | 7:34 | 6:04 | **5:29** | 7:22 |
| 25 | 25 | Tu. | | 7:33 | 6:05 | **6:26** | 8:01 |
| 26 | 26 | We. | | 7:33 | 6:06 | **7:24** | 8:36 |
| 27 | 27 | Th. | | 7:32 | 6:07 | **8:21** | 9:07 |
| 28 | 28 | Fr. | | 7:32 | 6:08 | **9:17** | 9:35 |
| 29 | 29 | Sa. | | 7:31 | 6:09 | **10:13** | 10:01 |
| 30 | 30 | Su. | | 7:31 | 6:10 | **11:10** | 10:28 |
| 31 | 31 | Mo. | ♃ ☌ ☾ | 7:30 | 6:11 | **11:22** | 10:56 |

**2nd Month** — **February 2005** — **28 Days**

Moon's Phases — Last Qtr., Feb. 2, 1:27 a.m.; New, Feb. 8, 4:28 p.m.; First Qtr., Feb. 15, 6:16 p.m.; Full, Feb. 23, 10:54 p.m.

| Year | Month | Week | Planetary Configurations and Phenomena | Sunrise | Sunset | Moon-rise | Moon-set |
|---|---|---|---|---|---|---|---|
| 32 | 1 | Tu. | | 7:29 | 6:11 | 12:10 | 11:26 |
| 33 | 2 | We. | ♃ stationary | 7:29 | 6:12 | 1:13 | **12:01** |
| 34 | 3 | Th. | ♆ ☌ ☉ | 7:28 | 6:13 | 2:20 | **12:42** |
| 35 | 4 | Fr. | | 7:27 | 6:14 | 3:30 | **1:33** |
| 36 | 5 | Sa. | ♂ ☌ ☾ | 7:27 | 6:15 | 4:39 | **2:34** |
| 37 | 6 | Su. | | 7:26 | 6:16 | 5:45 | **3:44** |
| 38 | 7 | Mo. | ☾ at perigee | 7:25 | 6:17 | 6:42 | **4:59** |
| 39 | 8 | Tu. | | 7:24 | 6:18 | 7:31 | **6:14** |
| 40 | 9 | We. | | 7:24 | 6:19 | 8:12 | **7:26** |
| 41 | 10 | Th. | | 7:23 | 6:19 | 8:47 | **8:35** |
| 42 | 11 | Fr. | | 7:22 | 6:20 | 9:19 | **9:40** |
| 43 | 12 | Sa. | | 7:21 | 6:21 | 9:49 | **10:43** |
| 44 | 13 | Su. | | 7:20 | 6:22 | 10:19 | **11:44** |
| 45 | 14 | Mo. | ☿ superior; ♀ ☌ ♆ | 7:19 | 6:23 | 10:50 | ... |
| 46 | 15 | Tu. | | 7:18 | 6:24 | 11:24 | 12:45 |
| 47 | 16 | We. | | 7:17 | 6:24 | **12:02** | 1:46 |
| 48 | 17 | Th. | | 7:17 | 6:25 | **12:44** | 2:45 |
| 49 | 18 | Fr. | | 7:16 | 6:26 | **1:32** | 3:41 |
| 50 | 19 | Sa. | ☾ at apogee | 7:15 | 6:27 | **2:25** | 4:33 |
| 51 | 20 | Su. | ♄ ☌ ☾ | 7:14 | 6:28 | **3:21** | 5:19 |
| 52 | 21 | Mo. | | 7:13 | 6:29 | **4:19** | 6:01 |
| 53 | 22 | Tu. | | 7:11 | 6:29 | **5:17** | 6:37 |
| 54 | 23 | We. | | 7:10 | 6:30 | **6:14** | 7:09 |
| 55 | 24 | Th. | | 7:09 | 6:31 | **7:11** | 7:38 |
| 56 | 25 | Fr. | ♅ ☌ ☉ | 7:08 | 6:32 | **8:08** | 8:05 |
| 57 | 26 | Sa. | | 7:07 | 6:32 | **9:05** | 8:32 |
| 58 | 27 | Su. | ♃ ☌ ☾ | 7:06 | 6:33 | **10:05** | 8:59 |
| 59 | 28 | Mo. | | 7:05 | 6:34 | **11:06** | 9:28 |

**3rd Month** — **March 2005** — **31 Days**

Moon's Phases — Last Qtr., March 3, 11:36 a.m.; New, March 10, 3:10 a.m.; First Qtr., March 17, 1:19 p.m.; Full, March 25, 2:58 p.m.

| Year | Month | Week | Planetary Configurations and Phenomena | Sunrise | Sunset | Moon-rise | Moon-set |
|---|---|---|---|---|---|---|---|
| 60 | 1 | Tu. | | 7:04 | 6:35 | 12:11 | 10:01 |
| 61 | 2 | We. | | 7:03 | 6:35 | 1:18 | 10:39 |
| 62 | 3 | Th. | | 7:02 | 6:36 | 2:26 | 11:25 |
| 63 | 4 | Fr. | | 7:00 | 6:37 | 3:32 | **12:21** |
| 64 | 5 | Sa. | | 6:59 | 6:38 | 4:30 | **1:25** |
| 65 | 6 | Su. | ♂ ☌ ☾ | 6:58 | 6:38 | 5:21 | **2:35** |
| 66 | 7 | Mo. | ♆ ☌ ☾; ☾ at perigee | 6:57 | 6:39 | 6:04 | **3:49** |
| 67 | 8 | Tu. | | 6:56 | 6:40 | 6:41 | **5:01** |
| 68 | 9 | We. | | 6:55 | 6:41 | 7:14 | **6:11** |
| 69 | 10 | Th. | | 6:53 | 6:41 | 7:45 | **7:18** |
| 70 | 11 | Fr. | ☿ ☌ ☾ | 6:52 | 6:42 | 8:15 | **8:23** |
| 71 | 12 | Sa. | ☿ greatest elongation E | 6:51 | 6:43 | 8:46 | **9:27** |
| 72 | 13 | Su. | | 6:50 | 6:43 | 9:20 | **10:30** |
| 73 | 14 | Mo. | | 6:48 | 6:44 | 9:57 | **11:32** |
| 74 | 15 | Tu. | | 6:47 | 6:45 | 10:38 | ... |
| 75 | 16 | We. | | 6:46 | 6:45 | 11:25 | 12:33 |
| 76 | 17 | Th. | | 6:45 | 6:46 | **12:16** | 1:32 |
| 77 | 18 | Fr. | | 6:43 | 6:47 | **1:11** | 2:26 |
| 78 | 19 | Sa. | ☿ stationary; ♄ ☌ ☾ | 6:42 | 6:47 | **2:08** | 3:15 |
| 79 | 20 | Su. | **Spring equinox** | 6:41 | 6:48 | **3:06** | 3:58 |
| 80 | 21 | Mo. | ♄ stationary | 6:40 | 6:49 | **4:04** | 4:36 |
| 81 | 22 | Tu. | | 6:38 | 6:49 | **5:02** | 5:10 |
| 82 | 23 | We. | | 6:37 | 6:50 | **5:59** | 5:40 |
| 83 | 24 | Th. | | 6:36 | 6:51 | **6:57** | 6:07 |
| 84 | 25 | Fr. | | 6:35 | 6:51 | **7:57** | 6:34 |
| 85 | 26 | Sa. | ♃ ☌ ☾ | 6:33 | 6:52 | **8:59** | 7:01 |
| 86 | 27 | Su. | ♇ stationary | 6:32 | 6:53 | **10:03** | 7:30 |
| 87 | 28 | Mo. | | 6:31 | 6:53 | **11:11** | 8:02 |
| 88 | 29 | Tu. | ☿ inferior | 6:30 | 6:54 | ... | 8:39 |
| 89 | 30 | We. | ♀ superior | 6:28 | 6:55 | **12:19** | 9:23 |
| 90 | 31 | Th. | | 6:27 | 6:55 | **12:11** | 10:15 |

**4th Month** — **April 2005** — **30 Days**

Moon's Phases - Last Qtr., April 1, 6:50 p.m; New, April 8, 3:32 p.m.; First Qtr., April 16, 9:37 a.m.; Full, April 24, 5:06 a.m.

| Year | Month | Week | Planetary Configurations and Phenomena | Sunrise | Sunset | Moon-rise | Moon-set |
|---|---|---|---|---|---|---|---|
| 91 | 1 | Fr. | | 6:26 | 6:56 | 1:25 | 11:16 |
| 92 | 2 | Sa. | | 6:25 | 6:57 | 2:25 | **12:23** |
| 93 † | 3 | Su. | ♃ ☍; ♂ ☌ ☾ | 6:23 | 6:57 | 4:17 | **2:34** |
| 94 | 4 | Mo. | ♆ ☌ ☾; ☾ at perigee | 6:22 | 6:58 | 5:01 | **3:45** |
| 95 | 5 | Tu. | ♅ ☌ ☾ | 6:21 | 6:59 | 5:39 | **4:53** |
| 96 | 6 | We. | | 7:20 | 7:59 | 6:12 | **6:00** |
| 97 | 7 | Th. | ☿ ☌ ☾ | 7:18 | 8:00 | 6:43 | **7:04** |
| 98 | 8 | Fr. | Eclipse ☉ | 7:17 | 8:01 | 7:13 | **8:08** |
| 99 | 9 | Sa. | | 7:16 | 8:01 | 7:43 | **9:11** |
| 100 | 10 | Su. | ☿ stationary | 7:15 | 8:02 | 8:15 | **10:15** |
| 101 | 11 | Mo. | | 7:14 | 8:02 | 8:51 | **11:18** |
| 102 | 12 | Tu. | ♂ ☌ ♆ | 7:12 | 8:03 | 9:31 | ... |
| 103 | 13 | We. | | 7:11 | 8:04 | 10:16 | 12:19 |
| 104 | 14 | Th. | | 7:10 | 8:04 | 11:06 | 1:16 |
| 105 | 15 | Fr. | ♄ ☌ ☾ | 7:09 | 8:05 | **12:00** | 2:08 |
| 106 | 16 | Sa. | ☾ at apogee | 7:08 | 8:06 | **12:57** | 2:54 |
| 107 | 17 | Su. | | 7:07 | 8:06 | **1:55** | 3:34 |
| 108 | 18 | Mo. | | 7:05 | 8:07 | **2:52** | 4:09 |
| 109 | 19 | Tu. | | 7:04 | 8:08 | **3:50** | 4:40 |
| 110 | 20 | We. | | 7:03 | 8:08 | **4:47** | 5:08 |
| 111 | 21 | Th. | | 7:02 | 8:09 | **5:44** | 5:35 |
| 112 | 22 | Fr. | ♃ ☌ ☾ | 7:01 | 8:10 | **6:44** | 6:02 |
| 113 | 23 | Sa. | | 7:00 | 8:11 | **7:45** | 6:30 |
| 114 | 24 | Su. | Eclipse ☾ | 6:59 | 8:11 | **8:50** | 7:01 |
| 115 | 25 | Mo. | | 6:58 | 8:12 | **9:59** | 7:37 |
| 116 | 26 | Tu. | ☿ greatest elongation W | 6:57 | 8:13 | **11:09** | 8:19 |
| 117 | 27 | We. | | 6:56 | 8:13 | ... | 9:10 |
| 118 | 28 | Th. | | 6:55 | 8:14 | **12:17** | 10:09 |
| 119 | 29 | Fr. | ☾ at perigee | 6:54 | 8:15 | **1:20** | 11:15 |
| 120 | 30 | Sa. | | 6:53 | 8:15 | **2:15** | **12:25** |

*See text before January calendar for explanation.

† Daylight Saving Time begins at 2:00 a.m.

# Calendar for 2005 (Cont'd.)

**5th Month** — **May 2005** — **31 Days**

**Moon's Phases** — Last Qtr., May 1, 1:24 a.m., New, May 8, 3:45 a.m; First Qtr., May 16, 3:56 a.m.; Full, May 23, 3:18 p.m.; Last Qtr., May 30, 6:47 a.m.

| Day of Year | Day of Month | Day of Week | Planetary Configurations and Phenomena | *Hour of Sunrise | *Hour of Sunset | *Hour of Moon-rise | *Hour of Moon-set |
|---|---|---|---|---|---|---|---|
| 121 | 1 | Su. | ♆ ☌ ☾ | 6:52 | 8:16 | 3:01 | **1:36** |
| 122 | 2 | Mo. | ♂ ☌ ☾; ♅ ☌ ☾ | 6:51 | 8:17 | 3:40 | **2:44** |
| 123 | 3 | Tu. | | 6:50 | 8:17 | 4:13 | **3:49** |
| 124 | 4 | We. | | 6:49 | 8:18 | 4:44 | **4:53** |
| 125 | 5 | Th. | | 6:48 | 8:19 | 5:13 | **5:55** |
| 126 | 6 | Fr. | ☿ ☌ ☾ | 6:48 | 8:19 | 5:43 | **6:57** |
| 127 | 7 | Sa. | | 6:47 | 8:20 | 6:14 | **8:00** |
| 128 | 8 | Su. | | 6:46 | 8:21 | 6:47 | **9:03** |
| 129 | 9 | Mo. | | 6:45 | 8:22 | 7:25 | **10:05** |
| 130 | 10 | Tu. | | 6:44 | 8:22 | 8:08 | **11:04** |
| 131 | 11 | We. | | 6:44 | 8:23 | 8:57 | **11:59** |
| 132 | 12 | Th. | | 6:43 | 8:24 | 9:50 | . . . |
| 133 | 13 | Fr. | ♄ ☌ ☾ | 6:42 | 8:24 | 10:46 | 12:48 |
| 134 | 14 | Sa. | ☾ at apogee; ♂ ☌ ♅ | 6:41 | 8:25 | 11:44 | 1:30 |
| 135 | 15 | Su. | | 6:41 | 8:26 | **12:41** | 2:07 |
| 136 | 16 | Mo. | | 6:40 | 8:26 | **1:38** | 2:39 |
| 137 | 17 | Tu. | | 6:40 | 8:27 | **2:34** | 3:08 |
| 138 | 18 | We. | | 6:39 | 8:28 | **3:31** | 3:35 |
| 139 | 19 | Th. | ♃ ☌ ☾; ♆ stationary | 6:38 | 8:28 | **4:28** | 4:01 |
| 140 | 20 | Fr. | | 6:38 | 8:29 | **5:28** | 4:29 |
| 141 | 21 | Sa. | | 6:37 | 8:30 | **6:32** | 4:58 |
| 142 | 22 | Su. | | 6:37 | 8:30 | **7:39** | 5:32 |
| 143 | 23 | Mo. | | 6:36 | 8:31 | **8:50** | 6:11 |
| 144 | 24 | Tu. | | 6:36 | 8:32 | **10:02** | 6:59 |
| 145 | 25 | We. | | 6:35 | 8:32 | **11:09** | 7:57 |
| 146 | 26 | Th. | ☾ at perigee | 6:35 | 8:33 | . . . | 9:03 |
| 147 | 27 | Fr. | | 6:35 | 8:33 | 12:09 | 10:14 |
| 148 | 28 | Sa. | ♆ ☌ ☾ | 6:34 | 8:34 | 12:59 | 11:26 |
| 149 | 29 | Su. | | 6:34 | 8:35 | 1:40 | **12:36** |
| 150 | 30 | Mo. | ♅ ☌ ☾ | 6:34 | 8:35 | 2:16 | **1:43** |
| 151 | 31 | Tu. | ♂ ☌ ☾ | 6:33 | 8:36 | 2:47 | **2:46** |

**6th Month** — **June 2005** — **30 Days**

**Moon's Phases** — New, June 6, 4:55 p.m., First Qtr., June 14, 8:22 p.m.; Full, June 21, 11:14 p.m.; Last Qtr., June 28, 1:23 p.m.

| Day of Year | Day of Month | Day of Week | Planetary Configurations and Phenomena | *Hour of Sunrise | *Hour of Sunset | *Hour of Moon-rise | *Hour of Moon-set |
|---|---|---|---|---|---|---|---|
| 152 | 1 | We. | | 6:33 | 8:36 | 3:16 | **3:48** |
| 153 | 2 | Th. | | 6:33 | 8:37 | 3:45 | **4:49** |
| 154 | 3 | Fr. | ☿ superior | 6:32 | 8:37 | 4:15 | **5:51** |
| 155 | 4 | Sa. | | 6:32 | 8:38 | 4:47 | **6:52** |
| 156 | 5 | Su. | ♃ stationary | 6:32 | 8:38 | 5:23 | **7:54** |
| 157 | 6 | Mo. | | 6:32 | 8:39 | 6:04 | **8:54** |
| 158 | 7 | Tu. | | 6:32 | 8:39 | 6:50 | **9:51** |
| 159 | 8 | We. | ♀ ☌ ☾ | 6:32 | 8:40 | 7:42 | **10:42** |
| 160 | 9 | Th. | ♄ ☌ ☾ | 6:32 | 8:40 | 8:37 | **11:26** |
| 161 | 10 | Fr. | ☾ at apogee | 6:32 | 8:41 | 9:34 | . . . |
| 162 | 11 | Sa. | | 6:32 | 8:41 | 10:32 | 12:05 |
| 163 | 12 | Su. | | 6:32 | 8:41 | 11:28 | 12:39 |
| 164 | 13 | Mo. | ♇ ☍ | 6:32 | 8:42 | **12:24** | 1:08 |
| 165 | 14 | Tu. | | 6:32 | 8:42 | **1:19** | 1:36 |
| 166 | 15 | We. | ♅ stationary | 6:32 | 8:43 | **2:15** | 2:02 |
| 167 | 16 | Th. | ♃ ☌ ☾ | 6:32 | 8:43 | **3:13** | 2:28 |
| 168 | 17 | Fr. | | 6:32 | 8:43 | **4:13** | 2:56 |
| 169 | 18 | Sa. | | 6:32 | 8:43 | **5:18** | 3:26 |
| 170 | 19 | Su. | | 6:32 | 8:44 | **6:27** | 4:03 |
| 171 | 20 | Mo. | | 6:32 | 8:44 | **7:39** | 4:46 |
| 172 | 21 | Tu. | **Summer solstice** | 6:33 | 8:44 | **8:49** | 5:39 |
| 173 | 22 | We. | | 6:33 | 8:44 | **9:54** | 6:43 |
| 174 | 23 | Th. | ☾ at perigee | 6:33 | 8:45 | **10:50** | 7:54 |
| 175 | 24 | Fr. | ♆ ☌ ☾ | 6:33 | 8:45 | **11:37** | 9:09 |
| 176 | 25 | Sa. | ♀ ☌ ♄; ☿ ☌ ♄ | 6:34 | 8:45 | . . . | 10:23 |
| 177 | 26 | Su. | ♅ ☌ ☾ | 6:34 | 8:45 | 12:15 | 11:33 |
| 178 | 27 | Mo. | ☿ ☌ ♀ | 6:34 | 8:45 | 12:49 | **12:39** |
| 179 | 28 | Tu. | ♂ ☌ ☾ | 6:35 | 8:45 | 1:19 | **1:42** |
| 180 | 29 | We. | | 6:35 | 8:45 | 1:48 | **2:44** |
| 181 | 30 | Th. | | 6:35 | 8:45 | 2:18 | **3:45** |

*See text before January calendar for explanation.

**7th Month** — **July 2005** — **31 Days**

**Moon's Phases** — New, July 6, 7:02 a.m.; First Qtr., July 14, 10:20 a.m.; Full, July 21, 6:00 a.m.; Last Qtr., July 27, 10:19 p.m.

| Day of Year | Day of Month | Day of Week | Planetary Configurations and Phenomena | *Hour of Sunrise | *Hour of Sunset | *Hour of Moon-rise | *Hour of Moon-set |
|---|---|---|---|---|---|---|---|
| 182 | 1 | Fr. | | 6:36 | 8:45 | 2:49 | **4:46** |
| 183 | 2 | Sa. | | 6:36 | 8:45 | 3:23 | **5:47** |
| 184 | 3 | Su. | | 6:37 | 8:45 | 4:02 | **6:48** |
| 185 | 4 | Mo. | | 6:37 | 8:45 | 4:47 | **7:45** |
| 186 | 5 | Tu. | ● at aphelion | 6:37 | 8:45 | 5:36 | **8:37** |
| 187 | 6 | We. | | 6:38 | 8:45 | 6:30 | **9:24** |
| 188 | 7 | Th. | ☿ ☌ ♀ | 6:38 | 8:45 | 7:27 | **10:04** |
| 189 | 8 | Fr. | ☿ ♀ ☌ ☾; ☾ at apogee; ☿ greatest elongation E | 6:39 | 8:44 | 8:25 | **10:39** |
| 190 | 9 | Sa. | | 6:39 | 8:44 | 9:22 | **11:10** |
| 191 | 10 | Su. | | 6:40 | 8:44 | 10:17 | **11:38** |
| 192 | 11 | Mo. | | 6:40 | 8:44 | 11:12 | . . . |
| 193 | 12 | Tu. | | 6:41 | 8:43 | **12:07** | 12:04 |
| 194 | 13 | We. | ♃ ☌ ☾ | 6:41 | 8:43 | **1:02** | 12:29 |
| 195 | 14 | Th. | | 6:42 | 8:43 | **2:00** | 12:56 |
| 196 | 15 | Fr. | | 6:43 | 8:42 | **3:01** | 1:24 |
| 197 | 16 | Sa. | | 6:43 | 8:42 | **4:06** | 1:57 |
| 198 | 17 | Su. | | 6:44 | 8:42 | **5:15** | 2:35 |
| 199 | 18 | Mo. | | 6:44 | 8:41 | **6:26** | 3:23 |
| 200 | 19 | Tu. | | 6:45 | 8:41 | **7:34** | 4:20 |
| 201 | 20 | We. | | 6:45 | 8:40 | **8:34** | 5:29 |
| 202 | 21 | Th. | ☾ at perigee; ☿ stationary | 6:46 | 8:40 | **9:26** | 6:43 |
| 203 | 22 | Fr. | ♆ ☌ ☾ | 6:47 | 8:39 | **10:09** | 8:00 |
| 204 | 23 | Sa. | ♄ ☌ ☉; ♅ ☌ ☾ | 6:47 | 8:39 | **10:46** | 9:14 |
| 205 | 24 | Su. | | 6:48 | 8:38 | **11:19** | 10:24 |
| 206 | 25 | Mo. | | 6:49 | 8:37 | **11:49** | 11:30 |
| 207 | 26 | Tu. | | 6:49 | 8:37 | . . . | **12:35** |
| 208 | 27 | We. | ♂ ☌ ☾ | 6:50 | 8:36 | 12:19 | **1:37** |
| 209 | 28 | Th. | | 6:50 | 8:36 | 12:50 | **2:40** |
| 210 | 29 | Fr. | | 6:51 | 8:35 | 1:24 | **3:42** |
| 211 | 30 | Sa. | | 6:52 | 8:34 | 2:02 | **4:42** |
| 212 | 31 | Su. | | 6:52 | 8:33 | 2:44 | **5:40** |

**8th Month** — **August 2005** — **31 Days**

**Moon's Phases** — New, Aug. 4, 10:05 p.m.; First Qtr., Aug. 12, 9:38 p.m.; Full, Aug. 19, 12:53 p.m.; Last Qtr., Aug. 26, 10:18 a.m.

| Day of Year | Day of Month | Day of Week | Planetary Configurations and Phenomena | *Hour of Sunrise | *Hour of Sunset | *Hour of Moon-rise | *Hour of Moon-set |
|---|---|---|---|---|---|---|---|
| 213 | 1 | Mo. | | 6:53 | 8:33 | 3:32 | **6:34** |
| 214 | 2 | Tu. | | 6:54 | 8:32 | 4:25 | **7:22** |
| 215 | 3 | We. | | 6:54 | 8:31 | 5:21 | **8:04** |
| 216 | 4 | Th. | ☾ at apogee | 6:55 | 8:30 | 6:18 | **8:41** |
| 217 | 5 | Fr. | ☿ inferior | 6:56 | 8:29 | 7:16 | **9:13** |
| 218 | 6 | Sa. | | 6:56 | 8:29 | 8:12 | **9:41** |
| 219 | 7 | Su. | ♀ ☌ ☾ | 6:57 | 8:28 | 9:07 | **10:07** |
| 220 | 8 | Mo. | ♆ ☍ | 6:58 | 8:27 | 10:02 | **10:33** |
| 221 | 9 | Tu. | | 6:58 | 8:26 | 10:57 | **10:58** |
| 222 | 10 | We. | ♃ ☌ ☾ | 6:59 | 8:25 | 11:53 | **11:25** |
| 223 | 11 | Th. | | 6:59 | 8:24 | **12:51** | **11:55** |
| 224 | 12 | Fr. | | 7:00 | 8:23 | **1:53** | . . . |
| 225 | 13 | Sa. | | 7:01 | 8:22 | **2:59** | 12:30 |
| 226 | 14 | Su. | | 7:01 | 8:21 | **4:06** | 1:12 |
| 227 | 15 | Mo. | ☿ stationary | 7:02 | 8:20 | **5:14** | 2:04 |
| 228 | 16 | Tu. | | 7:03 | 8:19 | **6:17** | 3:05 |
| 229 | 17 | We. | | 7:03 | 8:18 | **7:12** | 4:16 |
| 230 | 18 | Th. | ♆ ☌ ☾; ☾ at perigee | 7:04 | 8:17 | **7:59** | 5:31 |
| 231 | 19 | Fr. | | 7:04 | 8:16 | **8:39** | 6:47 |
| 232 | 20 | Sa. | ♅ ☌ ☾ | 7:05 | 8:15 | **9:14** | 8:00 |
| 233 | 21 | Su. | | 7:06 | 8:13 | **9:46** | 9:10 |
| 234 | 22 | Mo. | | 7:06 | 8:12 | **10:17** | 10:18 |
| 235 | 23 | Tu. | ☿ greatest elongation W | 7:07 | 8:11 | **10:49** | 11:23 |
| 236 | 24 | We. | | 7:08 | 8:10 | **11:22** | **12:28** |
| 237 | 25 | Th. | ♂ ☌ ☾ | 7:08 | 8:09 | **11:59** | **1:32** |
| 238 | 26 | Fr. | | 7:09 | 8:08 | . . . | **2:34** |
| 239 | 27 | Sa. | | 7:09 | 8:07 | 12:41 | **3:35** |
| 240 | 28 | Su. | | 7:10 | 8:05 | 1:28 | **4:30** |
| 241 | 29 | Mo. | | 7:11 | 8:04 | 2:19 | **5:20** |
| 242 | 30 | Tu. | | 7:11 | 8:03 | 3:15 | **6:04** |
| 243 | 31 | We. | ♄ ☌ ☾; ☾ at apogee; ♅ ☍ | 7:12 | 8:02 | 4:12 | **6:42** |

# Calendar for 2005 (Cont'd.)

**9th Month** — **September 2005** — **30 Days**

**Moon's Phases** — New, Sept. 3, 1:45 p.m., First Qtr., Sept. 11, 6:37 a.m.; Full, Sept. 17, 9:01 p.m.; Last Qtr., Sept. 25, 1:41 a.m.

| Day of Year | Day of Month | Day of Week | Planetary Configurations and Phenomena | *Hour of Sunrise | *Hour of Sunset | *Hour of Moon-rise | *Hour of Moon-set |
|---|---|---|---|---|---|---|---|
| 244 | 1 | Th. | | 7:12 | 8:01 | 5:10 | **7:15** |
| 245 | 2 | Fr. | ♀ ☌ ♃; ♇ stationary | 7:13 | 7:59 | 6:06 | **7:45** |
| 246 | 3 | Sa. | | 7:14 | 7:58 | 7:02 | **8:11** |
| 247 | 4 | Su. | | 7:14 | 7:57 | 7:57 | **8:37** |
| 248 | 5 | Mo. | | 7:15 | 7:56 | 8:52 | **9:02** |
| 249 | 6 | Tu. | ♃ ☌ ☾ | 7:15 | 7:54 | 9:48 | **9:29** |
| 250 | 7 | We. | ♀ ☌ ☾ | 7:16 | 7:53 | 10:46 | **9:58** |
| 251 | 8 | Th. | | 7:17 | 7:52 | 11:46 | **10:31** |
| 252 | 9 | Fr. | | 7:17 | 7:51 | **12:50** | **11:09** |
| 253 | 10 | Sa. | | 7:18 | 7:49 | **1:55** | **11:56** |
| 254 | 11 | Su. | | 7:18 | 7:48 | **3:01** | . . . |
| 255 | 12 | Mo. | | 7:19 | 7:47 | **4:04** | 12:52 |
| 256 | 13 | Tu. | | 7:19 | 7:45 | **5:01** | 1:57 |
| 257 | 14 | We. | | 7:20 | 7:44 | **5:50** | 3:08 |
| 258 | 15 | Th. | ♆ ☌ ☾ | 7:21 | 7:43 | **6:32** | 4:22 |
| 259 | 16 | Fr. | ☾ at perigee; ♅ ☌ ☾ | 7:21 | 7:41 | **7:08** | 5:35 |
| 260 | 17 | Sa. | ☿ superior | 7:22 | 7:40 | **7:42** | 6:46 |
| 261 | 18 | Su. | | 7:22 | 7:39 | **8:13** | 7:55 |
| 262 | 19 | Mo. | | 7:23 | 7:38 | **8:45** | 9:02 |
| 263 | 20 | Tu. | | 7:24 | 7:36 | **9:18** | 10:09 |
| 264 | 21 | We. | | 7:24 | 7:35 | **9:54** | 11:15 |
| 265 | 22 | Th. | ♂ ☌ ☾; **fall equinox** | 7:25 | 7:34 | **10:35** | **12:20** |
| 266 | 23 | Fr. | | 7:25 | 7:32 | **11:21** | **1:23** |
| 267 | 24 | Sa. | | 7:26 | 7:31 | . . . | **2:22** |
| 268 | 25 | Su. | | 7:27 | 7:30 | 12:11 | **3:15** |
| 269 | 26 | Mo. | | 7:27 | 7:28 | 1:06 | **4:02** |
| 270 | 27 | Tu. | ♄ ☌ ☾ | 7:28 | 7:27 | 2:04 | **4:42** |
| 271 | 28 | We. | ☾ at apogee | 7:28 | 7:26 | 3:01 | **5:17** |
| 272 | 29 | Th. | | 7:29 | 7:25 | 3:59 | **5:47** |
| 273 | 30 | Fr. | | 7:30 | 7:23 | 4:55 | **6:15** |

**10th Month** — **October 2005** — **31 Days**

**Moon's Phases** — New, Oct. 3, 5:28 a.m.; First Qtr., Oct. 10, 2:01 p.m.; Full, Oct. 17, 7:14 a.m.; Last Qtr., Oct. 24, 8:17 p.m.

| Day of Year | Day of Month | Day of Week | Planetary Configurations and Phenomena | *Hour of Sunrise | *Hour of Sunset | *Hour of Moon-rise | *Hour of Moon-set |
|---|---|---|---|---|---|---|---|
| 274 | 1 | Sa. | ♂ stationary | 7:30 | 7:22 | 5:50 | **6:41** |
| 275 | 2 | Su. | | 7:31 | 7:21 | 6:46 | **7:06** |
| 276 | 3 | Mo. | Eclipse ☉ | 7:32 | 7:20 | 7:42 | **7:32** |
| 277 | 4 | Tu. | | 7:32 | 7:18 | 8:39 | **8:01** |
| 278 | 5 | We. | | 7:33 | 7:17 | 9:40 | **8:32** |
| 279 | 6 | Th. | ☿ ☌ ♃ | 7:33 | 7:16 | 10:43 | **9:09** |
| 280 | 7 | Fr. | ♀ ☌ ☾ | 7:34 | 7:15 | 11:48 | **9:53** |
| 281 | 8 | Sa. | | 7:35 | 7:13 | **12:54** | **10:46** |
| 282 | 9 | Su. | | 7:35 | 7:12 | **1:57** | **11:47** |
| 283 | 10 | Mo. | | 7:36 | 7:11 | **2:55** | . . . |
| 284 | 11 | Tu. | | 7:37 | 7:10 | **3:45** | 12:54 |
| 285 | 12 | We. | ♆ ☌ ☾ | 7:37 | 7:09 | **4:28** | 2:05 |
| 286 | 13 | Th. | | 7:38 | 7:07 | **5:05** | 3:16 |
| 287 | 14 | Fr. | ♅ ☌ ☾; ☾ at perigee | 7:39 | 7:06 | **5:38** | 4:26 |
| 288 | 15 | Sa. | | 7:39 | 7:05 | **6:10** | 5:34 |
| 289 | 16 | Su. | | 7:40 | 7:04 | **6:41** | 6:41 |
| 290 | 17 | Mo. | Eclipse ☾ | 7:41 | 7:03 | **7:13** | 7:47 |
| 291 | 18 | Tu. | | 7:42 | 7:02 | **7:48** | 8:54 |
| 292 | 19 | We. | ♂ ☌ ☾ | 7:42 | 7:01 | **8:27** | 10:01 |
| 293 | 20 | Th. | | 7:43 | 7:00 | **9:11** | 11:07 |
| 294 | 21 | Fr. | | 7:44 | 6:59 | **10:01** | **12:09** |
| 295 | 22 | Sa. | ♃ ☌ ☉ | 7:44 | 6:57 | **10:55** | **1:06** |
| 296 | 23 | Su. | | 7:45 | 6:56 | **11:53** | **1:56** |
| 297 | 24 | Mo. | | 7:46 | 6:55 | . . . | **2:39** |
| 298 | 25 | Tu. | ♄ ☌ ☾ | 7:47 | 6:54 | 12:51 | **3:16** |
| 299 | 26 | We. | ☾ at apogee; ♆ stationary | 6:48 | 5:53 | 1:48 | **3:48** |
| 300 | 27 | Th. | | 6:48 | 5:52 | 2:45 | **4:16** |
| 301 | 28 | Fr. | ♂ closest approach | 6:49 | 5:52 | 3:40 | **4:43** |
| 302 | 29 | Sa. | | 6:50 | 5:51 | 4:36 | **5:08** |
| 303 | †30 | Su. | | 6:51 | 5:50 | 4:31 | **4:34** |
| 304 | 31 | Mo. | | 6:51 | 5:49 | 5:29 | **5:02** |

*See text before January calendar for explanation.
† Daylight Saving Time ends at 2:00 a.m.

**11th Month** — **November 2005** — **30 Days**

**Moon's Phases** — New, Nov. 1, 7:24 p.m; First Qtr., Nov. 8, 7:57 p.m.; Full, Nov. 15, 6:57 p.m.; Last Qtr., Nov. 23, 4:11 p.m.

| Day of Year | Day of Month | Day of Week | Planetary Configurations and Phenomena | *Hour of Sunrise | *Hour of Sunset | *Hour of Moon-rise | *Hour of Moon-set |
|---|---|---|---|---|---|---|---|
| 305 | 1 | Tu. | | 6:52 | 5:48 | 6:29 | **5:32** |
| 306 | 2 | We. | | 6:53 | 5:47 | 7:32 | **6:08** |
| 307 | 3 | Th. | ☿ ♀ greatest elongation E; ☿ ☌ ☾; | 6:54 | 5:46 | 8:38 | **6:50** |
| 308 | 4 | Fr. | | 6:55 | 5:45 | 9:45 | **7:41** |
| 309 | 5 | Sa. | ♀ ☌ ☾; | 6:56 | 5:45 | 10:51 | **8:40** |
| 310 | 6 | Su. | | 6:56 | 5:44 | 11:51 | **9:47** |
| 311 | 7 | Mo. | ♂ ☍ | 6:57 | 5:43 | **12:43** | **10:56** |
| 312 | 8 | Tu. | ♆ ☌ ☾; | 6:58 | 5:42 | **1:27** | . . . |
| 313 | 9 | We. | ☾ at perigee | 6:59 | 5:42 | **2:05** | 12:06 |
| 314 | 10 | Th. | ♅ ☌ ☾; | 7:00 | 5:41 | **2:39** | 1:15 |
| 315 | 11 | Fr. | | 7:01 | 5:41 | **3:09** | 2:21 |
| 316 | 12 | Sa. | | 7:01 | 5:40 | **3:40** | 3:26 |
| 317 | 13 | Su. | | 7:02 | 5:39 | **4:10** | 4:31 |
| 318 | 14 | Mo. | ☿ stationary | 7:03 | 5:39 | **4:43** | 5:36 |
| 319 | 15 | Tu. | ♂ ☌ ☾ | 7:04 | 5:38 | **5:20** | 6:42 |
| 320 | 16 | We. | ♅ stationary | 7:05 | 5:38 | **6:02** | 7:48 |
| 321 | 17 | Th. | | 7:06 | 5:37 | **6:50** | 8:52 |
| 322 | 18 | Fr. | | 7:07 | 5:37 | **7:43** | 9:53 |
| 323 | 19 | Sa. | | 7:07 | 5:36 | **8:40** | 10:46 |
| 324 | 20 | Su. | | 7:08 | 5:36 | **9:39** | 11:33 |
| 325 | 21 | Mo. | ♄ ☌ ☾ | 7:09 | 5:36 | **10:37** | **12:13** |
| 326 | 22 | Tu. | ♄ stationary | 7:10 | 5:35 | **11:34** | **12:46** |
| 327 | 23 | We. | ☾ at apogee | 7:11 | 5:35 | . . . | **1:16** |
| 328 | 24 | Th. | ☿ inferior | 7:12 | 5:35 | 12:29 | **1:43** |
| 329 | 25 | Fr. | | 7:13 | 5:34 | 1:24 | **2:09** |
| 330 | 26 | Sa. | | 7:14 | 5:34 | 2:19 | **2:34** |
| 331 | 27 | Su. | | 7:14 | 5:34 | 3:15 | **3:01** |
| 332 | 28 | Mo. | | 7:15 | 5:34 | 4:13 | **3:30** |
| 333 | 29 | Tu. | ♃ ☌ ☾ | 7:16 | 5:34 | 5:15 | **4:03** |
| 334 | 30 | We. | | 7:17 | 5:34 | 6:21 | **4:43** |

**12th Month** — **December 2005** — **31 Days**

**Moon's Phases** — New, Dec. 1, 9:01 a.m.; First Qtr., Dec. 8, 3:36 a.m.; Full, Dec. 15, 10:15 a.m.; Last Qtr., Dec. 23, 1:36 p.m.; New, Dec. 30, 9:12 p.m.

| Day of Year | Day of Month | Day of Week | Planetary Configurations and Phenomena | *Hour of Sunrise | *Hour of Sunset | *Hour of Moon-rise | *Hour of Moon-set |
|---|---|---|---|---|---|---|---|
| 335 | 1 | Th. | | 7:18 | 5:33 | 7:29 | **5:32** |
| 336 | 2 | Fr. | | 7:19 | 5:33 | 8:37 | **6:29** |
| 337 | 3 | Sa. | ☿ stationary | 7:19 | 5:33 | 9:42 | **7:35** |
| 338 | 4 | Su. | ♀ ☌ ☾; ☾ at perigee | 7:20 | 5:33 | 10:38 | **8:46** |
| 339 | 5 | Mo. | ♆ ☌ ☾ | 7:21 | 5:33 | 11:26 | **9:58** |
| 340 | 6 | Tu. | | 7:22 | 5:34 | **12:06** | **11:07** |
| 341 | 7 | We. | ♅ ☌ ☾ | 7:22 | 5:34 | **12:41** | . . . |
| 342 | 8 | Th. | | 7:23 | 5:34 | **1:12** | 12:14 |
| 343 | 9 | Fr. | ♀ greatest brilliancy | 7:24 | 5:34 | **1:42** | 1:19 |
| 344 | 10 | Sa. | ♂ stationary | 7:25 | 5:34 | **2:12** | 2:22 |
| 345 | 11 | Su. | ♂ ☌ ☾ | 7:25 | 5:34 | **2:43** | 3:25 |
| 346 | 12 | Mo. | ☿ greatest elongation W | 7:26 | 5:35 | **3:17** | 4:30 |
| 347 | 13 | Tu. | | 7:27 | 5:35 | **3:57** | 5:34 |
| 348 | 14 | We. | | 7:27 | 5:35 | **4:42** | 6:39 |
| 349 | 15 | Th. | ♇ ☌ ☉ | 7:28 | 5:35 | **5:32** | 7:40 |
| 350 | 16 | Fr. | | 7:29 | 5:36 | **6:28** | 8:36 |
| 351 | 17 | Sa. | | 7:29 | 5:36 | **7:27** | 9:26 |
| 352 | 18 | Su. | | 7:30 | 5:37 | **8:26** | 10:08 |
| 353 | 19 | Mo. | ♄ ☌ ☾ | 7:30 | 5:37 | **9:23** | 10:45 |
| 354 | 20 | Tu. | ☾ at apogee | 7:31 | 5:37 | **10:20** | 11:16 |
| 355 | 21 | We. | **Winter solstice** | 7:32 | 5:38 | **11:14** | 11:44 |
| 356 | 22 | Th. | ♀ stationary | 7:32 | 5:38 | . . . | **12:09** |
| 357 | 23 | Fr. | | 7:33 | 5:39 | 12:08 | **12:34** |
| 358 | 24 | Sa. | | 7:33 | 5:39 | 1:02 | **1:00** |
| 359 | 25 | Su. | | 7:33 | 5:40 | 1:58 | **1:27** |
| 360 | 26 | Mo. | ♃ ☌ ☾ | 7:34 | 5:41 | 2:57 | **1:58** |
| 361 | 27 | Tu. | | 7:34 | 5:41 | 4:00 | **2:34** |
| 362 | 28 | We. | | 7:35 | 5:42 | 5:07 | **3:18** |
| 363 | 29 | Th. | ☿ ☌ ☾ | 7:35 | 5:43 | 6:16 | **4:11** |
| 364 | 30 | Fr. | | 7:35 | 5:43 | 7:23 | **5:15** |
| 365 | 31 | Sa. | | 7:35 | 5:44 | 8:25 | **6:26** |

# 201-Year Calendar, A.D. 1894-2094, Inclusive

Using this calendar, you can find the day of the week for any day of the month and year for the period 1894-2094, inclusive. To find any day of the week, first look in the table of common years or leap years for the year required. Under the months are figures that refer to the corresponding figures at the heads of the columns of days below. For example, To know on what day of the week March 2 fell in the year 1918, find 1918 in the table of years. In a parallel line under March is Fig. 5, which directs you to Col. 5 in the table of days, in which it will be seen that March 2 fell on Saturday.

## Common Years, 1894 to 2094

| | | | | | | | | | | | Jan. | Feb. | Mar. | Apr. | May | June | July | Aug. | Sept. | Oct. | Nov. | Dec. |
|---|---|---|---|---|---|---|---|---|---|---|---|---|---|---|---|---|---|---|---|---|---|---|
| 1894 | 1900 | ... | ... | ... | ... | ... | ... | ... | | | | | | | | | | | | | | |
| 1906 | 1917 | 1923 | 1934 | 1945 | 1951 | 1962 | 1973 | 1979 | 1990 | ... | 1 | 4 | 4 | 7 | 2 | 5 | 7 | 3 | 6 | 1 | 4 | 6 |
| 2001 | 2007 | 2018 | 2029 | 2035 | 2046 | 2057 | 2063 | 2074 | 2085 | 2091 | | | | | | | | | | | | |
| 1895 | ... | ... | ... | ... | ... | ... | ... | | | | | | | | | | | | | | | |
| 1901 | 1907 | 1918 | 1929 | 1935 | 1946 | 1957 | 1963 | 1974 | 1985 | 1991 | 2 | 5 | 5 | 1 | 3 | 6 | 1 | 4 | 7 | 2 | 5 | 7 |
| 2002 | 2013 | 2019 | 2030 | 2041 | 2047 | 2058 | 2069 | 2075 | 2086 | 2097 | | | | | | | | | | | | |
| 1897 | ... | ... | ... | ... | ... | ... | ... | | | | | | | | | | | | | | | |
| 1909 | 1915 | 1926 | 1937 | 1943 | 1954 | 1965 | 1971 | 1982 | 1993 | 1999 | 5 | 1 | 1 | 4 | 6 | 2 | 4 | 7 | 3 | 5 | 1 | 3 |
| 2010 | 2021 | 2027 | 2038 | 2049 | 2055 | 2066 | 2077 | 2083 | 2094 | 2100 | | | | | | | | | | | | |
| 1898 | 1910 | 1921 | 1927 | 1938 | 1949 | 1955 | 1966 | 1977 | 1983 | 1994 | 6 | 2 | 2 | 5 | 7 | 3 | 5 | 1 | 4 | 6 | 2 | 4 |
| 2005 | 2011 | 2022 | 2033 | 2039 | 2050 | 2061 | 2067 | 2078 | 2089 | 2095 | | | | | | | | | | | | |
| 1899 | 1905 | 1911 | 1922 | 1933 | 1939 | 1950 | 1961 | 1967 | 1978 | 1989 | 7 | 3 | 3 | 6 | 1 | 4 | 6 | 2 | 5 | 7 | 3 | 5 |
| 1995 | 2006 | 2017 | 2023 | 2034 | 2045 | 2051 | 2062 | 2073 | 2079 | 2090 | | | | | | | | | | | | |
| 1902 | 1913 | 1919 | 1930 | 1941 | 1947 | 1958 | 1969 | 1975 | 1986 | 1997 | 3 | 6 | 6 | 2 | 4 | 7 | 2 | 5 | 1 | 3 | 6 | 1 |
| 2003 | 2014 | 2025 | 2031 | 2042 | 2053 | 2059 | 2070 | 2081 | 2087 | 2098 | | | | | | | | | | | | |
| 1903 | 1914 | 1925 | 1931 | 1942 | 1953 | 1959 | 1970 | 1981 | 1987 | 1998 | 4 | 7 | 7 | 3 | 5 | 1 | 3 | 6 | 2 | 4 | 7 | 2 |
| 2009 | 2015 | 2026 | 2037 | 2043 | 2054 | 2065 | 2071 | 2082 | 2093 | 2099 | | | | | | | | | | | | |

## Leap Years, 1894 to 2094

| | | | | | | | | | 29 | | | | | | | | | | | |
|---|---|---|---|---|---|---|---|---|---|---|---|---|---|---|---|---|---|---|---|---|
| ... | ... | 1920 | 1948 | 1976 | 2004 | 2032 | 2060 | 2088 | 4 | 7 | 1 | 4 | 6 | 2 | 4 | 7 | 3 | 5 | 1 | 3 |
| ... | ... | 1924 | 1952 | 1980 | 2008 | 2036 | 2064 | 2092 | 2 | 5 | 6 | 2 | 4 | 7 | 2 | 5 | 1 | 3 | 6 | 1 |
| ... | ... | 1928 | 1956 | 1984 | 2012 | 2040 | 2068 | 2096 | 7 | 3 | 4 | 7 | 2 | 5 | 7 | 3 | 6 | 1 | 4 | 6 |
| ... | 1904 | 1932 | 1960 | 1988 | 2016 | 2044 | 2072 | ... | 5 | 1 | 2 | 5 | 7 | 3 | 5 | 1 | 4 | 6 | 2 | 4 |
| 1896 | 1908 | 1936 | 1964 | 1992 | 2020 | 2048 | 2076 | ... | 3 | 6 | 7 | 3 | 5 | 1 | 3 | 6 | 2 | 4 | 7 | 2 |
| ... | 1912 | 1940 | 1968 | 1996 | 2024 | 2052 | 2080 | ... | 1 | 4 | 5 | 1 | 3 | 6 | 1 | 4 | 7 | 2 | 5 | 7 |
| ... | 1916 | 1944 | 1972 | 2000 | 2028 | 2056 | 2084 | ... | 6 | 2 | 3 | 6 | 1 | 4 | 6 | 2 | 5 | 7 | 3 | 5 |

| 1 | | 2 | | 3 | | 4 | | 5 | | 6 | | 7 | |
|---|---|---|---|---|---|---|---|---|---|---|---|---|---|
| Mon. | 1 | Tues | 1 | Wed. | 1 | Thurs. | 1 | Fri. | 1 | Sat. | 1 | SUN. | 1 |
| Tues. | 2 | Wed. | 2 | Thurs. | 2 | Fri. | 2 | Sat. | 2 | SUN. | 2 | Mon. | 2 |
| Wed. | 3 | Thurs. | 3 | Fri. | 3 | Sat. | 3 | SUN. | 3 | Mon. | 3 | Tues. | 3 |
| Thurs. | 4 | Fri. | 4 | Sat. | 4 | SUN. | 4 | Mon. | 4 | Tues. | 4 | Wed. | 4 |
| Fri. | 5 | Sat. | 5 | SUN. | 5 | Mon. | 5 | Tues. | 5 | Wed. | 5 | Thurs. | 5 |
| Sat. | 6 | SUN. | 6 | Mon. | 6 | Tues. | 6 | Wed. | 6 | Thurs. | 6 | Fri. | 6 |
| SUN. | 7 | Mon. | 7 | Tues. | 7 | Wed. | 7 | Thurs. | 7 | Fri. | 7 | Sat. | 7 |
| Mon. | 8 | Tues. | 8 | Wed. | 8 | Thurs. | 8 | Fri. | 8 | Sat. | 8 | SUN. | 8 |
| Tues. | 9 | Wed. | 9 | Thurs. | 9 | Fri. | 9 | Sat. | 9 | SUN. | 9 | Mon. | 9 |
| Wed. | 10 | Thurs. | 10 | Fri. | 10 | Sat. | 10 | SUN. | 10 | Mon. | 10 | Tues. | 10 |
| Thurs. | 11 | Fri. | 11 | Sat. | 11 | SUN. | 11 | Mon. | 11 | Tues. | 11 | Wed. | 11 |
| Fri. | 12 | Sat. | 12 | SUN. | 12 | Mon. | 12 | Tues. | 12 | Wed. | 12 | Thurs. | 12 |
| Sat. | 13 | SUN. | 13 | Mon. | 13 | Tues. | 13 | Wed. | 13 | Thurs. | 13 | Fri. | 13 |
| SUN. | 14 | Mon. | 14 | Tues. | 14 | Wed. | 14 | Thurs. | 14 | Fri. | 14 | Sat. | 14 |
| Mon. | 15 | Tues. | 15 | Wed. | 15 | Thurs. | 15 | Fri. | 15 | Sat. | 15 | SUN. | 15 |
| Tues. | 16 | Wed. | 16 | Thurs. | 16 | Fri. | 16 | Sat. | 16 | SUN. | 16 | Mon. | 16 |
| Wed. | 17 | Thurs. | 17 | Fri. | 17 | Sat. | 17 | SUN. | 17 | Mon. | 17 | Tues. | 17 |
| Thurs. | 18 | Fri. | 18 | Sat. | 18 | SUN. | 18 | Mon. | 18 | Tues. | 18 | Wed. | 18 |
| Fri. | 19 | Sat. | 19 | SUN. | 19 | Mon. | 19 | Tues. | 19 | Wed. | 19 | Thurs. | 19 |
| Sat. | 20 | SUN. | 20 | Mon. | 20 | Tues. | 20 | Wed. | 20 | Thurs. | 20 | Fri. | 20 |
| SUN. | 21 | Mon. | 21 | Tues. | 21 | Wed. | 21 | Thurs. | 21 | Fri. | 21 | Sat. | 21 |
| Mon. | 22 | Tues. | 22 | Wed. | 22 | Thurs. | 22 | Fri. | 22 | Sat. | 22 | SUN. | 22 |
| Tues. | 23 | Wed. | 23 | Thurs. | 23 | Fri. | 23 | Sat. | 23 | SUN. | 23 | Mon. | 23 |
| Wed. | 24 | Thurs. | 24 | Fri. | 24 | Sat. | 24 | SUN. | 24 | Mon. | 24 | Tues. | 24 |
| Thurs. | 25 | Fri. | 25 | Sat. | 25 | SUN. | 25 | Mon. | 25 | Tues. | 25 | Wed. | 25 |
| Fri. | 26 | Sat. | 26 | SUN. | 26 | Mon. | 26 | Tues. | 26 | Wed. | 26 | Thurs. | 26 |
| Sat. | 27 | SUN. | 27 | Mon. | 27 | Tues. | 27 | Wed. | 27 | Thurs. | 27 | Fri. | 27 |
| SUN. | 28 | Mon. | 28 | Tues. | 28 | Wed. | 28 | Thurs. | 28 | Fri. | 28 | Sat. | 28 |
| Mon. | 29 | Tues. | 29 | Wed. | 29 | Thurs. | 29 | Fri. | 29 | Sat. | 29 | SUN. | 29 |
| Tues. | 30 | Wed. | 30 | Thurs. | 30 | Fri. | 30 | Sat. | 30 | SUN. | 30 | Mon. | 30 |
| Wed. | 31 | Thurs. | 31 | Fri. | 31 | Sat. | 31 | SUN. | 31 | Mon. | 31 | Tues. | 31 |

## Beginning of the Year

The Athenians began the year in June, the Macedonians in September, the Romans first in March and later in January, the Persians on Aug. 11, and the ancient Mexicans on Feb. 23. The Chinese year, which begins in late January or early February, is similar to the Mohammedan year. Both have 12 months of 29 and 30 days alternating, while in every 19 years, there are seven years that have 13 months. This does not quite fit the planetary movements, hence the Chinese have formed a cycle of 60 years, in which period 22 intercalary (added to the calendar) months occur.

# Recreation

Information about recreational opportunities in state and national parks and forests and at U.S. Army Corps of Engineers Lakes, a representative list of festivals and celebrations in individual towns and communities across the state, as well as information on hunting and fishing opportunities and regulations is found in the following pages. Information about hunting, fishing and other recreation on State Wildlife Management Areas and National Wildlife Refuges can be found in the Environment section. Recreation and special events in each county are also mentioned in the Counties section.

## Texas State Parks

Texas' diverse system of state parks offers contrasting attractions — mountains and canyons, arid deserts and lush forests, spring-fed streams, sandy dunes, saltwater surf and fascinating historic sites.

The state park information below was provided by **Texas Parks and Wildlife** (TPW). Additional information and brochures on individual parks are available from the TPW's Austin headquarters, 4200 Smith School Rd., Austin 78744; 1-800-792-1112; **www.tpwd.state.tx.us/park/.**

The TPW's **Central Reservation Center** can take reservations for almost all parks that accept reservations. Exceptions are Indian Lodge, the Texas State Railroad and facilities not operated by the TPW. Call the center during usual business hours at 512-389-8900. The TDD line is 512-389-8915.

Guests at Big Bend Ranch State Park round up longhorn cattle in a semi-annual cattle drive. The park, in Presidio and Brewster counties, comprises 280,280 acres; it more than doubled the size of the Texas park system when it was purchased in 1988. File photo.

The **Texas Conservation Passport**, currently costing $50 per year, waives entrance fees for all members and all passengers in member's vehicle in state parks when entrance fees are required, as well as other benefits. For further information, contact TPW at numbers or address above.

**Texas State Parklands Passport** is a windshield decal granting discounted entrance to state parks for Texas residents who are senior citizens or are collecting Social Security disability payments and free entrance for disabled U.S. veterans. Available at state parks with proper identification. Details can be obtained at numbers or addresses above.

The following information is a brief glimpse of what each park has to offer. Refer to the chart on pages 112-113 for a more complete list of available activities and facilities. Entrance fees to state parks range from $1 to $5 per person. There are also fees for tours and some activities. For up-to-date information, call the information number listed above before you go. Road abbreviations used in this list are: IH - interstate highway, US - U.S. Highway, TX - state highway, FM - farm-to-market road, RM - ranch-to-market road, PR - park road.

### List of State Parks

**Abilene State Park**, 16 miles southwest of Abilene on FM 89 and PR 32 in Taylor County, consists of 529.4 acres that were deeded by the City of Abilene in 1933. A part of the **official Texas longhorn herd** and bison are located in the park. Large groves of pecan trees that once shaded bands of Comanches now shade visitors at picnic tables. Activities include camping, hiking, picnicking, nature study, biking, lake swimming and fishing. In addition to **Lake Abilene, Buffalo Gap**, the original Taylor County seat (1878) and one of the early frontier settlements, is nearby. Buffalo Gap was on the **Western**, or **Goodnight-Loving, Trail**, over which pioneer Texas cattlemen drove herds to railheads in Kansas.

**Acton State Historic Site** is a .01-acre cemetery plot in Hood County where **Davy Crockett's** second wife, Elizabeth, was buried in 1860. It is 4.5 miles east of Granbury on US 377 to FM 167 south, then 2.4 miles south to Acton. Nearby attractions include Cleburne, Dinosaur Valley and

Lake Whitney state parks.

**Admiral Nimitz Museum State Historic Site** (see **National Museum of the Pacific War**).

**Atlanta State Park** is 1,475 acres located 11 miles northwest of Atlanta on FM 1154 in Cass County; adjacent to **Wright Patman Dam and Reservoir.** Land acquired from the U.S. Army in 1954 by license to 2004 with option to renew to 2054. Camping, biking and hiking in pine forests, as well as water activities, such as boating, fishing, lake swimming. Nearby are historic town of **Jefferson** and **Caddo Lake and Daingerfield state parks.**

**Balmorhea State Park** is 45.9 acres four miles southwest of Balmorhea on TX 17 between Balmorhea and Toyahvale in Reeves County. Deeded in 1934-35 by private owners and Reeves Co. Water Imp. Dist. No. 1 and built by the Civilian Conservation Corps (CCC). Swimming pool (1-3/4 acres) fed by artesian **San Solomon Springs;** also provides water to **aquatic refuge** in park. Activities include swimming, picnicking, camping, scuba and skin diving. Motel rooms available at **San Solomon Springs Courts.** Nearby are city of Pecos, **Fort Davis National Historic Site, Davis Mountains State Park** and **McDonald Observatory.**

**Barton Warnock Environmental Education Center** consists of 99.9 acres in Brewster County. Originally built by the Lajitas Foundation in 1982 as the Lajitas Museum Desert Gardens, the TPW purchased it in 1990 and renamed it for Texas botanist Dr. Barton Warnock. The center is also the eastern entrance station to **Big Bend Ranch State Park.** Self-guiding botanical and museum tours. On FM 170 one mile east of Lajitas.

**Bastrop State Park** is 3,503.7 acres one mile east of Bastrop on TX 21 or from TX 71. The park was acquired by deeds from the City of Bastrop and private owners in 1933-35; additional acreage acquired in 1979. Site of famous **"Lost Pines,"** isolated region of loblolly pine and hardwoods. **Swimming pool, cabins** and **lodge** are among facilities. Fishing at Lake Bastrop, backpacking, picnicking, canoeing, bicycling, hiking. Golf course adjacent to park. **State capitol** at Austin 32 miles away; 13-mile drive through forest leads to **Buescher State Park.**

**Battleship Texas State Historic Site** (see **San Jacinto**

Battleground State Historic Site and Battleship Texas)

**Bentsen-Rio Grande Valley State Park,** a scenic park, is along the Rio Grande five miles southwest of Mission off FM 2062 in Hidalgo County. The 587.7 acres of **subtropical resaca woodlands and brushlands** were acquired from private owners in 1944. Park is excellent base from which to tour **Lower Rio Grande Valley** of Texas and adjacent **Mexico;** most attractions within an hour's drive. Hiking trails provide chance to study unique plants and animals of park. Many birds unique to southern United States found here, including **pauraque, groove-billed ani, green kingfisher, rose-throated becard** and **tropical parula.** Birdwatching tours guided by park naturalists offered daily December –March. Park is one of last natural refuges in Texas for **ocelot** and **jaguarundi.** Trees include **cedar elm, anaqua, ebony** and **Mexican ash.** Camping, hiking, picnicking, boating, fishing also available. Nearby are **Santa Ana National Wildlife Refuge, Falcon State Park** and **Sabal Palm Sanctuary.**

**Big Bend Ranch State Park,** 280,280 acres of **Chihuahuan Desert wilderness** in Brewster and Presidio counties along the Rio Grande, was purchased from private owners in 1988. The purchase more than doubled the size of the state park system, which comprised at that time 220,000 acres. Eastern entrance at Barton Warnock Environmental Education Center one mile east of Lajitas on FM 170; western entrance is at **Fort Leaton State Historical Park** four miles east of Presidio on FM 170. The area includes **extinct volcanoes,** several **waterfalls,** two **mountain ranges,** at least **11 rare species of plants and animals,** and **90 major archaeological sites.** There is little development. Vehicular access limited; wilderness backpacking, hiking, scenic drive, picnicking, fishing and swimming. There are longhorns in the park, although they are not part of the official **state longhorn herd.**

**Big Spring State Park** is 382 acres located on FM 700 within the city limits of Big Spring in Howard County. Both city and park were named for a natural spring that was replaced by an artificial one. The park was deeded by the City of Big Spring in 1934 and 1935. Drive to top of **Scenic Mountain** provides panoramic view of surrounding country and look at **prairie dog colony.** The "big spring," nearby in a city park, provided watering place for herds of bison, antelope and wild horses. Used extensively also as campsite for early Indians, explorers and settlers.

**Blanco State Park** is 104.6 acres along the Blanco River four blocks south of Blanco's town square in Blanco County. The land was deeded by private owners in 1933. Park area was used as campsite by early explorers and settlers. Fishing, camping, swimming, picnicking, boating. **LBJ Ranch** and **LBJ State Historic Site, Pedernales Falls** and **Guadalupe River** state parks are nearby.

**Boca Chica State Park** is 1,054.92 acres of open beach located at the mouth of the Rio Grande in southeastern Cameron County. Park was acquired in May 1994. From US 77/83 at Olmito, take FM 511 12 miles to TX 4, then 17 miles east to park. Picnicking, wading, swimming, birding, camping, fishing allowed. No facilities provided.

**Bonham State Park** is a 261-acre park located two miles southeast of Bonham on TX 78, then two miles southeast on FM 271 in Fannin County. It includes a 65-acre lake, **rolling prairies** and **woodlands.** The land was acquired in 1933 from the city of Bonham. Swimming, camping, mountain-bike trail, lighted fishing pier, boating. **Sam Rayburn Memorial Library** in Bonham. **Sam Rayburn Home** and **Valley Lake** nearby.

**Brazos Bend State Park** in Fort Bend County, seven miles west of Rosharon off FM 1462 on FM 762, approximately 28 miles south of Houston. The 4,897-acre park was purchased from private owners in 1976–77. **George**

**Observatory** in park. **Observation platform** for spotting and photographing the **270 species of birds, 23 species of mammals, and 21 species of reptiles and amphibians, including American alligator,** that frequent the park. Interpretive and educational programs every weekend. Backpacking, camping, hiking, biking, fishing. Creekfield Lake Nature Trail.

**Buescher State Park,** a scenic area, is 1,016.7 acres 2 miles northwest of Smithville off TX 71 to FM 153 in Bastrop County. Acquired between 1933 and 1936, about one-third deeded by private owner; heirs donated a third; balance from City of Smithville. **El Camino Real** once ran near park, connecting **San Antonio de Béxar** with **Spanish missions in East Texas.** Parkland was part of **Stephen F. Austin's colonial grant.** Some **250 species of birds** can be seen. Camping, fishing, hiking, boating. Scenic park road connects with **Bastrop State Park** through **Lost Pines** area.

**Caddo Lake State Park,** north of Karnack one mile off TX 43 to FM 2198 in Harrison County, consists of 483.85 acres along **Cypress Bayou,** which runs into Caddo Lake. A scenic area, it was acquired from private owners in 1933. Nearby Karnack is childhood home of Mrs. Lyndon B. Johnson. Close by is old city of **Jefferson,** famous as commercial center of Northeast Texas during last half of 19th century. Caddo Indian legend attributes formation of Caddo Lake to **a huge flood.** Lake originally only natural lake of any size in state; dam added in 1914 for flood control; new dam replaced old one in 1971. **Cypress trees, American lotus** and **lily pads,** as well as **71 species of fish,** predominate in lake. **Nutria, beaver, mink, squirrel, armadillo, alligator** and **turtle** abound. Activities include camping, hiking, swimming, fishing, canoeing. Screened shelters, cabins.

**Caddoan Mounds State Historic Site** in Cherokee County six miles southwest of Alto on TX 21. Total of 93.8 acres acquired in 1975. Open for day visits only, park offers exhibits and interpretive trails through reconstructed **Caddo dwellings and ceremonial areas,** including two temple mounds, a burial mound and a village area typical of people who lived in region for 500 years beginning about A.D. 800. Closed Tuesday and Wednesday. Nearby are **Jim Hogg State Historic Site, Mission Tejas State Historic Site** and **Texas State Railroad.**

**Caprock Canyons State Park,** 100 miles southeast of Amarillo and 3.5 miles north of Quitaque off FM 1065 and TX 86 in Briscoe, Floyd and Hall counties, has 15,313 acres. Purchased in 1975. Scenic escarpment's **canyons** provided camping areas for **Indians of Folsom culture** more than 10,000 years ago. **Mesquite** and **cacti** in the **badlands** give way to **tall grasses, cottonwood** and **plum thickets** in the bottomlands. Wildlife includes **aoudad sheep, coyote, bobcat, porcupine** and **fox.** Activities include scenic drive, camping, hiking, mountain-bike riding, horse riding and horse camping. A 64.25-mile trailway (hike, bike and equestrian trail) extends from South Plains to Estelline.

**Casa Navarro State Historic Site,** on .7 acre at corner of S. Laredo and W. Nueva streets in downtown San Antonio, was acquired by donation from San Antonio Conservation Society Foundation in 1975. Has furnished **Navarro House** three-building complex built about 1848, home of the statesman, rancher and Texas patriot **José Antonio Navarro.** Guided tours; exhibits. Open Wednesday through Sunday.

**Cedar Hill State Park,** an urban park on 1,826 acres 10 miles southwest of Dallas via US 67 and FM 1382 on **Joe Pool Reservoir,** was acquired by long-term lease from the Corp of Engineers in 1982. Camping mostly in wooded areas. Fishing from two lighted jetties and a perch pond for

children. Swimming, boating, bicycling, bird-watching and picnicking. Vegetation includes several sections of **tall-grass prairie.** Penn Farm Agricultural History Center includes reconstructed buildings of the **19th-century Penn Farm** and exhibits; self-guided tours.

**Choke Canyon State Park** consists of two units, South Shore and Calliham, located on 26,000-acre **Choke Canyon Reservoir.** Park acquired in 1981 in a 50-year agreement among Bureau of Reclamation, City of Corpus Christi and

Spring-blooming golden poppies cover the eastern approach to Franklin Mountains State Park in El Paso. The 24,247-acre park is the largest urban park in the United States. File photo.

Nueces River Authority. Thickets of **mesquite** and **blackbrush acacia** predominate, supporting populations of **javelina, coyote, skunk** and **alligator,** as well as the **crested caracara.** The 385-acre South Shore Unit is located 3.5 miles west of Three Rivers on TX 72 in Live Oak County; the 1,100-acre Calliham Unit is located 12 miles west of Three Rivers, on TX 72, in McMullen County. Both units offer camping, picnicking, boating, fishing, lake swimming, and baseball and volleyball areas. The Calliham Unit also has a hiking trail, wildlife educational center, screened shelters, rentable **gym and kitchen. Sports complex** includes swimming pool and tennis, volleyball, shuffleboard and basketball courts. Across dam from South Shore is North Shore Equestrian and Camping Area; 18 miles of horseback riding trails.

**Cleburne State Park** is a 528-acre park located 10 miles southwest of Cleburne via US 67 and PR 21 in Johnson County with 116-acre spring-fed lake; acquired from the City of Cleburne and private owners in 1935 and 1936. **Oak, elm, mesquite, cedar** and **redbud** cover white rocky hills. Bluebonnets in spring. Activities include camping, picnicking, hiking, bicycling, canoeing, swimming, boating, fishing. Nearby are **Fossil Rim Wildlife Center** and **dinosaur tracks** in Paluxy River at **Dinosaur Valley State Park.**

**Colorado Bend State Park,** a 5,328.3-acre facility, is 28 miles west of Lampasas in Lampasas and San Saba counties. Access is from Lampasas to Bend on FM 580 west, then follow signs (access road subject to flooding). Park site was purchased partly in 1984, with balance acquired in 1987. Primitive camping, fishing, swimming, hiking, biking and picnicking; guided tours to Gorman Falls. Rare and endangered species here include **golden-cheeked warbler, black-capped vireo** and **bald eagle.**

**Confederate Reunion Grounds State Historic Site,** located in Limestone County on the Navasota River, is 77.1 acres in size. Acquired 1983 by deed from Joseph E. Johnston Camp No. 94 CSA. Entrance is 6 miles south of Mexia on TX 14, then 2.5 miles west on FM 2705. **Historic buildings,** two **scenic footbridges** span creek; hiking trail. Nearby are **Fort Parker State Park** and **Old Fort Parker State Historic Site.**

**Cooper Lake State Park,** comprises 3,026 acres three miles southeast of Cooper in Delta and Hopkins counties acquired in 1991 by 25-year lease from Corps of Engineers. Two units, Doctors Creek and South Sulphur, adjoin 19,300-surface-acre Cooper Lake. Fishing, boating, camping, picnicking, swimming. Screened shelters and cabins. South Sulpher offers equestrian camping and horseback riding trails. Access to Doctors Creek Unit is via TX 24 east from Commerce to Cooper, then east on TX 154 to FM 1529 to park. To South Sulphur Unit, take IH 30 to Exit 122 west of Sulphur Springs to TX 19, then TX 71, then FM 3505.

**Copano Bay State Fishing Pier,** a 5.9-acre park, is located 5 miles north of Rockport on TX 35 in Aransas County. Acquired by transfer of jurisdiction from state highway department in 1967. Picnicking, saltwater fishing, boating and swimming. Operated by leased concession.

**Copper Breaks State Park,** 12 miles south of Quanah

on TX 6 in Hardeman County, was acquired by purchase from private owner in 1970. Park features rugged scenic beauty on 1,898.8 acres, two lakes, **grass-covered mesas** and juniper breaks. Nearby **medicine mounds** were important ceremonial sites of Comanche Indians. Nearby **Pease River** was site of 1860 battle in which **Cynthia Ann Parker** was recovered from Comanches. Part of **state longhorn herd** lives at park. Abundant wildlife. Nature, hiking and equestrian trails; natural and historical exhibits; summer programs; horseback riding; camping, equestrian camping.

**Daingerfield State Park,** off TX 49 and PR 17 southeast of Daingerfield in Morris County, is a 550.9-acre recreational area that includes an 80-surface-acre lake; deeded in 1935 by private owners. This area is center of iron industry in Texas; nearby is Lone Star Steel Co. In spring, **dogwood, redbuds** and **wisteria** bloom; in fall, brilliant foliage of **sweetgum, oaks** and **maples** contrast with dark green pines. Campsites, lodge and cabins.

**Davis Mountains State Park** is 2,709 acres in Jeff Davis County, 4 miles northwest of Fort Davis via TX 118 and PR 3. The scenic area was deeded in 1933-1937 by private owners. **First European, Antonio de Espejo,** came to area in 1583. Extremes of altitude produce both **plains grasslands** and **piñon-juniper-oak woodlands. Montezuma quail,** rare in Texas, visit park. Scenic drives, camping and hiking. **Indian Lodge,** built by the Civilian Conservation Corps during the early 1930s, has 39 rooms, restaurant and swimming pool (reservations: 915-426-3254). Four-mile hiking trail leads to **Fort Davis National Historic Site.** Other nearby points of interest include **McDonald Observatory** and 74-mile scenic loop through **Davis Mountains.** Nearby are scenic **Limpia, Madera, Musquiz** and **Keesey** canyons; **Camino del Rio;** ghost town of **Shafter; Big Bend National Park; Big Bend Ranch State Park; Fort Davis National Historic Site;** and **Fort Leaton State Historic Site.**

**Devil's River State Natural Area** comprises 19,988.6 acres in Val Verde County, 22 miles off US 277, about 65 miles north of Del Rio on graded road. It is an **ecological and archaeological crossroads.** Ecologically, it is in a **transitional area** between the **Edwards Plateau,** the **Trans-Pecos desert** and the **South Texas brush country.** Archaeological studies suggest occupation and/or use by cultures from both east and west. Camping, hiking and mountain biking. Canyon and pictograph-site tours by prearrangement only. Park accessible by reservation only. **Dolan Falls,** owned by The Nature Conservancy of Texas and open only to its members, is nearby.

**Devil's Sinkhole State Natural Area,** comprising 1,859.7 acres about 6 miles northeast of Rocksprings in Edwards County, is a **vertical cavern.** The sinkhole, discovered by Anglo settlers in 1867, is a registered **National Natural Landmark;** it was purchased in 1985 from private owners. The cavern opening is about 40 by 60 feet, with a vertical drop of about 140 feet. Access by prearranged tour with Devil's Sinkhole Society (830-683-BATS). Bats can be viewed in summer leaving cave at dusk; no access to cave itself. Access to the park is made by contacting **Kickapoo Cavern State Park** to arrange a tour.

**Dinosaur Valley State Park,** located off US 67 four miles west of Glen Rose in Somervell County, is a 1,524.72-acre scenic park. Land was acquired from private owners in 1968. **Dinosaur tracks** in bed of Paluxy River and two full-scale dinosaur models, originally created for New York World's Fair in 1964-65, on display. Part of state **longhorn herd** is in park. Camping, picnicking,

*Parks text continues on page 124.*

# ☆ Texas State Parks ☆

| Park/†Type of Park/Special Features | NEAREST TOWN | Day Use Only | Historic Site/Museum | Exhibit/Interpretive Center | Restrooms | Showers | Trailer Dump Stn. | ††Camping | Screened Shelters | Cabins | Group Facilities | Nature Trail | Hiking Trail | Picnicking | Boat Ramp | Fishing | Swimming | Water Skiing | Miscellaneous |
|---|---|---|---|---|---|---|---|---|---|---|---|---|---|---|---|---|---|---|---|
| Abilene SP | BUFFALO GAP | | | | ★ | ★ | ★ | 15 | ★ | | BG | ★ | | ★ | | | ☆ | ★ | L |
| Acton SHS (Grave of Davy Crockett's wife) | GRANBURY | ★ | ★ | | | | | | | | | | | | | | | | |
| Atlanta SP | ATLANTA | | | | ★ | ★ | ★ | 14 | | | DG | ★ | ★ | ★ | ★ | | ☆ | ☆ | ☆ |
| Balmorhea SP (San Solomon Springs Courts) | BALMORHEA | | | ★ | ★ | ★ | ★ | 14 | | | DG | | | ★ | | | ★ | | I |
| Barton Warnock Environmental Education Ctr. | LAJITAS | ★ | | ★ | ★ | ★ | | | | | | | | ★ | | | | | |
| Bastrop SP | BASTROP | | | | ★ | ★ | ★ | 10 | | ★ | BG | | | ★ | ★ | | ☆ | ★ | G |
| Battleship Texas HS (At San Jacinto Battleground) | DEER PARK | ★ | ★ | ★ | | | | | | | | | | | | | | | |
| Bentsen-Rio Grande Valley SP | MISSION | | | | ★ | ★ | | 10 | | | BG | ★ | ★ | ★ | ★ | ☆ | | | |
| Big Bend Ranch SP Complex | PRESIDIO | | | ★ | ★ | ★ | | 1 | | | NG | ★ | ★ | ★ | | | ☆ | ☆ | B1, L, E |
| Big Spring SP | BIG SPRING | | | | ★ | ★ | | 13 | | | BG | ★ | ★ | ★ | | | | | |
| Blanco SP | BLANCO | | | | ★ | ★ | ★ | 16 | ★ | | DG | | | ★ | ★ | | ☆ | ☆ | |
| Boca Chica SP (Open Beach) | BROWNSVILLE | | | | | | | 1 | | | | | | | | ☆ | ☆ | ☆ | |
| Bonham SP | BONHAM | | | | ★ | ★ | ★ | 14 | | | BG | | ★ | ★ | ★ | ★ | ☆ | | B1 |
| Brazos Bend SP (George Observatory) | RICHMOND | | | ★ | ★ | ★ | ★ | 4 | ★ | | BG | ★ | ★ | ★ | | ★ | | | B1, B2 |
| Buescher SP | SMITHVILLE | | | | ★ | ★ | ★ | 14 | ★ | | BG | | | ★ | ★ | ★ | ☆ | | B2 |
| Caddo Lake SP | KARNACK | | | ★ | ★ | ★ | ★ | 15 | ★ | ★ | BG | ★ | ★ | ★ | ★ | ★ | ☆ | ☆ | |
| Caddoan Mounds SHS | ALTO | ★ | ★ | ★ | ★ | | | | | | | ★ | | | | | | | |
| Caprock Canyons SP and Trailway | QUITAQUE | | | ★ | ★ | ★ | ★ | 8 | | | BG | ★ | ★ | ★ | ★ | ★ | ☆ | | B1, E |
| Casa Navarro SHS | SAN ANTONIO | ★ | ★ | ★ | ★ | | | | | | | | | | | | | | |
| Cedar Hill SP | CEDAR HILL | | | | ★ | ★ | ★ | 12 | | | DG | ★ | ★ | ★ | ★ | ★ | ☆ | ☆ | B1 |
| Choke Canyon SP, Calliham Unit | CALLIHAM | | | | ★ | ★ | ★ | 10 | ★ | | BG | ★ | | ★ | ★ | ★ | ☆ | ☆ | |
| Choke Canyon SP, South Shore Unit | THREE RIVERS | | | | ★ | ★ | ★ | 8 | | | DG | | | ★ | ★ | ★ | ☆ | ☆ | B1, E |
| Cleburne SP | CLEBURNE | | | | ★ | ★ | ★ | 16 | ★ | | BG | ★ | ★ | ★ | ★ | | ☆ | ☆ | |
| Colorado Bend SP (Cave Tours) | BEND | | | | ★ | | | 1 | | | | ★ | ★ | ★ | ★ | ★ | ☆ | | B1 |
| Confederate Reunion Grounds SHS | MEXIA | ★ | | ★ | ★ | | | 1 | | | BG | ★ | ★ | | | | ☆ | | |
| Cooper Lake SP (Doctors Creek Unit) | COOPER | | | | ★ | ★ | ★ | 4 | ★ | | DG | ★ | ★ | ★ | ★ | ★ | ★ | ☆ | |
| Cooper Lake SP (South Sulphur Unit) | SULPHUR SPRINGS | | | | ★ | ★ | ★ | 14 | ★ | ★ | DG | ★ | ★ | ★ | ★ | ★ | ★ | ☆ | B1, E |
| Copano Bay SFP ▲ | FULTON | | | | ★ | | | | | | | | | ★ | ★ | | | | |
| Copper Breaks SP | QUANAH | | | ★ | ★ | ★ | ★ | 10 | | | BG | ★ | ★ | | ★ | ★ | ☆ | | B1, E, L |
| Daingerfield SP | DAINGERFIELD | | | | ★ | ★ | ★ | 15 | | ★ | BG | ★ | ★ | ★ | ★ | ★ | ☆ | | |
| Davis Mountains SP (Indian Lodge) | FORT DAVIS | | | ★ | ★ | ★ | ★ | 11 | | | DG | ★ | ★ | | | | | | I, E |
| Devils River SNA (Use by reservation only) | DEL RIO | | | | ★ | | | 1 | | | BG | | | | | | | | B1, E |
| Devil's Sinkhole SNA | ROCKSPRINGS | colspan note → *(No access to cavern. Tours of SNA by special request only.)* | | | | | | | | | | | | | | | | | |
| Dinosaur Valley SP (Dinosaur Footprints) | GLEN ROSE | | | ★ | ★ | ★ | ★ | 12 | | | DG | ★ | ★ | ★ | | | ☆ | ☆ | B1, E, L |
| Eisenhower SP (Marina) | DENISON | | | | ★ | ★ | ★ | 15 | ★ | | BG | ★ | ★ | ★ | ★ | ★ | ☆ | ☆ | B1 |
| Eisenhower Birthplace SHS | DENISON | ★ | ★ | ★ | ★ | | | | | | DG | | | | | | | | |
| Enchanted Rock SNA | FREDERICKSBURG | | | ★ | ★ | ★ | | 9 | | | DG | ★ | ★ | ★ | | | | | R |
| Fairfield Lake SP | FAIRFIELD | | | | ★ | ★ | ★ | 11 | | | DG | ★ | ★ | ★ | ★ | ★ | ☆ | ☆ | B1 |
| Falcon SP (Airstrip) | ZAPATA | | | | ★ | ★ | ★ | 15 | ★ | | BG | ★ | | ★ | ★ | ☆ | ☆ | ☆ | B1 |
| Fannin Battleground SHS | GOLIAD | ★ | ★ | ★ | ★ | | | | | | DG | | | ★ | | | | | |
| Fanthorp Inn SHS | ANDERSON | ★ | ★ | ★ | ★ | | | | | | | | | ★ | | | | | |
| Fort Boggy SP | | ★ | | | ★ | | | | | | DG | ★ | | ★ | | ★ | ☆ | | |
| Fort Griffin SHS | ALBANY | | ★ | ★ | ★ | ★ | ★ | 10 | | | BG | ★ | ★ | ★ | | | ☆ | | L, E |
| Fort Lancaster SHS | OZONA | ★ | ★ | ★ | ★ | | | | | | | | | ☆ | | | | | |
| Fort Leaton SHS | PRESIDIO | ★ | ★ | ★ | ★ | | | | | | | ★ | | ★ | | | | | |
| Fort McKavett SHS | FORT McKAVETT | ★ | ★ | ★ | ★ | | | | | | | ★ | | ★ | | | | | |
| Fort Parker SP | MEXIA | | | | ★ | ★ | ★ | 14 | ★ | | BG | ★ | ★ | ★ | ★ | ★ | ☆ | | B1 |
| Fort Richardson SHS and Lost Creek Res. TW | JACKSBORO | | ★ | ★ | ★ | ★ | ★ | 10 | ★ | | DG | ★ | ★ | ★ | | ★ | ★ | | E |
| Franklin Mountains SP | EL PASO | | | | ★ | | | 6 | | | DG | ★ | ★ | | | | | | B1, E, R |
| Fulton Mansion SHS | FULTON | ★ | ★ | ★ | | | | | | | | | | ★ | | | | | |
| Galveston Island SP (Summer Theater) | GALVESTON | | | ★ | ★ | ★ | ★ | 4 | ★ | | | ★ | | ★ | | | ☆ | ☆ | B1 |
| Garner SP | CONCAN | | | | ★ | ★ | ★ | 14 | ★ | ★ | BG | ★ | ★ | ★ | | | ☆ | ☆ | B2 |
| Goliad SHS | GOLIAD | | ★ | ★ | ★ | ★ | ★ | 11 | ★ | | DG | ★ | ★ | ★ | | | ☆ | ★ | |
| Goose Island SP | ROCKPORT | | | | ★ | ★ | ★ | 14 | | | BG | | | ★ | ★ | ★ | | | |
| Governor Hogg Shrine SHS | QUITMAN | ★ | ★ | ★ | ★ | | | | | | DG | ★ | | ★ | | | | | |
| Guadalupe River SP/Honey Creek SNA | BOERNE | | | | ★ | ★ | ★ | 13 | | | | | | ★ | ★ | | ☆ | ☆ | E |
| Hill Country SNA | BANDERA | | | | | | | 6 | | | NG | | | | | | ☆ | ☆ | B1, E |
| Hueco Tanks SHS (Indian Pictographs) | EL PASO | | ★ | ★ | ★ | ★ | ★ | 14 | | | DG | ★ | ★ | ★ | | | | | R |
| Huntsville SP | HUNTSVILLE | | | ★ | ★ | ★ | ★ | 14 | ★ | | DG | ★ | ★ | ★ | ★ | ★ | ☆ | | B1, B2 |
| Inks Lake SP | BURNET | | | | ★ | ★ | ★ | 10 | ★ | | BG | ★ | ★ | ★ | ★ | ★ | ☆ | ☆ | G |
| Jim Hogg SHS | | ★ | ★ | ★ | ★ | | | | | | | ★ | | ★ | | | | | |
| Kerrville-Schreiner SP | KERRVILLE | | | ★ | ★ | ★ | ★ | 11 | ★ | | BG | ★ | ★ | ★ | ★ | ★ | ☆ | | B1 |
| Kickapoo Cavern SP (Use by reservation only) | BRACKETTVILLE | | | | ★ | ★ | | 6 | | | NG | ★ | ★ | | | | | | B1 |

## †Types of Parks

| | | | |
|---|---|---|---|
| SP | State Park | SFP | State Fishing Pier |
| SHS | State Historic Site | TW | Trailway |
| SNA | State Natural Area | | |

## ††Type(s) of Camping

1-Primitive; 2-Walk-in tent; 3-Tent; 4-Water and Electric; 5-Water, Electric, Sewer; 6-1 & 2; 7-1, 2 & 4; 8-1, 2, 3 & 4; 9-1 & 3; 10-1, 3 & 4; 11-1, 3, 4 & 5; 12-1 & 4; 13-2, 3 & 4; 14- 3 & 4; 15-3, 4 & 5; 16-4 & 5; 17-1, 3 & 5.

# ☆ Texas State Parks ☆

| Park/†Type of Park/Special Features | NEAREST TOWN | Day Use Only | Historic Site/Museum | Exhibit/Interpretive Center | Restrooms | Showers | Trailer Dump Stn. | ††Camping | Screened Shelters | Cabins | Group Facilities | Nature Trail | Hiking Trail | Picnicking | Boat Ramp | Fishing | Swimming | Water Skiing | Miscellaneous |
|---|---|---|---|---|---|---|---|---|---|---|---|---|---|---|---|---|---|---|---|
| Lake Arrowhead SP | WICHITA FALLS | | | | ★ | ★ | ★ | 10 | | | DG | ★ | ★ | ★ | ★ | ★ | ☆ | ☆ | E |
| Lake Bob Sandlin SP | MOUNT PLEASANT | | | | ★ | ★ | ★ | 10 | ★ | | DG | | ★ | ★ | ★ | ★ | ☆ | ☆ | B1 |
| Lake Brownwood SP | BROWNWOOD | | | | ★ | ★ | ★ | 15 | ★ | ★ | BG | ★ | ★ | ★ | ★ | ★ | ☆ | ☆ | |
| Lake Casa Blanca International SP | LAREDO | | | | ★ | ★ | ★ | 14 | | | DG | | | ★ | ★ | ☆ | ☆ | ☆ | B1 |
| Lake Colorado City SP | COLORADO CITY | | | | ★ | ★ | ★ | 14 | | ★ | BG | ★ | ★ | ★ | ★ | ★ | ☆ | ☆ | |
| Lake Corpus Christi SP | MATHIS | | | | ★ | ★ | ★ | 15 | ★ | | DG | | | ★ | ★ | ★ | ☆ | ☆ | |
| Lake Houston SP | NEW CANEY | | | | ★ | ★ | | 9 | | | BG | ★ | ★ | ★ | | ★ | | | B1, E |
| Lake Livingston SP | LIVINGSTON | | | | ★ | ★ | ★ | 15 | ★ | | DG | ★ | ★ | ★ | ★ | ★ | ★ | ☆ | B1, B2, E |
| Lake Mineral Wells SP and TW | MINERAL WELLS | | | | ★ | ★ | ★ | 10 | ★ | | DG | ★ | ★ | ★ | ★ | ★ | ★ | ☆ | B1, E, R |
| Lake Rita Blanca SP | DALHART | ★ | | | | | | | | | | | | ★ | | | | | B1, E |
| Lake Somerville SP and TW, Birch Creek Unit | SOMERVILLE | | | ★ | ★ | ★ | ★ | 10 | | | BG | ★ | ★ | ★ | ★ | ★ | ☆ | ☆ | B1, E |
| Lake Somerville SP and TW, Nails Creek Unit | | | | ★ | ★ | ★ | ★ | 10 | | | DG | ★ | ★ | ★ | ★ | ★ | ☆ | ☆ | B1, E |
| Lake Tawakoni SP | WILLS POINT | | | | ★ | ★ | ★ | 4 | | | | ★ | ★ | ★ | ☆ | ☆ | ☆ | ☆ | |
| Lake Texana SP | EDNA | | | ★ | ★ | ★ | ★ | 14 | | | DG | ★ | ★ | ★ | ★ | ★ | ☆ | ☆ | B1 |
| Lake Whitney SP (Airstrip) | WHITNEY | | | | ★ | ★ | ★ | 15 | ★ | | BG | | ★ | ★ | ★ | ☆ | ☆ | ☆ | B1 |
| Landmark Inn SHS (Hotel Rooms) | CASTROVILLE | | ★ | ★ | ★ | | | | | | DG | ★ | | ★ | | ☆ | | | I |
| Lipantitlan SHS | SAN PATRICIO | ★ | | | | | | | | | | | | ★ | | | | | |
| Lockhart SP | LOCKHART | | | | ★ | ★ | | 16 | | | BG | | | ★ | | ★ | | | G |
| Longhorn Cavern SP (Cavern Tours) ▲ | BURNET | ★ | ★ | ★ | ★ | | | | | | | ★ | ★ | ★ | | | | | |
| Lost Maples SNA | VANDERPOOL | | | ★ | ★ | ★ | ★ | 12 | | | | ★ | ★ | ★ | | ☆ | ★ | | L |
| Lyndon B. Johnson SHS | STONEWALL | ★ | ★ | ★ | ★ | | | | | | DG | ★ | | ★ | | | ☆ | ★ | L |
| Magoffin Home SHS | EL PASO | ★ | ★ | ★ | ★ | | | | | | | | | | | | | | |
| Martin Creek Lake SP | TATUM | | | | ★ | ★ | ★ | 12 | ★ | ★ | DG | | ★ | ★ | ★ | ★ | ☆ | ☆ | B1 |
| Martin Dies Jr. SP | JASPER | | | | ★ | ★ | ★ | 14 | ★ | | BG | ★ | ★ | ★ | ★ | ★ | ☆ | ☆ | B1 |
| Matagorda Island SP (Boat or Air Access Only) | PORT O'CONNOR | | ★ | ★ | ★ | | | 1 | | | NG | | ★ | ★ | | ☆ | ☆ | ☆ | B1 |
| McKinney Falls SP | AUSTIN | | ★ | ★ | ★ | ★ | ★ | 13 | ★ | | BG | ★ | ★ | ★ | | ☆ | ☆ | | B1, B2 |
| Meridian SP | MERIDIAN | | | | ★ | ★ | ★ | 15 | ★ | | BG | ★ | ★ | ★ | ★ | ★ | ☆ | | |
| Mission Tejas SHS | WECHES | | ★ | | ★ | ★ | ★ | 15 | | | BG | ★ | ★ | ★ | | ☆ | | | |
| Monahans Sandhills SP | MONAHANS | | | ★ | ★ | ★ | ★ | 14 | | | DG | ★ | | ★ | | | | | E |
| Monument Hill/Kreische Brewery SHS | LA GRANGE | ★ | ★ | ★ | ★ | | | | | | | ★ | | ★ | | | | | |
| Mother Neff SP | MOODY | | | | ★ | ★ | ★ | 10 | | | BG | ★ | ★ | ★ | | | ☆ | | |
| Mustang Island SP | PORT ARANSAS | | | | ★ | ★ | ★ | 12 | | | | | | ★ | | ☆ | ☆ | ☆ | B1 |
| National Museum of the Pacific War | FREDERICKSBURG | ★ | ★ | ★ | ★ | | | | | | | | ★ | | | | | | |
| Old Fort Parker SP (Managed by City of Groesbeck) | | ★ | ★ | ★ | | | | 1 | | | | | | | | | | | E |
| Palmetto SP | LULING | | | | ★ | ★ | ★ | 15 | | | BC | ★ | ★ | ★ | | ★ | ☆ | | |
| Palo Duro Canyon SP (Summer Drama: "Texas") | CANYON | | | ★ | ★ | ★ | ★ | 8 | | ★ | | | ★ | ★ | ★ | | | | B1, E, L |
| Pedernales Falls SP | JOHNSON CITY | | | | ★ | ★ | ★ | 9 | | | NG | ★ | ★ | ★ | | | ☆ | ☆ | B1, E |
| Port Isabel Lighthouse SHS | PORT ISABEL | ★ | ★ | | ★ | | | | | | | | | | | | | | |
| Port Lavaca SFP ▲ | PORT LAVACA | | | | ★ | | | | | | | | | ★ | ★ | | | | |
| Possum Kingdom SP | CADDO | | | | ★ | ★ | ★ | 10 | ★ | | | ★ | ★ | ★ | ★ | ★ | ☆ | ☆ | P |
| Purtis Creek SP | EUSTACE | | | | ★ | ★ | ★ | 10 | | | | ★ | ★ | ★ | ★ | ★ | ☆ | ☆ | |
| Ray Roberts Lake SP, Isle du Bois Unit | DENTON | | | | ★ | ★ | ★ | 13 | | | DG | ★ | ★ | ★ | ★ | ★ | ☆ | ☆ | B1, B2, E |
| Ray Roberts Lake SP, Johnson Unit | DENTON | | | | ★ | ★ | ★ | 7 | | | DG | ★ | ★ | ★ | ★ | ★ | ☆ | ☆ | B1, B2 |
| Rusk/Palestine SP (Texas State RR Terminals) | RUSK/PALESTINE | | | | ★ | ★ | ★ | 15 | | | DG | ★ | | ★ | | ★ | | | |
| Sabine Pass Battleground SHS | SABINE PASS | | ★ | ★ | ★ | | ★ | 12 | | | | | | ★ | ★ | ☆ | | | |
| Sam Bell Maxey House SHS | PARIS | ★ | ★ | ★ | ★ | | | | | | | | | | | | | | |
| San Angelo SP | SAN ANGELO | | | | ★ | ★ | ★ | 8 | | ★ | BG | ★ | ★ | ★ | ★ | ★ | ☆ | ☆ | B1, E, L |
| San Jacinto Battleground SHS (Battleship Texas) | HOUSTON | ★ | ★ | ★ | ★ | | | | | | DG | ★ | | ★ | ☆ | | | | |
| Sea Rim SP | PORT ARTHUR | | | | ★ | ★ | ★ | ★ | 10 | | | | ★ | | ★ | ★ | ☆ | ★ | | B1 |
| Sebastopol SHS | SEGUIN | ★ | ★ | ★ | | | | | | | | | | | | | | | |
| Seminole Canyon SHS (Indian Pictographs) | LANGTRY | | ★ | | ★ | ★ | ★ | 14 | | | | ★ | ★ | ★ | | | | | B1 |
| Sheldon Lake SP | HOUSTON | ★ | | | | | | | | | | ★ | ☆ | ★ | ★ | | | | |
| South Llano River SP | JUNCTION | | | ★ | ★ | ★ | ★ | 10 | | | | ★ | ★ | ★ | | | ☆ | ☆ | B1 |
| Starr Family SHS | MARSHALL | ★ | ★ | ★ | | | | | | | | | | | | | | | |
| Stephen F. Austin SHS | SAN FELIPE | | ★ | | ★ | ★ | ★ | 15 | ★ | | BG | ★ | ★ | ★ | | | ☆ | | G |
| Texas State Railroad SHS (Contact Park for Schedule) | PALESTINE/RUSK | ★ | ★ | ★ | ★ | | | | | | | | | | | | | | |
| Tyler SP | TYLER | | | | ★ | ★ | ★ | 15 | ★ | | BG | ★ | ★ | ★ | ★ | ★ | ★ | ☆ | B1 |
| Varner-Hogg Plantation SHS (Guided Tours) | WEST COLUMBIA | ★ | ★ | ★ | ★ | | | | | | | ★ | | ★ | | | ☆ | | |
| Village Creek SP | LUMBERTON | | | | ★ | ★ | ★ | 13 | | | BG | ★ | ★ | ★ | | ☆ | ☆ | | B1 |
| Walter Umphrey SP | | | | | | | | | | *(Managed by Jefferson County)* | | | | | | | | | |
| Washington-on-the-Brazos SHS (Anson Jones Home) | WASHINGTON | ★ | ★ | ★ | ★ | | | | | | DG | ★ | ★ | | | | | | |
| Wyler Aerial Tramway Franklin Mts. SP | | | ★ | | | | | | | | | | | | | | | | |

## Facilities

▲ Facilities not operated by Parks & Wildlife.
★ Facilities or services available for activity.
☆ Facilities or services not provided.

**Note: Contact individual parks for information on handicap facilities.**

## Miscellaneous Codes

| | | | |
|---|---|---|---|
| B1 | Mountain Biking | G | Golf |
| B2 | Surfaced Bike Trail | I | Hotel-Type Facilities |
| BG | Both Day & Night Group Facilities | L | Texas Longhorn Herd |
| DG | Day-Use Group Facilities | NG | Overnight Group Facilities |
| E | Equestrian Trails | R | Rock Climbing |

hiking, mountain biking, swimming, fishing.

**Eisenhower Birthplace State Historic Site** is 6 acres off US 75 at 609 S. Lamar, Denison, Grayson County. The property was acquired in 1958 from the Eisenhower Birthplace Foundation. Restoration of home of Pres. Dwight David "Ike" Eisenhower includes furnishings of period and some personal effects of Gen. Eisenhower. Guided tour; call for schedule. Park open daily, except Thanksgiving, Christmas Day and New Year's Day; call for hours. Town of Denison established on **Butterfield Overland Mail** Route in 1858.

**Eisenhower State Park,** 423.1 acres five miles northwest of Denison via US 75 to TX 91N to FM 1310 on the shores of **Lake Texoma** in Grayson County, was acquired by an Army lease in 1954. Named for the **34th U.S. president, Dwight David Eisenhower.** First Anglo settlers came to area in 1835; **Fort Johnson** was established in area in 1840; **Colbert's Ferry** established on Red River in 1853 and operated until 1931. Areas of **tall-grass prairie** exist. Hiking, camping, picnicking, fishing, swimming.

**Enchanted Rock State Natural Area** is 1,643.5 acres on Big Sandy Creek 18 miles north of Fredericksburg on RM 965 on the line between Gillespie and Llano counties. Acquired in 1978 by The Nature Conservancy of Texas; state acquired from TNCT in 1984. Enchanted Rock is huge **pink granite boulder** rising 425 feet above ground and covering 640 acres. It is **second-largest batholith** (underground rock formation uncovered by erosion) in the United States. Indians believed **ghost fires** flickered at top and were awed by weird creaking and groaning, which geologists say resulted from rock's heating and expanding by day, cooling and contracting at night. Enchanted Rock is a **National Natural Landmark** and is on the **National Register of Historic Places**. Activities include hiking, geological study, camping, **rock climbing** and star gazing.

**Fairfield Lake State Park** is 1,460 acres adjacent to Lake Fairfield, 6 miles northeast of the city of Fairfield off FM 2570 and FM 3285 in Freestone County. It was leased from Texas Utilities in 1971-72. Surrounding woods offer sanctuary for many species of birds and wildlife. Camping, hiking, backpacking, nature study, water-related activities available. Extensive schedule of tours, seminars and other activities.

**Falcon State Park** is 572.6 acres located 15 miles north of Roma off US 83 and FM 2098 at southern end of Falcon Reservoir in Starr and Zapata counties. Park leased from International Boundary and Water Commission in 1949. Gently rolling hills covered by **mesquite, huisache, wild olive, ebony, cactus**. Excellent **birding** and **fishing**. Camping and water activities also. Nearby are **Mexico, Fort Ringgold** in Rio Grande City and historic city of **Roma. Bentsen-Rio Grande Valley State Park** is 65 miles away.

**Fannin Battleground State Historic Site,** 9 miles east of Goliad in Goliad County off US 59 to PR 27. The 13.6-acre park site was acquired by the state in 1914; transferred to TPW by legislative enactment in 1965. At this site on March 20, 1836, **Col. J. W. Fannin** surrendered to Mexican **Gen. José Urrea** after **Battle of Coleto;** 342 massacred and 28 escaped near what is now **Goliad State Historic Site**. Near Fannin site is **Gen. Zaragoza's Birthplace** and partially restored **Mission Nuestra Señora del Espíritu Santo de Zúñiga** (see also **Goliad State Historic Site** in this list).

**Fanthorp Inn State Historic Site** includes a historic double-pen cedar-log dogtrot house and 1.4 acres in Anderson, county seat of Grimes County, on TX 90. Acquired by purchase in 1977 from a Fanthorp descendant and opened to the public in 1987. Inn records report visits from many prominent civic and military leaders, including **Sam Houston, Anson Jones, Ulysses S. Grant** and generals **Robert E. Lee** and **Stonewall Jackson**. Originally built in 1834, it has been restored to its 1850 usage as a family home and travelers' hotel. Tours available Friday, Saturday, Sunday. Call TPW for stagecoach-ride schedule. No dining or overnight facilities.

**Fort Boggy State Park** is 1,847 acres of wooded, rolling hills in Leon County near Boggy Creek, about 4 miles south of Centerville on TX 75. Land donated to TPWD in 1985 by Eileen Crain Sullivan. Area once home to Keechi and Kickapoo tribes. Log fort was built by settlers in 1840s; first settlement north of the Old San Antonio Road

**More Travel Information**

Call the **Texas Department of Transportation's** toll-free number: **1-800-888-8TEX** for:

• The **Texas State Travel Guide,** a free 288-page, full-color publication with a wealth of information about attractions, activities, history and historic sites.

• The official **Texas state highway map.**

On the Internet: **www.traveltex.com**

and between the Navasota and Trinity rivers. Swimming beach, fishing, picnicking, nature trails for hiking and mountain biking. Fifteen-acre lake open to small craft. Open-air group pavilion overlooking lake can be reserved ($50 per day). Nearby attractions include Rusk/Palestine State Park, Fort Parker State Park, Texas State Railroad, Old Fort Parker. Open Wed.–Sun. for day use only; entrance fee. For reservations, call 512-389-8900.

**Fort Griffin State Historic Site** is 506.2 acres 15 miles north of Albany off US 283 in Shackelford County. The state was deeded the land by the county in 1935. Portion of **state longhorn herd** resides in park. On bluff overlooking townsite of **Fort Griffin** and **Clear Fork of Brazos River** valley are partially restored ruins of **Old Fort Griffin,** restored bakery, replicas of enlisted men's huts. Fort constructed in 1867, deactivated 1881. Camping, equestrian camping, hiking. Nearby are **Albany** with restored courthouse square, **Abilene** and **Possum Kingdom State Park**. Albany annually holds **"Fandangle"** musical show in commemoration of frontier times.

**Fort Lancaster State Historic Site,** 81.6-acres located about 8 miles east of Sheffield on Interstate10 and US 290 in Crockett County. Acquired in 1968 by deed from Crockett County; Henry Meadows donated 41 acres in 1975. **Fort Lancaster** established Aug. 20, 1855, to guard San Antonio-El Paso Road and protect movement of supplies and immigrants from Indian hostilities. Site of part of Camel Corps experiment. Fort abandoned March 19, 1861, after Texas seceded from Union. Exhibits on history, natural history and archaeology; nature trail, picnicking. Open daily; day use only.

**Fort Leaton State Historic Site,** 4 miles southeast of Presidio in Presidio County on FM 170, was acquired in 1967 from private owners. Consists of 23.4 acres, 5 of which are on site of **pioneer trading post**. In 1848, **Ben Leaton** built fortified adobe trading post known as Fort Leaton near present Presidio. Ben Leaton died in 1851. Guided tours; exhibits trace history, natural history and archaeological history of area. Serves as western entrance to **Big Bend Ranch State Park**. Day use only.

**Fort McKavett State Historic Site,** 79.5 acres acquired from 1967 through the mid-1970s from Fort McKavett Restoration, Inc., Menard County and private individuals, is located 23 miles west of Menard off US 190 and FM 864. Originally called **Camp San Saba,** the fort was built by War Department in 1852 to protect frontier settlers and travelers on Upper El Paso Road from Indians. Camp later renamed for **Capt. Henry McKavett,** killed at Battle of Monterrey, Sept. 21, 1846. A **Buffalo Soldier post**. Fort abandoned March 1859; reoccupied April 1868; abandoned again June 30, 1883. Once called by Gen. Wm. T. Sherman, "the prettiest post in Texas." More than 25 restored buildings, ruins of many others. Interpretive exhibits. Day use only.

**Fort Parker State Park** includes 1,458.8 acres, including 758.78 land acres and 700-acre lake between Mexia and Groesbeck off TX 14 in Limestone County. Named for the former private fort built near present park in 1836, the site was acquired from private owners and the City of Mexia 1935-1937. Camping, fishing, swimming, canoeing, picnicking. Nearby is **Old Fort Parker Historic Site,** which is operated by the City of Groesbeck.

**Fort Richardson State Historic Site,** located one-half mile south of Jacksboro off US 281 in Jack County, contains 454 acres. Acquired in 1968 from City of Jacksboro. Fort founded in 1867, northernmost of line of federal forts established after Civil War for protection from Indians; originally named **Fort Jacksboro**. In April 1867, fort was

moved to its present location from 20 miles farther south; on Nov. 19, 1867, made permanent post at Jacksboro and named for **Israel Richardson**, who was fatally wounded at Battle of Antietam. Expeditions sent from Fort Richardson arrested Indians responsible for **Warren Wagon Train Massacre** in 1871 and fought Comanches in **Palo Duro Canyon.** Fort abandoned in May 1878. Park contains seven restored buildings and two replicas. Interpretive center, picnicking, camping, fishing; 10-mile trailway.

**Franklin Mountains State Park,** created by an act of the legislature in 1979 to protect the mountain range as a wilderness preserve and acquired by TPW in 1981, comprises 24,247.56 acres, all within El Paso city limits. **Largest urban park in the nation.** It includes virtually an entire **Chihuahuan Desert mountain range,** with an elevation of 7,192 feet at the summit. The park is habitat for many Chihuahuan Desert plants including **sotol, lechuguilla, ocotillo, cholla** and **barrel cactus,** and such animals as **mule deer, fox** and an occasional **cougar.** Camping, mountain biking, nature study, hiking, picnicking, rock-climbing.

**Fulton Mansion State Historic Site** is 3.5 miles north of Rockport off TX 35 in Aransas County. The 2.3 acre-property was acquired by purchase from private owner in 1976. Three-story wooden structure, built in 1874-1877, was home of **George W. Fulton,** prominent in South Texas for economic and commercial influence; mansion derives significance from its innovative construction and Victorian design. Call ahead for days and hours of guided tours; open Wednesday–Sunday.

**Galveston Island State Park,** on the west end of Galveston Island on FM 3005, is a 2,013.1-acre site acquired in 1969 from private owners. Camping, birding, nature study, swimming, bicycling and fishing amid **sand dunes and grassland.** Musical productions in **amphitheater** during summer.

**Garner State Park** is 1,419.8 acres of recreational facilities on US 83 on the Frio River in Uvalde County 9 miles south of Leakey. Named for **John Nance Garner,** U.S. Vice President, 1933-1941, the park was deeded in 1934-36 by private owners. Camping, hiking, picnicking, river recreation, miniature golf, biking, boat rentals. Cabins available. Nearby is **John Nance "Cactus Jack" Garner Museum** in Uvalde. Nearby also are ruins of historic **Mission Nuestra Señora de la Candelaria del Cañon,** founded in 1749; **Camp Sabinal** (a U.S. Cavalry post and later Texas Ranger camp) established 1856; **Fort Inge,** established 1849.

**Goliad State Historic Site** is 188.3 acres one-fourth mile south of Goliad on US 183 and 77A, along the San Antonio River in Goliad County. The land was deeded to state in 1931 by the City and County of Goliad; transferred to TPW 1949. Nearby are the sites of several battles in the Texas fight for independence from Mexico. The park includes a replica of **Mission Nuestra Señora del Espíritu Santo de Zúñiga,** originally established 1722 and settled at its present site in 1749. Park unit includes **Gen. Ignacio Zaragoza's Birthplace,** which is located near **Presidio la Bahía.** He was Mexican national hero who led troops against French at historic **Battle of Puebla** on May 5, 1862. Park also contains ruins of **Nuestra Señora del Rosario** mission, established 1754, located four miles west of Goliad on US 59. Camping, picnicking, historical exhibits, nature trail. Other nearby points of historical interest: restored **Nuestra Señora de Loreto de la Bahía** presidio, established 1721 and settled on site in 1749; it is located short distance south on US 183. Memorial shaft marking common burial site of **Fannin** and victims of **Goliad massacre** (1836) is near **Presidio la Bahía.** (See also **Fannin Battleground State Historic Site.**)

**Goose Island State Park,** 321.4 acres 10 miles northeast of Rockport on TX 35 and PR 13 on St. Charles and Aransas bays in Aransas County, was deeded by private owners in 1931-1935 plus an additional seven acres donated in the early 1990s by Sun Oil Co. Located here is "Big Tree" estimated to be more than 1,000 years old and listed as the **state champion coastal live oak.** Fishing, picnicking and camping, plus excellent birding; no swimming. Rare and endangered **whooping cranes** can be viewed during winter just across St. Charles Bay in **Aransas National Wildlife Refuge.**

Picnickers enjoy an outing at Lake Tawakoni State Park in Hunt County. The park opened in 2001 and is located on the southern end of its namesake lake in North Texas. File photo.

**Gov. Hogg Shrine State Historic Site** is a 26.7-acre tract on TX 37 about six blocks south of the Wood County Courthouse in Quitman. Named for **James Stephen Hogg, first native-born governor of Texas,** the park includes museums housing items that belonged to the Hogg and Stinson families. Seventeen acres deeded by the Wood County Old Settlers Reunion Association in 1946; 4.74 acres gift of Miss Ima Hogg in 1970; 3 acres purchased. **Gov. James Stephen Hogg Memorial Shrine** created in 1941. Three museums: Gov. Hogg's wedding held in **Stinson Home; Honeymoon Cottage; Miss Ima Hogg Museum** houses both park headquarters and display of representative history of entire Northeast Texas area. Operated by City of Quitman.

**Guadalupe River State Park** comprises 1,938.7 acres on cypress-shaded Guadalupe River in Kendall and Comal counties, 13 miles east of Boerne on TX 46. Acquired by deed from private owners in 1974. Park has four miles of river frontage with several **white-water rapids** and is located in a stretch of **Guadalupe River** noted for canoeing, tubing. Picnicking, camping, hiking, nature study. Trees include **sycamore, elm, basswood, pecan, walnut, persimmon, willow** and **hackberry** (see also **Honey Creek State Natural Area,** below).

**Hill Country State Natural Area** in Bandera and Medina counties, 9 miles west of Bandera on RM 1077. The 5,369.8-acre site acquired by gift from Merrick Bar-O-Ranch and purchase in 1976. Park is located in typical Texas Hill Country on West Verde Creek and contains several **spring-fed streams.** Primitive and equestrian camping, hiking, horseback riding, mountain biking, fishing. Group lodge.

**Honey Creek State Natural Area** consists of 2,293.7 acres adjacent to **Guadalupe River State Park** (above); entrance is in the park. Acquired from The Nature Conservancy of Texas in 1985 with an addition from private individual in 1988. Diverse plant life includes **agarita, Texas persimmon** and Ashe juniper in hills, and cedar elm, Spanish oak, pecan, walnut and **Mexican buckeye** in bottomlands. Abundant wildlife includes **ringtail, leopard frog, green kingfisher, golden-cheeked warbler** and **canyon wren.** Open Saturdays only for **guided naturalist tours;** call for details.

**Hueco Tanks State Historic Site,** located 32 miles northeast of El Paso in El Paso County on RM 2775 just north of US 62-180, was obtained from the county in 1969, with additional 121 acres purchased in 1970. Featured in this 860.3-acre park are large **natural rock basins** that provided water for archaic hunters, Plains Indians, Butterfield Overland Mail coach horses and passengers, and other travelers in this arid region. In park are **Indian pictographs, old ranch house** and relocated **ruins of stage station. Rock climbing,** picnicking, camping, hiking. Guided tours. Wildlife includes **gray fox, bobcat, prairie falcons, golden eagles.**

**Huntsville State Park** is 2,083.2-acre recreational area off IH 45 and PR 40 six miles south of Huntsville in Walker County, acquired by deeds from private owners in 1937. Heavily wooded park adjoins **Sam Houston National Forest** and encloses **Lake Raven.** Hiking, camping, fishing,

biking, paddle boats, canoeing. At nearby Huntsville are **Sam Houston's old homestead (Steamboat House)**, containing some of his personal effects, and **his grave.** Approximately 50 miles away is **Alabama-Coushatta Indian Reservation** in Polk County.

**Inks Lake State Park** is 1,201 acres of recreational facilities along Inks Lake, 9 miles west of Burnet on the Colorado River off TX 29 on PR 4 in Burnet County. Acquired by deeds from the Lower Colorado River Authority and private owners in 1940. Camping, hiking, fishing, swimming, boating, golf. **Deer, turkey** and other wildlife abundant. Nearby are **Longhorn Cavern State Park, LBJ Ranch, LBJ State Historic Site, Pedernales Falls State Park** and **Enchanted Rock State Natural Area. Granite Mountain** quarry at nearby Marble Falls furnished red granite for **Texas state capitol. Buchanan Dam,** largest multi-arch dam in world, located 4 miles from park.

Fishing enthusiasts try their luck at Lake Whitney State Park in Hill County. The park is noted for its display of bluebonnets in the spring. Camping, hiking and birding are also popular activities. File photo.

**Jim Hogg Historic Site** is 178.4 acres of East Texas Pineywoods in Cherokee County, 2 miles east of Rusk off U.S. 84 E. and Fire Tower Road. Memorial to Texas' first native born governor, James Stephen Hogg, 1891–1895. Remnants of 1880s iron ore mining. Scale replica of Hogg birthplace. Picnicking, historical study, nature study, hiking and bird watching. Self-guided and guided museum tours and nature trail tours. Operated by the City of Rusk; 903-683-4850. Area attractions: Caddoan Mounds, Mission Tejas State Historic Sites, Rusk/Palestine State Park, Texas State Railroad, Tyler State Parks and historic Nacogdoches. Day use only; entrance fee.

**Kerrville-Schreiner State Park** is a 517.2-acre area 3 miles southeast of Kerrville off TX 173 along the Guadalupe River in Kerr County. Land deeded by City of Kerrville in 1934. Trees include **redbud, sumac, buckeye, pecan, mesquite.** Birding, camping, fishing, picknicking, cycling. Near park is site of **Camp Verde,** active 1855–1869, which was a base for an army experiment using **camels** to haul equipment. **Bandera Pass,** 12 miles south of Kerrville, noted gap in chain of mountains through which passed camel caravans, wagon trains, Spanish conquistadores, immigrant trains. In nearby **Fredericksburg** is atmosphere of old country of Germany and famous **Nimitz Hotel** (see **Admiral Nimitz Museum Historic Site).**

**Kickapoo Cavern State Park** is located about 22 miles north of Brackettville on RM 674 on the Kinney/Edwards county line in the southern Edwards Plateau. The park (6,368.4 acres) contains **15 known caves,** two of which are large enough to be significant: **Kickapoo Cavern,** about 1/4 mile in length, has impressive formations, and **Green Cave,** slightly shorter, supports a nursery colony of **Brazilian freetail bats** in summer. Birds include rare species such as **black-capped vireo, varied bunting** and **Montezuma quail.** Reptiles and amphibians include **barking frog, mottled rock rattlesnake** and **Texas alligator lizard.** Tours of Kickapoo and observation of bats available only by special arrangement. Group lodge; primitive camping; hiking and mountain-biking trails. Open only by reservation.

**Kreische Brewery State Historic Site (see Monument Hill and Kreische Brewery State Historic Sites).**

**Lake Arrowhead State Park** consists of 524 acres in Clay County, about 7 miles south of Wichita Falls on US 281 to FM 1954, then 8 miles to park. Acquired in 1970 from the City of Wichita Falls. **Lake Arrowhead** is a reservoir on the Little Wichita River with 106 miles of shoreline. The land surrounding the lake is generally semiarid, gently rolling prairie, much of which has been invaded by mesquite in recent decades. Fishing, camping, lake swimming, picnicking, horseback-riding area.

**Lake Bob Sandlin State Park,** on the wooded shoreline of 9,400-acre Lake Bob Sandlin, is located 12 miles southwest of Mount Pleasant off FM 21 in Titus County.

Activities in the 639.8-acre park include picnicking, camping, mountain biking, hiking, swimming, fishing and boating. **Oak, hickory, dogwood, redbud, maple** and **pine** produce spectacular fall color. Eagles can sometimes be spotted in winter months.

**Lake Brownwood State Park** in Brown County is 537.5 acres acquired from Brown County Water Improvement District No. 1 in 1934. Park reached from TX 279 to PR 15, 16 miles northwest of Brownwood on Lake Brownwood near **geographical center of Texas.** Water sports, hiking, camping. Cabins available.

**Lake Casa Blanca International State Park,** located one mile east of Laredo off US 59 on Loop 20, was formerly operated by the City of Laredo and Webb County and was acquired by TPW in 1990. Park includes 371 acres on Lake Casa Blanca. **Recreation hall** can be reserved. Camping, picnicking, fishing, ball fields, playgrounds, amphitheater, and tennis courts. County-operated golf course nearby.

**Lake Colorado City State Park,** 500 acres leased for 99 years from a utility company. It is located in Mitchell County 11 miles southwest of Colorado City off IH 20 on FM 2836. Water sports, picnicking, camping, hiking. Part of **state longhorn herd** can be seen in park.

**Lake Corpus Christi State Park,** a 14,112-acre park in San Patricio, Jim Wells and Live Oak counties. Located 35 miles northwest of Corpus Christi and four miles southwest of Mathis off TX 359 and Park Road 25. Was leased from City of Corpus Christi in 1934. Camping, picnicking, birding, water sports. Nearby are **Padre Island National Seashore; Mustang Island, Choke Canyon, Goliad and Goose Island** state parks; **Aransas National Wildlife Refuge,** and **Fulton Mansion State Historic Site.**

**Lake Houston State Park** is situated at the confluence of Caney Creek and the East Fork of the San Jacinto River. The 4,919.5-acre site, purchased from Champion Paper Company in 1981, is northeast of Houston in Harris and Montgomery counties. Camping, birding, hiking, biking, horseback riding.

**Lake Livingston State Park,** in Polk County, about one mile southwest of Livingston on FM 3126 and PR 65, contains 635.5 acres along Lake Livingston. Acquired by deed from private landowners in 1971. Near ghost town of **Swartwout,** steamboat landing on Trinity River in 1830s and 1850s. Camping, picnicking, swimming pool, fishing, mountain biking and stables.

**Lake Mineral Wells State Park,** located 4 miles east of Mineral Wells on US 180 in Parker County, consists of 3,282.5 acres encompassing Lake Mineral Wells. In 1975, the City of Mineral Wells donated 1,095 land acres and the lake to TPW; the U.S. Government transferred additional land from Fort Wolters army post. Popular for **rock-climbing/rappelling.** Swimming, fishing, boating, camping; **Lake Mineral Wells State Trailway** (hiking, bicycling,

equestrian trail).

**Lake Somerville State Park,** northwest of Brenham in Lee and Burleson counties, was leased from the federal government in 1969. **Birch Creek Unit** (2,365 acres reached from TX 60 and PR 57) and **Nails Creek Unit** (3,155 acres reached from US 290 and FM 180), are connected by a **13-mile trailway system,** with **equestrian and primitive camp sites,** rest benches, shelters and drinking water. Also camping, birding, picnicking, volleyball and water sports. **Somerville Wildlife Management Area,** 3,180 acres is nearby.

**Lake Tawakoni State Park** is a 376.3-acre park in Hunt County along the shore of its namesake reservoir. It was acquired in 1984 through a 50-year lease agreement with the Sabine River Authority and opened in 2001. Includes a swimming beach, half-mile trail, picnic sites, boat ramp and campsites. A **40-acre tallgrass prairie** will be managed and enhanced in the post-oak woodlands. The park is reached from IH 20 on TX 47 north to FM 2475 about 20 miles past Wills Point.

**Lake Texana State Park** is 575 acres, 6.5 miles east of Edna on TX 111, half-way between Houston and Corpus Christi in Jackson County, with camping, boating, fishing and picnicking facilities. It was acquired by a 50-year lease agreement with the Bureau of Reclamation in 1977. Good birding in the **oak/pecan woodlands. Alligators** are often found in park coves.

**Lake Whitney State Park** is 955 acres along the east shore of Lake Whitney west of Hillsboro via TX 22 and FM 1244 in Hill County. Acquired in 1954 by a Department of the Army lease, effective through 2003. Located near ruins of **Towash,** early Texas settlement inundated by the lake. Towash Village named for chief of Hainai Indians. Park noted for **bluebonnets** in spring. Camping, hiking, birding, picnicking, water activities.

**Landmark Inn State Historic Site,** 4.7 acres in Castroville, Medina County, about 15 miles west of San Antonio, was acquired through donation by Miss Ruth Lawler in 1974. Castroville, settled in the 1840s by Alsatian farmers, is called **Little Alsace of Texas.** Landmark Inn built about 1844 as residence and store for **Cesar Monod,** mayor of Castroville 1851-1864. Special workshops, tours and events held at inn; grounds may be rented for receptions, family reunions and weddings. **Overnight lodging**; no phones; all rooms air-conditioned and nonsmoking.

**Lipantitlan State Historic Site** is 5 acres 9 miles east of Orange Grove in Nueces County off Texas 359, FM 624 and FM 70. The property was deeded by private owners in 1937. Fort constructed here in 1833 by Mexican government fell to Texas forces in 1835. Only facilities are picnic tables. **Lake Corpus Christi State Park** is nearby.

**Lockhart State Park** is 263.7 acres 4 miles south of Lockhart via US 183, FM 20 and PR 10 in Caldwell County. The land was deeded by private owners between 1934 and 1937. Camping, picnicking, hiking, fishing, **9-hole golf course.** After Comanche raid at Linnville, **Battle of Plum Creek** (1840) was fought in area.

**Longhorn Cavern State Park,** off US 281 and PR 4 about 6 miles west and 6 miles south of Burnet in Burnet County, is 645.62 acres dedicated as a natural landmark in 1971. It was acquired in 1932-1937 from private owners. The cave has been used as a shelter since prehistoric times. Among legends about the cave is that the outlaw **Sam Bass** hid stolen money there. Confederates made gunpowder in the cave during the Civil War. **Nature trail; guided tours** of cave; picnicking, hiking. Cavern operated by concession agreement. **Inks Lake State Park** and **Lyndon B. Johnson Ranch** located nearby.

**Lost Maples State Natural Area** consists of 2,174.2 scenic acres on the Sabinal River in Bandera and Real counties, 5 miles north of Vanderpool on RM 187. Acquired by purchase from private owners in 1973-1974. Outstanding example of Edwards Plateau flora and fauna, features isolated stand of uncommon **Uvalde bigtooth maple. Rare golden-cheeked warbler, black-capped vireo** and **green kingfisher** nest and feed in park. Fall foliage can be spectacular (late Oct. through early Nov.). Hiking trails, camping, fishing, picnicking, birding.

**Lyndon B. Johnson State Historic Site,** off US 290 in Gillespie County 14 miles west of Johnson City near Stonewall, contains 732.75 acres. Acquired in 1965 with private donations. **Home of Lyndon B. Johnson** located

*Lady Bird Johnson arrives for the annual wreath-laying ceremony at the Lyndon B. Johnson State Historical Park in Gillespie County in August 2002. The park includes the LBJ home, living history demonstrations, and the family cemetery where the former U.S. president is buried. File photo.*

north bank of **Pedernales River** across Ranch Road 1 from park; portion of **official Texas longhorn herd** maintained at park. Wildlife exhibit includes **turkey, deer** and **bison. Living-history demonstrations** at restored **Sauer-Beckmann house.** Reconstruction of **Johnson birthplace** is open to public. Historic structures, swimming pool, tennis courts, baseball field, picnicking. Day use only. Nearby is family cemetery where former president and relatives are buried. In Johnson City is **boyhood home of President Johnson.** (See also **National Parks.**)

**Magoffin Home State Historic Site,** in El Paso, is a 19-room territorial-style adobe on a 1.5-acre site. Purchased by the state and City of El Paso in 1976, it is operated by TPW. Home was built in 1875 by pioneer El Pasoan **Joseph Magoffin.** Furnished with original family artifacts. Guided tours; call for schedule. Day use only.

**Martin Creek Lake State Park,** 286.9 acres, is located 4 miles south of Tatum off TX 43 and CR 2183 in Rusk County. It was deeded to the TPW by Texas Utilities in 1976. Water activities; also cabins, camping, picnicking. Roadbed of **Trammel's Trace,** old Indian trail that became major route for settlers moving to Texas from Arkansas, can be seen. **Hardwood and pine** forest shelters abundant wildlife including **swamp rabbits, gophers, nutria** and numerous species of land birds and waterfowl.

**Martin Dies Jr. State Park,** until 1965 the **Dam B State Park,** is 705 acres in Jasper and Tyler counties on B. A. Steinhagen Reservoir between Woodville and Jasper via US 190. Land leased for 50 years from Corps of Engineers in 1964. Located at edge of **Big Thicket.** Plant and animal life varied and abundant. Winter **bald eagle census** conducted at nearby Sam Rayburn Reservoir. Camping, hiking, mountain biking, water activities. Wildscape/herb garden. Park is approximately 30 miles from **Alabama and Coushatta Indian Reservation.**

**Matagorda Island State Park and Wildlife Management Area** is separated from the mainland by San Antonio and Espíritu Santo bays. Matagorda Island is one of the **barrier islands** that border the Gulf and protect the mainland from the great tides and strong wave action of the open ocean. About 43,893 acres of park and WMA are managed by the TPW. The park occupies about 7,325 acres of the total. **La Salle** had a camp on the island in 1684. The first Matagorda Island **lighthouse** was constructed in 1852; the present cast-iron structure was a replacement built in 1873. It is listed on the National Register of Historic Places. Nineteen endangered or threatened species are found here, including **whooping crane, peregrine falcon, brown pelican** and **Ridley sea turtle.** More than **300 species of birds** use island during spring and fall migrations. Camping, birding, water activities, scheduled tours. Access only by boat; passenger **ferry operates** from Port O'Connor Thursday–Sunday.

**McKinney Falls State Park** is 744.4 acres 13 miles southeast of the state capitol in Austin off US 183. Acquired in 1970 by gift from private owners. Named for Thomas F. McKinney, **one of Stephen F. Austin's first**

**300 colonists**, who built his home here in the mid-1800s on Onion Creek. Ruins of his homestead can be viewed. Swimming, hiking, biking, camping, picnicking, fishing, guided tours.

**Meridian State Park** in Bosque County is a 505.4-acre park. The heavily wooded land, on TX 22 three miles southwest of Meridian, was acquired from private owners in 1933-1935. **Texas-Santa Fe expedition** of 1841 passed through Bosque County near present site of park on Bee Creek. **Endangered golden-cheeked warbler** nests here. Camping, picnicking, hiking, fishing, lake swimming, birding, bicycling.

**Mission Tejas State Historic Site** is a 363.5-acre park in Houston County. Situated 12 miles west of Alto via TX 21 and PR 44, the park was acquired from the Texas Forest Service in 1957. In the park is a replica of **Mission San Francisco de los Tejas**, the first mission in East Texas (1690). It was abandoned, then re-established 1716; abandoned again 1719; re-established again 1721; abandoned for last time in 1730 and moved to San Antonio. Also in park is restored **Rice Family Log Home**, built about 1828. Camping, hiking, fishing, picnicking.

**Monahans Sandhills State Park** consists of 3,840 acres of sand dunes, some up to 70 feet high, in Ward and Winkler counties 5 miles northeast of Monahans on IH 20 to PR 41. Land leased by state from private foundation until 2056. Dunes used as meeting place by raiding Indians. Camping, hiking, picnicking, **sand-surfing**. Scheduled tours. **Odessa meteor crater** is nearby, as is **Balmorhea State Park**.

**Monument Hill State Historic Site** and **Kreische Brewery State Historic Site** are operated as one park unit. Monument Hill consists of 40.4 acres one mile south of La Grange on US 77 to Spur Road 92 in Fayette County. Monument and tomb area acquired by state in 1907; additional acreage acquired from the Archbishop of San Antonio in 1956. Brewery and home purchased from private owners in 1977. Monument is dedicated to **Capt. Nicholas Dawson** and his men, who fought at **Salado Creek** in 1842, in Mexican **Gen. Woll's** invasion of Texas, and to the men of the **"black bean lottery"** (1843) of the **Mier Expedition**. Remains were brought to **Monument Hill** for reburial in 1848. Kreische Complex, on 36 acres, is linked to Monument Hill through interpretive trail. **Kreische Brewery State Historic Site** includes Kreische Brewery and stone-and-wood house built between 1850-1855 on Colorado River. One of **first commercial breweries** in state, it closed in 1884. Smokehouse and barn also in complex. Guided tours of brewery and house; call for schedule. Also picknicking, nature study.

**Mother Neff State Park** was the **first official state park** in Texas. It originated with 6 acres donated by Mrs. I. E. Neff, mother of **Pat M. Neff**, Governor of Texas from 1921 to 1925. Gov. Neff and Frank Smith donated remainder in 1934. The park, located 8 miles west of Moody on FM 107 and TX 236, now contains 259 acres along the Leon River in Coryell County. Heavily wooded. Camping, picnicking, fishing, hiking.

**Mustang Island State Park**, 3,954 acres on Gulf of Mexico in Nueces County, 14 miles south of Port Aransas on TX 361, was acquired from private owners in 1972. Mustang Island is a barrier island with a complicated ecosystem, dependent upon the sand dune. The foundation plants of the dunes are **sea oats, beach panic grass** and **soilbind morning glory**. Beach camping, picknicking; sun, sand and water activities. Excellent birding. **Padre Island National Seashore** 14 miles south.

**National Museum of the Pacific War** (formerly Admiral Nimitz Museum and Historical Center) is on 7 acres in downtown Fredericksburg. First established as a state agency in 1969 by Texas Legislature; transferred to TPW in 1981. George Bush Gallery opened in 1999. Named for **Adm. Chester W. Nimitz** of World War II fame, it includes the **Pacific War Museum** in the **Nimitz Steamboat Hotel**; the **Japanese Garden of Peace**, donated by the people of Japan; the **History Walk of the Pacific War**, featuring planes, boats and other equipment from World War II; and other special exhibits. Nearby is **Kerrville State Park**.

**Old Fort Parker** is a 37.5-acre park 4 miles north of Groesbeck on TX 14 in Limestone County. Deeded by private owners in 1936 and originally constructed by the Civilian Conservation Corps (CCC); rebuilt in 1967.

Reconstructed fort is pioneer memorial and site of Cynthia Ann Parker abduction on May 19, 1836, by Comanche Indians. Nearby Fort Parker Cemetery has graves of those killed at the Fort in the 1836 raid. Historical study and picnicking. Living History events throughout year. Primitive skills classes/campouts by appointment. Groups welcome. Operated by the City of Groesbeck, 254-729-5253.

**Palmetto State Park**, a scenic park, is 270.3 acres 8 miles southeast of Luling on US 183 and PR 11 along the San Marcos River in Gonzales County. Land deeded in 1934-1936 by private owners and City of Gonzales. Named for **tropical dwarf palmetto** found there. Diverse plant and animal life; excellent birding. Also picnicking, fishing, hiking, pedal boats, swimming. Nearby **Gonzales** and **Ottine** important in early Texas history. Gonzales settled 1825 as center of **Green DeWitt's colonies**.

**Palo Duro Canyon State Park** consists of 16,402.1 acres 12 miles east of Canyon on TX 217 in Armstrong and Randall counties. The land was deeded by private owners in 1933 and is the scene of the annual summer production of the musical drama, **"Texas."** Spectacular one-million-year-old **scenic canyon** exposes rocks spanning about 200 million years of geological time. **Coronado** may have visited canyon in 1541. Canyon officially discovered by **Capt. R. B. Marcy** in 1852. Scene of decisive battle in 1874 between Comanche and Kiowa Indians and U.S. Army troops under **Gen. Ranald Mackenzie**. Also scene of ranching enterprise started by **Charles Goodnight** in 1876. Part of **state longhorn herd** is kept here. Camping, mountain biking, scenic drives, horseback and hiking trails, horse rentals.

**Pedernales Falls State Park**, 5,211.7 acres in Blanco County about 9 miles east of Johnson City on FM 2766 along Pedernales River, was acquired from private owners in 1970. Typical **Edwards Plateau** terrain, with **live oaks, deer, turkey** and **stone hills**. Camping, picnicking, hiking, swimming, tubing. Falls main scenic attraction.

**Port Isabel Lighthouse State Historic Site** consists of 0.9 acre in Port Isabel, Cameron County. Acquired by purchase from private owners in 1950, site includes **lighthouse** constructed in 1852; visitors can climb to top. Park is near sites of Civil War battle of **Palmito Ranch** (1865), and Mexican War battles of **Palo Alto** and **Resaca de la Palma (1846)**. Operated by City of Port Isabel.

**Port Lavaca State Fishing Pier**, a 10.8-acre recreational area on Lavaca Bay in Calhoun County, was acquired by transfer of authority from state highway department in 1963. The 24-hour, lighted, 3,200-foot-long fishing pier was created from former causeway. **Port Lavaca City Park**, at base of pier, offers a boat ramp and picnicking facilities. Operated by City of Port Lavaca.

**Possum Kingdom State Park**, west of Mineral Wells via US 180 and PR 33 in Palo Pinto County, is 1,528.7 acres adjacent to **Possum Kingdom Lake**, in **Palo Pinto Mountains** and **Brazos River Valley**. Rugged canyons home to **deer**, other wildlife. Acquired from the Brazos River Authority in 1940. Camping, picnicking, swimming, fishing, boating. Cabins available.

**Purtis Creek State Park** is 1,582.4 acres in Henderson and Van Zandt counties 3.5 miles north of Eustace on FM 316. Acquired in 1977 from private owners. Fishing, camping, hiking, picnicking, paddle boats and canoes.

**Ray Roberts Lake State Park (Isle du Bois Unit)**, consists of 2,263 acres on the south side of Ray Roberts Lake on FM 455 in Denton County. **Johnson Branch Unit** contains 1,514 acres on north side of lake in Denton and Cooke counties 7 miles east of IH 30 on FM 3002. There are also six satellite parks. Land acquired in 1984 by lease from secretary of Army. Abundant and varied plant and animal life. Fishing, camping, picnicking, swimming, hiking, biking; tours of 19-century farm buildings at Johnson Branch. Includes Lantana Ridge Lodge on the east side of the lake. It is a full-service lodging facility with restaurant.

**Rusk/Palestine State Park**, a total of 136 acres, includes Rusk unit, adjacent to **Texas State Railroad Rusk Depot** off US 84 in Cherokee County, and Palestine unit, off US 84 adjacent to **Texas State Railroad Palestine Depot**. Fishing, picnicking, camping, tennis courts, playground. **Train rides** in restored passenger cars (see also **Texas State Railroad State Historic Site**).

**Sabine Pass Battleground State Historic Site** in Jefferson County 1.5 miles south of Sabine Pass on Dowlen

Road, contains 57.6 acres acquired from Kountze County Trust in 1972. Lt. **Richard W. Dowling,** with small Confederate force, repelled an attempted 1863 invasion of Texas by Union gunboats. **Monument, World War II ammunition bunkers.** Fishing, picnicking, camping.

**Sam Bell Maxey House State Historic Site,** at the corner of So. Church and Washington streets in Paris, Lamar County, was donated by City of Paris in 1976. Consists of .4 acre with 1868 Victorian Italianate-style frame house, plus outbuildings. Most of furnishings accumulated by Maxey family. Maxey served in Mexican and Civil wars and was two-term U.S. Senator. House is on the **National Register of Historic Places.** Open for tours Friday through Sunday.

**San Angelo State Park,** on **O.C. Fisher Reservoir** adjacent to the city of San Angelo in Tom Green County, contains 7,677 acres of land, most of which will remain undeveloped. Leased from U.S. Corps of Engineers in 1995. Access is from US 87 or 67, then FM 2288. Highly diversified plant and animal life. Activities include boating, water activities, hiking, mountain biking, horseback riding, camping, picnicking. Part of **state longhorn herd** in park. Nearby is **Fort Concho.**

**San Jacinto Battleground State Historic Site** and **Battleship Texas State Historic Site** are located 20 miles east of downtown Houston off TX 225 east to TX 134 to PR 1836 in east Harris County. The park is 1,200 acres with 570-foot-tall monument erected in 1936-1939 in honor of Texans who defeated Mexican **Gen. Antonio López de Santa Anna** on April 21, 1836, to win Texas' independence from Mexico. The park is original site of Texans' camp acquired in 1883. Subsequent acquisitions made in 1897, 1899 and 1985. Park transferred to TPW in 1965. Park registered as **National Historic Landmark.** Elevator ride to observation tower near top of monument; museum. Monument known as **tallest free-standing concrete structure in the world** at the time it was erected. Interpretive trail around battleground. Adjacent to park is the **U.S.S. Texas,** commissioned in 1914. The battleship, the only survivor of the dreadnought class and the only surviving veteran of two world wars, was donated to people of Texas by U.S. Navy. Ship was moored in the Houston Ship Channel at the **San Jacinto Battleground** on San Jacinto Day, 1948. Extensive repairs were done 1988-1990. Some renovation is on-going, but ship is open for tours. Ship closed Christmas Eve and Christmas Day.

**Sea Rim State Park** in Jefferson County, 20 miles south of Port Arthur, off TX 87, contains 4,141 acres of marshland and 5.2 miles of **Gulf beach** shoreline, acquired from private owners in 1972. It is prime wintering area for **waterfowl.** Wetlands also shelter such wildlife as river otter, nutria, alligator, mink, muskrat. Camping, fishing, swimming; wildlife observation; nature trail; boating. **Airboat tours of marsh.** Near **McFaddin National Wildlife Refuge.**

**Sebastopol State Historic Site** at 704 Zorn Street in Seguin, Guadalupe County, was acquired by purchase in 1976 from Seguin Conservation Society; approximately 2.2 acres. Built about 1856 by **Col. Joshua W. Young** of **limecrete,** concrete made from local gravel and lime, the Greek Revival-style house, which was restored to its 1880 appearance by the TPW, is on National Register of Historic Places. Tours available Saturday and Sunday. Also of interest in the area is historic **Seguin,** founded 1838.

**Seminole Canyon State Historic Site** in Val Verde County, 9 miles west of Comstock off US 90, contains 2,172.5 acres; acquired by purchase from private owners 1973-1977. **Fate Bell Shelter** in canyon contains several important **prehistoric Indian pictographs.** Historic interpretive center. Tours of rock-art sites Wednesday-Sunday; also hiking, mountain biking, camping.

**Sheldon Lake State Park and Wildlife Management Area,** 2,800 acres in Harris County on Garrett Road 20 miles east of Beltway 8. Acquired by purchase in 1952 from the City of Houston. Freshwater marsh habitat. Activities include nature study, birding and fishing. Wildscape gardens of native plants.

**South Llano River State Park,** 5 miles south of Junction in Kimble County off US 377, is a 524-acre site. Land donated to the TPW by private owner in 1977. Wooded

*Jet-skiers ride by Hell's Gate at Possum Kingdom State Park in Palo Pinto County. The 1,528-acre park in the Palo Pinto Mountains and the Brazos River Valley boasts rugged canyons and plenty of wildlife. File photo.*

bottomland along the winding South Llano River is **largest and oldest winter roosting site for the Rio Grande turkey** in Central Texas. Roosting area closed to visitors October-March. Other animals include **wood ducks, javelina, fox, beaver, bobcat** and **armadillo.** Camping, picnicking, tubing, swimming and fishing, hiking, mountain biking.

**Starr Family State Historic Site,** 3.1 acres at 407 W. Travis in Marshall, Harrison County. Greek Revival-style mansion, **Maplecroft,** built 1870-1871, was home to four generations of Starr family, powerful and economically influential Texans. Two other family homes also in park. Acquired by gift in 1976; additional land donated in 1982. Maplecroft is on National Register of Historic Places. Tours Friday-Sunday or by appointment. Special events during year.

**Stephen F. Austin State Historic Site** is 663.3 acres along the Brazos River in San Felipe, Austin County, named for the **"Father of Texas."** The area was deeded by the San Felipe de Austin Corporation and the San Felipe Park Association in 1940. Site of township of **San Felipe** was seat of government where conventions of 1832 and 1833 and Consultation of 1835 held. These led to **Texas Declaration of Independence.** San Felipe was home of **Stephen F. Austin** and other famous early Texans; home of **Texas' first Anglo newspaper (the Texas Gazette)** founded in 1829; postal system of Texas originated here. Area called **"Cradle of Texas Liberty."** Museum. Camping, picnicking, golf, fishing, hiking.

**Texas State Railroad State Historic Site,** in Anderson and Cherokee counties between the cities of Palestine and Rusk, adjacent to US 84, contains 499 acres. Acquired by Legislative Act in 1971. Trains run seasonal schedules on 25.5 miles of track. Call for information and reservations: In Texas 1-800-442-8951; outside 903-683-2561. Railroad built by the State of Texas to support the **state-owned iron works** at Rusk. Begun in 1893, and built largely by inmates from the state prison system, the railroad was gradually extended until it reached Palestine in 1909 and established regular rail service between the towns. (See also **Rusk/Palestine State Park.**)

**Tyler State Park** is 985.5 acres 2 miles north of IH 20 on FM 14 north of Tyler in Smith County. Includes 64-acre lake. The land was deeded by private owners in 1934-1935. Heavily wooded. Camping, hiking, fishing, boating, lake swimming. Nearby Tyler called **rose capital of world, with Tyler Rose Garden and annual Tyler Rose Festival.** Also in Tyler are **Caldwell Children's Zoo** and **Good-**

man Museum.

**Varner-Hogg Plantation State Historic Site** is 65 acres in Brazoria County two miles north of West Columbia on FM 2852. Land originally owned by Martin Varner, a member of Stephen F. Austin's **"Old Three Hundred"** colony; later was home of Texas governor **James Stephen Hogg**. Property was deeded to the state in 1957 by Miss Ima Hogg, Gov. Hogg's daughter. **First rum distillery** in Texas established in 1829 by Varner. Mansion tours Wednesday-Sunday. Also picnicking, fishing.

**Village Creek State Park**, comprising 1,004 heavily forested acres, is located in Lumberton, Hardin County, 10 miles north of Beaumont off US 69 and FM 3513. Purchased in 1979 from private owner, the park contains abundant flora and fauna typical of the Big Thicket area. The **200 species of birds** found here include wood ducks, egrets and herons. Activities include fishing, camping, canoeing, swimming, hiking and picnicking. Nearby is the **Big Thicket National Preserve**.

**Walter Umphrey State Park** is operated by Jefferson County. For RV site reservations, contact SGS Causeway Bait & Tackle, 361-552-5311.

**Washington-on-the-Brazos State Historic Site** consists of 293.1 acres 7 miles southwest of Navasota in Washington County on TX 105 and FM 1155. Land acquired by deed from private owners in 1916, 1976 and 1996. Park includes the site of the signing on March 2, 1836, of the **Texas Declaration of Independence** from Mexico, as well as the site of the later **signing of the Constitution of the Republic of Texas**. In 1842 and 1845, the land included the **capitol of the Republic**. Daily tours of Barrington, restored **home of Anson Jones, last president of the Republic of Texas**. **Star of the Republic Museum**. Activities include picnicking and birding.

**Wyler Aerial Tramway Franklin Mountains State Park** features an aerial cable-car tramway on 195 acres of rugged mountain on east side of Franklin Mountains in El Paso. Purchase tickets at tramway station on McKinley Avenue to ride in Swiss-made gondola to 5,632-foot Ranger Peak. Passengers view cacti, rock formations, wildlife and 7,000 square miles of Texas, New Mexico and Mexico. Accessible ramps and paved grounds at top lead to observation deck with 360-degree view. Check with park for fees and hours; 915-566-6622. Other area attractions include Franklin Mountains State Park, Hueco Tanks State Historic Site and Magoffin Home State Historic Site. ☆

# Birding in Texas

## World Birding Center

The World Birding Center comprises nine birding education centers and observation sites in the Lower Rio Grande Valley designed to protect wildlife habitat and offer visitors a view of more than 450 species of birds. The center has partnered with the Texas Parks and Wildlife Department, the U.S. Fish and Wildlife Service and nine communities to turn 10,000 acres back into natural areas for birds, butterflies and other wildlife.

This area in Cameron, Hidalgo and Starr counties is a natural migratory path for millions of birds that move between the Americas, but it has been affected by agricultural and urban development and a loss of wildlife habitat. The center wants to reconcile economic development, which will be derived from tourism, with environmental conservation.

The nine WBC sites are situated along the border with Mexico:

*Birders hike through Yellow Rail Prairie at Anahuac National Wildlife Refuge in Chambers County. The 34,000-acre preserve is one of the major stops on the Great Texas Coastal Birding Trail. File photo.*

- **Brownsville** — not yet open; to be constructed at Resaca de la Palma State Park and operated by TPWD;
- **Edinburg** — opened in March 2003 (first WBC site to open); located at Edinburg Scenic Wetlands;
- **Harlingen** — Arroyo Colorado is to open in 2004;
- **Hidalgo** — Old Hidalgo Pumphouse is open to the public with historical tours available. Official WBC opening set for summer 2004;
- **McAllen** — Quinta Mazatlan is open for birding groups by reservation or appointment through the McAllen Parks and Recreation Department. Official opening set for 2004;
- **Mission** — WBC headquarters; located at Bentsen–Rio Grande State Park; scheduled to open in Spring 2004 and be operated by TPWD;
- **Roma** — Roma Bluffs is open to public and prearranged tours; operated by U.S. Fish and Wildlife;
- **South Padre Island** — South Padre Island Birding and Nature Center to officially open in 2005. Nature trail boardwalk leading to Laguna Madre shore now open for birding.
- **Weslaco** — not yet open; to be constructed at Estero Llano Grande State Park and operated by TPWD.

For more information, contact World Birding Center, 900 N. Bryan Rd. Ste. 201, Mission, TX 78572; 956-584-9156. On the Web: www.worldbirdingcenter.org.

## Great Texas Coastal Birding Trail

The Great Texas Coastal Birding Trail winds its way through 43 Texas counties along the entire Texas coast. The trail, completed in April 2000, is divided into upper, central and lower coastal regions. It includes 308 wildlife-viewing sites and such amenities as boardwalks, parking pullouts, kiosks, observation platforms and landscaping to attract native wildlife.

Color-coded maps are available, and signs mark each site. Trail maps contain information about the birds and habitats likely to be found at each site, the best season to visit, and food and lodging.

For information, contact: Nature Tourism Coordinator, Texas Parks and Wildlife, 4200 Smith School Road, Austin, TX 78744; 512-389-4396. On the Web at www.tpwd.state.tx.us/birdingtrails/contact.phtml. ☆

# National Parks, Historical Sites, Recreation Areas in Texas

Below are listed the facilities in and the activities that can be enjoyed at the two national parks, a national seashore, a biological preserve, several historic sites, memorials and recreation areas in Texas. They are under supervision of the **U.S. Department of Interior.** On the Web: **www.nps.gov/parks/search.htm**; under "Select State," choose "Texas." In addition, the recreational opportunities in the national forests and national grasslands in Texas, under the jurisdiction of the **U.S. Department of Agriculture,** are listed at the end of the article.

**Alibates Flint Quarries National Monument** consists of 1,371 acres in Potter County. For more than 10,000 years, **pre-Columbian Indians** dug **agatized limestone** from the quarries to make projectile points, knives, scrapers and other tools. The area is presently undeveloped. You may visit the flint quarries on **guided walking tours** with a park ranger. Tours are at 10:00 a.m. and 2:00 p.m. from Memorial Day to Labor Day. Off-season tours can be arranged by writing to Lake Meredith National Recreation Area, Box 1460, Fritch 79036, or by calling 806-857-3151.

**Amistad National Recreation Area** is located on the U.S. side of **Amistad Reservoir**, an international reservoir on the Texas-Mexico border. The 57,292-acre park's attractions include **boating, water skiing, swimming, fishing, camping** and archaeological sites. If lake level is normal, visitors can see **4000-year-**

*The walking trail at Chamizal National Memorial in El Paso is lined with stone monuments erected in 1897 to mark the international border with Mexico. File photo.*

**old prehistoric pictographs** in Panther and Parida caves, which are accessible only by boat. Check with park before visiting. The area is **one of the densest concentrations of Archaic rock art in North America** — more than 300 sites. Commercial campgrounds, motels and restaurants nearby. Marinas located at Diablo East and Rough Canyon. Open year round. ANRA, HCR 3, Box 5-J, Del Rio 78840; 830-775-7491.

**Big Bend National Park,** established in 1944, has spectacular **mountain and desert scenery** and a variety of **unusual geological structures.** It is the **nation's largest** protected area of **Chihuahuan Desert.** Located in the great bend of the Rio Grande, the 801,000-acre park, which is part of the **international boundary** between the United States and Mexico, was designated a **U.S. Biosphere Reserve** in 1976. **Hiking, birding and float trips** are popular. Numerous campsites are located in park, and the **Chisos Mountain Lodge** has accommodations for approximately 345 guests. Write for reservations to National Park Concessions, Inc., Big Bend National Park, Texas 79834; 915-477-2291; www.chisosmountain-slodge.com. Park open year round; facilities most crowded during spring break. PO Box 129, Big Bend National Park 79834; 915-477-2251.

**Big Thicket National Preserve,** established in 1974, consists of 13 separate units totalling 97,000 acres of diverse flora and fauna, often nicknamed the **"biological crossroads of North America."** The preserve, which includes parts of seven East Texas counties, has been designated an **"International Biosphere Reserve"** by the United Nations Educational, Scientific and Cultural Organization (UNESCO). The preserve includes **four different ecological systems**: southeastern swamps, eastern forests, central plains and southwestern deserts. The visitor information station is located on FM 420, seven miles north of Kountze; phone 409-246-2337. Open daily from 9 a.m. to 5 p.m. Naturalist activities are available by reservation only; reservations are made through the station. **Nine trails,** ranging in length from one-half mile to 18 miles, visit a variety of forest communities. The two shortest trails are handicapped accessible. Trails are open year round,

but flooding may occur after heavy rains. Horses permitted on the **Big Sandy Horse Trail** only. Boating and canoeing are popular on preserve corridor units. Park headquarters are at 3785 Milam, Beaumont 77701; 409-246-2337.

**Chamizal National Memorial,** established in 1963 and opened to the public in 1973, stands as a monument to Mexican-American friendship and goodwill. The memorial, on 52 acres in El Paso, commemorates the peaceful settlement on Aug. 29, 1963, of a **99-year-old boundary dispute between the United States and Mexico.** Chamizal uses the visual and performing arts as a medium of interchange, helping people better understand not only other cultures but their own, as well. It hosts a variety of programs throughout the year, including: the fall **Chamizal Festival** musical event; the **Siglo de Oro** drama festival (early March); the **Oñate Historical Festival** celebrating the First Thanksgiving (April); and **Music Under the Stars** (Sundays, June-August). The park has a 1.8-mile walking trail and picnic areas. Phone: 915-532-7273.

**Fort Davis National Historic Site** in Jeff Davis County was a key post in the West Texas defense system, guarding immigrants and tradesmen on the San Antonio-El Paso road from 1854 to 1891. At one time, Fort Davis was manned by black troops, called **"Buffalo Soldiers"** (because of their curly hair) who fought with great distinction in the Indian Wars. **Henry O. Flipper, the first black graduate of West Point,** served at Fort Davis in the early 1880s. The 474-acre historic site is located on the north edge of the town of Fort Davis in the **Davis Mountains,** the second-highest mountain range in the state. The site includes a museum, an auditorium with daily audio-visual programs, restored and refurnished buildings, picnic area and hiking trails. Open year round except Christmas Day. PO Box 1456, Fort Davis 79734; 915-426-3224.

**Guadalupe Mountains National Park,** established in 1972, includes 86,416 acres in Hudspeth and Culberson counties. The Park contains one of the most extensive **fossil reefs** on record. Deep **canyons** cut through this reef and provide a rare opportunity for geological study. Special points of interest are **McKittrick Canyon,** a fragile riparian environment, and **Guadalupe Peak,** the highest

*Windsurfers glide along Bird Island Basin in Padre Island National Seashore near Corpus Christi. File photo.*

in Texas. Camping, hiking on 80 miles of trails, Frijole Ranch Museum, summer amphitheater programs. Orientation, free information and natural history exhibits available at Visitor Center. Open year round. Lodging at Van Horn, Texas, and White's City or Carlsbad, NM. HC 60, Box 400, Salt Flat 79847; 915-828-3251.

**Lake Meredith National Recreation Area,** 30 miles northeast of Amarillo, centers on a reservoir on the Canadian River, in Moore, Hutchinson and Potter counties. The 44,978-acre park is popular for water-based activities. Boat ramps, picnic areas, unimproved campsites. Commercial lodging and trailer hookups available in nearby towns. Open year round. PO Box 1460, Fritch 79036; 806-857-3151.

**Lyndon B. Johnson National Historic Site** includes two separate districts 14 miles apart. The **Johnson City District** comprises the **boyhood home of the 36th President of United States** and the **Johnson Settlement,** where his grandparents resided during the late 1800s. The **LBJ Ranch District** can be visited only by taking the National Park Service bus tour starting at the LBJ State Historic Site. The tour includes the reconstructed **LBJ Birthplace,** old school, family cemetery, show barn and a view of the **Texas White House.** Site in Blanco and Gillespie counties was established in 1969, and contains 1,570 acres, 674 of which are federal. Open year round except Christmas Day and New Year's Day. No camping on site; commercial campgrounds, motels in area. PO Box 329, Johnson City 78636; 830-868-7128.

**Padre Island National Seashore** consists of a 67.5-mile stretch of a barrier island along the Gulf Coast; noted for white-sand beaches, excellent fishing and abundant bird and marine life. Contains 133,000 acres in Kleberg, Willacy and Kenedy counties. Open year round. One paved campground (fee charged) located north of Malaquite Beach; unpaved (primitive) campground area south on beach. Five miles of beach are accessible by regular vehicles; 55 miles are accessible only by 4x4 vehicles. Off-road vehicles prohibited. Camping permitted in two designated areas. Commercial lodging available on the island outside the National Seashore boundaries. PO Box 181300, Corpus Christi 78480; 361-949-8068.

**Palo Alto Battlefield National Historic Site,** Brownsville, preserves the site of the **first major battle in the Mexican-American War.** Fought on May 8, 1846, it is recognized for the innovative use of light or "flying" artillery. Participating in the battle were three future presidents: **General Zachary Taylor and Ulysses S. Grant** on the U.S. side, and **Gen. Mariano Arista** on the Mexican. Historical markers are located at the junction of Farm-to-Market roads 1847 and 511. Access to the 3,400-acre site is currently limited. Exhibits at the park's interim visitor center, at 1623 Central Blvd., Ste. 213 in Brownsville (78520), interpret the battle as well as the causes and consequences of the war. Phone 956-541-2785.

**Rio Grande Wild and Scenic River** is a 196-mile strip on the U.S. shore of the Rio Grande in the **Chihuahuan Desert,** beginning in Big Bend National Park and continuing downstream to the Terrell-Val Verde County line. There are federal facilities in Big Bend National Park only. Contact Big Bend National Park (above) for more information.

**San Antonio Missions National Historic Site** preserves four Spanish Colonial Missions — **Concepción, San José, San Juan and Espada** — as well as the Espada dam and aqueduct, which are two of the best-preserved remains in the United States of the **Spanish Colonial irrigation system,** and Rancho de las Cabras, the colonial ranch of Mission Espada. All were crucial elements to Spanish settlement on the Texas frontier. When Franciscan attempts to establish a chain of missions in East Texas in the late 1600s failed, the Spanish Crown ordered three missions transferred to the San Antonio River valley in 1731.

**The missions** are located within the city limits of **San Antonio,** while **Rancho de las Cabras** is located 25 miles south in Wilson County near **Floresville.** The four missions, which are still in use as active parishes, are open to the public from 9 a.m. to 5 p.m. daily except Thanksgiving, Christmas and New Year's. Public roadways connect the sites; a hike-bike trail is being developed. The Rancho de las Cabras site is closed to the public pending development; guided tours are available on first Saturday of each month. Call visitor center for details. The visitor center for the mission complex is at San José. For more information, write to 2202 Roosevelt Ave., San Antonio 78210; 210-534-8833 or 210-932-1001 (Visitor Center).

## Recreation on the National Forests

For general information about the National Forests and National Grasslands, see the Environment chapter.

An estimated 3 million people visit the National Forests in Texas for recreation annually. These visitors use established recreation areas primarily for hiking, picnicking, swimming, fishing, camping, boating and nature enjoyment. In the following list of some of these areas, FSR means Forest Service Road:

**Angelina NF: Bouton Lake**, 7 miles southeast of Zavalla off Texas Highway 63 and FSR 303, has a 9-acre natural lake with primitive facilities for camping, picnicking and fishing. **Boykin Springs**, 11 miles southeast of Zavalla, has a 6-acre lake and facilities for hiking, swimming, picnicking, fishing and camping. **Caney Creek**, on Sam Rayburn Reservoir 10 miles southeast of Zavalla off FM 2743, also has an amphitheater. **Sandy Creek**, 15.5 miles east of Zavalla on Sam Rayburn, offers fishing, sailing and picnicking.

The **Sawmill Hiking Trail** is 5 miles long and spans from Bouton Lake to Boykin Springs Recreation Area.

**Davy Crockett NF: Ratcliff Lake**, 25 miles west of Lufkin on Highway 7, includes a 45-acre lake and facilities for picnicking, hiking, swimming, boating, fishing and camping. There is also an amphitheater.

The 20-mile-long **4C National Recreation Trail** con-

*The Chihuahuan Desert surrounds Guadalupe Mountains National Park, located in Hudspeth and Culberson counties. They are Texas' highest mountains. File photo.*

nects Ratcliff Recreation Area to the Neches Bluff overlook. The **Piney Creek Horse Trail**, 54 miles long, can be entered approximately 5.5 miles south of Kennard off FSR 514. There are two horse camps along the trail.

**Sabine NF: Indian Mounds Recreation Area,** accessible via FM 83 3.5 miles east of Hemphill, has camping facilities and a boat-launch ramp. **Lakeview,** on Toledo Bend Reservoir 16 miles from Pineland, offering camping, hiking, boating and fishing, can be reached via TX 87, FM 2928 and FSR 120. **Ragtown,** 21 miles southeast of Center and accessible by TX 87 and TX 139, CR 3184 and FSR 132, is also on Toledo Bend and has facilities for hiking, camping and boating. **Red Hills Lake,** 3 miles north of Milam on TX 87, has facilities for hiking, fishing, swimming, camping and picnicking. **Willow Oak Recreation Area,** on Toledo Bend 11 miles south of Hemphill off TX 87, offers fishing, picnicking, camping and boating.

**Trail Between the Lakes** is 28 miles long from Lakeview Recreation Area on Toledo Bend to US 96 near Sam Rayburn Reservoir.

**Sam Houston NF: Double Lake**, 3 miles south of Coldspring on FM 2025, has facilities for picnicking, hiking, camping, swimming and fishing. **Stubblefield Lake,** 15 miles west-northwest of New Waverly off TX 1375 on the shores of Lake Conroe, has facilities for camping, hiking, picnicking and fishing.

The **Lone Star Hiking Trail**, approximately 128 miles long, is located in Sam Houston National Forest in Montgomery, Walker and San Jacinto counties.

## Recreation on the National Grasslands

**East and North Texas: Lake Davy Crockett Recreation Area**, 12 miles north of Honey Grove on FM 100, has a boat-launch ramp and camping sites on a 450-acre lake. **Coffee Mill Lake Recreation Area** has camping and picnic facilities on a 750-acre lake. This area is 4 miles west of Lake Davy Crockett Recreation Area.

The **Caddo Multi-Use Trail system**, also 4 miles west of Lake Davy Crockett, offers camping, hiking and horseback riding on 3.5 miles of trails.

**Black Creek Lake Picnic Area** is 8 miles southeast of Alvord. It has camping, picnic facilities and a boat-launch ramp on a 30-acre lake. **Cottonwood Lake**, 10 miles north of Decatur, offers hiking, boating and fishing.

**TADRA Horse Trail**, 13 miles north of Decatur, offers camping and 35 miles of horse trails.

**West Texas: Lake McClellan** in Gray County and **Lake Marvin**, which is part of the **Black Kettle National Grassland** in Hemphill County, receive over 28,000 recreation visitors annually. These areas provide camping, picnicking, fishing and boating facilities. Concessionaires operate facilities at Lake McClellan, and a nominal fee is charged for use of the areas.

At the **Rita Blanca National Grassland**, about 4,500 visitors a year enjoy picnicking and hunting. ☆

## Recreational Facilities, Corps of Engineers Lakes, 2002

*Source: Southwestern Division, Corps of Engineers, Dallas*

| Reservoir | Swim Areas | Boat Ramps | Picnic Sites | Camp Sites | Rental Units | Visitor Hours, 2002 |
|---|---|---|---|---|---|---|
| Addicks* | 0 | 0 | 721 | 0 | 0 | 6,722,500 |
| Aquilla | 0 | 2 | 0 | 0 | 0 | 296,300 |
| Bardwell | 2 | 7 | 49 | 154 | 0 | 924,600 |
| Barker* | 0 | 0 | 50 | 0 | 0 | 1,623,000 |
| Belton | 5 | 21 | 435 | 245 | 10 | 14,384,400 |
| Benbrook | 1 | 17 | 113 | 179 | 0 | 4,104,100 |
| Canyon | 6 | 22 | 411 | 468 | 44 | 1,961,900 |
| Cooper | 2 | 5 | 98 | 177 | 30 | 3,281,500 |
| Georgetown | 1 | 3 | 118 | 234 | 0 | 3,640,300 |
| Granger | 2 | 5 | 125 | 133 | 0 | 1,512,500 |
| Grapevine | 4 | 17 | 140 | 178 | 0 | 6,052,700 |
| Hords Creek | 2 | 8 | 15 | 140 | 0 | 2,652,500 |
| Joe Pool | 3 | 7 | 315 | 556 | 0 | 6,081,400 |
| Lake O' the Pines | 8 | 34 | 197 | 525 | 0 | 7,958,500 |
| Lavon | 3 | 22 | 285 | 282 | 0 | 4,569,900 |
| Lewisville | 8 | 25 | 331 | 567 | 0 | 11,823,400 |
| Navarro Mills | 3 | 6 | 16 | 267 | 0 | 2,069,100 |
| O.C. Fisher | 0 | 17 | 90 | 61 | 0 | 4,966,500 |
| Pat Mayse** | 6 | 11 | 14 | 317 | 0 | 1,438,800 |
| Proctor | 0 | 6 | 44 | 215 | 0 | 1,782,100 |
| Ray Roberts | 2 | 11 | 294 | 371 | 0 | 21,812,600 |
| Sam Rayburn | 4 | 29 | 30 | 775 | 98 | 15,071,000 |
| Somerville | 2 | 12 | 229 | 827 | 22 | 21,396,300 |
| Stillhouse Hollow | 3 | 5 | 91 | 65 | 0 | 2,919,100 |
| Texoma**† | 9 | 37 | 190 | 1,222 | 244 | 90,457,500 |
| Town Bluff | 1 | 13 | 126 | 392 | 0 | 4,778,400 |
| Waco | 8 | 9 | 112 | 253 | 0 | 3,026,300 |
| Wallisville* | 0 | 0 | 0 | 0 | 0 | 177,600 |
| Whitney | 5 | 30 | 40 | 701 | 0 | 5,837,900 |
| Wright Patman | 4 | 22 | 209 | 601 | 0 | 11,005,100 |
| **Totals** | **94** | **403** | **4,888** | **9,905** | **448** | **264,327,800** |

*All above lakes managed by the Fort Worth District, U.S. Army Corps of Engineers, with the following exceptions:*
*\*Managed by Galveston District, USACE.*
*\*\*Managed by Tulsa District, USACE.*
*†Figures for facilities on Texas side of lake. Visitation is for entire lake.*

# Freshwater and Saltwater Fish and Fishing

*Source: Texas Parks and Wildlife Department*

## Freshwater Fish and Fishing

In Texas, **247 species of freshwater fish** are found. This includes 78 species that inhabit areas with low salinity and can be found in rivers entering the Gulf of Mexico. Also included in that total are 18 species that are not native, but were introduced into the state.

The estimated **number of freshwater recreational anglers** is 1.84 million, with annual expenditures of $1.49 billion annually. Catch-and-release fishing has emerged on the Texas scene as the conservation theme of anglers who desire continued quality fishing.

The **most popular fish** for recreational fishing are largemouth bass; catfish; crappie; and striped, white and hybrid striped bass.

The **Texas Parks and Wildlife Department** (TPWD) operates field stations, fish hatcheries and research facilities to support the conservation and management of fishery resources.

*Children fish at the B.A. Steinhagen Reservoir at Martin Dies Jr. State Park, located in Jasper and Tyler counties. Photo courtesy of Texas Parks and Wildlife Dept.*

TPW has continued its programs of stocking fish in public waters to increase angling opportunities. The hatcheries operated by TPW raise largemouth and smallmouth bass, as well as catfish, striped and hybrid striped bass, crappie, sunfish and paddlefish.

### Texas Freshwater Fisheries Center

The Texas Freshwater Fisheries Center in Athens, about 75 miles southeast of Dallas, is an $18 million hatchery, research laboratory, aquarium and educational center, where visitors can learn about the underwater life in Texas' freshwater streams, ponds and lakes.

The 24,000-square-foot hatchery and research facility concentrates on genetic research and the production of 5 to 6 million Florida largemouth bass for restocking Texas rivers and reservoirs.

The interactive Cox Visitors Center includes aquarium-displays of fish in their natural environment. Visitors get an "eye-to-eye" view of three authentically-designed Texas freshwater habitats: a Hill Country stream, an East Texas pond and a reservoir. A marsh exhibit features live American alligators.

Through touch-screen computer exhibits, visitors can learn more about fish habitats and life cycles and the importance of catch-and-release fishing. Films, seminars and demonstrations are also offered.

A casting pond stocked with rainbow trout in the winter and catfish in the summer provides a place for children to learn how to bait a hook, cast a line and land a fish. The center also has an active schedule of special programs and events.

The center is a cooperative effort of Texas Parks and Wildlife, the U.S. Fish and Wildlife Service, the City of Athens and private organizations.

The Texas Freshwater Fisheries Center is open Tuesday through Saturday, 9:00 a.m. to 4:00 p.m., and Sunday, 1:00 to 4:00 p.m. It is closed on Monday. Admission is charged. The Center is located four-and-a-half miles east of Athens on FM 2495 at Lake Athens. Address: 5550 Flat Creek Road, Athens 75751, or call 903-676-2277.

## Saltwater Fish and Fishing

There are approximately 1 million saltwater anglers in Texas (6 years old and older) who have a $1.328 billion economic impact annually. Catch averaged 2,054,700 fish annually in the ten years between 1988–98 for both Texas bays and the Gulf of Mexico off Texas combined.

The most popular **saltwater sport fish** in Texas bays are spotted seatrout, sand seatrout, Atlantic croaker, red drum, southern flounder, black drum, sheepshead and gafftopsail catfish. **Offshore,** some of the fish anglers target are red snapper, king mackerel, dolphin (fish), spotted seatrout, tarpon and yellowfin tuna.

# Commercial Fisheries

Total coastwide landings in 2000 were more than 101 million pounds, valued at more than $266 million. Shrimp accounted for 83 percent of the weight and 90 percent of the value of all seafood landed during 2000. The approximately *5,800 licensed saltwater commercial fishermen in Texas in 2000 made an economic impact of more than $809 million.

### Commercial Landings, 2000

| Finfish | Pounds | Value |
|---|---|---|
| Drum, Black | 2,837,100 | $2,350,300 |
| Flounder | 159,500 | 321,600 |
| Sheepshead | 106,000 | 38,900 |
| Snapper | 1,553,600 | 3,287,900 |
| Other | 1,719,200 | 3,305,000 |
| **Total Finfish** | **6,376,400** | **$9,303,800** |
| **Shellfish** | | |
| Shrimp (Heads On): | | |
|   Brown and Pink | 58,621,800 | $162,138,800 |
|   White | 24,975,800 | 77,260,600 |
|   Other | 793,300 | 580,700 |
| Crabs, Blue | 4,653,800 | 3,300,800 |
| Oyster, Eastern | 6,187,800 | 13,846,600 |
| Other | 106,300 | 244,100 |
| **Total Shellfish** | **95,338,300** | **$257,371,700** |
| **Grand Total** | **101,714,700** | **$266,675,400** |

\* Deck hands and other crew members no longer need a license to work on commercial boats, so total number of commercial fishermen will vary from previous years.
*Source: Trends in Texas Commercial Fishery Landings, 1972–2000, Texas Parks and Wildlife Department Coastal Fisheries Div., Management Data Series, Austin, 2002.*

## Sea Center Texas

Sea Center Texas is a marine aquarium, fish hatchery and nature center operated by the Texas Parks and Wildlife Department to educate and entertain visitors. The visitor center opened in 1996 and educates through interpretive displays, a "touch tank" and native Texas habitat exhibits depicting a salt marsh, jetty, reef and open Gulf waters. The aquarium features "Gordon," a 300-pound grouper, and sharks. The "Coastal Kids" educational program offers students on field trips hands-on learning activities.

Touted as the **world's largest redfish hatchery,** the facility is one of three marine hatcheries on the Texas coast that produces juvenile red drum and spotted speckled trout for enhancing natural populations in Texas bays. The hatchery has the capability to produce 20 million juvenile fish yearly. It also serves as a testing ground for production of other marine species, such as flounder and tarpon.

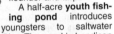

*Youngsters watch Gordon the Grouper, a Sea Center favorite.*

A half-acre **youth fishing pond** introduces youngsters to saltwater fishing through scheduled activities. The pond is handicap accessible and stocked with a variety of marine fish.

The center's **wetland area** is part of the Great Texas Coastal Birding Trail, where more than 150 species of birds have been identified. The wetland consists of a one-acre salt marsh and a three-acre freshwater marsh. Damselflies, dragonflies, butterflies and frogs are frequently sited off the boardwalk. A small outdoor pavilion provides a quiet resting place for lunch adjacent to the butterfly and hummingbird gardens.

Sea Center Texas is operated in partnership with The Dow Chemical Company and the Coastal Conservation Association. It is located in Lake Jackson, 50 miles south of Houston off of Texas 288. Admission and parking are free. Open 9 a.m. to 4 p.m. Tuesday through Friday; 10

*Sea Center's "touch tank," above, is popular with kids. The facility, below, is one of three marine hatcheries on the Texas coast. Photos courtesy of Texas Parks and Wildlife Dept.*

a.m. to 5 p.m. Saturday, and 1 p.m. to 4 p.m. Sunday. Closed Monday and some holidays. Reservations are required for some group tours, nature tours and hatchery tours. For more information call 979-292-0100. On the web: www.tpwd.state.tx.us/fish. ☆

# Hunting and Fishing Licenses

A **hunting license** is required of Texas residents and nonresidents of Texas who hunt any bird or animal. Hunting licenses and stamps are valid during the period September 1 through the following August 31 of each year, except lifetime licenses and licenses issued for a specific number of days. A hunting license (except the nonresident special hunting license and non-resident 5-day special hunting license) is valid for taking all legal species of wildlife in Texas including **deer, turkey, javelina, antelope, aoudad (sheep)** and all **small game and migratory game birds**. **Special licenses and tags** are required for taking **alligators**, and a **trapper's license** is required to hunt **fur-bearing animals**.

All **sport fishing licenses and stamps** are valid only during the period September 1 through August 31, except lifetime licenses and licenses issued for a specific number of days. In addition to sports hunting and fishing licenses, **hunting/fishing stamps** are required for special hunting/fishing privileges.

Detailed information concerning licenses, stamps, seasons, regulations and related information can be obtained from **Texas Parks and Wildlife, 4200 Smith School Road, Austin 78744; (800) 792-1112 or 512-389-4800.** On the Web, information from TPW on hunting: **www.tpwd.state.tx.us/hunt/hunt.htm;** on fishing:

**www.tpwd.state.tx.us/fish/fish.htm.**

Texas Parks and Wildlife Department reported that for the year ending **August 31, 2001,** there were 1,265,946 paid **hunting-license holders** and 1,642,012 **sport or recreation fishing-license holders**. These licenses, plus stamps, tags or permits, resulted in revenue to the state of $35,509,918 from hunting and $24,184,451 from fishing.

For the year ending **August 31, 2002,** there were 1,331,131 paid **hunting-license holders** and 1,584,805 paid **sport or recreation fishing-license holders**. These licenses, plus stamps, tags or permits, resulted in revenue to the state of $36,075,142 from hunting and $23,612,276 from fishing.

During the 2000–2001 license year, hunters killed 424,533 **white-tailed deer**; 23,275 **wild turkey** in the fall and 23,982 in the spring; 4,346 **mule deer**; and 22,794 **javelina**. In addition, 196,924 **rabbits**; 323,347 **squirrels**; 4,531,714 **mourning dove**; and 542,691 **bobwhite quail** were killed.

During the 2001–2002 license year, hunters killed 395,726 **white-tailed deer**; 35,417 **wild turkey** in the fall and 28,948 in the spring; 3,104 **mule deer**; and 17,026 **javelina**. In addition, 172,690 **rabbits**; 230,265 **squirrels**; 4,496,650 **mourning dove**; and 438,987 **bobwhite quail** were killed. ☆

# Fairs, Festivals and Special Events

Fairs, festivals and other special events provide year-round recreation in Texas. Some are of national interest, while many attract visitors from across the state. In addition to those listed here, the recreational paragraphs in the Counties section list numerous events. Information was furnished by the event sponsors. You can find more events on the Web at: **www.traveltex.com/events_listing.asp**.

**Albany** — Fort Griffin Fandangle; June; PO Box 155; 76430-0155; www.albany-texas.com.

**Alvarado** — Pioneers & Old Settlers Reunion; August; PO Box 217; 76009-0217.

**Amarillo** — Tri-State Fair; September; PO Box 31087; 79120.

**Anderson** — Grimes County Fair; June; PO Box 435; 77830.

**Angleton** — Brazoria County Fair; October; PO Box 818; 77516; www.bcfa.org.

**Arlington** — Texas Scottish Festival; June; PO Box 511; Clifton; 76634; www.texasscottishfestival.com.

**Athens** — Old Fiddlers Reunion; May; PO Box 1441; 75751-1441.

**Austin** — Austin Fine Arts Festival; April; PO Box 5705; 78763-5705; www.austinfineartsfestival.org.

**Bay City** — Bay City Rice Festival; October; PO Box 867; 77404; www.baycitylions.org.

**Bay City** — Matagorda County Fair & Livestock Show; February; PO Box 1803; 77404; www.matagordacountyfair.com.

The Butterfield Wagon Festival in Monahans at the Ward County Fairgrounds features bull rides, dances, a kids' rodeo, wagon displays and a parade. File photo.

**Beaumont** — South Texas State Fair; October; PO Box 3207; 77704-3207; www.ymbl.org/fair.htm.

**Bellville** — Austin County Fair; October; PO Box 141; 77418; www.austincountyfair.com.

**Big Spring** — Howard County Fair; August; PO Box 2356; 79720-2356.

**Boerne** — Boerne Berges Fest; June; PO Box 748; 78006.

**Boerne** — Kendall County Fair; September; PO Box 954; 78006-0954; www.hillcountrytourism.com/attractions/kendall.html.

**Brackettville** — Gunfighter Competition; July 4 weekend (Saturday); PO Box 528; 78832; www.alamovillage.com.

**Brackettville** — Western Horse Races & BBQ; September (Labor Day); PO Box 528; 78832; www.alamovillage.com.

**Brenham** — Washington County Fair; September; PO Box 1257; 77833.

**Brownsville** — Charro Days Fiesta; February (last Thursday); PO Box 3247; 78520; www.charrodays.org.

**Burton** — Burton Cotton Gin Festival; April; PO Box 98; 77835-0098; www.cottonginmuseum.org.

**Canyon** — "TEXAS Legacies" Outdoor Epic Theatre; June–August; 1514 5th Ave.; 79015; www.epictexas.com.

**Clute** — Great Texas Mosquito Festival; July; PO Box 997; 77531-0997; www.mosquitofestival.com.

**Columbus** — Colorado County Fair; September; PO Box 506; 78933; www.coloradocountyfair.org.

**Conroe** — Montgomery County Fair; March–April; PO Box 869; 77305-0869; www.mcfa.org.

**Corpus Christi** — Bayfest; September; PO Box 1858; 78403-1858; www.bayfesttexas.com.

**Corpus Christi** — Buccaneer Days; April–May; PO Box 30404; 78404-0404; www.bucdays.com.

**Dallas** — State Fair of Texas; September–October; PO Box 150009; 75315-0009; www.bigtex.com.

**De Leon** — De Leon Peach & Melon Festival; August; PO Box 44; 76444-0044.

**Denton** — North Texas State Fair & Rodeo; August; PO Box 1695; 76202-1695; www.northtexasstatefair.com.

**Edna** — Jackson County Fair; October; PO Box 457; 77957; www.jcyf.org.

**Ennis** — National Polka Festival; May; PO Box 1177; 75120-1237; www.visitennis.org/festivals.html.

**Fairfield** — Freestone County Fair; June; PO Box 196; 75840.

**Flatonia** — Czhilispiel; October; PO Box 610; 78941-0610; www.flatonia-tx.com/czhilispiel.htm.

**Fort Worth** — Pioneer Days; September; 131 E. Exchange Ave., Ste 100B; 76106; www.fortworthstockyards.org.

**Fort Worth** – Southwestern Expo. & Livestock Show; Jan.-Feb.; PO Box 150; 76101-0150; www.fwssr.com.

**Fredericksburg** — Easter Fires Pageant; Easter Eve; PO Box 526; 78624-0526; www.gillespiefair.com.

**Fredericksburg** — Fredericksburg Food & Wine Fest; October; 703 N Llano; 78624; www.fbgfoodandwinefest.com.

**Fredericksburg** — Night in Old Fredericksburg; July; 302 E. Austin; 78624; www.fredericksburg-texas.com.

**Fredericksburg** — Oktoberfest; October (1st weekend); PO Box 222; 78624; www.Oktoberfestinfbg.com.

**Freer** — Freer Rattlesnake Roundup; April; PO Box 717; 78357-0717; www.freerrattlesnake.com.

**Galveston** — Dickens on The Strand; December; 502 20th St.; 77550-2014; www.dickensonthestrand.org.

**Galveston** — Galveston Historic Homes Tour; May; 502 20th St.; 77550-2014; www.foundation@galvestonhistory.org.

**Gilmer** — East Texas Yamboree; October; PO Box 854; 75644-0854; www.yamboree.com.

**Glen Flora** — Wharton County Youth Fair; April; PO Box 167; 77443-0167; www.wcnet.net/wcyf.

**Graham** — Art Splash on the Square; May; PO Box 299; 76450; www.visitgraham.com.

**Graham** — Christmas Stroll & Lighted Parade; December; PO Box 299; 76450; www.visitgraham.com.

**Graham** — Red, White & You Parade & Festivities; July 4; PO Box 299; 76450; www.visitgraham.com.

**Grand Prairie** — National Championship Pow-Wow; Sept.; 2602 Mayfield Rd; 75052-7299; www.tradersvillage.com.

**Greenville** — Hunt County Fair; June; PO Box 1071; 75401; www.huntcountyfair.com.

**Hallettsville** — Hallettsville Kolache Fest; September; PO Box 313; 77964-0313; www.hallettsville.com.

**Helotes** — Helotes Cornyval; May (1st weekend); PO Box 376; 78023-0376; www.cornyval.com.

**Hempstead** — Waller County Fair; September–October; PO Box 911; 77445.

**Hico** — Hico Old Settler Reunion; July (last weekend); PO Box 93; 76457; www.hico-tx.com.

**Hidalgo** — BorderFest; March; PO 611 E. Coma; 78557; hidalgotexas.com.

**Hondo** — Medina County Fair; September (3rd weekend); PO Box 4; 78861.

**Houston** — Harris County Fair; October; 1 Abercrombie

Dr; 77084-4233.

**Houston** —Houston Livestock Show and Rodeo; February–March; PO Box 20070; 77225-0070; www.rodeohouston.com, www.hlsr.com.

**Houston** — Houston International Festival; April; 7413 Westview Dr., Ste. B; 77055-5100; www.ifest.org.

**Hughes Springs** — Wildflower Trails of Texas; April (last weekend); PO Box 805; 75656.

**Jefferson** — Historical Pilgrimage: Historical Home Tours and Spring Festival; May (first weekend); PO Box 301; 75657-0301; www.theexcelsiorhouse.com.

**Johnson City** — Blanco County Fair; August; PO Box 261; 78636-0261.

*Yorktown Western Days has been held annually for 45 years. The festival in DeWitt County includes arts, crafts, street dances, parades, music, a quilt show and cook-offs. File photo.*

**Kenedy** — Bluebonnet Days; April; 205 South 2nd St.; 78119-2729.

**Kerrville** — Kerr County Fair; October; PO Box 290842; 78029; www.kerrcountyfair.com.

**Kerrville** — Kerrville Folk Festival; May–June; PO Box 291466; 78029-1466; www.kerrville-music.com.

**Kerrville** — The Official Texas State Arts & Crafts Fair; May (Memorial weekend); PO Box 291527; 78029; www.tacef.org.

**Kerrville** — Kerrville Wine and Music Festival; September; PO Box 291466; 78029-1466; www.kerrville-music.com.

**Lamesa** — Dawson County Fair; September; PO Box 1268; 79331.

**Laredo** — Laredo International Fair & Exposition; March; PO Box 1770; 78043; www.laredofair.com.

**Laredo** — Washington's Birthday Celebration; February; 1819 E. Hillside Rd.; 78041-3383; www.wbcalaredo.com.

**Longview** — Gregg County Fair & Exposition; September; PO Box 1124; 75606; www.greggcountyfair.com.

**Lubbock** — Panhandle-South Plains Fair; September; PO Box 208; 79408-0208; www.southplainsfair.com.

**Lufkin** — Texas Forest Festival; September; 1615 S. Chestnut St.; 75901; www.lufkintexas.org.

**Luling** — Luling Watermelon Thump; June (last weekend); PO Box 710; 78648-0710; www.watermelonthump.com.

**Mercedes** — Rio Grande Valley Livestock Show; March; PO Box 867; 78570-0867; www.rgvlivestockshow.com.

**Mesquite** — Mesquite Championship Rodeo; April–September; 1818 Rodeo Dr; 75149-3800; www.mesquiterodeo.com.

**Monahans** — Butterfield-Overland Stage Coach and Wagon Festival; August; www.monahans.org.

**Mount Pleasant** — Titus County Fair; September (last full week); PO Box 1232; 75456-1232; www.tituscountyfair.com.

**Nacogdoches** — Piney Woods Fair; October; 3805 NW Stallings Dr.; 75961; www.nacexpo.net.

**Nederland** — Nederland Heritage Festival; March; PO Box 1176; 77627-1176; www.nederlandhf.com/.

**New Braunfels** — Comal County Fair; September; PO Box 310403; 78131-0223.

**New Braunfels** — Wurstfest; October–November; PO Box 310309; 78131-0309; www.wurstfest.com.

**Odessa** — Permian Basin Fair & Expo; September; PO Box 4812; 79760; www.pb-fair.com.

**Palestine** — Dogwood Trails Festival; March–April; PO Box 2828; 75802-2828; www.visitpalestine.com.

**Paris** — Red River Valley Fair; August; 570 E. Center St.; 75460-2680; www.rrvfair.org.

**Pasadena** — Pasadena Livestock Show & Rodeo; October; 7601 Red Bluff Rd.; 77507-1035; www.pasadenarodeo.com.

**Plantersville** — Texas Renaissance Festival; October–November; 21778 FM 1774; 77363-7722; www.texrenfest.com.

**Port Lavaca** — Calhoun County Fair; October; PO Box 42; 77979-0042.

**Poteet** — Poteet Strawberry Festival; April; PO Box 227; 78065-0227; www.strawberry-festival.com.

**Refugio** — Refugio County Fair & Rodeo; March; PO Box 88; 78377; www.rcfaonline.com.

**Richmond** — Texas Czech Heritage Celebrations; May, October, December; PO Box 6; 789457; www.czechtexas.com.

**Rio Grande City**— Starr County Fair; March; PO Box 841; 78582.

**Rosenberg** — Fort Bend County Fair; September–October; PO Box 428; 77471; www.fbcfa.org.

**Salado** — Gathering of the Clans; November; PO Box 36; 76571-0036.

**San Angelo** — San Angelo Stock Show & Rodeo; February, July, November; 200 W 43rd St.; 76903-1675; www.sanangelorodeo.com.

**San Antonio** — Fiesta San Antonio; April; 2611 Broadway St.; 78215-1022; www.fiesta-sa.org.

**San Antonio** — Texas Folklife Festival; June; 801 S. Bowie St.; 78205-3296; www.texasfolklifefestival.org.

**Sanderson** — Cinco de Mayo Celebration; May; PO Box 686; 79848.

**Sanderson** — Independence Day Celebration; July; PO Box 4810; 79848-4810; www.co.terrell.tx.us.

**Sanderson** — Prickly Pear Pachanga; October; PO Box 4810; 79848; www.co.terrell.tx.us.

**Sanderson** — Terrell County Fair; January; PO Box 686; 79848.

**Santa Fe** — Galveston County Fair & Rodeo; April; PO Box 889; 77510-0889; www.galvestoncountyfair.com.

**Seguin** — Guadalupe Agricultural & Livestock Fair; October (2nd weekend); PO Box 334; 78156; www.guadalupecountyfairandrodeo.com.

**Shamrock** — St. Patrick's Day Celebration; March; PO Box 588; 79079-0588.

**Stamford** — Texas Cowboy Reunion; July; PO Box 948; 79553-0928; www.tcrrodeo.com.

**Sulphur Springs** — Hopkins County Fall Festival; September; PO Box 177; 75483-0177.

**Sweetwater** — Rattlesnake Roundup; March (2nd weekend); PO Box 416; 79556-0416; www.rattlesnakeroundup.com.

**Texarkana** — Four States Fair; September; PO Box 1915; Texarkana AR; 75504; www.fourstatesfair.com.

**Tyler** — East Texas State Fair; September; 2112 W. Front St.; 75702-6828; www.statefair.tyler.com.

**Tyler** — Texas Rose Festival; Ocober; PO Box 8224; 75711-8224; www.texasrosefestival.com.

**Victoria** — Victoria Jaycee's Livestock Show; February; PO Box 2255; 77902-2255.

**Waco** — Brazos River Festival; April; 810 S. 4th St.; 76706-1036.

**Waco** — Heart O' Texas Fair & Rodeo; Oct.; PO Box 7581; 76714-7581; www.hotfair.com.

**Waxahachie** — Scarborough Faire the Renaissance Festival; April–June; PO Box 538; 75168-0538; www.scarboroughrenfest.com.

**Waxahachie** — Gingerbread Trail Tour of Homes; June (1st weekend); PO Box 706; 75168; www.rootsweb.com/~txecm/ginger.htm.

**Weatherford** — Parker County Peach Festival; July (2nd Saturday); PO Box 310; 76086-0310; www.visitweatherford.com.

**Winnsboro** — Autumn Trails Festival; October; 201 W. Broadway St.; 75494-2608.

**Woodville** — Tyler County Dogwood Festival; March–April; PO Box 2151; 75979-2151; www.woodvilletx.com.

**Yorktown** — Western Days; October (3rd weekend); PO Box 488; 78164-0488; www.yorktowntx.com. ☆

# Counties of Texas

These pages describe Texas' 254 counties and hundreds of towns. Descriptions are based on reports from chambers of commerce, the Texas Cooperative Extension, federal and state agencies, the *New Handbook of Texas* and other sources. Consult the index for other county information.

County maps are based on those of the Texas Department of Transportation and are copyrighted, 2003, as are the entire contents.

**Physical Features:** Descriptions are from U.S. Geological Survey and local sources.

**Economy:** From information provided by local chambers of commerce and county extension agents.

**History:** From Texas statutes, *Fulmore's History and Geography of Texas as Told in County Names*, WPA Historical Records Survey, Texas Centennial Commission Report and the *New Handbook of Texas*.

**Ethnicity:** Percentages from the 2000 Census of Population, U.S. Bureau of the Census, as compiled by the Texas State Data Center, Texas A&M University. **Anglo** refers to non-Hispanic whites; **Black** refers to non-Hispanic blacks; **Hispanic** refers to Hispanics of all races; **Other** is composed of persons from all other racial groups who are non-Hispanic.

**Vital Statistics, 2001**: From the Texas Department of Health Annual Report, 2001.

**Recreation:** From information provided by local chambers of commerce and county extension agents. Attempts were made to note activities unique to the area or that point to ethnic or cultural heritage.

**Minerals**: From extension agents.

**Agriculture**: Condensed from information provided to the *Texas Almanac* by county extension agents in 2002. **Market value** (total cash receipts from marketings) of agricultural products sold are from the **Bureau of Economic Analysis** of the U.S. Department of Commerce for 2000.

**Cities:** The county seat, incorporated cities and towns with post offices are listed. Population for incorporated towns are 2002 estimates from the State Data Center. (NA) means a population count is not available. When figures for a small part of a city are given, such as **part (45,155) of Dallas** in Collin County, they are from the 2000 U.S. census because more recent estimates are not available.

### Sources of DATA LISTS

**Population:** The county population estimate as of July 1, 2002, U.S. Census Bureau. The line following gives the percentage of increase or decrease from the 2000 U.S. census count.

**Area:** Total area in square miles, including water surfaces, as determined in the 2000 U.S. census.

**Land Area:** The land area in square miles as determined by the census bureau in 2000.

**Altitude** (ft.): From the U.S. Geological Survey. Not all of the surface of Texas has been precisely surveyed for elevation; in some cases data are from the Texas Railroad Commission or the Texas Department of Transportation.

**Climate:** Provided by the National Oceanic and Atmospheric Administration state climatologist, College Station. Data are revised at 10-year intervals. Listed are the latest compilations, as of Jan. 1, 1993, and pertain to a particular site within the county (usually the county seat). The data include: **Rainfall** (annual in inches); **January** mean minimum temperature; **July** mean maximum temperature.

**Workforce/Wages**: Prepared by the Texas Workforce Commission, Austin, in cooperation with the Bureau of Labor Statistics of the U.S. Department of Labor. The data are computed from reports by all establishments subject to the Texas Unemployment Compensation Act.

(Agricultural employers are subject to the act if they employ as many as three workers for 20 weeks or pay cash wages of $6,250 in a quarter. Employers who pay $1,000 in

wages in a quarter for domestic services are subject also. Still not mandatorily covered are self-employed, unpaid family workers, and those employed by churches and some small nonprofit organizations.)

**The work/wage data include:**

**Civilian labor force** as of March 2003 (state total, lowest county and highest county included here). Texas, 10,885,333; Loving County, 47; Harris County, 1,871,909.

**Unemployed:** The unemployment rate (percentage of workforce) for March 2003. Texas, 6.5; Kenedy County, 1.0; Maverick County, 29.7.

Total **Wages** paid in the **third quarter**, 2002. Texas, $81,366,890,382; Loving County $165,467; Harris County, $19,336,149,443.

**Average Weekly Wage** as of the third quarter of 2002. Texas, $676.90; Zavala County, $335.16; Carson County, $918.20.

**Property Values**: The appraised gross market value of real and personal property in each county appraisal district in 2001 as reported to the State Property Tax Board.

**Retail Sales**: Preliminary figures for 2002 as reported to the state Comptroller of Public Accounts. The figures are subject to change in the comptroller's final report.

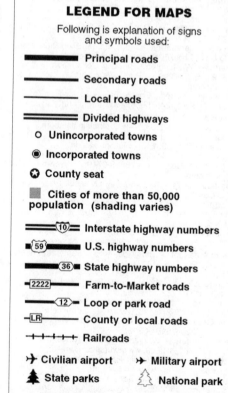

## LEGEND FOR MAPS

Following is explanation of signs and symbols used:

━━━━ **Principal roads**

──── **Secondary roads**

──── **Local roads**

═══ **Divided highways**

○ **Unincorporated towns**

◉ **Incorporated towns**

✪ **County seat**

▨ **Cities of more than 50,000 population** (shading varies)

═⟨10⟩═ **Interstate highway numbers**

◀59▶ **U.S. highway numbers**

⟨36⟩ **State highway numbers**

─⟨2222⟩─ **Farm-to-Market roads**

──⟨12⟩─ **Loop or park road**

─⟨LR⟩── **County or local roads**

┼┼┼┼┼ **Railroads**

✈ **Civilian airport**      ✦ **Military airport**

🌲 **State parks**      🌲 **National park**

▲ **Historic site**      ◆ **Other features**

A foldout map of Texas with the counties named follows **page 160.** A small outline map of the counties accompanies each county article.

# Anderson County

**Physical Features:** Forested, hilly East Texas county, slopes to Trinity and Neches rivers; sandy, clay, black soils; pines, hardwoods.

**Economy:** Manufacturing, distribution, agribusiness, tourism; hunting and fishing leases; prison units.

**History:** Comanche, Waco, other tribes. Anglo-American settlers arrived in 1830s. Antebellum slaveholding area. County created from Houston County in 1846; named for K.L. Anderson, last vice president of the Republic of Texas.

**Race/Ethnicity, 2000:** (In percent) Anglo, 63.45; Black, 23.60; Hispanic, 12.17; Other, 0.78.

**Vital Statistics, 2001:** Births, 650; deaths, 573; marriages, 439; divorces, 264.

**Recreation:** Fishing, hunting, streams, lakes; dogwood trails; historic sites; railroad park; museum. Tourist information at 1890 depot.

**Minerals:** Oil and gas.

**Agriculture:** Cattle, hay, truck vegetables, melons, pecans, peaches. Market value $28.8 million. Timber sold.

**PALESTINE** (17,632), county seat; clothing, metal, wood products; transportation and agribusiness center; scientific balloon station; historic bakery; library; vocational-technical facilities; hospitals; community college; dulcimer festival in March, hot pepper festival in October.

Other towns include: **Cayuga** (200) **Elkhart** (1,246); **Frankston** (1,243); **Montalba** (110); **Neches** (175); and **Tennessee Colony** (300) site of state prisons.

| | |
|---|---|
| Population | 54,585 |
| Change fm 2000 | -1.0 |
| Area (sq. mi.) | 1,077.95 |
| Land Area (sq. mi.) | 1,070.79 |
| Altitude (ft.) | 198-725 |
| Rainfall (in.) | 43.3 |
| Jan. mean min. | 36 |
| July mean max | 94 |
| Civ. Labor | 19,155 |
| Unemployed | 5.4 |
| Wages | $120,422,591 |
| Av. Weekly Wage | $561.92 |
| Prop. Value | $2,155,964,130 |
| Retail Sales | $833,694,022 |

# Railroad Abbreviations

AAT ....................................Austin Area Terminal Railroad
AGC .................................. Alamo Gulf Coast Railway Co.
ATK ..............................................................AMTRAK
ANR ................... Angelina & Neches River Railroad Co.
ATCX...............................Austin & Texas Central Railroad
BLR......................................... Blacklands Railroad
BNSF ........... Burlington Northern Santa Fe Railroad Co.
BOP ......................................Border Pacific Railroad Co.
BRG .............Brownsville & Rio Grande Int'l Railroad Co.
CMC...............................................CMC Railroad, Inc.
DART .............................. Trinity Railway Express
DGNO ............. Dallas, Garland & Northeastern Railroad
FWWR ............. Fort Worth & Western Railroad/Tarantula
GCSR ..............Gulf, Colorado & San Saba RailwayCorp.
GRR....................................Georgetown Railroad Co.
GVSR...........................................Galveston Railroad, L.P.
KCS ................... Kansas City Southern Railway Co., The
KRR ......................... Kiamichi Railroad Company, Inc.
MCSA ......... Moscow, Camden & San Augustine RR Co.
PCN ....................Point Comfort & Northern Railway Co.
PNR ..................Panhandle Northern Railroad Company

PTRA .......................Port Terminal Railroad Association
PVS.................. Pecos Valley Southern Railway Co., Inc.
RSS............. Rockdale, Sandow & Southern Railroad Co.
RVSC ................................................Rio Valley Switching
SAW .................................South Plains Switching LTD, Co.
SRN ........... Sabine River & Northern Railroad Company
SSC............ Southern Switching Co. (Lone Star Railroad)
SW ................................Southwestern Shortline Railroad
TCT ................................. Texas City Terminal Railway Co.
TIBR .......................... Timber Rock Railroad, Inc.
TM........................ The Texas Mexican Railway Company
TN ....................................Texas & Northern Railway Co.
TNER ................................ Texas Northeastern Railroad
TNMR ................. Texas & New Mexico Railroad
TNW............................. Texas North Western Railway Co.
TP ...............................Texas Pacifico Transportation Co.
TSE ................Texas South-Eastern Railroad Company
TXGN ..............Texas, Gonzales & Northern Railway Co.
TXR................................Texas Rock Crusher Railway Co.
TSSR .............................................Texas State Railroad
UP ..............................Union Pacific Railroad Company
WTJR................ Wichita, Tillman & Jackson Railway Co.
WTLR............... West Texas & Lubbock Railroad Co. Inc.

# Andrews County

**Physical Features:** South Plains, drain to playas; grass, mesquite, shin oak; red clay, sandy soils.

**Economy:** Oil; government/services; manufacturing; agribusiness.

**History:** Apache, Comanche area until U.S. Army campaigns of 1875. Ranching developed around 1900. Oil boom in 1940s. County created 1876 from Bexar Territory; organized 1910; named for Texas Revolutionary soldier Richard Andrews.

**Race/Ethnicity, 2000:** (In percent) Anglo, 57.07; Black, 1.62; Hispanic, 40.00; Other, 1.31.

**Vital Statistics, 2001:** Births, 203; deaths, 99; marriages, 106; divorces, 65.

**Recreation:** Prairie dog town; museum; camper facilities; Fall Fiesta in September.

**Minerals:** Oil and gas.

**Agriculture:** Beef cattle, cotton, sorghums, grains, corn, hay; significant irrigation. Market value $7.6 million.

**ANDREWS** (9,617) county seat; trade center, amphitheatre, hospital, parks.

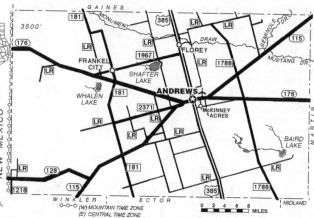

| | |
|---|---|
| Population ........................ 12,951 | July mean max. ...................... 94 |
| Change fm 2000 .................... -0.4 | Civ. Labor ......................... 5,202 |
| Area (sq. mi.) ................. 1,500.99 | Unemployed ........................... 5.9 |
| Land Area (sq. mi.) ......... 1,500.64 | Wages ..................... $31,878,439 |
| Altitude (ft.) ................. 2,900-3,500 | Av. Weekly Wage ............. $571.74 |
| Rainfall (in.) ....................... 15.4 | Prop. Value ......... $1,917,785,920 |
| Jan. mean min. ...................... 29 | Retail Sales ............... $82,351,030 |

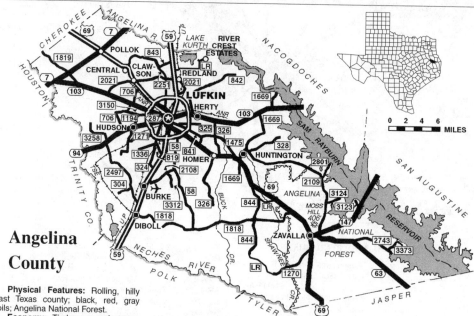

# Angelina County

**Physical Features:** Rolling, hilly East Texas county; black, red, gray soils; Angelina National Forest.

**Economy:** Timber; manufacturers of oil-field pumping units, iron and steel castings, truck trailers, mobile homes, horse stables; government/services; newsprint, other paper products, wood products, commercial printing; concrete products; cabinet works.

**History:** Caddoan area. First land deed to Vicente Micheli 1801. Anglo-American setters arrived in 1820s. County created 1846 from Nacogdoches County; named for legendary Indian maiden Angelina.

**Race/Ethnicity, 2000:** (In percent) Anglo, 69.87; Black, 14.78; Hispanic, 14.35; Other, 1.00.

**Vital Statistics, 2001:** Births, 1,264; deaths, 806; marriages, 842; divorces, 308.

**Recreation:** Sam Rayburn Reservoir; national, state forests, parks; locomotive exhibit; Forest Festival, bike ride in fall.

**Minerals:** Limited output of natural gas and oil.

**Agriculture:** Poultry, beef, horses; hay, melons, peaches, pecans. Market value $18.6 million. A leading timber-producing county.

**LUFKIN** (33,381) county seat; manufacturing; Angelina College; hospitals; U.S., Texas Forest centers; zoo; Museum of East Texas, civic center.

Other towns include: **Burke** (319); **Diboll** (5,566); **Hudson** (4,009); **Huntington** (2,096); **Pollok** (300); **Zavalla** (651).

| | |
|---|---|
| Population............................... 80,582 | |
| Change from 2000 ........................... 0.6 | |
| Area (sq. mi.)..................... 864.45 | |
| Land Area (sq. mi.).................... 801.56 | |
| Altitude (ft.) ........................ 139-406 | |
| Rainfall (in.) ........................... 38.9 | |
| Jan. mean min............................. 37 | |
| July mean max. ............................ 93 | |
| Civ. Labor............................. 36,967 | |
| Unemployed ............................... 6.6 | |
| Wages ............................. $239,715,657 | |
| Av. Weekly Wage................... $518.03 | |
| Prop. Value ............... $3,319,189,345 | |
| Retail Sales .................... $760,632,162 | |

*For explanation of sources, abbreviations and symbols, see p. 138.*

# Aransas County

**Physical Features**: Coastal plains; sandy loam, coastal clays; bays, inlets; mesquites, oaks.

**Economy:** Tourism, fishing and shrimping; oil production, refining; agriculture, offshore equipment fabricated; carbon plant.

**History:** Karankawa, Coahuiltecan area. Settlement by Irish and Mexicans began in 1829. County created 1871 from Refugio County; named for Rio Nuestra Señora de Aranzazu, derived from a Spanish palace.

**Race/Ethnicity, 2000:** (In percent) Anglo, 74.72; Black, 1.53; Hispanic, 20.32; Other, 3.43.

**Vital Statistics, 2001:** Births, 231; deaths, 262; marriages, 251; divorces, 107.

**Recreation:** Fishing, hunting, tourist facilities; Fulton Mansion; state marine lab; state park; Texas Maritime Museum; bird sanctuaries (a nationally known birding hotspot); Rockport Art Center.

**Minerals:** Oil and gas, also oyster-shell and sand.

**Agriculture:** Cow-calf operations; major crops are cotton, sorghum, corn. Market value $207,000. Fishing; redfish hatchery.

**ROCKPORT** (7,940) county seat; tourism, commercial, sport fishing; commuting to Corpus Christi and Victoria, retirement residences; Festival of Wines in May.

**Fulton** (1,593) Oysterfest in March. Part (867) of **Aransas Pass,** deepwater port on Intracoastal Waterway; oil production, refining; industrial plants; tourism; hospital.

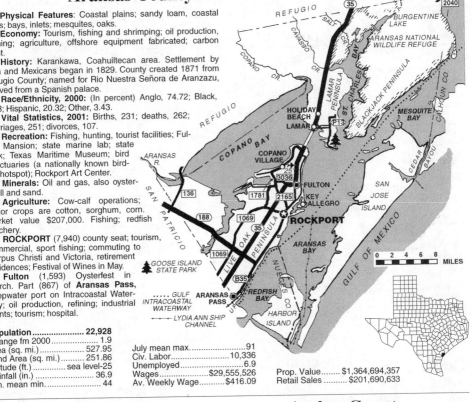

| | |
|---|---|
| Population | 22,928 |
| Change fm 2000 | 1.9 |
| Area (sq. mi.) | 527.95 |
| Land Area (sq. mi.) | 251.86 |
| Altitude (ft.) | sea level-25 |
| Rainfall (in.) | 36.9 |
| Jan. mean min. | 44 |

| | | | |
|---|---|---|---|
| July mean max. | 91 | | |
| Civ. Labor | 10,336 | | |
| Unemployed | 6.9 | | |
| Wages | $29,555,526 | Prop. Value | $1,364,694,357 |
| Av. Weekly Wage | $416.09 | Retail Sales | $201,690,633 |

# Archer County

**Physical Features:** North Central county, rolling to hilly, drained by Wichita, Trinity River forks; black, red loams, sandy soils; mesquites, post oaks.

**Economy:** Cattle; oil services. Part of Wichita Falls metropolitan area.

**History:** Caddo, Comanche, Kiowas and other tribes in area until 1875; Anglo-American settlement developed soon afterward. County created from Fannin Land District, 1858; organized 1880. Named for Dr. B.T. Archer, Republic commissioner to United States.

**Race/Ethnicity, 2000:** (In percent) Anglo, 94.19; Black, 0.15; Hispanic, 4.87; Other, 0.79.

**Vital Statistics, 2001:** Births, 102; deaths, 66; marriages, 40; divorces, 45.

**Recreation:** Lakes; hunting of dove, quail, deer, feral hog, coyote.

**Minerals:** Oil and natural gas.

**Agriculture:** Dairy, cow/calf, stocker cattle; swine; poultry; wheat, cotton. Market value $69.4 million.

**ARCHER CITY** (1,890) county seat; cattle, oil field service center; museum; book center; some manufacturing.

Other towns include: **Holliday** (1,685) Mayfest in spring; **Lakeside City** (1,017); **Megargel** (239); **Scotland** (445); **Windthorst** (441), biannual German sausage festival (also in Scotland).

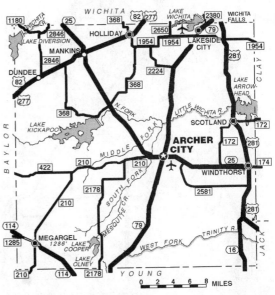

| | |
|---|---|
| Population | 8,996 |
| Change fm 2000 | 1.6 |
| Area (sq. mi.) | 925.78 |
| Land Area (sq. mi.) | 909.70 |
| Altitude (ft.) | 900-1,286 |
| Rainfall (in.) | 29.3 |

| | | | |
|---|---|---|---|
| Jan. mean min. | 29 | | |
| July mean max. | 98 | | |
| Civ. Labor | 4,422 | | |
| Unemployed | 3.0 | Prop. Value | $577,057,792 |
| Wages | $11,200,113 | Retail Sales | $44,008,665 |
| Av. Weekly Wage | $432.72 | | |

For explanation of sources, abbreviations and symbols, see p. 138.

# Armstrong County

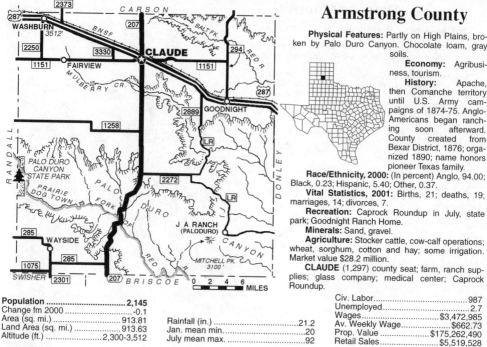

**Physical Features:** Partly on High Plains, broken by Palo Duro Canyon. Chocolate loam, gray soils.

**Economy:** Agribusiness, tourism.

**History:** Apache, then Comanche territory until U.S. Army campaigns of 1874-75. Anglo-Americans began ranching soon afterward. County created from Bexar District, 1876; organized 1890; name honors pioneer Texas family.

**Race/Ethnicity, 2000:** (In percent) Anglo, 94.00; Black, 0.23; Hispanic, 5.40; Other, 0.37.

**Vital Statistics, 2001:** Births, 21; deaths, 19; marriages, 14; divorces, 7.

**Recreation:** Caprock Roundup in July, state park; Goodnight Ranch Home.

**Minerals:** Sand, gravel.

**Agriculture:** Stocker cattle, cow-calf operations; wheat, sorghum, cotton and hay; some irrigation. Market value $28.2 million.

**CLAUDE** (1,297) county seat; farm, ranch supplies; glass company; medical center; Caprock Roundup.

| | |
|---|---|
| Population | 2,145 |
| Change fm 2000 | -0.1 |
| Area (sq. mi.) | 913.81 |
| Land Area (sq. mi.) | 913.63 |
| Altitude (ft.) | 2,300-3,512 |

| | |
|---|---|
| Rainfall (in.) | 21.2 |
| Jan. mean min. | 20 |
| July mean max. | 92 |

| | |
|---|---|
| Civ. Labor | 987 |
| Unemployed | 2.7 |
| Wages | $3,472,985 |
| Av. Weekly Wage | $662.73 |
| Prop. Value | $175,262,490 |
| Retail Sales | $5,519,528 |

# Atascosa County

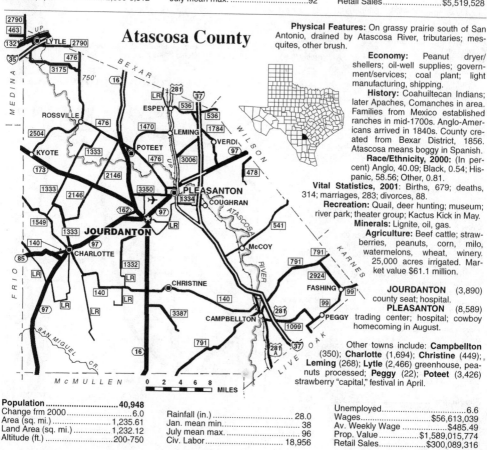

**Physical Features:** On grassy prairie south of San Antonio, drained by Atascosa River, tributaries; mesquites, other brush.

**Economy:** Peanut dryer/shellers; oil-well supplies; government/services; coal plant; light manufacturing, shipping.

**History:** Coahuiltecan Indians; later Apaches, Comanches in area. Families from Mexico established ranches in mid-1700s. Anglo-Americans arrived in 1840s. County created from Bexar District, 1856. Atascosa means boggy in Spanish.

**Race/Ethnicity, 2000:** (In percent) Anglo, 40.09; Black, 0.54; Hispanic, 58.56; Other, 0.81.

**Vital Statistics, 2001:** Births, 679; deaths, 314; marriages, 283; divorces, 88.

**Recreation:** Quail, deer hunting; museum; river park; theater group; Kactus Kick in May.

**Minerals:** Lignite, oil, gas.

**Agriculture:** Beef cattle; strawberries, peanuts, corn, milo, watermelons, wheat, winery. 25,000 acres irrigated. Market value $61.1 million.

**JOURDANTON** (3,890) county seat; hospital.

**PLEASANTON** (8,589) trading center; hospital; cowboy homecoming in August.

Other towns include: **Campbellton** (350); **Charlotte** (1,694); **Christine** (449); **Leming** (268); **Lytle** (2,466) greenhouse, peanuts processed; **Peggy** (22); **Poteet** (3,426) strawberry "capital," festival in April.

| | |
|---|---|
| Population | 40,948 |
| Change fm 2000 | 6.0 |
| Area (sq. mi.) | 1,235.61 |
| Land Area (sq. mi.) | 1,232.12 |
| Altitude (ft.) | 200-750 |

| | |
|---|---|
| Rainfall (in.) | 28.0 |
| Jan. mean min. | 38 |
| July mean max. | 96 |
| Civ. Labor | 18,956 |

| | |
|---|---|
| Unemployed | 6.6 |
| Wages | $56,613,039 |
| Av. Weekly Wage | $485.49 |
| Prop. Value | $1,589,015,774 |
| Retail Sales | $300,089,316 |

# Austin County

**Physical Features:** Southeast county; level to hilly, drained by San Bernard, Brazos rivers; black prairie to sandy upland soils.

**Economy:** Agribusiness; tourism, government/services; metal, other manufacturing; commuting to Houston.

**History:** Tonkawa Indians; reduced by diseases. Birthplace of Anglo-American colonization, 1821, and German mother colony at Industry, 1831. County created 1837; named for Stephen F. Austin, father of Texas.

**Race/Ethnicity, 2000:** (In percent) Anglo, 72.39; Black, 10.81; Hispanic, 16.13; Other, 0.67.

**Vital Statistics, 2001:** Births, 317; deaths, 285; marriages, 181; divorces, 110.

**Recreation:** Fishing, hunting; state park, Pioneer Trail; Country Livin' festival in May; Lone Star Raceway Park.

**Minerals:** Oil and natural gas.

**Agriculture:** Beef production and hay. Also, rice, corn, sorghum, nursery crops, grapes, pecans. Market value $35.1 million.

**BELLVILLE** (3,870) county seat; varied manufacturing; hospital; oil.

**SEALY** (5,510) oil-field and military vehicle manufacturing, varied industries; polka fest.

Other towns include: **Bleiblerville** (71); **Brazos Country** (450); **Cat Spring** (76); **Frydek** (150) Grotto celebration in April; **Industry** (300); **Kenney** (200); **New Ulm** (650) retail, art festival in April; **San Felipe** (913) colonial capital of Texas; **Wallis** (1,236).

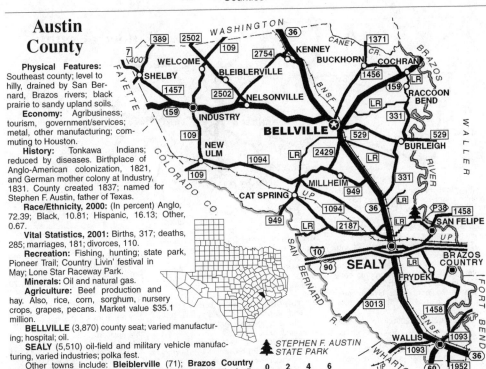

STEPHEN F. AUSTIN STATE PARK

0   2   4   6   MILES

| Population | 24,596 | | |
|---|---|---|---|
| Change fm 2000 | 4.3 | Rainfall (in.) | 40.4 |
| Area (sq. mi.) | 656.37 | Jan. mean min. | 39 |
| Land Area (sq. mi.) | 652.59 | July mean max. | 94 |
| Altitude (ft.) | 96-400 | Civ. Labor | 15,329 |

| | |
|---|---|
| Unemployed | 4.3 |
| Wages | $69,327,997 |
| Av. Weekly Wage | $618.45 |
| Prop. Value | $2,095,881,412 |
| Retail Sales | $185,400,299 |

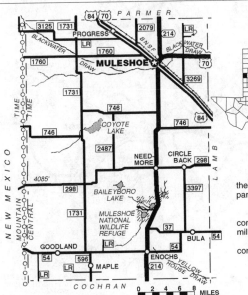

# Bailey County

**Physical Features:** High Plains county, sandy loam soils; mesquite brush; drains to draws forming upper watershed of Brazos River, playas.

**Economy:** Farm supply manufacturing; electric generating plant; food-processing plants; muffler manufacturing.

**History:** Settlement began after 1900. County created from Bexar 1876, organized 1917. Named for Alamo hero Peter J. Bailey.

**Race/Ethnicity, 2000:** (In percent) Anglo, 50.94; Black, 1.29; Hispanic, 47.30; Other, 0.47.

**Vital Statistics, 2001:** Births, 138; deaths, 56; marriages, 53; divorces, 16.

**Recreation:** Muleshoe National Wildlife Refuge; "Old Pete," the national mule memorial; outdoor drama; historical building park; museum; motorcycle rally; pheasant hunting.

**Minerals:** Insignificant.

**Agriculture:** Feedlot, dairy cattle; cotton, wheat, sorghum, corn, vegetables; 100,000 acres irrigated. Market value $150.1 million.

**MULESHOE** (4,432) county seat; agribusiness center; feed-corn milling; hospital; livestock show.

Other towns include: **Bula** (35); **Enochs** (80); **Maple** (75).

| Population | 6,480 | | |
|---|---|---|---|
| Change fm 2000 | -1.7 | Rainfall (in.) | 16.8 |
| Area (sq. mi.) | 827.38 | Jan. mean min. | 19 |
| Land Area (sq. mi.) | 826.69 | July mean max. | 92 |
| Altitude (ft.) | 3,700-4,085 | Civ. Labor | 3,412 |

| | |
|---|---|
| Unemployed | 7.1 |
| Wages | $15,176,209 |
| Av. Weekly Wage | $439.86 |
| Prop. Value | $340,304,460 |
| Retail Sales | $51,145,114 |

*For explanation of sources, abbreviations and symbols, see p. 138.*

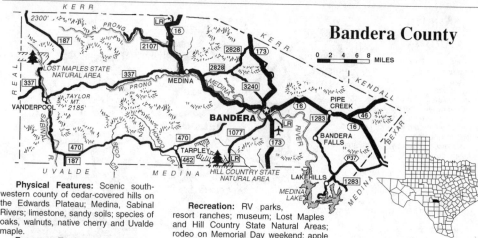

# Bandera County

**Physical Features:** Scenic south-western county of cedar-covered hills on the Edwards Plateau; Medina, Sabinal Rivers; limestone, sandy soils; species of oaks, walnuts, native cherry and Uvalde maple.

**Economy:** Tourism, hunting, fishing, ranching supplies, forest products.

**History:** Apache, then Comanche territory. White settlement began in early 1850s, including Mormons and Poles. County created from Bexar, Uvalde counties, 1856; named for Bandera (flag) Mountains.

**Race/Ethnicity, 2000:** (In percent) Anglo, 85.03; Black, 0.35; Hispanic, 13.51; Other, 1.11.

**Vital Statistics, 2001:** Births, 190; deaths, 160; marriages, 112; divorces, 79.

**Recreation:** RV parks, resort ranches; museum; Lost Maples and Hill Country State Natural Areas; rodeo on Memorial Day weekend; apple festival in August, Cajun festival in September; Medina Lake.

**Agriculture:** Beef cattle, sheep, goats, horses, apples. Market value $5.3 million. Hunting and nature tourism important.

**BANDERA** (1,000) county seat; "cowboy capital of the world"; cedar mill, shingle factory; purse factory; spurs, bits manufactured.

Other towns include: **Medina** (515) apple growing; **Pipe Creek** (NA); **Tarpley** (30); **Vanderpool** (20). Also, the community of **Lakehills** (4,856) on Medina Lake.

| | |
|---|---|
| Population | **19,153** |
| Change fm 2000 | 8.5 |
| Area (sq. mi.) | 797.54 |
| Land Area (sq. mi.) | 791.73 |
| Altitude (ft.) | 1,064-2,300 |
| Rainfall (in.) | 35.1 |
| Jan. mean min. | 31 |
| July mean max. | 94 |
| Civ. Labor | 9,177 |
| Unemployed | 3.1 |
| Wages | $ 14,087,130 |
| Av. Weekly Wage | $ 430.01 |
| Prop. Value | $1,382,376,680 |
| Retail Sales | $91,877,168 |

---

# Bastrop County

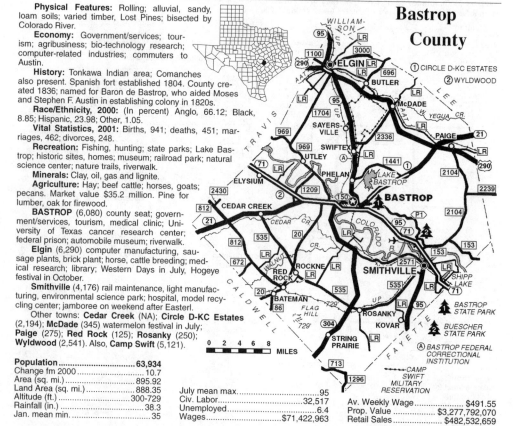

**Physical Features:** Rolling; alluvial, sandy, loam soils; varied timber, Lost Pines; bisected by Colorado River.

**Economy:** Government/services; tourism; agribusiness; bio-technology research; computer-related industries; commuters to Austin.

**History:** Tonkawa Indian area; Comanches also present. Spanish fort established 1804. County created 1836; named for Baron de Bastrop, who aided Moses and Stephen F. Austin in establishing colony in 1820s.

**Race/Ethnicity, 2000:** (In percent) Anglo, 66.12; Black, 8.85; Hispanic, 23.98; Other, 1.05.

**Vital Statistics, 2001:** Births, 941; deaths, 451; marriages, 462; divorces, 248.

**Recreation:** Fishing, hunting; state parks; Lake Bastrop; historic sites, homes; museum; railroad park; natural science center; nature trails, riverwalk.

**Minerals:** Clay, oil, gas and lignite.

**Agriculture:** Hay; beef cattle; horses, goats; pecans. Market value $35.2 million. Pine for lumber, oak for firewood.

**BASTROP** (6,080) county seat; government/services, tourism, medical clinic; University of Texas cancer research center; federal prison; automobile museum; riverwalk.

**Elgin** (6,290) computer manufacturing, sausage plants, brick plant; horse, cattle breeding; medical research; library; Western Days in July, Hogeye festival in October.

**Smithville** (4,176) rail maintenance, light manufacturing, environmental science park; hospital, model recycling center; jamboree on weekend after Easter!.

Other towns: **Cedar Creek** (NA); **Circle D-KC Estates** (2,194); **McDade** (345) watermelon festival in July; **Paige** (275); **Red Rock** (125); **Rosanky** (250); **Wyldwood** (2,541). Also, **Camp Swift** (5,121).

| | |
|---|---|
| Population | **63,934** |
| Change fm 2000 | 10.7 |
| Area (sq. mi.) | 895.92 |
| Land Area (sq. mi.) | 888.35 |
| Altitude (ft.) | 300-729 |
| Rainfall (in.) | 38.3 |
| Jan. mean min. | 35 |
| July mean max. | 95 |
| Civ. Labor | 32,517 |
| Unemployed | 6.4 |
| Wages | $71,422,963 |
| Av. Weekly Wage | $491.55 |
| Prop. Value | $3,277,792,070 |
| Retail Sales | $482,532,659 |

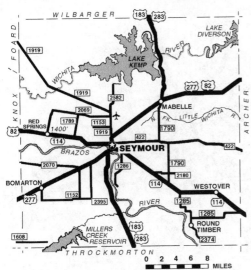

# Baylor County

**Physical Features:** North Central county; level to hilly; drains to Brazos, Wichita rivers; sandy, loam, red soils; grassy, mesquites, cedars.

**Economy:** Agribusiness; retail/service; health services.

**History:** Comanches, with Wichitas and other tribes; removed in 1874-75. Anglo-Americans settled in the 1870s. County created from Fannin County 1858; organized 1879. Named for H.W. Baylor, Texas Ranger surgeon.

**Race/Ethnicity, 2000:** (In percent) Anglo, 86.22; Black, 3.40; Hispanic, 9.33; Other, 1.05.

**Vital Statistics, 2001:** Births, 42; deaths, 79; marriages, 28; divorces, 9.

**Recreation:** Lakes; hunting; park, pavilions; settlers reunion, fish day in spring, autumn leaves festival in October.

**Minerals:** Oil, gas produced.

**Agriculture:** Cattle, cow-calf operations; wheat, cotton, grain sorghum, hay. Market value $32.2 million.

**SEYMOUR** (2,904) county seat; agribusiness; hospital; dove hunters' breakfast in September.

| | | |
|---|---|---|
| Population ................................... 3,929 | Rainfall (in.) ................................. 27.3 | Wages ............................. $5,461,094 |
| Change fm 2000 ........................... -4.0 | Jan. mean min. .............................. 26 | Av. Weekly Wage .................. $371.76 |
| Area (sq. mi.) ............................ 901.01 | July mean max. .............................. 97 | Prop. Value................... $263,985,403 |
| Land Area (sq. mi.) .................. 870.77 | Civ. Labor ................................. 1,676 | Retail Sales .................... $27,274,185 |
| Altitude (ft.) ....................... 1,053-1,400 | Unemployed ................................. 4.9 | |

# Bee County

**Physical Features:** South Coastal Plain, level to rolling; black clay, sandy, loam soils; brushy.

**Economy:** Agricluture, government/ services; hunting leases; oil and gas business.

**History:** Karankawa, Apache, Pawnee territory. First Spanish land grant, 1789. Irish settlers arrived 1826-29. County created from Karnes, Live Oak, Goliad, Refugio, San Patricio, 1857; organized 1858; named for Gen. Barnard Bee.

**Race/Ethnicity, 2000:** (In percent) Anglo, 35.53; Black, 9.79; Hispanic, 53.93; Other, 0.75.

**Vital Statistics, 2001:** Births, 394; deaths, 246; marriages, 223; divorces, 110.

**Recreation:** Hunting, camping; historical sites, antiques; Family Fall Fest.

**Minerals:** Oil, gas produced.

**Agriculture:** Beef cattle, corn, cotton and grain sorghhum. Market value $31.1 million. Hunting leases.

**BEEVILLE** (13,118) county seat; retail center; prison units, training academy; Costal Bend College; hospital, art museum; Cinco de Mayo, Diez y Seis festivals.

Other towns and places include: **Blue Berry Hill** (1,009); **Mineral** (50); **Normanna** (125); **Pawnee** (207); **Pettus** (625); **Skidmore** (1,041); **Tuleta** (301); **Tynan** (309).

| | |
|---|---|
| Population................................ 32,277 | Rainfall (in.) ................................. 32.1 |
| Change fm 2000........................... -0.3 | Jan. mean min. .............................. 41 |
| Area (sq. mi.) ........................... 880.31 | July mean max. .............................. 94 |
| Land Area (sq. mi.).................... 880.14 | Civ. Labor .............................. 10,732 |
| Altitude (ft.)................................ 87-500 | Unemployed ................................. 6.3 |
| | Wages ......................... $49,985,059 |
| | Av. Weekly Wage.................. $469.42 |
| | Prop. Value ................... $971,928,880 |
| | Retail Sales .................. $161,666,557 |

① BLUE BERRY HILL

For explanation of sources, abbreviations and symbols, see p. 138.

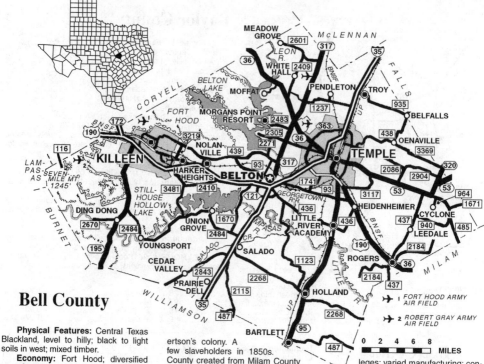

# Bell County

**Physical Features:** Central Texas Blackland, level to hilly; black to light soils in west; mixed timber.

**Economy:** Fort Hood; diversified manufacturing includes computers, plastic goods, furniture, clothing; agribusiness; distribution center; tourism.

**History:** Tonkawas, Lipan Apaches; reduced by disease and advancing frontier by 1840s. Comanches raided into 1870s. Settled in 1830s as part of Robertson's colony. A few slaveholders in 1850s. County created from Milam County in 1850; named for Gov. P.H. Bell.

| | |
|---|---|
| Population | 244,668 |
| Change fm 2000 | 2.8 |
| Area (sq. mi.) | 1,087.93 |
| Land Area (sq. mi.) | 1,059.72 |
| Altitude (ft.) | 400-1,245 |
| Rainfall (in.) | 34.9 |
| Jan. mean min. | 35 |
| July mean max. | 95 |
| Civ. Labor | 101,991 |
| Unemployed | 5.4 |
| Wages | $617,254,429 |
| Av. Weekly Wage | $534.49 |
| Prop. Value | $7,479,147,782 |
| Retail Sales | $2,476,711,577 |

**Race/Ethnicity, 2000:** (In percent) Anglo, 58.38; Black, 20.93; Hispanic, 16.68; Other, 4.01.

**Vital Statistics, 2001:** Births, 5,328; deaths, 1,540; marriages, 3,720; divorces, 1,821.

**Recreation:** Fishing, hunting; lakes; historic sites; exposition center; Salado gathering of Scottish clans in November.

**Minerals:** Gravel.

**Agriculture:** Beef, corn, sorghum, wheat, cotton. Market value $60 million.

**BELTON** (15,078) county seat; University of Mary Hardin-Baylor; manufactures include school and office furniture, roofing felt, athletic equipment; museum; Festival on Nolan Creek in July.

**KILLEEN** (91,852) Fort Hood; colleges; varied manufacturing; convention facilities; medical center, psychiatric center; plantetarium.

**TEMPLE** (55,437) Major medical center with two hospitals and VA hospital; diversified industries; rail, wholesale distribution center; retail center; Temple College; Czech museum; early-day tractor, engine show in October.

Other towns include: **Harker Heights** (17,872) Founder's Day in October; **Heidenheimer** (144); **Holland** (1,120) corn festival in June; **Little River-Academy** (1,763); **Morgan's Point Resort** (3,236); **Nolanville** (2,166); **Pendelton** (60); **Rogers** (1,124); **Salado** (3,606) tourism, art fair in August; library; **Troy** (1,384).

Also, part of **Bartlett** (1,699) is in Bell County.

**Fort Hood** has a population of 33,501.

# Bexar County

**Physical Features:** On edge of Balcones Escarpment, Coastal Plain; heavy black to thin limestone soils; spring-fed streams; underground water; mesquite, other brush.

**Economy:** Government center with large federal payroll, military bases; tourism second-largest industry; developing high-tech industrial park, research center; education center with 14 colleges.

**History:** Coahuiltecan Indian area; also Lipan Apaches and Tonkawas present. Mission San Antonio de Valero (Alamo) founded in 1718. Canary Islanders arrived in 1731. Anglo-Ameri-

*Dancers perform in Alamo Plaza during Fiesta. File photo.*

*For explanation of sources, abbreviations and symbols, see p. 138.*

can settlers began arriving in late 1820s. County created 1836 from Spanish municipality named for Duke de Bexar; a colonial capital of Texas.

**Race/Ethnicity, 2000:** (In percent) Anglo, 36.33; Black, 7.20; Hispanic, 54.35; Other, 2.12.

**Vital Statistics, 2001:** Births, 23,742; deaths, 9,995; marriages, 12,886; divorces, 4,386.

**Recreation:** Historic sites include the Alamo, other missions, Casa Navarro, La Villita; Riverwalk; El Mercado (market); Tower of the Americas; Brackenridge Park; zoo; Seaworld; symphony orchestra; HemisFair Plaza; Fiesta in April; Institute of Texan Cultures; Folklife Festival in June; parks, museums; hunting, fishing.

**Minerals:** Gravel, sand, limestone, some oil & gas.

**Agriculture:** Nursery crops, hay, beef cattle, corn, grain sorghum, small grains, peanuts, vegetables; some irrigation. Market value $126.6 million.

**Education:** Fourteen colleges

including Our Lady of the Lake, St. Mary's University, Trinity University and the University of Texas at San Antonio.

**SAN ANTONIO** (1,182,840) county seat; Texas' third largest city; varied manufacturing with emphasis on high-tech industries; other products include construction equipment, concrete and dairy products; industrial warehousing.

Other towns include: **Alamo Heights** (7,330); **Balcones Heights** (2,853); **Castle Hills** (4,228); **China Grove** (1,308); **Converse** (11,932);

**Elmendorf** (662); **Fair Oaks Ranch** (5,042); **Grey Forest** (443) **Helotes** (4,645); **Hill Country Village** (1,121); **Hollywood Park** (3,021); **Kirby** (8,761); **Leon Valley** (9,213); **Live Oak** (9,052); **Olmos Park** (2,373); **St. Hedwig** (1,931); **Selma** (961, parts in Guadalupe and Comal counties); **Shavano Park** (1,809); **Somerset** (1,628); **Terrell Hills** (4,970); **Universal City** (15,190); **Windcrest** (5,072). Part (1,045) of **Schertz**.

| | |
|---|---|
| Population | 1,446,333 |
| Change fm 2000 | 3.8 |
| Area (sq. mi.) | 1,256.66 |
| Land Area (sq. mi.) | 1,246.82 |
| Altitude (ft.) | 486-1,892 |
| Rainfall (in.) | 31.0 |
| Jan. mean min. | 38 |
| July mean max. | 95 |
| Civ. Labor | 714,487 |
| Unemployed | 5.2 |
| Wages | $5,032,418,687 |
| Av. Weekly Wage | $591.71 |
| Fed. Wages | $347,876,629 |
| Prop. Value | $55,949,036,296 |
| Retail Sales | $17,787,076,678 |

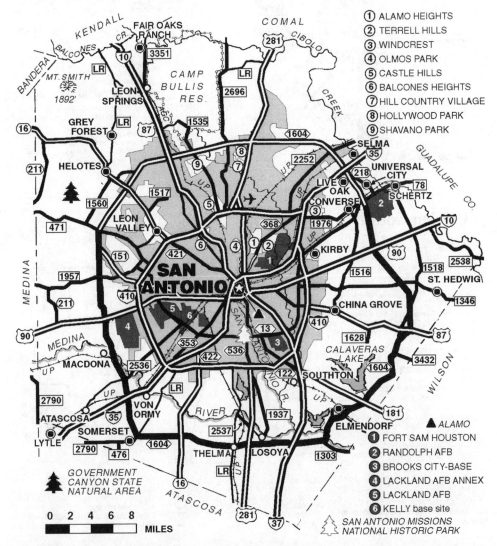

① ALAMO HEIGHTS
② TERRELL HILLS
③ WINDCREST
④ OLMOS PARK
⑤ CASTLE HILLS
⑥ BALCONES HEIGHTS
⑦ HILL COUNTRY VILLAGE
⑧ HOLLYWOOD PARK
⑨ SHAVANO PARK

▲ ALAMO

❶ FORT SAM HOUSTON
❷ RANDOLPH AFB
❸ BROOKS CITY-BASE
❹ LACKLAND AFB ANNEX
❺ LACKLAND AFB
❻ KELLY base site

SAN ANTONIO MISSIONS NATIONAL HISTORIC PARK

GOVERNMENT CANYON STATE NATURAL AREA

0 2 4 6 8 MILES

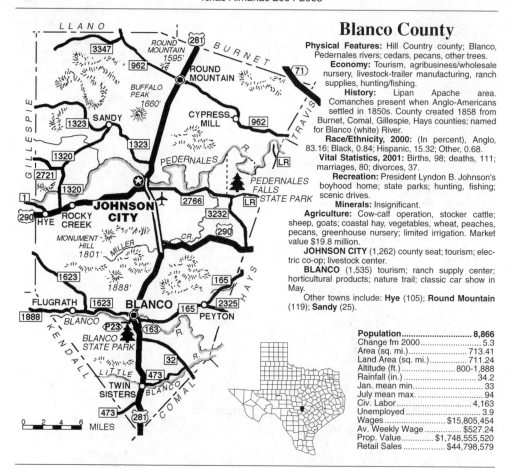

# Blanco County

**Physical Features:** Hill Country county; Blanco, Pedernales rivers; cedars, pecans, other trees.

**Economy:** Tourism, agribusiness/wholesale nursery, livestock-trailer manufacturing, ranch supplies, hunting/fishing.

**History:** Lipan Apache area. Comanches present when Anglo-Americans settled in 1850s. County created 1858 from Burnet, Comal, Gillespie, Hays counties; named for Blanco (white) River.

**Race/Ethnicity, 2000:** (In percent), Anglo, 83.16; Black, 0.84; Hispanic, 15.32; Other, 0.68.

**Vital Statistics, 2001:** Births, 98; deaths, 111; marriages, 80; divorces, 37.

**Recreation:** President Lyndon B. Johnson's boyhood home; state parks; hunting, fishing; scenic drives.

**Minerals:** Insignificant.

**Agriculture:** Cow-calf operation, stocker cattle; sheep, goats; coastal hay, vegetables, wheat, peaches, pecans, greenhouse nursery; limited irrigation. Market value $19.8 million.

**JOHNSON CITY** (1,262) county seat; tourism; electric co-op; livestock center.

**BLANCO** (1,535) tourism; ranch supply center; horticultural products; nature trail; classic car show in May.

Other towns include: **Hye** (105); **Round Mountain** (119); **Sandy** (25).

| | |
|---|---|
| Population | **8,866** |
| Change fm 2000 | 5.3 |
| Area (sq. mi.) | 713.41 |
| Land Area (sq. mi.) | 711.24 |
| Altitude (ft.) | 800-1,888 |
| Rainfall (in.) | 34.2 |
| Jan. mean min. | 33 |
| July mean max. | 94 |
| Civ. Labor | 4,163 |
| Unemployed | 3.9 |
| Wages | $15,805,454 |
| Av. Weekly Wage | $527.24 |
| Prop. Value | $1,748,555,520 |
| Retail Sales | $44,798,579 |

# Borden County

**Physical Features:** West Texas county of rolling surface, broken by Caprock Escarpment; drains to Colorado River; sandy loam, clay soils.

**Economy:** Agriculture and hunting leases; oil.

**History:** Comanche area. Anglo-Americans settled in 1870s. County created 1876 from Bexar District, organized 1891; named for Gail Borden, patriot, inventor, editor.

**Race/Ethnicity, 2000:** (In percent) Anglo, 87.52; Black, 0.14; Hispanic, 11.93; Other, 0.41.

**Vital Statistics, 2001:** Births, 2; deaths, 4; marriages, 2; divorces, 3.

**Recreation:** Fishing and quail, deer hunting; Lake J.B. Thomas; museum; Coyote Opry in September; junior livestock show in January.

**Minerals:** Oil, gas, caliche, sand, gravel.

**Agriculture:** Beef cattle, cotton, milo, oats, hay, pecans; some irrigation. Market value $9.6 million.

**GAIL** (189) county seat; museum; antique shop, ambulance service; "star" construction atop Gail Mountain.

| | |
|---|---|
| Population | **701** |
| Change fm 2000 | -3.8 |

*For explanation of sources, abbreviations and symbols, see p. 138.*

| | |
|---|---|
| Area (sq. mi.) | 906.04 |
| Land Area (sq. mi.) | 898.80 |
| Altitude (ft.) | 2,258-3,000 |
| Rainfall (in.) | 16.9 |
| Jan. mean min. | 31 |
| July mean max. | 94 |

| | |
|---|---|
| Civ. Labor | 364 |
| Unemployed | 6.0 |
| Wages | $825,094 |
| Av. Weekly Wage | $456.61 |
| Prop. Value | $375,436,196 |
| Retail Sales | $245,308 |

# Bosque County

**Physical Features:** North Central county; hilly, broken by Brazos, Bosque rivers; limestone to alluvial soils; cedars, oaks, mesquites.

**Economy:** Agribusiness, government/services, tourism, small industries.

**History:** Tonkawa, Waco and Tawakoni Indians. Settlers from England and Norway arrived in 1850s. County created 1854 from Milam District, McLennan County; named for Bosque (woods) River.

**Race/Ethnicity, 2000:** (In percent) Anglo, 85.10; Black, 2.02; Hispanic, 12.23; Other, 0.65.

**Vital Statistics, 2001:** Births, 215; deaths, 276; marriages, 116; divorces, 86.

**Recreation:** Lake, state park, museum at Clifton, conservatory of fine art; fishing, hunting; scenic routes, Norwegian smorgasbord at Norse in November.

**Minerals:** Limestone.

**Agriculture:** Cattle, hunting, wheat and oats, forages, turkeys, feed grains, horses. Market value $54.5 million.

**MERIDIAN** (1,529) county seat; distribution center; varied manufacturing.

**CLIFTON** (3,602) tourism; trade center; light manufacturing; hospital; library.

Other towns include: **Cranfills Gap** (354) Lutefisk dinner in December; **Iredell** (380); **Kopperl** (225); **Morgan** (498); **Valley Mills** (1,124); **Walnut Springs** (784).

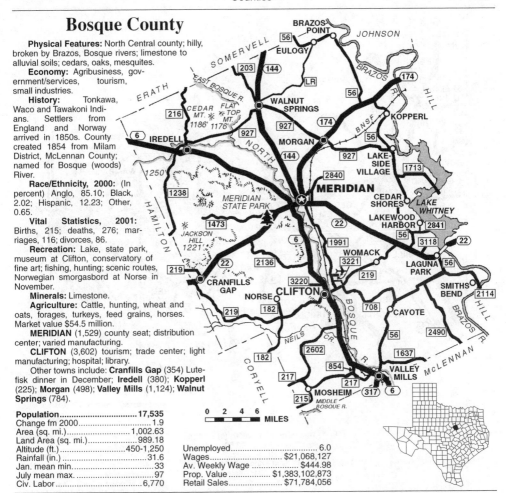

| | |
|---|---|
| Population | 17,535 |
| Change fm 2000 | 1.9 |
| Area (sq. mi.) | 1,002.63 |
| Land Area (sq. mi.) | 989.18 |
| Altitude (ft.) | 450-1,250 |
| Rainfall (in.) | 31.6 |
| Jan. mean min. | 33 |
| July mean max. | 97 |
| Civ. Labor | 6,770 |

| | |
|---|---|
| Unemployed | 6.0 |
| Wages | $21,068,127 |
| Av. Weekly Wage | $444.98 |
| Prop. Value | $1,383,102,873 |
| Retail Sales | $71,784,056 |

*U.S. Highway 180 runs through Gail in Borden County. File photo.*

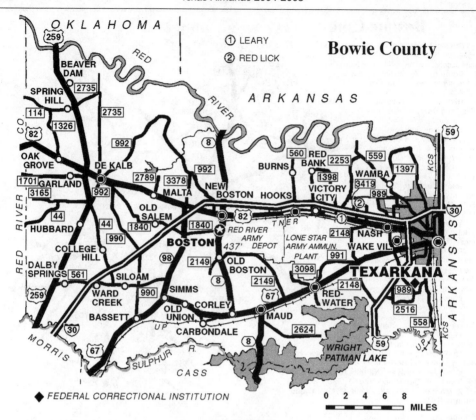

① LEARY
② RED LICK

# Bowie County

◆ FEDERAL CORRECTIONAL INSTITUTION

0  2  4  6  8
MILES

**Physical Features:** Forested hills at northeast corner of state; clay, sandy, alluvial soils; drained by Red and Sulphur rivers.

**Economy:** Government/services, lumber mills, manufacturing, agribusiness.

**History:** Caddo area, abandoned in 1790s after trouble with Osage tribe. Anglo-Americans began arriving 1815-20. County created 1840 from Red River County; named for Alamo hero James Bowie.

**Race/Ethnicity, 2000:** (In percent) Anglo, 70.83; Black, 23.58; Hispanic, 4.47; Other, 1.12.

**Vital Statistics, 2001:** Births, 1,105; deaths, 984; marriages, 634; divorces, 500.

**Recreation:** Lakes, Crystal Springs beach; hunting, fishing, historic sites; Four-States Fair in September, Red Neck Day in July, Octoberfest.

**Minerals:** Oil, gas, sand, gravel.

**Agriculture:** Beef cattle, hay, dairy, corn, soybeans, wheat, poultry, pecans, milo, rice, nurseries, truck crops, horses, goats. Market value $46.3 million. Pine timber, hardwoods, pulpwood harvested.

**BOSTON** (200) county seat (but courthouse now located in New Boston).

**TEXARKANA** (35,037 in Texas, 26,448 in Arkansas) distribution, manufacturing, hospitals; tourism; colleges; federal correctional unit; Quadrangle Festival in September, Perot Theatre.

**New Boston** (4,820) site of county courthouse; steel manufactured; agri-business; lumber mill; state prison unit; Pioneer Days in August.

Other towns include: **De Kalb** (1,748) agriculture, government/services, commuting to Texarkana, Oktoberfest; **Hooks** (3,020); **Leary** (559); **Maud** (1,035); **Nash** (2,138); **Red Lick** (878); **Redwater** (886); **Simms** (240); **Wake Village** (5,340).

| | |
|---|---|
| **Population** | **89,894** |
| Change fm 2000 | 0.7 |
| Area (sq. mi.) | 922.77 |
| Land Area (sq. mi.) | 887.87 |
| Altitude (ft.) | 200-437 |
| Rainfall (in.) | 45.3 |
| Jan. mean min. | 35 |
| July mean max. | 93 |
| Civ. Labor | 40,990 |
| Unemployed | 5.2 |
| Wages | $271,864,420 |
| Av. Weekly Wage | $539.76 |
| Prop. Value | $3,437,171,741 |
| Retail Sales | $1,024,381,299 |

*For explanation of sources, abbreviations and symbols, see p.138.*

# Brazoria County

**Physical Features:** Flat Coastal Plain, coastal soils, drained by Brazos and San Bernard rivers.

**Economy:** Petroleum and chemical industry; fishing; tourism; agribusiness. Part of Houston metropolitan area.

**History:** Karankawa area. Part of Austin's "Old Three Hundred" colony of families arriving in early 1820s. County created 1836 from Municipality of Brazoria; name derived from Brazos River.

**Race/Ethnicity, 2000:** (In percent) Anglo, 66.09; Black, 8.58; Hispanic, 22.78; Other, 2.55.

**Vital Statistics, 2001:** Births, 4,146; deaths, 1,692; marriages, 1,616; divorces, 1,260.

**Recreation:** Water sports; fishing; hunting; wildlife refuges, historic sites; state and county parks; replica of the first capitol of the Republic of Texas at West Columbia.

**Minerals:** Oil, gas, sand, gravel.

**Agriculture:** Cattle, hay, rice, soybeans, sorghum, nursery, corn, cotton, aquaculture. 20,000 acres of rice irrigated. Market value $53.6 million.

**ANGLETON** (18,370) county seat; banking, distribution center for oil, chemical, agricultural area; fish-processing plant; hospital.

**BRAZOSPORT** (57,469) is a community of eight cities; chemical complex; deepwater seaport; commercial fishing; tourism; college; hospital; Brazosport cities include: **Clute** (10,453) mosquito festival in July, **Freeport** (12,773) fishing fiesta in July, **Jones Creek** (2,032), **Lake Jackson** (26,970), **Oyster Creek** (1,197), **Quintana** (38), **Richwood** (3,139), **Surfside Beach** (817).

**ALVIN** (21,608) petrochemical processing; agribusiness; rail, trucking; junior college; hospital; Rice & Crawfest in March; Nolan Ryan museum.

**PEARLAND** (40,951, partly in Harris County) rail, trucking, oilfield, chemical production; commuting to Houston, NASA; community college.

Other towns include: **Bailey's Prairie** (729); **Bonney** (387); **Brazoria** (2,740), library; No-Name Festival in June; **Brookside Village** (2,005); **Damon** (562); **Danbury** (1,699), **Danciger** (357); **Hillcrest Village** (727); **Holiday Lakes** (1,147); **Iowa Colony** (799); **Liverpool** (416); **Manvel** (3,153), **Old Ocean** (915); **Rosharon** (435); **Sweeny** (3,668) petrochemicals, agriculture, grass farming, hospital, library, Pride Day in May, Levi Jordan Plantation; **West Columbia** (4,258) chemical companies; cattle, rice farming; museum, historic sites, plantation; San Jacinto Festival.

| | |
|---|---|
| **Population** | **257,256** |
| Change fm 2000 | 6.4 |
| Area (sq. mi.) | 1,597.44 |
| Land Area (sq. mi.) | 1,386.40 |
| Altitude (ft.) | sea level-146 |
| Rainfall (in.) | 56.4 |
| Jan. mean min. | 41 |
| July mean max. | 92 |
| Civ. Labor | 112,362 |
| Unemployed | 8.3 |
| Wages | $667,650,616 |
| Av. Weekly Wage | $682.75 |
| Prop. Value | $16,718,773,284 |
| Retail Sales | $2,078,650,390 |

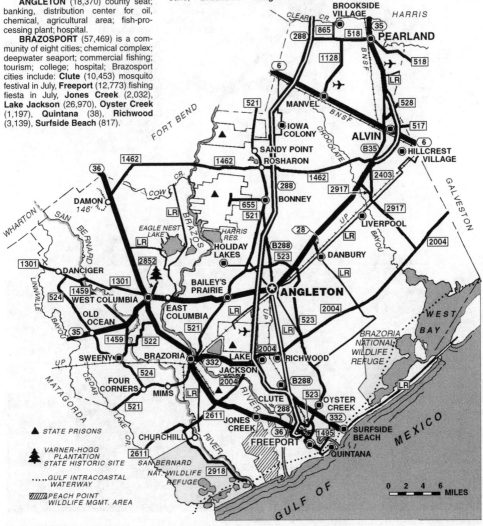

▲ STATE PRISONS

🌲 VARNER-HOGG PLANTATION STATE HISTORIC SITE

..... GULF INTRACOASTAL WATERWAY

▨▨▨ PEACH POINT WILDLIFE MGMT. AREA

# Brazos County

**Physical Features:** South Central county between Brazos, Navasota rivers; rich bottom soils, sandy, clays on rolling uplands; oak trees.

**Economy:** Texas A&M University; market and medical center; agribusiness; computers, research and development; government/services; winery; industrial parks; tourism.

**History:** Bidais and Tonkawas; Comanches hunted in area. Part of Stephen F. Austin's second colony, late 1820s. County created 1841 from Robertson, Washington counties and named Navasota; renamed for Brazos River in 1842, organized 1843.

**Race/Ethnicity, 2000:** (In percent) Anglo, 66.79; Black, 10.80; Hispanic, 17.88; Other, 4.53.

**Vital Statistics, 2001:** Births, 2,210; deaths, 748; marriages, 1,444; divorces, 305.

**Recreation:** Fishing, hunting; raceway; many events related to Texas A&M activities; George Bush Presidential Library and Museum; winery harvest weekends in August.

**Minerals:** Sand and gravel, lignite, gas, oil.

**Agriculture:** Cattle, eggs; cotton, hay, corn, sorghum; horses. Market value $40.5 million.

**BRYAN** (66,754) county seat; defense electronics, other varied manufacturing; agribusiness center; hospital, psychiatric facilities; Blinn College extension.

**COLLEGE STATION** (70,607) home of Texas A&M University, varied high-tech manufacturing; research; hospitals.

Other towns include: **Kurten** (231); **Millican** (104); **Wellborn** (100); **Wixon Valley** (241).

| | |
|---|---|
| Population | 156,099 |
| Change fm 2000 | 2.4 |
| Area (sq. mi.) | 590.29 |
| Land Area (sq. mi.) | 585.78 |
| Altitude (ft.) | 197-400 |
| Rainfall (in.) | 39.1 |
| Jan. mean min. | 39 |
| July mean max. | 94 |
| Civ. Labor | 84,289 |
| Unemployed | 1.9 |
| Wages | $486,544,770 |
| Av. Weekly Wage | $499.70 |
| Prop. Value | $6,106,973,134 |
| Retail Sales | $1,688,912,207 |

*The Agua Adentro Mountains rise over some saddles in Big Bend Ranch State Park. File photo.*

# Brewster County

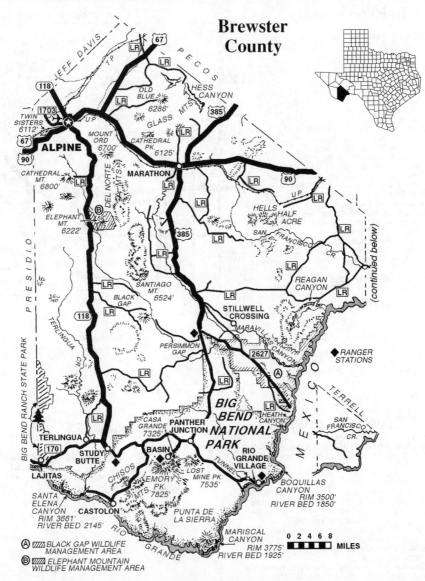

Ⓐ ▨ BLACK GAP WILDLIFE
      MANAGEMENT AREA
Ⓑ ▨ ELEPHANT MOUNTAIN
      WILDLIFE MANAGEMENT AREA

**Physical Features:** Largest county, with area slightly less than that of Connecticut plus Rhode Island; mountains, canyons, distinctive geology, plant life, animals.

**Economy:** Tourism, Sul Ross State University; ranching; government/services; retirement developments; hunting leases.

**History:** Pueblo culture had begun when Spanish explored in 1500s. Mescalero Apaches in Chisos; Comanches raided in area. Ranching developed in northern part 1880s; Mexican agricultural communites along river. County created 1887 from Presidio County; named for Henry P. Brewster, Republic secretary of war.

**Race/Ethnicity, 2000:** (In percent) Anglo, 54.08; Black, 1.12; Hispanic, 43.62; Other, 1.18.

**Vital Statistics, 2001:** Births, 114; deaths, 81; marriages, 98; divorces, 0.

**Recreation:** Big Bend National Park; Big Bend Ranch State Park; ghost towns; scenic drives; museum; rockhound areas; November chili cookoff at Terlingua; cavalry post, Barton Warnock Environmental Education Center at Lajitas; hunting.

**Minerals:** Bentonite.

**Agriculture:** Beef cattle, pecans, apples, hunting. Market value $12.2 million.

**ALPINE** (5,848) county seat; ranch trade center; tourism; Sul Ross State University; hospital; varied manufacturing.

**Marathon** (483) tourism, ranching center, Marathon Basin quilt show in October. Also, **Big Bend National Park** (194) and **Study Butte-Terlingua** (271).

| | |
|---|---:|
| Population | 9,009 |
| Change fm 2000 | 1.6 |
| Area (sq. mi.) | 6,192.78 |
| Land Area (sq. mi.) | 6,192.61 |
| Altitude (ft.) | 1,700-7,825 |
| Rainfall (in.) | 16.9 |
| Jan. mean min. | 30 |
| July mean max. | 89 |
| Civ. Labor | 6,169 |
| Unemployed | 2.0 |
| Wages | $25,691,961 |
| Av. Weekly Wage | $466.11 |
| Prop. Value | $534,986,821 |
| Retail Sales | $76,255,181 |

*For explanation of sources, abbreviations and symbols, see p. 138.*

# Briscoe County

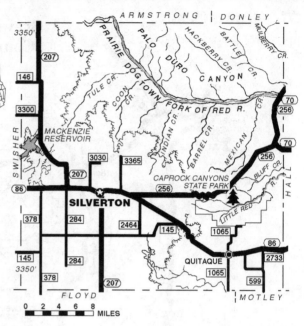

**Physical Features:** Partly on High Plains, broken by Caprock Escarpment, fork of Red River; sandy, loam soils.

**Economy:** Agribusiness, government/services.

**History:** Apaches, displaced by Comanches around 1700. Ranchers settled in 1880s. County created from Bexar District, 1876, organized 1892; named for Andrew Briscoe, Republic of Texas soldier.

**Race/Ethnicity, 2000:** (In percent) Anglo, 74.58; Black, 2.40; Hispanic, 22.74; Other, 0.28.

**Vital Statistics, 2001:** Births, 22; deaths, 21; marriages, 14; divorces, 7.

**Recreation:** Hunting, fishing; scenic drives; museum; state park, Mackenzie Reservoir.

**Minerals:** Insignificant.

**Agriculture:** Cotton, cow/calf, stocker cattle, sorghum, wheat, hay. Some 32,000 acres irrigated. Market value $17 million.

**SILVERTON** (773) county seat; agribusiness center; irrigation supplies manufactured; clinics.

**Quitaque** (433) trade center.

| | | |
|---|---|---|
| Population ................................. 1,716 | Rainfall (in.) ................................. 21.4 | Unemployed ................................. 4.3 |
| Change fm 2000 ........................... -4.1 | Jan. mean min. ................................. 20 | Wages ............................... $2,106,653 |
| Area (sq. mi.) ........................... 901.59 | July mean max. ................................. 91 | Av. Weekly Wage .................. $350.00 |
| Land Area (sq. mi.) ................... 900.25 | Civ. Labor ..................................... 811 | Prop. Value ................... $107,182,090 |
| Altitude (ft.) ...................... 2,100-3,350 | | Retail Sales ..................... $5,077,411 |

# Brooks County

**Physical Features:** On Rio Grande plain near Gulf; level to rolling; brushy; light to dark sandy loam soils.

**Economy:** Oil, gas, cattle, hunting leases, watermelons.

**History:** Coahuiltecan Indians. Spanish land grants date to around 1800. County created from Hidalgo, Starr, Zapata counties, 1911. Named for J.A. Brooks, Texas Ranger and legislator.

**Race/Ethnicity, 2000:** (In percent) Anglo, 8.04; Black, 0.06; Hispanic, 91.57; Other, 0.33.

**Vital Statistics, 2001:** Births, 131; deaths, 71; marriages, 40; divorces, 4.

**Recreation:** Hunting, fishing; Heritage Museum, Don Pedrito Shrine; fiestas, May and October.

**Minerals:** Oil, gas production.

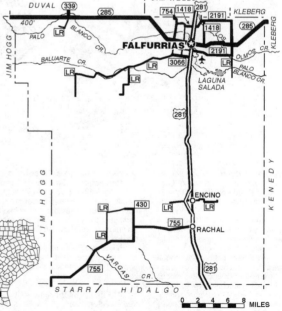

**Agriculture:** Beef cowcalf operations, stocker; crops include watermelons, grain sorghums, hay. Market value $15.2 million.

**FALFURRIAS** (5,186) county seat; agricultural market center, cattle, watermelons; government/services; heritage museum.

Other towns include: **Encino** (169).

| | | |
|---|---|---|
| Population ................................. 7,766 | Jan. mean min. ................................. 43 | Prop. Value ................... $705,718,493 |
| Change fm 2000 ........................... - 2.6 | July mean max. ................................. 97 | Retail Sales ..................... $53,143,450 |
| Area (sq. mi.) ........................... 943.61 | Civ. Labor ................................... 3,611 | |
| Land Area (sq. mi.) ................... 943.28 | Unemployed ................................... 7.4 | |
| Altitude (ft.) ............................... 46-400 | Wages ............................. $13,111,749 | *For explanation of sources, abbreviations* |
| Rainfall (in.) ................................. 25.9 | Av. Weekly Wage ................... $400.40 | *and symbols, see p. 138.* |

# Brown County

**Physical Features:** Rolling, hilly; drains to Colorado River; varied soils, timber.

**Economy:** Manufacturing plants, distribution center; government/services; agribusiness.

**History:** Apaches; displaced by Comanches who were removed by U.S. Army in 1874-75. Anglo-Americans first settled in mid-1850s. County created 1856 from Comanche, Travis counties, organized in 1857. Named for frontiersman Henry S. Brown.

**Race/Ethnicity, 2000:** (In percent) Anglo, 79.66; Black, 4.11; Hispanic, 15.38; Other, 0.85.

**Vital Statistics, 2001:** Births, 461; deaths, 451; marriages, 346; divorces, 138.

**Recreation:** State park; museum; fishing, hunting.

**Minerals:** Oil, gas, paving materials, gravel, clays.

**Agriculture:** Cattle, dairies, poultry, hay, peanuts, pecans, hogs, wheat, goats. Market value $36.1 million.

**BROWNWOOD** (19,400) county seat; manufacturing, retail trade; distribution center; Howard Payne University, MacArthur Academy of Freedom; state substance abuse treatment center; state 4-H Club center; hospital; bluegrass festival in June.

**Early** (2,664) varied manufacturing, retail, distribution center; Easter egg hunt.

Other towns include: **Bangs** (1,635); **Blanket** (406); **Brookesmith** (61); **May** (285); **Zephyr** (198). **Lake Brownwood** area has 1,716.

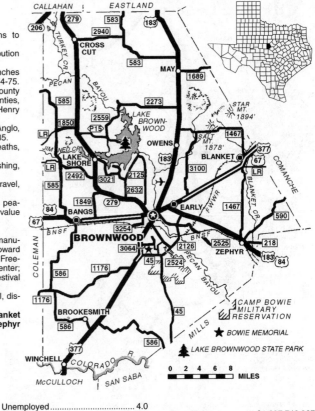

| | |
|---|---|
| Population | 37,957 |
| Change fm 2000 | 0.8 |
| Area (sq. mi.) | 956.94 |
| Land Area (sq. mi.) | 943.85 |
| Altitude (ft.) | 1,300-1,894 |
| Rainfall (in.) | 27.3 |
| Jan. mean min. | 33 |
| July mean max. | 97 |
| Civ. Labor | 17,321 |

| | |
|---|---|
| Unemployed | 4.0 |
| Wages | $95,669,210 |
| Av. Weekly Wage | $493.80 |

| | |
|---|---|
| Prop. Value | $1,637,746,927 |
| Retail Sales | $390,723,273 |

---

# Burleson County

**Physical Features:** Rolling to hilly; drains to Brazos, Yegua Creek, Somerville Lake; loam and heavy bottom soils; oaks, other trees.

**Economy:** Oil and gas; tourism; commuters to Texas A&M University; agribusiness.

**History:** Tonkawas and Caddoes roamed the area. Mexicans and Anglo-Americans settled around fort in 1830. Black freedmen migration increased until 1910. Germans, Czechs, Italians migrated in 1870s-80s. County created 1846 from Milam, Washington counties; named for Edward Burleson, a hero of the Texas Revolution.

**Race/Ethnicity, 2000:** (In percent) Anglo, 69.68; Black, 15.06; Hispanic, 14.64; Other, 0.62.

**Vital Statistics, 2001:** Births, 205; deaths, 144; marriages, 79; divorces, 72.

**Recreation:** Fishing, hunting; lake recreation; historic sites; Czech heritage museum; Kolache Festival in September.

**Minerals:** Oil, gas, sand, gravel.

**Agriculture:** Cattle, cotton, corn, hay, sorghum, broiler production, soybeans; some irrigation. Market value $29.7 million.

**CALDWELL** (3,643) county seat; agribusiness, oil & gas; manufacturing; distribution center; tourism; hospital, library, museum.

**Somerville** (1,722) tourism, railroad center, some manufacturing.

Other towns include: **Chriesman** (30); **Deanville** (130); **Lyons** (360); **Snook** (589), Snookfest in June.

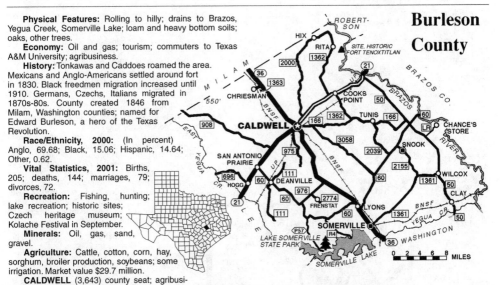

| | |
|---|---|
| Population | 16,874 |
| Change fm 2000 | 2.5 |
| Area (sq. mi.) | 677.78 |
| Land Area (sq. mi.) | 665.54 |
| Altitude (ft.) | 200-550 |
| Rainfall (in.) | 39.1 |
| Jan. mean min. | 37 |

| | |
|---|---|
| July mean max. | 94 |
| Civ. Labor | 8,185 |
| Unemployed | 3.9 |
| Wages | $22,282,627 |
| Av. Weekly Wage | $490.43 |
| Prop. Value | $1,057,030,895 |
| Retail Sales | $109,481,850 |

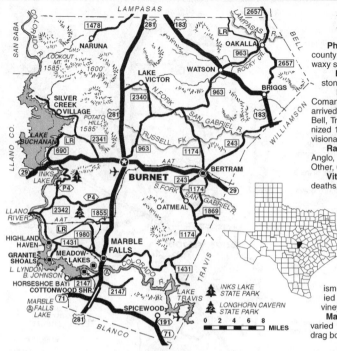

# Burnet County

**Physical Features:** Scenic Hill Country county with lakes; caves; sandy, red, black waxy soils; cedars, other trees.

**Economy:** Tourism, manufacturing, stone processing, hunting leases.

**History:** Tonkawas, Lipan Apaches. Comanches raided in area. Frontier settlers arrived in the late 1840s. County created from Bell, Travis, Williamson counties, 1852; organized 1854; named for David G. Burnet, provisional president of the Republic.

**Race/Ethnicity, 2000:** (In percent) Anglo, 82.76; Black, 1.61; Hispanic, 14.77; Other, 0.86.

**Vital Statistics, 2001:** Births, 499; deaths, 411; marriages, 270; divorces, 186.

**Recreation:** Water sports on lakes; sites of historic forts; hunting; state parks; wildflowers; birding.

**Minerals:** Granite capital of Texas, limestone, graphite.

**Agriculture:** Beef cattle, deer hunting, goats, hay. Market value $14.2 million.

**BURNET** (4,936) county seat; tourism; government/services; ranching; varied industries; hospitals; museums; vineyards; Bluebonnet festival in April.

**Marble Falls** (5,200) tourism; ranching; varied manufacturing; stone quarry; August drag boat race.

Other towns include: **Bertram** (1,220) Oatmeal festival on Labor Day; **Briggs** (92); **Cottonwood Shores** (960); **Granite Shoals** (2,062); **Highland Haven** (467); **Meadowlakes** (1,459); **Spicewood** (NA). Also, part of **Horseshoe Bay** (3,399).

| | |
|---|---|
| Population | 36,889 |
| Change fm 2000 | 8.0 |
| Area (sq. mi.) | 1,020.96 |
| Land Area (sq. mi.) | 996.04 |
| Altitude (ft.) | 700-1,600 |
| Rainfall (in.) | 31.2 |
| Jan. mean min. | 32 |
| July mean max. | 93 |
| Civ. Labor | 18,035 |
| Unemployed | 5.1 |
| Wages | $71,959,347 |
| Av. Weekly Wage | $515.39 |
| Prop. Value | $3,315,015,061 |
| Retail Sales | $464,420,572 |

# Caldwell County

**Physical Features:** Varied soils ranging from black clay to waxy; level, draining to San Marcos River.

**Economy:** Petroleum, agribusiness, varied manufacturing; part of Austin metro area, also near San Antonio.

**History:** Tonkawa area. Part of the DeWitt colony, Anglo-Americans settled in the 1830s. Mexican migration increased after 1890. County created from Bastrop, Gonzales counties, 1848; named for frontiersman Mathew Caldwell.

**Race/Ethnicity, 2000:** (In percent) Anglo, 50.15; Black, 8.58; Hispanic, 40.44; Other, 0.83.

**Vital Statistics, 2001:** Births, 519; deaths, 283; marriages, 212; divorces, 136.

**Recreation:** Fishing; state park; Luling Watermelon Thump; Chisholm Trail roundup at Lockhart; museums; nature trails; rodeo.

**Minerals:** Oil, gas, sand, gravel.

**Agriculture:** Beef cattle, turkeys, eggs; cotton, grain sorghums, corn, hay. Market value $36.7 million.

**LOCKHART** (12,601) county seat, petroleum, agribusiness center, tourism; light manufacturing; prison.

**Luling** (5,181) oil-industry center, oil museum; hospital. Other towns include: **Dale** (500); **Fentress** (291); **Martindale** (980); **Maxwell** (500); part of **Mustang Ridge** (838, mostly in Travis County), and **Prairie Lea** (255). Also, part of **Niederwald** (618), part of **Uhland** (401) and a small part of **San Marcos** (39,936), all mostly in Hays County.

| | |
|---|---|
| Population | 35,050 |
| Change fm 2000 | 8.9 |
| Area (sq. mi.) | 547.41 |
| Land Area (sq. mi.) | 545.73 |
| Altitude (ft.) | 350-705 |
| Rainfall (in.) | 35.3 |
| Jan. mean min. | 36 |
| July mean max. | 96 |
| Civ. Labor | 16,515 |
| Unemployed | 7.3 |
| Wages | $36,550,342 |
| Av. Weekly Wage | $445.78 |
| Prop. Value | $1,418,347,616 |
| Retail Sales | $204,793,403 |

# Calhoun County

**Physical Features:** Sandy, broken by bays; partly on Matagorda Island.

**Economy:** Aluminum manufacturing, plastics plant, marine construction, agribusinesses; petroleum; tourism; fish processing.

**History:** Karankawa area. Empresario Martín De León brought 41 families in 1825. County created from Jackson, Matagorda, Victoria counties, 1846. Named for John C. Calhoun, U.S. statesman.

**Race/Ethnicity, 2000:** (In percent) Anglo, 52.29; Black, 2.67; Hispanic, 40.92; Other, 3.72.

**Vital Statistics, 2001:** Births, 311; deaths, 169; marriages, 182; divorces, 61.

**Recreation:** Beaches, fishing, water sports, duck, goose hunting; historic sites, county park; La Salle Days in April.

**Minerals:** Oil, gas.

**Agriculture:** Cotton, cattle, corn, grain sorghum. Market value $24.5 million. Commercial fishing.

**PORT LAVACA** (11,978) county seat; commercial seafood operations; offshore drilling operations; tourist center; some manufacturing; convention center; hospital.

Other towns include: **Long Mott** (76); **Point Comfort** (772) aluminum, plastic plants, deepwater port; **Port O'Connor**, (1,184), tourist center; seafood processing; manufacturing; **Seadrift** (1,348), commercial fishing, processing plants; Bayfront Park; Shrimpfest in June.

| | |
|---|---|
| Population | 20,595 |
| Change fm 2000 | -0.3 |
| Area (sq. mi.) | 1,032.16 |
| Land Area (sq. mi.) | 512.31 |
| Altitude (ft.) | sea level-50 |
| Rainfall (in.) | 39.4 |
| Jan. mean min. | 46 |
| July mean max. | 90 |
| Civ. Labor | 7,716 |
| Unemployed | 9.0 |
| Wages | $96,027,575 |
| Av. Weekly Wage | $787.25 |
| Prop. Value | $4,392,800,946 |
| Retail Sales | $167,270,838 |

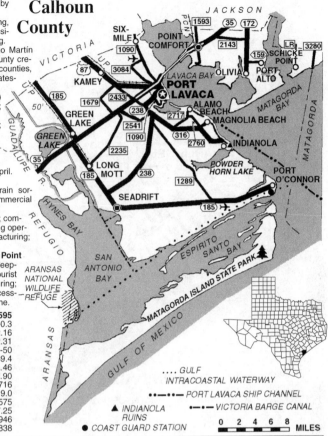

.... GULF INTRACOASTAL WATERWAY

■—■—■— PORT LAVACA SHIP CHANNEL

■—■—■— VICTORIA BARGE CANAL

▲ INDIANOLA RUINS

● COAST GUARD STATION

0  2  4  6  8  MILES

# Callahan County

**Physical Features:** West Texas county on divide between Brazos, Colorado rivers; level to rolling.

**Economy:** Manufacturing; feed and fertilizer business; many residents commute to Abilene; 200,000 acres in hunting leases.

**History:** Comanche territory until 1870s. Anglo-American settlement began around 1860. County created 1858 from Bexar, Bosque, Travis counties; organized 1877. Named for Texas Ranger J.H. Callahan.

**Race/Ethnicity, 2000:** (In percent) Anglo, 92.31; Black, 0.32; Hispanic, 6.29; Other, 1.08.

**Vital Statistics, 2001:** Births, 132; deaths, 143; marriages, 68; divorces, 64.

**Recreation:** Hunting; museums; lake; Hunters' Supper at deer season.

**Minerals:** Oil and gas.

**Agriculture:** Cattle; wheat, dairy, hay, peanuts, sorghum; goats, horses. Market value $21.6 million.

**BAIRD** (1,610) county seat; ranching and supplies; antiques shops; some manufacturing, shipping; historic sites.

**Clyde** (3,439) steel water systems manufacturing; government/services; library; Pecan Festival in October.

Other towns include: **Cross Plains** (1,055) government/services, agriculture, home of creator of Conan the Barbarian; **Putnam** (90).

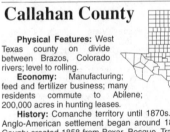

| | |
|---|---|
| Population | 12,762 |
| Change fm 2000 | -1.1 |
| Area (sq. mi.) | 901.26 |
| Land Area (sq. mi.) | 898.62 |

| | |
|---|---|
| Altitude (ft.) | 1,400-2,204 |
| Rainfall (in.) | 25.2 |
| Jan. mean min. | 32 |
| July mean max. | 96 |
| Civ. Labor | 6,714 |

| | |
|---|---|
| Unemployed | 3.8 |
| Wages | $12,484,886 |
| Av. Weekly Wage | $508.67 |
| Prop. Value | $740,068,438 |
| Retail Sales | $38,605,113 |

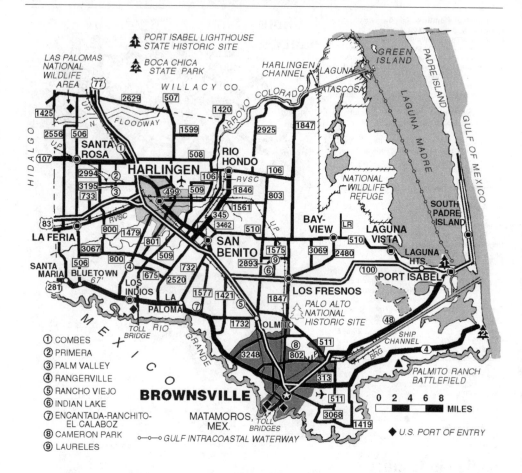

**Legend:**
- ① COMBES
- ② PRIMERA
- ③ PALM VALLEY
- ④ RANGERVILLE
- ⑤ RANCHO VIEJO
- ⑥ INDIAN LAKE
- ⑦ ENCANTADA-RANCHITO-EL CALABOZ
- ⑧ CAMERON PARK
- ⑨ LAURELES
- ◆ U.S. PORT OF ENTRY
- ○—○ GULF INTRACOASTAL WATERWAY

MILES: 0 2 4 6 8

# Cameron County

**Physical Features:** Southernmost county in rich Rio Grande Valley soils; flat landscape; semitropical climate.

**Economy:** Agribusiness; tourism; seafood processing; shipping, manufacturing; government/services.

**History:** Coahuiltecan Indian area. Spanish land grants date to 1781. County created from Nueces County, 1848; named for Capt. Ewen Cameron of Mier Expedition.

**Race/Ethnicity, 2000:** (In percent) Anglo, 14.73; Black, 0.30; Hispanic, 84.34; Other, 0.63.

**Vital Statistics, 2001:** Births, 8,381; deaths, 1,996; marriages, 3,418; divorces, 1,175.

**Recreation:** South Padre Island: year-round resort; fishing, hunting, water sports; historical sites; gateway to Mexico, state parks; wildlife refuge; recreational vehicle center; Birding Festival in mid-November.

**Minerals:** Natural gas, oil.

**Agriculture:** Cotton top crop with grain sorghums, vegetables, and sugar cane raised; wholesale nursery plants raised; small feedlot and cow-calf operations; 200,000 acres irrigated, mostly cotton and grain sorghums. Market value $119.5 million.

**BROWNSVILLE** (147,545) county seat; varied industries, shipping, college, hospitals, crippled children health center; Gladys Porter Zoo; University of Texas at Brownsville.

**Harlingen** (59,253) government/services; hospitals; garment, apparel industries; agribusiness; college; Riofest in April.

**San Benito** (24,079) varied manufacturing, bottling; tourism; hospital; recreation facilities.

Other towns include: **Bayview** (329); **Bluetown-Iglesia Antigua** (747); **Cameron Park** (6,055); **Combes** (2,667); **Encantada-Ranchito-El Calaboz** (2,149); **Indian Lake** (545); **La Feria** (6,336); **Laguna Heights** (2,008); **Laguna Vista** (1,883); **Laureles** (3,429); **Los Fresnos** (4,808); **Los Indios** (1,142); **Olmito** (1,244); **Palm Valley** (1,258).

Also, **Port Isabel** (5,067) tourist center, fishing, Shrimp Cook-Off in November, museums, lighthouse; **Primera** (2,834); **Rancho Viejo** (1,734); **Rangerville** (205); **Rio Hondo** (1,995); **Santa Maria** (848); **Santa Rosa** (2,897); **South Padre Island** (2,490).

| | |
|---|---|
| Population | 353,561 |
| Change fm 2000 | 5.5 |
| Area (sq. mi.) | 1,276.33 |
| Land Area (sq. mi.) | 905.76 |
| Altitude (ft.) | sea level-67 |
| Rainfall (in.) | 26.6 |
| Jan. mean min. | 50 |
| July mean max. | 93 |
| Civ. Labor | 144,790 |
| Unemployed | 10.1 |
| Wages | $652,981,409 |
| Av. Weekly Wage | $435.82 |
| Prop. Value | $9,240,940,293 |
| Retail Sales | $2,847,784,841 |

*For explanation of sources, abbreviations and symbols, see p. 138.*

# Camp County

**Physical Features:** East Texas county with forested hills; drains to Cypress Creek on north; Lake O' the Pines, Lake Bob Sandlin; third smallest county in Texas.

**Economy:** Agribusiness, chicken processing; timber industries; light manufacturing; retirement center.

**History:** Caddo area. Anglo-American settlers arrived in late 1830s. Antebellum slaveholding area. County created from Upshur County 1874; named for jurist J.L. Camp.

**Race/Ethnicity, 2000:** (In percent) Anglo, 65.45; Black, 19.24; Hispanic, 14.78; Other, 0.53.

**Vital Statistics, 2001:** Births, 170; deaths, 132; marriages, 110; divorces, 46.

**Recreation:** Water sports, fishing on lakes; farmstead and airship museum; Chickfest in September, Pittsburg hot links.

**Minerals:** Oil, gas, clays, coal.

**Agriculture:** Poultry and products important; beef, dairy cattle, horses; peaches, hay, blueberries, vegetables. Market value $164.9 million. Forestry.

**PITTSBURG** (4,461) county seat; agribusiness; timber; tourism; food processing; light manufacturing; community college; Prayer Tower.

Other towns include: **Leesburg** (115) and **Rocky Mound** (97).

| | |
|---|---|
| Population | 11,643 |
| Change fm 2000 | 0.8 |
| Area (sq. mi.) | 203.20 |
| Land Area (sq. mi.) | 197.51 |
| Altitude (ft.) | 277-538 |
| Rainfall (in.) | 43.3 |
| Jan. mean min. | 32 |
| July mean max. | 94 |
| Civ. Labor | 5,852 |
| Unemployed | 7.7 |
| Wages | $24,191,524 |
| Av. Weekly Wage | $424.47 |
| Prop. Value | $512,358,455 |
| Retail Sales | $92,796,972 |

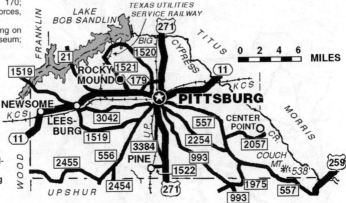

---

# Carson County

**Physical Features:** In center of Panhandle on level, some broken land; loam soils.

**Economy:** Pantex nuclear weapons assembly/disassembly facility (U.S. Department of Energy), commuting to Amarillo, petrochemical plants; agribusiness.

**History:** Apaches, displaced by Comanches. Anglo-American ranchers settled in 1880s. German, Polish farmers arrived around 1910. County created from Bexar District, 1876; organized 1888. Named for Republic secretary of state S.P. Carson.

**Race/Ethnicity, 2000:** (In percent) Anglo, 91.22; Black, 0.81; Hispanic, 7.03; Other, 0.94.

**Vital Statistics, 2001:** Births, 80; deaths, 62; marriages, 42; divorces, 40.

**Recreation:** Museum, Square House Barbecue in fall.

**Minerals:** Oil, gas production.

**Agriculture:** Wheat, sorghum, corn, cattle, soybeans, hay; some irrigation. Market value $85.4 million.

**PANHANDLE** (2,594) county seat; government/services; agribusiness, petroleum center; Veterans Day celebration.

Other towns include: **Groom** (566) Day festival in August, **Skellytown** (592), **White Deer** (1,020) Polish Sausage festival in November.

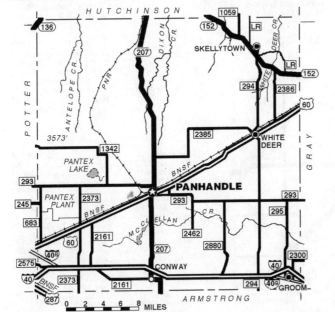

| | |
|---|---|
| Population | 6,582 |
| Change fm 2000 | 1.0 |
| Area (sq. mi.) | 924.10 |
| Land Area (sq. mi.) | 923.19 |
| Altitude (ft.) | 3,000-3,573 |
| Rainfall (in.) | 20.8 |
| Jan. mean min. | 22 |
| July mean max. | 93 |
| Civ. Labor | 3,347 |
| Unemployed | 4.2 |
| Wages | $56,459,996 |
| Av. Weekly Wage | $918.20 |
| Prop. Value | $812,525,282 |
| Retail Sales | $19,142,120 |

For explanation of sources, abbreviations and symbols, see p. 138.

# Cass County

| | |
|---|---|
| Population | 30,133 |
| Change fm 2000 | -1.0 |
| Area (sq. mi.) | 960.35 |
| Land Area (sq. mi.) | 937.35 |
| Altitude (ft.) | 200-600 |
| Rainfall (in.) | 48.3 |
| Jan. mean min. | 31 |
| July mean max. | 93 |
| Civ. Labor | 15,339 |

| | |
|---|---|
| Unemployed | 6.7 |
| Wages | $53,151,725 |
| Av. Weekly Wage | $486.91 |
| Prop. Value | $1,569,594,490 |
| Retail Sales | $177,478,326 |

**Physical Features:** Forested Northeast county rolling to hilly; drained by Cypress Bayou, Sulphur River.

**Economy:** Timber, paper industries; varied manufacturing; agribusiness; government/services.

**History:** Caddoes, displaced by other tribes in 1790s. Anglo-Americans arrived in 1830s. Antebellum slaveholding area. County created 1846 from Bowie County; named for U.S. Sen. Lewis Cass.

**Race/Ethnicity, 2000:** (In percent) Anglo, 77.89; Black, 19.71; Hispanic, 1.73; Other, 0.67.

**Vital Statistics, 2001:** Births, 327; deaths, 380; marriages, 194; divorces, 139.

**Recreation:** Fishing, hunting, water sports; state, county parks; lake, wildflower trails.

**Minerals:** Oil, iron ore.

**Agriculture:** Poultry, cattle; nursery; forage; watermelons. Market value $27.1 million. Timber important.

**LINDEN** (2,214) county seat, wood-treating plants, timber, oldest courthouse still in use as courthouse, hospital.

**ATLANTA** (5,704) Paper and timber industries, government/services, varied manufacturing, hospital, library; Forest festival in August.

Other towns include: **Avinger** (456); **Bivins** (195); **Bloomburg** (380); **Domino** (52); **Douglassville** (183); **Hughes Springs** (1,846) varied manufacturing, warehousing; trucking school; Pumpkin Glow in October; **Kildare** (49); **Marietta** (111); **McLeod** (230); **Queen City** (1,562).

# Castro County

**Physical Features:** Flat northwest county, drains to creeks, draws and playas; underground water.

**Economy:** Agribusiness.

**History:** Apaches, displaced by Comanches in 1720s. Anglo-American ranchers began settling in 1880s. Germans settled after 1900. Mexican migration increased after 1950. County created 1876 from Bexar, organized 1891. Named for Henri Castro, Texas colonizer.

**Race/Ethnicity, 2000:** (In percent) Anglo, 45.58; Black, 2.37; Hispanic, 51.65; Other, 0.40.

**Vital Statistics, 2001:** Births, 130; deaths, 71; marriages, 54; divorces, 20.

**Recreation:** Pheasant hunting; Harvest Days celebrated in August; Italian POW camp site.

**Minerals:** Not significant.

**Agriculture:** Feeder, stocker cattle; corn, cotton, wheat, sheep. Market value $601.7 million; second in state.

**DIMMITT** (4,213) county seat; agribusiness center; library, geriatric-care facility; Fiestas Patrias in September.

Other towns include: **Hart** (1,148), **Nazareth** (348), **Summerfield** (60).

| | |
|---|---|
| Population | 8,075 |
| Change fm 2000 | -2.5 |
| Area (sq. mi.) | 899.32 |
| Land Area (sq. mi.) | 898.31 |
| Altitude (ft.) | 3,600-4,000 |
| Rainfall (in.) | 18.0 |
| Jan. mean min. | 19 |
| July mean max. | 91 |
| Civ. Labor | 3,115 |
| Unemployed | 5.2 |
| Wages | $13,660,732 |
| Av. Weekly Wage | $435.49 |
| Prop. Value | $506,604,521 |
| Retail Sales | $39,276,724 |

*For explanation of sources, abbreviations and symbols, see p. 138.*

# COUNTIES
# OF TEXAS
# BY NAME

Close-up map and
locator map
with each county
article

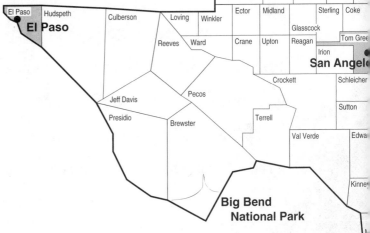

| Dallam | | Sherman | Hansford | Ochiltree | Li cc |
| Hartley | | Moore | Hutchin-son | Roberts | He |
| Oldham | | Potter | Carson | Gray | W |
| | | | Amarillo | | |
| Deaf Smith | | Randall | Armstrong | Donley | C w |
| Parmer | Castro | Swisher | Briscoe | Hall | |
| Bailey | Lamb | Hale | Floyd | Motley | C |
| Cochran | Hockley | Lubbock | Crosby | Dickens | Ki |
| | | Lubbock | | | |
| Yoakum | Terry | Lynn | Garza | Kent | St wa |
| Gaines | | Dawson | Borden | Scurry | Fishe |
| Andrews | | Martin | Howard | Mitchell | Nola |

| El Paso | Hudspeth | Culberson | Loving | Winkler | Ector | Midland | | Sterling | Coke |
| El Paso | | | | | | | Glasscock | | |
| | | | Reeves | Ward | Crane | Upton | Reagan | | Tom Gree |
| | | | | | | | | Irion | |
| | | | | | | | | | San Angel |
| | | | | | Crockett | | | Schleicher |
| | Jeff Davis | | Pecos | | | | | Sutton |
| | Presidio | | Brewster | | Terrell | | | |
| | | | | | | | Val Verde | Edwa |
| | | | | | | | | Kinne |

Big Bend
National Park

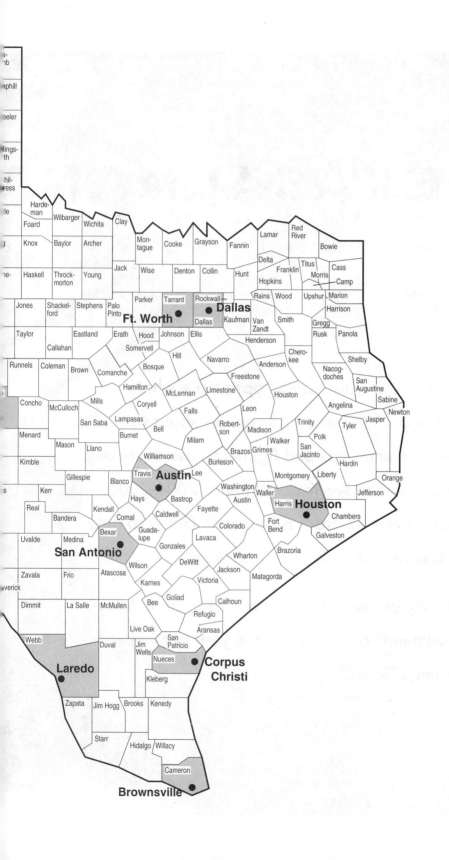

# Chambers County

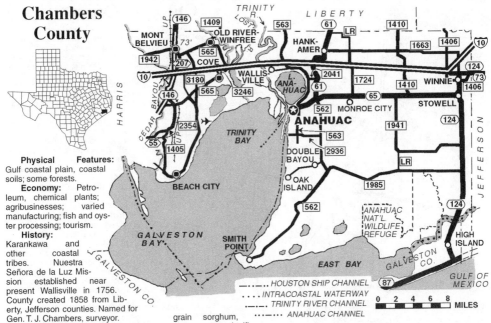

**Physical Features:** Gulf coastal plain, coastal soils; some forests.

**Economy:** Petroleum, chemical plants; agribusinesses; varied manufacturing; fish and oyster processing; tourism.

**History:** Karankawa and other coastal tribes. Nuestra Señora de la Luz Mission established near present Wallisville in 1756. County created 1858 from Liberty, Jefferson counties. Named for Gen. T. J. Chambers, surveyor.

**Race/Ethnicity, 2000:** (In percent) Anglo, 78.14; Black, 9.88; Hispanic, 10.79; Other, 1.19.

**Vital Statistics, 2001:** Births, 316; deaths, 192; marriages, 165; divorces, 150.

**Recreation:** Fishing, hunting; water sports; camping; county parks; wildlife refuge; historic sites; Wallisville Heritage Park; Texas Rice Festival, Texas Gatorfest in September.

**Minerals:** Oil, gas.

**Agriculture:** Rice, cattle and forage, soybeans, aquaculture, corn, grain sorghum, sugar cane; significant irrigation. Market value $11.6 million.

**ANAHUAC** (2,240) county seat; canal connects with Houston Ship Channel; agribusiness; hospital, library.

**Winnie** (2,999) fertilizer manufacturing; wholesale greenhouse; medical center; depot museum.

Other towns include: **Beach City** (1,760), **Cove** (324), **Hankamer** (525), **Mont Belvieu** (2,510), **Old River-Winfree** (1,380), **Stowell** (1,585) and **Wallisville** (460).

| | |
|---|---|
| Population | 27,244 |
| Change fm 2000 | 4.7 |
| Area (sq. mi.) | 871.99 |
| Land Area (sq. mi.) | 599.31 |
| Altitude (ft.) | sea level-73 |
| Rainfall (in.) | 51.7 |
| Jan. mean min. | 41 |
| July mean max. | 92 |
| Civ. Labor | 13,032 |
| Unemployed | 5.6 |
| Wages | $63,742,689 |
| Av. Weekly Wage | $702.98 |
| Prop. Value | $5,052,400,600 |
| Retail Sales | $484,389,638 |

*A cargo ship passes out of Galveston Bay into the Gulf of Mexico. File photo.*

# Cherokee County

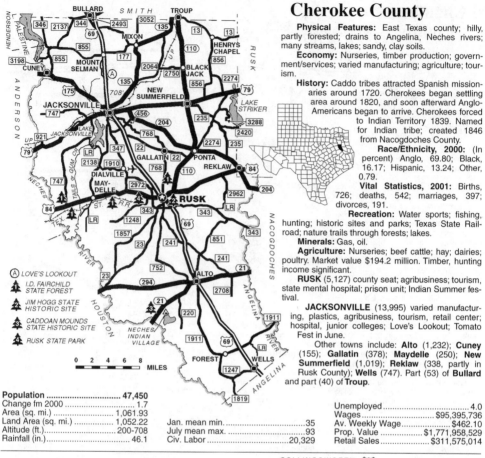

**Physical Features:** East Texas county; hilly, partly forested; drains to Angelina, Neches rivers; many streams, lakes; sandy, clay soils.

**Economy:** Nurseries, timber production; government/services; varied manufacturing; agriculture; tourism.

**History:** Caddo tribes attracted Spanish missionaries around 1720. Cherokees began settling area around 1820, and soon afterward Anglo-Americans began to arrive. Cherokees forced to Indian Territory 1839. Named for Indian tribe; created 1846 from Nacogdoches County.

**Race/Ethnicity, 2000:** (In percent) Anglo, 69.80; Black, 16.17; Hispanic, 13.24; Other, 0.79.

**Vital Statistics, 2001:** Births, 726; deaths, 542; marriages, 397; divorces, 191.

**Recreation:** Water sports; fishing, hunting; historic sites and parks; Texas State Railroad; nature trails through forests; lakes.

**Minerals:** Gas, oil.

**Agriculture:** Nurseries; beef cattle; hay; dairies; poultry. Market value $194.2 million. Timber, hunting income significant.

**RUSK** (5,127) county seat; agribusiness; tourism; state mental hospital; prison unit; Indian Summer festival.

**JACKSONVILLE** (13,995) varied manufacturing, plastics, agribusiness, tourism, retail center; hospital, junior colleges; Love's Lookout; Tomato Fest in June.

Other towns include: **Alto** (1,232); **Cuney** (155); **Gallatin** (378); **Maydelle** (250); **New Summerfield** (1,019); **Reklaw** (338, partly in Rusk County); **Wells** (747). Part (53) of **Bullard** and part (40) of **Troup.**

| | | |
|---|---|---|
| Population .............................. 47,450 | | |
| Change fm 2000 ............................. 1.7 | | |
| Area (sq. mi.) ........................ 1,061.93 | | |
| Land Area (sq. mi.) ................. 1,052.22 | Jan. mean min. ............................35 | Unemployed .....................................4.0 |
| Altitude (ft.) .......................... 200-708 | July mean max. .............................93 | Wages ............................ $95,395,736 |
| Rainfall (in.) ................................ 46.1 | Civ. Labor ..............................20,329 | Av. Weekly Wage ................... $462.10 |
| | | Prop. Value ................. $1,771,958,529 |
| | | Retail Sales ................... $311,575,014 |

# Childress County

**Physical Features:** Rolling prairie, at corner of Panhandle, draining to fork of Red River; mixed soils.

**Economy:** Government/services; trade; tourism, agriculture.

**History:** Apaches, displaced by Comanches. Ranchers arrived around 1880. County created 1876 from Bexar, Young districts; organized 1887; named for author of Texas Declaration of Independence, George C. Childress.

**Race/Ethnicity, 2000:** (In percent) Anglo, 64.50; Black, 14.30; Hispanic, 20.47; Other, 0.73.

**Vital Statistics, 2001:** Births, 109; deaths, 88; marriages, 58; divorces, 23.

**Recreation:** Recreation on lakes and creek, fishing, hunting of deer, turkey, wild hog, quail, dove; parks; county museum.

**Agriculture:** Cotton, beef cattle, wheat, hay, sorghum, peanuts; 6,000 acres irrigated. Market value $11 million. Hunting leases.

**CHILDRESS** (6,861) county seat; agribusiness, hospital, prison unit; settlers reunion and rodeo in July. Other towns include: **Tell** (63).

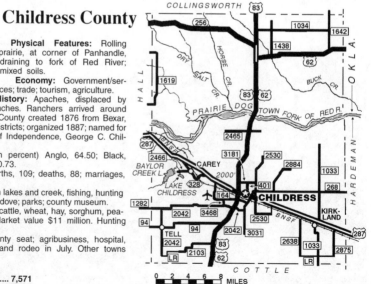

| | | |
|---|---|---|
| Population .............................. 7,571 | | |
| Change fm 2000 ............................ -1.5 | | |
| Area (sq. mi.) ........................... 713.61 | Jan. mean min. ...............................26 | Wages ...........................$13,787,680 |
| Land Area (sq. mi.) .................. 710.34 | July mean max. ..............................96 | Av. Weekly Wage ...................$420.70 |
| Altitude (ft.) ....................... 1,600-2,000 | Civ. Labor .....................................3,036 | Prop. Value ....................$221,909,093 |
| Rainfall (in.) ................................. 20.7 | Unemployed ...................................3.9 | Retail Sales ......................$59,989,487 |

# Clay County

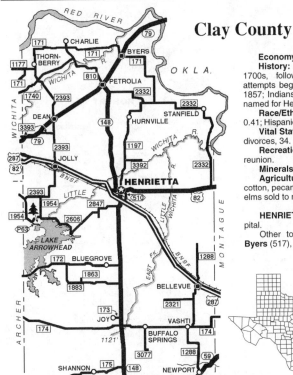

**Physical Features:** Hilly, rolling; north central county drains to Red, Trinity rivers, lake; sandy loam, chocolate soils; mesquites, post oaks.

**Economy:** Oil; agribusiness; varied manufacturing.

**History:** Wichitas arrived from north-central plains in mid-1700s, followed by Apaches and Comanches. Ranching attempts began in 1850s. County created from Cooke County, 1857; Indians forced disorganization, 1862; reorganized, 1873; named for Henry Clay, U.S. statesman.

**Race/Ethnicity, 2000:** (In percent) Anglo, 94.81; Black, 0.41; Hispanic, 3.67; Other, 1.11.

**Vital Statistics, 2001:** Births, 83; deaths, 91; marriages, 84; divorces, 34.

**Recreation:** Fishing, water sports; state park; pioneer reunion.

**Minerals:** Oil and gas, stone.

**Agriculture:** Beef and dairy cattle, horses raised; wheat, cotton, pecan, peaches. Market value $45.7 million. Oaks, cedar, elms sold to nurseries, mesquite cut for firewood.

**HENRIETTA** (3,267) county seat; agribusiness center; hospital.

Other towns include: **Bellevue** (386), **Bluegrove** (125), **Byers** (517), **Dean** (341), **Jolly** (187), **Petrolia** (780).

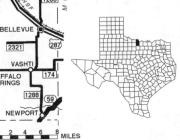

| | |
|---|---|
| Population | 11,396 |
| Change fm 2000 | 3.5 |
| Area (sq. mi.) | 1,116.17 |
| Land Area (sq. mi.) | 1,097.82 |
| Altitude (ft.) | 800-1,121 |
| Rainfall (in.) | 31.9 |
| Jan. mean min. | 26 |
| July mean max. | 97 |
| Civ. Labor | 5,830 |
| Unemployed | 3.5 |
| Wages | $12,450,980 |
| Av. Weekly Wage | $504.35 |
| Prop. Value | $687,587,401 |
| Retail Sales | $75,487,299 |

# Cochran County

**Physical Features:** South Plains bordering New Mexico with small lakes (playas); underground water; loam, sandy loam soils.

**Economy:** Agribusiness, government/services, oil.

**History:** Hunting area for various Indian tribes. Ranches operated in 1880s but population in 1900 was still only 25. Farming began in 1920s. County created from Bexar, Young districts, 1876; organized 1924; named for Robert Cochran, who died at the Alamo.

**Race/Ethnicity 2000:** (In percent) Anglo, 50.18; Black, 4.91; Hispanic, 44.13; Other, 0.78.

**Vital Statistics, 2001:** Births, 70; deaths, 45; marriages, 28; divorces, 12.

**Recreation:** Rodeo; Last Frontier days in July; museum.

**Minerals:** Oil, gas.

**Agriculture:** Cotton, sorghum, wheat, peanuts, sunflowers. Crops 60 percent irrigated. Cattle, swine, sheep. Market value $34.1 million.

**MORTON** (2,271) county seat; oil, farm center, meat packing; light manufacture; hospital.

Other towns include: **Bledsoe** (125), **Whiteface** (457).

| | |
|---|---|
| Population | 3,482 |
| Change fm 2000 | -6.6 |
| Area (sq. mi.) | 775.31 |

*For explanation of sources, abbreviations and symbols, see p. 138.*

| | |
|---|---|
| Land Area (sq. mi.) | 775.22 |
| Altitude (ft.) | 3,600-4,000 |
| Rainfall (in.) | 18.6 |
| Jan. temp. min. | 22 |
| July temp. max. | 91 |

| | |
|---|---|
| Civ. Labor | 1,431 |
| Unemployed | 11.6 |
| Wages | $5,695,022 |
| Av. Weekly Wage | $468.03 |
| Prop. Value | $488,910,210 |
| Retail Sales | $21,905,723 |

○–○–○ (W) MOUNTAIN TIME ZONE
(E) CENTRAL TIME ZONE

0  2  4  6 MILES

# Coke County

**Physical Features:** West Texas prairie, hills, Colorado River valley; sandy loam, red soils; reservoir.

**Economy:** Government/services, oil and gas, agriculture.

**History:** From 1700 to 1870s, Comanches roamed the area. Ranches began operating after the Civil War. County created 1889 from Tom Green County; named for Gov. Richard Coke.

**Race/Ethnicity, 2000:** (In percent) Anglo, 80.18; Black, 1.99; Hispanic, 16.90; Other, 0.93.

**Vital Statistics, 2001:** Births, 26; deaths, 63; marriages, 20; divorces, 4.

**Recreation:** Hunting, fishing; lakes; historic sites, Fort Chadbourne, county museum; Ole Coke County Pageant, July 4.

**Minerals:** Oil, gas.

**Agriculture:** Beef cattle; sheep; hay; goats. Market value $8.6 million.

**ROBERT LEE** (1,134) county seat; government/services, petroleum center, ranching.

**Bronte** (1,057) ranching, oil.

Other towns include: **Silver** (60) and **Tennyson** (35). Also, a small part of **Blackwell** (360).

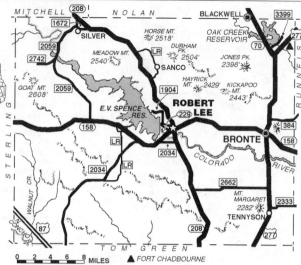

| | |
|---|---|
| Population | 3,844 |
| Change fm 2000 | -0.5 |
| Area (sq. mi.) | 927.97 |
| Land Area (sq. mi.) | 898.81 |
| Altitude (ft.) | 1,700-2,608 |
| Rainfall (in.) | 23.2 |
| Jan. mean min. | 28 |
| July mean max. | 96 |
| Civ. Labor | 1,460 |
| Unemployed | 3.1 |
| Wages | $5,685,051 |
| Av. Weekly Wage | $425.81 |
| Prop. Value | $388,804,240 |
| Retail Sales | $21,887,692 |

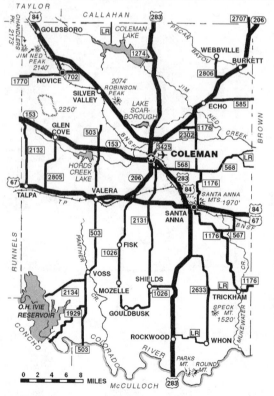

| | |
|---|---|
| Population | 8,906 |
| Change fm 2000 | -3.6 |
| Area (sq. mi.) | 1,281.45 |
| Land Area (sq. mi.) | 1,260.20 |
| Altitude (ft.) | 1,400-2,250 |
| Rainfall (in.) | 28.0 |

# Coleman County

**Physical Features:** Hilly, rolling; drains to Colorado River, Pecan Bayou; lakes; mesquite, oaks.

**Economy:** Agribusiness, petroleum, ecotourism; varied manufacturing.

**History:** Presence of Apaches and Comanches brought military outpost, Camp Colorado, before the Civl War. Settlers arrived after organization. County created 1858 from Brown, Travis counties; organized 1864; named for Houston's aide, R.M. Coleman.

**Race/Ethnicity, 2000:** (In percent), Anglo, 82.95; Black, 2.35; Hispanic, 13.96; Other, 0.74.

**Vital Statistics, 2001:** Births, 99; deaths, 145; marriages, 74; divorces, 46.

**Recreation:** Fishing, hunting; water sports; city park, historic sites; lakes; Santa Anna Peak.

**Minerals:** Oil, gas, stone, clays.

**Agriculture:** Cattle, wheat, sheep, hay, grain sorghum, goats, oats, cotton. Market value $21 million. Mesquite for firewood and furniture.

**COLEMAN** (5,081) county seat; agribusiness, petroleum center; varied manufacturing; hospital, library, museum, Fiesta de la Paloma in October.

**Santa Anna** (1,041) agribusiness; some manufacturing; tourism.

Other towns include: **Burkett** (30), **Goldsboro** (30), **Gouldbusk** (70), **Novice** (139), **Rockwood** (80), **Talpa** (127), **Valera** (80), and **Voss** (20).

| | |
|---|---|
| Jan. mean min. | 32 |
| July mean max. | 96 |
| Civ. Labor | 3,383 |
| Unemployed | 6.1 |
| Wages | $10,408,129 |
| Av. Weekly Wage | $364.09 |
| Prop. Value | $623,878,910 |
| Retail Sales | $56,398,514 |

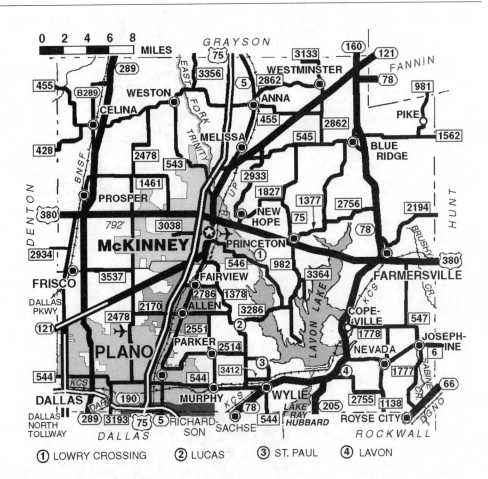

① LOWRY CROSSING    ② LUCAS    ③ ST. PAUL    ④ LAVON

# Collin County

**Physical Features:** North Texas county with heavy, black clay soil; level to rolling; drains to Trinity, Lavon Lake.

**Economy:** Government/services; manufacturing plants, retail and wholesale center; many residents work in Dallas.

**History:** Caddo area until 1850s. Settlers of Peters colony arrived in early 1840s. County created from Fannin County 1846. Named for pioneer settler Collin McKinney.

**Race/Ethnicity, 2000:** (In percent) Anglo, 77.11; Black, 4.98; Hispanic, 10.27; Other, 7.64.

**Vital Statistics, 2001:** Births, 9,445; deaths, 1,945; marriages, 4,166; divorces, 2,351.

**Recreation:** Fishing, water sports; historic sites; old homes restoration, tours; natural science museum; hot-air balloon festival.

**Minerals:** Stone production.

**Agriculture:** Greenhouse/nurseries, beef cattle, corn, horses, wheat, grain sorghum, hay. Market value $45.7 million.

**McKINNEY** (65,539) county seat; agribusiness, trade center; varied

For explanation of sources, abbreviations and symbols, see p. 138.

industry; hospital, community college; museums.

**PLANO** (237,495) telecommunications; manufacturing; newspaper printing; medical services, research center; community college; commercial and financial center; hospitals.

Other towns include: **Allen** (54,027) retail outlets, hospital, conservatory, natatorium; **Anna** (1,266); **Blue Ridge** (739); **Celina** (2,097) museum, historic town square; **Copeville** (106); **Fairview** (3,378); **Farmersville** (3,249) agriculture, light industries, Audie Murphy Day; **Frisco** (44,000) technical, areospace

industry, community college.

Also, **Josephine** (641); **Lavon** (402); **Lowry Crossing** (1,448); **Lucas** (3,141); **Melissa** (1,558); **Murphy** (5,820); **Nevada** (584); **New Hope** (685); **Parker** (1,592); **Princeton** (3,672); **Prosper** (2,466); **St. Paul** (700); **Westminster** (401); **Weston** (666); **Wylie** (17,410).

Also, part (45,155) of **Dallas**, part (20,873) of **Richardson** and part (1,660) of **Sachse**.

| | |
|---|---|
| **Population** | **566,798** |
| Change fm 2000 | 15.3 |
| Area (sq. mi.) | 885.85 |
| Land Area (sq. mi.) | 847.56 |
| Altitude (ft.) | 434-792 |
| Rainfall (in.) | 40.0 |
| Jan. mean min. | 32 |
| July mean max. | 95 |
| Civ. Labor | 320,938 |
| Unemployed | 6.5 |
| Wages | $1,850,021,319 |
| Av. Weekly Wage | $762.13 |
| Prop. Value | $50,924,006,394 |
| Retail Sales | $8,067,393,195 |

# Collingsworth County

**Physical Features:** Panhandle county of rolling, broken terrain, draining to Red River forks; sandy and loam soils.

**Economy:** Agribusiness.

**History:** Apaches, displaced by Comanches. Ranchers from England arrived in late 1870s. County created 1876, from Bexar and Young districts, organized 1890. Named for Republic of Texas' first chief justice, James Collinsworth (name misspelled in law).

**Race/Ethnicity, 2000:** (In percent) Anglo, 72.46; Black, 5.33; Hispanic, 20.43; Other, 1.78.

**Vital Statistics, 2001:** Births, 31; deaths, 53; marriages, 43; divorces, 10.

**Recreation:** Deer, quail hunting; children's camp, county museum, peanut festival; pioneer park.

**Minerals:** Gas, oil production.

**Agriculture:** Peanuts (leader in acreage), cotton; cow-calf operations, stocker cattle; alfalfa, wheat; 22,000 acres irrigated. Market value $29.4 million.

**WELLINGTON** (2,233) county seat; peanut-processing plants, varied manufacturing; agriculture; hospital, library.

Other towns include: **Dodson** (119), **Quail** (36), **Samnorwood** (49).

| | |
|---|---|
| Population | 3,103 |
| Change fm 2000 | -3.2 |
| Area (sq. mi.) | 919.44 |
| Land Area (sq. mi.) | 918.80 |

| | |
|---|---|
| Altitude (ft.) | 1,789-2,600 |
| Rainfall (in.) | 21.5 |
| Jan. mean min. | 26 |
| July mean max. | 97 |
| Civ. Labor | 1,592 |

| | |
|---|---|
| Unemployed | 4.8 |
| Wages | $4,759,803 |
| Av. Weekly Wage | $382.99 |
| Prop. Value | $264,460,171 |
| Retail Sales | $10,666,232 |

# Colorado County

**Physical Features:** South central county in three soil areas; level to rolling; bisected by Colorado River; oaks.

**Economy:** Agribusiness; oil-field services and equipment manufacturing; plants process minerals.

**History:** Karankawa and other tribes. Anglo settlers among Stephen F. Austin's Old Three Hundred families. First German settlers arrived around 1840. Antebellum slaveholding area. County created 1836, organized 1837; named for river.

**Race/Ethnicity, 2000:** (In percent) Anglo, 65.01; Black, 14.72; Hispanic, 19.74; Other, 0.53.

**Vital Statistics, 2001:** Births, 260; deaths, 290; marriages, 127; divorces, 51.

**Recreation:** Hunting, historic sites; prairie chicken refuge; opera house in Columbus.

**Minerals:** Gas, oil.

**Agriculture:** Rice (second in state in acres, sales), cattle, corn, nursery, poultry, hay, sorghum; significant irrigation for rice. Market value $50.4 million.

**COLUMBUS** (3,876) county seat; mining, agribusiness center; tourism; oil-field servicing; timber-treating center; hospital; historical sites, homes, walking tour; Live Oak festival in May.

**Eagle Lake** (3,667) rice drying center, wildflower celebration; goose hunting; hospital.

**Weimar** (1,982) ranching and rice center, feed mill, light industry, sausage company; hospital, library; "Gedenke" (remember) celebration on Mother's Day.

Other towns include: **Altair** (30), **Frelsburg** (75), **Garwood** (975), **Glidden** (255), **Nada** (165), **Oakland** (80), **Rock Island** (160), **Sheridan** (225).

ATTWATER PRAIRIE CHICKEN NATIONAL WILDLIFE REFUGE

| | |
|---|---|
| Population | 20,384 |
| Change fm 2000 | 0.0 |
| Area (sq. mi.) | 973.59 |
| Land Area (sq. mi.) | 962.95 |
| Altitude (ft.) | 150-450 |
| Rainfall (in.) | 41.8 |
| Jan. mean min. | 37 |

| | |
|---|---|
| July mean max. | 95 |
| Civ. Labor | 8,223 |
| Unemployed | 4.6 |

| | |
|---|---|
| Wages | $37,439,478 |
| Av. Weekly Wage | $462.79 |
| Prop. Value | $1,846,431,412 |
| Retail Sales | $247,948,755 |

# Comal County

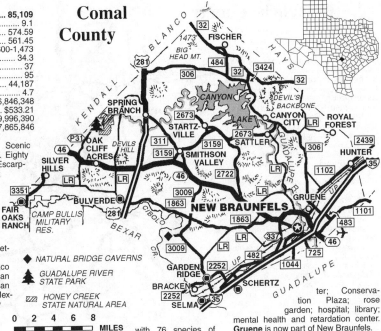

| | |
|---|---|
| Population | 85,109 |
| Change fm 2000 | 9.1 |
| Area (sq. mi.) | 574.59 |
| Land Area (sq. mi.) | 561.45 |
| Altitude (ft.) | 600-1,473 |
| Rainfall (in.) | 34.3 |
| Jan. mean min. | 37 |
| July mean max. | 95 |
| Civ. Labor | 44,187 |
| Unemployed | 4.7 |
| Wages | $216,846,348 |
| Av. Weekly Wage | $533.21 |
| Prop. Value | $6,629,996,390 |
| Retail Sales | $1,157,865,846 |

**Physical Features:** Scenic Southwest county of hills. Eighty percent above Balcones Escarpment. Spring-fed streams; 2.5-mile-long Comal River, Guadalupe River; Canyon Lake.

**Economy:** Varied manufacturing; tourism; government/services; agriculture; county in San Antonio metropolitan area.

**History:** Tonkawa, Waco Indians. A pioneer German settlement 1845. Mexican migration peaked during Mexican Revolution. County created from Bexar, Gonzales, Travis counties and organized in 1846; named for river, a name for Spanish earthenware or metal pan used for cooking tortillas.

**Race/Ethnicity, 2000:** (In percent) Anglo, 75.46; Black, 1.01; Hispanic, 22.57; Other, 0.96.

**Vital Statistics, 2001:** Births, 1,112; deaths, 668; marriages, 741; divorces, 325.

**Recreation:** Fishing, hunting; historic sites, Hummel museum; scenic drives; lake facilities; Prince Solms Park, other county parks; Landa Park with 76 species of trees; Gruene historic area; caverns; river resorts; river tubing; Schlitterbahn water park; Wurstfest in October-November.

**Minerals:** Stone, lime, sand and gravel.

**Agriculture:** Cattle, goats, sheep, hogs, horses; nursery, hay, corn, sorghum, wheat. Market value $6.2 million.

**NEW BRAUNFELS** (39,742) county seat; manufacturing; retail, distribution; one of the most picturesque cities in Texas, making it a tourist center; Conservation Plaza; rose garden; hospital; library; mental health and retardation center. **Gruene** is now part of New Braunfels.

Other towns include: **Bulverde** (4,038), **Fischer** (20), **Garden Ridge** (2,090), **Spring Branch** (NA), and the retirement/recreation community around **Canyon Lake** (17,924).

Also, small parts of **Fair Oaks Ranch** (5,042) and **Selma** (961), both mostly in Bexar County, and a small part of **Schertz** (20,336), mostly in Guadalupe County.

*For explanation of sources, abbreviations and symbols, see p. 138.*

♦ *NATURAL BRIDGE CAVERNS*
🌲 *GUADALUPE RIVER STATE PARK*
*HONEY CREEK STATE NATURAL AREA*

0 2 4 6 8 MILES

*A youth swings out over the Guadalupe River near the Highway 281 bridge. File photo.*

# Comanche County

**Physical Features:** West central county with rolling, hilly terrain; sandy, loam, waxy soils; drains to Leon River, Proctor Lake; pecans, oaks, mesquites, cedars.

**Economy:** Dairies, other agribusiness; peanut- and pecan-shelling plants; food processing; manufacturing.

**History:** Comanche area. Anglo-American settlers arrived in 1854 on land granted earlier to Stephen F. Austin and Samuel May Williams. County created 1856 from Bosque, Coryell counties; named for Indian tribe.

**Race/Ethnicity, 2000:** (In percent) Anglo, 78.10; Black, 0.49; Hispanic, 20.88; Other, 0.53.

**Vital Statistics, 2001:** Births, 158; deaths, 203; marriages, 106; divorces, 51.

**Recreation:** Hunting, fishing, water sports; parks, community center, museums; Comanche Pow-Wow in September, rodeo in July.

**Minerals:** Limited gas, oil, stone, clay.

**Agriculture:** Dairy (third in milk production), beef cattle; hay, peanuts, pecans, silage, melons; 20,000 acres irrigated. Market value $105.7 million.

**COMANCHE** (4,480) county seat; plants process feed, food; varied manufacturing; agribusiness; hospital; Ranger College branch; library; state's oldest courthouse, "Old Cora," on display on town square.

**De Leon** (2,436) marketing center for peanuts, pecans.

Other towns include: **Energy** (65), **Gustine** (457), **Proctor** (220), and **Sidney** (196).

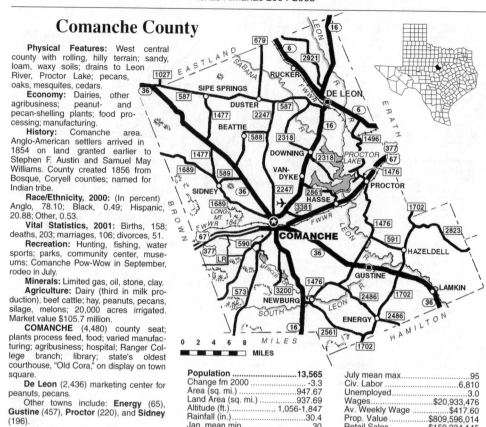

| | |
|---|---|
| Population ...........................13,565 | July mean max..............................95 |
| Change fm 2000 .......................-3.3 | Civ. Labor ..............................6,810 |
| Area (sq. mi.) ........................947.67 | Unemployed..............................3.0 |
| Land Area (sq. mi.) ...............937.69 | Wages..........................$20,933,476 |
| Altitude (ft.)...................1,056-1,847 | Av. Weekly Wage ................$417.60 |
| Rainfall (in.)................................30.4 | Prop. Value ................$809,596,014 |
| Jan. mean min. .............................30 | Retail Sales...............$159,934,145 |

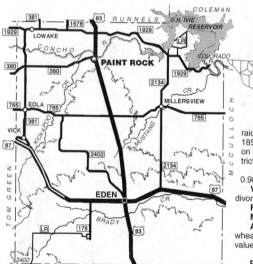

# Concho County

**Physical Features:** West central county on Edwards Plateau, rough, broken to south; level in north; sandy, loam and dark soils; drains to creeks and Colorado River.

**Economy:** Agribusinesses.

**History:** Athabascan-speaking Plains Indians, then Jumanos in 1600s, absorbed by Lipan Apaches 1700s. Comanches raided after 1800. Anglo-Americans began ranching around 1850; farming after the Civil War. Mexican-Americans employed on sheep ranches 1920s-30s. County created from Bexar District, 1858, organized 1879; named for river.

**Race/Ethnicity, 2000:** (In percent) Anglo, 57.39; Black, 0.98; Hispanic, 41.33; Other, 0.30.

**Vital Statistics, 2001:** Births, 17; deaths, 39; marriages, 20; divorces, 11.

**Recreation:** Famed for 1,500 Indian pictographs; reservoir.

**Minerals:** Oil, gas, stone.

**Agriculture:** A leading sheep-raising county; cattle, goats; wheat, feed grains; 10,000 acres irrigated for cotton. Market value $13.5 million.

**PAINT ROCK** (318) county seat; named for Indian pictographs nearby; farming, ranching center.

**EDEN** (2,575) steel fabrication, detention center; hospital; fall fest.

Other towns include: **Eola** (218), **Lowake** (40) and **Millersview** (75).

| | |
|---|---|
| Population................................3,854 | July mean max..............................98 |
| Change fm 2000..........................-2.8 | Civ. Labor...............................1,412 |
| Area (sq. mi.).........................993.69 | Unemployed..............................2.1 |
| Land Area (sq. mi.)..................991.45 | Wages...........................$4,455,926 |
| Altitude (ft.)......................1,500-2,400 | Av. Weekly Wage................$398.56 |
| Rainfall (in.)................................24.8 | Prop. Value ................$398,403,315 |
| Jan. mean min................................31 | Retail Sales...................$16,698,275 |

*For explanation of sources, abbreviations and symbols, see p. 138.*

# Cooke County

**Physical Features:** North central county; drains to Red, Trinity rivers, lakes; sandy, red, loam soils.

**Economy:** Tourism, agribusiness, varied manufacturing.

**History:** Frontier between Caddoes and Comanches. Anglo-Americans arrived in late 1840s. Germans settled western part around 1890. County created 1848 from Fannin County; named for Capt. W.G. Cooke of the Texas Revolution.

**Race/Ethnicity, 2000:** (In percent) Anglo, 85.55; Black, 3.19; Hispanic, 9.97; Other, 1.29.

**Vital Statistics, 2001:** Births, 513; deaths, 383; marriages, 718; divorces, 188.

**Recreation:** Water sports; hunting, fishing; zoo; museum; park, Depot Day/car show in October.

**Minerals:** Oil, sand, gravel.

**Agriculture:** Beef, dairy operations, wheat, grain sorghum, stocker cattle, horses. Market value $40.7 million.

**GAINESVILLE** (15,800) county seat; tourism, plastics, agribusiness; aircraft, steel fabrication; Victorian homes, walking tours; hospital; community college, juvenile correction unit; Camp Sweeney for diabetic children.

**Muenster** (1,582) oil, food processing, tourism, varied manufacturing; hospital, Germanfest in April.

Other towns include: **Callisburg** (380), **Era** (200), **Lindsay** (853), **Myra** (300), **Oak Ridge** (233), **Rosston** (75), **Valley View** (757) and the residential community around **Lake Kiowa** (1,903).

| | | |
|---|---|---|
| Population ................................. 37,634 | Rainfall (in.) ..................................... 35.8 | Wages ............................. $80,049,650 |
| Change fm 2000 ............................. 3.5 | Jan. mean min. ....................................27 | Av. Weekly Wage ................... $527.65 |
| Area (sq. mi.) ............................ 898.81 | July mean max. ...................................95 | Prop. Value ................. $2,037,627,387 |
| Land Area (sq. mi.) ................... 873.64 | Civ. Labor .................................... 16,037 | Retail Sales .................... $447,563,080 |
| Altitude (ft.) ........................... 617-1,200 | Unemployed ........................................4.7 | |

# Coryell County

**Physical Features:** Leon Valley in center, remainder rolling, hilly.

**Economy:** Fort Hood, agribusiness, state prisons, plastics and other manufacturing.

**History:** Tonkawa area, later various other tribes. Anglo-Americans settled around Fort Gates in late 1840s. Permanent establishment of Fort Hood in 1950 changed cultural geography. County created from Bell County 1854; named for local pioneer James Coryell.

**Race/Ethnicity, 2000:** (In percent) Anglo, 61.74; Black, 22.30; Hispanic, 12.57; Other, 3.39.

**Vital Statistics, 2001:** Births, 976; deaths, 329; marriages, 517; divorces, 215.

**Recreation:** state park; deer, turkey hunting; fishing; nearby lakes and Leon River, bluebonnet area. Historic homes; log jail; Shivaree in June.

**Minerals:** Small stone, sand and gravel production.

**Agriculture:** Beef cattle, forage, oats, wheat, corn, grain sorghum. Market value $38 million. Hunting leases.

**GATESVILLE** (15,587) county seat; varied manufacturing; prisons; hospital; refurbished courthouse; museum; antique shows; branch Central Texas College.

**COPPERAS COVE** (30,001) business center for Fort Hood; industrial filters, other manufacturing; hospital, library; Central Texas College; Rabbit Fest in May.

Other towns include: **Bee House** (40), **Evant** (394, partly in Hamilton County), **Flat** (210), **Jonesboro** (200), **Mound** (75), **Oglesby** (457), **Purmela** (61), **South Mountain** (416). Part (16,429) of **Fort Hood**.

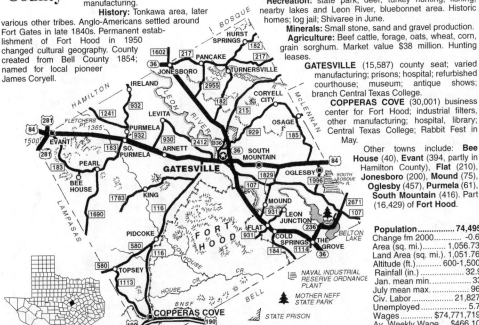

| | |
|---|---|
| Population ................ 74,495 | |
| Change fm 2000 ........... -0.6 | |
| Area (sq. mi.) ........... 1,056.73 | |
| Land Area (sq. mi.) . 1,051.76 | |
| Altitude (ft.) ........... 600-1,500 | |
| Rainfall (in.) ............... 32.9 | |
| Jan. mean min. ............... 33 | |
| July mean max. ............... 96 | |
| Civ. Labor ................. 21,827 | |
| Unemployed ................... 5.7 | |
| Wages ................. $74,771,719 | |
| Av. Weekly Wage .... $466.10 | |
| Prop. Value . $1,658,825,610 | |
| Retail Sales .... $355,110,904 | |

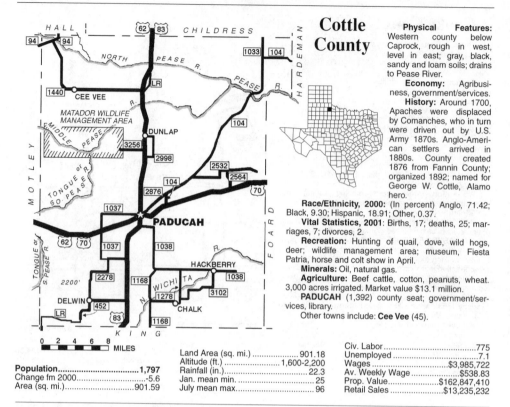

# Cottle County

**Physical Features:** Western county below Caprock, rough in west, level in east; gray, black, sandy and loam soils; drains to Pease River.

**Economy:** Agribusiness, government/services.

**History:** Around 1700, Apaches were displaced by Comanches, who in turn were driven out by U.S. Army 1870s. Anglo-American settlers arrived in 1880s. County created 1876 from Fannin County; organized 1892; named for George W. Cottle, Alamo hero.

**Race/Ethnicity, 2000:** (In percent) Anglo, 71.42; Black, 9.30; Hispanic, 18.91; Other, 0.37.

**Vital Statistics, 2001:** Births, 17; deaths, 25; marriages, 7; divorces, 2.

**Recreation:** Hunting of quail, dove, wild hogs, deer; wildlife management area; museum, Fiesta Patria, horse and colt show in April.

**Minerals:** Oil, natural gas.

**Agriculture:** Beef cattle, cotton, peanuts, wheat. 3,000 acres irrigated. Market value $13.1 million.

**PADUCAH** (1,392) county seat; government/services, library.

Other towns include: **Cee Vee** (45).

| | |
|---|---|
| Population | 1,797 |
| Change fm 2000 | -5.6 |
| Area (sq. mi.) | 901.59 |

| | |
|---|---|
| Land Area (sq. mi.) | 901.18 |
| Altitude (ft.) | 1,600-2,200 |
| Rainfall (in.) | 22.3 |
| Jan. mean min. | 25 |
| July mean max | 96 |

| | |
|---|---|
| Civ. Labor | 775 |
| Unemployed | 7.1 |
| Wages | $3,985,722 |
| Av. Weekly Wage | $538.83 |
| Prop. Value | $162,847,410 |
| Retail Sales | $13,235,232 |

# Crane County

**Physical Features:** Rolling prairie, Pecos Valley, some hills; sandy, loam soils; Juan Cordona Lake (intermittent).

**Economy:** Oil and gas; commuting to Odessa.

**History:** Lipan Apache area. Ranching developed in 1890s. Oil discovered in 1926. County created from Tom Green County 1887, organized 1927; named for Baylor University president W. C. Crane.

**Race/Ethnicity, 2000:** (In percent) Anglo, 52.42; Black, 2.98; Hispanic, 43.87; Other, 0.73.

**Vital Statistics, 2001:** Births, 33; deaths, 28; marriages, 37; divorces, 5.

**Recreation:** Sites of pioneer trails and historic Horsehead Crossing on Pecos River; county stock show in January; camping park.

**Minerals:** Among leaders in oil, gas production.

**Agriculture:** Cattle ranching, goats. Market value $2 million.

**CRANE** (2,961) county seat; oil-well servicing, production; foundry; steel, surfboard manufacturing; hospital.

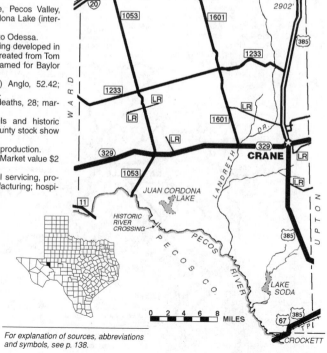

| | |
|---|---|
| Population | 3,874 |
| Change fm 2000 | -3.1 |
| Area (sq. mi.) | 785.59 |
| Land Area (sq. mi.) | 785.56 |
| Altitude (ft.) | 2,300-2,902 |
| Rainfall (in.) | 14.8 |
| Jan. mean min. | 31 |
| July mean max. | 97 |
| Civ. Labor | 1,811 |
| Unemployed | 6.2 |
| Wages | $9,902,005 |
| Av. Weekly Wage | $573.13 |
| Prop. Value | $1,077,873,130 |
| Retail Sales | $16,918,377 |

*For explanation of sources, abbreviations and symbols, see p. 138.*

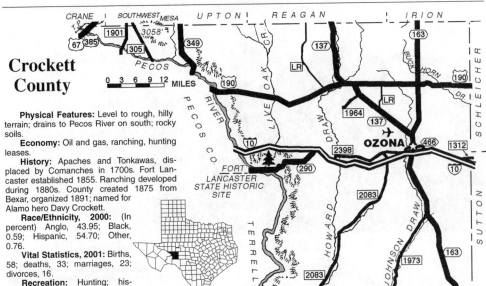

# Crockett County

**Physical Features:** Level to rough, hilly terrain; drains to Pecos River on south; rocky soils.

**Economy:** Oil and gas, ranching, hunting leases.

**History:** Apaches and Tonkawas, displaced by Comanches in 1700s. Fort Lancaster established 1855. Ranching developed during 1880s. County created 1875 from Bexar, organized 1891; named for Alamo hero Davy Crockett.

**Race/Ethnicity, 2000:** (In percent) Anglo, 43.95; Black, 0.59; Hispanic, 54.70; Other, 0.76.

**Vital Statistics, 2001:** Births, 58; deaths, 33; marriages, 23; divorces, 16.

**Recreation:** Hunting; historic sites; museum; Davy Crockett statue in park; Deerfest in December; world championship goat roping in June.

**Minerals:** Oil, gas production.

**Agriculture:** Sheep, goats; beef cattle. Market value $15.1 million.

**OZONA** (3,444) county seat; trade center for ranching; hunting leases; tourism.

| | | | |
|---|---|---|---|
| Population | 3,807 | July mean max. | 94 |
| Change fm 2000 | -7.1 | Civ. Labor | 1,961 |
| Area (sq. mi.) | 2,807.43 | Unemployed | 3.3 |
| Land Area (sq. mi.) | 2,807.42 | Wages | $7,667,422 |
| Altitude (ft.) | 1,700-3,058 | Av. Weekly Wage | $407.60 |
| Rainfall (in.) | 19.2 | Prop. Value | $1,437,856,214 |
| Jan. mean min. | 30 | Retail Sales | $25,436,325 |

# Crosby County

**Physical Features:** Flat, rich soil above Caprock, broken below; drains into Brazos River forks and playas.

**Economy:** Agribusiness, tourism, commuters to Lubbock.

**History:** Comanches, driven out by U.S. Army in 1870s; ranching developed soon afterward. Quaker colony founded in 1879. County created from Bexar District 1876, organized 1886; named for Texas Land Commissioner Stephen Crosby.

**Race/Ethnicity, 2000:** (In percent) Anglo, 46.93; Black, 3.83; Hispanic, 48.93; Other, 0.31.

**Vital Statistics, 2001:** Births, 103; deaths, 75; marriages, 35; divorces, 21.

**Recreation:** Lake; Silver Falls Park; outdoor theater in August; hunting.

**Minerals:** Sand, gravel, oil, gas.

**Agriculture:** Cotton, beef cattle; sorghum, peanuts, sunflowers, sesame; about 200,000 acres irrigated. Market value $46.3 million.

**CROSBYTON** (1,860) county seat; agribusiness center; hospital, Pioneer Museum, library; Prairie Trade Days in March and October.

Other towns include: **Lorenzo** (1,388); **Ralls** (2,215) government/services, agribusiness; museum of Indian artifacts; Cotton Boll Fest in September.

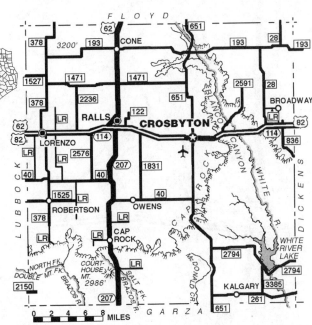

*For explanation of sources, abbreviations and symbols, see p. 138.*

| | | | |
|---|---|---|---|
| Population | 6,865 | July mean max. | 93 |
| Change fm 2000 | -2.9 | Civ. Labor | 2,950 |
| Area (sq. mi.) | 901.69 | Unemployed | 8.0 |
| Land Area (sq. mi.) | 899.51 | Wages | $9,510,873 |
| Altitude (ft.) | 2,300-3,200 | Av. Weekly Wage | $383.84 |
| Rainfall (in.) | 22.6 | Prop. Value | $347,584,514 |
| Jan. mean min. | 23 | Retail Sales | $49,735,360 |

*Guadalupe Peak and its twin peak, El Capitan, which are part of the Guadalupe Mountains National Park, tower over small hills in the foreground.*

*File photo.*

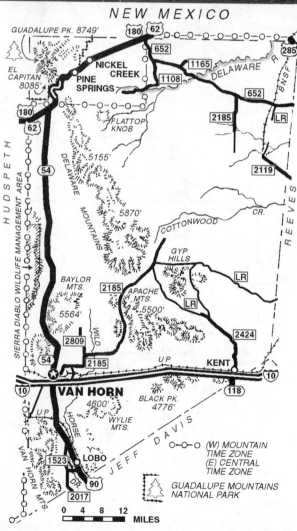

NEW MEXICO

GUADALUPE PK. 8749'
EL CAPITAN 8085'
NICKEL CREEK
PINE SPRINGS
DELAWARE R.
BNSF
FLATTOP KNOB
5155'
HUDSPETH
DELAWARE MOUNTAINS
SIERRA DIABLO WILDLIFE MANAGEMENT AREA
5870'
COTTONWOOD
REEVES
CR.
GYP HILLS
BAYLOR MTS.
5564'
APACHE MTS.
5500'
WILD
KENT
UP
VAN HORN
4600'
BLACK PK. 4776'
WYLIE MTS.
JEFF DAVIS
LOBO
HORSE
VAN HORN MTS.

O—O—O  (W) MOUNTAIN TIME ZONE
(E) CENTRAL TIME ZONE

GUADALUPE MOUNTAINS NATIONAL PARK

0  4  8  12  MILES

Population .................................. 2,839
Change fm 2000 ............................ -4.6
Area (sq. mi.) ......................... 3,812.71

# Culberson County

**Physical Features:** Contains Texas' highest mountain; slopes toward Pecos Valley on east, Diablo Bolson on west; salt lakes; unique vegetation in canyons.

**Economy:** Tourism; government/services; talc mining, processing; agribusiness.

**History:** Apaches arrived about 600 years ago. U.S. military frontier after Civil War. Ranching developed after 1880. Mexican migration increased after 1920. County created from El Paso County 1911, organized 1912; named for D.B. Culberson, Texas congressman.

**Race/Ethnicity, 2000:** (In percent) Anglo, 25.98; Black, 0.64; Hispanic, 72.24; Other, 1.14.

**Vital Statistics, 2001:** Births, 42; deaths, 21; marriages, 0; divorces, 1.

**Recreation:** National park; Guadalupe and El Capitan, twin peaks; scenic canyons and mountains; classic car museum; antique saloon bar; frontier days in June, big buck tournament.

**Minerals:** Sulfur, talc, marble, oil.

**Agriculture:** Beef cattle; crops include cotton, vegetables, melons, pecans; 4,000 acres in irrigation. Market value $8.7 million.

**VAN HORN** (2,310) county seat; agribusiness; tourism; rock crushing; government/services, hospital.

Other towns: **Kent** (60).

| | |
|---|---|
| Land Area (sq. mi.) | 3,812.46 |
| Altitude (ft.) | 3,000-8,749 |
| Rainfall (in.) | 13.1 |
| Jan. mean min. | 28 |
| July mean max. | 94 |
| Civ. Labor | 1,064 |
| Unemployed | 10.2 |
| Wages | $5,264,131 |
| Av. Weekly Wage | $390.49 |
| Prop. Value | $298,203,680 |
| Retail Sales | $58,067,852 |

# Dallam County

**Physical Features:** Prairie, broken by creeks; playas; sandy, loam soils; Rita Blanca National Grassland.

**Economy:** Agribusiness, tourism.

**History:** Earliest Plains Apaches; displaced by Comanches and Kiowas. Ranching developed in late 19th century. Farming began after 1900. County created from Bexar District, 1876, organized 1891. Named for lawyer-editor James W. Dallam.

**Race/Ethnicity, 2000:** (In percent) Anglo, 68.95; Black, 1.69; Hispanic, 28.38; Other, 0.98.

**Vital Statistics, 2001:** Births, 81; deaths, 40; marriages, 49; divorces, 34.

**Recreation:** Interstate Fair in September; XIT Museum; XIT Rodeo in August; hunting, wildlife; grasslands; La Rita Theater in June-August.

**Minerals:** Petroleum.

**Agriculture:** Cattle; hogs (leader in sales, inventory); corn (first in production for grain), wheat, grain sorghum, sugar beets, potatoes, sunflowers, beans; substantial irrigation. Market value $394.6 million.

**DALHART** (7,210, partly in Hartley County) county seat; government/services; agribusiness center for parts of Texas, New Mexico, Oklahoma; railroad; grain operations; hospital; prison.

Other towns include: **Kerrick** (60) and **Texline** (500).

| | |
|---|---|
| Population | 6,184 |
| Change fm 2000 | -0.6 |
| Area (sq. mi.) | 1,505.26 |
| Land Area (sq. mi.) | 1,504.69 |
| Altitude (ft.) | 3,700-4,700 |
| Rainfall (in.) | 17.9 |
| Jan. mean min. | 19 |
| July mean max. | 92 |
| Civ. Labor | 3,445 |
| Unemployed | 2.9 |
| Wages | $20,597,996 |
| Av. Weekly Wage | $472.13 |
| Prop. Value | $659,292,323 |
| Retail Sales | $82,360,550 |

The Texas Panhandle, where the high plains stretch all the way to the horizon. File photo.

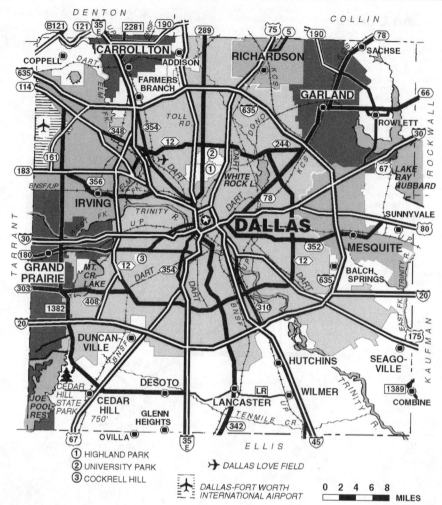

① HIGHLAND PARK
② UNIVERSITY PARK
③ COCKRELL HILL

↗ DALLAS LOVE FIELD

DALLAS-FORT WORTH
INTERNATIONAL AIRPORT

0  2  4  6  8
MILES

# Dallas County

**Physical Features:** Mostly flat, heavy blackland soils, sandy clays in west; drains to Trinity River.

**Economy:** A national center for telecommunications, transportation, electronics manufacturing, data processing, conventions and trade shows; foreign-trade zone located at D/FW International Airport, U.S. Customs port of entry; government/services.

**History:** Caddoan area. Anglo-Americans began arriving in 1840. Antebellum slaveholding area. County created 1846 from Nacogdoches, Robertson counties; named for U.S. Vice President George Mifflin Dallas.

**Race/Ethnicity, 2000:** (In percent) Anglo, 44.99; Black, 20.47; Hispanic, 29.87; Other, 4.67.

**Vital Statistics, 2001:** Births, 42,902; deaths, 14,063; marriages, 18,068; divorces, 10,094.

**Recreation:** One of the state's top tourist destinations and one of the nation's most popular convention centers; State Fair, museums, zoo, West End shopping and tourist district, historical sites, including Sixth Floor museum in the old Texas School Book Depository, site of the assassination of President Kennedy.

Other important attractions include the Morton H. Meyerson Symphony Center; performing arts; professional sports; Texas broadcast museum; lakes; theme and amusement parks.

**Minerals:** Sand, gravel.

**Agriculture:** Horticultural crops; wheat, hay, corn; horses. Market value $40.9 million.

**Education:** Southern Methodist University, University of Dallas, Dallas Baptist University, University of Texas at Dallas, University of Texas Southwest-ern Medical Center and many other education centers.

**DALLAS** (1,201,759) county seat; center of state's largest consolidated metropolitan area and second-largest city in Texas; D/FW International Airport is one of the world's busiest; headquarters for the U.S. Army and Air Force Exchange Service; Federal Reserve Bank; a leader in fashions and in computer operations; Infomart, a large computer-sales complex; many hotels in downtown area offer adequate accomodations for most conventions.

**Garland** (219,010) varied manufacturing, community college branch, hospital, performing arts center.

**Irving** (194,746) Texas Stadium, home of the Dallas Cowboys; telecommunications; varied light manufacturing, food processing; distribution center; Boy Scout headquarters and museum; North Lake College; hospitals.

Other large cities include: **Addison** (14,265) general aviation airport; **Balch Springs** (19,577); part (49,822) of **Carrollton** (115,656 total) residential community, distribution center; **Cedar Hill** (34,904) residential community,

Northwood University, Country Day on the Hill in October; **Cockrell Hill** (4,423); **Coppell** (37,091) distribution, varied manufacturing; office center; **DeSoto** (39,316) residential community, light industry and distribution, hospitals.

Also, **Duncanville** (36,779) varied manufacturing, residential community; **Farmers Branch** (27,572) distribution center, varied manufacturing, Brookhaven College, hospital; **Glenn Heights** (7,597, partly in Ellis County); most (99,760) of **Grand Prairie** (131,688 total) wholesale trade, aerospace, entertainment, plastics; library, Joe Pool Reservoir, Indian pow-wow in September, Lone Star horse-racing track; **Highland Park** (8,932); **Hutchins** (2,799) varied manufacturing; **Lancaster** (26,779) residential, industrial, distribution center, Cedar Valley College, airport, hospital, park, depot; Musicfests monthly in spring.

Also, **Mesquite** (127,584) varied industries; hospitals; championship rodeo, rodeo parade in spring; community college, historical parks; most (70,929) of **Richardson** (95,229 total) telecommunications, software development, Richland College, hospital, Owens Spring Creek Farm; **Rowlett** (47,588) residential, varied manufacturing, government/services, hospital, library, park; **Sachse** (11,703, partly in Collin County); **Seagoville** (10,966) rural/suburban setting, federal prison; **Sunnyvale** (3,043); **University Park** (23,682); **Wilmer** (3,517).

Part of **Combine** (1,956) and part of **Ovilla** (3,608).

The Magnolia Building's Flying Red Horse has become a symbol of Dallas. File photo.

| | | | |
|---|---|---|---|
| Population | 2,283,953 | July mean max. | 96 |
| Change fm 2000 | 2.9 | Civ. Labor | 1,265,409 |
| Area (sq. mi.) | 908.56 | Unemployed | 7.6 |
| Land Area (sq. mi.) | 879.60 | Wages | $16,188,608,031 |
| Altitude (ft.) | 382-750 | Av. Weekly Wage | $840.44 |
| Rainfall (in.) | 36.1 | Prop. Value | $144,616,171,010 |
| Jan. mean min | 35 | Retail Sales | $38,108,179,832 |

# Dawson County

**Physical Features:** South High Plains county in West Texas, broken on the east; loam and sandy soils.

**Economy:**
Agriculture; farm, gin equipment manufacturing; peanut plant; government/services.

**History:** Comanche, Kiowa area. Ranching developed in 1880s. Farming began after 1900. Hispanic population increased after 1940. County created from Bexar District, 1876, organized 1905; named for Nicholas M. Dawson, San Jacinto veteran.

**Race/Ethnicity, 2000:** (In percent) Anglo, 42.65; Black, 8.69; Hispanic, 48.19; Other, 0.47.

**Vital Statistics, 2001:** Births, 195; deaths, 157; marriages, 94; divorces, 74.

**Recreation:** Parks; museum; campground; May Fun Fest; July 4 celebration.

**Minerals:** Oil, natural gas.

**Agriculture:** A major cotton-producing county; also peanuts, sorghums, watermelons, alfalfa, grapes. 70,000 acres irrigated. Market value $58.9 million.

**LAMESA** (9,822) county seat; agribusiness; food processing, oil-field services; some manufacturing; computerized cotton-classing office; hospital; campus of Howard College; prison unit.

Other towns include: **Ackerly** (248, partly in Martin County), **Los Ybañez** (32) and **Welch** (110). Also, **O'Donnell** (980, mostly in Lynn County).

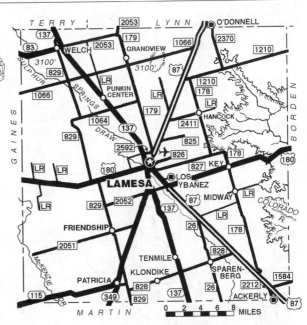

| | | | |
|---|---|---|---|
| Population | 14,712 | July mean max | 95 |
| Change fm 2000 | -1.8 | Civ. Labor | 4,947 |
| Area (sq. mi.) | 902.12 | Unemployed | 7.9 |
| Land Area (sq. mi.) | 902.06 | Wages | $26,703,321 |
| Altitude (ft.) | 2,600-3,100 | Av. Weekly Wage | $426.87 |
| Rainfall (in.) | 16.2 | Prop. Value | $979,169,045 |
| Jan. mean min | 25 | Retail Sales | $85,336,864 |

# Deaf Smith County

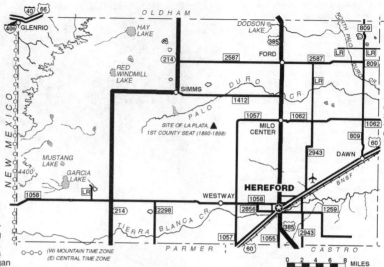

**Physical Features:** Panhandle High Plains county, partly broken; chocolate and sandy loam soils; drains to Palo Duro and Tierra Blanca creeks.

**Economy:** Agriculture, varied industries, meat packing, offset printing.

**History:** Apaches, displaced by Comanches, Kiowas. Ranching developed after U.S. Army drove out Indians 1874-75. Farming began after 1900. Hispanic settlement increased after 1950. County created 1876, from Bexar District; organized 1890. Named for famed scout in Texas Revolution, Erastus (Deaf) Smith.

**Race/Ethnicity, 2000:** (In percent) Anglo, 40.60; Black, 1.40; Hispanic, 57.40; Other, 0.60.

**Vital Statistics, 2001:** Births, 353; deaths, 158; marriages, 178; divorces, 52.

**Recreation:** Museum, tours, POW camp chapel; Cinco de Mayo, Pioneer Days in May.

**Minerals:** Not significant.

**Agriculture:** Leading farm county; cotton, dairies, feedlot operations; wheat, sorghum, corn, other vegetables, sun-

flowers; 50 percent irrigated. Market value $746.6 million, first in state.

**HEREFORD** (14,391) county seat; agribusinesses, food processing; varied manufacturing; trucking; hospital, aquatic center.

Other towns include: **Dawn** (52).

| | |
|---|---|
| Population | 18,396 |
| Change fm 2000 | -0.9 |
| Area (sq. mi.) | 1,498.26 |
| Land Area (sq. mi.) | 1,497.34 |
| Altitude (ft.) | 3,700-4,400 |
| Rainfall (in.) | 17.2 |
| Jan. mean min. | 20 |
| July mean max. | 90 |
| Civ. Labor | 7,102 |
| Unemployed | 6.0 |
| Wages | $34,506,958 |
| Av. Weekly Wage | $470.22 |
| Prop. Value | $836,163,832 |
| Retail Sales | $110,587,889 |

# Delta County

**Physical Features:** Northeast county between two forks of Sulphur River; Cooper Lake (also designated Jim Chapman Lake); black, sandy loam soils.

**Economy:** Agribusiness; tourism; manufacturing.

**History:** Caddo area, but disease, other tribes caused displacement around 1790. Anglo-Americans arrived in 1820s. County created from Lamar, Hopkins counties 1870. Greek letter delta origin of name, because of shape of the county.

**Race/Ethnicity, 2000:** (In percent) Anglo, 87.55; Black, 8.62; Hispanic, 3.10; Other, 0.73.

**Vital Statistics, 2001:** Births, 54; deaths, 59; marriages, 42; divorces, 17.

**Recreation:** Fishing, hunting; lakes, state park; Chiggerfest in October.

**Minerals:** Not significant.

**Agriculture:** Beef, dairy cattle; crops include hay, soybeans, corn, sorghum, cotton, wheat. Market value $10.7 million.

**COOPER** (2,150) county seat; industrial park, some manufacturing; agribusiness; museum.

Other towns include: **Ben Franklin** (75), **Enloe** (113), **Klondike** (135), **Lake Creek** (60) and **Pecan Gap** (225).

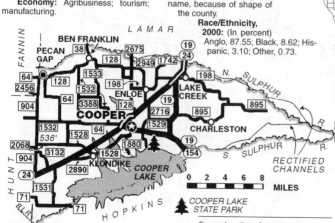

COOPER LAKE STATE PARK

*For explanation of sources, abbreviations and symbols, see p. 138.*

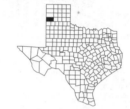

| | |
|---|---|
| Population | 5,362 |
| Change fm 2000 | 0.7 |
| Area (sq. mi.) | 277.92 |
| Land Area (sq. mi.) | 277.08 |
| Altitude (ft.) | 350-536 |
| Rainfall (in.) | 42.7 |
| Jan. mean min. | 30 |
| July mean max. | 94 |
| Civ. Labor | 2,836 |
| Unemployed | 4.5 |
| Wages | $7,054,393 |
| Av. Weekly Wage | $480.64 |
| Prop. Value | $185,304,985 |
| Retail Sales | $12,338,600 |

**Physical Features:** North Texas county; partly hilly, draining to Elm Fork of Trinity River, two lakes; Blackland and Grand Prairie soils and terrain.

**Economy:** Varied industries; colleges; tourism; government/services; part of Dallas-Fort Worth metropolitan area.

**History:** Land grant from Texas Congress 1841 for Peters colony. County created out of Fannin County 1846; named for John B. Denton, pioneer Methodist minister.

**Race/Ethnicity, 2000:** (In percent) Anglo, 76.93; Black, 6.07; Hispanic, 12.15; Other, 4.85.

**Vital Statistics, 2001:** Births, 7,899; deaths, 1,805; marriages, 4,069; divorces, 2,128.

**Recreation:** Water sports at Lewisville, Grapevine lakes, seven U.S. Corps of Engineers parks; Ray Roberts lake; universities' cultural, athletic activities, including "Texas Women; A Celebration of History'" exhibit at TWU library; State D.A.R. Museum "First Ladies of Texas" collection of gowns and memorabilia; Little Chapel in the Woods; Denton Jazzfest in April.

**Minerals:** Salt, sand, gravel.

**Education:** University of North Texas and Texas Woman's University.

**Agriculture:** Important horse-raising area. Eggs, nurseries, turf, cattle; also, hay, sorghum, wheat, peanuts also grown. Market value $60.7 million.

**DENTON** (89,379) county seat; uni-

# Denton County

versities; Denton State School (for the retarded); manufacturers of trucks (Peterbilt), bricks; milling; hospitals; Blues Festival in September, storytelling festival in March.

**LEWISVILLE** (85,081) commuting to Dallas and Fort Worth, retail center, electronics and varied industries including missile manufacturing; Lewisville Lake, hospital, library; Celtic Feis & Scottish Highland Games in March.

**Flower Mound** (56,230) residential community, library, bike classic in May.

**Carrollton** (115,656, also in Dallas County).

Other towns include: **The Colony** (31,556) on eastern shore of Lewisville Lake, tourism, IBM offices, chili cook-off in June, Las Vegas Night in April.

Also, **Argyle** (2,620); **Aubrey** (1,715) horse farms, training, Death by Chocolate event in November; **Barton-ville** (1,235); **Clark** (345); **Copper Can-**

yon (1,330); **Corinth** (13,690); **Corral City** (91); **Cross Roads** (679); **Double Oak** (2,394); **Hackberry** (593); **Hebron** (873); **Hickory Creek** (2,392); **Highland Village** (13,749); **Justin** (2,190); **Krugerville** (1,021); **Krum** (2,213); **Lake Dallas** (6,710) light manufacturing, marina.

Also, **Lakewood Village** (348); **Lincoln Park** (568); **Little Elm** (8,202); light manufacturing, lake activities; **Marshall Creek** (440); **Northlake** (974); **Oak Point** (1,961); **Pilot Point** (3,871) light manufacturing, agribusinesses, near Lake Ray Roberts, Country Fair on the Square in September; **Ponder** (572); **Roanoke** (3,166); **Sanger** (4,950) lake recreation enterprises; **Shady Shores** (1,628); **Trophy Club** (6,947).

Part (22,273) of **Dallas**, part (3,402) of **Frisco**, part (2,140) of **Plano** Small part (44) of **Fort Worth**.

| | |
|---|---|
| **Population** | .......................**488,481** |
| Change fm 2000 | ...........................12.8 |
| Area (sq. mi.) | ..........................957.88 |
| Land Area (sq. mi.) | ...................888.54 |
| Altitude (ft.) | ........................450-950 |
| Rainfall (in.) | .................................37.3 |
| Jan. mean min. | ...............................30 |
| July mean max. | ...............................94 |
| Civ. Labor | ............................275,568 |
| Unemployed | .....................................4.9 |
| Wages | ...................$962,708,737 |
| Av. Weekly Wage | ....................$601.20 |
| Prop. Value | ...............$34,599,554,151 |
| Retail Sales | ...............$4,611,990,649 |

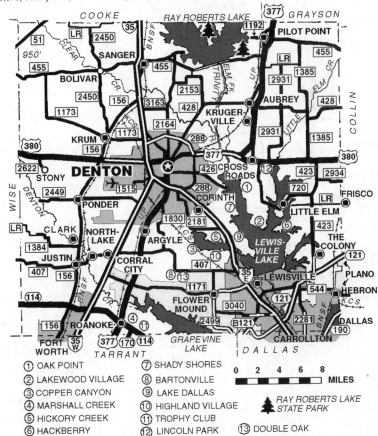

(1) OAK POINT
(2) LAKEWOOD VILLAGE
(3) COPPER CANYON
(4) MARSHALL CREEK
(5) HICKORY CREEK
(6) HACKBERRY
(7) SHADY SHORES
(8) BARTONVILLE
(9) LAKE DALLAS
(10) HIGHLAND VILLAGE
(11) TROPHY CLUB
(12) LINCOLN PARK
(13) DOUBLE OAK

0  2  4  6  8
MILES

RAY ROBERTS LAKE
STATE PARK

# DeWitt County

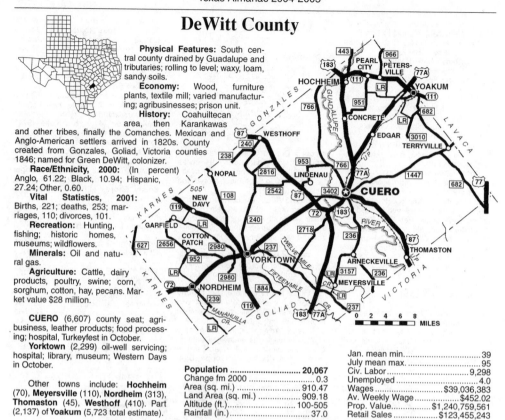

**Physical Features:** South central county drained by Guadalupe and tributaries; rolling to level; waxy, loam, sandy soils.

**Economy:** Wood, furniture plants, textile mill; varied manufacturing; agribusinesses; prison unit.

**History:** Coahuiltecan area, then Karankawas and other tribes, finally the Comanches. Mexican and Anglo-American settlers arrived in 1820s. County created from Gonzales, Goliad, Victoria counties 1846; named for Green DeWitt, colonizer.

**Race/Ethnicity, 2000:** (In percent) Anglo, 61.22; Black, 10.94; Hispanic, 27.24; Other, 0.60.

**Vital Statistics, 2001:** Births, 221; deaths, 253; marriages, 110; divorces, 101.

**Recreation:** Hunting, fishing; historic homes, museums; wildflowers.

**Minerals:** Oil and natural gas.

**Agriculture:** Cattle, dairy products, poultry, swine; corn, sorghum, cotton, hay, pecans. Market value $28 million.

**CUERO** (6,607) county seat; agribusiness, leather products; food processing; hospital, Turkeyfest in October.

**Yorktown** (2,299) oil-well servicing; hospital; library, museum; Western Days in October.

Other towns include: **Hochheim** (70), **Meyersville** (110), **Nordheim** (313), **Thomaston** (45), **Westhoff** (410). Part (2,137) of **Yoakum** (5,723 total estimate).

| | |
|---|---|
| Population | 20,067 |
| Change fm 2000 | 0.3 |
| Area (sq. mi.) | 910.47 |
| Land Area (sq. mi.) | 909.18 |
| Altitude (ft.) | 100-505 |
| Rainfall (in.) | 37.0 |

| | |
|---|---|
| Jan. mean min. | 39 |
| July mean max. | 95 |
| Civ. Labor | 9,298 |
| Unemployed | 4.0 |
| Wages | $39,036,383 |
| Av. Weekly Wage | $452.02 |
| Prop. Value | $1,240,759,561 |
| Retail Sales | $123,455,243 |

# Dickens County

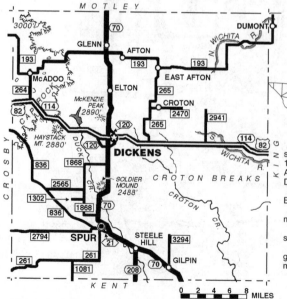

**Physical Features:** West Texas county; broken land, Caprock in northwest; sandy, chocolate, red soils; drains to Croton, Duck creeks.

**Economy:** Services/prison unit, agribusiness, hunting leases.

**History:** Comanches driven out by U.S. Army 1874-75. Ranching and some farming began in late 1880s. County created 1876, from Bexar District; organized 1891; named for Alamo hero who is variously listed as James R. Demkins or Dimpkins and J. Dickens.

**Race/Ethnicity, 2000:** (In percent) Anglo, 67.67; Black, 8.07; Hispanic, 23.90; Other, 0.36.

**Vital Statistics, 2001:** Births, 26; deaths, 44; marriages, 15; divorces, 5.

**Recreation:** Hunting, fishing; Soldiers Mound site, Dickens Springs; downtown Spur.

**Agriculture:** Cattle, cotton, forages, small grains, horses. Some irrigation. Market value $11.8 million. Hunting leases important.

**Minerals:** Oil, gas.

**DICKENS** (330) county seat, market for ranching country.

**SPUR** (1,076) agribusiness and shipping center, homecoming in October; state prison.

Other towns include: **Afton** (15) and **McAdoo** (75).

| | |
|---|---|
| Population | 2,702 |
| Change fm 2000 | -2.2 |
| Area (sq. mi.) | 905.21 |
| Land Area (sq. mi.) | 904.21 |
| Altitude (ft.) | 1,800-3,000 |
| Rainfall (in.) | 20.7 |
| Jan. mean min. | 26 |

| | |
|---|---|
| July mean max. | 95 |
| Civ. Labor | 859 |
| Unemployed | 4.9 |
| Wages | $2,850,825 |
| Av. Weekly Wage | $412.21 |
| Prop. Value | $182,568,750 |
| Retail Sales | $9,591,989 |

*For explanation of sources, abbreviations and symbols, see p. 138.*

# Dimmit County

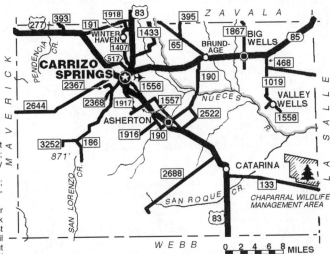

**Physical Features:** Southwest county; level to rolling; much brush; sandy, loam, red soils; drained by Nueces River.

**Economy:** Government/services; agribusiness; petroleum products; tourism.

**History:** Coahuiltecan area, later Comanches. John Townsend, a black man from Nacogdoches, led first attempt at settlement before the Civil War. Texas Rangers forced Indians out in 1877. Mexican migration increased after 1910. County created 1858 from Bexar, Maverick, Uvalde, Webb counties; organized 1880. Named for Philip Dimitt of Texas Revolution; law misspelled name.

**Race/Ethnicity, 2000:** (In percent) Anglo, 13.39; Black, 0.74; Hispanic, 84.97; Other, 0.90.

**Vital Statistics, 2001:** Births, 191; deaths, 92; marriages, 50; divorces, 9.

**Recreation:** Hunting, fishing, campsites, wildlife area; winter haven for tourists.

**Minerals:** Oil, natural gas.

**Agriculture:** Among leading irrigated vegetable-growing counties; cattle, poultry raised; nursery, hay, pecans. Market value $26.3 million.

**CARRIZO SPRINGS** (5,624) county seat; agribusiness center, feedlot, food processing; oil, gas processing; hunting center; hospital; Brush Country Day in October.

Other towns include: **Asherton** (1,330), **Big Wells** (717) Cinco de Mayo, and **Catarina** (141) Camino Real festival in April.

| | |
|---|---|
| Population | **10,200** |
| Change fm 2000 | -0.5 |
| Area (sq. mi.) | 1,334.48 |
| Land Area (sq. mi.) | 1,330.91 |
| Altitude (ft.) | 400-871 |
| Rainfall (in.) | 21.7 |
| Jan. mean min. | 41 |
| July mean max. | 99 |
| Civ. Labor | 3,760 |
| Unemployed | 11.9 |
| Wages | $15,508,034 |
| Av. Weekly Wage | $449.99 |
| Prop. Value | $759,286,390 |
| Retail Sales | $55,325,577 |

# Donley County

**Physical Features:** Northwest county bisected by Red River Salt Fork; rolling to level; clay, loam, sandy soils.

**Economy:** Agribusiness; tourism; varied manufacturing.

**History:** Apaches displaced by Kiowas and Comanches, who were driven out in 1874-75 by U.S. Army. Methodist colony from New York settled in 1878. County created in 1876, organized 1882, out of Bexar District; named for Texas Supreme Court Justice S.P. Donley.

**Race/Ethnicity, 2000:** (In percent) Anglo, 88.43; Black, 4.36; Hispanic, 6.35; Other, 0.86.

**Vital Statistics, 2001:** Births, 30; deaths, 55; marriages, 29; divorces, 14.

**Recreation:** Lake, hunting, fishing, camping, water sports; Col. Goodnight Chuckwagon cook-off, late September.

**Minerals:** Small amount of natural gas.

**Agriculture:** Cattle top revenue source; cotton, peanuts, wheat, alfalfa, hay; 11,000 acres irrigated. Market value $84.3 million.

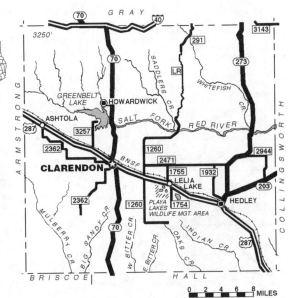

**CLARENDON** (1,878) county seat; junior college; Saints Roost museum; library; agribusiness; tourism; medical center.

Other towns include: **Hedley** (365) cotton festival in October, **Howardwick** (423) and **Lelia Lake** (125).

| | |
|---|---|
| Population | **3,887** |
| Change fm 2000 | 1.5 |
| Area (sq. mi.) | 933.05 |
| Land Area (sq. mi.) | 929.77 |
| Altitude (ft.) | 2,200-3,250 |
| Rainfall (in.) | 22.0 |
| Jan. mean min. | 21 |
| July mean max. | 94 |
| Civ. Labor | 1,690 |
| Unemployed | 3.0 |
| Wages | $5,030,250 |
| Av. Weekly Wage | $390.46 |
| Prop. Value | $262,074,710 |
| Retail Sales | $15,166,239 |

# Duval County

**Physical Features:** Southwestern county; level to hilly, brushy in most areas; varied soils.

**Economy:** Ranching; petroleum; tourism; government/services.

**History:** Coahuiltecans, displaced by Comanche bands. Mexican settlement began in 1812. County created from Live Oak, Nueces, Starr counties, 1858, organized 1876; named for Burr H. Duval, a victim of Goliad massacre.

**Race/Ethnicity, 2000:** (In percent) Anglo, 11.22; Black, 0.44; Hispanic, 87.99; Other, 0.35.

**Vital Statistics, 2001:** Births, 195; deaths, 137; marriages, 71; divorces, 44.

**Recreation:** Hunting, tourist crossroads, rattlesnake roundup.

**Minerals:** Production of oil, gas, salt, sand and gravel.

**Agriculture:** Most income from beef cattle; grains, cotton, vegetables, hay, dairy. Market value $14.3 million.

**SAN DIEGO** (4,792, part [825] in Jim Wells County) county seat; ranching, oil field, tourist center; hospital.

**Freer** (3,250) center of oil and livestock-raising; rattlesnake roundup in April.

**Benavides** (1,685) serves truck farming area.

Other towns include: **Concepcion** (64) and **Realitos** (216).

| | |
|---|---|
| Population | 12,811 |
| Change fm 2000 | -2.4 |
| Area (sq. mi.) | 1,795.67 |
| Land Area (sq. mi.) | 1,792.71 |
| Altitude (ft.) | 150-833 |
| Rainfall (in.) | 24.8 |
| Jan. mean min. | 41 |
| July mean max. | 96 |
| Civ. Labor | 4,692 |
| Unemployed | 9.6 |
| Wages | $18,534,583 |
| Av. Weekly Wage | $449.48 |
| Prop. Value | $983,427,159 |
| Retail Sales | $31,479,790 |

# Eastland County

**Physical Features:** West central county; hilly, rolling; sandy, loam soils; drains to Leon River forks.

**Economy:** Agribusinesses; education; petroleum industries; varied manufacturing.

**History:** Plains Indian area. Frank Sánchez among first settlers in 1850s. County created from Bosque, Coryell, Travis counties, 1858, organized 1873; named for W.M. Eastland, Mier Expedition casualty.

**Race/Ethnicity, 2000:** (In percent) Anglo, 86.26; Black, 2.30; Hispanic, 10.80; Other, 0.64.

**Vital Statistics, 2001:** Births, 199; deaths, 312; marriages, 144; divorces, 52.

**Recreation:** Lakes, water sports; fishing, hunting; festivals; historic sites and displays.

**Minerals:** Oil, gas, gravel and sand.

**Agriculture:** Beef cattle, forage. 20,000 acres irrigated. Market value $29.1 million.

**EASTLAND** (3,760) county seat; tourism; government/services, petroleum industries, varied manufacturing; hospital, library; Old Ripfest in September.

**CISCO** (3,813) agribusiness; clothing, molding plants; Conrad Hilton's first hotel restored, museums; junior college; folklife festival in April; Kendrick Religious Diorama.

**RANGER** (2,510) oil center, varied manufacturing, junior college, hospital.

Other towns include: **Carbon** (210) livestock equipment manufacturing; **Desdemona** (180); **Gorman** (1,200) peanut processing, agribusiness, hospital; and **Rising Star** (844) cap manufacturing, plant nursery; Octoberfest.

| | |
|---|---|
| Population | 18,210 |
| Change fm 2000 | -0.5 |
| Area (sq. mi.) | 931.90 |
| Land Area (sq. mi.) | 926.01 |
| Altitude (ft.) | 1,000-1,882 |
| Rainfall (in.) | 29.7 |
| Jan. mean min. | 29 |
| July mean max. | 94 |
| Civ. Labor | 9,936 |
| Unemployed | 4.3 |
| Wages | $42,508,440 |
| Av. Weekly Wage | $476.17 |
| Prop. Value | $773,350,888 |
| Retail Sales | $171,491,144 |

*For explanation of sources, abbreviations and symbols, see p. 138.*

# Ector County

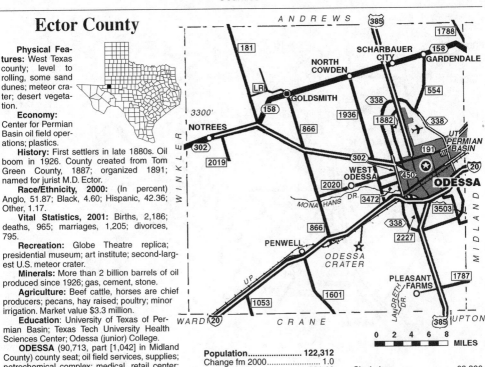

**Physical Features:** West Texas county; level to rolling, some sand dunes; meteor crater; desert vegetation.

**Economy:** Center for Permian Basin oil field operations; plastics.

**History:** First settlers in late 1880s. Oil boom in 1926. County created from Tom Green County, 1887; organized 1891; named for jurist M.D. Ector.

**Race/Ethnicity, 2000:** (In percent) Anglo, 51.87; Black, 4.60; Hispanic, 42.36; Other, 1.17.

**Vital Statistics, 2001:** Births, 2,186; deaths, 965; marriages, 1,205; divorces, 795.

**Recreation:** Globe Theatre replica; presidential museum; art institute; second-largest U.S. meteor crater.

**Minerals:** More than 2 billion barrels of oil produced since 1926; gas, cement, stone.

**Agriculture:** Beef cattle, horses are chief producers; pecans, hay raised; poultry; minor irrigation. Market value $3.3 million.

**Education:** University of Texas of Permian Basin; Texas Tech University Health Sciences Center; Odessa (junior) College.

**ODESSA** (90,713, part [1,042] in Midland County) county seat; oil field services, supplies; petrochemical complex; medical, retail center; cultural center; Permian Basin Fair and Expo in September.

Other towns include: **Gardendale** (1,228), **Goldsmith** (251), **Notrees** (338), **Penwell** (74), and **West Odessa** (17,874).

| | |
|---|---|
| Population...................... | 122,312 |
| Change fm 2000...................... | 1.0 |
| Area (sq. mi.)...................... | 901.68 |
| Land Area (sq. mi.)........... | 901.06 |
| Altitude (ft.)................... | 2,800-3,300 |
| Rainfall (in.)........................... | 13.1 |
| Jan. mean min......................... | 28 |
| July mean max........................ | 95 |

| | |
|---|---|
| Civ. Labor........................... | 62,800 |
| Unemployed........................... | 7.0 |
| Wages.................... | $364,496,208 |
| Av. Weekly Wage............. | $565.45 |
| Prop. Value.......... | $5,311,561,686 |
| Retail Sales......... | $1,404,552,001 |

---

# Edwards County

**Physical Features:** Rolling, hilly; caves; spring-fed streams; rocky, thin soils; drained by Llano, Nueces rivers; varied timber.

**Economy:** Ranching; hunting leases; tourism; oil, gas production.

**History:** Apache area. First land sold in 1876. County created from Bexar District, 1858; organized 1883; named for Nacogdoches empresario Hayden Edwards.

**Race/Ethnicity, 2000:** (In percent) Anglo, 54.25; Black, 0.14; Hispanic, 45.05; Other, 0.56.

**Vital Statistics, 2001:** Births, 24; deaths, 15; marriages, 17; divorces, 7.

**Recreation:** Hunting, fishing; scenic drives; state park.

**Minerals:** Gas.

**Agriculture:** Center for mohair-wool production; Angora goats, sheep, cattle; some pecans. Market value $9.6 million. Cedar for oil.

**ROCKSPRINGS** (1,269) county seat; ranching, tourism, Top of the World Festival, July 4.

Other towns include: **Barksdale** (1,081).

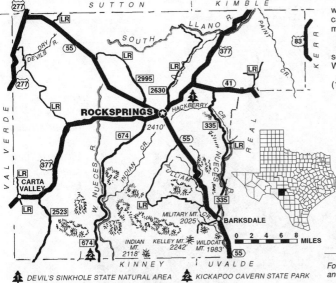

🌲 DEVIL'S SINKHOLE STATE NATURAL AREA   🌲 KICKAPOO CAVERN STATE PARK

| | |
|---|---|
| Population .............................. | 2,081 |
| Change fm 2000 ...................... | -3.7 |
| Area (sq. mi.) ...................... | 2,119.95 |
| Land Area (sq. mi.) ............. | 2,119.75 |
| Altitude (ft.) ................. | 1,507-2,410 |
| Rainfall (in.).............................. | 22.0 |
| Jan. mean min. ........................... | 35 |
| July mean max........................... | 95 |
| Civ. Labor............................... | 913 |
| Unemployed.............................. | 3.8 |
| Wages................... | $2,327,626 |
| Av. Weekly Wage .............. | $422.28 |
| Prop. Value ............... | $395,149,312 |
| Retail Sales................. | $10,370,043 |

*For explanation of sources, abbreviations and symbols, see p. 138.*

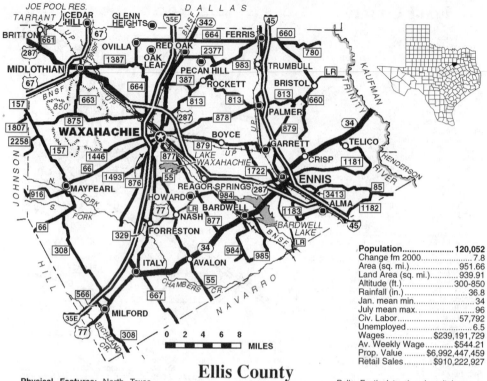

| | |
|---|---|
| Population | 120,052 |
| Change fm 2000 | 7.8 |
| Area (sq. mi.) | 951.66 |
| Land Area (sq. mi.) | 939.91 |
| Altitude (ft.) | 300-850 |
| Rainfall (in.) | 36.8 |
| Jan. mean min. | 34 |
| July mean max. | 96 |
| Civ. Labor | 57,792 |
| Unemployed | 6.5 |
| Wages | $239,191,729 |
| Av. Weekly Wage | $544.21 |
| Prop. Value | $6,992,447,459 |
| Retail Sales | $910,222,927 |

# Ellis County

**Physical Features:** North Texas Blackland soils; level to rolling; Chambers Creek, Trinity River.

**Economy:** Cement, steel production; warehousing & distribution; government/services, agriculture; many residents work in Dallas.

**History:** Tonkawa area. Part of Peters colony settled in 1843. County created 1849, organized 1850, from Navarro County. Named for Richard Ellis, president of convention that declared Texas' independence.

**Race/Ethnicity, 2000:** (In percent) Anglo, 71.94; Black, 8.73; Hispanic, 18.42; Other, 0.91.

**Vital Statistics, 2001:** Births, 1,815; deaths, 936; marriages, 1,088; divorces, 242.

**Recreation:** Medieval-theme Scarborough Faire; Gingerbread Trail homes tour, fall festival; lakes, fishing, hunting.

**Minerals:** Cement, gas.

**Agriculture:** Cotton, wheat, cattle, hay, turf grass, nursery plants, horses, sorghum. Market value $49.9 million.

**WAXAHACHIE** (22,710) county seat; manufacturing; transportation; steel, aluminum; tourism; hospital; colleges; museum; hike & bike trail; Crape Myrtle festival in July.

**Ennis** (17,150) agribusiness; manufacturing; bluebonnet trails, National Polka Festival; tourism; hospital.

**Midlothian** (9,131) trade zone, cement plant, steel manufacturing; other factories; fall festival.

Other towns include: **Alma** (311); **Avalon** (130); **Bardwell** (609); **Ferris** (2,246); **Forreston** (200); **Garrett** (480); **Howard** (NA); **Italy** (2,071); **Maypearl** (795); **Milford** (677); **Oak Leaf** (1,315); **Ovilla** (3,608); **Palmer** (1,799); **Pecan Hill** (670); and **Red Oak** (4,597) manufacturing, Founders Day in September. Also, **Glenn Heights** (7,597, mostly in Dallas County).

*For explanation of sources, abbreviations and symbols, see p. 138.*

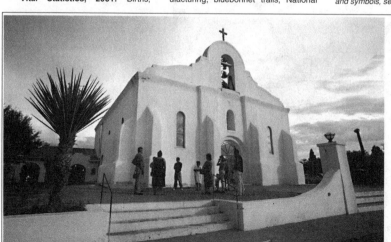

*Church members gather around the San Elizario Chapel near El Paso.*

*File photo.*

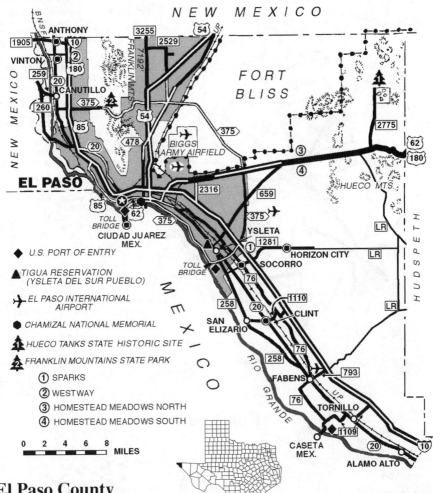

**EL PASO**

◆ U.S. PORT OF ENTRY

▲ TIGUA RESERVATION
(YSLETA DEL SUR PUEBLO)

✈ EL PASO INTERNATIONAL
AIRPORT

⬡ CHAMIZAL NATIONAL MEMORIAL

⬆ HUECO TANKS STATE HISTORIC SITE

⬆ FRANKLIN MOUNTAINS STATE PARK

① SPARKS

② WESTWAY

③ HOMESTEAD MEADOWS NORTH

④ HOMESTEAD MEADOWS SOUTH

0   2   4   6   8
▬▬▬▬▬▬▬▬  MILES

# El Paso County

**Physical Features:** Westernmost county in fertile Rio Grande Valley; 7,000-foot mountains; desert vegetation except where irrigated.

**Economy:** Government, military are major economic factors; wholesale, retail distribution center; education; tourism; maquiladora plants, varied manufacturers; ore smelting, refining, cotton, food processing.

**History:** Various Indian tribes inhabited the valley before Spanish civilization arrived in late 1650s. Spanish and Tigua and Piro tribes fleeing Santa Fe uprising of 1680 sought refuge at Ysleta and Socorro. County created from Bexar District, 1849; organized 1850; named for historic pass (Paso del Norte), lowest all-weather pass through Rocky Mountains.

**Race/Ethnicity, 2000:** (In percent) Anglo, 17.41; Black, 2.93; Hispanic, 78.23; Other, 1.43.

**Vital Statistics, 2001:** Births, 14,189; deaths, 4,035; marriages, 7,126; divorces, 482.

**Recreation:** Gateway to Mexico; Chamizal Museum; major tourist center; December Sun Carnival with foot-

ball game; state parks, mountain tramway, missions and other historic sites.

**Minerals:** Production of cement, stone, sand and gravel.

**Agriculture:** Dairy products (fourth in state in milk production); cattle; cotton, pecans, onions, forage, peppers also raised; 50,000 acres irrigated, mostly cotton. Market value $102.8 million.

**Education:** University of Texas at El Paso; UT School of Nursing at El Paso; Texas Tech University Health Sciences Center; El Paso Community College.

**EL PASO** (573,787) county seat; fifth-largest Texas city, largest U.S. city on Mexican border.

A center for government operations. Federal installations include Fort Bliss, William Beaumont General Hospital, La Tuna federal prison, and headquarters of the U.S. Army Air Defense Command;

Manufactured products include clothing, electronics, auto equipment,

plastics; trade and distribution; refining; processing of ore, oil, food, cotton, and other farm products.

Hospitals; museums; convention center; theater, symphony orchestra.

Other towns include: **Anthony** (3,898); **Canutillo** (5,079); **Clint** (998); **Fabens** (8,091); **Homestead Meadows North** (4,263); **Homestead Meadows South** (7,009); **Horizon City** (5,942); (216); **San Elizario** (11,364); **Socorro** (27,892); **Sparks** (3,047); **Tornillo** (1,591); **Vinton** (1,949); **Westway** (3,983), and **Ysleta**, (now within El Paso) settled in 1680, perhaps the oldest town in Texas.

**Fort Bliss** (8,128) and **Biggs Field** (4,226).

| | |
|---|---|
| Population | 697,562 |
| Change fm 2000 | 2.6 |
| Area (sq. mi.) | 1,014.68 |
| Land Area (sq. mi.) | 1,013.11 |
| Altitude (ft.) | 3,582-7,192 |
| Rainfall (in.) | 8.8 |
| Jan. mean min. | 29 |
| July mean max. | 96 |
| Civ. Labor | 294,852 |
| Unemployed | 8.9 |
| Wages | $1,628,328,218 |
| Av. Weekly Wage | $498.16 |
| Prop. Value | $21,464,784,707 |
| Retail Sales | $6,335,884,132 |

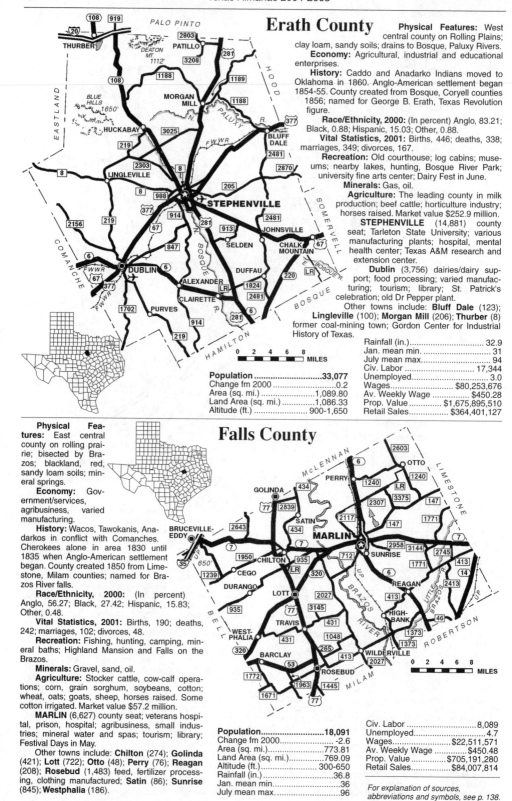

# Erath County

**Physical Features:** West central county on Rolling Plains; clay loam, sandy soils; drains to Bosque, Paluxy Rivers.

**Economy:** Agricultural, industrial and educational enterprises.

**History:** Caddo and Anadarko Indians moved to Oklahoma in 1860. Anglo-American settlement began 1854-55. County created from Bosque, Coryell counties 1856; named for George B. Erath, Texas Revolution figure.

**Race/Ethnicity, 2000:** (In percent) Anglo, 83.21; Black, 0.88; Hispanic, 15.03; Other, 0.88.

**Vital Statistics, 2001:** Births, 446; deaths, 338; marriages, 349; divorces, 167.

**Recreation:** Old courthouse; log cabins; museums; nearby lakes, hunting, Bosque River Park; university fine arts center; Dairy Fest in June.

**Minerals:** Gas, oil.

**Agriculture:** The leading county in milk production; beef cattle; horticulture industry; horses raised. Market value $252.9 million.

**STEPHENVILLE** (14,881) county seat; Tarleton State University; various manufacturing plants; hospital, mental health center; Texas A&M research and extension center.

**Dublin** (3,756) dairies/dairy support; food processing; varied manufacturing; tourism; library; St. Patrick's celebration; old Dr Pepper plant.

Other towns include: **Bluff Dale** (123); **Lingleville** (100); **Morgan Mill** (206); **Thurber** (8) former coal-mining town; Gordon Center for Industrial History of Texas.

| | |
|---|---|
| Population | 33,077 |
| Change fm 2000 | 0.2 |
| Area (sq. mi.) | 1,089.80 |
| Land Area (sq. mi.) | 1,086.33 |
| Altitude (ft.) | 900-1,650 |
| Rainfall (in.) | 32.9 |
| Jan. mean min. | 31 |
| July mean max. | 94 |
| Civ. Labor | 17,344 |
| Unemployed | 3.0 |
| Wages | $80,253,676 |
| Av. Weekly Wage | $450.28 |
| Prop. Value | $1,675,895,510 |
| Retail Sales | $364,401,127 |

# Falls County

**Physical Features:** East central county on rolling prairie; bisected by Brazos; blackland, red, sandy loam soils; mineral springs.

**Economy:** Government/services, agribusiness, varied manufacturing.

**History:** Wacos, Tawokanis, Anadarkos in conflict with Comanches. Cherokees alone in area 1830 until 1835 when Anglo-American settlement began. County created 1850 from Limestone, Milam counties; named for Brazos River falls.

**Race/Ethnicity, 2000:** (In percent) Anglo, 56.27; Black, 27.42; Hispanic, 15.83; Other, 0.48.

**Vital Statistics, 2001:** Births, 190; deaths, 242; marriages, 102; divorces, 48.

**Recreation:** Fishing, hunting, camping, mineral baths; Highland Mansion and Falls on the Brazos.

**Minerals:** Gravel, sand, oil.

**Agriculture:** Stocker cattle, cow-calf operations; corn, grain sorghum, soybeans, cotton; wheat, oats; goats, sheep, horses raised. Some cotton irrigated. Market value $57.2 million.

**MARLIN** (6,627) county seat; veterans hospital, prison, hospital; agribusiness, small industries; mineral water and spas; tourism; library; Festival Days in May.

Other towns include: **Chilton** (274); **Golinda** (421); **Lott** (722); **Otto** (48); **Perry** (76); **Reagan** (208); **Rosebud** (1,483) feed, fertilizer processing, clothing manufactured; **Satin** (86); **Sunrise** (845); **Westphalia** (186).

| | |
|---|---|
| Population | 18,091 |
| Change fm 2000 | -2.6 |
| Area (sq. mi.) | 773.81 |
| Land Area (sq. mi.) | 769.09 |
| Altitude (ft.) | 300-650 |
| Rainfall (in.) | 36.8 |
| Jan. mean min. | 36 |
| July mean max. | 96 |
| Civ. Labor | 8,089 |
| Unemployed | 4.7 |
| Wages | $22,511,571 |
| Av. Weekly Wage | $450.48 |
| Prop. Value | $705,191,280 |
| Retail Sales | $84,007,814 |

*For explanation of sources, abbreviations and symbols, see p. 138.*

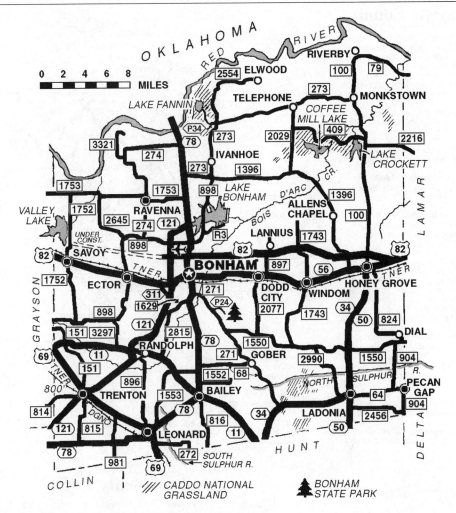

0  2  4  6  8
MILES

## Fannin County

**Physical Features:** North Texas county of rolling prairie, drained by Red River, Bois d'Arc Creek; mostly black-land soils; national grassland.

**Economy:** Communications; agriculture; government/services, prisons; petroleum distribution, tourism; varied manufacturing.

**History:** Caddoes who joined with Cherokees. Anglo-American settlement began in 1836. County created from Red River County, 1837, organized 1838; named for James W. Fannin, a victim of Goliad massacre.

**Race/Ethnicity, 2000:** (In percent) Anglo, 85.12; Black, 8.12; Hispanic, 5.61; Other, 1.15.

**Vital Statistics, 2001:** Births, 340; deaths, 411; marriages, 239; divorces, 149.

**Recreation:** Water activities on lakes; hunting; state park, fossil beds; winery; Sam Rayburn home, memorial library; Bois D'Arc festival in May.

**Minerals:** Not significant; some sand produced.

**Agriculture:** Beef cattle, wheat, corn, grain sorghum, hay, horses, pecans. Market value $45.3 million.

**BONHAM** (10,255) county seat; varied manufacturing; veterans hospital and private hospital; state jail; Sam Rayburn birthday celebration in January.

Other towns include: **Bailey** (239); **Dodd City** (406); **Ector** (641); **Gober** (146); **Honey Grove** (1,791) agribusiness center, varied manufacturing, tourism, historic buildings, library, Davy Crockett Day in October; **Ivanhoe** (110); **Ladonia** (674) restored historical downtown, tourism; varied manufacturing, commuters, rodeo; **Leonard** (1,900) varied manufacturing; **Randolph** (70); **Ravenna** (223); **Savoy** (850); **Telephone** (210); **Trenton** (687); **Windom** (244).

| | |
|---|---|
| Population | 31,672 |
| Change fm 2000 | 1.4 |
| Area (sq. mi.) | 899.16 |
| Land Area (sq. mi.) | 891.45 |
| Altitude (ft.) | 450-800 |
| Rainfall (in.) | 44.0 |
| Jan. mean min. | 29 |
| July mean max. | 94 |
| Civ. Labor | 12,586 |
| Unemployed | 6.4 |
| Wages | $49,783,833 |
| Av. Weekly Wage | $525.38 |
| Prop. Value | $1,115,001,700 |
| Retail Sales | $198,464,505 |

*For explanation of sources, abbreviations and symbols, see p. 138.*

# Fayette County

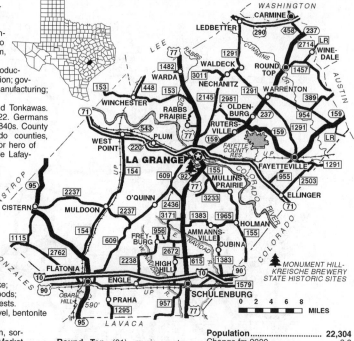

**Physical Features:** Southeast county bisected by Colorado River; rolling to level; sandy loam, black waxy soils.

**Economy:** Agribusiness; production of electricity; mineral production; government/services; small manufacturing; tourism.

**History:** Lipan Apaches and Tonkawas. Austin's colonists arrived in 1822. Germans and Czechs began arriving in 1840s. County created from Bastrop, Colorado counties, 1837; organized, 1838; named for hero of American Revolution, Marquis de Lafayette.

**Race/Ethnicity, 2000:** (In percent) Anglo, 79.61; Black, 6.98; Hispanic, 12.78; Other, 0.63.

**Vital Statistics, 2001:** Births, 270; deaths, 317; marriages, 140; divorces, 84.

**Recreation:** Monument Hill, Kreische brewery, Faison Home Museum, other historic sites including "Painted Churches"; hunting, fishing, lake; German and Czech ethnic foods; Prazska Pout in August, Octoberfests.

**Minerals:** Oil, gas, sand, gravel, bentonite clay.

**Agriculture:** Beef cattle; corn, sorghum, peanuts, hay, pecans. Market value $68 million. Firewood sold.

**LA GRANGE** (4,619) county seat; electric-power generation; varied manufacturing; food processing; retail trade center; tourism; hospital, library, museum, archives; Czech heritage center; Texas Independence Day observance.

**Schulenburg** (2,794) varied manufacturing; food processing; Bluebonnet Festival.

**Round Top** (81) music center, museums, tourism, old Bethlehem Lutheran church, and **Winedale** (41), historic restorations including Winedale Inn.

Other towns include: **Carmine** (241); **Ellinger** (200); **Fayetteville** (272); **Flatonia** (1,403) farm market, varied manufacturing, antiques, Czhilispiel in October; **Ledbetter** (76); **Muldoon** (98); **Plum** (95); **Warda** (98); **Warrenton** (65), and **West Point** (205).

| | |
|---|---|
| Population | **22,304** |
| Change fm 2000 | 2.3 |
| Area (sq. mi.) | 959.84 |
| Land Area (sq. mi.) | 950.03 |
| Altitude (ft.) | 200-590 |
| Rainfall (in.) | 37.1 |
| Jan. mean min. | 40 |
| July mean max. | 95 |
| Civ. Labor | 11,722 |
| Unemployed | 3.3 |
| Wages | $54,130,453 |
| Av. Weekly Wage | $486.04 |
| Prop. Value | $2,294,266,705 |
| Retail Sales | $281,575,654 |

MONUMENT HILL-KREISCHE BREWERY STATE HISTORIC SITES

---

# Fisher County

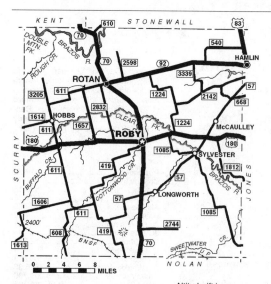

**Physical Features:** West central county on rolling prairie; mesquite; red, sandy loam soils; drains to forks of Brazos River.

**Economy:** Agribusiness; electric co-op; gypsum; hunting.

**History:** Lipan Apaches, disrupted by Comanches and other tribes around 1700. Ranching began in 1876. County created from Bexar District, 1876; organized 1886; named for S.R. Fisher, Republic of Texas secretary of navy.

**Race/Ethnicity, 2000:** (In percent) Anglo, 75.30; Black, 2.72; Hispanic, 21.36; Other, 0.62.

**Vital Statistics, 2001:** Births, 24; deaths, 59; marriages, 29; divorces, 25.

**Recreation:** Quail, dove, turkey hunting; wildlife viewing; fair, rodeo in August,

**Minerals:** Gypsum, oil.

**Agriculture:** Cattle, cotton, hay, wheat, sorghum, horses, sheep, goats. Irrigation for cotton and alfalfa. Market value $15.1 million.

**ROBY** (650) county seat; agribusiness, cotton gin; hospital between Roby and Rotan.

**ROTAN** (1,551) gypsum plant; oil mill; agribusinesses. Other towns include: **McCaulley** (96) and **Sylvester** (79). Part of **Hamlin** (2,196).

| | |
|---|---|
| Population | **4,246** |
| Change fm 2000 | -2.3 |
| Area (sq. mi.) | 901.74 |
| Land Area (sq. mi.) | 901.16 |
| Altitude (ft.) | 1,723-2,400 |
| Rainfall (in.) | 24.3 |
| Jan. mean min. | 30 |
| July mean max. | 96 |
| Civ. Labor | 1,901 |
| Unemployed | 7.6 |
| Wages | $5,407,899 |
| Av. Weekly Wage | $435.59 |
| Prop. Value | $321,332,843 |
| Retail Sales | $10,180,372 |

# Floyd County

**Physical Features:** Flat High Plains, broken by Caprock on east, by White River on south; many playas; red, black loam soils.

**Economy:** Cotton; livestock feedlots; varied manufacturing; government/services.

**History:** Plains Apaches and later Comanches. First white settlers arrived in 1884. County created from Bexar District, 1876; organized 1890. Named for Dolphin Ward Floyd, who died at Alamo.

**Race/Ethnicity, 2000:** (In percent) Anglo, 50.05; Black, 3.35; Hispanic, 45.93; Other, 0.67.

**Vital Statistics, 2001:** Births, 110; deaths, 95; marriages, 45; divorces, 27.

**Recreation:** Hunting, fishing; Blanco Canyon; Pumpkin Days; museum.

**Minerals:** Not significant.

**Agriculture:** Cotton, wheat, sorghum; beef cattle; 260,000 acres irrigated. Market value $151.5 million.

**FLOYDADA** (3,617) county seat; some manufacturing; meat, vegetable processing; distribution center; Old Settlers Reunion; Texas A&M engineering extension.

**Lockney** (2,030) agriculture center; manufacturing; hospital.

Other towns include: **Aiken** (57), **Dougherty** (109), and **South Plains** (92).

| | | |
|---|---|---|
| Population ................................... 7,455 | Rainfall (in.) ................................... 20.5 | Wages ................................ $12,310,865 |
| Change fm 2000 ............................. -4.1 | Jan. mean min. ................................... 22 | Av. Weekly Wage ................... $390.67 |
| Area (sq. mi.) ............................ 992.51 | July mean max. .................................... 92 | Prop. Value ................... $359,896,575 |
| Land Area (sq. mi.) ................... 992.19 | Civ. Labor ..................................... 2,994 | Retail Sales ..................... $38,089,851 |
| Altitude (ft.) ........................ 2,574-3,316 | Unemployed ..................................... 10.0 | |

# Foard County

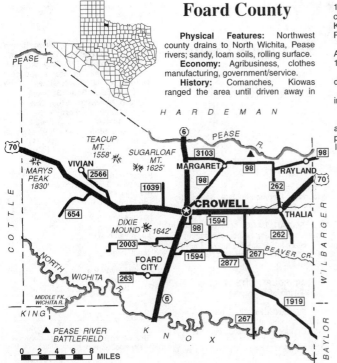

**Physical Features:** Northwest county drains to North Wichita, Pease rivers; sandy, loam soils, rolling surface.

**Economy:** Agribusiness, clothes manufacturing, government/service.

**History:** Comanches, Kiowas ranged the area until driven away in 1870s. Ranching began in 1880. County created out of Cottle, Hardeman, King, Knox counties, 1891; named for Maj. Robert L. Foard of Confederate army.

**Race/Ethnicity, 2000:** (In percent) Anglo, 79.53; Black, 3.39; Hispanic, 16.34; Other, 0.74

**Vital Statistics, 2001:** Births, 14; deaths, 15; marriages, 0; divorces, 2.

**Recreation:** Three museums; hunting; wild hog cookoff in November.

**Minerals:** Oil, gas.

**Agriculture:** Wheat; cow-calf operations, stocker cattle, alfalfa, dairies, peanuts; cotton. Market value $10.5 million.

**CROWELL** (1,101) county seat; agriculture/retail center; clothing manufacturing, library.

| | |
|---|---|
| Population ................................. 1,545 | |
| Change fm 2000 .......................... -4.7 | |
| Area (sq. mi.) ........................... 707.69 | |
| Land Area (sq. mi.) ................. 706.68 | |
| Altitude (ft.) ...................... 1,300-1,830 | |
| Rainfall (in.) ................................ 23.9 | |
| Jan. mean min. ............................... 24 | |
| July mean max. .............................. 97 | |
| Civ. Labor ..................................... 864 | |
| Unemployed .................................... 4.6 | |
| Wages .............................. $1,657,328 | |
| Av. Weekly Wage ................ $340.87 | |
| Prop. Value ................. $133,151,602 | |
| Retail Sales .................... $5,188,815 | |

*For explanation of sources, abbreviations and symbols, see p. 138.*

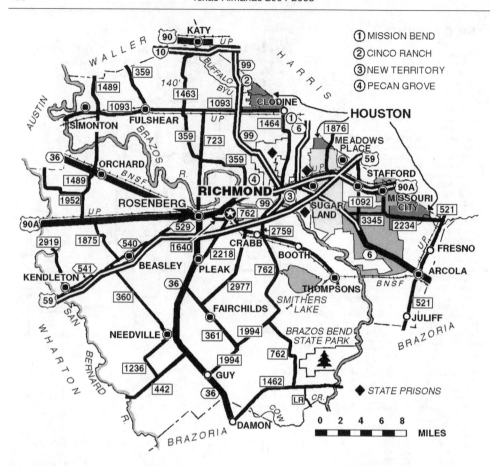

① MISSION BEND
② CINCO RANCH
③ NEW TERRITORY
④ PECAN GROVE

STATE PRISONS

0  2  4  6  8  MILES

**Physical Features:** On Gulf Coastal Plain; drained by Brazos, San Bernard rivers; level to rolling; rich alluvial soils.

**Economy:** Agribusiness, petrochemicals, sulfur; government/service; many residents work in Houston; part of Houston metropolitan area.

**History:** Karankawas retreated to Mexico by 1850s. Named for river bend where some of Austin's colonists settled 1824. Antebellum plantations made it one of six Texas counties with black majority in 1850. County created 1837 from Austin County; organized 1838.

**Race/Ethnicity, 2000:** (In percent) Anglo, 47.05; Black, 19.98; Hispanic, 21.12; Other, 11.85.

**Vital Statistics, 2001:** Births, 5,289; deaths, 1,533; marriages, 1,919; divorces, 1,250.

**Recreation:** Many historic sites, museums, memorials; George Ranch historical park; state park with George Observatory; fishing, waterfowl hunting.

**Minerals:** Oil, gas, sulphur, salt, clays, sand and gravel.

**Agriculture:** A leading county in nursery crops; cotton, sorghum, hay, soybeans; cattle, horses; irrigation for rice. Market value $138 million.

**RICHMOND** (11,555) county seat;

# Fort Bend County

foundry, Richmond State School (for mentally retarded), hospital.

**SUGAR LAND** (68,954) government/services, prisons; commuting to Houston; hospital; Museum of Southern History. **First Colony** is now part of Sugar Land.

**MISSOURI CITY** (57,239, part [5,494] in Harris County).

**ROSENBERG** (25,889) varied industry; annual Czech festival; Wharton County Junior College campus.

Other towns include: **Arcola**

(1,119); **Beasley** (607); **Cinco Ranch** (11,808); **Fairchilds** (723); **Fresno** (6,854); **Fulshear** (778); **Guy** (60); **Katy** (12,909, mostly in Harris County); **Kendleton** (466); **Meadows Place** (5,063); **Mission Bend** (31,968).

Also, **Needville** (2,769); **New Territory** (14,306); **Orchard** (426); **Pecan Grove** (14,406); **Pleak** (1,056); **Simonton** (728); **Stafford** (16,809, partly in Harris County); **Thompsons** (241).

Also, part (33,384) of **Houston**.

| | |
|---|---|
| Population | **399,537** |
| Change fm 2000 | 12.7 |
| Area (sq. mi.) | 886.05 |
| Land Area (sq. mi.) | 874.64 |
| Altitude (ft.) | 46-140 |
| Rainfall (in.) | 45.3 |
| Jan. mean min. | 41 |
| July mean max. | 93 |
| Civ. Labor | 202,761 |
| Unemployed | 5.4 |
| Wages | $875,039,771 |
| Av. Weekly Wage | $708.80 |
| Prop. Value | $22,693,470,176 |
| Retail Sales | $3,552,948,481 |

*For explanation of sources, abbreviations and symbols, see p. 138.*

# Franklin County

**Physical Features:** Small Northeast county with many wooded hills; drained by numerous streams; alluvial to sandy clay soils; two lakes.

**Economy:** Agribusiness; government/services; retirement center; manufacturing; distribution.

**History:** Caddoes abandoned the area in 1790s because of disease and other tribes. White settlement began in 1830s. County created 1875 from Titus County; named for jurist B.C. Franklin.

**Race/Ethnicity, 2000:** (In percent) Anglo, 86.40; Black, 3.96; Hispanic, 8.90; Other, 0.74.

**Vital Statistics, 2001:** Births, 118; deaths, 110; marriages, 71; divorces, 36.

**Recreation:** Fishing, water sports; Countryfest/stew cookoff in October; historic homes; wild hog hunting, horse stables.

**Minerals:** Lignite, oil and gas.

**Agriculture:** Dairy and broiler production; beef cattle; hay. Market value $54.1 million. Timber marketed.

**MOUNT VERNON** (2,290) county seat; distribution center, manufacturing; tourism; antiques; Labor Day rodeo.

Other towns include: **Scroggins** (125), and **Winnsboro** (3,563, mostly in Wood County) commercial center, Autumn Trails.

| | |
|---|---|
| Population | 9,699 |
| Change fm 2000 | 2.5 |
| Area (sq. mi.) | 294.77 |
| Land Area (sq. mi.) | 285.66 |
| Altitude (ft.) | 300-600 |
| Rainfall (in.) | 46.8 |
| Jan. mean min. | 33 |
| July mean max. | 93 |
| Civ. Labor | 4,536 |
| Unemployed | 3.9 |
| Wages | $16,214,830 |
| Av. Weekly Wage | $455.88 |
| Prop. Value | $796,939,645 |
| Retail Sales | $59,866,340 |

*Scientists and forest service personnel confirm a tree as the largest live oak in Texas. The tree is located in the San Bernard National Wildlife Refuge in Brazoria County. File photo.*

# Freestone County

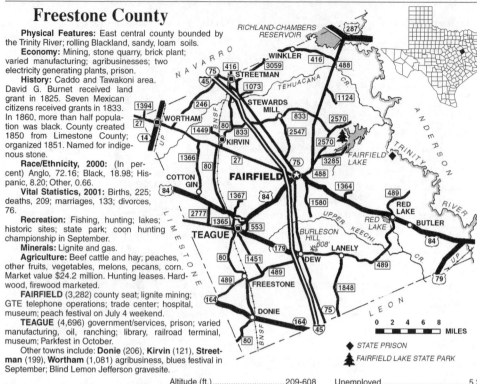

**Physical Features:** East central county bounded by the Trinity River; rolling Blackland, sandy, loam soils.

**Economy:** Mining, stone quarry, brick plant; varied manufacturing; agribusinesses; two electricity generating plants, prison.

**History:** Caddo and Tawakoni area. David G. Burnet received land grant in 1825. Seven Mexican citizens received grants in 1833. In 1860, more than half population was black. County created 1850 from Limestone County; organized 1851. Named for indigenous stone.

**Race/Ethnicity, 2000:** (In percent) Anglo, 72.16; Black, 18.98; Hispanic, 8.20; Other, 0.66.

**Vital Statistics, 2001:** Births, 225; deaths, 209; marriages, 133; divorces, 76.

**Recreation:** Fishing, hunting; lakes; historic sites; state park; coon hunting championship in September.

**Minerals:** Lignite and gas.

**Agriculture:** Beef cattle and hay; peaches, other fruits, vegetables, melons, pecans, corn. Market value $24.2 million. Hunting leases. Hardwood, firewood marketed.

**FAIRFIELD** (3,282) county seat; lignite mining; GTE telephone operations; trade center; hospital; museum; peach festival on July 4 weekend.

**TEAGUE** (4,696) government/services, prison; varied manufacturing, oil, ranching; library, railroad terminal, museum; Parkfest in October.

Other towns include: **Donie** (206), **Kirvin** (121), **Streetman** (199), **Wortham** (1,081) agribusiness, blues festival in September; Blind Lemon Jefferson gravesite.

| | | |
|---|---|---|
| Population | | 18,595 |
| Change fm 2000 | | 4.1 |
| Area (sq. mi.) | | 892.13 |
| Land Area (sq. mi.) | | 877.43 |
| Altitude (ft.) | | 209-608 |
| Rainfall (in.) | | 39.8 |
| Jan. mean min. | | 36 |
| July mean max. | | 95 |
| Civ. Labor | | 9,171 |
| Unemployed | | 5.2 |
| Wages | | $30,755,158 |
| Av. Weekly Wage | | $468.29 |
| Prop. Value | | $2,330,850,500 |
| Retail Sales | | $249,898,191 |

# Frio County

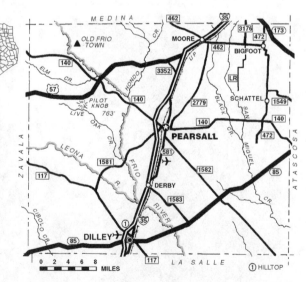

**Physical Features:** South Texas county of rolling terrain with much brush; bisected by Frio River; sandy, red sandy loam soils.

**Economy:** Agribusiness; oil-field services; hunting leases.

**History:** Coahuiltecans; many taken into San Antonio missions. Comanche hunters kept settlers out until after the Civil War. Mexican citizens recruited for labor after 1900. County created 1858 from Atascosa, Bexar, Uvalde counties, organized in 1871; named for Frio (cold) River.

**Race/Ethnicity, 2000:** (In percent) Anglo, 20.79; Black, 4.79; Hispanic, 73.76; Other, 0.66.

**Vital Statistics, 2001:** Births, 260; deaths, 128; marriages, 108; divorces, 23.

**Recreation:** Hunting; Big Foot Wallace Museum; Winter Garden area; potato festival in March.

**Minerals:** Oil, natural gas, stone.

**Agriculture:** A leading peanut-producing county; other crops: potatoes, spinach, cucumbers, watermelons; beef cattle, goats raised. Market value $85.7 million. Hunting leases.

**PEARSALL** (7,204) county seat; agriculture center; oil, gas; food processing, shipping; old jail museum; hospital; Pioneer days in April.

**Dilley** (3,745) shipping center for melons, peanuts.

Other towns include: **Bigfoot** (315), **Derby** (50), **Hilltop** (311); **Moore** (665); **North Pearsall** (582) and **West Pearsall** (361).

| | | |
|---|---|---|
| Population | | 16,249 |
| Change fm 2000 | | 0.0 |
| Area (sq. mi.) | | 1,134.28 |
| Land Area (sq. mi.) | | 1,133.02 |
| Altitude (ft.) | | 400-763 |
| Rainfall (in.) | | 25.4 |
| Jan. mean min. | | 38 |
| July mean max. | | 97 |
| Civ. Labor | | 5,866 |
| Unemployed | | 7.5 |
| Wages | | $19,946,953 |
| Av. Weekly Wage | | $406.24 |
| Prop. Value | | $718,370,750 |
| Retail Sales | | $73,014,128 |

# Gaines County

**Physical Features:** On South Plains, drains to draws; playas; underground water.

**Economy:** Oil and gas production, cotton and peanut farming.

**History:** Comanche country until U.S. Army campaigns of 1875. Ranchers arrived in 1880s; farming began around 1900. County created from Bexar District, 1876; organized 1905; named for James Gaines, signer of Texas Declaration of Independence.

**Race/Ethnicity, 2000:** (In percent) Anglo, 61.48; Black, 2.19; Hispanic, 35.77; Other, 0.56.

**Vital Statistics, 2001:** Births, 239; deaths, 81; marriages, 126; divorces, 29.

**Recreation:** Cedar Lake one of largest alkali lakes on Texas plains; Ag and Oil Day in September.

**Minerals:** One of leading oil-producing counties; gas.

**Agriculture:** Cotton, peanuts, small grains, pecans, vegetables raised; cattle, sheep, hogs; substantial irrigation. Market value $188.8 million.

**SEMINOLE** (5,867) county seat; oil & gas, market center; hospital, library; county airport.

**Seagraves** (2,299) market for three-county area; cotton, peanut farming; library, museum; Celebrate Seagraves in July.

Other towns include: **Loop** (315).

| Population | 14,312 |
|---|---|
| Change fm 2000 | -1.1 |
| Area (sq. mi.) | 1,502.84 |
| Land Area (sq. mi.) | 1,502.35 |
| Altitude (ft.) | 3,000-3,625 |
| Rainfall (in.) | 17.5 |
| Jan. mean min. | 25 |
| July mean max. | 94 |
| Civ. Labor | 6,592 |
| Unemployed | 5.4 |
| Wages | $29,218,645 |
| Av. Weekly Wage | $461.61 |
| Prop. Value | $2,600,248,524 |
| Retail Sales | $108,009,513 |

*For explanation of sources, abbreviations and symbols, see p. 138.*

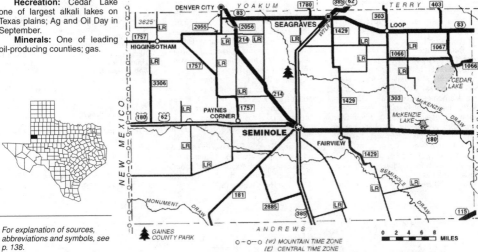

*A farmer checks the soil on his farm in Terry County. File photo.*

# Galveston County

**Physical Features:** Partly island, partly coastal; flat, artificial drainage; sandy, loam, clay soils; broken by bays.

**Economy:** Port activities dominate economy; insurance and finance center; petrochemical plants; varied manufacturing; tourism; medical education center; oceanographic research center; ship building; commercial fishing.

**History:** Karankawa and other tribes roamed the area until 1850. French, Spanish and American settlement began in 1815 and reached 1,000 by 1817. County created from Brazoria County 1838; organized 1839; named for Spanish governor of Louisiana Count Bernardo de Gálvez.

**Race/Ethnicity, 2000:** (In percent) Anglo, 63.80; Black, 15.54; Hispanic, 17.96; Other, 2.70.

**Vital Statistics, 2001:** Births, 3,720; deaths, 2,183; marriages, 2,190; divorces, 1,050.

**Recreation:** One of Texas' most historic cities; popular tourist and convention center; fishing, surfing, boating, sailing and other water sports; state park; Historical District tour in spring includes homes, sites, Moody Gardens; Mardi Gras celebration; Rosenberg Library; museums, drama *Lone Star* presented in outdoor amphitheater in summer; restored sailing ship, "Elissa," railroad museum; Dickens on the Strand in early December.

**Minerals:** Production of oil, gas, clays, sand and gravel.

**Agriculture:** Cattle, aquaculture, nursery crops, rice, hay, horses, soybeans, grain sorghum. Market value $8.4 million.

**GALVESTON** (57,027) county seat; tourist center; shipyard; other industries; insurance; port container facility; University of Texas Medical Branch; National Maritime Research Center; Texas A&M University at Galveston; Galveston College; hospitals.

**Texas City** (42,611) refining, petrochemical plants; port, rail shipping; College of the Mainland; hospital, library; dike; Cinco de Mayo, Shrimp Boil in August.

**Bolivar Peninsula** (3,991) includes: **Port Bolivar** (1,200) lighthouse, free ferry; **Crystal Beach** (787) seafood industry; sport fishing; tourism, Fort Travis Seashore Park, shorebird sanctuary; Crab Festival in May; **Gilchrist** (750) and **High Island** (500).

Other towns include: **Bacliff** (6,981); **Bayou Vista** (1,651); **Clear Lake Shores** (1,230).

Also, **Dickinson** (17,644) manufacturing, commuters; strawberry festival in May; **Friendswood** (30,740, partly [7,800] in Harris County); **Hitchcock** (6,628) residential community, tourism, fishing and shrimping, Good Ole Days in August, WWII blimp base, museum.

Also, **Jamaica Beach** (1,094); **Kemah** (2,425) fishing; **La Marque** (13,804) refining, greyhound racing, farming; hospital, library; Seafood Grill-off in October; **League City** (48,647); **San Leon** (4,436); **Santa Fe** (9,947); **Village of Tiki Island** (1,060).

| | |
|---|---|
| Population | 261,219 |
| Change fm 2000 | 4.4 |
| Area (sq. mi.) | 872.93 |
| Land Area (sq. mi.) | 398.47 |
| Altitude (ft.) | sea level-35 |
| Rainfall (in.) | 42.3 |
| Jan. mean min. | 47 |
| July mean max. | 87 |
| Civ. Labor | 123,394 |
| Unemployed | 7.7 |
| Wages | $673,226,218 |
| Av. Weekly Wage | $593.64 |
| Prop. Value | $22,340,197,004 |
| Retail Sales | $2,055,201,502 |

*For explanation of sources, abbreviations and symbols, see p. 138.*

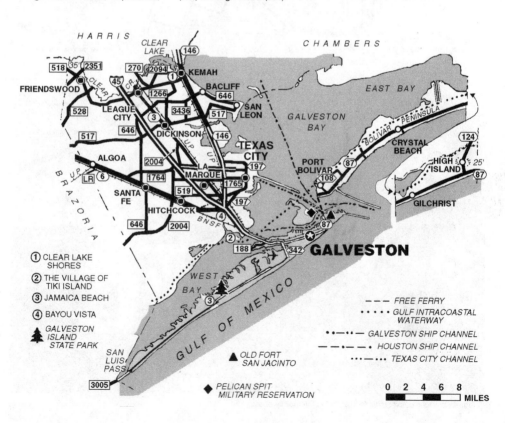

① CLEAR LAKE SHORES
② THE VILLAGE OF TIKI ISLAND
③ JAMAICA BEACH
④ BAYOU VISTA
🌲 GALVESTON ISLAND STATE PARK

– – – FREE FERRY
• • • • • GULF INTRACOASTAL WATERWAY
• — • • — GALVESTON SHIP CHANNEL
— • — • — HOUSTON SHIP CHANNEL
• • • — • • • TEXAS CITY CHANNEL

▲ OLD FORT SAN JACINTO

◆ PELICAN SPIT MILITARY RESERVATION

0  2  4  6  8 MILES

# Garza County

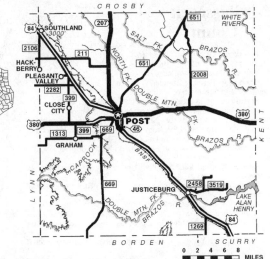

**Physical Features:** On edge of Caprock; rough, broken land, with playas, gullies, canyons, Brazos River forks, lake; sandy, loam, clay soils.

**Economy:** Agriculture, oil & gas, trade, government/services, hunting leases.

**History:** Kiowas and Comanches yielded to U.S. Army in 1875. Ranching began in 1870s, farming in the 1890s. C.W. Post, the cereal millionaire, established enterprises in 1906. County created from Bexar District, 1876; organized 1907; named for early Texas family.

**Race/Ethnicity, 2000:** (In percent) Anglo, 57.44; Black, 4.86; Hispanic, 37.15; Other, 0.55.

**Vital Statistics, 2001:** Births, 66; deaths, 57; marriages, 37; divorces, 15.

**Recreation:** Founders Day in September, scenic areas; lake activities; Post-Garza Museum.

**Minerals:** Oil, gas, sand, gravel.

**Agriculture:** Cotton, beef cattle, hay; 12,800 acres irrigated. Market value $10.6 million. Hunting leases.

**POST** (3,800) county seat; founded by C.W. Post; agriculture, tourism, government/services, prisons; Garza Theatre.

Other towns include: **Justiceburg** (76).

| | |
|---|---|
| Population | 4,976 |
| Change fm 2000 | 2.1 |
| Area (sq. mi.) | 896.19 |
| Land Area (sq. mi.) | 895.56 |
| Altitude (ft.) | 2,176-3,000 |
| Rainfall (in.) | 20.9 |
| Jan. mean min. | 27 |
| July mean max. | 94 |
| Civ. Labor | 2,368 |
| Unemployed | 4.7 |
| Wages | $9,151,368 |
| Av. Weekly Wage | $470.87 |
| Prop. Value | $536,087,500 |
| Retail Sales | $24,812,058 |

---

# Gillespie County

**Physical Features:** Picturesque Edwards Plateau area with hills, broken by spring-fed streams.

**Economy:** Agribusiness; tourism; government/services; food processing; hunting leases; small manufacturing; granite for markers.

**History:** German settlement founded 1846 in heart of Comanche country. County created 1848 from Bexar, Travis counties; named for Texas Ranger Capt. R.A. Gillespie. Birthplace of President Lyndon B. Johnson and Fleet Admiral Chester W. Nimitz.

**Race/Ethnicity, 2000:** (In percent) Anglo, 83.39; Black, 0.17; Hispanic, 15.90; Other, 0.54.

**Vital Statistics, 2001:** Births, 232; deaths, 266; marriages, 155; divorces, 86.

**Recreation:** Among leading deer-hunting areas; fishing; numerous historic sites and tourist attractions include LBJ Ranch, Nimitz Hotel and Pacific war museum; Pioneer Museum Complex, Enchanted Rock.

**Minerals:** Sand, gravel, gypsum, limestone rock.

**Agriculture:** Income mostly from beef cattle, turkeys, sheep and goats; a leading peach-producing county; hay, grain sorghum, oats, wheat, grapes also raised. Market value $31.9 million. Hunting leases.

**FREDERICKSBURG** (9,306) county seat; government/services; varied manufacturing; wine production; food processing; museum; tourist attractions; hospital; Easter Fires.

Other towns include: **Doss** (75); **Harper** (1,046) ranching, deer hunting; Dachshund Hounds Downs race and Trades Day in October; **Luckenbach** (25); **Stonewall** (487) agribusiness, wineries, tourism, Peach Jamboree in June, and **Willow City** (75).

| | |
|---|---|
| Population | 21,607 |
| Change fm 2000 | 3.8 |
| Area (sq. mi.) | 1,061.48 |
| Land Area (sq. mi.) | 1,061.06 |
| Altitude (ft.) | 1,400-2,244 |
| Rainfall (in.) | 30.0 |
| Jan. mean min. | 35 |
| July mean max. | 93 |
| Civ. Labor | 11,184 |
| Unemployed | 2.2 |
| Wages | $42,898,957 |
| Av. Weekly Wage | $444.19 |
| Prop. Value | $2,855,416,390 |
| Retail Sales | $278,319,475 |

*For explanation of sources, abbreviations and symbols, see p. 138.*

# Glasscock County

**Physical Features**: Western county on rolling plains, broken by small streams; sandy, loam soils.

**Economy:** Farming, ranching, hunting leases, oil and gas; quarries.

**History:** Hunting area for Kickapoos and Lipan Apaches. Anglo-American sheep ranchers and Mexican-American shepherds or *pastores* moved into the area in 1880s. County created 1887, from Tom Green County; organized, 1893; named for Texas pioneer George W. Glasscock.

**Race/Ethnicity, 2000:** (In percent) Anglo, 69.56; Black, 0.50; Hispanic, 29.87; Other, 0.07.

**Vital Statistics, 2001:** Births, 19; deaths, 4; marriages, 9; divorces, 3.

**Recreation:** Hunting of deer, quail, turkey; St. Lawrence Fall Festival.

**Minerals:** Oil, gas, stone/rock.

**Agriculture:** Cattle, goats, sheep, hogs raised. Cotton, sorghum, wheat, peanuts, hay. 55,000 acres irrigated. Market value $13.9 million.

**GARDEN CITY** (293), county seat; serves sparsely settled ranching, oil area.

| | | | |
|---|---|---|---|
| Population | 1,369 | Altitude (ft.) | 2,495-2,727 |
| Change fm 2000 | -2.6 | Rainfall (in.) | 18.0 |
| Area (sq. mi.) | 900.93 | Jan. mean min. | 25 |
| Land Area (sq. mi.) | 900.75 | July mean max. | 94 |
| | | Civ. Labor | 608 |

| | |
|---|---|
| Unemployed | 3.6 |
| Wages | $1,876,261 |
| Av. Weekly Wage | $436.04 |
| Prop. Value | $549,582,870 |
| Retail Sales | $1,793,162 |

# Goliad County

**Physical Features:** South Texas county; rolling, brushy; bisected by San Antonio River; sandy, loam, alluvial soils.

**Economy:** Government/services; oil/gas; agriculture, electricity-generating plant.

**History:** Karankawas, Comanches and other tribes in area in historic period. La Bahía presidio/mission established 1749. County created 1836 from Spanish municipality; organized 1837; name is anagram of (H)idalgo. Birthplace of Gen. Ignacio Zaragoza, hero of Battle of Puebla (Mexico).

**Race/Ethnicity, 2000:** (In percent) Anglo, 59.75; Black, 4.69; Hispanic, 35.20; Other, 0.36.

**Vital Statistics, 2001:** Births, 84; deaths, 62; marriages, 33; divorces, 20.

**Recreation:** Missions, restored Presidio La Bahía, Fannin Battleground; Old Market House museum; lake, fishing, hunting (deer, quail, dove, hogs), camping.

**Minerals:** Production of oil, gas.

**Agriculture:** Beef cattle, stocker operations and fed cattle are top revenue producers; corn, grain sorghums, hay; minor irrigation for pasture, fruit trees. Market value $15.3 million. Hunting leases.

**GOLIAD** (2,041) county seat; one of state's oldest towns; oil, gas center; agriculture; tourism; library; Goliad Massacre re-enactment in March; Zaragoza Birthplace State Historic Site, statue.

Other towns include: **Berclair** (253), **Fannin** (359) and **Weesatche** (411).

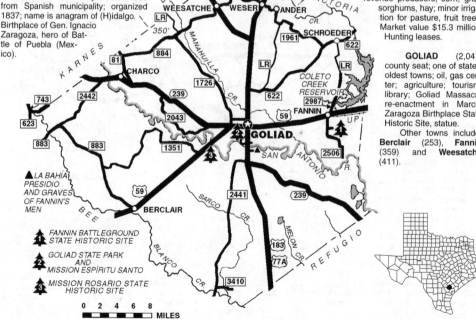

| | |
|---|---|
| Population | 7,075 |
| Change fm 2000 | 2.1 |
| Area (sq. mi.) | 859.35 |
| Land Area (sq. mi.) | 853.52 |

| | |
|---|---|
| Altitude (ft.) | 50-350 |
| Rainfall (in.) | 36.5 |
| Jan. mean min. | 43 |
| July mean max. | 95 |
| Civ. Labor | 2,735 |

| | |
|---|---|
| Unemployed | 4.5 |
| Wages | $7,446,887 |
| Av. Weekly Wage | $460.85 |
| Prop. Value | $902,167,700 |
| Retail Sales | $29,636,433 |

# Gonzales County

**Physical Features:** South Texas county; rolling, rich bottom soils along Guadalupe River and its tributaries; some sandy areas; many oaks, pecans.

**Economy:** Agribusiness, hunting leases.

**History:** Coahuiltecan area. Among first Anglo-American settlements; the De-Witt colony late 1820s. County created 1836; organized 1837; named for Coahuila y Texas Gov. Rafael Gonzales.

**Race/Ethnicity, 2000:** (In percent) Anglo, 51.56; Black, 8.15; Hispanic, 39.62; Other, 0.67.

**Vital Statistics, 2001:** Births, 310; deaths, 213; marriages, 151; divorces, 65.

**Recreation:** Historic sites, 86 officially recognized homes or historical markers; Pioneer Village Living History Center; state park; museums, Independence Park.

**Minerals:** Gas, oil, clay, gravel.

**Agriculture:** Major poultry county (leader in turkeys sold); cattle, hogs; hay, corn, sorghum, pecans. Market value $335.8 million.

**GONZALES** (7,339) county seat; first shot in Texas Revolution fired here; shipping, processing center; manufacturing; hospitals; "Come and Take It" festival.

Other towns include: **Bebe** (52); **Belmont** (60); **Cost** (62); **Harwood** (112); **Leesville** (150); **Nixon** (2,241) Feather Fest; **Ottine** (90), crippled children's hospital, Gonzales Warm Springs Foundation Hospital; **Smiley** (449) Settlers Set-To; **Waelder** (984) Guacamole Fest; **Wrightsboro** (76).

| | |
|---|---|
| Population | 18,884 |
| Change fm 2000 | 1.4 |
| Area (sq. mi.) | 1,069.82 |
| Land Area (sq. mi.) | 1,067.75 |
| Altitude (ft.) | 200-600 |
| Rainfall (in.) | 32.4 |
| Jan. mean min. | 40 |
| July mean max. | 95 |
| Civ. Labor | 8,188 |
| Unemployed | 4.5 |
| Wages | $36,400,831 |
| Av. Weekly Wage | $460.76 |
| Prop. Value | $1,206,391,840 |
| Retail Sales | $135,211,457 |

# Gray County

**Physical Features:** Panhandle High Plains, broken by Red River forks, tributaries; sandy loam, waxy soils.

**Economy:** Petroleum, agriculture, feedlot operations, chemical plant, other manufacturing.

**History:** Apaches, displaced by Comanches and Kiowas. Ranching began in late 1870s. Farmers arrived around 1900. Oil discovered 1926. County created 1876, from Bexar District; organized 1902; named for Peter W. Gray, member of first Legislature.

**Race/Ethnicity, 2000:** (In percent) Anglo, 79.61; Black, 6.03; Hispanic, 13.01; Other, 1.35.

**Vital Statistics, 2001:** Births, 251; deaths, 283; marriages, 177; divorces, 132.

**Recreation:** Water sports, Lake McClellan and grassland; White Deer Land Museum; barbed-wire museum, Chautauqua on Labor Day.

**Minerals:** Production of oil, gas.

**Agriculture:** Cattle, wheat, sorghum, hay, corn, soybeans. Market value $109.2 million.

**PAMPA** (17,659) county seat; petroleum and agriculture; chemical plant; hospital; college; prison unit.

Other towns include: **Alanreed** (48); **Lefors** (563); **McLean** (811) commercial center for southern part of county.

| | |
|---|---|
| Population | 22,088 |
| Change fm 2000 | -2.9 |
| Area (sq. mi.) | 929.25 |
| Land Area (sq. mi.) | 928.28 |
| Altitude (ft.) | 2,500-3,300 |
| Rainfall (in.) | 21.0 |
| Jan. mean min. | 21 |
| July mean max. | 92 |
| Civ. Labor | 9,430 |
| Unemployed | 5.2 |
| Wages | $57,070,632 |
| Av. Weekly Wage | $587.61 |
| Prop. Value | $1,211,579,830 |
| Retail Sales | $244,101,778 |

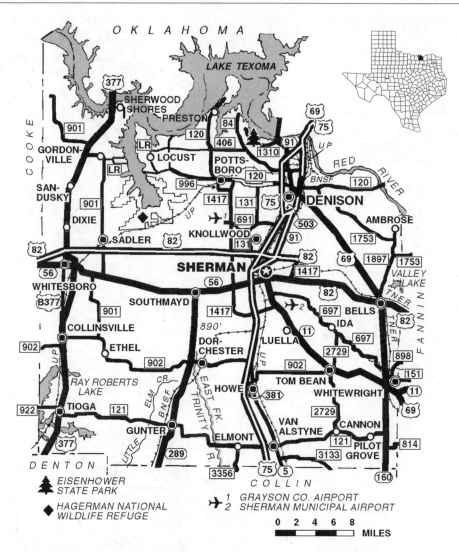

1 GRAYSON CO. AIRPORT
2 SHERMAN MUNICIPAL AIRPORT

0  2  4  6  8  MILES

EISENHOWER STATE PARK

HAGERMAN NATIONAL WILDLIFE REFUGE

# Grayson County

**Physical Features:** North Texas county; level, some low hills; sandy loam, blackland soils; drains to Red River and tributaries of Trinity River.

**Economy:** A manufacturing, distribution and trade center for northern Texas and southern Oklahoma; tourism; agriculture; prisons.

**History:** Caddo and Tonkawa area. Preston Bend trading post established 1836-37. Peters colony settlers arrived in 1840s. County created 1846 from Fannin County; named for Republic Atty. Gen. Peter W. Grayson.

**Race/Ethnicity, 2000:** (In percent) Anglo, 85.10; Black, 6.14; Hispanic, 6.80; Other, 1.96.

**Vital Statistics, 2001:** Births, 1,602; deaths, 1,280; marriages, 1,146; divorces, 696.

**Recreation:** Lakes; fishing; pheasant hunting; water sports; state park; cultural activities; wildlife refuge; Pioneer Village; railroad museum.

**Minerals:** Oil, gas.

**Agriculture:** Beef cattle, corn, wheat, hogs, sorghum. Irrigation of 145,000 acres. Market value $42.1 million.

**Education:** Austin College in Sherman and Grayson County College located between Sherman and Denison.

**SHERMAN** (35,920) county seat; varied manufacturing; processors, distributors for major companies; Austin College; hospitals.

**DENISON** (23,133) Tourism, hospital, food processing; transportation center; Eisenhower birthplace; Main Street Fall festival.

Other towns include: **Bells** (1,198); **Collinsville** (1,309); **Dorchester** (110); **Gordonville** (165); **Gunter** (1,339); **Howe** (2,570) distribution; varied manufacturing; museum, Founders' Day in

May; **Knollwood** (382); **Pottsboro** (1,605); **Sadler** (410); **Southmayd** (1,015); **Tioga** (798); **Tom Bean** (952); **Van Alstyne** (2,563) window screen, electronics, saddle, tack manufacturing; **Whitesboro** (3,830) agribusiness, tourism, library, Peanut Festival in October; **Whitewright** (1,755) varied manufacturing, government/services.

| | |
|---|---|
| Population | 113,860 |
| Change fm 2000 | 3.0 |
| Area (sq. mi.) | 979.19 |
| Land Area (sq. mi.) | 933.51 |
| Altitude (ft.) | 500-890 |
| Rainfall (in.) | 40.4 |
| Jan. mean min. | 30 |
| July mean max. | 95 |
| Civ. Labor | 52,292 |
| Unemployed | 6.7 |
| Wages | $315,405,302 |
| Av. Weekly Wage | $573.30 |
| Prop. Value | $4,978,908,233 |
| Retail Sales | $1,234,878,210 |

**Physical Features:** A populous, leading petroleum county, heart of the famed East Texas oil field; bisected by the Sabine River; hilly, timbered; with sandy, clay, alluvial soils.

**Economy:** Oil but with significant other manufacturing; tourism, conventions; agribusiness and lignite coal production.

**History:** Caddoes; later Cherokees, who were driven out in 1838 by President Lamar. First land grants issued in 1835 by Republic of Mexico. County created and organized in 1873 from Rusk, Upshur counties; named for Confederate Gen. John Gregg. In U.S. censuses 1880-1910, blacks were more numerous than whites. Oil discovered in 1931.

**Race/Ethnicity, 2000:** (In percent) Anglo, 69.59; Black, 20.07; Hispanic, 9.14; Other, 1.20.

**Vital Statistics, 2001:** Births, 1,766; deaths, 1,213; marriages, 1,467; divorces, 573.

**Recreation:** Water activities on lakes; hunting; varied cultural events; the East Texas Oil Museum, Glory Days in Kilgore in May, Depot Fest and

# Gregg County

Loblolly Festival in October.

**Minerals:** Leading oil-producing county with more than 3 billion barrels produced since 1931; also, sand, gravel and natural gas.

**Agriculture:** Cattle, horses, hay, nursery crops. Market value $3.7 million. Timber sales.

**LONGVIEW** (74,021) county seat; chemical manufacturing, oil industry,

distribution and retail center; hospitals; LeTourneau University, UT-Tyler Longview center; convention center; balloon race in July.

**Kilgore** (11,524, part [2,580] in Rusk County), oil center; manufacturing; hospital; Kilgore College (junior college); East Texas Treatment Center; Shakespeare festival in summer; Celtic Heritage festival in April.

**Gladewater** (6,113, part [2,454] in Upshur County) Oil, manufacturing, tourism, agriculture, antiques center; library, airport; Gusher Days in April; daffodil gardens in Feburary-March.

Other towns include: **Clarksville City** (821); **Easton** (536, partly in Rusk County); **Judson** (650); **Lakeport** (897); **Liberty City** (1,992) oil, tourism, government/services; Christmas parade; **Rolling Meadows** (362); **Warren City** (348); **White Oak** (5,820) petroleum, government/services, commuting to Longview; Roughneck Days in April.

*For explanation of sources, abbreviations and symbols, see p. 138.*

| | |
|---|---|
| **Population** | **113,255** |
| Change fm 2000 | 1.7 |
| Area (sq. mi.) | 276.37 |
| Land Area (sq. mi.) | 274.03 |
| Altitude (ft.) | 280-500 |
| Rainfall (in.) | 47.0 |
| Jan. mean min. | 33 |
| July mean max. | 93 |
| Civ. Labor | 61,344 |
| Unemployed | 6.8 |
| Wages | $426,647,555 |
| Av. Weekly Wage | $518.39 |
| Prop. Value | $6,245,205,264 |
| Retail Sales | $2,022,971,612 |

# Grimes County

**Physical Features:** Rich bottom soils along Brazos, Navasota rivers; remainder hilly, partly forested.

**Economy:** Varied manufacturing; agribusiness; tourism.

**History:** Bidais (customs similar to the Caddoes) lived peacefully with Anglo-American settlers who arrived in 1820s, but tribe was removed to Indian Territory. Planter agriculture reflected in 1860 census, which listed 77 persons owning 20 or more slaves. County created from Montgomery County 1846; named for Jesse Grimes, who signed Texas Declaration of Independence.

**Race/Ethnicity, 2000:** (In percent) Anglo, 63.28; Black, 20.02; Hispanic, 16.08; Other, 0.62.

**Vital Statistics, 2001:** Births, 321; deaths, 254; marriages, 181; divorces, 38.

**Recreation:** Hunting, fishing; Gibbons Creek Reservoir; historic sites; fall Renaissance Festival at Plantersville.

**Minerals:** Lignite coal, natural gas.

**Agriculture:** Cattle, forage, horses, poultry; berries, pecans, honey sales significant. Market value $33.1 million. Some timber sold, Christmas tree farms.

**ANDERSON** (273) county seat; rural center; Fanthorp Inn historic site; Go-Texan weekend in February.

**NAVASOTA** (7,027) agribusiness center for parts of three counties; varied manufacturing; food, wood processing; hospital; La Salle statue; blues festival in May.

Other towns include: **Bedias** (301); **Iola** (331); **Plantersville** (212); **Richards** (296); **Roans Prairie** (56); **Shiro** (205); **Todd Mission** (153).

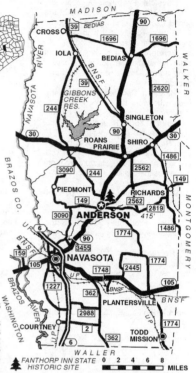

| | |
|---|---|
| Population ............................**24,740** | July mean max.............................96 |
| Change fm 2000 .........................5.0 | Civ. Labor ..............................8,531 |
| Area (sq. mi.) ........................801.16 | Unemployed...............................9.8 |
| Land Area (sq. mi.) ................793.60 | Wages....................$44,220,118 |
| Altitude (ft.) ........................150-415 | Av. Weekly Wage ................$576.92 |
| Rainfall (in.) ..............................40.4 | Prop. Value .............$1,847,709,036 |
| Jan. mean min. ............................40 | Retail Sales...............$324,088,228 |

# Guadalupe County

**Physical Features:** South central county bisected by Guadalupe River; level to rolling surface; sandy, loam, blackland soils.

**Economy:** Varied manufacturing; many residents work in San Antonio; agribusiness, tourism.

**History:** Karankawas, Comanches, other tribes until 1850s. Spanish land grant in 1806 to José de la Baume. DeWitt colonists arrived in 1827. County created 1846 from Bexar, Gonzales counties; named for river.

**Race/Ethnicity, 2000:** (In percent) Anglo, 60.21; Black, 5.10; Hispanic, 33.21; Other, 1.48.

**Vital Statistics, 2001:** Births, 1,147; deaths, 616; marriages, 606; divorces, 360.

**Recreation:** Fishing, hunting, river floating; Sebastopol historic site, other historic sites; river drive, Freedom Fiesta in July, Diez y Seis.

**Minerals:** Oil, gas, gravel, clays.

**Agriculture:** Nursery crops, cattle, hay, sorghum, corn, pecans, wheat, hogs. Market value $43.3 million.

**SEGUIN** (22,808) county seat; electronics, steel, other manufacturing; government/services; hospital, museums, Sebastopol park; Texas Lutheran University.

Other towns include: **Cibolo** (3,572), **Geronimo** (645), **Kingsbury** (688), **Marion** (1,155), **McQueeney** (2,640), **New Berlin** (512), **Northcliff** (1,879); **Redwood** (3,808); **Santa Clara** (955); **Schertz** (20,336, parts in Bexar and Comal counties), **Staples** (350).

Also, part (1,166) of **New Braunfels** and part (50) of **Selma**.

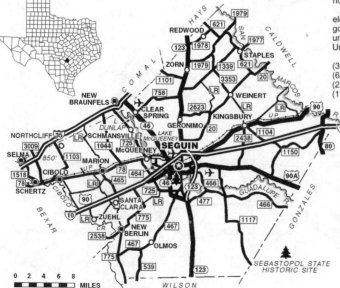

| | |
|---|---|
| Population ............................**94,215** | |
| Change fm 2000 .........................5.8 | |
| Area (sq. mi.) ........................714.17 | |
| Land Area (sq. mi.) ................711.14 | |
| Altitude (ft.) ........................350-850 | |
| Rainfall (in.)...............................31.4 | |
| Jan. mean min. ............................40 | |
| July mean max...............................96 | |
| Civ. Labor..............................49,704 | |
| Unemployed...............................4.0 | |
| Wages....................$160,361,509 | |
| Av. Weekly Wage ................$545.87 | |
| Prop. Value .............$4,854,613,814 | |
| Retail Sales...............$564,685,483 | |

# Hale County

**Physical Features:** High Plains; fertile sandy, loam soils; many playas; large underground water supply.

**Economy:** Agribusiness, food-processing plants; manufacturing; government/services.

**History:** Comanche hunters driven out by U.S. Army in 1875. Ranching began in 1880s. First motor-driven irrigation well drilled in 1911. County created from Bexar District, 1876; organized 1888; named for Lt. J.C. Hale, who died at San Jacinto.

**Race/Ethnicity, 2000:** (In percent), Anglo, 45.54; Black, 5.77; Hispanic, 47.90; Other, 0.79.

**Vital Statistics, 2001:** Births, 648; deaths, 310; marriages, 322; divorces, 115.

**Recreation:** Llano Estacado Museum; art gallery, antiques stores; Plainview Cattle Drive in September.

**Minerals:** Production of oil, gas.

**Agriculture:** Leading cotton-producing county, cattle, sheep, hogs. Other crops, corn, sorghum, wheat, soybeans, sunflowers. Market value $239.3 million. Irrigation of 448,000 acres.

**PLAINVIEW** (22,257) county seat; packing plants, distribution center; food processing, other industries; Wayland Baptist University; hospital, library, mental health center; state prisons.

**Hale Center** (2,255) farming trade center; food processing plants; hospital, wildlife museum, library, parks, murals; car/motorcycle show, July 4.

**Abernathy** (2,850, part [708] in Lubbock County), government/services, farm supplies, textile plant, gins.

Other towns include: **Cotton Center** (205), **Edmonson** (121), **Petersburg** (1,250), **Seth Ward** (1,933).

| | |
|---|---|
| Population | 35,900 |
| Change fm 2000 | -1.9 |
| Area (sq. mi.) | 1,004.77 |
| Land Area (sq. mi.) | 1,004.65 |
| Altitude (ft.) | 3,315-3,600 |
| Rainfall (in.) | 19.8 |
| Jan. mean min. | 24 |
| July mean max. | 92 |

| | |
|---|---|
| Civ. Labor | 15,990 |
| Unemployed | 6.6 |
| Wages | $92,134,069 |
| Av. Weekly Wage | $487.63 |
| Prop. Value | $1,506,544,690 |
| Retail Sales | $549,371,138 |

# Hall County

**Physical Features:** Rolling to hilly, broken by Red River forks, tributaries; red and black sandy loam.

**Economy:** Grain, cotton processing; farm, ranch supplies, marketing for large rural area.

**History:** Apaches displaced by Comanches, who were removed to Indian Territory in 1875. Ranching began in 1880s. Farming expanded after 1910. County created 1876 from Bexar, Young districts; organized 1890; named for Republic of Texas secretary of war W.D.C. Hall.

**Race/Ethnicity, 2000:** (In percent) Anglo, 63.88; Black, 8.12; Hispanic, 27.50; Other, 0.50.

**Vital Statistics, 2001:** Births, 65; deaths, 58; marriages, 19; divorces, 8.

**Recreation:** Fishing, hunting; museum; Old Settlers reunion in September.

**Minerals:** Not significant.

**Agriculture:** Most income from crops including cotton, peanuts; also beef cattle, hogs; some irrigation. Market value $12 million.

**MEMPHIS** (2,496) county seat; cotton gins; food processing.

Other towns include: **Estelline** (170), **Lakeview** (153), **Turkey** (500) Bob Wills Day in April.

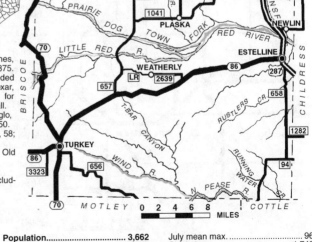

| | |
|---|---|
| Population | 3,662 |
| Change fm 2000 | -3.2 |
| Area (sq. mi.) | 904.08 |
| Land Area (sq. mi.) | 903.09 |
| Altitude (ft.) | 1,799-2,400 |
| Rainfall (in.) | 20.5 |
| Jan. mean min. | 24 |

| | |
|---|---|
| July mean max. | 96 |
| Civ. Labor | 1,743 |
| Unemployed | 5.7 |
| Wages | $5,689,515 |
| Av. Weekly Wage | $397.51 |
| Prop. Value | $187,813,827 |
| Retail Sales | $16,811,360 |

# Hamilton County

**Physical Features:** Hilly north central county broken by scenic valleys; loam soils.

**Economy:** Varied manufacturing; agribusiness; hunting leases; tourism; many residents work outside county.

**History:** Waco and Tawakoni Indian area. Anglo-American settlers arrived in mid-1850s. County created, organized 1858, from Bosque, Comanche, Lampasas counties; named for South Carolina Gov. James Hamilton, who aided Texas Revolution and Republic.

**Race/Ethnicity, 2000:** (In percent) Anglo, 91.68; Black, 0.16; Hispanic, 7.41; Other, 0.75.

**Vital Statistics, 2001:** Births, 94; deaths, 143; marriages, 60; divorces, 49.

**Recreation:** Deer, quail, duck hunting; dove festival on Labor Day; July arts and crafts show.

**Minerals:** Limited oil, gas.

**Agriculture:** Dairies, beef cattle top revenue sources. Hay, wheat, oats, sorghum. Also, pecans, sheep, horses. Market value $55.7 million.

**HAMILTON** (2,990) county seat; dairies, hunting, antiques shops, historical homes; varied manufacturing; hospital; library.

**Hico** (1,347) farm center, antiques, Old Settlers Reunion in July.

Other towns include: **Carlton** (70), **Evant** (394, partly in Coryell County), **Jonesboro** (200, partly in Coryell County); **Pottsville** (100).

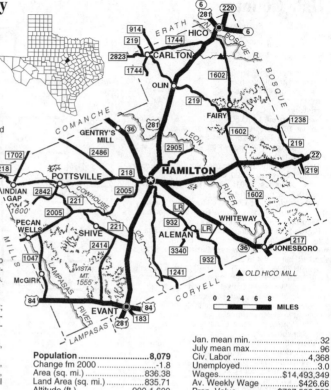

▲ OLD HICO MILL

| Population | 8,079 |
|---|---|
| Change fm 2000 | -1.8 |
| Area (sq. mi.) | 836.38 |
| Land Area (sq. mi.) | 835.71 |
| Altitude (ft.) | 900-1,600 |
| Rainfall (in.) | 31.8 |

| | |
|---|---|
| Jan. mean min. | 32 |
| July mean max. | 96 |
| Civ. Labor | 4,368 |
| Unemployed | 3.0 |
| Wages | $14,493,349 |
| Av. Weekly Wage | $426.66 |
| Prop. Value | $707,582,782 |
| Retail Sales | $53,376,633 |

# Hansford County

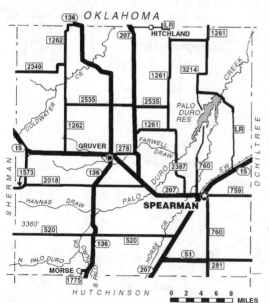

**Physical Features:** High Plains, many playas, creeks, draws; sandy, loam, black soils; underground water.

**Economy:** Agribusinesses; oil, gas operations.

**History:** Apaches, pushed out by Comanches around 1700. U.S. Army removed Comanches in 1874-75 and ranching began soon afterward. Farmers, including some from Norway, moved in around 1900. County created 1876, from Bexar, Young districts; organized 1889; named for jurist J.M. Hansford.

**Race/Ethnicity, 2000:** (In percent) Anglo, 67.64; Black, 0.17; Hispanic, 31.48; Other, 0.71.

**Vital Statistics, 2001:** Births, 71; deaths, 56; marriages, 54; divorces, 6.

**Recreation:** Stationmasters House Museum; hunting; lake activities; ecotourism; Heritage Days in June.

**Minerals:** Production of gas, oil.

**Agriculture:** Large cattle-feeding operations; corn, wheat, sorghum; hogs. Substantial irrigation. Market value $397.1 million.

**SPEARMAN** (2,937) county seat; grain marketing, storage center; oil; gas processing; feedlots; hospital; library, windmill collection. Other towns include: **Gruver** (1,131) farm-ranch market, natural gas production; Fourth of July barbecue; **Morse** (171).

| Population | 5,288 |
|---|---|
| Change fm 2000 | -1.5 |
| Area (sq. mi.) | 920.40 |
| Land Area (sq. mi.) | 919.80 |
| Altitude (ft.) | 2,800-3,360 |
| Rainfall (in.) | 19.4 |

| | |
|---|---|
| Jan. mean min. | 21 |
| July mean max. | 95 |
| Civ. Labor | 2,504 |
| Unemployed | 3.4 |
| Wages | $13,015,918 |
| Av. Weekly Wage | $501.62 |
| Prop. Value | $777,370,182 |
| Retail Sales | $37,670,798 |

# Hardeman County

**Physical Features:** Rolling, broken area on divide between Pease, Red rivers' forks; sandy loam soils.

**Economy:** Agribusiness; some manufacturing, tourism.

**History:** Apaches, later the semi-sedentary Wichitas and Comanche hunters. Ranching began in late 1870s. Farming expanded after 1900. County created 1858 from Fannin County; re-created 1876, organized 1884; named for pioneer brothers Bailey and T.J. Hardeman.

**Race/Ethnicity, 2000:** (In percent) Anglo, 79.64; Black, 4.97; Hispanic, 14.50; Other, 0.89.

**Vital Statistics, 2001:** Births, 46; deaths, 61; marriages, 39; divorces, 17.

**Recreation:** state park; lake activities; Medicine Mound aborigine gathering site; Quanah Parker monument; old railroad depot.

**Minerals:** Oil, gypsum, gravel.

**Agriculture:** Beef cattle, cotton, wheat, hay, feed products. Market value $13.4 million. Hunting leases.

**QUANAH** (2,951) county seat; agribusiness; cotton oil mill; manufacturing; hospital; historical sites; Fall Festival in September.

Other towns include: **Chillicothe** (760) farm market center, hospital.

| | | |
|---|---|---|
| Population .................................. 4,490 | | Unemployed ................................. 7.2 |
| Change fm 2000 ............................. -5.0 | | Wages ............................ $7,525,413 |
| Area (sq. mi.) ............................ 697.00 | Rainfall (in.) .................................... 24.5 | Av. Weekly Wage ................. $441.55 |
| Land Area (sq. mi.) .................. 695.38 | Jan. mean min. ................................ 23 | Prop. Value .............. $358,008,182 |
| Altitude (ft.) ...................... 1,287-1,749 | July mean max. ................................ 97 | Retail Sales ................... $16,233,258 |
| | Civ. Labor .................................... 1,795 | |

# Hardin County

**Physical Features:** Southeast county; timbered; many streams; sandy, loam soils; Big Thicket covers much of area.

**Economy:** Paper manufacturing; wood processing; minerals; food processing; oil, gas; county in Beaumont-Port Arthur-Orange metropolitan area.

**History:** Lorenzo de Zavala received first land grant in 1829. Anglo-American settlers arrived in 1830. County created 1858 from Jefferson, Liberty counties. Named for Texas Revolutionary leader William Hardin.

**Race/Ethnicity, 2000:** (In percent) Anglo, 89.93; Black, 6.95; Hispanic, 2.54; Other, 0.58.

**Vital Statistics, 2001:** Births, 658; deaths, 465; marriages, 499; divorces, 336.

**Recreation:** Big Thicket with rare plant, animal life; national preserve; Red Cloud Water Park; hunting, fishing; state park.

**Minerals:** Oil, gas, sand, gravel.

**Agriculture:** Beef cattle, hay, blueberries and rice; market value $3.6 million. Timber provides most income; more than 85 percent of county forested. Hunting leases.

**KOUNTZE** (2,150) county seat; sawmill; some manufacturing; tourism; library.

**SILSBEE** (6,489) trade, manufacturing, rail center; oil, gas processing;

library, Christmas in the Big Thicket festival.

**LUMBERTON** (8,937) construction company; government/services; tourism, library, Village Creek Festival in April.

Other towns and places include: **Batson** (140); **Grayburg** (315); **Pinewood Estates** (1,668); **Rose Hill Acres** (487); **Saratoga** (1,000) Big Thicket Museum; **Sour Lake** (1,694) oil, lumbering; Old Timer's Day in September; **Thicket** (306); **Village Mills** (1,700); **Votaw** (160).

| | |
|---|---|
| Population .................................. 48,988 | |
| Change fm 2000 ............................. 1.9 | |
| Area (sq. mi.) ............................ 897.37 | |
| Land Area (sq. mi.) .................. 894.33 | |
| Altitude (ft.) .............................. 25-150 | |
| Rainfall (in.) .................................. 55.7 | |
| Jan. mean min. ................................ 37 | |
| July mean max. ................................ 93 | |
| Civ. Labor .................................. 22,861 | |
| Unemployed ................................. 8.1 | |
| Wages ........................... $64,528,438 | |
| Av. Weekly Wage ................. $483.70 | |
| Prop. Value ............. $2,170,358,200 | |
| Retail Sales .............. $432,873,535 | |

For explanation of sources, abbreviations and symbols, see p. 138.

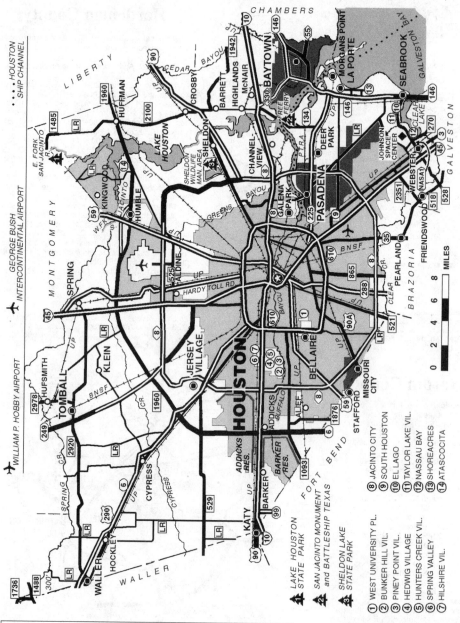

① LAKE HOUSTON STATE PARK
② SAN JACINTO MONUMENT and BATTLESHIP TEXAS
③ SHELDON LAKE STATE PARK

① WEST UNIVERSITY PL.
② BUNKER HILL VIL.
③ PINEY POINT VIL.
④ HEDWIG VILLAGE
⑤ HUNTERS CREEK VIL.
⑥ SPRING VALLEY
⑦ HILSHIRE VIL.

⑧ JACINTO CITY
⑨ SOUTH HOUSTON
⑩ EL LAGO
⑪ TAYLOR LAKE VIL.
⑫ NASSAU BAY
⑬ SHOREACRES
⑭ ATASCOCITA

| U.S. Metro Areas 2000 | Rank | Population |
|---|---|---|
| | 1. New York | 21.20 million |
| | 2. Los Angeles | 16.37 million |
| | 3. Chicago | 9.16 million |
| | 4. Washington/Baltimore | 7.61 million |
| | 5. San Francisco | 7.04 million |
| | 6. Philadelphia | 6.19 million |
| | 7. Boston | 5.82 million |
| | 8. Detroit | 5.46 million |
| | **9. Dallas/Fort Worth** | **5.22 million** |
| | **10. Houston** | **4.67 million** |

*Source: U.S. Bureau of the Census*

| | |
|---|---|
| Population | 3,557,055 |
| Change fm 2000 | 4.6 |
| Area (sq. mi.) | 1,777.69 |
| Land Area (sq. mi.) | 1,728.83 |
| Altitude (ft.) | sea level-300 |
| Rainfall (in.) | 46.1 |
| Jan. mean min. | 43 |
| July mean max. | 92 |
| Civ. Labor | 1,871,909 |
| Unemployed | 6.5 |
| Wages | $19,336,149,443 |
| Av. Weekly Wage | $803.29 |
| Fed. Wages | $344,772,523 |
| Prop. Value | $201,135,448,968 |
| Retail Sales | $47,944,789,895 |

*For explanation of sources, abbreviations and symbols, see p. 138.*

**Physical Features:** Largest county in eastern half of state; level; typically coastal surface and soils; many bayous, lakes, canals for artificial drainage; partly forested.

**Economy:** Highly industrialized county with largest population; more than 55 foreign governments maintain offices in Houston; corporate management center; nation's largest concentration of petrochemical plants; largest U.S wheat-exporting port, among top U.S. ports in the value of foreign trade and total tonnage.

Petroleum refining, chemicals, food, fabricated metal products, non-electrical machinery, primary metals, scientific instruments; paper and allied products, printing and publishing; center for energy, space and medical research; center of international business.

**History:** Orcoquiza villages visited by Spanish authorities in 1746. Pioneer settlers arrived by boat from Louisiana in 1822. Antebellum planters brought black slaves. Mexican migration increased after Mexican Revolution. County created 1836, organized 1837; named for John R. Harris, founder of Harrisburg (now part of Houston) in 1824.

**Race/Ethnicity, 2000:** (In percent) Anglo, 42.84; Black, 18.53; Hispanic, 32.93; Other, 5.70.

**Vital Statistics, 2001:** Births, 63,411; deaths, 20,652; marriages, 33,897; divorces, 14,592.

**Recreation:** Professional baseball, basketball, football; rodeo and livestock show; Jones Hall for the Performing Arts; Nina Vance Alley Theatre; Houston Theatre Center; Convention Center; the Summit, a 17,000-seat sports and entertainment center; Astroworld and WaterWorld amusement parks; Reliant Stadium and downtown ballpark.

Sam Houston Park, with restored early Houston homes, church, stores; Museum of Fine Arts, Contemporary Arts Museum, Rice Museum; Wortham Theater; Hobby Center for Performing Arts (fall 2002); museum of natural science, planetarium, zoo in Hermann Park.

San Jacinto Battleground, Battleship Texas; Johnson Space Center.

Fishing, boating, other freshwater and saltwater activities.

**Minerals:** Among leading oil, gas, petrochemical areas; production of petroleum, cement, natural gas, liquids, salt, lime, sulfur, sand and gravel, clays, stone.

**Agriculture:** Nursery crops, cattle, horses, turfgrass, hay, vegetables, corn. Irrigation for rice and turfgrass. Market value $77.5 million. Substantial income from forest products.

# Harris County

**Education:** Houston is a major center of higher education, with more than 140,000 students enrolled in 28 colleges and universities in the county. Among these are Rice University, University of Houston, Texas Southern University, University of St. Thomas, Houston Baptist University.

Medical schools include University of St. Thomas and Houston Baptist University Schools of Nursing, University of Texas Health Science Center, Baylor College of Medicine, Institute of Religion and Human Development, Texas Chiropractic College, Texas Woman's University-Houston Center.

**HOUSTON** (1,980,950) county seat; largest Texas city; fourth-largest in nation.

Ranks first in manufacture of petroleum equipment, agricultural chemicals, fertilizers, pesticides, oil and gas pipeline transmission; a leading scientific center; ranks high in manufacture of machinery, fabricated metals; a major

distribution, shipping center; engineering and research center; food processing and textile mills.

Plants make apparel, lumber and wood products; furniture, paper, chemical, petroleum and coal products; publishing center; one of the nation's largest public school systems; prominent corporate center, with more than 200 firms relocating corporate headquarters, divisions or subsidaries to county since 1970; Go Texan Days in February.

**Pasadena** (143,527) residential city with large industrial area manufacturing petrochemicals and other petroleum-related products; civic center; San Jacinto College, Texas Chiropractic College; four hospitals; historical museum; Strawberry Festival.

**Baytown** (66,646) refining, petrochemical center; Lee College; hospitals; historical homes; youth fair in April.

**Bellaire** (15,637) residential city with several major office buildings.

The **Clear Lake Area**, which includes **El Lago** (3,029); **Nassau Bay** (4,230); **Seabrook** (9,950); **Taylor Lake Village** (3,798); **Webster** (9,029); Johnson Space Center, University of Houston-Clear Lake; Bayport Industrial Complex includes Port of Bayport; 12 major marinas; hospitals; Christmas lighted boat parade.

Other towns include: **Aldine** (14,040); **Atascocita** (36,923); **Barrett** (2,835); **Bunker Hill Village** (3,776); **Channelview** (29,814); **Crosby** (1,681); **Deer Park** (29,387) ship-channel industries, fall festival; hospital; **Galena Park** (10,678); **Hedwig Village** (2,327); **Highlands** (7,194); **Hilshire Village** (737); **Hockley** (300); **Humble** (14,823) oil-field equipment manufactured, retail center, hospital; **Hunters Creek Village** (4,456); **Jacinto City** (10,343); **Jersey Village** (7,207).

Also, **Katy** (12,909, partly in Fort Bend, Waller counties) varied manufacturing, hospital; rice harvest festival in October, rice museum, G.I. Joe museum; **La Porte** (32,826) varied manufacturing; Sylvan Beach Festival in April; Galveston Bay; **Morgan's Point** (362); **Piney Point Village** (3,472); **Sheldon** (1,834); **Shoreacres** (1,525); **South Houston** (15,765).

Also, **Southside Place** (1,585); **Spring** (36,948); **Spring Valley** (3,528); **Tomball** (9,544) computers, oil equipment, retail center; antiques; hospital; sports medical center; museum, junior college, parks; **West University Place** (14,430).

Parts of **Friendswood**, **Missouri City**, **Pearland**, **Stafford** and **Waller**.

**Addicks**, **Alief** and **Kingwood** are now within the city limits of Houston.

*A ship on the Houston Ship Channel. In the background is the Fred Hartman Bridge between Baytown and La Porte. File photo.*

# Harrison County

**Physical Features:** East Texas county; hilly, rolling; over half forested; Sabine River; Caddo Lake.

**Economy:** Oil, gas processing; lumbering; pottery, other varied manufacturing.

**History:** Agriculturist Caddo Indians whose numbers were reduced by disease. Anglo-Americans arrived in 1830s. In 1850, the county had more slaves than any other in the state. County created 1839 from Shelby County; organized 1842. Named for eloquent advocate of Texas Revolution, Jonas Harrison.

**Race/Ethnicity, 2000:** (In percent) Anglo, 69.81; Black, 24.13; Hispanic, 5.34; Other, 0.72.

**Vital Statistics, 2001:** Births, 792; deaths, 641; marriages, 541; divorces, 150.

**Recreation:** Fishing, other water activities on Caddo and other lakes; hunting; plantation homes, historic sites; Stagecoach Days in May; Old Courthouse Museum; Old World Store; state park, performing arts; Fire Ant festival in October.

**Minerals:** Oil, gas, lignite coal, clays, sand and gravel.

**Agriculture:** Cattle, hay. Also, poultry, nursery plants, horses, vegetables, watermelons. Market value $14.1 million. Hunting leases important. Substantial timber industry.

**MARSHALL** (23,791) county seat; petroleum, lumber processing; varied manufacturing; Wonderland of Lights in December; civic center; historic sites, including Starr Family State Historic Site; hospital; Wiley College; East Texas Baptist University.

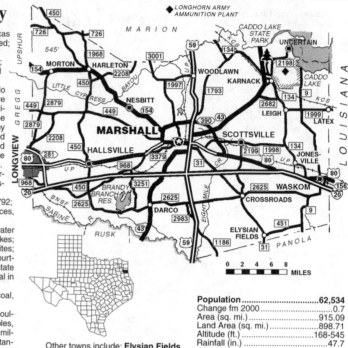

Other towns include: **Elysian Fields** (300); **Hallsville** (2,846) Western Days in October, museum; **Harleton** (260); **Jonesville** (28); **Karnack** (775); **Nesbitt** (294); **Scottsville** (251); **Uncertain** (141); **Waskom** (2,110) oil, gas; ranching; Armadillo Daze in April; **Woodlawn** (370). Also, part (1,598) of **Longview**.

| | |
|---|---|
| Population | **62,534** |
| Change fm 2000 | 0.7 |
| Area (sq. mi.) | 915.09 |
| Land Area (sq. mi.) | 898.71 |
| Altitude (ft.) | 168-545 |
| Rainfall (in.) | 47.7 |
| Jan. mean min. | 32 |
| July mean max. | 93 |
| Civ. Labor | 30,030 |
| Unemployed | 6.3 |
| Wages | $163,028,941 |
| Av. Weekly Wage | $583.72 |
| Prop. Value | $4,718,968,712 |
| Retail Sales | $481,142,555 |

# Hartley County

**Physical Features:** Panhandle High Plains; drains to Canadian River tributaries, playas; sandy, loam, chocolate soils; lake.

**Economy:** Agriculture, gas production; varied manufacturing.

**History:** Apaches, pushed out by Comanches around 1700. U.S. Army removed Indians in 1875. *Pastores* (Hispanic sheepmen) in area until 1880s. Cattle ranching began in 1880s. Farming expanded after 1900. County created 1876 from Bexar, Young districts; organized 1891; named for Texas pioneers O.C. and R.K. Hartley.

**Race/Ethnicity, 2000:** (In percent) Anglo, 77.59; Black, 8.11; Hispanic, 13.69; Other, 0.61.

**Vital Statistics, 2001:** Births, 70; deaths, 35; marriages, 4; divorces, 16.

**Recreation:** Rita Blanca Lake activities; ranch museum; local events; XIT Rodeo and Reunion at Dalhart.

**Minerals:** Sand, gravel, natural gas.

**Agriculture:** Cattle, corn, wheat, hay, dairy cows, vegetables. 110,000 acres irrigated. Market value $401.2 million. Hunting leases.

**CHANNING** (359) county seat, Roundup.

**DALHART** (7,210, mostly in Dallam County), feedlots; feed, meat processing; other industries. Also, **Hartley** (478).

| | |
|---|---|
| Population | **5,464** |
| Change fm 2000 | -1.3 |
| Area (sq. mi.) | 1,463.20 |
| Land Area (sq. mi.) | 1,462.25 |
| Altitude (ft.) | 3,400-4,470 |
| Rainfall (in.) | 16.1 |
| Jan. mean min. | 21 |
| July mean max. | 92 |
| Civ. Labor | 3,157 |
| Unemployed | 1.2 |
| Wages | $5,757,562 |
| Av. Weekly Wage | $440.25 |
| Prop. Value | $628,924,974 |
| Retail Sales | $13,359,875 |

# Haskell County

**Physical Features:** West central county; rolling; broken areas; drained by Brazos tributaries; lake; sandy loam, gray, black soils.

**Economy:** Agribusiness, oil-field operations.

**History:** Apaches until 1700, then Comanche area. Ranching began in late 1870s after Indians removed. Farming expanded after 1900. County created 1858, from Milam, Fannin counties; re-created 1876; organized 1885; named for Goliad victim C.R. Haskell.

**Race/Ethnicity,2000:** (In percent) Anglo, 76.02; Black, 2.86; Hispanic, 20.50; Other, 0.62.

**Vital Statistics, 2001:** Births, 78; deaths, 85; marriages, 36; divorces, 29.

**Recreation:** Lake Stamford activities; bass tournament, arts & crafts show; hunting of deer, geese, wild hog.

**Minerals:** Oil and gas.

**Agriculture:** Wheat, cotton, peanuts; 28,000 acres irrigated. Beef cattle raised. Market value $23.5 million.

**HASKELL** (3,084) county seat; farming center; hospital; city park; Wild Horse Prairie Days in June.

Other towns include: **O'Brien** (131), **Rochester** (377), **Rule** (693), **Sagerton** (115), **Weinert** (175). Also, **Stamford** (3,530, mostly in Jones County),

| | | | |
|---|---|---|---|
| Population | 5,909 | Altitude (ft.) | 1,400-1,681 |
| Change fm 2000 | -3.0 | Rainfall (in.) | 26.1 |
| Area (sq. mi.) | 910.25 | Jan. mean min. | .27 |
| Land Area (sq. mi.) | 902.97 | July mean max. | .96 |
| | | Civ. Labor | 2,739 |

| | |
|---|---|
| Unemployed | 5.3 |
| Wages | $8,473,212 |
| Av. Weekly Wage | $386.36 |
| Prop. Value | $364,971,123 |
| Retail Sales | $56,355,744 |

# Hays County

**Physical Features:** Hilly in west, blackland in east; on edge of Balcones Escarpment.

**Economy:** Education, tourism, retirement area, some manufacturing; part of Austin metropolitan area.

**History:** Tonkawa area, also Apache and Comanche presence. Spanish authorities attempted first permanent settlement in 1807. Mexican land grants in early 1830s to Juan Martín Veramendi, Juan Vicente Campos and Thomas Jefferson Chambers. County created 1843 from Travis County; named for Capt. Jack Hays, famous Texas Ranger.

**Race/Ethnicity, 2000:** (In percent) Anglo, 65.26; Black, 3.74; Hispanic, 29.57; Other, 1.43.

**Vital Statistics, 2001:** Births, 1,538; deaths, 542; marriages, 792; divorces, 298.

**Recreation:** Fishing, hunting; college cultural, athletic events; Cypress Creek and Blanco River resorts; guest ranches.

**Minerals:** Sand and gravel, cement produced.

**Agriculture:** Beef cattle, goats, exotic wildlife; greenhouse nurseries; hay, corn, sorghum, wheat and cotton. Market value $13.4 million.

**SAN MARCOS** (39,936) county seat; Texas State University, San Marcos Baptist Academy, Gary Job Corps Training Center; government/services; distribution center; outlet centers; hospital, sports medicine, physical therapy center; Scheib Center for mentally handicapped; Republic of Texas Chilympiad in September.

Other towns include: **Bear Creek** (389); **Buda** (2,700); **Driftwood** (1,253); **Dripping Springs** (1,636); **Hays** (244); **Kyle** (6,966); **Mountain City** (709); **Niederwald** (618, partly in Caldwell County); **Uhland** (401, partly in Caldwell County); **Wimberley** (4,004) tourism, retirement community, artists, concert series; Country Pie Social and Fair in April; **Woodcreek** (1,399).

| | |
|---|---|
| Population | 109,570 |
| Change fm 2000 | 12.3 |
| Area (sq. mi.) | 679.79 |
| Land Area (sq. mi.) | 677.87 |
| Altitude (ft.) | 550-1,501 |
| Rainfall (in.) | 34.6 |
| Jan. mean min. | 36 |
| July mean max. | 95 |
| Civ. Labor | 57,772 |
| Unemployed | 5.2 |
| Wages | $227,780,824 |
| Av. Weekly Wage | $496.17 |
| Prop. Value | $6,609,831,197 |
| Retail Sales | $1,187,600,503 |

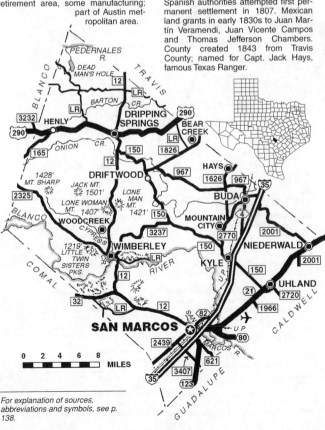

For explanation of sources, abbreviations and symbols, see p. 138.

# Hemphill County

**Physical Features:** Panhandle county; sloping surface, broken by Canadian, Washita rivers; sandy, red, dark soils.

**Economy:** Petroleum production and refining, livestock production, tourism, government/services.

**History:** Apaches, who were pushed out by Comanches, Kiowas. Tribes removed to Indian Territory in 1875. Ranching began in late 1870s. Farmers began to arrive after 1900. County created from Bexar, Young districts, 1876; organized 1887; named for Republic of Texas Justice John Hemphill.

**Race/Ethnicity, 2000:** Anglo, 81.42; Black, 1.55; Hispanic, 15.58; Other, 1.13.

**Vital Statistics, 2001:** Births, 40; deaths, 36; marriages, 48; divorces, 5.

**Recreation:** Lake Marvin activities; fall foliage tours; hunting, fishing; Buffalo Wallow Indian Battleground, wildlife management area; 4th of July rodeo.

**Minerals:** Oil, natural gas, caliche.

**Agriculture:** Beef cattle top revenue source; crops include hay, wheat, improved pastures; some irrigation. Market value $105.5 million. Hunting leases, nature tourism.

**CANADIAN** (2,173) county seat; oil, gas production; feedlot; hospital.

| | | | |
|---|---|---|---|
| Population | 3,332 | Altitude (ft.) | 2,185-3,000 |
| Change fm 2000 | -0.6 | Rainfall (in.) | 20.1 |
| Area (sq. mi.) | 912.06 | Jan. mean min. | 22 |
| Land Area (sq. mi.) | 909.68 | July mean max. | 96 |
| | | Civ. Labor | 2,090 |

| | |
|---|---|
| Unemployed | 1.3 |
| Wages | $10,403,186 |
| Av. Weekly Wage | $508.74 |
| Prop. Value | $1,095,634,480 |
| Retail Sales | $19,003,871 |

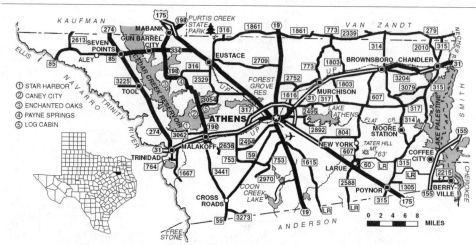

① STAR HARBOR
② CANEY CITY
③ ENCHANTED OAKS
④ PAYNE SPRINGS
⑤ LOG CABIN

# Henderson County

**Physical Features:** East Texas county bounded by Neches, Trinity rivers; hilly, rolling; one-third forested; sandy, loam, clay soils; commercial timber; Cedar Creek, other lakes.

**Economy:** Agibusiness, retail trade; varied manufacturing; minerals; recreation; tourism.

**History:** Caddo area. Cherokee, other tribes migrated into the area in 1819-20 ahead of white settlement. Cherokees forced into Indian Territory in 1839. Anglo-American settlers arrived in 1840s. County created 1846 from Nacogdoches, Houston counties and named for Gov. J. Pinckney Henderson.

**Race/Ethnicity, 2000:** (In percent) Anglo, 85.49; Black, 6.72; Hispanic, 6.92; Other, 0.87.

**Vital Statistics, 2001:** Births, 930; deaths, 932; marriages, 608; divorces, 28.

**Recreation:** Cedar Creek Reservoir, Lake Palestine, and other lakes; Purtis Creek State Park; hunting, fishing, bird-watching.

**Minerals:** Oil, gas, clays, lignite, sulfur, sand and gravel.

**Agriculture:** Greenhouse/nurseries, beef cattle, forages, horses. Market value $43.7 million. Timber marketed.

**ATHENS** (11,405) county seat; agribusiness center; varied manufacturing; tourism; state fish hatchery and museum; hospital, mental health-center; Trinity Valley Community College; Texas Fiddlers' Contest in May.

**Gun Barrel City** (5,300) recreation, retirement, retail center.

**Malakoff** (2,281) brick factory, varied industry, tourism, library, Cornbread Festival in April.

Other towns include: **Berryville** (901); **Brownsboro** (810); **Caney City** (238); **Chandler** (2,173); **Coffee City** (202); **Enchanted Oaks** (361); **Eustace** (833); **Larue** (160); **Log Cabin** (761); **Moore Station** (178); **Murchison** (589); **Payne Springs** (720); **Poynor** (316); **Seven Points** (1,210) agribusiness, retail trade, recreation, Monte Carlo celebration in November; **Star Harbor** (423); **Tool** (2,301), and **Trinidad** (1,132). **Mabank** (2,305, mostly in Kaufman County).

| | |
|---|---|
| Population | 75,797 |
| Change fm 2000 | 3.4 |
| Area (sq. mi.) | 949.00 |
| Land Area (sq. mi.) | 874.24 |
| Altitude (ft.) | 256-763 |
| Rainfall (in.) | 39.7 |
| Jan. mean min. | 35 |
| July mean max. | 95 |
| Civ. Labor | 30,414 |
| Unemployed | 5.9 |
| Wages | $92,453,154 |
| Av. Weekly Wage | $446.19 |
| Prop. Value | $3,907,318,430 |
| Retail Sales | $602,913,094 |

# Hidalgo County

**Physical Features:** Rich alluvial soils along Rio Grande; sandy, loam soils in north; semitropical vegetation.

**Economy:** Food processing, shipping; other agribusinesses; tourism; mineral operations.

**History:** Coahuiltecan and Karankawa area. Comanches forced Apaches southward into valley in 1700s; Comanches arrived in valley in 1800s. Spanish settlement occurred 1750-1800. County created 1852 from Cameron, Starr counties; named for leader of Mexico's independence movement, Father Miguel Hidalgo y Costillo.

**Race/Ethnicity, 2000:** (In percent) Anglo, 10.59; Black, 0.36; Hispanic, 88.35; Other, 0.70.

**Vital Statistics, 2001:** Births, 15,083; deaths, 2,985; marriages, 5,069; divorces, 146.

**Recreation:** Winter resort, retirement area; fishing, hunting; gateway to Mexico; historical sites; Bentsen-Rio Grande Valley State Park; museums; All-Valley Winter Vegetable Show at Pharr.

**Minerals:** Oil, gas, stone, sand and gravel.

**Agriculture:** Ninety percent of farm cash receipts from crops, principally from sugar cane, grain, vegetables, citrus, cotton; livestock includes cattle; 270,000 acres irrigated. Market value $272.5 million.

**EDINBURG** (51,935) county seat; vegetable processing, packing; petroleum operations; clothing; tourism; planetarium; the University of Texas-Pan American; hospital; mental health center; museum; Fiesta Hidalgo in February.

**McALLEN** (112,395) food processing, packing, shipping; foreign trade zone; agriculture; tourism; varied manufacturing; new air terminal; community college; cancer center.

**Mission** (50,515) citrus groves, with Citrus Fiesta in January; agricultural processing and distribution; hospital; community college.

**Pharr** (49,655) agriculture, trading center; trucking; tourism; old clock, juke box museums; folklife festival in February.

Other towns include: **Abram-Perezville** (5,477); **Alamo** (15,456) live steam museum; **Alton** (4,690); **Alton North** (5,215); **Doffing** (4,366); **Donna** (15,334) citrus center, varied manufacturing; lamb, sheep show; **Edcouch** (3,604); **Elsa** (5,760); **Granjeno** (335); **Hargill** (1,349); **Hidalgo** (8,190) trade zone, shipping; winter resort, agribusiness, historical sites, library; Borderfest in March; **La Blanca** (2,438); **La Homa** (10,765); **La Joya** (3,589); **Los Ebanos** (425).

Also, **Mercedes** (14,016) "boot capital," citrus, vegetable center; food processing; tourism; recreation vehicle show in January, Hispanic Fest July 4; **Mila Doce** (5,102); **Monte Alto** (1,676); **North Alamo** (2,107); **Nurillo** (5,200); **Palmhurst** (5,122); **Palmview** (4,336); **Palmview South** (6,421); **Peñitas** (1,158); **Progreso** (5,107); **Progreso Lakes** (238); **San Carlos** (2,718); **San Juan** (27,777); **San Manuel-Linn** (971); **South Alamo** (3,194); **Sullivan City** (4,124); **Weslaco** (28,007) Bicultural Museum.

| | |
|---|---|
| Population | **614,474** |
| Change fm 2000 | 7.9 |
| Area (sq. mi.) | 1,582.66 |
| Land Area (sq. mi.) | 1,569.75 |
| Altitude (ft.) | 28-350 |
| Rainfall (in.) | 23.4 |
| Jan. mean min. | 49 |
| July mean max. | 96 |
| Civ. Labor | 224,741 |
| Unemployed | 13.5 |
| Wages | $972,160,629 |
| Av. Weekly Wage | $447.89 |
| Prop. Value | $15,676,825,766 |
| Retail Sales | $5,565,163,646 |

*For explanation of sources, abbreviations and symbols, see p. 138.*

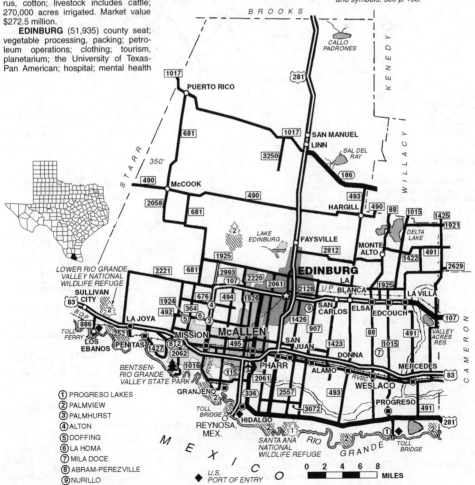

① PROGRESO LAKES
② PALMVIEW
③ PALMHURST
④ ALTON
⑤ DOFFING
⑥ LA HOMA
⑦ MILA DOCE
⑧ ABRAM-PEREZVILLE
⑨ NURILLO

# Hill County

**Physical Features:** North central county; level to rolling; blackland soils, some sandy loams; drains to Brazos; lakes.

**Economy:** Agribusiness, varied manufacturing, tourism.

**History:** Waco and Tawakoni area, later Comanches. Believed to be Indian "council spot," without evidence of raids and a place of safe passage. Anglo-Americans of the Robertson colony arrived in early 1830s. County created from Navarro County 1853; named for G.W. Hill, Republic of Texas official.

**Race/Ethnicity, 2000:** (In percent) Anglo, 78.40; Black, 7.51; Hispanic, 13.49; Other, 0.60.

**Vital Statistics, 2001:** Births, 514; deaths, 430; marriages, 312; divorces, 137.

**Recreation:** Lake activities; excursion boat on Whitney; Confederate Museum, Audie Murphy Gun Museum, historic structures; art festival; motorcycle track.

**Minerals:** Limestone, gas, oil.

**Agriculture:** Cattle, nursery crops, sorghum, dairies, wheat, hay, turkeys, cotton. Market value $63.6 million. Some firewood marketed.

**HILLSBORO** (8,475) county seat; retail, outlet center; tourism; manufacturing, agribusiness; antique malls; Hill College; hospital; crafts fair; restored courthouse.

**Whitney** (1,919) tourist center; hospital, varied manufacturing.

Other towns include: **Abbott** (309); **Aquilla** (138); **Blum** (410); **Brandon** (80); **Bynum** (230); **Carl's Corner** (137); **Covington** (298); **Hubbard** (1,626) retail center; government/services, lakes, baseball museum; **Irene** (160); **Itasca** (1,544); **Malone** (286); **Mertens** (150); **Mount Calm** (319); **Penelope** (216).

| | | |
|---|---|---|
| Population ...............................**33,701** | Rainfall (in.) .................................. 35.1 | Unemployed...................................7.1 |
| Change fm 2000 ...........................4.3 | Jan. mean min.................................. 34 | Wages...............................$49,623,543 |
| Area (sq. mi.) ..........................985.65 | July mean max............................... 95 | Av. Weekly Wage ....................$434.96 |
| Land Area (sq. mi.) ...................962.36 | Civ. Labor.............................. 16,351 | Prop. Value...............$1,343,433,162 |
| Altitude (ft.) ............................ 450-880 | | Retail Sales..................$320,248,539 |

# Hockley County

**Physical Features:** West Texas High Plains, numerous playas, drains to Yellow House Draw; loam, sandy loam soils.

**Economy:** Extensive oil, gas production and services; manufacturing; varied agribusiness.

**History:** Comanches displaced Apaches in early 1700s. Large ranches of 1880s brought few residents. Homesteaders arrived after 1900. County created 1876, from Bexar, Young districts; organized 1921. Named for Republic of Texas secretary of war Gen. G.W. Hockley.

**Race/Ethnicity, 2000:** Anglo, 58.37; Black, 3.79; Hispanic, 37.24; Other, 0.60.

**Vital Statistics, 2001:** Births, 328; deaths, 202; marriages, 146; divorces, 85.

**Recreation:** Early Settlers' Day in July; Marigolds Arts, Crafts Festival in November.

**Minerals:** Oil, gas, stone; one of leading oil counties with more than 1 billion barrels produced.

**Agriculture:** Cotton, grain sorghum are top crops; cattle, hogs raised; substantial irrigation. Market value $76.8 million.

**LEVELLAND** (12,667) county seat; oil, cotton, cattle center; government/services; hospital; South Plains College; Hot Burrito & Bluegrass Music Festival in July.

Other towns include: **Anton** (1,179); **Opdyke West** (187); **Pep** (35); **Ropesville** (516); **Smyer** (474); **Sundown** (1,505); **Whitharral** (175).

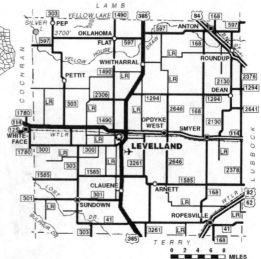

| | | |
|---|---|---|
| Population ..........................**22,838** | July mean max. ...........................92 |
| Change fm 2000 ....................... 0.5 | Civ. Labor .............................10,415 |
| Area (sq. mi.) ......................908.55 | Unemployed ...............................5.1 |
| Land Area (sq. mi.) ..............908.28 | Wages..............$46,920,728 |
| Altitude (ft.)...................3,300-3,700 | Av. Weekly Wage ...............$469.59 |
| Rainfall (in.)..............................19.3 | Prop. Value.............$2,293,554,373 |
| Jan. mean min. ..........................22 | Retail Sales ...............$166,475,249 |

# Hood County

**Physical Features:** Hilly; broken by Paluxy, Brazos rivers; sandy loam soils.

**Economy:** Tourism; nuclear power plant; commuting to Fort Worth; agriculture.

**History:** Lipan Apache and Comanche area. Anglo-American settlers arrived in late 1840s. County created 1866 from Johnson and Erath counties; named for Confederate Gen. John B. Hood.

**Race/Ethnicity, 2000:** (In percent), Anglo, 91.22; Black, 0.36; Hispanic, 7.24; Other, 1.18.

**Vital Statistics, 2001:** Births, 451; deaths, 496; marriages, 371; divorces, 218.

**Recreation:** Lakes, fishing, scenic areas; summer theater; Gen. Granbury's Bean & Rib cookoff in March; Acton historic site.

**Minerals:** Oil, stone.

**Agriculture:** Hay, turfgrass, beef cattle, nursery crops, pecans, peanuts; some irrigation. Market value $29.8 million.

**GRANBURY** (6,027) county seat; tourism; real estate; power plants; historic downtown area; opera house; hospital, library; Civil War re-enactment in October.

Other towns include: **Acton** (1,129) grave of Elizabeth Crockett, wife of Davy; **Cresson** (208), **DeCordova** (3,693), **Lipan** (428), **Oak Trail Shores** (2,563), **Paluxy** (76), **Pecan Plantation** (3,593); **Tolar** (524).

| | |
|---|---|
| Population | 44,149 |
| Change fm 2000 | 7.4 |
| Area (sq. mi.) | 436.80 |
| Land Area (sq. mi.) | 421.61 |
| Altitude (ft.) | 600-1,230 |
| Rainfall (in.) | 30.9 |
| Jan. mean min. | 33 |
| July mean max | 97 |
| Civ. Labor | 19,170 |
| Unemployed | 6.1 |
| Wages | $65,201,715 |
| Av. Weekly Wage | $484.97 |
| Prop. Value | $2,433,347,260 |
| Retail Sales | $381,247,574 |

---

# Hopkins County

**Physical Features:** Northeast Texas county of varied timber, including pines; drains north to South Sulphur River; Cooper Lake (also known as Jim Chapman Lake); light, sandy to heavier black soils.

**Economy:** Dairies, large milk-processing plants; agribusiness, feed mills; varied manufacturing.

**History:** Caddo area, displaced by Cherokees, who in turn were forced out by President Lamar in 1839. First Anglo-American settlement in 1837. County created 1846 from Lamar, Nacogdoches counties; named for pioneer Hopkins family.

**Race/Ethnicity, 2000:** (In percent) Anglo, 81.74; Black, 8.07; Hispanic, 9.28; Other, 0.91.

**Vital Statistics, 2001:** Births, 479; deaths, 357; marriages, 301; divorces, 206.

**Recreation:** Fishing, hunting; lake activities; stew contest in September; dairy museum; dairy festival in June.

**Minerals:** Lignite coal.

**Agriculture:** A leading county in dairies and hay; beef cattle; horses. Market value $137.4 million. Firewood and hardwood lumber marketed.

**SULPHUR SPRINGS** (14,606) county seat; dairy farming; equine center; food processing, distribution; varied manufacturing; tourism; hospital; library, heritage park; music box gallery; civic center.

Other towns include: **Brashear** (280), **Como** (617), **Cumby** (613), **Dike** (170), **Pickton** (90), **Saltillo** (200), **Sulphur Bluff** (280), **Tira** (245).

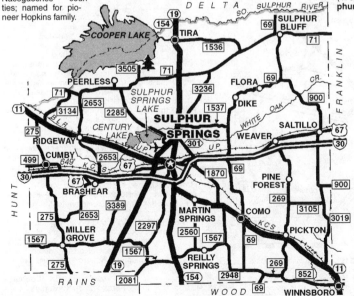

| | |
|---|---|
| Population | 32,299 |
| Change fm 2000 | 1.1 |
| Area (sq. mi.) | 792.74 |
| Land Area (sq. mi.) | 782.40 |
| Altitude (ft.) | 350-649 |
| Rainfall (in.) | 46.0 |
| Jan. mean min. | 30 |
| July mean max. | 94 |
| Civ. Labor | 15,015 |
| Unemployed | 5.5 |
| Wages | $66,364,667 |
| Av. Weekly Wage | $471.03 |
| Prop. Value | $1,461,884,962 |
| Retail Sales | $357,186,538 |

For explanation of sources, abbreviations and symbols, see p. 138.

# Houston County

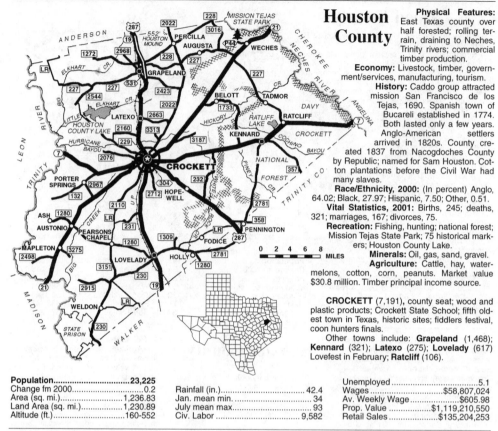

**Physical Features:** East Texas county over half forested; rolling terrain, draining to Neches, Trinity rivers; commercial timber production.

**Economy:** Livestock, timber, government/services, manufacturing, tourism.

**History:** Caddo group attracted mission San Francisco de los Tejas, 1690. Spanish town of Bucareli established in 1774. Both lasted only a few years. Anglo-American settlers arrived in 1820s. County created 1837 from Nacogdoches County by Republic; named for Sam Houston. Cotton plantations before the Civil War had many slaves.

**Race/Ethnicity, 2000:** (In percent) Anglo, 64.02; Black, 27.97; Hispanic, 7.50; Other, 0.51.

**Vital Statistics, 2001:** Births, 245; deaths, 321; marriages, 167; divorces, 75.

**Recreation:** Fishing, hunting; national forest; Mission Tejas State Park; 75 historical markers; Houston County Lake.

**Minerals:** Oil, gas, sand, gravel.

**Agriculture:** Cattle, hay, watermelons, cotton, corn, peanuts. Market value $30.8 million. Timber principal income source.

**CROCKETT** (7,191), county seat; wood and plastic products; Crockett State School; fifth oldest town in Texas, historic sites; fiddlers festival, coon hunters finals.

Other towns include: **Grapeland** (1,468); **Kennard** (321); **Latexo** (275); **Lovelady** (617) Lovefest in February; **Ratcliff** (106).

| | |
|---|---|
| Population | 23,225 |
| Change fm 2000 | 0.2 |
| Area (sq. mi.) | 1,236.83 |
| Land Area (sq. mi.) | 1,230.89 |
| Altitude (ft.) | 160-552 |
| Rainfall (in.) | 42.4 |
| Jan. mean min. | 34 |
| July mean max. | 93 |
| Civ. Labor | 9,582 |
| Unemployed | 5.1 |
| Wages | $58,807,024 |
| Av. Weekly Wage | $605.98 |
| Prop. Value | $1,119,210,550 |
| Retail Sales | $135,204,253 |

# Howard County

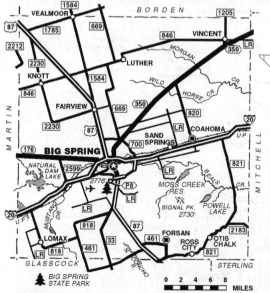

**Physical Features:** On edge of Llano Estacado; sandy loam soils.

**Economy:** Government/services; agribusiness; oil, gas; varied manufacturing, including clothing.

**History:** Pawnee and Comanche area. Anglo-American settlement began in 1870. Oil boom in mid-1920s. County named for V.E. Howard, legislator; created 1876 from Bexar, Young districts; organized 1882.

**Race/Ethnicity, 2000:** (In percent), Anglo, 57.47; Black, 4.04; Hispanic, 37.46; Other, 1.03.

**Vital Statistics, 2001:** Births, 430; deaths, 383; marriages, 256; divorces, 40.

**Recreation:** Lakes; state park; campground in Comanche Trail Park; Native Plant Trail; museum; historical sites; West Texas agricultural expo in March; Cranefest in February.

**Minerals:** Oil, gas, sand, gravel and stone.

**Agriculture:** Principally dry-land cotton; also, beef, stocker cattle, horses, peanuts, sorghum. Market value $12.2 million.

**BIG SPRING** (25,477) county seat; agriculture, petrochemicals produced; hospitals, including a state institution and Veterans Administration hospital; federal prison; varied manufacturing; Howard College; railroad plaza.

Other towns include: **Coahoma** (911), **Forsan** (223), **Knott** (685).

*For explanation of sources, abbreviations and symbols, see p. 138.*

| | |
|---|---|
| Population | 33,215 |
| Change fm 2000 | -1.2 |
| Area (sq. mi.) | 904.19 |
| Land Area (sq. mi.) | 902.84 |
| Altitude (ft.) | 2,200-2,776 |
| Rainfall (in.) | 19.2 |
| Jan. mean min. | 28 |
| July mean max. | 94 |
| Civ. Labor | 14,369 |
| Unemployed | 5.1 |
| Wages | $82,346,268 |
| Av. Weekly Wage | $516.20 |
| Prop. Value | $1,407,789,625 |
| Retail Sales | $280,521,382 |

# Hudspeth County

**Physical Features:** Plateau, basin terrain, draining to salt lakes; Rio Grande; mostly rocky, alkaline, clay soils and sandy loam soils, except alluvial along Rio Grande; desert, mountain vegetation. Fertile agricultural valleys.

**Economy:** Agribusiness, mining, tourism, hunting leases.

**History:** Mescalero Apache area. Fort Quitman established in 1858 to protect routes to west. Railroad in 1881 brought Anglo-American settlers. Political turmoil in Mexico (1912-29) brought more settlers from Mexico. County named for Texas political leader Claude B. Hudspeth; created 1917 from El Paso County.

**Race/Ethnicity, 2000:** (In percent) Anglo, 23.50; Black, 0.21; Hispanic, 75.03; Other, 1.26.

**Vital Statistics, 2001:** Births, 41; deaths, 16; marriages, 13; divorces, 0.

**Recreation:** Scenic drives; fort ruins; hot springs; salt basin; white sands; hunting; birding; part of Guadalupe Mountains National Park, containing unique plant life, canyons.

**Minerals:** Talc, stone, gypsum.

**Agriculture:** Most income from cotton, vegetables, hay, alfalfa; beef cattle raised; 35,000 acres irrigated. Market value $37 million.

**SIERRA BLANCA** (549) county seat; ranching center; tourist stop on interstate highway; adobe courthouse; 4th of July fair; livestock show in January.

Other towns include: **Dell City** (425) feedlots; vegetable packing; gypsum processing; clinic; trade center; airport; some of largest water wells in state; **Fort Hancock** (1,764), and **Salt Flat** (35).

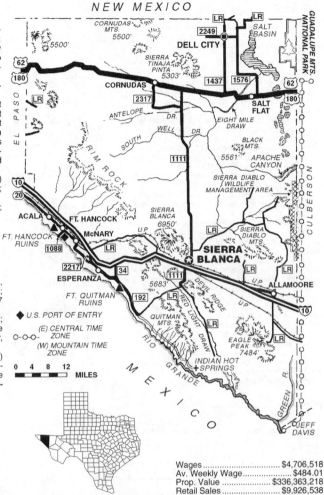

| | |
|---|---|
| Population | 3,341 |
| Change fm 2000 | -0.1 |
| Area (sq. mi.) | 4,571.93 |
| Land Area (sq. mi.) | 4,571.00 |
| Altitude (ft.) | 3,200-7,484 |
| Rainfall (in.) | 10.0 |
| Jan. mean min. | 25 |
| July mean max. | 95 |
| Civ. Labor | 1,343 |
| Unemployed | 6.6 |

| | |
|---|---|
| Wages | $4,706,518 |
| Av. Weekly Wage | $484.01 |
| Prop. Value | $336,363,218 |
| Retail Sales | $9,926,538 |

*Wind turbines on a site just south of the Guadalupe National Park. File photo.*

# Hunt County

**Physical Features:** North Texas county; level to rolling surface; Sabine, Sulphur rivers; Lake Tawakoni; mostly heavy Blackland soil, some loam, sandy loams.

**Economy:** Education, varied manufacturing, agribusiness; several Fortune 500 companies in county; many residents employed in Dallas area.

**History:** Kiowa Indians who left soon after Anglo-American settlers arrived in 1839. County named for Memucan Hunt, Republic secretary of navy; created 1846 from Fannin, Nacogdoches counties.

**Race/Ethnicity, 2000:** (In percent) Anglo, 80.61; Black, 9.67; Hispanic, 8.31; Other, 1.41.

**Vital Statistics, 2001:** Births, 1,116; deaths, 716; marriages, 696; divorces, 461.

**Recreation:** Lake sports; Texas A&M University-Commerce events; museum; Audie Murphy exhibit.

**Minerals:** Sand and white rock, gas, oil.

**Agriculture:** Cattle, forage, greenhouse crops, top revenue sources; horses, wheat, oats, cotton, grain sorghum. Market value $27.6 million. Some firewood sold.

**GREENVILLE** (24,514) county seat; aircraft electronics; plastics distribution; varied manufacturing; government/services; hospital; branch of Paris Junior College; Native American Pow-wow in January; cotton museum.

**Commerce** (7,712) Texas A&M University-Commerce; varied manufacturing; tourism; Bois d'Arc Bash in September; hospital.

Other towns include: **Caddo Mills** (1,181); **Campbell** (749); **Celeste** (836); **Hawk Cove** (478); **Lone Oak** (531); **Merit** (215); **Mount Bethel** (NA); **Neylandville** (56); **Quinlan** (1,405); **West Tawakoni** (1,489) tourist center, light industry, catfish tournament, Lakefest; **Wolfe City** (1,597).

| | | |
|---|---|---|
| Population | 79,361 | |
| Change fm 2000 | 3.6 | |
| Area (sq. mi.) | 882.02 | |
| Land Area (sq. mi.) | 841.16 | |
| Altitude (ft.) | 437-692 | |
| Rainfall (in.) | 41.6 | |
| Jan. mean min. | 29 | |
| July mean max. | 94 | |
| Civ. Labor | 37,537 | |
| Unemployed | 6.6 | |
| Wages | $168,461,035 | |
| Av. Weekly Wage | $543.38 | |
| Prop. Value | $2,653,068,205 | |
| Retail Sales | $911,737,882 | |

# Hutchinson County

**Physical Features:** High Plain, broken by Canadian River and tributaries, Lake Meredith; fertile valleys along streams.

**Economy:** Oil, gas, petrochemicals; agribusiness; varied manufacturing; tourism.

**History:** Antelope Creek Indian area. Later Comanches were driven out in U.S. cavalry campaigns of 1874-75. Adobe Walls site of two Indian attacks, 1864 and 1874. Ranching began in late 1870s. Oil boom in early 1920s. County created 1876 from Bexar Territory; organized 1901; named for pioneer jurist Anderson Hutchinson.

**Race/Ethnicity, 2000:** (In percent) Anglo, 81.15; Black, 2.47; Hispanic, 14.70; Other, 1.68.

**Vital Statistics, 2001:** Births, 340; deaths, 283; marriages, 211; divorces, 123.

**Recreation:** Lake activities; fishing, camping; Adobe Walls, historic Indian battle site; fish fry in June.

**Minerals:** Gas, oil, sand, gravel.

**Agriculture:** Cattle, corn, wheat, grain sorghum; about 45,000 acres irrigated. Market value $43.3 million.

**STINNETT** (1,920) county seat; petroleum refining; farm center.

**BORGER** (14,169) petroleum refining, petrochemicals; agribusiness; carbon-black production, oilfield servicing; varied manufacturing; retail center; Frank Phillips College; hospital.

Other cities include: **Fritch** (2,220), **Sanford** (201).

| | | |
|---|---|---|
| Population | 23,061 | |
| Change fm 2000 | -3.3 | |
| Area (sq. mi.) | 894.95 | |
| Land Area (sq. mi.) | 887.37 | |
| Altitude (ft.) | 2,700-3,350 | |
| Rainfall (in.) | 20.3 | |
| Jan. mean min. | 23 | |
| July mean max. | 93 | |
| Civ. Labor | 8,480 | |
| Unemployed | 8.4 | |
| Wages | $70,977,974 | |
| Av. Weekly Wage | $658.45 | |
| Prop. Value | $1,832,747,518 | |
| Retail Sales | $143,182,328 | |

# Irion County

**Physical Features:**
West Texas county with hilly surface, broken by Middle Concho, tributaries; clay, sandy soils.

**Economy:**
Ranching; oil, gas production, wildlife recreation.

**History:** Tonkawa Indian area. Anglo-American settlement began in late 1870s. County named for Republic leader R.A. Irion; created 1889 from Tom Green County.

**Race/Ethnicity, 2000:** (In percent) Anglo, 74.81; Black, 0.23; Hispanic, 24.62; Other, 0.34.

**Vital Statistics, 2001:** Births 10; deaths, 11; marriages, 9; divorces, 5.

**Recreation:** Hunting; historic sites, including Dove Creek battlefield and stagecoach stops, old Sherwood courthouse built 1900; hunters appreciation dinner in November.

**Minerals:** Oil, gas.

**Agriculture:** Beef cattle, sheep, goats; wheat, cotton, hay. Market value $5.8 million.

**MERTZON** (836) county seat; farm center; wool warehousing.

Other towns include: **Barnhart** (160).

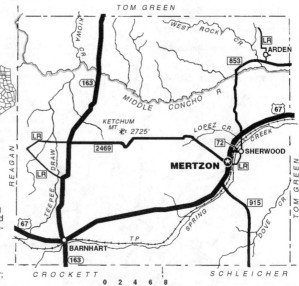

| | | |
|---|---|---|
| Population | | 1,757 |
| Change fm 2000 | | -0.8 |
| Area (sq. mi.) | | 1,051.59 |
| Land Area (sq. mi.) | | 1,051.48 |

| | | |
|---|---|---|
| Altitude (ft.) | | 2,000-2,725 |
| Rainfall (in.) | | 21.1 |
| Jan. mean min. | | 32 |
| July mean max. | | 95 |
| Civ. Labor | | 758 |

| | | |
|---|---|---|
| Unemployed | | 3.6 |
| Wages | | $3,288,744 |
| Av. Weekly Wage | | $563.43 |
| Prop. Value | | $321,309,380 |
| Retail Sales | | $2,555,356 |

# Jack County

**Physical Features:** Rolling Cross Timbers, broken by West Fork of the Trinity, other streams; sandy, dark brown, loam soils; lakes.

**Economy:** Petroleum production, oil-field services, livestock, manufacturing, tourism.

**History:** Caddo and Comanche borderland. Anglo-American settlers arrived in 1855, part of Peters Colony. County named for brothers P.C. and W.H. Jack, leaders in Texas' independence effort; created 1856 from Cooke County; organized 1857 with Mesquiteville (orginal name of Jacksboro) as county seat.

**Race/Ethnicity, 2000:** (In percent) Anglo, 85.75; Black, 5.50; Hispanic, 7.89; Other, 0.86.

**Vital Statistics, 2001:** Births, 95; deaths, 95; marriages, 66; divorces, 45.

**Recreation:** Hunting, wildlife leases; fishing; Lake activities; Fort Richardson, museum, other historic sites; Lost Creek Reservoir State Trailway; rattlesnake roundup in March.

**Minerals:** Oil, gas.

**Agriculture:** Cattle, hay, wheat, goats, sheep. Market value $20 million. Firewood sold.

**JACKSBORO** (4,535) county seat; agribusiness; manufacturing; tourism; petroleum production and services; hospital; hospice; library; Old Mesquiteville Festival in fall.

Other towns include: **Bryson** (529), **Jermyn** (75), **Perrin** (300).

| | | |
|---|---|---|
| Population | | 8,965 |
| Change fm 2000 | | 2.3 |
| Area (sq. mi.) | | 920.11 |
| Land Area (sq. mi.) | | 916.61 |
| Altitude (ft.) | | 836-1,350 |
| Rainfall (in.) | | 30.7 |

| | | |
|---|---|---|
| Jan. mean min. | | 29 |
| July mean max. | | 95 |
| Civ. Labor | | 4,178 |
| Unemployed | | 3.4 |
| Wages | | $15,157,824 |
| Av. Weekly Wage | | $556.03 |

| | | |
|---|---|---|
| Prop. Value | | $831,764,999 |
| Retail Sales | | $31,169,502 |

*For explanation of sources, abbreviations and symbols, see p. 138.*

# Jackson County

**Physical Features:** Southeastern county of prairie and motts of trees; loam, clay, black soils; drains to creek, rivers, bays.

**Economy:** Petroleum production

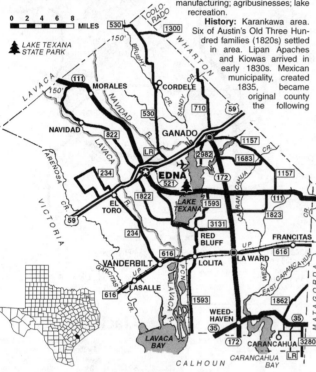

and operation; metal fabrication and tooling, sheet-metal works, plastics manufacturing; agribusinesses; lake recreation.

**History:** Karankawa area. Six of Austin's Old Three Hundred families (1820s) settled in area. Lipan Apaches and Kiowas arrived in early 1830s. Mexican municipality, created 1835, became original county the following year; named for U.S. President Andrew Jackson. Oil discovered in 1934.

**Race/Ethnicity, 2000:** (In percent) Anglo, 66.82; Black, 7.66; Hispanic, 24.68; Other, 0.84.

**Vital Statistics, 2001:** Births, 174; deaths, 138; marriages, 97; divorces, 43.

**Recreation:** Hunting, fishing, birding; historic sites; Texana Museum; Lake Texana, Brackenridge Plantation campground, state park; county fair, rodeo in October.

**Minerals:** Oil and natural gas.

**Agriculture:** Cotton, corn, rice; also, sorghums, beef cattle, soybeans; 13,000 acres of rice irrigated. Market value $51 million.

**EDNA** (5,921) county seat; oil, gas; agriculture; tourism; varied manufacturing; hospital, library; Texana Day in April with community bands.

Other towns include: **Francitas** (143), **Ganado** (1,923), **LaSalle** (103), **La Ward** (200), **Lolita** (564), **Vanderbilt** (424).

| | |
|---|---|
| Population | 14,364 |
| Change fm 2000 | -0.2 |
| Area (sq. mi.) | 857.03 |
| Land Area (sq. mi.) | 829.49 |
| Altitude (ft.) | sea level-150 |
| Rainfall (in.) | 40.9 |
| Jan. mean min. | 42 |
| July mean max. | 94 |
| Civ. Labor | 7,542 |
| Unemployed | 3.8 |
| Wages | $32,482,213 |
| Av. Weekly Wage | $511.28 |
| Prop. Value | $1,488,427,224 |
| Retail Sales | $110,051,963 |

# Jasper County

**Physical Features:** East Texas county; hilly to level; national forests; lakes; Neches River.

**Economy:** Timber industries; oil; tourism; fishing; aircraft manufacturer; agriculture.

**History:** Caddo and Atakapa Indian area. Land grants to John R. Bevil and Lorenzo de Zavala in 1829. County created 1836, organized 1837, from Mexican municipality; named for Sgt. William Jasper of American Revolution.

**Race/Ethnicity, 2000:** (In percent) Anglo, 77.38; Black, 17.94; Hispanic, 3.89; Other, 0.79.

**Vital Statistics, 2001:** Births, 459; deaths, 353; marriages, 355; divorces, 238.

**Recreation:** Lake activities; hunting; state park; azalea trail.

**Minerals:** Oil, gas produced.

**Agriculture:** Cattle, hogs, poultry, major revenue source; vegetables, fruit, pecans. Market value $4 million. Timber is major income producer.

**JASPER** (8,295) county seat; wood industries; plywood mill, sawmills; tourism; oil, gas production; hospitals; prison; fall fest.

Other towns include: **Browndell** (222), **Buna** (2,272), **Evadale** (1,434), **Kirbyville** (2,098), **Magnolia Springs** (80).

| | | | |
|---|---|---|---|
| Population | 35,776 | July mean max. | 93 |
| Change fm 2000 | 0.5 | Civ. Labor | 14,987 |
| Area (sq. mi.) | 969.62 | Unemployed | 12.1 |
| Land Area (sq. mi.) | 937.40 | Wages | $72,782,686 |
| Altitude (ft.) | 25-550 | Av. Weekly Wage | $529.53 |
| Rainfall (in.) | 52.7 | Prop. Value | $2,126,846,374 |
| Jan. mean min. | 36 | Retail Sales | $319,474,088 |

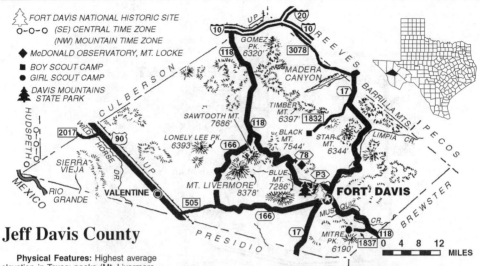

FORT DAVIS NATIONAL HISTORIC SITE
o–o–o  (SE) CENTRAL TIME ZONE
        (NW) MOUNTAIN TIME ZONE
◆ McDONALD OBSERVATORY, MT. LOCKE
■ BOY SCOUT CAMP
● GIRL SCOUT CAMP
▲ DAVIS MOUNTAINS
   STATE PARK

# Jeff Davis County

**Physical Features:** Highest average elevation in Texas; peaks (Mt. Livermore, 8,378 ft.), canyons, plateaus; intermountain wash, clay, loam soils; cedars, oaks in highlands.

**Economy:** Tourism, ranching, greenhouse/nurseries.

**History:** Mescalero Apaches in area when Antonio de Espejo explored in 1583. U.S. Army established Fort Davis in 1854 to protect routes to west. Civilian settlers followed, including Manuel Músquiz, a political refugee from Mexico. County named for Jefferson Davis, U.S. war secretary, Confederate president; created 1887 from Presidio County.

**Race/Ethnicity, 2000:** (In percent) Anglo, 63.20; Black, 0.82; Hispanic, 35.48; Other, 0.50.

**Vital Statistics, 2001:** Births, 18; deaths, 24; marriages, 10; divorces, 0.

**Recreation:** Scenic drives including scenic loop along Limpia Creek, Mt. Livermore, Blue Mountain; hunting; Fort Davis National Historic Site (with Restoration Festival on Columbus Day weekend); state park; McDonald Observatory; solar power park; Chihuahuan Desert Research Institute.

**Minerals:** bentonite.

**Agriculture:** Greenhouse nurseries, beef cattle, apples, grapes. Market value $8.8 million.

**FORT DAVIS** (1,098), county seat; ranch center; trade, tourism; government/ services; library; "Coolest July 4th in Texas".

Other town: **Valentine** (190).

| | |
|---|---|
| **Population** | **2,211** |
| Change fm 2000 | 0.2 |
| Area (sq. mi.) | 2,264.60 |
| Land Area (sq. mi.) | 2,264.43 |
| Altitude (ft.) | 3,500-8,378 |
| Rainfall (in.) | 20.8 |
| Jan. mean min. | 30 |
| July mean max. | 82 |
| Civ. Labor | 1,569 |
| Unemployed | 1.3 |
| Wages | $6,019,625 |
| Av. Weekly Wage | $466.31 |
| Prop. Value | $311,539,732 |
| Retail Sales | $7,954,412 |

*For explanation of sources, abbreviations and symbols, see p. 138.*

*The Davis Mountains in Jeff Davis County. Texas Parks and Wildlife photo.*

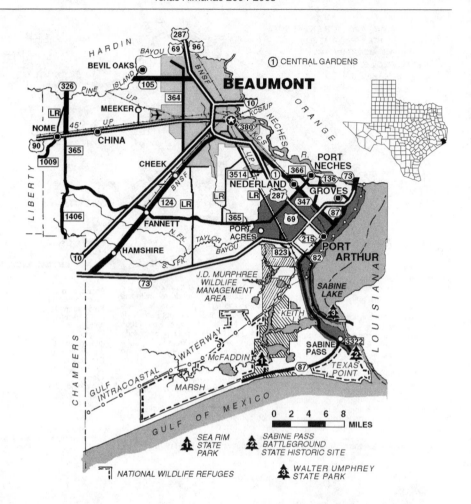

SEA RIM STATE PARK

SABINE PASS BATTLEGROUND STATE HISTORIC SITE

NATIONAL WILDLIFE REFUGES

WALTER UMPHREY STATE PARK

**Physical Features:** Gulf Coast grassy plain, with timber in northwest; beach sands, sandy loams, black clay soils; drains to Neches River, Gulf of Mexico.

**Economy:** Government/services; petrochemical, other chemical plants; shipbuilding; steel mill; port activity; oil-field supplies; .

**History:** Atakapas and Orcoquizas, whose numbers were reduced by epidemics or migration before Anglo-American settlers arrived in 1820s. Cajuns arrived in 1840s; Europeans in 1850s. Antebellum slaveholding area. County created 1836 from Mexican municipality; organized 1837; named for U.S. President Thomas Jefferson.

**Race/Ethnicity, 2000:** (In percent) Anglo, 52.27; Black, 33.83; Hispanic, 10.53; Other, 3.37.

**Vital Statistics, 2001:** Births, 3,309; deaths, 2,517; marriages, 2,396; divorces, 1,227.

**Recreation:** Beaches, fresh and saltwater fishing; duck, goose hunting; water activities; Dick Dowling Monument and Park; Spindletop site, museums; saltwater lake; wildlife refuge; Lamar University events; historic sites; South Texas Fair.

# Jefferson County

**Minerals:** Large producer of oil, gas, sulfur, salt, sand and gravel.

**Agriculture:** Rice, soybeans; crawfish; beef cattle; hay; considerable rice irrigated. Market value $24.6 million. Timber sales significant.

**BEAUMONT** (114,067) county seat; government/services; petrochemical production; shipbuilding; port activities; rice milling; Lamar University; hospital; entertainment district; Main Street on the Neches.

**Port Arthur** (57,313) oil, chemical activities; shrimping and crawfishing; shipping; offshore marine; tourism; hospitals; museum; prison. Asian New Year Tet, Janis Joplin Birthday Bash in January. **Sabine Pass** and **Port Acres** are now within the city limits of Port Arthur.

Other towns include: **Bevil Oaks** (1,339); **Central Gardens** (4,082); **China** (1,104); **Fannett** (105); **Groves** (15,671) retail center, some manufacturing, government/services, tourism; hospital, pecan festival in September; **Hamshire** (350).

Also, **Nederland** (17,548) marine manufacturing; tourism, Windmill and French museums; hospital; Tex Ritter memorial and park, heritage festival (city founded by Dutch immigrants in 1898); **Nome** (512); **Port Neches** (13,533) chemical and synthetic rubber industry, manufacturing, library, riverfront park with La Maison Beausoleil; RiverFest in May.

| | |
|---|---|
| Population | **248,890** |
| Change fm 2000 | -1.3 |
| Area (sq. mi.) | 1,111.26 |
| Land Area (sq. mi.) | 903.55 |
| Altitude (ft.) | sea level-45 |
| Rainfall (in.) | 57.2 |
| Jan. mean min. | 42 |
| July mean max. | 92 |
| Civ. Labor | 118,786 |
| Unemployed | 8.4 |
| Wages | $936,239,560 |
| Av. Weekly Wage | $620.05 |
| Prop. Value | $15,189,833,460 |
| Retail Sales | $2,838,632,356 |

*For explanation of sources, abbreviations and symbols, see p. 138.*

# Jim Hogg County

**Physical Features:** South Texas county on rolling plain, with heavy brush cover; white blow sand and sandy loam; hilly, broken.

**Economy:** Oil, cattle operations.

**History:** Coahuiltecan area, then Lipan Apache. Spanish land grant in 1805 to Xavier Vela. County named for Gov. James Stephen Hogg; created, organized 1913 from Brooks, Duval counties.

**Race/Ethnicity, 2000:** (In percent) Anglo, 9.07; Black, 0.42; Hispanic, 89.98; Other, 0.53.

**Vital Statistics, 2001:** Births, 81; deaths, 61; marriages, 35; divorces, 0.

**Recreation:** White-tailed deer and bobwhite hunting.

**Minerals:** Oil and gas.

**Agriculture:** Cattle, hay, milk goats; some irrigation. Market value $7 million.

**HEBBRONVILLE** (4,537) county seat; ranching, oil-field center.

Other towns include: **Guerra** (8), **Las Lomitas** (274) and **South Fork Estates** (49).

| | |
|---|---|
| Population | 5,173 |
| Change fm 2000 | -2.0 |
| Area (sq. mi.) | 1,136.16 |
| Land Area (sq. mi.) | 1,136.11 |
| Altitude (ft.) | 249-886 |
| Rainfall (in.) | 22.7 |
| Jan. mean min. | 42 |
| July mean max. | 97 |
| Civ. Labor | 2,336 |
| Unemployed | 7.1 |
| Wages | $8,197,507 |
| Av. Weekly Wage | $406.56 |
| Prop. Value | $566,930,151 |
| Retail Sales | $29,906,926 |

# Jim Wells County

| | |
|---|---|
| Population | 39,945 |
| Change fm 2000 | 1.6 |
| Area (sq. mi.) | 868.22 |
| Land Area (sq. mi.) | 864.52 |
| Altitude (ft.) | 50-400 |
| Rainfall (in.) | 27.8 |
| Jan. mean min. | 43 |
| July mean max. | 96 |
| Civ. Labor | 17,033 |
| Unemployed | 7.5 |
| Wages | $85,264,675 |
| Av. Weekly Wage | $466.09 |
| Prop. Value | $1,196,912,694 |
| Retail Sales | $319,834,326 |

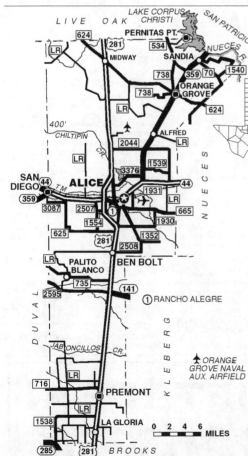

**Physical Features:** South Coastal Plains; level to rolling; sandy to dark soils; grassy with mesquite brush.

**Economy:** Oil, gas production, sorghum and cattle.

**History:** Coahuiltecans, driven out by Lipan Apaches in 1775. Tomás Sánchez established settlement in 1754. Anglo-American settlement in 1878. County created 1911 from Nueces County; organized 1912; named for developer J.B. Wells Jr.

**Race/Ethnicity, 2000:** (In percent) Anglo, 23.10; Black, 0.48; Hispanic, 75.71; Other, 0.71.

**Vital Statistics, 2001:** Births, 607; deaths, 353; marriages, 279; divorces, 63.

**Recreation:** Hunting; fiestas; Tejano Roots hall of fame; South Texas museum.

**Minerals:** Oil, gas, caliche.

**Agriculture:** Cattle, dairy products, goats; grain sorghum, wheat, corn, cotton; some irrigation for coastal Bermuda, vegetables. Market value $35.9 million.

**ALICE** (19,156) county seat; oil-field service center; agri-business; government/services; hospital; Fiesta Bandana (from original name of city) in May; Bee County College extension.

Other towns include: **Alfred-South La Paloma** (461); **Ben Bolt** (110); **Orange Grove** (1,300); **Pernitas Point** (271, partly in Live Oak County); **Premont** (2,879) wildflower tour, youth rodeo; **Rancho Alegre** (1,860); **Sandia** (462). Also, a small part of **San Diego** (4,972).

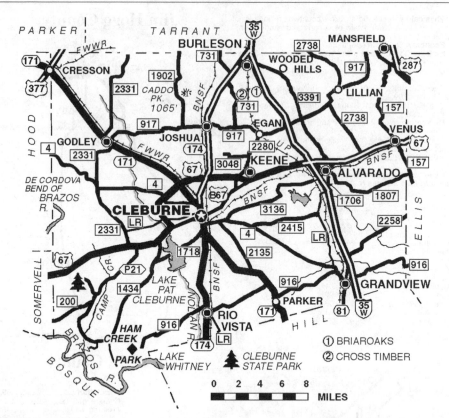

① BRIAROAKS
② CROSS TIMBER

CLEBURNE
STATE PARK

LAKE
WHITNEY

0   2   4   6   8
MILES

## Johnson County

**Physical Features:** North central county drained by tributaries of Trinity, Brazos rivers; lake; hilly, rolling, many soil types.

**Economy:** Agribusiness; railroad shops; manufacturing; distribution; lake activities; many residents employed in Fort Worth; part of Fort Worth-Arlington metropolitan area.

**History:** No permanent Indian villages existed in area. Anglo-American settlers arrived in 1840s. County named for Col. M.T. Johnson of Mexican War, Confederacy; created, organized 1854. Formed from McLennan, Hill, Navarro counties.

**Race/Ethnicity, 2000:** (In percent) Anglo, 83.91; Black, 2.58; Hispanic, 12.12; Other, 1.39.

**Vital Statistics, 2001:** Births, 1,907; deaths, 1,042; marriages, 1,115; divorces, 533.

**Recreation:** Bird, deer hunting; water activities on Lake Pat Cleburne; state park; museum; Chisholm Trail; Goatneck bike ride in July.

**Minerals:** Limestone, sand and gravel.

**Agriculture:** A leading dairy county, cattle, hay, horses (a leader in number sold), cotton, sorghum, wheat, oats, hogs. Market value $50.3 million.

**CLEBURNE** (27,314) county seat; dairy center; rail-shipping terminal; varied manufacturing; tourism; hospital, library, museum; Hill College, Cleburne campus; Cinco de Mayo.

**BURLESON** (23,351, part [3,462] in Tarrant County) agriculture, retail center; hospital.

Other towns include: **Alvarado** (3,535) County Pioneer Days; **Briaroaks** (510); **Cresson** (208); **Cross Timber** (294); **Godley** (918); **Grandview** (1,438); **Joshua** (4,835) many residents work in Fort Worth; **Keene** (5,268) Southwestern Adventist University; **Lillian** (105); **Rio Vista** (682), and **Venus** (970).

Also, part (622) of **Mansfield**.

| | |
|---|---|
| Population | **136,332** |
| Change fm 2000 | 7.5 |
| Area (sq. mi.) | 734.46 |
| Land Area (sq. mi.) | 729.42 |
| Altitude (ft.) | 600-1,065 |
| Rainfall (in.) | 34.0 |
| Jan. mean min. | 33 |
| July mean max. | 97 |
| Civ. Labor | 67,368 |
| Unemployed | 6.9 |
| Wages | $217,429,815 |
| Av. Weekly Wage | $509.36 |
| Prop. Value | $5,659,932,593 |
| Retail Sales | $855,371,988 |

*For explanation of sources, abbreviations and symbols, see p. 138.*

# Jones County

**Physical Features:** West Texas Rolling Plains; drained by Brazos River fork, tributaries; Lake Fort Phantom Hill.

**Economy:** Agribusiness; government/services; varied manufacturing.

**History:** Comanches and other tribes hunted in area. Military presence began in 1851. Ranching established in 1870s. County named for the last president of the Republic, Anson Jones; created 1858 from Bexar, Bosque counties; re-created 1876; organized 1881.

**Race/Ethnicity, 2000:** (In percent) Anglo, 66.67; Black, 11.53; Hispanic, 20.91; Other, 0.89.

**Vital Statistics, 2001:** Births, 196; deaths, 250; marriages, 89; divorces, 82.

**Recreation:** Lake activities; Fort Phantom Hill site, museum; Cowboys Christmas Ball; Cowboy Reunion on July 4 weekend; old courthouse, opera house, museum, art show.

**Minerals:** Oil, gas, sand and gravel, stone.

**Agriculture:** Cotton, wheat, sesame and peanuts; cattle. Some 10,000 acres irrigated for peanuts and hay. Market value $19.6 million.

**ANSON** (2,552) county seat; farming center; boat-trailer factory, Western clothing manufacturing; hospital; historic buildings.

**STAMFORD** (3,530) trade center for three counties.

**HAMLIN** (2,196) trade center for farm and oil, gas area; government/services; feed mills; hospital; historical festival in June.

Other towns include: **Hawley** (591), **Lueders** (304) limestone quarries.

Part (5,488) of **Abilene**.

| | |
|---|---|
| Population | 20,284 |
| Change fm 2000 | -2.4 |
| Area (sq. mi.) | 937.13 |
| Land Area (sq. mi.) | 930.99 |
| Altitude (ft.) | 1,500-1,950 |
| Rainfall (in.) | 25.8 |
| Jan. mean min. | 31 |
| July mean max. | 96 |

| | |
|---|---|
| Civ. Labor | 9,868 |
| Unemployed | 3.3 |
| Wages | $29,112,256 |
| Av. Weekly Wage | $454.52 |
| Prop. Value | $615,777,766 |
| Retail Sales | $179,974,350 |

# Karnes County

**Physical Features:** Sandy loam, dark clay, alluvial soils in rolling terrain; traversed by San Antonio River; mesquite, oak trees.

**Economy:** Government/services; agribusiness; oil, gas, mineral production, tourism; commuting to San Antonio.

**History:** Coahuiltecan Indian area. Spanish ranching began around 1750. Anglo-Americans arrived in 1840s; Polish in 1850s. County created 1854 from Bexar, Goliad, San Patricio counties; named for Texas Revolutionary figure Henry W. Karnes.

**Race/Ethnicity, 2000:** (In percent) Anglo, 41.29; Black, 10.53; Hispanic, 47.42; Other, 0.76.

**Vital Statistics, 2001:** Births, 158; deaths, 175; marriages, 93; divorces, 21.

**Recreation:** Panna Maria, nation's oldest Polish settlement, founded Dec. 24, 1854; Old Helena restored courthouse, museum; bird hunting, guest ranches.

**Minerals:** Oil, gas, stone.

**Agriculture:** Beef cattle, hay, wheat, corn, sorghum. Market value $17.7 million.

**KARNES CITY** (3,428) county seat; agribusiness; tourism; processing center; oil-field servicing; varied manufacturing; hospital; library; Lonesome Dove Fest in September.

**KENEDY** (3,462) farm and oil center, library, dove and quail hunting leases, prison; Bluebonnet Days in April.

Other towns include: **Falls City** (625) ranching, sausage making, library, city park on river; **Gillett** (120); **Hobson** (135); **Panna Maria** (96); **Runge** (1,075) farm center, library.

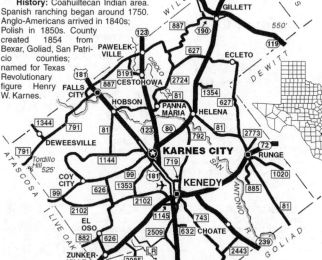

| | |
|---|---|
| Population | 15,411 |
| Change fm 2000 | -0.2 |
| Area (sq. mi.) | 753.58 |
| Land Area (sq. mi.) | 750.32 |
| Altitude (ft.) | 180-550 |
| Rainfall (in.) | 33.2 |
| Jan. mean min. | 41 |
| July mean max. | 97 |
| Civ. Labor | 5,679 |
| Unemployed | 5.1 |
| Wages | $22,108,353 |
| Av. Weekly Wage | $440.47 |
| Prop. Value | $699,502,540 |
| Retail Sales | $101,785,527 |

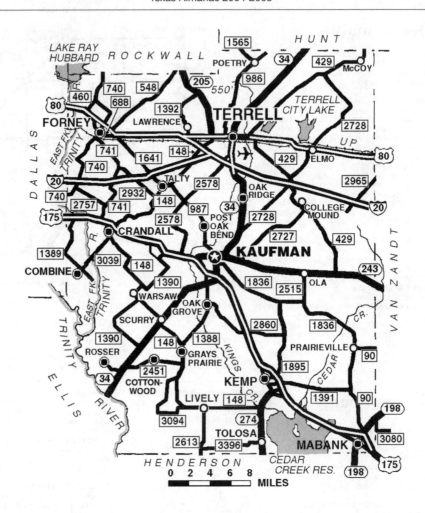

# Kaufman County

**Physical Features:** North Blackland prairie, draining to Trinity River, Cedar Creek and Lake.

**Economy:** varied manufacturing; trade center; government/services; antique center; commuting to Dallas.

**History:** Caddo and Cherokee Indians; removed by 1840 when Anglo-American settlement began. County created from Henderson County and organized, 1848; named for member of Texas and U.S. congresses D.S. Kaufman.

**Race/Ethnicity, 2000:** (In percent) Anglo, 76.97; Black, 10.76; Hispanic, 11.11; Other, 1.16.

**Vital Statistics, 2001:** Births, 1,102; deaths, 711; marriages, 719; divorces, 331.

**Recreation:** Lake activities; Porter Farm near Terrell is site of origin of U.S.-Texas Agricultural Extension program; antique centers near Forney; historic homes at Terrell.

**Minerals:** Oil, gas, stone, sand.

**Agriculture:** Nursery crops; beef cattle, horses, goats, hogs, sheep; wheat, hay, sorghum, oats, cotton, peaches. Market value $37.4 million.

**KAUFMAN** (7,246) county seat; varied manufacturing; commuters to Dallas; hospital; Scarecrow Festival in October.

**TERRELL** (15,046) agribusiness, varied manufacturing; outlet center; private hospital, state hospital; community college, Southwestern Christian College.

Other towns include: **College Mound** (350); **Combine** (1,956, partly in Dallas County); **Cottonwood** (204);

**Crandall** (3,016); **Elmo** (90); **Forney** (6,271) antiques, light manufacturing, historic homes, Jackrabbit Stampede bike race in September; **Grays Prairie** (313); **Kemp** (1,200); **Lawrence** (279); **Mabank** (2,305, partly in Henderson County) tourism; manufacturing, retail trade; **Oak Grove** (777); **Oak Ridge** (426); **Ola** (50); **Post Oak Bend** (430); **Prairieville** (50); **Rosser** (396); **Scurry** (315); **Talty** (1,113).

| | |
|---|---|
| Population | **77,954** |
| Change fm 2000 | 9.3 |
| Area (sq. mi.) | 806.81 |
| Land Area (sq. mi.) | 786.04 |
| Altitude (ft.) | 300-550 |
| Rainfall (in.) | 38.9 |
| Jan. mean min. | 32 |
| July mean max. | 95 |
| Civ. Labor | 36,584 |
| Unemployed | 9.8 |
| Wages | $144,089,674 |
| Av. Weekly Wage | $511.95 |
| Prop. Value | $3,569,116,258 |
| Retail Sales | $869,340,643 |

*For explanation of sources, abbreviations and symbols, see p. 138.*

# Kendall County

**Physical Features:** Hill Country, plateau, with springfed streams; caves; scenic drives.

**Economy:** Government/services, commuters to San Antonio, tourism, agribusiness, some manufacturing.

**History:** Lipan Apaches, Kiowas and Comanches in area when German settlers arrived in 1840s. County created from Blanco, Kerr counties 1862; named for pioneer journalist-sheepman and early contributor to Texas Almanac, George W. Kendall.

**Race/Ethnicity, 2000:** (In percent) Anglo, 81.06; Black, 0.32; Hispanic, 17.89; Other, 0.73.

**Vital Statistics, 2001:** Births, 295; deaths, 243; marriages, 278; divorces, 75.

**Recreation:** Hunting, fishing, state park; tourist center; Cascade Cavern; historic sites.

**Minerals:** None.

**Agriculture:** Cattle, sheep, meat goats, Angora goats; hay, small grains. Market value $7.5 million. Cedar posts, firewood sold.

**BOERNE** (6,462) county seat; tourism, antiques; some manufacturing; ranching; commuting to San Antonio; library; Berges Fest on Father's Day weekend.

Other towns include: **Comfort** (2,397) ranching, tourism, Civil War monument honoring Unionists; **Kendalia** (76); **Sisterdale** (63); **Waring** (73). Part of **Fair Oaks Ranch** (5,042).

| | |
|---|---|
| Population | 25,390 |
| Change fm 2000 | 6.9 |
| Area (sq. mi.) | 663.04 |
| Land Area (sq. mi.) | 662.44 |
| Altitude (ft.) | 1,000-2,025 |
| Rainfall (in.) | 34.2 |
| Jan. mean min. | 33 |

| | |
|---|---|
| July mean max. | 93 |
| Civ. Labor | 17,619 |
| Unemployed | 2.9 |
| Wages | $58,782,215 |
| Av. Weekly Wage | $507.15 |
| Prop. Value | $3,225,711,382 |
| Retail Sales | $511,999,938 |

---

# Kenedy County

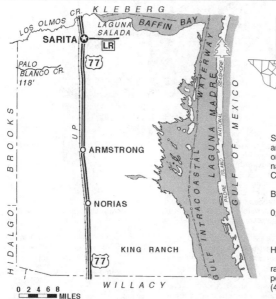

**Physical Features:** Gulf coastal county; flat, sandy terrain, some loam soils; motts of live oaks.

**Economy:** Oil, ranching; hunting leases/eco-tourism.

**History:** Coahuiltecan Indians who assimilated or were driven out by Lipan Apaches. Spanish ranching began in 1790s. Anglo-Americans arrived after Mexican War. Among last counties created, organized 1921, from Cameron, Hidalgo, Willacy counties; named for pioneer steamboat operator and cattleman, Capt. Mifflin Kenedy.

**Race/Ethnicity, 2000:** (In percent) Anglo, 20.29; Black, 0.00; Hispanic, 78.99; Other, 0.72.

**Vital Statistics, 2001:** Births, 8; deaths, 3; marriages, 0; divorces, 0.

**Recreation:** Hunting; fishing; bird watching.

**Minerals:** Oil, gas.

**Agriculture:** Beef cattle. Market value $10.7 million. Hunting leases.

**SARITA** (250) county seat; cattle-shipping point; ranch headquarters; gas processing; one of state's least populous counties. Also, **Armstrong** (20) and **Norias** (45).

| | |
|---|---|
| Population | 419 |
| Change fm 2000 | 1.2 |
| Area (sq. mi.) | 1,945.60 |
| Land Area (sq. mi.) | 1,456.77 |

| | |
|---|---|
| Altitude (ft.) | sea level-118 |
| Rainfall (in.) | 29.7 |
| Jan. mean min. | 45 |
| July mean max. | 95 |
| Civ. Labor | 207 |

| | |
|---|---|
| Unemployed | 1.0 |
| Wages | $2,005,655 |
| Av. Weekly Wage | $463.31 |
| Prop. Value | $510,335,512 |
| Retail Sales | $0 |

# Kent County

**Physical Features:** West central county of rolling, broken terrain; lake; drains to Salt and Double Mountain forks of Brazos River; sandy, loam soils.

**Economy:** Agribusiness, oil-field operations, hunting leases.

**History:** Comanches driven out by U.S. Army in 1870s. Ranching developed in 1880s. County created 1876 from Bexar, Young territories; organized 1892. Name honors Andrew Kent, one of 32 volunteers from Gonzales who died at the Alamo.

**Race/Ethnicity, 2000:** (In percent) Anglo, 90.57; Black, 0.23; Hispanic, 9.08; Other, 0.12.

**Vital Statistics, 2001:** Births, 7; deaths, 19; marriages, 43; divorces, 3.

**Recreation:** Hunting, fishing; scenic croton breaks and salt flat; wildlife festival in November.

**Minerals:** Oil, gas.

**Agriculture:** Cattle, cotton, wheat, sorghum. Market value $8.9 million.

**JAYTON** (508) county seat; oil-field services; farming center; fun fest in August.

Other towns include: **Girard** (64).

| | | |
|---|---|---|
| Population ..................................807 | Rainfall (in.) ..................................21.8 | Wages..............................$1,310,904 |
| Change fm 2000 ..........................-6.1 | Jan. mean min...............................25 | Av. Weekly Wage..................$374.87 |
| Area (sq. mi.) ..........................902.91 | July mean max. ..............................96 | Prop. Value ..................$462,437,654 |
| Land Area (sq. mi.) ..................902.33 | Civ. Labor ......................................416 | Retail Sales....................$11,982,490 |
| Altitude (ft.)........................1,823-2,830 | Unemployed ..................................7.2 | |

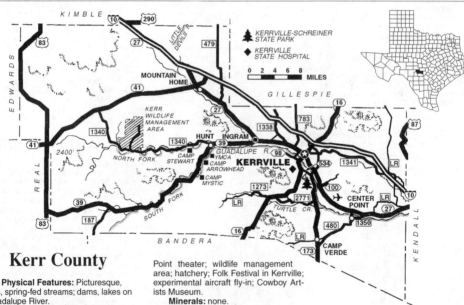

# Kerr County

**Physical Features:** Picturesque, hills, spring-fed streams; dams, lakes on Guadalupe River.

**Economy:** Tourism; medical services; retirement area; agribusiness; manufacturing; hunting leases.

**History:** Lipan Apaches, Kiowas and Comanches in area. Anglo-American settlers arrived in late 1840s. County created 1856 from Bexar County; named for member of Austin's Colony, James Kerr.

**Race/Ethnicity, 2000:** (In percent) Anglo, 78.11; Black, 1.78; Hispanic, 19.13; Other, 0.98.

**Vital Statistics, 2001:** Births, 516; deaths, 629; marriages, 405; divorces, 209.

**Recreation:** Popular area for tourists, hunters, fishermen; private and youth camps; dude ranches; state park; Point theater; wildlife management area; hatchery; Folk Festival in Kerrville; experimental aircraft fly-in; Cowboy Artists Museum.

**Minerals:** none.

**Agriculture:** Cattle, sheep, goats for wool, mohair; meat and breeding goats on increase; crops include hay, pecans. Market value $8 million.

**KERRVILLE** (20,878) county seat; tourist center; youth camps; agribusiness; aircraft and parts and varied manufacturing; Schreiner University; Kerrville State Hospital; Veterans Administration Medical Center; retirement center; retail trade; state arts, crafts show in May-June; experimental aircraft fly-in during October.

Other towns include: **Camp Verde** (41); **Center Point** (800); **Hunt** (708), youth camps; **Ingram** (1,773) camps, cabins; **Mountain Home** (96).

| | |
|---|---|
| Population ............................44,857 | |
| Change fm 2000 ..........................2.8 | |
| Area (sq. mi.) ......................1,107.66 | |
| Land Area (sq. mi.) .............1,106.12 | |
| Altitude (ft.) .....................1,450-2,400 | |
| Rainfall (in.)..................................29.8 | |
| Jan. mean min. ............................32 | |
| July mean max..............................94 | |
| Civ. Labor .............................18,546 | |
| Unemployed................................3.0 | |
| Wages.......................$101,781,395 | |
| Av. Weekly Wage ...............$506.75 | |
| Prop. Value ...............$2,612,303,899 | |
| Retail Sales................$600,942,886 | |

*For explanation of sources, abbreviations and symbols, see p. 138.*

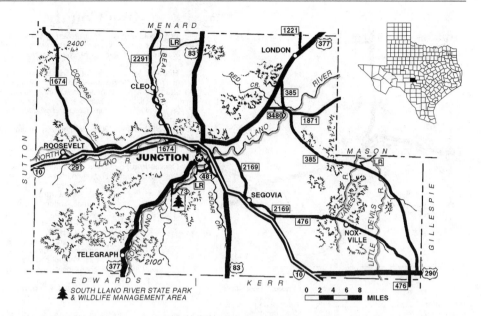

SOUTH LLANO RIVER STATE PARK
& WILDLIFE MANAGEMENT AREA

0  2  4  6  8
MILES

## Kimble County

**Physical Features:** Picturesque southwestern county; rugged, broken by numerous streams; drains to Llano River; sandy, gray, chocolate loam soils.

**Economy:** Livestock production, market; tourism, hunting, fishing; cedar oil and wood products sold; metal building materials manufactured.

**History:** Apache, Kiowas and Comanche stronghold until 1870s. Military outposts protected first Anglo-American settlers in 1850s. County created from Bexar County 1858; organized 1876. Named for George C. Kimble, a Gonzales volunteer who died at the Alamo.

**Race/Ethnicity, 2000:** (In percent) Anglo, 78.37; Black, 0.09; Hispanic, 20.73; Other, 0.81.

**Vital Statistics, 2001:** Births, 62; deaths, 76; marriages, 31; divorces, 14.

**Recreation:** Hunting, fishing in spring-fed streams, ecotourism; among leading deer counties; state park; Kimble Kounty Kow Kick on Labor Day, Wild Game dinner on Thanksgiving Saturday.

**Minerals:** gravel.

**Agriculture:** Cattle, meat goats, sheep, Angora goats. Market value $8.1 million. Hunting leases important. Firewood, cedar sold.

**JUNCTION** (2,622) county seat; tourism; varied manufacturing; livestock production; two museums; Texas Tech University center; hospital; library; airport.

Other towns include: **London** (180); **Roosevelt** (14); **Telegraph** (3).

| | |
|---|---|
| Population | 4,502 |
| Change fm 2000 | 0.8 |
| Area (sq. mi.) | 1,250.92 |
| Land Area (sq. mi.) | 1,250.70 |
| Altitude (ft.) | 1,500-2,400 |
| Rainfall (in.) | 23.8 |
| Jan. mean min. | 31 |
| July mean max. | 96 |
| Civ. Labor | 2,333 |
| Unemployed | 2.2 |
| Wages | $7,728,019 |
| Av. Weekly Wage | $397.63 |
| Prop. Value | $606,809,741 |
| Retail Sales | $52,056,530 |

## Largest Counties by Population 2002

| Rank | County (Largest city) | Population |
|---|---|---|
| 1. | Harris County (Houston) | 3,557,055 |
| 2. | Dallas County (Dallas) | 2,283,953 |
| 3. | Tarrant County (Fort Worth) | 1,527,366 |
| 4. | Bexar County (San Antonio) | 1,446,333 |
| 5. | Travis County (Austin) | 850,813 |
| 6. | El Paso County (El Paso) | 697,562 |
| 7. | Hidalgo County (McAllen) | 614,474 |
| 8. | Collin County (Plano) | 566,798 |
| 9. | Denton County (Denton) | 488,481 |
| 10. | Fort Bend County (Sugar Land) | 399,537 |
| 11. | Cameron County (Brownsville) | 353,561 |
| 12. | Montgomery County (Conroe) | 328,449 |
| 13. | Nueces County (Corpus Christi) | 314,696 |
| 14. | Williamson County (Round Rock) | 289,924 |
| 15. | Galveston County (Galveston) | 261,219 |
| 16. | Brazoria County (Brazosport) | 257,256 |
| 17. | Jefferson County (Beaumont) | 248,890 |
| 18. | Lubbock County (Lubbock) | 247,574 |
| 19. | Bell County (Killeen) | 244,668 |
| 20. | McLennan County (Waco) | 217,713 |
| 21. | Webb County (Laredo) | 207,611 |
| 22. | Smith County (Tyler) | 181,437 |
| 23. | Brazos County (College Station) | 156,099 |
| 24. | Johnson County (Cleburne) | 136,332 |
| 25. | Wichita County (Wichita Falls) | 129,964 |
| 26. | Taylor County (Abilene) | 125,647 |
| 27. | Ector County (Odessa) | 122,312 |
| 28. | Ellis County (Waxahachie) | 120,052 |
| 29. | Midland County (Midland) | 117,669 |
| 30. | Potter County (Amarillo) | 116,093 |

*Source: Estimates from the U.S. Bureau of the Census.*

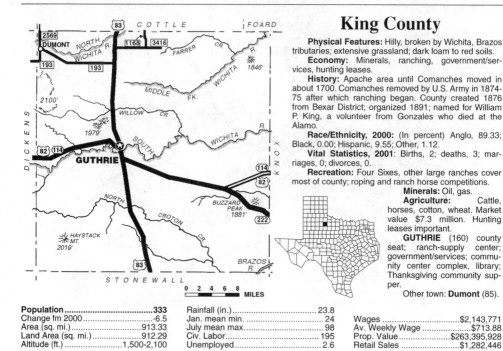

# King County

**Physical Features:** Hilly, broken by Wichita, Brazos tributaries; extensive grassland; dark loam to red soils.

**Economy:** Minerals, ranching, government/services, hunting leases.

**History:** Apache area until Comanches moved in about 1700. Comanches removed by U.S. Army in 1874-75 after which ranching began. County created 1876 from Bexar District; organized 1891; named for William P. King, a volunteer from Gonzales who died at the Alamo.

**Race/Ethnicity, 2000:** (In percent) Anglo, 89.33; Black, 0.00; Hispanic, 9.55; Other, 1.12.

**Vital Statistics, 2001:** Births, 2; deaths, 3; marriages, 0; divorces, 0.

**Recreation:** Four Sixes, other large ranches cover most of county; roping and ranch horse competitions.

**Minerals:** Oil, gas.

**Agriculture:** Cattle, horses, cotton, wheat. Market value $7.3 million. Hunting leases important.

**GUTHRIE** (160) county seat; ranch-supply center; government/services; community center complex, library; Thanksgiving community supper.

Other town: **Dumont** (85).

| | | |
|---|---|---|
| Population | | 333 |
| Change fm 2000 | | -6.5 |
| Area (sq. mi.) | | 913.33 |
| Land Area (sq. mi.) | | 912.29 |
| Altitude (ft.) | | 1,500-2,100 |

| | | |
|---|---|---|
| Rainfall (in.) | | 23.8 |
| Jan. mean min. | | 24 |
| July mean max. | | 98 |
| Civ. Labor | | 195 |
| Unemployed | | 2.6 |

| | | |
|---|---|---|
| Wages | | $2,143,771 |
| Av. Weekly Wage | | $713.88 |
| Prop. Value | | $263,395,928 |
| Retail Sales | | $1,282,446 |

# Kinney County

**Physical Features:** Hilly, broken by Rio Grande tributaries; Anacacho Mountains; Nueces Canyon.

**Economy:** Agribusinesses, tourism, government/services, hunting leases.

**History:** Coahuiltecans, Apaches, Comanches in area. Spanish Franciscans established settlement in late 1700s. English empresarios John Beales and James Grant established English-speaking colony in 1834. Black Seminoles served as army scouts in 1870s. County created from Bexar County 1850; organized 1874; named for H.L. Kinney, founder of Corpus Christi.

**Race/Ethnicity, 2000:** (In percent) Anglo, 47.79; Black, 1.39; Hispanic, 50.52; Other, 0.30.

**Vital Statistics, 2001:** Births, 38; deaths, 42; marriages, 16; divorces, 2.

**Recreation:** Hunting; replica of Alamo; old Fort Clark Springs; state park; Seminole Days.

**Minerals:** Not significant.

**Agriculture:** Cattle, meat goats, Angora goats; hay, pecans, wheat, cotton. Market value $7.6 million.

**BRACKETTVILLE** (1,905) county seat; agriculture, tourism; museum; cowboy cauldron.

Other towns include: **Fort Clark Springs** (1,070); **Spofford** (77).

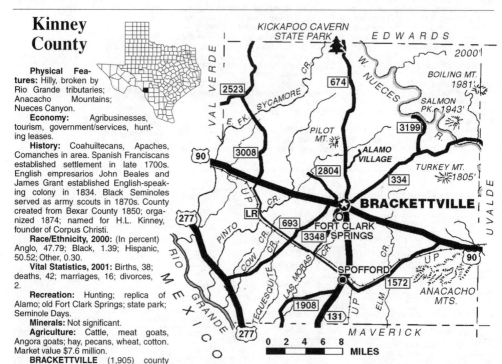

*For explanation of sources, abbreviations and symbols, see p. 138.*

| | | |
|---|---|---|
| Population | | 3,447 |
| Change fm 2000 | | 2.0 |
| Area (sq. mi.) | | 1,365.31 |
| Land Area (sq. mi.) | | 1,363.44 |
| Altitude (ft.) | | 850-2,000 |
| Rainfall (in.) | | 21.7 |
| Jan. mean min. | | 36 |

| | | |
|---|---|---|
| July mean max. | | 95 |
| Civ. Labor | | 1,395 |
| Unemployed | | 9.6 |
| Wages | | $4,315,679 |
| Av. Weekly Wage | | $469.55 |
| Prop. Value | | $326,780,338 |
| Retail Sales | | $8,907,334 |

**Physical Features:** Coastal plain, broken by bays; sandy, loam, clay soils; tree motts.

**Economy:** Oil and gas; Naval air station; chemicals and plastics; agriculture; Texas A&M University-Kingsville.

**History:** Coahuiltecan and Karankawa area. Spanish land grants date to 1750s. In 1853 Richard King

# Kleberg County

purchased Santa Gertrudis land grant. County created 1913 from Nueces County; named for San Jacinto veteran and rancher Robert Kleberg.

**Race/Ethnicity, 2000:** (In percent) Anglo, 29.03; Black, 3.59; Hispanic, 65.41; Other, 1.97.

**Vital Statistics, 2001:** Births, 513; deaths, 273; marriages, 248; divorces, 143.

**Recreation:** Fishing, hunting, water sports, park on Baffin Bay; wildlife sanctuary; winter bird watching; university events, museum; King Ranch headquarters, tours; La Posada celebration in November.

**Minerals:** Oil, gas.

**Agriculture:** Cotton, beef cattle, grain sorghum. Market value $72.2 million. Hunting leases/eco-tourism.

**KINGSVILLE** (25,427) county seat; government/services; oil, gas; agribusiness; tourism; chemical plant; university, Coastal Bend College branch; hospital; ranching heritage festival in February.

Other towns include: **Riviera** (1,064).

| | | |
|---|---|---|
| Population .................................31,145 | Rainfall (in.) ....................................27.6 | Wages .........................$60,190,686 |
| Change fm 2000 ............................-1.3 | Jan. mean min....................................45 | Av. Weekly Wage.....................$454.55 |
| Area (sq. mi.) .........................1,090.29 | July mean max. ...................................95 | Prop. Value ................$1,464,470,949 |
| Land Area (sq. mi.) ...................870.97 | Civ. Labor ....................................13,117 | Retail Sales...................$293,989,091 |
| Altitude (ft.) .....................sea level-151 | Unemployed .......................................6.0 | |

# Knox County

**Physical Features:** Eroded breaks on West Texas Rolling Plains; Brazos, Wichita rivers; sandy, loam soils.

**Economy:** Oil, agribusiness, government/services.

**History:** Indian conscripts used during Spanish period to mine copper deposits along the Brazos. Ranching, farming developed in 1880s. German colony settled in 1895. County created from Bexar, Young territories 1858; re-created 1876; organized 1886; named for U.S. Secretary of War Henry Knox.

**Race/Ethnicity, 2000:** (In percent) Anglo, 67.06; Black, 7.24; Hispanic, 25.09; Other, 0.61.

**Vital Statistics, 2001:** Births, 42; deaths, 73; marriages, 31; divorces, 11.

**Recreation:** Lake activities, fishing; hunting; Knox City seedless watermelon festival in July.

**Minerals:** Oil, gas.

**Agriculture:** Stocker cattle, cow/calf; wheat, cotton. Cotton irrigated. Market value $45.5 million.

**BENJAMIN** (253) county seat; ranching, farm center.

**MUNDAY** (1,459) portable buildings, other manufacturing; Texas A&M Vegetable Research Station; vegetable festival.

**KNOX CITY** (1,161) agribusiness, petroleum center; USDA Plant Materials Research Center; veterans memorial; hospital.

Other towns include: **Goree** (305); **Rhineland** (100) old church established by German immigrants; **Truscott** (50); **Vera** (50).

| | |
|---|---|
| Population...........................4,061 | July mean max. ..........................98 |
| Change fm 2000......................-4.5 | Civ. Labor..............................1,769 |
| Area (sq. mi.).......................855.43 | Unemployed ..............................4.4 |
| Land Area (sq. mi.)...............849.00 | Wages...........................$7,205,752 |
| Altitude (ft.) ..................1,300-1,700 | Av. Weekly Wage...............$425.72 |
| Rainfall (in.) ..............................26.2 | Prop. Value................$227,431,154 |
| Jan. mean min...............................28 | Retail Sales .................$18,031,012 |

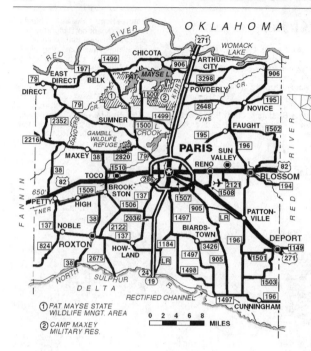

① PAT MAYSE STATE
WILDLIFE MNGT. AREA

② CAMP MAXEY
MILITARY RES.

0 2 4 6 8
MILES

# Lamar County

**Physical Features**: North Texas county on divide between Red, Sulphur rivers; soils chiefly blackland, except along Red; pines, hardwoods.

**Economy**: Varied manufacturing; agribusiness; medical, government/services.

**History**: Caddo Indian area. First Anglo-American settlers arrived about 1815. County created 1840 from Red River County; organized 1841; named for second president of Republic, Mirabeau B. Lamar.

**Race/Ethnicity, 2000**: (In percent) Anglo, 81.43; Black, 13.72; Hispanic, 3.33; Other, 1.52.

**Vital Statistics, 2001**: Births, 621; deaths, 572; marriages, 549; divorces, 329.

**Recreation**: Lake activities; Gambill goose refuge; hunting, fishing; state park; Sam Bell Maxey Home; State Sen. A.M. Aikin Archives, other museums.

**Minerals**: Negligible.

**Agriculture**: Beef, hay, dairy, soybeans, wheat, corn, sorghum, cotton. Market value $40.7 million.

**PARIS** (26,120) county seat; varied manufacturing; food processing; government/services; hospital; junior college; Tour de Paris bicycle rally in July; square dance weekend Labor Day.

Other towns include: **Arthur City** (200), **Blossom** (1,450), **Brookston** (70), **Chicota** (125), **Cunningham** (110), **Deport** (708, partly in Red River County), **Pattonville** (180), **Petty** (100), **Powderly** (185), **Reno** (2,831), **Roxton** (699), **Sumner** (80), **Sun Valley** (50), **Toco** (89).

| | |
|---|---|
| Population.......................... **49,079** | July mean max. ........................ 94 |
| Change fm 2000 ..................... 1.2 | Civ. Labor ........................... 21,948 |
| Area (sq. mi.)..................... 932.47 | Unemployed ............................. 8.0 |
| Land Area (sq. mi.)............. 916.81 | Wages .................... $135,184,680 |
| Altitude (ft.)..................... 350-650 | Av. Weekly Wage ............ $523.58 |
| Rainfall (in.)............................ 46.1 | Prop. Value.......... $2,860,106,788 |
| Jan. mean min.......................... 30 | Retail Sales ............ $579,601,352 |

# Lamb County

**Physical Features**: Rich, red, brown soils on West Texas High Plains; some hills; drains to upper Brazos River tributaries; numerous playas.

**Economy**: Agribusiness; distribution center; denim textiles.

**History**: Apaches, displaced by Comanches around 1700. U.S. Army pushed Comanches into Indian Territory in 1875. Ranching began in 1880s; farming after 1900. County created 1876 from Bexar District; organized 1908; named for Lt. G.A. Lamb, who died in battle of San Jacinto.

**Race/Ethnicity, 2000**: (In percent) Anglo, 51.71; Black, 4.32; Hispanic, 43.46; Other, 0.51.

**Vital Statistics, 2001**: Births, 227; deaths, 169; marriages, 80; divorces, 46.

**Recreation**: Pioneer celebration in August; Caprock Soaring glider competition.

**Minerals**: Oil, stone, gas.

**Agriculture**: Fed cattle; cotton, corn, wheat, grain sorghum, vegetables, soybeans, hay; sheep. 385,000 acres irrigated. Market value $277.8 million.

**LITTLEFIELD** (6,567) county seat; tourism; agribusiness; varied manufacturing; hospital; prison.

**Olton** (2,325) agribusiness, commercial center for northeast part of county; pheasant hunt in winter; Sandhills Celebration in summer.

Other towns include: **Amherst** (799); **Earth** (1,087) farming center, manufacturing, feed lot, supplies; **Fieldton** (126); **Spade** (103); **Springlake** (136); **Sudan** (1,050) farming center, government/services, Homecoming Day in fall.

| | |
|---|---|
| Population ...........................**14,662** | July mean max. ........................91 |
| Change fm 2000 .......................- 0.3 | Civ. Labor ..............................6,645 |
| Area (sq. mi.).................... 1,017.73 | Unemployed ..............................6.4 |
| Land Area (sq. mi.)............. 1,016.21 | Wages ........................$25,853,649 |
| Altitude (ft.) ....................3,400-3,849 | Av. Weekly Wage ..............$407.95 |
| Rainfall (in.)............................18.7 | Prop. Value..............$1,067,927,799 |
| Jan. mean min............................22 | Retail Sales ................$53,348,376 |

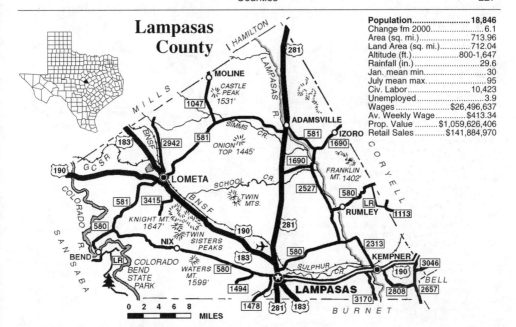

# Lampasas County

| | |
|---|---|
| Population | 18,846 |
| Change fm 2000 | 6.1 |
| Area (sq. mi.) | 713.96 |
| Land Area (sq. mi.) | 712.04 |
| Altitude (ft.) | 800-1,647 |
| Rainfall (in.) | 29.6 |
| Jan. mean min. | 30 |
| July mean max. | 95 |
| Civ. Labor | 10,423 |
| Unemployed | 3.9 |
| Wages | $26,496,637 |
| Av. Weekly Wage | $413.34 |
| Prop. Value | $1,059,626,406 |
| Retail Sales | $141,884,970 |

**Physical Features:** Central Texas on edge of Hill Country; Colorado, Lampasas rivers; cedars, oaks, pecans.

**Economy:** Many employed at Fort Hood; several industrial plants; tourism; agribusinesses.

**History:** Mineral springs attracted first Anglo-Americans in 1853. Frontier confrontations between settlers, Comanches continued into 1870s. County created 1856 from Bell, Travis counties. Named for river. Some have speculated that an early expedition named river for city of Lampazos in Mexico.

**Race/Ethnicity, 2000:** (In percent) Anglo, 80.40; Black, 3.12; Hispanic, 15.07; Other, 1.41.

**Vital Statistics, 2001:** Births, 248; deaths, 193; marriages, 164; divorces, 113.

**Recreation:** Scenic drives; state park; deer hunting, fishing in streams.

**Minerals:** Sand and gravel, building stone.

**Agriculture:** Beef cattle, hay, sheep, goats; pecans. Market value $13.9 million. Hunting leases, ecotourism.

**LAMPASAS** (7,110) county seat; varied manufacturing; government/services; ranching, hunting center; historic downtown; hospital; Spring Ho in July.

Other towns include: **Adamsville** (41); **Bend** (115, partly in San Saba County); **Izoro** (17); **Kempner** (1,070); **Lometa** (811) market and shipping point; Diamondback Jubilee in March.

*For explanation of sources, abbreviations and symbols, see p. 138.*

*A surfer rides in on a wave in the Gulf of Mexico near Corpus Christi. File photo.*

# La Salle County

**Physical Features:** Southwestern county on brushy plain, broken by Nueces, Frio rivers and their tributaries; chocolate, dark gray, sandy loam soils.

**Economy:** Agribusiness, hunting leases; tourism; government services.

**History:** Coahuiltecans, squeezed out by migrating Apaches. U.S. military outpost in 1850s; settlers of Mexican descent established nearby village. Anglo-American ranching developed in 1870s. County created from Bexar County 1858; organized 1880; named for Robert Cavelier Sieur de La Salle, French explorer who died in Texas.

**Race/Ethnicity, 2000:** (In percent) Anglo, 19.15; Black, 3.29; Hispanic, 77.12; Other, 0.44.

**Vital Statistics, 2001:** Births, 98; deaths, 50; marriages, 29; divorces, 3.

**Recreation:** Nature trails; Cotulla school where Lyndon B. Johnson taught; wildlife management area; deer, bird, javelina hunting; wild hog cookoff in March; fishing.

**Minerals:** Oil, gas.

**Agriculture:** Beef cattle, peanuts, watermelons, grain sorghum. Market value $24.1 million.

**COTULLA** (3,591) county seat; livestock, state prison; hunting center; Brush Country museum; Cinco de Mayo celebration.

Other towns include: **Encinal** (619), **Fowlerton** (58).

| | |
|---|---|
| Population | 5,876 |
| Change fm 2000 | 0.2 |
| Area (sq. mi.) | 1,494.23 |
| Land Area (sq. mi.) | 1,488.85 |

| | |
|---|---|
| Altitude (ft.) | 250-600 |
| Rainfall (in.) | 22.5 |
| Jan. mean min. | 38 |
| July mean max. | 99 |
| Civ. Labor | 2,780 |

| | |
|---|---|
| Unemployed | 5.9 |
| Wages | $7,824,775 |
| Av. Weekly Wage | $486.98 |
| Prop. Value | $470,361,881 |
| Retail Sales | $38,577,330 |

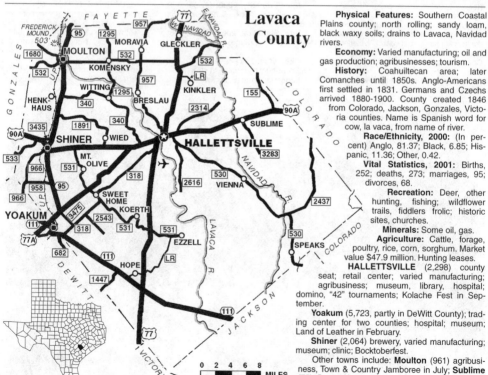

# Lavaca County

**Physical Features:** Southern Coastal Plains county; north rolling; sandy loam, black waxy soils; drains to Lavaca, Navidad rivers.

**Economy:** Varied manufacturing; oil and gas production; agribusinesses; tourism.

**History:** Coahuiltecan area; later Comanches until 1850s. Anglo-Americans first settled in 1831. Germans and Czechs arrived 1880-1900. County created 1846 from Colorado, Jackson, Gonzales, Victoria counties. Name is Spanish word for cow, la vaca, from name of river.

**Race/Ethnicity, 2000:** (In percent) Anglo, 81.37; Black, 6.85; Hispanic, 11.36; Other, 0.42.

**Vital Statistics, 2001:** Births, 252; deaths, 273; marriages, 95; divorces, 68.

**Recreation:** Deer, other hunting, fishing; wildflower trails, fiddlers frolic; historic sites, churches.

**Minerals:** Some oil, gas.

**Agriculture:** Cattle, forage, poultry, rice, corn, sorghum. Market value $47.9 million. Hunting leases.

**HALLETTSVILLE** (2,298) county seat; retail center; varied manufacturing; agribusiness; museum, library, hospital; domino, "42" tournaments; Kolache Fest in September.

**Yoakum** (5,723, partly in DeWitt County); trading center for two counties; hospital; museum; Land of Leather in February.

**Shiner** (2,064) brewery, varied manufacturing; museum; clinic; Bocktoberfest.

Other towns include: **Moulton** (961) agribusiness, Town & Country Jamboree in July; **Sublime** (75); **Sweet Home** (360).

| | |
|---|---|
| Population | 18,935 |
| Change fm 2000 | -1.4 |
| Area (sq. mi.) | 970.35 |
| Land Area (sq. mi.) | 969.90 |
| Altitude (ft.) | 100-503 |

| | |
|---|---|
| Rainfall (in.) | 39.1 |
| Jan. mean min. | 41 |
| July mean max. | 95 |
| Civ. Labor | 9,164 |

| | |
|---|---|
| Unemployed | 1.9 |
| Total Wages | $29,389,039 |
| Av. Weekly Wage | $409.84 |
| Prop. Value | $1,632,936,514 |
| Retail Sales | $170,068,199 |

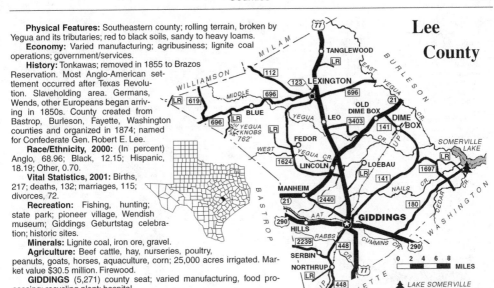

## Lee County

**Physical Features:** Southeastern county; rolling terrain, broken by Yegua and its tributaries; red to black soils, sandy to heavy loams.

**Economy:** Varied manufacturing; agribusiness; lignite coal operations; government/services.

**History:** Tonkawas; removed in 1855 to Brazos Reservation. Most Anglo-American settlement occurred after Texas Revolution. Slaveholding area. Germans, Wends, other Europeans began arriving in 1850s. County created from Bastrop, Burleson, Fayette, Washington counties and organized in 1874; named for Confederate Gen. Robert E. Lee.

**Race/Ethnicity, 2000:** (In percent) Anglo, 68.96; Black, 12.15; Hispanic, 18.19; Other, 0.70.

**Vital Statistics, 2001:** Births, 217; deaths, 132; marriages, 115; divorces, 72.

**Recreation:** Fishing, hunting; state park; pioneer village, Wendish museum; Giddings Geburtstag celebration; historic sites.

**Minerals:** Lignite coal, iron ore, gravel.

**Agriculture:** Beef cattle, hay, nurseries, poultry, peanuts, goats, horses, aquaculture, corn; 25,000 acres irrigated. Market value $30.5 million. Firewood.

**GIDDINGS** (5,271) county seat; varied manufacturing, food processing; recycling plant; hospital.

Other towns include: **Dime Box** (313); **Lexington** (1,260) livestock-marketing center; **Lincoln** (276); **Serbin** (90) Wendish museum.

| | | |
|---|---|---|
| **Population** ............................. **16,329** | Altitude (ft.) ............................. 238-762 | Unemployed ...................................... 5.3 |
| Change fm 2000 ............................. 4.3 | Rainfall (in.) ................................... 35.6 | Wages ............................. $31,807,353 |
| Area (sq. mi.) ............................ 634.03 | Jan. mean min. ............................... 36 | Av. Weekly Wage ................. $473.99 |
| Land Area (sq. mi.) .................... 628.50 | July mean max. ................................ 94 | Prop. Value ................. $1,174,960,794 |
| | Civ. Labor ................................. 7,170 | Retail Sales ................. $163,207,560 |

## Leon County

**Physical Features:** East central county; hilly, rolling, almost half covered by timber; drains to Navasota, Trinity rivers and tributaries; sandy, dark, alluvial soils.

**Economy:** Oil, gas production; agribusiness.

**History:** Bidais band, absorbed into Kickapoos and other groups. Permanent settlement by Anglo-Americans occurred after Texas Revolution; Germans in 1870s. County created 1846 from Robertson County; named for founder of Victoria, Martín de León.

**Race/Ethnicity, 2000:** (In percent) Anglo, 81.04; Black, 10.41; Hispanic, 7.91; Other, 0.64.

**Vital Statistics, 2001:** Births, 181; deaths, 212; marriages, 106; divorces, 53.

**Recreation:** Hilltop Lakes resort area; sites of Camino Real, Fort Boggy State Park; deer hunting.

**Minerals:** Oil, gas, iron ore, lignite.

**Agriculture:** A leading county in cow-calf production; hogs, poultry raised; hay, watermelons, vegetables, small grains; Christmas trees. Market value $31.2 million. Hardwoods, pine marketed value $10 million.

**CENTERVILLE** (911) county seat; farm center; hunting; tourism; oil, gas; timber.

**BUFFALO** (1,822) farm center; clinic; library; stampede in September.

Other towns include: **Flynn** (81); **Hilltop Lakes** (300), resort, retirement center; **Jewett** (872) electricity-generating plant, civic center, barbecue in March; **Leona** (183) candle factory; **Marquez** (218); **Normangee** (724, partly in Madison County) farming, tourism; library, museum, city park; **Oakwood** (475).

| | | |
|---|---|---|
| **Population** ............................. **15,885** | Jan. mean min. ................................ 34 | Prop. Value ................. $1,576,439,951 |
| Change fm 2000 ............................. 3.6 | July mean max. ................................ 95 | Retail Sales ................. $106,034,563 |
| Area (sq. mi.) ......................... 1,080.38 | Civ. Labor ................................. 7,046 | |
| Land Area (sq. mi.) ................. 1,072.04 | Unemployed ...................................... 6.6 | *For explanation of sources, abbreviations* |
| Altitude (ft.) ............................. 150-600 | Wages ............................. $39,573,312 | *and symbols, see p. 138.* |
| Rainfall (in.) ..................................... 40.5 | Av. Weekly Wage ................. $617.09 | |

# Liberty County

Population.............................73,739
Change fm 2000...........................5.1
Area (sq. mi.)......................1,176.22
Land Area (sq. mi.)..............1,159.68
Altitude (ft.)............................23-261
Rainfall (in.)..............................54.1
Jan. mean min....................39
July mean max.......................93
Civ. Labor...............................31,666
Unemployed...............................8.9
Wages............................$99,905,147
Av. Weekly Wage..................$490.37
Prop. Value................$3,058,982,706
Retail Sales.................$612,626,014

**Physical Features:** Coastal Plain county east of Houston; 60 percent in pine, hardwood timber; bisected by Trinity River; sandy, loam, black soils; Big Thicket.

**Economy:** Agribusiness; chemical plants; varied manufacturing; tourism; forest industries; prisons; many residents work in Houston; part of Houston metropolitan area.

**History:** Karankawa area until 1740s. Nuestra Señora de la Luz Mission established in 1746 and Atascosito settlement developed. Settlers from Louisiana began arriving in 1810s. County named for Spanish municipality, Libertad; created 1836, organized 1837.

**Race/Ethnicity, 2000:** (In percent) Anglo, 75.17; Black, 12.99; Hispanic, 10.92; Other, 0.92.

**Vital Statistics, 2001:** Births, 1,039; deaths, 702; marriages, 663; divorces, 325.

**Recreation:** Big Thicket; hunting, fishing; historic sites; Trinity Valley exposition; Liberty Opry.

**Minerals:** Oil, gas.

**Agriculture:** Beef cattle; rice is principal crop. Also nursery crops, corn, hay, sorghum. Market value $22.6 million. Some lumbering.

**LIBERTY** (8,312) county seat; petroleum-related industry; agribusiness; library; museum; regional historical resource depository; Liberty Bell; hospital; Jubilee in March.

**Cleveland** (7,858) forest products processed, shipped; tourism; library; museum; hospital.

**Dayton** (5,996) rice, oil center.

Other towns include: **Ames** (1,116); **Daisetta** (1,067); **Dayton Lakes** (101); **Devers** (429); **Hardin** (787); **Hull** (1,800); **Kenefick** (694); **North Cleveland** (272); **Plum Grove** (974); **Raywood** (231); **Romayor** (96); **Rye** (76).

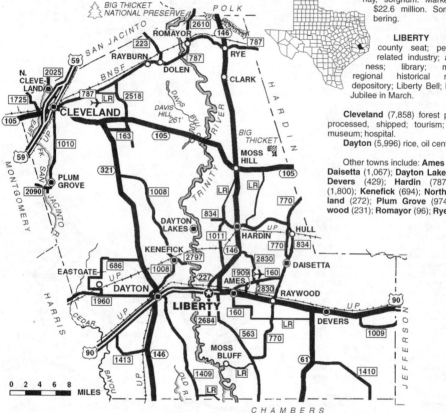

# Limestone County

**Physical Features:** East central county on divide between Brazos and Trinity rivers; borders Blacklands, level to rolling; drained by Navasota and tributaries.

**Economy:** Varied manufacturing; agribusiness; tourism; mineral operations.

**History:** Tawakoni (Tehuacana) and Waco area, later Comanche raiders. First Anglo-Americans arrived in 1833. Antebellum slaveholding area. County created from Robertson County and organized 1846; named for indigenous rock.

*For explanation of sources, abbreviations and symbols, see p. 138.*

**Race/Ethnicity, 2000:** (In percent) Anglo, 67.20; Black, 19.33; Hispanic, 12.97; Other, 0.50.

**Vital Statistics, 2001:** Births, 306; deaths, 291; marriages, 188; divorces, 0.

**Recreation:** Fishing, lake activities; Fort Parker; Confederate Reunion Grounds; historic sites; museum; hunting; Christmas at the Fort.

**Minerals:** Lignite, crushed rock, sand, oil, gas.

**Agriculture:** Cow-calf, stocker cattle operations; dairies; horses, goats, sheep, some exotic animals; crops include hay, corn, cotton, wheat, peaches. Market value $31 million.

**GROESBECK** (4,415) county seat, agribusiness, tourism, hunting, mining, prison, power generating, hospital.

**MEXIA** (6,571) agribusiness, grocery distribution, state school, hospital.

Other towns include: **Coolidge** (866), **Kosse** (507), **Prairie Hill** (150), **Tehuacana** (315), **Thornton** (536).

continued on next page

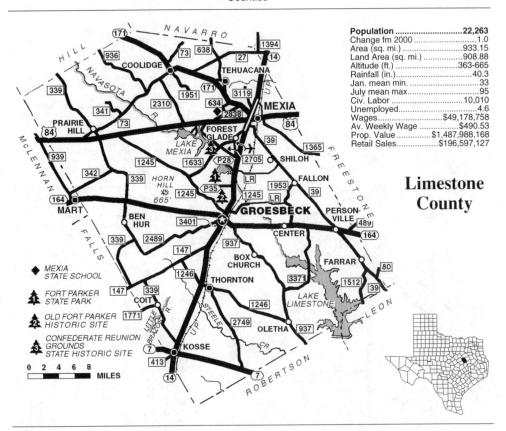

## Limestone County

| Population | 22,263 |
| --- | --- |
| Change fm 2000 | 1.0 |
| Area (sq. mi.) | 933.15 |
| Land Area (sq. mi.) | 908.88 |
| Altitude (ft.) | 363-665 |
| Rainfall (in.) | 40.3 |
| Jan. mean min. | 33 |
| July mean max. | 95 |
| Civ. Labor | 10,010 |
| Unemployed | 4.6 |
| Wages | $49,178,758 |
| Av. Weekly Wage | $490.53 |
| Prop. Value | $1,487,988,168 |
| Retail Sales | $196,597,127 |

# Lipscomb County

**Physical Features:** High Plain, broken in east; drains to tributaries of Canadian, Wolf Creek; sandy loam, black soils.

**Economy:** Oil, gas operations; agribusinesses; government/ services.

**History:** Apaches, later Kiowas and Comanches who were driven into Indian Territory in 1875. Ranching began in late 1870s. County created 1876 from Bexar District; organized 1887; named for A.S. Lipscomb, Republic of Texas leader.

**Race/Ethnicity, 2000:** (In percent) Anglo, 77.46; Black, 0.46; Hispanic, 20.71; Other, 1.37.

**Vital Statistics, 2001:** Births, 36; deaths, 30; marriages, 51; divorces, 12.

**Recreation:** Hunting; Will Rogers Day; Wolf Creek museum.

**Minerals:** Oil, natural gas.

**Agriculture:** Cattle; wheat, sorghum, corn; 19,000 acres irrigated. Market value $41.7 million.

**LIPSCOMB** (44), county seat; livestock center.

**Booker** (1,279, partly in Ochiltree County) trade center, library.

Other towns include: **Darrouzett** (295) Deutsches Fest, **Follett** (402); **Higgins** (414) library.

| Population | 3,103 |
| --- | --- |
| Change fm 2000 | 1.5 |
| Area (sq. mi.) | 932.22 |
| Land Area (sq. mi.) | 932.11 |
| Altitude (ft.) | 2,300-2,837 |

| Rainfall (in.) | 22.8 |
| --- | --- |
| Jan. mean min. | 20 |
| July mean max. | 93 |
| Civ. Labor | 1,731 |
| Unemployed | 2.6 |

| Wages | $7,866,906 |
| --- | --- |
| Av. Weekly Wage | $631.02 |
| Prop. Value | $506,274,259 |
| Retail Sales | $7,989,771 |

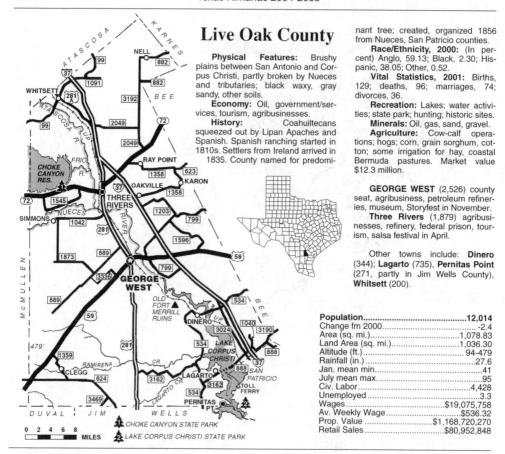

# Live Oak County

**Physical Features:** Brushy plains between San Antonio and Corpus Christi, partly broken by Nueces and tributaries; black waxy, gray sandy, other soils.

**Economy:** Oil, government/services, tourism, agribusinesses.

**History:** Coahuiltecans squeezed out by Lipan Apaches and Spanish. Spanish ranching started in 1810s. Settlers from Ireland arrived in 1835. County named for predomi-nant tree; created, organized 1856 from Nueces, San Patricio counties.

**Race/Ethnicity, 2000:** (In percent) Anglo, 59.13; Black, 2.30; Hispanic, 38.05; Other, 0.52.

**Vital Statistics, 2001:** Births, 129; deaths, 96; marriages, 74; divorces, 36.

**Recreation:** Lakes; water activities; state park; hunting; historic sites.

**Minerals:** Oil, gas, sand, gravel.

**Agriculture:** Cow-calf operations; hogs; corn, grain sorghum, cotton; some irrigation for hay, coastal Bermuda pastures. Market value $12.3 million.

**GEORGE WEST** (2,526) county seat, agribusiness, petroleum refineries, museum, Storyfest in November.

**Three Rivers** (1,879) agribusinesses, refinery, federal prison, tourism, salsa festival in April.

Other towns include: **Dinero** (344); **Lagarto** (735), **Pernitas Point** (271, partly in Jim Wells County), **Whitsett** (200).

| | |
|---|---|
| Population | 12,014 |
| Change fm 2000 | -2.4 |
| Area (sq. mi.) | 1,078.83 |
| Land Area (sq. mi.) | 1,036.30 |
| Altitude (ft.) | 94-479 |
| Rainfall (in.) | 27.6 |
| Jan. mean min. | 41 |
| July mean max. | 95 |
| Civ. Labor | 4,428 |
| Unemployed | 3.3 |
| Wages | $19,075,758 |
| Av. Weekly Wage | $536.32 |
| Prop. Value | $1,168,720,270 |
| Retail Sales | $80,952,848 |

*Enchanted Rock, a massive granite outcrop, rises at the Llano-Gillespie county line. Texas Parks & Wildlife photo.*

# Llano County

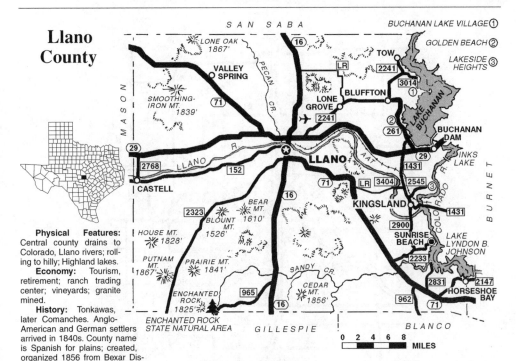

**Physical Features:** Central county drains to Colorado, Llano rivers; rolling to hilly; Highland lakes.

**Economy:** Tourism, retirement; ranch trading center; vineyards; granite mined.

**History:** Tonkawas, later Comanches. Anglo-American and German settlers arrived in 1840s. County name is Spanish for plains; created, organized 1856 from Bexar District, Gillespie County.

**Race/Ethnicity, 2000:** (In percent) Anglo, 93.74; Black, 0.34; Hispanic, 5.13; Other, 0.79.

**Vital Statistics, 2001:** Births, 154; deaths, 259; marriages, 101; divorces, 83.

**Recreation:** Leading deer-hunting county; fishing; lake activities; major tourist area; Enchanted Rock; bluebonnet festival; hang gliding.

**Minerals:** Granite, vermiculite, llanite.

**Agriculture:** Beef cattle, sheep, goats. Market value $11.5 million. Deer-hunting, wildlife leases.

**LLANO** (3,428) county seat; varied manufacturing; hunting center; government/services; hospital; livestock trading; historic district; museum.

**Kingsland** (4,604) tourism, retirement community, fishing and water sports; metal fabrication; wood work; library; AquaBoom on July 4.

Other towns include: **Bluffton** (75); **Buchanan Dam** (1,703) dam museum; **Castell** (72); **Horseshoe Bay** (3,399, partly in Burnet County); **Sunrise Beach** (720); **Tow** (305); **Valley Spring** (50).

| | |
|---|---|
| Population | 17,758 |
| Change fm 2000 | 4.2 |
| Area (sq. mi.) | 966.18 |
| Land Area (sq. mi.) | 934.76 |
| Altitude (ft.) | 825-1,867 |
| Rainfall (in.) | 26.4 |
| Jan. mean min. | 31 |
| July mean max. | 96 |
| Civ. Labor | 6,129 |
| Unemployed | 4.3 |
| Wages | $26,057,651 |
| Av. Weekly Wage | $468.76 |
| Prop. Value | $2,316,958,772 |
| Retail Sales | $107,737,116 |

# Loving County

**Physical Features:** Western county of dry, rolling prairies; slopes to Pecos River; Red Bluff Reservoir; sandy, loam, clay soils.

**Economy:** Petroleum operations; cattle.

**History:** Land developers began operations in late 19th century. Oil discovered in 1925. County created 1887 from Tom Green; organized 1931, last county organized. Named for Oliver Loving, trail driver. Loving is Texas' least populous county.

**Race/Ethnicity, 2000:** (In percent) Anglo, 89.55; Black, 0.00; Hispanic, 10.45; Other, 0.00.

**Vital Statistics, 2001:** Births, 1; deaths, 0; marriages, 4; divorces, 0.

**Recreation:** NA.

**Minerals:** Oil, gas.

**Agriculture:** Some cattle. Market value $747,000.

**MENTONE** (15) county seat, oil-field supply center; only town.

For explanation of sources, abbreviations and symbols, see p. 138.

| | |
|---|---|
| Population | 64 |
| Change fm 2000 | -4.5 |
| Area (sq. mi.) | 676.85 |
| Land Area (sq. mi.) | 673.08 |
| Altitude (ft.) | 2,685-3,311 |
| Rainfall (in.) | 9.1 |
| Jan. mean min. | 28 |
| July mean max. | 96 |
| Civ. Labor | 47 |
| Unemployed | 10.6 |
| Wages | $165,467 |
| Av. Weekly Wage | $397.76 |
| Prop. Value | $219,677,542 |
| Retail Sales | $0 |

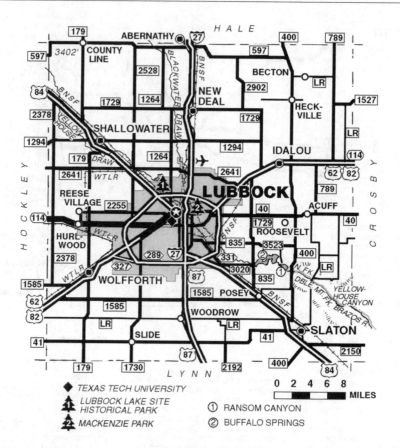

◆ TEXAS TECH UNIVERSITY
🌲 LUBBOCK LAKE SITE
    HISTORICAL PARK
🌲 MACKENZIE PARK

① RANSOM CANYON
② BUFFALO SPRINGS

0  2  4  6  8
████████  MILES

**Physical Features:** High Plains of West Texas, broken by 1,500 playas, upper Brazos River tributaries; rich soils with underground water.

**Economy:** Among world's largest cottonseed processing centers; a leading agribusiness center; cattle feedlots; manufacturing; higher education center; medical center; government/services.

**History:** Evidence of human habitation for 12,000 years. In historic period, Apache Indians, followed by Comanche hunters. Sheep raisers from Midwest arrived in late 1870s. Cotton farms brought in Mexican laborers in 1940s-60s. County named for Col. Tom S. Lubbock, an organizer of Confederate Terry's Rangers; county created 1876 from Bexar District; organized 1891.

**Race/Ethnicity, 2000:** (In percent) Anglo, 63.06; Black, 7.71; Hispanic, 27.45; Other, 1.78.

**Vital Statistics, 2001:** Births, 3,826; deaths, 1,961; marriages, 2,036; divorces, 1,257.

**Recreation:** Lubbock Lake archaeological site, park; Texas Tech events; civic center; Buddy Holly statue, Walk of Fame, festival in September; planetarium; Ranching Heritage Center; Panhandle-South Plains Fair; wine festivals; Buffalo Springs Lake.

**Minerals:** Oil, gas, stone, sand and gravel.

# Lubbock County

**Agriculture:** A leading cotton-producing county. Fed beef, cow-calf operations; poultry, eggs; hogs. Other crops, nursery, grain sorghum, wheat, sunflowers, soybeans, hay, vegetables; more than 230,000 acres irrigated, mostly cotton. Market value $97.8 million.

**Education:** Texas Tech University with law and medical schools; Lubbock Christian University; South Plains College branch; Wayland Baptist University off-campus center.

**LUBBOCK** (201,855) county seat; center for large agricultural area; manufacturing includes electronics, earth-moving equipment, food containers, fire-protection equipment, clothing, other products; distribution center for South Plains; feedlots; museum; gov-

ernment/services; hospitals, psychiatric hospital; state school for retarded; wind power center.

Other towns include: **Buffalo Springs** (506); **Idalou** (2,166); **New Deal** (760); **Ransom Canyon** (1,021); **Shallowater** (2,151); **Slaton** (6,092) agribusiness, government/services, prison, varied manufacturing, railroad, sausagefest in October; **Wolfforth** (2,653) retail, government/services, harvest festival in September.

Also, part of **Abernathy** (2,850).

| Population | 247,574 |
|---|---|
| Change fm 2000 | 2.0 |
| Area (sq. mi.) | 900.70 |
| Land Area (sq. mi.) | 899.49 |
| Altitude (ft.) | 2,900-3,402 |
| Rainfall (in.) | 18.7 |
| Jan. mean min. | 25 |
| July mean max. | 92 |
| Civ. Labor | 131,067 |
| Unemployed | 3.1 |
| Wages | $814,402,003 |
| Av. Weekly Wage | $534.61 |
| Prop. Value | $8,780,550,519 |
| Retail Sales | $3,092,492,555 |

*For explanation of sources, abbreviations and symbols, see p. 138.*

# Lynn County

**Physical Features:** South High Plains, broken by Caprock Escarpment, playas, draws; sandy loam, black, gray soils.

**Economy:** Agribusiness.

**History:** Apaches, ousted by Comanches who were removed to Indian Territory in 1875. Ranching began in 1880s. Farming developed after 1900. County created 1876 from Bexar District; organized 1903; named for Alamo victim W. Lynn.

**Race/Ethnicity, 2000:** (In percent) Anglo, 51.95; Black, 2.63; Hispanic, 44.63; Other, 0.79.

**Vital Statistics, 2001:** Births, 75; deaths, 55; marriages, 26; divorces, 13.

**Recreation:** Pioneer museum in Tahoka; Dan Blocker museum in O'Donnell.

**Minerals:** Oil, natural gas, stone.

**Agriculture:** Cotton produces largest income; 74,000 acres irrigated. Market value $34.9 million.

**TAHOKA** (2,848) county seat; agribusiness center; cotton compress; some manufacturing; hospital; harvest festival.

**O'Donnell** (980, partly in Dawson County), commercial center.

Other towns include: **New Home** (322); **Wilson** (518).

| | | |
|---|---|---|
| Population..................................6,325 | | Unemployed.................................5.9 |
| Change fm 2000..........................-3.4 | Rainfall (in.) .................................19.7 | Wages..................................$8,553,983 |
| Area (sq. mi.) ...........................893.46 | Jan. mean min. .................................24 | Av. Weekly Wage...................$395.91 |
| Land Area (sq. mi.)...................891.88 | July mean max. .................................92 | Prop. Value .....................$386,724,991 |
| Altitude (ft.) .......................2,800-3,300 | Civ. Labor ...................................2,689 | Retail Sales.....................$13,512,483 |

# Madison County

**Physical Features:** East central county; hilly, draining to Trinity, Navasota rivers, Bedias Creek; one-fifth of area timbered; alluvial, loam, sandy soils.

**Economy:** Prison; government/services; varied manufacturing; agribusinesses; oil production.

**History:** Caddo and Bidai Indian area; Kickapoos migrated from east. Spanish settlements established in 1774 and 1805. Anglo-Americans arrived in 1829. Census of 1860 showed 30 percent of population was black. County named for U.S. President James Madison; created from Grimes, Leon, Walker counties 1853; organized 1854.

**Race/Ethnicity, 2000:** (In percent) Anglo, 60.72; Black, 22.76; Hispanic, 15.78; Other, 0.74.

**Vital Statistics, 2001:** Births, 163; deaths, 142; marriages, 105; divorces, 50.

**Recreation:** Fishing, hunting; Spanish Bluff where survivors of the Gutiérrez-Magee expedition were executed in 1813; other historic sites.

**Minerals:** sand, oil.

**Agriculture:** Nursery crops, cattle, horses, poultry raised; forage for livestock. Market value $84.3 million.

**MADISONVILLE** (4,213) county seat; farm-trade center; varied manufacturing; hospital; library; Spring Fling in April.

Other towns include, **Midway** (285); **Normangee** (724, mostly in Leon County); **North Zulch** (150).

◆ STATE PRISON
▲ SITE OF SPANISH BLUFF
OSR OLD SAN ANTONIO ROAD

| |
|---|
| Population ................................13,105 |
| Change fm 2000 .............................1.3 |
| Area (sq. mi.) ............................472.44 |
| Land Area (sq. mi.) ...................469.65 |
| Altitude (ft.)...........................150-364 |
| Rainfall (in.)....................................41.6 |
| Jan. mean min. .................................38 |
| July mean max. .................................96 |
| Civ. Labor....................................4,462 |
| Unemployed......................................3.9 |
| Wages.............................$23,167,000 |
| Av. Weekly Wage...................$461.03 |
| Prop. Value .....................$660,689,387 |
| Retail Sales....................$158,723,144 |

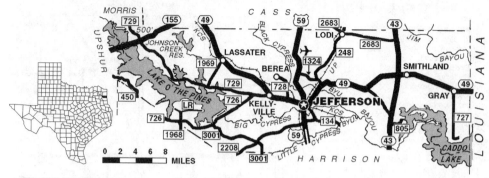

## Marion County

**Physical Features:** Northeastern county; hilly, three-quarters forested with pines, hardwoods; drains to Caddo Lake, Lake O' the Pines, Cypress Bayou.

**Economy:** Tourism; timber; food processing.

**History:** Caddoes forced out in 1790s. Kickapoo in area when settlers arrived from Deep South around 1840. Antebellum slaveholding area. County created 1860 from Cass County; named for Gen. Francis Marion of American Revolution.

**Race/Ethnicity, 2000:** (In percent) Anglo, 72.38; Black, 24.17; Hispanic, 2.40; Other, 1.05.

**Vital Statistics, 2001:** Births, 117; deaths, 152; marriages, 84; divorces, 39.

**Recreation:** Lake activities; hunting; Excelsior Hotel; 84 medallions on historic sites including Jay Gould railroad car; museum; Mardi Gras; historical pilgrimage in May, founder's day in October.

**Minerals:** Iron ore.

**Agriculture:** Beef cattle, hay, goats. Market value $2.1 million. Forestry is most important industry.

**JEFFERSON** (2,040) county seat; tourism; board plant; agriculture center; timber; museums, library; historical sites.

Other towns include: **Lodi** (164).

| | |
|---|---|
| Population | 11,081 |
| Change fm 2000 | 1.3 |
| Area (sq. mi.) | 420.36 |
| Land Area (sq. mi.) | 381.21 |
| Altitude (ft.) | 168-500 |
| Rainfall (in.) | 44.7 |
| Jan. mean min. | 32 |
| July mean max. | 94 |
| Civ. Labor | 3,505 |
| Unemployed | 9.5 |
| Wages | $9,068,599 |
| Av. Weekly Wage | $383.92 |
| Prop. Value | $565,266,500 |
| Retail Sales | $59,977,451 |

---

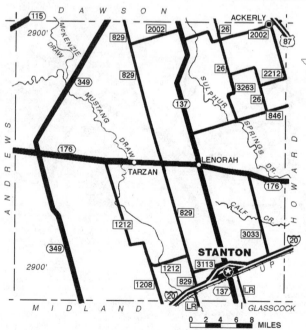

## Martin County

**Physical Features:** Western county on South Plains; sandy, loam soils, broken by playas, creeks.

**Economy:** Petroleum production, agribusiness.

**History:** Apaches, ousted by Comanches who in turn were forced out by U.S. Army 1875. Farming began in 1881. County created from Bexar District 1876; organized 1884; named for Wylie Martin, senator of Republic of Texas.

**Race/Ethnicity, 2000:** (In percent) Anglo, 57.37; Black, 1.73; Hispanic, 40.56; Other, 0.34.

**Vital Statistics, 2001:** Births, 71; deaths, 52; marriages, 82; divorces, 25.

**Recreation:** Museum, settlers reunion, restored monastery.

**Minerals:** Oil, gas.

**Agriculture:** Cotton, milo, wheat; Beef cattle, horses, meat goats, sheep raised. Market value $16 million.

**STANTON** (2,552) county seat; farm, ranch, oil center; varied manufacturing; electric co-op; communting to Midland, Big Spring; hospital, restored convent, other historic buildings; Old Sorehead trade days three times a year.

Other towns include: **Ackerly** (248, partly in Dawson County); **Lenorah** (70); **Tarzan** (80).

*For explanation of sources, abbreviations and symbols, see p. 138.*

| | |
|---|---|
| Population | 4,673 |
| Change fm 2000 | -1.5 |
| Area (sq. mi.) | 915.62 |
| Land Area (sq. mi.) | 914.78 |
| Altitude (ft.) | 2,500-2,900 |
| Rainfall (in.) | 17.2 |
| Jan. mean min. | 30 |
| July mean max. | 94 |
| Civ. Labor | 1,708 |
| Unemployed | 4.8 |
| Wages | $8,420,574 |
| Av. Weekly Wage | $495.97 |
| Prop. Value | $718,413,371 |
| Retail Sales | $29,787,332 |

# Mason County

**Physical Features:** Central county; hilly, draining to Llano and San Saba rivers and their tributaries; limestone, red soils; varied timber.

**Economy:** Ranching; hunting; tourism; soft-drink bottling.

**History:** Lipan Apaches, driven south by Comanches around 1790. German settlers arrived in mid-1840s, followed by Anglo-Americans. Mexican immigration increased after 1930. County created from Bexar, Gillespie counties 1858; named for Mexican War victim U.S. Army Lt. G.T. Mason.

**Race/Ethnicity, 2000:** (In percent) Anglo, 78.25; Black, 0.16; Hispanic, 20.95; Other, 0.64.

**Vital Statistics, 2001:** Births, 35; deaths, 57; marriages, 26; divorces, 27.

**Recreation:** Outstanding deer, turkey hunting, river fishing; camping; historic homes of stone; Fort Mason, where Robert E. Lee served; wildflower drives in spring.

**Minerals:** Topaz, granite.

**Agriculture:** Cattle, sheep, goats, exotic wildlife; peanuts, hay, watermelons, grapes. Market value $21.5 million. Hunting leases important.

**MASON** (2,176) county seat; ranching center; camping; tourism; museum; historical district, homes, rock fences built by German settlers; wild game dinner in November.

Other towns include: **Art** (18), **Fredonia** (50), **Pontotoc** (125).

▲ OLD FORT MASON

| | |
|---|---|
| Population | 3,771 |
| Change fm 2000 | 0.9 |
| Area (sq. mi.) | 932.18 |
| Land Area (sq. mi.) | 932.07 |
| Altitude (ft.) | 1,200-2,217 |
| Rainfall (in.) | 26.8 |
| Jan. mean min. | 31 |
| July mean max. | 95 |
| Civ. Labor | 1,781 |
| Unemployed | 1.5 |
| Wages | $4,913,843 |
| Av. Weekly Wage | $388.08 |
| Prop. Value | $617,180,200 |
| Retail Sales | $18,802,470 |

# Matagorda County

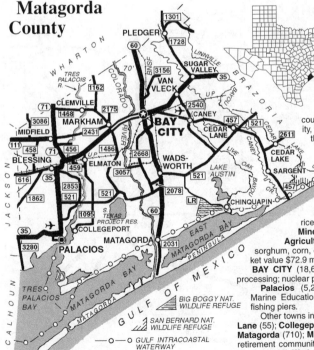

**Physical Features:** Gulf Coast county; flat, broken by bays; contains part of Matagorda Island; many different soils; drains to Colorado River, creeks, coast.

**Economy:** Petroleum operations, petrochemicals, agribusiness; varied manufacturing; tourism.

**History:** Karankawa Indian area, Tonkawas later. Anglo-Americans arrived in 1822. Mexican immigration increased after 1920. An original county, created 1836 from Spanish municipality, named for canebrake; organized 1837; settled by Austin colonists.

**Race/Ethnicity, 2000:** (In percent) Anglo, 53.00; Black, 12.84; Hispanic, 31.35; Other, 2.81.

**Vital Statistics, 2001:** Births, 562; deaths, 367; marriages, 346; divorces, 179.

**Recreation:** Fishing, water sports, hunting; historic sites, museums; rice festival in October.

**Minerals:** Gas, oil, salt.

**Agriculture:** Turfgrass, cattle, cotton, rice, grain sorghum, corn, catfish; 24,000 acres irrigated for rice. Market value $72.9 million.

**BAY CITY** (18,666) county seat; petrochemicals; oil, gas processing; nuclear power plant; commercial fishing; hospital.

**Palacios** (5,235) tourism; seafood industry; hospital; Marine Education Center; Bay Festival Labor Day; public fishing piers.

Other towns include: **Blessing** (892), historic sites; **Cedar Lane** (55); **Collegeport** (85); **Elmaton** (140); **Markham** (1,145); **Matagorda** (710); **Midfield** (70); **Pledger** (159); **Sargent** (300), retirement community, fishing, birding, commercial fishing; **Van Vleck** (1,426); **Wadsworth** (160).

| | |
|---|---|
| Population | 37,954 |
| Change fm 2000 | 0.0 |
| Area (sq. mi.) | 1,612.19 |
| Land Area (sq. mi.) | 1,114.46 |
| Altitude (ft.) | sea level-70 |
| Rainfall (in.) | 44.7 |
| Jan. mean min. | 45 |
| July mean max. | 91 |
| Civ. Labor | 15,006 |
| Unemployed | 13.0 |
| Wages | $85,909,307 |
| Av. Weekly Wage | $604.22 |
| Prop. Value | $3,455,447,979 |
| Retail Sales | $270,707,094 |

# Maverick County

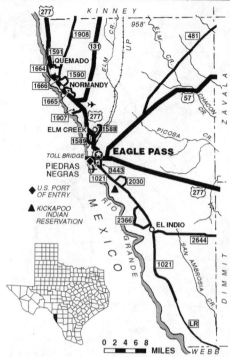

**Physical Features:** Southwestern county on Rio Grande; broken, rolling surface, with dense brush; clay, sandy, alluvial soils.

**Economy:** Oil; government/services; agribusinesses; feedlots; tourism.

**History:** Coahuiltecan Indian area; later Comanches in area. Spanish ranching began in 1760s. First Anglo-Americans arrived in 1834. County named for Sam A. Maverick, whose name is now a synonym for unbranded cattle; created 1856 from Kinney County; organized 1871.

**Race/Ethnicity, 2000:** (In percent) Anglo, 3.54; Black, 0.12; Hispanic, 95.01; Other, 1.33.

**Vital Statistics, 2001:** Births, 1,108; deaths, 266; marriages, 661; divorces, 112.

**Recreation:** Tourist gateway to Mexico; white-tailed deer, bird hunting; fishing; historic sites.

**Minerals:** Oil, gas, sand, gravel.

**Agriculture:** Cattle feedlots; pecans, vegetables, sorghum, wheat; goats, sheep. Some irrigation from Rio Grande. Market value $26.3 million.

**EAGLE PASS** (23,450) county seat; varied manufacturing; tourism center; rail, highway entry point to Piedras Negras, Mex.; hospital.

Other communities include: **Eidson Road** (9,713), **El Indio** (265), **Las Quintas Fronterizas** (2,101), **Rosita North** (3,488); **Rosita South** (2,689), all immediately south of Eagle Pass.

Also, **Elm Creek** (1,987) and **Quemado** (259).

| | |
|---|---|
| Population | 48,651 |
| Change fm 2000 | 2.9 |
| Area (sq. mi.) | 1,291.74 |
| Land Area (sq. mi.) | 1,280.08 |
| Altitude (ft.) | 600-958 |
| Rainfall (in.) | 21.5 |
| Jan. mean min. | 38 |
| July mean max. | 98 |
| Civ. Labor | 19,980 |
| Unemployed | 29.7 |
| Wages | $62,379,374 |
| Av. Weekly Wage | $439.01 |
| Prop. Value | $1,266,341,377 |
| Retail Sales | $418,840,369 |

# McCulloch County

**Physical Features:** Central county; hilly and rolling; drains to Colorado, Brady Creek and Lake, San Saba River; black loams to sandy soils.

**Economy:** Agribusiness; manufacturing; tourism; hunting leases.

**History:** Apache area. First Anglo-American settlers arrived in late 1850s, but Comanche raids delayed further settlement until 1870s. County created from Bexar District 1856; organized 1876; named for San Jacinto veteran Gen. Ben McCulloch.

**Race/Ethnicity, 2000:** (In percent) Anglo, 70.93; Black, 1.52; Hispanic, 27.04; Other, 0.51.

**Vital Statistics, 2001:** Births, 89; deaths, 119; marriages, 69; divorces, 51.

**Recreation:** Hunting; lake activities; museum, restored Santa Fe depot, goat cookoff on Labor Day, muzzle-loading rifle association state championship; rodeos; golf, tennis tournaments.

**Minerals:** Sand, gravel, gas and oil.

**Agriculture:** Beef cattle provide most income; wheat, sheep, goats, hay, cotton, sorghum, hogs, dairy cattle; some irrigation for peanuts. Market value $15.4 million.

**BRADY** (5,443) county seat; silica sand, oil-field equipment, ranching, tourism, other manufacturing; hospital; Heart of Texas car show in April, Cinco de Mayo.

Other towns: **Doole** (74), **Lohn** (149), **Melvin** (152), **Mercury** (166); **Pear Valley** (37), **Rochelle** (163) and **Voca** (56).

*For explanation of sources, abbreviations and symbols, see p. 138.*

◆ GEOGRAPHICAL CENTER OF TEXAS

| | |
|---|---|
| Population | 7,885 |
| Change fm 2000 | -3.9 |
| Area (sq. mi.) | 1,073.35 |
| Land Area (sq. mi.) | 1,069.31 |
| Altitude (ft.) | 1,300-2,021 |
| Rainfall (in.) | 26.1 |
| Jan. mean min. | 30 |
| July mean max. | 95 |
| Civ. Labor | 3,631 |
| Unemployed | 4.9 |
| Wages | $16,214,989 |
| Av. Weekly Wage | $479.36 |
| Prop. Value | $597,664,950 |
| Retail Sales | $93,117,264 |

# McLennan County

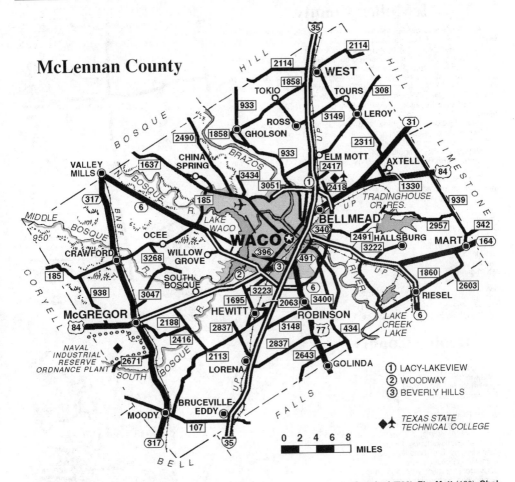

① LACY-LAKEVIEW
② WOODWAY
③ BEVERLY HILLS

◆✈ TEXAS STATE
   TECHNICAL COLLEGE

0  2  4  6  8
▬▬▬▬▬▬ MILES

**Physical Features:** Central Texas county of mostly Blackland prairie, but rolling hills in west; drains to Bosque, Brazos rivers and Lake Waco; heavy, loam, sandy soils.

**Economy:** A leading distribution, government center for Central Texas; diversified manufacturing; agribusiness; education.

**History:** Tonkawas, Wichitas and Wacos in area. Anglo-American settlers arrived in 1840s. Indians removed to Brazos reservations in 1854. County created from Milam County in 1850; named for settler, Neil McLennan Sr.

**Race/Ethnicity, 2000:** (In percent) Anglo, 65.19; Black, 15.33; Hispanic, 17.91; Other, 1.57.

**Vital Statistics, 2001:** Births, 3,225; deaths, 1,951; marriages, 1,978; divorces, 1,037.

**Recreation:** Varied metropolitan activies; Texas Ranger Hall of Fame; Texas Sports Hall of Fame; Dr Pepper Museum; Cameron Park; drag boat races April and May; zoo; historic sites, homes; museums; libraries, art center; symphony; civic theater; Baylor University events; Heart o' Texas Fair.

**Minerals:** Sand and gravel, limestone, oil, gas.

**Agriculture:** Poultry, beef cattle, corn, wheat, hay, grain sorghum, soybeans, dairy cattle. Market value $114.8 million.

**Education:** Baylor University; community college; Texas State Technical College.

**WACO** (114,743) county seat; varied manufacturing; tourism center, conventions; agribusiness; aerospace firms; hospitals; Veterans Administration regional office, hospital.

**Hewitt** (11,548) iron works, other manufacturing; hamburger cookoff.

**West** (2,695) famous for Czech foods; varied manufacturing; Westfest.

Other towns include: **Axtell** (300); **Bellmead** (9,285); **Beverly Hills** (2,068); **Bruceville-Eddy** (1,549, partly in Falls County); **China Spring** (1,000);

Crawford (732); **Elm Mott** (190); **Gholson** (969); **Hallsburg** (536); **Lacy-Lakeview** (5,834); **Leroy** (335); **Lorena** (1,502); **Mart** (2,272) agricultural center, some manufacturing, museum, juvenile correction facility; **McGregor** (4,763) agriculture, manufacturing, distribution; private telephone museum; Frontier Founders Day in September; **Moody** (1,428) agriculture, commuting to Waco, Temple; library; Cotton Harvest fest in September; **Riesel** (958); **Robinson** (8,182); **Ross** (230); **Woodway** (8,895).

Part of **Golinda** (421, mostly in Falls County) and part of **Valley Mills** (1,124, mostly in Bosque County).

| Population | 217,713 |
|---|---|
| Change fm 2000 | 2.0 |
| Area (sq. mi.) | 1,060.23 |
| Land Area (sq. mi.) | 1,041.88 |
| Altitude (ft.) | 350-950 |
| Rainfall (in.) | 32.0 |
| Jan. mean min. | 34 |
| July mean max. | 97 |
| Civ. Labor | 105,873 |
| Unemployed | 4.8 |
| Wages | $696,613,199 |
| Av. Weekly Wage | $546.03 |
| Prop. Value | $7,276,637,892 |
| Retail Sales | $2,481,518,509 |

# McMullen County

**Physical Features:** Southern county of brushy plain, sloping to Frio, Nueces rivers and tributaries; saline clay soils.

**Economy:** Livestock, hunting leases, oil and gas.

**History:** Coahuiltecans, squeezed out by Lipan Apaches and other tribes. Anglo-American settlers arrived in 1858. Sheep ranching of 1870s attracted Mexican laborers. County created from Atascosa, Bexar, Live Oak counties 1858; organized 1862, reorganized 1877; named for Nueces River pioneer-empresario John McMullen.

**Race/Ethnicity, 2000:** (In percent) Anglo, 65.44; Black, 1.18; Hispanic, 33.14; Other, 0.24.

**Vital Statistics, 2001:** Births, 5; deaths, 3; marriages, 5; divorces, 3.

**Recreation:** Deer hunting; lake activities, state park; Labor Day rodeo; Dogtown Day cook-off in October.

**Minerals:** Gas, oil, lignite coal, zeolite-kaline.

**Agriculture:** Beef cattle, hay, grain sorghum. Market value $10 million.

**TILDEN** (450), county seat; oil, gas, lignite mining; ranch center; government/services.

Other towns include: **Calliham** (200).

| | |
|---|---|
| Population | 856 |
| Change fm 2000 | 0.6 |
| Area (sq. mi.) | 1,142.60 |
| Land Area (sq. mi.) | 1,113.00 |
| Altitude (ft.) | 200-642 |
| Rainfall (in.) | 23.4 |
| Jan. mean min. | 40 |
| July mean max. | 98 |
| Civ. Labor | 273 |
| Unemployed | 5.5 |
| Wages | $1,632,731 |
| Av. Weekly Wage | $512.63 |
| Prop. Value | $514,160,096 |
| Retail Sales | $2,423,755 |

# Medina County

**Physical Features:** Southwestern county with scenic hills in north; south has fertile valleys, rolling surface; Medina River, Lake.

**Economy:** Agribusinesses; tourism; varied manufacturing; commuters to San Antonio; government/services.

**History:** Lipan Apaches and Comanches. Settled by Alsatians led by Henri Castro in 1844. Mexican immigration increased after 1900. County created 1848 from Bexar; named for river, probably for Spanish engineer Pedro Medina.

**Race/Ethnicity, 2000:** (In percent) Anglo, 51.44; Black, 2.13; Hispanic, 45.47; Other, 0.96.

**Vital Statistics, 2001:** Births, 572; deaths, 313; marriages, 237; divorces, 117.

**Recreation:** A leading deer area; scenic drives; camping, fishing; historic buildings, museum; market trail days most months.

**Minerals:** Oil, gas, clay, sand, gravel.

**Agriculture:** Most income from cattle; crops include corn, grains, peanuts, hay, vegetables; 40,000 acres irrigated. Market value $64.8 million.

**HONDO** (8,065) county seat; Air Force screening center; aerospace industry; agribusiness; varied manufacturing; hunting leases; hospital; prisons.

**Castroville** (2,792) farm center; tourism; government/services; commuting to San Antonio; Landmark Inn; St. Louis Day celebration in August.

**Devine** (4,171) commuters to San Antonio, shipping for truck crop-livestock; fall festival in October.

Other towns include: **D'Hanis** (548); **La Coste** (1,306); **Natalia** (1,697); **Riomedina** (53); **Yancey** (202). Also, **Lytle** (2,466, mostly in Atascosa County).

| | | | |
|---|---|---|---|
| Population | 40,924 | July mean max. | 94 |
| Change fm 2000 | 4.1 | Civ. Labor | 15,954 |
| Area (sq. mi.) | 1,334.53 | Unemployed | 5.1 |
| Land Area (sq. mi.) | 1,327.76 | Wages | $47,585,253 |
| Altitude (ft.) | 635-1,995 | Av. Weekly Wage | $443.42 |
| Rainfall (in.) | 27.3 | Prop. Value | $1,914,147,423 |
| Jan. mean min. | 37 | Retail Sales | $316,988,682 |

# Menard County

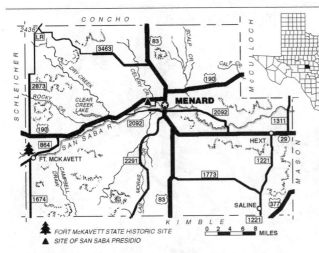

**Physical Features:** West central county of rolling topography, draining to San Saba River and tributaries; limestone soils.

**Economy:** Agribusiness; tourism; oil, gas production.

**History:** Apaches, followed by Comanches in 18th century. Mission Santa Cruz de San Sabá established in 1757. A few Anglo-American and German settlers arrived in 1840s. County created from Bexar County in 1858, organized, 1871; named for Galveston's founder, Michel B. Menard.

**Race/Ethnicity, 2000:** (In percent) Anglo, 66.83; Black, 0.42; Hispanic, 31.69; Other, 1.06.

**Vital Statistics, 2001:** Births, 27; deaths, 32; marriages, 14; divorces, 3.

**Recreation:** Hunting, fishing; historic sites, including Spanish presidio, mission, U.S. fort; museum; Jim Bowie days in June.

**Minerals:** Oil, gas.

**Agriculture:** Sheep, goats, cattle; pecans, wheat, alfalfa, peaches, melons, grapes. Market value $11.8 million.

**MENARD** (1,690) county seat; hunting, ranching center; chili cookoff in September. Other towns include: **Fort McKavett** (15); **Hext** (73).

| | |
|---|---|
| Population | 2,329 |
| Change fm 2000 | -1.3 |
| Area (sq. mi.) | 902.25 |
| Land Area (sq. mi.) | 901.91 |
| Altitude (ft.) | 1,690-2,436 |
| Rainfall (in.) | 24.3 |
| Jan. mean min. | 30 |
| July mean max. | 95 |
| Civ. Labor | 972 |
| Unemployed | 5.1 |
| Wages | $2,532,539 |
| Av. Weekly Wage | $368.96 |
| Prop. Value | $319,604,160 |
| Retail Sales | $10,098,497 |

FORT McKAVETT STATE HISTORIC SITE
SITE OF SAN SABÁ PRESIDIO

# Midland County

**Physical Features:** Flat western county, broken by draws; sandy, loam soils with native grasses.

**Economy:** Among leading petroleum-producing counties; distribution, administrative center for oil industry; varied manufacturing; government/services.

**History:** Comanches in area in 19th century. Sheep ranching developed in 1880s. Permian Basin oil boom began in 1920s. County created from Tom Green County 1885; name came from midway location on railroad between El Paso and Fort Worth. Chihuahua Trail and Emigrant Road were pioneer trails that crossed county.

**Race/Ethnicity, 2000:** (In percent) Anglo, 62.54; Black, 7.05; Hispanic, 29.03; Other, 1.38.

**Vital Statistics, 2001:** Births, 1,791; deaths, 922; marriages, 940; divorces, 544.

**Recreation:** Permian Basin Petroleum Museum, Library, Hall of Fame; Museum of Southwest; Confederate Air Force and Museum; community theater; metropolitan events; Cinco de Mayo International soccer tournament.

**Minerals:** Oil, natural gas.

**Agriculture:** Beef cattle, horses, sheep and goats; cotton, hay, pecans; 20,000 acres irrigated. Market value $18.7 million.

**MIDLAND** (95,222) county seat; petroleum, petrochemical center; varied manufacturing; livestock sale center; hospitals; cultural activities; junior college; Celebration of the Arts in May; polo club, Texas League baseball. Part (1,042) of **Odessa**.

1 MIDLAND AIRPARK
2 MIDLAND INTERNATIONAL AIRPORT

| | |
|---|---|
| Population | 117,669 |
| Change fm 2000 | 1.4 |
| Area (sq. mi.) | 901.97 |
| Land Area (sq. mi.) | 900.25 |
| Altitude (ft.) | 2,600-2,985 |
| Rainfall (in.) | 15.2 |
| Jan. mean min. | 29 |
| July mean max. | 95 |
| Civ. Labor | 63,787 |
| Unemployed | 4.4 |
| Wages | $419,437,918 |
| Av. Weekly Wage | $613.04 |
| Prop. Value | $5,905,521,520 |
| Retail Sales | $1,541,108,458 |

For explanation of sources, abbreviations and symbols, see p. 138.

# Milam County

**Physical Features:** East central county of partly level Blackland; southeast rolling to Post Oak Belt; Brazos, Little rivers.

**Economy:** Aluminum manufacturing; other varied manufacturing; lignite mining; agribusiness.

**History:** Lipan Apaches, Tonkawas and Comanches in area. Mission San Francisco Xavier established in 1746. Anglo-American settlers arrived in 1834. County created 1836 from municipality named for Ben Milam, a leader who died at the battle for San Antonio in December 1835; organized 1837.

**Race/Ethnicity, 2000:** (In percent) Anglo, 69.64; Black, 11.01; Hispanic 18.63; Other, 0.72.

**Vital Statistics, 2001:** Births, 359; deaths, 306; marriages, 179; divorces, 78.

**Recreation:** Fishing, hunting; historic sites include Fort Sullivan, Indian battlegrounds, mission site; museum in old jail at Cameron.

**Minerals:** Large lignite deposits; limited oil, natural gas production.

**Agriculture:** Cattle, poultry, hay, corn, sorghum, cotton. Market value $70.6 million.

**CAMERON** (5,805) county seat; government/services; manufacturing; hospital; library; restored courthouse; dewberry festival in April.

**Rockdale** (5,615) aluminum plant, utility company; agribusiness; hospital; Milam Opry monthly, Jubilee Days in June.

Other towns include: **Ben Arnold** (148); **Buckholts** (401); **Burlington** (140); **Davilla** (200); **Gause** (400); **Maysfield** (140); **Milano** (414); **Thorndale** (1,323) market center.

| | |
|---|---|
| Population | 24,880 |
| Change fm 2000 | 2.6 |
| Area (sq. mi.) | 1,021.67 |
| Land Area (sq. mi.) | 1,016.71 |
| Altitude (ft.) | 250-648 |
| Rainfall (in.) | 34.2 |
| Jan. mean min. | 38 |
| July mean max. | 95 |
| Civ. Labor | 9,747 |
| Unemployed | 6.8 |
| Wages | $50,878,140 |
| Av. Weekly Wage | $587.47 |
| Prop. Value | $1,483,232,866 |
| Retail Sales | $155,739,195 |

# Mills County

**Physical Features:** West central county of hills, plateau draining to Colorado River; sandy, loam soils.

**Economy:** Agribusiness, hunting leases.

**History:** Apache-Comanche area of conflict. Anglo-Americans and a few Germans settled in 1850s. County created 1887 from Brown, Comanche, Hamilton, Lampasas counties; named for pioneer jurist John T. Mills.

**Race/Ethnicity, 2000:** (In percent) Anglo, 85.32; Black, 1.30; Hispanic, 13.03; Other, 0.35.

**Vital Statistics, 2001:** Births, 41; deaths, 95; marriages, 32; divorces, 16.

**Recreation:** Fishing; deer, dove and turkey hunting; Regency suspension bridge; rangeland recreation.

**Minerals:** Not significant.

**Agriculture:** Beef cattle, goats, sheep; some irrigation for pecans. Market value $24.7 million.

**GOLDTHWAITE** (1,803) county seat; agribusiness, livestock center; light manufacturing; tourism; barbecue & goat cook-off in April.

Other towns include: **Mullin** (174); **Priddy** (215); **Star** (85).

*For explanation of sources, abbreviations and symbols, see p. 138.*

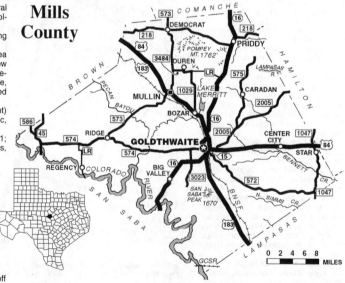

| | |
|---|---|
| Population | 5,133 |
| Change fm 2000 | -0.3 |
| Area (sq. mi.) | 749.89 |
| Land Area (sq. mi.) | 748.11 |
| Altitude (ft.) | 1,200-1,762 |
| Rainfall (in.) | 27.6 |
| Jan. mean min. | 34 |
| July mean max. | 95 |
| Civ. Labor | 2,412 |
| Unemployed | 1.9 |
| Wages | $8,351,563 |
| Av. Weekly Wage | $422.09 |
| Prop. Value | $534,662,904 |
| Retail Sales | $52,144,812 |

# Mitchell County

**Physical Features:** Rolling, draining to Colorado and tributaries; sandy, red, dark soils; Lake Colorado City and Champion Creek Reservoir.

**Economy:** Government/services; agribusiness, oil, some manufacturing.

**History:** Jumano Indians in area; Comanches arrived about 1780. Anglo-American settlers arrived in late 1870s after Comanches were forced into Indian Territory. County created 1876 from Bexar District; organized 1881; named for pioneer brothers Asa and Eli Mitchell.

**Race/Ethnicity, 2000:** (In percent) Anglo, 55.39; Black, 12.79; Hispanic, 31.03; Other, 0.79.

**Vital Statistics, 2001:** Births, 83; deaths, 100; marriages, 67; divorces, 35.

**Recreation:** Lake activities; state park; museums, hunting; railhead arts, crafts show, Colorado City playhouse.

**Minerals:** Oil.

**Agriculture:** Cotton principal crop, grains also produced. Cattle, sheep, goats, hogs raised. Market value $10.1 million.

**COLORADO CITY** (4,304) county seat; prisons; varied manufacturing; tourism; electric service center; hospital; bluegrass festival.

Other towns include: **Loraine** (660) and **Westbrook** (202), trade centers.

LAKE COLORADO CITY STATE PARK

| | | | |
|---|---|---|---|
| Population .................................. 9,348 | Altitude (ft.) ....................... 2,000-2,574 | Unemployed .................................. 4.9 |
| Change fm 2000 ........................... -3.6 | Rainfall (in.) ..................................... 19.8 | Wages .............................. $14,174,013 |
| Area (sq. mi.) ........................... 915.90 | Jan. mean min. ................................. 30 | Av. Weekly Wage ................... $473.22 |
| Land Area (sq. mi.) ................... 910.04 | July mean max. .................................. 97 | Prop. Value ................... $524,921,968 |
| | Civ. Labor .................................... 3,050 | Retail Sales ..................... $34,113,263 |

# Montague County

**Physical Features:** Rolling, draining to tributaries of Trinity, Red rivers; sandy loams, red, black soils; Lake Nocona, Lake Amon G. Carter.

**Economy:** Agribusiness; oil production; varied manufacturing; government/services.

**History:** Kiowas and Wichitas who allied with Comanches. Anglo-American settlements developed in 1850s. County created from Cooke County 1857, organized 1858; named for pioneer Daniel Montague.

**Race/Ethnicity, 2000:** (In percent) Anglo, 93.42; Black, 0.17; Hispanic, 5.41; Other, 1.00.

**Vital Statistics, 2001:** Births, 228; deaths, 278; marriages, 148; divorces, 84.

**Recreation:** Lake activities; quail, turkey, deer hunting; scenic drives; museums; historical sites; Chisholm Trail Days in September, Jim Bowie Days in June.

**Minerals:** Oil, rock, limestone.

**Agriculture:** Beef, dairy cattle; hay, wheat, grasses, pecans, peaches, melons. Some irrigation for peanuts, fruits. Market value $35 million.

**MONTAGUE** (400), county seat.

**BOWIE** (5,220) varied manufacturing, livestock, hospital, library; Second Monday trade day.

**NOCONA** (3,241) athletic goods, boot manufacturing; hospital; Fun Day each May.

Other towns include: **Forestburg** (50); **Ringgold** (100); **Saint Jo** (964) farm center; Pioneer Days on last weekend in May, saloon; **Sunset** (352).

| | | | |
|---|---|---|---|
| Population .............................. 19,237 | Rainfall (in.) ..................................... 32.9 | Wages .............................. $22,680,144 |
| Change fm 2000 ............................ 0.6 | Jan. mean min. ................................. 31 | Av. Weekly Wage ................... $421.81 |
| Area (sq. mi.) ........................... 938.44 | July mean max. .................................. 96 | Prop. Value ............... $1,284,577,184 |
| Land Area (sq. mi.) ................... 930.66 | Civ. Labor .................................... 6,999 | Retail Sales ................. $151,004,336 |
| Altitude (ft.) ......................... 750-1,318 | Unemployed .................................. 6.3 | |

**Physical Features:** Rolling, three-fourths timbered; Sam Houston National Forest; loam, sandy, alluvial soils.

**Economy:** Many residents work in Houston; lumber, oil production; government/services; part of Houston metropolitan area.

**History:** Orcoquisacs and Bidais, removed from area by 1850s. Anglo-Americans arrived in 1820s as part of Austin's colony. County created 1837 from Washington County; named for Richard Montgomery, American Revolution general.

**Race/Ethnicity, 2000:** (In percent) Anglo, 82.09; Black, 3.57; Hispanic, 12.65; Other, 1.69.

**Vital Statistics, 2001:** Births, 4,801; deaths, 2,104; marriages, 2,515; divorces, 1,375.

**Recreation:** Hunting, fishing; Lake Conroe activities; national and state forests; hiking, boating, horseback riding; historic sites.

**Minerals:** Natural gas.

**Agriculture:** Greenhouse crops, forage, beef cattle, horses. Also, Christmas trees and blueberries. Market value $29.3 million. Timber is primary industry.

# Montgomery County

**CONROE** (38,727) county seat; retail/wholesale center; government/services; manufacturing; commuters to Houston; hospital; community college; Cajun Catfish festival in October.

**The Woodlands** (59,603) commuters to Houston, research and biotech businesses, hospital, parks; concerts, festivals at Mitchell Pavilion.

Other towns include: **Cut and Shoot** (1,159); **Dobbin** (170); **Magnolia** (1,198); **Montgomery** (515) historic buildings, antique stores;

New Caney (2,771); Oak Ridge North (3,191); Panorama (2,089); Patton Village (1,445); Pinehurst (4,669); Porter (2,146); Porter Heights (1,549); Roman Forest (1,695); Shenandoah (1,537); Splendora (1,330); Stagecoach (470); Willis (4,153); Woodbranch (1,393); Woodloch (253).

Also, part (458) of **Houston**.

| | |
|---|---|
| Population | 328,449 |
| Change fm 2000 | 11.8 |
| Area (sq. mi.) | 1,076.81 |
| Land Area (sq. mi.) | 1,044.03 |
| Altitude (ft.) | 50-415 |
| Rainfall (in.) | 47.3 |
| Jan. mean min. | 38 |
| July mean max. | 94 |
| Civ. Labor | 156,997 |
| Unemployed | 5.1 |
| Wages | $661,467,694 |
| Av. Weekly Wage | $624.00 |
| Prop. Value | $16,521,663,878 |
| Retail Sales | $3,491,655,569 |

*For explanation of sources, abbreviations and symbols, see p. 138.*

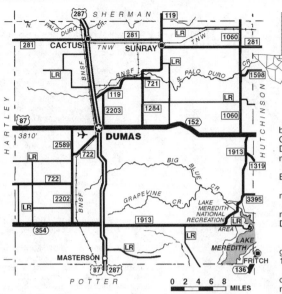

# Moore County

**Physical Features**: Northern Panhandle county; flat to rolling, broken by creeks; sandy loams; lake.

**Economy:** Extensive petroleum operations; major natural gas producing county; varied agribusiness.

**History:** Comanches, removed to Indian Territory in 1874-75; ranching began soon afterward. Farming developed after 1910. Oil boom in 1920s. County created 1876 from Bexar District; organized 1892; named for Republic of Texas navy commander E.W. Moore.

**Race/Ethnicity, 2000:** (In percent) Anglo, 50.54; Black, 0.48; Hispanic, 47.50; Other, 1.48.

**Vital Statistics, 2001:** Births, 391; deaths, 132; marriages, 185; divorces, 82.

**Recreation:** Lake Meredith activities; historical museum; arts center; free overnight RV park; Dogie Days in June.

**Minerals:** Natural gas, oil.

**Agriculture:** Fed beef, corn, wheat, stocker cattle, grain sorghum. Market value $353 million. Irrigation of 162,000 acres.

**DUMAS** (13,917) county seat; tourist, retail trade center; varied agribusiness; hospital, hospice, retirement complex. Other towns include: **Cactus** (2,588), **Sunray** (1,973). Small part of **Fritch**.

| | |
|---|---|
| Population | 20,350 |
| Change fm 2000 | 1.1 |
| Area (sq. mi.) | 909.61 |
| Land Area (sq. mi.) | 899.66 |
| Altitude (ft.) | 2,900-3,810 |
| Rainfall (in.) | 17.4 |
| Jan. mean min. | 20 |
| July mean max. | 92 |
| Civ. Labor | 9,810 |
| Unemployed | 3.9 |
| Wages | $59,992,606 |
| Av. Weekly Wage | $524.29 |
| Prop. Value | $1,758,454,010 |
| Retail Sales | $103,487,137 |

# Morris County

**Physical Features:** East Texas county of forested hills; drains to streams, lakes.

**Economy:** Steel manufacturing, agriculture, timber, government/services.

**History:** Caddo Indians until 1790s. Kickapoo and other tribes in area 1820s-30s. Anglo-American settlement began in mid-1830s. Antebellum slaveholding area. County named for legislator-jurist W.W. Morris; created from Titus County and organized in 1875.

**Race/Ethnicity, 2000:** (In percent) Anglo, 71.26; Black, 24.26; Hispanic, 3.66; Other, 0.82.

**Vital Statistics, 2001:** Births, 149; deaths, 190; marriages, 148; divorces, 57.

**Recreation:** Activities on Lake O' the Pines, small lakes; fishing, hunting; state park.

**Minerals:** Iron ore.

**Agriculture:** Beef cattle, broiler production; hay. Market value $16.4 million. Timber industry significant.

**DAINGERFIELD** (2,499) county seat; varied manufacturing; library, city park; Northeast Texas Community College; Captain Daingerfield Day in October.

Other towns include: **Cason** (173); **Lone Star** (1,624) oil-field equipment manufactured, catfish farming, Starfest in September; **Naples** (1,401) trailer manufacturing, livestock, watermelon festival in July; **Omaha** (999).

| | |
|---|---|
| Population | 13,240 |
| Change fm 2000 | 1.5 |
| Area (sq. mi.) | 258.64 |
| Land Area (sq. mi.) | 254.51 |
| Altitude (ft.) | 228-598 |
| Rainfall (in.) | 44.6 |
| Jan. mean min. | 35 |
| July mean max. | 95 |
| Civ. Labor | 6,322 |
| Unemployed | 8.2 |
| Wages | $38,618,997 |
| Av. Weekly Wage | $657.67 |
| Prop. Value | $692,202,333 |
| Retail Sales | $85,939,443 |

*For explanation of sources, abbreviations and symbols, see p. 138.*

# Motley County

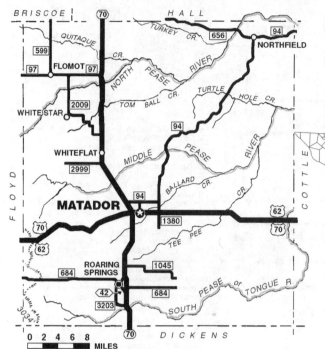

**Physical Features:** Western county just below Caprock; rough terrain, broken by Pease tributaries; sandy to red clay soils.

**Economy:** Government/services; ranching; cotton; light manufacturing; hunting.

**History:** Comanches, removed to Indian Territory by U.S. Army in 1874-75. Ranching began in late 1870s. County created out of Bexar District 1876; organized 1891; named for Dr. J.W. Mottley, signer of Texas Declaration of Independence (name misspelled in statute).

**Race/Ethnicity, 2000:** (In percent) Anglo, 83.17; Black, 4.00; Hispanic, 12.13; Other, 0.70.

**Vital Statistics, 2001:** Births, 14; deaths, 19; marriages, 5; divorces, 3.

**Recreation:** Quail, dove, turkey, deer hunting; Matador Ranch headquarters; spring-fed pool at Roaring Springs; camp grounds; settlers reunion in August.

**Minerals:** Minimal.

**Agriculture:** Beef cattle, cotton, peanuts, hunting leases. Also vegetables, wheat, hay produced. Extensive irrigation. Market value $12.8 million.

**MATADOR** (738) county seat; farm trade center; museum; pony express days in June.

Other towns include: **Flomot** (181) and **Roaring Springs** (274).

| | | | |
|---|---|---|---|
| Population | 1,336 | July mean max | 95 |
| Change fm 2000 | -6.3 | Civ. Labor | 712 |
| Area (sq. mi.) | 989.81 | Unemployed | 2.1 |
| Land Area (sq. mi.) | 989.38 | Wages | $1,696,523 |
| Altitude (ft.) | 1,900-3,034 | Av. Weekly Wage | $367.61 |
| Rainfall (in.) | 21.2 | Prop. Value | $122,764,359 |
| Jan. mean min. | 26 | Retail Sales | $5,763,827 |

*Bass fishermen move out on Sam Rayburn Reservoir. File photo.*

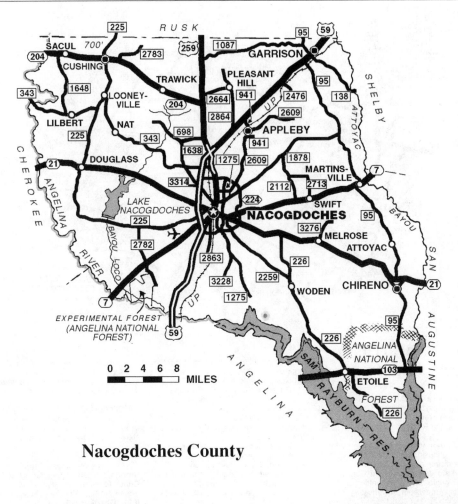

## Nacogdoches County

**Physical Features:** East Texas county on divide between streams; hilly; two-thirds forested; red, gray, sandy soils; Sam Rayburn Reservoir.

**Economy:** Agribusiness; timber; manufacturing; education; tourism.

**History:** Caddo tribes, joined by displaced Cherokees in 1820s. Indians moved west of Brazos by 1840. Spanish missions established in 1716. Spanish settlers in mid-1700s. Anglo-Americans arrived in 1820s. Original county of Republic 1836, organized 1837.

**Race/Ethnicity, 2000:** (In percent) Anglo, 70.83; Black, 16.80; Hispanic, 11.25; Other, 1.12.

**Vital Statistics, 2001:** Births, 813; deaths, 515; marriages, 549; divorces, 130.

**Recreation:** Lake, river activities; Stephen F. Austin State University events; Angelina National Forest; historic sites; major tourist attractions include the Old Stone

Fort, pioneer homes, museums; Piney Woods Fair, Blueberry Festival in June.

**Minerals:** First Texas oil found here, 1866; gas, oil, clay, stone.

**Agriculture:** A leading poultry-producing county; beef cattle raised. Market value $182.8 million. Substantial timber sold.

**NACOGDOCHES** (30,037) county seat; varied manufacturing; lumber mills, wood products; trade center; hospitals; Stephen F. Austin State University.

Other towns include: **Appleby** (449), **Chireno** (410), **Cushing** (635), **Douglass** (75), **Etoile** (70), **Garrison** (859), **Martinsville** (126), **Sacul** (170), **Woden** (70).

| | |
|---|---:|
| **Population** | 59,514 |
| Change fm 2000 | 0.5 |
| Area (sq. mi.) | 981.33 |
| Land Area (sq. mi.) | 946.77 |
| Altitude (ft.) | 164-700 |
| Rainfall (in.) | 47.5 |
| Jan. mean min. | 36 |
| July mean max. | 94 |
| Civ. Labor | 26,441 |
| Unemployed | 4.2 |
| Wages | $134,386,960 |
| Av. Weekly Wage | $475.85 |
| Prop. Value | $2,426,555,240 |
| Retail Sales | $600,571,069 |

*For explanation of sources, abbreviations and symbols, see p. 138.*

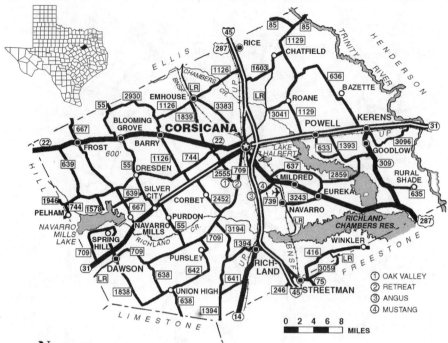

# Navarro County

**Physical Features:** North central county of level Blackland, some rolling; drains to creeks, Trinity River; Navarro Mills Lake, Richland-Chambers Reservoir.

**Economy:** Diversified manufacturing; agribusinesses; oil-field operations, distribution.

**History:** Kickapoo and Comanche area. Anglo-Americans settled in late 1830s. Antebellum slaveholding area.

County created from Robertson County, organized in 1846; named for Republic of Texas leader José Antonio Navarro.

**Race/Ethnicity, 2000:** (In percent) Anglo, 66.12; Black, 16.96; Hispanic, 15.76; Other, 1.16.

**Vital Statistics, 2001:** Births, 721; deaths, 539; marriages, 457; divorces, 209.

**Recreation:** Lake activities; Pioneer Village; historic buildings; youth exposition, Derrick Days in April.

**Minerals:** Longest continuous Texas oil flow; more than 200 million barrels produced since 1895; natural

gas, sand and gravel also produced.

**Agriculture:** Beef cattle, hay, grain sorghum, horses, dairy, cotton, wheat, herbs. Market value $41.5 million.

**CORSICANA** (24,950) county seat; major distribution center; varied manufacturing; agribusiness; hospital; Navarro College; Texas Youth Commission facility.

Other towns include: **Angus** (349); **Barry** (214); **Blooming Grove** (871); **Chatfield** (40); **Dawson** (908); **Emhouse** (162); **Eureka** (350); **Frost** (683); **Goodlow** (267).

Also, **Kerens** (1,739) some manufacturing; **Mildred** (422); **Mustang** (49); **Navarro** (203); **Oak Valley** (410); **Powell** (106); **Purdon** (133); **Retreat** (359); **Rice** (835); **Richland** (307).

| | |
|---|---|
| Population | **46,792** |
| Change fm 2000 | 3.7 |
| Area (sq. mi.) | 1,086.17 |
| Land Area (sq. mi.) | 1,070.66 |
| Altitude (ft.) | 250-600 |
| Rainfall (in.) | 37.9 |
| Jan. mean min. | 33 |
| July mean max. | 94 |
| Civ. Labor | 22,306 |
| Unemployed | 6.1 |
| Wages | $99,644,236 |
| Av. Weekly Wage | $470.53 |
| Prop. Value | $1,892,261,971 |
| Retail Sales | $381,676,496 |

*A statue of José Antonio Navarro sits in front of the Navarro County Courthouse in Corsicana. File photo.*

*For explanation of sources, abbreviations and symbols, see p. 138.*

# Newton County

**Physical Features:** East Texas county of densely forested hills, valleys; spring-fed streams; Toledo Bend Reservoir; Sabine River; mostly sandy soils.

**Economy:** Forestry, government/services, tourism.

**History:** Caddo Indian area. Displaced Coushattas moved across area from South. Anglo-American settlement established in 1830s. Antebellum slaveholding area. County created 1846 from Jasper County; named for American Revolutionary soldier John Newton.

**Race/Ethnicity, 2000:** (In percent) Anglo, 74.57; Black, 20.73; Hispanic, 3.79; Other, 0.91.

**Vital Statistics, 2001:** Births, 150; deaths, 142; marriages, 116; divorces, 97.

**Recreation:** Toledo Bend Reservoir; water sports; fishing, hunting; birding; tourism; state forest; Azalea Canyons. Belgrade, site of early town.

**Minerals:** Oil, gas.

**Agriculture:** Cattle, hay, nursery crops, vegetables, goats, hogs. Market value $1.7 million. Hunting leases. Major forestry area.

**NEWTON** (2,451) county seat; lumber manufacturing; plywood mill; private prison unit; tourist center; genealogical library; Wild Azalea festival in March.

**Deweyville** (1,170) power plant; commercial center for forestry, farming area.

Other towns include: **Bon Wier** (475); **Burkeville** (515); **Call** (170); **South Toledo Bend** (598); **Wiergate** (461).

| | |
|---|---|
| Population | 14,946 |
| Change fm 2000 | -0.8 |
| Area (sq. mi.) | 939.51 |
| Land Area (sq. mi.) | 932.69 |
| Altitude (ft.) | 23-510 |
| Rainfall (in.) | 56 |
| Jan. mean min. | 40 |
| July mean max. | 93 |
| Civ. Labor | 6,024 |
| Unemployed | 15.8 |
| Wages | $12,593,501 |
| Av. Weekly Wage | $507.45 |
| Prop. Value | $809,299,894 |
| Retail Sales | $72,116,509 |

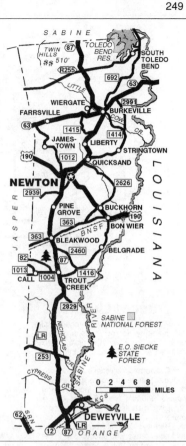

# Nolan County

**Physical Features:** On divide between Brazos, Colorado watersheds; mostly red sandy loams, some waxy, sandy soils; lakes.

**Economy:** Varied manufacturing; oil and gas production; ranching;.

**History:** Anglo-American settlement began in late 1870s. County created from Bexar, Young districts 1876; organized 1881; named for adventurer Philip Nolan, who was killed near Waco.

**Race/Ethnicity, 2000:** (In percent) Anglo, 66.64; Black, 4.85; Hispanic, 28.04; Other, 0.47.

**Vital Statistics, 2001:** Births, 207; deaths, 179; marriages, 153; divorces, 76.

**Recreation:** Lakes; hunting; rattlesnake roundup; pioneer museum; national junior rodeo finals in summer.

**Minerals:** Oil, gas, sand, gravel.

**Agriculture:** Cotton is the principal crop, wheat, sorghum also raised. Beef cattle and dairies. Market value $17.3 million. Twenty percent irrigated.

**SWEETWATER** (11,213) county seat; varied manufacturing, tourism, oil and gas, ranching; hospital; Texas State Technical College.

Other towns include: **Blackwell** (360, partly in Coke County), Oak Creek Reservoir to south; **Maryneal** (61); **Nolan** (47); **Roscoe** (1,323).

| | | | |
|---|---|---|---|
| Population | 15,172 | Rainfall (in.) | 24.4 | Wages | $34,836,854 |

| | |
|---|---|
| Population | 15,172 |
| Change fm 2000 | -4.0 |
| Area (sq. mi.) | 913.93 |
| Land Area (sq. mi.) | 911.98 |
| Altitude (ft.) | 1,990-2,603 |

| | |
|---|---|
| Rainfall (in.) | 24.4 |
| Jan. mean min. | 30 |
| July mean max. | 94 |
| Civ. Labor | 7,002 |
| Unemployed | 5.4 |

| | |
|---|---|
| Wages | $34,836,854 |
| Av. Weekly Wage | $463.87 |
| Prop. Value | $867,417,606 |
| Retail Sales | $135,791,494 |

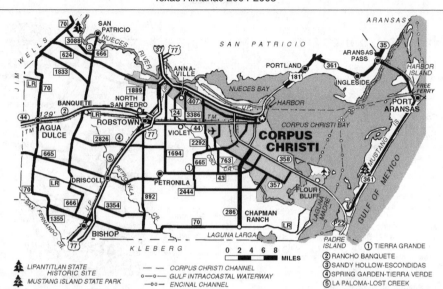

# Nueces County

**Physical Features:** Southern Gulf Coast county; flat, rich soils, broken by bays, Nueces River, Petronila Creek; includes Mustang Island, north tip of Padre Island.

**Economy:** Diversified economy includes petroleum processing and production; deepwater port facilities; agriculture; tourism, conventions; coastal shipping; manufacturing; military complex.

**History:** Coahuiltecan, Karankawa and other tribes who succumbed to disease or fled by 1840s. Spanish settlers arrived in 1760s. Settlers from Ireland arrived around 1830. County name is Spanish for nuts; county named for river; created 1846 out of San Patricio County.

**Race/Ethnicity, 2000:** (In percent) Anglo, 38.32; Black, 4.24; Hispanic, 55.78; Other, 1.66.

**Vital Statistics, 2001:** Births, 5,186; deaths, 2,524; marriages, 2,643; divorces, 1,541.

**Recreation:** Major resort area; fishing, water sports, birding; Padre Island National Seashore; Mustang Island State Park; Lipantitlan State Historic Site; Art Museum of South Texas, Corpus Christi Museum of Science and History; Texas State Aquarium; various metropolitan events; greyhound race track.

**Minerals:** Sand and gravel, oil and gas.

**Agriculture:** Grain sorghum (a leader in sales, acreage); cotton, corn, nursery crops. Beef cattle, hogs, goats. Market value $71.9 million.

**CORPUS CHRISTI** (279,241) county seat; varied manufacturing; petroleum processing; seaport; hospitals; museums; recreation centers; tourist destination; Naval Air Station; Army depot; Texas A&M University-Corpus Christi; Del Mar College; Buccaneer Days; replicas of Columbus' ships on display, U.S.S. Lexington museum.

**Port Aransas** (3,486) tourism, sea research institute, fishing accomodations, fisheries management, deep sea roundup, birding facility, ferry to Aransas Pass; Celebration of Whooping Cranes in Febuary.

**Robstown** (12,677) market center for oil, farm area; Cottonfest in October; Fiesta Mexicana in March.

Other towns include: **Agua Dulce** (745); **Banquete** (449); **Bishop** (3,320) petrochemicals, agriculture, pharmaceuticals, plastics; nature trail; Old Tyme Faire in April; **Chapman Ranch** (100); **Driscoll** (818); **La Paloma-Lost Creek** (351); **North San Pedro** (926); **Petronila** (87); **Rancho Banquete** (473); **Sandy Hollow-Escondidas** (459); **Spring Garden-Tierra Verde** (718); **Tierra Grande** (345).

Also, part of **San Patricio** and a small part of **Aransas Pass** on Harbor Island; both cities mostly in San Patricio County.

**Flour Bluff** and **Annaville** are now part of Corpus Christi.

| | |
|---|---:|
| **Population** | **314,696** |
| Change fm 2000 | 0.3 |
| Area (sq. mi.) | 1,166.42 |
| Land Area (sq. mi.) | 835.82 |
| Altitude (ft.) | sea level-129 |
| Rainfall (in.) | 30.1 |
| Jan. mean min. | 45 |
| July mean max. | 93 |
| Civ. Labor | 150,836 |
| Unemployed | 6.3 |
| Wages | $1,042,041,716 |
| Av. Weekly Wage | $563.61 |
| Prop. Value | $13,309,416,897 |
| Retail Sales | $3,258,939,348 |

*For explanation of sources, abbreviations and symbols, see p. 138.*

*Riders drive cattle along the beach on Matagorda Island. File photo.*

# Ochiltree County

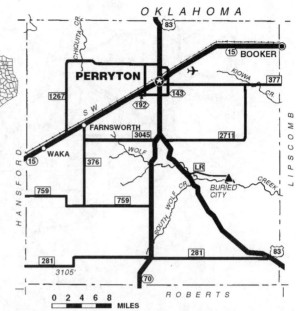

**Physical Features:** Panhandle county bordering Oklahoma; level, broken by creeks; deep loam, clay soils.

**Economy:** Oil and gas; agribusiness, center of large feedlot and swine operations.

**History:** Apaches, pushed out by Comanches in late 1700s. Comanches removed to Indian Territory in 1874-75. Ranching developed in 1880s; farming after 1900. County created from Bexar District 1876, organized 1889; named for Republic of Texas leader W.B. Ochiltree.

**Race/Ethnicity, 2000:** (In percent) Anglo, 66.95; Black, 0.11; Hispanic, 31.79; Other, 1.15.

**Vital Statistics, 2001:** Births, 158; deaths, 70; marriages, 151; divorces, 45.

**Recreation:** Wolf Creek park; Wheatheart of the Nation celebration in August; Museum of the Plains; Indian "Buried City" site; pheasant hunting, also deer and dove.

**Minerals:** Oil, natural gas, caliche.

**Agriculture:** Cattle, swine, wheat, soybeans, grain sorghum, corn; 80,000 acres irrigated. Market value $176.1 million.

**PERRYTON** (7,922) county seat; oil and gas, cattle feeding; grain center; hospital; convention center.

Other towns include: **Farnsworth** (130); **Waka** (65). Also, **Booker** (1,259, mostly in Lipscomb County.

| | |
|---|---|
| Population | **9,048** |
| Change fm 2000 | 0.5 |
| Area (sq. mi.) | 918.07 |
| Land Area (sq. mi.) | 917.56 |
| Altitude (ft.) | 2,642-3,105 |
| Rainfall (in.) | 19.5 |
| Jan. mean min. | 17 |
| July mean max. | 94 |
| Civ. Labor | 4,611 |
| Unemployed | 2.9 |
| Wages | $24,929,234 |
| Av. Weekly Wage | $527.69 |
| Prop. Value | $710,755,689 |
| Retail Sales | $66,001,495 |

# Oldham County

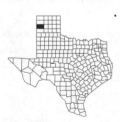

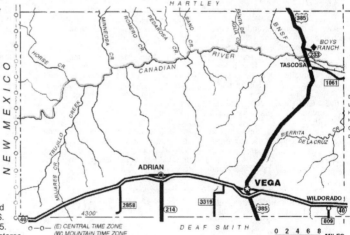

**Physical Features:** Northwestern Panhandle county; level, broken by Canadian River and tributaries.

**Economy:** Ranching center.

**History:** Apaches; followed later by Comanches, Kiowas. U.S. Army removed Indians in 1875. Anglo ranchers and Spanish *pastores* (sheep men) from New Mexico were in area in 1870s. County created 1876 from Bexar District; organized 1880; named for editor-Confederate senator W.S. Oldham.

**Race/Ethnicity, 2000:** (In percent) Anglo, 85.13; Black, 2.24; Hispanic, 11.03; Other, 1.60.

**Vital Statistics, 2001:** Births, 16; deaths, 22; marriages, 14; divorces, 7.

**Recreation:** Old Tascosa with Boot Hill Cemetery nearby, pioneer town; County Roundup in August; youth cowboy poetry gathering in June; midway point on old Route 66.

**Minerals:** Sand and gravel, oil, natural gas, stone.

**Agriculture:** Beef cattle; crops include wheat, grain sorghum. Market value $90.7 million.

**VEGA** (907) county seat; ranch trade center; museums.

Other towns include: **Adrian** (156); **Wildorado** (180). Cal Farley's Boys Ranch.

*For explanation of sources, abbreviations and symbols, see p. 138.*

| | |
|---|---|
| Population | **2,156** |
| Change fm 2000 | -1.3 |
| Area (sq. mi.) | 1,501.42 |
| Land Area (sq. mi.) | 1,500.63 |
| Altitude (ft.) | 3,200-4,300 |
| Rainfall (in.) | 17.4 |
| Jan. mean min. | 19 |
| July mean max. | 91 |
| Civ. Labor | 1,270 |
| Unemployed | 2.8 |
| Wages | $6,131,912 |
| Av. Weekly Wage | $483.78 |
| Prop. Value | $252,726,254 |
| Retail Sales | $9,633,568 |

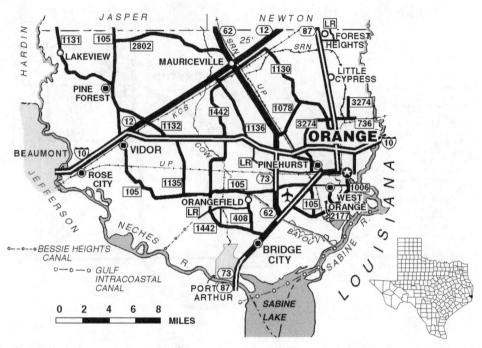

# Orange County

**Physical Features:** In southeastern corner of the state; bounded by Sabine, Neches rivers, Sabine Lake; coastal soils; two-thirds timbered.

**Economy:** Petrochemicals; varied manufacturing; agribusiness; tourism; lumber processing.

**History:** Atakapan Indian area. French traders in area by 1720. Anglo-American settlement began in 1820s. County created from Jefferson County in 1852; named for early orange grove.

**Race/Ethnicity, 2000:** (In percent) Anglo, 86.54; Black, 8.50; Hispanic, 3.62; Other, 1.34.

**Vital Statistics, 2001:** Births, 1,054; deaths, 911; marriages, 756; divorces, 487.

**Recreation:** Fishing, hunting; water sports; birding; county park; museums; historical homes; crawfish and crab festivals in spring.

**Minerals:** Salt, oil, gas, clays, sand and gravel.

**Agriculture:** Cattle, hay, Christmas trees and rice are top revenue sources; honey a significant revenue producer; fruits, berries, vegetables. Also, crawfishing. Market value $4.6 million. Hunting leases. Timber important.

**ORANGE** (18,352) county seat; seaport; petrochemical plants; varied manufacturing; food, timber processing; shipping; hospital, theater, museums; Lamar State College-Orange; gumbo festival in May.

**Bridge City** (8,691) varied manufacturing; ship repair yard; steel fabrication; fish farming; government/services; library; tall bridge and newer suspension bridge over Neches; stop for Monarch butterfly in fall during its migration to Mexico.

**Vidor** (11,466) steel processing; railroad-car refinishing; library; barbecue festival in April.

Other towns include: **Mauriceville** (2,786); **Pine Forest** (627); **Pinehurst** (2,167); **Rose City** (523); **West Orange** (4,023).

| | |
|---|---|
| Population | **84,364** |
| Change fm 2000 | -0.7 |
| Area (sq. mi.) | 379.54 |
| Land Area (sq. mi.) | 356.40 |
| Altitude (ft.) | sea level-25 |
| Rainfall (in.) | 58.3 |
| Jan. mean min. | 39 |
| July mean max. | 91 |
| Civ. Labor | 40,788 |
| Unemployed | 10.6 |
| Wages | $186,330,301 |
| Av. Weekly Wage | $593.75 |
| Prop. Value | $4,495,332,210 |
| Retail Sales | $595,626,116 |

# Palo Pinto County

**Physical Features:** North central county west of Fort Worth; broken, hilly, wooded in parts; Possum Kingdom Lake, Lake Palo Pinto; sandy, gray, black soils.

**Economy:** Varied manufacturing; tourism; petroleum; agribusiness.

**History:** Anglo-American ranchers arrived in 1850s. Conflicts between settlers and numerous Indian tribes who had sought refuge on Brazos resulted in Texas Rangers removing Indians in 1856. County created 1856 from Bosque, Navarro counties; organized 1857; named for creek (in Spanish name means painted stick).

**Race/Ethnicity, 2000:** (In percent) Anglo, 82.77; Black, 2.51; Hispanic, 13.57; Other, 1.15.

**Vital Statistics, 2001:** Births, 371; deaths, 399; marriages, 256; divorces, 137.

**Recreation:** Lake activities; hunting, fishing, water sports; state park; Rails to Trails conversion for hiking, biking.

**Minerals:** Oil, gas, clays, sand and gravel.

**Agriculture:** Cattle, dairy products, nursery crops, hay, wheat. Market value $17.5 million. Cedar fence posts marketed.

**PALO PINTO** (411) county seat; old settlers reunion; government center.

**MINERAL WELLS** (17,163, small part [2,176] in Parker County) varied manufacturing; tourism; agriculture; hospital, prison; Weatherford College extension; Crazy Water Festival in October; state park east of city in Parker County.

Other towns include: **Gordon** (473), **Graford** (589) retirement and recreation area; Mardi Gras along the Brazos; **Mingus** (259), **Santo** (445), **Strawn** (756).

**(Map on next page.)**

For explanation of sources, abbreviations and symbols, see p. 138.

# Palo Pinto County

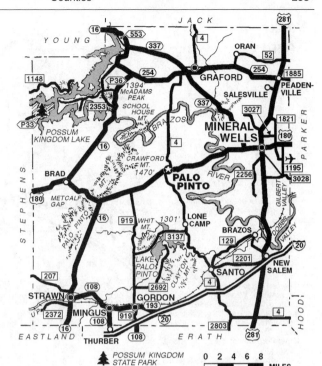

| | |
|---|---|
| Population | 27,306 |
| Change fm 2000 | 1.0 |
| Area (sq. mi.) | 985.50 |
| Land Area (sq. mi.) | 952.93 |
| Altitude (ft.) | 782-1,470 |
| Rainfall (in.) | 32.2 |
| Jan. mean min. | 30 |
| July mean max. | 96 |
| Civ. Labor | 11,674 |
| Unemployed | 5.8 |
| Wages | $46,728,316 |
| Av. Weekly Wage | $453.73 |
| Prop. Value | $1,593,105,301 |
| Retail Sales | $270,061,072 |

🌲 POSSUM KINGDOM STATE PARK

0 2 4 6 8 MILES

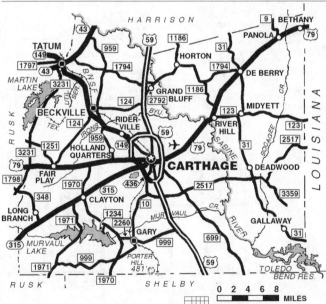

0 2 4 6 8 MILES

| | |
|---|---|
| Population | 22,734 |
| Change fm 2000 | -0.1 |
| Area (sq. mi.) | 821.34 |
| Land Area (sq. mi.) | 800.92 |
| Altitude (ft.) | 172-481 |
| Rainfall (in.) | 48.0 |
| Jan. mean min. | 33 |
| July mean max. | 94 |
| Civ. Labor | 7,897 |
| Unemployed | 7.9 |
| Wages | $41,182,319 |
| Av. Weekly Wage | $484.90 |

| | |
|---|---|
| Prop. Value | $3,107,320,715 |
| Retail Sales | $159,124,508 |

# Panola County

**Physical Features:** East Texas county; sixty percent forested, rolling plain; broken by Sabine, Murvaul Creek and Lake, Toledo Bend Reservoir.

**Economy:** Gas processing; oilfield operation; agribusinesses; food processing; varied manufacturing; forest industries.

**History:** Caddo area. Anglo-American settlement established in 1833. Antebellum slaveholding area. County name is Indian word for cotton; created from Harrison, Shelby counties 1846.

**Race/Ethnicity, 2000:** (In percent) Anglo, 77.97; Black, 17.85; Hispanic, 3.51; Other, 0.67.

**Vital Statistics, 2001:** Births, 275; deaths, 251; marriages, 207; divorces, 77.

**Recreation:** Lake fishing, other water activities; hunting; scenic drives; Jim Reeves memorial and Tex Ritter museum; historic sites, homes.

**Minerals:** Oil, gas.

**Agriculture:** A leading broiler-producing county; beef cattle, forages; market value $51.2 million. Timber sales significant.

**CARTHAGE** (6,629) county seat; petroleum processing; poultry; sawmills; hospital; junior college.

Other towns include: **Beckville** (745), **Clayton** (79), **DeBerry** (191), **Gary** (300), **Long Branch** (181), **Panola** (296). Also, **Tatum** (1,182, mostly in Rusk County).

For explanation of sources, abbreviations and symbols, see p. 138.

# Parker County

**Physical Features:** Hilly, broken by Brazos, Trinity tributaries, lakes; varied soils.

**Economy:** Agribusiness; varied manufacturing; government/services; many residents work in Fort Worth; county part of Fort Worth-Arlington metropolitan area.

**History:** Comanche and Kiowa area in late 1840s when Anglo-American settlers arrived. County named for pioneer legislator Isaac Parker; created 1855 from Bosque, Navarro counties.

**Race/Ethnicity, 2000:** (In percent) Anglo, 90.05; Black, 1.87; Hispanic, 7.02; Other, 1.06.

**Vital Statistics, 2001:** Births, 1,110; deaths, 741; marriages, 679; divorces, 361.

**Recreation:** Water sports; state park; nature trails; hunting; horse racing at Trinity Meadows; Peach Festival in July and frontier days; first Monday trade days monthly.

**Minerals:** Natural gas, oil, stone, sand and gravel, clays.

**Agriculture:** Cattle, horticultural plants, horses, dairies, peaches, peanuts, pecans. Market value $59.2 million.

**WEATHERFORD** (20,260) county seat; agribusiness center; varied manufacturing; government/services; commuting; hospital; Weatherford College; Civil War weekend in September.

Other towns include: **Aledo** (1,909); **Annetta** (1,189), **Annetta North** (503) and **Annetta South** (582); **Cool** (161); **Dennis** (90); **Hudson Oaks** (1,686); **Millsap** (367); **Peaster** (102); **Poolville** (520); **Reno** (2,493); **Sanctuary** (376);

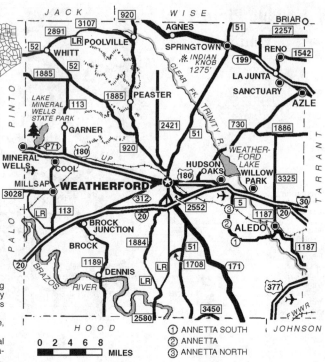

① ANNETTA SOUTH
② ANNETTA
③ ANNETTA NORTH

0 2 4 6 8 MILES

**Springtown** (2,221) government/services, manufacturing; **Whitt** (38); **Willow Park** (3,043).

Also, part of **Azle** (9,971) and **Briar**, (5,531), both mostly in Tarrant County, and part (2,176) of **Mineral Wells.**

Population ............................. 94,618
Change fm 2000 ........................... 6.9
Area (sq. mi.) ........................... 910.09

Land Area (sq. mi.) ..................... 903.51
Altitude (ft.) ........................ 700-1,275
Rainfall (in.) ............................. 32.9
Jan. mean min. .............................. 28
July mean max. .............................. 96
Civ. Labor .............................. 45,912
Unemployed .................................. 5.0
Wages ............................ $123,953,087
Av. Weekly Wage ..................... $507.42
Prop. Value ................... $4,785,993,400
Retail Sales ................. $1,055,186,888

# Parmer County

Population ........................................ 9,877
Change fm 2000 .................................... -1.4
Area (sq. mi.) ................................. 885.17
Land Area (sq. mi.) ........................... 881.66
Altitude (ft.) ........................... 3,850-4,400
Rainfall (in.) ................................... 16.8
Jan. mean min. ..................................... 21
July mean max. ..................................... 90
Civ. Labor ...................................... 4,338
Unemployed ........................................ 2.9
Wages ..................................... $31,369,904
Av. Weekly Wage ........................... $508.98
Prop. Value ........................... $535,159,790
Retail Sales ........................... $43,832,987

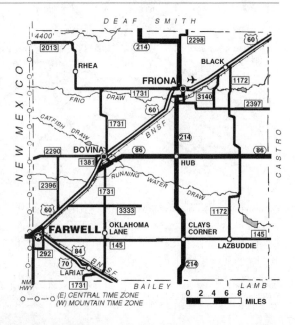

(E) CENTRAL TIME ZONE
(W) MOUNTAIN TIME ZONE

0 2 4 6 8 MILES

**Physical Features:** Western High Plains, broken by draws, playas; sandy, clay, loam soils.

**Economy:** Cattle feeding; grain elevators; meat-packing plant; other agribusiness.

**History:** Apaches, pushed out in late 1700s by Comanches, Kiowas. U.S. Army removed Indians in 1874-75. Anglo-Americans arrived in 1880s. Mexican migration increased after 1950. County named for Republic figure

**(Map on preceding page.)**

# Parmer County

Martin Parmer; created from Bexar District 1876, organized 1907.

**Race/Ethnicity, 2000:** (In percent) Anglo, 49.17; Black, 1.01; Hispanic, 49.19; Other, 0.63.

**Vital Statistics, 2001:** Births, 150; deaths, 85; marriages, 53; divorces, 28.

**Recreation:** Hunting, Border Town Days in July.

**Minerals:** Not significant.

**Agriculture:** Among leading counties in total farm income. Beef cattle;

crops include wheat, corn, cotton, grain sorghum, alfalfa; apples and potatoes also raised; 190,000 acres irrigated. Market value $574 million.

**FARWELL** (1,313) county seat; agribusiness center; grain storage; plants make farm equipment.

**FRIONA** (3,812) feedlots, meat packing, trucking, grain elevators, hospital; Maize Days in September.

Other towns include: **Bovina** (1,817) farm trade center; **Lazbuddie** (248).

## Pecos County

**Physical Features:** Second largest county; high, broken plateau in West Texas; draining to Pecos and tributaries; sandy, clay, loam soils.

**Economy:** Oil, gas; tourism; government/services; agriculture; wind turbines.

**History:** Comanches in area when military outpost established in 1859. Settlement began after Civil War. County created from Presidio 1871; organized 1872; named for Pecos River, name origin uncertain.

**Race/Ethnicity, 2000:** (In percent) Anglo, 33.98; Black, 4.21; Hispanic, 61.05; Other, 0.76.

**Vital Statistics, 2001:** Births, 223; deaths, 128; marriages, 86; divorces, 10.

**Recreation:** Old Fort Stockton, Annie Riggs Museum, stagecoach stop; scenic drives; Dinosaur Track Roadside Park; cattle-trail sites; archaeological museum with oil, ranch-heritage collec-

tions; Cinco de Mayo.

**Minerals:** Natural gas, oil.

**Agriculture:** Cotton, alfalfa, hay, pecans, onions, melons, vineyard; 10,000 acres irrigated. Cattle, sheep, goats, horses. Market value $42 million. Aquaculture firm producing shrimp. Hunting leases.

**FORT STOCKTON** (7,693) county seat, distribution center for petroleum industry, government/services, agriculture, tourism, varied manufacturing, winery, hospital, historical tours, prison units, spaceport launching small satellites.

**Iraan** (1,211) oil, gas center, tourism; ranching, meat processing, hospital, birthplace of Alley Oop comic strip, chili, brisket cookoff.

Other towns include: **Coyanosa** (138); **Girvin** (30); **Imperial** (432), center for irrigated farming; **Sheffield** (400), oil, gas center.

| | |
|---|---|
| Population | 16,421 |
| Change fm 2000 | -2.3 |
| Area (sq. mi.) | 4,764.73 |
| Land Area (sq. mi.) | 4,763.66 |
| Altitude (ft.) | 2,168-5,200 |
| Rainfall (in.) | 13.9 |
| Jan. mean min. | 30 |
| July mean max. | 95 |
| Civ. Labor | 6,314 |
| Unemployed | 6.1 |
| Wages | $28,974,008 |
| Av. Weekly Wage | $459.45 |
| Prop. Value | $2,364,902,795 |
| Retail Sales | $100,108,038 |

*For explanation of sources, abbreviations and symbols, see p. 138.*

# Polk County

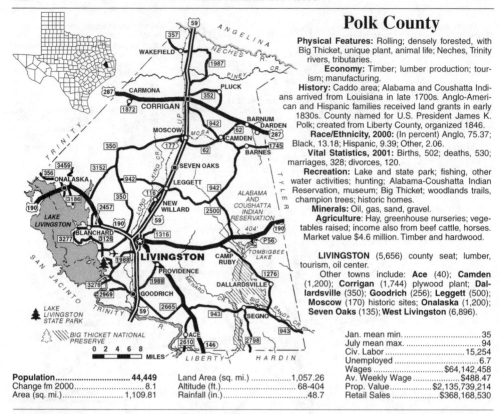

**Physical Features:** Rolling; densely forested, with Big Thicket, unique plant, animal life; Neches, Trinity rivers, tributaries.

**Economy:** Timber; lumber production; tourism; manufacturing.

**History:** Caddo area; Alabama and Coushatta Indians arrived from Louisiana in late 1700s. Anglo-American and Hispanic families received land grants in early 1830s. County named for U.S. President James K. Polk; created from Liberty County, organized 1846.

**Race/Ethnicity, 2000:** (In percent) Anglo, 75.37; Black, 13.18; Hispanic, 9.39; Other, 2.06.

**Vital Statistics, 2001:** Births, 502; deaths, 530; marriages, 328; divorces, 120.

**Recreation:** Lake and state park; fishing, other water activities; hunting; Alabama-Coushatta Indian Reservation, museum; Big Thicket; woodlands trails, champion trees; historic homes.

**Minerals:** Oil, gas, sand, gravel.

**Agriculture:** Hay, greenhouse nurseries; vegetables raised; income also from beef cattle, horses. Market value $4.6 million. Timber and hardwood.

**LIVINGSTON** (5,656) county seat; lumber, tourism, oil center.

Other towns include: **Ace** (40); **Camden** (1,200); **Corrigan** (1,744) plywood plant; **Dallardsville** (350); **Goodrich** (256); **Leggett** (500); **Moscow** (170) historic sites; **Onalaska** (1,200); **Seven Oaks** (135); **West Livingston** (6,896).

| | |
|---|---|
| Jan. mean min. | 35 |
| July mean max. | 94 |
| Civ. Labor | 15,254 |
| Unemployed | 6.7 |
| Wages | $64,142,458 |
| Av. Weekly Wage | $488.47 |
| Prop. Value | $2,135,739,214 |
| Retail Sales | $368,168,530 |

| | | | |
|---|---|---|---|
| Population | 44,449 | Land Area (sq. mi.) | 1,057.26 |
| Change fm 2000 | 8.1 | Altitude (ft.) | 68-404 |
| Area (sq. mi.) | 1,109.81 | Rainfall (in.) | 48.7 |

# Potter County

**Physical Features:** Panhandle county; mostly level, part rolling; broken by Canadian River and tributaries; sandy, sandy loam, chocolate loam, clay soils; Lake Meredith.

**Economy:** Transportation, distribution hub for large area; manufacturing; agribusinesses; tourism; government/services; petrochemicals; gas processing; .

**History:** Apaches, pushed out by Comanches in 1700s. Comanches removed to Indian Territory in 1874-75. Ranching began in late 1870s. Oil boom in 1920s. County named for Robert Potter, Republic leader; created 1876 from Bexar District; organized 1887.

**Race/Ethnicity, 2000:** (In percent) Anglo, 58.49; Black, 10.15; Hispanic, 28.11; Other, 3.25.

**Vital Statistics, 2001:** Births, 2,182; deaths, 1,199; marriages, 1,639; divorces, 429.

**Recreation:** Metropolitan activities, events; lake activities; Alibates Flint Quarries National Monument; hunting, fishing; Tri-State Fair.

**Minerals:** Natural gas, oil, helium.

**Agriculture:** Beef cattle production and processing; wheat, sorghum, cotton. Market value $21.7 million.

**AMARILLO** (176,066 total, part (73,794) in Randall County) county seat; hub for northern Panhandle and ranching; distribution, marketing center; tourism; varied manufacturing; food processing; hospitals; prison; museum; varied cultural, recreational events; junior college, Texas Tech University medical, engineering schools; Texas State Technical College branch; Quarter Horse Heritage Center; *Texas Legacies* outdoor drama,

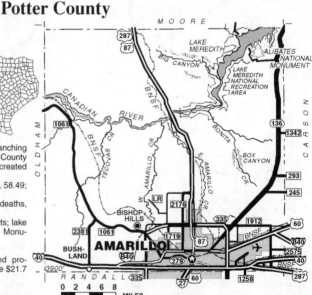

cowboy breakfasts during summer.

Other towns include: **Bishop Hills** (202) and **Bushland** (130).

| | |
|---|---|
| Population | 116,093 |
| Change fm 2000 | 2.2 |
| Area (sq. mi.) | 921.98 |
| Land Area (sq. mi.) | 909.24 |

| | |
|---|---|
| Altitude (ft.) | 2,915-3,900 |
| Rainfall (in.) | 19.6 |
| Jan. mean min. | 21 |
| July mean max. | 92 |
| Civ. Labor | 56,273 |
| Unemployed | 6.1 |
| Wages | $530,318,201 |
| Av. Weekly Wage | $547.94 |
| Prop. Value | $4,711,543,038 |
| Retail Sales | $2,020,321,402 |

# Presidio County

**Physical Features:** Rugged, some of Texas' tallest mountains; scenic drives; clays, loams, sandy loams on uplands; intermountain wash; timber sparse; Capote Falls, state's highest.

**Economy:** Government/services; ranching; hunting leases; tourism.

**History:** Area around Presidio believed to be oldest continuously cultivated farmland in Texas, since 1500 B.C. Jumanos, Apaches and Comanches in area when Spanish arrived in 1680s. Anglo-Americans arrived in 1840s. County created 1850 from Bexar District; organized 1875; named for Spanish Presidio del Norte (fort of the north).

**Race/Ethnicity, 2000:** (In percent) Anglo, 15.03; Black, 0.21; Hispanic, 84.36; Other, 0.40.

**Vital Statistics, 2001:** Births, 149; deaths, 27; marriages, 66; divorces, 0.

**Recreation:** Mild climate and scenic surroundings; hunting; scenic drives along Rio Grande, in mountains; ghost towns, mysterious Marfa Lights; Fort D.A. Russell; Big Bend Ranch State Park; hot springs; Chinati Foundation art festival in fall.

**Minerals:** Sand, gravel, silver, zeolite.

**Agriculture:** Cattle, tomatoes, hay, onions, melons. 5,500 acres irrigated near Rio Grande. Market value $16.5 million.

**MARFA** (2,078) county seat; ranching supply, Border Patrol sector headquarters; tourist center; gateway to mountainous area; Paisano Hotel, headquarters for movie, "Giant"; Old Timers Roping on Memorial Day weekend.

**PRESIDIO** (4,334) international bridge to Ojinaga, Mex., gateway to Mexico's West Coast by rail; Fort Leaton historic site; Onion Festival in May.

Other towns include: **Redford** (132); **Shafter** (26) old mining town.

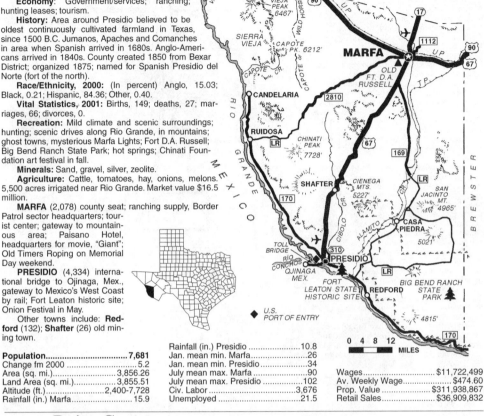

| | |
|---|---|
| Population....................................7,681 | Rainfall (in.) Presidio .....................10.8 |
| Change fm 2000 .............................5.2 | Jan. mean min. Marfa......................26 |
| Area (sq. mi.)............................3,856.26 | Jan. mean min. Presidio...................34 |
| Land Area (sq. mi.)................3,855.51 | July mean max. Marfa .....................90 |
| Altitude (ft.).........................2,400-7,728 | July mean max. Presidio ...............102 |
| Rainfall (in.) Marfa.........................15.9 | Civ. Labor .................................3,676 |
| | Unemployed ...................................21.5 |

| | |
|---|---|
| Wages..............................$11,722,499 |
| Av. Weekly Wage....................$474.60 |
| Prop. Value .........................$311,938,867 |
| Retail Sales.......................$36,909,832 |

# Rains County

**Physical Features:** Northeastern county; rolling; partly Blackland, sandy loams, sandy soils; Sabine River, Lake Tawakoni.

**Economy:** Oil, tourism, agribusinesses, some manufacturing.

**History:** Caddo area. In 1700s, Tawakoni Indians entered the area. Anglo-Americans arrived in 1840s. County, county seat named for Emory Rains, Republic leader; created 1870 from Hopkins, Hunt and Wood counties; birthplace of National Farmers Union, 1902.

**Race/Ethnicity, 2000:** (In percent) Anglo, 90.25; Black, 2.98; Hispanic, 5.53; Other, 1.24.

**Vital Statistics, 2001:** Births, 100; deaths, 112; marriages, 81; divorces, 42.

**Recreation:** Lake Tawakoni and Lake Fork Reservoir activities; Eagle Fest in January.

**Minerals:** Gas, oil.

**Agriculture:** Beef, dairy cattle, horses; crops are vegetables, hay, small grains. Market value $18.5 million.

**EMORY** (1,151) county seat; local trade; tourism; government/services; commuting to Greenville, Dallas; African-American museum.

Other towns include: **East Tawakoni** (806) and **Point** (885), manufacturing, tourism, tamale fest on July 4. Part of **Alba** (439), mostly in Wood County.

*For explanation of sources, abbreviations and symbols, see p. 138.*

| | |
|---|---|
| Population .............................. 10,236 | July mean max. ...............................94 |
| Change fm 2000 ...........................12.0 | Civ. Labor .................................4,006 |
| Area (sq. mi.) ..............................258.87 | Unemployed ...................................6.4 |
| Land Area (sq. mi.) ..................232.05 | Wages .................................$7,109,991 |
| Altitude (ft.) ............................345-600 | Av. Weekly Wage ..................$402.44 |
| Rainfall (in.) ..................................42.9 | Prop. Value..................$407,018,990 |
| Jan. mean min. ..............................31 | Retail Sales ...................$55,668,757 |

# Randall County

**Physical Features:** Northwestern county; level, but broken by scenic Palo Duro Canyon, Buffalo Lake; silty clay, loam soils.

**Economy:** Agribusinesses; education; some manufacturing; tourism; part of Amarillo metropolitan area.

**History:** Comanche Indians removed in mid-1870s; ranching began soon afterward. County created 1876 from Bexar District; organized 1889; named for Confederate Gen. Horace Randal (name misspelled in statute).

**Race/Ethnicity, 2000:** (In percent) Anglo, 86.48; Black, 1.60; Hispanic, 10.27; Other, 1.65.

**Vital Statistics, 2001:** Births, 1,284; deaths, 716; marriages, 324; divorces, 503.

**Recreation:** Palo Duro Canyon State Park, with *Texas Legacies* musical drama a tourist attraction each summer; Panhandle-Plains Historical Museum; West Texas A&M University events; aoudad sheep, migratory waterfowl hunting in season; Buffalo Lake National Wildlife Refuge.

**Minerals:** Not significant.

**Agriculture:** Beef cattle, wheat, sorghum, corn, hay, cotton; 50,000 acres irrigated. Market value $207 million.

**CANYON** (13,245) county seat; West Texas A&M University; tourism; commuting to Amarillo; ranching, farm center; light manufacturing; gateway to state park.

Other towns include: **Lake Tanglewood** (854); **Palisades** (370); **Timbercreek Canyon** (437); **Umbarger** (327). Part (73,794) of **Amarillo** (176,066 total); also, **Happy** (652, mostly in Swisher County).

**① TIMBERCREEK CANYON**
**② PALISADES**
**③ LAKE TANGLEWOOD**

| | |
|---|---|
| Population ........................... 106,822 | July mean max. ............................92 |
| Change fm 2000 ......................... 2.4 | Civ. Labor ............................59,511 |
| Area (sq. mi.) ....................... 922.42 | Unemployed .............................1.4 |
| Land Area (sq. mi.) ................. 914.43 | Wages ................$134,950,492 |
| Altitude (ft.) ................... 2,700-3,900 | Av. Weekly Wage ............$518.99 |
| Rainfall (in.) ............................ 18.9 | Prop. Value...............$4,616,331,885 |
| Jan. mean min. ............................ 23 | Retail Sales .................$705,868,509 |

# Reagan County

**Physical Features:** Western county; level to hilly, broken by draws, Big Lake (intermittent); sandy, loam, clay soils.

**Economy:** Oil production; natural gas; ranching.

**History:** Comanches in area until mid-1870s. Ranching began in 1880s. Hispanic migration increased after 1950. County named for Sen. John H. Reagan, first chairman, Texas Railroad Commission; county created 1903 from Tom Green County.

**Race/Ethnicity, 2000:** (In percent) Anglo, 46.84; Black, 3.04; Hispanic, 49.49; Other, 0.63.

**Vital Statistics, 2001:** Births, 36; deaths, 21; marriages, 30; divorces, 9.

**Recreation:** Texon reunion; rodeo; site of 1923 discovery well Santa Rita No. 1 on University of Texas land.

**Minerals:** Gas, oil.

**Agriculture:** Cotton, cattle, sheep, goats, sheep; cotton, grains principal crops; 36,000 acres irrigated. Market value $9.5 million.

**BIG LAKE** (2,752) county seat; center for oil activities, farming, ranching; hospital; Blue Grass Festival in April.

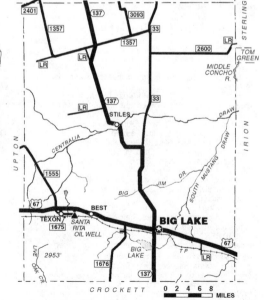

| | |
|---|---|
| Population .....................................3,182 | |
| Change fm 2000 ............................-4.3 | |
| Area (sq. mi.) ...........................1,175.98 | |
| Land Area (sq. mi.) .................1,175.30 | |
| Altitude (ft.) .......................2,400-2,953 | |
| Rainfall (in.).................................19.2 | |

| | |
|---|---|
| Jan. mean min. ................................ 28 | Wages.................................$7,648,575 |
| July mean max. ............................... 94 | Av. Weekly Wage ....................$514.29 |
| Civ. Labor .....................................1,542 | Prop. Value ....................$579,392,300 |
| Unemployed .................................. 2.7 | Retail Sales.....................$18,302,832 |

# Real County

**Physical Features:** Hill Country, spring-fed streams, scenic canyons; Frio, Nueces rivers; cedars, pecans, walnuts, many live oaks.

**Economy:** Ranching; tourism, government/services; cedar cutting.

**History:** Tonkawa area; Lipan Apaches arrived in early 1700s; later, Comanche hunters in area. Spanish mission established 1762. Anglo-Americans arrived in 1850s. County created 1913 from Bandera, Edwards, Kerr counties; named for legislator-ranchman Julius Real.

**Race/Ethnicity, 2000:** (In percent) Anglo, 76.53; Black, 0.23; Hispanic, 22.58; Other, 0.66.

**Vital Statistics, 2001:** Births, 23; deaths, 40; marriages, 24; divorces, 13.

**Recreation:** Tourist, hunting center; many deer killed each season; fishing; camping; scenic drives; state natural area.

**Minerals:** Not significant.

**Agriculture:** Goats, sheep, beef cattle produce most income. Market value $4.1 million. Cedar posts processed.

**LEAKEY** (374) county seat; center for ranching, tourism; cedar-oil mill; medical facilities; July Jubilee.

**CAMP WOOD** (817) San Lorenzo de la Santa Cruz mission site; museum; settlers reunion in August; a tourist, ranching hub for parts of three counties.

Other towns include: **Rio Frio** (50).

| | | | |
|---|---|---|---|
| Population | 2,999 | Rainfall (in.) | 25.7 |
| Change fm 2000 | -1.7 | Jan. mean min. | 29 |
| Area (sq. mi.) | 700.04 | July mean max. | 92 |
| Land Area (sq. mi.) | 699.91 | Civ. Labor | 1,108 |
| Altitude (ft.) | 1,450-2,381 | Unemployed | 3.8 |

| | |
|---|---|
| Wages | $2,838,220 |
| Av. Weekly Wage | $338.49 |
| Prop. Value | $371,313,399 |
| Retail Sales | $10,961,890 |

# Red River County

**Physical Features:** On Red-Sulphur rivers' divide; 39 different soil types; half timbered.

**Economy:** Agribusinesses; lumbering; manufacturing.

**History:** Caddo Indians abandoned area in 1790s. One of the oldest counties; settlers were moving in from the United States in 1810s. Kickapoo and other tribes arrived in 1820s. Antebellum slaveholding area. County created 1836 as original county of the Republic; organized 1837; named for Red River, its northern boundary.

**Race/Ethnicity, 2000:** (In percent) Anglo, 76.65; Black, 17.93; Hispanic, 4.67; Other, 0.75.

**Vital Statistics, 2001:** Births, 162; deaths, 224; marriages, 97; divorces, 41.

**Recreation:** Historical sites include pioneer homes, birthplace of John Nance Garner; water activities; hunting of deer, turkey, duck, small game.

**Minerals:** Small oil flow.

**Agriculture:** Beef cattle, hay, cotton, soybeans, wheat. Market value $46 million. Timber sales substantial.

**CLARKSVILLE** (3,879) county seat; varied manufacturing; hospital; library; century-old courthouse; Historical Society bazaar in October.

Other towns include: **Annona** (280); **Avery** (458); **Bagwell** (150); **Bogata** (1,384); **Detroit** (775) commercial center in west. Part of **Deport** (708).

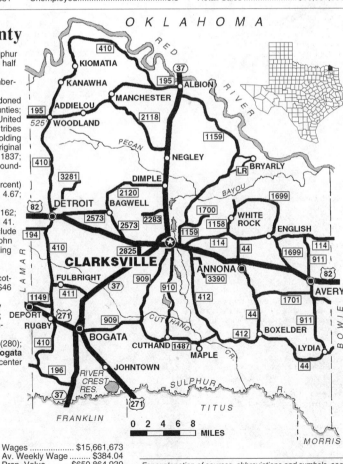

| | |
|---|---|
| Population | 13,941 |
| Change fm 2000 | -2.6 |
| Area (sq. mi.) | 1,057.61 |
| Land Area (sq. mi.) | 1,050.18 |
| Altitude (ft.) | 287-525 |
| Rainfall (in.) | 44.9 |
| Jan. mean min. | 28 |
| July mean max. | 92 |
| Civ. Labor | 5,263 |
| Unemployed | 8.1 |

| | |
|---|---|
| Wages | $15,661,673 |
| Av. Weekly Wage | $384.04 |
| Prop. Value | $650,864,930 |
| Retail Sales | $54,985,202 |

*For explanation of sources, abbreviations and symbols, see p. 138.*

# Reeves County

| | |
|---|---|
| Population | **12,478** |
| Change fm 2000 | -5.0 |
| Area (sq. mi.) | 2,641.95 |
| Land Area (sq. mi.) | 2,635.88 |
| Altitude (ft.) | 2,500-5,000 |
| Rainfall (in.) | 11.0 |
| Jan. mean min. | 27 |
| July mean max. | 99 |
| Civ. Labor | 5,978 |
| Unemployed | 13.0 |
| Wages | $21,767,939 |
| Av. Weekly Wage | $398.68 |
| Prop. Value | $638,172,901 |
| Retail Sales | $80,101,013 |

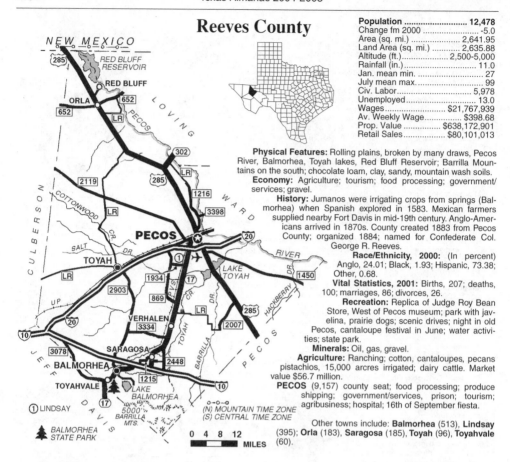

**Physical Features:** Rolling plains, broken by many draws, Pecos River, Balmorhea, Toyah lakes, Red Bluff Reservoir; Barrilla Mountains on the south; chocolate loam, clay, sandy, mountain wash soils.

**Economy:** Agriculture; tourism; food processing; government/services; gravel.

**History:** Jumanos were irrigating crops from springs (Balmorhea) when Spanish explored in 1583. Mexican farmers supplied nearby Fort Davis in mid-19th century. Anglo-Americans arrived in 1870s. County created 1883 from Pecos County; organized 1884; named for Confederate Col. George R. Reeves.

**Race/Ethnicity, 2000:** (In percent) Anglo, 24.01; Black, 1.93; Hispanic, 73.38; Other, 0.68.

**Vital Statistics, 2001:** Births, 207; deaths, 100; marriages, 86; divorces, 26.

**Recreation:** Replica of Judge Roy Bean Store, West of Pecos museum; park with javelina, prairie dogs; scenic drives; night in old Pecos, cantaloupe festival in June; water activities; state park.

**Minerals:** Oil, gas, gravel.

**Agriculture:** Ranching; cotton, cantaloupes, pecans pistachios, 15,000 arcres irrigated; dairy cattle. Market value $56.7 million.

**PECOS** (9,157) county seat; food processing; produce shipping; government/services; prison; tourism; agribusiness; hospital; 16th of September fiesta.

Other towns include: **Balmorhea** (513), **Lindsay** (395); **Orla** (183), **Saragosa** (185), **Toyah** (96), **Toyahvale** (60).

*Hills west of Toyah in Reeves County. File photo.*

# Refugio County

**Physical Features:** Coastal plain, broken by streams, bays; sandy, loam, black soils; mesquite, oak, huisache motts.

**Economy:** Petroleum, petrochemical production, agribusinesses, tourism, commuting to Corpus Christi, Victoria.

**History:** Karankawa area. Spanish mission, for which the county is named, Our Lady of Refuge, established in 1793. Colonists from Ireland and United States arrived in 1830s. Original county of the Republic created 1836, organized 1837.

**Race/Ethnicity, 2000:** (In percent) Anglo, 47.78; Black, 6.80; Hispanic, 44.58; Other, 0.84.

**Vital Statistics, 2001:** Births, 105; deaths, 90; marriages, 51; divorces, 17.

**Recreation:** Water activities; hunting, fishing; historic sites; chili cook-off in August; wildlife refuge, home of the whooping crane; Festival of Flags in October.

**Minerals:** Oil, natural gas.

**Agriculture:** Cotton, beef cattle, sorghum, corn, soybeans, horses. Market value $40.1 million. Hunting leases.

REFUGIO (2,886) county seat; petroleum, agribusiness center; hospital; museum, historic homes.

Other towns include: **Austwell** (189); **Bayside** (351) resorts; **Tivoli** (550); **Woodsboro** (1,666) commercial center.

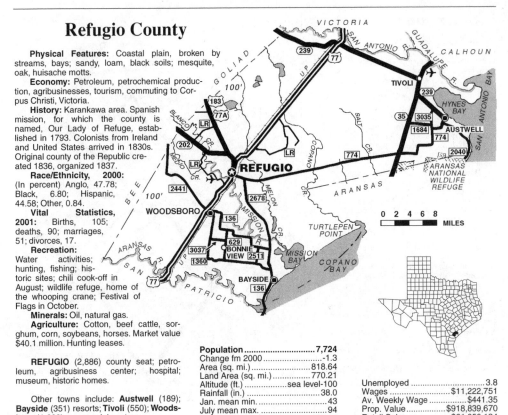

| Population | 7,724 |
| --- | --- |
| Change fm 2000 | -1.3 |
| Area (sq. mi.) | 818.64 |
| Land Area (sq. mi.) | 770.21 |
| Altitude (ft.) | sea level-100 |
| Rainfall (in.) | 38.0 |
| Jan. mean min. | 43 |
| July mean max. | 94 |
| Civ. Labor | 2,689 |

| | |
| --- | --- |
| Unemployed | 3.8 |
| Wages | $11,222,751 |
| Av. Weekly Wage | $441.35 |
| Prop. Value | $918,839,670 |
| Retail Sales | $61,856,194 |

# Roberts County

**Physical Features:** Rolling, broken by Canadian and tributaries; Red Deer Creek; black, sandy loam, alluvial soils.

**Economy:** Oil-field operations; agribusiness.

**History:** Apaches; pushed out by Comanches who were removed in 1874-75 by U.S. Army. Ranching began in late 1870s. County created 1876 from Bexar District; organized 1889; named for Texas leaders John S. Roberts and Gov. O.M. Roberts.

**Race/Ethnicity, 2000:** (In percent) Anglo, 96.39; Black, 0.34; Hispanic, 3.16; Other, 0.11.

**Vital Statistics, 2001:** Births, 5; deaths, 2; marriages, 1; divorces, 5.

**Recreation:** National cow-calling contest in June; scenic drives; museum.

**Minerals:** Production of gas, oil.

**Agriculture:** Beef cattle; wheat, sorghum, corn, soybeans, hay; 10,000 acres irrigated. Market value $17.6 million.

MIAMI (557) county seat; ranching, oil center; some manufacturing.

| Population | 857 |
| --- | --- |
| Change fm 2000 | -3.4 |
| Area (sq. mi.) | 924.19 |
| Land Area (sq. mi.) | 924.09 |
| Altitude (ft.) | 2,400-3,250 |
| Rainfall (in.) | 21.6 |

| | |
| --- | --- |
| Jan. mean min. | 20 |
| July mean max. | 93 |
| Civ. Labor | 421 |
| Unemployed | 3.3 |
| Wages | $1,048,664 |
| Av. Weekly Wage | $409.47 |

| | |
| --- | --- |
| Prop. Value | $356,189,998 |
| Retail Sales | $2,243,136 |

*For explanation of sources, abbreviations and symbols, see p. 138.*

# Robertson County

**Physical Features:** Rolling in north and east, draining to bottoms along Brazos, Navasota rivers; sandy soils, heavy in bottoms.

**Economy:** Agribusiness; small manufacturing; power-generating plant.

**History:** Tawakoni, Waco, Comanche and other tribes. Anglo-Americans arrived in 1820s. Antebellum slaveholding area. County created 1837, organized 1838, subdivided into many others later; named for pioneer Sterling Clack Robertson.

**Race/Ethnicity, 2000:** (In percent) Anglo, 60.55; Black, 24.11; Hispanic, 14.74; Other, 0.60.

**Vital Statistics, 2001:** Births, 215; deaths, 209; marriages, 102; divorces, 43.

**Recreation:** Hunting, fishing; historic sites; historic-homes tour; dogwood trails, wildlife preserves.

**Minerals:** Gas, oil, lignite coal.

**Agriculture:** Most revenue from beef cattle, cotton, hay, corn; 20,000 acres of cropland irrigated. Market value $30.7 million.

**FRANKLIN** (1,474) county seat; farm-trade center, power plants.

**HEARNE** (4,655) agribusiness; varied manufacturing; depot museum; music festival in October.

Other towns include: **Bremond** (873) power plant, coal mining, Polish Days in June; **Calvert** (1,427) agriculture, tourism, antiques, Maypole festival, tour of homes; **Mumford** (170); **New Baden** (150); **Wheelock** (225).

| | |
|---|---|
| Population | 16,044 |
| Change fm 2000 | 0.3 |
| Area (sq. mi.) | 865.67 |
| Land Area (sq. mi.) | 854.56 |
| Altitude (ft.) | 250-550 |
| Rainfall (in.) | 37.5 |
| Jan. mean min. | 37 |

| | |
|---|---|
| July mean max. | 95 |
| Civ. Labor | 6,246 |
| Unemployed | 5.4 |

| | |
|---|---|
| Wages | $22,294,805 |
| Av. Weekly Wage | $490.70 |
| Prop. Value | $1,400,983,330 |
| Retail Sales | $70,771,599 |

---

# Rockwall County

**Physical Features:** Rolling prairie, mostly Blackland soil; Lake Ray Hubbard. Texas' smallest county.

**Economy:** Industrial employment in local plants and in Dallas; in Dallas metropolitan area; residential development around Lake Ray Hubbard.

**History:** Caddo area. Cherokees arrived in 1820s. Anglo-American settlers arrived in 1840s. County created 1873 from Kaufman; named for wall-like rock formation.

**Race/Ethnicity, 2000:** (In percent) Anglo, 83.77; Black, 3.32; Hispanic, 11.07; Other, 1.84.

**Vital Statistics, 2001:** Births, 708; deaths, 302; marriages, 1,714; divorces, 203.

**Recreation:** Lake activities; proximity to Dallas; unusual rock outcrop.

**Minerals:** Not significant.

**Agriculture:** Small grains, cattle, horticulture, horses. Market value $5.9 million.

**ROCKWALL** (21,529) county seat; varied manufacturing; hospital; youth fair in April.

Other towns include: **Fate** (891); **Heath** (4,996); **McLendon-Chisholm** (1,013) chili cookoff in October; **Mobile City** (189); **Royse City** (3,496) varied manufacturing, agribusiness, Funfest in April, North Texas Speedway. Part (7,041) of **Rowlett** and a small part (315) of **Wylie**.

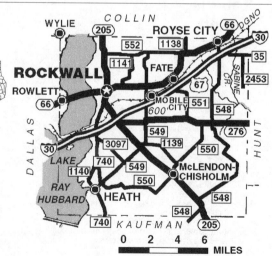

| | |
|---|---|
| Population | 50,858 |
| Change fm 2000 | 18.1 |
| Area (sq. mi.) | 148.70 |
| Land Area (sq. mi.) | 128.79 |
| Altitude (ft.) | 450-600 |
| Rainfall (in.) | 36.9 |
| Jan. mean min. | 33 |
| July mean max. | 96 |
| Civ. Labor | 26,374 |

| | |
|---|---|
| Unemployed | 5.6 |
| Wages | $96,380,763 |
| Av. Weekly Wage | $534.30 |
| Prop. Value | $3,521,951,751 |
| Retail Sales | $636,507,273 |

*For explanation of sources, abbreviations and symbols, see p. 138.*

# Runnels County

**Physical Features:** West central county; level to rolling; bisected by Colorado and tributaries; sandy loam, black waxy soils.

**Economy:** Agribusiness; oil activity; government/services; manufacturing.

**History:** Spanish explorers found Jumanos in area in 1650s; later, Apaches and Comanches driven out in 1870s by U.S. military. First Anglo-Americans arrived in 1850s; Germans, Czechs around 1900. County named for planter-legislator H.G. Runnels; created 1858 from Bexar, Travis counties; organized 1880.

**Race/Ethnicity, 2000:** (In percent) Anglo, 68.32; Black, 1.57; Hispanic, 29.33; Other, 0.78.

**Vital Statistics, 2001:** Births, 150; deaths, 137; marriages, 68; divorces, 34.

**Recreation:** Deer, dove and turkey hunting; O.H. Ivie Reservoir; fishing; historical markers in county.

**Minerals:** Oil, gas, sand.

**Agriculture:** Cattle, cotton, wheat, sorghum, dairy products, sheep and goats. Market value $19.4 million.

**BALLINGER** (4,235) county seat; varied manufacturing; oil-field services; meat processing; fertilizer produced; Carnegie Library; hospital; Western Texas College extension; the Cross, 100-ft. tall atop hill south of city; Festival of Ethnic Cultures in April.

Other towns include: **Miles** (857); **Norton** (76); **Rowena** (466); **Wingate** (216); **Winters** (2,869) manufacturing, museum; hospital.

| | | |
|---|---|---|
| Population.................................. **11,123** | Rainfall (in.)....................................23.3 | Wages .............................$20,447,735 |
| Change fm 2000............................-3.2 | Jan. mean min. ................................30 | Av. Weekly Wage....................$436.07 |
| Area (sq. mi.)...........................1,057.13 | July mean max...................................95 | Prop. Value.....................$576,478,370 |
| Land Area (sq. mi.)..................1,050.73 | Civ. Labor ..................................5,239 | Retail Sales .....................$55,760,112 |
| Altitude (ft.)........................1,600-2,301 | Unemployed.......................................3.3 | |

# Rusk County

**Physical Features:** East Texas county on Sabine-Angelina divide; varied deep, sandy soils; over half in pines, hardwoods; lakes.

**Economy:** Lignite mining, oil and gas, lumbering, agribusiness, government/services, brick production.

**History:** Caddo area. Cherokees settled in 1820s; removed in 1839. First Anglo-Americans arrived in 1829. Antebellum slaveholding area. County named for Republic, state leader Thomas J. Rusk; created from Nacogdoches County 1843.

**Race/Ethnicity, 2000:** (In percent) Anglo, 71.61; Black, 19.31; Hispanic, 8.44; Other, 0.64.

**Vital Statistics, 2001:** Births, 580; deaths, 542; marriages, 380; divorces, 256.

**Recreation:** Water sports, state park; historic homes, sites; scenic drives; marked site of East Texas Field discovery oil well; syrup festival in November.

**Minerals:** Oil, natural gas, lignite, clays.

**Agriculture:** Beef cattle, hay, broilers, nursery plants. Market value $42.5 million. Timber income substantial.

**HENDERSON** (11,369) county seat; center for agribusiness, oil activities; varied manufacturing; hospital; state jail.

Other towns include: **Joinerville** (140); **Laird Hill** (405); **Laneville** (200); **Minden** (350); **Mount Enterprise** (528); **New London** (992) site of 1937 school explosion that killed 293 students and faculty; **Overton** (2,383, partly in Smith County) oil, lumbering center, petroleum processing, A&M research unit, blue grass festival in July, prison unit; **Price** (275); **Selman City** (271); **Tatum** (1,182, partly in Panola County).

Also, part of **Easton** (536, mostly in Gregg County), part of **Reklaw** (338, mostly in Cherokee County) and part (2,580) of **Kilgore** (11,524 total).

| | | |
|---|---|---|
| Population........................... **47,541** | July mean max..............................93 | |
| Change fm 2000.........................0.4 | Civ. Labor ..............................23,160 | |
| Area (sq. mi.).........................938.62 | Unemployed.................................5.4 | |
| Land Area (sq. mi.)................923.55 | Wages.........................$93,086,338 | |
| Altitude (ft.).......................280-662 | Av. Weekly Wage ..............$537.70 | |
| Rainfall (in.)............................45.6 | Prop. Value ............$3,174,600,570 | |
| Jan. mean min..........................33 | Retail Sales................$297,641,444 | |

# Sabine County

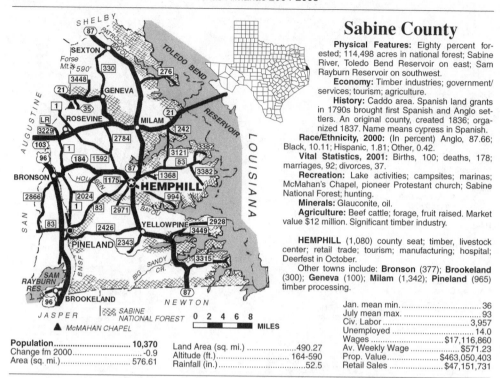

**Physical Features:** Eighty percent forested; 114,498 acres in national forest; Sabine River, Toledo Bend Reservoir on east; Sam Rayburn Reservoir on southwest.

**Economy:** Timber industries; government/services; tourism; agriculture.

**History:** Caddo area. Spanish land grants in 1790s brought first Spanish and Anglo settlers. An original county, created 1836; organized 1837. Name means cypress in Spanish.

**Race/Ethnicity, 2000:** (In percent) Anglo, 87.66; Black, 10.11; Hispanic, 1.81; Other, 0.42.

**Vital Statistics, 2001:** Births, 100; deaths, 178; marriages, 92; divorces, 37.

**Recreation:** Lake activities; campsites; marinas; McMahan's Chapel, pioneer Protestant church; Sabine National Forest; hunting.

**Minerals:** Glauconite, oil.

**Agriculture:** Beef cattle; forage, fruit raised. Market value $12 million. Significant timber industry.

**HEMPHILL** (1,080) county seat; timber, livestock center; retail trade; tourism; manufacturing; hospital; Deerfest in October.

Other towns include: **Bronson** (377); **Brookeland** (300); **Geneva** (100); **Milam** (1,342); **Pineland** (965) timber processing.

| | |
|---|---|
| Jan. mean min. | 36 |
| July mean max. | 93 |
| Civ. Labor | 3,957 |
| Unemployed | 14.0 |
| Wages | $17,116,860 |
| Av. Weekly Wage | $571.23 |
| Prop. Value | $463,050,403 |
| Retail Sales | $47,151,731 |

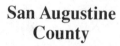

| | | | |
|---|---|---|---|
| Population | 10,370 | Land Area (sq. mi.) | 490.27 |
| Change fm 2000 | -0.9 | Altitude (ft.) | 164-590 |
| Area (sq. mi.) | 576.61 | Rainfall (in.) | 52.5 |

# San Augustine County

**Physical Features:** Hilly East Texas county, 80 percent forested with 66,799 acres in Angelina National Forest, 4,317 in Sabine National Forest; Sam Rayburn Reservoir; varied soils, sandy to black alluvial.

**Economy:** Lumbering; shipping; varied manufacturing.

**History:** Presence of Caddoes attracted Spanish mission in 1717. First Anglos and Indians from U.S. southern states arrived around 1800. Antebellum slaveholding area. County created and named for Mexican municipality in 1836; an original county; organized 1837.

**Race/Ethnicity, 2000:** (In percent) Anglo, 68.13; Black, 27.93; Hispanic, 3.58; Other, 0.36.

**Vital Statistics, 2001:** Births, 111; deaths, 109; marriages, 74; divorces, 11.

**Recreation:** Lake activities; pine fest, annual tour of homes in April, sassafras festival in October; many historic homes; tourist facilities in national forests.

**Minerals:** Small amount of oil.

**Agriculture:** Poultry, cattle, horses; watermelons, peas, corn, truck crops. Market value $28.8 million. Timber sales significant.

**SAN AUGUSTINE** (2,481) county seat; tourism; livestock center; varied manufacturing; Deep East Texas Electric Cooperative; lumbering; hospital; Tour of Homes.

Other towns include: **Broaddus** (190).

| | |
|---|---|
| Population | 8,922 |
| Change fm 2000 | -0.3 |
| Area (sq. mi.) | 592.21 |
| Land Area (sq. mi.) | 527.87 |
| Altitude (ft.) | 164-550 |
| Rainfall (in.) | 48.6 |
| Jan. mean min. | 35 |

| | | | |
|---|---|---|---|
| July mean max. | 93 | Av. Weekly Wage | $420.20 |
| Civ. Labor | 3,153 | Prop. Value | $350,227,082 |
| Unemployed | 5.7 | Retail Sales | $43,083,203 |
| Wages | $10,116,828 | | |

*For explanation of sources, abbreviations and symbols, see p. 138.*

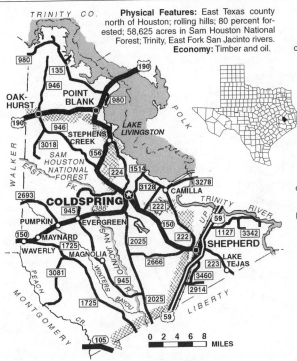

**Physical Features:** East Texas county north of Houston; rolling hills; 80 percent forested; 58,625 acres in Sam Houston National Forest; Trinity, East Fork San Jacinto rivers.
**Economy:** Timber and oil.

# San Jacinto County

**History:** Atakapa Indian area. Anglo-Americans arrived in 1820s. Land grants issued to Mexican families in early 1830s. County created from Liberty, Montgomery, Polk, Walker counties 1869; organized 1870; named for the battle.

**Race/Ethnicity, 2000:** (In percent) Anglo, 81.60; Black, 12.72; Hispanic, 4.87; Other, 0.81.

**Vital Statistics, 2001:** Births, 288; deaths, 213; marriages, 137; divorces, 145.

**Recreation:** Lake activities; hunting; old courthouse and jail are tourist attractions. Approximately 60 percent of county in national forest.

**Minerals:** Oil, rock, gravel and iron ore.

**Agriculture:** Beef cattle and forages. Market value $5.4 million. Timber principal product.

**COLDSPRING** (721) county seat; lumbering; oil; farming center; tourism; historic sites.

**SHEPHERD** (2,132) lumbering.

Other towns include: **Oakhurst** (241); **Point Blank** (582) logging, agribusiness, construction.

| | |
|---|---|
| Population | 23,247 |
| Change fm 2000 | 4.5 |
| Area (sq. mi.) | 627.90 |
| Land Area (sq. mi.) | 570.65 |
| Altitude (ft.) | 74-386 |
| Rainfall (in.) | 48.3 |
| Jan. mean min. | 36 |
| July mean max. | 93 |
| Civ. Labor | 9,186 |
| Unemployed | 5.5 |
| Wages | $12,060,836 |
| Av. Weekly Wage | $455.90 |
| Prop. Value | $965,299,173 |
| Retail Sales | $62,116,457 |

# San Patricio County

| | |
|---|---|
| Population | 67,492 |
| Change fm 2000 | 0.5 |
| Area (sq. mi.) | 707.06 |
| Land Area (sq. mi.) | 691.65 |
| Altitude (ft.) | sea level-200 |
| Rainfall (in.) | 35.0 |
| Jan. mean min. | 43 |
| July mean max. | 94 |
| Civ. Labor | 29,740 |
| Unemployed | 7.2 |
| Wages | $132,141,996 |
| Av. Weekly Wage | $631.00 |
| Prop. Value | $3,221,331,402 |
| Retail Sales | $499,999,204 |

**Physical Features:** Grassy, coastal prairie draining to Aransas, Nueces rivers, and to bays; sandy loam, clay, black loam soils; lake.

**Economy:** Oil, petrochemicals; agribusiness; manufacturing; tourism, naval base; in Corpus Christi metropolitan area.

**History:** Karankawa area. Mexican sheep herders in area before colonization. Settled by Irish families in 1830 (name is Spanish for St. Patrick). Created, named for municipality 1836; organized 1837, reorganized 1847.

**Race/Ethnicity, 2000:** (In percent) Anglo, 46.48; Black, 2.84; Hispanic, 49.42; Other, 1.26.

**Vital Statistics, 2001:** Births, 1,181; deaths, 533; marriages 338; divorces, 307.

**Recreation:** Water activities; hunting; Corpus Christi Bay; state park; Welder Wildlife Foundation and Park; shrimporee; birdwatching.

**Minerals:** Production of oil, gas, iron ore.

**Agriculture:** Cotton, grain sorghum, beef cattle, corn. Market value $91.2 million. Fisheries income significant.

**SINTON** (5,653) county seat; oil, agribusiness; tourism; Go Texan Days in October.

**ARANSAS PASS** (8,234, parts in Aransas, Nueces counties) shrimping, tourist center; offshore oil-well servicing; aluminum, chemical plants; hospitals.

**PORTLAND** (15,033) petrochemicals; many residents work in Corpus Christi, naval bases; Indian Point pier; Windfest in April.

Other towns include: **Edroy** (429); **Gregory** (2,294); **Ingleside** (9,516) naval base, chemical and manufacturing plants, ship repair, birding, Round Up Day in May; **Ingleside-on-the-Bay** (679); **Lake City** (523); **Lakeside** (325); **Mathis** (4,941); **Odem** (2,544); **St. Paul** (549); **San Patricio** (323, partly in Nueces County); **Taft** (3,423) manufacturing, processing, drug rehabilitation center, hospital; Christmas parade; **Taft Southwest** (1,678).

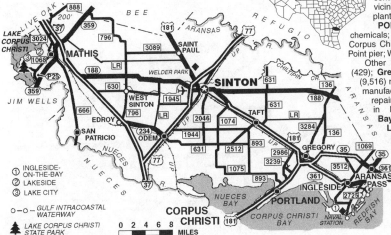

# San Saba County

**Physical Features:** West central county; hilly, rolling; bisected by San Saba River; Colorado River on east; black, gray sandy loam, alluvial soils.

**Economy:** Government/services; retail pecan industry; tourism, hunting leases.

**History:** Apaches and Comanches in area when Spanish explored. Anglo-American settlers arrived in 1850s. County created from Bexar 1856; named for river.

**Race/Ethnicity, 2000:** (In percent) Anglo, 75.19; Black, 2.63; Hispanic, 21.55; Other, 0.63.

**Vital Statistics, 2001:** Births, 69; deaths, 97; marriages, 41; divorces, 11.

**Recreation:** State park; deer hunting; historic sites; log cabin museum; fishing; scenic drives; wildflower trail; Gorman Falls.

**Minerals:** Limestone, rock quarry.

| | |
|---|---|
| Population | 6,148 |
| Change fm 2000 | -0.6 |
| Area (sq. mi.) | 1,138.25 |
| Land Area (sq. mi.) | 1,134.47 |
| Altitude (ft.) | 1,100-1,971 |
| Rainfall (in.) | 26.3 |
| Jan. mean min. | 32 |
| July mean max. | 96 |
| Civ. Labor | 2,325 |
| Unemployed | 3.0 |
| Wages | $10,460,933 |
| Av. Weekly Wage | $424.64 |
| Fed. Wages | $193,542 |
| Prop. Value | $720,832,850 |
| Retail Sales | $28,362,801 |

**Agriculture:** Cattle, pecans, hay, sheep and goats, wheat. Market value $28 million. Hunting, wildlife leases.

**SAN SABA** (2,648) county seat; claims title "Pecan Capital of the World"; stone processing; varied manufacturing; state prison; Cow Camp cookoff in May.

Other towns include: **Bend** (115, partly in Lampasas County); **Cherokee** (175); **Richland Springs** (360).

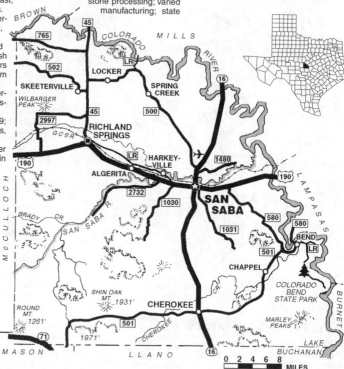

# Schleicher County

**Physical Features:** Southwestern county on edge of Edwards Plateau, broken by Devils, Concho, San Saba tributaries; part hilly; black soils.

**Economy:** Oil, ranching; hunting.

**History:** Jumanos in area in 1630s. Later, Apaches and Comanches; re-moved in 1870s. Ranching began in 1870s. Census of 1890 showed third of population from Mexico. County named for Gustav Schleicher, founder of German colony; county created from Crockett 1887, organized 1901.

**Race/Ethnicity, 2000:** (In percent) Anglo, 54.59; Black, 1.26; Hispanic, 43.54; Other, 0.61.

**Vital Statistics, 2001:** Births, 47; deaths, 30; marriages, 18; divorces, 6.

**Recreation:** Hunting; livestock show in January, youth, open rodeos; mountain bike events; playhouse "Way off Broadway".

**Minerals:** Oil, natural gas.

**Agriculture:** Beef cattle, goats, sheep; crops include cotton, milo, hay, small grains. Market value $10.8 million. Hunting leases important.

**ELDORADO** (1,977) county seat; oil activities; center for livestock, mohair marketing, woolen mill; government/services, medical center.

| | |
|---|---|
| Population | 2,944 |
| Change fm 2000 | 0.3 |
| Area (sq. mi.) | 1,310.65 |
| Land Area (sq. mi.) | 1,310.61 |
| Altitude (ft.) | 2,100-2,600 |
| Rainfall (in.) | 19.0 |
| Jan. mean min. | 28 |
| July mean max. | 93 |
| Civ. Labor | 1,169 |
| Unemployed | 3.4 |
| Wages | $4,386,429 |
| Av. Weekly Wage | $437.64 |
| Prop. Value | $386,098,050 |
| Retail Sales | $8,533,663 |

*For explanation of sources, abbreviations and symbols, see p. 138.*

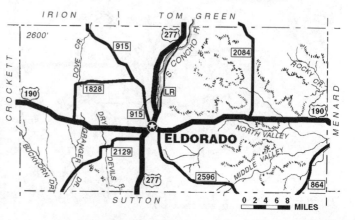

# Scurry County

**Physical Features:** Plains county below Caprock, some hills; drained by Colorado, Brazos tributaries; lake; sandy, loam soils.

**Economy:** Oil production; government/services; agribusinesses, manufacturing.

**History:** Apaches; displaced later by Comanches who were relocated to Indian Territory in 1875. Ranching began in late 1870s. County created from Bexar 1876; organized 1884; named for Confederate Gen. W.R. Scurry.

**Race/Ethnicity, 2000:** (In percent) Anglo, 65.55; Black, 6.14; Hispanic, 27.77; Other, 0.54.

**Vital Statistics, 2001:** Births, 229; deaths, 178; marriages, 123; divorces, 83.

**Recreation:** Lake J.B. Thomas water recreation; Towle Memorial Park; museums, community theater, White Buffalo festival in October.

**Minerals:** Oil, gas.

**Agriculture:** Cotton, wheat, cattle, hay. Market value 14.8 million.

**SNYDER** (10,506) county seat; textiles, brick plant, cotton, oil center; Western Texas (Jr.) College; hospital; prison; walking trail; Western Swing days in June.

Other towns include: **Dunn** (75); **Fluvanna** (180); **Hermleigh** (430); **Ira** (250).

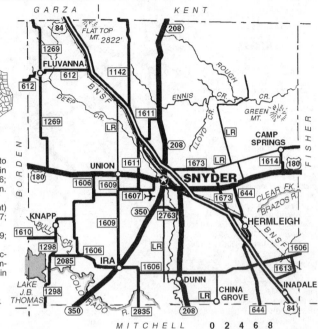

| | |
|---|---|
| Population | 15,877 |
| Change fm 2000 | -3.0 |
| Area (sq. mi.) | 907.53 |
| Land Area (sq. mi.) | 902.50 |
| Altitude (ft.) | 2,000-2,822 |
| Rainfall (in.) | 22.2 |
| Jan. mean min. | 25 |
| July mean max. | 93 |
| Civ. Labor | 6,668 |
| Unemployed | 4.5 |
| Wages | $38,266,210 |
| Av. Weekly Wage | $523.48 |
| Prop. Value | $965,315,300 |
| Retail Sales | $113,665,203 |

# Shackelford County

**Physical Features:** Rolling, hilly, drained by tributaries of Brazos; sandy and chocolate loam soils; lake.

**Economy:** Oil and ranching; some manufacturing; hunting leases.

**History:** Apaches; driven out by Comanches. First Anglo-American settlers arrived soon after establishment of military outpost in 1850s. County created from Bosque County 1858; organized 1874; named for Dr. Jack Shackelford (sometimes referred to as John), Texas Revolutionary hero.

**Race/Ethnicity, 2000:** (In percent) Anglo, 91.68; Black, 0.33; Hispanic, 7.60; Other, 0.39.

**Vital Statistics, 2001:** Births, 43; deaths, 34; marriages, 28; divorces, 14.

**Recreation:** Fort Griffin State Park, June Fandangle musical about area history; courthouse historical district; hunting, lake, outdoor activities.

**Minerals:** Oil, natural gas.

**Agriculture:** Beef cattle, wheat, hay, cotton. Market value $13.6 million. Hunting leases.

**ALBANY** (1,931) county seat; tourism; oil, agriculture center; quarter-horse breeding; hospital; historical district; Old Jail art center.

| | |
|---|---|
| Population | 3,338 |
| Change fm 2000 | 1.1 |
| Area (sq. mi.) | 915.54 |
| Land Area (sq. mi.) | 913.95 |
| Altitude (ft.) | 1,200-2,000 |
| Rainfall (in.) | 28.6 |
| Jan. mean min. | 31 |
| July mean max. | 97 |
| Civ. Labor | 1,645 |
| Unemployed | 3.0 |
| Wages | $5,497,149 |
| Av. Weekly Wage | $433.26 |
| Prop. Value | $393,474,903 |
| Retail Sales | $11,794,285 |

# Shelby County

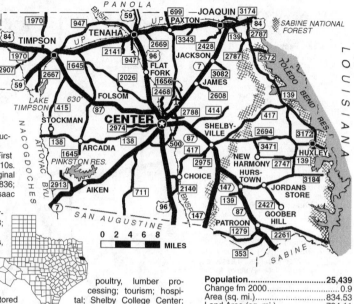

**Physical Features:** East Texas county; partly hills, much bottomland; well-timbered, 67,762 acres in national forest; Attoyac Bayou and Toledo Bend, other streams; sandy, clay, alluvial soils.

**Economy:** Broiler, egg production; cattle; timber; tourism.

**History:** Caddo Indian area. First Anglo-Americans settled in 1810s. Antebellum slaveholding area. Original county of Republic, created 1836; organized 1837; named for Isaac Shelby of American Revolution.

**Race/Ethnicity, 2000:** (In percent) Anglo, 69.95; Black, 19.53; Hispanic, 9.87; Other, 0.65.

**Vital Statistics, 2001:** Births, 400; deaths, 295; marriages, 249; divorces, 54.

**Recreation:** Toledo Bend Reservoir activities; Sabine National Forest; hunting, fishing; camping; historic sites, restored 1885 courthouse; What-a-Melon festival in July, fox hunt.

**Minerals:** Natural gas, oil.

**Agriculture:** A leader in broiler and egg production; cattle; hay, vegetables, watermelons. Market value $200.7 million. Timber sales significant.

**CENTER** (5,660) county seat; poultry, lumber processing; tourism; hospital; Shelby College Center; Poultry festival in October; fall fox hunt.

Other towns: **Arcadia** (20); **Huxley** (303); **Joaquin** (927); **Shelbyville** (215); **Tenaha** (1,031); **Timpson** (1,138) livestock, timber, farming, commuters; genealogy library; So-So festival in fall.

| | |
|---|---|
| Population | 25,439 |
| Change fm 2000 | 0.9 |
| Area (sq. mi.) | 834.53 |
| Land Area (sq. mi.) | 794.11 |
| Altitude (ft.) | 174-630 |
| Rainfall (in.) | 50.2 |
| Jan. mean min. | 33 |
| July mean max. | 94 |
| Civ. Labor | 10,028 |
| Unemployed | 8.0 |
| Wages | $41,911,156 |
| Av. Weekly Wage | $441.63 |
| Prop. Value | $931,687,004 |
| Retail Sales | $184,360,490 |

# Sherman County

**Physical Features:** A northernmost Panhandle county; level, broken by creeks, playas; sandy to dark loam soils; underground water.

**Economy:** Agribusiness, tourism.

**History:** Apaches; pushed out by Comanches in 1700s. Comanches removed to Indian Territory in 1875. Ranching began around 1880; farming after 1900. County named for Texas Gen. Sidney Sherman; created from Bexar District 1876; organized 1889.

**Race/Ethnicity, 2000:** (In percent) Anglo, 71.54; Black, 0.50; Hispanic, 27.43; Other, 0.53.

**Vital Statistics, 2001:** Births, 40; deaths, 30; marriages, 28; divorces, 4.

**Recreation:** Depot museum; jamboree and ranch rodeo in August; pheasant hunting.

**Minerals:** Natural gas, oil.

**Agriculture:** Beef and stocker cattle important; wheat, corn, grain sorghum, alfalfa; swine; 145,000 acres irrigated. Market value $321.6 million.

**STRATFORD** (2,033) county seat; agribusiness center; feedlot operations; industrial authority; birdseed packaging; some manufacturing; German sausage festival in February.

**Texhoma** (383 in Texas, 985 in Oklahoma) other principal town.

| | | | |
|---|---|---|---|
| Population | 3,285 | Jan. mean min. | 18 |
| Change fm 2000 | 3.1 | July mean max. | 92 |
| Area (sq. mi.) | 923.20 | Civ. Labor | 1,498 |
| Land Area (sq. mi.) | 923.03 | Unemployed | 1.3 |
| Altitude (ft.) | 3,200-3,800 | Wages | $7,166,652 |
| Rainfall (in.) | 17.2 | Av. Weekly Wage | $540.47 |

| | |
|---|---|
| Prop. Value | $627,850,709 |
| Retail Sales | $13,076,254 |

*For explanation of sources, abbreviations and symbols, see p. 138.*

# Smith County

**Physical Features:** Populous East Texas county of rolling hills, many timbered; Sabine, Neches, other streams; Tyler, Palestine lakes; alluvial, gray, sandy loam, clay soils.

**Economy:** Medical facilities, education, government/services; agribusiness; petroleum production; manufacturing, distribution center; tourism.

**History:** Caddoes of area reduced by disease and other tribes in 1790s. Cherokees settled in 1820s; removed in 1839. In late 1820s, first Anglo-American settlers arrived. Antebellum slaveholding area. County named for Texas Revolutionary Gen. James Smith; county created 1846 from Nacogdoches.

**Race/Ethnicity, 2000:** (In percent) Anglo, 68.40; Black, 19.24; Hispanic, 11.17; Other, 1.19

**Vital Statistics, 2001:** Births, 2,678; deaths, 1,819; marriages, 1,814; divorces, 691.

**Recreation:** Activities on Palestine, Tyler lakes and others; famed Rose Garden; Texas Rose Festival in October; Azalea Trail; state park; Goodman Museum; Juneteenth celebration, East Texas Fair in Sept./Oct.; Caldwell Zoo; collegiate events.

**Minerals:** Oil, gas, iron ore, gravel and soils.

**Agriculture:** Horticultural crops and roses; beef cattle, hay, melons, horses. Market value $65.6 million. Timber sales substantial.

**TYLER** (85,807) county seat; claims title, "Rose Capital of the Nation"; administrative center for oil production; varied manufacturing; University of Texas at Tyler, Tyler Junior College; Texas College, University of Texas Health Center; hospitals, nursing school.

Other towns include: **Arp** (940) Strawberry Festival in April; **Bullard** (1,380, part in Cherokee County); **Flint** (700); **Hideaway** (2,672); **Lindale** (3,156) rose distribution, food processing; Country Fest in October, youth rodeo in August; **New Chapel Hill** (604); **Noonday** (523) Sweet Onion festival in June; **Troup** (2,021, part in Cherokee County); **Whitehouse** (6,107) commuters to Tyler, government/services, Yesteryear festival in June; **Winona** (601).

Part of **Overton** (2,383, mostly in Rusk County).

| | |
|---|---|
| Population | 181,437 |
| Change fm 2000 | 3.9 |
| Area (sq. mi.) | 949.45 |
| Land Area (sq. mi.) | 928.38 |
| Altitude (ft.) | 300-631 |
| Rainfall (in.) | 43.1 |
| Jan. mean min. | 33 |
| July mean max. | 94 |
| Civ. Labor | 96,947 |
| Unemployed | 4.3 |
| Wages | $648,977,276 |
| Av. Weekly Wage | $587.32 |
| Prop. Value | $9,114,225,897 |
| Retail Sales | $2,379,486,766 |

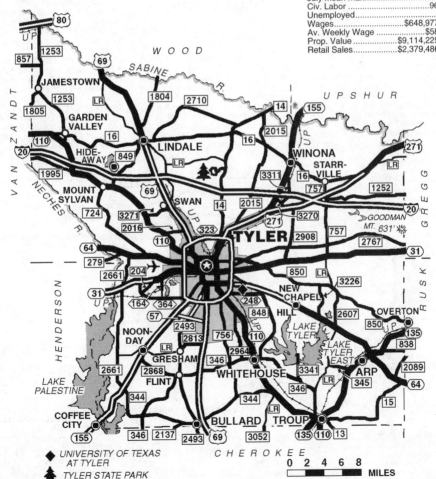

♦ UNIVERSITY OF TEXAS AT TYLER

🌲 TYLER STATE PARK

0 2 4 6 8 MILES

# Somervell County

**Physical Features:** Hilly terrain southwest of Fort Worth; Brazos, Paluxy rivers; gray, dark, alluvial soils; second-smallest county.

**Economy:** Nuclear power plant; tourism, agribusiness.

**History:** Wichita, Tonkawa area; Comanches later. Anglo-Americans arrived in 1850s. County created as Somerville County 1875 from Hood County. Spelling was changed 1876; named for Republic of Texas Gen. Alexander Somervell.

**Race/Ethnicity, 2000:** (In percent) Anglo, 85.29; Black, 0.32; Hispanic, 13.44; Other, 0.95.

**Vital Statistics, 2001:** Births, 95; deaths, 81; marriages, 95; divorces, 27.

**Recreation:** Fishing, hunting; unique geological formations; dinosaur tracks in state park; Glen Rose Big Rocks Park; Fossil Rim Wildlife Center; nature trails, museum; exposition center; Passion play at amphitheatre June-October.

**Minerals:** Sand, gravel, silica.

**Agriculture:** Cattle, hay, small grains, goats. Market value $2.1 million.

**GLEN ROSE** (2,265) county seat; nuclear power plant, tourism, farm trade center; hospital. Other towns include: **Nemo** (56); **Rainbow** (76).

| | |
|---|---|
| Population | 7,224 |
| Change fm 2000 | 6.1 |
| Area (sq. mi.) | 191.90 |
| Land Area (sq. mi.) | 187.17 |
| Altitude (ft.) | 600-1,200 |
| Rainfall (in.) | 33.3 |
| Jan. mean min. | 30 |
| July mean max. | 98 |

| | |
|---|---|
| Civ. Labor | 2,063 |
| Unemployed | 9.5 |
| Wages | $35,809,462 |
| Av. Weekly Wage | $757.58 |
| Prop. Value | $2,377,366,566 |
| Retail Sales | $48,229,055 |

# Starr County

**Physical Features:** Rolling, some hills; dense brush; clay, loam, sandy soils; alluvial on Rio Grande; Falcon Reservoir.

**Economy:** Vegetable packing, shipping, other agribusiness; oil processing; tourism; government/services.

**History:** Coahuiltecan Indian area. Settlers from Spanish villages that were established in 1749 on south bank began to move across river soon afterward. County named for Dr. J.H. Starr, secretary of treasury of the Republic; county created from Nueces 1848.

**Race/Ethnicity, 2000:** (In percent) Anglo, 2.08; Black, 0.01; Hispanic, 97.54; Other, 0.37.

**Vital Statistics, 2001:** Births, 1,460; deaths, 272; marriages, 600; divorces, 2.

**Recreation:** Falcon Reservoir activities; deer, white-wing dove hunting; access to Mexico; historic houses; grotto at Rio Grande City; Roma Fest in November.

**Minerals:** Oil, gas, sand, gravel.

**Agriculture:** Beef and fed cattle; vegetables, cotton, sorghum; 18,000 acres irrigated for vegetables. Market value $65.1 million.

**RIO GRANDE CITY** (12,305) county seat; agriculture center; food processing; exports to Mexico; hospital.

**ROMA-Los Saenz** (9,969) agriculture center; La Purisima Concepcíon Visita.

Other towns include: **Delmita** (50); **Escobares** (2,046); **Falcon Heights** (348); **Fronton** (623); **Garceño** (1,491); **La Casita-Garciasville** (2,287); **La Grulla** (1,192); **La Puerta** (1,702); **La Rosita** (1,757); **Las Lomas** (2,738); **La Victoria** (1,738); **Los Alvarez** (1,451); **Los Villareales** (950); **North Escobares** (1,762); **Salineno** (308); **San Isidro** (273); **Santa Elena** (64).

| | |
|---|---|
| Population | 56,686 |
| Change fm 2000 | 5.8 |
| Area (sq. mi.) | 1,229.28 |
| Land Area (sq. mi.) | 1,223.02 |
| Altitude (ft.) | 125-531 |
| Rainfall (in.) | 22.3 |
| Jan. mean min. | 43 |
| July mean max. | 99 |
| Civ. Labor | 25,391 |
| Unemployed | 22.1 |
| Wages | $49,649,117 |
| Av. Weekly Wage | $352.06 |
| Prop. Value | $1,606,301,512 |
| Retail Sales | $304,022,859 |

# Stephens County

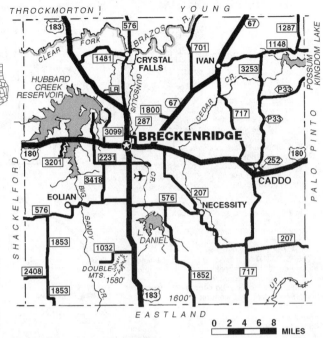

**Physical Features:** West central county; broken, hilly; Hubbard Creek Reservoir, Possum Kingdom, Daniel lakes; Brazos River; loam, sandy soils.

**Economy:** Oil, agribusinesses, recreation, some manufacturing.

**History:** Comanches, Tonkawas in area when Anglo-American settlement began in 1850s. County created as Buchanan 1858 from Bosque; renamed 1861 for Confederate Vice President Alexander H. Stephens; organized 1876.

**Race/Ethnicity, 2000:** (In percent) Anglo, 81.76; Black, 3.04; Hispanic, 14.66; Other, 0.54.

**Vital Statistics, 2001:** Births, 148; deaths, 112; marriages, 87; divorces, 31.

**Recreation:** Lakes activities; hunting; campsites; historical points; Swenson Museum; Sandefer Oil Museum; aviation museum; drag boat races in June.

**Minerals:** Oil, natural gas, stone.

**Agriculture:** Beef cattle, hogs, goats, sheep; wheat, oats, hay, peanuts, grain sorghums, cotton, pecans. Market value $8.1 million.

**BRECKENRIDGE** (5,974) county seat; oil, agriculture center; mobile home, aircraft parts manufacturing; petrochemical production; hospital; prison unit; arts center, library.

Other towns include: **Caddo** (40), gateway to Possum Kingdom State Park.

| Population | 9,453 |
|---|---|
| Change fm 2000 | -2.3 |
| Area (sq. mi.) | 921.48 |
| Land Area (sq. mi.) | 894.64 |
| Altitude (ft.) | 995-1,600 |
| Rainfall (in.) | 27.6 |
| Jan. mean min. | 28 |
| July mean max. | 97 |

| | |
|---|---|
| Civ. Labor | 4,097 |
| Unemployed | 8.7 |
| Wages | $17,696,791 |
| Av. Weekly Wage | $451.66 |
| Prop. Value | $619,437,900 |
| Retail Sales | $66,139,789 |

# Sterling County

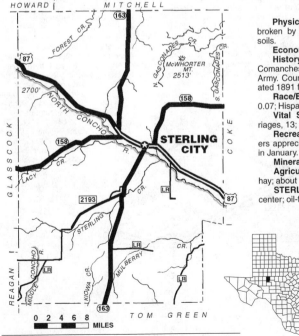

**Physical Features:** Central prairie, surrounded by hills, broken by Concho River and tributaries; sandy to black soils.

**Economy:** Ranching; oil & gas; hunting leases.

**History:** Ranching began in late 1870s after Comanches, Kickapoos and other tribes removed by U.S. Army. County named for buffalo hunter W.S. Sterling; created 1891 from Tom Green County.

**Race/Ethnicity, 2000:** (In percent) Anglo, 68.63; Black, 0.07; Hispanic, 31.01; Other, 0.29.

**Vital Statistics, 2001:** Births, 17; deaths, 12; marriages, 13; divorces, 11.

**Recreation:** Hunting of deer, quail, turkey, dove; hunters appreciation dinner in November; junior livestock show in January.

**Minerals:** Oil, natural gas.

**Agriculture:** Beef cattle, meat goats, sheep; wheat, hay; about 1,000 acres irrigated. Market value $9.2 million.

**STERLING CITY** (1,105) county seat; farm, ranch trade center; oil-field services.

| Population | 1,346 |
|---|---|
| Change fm 2000 | -3.4 |
| Area (sq. mi.) | 923.49 |
| Land Area (sq. mi.) | 923.36 |
| Altitude (ft.) | 2,100-2,700 |
| Rainfall (in.) | 20.3 |
| Jan. mean min. | 29 |
| July mean max. | 96 |
| Civ. Labor | 774 |
| Unemployed | 3.2 |
| Wages | $3,623,017 |
| Av. Weekly Wage | $509.49 |
| Prop. Value | $360,445,930 |
| Retail Sales | $5,111,151 |

# Stonewall County

**Physical Features:** Western county on rolling plains below Caprock, bisected by Brazos forks; sandy loam, sandy, other soils; some hills.

**Economy:** Agribusiness, light fabrication, government/services.

**History:** Anglo-American ranchers arrived in 1870s after Comanches and other tribes removed by U.S. Army. German farmers settled after 1900. County named for Confederate Gen. T.J. (Stonewall) Jackson; created from Bexar 1876, organized 1888.

**Race/Ethnicity, 2000:** (In percent) Anglo, 84.17; Black, 3.37; Hispanic, 11.75; Other, 0.71.

**Vital Statistics, 2001:** Births, 25; deaths, 30; marriages, 17; divorces, 1.

**Recreation:** Deer, quail, feral hog, turkey hunting; rodeos in June, September; livestock show.

**Minerals:** Gypsum, gravel, oil.

**Agriculture:** Beef cattle, wheat, cotton, peanuts, hay. Also, grain sorghum, meat goats and swine. Market value $9.9 million.

**ASPERMONT** (1,038) county seat; oil field; ranching center; light fabrication; hospital; springfest; livestock show in February.

Other towns include: **Old Glory** (125), farming center; **Peacock** (125); **Swenson** (185).

| | |
|---|---|
| Population | 1,493 |
| Change fm 2000 | -11.8 |
| Area (sq. mi.) | 920.23 |
| Land Area (sq. mi.) | 918.67 |

| | |
|---|---|
| Altitude (ft.) | 1,500-2,500 |
| Rainfall (in.) | 23.3 |
| Jan. mean min. | .27 |
| July mean max. | 97 |
| Civ. Labor | 691 |

| | |
|---|---|
| Unemployed | 2.5 |
| Wages | $3,095,154 |
| Av. Weekly Wage | $412.63 |
| Prop. Value | $199,576,226 |
| Retail Sales | $7,787,450 |

| | |
|---|---|
| Population | 4,117 |
| Change fm 2000 | 1.0 |
| Area (sq. mi.) | 1,454.40 |
| Land Area (sq. mi.) | 1,453.76 |
| Altitude (ft.) | 1,900-2,500 |
| Rainfall (in.) | 22.4 |
| Jan. mean min. | 30 |
| July mean max. | 96 |
| Civ. Labor | 2,190 |
| Unemployed | 2.5 |
| Wages | $13,941,072 |
| Av. Weekly Wage | $570.42 |
| Prop. Value | $746,777,964 |
| Retail Sales | $30,582,632 |

# Sutton County

**Physical Features:** Southwestern county; level in west, rugged terrain in east, broken by tributaries of Devils, Llano rivers; black, red loam soils.

**Economy:** Oil and gas; agribusiness; hunting; tourism.

**History:** Lipan Apaches drove out Tonkawas in 1600s. Comanches, military outpost and disease forced Apaches south. Anglo-Americans settled in 1870s. Mexican immigration increased after 1890. County created from Crockett 1887; organized 1890; named for Confederate officer Col. John S. Sutton.

**Race/Ethnicity, 2000:** (In percent) Anglo, 47.51; Black, 0.29; Hispanic, 51.66; Other, 0.54.

**Vital Statistics, 2001:** Births, 70; deaths, 25; marriages, 20; divorces, 20.

**Recreation:** Hunting; Meirs Museum; Caverns of Sonora; goat cookoff; Diez y Seis in September.

**Minerals:** Oil, natural gas.

**Agriculture:** Cattle, sheep, meat goats, Angora goats, cashmere goats, mohair. Exotic wildlife. Wheat raised for grazing, hay; minor irrigation. Market value $9.6 million. Hunting leases important.

**SONORA** (2,977) county seat; oil, gas production; ranching; tourism; hospital; wool, mohair show in June.

For explanation of sources, abbreviations and symbols, see p. 138.

# Swisher County

**Physical Features:** High Plains county; level, broken by Tule Canyon and Creek; playas; large underground water supply; rich soils.

**Economy:** Feedlots, grain storage, other agribusinesses; varied manufacturing; tourism; prison unit.

**History:** Apaches; displaced by Comanches around 1700. U.S. Army removed Comanches in 1874. Ranching began in late 1870s. Farming developed after 1900. County named for J.G. Swisher of Texas Revolution; county created from Bexar, Young territories 1876; organized 1890.

**Race/Ethnicity, 2000:** (In percent) Anglo, 58.37; Black, 5.91; Hispanic, 35.22; Other, 0.50.

**Vital Statistics, 2001:** Births, 150; deaths, 76; marriages, 44; divorces, 22.

**Recreation:** Tule Lake activities; museum; county picnic in July; "Rogue of the Railways" melodrama in March.

**Minerals:** Not significant.

**Agriculture:** A major agricultural county. Stocker cattle, feed lots. Cotton, corn, wheat, sorghum raised. Some 400,000 acres irrigated. Market value $361 million.

**TULIA** (5,148) county seat; farming center; government/services; food processing; hospital; library; museum; prison; Tule Creek bluegrass festival in July.

Other towns include: **Happy** (652, partly in Randall County), **Kress** (839).

| | |
|---|---|
| Population ............................. 8,082 | July mean max. ........................... 91 |
| Change fm 2000 ....................... -3.5 | Civ. Labor ............................... 3,636 |
| Area (sq. mi.) ........................ 900.68 | Unemployed ............................... 4.4 |
| Land Area (sq. mi.) ............... 900.43 | Wages ......................... $12,935,929 |
| Altitude (ft.).................... 3,100-3,700 | Av. Weekly Wage ............... $421.46 |
| Rainfall (in.) .............................. 19.4 | Prop. Value............... $395,177,882 |
| Jan. mean min. ............................ 22 | Retail Sales ................. $32,067,903 |

*A ranch hand works with horses near Guthrie in King County. File photo.*

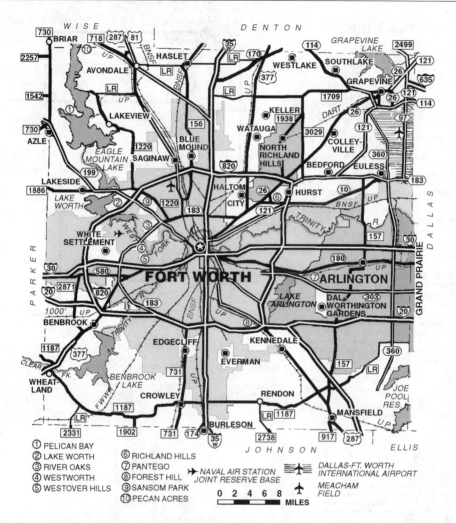

① PELICAN BAY
② LAKE WORTH
③ RIVER OAKS
④ WESTWORTH
⑤ WESTOVER HILLS
⑥ RICHLAND HILLS
⑦ PANTEGO
⑧ FOREST HILL
⑨ SANSOM PARK
⑩ PECAN ACRES

✈ NAVAL AIR STATION
JOINT RESERVE BASE

DALLAS-FT. WORTH
INTERNATIONAL AIRPORT

✈ MEACHAM
FIELD

0 2 4 6 8
MILES

# Tarrant County

**Physical Features:** Part Blackland, level to rolling; drains to Trinity; Worth, Grapevine, Eagle Mountain, Benbrook lakes.

**Economy:** Tourism; planes, helicopters, foods, mobile homes, electronic equipment, chemicals, plastics among products of more than 1,000 factories; large federal expenditure; D/FW International Airport; economy closely associated with Dallas urban area.

**History:** Caddoes in area. Comanches, other tribes arrived about 1700. Anglo-Americans settled in 1840s. Named for Gen. Edward H. Tarrant, who helped drive Indians from area. County created 1849 from Navarro County; organized 1850.

**Race/Ethnicity, 2000:** (In percent) Anglo, 62.79; Black, 13.01; Hispanic, 19.73; Other, 4.47.

**Vital Statistics, 2001:** Births, 26,367; deaths, 9,679; marriages, 13,600; divorces, 7,409.

**Recreation:** Scott Theatre; Amon G. Carter Museum; Kimbell Art Museum; Modern Art Museum; Museum of Science and History; Casa Manana; Botanic Gardens; Fort Worth Zoo; Log Cabin Village; Six Flags Over Texas at Arlington; Southwestern Exposition, Stock Show; Convention Center; Stockyards Historical District; Texas Rangers major-league baseball at Arlington, other athletic events.

**Minerals:** Production of cement, sand, gravel, stone, gas.

**Agriculture:** Hay, beef cattle, wheat, horses, horticulture. Market value $34.9 million. Firewood marketed.

**Education:** Texas Christian University, University of Texas at Arlington, Texas Wesleyan University, Southwestern Baptist Theological Seminary and several other academic centers including a junior college system (three campuses).

**FORT WORTH** (555,110) county seat; a major mercantile, commercial and financial center; wholesale trade center for much of West Texas; airplane, helicopter and other plants.

A cultural center with renowned art museums, Bass Performance Hall; many conventions held in downtown center; agribusiness center for wide area with grain-storage and feed-mill operations; adjacent to D/FW International Airport; hospitals).

**ARLINGTON** (344,751) industrial and distribution center for automobiles, food products, electronic

components, aircraft and parts, rubber and plastic products; medical center, hospitals. A tourist center with Six Flags Over Texas, the Texas Rangers baseball team, numerous restaurants; educational facilities; Scottish Highland games in June.

Other towns include: **Hurst** (36,895); **Euless** (47,638); **Bedford** (48,481) helicopter plant, hospital; **North Richland Hills** (58,265).

**Azle** (9,971, partly in Parker County) varied industries, Jumpin' Jack Jamboree in October; **Benbrook** (20,500) varied manufacturing; hospitals; **Blue Mound** (2,404); **Briar** (5,531, parts in Wise and Parker counties); **Colleyville** (20,915) major residential development, some retail, manufacturing; **Crowley** (7,997), varied manufacturing, government/services; hospital; **Dalworthington Gardens** (2,260); **Edgecliff** (2,579); **Everman** (5,907); **Forest Hill** (13,338).

Also, **Grapevine** (43,852), varied manufacturing, distribution; near the D/FW International Airport; tourist center; hospital; Grapefest in September; **Haltom City** (39,913) light

manufacturing, food processing, medical center; library; **Haslet** (1,254); **Keller** (31,115) Bear Creek Park, Wild West Fest.

Also, **Kennedale** (6,191) printing manufacturing; **Lakeside** (1,079); **Lake Worth** (4,766); **Mansfield** (30,102, partly in Johnson County) varied manufacturing; hospital; Frontier Days, hometown celebration in fall; **Pantego** (2,378); **Pelican Bay** (1,543); **Rendon** (9,399); **Richland Hills** (8,268).

Also, **River Oaks** (7,102); **Saginaw** (14,338) grain milling, manufacturing, distribution; Train and Grain festival in October; library; **Sansom Park** (4,233); **Southlake** (22,872) technology, financial, retail center,

hospital, parks, Oktoberfest; **Watauga** (22,707); **Westlake** (206); **Westover Hills** (665); **Westworth Village** (2,075); **White Settlement** (14,948) near aircraft manufacturing, museum, parks, historical sites; industrial park; White Settlement Day parade in fall.

Also, part (3,462) of **Burleson** (23,351 total); part (27,621) of **Grand Prairie** (131,688 total), and part of **Pecan Acres** (2,434).

| | |
|---|---|
| Population | 1,527,366 |
| Change fm 2000 | 5.6 |
| Area (sq. mi.) | 897.48 |
| Land Area (sq. mi.) | 863.42 |
| Altitude (ft.) | 450-1,000 |
| Rainfall (in.) | 31.3 |
| Jan. mean min. | 35 |
| July mean max. | 96 |
| Civ. Labor | 834,147 |
| Unemployed | 6.2 |
| Wages | $6,468,996,091 |
| Av. Weekly Wage | $711.16 |
| Prop. Value | $104,051,657,216 |
| Retail Sales | $20,459,751,131 |

*For explanation of sources, abbreviations and symbols, see p. 138.*

*Runners make their way under an overpass along the Trinity River in Fort Worth.*

*File photo.*

**Physical Features:** Prairies, with Callahan Divide, draining to Colorado tributaries, Brazos forks; Lakes Abilene, Kirby; mostly loam soils.

**Economy:** Dyess Air Force Base, feedlots, agribusinesses, diversified manufacturing and education; government/services.

**History:** Comanches in area about 1700. Anglo-American settlers arrived in 1870s. Named for Alamo heroes Edward, James and George Taylor, brothers; county created from Bexar, Travis 1858; organized 1878.

**Race/Ethnicity, 2000:** (In percent) Anglo, 73.54; Black, 6.95; Hispanic, 17.64; Other, 1.87.

**Vital Statistics, 2001:** Births, 2,023; deaths, 1,176; marriages, 1,324; divorces, 801.

**Recreation:** Abilene State Park; lake activities; Nelson Park Zoo; Texas Cowboy Reunion, West Texas Fair; Buffalo Gap historical tour and art festival; rodeo, college events.

**Minerals:** Oil, natural gas, stone, caliche, clays, sand and gravel.

# Taylor County

**Agriculture:** Wheat; cattle, fed, cow/calf, and stocker; cotton; milo. Market value $55.9 million.

**Education:** Abilene Christian University, Hardin-Simmons University, McMurry University, Cisco Junior College branch.

**ABILENE** (116,097, partly in Jones County) county seat; distribution center; plants make a variety of products; meat, dairy processing; oil-field service center; hospitals; Abilene State School; West Texas Rehabilitation Center; Fort Phantom

Hill (in Jones County). **Wylie** is now part of Abilene.

Other communities include: **Buffalo Gap** (464) historic sites; **Impact** (34); **Lawn** (379); **Merkel** (2,643) agribusiness center, clothing manufacturing, oil-field services; **Ovalo** (225); **Potosi** (1,723); **Trent** (321); **Tuscola** (712); **Tye** (1,165).

| | |
|---|---|
| Population | **125,647** |
| Change fm 2000 | -0.7 |
| Area (sq. mi.) | 919.25 |
| Land Area (sq. mi.) | 915.63 |
| Altitude (ft.) | 1,670-2,500 |
| Rainfall (in.) | 24.4 |
| Jan. mean min. | 31 |
| July mean max. | 95 |
| Civ. Labor | 60,610 |
| Unemployed | 4.2 |
| Wages | $341,051,544 |
| Av. Weekly Wage | $493.32 |
| Prop. Value | $4,975,948,703 |
| Retail Sales | $1,562,664,493 |

*For explanation of sources, abbreviations and symbols, see p. 138.*

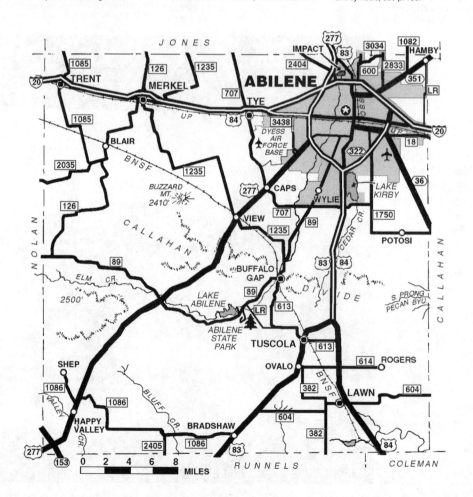

# Terrell County

**Physical Features:** Trans-Pecos southwestern county; semi-mountainous, many canyons; rocky, limestone soils.

**Economy:** Ranching; oil and natural gas exploration; farm services; tourism, hunting leases.

**History:** Coahuiltecans, Jumanos and other tribes left many pictographs in area caves. Sheep ranching began in 1880s. Named for Confederate Gen. A.W. Terrell; county created 1905 from Pecos County.

**Race/Ethnicity, 2000:** (In percent) Anglo, 49.02; Black, 0.00; Hispanic, 48.57; Other, 2.41.

**Vital Statistics, 2001:** Births, 6; deaths, 4; marriages, 5; divorces, 1.

**Recreation:** Hunting, especially white-tailed, mule deer; Rio Grande Wild and Scenic River; varied wildlife; Cinco de Mayo, Prickly Pear Pachanga in October.

**Minerals:** Gas, oil, limestone.

**Agriculture:** Goats (meat, Angora); sheep (meat, wool); some beef cattle. Market value $4.3 million.

**SANDERSON** (810) county seat; ranching, petroleum center; government/services. Other town: **Dryden** (13).

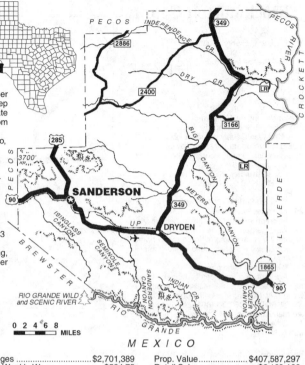

| | |
|---|---|
| Population | **998** |
| Change fm 2000 | -7.7 |
| Area (sq. mi.) | 2,357.75 |
| Land Area (sq. mi.) | 2,357.72 |
| Altitude (ft.) | 1,400-3,700 |
| Rainfall (in.) | 14.3 |
| Jan. mean min. | 29 |
| July mean max. | 92 |
| Civ. Labor | 823 |
| Unemployed | 4.3 |

| | | | |
|---|---|---|---|
| Wages | $2,701,389 | Prop. Value | $407,587,297 |
| Av. Weekly Wage | $524.75 | Retail Sales | $2,169,166 |

# Terry County

**Physical Features:** Western county on South Plains, broken by draws, playas; sandy, sandy loam, loam soils.

**Economy:** Agribusiness, government/services, trade, commuting to Lubbock.

**History:** Comanches removed in 1870s by U.S. Army. Ranching developed in 1890s; farming after 1900. Oil discovered in 1940. County named for head of famed Texas Ranger troop, Col. B.F. Terry. County created from Bexar District 1876; organized 1904.

**Race/Ethnicity, 2000:** (In percent), Anglo, 50.32; Black, 5.02; Hispanic, 44.09; Other, 0.57.

**Vital Statistics, 2001:** Births, 186; deaths, 120; marriages, 89; divorces, 42.

**Recreation:** Museum; harvest festival in October; Brisket and Bean cook-off in April.

**Minerals:** Oil, gas, salt mining.

**Agriculture:** Cotton is principal crop; peanuts, grain sorghum, guar, wheat, melons, cucumbers, sesame. 170,000 acres irrigated. Market value $69.7 million.

**BROWNFIELD** (9,218) county seat; oilfield services; agribusiness; minerals processed; hospital; prison.

Other towns include: **Meadow** (626); **Tokio** (24); **Wellman** (205).

| | |
|---|---|
| Population | **12,723** |
| Change fm 2000 | -0.3 |
| Area (sq. mi.) | 890.93 |
| Land Area (sq. mi.) | 889.88 |
| Altitude (ft.) | 3,100-3,600 |
| Rainfall (in.) | 19.0 |
| Jan. mean min. | 24 |
| July mean max. | 93 |
| Civ. Labor | 4,852 |
| Unemployed | 8.4 |
| Wages | $22,919,764 |
| Av. Weekly Wage | $465.06 |
| Prop. Value | $708,842,201 |
| Retail Sales | $93,708,158 |

# Throckmorton County

**Physical Features:** North Central county southwest of Wichita Falls; rolling, between Brazos forks; red to black soils.

**Economy:** Oil, agribusiness, hunting leases.

**History:** Site of Comanche Indian Reservation 1854-59. Ranching developed after Civil War. County named for Dr. W.E. Throckmorton, father of Gov. J.W. Throckmorton; county created from Fannin 1858; organized 1879.

**Race/Ethnicity, 2000:** (In percent) Anglo, 90.11; Black, 0.05; Hispanic, 9.35; Other, 0.49.

**Vital Statistics, 2001:** Births, 19; deaths, 25; marriages, 8; divorces, 5.

**Recreation:** Hunting, fishing; historic sites include Camp Cooper, site of former Comanche reservation; restored ranch home, Miller's Creek Reservoir; wild game dinner in January.

**Minerals:** Natural gas, oil.

**Agriculture:** Beef cattle, horses, wheat, hay. Market value $18.7 million. Mesquite firewood sold. Hunting leases important.

**THROCKMORTON** (867) county seat; varied manufacturing; oil-field services; hospital.

Other towns include: **Elbert** (53), **Woodson** (311).

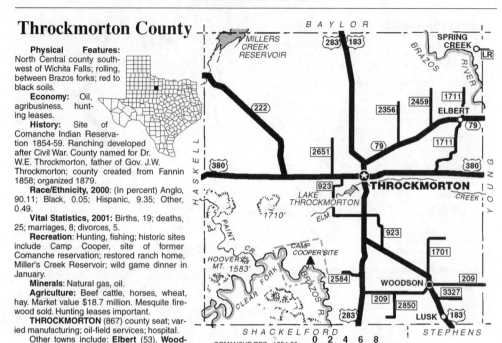

| | |
|---|---|
| Population | 1,711 |
| Change fm 2000 | -7.5 |
| Area (sq. mi.) | 915.47 |
| Land Area (sq. mi.) | 912.34 |
| Altitude (ft.) | 1,140-1,710 |
| Rainfall (in.) | 27.1 |
| Jan. mean min. | 27 |
| July mean max. | 96 |
| Civ. Labor | 862 |
| Unemployed | 3.5 |
| Wages | $2,031,132 |
| Av. Weekly Wage | $335.28 |
| Prop. Value | $287,848,367 |
| Retail Sales | $4,771,720 |

# Titus County

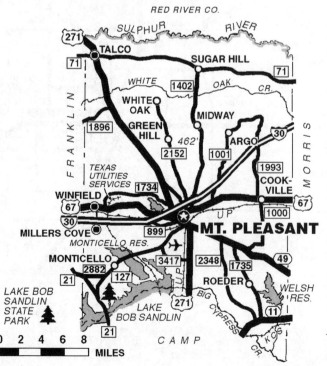

| | |
|---|---|
| Population | 28,405 |
| Change fm 2000 | 1.0 |
| Area (sq. mi.) | 425.69 |
| Land Area (sq. mi.) | 410.54 |
| Altitude (ft.) | 300-462 |
| Rainfall (in.) | 46.8 |
| Jan. mean min. | 29 |
| July mean max. | 94 |
| Civ. Labor | 14,129 |
| Unemployed | 4.9 |
| Wages | $108,369,610 |
| Av. Weekly Wage | $504.03 |
| Prop. Value | $2,209,520,504 |
| Retail Sales | $368,907,203 |

*For explanation of sources, abbreviations and symbols, see p. 138.*

**Physical Features:** East Texas county; hilly, timbered; drains to Big Cypress Creek, Sulphur River.

**Economy:** Agribusinesses; lignite mining and power generation; trailer manufacturing.

**History:** Caddo area. Cherokees and other tribes settled in 1820s. Anglo-American settlers arrived in 1840s. Named for pioneer settler A.J. Titus; county created from Bowie, Red River counties 1846.

**Race/Ethnicity, 2000:** (In percent)

# Titus County

Anglo, 60.03; Black, 10.72; Hispanic, 28.31; Other, 0.94.

**Vital Statistics, 2001:** Births, 514; deaths, 287; marriages, 316; divorces, 45.

**Recreation:** Fishing, hunting; lake activities; state park; railroad museum; riverboat; flower gardens.

**Minerals:** Lignite coal, oil, gas.

**Agriculture:** Poultry, beef cattle,

hay, horses, watermelons. Market value $45.6 million. Timber sales significant.

**MOUNT PLEASANT** (14,139) county seat; tourism; varied manufacturing; food-processing plants; hospital; Northeast Texas Community College; WranglerFest in October.

Other towns include: **Cookville** (105), **Millers Cove** (122), **Talco** (577), **Winfield** (509).

**(Map on previous page.)**

**Physical Features:** West central county of plains, rolling hills, broken by Concho forks; loams in basin, stony hillsides; lakes.

**Economy:** "Sheep and Wool Capital"; varied agribusinesses, manufacturing; trade center for area, education center, medical center; government/services.

**History:** Jumano Indians attracted Spanish missionaries around 1630. Comanches controlled area when U.S. military established outposts in 1850s. Anglo-American settlement occurred after Civil War. County created from Bexar District 1874, named for Gen. Tom Green of Texas Revolution; organized 1875; 12 other counties created from this original area.

**Race/Ethnicity, 2000:** (In percent) Anglo, 63.65; Black, 4.22; Hispanic, 30.71; Other, 1.42.

**Vital Statistics, 2001:** Births, 1,533; deaths, 1,014; marriages, 1,059; divorces, 490.

**Recreation:** Water sports; hunting; Fort Concho museum; urban, collegiate activities; roping fiesta in Novem-

# Tom Green County

ber; February rodeo; minor league hockey, baseball teams.

**Minerals:** Oil, natural gas.

**Agriculture:** Cattle; cotton; a leading sheep-raising county; goats; dairy products. Also, sorghum, wheat, swine, horses. About 30,000 acres irrigated. Market value $78.6 million.

**SAN ANGELO** (88,608) county seat; manufacturing of medical devices; distribution center; varied agri-

business; oil and gas; airbase; riverwalk; hospitals; Angelo State University, A&M extension center; Museum of Fine Arts.

Other towns include: **Carlsbad** (100); **Christoval** (433); **Grape Creek** (3,203); **Knickerbocker** (50); **Mereta** (75); **Vancourt** (125); **Veribest** (40); **Wall** (200); **Water Valley** (120).

| | |
|---|---|
| Population | 103,018 |
| Change fm 2000 | -1.0 |
| Area (sq. mi.) | 1,540.54 |
| Land Area (sq. mi.) | 1,522.10 |
| Altitude (ft.) | 1,700-2,600 |
| Rainfall (in.) | 20.5 |
| Jan. mean min. | 31 |
| July mean max. | 96 |
| Civ. Labor | 51,276 |
| Unemployed | 3.7 |
| Wages | $287,153,132 |
| Av. Weekly Wage | $498.26 |
| Prop. Value | $3,545,279,424 |
| Retail Sales | $1,180,327,783 |

*For explanation of sources, abbreviations and symbols, see p. 138.*

**Physical Features:** Central county of scenic hills, broken by Colorado River and lakes; cedars, pecans, other trees; diverse soils, mineral deposits.

**Economy:** Education, state government, tourism, research and industry; conventions.

**History:** Tonkawa and Lipan Apache area; Comanches, Kiowas arrived about 1700. Spanish missions from East Texas temporarily relocated near Barton Springs in 1730 before removing to San Antonio. Anglo-Americans arrived in early 1830s. County created 1840, when Austin became Republic's capital, from Bastrop County; organized 1843; named for Alamo commander Col. William B. Travis; many other counties created from its original area.

**Race/Ethnicity, 2000:** (In percent) Anglo, 57.28; Black, 9.38; Hispanic, 28.20; Other, 5.14.

**Vital Statistics, 2001:** Births, 14,599; deaths, 4,002; marriages, 8,187; divorces, 2,163.

**Recreation:** Colorado River lakes; hunting, fishing; McKinney Falls State Park; Lady Bird Johnson Wildflower Center; Austin Aqua Festival; collegiate, metropolitan, governmental events; official buildings and historic sites; museums; Sixth St. restoration area; scenic drives; city parks.

# Travis County

**Minerals:** Production of lime, stone, sand, gravel, oil and gas.

**Agriculture:** Cattle, nursery crops, hogs; sorghum, corn, cotton, small grains, pecans. Market value $21.4 million.

**Education:** University of Texas main campus; St. Edward's University, Concordia Lutheran University, Huston-Tillotson College, Austin Community College, Episcopal and Presbyterian seminaries; state schools and institutions for blind, deaf, mental illnesses.

**AUSTIN** (678,198, part [11,810] in Williamson County) county seat and state capital; state and federal payrolls; IRS center; a leading convention, tourist city; Lyndon B. Johnson Library; research, high-tech industries; hospitals, including state institutions; popular retirement area.

Other towns include: **Bee Cave** (1,109); **Briarcliff** (956); **Creedmoor** (228); **Del Valle** (2,476); **Garfield** (1,735); **Jonestown** (1,746); **Lago Vista** (4,762); **Lakeway** (8,368); **Manchaca** (2,259); **Manor** (1,248); **McNeil** (70); **Mustang Ridge** (838, partly in Caldwell County).

Also, **Pflugerville** (19,298) high-tech industries, agriculture, government/services, Deutchenfest in May; **Point Venture** (470); **Rollingwood** (1,410); **San Leanna** (412); **Sunset Valley** (398); **The Hills** (1,536); **Volente** (NA); **Webberville** (NA); **Wells Branch** (11,396); **West Lake Hills** (3,284).

Also, part of **Anderson Mill**, part of **Cedar Park**, part of **Jollyville** and part of **Round Rock**, all mostly in Williamson County.

| Population | 850,813 |
|---|---|
| Change fm 2000 | 4.7 |
| Area (sq. mi.) | 1,022.06 |
| Land Area (sq. mi.) | 989.30 |
| Altitude (ft.) | 400-1,330 |
| Rainfall (in.) | 31.9 |
| Jan. mean min. | 39 |
| July mean max. | 95 |
| Civ. Labor | 516,473 |
| Unemployed | 5.7 |
| Wages | $5,195,947,087 |
| Av. Weekly Wage | $774.95 |
| Prop. Value | $73,279,137,188 |
| Retail Sales | $12,630,214,827 |

*For explanation of sources, abbreviations and symbols, see p. 138.*

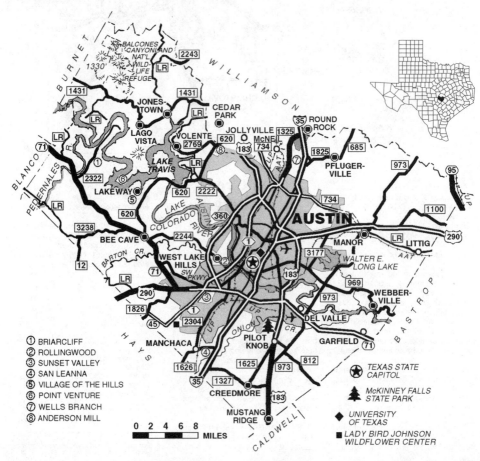

① BRIARCLIFF
② ROLLINGWOOD
③ SUNSET VALLEY
④ SAN LEANNA
⑤ VILLAGE OF THE HILLS
⑥ POINT VENTURE
⑦ WELLS BRANCH
⑧ ANDERSON MILL

0 2 4 6 8 MILES

⭐ *TEXAS STATE CAPITOL*

🌲 *McKINNEY FALLS STATE PARK*

◆ *UNIVERSITY OF TEXAS*

■ *LADY BIRD JOHNSON WILDFLOWER CENTER*

# Trinity County

**Physical Features:** Heavily forested East Texas county of hills, between Neches and Trinity (Lake Livingston) rivers; rich alluvial soils, sandy upland; 67,910 acres in national forest.

**Economy:** Forestry, cattle, tourism, government/services.

**History:** Caddoes, reduced by disease in late 1700s. Kickapoo, Alabama, Coushatta in area when Anglo-Americans settled in 1840s. Named for river; county created 1850 out of Houston County.

**Race/Ethnicity, 2000:** (In percent) Anglo, 82.46; Black, 12.04; Hispanic, 4.85; Other, 0.65.

**Vital Statistics, 2001:** Births, 162; deaths, 195; marriages, 80; divorces, 41.

**Recreation:** Lake activities; fishing, hiking, hunting; Davy Crockett National Forest; historic sites; Timber Festival in March; Scottish festival at Thanksgiving.

**Minerals:** Limited oil, gas, sand and gravel.

**Agriculture:** Beef cattle. Market value $6.3 million. Timber sales significant. Hunting leases.

**GROVETON** (1,122) county seat; lumber center; petroleum processing; varied manufacturing; government/services.

**TRINITY** (2,831) steel fabrication; forest-industries center; government/services; hospital; near Lake Livingston.

Other towns include: **Apple Springs** (185); **Centralia** (53); **Pennington** (67); **Sebastopol** (120) historic town; **Woodlake** (98).

| | |
|---|---|
| Population | 14,088 |
| Change fm 2000 | 2.2 |
| Area (sq. mi.) | 714.00 |

| | |
|---|---|
| Land Area (sq. mi.) | 692.84 |
| Altitude (ft.) | 131-400 |
| Rainfall (in.) | 44.9 |
| Jan. mean min. | 36 |

| | |
|---|---|
| July mean max. | 94 |
| Civ. Labor | 7,425 |
| Unemployed | 3.8 |
| Wages | $12,134,195 |
| Av. Weekly Wage | $412.83 |
| Prop. Value | $671,974,312 |
| Retail Sales | $64,160,182 |

# Tyler County

**Physical Features:** Hilly East Texas county; densely timbered; drains to Neches River; B.A. Steinhagen Lake; Big Thicket is unique plant and animal area.

**Economy:** Lumbering; government/services, some manufacturing; tourism, hunting leases.

**History:** Caddoan area. Cherokees, Alabama and Coushatta pushed into area from U.S. South in 1820s. Anglo-Americans settled in 1830s. Named for U.S. President John Tyler; county created 1846 from Liberty.

**Race/Ethnicity, 2000:** (In percent) Anglo, 83.49; Black, 12.16; Hispanic, 3.56; Other, 0.79.

**Vital Statistics, 2001:** Births, 214; deaths, 253; marriages, 149; divorces, 133.

**Recreation:** Big Thicket National Preserve; Heritage Village; lake activities; Allan Shivers Museum; state forest; historic sites; dogwood festival; rodeo; frontier frolics in September; gospel music fest in June.

**Minerals:** Oil, natural gas.

**Agriculture:** Cattle, hay, nursery crops, blueberries, horses. Market value $4 million. Timber sales significant.

**WOODVILLE** (2,408) county seat; lumber, cattle market; varied manufacturing; tourism; hospital; prison unit.

Other towns include: **Chester** (264) **Colmesneil** (638), **Doucette** (131), **Fred** (239), **Hillister** (200), **Spurger** (472), **Warren** (304).

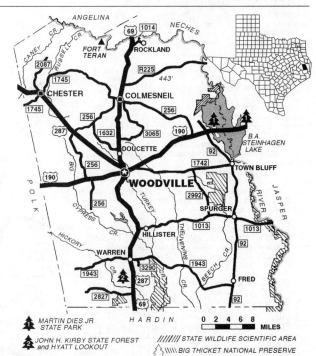

MARTIN DIES JR. STATE PARK

JOHN H. KIRBY STATE FOREST and HYATT LOOKOUT

////// STATE WILDLIFE SCIENTIFIC AREA

\\\\\ BIG THICKET NATIONAL PRESERVE

| | |
|---|---|
| Population | 20,743 |
| Change fm 2000 | -0.6 |
| Area (sq. mi.) | 935.71 |
| Land Area (sq. mi.) | 922.90 |
| Altitude (ft.) | 50-443 |

| | |
|---|---|
| Rainfall (in.) | 54.3 |
| Jan. mean min. | 38 |
| July mean max. | 93 |
| Civ. Labor | 7,218 |
| Unemployed | 10.7 |

| | |
|---|---|
| Wages | $22,625,515 |
| Av. Weekly Wage | $450.19 |
| Prop. Value | $977,813,830 |
| Retail Sales | $93,898,321 |

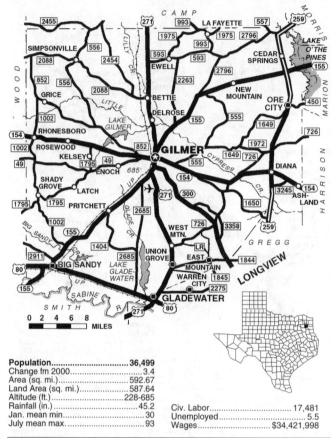

## Upshur County

**Physical Features:** East Texas county; rolling to hilly, over half forested; drains to Sabine River, Little Cypress Creek, Lake O' the Pines, Lake Gilmer, Lake Gladewater.

**Economy:** Manufacturing, agribusinesses, government/services, petroleum products and lumber mill; many residents work at area plants.

**History:** Caddoes; reduced by epidemics in 1700s. Cherokees in area in 1820s. Anglo-American settlement in mid-1830s. County created from Harrison, Nacogdoches counties 1846; named for U.S. Secretary of State A.P. Upshur.

**Race/Ethnicity, 2000:** (In percent) Anglo, 84.82; Black, 10.31; Hispanic, 3.95; Other, 0.92.

**Vital Statistics, 2001:** Births, 507; deaths, 413; marriages, 235; divorces, 235.

**Recreation:** Scenic trails; hunting, fishing; Cherokee Rose Festival, Fall Foliage, East Texas Yamboree in October.

**Minerals:** Oil, gas, sand, gravel.

**Agriculture:** Poultry (among leading broiler counties), dairies, beef cattle; vegetable crops, hay, peaches raised. Market value $34.3 million. Timber a major product.

**GILMER** (4,932) county seat; varied manufacturing; timber, ceramics produced; vegetable processing; civic center.

Other towns include: **Big Sandy** (1,331); **Diana** (585); **East Mountain** (580); **Ore City** (1,144); **Union Grove** (364). Part (2,454) of Gladewater (6,113 total).

| | | |
|---|---|---|
| Population | | 36,499 |
| Change fm 2000 | | 3.4 |
| Area (sq. mi.) | | 592.67 |
| Land Area (sq. mi.) | | 587.64 |
| Altitude (ft.) | | 228-685 |
| Rainfall (in.) | | 45.2 |
| Jan. mean min | | 30 |
| July mean max. | | 93 |

| | | |
|---|---|---|
| Civ. Labor | | 17,481 |
| Unemployed | | 5.5 |
| Wages | | $34,421,998 |

| | | |
|---|---|---|
| Av. Weekly Wage | | $445.32 |
| Prop. Value | | $1,833,844,060 |
| Retail Sales | | $211,505,313 |

## Upton County

**Physical Features:** Western county; north flat, south rolling, hilly; limestone, sandy loam soils, drains to creeks.

**Economy:** Oil, electric power plant, wind turbines, cotton, ranching.

**History:** Apache and Comanche area until tribes removed by U.S. Army in 1870s. Sheep and cattle ranching developed in 1880s. Oil discovered in 1925. County created in 1887 from Tom Green County; organized 1910; name honors brothers John and William Upton, Confederate colonels.

**Race/Ethnicity, 2000:** (In percent) Anglo, 54.93; Black, 1.62; Hispanic, 42.57; Other, 0.88.

**Vital Statistics, 2001:** Births, 40; deaths, 45; marriages, 44; divorces, 8.

**Recreation:** Historic sites, Mendoza Trail Museum; scenic areas; chili cookoff in October, Christmas bazaar.

**Minerals:** Oil, natural gas.

**Agriculture:** Cotton, sheep, goats, beef and feeder cattle, pecans. Extensive irrigation. Market value $5.8 million.

**RANKIN** (764) county seat, oil, ranching; Barbados cookoff on Memorial Day weekend, All Kid rodeo in June.

**McCAMEY** (1,707) oil, ranching; hospital; pecan show. Other town: **Midkiff** (98).

| | |
|---|---|
| Population | 3,287 |
| Change fm 2000 | -3.4 |
| Area (sq. mi.) | 1,241.83 |
| Land Area (sq. mi.) | 1,241.68 |
| Altitude (ft.) | 2,400-3,141 |
| Rainfall (in.) | 14.3 |
| Jan. mean min. | 31 |
| July mean max. | 95 |
| Civ. Labor | 1,363 |
| Unemployed | 5.6 |
| Wages | $7,889,699 |
| Av. Weekly Wage | $557.81 |
| Prop. Value | $1,033,679,595 |
| Retail Sales | $11,877,640 |

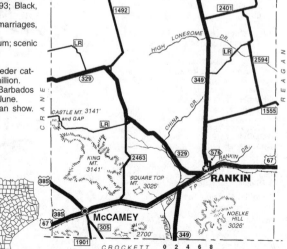

# Uvalde County

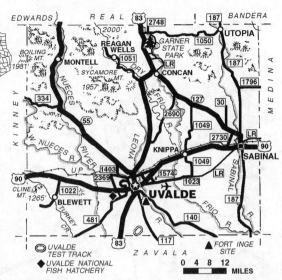

**Physical Features:** Edwards Plateau, rolling hills below escarpment; spring-fed Sabinal, Frio, Leona, Nueces rivers; cypress, cedar, other trees; unique maple groves.

**Economy:** Agribusinesses; hunting leases; light manufacturing; tourism.

**History:** Spanish mission Nuestra Señora de la Candelaria founded in 1762 for Lipan Apaches near present-day Montell; Comanches harassed mission. U.S. military outpost established in 1849. County created from Bexar 1850; re-created, organized 1856; named for 1778 governor of Coahuila, Juan de Ugalde, with name Anglicized.

**Race/Ethnicity, 2000:** (In percent) Anglo, 33.08; Black, 0.34; Hispanic, 65.91; Other, 0.67.

**Vital Statistics, 2001:** Births, 509; deaths, 256; marriages, 145; divorces, 73.

**Recreation:** Deer, turkey hunting area; Garner State Park; water activities on rivers; John Nance Garner Museum; Uvalde Memorial Park; scenic trails; historic sites; recreational homes.

**Minerals:** Asphalt, stone, sand and gravel.

**Agriculture:** Beef cattle, vegetables, corn, cotton, grain sorghum; sheep, goats; hay, wheat. Substantial irrigation. Market value $70.5 million.

**UVALDE** (15,144) county seat; vegetable, wool, mohair processing; tourism, opera house; junior college; A&M research center; hospital; Fort Inge Day in April.

**Sabinal** (1,592) farm, ranch center; gateway to Frio and Sabinal canyons; tourist, retirement area.

Other towns include: **Concan** (225); **Knippa** (769); **Utopia** (251), resort; **Uvalde Estates** (2,050).

| | |
|---|---|
| Population | 26,508 |
| Change fm 2000 | 2.2 |
| Area (sq. mi.) | 1,558.60 |
| Land Area (sq. mi.) | 1,556.55 |
| Altitude (ft.) | 699-2,000 |

| | |
|---|---|
| Rainfall (in.) | 24.8 |
| Jan. mean min. | 36 |
| July mean max. | 96 |
| Civ. Labor | 11,167 |
| Unemployed | 8.0 |
| Wages | $50,498,622 |
| Av. Weekly Wage | $409.59 |
| Prop. Value | $1,532,816,985 |
| Retail Sales | $250,352,689 |

# Val Verde County

**Physical Features:** Southwestern county bordering Mexico; rolling, hilly; brushy; Devils, Pecos rivers, Amistad Reservoir; limestone, alluvial soils.

**Economy:** Agribusiness; tourism; area trade center; large military, other federal expenditures; hunting leases.

**History:** Apaches, Coahuiltecans, Jumanos present when Spanish explored area 1535. Comanches arrived later. U.S. military outposts established in 1850s to protect settlers. Only county named for Civil War battle; Val Verde means green valley. Created 1885 from Crockett, Kinney, Pecos counties.

**Race/Ethnicity, 2000:** (In percent) Anglo, 22.11; Black, 1.46; Hispanic, 75.46; Other, 0.97.

**Vital Statistics, 2001:** Births, 860; deaths, 315; marriages, 463; divorces, 147.

**Recreation:** Gateway to Mexico; deer hunting, fishing; Amistad lake activities; two state parks; Langtry restoration of Judge Roy Bean's saloon; San Felipe Springs; winery.

**Minerals:** Production sand and gravel, gas, oil.

**Agriculture:** Major sheep-raising county, Angora goats, cattle, meat goats; minor irrigation. Market value $19.2 million.

**DEL RIO** (34,631) county seat; tourism and trade with Mexico; government/services, including federal agencies and military; varied manufacturing, winery; hospital; extension colleges; Fiesta de Amistad in October.

**Laughlin Air Force Base** (2,176).

Other towns and places include: **Cienegas Terrace** (2,999); **Comstock** (375); **Langtry** (30); **Val Verde Park** (2,025).

| | |
|---|---|
| Population | 45,903 |
| Change fm 2000 | 2.3 |
| Area (sq. mi.) | 3,232.40 |
| Land Area (sq. mi.) | 3,170.38 |
| Altitude (ft.) | 900-2,300 |
| Rainfall (in.) | 18.2 |
| Jan. mean min. | 39 |

| | |
|---|---|
| July mean max. | 96 |
| Civ. Labor | 20,458 |
| Unemployed | 7.8 |
| Wages | $89,002,994 |
| Av. Weekly Wage | $458.53 |
| Prop. Value | $1,292,780,717 |
| Retail Sales | $418,051,038 |

*For explanation of sources, abbreviations and symbols, see p. 138.*

# Van Zandt County

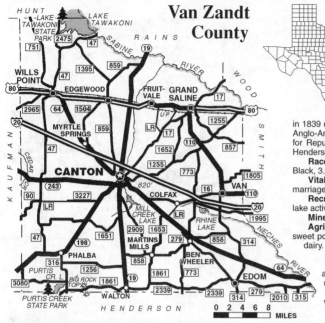

**Physical Features:** Northeastern county in three soil belts; level to rolling; Sabine, Neches rivers; Lake Tawakoni; partly forested.

**Economy:** Agribusiness, tourism, oil & gas; light manufacturing; many commute to jobs in Dallas.

**History:** Caddo tribes, reduced by epidemics before settlers arrived. Cherokees settled in 1820s; removed in 1839 under policies of Republic President Lamar; Anglo-American settlement followed. County named for Republic leader Isaac Van Zandt; created from Henderson County 1848.

**Race/Ethnicity, 2000:** (In percent) Anglo, 89.57; Black, 3.05; Hispanic, 6.65; Other, 0.73.

**Vital Statistics, 2001:** Births, 583; deaths, 589; marriages, 357; divorces, 135.

**Recreation:** Canton First Monday trades days; lake activities; state parks; historic sites.

**Minerals:** Oil, gas, salt, iron ore, clays.

**Agriculture:** Nursery crops. A major hay and sweet potato producer, also vegetables. Beef cattle, dairy. Market value $78 million.

**CANTON** (3,357) county seat; tourism; agribusiness; commuters to Dallas, Tyler; museums, bluegrass festival in June.

**Wills Point** (3,563) government/services, some manufacturing, retail center, Bluebird festival in April.

Other towns include: **Ben Wheeler** (400); **Edgewood** (1,379) commuters to Dallas; heritage park, antiques; **Edom** (316); **Fruitvale** (430); **Grand Saline** (3,135) salt plant, manufacturing, hospital, salt palace; **Van** (2,459) oil center, hay, cattle; oil festival in October.

| | |
|---|---|
| Population | 50,124 |
| Change fm 2000 | 4.1 |
| Area (sq. mi.) | 859.48 |
| Land Area (sq. mi.) | 848.64 |
| Altitude (ft.) | 400-620 |
| Rainfall (in.) | 43.0 |
| Jan. mean min. | 32 |
| July mean max. | 95 |
| Civ. Labor | 23,355 |
| Unemployed | 5.4 |
| Wages | $53,288,846 |
| Av. Weekly Wage | $427.97 |
| Prop. Value | $2,454,439,570 |
| Retail Sales | $311,777,177 |

# Victoria County

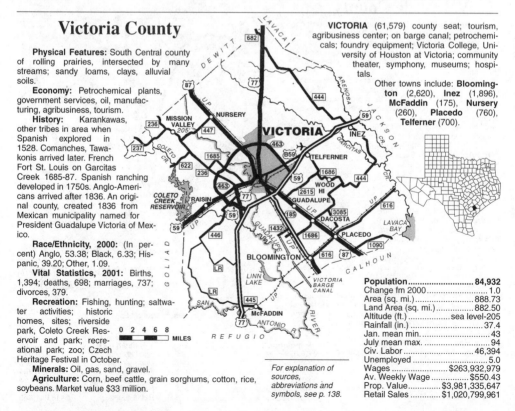

**Physical Features:** South Central county of rolling prairies, intersected by many streams; sandy loams, clays, alluvial soils.

**Economy:** Petrochemical plants, government services, oil, manufacturing, agribusiness, tourism.

**History:** Karankawas, other tribes in area when Spanish explored in 1528. Comanches, Tawakonis arrived later. French Fort St. Louis on Garcitas Creek 1685-87. Spanish ranching developed in 1750s. Anglo-Americans arrived after 1836. An original county, created 1836 from Mexican municipality named for President Guadalupe Victoria of Mexico.

**Race/Ethnicity, 2000:** (In percent) Anglo, 53.38; Black, 6.33; Hispanic, 39.20; Other, 1.09.

**Vital Statistics, 2001:** Births, 1,394; deaths, 698; marriages, 737; divorces, 379.

**Recreation:** Fishing, hunting; saltwater activities; historic homes, sites; riverside park, Coleto Creek Reservoir and park; recreational park; zoo; Czech Heritage Festival in October.

**Minerals:** Oil, gas, sand, gravel.

**Agriculture:** Corn, beef cattle, grain sorghums, cotton, rice, soybeans. Market value $33 million.

**VICTORIA** (61,579) county seat; tourism, agribusiness center; on barge canal; petrochemicals; foundry equipment; Victoria College, University of Houston at Victoria; community theater, symphony, museums; hospitals.

Other towns include: **Bloomington** (2,620), **Inez** (1,896), **McFaddin** (175), **Nursery** (260), **Placedo** (760), **Telferner** (700).

*For explanation of sources, abbreviations and symbols, see p. 138.*

| | |
|---|---|
| Population | 84,932 |
| Change fm 2000 | 1.0 |
| Area (sq. mi.) | 888.73 |
| Land Area (sq. mi.) | 882.50 |
| Altitude (ft.) | sea level-205 |
| Rainfall (in.) | 37.4 |
| Jan. mean min. | 43 |
| July mean max. | 94 |
| Civ. Labor | 46,394 |
| Unemployed | 5.0 |
| Wages | $263,932,979 |
| Av. Weekly Wage | $550.43 |
| Prop. Value | $3,981,335,647 |
| Retail Sales | $1,020,799,961 |

# Walker County

**Physical Features:** Southeastern county north of Houston of rolling hills; more than 70 percent forested; national forest; San Jacinto, Trinity rivers.

**Economy:** State employment in prison system, education; tourism; timber; beef cattle.

**History:** Coahuiltecans, Bidais in area when Spanish explored around 1690. Later, area became trading ground for many Indian tribes. Anglo-Americans settled in 1830s. Antebellum slaveholding area. County created 1846 from Montgomery County; first named for U.S. Secretary of Treasury R.J. Walker; renamed 1863 for Texas Ranger Capt. S.H. Walker.

**Race/Ethnicity, 2000:** (In percent) Anglo, 60.55; Black, 24.04; Hispanic, 14.11; Other, 1.30.

**Vital Statistics, 2001:** Births, 603; deaths, 419; marriages, 489; divorces, 214.

**Recreation:** Fishing, hunting; lake activities; Sam Houston Museum, homes, grave; prison museum; other historic sites; state park; Sam Houston National Forest; Cinco de Mayo celebration, Sam Houston folk festival in April.

**Minerals:** Clays, natural gas, oil, sand and gravel, stone.

**Agriculture:** Cattle, nursery plants, poultry, cotton, hay. Market value $13.9 million. Timber sales substantial; Christmas trees.

**HUNTSVILLE** (35,682) county seat; Texas Department of Criminal Justice headquarters, prisons; Sam Houston State University, forest products; museum; varied manufacturing; hospital.

Other towns include: **Dodge** (150), **New Waverly** (918), **Riverside** (417).

| | | | |
|---|---|---|---|
| Population | 62,388 | Rainfall (in.) | 45.0 |
| Change fm 2000 | 1.0 | Jan. mean min. | 38 |
| Area (sq. mi.) | 801.44 | July mean max. | 94 |
| Land Area (sq. mi.) | 787.45 | Civ. Labor | 23,558 |
| Altitude (ft.) | 131-404 | Unemployed | 2.9 |

| | |
|---|---|
| Wages | $151,590,574 |
| Av. Weekly Wage | $522.60 |
| Prop. Value | $1,565,557,770 |
| Retail Sales | $498,240,466 |

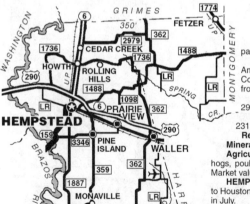

# Waller County

**Physical Features:** Southeastern county near Houston on rolling prairie; drains to Brazos; alluvial soils; about 20 percent forested.

**Economy:** Agribusiness, manufacturing, education, county part of Houston metropolitan area; oil.

**History:** Bidais Indians reduced to about 100 when Anglo-Americans settled in 1820s. Antebellum slaveholding area. County named for Edwin Waller, Republic leader; created 1873 from Austin, Grimes counties.

**Race/Ethnicity, 2000:** (In percent), Anglo, 50.36; Black, 29.40; Hispanic, 19.42; Other, 0.82.

**Vital Statistics, 2001:** Births, 484; deaths, 239; marriages, 231; divorces, 115.

**Recreation:** Fishing, hunting; historic sites; museum.

**Minerals:** Oil, gas, sand, gravel.

**Agriculture:** Cattle, rice, nursery crops, aquaculture, corn; also, hogs, poultry, horses, goats; hay, watermelons. 10,000 acres irrigated. Market value $34.3 million. Some timber marketed.

**HEMPSTEAD** (5,213) county seat; varied manufacturing; commuting to Houston; agribusiness center, large vegetable market; watermelon fest in July.

**Prairie View** (4,479) home of Prairie View A&M University.

Other towns include: **Brookshire** (3,498), **Pattison** (451), **Pine Island** (856), **Waller** (2,129, partly in Harris County). Also, part of **Katy** (12,909, mostly in Harris County).

| | |
|---|---|
| Population | 34,057 |
| Change fm 2000 | 4.3 |
| Area (sq. mi.) | 518.49 |
| Land Area (sq. mi.) | 513.63 |
| Altitude (ft.) | 100-350 |
| Rainfall (in.) | 38.2 |
| Jan. mean min. | 38 |
| July mean max. | 95 |
| Civ. Labor | 15,232 |
| Unemployed | 6.3 |
| Wages | $68,496,281 |
| Av. Weekly Wage | $516.31 |
| Prop. Value | $12,007,462,264 |
| Retail Sales | $544,468,407 |

*For explanation of sources, abbreviations and symbols, see p. 138.*

# Ward County

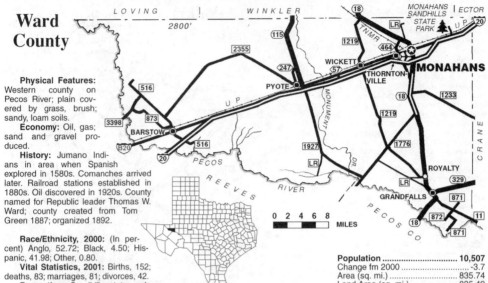

**Physical Features:** Western county on Pecos River; plain covered by grass, brush; sandy, loam soils.

**Economy:** Oil, gas; sand and gravel produced.

**History:** Jumano Indians in area when Spanish explored in 1580s. Comanches arrived later. Railroad stations established in 1880s. Oil discovered in 1920s. County named for Republic leader Thomas W. Ward; county created from Tom Green 1887; organized 1892.

**Race/Ethnicity, 2000:** (In percent) Anglo, 52.72; Black, 4.50; Hispanic, 41.98; Other, 0.80.

**Vital Statistics, 2001:** Births, 152; deaths, 83; marriages, 81; divorces, 42.

**Recreation:** Sandhills state park, museum; Pyote Rattlesnake museum; Million Barrel museum; county park; stagecoach festival in August.

**Minerals:** Oil, gas, caliche, sand, gravel.

**Agriculture:** Beef cattle; cotton, alfalfa, pecans, nursery crops. Goats also raised. Some irrigation for cotton. Market value $2.2 million.

**MONAHANS** (6,647) county seat; center for oil, gas; sand, gravel; agribusiness; tourism; hospital; fajita festival in May.

Other towns: **Barstow** (395); **Grandfalls** (380); **Pyote** (127) West Texas Children's Home; **Thorntonville** (426); **Wickett** (442).

| | |
|---|---|
| Population | 10,507 |
| Change fm 2000 | -3.7 |
| Area (sq. mi.) | 835.74 |
| Land Area (sq. mi.) | 835.49 |
| Altitude (ft.) | 2,400-2,800 |
| Rainfall (in.) | 12.7 |
| Jan. mean min. | 27 |
| July mean max. | 96 |
| Civ. Labor | 3,546 |
| Unemployed | 8.5 |
| Wages | $21,681,412 |
| Av. Weekly Wage | $538.00 |
| Prop. Value | $1,055,568,668 |
| Retail Sales | $59,024,572 |

# Washington County

| | |
|---|---|
| Population | 30,626 |
| Change fm 2000 | 0.8 |
| Area (sq. mi.) | 621.35 |
| Land Area (sq. mi.) | 609.22 |
| Altitude (ft.) | 150-505 |
| Rainfall (in.) | 41.4 |
| Jan. mean min. | 41 |
| July mean max. | 96 |
| Civ. Labor | 16,084 |
| Unemployed | 3.5 |
| Wages | $85,920,282 |
| Av. Weekly Wage | $494.00 |
| Prop. Value | $2,377,764,103 |
| Retail Sales | $332,579,222 |

WASHINGTON-ON-THE-BRAZOS STATE HISTORIC SITE

**Physical Features:** Southeastern county in Brazos valley; rolling prairie of sandy loam, alluvial soils.

**Economy:** Agribusinesses, oil, tourism, manufacturing; government/services.

**History:** Coahuiltecan tribes and Tonkawas in area when Anglo-American settlers arrived in 1821. Antebellum slaveholding area. Germans arrived around 1870. County named for George Washington; an original county, created 1836, organized 1837.

**Race/Ethnicity, 2000:** (In percent), Anglo, 71.15; Black, 18.67; Hispanic, 8.71; Other, 1.47.

**Vital Statistics, 2001:** Births, 395; deaths, 340; marriages, 245; divorces, 93.

**Recreation:** Many historic sites; Washington-on-the-Brazos; Texas Bap-

# Washington County

tist Historical Museum; Star of Republic Museum; Somerville Lake; fishing, hunting; antique rose nursery, spring fling.

**Minerals:** Oil, gas and stone.

**Agriculture:** Beef cattle, poultry, dairy products, hogs, horses; hay, corn, sorghum, cotton, small grains, nursery crops. Market value $37.2 million.

**BRENHAM** (13,543) county seat; cotton processing; varied manufacturing including ceramics, mattresses, computers, Blue Bell creamery; wholesale distribution center; tourism; Blinn College, Brenham State School; Maifest.

Other towns include: **Burton** (364) agriculture, tourism, national landmark cotton gin, festival in April; **Chappell Hill** (600) historic homes; **Washington** (265), site of signing of Texas Declaration of Independence.

**(Map on previous page.)**

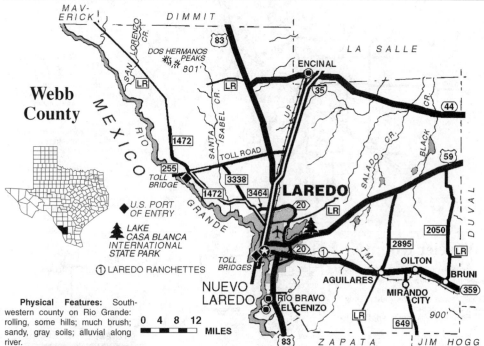

Webb County

**Physical Features:** Southwestern county on Rio Grande: rolling, some hills; much brush; sandy, gray soils; alluvial along river.

**Economy:** International trade, manufacturing, tourism, government/services, natural gas, oil.

**History:** Coahuiltecan groups squeezed out by Comanches, Apaches and Spanish settlers. Laredo founded in 1755 by Tomás Sánchez. County named for Republic leader James Webb; created 1848 from Nueces and Bexar counties.

**Race/Ethnicity, 2000:** (In percent) Anglo, 5.02; Black, 0.17; Hispanic, 94.28; Other, 0.53.

**Vital Statistics, 2001:** Births, 5,936; deaths, 1,016; marriages, 1,789; divorces, 240.

**Recreation:** Major tourist gateway to Mexico; top hunting, fishing; Lake Casa Blanca park, water recreation; art festival; Washington's Birthday celebration; historic sites; museum; Fort McIntosh.

**Minerals:** Natural gas, oil, coal.

**Agriculture:** Onions, melons, nursery crops, cattle, horses, goats. About 4,500 acres irrigated. Market value $32.2 million. Mesquite sold. Hunting leases important.

**LAREDO** (188,135) county seat; international trade; retail; tourism; manufacturing; meat packing; rail, highway gateway to Mexico; agribusiness; junior college, Texas A&M International University; hospitals; detention centers; "El Grito" on Sept. 15; Jalapeño festival in February.

Other towns and places include: **Bruni** (422); **El Cenizo** (3,597); **Laredo Ranchettes** (1,892); **Mirando City** (505); **Oilton** (319); **Rio Bravo** (5,693).

| | |
|---|---|
| Population | 207,611 |
| Change fm 2000 | 7.5 |
| Area (sq. mi.) | 3,375.53 |
| Land Area (sq. mi.) | 3,356.83 |
| Altitude (ft.) | 300-900 |
| Rainfall (in.) | 21.4 |
| Jan. mean min. | 43 |
| July mean max. | 99 |
| Civ. Labor | 81,816 |
| Unemployed | 7.6 |
| Wages | $445,043,439 |
| Av. Weekly Wage | $466.39 |
| Prop. Value | $7,681,492,032 |
| Retail Sales | $2,404,567,290 |

*For explanation of sources, abbreviations and symbols, see p. 138.*

# Wharton County

**Population** ..................... 41,329
Change fm 2000 ................... 0.3
Area (sq. mi.) ............... 1,094.43
Land Area (sq. mi.) ..... 1,090.13
Altitude (ft.) ...................... 50-150
Rainfall (in.) ........................ 42.3
Jan. mean min. .................... 41
July mean max. .................... 92
Civ. Labor ...................... 19,188
Unemployed ........................ 6.1
Wages ................. $93,107,787
Av. Weekly Wage ........ $481.20
Prop. Value ....... $2,167,215,194
Retail Sales ........ $370,333,629

**Physical Features:** Southeastern county near Houston on prairie; bisected by Colorado River; alluvial, black, sandy loam soils.

**Economy:** Oil; agribusiness, hunting leases, varied manufacturing; government/services.

**History:** Karankawas in area until 1840s. Anglo-American colonists settled in 1823. Czechs, Germans arrived in 1880s. Mexican migration increased after 1950. County named for John A. and William H. Wharton, brothers active in the Texas Revolution; created 1846 from Jackson, Matagorda counties.

**Race/Ethnicity, 2000:** (In percent) Anglo, 53.29; Black, 14.84; Hispanic, 31.29; Other, 0.58.

**Vital Statistics, 2001:** Births, 598; deaths, 424; marriages, 291; divorces, 160.

**Recreation:** Waterfowl hunting, fishing, big-game, birding; art and historical museums; river-front park in Wharton; historic sites; Fiesta Hispano Americana in September.

**Minerals:** Oil, gas.

**Agriculture:** Leading rice-producing county; other crops are cotton, milo, corn, grain sorghum, soybeans; about 130,000 acres irrigated, mostly rice. Also, eggs, turfgrass, beef cattle, aquaculture. Market value $167 million.

**WHARTON** (9,285) county seat; plastics manufacturing; agriculture; distribution; government/services; hospital; Wharton County Junior College; Riverfront park; Shanghai Days in March.

**EL CAMPO** (11,098) rice processing, storage; plastic, styrofoam processing; wholesale nursery; hospital; Polka Expo in November.

Other towns include: **Boling-Iago** (1,240); **Danevang** (61); **East Bernard** (1,781) agribusiness, varied manufacturing; **Egypt** (26); **Glen Flora** (210); **Hungerford** (664); **Lane City** (111); **Lissie** (70); **Louise** (1,032); **Pierce** (49).

# Wheeler County

**Physical Features:** Panhandle county adjoining Oklahoma. Plain, on edge of Caprock; Red River, Sweetwater Creek; some canyons; red sandy loam, black clay soils.

**Economy:** Oil, agribusinesses, tourism.

**History:** Apaches, displaced by Kiowas, Comanches around 1700. Military outpost established in 1875 after Indians forced into Oklahoma. Ranching began in late 1870s. Oil boom in 1920s. County named for pioneer jurist R.T. Wheeler; county created from Bexar, Young districts 1876; organized 1879.

**Race/Ethnicity, 2000:** (In percent) Anglo, 83.55; Black, 2.63; Hispanic, 12.57; Other, 1.25.

**Vital Statistics, 2001:** Births, 40; deaths, 99; marriages, 157; divorces, 8.

**Recreation:** Pioneer West museum at Shamrock; historic sites; Old Mobeetie trading post, Fort Elliott; ostrich depot.

**Minerals:** Oil, natural gas.

**Agriculture:** Fed beef, cow-calf and stocker cattle, swine, horses; crops include wheat, grain sorghum, cotton. Market value $93.3 million.

**WHEELER** (1,368) county seat; agribusiness; petroleum center; tourism; slaughter plant; hospital; library.

**SHAMROCK** (1,959) tourism; agribusiness; hospital; library; St. Patrick's Day event; Octoberfest.

Other towns include: **Allison** (135); **Briscoe** (135); **Mobeetie** (98).

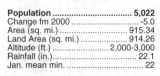

**Population** ................................. 5,022
Change fm 2000 ........................... -5.0
Area (sq. mi.) .......................... 915.34
Land Area (sq. mi.) ................ 914.26
Altitude (ft.) .................. 2,000-3,000
Rainfall (in.) .............................. 22.1
Jan. mean min. ........................... 22
July mean max. ............................. 95
Civ. Labor ................................. 2,745
Unemployed ................................ 2.7
Wages ............................... $9,169,338
Av. Weekly Wage .................... $388.40
Prop. Value .................... $747,209,870
Retail Sales ..................... $30,809,736

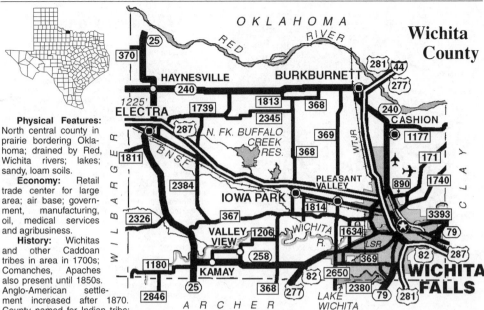

# Wichita County

**Physical Features:** North central county in prairie bordering Oklahoma; drained by Red, Wichita rivers; lakes; sandy, loam soils.

**Economy:** Retail trade center for large area; air base; government, manufacturing, oil, medical services and agribusiness.

**History:** Wichitas and other Caddoan tribes in area in 1700s; Comanches, Apaches also present until 1850s. Anglo-American settlement increased after 1870. County named for Indian tribe; created from Young Territory 1858; organized 1882.

**Race/Ethnicity, 2000:** (In percent) Anglo, 74.34; Black, 10.57; Hispanic, 12.23; Other, 2.86.

**Vital Statistics, 2001:** Births, 1,893; deaths, 1,298; marriages, 2,542; divorces, 823.

**Recreation:** Metropolitan events; museums; historic sites; Texas-Oklahoma High School Oil Bowl football game; collegiate activities; water sports on lakes; Fiestas Patrias parade; Ranch Round-up in August.

**Minerals:** Oil, natural gas, sand, gravel, stone.

**Agriculture:** Stocker, cow-calf production important; wheat, other small grains; hay; cotton. Seventy-five percent of hay irrigated; 10 percent of wheat/cotton. Market value $21.8 million.

**WICHITA FALLS** (104,544) county seat; distribution center for large area in Texas, Oklahoma; government/services; varied manufacturing; oil-field services; hospitals; state prison; Midwestern State University, vocational-technical training center; North Texas State Hospital; hiking trails, major bicycle race in August; Zephyr Days in October; **Sheppard Air Force Base**.

Other cities include: **Burkburnett** (10,963) some manufacturing; **Cashion** (342); **Electra** (3,152) oil, agriculture, some manufacturing, commuters to Wichita Falls; hospital; Goat barbecue in May; **Iowa Park** (6,473) some manufacturing, clinic; **Kamay** (642); **Pleasant Valley** (407).

| Population | 129,964 |
| --- | --- |
| Change fm 2000 | -1.3 |
| Area (sq. mi.) | 633.01 |
| Land Area (sq. mi.) | 627.66 |
| Altitude (ft.) | 954-1,225 |
| Rainfall (in.) | 28.9 |
| Jan. mean min. | 28 |
| July mean max. | 97 |
| Civ. Labor | 60,462 |
| Unemployed | 4.4 |
| Wages | $362,680,659 |
| Av. Weekly Wage | $510.03 |
| Prop. Value | $4,859,381,229 |
| Retail Sales | $1,275,266,791 |

*For explanation of sources, abbreviations and symbols, see p. 138.*

*A view of U.S. Highway 281 as it runs through Windthorst in Archer County. File photo.*

# Wilbarger County

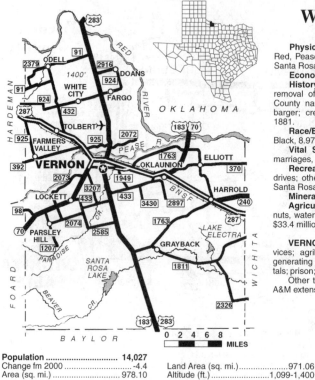

**Physical Features:** Gently rolling prairie draining to Red, Pease rivers, tributaries; sandy, loam, waxy soils; Santa Rosa Lake.

**Economy:** Government/services, agribusinesses.

**History:** Anglo-American settlement developed after removal of Comanches into Indian Territory in 1875. County named for pioneers Josiah and Mathias Wilbarger; created from Bexar District 1858; organized 1881.

**Race/Ethnicity, 2000:** (In percent) Anglo, 69.18; Black, 8.97; Hispanic, 20.54; Other, 1.31.

**Vital Statistics, 2001:** Births, 207; deaths, 178; marriages, 328; divorces, 41.

**Recreation:** Doan's Crossing, on route of cattle drives; other historic sites; Red River Valley Museum; Santa Rosa roundup in May; hunting, fishing.

**Minerals:** Oil, natural gas.

**Agriculture:** Wheat, alfalfa, beef cattle, cotton, peanuts, watermelons; 25,000 acres irrigated. Market value $33.4 million.

**VERNON** (11,474) county seat; government/services; agribusiness; varied manufacturing; electricity-generating plant; college; mental health center, hospitals; prison; downtown antiques retailers.

Other towns include: **Harrold** (320); **Lockett** (200), A&M extension center; **Odell** (131); **Oklaunion** (138).

| | |
|---|---|
| Population | 14,027 |
| Change fm 2000 | -4.4 |
| Area (sq. mi.) | 978.10 |
| Land Area (sq. mi.) | 971.06 |
| Altitude (ft.) | 1,099-1,400 |
| Rainfall (in.) | 25.7 |
| Jan. mean min. | 25 |
| July mean max. | 97 |
| Civ. Labor | 7,474 |
| Unemployed | 3.5 |
| Wages | $40,747,855 |
| Av. Weekly Wage | $480.23 |
| Prop. Value | $942,323,550 |
| Retail Sales | $106,159,358 |

# Willacy County

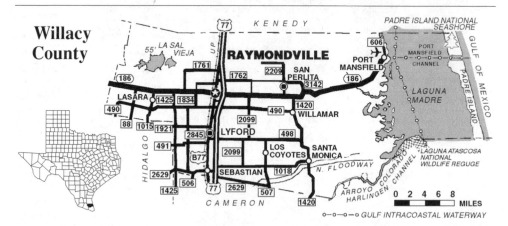

**Physical Features:** Flat coastal prairie sloping toward Gulf; alluvial, sandy, marshy soils; Padre Island; La Sal Vieja, salt lake; wildlife refuge.

**Economy:** Oil, agribusinesses; tourism; shipping.

**History:** Coahuiltecan area when Spanish explored in 1500s. Spanish ranching began in 1790s. County named for Texas legislator John G. Willacy; created 1911 from Cameron, Hidalgo counties; reorganized 1921.

**Race/Ethnicity, 2000:** (In percent) Anglo, 11.98; Black, 2.02; Hispanic, 85.69; Other, 0.31.

**Vital Statistics, 2001:** Births, 399; deaths, 102; marriages, 137; divorces, 31.

**Recreation:** Fresh and saltwater fishing, hunting of deer, turkey, dove; mild climate attracts many winter tourists; Port Mansfield fishing tournament.

**Minerals:** Oil, natural gas.

**Agriculture:** Cotton, sorghum, corn, vegetables, sugar cane; 20 percent of cropland irrigated. Livestock includes cattle, horses, goats, hogs. Market value $52.5 million.

**RAYMONDVILLE** (9,760) county seat; agribusiness, oil center; clothing manufacturing; food processing, shipping; tourist center; museum; hospital; enterprise zone; prison unit.

Other towns include: **Lasara** (1,049); **Lyford** (2,005); **Port Mansfield** (416), popular fishing port; shrimp processing; fishing tournament in late July; **San Perlita** (685); **Sebastian** (1,882).

| | |
|---|---|
| Population | 19,990 |
| Change fm 2000 | -0.5 |
| Area (sq. mi.) | 784.23 |
| Land Area (sq. mi.) | 596.68 |
| Altitude (ft.) | sea level-55 |
| Rainfall (in.) | 27.6 |
| Jan. mean min. | 46 |
| July mean max. | 96 |
| Civ. Labor | 6,130 |
| Unemployed | 18.4 |
| Wages | $17,942,614 |
| Av. Weekly Wage | $414.35 |
| Prop. Value | $798,950,079 |
| Retail Sales | $58,659,159 |

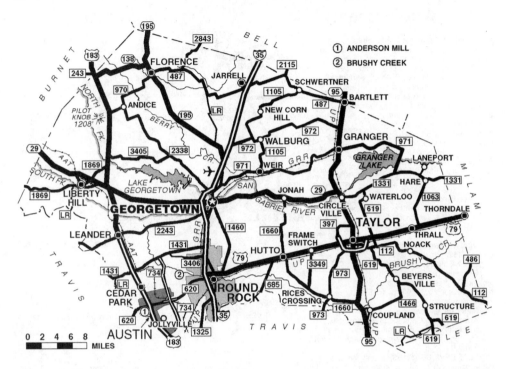

① ANDERSON MILL
② BRUSHY CREEK

0 2 4 6 8 MILES

# Williamson County

**Physical Features:** Central county near Austin. Level to rolling; mostly Blackland soil, some loam, sand; drained by San Gabriel River and tributaries.

**Economy:** Agribusinesses, varied manufacturing, education center, government/services; the county is part of Austin metropolitan area.

**History:** Tonkawa area; later, other tribes. Comanches raided until 1860s. Anglo-American settlement began in late 1830s. County named for Robert M. Williamson, pioneer leader; created from Milam and organized in 1848.

**Race/Ethnicity, 2000:** (In percent) Anglo, 74.33; Black, 5.27; Hispanic, 17.20; Other, 3.20.

**Vital Statistics, 2001:** Births, 4,784; deaths, 1,159; marriages, 1,864; divorces, 1,211.

**Recreation:** Lake recreation; Inner Space Cavern; historic sites; deer hunting, fishing; Gov. Dan Moody Museum at Taylor; San Gabriel Park; old settlers park; walking tours, rattlesnake sacking, barbecue cookoff, frontier days in summer.

**Minerals:** Building stone, sand and gravel.

**Agriculture:** Corn, cattle, grain sorghum, cotton, wheat. Market value $53.4 million.

**GEORGETOWN** (32,128) county seat; agribusiness, manufac-turing, education, tourism, mining; hospital; Southwestern University; Mayfair; Christmas Stroll.

**ROUND ROCK** (70,036, part [1,076] in Travis County) semiconductor, varied manufacturing; tourism and distribution center; hospital; Texas Baptist Children's Home.

**Taylor** (14,393) agribusiness, publishing center; varied manufacturing including cottonseed and meat processing; hospital; movie location.

Other towns include: **Andice** (NA); **Bartlett** (1,699, partly in Bell County) cotton, corn production; commuters; prison; first rural electrification in nation in 1933, clinic; library; Friendship Fest in September; **Brushy Creek** (16,341); **Cedar Park** (31,876, partly in Travis County) varied manufacturing, communting to Austin, steam-engine train; **Coupland** (NA), **Florence** (1,101).

Also, **Granger** (1,317); **Hutto** (2,284) agriculture, manufacturing, government/services; commuters to Austin; museum; Olde Tyme Days in October; **Jarrell** (1,384); **Jollyville** (15,920, partly in Travis County); **Leander** (10,895); **Liberty Hill** (1,468), artisans center; **Schwertner** (150); **Thrall** (774); **Walburg** (250); **Weir** (608).

Also, the residential community of **Anderson Mill** (9,051), which extends into Travis County, and part (11,810) of **Austin**.

| Population | 289,924 |
|---|---|
| Change fm 2000 | 16.0 |
| Area (sq. mi.) | 1,134.74 |
| Land Area (sq. mi.) | 1,122.77 |
| Altitude (ft.) | 400-1,208 |
| Rainfall (in.) | 34.4 |
| Jan. mean min. | 34 |
| July mean max. | 96 |
| Civ. Labor | 166,616 |
| Unemployed | 5.2 |
| Wages | $747,958,539 |
| Av. Weekly Wage | $725.87 |
| Prop. Value | $ 26,375,536,513 |
| Retail Sales | $ 3,325,675,185 |

*For explanation of sources, abbreviations and symbols, see p. 138.*

# Wilson County

**Physical Features:** South central county on rolling plains; mostly sandy soils, some heavier; San Antonio River, Cibolo Creek.

**Economy:** Agribusiness; some residents employed in San Antonio; part of San Antonio metropolitan area.

**History:** Coahuiltecan Indians in area when Spanish began ranching around 1750. Anglo-American settlers arrived in 1840s. German, Polish settled in 1850s. County created from Bexar, Karnes counties 1860; named for James C. Wilson, member of the Mier Expedition.

**Race/Ethnicity, 2000:** (In percent) Anglo, 61.51; Black, 1.21; Hispanic, 36.52; Other, 0.76.

**Vital Statistics, 2001:** Births, 442; deaths, 242; marriages, 214; divorces, 101.

**Recreation:** Mission ranch ruins, historic homes; Stockdale watermelon festival; Floresville peanut festival in October.

**Minerals:** Oil, gas, clays.

**Agriculture:** Cattle, dairy products, hogs, poultry; peanuts, sorghum, corn, small grains, vegetables, watermelons, fruit. Market value $53.9 million.

**FLORESVILLE** (6,193) county seat; agribusiness center; hospital; veterans home; Heritage Days in spring; annual Pony Express ride.

Other towns include: **La Vernia** (976); **Pandora** (125); **Poth** (1,910) agriculture, commuting to San Antonio; Mayfest; **Stockdale** (1,466) food processing; medical center; recreation facilities; **Sutherland Springs** (362). Part of **Nixon** (2,241, mostly in Gonzales County).

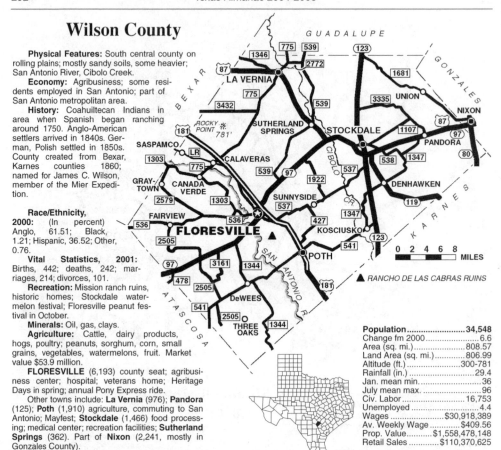

RANCHO DE LAS CABRAS RUINS

| | |
|---|---|
| Population | 34,548 |
| Change fm 2000 | 6.6 |
| Area (sq. mi.) | 808.57 |
| Land Area (sq. mi.) | 806.99 |
| Altitude (ft.) | 300-781 |
| Rainfall (in.) | 29.4 |
| Jan. mean min. | 36 |
| July mean max. | 96 |
| Civ. Labor | 16,753 |
| Unemployed | 4.4 |
| Wages | $30,918,389 |
| Av. Weekly Wage | $409.56 |
| Prop. Value | $1,558,478,148 |
| Retail Sales | $110,370,625 |

# Winkler County

**Physical Features:** Western county adjoining New Mexico on plains, partly sandy hills.

**Economy:** Oil, natural gas; ranching; prison.

**History:** Apache area until arrival of Comanches in 1700s. Anglo-Americans began ranching in 1880s. Oil discovered 1926. Mexican migration increased after 1960. County named for Confederate Col. C.M. Winkler; created from Tom Green 1887; organized 1910.

**Race/Ethnicity, 2000:** (In percent) Anglo, 53.60; Black, 1.87; Hispanic, 44.00; Other, 0.53.

**Vital Statistics, 2001:** Births, 105; deaths, 77; marriages, 46; divorces, 13.

**Recreation:** Sandhills Park; museum; zoo; wooden oil derrick; Roy Orbison festival in June at Wink; Wink Sink, large sinkhole.

**Minerals:** Oil, gas.

**Agriculture:** Beef cattle, potatoes, meat goats. Market value $1.9 million.

**KERMIT** (5,586) the county seat, and **Wink** (918) oil, gas, ranching; hospital.

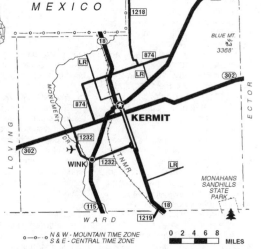

N & W - MOUNTAIN TIME ZONE
S & E - CENTRAL TIME ZONE

| | | | |
|---|---|---|---|
| Population | 6,892 | Rainfall (in.) | 12.6 |
| Change fm 2000 | -3.9 | Jan. mean min. | 28 |
| Area (sq. mi.) | 841.24 | July mean max. | 97 |
| Land Area (sq. mi.) | 841.05 | Civ. Labor | 2,902 |
| Altitude (ft.) | 2,671-3,368 | Unemployed | 8.2 |

| | |
|---|---|
| Wages | $13,713,976 |
| Av. Weekly Wage | $536.58 |
| Prop. Value | $836,504,341 |
| Retail Sales | $31,626,998 |

# Wise County

**Physical Features:** North central county of rolling prairie, some oaks; clay, loam, sandy soils; lakes.

**Economy:** Agribusiness; petroleum; recreation; sand and gravel; hunting leases; many residents work in Fort Worth.

**History:** Caddo Indian groups. Delaware tribe present when Anglo-Americans arrived in 1850s. County created 1856 from Cooke County; named for Virginian, U.S. Sen. Henry A. Wise, who favored annexation of Texas.

**Race/Ethnicity, 2000:** (In percent) Anglo, 86.88; Black, 1.33; Hispanic, 10.76; Other, 1.03.

**Vital Statistics, 2001:** Births, 685; deaths, 395; marriages, 421; divorces, 328.

**Recreation:** Lake activities; hunting; exotic deer preserve; historical sites; Lyndon B. Johnson National Grasslands; Chisholm trail days in June, antique auto swap meet; Butterfield stage days in July; heritage museum, old courthouse.

**Minerals:** Gas, oil, sand, gravel.

**Agriculture:** Beef cattle, dairy operations, forages, horses, wheat, pecans, peanuts. Market value $42.8 million.

**DECATUR** (5,393) county seat; petroleum center; dairying; cattle marketing; some manufacturing; hospital.

**BRIDGEPORT** (4,518) trade center for lake resort; oil, gas production; timeshare housing; artistic community; manufacturing.

Other towns include: **Alvord** (1,028); **Aurora** (888); **Boyd** (1,145); **Briar** (5,531, mostly in Tarrant County);

**Chico** (977); **Greenwood** (76); **Lake Bridgeport** (390); **Newark** (939); **New Fairview** (886); **Paradise** (492); **Pecan Acres** (2,434, partly in Tarrant County); **Rhome** (626); **Runaway Bay** (1,199); **Slidell** (175).

| | |
|---|---|
| Population | 52,926 |
| Change fm 2000 | 8.5 |
| Area (sq. mi.) | 922.77 |

| | |
|---|---|
| Land Area (sq. mi.) | 904.61 |
| Altitude (ft.) | 649-1,180 |
| Rainfall (in.) | 32.6 |
| Jan. mean min. | 30 |
| July mean max. | 99 |
| Civ. Labor | 29,116 |
| Unemployed | 4.3 |
| Wages | $95,665,004 |
| Av. Weekly Wage | $539.23 |
| Prop. Value | $3,592,867,265 |
| Retail Sales | $407,371,656 |

# Wood County

**Physical Features:** Hilly northeastern county almost half forested; sandy to alluvial soils; drained by Sabine and tributaries; many lakes.

**Economy:** Agribusiness, oil and gas; tourism.

**History:** Caddo Indians; reduced by disease. Anglo-American settlement developed in 1840s. County created from Van Zandt County 1850; named for Gov. George T. Wood.

**Race/Ethnicity, 2000:** (In percent) Anglo, 87.23; Black, 6.27; Hispanic, 5.72; Other, 0.78.

**Vital Statistics, 2001:** Births, 441; deaths, 525; marriages, 261; divorces, 148.

**Recreation:** Autumn trails; lake activities; hunting; Gov. Hogg shrine and museum; historic sites; scenic drives; Mineola May Days & Bean Fest; railroad heritage days; autumn trails.

**Minerals:** Natural gas, oil, sand, gravel.

**Agriculture:** Poultry, dairy, beef cattle, forage, horses. Market value $91.9 million. Timber production. Timber significant.

**QUITMAN** (2,077) county seat; tourism; food processing; some manufacturing; hospital; Dogwood Fiesta.

**MINEOLA** (4,694) farm, railroad center, Amtrak stop; food processing; some manufacturing; museum, Iron Horse festival in October.

**Winnsboro** (3,622, partly in Franklin County) gas and oil, dairies, tourism; hospital; prison. Other towns include: **Alba** (439, partly in Rains County); **Golden** (156) Sweet Potato festival; **Hawkins** (1,337) refinery, water bottling, Jarvis Christian College; oil festival in October; **Yantis** (332).

▲ GOV. HOGG SHRINE
STATE HISTORIC SITE

| | |
|---|---|
| Population | 38,053 |
| Change fm 2000 | 3.5 |
| Area (sq. mi.) | 695.80 |
| Land Area (sq. mi.) | 650.22 |
| Altitude (ft.) | 299-630 |
| Rainfall (in.) | 45.0 |
| Jan. mean min. | 31 |
| July mean max. | 94 |
| Civ. Labor | 14,827 |

| | |
|---|---|
| Unemployed | 5.7 |
| Wages | $49,722,044 |
| Av. Weekly Wage | $447.97 |
| Prop. Value | $2,159,678,694 |
| Retail Sales | $341,827,151 |

*For explanation of sources, abbreviations and symbols, see p. 138.*

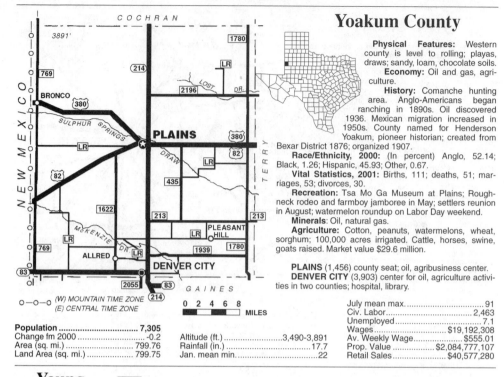

# Yoakum County

**Physical Features:** Western county is level to rolling; playas, draws; sandy, loam, chocolate soils.

**Economy:** Oil and gas, agriculture.

**History:** Comanche hunting area. Anglo-Americans began ranching in 1890s. Oil discovered 1936. Mexican migration increased in 1950s. County named for Henderson Yoakum, pioneer historian; created from Bexar District 1876; organized 1907.

**Race/Ethnicity, 2000:** (In percent) Anglo, 52.14; Black, 1.26; Hispanic, 45.93; Other, 0.67.

**Vital Statistics, 2001:** Births, 111; deaths, 51; marriages, 53; divorces, 30.

**Recreation:** Tsa Mo Ga Museum at Plains; Roughneck rodeo and farmboy jamboree in May; settlers reunion in August; watermelon roundup on Labor Day weekend.

**Minerals:** Oil, natural gas.

**Agriculture:** Cotton, peanuts, watermelons, wheat, sorghum; 100,000 acres irrigated. Cattle, horses, swine, goats raised. Market value $29.6 million.

**PLAINS** (1,456) county seat; oil, agribusiness center.
**DENVER CITY** (3,903) center for oil, agriculture activities in two counties; hospital, library.

○—○—○ (W) MOUNTAIN TIME ZONE
(E) CENTRAL TIME ZONE

0 2 4 6 8 MILES

| | |
|---|---|
| Population | 7,305 |
| Change fm 2000 | -0.2 |
| Area (sq. mi.) | 799.76 |
| Land Area (sq. mi.) | 799.75 |

| | |
|---|---|
| Altitude (ft.) | 3,490-3,891 |
| Rainfall (in.) | 17.7 |
| Jan. mean min. | 22 |

| | |
|---|---|
| July mean max. | 91 |
| Civ. Labor | 2,463 |
| Unemployed | 7.1 |
| Wages | $19,192,308 |
| Av. Weekly Wage | $555.01 |
| Prop. Value | $2,084,777,107 |
| Retail Sales | $40,577,280 |

# Young County

**Physical Features:** Hilly, broken; drained by Brazos and tributaries; Possum Kingdom Lake, Lake Graham.

**Economy:** Oil, agribusiness, tourism; hunting leases.

**History:** U.S. military outpost established 1851. Site of Brazos Indian Reservation 1854-59 with Caddoes, Wacos, other tribes. Anglo-American settlers arrived in 1850s. County named for early Texan, Col. W.C. Young; created 1856 from Bosque, Fannin counties; reorganized 1874.

**Race/Ethnicity, 2000:** (In percent) Anglo, 87.25; Black, 1.32; Hispanic, 10.62; Other, 0.81.

**Vital Statistics, 2001:** Births, 225; deaths, 257; marriages, 151; divorces, 79.

**Recreation:** Lake activities; hunting; Fort Belknap restoration; marker at oak tree in Graham where ranchers formed forerunner of Texas and Southwestern Cattle Raisers Association; vintage auto club tour, antique tractor show in April.

**Minerals:** Oil, gas, sand, gravel.

**Agriculture:** Beef cattle; wheat chief crop, also hay, cotton, pecans, nursery plants. Market value $24.3 million.

**GRAHAM** (8,686) county seat; oil, agribusiness, manufacturing, tourism, hunting; hospital, mental health clinic; celebrity rodeo in fall.

Other towns include: **Eliasville** (150); **Loving** (300); **Newcastle** (589); **Olney** (3,372) aluminum, varied manufacturing, hospital; Mayfest; **South Bend** (140).

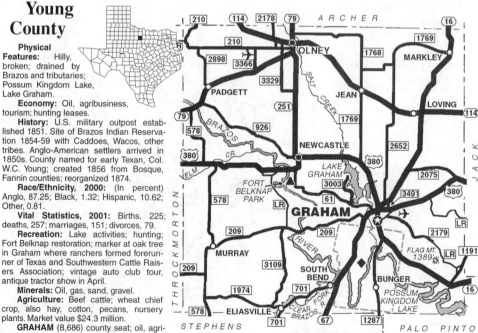

◆ BRAZOS RES. 1854-59

0 2 4 6 8 MILES

*For explanation of sources, abbreviations and symbols, see p. 138.*

| | |
|---|---|
| Population | 17,725 |
| Change fm 2000 | -1.2 |
| Area (sq. mi.) | 930.84 |
| Land Area (sq. mi.) | 922.33 |
| Altitude (ft.) | 995-1,389 |
| Rainfall (in.) | 30.6 |
| Jan. mean min. | 26 |

| | |
|---|---|
| July mean max. | 96 |
| Civ. Labor | 8,518 |
| Unemployed | 5.0 |
| Wages | $36,943,865 |
| Av. Weekly Wage | $461.34 |
| Prop. Value | $975,741,960 |
| Retail Sales | $149,714,474 |

# Zapata County

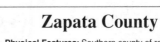

**Physical Features:** Southern county of rolling, brushy topography; broken by tributaries of Rio Grande; Falcon Reservoir.

**Economy:** Oil and gas, ranching, Falcon Reservoir activities, government/services.

**History:** Coahuiltecan Indians in area when mission visita of Nuestra Señora de los Dolores established in 1750. Anglo-American migration increased after 1980. County named for Col. Antonio Zapata, pioneer rancher; created 1858 from Starr, Webb counties.

**Race/Ethnicity, 2000:** (In percent) Anglo, 14.78; Black, 0.18; Hispanic, 84.78; Other, 0.26.

**Vital Statistics, 2001:** Births, 266; deaths, 89; marriages, 57; divorces, 0.

**Recreation:** Lake; state park; historic sites; Nuestra Señora de los Dolores Hacienda; winter tourist center.

**Minerals:** Natural gas, oil.

**Agriculture:** Beef cattle, goats; onions, cantaloupes and melons. Market value $7.2 million. Hunting/wildlife leases.

**ZAPATA** (5,056) county seat; tourism, agribusiness, oil center; retirement, winter tourist center; clinic; Fajita Cook-off in November.

Other towns and places include: **Bustamante** (15); **Chihuahua Farm** (25); **Escobas** (3); **Falcon** (376); **Lopeño** (142); **Medina** (3,069); **Ramireno** (25), and **San Ygnacio** (932).

| Population | 12,788 |
|---|---|
| Change fm 2000 | 5.0 |
| Area (sq. mi.) | 1,058.10 |
| Land Area (sq. mi.) | 996.76 |
| Altitude (ft.) | 301-800 |
| Rainfall (in.) | 19.7 |
| Jan. mean min. | 43 |
| July mean max. | 99 |
| Civ. Labor | 5,305 |
| Unemployed | 8.2 |
| Wages | $17,885,910 |
| Av. Weekly Wage | $483.60 |
| Prop. Value | $1,963,102,732 |
| Retail Sales | $59,650,053 |

# Zavala County

**Physical Features:** Southwestern county near Mexican border of rolling plains broken by much brush; Nueces, Leona, other streams.

**Economy:** Agribusiness, food packaging, leading county in Winter Garden truck-farming area; government/services.

**History:** Coahuiltecan area; Apaches, Comanches arrived later. Ranching developed in late 1860s. County created from Maverick, Uvalde counties 1858; organized 1884; named for Texas Revolutionary leader Lorenzo de Zavala.

**Race/Ethnicity, 2000:** (In percent) Anglo, 8.15; Black, 0.40; Hispanic, 91.22; Other, 0.23.

**Vital Statistics, 2001:** Births, 202; deaths, 102; marriages, 41; divorces, 1.

**Recreation:** Hunting, fishing; spinach festival in November.

**Minerals:** Oil, natural gas.

**Agriculture:** Cattle, grains, vegetables, cotton, pecans. About 50,000 acres irrigated. Market value $48.7 million. Hunting leases important.

**CRYSTAL CITY** (7,196) county seat; agribusiness; food processing; oil-field services; site of Japanese detention center. Home of Popeye statue.

Other towns include: **Batesville** (1,348) and **La Pryor** (1,449).

| Population | 11,556 |
|---|---|
| Change fm 2000 | -0.4 |
| Area (sq. mi.) | 1,301.72 |
| Land Area (sq. mi.) | 1,298.48 |
| Altitude (ft.) | 540-956 |
| Rainfall (in.) | 21.0 |
| Jan. mean min. | 42 |
| July mean max. | 97 |
| Civ. Labor | 4,716 |

| Unemployed | 16.3 |
|---|---|
| Wages | $11,402,529 |
| Av. Weekly Wage | $335.16 |
| Prop. Value | $603,755,417 |
| Retail Sales | $30,114,671 |

*For explanation of sources, explanations and symbols, see p. 138.*

# Texas Population: It's Growing, Although More Slowly

By Steve H. Murdock, Beverly Pecotte, Md. Nazrul Hoque, of the Texas State Data Center

Texas' population change was substantial in the 1990s and has remained large in the first years of the 21st century. At the same time, there are signs of at least a short-term slowing of rates of population growth.

Coupled with changes in the number of persons in Texas are data released from the 2000 census since the last issue of the Almanac which show that the 1990s brought substantial change in the socioeconomic characteristics of Texas, change which current economic conditions may threaten to, at least partially, stall or reverse.

## Post-2000 Patterns Suggest Continued Growth

U.S. Bureau of the Census estimates for July 1, 2002 showed Texas' population increasing to 21,779,893 by that date. This represents a 928,073, or 4.5 percent increase from the 2000 census count of 20,851,820. As in the 1990s (when the population increased by nearly 3.9 million persons), in the first years of this century the state was showing a net increase of roughly 100,000 persons per quarter (there were nine quarters between April 1, 2000 [the census date] and July 1, 2002 [the estimate date] and forty between the 1990 and 2000 Censuses).

From 2000 to 2002, Texas was the second fastest growing state in numerical terms (behind California as it had been in the 1990s) and the sixth fastest growing in percentage terms (it was the eighth-fastest growing in the 1990s). Thus, these estimates suggest that growth has continued to characterize Texas' population change.

In fact, the 2002 estimates suggest that growth was quite pervasive, with 140 of Texas' 254 counties showing population increases from 2000 to 2002. Nine counties increased their population by more than 10 percent and 37 by at least 5 percent from 2000 to 2002.

Of the state's 27 metropolitan areas, 23 continued to show increases from 2000 to 2002 (there were declines in Abilene, Beaumont-Port Arthur, San Angelo, and Wichita Falls), as did 19 of 24 Council of Governments (COG) regions. A total of 57 counties showed faster

*It is in rural counties that declines in rates of growth are particularly evident*

rates of growth from 2000 to 2002 than in the 1990s.

## Slower Rates of Growth

The apparent continuing rapid growth of Texas' population may be surprising to many who sense that the recent slowdown in the Texas economy must also bring decreased rates of population growth. There are several reasons why slowdown in the Texas population has been less immediately apparent than that in the economy.

First, population change simply responds more slowly to economic downturns than other factors. Even those who lose jobs and must relocate often have homes to sell, children who need to finish school, spouses who are still employed and similar factors that delay their response to economic change. As a result, population growth rates, although responding to economic change, tend to lag such change.

Second, population growth is not totally determined by economic growth. Texas increases its population by about 200,000 persons per year just as a result of natural increase (the excess of births relative to deaths), and rates of natural increase are much less impacted by the economy than the other driver of population growth, migration. In yet other areas where growth has resulted largely from non-economic factors, such as in retirement communities, economic patterns may have less direct and immediate effects on population growth.

Although lagging economic change, the slowdown in population growth is apparent particularly when rates of change are examined. The state's annualized rate of population change declined from 2.3 percent during the 1990s to 2.0 percent from 2000 to 2001 to 1.9 percent from 2001 to 2002. This represents a decline in the rate of growth of 17.4 percent from 1990-2000 to 2000-2002.

The slowdown is also evident when the trends for metropolitan areas, Council of Governments regions and counties for the 2000-2002 period are compared to those from 1990-2000. In 23 of Texas' 27 metropolitan areas, annualized rates of growth for 2000 to 2002 are slower or equal to those for the 1990s and in 22 of 24 Council of Governments regions growth was slower in the 2000 to 2002 period than from 1990 to 2000.

In the 1990s, 68 counties lost population, but, between April 1, 2000 and July 1, 2002, 114 counties lost population. Even more evident is the slowdown in rates of growth. Of the state's 254 counties, 197 showed slower rates of growth (when rates are annualized) from 2000 to 2002 than from 1990 to 2000.

Although continuing to grow substantially, rates of growth have markedly decreased for some of the state's fastest growing counties in the 2000 to 2002 period compared to the 1990s. For example, Collin County, the fastest growing county in Texas in the 1990s, still increased at an annualized rate of 6.8 percent from 2000 to 2002, but that is a nearly 21 percent reduction from its annual 8.6 percent rate of growth during the 1990s. Similar patterns of slower but yet substantial growth

| Fastest Growing Counties in Texas 2000-2002 by percentage of increase in population | Fastest Declining Counties in Texas 2000-2002 by percentage of decrease in population |
|---|---|
| 1. Rockwall ......... 18.1 | 1. Stonewall ....... -11.8 |
| 2. Williamson ...... 16.0 | 2. Terrell .............. -7.7 |
| 3. Collin ............... 15.3 | 3. Throckmorton .. -7.5 |
| 4. Denton ............ 12.8 | 4. Crockett .......... -7.1 |
| 5. Fort Bend ....... 12.7 | 5. Cochran .......... -6.6 |
| 6. Hays ............... 12.3 | 6. King ................ -6.5 |
| 7. Rains .............. 12.0 | 7. Motley ............. -6.3 |
| 8. Montgomery ... 11.8 | 8. Kent ................ -6.1 |
| 9. Bastrop .......... 10.7 | 9. Cottle .............. -5.6 |
| 10. Kaufman ......... 9.3 | 10. Reeves .......... -5.0 |

*Source: U.S. Bureau of the Census.*

are evident for Williamson County, which increased its population at an annualized rate of 7.1 percent from 2000 to 2002 compared to 7.9 percent in the 1990s, and Montgomery County which increased by 5.2 percent from 2000 to 2002 compared to 6.1 percent during the 1990s.

Among the state's largest counties, the change in the Travis County rate was the most substantial with the annualized rate of growth declining from 4.1 percent in the 1990s to 2.1 percent from 2000-2002. This is still a rapid rate of growth, but growth is also clearly slowing.

It is in rural counties that declines in rates of growth are particularly evident, however. Of the 24 counties with reductions in absolute annualized rates of growth of 2.0 percent or more between the 1990s and the 2000-2002 rates, only Travis is an urban county, all of the remaining are rural counties. These include such counties as Hartley, Concho, Live Oak, Mitchell, and Jones.

Care must always be taken in generalizing from data from any source for a relatively short period of time (such as a single year or even a couple of years). However, the available data clearly show sufficiently pervasive trends to suggest that the demographic clouds of slower growth are gathering.

Population growth is likely to slow (although not totally disappear because of high rates of natural increase) for a period of time and, because population change tends to lag economic change, to continue to be slower than in the past even after the economy begins to recover. Slower population growth is occurring and is likely to continue in the near term.

### Socioeconomic Characteristics

The 2000 census data reveal that the 1990s brought substantial socioeconomic change to Texas but also indicated that much of the socioeconomic diversity among demographic groups and regions of Texas remains.

### Increases in Income

Because the year preceding the census is the reference year for income data, 2000 census data refer to the income year 1999 and 1990 census data to 1989. Median household income in Texas increased by 47.8 percent from $27,016 in 1989 to $39,927 in 1999, median family income by 45.3 percent from $31,553 to $45,861, and per capita income by 52.0 percent from $12,904 to $19,617. When adjusted for inflation from 1989 to 1999 these represented real income increases of 13.9, 12.0, and 17.1 percent respectively.

These real income increases exceeded those for the nation which showed increases of 7.7, 9.5 and 15.3 percent respectively, from 1989 to 1999.

Nevertheless, Texas' income levels remained lower than those for the nation, with the nation having a median household income of $41,994 in 1999, a median family income of $50,046, and a per capita income level of $21,587.

Texas' median household income level was 95.1 percent of that for the nation in 1999, while Texas' median family income level was 91.6 percent of the national level, and the per capita income level was 90.9 percent of the nation's per capita income.

These represented increases from the 89.9 percent for median household income, 89.6 percent for median family income, and 89.5 percent for per capita income

## Population change, 1850-2002

| Year | Total Population | | Percent change | |
|---|---|---|---|---|
| | Texas | U.S. | Texas | U.S. |
| 1850 | 212,592 | 23,191,876 | ... | ... |
| 1860 | 604,215 | 31,443,321 | 184.2 | 35.6 |
| 1870 | 818,579 | 39,181,449 | 35.5 | 26.6 |
| 1880 | 1,591,749 | 50,155,783 | 94.5 | 26.0 |
| 1890 | 2,235,527 | 62,947,714 | 40.4 | 25.5 |
| 1900 | 3,048,710 | 75,994,575 | 36.4 | 20.7 |
| 1910 | 3,896,542 | 91,972,266 | 27.8 | 21.0 |
| 1920 | 4,663,228 | 105,710,620 | 19.7 | 14.9 |
| 1930 | 5,824,715 | 122,775,046 | 24.9 | 16.1 |
| 1940 | 6,414,824 | 131,669,275 | 10.1 | 7.2 |
| 1950 | 7,711,194 | 150,697,361 | 20.2 | 14.5 |
| 1960 | 9,579,677 | 179,323,175 | 24.2 | 19.0 |
| 1970 | 11,196,730 | 203,302,031 | 16.9 | 13.4 |
| 1980 | 14,229,191 | 226,545,805 | 27.1 | 11.4 |
| 1990 | 16,986,510 | 248,709,873 | 19.4 | 9.8 |
| 2000 | 20,851,820 | 281,421,906 | 22.8 | 13.2 |
| **2002** | **21,779,893** | **288,368,698** | **4.5** | **2.5** |

*U.S. Bureau of the Census, compiled by the Texas State Data Center, Texas A&M University.*

that Texas' incomes represented of national incomes in 1989. Nevertheless Texas' income levels continued to lag those for the nation in 1999.

There were substantial differences in incomes among population subgroups and regions of Texas. Black and Hispanic incomes, although increasing more rapidly than those for Anglos in percentage terms, continued to be less than two-thirds of those for Anglos and the absolute dollar differences in incomes actually increased.

For example, the difference between Anglo and black median household incomes increased from $13,602 in 1989 to $17,857 in 1999, while Anglo and Hispanic median household income differences increased from $12,242 in 1989 to $17,289 in 1999.

Geographical differences also remained large.

• Median household incomes in 1999 ranged from $70,835 in Collin County to $16,504 in Starr County. Suburban counties tended to have the highest incomes and South Texas counties the lowest incomes.

• Collin, Rockwall, Fort Bend, Williamson, Denton, Montgomery, and Ellis all showed median household incomes of more than $50,000 while Duval, Willacy, Dimmit, La Salle, Maverick, Hudspeth, Presidio, Brooks, Zavala, and Starr all had median household incomes of less than $23,000.

• Similarly, Collin had the highest per capita income at $33,345 while the lowest was in Starr at $7,069. Highest per capita incomes were in the large central-city and suburban counties and the lowest in parts of the Panhandle, West Texas and South Texas.

### Decreases in Poverty

The state's poverty rate for individuals fell from 18.1 percent in 1989 to 15.4 percent in 1999, a decrease of 14.9 percent. Again this was a greater decline than in the United States as a whole where the poverty rate for

individuals decreased from 13.1 to 12.4, a decrease of 5.3 percent. But, as with income, Texas levels tended to be less positive than those for the nation, with Texas' poverty rate being 138.2 percent of the U.S. rate in 1989 and still 124.2 percent of the national rate in 1999.

In fact, despite the decline in poverty rates, the absolute numbers of persons in poverty in Texas increased by more than 117,000 from 1989 to 1999. Such differences were evident across age groups.

Poverty, although declining faster for blacks and Hispanics in the 1990s, was still substantially higher for these groups than for Anglos. Although the percentage of persons in poverty declined by 24.5 percent for blacks and by 23.0 percent for Hispanics (compared to a 17.9 percent decline in the Anglo rate), 23.4 percent of blacks and 25.4 percent of Hispanics lived in poverty in 1999 compared to 7.8 percent of Anglos.

Similar geographical distributions to those for income were also evident. For example, poverty rates were highest in Starr County where 50.9 percent of all individuals lived in poverty and lowest in Rockwall County (the rate in Loving County is 0 percent but that value results from the small population size and small census sample size for the county) where only 4.7 percent of individuals lived in poverty.

Starr, Zavala, Brooks, Presidio, Hidalgo, Zapata, Hudspeth, and Maverick counties all had poverty rates above 33.3 percent while Rockwall, Williamson, and Collin all had fewer than 5 percent of their persons living in poverty. The concentration of high rates of poverty in South Texas, with scattered pockets of poverty in the Panhandle, South Plains, and East Texas, is evident as are the relatively lower rates of poverty around such major population centers as Dallas-Fort Worth, Austin, and Houston.

### Increases in Education

The 1990s also witnessed improvements in educational attainment in Texas. The percentage of adults (25 years of age or older) who are high school graduates increased from 72.1 percent in 1990 to 75.7 percent in 2000, an absolute percentage increase of 3.6 percent and a percentage increase in the overall percent with this level of education of 5.0 percent.

Similarly, the percentage of college graduates increased from 20.3 percent to 23.2 percent, an absolute increase of 2.9 percent, and a percentage increase in the attainment rate of 14.3 percent.

Again, Texas' patterns are less positive than those for the nation with the percent of high school graduates being 80.4 percent and the percent of college graduates 24.4 percent. Texas ranked 45 among all the states on the percentage of its adult population who are high school graduates and 27 relative to the percent of adults who are college graduates or higher in 2000, and these represented declines in ranking from 39th and 23rd in 1990 respectively.

The percent of Anglos with a high school degree increased by 5.7 percent, the percent of blacks with a high school degree by 9.6 percent and the percent of Hispanics with a high school degree by 4.7 percent. The percent of Anglos with a college degree increased by 4.8 percent, the percent of blacks with a college degree by 3.3 percent and the percent of Hispanics with a college degree by 1.6 percent.

Attainment differences remained large, however, with the percentage of high school graduates among Anglo adults being 87.2 percent in 2000 compared to 75.8 percent for blacks and 49.3 percent for Hispanics and whereas 30.0 percent of Anglo adults were college graduates only 15.3 percent of blacks and 8.9 percent of Hispanics were college graduates.

When viewed geographically, it is evident that those counties with high incomes and low levels of poverty also tend to have higher levels of educational attainment and those with the lowest incomes and highest levels of poverty tend to have the lowest levels of attainment.

• Collin County had the highest percentage of high school graduates, 91.8 percent, while Starr County had the lowest percentages with only 34.7 percent of adults being high school graduates. Collin County also had the highest percentage of college graduates at 47.3 percent, while Newton County with 5.5 percent had the lowest percentage of college graduates.

• Among those counties with 85 percent or more of their adult populations with high school degrees were Collin, Roberts, Randall, Loving, Rockwall, Denton, Williamson, and Kendall while those with less than 50 percent with high school degrees included Brooks, Willacy, Reeves, Hudspeth, Presidio, Zavala, Maverick, and Starr.

• Those counties with 35 percent or more of their population that were college graduates included Collin, Travis, Brazos, Fort Bend, Denton, and Jeff Davis and those with less than 8.0 percent college graduates included Zavala, Willacy, Starr, Brooks, La Salle, and Newton. Generally the highest levels of education are among populations in suburban counties and the lowest levels in South and rural Texas.

Overall, then, the 1990s showed substantial socioeconomic progress. This progress occurred across racial/ethnic groups but large differentials in income, poverty, and educational attainment continue among these groups. Similarly, large geographical differences in such factors remain with South, and to a lesser extent, rural Texas having lower levels of income and educational attainment and higher rates of poverty than other parts of Texas, particularly suburban Texas.

### Conclusions

Texas' relatively high level of natural increase, as well as continuing growth in many parts of Texas seem likely to maintain statewide population growth in the coming years, albeit at slower rates than in the 1990s.

The future socioeconomic characteristics of Texas are even more difficult to project than its level of population change. The progress of the1990s occurred in a period of unprecedented economic growth in Texas and the nation as a whole. Despite progress, demographic and regional disparities remained in 2000.

If these disparities are to be reduced, continued economic growth and development are clearly necessary. This may be more difficult with the economic conditions that have prevailed in the early years of this century but providing the education and training necessary to reduce such disparities is seen by many Texans as the major challenge that must be met in the 21st century to ensure a positive socioeconomic future for Texas. ☆

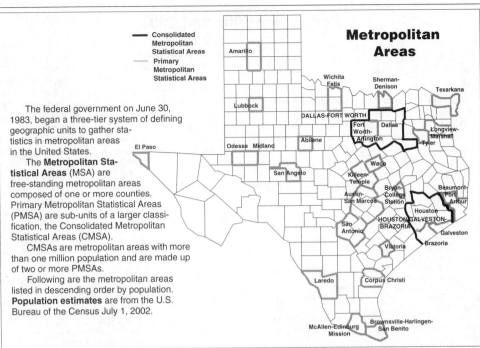

The federal government on June 30, 1983, began a three-tier system of defining geographic units to gather statistics in metropolitan areas in the United States.

The **Metropolitan Statistical Areas** (MSA) are free-standing metropolitan areas composed of one or more counties. Primary Metropolitan Statistical Areas (PMSA) are sub-units of a larger classification, the Consolidated Metropolitan Statistical Areas (CMSA).

CMSAs are metropolitan areas with more than one million population and are made up of two or more PMSAs.

Following are the metropolitan areas listed in descending order by population. **Population estimates** are from the U.S. Bureau of the Census July 1, 2002.

| Consolidated Metropolitan Statistical Areas (CMSA) | | Percent change 2000-2002 |
|---|---|---|
| **Dallas-Fort Worth** (Dallas and Fort Worth-Arlington PMSAs) | 5,545,719 | 6.2 |
| **Houston** (Houston, Galveston and Brazoria PMSAs) | 4,938,556 | 5.7 |

**Metropolitan Statistical Areas (MSA) and Primary Metropolitan Statistical Areas (PMSA)**

| | | |
|---|---|---|
| *Level A — Population 1,000,000 or More:* | | |
| 1. **Houston** PMSA (Chambers, Fort Bend, Harris, Liberty, Montgomery and Waller counties) | 4,420,081 | 5.8 |
| 2. **Dallas** PMSA(Collin, Dallas, Denton, Ellis, Henderson, Hunt, Kaufman, Rockwall counties) | 3,743,254 | 6.4 |
| 3. **Fort Worth-Arlington** PMSA (Hood, Johnson, Parker and Tarrant counties) | 1,802,465 | 5.7 |
| 4. **San Antonio** MSA (Bexar, Comal, Guadalupe and Wilson counties) | 1,660,205 | 4.3 |
| 5. **Austin-San Marcos** MSA (Bastrop, Caldwell, Hays, Travis and Williamson counties) | 1,349,291 | 8.0 |
| *Level B — Population 250,000 to 1,000,000* | | |
| 6. **El Paso** MSA (El Paso County) | 697,562 | 2.6 |
| 7. **McAllen-Edinburg-Mission** MSA (Hidalgo County) | 614,474 | 7.9 |
| 8. **Beaumont-Port Arthur** MSA (Hardin, Jefferson and Orange counties) | 382,242 | -0.7 |
| 9. **Corpus Christi** MSA (Nueces and San Patricio counties) | 382,188 | 0.4 |
| 10. **Brownsville-Harlingen-San Benito** MSA (Cameron County) | 353,561 | 5.5 |
| 11. **Killeen-Temple** MSA (Bell and Coryell counties) | 319,163 | 2.0 |
| 12. **Galveston-Texas City** PMSA (Galveston County) | 261,219 | 4.4 |
| 13. **Brazoria** PMSA (Brazoria County) | 257,256 | 6.4 |
| *Level C — Population 100,000 to 250,000* | | |
| 14. **Lubbock** MSA (Lubbock County) | 247,574 | 2.0 |
| 15. **Odessa-Midland** MSA (Ector and Midland County) | 239,981 | 1.2 |
| 16. **Amarillo** MSA (Potter and Randall counties) | 222,915 | 2.3 |
| 17. **Waco** MSA (McLennan County) | 217,713 | 2.0 |
| 18. **Longview-Marshall** MSA (Gregg, Harrison and Upshur counties) | 212,288 | 1.7 |
| 19. **Laredo** MSA (Webb County) | 207,611 | 7.5 |
| 20. **Tyler** MSA (Smith County) | 181,437 | 3.9 |
| 21. **Bryan-College Station** MSA (Brazos County) | 156,099 | 2.4 |
| 22. **Wichita Falls** MSA (Archer and Wichita counties) | 138,960 | -1.1 |
| 23. **Texarkana** MSA (Bowie County, TX, and Miller County, AR) | 131,027 | 1.0 |
| 24. **Abilene** MSA (Taylor County) | 125,647 | -0.7 |
| 25. **Sherman-Denison** MSA (Grayson County) | 113,860 | 3.0 |
| 26. **San Angelo** MSA (Tom Green County) | 103,018 | -1.0 |
| *Level D — Population Under 100,000* | | |
| 27. **Victoria** MSA (Victoria County) | 84,932 | 1.0 |

# Population 2000 and 2002

Existing towns are in **bold type**.
Towns that no longer exist or town names no longer in use are in *italics*.

**Population:** Numbers in parentheses are from the 2000 count by the U.S. Bureau of the Census.

The U.S. census counts only incorporated cities and some unincorporated towns called Census Designated Places (CDPs).

Population figures to the right for those same cities are Texas State Data Center estimates as of Jan. 1, 2002. Names of the incorporated places are in capital letters, e.g., "ABBOTT."

The population figure given for all other towns is an estimate received from local officials through a

Texas Almanac survey. In some cases, we could not obtain a population estimate; these places show "NA" (Not Available) in place of a population figure.

**Location:** The county in which the town is/was located follows the name of town. If more than one county is listed, the town is principally in the first-named county, e.g., "ABERNATHY, Hale-Lubbock." A town-county reference is listed twice for different locations within the same county, e.g., "Alabama, Trinity."

**Businesses:** The number following the county name indicates the number of business that have been given a credit rating by Dun & Bradstreet as of November 2002. For example, "ABBOTT, Hill, 23" means that Abbott in Hill County had 23 businesses.

**Post Offices:** Places with post offices, as of Nov. 2002, are marked with an asterisk (*) e.g., "*Ace".

---

| Town, County . . . . . . . . . . . Pop. 2002 | Town, County . . . . . . . . . . . Pop. 2002 | Town, County . . . . . . . . . . . Pop. 2002 |
|---|---|---|
| *Abbie, Jones* | *Ada, Lampasas* | *Agee, Hamilton* |
| *Abbieville, Denton* | *Ada, Montgomery* | *Agistha, Gregg* |
| *Abbington, Childress* | *Ada, Nolan* | **Agnes, Parker, . . . . . . . . . . . . . . . NA** |
| **\*ABBOTT, Hill, 23 (300) . . . . . . . 309** | *Ada, Upshur* | *Agricola, Parker* |
| *Abe, Houston* | *Adair, Fisher* | **Agua Dulce, El Paso, (738) . . . . . .770** |
| *Abell, Carson* | *Adair, Swisher* | **\*AGUA DULCE, Nueces,** |
| *Abell City, Pecos* | *Adalia, Caldwell* | **28 (737). . . . . . . . . . . . . . . . .745** |
| *Abercrombie, Travis* | *Adams, Fort Bend* | *Agua Negra, Atascosa* |
| *Aberdeen, Collingsworth* | *Adams, Lamar* | *Agua Negra, Cameron* |
| *Aberdeen, Henderson-Smith* | *Adams, Panola* | **Agua Nueva, Jim Hogg, . . . . . . . . .20** |
| *Aberdeen, Medina* | *Adams, Pecos* | *Ague, Walker* |
| **Aberfoyle, Hunt, . . . . . . . . . . . . . . 35** | *Adams, Schleicher* | **Aguilares, Webb, . . . . . . . . . . . . . .37** |
| **\*ABERNATHY, Hale-Lubbock,** | *Adams Bayou, Orange* | *Aid, Grimes* |
| **126 (2,839) . . . . . . . . . . . . . 2,850** | **Adams Gardens, Cameron, . . . . . 200** | *Aiken, Bell* |
| *Abex, Navarro* | *Adams Hill, Bexar* | **\*Aiken, Floyd, 4 . . . . . . . . . . . . . . .57** |
| **\*ABILENE, Taylor-Jones,** | *Adams Spring, Falls* | **Aiken, Shelby, . . . . . . . . . . . . . . . .75** |
| **5,559 (115,930). . . . . . . . 116,097** | **Adams Store, Panola, . . . . . . . . . NA** | **Aikin Grove, Red River, . . . . . . . . .26** |
| *Ables, Hudspeth* | *Adamston, Brazoria* | *Air Hall, Bell* |
| *Ables Springs, Hudspeth* | **Adamsville, Lampasas, . . . . . . . . . 41** | *Airline, Harris* |
| **Ables Springs, Kaufman, . . . . . . . NA** | **Addran, Hood . . . . . . . . . . . . . . . . NA** | **Airport City, Bexar, . . . . . . . . . . .106** |
| **Abner, Kaufman, . . . . . . . . . . . . . NA** | *Addicks, Harris* | **Airport Road Addition, Brooks,** |
| *Abner, Rusk* | **Addielou, Red River, . . . . . . . . . . . 31** | **(132) . . . . . . . . . . . . . . . . . . .132** |
| *Abney, Cameron* | *Addingtonville, Karnes* | **Airville, Bell, . . . . . . . . . . . . . . . . .10** |
| *Abney's Farm, Denton* | **\*ADDISON, Dallas, 2,564** | *Ajax, Panola* |
| *Abney's Farm, Falls* | **(14,166) . . . . . . . . . . . . . .14,265** | *Akers, Schleicher* |
| *Abra, Collingsworth* | *Addran, Hopkins* | *Akin, Sabine* |
| **Abram-Perezville, Hidalgo,** | *Adelaide, Harrison* | *Akron, Smith* |
| **(5,444). . . . . . . . . . . . . . . . .5,477** | **Adell, Parker, . . . . . . . . . . . . . . . . NA** | *Alabama, Callahan* |
| *Acacia, Cameron* | *Ad Hall, Milam* | *Alabama, Houston* |
| **\*ACADEMY [Little River-], Bell,** | *Adieu, Jack* | *Alabama, Trinity* |
| **36 (1,645) . . . . . . . . . . . . . .1,763** | *Adina, Lee* | *Alabama, Trinity* |
| **Acala, Hudspeth, . . . . . . . . . . . . . 25** | **\*Adkins, Bexar, 158. . . . . . . . . . . 241** | **Alabama-Coushatta, Polk,** |
| *Acampo, Shackelford* | *Adkins' Store, Grimes* | **(480) . . . . . . . . . . . . . . . . . . .480** |
| **\*Ace, Polk, 3 . . . . . . . . . . . . . . . . . 40** | **Admiral, Callahan, . . . . . . . . . . . . 18** | *Alameda, Brooks* |
| *Acker's Ferry, Henderson* | *Adobe, Hutchinson* | *Alameda, Eastland* |
| **\*ACKERLY, Dawson-Martin,** | **Adobes, Presidio, . . . . . . . . . . . . NA** | *Alamita, Karnes* |
| **24 (245). . . . . . . . . . . . . . . . 248** | *Adobe Walls, Hutchinson* | *Alamito, Presidio* |
| *Ackersville, Cherokee* | *Adora, Montague* | **\*ALAMO, Hidalgo, 325** |
| **Acme, Hardeman, . . . . . . . . . . . . . 14** | *Adora, Titus* | **(14,760). . . . . . . . . . . . . . .15,456** |
| *Acme, Henderson-Van Zandt* | **\*ADRIAN, Oldham, 13 (159) . . . . . 156** | *Alamo, Reeves* |
| *Acme, Hudspeth* | *Adrian, Orange* | *Alamo, Wharton* |
| *Acol, Angelina* | *Adsul, Newton* | **Alamo Alto, El Paso, . . . . . . . . . . .25** |
| *Acol, Polk* | *Adullam, Mason* | **Alamo Beach, Calhoun, . . . . . . . .100** |
| *Acol, Tyler* | **Advance, Parker, . . . . . . . . . . . . . NA** | **ALAMO HEIGHTS, Bexar,** |
| *Acomb, McLennan* | *Ady, Potter* | **(7,319). . . . . . . . . . . . . . . . 7,330** |
| *Acona, Guadalupe* | *Affie, Wheeler* | *Alamo Mills, Cass* |
| *Acorn, Robertson* | *Afra, Scurry* | *Alamositas, Oldham* |
| *Acres Homes, Harris* | *Africa, Liberty* | **\*Alanreed, Gray, 4 . . . . . . . . . . . . .48** |
| *Acrey, Burleson* | *Africa, Shelby* | *Alarm Creek, Erath* |
| *Acrey, Erath* | **\*Afton, Dickens, 4 . . . . . . . . . . . . . 15** | *Alayone, Deaf Smith* |
| **Acton, Hood, . . . . . . . . . . . . . .1,129** | *Afton, Fisher* | **Alazan, Nacogdoches, . . . . . . . . . NA** |
| **Acuff, Lubbock, . . . . . . . . . . . . . . 30** | *Afton, Lubbock* | **\*ALBA, Wood-Rains, 87 (430) . . . .439** |
| **Acworth, Red River, . . . . . . . . . . . 52** | *Agathos, Bell* | *Albade, Caldwell* |
| *Ada, Camp* | *Agatite, Hardeman* | **\*ALBANY, Shackelford,** |

| Town,County . . . . . . . . . . .Pop. 2002 | Town,County . . . . . . . . . . .Pop. 2002 | Town,County . . . . . . . . . . . Pop. 2002 |
|---|---|---|
| 160 (1,921). . . . . . . . . . . . . 1,931 | *ALLEN, Collin, 1,879 | Alsa, Van Zandt, . . . . . . . . . . . . . . 30 |
| Albert, Angelina | (43,554). . . . . . . . . . . . . .54,027 | Alsdorf, Ellis |
| Albert, Gillespie, 1 . . . . . . . . . . . . .25 | Allen's Chapel, Fannin, . . . . . . . . 41 | Alsobrooks, Tyler |
| Albion, Red River, . . . . . . . . . . . . .50 | Allen's Creek, Austin | Alsonia, Hidalgo |
| Albritten, Cherokee | Allen's Gin, Angelina | *Altair, Colorado, 7 . . . . . . . . . . . . 30 |
| Albuquerque, Wilson | Allen's Grove, Grayson | Alta Loma, Galveston |
| Alcedo, Angelina | Allen's Landing, Harris | Alta Mesa, Dallas |
| Alcino, Floyd | Allen's Point, Fannin, . . . . . . . . . . 76 | Alta Mira, Grimes |
| Alco, Angelina | Allen Bend, Bosque | Altavista, Jim Hogg |
| Alcorn, Washington | Allen Chapel, Houston | Althea, Bell |
| Alcott, Falls | Allendale, Montgomery | Altman, Erath |
| Alderbranch, Anderson, . . . . . . . . .5 | Allendale, San Patrico | Altman, Moore |
| Aldie, Yoakum | Allendale, Wichita | *ALTO, Cherokee, 85 (1,190). . . .1,232 |
| Aldine, Harris, (13,979) . . . . . . 14,040 | Allenfarm, Brazos, . . . . . . . . . . . . 30 | Alto Bonito, Starr, (569) . . . . . . . . 579 |
| Aldine, Uvalde | Allenhurst, Matagorda, . . . . . . . . 50 | Altoga, Collin, . . . . . . . . . . . . . . . 367 |
| Aldridge, Angelina | Allentown, Angelina, . . . . . . . . . 110 | Alton, Denton |
| Aldridge, Cooke | Allentown, Ward | *ALTON, Hidalgo, (4,384) . . . . . .4,690 |
| Aldridge, Jasper | Allenville, Milam | Altonia, San Augustine |
| Aldridge's, Nacogdoches | Alley, Hale | Alton North, Hidalgo, (5,051) . . .5,215 |
| Aleck, Tyler | Alleys Mill, Marion | Alto Springs, Falls |
| *ALEDO, Parker, 334 (1,726) . . . 1,909 | Alleyton, Colorado, 20 . . . . . . . . 165 | Altuda, Brewster |
| Aleman, Hamilton, . . . . . . . . . . . . .60 | Alliance, Hunt | Altura, El Paso |
| Aleo, Collin | Alliance Hall, Navarro | Alum, Wilson |
| Alethia, Montgomery | Alligator, Brazos | Alum Creek, Bastrop, . . . . . . . . . . NA |
| Alexander, Erath, . . . . . . . . . . . . .40 | Alligator Head, Calhoun | Alum Wells, Houston |
| Alexander's, Fayette | Alligator School House, Navarro | *ALVARADO, Johnson, 360 |
| Alexander Spur, Orange | *Allison, Wheeler, 7 . . . . . . . . . . 135 | (3,288) . . . . . . . . . . . . . . . . .3,535 |
| Alexanders Store, Shelby | Allison, Williamson | Alverde, Lampasas |
| Aley, Henderson, . . . . . . . . . . . . . .20 | Allison, Wise | *ALVIN, Brazoria, 1,366 |
| Alfalfa, El Paso | Allisonville, Tyler | (21,413) . . . . . . . . . . . . . . .21,608 |
| Alfalfa, Ochiltree | Allis School, Lavaca | Alvin, Henderson |
| Alford, Sabine | Allmon, Floyd, . . . . . . . . . . . . . . . 24 | Alvis, Ellis |
| Alfred, Henderson | Allred, Yoakum, . . . . . . . . . . . . . . 90 | *ALVORD, Wise, 74 (1,007) . . . . .1,028 |
| Alfred-South La Paloma, | Alluvia, Stonewall | Alwoodco, Ellis |
| Jim Wells, (451) . . . . . . . . . . .461 | Alma, Clay | Amanda, Kinney |
| Alfred, Nueces | ALMA, Ellis, (302). . . . . . . . . . . . 311 | Amanda, McLennan |
| Alfred, Shelby | Alma, Houston | Amarada, Brown |
| Algana, Coryell | Alma, Rusk | Amargosa [Owl Ranch-], Jim Wells, |
| Algereta, Menard | Almeda, Harris | (527). . . . . . . . . . . . . . . . . . . .546 |
| Algeria, Travis | Almedes, Anderson | *AMARILLO, Potter-Randall, |
| Algerita, San Saba, . . . . . . . . . . . .48 | Almira, Cass, . . . . . . . . . . . . . . . 30 | 9,296 (173,627) . . . . . . . .176,066 |
| Algoa, Galveston, . . . . . . . . . . . .135 | Almon, Llano | Ambia, Lamar, . . . . . . . . . . . . . . . 20 |
| Algoma, Stephens | Almond Grove, Red River | Ambrose, Grayson, . . . . . . . . . . . 90 |
| Alguna, San Patricio | Almont, Bowie | Amelbulk, Jefferson |
| Alhambra, Hutchinson | Aloe, Victoria | Amelia, Jefferson |
| *ALICE, Jim Wells, | Alon, Limestone | Ames, Coryell, . . . . . . . . . . . . . . . 10 |
| 1,054 (19,010) . . . . . . . . . 19,156 | Alp, Montague | AMES, Liberty, (1,079) . . . . . . . .1,116 |
| Alice Acres, Jim Wells, (491). . . . .525 | Alpha, Bowie | Ameus, Cherokee |
| Alice Southwest, Jim Wells | Alpha, Coke | Amherst, Lamar, . . . . . . . . . . . . . 125 |
| *Alief, Harris, 36 . . . . . (part of Houston) | Alpha, Dallas | *AMHERST, Lamb, 27 (791) . . . . . 799 |
| Alkali, Fisher | Alpha, Fannin | Amicus, Marion |
| Allah, Hunt | Alpha, Hutchinson | Amigo, Smith |
| Allamoore, Hudspeth, . . . . . . . . . . .25 | Alpha, Upshur | Amistad [Box Canyon-], Val Verde, |
| Allard, Erath | *ALPINE, Brewster, 431 | (76). . . . . . . . . . . . . . . . . . . . 76 |
| Allardale, Newton | (5,786). . . . . . . . . . . . . . . .5,848 | Amity, Comanche |
| Allarton, Newton | Alpine, Gregg | Ammann's, Kendall |
| Allcorn's, Washington | Alredge, Angelina | Ammannsville, Fayette, . . . . . . . . 42 |

## Sources for town names

Sources used by the Texas Almanac in compiling the accompanying list of Texas communities, including previous names of existing towns:

— The U.S. Bureau of the Census.
— Earlier Texas Almanacs.
— *Texas Post Offices by County*, John J. Germann and Myron R. Janzen, 1986, unpublished.
— *The New Handbook of Texas*, six volumes, Austin, The Texas State Historical Association, 1996.
— *Geographic Names Information System*, U.S. Geological Survey.

— Texas Department of Transportation.
— Local officials who were asked periodically to provide information on the existence and population of smaller, unincorporated towns and communities.

Some places no longer exist as towns because they have been taken in or annexed by cities. However, they are recognized now as areas or neighborhoods of the larger city.

In some cases, a town name is listed more than once in one county because it is believed these were different communities existing at different times or at different locations. — RP

CITIES & TOWNS

| Town,County . . . . . . . . . . . .Pop. 2002 | Town,County . . . . . . . . . . . .Pop. 2002 | Town,County . . . . . . . . . . . . Pop. 2002 |
|---|---|---|
| *Amo, Freestone* | *Antioch, Fannin* | *Ariola, Hardin* |
| *Amo, Montague* | *Antioch, Freestone* | *Arion, Liberty* |
| **Amphion, Atascosa, . . . . . . . . . . 26** | *Antioch, Harrison* | *Arispie, Hudspeth* |
| **Amsterdam, Brazoria, . . . . . . . . 193** | *Antioch, Houston* | *Aristo, Coryell* |
| *Amy, Delta* | *Antioch, Johnson* | *Arizona, Walker* |
| *Anacacho, Kinney* | *Antioch, Lavaca* | *Arkada, Fannin* |
| *Anacostia, Panola* | *Antioch, Lee* | *Arkadelphia, Bowie* |
| *Anadarco, Rusk* | **Antioch, Madison, . . . . . . . . . . . . 15** | *Arkansas, Gonzales* |
| **Anadarko, Rusk,. . . . . . . . . . . . . . 30** | *Antioch, Navarro* | *Arkansas, Young* |
| ***ANAHUAC, Chambers,*** | **Antioch, Panola, . . . . . . . . . . . . 121** | *Arkansas City, Starr* |
| **154 (2,210) . . . . . . . . . . . . . 2,240** | *Antioch, Shelby* | *Arkansas Colony, Baylor* |
| *Anaqua, Victoria* | **Antioch, Smith,. . . . . . . . . . . . . . .NA** | *Arlam, Rusk* |
| *Anarene, Archer* | *Antioch, Stonewall* | *Arles, Burleson* |
| *Ancaster, La Salle* | *Antioch, Trinity* | *Arleston, Panola* |
| *Anchor, Brazoria* | *Antioch, Van Zandt* | *Arlie, Childress* |
| *Anchor, Hale* | *Antioch Church, Freestone* | ***ARLINGTON,Tarrant, 13,573*** |
| *Anchorage, Atascosa* | **Antioch Colony, Hays, . . . . . . . . . 20** | **(332,969) . . . . . . . . . . . . . 344,751** |
| *Ander, Goliad* | *Antiquity, Anderson* | *Arlington Downs, Tarrant* |
| **Ander-Weser-Kilgore, Goliad,. . . 322** | *Antlers, Fannin* | *Arlington Heights, Nueces* |
| ***ANDERSON, Grimes, 65*** | ***ANTON, Hockley, 48 (1,200) . . .1,179*** | *Arlo, Walker* |
| **(257) . . . . . . . . . . . . . . . . . . 273** | *Apache Ranch, Webb* | *Armaglas, Ellis* |
| **Anderson Mill, Williamson-Travis,** | *Apex, San Saba* | *Armco, Harris* |
| **(8,953). . . . . . . . . . . . . . . . .9,051** | *Apolonia, Grimes* | *Armenderez, Mitchell* |
| *Andersonville, Williamson* | *Apperson's, Bowie* | *Armide, Denton* |
| ***Andice, Williamson, 15. . . . . . . .NA*** | **APPLEBY, Nacogdoches,** | *Armo, Dallas* |
| *Andressville, Polk* | **(444) . . . . . . . . . . . . . . . . . . . 449** | *Armour, Limestone* |
| ***ANDREWS, Andrews,*** | *Applegate, Jasper* | **Armstrong, Bell, . . . . . . . . . . . . . 22** |
| **529 (9,652) . . . . . . . . . . . . .9,617** | ***Apple Springs,Trinity, 18 . . . . . . 185*** | *Armstrong, Erath* |
| *Andrews, Wood* | *Apple Springs, Trinity* | ***Armstrong, Kenedy, 1 . . . . . . . . . . 20*** |
| *Andrews Chapel, Bosque* | *Appleton, Hansford* | *Armstrong, Washington* |
| *Andy, Cherokee* | *Appleville, Karnes* | *Armstrong City, Armstrong* |
| *Angel City, Goliad* | *Appling, Guadalupe* | **Arneckeville, DeWitt, . . . . . . . . . . 50** |
| *Angeles, Reeves* | *Aqua, Moore-Potter* | **Arnett, Coryell, . . . . . . . . . . . . . . 20** |
| *Angelina, Angelina* | ***AQUILLA, Hill, 17 (136) . . . . . . . 138*** | **Arnett, Hockley,. . . . . . . . . . . . . . 10** |
| *Angelina, Angelina* | *Arab, Smith* | *Arney, Castro* |
| *Angelina, Angelina* | *Aragon, Presidio* | *Arnim, Wharton* |
| *Angelina, Cherokee* | *Arah, Scurry* | *Arno, Burnet* |
| *Angelita, San Patricio* | *Aransas, Aransas* | *Arno, Reeves* |
| *Angle, Walker* | *Aransas, Aransas* | *Arnold, Collin* |
| *Angler, Wood* | *Aransas, Bee* | *Arnold, Dallas* |
| ***ANGLETON, Brazoria, 1,086*** | *Aransas City, Aransas* | *Arnold, Montgomery* |
| **(18,130). . . . . . . . . . . . . . . 18,370** | *Aransas Harbor, San Patricio* | *Arnold's, Waller* |
| *Anglin's, Anderson* | *Aransas Pass, Aransas* | *Arnold Mills, Montgomery* |
| *Anglo American, Bowie* | ***ARANSAS PASS, San Patricio-*** | *Arnottville, Hill* |
| *Angoria, Palo Pinto* | **Aransas-Nueces, 490** | *Aroya, Ward* |
| **ANGUS, Navarro, (334) . . . . . . . . 349** | **(8,138). . . . . . . . . . . . . . . .8,234** | *Arp, Atascosa* |
| *Anhalt, Comal* | *Aransas Pass Light House, Aransas* | ***ARP, Smith, 80 (901) . . . . . . . . . . 940*** |
| *Anita, Palo Pinto* | *Ararat, Comanche* | **Arrowhead Shores, Hood, . . . . . . 518** |
| ***ANNA, Collin, 104 (1,225). . . . . 1,266*** | **Arbala, Hopkins,. . . . . . . . . . . . . . 41** | *Arroyo, Willacy* |
| *Annadale, Callahan* | *Arbor , Houston* | **Arroyo Alto, Cameron, (320). . . . . 327** |
| *Annarose, Live Oak* | *Arbor, Navarro* | *Arroyo Bonito, Cameron* |
| *Annaville, Nueces* | *Arby, Swisher* | **Arroyo Colorado Estates,** |
| *Ann Eliza, Grayson* | *Arcade, Cooke* | **Cameron, (755) . . . . . . . . . . . 790** |
| **ANNETTA, Parker, (1,108) . . . . . 1,189** | *Arcade, Ector* | **Arroyo Gardens-La Tina Ranch,** |
| **ANNETTA NORTH, Parker,** | *Arcadia, Galveston* | **Cameron, (732). . . . . . . . . . . . 756** |
| **(467) . . . . . . . . . . . . . . . . . . 503** | *Arcadia, Milam* | ***Art, Mason, 1 . . . . . . . . . . . . . . . . . 18*** |
| **ANNETTA SOUTH, Parker,** | **Arcadia, Shelby, 15. . . . . . . . . . . . 20** | *Artesia, La Salle* |
| **(555) . . . . . . . . . . . . . . . . . . 582** | *Arcadia Park, Dallas* | *Artesia, McLennan* |
| *Anneville, Wise* | *Archer, Chambers* | *Artesian, Mitchell* |
| *Annie, Bowie* | ***ARCHER CITY, Archer, 85*** | ***Artesia Wells, La Salle, 3. . . . . . . . 35*** |
| ***ANNONA, Red River, 14*** | **(1,848). . . . . . . . . . . . . . . .1,890** | *Arthur, Nacogdoches* |
| **(282) . . . . . . . . . . . . . . . . . . 280** | **ARCOLA, Fort Bend, (1,048) . . .1,119** | ***Arthur City, Lamar, 17 . . . . . . . . . 200*** |
| ***ANSON, Jones, 144 (2,556) . . . 2,552*** | *Arctic, Jack* | *Arum, Johnson* |
| *Antelope, Coryell* | *Ard, Angelina* | *Arundel, Medina* |
| *Antelope, Culberson* | *Ardath, Collin* | **Arvana, Dawson,. . . . . . . . . . . . . . 25** |
| *Antelope, Foard* | *Ardelia, Dallas* | *Arwine, Tarrant* |
| **Antelope, Jack, 1 . . . . . . . . . . . . . 65** | *Ardell, Cooke* | *Asa, Fannin* |
| *Antelope Flats, Briscoe* | **Arden, Irion, . . . . . . . . . . . . . . . . . 1** | **Asa, McLennan,. . . . . . . . . . . . . . 46** |
| *Antelope Gap, Mills-Lampasas* | *Ardis, Hunt* | *Asadores Ranch, Hidalgo* |
| *Antelope Mesa, Carson* | *Arena, Colorado* | *Asander, Titus* |
| *Anthony, Bexar* | *Arenosa, Victoria* | *Asbury, Upshur* |
| ***ANTHONY, El Paso, 147*** | *Arey, Wharton* | *Ascarate, El Paso* |
| **(3,850). . . . . . . . . . . . . . . .3,898** | *Argenta, Live Oak* | *Ash, Henderson* |
| *Anthony, Fannin* | *Argenta, Tom Green* | **Ash, Houston, . . . . . . . . . . . . . . . 19** |
| **Antioch, Cass, . . . . . . . . . . . . . . 45** | **Argo, Titus, . . . . . . . . . . . . . . . . 200** | *Ashby, Houston* |
| **Antioch, Delta, . . . . . . . . . . . . . . 25** | ***ARGYLE, Denton, 265*** | **Ashby, Matagorda, . . . . . . . . . . . . 60** |
| | **(2,365). . . . . . . . . . . . . . . .2,620** | *Ashcraft, Smith* |

| Town,County . . . . . . . . . . .Pop. 2002 | Town,County . . . . . . . . . . .Pop. 2002 | Town,County . . . . . . . . . . . Pop. 2002 |
|---|---|---|
| Ash Creek, Hill | Authon, Parker, . . . . . . . . . . . . . . . 15 | Baker, Cooke |
| *ASHERTON, Dimmit, 11 | Auto, Howard | Baker, Cottle |
| (1,342). . . . . . . . . . . . . . . . .1,330 | Autryville, Newton | Baker, Floyd, . . . . . . . . . . . . . . . . 46 |
| Ashford, Harris | Autumn, Ellis | Baker, Parker |
| Ashland, Brazoria | *Avalon, Ellis, 15. . . . . . . . . . . . . 130 | Baker, Polk |
| Ashland, Hunt | Avalon, Fisher | Baker's Mill, Houston |
| Ashland, Tarrant | Avant, Freestone | Baker's Prairie, Kaufman |
| Ashland, Upshur, . . . . . . . . . . . . . 45 | Avaton, Harrison | Baker's Store, Fayette |
| Ashley, El Paso | Averitt, Tom Green | Bakersfield, Pecos,. . . . . . . . . . . . 30 |
| Ashmore, Gaines | *AVERY, Red River, 33 | Bakersfield Valley, Pecos |
| Ash Springs, Harrison | (462) . . . . . . . . . . . . . . . . . 458 | Bala, Cottle |
| Ashtola, Donley,. . . . . . . . . . . . . 25 | *AVINGER, Cass, 65 | Bala, King |
| Ashton, San Augustine | (464) . . . . . . . . . . . . . . . . . 456 | Balch, Hockley |
| Ashton, Shelby | Avis, Jack | Balch, Parker |
| Ashville, Harrison | *Avoca, Jones, 9. . . . . . . . . . . . . 121 | *BALCH SPRINGS, Dallas, |
| Ashville, Hunt | Avoca, Wilbarger | (19,375) . . . . . . . . . . . . . . 19,577 |
| Ashville, King | Avon, Wichita | BALCONES HEIGHTS, Bexar, |
| Ashville, Parker | Avonak, Harris | (3,016) . . . . . . . . . . . . . . . 2,853 |
| Ashwood, Matagorda, . . . . . . . . 120 | Avondale, Cameron | Baldaras, Jim Hogg |
| Ashworth, Kaufman | Avondale, Tarrant,. . . . . . . . . . . . .NA | Bald Eagle, Taylor |
| Ashworth Settlement, Trinity | Avon Park, McLennan | Bald Hill, Angelina, . . . . . . . . . . . 100 |
| Asia, Polk,. . . . . . . . . . . . . . . . . .NA | Awalt, Gregg | Bald Hill, Limestone |
| Askew, Hopkins | Axine, Cass | Bald Knob, Wise |
| *ASPERMONT, Stonewall, 79 | *Axtell, McLennan, 50 . . . . . . . . . 300 | Bald Prairie, Robertson,. . . . . . . . 40 |
| (1,021). . . . . . . . . . . . . . . .1,038 | Ayers, Anderson | Baldridge, Ellis |
| Astin, Robertson | Ayish Bayou, San Augustine | Baldridge, Pecos |
| Astonia, Ellis | Ayr, Deaf Smith | Baldwin, Harrison |
| Atascocita, Harris, (35,757). . .36,923 | Ayres, Washington | Baldwin, Medina |
| *Atascosa, Bexar, 69 . . . . . . . . . 300 | Ayres Retreat, Bell | Baldwin, Polk |
| Atascosito, Liberty | *AZLE, Tarrant-Parker, 838 | Ball, Floyd |
| Atchison's Point, Tarrant | (9,600). . . . . . . . . . . . . . . .9,971 | Ballard, Motley |
| Atco, McLennan | | Ballards, Lamar |
| Ater, Coryell, . . . . . . . . . . . . . . 25 | **B** | Ballew, Parker |
| *ATHENS, Henderson, 1,092 | Babbville, Coryell | Ball Hill, Bowie |
| (11,297). . . . . . . . . . . . . . 11,405 | Baber, Angelina | Ballie, Ellis |
| Atherton, Lampasas | Babyhead, Llano | *BALLINGER, Runnels, 276 |
| Athol, Tarrant | Babylon, Navarro | (4,243) . . . . . . . . . . . . . . . 4,235 |
| Atkins, Dallas | Bacchus, Hopkins | Ball Knob, Hood |
| Atkinson, Erath | Bachman, Dallas | Ballowe, Brazoria |
| Atlanta, Caldwell | Back, Gray, . . . . . . . . . . . . . . . . . 6 | Balm, Cooke |
| *ATLANTA, Cass, 517 | Backbone Valley, Burnet | *BALMORHEA, Reeves, 26 |
| (5,745). . . . . . . . . . . . . . . .5,704 | *Bacliff, Galveston, | (527). . . . . . . . . . . . . . . . .513 |
| Atlanta, Cass | 210 (6,962) . . . . . . . . . . . . .6,981 | Balsora, Wise, . . . . . . . . . . . . . . 50 |
| Atlas, Lamar,. . . . . . . . . . . . . . . 20 | Bacon, Bell | Baltic, Cherokee |
| At Last, Matagorda | Bacon, Panola | Bammel, Harris |
| Atlee, La Salle | Bacon, Wichita | Banckers, Cass |
| Atoka, Coleman | Bacontown, Jackson | Bancroft, Chambers |
| Atoy, Cherokee, . . . . . . . . . . . . . 50 | Baden, Martin | Bancroft, Orange |
| Atreco, Jefferson | Bader, Medina | Bandana, Jim Wells |
| Attoyac, Nacogdoches, . . . . . . . . .NA | Badger, Ector | *BANDERA, Bandera, 292 |
| Attoyac, San Augustine | Badgett, Martin | (957). . . . . . . . . . . . . . . . 1,000 |
| Atwell, Callahan, . . . . . . . . . . . . . 8 | Baer, Orange | Bandera Falls, Bandera,. . . . . . . . NA |
| Atwood, Archer | Bagby, Fannin | Bangor, Cherokee |
| *AUBREY, Denton, 272 | Bagdad, Cameron | *BANGS, Brown, 72 |
| (1,500). . . . . . . . . . . . . . . .1,715 | Bagdad, Taylor | (1,620) . . . . . . . . . . . . . . . 1,635 |
| Auburn, Ellis, . . . . . . . . . . . . . . . 12 | Bagdad, Williamson | Bankersmith, Kendall-Gillespie |
| Auburn, Johnson | Baggett, McLennan | Banks, McLennan |
| Auburn, Swisher | Bagley, Delta | Banner, Jones |
| Auburn, Walker | Bagley, Swisher | Bannister, San Augustine |
| Audelia, Dallas | *Bagwell, Red River, 11 . . . . . . . . 150 | *Banquete, Nueces, 17. . . . . . . . 449 |
| Audra, Taylor | *BAILEY, Fannin, 4 (213) . . . . . . . 239 | Banquete, Nueces |
| Audrey, Liberty | Bailey's, Johnson | Bantam, Fannin |
| Audubon, Wise | BAILEY'S PRAIRIE, Brazoria, | Bar-X, Brazoria,. . . . . . . . . . . . . 340 |
| Augusta, Houston,. . . . . . . . . . . . 20 | (694) . . . . . . . . . . . . . . . . . 729 | Barado, Walker |
| Augustus, Garza | Baileyboro, Bailey | Barbarosa, Guadalupe,. . . . . . . . . 25 |
| Auld, Real | Bailey Junction, Grayson | Barber, Llano |
| Auranti, Fannin | Bailey Ranch, Schleicher | Barber Mountain, Palo Pinto |
| Aurora, Jefferson | Baileyville, Milam,. . . . . . . . . . . . . 45 | Barbers Hill, Chambers |
| AURORA, Wise, (853). . . . . . . . . 888 | Bailie, Milam | Barcee, Ochiltree |
| Ausley, Kaufman | Bain, Coryell | Barclay, Falls, . . . . . . . . . . . . . . 58 |
| Austin, Matagorda | Bain, Grayson | Barclay, Jasper |
| *AUSTIN, Travis-Williamson, | Bainer, Lamb, . . . . . . . . . . . . . . . 10 | Barclay's, Tyler |
| 39,352 (656,562). . . . . . .678,198 | Bainville, Karnes, . . . . . . . . . . . . . 8 | Bardsdale, Denton |
| Austin Hill, Comal | *BAIRD, Callahan, | *BARDWELL, Ellis, 14 (583) . . . . . 609 |
| Austinia, Galveston | 116 (1,623) . . . . . . . . . . . . .1,610 | Barera, Maverick |
| Austonio, Houston, 13. . . . . . . . . 37 | Baird, Lamar | Barge, Angelina |
| *AUSTWELL, Refugio, 8 (192). . . 189 | Baker, Angelina | Barker, Ellis |

CITIES & TOWNS

| Town, County | Pop. 2002 |
|---|---|

*Barker, Harris, 19 . . . . . . . . . . . . . NA
Barker's Store, Dallas
Barker Springs, Hopkins
*Barksdale, Edwards, 14 . . . . . . 1,081
Barlow, Cooke
Barlow, Rusk
Barlow's Ferry, Live Oak
Barnard, Colorado
Barnard's Mill, Somervell
Barnard's Store, Parker
Barnardville, Hood
Barnes, Polk, . . . . . . . . . . . . . . . . . 75
Barnes, Rockwall
Barnes, Trinity
Barnes Store, Shelby
Barnesville, Johnson
Barnett, Lamar
*Barnhart, Irion, 7. . . . . . . . . . . . 160
Barnhart, Rusk
Barnum, Polk, 1 . . . . . . . . . . . . . 50
Baronsville, Runnels
Barreda, Cameron
Barren Ridge, Van Zandt
Barrens, Wood
*Barrett, Harris, (2,872) . . . . . . . 2,835
Barrett, Titus
Barron, Brazos
Barron, Milam
Barroso, Brooks
Barrowdale, Guadalupe
*BARRY, Navarro, 17 (209). . . . . . 214
Barsola, Cherokee
*BARSTOW, Ward, 8 (406) . . . . . . 395
Bart, Bastrop
Bart, La Salle
Bartek, Gonzales
Bartholomew, Trinity
*BARTLETT, Williamson-Bell,
   70 (1,675) . . . . . . . . . . . . . . 1,699
Bartley Woods, Fannin
Barton, Anderson
Barton, Delta
Barton, Hale
Barton, Lubbock
Barton, Robertson
Barton's Creek, Bastrop
Barton Corners, Lipscomb,. . . . . . . 4
Barton Creek, Hays
Barton Creek, Travis, (1,589). . . 1,573
Bartons Chapel, Jack,. . . . . . . . . . NA
Barton Springs, Mason
BARTONVILLE, Denton,
   (1,093). . . . . . . . . . . . . . . . . 1,235
Barwise, Floyd,. . . . . . . . . . . . . . . 16
Bascom, Smith, . . . . . . . . . . . . . . NA
*Basin, Brewster, . . . . . . . . . . . . . 22
Basin Springs, Grayson
Baskin, Dallas
Bason, Red River
Bass, Houston
Bass, Smith
Bassett, Bowie, . . . . . . . . . . . . . 373
Bassett & Blakeley's Store, Fort Bend
*BASTROP, Bastrop, 736
   (5,340). . . . . . . . . . . . . . . . . 6,080
Bastrop Beach, Brazoria
Bat, Hill
Bateman, Bastrop,. . . . . . . . . . . . NA
Bates, Denton
Bates, Hidalgo
Batesville, Red River, . . . . . . . . . 14
*Batesville, Zavala, 20
   (1,298). . . . . . . . . . . . . . . . . 1,348
Bath, Walker
Bath, Walker
Batson, Hardeman
*Batson, Hardin, 25 . . . . . . . . . . 140

Batte, Milam
Battle, McLennan,. . . . . . . . . . . 100
Battle Creek, Shackelford
Battle Ridge, Shelby
Baty, Freestone
Baucis, Trinity
Baum, Cooke
Baurs, Harris
Baurs, Lavaca
Bausell-Ellis, Willacy, (112) . . . . . 121
Bautista, Moore
Baxter, Archer
Baxter, Henderson,. . . . . . . . . . . . 20
Bay, Grimes
Bay, Matagorda
*BAY CITY, Matagorda, 987
   (18,667). . . . . . . . . . . . . . . .18,666
Bayland, Harris
Baylor, San Patricio
Baylor Lake, Childress, . . . . . . . . 27
Bay Oaks, Harris
Bayou, Sabine
Bayou, San Patricio
BAYOU VISTA, Galveston,
   (1,644). . . . . . . . . . . . . . . . . .1,651
Bayside, Cameron
*BAYSIDE, Refugio, 11 (360) . . . . 351
*BAYTOWN, Harris, 2,818
   (66,430). . . . . . . . . . . . . . . .66,646
BAYVIEW, Cameron, (323) . . . . . 329
Bay View, Galveston
Bay View, Harris
Bazette, Navarro, . . . . . . . . . . . . . 30
Beach, Edwards
Beach, Montgomery, . . . . . . . . . .NA
Beach's, San Jacinto
BEACH CITY, Chambers,
   (1,645). . . . . . . . . . . . . . . . . .1,760
Beachy, Dimmit
Beadle, Matagorda
Bean, Kent
Bean's Saline, Smith
Bean Creek, Hunt
Bean Hill, Bell
Beans, Jasper, . . . . . . . . . . . . . . .NA
Beans Creek, Cherokee
Bear Bayou, Shelby
Bear Branch Mills, Stephens
Bear Creek, Cass
Bear Creek, Comal
Bear Creek, Dallas,. . . . . . . . . . .1,000
Bear Creek, DeWitt
Bear Creek, Harris
BEAR CREEK, Hays, (360). . . . . . 389
Bear Creek, Kimble
Bear Creek, Polk
Bear Creek, Sabine
Bear Creek, Sabine
Bear Creek, San Jacinto
Bear Creek, Tarrant-Parker
Bear Creek, Uvalde
Beard, Austin
Beard, Van Zandt
Bearden, Lavaca
Bear Grass, Leon-Limestone
Bear Hill, Clay
Bear Hill, Montague
*BEASLEY, Fort Bend,
   31 (590). . . . . . . . . . . . . . . . . 607
Beasley's Store, Sabine
Beasley's Store, Trinity
Beason's, Colorado
Beatrice, Frio
Beatriz, Hidalgo
Beattie, Comanche, . . . . . . . . . . . 50
Beauchamps Springs, Harris
Beaukiss, Williamson

*BEAUMONT, Jefferson, 6,730
   (113,866) . . . . . . . . . . . . 114,067
Beaumont Place, Harris
Beaux Art Gardens, Jefferson, . . NA
Beavens, Leon
Beaver, Anderson
Beaver, Wichita
Beaver Creek, Clay
Beaver Creek, Mason
Beaver Dam, Bowie, . . . . . . . . . . . 55
Beaver Lake, Val Verde
Beaver Valley, Anderson
*Bebe, Gonzales,. . . . . . . . . . . . . . 52
Bebe, Hale
Beck, Lamb
Beck's Chapel, Henderson
Beck's Store, Guadalupe
Becker, Grimes
Becker, Kaufman, . . . . . . . . . . . . NA
Beckham, Hopkins
Beckley Heights, Dallas
Beckman, Bexar
Becknal Gap, Franklin
Beck Prairie, Robertson
Beckton, Dickens
*BECKVILLE, Panola, 45 (752). . . 745
Becton, Lubbock, . . . . . . . . . . . . 125
*BEDFORD, Tarrant, 2,428
   (47,152) . . . . . . . . . . . . . . 48,481
*Bedias, Grimes, 39 . . . . . . . . . . .301
Bee Branch, Coleman
BEE CAVE, Travis, (656) . . . . . . 1,109
Beech, Shelby
Beech Creek, Tyler
Beech Grove, Jasper
Bee Creek, Ellis
Bee House, Coryell, . . . . . . . . . . . 40
Beeman's School House, Navarro
Beene, Freestone
*BEEVILLE, Bee, 755
   (13,129) . . . . . . . . . . . . . . 13,118
Beeville, Bee
Behamon, Angelina
Behrens, Mason
Behring Store, Guadalupe
Behrnville, Williamson
Belcherville, Montague, . . . . . . . . 34
Belco, Gray
Belden, Morris
Belding, Pecos
Belen, El Paso
Belen, Mitchell
Belfalls, Bell, . . . . . . . . . . . . . . . 20
Belgrade, Newton,. . . . . . . . . . . . NA
Belk, Lamar,. . . . . . . . . . . . . . . . 55
Belknap, Young
Bell, Montgomery
Bell's Ferry, Jasper
Bell's Landing, Brazoria
Belladonna, Bastrop
Bellah, Baylor
*BELLAIRE, Harris, 1,312
   (15,642) . . . . . . . . . . . . . . 15,637
Bell Bottom, Matagorda
Bell Bottom, Waller
Bell Branch, Atascosa
Bell Branch, Callahan
Bell Branch, Ellis, . . . . . . . . . . . . 20
Bell Chapel, Shelby
Bellco, Wheeler
Belle Plain, Callahan
Belle Plain, Moore
Belle Point, Navarro
Belleview, Rusk
Belleville, Gonzales
*BELLEVUE, Clay, 18 (386). . . . . .386
Bell Fountain, Panola

| Town,County .......... Pop. 2002 | Town,County .......... Pop. 2002 | Town,County.......... Pop. 2002 |
|---|---|---|
| *Bell Founte, Wood* | *Berg's Mill, Bexar* | *Bettina, Llano* |
| **\*BELLMEAD, McLennan, 93** | *Berger, Bell* | *Betts, Bastrop* |
| **(9,214)**.................. **9,285** | *Berger, Bell* | *Betts, Grimes* |
| *Bello, DeWitt* | **\*Bergheim, Kendall, 17**..........**NA** | *Betts Chapel, Lee* |
| *Bellona, Falls* | *Bergs, Bexar* | *Beulah, Angelina* |
| *Bell Plain, Grayson* | *Bering, Polk* | *Beulah, Armstrong* |
| **\*BELLS, Grayson, 68** | *Berlin, Erath* | *Beulah, Fannin* |
| **(1,190)**................**1,198** | **Berlin, Washington,** ...........**NA** | *Beulah, Hamilton* |
| *Bell Springs, Hill* | *Berlin, Wilbarger* | *Beulah, Johnson* |
| **\*BELLVILLE, Austin,** | *Bermuda, Chambers* | *Beulah, Lee* |
| **429 (3,794)** ............. **3,870** | *Bermuda, Dimmit* | **Beulah, Limestone,**............ **12** |
| *Bellville, Zapata* | *Bermuda, Shelby* | *Beulah, Moore* |
| *Bellwood, Smith* | *Bermuda, Webb* | *Beulah, Palo Pinto* |
| **Belmena, Milam,**............... **15** | **Bernardo, Colorado,**.......... **155** | *Beulah, Wilbarger* |
| **\*Belmont, Gonzales, 5**......... **60** | *Bernecker, Fisher* | *Beverly, Briscoe-Swisher* |
| *Belone, Austin-Waller* | *Bernhardsville, Guadalupe* | *Beverly, Coryell* |
| **Belott, Houston,**............. **101** | *Bernice, Andrews* | *Beverly, Llano* |
| *Belt's Ferry, Tyler* | *Bernstein, Hansford* | *Beverly, McLennan* |
| *Belt's Store, Navarro* | *Berrien, Smith* | *Beverly Hill, Collin* |
| **\*BELTON, Bell, 984** | *Berry's Creek, Williamson* | **BEVERLY HILLS, McLennan,** |
| **(14,623)**.............. **15,078** | *Berry's Creek, Williamson* | **(2,113)** ................. **2,068** |
| *Belvey, Borden* | **Berryhill, Shackelford,** .......... **5** | **BEVIL OAKS, Jefferson,** |
| *Belview, Marion* | **BERRYVILLE, Henderson,** | **(1,346)** ................ **1,339** |
| *Belzora, Smith* | **(891)** ................... **901** | **Bevilport, Jasper,** ............ **NA** |
| *Ben, Wood* | *Bertie, Hardeman* | *Bevil Settlement, Jasper* |
| *Benada, DeWitt* | **\*BERTRAM, Burnet, 103** | *Bexar, Bexar* |
| **\*Ben Arnold, Milam, 6** ........ **148** | **(1,122)**................**1,220** | *Bexar, Bexar* |
| **\*BENAVIDES, Duval,** | *Berwick, Jack* | *Beyer, Bexar* |
| **36 (1,686)** ............. **1,685** | *Bess, Dallas* | **Beyersville, Williamson,** ......... **75** |
| *Benavides Hill, Webb* | *Bess, Delta* | **Biardstown, Lamar,**............. **75** |
| **\*Ben Bolt, Jim Wells, 7**........ **110** | *Bess, Duval* | *Bibb, Comanche* |
| **\*BENBROOK, Tarrant,** | *Bessemer, Llano* | *Bibles, Hardeman* |
| **(20,208)**.............. **20,500** | *Bessie, Cameron* | *Biddle, Scurry* |
| **Benchley, Robertson,** ........ **110** | *Bessie, Gaines* | *Biegel, Fayette* |
| *Bencini, Newton* | **Bessmay, Jasper,** .............**NA** | *Biff Springs, Harrison* |
| **\*Bend, San Saba-Lampasas, 6** .. **115** | *Best, Hays* | *Bigbend, Brewster* |
| *Bender, Harris* | **Best, Reagan, 2.**................ **2** | **\*Big Bend National Park,** |
| *Bendetsen, Liberty* | *Beth, Collin* | **Brewster, 7** ..............**194** |
| *Bendy's Landing, Tyler* | *Beth, Palo Pinto* | *Bigby Corner, Glasscock* |
| *Ben Ficklen, Tom Green* | *Bethany, Collin* | *Big Creek, Burleson* |
| *Benford, Polk* | *Bethany, Fayette* | *Big Creek, Fort Bend* |
| **\*Ben Franklin, Delta, 6**......... **75** | **Bethany, Panola,**.............. **50** | *Big Creek, Hutchinson* |
| **Ben Hur, Limestone,** .......... **100** | *Bethany, Tyler* | *Big Creek, Jasper* |
| *Benina, San Augustine* | *Bethard, Dallas* | *Big Creek, Liberty* |
| **\*BENJAMIN, Knox, 16 (264).**.... **253** | **Bethel, Anderson,**............. **50** | *Big Creek, San Jacinto* |
| *Benner, Gillespie* | *Bethel, Brazos* | *Big Cut, Panola* |
| *Bennett, Frio* | *Bethel, Burnet* | *Big Cypress, Camp* |
| *Bennett, Llano* | **Bethel, Ellis,** .................. **25** | *Big Cypress, Harris* |
| **Bennett, Parker,** .............. **40** | *Bethel, Fannin* | *Big Dollar, Wood* |
| *Bennett, Red River* | *Bethel, Freestone* | **\*Bigfoot, Frio, 9 (304)** ......... **315** |
| *Bennett, Sabine* | *Bethel, Gregg* | *Big Four, Hunt* |
| *Bennett, San Saba* | **Bethel, Henderson,**............ **25** | *Biggers, Collin* |
| *Bennett, Trinity* | *Bethel, Hopkins* | *Biggs, Panola* |
| *Bennett, Yoakum* | *Bethel, Houston* | *Biggs, Shelby* |
| *Bennett's, Houston* | *Bethel, Mason* | **Biggs Field, El Paso,**........ **4,226** |
| *Bennett's Bridge, Brazoria* | *Bethel, Montague* | *Big Head Village, Gregg* |
| *Bennett's Ferry, Brazoria* | **Bethel, Runnels,**.............. **12** | *Big Hill, Gonzales* |
| *Bennette, Montgomery* | *Bethel, Rusk* | *Big Hill, Jefferson* |
| *Bennett Station, Frio* | *Bethel, San Saba* | **Big Hill, Limestone,** ............. **9** |
| *Bennie, Moore* | *Bethel, Tarrant* | *Big Hill, Matagorda* |
| *Bennview, Jackson* | *Bethel, Tarrant* | **\*BIG LAKE, Reagan, 177** |
| **Benoit, Runnels,**.............. **22** | *Bethel, Van Zandt* | **(2,885)** ................ **2,752** |
| *Benonine, Wheeler* | *Bethel, Wheeler* | *Big Lump, Milam* |
| *Benson, Hunt* | *Bethelder, Brazoria* | *Big Motte, Jackson* |
| *Benton, Atascosa* | *Bethesda, Grayson* | *Big Oaks, Marion* |
| *Benton, Harrison* | *Bethesda, Titus* | *Big Paint, Real* |
| *Bentonville, Fannin* | *Bethlehem, Hill* | *Big Ridge, Liberty* |
| **Bentonville, Jim Wells,** ........ **15** | *Bethlehem, Leon* | *Big Rock, Van Zandt* |
| *Benvanue, Clay* | *Bethlehem, Limestone* | *Big Sandy, Polk* |
| *Benville, Eastland* | *Bethlehem, Marion* | **\*BIG SANDY, Upshur, 162** |
| **\*Ben Wheeler, Van Zandt, 113** ... **400** | *Bethlehem, Milam* | **(1,288)** ................ **1,331** |
| *Benz, Bexar* | *Bethlehem, Smith* | **\*BIG SPRING, Howard,** |
| *Benzine, Jackson* | **Bethlehem, Upshur,** ............ **75** | **1,195 (25,233)** ......... **25,477** |
| **\*Berclair, Goliad, 7** ............ **253** | *Bethlehem, Van Zandt* | *Big Spring, Polk* |
| *Berea, Bell* | *Betner, Lamar* | **Big Square, Castro,**............. **3** |
| **Berea, Houston,**............... **41** | *Betsada, Matagorda* | *Big Thicket, Liberty* |
| **Berea, Marion,** ............... **74** | **Bettie, Upshur,** ............... **110** | *Big Valley, Comanche* |

| Town,County . . . . . . . . . .Pop. 2002 | Town,County . . . . . . . . . . .Pop. 2002 | Town,County . . . . . . . . . . . Pop. 2002 |
|---|---|---|

**Big Valley, Mills, . . . . . . . . . . . . . 35**
*Big Valley, Parker*
**Big Valley Ranchettes,**
　**Coryell,. . . . . . . . . . . . . . . 220**
***BIG WELLS, Dimmit, 12**
　**(704) . . . . . . . . . . . . . . . . . 717**
*Big Wichita, Clay*
*Big Woods, Upshur*
*Bila Hora, Lavaca*
*Billie, Wilson*
*Billingsley, Johnson*
*Billington, Limestone*
*Billpark, Harris*
*Billum's Creek, Tyler*
*Biloxi, Angelina*
**Biloxi, Newton, . . . . . . . . . . . . . . NA**
*Biloxi, Newton*
*Bins, Edwards*
*Bippus, Deaf Smith*
**Birch, Burleson, . . . . . . . . . . . . . . NA**
*Birch, Erath*
*Birch Creek, Leon*
*Birchville, Hudspeth*
*Bird, Houston*
*Bird, Wichita*
*Birds, Tarrant*
*Birdsdale, Bell*
*Birdston, Navarro*
*Bird Town, Blanco*
*Birdville, Tarrant*
*Birmingham, Palo Pinto*
*Birmingham, Red River*
**Birome, Hill, 4 . . . . . . . . . . . . . . . 31**
**Birthright, Hopkins, . . . . . . . . . . . 40**
**Biry, Medina,. . . . . . . . . . . . . . . . NA**
*Bisbee, Tarrant*
*Bisco, Howard*
*Bishop, Collin*
*Bishop, Erath*
*Bishop, McLennan*
***BISHOP, Nueces, 126**
　**(3,305). . . . . . . . . . . . . . . . 3,320**
*Bishop's Hill, Wise*
**BISHOP HILLS, Potter, (210) . . . . 202**
*Bishop Hollow, Frio*
*Bishop Spur, Bastrop*
*Bismark, Wichita*
*Bison, Scurry*
*Bissell, Armstrong*
*Bissell, Hunt*
*Bissell, Trinity*
*Bissell, Upshur*
*Bitter Creek, Nolan*
*Bitter Creek, Young*
*Bitter Lake, Motley*
*Bitting, Travis*
***Bivins, Cass, 15 . . . . . . . . . . . . 195**
*Bivouac, Stephens*
**Bixby, Cameron, (356) . . . . . . . . 369**
*Black, Milam*
**Black, Parmer, 4 . . . . . . . . . . . . . 100**
*Black, Titus*
*Black's Store, Freestone*
*Black Ankle, Caldwell*
*Black Ankle, San Augustine*
*Blackberry Plains, Fannin*
*Black Bridge, Robertson*
*Blackburn, Angelina*
*Black Cat, Hunt*
*Black Colony, Hays*
*Black Creek, Medina*
*Black Flat, Archer*
**Blackfoot, Anderson,. . . . . . . . . . 33**
**Black Hill, Atascosa, . . . . . . . . . . 60**
*Black Hill, Collin*
*Black Hill, Rockwall*
**Black Hills, Navarro, . . . . . . . . . . 80**

**Black Jack, Cherokee, . . . . . . . . . 47**
*Black Jack, Fayette*
*Blackjack, Henderson*
*Black Jack, Nacogdoches*
**Black Jack, Robertson, . . . . . . . . 45**
*Blackjack, Rusk*
**Blackjack, Smith, . . . . . . . . . . . . .NA**
*Black Jack, Walker*
*Black Jack, Wood*
*Black Jack Grove, Hopkins*
*Blackland, McLennan*
*Black Land, Milam*
*Blackland, Rockwall*
*Blackmonk, Fannin*
**Black Oak, Hopkins,. . . . . . . . . . .NA**
*Black Point, Refugio*
*Black Rock, Anderson*
*Blacks Fort, Burnet*
*Black Springs, Palo Pinto*
***BLACKWELL, Nolan-Coke,**
　**20 (360) . . . . . . . . . . . . . . . . 360**
*Blaine, Falls*
*Blaine, Van Zandt*
*Blair, Childress*
*Blair, Shelby*
**Blair, Taylor,. . . . . . . . . . . . . . . . . 25**
*Blair's, DeWitt*
*Blake, Brown*
*Blakeney, Red River*
*Blalack, Cameron*
*Blalock, Titus*
**Blanchard, Polk, . . . . . . . . . . . . . 200**
*Blanche, Cottle*
*Blanchette, Jefferson*
*Blanco, Bee*
***BLANCO, Blanco, 194**
　**(1,505). . . . . . . . . . . . . . . .1,535**
*Blanco, Hays*
**Blanconia, Bee,. . . . . . . . . . . . . . . 30**
*Bland, Bell*
**Bland Lake, San Augustine, . . . . . 25**
***BLANKET, Brown, 25**
　**(402). . . . . . . . . . . . . . . . . . . 406**
*Blankinship, Van Zandt*
**Blanton, Hill, . . . . . . . . . . . . . . . . . 8**
*Blanton, Runnels*
*Blanton, Wilbarger*
*Blanton's Gin, Grayson*
*Bleakley, Hidalgo*
**Bleakwood, Newton,. . . . . . . . . . 300**
***Bledsoe, Cochran, 5 . . . . . . . . . 125**
*Bledsoe, Lubbock*
***Bleiblerville, Austin, 7. . . . . . . . . 71**
***Blessing, Matagorda, 35**
　**(861) . . . . . . . . . . . . . . . . . . . 892**
**Blevins, Falls, . . . . . . . . . . . . . . . . 36**
**Blewett, Uvalde, . . . . . . . . . . . . . . 10**
*Blewett, Wise*
*Bliss, Grayson*
*Bliss, Sterling-Coke*
*Blix, Angelina*
*Block Creek, Kendall*
*Blocker, Harrison*
*Blocker, Harrison*
*Block House, Williamson*
*Block Twenty, Lubbock*
**Blodgett, Titus, . . . . . . . . . . . . . . 60**
***BLOOMBURG, Cass, 19**
　**(375) . . . . . . . . . . . . . . . . . . 380**
*Bloomdale, Collin*
*Bloomfield, Cooke*
***BLOOMING GROVE, Navarro,**
　**33 (833). . . . . . . . . . . . . . . . 871**
*Bloomington, Fannin*
***Bloomington, Victoria, 23**
　**(2,562). . . . . . . . . . . . . . . . .2,620**
*Bloomington, Wheeler*

***BLOSSOM, Lamar, 66**
　**(1,439). . . . . . . . . . . . . . . 1,450**
*Blossom Hill, Rusk*
*Blowout, Blanco*
*Blox, Jasper*
*Blucher, Mason*
**Blue, Lee,. . . . . . . . . . . . . . . . . . . 50**
**Blue Berry Hill, Bee,**
　**(982). . . . . . . . . . . . . . . . . 1,009**
*Blueberry Hill, Montgomery*
*Bluebird, Lamar*
*Blue Bluff, McLennan*
*Bluebonnet, McLennan*
*Blue Camp, Coleman*
*Blue Gap, Runnels*
*Blue Goose, Gaines*
*Blue Goose, Nolan*
***Bluegrove, Clay, 1 . . . . . . . . . . . 125**
*Blue Hill, Williamson*
*Blue Mott, Victoria*
*Blue Mound, Denton*
**BLUE MOUND, Tarrant,**
　**(2,388) . . . . . . . . . . . . . . . 2,404**
*Blue Mountain, Mason*
*Blue Prairie, Fannin*
***BLUE RIDGE, Collin, 65**
　**(672). . . . . . . . . . . . . . . . . . 739**
*Blue Ridge, Falls*
*Blue Ridge, Fort Bend*
*Blue Ridge, Hamilton*
*Blue Roan, Colorado*
*Blue Spring, San Augustine*
*Blue Springs, Nacogdoches*
*Blue Springs, Van Zandt*
*Blue Stretch, Mason*
**Bluetown-Iglesia Antigua, Cameron,**
　**(692). . . . . . . . . . . . . . . . . . 747**
*Bluewater, Bandera*
*Blue Water, Deaf Smith*
*Bluewater, Polk*
*Blue Water, Polk*
*Bluff, Bandera*
*Bluff, Bell*
*Bluff, Fayette*
*Bluff Branch, Eastland*
*Bluff City, Parker*
*Bluff Creek, Lee*
*Bluff Creek, Mason*
*Bluff Creek, Polk*
***Bluff Dale, Erath, 19 . . . . . . . . . 123**
*Bluff Grove, Ellis*
**Bluff Springs, Travis, . . . . . . . . . . NA**
***Bluffton, Llano, 4. . . . . . . . . . . . . 75**
*Blum, Freestone*
***BLUM, Hill, 24 (399). . . . . . . . . . 410**
*Blumberg, Guadalupe*
*Blumberg Spur, Guadalupe*
*Blumenthal, Colorado*
*Blumenthal, Gillespie*
*Blum Hill, Fayette*
*Blunt, Fannin*
*Blunt, Freestone*
**Bluntzer, Nueces, . . . . . . . . . . . . 150**
*Bly, Titus*
*Blythe, Gaines*
*Board, Navarro*
*Board, Van Zandt*
*Board's Ferry, Harrison*
*Board Church, Comanche*
*Board House, Blanco*
*Boaz, Coryell*
*Boaz, Coryell*
*Bob, Borden*
*Bobbin, Montgomery*
*Bobo, Shelby*
*Bobos, Tarrant*
*Bobsher, Orange*

Town,County . . . . . . . . . . .Pop. 2002

Bob Town, Jack, . . . . . . . . . . . . . . NA
Bobville, Montgomery
Bobwyn, Dallas
Boca Chica, Cameron
Boca Del Rio, Cameron
Bodan, Angelina
Boddie, Grayson
Boden, Potter
Bodie, Gregg
Boedecker Junction, Colorado
*BOERNE, Kendall, 1,312
　(6,178). . . . . . . . . . . . . . . . .6,462
*BOGATA, Red River, 58
　(1,396). . . . . . . . . . . . . . . .1,384
Boggy, Lamar
Boggy, Leon
Boggy Station, Hemphill
Bogus Springs, Cass
Bohemia, Tom Green
Bohemian, Trinity
Boiling Spring, Deaf Smith
Bois d'Arc, Anderson, . . . . . . . . . 10
Bois d'Arc, Fannin
Bois d'Arc, Rains, . . . . . . . . . . . . 10
Bois d'Arc Mills, Fannin
Boiše, Oldham
Bola, Hudspeth
Bolder, Van Zandt
Bold Springs, McLennan
Bold Springs, Polk, . . . . . . . . . . 100
Bold Springs, Trinity
Boldtville, Bexar, . . . . . . . . . . . . 20
Bolen Switch, Van Zandt
Bolf, Runnels
Bolin, Dallam
*Boling-Iago, Wharton, 68
　(1,271). . . . . . . . . . . . . . . . .1,240
Bolivar, Brazoria
Bolivar, Denton, . . . . . . . . . . . . . 40
Bolivar Peninsula, Galveston,
　(3,853). . . . . . . . . . . . . . . . .3,991
Bolt, San Saba
Bolton Switch, La Salle
Bomar, San Saba
Bomarton, Baylor, . . . . . . . . . . . . 15
Bona, Grayson
Bon Ami, Jasper, . . . . . . . . . . . . . NA
*Bonanza, Hill, . . . . . . . . . . . . . . . NA
Bonanza, Hopkins,. . . . . . . . . . . . 26
Bond, Brazoria
Bond, Morris
Bond's Prairie, Freestone
*BONHAM, Fannin, 557
　(9,990). . . . . . . . . . . . . . . .10,255
Bonham's Store , Jackson
Bonita, Comal
Bonita, Crockett
Bonita, Guadalupe
Bonita, Jones
Bonita, Montague, . . . . . . . . . . . . 25
Bonito, Atascosa
Bonner, Freestone
Bonner's Ferry, Cherokee
Bonner's Mills, Angelina
Bonnersville, Angelina
Bonnerville, Freestone,. . . . . . . . NA
BONNEY, Brazoria, (384). . . . . . . 387
Bonnie View, Refugio, . . . . . . . . 135
Bono, Johnson
Bonton, Kendall
Bonus, Wharton, . . . . . . . . . . . . . 42
*Bon Wier, Newton, 17 . . . . . . . . 475
Booker, Bowie
*BOOKER, Lipscomb-Ochiltree,
　79 (1,315) . . . . . . . . . . . . . .1,279
Booker, Panola
Bookout, Scurry

Town,County . . . . . . . . . . . .Pop. 2002

Boom, Castro
Boon, Blanco
Boone, Hale
Boone, Walker
Boone, Williamson
Boone's Ferry, Tyler
Boone's Rock, Floyd
Boone Prairie, Robertson
Booner, Hidalgo
Boonesboro, Uvalde
Boonetown, Trinity
Booneville, Hopkins
Boonsville, Wise, . . . . . . . . . . . . . 52
Boonville, Brazos
Boory, Cameron
Booth, Fort Bend, 24 . . . . . . . . . .NA
Booth, Walker
Boot Hill, Oldham
Booth Spur, Floyd
Bootleg, Deaf Smith
Booton, Caldwell
Boquillas, Brewster
Boquillas Hot Springs, Brewster
Boracho, Culberson
Borden, Colorado, . . . . . . . . . . . . 60
Borden's, Fort Bend
Border, Harrison
Borders Chapel, Taylor
Bordersville, Harris
Boren, Panola
Borens Mills, San Augustine
*BORGER, Hutchinson, 798
　(14,302). . . . . . . . . . . . . . .14,169
Borjas, Duval
Borrego, Bexar
Borrillo, Pecos
Bosman, Anderson
Bosque, Bosque
Bosqueville, McLennan, . . . . . . . 200
Boss, Tarrant
Bossier, Fisher
Bostick, Smith
Bostick's Crossing, Austin
Boston, Bowie, 15 . . . . . . . . . . . 200
Boston, Houston
Boston Ranch, Oldham
Boswell, Walker
Botha, Gonzales
Botines, Webb, (132). . . . . . . . . . 135
Bottle Springs, Bowie
Bottom, Bell
Botts, Gonzales
Boudreaux Estates, Harris
Boulevard Junction, Cameron
Bourland, Floyd
*BOVINA, Parmer, 36
　(1,874). . . . . . . . . . . . . . . . .1,817
Bovine, Lavaca
Bovine Bend, Austin
Bowden, Red River
Bowen, Coleman
Bowen, Erath
Bowers, Milam
Bowers, Polk, . . . . . . . . . . . . . . .NA
Bowers, Scurry
Bowers City, Gray, . . . . . . . . . . . 26
Bowery, Leon
*BOWIE, Montague, 505
　(5,219). . . . . . . . . . . . . . . . .5,220
Bowie Hill, Cass
Bowieville, Matagorda
Bowlder, Mills
Bowles, Uvalde
Bowling, Freestone
Bowling, Leon
Bowling Green, McLennan
Bowman, Archer, . . . . . . . . . . . . 200

Town,County . . . . . . . . . . . . Pop. 2002

Bowman, Taylor
Bowman's Springs, Tarrant
Bowser, San Saba, . . . . . . . . . . . . 20
Bowser Bend, San Saba
Box, Lamar
Box, Wilbarger
Box Canyon-Amistad, Val Verde,
　(76). . . . . . . . . . . . . . . . . . . . .76
Box Church, Limestone,. . . . . . . . 45
Box Creek, Cherokee
Boxelder, Red River, . . . . . . . . . . 258
Box Quarter, Robertson
Boxville, Lavaca
Boxwood, Upshur,. . . . . . . . . . . . 20
Boy, Montgomery
Boyce, Ellis,. . . . . . . . . . . . . . . . . 75
Boyd, Fannin, . . . . . . . . . . . . . . . 40
*BOYD, Wise, 158
　(1,099). . . . . . . . . . . . . . . .1,145
Boyd's Cove, Coryell
Boyd's Mill, Wise
Boyd Ranch, Gonzales
Boyds Chapel, Jones
Boydston, Gray-Donley
Boyle, Bastrop
Boyles, Falls
Boynton, Angelina
Boynton, Comanche
*Boys Ranch, Oldham, 12 . . . . . . 435
Boyt, Jefferson
Boz, Ellis
Bozar, Mills,. . . . . . . . . . . . . . . . . .9
Bozeman's Corner, Gregg
Bracewell, Polk
Brachfield, Rusk,. . . . . . . . . . . . . 40
Brack, Hutchinson
Bracken, Comal, . . . . . . . . . . . . . 76
Bracken, Panola
Brackenridge, Karnes
Brackenville, Milam
*BRACKETTVILLE, Kinney,
　72 (1,876). . . . . . . . . . . . . . 1,902
Bracy's Ferry, Waller
Brad, Palo Pinto,. . . . . . . . . . . . . 16
Bradburn, Hunt
Braden, Colorado
Bradfield, Kaufman
Bradford, Anderson,. . . . . . . . . . . 30
Bradley, Angelina
Bradley, Houston
Bradley, Johnson
Bradley, Sherman
Bradleys Corner, Wichita
Bradshaw, Rusk
Bradshaw, Taylor, 1 . . . . . . . . . . . 61
Bradville, Waller
*BRADY, McCulloch, 381
　(5,523). . . . . . . . . . . . . . . . 5,443
Brady, Shelby
Bragg, Hardin
Bragg, Navarro
Brambleton, Tarrant
Branch, Collin,. . . . . . . . . . . . . . 447
Branchtown, Cherokee
Branchville, Milam, . . . . . . . . . . . 200
Brand, Scurry
Brandenburg, Harris
Brandenburg, Stonewall
*Brandon, Hill, 3 . . . . . . . . . . . . . 80
Brand Rock, Frio
Branham's Store, Cherokee
Brannon's Store, Parker
Branom, Hopkins
Branon, Lavaca
Bransford, Tarrant
Brantley, Montgomery
Branton, Eastland

CITIES & TOWNS

| Town,County ...........Pop. 2002 | Town,County ...........Pop. 2002 | Town,County ...........Pop. 2002 |
|---|---|---|
| **\*Brashear, Hopkins, 16** ........ 280 | *Bristow, Nacogdoches* | (219)..................... 222 |
| *Bratton, Harris* | *Bristow's Ferry, Panola* | **\*BROWNFIELD, Terry, 465** |
| *Bravo, Bastrop* | *Brit, Anderson* | (9,488) ................. 9,218 |
| *Bravo, Hartley* | *Britamer, Baylor* | *Brown Hill, Gonzales* |
| *Bray, Donley* | *Brite, Presidio* | **Browning, Smith,** ............. 25 |
| *Bray, Navarro* | *Britt, Leon* | *Brownlee, Martin* |
| *Bray, Stephens* | *Britt, Scurry* | *Browns Bend, San Saba* |
| *Brazlime, Hill* | *Brittain, Shelby* | **Brownsboro, Caldwell,** ......... 50 |
| **\*BRAZORIA, Brazoria, 289** | **Britton, Ellis,**...................**NA** | **\*BROWNSBORO, Henderson,** |
| (2,787)................. 2,740 | *Brizendine Mills, Williamson* | 82 (796) ................. 810 |
| **Brazos, Palo Pinto,** ............ 97 | **\*BROADDUS, San Augustine,** | *Brownsboro,Kendall* |
| *Brazos Agency, Young* | 35 (189)................. 190 | *Brownsborough, Kerr* |
| *Brazos Bottom, Burleson* | *Broadmoor, McCulloch* | *Brown School Settlement, San Jacinto* |
| **BRAZOS COUNTRY, Austin,** .... 450 | *Broad Oak, Kaufman-Rockwall* | *Brown Springs, Robertson* |
| **Brazos Point, Bosque,**..........**NA** | *Broadtown, Brown* | *Browns Spring, Rockwall* |
| **Brazosport, Brazoria,** ....... 57,469 | *Broadview, Lubbock* | *Brownstown, Bowie* |
| *Brazos Santiago, Cameron* | *Broadway, Armstrong* | *Browns Valley, Navarro* |
| *Breaker, Angelina* | **Broadway, Crosby,** ............. 20 | *Brownsville, Anderson* |
| *Breckenridge, Medina* | **Broadway, Lamar,** ............. 25 | **\*BROWNSVILLE , Cameron,** |
| **\*BRECKENRIDGE, Stephens,** | *Broadway Junction, Lamar* | 4,391 (139,722) ........ 147,545 |
| 534 (5,868) .............. 5,974 | **Brock, Parker,** .................. 80 | *Brown Town, Brown* |
| *Breckenridge Springs, Panola* | **Brock Junction, Parker,** .........**NA** | *Brown Town, McCulloch* |
| *Breckinridge, Dallas* | *Brocksville, Ellis* | *Browntown, Morris* |
| *Breckwalker, Stephens* | *Brodie, Lamar* | **\*BROWNWOOD, Brown,** |
| *Breedlove, Cooke* | *Brogado, Reeves* | 1,438 (18,813) .......... 19,400 |
| *Bremen, Callahan* | *Broncho, Tom Green* | *Brownwood-Oakland, Orange* |
| **\*BREMOND, Robertson, 61** | *Bronco, Coke* | *Broxson, Houston* |
| (876) .................... 873 | **Bronco,Yoakum,**............... 30 | **Broyles Chapel, Anderson,** ...... 40 |
| **\*BRENHAM, Washington,** | **\*Bronson, Sabine, 17** .......... 377 | *Bruce, Johnson* |
| 1,307 (13,507).......... 13,543 | **\*BRONTE, Coke, 59** | *Bruce, Orange* |
| *Brenner, Guadalupe* | (1,076).................1,057 | *Bruce, Wilbarger* |
| *Bresford, Garza* | *Brooke, San Augustine* | *Bruceton, Hunt* |
| **Breslau, Lavaca,**............... 65 | **\*Brookeland, Sabine, 46** ....... 300 | **\*BRUCEVILLE-EDDY, McLennan-** |
| *Brethern Farm, Brooks* | **\*Brookesmith, Brown, 7** ........ 61 | Falls, 90 (1,490).......... 1,549 |
| *Brewer, Freestone* | *Brookhaven, Bell* | *Brueggerhoff, Williamson* |
| *Brewer's Station, Taylor* | *Brooklyn, Kaufman* | *Bruin, Montgomery* |
| *Brewster, Brown* | *Brooklyn, Shelby* | *Brumberg, Houston* |
| *Brewster's Bluff, Panola* | *Brooklyn Heights, Tarrant* | **Brumley, Upshur,** ............. 75 |
| *Briar, Archer* | *Brooks, Burleson* | *Brumley's Mill, Hunt* |
| **Briar, Tarrant-Wise-Parker,** | *Brooks, Coleman* | *Brumlow, Wise* |
| (5,350)................. 5,531 | *Brooks, Jefferson* | *Brummersville, Lampasas* |
| *Briar Branch, Medina* | **Brooks, Panola,** .............. 40 | *Brummet, Frio* |
| **BRIARCLIFF,Travis, (895)** ...... 956 | *Brooks, Wharton* | *Brummets Ranch, Jack* |
| **BRIAROAKS, Johnson,** | *Brooks' Saline, Smith* | **Brundage, Dimmit, (31).** ......... 31 |
| (493) ..................... 510 | **\*Brooks Air Force Base, Bexar,** .. 720 | **\*Bruni, Webb, 17 (412)** ......... 422 |
| *Briary, Milam* | *Brooks Chapel, Panola* | *Brunner, Harris* |
| *Brice, Briscoe* | **Brookshier, Runnels,** ........... 18 | *Brunson, Leon* |
| **Brice, Hall,** .................. 37 | **\*BROOKSHIRE, Waller, 245** | *Brunswick, Cherokee* |
| *Brick, Liberty* | (3,450).................3,498 | *Brush, Young* |
| *Bridge, Kaufman* | **BROOKSIDE VILLAGE, Brazoria,** | **Brushie Prairie, Navarro,** ........ 35 |
| **\*BRIDGE CITY, Orange, 347** | (1,960).................2,005 | *Brush Prairie, Trinity* |
| (8,651)................. 8,691 | *Brooks Store, Marion* | *Brushy, DeWitt* |
| *Bridge Port, Trinity* | **\*Brookston, Lamar, 12** .......... 70 | *Brushy, Hood* |
| **\*BRIDGEPORT, Wise, 428** | *Brooksville, Ellis* | *Brushy, Panola* |
| (4,309)................. 4,518 | *Brooksville, Williamson* | **Brushy Creek, Anderson,** ....... 50 |
| *Bridges, Polk* | **Broom City, Anderson,** ......... 20 | *Brushy Creek, Bastrop* |
| **Bridges Chapel, Titus,** .......... 90 | **Broome, Panola,** .............. 21 | **Brushy Creek, Brazos,** ......... **NA** |
| *Bridgetown, Wichita* | *Broome, Sterling* | *Brushy Creek, Delta* |
| *Bridgevalley, Fayette* | *Broomtown, Austin* | *Brushy Creek, Trinity* |
| *Briggs, Bexar* | *Brouchard, Dallas* | *Brushy Creek, Williamson* |
| **\*Briggs, Burnet, 6.** ............. 92 | *Broughton, Cherokee* | **Brushy Creek, Williamson,** |
| *Briggs, Dallas* | *Broussard's Store, Jefferson* | (15,371) .............. 16,341 |
| *Bright, Navarro* | *Browder, Dallas* | *Brushy Knob, Hill* |
| *Brighton, Harris* | *Browder, Montgomery* | *Brushy Mound, Johnson-Tarrant* |
| *Brighton, Nueces* | *Brown, DeWitt* | *Brushy Settlement, Lavaca* |
| *Bright Star, Hopkins* | *Brown, Jack* | *Brushyville, Lavaca* |
| **Bright Star, Rains,** ............ 592 | *Brown, Martin* | *Brussel, Rusk-Gregg* |
| *Bright Star, Van Zandt* | *Brown's, Brazoria* | *Bruton, Dimmit* |
| *Brigman, Hill* | *Brown's Addition, Calhoun* | *Bruton, Rains* |
| **Brinker, Hopkins,** ..............**NA** | *Brown's Bluff, Gregg* | *Bruton, Wood* |
| *Briquette, Milam* | *Brown's Creek, Coryell* | **\*BRYAN, Brazos, 3,383** |
| **\*Briscoe, Wheeler, 10.** .......... 135 | *Brown's Ferry, Nacogdoches* | (65,660) .............. 66,754 |
| **Bristol, Ellis,**.................. 94 | *Brown's Gin, Lee* | **Bryans Mill, Cass,**.............. 71 |
| *Bristol City, Collin* | *Brown's Mill, Lee* | **Bryan Beach, Brazoria,**......... 14 |
| *Bristow, Hamilton* | *Brown Chapel, Navarro* | *Bryan Junction, Brazos* |
| *Bristow, Llano* | **Brown College, Washington,**..:..**NA** | *Bryan Mound, Brazoria* |
| *Bristow, Montgomery* | **BROWNDELL, Jasper,** | *Bryant Station, Milam* |

Town,County . . . . . . . . . . .Pop. 2002

Bryarly, Red River,. . . . . . . . . . . . . 5
Bryce, Rusk,. . . . . . . . . . . . . . . . . 15
Bryden, Moore
Brymer, Burleson
*BRYSON, Jack, 13 (528). . . . . . 529
Buaas, Travis
Bucareli, Madison
Buchanan, Bowie
Buchanan, Johnson
Buchanan, Lipscomb
Buchanan, Morris-Titus
*Buchanan Dam, Llano, 74
   (1,688). . . . . . . . . . . . . . . . .1,703
Buchanan Lake Village, Llano, . . . NA
Buchanan Springs, Coryell
Buchel, DeWitt,. . . . . . . . . . . . . . 45
Buchell's Store, Lavaca
Buchen's Store, Callahan
Buck, Polk,. . . . . . . . . . . . . . . . . .NA
Buck, Trinity
Buck & Breck, Dallas
Buck Creek, Angelina
Buck Creek, Childress
Buck Creek, Cottle, . . . . . . . . . . . . 7
Buck Den, Real
Buckeye, Matagorda,. . . . . . . . . . . 25
Buck Hills, Montgomery
Buck Hollow, Kimble
*BUCKHOLTS, Milam, 24 (387) . . 401
Buckhorn, Austin, . . . . . . . . . . . . 20
Buckhorn, Bell
Buckhorn, Frio
Buckhorn, Newton, . . . . . . . . . . . NA
Buckingham, Dallas
Buckley, LaSalle
Buckner, Collin
Buckner, Fayette
Buckner, Kinney
Buckner, Parker,. . . . . . . . . . . . . . NA
Bucks Bayou, Matagorda
Bucksnort, Falls
Buck Snort, Shelby
*BUDA, Hays, 471 (2,404). . . . . . 2,700
Bud Conner, Hardin
Budmatthews, Shackelford
Buel, Johnson
Buena Suerte, Brooks
Buena Suerte, Presidio
Buena Vista, Bexar
Buena Vista, Cameron, . . . . . . . . NA
Buena Vista, Ellis
Buenavista, Pecos
Buena Vista, Shelby
Buena Vista, Starr
Buenos, Garza
Buenos Aires, Brewster
Buescher, Colorado
Buesing, DeWitt
Buffalo, Coleman
Buffalo, Fisher
Buffalo, Henderson
*BUFFALO, Leon, 203
   (1,804). . . . . . . . . . . . . . . . .1,822
Buffalo, Mills
Buffalo Camp, Brazoria, . . . . . . 1098
*BUFFALO GAP, Taylor, 46
   (463) . . . . . . . . . . . . . . . . . . . 464
Buffalo Gap, Travis
Buffalo Mop, Limestone,. . . . . . . . 21
Buffalo Mott, Limestone
Buffalo Springs, Clay, . . . . . . . . . 51
Buffalo Springs, Comal
BUFFALO SPRINGS, Lubbock,
   (493) . . . . . . . . . . . . . . . . . . . 506
Buffalo Springs, Williamson
Bufkin, Robertson
Buford, El Paso

Town,County . . . . . . . . . . .Pop. 2002

Buford, Mitchell, . . . . . . . . . . . . . 25
Bugbee, Hutchinson
Bug Eye, Dallas
Bugscuffle, Bandera
Bugscuffle, Llano
Bugscuffle, Wilbarger
Bugtown, Denton
Bug Tussle, Fannin
Bug Tussle, Grayson
Buhler, Jackson
*Bula, Bailey, 2 . . . . . . . . . . . . . . 35
Bula, Brown
Bula, Lampasas
Bulah, Cherokee
Bulcher, Cooke, . . . . . . . . . . . . . . 6
Buler, Ochiltree
Bullard, Johnson
*BULLARD, Smith-Cherokee,
   214 (1,150) . . . . . . . . . . . . . .1,380
Bull Creek, Eastland
Bull Head, Real
Bullis, Val Verde
Bullisford, Val Verde
Bullock, Eastland
Bullock, Young
Bull Run, Newton,. . . . . . . . . . . . .NA
Bull Rush, Van Zandt
Bullseye, Webb
Bull Town, Parmer
Bulverde, Bexar
*BULVERDE, Comal, 301
   (3,761). . . . . . . . . . . . . . . . .4,038
*Buna, Jasper, 155 (2,269). . . . .2,272
Bunavista, Hutchinson
Bunch, Jefferson
Buncombe, Panola, . . . . . . . . . . . 87
Bundy, Motley
Bunger, Young, . . . . . . . . . . . . . . 40
Bunker Hill, Bowie
Bunker Hill, Jasper, . . . . . . . . . . .NA
Bunker Hill, Lamar
Bunker Hill, Rusk
BUNKER HILL VILLAGE, Harris,
   (3,654). . . . . . . . . . . . . . . . .3,776
Bunkesville, Gillespie
Bunn's Bluff, Orange
Bunsen, El Paso
Bunyan, Erath, . . . . . . . . . . . . . . 20
Buran, Hansford
Burbank Gardens, Dallas
Burden, Moore
Burdette, Hill
Burdette Wells, Caldwell
Burell, Medina
Burgess, Bell
Buriton, Wood
*BURKBURNETT, Wichita, 375
   (10,927). . . . . . . . . . . . . . . .10,963
BURKE, Angelina, (315). . . . . . . . 319
Burke Town, Trinity
*Burkett, Coleman, 11 . . . . . . . . . 30
Burkett, Stephens
*Burkeville, Newton, 42 . . . . . . . . 515
Burkland, Williamson
Burks, Cass
Burks, La Salle
Burk Station, Wichita
Burl, Guadalupe
Burleigh, Austin,. . . . . . . . . . . . . 69
Burleson, Bastrop
Burleson, Freestone
*BURLESON, Johnson-Tarrant,
   1,494 (20,976). . . . . . . . . . .23,351
Burleson, Lampasas
Burleson's Springs, Williamson
*Burlington, Milam, 7 . . . . . . . . . . 140
Burlington, Montague

Town,County. . . . . . . . . . . Pop. 2002

Burn's Ford, Burnet
Burnam, Callahan
Burnam, Ellis
Burnell, Karnes
Burnell Switch, Bee
*BURNET, Burnet, 498
   (4,735). . . . . . . . . . . . . . . . . 4,936
Burney's Bridge, Navarro
Burning Bush, Smith-Cherokee
Burns, Bowie, . . . . . . . . . . . . . . . 400
Burns, Van Zandt
Burns City, Cooke, . . . . . . . . . . . . 60
Burnside, Ochiltree
Burns Mill, Panola
Burns Siding, Rusk
Burns Station, DeWitt
Burns Valley, Jack
Burr, Tarrant
Burr, Wharton
Burrantown, Houston, . . . . . . . . . . 70
Burris, Irion
Burris Prairie, Angelina
Burrough, Austin
Burroughsville, Victoria
Burrow, Hunt, . . . . . . . . . . . . . . . NA
Burt, Comal
*BURTON, Washington, 62
   (359). . . . . . . . . . . . . . . . . . . 364
Burton Springs, Jack
Burtonsville, Shelby
Busby, Fisher
Busco, Harris
Bush, Anderson
Bush, Bowie
Bush, Coryell
Bush, Jones
Bush's Store, Waller
*Bushland, Potter, 19 . . . . . . . . . . 130
Bustamante, Zapata,. . . . . . . . . . . 15
Buster, Coryell
Buster's, Washington
Busterville, Hockley,. . . . . . . . . . . . 6
Busyton, Hamilton
Bute, Henderson
Butler, Bastrop,. . . . . . . . . . . . . . NA
Butler, Freestone, . . . . . . . . . . . . 67
Butler's Ranch, Galveston
Butlerberg, Montgomery
Butlers, Bee
Buttercup, Williamson
Butterfield, Cherokee
Butterfield, El Paso, (61). . . . . . . . 66
Butter Krust, Travis
Buttermilk Station, Brazoria
Buttermilk Station, Galveston
Buttfield, Jefferson
Button Prairie, Milam
Butts, Gregg
Buzzard Roost, Llano
Byerly's Gin, Jasper
*BYERS, Clay, 13 (517) . . . . . . . . 517
Byfield, Panola
Byfield's Store, Llano
*BYNUM, Hill, 5 (225) . . . . . . . . . . 230
Byran, Duval
Byrd, Dimmit
Byrd, Ellis, . . . . . . . . . . . . . . . . . .15
Byrd, Houston
Byrd, Tom Green
Byrds, Brown, . . . . . . . . . . . . . . . NA
Byrdtown, Lamar, . . . . . . . . . . . . . 22
Byrne, Tom Green
Byron, Anderson
Byron, Ellis
Byspot, San Jacinto
Byzone, Hunt

| Town,County . . . . . . . . . . .Pop. 2002 | Town,County . . . . . . . . . . .Pop. 2002 | Town,County . . . . . . . . . . . Pop. 2002 |
|---|---|---|
| **C** | Calloway, Upshur | Cana, Van Zandt |
| Cabell, Fort Bend | Calloway's Gin, Wood | Canaan, Harrison |
| Cabeza, DeWitt | Calvary, Trinity | Canaan, Limestone |
| Cabot, Cherokee | Calvary, Wood | **Canada Verde, Wilson, . . . . . . . . . 23** |
| Cabot Kingsmill, Gray | **\*CALVERT, Robertson, 45** | Canaday, Franklin |
| **\*CACTUS, Moore, 34** | **(1,426). . . . . . . . . . . . . . . . .1,427** | **\*CANADIAN, Hemphill, 272** |
| **(2,538). . . . . . . . . . . . . . . . 2,588** | Calvert Junction, Robertson | **(2,233) . . . . . . . . . . . . . . . 2,173** |
| Cactus, Webb | Calvin, Bastrop | **Canary, Leon, . . . . . . . . . . . . . NA** |
| Cactus Flat, Stonewall-Fisher | Calvin, Red River | Canary, Madison |
| Cactus Hill, Wise | Calvin City, Nueces | Canary, Polk |
| Caddell, San Augustine | Camada Ranch, Jim Wells | Cana School, Wood |
| Caddo, Milam | Camanche Peak, Hood | Canby, Angelina |
| **\*Caddo, Stephens, 6 . . . . . . . . . . 40** | Camanche Springs, Blanco | **Candelaria, Presidio, . . . . . . . . . . 55** |
| Caddo, Wilson | Cambridge, Clay | Candlish, Bee |
| Caddo Camp, Hunt | Cambridge, Rusk-Gregg | Candon, Tarrant |
| Caddo Grove, Johnson | Camden, Comanche | Cane Branch, Leon |
| **\*CADDO MILLS, Hunt,** | Camden, Falls | Cane Island, Harris |
| **113 (1,149) . . . . . . . . . . . . .1,181** | Camden, Gregg | Caney, Freestone |
| Caddo Peak, Callahan | **\*Camden, Polk, 4 . . . . . . . . . . .1,200** | Caney, Hopkins |
| Caddo Peak, Johnson | Camden, Rusk | **Caney, Matagorda, . . . . . . . . . . . 300** |
| Caddo Villa, Hunt | Camel, Houston | **CANEY CITY, Henderson,** |
| Caddo Village, Wise | Cameo, Guadalupe | **(236). . . . . . . . . . . . . . . . . . . 238** |
| **Cade Chapel, Navarro, . . . . . . . . . 25** | Cameron, DeWitt | Caney Creek, Fannin |
| Cade Lake, Burleson | **\*CAMERON, Milam, 326** | Caney Creek, Henderson |
| **Cadiz, Bee, . . . . . . . . . . . . . . . . . . 15** | **(5,634). . . . . . . . . . . . . . . .5,805** | Caney Creek, Newton |
| Caesar, Bee | Cameron Flatt, Travis | Caney Head, Hardin |
| Caesar, Kleberg | **Cameron Park, Cameron,** | Cann, Hemphill |
| Cage, San Patricio | **(5,961). . . . . . . . . . . . . . . .6,055** | Cannel, Webb |
| Cain, Dallas | Camey Spur, Denton | Cannett, Orange |
| Cain, Lee | **Camilla, San Jacinto, . . . . . . . . . 200** | **Cannon, Grayson, . . . . . . . . . . . . 50** |
| **Cain City, Gillespie, . . . . . . . . . . . NA** | **Camp Air, Mason, . . . . . . . . . . . . . 15** | Cannon Switch, Camp |
| Cairo, Jasper | Camp Allison, Sutton | Cannonville, Hays |
| Cairo, Leon | Camp Barkley, Taylor | Canton, Smith |
| Caisons, Rusk | **\*CAMPBELL, Hunt, 61 (734). . . . . 749** | **\*CANTON, Van Zandt, 534** |
| Calallen, Nueces | Campbell, Navarro | **(3,292) . . . . . . . . . . . . . . . . 3,357** |
| **Calaveras, Wilson, . . . . . . . . . . . 100** | Campbell's Bayou, Galveston | Cantrell, Anderson |
| Calcote, San Augustine | Campbell's Retreat, Refugio | **Cantu Addition, Brooks, (217) . . . 220** |
| Calder, Cherokee | **\*Campbellton, Atascosa, 6 . . . . . 350** | **\*Canutillo, El Paso, 267** |
| Caldren, Bailey | Camp Charlotte, Irion | **(5,129) . . . . . . . . . . . . . . . 5,079** |
| **\*CALDWELL, Burleson,** | Camp Colorado, Coleman | **Canyon, Lubbock, . . . . . . . . . . . . 40** |
| **345 (3,449) . . . . . . . . . . . . .3,643** | Camp Concordia, El Paso | **\*CANYON, Randall, 607** |
| Caldwell, Lubbock | Camp Cooper, Throckmorton | **(12,875) . . . . . . . . . . . . . . 13,245** |
| Caldwell's Hill, Gillespie | Camp Creek, Bell | **Canyon City, Comal, . . . . . . . . . . 100** |
| Caldwell's Store, Bastrop | Camp Creek, Coleman | **\*Canyon Lake, Comal,** |
| Caldwell's Store, Leon | Camp Creek, Johnson | **(16,870) . . . . . . . . . . . . . . 17,924** |
| Caleb, Johnson | **Camp Creek Lake, Robertson, . . 350** | Canyon Valley, Crosby |
| **Caledonia, Rusk, . . . . . . . . . . . . . 75** | Camp Dallas, Denton | Capiote, Gonzales |
| Calef, Tarrant | Camp Ford, Smith | Capisallo, Hidalgo |
| Calera, Hill | Campground, Cherokee | Capitola, Fisher |
| Caleta, Polk | Camp Henderson, Johnson | Capitola, Mason |
| **Calf Creek, McCulloch, . . . . . . . . 23** | Camp Hudson, Val Verde | **Caplen, Galveston, . . . . . . . . . . . . 30** |
| Calgando, Palo Pinto | Camp Hulen, Matagorda | Caples, DeWitt |
| Calgary, San Augustine | Camp Lucille, Denton | Capote, Guadalupe |
| Calhoun, Calhoun | Camp Maxey, Lamar | Capote, Hidalgo |
| Calhoun, Colorado | Camp Melbourne, Crockett | Capps, Moore |
| Calhoun, Dallas | Camp Melvin, Crockett | **Capps Corner, Montague, . . . . . . NA** |
| Calhoun, Gregg | **Campo Alto, Hidalgo, . . . . . . . . . . .NA** | **Cap Rock, Crosby, . . . . . . . . . . . . 25** |
| Calhoun, Rusk | Camp on San Pedro, Val Verde | Caprock, Ector |
| Calhoun's Ferry, Houston | Camp Rice, Hudspeth | **Caps, Taylor, . . . . . . . . . . . . . . . . 100** |
| Calhoun School, DeWitt | **Camp Ruby, Polk, . . . . . . . . . . . . . 35** | Caps Sides, Taylor |
| Caliche, San Patricio | **Camp San Saba, McCulloch, . . . . . 36** | Capt's Mill, Hays |
| California, Jones | Camp San Saba, Menard | Caput, Gaines |
| California Store, Hidalgo | Camp Scenic, Kerr | Car, Mitchell |
| **Calina, Limestone, . . . . . . . . . . . . 10** | **Camp Seale, Polk, . . . . . . . . . . . . .NA** | Cara Blanca, Baylor |
| **\*Call, Newton, 14 . . . . . . . . . . . . 170** | **Camp Springs, Scurry, . . . . . . . . . 10** | **Caradan, Mills, . . . . . . . . . . . . . . . 20** |
| Calla, Brazos | **Camp Swift, Bastrop** | **Carancahua, Jackson, . . . . . . . . . 301** |
| Callahan, Callahan | **(4,731). . . . . . . . . . . . . . . .5,121** | Caranchua, Jackson |
| Callahan, Callahan | **Camp Switch, Gregg, . . . . . . . . . . 70** | Carbody, Bosque |
| Callahan, DeWitt | **Campti, Shelby, . . . . . . . . . . . . . .NA** | **\*CARBON, Eastland, 20** |
| Callahan, Webb | Camptown, Newton | **(224). . . . . . . . . . . . . . . . . . . 210** |
| Callan, Menard | **\*Camp Verde, Kerr, 2 . . . . . . . . . . 41** | Carbon, Webb |
| CallField, Wichita | Camp Willow, Guadalupe | **Carbondale, Bowie, . . . . . . . . . . . . 30** |
| Callie, Montgomery | **\*CAMP WOOD, Real, 57** | Carbondale, Young |
| **\*Calliham, McMullen, 3 . . . . . . . . 200** | **(822) . . . . . . . . . . . . . . . . . . 817** | Carbonville, Uvalde |
| Callis, Collin | **Camp Worth, San Augustine, . . . .NA** | Carden, Coryell |
| **CALLISBURG, Cooke, (365) . . . . 380** | Camp Wright, Cherokee | Cardiff, Bastrop |
| **Call Junction, Jasper, . . . . . . . . . 50** | Cana, Bandera | Cardiff, Waller |

| Town,County ........... Pop. 2002 | Town,County ........... Pop. 2002 | Town,County ........... Pop. 2002 |
|---|---|---|
| *Cardova, Guadalupe* | *Carter's Mill, Gregg* | *Cedar, Limestone* |
| *Carew, Van Zandt* | *Carter's Prairie, Washington* | *Cedar Bayou, Chambers* |
| **Carey, Childress, 7............. 60** | *Carter's Woods, Jefferson* | **Cedar Bayou, Harris, ........ 1,287** |
| *Cargray, Carson* | *Carter Lake, Brazos* | *Cedar Bayou, Liberty* |
| *Cariker, Panola* | *Carter Station ,Liberty* | *Cedar Bluff, Harris* |
| *Carl, Navarro* | **Carterville, Cass, ............. 39** | *Cedar Bluff, Nacogdoches* |
| **Carl, Travis,.................. NA** | *Carterville, Harrison* | *Cedar Bluff, Polk-San Jacinto* |
| **CARL'S CORNER, Hill,** | ***CARTHAGE, Panola, 669** | *Cedar Brakes, Brazoria* |
| **(134) ................... 137** | **(6,664)................6,629** | *Cedar Creek, Anderson* |
| *Carleton, Cass* | *Cartwright, Kaufman* | ***Cedar Creek, Bastrop, 150 ..... NA** |
| *Carley, Freestone* | **Cartwright, Wood,............. 61** | *Cedar Creek, Delta* |
| *Carley, Robertson* | *Caruth, Dallas* | *Cedar Creek, Trinity* |
| *Carlisle, Lubbock* | *Caruthers, Angelina* | **Cedar Creek, Waller,.......... NA** |
| *Carlisle, Rusk* | *Carvajal Crossing, Karnes* | *Cedar Creek, Washington* |
| **Carlisle, Trinity,.............. 68** | **Carver, Leon,..................NA** | *Cedar Creek Park, Hill* |
| **Carlos, Grimes, .............. 50** | *Carver Park, Bexar* | *Cedarfield, Grayson* |
| *Carlos, Victoria* | *Casa Blanca, Jim Wells* | *Cedar Fork, Kaufman* |
| *Carlos City, Aransas* | **Casa Piedra, Presidio, .........NA** | *Cedar Grove, Brazoria* |
| *Carlota, Hidalgo* | *Casas Blancas, Starr* | *Cedar Grove, Harris* |
| ***Carlsbad, Tom Green, 7 ....... 100** | *Casco, Dickens* | *Cedar Grove, Kaufman-Van Zandt* |
| **Carlson, Travis,................ NA** | *Case's, Travis* | *Cedar Grove, Matagorda* |
| ***Carlton, Hamilton, 9 .......... 70** | *Casey, Bell* | ***CEDAR HILL, Dallas-Ellis,** |
| *Carlville, Williamson* | **Casey, El Paso,.............. 115** | **1,229 (32,093) .......... 34,904** |
| *Carmargo, Burleson* | *Casey, Harris* | **Cedar Hill, Floyd,.............. 36** |
| *Carmel, Bexar* | *Casey, Jeff Davis* | *Cedar Hill, Washington* |
| *Carmel, Pecos* | *Caseyville, Young* | *Cedar Island, Limestone* |
| *Carmel, San Jacinto-Walker* | *Cash, Goliad* | *Cedar Island, Matagorda* |
| ***CARMINE, Fayette, 27** | **Cash, Hunt,.................. 56** | *Cedar Knob, Bell* |
| **(228) .................... 241** | **CASHION, Wichita, (346) ....... 342** | *Cedar Knob, Palo Pinto* |
| **Carmona, Polk,................ 50** | ***Cason, Morris, 7 ............. 173** | *Cedar Lake, Brazoria* |
| *Carnell, Refugio* | *Cason Town, Rains* | *Cedar Lake, Gaines* |
| *Carnes, Hardeman* | **Cass, Cass,.................. 60** | **Cedar Lake, Matagorda, ........ 160** |
| *Carney, Haskell* | **Cassie, Burnet,.............. 446** | ***Cedar Lane, Matagorda, 3...... 55** |
| **Caro, Nacogdoches, .......... 113** | **Cassin, Bexar,................NA** | *Cedar Mill, Burnet* |
| *Carolina, Falls* | ***Castell, Llano, 4.............. 72** | *Cedar Mills, Grayson* |
| *Carolina, Walker-San Jacinto* | *Castine, Karnes* | ***CEDAR PARK, Williamson-Travis,** |
| *Carp, Falls* | *Castle, DeWitt* | **1,323 (26,049) .......... 31,876** |
| *Carpenter, Bexar* | *Castleberry, Tarrant* | *Cedar Point, Brown* |
| *Carpenter, Wilson* | *Castle Heights, McLennan* | *Cedar Point, Chambers* |
| *Carpenters Bluff, Grayson* | **CASTLE HILLS, Bexar,** | *Cedar Point, Collin* |
| *Carr, Titus* | **(4,202)................4,228** | *Cedar Point, Erath* |
| *Carr, Victoria* | **Castolon, Brewster, ............ 8** | *Cedar Point, Erath* |
| *Carr's, Hill* | *Castor, Mills* | *Cedar Point, Falls* |
| *Carriage, Cooke* | ***CASTROVILLE, Medina, 240** | *Cedar Point, Llano* |
| **Carricitos, Cameron, .......... 25** | **(2,664)................2,792** | **Cedar Shores, Bosque, ........170** |
| *Carrizo, Hudspeth* | *Cataline, Hemphill* | *Cedar Spring, Leon* |
| *Carrizo, Zapata* | ***Catarina, Dimmit, 7 (135) ...... 141** | *Cedar Spring, Washington* |
| **Carrizo Hill, Dimmit, (548) ...... 562** | *Cat Claw, Callahan* | *Cedar Springs, Dallas* |
| ***CARRIZO SPRINGS, Dimmit,** | *Catfish, Henderson* | **Cedar Springs, Falls, ...........90** |
| **265 (5,655) .............5,624** | *Cathedral, Brewster* | **Cedar Springs, Upshur, ........100** |
| *Carroll, Bastrop* | *Cathrons Store, Lamar* | *Cedar Station, Liberty* |
| *Carroll, Hardin* | *Catlett's Creek, Wise* | *Cedarton, Brown* |
| **Carroll, Smith, .............. 60** | *Cato, McLennan* | **Cedarvale, Kaufman, .......... NA** |
| *Carroll, Stephens* | *Caton, Red River* | **Cedar Valley, Bell,.............. 4** |
| *Carroll's Prairie, Hopkins* | ***Cat Spring, Austin, 27.......... 76** | **Cedar Valley, Travis, ........... 70** |
| *Carroll's Store, Shelby* | *Cat Town, Llano* | *Cedar Yard, Shelby* |
| *Carrolla, Jasper* | *Caufield Mountain, Coryell* | *Cedric, Crosby* |
| *Carroll Chapel, Navarro* | *Causey Hill, Lubbock* | *Cedron, Bosque* |
| **Carroll Springs, Anderson, ...... 20** | *Cavan, Sterling* | ***Cee Vee, Cottle, 5.............. 45** |
| *Carroll Springs, Henderson* | **Cavazos, Cameron, .......... 201** | **Cego, Falls, .................. 42** |
| *Carroll Switch, Tyler* | *Cave, Bosque* | **Cele, Travis,.................. NA** |
| ***CARROLLTON, Dallas-Denton,** | *Cave Creek, Coryell* | ***CELESTE, Hunt, 46** |
| **5,407 (109,576)........ 115,656** | **Cave Creek, Gillespie, ..........NA** | **(817)...................... 836** |
| *Carrollton, Upshur* | *Cavender, Dimmit* | *Celeste, Montague* |
| *Carruth, Caldwell* | *Cave Spring, Harrison* | *Celia, Fannin* |
| *Carsner, Victoria* | *Caves Springs, Cass* | ***CELINA, Collin, 175** |
| **Carson, Fannin, .............. 22** | **Caviness, Lamar, .............. 80** | **(1,861) ................. 2,097** |
| *Carson, Midland* | *Cavins Mill, Newton* | *Celotex, Fisher* |
| *Carson, Upshur* | *Cavitt, Coryell* | *Celtic, Briscoe* |
| *Carson City, Carson* | **Cawthon, Brazos,.............. 75** | *Cely's Store, Anderson* |
| **Carswell Base, Tarrant, ....... 3,162** | *Cawthorn, Grimes* | *Celynda, Lee* |
| **Carta Valley, Edwards,.......... 12** | **Cayote, Bosque,.............. 75** | *Cement, Dallas* |
| *Carter, Denton* | ***Cayuga, Anderson, 9 ......... 200** | *Cement, Hardeman* |
| *Carter, Parker* | *Caywood, Brazos* | *Ceniza, Hidalgo* |
| *Carter, Polk* | *Cecil, Walker* | *Cenizal, Hidalgo* |
| *Carter, Stephens* | *Cedar, Fayette* | *Centenary, Titus* |
| *Carter's Flat, Edwards* | *Cedar, Kaufman* | *Centennial, Panola* |

| Town,County ............Pop. 2002 | Town,County ............Pop. 2002 | Town,County ............ Pop. 2002 |
|---|---|---|
| *Centennial City, Cooke* | *Chaha, Dallas* | **Chateau Woods, Montgomery,** |
| *Center, Fisher* | *Chaille, Grimes* | ...................... 1,091 |
| *Center, Houston* | *Chaison, Jefferson* | *Chatfield, Navarro, 7 .......... 40 |
| **Center, Limestone,............. 76** | **Chalk, Cottle, 11 .............. 17** | *Chatfield, Uvalde* |
| *Center, Lubbock* | *Chalk Bluff, McLennan* | *Chatt, Hill* |
| *CENTER, Shelby, 489 | **Chalk Hill, Rusk, ............. 200** | *Chatterton Spur, Harrison* |
| (5,678)................. 5,660 | **Chalk Mountain, Erath, ........ 25** | *Chauncey, Eastland* |
| *Center, Wilbarger* | *Chalk Mountain, Somervell* | *Chautaugua, Callahan* |
| *Center, Wood* | *Chalkton, Howard* | *Chautauqua, Callahan* |
| **Center City, Mills,............. 15** | *Chalmers, Harris* | **Cheapside, Gonzales, 1 ......... 24** |
| *Center Grove, Franklin* | *Chalmers, Matagorda* | **Cheek, Jefferson, ............. 62** |
| **Center Grove, Houston,........ 108** | *Chalybeate, Wood* | *Cheeseburg, Jackson* |
| **Center Grove, Titus,............ 65** | *Chalybeate Springs, Cass* | *Cheeseland, Angelina* |
| **Center Hill, Houston, .......... 105** | *Chamberlain, Dallam* | *Cheetham, Colorado* |
| *Center Line, Burleson* | *Chambers, Angelina* | *Cheisa, Dallas* |
| *Centerline, Jones* | *Chambersburgh, Jasper* | *Chek, Falls* |
| *Center Mills, Johnson* | *Chambers Creek, Ellis* | *Cheley, Upshur-Camp* |
| *Center Plains, Hale* | *Chambersea, Chambers* | *Chelsea, Angelina* |
| **Center Plains, Swisher, ......... 40** | **Chambersville, Collin, .......... 40** | *Chelsea, Upshur* |
| *Center Point, Bexar* | *Chambersville, Grayson* | *Chemcel, Nueces* |
| **Center Point, Camp,............. 41** | **Chambliss, Collin, ............. 25** | *Chenango, Brazoria* |
| *Center Point, Ellis* | *Champ, Borden* | *Chenango Junction, Brazoria* |
| *Center Point, Fisher* | *Champ d'Asile, Liberty* | **Cheneyboro, Navarro,.......... 100** |
| *Centerpoint, Hays* | **Champion, Nolan,............... 8** | *Cheneyville, Harris* |
| *Center Point, Hopkins* | **Champions, Harris, ........17,125** | *Cherokee, San Saba, 25 ....... 175 |
| *Center Point, Hunt* | *Chance, Hardin* | *Cherokee, Tyler* |
| *Center Point, Kerr, 69 ........ 800 | *Chancellor, Pecos* | **Cherokee Hill, Smith, .......... NA** |
| *Center Point, Mitchell* | *Chance Prairie, Burleson* | *Cherry, Callahan* |
| *Center Point, Navarro* | *Chances Prairie, Brazoria* | *Cherry, Red River* |
| **Center Point, Panola,........... NA** | **Chance's Store, Burleson,.......NA** | *Cherry Grove, Hopkins* |
| *Center Point, Tarrant* | *Chanceville, Cherokee* | *Cherry Mound ,Grayson* |
| *Center Point, Trinity* | *Chanceville, Hardin* | **Cherry Spring, Gillespie, ........ 75** |
| **Center Point, Upshur, .......... 50** | *Chancey, Angelina* | *Chesnutt, Navarro* |
| *Center Star, Williamson* | *Chancey, Bowie* | *Chester, Hansford* |
| *Center Union, Bastrop* | *CHANDLER, Henderson, 186 | *CHESTER ,Tyler, 15 (265) ...... 264 |
| *Centerview, Henderson* | (2,099)...................2,173 | *Chesterfield, Winkler* |
| **Centerview, Leon, ............. NA** | *Chandler, Houston* | **Chesterville, Colorado,.......... 50** |
| *Centerview, Nolan* | *Chandler, Terrell* | *Chevo, Terrell* |
| *Centerville, Dallas* | **Chaney, Eastland,............. 35** | *Cheyenne, Edwards* |
| *Centerville, Goliad* | *Channel, Harris* | *Cheyenne, Oldham* |
| *CENTERVILLE, Leon, 123 | *Channelview, Harris, 827 | *Cheyenne, Winkler* |
| (903).................... 911 | (29,685)................29,814 | *Chicago, Brown* |
| *Centerville, Travis* | *CHANNING, Hartley, 24 | *Chicago, Dawson* |
| **Centerville, Trinity, ............. 60** | (356) .................... 359 | *Chickenfoot, Fisher* |
| *Centerville, Trinity* | *Chapa, Duval* | *CHICO, Wise, 98 (947) ........ 977 |
| *CenterVine, Morris* | **Chapel Hill, Smith, .............NA** | *Chicolete, DeWitt* |
| *Centex, Hays* | *Chapel Hill, Upshur* | *Chico South, Medina* |
| **Central, Angelina, ........... 200** | *Chapena, Starr* | *Chicota, Lamar, 5............. 125 |
| *Central, Bee* | *Chapin, Hidalgo* | *Chief, Kaufman* |
| *Central, Dawson* | *Chapin, Hood* | **Chihuahua, Hidalgo,........... NA** |
| *Central, Lynn* | **Chapman, Rusk,.............. 20** | *Chihuahua, Jeff Davis* |
| *Central, Van Zandt* | *Chapman, Trinity* | **Chihuahua Farm, Zapata,........ 25** |
| *Central Academy, Harrison* | *Chapman, Wood* | *Childer's Mill, Bell* |
| **Central Gardens, Jefferson,** | *Chapman Arm, Hopkins* | *CHILDRESS, Childress, |
| (4,106)...................4,082 | *Chapman City, Williamson* | 313 (6,778).............. 6,861 |
| *Central Heights, Nacogdoches* | *Chapman Ranch, Nueces, 6.... 100 | *Childress, Cooke* |
| **Central High, Cherokee, ........ 30** | *Chapparal Park, Hays* | *CHILLICOTHE, Hardeman, |
| *Centralia, Trinity,............ 53 | *Chappel, Burnet* | 32 (798) ................760 |
| *Central Institute, Limestone* | **Chappel, San Saba, ............ 25** | *Chiltipin, San Patricio* |
| *Central Plains,Hale* | *Chappell, Hopkins* | *Chilton, Falls, 30 ............. 274 |
| *Centre, Cass* | *Chappell Hill, Washington, 59 .. 600 | *Chilton, Wood* |
| *Centre, Rusk* | **Charco, Goliad,................ 96** | *Chimney, Shackelford* |
| *Centre Hill, Austin* | *Charcoal City, Kendall* | *CHINA, Jefferson, 40 |
| *Centre Mill, Hood* | *Charco Hondo, Cameron* | (1,112) ................. 1,104 |
| *Centre Spring, Lamar* | *Charity, Parker* | *China Creek, San Saba* |
| *Centreville, Gonzales* | *Charity, Polk* | **CHINA GROVE, Bexar,** |
| *Centreville, Henderson* | *Charles, Travis* | (1,247) ................. 1,308 |
| *Century City, Webb* | *Charles Barker, Ellis* | *China Grove, Brazoria* |
| *Cereal, Floyd* | *Charleston, Dallas* | *China Grove, Dallas* |
| *Ceres, Brown* | **Charleston, Delta,............. 120** | *China Grove, Gonzales* |
| *Ceries, Red River* | **Charlie, Clay,................. 65** | **China Grove, Scurry, .......... 15** |
| **Cesar Chavez, Hidalgo,** | *CHARLOTTE, Atascosa, 33 | *China Grove, Trinity* |
| (1,469).................1,530 | (1,637).................1,694 | *China Grove, Van Zandt* |
| **Cestohowa, Karnes,.......... 110** | *Charlton, Denton* | *China Lake, Knox* |
| *Ceta, Randall* | *Charter Oak, Bell* | *China Pond, Andrews* |
| *Ceyola, Limestone* | *Chase, Bosque* | *China Spring, McLennan, 100 |
| *Chadwick, Lampasas* | *Chase, McLennan* | ...................... 1,000 |

| Town,County | Pop. 2002 | Town,County | Pop. 2002 | Town,County | Pop. 2002 |
|---|---|---|---|---|---|
| **Chinati, Presidio,** | **NA** | *Clabbertown, Gonzales* | | **Clegg, Live Oak,** | **125** |
| *Chinita, Nacogdoches* | | *Clair, Hunt* | | *Clem, Delta* | |
| *Chinn's Chapel, Denton* | | *Clair, Red River* | | *Clemens, Brazoria* | |
| **Chinquapin, Matagorda,** | **30** | **Clairemont, Kent,** | **15** | *Clemens, Guadalupe* | |
| **Chinquapin, San Augustine** | **NA** | **Clairette, Erath,** | **55** | *Clements, Mills* | |
| *Chinquapin, San Jacinto* | | *Clanton, Caldwell* | | *Clemma, Ellis* | |
| *Chinquapin, Van Zandt* | | *Clapp's Creek, Leon* | | **Clemons, Waller,** | **NA** |
| *Chio, Cooke* | | *Clara, Bee* | | **Clemville, Matagorda, 1** | **45** |
| *Chipley, Cochran* | | **Clara, Wichita,** | **100** | *Cleo, Castro* | |
| *Chipley, Victoria* | | **Clardy, Lamar,** | **160** | *Cleo, Harris* | |
| **\*CHIRENO, Nacogdoches,** | | **\*CLARENDON, Donley,** | | **Cleo, Kimble,** | **3** |
| **16 (405).** | **410** | **146 (1,974)** | **1,878** | *Cleon, Shelby* | |
| **CHISHOLM [McLendon-], Rockwall,** | | *Clareno, Zapata* | | *Clermont, San Jacinto* | |
| **(914)** | **1,013** | **Clareville, Bee,** | **23** | *Cleta, Randall* | |
| *Chisholm's Ferry, DeWitt* | | *Clark, Bell* | | *Cleto, Karnes* | |
| *Chisos Basin, Brewster* | | **CLARK, Denton,** | **345** | **Cleveland, Austin,** | **78** |
| *Chisos Mines, Brewster* | | *Clark, Johnson* | | *Cleveland, Delta* | |
| *Chispa, Jeff Davis* | | *Clark, Lee* | | *Cleveland, Fort Bend* | |
| **Chita, Trinity,** | **81** | **Clark, Liberty,** | **NA** | **\*CLEVELAND, Liberty, 761** | |
| *Choat, Shelby* | | *Clark, Rockwall* | | **(7,605)** | **7,858** |
| **Choate, Karnes,** | **20** | *Clark, Rusk* | | *Clevenger, Nacogdoches* | |
| *Chocolate, Calhoun* | | *Clark, Van Zandt* | | *Clevilas, Polk* | |
| **Chocolate Bayou, Brazoria,** | **60** | *Clark, Victoria* | | *Click, Llano* | |
| *Choctaw, Grayson* | | *Clark's Chapel, Caldwell* | | *Clifden, Medina* | |
| *Choctaw, Red River* | | *Clark's Store, Fannin* | | *Cliff, Haskell* | |
| **Choice, Shelby,** | **21** | *Clark's Store, Newton* | | *Cliff, Medina* | |
| **\*Chriesman, Burleson,** | **30** | *Clarkridge, Eastland* | | *Cliffdale, Kimble* | |
| *Chriesman Chapel School, Burleson* | | *Clarks, Calhoun* | | *Clifford, Collingsworth* | |
| *Christel, Gillespie* | | **Clarkson, Milam,** | **10** | *Clifford, Eastland* | |
| *Christen, Webb* | | *Clarksville, Cameron* | | **Cliffside, Potter,** | **206** |
| *Christian, Palo Pinto* | | **\*CLARKSVILLE, Red River,** | | *Clifstone, Bosque* | |
| *Christian Valley, Dallas* | | **234 (3,883)** | **3,879** | **\*CLIFTON, Bosque, 310** | |
| **\*CHRISTINE, Atascosa, 9** | | *Clarksville, Tom Green* | | **(3,542)** | **3,602** |
| **(436)** | **449** | *Clarksville, Travis* | | *Clifton, Van Zandt* | |
| **\*Christoval, Tom Green,** | | **CLARKSVILLE CITY, Gregg,** | | *Clifton's Prairie, Hopkins* | |
| **26 (422).** | **433** | **(806)** | **821** | *Clifton-by-the-Sea, Galveston* | |
| *Chronister, Cherokee* | | *Clarkwood, Nueces* | | **Climax, Collin,** | **40** |
| *Chuckville, Eastland* | | **\*CLAUDE, Armstrong, 85** | | *Climax, Nacogdoches* | |
| **Chula Vista-Orason, Cameron,** | | **(1,313)** | **1,297** | **Cline, Uvalde,** | **15** |
| **(394)** | **403** | *Claudine, Fort Bend* | | *Cline's Corner, Cottle* | |
| **Chula Vista-River Spur, Zavala,** | | **Clauene, Hockley,** | **10** | *Cline's Prairie, Walker* | |
| **(400)** | **403** | **Clawson, Angelina,** | **195** | *Clinesburg, Montgomery* | |
| *Chumley San Augustine* | | **Clay, Burleson,** | **61** | *Clint, Dallas* | |
| *Chunky, Potter* | | *Clay's Mound, Shelby* | | **\*CLINT, El Paso, 83 (980)** | **998** |
| *Church, Refugio* | | *Claybank, Gregg* | | *Clinton, DeWitt* | |
| **Church Hill, Rusk,** | **20** | *Clay Hill, Limestone* | | *Clinton, Harris* | |
| **Churchill, Brazoria,** | **NA** | *Clay Hill, Titus* | | **Clinton, Hunt,** | **NA** |
| *Cibolo, Bexar* | | **Clays Corner, Parmer,** | **15** | *Clinton, Johnson* | |
| *Cibolo, Caldwell* | | *Clayton, Grayson* | | *Clio, Brown* | |
| *Cibolo, Frio* | | **\*Clayton, Panola, 4** | **79** | *Clio, Shelby* | |
| **\*CIBOLO, Guadalupe, 199** | | *Claytonville, Fisher* | | *Clip, Goliad* | |
| **(3,035).** | **3,572** | **Claytonville, Swisher,** | **116** | *Clipper, Kent* | |
| *Cibolo Settlement, Comal* | | *Claywell, Wichita* | | *Clisbee, Hale* | |
| *Cibolo Station, La Salle* | | **Clear Creek, Burnet,** | **28** | **Clodine, Fort Bend,** | **NA** |
| *Ciel, Dallas* | | *Clear Creek, Cooke* | | *Clopper's Point, Harris* | |
| **Cienegas Terrace, Val Verde,** | | *Clear Creek, Denton* | | **Clopton, Franklin,** | **15** |
| **(2,878).** | **2,999** | *Clear Creek, DeWitt* | | *Clopton, Smith* | |
| *Cima, Tyler* | | *Clear Creek, Galveston* | | **Close City, Garza,** | **94** |
| *Cimarron Springs, Archer* | | *Clear Creek, Hemphill* | | *Closner, Hidalgo* | |
| *Cincinnati, Walker* | | *Clear Creek, Henderson* | | *Cloud, Freestone* | |
| **Cinco Ranch, Fort Bend-Harris,** | | *Clear Creek, Jasper* | | *Cloudy, Dallas* | |
| **(11,196).** | **11,808** | *Clear Fork, Caldwell* | | *Clough, Van Zandt* | |
| *Cinonia, Zavala* | | *Clear Fork, Parker* | | *Clover, Burnet* | |
| **Cipres, Hidalgo,** | **20** | *Clear Fork, Tarrant* | | *Clover, Travis* | |
| *Circle, Cherokee* | | *Clearlake, Collin* | | *Cloverhill, Wood* | |
| **Circle, Lamb,** | **6** | *Clear Lake, Fort Bend* | | **Cloverleaf, Harris, (23,508).** | **23,685** |
| **Circleback, Bailey,** | **10** | *Clear Lake City, Harris* | | *Clovis, Parker* | |
| *Circle City, Clay* | | **CLEAR LAKE SHORES, Galveston,** | | *Clower, Van Zandt* | |
| **Circle D-KC Estates, Bastrop,** | | **(1,205)** | **1,230** | *Cloyd, Jack* | |
| **(2,010).** | **2,194** | *Clear Lake Station, Fort Bend* | | *Club Lake, Collingsworth* | |
| *Circleville, Travis* | | *Clearning, Rains* | | **\*CLUTE, Brazoria, 602** | |
| **Circleville, Williamson,** | **42** | **Clear Spring, Guadalupe,** | **200** | **(10,424).** | **10,453** |
| **\*CISCO, Eastland, 231** | | *Clear Springs, Smith* | | **\*CLYDE, Callahan, 232** | |
| **(3,851).** | **3,813** | *Clearwater, Franklin* | | **(3,345)** | **3,439** |
| **Cistern, Fayette,** | **75** | **\*CLEBURNE, Johnson, 1,500** | | *Clymore, Milam* | |
| **Citrus City, Hidalgo, (941)** | **956** | **(26,005)** | **27,314** | *Coady, Harris* | |
| **Citrus Grove, Matagorda,** | **15** | *Cleere, Lamar* | | **\*COAHOMA, Howard, 42** | |

CITIES & TOWNS

| Town, County .......... Pop. 2002 | Town, County .......... Pop. 2002 | Town, County .......... Pop. 2002 |
|---|---|---|
| **(932)** ..................... **911** | *Coleto Creek, Goliad* | *Comanche Springs, Pecos* |
| *Coal, Frio* | *Coletoville, Victoria* | ***COMBES, Cameron, 19*** |
| *Coal, Limestone* | *Coletown, Montgomery* | **(2,553)** .................... **2,667** |
| *Coaling Camp, Cherokee* | *Coletto, DeWitt* | **COMBINE, Kaufman-Dallas,** |
| *Coal Mine, Medina* | *Coleville, Cooke* | **(1,788)** ................. **1,956** |
| *Coalson, Fort Bend* | *Coley Creek, San Jacinto* | *Comer, Eastland* |
| *Coalville, Palo Pinto* | *Coleyville, Cottle* | *Comet, Marion* |
| *Coats, Taylor* | *Colfax, McMullen* | **Cometa, Zavala,** .............. **10** |
| *Coats City, Karnes* | **Colfax, Van Zandt,** ............. **35** | ***Comfort, Kendall, 186*** |
| *Cobb, Archer* | **Colita, Polk,** ................... **50** | **(2,358)** ............... **2,397** |
| *Cobb, Cass* | *Collado, Culberson* | *Comitas, Zapata* |
| *Cobb, Freestone* | *Collard's, Madison* | ***COMMERCE, Hunt, 342*** |
| **Cobb, Kaufman,** ............... **NA** | **College Hill, Bowie** ........... **116** | **(7,669)** ............... **7,712** |
| *Cobb, Smith* | **College Mound, Kaufman,** ...... **350** | *Community, Swisher* |
| *Cobb, Stephens* | ***Collegeport, Matagorda, 2*** ...... **85** | *Como, Bastrop* |
| **Coble, Hockley,** ............... **11** | ***COLLEGE STATION, Brazos,*** | ***COMO, Hopkins, 45 (621)*** ...... **617** |
| *Coburn, Lipscomb* | **2,775 (67,890)** .......... **70,607** | *Como, Jack* |
| *Cochina, La Salle* | *Colletto, DeWitt* | **Compass, Lamar** |
| **Cochran, Austin,** ............. **116** | ***COLLEYVILLE, Tarrant, 1,027*** | **Compton, Rusk,** ............. **NA** |
| *Cochran, Cochran* | **(19,636)** ................ **20,915** | ***Comstock, Val Verde, 10*** ....... **375** |
| *Cochran, Hill* | *Collier, Hardin* | **Comyn, Comanche,** ............ **40** |
| *Cochran's Peak, Floyd* | *Collier, Milam* | ***Concan, Uvalde, 28*** ........... **225** |
| *Cochran's Retreat, Newton* | *Collier Spur, Reeves* | ***Concepcion, Duval, 7 (61)*** ...... **64** |
| *Cochranville, Angelina* | *Collin, Collin* | *Concho, Concho* |
| *Cockrell, El Paso* | *Collingsworth, Collingsworth* | *Concho, Tom Green* |
| **COCKRELL HILL, Dallas,** | *Collins, Jasper* | *Concord, Angelina* |
| **(4,443).** ................. **4.423** | *Collins, Jim Wells* | **Concord, Cherokee,** ........... **50** |
| *Cockrells Hill, Fayette* | *Collinsburg, Cass* | *Concord, Hardin* |
| *Codman, Roberts* | *Collinsburgh, El Paso* | *Concord, Harrison* |
| *Cody, Navarro* | *Collins City, Cherokee* | *Concord, Houston* |
| *Cody, Waller* | *Collins Mill, Montgomery* | **Concord, Hunt,** ................ **30** |
| *Coesfield, Cooke* | ***COLLINSVILLE, Grayson,*** | *Concord, Jefferson* |
| *Coesville, Limestone* | **67 (1,235)** .............. **1,309** | *Concord, Johnson* |
| *Coffee, Hopkins* | *Collwood, Angelina* | ***Concord, Leon, 2*** ............ **28** |
| *Coffee's Station, Grayson* | ***COLMESNEIL, Tyler, 37*** | **Concord, Liberty,** ............ **26** |
| **COFFEE CITY, Henderson,** | **(638)** .................... **638** | **Concord, Madison,** ............ **50** |
| **(193)** .................... **202** | *Cologne, Goliad* | *Concord, McLennan* |
| *Coffee Creek, Baylor* | *Coloney, Dallam* | **Concord, Rusk,** ................ **23** |
| **Coffeeville, Upshur,** ........... **50** | *Colony, Bee* | *Concord, Upshur* |
| **Cofferville, Lamb,** ............ **4** | *Colony, Fayette* | *Concord, Wood* |
| *Coffey, Coryell* | *Colony, Goliad* | *Concord Church, Anderson* |
| *Cogniac, Jasper* | **Colony, Rains,** ................ **70** | *Concord Church, Brown* |
| *Coin, Cherokee* | *Colony City, Victoria* | *Concordia, El Paso* |
| **Coit, Limestone,** .............. **25** | *Colony Hill, Taylor* | *Concordia, Nueces* |
| *Coke, McLennan* | *Colorado, Bastrop* | *Concordia, Williamson* |
| **Coke, Wood,** ................. **105** | *Colorado, Jim Hogg* | **Concrete, DeWitt,** ............. **46** |
| *Cokelan, Palo Pinto* | *Colorado, Wharton* | *Condor, Limestone* |
| *Coker, Limestone* | *Colorado City, Fayette* | **Cone, Crosby, 2** ............... **70** |
| *Colbay Settlement, Bee* | ***COLORADO CITY, Mitchell,*** | *Cone, Milam* |
| *Colberg, Travis* | **271 (4,281)** ............. **4,304** | *Cone, Webb* |
| *Colbert, Erath* | **Colquitt, Kaufman,** ........... **.NA** | *Cone's Switch, Milam* |
| *Colbert's Ferry, Grayson* | *Coltexo, Gray* | *Conel, Williamson* |
| *Colburn, Wharton* | **Coltharp, Houston,** ............ **40** | *Cone Springs, Hall* |
| *Colby, Harris* | **Colton, Travis,** ................ **50** | *Congreve Station, Jefferson* |
| *Cold Creek, San Saba* | *Columbia, Brazoria* | **Conlen, Dallam,** ............... **69** |
| *Cold Hill, Hopkins* | **Columbia Lakes, Brazoria,** ..... **646** | *Conn, Newton* |
| *Coldris, Nueces* | ***COLUMBUS, Colorado,*** | *Connally's Store, Frio* |
| *Cold Spring, Mason* | **392 (3,916)** ............. **3,876** | *Connell, Orange* |
| ***COLDSPRING, San Jacinto,*** | *Colville, Grayson* | *Connelley's Crossing, Crockett* |
| **144 (691).** ................ **721** | *Colville, Newton* | *Conner, Navarro* |
| *Cold Springs, Cherokee* | *Colvin, Hood* | *Connor, Collin* |
| **Cold Springs, Coryell,** .......... **4** | *Colvin, Lee* | *Connor, Leon* |
| *Cold Springs, Mills* | **Comal, Comal,** ............... **40** | **Connor, Madison,** .............. **20** |
| *Cold Springs, Red River* | *Comal, Knox* | *Connor Creek, Young* |
| *Coldwater, Bastrop* | *Comal Creek Settlement, Comal* | *Connville, Sabine* |
| *Cold Water, Bastrop* | *Comal Ranche, Comal* | *Conoley, Milam* |
| **Coldwater, Dallam,** ............ **53** | *Comal Town, Comal* | *Conrad, Wheeler* |
| *Coldwater, Sherman* | ***COMANCHE, Comanche,*** | ***CONROE, Montgomery,*** |
| *Cold Water, Van Zandt* | **339 (4,482)** ............. **4,480** | **4,215 (36,811)** ......... **38,727** |
| *Coldwater, Wood* | *Comanche, Concho* | *Conroy, DeWitt* |
| *Cole, Cherokee* | *Comanche, Travis* | *Conroy, Lavaca* |
| *Cole, Erath* | **Comanche Cove, Hood,** ........ **501** | **Content, Bell,** .................. **25** |
| ***COLEMAN, Coleman, 325*** | *Comanche Crossing, Anderson* | *Content, Coleman* |
| **(5,127).** ................. **5,081** | **Comanche Harbor, Hood,** ...... **325** | *Content, Colorado* |
| *Coleman Junction, Coleman* | *Comanche Pass, Travis* | *Content, Fayette* |
| *Coles', Washington* | *Comanche Spring, Blanco* | *Content, Runnels* |
| *Cole Springs, Lee* | *Comanche Springs, McLennan* | ***CONVERSE, Bexar, 479*** |

| Town,County . . . . . . . . . . .Pop. 2002 | Town,County . . . . . . . . . . .Pop. 2002 | Town,County . . . . . . . . . . . Pop. 2002 |
|---|---|---|
| (11,508). . . . . . . . . . . . . .11,932 | Corinth, Navarro | Cottonwood, McLennan, . . . . . . . .50 |
| Conville, San Augustine | Corinth, Panola | Cottonwood, Nolan |
| Conway, Carson, . . . . . . . . . . . . . 20 | Corinth, Van Zandt | Cottonwood, Somervell,. . . . . . . . 24 |
| Conway, Hidalgo | Corinth School Community, Ellis | Cottonwood, Travis |
| Cook's, Matagorda | Corlena, Dallam | Cottonwood, Wilbarger |
| Cook's Mill, DeWitt | Corley, Bowie,. . . . . . . . . . . . . . . 35 | Cottonwood, Wood |
| Cook's Schoolhouse, Navarro | Cornelia, Armstrong | Cottonwood Flat, Scurry |
| Cooks Ferry, Austin | Cornelia, Live Oak | COTTONWOOD SHORES, Burnet, |
| Cooks Fort, Cherokee | Cornell, Angelina | (877). . . . . . . . . . . . . . . . . . .960 |
| Cooks Point, Burleson, . . . . . . . . 60 | Cornell, Kinney | Cottonwood Springs, Young |
| Cooks Springs, Grayson | Corner, Hutchinson | *COTULLA, La Salle, 139 |
| Cooks Store, Anderson | Corners, Dickens-King | (3,614) . . . . . . . . . . . . . . . 3,591 |
| Cooksville, Goliad | Corners, Taylor | Couch, Coleman |
| *Cookville, Titus, 27 . . . . . . . . . . 105 | Cornersville, Hopkins, . . . . . . . . . .NA | Couch, Dallas |
| COOL, Parker, (162) . . . . . . . . . . 161 | Cornett, Cass, . . . . . . . . . . . . . . 30 | Couch, Karnes, . . . . . . . . . . . . . . 10 |
| *COOLIDGE, Limestone, | Corn Hill, Williamson | Couch, Roberts |
| 30 (848). . . . . . . . . . . . . . . . 866 | Cornstreet, Jefferson | Cougar, Parker |
| Cool Springs, Van Zandt | Cornudas, Hudspeth, . . . . . . . . . . 19 | Coughran, Atascosa, . . . . . . . . . . 20 |
| Coon Creek, Bosque | *CORPUS CHRISTI, Nueces, | Coulterville, Matagorda |
| Coonskin, San Jacinto | 11,820 (277,454) . . . . . . .279,241 | Council Creek, Burnet |
| Coonville, Shelby | Corpus Christi NAS, Nueces, . . . 500 | Country Campus, Walker |
| *COOPER, Delta, 157 (2,150). . . 2,150 | CORRAL CITY, Denton, | County Acres [Falman-], |
| Cooper, Hansford | (89) . . . . . . . . . . . . . . . . . . . . 91 | San Patricio, (289) . . . . . . . . 282 |
| Cooper, Houston,. . . . . . . . . . . . . 27 | Corrie, Polk | County Line, Anderson |
| Cooper Creek, Denton | Corrigan, Bee | County Line, Austin |
| Coopers Chapel, Titus | *CORRIGAN, Polk, 97 | County Line, Camp |
| Cootsville, Mason | (1,721). . . . . . . . . . . . . . . . .1,744 | County Line, Cochran |
| Copano, Refugio | Corry, Lamb | Countyline, Cooke |
| Copano Village, Aransas, . . . . . . 210 | *CORSICANA, Navarro, | County Line, Lubbock, . . . . . . . . . . 15 |
| Cope's Store, Bastrop | 1,413 (24,485). . . . . . . . . . .24,950 | County Line, Rains, . . . . . . . . . . . 40 |
| Copeland, Leon | Cortelyou, Edwards | County Line, Runnels |
| Copeland, Montgomery | Cortes, Matagorda | County Line, Sterling-Coke |
| Copeland, Smith,. . . . . . . . . . . . . NA | Corvey, Webb | County Line, Wood |
| Copeland's Store, Terry | Corwin, Burnet | *Coupland, Williamson, 22 . . . . . . NA |
| Copeland Creek, Marion | Coryell Church, Coryell | Coursey, Lamar |
| Copenhagen, Hale | Coryell City, Coryell,. . . . . . . . . . 125 | Courtland, Cass |
| Coperas, Eastland | Coryell Valley, Coryell | Courtland, Shelby |
| *Copeville, Collin, 7 . . . . . . . . . . 106 | Coshatte Bluff, Polk | Courtney, Grimes,. . . . . . . . . . . . . 55 |
| Copita, Duval | Cosmos, Madison | Courtney, Martin |
| Coplen, Smith | Cosner, Denton | Cousinville, Knox |
| Coppage, Bell | *Cost, Gonzales, 12 . . . . . . . . . . . 62 | Coutchman, Freestone |
| *COPPELL, Dallas-Denton, | Coth, Montague | COVE, Chambers, (323) . . . . . . . 324 |
| 1,313 (35,958). . . . . . . . . . .37,091 | Cotland, Newton | Cove, Coryell |
| Copperas Bluff, Cooke | Cottage, Angelina | Cove, Palo Pinto |
| *COPPERAS COVE, Coryell, | Cottage, Henderson | Cove, San Patricio |
| 736 (29,592) . . . . . . . . . . . 30,001 | Cottage Hill, Bexar | Cove City, Fort Bend |
| COPPER CANYON, Denton, | Cottage Hill, Titus | Cove City, Orange |
| (1,216). . . . . . . . . . . . . . . . .1,330 | Cottage Home, Grimes | Cove Spring, Nacogdoches |
| Copper City, King | Cottle, Cottle | Cove Springs, Cherokee, . . . . . . . . 40 |
| Copper Hill, Parker | Cotton, Grimes | Covey, Frio |
| Cora, Comanche | Cotton, Travis | *COVINGTON, Hill, 30 (282) . . . . . 298 |
| Cora, Ochiltree | Cotton's Crossing, Gregg | Cowan, Bee |
| Cora, Shelby | Cotton Center, Fannin,. . . . . . . . . . 5 | Cowan, Erath |
| Cora, Titus | *Cotton Center, Hale, 13. . . . . . . 205 | Cow Bayou, McLennan |
| Corbet, Navarro,. . . . . . . . . . . . . 80 | Cottondale, Wise,. . . . . . . . . . . . .NA | Cow Bayou, Orange |
| Corbett, McLennan | Cotton Flat, Midland | Cowboy, McCulloch |
| Corbinville, Jefferson | Cotton Gin, Freestone,. . . . . . . . . 28 | Cow Creek, Burnet |
| Corbyn, Comal | Cotton Mill Spur, Grayson | Cow Creek, Erath,. . . . . . . . . . . . .14 |
| Cordaro, Sherman | Cotton Patch, DeWitt,. . . . . . . . . . 11 | Cow Creek, Newton |
| Cordel, Cottle | Cotton Plant, Gregg | Cow Creek, Newton |
| Cordele, Jackson, . . . . . . . . . . . . 51 | Cotton Plant, Lamar | Cowen, Bowie |
| Corder, Franklin | Cotton Plant, Rusk | Cowen, Wise |
| Cordova, Gonzales | Cotton Plant, Stephens | Cowhill, Hunt |
| Cordova, McLennan | Cottonwood, Brazos, . . . . . . . . . .NA | Cowl Spur, Montgomery |
| Cordull, Jackson | Cottonwood, Callahan, . . . . . . . . 65 | Cow Prairie, Van Zandt |
| Cordwood Junction, Comanche | Cottonwood, Dickens | Cow Spur, Garza |
| Corine, Cherokee | Cottonwood, Erath, . . . . . . . . . . 23 | Cox, Coleman |
| CORINTH, Denton, (11,325). . . 13,690 | Cottonwood, Falls | Cox, Lamar |
| Corinth, Eastland | Cottonwood, Fayette | Cox, Milam |
| Corinth, Henderson | Cottonwood, Foard | Cox, Titus |
| Corinth, Hopkins | Cottonwood, Jack | Cox, Upshur, . . . . . . . . . . . . . . . .30 |
| Corinth, Houston | COTTONWOOD, Kaufman, | Cox's, Lamar |
| Corinth, Jones,. . . . . . . . . . . . . . 10 | (181) . . . . . . . . . . . . . . . . . . 204 | Cox's Colony, Lubbock-Crosby |
| Corinth, Lee | Cottonwood, Lamar | Cox's Gin, Van Zandt |
| Corinth, Leon,. . . . . . . . . . . . . . .NA | Cottonwood, Limestone | Cox's Mill, Coryell |
| Corinth, Marion | Cottonwood, Madison,. . . . . . . . . 40 | Cox's Store, Coleman |
| Corinth, Milam | Cottonwood, Martin | Cox's Switch, Montgomery |

CITIES & TOWNS

CITIES & TOWNS

Coxey, Montgomery
Cox Point, Calhoun
Coxton, Jack
Coxville, Bastrop
Coxville, Hill
Coxville, Travis
Coy, Mills
*Coyanosa, Pecos, 11 (138). . . . . 138
Coy City, Karnes, . . . . . . . . . . . . . 30
Coymack, Falls
Coyote, Knox
Coyote Acres, Jim Wells, (389) . . 418
Cozart, Panola
Crab Apple, Gillespie
Crabb, Fort Bend, . . . . . . . . . . . 125
Crabbs Prairie, Walker, . . . . . . . . NA
Cracker's Neck, Chambers
Cracker's Prairie, Trinity
Craddock, Gaines
Craft, Cherokee, . . . . . . . . . . . . . 21
Craft, Ellis
Crafton, Wise, . . . . . . . . . . . . . . . 20
Craig, Lamar
Craig, Rusk, . . . . . . . . . . . . . . . . NA
Craig, Victoria
Craig-Tranquil, Delta
Crain, DeWitt
Crain, Maverick-Zavala
*CRANDALL, Kaufman, 111
   (2,774). . . . . . . . . . . . . . . . . 3,016
*CRANE, Crane, 169 (3,191) . . . 2,961
Cranes Mill, Comal
*CRANFILLS GAP, Bosque, 28
   (335) . . . . . . . . . . . . . . . . . . . 354
Cranz, Gonzales
Crasco, Colorado
Cravens, Red River
Cravensville, Bee
Crawfish, Floyd
Crawfish, Hale
*CRAWFORD, McLennan,
   70 (705). . . . . . . . . . . . . . . . . 732
Crawford, Titus
Creagleville, Van Zandt
Cream, Parker
Creamer, Comanche
Cream Level, Parker
Creamlevel, Van Zandt
Creasy, Houston
Creath, Houston, . . . . . . . . . . . . . 20
Creath, Houston
Crecy, Trinity, . . . . . . . . . . . . . . . 15
Creech, San Augustine
Creechville, Ellis, . . . . . . . . . . . . . 15
Creed, Cooke
CREEDMOOR, Travis, 13
   (211) . . . . . . . . . . . . . . . . . . . 228
Creek, Houston
Crenshaw, Falls
Creole, Lavaca
Crescent, Titus
Crescent Heights, Henderson, . . . 35
Crescent Lake, Leon
Crescent Village, Refugio
Cresco, Hale
Cresco, Palo Pinto
*Cresson, Hood-Johnson, 30 . . . 208
Cresswell, Ochiltree
Crestonio, Duval
Crestwood, Llano
Crestwood, Marion
Creswell, Houston
Crete, Trinity
Crews, Gregg
Crews, Runnels, . . . . . . . . . . . . . . 40
Crewville, McCulloch
Crib Creek, Trinity

Cricket, Harrison
Crim, Rusk
Crimea, Hill
Crims Chapel, Rusk
Cring, Harris
Crisp, Ellis. . . . . . . . . . . . . . . . . . 90
Crisp, Hopkins
Criswell's, Polk
Crockett, Bandera
*CROCKETT, Houston, 479
   (7,141). . . . . . . . . . . . . . . . .7,191
Crockett's Bluff, Smith
Crockett's Bluff, Van Zandt
Crockettsville, Panola
Croft's Mills, Harris
Cromwell, Harrison
Cronin, Anderson
Cronje, Bell
*Crosby, Harris, 616
   (1,714). . . . . . . . . . . . . . . . .1,681
*CROSBYTON, Crosby,
   106 (1,874) . . . . . . . . . . . . . .1,860
Crosbyville, Brazoria
Cross, Grimes, . . . . . . . . . . . . . . 49
Cross, Jasper
Cross, McMullen, . . . . . . . . . . . . . 60
Cross Creek, Travis
Cross Cut, Brown, . . . . . . . . . . . .NA
Crossenville, DeWitt
Crossett, Upton
Cross Gin, Cooke
Crossland, Gray
Crossland, Young
Cross Mountain, Bexar,
   (1,524). . . . . . . . . . . . . . . . .1,533
Cross Out, Brown
*CROSS PLAINS, Callahan,
   88 (1,068) . . . . . . . . . . . . . . .1,055
Cross Roads, Anderson
Cross Roads, Bastrop
Crossroads, Camp
Crossroads, Cass, . . . . . . . . . . . . 40
Cross Roads, Comanche
Crossroads, Delta, . . . . . . . . . . . . 10
CROSS ROADS, Denton,
   (603) . . . . . . . . . . . . . . . . . . . 679
Cross Roads, Grayson
Crossroads, Harrison, . . . . . . . . . 100
Cross Roads, Henderson, . . . . . . 135
Crossroads, Hopkins, . . . . . . . . . .NA
Crossroads, Jackson
Cross Roads, Madison. . . . . . . . . .,75
Cross Roads, Milam, . . . . . . . . . . 35
Crossroads, Montgomery
Crossroads, Nacogdoches
Cross Roads, Nacogdoches
Cross Roads, Navarro
Crossroads, Panola
Cross Roads, Robertson
Cross Roads, Rusk, . . . . . . . . . . .NA
Cross Roads, Upshur
Cross Roads, Wheeler
Cross Roads, Williamson
Cross Roads, Williamson
CROSS TIMBER, Johnson,
   (277) . . . . . . . . . . . . . . . . . . . 294
Cross Timbers, Tarrant
Crossville, Bell
Crossville, Cooke
Crotan, Stonewall
Crothers, McCulloch
Croton, Dickens, . . . . . . . . . . . . . . 5
Crouch, Atascosa
Crow, Cass
Crow, Madison
Crow, Wood, . . . . . . . . . . . . . . . . 25
*CROWELL, Foard, 67

   (1,141) . . . . . . . . . . . . . . . . . 1,101
*CROWLEY, Tarrant, 407
   (7,467) . . . . . . . . . . . . . . . . . 7,997
Crown, Atascosa, . . . . . . . . . . . . . 10
Crowther, McMullen
Crozier, Young
Crunk's Lake, Lee-Burleson
Cruseville, Nacogdoches
Crush, Hopkins
Crush, McLennan
Crush, Milam
Crusher, Hudspeth
Crutcher, Nolan
Crutchfield, Fannin
Cruz Calle, Duval, . . . . . . . . . . . . NA
Cryer Creek, Navarro, . . . . . . . . . . 15
Crystal Beach, Galveston, . . . . . . 787
*CRYSTAL CITY, Zavala,
   183 (7,190). . . . . . . . . . . . . . 7,196
Crystal Falls, Stephens, . . . . . . . . 10
Crystal Lake, Anderson, . . . . . . . . 20
Crystal Springs, Wood
Crystal Water, Reeves
Cuadrilla, El Paso, . . . . . . . . . . . . . 40
Cuba, Colorado
Cuba, Delta
Cuba, Johnson
Cuba, Live Oak
Cuba, Wise
Cude's Mill, Hays
Cudlip Switch, Montgomery
Cuellar Store, Zapata
*CUERO, DeWitt, 393
   (6,571) . . . . . . . . . . . . . . . . . 6,607
Cuevitas, Hidalgo, (37) . . . . . . . . . 41
Cuevitas, Jim Hogg, . . . . . . . . . . . 12
Culberson, Cass
Culberson, Hunt
Culberson, Titus
Culebra, Bexar
Culleoka, Collin
Cullinan, Leon
Culp, Hill
Culver, Matagorda
*CUMBY, Hopkins, 41 (616) . . . . . 613
Cumings, Fort Bend, (683) . . . . . . 743
Cummin's Creek, Colorado
Cummingsville, Bee
Cummingsville, Goliad
Cummins, Sterling
Cummins' Creek, Ellis
Cundiff, Jack, . . . . . . . . . . . . . . . . 45
*CUNEY, Cherokee, 7 (145). . . . . . 155
*Cunningham, Lamar, 2 . . . . . . . . 110
Cunningham's, Fayette
Cunninghams, Bastrop
Cunninghams Store, Fannin
Cupp, San Augustine
Curds Prairie, Brazos
Curlew, Floyd
Currey, Collin
Currie, Navarro, . . . . . . . . . . . . . . 25
Currie, Travis
Curry, Henderson
Curry, Milam
Curry, Stephens
Currys, Kendall
Curtis, Childress
Curtis, Dallas
Curtis, Eastland
Curtis, Jasper, . . . . . . . . . . . . . . . NA
Curtright, Cass
*CUSHING, Nacogdoches, 46
   (637). . . . . . . . . . . . . . . . . . . . 635
Cushman, Wilbarger
Cusseta, Cass, . . . . . . . . . . . . . . . 30
Custer, Brazoria

| Town,County ........... Pop. 2002 | Town,County ........... Pop. 2002 | Town,County ........... Pop. 2002 |
|---|---|---|

*Custer City, Cooke*
*Cut, Houston*
**\*CUT AND SHOOT, Montgomery,**
    **(1,158)................. 1,159**
**Cuthand, Red River,.......... 116**
*Cuthbert, Mitchell*
*Cutler, Grayson*
*Cutoff, Guadalupe*
*Cuyler, Carson*
**Cyclone, Bell,................ 45**
**Cypress, Franklin,............. 20**
*Cypress, Harrison*
*Cypress, Upshur*
**\*Cypress(-Fairbanks), Harris,**
    **1,462.................. 18,527**
**Cypress Creek, Kerr,......... 200**
*Cypress Crossings, Newton*
*Cypress Grove, Harris*
*Cypress Grove, Victoria*
**Cypress Mill, Blanco,.......... 56**
*Cyril, Rusk*
*Cyrus, Bosque*

**D**
**\*D'Hanis, Medina, 28 ......... 548**
*Dabney, Uvalde*
*Dabney Hill, Burleson*
*Dacha, Shelby*
**Dacosta, Victoria,............. 89**
**Dacus, Montgomery,......... 161**
*Dacus, Williamson*
*Daddy Hollow, Freestone*
*Dads Corner, Archer*
**Daffan, Travis,................ NA**
*Daggett's Switch, Wichita*
*Da Honey, Lamar*
*Daileyville, Karnes*
**\*DAINGERFIELD, Morris, 191**
    **(2,517)................. 2,499**
*Dairy, Harris*
**\*DAISETTA, Liberty, 16**
    **(1,034).................. 1,067**
*Daisy, Hopkins*
*Daisy, Rains*
*Dakin, Young*
*Dalberg, Hudspeth*
**Dalby Springs, Bowie,......... 141**
**\*Dale, Caldwell, 74 ............ 500**
*Dale Crest, Van Zandt*
**\*DALHART, Dallam-Hartley,**
    **503 (7,237) .............. 7,210**
*Dallam, Brazos*
**\*Dallardsville, Polk, 5.......... 350**
**\*DALLAS, Dallas-Collin-Denton,**
    **65,819 (1,188,580) .... 1,201,759**
*Dalmoor, Hartley*
*Dalmus, Coleman*
*DalNor, Dallas*
*Dalrock, Dallas*
**Dalton, Cass, ................ 50**
*Dalworth, Tarrant*
**DALWORTHINGTON GARDENS,**
    **Tarrant, (2,186).......... 2,260**
*Dalworth Park, Dallas*
*Dalys, Houston*
*Dalzell, Brown*
*Damascus, Titus*
**\*Dam B (Dogwood Station), Tyler,**
    **...................... 56**
*Dameron City, Midland*
**\*Damon, Brazoria, 56**
    **(535)................... 562**
*Damon's Mills, Fort Bend*
*Damon Junction, Fort Bend*
*Damsite, Hardeman*
*Damson's Prairie, Kaufman*
*Dan, Clay*

*Dan, Coleman*
*Dan, Wise*
*Dana, Angelina*
**\*DANBURY, Brazoria, 53**
    **(1,611).................. 1,699**
**\*Danciger, Brazoria, 1.......... 357**
*Dancl, Johnson*
**\*Danevang, Wharton, 8......... 61**
*Danforth Switch, Hockley*
*Dan Horn Community, Eastland*
*Daniel, Houston*
*Daniel, Kaufman*
*Daniel, Presidio*
**Daniels, Panola, ...............NA**
*Daniels, Washington*
*Daniels Chapel, Bowie*
*Danner, Fannin*
*Dannie, Scurry*
*Dante, Austin*
*Danube, Culberson*
*Danville, Collin*
*Danville, Comal*
**Danville, Gregg, ............. 200**
*Danville, Montgomery-Walker*
*Daphne, Franklin*
*Darby, Bee*
*Darby, Grimes*
*Darby, Polk*
**Darby Hill, San Jacinto, ........ 50**
**Darco, Harrison,.............. 85**
*Dar Corner, Jack*
*Darden, Bowie*
**Darden, Polk,..................NA**
*Darden Spring, Lee*
*Dargan, Panola*
*Dar Junction, Colorado*
*Dark, Scurry*
*Dark Corners, Bee*
*Darling, Maverick*
*Darlington, Frio*
*Darnell, Van Zandt*
**\*DARROUZETT, Lipscomb,**
    **23 (303)................. 295**
*Darwin, Limestone*
*Darwin, Webb*
*Daryl, Harrison*
**Datura, Limestone,............. 2**
*Daugherty, Culberson*
*Daugherty, Kaufman*
*Dauphin, Henderson*
*Davenport, Anderson*
*Davenport, Comal*
*Davenport, Cooke*
*Davenport, Coryell*
*Davenport, Red River*
*Davenport's Mill, Denton*
*David Rusk Ferry, Cherokee*
*Davidson, Burleson*
*Davidson, Van Zandt*
*Davidsonville, Palo Pinto*
*Davies, Garza*
**\*Davilla, Milam, 6 ............ 200**
**Davis, Atascosa,............... 8**
*Davis, Lamar*
*Davis, Panola*
*Davis' Mills, Dallas*
*Davis Community, Newton*
*Davis Gin, Milam*
*Davis Hill, Liberty*
**Davis Prairie, Limestone,........ 17**
*Davisville, Angelina*
*Davisville, Grimes*
*Davisville, Leon*
*Davisville, San Jacinto*
*Davy, Denton*
*Davy, DeWitt*
*Davy's, Madison*

*Dawes, Harris*
**\*Dawn, Deaf Smith, 9 .......... 52**
*Dawning, Comanche*
**\*DAWSON, Navarro, 40 (852) .... 908**
*Day, Bosque*
*Day, Grayson*
*Day, Scurry*
*Day, Washington*
*Day, Wichita*
*Daylea, Coleman*
*Days Chapel, Anderson*
*Daystown, Liberty*
**\*DAYTON, Liberty, 445**
    **(5,709) ................ 5,996**
*Dayton, San Jacinto*
**DAYTON LAKES, Liberty,**
    **(101)..................... 101**
*Deacon, Parker*
**Deadwood, Panola,........... 106**
*Deal, Carson*
*Dealey, Rusk*
*DeAlva, Erath*
**DEAN, Clay, (341) ............ 341**
*Dean, Deaf Smith*
**Dean, Hockley,................ 20**
*Dean, Jones*
*Dean, Leon*
*Dean, Madison*
**\*Deanville, Burleson, 12........ 130**
*Deanville, Dallas*
*Deanville, Smith*
*Deanwright, Anderson*
*Dearborn, Hardin*
*Dearing, Gillespie*
*Dearmore, Young*
*Deason, Polk*
*Deaton, Polk*
*Deaton, Trinity*
*Deaver, Grayson*
*Debard's, Smith*
*Debbie, Wood*
**\*DeBerry, Panola, 26.......... 191**
*Decatur, Collin*
**\*DECATUR, Wise, 647**
    **(5,201) ................ 5,393**
*Decker, Nolan*
*Decker, Travis*
**Decker Prairie, Montgomery, .... NA**
*Deckman, Dallas*
*Deco, Harris*
*Decorah, Hunt*
**DeCORDOVA, Hood,......... 3,693**
*Decoy, Nacogdoches*
*DeCros Point, Matagorda*
*Dee, Jones*
*Dee, Randall*
*Deep Creek, Baylor*
*Deep Creek, Callahan*
*Deep Creek, McCulloch*
*Deep Lake, Hall*
*Deep Lake, Hall*
*Deepwater, Harris*
*Deer, Childress*
*Deer Creek, Clay*
*Deer Creek, Falls*
*Deer Creek, Medina*
*Deer Haven, Llano*
**\*DEER PARK, Harris, 1,004**
    **(28,520) .............. 29,387**
*Deerton, Mason-San Saba*
*Deeville, Lamar*
*Defense, Bowie*
*Defo, Van Zandt*
*DeGraffenreid, Henderson*
*DeGress, Jack*
**\*DE KALB, Bowie, 165**
    **(1,769) ................ 1,748**

| Town,County | Pop. 2002 |
|---|---|
| Deland, McCulloch | |
| Delaware, Brown | |
| Delaware, Cooke | |
| Delba, Fannin | |
| *DE LEON, Comanche, 207 | |
| (2,433). . . . . . . . . . . . . . . | 2,436 |
| Delfina, Hidalgo | |
| Delgado, Brown | |
| Delhi, Bosque | |
| Delhi, Caldwell,. . . . . . . . . . . . . | 300 |
| Delia, Limestone, . . . . . . . . . . . . | 20 |
| Delight, Kerr | |
| Delk, Jones | |
| Dell, Bosque | |
| Della Plain, Floyd | |
| *DELL CITY, Hudspeth, 35 | |
| (413) . . . . . . . . . . . . . . . . . | 425 |
| Dellwood, Webb | |
| Delma, Newton | |
| Del Mar, Cameron | |
| Delmar, Eastland | |
| Del Mar Heights, Cameron, | |
| (259) . . . . . . . . . . . . . . . . . | 278 |
| Del Mar Hills, Webb | |
| Delmer, Cherokee | |
| *Delmita,Starr, 4 . . . . . . . . . . . . . | 50 |
| Delong, Tom Green | |
| Delphi, Taylor | |
| Delphine, Jefferson | |
| Delphine, Parker | |
| Delray, Panola, . . . . . . . . . . . . . . | 40 |
| *DEL RIO, Val Verde, 1,358 | |
| (33,867). . . . . . . . . . . . . . | 34,631 |
| Delrose, Upshur, . . . . . . . . . . . . . | 35 |
| Del Sol-Loma Linda, San Patricio, | |
| (726) . . . . . . . . . . . . . . . . . | 751 |
| Delta, Hamilton | |
| *Del Valle, Travis, 225 . . . . . . . . | 2,476 |
| Delvin, Floyd | |
| Delwau, Travis | |
| Delwin,Cottle,. . . . . . . . . . . . . . . | 12 |
| Demarco, Burnet | |
| Dement, Gonzales | |
| Demi-John Island, Brazoria, . . . . . | 18 |
| Demijohn Bend, Comal | |
| Demings Bridge, Matagorda | |
| Democrat, Mills, . . . . . . . . . . . . . . | 8 |
| Democrat, Wood | |
| DeMoss, Matagorda | |
| Dempsey, Cass | |
| Denhawken, Wilson, . . . . . . . . . . | 46 |
| *DENISON, Grayson, 1,351 | |
| (22,773). . . . . . . . . . . . . . | 23,133 |
| Denman, Kimble | |
| Denman Crossroads, Van Zandt, . NA | |
| Denman Springs, Angelina | |
| Denmark, Anderson | |
| Denning, San Augustine, . . . . . . | 361 |
| *Dennis, Parker, 3. . . . . . . . . . . . | 90 |
| Dennis Chapel, Hopkins | |
| Denny, Dallas | |
| Denny, Falls | |
| Denrock, Dallam | |
| Denson, Williamson | |
| Denson Springs, Anderson, . . . . | 100 |
| Dent, Hunt | |
| Denton, Callahan,. . . . . . . . . . . . . | 6 |
| *DENTON, Denton, 3,954 | |
| (80,537). . . . . . . . . . . . . . | 89,379 |
| Denton, Franklin | |
| Denton Creek, Montague | |
| Denton Creek, Denton | |
| Denton Creek, Denton | |
| Dentonio, Dimmit | |
| Denver, Montague | |
| *DENVER CITY, Yoakum, | |
| 255 (3,985) . . . . . . . . . . . . | 3,903 |

| Town,County | Pop. 2002 |
|---|---|
| Denworth, Gray | |
| *DEPORT, Lamar-Red River, | |
| 38 (718) . . . . . . . . . . . . . . | 708 |
| Derby, Frio, . . . . . . . . . . . . . . . | 50 |
| Derden, Hill | |
| Dermott, Scurry . . . . . . . . . . . . . | 5 |
| Dernal, Victoria | |
| *Desdemona, Eastland, 15. . . . . | 180 |
| Desert, Collin,. . . . . . . . . . . . . . | 25 |
| *DESOTO, Dallas, 1,519 | |
| (37,646). . . . . . . . . . . . . . | 39,316 |
| Dessau, Travis, . . . . . . . . . . . . | NA |
| Detmold, Milam | |
| *DETROIT, Red River, 36 | |
| (776) . . . . . . . . . . . . . . . . . | 775 |
| Dety, Leon | |
| Deuce of Hearts, Lynn | |
| Devenport, Hunt | |
| *DEVERS, Liberty, 15 | |
| (416) . . . . . . . . . . . . . . . . . | 429 |
| Devil's Drag, Jackson | |
| Devil's Pocket, Wharton | |
| Devil's River, Val Verde | |
| DeVilbiss Ranch, Frio | |
| Devillia, Angelina | |
| Devils Bend, Milam | |
| *DEVINE, Medina, 266 | |
| (4,140) . . . . . . . . . . . . . . . | 4,171 |
| Dew, Freestone, . . . . . . . . . . . . | 71 |
| Dewalt, Fort Bend | |
| Dewdrop, Liberty | |
| Dewees, Waller | |
| DeWees, Wilson, . . . . . . . . . . . . | 35 |
| Deweesville, Karnes, . . . . . . . . . | 12 |
| Dewet, Gonzales | |
| Dewey, Comanche | |
| Dewey, Hunt | |
| Dewey, Liberty | |
| Dewey, Montague | |
| Dewey, Rusk | |
| Dewey Prairie, Freestone | |
| *Deweyville, Newton, 28 | |
| (1,190). . . . . . . . . . . . . . . | 1,170 |
| Dewville, Gonzales, . . . . . . . . . . | 15 |
| Dexter, Cooke, . . . . . . . . . . . . . | 18 |
| Dextra, Nacogdoches | |
| Dial, Fannin, . . . . . . . . . . . . . . . | 76 |
| Dial, Hutchinson | |
| Dialville, Cherokee, 1 . . . . . . . . . | 200 |
| Diamond, Scurry | |
| Diamond City, Lamar | |
| Diana, Orange | |
| Diana, Upshur | |
| Diana, Upshur | |
| *Diana, Upshur, 66 . . . . . . . . . . | 585 |
| Diantha, Foard | |
| Diaz, Cameron | |
| Diaz, Hidalgo | |
| *DIBOLL, Angelina, 167 | |
| (5,470) . . . . . . . . . . . . . . . | 5,566 |
| Dice, Bell | |
| Dicey, Parker, . . . . . . . . . . . . . . | NA |
| Dick, Jack | |
| *DICKENS, Dickens, 16 (332). . . . | 330 |
| Dickey, Leon | |
| Dickie, Lamar | |
| *DICKINSON, Galveston, | |
| 937 (17,093) . . . . . . . . . . . | 17,644 |
| Dickworsham, Clay | |
| Dido, Tarrant | |
| Dido, Tarrant | |
| Dido, Walker | |
| Dierlam, Calhoun | |
| Dies, Hardin | |
| Dies, Tyler | |
| Dietz, Guadalupe | |
| *Dike, Hopkins, 5 . . . . . . . . . . . | 170 |

| Town,County | Pop. 2002 |
|---|---|
| Dillard, Erath | |
| Dillard, Floyd | |
| Dillard's, Falls | |
| *DILLEY, Frio, 105 (3,674). . . . . | 3,745 |
| Dillingham Prairie, Jack | |
| Dillon, Hopkins | |
| Dilworth, Gonzales,. . . . . . . . . . . | 15 |
| Dilworth, Red River, . . . . . . . . . . | 22 |
| *Dime Box, Lee, 30 . . . . . . . . . . | 313 |
| Dimitt's Landing, Jackson | |
| *DIMMITT, Castro, 259 | |
| (4,375) . . . . . . . . . . . . . . . | 4,213 |
| Dimple, Red River, . . . . . . . . . . . | 60 |
| *Dinero, Live Oak, 2 . . . . . . . . . . | 344 |
| Ding Dong, Bell, . . . . . . . . . . . . . | 22 |
| Dingler, Comanche | |
| Dinkins, Brazos | |
| Dinsmore, Nolan | |
| Dinsmore, Wharton | |
| Direct, Lamar, . . . . . . . . . . . . . . | 70 |
| Dirgin, Rusk, . . . . . . . . . . . . . . . | 12 |
| Discord, Coleman | |
| Discus, Culberson | |
| Dittlinger, Comal | |
| Ditto, Atascosa | |
| Divide, Coke | |
| Divide, Guadalupe | |
| Divide, Hopkins, . . . . . . . . . . . . . | NA |
| Divide, Nolan | |
| Divot, Frio | |
| Dix, Martin | |
| Dixico, Harris | |
| Dixie, Brooks | |
| Dixie, Edwards | |
| Dixie, Grayson, . . . . . . . . . . . . . | 17 |
| Dixie, Jackson | |
| Dixie, Lamar | |
| Dixie, Lynn | |
| Dixie, Panola | |
| Dixie, San Jacinto | |
| Dixie, Smith | |
| Dixieland, Reeves | |
| Dixon, Fannin | |
| Dixon, Hunt,. . . . . . . . . . . . . . . . | 31 |
| Dixon-Hopewell, Houston, . . . . . . | 49 |
| Dixon Prairie, Bastrop | |
| Dixson, Cooke | |
| Doak Springs, Lee, . . . . . . . . . . . | 50 |
| Doans, Wilbarger, . . . . . . . . . . . . | 20 |
| *Dobbin, Montgomery, 8. . . . . . . | 170 |
| Dobbs City, Dickens | |
| Dobrowolski, Atascosa, . . . . . . . . | 10 |
| Dobskyville, Goliad | |
| Dobyville, Burnet | |
| Dock, Scurry | |
| Dock, Tyler-Polk | |
| Dockery, Lee | |
| Dockum Ranch, Dickens | |
| Doctors Creek, Delta | |
| Dodd, Castro, . . . . . . . . . . . . . . | 15 |
| Dodd, Webb | |
| Dodd's Store, Williamson | |
| *DODD CITY, Fannin, 17 | |
| (419). . . . . . . . . . . . . . . . . | 406 |
| Dodd City, Travis | |
| Doddville, Lee | |
| Doddville, Washington | |
| Dode, Floyd-Crosby | |
| Dodge, McCulloch | |
| *Dodge, Walker, 5 . . . . . . . . . . . | 150 |
| *DODSON, Collingsworth, | |
| 6 (115) . . . . . . . . . . . . . . . | 119 |
| Dodson, Houston | |
| Dodson, Tarrant | |
| Dodson's Store, Coryell | |
| Dodson Prairie, Palo Pinto, . . . . . | 18 |
| Doffing, Hidalgo, (4,256). . . . . . | 4,366 |

**CITIES & TOWNS**


...........................Pop. 2002

3. .......................... 200
, Marion
nan
Jones, ............ 35
r, ............... 40
nzales
ard-Mason
avis
cres, Brazoria, ........NA
st, Atascosa
nst's Place, Austin
os, Marion
rskine, Concho
rudia, Collin
**Erwin, Grimes,** ............... 50
Esbon, Llano
Escarbada, Deaf Smith
**Escobares, Starr, (1,954)** ...... 2,046
**Escobas, Zapata,** ............... 3
**Escondidas [Sandy Hollow-],**
   **Nueces, (433)** ............ 459
Eshman, Erath
Eskota, Fisher
Esoes, Cameron
Esom Hill, Trinity
Esparanza, Smith
Esperanza, Brooks
**Esperanza, Hudspeth,** .......... 75
Esperanza, Montgomery
Esperanza Ranch, Hidalgo
Esperson, Liberty
**Espey, Atascosa,** ............. 55
Espuela, Dickens
Esser Crossing, Comal
Esseville, Atascosa
Esseville, Live Oak
Essex, Upshur
Essie, Jones
**Estacado, Lubbock-Crosby,** ..... 80
Estelle, Dallas
Estelle, Tarrant
**\*ESTELLINE, Hall, 5 (168)** ...... 170
**Estes, Aransas,** ............... 50
Estes, Harrison
Estill's Station, Tarrant
Estrella, Kimble
**Ethel, Grayson,** ............... 40
Ethel, Wharton
Etholen, Hudspeth
Etna, Cherokee-Smith
Etna, Franklin
**\*Etoile, Nacogdoches, 13** ....... 70
Etta, Baylor
Etta, Bowie
Etta, Harris
Etta, Red River
Etter, Moore
Ettowa, Gonzales
Ettra, Lamar
Eudor, Sterling
Eudora, Angelina
Eufaula, Hill
**Eula, Callahan,** ............... 125
Eula, Kaufman
Eulalie, Rusk
**\*EULESS, Tarrant, 1,725**
   **(46,005)** .................. 47,638
**Eulogy, Bosque,** ............... 45
**Eunice, Leon,** ............... NA
Eunice, Swisher
Eunice, Titus
Eunice, Walker
Eura, Kerr
Eureka, Collin


Town,County ............ Pop. 2002

Eureka, Delta
**Eureka, Franklin,** ............... 18
Eureka, Kaufman
**EUREKA, Navarro, (340)** ....... 350
Eureka, Stephens
Eureka, Tarrant
Eureka Mills, Harris
Eureka Mills, Williamson
Europe, Madison
**\*EUSTACE, Henderson, 77**
   **(798)** .................... 833
Eutaw, Limestone
Eutaw, Robertson
Eva, Caldwell
Eva, Jim Wells
Eva, Leon
Eva, San Augustine
**\*Evadale, Jasper, 31 (1,430)** .... 1,434
Evan, Cameron
Evana, Wood
Evans, Fannin
Evans, Hardeman
Evans, Hardin
Evans, Williamson
Evans Cross Roads, Bosque
Evans Ferry, Burleson
Evans Point, Hopkins
Evansville, Leon
**\*EVANT, Coryell-Hamilton, 37**
   **(393)** .................... 394
Evelena, Dawson
Evelyn, Travis
Everett, Milam
Everett, Oldham
Everett, Williamson
Everettsville, Starr
Evergreen, Bexar
Evergreen, Comanche
Evergreen, Galveston
Evergreen, Hamilton
Evergreen, Houston
Evergreen, Lee
Evergreen, McLennan
Evergreen, Panola
**Evergreen, San Jacinto,** ........ 150
Evergreen, Smith
Evergreen, Titus
Everitt, San Jacinto
**EVERMAN, Tarrant,**
   **(5,836)** .................. 5,907
Everton, Palo Pinto
Evie, San Augustine
Evora, Jefferson
Ewelder, San Patricio
**Ewell, Upshur,** ................. 20
Ewen, Palo Pinto
Ewing, Angelina
Ewing, Coryell
Ewing, Hopkins
Exall, Dallas
Excel, Potter
Excell, Moore
Excelsior, Liberty
Excelsior Mill, Williamson
Exie, Kaufman
Exile, Uvalde-Real
Exit, Hartley
Exray, Erath
Exum, Hartley
Exum, Wheeler
Exum, Wheeler
Eylau, Bowie
Eyle, Harris
Eyrie, Ellis
**Ezzell, Lavaca,** ................ 55

F


Town,County ........... Pop. 2002

**\*Fabens, El Paso, 134**
   **(8,043)** ................ 8,091
Faber, Colorado
Fabien, Lavaca
Fabius, Hopkins
Fagan, Bandera
Fails, Walker
Fain, Nolan
Fairbanks, Harris
**FAIRCHILDS, Fort Bend, (678)** ... 723
Faircloth, Jasper
Fairdale, Sabine
**\*FAIRFIELD, Freestone,**
   **407 (3,094)** .............. 3,282
Fair Hill, Travis
Fair Home, Grayson
**Fairland, Burnet,** .............. 290
Fairlawn, Lamb
**Fairlie, Hunt,** ................. 80
Fairmont, Floyd
**Fairmount, Sabine,** ............. 45
Fair Oaks, Freestone
**Fair Oaks, Limestone,** .......... 15
**\*FAIR OAKS RANCH, Bexar-Comal-**
   **Kendall, (4,695)** ......... 5,042
Fair Park, Dallas
Fair Plains, Cooke
**Fair Play, Panola,** ............. 80
**Fairview, Angelina,** ............ 10
**Fairview, Armstrong,** .......... 75
Fairview, Bailey
Fairview, Bosque
**Fairview, Brazos,** ............. NA
Fairview, Brown
Fairview, Camp
**Fairview, Cass,** ............... 20
**FAIRVIEW, Collin, (2,644)** ..... 3,378
Fairview, Comanche
Fairview, Crosby
Fairview, Floyd
Fairview, Franklin
**Fairview, Gaines,** ............. NA
Fairview, Grimes
Fairview, Grimes
Fairview, Hays
Fair View, Hill
**Fairview, Hockley,** ............. 10
**Fairview, Hood,** ................ 30
**Fairview, Howard,** ............. 85
Fairview, Milam
Fairview, Rusk
Fairview, Smith
Fairview, Taylor
Fairview, Tom Green
Fairview, Travis
Fairview, Van Zandt
**Fairview, Wilson,** ............. 322
**Fairy, Hamilton,** ............... 31
Fairyland, Hopkins
Falba, Walker
Falcon, Crosby
Falcon, Wood
**Falcon, Zapata,** ............... 376
**\*Falcon Heights, Starr,**
   **18 (335)** ................ 348
**Falcon Lake Estates, Zapata,**
   **(830)** ................... 874
**Falcon Mesa, Zapata,**
   **(506)** ................... 524
**Falcon Village, Starr, (78)** ....... 71
**\*FALFURRIAS, Brooks,**
   **265 (5,297)** .............. 5,186
Falkner, Aransas
**Fallon, Limestone,** ............ 100
Falls, Johnson
Falls, Walker
**\*FALLS CITY, Karnes, 40**


Town,County ............ Pop. 2002

Dofin, San Patricio
**Dog Ridge, Bell,** ............ 125
Dogtown, Burleson
Dog Town, Falls
Dog Town, McMullen
**Dogwood City, Smith,** ........ 800
Dogwood Grove, San Augustine
Doke, Llano
Dolan, Angelina
Dolce, Shelby
Dolchburg, Maverick
**Dolen, Liberty,** ............... NA
Dolive, San Jacinto
Dollarhide, Andrews
Dollarhide, Atascosa
Dolman, Stonewall
Dolores, Kinney
Dolores, Webb
Dolph, Grimes
Dome, Mitchell
Dominion, Bexar
Dominion, Lipscomb
**DOMINO, Cass, (52)** ........... 52
Donahoe, Bell
Donald, Denton
Donald, Johnson
Donelton, Hunt
**\*Donie, Freestone, 13** ......... 206
Doniphan, Fannin
Donley, Donley
Donna, Collin
**\*DONNA, Hidalgo, 395**
   **(14,768)** ............... 15,334
Donnell, Wilbarger
Donnell's Mill, Young
Donnybrook Place, Harris
Donoho, Cherokee
Donovan, Angelina
Don Tol, Wharton
**\*Doole, McCulloch, 2** ........... 74
Dooley, Limestone
**Doolittle, Hidalgo, (2,358)** ..... 2,500
Dora, Nolan
Dorado, Cherokee
**DORCHESTER, Grayson,**
   **2 (109)** .................. 110
Dorman, Wharton
Dorne, Liberty
**Dorras, Stonewall,** ............. 30
Dorr Junction, Nacogdoches
Dorsey, Montague
Dorsey, Titus
Dorso, Val Verde
**Doss, Cass,** ................... NA
Doss, Clay
**\*Doss, Gillespie, 11** ........... 75
**Dot, Falls,** ................... 17
**Dothan, Eastland,** ............. 20
Dothan, Hall
**Dotson, Panola,** ............... 40
Dott, Anderson
Doty, Orange
**Double Bayou, Chambers,** ..... 400
Double Gates, Coleman
Double Header, Bell
Double Horn, Burnet
Double Knobbs, Mason
Double Mountain, Stonewall
**DOUBLE OAK, Denton,**
   **(2,179)** .................. 2,394
Double Oak, Denton
Double Springs, Tarrant
Double Springs, Upshur
Double Tanks, Val Verde
**\*Doucette, Tyler, 7** ............ 131
**\*Dougherty, Floyd, 5** .......... 109
**Dougherty, Rains,** ........... 342


Town,County ............ Pop. 2002

**Douglas, Smith,** ............... NA
Douglas, Smith
Douglas Chapel, Marion
**\*Douglass, Nacogdoches, 17** .... 75
Douglass, Red River
Douglas Store, Van Zandt
**\*DOUGLASSVILLE, Cass, 14**
   **(175)** ................... 183
Douro, Ector
Dove, Tarrant
Dover, Fannin
Dover, Navarro
Dovie, Wise
Dow, Brazoria
Dow, Gray
Dowco, Smith
Dowden, Polk
Dowell, Fisher
Dowlin, Lamar
Dowling, Jefferson
**Downing, Comanche,** .......... 30
Downs, McLennan
**Downsville, McLennan,** ........ 150
Dowson Springs, Anderson
Doxey, Travis
Doxie, Houston
**Doyle, Limestone,** ............. 50
Doyle, Limestone
**Doyle, San Patricio, (285)** ...... 293
**Dozier, Collingsworth,** .......... 30
Draco, Williamson
Draco, Wise
Dragoo, Burnet
Drake, Liberty
**Drane, Navarro,** ............... 16
Draper, Bowie
Draper, Dickens
Draper, Jack
**Drasco, Runnels,** .............. 20
**Draw, Lynn,** ................... 39
Dreamland, Starr
**Dreka, Shelby,** ................ NA
Dreka, Swisher
Drennan, Sterling
Drennen's Store, Coryell
**Dresden, Navarro,** ............ 25
Dresser, Bell
Dressy, Callahan
Drew, Kaufman
Drews Landing, Polk
**Dreyer, Gonzales,** ............. 20
Dreyfoos, Hemphill
**\*Driftwood, Hays, 53** .......... 1,253
**\*DRIPPING SPRINGS, Hays,**
   **483 (1,548)** ............. 1,636
Driscoll, Jim Wells
Driscoll, Nueces
**\*DRISCOLL, Nueces, 19**
   **(825)** ................... 818
Driskell, Houston
Driskill, Travis
Driver, Freestone
Driver's Store, Cass
Drop, Denton
Drum, Terrell
Drummond, Cottle
Drummond, Young
Drumright, Glasscock
Drury, San Jacinto
Drusilla, Wood
Druso, Houston
Dry Branch, Bosque
Dryburg, Jasper
Dry Creek, Parker
Dry Creek, Parker
**\*Dryden, Terrell,** .............. 13
Dry Medio, Bee


Town,County ........... Pop. 2002

Dry Valley, Montague
**Dubina, Fayette,** ............... 44
**\*DUBLIN, Erath, 269 (3,754)** ... 3,756
Dubois, Aransas
Dubois, Refugio
Dubose, Duval
Dubwright, Taylor
Duck, Kent
Duck Creek, Dallas
Duck Creek, Dallas
Dudeville, Milam
**Dudley, Callahan,** ............. 25
Dudley Place, Grayson
Duff, Foard
Duff, Shelby
Duff's Settlement, Austin
**Duffau, Erath, 1** ............... 76
Duffau Wells, Erath
Duffin, Upshur
Duff Prairie, Stephens
Dugan's Chapel, Grayson
Dugansville, Grayson
**Dugger, Guadalupe,** ........... 20
Dugout, Fisher
Dugout, McCulloch
Duke, Fort Bend
Duke, Panola
Dulaney, Hunt
Duley, Jones
Dulin, Brown
Dull, La Salle
Dull, Madison
**\*DUMAS, Moore, 709**
   **(13,747)** ............... 13,917
Dumas, Wood
Dumont, Harris
**\*Dumont, King, 2** .............. 85
Dump, Collin
Dump, Limestone
Dunagan, Angelina
Dunbar, Matagorda
**Dunbar, Rains,** ................ 40
Dunbar, Smith
Dunbar, Trinity
Duncan, Hartley
Duncan, Jasper
Duncan, Milam
Duncan, Smith
Duncan, Wharton
Duncan's Woods, Orange
Duncan Ferry, Tyler
**\*DUNCANVILLE, Dallas,**
   **1,711 (36,081)** .......... 36,779
**Dundee, Archer,** ............... 12
Dunkin, Angelina
Dunlap, Brazos
**Dunlap, Cottle,** ................ 10
**Dunlap, Travis,** ................ 80
**Dunlay, Medina, 6** ............ 119
Dunlay, Travis
**\*Dunn, Scurry, 1** ............... 75
Dunn's, Robertson
Dunn's House, Coryell
Dunnville, Tarrant
Dunstan ,Bastrop
**Duplex, Fannin,** ............... 25
DuPont, Denton
Dupree, Hays
Dupree, Wood
Dura, Brazoria
Duraglas, McLennan
**Durango, Falls,** ............... 54
Durant, Angelina
Durant, Robertson
Durant, Van Zandt
Durban, Atascosa
**Duren, Mills,** .................. 15

| Town,County | Pop. 2002 |
|---|---|

Durham, Borden
Durham, Freestone
Durie, Bell
Duroc, Brazoria
Durst, Angelina
Durst's, Leon
**Duster, Comanche,** ........... 25
Dutch, Smith
Dutch Colony, Cottle
Dutchman, Motley
Dutch Settlement, Matagorda
Dutchtown, DeWitt
Dutch Waterhole, Travis
Duval, Duval
Duval, Travis
Duval, Winkler
Duxbury, Montague
Dwire, San Augustine
Dye, Cooke
**Dye, Montague,** .............. 200
Dyer, Fort Bend
Dyer, Fort Bend
Dyer, Hunt
Dyer, Limestone
Dyersdale, Harris
Dyersville, Bosque
**\*Dyess Air Force Base, Taylor,**
    9 ..................... 4,676
Dyess Grove, Bell
Dysart, Presidio

**E**

Eads, Smith
**Eagle, Chambers,** .......... 50
Eagle, Milam
Eagle, San Saba
Eagle, Wood
Eagle's Nest, Val Verde
Eagle Branch, Bastrop
Eagle Cove, Callahan
Eagle Flat, Hudspeth
Eagle Flat, Wilbarger
Eagle Ford, Dallas
**\*EAGLE LAKE, Colorado,**
    195 (3,664) ........... 3,667
Eagle Mills, Shelby
**Eagle Mountain, Tarrant,**
    (6,599) .............. 6,961
**\*EAGLE PASS, Maverick,**
    1,167 (22,413) ........ 23,450
Eagle Point, Montague
Eagle Rock, Bandera
Eagle Rock, Parker
Eagle Springs, Coryell
Eagleton, Harrison
Eagle Valley, Leon
Eagleville, Parker
Eanes, Travis
Earl, Cherokee
Earl, Freestone
Earl, Terry
Earle, Bexar
**\*EARLY, Brown, (2,588)** ...... 2,664
Early, Cooke
Early Grove, Titus
**Earlywine, Washington,** ........ NA
Earnest, Sterling
Earpville, Gregg
**\*EARTH, Lamb, 47 (1,109)** ..... 1,087
Easley Chapel, Houston
Easom, Polk
**East Afton, Dickens,** .......... 11
East Beaumont, Orange
**\*East Bernard, Wharton,**
    146 (1,729) ............. 1,781
East Caddo, Callahan
**East Caney, Hopkins,** ........... NA

East Center, Van Zandt
**East Columbia, Brazoria,** ........ 95
East Dallas, Dallas
**East Delta, Delta,** ........... 50
**East Direct, Lamar,** ........... 45
East Donna, Hidalgo
East El Paso, El Paso
**Easter, Castro,** ................ 30
Easterling, Wilson
**Easterly, Robertson,** ........... 61
East Fork, Collin
East Fort Worth, Tarrant
**Eastgate, Liberty,** ............. NA
**East Hamilton, Shelby,** ......... NA
East Houston, Harris
East Jefferson, Orange
**\*EASTLAND, Eastland,**
    377 (3,769) ............. 3,760
East Liberty, Shelby
Eastman, Hardin
East Mayfield, Sabine
**EAST MOUNTAIN Upshur,**
    (580) ................... 580
**\*EASTON, Gregg-Rusk,**
    5 (524) ................. 536
**East Point, Wood,** ............. 40
East Prairie, Trinity
East Side, Zavala
East Stamford, Jones
**East Sweden, McCulloch,** ....... 40
**EAST TAWAKONI, Rains,**
    (775) ................... 806
**East Tempe, Polk,** ............ 200
Eastvale, Denton
East Waco, McLennan
Eaton, Jones
Eaton, Limestone
**Eaton, Robertson,** ............. NA
**Ebenezer, Camp,** .............. 55
Ebenezer, Hidalgo
**Ebenezer, Jasper,** ............. NA
Ebenezer, Walker
Ebenezer, Walker
Eblin's, Bastrop
Ebony, Mills
Echo, Bell
**Echo, Coleman,** ............... 16
Echo, Jack
Echo, Live Oak
Echo, Orange
Echols, Limestone
Eck, Travis
**Eckert, Gillespie,** ............. NA
Ecla, Gray
Eclectic Grove, Fannin
Ecleto, Karnes
**Ecleto, Karnes,** ............... 22
Eclipse, Gaines
Eclipse, Jasper
**\*ECTOR, Fannin, 18 (600),** ...... 641
Ector, Harrison
Ector, Rusk
Edclauder, Harris
**\*EDCOUCH, Hidalgo, 74**
    (3,342) ................ 3,604
**\*EDDY [Bruceville-], McLennan-**
    Falls, 36 (1,490) ......... 1,549
Eden, Clay
Eden, Collin
**\*EDEN, Concho, 75 (2,561)** .... 2,575
Eden, Guadalupe
Eden, Harris
**Eden, Nacogdoches,** ........... NA
Eden, Tarrant
Edenville, Hale
Ederville, Tarrant
Edey, Comanche

**Edgar, DeWitt,** ................. 8
Edgar School, Delta
**Edge, Brazos,** ............... 100
**EDGECLIFF, Tarrant,**
    (2,550) ............... 2,579
Edge Hill, Tom Green
Edgewater, Galveston
**Edgewater-Paisano, San Patricio,**
    (182) .................. 187
**\*EDGEWOOD, Van Zandt,**
    105 (1,348) ............. 1,379
**Edgeworth, Bell,** .............. 20
Edgeworth, Milam
Edgin, Floyd
Edhobby, Eastland
**Edhube, Fannin,** ............... 25
**\*EDINBURG, Hidalgo,**
    1,898 (48,465) ......... 51,935
Edinburgh, Hidalgo
Edison, Montgomery
Edison, Zavala
Edith, Coke
Edleona, Nolan
Edmond, Houston
**\*EDMONSON, Hale, 16 (123)** .... 121
Edmund, Sherman
Edmunds, Brazoria
**\*EDNA, Jackson, 377**
    (5,899) ............... 5,921
Edna, Tarrant
**Edna Hill, Erath,** .............. 32
Ednaville, Palo Pinto
**EDOM, Van Zandt, (322)** ....... 316
Ed Pit, Tarrant
**\*Edroy, San Patricio, 8 (420),** .... 429
Edruvera, Crane
Edson, Hamilton
Edward, Stephens
Edward's Point, Galveston
Edwards, Clay
Edwards, Cochran
Edwardsville, Gregg
Effie, Wilbarger
**Egan, Johnson,** ................ 21
Ego, Live Oak
Egypt, Johnson
Egypt, Kaufman
**Egypt, Leon,** .................. NA
**Egypt, Montgomery,** ........... NA
Egypt, Montgomery
**\*Egypt, Wharton, 5** ............ 26
Eickhoff, Titus
**Eidson Road, Maverick,**
    (9,348) ............... 9,713
Eight Mile Creek, Comal
Eight Mile Creek, Harrison
El Acha, Starr
El Alamo de San Juan, Jeff Davis
Elam, Dallas
**Elam Springs, Upshur,** ......... 50
Elandel, Caldwell
**El Arroyo, Starr,** ............. 500
El Atascoso, Nacogdoches
Elba, Hardeman
Elbee, Burleson
El Bernardo, Brazoria
Elbert, Polk
**Elbert, Throckmorton, 9 (56)** ..... 53
Elberta, Smith
Elberta, Wood
Elbow, Howard
**El Calaboz [Encantado-Ranchito-],**
    Cameron, (2,100) ........ 2,149
**El Camino Angosto, Cameron,**
    (254) .................. 268
**\*EL CAMPO, Wharton,**
    812 (10,945) ........... 11,098

| Town,County | Pop. 2002 |
|---|---|

El Carro, Jim Wells
**EL CENIZO, Webb,**
    (3,545) ............... 3,597
**El Centro, Starr,** .............. 10
Elder, Hardeman
Elder, Schleicher
Elderville, Gregg
Eldon, Harris
**\*ELDORADO, Schleicher,**
    127 (1,951) ............ 1,977
Eldorado, Wise
**Eldorado Center, Navarro,** ...... 20
**Eldridge, Colorado,** ........... 20
Eldridge, Gray
El Ebano, Cameron
Electra, Fayette
**\*ELECTRA, Wichita, 170**
    (3,168) ............... 3,152
Electric City, Hutchinson
Elena, Harris
**Elevation, Milam,** .............. 12
Elfco, Gray
Elfin Grove, Gray
El Frieda, Matagorda
**El Gato, Hidalgo,** .............. NA
**\*ELGIN, Bastrop, 402**
    (5,700) ............... 6,290
Eli, Bowie
Eli, Hall
**Eliasville, Young, 4** ........... 150
Eliga, Coryell
Elijah, Coryell
**\*El Indio, Maverick, 2 (263)** ..... 265
Elite, Hall
Eliza, Houston
Elizabeth, Denton
Elizabeth, Jefferson
Elizabethtown, Denton
El Jardin, Dimmit
**Elk, McLennan,** ............... 150
**\*ELKHART, Anderson,**
    115 (1,215) ............ 1,246
Elkhart, Houston
Elkheart, Anderson
Elkhorn, Jack
Elkhorn, Red River
Elkins, Brown
Elkins, Houston
Elkton, Smith
Elkton, Smith
Ella, Brazos
Ella, Duval
Ella, Franklin
Ella, Jim Wells
**EL LAGO, Harris, (3,075)** ...... 3,029
Ellen, Hale
Ellendale, Harris
Ellinger, Colorado
**\*Ellinger, Fayette, 10** .......... 200
Elliot, Trinity
Elliot's Ferry, Panola
Elliott, Matagorda
**Elliott, Robertson,** ............. 55
**Elliott, Wilbarger,** ............. 50
Elliott's Mill, Morris
Elliott Flats, Collingsworth
Ellis, Austin
Ellis, Edwards
Ellis, Johnson
Ellis, Navarro
**Ellis [Bausell-], Willacy, (112)** ... 121
Ellis Chapel, Van Zandt
Ellison Springs, Eastland
Ellis Prairie, Trinity
Ellpleasant, Austin
Ellsworth, Grayson
Elm, Collingsworth

Elm, Karnes
Elm, Limestone
Elm, Rains
**\*Elmaton, Matagorda, 6** ........ 140
Elm Creek, Bell
Elm Creek, Guadalupe
Elm Creek, Hunt
**Elm Creek, Maverick, (1,928)** ...1,987
Elm Creek, Taylor
**Elmdale, Taylor,** ............... 50
**\*ELMENDORF, Bexar, 95**
    (664) ................... 662
Elmer, Guadalupe
Elm Flat, Navarro
Elm Grove, Burnet
Elm Grove, Caldwell
**Elm Grove, Cherokee,** .......... 50
Elm Grove, Dallas
Elmgrove, Erath
Elm Grove, Fayette
Elm Grove, Fort Bend
Elm Grove, Hays
Elm Grove, Johnson
Elm Grove, Limestone
**Elm Grove, San Saba,** .......... 15
Elm Grove, Van Zandt
**Elm Grove, Wharton,** .......... 75
Elm Grove, Williamson
**Elm Grove Camp, Guadalupe,** ... 150
Elm Hill, Navarro
Elmina, Walker
**\*Elm Mott, McLennan, 99** ....... 190
Elmo, Bandera
**\*Elmo, Kaufman, 4** ............. 90
Elmore, Hall
Elm Ridge, Denton
Elm Ridge, Hopkins
**Elm Ridge, Milam,** ............. 25
Elms, Bexar
Elmtown, Anderson
Elmview, Grayson
**Elmwood, Anderson,** ........... 25
Elmwood, Harrison
**Eloise, Falls,** .................. 29
El Ojito, Brewster
**El Oso, Karnes,** ............... 35
El Par, Jim Wells
**\*EL PASO, El Paso, 19,342**
    (563,662) ............. 573,787
El Pleasant, Austin
**El Refugio, Starr, (221)** ........ 219
Elrod, Anderson
Elrod, McLennan
**Elroy, Travis,** ................ 125
**\*ELSA, Hidalgo, 126 (5,549)** ...5,760
El Salde Rey, Hidalgo
El Sauz, Hidalgo
**El Sauz, Starr, 2** .............. 50
El Sauz, Willacy
El Sordo, Jim Hogg
Elstone, Medina
**El Tacalote, Jim Wells** ......... 100
El Tigre, Zapata
**Elton, Dickens,** ................ 1
**El Toro, Jackson,** ............. 126
Elva, Ellis
Elva, Uvalde
**El Venadito, Cameron,** ........ 207
El Vista, Jefferson
**Elwood, Fannin,** ............... 31
Elwood, Hockley
Elwood, Jefferson
**Elwood, Madison,** ............. 50

| Town,County |
|---|

**\*Era, Cooke** ...
Eramter's M...
Erath...rath
Erath...Le...
Erickh...
Erie, K...
Erin, p...
Erin, ...
Ermin...
Erns...
Ern...
Ern...
Ern...
**\*Ely...**
Elysiu...
**Elysiun...**
**Embersо...**
**Emblem, H...**
Embree, Dalla...
Embrey, Menar...
Embryfield, San ...
Emelia, Fort Bend
Emerald, Crockett
Emerald Bay, Smith, ...
Emerson, Collin
Emerson, Terrell
**EMHOUSE, Navarro, (159)** ...
Emille, Tyler
Eminence, Chambers
Emma, Crosby
Emmaus, Cherokee
**Emmett, Navarro,** ...
Emmett, Red River
Emmit, Polk
**\*EMORY, Rains, 190 (1,021)** .... 1,151
Empire, Collin
Emporia, Angelina
Enal, Angelina
Encantada, Brooks
**Encantada-Ranchito-El Calaboz,**
    Cameron, (2,100) ....... 2,149
**ENCHANTED OAKS, Henderson,**
    (357) .................. 361
Encina, Uvalde
**\*ENCINAL, La Salle, 19 (629)** .. 619
**\*Encino, Brooks, 16 (177)** ...... 169
Endolynn, Lynn
**\*Energy, Comanche, 2** .......... 65
Engelwood, Robertson
England, Baylor
**Engle, Fayette,** ............... 106
Englehart, Colorado
Engleman, Collin
English, Brazoria
**English, Red River,** ............ 92
English Prairie, Trinity
**\*Enloe, Delta, 4** .............. 113
**\*ENNIS, Ellis, 861 (16,045)** ... 17,150
Ennis, Scurry
Enoch, Clay
**Enoch, Upshur,** ................ 25
**\*Enochs, Bailey, 2** ............. 80
Enon, Houston
Enon, Rusk
Enon, Tarrant
Enon, Upshur
Enos, Waller
**Enright, Brazos,** .............. NA
Ensign, Ellis
Enso, Comanche
Enterprise, Medina
Enterprise, Red River
**Enterprise, Van Zandt,** ......... 90
Enterprise Farm, Liberty
Entre, Montgomery
**\*Eola, Concho, 9** ............. 218
**Eolian, Stephens,** .............. 9
Ephesus, Leon
Ephraim, Hall
Epperson, Marion
Epperson's Ferry, Bowie
Eppler, Bastrop
Epworth, Hale
Equality, Harrison
Equestria, Johnson

| Town,County | Pop. 2002 |
|---|---|

(591) .................... 625
*Falls Creek, Lampasas*
*Falls of Brazos, Falls*
**Falman-County Acres, San Patricio,**
(289) .................... 282
*Fambrough, Stephens*
**Famuliner, Cochran,............. 5**
*Fancher, Baylor*
*Fanchon, Swisher*
**Fannett, Jefferson,............. 105**
***Fannin, Goliad, 8.............. 359**
*Fannin Court House, Fannin*
*Fanninsdefeat, Victoria*
*Fannintown, Clay*
*Fant, Cass*
*Fant, Polk*
*Fant City, Live Oak*
*Fanthorp's, Grimes*
**Fargo, Wilbarger, ............. 161**
*Farias, Webb*
*Farish, Carson*
*Farmer, Crosby*
*Farmer, McLennan*
*Farmer, Young*
*Farmers' Point, Hill*
**Farmers Academy, Titus,........ 75**
***FARMERS BRANCH, Dallas,***
(27,508)............... 27,572
*Farmers Institute, Rusk*
*Farmers Spring, Coryell*
**Farmers Valley, Wilbarger,....... 50**
***FARMERSVILLE, Collin, 233***
(3,118)................. 3,249
*Farm Home, Hockley*
**Farmington, Grayson, .......... 38**
*Farmington, La Salle*
*Farm Town, Bell*
***Farnsworth, Ochiltree, 9 ...... 130**
*Farr, McLennan*
**Farrar, Limestone, ............. 51**
*Farrell, Angelina*
*Farris, Uvalde*
*Farris Store, Walker*
**Farrsville, Newton,............. 150**
*Farwell, Hansford*
***FARWELL, Parmer, 109***
(1,364)................. 1,313
*Farwell Heights, McLennan*
*Farwell Park, Dallam*
**Fashing, Atascosa, ............. 35**
*Fasken, Andrews*
*Fastrill, Cherokee*
**Fawil, Newton, ................ NA**
*Fay, Culberson*
*Fay, Leon*
*Fay, Van Zandt*
*Fayburg, Collin*
***FAYETTEVILLE, Fayette, 60***
(261) .................... 272
*Fayetteville, Fort Bend*
**Faysville, Hidalgo, (348) ....... 369**
*Fazenda, Upshur*
**Fedor, Lee, ................... 76**
*Fedora, Terrell*
*Feely, Val Verde*
*Fehlis, Kinney*
*Feld, Williamson*
*Felder, Washington*
*Felicia, Liberty*

*Felix, Glasscock*
*Felix, Hall*
*Felix, Limestone*
*Feliz, Webb*
*Felton, Camp*
*Felton, Walker*
*Fenella, Waller*
*Fenn Lake, Fort Bend*
***Fentress, Caldwell, 11 ........ 291**
*Fergus, Hunt*
*Ferguson, Grayson*
*Ferguson, Jasper*
*Ferguson, Montague*
*Ferguson, Tarrant*
*Ferguson's, Grayson*
*Fermina, Cameron*
*Fern, Harris*
*Fern, Nacogdoches*
*Fernando, Cameron*
*Fernando, Medina*
*Ferns, Harrison*
***FERRIS, Ellis, 156 (2,175).....2,246**
*Ferrissa, Matagorda*
*Fertile Hill, Falls*
*Festus, Moore*
**Fetzer, Waller, .................NA**
*Ficklin, Crockett*
*Fiddlers Green, Denton*
*Field, Van Zandt*
*Field's Point, Van Zandt*
*Field City, Dallas*
*Field Creek, Llano*
*Fields, Harrison*
*Fields, Liberty*
**Field Schoolhouse, Erath,....... 12**
*Field Senate, Jack*
*Fields Spur, Lee*
**Fields Store, Waller, ...........NA**
***Fieldton, Lamb, 1 ............ 126**
*Fife, Houston*
**Fife, McCulloch, ............... 32**
**Fifth Street, Fort Bend,**
(2,059)................. 1,773
*Figridge, Chambers*
*Figure 2 Ranch, Culberson*
**Files Valley, Hill, .............. 50**
*Filigonio, Hidalgo-Willacy*
**Fincastle, Henderson, .......... 25**
*Finch, Lamar*
*Finch, Navarro*
*Findit, Smith*
*Fineza, Shelby*
*Finis, Jack*
*Fink, Grayson*
*Finks, Bell*
*Finland, Bell*
*Finlay, Bowie*
*Finlay, Hudspeth*
*Finlay, McCulloch*
*Finley, Dallas*
*Finley, Liberty*
*Finley Point, Stephens*
**Finney, Hale, .................. 15**
*Finney, King*
*Fireman's Hill, San Jacinto*
*First Colony, Fort Bend*
***Fischer, Comal, 16 ........... 20**
*Fish Branch, San Jacinto*
*Fish Creek, Cooke*
*Fish Creek, Nolan*
*Fish Creek, Young*
*Fisher, Dallas*
*Fisher, Fisher*
*Fisher, Nacogdoches*
*Fisher's Gin, Collin*
*Fisherburgh, Cooke*
*Fisherville, Tom Green*

**Fisk, Coleman,................. 40**
*Fiskville, Travis*
*Fite, Cass*
*Fitze, Nacogdoches*
*Fitzgerald, Anderson*
*Fitzhugh, Collin*
*Fitzhugh, Hays*
*Fitzpatrick, Harrison*
*Five Mile, Dallas*
*Five Mile, DeWitt*
*Five Notch, Harrison*
*Five Points, Dallas*
**Five Points, Ellis, ............. 10**
*Five Points, Nueces*
**Flaccus, Karnes,............... 15**
**Flagg, Castro, ................ 30**
*Flag Pond, Bosque*
*Flag Springs, Callahan*
*Flanagan, Rusk*
*Flanagan's Mills, Rusk*
*Flannagan's Ranch, Eastland*
*Flap Top, Scurry*
***Flat, Coryell, 5 ............... 210**
*Flat Creek, Comanche*
*Flat Creek, Erath*
*Flat Foot, Henderson*
**Flat Fork, Shelby, ............. NA**
***FLATONIA, Fayette, 117***
(1,377)................. 1,403
**Flat Prairie, Trinity, ............ 33**
*Flatprairie, Washington*
*Flatrock, Brown*
*Flat Rock Spring, Clay*
**Flats, Rains,.................. 646**
*Flatt, Travis*
*Flat Top, Coleman*
**Flat Top, Stonewall,............ 10**
*Flatwood, Van Zandt*
**Flatwoods, Eastland, .......... 56**
*Flat Woods, Erath*
*Flat Woods, Nacogdoches*
*Fleerton, Archer*
*Fleetwood, Stephens*
*Fleig, El Paso*
*Fleming, Comanche*
*Fleming Station, Bowie*
*Fleming Station, Tyler*
*Flemingville, Mason*
*Fletcher, Hardin*
*Fletcher, Milam*
*Flewellen, Fort Bend*
*Flinn, Erath*
***Flint, Smith, 236.............. 700**
*Flintham's Tan Yard, Red River*
*Flint Hill, Anderson*
*Flint Hill, Medina*
*Flintrock, Travis*
**Flo, Leon,.................... 20**
*Flo, Moore*
*Floco, Floyd*
*Flomot, Floyd*
***Flomot, Motley, 5 ............ 181**
*Flora, Fort Bend*
**Flora, Hopkins, ............... NA**
*Flora, Smith*
*Flora Bluff, Franklin*
*Floral, Real*
*Floral Park, Brazoria*
*Florence, Smith*
***FLORENCE, Williamson, 129***
(1,054)................. 1,101
*Florence Hill, Dallas*
*Flores, Atascosa*
***FLORESVILLE, Wilson, 416***
(5,868)................. 6,193
**Florey, Andrews,............... 25**
*Florida, Fayette*

| Town,County . . . . . . . . . . .Pop. 2002 | Town,County . . . . . . . . . . .Pop. 2002 | Town,County . . . . . . . . . . . Pop. 2002 |
|---|---|---|
| Flour Bluff, Nueces | Forest Lake, Gregg | Foster Station, Hunt |
| Flour Bluff, Nueces | Foresville, DeWitt | Fosterville, Anderson |
| Flournoy, Angelina | Fork Point, Panola | Fostoria, Liberty |
| Flournoy's, Nacogdoches | Forks of the Creek, Navarro | Fostoria, Montgomery, . . . . . . . . NA |
| Flowella, Brooks, (134) . . . . . . . . 132 | Fork Valley, Comanche | Fouke, Wood, . . . . . . . . . . . . . . . 30 |
| Flowerdale, Freestone | Forman's, Llano | Fountain, Brazos |
| Flower Grove, Martin | *FORNEY, Kaufman, 516 | Four, Red River |
| Flower Hill, Bastrop | (5,588) . . . . . . . . . . . . . . . . . .6,271 | Four Corners, Archer |
| Flower Hill, Colorado, . . . . . . . . . 20 | *Forreston, Ellis, 7 . . . . . . . . . . . . 200 | Four Corners, Brazoria, . . . . . . . NA |
| *FLOWER MOUND, Denton, | *FORSAN, Howard, 14 (226) . . . . 223 | Four Corners, Chambers, . . . . . . . 18 |
| 682 (50,702) . . . . . . . . . . . 56,230 | Fort Belknap, Young | Four Corners, Fort Bend, |
| Flowery Mountain, Nacogdoches | Fort Bend, Fort Bend | (2,954) . . . . . . . . . . . . . . . . 3,133 |
| Flox, Walker | Fort Bennett, Houston | Four Corners, Harris |
| Floy, Fayette | Fort Bliss, El Paso, (8,264). . . . .8,128 | Four Corners, Montgomery, . . . . . NA |
| Floy, Jasper | Fort Boggy, Leon | Four Corners, Motley |
| Floyd, Denton | Fort Chadbourne, Coke | Four Mile Branch, Marion |
| Floyd, Hunt, 1 . . . . . . . . . . . . . . . 220 | Fort Clark, Kinney | Four Mile Creek, Comal |
| Floyd's Lane, Wharton | Fort Clark Springs, Kinney, . . . .1,070 | Four Mile Prairie, Van Zandt |
| *FLOYDADA, Floyd, 205 | Fort Colorado, Travis | Four Notch, Walker |
| (3,676). . . . . . . . . . . . . . . . . .3,617 | Fort Concho, Tom Green | Four Points, Travis |
| Floyd Hill, Cass | Fort Crawford, Harrison | Four Way, Moore |
| Flugrath, Blanco, . . . . . . . . . . . . . 20 | *Fort Davis, Jeff Davis, 103 | Fouts, Liberty |
| *Fluvanna, Scurry, 4. . . . . . . . . . 180 | (1,050) . . . . . . . . . . . . . . . . .1,098 | Fowler, Bosque |
| Fly, Medina | Fort Duncan, Maverick | Fowler's Gin, Bell |
| Fly Gap, Mason | Fort Elliott, Wheeler | Fowler's Store, Hopkins |
| Flynn, Cass | Fort Ewell, La Salle | Fowlers Store, Lamar |
| *Flynn, Leon, 6 . . . . . . . . . . . . . . . 81 | Fort Gall, Pecos | *Fowlerton, La Salle, 3 (62) . . . . . . 58 |
| Foard City, Foard, . . . . . . . . . . . . 10 | Fort Gates, Coryell | Fowlkes, Wichita |
| Foch, Scurry | Fort Graham, Hill | Fox, Dallas |
| Fodice, Houston, . . . . . . . . . . . . . 49 | Fort Griffin, Bell | Fox, Eastland |
| Fojt, Burleson | Fort Griffin, Shackelford, . . . . . . . . 4 | Fox, Gonzales |
| Folger, Palo Pinto | *Fort Hancock, Hudspeth, | Fox, Harrison |
| *FOLLETT, Lipscomb, 41 | 22 (1,713) . . . . . . . . . . . . . .1,764 | Fox, Henderson |
| (412) . . . . . . . . . . . . . . . . . . 402 | *Fort Hood, Bell-Coryell, | Fox, Hunt |
| Follett's Island, Brazoria | 121 (33,711) . . . . . . . . . . .33,501 | Fox, Liberty |
| Folley, Motley | Fort Houston, Anderson | Fox, Parker |
| Folsom, Potter | Fort Inge, Uvalde | Fox City, Gregg |
| Folsom, Shelby, . . . . . . . . . . . . . NA | Fort Inglish, Fannin | Fox Nation, Live Oak |
| Foncine, Collin | Fort Kitchen, Fannin | Foy, Collin |
| Fondren, Harris | Fort Lacy, Cherokee | Fraimville, Burleson |
| Fondren's Store, Parker | Fort Lancaster, Crockett | Frame, Clay |
| Fontana, Harrison | Fort Lindsey, Tyler | Frame Switch, Williamson, . . . . . . 20 |
| Fontella, Sabine | Fort McIntosh, Webb | Frances, Henderson |
| Foot, Collin | *Fort McKavett, Menard, 9 . . . . . . 15 | Frances, Zavala |
| Footes, Gregg | Fort Merrill, Live Oak | Francis, Dallas |
| Footout, Bosque | Fort Murray, Young | Francis, Franklin |
| Foots Switch, Gregg | Fort Oldham, Burleson-Washington | Francis, Orange |
| Forbes, Jasper | Fort Parker, Limestone, . . . . . . . . . 2 | *Francitas, Jackson, 1 . . . . . . . . 143 |
| Ford, Deaf Smith, . . . . . . . . . . . . 15 | Fort Parker State Park, | Franco, Parker |
| Ford, Frio | Limestone, . . . . . . . . . . . . . . . 30 | Frank, Fannin |
| Ford, Van Zandt | Fort Phantom Hill, Jones | Frankel City, Andrews, . . . . . . . . . . 2 |
| Ford's Bluff, Jasper | Fort Prairie, Travis | Frankell, Stephens, . . . . . . . . . . . NA |
| Ford's Mill, Jasper | Fort Quitman, Hudspeth | Frankford, Collin |
| Ford Oaks, Travis | Fort Riley, Kinney | Frankford, Dallas |
| Fords Corner, San Augustine, . . . 30 | Fort Ringgold, Starr | Frankfort, Anderson |
| Fordtran, Victoria, . . . . . . . . . . . . 18 | *Fort Sam Houston, Bexar, . . .10,000 | Frankfort, Dickens |
| Forest, Cherokee, . . . . . . . . . . . . 85 | Fort Shelton, Lamar | Frankfort, Guadalupe |
| Forest Academy, Hopkins | Fort Spunky, Hood, . . . . . . . . . . . 15 | Franklin, El Paso |
| *Forestburg, Montague, 17 . . . . . . 50 | Fort Stanley Creek, Angelina, . . . 100 | Franklin, Lamar |
| Forest Chapel, Lamar, . . . . . . . . . 85 | *FORT STOCKTON, Pecos, | Franklin, Liberty |
| Forest Glade, Limestone, . . . . . . 340 | 465 (7,846) . . . . . . . . . . . . .7,693 | *FRANKLIN, Robertson, |
| Forest Grove, Collin | Fort Tenoxtitlan, Burleson | 124 (1,470). . . . . . . . . . . . . 1,474 |
| Forest Grove, Henderson | Fort Teran, Tyler-Angelina | Franklin Center, Scurry |
| Forest Grove, Milam, . . . . . . . . . . 60 | Fort Travis, Galveston | Franklin Settlement, McMullen |
| Forest Grove, Titus | Fortune, Harris | Franklinville, Anderson |
| Forest Heights, Orange, . . . . . . . 250 | Fort Warren, Fannin | *FRANKSTON, Anderson, |
| Forest Hill, Bell | *FORT WORTH, Tarrant-Denton, | 198 (1,209). . . . . . . . . . . . . 1,243 |
| Forest Hill, Lamar, . . . . . . . . . . . . 40 | 32,429 (534,694) . . . . . . . .555,110 | Frankston, Jefferson |
| FOREST HILL, Tarrant, | Forum, Hidalgo | Frankville, Leon |
| (12,949). . . . . . . . . . . . . . .13,338 | Forward, Lamar | Fraser, Hill |
| Forest Hill, Upshur | Fossil, Tarrant | Fratt, Bexar |
| Forest Hill, Wood, . . . . . . . . . . . . 30 | Foster, Fort Bend | Frazier, Hopkins |
| Forest Hill Estates, Coryell, . . . . 125 | Foster, Sterling | Frazier, Marion |
| Forest Home, Cass | Foster, Terry, . . . . . . . . . . . . . . . 25 | Frean, Lamar |
| Forest Home, Cass | Foster, Wise | *Fred, Tyler, 12. . . . . . . . . . . . . .239 |
| Forest Home, Wood | Foster's, Childress | *FREDERICKSBURG, Gillespie, |
| Forest Lake, Brazos | Fosters Store, Burleson | 1,145 (8,911) . . . . . . . . . . . 9,306 |

| Town,County . . . . . . . . . . .Pop. 2002 | Town,County . . . . . . . . . . .Pop. 2002 | Town,County . . . . . . . . . . . Pop. 2002 |
|---|---|---|
| Fredonia, Gregg | 1,726 (29,037) . . . . . . . . . .30,740 | Fussell, Rusk |
| *Fredonia, Mason, 5 . . . . . . . . . . . 50 | Frier, Guadalupe | |
| Free, Polk | Frijole, Culberson | **G** |
| Free, Terrell | **Frio, Castro, . . . . . . . . . . . . . . . . 15** | Gabion, Galveston |
| Freedman's Ridge, Gregg | Frio, Frio | Gable, Navarro |
| Freedmen's Colony, Blanco | Frio, McMullen | Gabriel Mills, Williamson |
| Freedom, Harrison | Frio, Parmer | Gabriel River, Williamson |
| Freedom, McLennan | *FRIONA, Parmer, 174 | **Gadston, Lamar, . . . . . . . . . . . . . . 35** |
| **Freedom, Rains, . . . . . . . . . . . . . . 60** | (3,854) . . . . . . . . . . . . . . . . .3,812 | **Gafford, Hopkins, . . . . . . . . . . . . NA** |
| Freeland, Johnson | Frio Water Hole, Real | Gage, Grayson |
| Freeman, Brown | *FRISCO, Collin-Denton, 1,801 | Gage's, Bastrop |
| Freeman, Panola | (33,714) . . . . . . . . . . . . . . .44,000 | Gage's, Rusk |
| Freeman, Polk | Frisco, Lamar | Gageby, Wheeler-Hemphill |
| Freeman's Store, Nacogdoches | Frisco, Sherman | Gagne, Shelby |
| Freeman Town, Denton | Frisco Junction, Newton | *Gail, Borden, 14 . . . . . . . . . . . . .189 |
| Freemound, Cooke | *FRITCH, Hutchinson-Moore, | Gail, Concho |
| Freeneytown, Rusk | 105 (2,235) . . . . . . . . . . . . .2,220 | Gaines Ferry, Sabine |
| *FREEPORT, Brazoria, 810 | Fritzvann, Trinity | Gainesmore, Matagorda |
| (12,708) . . . . . . . . . . . . . . 12,773 | **Frog, Kaufman, . . . . . . . . . . . . . .NA** | *GAINESVILLE, Cooke, |
| Freeport, Brazoria | Frog Hollow, Motley | 1,242 (15,538) . . . . . . . . . 15,800 |
| Freeport, Hale | Frog Liver, Hill | Gainesville, Llano |
| Freeport, Jackson | Frogmore, Kimble | Gainey, Fort Bend |
| *FREER, Duval, 117 (3,241) . . . . 3,250 | Frognot, Collin | Galatea, Harrison |
| Free State, Van Zandt | Frogpond, Panola | **Galena, Smith, . . . . . . . . . . . . . . NA** |
| **Freestone, Freestone, . . . . . . . . . . 35** | Fromme, Travis | *GALENA PARK, Harris, |
| Free Timbers, Wilson | Fromme's Store, Guadalupe | 222 (10,592). . . . . . . . . . . 10,678 |
| **Freheit, Comal, . . . . . . . . . . . . . . NA** | **Front, Panola, . . . . . . . . . . . . . . .NA** | Galesville, Kaufman |
| Frells, Fort Bend | Frontera, El Paso | **Galilee, Smith, . . . . . . . . . . . . . . .150** |
| Frels, Colorado | Fronton, Cameron | Galilee, Walker |
| **Frelsburg, Colorado, . . . . . . . . . . 75** | **Fronton, Starr, (599) . . . . . . . . . . 623** | Gallagher, Shelby |
| Fremont, Parker | Frosa, Limestone | Gallagher's Ranch, Medina |
| French, Callahan | *FROST, Navarro, 28 (648) . . . . . . 683 | Gallalia, Harrison |
| French, Denton | Frost, Navarro | *GALLATIN, Cherokee, |
| French, Falls | Frost, Navarro | 5 (378) . . . . . . . . . . . . . . . . .378 |
| French, Madison | Frostown, Harris | **Galle, Guadalupe, . . . . . . . . . . . .130** |
| French, Marion | Fruit, Smith | Gallina, Presidio |
| French, Navarro | Fruitdale, Dallas | Gallinas, Atascosa |
| French Mills, Jefferson | Fruitland, Brazoria | Galloway, Cass |
| French Settlement, Medina | Fruitland, Fort Bend | Galloway, Jefferson |
| Frenchtown, Harris | **Fruitland, Montague, . . . . . . . . . . 20** | **Galloway, Panola, . . . . . . . . . . . . 71** |
| **Frenstat, Burleson, . . . . . . . . . . . NA** | *FRUITVALE, Van Zandt, | *GALVESTON, Galveston, |
| Fresenius, Hardin | 21 (418) . . . . . . . . . . . . . . . . 430 | 2,701 (57,247) . . . . . . . . . 57,027 |
| Fresnal, Cameron | Fry, Brown | Galvez, Jim Wells |
| Fresnito, Maverick | Fry, Coleman | Gamble, Ellis |
| **Fresno, Collingsworth, . . . . . . . . NA** | Fryar, McLennan | Gamma, Coke |
| *Fresno, Fort Bend, 136 | **Frydek, Austin, . . . . . . . . . . . . . . 150** | Gamma, Parker |
| (6,603) . . . . . . . . . . . . . . . . 6,854 | Frye, Wheeler | *GANADO, Jackson, 100 |
| **Freyburg, Fayette, . . . . . . . . . . . . 45** | Frys Gap, Cherokee | (1,915) . . . . . . . . . . . . . . . . 1,923 |
| Friar, Rusk | Fuch's Mill, Blanco | Ganahl, Kerr |
| **Friday, Trinity, . . . . . . . . . . . . . . . 99** | Fuchs, Milam | Gander Slu, Guadalupe |
| Frieden, Washington | Fueldale, Bastrop | Gandertown, Bell |
| Friendly, Van Zandt | **Fulbright, Red River, . . . . . . . . . 150** | Gandy, Burnet |
| Friendship, Cherokee | Fulda, Baylor | Gandy, Jackson |
| Friendship, Coryell | Fuller, Wheeler | Gandy, Lavaca |
| **Friendship, Dawson, . . . . . . . . . . . 5** | Fuller, Wichita | Gannon, Fisher |
| Friendship, Delta | Fuller Springs, Angelina | Gano, Van Zandt |
| Friendship, Denton | Fullerton, Andrews | Gano, Williamson |
| Friendship, Falls | Fullerton, Liberty | Gansel, McCulloch |
| Friendship, Franklin | Fullerville, Scurry | Gantt, Lamar |
| Friendship, Freestone | Fulp, Fannin | Gap, Coleman |
| Friendship, Hardin | *FULSHEAR, Fort Bend, | Gap, Comanche |
| Friendship, Harrison | 87 (716) . . . . . . . . . . . . . . . . 778 | **Garceño, Starr, (1,438) . . . . . . . 1,491** |
| Friendship, Jack | Fulsher, Fort Bend | Garcia, Deaf Smith |
| Friendship, Jasper | *FULTON, Aransas, | **Garcias, Starr, . . . . . . . . . . . . . . .200** |
| Friendship, Lamar | 61 (1,553) . . . . . . . . . . . . . .1,593 | Garcias, Zapata |
| Friendship, Lamb | Fulton, Lamar | Garcias Ranch, Starr |
| **Friendship, Leon, . . . . . . . . . . . . . NA** | Fulton, Van Zandt | *Garciasville [La Casita]-, Starr, |
| Friendship, Marion | Fulton, Wharton | 13 (2,177). . . . . . . . . . . . . . 2,287 |
| Friendship, Milam | Funston, Jefferson | Garcitas, Victoria |
| **Friendship, Smith, . . . . . . . . . . . 200** | **Funston, Jones, . . . . . . . . . . . . . . 26** | Garden Center, Denton |
| Friendship, Trinity | Funston, Mason | *Garden City, Glasscock, 60. . . . . 293 |
| **Friendship, Upshur, . . . . . . . . . . . 25** | Funston, Taylor | Gardendale, Bexar |
| Friendship, Van Zandt | Fuqua, Grimes | *Gardendale, Ector, 40 |
| Friendship, Williamson | Fuqua, Liberty | (1,197) . . . . . . . . . . . . . . . . 1,228 |
| Friendship, Wood | Furguson, Hale | **Gardendale, La Salle, . . . . . . . . . . 40** |
| **Friendship Village, Bowie, . . . . . . 200** | Furman, Panola | Gardendale, Nueces |
| *FRIENDSWOOD, Galveston-Harris, | **Furrh, Panola, . . . . . . . . . . . . . . . 40** | Garden Oaks, Harris |

CITIES & TOWNS

| Town,County | Pop. 2002 |
|---|---|

**GARDEN RIDGE, Comal,**
  **(1,882)** . . . . . . . . . . . . . . . . 2,090
*Gardentown, Harris*
*Garden Valley, Childress*
**Garden Valley, Smith,** . . . . . . . . 150
*Gardner, Milam*
*Gardner, Roberts*
*Gardner's Saline, Smith*
**Garfield, DeWitt,** . . . . . . . . . . . . 16
**Garfield, Travis, (1,660)** . . . . . . . 1,735
**Garland, Bowie,** . . . . . . . . . . . . . 125
**\*GARLAND, Dallas,**
  **7,584 (215,768)** . . . . . . . . 219,010
*Garlock, Grayson*
*Garner, Frio*
*Garner, Lavaca*
**Garner, Parker,** . . . . . . . . . . . . . 196
*Garner's, Jefferson*
**Garner State Park, Uvalde,** . . . . . . 50
*Garnersville, Bosque*
*Garnett's Bluff, Fannin*
**GARRETT, Ellis, (448)** . . . . . . . . 480
*Garrett, Panola*
*Garrett's Mills, McLennan*
*Garrett's Store, Marion*
**Garretts Bluff, Lamar,** . . . . . . . . . 20
**\*GARRISON, Nacogdoches,**
  **76 (844)** . . . . . . . . . . . . . . . . 859
*Garry, Henderson*
*Garth, Cherokee*
*Garth, Harris*
*Garthright, Calhoun*
*Garvin, Wise*
*Garvinsville, Red River*
**\*Garwood, Colorado, 37** . . . . . . . 975
*Gary, Montgomery*
**\*GARY, Panola, 28 (303)** . . . . . . . 300
*Garza, Denton*
*Garza's Crossing, Bexar*
*Gasca, San Jacinto*
*Gasco, Dallas*
*Gasoline, Briscoe*
*Gas Plant, Terrell*
*Gaston, Dallas*
*Gaston, Fort Bend*
*Gaston, Rusk*
*Gaston, Trinity*
**Gastonia, Kaufman,** . . . . . . . . . . . 30
*Gates, Dallas*
*Gates Chapel, Shelby*
*Gates Valley, Atascosa*
**\*GATESVILLE, Coryell, 464**
  **(15,591)** . . . . . . . . . . . . . . 15,587
*Gatlin, Hays*
*Gatling, Stonewall*
*Gaultville, McCulloch*
**\*Gause, Milam, 6** . . . . . . . . . . . . 400
*Gavett, Morris*
*Gavilan, Terrell*
*Gay, San Augustine*
*Gay's Mill, Hopkins*
*Gay Assembly, Marion*
*Gay Hill, Fayette*
*Gay Hill, Milam*
**Gay Hill, Washington,** . . . . . . . . 145
**Gayle Estates, Brazoria,** . . . . . . . 102
*Gaylord, Lipscomb*
*Gazelle, Hall*
*Gear's Tanyard, Red River*
*Gee's Store, Anderson*
*Gee Prairie, Burleson*
*Gem, Collin*
*Gem, Hemphill*
*Gemmer & Tanner, Colorado*
*Gene, Colorado*
*Gene, Gonzales*
*Geneva, McLennan*

*Geneva, Polk*
**\*Geneva, Sabine, 2** . . . . . . . . . . . 100
*Geneva, San Jacinto*
*Genevie Switch, Wood*
**Geneview, Stonewall,** . . . . . . . . . . 6
*Genoa, Harris*
*Gent, Cherokee*
*Gentry, Fannin*
*Gentry, Harris*
*Gentry, Potter*
*Gentry, Stephens*
*Gentry, Wise*
**Gentry's Mill, Hamilton,** . . . . . . . . 17
*George, Madison*
**George's Creek, Somervell,** . . . . . . 66
*Georgetown, Grayson*
*Georgetown, Van Zandt*
**\*GEORGETOWN, Williamson,**
  **1,996 (28,339)** . . . . . . . . . . 32,128
**\*GEORGE WEST, Live Oak,**
  **190 (2,524)** . . . . . . . . . . . . . 2,526
**Georgia, Lamar,** . . . . . . . . . . . . . . 48
*Georgia Camp, Houston*
*Georgia Colony, Hays*
*Gerald, Denton*
*Gerald, McLennan*
*Geraldine, Archer*
*Germania, Lee*
*Germania, Midland*
*German Settlement, Fayette*
*German Settlement, Matagorda*
*Germantown, Goliad*
*Germantown, Hamilton*
*Germantown, Harris*
**Germany, Houston,** . . . . . . . . . . . . 43
*Germany, Navarro*
*Gerome, Henderson*
**\*Geronimo, Guadalupe, 18**
  **(619)** . . . . . . . . . . . . . . . . . . 645
*Gerron, Bell*
*Gertie, Tarrant*
*Gertrude, Jack*
*Gertrude, Wise*
*Gethsemane, Marion*
*Gewhitt, Hutchinson*
*Gholson, Brown*
*Gholson, Lampasas*
**GHOLSON, McLennan, (922)** . . . . 969
*Ghost Hill, Ellis*
*Gibbons Creek, Grimes*
*Gibbs, Dallas*
*Gibbs, Smith*
*Gibbs, Sterling*
*Gibson, King*
*Gibson, Lamar*
*Gibson Chapel, Freestone*
*Gibsontown, Rusk*
*Gibson Town, Rusk*
**Gibtown, Jack,** . . . . . . . . . . . . . . NA
**\*GIDDINGS, Lee, 480**
  **(5,105)** . . . . . . . . . . . . . . . . 5,271
*Giesecke's Store, Burnet*
*Giesinger, Grimes*
*Gifco, Ellis*
*Gifford, Dallas*
*Gilaloo, Ochiltree*
*Gilbert, Angelina*
*Gilbert, Eastland*
*Gilbert, McLennan*
*Gilbert, Wichita*
*Gilbreth, Wood*
*Gilburg, Jefferson*
**\*Gilchrist, Galveston, 24** . . . . . . . 750
*Gilead, Callahan*
*Gilead, Gregg*
*Giles, Delta*
*Giles, Donley*

*Gilesburg, Travis*
*Gilford, Shelby*
*Gilking, Stephens*
*Gill, Harrison*
*Gilleland Creek, Travis*
**\*Gillett, Karnes, 8** . . . . . . . . . . . . 120
*Gilley, Burleson*
*Gilliam, Webb*
*Gilliamsville, Lampasas-Coryell*
*Gilliland, Callahan*
**Gilliland, Knox,** . . . . . . . . . . . . . . 25
*Gilliland, Parker*
*Gillis, Morris*
*Gilmer, Orange*
**\*GILMER, Upshur, 520**
  **(4,799)** . . . . . . . . . . . . . . . 4,932
*Gilmerville, Jasper*
*Gilmore, Carson*
*Gilmore, Erath*
*Gilmore, Tarrant*
*Gilpin, Childress*
**Gilpin, Dickens,** . . . . . . . . . . . . . . . 3
*Gilpin, McLennan*
*Gilpin, Motley*
*Gilpin, Titus*
*Gindale, Bell*
*Giner, Rains*
**Ginger, Rains,** . . . . . . . . . . . . . . . 96
*Ginsite, Cottle*
*Gipaw, Hall*
**\*Girard, Kent, 2 (62)** . . . . . . . . . . . 64
**Girlstown USA, Cochran,** . . . . . . . 95
**\*Girvin, Pecos, 2** . . . . . . . . . . . . . 30
*Gish, Harris*
*Gist, Hill*
**Gist, Jasper,** . . . . . . . . . . . . . . . . NA
*Gist, Jones*
*Gist, Upshur*
**Givens, Lamar,** . . . . . . . . . . . . . 135
*Givensville, Bastrop*
*Glade, Polk*
*Glade, Tarrant*
*Glade Branch, Franklin*
*Glade Creek, Hopkins*
*Glade Spring, Harrison*
*Glade Spring, Upshur*
**\*GLADEWATER, Gregg-Upshur,**
  **456 (6,078)** . . . . . . . . . . . . . 6,113
*Gladewater, Titus*
*Gladish, Waller*
*Gladstell, Liberty*
*Gladstone, Walker*
*Gladys, Jefferson*
*Gladys, Montague*
*Glasgow, Gray*
*Glasgow, Wilbarger*
*Glass, Bastrop*
*Glass, Robertson*
**Glass, Somervell,** . . . . . . . . . . . . NA
*Glasscock, Bastrop*
**Glaze City, Gonzales,** . . . . . . . . . . 10
**Glazier, Hemphill,** . . . . . . . . . . . . 48
*Gleam, Lee*
**Glecker, Lavaca,** . . . . . . . . . . . . . NA
*Glen, Chambers*
*Glen, Parker*
*Glen, Smith*
*Glenbelto, Bastrop*
*Glencoe, Ellis*
*Glencoe, Houston*
**Glen Cove, Coleman,** . . . . . . . . . . 40
*Glencross, Donley*
*Glendale, Dallas*
**Glendale, Trinity,** . . . . . . . . . . . . 175
**Glenfawn, Rusk,** . . . . . . . . . . . . . 16
**\*Glen Flora, Wharton, 12** . . . . . . . 210
*Glen Flora Place, Wharton*

CITIES & TOWNS

| Town,County ...........Pop. 2002 | Town,County ...........Pop. 2002 | Town,County...........Pop. 2002 |
|---|---|---|
| *Glenham, Bastrop* | *Good Luck Colony, Dimmit* | *Graham, Garza,* ............... 139 |
| *Glenmore, Tom Green* | *Goodman, Bastrop* | *Graham, Jasper* |
| **Glenn, Dickens,** ............... 7 | *Goodman's Crossing, Nacogdoches* | *Graham, Wood* |
| *Glenn, Hutchinson* | **Good Neighbor, Hopkins,** .......NA | *****GRAHAM, Young, 836** |
| *Glenn, Liberty* | **Goodnight, Armstrong,** ......... 18 | **(8,716)** ........ 8,686 |
| **GLENN HEIGHTS, Dallas-Ellis,** | **Goodnight, Navarro,** ........... 25 | *Graham's Chapel, Comanche* |
| **(7,224).** ................. 7,597 | *****GOODRICH, Polk, 48 (243)** ..... 256 | *Graham's Mills, Shelby* |
| *Glenn Spring, Brewster* | *Goods Chapel, Delta* | *Graham Prairie, Hunt* |
| *Glen Oaks, Kerr* | *Goodson, Smith* | *Granada, Hutchinson* |
| *Glenpark, Yoakum* | *Goodsonville, Anderson* | *Granada, Pecos* |
| **Glenrio, Deaf Smith,.** ........... 5 | **Goodsprings, Rusk,** ........... 40 | *****GRANBURY, Hood, 1,773** |
| *****GLEN ROSE, Somervell, 301** | *Goodville, Falls* | **(5,718)** ............... 6,027 |
| **(2,122).** ................. 2,265 | **Goodwill, Burleson,** ...........NA | *Granby, Hunt* |
| **Glenwood, Upshur,** .......... 150 | *Goodwin, Comal* | *Granda, Mason* |
| *****Glidden, Colorado, 4** ....... 255 | **Goodwin, San Augustine,** .......NA | **Grand Acres, Cameron,** |
| **Globe, Lamar,.** ............... 62 | *Goolesboro, Titus* | **(203).** ....... 217 |
| *Globe Hill, Lee* | *Goose Creek, Harris* | *Grand Bluff, Orange* |
| **Glory, Lamar,** ................ 30 | *Gooseneck, Young* | **Grand Bluff, Panola,** ........... 97 |
| *Glover, Houston* | *Gorbett, Dallas* | *Grand Cane, Liberty* |
| *Glover, Leon* | *Gordon, Lynn* | *****GRANDFALLS, Ward, 13** |
| *Gloyna, Lee* | *****GORDON, Palo Pinto, 36** | **(391).** .................... 380 |
| *Gluck, Potter* | **(451)** .................... 473 | *Grand Lake, Montgomery* |
| *Gnarled Oak, Washington* | *Gordon, Wood* | *Grand Prairie, Bastrop* |
| *Goather's, Erath* | *Gordon Coal Mines, Palo Pinto* | *****GRAND PRAIRIE, Dallas-Tarrant,** |
| *Goatneck, Johnson* | *Gordon Junction, Palo Pinto* | **4,652 (127,427)** ....... 131,688 |
| *****Gober, Fannin, 2** ............. 146 | *****Gordonville, Grayson, 47** ...... 165 | *Grand Ranche, Palo Pinto* |
| *****GODLEY, Johnson, 70 (879)** ... 918 | *Gore, Anderson* | *****GRAND SALINE, Van Zandt,** |
| *Goetz, Freestone* | *****GOREE, Knox, 7 (321)** ........ 305 | **218 (3,028).** ............. 3,135 |
| *Goff, Rains* | *Gorey, Lampasas* | **Grandview, Dawson,.** ........... 12 |
| *Goforth, Gregg* | *Gorey, Mills* | **Grandview, Gray,.** ............. 13 |
| *Goforth, Hays* | *Gorgona, Montague* | *****GRANDVIEW, Johnson,** |
| *Golan, Jones* | *****GORMAN, Eastland, 58** | **119 (1,358).** ........... 1,438 |
| *Golconda, Palo Pinto* | **(1,236).** ................1,200 | *Grand Vista, Armstrong* |
| *Gold, Gillespie* | *Gose City, Archer* | *Grange, Jasper-Newton* |
| *Gold Dollar, Hopkins* | *Goshen, Henderson* | *Grange Hall, Harrison* |
| *****Golden, Wood, 18.** ........... 156 | *Goshen, Parker* | *Grange Hall, Johnson* |
| *Golden Acres, Harris* | **Goshen, Walker,** ...............NA | *Grange Hall, Navarro* |
| **Golden Beach, Llano,** ..........NA | *Gospel Ridge, Grayson* | *Grange Hall, Upshur* |
| *Golden Drain, Rusk* | *Goss, Fannin* | *Grange Hill, Upshur* |
| *Golden Pond, Stonewall* | *Gossett, Kaufman* | *****GRANGER, Williamson, 60** |
| *Goldenrod, Colorado* | **Gossett, Kaufman,** .............NA | **(1,299)** ................ 1,317 |
| *Goldenrod, Lavaca* | *Gossett Switch, Henderson* | *****Grangerland, Montgomery,** ..... NA |
| *Goldenrod, Wharton* | *Gossip, Johnson* | *Grangerville, Hemphill* |
| *Golden Rule, Wood* | *Gotiers, Bastrop* | *Granite, Burnet* |
| *Golden Vale, Panola* | *Gouge Eye, Gray* | *****GRANITE SHOALS, Burnet,** |
| **Goldfinch, Frio,** ............... 35 | *Gough, Delta* | **(2,040).** .............. 2,062 |
| *Gold Hill, Hopkins* | *Gould, Bell* | **GRANJENO, Hidalgo, (313)** ..... 335 |
| *****Goldsboro, Coleman, 1** ........ 30 | **Gould, Cherokee,** .............. 20 | *Grannys Neck, Delta* |
| *****GOLDSMITH, Ector, 30 (253)** ... 251 | *Gould, Rusk* | *Gran Sabana, Burnet* |
| *****GOLDTHWAITE, Mills,** | *****Gouldbusk, Coleman, 10** ....... 70 | *Grant, Burleson* |
| **180 (1,802)** ............. 1,803 | *Gould City, Callahan* | *Grant, Eastland* |
| *****GOLIAD, Goliad, 193** | *Gourd Neck, Freestone* | *Grant, Marion* |
| **(1,975).** ................. 2,041 | **Gourdneck, Panola,** ........... 30 | *Grant's Bluff, Jasper* |
| **GOLINDA, Falls-McLennan,** | *Gourdneck, Rusk* | *Grant's Colony, Walker* |
| **(423)** .................... 421 | *Gover, Grayson* | *Grantville, Red River* |
| **Golly, DeWitt,** ................. 41 | *Government Wells, Duval* | *Granville, Angelina* |
| **Gomez, Terry,** ................. 12 | *Gower, Williamson* | *Grape Creek, Borden* |
| *Gonzalena, Brooks* | *Gozar, Reeves* | *Grape Creek, Gillespie* |
| *****GONZALES, Gonzales,** | **Graball, Washington,** ...........NA | **Grape Creek, Tom Green,** |
| **497 (7,202)** ............. 7,339 | *Grace, Baylor* | **(3,138)** ................ 3,203 |
| **Goober Hill, Shelby,** ..........NA | **Grace, King,** ................... 20 | *****GRAPELAND, Houston,** |
| *Gooch's Mill Shop, Hamilton* | *Grace Hill, Polk* | **121 (1,451).** ............. 1,468 |
| *Good, Hays* | *Graceland, Llano* | *Grapetown, Gillespie* |
| *Good Creek, Foard* | **Graceton, Upshur,** ........... 100 | **Grapetown, Gillespie,.** ......... NA |
| *Good Exchange, Cass* | *Grady, Briscoe* | *Grapevine, Dickens* |
| *****Goodfellow Air Force Base,** | *Grady, Fisher* | *Grapevine, San Augustine* |
| **Tom Green, 10** .............NA | *Grady, Harrison* | *****GRAPEVINE, Tarrant,** |
| *Good Hope, Denton* | *Grady, Liberty* | **3,318 (42,059)** ......... 43,852 |
| *Good Hope, Franklin* | *Grady, Marion* | *Graphite, Llano* |
| *Good Hope, Lavaca* | *Grady, Smith* | *Grassbur, DeWitt* |
| *Goodhope, Navarro* | *Grady's Mill, Ellis* | *Grassdale, Travis* |
| *Good Hope, Val Verde* | **Grady, Martin** ................NA | **Grassland, Lynn,.** ............... 61 |
| *****Goodland, Bailey,.** ............. 10 | *Gradyville, Ellis* | *Grassmyers, Fayette* |
| *Goodland, Robertson* | *Gradyville, Navarro* | **Grassyville, Bastrop,** ........... 50 |
| **Goodlett, Hardeman,** .......... 80 | *Graeb, Guadalupe* | *Gratis, Orange* |
| **GOODLOW, Navarro, (264)** ..... 267 | *****GRAFORD, Palo Pinto,** | *Gravel, Cottle* |
| *Good Luck, Uvalde* | **128 (578)** ................ 589 | *Gravel, Floyd* |

| Town,County ..........Pop. 2002 | Town,County ..........Pop. 2002 | Town,County ..........Pop. 2002 |
|---|---|---|
| Gravel Hill, Sabine | Greggton, Gregg | *GROVETON, Trinity, 87 |
| Gravel Spur, Cooke | *GREGORY, San Patricio, | (1,107) ................. 1,122 |
| Gravis, Duval | 45 (2,318) ..............2,294 | Groveton Front, Trinity |
| Gravis, Williamson | Grelton, Martin | Grow, Jones |
| Gravity, Brown | Grenada, Deaf Smith | Grow, King, ................... 70 |
| Gray, Eastland | Grenada, Jefferson | Groyan, Harrison |
| Gray, Marion, ................. NA | Gresham, Runnels | Grubbe, Hopkins |
| Gray's Gin, Dallas | Gresham, Smith,............. 100 | Gruenau, DeWitt,............. 18 |
| Grayback, Wilbarger, .......... 25 | Greta, Refugio | Gruene, Comal |
| Graybill, Cameron | GREY FOREST, Bexar, (418) .... 443 | Gruhlkey, Oldham |
| Graybill, Collin | Grey Mule, Floyd | *Grulla, Starr (see La Grulla) |
| GRAYBURG, Hardin, .......... 315 | Gribble, Dallas | Grundyville, Lampasas |
| Grayco, Grayson | Gribble Springs, Denton | *GRUVER, Hansford, 101 |
| Graydale, Stonewall | Grice, Upshur,................. 20 | (1,162) ................. 1,131 |
| Graydon, Chambers | Griffhill, Denton | Guadalupe, Kendall |
| Grayflat, Stonewall | Griffin, Cherokee | Guadalupe, Victoria, .......... 106 |
| Gray Hill, Washington | Griffing Park, Jefferson | Guadalupe, Zapata |
| Gray Rock, Franklin | Griffin Store, Rusk | Guadalupe Ranch, Hidalgo |
| GRAYS PRAIRIE, Kaufman, | Griffinsville, Bosque | Guadalupe Station, Culberson, ... 80 |
| (296) .................... 313 | Griffith, Cochran, ............. 12 | Guadalupe Valley, Comal |
| Grayton, Hudspeth | Griffith, Ellis,................. 10 | Guadalupe Victoria, Victoria |
| Graytown, Wilson-Bexar,........ 64 | Griggs, Newton | Guadelupe, Victoria |
| Greasy Bend, Wise | Grigsby, Jefferson | Guajillo, Duval |
| Greasy Neck, Hall | Grigsby, Shelby, .............. 45 | Guajoco, La Salle |
| Greathouse, Ellis | Grimes, Nolan | Guda, Falls |
| Greathouse, Jack | Grimes, Tyler | Gude, Limestone |
| Greatwood, Fort Bend, | Grimes' Gin, Navarro | Gudger, Stephens |
| (6,640)................. 6,492 | Grimes Prairie, Grimes | Guelph, Polk |
| Green, Karnes, .............. 35 | Grimes Switch, Grimes | *Guerra, Jim Hogg, 1 (8).......... 8 |
| Green, Kaufman | Grimesville, Grimes | Guerrero, Maverick |
| Green's, Liberty | Grimshaw, Young | Guest, Stonewall |
| Green's, Polk | Grindale, Bell | Guest's Station, Runnels |
| Green's Bluff, Orange | Grindstone, Parker | Guffey, Jefferson |
| Green's Creek, Erath,.......... 75 | Grisham, Castro | Guffeyola, McMullen |
| Green's Point, Hunt | Griswold, Polk | Guiceland, Houston |
| Green's Store, Cass | Grit, Mason,.................. 30 | Guide, Ellis |
| Green Bay, Anderson | Grit, Medina | Guilford, DeWitt |
| Greenberry, Fannin | Grit, Rains | Guion, Taylor,.................18 |
| Greenbriar, Smith | Grittersville, Fannin | Gulf, Austin |
| Green DeWitt, DeWitt | Groce's Retreat, Grimes | Gulf, Matagorda |
| Green Grove, Lavaca | Groceville, Montgomery | Gulf Camp, Ward |
| Green Grove, Wood | Groesbeck, Hardeman | Gulf Dial, Hutchinson |
| Green Hill, Brazoria | *GROESBECK, Limestone, | Gulf Hill, Matagorda |
| Green Hill, Titus,.............. 150 | 247 (4,291) .............4,415 | Gulf Park, Brazoria |
| Green Lake, Calhoun, .......... 51 | Grogan, Ochiltree | Gulf Prairie, Brazoria |
| Green Lake, Edwards | *GROOM, Carson, 47 (587) ..... 566 | Gum, Wise |
| Greenock, Bosque | Groos, Fayette | Gum Branch, Hamilton |
| Greenpond, Hopkins,........... NA | Groschkeville, Harris | Gum Creek ,Cherokee |
| Greens Bayou, Harris | Grossville, Mason, ............NA | Gum Island, Harris |
| Greensborough, Harrison | Grosvenor, Brown | Gum Pole, Hopkins |
| Green Valley, Denton | Grotto, Hopkins | Gum Spring, Comal |
| Green Valley, Guadalupe | Grounds, Houston | Gum Spring, Smith |
| Green Valley, Jones | Grove, Collin | Gum Spring, Wilson |
| Green Valley Farms, Cameron, | Grove, Jack | Gum Spring[s], Harrison |
| (720) .................... 722 | Grove, Lamar | Gum Springs, Burnet |
| Greenview, Hopkins, ........... NA | Grove Controls, Harrison | Gum Springs, Cass, ............ 50 |
| Greenville, Gregg | Grovedale, Matagorda | Gum Springs, Fannin |
| *GREENVILLE, Hunt, 1,493 | Grove Hill, Fannin | Gumwood, Smith |
| (23,960). ...............24,514 | Grove Hill, Matagorda | GUN BARREL CITY, Henderson, |
| Greenvine, Washington, ........ 35 | Grove Island, Freestone | 165 (5,145).............. 5,300 |
| Greenwade's Mills, Hill | Groveland, Jack | Gunn, Gonzales |
| Greenway, Bexar | Grover, Bell | Gunsight, Stephens,............. 6 |
| Greenway, Johnson | Grover, Coke | *GUNTER, Grayson, 48 |
| Greenwood, Hopkins, ........ 35 | Grover, Comanche | (1,230) ................. 1,339 |
| Greenwood, Midland,........ 2,000 | Grover, Comanche | Gunter, Wood |
| Greenwood, Nacogdoches | Grover, Guadalupe | Gurley, Falls |
| Greenwood, Parker | Grover, Harrison | Gus, Burleson, ............... NA |
| Greenwood, Red River, ......... 20 | Grover, Hays | Gusher, Hardin |
| Greenwood, Van Zandt | Grover, Montgomery | Gussettville, Live Oak |
| *Greenwood, Wise, 2 ........... 76 | Grover, Navarro | *GUSTINE, Comanche, 20 |
| Greer, McLennan | Grover, Panola | (457)..................... 457 |
| Greer's, Brazos | Grover, Shelby | Guthrie, Jack |
| Greer's Horsepen, Falls | Grover, Williamson | *Guthrie, King, 15 ............. 160 |
| Greer's Neighborhood, Wood | Grove Ranch, Williamson | *Guy, Fort Bend, 14. ............ 60 |
| Greeson, Henderson | *GROVES, Jefferson, | Guy, Van Zandt |
| Gregerville, Falls | 473 (15,733) ...........15,671 | Guys Store, Leon,............. NA |
| Gregg, Travis | Grovesville, Lubbock | Guyer, Wilbarger |

| Town,County ..........Pop. 2002 | Town,County ..........Pop. 2002 | Town,County..........Pop. 2002 |
|---|---|---|
| Guyler, Montgomery | Hall's Bluff, Houston, .......... 67 | Hanna, Wise |
| Gwynn, Schleicher | Hall's Station,Galveston | Hannah Land, Bastrop |
| Gyp, Collingsworth | Halladay, Liberty | Hanna Valley, Mills |
| Gyp, Fisher | *HALLETTSVILLE, Lavaca, | Hanner, Polk |
| Gypmine, Brooks | 306 (2,345) ...........2,298 | Hannes' Gin, Burleson |
| Gypsum, Hardeman | Hallmark Prairie, Bastrop | Hannibal, Erath,.............. NA |
| Gypsum, Hudspeth | Halls Bayou, Brazoria | Hanover, Goliad |
| | HALLSBURG, McLennan, | Hanover, Hill |
| **H** | (518) .............. 536 | Hanover, Milam,............27 |
| H.S. Ranch, Mitchell | Halls Store, Panola, ...........NA | Hanrahan, Grimes |
| Habermacher, Harris | *HALLSVILLE, Harrison, | Hansford, Hansford |
| Habern's Chapel, Delta | 143 (2,772) ...........2,846 | Hanson, Fort Bend |
| Habitacion, Zapata | Halltown, San Augustine | Hanson, Shelby |
| Haby, Medina | Halsell, Clay | Hanson's, Rusk |
| Hacienda, Uvalde | Halsey, Navarro | Happiness, Newton |
| Hacienda Glorieta, Crosby | Halsted, Fayette,.............. 26 | Happle, La Salle |
| Haciendito, Presidio, ...........NA | Haltom's, Montgomery | *HAPPY, Swisher-Randall, |
| Hackberry, Collin | *HALTOM CITY, Tarrant, | 49 (647) ..................652 |
| Hackberry, Cottle, ............. 30 | (39,018)...............39,913 | Happy Hill, Johnson |
| Hackberry, Cottle | Ham, Henderson | Happy Hollow, Burnet |
| HACKBERRY, Denton, (544) .... 593 | Ham's Creek, Johnson | Happy Hollow, Uvalde |
| Hackberry, Edwards, ........... 3 | Haman's, Lamar | Happy Land, Nolan |
| Hackberry, Garza,............. 5 | Hamblin's, Harris | Happy Landing, Shelby |
| Hackberry, Lavaca,............NA | Hamburg, Red River | Happy Union, Hale,............. 15 |
| Hackberry, Madison | Hamburg, Travis | Happy Valley, Taylor, ......... 10 |
| Hackberry Bluff, Collin | Hamburg[h], Van Zandt | Harbin, Erath, ............. 21 |
| Hackberry Grove, Grayson | Hamby, Taylor,............... 100 | Harbor City, San Patricio |
| Hackberry Grove, Wise | Hamco, Coryell | Hardeman, Matagorda |
| Hackney's Mill, Montgomery | Hamil's Chapel, Cass | Hardeman's, Nacogdoches |
| Hackneyville, Polk | Hamil's Chapel, Upshur | Hardin, Coleman |
| Hadacol Corner, Upton | Hamilton, Burnet | Hardin, Hardin |
| Hadley's Prairie, Grimes | Hamilton, Franklin | *HARDIN, Liberty, 28 (755) .....787 |
| Hagan's Mill, Kent | *HAMILTON, Hamilton, 254 | Hardins Store, Leon |
| Hagansport, Franklin, .......... 40 | (2,977)..................2,990 | Hardman's, Anderson |
| Hager, Hopkins | Hamilton, Harris | Hardwick, Hudspeth |
| Hagerman, Grayson | Hamilton, Milam | Hardy, Harris |
| Hagertown, Reeves | Hamiltonburg, Live Oak | Hardy, Matagorda |
| Hagerville, Houston, .......... 70 | Hamilton Dam, Llano | Hardy, Montague, .............. 6 |
| Hagg's Settlement, Comal | Hamilton Park, Dallas | Hardys Chapel, Navarro |
| Haggerty's Bluff, Harrison | Hamilton Pool, Travis | Hare, Medina |
| Hagler, Freestone | Hamilton Springs, Hill | Hare, Williamson, .............70 |
| Hagler's Store, Montague | Hamlet, Angelina | *Hargill, Hidalgo, 8 .......... 1,349 |
| Hague, McLennan | Hamlin, Frio | Hargrave, Roberts |
| Hahn Prairie, Wharton | *HAMLIN, Jones-Fisher, | Hargrove, Somervell |
| Haiduk, Atascosa | 118 (2,248) ............2,196 | *HARKER HEIGHTS, Bell, |
| Hail, Fannin, .................. 30 | Hammels Branch, Hill | 265 (17,308)...........17,872 |
| Hailey, Harrison | Hammer, Uvalde | Harkeyville, San Saba, ......... 12 |
| Hailsburg, Houston | Hammer's Station, Uvalde | Harland, Robertson |
| Haines, Tarrant | Hammock, Polk | Harlanville, Falls |
| Hainesville, Wood, ............. 74 | Hammond, Robertson,.......... 44 | Harlem, Fort Bend |
| Hairston Creek, Burnet | Hamon, Gonzales, ............. 15 | *Harleton, Harrison, 45........ 260 |
| Hajek, Baylor | Hampton, Coryell | *HARLINGEN, Cameron, |
| Halamiceks Store, Fayette | Hampton, Hamilton | 2,852 (57,564) ......... 59,253 |
| Halbert, Shelby | Hampton, Nacogdoches | Harlow, Eastland |
| Hale, Dallas | Hampton, Palo Pinto | Harlow, Hunt,................. NA |
| Hale, Fannin | Hampton, Tyler | Harman, Coryell |
| Hale's Store, Runnels | Hamrick, Coleman | Harmaston, Harris |
| *HALE CENTER, Hale, 84 | *Hamshire, Jefferson, 58 ....... 350 | Harmon, Chambers |
| (2,263)..................2,255 | Han's Settlement, Bandera | Harmon, Lamar,.................35 |
| Halesboro, Red River | Hancock, Collin | Harmon, Waller |
| Haley, Jack | Hancock, Comal, .............NA | Harmony, Floyd, .............42 |
| Haley's Mill, Erath | Hancock, Dawson, ............. 30 | Harmony, Gonzales |
| Haley Springs, Jack | Hancock, Houston | Harmony, Grimes,..............12 |
| Half-Way House, Parker | Hancock, Limestone | Harmony, Hutchinson |
| Halfmoon, Lavaca | Hander, Falls | Harmony, Karnes |
| Halfway, Hale,................ 58 | Handley, Tarrant | Harmony, Kent, ................7 |
| Halfway, Hill | Handville, Randall | Harmony, Limestone |
| Half Way, Hunt | Handy, Jack | Harmony, Milam |
| Halfway, Shelby | Handy, Milam | Harmony, Nacogdoches, ....... NA |
| Halfway House, Archer | Handy, Nolan | Harmony, Panola |
| Halfway House, Nacogdoches | Handy Stop, Kendall | Harmony, San Augustine |
| Halfway House, Ochiltree | Haney, Hunt | Harmony, Tyler |
| Halifax, Polk | Haney, Randall | Harmony Hill, Rusk |
| Hall, Fayette-Lee | Hanger, Grayson | Harmony Settlement, Walker |
| Hall, Marion | *Hankamer, Chambers, 17...... 525 | Harold County Line, Lubbock |
| Hall, San Saba,............... 15 | Hanks, Anderson | Harp, Freestone |
| Hall's Bluff, Freestone | Hanks, Titus | Harp, Montague |

**CITIES & TOWNS**

| Town,County . . . . . . . . . . .Pop. 2002 | Town,County . . . . . . . . . .Pop. 2002 | Town,County . . . . . . . . . . . Pop. 2002 |
|---|---|---|
| *Harper, Gillespie, 54 | Hatchetville, Hopkins, . . . . . . . . . .NA | Heard, Uvalde |
|   (1,006). . . . . . . . . . . . . . . . 1,046 | Hatchton ,Gaines | *HEARNE, Robertson, |
| Harper, Medina | Hathaway, Hardin |   275 (4,690) . . . . . . . . . . . 4,655 |
| Harper's Crossing, Delta | Hattersville, Dallas | Heath, Fayette |
| Harper's Mill, Erath | Hatti, Cooke | Heath, Kaufman |
| Harpersville, Stephens, . . . . . . . . NA | Hattie, Taylor | HEATH, Rockwall, 72 |
| Harper Valley, Freestone | Hatton, Polk |   (4,149) . . . . . . . . . . . . . . . . 4,996 |
| Harrell, Hunt | Hatton, Van Zandt | Heaton, DeWitt |
| Harrell's Chapel, San Saba | Haught's Store, Dallas | Heaton, Gray |
| Harrells, Newton | Haulk, Wilbarger | *Hebbronville, Jim Hogg, |
| Harrellton, Lamar | Hauser, Hidalgo |   201 (4,498). . . . . . . . . . . . 4,537 |
| Harriet, Tom Green | Hausler City, Archer | Hebert, Hardin |
| Harrington, Nacogdoches | Havana, Cass | Hebert, Jefferson |
| Harris, Edwards | Havana, Hidalgo, (452) . . . . . . . . 455 | HEBRON, Denton, (874) . . . . . . . 873 |
| Harris, Hudspeth | Havanna, Dallas | Hebron, DeWitt |
| Harris, Terry | Haven, Cochran | Hebron, Jefferson |
| Harrisburg, Jasper | Haw Creek, Fayette | Hebron, Smith |
| Harrisburg[h], Harris | Hawdon, Fort Bend | Heckel, Hockley |
| Harris Chapel, Panola, . . . . . . . . 180 | Haw Grove, Cass | Heckler, Hill |
| Harris Chapel, Rusk | HAWK COVE, Hunt, (457) . . . . . . 478 | Heckville, Lubbock, . . . . . . . . . . . NA |
| Harris Chapel, Smith | Hawkeye, Bastrop | *HEDLEY, Donley,16 (379) . . . . . . 365 |
| Harris Creek, McLennan | Hawkeye, Denton | Hedwigs Hill, Mason, . . . . . . . . . . . 10 |
| Harris Creek, Smith | Hawkins, Denton | HEDWIG VILLAGE, Harris, |
| Harris Ferry, Red River | *HAWKINS, Wood, 163 |   (2,334) . . . . . . . . . . . . . . . . 2,327 |
| Harrison, Foard |   (1,331). . . . . . . . . . . . . . . .1,337 | Heelstring, Ellis |
| Harrison, McLennan, . . . . . . . . . . 100 | Hawkins Prairie, Fannin | Heffron, Galveston |
| Harrison Chapel, Freestone | Hawkins Springs, Ellis | Hefner, Knox, . . . . . . . . . . . . . . . . . 5 |
| Harrisonia, Montague | Hawkinsville, Matagorda | Hegar, Walker |
| Harris Valley, La Salle | Hawkinsville, Tarrant | Hegar, Waller, . . . . . . . . . . . . . . . . NA |
| Harrisville, Bell | Hawks Chapel, Dallas | Heidelberg, Hidalgo, (1,586). . . 1,636 |
| *Harrold, Wilbarger, 8. . . . . . . . . 320 | Hawks Store, Anderson | *Heidenheimer, Bell, 8 . . . . . . . . .144 |
| Harrows, Matagorda | Hawley, Hunt | Heilbrun, Bowie |
| Harrys, Dallas | *HAWLEY, Jones, 72 (646) . . . . . . 591 | Heinzeville, DeWitt |
| *HART, Castro, 72 (1,198) . . . . . 1,148 | Hawley, Matagorda | Heise, Tom Green |
| Hart, Marion | Haws, Dallas | Helbig, Jefferson |
| Hart's, Bee | Hawthorn, Trinity | Helena, Karnes, . . . . . . . . . . . . . . .35 |
| Hartburg, Newton, . . . . . . . . . . . 275 | Hawthorne, Shelby | Helinora, Fort Bend |
| Hart Camp, Lamb, . . . . . . . . . . . . . 8 | Hawthorne, Walker, . . . . . . . . . . . .NA | Hellandville, Ellis |
| Hartex, Archer | Hay, Deaf Smith | Hellemans, Bexar |
| Hartland, Brooks | Hay, Eastland | Helmic, Trinity, . . . . . . . . . . . . . . . .86 |
| *Hartley, Hartley, 32 (441) . . . . . . 478 | Hayden, Van Zandt | Helms, Colorado |
| Hartley, Montgomery | Hayes, Jefferson | *HELOTES, Bexar, 368 |
| Hartman, Bowie | Hayes, Oldham |   (4,285) . . . . . . . . . . . . . . . . 4,645 |
| Harts Bluff, Red River | Hayes, Robertson | Help, Bosque |
| Hart Spur, Tarrant | Hayflat, Loving | Hembrie, Crockett |
| Harts Ranch, Atascosa | 'Hayflat, Winkler | Hemming, Cooke |
| Hartsville, Austin | Hayhurst, Grayson | Hemphill, Hays |
| Hartsville, Callahan | Haymond, Brewster | *HEMPHILL, Sabine, 206 |
| Hartzo, Marion | Haynes, Lamar |   (1,106) . . . . . . . . . . . . . . . . 1,080 |
| Harvard Switch, Camp, . . . . . . . . 48 | Haynesburgh, Hood | *HEMPSTEAD, Waller, |
| Harvester, Waller | Haynesville, Wichita, . . . . . . . . . . 60 |   314 (4,691). . . . . . . . . . . . 5,213 |
| Harvey, Brazos, . . . . . . . . . . . . . 310 | Haynie's Chapel, Travis-Bastrop | *HENDERSON, Rusk, |
| Harvey's Creek Settlement, Colorado | Haynie Flat, Burnet |   913 (11,273). . . . . . . . . . . 11,369 |
| Harvey's Mill, Red River | Haynie Flat, Travis, . . . . . . . . . . . .NA | Henderson Chapel, Concho |
| Harwell, Kaufman | Hayrick, Coke | Henderson Crossing, Comal |
| Harwell Point, Burnet, . . . . . . . . . 88 | HAYS, Hays, (233) . . . . . . . . . . . . 244 | Hendersonville, Anderson |
| *Harwood, Gonzales, 17 . . . . . . . 112 | Hays City, Hays | Hendricks, Hunt, . . . . . . . . . . . . . . NA |
| Hash Knife, Taylor | Haysland, Panola | Hendricks, Rusk |
| Hasima, Brazoria | Hays Station, Panola | Henkhaus, Lavaca, . . . . . . . . . . . NA |
| Hasima, Matagorda | Hayter, Tarrant | Henly, Hays, . . . . . . . . . . . . . . . . .55 |
| *HASKELL, Haskell, | Hay Valley, Coryell | Hennen, Gillespie |
|   211 (3,106) . . . . . . . . . . . . .3,084 | Hayward, Nacogdoches | Hennessey, Harris |
| Haskins Mill, Leon | Haywood, Jasper | Hennessy, Madison |
| Haslam, Shelby, . . . . . . . . . . . . . 101 | Haywood, Panola | Henning, Nacogdoches |
| *HASLET, Tarrant, 132 | Haywood, Rains | *HENRIETTA, Clay, 206 |
|   (1,134). . . . . . . . . . . . . . . .1,254 | Hazel, Hardeman |   (3,264) . . . . . . . . . . . . . . . . 3,267 |
| Hasse, Comanche, 1 . . . . . . . . . . 43 | Hazel, Montgomery | Henry, Bastrop |
| Hassell, Anderson | Hazel Chapel, Houston | Henry, Childress |
| Hassett, Polk | Hazeldell, Comanche, . . . . . . . . . .NA | Henry, Ellis |
| Hasslers, Coleman | Hazel Dell, Lamar | Henry, Freestone |
| Hastings, Brazoria | Heacker, Harris | Henry, Rusk-Gregg |
| Hastings, Kendall | Head, Mills | Henry, Swisher |
| Hastings, Titus | Head of California, Fisher | Henry's Chapel, Cherokee, . . . . . . 75 |
| Hatch, Kaufman | Head of Elm, Montague | Henry Chapel, Young |
| Hatchel, Runnels, . . . . . . . . . . . . . 25 | Headsville, Robertson, . . . . . . . . . .NA | Henry County Settlement, Polk |
| Hatcher's, Bee | Heald, Wheeler | Hensley, Jack |
| Hatchett Ferry, Cherokee | Heard, Galveston | Henson's, Cherokee |

| Town,County . . . . . . . . . . .Pop. 2002 | Town,County . . . . . . . . . . .Pop. 2002 | Town,County . . . . . . . . . . . Pop. 2002 |
|---|---|---|
| Henson's Creek, Coryell | Hickory Hill, Cass | Hilburn, Castro |
| Henze, Edwards | Hickory Hollow, Hunt | Hilburn, Eastland |
| Herbert, Fort Bend | Hickory Plains, Wise | Hilda, Guadalupe |
| Herbert, Mitchell | Hickory Point, Washington | Hilda, Mason |
| Hereford, Calhoun | Hickory Ridge, Sabine | Hill, Bastrop |
| *HEREFORD, Deaf Smith, | Hicks, Lee | Hill, Callahan |
| 805 (14,597) . . . . . . . . . . . 14,391 | Hicks, Shackelford | Hill, Matagorda |
| Herg, Hardeman | Hicks, Tarrant | Hill, Travis |
| Heritage, Hill | Hicksbaugh, Tyler | Hill's Ferry, Clay |
| Herman, Wise | Hickson, Coryell | Hillard, Carson |
| Hermans, Fort Bend | Hickston, Gonzales | Hillard, Dallas |
| Hermia, Kerr | *HICO, Hamilton, 107 | Hill City, Hood |
| Hermis, Gonzales | (1,341) . . . . . . . . . . . . . . . .1,347 | Hillcoat, Kinney |
| Hermitage, Cass | *HIDALGO, Hidalgo, 393 | HILL COUNTRY VILLAGE, Bexar, |
| Hermits Cove, Rains, . . . . . . . . . . 40 | (7,322) . . . . . . . . . . . . . . . .8,190 | (1,028) . . . . . . . . . . . . . . . . 1,121 |
| *Hermleigh, Scurry, 17 (393) . . . . 430 | Hidalgo, Washington | Hill Creek, Bosque |
| Hermosa, Reeves | Hidalgo Park, Hidalgo | Hillcrest, Colorado, . . . . . . . . . . . . 25 |
| Hermoson, McLennan | Hidden Acres [Lakshore Gardens-], | Hillcrest, Floyd |
| Herndon, Nolan | San Patricio, (720) . . . . . . . . . 762 | Hillcrest, Hunt |
| Hero, Mills | HIDEAWAY, Smith, (2,619) . . . . .2,672 | Hillcrest, Wichita |
| Heron, Montgomery | Hide Away, Brazoria, . . . . . . . . . . 69 | HILLCREST VILLAGE, Brazoria, |
| Herrera, Comal | Hide Bug, Motley | (722). . . . . . . . . . . . . . . . . . . .727 |
| Herring, Anderson | Hidesville, Lavaca | Hill Dale, Hopkins |
| Herring, Bell | Hidetown, Scurry | Hillebrand, Colorado |
| Herring, Oldham | Hide Town, Stonewall | Hillendahl, Harris |
| Herrington, Angelina | Hidetown, Wheeler | Hillger, Bastrop |
| Herrington, Brazos | Higginbotham, Gaines, . . . . . . . . .NA | Hillger, Fannin |
| Herron City, Young | Higgins, Jefferson | Hilliard's, Shelby |
| Hersfeld, Mason | *HIGGINS, Lipscomb, 25 | *Hillister, Tyler, 12 . . . . . . . . . . . . 200 |
| Herty, Angelina, . . . . . . . . . . . . . 605 | (425) . . . . . . . . . . . . . . . . . 414 | Hillje, Wharton, . . . . . . . . . . . . . . .51 |
| Herwig, Blanco | Higgins Gap, Lampasas | Hills, Lee, . . . . . . . . . . . . . . . . . . . 20 |
| Hess, Tom Green | High, Lamar, . . . . . . . . . . . . . . . . 55 | Hillsboro, Guadalupe |
| Hesse, Webb | High, Van Zandt | *HILLSBORO, Hill, 590 |
| Hester, Dimmit | Highbank, Falls, . . . . . . . . . . . . . . 68 | (8,232) . . . . . . . . . . . . . . . . 8,475 |
| Hester, Hardin | High Grove, Bastrop | Hillsborough, Bexar |
| Hester, Navarro, . . . . . . . . . . . . . . 35 | High Hill, Fayette, . . . . . . . . . . . . 116 | Hillsdale, Coryell |
| Hesterville, DeWitt | *High Island, Galveston, 12 . . . . . 500 | Hillsdale Pit, Nolan |
| Hetty, Hunt | Highland, Collin | Hillside, Culberson |
| Heugh, Johnson | Highland, Erath, . . . . . . . . . . . . . . 60 | Hillside, McLennan |
| Hewett's Store, Cooke | Highland, Galveston | Hills Prairie, Bastrop, . . . . . . . . . . 50 |
| *HEWITT, McLennan, 375 | Highland, Lamar | Hillspur, Lee |
| (11,085). . . . . . . . . . . . . . 11,548 | Highland, McLennan | Hilltop, Coryell |
| Hewitt, Titus | Highland, Montgomery | Hilltop, Frio, (300) . . . . . . . . . . . .311 |
| Hewsville, Smith | Highland, Randall | Hilltop, Gillespie |
| *Hext, Menard, 3 . . . . . . . . . . . . . . 73 | Highland, Scurry | Hill Top, Milam |
| Hey, Mason | Highland, Smith, . . . . . . . . . . . . . .NA | *Hilltop Lakes, Leon, . . . . . . . . . . 300 |
| Heynville, Harrison | Highland, Young | Hilltown, Denton |
| Heyser, Randall | Highland Bayou, Galveston, . . .1,209 | Hillville, Hunt |
| Hiawatha, Newton | HIGHLAND HAVEN, Burnet, | Hilo, Stephens |
| Hibbetsville, San Jacinto | (450) . . . . . . . . . . . . . . . . . 467 | HILSHIRE VILLAGE, Harris, |
| Hickey, Fort Bend | HIGHLAND PARK, Dallas, | (720). . . . . . . . . . . . . . . . . . . .737 |
| Hickey, Panola | (8,842) . . . . . . . . . . . . . . . .8,932 | Hilton, Cherokee |
| Hickey's Store, Panola | *Highlands, Harris, 273 | Hilton, Grayson |
| Hickman, Collin | (7,089) . . . . . . . . . . . . . . . .7,194 | Himmons, Erath |
| Hickmuntown, Travis | HIGHLAND VILLAGE, Denton, | Hinckley, Hunt |
| Hickok, Atascosa | (12,173) . . . . . . . . . . . . . .13,749 | Hinckley, Lamar, . . . . . . . . . . . . . . 40 |
| Hickory, Blanco | High Lonesome, Reagan | Hinde, Crockett |
| Hickory, Denton | Highpoint, Childress | Hindenburg, Atascosa |
| Hickory, Llano | High Point, Collin | Hindes, Atascosa, . . . . . . . . . . . . . 14 |
| Hickory Creek, Burnet | High Point, Grimes | Hindman, Dawson |
| Hickory Creek, Cooke | High Prairie, Fannin | Hinds', Brazoria |
| HICKORY CREEK, Denton, | High Prairie, Hays | Hiner, Parker |
| (2,078). . . . . . . . . . . . . . . . 2,392 | High Prairie, Houston | Hines, Ellis |
| Hickory Creek, Fannin | High Prairie, Madison | Hines, Johnson |
| Hickory Creek, Houston, . . . . . . . . 31 | Highsmith's, Bastrop | Hines,Taylor |
| Hickory Creek, Hunt, . . . . . . . . . .NA | Hight, Stephens | Hines, Walker |
| Hickory Creek, Limestone | Hightop, Cottle | Hinkles Ferry, Brazoria, . . . . . . . . 35 |
| Hickory Forrest, Guadalupe, . . . . 300 | Hightower, Liberty, . . . . . . . . . . . . 30 | Hippie Ridge, Wise |
| Hickory Grove, Delta | Hightower, Parker | Hiram, Kaufman, . . . . . . . . . . . . . . 34 |
| Hickory Grove, Freestone | Hightown, Polk | Hirams', Polk |
| Hickory Grove, Lamar | High Valley, San Saba | *HITCHCOCK, Galveston, |
| Hickory Grove, Limestone | Highway, Dallas | 292 (6,386). . . . . . . . . . . . . 6,628 |
| Hickory Grove, Milam | Highway, Grayson | Hitchland, Hansford, . . . . . . . . . . . 27 |
| Hickory Grove, Smith | Highway Village, Nueces | Hitson, Fisher |
| Hickory Grove, Travis | Hiland, Dallas | Hitson's Crossing, Palo Pinto |
| Hickory Grove, Van Zandt | Hilbigville, Bastrop | Hitt, Dallam |
| Hickory Grove, Washington | Hilburn, Atascosa | Hix, Burleson, . . . . . . . . . . . . . . . . 35 |

CITIES & TOWNS

| Town,County . . . . . . . . . . . Pop. 2002 | Town,County . . . . . . . . . . . Pop. 2002 | Town,County . . . . . . . . . . . Pop. 2002 |
|---|---|---|
| Hixon, Austin | Hollis, Madison | Hoopand Holler, Liberty |
| **Hoard, Wood,** . . . . . . . . . . . . . . . 45 | Hollis Prairie, Bosque | Hooper, Brown |
| Hoban, Reeves | Hollomon, Tyler | Hoot, Bowie |
| Hobart, Eastland | Holloway, Upshur | Hootsville, Cass |
| Hobart, Llano | Holloways Store, Walker | Hoover, Burnet |
| Hobbs, Delta | Hollub, Victoria | **Hoover, Gray,** . . . . . . . . . . . . . . . . . 5 |
| **Hobbs, Fisher,** . . . . . . . . . . . . . . . 91 | **Holly, Houston,** . . . . . . . . . . . . . . 112 | Hoover, Guadalupe |
| Hobbs, Van Zandt | Holly Acres, Angelina | **Hoover, Lamar,** . . . . . . . . . . . . . . . 20 |
| Hobbs Spur, Bell | **Holly Beach, Cameron,** . . . . . . . . .NA | Hoover's Gin, Hunt |
| Hobby, Fort Bend | Holly Grove, Freestone | Hoovers Valley, Burnet |
| Hobby's Mills, Cass | **Holly Grove, Polk,** . . . . . . . . . . . . . 20 | Hoovers Valley, Llano |
| Hobson, Franklin | Holly Springs, Anderson | Hope, Cooke |
| *Hobson, Karnes, 8 . . . . . . . . . . 135 | Holly Springs, Camp | **Hope, Lavaca,** . . . . . . . . . . . . . . . . 45 |
| Hobson, Van Zandt | **Holly Springs, Jasper,** . . . . . . . . . 50 | Hope, Ochiltree |
| *Hochheim, DeWitt, 2. . . . . . . . . . 70 | Holly Springs, Nacogdoches | Hope Church, Falls |
| Hochkirk, Williamson | Holly Springs, Robertson | Hopewell, Camp |
| Hochheim Prairie, DeWitt | Holly Springs, Van Zandt | **Hopewell, Franklin,** . . . . . . . . . . . . 35 |
| *Hockley, Harris, 160 . . . . . . . . . 300 | Holly Springs, Wood | **Hopewell, Houston,** . . . . . . . . . . . . 22 |
| Hockley City, Hockley | Hollywood, Atascosa | Hopewell [Dixon-], Houston, . . . . . 49 |
| Hodge, Burnet | **HOLLYWOOD PARK, Bexar,** | Hopewell, Lamar |
| Hodge, Tarrant | (2,983) . . . . . . . . . . . . . . . . . .3,021 | Hopewell, Leon-Madison |
| Hodge's Bend, Fort Bend | **Holman, Fayette,** . . . . . . . . . . . . . 116 | Hopewell, Montgomery |
| **Hodges, Jones,** . . . . . . . . . . . . . 150 | Holmes, Caldwell | Hopewell, Navarro |
| Hodges, Kendall | Holmes, Foard | **Hopewell, Red River,** . . . . . . . . . . 150 |
| Hodgins, Pecos | Holmes', Jasper | Hopewell, Smith |
| Hodgson, Bowie | Holmes, Panola | Hopewell, Somervell |
| Hoefer, Colorado | Holt, Mason | Hopewell, Upshur |
| Hoen, McLennan | Holt, San Saba | Hopewell, Williamson-Burnet |
| Hogan Acres, Johnson | Holt, Smith | Hopkins, Hemphill |
| **Hogansville, Rains,** . . . . . . . . . . 200 | Holton, Randall | Hopkins Store, Walker |
| Hog Creek, Bosque | Home, Coleman | Hopkinsville, DeWitt |
| Hog Creek, Comanche | Home, Red River | Hopkinsville, Gonzales |
| Hog Creek, McLennan | Home, Titus | Horace, Hutchinson |
| Hogeye, Bastrop | Home, Walker | Horace, Upshur |
| Hogeye, Bastrop | Home Creek, Coleman | Hord, Milam |
| Hog Eye, Gregg | Home Place, Karnes | Hord's Ridge, Dallas |
| Hogeye, Hunt | **Homer, Angelina,** . . . . . . . . . . . . 360 | Horger, Jasper |
| Hogeye, Jack | Homestead, Floyd | **HORIZON CITY, El Paso,** |
| Hogeye, Travis | **Homestead Meadows North,** | (5,233) . . . . . . . . . . . . . . . . . 5,942 |
| Hog Fork, Henderson | El Paso, (4,232) . . . . . . . . . .4,263 | Horn, Jones |
| Hogg, Borden | **Homestead Meadows South,** | Hornbeck, Sabine |
| **Hogg, Burleson,** . . . . . . . . . . . . . .NA | El Paso, (6,807) . . . . . . . . .7,009 | Horn Hill, Limestone |
| Hogg, Coke | Home Valley, Karnes | Horn Hill, Montague |
| Hogg, Ellis | Homewood, Leon | Hornsby, Travis |
| Hogg, Fannin | Hondo, Gillespie | **Hornsby Bend, Travis,** . . . . . . . . . . 20 |
| Hogg, Kaufman | Hondo, Llano | Horsehead, Rusk-Gregg |
| Hogg, Leon | *HONDO, Medina, 369 | Horseshoe, Erath |
| Hogg, Robertson | (7,897) . . . . . . . . . . . . . . . . .8,065 | **Horseshoe Bay, Llano-Burnet,** |
| Hogjaw, Cherokee | Hondo Cañon, Bandera | 55 (3,337) . . . . . . . . . . . . . . 3,399 |
| Hogtown, Eastland | Honea, Montgomery | Horse Shoe Bend, Cooke |
| Hogtown, Hemphill | Honest, Delta | Horse Shoe Bend, Parker |
| Hog Valley, Brown | Honey Bend, Young | Horse Valley, Bandera |
| Hohenstein, Mason | Honey Creek, Bandera | **Hortense, Polk,** . . . . . . . . . . . . . . . 20 |
| Hokah, Red River | Honey Creek, Comal | **Horton, Delta,** . . . . . . . . . . . . . . . . 25 |
| Holbrook, Bowie | Honey Creek, Hamilton | Horton, Jasper |
| Holcombs Store, Cherokee | Honey Creek, Llano | **Horton, Panola,** . . . . . . . . . . . . . . . NA |
| Holden, Limestone | Honey Creek, Mason | Hortonville, Karnes |
| Holden Springs, Van Zandt | *HONEY GROVE, Fannin, | Horton Town, Comal |
| Holder, Brown | 115 (1,746) . . . . . . . . . . . . . .1,791 | Hortonville, Red River |
| Holder's Gin, Bastrop | **Honey Island, Hardin,** . . . . . . . . . 401 | Hoshall, Angelina |
| Holford Prairie, Denton | Honey Springs, Dallas | Hoskins, Brazoria |
| **Holiday Beach, Aransas,** . . . . . . 1,000 | **Hood, Cooke,** . . . . . . . . . . . . . . . . 20 | Hoskins Junction, Brazoria |
| **HOLIDAY LAKES, Brazoria,** | Hoodville, Marion | Hostyn, Fayette |
| (1,095) . . . . . . . . . . . . . . . . .1,147 | Hooker, Hunt | Hot, Shelby |
| Holik, Waller | Hooker, Stonewall | Hot Springs, Brewster |
| Holiness, Hunt | Hooker's, Tyler | Hottentot, Fayette |
| *HOLLAND, Bell, 54 (1,102) . . . . 1,120 | **Hooker Ridge, Rains,** . . . . . . . . . 250 | Hot Wells, Harris |
| Holland, Hardin | Hookers, Rains | Hot Wells, Hudspeth |
| Holland Hill, San Saba | Hookerville, Burleson | Houghton, Fannin |
| Hollandale, Grimes | *HOOKS, Bowie, 131 | Houmont Park, Harris |
| **Holland Quarters, Panola,** . . . . . . . 40 | (2,973) . . . . . . . . . . . . . . . . .3,020 | House, Fort Bend |
| Holland Springs, Burnet | Hooks, Hidalgo | House's Ranch, Coke |
| Hollebeke, Andrews | Hooks Ferry, Red River | Houseville, Harris |
| *HOLLIDAY, Archer, 52 | Hooks Switch, Hardin | Housh, Palo Pinto |
| (1,632) . . . . . . . . . . . . . . . . .1,685 | Hooks Switch, Matagorda | Housley, Dallas |
| Holliman, Milam | Hooleyan, Hardeman | Houston, Anderson |
| Hollimon, Colorado | | **HOUSTON, Harris-Fort Bend-** |

| Town,County . . . . . . . . . . .Pop. 2002 | Town,County . . . . . . . . . . .Pop. 2002 | Town,County . . . . . . . . . . . Pop. 2002 |
|---|---|---|
| Montgomery, 123,141 | Hughes Town, Shelby | Hutton, DeWitt |
| (1,953,631) . . . . . . . . . 1,980,950 | Hughey, Gregg | HUXLEY, Shelby, (298) . . . . . . . . 303 |
| Houston Creek, Ellis | Hughlett, Armstrong | Hyatt, Tyler |
| Houston Heights, Harris | Hugo, Bell | Hyde, Kimble |
| Houston Terminals, Harris | Hugo, Hays | Hydesport, Mills |
| Hovey, Brewster-Pecos | Hulda, Gillespie | Hydro, Eastland |
| Howard, Archer | Hulen, Galveston | *Hye, Blanco, 5 . . . . . . . . . . . . . . 105 |
| Howard, Bell | Hulin, Denton | Hylton, Nolan, . . . . . . . . . . . . . . . . 6 |
| Howard, Eastland | Hulky, Franklin | Hyman, Mitchell |
| HOWARD, Ellis . . . . . . . . . . . . . NA | *Hull, Liberty, 23 . . . . . . . . . . . .1,800 | Hynds City, Montague |
| Howard, Freestone | Hull's Store, Panola | Hynesville, Refugio |
| Howard, Wichita | Hulldale, Schleicher | Hynson Springs, Harrison |
| Howard Lake, Frio | Hulltown, Shackelford | |
| Howards, Newton | Hulsey, Hopkins | I |
| Howardsville, Bosque | Hulver, Hall | *Iago [Boling-], Wharton, 68 |
| Howard Valley, Jack | *HUMBLE, Harris, 4,774 | (1,271) . . . . . . . . . . . . . . . . 1,240 |
| HOWARDWICK, Donley, (437) . . . 423 | (14,579) . . . . . . . . . . . . . .14,823 | Iatan, Mitchell |
| *HOWE, Grayson, 108 | Humble, Wilbarger | Iberis, Taylor |
| (2,478) . . . . . . . . . . . . . . . 2,570 | Humble Camp, Harris | Ibex, Shackelford |
| Howell, Jasper | Humble Camp, Kleberg | Icarian Colony, Denton |
| Howell's Store, Wise | Humble Camp, Refugio | Ida, Andrews |
| Howellville, Harris | Humble Colorado Camp, | Ida, Gaines |
| Howerton's Ranch, Kinney | Jim Hogg, . . . . . . . . . . . . . . . .NA | Ida, Grayson, . . . . . . . . . . . . . . . . 30 |
| Howe Settlement, Ellis | Humble Government Wells Camp, | Ida, Harris |
| Howland, Lamar, . . . . . . . . . . . . . 90 | Duval | Ida, Scurry |
| Howth, Waller, . . . . . . . . . . . . . . 65 | Humboldt, Hunt | Idaho, Collingsworth |
| Hoxie, Cass | Humbra, Motley | Idaho, Dawson |
| Hoxie, Palo Pinto | Hume, Cherokee | Idalia, Newton |
| Hoxie, Williamson, . . . . . . . . . . . . 50 | Hume, Travis | *IDALOU, Lubbock, 102 |
| Hoya, Nacogdoches | Humline, Bee | (2,157) . . . . . . . . . . . . . . . 2,166 |
| Hoyt, Wood | Humphrey, Hunt | Ideal, Sherman-Hutchinson |
| Hoyte, Milam, . . . . . . . . . . . . . . . 20 | *Hungerford, Wharton, 24 | Idlewild, Bexar |
| Hranice, Lee | (645) . . . . . . . . . . . . . . . . . . . 664 | Idlewild, Dallas |
| Huaca, Hays | Hunt, Hunt | Igie, Hopkins |
| Huajuco, La Salle | *Hunt, Kerr, 72. . . . . . . . . . . . . . . 708 | Iglesia Antigua [Bluetown-], |
| Hub, Parmer, . . . . . . . . . . . . . . . . 25 | Hunt, Webb | Cameron, (692) . . . . . . . . . . . 747 |
| Hubb, Cherokee | Hunter, Comal, . . . . . . . . . . . . . . 30 | Ike, Ellis, . . . . . . . . . . . . . . . . . . . 10 |
| Hubbard, Bowie, . . . . . . . . . . . . 269 | Hunter, Grayson | Ike, Live Oak |
| Hubbard, Coryell | Hunter's, Fort Bend | Ila, King |
| *HUBBARD, Hill, 95 (1,586) . . . . 1,626 | Hunter's Point, Harris | Ilah, Polk |
| Huber, Shelby, . . . . . . . . . . . . . . NA | Hunter's Store, Taylor | Ilka, Guadalupe |
| Hubert, San Patricio | HUNTERS CREEK VILLAGE, Harris, | Illinois Bend, Montague, . . . . . . . . 30 |
| Hucal, Somervell | (4,374) . . . . . . . . . . . . . . . . .4,456 | Illinois Colony, Clay |
| Huckabay, Erath, . . . . . . . . . . . . 150 | Hunters Retreat, Montgomery | Illinois Colony, Matagorda |
| Hud, Scurry | Huntersville, Travis | Illinois Torpedo Company, Eastland |
| Huddleston, Montague | *HUNTINGTON, Angelina, | Ima, Red River |
| Hudgins, Matagorda | 106 (2,068) . . . . . . . . . . . . .2,096 | Immermere, Erath |
| HUDSON, Angelina, (3,792). . . . 4,009 | Huntley, Orange | Imogene, Atascosa |
| Hudson, Carson | Huntoon, Ochiltree | IMPACT, Taylor, (39). . . . . . . . . . . . 34 |
| Hudson, Harris | Hunts Store, Leon | Imperial, Fort Bend |
| Hudson, Panola | *HUNTSVILLE, Walker, | *Imperial, Pecos, 17 (428). . . . . . . 432 |
| Hudson, Red River | 1,389 (35,078) . . . . . . . . . .35,682 | Imperial Valley, Travis |
| Hudson, Red River | Hurley, Bailey | Inadale, Scurry, . . . . . . . . . . . . . . . 8 |
| Hudson's Chapel, Cherokee | Hurley, Wood, . . . . . . . . . . . . . . . 30 | Inari, Refugio |
| Hudson Bend, Travis, (2,369) . . 2,423 | Hurley Station, Ellis | Independence, Cherokee |
| HUDSON OAKS, Parker, | Hurlwood, Lubbock, . . . . . . . . . . 115 | Independence, Hopkins |
| (1,637) . . . . . . . . . . . . . . . .1,686 | Hurnville, Clay, . . . . . . . . . . . . . . 15 | Independence, Martin |
| Hudsonville, Fannin | Huron, Hill | Independence, Smith |
| Hudsonville, Henderson | *HURST, Tarrant, 2,435 | Independence, Terrell |
| Huelster, Jeff Davis | (36,273) . . . . . . . . . . . . . . .36,895 | Independence, Washington, . . . . . 140 |
| Huff, Archer | Hurst, Tarrant | Independence Heights, Harris |
| Huff, Wichita | Hurstland, McLennan | Independent, Leon |
| Huff, Williamson | Hurstown, Shelby, . . . . . . . . . . . .NA | Index, Bowie |
| Huffines, Cass, . . . . . . . . . . . . . . 140 | Hurst Springs, Coryell, . . . . . . . . . 8 | Index, Van Zandt |
| *Huffman, Harris, 262. . . . . . . . . .NA | Hustler, Eastland | Index, Wheeler |
| Huff Valley, Wise | Hutcherson, Wilbarger | India, Ellis, . . . . . . . . . . . . . . . . . . 12 |
| Hufsmith, Harris, . . . . . . . . . . . . 250 | Hutcheson, Walker | India, Polk |
| Huggins, Clay | Hutchings, Runnels | India, Reeves |
| Hughes', Cass | Hutchingsville, Titus | Indianapolis, Mason-Menard |
| Hughes, Galveston | *HUTCHINS, Dallas, 141 | Indian Camp Springs, Trinity |
| Hughes, Irion | (2,805) . . . . . . . . . . . . . . . .2,799 | Indian Creek, Brown |
| Hughes, Newton | Hutchison's Ranch, Kinney | Indian Creek, Fayette |
| Hughes, Tom Green | Hutson, Brown | Indian Creek, Smith, . . . . . . . . . . 300 |
| Hughes, Victoria | *HUTTO, Williamson, 221 | Indian Creek, Tarrant |
| Hughes' Store, Mills | (1,250) . . . . . . . . . . . . . . . .2,284 | Indian Gap, Hamilton, . . . . . . . . . . 36 |
| *HUGHES SPRINGS, Cass, | Hutto's Grove, Polk | Indian Grove, Grayson |
| 121 (1,856) . . . . . . . . . . . . . 1,846 | Hutton, Archer | Indian Harbor Estates, Hood, . . 2,620 |

CITIES & TOWNS

| Town,County ..........Pop. 2002 | Town,County ..........Pop. 2002 | Town,County ..........Pop. 2002 |
|---|---|---|
| **Indian Hill, Newton,** ........... **NA** | *Ironwood, Liberty* | *Jackwood, Falls* |
| **Indian Hills, Hidalgo,** | *Irvin, Hopkins* | *Jacob's Well, Hays* |
| (2,036)................. 2,061 | *Irvine, Navarro* | **Jacobia, Hunt,** ............... 60 |
| *Indian Hills, Llano* | ***IRVING, Dallas, 9,287** | *Jacobs, Cottle* |
| **INDIAN LAKE, Cameron,** | (191,615) ............. 194,746 | *Jacobs, Nacogdoches* |
| (541) .................. 545 | *Irwin, Dallam* | *Jacobs, Rusk* |
| *Indian Mound, Denton* | *Irwin, Rusk* | *Jagoe, Denton* |
| *Indian Mound, Young* | *Irwin's Chapel, Rusk* | *Jahuey Ranch, La Salle* |
| *Indian Oaks, Tarrant* | *Isaac, Reagan* | *Jake, Angelina* |
| **Indianola, Calhoun,** .......... 200 | *Isaacs, Hemphill* | *Jakehamon, Comanche* |
| *Indian Point, Calhoun* | *Isabel, Webb* | **Jakes Colony, Guadalupe,** ....... 60 |
| **Indian Rock, Upshur,** .......... 45 | *Isaca, Red River* | *Jakin, Shelby* |
| *Indian Spring, Polk* | *Isbelle, Shelby* | **JAMAICA BEACH, Galveston,** |
| *Indian Springs, Dallas* | *Iser, Hudspeth* | (1,075) ................. 1,094 |
| **Indian Springs, Polk,** ......... 250 | **Isla, Sabine,**.................. 29 | *James, Houston* |
| **Indio, Presidio,**............... **NA** | *Islana, Madison* | *James, Nolan* |
| *Indio, Zavala* | *Island, Galveston* | *James, Potter* |
| *Indpark, Brazos* | *Island, Limestone* | **James, Shelby,** .............. **NA** |
| ***INDUSTRY, Austin, 42 (304)** .... 300 | *Island, Madison* | *James, Upshur* |
| ***Inez, Victoria, 42 (1,787)** ...... 1,896 | *Isle Haute, Galveston* | *Jameson, Grayson* |
| *Inge, Uvalde* | *Islitas, Webb* | **Jamestown, Newton,** ........... 70 |
| *Ingemal, Dimmit* | *Isom, Hutchinson* | **Jamestown, Smith,** ............. 75 |
| *Ingersoll, Bowie* | *Israel, Freestone* | *Jamestown, Smith* |
| *Ingerton, Hutchinson* | **Israel, Polk,** .................. 25 | *Jamestown, Tarrant* |
| *Ingleside, Panola* | ***ITALY, Ellis, 71 (1,993)** ....... 2,071 | *Jamesville, Fisher* |
| ***INGLESIDE, San Patricio,** | ***ITASCA, Hill, 77 (1,503)** ...... 1,544 | *Janes, Bailey* |
| 225 (9,388) ............. 9,516 | *Iuka, Atascosa* | *Janes, Lamb* |
| **INGLESIDE-ON-THE-BAY,** | *Iuka, La Salle* | *Janet, Wharton* |
| San Patricio, (659) ......... 679 | **Ivan, Stephens,**............... 15 | *Janice, Gonzales* |
| *Ingleside Park, San Patricio* | *Ivanhoe, Bexar* | *Janson, Kaufman* |
| *Inglewood, Lamar* | ***Ivanhoe, Fannin, 16.** .......... 110 | *Janus, Nolan* |
| ***INGRAM, Kerr, 188 (1,740)** .... 1,773 | *Ivanhoe, Yoakum* | *Japan, Montgomery* |
| *Ingram, Randall* | *Iverson, Hill* | *Japonica, Kerr* |
| *Ingrams Prairie, Fayette* | *Ives', Lavaca* | *Jaques Spur, Grayson* |
| *Inkum, Taylor* | *Ivory, Freestone* | *Jara China, Hidalgo* |
| *Inman, Moore* | *Ivy, Angelina* | *JA Ranch, Armstrong* |
| *International, Milam* | *Ivy, Hale* | **Jardin, Hunt,** ................. 22 |
| *Inwood, Dallas* | ***Izoro, Lampasas,**............. 17 | ***JARRELL, Williamson, 65** |
| *Inwood, San Patricio* | | (1,319) ................. 1,384 |
| ***Iola, Grimes, 36.**............. 331 | **J** | *Jarvis, Anderson* |
| *Iola, Kerr* | *J.P. Rodriguez Settlement, Bandera* | *Jarvis, Liberty* |
| *Iola, Van Zandt* | *Jabco, Hood* | *Jarvis, Smith* |
| *Iolanthe, Sterling* | *Jacinto, Rusk* | *Jarvis, Wood* |
| *Iona, Parker* | ***JACINTO CITY, Harris,** | *Jasmine, Hardin* |
| *Ioni, Anderson* | (10,302) ............... 10,343 | *Jasmine, Victoria* |
| *Ioni, Palo Pinto* | *Jacintoport, Harris* | *Jason, Trinity* |
| *Iota, Jones* | *Jack, Borden* | ***JASPER, Jasper, 831** |
| **IOWA COLONY, Brazoria, (804).. 799** | *Jack, Haskell* | (8,247) ................ 8,295 |
| *Iowa Colony, Matagorda* | *Jack Camp, Polk* | *Jasper Mills, Jasper* |
| ***IOWA PARK, Wichita,** | *Jacks, Newton* | *Java, Cherokee* |
| 311 (6,431) ............. 6,473 | ***JACKSBORO, Jack, 276** | *Jay, Upshur* |
| *Iowa Point, Clay* | (4,533) ................. 4,535 | *Jaybart, Cass* |
| *Ira, Goliad* | *Jackson, Brazos* | *Jaybird, Panola* |
| *Ira, Red River* | *Jackson, Colorado* | *Jayell, Callahan* |
| ***Ira, Scurry, 25** ............... 250 | *Jackson, Hill* | *Jaynes, McLennan* |
| ***IRAAN, Pecos, 66 (1,238)** ..... 1,211 | *Jackson, Marion* | *Jayray, Colorado* |
| *Irby, Haskell* | *Jackson, McLennan* | ***JAYTON, Kent, 32 (513)** ........ 508 |
| ***IREDELL, Bosque, 14 (360)** .... 380 | *Jackson, Montgomery* | *J Bob, Brown* |
| **Ireland, Coryell,** ............... 60 | **Jackson, Shelby,**............... **NA** | **Jean, Young,** ................. 110 |
| *Ireland, Frio* | **Jackson, Smith,** ............... **NA** | *Jeannetta, Harris* |
| ***Irene, Hill, 3** ................. 160 | *Jackson, Stonewall* | *Jeannette, Jack* |
| *Irion City, Irion* | *Jackson, Swisher* | **Jeddo, Bastrop,**................ 75 |
| *Iris, Trinity* | **Jackson, Van Zandt,**............ **NA** | *Jeddo, Dallas* |
| *Irish Creek, DeWitt* | *Jackson, Zavala* | ***JEFFERSON, Marion,** |
| *Irish Ridge, Kaufman* | *Jackson & Ake Ranch, Schleicher* | 350 (2,024). ............. 2,040 |
| *Irish Settlement, Milam* | *Jackson's Chapel, Delta* | *Jefferson, Orange* |
| *Irishtown, Brazos* | *Jackson's Crossing, Coryell* | *Jeffries, Wise* |
| *Irma, Brown* | *Jackson's Gin, Fannin* | *Jeffry, Hutchinson* |
| *Iron Bluff, Morris* | *Jackson's Gin, Jack* | *Jehoy, Travis* |
| *Iron Bridge, Gregg* | *Jackson's Gin, Williamson* | *Jellico, Tarrant* |
| *Iron Clad, Limestone* | *Jackson Chapel, Henderson* | *Jena, Falls* |
| *Iron Creek, Waller* | *Jackson School House, Dallas* | **Jenkins, Morris,**................ 350 |
| *Iron Mountain, Caldwell* | ***JACKSONVILLE, Cherokee,** | *Jenkins' Store, Tarrant* |
| *Iron Mountain, Rusk* | 978 (13,868) ........... 13,995 | *Jenkins Prairie, Bastrop* |
| *Ironosa, San Augustine* | *Jacksonville, Hopkins* | *Jenkins Ranch, Mason* |
| *Iron Springs, Harrison* | *Jacksonville, Montague* | **Jennings, Lamar,**............... 85 |
| **Ironton, Cherokee,**........... 110 | *Jacksonville, Washington* | *Jennings, Lamar* |

| Town,County ........Pop. 2002 | Town,County ........Pop. 2002 | Town,County ........Pop. 2002 |
|---|---|---|
| Jennings Lake, Cass | Joiel, Winkler | Jud, Lynn |
| Jensen, Frio | Joiner, Fayette | Jude, Oldham |
| Jerehart, Palo Pinto | *Joinerville, Rusk, 2 ......... 140 | Judea, Marion |
| Jericho, Donley | Joliet, Caldwell, ............. 192 | Judkins, Ector |
| Jericho, Shelby | JOLLY, Clay, (188) ........... 187 | *Judson, Gregg, 5 ............ 650 |
| *Jermyn, Jack, 3 ............. 75 | Jollyville, Williamson-Travis, | Julia, Borden |
| Jerrys Quarters, Washington | (15,813) ............... 15,920 | Julia, Nueces |
| Jersey, Caldwell | Jolo, Henderson | Julia, Wilbarger |
| JERSEY VILLAGE, Harris, | Jonah, Williamson, ........... 60 | Julian, Houston |
| (6,880). ............... 7,207 | Jones, Fayette | Julia Pens, Victoria |
| Jerusalem, Brazoria | Jones, Hood | Julietta, Floyd |
| Jerusalem, Freestone | Jones, Mills | Juliff, Fort Bend, ............. NA |
| Jessamine, Kerr | Jones', Panola | Julliard, Potter |
| Jessie, Hill | Jones, Van Zandt | Jumbo, Cass |
| Jessie, Kaufman | *Jonesboro, Coryell-Hamilton, | Jumbo, Castro, ................ 3 |
| Jester, Navarro | 18. ................... 200 | Jumbo, Panola, .............. NA |
| Jetero, Harris | Jonesborough, Red River | Junction, Coleman |
| Jetie, Bowie | Jones Chapel, Cass | *JUNCTION, Kimble, 224 |
| Jewell, Eastland | Jones City, Jones | (2,618) ............... 2,622 |
| Jewell, McLennan | Jones City, Kinney | June, Rusk |
| Jewell, Waller | Jones Colony, Lee | Junior, Guadalupe |
| *JEWETT, Leon, 100 (861) ..... 872 | JONES CREEK, Brazoria, | Junker's Cove, Harris |
| Jiba, Kaufman, ............... NA | (2,130) ............... 2,082 | Juno, Val Verde, ............. 10 |
| Jim Hogg, Wood | Jones Creek, Wharton | Jupiter, Coke |
| Jimkurn, Stephens | Jonesdale, Wichita | Jury, Bowie |
| Jimmie's Creek, Comanche | Jones Gin, Bell | Justiceburg, Garza, 2 .......... 76 |
| Jim Ned, Brown | Jones Gin, Kaufman | *JUSTIN, Denton, 178 |
| Jimned, Wise | Jones Mound, Frio | (1,891) ............... 2,190 |
| Jim Rogers, Cameron | Jones Prairie, Milam, .......... 35 | |
| Jimtown, Burleson | Jones Prairie, Polk | **K** |
| Jim Town, Dallas | Jones Ranch, Jim Hogg | K-Bar Ranch, Jim Wells, (350) ... 376 |
| Jim Town, Sabine | Jones School House, Houston | Ka, Dallas |
| Jines, Ochiltree | Jones Store, Grimes | Kadane Corner, Wichita |
| Jink, Coryell | Jonestown, Travis | Kaffir, Schleicher |
| *JOAQUIN, Shelby, 55 (925)..... 927 | *JONESTOWN, Travis, | Kaffir, Swisher |
| Jo Bailey, Floyd | (1,681) ............... 1,746 | Kaleta, San Patricio |
| Joe, Grayson | Jonesville, Angelina | Kalgary, Crosby, ............. 70 |
| Joe, Houston | Jonesville, Dallas | *Kamay, Wichita, 7. ........... 642 |
| Joe, Montague | *Jonesville, Harrison, 12 ....... 28 | Kamey, Calhoun, ............. 25 |
| Joe's Branch, Dallas | Joni, Throckmorton | Kanawha, Red River, .......... 149 |
| Joel, Deaf Smith | Joplin, Jack, .................. NA | Kane, Hidalgo |
| Joe Lee, Bell, ................ 2 | Joppa, Burnet, ............... 34 | Kane, Scurry-Mitchell |
| Joentz, Liberty | Jordan, Bastrop | Karen, Montgomery |
| John, Travis | Jordan, Brazoria | Karlshaven, Calhoun |
| John's, Chambers | Jordan, Collin | *Karnack, Harrison, 55 ........ 775 |
| John Adams' Mill ,Sabine | Jordan, Concho | *KARNES CITY, Karnes, |
| Johnfarris, Floyd | Jordan, DeWitt | 154 (3,457). ........... 3,428 |
| Johnnie, Lamar | Jordan, Walker | Karney, Gonzales |
| Johnson, Jasper | Jordan's Saline, Van Zandt | Karney, Lavaca |
| Johnson, Montgomery | Jordan Springs, Brown | Karon, Live Oak, .............. 25 |
| Johnson, Somervell | Jordans Store, Shelby, ......... NA | Kasoga, Knox |
| Johnson, Terry, .............. 21 | Joseph, Waller | Kasota, Armstrong |
| Johnson's Bluff, San Jacinto | *JOSEPHINE, Collin, | Kate, Delta |
| Johnson's Chapel, Stonewall | 4 (594). ................ 641 | Katemcy, Mason, ............. 90 |
| Johnson's Chapel, Walker | Joseway, Kendall | Katherine, Kenedy |
| Johnson's Gin, Navarro | *JOSHUA, Johnson, 322 | Kathleen, Brown |
| Johnson's Institute, Hays | (4,528). .............. 4,835 | Katula, Nolan |
| Johnson's Mill, Erath | Josie, Tyler | *KATY, Harris-Waller-Fort Bend, |
| Johnson's Point, Kaufman | Josselet, Haskell | 3,995 (11,775) ......... 12,909 |
| Johnson Chapel, Upshur | Josserand, Trinity, ............ 29 | *KAUFMAN, Kaufman, |
| *JOHNSON CITY, Blanco, | Jot-Em-Down, Delta, .......... 10 | 506 (6,490). ........... 7,246 |
| 158 (1,191) ............ 1,262 | Jouett's, Fannin | Kay, Trinity |
| Johnson Creek, Marion | *JOURDANTON, Atascosa, | Kayare, Cameron |
| Johnson Mines, Erath | 167 (3,732) ............ 3,890 | Kayser's Prairie, Trinity |
| Johnsons, Lamar | Joy, Cass | Kayville, Falls |
| Johnsons Station, Tarrant | Joy, Clay, ................... 100 | Keahey, Liberty |
| Johnsonton, Van Zandt | Joy, Smith | Keck, Gonzales |
| Johnsonville, Gregg | Joyce, Bowie | Keechi, Freestone |
| Johnsonville, Williamson | Joyce, Harris | Keechi, Jack |
| Johnstone, Val Verde | Joyce, Webb | Keechi, Leon, ................ 67 |
| Johnston Store, Nacogdoches | Joys Store, Kerr | Keechil, Freestone |
| Johnstonville, Upshur | Jozye, Madison | Keefer, Montgomery |
| Johnstown, Travis | Juanita, Loving | Keeler, Johnson |
| Johnsue, Waller | Juan Saenz, Nueces | Keenan, Montgomery |
| Johnsville, Erath, ............. 25 | Juarez [Las Palmas-], Zapata, | *KEENE, Johnson, 109 |
| Johntown, Red River, ........ 175 | (1,666) ............... 1,649 | (5,003) ............... 5,268 |
| John Tucker, Erath | Jud, Haskell, ................. 40 | Keeney's, San Saba |

| Town,County | Pop. 2002 |
|---|---|

*Keeran, Victoria*
**Keeter, Wise,** ................ NA
*Keisler, Montgomery*
*Keith, Franklin*
**Keith, Grimes,** ............... 50
*Keith, Tom Green*
*Keith Lake, Jefferson*
*Keithton, Jasper*
*Kelat, Navarro*
*Keliehor, Williamson*
**\*KELLER, Tarrant, 1,153**
   **(27,345)** ............. 31,115
**Kellers Corner, Cameron,** ...... 123
**Kellerville, Wheeler,** ........... 50
*Kelley, Angelina*
*Kelley's, Walker*
*Kellner, Waller*
**Kellogg, Hunt,** ................ NA
*Kellogg's, Robertson*
*Kellum's Springs, Grimes*
*Kelly, Bexar*
*Kelly, Carson*
*Kelly, Collin*
*Kelly, Uvalde*
*Kelly Store, San Jacinto*
**Kellyville, Marion,** ............. NA
*Kelm, Navarro*
*Kelow, Walker*
*Kelsay, Starr*
**Kelsey, Upshur,** ............... 50
*Kelso, Deaf Smith*
*Kelsoville, Bell*
**Kelton, Wheeler,** .............. 20
*Keltys, Angelina*
**\*KEMAH, Galveston,**
   **416 (2, 330).** ............. 2,425
**\*KEMP, Kaufman, 349**
   **(1,133).** ................. 1,200
*Kemp City, Wichita*
**Kemper City, Victoria,** ......... 16
**\*KEMPNER, Lampasas,**
   **67 (1,004)** .............. 1,070
*Kemp Newby, Wichita*
*Ken, Hidalgo*
**\*Kendalia, Kendall, 13** ......... 76
*Kendall, Grayson*
*Kendall Valley, Comal*
**\*KENDLETON, Fort Bend,**
   **11 (466).** ................ 466
*Kendrick's, San Augustine*
**\*KENEDY, Karnes, 212**
   **(3,487).** ................. 3,462
*Kenedy, Karnes*
**KENEFICK, Liberty, (667)** ...... 694
*Kenelm, Henderson*
*Kenerly, Jasper*
**\*KENNARD, Houston, 19**
   **(317)** ................... 321
*Kennebunk, Hale*
**\*KENNEDALE, Tarrant,**
   **389 (5,850)** ............. 6,191
*Kenner, Matagorda*
*Kenneth, Walker*
**\*Kenney, Austin, 3** ........... 200
*Kennon City, Wilson*
*Keno, Liberty*
**Kenser, Hunt,** ................ NA
**Kensing, Delta,** ............... 35
*Kent, Bosque*
**\*Kent, Culberson, 5** ........... 60
*Kent, Houston*
*Kenton, Bastrop*
*Kentuck, Live Oak*
**Kentucky Town, Grayson,** ....... 20
*Kerby, Hill*
**\*KERENS, Navarro, 91**
   **(1,681).** ................. 1,739

| Town,County | Pop. 2002 |
|---|---|

**\*KERMIT, Winkler, 262**
   **(5,714)** ................. 5,586
*Kern, Polk*
*Kerr, Collin*
*Kerr, Williamson*
*Kerr's, Jackson*
*Kerrdale, Newton*
**Kerrick, Dallam, 7** ............. 60
*Kerr Settlement, Washington*
**\*KERRVILLE, Kerr,**
   **2,098 (20,425)** .......... 20,878
**Kerrville South, Kerr,** ........ 6,600
*Kertman, Angelina*
*Kesler's Bluffs, Colorado*
*Kessler, Collingsworth*
*Ketch, Stephens*
*Kevin, Liberty*
**Key, Dawson,** ................ 20
*Key, Grayson*
*Key, Grimes*
*Key, Navarro*
**Key Allegro, Aransas,** ........ 600
*Key Stone, Frio*
*Key West, Montague*
*Keziah, Madison*
**Kiam, Polk,** ................... NA
*Kiber, Brazoria*
**Kicaster, Wilson,** ............. 100
*Kickapoo, Anderson*
*Kickapoo, Polk*
*Kickapoo Springs, Concho*
*Kickapoo Springs, Edwards*
*Kidd, Burleson*
*Kidd's Mills, Leon*
*Kiel, Washington*
*Kiesling, Tom Green*
**\*Kildare, Cass, 1** .............. 49
*Kilgore, Goliad*
**\*KILGORE, Gregg-Rusk,**
   **1,116 (11, 301)** ......... 11,524
**\*KILLEEN, Bell, 3,268**
   **(86, 911)** .............. 91,852
*Killen, Shelby*
*Killingsworth, Gregg*
*Kilowatt, Orange*
*Kilraven, Cherokee*
*Kimball, Bosque*
*Kimble, Johnson*
*Kimbleville, Kimble*
*Kimbro, Travis*
*Kincaid, Taylor*
*Kincaid, Uvalde*
*Kincheloe's Crossing, Wharton*
*Kincheloe's Store, Uvalde*
*Kincheonville, Travis*
*Kinder, Briscoe*
**King, Coryell,** ................ 25
*King's Store, Nacogdoches*
*Kingola, Wilbarger*
**King Ranch Headquarters,**
   **Kleberg,** ................ 191
*Kings, Val Verde*
*Kingsboro, Kaufman*
**\*Kingsbury, Guadalupe,**
   **40 (652).** ................ 688
*Kings Crossing, Denton*
*Kings Farm, Cass*
**\*Kingsland, Llano, 239**
   **(4,584).** ................. 4,604
*Kingsley, Dallas*
*Kingsmere, Borden*
*Kings Mill, Gray*
*Kings Point, Grayson*
*King Spring, Burnet*
**Kingston, Hunt,** ............... 140
*Kingsville, Bowie*
*Kingsville, Frio*

| Town,County | Pop. 2002 |
|---|---|

**\*KINGSVILLE, Kleberg,**
   **987 (25,575).** .......... 25,427
*Kingsville, Wise*
**\*Kingsville Naval Air Sta.,**
   **Kleberg,** ................ NA
**Kingtown, Nacogdoches,** ....... NA
*Kingwillow, Navarro*
*Kingwood, Harris*
*Kinkead, Galveston*
**Kinkler, Lavaca,** ............... 75
*Kinley's, Bexar*
*Kinlock, Panola*
*Kinney, Kinney*
*Kinney, Rusk*
*Kinney Point, Franklin*
*Kinwood, Harris*
**Kiomatia, Red River,** ........... 61
*Kiowa, Lipscomb*
*Kipfer, Cameron*
*Kipling, Kaufman*
**KIRBY, Bexar, (8,673)** ........ 8,761
*Kirby, Edwards*
*Kirby Chapel, Waller*
*Kirby Town, Hardin*
**\*KIRBYVILLE, Jasper,**
   **195 (2,085).** ............. 2,098
*Kirk, Bexar*
**Kirk, Limestone,** ............... 10
*Kirk, Smith*
*Kirkham, Liberty*
**Kirkland, Childress, 1** .......... 102
*Kirkpatrickville, Robertson*
*Kirksey, Hansford*
*Kirkwood, Bell*
*Kirkwood, Harris*
*Kirkwood, Tarrant*
*Kirkwood, Wood*
**Kirtley, Fayette,** ................ 43
**\*KIRVIN, Freestone, 8 (122)** ..... 121
*Kishi Colony, Orange*
*Kit, Dallas*
*Kitalou, Lubbock*
*Kitsee Ridge, Hunt*
*Kittie, Live Oak*
**Kittrell, Walker,** ............... 126
*Klattenhoff, Tom Green*
*Kleberg, Dallas*
*Kleberg, Jim Wells*
**Klein, Harris,** ................. NA
*Klimek, Colorado*
**Klondike, Dawson,** ............. 50
**\*Klondike, Delta, 11** ........... 135
*Klondike, Grimes*
*Klondike, Newton*
*Klumco, Liberty*
**Klump, Washington,** ........... NA
**Knapp, Scurry,** ................ 10
*Kneitz, Fort Bend*
**\*Knickerbocker, Tom Green, 1** .... 50
*Knight, Bowie*
**Knight, Polk,** .................. NA
*Knight's Ranch, Travis*
*Knight Spur, Dallas*
**\*Knippa, Uvalde, 16 (739)** ....... 769
*Knittel, Burleson*
*Knob, Parker*
*Knob, San Saba*
**Knobbs Springs, Lee,** ........... 20
*Knob Hill, Denton*
*Knobs, Bell*
*Knobview, Callahan*
*Knolle, Nueces*
*Knollee Nueces, Jim Wells*
**KNOLLWOOD, Grayson, (375)** ... 382
*Knollwood, Smith*
*Knott, Foard*
**\*Knott, Howard, 9** ............. 685

| Town,County .......... Pop. 2002 | Town,County .......... Pop. 2002 | Town,County .......... Pop. 2002 |
|---|---|---|
| Know, Upshur | La Bahia, Washington | Laird, Montgomery |
| Knox, Collin | La Bahia, Washington | Laird, Tyler |
| Knox, Ellis | Laban, Colorado | *Laird Hill, Rusk, 8 ........... 405 |
| Knox, Falls | Labatt, Wilson | La Isla, El Paso,............... 29 |
| Knox, Hamilton | LaBelle, Jefferson, | Lajitas, Brewster, ............. 75 |
| *KNOX CITY, Knox, 75 | *La Blanca, Hidalgo, 8 | *LA JOYA, Hidalgo, 60 |
|   (1,219)................. 1,161 |   (2,351)................. 2,438 |   (3,303) ................. 3,589 |
| Knoxville, Cherokee | La Casa, Stephens, | La Junta, Parker |
| Kodal, Henderson | *La Casita-Garciasville, Starr, | La Junta de los Rios, Presidio |
| Kodol, Hidalgo |   13 (2,177) ............... 2,287 | Lake, Robertson |
| Koerth, Lavaca, .............. 45 | Laceola, Madison, ............ 10 | Lake, Trinity |
| Kohrville, Harris | La Cerda, Nacogdoches | Lake, Wise |
| Kokernot, DeWitt | Laceyville, Nacogdoches | Lake Arrowhead, Clay, ........ 250 |
| Kokernot, Gonzales | Lache's Mill, Upshur | LAKE BRIDGEPORT, Wise, |
| Kokomo, Eastland,............. 25 | Lackawanna, Eastland |   (372)..................... 390 |
| Kola, Childress | *Lackland Air Force Base, Bexar, | Lake Brownwood, Brown, |
| Kola, Clay |   (7,123)................. 7,096 |   (1,694) ............... 1,716 |
| Kolbs, Milam | Lacoma, Cameron | Lake Charlotte, Chambers |
| Kolls, Bell | La Copita, Starr | Lake Charlotte, Liberty |
| Komensky, Lavaca, ........... NA | *LA COSTE, Medina, 33 | Lake Cisco, Eastland,......... 105 |
| Konohasset, Glasscock |   (1,255)................. 1,306 | LAKE CITY, San Patricio, |
| Koocksville, Mason | La Coyota, Brewster |   (526)..................... 523 |
| Koonce, Shelby | Lacus, Gray | *Lake Creek, Delta, 9........... 60 |
| Kopernik Shores, Cameron, ..... 26 | Lacy, Burnet | Lake Creek, Donley |
| Koppe, Brazos | Lacy, Cass | Lake Creek, McLennan |
| *Kopperl, Bosque, 17 ......... 225 | Lacy, Trinity, .................. 44 | Lake Crockett Estates, Fannin, .... 5 |
| Korf, Orange | Lacy, Young | *LAKE DALLAS, Denton, |
| Kosarek, Brazos | LACY-LAKEVIEW, McLennan, |   284 (6,166)............. 6,710 |
| Kosciusko, Wilson ........... 390 |   (5,764)................. 5,834 | Lake Dunlap, Guadalupe,..... 1,000 |
| Kosmos, Aransas | Ladd, Liberty | Lake Fork, Hopkins |
| *KOSSE, Limestone, 24 (497) ... 507 | Ladig, Austin | Lake Fork, Wood |
| Kossuth, Anderson | *LADONIA, Fannin, 32 (667)..... 674 | Lake Fork, Wood |
| Kostoryz, Nueces | Lafayette, Dallas | Lake Gardens, Tom Green |
| *KOUNTZE, Hardin, 233 | Lafayette, Lamar | Lake Grove, Grimes |
|   (2,115)................. 2,150 | LaFayette, Upshur, ............ 80 | *Lakehills, Bandera, (4,668) ... 4,856 |
| Koury, Angelina | *LA FERIA, Cameron, 168 | *LAKE JACKSON, Brazoria, |
| Kovar, Bastrop,............... NA |   (6,115)................. 6,336 |   1,141 (26,386).......... 26,970 |
| Krajina, Lavaca | La Feria North, Cameron, | Lake James, Hidalgo |
| Krauseland, Bell |   (168) ................... 167 | Lake June, Dallas |
| Krause Settlement, Comal | Lafitte, Colorado | Lake Kiowa, Cooke, (1,883) ... 1,903 |
| Krausse, Willacy | Lafitte Grove, Galveston | Lakeland, Gonzales |
| *KRESS, Swisher, 41 (826) ..... 839 | Lafruta, San Patricio | Lakeland, Liberty |
| Kreutsberg, Kendall | Lagarto, Live Oak, ............ 735 | Lakeland, Montgomery |
| Kriegel, Wharton | La Gloria, Cameron | Lakeland, Nacogdoches |
| Kristenstad, Hood | La Gloria, Jim Wells, | Lake Leon, Eastland, ........... 75 |
| Krohne, Burleson | La Gloria, Maverick | Lake Mills, Collin |
| Krub, Angelina | La Gloria, Starr,............... 102 | Lakenon, Hill |
| Krueger's Store, Blanco | Lago, Cameron, (246)......... 242 | Lake Nueces, Uvalde,.......... 60 |
| Krug, Washington | Lagonda, Midland | Lake Pauline, Hardeman |
| Kruger, Kaufman | *LAGO VISTA, Travis, 105 | Lake Placid, Brazos |
| KRUGERVILLE, Denton, |   (4,507)................. 4,762 | Lake Placid, Guadalupe, ....... 400 |
|   (903)................... 1,021 | La Grange, Fannin | Lakeport, Freestone |
| *KRUM, Denton, 144 (1,979) ... 2,213 | *LA GRANGE, Fayette, 638 | LAKEPORT, Gregg, (861) ...... 897 |
| Kruse, Lee |   (4, 478) ............... 4,619 | Lake Providence, Upshur |
| Kubala Store, DeWitt | La Grange, Red River | Lakes Chapel, Freestone |
| Kuchton, Jack | *LA GRULLA, Starr, 14 | Lake Shore, Brown, .......... NA |
| Kulhanek, Waller |   (1, 211) ............... 1,192 | Lakeshore Gardens-Hidden Acres, |
| Kunz Settlement, Comal | Laguna, Atascosa |   San Patricio, (720) ........ 762 |
| *KURTEN, Brazos, 5 (227)...... 231 | Laguna, Falls | Lakeside, Brazoria |
| Kurth, Angelina | Laguna, Uvalde, ............... 20 | Lakeside, Colorado |
| Kus, Ellis | Laguna de Escobas, Zapata | Lakeside, Hansford |
| Kushla, Hays | Laguna Heights, Cameron, | Lakeside, Harris |
| Kuter, Wise |   (1,990)................. 2,008 | LAKESIDE, San Patricio, (333)... 325 |
| *KYLE, Hays, 286 (5,314)...... 6,966 | *Laguna Park, Bosque, ........ 550 | LAKESIDE, Tarrant, (1,040).... 1,079 |
| Kyle's, Victoria | Laguna Seca, Hidalgo, (251) .... 272 | LAKESIDE CITY, Archer, |
| Kyle's Station, Parker | Laguna Tres Estates, Hood,..... 377 |   (984)................... 1,017 |
| Kyles Quarry, Jasper | Laguna Vista, Burnet,........... 44 | Lakeside Heights, Llano |
| Kyleville, Houston | LAGUNA VISTA, Cameron, | Lakeside Village, Bosque, ...... 226 |
| Kyley, Tarrant |   (1,658)................. 1,883 | LAKE TANGLEWOOD, Randall, |
| Kymo, Bee | Lagunillas, Atascosa |   (825)..................... 854 |
| Kyote, Atascosa, .............. 34 | La Habitacion, Hidalgo | Lake Tejas, San Jacinto,......... 50 |
|  | La Hacha, Starr | Laketon, Gray,................. 12 |
| L | Lahai, Burnet | Lake Valley, Montague |
| La Aurora, Brooks | Lahey, Terry | Lake Victor, Burnet, .......... 215 |
| La Baca, Jackson | La Homa, Hidalgo, (10,433) ...10,765 | Lake View, Armstrong |
| La Bahia, Goliad | Lair, Wheeler | Lakeview, Dallas |
| La Bahia, Goliad |  | Lakeview, Floyd, ............... 44 |

**CITIES & TOWNS**

| Town,County | Pop. 2002 |
|---|---|

**Lakeview, Franklin,** ............ 30
Lakeview, Hale
*****LAKEVIEW, Hall, 9 (152)...... 153
Lakeview, Jefferson
**Lakeview, Lynn,** .............. 20
Lakeview, Marion
**LAKEVIEW [LACY-], McLennan,**
  (5,764)................. 5,834
Lakeview, Midland
**Lakeview, Orange,** ............ 75
Lakeview, Parmer
Lake View, San Augustine
Lakeview, Swisher
Lakeview, Tom Green
**Lake View, Val Verde, (167)** ..... 176
**Lake Water Wheel, San Jacinto,** .. 75
**LAKEWAY, Travis,**
  (8,002)................. 8,368
Lake Wichita, Wichita
Lakewood, Harris
Lakewood, Travis,
Lakewood Harbor, Bosque
**LAKEWOOD VILLAGE, Denton,**
  (342) ................... 348
**LAKE WORTH, Tarrant,**
  (4,618)................. 4,766
Lakota, Parker
La Leona, Cameron,
La Lomita, Hidalgo
Laman, Morris
**Lamar, Aransas,** ............ 1,600
Lamar, Falls
Lamar, Maverick
Lamar, Shelby
Lamar Court House, Lamar
*****LA MARQUE, Galveston,**
  580 (13,682) ............ 13,804
**Lamasco, Fannin,** .............. 32
Lamb, Kimble
Lamb, Liberty
Lamb's Mill, Montague
Lamb's Shop, Caldwell
Lambert, Parker
La Merle, Sabine
La Mesa, Brooks
*****LAMESA, Dawson, 584**
  (9,952)................. 9,822
Lamesa, Schleicher
**Lamkin, Comanche,** ........... 88
Lammburg, Atascosa
Lamont, Eastland
Lamont, Polk
*****LAMPASAS, Lampasas,**
  492 (6,786) ............. 7,110
Lamson, Callahan
La Nana, Nacogdoches
**Lanark, Cass,** ................. 30
La Navidad en las Cruces, Presidio
*****LANCASTER, Dallas,**
  919 (25,894) ........... 26,779
Lancaster, Washington
Lancing, Hamilton
Land, Callahan-Eastland
Land, Collin
Landa, Bexar
Lander, DeWitt
Landergin, Oldham
Landes, Washington
Landrum, Cherokee
Landrum, Falls
Landrum, Jefferson
**Landrum Station, Cameron,** .... 125
Lane, Bowie
Lane, Fannin
Lane, Hunt
Lane's, Bowie

*****Lane City, Wharton, 4** ........ 111
Lane Community, Van Zandt
**Lanely, Freestone,** ............. 27
**Laneport, Williamson,** .......... 60
Lanes Chapel, Bosque
Lanes Chapel, Smith
*****Laneville, Rusk, 19** ........... 200
Lang, Falls
Lange, Gillespie
Langford Cove, Coryell
Langley, DeWitt
Langston, Franklin
*****Langtry, Val Verde, 2** ......... 30
Langum Quarter, Houston
Lanham, Coryell
Lanham, Hamilton
Lanham, Palo Pinto
Lanham Mill, Somervell
**Lanier, Cass,** .................. 43
Lanius, Taylor
**Lannius, Fannin,** ............... 79
Lansdale, Robertson
Lansing, Harrison
**Lantana, Cameron,** ........... 137
Lantier, Tarrant
**La Paloma, Cameron, (354)** ... 329
**La Paloma-Lost Creek, Nueces,**
  (323) ................... 351
La Paloma Junction, Cameron
Lapara, Bee
Lapara, Live Oak
**La Parita, Atascosa,** ........... 48
La Peñusca, Cameron
La Plata, Deaf Smith
*****LA PORTE, Harris, 1,278**
  (31,880)............... 32,826
La Posta, Live Oak
**La Presa, Webb, (508)**.......... 520
La Presa, Zapata
*****La Pryor, Zavala, 22 (1,491)** ... 1,449
**La Puerta, Starr, (1,636)** ....... 1,702
Larch, Newton
*****LAREDO, Webb, 6,965**
  (176,576)............. 188,135
**Laredo Ranchettes, Webb,**
  (1,845) ................. 1,892
**La Reforma, Starr,** ............. 45
Largacinto, Walker
**Larga Vista, Webb, (742)** ....... 759
**Lariat, Parmer,** ............... 100
Larimer, Grimes
Larissa, Cherokee
Lark, Carson
Larkspur, Wheeler
**La Rosa, Nueces,** .............. 20
**La Rosita, Starr, (1,729)** ....... 1,757
Larremore, Caldwell
Larrison, Madison
*****Larue, Henderson, 42** ........ 160
La Salle, Calhoun
*****LaSalle, Jackson, 2** ........... 103
La Salle, La Salle
La Salle, Limestone
**Lasana, Cameron, (135)** ....... 150
*****Lasara, Willacy, 9 (1,024)** ..... 1,049
Lasca, Hudspeth
Las Colinas, Dallas
**Las Colonias, Zavala, (283)** ..... 304
Las Cuatas, Brooks
Las Cuevas, Hidalgo
**Las Escobas, Starr,** ........... 10
Lasher, Bastrop
Las Hermanitas, Duval
Las Islitas, Bexar
**Las Lomas, Starr, (2,684)**...... 2,738
**Las Lomitas, Jim Hogg, (267)** ... 274
Las Milpas-Hidalgo Park, Hidalgo

Las Moras, Kinney
**Las Palmas-Juarez, Cameron,**
  (1,666).................. 1,649
Las Playas, Brazoria
**Las Quintas Fronterizas,**
  Maverick, (2,030)........ 2,101
**Las Rusias, Cameron,** ......... 225
**Lassater, Marion,**............... 48
Las Tiendas, Webb
Las Vegas, Dimmit
**Las Yescas, Cameron,**......... 221
Latan, Mitchell
**Latch, Upshur,**................. 50
Lateiner Settlement, DeWitt
**Latex, Harrison,**............... 75
Latex, Panola
*****LATEXO, Houston, 11 (272)**..... 275
**Latham Prairie, Coryell**
Lathrop, Oldham
Laticia[Leticia], Harris
**La Tina Ranch [Arroyo Gardens-],**
  Cameron, (732)............ 756
**Latium, Washington,**........... 30
Lato, Shelby
Latona, Childress
Lattington, Bee
La Tuna, El Paso
**Laubach, Guadalupe,** .......... 20
*****Laughlin Air Force Base,**
  Val Verde, (2,225)** ....... 2,176
La Union, Cameron
Laura, Harris
Laura, Johnson
Laura, Knox
**Laurel, Newton,**.............. 125
Laurel, Webb
**Laureles, Cameron, (3,285)** .... 3,429
Laurel Hill, Newton
Laurelia, Polk
Lautz, Sherman
Lavada, Franklin
Lavada, Johnson
La Valley, Hudspeth
**Lavender, Limestone,**........... 30
Laverne, Crockett
*****LA VERNIA, Wilson, 154**
  (931)................... 976
La Verte, Jasper
**La Victoria, Starr, (1,683)** ..... 1,738
La Vierne, Runnels
*****LA VILLA, Hidalgo, 17**
  (1,305) ................. 1,330
La Villa de los Jacallas, Refugio
*****LAVON, Collin, 17 (387)**........ 402
Law, Brazos,
*****LA WARD, Jackson, 12 (200)**.... 200
Lawhon's Mills, Newton
Lawhon Springs, Lee
Lawn, Coleman
*****LAWN, Taylor, 16 (353)**........ 379
Lawndale, Kaufman
**Lawrence, Kaufman,**........... 279
Lawrence Chapel, Williamson
Lawrence Key, Waller
Lawrence Springs, Van Zandt
Lawrenceville, Gregg
Laws, Franklin
Lawson, Dallas
Lawson, Wharton
Lawsonville, Rusk,
Lawther, Dallas
Lay, Angelina
Layden's Ridge, Kaufman
Laytonia, Brazoria
Lazare, Cottle-Hardeman
Lazarus, Archer
*****Lazbuddie, Parmer, 20**........ 248

| Town,County ...........Pop. 2002 | Town,County ...........Pop. 2002 | Town,County...........Pop. 2002 |
|---|---|---|

Leachville, Milam
Leaday, Coleman
League, Crosby
League, Ellis
*LEAGUE CITY, Galveston-Harris
   1,655 (45,444)...........48,647
League Settlement, Comal
Leagueville, Henderson, ........ 32
Leah, Tyler
Leake's, Ellis
*LEAKEY, Real, 78 (387) ....... 374
Leal, Bexar
*LEANDER, Williamson,
   936 (7,596) .............10,895
LEARY, Bowie, (555) .......... 559
Leasville, Coleman
Leatherwood, Crosby
Leavitt, Haskell
Lebanon, Bee
Lebanon, Collin
Lebanon, Ellis
Lebanon, Hill
Lebanon, Live Oak
Lecomteville, Bexar
*Ledbetter, Fayette, 22.......... 76
Ledford, Caldwell
Ledwig, Hockley
Lee, Bell
Lee, Carson
Lee, Childress
Lee, Comanche
Lee, Eastland
Lee, Fannin
Lee, Freestone
Lee, Hamilton
Lee, Hill
Lee, Upshur
Lee, Van Zandt
Lee's Hill, Freestone
Leedale, Bell, ................. 16
Leeray, Stephens
Lees, Glasscock
*Leesburg, Camp, 19 .......... 115
Leesburg, Gonzales
Lees Mill, Newton
Lee Spring, Smith,
*Leesville, Gonzales, 6 ........ 150
Leeton, Jasper
Leevan, Fayette
Lefman, Wharton
LeForest, Garza
*LEFORS, Gray, 16 (559) ....... 563
Legard's Ranch, Jeff Davis
*Leggett, Polk, 15............. 500
Leggs Store, Nacogdoches
Legion, Kerr
Legion, Llano
Lehigh, Wilbarger
Lehman, Bastrop
Lehman, Cochran, .............. 8
Lehmann's Ranch, Maverick
Lehmberg, Llano
Leida, Edwards
Leigh, Harrison, .............. 100
Leiningen, Llano
Leisure Acres, Coryell, ........ 25
Lela, Wheeler, ................ 135
Lelan, Montague
Leland, Ellis
Leland, Franklin
Leland, McLennan
Lelavale, Hardin
*Lelia Lake, Donley, 7 ........ 125
Lellan, Cameron
*Leming, Atascosa, 5.......... 268
Lemit, Shelby
Lemley, Parker

Lemo, Harrison
Lemon, Orange
Lemons Gap, Taylor
Len, Fisher
Lena, Fayette
Lena, Henderson
Lenley's, Montgomery
Leno, Falls
Lenoir, Lamar
Lenor, San Augustine
Lenora, Harris
*Lenorah, Martin, 9............. 70
Lenore, Frio
Lenore, Jones
Lenox, Brewster
Lenoxville, Bowie
Lent, Taylor
Lenz, Colorado
Lenz, Karnes, ................. 20
Leo, Cooke,................... 20
Leo, Lee, ..................... 10
Leon, Leon
Leona, Frio
*LEONA, Leon, 18 (181) ....... 183
Leona Ditch, Uvalde
Leona Mills, Leon
*LEONARD, Fannin, 108
   (1,846)..................1,900
Leonardville, Tarrant
Leona Schroder, Nueces,........ 40
Leonhard, Kinney
Leonidas, Montgomery,
Leon Junction, Coryell, ........ 25
Leon Powell, Crockett
Leon River, Hamilton
Leon Springs, Bexar, ......... 137
*LEON VALLEY, Bexar,
   (9,239)..................9,213
Leonville, Coryell
Leota, Madison
Lera, Nacogdoches
Leroy, Llano
*LEROY, McLennan, 6 (335) ..... 335
Leroy, McLennan
Lesley, Hall, .................. 45
Leslie, Waller
Leslieville, Montgomery
Lester, Hunt
Leta, Hopkins
Letot, Dallas
Leubner, Williamson
Levada, Brown
*LEVELLAND, Hockley,
   786 (12,866) ...........12,667
Leverett's Chapel, Rusk, ....... 450
Levi, McLennan, .............. 50
Levin, Grimes
Levin, Pecos
Levinson, Culberson
Levita, Coryell, ............... 70
Lewalt, Stephens
Lewis, Anderson
Lewis, Cass
Lewis, Henderson
Lewis', Houston
Lewis' Wharf, Jackson
Lewis Chapel, Marion
Lewis Ferry, Jasper
Lewiston, Burnet
*LEWISVILLE, Denton,
   5,459 (77,737)...........85,081
Lewisville, Limestone
Lewisville, Waller
Lexington, Denton
Lexington, Fannin
Lexington, Hill
*LEXINGTON, Lee, 86

   (1,178) ................. 1,260
Leyendecker, Webb
Libby, Nacogdoches
Liberty, Coleman
Liberty, Ellis
Liberty, Falls
Liberty, Freestone
Liberty, Hamilton
Liberty, Hopkins
Liberty, Lee
*LIBERTY, Liberty, 585
   (8,033) ................. 8,312
Liberty, Lubbock, .............. 10
Liberty, Milam,................ 40
Liberty, Newton,
Liberty, Rusk
Liberty, Smith
Liberty, Van Zandt
Liberty, Wood
Liberty Chapel, Johnson
Liberty Chapel, Panola
Liberty City, Gregg, (1,935).... 1,992
Liberty Grove, Collin
Liberty Grove, Dallas
Liberty Grove, Delta
Liberty Grove, Hill
Liberty Hill, Bowie
Liberty Hill, Hays
Liberty Hill, Houston, ........... 73
Liberty Hill, Milam, ............. 25
Liberty Hill, Navarro
Liberty Hill, Rusk
Liberty Hill, San Jacinto
*LIBERTY HILL, Williamson,
   258 (1,409) ............ 1,468
Liberty Hill, Wood
Liberty Point, Wise
Liberty Springs, Collin
Licke, Fannin
Lick Skillet, Fayette
Lickskillet, Grayson
Lick-Skillet, Rusk
Lieb, Hutchinson
Liendo, Waller
Lieu, Collin
Liggett, Dallas
Light, Dimmit
Light, Howard
Light, Scurry
Lightfoot, Lampasas
Lightner, Concho
Ligon, Cochran
Ligonville, Guadalupe
Lilac, Milam
Lilbert, Nacogdoches,
Liles, Rusk
Lilla, Lavaca
Lillard, Hardin
Lilley, Morris
*Lillian, Johnson, 12........... 105
Lillie, Collingsworth
Lillie, Newton
Lillie, Upshur
Lilly, Camp
Lilly, Hunt
Lilly, Wilbarger
Lilly Grove, Nacogdoches
Lily Island, Polk
Lily White, Harris
Lima, Bandera
Lime City, Coryell
Limestone, Limestone
Limpia, Jeff Davis
Limpia Cañon, Jeff Davis
Lin, Young
Linberg, Tarrant
*Lincoln, Lee, 19 ............. 276

| Town, County . . . . . . . . . . . Pop. 2002 | Town, County . . . . . . . . . . . Pop. 2002 | Town, County . . . . . . . . . . . Pop. 2002 |
|---|---|---|
| *Lincoln, San Jacinto* | *Little St. Louis, DeWitt* | *Locust Grove, Upshur* |
| *Lincoln City, Harris* | *Littleton's Springs, Parker* | *Locust Shade, Dallas* |
| **LINCOLN PARK, Denton,** | *Littleville, Hamilton* | *Loden, Upshur* |
| (517) . . . . . . . . . . . . . . . . . . . 568 | *LittleYork, Harris* | *Lodge, Clay* |
| *Lincoln Park, Grayson* | *Litwalton, Garza* | *Lodge, Hall* |
| *Lincoln Springs, Smith* | *Lively, Kaufman,* | *Lodge Valley, Burnet* |
| *Lincolnville, Coryell* | *Livelyville, Houston* | ***Lodi, Marion, 3** . . . . . . . . . . . . . . 164* |
| ***LINDALE, Smith, 498** | *Live Oak, Bee* | *Lodi, Wilson* |
| (2,954). . . . . . . . . . . . . . . . 3,156 | *Live Oak, Bell* | *Lodwick, Harrison* |
| ***LINDEN, Cass, 169 (2,256)** . . . . 2,214 | **LIVE OAK, Bexar, (9,156)** . . . . . . 9,052 | *Lodwick, Marion* |
| **Lindenau, DeWitt,** . . . . . . . . . . . . . 50 | *Live Oak, Blanco* | *Loeb, Hardin* |
| **Lindendale, Kendall,** . . . . . . . . . . . 10 | *Live Oak, Bosque* | **Loebau, Lee,** . . . . . . . . . . . . . . . . . 20 |
| *Lindley, Comanche* | *Liveoak, Brazoria* | *Loftin, Smith* |
| ***LINDSAY, Cooke, 21 (788)** . . . . . 853 | *Live Oak, Burnet* | *Logan, Brazoria* |
| *Lindsay, Fannin* | *Live Oak, Caldwell* | *Logan, Marion* |
| **Lindsay, Reeves, (394)** . . . . . . . . . 395 | *Live Oak, Concho* | **Logan, Panola,** . . . . . . . . . . . . . . . 40 |
| *Lindsay Gardens, Hidalgo* | *Live Oak, Crockett* | **LOG CABIN, Henderson,** |
| *Lindsey, Henderson* | *Live Oak, DeWitt* | (733). . . . . . . . . . . . . . . . . . . 761 |
| *Line, Hopkins* | *Live Oak, Falls* | *Logco, Karnes* |
| *Line Creek, McLennan* | *Live Oak, Guadalupe* | *Loggins, Cameron* |
| *Liner, Swisher* | *Live Oak, Hays* | *Logsdon, Andrews* |
| *Lineville, Panola* | *Live Oak, Kinney* | *Logsdon, Gaines* |
| ***Lingleville, Erath, 2** . . . . . . . . . . 100 | *Live Oak, Medina* | *Logtown, Newton* |
| *Lingo, Hill* | *Live Oak, Milam* | *Logville, San Augustine* |
| *Lingo, Stonewall* | *Liveoak, Newton* | ***Lohn, McCulloch, 7** . . . . . . . . . . 149 |
| *Link, Limestone* | *Live Oak Bend, Matagorda* | **Loire, Wilson,** . . . . . . . . . . . . . . . . 50 |
| *Link, Scurry-Mitchell* | *Liveoak Community, Matagorda* | **Lois, Cooke,** . . . . . . . . . . . . . . . . 20 |
| *Linksville, Jones* | *Live Oak Grove, Wilson* | *Lois, Harris* |
| ***Linn [San Manuel-], Hidalgo,** | *Live Oak Hill, Fayette* | *Lolaville, Collin* |
| 13 (958). . . . . . . . . . . . . . . 971 | *Live Oak Point, Aransas* | ***Lolita, Jackson, 18 (548)** . . . . . . 564 |
| *Linn Flat, Nacogdoches* | *Live Oak Point, Aransas* | *Loma, San Patricio* |
| *Linnie, Fisher* | *Live Oaks, Bastrop* | *Loma, Walker* |
| *Linnville, Brazoria* | *Live Oak Springs, Travis* | **Loma Alta, McMullen,** . . . . . . . . . . 100 |
| *Linnville, Calhoun* | ***LIVERPOOL, Brazoria,** | **Loma Alta, Val Verde,** . . . . . . . . . . 30 |
| *Lint, Collin* | 25 (404) . . . . . . . . . . . . . . . . . 416 | **Loma Linda [Del Sol-],** |
| *Linus, Panola* | *Living Green, Camp* | San Patricio, (726) . . . . . . . . 751 |
| **Linwood, Cherokee,** . . . . . . . . . . . 40 | ***LIVINGSTON, Polk,** | **Loma Linda East, Jim Wells,** |
| *Linwood, Shelby* | 969 (5,433) . . . . . . . . . . . . . 5,656 | (214). . . . . . . . . . . . . . . . . . 226 |
| *Lipan, Atascosa* | *Livonia, Newton* | *Loma Prieta, Atascosa* |
| ***LIPAN, Hood, 73 (425).** . . . . . . . 428 | *Llano, Armstrong* | *Loma Vista, Zavala* |
| *Lipan, Tom Green* | ***LLANO, Llano, 328** | *Lomax, Harris* |
| *Lipan, Tom Green* | (3,325) . . . . . . . . . . . . . . . . 3,428 | **Lomax, Howard,** . . . . . . . . . . . . . . 500 |
| ***Lipscomb, Lipscomb, 7 (44)** . . . . 44 | **Llano Grande, Hidalgo,** | ***LOMETA, Lampasas,** |
| *Lisbon, Dallas* | (3,333). . . . . . . . . . . . . . . . 3,490 | 41 (782) . . . . . . . . . . . . . . . 811 |
| *Lisle, Young* | *Lloyd, Brown* | *Lomita, Bee* |
| ***Lissie, Wharton, 3** . . . . . . . . . . . 70 | *Lloyd, Denton* | ***London, Kimble, 5** . . . . . . . . . . . 180 |
| ***Littig, Travis,** . . . . . . . . . . . . . . . 37 | *Lloyd, Falls* | *London, Nueces* |
| *Little Arkansas, Gregg* | *Lloyd Mountain, Scurry* | *London, Rusk,* |
| *Little Brazos, Robertson* | *Lo, Limestone* | *Londonderry, Harris* |
| *Little Chicago, DeWitt* | *Lobo, Briscoe* | *Londy, Van Zandt* |
| *Little Cow Creek, Newton* | **Lobo, Culberson,** . . . . . . . . . . . . . 40 | **Lone Camp, Palo Pinto,** . . . . . . . . 110 |
| **Little Cypress, Orange,** . . . . . . . 1,050 | *Lochridge, Brazoria,* | **Lone Cedar, Ellis,** . . . . . . . . . . . . . 18 |
| *Little Egypt, Dallas* | *Lock, Smith* | *Lone Cottonwood, Hunt* |
| ***LITTLE ELM, Denton, 221** | *Locke Hill, Bexar* | *Lone Elm, Collin* |
| (3,646). . . . . . . . . . . . . . . . 8,202 | **Locker, San Saba,** . . . . . . . . . . . . . 16 | *Lone Elm, Delta* |
| ***LITTLEFIELD, Lamb, 315** | *Locker Spur, Reeves* | *Lone Elm, Ellis* |
| (6,507). . . . . . . . . . . . . . . . 6,567 | *Locket, Navarro* | *Lone Elm, Kaufman,* |
| *Little Flock, Bell* | *Lockett, Jones* | *Lone Grove, Falls* |
| *Little Flock, Leon* | *Lockett, Marion* | **Lone Grove, Llano,** . . . . . . . . . . . . 50 |
| *Little Georgia, Brazos* | **Lockett, Wilbarger,** . . . . . . . . . . . 200 | *Lone Hand, San Saba* |
| *Littleglade, Limestone* | **Lockettville, Hockley,** . . . . . . . . . . 20 | *Lone Mill, Sterling* |
| **Little Hope, Wood,** . . . . . . . . . . . . 25 | ***LOCKHART, Caldwell,** | *Lone Mountain, Upshur* |
| *Little Hope-Moore Community,* | 486 (11,615) . . . . . . . . . . . 12,601 | *Lone Oak, Bexar* |
| *Van Zandt* | *Lockhart, DeWitt* | **Lone Oak, Colorado,** . . . . . . . . . . . 50 |
| *Little Hope Church, Freestone* | *Lockhart's Switch, Upshur* | *Lone Oak, Erath* |
| *Little Indiana, Wood* | *Lockland, Henderson* | ***LONE OAK, Hunt, 56 (521)** . . . . . 531 |
| *Little Lost Valley, Jack* | *Locklin, Rusk* | *Lone Oak, Montgomery* |
| **Little Midland, Burnet,** . . . . . . . . . . 32 | ***LOCKNEY, Floyd, 87 (2,056).** . . . 2,030 | *Lone Oak, Navarro* |
| *Little Mineral, Grayson* | *Lockranzie, Cherokee* | **Lone Pine, Houston,** . . . . . . . . . . . . 81 |
| *Little Mississippi, Robertson* | *Loco, Childress* | *Lonepine, Milam* |
| *Little Mound, Upshur* | *Locus, Hall* | *Lonesome Dove, Tarrant* |
| **Little New York, Gonzales,** . . . . . . . 20 | *Locus, Limestone* | *Lone Spring, Lamar* |
| *Little River, Milam* | **Locust, Grayson,** . . . . . . . . . . . . . 118 | *Lone Star, Bastrop* |
| ***LITTLE RIVER-ACADEMY, Bell,** | *Locust, Kaufman* | *Lone Star, Bell* |
| 36 (1,645) . . . . . . . . . . . . . 1,763 | *Locust Grove, Brazos* | *Lone Star, Burnet* |
| *Littles Chapel, Nacogdoches* | *Locust Grove, Navarro* | **Lone Star, Cherokee,** . . . . . . . . . . . 20 |
| *Little School, Tom Green* | *Locust Grove, Rusk* | *Lonestar, Collingsworth* |

| Town,County | Pop. 2002 |
|---|---|

Lone Star, Comal
Lone Star, Delta
Lonestar, Falls
**Lone Star, Floyd, . . . . . . . . . . . . . 42**
Lone Star, Franklin
Lone Star, Hopkins
Lone Star, Kaufman
**Lone Star, Lamar,. . . . . . . . . . . . . 35**
Lone Star, Llano
**\*LONE STAR, Morris,**
**    81 (1,631) . . . . . . . . . . . . . . 1,624**
Lone Star, Polk
Lone Star, Titus
Lone Star, Van Zandt
Lone Star, Wise
Lone Star, Wood
Lone Tree, Collin
Lone Willow, Johnson
Lone Wolf, Tom Green
Long Bottom, Freestone
Longbranch, Eastland
Long Branch, Ellis
**\*Long Branch, Panola, 7 . . . . . . . 181**
Long Branch, Rockwall
Long Bridge, Polk
Long Creek, Dallas
Long Creek, Fannin
Longfellow, Pecos
Long Hollow, Jack
Long Hollow, Leon
Long King, Polk
**Long Lake, Anderson,. . . . . . . . . 15**
Long Leaf, San Augustine
**\*Long Mott, Calhoun, 4 . . . . . . . . 76**
Long Mount, Mason
Long Mountain, Llano
Longoria, Brooks
Longorio, Jones
Long Point, Fort Bend
**Longpoint, Washington, . . . . . . . . 80**
Long Prairie, Fayette
Long Prairie, Lee
Long Prairie, Navarro
Long Station, Hardin
Longstreet, Houston
Longstreet, Montgomery
Long Taw, Delta
**\*LONGVIEW, Gregg-Harrison,**
**    5,310 (73,344). . . . . . . . . . 74,021**
Longview, Medina
Longview, Midland
Longview Heights, Harrison
Longview Junction, Gregg
Longwood, Sabine
**Longworth, Fisher,. . . . . . . . . . . . 65**
Lon Hill, Nueces
Lon Hill's Town, Cameron
Lonnie, Childress
Lonsboro, Hidalgo
Lonsdale, Nacogdoches
Lookout, Bexar
Lookout, Lamar
Lookout, Leon
Lookout, Mills
Look Out, Upshur
Look Out Point, Aransas
Looneyville, Nacogdoches,
Loop, Clay
**\*Loop, Gaines, 22. . . . . . . . . . . . . 315**
Loop, Gaines
**\*Lopeno, Zapata, 3 (140) . . . . . . . 142**
Loper, Henderson
**Lopezville, Hidalgo, (4,476). . . . 4,645**
Lora, Roberts
**\*LORAINE, Mitchell, 16 (656). . . . 660**
Lord, Harris
Lord, Ochiltree

**\*LORENA, McLennan,**
**    182 (1,433) . . . . . . . . . . . . . 1,502**
Lorenz, Wilson
**\*LORENZO, Crosby, 46**
**    (1,372). . . . . . . . . . . . . . . . . 1,388**
Loring, Cooke
**Los Alvarez, Starr, (1,434) . . . . . 1,451**
**Los Angeles, LaSalle, . . . . . . . . . 20**
**Los Angeles Subdivision,**
**    Willacy, (86) . . . . . . . . . . . . . . 86**
Los Apaches, Webb
Los Arrieros, Starr
**Los Barreras, Starr, . . . . . . . . . . . 75**
**Los Coyotes, Willacy,. . . . . . . . . . . 4**
Los Cuates, Cameron
Los Dinero, Mills
**\*Los Ebanos, Hidalgo,**
**    5 (403). . . . . . . . . . . . . . . . . . 425**
**Los Escondidos, Burnet,. . . . . . . 30**
Los Federales, Brooks
**\*LOS FRESNOS, Cameron,**
**    176 (4,512) . . . . . . . . . . . . . 4,808**
Los Fresnos, Presidio
Los Horconsitos, Liberty
**\*LOS INDIOS, Cameron,**
**    12 (1,149) . . . . . . . . . . . . . . 1,142**
Los Machos, Jim Wells
Los Nogales, Guadalupe
Los Ojuelos, Webb
Los Olmos, Brooks
**Losoya, Bexar, . . . . . . . . . . . . . . 322**
Los Preseños, Jim Wells
**LOS SAENZ [Roma-], Starr, 272**
**    (9,617). . . . . . . . . . . . . . . . . 9,969**
Loss Creek, Coleman
Lost, Montague
Lost Creek, Jack
Lost Creek, McCulloch
**Lost Creek [La Paloma-],**
**    Nueces, (323) . . . . . . . . . . . 351**
**Lost Creek, Travis, (4,729) . . . . 4,872**
Lost Prairie, Bell
**Lost Prairie, Limestone,. . . . . . . . . 2**
Lost Prairie, Limestone
Lostprong, Wharton
**Los Villareales, Starr, (930) . . . . . 950**
**LOS YBANEZ, Dawson, (32). . . . . . 32**
**\*LOTT, Falls, 57 (724) . . . . . . . . . 722**
Lott, Washington
Lotta, Harrison
Lotta, Kaufman
Lotta, Parker
Lottie, Wood
Lotus, Harris
Lou, Dawson
Louetta, Harris
Louis, Limestone
**\*Louise, Wharton, 56 (977). . . . . 1,032**
Louisiana Settlement, Polk
Louisville, Bowie
Louisville, Fort Bend
Louisville, Limestone
Loulynn, Lynn
Lourwood, Lipscomb
Love, Goliad
Love Branch, Eastland
**Lovelace, Hill, . . . . . . . . . . . . . . . 12**
**\*LOVELADY, Houston**
**    33 (608) . . . . . . . . . . . . . . . 617**
Loveless, Concho
Loveless, Hill
**\*Loving, Young, 11 . . . . . . . . . . . 300**
Loving Valley, Palo Pinto
Low, Wood
**\*Lowake, Concho, 2 . . . . . . . . . . . 40**
Lowe, Upshur
Lowell, Erath

Lowell, Guadalupe-DeWitt
Lower Medio, Bee
Lower Mott, Calhoun
Lower Station, Grayson
Lower Taylor Bayou, Jefferson
Lower Valley, Guadalupe
Lowery, Grimes
Lowery, Nacogdoches
Lowes Chapel, Cherokee
Lowesville, Guadalupe
Lowman, Lamar
Low Pin Oak, Lee
Lowry, Panola
**LOWRY CROSSING, Collin,**
**    (1,229) . . . . . . . . . . . . . . . . . 1,448**
**Loyal Valley, Mason, . . . . . . . . . . . 50**
Loyola, Martin
**Loyola Beach, Kleberg, . . . . . . . . 195**
**\*Lozano, Cameron, 1 (324). . . . . 326**
Lozier, Terrell
Luanna, Cass
Lubbock, Hardeman
**\*LUBBOCK, Lubbock, 10,909**
**    (199,564) . . . . . . . . . . . . 201,855**
**LUCAS, Collin, (2,890) . . . . . . . 3,141**
Lucas, Milam
Lucas, Wilson
Lucas City, Atascosa
Lucas Spring, Bexar
Luce, Trinity
Lucern, Hansford
Lucero, Brooks
Lucile, Lampasas
Luck, Collin
**Luckenbach, Gillespie,. . . . . . . . . 25**
Luckey, Coryell
Lucknow, Nacogdoches
Lucky, Montague
Lucky, Polk
Lucy, Atascosa
Lucy, Victoria
**\*LUEDERS, Jones, 16 (300) . . . . . 304**
**Luella, Grayson, . . . . . . . . . . . . . 639**
**\*LUFKIN, Angelina, 2,499**
**    (32,709) . . . . . . . . . . . . . . 33,381**
Luke, Atascosa
Luke Wilson, Archer
Lula, Culberson
Lula, Real
**\*LULING, Caldwell, 293**
**    (5,080) . . . . . . . . . . . . . . . . 5,181**
**Lull, Hidalgo, . . . . . . . . . . . . . . . 999**
Lumber, Marion
**\*LUMBERTON, Hardin, 474**
**    (8,731) . . . . . . . . . . . . . . . 8,937**
**Lumkins, Ellis,. . . . . . . . . . . . . . . 20**
Lumm, Liberty
Lumpkin, Smith
**Lums Chapel, Lamb,. . . . . . . . . . . . 6**
Luna, Freestone
Lunarville, Jack
Lund, Travis
Lundy, Houston
Lunette, Eastland
Luray, Houston
Lusk, McLennan
**Lusk, Throckmorton,. . . . . . . . . . . 10**
Luster, Van Zandt
Lutes, Henderson
Luther, Briscoe
**Luther, Howard,. . . . . . . . . . . . . . 335**
Luther, Lamar
Luther, Limestone
**Lutie, Collingsworth, . . . . . . . . . . 35**
Luvial, Colorado
Luxello, Bexar
Luzon, Kent

CITIES & TOWNS

| Town,County . . . . . . . . . . .Pop. 2002 | Town,County . . . . . . . . . . .Pop. 2002 | Town,County . . . . . . . . . . . Pop. 2002 |
|---|---|---|
| Luzon, Van Zandt | Madden, Hudspeth | Manchester, Red River,. . . . . . . . 185 |
| **Lydia, Red River,** . . . . . . . . . . . . 109 | Madera Springs, Jeff Davis | Manchester Mills, Tarrant |
| Lyford, Navarro | **Madero, Hidalgo,** . . . . . . . . . . . . 720 | Manda, Travis |
| *LYFORD, Willacy, 40 | Madge, Coleman | Manestee, Tom Green |
| (1,973). . . . . . . . . . . . . . . . .2,005 | Madison, Madison | Mangold, Archer |
| **Lyford South, Willacy, (172). . . . . 180** | Madison, Orange | **Mangum, Eastland,** . . . . . . . . . . . 15 |
| Lyle, Rusk | Madison, Swisher | Mangus Corner, Bexar |
| Lyles, Reeves | *MADISONVILLE, Madison, | Manhattan, Matagorda |
| Lyman, Motley | 340 (4,159) . . . . . . . . . . . . .4,213 | **Manheim, Lee,** . . . . . . . . . . . . . . . 40 |
| Lynch, Hopkins | **Madras, Red River,** . . . . . . . . . . . . 61 | Manila, Cherokee |
| Lynch, Rains | Mae, Jim Wells | Manila, Crosby |
| Lynchburg, Harris | Magasco, Sabine | Manila, Freestone |
| Lynches Chapel, Cherokee | Magee Bend, Trinity | Manila, Grimes |
| Lynchs Creek, Lampasas | Magenta, Oldham | **Mankin, Henderson,** . . . . . . . . . . . 20 |
| Lynn, King | Maggie, Montgomery | **Mankins, Archer,** . . . . . . . . . . . . . 10 |
| Lynn, Lynn | Maggie Murph, Smith | Manle, Young |
| Lynnell, Sterling | Magic City, Wheeler | Mann, Navarro |
| **Lynn Grove, Grimes,** . . . . . . . . . . 25 | Magill, Milam | Mann, Reeves |
| Lynox, Bowie | Maginnis, Bowie | Mann's Crossing, Bexar |
| Lyon, Grayson | Maglab, Dallas | Manning, Angelina |
| *Lyons, Burleson, 15 . . . . . . . . . 360 | Magnesium, Brazoria | Manning, Bexar |
| Lyons, Fayette | Magnet, Smith | *MANOR, Travis, 227 |
| Lyra, Palo Pinto | **Magnet, Wharton,** . . . . . . . . . . . . . 42 | (1,204) . . . . . . . . . . . . . . . 1,248 |
| Lyric, Liberty | Magnolia, Anderson | *MANSFIELD, Tarrant-Johnson, |
| Lystra, Jones | Magnolia, Borden | 1,391 (28,031) . . . . . . . . . 30,102 |
| *LYTLE, Atascosa-Medina-Bexar, | Magnolia, Montague | Mansker Lake, Eastland |
| 133 (2,383) . . . . . . . . . . . . .2,466 | Magnolia, Montgomery | Manson, Anderson |
| Lytle, Tarrant | *MAGNOLIA, Montgomery, | Manson, Jackson |
| Lytle, Taylor | 1,057 (1,111) . . . . . . . . . . . .1,198 | Mantha, Camp |
| Lytle Cove, Taylor | **Magnolia, San Jacinto,** . . . . . . . . 330 | Mantha, Upshur |
| Lyttle's, Burleson | Magnolia, Wilbarger | Manton, Angelina |
| **Lytton Springs, Caldwell,** . . . . . . 500 | **Magnolia Beach, Calhoun,** . . . . . 250 | Manton's, Fayette |
|  | Magnolia Gardens, Harris | Mantu, Harris |
| **M** | Magnolia Mills, Sabine | Mantua, Collin |
| *MABANK, Kaufman-Henderson, | Magnolia Park, Harris | Mantua, Grayson |
| 714 (2,151) . . . . . . . . . . . . .2,305 | Magnolia Point, Harris | *MANVEL, Brazoria, |
| Mabel, Bexar | **Magnolia Springs, Jasper, 2** . . . . . 80 | 257 (3,046). . . . . . . . . . . . . 3,153 |
| Mabel, Fisher | Magoffinsville, El Paso | Mapes, Wood |
| **Mabelle, Baylor,** . . . . . . . . . . . . . . 9 | Magoun, Lipscomb | *Maple, Bailey, 4 . . . . . . . . . . . . . .75 |
| Mable, Lipscomb | Magpetco, Jefferson | Maple, Collin |
| Mabledean, Clay | Maguire, Robertson | **Maple, Red River,** . . . . . . . . . . . . .30 |
| Mabry, Harris | Magwalt, Winkler | Maples, Wichita |
| **Mabry, Red River,** . . . . . . . . . . . . . 60 | **Maha, Travis,** . . . . . . . . . . . . . . . .NA | Maple Springs, Red River |
| Macaroni Station, Jackson | Mahala, Live Oak | **Maple Springs, Titus,** . . . . . . . . . . 25 |
| MacBain, Motley | **Mahl, Nacogdoches,** . . . . . . . . . . .NA | Maple Springs, Titus |
| *Macdona, Bexar, 4 . . . . . . . . . . 297 | **Mahomet, Burnet,** . . . . . . . . . . . . . 47 | **Mapleton, Houston,** . . . . . . . . . . . 32 |
| Mace, Lampasas | Mahon, Panola | Mara, Tarrant |
| Macedonia, Bowie | Mahoney, Hopkins | Marak, Milam |
| Macedonia, Harrison | Mahoney, Hopkins | *Marathon, Brewster, 37 |
| Macedonia, Henderson | Mainz, Kendall | (455). . . . . . . . . . . . . . . . . . .483 |
| Macedonia, Liberty | Mainzer, Dallas | *MARBLE FALLS, Burnet, |
| Macedonia, Marion | Maize, Scurry | 1,021 (4,959) . . . . . . . . . . . 5,200 |
| Macedonia, Panola | Major, Limestone | Marble Hill, Burnet |
| Macedonia, Walker | **Majors, Franklin,** . . . . . . . . . . . . . 13 | Marble Mountain, Brewster |
| Macedonia, Waller | *MALAKOFF, Henderson, | Marcelena, Wilson |
| Macedonia, Williamson | 203 (2,257) . . . . . . . . . . . . .2,281 | Marcelena, Wilson |
| Macedonia, Wood | Malcom, Smith | Marcelina, Karnes |
| **Macey, Brazos,** . . . . . . . . . . . . . . .NA | Malden, Armstrong | March, Rusk |
| MacGrath, Tom Green | **Mallard, Montague,** . . . . . . . . . . . . 12 | Marco, McCulloch |
| Machos, La Salle | Mallard Prairie, Henderson | Marcy, Haskell |
| Machovec, Moore | Mallett, Sherman | Marekville, Bell |
| Macie, Kinney | Mallie, Hudspeth | Marekville, Calhoun |
| Mack, Polk | *MALONE, Hill, 17 (278) . . . . . . . . 286 | Marengo, Menard |
| Mack, Wilbarger | Maloney, Ellis | *MARFA, Presidio, 120 |
| Mackay, Wharton | **Malta, Bowie,** . . . . . . . . . . . . . . . . 297 | (2,121) . . . . . . . . . . . . . . . 2,078 |
| Mackie, Ellis | Malta, King | **Margaret, Foard,** . . . . . . . . . . . . . .51 |
| Mackiesville, Caldwell | Malvado, Terrell | Margie, Leon |
| Macksville, Comanche | Malvern, Fort Bend | Mari Ann, Harris |
| Macksville, Harrison | **Malvern, Leon,** . . . . . . . . . . . . . . .NA | Marianna, Polk |
| Mackville, Collin | **Mambrino, Hood,** . . . . . . . . . . . . . 74 | Marianna, Victoria |
| Macomb, Grayson | Mammoth, Lipscomb | **Marie, Runnels,** . . . . . . . . . . . . . . . 12 |
| **Macon, Franklin,** . . . . . . . . . . . . . 21 | Mamre, Atascosa | Marienfeld, Martin |
| Macon, Harrison | Mance, Henderson | Marienthal, Comal |
| Macrae, Fannin | Manchac, Hays | Marietta, Anderson |
| Macrod, Cameron | *Manchaca, Travis, 171 . . . . . . . .2,259 | *MARIETTA, Cass, 12 (112) . . . . . 111 |
| **Macune, San Augustine,** . . . . . . . 100 | Manchester, Fort Bend | Marietta, Lubbock-Crosby |
| Mada, Milam | Manchester, Harris | Marietta, Van Zandt |

| Town,County .......... Pop. 2002 | Town,County .......... Pop. 2002 | Town,County .......... Pop. 2002 |
|---|---|---|
| Marilee, Collin | Mary, Montague | Mayfield, Hutchinson |
| Marilla, Collingsworth | Mary's Creek, Tarrant-Parker | **Mayflower, Newton,.......... 100** |
| Marine, Tarrant | **Maryetta, Jack, ................. 7** | Mayflower, Rusk |
| Marion, Angelina | ***Maryneal, Nolan, 3 ........... 61** | Mayflower, Wilbarger |
| Marion, Brazoria | Marys Creek, Baylor | **Mayhill, Denton, ............. 150** |
| ***MARION, Guadalupe,** | Marysee, Liberty | **Maynard, San Jacinto, ........ 150** |
| **98 (1,099) .............. 1,155** | Marystown, Johnson | Mayo, Freestone |
| Marion Ferry Park, Angelina | **Marysville, Cooke, ............ 15** | Mayo, Karnes |
| Mariposa, Kinney | Maryville, Bee | Mayotown, Nacogdoches |
| Mariscal, Brewster | ***MASON, Mason, 189** | ***MAYPEARL, Ellis, 31 (746) ..... 795** |
| Marith, Dallas | **(2,134)................2,176** | ***Maysfield, Milam,............ 140** |
| Marjorie, Milam | Mason's Ranch, Terry | Mayshaw, Floyd |
| Mark, McCulloch | Masons, Reeves | Maysville, Karnes |
| Markbelt, Brazoria | Masontown, Travis | Mazatlan, Duval |
| Market, Polk | Massey, Hill | Mazeland, Runnels |
| ***Markham, Matagorda,** | Massey Lake, Anderson, ........NA | McAdams, Walker |
| **23 (1,138) ............. 1,145** | Massie, San Augustine | ***McAdoo, Dickens, 6........... 75** |
| **Markley, Young, ............... 50** | Massie, Trinity | McAfee, Tarrant |
| **Markout, Kaufman,........... 80** | Masters', Houston | ***McALLEN, Hidalgo, 5,721** |
| Marks, Frio | Masters, Throckmorton | **(106,414) ............. 112,395** |
| Marley, Fayette | Masterson, Brazoria | McAllister, Navarro |
| Marley Springs, Burnet | **Masterson, Moore, 6........... 15** | McAnelly's Bend, Lampasas-San Saba |
| ***MARLIN, Falls, 299 (6,628).... 6,627** | Masterville, McLennan | McBeth, Brazoria |
| Marlow, Anderson | Maston, Comanche | McBride, Carson |
| Marlow, Fort Bend | ***MATADOR, Motley, 49 (740) .... 738** | McCain Point, Palo Pinto |
| **Marlow, Milam, ................ 45** | ***Matagorda, Matagorda, 31 ..... 710** | McCamant, Jones |
| Marmaduke, Jack | Matalfos, Coke | ***McCAMEY, Upton, 83** |
| Marmion, Brazoria | Matejowsky, Washington | **(1,805) ................ 1,707** |
| Marnels, Lubbock | Mather Mills, Williamson | McCampbell Switch, San Patricio |
| ***MARQUEZ, Leon, 44 (220) ..... 218** | ***MATHIS, San Patricio,** | McCardy, Harrison-Marion |
| Marr, Polk | **221 (5,034) .............4,941** | McCarty, La Salle |
| Mars, Franklin | Matilda, Jackson | McCarys Chapel, Gregg |
| **Mars, Van Zandt,.............. NA** | Matile, Hardin | McCaslin, Webb |
| Marsh, Bowie | Matinburg, Camp | ***McCauley, Fisher, 4 .......... 96** |
| Marsh, Polk | Matlock, Dallam | **McClanahan, Falls,............ 42** |
| Marsh, Potter | Matson, Hill | McClellan's, Guadalupe |
| ***MARSHALL, Harrison,** | **Matthews, Colorado, .......... 25** | McClelland, Shelby |
| **1,441 (23,935).......... 23,791** | Mattie, Stonewall | McClung, Lubbock |
| Marshall's Store, Jack | Mattox, Newton | McClure's Hill, Gonzales |
| **MARSHALL CREEK, Denton,** | Mattson, Haskell | McClures, Nacogdoches |
| **(431) ................. 440** | ***MAUD, Bowie, 50 (1,028)......1,035** | McColl, Hidalgo |
| **Marshall Ford, Travis,.......... NA** | Maud, Knox | McCollum, Montague |
| **Marshall Northeast, Harrison,.. 1,500** | Maud, Parker | McCombs, El Paso |
| Marshall Springs, Harrison | Maud, Wise | McConnell, Haskell |
| **Marston, Polk,................. 25** | Maudlowe, Refugio | McConnellsville, Parker |
| ***MART, McLennan, 107** | ***Mauriceville, Orange, 58** | McConnico, Angelina |
| **(2,273).................2,272** | **(2,743).................2,786** | **McCook, Hidalgo, ............. 91** |
| Martha, Liberty | Maurin, Gonzales | McCormack, Grimes |
| Martha's Chapel, Walker | Maverick, Medina | McCormick, Archer |
| Martin, Angelina | **Maverick, Runnels,............ 31** | McCowanville, Fannin |
| Martin, Coryell | Maxbury, Stephens-Palo Pinto | McCowen, Bowie |
| Martin, Frio | **Maxdale, Bell,.................. 4** | **McCoy, Atascosa, 4............. 30** |
| Martin, Hill | **Maxey, Lamar,................. 55** | **McCoy, Floyd, ..................2** |
| Martin, Lamar | Maxey, Travis | **McCoy, Kaufman, ............. 20** |
| Martin, Lamar | Maxon, Brewster | **McCoy, Panola, .............. NA** |
| Martin, Red River | Maxson, Liberty | **McCoy, Red River,............ 175** |
| Martin's Creek, Panola | ***Maxwell, Caldwell, 27 ........ 500** | McCraven, Washington |
| ***MARTINDALE, Caldwell,** | Maxwell, Collin | McCrawville, Cooke |
| **35 (953)................. 980** | Maxwells Branch, Collin | McCreaville, Lampasas |
| Martinez, Bexar | Maxwelton, San Saba | McCroskey, Matagorda |
| Martin Lake Junction, Panola | ***May, Brown, 26 ............. 285** | McCrossin, Cherokee |
| Martin Prairie, Grimes | May, Cottle | McCulloch, McCulloch |
| Martinsburg, Gillespie | May, Ellis | McCulloch, Red River |
| Martinsburgh, Blanco | May, Lamar | McCullough, Ellis |
| Martins Gap, Hamilton | May, Tarrant | ***McDade, Bastrop, 25.......... 345** |
| **Martins Mills, Van Zandt,....... 125** | May Apple Springs, Trinity | McDaniel, Grimes |
| Martin Springs, Grayson | ***Maydelle, Cherokee, 9 ........ 250** | McDaniel, Limestone |
| **Martin Springs, Hopkins, ..... 115** | Mayer, Lamar | **McDaniels, Brown, ............ NA** |
| ***Martinsville, Nacogdoches, 3 .. 126** | Mayer, Potter | McDonald, Hill |
| Marvel Wells, Milam | Mayer, Schleicher | McDonald, Montague |
| Marville, Panola | Mayers Spring, Terrell | McDonald's Store, Bastrop |
| **Marvin, Lamar, ................ 48** | Mayes' Store, Tom Green | McDonough, Harris |
| Marvin, McLennan | Mayfair Park, Fort Bend | McDow, Wharton |
| Marvin, Robertson | Mayfield, Erath | McDowell, Austin |
| Marvin, Van Zandt | **Mayfield, Hale, ................NA** | McDowell, Jackson |
| Marx, Limestone | **Mayfield, Hill, ................. 12** | McDuff, Bastrop |
| Mary, Jim Wells | Mayfield, Houston | McElroy, Sabine |

CITIES & TOWNS

| Town,County ..........Pop. 2002 | Town,County ...........Pop. 2002 | Town,County ........... Pop. 2002 |
|---|---|---|
| McFaddens Store, Rusk | (1,293)................1,459 | Merito, Hidalgo |
| *McFaddin, Victoria, 3 ......... 175 | MEADOWS PLACE, Fort Bend, | Meritt's, Jasper |
| McFarland, Jackson | (4,912)................5,063 | *MERKEL, Taylor, 165 |
| McFarland, Parker | Meadowview, Hunt | (2,637) ................ 2,643 |
| McGarrah's, Collin | Meadville, Denton | Merle, Burleson, ............. NA |
| McGee, Montague | Meansville, San Patricio | Merret, Red River |
| McGee's, San Jacinto | Mecca, Madison,.............. 48 | Merriam, Eastland |
| McGeeMill, Gonzales | Mechanicsville, Harris | Merrick, Martin |
| McGill, Tom Green | Mechanicsville, Smith | Merrill's, Fannin |
| McGinnis, Bowie | Medicine Mound, Hardeman,..... 50 | Merrilltown, Travis |
| McGinty, Trinity | Medill, Lamar, ................ 50 | Merrimac, Wood |
| McGirk, Hamilton, .............. 9 | *Medina, Bandera, 52 ........ 515 | Merriman, Eastland, .............14 |
| McGlasson, Lamar | Medina, Zapata, (2,960) .......3,069 | Merrivale, Bosque |
| McGonogil's Mill, Lavaca | Medina Base, Bexar | Merry Flat, Wheeler |
| McGough Springs, Eastland | Medina Lake, Medina | *MERTENS, Hill, 3 (146) ........ 150 |
| *McGREGOR, McLennan, | Medina Station, Bexar | *MERTZON, Irion, 60 (839) ...... 836 |
| 284 (4,727) .............. 4,763 | Medinaville, Bexar | Merv, Henderson |
| McGue Springs, Eastland | Medio, Bee | Mesa, El Paso,.................50 |
| McGuffin's, Grimes | Medio, Harris | Mesa, Grimes |
| McGuire, Stephens | Medio Hill, Bee | Mesa, Randall |
| McHall, Ochiltree | Medio Hill, Bee | Meshaw, Cherokee |
| McHattie, Fort Bend | Medlarsville, Fannin | Mesquital, San Patricio |
| McIntosh, Parker | Medley, Montgomery | Mesquite, Borden |
| McKamey, Calhoun | Medmill, Medina | *MESQUITE, Dallas, 5,107 |
| McKandles' Store, Runnels | Medo, Bell | (124,523) ............. 127,584 |
| McKay, Irion | Meeker, Jefferson, .............NA | Mesquite Flat, Coryell |
| McKee Colony, Cherokee | Meeks, Bell,................... 15 | Mesquiteville, Jack |
| McKees, Val Verde | *MEGARGEL, Archer, 8 | Metcalf Gap, Palo Pinto,.......... 6 |
| McKenzie, Mitchell | (248) .................... 239 | Meteor, Floyd |
| McKenzie, Swisher | Meldavis, Gray | Methodist Colony, Donley |
| McKenzie, Walker | Meldrum, Shelby, .............NA | Mettina, Falls |
| McKibben, Hansford | Melendy, Harris | Metz, Denton |
| McKinley, Parker | *MELISSA, Collin, 100 | Metz, Ector |
| *McKINNEY, Collin, 2,785 | (1,350)................1,558 | Metz, Gonzales |
| (54,369)............... 65,539 | Melo, Goliad | *MEXIA, Limestone, 424 |
| McKinney Acres, Andrews,..... 197 | Melon, Frio | (6,563) ................ 6,571 |
| McKinney Springs, Brewster | Melrose, Gregg | Mexico, Hunt |
| McKnight, Robertson | Melrose, Nacogdoches, ........ 150 | Mexline, Cochran |
| McKnight, Rusk | Melton, Hunt | Meyer City, Mills |
| McLainsboro, Hill | Melton, Montgomery | *Meyersville, DeWitt, 8 .........110 |
| *McLean, Gray, 63 (830)........ 811 | Melton, Navarro | *MIAMI, Roberts, 39 (588).......557 |
| McLeary, Brewster | *MELVIN, McCulloch, 7 | Mica, Hudspeth |
| McLENDON-CHISHOLM, Rockwall, | (155) .................... 152 | Micars, Caldwell |
| (914)................1,013 | Melvin, Montgomery | Micheli, Angelina |
| McLennan, Eastland | Melvine, Duval | Michelle, Angelina |
| *McLeod, Cass, 8............. 230 | *MEMPHIS, Hall, 137 | Michies, Dawson |
| McMahan, Caldwell,........... 125 | (2,479)................2,496 | Mickey, Floyd |
| McMahan Chapel, Sabine | Mena, Red River | Mico, Medina, 11 .............. 98 |
| McMannis' Store, Young | Menard, Liberty | Micolithic, Culberson |
| McMillan, San Saba,........... 15 | *MENARD, Menard, 87 | Micomber, Floyd |
| McMillans, Panola | (1,653)................1,690 | Mid, Haskell |
| McMillin, Bell | Menard, Polk | Midcity, Lamar, ................50 |
| McMinn, Eastland | Menard's Mills, Polk | Middle Bayou, Harris |
| McNair, Harris, ..............2,039 | Mendota, Hemphill | Middle Bosque, McLennan |
| McNairy, Dallas | Mendoza, Caldwell, .......... 100 | Middle Bosque, McLennan |
| McNamara, Goliad | Menefee's, Jackson | Middle Caddo, Hunt |
| McNary, Hudspeth ............ 250 | Menlow, Hill, .................. 10 | Middle Gabriel, Burnet |
| McNeece, Panola | Mennonite Colony, Bee | Middleton, Leon, ...............26 |
| McNeel, Brazoria,............. NA | *Mentone, Loving, 7 ............ 15 | Middletown, Blanco |
| McNeil, Caldwell, ............. 200 | Mentone, Loving | Middletown, Goliad |
| *McNeil, Travis,.............. 70 | Mentz, Colorado,............. 100 | Middletown, Harris |
| McNeills Landing, Angelina | *MERCEDES, Hidalgo, 400 | Middletown, Kendall |
| McNeil Switch, Angelina | (13,649)................14,016 | Middle Valley, Schleicher |
| McNorton, Nueces | Mercer's, Wharton | Middle Water, Hartley |
| McNulty, Rusk | Mercer's Bluff, Milam | *Midfield, Matagorda, 3.......... 70 |
| McPeek, Upshur | Mercer's Gap, Brown | Midkiff, Midland |
| *McQueeney, Guadalupe, | Mercer's Gap, Comanche | *Midkiff, Upton, 20.............. 98 |
| 65 (2,527) ..............2,640 | Mercier, Hidalgo | *MIDLAND, Midland, 6,680 |
| McRae, Montgomery | Mercury, McCulloch .......... 166 | (94,996) .............. 95,222 |
| McShane, Hardin | Mercy, Parker | Midlin, Denton |
| McWhorter, Madison | Mercy, San Jacinto | Midline, Montgomery |
| Meaders, Dallas | Meredith, Johnson | *MIDLOTHIAN, Ellis, 640 |
| *MEADOW, Terry, 19 (658) ...... 626 | *Mereta, Tom Green, 3 .......... 75 | (7,480) ................ 9,131 |
| Meadow Brook, Coryell | Meriam, Liberty | Midway, Bell, .................122 |
| Meadow Grove, Bell, ........... 10 | *MERIDIAN, Bosque, 128 | Midway, Bexar |
| Meadow Lake, Guadalupe, ..... 450 | (1,491)................1,529 | Midway, Bosque |
| MEADOW LAKES, Burnet, | *Merit, Hunt, 10............... 215 | Midway, Dawson,................ 20 |

CITIES & TOWNS

| Town,County . . . . . . . . . . .Pop. 2002 | Town,County . . . . . . . . . . .Pop. 2002 | Town,County . . . . . . . . . . . Pop. 2002 |
|---|---|---|
| Midway, Dickens | Millerton, San Augustine | Minnie, Jackson |
| **Midway, Fannin,** . . . . . . . . . . . . . . 7 | Millerville, Erath | Minnis, Wilbarger |
| Midway, Franklin | **Millett, La Salle,** . . . . . . . . . . . 40 | Minnocks, Montgomery |
| Midway, Hamilton | Millett's, Baylor | Minor, Lynn |
| Midway, Hemphill | Mill Grove, Fannin | Minor, Mills |
| Midway, Henderson | **Millheim, Austin,** . . . . . . . . . . . . 150 | Minora, Liberty |
| Midway, Hill | Millheim Station, Austin | **Minter, Lamar,** . . . . . . . . . . . . . . . .78 |
| Midway, Howard | Mill Hollow, Williamson | Minter, Tarrant |
| **Midway, Jim Wells,** . . . . . . . . . . . . NA | **\*MILLICAN, Brazos, 7 (108)** . . . . . 104 | Minters, Kerr |
| Midway, Johnson | Milligan, Collin | Minterville, Howard |
| Midway, Jones | Milliken, Runnels | Mirage, Deaf Smith |
| **Midway, Lavaca,** . . . . . . . . . . . . . . NA | Millino, Colorado | Miranda, Tarrant |
| Midway, Leon | Mill Lake, Freestone | **\*Mirando City, Webb, 19 (493)** . . . 505 |
| **Midway, Limestone,** . . . . . . . . . . . . 9 | Mill Prairie, Wood | Miriam, Liberty |
| Midway, Lubbock | Mill Run, Henderson | Mirror, Floyd |
| **\*MIDWAY, Madison, 23 (288)** . . . . 285 | Mills, Dallas | **\*MISSION, Hidalgo, 1,903** |
| Midway, Montgomery | Mills, Freestone | **(45,408)** . . . . . . . . . . . . . . . 50,515 |
| Midway, Navarro | Mills, Grayson | Mission, Hidalgo |
| Midway, Newton | Mills', San Jacinto | Mission, Moore |
| Midway, Nueces | **\*MILLSAP, Parker, 67 (353)** . . . . . . 367 | **Mission Bend, Fort Bend-Harris,** |
| **Midway, Polk,** . . . . . . . . . . . . . . . . NA | Mills Bennett, Webb | **(30,831)** . . . . . . . . . . . . . . . 31,968 |
| **Midway, Red River,** . . . . . . . . . . . . 40 | Millseat, Hays | Mission Grove, Panola |
| Midway, San Patricio | Mills Store, Brown | Mission Hill, Comal |
| Midway, Scurry | Millsville, San Patricio | Mission Valley, Comal |
| **Midway, Smith,** . . . . . . . . . . . . . . . NA | Mill Town, Fannin | Mission Valley, Medina |
| Midway, Starr | Mill Town, Hardin | **Mission Valley, Victoria,** . . . . . . . . 225 |
| **Midway, Titus,** . . . . . . . . . . . . . . . 110 | Mill Tract, Falls | Mississippi Colony, Fayette |
| Midway, Tom Green | Millville, Gillespie | Missoula, Fort Bend |
| **Midway, Upshur,** . . . . . . . . . . . . . . 20 | Millville, Rusk | **\*MISSOURI CITY, Fort Bend-Harris,** |
| **Midway, Van Zandt,** . . . . . . . . . . . 31 | Millwood, Collin | **2,104 (52,913)** . . . . . . . . . . 57,239 |
| Midway Center, Grayson | Milner, Cass | Mitcham, Henderson |
| **Midway North, Hidalgo,** | Milo, Baylor | Mitchell, Cameron |
| **(3,946).** . . . . . . . . . . . . . . . .4,137 | Milo, Briscoe | **Mitchell, Eastland,** . . . . . . . . . . . . . 46 |
| **Midway South, Hidalgo,** | Milo, Wood | Mitchell, Lipscomb |
| **(1,711).** . . . . . . . . . . . . . . . .1,782 | **Milo Center, Deaf Smith,** . . . . . . . . 5 | Mitchell, Panola |
| Midwest, Wheeler | Milred, Navarro | Mitchell, Swisher |
| **Midyett, Panola,** . . . . . . . . . . . . . . NA | Milton, Freestone | Mitchell's, Cooke |
| Mifflin, Donley | **Milton, Lamar,** . . . . . . . . . . . . . . . 80 | Mitchell's Valley, Limestone |
| Mifflin, Kenedy | Milton, Red River | Mitchell Hill, Tyler |
| Miguel, Frio | Milton, Shelby | Mitchell Pens, Victoria |
| Mikado, Wood | Milton, Tyler | Mitchells, Madison |
| **Mikeska, Live Oak,** . . . . . . . . . . . . 10 | Milvid, Liberty | Mittie, Cherokee |
| **Mila Doce, Hidalgo, (4,907)** . . . . 5,102 | Milvid, Montgomery | Mitto, Anderson |
| Milam, Falls | **Mims, Brazoria,** . . . . . . . . . . . . . . . .NA | **Mixon, Cherokee,** . . . . . . . . . . . . . . 50 |
| Milam, Milam | Mims, Rusk | Mixon, Lavaca |
| **\*Milam, Sabine, 19 (1,329)** . . . . . 1,342 | **Mims Chapel, Marion,** . . . . . . . . . .NA | Mizpah, Anderson |
| **\*MILANO, Milam, 22 (400)** . . . . . . 414 | Mims Chapel, Panola | Moab, Lee |
| **Milburn, McCulloch,** . . . . . . . . . . . . 8 | Mina, Bastrop | Mobberly, Red River |
| Milby, Travis | Mina, Eastland | **\*MOBEETIE, Wheeler, 9 (107)** . . . . .98 |
| **MILDRED, Navarro, (405)** . . . . . . . 422 | Mina, Hunt | Mobile, Crockett |
| Miles, Gonzales | Mina, Wise | Mobile, Tyler |
| **\*MILES, Runnels, 42 (850)** . . . . . . 857 | Minchin, Denton | **MOBILE CITY, Rockwall, (196)** . . . 189 |
| Miley, Bastrop | **\*Minden, Rusk, 5.** . . . . . . . . . . . . . 350 | Moccasin, Coryell |
| **\*MILFORD, Ellis, 14 (685).** . . . . . . 677 | Mindiette, Duval | Moccasin Gap, Trinity |
| Millay, Denton | Minear, Gonzales | Mode, Floyd |
| Mill Creek, Bowie | Mineola, Cooke | Modera, Bandera |
| Mill Creek, Guadalupe | **\*MINEOLA, Wood, 504** | Modern, Jim Wells |
| Mill Creek, Harrison | **(4,550).** . . . . . . . . . . . . . . . .4,694 | Modeville, Wise |
| Mill Creek, Red River | Minera, Webb | Modisett, Angelina |
| Mill Creek, San Jacinto | **\*Mineral, Bee,** . . . . . . . . . . . . . . . . 50 | Modoc, Henderson |
| Mill Creek, Waller | Mineral Heights, Hunt | Mofeta, Terrell |
| **Mill Creek, Washington,** . . . . . . . . 40 | Mineral Spring, Karnes | **Moffat, Bell,** . . . . . . . . . . . . . . . . . 150 |
| Milledge, San Jacinto | Mineral Springs, Gray | **Moffett, Angelina,** . . . . . . . . . . . . . 100 |
| Miller, Bastrop | Mineral Springs, Kendall | Moglia, Webb |
| Miller, Bell | Mineral Springs, Panola | Mogul, Tom Green |
| Miller, Dallas | Mineral Springs, Wilson | Mohair, Blanco |
| Miller, Rusk | **\*MINERAL WELLS, Palo Pinto-Parker,** | Mohat, Colorado |
| Miller's, Fannin | **878 (16,946)** . . . . . . . . . . .17,163 | Mohecan, Cherokee |
| Miller's, Fayette | Minerva, Foard | Mohegan, Hunt-Delta |
| Miller's, Lamar | **Minerva, Milam, 2** . . . . . . . . . . . . . 60 | Moistown, Cameron |
| Miller's, Panola | Minerva, Travis | **Moline, Lampasas,** . . . . . . . . . . . . . 12 |
| Miller's Farm, Lavaca | Mingo, Denton | Mollie, Red River |
| Miller Grove, Camp | **Mings Chapel, Upshur,** . . . . . . . . . 50 | Monadale, Williamson |
| **Miller Grove, Hopkins,** . . . . . . . . . 115 | **\*MINGUS, Palo Pinto, 19** | **\*MONAHANS, Ward, 413** |
| **MILLERS COVE, Titus, (120)** . . . . 122 | **(246)** . . . . . . . . . . . . . . . . . 259 | **(6, 821).** . . . . . . . . . . . . . . . .6,647 |
| **\*Millersview, Concho, 6** . . . . . . . . 75 | Mink, Montgomery | **Monaville, Waller,** . . . . . . . . . . . . . 180 |
| Millerton, Milam | Minnetex, Harris | Moncass, Cass |

**CITIES & TOWNS**

| Town, County ........ Pop. 2002 | Town, County ........ Pop. 2002 | Town, County ........ Pop. 2002 |
|---|---|---|
| Monico, Van Zandt | Mooring, Brazos, ............. 80 | Mosier Valley, Tarrant |
| Monington, Anderson | Moorman, Comanche | Mosley, Montgomery |
| Monkeyville, Hays | Morales, Jackson, ........... 72 | Mosquito Prairie, Lee |
| Monkstown, Fannin, .......... 35 | Morales-Sanchez, Zapata, (95) ... 95 | Moss, Medina |
| Monroe, Dallas | Morales de Lavaca, Jackson | Moss, Smith |
| Monroe, Eastland | Moran, Dallas | Moss Bluff, Liberty, ........... 65 |
| Monroe, Lubbock | *MORAN, Shackelford, 13 | Moss Hill, Liberty, ............ 49 |
| Monroe, Rusk, ............... 96 | (233) .................... 226 | Mossville, Cooke |
| Monroe City, Chambers, ....... 90 | Morard, Liberty | Mossy, Trinity |
| Monserate, Lavaca | Moravia, Lavaca, ............ 165 | Mossy Creek, Jefferson-Hardin |
| Mont, Lavaca, ............... 30 | Morceville, El Paso | Mossy Grove, Walker |
| Montadale, Williamson | Moreland, Collin | Mostyn, Montgomery, ......... NA |
| Montague, Fannin | Moreland, Navarro | Mote's Mill, Delta |
| *Montague, Montague, 26 ...... 400 | Morey, Jefferson | Motley, Rusk |
| Montague Village, Coryell, .... 1,410 | Morg, Stephens | Mott, Angelina |
| *Montalba, Anderson, 24 ...... 110 | *MORGAN, Bosque, 30 (485) .... 498 | Mottomosa, Atascosa |
| Montana, Uvalde | Morgan, Brazoria | Mott Springs, Shelby |
| *MONT BELVIEU, Chambers, | Morgan, Ellis | *MOULTON, Lavaca, 65 |
| 119 (2,324) ............. 2,510 | Morgan, Lynn | (944). ................... 961 |
| Mont Clair, Reeves | Morgan, Robertson | Moulton Institute, Lavaca |
| Monte Alto, Hidalgo, (1,611) ... 1,676 | Morgan, Williamson | *Mound, Coryell, 3. ............ 75 |
| Monte Christo, Hidalgo | Morgan, Young | Mound, Gonzales |
| Monte Grande, Cameron, ....... 97 | MORGAN'S POINT, Harris, | Mound City, Anderson-Houston, . 127 |
| Montell, Uvalde, ............. 20 | (336) .................. 362 | Mound City, Red River |
| Monteola, Bee | MORGAN'S POINT RESORT, | Mound Creek, Karnes |
| Monterey, Angelina | Bell, (2,989). ............ 3,236 | Mound Prairie, Anderson |
| Monterey, Hill | Morgan's Store, Shelby | Mound Prairie, Burleson |
| Monterey, Hockley | Morgan Center, Wichita | Mound Prairie, Freestone |
| Monterey, Lubbock | Morgan Creek, Burnet, ......... 76 | Mound Prairie, Lamar |
| Monterey, Marion-Harrison | Morgan Farm Area, San Patricio, | Mount, Hamilton |
| Monterey, Red River | (484) ................... 531 | Mountain, Coryell, ........... 300 |
| Monterey Station, Marion | Morganlea, Robertson | MOUNTAIN CITY, Hays, (671) .... 709 |
| Montero, McLennan | *Morgan Mill, Erath, 8. ........ 206 | Mountain Creek, Dallas |
| Monte Robles Park, Bexar | Morgan Springs, Parker | Mountain Creek, Tarrant |
| Montezuma, Bailey | Morganville, Polk | Mountain Home, Bell |
| Montezuma, Colorado | Morince, Van Zandt | *Mountain Home, Kerr, 19 ....... 96 |
| Montfort, Navarro | Morita, Howard | Mountain Peak, Ellis, ........... 20 |
| *MONTGOMERY, Montgomery, | Morita, Presidio | Mountain Spring, Cooke |
| 854 (489). ............... 515 | Morman, Falls | Mountain Springs, Cooke, ...... 100 |
| Monthalia, Gonzales, .......... 65 | Mormon Grove, Grayson | Mountain Springs, Hill |
| Monticello, Titus, ............. 20 | Mormon Mills, Burnet | Mountain Top, Eastland, ........ 22 |
| Montopolis, Travis | Mornack, Bosque | Mountain Valley, Comal |
| Montoya, El Paso | Morning Glory, El Paso, (627) ... 647 | Mountain Valley, Medina |
| Mont Truby, Jones | Moro, Tarrant | Mountain View, Blanco |
| Montvale, Hamilton | Moro, Taylor | Mountain View, Travis, ........ 393 |
| Montvale, Lampasas | Morrill, Cherokee | Mount Airy, Cherokee |
| Montvale, Sterling | Morris, Borden | Mount Airy, Erath |
| Montville, Washington | Morris, Dallas | MOUNT BETHEL, Hunt, ........ NA |
| Monument Switch, Irion | Morris, DeWitt | Mount Bethel, Panola, .......... 62 |
| Moody, Bell | Morris, Falls | Mount Blanco, Crosby |
| *MOODY, McLennan, 100 | Morris, Howard | *MOUNT CALM, Hill, 14 (310) .... 319 |
| (1,400). ................ 1,428 | Morris, Morris | Mount Calm, Limestone |
| Moody's Cross Roads, Leon | Morris Ferry, Jasper | Mount Carmel, Marion |
| Moody Store, Lubbock | Morrison, Fort Bend | Mount Carmel, Smith |
| Moon, Baylor | Morrison's Chapel, Leon | Mount Carmel, Wichita |
| Moon Chapel, Sterling | Morrison Chapel, Henderson | Mount Comfort, Cherokee |
| Mooney, Harris | Morris Ranch, Gillespie, ........ NA | Mount Eden, Gonzales |
| Moonshine Colony, Baylor | Morrisstown, Harris | *MOUNT ENTERPRISE, Rusk, |
| Moonshine Hill, Harris | *Morse, Hansford, 11 (172). ..... 171 | 65 (525) ................. 528 |
| Moore, Brazos, ............... NA | Mortimer, Milam | Mount Enterprise, Wood |
| Moore, Clay | Morton, Cherokee | Mount Gainor, Hays |
| *Moore, Frio, 16 (644). ......... 665 | *MORTON, Cochran, 118 | Mount Gilead, Upshur |
| Moore's Crossing, Travis, ....... 25 | (2,249) ................. 2,271 | Mount Gilead, Washington |
| Moore's Fort, Fayette | Morton, Grayson | Mount Gillion, Nacogdoches |
| Moore's Hill, Martin | Morton, Harrison, ............. 75 | Mount Gillion, Shelby |
| Moore Chapel, Fannin | Morton, Lipscomb | Mount Green, Bell |
| Mooredale, Fort Bend | Morton Valley, Eastland, ........ 46 | Mount Harrison, Dallas |
| Moore Hill, Polk | Moscow, Falls | Mount Haven, Cherokee, ........ 30 |
| Moores', Bowie | *Moscow, Polk, 8. ............. 170 | Mount Hecla, Jack |
| Moores' Landing, Bowie | Mosel, Gillespie | Mount Hermon, Shelby, ......... 56 |
| MOORE STATION, Henderson, | Moseley, Henderson | Mount Holland, Hardin |
| (184) .................... 178 | Mosely, Red River | Mount Hope, Cherokee |
| Mooresville, Comanche | Mosely, Upton | Mount Hope, Cooke |
| Mooresville, Wood | Moses, Stephens | Mount Hope, SanJacinto |
| Mooreville, Falls, ............. 96 | Moses Bluff, Angelina | Mount Hope, Tyler |
| Moorhead, Freestone | Moseville, Cameron | Mount Houston, Harris |
| Moorhead, Val Verde | Mosheim, Bosque, 1. ........... 75 | Mount Huling, Nacogdoches |

| Town,County . . . . . . . . . . .Pop. 2002 | Town,County . . . . . . . . . . .Pop. 2002 | Town,County. . . . . . . . . . . Pop. 2002 |
|---|---|---|
| Mount Jordan, Jasper | Muddig Prairie, Delta | Mustang, Van Zandt |
| Mount Joy, Delta | Muddy Creek Church, Wood | Mustang, Washington |
| Mount Juliet, Travis | Mud Spring, Denton | Mustang, Wharton |
| Mount Lebanon, Upshur | Mud Springs, Bell | Mustang Branch, Dallas |
| Mount Lucas, Live Oak | Mud Town, Bell | Mustang Creek, Johnson |
| Mount Margaret, Coke | Mud Town, Hill | Mustang Hill, Comal |
| Mount Mariah [Moriah], Gregg | Mudville, Brazos | Mustang Island, Nueces |
| Mount Mitchell, Morris | Muela, Maverick-Zavala | **Mustang Mott, DeWitt, . . . . . . . . . 20** |
| Mount Moriah, Anderson | **Muellersville, Washington,. . . . . . . 40** | Mustang Prairie, Falls |
| Mount Mourne, Panola | **\*MUENSTER, Cooke, 166** | Mustang Prairie, Houston |
| Mount Nebo, Navarro | **(1,556). . . . . . . . . . . . . . . . .1,582** | Mustang Prairie, Walker |
| Mount Olive, Cherokee | Muerto, Cameron | **MUSTANG RIDGE, Travis-Caldwell,** |
| **Mount Olive, Lavaca,. . . . . . . . . . . NA** | **Mulberry, Fannin, . . . . . . . . . . . . . 17** | **(785). . . . . . . . . . . . . . . . . . . . .838** |
| Mount Olive, Mills | Mulberry, Fayette | Mustang Settlement, Jackson |
| Mount Olive, Shelby | Mulberry, Red River | Mustang Springs, Williamson |
| Mount Olive, Smith | Mulberry Flats, Armstrong | Muster Point, Jasper |
| Mount Olivet, McLennan | Mulberry Grove, Grayson | Mutt and Jeff, Wood |
| Mount Pesrea, DeWitt | Mulberry Grove, Rusk | Myers, Burleson |
| Mount Pilgrim, Matagorda | **\*Muldoon, Fayette, 9. . . . . . . . . . . 98** | Myers, Collingsworth |
| Mount Pilgrim, Wharton | Mule Creek, Coke | Myers' Mill, Bell |
| Mount Pisgah, Hopkins | Mule Creek, Gonzales | Myers Settlement, Johnson |
| Mount Pisgah, Leon | **\*MULESHOE, Bailey, 345** | Mykawa, Harris |
| Mount Pisgah, Van Zandt | **(4,530). . . . . . . . . . . . . . . . .4,432** | **\*Myra, Cooke, 3. . . . . . . . . . . . . .300** |
| Mount Pisgah, Wood | Mulford, Orange | Myricks, Shelby |
| Mount Pleasant, Bastrop | Mulkey, Hill | Myrtle, Childress |
| Mount Pleasant, Comanche | **\*MULLIN, Mills, 26 (175). . . . . . . . 174** | Myrtle, Clay |
| Mount Pleasant, Freestone | Mullins, Falls | Myrtle, Harris |
| Mount Pleasant, Freestone | Mullins, Tom Green | Myrtle, Marion |
| Mount Pleasant, Grimes | **Mullins Prairie, Fayette, . . . . . . . . 52** | Myrtle Springs, Anderson |
| Mount Pleasant, Panola | Mulloy's, Robertson | Myrtle Springs, Bowie |
| Mount Pleasant, San Saba | Mulock, Hansford | Myrtle Springs, Bowie |
| Mount Pleasant, Taylor | Mulvey, Polk | Myrtle Springs, Camp |
| **\*MOUNT PLEASANT, Titus,** | **\*Mumford, Robertson, 4. . . . . . . . 170** | Myrtle Springs, Cherokee |
| **1,000 (13,935). . . . . . . . . . 14,139** | Muncy, Floyd | Myrtle Springs, Henderson |
| Mount Pleasant, Wharton | **\*MUNDAY, Knox, 88 (1,527) . . . .1,459** | **Myrtle Springs, Van Zandt,. . . . . . 131** |
| **Mount Rose, Falls,. . . . . . . . . . . . . 26** | **Munger, Limestone, . . . . . . . . . . . . 5** | Myrtle Springs, Wood |
| Mount Rose, Polk | **Mungerville, Dawson,. . . . . . . . . . 25** | |
| Mount Scopus, Atascosa | **Muniz, Hidalgo, (1,106). . . . . . .1,173** | **N** |
| **Mount Selman, Cherokee,. . . . . . 200** | Munn, Eastland | Naaman, Dallas |
| Mount Sharp, Hays | Munson, Rockwall | Nabors, Haskell-Jones |
| Mount Sterling, Hopkins | Munsonville, Polk | Nacalina, Nacogdoches-Angelina |
| Mount Sterling, Nacogdoches | Munz, Cass | Naches, Houston |
| **Mount Sylvan, Smith,. . . . . . . . . 181** | **\*MURCHISON, Henderson, 65** | **\*NACOGDOCHES, Nacogdoches,** |
| Mount Tabor, Lamar | **(592) . . . . . . . . . . . . . . . . . . . 589** | **1,971 (29,914) . . . . . . . . . 30,037** |
| Mount Union, Jasper | Murchison's Prairie, Houston | **\*Nada, Colorado, 13 . . . . . . . . . . . 165** |
| Mountvale, Coleman | Murdo, Oldham | Nadine, Rockwall |
| Mount Vernon, Anderson | Murdock Place, Bee | Nagiller, Potter |
| **\*MOUNT VERNON, Franklin,** | Murdocks Landing, Kenedy | Nag Park, Cherokee |
| **243 (2,286) . . . . . . . . . . . . . 2,290** | Muriel, Tarrant | Nailer, Fannin |
| Mount Vernon, Gonzales | **MURPHY, Collin, (3,099). . . . . . .5,820** | Nailton, Lipscomb |
| **Mount Vernon, Houston, . . . . . . . . 43** | Murphy, Medina | Naizerville, Williamson |
| Mount Vernon, Lamar | Murphy's Store, Burnet | Nall, Howard |
| Mount Vernon, Limestone | Murphyville, Brewster | Nalley, Lee |
| Mount Vernon, Montgomery | Murray, Cameron | Nalley, McLennan |
| Mount Vernon, Washington | Murray, Dallam | Nalyon, Bandera |
| Mount Zion, Coryell | Murray, Lubbock | Nameless, Travis |
| Mount Zion, Freestone | Murray, Medina | Nan, Fort Bend |
| Mount Zion, Hopkins | Murray, Panola | Nance's Mill, Hays |
| Mount Zion, Houston | **Murray, Young, . . . . . . . . . . . . . . 45** | Nancy, Angelina |
| Mount Zion, Montgomery | Murray's Store, Tom Green | Nancy, Colorado |
| Mount Zion, Rockwall | Murrey League, Marion | Nanhattie, Coke-Sterling |
| Mount Zora, Haskell | Murry League, Upshur | Napier, Bastrop |
| Moursund, Victoria | Murryville, Reeves | Napier, San Jacinto |
| Mouth of Pedernales, Travis | Murval, Rusk | **\*NAPLES, Morris, 76** |
| Mowatt, Bastrop | **Murvaul, Panola,. . . . . . . . . . . . . 110** | **(1,410) . . . . . . . . . . . . . . . . . 1,401** |
| Moyer, Childress | Muse, Wise | Narcisso, Cottle |
| Mozart, Crockett | Musgrove, Wood-Franklin | **Naruna, Burnet,. . . . . . . . . . . . . . . 45** |
| Mozelle, Cochran | Music, Frio | **\*NASH, Bowie, 103 (2,169) . . . . 2,138** |
| **Mozelle, Coleman, . . . . . . . . . . . . NA** | Muskegon, Orange | **Nash, Ellis,. . . . . . . . . . . . . . . . . . 25** |
| Mozo, Williamson | Muskete, Navarro | Nash's Foundry, Marion |
| Muckymuck, Travis | Musquis, Jeff Davis | Nash's Mill, Gonzales |
| Mud, Travis | Mustang, Bosque | Nashland, Jefferson |
| Mud City, Travis | **Mustang, Denton,. . . . . . . . . . . . . .NA** | Nashville, Milam |
| Mud Creek, Cherokee | Mustang, Falls | Nashville, Shelby |
| Mud Creek, Kinney | Mustang, Lavaca | Nassau, Fayette |
| Mud Creek, Smith | Mustang, Limestone | **NASSAU BAY, Harris, (4,170) . . 4,230** |
| Muddig, Hunt | **MUSTANG, Navarro, (47) . . . . . . . 49** | **Nat, Nacogdoches, . . . . . . . . . . . . 25** |

**CITIES & TOWNS**

| Town,County . . . . . . . . . . .Pop. 2002 | Town,County . . . . . . . . . . .Pop. 2002 | Town,County. . . . . . . . . . . Pop. 2002 |
|---|---|---|

*Natali, Fort Bend*
**\*NATALIA, Medina, 49**
   **(1,663). . . . . . . . . . . . . . . . 1,697**
*Natalie, Dawson*
*Natalie, Palo Pinto*
*Natches, Tyler*
*Nathan, Johnson*
*Nathan, Trinity*
*Nathen, Caldwell*
*Nations, Pecos*
*Nationsville, Coleman*
*Naught, Henderson*
*Navarro, Atascosa*
*Navarro, Guadalupe*
*Navarro, Leon*
**NAVARRO, Navarro, (191) . . . . . . 203**
*Navarro County Town, Ellis*
**Navarro Mills, Navarro, . . . . . . . . 50**
**\*NAVASOTA, Grimes, 474**
   **(6,789). . . . . . . . . . . . . . . . .7,027**
*Navasota, Robertson-Leon*
*Navidad, Fayette*
*Navidad, Fayette*
*Navidad, Jackson*
**Navidad, Jackson. . . . . . . . . . . . 227**
**Navo, Denton . . . . . . . . . . . . . . . 35**
*Nay, Hunt*
*Naylor, Donley*
**\*NAZARETH, Castro, 34**
   **(356) . . . . . . . . . . . . . . . . . . 348**
*Nazro, Limestone*
*Neal, Hill*
*Neal, Madison*
*Neale, McLennan*
*Neals, Upshur*
*Neals Valley, Ellis*
*Neason, Grimes*
*Nebo, Cherokee*
*Nebo, Denton*
*Nebo, Gillespie*
*Nebo, Hall*
*Nebo, Parker*
*Nebo, Smith*
*Nebraska, Cameron*
**Necessity, Stephens, . . . . . . . . . . 10**
**Nechanitz, Fayette, . . . . . . . . . . . 21**
*Neche, Houston*
**\*Neches, Anderson, 13 . . . . . . . . 175**
*Neches, Cherokee*
*Neches River Settlement, Jefferson*
*Neches Saline, Smith*
*Ned, Taylor*
**\*NEDERLAND, Jefferson,**
   **1,080 (17,422). . . . . . . . . . 17,548**
*Nedra, Wharton*
*Need, Lamar*
**Needmore, Bailey, . . . . . . . . . . . . 45**
*Needmore, Bowie*
*Needmore, Cherokee*
*Needmore, Cooke*
*Needmore, Delta*
*Needmore, Erath*
*Needmore, Falls*
*Needmore, Nacogdoches*
*Needmore, Rusk*
**Needmore, Terry, . . . . . . . . . . . . . 55**
*Needmore, Van Zandt*
*Needmore Store, Archer*
**\*NEEDVILLE, Fort Bend, 250**
   **(2,609). . . . . . . . . . . . . . . . 2,769**
*Neelie, Live Oak*
*Neely, Nolan*
*Neely, San Augustine*
**Neely Ward, Cochran, . . . . . . . . . . 5**
*Neese's Store, Fayette*
*Neff, Erath*
*Neff, Stonewall*

**Negley, Red River, . . . . . . . . . . . 136**
*Neighborsville, Comal*
*Neill's Creek, Bosque*
*Neill's Creek, Hamilton*
**Neinda, Jones, . . . . . . . . . . . . . . . 21**
*Nell, Henderson*
**Nell, Live Oak, . . . . . . . . . . . . . . . 60**
**Nelleva, Brazos, . . . . . . . . . . . . . .NA**
*Nelleville, Travis*
*Nelson, Ellis*
*Nelson, Kerr*
*Nelsonberg, Bexar*
*Nelson City, Kendall*
**Nelsonville, Austin, . . . . . . . . . . . 110**
**Nelta, Hopkins, . . . . . . . . . . . . . . . 36**
**\*Nemo, Somervell, 7. . . . . . . . . . . 56**
*Nena, Ellis*
*Neola, Hunt*
*Neosho, Henderson*
*Neri, Hood*
**NESBITT, Harrison, (302) . . . . . . . 294**
**Nesbitt, Robertson, . . . . . . . . . . . .NA**
*Nesmith, Brewster*
*Nesterville, Wichita*
*Nestorville, Navarro*
*Nettaville, LaSalle*
*Nettie, Polk*
*Nettleridge, Shelby*
*Neugent, Hill*
*Neuse Store, Comal*
*Neusser, Williamson*
*Neut, Fannin*
**Neuville, Shelby, . . . . . . . . . . . . . . 43**
*Neva, Stonewall*
**\*NEVADA, Collin, 68 (563) . . . . . . 584**
*Neville, Gonzales*
*New Anhalt, Lee*
**\*NEWARK, Wise, 53 (887). . . . . . . 939**
*New Artesia, Atascosa*
**\*New Baden, Robertson, 6. . . . . . 150**
**NEW BERLIN, Guadalupe,**
   **(467) . . . . . . . . . . . . . . . . . . 512**
*New Bern, Williamson*
*New Bethel, Jefferson*
*New Bethel, Smith*
*New Bethlehem, Titus*
*New Bethlehem, Upshur*
**New Bielau, Colorado, . . . . . . . . . 75**
*New Birmingham, Cherokee*
**New Birthright, Hopkins, . . . . . . . .NA**
**New Blox, Jasper, . . . . . . . . . . . . .NA**
*New Bolivar, Denton*
**\*NEW BOSTON, Bowie, 340**
   **(4,808). . . . . . . . . . . . . . . . .4,820**
*New Boston, Chambers*
**\*NEW BRAUNFELS, Comal-**
   **Guadalupe, 2,977**
   **(36,494) . . . . . . . . . . . . . . .39,742**
**New Bremen, Austin, . . . . . . . . . . 75**
*New Bremen, Karnes*
**Newburg, Comanche, . . . . . . . . . . 35**
*Newburg, Parker*
**Newby, Leon, . . . . . . . . . . . . . . . . 40**
*New California, Glasscock*
*New California, Zavala*
*New Camp, Nacogdoches*
*New Camp Ruby, Polk*
**\*New Caney, Montgomery, 461**
   **. . . . . . . . . . . . . . . . . . . . . .2,771**
*New Carlisle, Rusk*
**\*NEWCASTLE, Young, 13**
   **(575) . . . . . . . . . . . . . . . . . . 589**
*New Center, Blanco*
**NEW CHAPEL HILL, Smith,**
   **(553) . . . . . . . . . . . . . . . . . . 604**
*New Cincinnati, Walker*
*New Clarkson, Milam*

**New Colony, Bell, . . . . . . . . . . . . . . 4**
**New Colony, Cass, . . . . . . . . . . . . 65**
*New Columbia, Newton*
*Newcomb, Shackelford*
**New Corn Hill, Williamson, . . . . . . NA**
*New Danville, Rusk*
**New Davy, DeWitt, . . . . . . . . . . . . 20**
**\*NEW DEAL, Lubbock, 16**
   **(708). . . . . . . . . . . . . . . . . . . 760**
*New Diana, Upshur*
*Newell, Kinney*
*New Emmaus, Cherokee*
*New Epworth, Hale*
*New Era, Bowie*
**NEW FAIRVIEW, Wise, (877) . . . . 886**
**New Falcon, Zapata, (184) . . . . . . 199**
**New Fountain, Medina, . . . . . . . . . NA**
**\*Newgulf, Wharton, 1 . . . . . . . . . . . 10**
**New Harmony, Shelby, . . . . . . . . . NA**
**New Harmony, Smith, . . . . . . . . . . 350**
**New Harp, Montague, . . . . . . . . . . . 8**
*New Henrietta, Clay*
*New Home, Hays*
*New Home, Limestone*
**\*NEW HOME, Lynn, 18**
   **(320). . . . . . . . . . . . . . . . . . . 322**
*New Home, Smith*
*New Hope, Angelina*
**New Hope, Cherokee, . . . . . . . . . . 50**
**NEW HOPE, Collin, (662) . . . . . . . 685**
*New Hope, Coryell*
*New Hope, Dallas*
*New Hope, Denton*
*New Hope, Eastland*
*New Hope, Franklin*
*New Hope, Freestone*
**New Hope, Jones, . . . . . . . . . . . . . . 9**
*New Hope, Leon*
*New Hope, Liberty*
*New Hope, Limestone*
*New Hope, Mitchell*
*New Hope, Polk*
*New Hope, Runnels*
*New Hope, Rusk*
**New Hope, San Augustine, . . . . . . 75**
*New Hope, San Jacinto*
**New Hope, Smith, . . . . . . . . . . . . . 75**
*New Hope, Smith*
*New Hope, Wilson*
**New Hope, Wood, . . . . . . . . . . . . . 15**
*New Hope City, Jack*
*New Katy, Travis*
*New Leon, Comanche*
**Newlin, Hall, . . . . . . . . . . . . . . . . . 31**
*Newline, Marion*
*New Loco, Collingsworth*
**\*NEW LONDON, Rusk, 21**
   **(987). . . . . . . . . . . . . . . . . . . 992**
*New Loven, Dallas*
**New Lynn, Lynn, . . . . . . . . . . . . . . 18**
*New Mainz, Colorado*
**Newman, ElPaso, . . . . . . . . . . . . . 60**
*Newman, Fisher*
*Newmanville, Jones*
*New Martindale, Caldwell*
*New Mesquite, Collin*
*New Mine, Camp*
**New Moore, Lynn, . . . . . . . . . . . . . 10**
**New Mountain, Upshur, . . . . . . . . . 20**
*New Philadelphia, Wharton*
*New Pittsburg, Blanco*
*New Pleasanton, Atascosa*
*New Port, Calhoun*
**Newport, Clay-Jack, . . . . . . . . . . . 70**
*Newport, San Jacinto*
*Newport, Trinity*
*Newport, Walker*

| Town,County . . . . . . . . . . . .Pop. 2002 | Town,County . . . . . . . . . . .Pop. 2002 | Town,County . . . . . . . . . . . Pop. 2002 |
|---|---|---|
| New Prague, Fayette | Nine, McCulloch | Norse, Bosque, . . . . . . . . . . . . . . .110 |
| New Prospect, Delta | Nineveh, Leon, . . . . . . . . . . . . . . 101 | Norse Grove, Bosque |
| New Prospect, Denton | Nip'n Tuck, Freestone | North Abilene, Jones |
| New Prospect, Fannin | Nip and Tuck, Rusk | North Alamo, Hidalgo, |
| New Prospect, Houston | Nisbet, Swisher | (2,601) . . . . . . . . . . . . . . . . 2,107 |
| New Prospect, Rusk | Nivac, Nacogdoches | North Bennett, Mills |
| New Salem, Falls | Niwot, Coleman | North Cedar, Trinity |
| New Salem, Leon | Nix, Lampasas, . . . . . . . . . . . . . . . 6 | North Chapel, Gregg |
| New Salem, Milam | Nix's Ranch, Crockett | North China, Jefferson |
| New Salem, Palo Pinto, . . . . . . . . 89 | Nix Chapel, Upshur | NORTH CLEVELAND, Liberty, |
| New Salem, Rusk, . . . . . . . . . . . . 55 | *NIXON, Gonzales-Wilson, 98 | (263). . . . . . . . . . . . . . . . . . . . 272 |
| New Serbin, Lee | (2,186) . . . . . . . . . . . . . . . . .2,241 | Northcliff, Guadalupe, |
| Newsom, Jones | Nixon, Guadalupe | (1,819) . . . . . . . . . . . . . . . . 1,879 |
| Newsom, Upshur | Nixon, Lamar | North Cowden, Ector, . . . . . . . . . . 80 |
| Newsome, Bailey | Noack, Williamson . . . . . . . . . . . . 60 | Northcrest, McLennan |
| Newsome, Camp, . . . . . . . . . . . . 100 | Noah, Upshur | North Elm, Milam |
| New Sour Lake, Hardin | Nobel, Lamar | Northern Headquarters, Matagorda |
| *NEW SUMMERFIELD, Cherokee, | Nob Hill, Llano | North Escobares, Starr, |
| 27 (998). . . . . . . . . . . . . . . .1,019 | Nobility, Fannin, . . . . . . . . . . . . . 21 | (1,692) . . . . . . . . . . . . . . . 1,762 |
| New Sweden, Travis, . . . . . . . . . 60 | Noble, Hardin | Northfield, Motley, . . . . . . . . . . . . 15 |
| New Taiton, Wharton, . . . . . . . . . NA | Noble, Lamar, . . . . . . . . . . . . . . . 40 | Northfork, Gray |
| New Territory, Fort Bend, | Noble, Lynn | North Fort Hood, Coryell |
| (13,861). . . . . . . . . . . . . . . 14,306 | Noble, Potter | North Fort Worth, Tarrant |
| New Tira, Hopkins | Nockenut, Wilson, . . . . . . . . . . . . 10 | North Galveston, Galveston |
| Newton, Fannin | *NOCONA, Montague, 256 | North Goree, Knox |
| *NEWTON, Newton, 116 | (3,198) . . . . . . . . . . . . . . . .3,241 | North Groesbeck, Hardeman |
| (2,459). . . . . . . . . . . . . . . . 2,451 | Nod, Cooke | North Heights, Potter |
| Newton, Newton | Nodena, Titus | North Hopkins, Hopkins, . . . . . . . NA |
| Newton, Rockwall | Noel, Harrison | North Houston, Harris, 3 . . . . . . . NA |
| Newtonville, Gonzales | Noelette, Carson | North Jericho, Shelby |
| Newtonville, Jasper | Noelke, Irion | NORTHLAKE, Denton, (921). . . . . 974 |
| Newtown, Harris | Noell, Dallas | North Liberty, Hopkins |
| New Town, Throckmorton | Nogal, Ochiltree | North Llano, Kimble |
| Newtown, Wichita | Nogalus Prairie, Trinity, . . . . . . . . 109 | North Mesquite, Dallas |
| Newtown, Wichita | Nola, Cooke | North Olney, Archer |
| *New Ulm, Austin, 53 . . . . . . . . . . 650 | *Nolan, Nolan, 7 . . . . . . . . . . . . . 47 | North Park, Taylor |
| New Washington, Harris | Nolands River, Johnson | North Pearsall, Frio, (561). . . . . . . 582 |
| *NEW WAVERLY, Walker, 93 | Noland Valley, Bell | North Pleasanton, Atascosa |
| (950) . . . . . . . . . . . . . . . . . . . 918 | Nolansville, Bell | North Pole, Nueces |
| New Wehdem, Austin, . . . . . . . . 100 | *NOLANVILLE, Bell, 46 | North Prairie, Falls |
| New Wied, Comal | (2,150) . . . . . . . . . . . . . . . .2,166 | *NORTH RICHLAND HILLS, |
| New Willard, Polk, . . . . . . . . . . . 160 | Nolanville, Grimes | Tarrant, (55,635) . . . . . . . . 58,265 |
| New York, Henderson, . . . . . . . . . 15 | Noleda, Duval | North Roby, Fisher |
| New Zion, Marion | Nolia, Sabine | Northrup, Lee, . . . . . . . . . . . . . . . 71 |
| Neyland, Hardin | Nolte, Guadalupe, . . . . . . . . . . . . 25 | North Rusk, Cherokee |
| Neyland, Hunt | Noma, Nueces | North San Antonio Hills, Bexar |
| NEYLANDVILLE, Hunt, (56) . . . . . 56 | *NOME, Jefferson, 22 (515) . . . . . 512 | North San Pedro, Nueces, |
| Nibletts Bluff, Newton | Nona, Hardin | (920). . . . . . . . . . . . . . . . . . . 926 |
| Niblock, McCulloch | Noodle, Jones, . . . . . . . . . . . . . . 40 | North Seadrift, Calhoun |
| Nicaragua, Karnes | Noon, Falls | North Star, Archer, . . . . . . . . . . . . 4 |
| Nicholas, Robertson | Noonan, Medina | North Sulphur, Fannin |
| Nichols, Bell | Noonday, Harrison | North Texarkana, Bowie |
| Nichols, Karnes | NOONDAY, Smith, (515) . . . . . . . 523 | North Uvalde, Uvalde |
| Nicholson, Fannin | Nopal, DeWitt, . . . . . . . . . . . . . . . 25 | North Vernon, Wilbarger |
| Nicholsville, McLennan | Nopal, Dimmit | North Waco, McLennan |
| Nickel, Gonzales | Nopal, La Salle | Northwood, Grimes |
| Nickel Creek, Culberson, . . . . . . . 16 | Nopal, McMullen | *North Zulch, Madison, 35 . . . . . . 150 |
| Nickelville, Collin | Nopal, Presidio | Norton, Grayson |
| Nickle, Burleson | Nopal, Willacy | *Norton, Runnels, 3 . . . . . . . . . . . 76 |
| Nickleberry, Cass | Norcross, Wilbarger | Norton's Grove, Tarrant |
| Nickleville, Wise | *NORDHEIM, DeWitt, 12 | Norvall, Cherokee |
| Nickols, Colorado | (323) . . . . . . . . . . . . . . . . . . 313 | Norvell's, Sabine |
| Nicks, Red River | Norfleet, Hale | Norway, Bosque |
| Nicolia, Kimble | Norfolk, Rusk | Norway, Duval |
| NIEDERWALD, Hays-Caldwell, | Norias, Kenedy, . . . . . . . . . . . . . . 45 | Norway Hills, Bosque |
| (584) . . . . . . . . . . . . . . . . . . . 618 | Norma, Polk | Norwegian Colony, Bee |
| Nigh, Colorado | Norman, Williamson, . . . . . . . . . . 20 | Norwood, Dallas |
| Nigton, Trinity, . . . . . . . . . . . . . . 87 | Norman, Winkler | Norwood, Harrison |
| Niland, Lamar | Normandy, Henderson | Norwood, McLennan |
| Nilar, Floyd | Normandy, Maverick, . . . . . . . . . . 98 | Norwood, Montague |
| Nile, Milam | *NORMANGEE, Leon-Madison, | Norwood, Runnels |
| Niles, Lee | 86 (719) . . . . . . . . . . . . . . . 724 | Norwood, San Augustine |
| Niles City, Tarrant | Norman Hill, Bosque | Norwood, Uvalde |
| Nimrod, Eastland, . . . . . . . . . . . . 85 | *Normanna, Bee, 4 (121) . . . . . . . 125 | Notla, Ochiltree, . . . . . . . . . . . . . 20 |
| Nimrod, Liberty | Normanville, San Jacinto | *Notrees, Ector, 3 . . . . . . . . . . . . 338 |
| Nina, Castro | Norrick, Wheeler | Nottawa, Wharton |
| Nina, Wise | Norris, Val Verde | Nottingham, Galveston |

CITIES & TOWNS

| Town,County | Pop. 2002 |
|---|---|


*NOVICE, Coleman, 10 (142) . . . . 139
Novice, Lamar, . . . . . . . . . . . . . . . 35
Noview, Dickens
Novoco, Fannin
Novohrad, Lavaca
Nowell, Lamar
Nox, Cooke
Noxville, Kimble, . . . . . . . . . . . . . . 3
Nubbin Ridge, Leon
Nubbin Ridge, Upshur
Nubbin Ridge, Wheeler-Hemphill
Nubia, Taylor, . . . . . . . . . . . . . . . . 2
Nueces, Nueces
Nueces Cañon, Edwards
Nueva Dolores, Zapata
Nueve, Dawson
Nugent, Chambers
Nugent, Jones, . . . . . . . . . . . . . . . 41
Nulo, Hudspeth
Nun, Hockley
Nunelee, Fannin, . . . . . . . . . . . . . 25
Nunn, Wilbarger
Nunnsville, Lee
Nurillo, Hidalgo, (5,056). . . . . . . 5,200
Nurmoore, Lynn
Nursery, Dallas
*Nursery, Victoria, 11 . . . . . . . . . 260
Nus, Limestone
Nussbaumer, Dallas
Nutsford, Lampasas
Nye, Webb

**O**

Oak, Ellis
Oakalla, Burnet, . . . . . . . . . . . . . . 45
Oak Bluff, Matagorda
Oak Cliff, Dallas
Oak Cliff Acres, Comal, . . . . . . . . NA
Oakdale, Hopkins, . . . . . . . . . . . . NA
Oakdale, Liberty
Oakdale, Polk, . . . . . . . . . . . . . . . 25
Oakdale, Sabine
Oakdale, Van Zandt
Oak Flat, Nacogdoches
Oak Flats, Rusk
Oakflatt, Comanche
Oak Forest, Gonzales, . . . . . . . . . 25
Oak Forest, Harris
Oak Glen, Jack
Oak Grove, Bowie, . . . . . . . . . . . 294
Oak Grove, Collin
Oak Grove, Colorado, . . . . . . . . . 40
Oak Grove, Coryell
Oak Grove, Denton
Oak Grove, Ellis, . . . . . . . . . . . . . 10
Oak Grove, Freestone
Oak Grove, Grayson
Oak Grove, Hopkins, . . . . . . . . . . NA
OAK GROVE, Kaufman,
  (710) . . . . . . . . . . . . . . . . . . . 777
Oak Grove, McLennan
Oak Grove, Morris
Oak Grove, Navarro
Oak Grove, Newton
Oak Grove, Tarrant
Oak Grove, Tarrant
Oak Grove, Terrell
Oak Grove, Titus
Oak Grove, Washington
Oak Grove, Wood, . . . . . . . . . . . . 74
Oak Hill, Bastrop
Oak Hill, Fannin
Oak Hill, Harrison
Oak Hill, Hemphill
Oak Hill, Hood, . . . . . . . . . . . . . . 247
Oak Hill, Houston
Oak Hill, Lamar


Oak Hill, Milam
Oakhill, Newton
Oak Hill, Rusk . . . . . . . . . . . . . . . 24
Oak Hill, Shelby
Oak Hill, Travis
*OAKHURST, San Jacinto, 8
  (230) . . . . . . . . . . . . . . . . . . 241
Oak Island, Bexar
Oak Island, Chambers, . . . . . . . . 255
Oak Knoll, Tarrant
Oaklake, McLennan, . . . . . . . . . . 60
Oakland, Brazoria, . . . . . . . . . . . NA
Oakland, Cherokee, . . . . . . . . . . 50
*Oakland, Colorado, 3 . . . . . . . . . 80
Oakland, Hopkins
Oakland, Houston
Oakland, Jack
Oakland, Lamar
Oakland, Red River
Oakland, Van Zandt, . . . . . . . . . . 26
Oakland Church, Grimes
OAK LEAF, Ellis, (1,209). . . . . . .1,315
Oakley, Bexar
Oakley, Falls
Oakley, Harris
Oak Manor, Brazoria, . . . . . . . . . 119
Oak Moss, Bexar
Oak Mott, Milam
Oak Park, Kerr
Oak Park, Travis
OAK POINT, Denton,
  (1,747) . . . . . . . . . . . . . . . . .1,961
Oak Point, Milam
Oak Ridge, Cass
OAK RIDGE, Cooke, (224) . . . . . . 233
Oakridge, Eastland
Oak Ridge, Fannin, . . . . . . . . . . . 90
Oak Ridge, Grayson, . . . . . . . . . 161
OAK RIDGE, Kaufman, (400) . . . . 426
Oak Ridge, Llano
Oak Ridge, Nacogdoches, . . . . . .NA
Oak Ridge, Rusk
OAK RIDGE NORTH, Montgomery,
  (2,991) . . . . . . . . . . . . . . . . .3,191
Oaks, Bee
Oaks, Tarrant
Oak Shade, Liberty
Oak Shade, Polk
Oak Springs, Hill
Oakton, Coryell
Oak Trail Shores, Hood,
  (2,475) . . . . . . . . . . . . . . . . .2,563
Oak Vale, Coleman
Oak Valley, Cooke
Oak Valley, Hill
Oak Valley, McLennan
OAK VALLEY, Navarro, (401) . . . . 410
Oak Valley, Wood
Oak Village, Bexar
Oakville, Live Oak, 1 . . . . . . . . . . 260
Oakville, Milam
Oakwood, Lavaca
*OAKWOOD, Leon, 49 (471). . . . . 475
Oasis, Cochran
Oasis, Dallas
Oatmanville, Travis
Oatmeal, Burnet, . . . . . . . . . . . . . 20
Obal, Cooke
Obal, Jefferson
O'Bar, Tarrant
O'Barr's, Fayette
Obe, Harrison
Ober, Grayson
Obi, Uvalde
Oblate, Hidalgo
Obregon, Coleman
*O'BRIEN, Haskell, 4 (132) . . . . . . 131


Oby, Camp
Ocaw, McLennan
Ocean Shore, Galveston
Ocee, McLennan, . . . . . . . . . . . . 35
Ochiltree, Ochiltree
Ochoa, Presidio
Ochoa, Webb
Ocie, Llano
Ocker, Bell
O'Daniel, Guadalupe
Odd's Creek, Delta-Lamar
Odds, Limestone, . . . . . . . . . . . . 24
Odelia, Jefferson
Odell, Angelina
Odell, Rockwall
Odell, Washington
*Odell, Wilbarger, 1 . . . . . . . . . . . 131
*ODEM, San Patricio, 65
  (2,499) . . . . . . . . . . . . . . . 2,544
Oden, Leon
Odesco, Panola
*ODESSA, Ector-Midland,
  5,579 (90,943) . . . . . . . . . 90,731
Odessa, Wise
Odlaw, Kinney
Odom, Van Zandt
Odom Store, Cherokee
*O'DONNELL, Lynn-Dawson, 55
  (1,011) . . . . . . . . . . . . . . . . . 980
Odum's Town, Angelina
Oenaville, Bell, . . . . . . . . . . . . . . 120
O'Farrell, Cass, . . . . . . . . . . . . . . 20
Ogan, Erath
Ogarita, Travis
Ogburn, Smith
Ogburn, Wood, . . . . . . . . . . . . . . 10
Ogden, Comal
Ogden, Cottle
Ogden, Falls
Ogden, Tyler
Ogg, Randall
Ogles, Lampasas
*OGLESBY, Coryell, 19 (458) . . . . 457
Ogletree, Coryell
O'Hair, Johnson
O'Hair's Hill, Burnet
Ohio, Cameron
Ohio, Hamilton
Ohio Colony, Matagorda
Oil, Cherokee
Oil Center, Eastland
Oil City, Clay
Oil City, Hutchinson
Oil City, Young
Oildom, Wichita
Oilla, Orange
Oil Spring, Taylor
Oil Springs, Nacogdoches
*Oilton, Webb, 8 (310) . . . . . . . . . 319
Ojo de Agua, Hidalgo
Ojo de Veranda, Presidio
Okay, Bell
Oklahoma, Cooke
Oklahoma, Karnes
Oklahoma, Montgomery, . . . . . . . NA
Oklahoma Flat, Hockley, . . . . . . . . 8
Oklahoma Lane, Parmer, . . . . . . . 25
*Oklaunion, Wilbarger, 4 . . . . . . . 138
Okra, Eastland, . . . . . . . . . . . . . . 20
Ola, Dallas
Ola, Kaufman, . . . . . . . . . . . . . . . 50
Ola, Taylor
Olcott, Harris
Old Aiken, Bell
Old Boston, Bowie, . . . . . . . . . . . 100
Old Bowling, Leon, . . . . . . . . . . . 20
Old Carolina, Walker

| Town,County | Pop. 2002 | Town,County | Pop. 2002 | Town,County | Pop. 2002 |
|---|---|---|---|---|---|

**Old Center, Panola,** . . . . . . . . . . . 83
*Old Cuero, DeWitt*
*Old Decatur, Collin*
*Old Diana, Upshur*
**Old Dime Box, Lee,** . . . . . . . . . . 200
*Old Emma, Crosby*
***Olden, Eastland, 7** . . . . . . . . . . 110
**Oldenburg, Fayette,** . . . . . . . . . . . 30
*Oldenburg, Fayette*
*Oldenburg, Smith*
*Old Evergreen, Lee*
*Old Ferry, Travis*
*Old Franklin, Robertson*
*Old Friendship, Williamson*
*Old Frio Town, Frio*
*Old Gay Hill, Washington*
***Old Glory, Stonewall, 3.** . . . . . . . 125
*Old Glover, Houston*
*Old Graball, Milam*
*Old Gulf, Matagorda*
*Oldham, Houston*
*Oldham, Tyler*
*Old Hope, Polk*
*Old Howard, Bell*
*Old Lubbock, Lubbock*
**Old Midway, Leon,** . . . . . . . . . . . NA
*Old Milsap, Parker*
*Old Minden, Rusk*
*Old Moulton, Lavaca*
***Old Ocean, Brazoria, 21** . . . . . . . 915
*Old Palestine, Cherokee*
*Old Philadelphia, Nacogdoches*
*Old Red Rock, Bastrop*
**OLD RIVER-WINFREE, Chambers,**
    **(1,364).** . . . . . . . . . . . . . . . . 1,380
*Old River Lake, Chambers*
*Old River Lake, Liberty*
*Old Rock Church, Atascosa*
*Old Round Rock, Williamson*
*Old Roxton, Lamar*
*Olds, Kinney*
*Olds, Ochiltree*
*Old Sabinetown, Sabine*
**Old Salem, Bowie,** . . . . . . . . . . . 50
*Old San Antonio, Jim Hogg*
*Old Snake River, Liberty*
*Old Spanish Trail Acres, Harris*
*Old Springfield, Limestone*
*Old Sutherland, Wilson*
*Old Tarrant, Hopkins*
*Old Tascosa, Oldham*
*Old Towash, Hill*
*Old Town, Harris*
*Old Troy, Bell*
*Old Union, Angelina*
**Old Union, Bowie,** . . . . . . . . . . . 238
**Old Union, Limestone,** . . . . . . . . . 25
*Old Union, Tarrant*
**Oletha, Limestone,** . . . . . . . . . . . . 53
**Olfen, Runnels,** . . . . . . . . . . . . . . 50
*Olga, Nolan*
*Olga, Swisher*
**Olin, Hamilton,** . . . . . . . . . . . . . . 12
*Olio, Fisher*
*Oliphint, Walker*
**Olivarez, Hidalgo, (2,445).** . . . . . 2,529
*Olive, Hardin*
*Olive, Hays*
*Olive Branch, McLennan*
*Olive Branch, Parker*
*Oliver, Denton*
*Oliver, Limestone*
*Oliver, Montague*
*Oliverea, Hunt*
*Oliverea, Hunt*
*Oliver Springs, Comanche*
**Olivia, Calhoun,** . . . . . . . . . . . . 215

**Ollie, Polk,** . . . . . . . . . . . . . . . . . . . 5
*Ollis, Falls*
***Olmito, Cameron, 59**
    **(1,198).** . . . . . . . . . . . . . . . . 1,244
*Olmos, Bee*
**Olmos, Guadalupe,** . . . . . . . . . . . 75
*Olmos, Maverick*
*Olmos, Starr*
**OLMOS PARK, Bexar, (2,343)** . . 2,373
***OLNEY, Young, 201**
    **(3,396).** . . . . . . . . . . . . . . . . 3,372
***OLTON, Lamb, 116**
    **(2,288).** . . . . . . . . . . . . . . . . 2,325
*Olympus, Childress*
*Olympus, Smith*
*Oma, Fisher*
***OMAHA, Morris, 48 (999)** . . . . . . 999
*Omega, Gregg*
*Omega, Upshur*
**Omen, Smith,** . . . . . . . . . . . . . . 150
***ONALASKA, Polk, 130**
    **(1,174).** . . . . . . . . . . . . . . . . 1,200
*Ondee, Hamilton*
*Oneal, Morris*
*Onega, Denton*
*Oneida, Orange*
*Oneida, Potter*
*Oneta, Leon*
*Oneta, Leon*
*Onie, Floyd*
*Onion, Ellis*
*Onion, Jones*
*Onion Creek, Ellis*
**Onion Creek, Travis, (2,116).** . . . 2,071
*Onslow, Edwards*
*Ontario, Gray*
*Ontario, Kimble*
*Ontario, Oldham*
*Onward, Taylor*
*Opah, Red River*
*Opal, Wise*
**Opdyke, Hockley,** . . . . . . . . . . . . 20
**OPDYKE WEST, Hockley, (188)** . . 187
*Opelika, Henderson*
*Ophelia, Caldwell*
*Ophelia, Rains*
*Ophir, Cooke*
*Ophir, Lubbock*
**Oplin, Callahan,** . . . . . . . . . . . . . 75
**O'Quinn, Fayette,** . . . . . . . . . . . . 25
*Ora, Angelina*
*Oral, Hays*
**Oran, Palo Pinto,** . . . . . . . . . . . . 61
*Oran, Roberts*
***ORANGE, Orange, 1,635**
    **(18,643).** . . . . . . . . . . . . . . 18,352
**Orangedale, Bee,** . . . . . . . . . . . . 35
***Orangefield, Orange, 16** . . . . . . . 725
*Orange Grove, Harris*
***ORANGE GROVE, Jim Wells,**
    **72 (1,288)** . . . . . . . . . . . . . . 1,300
*Orange Hill, Austin*
*Orangeville, Fannin*
**Oranson [Chula Vista-], Cameron,**
    **(394)** . . . . . . . . . . . . . . . . . . . 403
***ORCHARD, Fort Bend, 10**
    **(408)** . . . . . . . . . . . . . . . . . . . 426
*Orchard, Guadalupe*
*Orchard City, Cherokee*
*Orchard Park, Harrison*
*Ore, Morris*
*O'Rear's Mill, Cass*
***ORE CITY, Upshur, 85**
    **(1,106).** . . . . . . . . . . . . . . . . 1,144
*Oregon City, Baylor*
*Orelia, Frio*
*Oriana, Stonewall*

*Orient, Knox*
*Orient, Stonewall*
**Orient, Tom Green,** . . . . . . . . . . . 40
*Orient, Wichita*
*Orio, Van Zandt*
*Oriole, Houston*
*Orion, Hunt*
*Orizaba, Fayette*
***Orla, Reeves, 4.** . . . . . . . . . . . . . 183
*Orland, Stephens*
*Orleans, Hunt*
*Orlena, Cooke*
*Orme, Ellis*
*Orme, Tarrant*
*Ormel, Tarrant*
*Ornaville, Bell*
*Orozimbo, Brazoria*
*Orphans Home, Dallas*
*Orr, Dallas*
*Orr, Harris*
*Orr, Johnson*
*Orr, Rusk*
*Orrs, Marion*
*Orsack, Lavaca*
*Orth, Young*
*Orvil, Webb*
**Osage, Colorado,** . . . . . . . . . . . . 50
**Osage, Coryell,** . . . . . . . . . . . . . 30
*Osborne, Brewster*
*Osborne, Montgomery*
*Osborne, Wheeler*
*Osborne, Wilbarger*
*Osburnville, Eastland*
**Oscar, Bell,** . . . . . . . . . . . . . . . . 40
*Oscar, Bexar*
*Oscar, Kaufman*
**Osceola, Hill,** . . . . . . . . . . . . . . . 90
*Osceola, Madison*
*Osceola, Walker*
*Oslo, Hansford*
*Oso, Coke*
*Oso, Fayette*
*Oso, Fayette*
*Oso, Gonzales*
*Ossaba, Grayson*
*Ossey, Tarrant*
*Ostella, Hall*
*Oswego, Travis*
**Otey, Brazoria,** . . . . . . . . . . . . . 318
*Otho, Shelby*
*Otis, Bastrop*
*Otis, Red River*
*Otis, Van Zandt*
**Otis Chalk, Howard,** . . . . . . . . . . 79
*Otley, Frio*
*Otta, Cottle*
*Otta, Lubbock*
*Ottawa, Madison*
*Ottillie, Armstrong*
***Ottine, Gonzales, 2** . . . . . . . . . . . 90
***Otto, Falls, 2.** . . . . . . . . . . . . . . . 48
*Otto, Gonzales*
*Otto, Hardin*
*Otwell, Ellis*
*Ouida, Moore*
*Oval, Nacogdoches*
***Ovalo, Taylor, 17.** . . . . . . . . . . . 225
*Overall, Coleman*
*Overby, Karnes*
*Overland, Hopkins*
***OVERTON, Rusk-Smith,**
    **158 (2,350).** . . . . . . . . . . . . . 2,383
*Ovid, Jack*
***OVILLA, Ellis-Dallas,**
    **(3,405)** . . . . . . . . . . . . . . . . 3,608
*Owego, Pecos*
**Owens, Brown** . . . . . . . . . . . . . . NA

CITIES & TOWNS

| Town,County .......... Pop. 2002 | Town,County .......... Pop. 2002 | Town,County .......... Pop. 2002 |
|---|---|---|
| **Owens, Crosby,** .............. 40 | *Palmetto, Newton* | *Parker's Mills, Houston* |
| *Owens, Fannin* | *Palmetto, San Jacinto* | *Parker's Point, Limestone* |
| *Owensburg, Bowie* | **Palm Harbor, Aransas,** ........ 125 | *Parker's Shop, Parker* |
| **Owensville, Robertson,** ........ NA | **PALMHURST, Hidalgo,** | *Parker's Voting Box, Lamar* |
| **Owentown, Smith,** ........... 100 | (4,872) ................. 5,122 | *Parkers, Jasper* |
| *Owenville, Sutton* | *Palm Park, Bexar* | *Parkerton, Lamar* |
| *Owl, Camp* | **PALM VALLEY, Cameron,** | *Parkhurst, Wise* |
| *Owl, Wise* | (1,298) ................. 1,258 | *Parkinson, Gaines* |
| **Owl Creek, Bell,** .............. 45 | *Palm Valley, Williamson* | *Parks, Williamson* |
| *Owl Creek, Burnet* | **PALMVIEW, Hidalgo, (4,107)** ... 4,336 | *Parks Bluff, Red River* |
| **Owl Ranch-Amargosa, Jim Wells,** | **Palmview South, Hidalgo,** | **Parks Camp, Stephens,** ........ NA |
| (527) .................... 546 | (6,219) ................. 6,421 | *Parksdale, Hutchinson* |
| *Oxford, Fayette-Lee* | *Palo, Llano* | **Park Springs, Wise,** ........... NA |
| *Oxford, Llano* | *Palo Alto, Bell* | *Parksville, Polk-San Jacinto* |
| *Oxford, Milam* | *Palo Alto, Gonzales* | **Parkview Estates, Guadalupe,** ... 500 |
| *Oxford, Palo Pinto* | **Palo Alto, Nueces,** ............ 15 | *Parkville, Madison* |
| *Oxidine, Falls* | *Palo Alto Park, Bexar* | *Parmerton, Parmer* |
| *Oxien, Runnels* | *Palo Blanco, Willacy* | *Parmley, Montague* |
| **OYSTER CREEK, Brazoria,** | *Palo Blanco, Zavala* | *Parnell, Hall* |
| (1,192) ................. 1,197 | **Paloduro, Armstrong,** ......... 10 | *Parnell, Roberts* |
| *Oyster Creek, Brazoria* | *Palo Duro Creek, Hansford* | *Parris, Collin* |
| *Oyster Creek, Brazoria* | *Paloma, Edwards* | *Parrita Ranch, Brooks* |
| *Oyster Point, Nueces* | *Paloma, Matagorda* | *Parrott, Castro* |
| *Ozark, Lamar* | *Paloma, Maverick* | *Parrsville, Galveston* |
| *Ozarking, Ward* | *Paloma Ranch, Presidio* | *Parry's, Panola* |
| *Ozias, Angelina* | *Palomas, San Patricio* | *Parsell's Ranch, Roberts* |
| ***Ozona, Crockett, 182** | ***Palo Pinto, Palo Pinto, 30** ..... 411 | **Parsley Hill, Wilbarger,** ......... 40 |
| (3,436) ................. 3,444 | ***Paluxy, Hood, 3** ............... 76 | *Parson's Seminary, Travis* |
| *Ozro, Ellis* | ***PAMPA, Gray, 1,143** | *Parsons, Parker* |
| | (17,887) ................. 17,659 | **Parvin, Denton,** ................ 44 |
| | *Pamplin's Creek, Tyler* | ***PASADENA, Harris, 4,588** |
| **P** | *Panama, Reeves* | (141,674) ............. 143,527 |
| *Pace, Webb* | *Pan American Camp, Willacy* | *Pascal, Comanche* |
| *Pace's Chapel, Anderson* | **Pancake, Coryell,** .............. 11 | *Paschall, Wise* |
| *Pace's Ferry, Jasper* | *Panchita, Brooks* | *Pasche, Concho* |
| *Pacific, La Salle* | *Panchita, Hidalgo* | *Paso del Chalan, Sabine* |
| **Pacio, Delta,** ................. 15 | *Pancho, El Paso* | *Paso Real, Willacy* |
| *Pacita, Lubbock* | **Pandale, Val Verde,** ............ 20 | *Paso Station, Houston* |
| *Pack Saddle, Llano* | ***Pandora, Wilson,** ............. 125 | *Pastura, Jones* |
| *Pacono, Camp* | ***PANHANDLE, Carson, 123** | *Pate, McLennan* |
| *Pad's Chapel, Titus* | (2,589) ................. 2,594 | *Patella, Walker* |
| **Padgett, Young,** .............. 28 | *Pankey, Grimes* | **Patillo, Erath,** .................. 10 |
| *Padreco, Cherokee* | ***Panna Maria, Karnes** ......... 96 | *Patman, Cass* |
| ***PADUCAH, Cottle, 73** | *Panola, Panola* | **Patman Switch, Cass,** ........... 40 |
| (1,498) ................. 1,392 | ***Panola, Panola, 12** ........... 296 | *Patmos, Hopkins* |
| *Page, Panola* | **PANORAMA, Montgomery,** | *Pato, Webb* |
| ***Paige, Bastrop, 42** .......... 275 | (1,965) ................. 2,089 | *Paton, Carson* |
| *Paint Creek, Edwards* | *Pansy, Crosby* | **Patonia, Polk,** .................. NA |
| **Paint Creek, Haskell,** .......... NA | *Pansy, Crosby* | **Patricia, Dawson,** .............. 60 |
| *Paint Creek, Haskell* | *Pansy, Navarro* | *Patrick, McLennan* |
| *Painted Comanche Camp, Jeff Davis* | ***PANTEGO, Tarrant,** | *Patrick, Rusk* |
| ***PAINT ROCK, Concho, 22** | (2,318) ................. 2,378 | *Patricks Ferry, San Jacinto* |
| (320) .................... 318 | *Panter, Hood* | *Patrol, Reeves* |
| *Paisano, Brooks* | *Pantex, Carson* | **Patroon, Shelby, 1** .............. 55 |
| *Paisano, Presidio* | *Pantex, Hutchinson* | *Pattengill, Cass* |
| **Paisano [Edgewater-],** | *Panther, Edwards* | *Patterson, Uvalde* |
| **San Patricio, (182)** ........ 187 | *Panther Chapel, Franklin* | *Patterson Settlement, Uvalde* |
| *Pakan, Wheeler* | *Panther Creek, Kendall* | *Pattie, Grayson* |
| *Palace, Van Zandt* | **Panther Junction, Brewster,** .... 112 | *Pattillos, Orange* |
| *Palace Hill, Dallas* | **Papalote, Bee,** ................. 70 | ***PATTISON, Waller, 24 (447)** ..... 451 |
| ***PALACIOS, Matagorda, 224** | *Paradise, Foard* | *Patton, Comanche* |
| (5,153) ................. 5,235 | ***PARADISE, Wise, 75 (459)** ..... 492 | *Patton, Galveston* |
| *Palacios Point, Matagorda* | *Pardo, Cameron* | *Patton, Hemphill* |
| *Palafox, Webb* | ***PARIS, Lamar, 1,869** | *Patton, McLennan* |
| *Palangana, Duval* | (25,898) ................. 26,120 | *Patton's Mill, Hill* |
| *Palava, Fisher* | **Parita, Bexar,** .................. NA | *Patton's Port, Smith* |
| ***PALESTINE, Anderson, 1,275** | *Park, Bowie* | **Pattonfield, Upshur,** ............ 20 |
| (17,598) .............. 17,632 | **Park, Fayette,** ................. 47 | *Pattonia, Nacogdoches* |
| *Palestine, Lamar* | *Park City, Throckmorton* | **PATTON VILLAGE, Montgomery,** |
| **PALISADES, Randall, (352)** ..... 370 | **Park Community, Navarro,** ...... 160 | (1,391) ................ 1,445 |
| **Palito Blanco, Jim Wells,** ........ 35 | *Parkdale, Bell* | ***Pattonville, Lamar, 12** ......... 180 |
| *Palm, Dimmit* | *Parker, Burleson* | *Paul, Midland* |
| ***PALMER, Ellis, 73 (1,774)** ..... 1,799 | *Parker, Clay* | *Paul's, Bexar* |
| *Palmer's, San Jacinto* | **PARKER, Collin, (1,379)** ...... 1,592 | *Paul's Store, Shelby* |
| *Palmer's Bridge, Franklin* | **Parker, Johnson,** .............. 21 | *Paul's Valley, Nacogdoches* |
| *Palmetal, Cameron* | *Parker, Parker* | *Pauldie, Cameron* |
| | *Parker's Bluff, Anderson* | *Pauli, Montgomery* |

| Town,County ...........Pop. 2002 | Town,County ...........Pop. 2002 | Town,County............ Pop. 2002 |
|---|---|---|
| Paulina, Childress | Pecan Hill, Fort Bend | (5,444) ................. 5,477 |
| Paulina, Jack | **Pecan Plantation, Hood,** | Perico, Dallam |
| Pauline, Collin | (3,544) .................3,593 | Perkins, Cass |
| Pauline, Hardeman | Pecan Point, Red River | Perkins, Dallas |
| Pauline, Henderson | Pecan Point, Red River | Perkins, Lamar |
| Pauline, Ochiltree | **Pecan Wells, Hamilton,.......... 7** | Perley, Cochran |
| Paulineville, Hardin | Peck, Harris | Perley, Henderson |
| Paul Wheeler, Jefferson | ***PECOS, Reeves, 372*** | Permian, Reeves |
| Pavo, Kinney | (9,501) .................9,157 | **PERNITAS POINT, Live Oak-** |
| **Pawelekville, Karnes,......... 105** | Pecosa, Maverick | Jim Wells, (269)...........271 |
| ***Pawnee, Bee, 6 (201) ........ 207** | Pecos High Bridge, Val Verde | Peron, Wood |
| **Paxton, Shelby,.............. 161** | Pecos Springs, Pecos | ***Perrin, Jack, 24 .............. 300** |
| Payne, Brown | Pecos Station, Crockett | ***Perry, Falls, 2 ................76** |
| Payne, Mills | Pedeco, Liberty | Perry, McLennan |
| Payne, Navarro | Peden, Tarrant | Perry's Landing, Brazoria |
| Payne, Shelby | Pedernales, Gillespie | Perry's Point, Chambers |
| Paynes, Fort Bend | Pedigo, Tyler | Perry Landing, Brazoria |
| **Paynes Corner, Gaines,......... NA** | Pedro, Coke | Perryman, Liberty |
| **PAYNE SPRINGS, Henderson,** | Peede, Kaufman | Perryman's, Waller |
| (683) ................... 720 | Peek, Stonewall | Perryman's Crossing, Guadalupe |
| Paynes Store, Hunt | Peeler, Dallas | ***PERRYTON, Ochiltree, 522** |
| Peacevale, Roberts-Hutchinson | Peeler, Leon | (7,774) ................. 7,922 |
| Peach, Cherokee | Peel Junction, Montgomery | Perryview, Bell |
| Peach, Wood | **Peeltown, Kaufman, ............NA** | Perryville, Bastrop |
| **Peach Creek, Brazos, ..........NA** | **Peerless, Hopkins, .............NA** | **Perryville, Wood,.............. 52** |
| Peach Creek, Gonzales | Peerless Spur, Brazoria | Pershing, Polk |
| Peach Creek, Wharton | Peeryville, Kaufman | Pershing, Travis |
| Peach Tree, Jasper | Pegasus, Midland | Persimmon Grove, Kaufman |
| Peach Tree, Medina | ***Peggy, Atascosa, 2 ............ 22** | Persimmon Point, Calhoun |
| Peach Tree Village, Tyler | Pegoda, Trinity | Personville, Freestone |
| **Peacock, Stonewall,.......... 125** | Pelham, Burleson | **Personville, Limestone, ......... 50** |
| **Peadenville, Palo Pinto,........ 15** | **Pelham, Navarro, .............. 75** | **Pert, Anderson,................ 20** |
| Peak, Castro | Pelican, Liberty | Peru, DeWitt |
| Peak, San Patricio | **PELICAN BAY, Tarrant,** | Peru, La Salle |
| Pealoreville, Foard | (1,505) .................1,543 | Peruna, Coryell |
| Pearl, Collingsworth | Pella, Wise | Pescadito, Webb |
| **Pearl, Coryell,............... 125** | Pelly, Harris | Pesch, Washington |
| Pearl, Orange | Pen, Shackelford | Pete, Nolan |
| Pearl, Swisher | Peña Station, Jim Hogg-Duval | Peter's Prairie, Mason |
| ***PEARLAND, Brazoria-Harris,** | Pencilville, Frio | **Peter's Prairie, Red River, ....... 40** |
| 2,126 (37,640).......... 40,951 | Pendell, Bosque | **Peters, Austin,................. 95** |
| **Pearl City, DeWitt, .............. 4** | Pendentia, Dimmit | ***PETERSBURG, Hale, 41** |
| Pearl City, Ellis | ***Pendleton, Bell, 5 ............. 60** | (1,262) ................. 1,250 |
| Pear Ridge, Jefferson | Pendleton, Sabine | Petersburg, Lavaca |
| ***PEARSALL, Frio, 289** | ***PENELOPE, Hill, 5 (211) ....... 216** | Peters Colony, Dallas |
| (7,157)..................7,204 | Penfield, Travis | Petersville, Cherokee |
| **Pearson, Medina,.............. NA** | Penick, Jones | **Petersville, DeWitt, ............. 38** |
| Pearson, Montague | Peniel, Hunt | Petersville, Fayette |
| Pearson's Ranch, Sterling | ***PEÑITAS, Hidalgo, 22** | Petersville, Polk |
| **Pearsons Chapel, Houston ...... 95** | (1,167)..................1,158 | Pether City, Bee |
| ***Pear Valley, McCulloch, 1 .......37** | Penitas, Jim Wells | Petroleum, Jim Hogg |
| Pearville, Houston | Penland, Grayson | ***PETROLIA, Clay, 14 (782) ......780** |
| Peary Place, Nueces | Penn, Hopkins | **PETRONILA, Nueces, (83) ....... 87** |
| Pease, Foard | Penn's, Harris | Petry Woods, Jefferson |
| ***Peaster, Parker, 7 ............ 102** | Penn City, Harris | **Petteway, Robertson, ........... 25** |
| Peatown, Gregg | ***Pennington, Trinity-Houston, 7 .. 67** | **Pettibone, Milam, .............. 25** |
| Peavy, Angelina | Penn Springs, Dallas | Pettit, Comanche |
| Pebble, Kerr | Pen Oak, Liberty | **Pettit, Hockley,................. 26** |
| Pebble Mound, Burnet | Penrose, Shackelford | Pettit's, Houston |
| Pecan, Callahan | ***Penwell, Ector, 11 ............. 74** | ***Pettus, Bee, 25 (608) .......... 625** |
| Pecan, Delta | **Peoria, Hill, ................... 81** | ***Petty, Lamar, 1 ............... 100** |
| Pecan, Fayette | ***Pep, Hockley, 4 ............... 35** | **Petty, Lynn, ................... 24** |
| **Pecan Acres, Tarrant-Wise,** | Pepper, Rusk | **Petty's Chapel, Navarro,......... 25** |
| (2,289)..................2,434 | Pepper's Ranch, Kent | Pettytown, Bastrop |
| Pecan City, Matagorda | Pepper Grove, Galveston | Petzel's Camp, Crosby |
| **Pecan Creek, Tom Green, .......NA** | Pera, Reeves | Peveto, Orange |
| ***PECAN GAP, Delta-Fannin,** | Perch, Falls | Pewitt, Morris |
| 11 (214).................. 225 | Percheron, Lynn | **Peyton, Blanco,................. 30** |
| Pecan Grove, Collin | Perch Hill, Wise | Peyton, Falls |
| Pecan Grove, Coryell | **Percilla, Houston, .............. 95** | Peyton, Williamson |
| **Pecan Grove, Fort Bend,** | Percy, Mills | ***PFLUGERVILLE, Travis, 1,085** |
| (13,551)..................14,406 | Perdenales, Travis | (16,335) .............. 19,298 |
| Pecan Grove, Gonzales | Perdido, Goliad | Phair, Brazoria |
| Pecan Grove, Jefferson | Perdido Community, Goliad | **Phalba, Van Zandt, ............. 58** |
| Pecan Grove, Navarro | Perdiz, Presidio | ***PHARR, Hidalgo, 1,476** |
| Pecan Grove, San Saba | Perezville, Duval | (46,660) .............. 49,655 |
| **PECAN HILL, Ellis, (672) ....... 670** | **Perezville [Abram-], Hidalgo,** | Phears, Lee |

**CITIES & TOWNS**

| Town,County . . . . . . . . . . .Pop. 2002 | Town,County . . . . . . . . . . .Pop. 2002 | Town,County . . . . . . . . . . Pop. 2002 |
|---|---|---|
| *Pheasant, Matagorda* | Pinehill, Rusk . . . . . . . . . . . . . . . . 49 | *Placedo, Victoria, 12 . . . . . . . . . 760 |
| Phelan, Bastrop, . . . . . . . . . . . . . NA | *Pine Hill, Walker* | Placid, McCulloch, . . . . . . . . . . . 32 |
| *Phelps, Walker* | *Pinehurst, Montgomery, 146 | *Placido, Hopkins-Delta* |
| Phelps, Walker, . . . . . . . . . . . . . . 98 | (4,266) . . . . . . . . . . . . . . . . .4,669 | Plain, Houston, . . . . . . . . . . . . . . 66 |
| *Phenix, Pecos* | PINEHURST, Orange, | *Plains, Borden* |
| *Philadelphia, Wood* | (2,274) . . . . . . . . . . . . . . . . .2,167 | *Plains, Lipscomb* |
| *Philippi, Gregg* | Pine Island, Jefferson, . . . . . . . . 350 | *PLAINS, Yoakum, 74 |
| *Philips, Navarro* | *Pine Island, Jefferson* | (1,450) . . . . . . . . . . . . . . . . 1,456 |
| *Phillips, Hutchinson* | PINE ISLAND, Waller, (849) . . . . . 856 | *Plainview, Coryell* |
| *Phillips, Montgomery* | *PINELAND, Sabine, 44 | *Plainview, Cottle* |
| *Phillips, Wharton* | (980) . . . . . . . . . . . . . . . . . . . 965 | *Plainview, Denton* |
| Phillipsburg, Washington, . . . . . . . 40 | Pine Mills, Wood, . . . . . . . . . . . . . 75 | *Plain View, Grayson* |
| *Phillipsburgh, Robertson* | Pine Prairie, Walker, . . . . . . . . . . .NA | *PLAINVIEW, Hale, 1,264 |
| *Phillips Camp, Hansford* | *Pine Ridge, Chambers* | (22,336) . . . . . . . . . . . . . . 22,257 |
| *Phillips Ranch, Llano* | *Pine Ridge, Hardin* | *Plainview, Haskell* |
| *Phillips Store, Ellis* | *Pine Ridge, Harrison* | *Plainview, Houston* |
| *Phillips Store, Wood* | *Pinery, Montgomery* | *Plainview, Martin* |
| *Phoenix, Polk* | *Pine Spring, Houston* | *Plainview, Sabine* |
| *Phosopolis, Waller* | *Pine Springs, Cherokee* | *Plainview, Scurry* |
| Pickens, Henderson, . . . . . . . . . . 20 | Pine Springs, Culberson, . . . . . . . 20 | *Plainview, Wharton* |
| *Pickering, Shelby* | Pine Springs, Smith, . . . . . . . . . . 150 | *Plainview, Wise* |
| *Pickett, Liberty* | *Pine Top, Leon* | *Planeport, El Paso* |
| Pickett, Navarro, . . . . . . . . . . . . . 30 | *Pine Town, Cherokee* | Plank, Hardin, . . . . . . . . . . . . . . . 205 |
| *Pickett, Wise* | *Pine Tree, Gregg* | *Plank House, Nacogdoches* |
| *Pickett Valley, Lampasas* | *Pinetucky, Jasper* | *PLANO, Collin-Denton, 11,018 |
| *Picketville, Stephens* | *Pine Valley, San Jacinto* | (222,030) . . . . . . . . . . . . . 237,495 |
| *Pickton, Hopkins, 14 . . . . . . . . . . 90 | *Pine Valley, Walker* | *Plano, Montague* |
| *Pickwick, Palo Pinto* | Pineview, Wood, . . . . . . . . . . . . . . 10 | *Plantersville, Grimes, 54 . . . . . . 212 |
| Pidcoke, Coryell, . . . . . . . . . . . . . 30 | *Pineville, Tyler* | *Plascido, Tarrant* |
| Piedmont, Grimes, . . . . . . . . . . . . 46 | Pinewood Estates, Hardin, | Plaska, Hall, . . . . . . . . . . . . . . . . . 28 |
| Piedmont, Upshur, . . . . . . . . . . . . 20 | (1,633) . . . . . . . . . . . . . . . . .1,668 | *Plasterco, Fisher* |
| *Piedras Pintas, Duval* | Piney, Austin, . . . . . . . . . . . . . . . . 50 | *Plasterville, Grimes* |
| *Piel, Taylor* | *Piney, Titus* | *Plata, Presidio* |
| *Pieper Settlement, Comal* | *Piney Grove, Gonzales* | *Plate's Store, Runnels* |
| *Pierce, Wharton, 8 . . . . . . . . . . . 49 | *Piney Point, Montgomery* | *Plateau, Culberson* |
| *Pierce Junction, Harris* | *Piney Point, Trinity* | *Plateau, Stephens* |
| *Pierces Chapel, Cherokee* | PINEY POINT VILLAGE, Harris, | *Platt, Angelina* |
| *Pierpont Place, DeWitt* | (3,380) . . . . . . . . . . . . . . . . .3,472 | *Platteville, Castro* |
| *Pigeon, Erath* | *Pinhead, Clay* | *Plaxco, Young* |
| *Piggtown, Hamilton* | *Pinhook, Lamar* | PLEAK, Fort Bend, (947) . . . . . 1,056 |
| Pike, Collin, . . . . . . . . . . . . . . . . . 80 | *Pin Hook, Lamar* | Pleasant Farms, Ector, . . . . . . . 1,400 |
| *Pikesville, Bosque* | *Pink, San Augustine* | *Pleasant Glade, Tarrant* |
| *Pila Blanca, Duval* | *Pinkerton, Haskell* | *Pleasant Glade, Van Zandt* |
| *Pilares, Presidio* | *Pinkham, Bowie* | *Pleasant Green, Gregg* |
| Pilgrim, Gonzales, . . . . . . . . . . . . 60 | *Pink Hill, Grayson* | Pleasant Grove, Bastrop, . . . . . . . NA |
| *Pilgrim Point, Grimes* | *Pinkston, Navarro* | *Pleasant Grove, Bowie* |
| Pilgrim Rest, Rains, . . . . . . . . . . . 72 | *Pin Oak, Fayette* | *Pleasant Grove, Brown* |
| *Pilot, Fort Bend* | *Pinoak, Freestone* | *Pleasant Grove, Dallas* |
| Pilot Grove, Grayson, . . . . . . . . . . 48 | *Pinoak, Hardin* | *Pleasant Grove, Delta* |
| *Pilot Knob, Denton* | *Pin Oak, Milam* | *Pleasant Grove, Eastland* |
| Pilot Knob, Travis, . . . . . . . . . . . . NA | *Pinta, Wilbarger* | Pleasant Grove, Falls, . . . . . . . . . . 35 |
| *PILOT POINT, Denton, 263 | *Pinto, Kinney* | *Pleasant Grove, Hardin* |
| (3,538) . . . . . . . . . . . . . . . . .3,871 | *Pinto, Presidio* | Pleasant Grove, Hopkins, . . . . . . . NA |
| *Pilotville, Harris* | *Pinyville, Tyler* | *Pleasant Grove, Houston* |
| *Pinchem, Red River* | Pioneer, Eastland, . . . . . . . . . . . . 40 | *Pleasant Grove, Lamar* |
| *Pinckney, Polk* | *Pioneer, Ochiltree* | *Pleasant Grove, Lee* |
| *Pinckneyville, Denton* | *Pipe Creek, Bandera, 192 . . . . . . .NA | Pleasant Grove, Limestone, . . . . . . 20 |
| Pine, Camp, . . . . . . . . . . . . . . . . . 78 | *Piper's Settlement, Bexar* | *Pleasant Grove, Mills* |
| *Pine Bluff, Freestone* | *Pirkey, Harrison* | *Pleasant Grove, Navarro* |
| *Pine Bluffs, Red River* | *Pirkle, Kent* | *Pleasant Grove, Panola* |
| *Pine Branch, Houston* | *Pirtle, Rusk* | *Pleasant Grove, Rusk* |
| Pine Branch, Red River, . . . . . . . . 40 | *Pisek, Colorado* | *Pleasant Grove, San Jacinto* |
| *Pine Creek, Lamar* | *Pisgah, Comanche* | *Pleasant Grove, Shelby* |
| *Pine Creek, Red River* | *Pisgah, Eastland* | *Pleasant Grove, Smith* |
| *Pinedale, Walker* | *Pisgah, Nacogdoches* | Pleasant Grove, Upshur, . . . . . . . . 35 |
| Pine Forest, Hopkins, . . . . . . . . . . 51 | *Pisgah, Navarro* | *Pleasant Grove, Washington* |
| PINE FOREST, Orange, (632) . . . 627 | *Pistol Hill, Rusk* | Pleasant Grove, Wood, . . . . . . . . . 30 |
| Pine Grove, Cherokee, . . . . . . . . . 30 | Pitner Junction, Rusk, . . . . . . . . . 20 | *Pleasant Hill, Cherokee* |
| *Pine Grove, Harris* | *Pitts, Motley* | *Pleasant Hill, Cottle* |
| *Pine Grove, Henderson* | *Pittsbridge, Burleson* | Pleasant Hill, Eastland, . . . . . . . . . 15 |
| *Pine Grove, Houston* | *PITTSBURG, Camp, 381 | *Pleasant Hill, Franklin* |
| *Pine Grove, Nacogdoches* | (4,347) . . . . . . . . . . . . . . . . .4,461 | *Pleasant Hill, Harrison* |
| Pine Grove, Newton, . . . . . . . . . 160 | *Pittsville, Fort Bend* | *Pleasant Hill, Hopkins* |
| *Pine Grove, Panola* | *Pittsville, Montgomery* | *Pleasant Hill, Houston* |
| *Pine Grove, Trinity* | *Pittsville Switch, Waller* | *Pleasant Hill, Lamar* |
| *Pine Grove, Upshur* | *Pizarro, Erath* | *Pleasant Hill, Live Oak* |
| *Pine Grove, Waller* | *Place, Cameron* | *Pleasant Hill, McLennan* |

| Town,County .......... Pop. 2002 | Town,County .......... Pop. 2002 | Town,County .......... Pop. 2002 |
|---|---|---|
| Pleasant Hill, Milam | Poe, Nacogdoches | Pool Branch, Burnet |
| **Pleasant Hill, Nacogdoches,..... NA** | Poer, Bowie | **Poole, Rains,.................. 50** |
| Pleasant Hill, San Augustine | Poesta, Bee | Poole Pens, Matagorda |
| Pleasant Hill, Smith | Poesville, Bosque | ***Poolville, Parker, 28.......... 520** |
| Pleasant Hill, Travis | Poet, Dickens | Poor, Leon |
| Pleasant Hill, Travis | Poet, Milam | Poor Farm, Travis |
| Pleasant Hill, Upshur ◦ | **Poetry, Kaufman, ..............NA** | Pope, Bowie |
| Pleasant Hill, Van Zandt | Pog, Winkler | Pope, Fannin |
| Pleasant Hill, Washington | Poindexter, Rusk | Pope, Hall |
| Pleasant Hill, Williamson | ***POINT, Rains, 55 (792) ....... 885** | Poperanch, Hall |
| **Pleasant Hill, Yoakum,.......... 40** | ***POINT BLANK, San Jacinto, 20** | Popes Crossing, Reeves |
| Pleasant Mound, Dallas | (559) ................... 582 | Popher, Angelina |
| Pleasant Oaks, Henderson | ***POINT COMFORT, Calhoun, 47** | Poplar, San Jacinto |
| ***PLEASANTON, Atascosa, 487** | (781) ................... 772 | Popp, Limestone |
| (8,266).................. 8,589 | Point Enterprise, Limestone,.... 200 | Porfirio, Willacy |
| Pleasant Plains, Cherokee | Pointers, Waller | Port-Au-Prince, Brazoria |
| Pleasant Point, Hamilton | Point Isabel, Cameron | ***Port Acres, Jefferson** |
| Pleasant Point, Johnson | Point Loma, San Patricio | .......... (part of Port Arthur) |
| Pleasant Retreat, Smith | Point Pleasant, Gregg | **Port Alto, Calhoun,............. 45** |
| **Pleasant Ridge, Leon,.......... NA** | Point Pleasant, Upshur-Camp | ***PORT ARANSAS, Nueces, 342** |
| Pleasant Ridge, Panola | **POINT VENTURE, Travis, ....... 470** | (3,370) ................. 3,486 |
| Pleasant Ridge, Van Zandt-Henderson | Pokerville, Bell | ***PORT ARTHUR, Jefferson,** |
| Pleasant Run, Dallas | **Polar, Kent, .................. 10** | 2,007 (57,755) ......... 57,313 |
| Pleasant Run, Tarrant | Polaris, Presidio | ***Port Bolivar, Galveston, 90... 1,200** |
| **Pleasant Springs, Leon, ........ NA** | Polish Village, Matagorda | Port Brownsville, Cameron |
| Pleasant Valley, Blanco | Polk, Caldwell | Port Caddo, Harrison |
| Pleasant Valley, Burnet | Polk, Grimes | Port Cavallo, Matagorda |
| Pleasant Valley, Coleman | Pollack, Williamson | ***Porter, Montgomery, 581..... 2,146** |
| Pleasant Valley, Collingsworth | Pollard, Hill | Porter, Somervell |
| Pleasant Valley, Dallas | Pollard, Palo Pinto | Porter's Chapel, Burleson |
| Pleasant Valley, Eastland | Pollard, Taylor | Porter's Prairie, Burleson |
| Pleasant Valley, Falls | ***Pollok, Angelina, 41 .......... 300** | **Porter Heights, Montgomery,** |
| Pleasant Valley, Fisher | Polly, Bandera | (1,490) ................. 1,549 |
| **Pleasant Valley, Garza,........... 5** | Pollygacho, San Augustine | Porters Bluff, Navarro |
| Pleasant Valley, Hall | Polonia, Caldwell | **Porter Springs, Houston, ........ 50** |
| Pleasant Valley, Hopkins | Polvo, El Paso | Porterville, Loving |
| Pleasant Valley, Hunt | Polytechnic, Tarrant | Portilla, Calhoun |
| Pleasant Valley, Jack | Pomeroy, Carson | ***PORT ISABEL, Cameron, 321** |
| Pleasant Valley, Jones | Pomona, Brazoria | (4,865) ................. 5,067 |
| Pleasant Valley, Kendall | Pomona, Burnet | Portland, Fannin |
| Pleasant Valley, Lamb | Pomona, Cherokee | ***PORTLAND, San Patricio, 433** |
| Pleasant Valley, Midland | Pompey, Mills | (14,827) .............. 15,033 |
| Pleasant Valley, Palo Pinto | ***PONDER, Denton, 74** | ***PORT LAVACA, Calhoun, 645** |
| Pleasant Valley, Potter | (507) ................... 572 | (12,035) .............. 11,978 |
| Pleasant Valley, Throckmorton | Pond Spring, Williamson | ***Port Mansfield, Willacy, 9** |
| Pleasant Valley, Travis | Pone, Rusk | (415)................... 416 |
| **PLEASANT VALLEY, Wichita,** | Ponetta, Johnson | ***PORT NECHES, Jefferson, 448** |
| (408) ................... 407 | **Ponta, Cherokee, .............. 50** | (13,601) .............. 13,533 |
| Pleasant Valley, Wilson | Pontiac, Tarrant | ***Port O'Connor, Calhoun, 70 .. 1,184** |
| Pleasant View, Henderson | Ponton, Williamson | Port Preston, Refugio |
| Pleasantville, DeWitt | Pontoon Bridge, Crockett | Portsmouth, Matagorda |
| Pleasure Point, Angelina | Pontotoc, Bastrop | Portsmouth, Randall |
| Pleasure Point, Marion | ***Pontotoc, Mason, 4........... 125** | **Port Sullivan, Milam,........... 15** |
| ***Pledger, Matagorda, 5 ........ 159** | Pony, Runnels | Porvenir, Presidio, ........... NA |
| Plehweville, Mason | Pool, Lamar | **Posey, Hopkins,.............. NA** |
| Plemons, Hutchinson | Pool's Crossing, Falls | **Posey, Lubbock, .............. 125** |
| Plemons, Randall | | |
| Plenitude, Anderson | | |
| Plover, Tarrant | | |
| **Pluck, Polk,....................NA** | | |
| ***Plum, Fayette, 6 .............. 95** | | |
| Plum Creek, Caldwell | | |
| Plum Creek, Caldwell | | |
| **Plum Creek, Freestone,......... NA** | | |
| Plum Grove, Ellis | | |
| **PLUM GROVE, Liberty,** | | |
| (930) ................... 974 | | |
| Plum Grove, Young | | |
| Plum Tree Village, Tyler | | |
| Plunkett, Madison | | |
| **Pluto, Ellis, ................... 15** | | |
| Plymouth, Collingsworth | | |
| Pocahontas, Montgomery | | |
| Pock, Coleman | | |
| Pocket, Wharton | | |
| Podo, Matagorda | | |
| Poe, Blanco | | |

*Downtown Post, the county seat of Garza County south of Lubbock. File photo.*

| Town,County . . . . . . . . . . .Pop. 2002 | Town,County . . . . . . . . . . .Pop. 2002 | Town,County . . . . . . . . . . . Pop. 2002 |
|---|---|---|
| Posideon, Palo Pinto | Prairie Creek, Van Zandt | Prickly Pear, Gonzales |
| Possum Bluff, Newton | Prairiedale, Hill | *Priddy, Mills, 10 . . . . . . . . . . . . .215 |
| Possum Trot, Ellis | Prairie Dell, Bell, . . . . . . . . . . . . . 12 | Pride, Dawson |
| Possum Trot, Gonzales | Prairie Dog Town, Gray | PRIMERA, Cameron, (2,723). . . 2,834 |
| Possum Trot, Red River | Prairie Grove, Cooke | Primm, Fayette |
| Possum Trot, Shelby | Prairie Grove, Franklin | Primrose, Hockley |
| Possum Walk, Trinity | Prairie Grove, Limestone | Primrose, Tarrant |
| Possum Walk, Walker | Prairie Hill, Hays | Primrose, Terry |
| *POST, Garza, 259 (3,708) . . . . . 3,800 | Prairie Hill, Hunt | Primrose, Van Zandt, . . . . . . . . . . 24 |
| Post Oak, Blanco, . . . . . . . . . . . . 10 | *Prairie Hill, Limestone, 6 . . . . . . 150 | Prince, McMullen |
| Post Oak, Delta | Prairie Hill, Washington, . . . . . . . .NA | Princeton, Cherokee |
| Postoak, Freestone | Prairie Home, Ector | *PRINCETON, Collin, 234 |
| Post Oak, Henderson | Prairie Home, Montgomery | (3,477) . . . . . . . . . . . . . . . . . . 3,672 |
| Post Oak, Houston | Prairie Home, Navarro | Princeton, Newton |
| Postoak, Jack, . . . . . . . . . . . . . . . 79 | *Prairie Lea, Caldwell, 4 . . . . . . . . 255 | Princeton, Newton |
| Postoak, Lamar, . . . . . . . . . . . . . . 65 | Prairie Lea, Williamson | Princeville, Gonzales |
| Post Oak, Lee, . . . . . . . . . . . . . . 100 | Prairie Lee, Midland | Prindle, Wise |
| Post Oak, Navarro | Prairie Mills, Coryell | Pringle, Hutchinson, . . . . . . . . . . . 40 |
| Post Oak, Robertson | Prairie Mount, Lamar | Prismoid, Montgomery |
| Post Oak, Washington | Prairie Mountain, Llano, . . . . . . . . .NA | Prismoid, Montgomery |
| Post Oak, Wilson | Prairie Plains, Grimes | Pritchett, Upshur, . . . . . . . . . . . . .125 |
| POST OAK BEND, Kaufman, | Prairie Point, Anderson | Privilege, Bandera |
| (404) . . . . . . . . . . . . . . . . . . . 430 | Prairie Point, Burnet | *Proctor, Comanche, 15 . . . . . . . . 220 |
| Post Oak Branch, Bell | Prairie Point, Colorado-Lavaca | Proffitt, Young |
| Post Oak Grove, Hopkins | Prairie Point, Cooke, . . . . . . . . . . 40 | *PROGRESO, Hidalgo, 41 |
| Post Oak Grove, Lavaca | Prairie Point, Wise | (4,851) . . . . . . . . . . . . . . . . . 5,107 |
| Post Oak Island, Williamson | Prairie Point, Wise | PROGRESO LAKES, Hidalgo, |
| Post Oak Point, Austin, . . . . . . . . . 40 | Prairie Springs, Van Zandt | (234). . . . . . . . . . . . . . . . . . . .238 |
| Post Oak School, Navarro | Prairie Springs, Williamson | Progress, Bailey, . . . . . . . . . . . . . .49 |
| Post Oak Springs, Coleman | Prairie Switch, Wharton | Progress, Hale |
| Post of El Paso, El Paso | Prairie Valley, Dallas | Progress, Montgomery |
| *POTEET, Atascosa, 124 | Prairie Valley, Hill, . . . . . . . . . . . . .NA | Proserpina, Jasper |
| (3,305). . . . . . . . . . . . . . . . . 3,426 | Prairie Valley, Hunt | Prospect, Atascosa |
| *POTH, Wilson, 49 (1,850) . . . . . 1,910 | Prairie View, Coryell | Prospect, Clay |
| Pothole City, Edwards | Prairie View, Dickens | Prospect, Collin |
| Potomac, Polk | Prairie View, Freestone | Prospect, Lee |
| Potosi, Taylor, (1,664). . . . . . . . 1,723 | Prairieview, Hale | Prospect, Marion |
| Potter's Creek, Harrison | Prairie View, Orange | Prospect, McLennan |
| Potter's Ranche, San Saba | Prairie View, Red River | Prospect, Milam |
| Potters Shop, Bastrop | Prairie View, Trinity | Prospect, Rains, . . . . . . . . . . . . . . 40 |
| Pottersville, Burleson | *PRAIRIE VIEW, Waller, 63 | Prospect Hill, Wood |
| Pottersville, Limestone | (4,410) . . . . . . . . . . . . . . . . .4,479 | *PROSPER, Collin, 118 |
| *POTTSBORO, Grayson, 244 | Prairie View, Young | (2,097) . . . . . . . . . . . . . . . . 2,466 |
| (1,579). . . . . . . . . . . . . . . . . 1,605 | Prairieville, Kaufman, . . . . . . . . . . 50 | Prosperity, Falls |
| Potts Mill, Gonzales | Prajedis, Hidalgo | Prosser, Angelina |
| *Pottsville, Hamilton, 4 . . . . . . . . 100 | Prather, Shelby | Providence, Anderson |
| Pottsville, Nueces | Pratt, Fannin | Providence, Angelina |
| Pounds, Smith | Prattville, Delta | Providence, Burnet |
| Pounds Mill, Shelby | Preceno Rancho, Cameron | Providence, Floyd, . . . . . . . . . . . . 85 |
| Povenir, Jeff Davis | Preloch, Sterling | Providence, Hardin |
| Poverty Flat, Childress | *PREMONT, Jim Wells, 92 | Providence, Navarro |
| Poverty Slope, Harrison | (2,772). . . . . . . . . . . . . . . . .2,879 | Providence, Polk, . . . . . . . . . . . . 350 |
| Povilas, Bell | Presidio, Maverick | Providence, Smith-Van Zandt |
| Powderhorn, Calhoun | *PRESIDIO, Presidio, 96 | Provident City, Colorado |
| *Powderly, Lamar, 61 . . . . . . . . . 185 | (4,167). . . . . . . . . . . . . . . . .4,334 | Pruitt, Cass, . . . . . . . . . . . . . . . . 25 |
| *POWELL, Navarro, 10 (105) . . . . 106 | Presley, Titus | Pruitt, Van Zandt, . . . . . . . . . . . . . NA |
| Powell, Shelby | Presswood, Montgomery | Pryor, Fort Bend |
| Powell Dale, Bosque | Prestidge, Angelina | Pryor, Navarro |
| Powell Grove, Bowie | Presto, Roberts | Pualetos, Duval |
| Powell Mills, Henderson | Preston, Grayson, . . . . . . . . . . . . 325 | Pueblo, Baylor |
| Powell Point, Fort Bend | Preston, Van Zandt | Pueblo, Callahan, . . . . . . . . . . . . . 46 |
| Powellton, Harrison | Preston, Wharton | Pueblo, McCulloch |
| Powell Well, Crockett | Preston Hollow, Dallas | Pueblo Nuevo, Webb, . . . . . . . . . 377 |
| Power, Parker | Prew's Place, Callahan | Puente, Potter |
| Powers, Bandera | Prewitt's Tan Yard, Anderson | Puente Piedra, Live Oak |
| *POYNOR, Henderson, 17 | Price, Anderson | Puerto Rico, Hidalgo, . . . . . . . . . . 91 |
| (314) . . . . . . . . . . . . . . . . . . . 316 | Price, Collin | Pugh, Parker |
| Prade Ranch, Real | Price, Delta | Pugh's, Harrison |
| Prado Verde, El Paso, (200). . . . . 216 | Price, McLennan | Pulaski, Panola |
| Praesel, Milam, . . . . . . . . . . . . . . 115 | Price, Randall | Pulliam, Tom Green |
| Praha, Fayette, . . . . . . . . . . . . . . . 25 | *Price, Rusk, 11 . . . . . . . . . . . . . 275 | Pulliam, Uvalde |
| Prairie, Houston | Price, Swisher | Pulliam, Zavala |
| Prairie Anna, Harris | Price's, Cherokee | Pullin, Karnes |
| Prairie Center, Matagorda, . . . . . . 25 | Price's Creek, DeWitt | Pullman, Potter, . . . . . . . . . . . . . . 31 |
| Prairie Chapel, McLennan, . . . . . . 35 | Price's Cross Roads, Ellis | Pull Tight, Bee |
| Prairie Cottage, Colorado | Price's Hill, San Augustine | Pull Tight, Erath |
| Prairie Creek, Dallas | Price's Store, Lamar | Pull Tight, Van Zandt |

| Town,County | Pop. 2002 |
| --- | --- |

Pulltype, Newton
Pulteville, Cooke
Pulvo, Presidio
**Pumphrey, Runnels,** .......... 15
**Pumpkin, San Jacinto,** ........ 150
Pumpkin Center, Brewster
Pumpkin Center, Matagorda
Pumpkinville, Gillespie
Pumps, Harrison
**Pumpville, Val Verde,** .......... 21
Punchard's, Austin
**Punkin Center, Dawson,** ........ 30
**Punkin Center, Eastland,** ....... 12
Punkin Center, Hardeman
Punkin Center, Lamb
Punkin Center, Wichita
Purdon, Henderson
*****Purdon, Navarro, 14** ......... 133
Purgatory, Hays
**Purley, Franklin,** .............. 81
*****Purmela, Coryell, 5** ........... 61
**Pursley, Navarro,** .............. 40
**Purves, Erath,** ................ 50
*****PUTNAM, Callahan, 9 (88)** ..... 90
Putnam, Llano
Putnam's Store, Caldwell
Puxico, Van Zandt
Pyburn, Freestone
Pyland, Marion
Pylas, Rusk
Pyle, Reeves
Pyle's Prairie, Kaufman
*****PYOTE, Ward, 8 (131)** ........ 127
Pyramid, Nolan
Pyron, Scurry

**Q**

*****Quail, Collingsworth, 5 (33)** .... 36
**Quail Creek, San Jacinto,** ....... 50
Quail Valley, Anderson
Quakertown, Denton
Quality, Harris
Qualls, Clay
*****QUANAH, Hardeman, 190**
(3,022)............... 2,951
Quanto, Bee
Quapaw, Harrison
Quaro, DeWitt
**Quarry, Washington,** .......... NA
**Quarterway, Hale,** ............. 12
Quarton, Moore
Quebec, Presidio
*****QUEEN CITY, Cass, 93**
(1,613)............... 1,562
Queen Peak, Montague
*****Quemado, Maverick, 16**
(243) .................. 259
Quicksand, Johnson
**Quicksand, Newton,** .......... NA
Quigley, Jasper
**Quihi, Medina,** .............. 104
Quillin's Store, Hill
Quinan, Wharton
Quincy, Bee
Quincy, Fannin
Quincy, Harrison
Quinif, Milam
*****QUINLAN, Hunt, 367**
(1,370)............... 1,405
Quinlan, Hunt
Quinntown, Lynn
Quintal, Harrison
Quintana, Bexar
**QUINTANA, Brazoria, (38)** ...... 38
*****QUITAQUE, Briscoe, 30**
(432) ................. 433
*****QUITMAN, Wood, 323**

(2,030)................ 2,077
Quito, Leon
Quito, Ward

**R**

**Rabb, Nueces,** ................ 20
Rabbit Creek, Gregg
Rabbit Creek, Rusk
Rabbit Hill, Navarro
**Rabbs Prairie, Fayette,** ......... 36
Rabb Switch, Lavaca
Rabke, DeWitt
**Raccoon Bend, Austin,** ....... 400
Race Track, Delta
**Rachal, Brooks,** .............. 36
Rachal, San Patricio
Rachel Station, Liberty
Rad, Kent
**Radar Base, Maverick, (162)** .... 164
Radford, Karnes
Radio Junction, Lampasas
**Radium, Jones,** ............... 10
Rafael, Cameron
Ragland, Lamar
Ragley, Marion
Ragley, Panola
Ragsdale, Fannin
Ragtown, Garza
**Ragtown, Lamar,** .............. 25
Ragtown, Motley
Ragtown, Wise
Rail, Hamilton
Rainbolt, Fisher
Rainbow, Newton
*****Rainbow, Somervell, 17** ....... 76
Rainey, Harrison
Rainey's Chapel, Van Zandt
Rainey's Creek, Coryell
Rains, Rains
Rainsville, Shelby
*****Raisin, Victoria** ............. 50
Rake Pocket, Rusk
Raleigh, Fannin
**Raleigh, Navarro,** ............. 40
*****RALLS, Crosby, 82**
(2,252)................ 2,215
Ralls, Randall
Ralph, Lamar
Ralph, Randall
Ralston, El Paso
Ramage, Guadalupe
Ramal, Kinney
Ramarito, Jim Hogg
Rambert, Marion
Rambo, Archer
Rambo, Cass
Ramirena, Live Oak
Ramirena, San Patricio
**Ramireno, Zapata,** ............ 25
Ramireno, Zapata
**Ramirez, Duval,** .............. 40
Ramirez, Jim Hogg
Ramona, Hidalgo
Ramsdell, Wheeler
Ramsey, Brazoria
Ramsey, Colorado
Ramsey, Loving
Ramsey, Shelby
Ranch, Crane
Ranch Branch, Mason
Ranchette, Fannin
**Ranchette Estates, Willacy,**
(133) .................. 144
**Ranchito [Encantada--El Calaboz],**
Cameron, (2,100) ........ 2,149
**Ranchitos Las Lomas, Webb,**
(334) ................. 344

Ranchland, Wilbarger
Rancho, Gonzales-Wilson
**Rancho Alegre, Jim Wells,**
(1,775) ............... 1,860
**Rancho Banquete, Nueces,**
(469)................... 473
**Rancho Chico, San Patricio,**
(309)................. 312
Rancho Davis, Starr
Rancho de la Parita, Jim Wells
**Rancho Penitas West, Webb,**
(520).................. 531
Rancho San Luis, Hidalgo
**RANCHO VIEJO, Cameron,**
(1,754) ............... 1,734
Ranch Prairie, Brazoria
Rand, Kaufman
**Randado, Jim Hogg,** ........... 15
Randal's Store, Stephens-Palo Pinto
Randalia, Walker
Randall, Grayson
Randall, Smith
Randol, Tarrant
*****Randolph, Fannin, 3** .......... 70
Randolph, Grimes
Randolph, Houston
Randolph, Madison
Randolph, Trinity
*****Randolph Air Force Base, Bexar,**
3..................... 3,015
Randolphsville, San Jacinto
Randon, Fort Bend
Rane, Eastland
Raney, Fannin
Raney, Hunt
Range Creek, Grayson
Rangel, Duval
*****RANGER, Eastland, 138**
(2,584) ............... 2,510
**RANGERVILLE, Cameron,**
(203).................. 205
Ranier, Coryell
**Rankin, Ellis,** ................. 12
*****RANKIN, Upton, 41 (800)** ...... 764
Rankin's, San Jacinto
Ransom, San Augustine
**RANSOM CANYON, Lubbock,**
54 (1,011).............. 1,021
Rast, Van Zandt
Rat, Burnet
Ratama, Frio
**Ratamosa, Cameron, (218)** ..... 219
*****Ratcliff, Houston, 2** .......... 106
Ratcliff, San Augustine
Ratcliff, Starr
Ratcliff's, Tyler
Ratcliffe, DeWitt
Rath City, Stonewall
Rather, Shelby
Rathjen Farm, Wheeler
**Ratibor, Bell,** ................. 10
Ratler, Mills
Ratliff's Store, Lamar
**Rattan, Delta,** ................ 10
Rattan, Williamson
Ratty Towns, Van Zandt
Raven Hill, San Jacinto
*****RAVENNA, Fannin, 18 (215)** .... 223
Ravenwood, Brazos
Rawlings, Coke
Rawlins, Dallas
Rawls, Brazoria
Ray, Ellis
Ray, Grayson
Ray, Tom Green
Ray's Bluff, Harrison
**Rayburn, Liberty,** .............. 30

| Town,County ........... Pop. 2002 | Town,County ........... Pop. 2002 | Town,County ........... Pop. 2002 |
|---|---|---|
| Rayford, Montgomery | Red Mount, Sabine | *RENO, Lamar, (2,767) ...... 2,831 |
| Raylake, Angelina | *RED OAK, Ellis, 756 | RENO, Parker, (2,441) ....... 2,493 |
| Rayland, Foard, ............... 30 | (4,301)................4,597 | Renova, Angelina |
| Ray Lee, Stephens | Red Oak, Kaufman | Republic, Johnson |
| Raymer, Colorado | Red Ranger, Bell, ............. 12 | Republic, Llano |
| Raymond, Brazos | Red River, Grayson | Res, Montague |
| Raymond, Carson | Red River, Hall | Rescue, Lampasas |
| Raymond, Clay | Red River, Hardeman | Reservation, Kerr |
| Raymond, Leon | Red River City, Grayson | Resley's Creek, Comanche |
| *RAYMONVILLE, Willacy, 299 | Red River Station, Montague | Resort, Kerr |
| (9,733)................. 9,760 | Red River Valley, Hall | Rest, Caldwell |
| Rayner, Stonewall | *Red Rock, Bastrop, 23 ........ 125 | Retama, Hidalgo |
| Ray Point, Live Oak,.......... 200 | Red Rock, Tarrant | Rethaville, Tom Green |
| Ray School, Parker | Red Rock, Upshur | Retina, Hopkins |
| Ray Town, Lubbock | Red Springs, Baylor, .......... 42 | Retreat, Grimes, ............... 25 |
| Rayville, Parker | Red Springs, Bowie | Retreat, Hill |
| *Raywood, Liberty, 14 ......... 231 | Red Springs, Smith,.......... 350 | RETREAT, Navarro, (339) ...... 359 |
| Razor, Lamar, ................. 15 | Red Star, Grimes | Retrieve, Angelina |
| Re, Navarro | Red Store, Travis | Retrieve, Brazoria |
| Readsville, Red River | Red Top, Brazos | Retta, Tarrant-Johnson, ........ NA |
| *Reagan, Falls, 4 ............. 208 | Red Top, Harrison-Marion | Rettig, San Jacinto |
| Reagan, Rusk | Red Top, Young | Reuben, Hopkins |
| Reaganview, Reagan | Redtown, Anderson ............ 30 | Reunion, Dallas |
| Reaganville, Fayette | Redtown, Angelina............. 50 | Rex, Foard |
| Reagan Wells, Uvalde,.......... 20 | Red Town, Fisher | Rex, Nolan |
| Reagor Springs, Ellis, ......... 45 | *REDWATER, Bowie, 25 | Rex, Nolan |
| *Realitos, Duval, 9 (209)........ 216 | (872) ................... 886 | Rex, Shelby |
| Rear, Red River | Redwine, Lynn | Rex, Wise |
| Reavesville, Grayson | Red Wing, Medina | Rexville, Austin |
| Rebe, Van Zandt | Redwood, Guadalupe, | Reyes, Duval |
| Rebecca, San Augustine | (3,586).................3,808 | Reynard, Houston, ............75 |
| Rebecca Creek, Comal | Reed, Cooke | Reynolds, Cherokee |
| Record, Hansford | Reed, Red River | Reynolds, Edwards |
| Rector, Denton | Reed's Settlement, Panola | Reynolds, Stonewall |
| Red, Dawson | Reeds, Rusk | Reynolds Siding, Fisher |
| Red Bank, Bowie,............. 125 | Reeds Lake, Bell | Reynolds Spur, Caldwell |
| Red Bank, Ellis | Reeds Settlement, Red River, .... 50 | Rhea, Parker |
| Red Barn, Castro | Reedsville, Wood | Rhea, Parmer, ................98 |
| Red Barn, Pecos | Reedville, Caldwell, .......... 432 | Rhea Mills, Collin,..............47 |
| Red Bluff, Burnet | Reedyville, Hidalgo | Rheingold, Gillespie |
| Red Bluff, Harris | Reel Foot, Harrison | Rhineland, Knox,..............100 |
| Red Bluff, Jackson, ............ 35 | Reep, Frio | Rhode's Store, Lavaca |
| Red Bluff, Reeves, ............. 40 | Reese, Cherokee, .............. 75 | Rhode Island, Freestone |
| Red Bluff, San Saba | Reese Center, Lubbock, (42) ..... 42 | Rhoden, Polk |
| Redbone, Gregg | Reeves, Briscoe | Rhodes, Angelina |
| Red Branch, Grayson | Reeves, Hardin | Rhodes, Brazoria |
| Red Branch, Leon ............ NA | Reeves Chapel, Camp | Rhodes, Hopkins |
| Red Branch, Trinity | Refuge, Coryell | Rhodes, Rusk |
| Redbuck, Rusk | Refuge, Houston. .............. 27 | Rhomberg, Stonewall |
| Redbud, Montague | *REFUGIO, Refugio, 207 | *RHOME, Wise, 102 (551) ....... 626 |
| Red Creek, Tom Green | (2,941).................2,886 | Rhonesboro, Upshur,...........40 |
| Red Cut Heights, Bowie, ....... 563 | Regency, Mills, ................ 25 | Rhymer, Collin |
| Reddam, Grayson | Regna, Zavala | Ricardo, Kleberg, ........... 1,641 |
| Red Deer, Roberts | Rehburg, Washington, ..........NA | *RICE, Navarro, 46 (798)........835 |
| Redfield, Nacogdoches | Rehm, Hartley | Rice, Polk |
| Redfish, San Patricio | Rehobeth, Panola | Rice, Smith |
| Redfish Bay, Willacy | Reid, Van Zandt | Rice's Crossing, Williamson, .... NA |
| Red Flat, Nacogdoches | Reid Hope King, Cameron, | Rice's Point, Rains |
| *Redford, Presidio, (132) ....... 132 | (802) ...... .............. 825 | Rice Chapel, Houston |
| Red Gap, Eastland | Reilly Springs, Hopkins, ........ 44 | Riceland, Colorado |
| Red Gate, Hidalgo,.............NA | Reinhardt, Dallas | Riceland, Liberty |
| Red Hill, Cass, ................ 28 | Reinhardt's Store, Leon | Rice Ranch, Sterling |
| Red Hill, Limestone, ........... 20 | Reinkin, Hale | Rice Springs, Haskell |
| Red Hill, Van Zandt | Reiser, Webb | Riceton, Fort Bend |
| Red Horse, Polk | Rek Hill, Fayette,............... 48 | Riceville, Harris |
| Red Lake, Freestone,...........NA | *REKLAW, Cherokee-Rusk, 9 | Riceville, Matagorda |
| Redland, Angelina, ........... 250 | (327) .................... 338 | Rich, Hunt |
| Redland, Leon,................ 35 | Relampago, Hidalgo, (104)...... 106 | Richards, Clay |
| Redland, Van Zandt,...........NA | Relda, Sterling | Richards, Collin |
| Redland, Wood | Reliance, Brazos | Richards, Cottle |
| Redlands, Pecos | Remlig, Jasper | *Richards, Grimes, 13.......... 296 |
| Redlawn, Cherokee | Rendham, Baylor | Richards, San Saba |
| Red Lawn, Cherokee | Rendon, Tarrant, (9,022).......9,399 | *RICHARDSON, Dallas-Collin, |
| Redlew, Refugio | Renfro, Castro | 6,377 (91,802) .......... 95,229 |
| RED LICK, Bowie, (853)........ 878 | Renfro Prairie, Angelina | Richardson's, Jasper |
| Redman, Kent | Renner, Collin | Richards Store, Wood |
| Red Mound, Sabine | Renner, Denton | Richardsville, Wood |

| Town,County ..........Pop. 2002 | Town,County ..........Pop. 2002 | Town,County ........... Pop. 2002 |
|---|---|---|

Rich Coffey, Coleman
Richers, Fayette
Richie, McLennan
Richland, Bee
Richland, Collin
Richland, Hopkins
*RICHLAND, Navarro, 5
   (291) .................... 307
Richland, Orange
Richland, Rains, ............. 100
Richland, Travis
Richland, Wilbarger
Richland Creek, San Saba
*RICHLAND HILLS, Tarrant,
   (8,132). ................8,268
*RICHLAND SPRINGS, San Saba,
   19 (350). ............. 360
Richlandville, Fannin
*RICHMOND, Fort Bend, 1,408
   (11,081). ..............11,555
Rich Row, Leon
Rich Valley, Cooke
RICHWOOD, Brazoria,
   (3,012). ...............3,139
Rickels, Wise
Ricker, Brown
Ricks, Colorado
Rico, Fisher
Riddleville, Karnes
Ridenhower, Hamilton
Riderville, Panola, ............ 50
Ridge, Colorado
Ridge, Mills, .................. 25
Ridge, Robertson, ............ 67
Ridgeway, Bastrop
Ridgeway, Hopkins, .......... 54
Ridings, Fannin, .............. 10
Ridion, Harris
Rienzi, Hill
*RIESEL, McLennan, 53
   (973) .................. 958
Rightor's Point, Harris
Riley, Hardeman
Riley, Montague
Riley, Van Zandt
Riley's, Leon
Riley Springs, Knox
Riman, Archer
Rincon, Hidalgo
Rincon, Nueces
Rincon, Starr, ................. 5
Ring, Collingsworth
Ringgold, Leon
*Ringgold, Montague, 3........ 100
Ringling Junction, Stephens
RIO BRAVO, Webb,
   (5,553). ................5,693
Rio del Sol, Cameron
*Rio Frio, Real, 9 ............. 50
*RIO GRANDE CITY, Starr,
   555 (11,923) ...........12,305
Rio Grande Station, El Paso
Rio Grande Village, Brewster,..... 9
*RIO HONDO, Cameron, 101
   (1,942). ...............1,995
*Riomedina, Medina, 7.......... 53
Rio Pecos, Crane
Rio Rico, Hidalgo
Rios, Duval, ................ 100
*RIO VISTA, Johnson, 62
   (656) .................... 682
Rip, Montague
Ripley, Lubbock
Ripley, San Saba
Ripley, Titus
Ripley, Titus
Rischer Town, Freestone

*RISING STAR, Eastland, 57
   (835) ..................... 844
Rising Sun, Jones-Shackelford
Rita, Burleson, ................ 50
Ritchen, Uvalde
Ritchie, McLennan
Rite-Care, Shelby
Ritter, Panola
River, Liberty
Rivera, Ellis
River Bend, Palo Pinto
Riverbottom, San Jacinto
Riverby, Fannin, .............. 15
River Crest, Red River
River Crest Estates, Angelina, .. 250
Riverdale, Goliad
Riverdale, Kent
River Fork, Nacogdoches
River Hill, Panola, .............NA
Riverland, Clay
River Oaks, Brazos
River Oaks, Harris
RIVER OAKS, Tarrant,
   (6,985). ................7,102
Rivers, Hartley
Rivers End, Brazoria
River Side, Bee
Riverside, Caldwell
Riverside, Collingsworth
Riverside, Comal
Riverside, Nueces
Riverside, Van Zandt
*RIVERSIDE, Walker, 27
   (425) .................. 417
River Spur [Chula Vista-],
   Zavala, (400) ............. 403
River Terrace, Harris
Riverton, Reeves
River View, Comal
River View, Red River
Rives, Fisher
*Riviera, Kleberg, 50. .........1,064
Riviera Beach, Kleberg, ....... 155
Roa, Garza
Roach, Austin
Roach, Cass, ................. 50
Roach, Gregg
Roadville, Anderson
Roadville, Houston
Roane, Navarro, ............. 120
*ROANOKE, Denton, 725
   (2,810). ................3,166
*Roans Prairie, Grimes, 3 ....... 56
*ROARING SPRINGS, Motley,
   23 (265). ................. 274
Roark, Karnes
Robards, Bexar
Robber's Roost, Scurry
Robberson, Starr
Robbins, Carson
Robbins, Leon, ............. 20
Robbins's Ferry, Madison-Houston
Robbinsville, Red River
Roberta, Limestone
*ROBERT LEE, Coke, 74
   (1,171). ................1,134
Roberts, Hunt
Roberts, Parker
Roberts, Wharton
Robertson, Crosby, ........... 35
Robertson, Hill
Robertson, Jasper
Robertson Mills, Van Zandt
Robinson, Denton
ROBINSON, McLennan,
   (7,845). ................8,182
Robinson, Montgomery

Robinson's, Bee
Robinson's, Madison
Robinson's Mills, Tarrant
Robinson's Settlement, Walker
Robinson Arms Landing, Reeves
Robison, Van Zandt
*ROBSTOWN, Nueces, 499
   (12,727) .............. 12,677
*ROBY, Fisher, 46 (673). ........ 650
Roca Springs, Kimble
Rochelle, Bowie
*Rochelle, McCulloch, 26 ....... 163
*ROCHESTER, Haskell, 19
   (378). .................... 377
Rock, Dallas
Rock Bluff, Burnet, ............ 40
Rock Church, Hood
Rock Creek, Briscoe
Rock Creek, Grayson
Rock Creek, Johnson
Rock Creek, McLennan, ......... 25
Rock Creek, Parker
Rock Creek, Somervell, ........ 38
Rock Crossing, Wilbarger
Rock Crusher, Coleman
*ROCKDALE, Milam, 357
   (5,439) ................ 5,615
Rock Dam, Falls
Rockett, Ellis, ................ 124
Rockett, Hamilton
Rockey, Blanco
Rockey Well, Fort Bend
Rock Falls, Erath
Rockford, Lamar, ............... 30
Rock Harbor, Hood, ........... 522
Rock Hill, Cherokee
Rock Hill, Collin
Rockhill, Franklin
Rock Hill, Henderson
Rock Hill, Panola
Rock Hill, Stephens
Rock Hill, Van Zandt
Rock Hill, Wood
Rockhouse, Austin, ........... 30
Rock House, Culberson
Rock House, Williamson
Rockingham, Tyler
*Rock Island, Colorado, 7....... 160
Rock Island, Marion
Rock Island, Polk
Rock Island, Waller-Washington
Rock Lake, Oldham
Rockland, Tyler, .............. 105
Rockne, Bastrop, ............. 400
Rockne, Bastrop
*ROCKPORT, Aransas, 850
   (7,385) ................ 7,940
Rock Shoals, San Saba
Rock Springs, Bosque
Rock Springs, Cass
*ROCKSPRINGS, Edwards, 58
   (1,285) ................ 1,269
Rock Springs, Gregg
Rock Springs, Marion
Rockvale, Burnet
Rockville, Henderson
Rockwall, Hill
*ROCKWALL, Rockwall, 1,775
   (17,976) .............. 21,529
Rockwell, Reeves
*Rockwood, Coleman, 1 ......... 80
Rocky, Erath
Rocky Branch, Morris, ......... 135
Rocky Cedar Creek, Kaufman
Rocky Creek, Blanco, ........... 20
Rocky Crossing, Limestone
Rocky Hill, Angelina

**CITIES & TOWNS**

| Town,County ..........Pop. 2002 | Town,County ..........Pop. 2002 | Town,County ..........Pop. 2002 |
|---|---|---|
| Rocky Hill, Colorado | *ROPESVILLE, Hockley, 27 | 18 (111) .................119 |
| Rocky Hill, Falls | (517) ...................516 | Round Mountain, Cass |
| Rocky Hill, Gillespie | Ropesville, Nueces | Round Mountain, Comanche |
| Rocky Hill, Lee | Rosalie, Red River,...........100 | Round Mountain, Eastland |
| Rocky Hollow, Williamson | *Rosanky, Bastrop, 20 ........250 | Round Mountain, Lampasas |
| Rocky Mills, Lavaca | Rosborough, Bowie | Round Mountain, McCulloch |
| ROCKY MOUND, Camp, (93).....97 | Rosborough Springs, Harrison | Round Mountain, Travis,........59 |
| Rocky Mound, Young | *ROSCOE, Nolan, 57 | Round Point, Chambers |
| Rocky Mount, Rusk | (1,378)...................1,323 | Round Prairie, Fayette |
| Rocky Mountain, Nacogdoches | Rose, Hamilton | Round Prairie, Lamar |
| Rocky Point, Burnet, ..........102 | Rose, Jackson | Round Prairie, Navarro, .........40 |
| Rocky Point, Delta | Rose, Lee | Round Prairie, Robertson |
| Rocky Point, Rains | *ROSEBUD, Falls, 71 | *ROUND ROCK, Williamson-Travis, |
| Rocky Point, Van Zandt | (1,493)...................1,493 | 3,052 (61,136)... 70,036 |
| Rocky Springs, Angelina | ROSE CITY, Orange, (519) .....523 | Round Timber, Baylor, ...........2 |
| Rocky Valley, Burnet | Rosedale, Falls | *ROUND TOP, Fayette, 55 |
| Rockyville, San Jacinto | Rosedale, Fannin | (77).......................81 |
| Roda, Limestone | Rosedale, Hardin | Round Top, Fisher |
| Roddy, Fannin | Rosedale, Jefferson | Roundtree, Bee |
| Roddy, McLennan | Rose Hill, Dallas | Roundup, Hockley, .............20 |
| Roddy, Van Zandt, .............NA | Rose Hill, Harris,..............NA | Round Valley, Blanco |
| Rodet, Mitchell | Rose Hill, San Jacinto,..........30 | Routon, Haskell |
| Rodney, Navarro, .............15 | Rose Hill, Travis | Rowan, Brazoria |
| Rodolph, Grimes | ROSE HILL ACRES, Hardin, | Rowden, Callahan, ............30 |
| Roebuck, Camp | (480) ...................487 | Rowe, Donley |
| Roebuck, Leon | Roseland, Collin | Rowe's Land, San Saba |
| Roeder, Titus, ...............110 | Roselawn, Dallas | Rowe's Store, Robertson |
| Roeder's Mill, Austin | Roseleaf, Val Verde | Rowena, Karnes |
| Roemerville, Calhoun | Rosenas, Van Zandt | *Rowena, Runnels, 27..........466 |
| Roeville, Brazoria | *ROSENBERG, Fort Bend, 1,230 | Roweville, Brazoria |
| Roganville, Jasper, 1 .........100 | (24,043)...............25,889 | Roweville, Montgomery |
| Rogatton, Young | Rosenfeld, Brewster | Rowland, Comanche |
| *ROGERS, Bell, 57 (1,117).....1,124 | Rosenthal, McLennan | Rowland, Montague |
| Rogers, Ochiltree | Roseville, DeWitt | Rowland, Red River |
| Rogers, Taylor, ..............151 | Rosevine, Sabine,..............50 | Rowland Springs, Collin |
| Rogers Ferry, Red River | Rosewood, Upshur, ..........100 | *ROWLETT, Dallas-Rockwall, |
| Rogers Hill, McLennan | Rosewood Hill, Harris | 1,421 (44,503)..........47,588 |
| Rogers Hill, Travis | *Rosharon, Brazoria, 237.......435 | Rowlett's Creek, Collin |
| Rogerslacy, Hidalgo | Rosita, Cameron | Roxana, Carson |
| Rogers Mill, Bowie | Rosita, Duval, .................25 | *ROXTON, Lamar, 20 (694) .....699 |
| Rogers Plantation, Brazos | Rosita, San Patricio | Roy, Castro |
| Rogers Prairie, Leon-Madison | Rosita North, Maverick, | Roy, Jasper |
| Rogers Ranch, Caldwell | (3,400).................3,488 | Roy, Lamar |
| Rogersville, Bastrop | Rosita South, Maverick, | Roy, Parker |
| Rogersville, Parker | (2,574).................2,689 | Roy, Tarrant |
| Rogersville, Waller | Rosita Valley, Duval | Royal, Calhoun |
| Rohde, Atascosa | Rosprim, Brazos | Royal, Carson |
| Roland, Clay | Ross, Brazoria | Royal, Lipscomb |
| Roland, Collin | *ROSS, McLennan, 7 (228)......230 | Royal, Shelby |
| Roland, Sabine | Ross City, Howard,.............81 | Royal Forest, Comal, ..........NA |
| Rolla, Collingsworth | *ROSSER, Kaufman, 8 | Royal Oaks, Llano |
| Rolling Hills, Potter,..........1,000 | (379) ...................396 | Royalty, Ward, ................29 |
| Rolling Hills, Waller,............NA | Rosslyn, Harris | Royder, Brazos |
| Rolling Hills Shores, Hood,.....421 | Rosson, Clay | *ROYSE CITY, Rockwall-Collin, |
| Rolling Meadows, Gregg, ......362 | Rosson, Jones | 315 (2,957)..............3,496 |
| ROLLINGWOOD, Travis, | Ross Prairie, Fayette | Royston, Fisher |
| (1,403)..................1,410 | *Rosston, Cooke, 7.............75 | Roznov, Fayette |
| Rollover, Galveston | Ross Valley, Coryell | Ruben, Fannin |
| Rolyat, Bowie | Ross Valley, Jack | Rubio, Jeff Davis |
| *ROMA-LOS SAENZ, Starr, | Rossville, Atascosa ...........200 | Ruby, Childress |
| 272 (9,617) ..............9,969 | Rossville, Fayette | Ruby, Jack |
| Roma Creek, Starr, (610) .......636 | Roswell, Bosque | Ruby, Karnes |
| ROMAN FOREST, Montgomery, | *ROTAN, Fisher, 102 (1,611)....1,551 | Ruby, McLennan |
| (1,279)..................1,695 | Rotando, Fisher | Ruby, Sherman |
| *Romayor, Liberty, 11...........96 | Rothe, Medina | Rucker, Comanche,.............30 |
| Rome, Milam | Rothwell, Hall | Rucker's Bridge, Lamar,........20 |
| Romero, Hartley | Rough Creek, Callahan | Rud's Ranch, Fisher |
| Romney, Eastland,.............12 | Rough Creek, Coleman | Rudd, Cherokee |
| Ronda, Wilbarger | Rough Creek, San Saba, ........15 | Rudd, Harrison |
| Rook, Rusk | Roughrock, Blanco | Rudd, Schleicher |
| *Roosevelt, Kimble, 3 ..........14 | Roughtown, Live Oak | Rudolph, Kenedy |
| Roosevelt, Lubbock, ...........NA | Round Flat, Van Zandt | Rudyville, Hidalgo |
| Roosevelt Heights, Dallas | Roundhill, Smith | Rue, Denton |
| Roosevlet, Polk | Round House, Navarro, ........40 | Rue, Shelby |
| Rooster Springs, Hays | Round Lake, Gonzales | Ruff, Hopkins |
| Roosterville, Shelby | Round Mott, Wharton | Rufinch, Robertson |
| Root, Fannin | *ROUND MOUNTAIN, Blanco, | Rufus, Kaufman |

| Town,County ..........Pop. 2002 | Town,County ..........Pop. 2002 | Town,County.......... Pop. 2002 |
|---|---|---|
| **Rugby, Red River,** ............ 24 | ***Sabine Pass, Jefferson, 55** | Salem, Waller |
| Rugeley, Matagorda | ..............(part of Port Arthur) | Salem, Washington |
| **Ruidosa, Presidio,** ............ 43 | Sabine Pass, Rains | Salem, Wood |
| ***RULE, Haskell, 26 (698)** ...... 693 | Sabinetown, Sabine | **Salesville, Palo Pinto,** .......... 88 |
| Ruliff, Newton | **SACHSE, Dallas-Collin,** | **Saline, Menard,** .................. 59 |
| **Rumley, Lampasas,** ............ 8 | (9,751) ..............11,703 | ***Salineno, Starr, 2 (304)** ....... 308 |
| **RUNAWAY BAY, Wise,** | Sacred Heart, Bastrop | Salisbury, Hall |
| (1,104)................ 1,199 | ***Sacul, Nacogdoches, 4**....... 170 | **Salmon, Anderson,** ............. 20 |
| ***RUNGE, Karnes, 35** | Sada, Webb | Salome, Hutchinson |
| (1,080)................ 1,075 | Saddle Creek, McCulloch | Salona, Montague |
| **Runn, Hidalgo,** ............... NA | Saddler's Bend, Cooke | Salt Branch, Bee |
| Runnells, Matagorda | Sadell, Tyler | Salt Branch, Denton |
| Runnels, Runnels | ***SADLER, Grayson, 23 (404)** .... 410 | Salt Creek, Cottle |
| Running Brushy, Williamson | Sage, Burnet | Salt Creek, Lampasas |
| Running Creek, Leon | ***Sagerton, Haskell, 2** .......... 115 | Salt Creek, Montague |
| Running Spring, Titus | ***SAGINAW, Tarrant, 125** | Salt Creek, Young |
| Running Water, Hale | (12,374)..............14,338 | Salter, Robertson |
| Rupee, Falls | St. Bernard, Baylor | ***Salt Flat, Hudspeth, 8** ......... 35 |
| Rural, Bosque | St. Charles, Aransas | **Salt Gap, McCulloch,** .......... 25 |
| **Rural Shade, Navarro,** ......... 30 | St. Clair, Caldwell | Salt Hill, Jack |
| Rush Creek, Navarro | St. Clair, Gregg | ***Saltillo, Hopkins, 12.** ......... 200 |
| **Rushing, Navarro,** ............ 10 | **St. Elmo, Freestone,** ...........NA | Salt Lake, Andrews |
| Rushing, Tarrant | St. Elmo, Sterling-Tom Green | Salt Spring, Comanche |
| Rush Prairie, Navarro | St. Elmo, Travis | Salt Spring, Erath |
| ***RUSK, Cherokee, 228** | **St. Francis, Potter,** ............ 30 | Salt Stream, Gonzales |
| (5,085)................ 5,127 | St. Francisville, Matagorda | Salty, Milam |
| Rusk, Grimes | St. Gall, Pecos | Saluria, Calhoun |
| **Russell, Leon,** ............... 27 | ***ST. HEDWIG, Bexar, 48** | Salvation, Liberty |
| Russell, Van Zandt | (1,875)................1,931 | Sam, Parker |
| Russell's Gap, Bosque | St. Helena, San Augustine | **Samaria, Navarro,** ............. 90 |
| Russell's Pocket, Palo Pinto | St. Holland, Grimes | Sambo, Taylor |
| Russell's Store, Palo Pinto | St. Jo, Collin | Samfordyce, Hidalgo |
| Russell Gabriel, Burnet | ***ST. JO, Montague, 52 (977)**..... 964 | Sammons, Montgomery |
| Russelltown, Cameron | St. Joe, Karnes | ***Samnorwood, Collingsworth,** |
| Russellville, Motley | St. John, Fayette | 1 (39) .................... 49 |
| Rustler, Eastland | St. John, Harrison | **Sample, Gonzales,** ............. 25 |
| Rustler Springs, Culberson | St. John's Mission, Bexar | Sampson, Bell |
| **Rutersville, Fayette,** ........... 52 | **St. John Colony, Caldwell,** ...... 150 | Sampson, Henderson |
| Ruth, Bowie | St. Johns Community, Travis | ***Sam Rayburn, Jasper,** ......... 600 |
| Ruth, Concho | St. Joseph's, Aransas | Samuel, Washington |
| Ruth, Coryell | **St. Lawrence, Glasscock,** ....... 35 | Samuels, Val Verde |
| Rutherford, Parker | St. Louis, Kimble | San Andres, Milam |
| Rutherford, Pecos | St. Louis, Smith | ***SAN ANGELO, Tom Green, 4,231** |
| Ruthford, Wichita | St. Luke, Wharton | (88,439).......... 88,608 |
| **Ruth Springs, Henderson,** ....... 15 | St. Martinville, McLennan | San Angelo Junction, Coleman |
| Ruthven's Gin, Lee | St. Mary, Grimes | ***SAN ANTONIO, Bexar, 44,958** |
| Rutland, Angelina | St. Mary, Harrison | (1,144,646)....... 1,182,840 |
| Rutledge, Williamson | St. Mary, Refugio | San Antonio Prairie, Burleson, .. NA |
| Ruvaldt's Gin, Kaufman | St. Mary's, Frio | Sanatorium, Tom Green |
| Ryals, Montgomery | **St. Mary's Colony, Bastrop,** ......NA | San Augustine, Atascosa |
| Ryan, Cottle | St. Matthew, Burleson | ***SAN AUGUSTINE, San Augustine,** |
| Ryan, McLennan | St. Olive, Walker | 214 (2,475)............. 2,481 |
| Ryan, Navarro | **ST. PAUL, Collin, (630)** ......... 700 | San Barnard, Colorado |
| Ryan, Presidio | St. Paul, Falls | San Bartolo, Zapata |
| Ryans Neighborhood, Bee | St. Paul, Leon | ***SAN BENITO, Cameron, 651** |
| Ryanville, Refugio | **St. Paul, San Patricio, (542)** ..... 549 | (23,444)............... 24,079 |
| Ryburn, Schleicher | Saints' Roost, Donley | San Bernard, Fort Bend |
| Rye, Brazos | St. Thomas Chapel, Cherokee | San Bernardo, Brazoria |
| ***Rye, Liberty, 11**............... 76 | St. Viola, Smith | Sanborn, Grayson |
| Rye, Scurry | ***Salado, Bell, 291 (3,475)**......3,606 | **San Carlos, Hidalgo, (2,650).**... 2,718 |
| Rylie, Dallas | Salado, Jim Hogg | **San Carlos, Starr,** .............. 10 |
| Rymers, Matagorda | Salado Creek, Bexar | Sanchez, Webb |
|  | Salcedo, Madison | **Sanchez [Morales-], Zapata,** |
| **S** | Salem, Bastrop | (95)....................... 95 |
| Sabana Creek, Comanche | Salem, Cass | **Sanco, Coke,** .................. 30 |
| **Sabanno, Eastland,** ............ 12 | **Salem, Cherokee,** .............. 20 | San Cosme, Rusk |
| Sabathany, Parker | Salem, Eastland | **SANCTUARY, Parker, (256)**...... 376 |
| ***SABINAL, Uvalde, 56** | Salem, Erath | Sand, Bastrop |
| (1,586)................ 1,592 | Salem, Freestone | Sand, Dawson |
| Sabinal Canyon, Uvalde | Salem, Freestone | Sand Branch, Atascosa |
| Sabine, Gregg | **Salem, Grimes,** ................ 50 | **Sand Branch, Dallas,** .......... 400 |
| Sabine, Jefferson | Salem, Hays | Sanders, Wharton |
| Sabine, Sabine | Salem, Lee | ***Sanderson, Terrell, 56** |
| Sabine, Smith | Salem, Milam | (861)..................... 810 |
| Sabine Farms, Harrison | **Salem, Newton,** ................ 85 | Sandersville, Jones |
| Sabine Lake, Hunt | Salem, Smith-Rusk | Sand Flat, Anderson |
| Sabine Mills, Gregg | Salem, Victoria | **Sand Flat, Johnson,** ........... NA |

**CITIES & TOWNS**

| Town,County ......... Pop. 2002 | Town,County ......... Pop. 2002 | Town,County ......... Pop. 2002 |
|---|---|---|
| **Sand Flat, Leon,** .............. 32 | San Francisco, Willacy | Santa Lucia, Pecos |
| **Sand Flat, Rains,** ............ 100 | **San Gabriel, Milam, 1** .......... 100 | Santa Margarita, Nueces |
| **Sand Flat, Smith,** ............ 100 | ***SANGER, Denton, 336*** | Santa Margarita, Willacy |
| Sand Flat, Van Zandt | (4,534) ................. 4,950 | ***Santa Maria, Cameron, 5** |
| Sand Fly, Bastrop-Lee | San Geronimo, Bexar | (846). .................... 848 |
| Sandgate, DeWitt | San Geronimo, Medina | **Santa Monica, Willacy, (78)** ...... 78 |
| Sand Grove, Milam | ***San Isidro, Starr, 10 (270)** ...... 273 | Santander, Cameron |
| Sand Hill, Burleson | San Jacinto, Harris | Santa Rita, Cameron |
| Sand Hill, Comanche | San Jacinto, Harris | Santarita, Hidalgo |
| **Sandhill, Floyd,** .............. 33 | San Jacinto, San Jacinto | Santa Rita, Reagan |
| Sand Hill, Freestone | San Jacinto, Walker | ***SANTA ROSA, Cameron, 36** |
| Sand Hill, Hopkins | San Jose, Bexar | (2,833) ................. 2,897 |
| Sand Hill, Shelby | **San Jose, Duval,** .............. 15 | Santa Rosa, Kenedy |
| Sand Hill, Smith | San Jose, El Paso | Santiago Carr, Webb |
| **Sand Hill, Upshur,** ............. 75 | San Jose, Hidalgo | ***Santo, Palo Pinto, 38** .......... 445 |
| Sand Hill[s], Rusk | San Jose, Reeves | Santo Tomas, Webb |
| Sand Hills, Ward | San Jose, Webb | San Vicente, Brewster |
| Sand Hollow, Frio | San Jose de Lopeno, Zapata | San Vicente, Cameron |
| ***Sandia, Jim Wells, 32** | San Juan, Bexar | ***San Ygnacio, Zapata, 10** |
| (431) ................... 462 | ***SAN JUAN, Hidalgo, 414** | (853). .................. 932 |
| ***SAN DIEGO, Duval-Jim Wells,*** | (26,229) ............... 27,777 | San Ysidro, El Paso, ........... 400 |
| 115 (4,753) ............. 4,792 | San Juan, Nueces | Sapoak, Erath |
| Sandies, Gonzales | San Juanito Ranch, Starr | ***Saragosa, Reeves, 6** .......... 185 |
| Sandies, Wharton | San Julian, Cameron | Saragosa, Reeves |
| Sandlake, Ellis | **SAN LEANNA, Travis, (384)** ..... 412 | Sarahville de Viesca, Falls |
| **Sandlin, Stonewall,** ............. 5 | ***San Leon, Galveston,*** | Saralvo, Ellis |
| Sand Mountain, Rusk | (4,365) ................. 4,436 | Sarat, Shelby |
| San Domingo, Bee | San Lorenzo, El Paso | ***Saratoga, Hardin, 14** ........ 1,000 |
| San Domingo, Starr | San Lucas Springs, Bexar | Sarber, Marion |
| **Sandoval, Williamson,** .......... 50 | San Luis, Brazoria | **Sarco, Goliad,** .................. 78 |
| Sandow, Milam | San Luisito, Hidalgo | Sarco Creek, Goliad |
| Sand Pit, Newton | ***San Manuel-Linn, Hidalgo,*** | Sardis, Cass |
| Sand Prairie, Kaufman | 13 (958) ................. 971 | Sardis, Cherokee |
| Sand Ridge, Houston | ***SAN MARCOS, Hays, 2,215*** | Sardis, Coryell |
| Sand Ridge, Wharton | (34,733) ............... 39,936 | **Sardis, Ellis,** .................. 20 |
| Sand Rock, Foard | San Martine, Reeves | Sardis, Fisher |
| Sand Rock Springs, Scurry | San Miguel, Frio | Sardis, Leon |
| Sand Spring, Anderson | San Miguel, McMullen | Sardis, Limestone |
| Sand Spring, Wood | **SAN PATRICIO, San Patricio-Nueces,** | Sardis, McLennan |
| **Sand Springs, Howard,** ........ 903 | (318) .................... 323 | Sardis, Rusk |
| Sand Spur, Fisher | **San Pedro, Cameron, (668)** ..... 679 | Sardis, Shelby |
| Sand Switch, Kaufman | San Pedro, Houston | Sargent, Dallas |
| Sand Town, Freestone | San Pedro, Jim Hogg | **Sargent, Matagorda,** ........... 300 |
| Sand Town, Titus | San Pedro, Nueces | ***Sarita, Kenedy, 8** ............. 250 |
| Sandtown, Washington | San Pedro, Zapata | Saron, Angelina |
| Sandune, Liberty | ***SAN PERLITA, Willacy, 5** | **Saron, Trinity,** ................... 5 |
| **Sandusky, Grayson,** ........... 15 | (680) .................... 685 | Saron Front, Trinity |
| Sandy, Bastrop | Sanramon, Hidalgo | Sartartia, Fort Bend |
| ***Sandy, Blanco, 1** .............. 25 | Sanramon, Hidalgo | Sartor, Guadalupe |
| **Sandy, Limestone,** ............. 5 | **San Roman, Starr,** .............. 5 | Sash, Fannin |
| Sandy, Llano | San Roman, Webb | **Saspamco, Wilson,** ........... 443 |
| Sandy Creek, Limestone | ***SAN SABA, San Saba, 245*** | Sasseville, DeWitt |
| Sandy Creek, Milam | (2,637) ................. 2,648 | Satan's Flat, Mitchell |
| Sandy Elm, Guadalupe | San Solomon, Jeff Davis | ***Satin, Falls, 5** ................. 86 |
| Sandy Fork, Gonzales | Sansom, Uvalde | Satren, Sherman |
| **Sandy Harbor, Llano,** .......... 85 | **SANSOM PARK, Tarrant,** | Satsuma, Harris |
| **Sandy Hill, Washington,** ........ 50 | (4,181) ................. 4,233 | Satsuma, Matagorda |
| **Sandy Hills, Montgomery,** ....... NA | Sans Souci, Montgomery | Satterfeild, Stephens |
| **Sandy Hollow-Escondidas,** | ***SANTA ANNA, Coleman, 81** | **Sattler, Comal,** ................. 30 |
| Nueces, (433) ............. 459 | (1,081) ................. 1,041 | Satuit, McCulloch |
| Sandy Hook, Panola | Santa Anna, Colorado | **Saturn, Gonzales,** .............. 15 |
| Sandy Mountain, Llano | Santa Anna, Jackson | Sauer, Milam |
| **Sandy Point, Brazoria,** .......... 30 | **Santa Anna, Starr,** .............. 20 | Saul's Mills, Williamson |
| Sandy Point, Colorado | **Santa Catarina, Starr,** ........... 15 | Sauls, Cass |
| Sandy Valley, Llano | **Santa Clara, Guadalupe,** | Saunders, Anderson |
| ***San Elizario, El Paso, 74** | (889) .................... 955 | Saunders, Bexar |
| (11,046). .............. 11,364 | Santa Cruz, Duval | Saunders, Trinity |
| San Esteban, Presidio | Santa Cruz, Hays | **Sauney Stand, Washington,** ..... NA |
| ***SAN FELIPE, Austin, 10** | **Santa Cruz, Starr, (630)** ........ 662 | Sauz, Willacy |
| (868) ................... 913 | Santa Elena, Cameron | Sava, Van Zandt |
| San Felipe del Rio, Val Verde | ***Santa Elena, Starr,** ............ 64 | Savage, Crosby |
| San Fernando, Llano | ***SANTA FE, Galveston, 471** | Savage, Fannin |
| San Fernando de Bexar, Bexar | (9,548). ............... 9,947 | Savage, Hidalgo |
| Sanford, Hill | Santa Fe, Zapata | Savanah, Upshur |
| ***SANFORD, Hutchinson, 9** | Santa Gertrudes, Kleberg | Savannah, Marion |
| (203) ................... 201 | Santa Helena, Brewster | Savannah, Red River |
| San Francisco, Medina | Santa Isabel, Webb | Savilla, Foard |

| Town,County . . . . . . . . . . .Pop. 2002 | Town,County . . . . . . . . . . .Pop. 2002 | Town,County . . . . . . . . . . Pop. 2002 |
|---|---|---|
| *SAVOY, Fannin, 40 (850) . . . . . . . 850 | Scoville, Harris | SELMA, Bexar-Guadalupe-Comal, |
| Saw Mill, Bastrop | Scranton, Eastland, . . . . . . . . . . . 40 | (788). . . . . . . . . . . . . . . . . . . . . . .961 |
| Sawyer, Irion | Scrap, Red River | Selman, McCulloch |
| Saxet, Shelby | Scrappin Valley, Newton | *Selman City, Rusk, 8 . . . . . . . . . 271 |
| Saxeton Shores, Galveston | Scratch Eye, Harrison | Selmer, Hansford |
| Sayers, Bexar,. . . . . . . . . . . . . . . . . NA | *Scroggins, Franklin, 46. . . . . . . 125 | Seltser, Tarrant |
| Sayersville, Bastrop, . . . . . . . . . . NA | Scroggins, Wood | Selvin, Houston |
| Sayles Cross Roads, Camp | Scroungeout, Anderson | Seminary Hill, Tarrant |
| Sayre, Harrison | Scrub Creek, Trinity | *SEMINOLE, Gaines, 438 |
| Scale, Upshur | Scruggs, Panola | (5,910) . . . . . . . . . . . . . . . . 5,867 |
| Scallorn, Bastrop | Scruggs, Wise | Seminole, Val Verde |
| Scallorn, Mills | Scurlock, Goliad | Seminole Camp, Kinney |
| Scalp Creek, Menard | *Scurry, Kaufman, 64 . . . . . . . . . 315 | Sempronius, Austin,. . . . . . . . . . . 15 |
| Scatter Branch, Hunt, . . . . . . . . . NA | Scyene, Dallas | Senate, Jack |
| Scenic Hills, Guadalupe,. . . . . . . 170 | Scyene Switch, Dallas | Seneca, Coryell |
| Scenic Oaks, Bexar, | Sea, Grayson | Seneca, Tyler |
| (3,279). . . . . . . . . . . . . . . . .3,391 | Sea, Houston | Senior, Bexar, . . . . . . . . . . . . . . . NA |
| Scharbauer City, Ector, . . . . . . . . 20 | Seaborn, Baylor | Senterfitt, Lampasas |
| Schattel, Frio,. . . . . . . . . . . . . . . . 85 | Seabreeze, Chambers | Sequoyah, Trinity |
| Schendelville, Fort Bend | *SEABROOK, Harris, 819 | Serbin, Lee, . . . . . . . . . . . . . . . . . 90 |
| Schermersville, Bexar | (9,443). . . . . . . . . . . . . . . . .9,950 | Serenada, Williamson, |
| *SCHERTZ, Guadalupe-Comal-Bexar, | Seabur, Tyler | (1,847). . . . . . . . . . . . . . . . 1,832 |
| 638 (18,694) . . . . . . . . . . . 20,336 | *SEADRIFT, Calhoun, 49 | Service, Ellis |
| Scherz, Tom Green | (1,352). . . . . . . . . . . . . . . . .1,348 | Servsand, Atascosa |
| Schicke Point, Calhoun, . . . . . . . . 70 | Seago, Duval | Setag, Polk |
| Schiller, Kendall | *SEAGOVILLE, Dallas, 442 | Seth, Hardin |
| Schindler, Austin | (10,823). . . . . . . . . . . . . . . .10,966 | Seth Ward, Hale, (1,926) . . . . . . 1,933 |
| Schkade, Lee | *SEAGRAVES, Gaines, 83 | Setler, Briscoe |
| Schleicher, Callahan | (2,334). . . . . . . . . . . . . . . . .2,299 | Settlement, Hall |
| Schleicher's Bend, San Saba | Seale, Robertson,. . . . . . . . . . . . . 60 | Settlers Village, Harris |
| Schley, Coryell | Seale's Chapel, Karnes | Seven D, Reagan |
| Schley, Harrison | *SEALY, Austin, 460 | Seven Leagues, Smith |
| Schley, Kent | (5,248). . . . . . . . . . . . . . . . .5,510 | Seven Oaks, Galveston |
| Schley, Smith | Sealy's, Falls | Seven Oaks, Hemphill |
| Schneider, Orange | Seaman, Liberty | SEVEN OAKS, Polk, (131). . . . . . 135 |
| Schoenau, Austin | Searcy, Madison | Seven Pines, Gregg-Upshur, . . . . . 50 |
| Schoenau, Austin | Sears, Scurry | Seven Points, Collin |
| Schoenburg, Llano | Searsville, Bosque-McLennan | *SEVEN POINTS, Henderson, |
| Schoenthal, Comal | Seaton, Bell, . . . . . . . . . . . . . . . . 60 | (1,145) . . . . . . . . . . . . . . . . 1,210 |
| School, Guadalupe | Seattle, Coryell | Seven Sisters, Duval, . . . . . . . . . . 60 |
| School Creek, Lampasas | Seawillow, Caldwell,. . . . . . . . . . 100 | Seventy-seven Ranch (77 Ranch), |
| Schooler's Store, Terry | *Sebastian, Willacy, 16 | Crockett |
| Schoolerville, Hamilton | (1,864). . . . . . . . . . . . . . . . .1,882 | Seven Wells, Mitchell |
| School Hill, Erath, . . . . . . . . . . . . 22 | Sebastopol, Trinity,. . . . . . . . . . . 120 | Sevier, Hill |
| Schoolland, Gonzales | Sebastopol, Wilson | Sevilla, Brown |
| School Land, Navarro | Sebesta, Burleson | Seward Junction, Williamson |
| Schraeder, Red River | Sebree, Jack | Sewell, Young |
| Schreiner, Kerr | Sebrick, Stephens | Sexton, Sabine,. . . . . . . . . . . . . . 27 |
| Schroeder, Goliad,. . . . . . . . . . . 347 | Seclusion, Lavaca | Sexton, Van Zandt |
| *SCHULENBURG, Fayette, 279 | Seco, Collin | Sexton City, Rusk,. . . . . . . . . . . . NA |
| (2,699). . . . . . . . . . . . . . . . .2,794 | Seco, Medina | Sexton Community, Matagorda |
| Schull, Bell | Seco Mines, Maverick, . . . . . . . . .NA | Seymore, Hopkins, . . . . . . . . . . . NA |
| Schumansville, Guadalupe, . . . . 650 | Second Creek, Lipscomb | *SEYMOUR, Baylor, 184 |
| Schussler, Gillespie | Second Corinth, Waller | (2,908) . . . . . . . . . . . . . . . . 2,904 |
| Schwab City, Polk, . . . . . . . . . . . 120 | Secret Springs, Clay | Seymour Colony, Baylor |
| *Schwertner, Williamson, 5 . . . . . 150 | Security, Montgomery, . . . . . . . . . 24 | Shackelford, Henderson |
| Science Hall, Hays | Sedalia, Collin, . . . . . . . . . . . . . . 25 | Shackelford Ranch, Real |
| Science Hall, Jasper, . . . . . . . . . . NA | Sedan, Gonzales | Shack Town, Dawson |
| Science Hill, Henderson | Sedwick, Shackelford | Shadeland, Lipscomb |
| Scissors, Hidalgo, (2,805) . . . . . 2,897 | Seefeld, Dimmit | Shadeville, Henderson |
| Scobee, Burnet | Seeligson, Jim Wells | Shadowland, Red River |
| Scofield, Burleson | Seelye, Tom Green | Shady, Baylor |
| Scooba, Rusk | Sefcikville, Bell | Shady, Smith |
| *SCOTLAND, Archer, 15 | Seger, Robertson | Shady Grove, Burnet, . . . . . . . . . . 64 |
| (438) . . . . . . . . . . . . . . . . . . 445 | Seglar, Bexar | Shady Grove, Cherokee,. . . . . . . . 30 |
| Scotland, Harrison | Segno, Polk, . . . . . . . . . . . . . . . . 80 | Shady Grove, Dallas |
| Scott, Lamar | Segovia, Kimble,. . . . . . . . . . . . . 12 | Shady Grove, Franklin |
| Scott, Panola | *SEGUIN, Guadalupe, 1,553 | Shady Grove, Hopkins |
| Scott, Van Zandt | (22,011). . . . . . . . . . . . . . .22,808 | Shady Grove, Houston, . . . . . . . . 83 |
| Scott's, Burleson | Sejita, Duval,. . . . . . . . . . . . . . . . 22 | Shady Grove, Lamar |
| Scott's, Rusk | Selden, Erath, . . . . . . . . . . . . . . . 7 | Shady Grove, Limestone |
| Scott's Mills, Cass | Self, San Saba | Shady Grove, Madison |
| Scottdale, Dallas | Self's, Brown | Shady Grove, Nacogdoches |
| Scotts Chapel, Hill | Selfs, Fannin, . . . . . . . . . . . . . . . 30 | Shady Grove, Panola, . . . . . . . . . . NA |
| *SCOTTSVILLE, Harrison, 20 | Selkirk Island, Matagorda | Shady Grove, Polk |
| (263) . . . . . . . . . . . . . . . . . . 251 | Sellers, Collin | Shady Grove, Smith,. . . . . . . . . . 250 |
| Scottsville, Henderson | Sellers, Harris | Shady Grove, Upshur, . . . . . . . . . 40 |

| Town,County . . . . . . . . . . .Pop. 2002 | Town,County . . . . . . . . . . .Pop. 2002 | Town,County . . . . . . . . . . . Pop. 2002 |
|---|---|---|
| *Shady Grove Church, Marion* | Shep, Taylor, . . . . . . . . . . . . . . . . . 60 | **Shovel Mountain, Burnet,. . . . . . . . 98** |
| **Shady Hollow, Travis,** | *****SHEPHERD, San Jacinto, 128** | *Shrum, Comanche* |
| (5,140). . . . . . . . . . . . . . . . .5,361 | (2,029). . . . . . . . . . . . . . .2,132 | *Shult's Store, Fayette* |
| *Shady Oaks, Brazoria* | *Shepherds Valley, Walker* | *Shumla, Val Verde* |
| **Shady Oaks, Henderson,. . . . . . . 100** | *****Sheppard Air Force Base, Wichita,** | *Siam, Leon* |
| **SHADY SHORES, Denton,** | 61. . . . . . . . . . . . . . . . . . .3,825 | *Siam, Terry* |
| (1,461). . . . . . . . . . . . . . . .1,628 | *Shepton, Collin* | *Sid, Hays* |
| *Shaeffer, Duval* | *Shepton, Denton* | *****Sidney, Comanche, 13. . . . . . . . 196** |
| *****Shafter, Presidio, 1 . . . . . . . . . . . 26** | *Sher-Han, Hansford* | *Sidney, Marion* |
| *Shafter Lake, Andrews* | *****Sheridan, Colorado, 12. . . . . . . 225** | *Sid Richardson, Ector* |
| *Shahan's Prairie, Collin* | *Sheridan, Houston* | **Sienna Plantation, Fort Bend,** |
| *Shaid's Chapel, Anderson* | *Sherlock, Lipscomb* | (1,896) . . . . . . . . . . . . . . . 1,936 |
| *Shake Rag, Rusk* | *****SHERMAN, Grayson, 2,235** | *Sieper's, Austin* |
| *Shale, Hill* | (35,082). . . . . . . . . . . . . . .35,920 | *****Sierra Blanca, Hudspeth, 27** |
| *****SHALLOWATER, Lubbock, 106** | **Sherry, Red River,. . . . . . . . . . . . . 15** | (533). . . . . . . . . . . . . . . . . .549 |
| (2,086). . . . . . . . . . . . . . . .2,151 | **Sherwood, Irion, . . . . . . . . . . . . . 150** | *Siesta, Atascosa* |
| *Shamrock, Castro* | *Sherwood, Wilbarger* | *Siesta Dara, Medina* |
| *****SHAMROCK, Wheeler, 175** | **Sherwood Shores, Bell, . . . . . . . . 600** | **Siesta Shores, Zapata, (890) . . . . 964** |
| (2,029). . . . . . . . . . . . . . . .1,959 | **Sherwood Shores, Burnet, . . . . . 870** | *Signal Hill, Hutchinson* |
| *Shanghai, Wharton* | **Sherwood Shores, Grayson, . . .1,590** | *Signal Peak, Culberson* |
| **Shangri La, Burnet, . . . . . . . . . . . 58** | **Shields, Coleman, . . . . . . . . . . . . 13** | *Sigsbee, Coryell* |
| **Shankleville, Newton, . . . . . . . . . NA** | *Shields Gin, Milam* | *Sikes, Hunt* |
| *Shanklin's Mill, Bell* | *Shilo, Clay* | **Silas, Shelby,. . . . . . . . . . . . . . . NA** |
| *Shanks, Freestone* | *Shiloh, Atascosa* | *Silesia, Bexar* |
| **Shannon, Clay,. . . . . . . . . . . . . . . 23** | **Shiloh, Bastrop, . . . . . . . . . . . . . .NA** | **Siloam, Bowie,. . . . . . . . . . . . . . . 50** |
| *Shannon, Madison* | *Shiloh, Burleson* | *Siloam, Comanche* |
| *Shannon, Montgomery* | *Shiloh, Dallas* | *Siloam, Williamson* |
| *Sharon, Bandera* | *Shiloh, Delta* | *Silone, Smith* |
| *Sharon, Hardin* | *Shiloh, Denton* | *****SILSBEE, Hardin, 586** |
| *Sharon, Panola* | *Shiloh, Denton* | (6,393) . . . . . . . . . . . . . . . 6,489 |
| *Sharon, Scurry* | *Shiloh, DeWitt* | *****Silver, Coke, 6 . . . . . . . . . . . . . . 60** |
| *Sharon, Smith* | *Shiloh, Erath* | *Silver City, Bell* |
| *Sharon, Wood* | *Shiloh, Freestone* | *Silver City, Fannin* |
| **Sharp, Milam, . . . . . . . . . . . . . . . 75** | *Shiloh, Freestone* | **Silver City, Milam,. . . . . . . . . . . . 25** |
| *Sharpsburg, San Patricio* | *Shiloh, Gregg* | *Silver City, Montgomery* |
| *Sharpstown, Harris* | *Shiloh, Houston* | **Silver City, Navarro, . . . . . . . . . . 100** |
| *Sharpville, San Augustine* | *Shiloh, Hunt* | **Silver City, Red River, . . . . . . . . . 25** |
| *Sharyland, Hidalgo* | *Shiloh, Lavaca* | **Silver Creek Village, Burnet, . . . . 250** |
| *Shaufler, Nolan* | *Shiloh, Lee* | *Silver Falls, Crosby* |
| *Shavano, Bexar* | **Shiloh, Leon,. . . . . . . . . . . . . . . . .NA** | *Silver Glade, Cooke* |
| **SHAVANO PARK, Bexar,** | **Shiloh, Limestone, . . . . . . . . . . . 250** | *Silver Hill, Polk* |
| (1,754). . . . . . . . . . . . . . . . 1,809 | *Shiloh, Madison* | **Silver Hills, Comal, . . . . . . . . . . . NA** |
| *Shaw, Bowie* | *Shiloh, Navarro* | *Silver Lake, Cochran* |
| *Shaw, Bowie* | *Shiloh, Rusk* | **Silver Lake, Van Zandt,. . . . . . . . . 42** |
| *Shaw, Fannin* | *Shiloh, Titus* | *Silver Pass, Eastland* |
| *Shaw, Kaufman* | *Shiloh, Travis* | **Silver Pines, Smith,. . . . . . . . . . . NA** |
| *Shaw, Robertson* | *Shiloh, Waller* | *Silver Springs, Limestone* |
| *Shaw, Terrell* | *Shiloh, Williamson* | *****SILVERTON, Briscoe, 52** |
| *Shaw's Ranch, Callahan* | *Shiloh Academy, Lamar* | (771). . . . . . . . . . . . . . . . . .773 |
| *Shaw Bend, San Saba* | *Shimek, Colorado* | **Silver Valley, Coleman, . . . . . . . . 20** |
| *Shawnee, Angelina* | *****SHINER, Lavaca, 150** | *Simmons, Delta* |
| *Shawnee, Concho* | (2,070). . . . . . . . . . . . . . . .2,064 | **Simmons, Live Oak, . . . . . . . . . . . 65** |
| *Shawnee, Red River* | *Shingle Arbor, Navarro* | *Simmons, Marion* |
| *Shawnee Creek, Angelina* | *Shinnery, Collingsworth* | *Simmons Bottom, Liberty* |
| **Shawnee Prairie, Angelina,. . . . . . 20** | *Shinnery Lake, Stonewall* | *Simmonsville, Bell* |
| *Shawnee Town, Rusk* | *Shinoak, Eastland* | *****Simms, Bowie, 30 . . . . . . . . . . . 240** |
| *Shawnee Village, Sabine* | *Ship, Montague* | **Simms, Deaf Smith, . . . . . . . . . . . 10** |
| **Shaws Bend, Colorado,. . . . . . . . 100** | **Shire, Rusk,. . . . . . . . . . . . . . . . . 200** | *Simms, Lipscomb* |
| *Shawville, Coke* | **Shirley, Hopkins,. . . . . . . . . . . . . .NA** | *Simms, Mills* |
| *Shea, Webb* | *Shirley Creek, Nacogdoches* | *Simon, Webb* |
| *Shealey, Brazos* | *****Shiro, Grimes, 8 . . . . . . . . . . . . 205** | *Simonds, Dallas* |
| *Shed, Panola* | **Shive, Hamilton,. . . . . . . . . . . . . . 61** | *****SIMONTON, Fort Bend, 36** |
| *Sheeks, Liberty* | *Shoal Point, Galveston* | (718). . . . . . . . . . . . . . . . . .728 |
| *Sheerin, Moore* | *Shockeys Prairie, Lamar* | *Simonville, Mason* |
| *Sheffield, Cass* | *Shockley, Hamilton* | *Simpkins Prairie, Wood* |
| *****Sheffield, Pecos, 16 . . . . . . . . . . 400** | *Shoe-Bar Ranch, Hall* | *Simpson, Webb* |
| *Sheid, McLennan* | *Shoe String, Harrison* | *Simpson's, Nacogdoches-Shelby* |
| **Shelby, Austin, . . . . . . . . . . . . . . 175** | *Sholar, Shelby* | *Simpson's Bend, Llano* |
| *****Shelbyville, Shelby, 35 . . . . . . . 215** | *Shook, Medina* | *Simpson's Ranch, Taylor* |
| **Sheldon, Harris, (1,831). . . . . . 1,834** | *Shook's Bluff, Cherokee* | *Simpsonville, Coryell* |
| *Shell Camp, Gregg* | *Shooks Chapel, Hopkins* | **Simpsonville, Matagorda,. . . . . . . 10** |
| *Shell Rock, Tarrant* | **SHORE ACRES, Harris,** | **Simpsonville, Upshur, . . . . . . . . 100** |
| *Shell Siding, Galveston* | (1,488). . . . . . . . . . . . . . . .1,525 | **Sims, Brazos, . . . . . . . . . . . . . . . NA** |
| *Shelton's, Lamar* | **Short, Shelby, . . . . . . . . . . . . . . .NA** | *Sims, Ellis* |
| *Shelton's Store, Shelby* | *Short Pone, Rusk* | *Sims, Tom Green* |
| **SHENANDOAH, Montgomery,** | *Shortview, Harrison* | **Simsboro, Freestone,. . . . . . . . . . NA** |
| (1,503). . . . . . . . . . . . . . . .1,537 | *Shoup, Jasper* | *Sims Colony, Limestone* |

| Town,County ......... Pop. 2002 | Town,County .......... Pop. 2002 | Town,County ......... Pop. 2002 |
|---|---|---|
| Sims Creek, Lampasas | Small, Hudspeth | Snyder, Hale |
| Sims Valley, Concho | Small, Van Zandt | *SNYDER, Scurry, 678 |
| Simtrott, Hunt | Small, Williamson | (10,783) ............. 10,506 |
| Sinclair, Jones | Smead, McLennan | Soash, Howard |
| Sinclair City, Smith, .......... NA | Smeltertown, El Paso | Soco, Victoria |
| Sinco, Harris | Smetana, Brazos, ............. 80 | *SOCORRO, El Paso, |
| Sines, Liberty | Smilax, Wood | (27,152) ............. 27,892 |
| Singer's Store, Lubbock | *SMILEY, Gonzales, 28 (453) .... 449 | Soda, Polk |
| Singleton, Grimes, 1 .......... 44 | Smith, Bell | Soda Springs, Caldwell |
| Singleton's, Ellis | Smith, Kaufman | Sodom, Hunt |
| Singleton Prairie, Wood | Smith, Parker | Sodom, Wood |
| *SINTON, San Patricio, 312 | Smith, Upshur | Sodville, San Patricio |
| (5,676)................ 5,653 | Smith, Wood | Soldier Mound, Dickens, ........ 12 |
| Sion, Walker | Smith's Landing, Marion | Soldiers' Camp, Medina |
| Sipe Springs, Comanche, ....... 75 | Smith's Ranch, Culberson | Solino, Hidalgo |
| Sipe Springs, Milam | Smith's Ranch, Hudspeth | Solis, Cameron, (545) ......... 565 |
| Sisk, Erath | Smith's Store, Cass | Solitude, Brazoria |
| *Sisterdale, Kendall, 3 ......... 63 | Smith's Tram, Jasper | Solitude, El Paso |
| Sister Grove, Collin | Smith Chapel, Limestone | Solms, Comal,................ 40 |
| Sivells Bend, Cooke, ........... 50 | Smith Creek, Clay | Solon, Wilbarger |
| Sixmile, Calhoun,............. 300 | Smithdale, Childress | Somerset, Atascosa |
| Six Mile, Hopkins | Smithers Lake, Fort Bend | *SOMERSET, Bexar, 66 |
| Sixmile, Llano | Smith Ferry, Tyler | (1,550) .............. 1,628 |
| Six Mile, Milam | Smithfield, Polk | Somerset, Williamson |
| Six Shooter Junction, Cameron | Smithfield, Tarrant | *SOMERVILLE, Burleson, 100 |
| Six Shooter Junction, Karnes | Smith Grove, Houston | (1,704)................ 1,722 |
| Skains, Trinity | Smithland, Marion,........... 179 | Sommer, Cottle |
| Skeen, Lynn | Smithland, Marion-Cass-Morris | Sommer's Mill, Bell, ............ 6 |
| Skeeterville, San Saba, ........ 10 | Smithland, Milam | Soncy, Potter |
| *SKELLYTOWN, Carson, 21 | Smith Oaks, Grayson | Sonoma, Ellis |
| (610) ................... 592 | Smith Point, Chambers,....... 150 | *SONORA, Sutton, 255 |
| Skellyville, Travis | Smiths Bend, Bosque,..........NA | (2,924) ............... 2,977 |
| *Skidmore, Bee, 29 (1,013) .... 1,041 | Smiths Bluff, Jefferson | Soon-over, Hopkins |
| Skiles, Karnes | Smithson Valley, Comal, .......NA | Sorghumville, Houston |
| Skinner, Tom Green | Smithton, Montague | Sorgo, Bandera |
| Skinner Springs, Clay | *SMITHVILLE, Bastrop, 288 | Sorrella, Wharton |
| Skin Tight, Cherokee | (3,901)................4,176 | Sorrels Creek, Comal |
| Skippers Gap, Erath | Smithville, Bosque | Sotol, Kinney |
| Skull Creek, Colorado | Smithwick, Burnet,............ 52 | Sotol, Val Verde |
| Skunk Hill, Nueces | Smithwick's, Travis | Sotol City, Val Verde |
| Sky, Madison | Smitty, Henderson | Souleman, Archer |
| Sky Harbor, Hood, ........... 687 | Smoot, Travis | Soules Chapel, Upshur |
| Sky Lakes, Walker | Smoothing Iron, Lavaca | Soumethun, Dallas |
| Slabtown, Lamar | Smoots, Denton | *SOUR LAKE, Hardin, 147 |
| Slack's Wells, Fayette | *SMYER, Hockley, 19 (480)...... 474 | (1,667) ............... 1,694 |
| Slade's Camp, Jasper | Smyna, Milam | Sour Lake, Jefferson |
| Slapfoot, Dallas | Smyrna, Cass,................ 215 | Sour Spring, Caldwell |
| Slap Out, Brown | Smyrna, Harrison | Sour Spring, Caldwell |
| Slap Out, Hill | Smyrna, Nacogdoches | Sour Well, Caldwell |
| Slater, Coryell | Smyrna, Rains, ............... 25 | South Alamo, Hidalgo, |
| Slate Shoals, Lamar, .......... 10 | Smyrna, Rusk | (3,101) ............... 3,194 |
| *SLATON, Lubbock, 221 | Smyrna, Wood | Southard, Donley |
| (6,109)................ 6,092 | Smyth, Uvalde | Southbank, Wichita |
| Slaughter, Lampasas | Snake Prairie, Bastrop | *South Bend, Young, 2 ......... 140 |
| Slaughter, Midland | Snap, Panola | South Bosque, McLennan,...... 500 |
| Slay, Ellis | Snead, Burnet | South Brice, Hall, ............. 15 |
| Slayden, Gonzales, ........... 15 | Sneed, Mills | South Camp, King, ............ 20 |
| Slayden, Lampasas | Sneed, Travis | South Concho, Tom Green |
| Slayden, Llano | Sneed Chapel, Milam | Southdown, Brazoria,........ 2,427 |
| Slayton, Harris | Sneedville, Cottle | South Elm, Milam |
| Sleepy Hollow, Montgomery | Sneedville, San Augustine | Southern Lumber Log Camp, Cherokee |
| Slick Hill, Comanche | Snell's, Newton | South Fork Estates, Jim Hogg, |
| Slide, Lubbock, .............. 44 | Snider Springs, Van Zandt | (47)...................... 49 |
| *Slidell, Wise, 3.............. 175 | Snipe, Brazoria | South Franklin, Franklin, ........ 30 |
| Sligo, Yoakum | *SNOOK, Burleson, 28 (568) .... 589 | South Gabriel, Burnet-Williamson |
| Slinkerts, Cameron | Snow, Leon | South Gale, Grayson |
| Sloan, Navarro | Snowball, Walker | South Galveston, Galveston |
| Sloan, Navarro | Snow Hill, Collin, ............. 20 | South Grape Creek, Kendall |
| Sloan, San Saba, ............. 30 | Snow Hill, Morris-Titus | South Groveton, Trinity |
| Slocum, Anderson, 1.......... 250 | Snow Hill, Upshur, ............ 75 | South Hanlon, Stephens |
| Slocum, Hood | Snow River, Jasper | South Haven, Howard |
| Slovanville, Waller | Snowsville, Hamilton | *SOUTH HOUSTON, Harris, 701 |
| Slover, Parker | Snowtown, San Jacinto | (15,833) ............. 15,765 |
| Slutter, Colorado | Snuff City, Smith | South Jericho, Shelby |
| Smackover, Andrews | Snuff Ridge, Liberty | *SOUTHLAKE, Tarrant-Denton, |
| Smada, Fort Bend | Snug Harbor, Brazoria, ....... 193 | 691 (21,519)........... 22,872 |
| Smada, Lee | Snyder, Bowie | Southland, Garza, 3 .......... 157 |

| Town,County . . . . . . . . . . Pop. 2002 | Town,County . . . . . . . . . . Pop. 2002 | Town,County . . . . . . . . . . Pop. 2002 |
|---|---|---|
| **South La Paloma [Alfred-],** | *Spencer, Montague* | (2,062) . . . . . . . . . . . . . . . . 2,221 |
| **Jim Wells (451). . . . . . . . . . . 461** | *Spencer, Parker* | *Springtown, Williamson* |
| *South Laredo, Webb* | *Spencer, Red River* | *Spring Vale, Fort Bend* |
| *South Leon, Comanche* | *Spencer's Ranch[o], Presidio* | **SPRING VALLEY, Harris,** |
| *South Liberty, Liberty* | *Sperry, Grayson* | **(3,611) . . . . . . . . . . . . . . . . 3,528** |
| *South Llano, Kimble* | ***Spicewood, Burnet, 242 . . . . . . .NA** | **Spring Valley, McLennan, . . . . . . . 400** |
| ***SOUTHMAYD, Grayson,** | **Spicewood Springs, Travis, . . . . . .NA** | *Spring Valley, Mitchell* |
| **(992) . . . . . . . . . . . . . . . . . 1,015** | **Spider Mountain, Burnet, . . . . . . . 42** | **Spring Valley, Travis, . . . . . . . . . . NA** |
| *Southmost, Cameron* | *Spiers', Fayette* | *Springville, Grayson* |
| **SOUTH MOUNTAIN, Coryell,** | **Spiller's Store, Leon, . . . . . . . . . .NA** | *Springville, Rains* |
| **(412) . . . . . . . . . . . . . . . . . . 416** | *Spillers Rancho, McCulloch* | **Sprinkle, Travis, . . . . . . . . . . . . . NA** |
| *South Nolan, Bell* | *Spilman's Island, Harris* | *Sprowls, Dallas* |
| ***SOUTH PADRE ISLAND,** | *Spindletop, Jefferson* | *Spunkie's Ridge, Ellis* |
| **Cameron, 388 (2,422) . . . . . 2,490** | *Spinks Switch, Cherokee* | *Spur, Crosby* |
| ***South Plains, Floyd, 5 . . . . . . . . 92** | *Spivey, Rusk* | ***SPUR, Dickens, 90** |
| *South Plains, Martin* | *Spivey, Shelby* | **(1,088) . . . . . . . . . . . . . . . . 1,076** |
| **South Point, Cameron,** | *Splawn, Milam* | *Spur, Dickens* |
| **(1,118). . . . . . . . . . . . . . . . 1,165** | ***SPLENDORA, Montgomery, 190** | ***Spurger, Tyler, 19 . . . . . . . . . . . . 472** |
| *South Prairie, Stephens* | **(1,275) . . . . . . . . . . . . . . . .1,330** | *Spurlin, Hamilton* |
| **South Purmela, Coryell, . . . . . . . . 3** | **SPOFFORD, Kinney, (75) . . . . . . . . 77** | *Spurlock, Sherman* |
| **Southridge Estates, Guadalupe, 125** | *Spooner, Orange* | *Squaw, Jack* |
| *South Riverside, Gonzales* | *Sport, Aransas* | *Squaw Creek, Gillespie* |
| *Southsan, Bexar* | **Spraberry, Midland, . . . . . . . . . . . 46** | *Squaw Creek, Hood* |
| *South San Antonio, Bexar* | ***Spring, Harris, 7,207** | *Squaw Creek Station, Hood* |
| *South San Pedro, Nueces* | **(36,385) . . . . . . . . . . . . . . .36,948** | *Sramek, Brazos* |
| **South Shore, Bell, . . . . . . . . . . . 40** | ***Spring Branch,** | *Stack, Shelby* |
| *South Side, Collingsworth* | **Comal, 255 . . . . . . . . . . . . . .NA** | *Stacks, Bastrop* |
| **SOUTHSIDE PLACE, Harris,** | *Spring Branch, Harris* | **Stacy, McCulloch, . . . . . . . . . . . . . 20** |
| **(1,547). . . . . . . . . . . . . . . . 1,585** | **Spring Branch, Smith, . . . . . . . . .NA** | **Staff, Eastland, . . . . . . . . . . . . . . 65** |
| **South Sulphur, Hunt, . . . . . . . . . . 60** | *Spring Creek, Blanco* | ***STAFFORD, Fort Bend-Harris,** |
| **South Texarkana, Bowie, . . . . . . . 370** | *Spring Creek, Bosque* | **2,185 (15,681) . . . . . . . 16,809** |
| *South Texarkana, Cass* | *Spring Creek, Burnet* | *Stafford's Ranch, Colorado* |
| **South Toledo Bend, Newton,** | *Spring Creek, Collin* | **Stag Creek, Comanche, . . . . . . . . . 50** |
| **(576) . . . . . . . . . . . . . . . . . . 598** | *Spring Creek, Harris* | **STAGECOACH, Montgomery,** |
| **Southton, Bexar, . . . . . . . . . . . . 113** | *Spring Creek, Harris* | **(455). . . . . . . . . . . . . . . . . . .470** |
| *South Town, Lubbock* | **Spring Creek, Hutchinson, . . . . . 139** | *Staggers Point, Robertson* |
| *South Vernon, Wilbarger* | *Spring Creek, Jones* | *Stag Mills, Franklin* |
| *Souz Creek, La Salle* | *Spring Creek, Parker* | *Stagner, Wood* |
| *Sowell, Nolan* | **Spring Creek, San Saba, . . . . . . . . 20** | **Stairtown, Caldwell, . . . . . . . . . . . 35** |
| *Sowells Bluff, Fannin* | **Spring Creek, Throckmorton, . . . . 13** | **Staley, San Jacinto, . . . . . . . . . . . . 55** |
| *Sowers, Dallas* | *Spring Creek, Tyler* | *Stallings, Colorado* |
| ***Spade, Lamb, 7 (100) . . . . . . . . 103** | *Spring Creek, Waller* | *Stalls, Marion* |
| *Spade, Mitchell* | **Springdale, Cass, . . . . . . . . . . . . . 55** | *Stalty, Milam* |
| *Spain's Settlement, Washington* | *Springdale, Crosby* | ***STAMFORD, Jones-Haskell,** |
| *Spangle Field, Bee* | *Springdale, Jack* | **198 (3,636). . . . . . . . . . . . . 3,530** |
| *Spanish Bluff, Madison* | *Springer, Waller* | *Stamp, Falls* |
| *Spanish Camp, Wharton* | *Springer Ranch, Hemphill* | **Stampede, Bell, . . . . . . . . . . . . . . 10** |
| **Spanish Fort, Montague, . . . . . . . 50** | **Springfield, Anderson, . . . . . . . . . 30** | *Stampede, Clay* |
| **Spanish Trail, Hood, . . . . . . . . . . 478** | **Springfield, Jim Wells, . . . . . . . . .NA** | *Stampede, Coryell* |
| *Spanky, Navarro* | *Springfield, Limestone* | *Stamper, Nolan* |
| **Sparenberg, Dawson, . . . . . . . . . 20** | *Springfield, Polk* | **Stamps, Upshur, . . . . . . . . . . . . . 45** |
| **Sparks, Bell, . . . . . . . . . . . . . . . 30** | *Spring Gap, Callahan* | *Standard, Grayson* |
| **Sparks, El Paso, (2,974). . . . . . 3,047** | *Spring Garden, Gillespie* | *Standart, Kinney* |
| *Sparks, Jefferson* | *Spring Garden, Tarrant* | *Standish, Gray* |
| *Sparks Colony, Aransas* | **Spring Garden-Tierra Verde,** | **Stanfield, Clay, . . . . . . . . . . . . . . 15** |
| *Sparksville, Childress* | **Nueces, (693) . . . . . . . . . . . 718** | *Stanford, McLennan* |
| *Sparksville, Leon* | **Spring Hill, Bowie, . . . . . . . . . . . 209** | *Stanford, Orange* |
| *Sparta, Bell* | *Spring Hill, Coryell* | *Stanger Springs, Van Zandt* |
| *Sparta, Palo Pinto* | *Springhill, Culberson* | *Stanley, Falls* |
| *Sparta, San Jacinto* | *Spring Hill, Falls* | *Stanley, Gaines* |
| *Spat, Montague* | *Spring Hill, Gregg* | *Stanley, Hill* |
| *Spaulding, Hidalgo* | *Spring Hill, Harrison* | *Stanley, Polk* |
| **Speaks, Lavaca, . . . . . . . . . . . . . 60** | *Spring Hill, Jasper* | *Stanley, Red River* |
| *Spear, Brazos* | *Spring Hill, Lamar* | *Stanley, Taylor* |
| ***SPEARMAN, Hansford, 237** | *Spring Hill, Nacogdoches* | *Stanolind Camp, Gray* |
| **(3,021). . . . . . . . . . . . . . . . 2,937** | **Spring Hill, Navarro, . . . . . . . . . . . 60** | *Stansel, Navarro* |
| *Spears Chapel, Newton* | *Spring Hill, Sabine* | ***STANTON, Martin, 133** |
| **Specht Store, Bexar, . . . . . . . . . . 20** | **Spring Hill, San Jacinto, . . . . . . . . 38** | **(2,556) . . . . . . . . . . . . . . . . 2,552** |
| *Speckville, Menard* | *Spring Hill, Smith* | ***Staples, Guadalupe, 4 . . . . . . . . .350** |
| *Speed, Burleson* | *Spring Hill, Upshur* | *Stapp, Williamson* |
| *Speed, Van Zandt* | ***SPRINGLAKE, Lamb, 22** | *Stapp's, Jackson* |
| *Speedwell, Hale* | **(135) . . . . . . . . . . . . . . . . . . 136** | *Star, Grimes* |
| **Speegleville, McLennan, . . . . . . . 111** | *Spring Place, Franklin* | *Star, Lavaca* |
| *Speer, Wood* | *Spring Ridge, San Augustine* | ***Star, Mills, 5 . . . . . . . . . . . . . . . 85** |
| *Speer's Mill, Denton* | **Springs Hill, Guadalupe, . . . . . . . 500** | *Star, Nueces* |
| *Spence, Harris* | *Springtown, Gray* | *Star, Walker* |
| *Spencer, Hunt* | ***SPRINGTOWN, Parker, 374** | *Stargas, Dallas* |

| Town,County .......... Pop. 2002 | Town,County .......... Pop. 2002 | Town,County .......... Pop. 2002 |
|---|---|---|
| **STAR HARBOR, Henderson,** | Stiles, Reagan, ................. 4 | (739)........................756 |
| **(416)** .................... **423** | Stiles Ranch, Williamson | **Straws Mill, Coryell** |
| Stark, Houston | Still's Creek, Anderson | **Streeter, Mason, 2** ............ **100** |
| Stark's Switch, Houston | Still's Creek, Anderson | ***STREETMAN, Freestone,** |
| Starkes, Llano | Stillman, Willacy | **51 (203)** ................. **199** |
| Starkesville, Red River-Lamar | Stillwater, Henderson | Streets, Harris |
| Starkey, Floyd | Stillwater, Lipscomb | Streichville, Williamson |
| Stark Grove, McLennan | **Stillwell Crossing, Brewster,** ...... 2 | Stribling, Navarro |
| Starling, Wilbarger | Stilson, Liberty | Strickland, Williamson |
| Starlong, Dallas | Stilwell, Crane | Strickland Crossing, Sabine |
| Starr's Mill, Smith | ***STINNETT, Hutchinson, 67** | Strickling, Burnet |
| Starrco, Starr | **(1,936)**.................. **1,920** | Striker Creek, Cherokee |
| Star Ridge, Clay | Stinson, Hunt | Striker Town, Cherokee |
| **Star Route, Cochran,** .......... **27** | Stinson, Wood | Stringer, Cherokee |
| **Starrville, Smith,** ............. **75** | Stinson's Ferry, Cherokee | Stringer, Floyd |
| **Startzville, Comal,** ............ **30** | **Stith, Jones,** ............... **50** | **String Prairie, Bastrop,** ........ **125** |
| Stasny, Bastrop | Stockard, Henderson | String Prairie, Lee |
| State Bank, Lamar | ***STOCKDALE, Wilson, 96** | Stringtown, Bell |
| **State Line, Culberson,** ......... **18** | **(1,398)** ............... **1,466** | Stringtown, Burnet |
| Station Creek, Coryell | **Stockholm, Hidalgo,** .......... **50** | Stringtown, Coryell |
| Steadmanville, Grimes | **Stockman, Shelby,** ........... **52** | Stringtown, Hays |
| Stedham's, San Augustine | Stockton, Johnson | Stringtown, Hunt |
| Steedman, Grayson | Stoker, Nacogdoches | **Stringtown, Newton,** .......... **NA** |
| Steel, Brazos | Stokes, Coke | Strip, Hale |
| Steel's Creek, Limestone | Stolz, Llano | Strobel, Brewster |
| Steelboro, Anderson | Stone, Hidalgo | Strobel, Hamilton |
| Steele, Fisher | Stone, Washington | Stroman, Gonzales |
| Steele's Creek, Bosque | Stone's Mill[s], Panola | Strong, Anderson |
| Steele Gin, Parker | **Stoneburg, Montague,** ......... **51** | Strong, Shelby |
| **Steele Hill, Dickens,** ........... **6** | **Stone City, Brazos,** ........... **NA** | Strong's Bluff, Orange |
| Steeles Grove, Tyler | Stone Creek, Harris | Strongfield, Rusk |
| Steeles Store, Brazos | Stone Gin, Bexar | Stroud, Hardeman |
| Steeltown, Jefferson | **Stoneham, Grimes,** ........... **12** | Stroud's, Limestone |
| Steen, DeWitt | **Stone Point, Van Zandt,** ........ **32** | **Structure, Williamson,** .......... **60** |
| Steenville, Bee | Stone Ranch, Maverick | Strumberg, Bexar |
| **Steep Creek, San Augustine,** .... **NA** | Stone Ranch, Schleicher | Stryker, Polk |
| Steep Hollow, Brazos | Stonetown, Comal | Stuart, Falls |
| Stegall, Bailey | Stonetown, Jefferson | Stuart's Rancho, La Salle |
| **Steiner, Bosque,** .............. **20** | **Stonewall, Denton** | **Stuart Place, Cameron,** ........ **990** |
| Steiner's Settlement, Victoria | Stonewall, Freestone | **Stubblefield, Houston,** .......... **15** |
| Stella, Fayette | ***Stonewall, Gillespie, 26** | Stubblefield, Johnson |
| Stella, Harris | **(469)** ................... **487** | Stubblefield's, Polk |
| Stella, Tom Green | Stonewall, Jackson | **Stubbs, Kaufman,** ........... **NA** |
| Stemmons, Dawson | Stonewall, Llano | ***Study Butte-Terlingua,** |
| Stephen's Gin, Montague | Stone Wall, McLennan | **Brewster, 48 (267)**.......... **271** |
| Stephensboro, Red River | Stonewall, Titus | Stuebner, Harris |
| **Stephens Creek, San Jacinto,** ... **385** | Stoney Point, Collin | Stump, Henderson |
| Stephensville, Fannin | **Stony, Denton,** ............... **25** | Stumpville, Houston |
| ***STEPHENVILLE, Erath, 952** | Stop, San Augustine | Sturdivant, Palo Pinto |
| **(14,921)** ............... **14,881** | Storey's Store, Travis | **Sturgeon, Cooke,** .............. **10** |
| Stepps Creek, Brown | Stormville, Wood | Sturgis, San Augustine |
| **Sterley, Floyd,** ................ **24** | Storrs, Limestone | **Styx, Kaufman,** .............. **NA** |
| Sterling, Robertson | Story, Hill | Sublett, Tarrant |
| Sterling, Sterling | Story, Wheeler | ***Sublime, Lavaca, 1** ............ **75** |
| ***STERLING CITY, Sterling, 56** | **Stout, Wood,** ................. **86** | ***SUDAN, Lamb, 55 (1,039)** .... **1,050** |
| **(1,081)**................. **1,105** | Stovall, Johnson | Sudduth, Burnet |
| Sterne, Nacogdoches | Stoveall, Fannin | Sue, Atascosa |
| **Sterrett, Ellis,** ................ **28** | Stove Foundry, Tarrant | Sue, Navarro |
| Stevens, Rusk | Stover, Terrell | Sueville, Wise |
| Stevens, Sherman | Stover's Cross Roads, Kaufman | Suez, Comanche |
| Stevenson, Hudspeth | Stoverville, Denton | Suffolk, Upshur |
| Stevenson, Van Zandt | ***Stowell, Chambers, 17** | Sugar Hill, Collin |
| **Stewards Mill, Freestone,** ....... **22** | **(1,572)** ................. **1,585** | Sugar Hill, Panola |
| Stewart, Cottle | Stracenter, Upshur | **Sugar Hill, Titus,** .............. **150** |
| Stewart, Dallas | Straddle, Chambers | ***SUGAR LAND, Fort Bend,** |
| Stewart, Henderson | Strain, Hardin | **4,187 (63,328)** .......... **68,954** |
| **Stewart, Rusk,** ................ **15** | Strang, Harris | Sugar Land, Matagorda |
| Stewart's Chapel, Van Zandt | **Stranger, Falls,** ............... **27** | Sugarland Junction, Fort Bend |
| Stewart's Creek, Denton | ***STRATFORD, Sherman, 110** | Sugar Loaf, Coryell |
| Stewart Heights, Harris | **(1,991)**................. **2,033** | **Sugar Mill, Brazoria,** .......... **523** |
| Stewarton, Jack | Stratton, Brazoria | **Sugar Valley, Matagorda,** ........ **35** |
| Stewartsville, Denton | **Stratton, DeWitt,** .............. **25** | Sullivan, Guadalupe |
| Stewart Town, Burnet | Stratton Ridge, Brazoria | Sullivan, Johnson |
| Stickley, Hemphill | Straw's, Shelby | Sullivan, Van Zandt |
| Stieren, Gonzales | Strawberry, Smith | Sullivan's Bluff, Houston |
| Stiff, Collin | Strawbridge, Terrell | ***Sullivan City, Hidalgo, 25** |
| | ***STRAWN, Palo Pinto, 38** | **(3,998)** ............... **4,124** |

| Town,County ........... Pop. 2002 | Town,County ........... Pop. 2002 | Town,County ........... Pop. 2002 |
|---|---|---|
| Sullivan Settlement, Denton | Superior, Brazoria | Tadella, Bell |
| Sulphur, Bowie | Surfside, Brazoria | Tadlock, Tarrant |
| Sulphur, Franklin | **SURFSIDE BEACH, Brazoria,** | **Tadmor, Houston,** ............... 67 |
| *Sulphur Bluff, Hopkins, 7...... 280 | (763) .................... 817 | *TAFT, San Patricio, 174 |
| Sulphur Docks, Brazoria | Surveyville, Newton | (3,396) ................ 3,423 |
| Sulphuria, Culberson | *Sutherland Springs, Wilson, 8 .. 362 | Taft Southwest, San Patricio, |
| Sulphur Spring, Karnes | Sutton, Gray | (1,721) ................ 1,678 |
| Sulphur Springs, Angelina | Sutton, Robertson | Tage, Montague |
| Sulphur Springs, Cherokee | Swain, Bastrop | Taggart, Swisher |
| Sulphur Springs, Grimes | Swain, Young | *TAHOKA, Lynn, 122 (2,910)... 2,848 |
| Sulphur Springs, Hood | Swallow, Hidalgo | Tait, Colorado |
| *SULPHUR SPRINGS, Hopkins, | Swamp City, Gregg, ............. 8 | Taiton, Wharton |
| 1,102 (14,551).......... 14,606 | Swan, Smith,................ 150 | Talbot, Navarro |
| Sulphur Springs, Rusk | Swan Lake, Jackson | Talbott Ridge, Milam |
| Sulphur Springs, San Saba | Swanntown, Red River | *TALCO, Titus, 36 (570)........ 577 |
| Sulphur Springs, Trinity | Swannville, San Augustine | Tallahassee, Colorado |
| Sulphur Springs, Wilson | Swanson, Falls | Talledega, Cherokee |
| Suman, Robertson | Swanson Hill Church, Anderson | Talley, Grayson |
| Sumatra, Montgomery | Swanville, Red River | Talltimber, Sabine |
| Summerall, Henderson | Swartwout, Polk | Tallulah, Childress |
| Summerfield, Castro, 3 ......... 60 | Swearingen, Collingsworth, .....NA | Tally, Harrison |
| Summerfield, Gregg | Swearingen, Cottle | Talma, Comanche |
| Summerfield, Upshur | Swearingen's, Austin | Talmage, Wilbarger |
| Summer Grove, Rusk | Swearingen's, Austin | Talo, Smith |
| Summer Grove, Smith | Swede Hill, Travis | *Talpa, Coleman, 10 ........... 127 |
| Summer Hill, Henderson | Sweden, Duval | TALTY, Kaufman, (1,028)...... 1,113 |
| Summerville, Gonzales, ........ 40 | Swedenborg Settlers Colony, Milam | Tama, Coryell |
| Summerville, Travis | Swedonia, Fisher | Tam Anne, Castro |
| Summit, Burnet | *SWEENY, Brazoria, 171 | Tamar, Bowie |
| Summit, Grayson | (3,624)................3,668 | Tamaulipas, Blanco |
| Summit, Medina | Sweeten, Panola | Tamberg, Fayette |
| Summit, Milam | Sweet Farms, Williamson | Tamega, Burnet |
| Summit, Motley | Sweet Home, Guadalupe, ....... 80 | Tamina, Montgomery,.......... NA |
| Summit, Tyler | *Sweet Home, Lavaca, 10....... 360 | Tampareka, Foard |
| Summit, Upshur | Sweet Home, Lee,............. 30 | Tampico, Hall |
| *Sumner, Lamar, 25 ........... 80 | Sweet Oak, Leon | Tanglefoot, Bell |
| Sumpter, Trinity | Sweet Union, Cherokee, ........ 40 | Tanglewood, Lee, 1............48 |
| Sumptner, Angelina | Sweetwater, Comanche | Tanglewood Forest, Travis |
| Sun, Bosque | Sweet Water, Dallas | Tankersley, Tom Green |
| Sun, Jefferson | *SWEETWATER, Nolan, 668 | Tank Hollow, Atascosa |
| Sunbeam, Grayson | (11,415)................11,213 | Tanks, Cottle |
| Sunday Creek, Erath | Sweetwater, Wheeler | Tannahill, Tarrant |
| Sunday School Grove, Falls | Swenson, Stonewall, ......... 185 | Tanner, Eastland |
| *SUNDOWN, Hockley, 78 | Swift, Nacogdoches, .......... 125 | Taopi, Fisher |
| (1,505)................1,505 | Swiftex, Bastrop, .............NA | Taos, Navarro |
| Sunflower Flat, Stonewall | Swindall, Van Zandt | Taos, Shackelford |
| Suniland, Live Oak | Swindells, Baylor | Tap, Dickens |
| Sunny Lane, Burnet | Swinney Switch, Live Oak | Tarbutton, Atascosa |
| Sunny Point, Coleman | Swinneytown, Smith | Tar Heel Flat, Collin |
| Sunny Point, Hopkins | Swinson, Travis | Tarkington Prairie, Liberty,..... NA |
| Sunny Point, Panola | Swiss Alp, Fayette,............ 46 | *Tarpley, Bandera, 8 ........... 30 |
| Sunnyside, Castro, ........... 80 | Switch, Ellis | Tarpon, Nueces |
| Sunnyside, Menard | Switch, Navarro | Tarrant, Hopkins |
| Sunnyside, Waller, ........... 120 | Swofford, Hockley | Tarrant, Tarrant |
| Sunnyside, Wilson, ........... 300 | Sycamore, Burnet | Tarver, Culberson |
| SUNNYVALE, Dallas, | Sycamore, Guadalupe | *Tarzan, Martin, 12 .......... 80 |
| (2,693).................3,043 | Sycamore, Kinney | Tascosa, Oldham,............. NA |
| Sun Oil Camp, Starr | Sycamore, Newton | Tascosa Hills, Potter, .......... 90 |
| *SUNRAY, Moore, 76 | Sycamore, Wise | Tasso, Rusk |
| (1,950).................1,973 | Sykes, Tom Green | Tata, Sherman |
| Sunrise, Falls,............... 845 | Sylvan, Fayette | Tate, Rusk |
| *SUNRISE BEACH, Llano, | Sylvan, Lamar, ............... 68 | Tate, Travis |
| (704) .................... 720 | Sylvania, Tarrant | Tate Springs, Tarrant |
| Sunset, Dawson | *Sylvester, Fisher, 4 ........... 79 | Tatsie, Robertson |
| Sunset, Hardin | Sylvester, Trinity | *TATUM, Rusk-Panola, 100 |
| *SUNSET, Montague, 19 | Sylvia, Hunt | (1,175)................ 1,182 |
| (339) .................... 352 | Syracuse, Harris | Tavener, Fort Bend |
| Sunset Heights, Harris | Syringa, Upshur | Tax, Leon |
| Sunset Oaks, Burnet,.......... 148 | | Taylor, Red River |
| Sunset Station, Harris | **T** | *TAYLOR, Williamson, 585 |
| SUNSET VALLEY, Travis, (365) .. 398 | Tabasco, Hidalgo | (13,575) .............. 14,393 |
| Sunshine, Freestone | Tabor, Brazos,................ 150 | Taylor's Bluff, Harrison |
| Sunshine, Houston | Tabor, Brewster | Taylor's Chapel, Cherokee |
| Sunshine, Nueces | Tacitus, Haskell | Taylor's Gin, Burnet |
| Sunshine Hill, Wichita | Tacker, Freestone | Taylor Bayou, Jefferson |
| SUN VALLEY, Lamar, (51) ....... 50 | Tacoma, Panola | TAYLOR LAKE VILLAGE, Harris, |
| Sunview, Marion | Tacubaya, Brooks | (3,694) ............... 3,798 |

| Town,County ...........Pop. 2002 | Town,County ...........Pop. 2002 | Town,County............ Pop. 2002 |
|---|---|---|


Taylors Creek, Lampasas
**Taylorsville, Caldwell, .........** 20
Taylorsville, Wise
**Taylor Town, Lamar, ...........** 40
Taylorville, San Saba
Taz, Ochiltree
Taza, Hudspeth
**Tazewell, Hopkins, .............NA**
TC Junction, Bowie
Tea Color, Freestone
Teacup, Kimble
**\*TEAGUE, Freestone, 163**
   **(4,557)................** 4,696
Teague, Upshur
Teas, Gonzales
**Teaselville, Smith, ............** 150
Tebo, Sabine
Tebo, Taylor
Tech, Lubbock
Teci, Wheeler
Teck, Travis
Teco, Clay
Tecula, Cherokee
Tecumseh, Callahan
Teddy, Montgomery
Teddy, San Jacinto
Tee Pee City, Motley
Teferville, Coke
Tegaco, Refugio
Tehuacana, Freestone
Tehuacana, Frio
**\*TEHUACANA, Limestone, 8**
   **(307) ...................** 315
Tehuacana, Medina
Tehuacana Station, Freestone
Tehuacana Valley, Limestone
Tejon, Cameron
Teka, McLennan
**\*Telegraph, Kimble, 2...........** 3
Telegraph Mills, Houston
**\*Telephone, Fannin, 18 ........** 210
**\*Telferner, Victoria, 13 .........** 700
**Telico, Ellis, ..................** 95
**\*Tell, Childress, 2 ..............** 63
Tell, Stonewall
Temco, Jasper
Tempest, Erath
**\*TEMPLE, Bell, 2,800**
   **(54,514)...............** 55,437
Temple Junction, Polk
Temple Springs, Jasper
Templeton, Cameron
Templeton, Ellis
Ten-Mile Board, Polk
Tenaha, Bexar
**\*TENAHA, Shelby, 51**
   **(1,046).................** 1,031
Tenark, Cass
Teneryville, Gregg
Ten Mile, Dallas
**Tenmile, Dawson,..............** 30
Ten Mile, Henderson
Tenmile, Madison
Ten Mile, Mason
Tennessee, Shelby
**\*Tennessee Colony, Anderson,**
   **33 .....................** 300
Tennessee Valley, Bell
Tennessee Valley, Cottle
**\*Tennyson, Coke, 2 ...........** 35
Teresita, Milam
**\*Terlingua [StudyButte-], Brewster,**
   **48 (267).................** 271
Terminal, Midland
Terrace, Bexar
Terrace, Grayson
Terrapin Neck, Harrison


Terrapin Neck, Shelby
Terrapin Neck, Wood
**\*TERRELL, Kaufman, 1,163**
   **(13,606)...............** 15,046
**TERRELL HILLS, Bexar,**
   **(5,019).................** 4,970
Terrell Wells, Bexar
Terrels, Brazos
Terry, Childress
Terry, Milam
Terry, Orange
Terry, Orange
**Terry Chapel, Falls, ...........** 30
Terrysville, Gonzales
**Terryville, DeWitt,..............** 40
Tesco, Nolan
Tesla, Houston
Tesnus, Brewster
Tessie, Pecos
Teville, Mitchell
Tevis Bluff, Jefferson
Tex-Harvey, Martin
Texaco, Fayette
Texana, Jackson
Texand, McLennan
**\*TEXARKANA, Bowie (Miller, Ark.),**
   **(61,230)...............** 61,485
**\*TEXAS CITY, Galveston, 1,455**
   **(41,512)...............** 42,611
Texas Elf Co Settlement, Gray
Texas Iron Works, Marion
Texas National, Montgomery
**TEXHOMA, Sherman, (371) .....** 383
Texhoma City, Archer
Texico, Parmer
Texla, Harrison
Texla, Orange
**\*TEXLINE, Dallam, 47 (511) .....** 500
**Texon, Reagan, 1 ..............** 12
Texroy, Hutchinson
Thackwell, Smith
**Thalia, Foard, ................** 104
Tharp, Montgomery
Thayer, Hidalgo
The Colony, Bosque
**\*THE COLONY, Denton,**
   **(26,531)...............** 31,556
**Thedford, Smith,..............** 65
The Ditch, Real
**The Divide, Kerr,..............** 250
The Flat, Shackelford
The Flat, Taylor
**The Grove, Coryell,...........** 65
**THE HILLS, Travis, (1,492) .....** 1,536
The Knobbs, Lee
**Thelma, Bexar, ...............** 45
**Thelma, Limestone, ...........** 20
The Motts, Nueces
Theny, Comanche
Theo, Falls
Theodocia, Hopkins
Theodore, Grayson
Theodore, Winkler
**Theon, Williamson,............** 20
The Point, Live Oak
**Thermo, Hopkins,.............NA**
The Rock, Marion
The Switch, Mills
Theta, Hunt
The Valley, Guadalupe
**\*The Woodlands, Montgomery,**
   **964 (55,649) ...........** 59,603
**\*Thicket, Hardin, 2 ...........** 306
Thicket, Polk
Thin Gravy, Dallas
Thomas, Burnet
Thomas, Denton


Thomas, Moore
Thomas, Panola
Thomas, Upshur
**\*Thomaston, DeWitt, 4 .........** 45
Thomasville, Bell
Thompson, Austin
Thompson, Harris
Thompson, Smith
Thompson, Trinity
Thompson's Mill, Henderson
Thompson Chapel, Fort Bend
Thompson Hills, Smith
**\*THOMPSONS, Fort Bend, 13**
   **(236)...................** 241
Thompsons Gin, Lee
Thompson Switch, Harris
**Thompsonville, Gonzales, .......** 30
Thompsonville, Harris
**Thompsonville, Jim Hogg, ......** NA
Thomson, Collin
**Thornberry, Clay,..............** 60
**\*THORNDALE, Milam, 65**
   **(1,278) ...............** 1,323
Thorn Hill, Comal
**\*THORNTON, Limestone, 22**
   **(525)..................** 536
Thornton, Trinity
**THORNTONVILLE, Ward,**
   **(442)..................** 426
Thorpe, Schleicher
**Thorp Spring, Hood,...........** 184
Thorpville, Dallas
Thors, Nacogdoches
**\*THRALL, Williamson, 26**
   **(710)..................** 774
Thrash, Nacogdoches
Thrasher, Victoria
Three League, Martin
**Three Oaks, Wilson, .........** 150
Three Points, Travis
**\*THREE RIVERS, Live Oak, 112**
   **(1,878) ................** 1,879
**Three States, Cass,............** 45
Three Way, Erath
Thrift, Wichita
**Thrifty, Brown,................** NA
**\*THROCKMORTON, Throckmorton,**
   **90 (905) ..............** 867
Thulemeyer's, Fayette
**Thurber, Erath, .................** 8
Thurber Junction, Palo Pinto
Thurman, Cherokee
Thurman, Hardin
Thurman, Panola
Thurman, Shelby
Thurman, Young
Thurst, Terrell
Tib, Collin
Tibb, Collin
Tibbie, Polk
Tickey, Collin
Ticklefoot, Grimes
Tidehaven, Matagorda
**Tidwell, Hunt,.................** NA
Tidwell, Limestone
Tidwell, Williamson
Tidwell Creek, Hunt
**Tidwell Prairie, Robertson, .....** NA
Tie City, Bastrop
Tiemann, Guadalupe
Tierra Alta, Schleicher
Tierra Blanca, Hidalgo
**Tierra Bonita, Cameron, (160) ...** 166
**Tierra Grande, Nueces, (362)....** 345
**Tierra Verde [Spring Garden-],**
   **Nueces, (693) ............** 718
Tiffin, Eastland

| Town,County | Pop. 2002 | Town,County | Pop. 2002 | Town,County | Pop. 2002 |
|---|---|---|---|---|---|
| Tige, Hopkins | | Todd's, Shelby | | Townley, Walker | |
| Tiger, Kaufman | | Todd City, Anderson, | 10 | Towns, Maverick | |
| Tiger Mill, Burnet | | TODD MISSION, Grimes, | | Towns' Mill, Williamson | |
| Tiger Point, Jefferson | | (146) | 153 | Townsend, Fayette | |
| Tiger Prairie, Limestone | | Todd Springs, Shelby | | Townsend, San Augustine | |
| Tigertown, Lamar, | 150 | Toddville, Upshur | | Townsen Mills, Lampasas | |
| Tigertown, Washington | | Todville, Harris | | Town West, Fort Bend | |
| Tigerville, Polk | | Togo, Bastrop | | Towson, Red River | |
| Tight Wad, Ellis | | Togo, Coleman | | *TOYAH, Reeves, 5 (100) | 96 |
| Tigua, El Paso | | Tokeen, Runnels | | *Toyahvale, Reeves, 3 | 60 |
| TIKI ISLAND VILLAGE, Galveston, | | Tokio, McLennan, | 250 | Tracy, Milam | |
| (1,016) | 1,060 | *Tokio, Terry, 4 | 24 | Tradewinds, San Patricio, | |
| *Tilden, McMullen, 28 | 450 | Toksana, Wichita | | (163) | 166 |
| Tilecrete, Smith | | *TOLAR, Hood, 72 (504) | 524 | Tradinghouse Creek, McLennan | |
| Tillis Prairie, Montgomery | | Tolbert, Wilbarger, | 30 | Traildust, Denton | |
| Tillman, Cherokee | | Toledo, Fayette | | Tram, Jasper | |
| Tilmon, Caldwell, | 117 | Toledo, Newton | | Trammells, Fort Bend | |
| Tilton, Montague | | Toledo Village, Newton | | Trap, Coleman | |
| Timber, Montgomery | | Tolette, Lamar, | 40 | Trapps Springs, Parker | |
| Timber Creek, Fannin | | Toliver, Nacogdoches | | Traprock, Uvalde | |
| Timber Creek, Hunt | | Tollett's Prairie, Lamar | | Traver, Terrell | |
| TIMBERCREEK CANYON, | | Toll Town, Denton | | Travis, Austin | |
| Randall, (406) | 437 | Tolosa, Henderson | | Travis, Falls, | 48 |
| Timber Lake, Burnet | | Tolosa, Kaufman, | 58 | Travis Peak, Travis | |
| Timberwood Park, Bexar, | | Toluca, Hidalgo | | Traweek, Freestone | |
| (5,889) | 6,067 | Tom, Sterling | | Trawick, Nacogdoches, | 100 |
| Time, Houston | | Tom, Wichita | | Treasure Island, Guadalupe, | 600 |
| Time, Sabine | | Tom, Wilson | | Tredway, Borden | |
| Timesville, Leon, | NA | Tomaha, Red River | | *TRENT, Taylor, 24 (318) | 321 |
| Timm's Store, Guadalupe | | Tomato, Callahan | | *TRENTON, Fannin, 44 | |
| Timm City, Lipscomb | | *TOMBALL, Harris, 1,761 | | (662) | 687 |
| Timme's Store, Austin | | (9,089) | 9,544 | Tres Norias, Cameron | |
| Timmons', Panola | | Tomball, Harris | | Tres Palacios, Matagorda | |
| Timothy, Hidalgo | | *TOM BEAN, Grayson, 35 | | Trespalacios, Matagorda | |
| Timothy, Navarro | | (941) | 952 | Trevat, Trinity | |
| *TIMPSON, Shelby, 89 | | Tomburnett, Wichita | | Trevino, Duval | |
| (1,094) | 1,138 | Tomday, Shelby | | Trexler, Bowie | |
| Tinaja, Presidio | | Tom Gill, Hidalgo | | Triangle, Dallas | |
| Tince, Henderson | | Tomlinson Hill, Falls, | 64 | Triangle, Falls | |
| Tindel, Henderson | | Tommie, Lavaca | | Triar, Bexar-Wilson | |
| Tinimax, Cherokee | | Tompkins Store, Williamson | | Tribune, Grayson | |
| Tinkle, Navarro | | Tomsonville, Briscoe | | Trice, Trinity | |
| Tinnenville, Robertson | | Tona, Kaufman | | Trickham, Coleman, | 12 |
| Tinney Creek, Caldwell | | Tonk, Young | | Trigg, Bastrop | |
| Tinnin, Lamar | | Tonkawa Springs, Williamson | | Trigg, Stephens | |
| Tinnin's, Lamar | | Tonk Creek, McLennan | | Trigger, Coleman | |
| Tinrag, Hopkins | | Tonqua, DeWitt | | Trimmier, Bell, | 90 |
| Tintop, Matagorda | | Tony, Hunt | | *TRINIDAD, Henderson, 50 | |
| Tin Top, Parker, | 31 | TOOL, Henderson, (2,275) | 2,301 | (1,091) | 1,132 |
| Tin Top, Polk | | Toombs, Runnels | | Trinidad, Kaufman | |
| Tio, Frio | | Toomey, Shelby | | Trinidad, Madison | |
| Tiocano, Cameron | | Topaz, Erath | | Trinity, Rockwall | |
| *TIOGA, Grayson, 36 (754) | 798 | Topeka Junction, Lavaca | | *TRINITY, Trinity, 244 | |
| Tippett's Crossing, Wood | | Topp, Hopkins | | (2,721) | 2,831 |
| Tipton's Grocery, Cherokee | | Topsey, Coryell, | 20 | Trinity Church, Walker | |
| Tip Top, Henderson | | Torbert, Hudspeth | | Trinity City, Dallas | |
| Tip Top, Polk | | Torbit, Dallas | | Trinity City, Ellis-Navarro | |
| TIRA, Hopkins, (248) | 245 | Torcer, Hudspeth | | Trinity Mills, Dallas | |
| Tirkle, Kent | | Tordia, Wilson | | Trinity River Spur, Liberty | |
| Titley, Brewster | | Tordilla, Atascosa | | Trinto, Kaufman | |
| Tittle, Hill | | Torian, Jim Wells | | Trio, Uvalde | |
| Titus, Titus | | *Tornillo, El Paso, 23 (1,609) | 1,591 | Trion, Palo Pinto | |
| *Tivoli, Refugio, 19 | 550 | Toro, Callahan | | Triplett, Wise | |
| Tivy, Kerr | | Toronto, Brewster | | Tripp, Dallas | |
| Tivydale, Gillespie | | Torpedo, Comanche | | Tritonia, Franklin | |
| Toadsuck, Grayson | | Torrecillas, Webb | | Trixie, Gaines | |
| Tobacco Patch, Polk | | Torres, Val Verde | | TROPHY CLUB, Denton, | |
| Tobey, Atascosa | | Tosca, Blanco-Gillespie | | (6,350) | 6,947 |
| Tobey, Burnet | | Toto, Parker | | Trot, Polk | |
| Tobin, ElPaso | | Tours, McLennan, | 100 | Trotti, Newton | |
| Tobin, Erath | | *Tow, Llano, 35 | 305 | Trouble, Washington | |
| Toccoa, Leon | | Towash, Hill | | Troup, Smith | |
| TOCO, Lamar, (89) | 89 | Tower Lake, Wilson, | 100 | *TROUP, Smith-Cherokee, 194 | |
| Todd, Grayson | | Towers, Panola | | (1,949) | 2,021 |
| Todd, Milam | | Towles, Van Zandt | | Troupe, Cass | |
| Todd, Montague | | Towles, Van Zandt | | Trout, Lamar | |
| Todd, Newton | | Town Bluff, Tyler, | 26 | Trout Creek, Newton, | NA |

CITIES & TOWNS

| Town,County .......... Pop. 2002 | Town,County .......... Pop. 2002 | Town,County .......... Pop. 2002 |
|---|---|---|
| Troutman, Cherokee | Turtle, Kerr | Union, Washington |
| *TROY, Bell, 69 (1,378) ....... 1,384 | Turtle Bay, Matagorda | Union, Wilson, ................. 22 |
| Troy, Comanche | Turtle Bayou, Chambers, ....... 42 | Union Bluff, Hill |
| Troy, Freestone | Turtle Bayou, Liberty | Union Bower, Dallas |
| Truby, Jones, ................. 26 | Turtle Cove, Brazoria,.......... 50 | Union Bridge, Titus |
| Truce, Jack | Tuscaloosa, Titus | Union Center, Eastland, ........ NA |
| True, Young | Tuscaloosa, Walker | Union Chapel, Camp |
| Truebsal, Washington | *TUSCOLA, Taylor, 68 | Union Chapel, Cherokee |
| Trueheart, Ward | (714) ................... 712 | Union Chapel, Freestone |
| Trueloves, Johnson | Tusculum, Kendall | Union Chapel, Smith |
| Truit's Store, Shelby | Tuscumbia, Harrison | Union Flat, Childress |
| Truitt, Erath | Tuttle's Store, Fayette | Union Flat, Titus |
| Truitt, Runnels | Tuxedo, Jones, ................ 42 | Union Grove, Bell,.............. 4 |
| Trukton, Rusk | Tweedle, Coleman | Union Grove, Brown |
| Truman, Dallas | 25 Mile Post, Montgomery | Union Grove, Cherokee |
| Trumble, Moore | Twichell, Ochiltree | Union Grove, Erath, ........... 12 |
| Trumbull, Ellis, ................ 65 | Twin Buttes, Hall | Union Grove, Houston |
| Truscott, Knox, 4 .............. 50 | Twin Creek, Webb | Union Grove, Kaufman |
| Truss, Fannin | Twin Groceries, Hopkins | Union Grove, McLennan |
| Trygillo, Oldham | Twin Mountain, Coryell | UNION GROVE, Upshur, |
| Tryon, Gregg | Twin Mountain, Hamilton | (346)..................... 364 |
| Tryon, Hardin | Twin Mountain, Tom Green | Union Grove, Upshur |
| Tubbes, Nacogdoches | Twin Oak, Falls | Union Hall, Swisher |
| Tubbs Corner, Crane | Twin Ranch & Farm, Lubbock | Union Hall, Williamson |
| Tucker, Anderson, ............ 304 | Twin Sisters, Blanco, ........... 78 | Union High, Navarro, ........... 30 |
| Tucker, McCulloch | Twist, Hartley | Union Hill, Bosque |
| Tucker's Mills, Limestone | Twist, Swisher | Union Hill, Kaufman |
| Tuckertown, Navarro | Twist Junction, Dallam | Union Hill, McLennan |
| Tuckertown, Van Zandt | Twitty, Wheeler,................ 12 | Union Hill, Titus |
| Tucumcari, Williamson | Twohig, La Salle | Union Hill, Upshur |
| Tudor, Eastland | Two Mile, Milam | Union Hill, Van Zandt |
| Tuff, Bandera | *TYE, Taylor, 48 (1,158)....... 1,165 | Union Hill, Walker |
| Tulane, Orange | *TYLER, Smith, 6,633 | Union Hope Church, Anderson |
| Tularosa, Kinney | (83,650) ................85,807 | Union Point, Jack |
| *Tuleta, Bee, 10 (292) ......... 301 | Tyler's Prairie, Trinity | Union Ridge, Upshur |
| *TULIA, Swisher, 271 | Tyler Bluff, Cooke | Union School House, Wilson |
| (5,117)................. 5,148 | Tyler Springs, Wise | Union Springs, Harrison |
| Tulip, Fannin, ................. 10 | *Tynan, Bee, 9 (301) .......... 309 | Union Springs, Nacogdoches |
| Tulip, Newton | Tyner, Blanco | Union Valley, Hopkins |
| Tulosa, Nueces | Type, Bastrop | Union Valley, Hunt, ............. 25 |
| Tulsa, Bee | Type, Williamson, .............. 40 | Union Valley, Rains |
| Tulsa, Lamb | Tyro, Coleman | Unionville, Cass |
| Tulsa, Winkler | Tyro, Parker | Unit, Waller |
| Tulsita, Bee, (20). .............. 20 | Tyro, San Saba | Unitia, Delta |
| Tulsy, Brazoria | Tyson, Hill | Unity, Collingsworth |
| Tuna, La Salle | | Unity, Colorado |
| Tundra, Van Zandt, ............. 34 | **U** | Unity, Henderson |
| Tunis, Burleson,.............. 150 | U. Auglin, Cherokee | Unity, Lamar, .................. 50 |
| Tunnell's Camp, Van Zandt | U.S. Factory, Lamar | Unity, Wilson |
| Tupelo, Navarro,............... NA | Ubell, Fannin | *UNIVERSAL CITY, Bexar, 628 |
| Turcotte, Kenedy | Udolpho, Madison | (14,849) .............. 15,190 |
| *TURKEY, Hall, 24 (494)....... 500 | Udston, Houston | Universe, Smith |
| Turkey, Wharton | Ufnau, Comal | University Community, Cottle |
| Turkey Bend, Burnet | UHLAND, Hays-Caldwell, (386) .. 401 | UNIVERSITY PARK, Dallas, |
| Turkey Creek, Callahan | Ula, Foard | (23,324) .............. 23,682 |
| Turkey Creek, Cass | Ulmer, Grimes | Uno, Stonewall |
| Turkey Creek, Henderson | Ultzville, Bexar | Upland, Upton |
| Turkey Creek, Hunt | *Umbarger, Randall, 10 ........ 327 | Upper Cuero Creek Settlement, DeWitt |
| Turkey Creek, San Jacinto | Una, Marion | Upper Hondo, Medina |
| Turkey Creek, Uvalde | Una, Robertson | Upper Medina Lake, Bandera |
| Turkey Creek, Washington | UNCERTAIN, Harrison, (150) .... 141 | Upper Medio, Bee |
| Turkey Creek, Williamson | Underwood, Delta | Upper Meyersville, DeWitt,....... 33 |
| Turlington, Freestone, .......... 27 | Underwood, Hale | Upper Quihi, Medina |
| Turnbaugh Corner, Ector | Uneva, Henderson | Upper Yorktown, DeWitt |
| Turner, Clay | Union, Brazos, ................NA | Upshaw, Nacogdoches, ........ NA |
| Turner, Van Zandt | Union, Camp | Upson, Maverick |
| Turner's Point, Kaufman | Union, Dawson | Upton, Bastrop,................. 25 |
| Turnerdale, Tom Green | Union, Eastland | Urban, Dallas |
| Turnersville, Coryell, .......... 155 | Union, Falls | Urbana, San Jacinto, ........... 25 |
| Turnersville, Travis, ........... 90 | Union, Freestone | Uriah, Coryell |
| Turnertown, Jefferson | Union, Hopkins | Uribeno, Zapata |
| Turnertown, Rusk, ............. 76 | Union, Jasper | Ury's Store, Cass |
| Turnerville, Matagorda | Union, Lubbock | Utah, Coleman |
| Turney, Cherokee | Union, Marion | Utah, Madison |
| Turney's Store, Travis | Union, San Augustine | Utica, Smith |
| Turnover, Coryell | Union, Scurry,................. 20 | Utley, Bastrop,................. 50 |
| Turpentine, Jasper | Union, Terry, .................. 55 | *Utopia, Uvalde, 64 (241) ....... 251 |

CITIES & TOWNS

**CITIES & TOWNS**

| Town,County .......... Pop. 2002 | Town,County .......... Pop. 2002 | Town,County .......... Pop. 2002 |
|---|---|---|
| *UVALDE, Uvalde, 799 (14,929)............... 15,144 | *Vanderbilt, Jackson, 11 (411)................... 424 | Veto, Jack |
| Uvalde Estates, Uvalde, (1,972)................ 2,050 | *Vanderpool, Bandera, 4 ....... 20 | Viboras, Starr,................ 22 |
| Uvalde Junction, Uvalde | Vandersville, Collin | Vick, Concho, ................ 20 |
| Uz, Montague | Vandyke, Comanche,.......... 20 | Vickery, Callahan |
|  | Vanetia, Leon | Vickery, Dallas |
| **V** | *VAN HORN, Culberson, 114 (2,435)................ 2,310 | Vicksburg, Montgomery |
| Vaca, Callahan | Vann, Navarro | Vicksburgh, Caldwell |
| Vahlsing, San Patricio | Vannoy's, Rusk | Victor, Erath |
| Vair, Trinity | Vann Settlement, Matagorda | Victor, Fannin |
| Valda, Polk | Van Pelt, Brazoria | Victor, Harris |
| Valdasta, Collin | Van Raub, Bexar, ............. NA | Victoria, Limestone, ........... 25 |
| Vale, Coleman | Van Sickle, Hunt, ............. NA | Victoria, Stonewall |
| Vale, Runnels | Van Slyke, Cooke | *VICTORIA, Victoria, 3,622 (60,603) .............. 61,579 |
| *VALENTINE, Jeff Davis, 2 (187).................. 190 | Van Syckles, Cameron | Victoria Peak, Montague |
| Valenzuela, Webb | *Van Vleck, Matagorda, 41 (1,411)................ 1,426 | Victoria Ranch, Oldham |
| *Valera, Coleman, 8 ........... 80 | Varela, Limestone | Victory City, Bowie,.......... 250 |
| Valletta Ranch, Denton | Varina, Haskell | Vida, Tyler |
| Valley, Grayson | Varisco, Brazos | Vidaurri, Refugio |
| Valley, Guadalupe | Vasco, Delta,.................. 20 | Vidette, Liberty |
| Valley Creek, Fannin,.......... 12 | Vashtel, Harrison | Vidor, Montgomery |
| Valley Farm, Reeves | Vashti, Clay,.................. 80 | *VIDOR, Orange, 835 (11,440) .............. 11,466 |
| Valley Farms, Navarro | Vashtie, Bosque | Viejo, Kimble |
| Valley Ford, Hays | Vattmann, Kleberg,............. 25 | Viejo Springs, Kimble |
| Valley Grove, Erath | Vaughan, Bosque | Vienna, Lavaca,................ 40 |
| Valley Grove, Rusk | Vaughan, Hill, ................ 70 | Viesca, Falls |
| Valley Grove, Young | Vaughan's Mill, Trinity | Viesca, Falls |
| Valley Hi, Bexar, ............ 3,000 | Veach, San Augustine,......... NA | View, Comal |
| Valley Home, Brown | Veal's Station, Parker | View, Taylor,.................. 75 |
| Valley Junction, Robertson | Vealmoor, Howard,........... 179 | Viewpoint, Lamar |
| *VALLEY MILLS, Bosque-McLennan, 79 (1,123)............ 1,124 | Veals, Morris | Vigo, Callahan |
| Valley Park, Lipscomb | *VEGA, Oldham, 65 (936)...... 907 | Vigo, Concho |
| Valley Pass, Bell | Vela, Hidalgo | *Vigo Park, Swisher,........... 31 |
| Valley Ridge, Brazos | Velasco, Brazoria | Vilas, Bell |
| *Valley Spring, Llano, 7 ........ 50 | Velasco, Brazoria | Vilas, Houston |
| Valley Springs, Hill | Velasco, Brazoria | Vilas, Panola |
| Valley View, Comal | Veldt, Kaufman | Villa, Hudspeth |
| *VALLEY VIEW, Cooke, 112 (737).................... 757 | Velehrad, Lavaca | Villa, Mills |
| Valley View, Cottle,............ 23 | Velma, San Saba | Villa Cavazos, Cameron |
| Valley View, DeWitt | Velma, Sherman | Villa del Sol, Cameron, (132) .... 136 |
| Valley View, Martin | Velpo, San Jacinto | Village Creek, Hardin |
| Valley View, McLennan | Venable, San Augustine | Village Creek, Tarrant |
| Valley View, Midland | Venadito, Cameron | *Village Mills, Hardin, 17...... 1,700 |
| Valley View, Mitchell | Venice, Coke | Villa Nueva, Hidalgo |
| Valley View, Rockwall | Venice, Nacogdoches | Villa Nueva, Nueces |
| Valley View, Runnels,........... 22 | Ventura, Montgomery | Villa Nueva North, Cameron, .... 374 |
| Valley View, Upshur,.......... 75 | *VENUS, Johnson, 103 (910) .................... 970 | Villa Nueva South, Cameron,.... 402 |
| Valley View, Wichita,.......... 200 | Vera, Gray | Villa Pancho, Cameron, (386).... 394 |
| Valley View, Williamson | Vera, Knox, ................... 50 | Villa Verde, Hidalgo, (891)....... 925 |
| Valley Wells, Dimmit, ........... 25 | Vera, Tyler | Villegas, Webb |
| Valmont, Bexar | Vera Cruz, Duval | Vilott, Cooke |
| Valota, Freestone | Verand, Schleicher | Vina, Clay |
| Valparaiso, Calhoun | Verbena, Garza | Vincent, Howard,............. 500 |
| Valparaiso, Hopkins | Vercal, Anderson | Vinegarone, Val Verde |
| Valton, Hopkins | Verdi, Atascosa, ............. 110 | Vinegarroon, Val Verde |
| Val Verde, Denton | Verdina, Medina | Vine Green, Washington |
| Val Verde, Hidalgo | Verhalen, Reeves,............. 52 | Vine Grove, Washington |
| Val Verde, Milam, ............. 25 | Verhelle, DeWitt | Vineland, Collin |
| Val Verde Park, Val Verde, (1,945)................ 2,025 | *Veribest, Tom Green, 7 ....... 40 | Viney, Collin |
| Van, Leon | Vermont Ranch, Schleicher | Vineyard, Morris |
| *VAN, Van Zandt, 129 (2,362)................ 2,459 | Vern, Liberty | Vineyard, Jack |
| Vanall, Henderson | Verna, Collin | Vineyard, Jack, ................ 37 |
| *VAN ALSTYNE, Grayson, 173 (2,502)................ 2,563 | Vernal, McLennan | Vinson, Travis |
| Van Camp, Young | Vernon, Gonzales | VINTON, El Paso, 2 (1,892).... 1,949 |
| Vance, Colorado | Vernon, Panola | Viola, Cass |
| Vance, Real, .................. 20 | *VERNON, Wilbarger, 627 (11,660)............... 11,474 | Viola, Milam |
| Vance, Taylor | Verona, Collin | Viola, Nueces |
| *Vancourt, Tom Green, 5 ....... 125 | Vesper, La Salle | Violet, Nueces, ............... 160 |
| Vandalia, Red River,........... 35 | Vesrue, Winkler | Virgie, Montgomery |
| Vandenburg, Medina | Vessey, Red River, ........... 14 | Virgile, Johnson |
|  | Vesta, Sabine | Virginia, Armstrong |
|  | Vesta, Shackelford | Virginia, Dallas |
|  | Veto, Gillespie | Virginia City, Bailey |
|  |  | Virginia Mills, Montague |
|  |  | Virginia Point, Galveston |
|  |  | Visco, Mitchell |

| Town,County ...........Pop. 2002 | Town,County ...........Pop. 2002 | Town,County ...........Pop. 2002 |
|---|---|---|
| Vista, Dickens | Waldrip, McCulloch, ........... 15 | Walton, Panola |
| Vista, Hamilton | Waldrop, Panola | Walton, Trinity |
| Vista, Mitchell | Waldrop's Gin, Stonewall | Walton, Van Zandt, ............ 35 |
| Vista, Nolan | Wales, Lamar | Wamba, Bowie, ............... 70 |
| Vistula, Houston, ............. 21 | Walhalla, Comal | Wanda, Henderson |
| Viterbo, Jefferson | Walhalla, Fayette, ............ 37 | Waneta, Houston. ........... 19 |
| Viva, Bexar | Walk, Lampasas | Waples, Hood, ............... 155 |
| Vivian, Foard, ................ NA | Walker, Howard | Warbonnet, Refugio |
| Vivian, Marion | Walker, Parker | Ward's, Red River |
| Vix, Kerr | Walker, Walker | Ward's Store, Cherokee |
| Vliets, Mitchell | Walker's, Gregg | *Warda, Fayette, 8 ............. 98 |
| *Voca, McCulloch, 7 ........... 56 | Walker's, Rusk | Ward Branch, Somervell |
| Voelkle, Grayson | Walker's Store, McLennan | Ward Chapel, Freestone |
| Vogel's Valley, Comal | Walker Chapel, Cherokee | Ward Creek, Bowie, ........... 164 |
| Vogelsang, Milam | Walkers Creek, Milam | Warden, Midland |
| Vogelsang, Runnels | Walkers Mill, Harrison | Wardlaw, McLennan |
| VOLENTE, Travis, ............. NA | Walker Station, Red River | Wards, Stephens |
| Volga, Houston, ............. 300 | Walkerton, Williamson | Ward Spur, Ellis |
| Vollmer, Harris | *Wall, Tom Green, 14 ......... 200 | Wardville, Hansford |
| Volney, Burleson | Wallace, Bandera | Wardville, Johnson |
| Volney, Delta | Wallace, Parker | Wardville, Montague |
| Volney, Robertson | Wallace, Travis | Wardville, Wichita |
| Volo, Bell | Wallace, Uvalde | Ware, Comanche |
| *Von Ormy, Bexar, 107 ......... NA | Wallace, Van Zandt, .........NA | Ware, Dallam |
| Vontress, Haskell | Wallace Chapel, Upshur | Ware's Settlement, Montgomery |
| *Voss, Coleman, 1 ............. 20 | Wallace Creek, San Saba | Waresville, Uvalde |
| Voss, Coryell | Wallace Grove, Nacogdoches | Warfield, Midland |
| Vossville, Fort Bend | Wallace Mill, Shelby | *Waring, Kendall, 5 ............ 73 |
| *Votaw, Hardin, 5 ............ 160 | Wallace Prairie, Grimes | Warlock, Marion |
| Votaw, Live Oak | *WALLER, Waller-Harris, 269 | Warner, Franklin |
| Voth, Jefferson, .............. NA | (2,092) ................2,129 | Warner Junction, Grayson |
| Vox Populi, Colorado | Waller's Store, Waller | Warren, Bell |
| Vox Populi, Colorado | Walles Store, Orange | Warren, Brown |
| Vreeland, Polk | Wallick, Schleicher | Warren, Cooke |
| Vsetin, Lavaca, .............. NA | Walling, Hill | Warren, Dickens |
| Vysehrad, Lavaca | Walling's Ferry, Gregg | Warren, Fannin |
| | Walling's Mills, Rusk | *Warren, Tyler, 25 ............ 304 |
| **W** | Walling Bend, Bosque | Warren, Washington |
| *WACO, McLennan, 6,610 | Wallings Ferry, Rusk | WARREN CITY, Gregg-Upshur, |
| (113,726) ............. 114,743 | Wallingville, Wood | (343) ................... 348 |
| Waco Spring, Lee | *WALLIS, Austin, 66 | Warren Springs, Cass |
| Waco Springs, Comal | (1,172) ................1,236 | *Warrenton, Fayette, 3 ......... 65 |
| Wade, Guadalupe | Wallisburgh, Smith | Warsaw, Harrison |
| Wade's, Fayette | Wallis Ranch, DeWitt | Warsaw, Kaufman, ............. 58 |
| Wade's Chapel, Parker | *Wallisville, Chambers, 23 ..... 460 | Warwick, Bexar |
| Wade's City, Jim Wells | Walnut Bend, Cooke, .......... 59 | Warwick, Brewster |
| Wade Mill, San Augustine | Walnut Creek, Bastrop | Warwick, Smith, .............. NA |
| Wadeville, Navarro | Walnut Creek, Bastrop | Washburn, Armstrong, ........ 120 |
| Wadis Post Office, Fayette | Walnut Creek, Henderson | Washburn, Grayson |
| Wadsworth, Hale | Walnut Creek, Palo Pinto | Washer, Zavala |
| *Wadsworth, Matagorda, 16 .... 160 | Walnut Grove, Collin, ......... 200 | Washington, Coleman |
| *WAELDER, Gonzales, 27 | Walnut Grove, Panola | *Washington, Washington, 33 ... 265 |
| (947) ................... 984 | Walnut Grove, Red River | Washington Mills, Polk |
| Wage, Kimble | Walnut Grove, San Jacinto | Washita, Grayson |
| Waggoner, Wichita | Walnut Grove, Smith, ..........NA | Washita, Hemphill |
| Waggoner's Colony, Wilbarger | Walnut Grove, Tom Green | *WASKOM, Harrison, 125 |
| Wagner, Hartley | Walnut Grove, Washington | (2,068) ................ 2,110 |
| Wagner, Hunt, ................ NA | Walnut Hill, Panola | Wasson, Hale |
| Wagram, Mason | Walnut Hill, Upshur | Wasson, Yoakum-Gaines |
| Waidville, Montague | Walnut Hills, Potter, ........... 60 | Wastella, Nolan, ............... 4 |
| Waintown, Denton | Walnut Run, Jasper | *WATAUGA, Tarrant, |
| Wainwright, Navarro | Walnut Springs, Bell | (21,908) ............. 22,707 |
| Waite, Hidalgo | *WALNUT SPRINGS, Bosque, | Water's Bluff, Smith |
| *Waka, Ochiltree, 3. ........... 65 | 24 (755) ................. 784 | Waterford, Milam |
| Wake, Crosby | Walnut Springs, Ellis | Waterloo, Grayson |
| Wakefield, Freestone | Walnut Springs, Guadalupe | Waterloo, Travis |
| Wakefield, Howard | Walnut Station, Travis | Waterloo, Williamson, .......... 60 |
| Wakefield, Polk, .............. 25 | Walsh, Gonzales | Waterman, Shelby, ............ 53 |
| Waketon, Denton | Walsh, San Jacinto | Waters, Navarro |
| WAKE VILLAGE, Bowie, | Walsh, Williamson-Travis | Waters Park, Travis |
| (5,129). ................5,340 | Walstad, Roberts | *Water Valley, Tom Green, 9 ..... 120 |
| *Walburg, Williamson, 6. ....... 250 | Walter, Liberty | Water Valley, Williamson |
| Walch, San Jacinto | Walter, Milam | Waterville, Wharton |
| Walcott, Martin | Walters, Karnes | Waterwood, San Jacinto, ....... 100 |
| Waldeck, Fayette, ............. 35 | Walters, San Patricio | Wathen, Marion |
| Walden, Jefferson | Walthall, Runnels | Watkins, Terrell |
| Waldo, McLennan | Walton, Bee | Watkins, Van Zandt, .......... NA |

CITIES & TOWNS

| Town,County . . . . . . . . . . .Pop. 2002 | Town,County . . . . . . . . . . .Pop. 2002 | Town,County . . . . . . . . . . . Pop. 2002 |
|---|---|---|
| **Watson, Burnet,** . . . . . . . . . . . . . . 98 | *Wehdem, Austin* | *Westfield, Harris* |
| *Watson, Clay* | **\*WEIMAR, Colorado, 218** | *Westfork, Archer* |
| *Watson, Comanche* |    **(1,981)**. . . . . . . . . . . . . . . . .**1,982** | *West Fork, Wise* |
| *Watson, Crosby* | *Weimer, Wood* | *West Hamilton, Shelby* |
| *Watson, Milam* | **Weinert, Guadalupe,**. . . . . . . . . . 10 | **\*Westhoff, DeWitt, 14** . . . . . . . . . 410 |
| *Watson, Red River* | **\*WEINERT, Haskell, 9 (177)** . . . . . 175 | *West Junction, Harris* |
| *Watson, Washington* | **Weir, Hopkins,** . . . . . . . . . . . . . .NA | **WESTLAKE, Tarrant, (207)** . . . . . . 206 |
| *Watson Branch, Milam* | **\*WEIR, Williamson, 6 (591)**. . . . . . 608 | **\*WEST LAKE HILLS, Travis,** |
| *Watsonville, Bexar* | *Weir's, Guadalupe* |    **(3,116)**. . . . . . . . . . . . . . . 3,284 |
| *Watsonville, Panola* | *Weisinger, Montgomery* | *Westland, Tarrant* |
| *Watsonville, Sabine* | **Weiss Bluff, Jasper,** . . . . . . . . . . .NA | *West Liberty, Liberty* |
| *Watsonville, Tarrant* | *Weland, Parker* | **West Livingston, Polk,** |
| **Watt, Limestone,** . . . . . . . . . . . . . 25 | **\*Welch, Dawson, 21** . . . . . . . . . . . 110 |    **(6,612)**. . . . . . . . . . . . . . . 6,896 |
| *Watters, Johnson* | *Welch, Rusk* | *West Mesquite, Dallas* |
| *Watters, Tom Green* | **Welcome, Austin,** . . . . . . . . . . . . 150 | **West Mineola, Wood,**. . . . . . . . . . . 20 |
| **Watterson, Bastrop,**. . . . . . . . . . . NA | *Welden Switch, DeWitt* | **\*WESTMINSTER, Collin, 5** |
| *Watts, Marion* | **Weldon, Houston,** . . . . . . . . . . . . 131 |    **(390)**. . . . . . . . . . . . . . . . . . .401 |
| *Watts, Robertson* | **Welfare, Kendall,**. . . . . . . . . . . . . . 36 | **West Mountain, Upshur,**. . . . . . . . 445 |
| *Watts, Van Zandt* | **\*Wellborn, Brazos, 8.** . . . . . . . . . . 100 | *West Nona, Hardin* |
| *Watts Creek, Coleman* | *Wellersburgh, Lavaca* | *West Nueces, Kinney* |
| *Wattsville, Rains* | **\*WELLINGTON, Collingsworth,** | **West Odessa, Ector,** |
| *Waugh's Rancho, La Salle* |    **157 (2,275)** . . . . . . . . . . . . .**2,233** |    **(17,799)** . . . . . . . . . . . . . . 17,874 |
| *Waukegan, Montgomery* | **\*WELLMAN, Terry, 6 (203)** . . . . . . 205 | **\*WESTON, Collin, 12 (635)** . . . . . . 666 |
| *Waverlan, Hansford* | **\*WELLS, Cherokee, 26** | **WEST ORANGE, Orange,** |
| **Waverly, San Jacinto,** . . . . . . . . 200 |    **(769)** . . . . . . . . . . . . . . . . . . 747 |    **(4,111)**. . . . . . . . . . . . . . . 4,023 |
| *Wawaka, Ochiltree* | *Wells, Gonzales* | *West Oso, Nueces* |
| **\*WAXAHACHIE, Ellis, 1,316** | **Wells, Lynn,**. . . . . . . . . . . . . . . . . 10 | **Westover, Baylor,** . . . . . . . . . . . . . 18 |
|    **(21,426)**. . . . . . . . . . . . . . . 22,710 | *Wells, Panola* | **WESTOVER HILLS, Tarrant,** |
| *Waxford, Refugio* | *Wells' Gin, Hunt* |    **(658)**. . . . . . . . . . . . . . . . . . 665 |
| *Way, Hall* | **Wells Branch, Travis,** | *West Paris, Lamar* |
| *Wayback, Coryell* |    **(11,271)**. . . . . . . . . . . . . . .**11,396** | *West Park, Harris* |
| *Wayland, Red River* | *Wells Creek, Anderson* | **West Pearsall, Frio, (349)** . . . . . . . 361 |
| *Wayland, Stephens* | *Wellswood, San Augustine* | **Westphalia, Falls,** . . . . . . . . . . . . 186 |
| **Wayne, Cass,** . . . . . . . . . . . . . . . 15 | *Welsh, Titus* | **\*West Point, Fayette, 12** . . . . . . . . 205 |
| *Wayne, Lamar* | *Welview, Concho* | *West Point, Freestone* |
| **\*Wayside, Armstrong, 6.** . . . . . . . . 35 | *Wenasco, Jasper* | *West Point, Hamilton* |
| *Wayside, Bastrop* | *Wendell, Jeff Davis* | *West Point, Hays* |
| *Wayside, Burleson* | *Weno, Grayson* | *West Point, Lynn* |
| *Wayside, Dawson* | *Wenona, Erath* | *West Port Arthur, Jefferson* |
| *Wayside, Lynn* | *Wentworth, Sutton* | *West Portland, San Patricio* |
| *Wayside, Marion* | **Wentworth, Van Zandt,**. . . . . . . . . 32 | *Westprong, Uvalde* |
| *Wayside, McLennan* | *Wentz, McMullen* | *West Saint Paul, San Patricio* |
| *Wayside, Panola* | *Werners Bluff, Walker* | *West Scrap, Red River* |
| **Wayside, Roberts,** . . . . . . . . . . . 105 | **Wesco, Gray,** . . . . . . . . . . . . . . . . 7 | **West Sharyland, Hidalgo,** |
| *Wayside, Wood* | *Weser, Goliad* |    **(2,947)** . . . . . . . . . . . . . . . 3,059 |
| *Weakley, Smith* | **\*WESLACO, Hidalgo, 1,198** | *Westside, Morris* |
| **Wealthy, Leon,** . . . . . . . . . . . . . .NA |    **(26,935)**. . . . . . . . . . . . . . .**28,007** | **West Sinton, San Patricio,** . . . . . . 318 |
| **\*WEATHERFORD, Parker,** | *Wesley, Austin* | *West Sweden, McCulloch* |
|    **2,081 (19,000).** . . . . . . . . . . 20,260 | **Wesley, Washington,** . . . . . . . . . . 60 | **WEST TAWAKONI, Hunt** |
| **Weatherly, Hall,**. . . . . . . . . . . . . . 20 | *Wesley Chapel, Houston* |    **(1,462)** . . . . . . . . . . . . . . . 1,489 |
| **Weaver, Hopkins,** . . . . . . . . . . . . . 35 | *Wesley Grove, Walker* | *West Tempe, Polk* |
| *Weaver, Kinney* | *Wessels, Fayette* | **WEST UNIVERSITY PLACE,** |
| *Weavers, Bowie* | *Wesson, Comal* |    **Harris, (14,211)** . . . . . . . . . 14,430 |
| *Weaver Springs, Nolan* | **\*WEST, McLennan, 217** | *West Vernon, Wilbarger* |
| *Webb, Houston* |    **(2,692)**. . . . . . . . . . . . . . . .**2,695** | *Westville, DeWitt* |
| *Webb, McLennan* | *West Bevilport, Jasper* | **Westville, Trinity,** . . . . . . . . . . . . . 46 |
| *Webb, Shelby* | *Westbrook, Blanco* | *West Waco, McLennan* |
| *Webb, Tarrant* | **Westbrook, Jack,** . . . . . . . . . . . . .NA | **Westway, Deaf Smith,**. . . . . . . . . . 15 |
| *Webb, Webb* | *Westbrook, Jasper* | **Westway, El Paso, (3,829).** . . . . . 3,983 |
| *Webb Chapel, Limestone* | *Westbrook, Johnson* | **WESTWORTH VILLAGE, Tarrant,** |
| **WEBBERVILLE, Travis,** . . . . . . . . .NA | **\*WESTBROOK, Mitchell, 13** |    **(2,124)** . . . . . . . . . . . . . . . 2,075 |
| **Webbville, Coleman,** . . . . . . . . . . 50 |    **(203)** . . . . . . . . . . . . . . . . . . 202 | *West Yegua, Lee* |
| *Webbville, Jones* | *Westbrook, Webb* | **\*Wetmore, Bexar, 1** . . . . . . . . . . . NA |
| *Web City, Jack* | *Westbrook, Wood* | *Wetsel, Collin* |
| **\*WEBSTER, Harris, 1,301** | *Westbrook Mill, Newton* | *Whaley, Bowie* |
|    **(9,083)**. . . . . . . . . . . . . . . . 9,029 | *Westbury, Jefferson* | **\*WHARTON, Wharton, 601** |
| *Webster, Wood* | *West Carlisle, Lubbock* |    **(9,237)** . . . . . . . . . . . . . . . 9,285 |
| *Webster's, Hall* | *West Chapel, Camp* | *Whatley, Marion* |
| **Weches, Houston,** . . . . . . . . . . . . 26 | **\*WEST COLUMBIA, Brazoria,** | *Wheat, Scurry* |
| *Weddington, Brazos* |    **321 (4,255)** . . . . . . . . . . . . .**4,258** | *Wheatland, Dallas* |
| *Wedemeyer, Falls* | **Westcott, San Jacinto,**. . . . . . . . . 25 | *Wheatland, Hardeman* |
| *Weed, Sabine* | **Westdale, Jim Wells, (295)** . . . . . . 313 | *Wheatland, Jackson* |
| **Weedhaven, Jackson,** . . . . . . . . . 35 | *West Delta, Delta* | **Wheatland, Tarrant,**. . . . . . . . . . . 175 |
| *Weedy, Karnes* | *West Eden, Wise* | *Wheatland, Wilbarger* |
| *Weeks Settlement, Newton* | *Western Lake, Parker* | *Wheatville, Morris* |
| **Weeping Mary, Cherokee,** . . . . . . 40 | *Westerville, Palo Pinto* | *Wheatville, Travis* |
| **\*Weesatche, Goliad, 4** . . . . . . . . 411 | *West Falls, Falls* | *Wheel City, Hidalgo* |

| Town,County ........... Pop. 2002 | Town,County ........... Pop. 2002 | Town,County ........... Pop. 2002 |
|---|---|---|
| *Wheeler, Potter* | *WHITESBORO, Grayson, 263 | *Wilder's Gin, Williamson* |
| *WHEELER, Wheeler, 88 | (3,760)..................3,830 | Wilderville, Falls,.............. 45 |
| (1,378)..................1,368 | *WHITE SETTLEMENT, Tarrant, | *Wildhorse, Culberson* |
| *Wheeler, Wheeler* | (14,831)...............14,948 | *Wild Horse Prairie, Wise* |
| *Wheeler's Hill, Trinity* | *Whiteside's Prairie, Fayette* | *Wildhurst, Cherokee* |
| *Wheeler's Store, Travis* | *Whitesides', Washington* | *Wildorado, Oldham, 23 ........ 180 |
| *Wheeler's Switch, Polk* | *Whitesmine, Uvalde* | Wild Peach, Brazoria, |
| Wheeler Springs, Houston,...... 89 | *Whites Ranch, Chambers* | (2,498)................. 2,490 |
| *Wheelock, Leon* | White Star, Motley, ............. 5 | *Wiles, Stephens* |
| *Wheelock, Lubbock* | *White Stone, Williamson* | *Wilford, Stonewall* |
| *Wheelock, Robertson, 5....... 225 | *White Sulphur Springs, Cass* | *Wilhite, Lamar* |
| *Wherry, Rusk* | *White Sulphur Springs, Grimes* | *Wilke, Burnet* |
| *Whig, Carson* | *Whitesville, Houston* | Wilkins, Upshur, ............... 75 |
| *Whistler, Kinney* | *White Swan, Tom Green* | *Wilkinson, Titus* |
| *Whistleville, Llano* | *Whitetail, Williamson* | *Wilkinson's, Bell* |
| *Whit, Harris* | *White Water Springs, Wheeler* | *Wilkinson's, Burleson* |
| *White, El Paso* | Whiteway, Hamilton,........... 10 | *Willaluce, Shelby* |
| *White, Milam* | *WHITEWRIGHT, Grayson-Fannin, | Willamar, Willacy, (15).......... 18 |
| *White, Uvalde* | 112 (1,740) ..............1,755 | *Willard, Jones* |
| *White's, Sabine* | *Whitfield, Swisher* | *Willard, Trinity* |
| *White's Chapel, Navarro* | *Whitfield's, Waller* | *Willa Walla, Montague* |
| *White's Grove, Collin* | *Whitham, Jones* | *Willett, Cottle* |
| *White's Store, Chambers* | *Whitharral, Hockley, 6........ 175 | *William's Chapel, Van Zandt* |
| *White's Switch, Fort Bend* | *Whiting's Farm, Washington* | William Penn, Washington, ..... 100 |
| *White's Wells, Hill* | *Whitley, Briscoe* | *William Routt, Fort Bend* |
| *White Church, Navarro* | Whitman, Washington,......... 25 | *Williams, Brown* |
| *White City, Chambers* | *WHITNEY, Hill, 305 | *Williams, Hardeman* |
| *White City, Gaines* | (1,833)..................1,919 | *Williams, Hardin* |
| White City, San Augustine, ...... 20 | *Whitsett, Live Oak, 4.... 200 | *Williams', Jefferson* |
| White City, Wilbarger,........... 40 | *Whitson, Coryell, ............. 30 | *Williams', Lamar* |
| *White City, Wise* | *Whitt, Parker, 2 ............... 38 | *Williams, Liberty* |
| *White Cottage, Shelby* | *Whittaker, Burleson* | *Williams, Matagorda* |
| *Whited, Gray* | *Whittenburg, Hutchinson* | *Williams' Settlement, Cherokee* |
| *WHITE DEER, Carson, 42 | Whitton, Van Zandt,...........NA | *Williams' Store, Guadalupe* |
| (1,060)..................1,020 | *Whittville, Comanche* | Williamsburg, Lavaca, ......... NA |
| *WHITEFACE, Cochran, 29 | *Whitworth, Kaufman* | *Williamsburg, Throckmorton* |
| (465)................... 457 | *Whizzerville, Caldwell* | *Williams Creek, Gillespie* |
| *Whitefish, Donley* | *Who'd-a-Thought-It, Van Zandt* | Williamson Settlement, Orange, . 175 |
| *White Flat, Fisher* | *Who'd Thought It, Hopkins* | *Williams Ranch, Mills* |
| *White Flat, Knox* | *Whon, Coleman, ............. 15 | *Williams Ranch, Montague* |
| Whiteflat, Motley, .............. 3 | *Whybark, Bowie* | *Williams Settlement, Rusk* |
| *Whiteflat, Nolan* | *Whynot, Hunt* | *Willingham, Smith* |
| White Hall, Bell, .............. 45 | *Wichita, Clay* | *Willingham Springs, Bell* |
| *White Hall, Cass* | *Wichita Colony, Baylor* | *Willingham Store, Martin* |
| *White Hall, Coryell* | *WICHITA FALLS, Wichita, | *WILLIS, Montgomery, 667 |
| *White Hall, Grimes* | 4,967 (104,197)........104,544 | (3,985) ................ 4,153 |
| *White Hall, Jackson* | Wicker, Brazos,...............NA | *Willman, Bastrop* |
| *Whitehall, Kaufman* | *Wickes Spur, Brazoria* | *Willow, Harris* |
| *Whitehead, Cherokee* | *WICKETT, Ward, 19 (455) ...... 442 | *Willow, Travis* |
| *Whitehead, Hunt* | Wied, Lavaca, .................. 65 | *Willow Bar, Colorado* |
| *WHITEHOUSE, Smith, 394 | *Wiedeville, Washington,........NA | *Willow City, Gillespie, 9........ 75 |
| (5,346)..................6,107 | Wieland, Hunt, ................NA | *Willow Creek, Howard* |
| *Whiteland, McCulloch* | *Wiergate, Newton, 8 .......... 461 | *Willow Creek, Mason* |
| *White League, Ellis* | *Wigfall, Houston* | *Willow Creek, Robertson* |
| *White Mound, Grayson* | *Wiggins, Cass* | *Willow Dale, Comanche* |
| *White Oak, Blanco* | *Wiggins, Houston* | Willow Grove, McLennan, ...... 100 |
| *WHITE OAK, Gregg, 207 | *Wiggins, McLennan* | *Willow Grove, Shelby* |
| (5,624)..................5,820 | *Wiggins, Rusk* | *Willow Hole, Madison* |
| *White Oak, Harris* | Wigginsville, Montgomery, ......NA | *Willow Oak, Upshur* |
| *Whiteoak, Hopkins* | *Wight, Val Verde* | WILLOW PARK, Parker, |
| *Whiteoak, Marion* | *Wightman, Newton* | (2,849) ................ 3,043 |
| White Oak, Titus, ............. 100 | *Wihan, Newton* | *Willow Point, Fannin* |
| *White Oak, Wood* | *Wilbarger, Bastrop* | *Willow Point, Wise* |
| White Oak Junction, Hopkins, ... NA | *Wilbarger, Wilbarger* | *Willow Pond, Ellis* |
| *White Point, Concho* | *Wilborn, Donley* | *Willow Pond, Palo Pinto* |
| *White Point, San Patricio* | *Wilbourn, Walker* | *Willow Pond Springs, Haskell* |
| White River, Crosby, ........... 35 | *Wilburton, Montgomery* | *Willow Prairie, Travis* |
| *White Rock, Dallas* | *Wilco, Hartley* | *Willow Spring, Travis* |
| *White Rock, Fannin* | Wilcox, Burleson,.............. 40 | *Willow Springs, Bell* |
| *White Rock, Grayson* | *Wilcox, Gray* | Willow Springs, Fayette,........ 35 |
| *White Rock, Hill* | *Wilcox, Somervell* | *Willow Springs, Gregg* |
| White Rock, Hunt, ............. 73 | *Wilda, Liberty* | *Willow Springs, McLennan* |
| White Rock, Red River, ........ 85 | *Wilda, Shelby* | *Willow Springs, Milam* |
| White Rock, Robertson, ........ 80 | *Wildcat, Eastland* | Willow Springs, Rains,.......... 50 |
| White Rock, San Augustine,..... 60 | *Wildcat, Henderson* | *Willow Springs, Rockwall* |
| *White Rock, Trinity* | *Wildcat, Wilbarger* | *Willow Springs, San Jacinto* |
| *Whites, Robertson* | *Wild Cat Bluff, Anderson* | *Willow Springs, Van Zandt* |

CITIES & TOWNS

| Town,County . . . . . . . . . . .Pop. 2002 | Town,County . . . . . . . . . . .Pop. 2002 | Town,County. . . . . . . . . . . Pop. 2002 |
|---|---|---|
| *WILLS POINT, Van Zandt, 380 (3,496) . . . . . . . . . . . . . 3,563 | Wintergreen, Karnes | Woodmyer, Newton |
| Willsville, Matagorda | Winter Haven, Dimmit, . . . . . . . . 112 | Wood Port, Jackson-Victoria |
| Willton, Williamson | *WINTERS, Runnels, 160 | Woodridge, Orange, . . . . . . . . . 1,000 |
| *WILMER, Dallas, 62 (3,393). . . . . . . . . . . . . . . . . 3,517 | (2,880). . . . . . . . . . . . . . . . . 2,869 | Woodridge Park, Bexar |
| | Win Town, Panola | Woodrow, Fort Bend |
| Wilmerding, Navarro | Wire, Trinity | Woodrow, Hardin |
| Wilmeth, Collin | Wisdom Temple, Van Zandt | Woodrow, Lubbock, . . . . . . . . . . . 85 |
| Wilmeth, Runnels, . . . . . . . . . . . . 25 | Wise, Liberty | Woodruff, Jefferson |
| Wilmington, Robertson | Wise, Van Zandt, . . . . . . . . . . . . . . 29 | Woods, Fannin |
| Wilmoth, Angelina | Wise, Webb | Woods, Navarro |
| Wilmoth, Montgomery | Witcher, Milam | Woods, Panola, . . . . . . . . . . . . . . 65 |
| Wilna, Bastrop | Witco, Reagan | *WOODSBORO, Refugio, 45 |
| Wilsey, Parmer | Witting, Lavaca, . . . . . . . . . . . . . 90 | (1,685) . . . . . . . . . . . . . . . . . 1,666 |
| Wilson, Collin | WIXON VALLEY, Brazos, (235). . . 241 | *WOODSON, Throckmorton, 13 |
| Wilson, Collingsworth | Wizard Wells, Jack, . . . . . . . . . . . . 69 | (296). . . . . . . . . . . . . . . . . . . 311 |
| Wilson, Comanche | *Woden, Nacogdoches, 15. . . . . . . 70 | Wood Springs, Smith, . . . . . . . . . 200 |
| Wilson, Cooke | Wofford, DeWitt | Woodstock, Bowie |
| Wilson, Cottle | Wofford, Henderson | Woodstock, Parker |
| Wilson, Falls, . . . . . . . . . . . . . . . . 42 | Wokaty, Milam | Woodswitch, Grimes |
| Wilson, Kaufman | Wolcott, Brown | Woodswitch, Montague |
| Wilson, Limestone | Wolf's Crossing, Burnet | Wood Valley, Limestone |
| *WILSON, Lynn, 24 (532) . . . . . . . 518 | Wolf Branch, Red River | Woodville, Cherokee, . . . . . . . . . . 20 |
| Wilson, Navarro | Wolf Creek, Ochiltree | Woodville, Parker |
| Wilson's, Tyler | Wolf Creek, Tyler | *WOODVILLE, Tyler, 352 |
| Wilson Chapel, Freestone | Wolfe's, Bee | (2,415) . . . . . . . . . . . . . . . . 2,408 |
| Wilson Creek, Matagorda | *WOLFE CITY, Hunt, 72 | Woodward, Kinney |
| Wilson Springs, Shelby | (1,566). . . . . . . . . . . . . . . . . 1,597 | Woodward, La Salle, . . . . . . . . . . . 10 |
| Wilson Springs, Williamson | *WOLFFORTH, Lubbock, 141 | WOODWAY, McLennan, |
| Wilson Station, Jack | (2,554). . . . . . . . . . . . . . . . . 2,653 | (8,733) . . . . . . . . . . . . . . . . 8,895 |
| Wilton, Cass | Wolf Hollow, Leon | Woody, Coleman |
| Wilton, Ellis | Wolfpen, Hopkins | Woody, Loving |
| Wilton, Tarrant | Wolf Point, Calhoun | Wooland, Tom Green |
| Wilton, Wilbarger | Wolf Point, Jefferson | Woosley, Rains, . . . . . . . . . . . . . . 47 |
| *WIMBERLEY, Hays, 622 (3,797). . . . . . . . . . . . . . . . 4,004 | Wolf Ridge, Cooke | Wooster, Harris |
| | Wolf Valley, Brown | Wootan Wells, Robertson |
| Wimberly, Fort Bend | Wolters Village, Palo Pinto | Wooten's, Rusk |
| Wims, Franklin | Womack, Bosque, . . . . . . . . . . . . . 25 | Wooters, Houston |
| Winchell, Brown, . . . . . . . . . . . . . NA | Womack, Colorado | Worbaino, Orange |
| *Winchester, Fayette, 1 . . . . . . . . . 50 | Womble, Collin | Word, Shelby |
| *WINDCREST, Bexar, (5,105). . . . . . . . . . . . . . . . . 5,072 | Wonderland Forest, San Jacinto, . 40 | Worley, Parker |
| | Wonders, Nacogdoches | Worleys, Baylor |
| Windemere, Travis, (6,868) . . . . 6,982 | Wood, Robertson | Worsham, Reeves |
| Windham, Callahan | Wood, Rusk | Worsham, Wilbarger |
| Windmill Town, Taylor | Wood's Creek, Polk | *WORTHAM, Freestone, 37 |
| Windom, Angelina | Wood's Prairie, Fayette | (1,082) . . . . . . . . . . . . . . . . 1,081 |
| *WINDOM, Fannin, 11 (245). . . . . 244 | Woodal, Cherokee | Worthing, Lavaca, . . . . . . . . . . . . 55 |
| Windom, Hutchinson | Woodal Farm, Milam | Worthy, Uvalde |
| Windsor, Cooke | Woodall, Harrison | Wragg's Hill, Rusk |
| Windsor, Kendall | Woodall, Van Zandt | Wren, Franklin |
| Windsor, McLennan | Woodard, Lamar | Wren, Washington |
| *WINDTHORST, Archer, 49 (440) . . . . . . . . . . . . . . . . . . . 441 | Woodbine, Cooke, . . . . . . . . . . . 250 | Wright, Hale |
| | Woodborough, Grayson | Wright, Swisher |
| Winedale, Fayette-Washington, . . 41 | WOODBRANCH, Montgomery, (1,305). . . . . . . . . . . . . . . . .1,393 | Wright, Wilson |
| Winfield, Bastrop | | Wright's, Jasper |
| *WINFIELD, Titus, 22 (499). . . . . 509 | Woodbury, Grayson | Wright's Bend, Colorado |
| WINFREE [Old River-], Chambers, (1,364). . . . . . . . 1,380 | Woodbury, Hill, . . . . . . . . . . . . . . 40 | Wright City, Smith, . . . . . . . . . . . 172 |
| | Wood City, Bastrop | *Wrightsboro, Gonzales, 1 . . . . . . . 76 |
| *Wingate, Runnels, 9 . . . . . . . . . 216 | WOODCREEK, Hays, (1,274). . . . . . . . . . . . . . . . .1,399 | Wrightsville, Lamar |
| *WINK, Winkler, 29 (919) . . . . . . . 918 | | Wrightsville, Red River |
| Winkler, Navarro-Freestone, . . . . . 26 | Wooded Hills, Johnson, . . . . . . . . 310 | Wurst, Comal |
| Winkler City, Winkler | Wood Hi, Victoria, . . . . . . . . . . . . . 35 | Wursten, Fayette |
| Winn, Robertson | Woodlake, Brazos | Wuthrich Hill, Williamson |
| Winn's Colony, Caldwell | Woodlake, Grayson | Wyatt, Ellis |
| *Winnie, Chambers, 230 (2,914). . . . . . . . . . . . . . . . . 2,999 | *Woodlake, Trinity, 3 . . . . . . . . . . . 98 | Wyattsville, Williamson |
| | Woodland, Bell | Wyche, Deaf Smith |
| Winningkoff, Collin | Woodland, Brazoria | Wyldwood, Bastrop, (2,310) . . . 2,541 |
| *WINNSBORO, Wood-Franklin, 434 (3,584) . . . . . . . . . . . . . 3,622 | Woodland, Freestone | *WYLIE, Collin-Rockwall-Dallas, 759 (15,132). . . . . . . . . . . 17,410 |
| | Woodland, Hopkins | |
| Winnton, Gonzales | Woodland, Limestone | Wylie, Franklin |
| *WINONA, Smith, 75 (582) . . . . . . 601 | Woodland, Red River, . . . . . . . . . 128 | Wylie, Taylor |
| Winscott, Tarrant | Woodland, Robertson | Wylieville, Erath |
| Winshire, Jefferson | Woodland Hills, Dallas | Wylma, Shelby |
| Winston, Dallas | Woodland Park, Nueces | Wyly, Gaines |
| Winston, Scurry-Mitchell | *Woodlawn, Harrison, . . . . . . . . . 370 | Wynder, Panola |
| Winter's Mill, Hays | Woodlawn, Jasper | Wynema, Foard |
| Winterfield, Hopkins | WOODLOCH, Montgomery, (247) . . . . . . . . . . . . . . . . . . 253 | Wynne, Swisher-Castro |
| | | Wynne, Van Zandt, . . . . . . . . . . . 175 |

| Town,County ...........Pop. 2002 | Town,County ...........Pop. 2002 | Town,County ...........Pop. 2002 |
|---|---|---|

Wynnewood, Walker
Wynton, Hunt
Wysers Bluff, Walker

**X**

X-ray, Erath

**Y**

Yager, Blanco
Yakima, Collin
Yakima, Grayson
Yale, Franklin
Yale Seminary, Henderson
Yam, Walker
Yampareka, Foard-Hamilton
*Yancey, Medina, 12............202
Yancey, Panola
Yancy, Hunt
Yancy, Smith
Yandell, Tom Green
Yanna, Franklin
*YANTIS, Wood, 102 (321) .......332
Yantis' Store, Brown
Yarboro, Grimes
Yarbrough Bend, McMullen
Yarbroville, Limestone
**Yard, Anderson,................18**
Yarnall, Carson
**Yarrellton, Milam,...............35**
Yaterville, Hill
Yates, Hill
Yates, Kimble
Yates Prairie, Delta
Yegua, Burleson
Yegua, Lee
Yegua, Lee
Yeldell, Freestone
Yellow Bank, Lavaca
Yellow Bank, Medina
Yellow Bush, Camp
Yellow House, Lamb
Yellow House Cañon, Crosby
Yellow Mound, Eastland
**Yellowpine, Sabine,.............74**
Yellow Prairie, Burleson
Yell Settlement, Hays
Yerby, Freestone
Yero, Walker
Yesner, Hopkins

Yew, Fannin
Yewpon, Bastrop
*YOAKUM, Lavaca-DeWitt, 330
   (5,731).................5,723
Yoca, Gaines
York, Wharton
York Creek, Guadalupe
*YORKTOWN, DeWitt, 127
   (2,271).................2,299
Youens, Montgomery
Yougeen, Bee
**Young, Freestone, ............. 27**
Young, Panola
Young's Settlement, Bastrop
Young's Store, Fayette
Youngblood, Panola
Younger, Navarro
Youngsboro, Smith
**Youngsport, Bell, ............. 40**
Younkin, Webb
**Yowell, Delta-Hunt,............ 15**
*Ysleta [del Sur Pueblo], El Paso,...
   (421) ................... 421
Yturria, Willacy
Yubadam, Harrison
Yucca, Uvalde
Yuma, Brazos
Yuno, Angelina
Yznaga, Cameron, (103)....... 100

**Z**

**Zabcikville, Bell,.............. 38**
Zack, Brazos
Zana, San Augustine
Zandt, Kaufman
Zanzenburg, Kerr
Zapalac, Fayette
*Zapata, Zapata, 264
   (4,856).................5,056
**Zapata Ranch, Willacy,**
   (88) ..................... 92
Zapp, Fayette
Zaragosa, Starr
Zareda, Sterling
Zavala, Jasper
Zavala, Smith
*ZAVALLA, Angelina, 44
   (647) .................... 651
Zavalla, Zavala

Zedlar's Mills, Gonzales
Zeevee, Hill
Zeirath, Jasper
Zelda, Leon
Zella, McMullen
Zelma, Stephens
Zelo, Jones
Zenith, Swisher
Zeno, Smith
*Zephyr, Brown, 22 ........... 198
Zig Zag, Medina
Ziler, Howard
Zim, Montague
**Zimerman, Pecos**
**Zimmerscheidt, Colorado, ....... 50**
Zink's Settlement, Kendall
Zinnia, Montague
Zint, Gonzales
Zion, Denton
Zion Grove, Rusk
**Zion Hill, Guadalupe, ........... 30**
Zion Hill, Jasper
Zion Hill, Trinity
Zion Hill, Upshur
Zionville, Washington
Zipp City, Dallas
**Zipperlandville, Falls,........... 22**
**Zippville, Guadalupe, ......... 110**
Zita, Randall
Zither, Montgomery
Zoar, Gonzales
Zobel's, DeWitt
Zodiac, Gillespie
Zollicoffer's Mill, Hill
**Zorn, Guadalupe, .............. 60**
Zourette, Brown
Zourette, Comanche
Zuber, Panola
**Zuehl, Guadalupe, (346)....... 378**
Zulch, Madison
Zulime, Presidio
Zulrich, Madison
Zulu, Hansford
Zummo, Jefferson
Zuniga, Nolan
**Zunkerville, Karnes,........... 15**
Zury, Cottle
Zybach, Hemphill
Zybach, Wheeler

CITIES & TOWNS

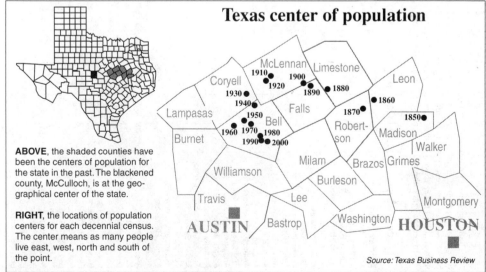

**Texas center of population**

ABOVE, the shaded counties have been the centers of population for the state in the past. The blackened county, McCulloch, is at the geographical center of the state.

RIGHT, the locations of population centers for each decennial census. The center means as many people live east, west, north and south of the point.

Source: Texas Business Review

# City Population History, 1850-2000

The table shows, for a selected list of cities, a complete record of population for each decennial year, insofar as such record exists. The official census record is presented below, with a few exceptions. Unofficial figures are given where census figures are unavailable. These, as well as other anomalies, are explained in footnotes. In recent years, the official census has included not only incorporated towns, but also unincorporated towns that meet certain federal criteria. These are called "Census Designated Places," and some are included in this list. At least one town from each county is listed. Where no figure is given, it means that no census was taken for it. It does not necessarily mean that the town did not exist. Some Texas towns were in existence many years before incorporating.

| City, County | 1850 | 1860 | 1870 | 1880 | 1890 | 1900 | 1910 | 1920 | 1930 | 1940 | 1950 | 1960 | 1970 | 1980 | 1990†† | 2000 | % Change 90-00 |
|---|---|---|---|---|---|---|---|---|---|---|---|---|---|---|---|---|---|
| Abernathy, Hale | | | | | | | | | 858 | 847 | 1,692 | 2,491 | 2,625 | 2,904 | 2,720 | 2,839 | 4.38 |
| Abilene, Taylor | | | | | 3,194 | 3,411 | 9,204 | 10,274 | 23,175 | 26,612 | 45,570 | 90,368 | 89,653 | 98,315 | 106,707 | 115,930 | 8.64 |
| Addison, Dallas | | | | | | | | | | | | 308 | 593 | 5,553 | 8,783 | 14,166 | 61.29 |
| Alamo, Hidalgo | | | | | | | | | 1,018 | 1,944 | 3,017 | 4,121 | 4,291 | 5,831 | 8,210 | 14,760 | 79.78 |
| Alamo Heights, Bexar | | | | | | 999 | | 1,469 | 3,874 | 5,700 | 8,000 | 7,552 | 6,933 | 6,252 | 6,502 | 7,319 | 12.57 |
| Albany, Shackelford | | | | 129 | 857 | | | | 2,422 | 2,230 | 2,255 | 2,200 | 1,978 | 2,450 | 1,962 | 1,921 | -2.09 |
| Alice, Jim Wells | | | | | | | 2,136 | 1,880 | 4,239 | 7,792 | 16,449 | 20,861 | 20,121 | 20,961 | 19,788 | 19,010 | -3.93 |
| Allen, Collin | | | | | | | | 931 | | | | 659 | 1,940 | 8,314 | 19,315 | 43,554 | 125.49 |
| Alpine, Brewster | | | | | | | | | 3,495 | 3,866 | 5,261 | 4,740 | 5,971 | 5,465 | 5,622 | 5,786 | 2.92 |
| Alton, Hidalgo | | | | | | | | | | | | | | 2,732 | 3,069 | 4,384 | 42.85 |
| Alvarado, Johnson | | | | | 1,543 | 1,342 | 1,155 | 1,284 | 1,210 | 1,324 | 1,656 | 1,907 | 2,129 | 2,701 | 2,918 | 3,288 | 12.68 |
| Alvin, Brazoria | | | | | 261 | 996 | 1,453 | 1,519 | 1,511 | 3,087 | 3,701 | 5,643 | 10,671 | 16,515 | 19,220 | 21,413 | 11.41 |
| Amarillo, Potter | | | | | 482 | 1,442 | 9,957 | 15,494 | 43,132 | 51,686 | 74,246 | 137,969 | 127,010 | 149,230 | 157,571 | 173,627 | 10.19 |
| Anahuac, Chambers | | | | | | | | ‡500 | ‡800 | ‡1,800 | 1,282 | 2,105 | 1,881 | 1,840 | 1,993 | 2,210 | 10.89 |
| Andrews, Andrews | | | | | | | | | | 611 | 3,294 | 11,135 | 8,625 | 11,061 | 10,678 | 9,652 | -9.61 |
| Angleton, Brazoria | | | | | | | 1,842 | | 1,229 | 1,763 | 3,399 | 7,312 | 9,770 | 13,929 | 17,140 | 18,130 | 5.78 |
| Anson, Jones | | | | | 1,764 | 1,301 | 1,043 | 1,425 | 2,093 | 2,338 | 2,708 | 2,890 | 2,615 | 2,831 | 2,644 | 2,556 | -3.33 |
| Anthony, El Paso | | | | | | | | | | | | 1,082 | 2,154 | 2,640 | 3,328 | 3,850 | 15.69 |
| Aransas Pass, San Patricio | | | | | | | 1,197 | 1,569 | 2,482 | 4,095 | 5,396 | 6,956 | 5,813 | 7,173 | 7,180 | 8,138 | 13.34 |
| Archer City, Archer | | | | | | 187 | 825 | 689 | 1,512 | 1,675 | 1,895 | 1,974 | 1,722 | 1,862 | 1,784 | 1,848 | 3.59 |
| Arlington, Tarrant | | | | | 664 | 1,079 | 1,794 | 3,031 | 3,661 | 4,240 | 7,692 | 44,775 | 89,723 | 160,123 | 261,717 | 332,969 | 27.22 |
| Aspermont, Stonewall | | | | | | 205 | | 436 | 769 | 1,041 | 1,060 | 1,275 | 1,198 | 1,357 | 1,214 | 1,021 | -15.90 |
| Athens, Henderson | *177 | | †500 | | | 1,604 | 2,261 | 3,176 | 4,342 | 4,765 | 5,194 | 7,086 | 9,582 | 10,197 | 10,982 | 11,297 | 2.87 |
| Atlanta, Cass | | | | | | | | 1,685 | 1,469 | 2,453 | 3,782 | 4,076 | 5,007 | 6,272 | 6,118 | 5,745 | -6.10 |
| Austin, Travis | 629 | 3,494 | 4,428 | 11,013 | 14,575 | 22,258 | 29,860 | 34,876 | 53,120 | 87,930 | 132,459 | 186,545 | 251,808 | 345,496 | 472,020 | 656,562 | 39.10 |
| Azle, Tarrant | | | | | | | | | | | | 2,969 | 4,493 | 5,822 | 8,868 | 9,600 | 8.25 |
| Balch Springs, Dallas | | | | | | | | | | | 376 | 6,821 | 10,464 | 13,746 | 17,406 | 19,375 | 11.31 |
| Balcones Heights, Bexar | | | | | | | | | | | | 950 | 2,504 | 2,853 | 3,022 | 3,016 | -0.20 |
| Ballinger, Runnels | | | | | 1,390 | 1,128 | 3,536 | 2,767 | 4,187 | 4,472 | 5,302 | 5,043 | 4,203 | 4,207 | 3,975 | 4,243 | 6.74 |
| Bandera, Bandera | | | | | 372 | 419 | | ‡700 | ‡580 | ‡1,250 | ‡1,325 | ‡1,065 | 891 | 947 | 877 | 957 | 9.12 |
| Barrett, Harris | | | | | | | | | | | | 2,364 | 2,750 | nc | 3,052 | 2,872 | -5.90 |
| Bastrop, Bastrop | | | | 1,546 | 1,634 | 2,145 | 1,707 | 1,828 | 1,895 | 1,976 | 3,176 | 3,001 | 3,112 | 3,789 | 4,044 | 5,340 | 32.05 |
| Bay City, Matagorda | | | | | | | 3,156 | 3,454 | 4,070 | 6,594 | 9,427 | 11,656 | 11,733 | 17,837 | 18,170 | 18,667 | 2.74 |
| **Baytown, Harris | | | | | | | | | | | 22,983 | 28,159 | 43,980 | 56,923 | 63,843 | 66,430 | 4.05 |
| Beaumont, Jefferson | *151 | | | | 3,296 | 9,427 | 20,640 | 40,422 | 57,732 | 59,061 | 94,014 | 119,175 | 115,919 | 118,102 | 114,323 | 113,866 | -0.40 |
| Bedford, Tarrant | | | | | | | | | | | | 2,706 | 10,049 | 20,821 | 43,762 | 47,152 | 7.75 |
| Beeville, Bee | | | | | ‡1,311 | ‡2,311 | 3,269 | 3,062 | 4,806 | 6,789 | 9,348 | 13,811 | 13,506 | 14,574 | 13,547 | 13,129 | -3.09 |
| Bellaire, Harris | | | | | | | | | 390 | 1,124 | 10,173 | 19,872 | 19,009 | 14,950 | 13,842 | 15,642 | 12.99 |

| City, County | 1850 | 1860 | 1870 | 1880 | 1890 | 1900 | 1910 | 1920 | 1930 | 1940 | 1950 | 1960 | 1970 | 1980 | 1990†† | % Change 90-00 | 2000 |
|---|---|---|---|---|---|---|---|---|---|---|---|---|---|---|---|---|---|
| Bellmead, McLennan | | | | | | | | | 1,533 | 1,347 | 2,112 | 5,127 | 7,698 | 7,569 | 8,336 | 10.53 | 9,214 |
| Bellville, Austin | | | | | | | | | | | | 2,218 | 2,371 | 2,860 | 3,378 | 12.31 | 3,794 |
| Belton, Bell | 300 | 305 | 777 | 1,797 | 3,000 | 3,700 | 4,164 | 5,098 | 3,779 | 3,572 | 6,246 | 8,163 | 8,696 | 10,660 | 12,463 | 17.33 | 14,623 |
| Benavides, Duval | | | | | | | | | | 3,081 | 3,016 | 2,459 | 2,112 | 1,978 | 1,788 | -5.70 | 1,686 |
| Benbrook, Tarrant | | | | | | | | | | | 617 | 3,254 | 8,169 | 13,579 | 19,564 | 3.29 | 20,208 |
| Benjamin, Knox | | | | | | 107 | | 500 | 485 | 599 | 531 | 308 | 308 | 257 | 225 | 17.33 | 264 |
| Big Lake, Reagan | | | | | | | | | 832 | 763 | 2,152 | 2,668 | 2,489 | 3,404 | 3,672 | -21.43 | 2,885 |
| Big Spring, Howard | | | | | | ‡1,255 | 4,102 | 4,273 | 13,735 | 12,604 | 17,286 | 31,230 | 28,735 | 24,804 | 23,093 | 9.27 | 25,233 |
| Bishop, Nueces | | | | | | | | | 953 | 1,329 | 2,731 | 3,722 | 3,466 | 3,706 | 3,337 | -0.96 | 3,305 |
| Boerne, Kendall | | | | | | | 886 | 1,153 | 1,117 | 1,271 | 1,802 | 2,169 | 2,432 | 3,229 | 4,361 | 41.66 | 6,178 |
| Bonham, Fannin | *477 | | | 1,880 | 3,361 | 5,042 | 4,844 | 6,008 | 5,655 | 6,349 | 7,049 | 7,357 | 7,698 | 7,338 | 6,688 | 49.37 | 9,990 |
| Borger, Hutchinson | | | | | | | | | 6,532 | 10,018 | 18,059 | 20,911 | 14,195 | 15,837 | 15,675 | -8.76 | 14,302 |
| Bowie, Montague | | | | | 1,486 | 2,600 | 2,874 | 3,179 | 3,131 | 3,470 | 4,544 | 4,566 | 5,185 | 5,610 | 4,990 | 4.59 | 5,219 |
| Brackettville, Kinney | | | | | | | | | 1,822 | 2,653 | 1,858 | 1,662 | 1,539 | 1,676 | 1,740 | 7.82 | 1,876 |
| Brady, McCulloch | | | | 115 | 560 | 690 | 2,669 | 2,197 | 3,983 | 5,002 | 5,944 | 5,338 | 5,557 | 5,969 | 5,946 | -7.11 | 5,523 |
| Brazoria, Brazoria | | | | | | | | 1,846 | | | 776 | 1,291 | 1,681 | 3,025 | 2,717 | 2.58 | 2,787 |
| Breckenridge, Stephens | | | | | | | | 5,066 | 7,569 | 5,826 | 6,610 | 6,273 | 5,944 | 6,921 | 5,665 | 3.58 | 5,868 |
| Brenham, Washington | | | 2,221 | 4,101 | 5,209 | 5,968 | 4,718 | | 5,974 | 6,435 | 6,941 | 7,740 | 8,922 | 10,966 | 11,952 | 13.01 | 13,507 |
| Bridge City, Orange | | | | | | | | | | | | 4,677 | 8,164 | 7,667 | 8,010 | 8.00 | 8,651 |
| Bridgeport, Wise | | | | | 498 | 900 | 2,000 | 1,872 | 2,464 | 1,735 | 2,049 | 3,218 | 3,614 | 3,737 | 3,581 | 20.33 | 4,309 |
| Brownfield, Terry | | | | | | | | | 1,907 | 4,009 | 6,161 | 10,286 | 9,647 | 10,387 | 9,560 | -0.75 | 9,488 |
| Brownsville, Cameron | | 2,734 | 4,905 | 4,938 | 6,134 | 6,305 | 10,517 | 11,791 | 22,021 | 22,083 | 36,066 | 48,040 | 52,522 | 84,997 | 107,027 | 30.55 | 139,722 |
| Brownwood, Brown | | | | 725 | 2,176 | 6,965 | 6,967 | 8,223 | 12,789 | 13,398 | 20,181 | 16,974 | 17,368 | 19,203 | 18,387 | 2.32 | 18,813 |
| Bryan, Brazos | | | | | 2,979 | 3,589 | 4,132 | 6,307 | 7,814 | 11,842 | 18,102 | 27,542 | 33,719 | 44,337 | 55,002 | 19.38 | 65,660 |
| Buffalo, Leon | | | | 190 | | 310 | | 510 | 470 | 737 | 966 | 1,108 | 1,242 | 1,507 | 1,555 | 16.01 | 1,804 |
| Bunker Hill Village, Harris | | | | | | | | | | | | 2,216 | 3,977 | 3,750 | 3,391 | 7.76 | 3,654 |
| Burkburnett, Wichita | | | | | | | | 5,300 | 3,281 | 2,814 | 4,555 | 7,621 | 9,230 | 10,668 | 10,145 | 7.71 | 10,927 |
| Burleson, Johnson | | | | | | | | 241 | 591 | 573 | 791 | 2,345 | 7,713 | 11,734 | 16,113 | 30.18 | 20,976 |
| Burnet, Burnet | | | | | 1,454 | 1,003 | 981 | 1,055 | 1,055 | 1,945 | 2,394 | 2,864 | 2,864 | 3,410 | 3,423 | 38.33 | 4,735 |
| Caldwell, Burleson | | | | | 1,250 | 1,535 | 1,476 | 1,689 | 1,724 | 2,165 | 2,109 | 2,204 | 2,308 | 2,953 | 3,181 | 8.43 | 3,449 |
| Calvert, Robertson | | | | 2,280 | 2,632 | 3,322 | 2,579 | 2,099 | 2,103 | 2,366 | 2,548 | 2,073 | 2,072 | 1,732 | 1,536 | -7.16 | 1,426 |
| Cameron, Milam | | | | | 1,608 | 3,341 | 3,263 | 4,298 | 4,565 | 5,040 | 5,052 | 5,640 | 5,546 | 5,721 | 5,635 | -0.02 | 5,634 |
| Canadian, Hemphill | | | | | | | 1,648 | 2,187 | 2,068 | 2,151 | 2,700 | 2,239 | 2,292 | 3,491 | 2,417 | -7.61 | 2,233 |
| Canton, Van Zandt | | | | | | | | 583 | 704 | 715 | 881 | 1,114 | 2,283 | 2,845 | 2,949 | 11.63 | 3,292 |
| Canyon, Randall | | | | | | | 1,400 | 1,618 | 2,821 | 2,622 | 4,364 | 5,864 | 8,333 | 10,724 | 11,365 | 13.29 | 12,875 |
| Carrizo Springs, Dimmit | | | | | | | | 954 | 2,171 | 2,494 | 4,316 | 5,699 | 5,374 | 6,886 | 5,745 | -1.57 | 5,655 |
| Carrollton, Dallas | | | | | | | | 573 | 689 | 921 | 1,610 | 4,242 | 13,855 | 40,591 | 82,169 | 33.35 | 109,576 |
| Carthage, Panola | | | | | | | | 1,366 | 1,651 | 2,178 | 4,750 | 5,262 | 5,392 | 6,447 | 6,496 | 2.59 | 6,664 |
| Castle Hills, Bexar | | | | | | | | | | | | 2,622 | 5,311 | 4,773 | 4,198 | 0.10 | 4,202 |
| Cedar Hill, Dallas | | | | | | | | | | 476 | 732 | 1,848 | 2,610 | 6,849 | 19,988 | 60.56 | 32,093 |
| Cedar Park, Williamson | | | | | | | | | | | | | | 3,474 | 5,161 | 404.73 | 26,049 |
| Center, Shelby | | | | 223 | 288 | 318 | 1,684 | 1,838 | 2,510 | 3,010 | 4,323 | 4,510 | 4,989 | 5,827 | 4,950 | 14.71 | 5,678 |
| Centerville, Leon | | | | | | | | ‡500 | 388 | 900 | 961 | 836 | 831 | 799 | 812 | 11.21 | 903 |
| Channing, Hartley | | | | | | 204 | | ‡475 | ‡500 | ‡475 | ‡300 | 390 | 336 | 304 | 277 | 28.52 | 356 |
| Childress, Childress | | | | | | 692 | 3,818 | 5,003 | 7,163 | 6,434 | 7,619 | 6,399 | 5,408 | 5,817 | 5,055 | 34.09 | 6,778 |
| Cisco, Eastland | | | | | 1,063 | 1,514 | 2,410 | 7,422 | 6,027 | 4,868 | 5,230 | 4,499 | 4,160 | 4,517 | 3,813 | 1.00 | 3,851 |

| City, County | 1850 | 1860 | 1870 | 1880 | 1890 | 1900 | 1910 | 1920 | 1930 | 1940 | 1950 | 1960 | 1970 | 1980 | 1990†† | % Change 90-00 | 2000 |
|---|---|---|---|---|---|---|---|---|---|---|---|---|---|---|---|---|---|
| Clarendon, Donley | | | | | | | 1,946 | 2,456 | 2,756 | 2,431 | 2,577 | 2,172 | 1,974 | 2,220 | 2,067 | -4.50 | 1,974 |
| Clarksville, Red River | ‡700 | *400 | | | 1,588 | 2,069 | 2,065 | 3,386 | 2,952 | 4,095 | 4,353 | 3,851 | 3,346 | 4,917 | 4,311 | -9.93 | 3,883 |
| Claude, Armstrong | | | | | 285 | 310 | 692 | 770 | 1,041 | 761 | 820 | 1,005 | 992 | 1,112 | 1,199 | 9.51 | 1,313 |
| Cleburne, Johnson | | | 683 | 1,855 | 3,278 | 7,493 | 10,364 | 12,820 | 11,539 | 10,558 | 12,905 | 15,381 | 16,015 | 19,218 | 22,205 | 17.11 | 26,005 |
| Cleveland, Liberty | | | | | | | | | 1,422 | 1,783 | 5,183 | 5,838 | 5,627 | 5,977 | 7,124 | 6.75 | 7,605 |
| Clifton, Bosque | | | | | | | 1,137 | 1,327 | 1,367 | 1,732 | 1,837 | 2,335 | 2,578 | 3,063 | 3,195 | 10.86 | 3,542 |
| Clute, Brazoria | | | | | | | | | | | | 4,501 | 6,023 | 9,577 | 9,467 | 10.11 | 10,424 |
| Clyde, Callahan | | | | | | | 495 | 610 | 706 | 800 | 908 | 1,116 | 1,635 | 2,562 | 3,002 | 11.43 | 3,345 |
| Cockrell Hill, Dallas | | | | | | | | | | 1,246 | 2,207 | 3,104 | 3,515 | 3,262 | 3,746 | 18.61 | 4,443 |
| Coldspring, San Jacinto | | | | ‡400 | 439 | | | ‡500 | ‡500 | ‡500 | ‡500 | ‡655 | ‡675 | 569 | 538 | 28.44 | 691 |
| Coleman, Coleman | | | | | 906 | 1,362 | 3,046 | 2,868 | 6,078 | 6,054 | 6,530 | 6,371 | 5,608 | 5,960 | 5,410 | -5.23 | 5,127 |
| College Station, Brazos | | | | | | | | | | 2,184 | 7,925 | 11,396 | 11,676 | 37,272 | 52,443 | 29.45 | 67,890 |
| Colleyville, Tarrant | | | | | | | | | | | | 1,491 | 3,368 | 6,700 | 12,724 | 54.32 | 19,636 |
| Colorado City, Mitchell | | | | ‡1,200 | | | 1,840 | 1,766 | 4,671 | 5,213 | 6,774 | 6,457 | 5,227 | 5,405 | 4,749 | -9.85 | 4,281 |
| Columbus, Colorado | | | | 1,959 | 1,226 | 2,070 | | | 2,054 | 2,422 | 2,878 | 3,656 | 3,342 | 3,923 | 3,367 | 16.31 | 3,916 |
| Comanche, Comanche | | | | 704 | 810 | 1,800 | 2,756 | 3,524 | 2,435 | 3,209 | 3,840 | 3,415 | 3,933 | 4,075 | 4,087 | 9.66 | 4,482 |
| Commerce, Hunt | | | | | | | 2,818 | 3,842 | 4,267 | 4,699 | 5,889 | 5,789 | 9,534 | 8,136 | 6,825 | 12.37 | 7,669 |
| Conroe, Montgomery | | | | | | | 1,374 | 1,858 | 2,457 | 4,624 | 7,298 | 9,192 | 11,969 | 18,034 | 27,675 | 33.01 | 36,811 |
| Converse, Bexar | | | | | | | | | | | | | 1,383 | 4,907 | 8,887 | 29.49 | 11,508 |
| Cooper, Delta | | | | | 629 | 1,518 | 1,513 | 2,563 | 2,023 | 2,537 | 2,350 | 2,213 | 2,258 | 2,338 | 2,153 | -0.14 | 2,150 |
| Coppell, Dallas | | | | | | | | 509 | 406 | 356 | | 666 | 1,728 | 3,826 | 16,881 | 113.01 | 35,958 |
| Copperas Cove, Coryell | | | | | | | | | | | 1,052 | 4,567 | 10,818 | 19,469 | 24,079 | 22.90 | 29,592 |
| Corpus Christi, Nueces | | 175 | 2,140 | 3,257 | 4,387 | 4,703 | 8,222 | 10,522 | 27,741 | 57,301 | 108,287 | 167,690 | 204,525 | 231,999 | 257,453 | 7.77 | 277,454 |
| Corsicana, Navarro | | | 80 | 3,373 | 6,285 | 9,313 | 9,749 | 11,356 | 15,202 | 15,232 | 19,211 | 20,344 | 19,972 | 21,712 | 22,911 | 6.87 | 24,485 |
| Cotulla, La Salle | | | | | | | 1,880 | 1,058 | 3,175 | 3,633 | 4,418 | 3,960 | 3,415 | 3,912 | 3,694 | -2.17 | 3,614 |
| Crane, Crane | | | | | | | | | | 1,420 | 2,154 | 3,796 | 3,427 | 3,622 | 3,533 | -9.68 | 3,191 |
| Crockett, Houston | ‡600 | ‡1,500 | | 599 | 1,445 | 2,612 | 3,947 | 3,061 | 4,441 | 4,536 | 5,932 | 5,356 | 6,616 | 7,405 | 7,024 | 1.67 | 7,141 |
| Crosbyton, Crosby | | | | | | | | 809 | 1,250 | 1,615 | 1,878 | 2,650 | 2,251 | 2,289 | 2,026 | -7.50 | 1,874 |
| Crowell, Foard | | | | | | 278 | 1,341 | 1,175 | 1,946 | 1,817 | 1,922 | 1,710 | 1,399 | 1,509 | 1,230 | -7.24 | 1,141 |
| Crowley, Tarrant | | | | | | | | | | | | 583 | 2,662 | 5,852 | 6,974 | 7.07 | 7,467 |
| Crystal City, Zavala | | | | | | | | 800 | 6,609 | 6,529 | 7,198 | 9,101 | 8,104 | 8,334 | 8,263 | -12.99 | 7,190 |
| Cuero, DeWitt | | | | 1,333 | 2,442 | 3,422 | 3,109 | 3,671 | 4,672 | 5,474 | 7,498 | 7,338 | 6,956 | 7,124 | 6,700 | -1.93 | 6,571 |
| Daingerfield, Morris | | | | | | | | | | 1,032 | 1,668 | 3,133 | 2,630 | 3,030 | 2,655 | -5.20 | 2,517 |
| Dalhart, Dallam | | | | | | | 2,580 | 2,676 | 4,691 | 4,682 | 5,918 | 5,160 | 5,705 | 6,854 | 6,246 | 15.87 | 7,237 |
| Dallas, Dallas | *430 | ‡2,000 | ‡3,000 | 10,358 | 38,067 | 42,638 | 92,104 | 158,976 | 260,475 | 294,734 | 434,462 | 679,684 | 844,401 | 904,078 | 1,007,618 | 17.96 | 1,188,580 |
| Dayton, Liberty | | | | | | | | | 1,207 | 1,279 | 1,820 | 3,367 | 3,804 | 4,908 | 5,042 | 13.23 | 5,709 |
| Decatur, Wise | | | | 579 | 1,746 | 1,562 | 1,651 | 2,205 | 2,037 | 2,578 | 2,922 | 3,563 | 3,240 | 4,104 | 4,245 | 22.52 | 5,201 |
| Deer Park, Harris | | | | | | | | | | | 736 | 4,865 | 12,773 | 22,648 | 27,424 | 4.00 | 28,520 |
| Del Rio, Val Verde | | | | 50 | 1,980 | | | 10,589 | 11,693 | 13,343 | 14,211 | 18,612 | 21,330 | 30,034 | 30,705 | 10.30 | 33,867 |
| Denison, Grayson | | | | 3,975 | 10,958 | 11,807 | 13,632 | 17,065 | 13,850 | 15,581 | 17,504 | 22,748 | 24,923 | 23,884 | 21,505 | 5.90 | 22,773 |
| Denton, Denton | | | | 1,194 | 2,558 | 4,187 | 4,732 | 7,626 | 9,587 | 11,192 | 21,372 | 26,844 | 39,874 | 48,063 | 66,270 | 21.53 | 80,537 |
| Denver City, Yoakum | | | | | | | | | | | 1,855 | 4,302 | 4,133 | 4,704 | 5,156 | -24.11 | 3,985 |
| DeSoto, Dallas | | | | | | | | | | | 298 | 1,969 | 6,617 | 15,538 | 30,544 | 23.25 | 37,646 |
| Devine, Medina | | | | | | | 1,042 | 995 | 1,093 | 1,398 | 1,672 | 2,522 | 3,311 | 3,756 | 3,928 | 5.40 | 4,140 |
| Diboll, Angelina | | | | | | | | ‡150 | 1,363 | | 2,391 | 2,506 | 3,557 | 5,227 | 4,341 | 26.01 | 5,470 |
| Dickens, Dickens | | | | | | 176 | | | ‡400 | 465 | 416 | 400 | 295 | 409 | 322 | 3.11 | 332 |

| City, County | 1850 | 1860 | 1870 | 1880 | 1890 | 1900 | 1910 | 1920 | 1930 | 1940 | 1950 | 1960 | 1970 | 1980 | 1990†† | % Change 90-00 | 2000 |
|---|---|---|---|---|---|---|---|---|---|---|---|---|---|---|---|---|---|
| Dickinson, Galveston | | | | | | | | | | | 2,704 | 4,715 | 10,776 | 7,505 | 11,692 | 46.19 | 17,093 |
| Dilley, Frio | | | | | | | | | 929 | 1,244 | 1,809 | 2,118 | 2,362 | 2,579 | 2,632 | 39.59 | 3,674 |
| Dimmitt, Castro | | | | | | | | | 829 | 943 | 1,461 | 2,935 | 4,327 | 5,019 | 4,408 | -0.75 | 4,375 |
| Donna, Hidalgo | | | | | | | | 1,579 | 4,103 | 4,712 | 7,171 | 7,522 | 7,365 | 9,952 | 12,652 | 16.72 | 14,768 |
| Dublin, Erath | | | | 2,025 | | 2,370 | 2,551 | 3,229 | 2,271 | 2,546 | 2,761 | 2,443 | 2,810 | 2,723 | 3,190 | 17.68 | 3,754 |
| Dumas, Moore | | | | | | | | | | 2,117 | 6,127 | 8,477 | 9,771 | 12,194 | 12,871 | 6.81 | 13,747 |
| Duncanville, Dallas | | | | | | | | | | | 841 | 3,774 | 14,105 | 27,781 | 35,008 | 3.07 | 36,081 |
| Eagle Lake, Colorado | | | | | 769 | 1,107 | 1,717 | 2,017 | 2,343 | 2,124 | 2,787 | 3,565 | 3,587 | 3,921 | 3,551 | 3.18 | 3,664 |
| Eagle Pass, Maverick | | | | | | | 3,536 | 5,765 | 5,059 | 6,459 | 7,276 | 12,094 | 15,364 | 21,407 | 20,651 | 8.53 | 22,413 |
| Eastland, Eastland | | | | | | 596 | 855 | 9,368 | 4,648 | 3,849 | 3,626 | 3,292 | 3,178 | 3,747 | 3,690 | 2.14 | 3,769 |
| Edcouch, Hidalgo | | | | | | | | 593 | 914 | 1,758 | 2,925 | 2,814 | 2,656 | 3,092 | 2,878 | 16.12 | 3,342 |
| Eden, Concho | | | | | | | | | 1,194 | 1,603 | 1,978 | 1,500 | 1,291 | 1,294 | 1,567 | 63.43 | 2,561 |
| Edgecliff, Tarrant | | | | | | | | | | | | 339 | 1,143 | 2,695 | 2,715 | -6.08 | 2,550 |
| Edinburg, Hidalgo | | | | | | | | 1,406 | 4,821 | 8,718 | 12,383 | 18,706 | 17,163 | 24,075 | 31,091 | 55.88 | 48,465 |
| Edna, Jackson | | | | | | | | | 1,752 | 2,724 | 3,855 | 5,038 | 5,332 | 5,650 | 5,343 | 10.41 | 5,899 |
| El Campo, Wharton | | | | | | | 1,778 | 1,766 | 2,034 | 3,906 | 6,237 | 7,700 | 9,332 | 10,462 | 10,511 | 4.13 | 10,945 |
| Eldorado, Schleicher | | | | | | 112 | | 850 | 1,404 | 1,530 | 1,653 | 1,850 | 1,446 | 2,061 | 2,019 | -3.37 | 1,951 |
| Electra, Wichita | | | | | | | 640 | 4,744 | 6,712 | 5,588 | 4,970 | 4,759 | 3,895 | 3,755 | 3,113 | 1.77 | 3,168 |
| Elgin, Bastrop | | | | | | | 1,707 | 1,630 | 1,823 | 2,008 | 3,168 | 3,511 | 3,832 | 4,535 | 4,846 | 17.62 | 5,700 |
| El Lago, Harris | | | | | | | | | | | | | 2,308 | 3,129 | 3,269 | -5.93 | 3,075 |
| El Paso, El Paso | | | | | 10,338 | 15,096 | 39,279 | 77,560 | 102,421 | 96,810 | 130,485 | 276,687 | 322,261 | 425,259 | 515,342 | 9.38 | 563,662 |
| Elsa, Hidalgo | | | | | | | | 800 | 750 | 1,006 | 3,179 | 3,847 | 4,400 | 5,061 | 5,242 | 5.86 | 5,549 |
| Emory, Rains | | | | | 353 | 426 | | | | 700 | 648 | 570 | 693 | 813 | 963 | 6.02 | 1,021 |
| Ennis, Ellis | | | | 1,351 | 2,171 | 4,919 | 5,669 | 7,224 | 7,069 | 7,087 | 7,815 | 9,347 | 11,046 | 12,110 | 13,869 | 15.69 | 16,045 |
| Euless, Tarrant | | | | | | | | | | | 451 | 4,263 | 19,316 | 24,002 | 38,149 | 20.59 | 46,005 |
| Everman, Tarrant | | | | | | | | | | | | 1,076 | 4,570 | 5,387 | 5,672 | 2.89 | 5,836 |
| Fabens, El Paso | | | | | | | | | 1,623 | 1,047 | | 3,089 | 3,241 | | 5,599 | 43.65 | 8,043 |
| Fairfield, Freestone | | | | | | | | | | | 1,742 | 3,134 | 2,074 | 3,505 | 3,234 | -4.33 | 3,094 |
| Falfurrias, Brooks | | | | | | | | 1,518 | 1,581 | 1,708 | 6,712 | 6,515 | 6,355 | 6,103 | 5,788 | -8.48 | 5,297 |
| Farmers Branch, Dallas | | | | | | | | | | | 915 | 13,441 | 27,492 | 24,863 | 24,250 | 13.44 | 27,508 |
| Floresville, Wilson | | | | | 913 | 895 | 1,398 | 1,384 | 2,637 | 2,726 | 1,949 | 2,126 | 3,707 | 4,381 | 5,247 | 11.84 | 5,868 |
| Flower Mound, Denton | | | | | | | | | | | | | 1,685 | 4,402 | 15,527 | 226.54 | 50,702 |
| Floydada, Floyd | | | | | | | 664 | ‡1,061 | ‡1,200 | ‡1,000 | 3,210 | 3,769 | 4,109 | 4,193 | 3,896 | -5.65 | 3,676 |
| Forest Hill, Tarrant | | | | | | | | | | | 1,519 | 3,221 | 8,236 | 11,684 | 11,482 | 12.78 | 12,949 |
| Fort Davis, Jeff Davis | | | 615 | 1,162 | | 1,061 | | | | | ‡1,200 | 850 | 896 | 900 | ‡1,212 | | 1,050 |
| Fort Stockton, Pecos | | | | | | | | 1,297 | 2,695 | 3,294 | 4,444 | 6,373 | 8,283 | 8,688 | 8,524 | -7.95 | 7,846 |
| Fort Worth, Tarrant | | | 500 | 6,663 | 23,076 | 26,688 | 73,312 | 106,482 | 163,447 | 177,662 | 278,778 | 356,268 | 393,476 | 385,141 | 447,619 | 19.45 | 534,694 |
| Fredericksburg, Gillespie | | | | | | | 1,061 | 1,798 | 3,544 | 3,544 | 3,854 | 4,629 | 5,326 | 6,412 | 6,934 | 28.51 | 8,911 |
| Freeport, Brazoria | | | | | | | | | 3,162 | 2,579 | 6,012 | 11,619 | 11,997 | 13,444 | 11,389 | 11.58 | 12,708 |
| Freer, Duval | | | | | | | | | | 2,346 | 2,280 | 2,724 | 2,804 | 3,213 | 3,271 | -0.92 | 3,241 |
| Friendswood, Galveston | | | | | | | | | | | | | 5,675 | 10,719 | 22,814 | 27.28 | 29,037 |
| Friona, Parmer | | | | | | | | | 731 | 803 | 1,202 | 2,048 | 3,111 | 3,809 | 3,688 | 4.50 | 3,854 |
| Frisco, Collin | | | | | | 126 | 332 | 733 | 618 | 670 | 736 | 1,184 | 1,845 | 3,420 | 6,138 | 449.27 | 33,714 |
| Gail, Borden | | | | | | | | ‡126 | ‡175 | ‡200 | ‡200 | ‡200 | ‡178 | ‡189 | ‡202 | | 202 |
| Gainesville, Cooke | | | | 2,667 | 6,594 | 7,874 | 7,624 | 8,643 | 8,915 | 9,651 | 11,246 | 13,083 | 13,830 | 14,081 | 14,256 | 8.99 | 15,538 |
| Galena Park, Harris | | | | | | | | | | 1,562 | 7,186 | 10,852 | 10,479 | 9,879 | 10,033 | 5.57 | 10,592 |

| City, County | 1850 | 1860 | 1870 | 1880 | 1890 | 1900 | 1910 | 1920 | 1930 | 1940 | 1950 | 1960 | 1970 | 1980 | 1990†† | % Change 90-00 | 2000 |
|---|---|---|---|---|---|---|---|---|---|---|---|---|---|---|---|---|---|
| Galveston, Galveston | 4,117 | 7,307 | 13,818 | 22,248 | 29,084 | 37,788 | 36,981 | 44,255 | 52,938 | 60,862 | 66,568 | 67,175 | 61,809 | 61,902 | 59,067 | -3.08 | 57,247 |
| Garden City, Glasscock | | | | | | | | ‡100 | ‡250 | ‡250 | ‡270 | ‡270 | ‡286 | ‡293 | ‡293 | | ‡293 |
| Garland, Dallas | | | | | 478 | 819 | 804 | 1,421 | 1,584 | 2,233 | 10,571 | 38,501 | 81,437 | 138,857 | 180,635 | 19.45 | 215,768 |
| Gatesville, Coryell | | | | 434 | 1,375 | 1,865 | 1,929 | 2,499 | 2,601 | 3,177 | 3,856 | 4,626 | 4,683 | 6,260 | 11,492 | 35.67 | 15,591 |
| Georgetown, Williamson | †200 | | †320 | 1,354 | 2,447 | 2,790 | 3,096 | 2,871 | 3,583 | 3,682 | 4,951 | 5,218 | 6,395 | 9,468 | 14,842 | 90.94 | 28,339 |
| George West, Live Oak | | | | | | | | 1,650 | 1,835 | 2,166 | 1,533 | 1,878 | 2,022 | 2,627 | 2,586 | -2.40 | 2,524 |
| Giddings, Lee | | | | 624 | | | 1,484 | 2,268 | 1,963 | 3,138 | 2,532 | 2,821 | 2,783 | 3,950 | 4,093 | 24.73 | 5,105 |
| Gilmer, Upshur | | | | | | | | | | | 4,096 | 4,312 | 4,196 | 5,167 | 4,824 | -0.52 | 4,799 |
| Gladewater, Gregg | | | | | | | | | | 4,454 | 5,305 | 5,742 | 5,574 | 6,548 | 6,027 | 0.85 | 6,078 |
| Glen Rose, Somervell | | | | 132 | 400 | 890 | | ‡1,000 | 983 | 1,050 | 1,248 | 1,495 | 1,554 | 2,075 | 1,949 | 8.88 | 2,122 |
| Goliad, Goliad | 648 | 1,212 | | | | 1,261 | | ‡2,500 | 1,424 | 1,446 | 1,580 | 1,750 | 1,709 | 1,990 | 1,946 | 1.49 | 1,975 |
| Gonzales, Gonzales | 1,072 | | | 1,581 | 1,641 | 4,297 | 3,139 | 3,128 | 3,859 | 4,722 | 5,659 | 5,829 | 5,854 | 7,152 | 6,527 | 10.34 | 7,202 |
| **Goose Creek, Harris | | | | | | | | | 5,208 | 6,929 | | | | | | | |
| Graham, Young | | | | | 667 | 878 | 1,569 | 2,544 | 4,981 | 5,175 | 6,742 | 8,505 | 7,477 | 9,055 | 8,986 | -3.00 | 8,716 |
| Granbury, Hood | | | | | 1,164 | 1,410 | 1,336 | 1,364 | 996 | 1,166 | 1,683 | 2,227 | 2,473 | 3,332 | 4,045 | 41.36 | 5,718 |
| Grand Prairie, Dallas | | | | | | | 994 | 1,263 | 1,529 | 1,595 | 14,594 | 30,386 | 50,904 | 71,462 | 99,606 | 27.93 | 127,427 |
| Grand Saline, Van Zandt | | | | | | | 1,065 | 1,528 | 1,799 | 1,641 | 1,810 | 2,006 | 2,257 | 2,709 | 2,630 | 15.13 | 3,028 |
| Grapevine, Tarrant | | | | | | | 681 | 821 | 936 | 1,043 | 1,824 | 2,821 | 7,023 | 11,801 | 29,198 | 44.05 | 42,059 |
| Greenville, Hunt | *246 | | | | 4,330 | 6,860 | 8,850 | 12,384 | 12,407 | 13,995 | 14,727 | 19,087 | 22,043 | 22,161 | 23,071 | 3.85 | 23,960 |
| Gregory, San Patricio | | | | | | | | | | | 2,182 | 1,970 | 2,246 | 2,739 | 2,458 | -5.70 | 2,318 |
| Groesbeck, Limestone | | | | | 663 | 1,462 | 1,454 | 1,522 | 2,059 | 2,272 | | 2,498 | 2,396 | 3,373 | 3,360 | 27.71 | 4,291 |
| Groves, Jefferson | | | | | | | | | | | | 17,304 | 18,067 | 17,090 | 16,744 | -6.04 | 15,733 |
| Guthrie, King | | | | | | 101 | | ‡101 | | ‡101 | ‡150 | ‡210 | ‡125 | ‡140 | ‡160 | | ‡160 |
| Hallettsville, Lavaca | | | | | 1,011 | 1,457 | 1,379 | 1,444 | 1,406 | 1,581 | 2,000 | 2,808 | 2,712 | 2,865 | 2,718 | -13.72 | 2,345 |
| Haltom City, Tarrant | | | | | | | | | | | 5,760 | 23,133 | 28,127 | 29,014 | 32,856 | 18.75 | 39,018 |
| Hamilton, Hamilton | | | | | | | 1,548 | 2,018 | 2,048 | 2,716 | 3,077 | 3,106 | 2,760 | 3,189 | 2,937 | 1.36 | 2,977 |
| Hamlin, Jones | | | | | | | 1,978 | 1,633 | 2,328 | 2,406 | 3,659 | 3,791 | 3,325 | 3,248 | 2,791 | -19.46 | 2,248 |
| Harker Heights, Bell | | | | | | | | | | | | | 4,216 | 7,345 | 12,932 | 33.84 | 17,308 |
| Harlingen, Cameron | | | | | | | 2,346 | 1,784 | 12,124 | 13,306 | 23,229 | 41,207 | 33,503 | 43,543 | 48,746 | 18.09 | 57,564 |
| Haskell, Haskell | | | | | | | 2,353 | 2,300 | 2,632 | 3,051 | 3,836 | 4,016 | 3,655 | 3,782 | 3,362 | -7.61 | 3,106 |
| Hearne, Robertson | | | | 1,421 | | | | 2,741 | 2,956 | 3,511 | 4,872 | 5,172 | 4,982 | 5,418 | 5,132 | -8.61 | 4,690 |
| Hebbronville, Jim Hogg | | | | | | | | | | | 4,302 | 3,987 | 4,079 | ‡4,050 | 4,465 | 0.74 | 4,498 |
| Hedwig Village, Harris | | | | | | | | | | | | 1,182 | 3,255 | 2,506 | 2,616 | -10.78 | 2,334 |
| Hemphill, Sabine | | | | | | | | | | 739 | 969 | 913 | 1,005 | 1,353 | 1,182 | -6.43 | 1,106 |
| Hempstead, Waller | | | | | | 279 | | ‡3,100 | 731 | 1,674 | 1,395 | | 1,891 | 3,456 | 3,556 | 31.92 | 4,691 |
| Henderson, Rusk | *705 | | | | 2,100 | | | 2,273 | 2,932 | 6,437 | 6,833 | 9,666 | 10,187 | 11,473 | 11,139 | 1.20 | 11,273 |
| Henrietta, Clay | | | | | | 1,614 | 2,104 | 2,563 | 2,020 | 2,391 | 2,813 | 3,062 | 2,897 | 3,149 | 2,896 | 12.71 | 3,264 |
| Hereford, Deaf Smith | | | | | | | 1,750 | 1,696 | 2,458 | 2,584 | 5,207 | 6,752 | 13,414 | 15,853 | 14,745 | -1.00 | 14,597 |
| Hewitt, McLennan | | | | | | | | | | | | | 569 | 5,247 | 8,983 | 23.40 | 11,085 |
| Highland Park, Dallas | | | | | | ‡800 | 2,129 | 2,321 | 8,422 | 10,288 | 11,405 | 10,411 | 10,133 | 8,909 | 8,739 | 1.18 | 8,842 |
| Highlands, Harris | | | | | | | | | | | | | | | 6,632 | 6.89 | 7,089 |
| Highland Village, Denton | | | | | | | | | | | | | 516 | 3,246 | 7,027 | 73.23 | 12,173 |
| Hillsboro, Hill | | | †313 | | 2,541 | 5,346 | 6,115 | 6,952 | 7,823 | 7,799 | 8,363 | 7,402 | 7,224 | 7,397 | 7,072 | 16.40 | 8,232 |
| Hitchcock, Galveston | | | | | | | | | | | 1,105 | 5,216 | 5,565 | 6,655 | 5,868 | 8.83 | 6,386 |
| Hollywood Park, Bexar | | | | | | | | | | | | 783 | 2,299 | 3,231 | 2,870 | 3.94 | 2,983 |
| Hondo, Medina | | | | | | | | | | | 4,188 | 4,992 | 5,487 | 6,057 | 6,018 | 31.22 | 7,897 |

| City, County | 1850 | 1860 | 1870 | 1880 | 1890 | 1900 | 1910 | 1920 | 1930 | 1940 | 1950 | 1960 | 1970 | 1980 | 1990†† | % Change 90-00 | 2000 |
|---|---|---|---|---|---|---|---|---|---|---|---|---|---|---|---|---|---|
| Hooks, Bowie | | | | | | | | | | | 2,319 | 2,048 | 2,545 | 2,507 | 2,684 | 10.77 | 2,973 |
| Houston, Harris | 2,396 | 4,845 | 9,382 | 16,513 | 27,557 | 44,633 | 78,800 | 138,276 | 292,352 | 384,514 | 596,163 | 938,219 | 1,232,802 | 1,594,086 | 1,637,859 | 19.28 | 1,953,631 |
| Humble, Harris | | | | | | | | | | 1,371 | 1,388 | 1,711 | 3,278 | 6,729 | 12,060 | 20.89 | 14,579 |
| Huntsville, Walker | *892 | | †1,600 | §2,536 | 1,509 | 2,485 | 2,072 | 4,689 | 5,028 | 5,108 | 9,820 | 11,999 | 17,610 | 23,936 | 27,925 | 25.62 | 35,078 |
| Hurst, Tarrant | | | | | | | | | | | | 10,165 | 27,215 | 31,420 | 33,574 | 8.04 | 36,273 |
| Hutchins, Dallas | | | | | | | | | | | 743 | 1,100 | 1,755 | 2,996 | 2,719 | 3.16 | 2,805 |
| Ingleside, San Patricio | | | | | | | | | | | 1,424 | 3,022 | 3,763 | 5,436 | 5,696 | 64.82 | 9,388 |
| Iowa Park, Wichita | | | | | | | 603 | 2,041 | 2,009 | 1,980 | 2,110 | 3,295 | 5,796 | 6,184 | 6,072 | 5.91 | 6,431 |
| Irving, Dallas | | | | | | | | | 731 | 1,089 | 2,621 | 45,985 | 97,260 | 109,943 | 155,037 | 23.59 | 191,615 |
| Jacinto City, Harris | | | | | | | | | | | 6,856 | 9,547 | 9,563 | 8,953 | 9,343 | 10.26 | 10,302 |
| Jacksboro, Jack | | | | | 751 | 1,311 | 1,480 | 1,373 | 1,837 | 2,368 | 2,951 | 3,816 | 3,554 | 4,000 | 3,350 | 35.31 | 4,533 |
| Jacksonville, Cherokee | | | | | 970 | 1,568 | 2,875 | 3,723 | 6,748 | 7,213 | 8,607 | 9,590 | 9,734 | 12,264 | 12,765 | 8.64 | 13,868 |
| Jasper, Jasper | | | †360 | ‡500 | ‡473 | | | ‡750 | 3,393 | 3,497 | 4,403 | 4,889 | 6,251 | 6,959 | 7,160 | 15.18 | 8,247 |
| Jayton, Kent | | | | | | | 314 | | 623 | 770 | 633 | 700 | 703 | 638 | 608 | -15.63 | 513 |
| Jefferson, Marion | | 988 | 4,190 | 3,260 | 3,072 | 2,850 | 2,515 | 2,549 | 2,329 | 2,797 | 3,164 | 3,082 | 2,866 | 2,643 | 2,199 | -7.96 | 2,024 |
| Jersey Village, Harris | | | | | | | | | | | | 493 | 765 | 4,084 | 4,826 | 42.56 | 6,880 |
| Johnson City, Blanco | | | | | | 344 | | ‡400 | ‡400 | ‡750 | 645 | 595 | 767 | 872 | 932 | 27.79 | 1,191 |
| Jones Creek, Brazoria | | | | | | | | | | | | | 1,763 | 2,634 | 2,160 | -1.39 | 2,130 |
| Jourdanton, Atascosa | | | | | | | | | 767 | 950 | 1,481 | 1,504 | 1,271 | 2,743 | 3,220 | 15.90 | 3,732 |
| Junction, Kimble | | | | | | | | 682 | 1,415 | 2,086 | 2,471 | 2,441 | 2,654 | 2,593 | 2,654 | -1.36 | 2,618 |
| Karnes City, Karnes | | | | | | | | 787 | 1,141 | 1,571 | 2,588 | 2,603 | 2,926 | 3,296 | 2,916 | 18.55 | 3,457 |
| Katy, Harris | | | | | | | | | | | 849 | 1,569 | 2,923 | 5,660 | 8,004 | 47.11 | 11,775 |
| Kaufman, Kaufman | | | | | 1,282 | 1,378 | 1,959 | 2,501 | 2,279 | 2,654 | 2,714 | 3,087 | 4,012 | 4,658 | 5,251 | 23.60 | 6,490 |
| Keene, Johnson | | | | | | | | | | | | 1,532 | 2,440 | 3,013 | 3,944 | 26.85 | 5,003 |
| Keller, Tarrant | | | | | | | | | | | | 827 | 1,474 | 4,143 | 13,683 | 99.85 | 27,345 |
| Kenedy, Karnes | | | | | | | 1,147 | 2,015 | 2,610 | 2,891 | 4,234 | 4,301 | 4,156 | 4,356 | 3,763 | -7.33 | 3,487 |
| Kennedale, Tarrant | | | | | | | | | | | 1,046 | 1,521 | 3,076 | 2,594 | 4,096 | 42.75 | 5,850 |
| Kermit, Winkler | | | | | | | | | | 2,584 | 6,912 | 10,465 | 7,884 | 8,015 | 6,875 | -16.89 | 5,714 |
| Kerrville, Kerr | | | †226 | | 1,044 | 1,423 | 1,834 | 2,353 | 4,546 | 5,572 | 7,691 | 8,901 | 12,672 | 15,276 | 17,384 | 17.49 | 20,425 |
| Kilgore, Gregg | | | | | | | | | 1,260 | 6,708 | 9,638 | 10,092 | 9,495 | 10,968 | 11,066 | 2.12 | 11,301 |
| Killeen, Bell | | | | 156 | 285 | 780 | 1,265 | 1,298 | | 1,263 | 7,045 | 23,377 | 35,507 | 46,296 | 63,535 | 36.79 | 86,911 |
| Kingsville, Kleberg | | | | | | | | 4,770 | 6,815 | 7,782 | 16,898 | 25,297 | 28,995 | 28,808 | 25,276 | 1.18 | 25,575 |
| Kirby, Bexar | | | | | | | | | | | | 680 | 2,558 | 6,385 | 8,326 | 4.17 | 8,673 |
| Kountze, Hardin | | | | | | | | | | 1,644 | 1,651 | 1,768 | 2,173 | 2,752 | 2,067 | 2.32 | 2,115 |
| Lacy-Lakeview, McLennan | | | | | | | | | | | | 2,272 | 2,558 | | 3,617 | 59.36 | 5,764 |
| La Feria, Cameron | | | | | | | | 236 | 1,594 | 2,531 | 2,952 | 3,047 | 2,642 | 3,495 | 4,360 | 40.25 | 6,115 |
| La Grange, Fayette | | | 1,165 | 1,325 | 1,626 | 2,392 | 1,850 | 1,669 | 2,354 | | 2,738 | 3,623 | 3,092 | 3,768 | 3,951 | 13.34 | 4,478 |
| Lake Dallas, Denton | | | | | | | | | | | | | 1,431 | 3,177 | 3,656 | 68.65 | 6,166 |
| Lake Jackson, Brazoria | | | | | | | | | | | 2,897 | 9,651 | 13,376 | 19,102 | 22,771 | 15.88 | 26,386 |
| Lakeway, Travis | | | | | | | | | | | | | | 790 | 4,044 | 97.87 | 8,002 |
| Lake Worth, Tarrant | | | | | | | | | | | 2,351 | 3,833 | 4,958 | 4,394 | 4,591 | 0.59 | 4,618 |
| La Marque, Galveston | | | | | | | | | | | 7,359 | 13,969 | 16,131 | 15,372 | 14,120 | -3.10 | 13,682 |
| Lamesa, Dawson | | | | | | | | | 3,528 | 6,038 | 10,704 | 12,438 | 11,559 | 11,790 | 10,809 | -7.93 | 9,952 |
| Lampasas, Lampasas | | | | | 2,408 | 2,107 | 2,119 | 2,107 | 2,709 | 3,426 | 4,869 | 5,061 | 5,922 | 6,165 | 6,382 | 6.33 | 6,786 |
| Lancaster, Dallas | | | †420 | 653 | 741 | 1,045 | 1,115 | 1,190 | 1,133 | 1,151 | 1,632 | 7,501 | 10,522 | 14,807 | 22,117 | 17.08 | 25,894 |
| La Porte, Harris | | | | | | 537 | 678 | 889 | 1,280 | 3,072 | 4,429 | 4,512 | 7,149 | 14,062 | 27,923 | 14.17 | 31,880 |
| Laredo, Webb | | 1,256 | 2,046 | 3,521 | 11,319 | 13,429 | 14,855 | 22,710 | 32,618 | 39,274 | 51,910 | 60,678 | 69,024 | 91,449 | 122,899 | 43.68 | 176,576 |

| City, County | 1850 | 1860 | 1870 | 1880 | 1890 | 1900 | 1910 | 1920 | 1930 | 1940 | 1950 | 1960 | 1970 | 1980 | 1990†† | % Change 90-00 | 2000 |
|---|---|---|---|---|---|---|---|---|---|---|---|---|---|---|---|---|---|
| League City, Galveston | | | | | | 318 | | ‡150 | ‡700 | ‡550 | 1,341 | 2,622 | 10,818 | 16,578 | 30,159 | 50.68 | 45,444 |
| Leakey, Real | | | | | | | | | | | ‡550 | 450 | 393 | 468 | 399 | -3.01 | 387 |
| Leon Valley, Bexar | | | | | | | | | | | | 536 | 2,487 | 8,951 | 9,581 | -3.57 | 9,239 |
| Levelland, Hockley | | | | | | | | | 1,661 | 3,091 | 8,264 | 10,153 | 11,445 | 13,809 | 13,986 | -8.01 | 12,866 |
| Lewisville, Denton | | | | | | 865 | 980 | | 853 | 873 | 1,516 | 3,956 | 9,264 | 24,273 | 46,521 | 67.10 | 77,737 |
| Liberty, Liberty | | 584 | 458 | 497 | | | | 1,117 | 2,187 | 3,087 | 4,163 | 6,127 | 5,591 | 7,945 | 7,690 | 4.46 | 8,033 |
| Littlefield, Lamb | | | | | | | | | 3,218 | 3,817 | 6,540 | 7,236 | 6,738 | 7,409 | 6,489 | 0.28 | 6,507 |
| Live Oak, Bexar | | | | | | | | | | | | | 2,779 | 8,183 | 10,023 | -8.65 | 9,156 |
| Livingston, Polk | | | | | | | 1,687 | 928 | 1,165 | 1,851 | 2,865 | 3,398 | 3,965 | 4,928 | 5,019 | 8.25 | 5,433 |
| Llano, Llano | | | | | | | | 1,645 | 2,124 | 2,658 | 2,954 | 2,656 | 2,608 | 3,071 | 2,962 | 12.26 | 3,325 |
| Lockhart, Caldwell | *423 | | †500 | 718 | 1,233 | 2,306 | 2,945 | 3,731 | 4,367 | 5,018 | 5,573 | 6,084 | 6,489 | 7,953 | 9,205 | 26.18 | 11,615 |
| Longview, Gregg | | | | 1,525 | 2,034 | 3,591 | 5,155 | 5,713 | 5,036 | 13,758 | 24,502 | 40,050 | 46,744 | 62,762 | 70,311 | 4.31 | 73,344 |
| Lubbock, Lubbock | | | | | | | 1,938 | 4,051 | 20,520 | 31,853 | 71,747 | 128,691 | 149,101 | 173,979 | 186,206 | 7.17 | 199,564 |
| Lufkin, Angelina | | | | | 1,792 | 1,527 | 2,749 | 4,878 | 7,311 | 9,567 | 15,135 | 17,641 | 23,049 | 28,562 | 30,206 | 8.29 | 32,709 |
| Luling, Caldwell | | | | | 529 | 1,349 | 1,404 | 1,502 | 5,970 | 4,437 | 4,297 | 4,412 | 4,719 | 5,039 | 4,661 | 8.99 | 5,080 |
| Madisonville, Madison | | | | | | | | 1,079 | 1,294 | 2,095 | 2,393 | 2,324 | 2,881 | 3,660 | 3,569 | 16.53 | 4,159 |
| Mansfield, Tarrant | | | | | 418 | 694 | 627 | 719 | 635 | 774 | 964 | 1,375 | 3,658 | 8,092 | 15,615 | 79.51 | 28,031 |
| Manvel, Brazoria | | | | | | | | | | | | | 106 | 3,549 | 3,733 | -18.40 | 3,046 |
| Marble Falls, Burnet | | | | | | | 1,061 | 639 | 865 | 1,021 | 2,044 | 2,161 | 2,209 | 3,252 | 4,007 | 23.76 | 4,959 |
| Marfa, Presidio | | | | | | | | 3,553 | 3,909 | 3,805 | 3,603 | 2,799 | 2,682 | 2,466 | 2,424 | -12.50 | 2,121 |
| Marlin, Falls | | | | | 2,058 | 3,092 | 3,878 | 4,310 | 5,338 | 6,542 | 7,099 | 6,918 | 6,351 | 7,099 | 6,386 | 3.79 | 6,628 |
| Marshall, Harrison | ‡1,189 | ‡4,000 | 1,920 | 5,624 | 7,207 | 7,855 | 11,452 | 14,271 | 16,203 | 16,410 | 22,327 | 23,846 | 22,937 | 24,921 | 23,682 | 1.07 | 23,935 |
| Mart, McLennan | | | | | | ‡300 | 2,939 | 3,105 | 2,853 | 2,856 | 2,269 | 2,197 | 2,183 | 2,324 | 2,004 | 13.42 | 2,273 |
| Mason, Mason | | | | 575 | | 1,137 | | 1,200 | 12,000 | 1,500 | 2,448 | 1,815 | 1,806 | 2,153 | 2,041 | -4.56 | 2,134 |
| Matador, Motley | | | | | | 158 | | 692 | 1,302 | 1,376 | 1,325 | 1,217 | 1,091 | 1,052 | 790 | -6.33 | 740 |
| Mathis, San Patricio | | | | | | | | | | 1,950 | 4,050 | 6,075 | 5,351 | 5,667 | 5,423 | -7.17 | 5,034 |
| McAllen, Hidalgo | | | | | | | | 5,331 | 9,074 | 11,877 | 20,067 | 32,728 | 37,636 | 67,042 | 84,021 | 26.65 | 106,414 |
| McCamey, Upton | | | | | | | | | 3,446 | 2,595 | 3,121 | 3,375 | 2,647 | 2,436 | 2,493 | -27.60 | 1,805 |
| McGregor, McLennan | | | | | 774 | 1,435 | 1,864 | 2,081 | 2,041 | 2,062 | 2,669 | 4,642 | 4,365 | 4,513 | 4,683 | 0.94 | 4,727 |
| McKinney, Collin | *523 | | | 1,479 | 2,489 | 4,342 | 4,714 | 6,677 | 7,307 | 8,555 | 10,560 | 13,763 | 15,193 | 16,249 | 21,283 | 155.46 | 54,369 |
| Memphis, Hall | | | | | | 1,209 | 1,936 | 2,839 | 4,257 | 3,869 | 3,810 | 3,332 | 3,227 | 3,352 | 2,465 | 0.57 | 2,479 |
| Menard, Menard | | | | | | | | 1,164 | 1,969 | 2,375 | 2,685 | 1,914 | 1,740 | 1,697 | 1,606 | 2.93 | 1,653 |
| Mentone, Loving | | | | | | | | | | ‡150 | ‡110 | ‡110 | ‡44 | ‡44 | ‡50 | | ‡15 |
| Mercedes, Hidalgo | | | | | | | 1,209 | 3,414 | 6,608 | 7,624 | 10,081 | 10,943 | 9,355 | 11,851 | 12,694 | 7.52 | 13,649 |
| Mertzon, Irion | | | | | | | | 400 | 684 | 869 | 765 | 594 | 513 | 687 | 778 | 7.84 | 839 |
| Mesquite, Dallas | | | | | 135 | 406 | 687 | 674 | 729 | 1,045 | 1,696 | 27,526 | 55,131 | 67,053 | 101,484 | 22.70 | 124,523 |
| Mexia, Limestone | | | | 1,298 | 1,674 | 2,393 | 2,694 | 3,482 | 6,579 | 6,410 | 6,627 | 6,121 | 5,943 | 7,094 | 6,933 | -5.34 | 6,563 |
| Miami, Roberts | | | | | | 286 | | 937 | 953 | 713 | 645 | 656 | 611 | 813 | 675 | -12.89 | 588 |
| Midland, Midland | | | | | | | 2,192 | 1,795 | 5,484 | 9,352 | 21,713 | 62,625 | 59,463 | 70,525 | 89,443 | 6.21 | 94,996 |
| Midlothian, Ellis | | | | | 297 | 832 | 868 | 1,298 | 1,168 | 1,027 | 1,177 | 1,521 | 2,322 | 3,219 | 5,040 | 48.41 | 7,480 |
| Mineola, Wood | | | | 1,175 | 1,323 | 1,725 | 1,706 | 2,299 | 3,304 | 3,223 | 3,626 | 3,810 | 3,926 | 4,346 | 4,321 | 5.30 | 4,550 |
| Mineral Wells, Palo Pinto | | | | | 577 | 2,048 | 3,950 | 7,890 | 5,986 | 6,303 | 7,801 | 11,053 | 18,411 | 14,468 | 14,935 | 13.47 | 16,946 |
| Mission, Hidalgo | | | | | | | | 3,847 | 5,120 | 5,982 | 10,765 | 14,081 | 13,043 | 22,589 | 28,653 | 58.48 | 45,408 |
| Missouri City, Fort Bend | | | | | | | | | | | | 604 | 4,136 | 24,533 | 36,176 | 46.27 | 52,913 |
| Monahans, Ward | | | | | | | | | 816 | 3,944 | 6,311 | 8,567 | 8,333 | 8,397 | 8,101 | -15.80 | 6,821 |
| Mont Belvieu, Chambers | | | | | | | | ‡20 | ‡600 | ‡600 | ‡500 | ‡500 | 1,144 | 1,730 | 1,323 | 75.66 | 2,324 |

| City, County | 1850 | 1860 | 1870 | 1880 | 1890 | 1900 | 1910 | 1920 | 1930 | 1940 | 1950 | 1960 | 1970 | 1980 | 1990†† | % Change 90-00 | 2000 |
|---|---|---|---|---|---|---|---|---|---|---|---|---|---|---|---|---|---|
| Morton, Cochran | *227 | | | | | | | | | 1,137 | 2,274 | 2,731 | 2,738 | 2,674 | 2,597 | -13.40 | 2,249 |
| Mount Pleasant, Titus | | | | | | | 3,137 | 4,099 | 3,541 | 4,528 | 6,342 | 8,027 | 9,459 | 11,003 | 12,291 | 13.38 | 13,935 |
| Mount Vernon, Franklin | | | | 311 | 589 | 972 | | 1,212 | 1,222 | 1,443 | 1,423 | 1,338 | 1,806 | 2,025 | 2,219 | 3.02 | 2,286 |
| Muleshoe, Bailey | | | | | | | | | 779 | 1,327 | 2,477 | 3,871 | 4,525 | 4,842 | 4,571 | -0.90 | 4,530 |
| Munday, Knox | ‡468 | | | | | | 956 | 998 | 1,318 | 1,545 | 2,270 | 1,978 | 1,726 | 1,738 | 1,600 | -4.56 | 1,527 |
| Nacogdoches, Nac. | | *383 | | | 1,138 | 1,827 | 3,369 | 3,546 | 5,687 | 7,538 | 12,327 | 12,674 | 22,544 | 27,149 | 30,872 | -3.10 | 29,914 |
| Nassau Bay, Harris | | | | | | | | | | | | | | 4,526 | 4,320 | -3.47 | 4,170 |
| Navasota, Grimes | | | | 1,611 | 2,997 | 3,857 | 3,284 | 5,060 | 5,128 | 6,138 | 5,188 | 4,937 | 5,111 | 5,971 | 6,296 | 7.83 | 6,789 |
| Nederland, Jefferson | | | | | | | | | 949 | 1,111 | 3,805 | 12,036 | 16,810 | 16,855 | 16,192 | 7.60 | 17,422 |
| New Boston, Bowie | | | | | | | | 869 | ‡1,000 | ‡1,200 | 2,688 | 2,773 | 4,034 | 4,628 | 5,057 | -4.92 | 4,808 |
| New Braunfels, Comal | **1,727 | ‡3,500 | 2,261 | 1,938 | 1,608 | 2,097 | 3,165 | 3,590 | 6,242 | 6,976 | 12,210 | 15,631 | 17,859 | 22,402 | 27,334 | 33.51 | 36,494 |
| Newton, Newton | | | | | | | | | | | 934 | 1,233 | 1,529 | 1,620 | 1,885 | 30.45 | 2,459 |
| Nocona, Montague | | | | 381 | 961 | 1,338 | 1,422 | 2,352 | 2,605 | 3,022 | 3,127 | 2,871 | 2,992 | 2,870 | 11.43 | 3,198 |
| North Richland Hills, Tarrant | | | | | | | | | | | 8,662 | 16,514 | 30,592 | 45,895 | | 21.22 | 55,635 |
| Odessa, Ector | | | | | | | | 2,407 | 9,573 | 29,495 | 80,338 | 78,380 | 90,027 | 89,699 | | 1.39 | 90,943 |
| Olmos Park, Bexar | | | | | | | | | 1,822 | 2,841 | 2,457 | 2,250 | 2,069 | 2,161 | | 8.42 | 2,343 |
| Olney, Young | | | | | | 1,095 | 1,164 | 4,138 | 3,497 | 3,765 | 3,872 | 3,624 | 4,060 | 3,519 | | -3.50 | 3,396 |
| Orange, Orange | | | | 3,173 | 3,835 | 5,527 | 9,212 | 7,913 | 7,472 | 21,174 | 25,605 | 24,457 | 23,628 | 19,370 | | -3.75 | 18,643 |
| Ozona, Crockett | | | | | | | | 1,318 | 2,677 | 2,885 | 3,361 | 2,864 | 3,766 | 3,181 | | 8.02 | 3,436 |
| Paducah, Cottle | | | | | | 1,389 | 1,335 | ‡1,000 | ‡800 | 2,952 | 2,392 | 2,052 | 2,216 | 1,788 | | -16.22 | 1,498 |
| Paint Rock, Concho | | | | 323 | 323 | | | | ‡800 | | | 193 | 256 | 227 | | 40.97 | 320 |
| Palacios, Matagorda | | | | | | 1,350 | ‡750 | 2,802 | 2,288 | 2,799 | 3,676 | 3,642 | 4,667 | 4,418 | | 16.64 | 5,153 |
| Palestine, Anderson | ‡2,000 | | | 2,997 | 5,838 | 8,297 | 10,482 | 11,039 | 11,445 | 12,144 | 12,503 | 13,974 | 14,525 | 15,948 | 18,042 | -2.46 | 17,598 |
| Pampa, Gray | | | | | | | 987 | 10,470 | 12,895 | 16,583 | 24,664 | 21,726 | 21,396 | 19,959 | | -10.38 | 17,887 |
| Panhandle, Carson | | | | | | 521 | 638 | 987 | 978 | 1,403 | 1,907 | 2,141 | 2,226 | 2,353 | | 10.03 | 2,589 |
| Paris, Lamar | *1,003 | ‡1,500 | | 3,980 | 8,254 | 9,358 | 11,269 | 15,040 | 15,649 | 18,678 | 21,643 | 20,977 | 23,441 | 25,498 | 24,799 | 4.43 | 25,898 |
| Pasadena, Harris | | | | | | | | 1,647 | 3,436 | 22,483 | 58,737 | 89,277 | 112,560 | 119,604 | | 18.45 | 141,674 |
| Pearland, Brazoria | | | | | | | | | | 1,497 | 6,444 | 13,248 | 18,927 | | 98.87 | 37,640 |
| Pearsall, Frio | | | | | | 1,799 | 2,161 | 2,536 | 3,164 | 4,481 | 4,957 | 5,545 | 7,383 | 6,924 | | 3.37 | 7,157 |
| Pecos, Reeves | | | | 393 | 639 | 1,856 | 1,445 | 3,304 | 3,712 | 8,054 | 12,728 | 12,682 | 12,855 | 12,069 | | -21.28 | 9,501 |
| **Pelly, Harris | | | | | | | | 3,442 | | | | | | | | | |
| Perryton, Ochiltree | | | | | | | ‡500 | 2,824 | 2,325 | 4,417 | 7,903 | 7,810 | 7,991 | 7,619 | | 2.03 | 7,774 |
| Pflugerville, Travis | | | | | | | | ‡580 | ‡500 | ‡380 | ‡380 | 549 | 745 | 4,444 | | 267.57 | 16,335 |
| Pharr, Hidalgo | | | | | | | 1,565 | 3,225 | 4,784 | 8,690 | 14,106 | 15,829 | 21,381 | 32,921 | | 41.73 | 46,660 |
| Pinehurst, Orange | | | | | | | | | | 1,703 | 2,198 | 3,055 | 2,682 | | -15.21 | 2,274 |
| Piney Point Village, Harris | | | | | | | | | | 1,790 | 2,548 | 2,958 | 3,197 | | 5.72 | 3,380 |
| Pittsburg, Camp | | | | | 1,203 | 1,783 | 1,916 | 2,540 | 2,640 | 2,916 | 3,142 | 3,796 | 3,844 | 4,245 | 4,007 | 8.49 | 4,347 |
| Plainview, Hale | | | | | | | 2,829 | 3,989 | 8,834 | 8,263 | 14,044 | 18,735 | 19,096 | 22,187 | 21,698 | 2.94 | 22,336 |
| Plano, Collin | | | | | 824 | 1,304 | 1,258 | 1,715 | 1,554 | 1,582 | 2,126 | 3,695 | 17,872 | 72,331 | 127,885 | 73.62 | 222,030 |
| Pleasanton, Atascosa | | | | | | | | 1,036 | 1,154 | 2,074 | 2,913 | 3,467 | 5,407 | 6,346 | 7,678 | 7.66 | 8,266 |
| Port Arthur, Jefferson | | | | | | 900 | 7,663 | 22,251 | 50,902 | 46,140 | 57,530 | 66,676 | 57,371 | 61,195 | 58,551 | -1.36 | 57,755 |
| Port Isabel, Cameron | | | | | | | | | 1,177 | 1,440 | 2,372 | 3,575 | 3,067 | 3,769 | 4,467 | 8.91 | 4,865 |
| Portland, San Patricio | | | | | | | | | | | 1,292 | 2,538 | 7,302 | 12,023 | 12,224 | 21.29 | 14,827 |
| Port Lavaca, Calhoun | | | | | | | 1,699 | 1,213 | 1,367 | 2,069 | 5,599 | 8,864 | 10,491 | 10,911 | 10,886 | 10.55 | 12,035 |
| Port Neches, Jefferson | | | | | | | | | 2,327 | 2,487 | 5,448 | 8,696 | 10,894 | 13,944 | 12,908 | 5.37 | 13,601 |
| Post, Garza | | | | | | | | 1,436 | 1,668 | 2,046 | 3,141 | 4,663 | 3,854 | 3,961 | 3,768 | -1.59 | 3,708 |

| City, County | 1850 | 1860 | 1870 | 1880 | 1890 | 1900 | 1910 | 1920 | 1930 | 1940 | 1950 | 1960 | 1970 | 1980 | 1990†† | % Change 90-00 | 2000 |
|---|---|---|---|---|---|---|---|---|---|---|---|---|---|---|---|---|---|
| Poteet, Atascosa | | | | | | | | | 1,231 | 2,315 | 2,487 | 2,811 | 3,013 | 3,086 | 3,206 | 3.09 | 3,305 |
| Prairie View, Waller | | | | | | | | | | | | 2,326 | 3,589 | 3,993 | 4,004 | 10.14 | 4,410 |
| Premont, Jim Wells | | | | | | | | | | 1,080 | 2,619 | 3,049 | 3,282 | 2,984 | 2,914 | -4.87 | 2,772 |
| Princeton, Collin | | | | | | | | 500 | 459 | 564 | 540 | 594 | 1,105 | 3,408 | 2,448 | 42.03 | 3,477 |
| Quanah, Hardeman | | | | | 1,477 | 1,651 | 3,127 | 3,691 | 4,464 | 3,767 | 4,589 | 4,564 | 3,948 | 3,890 | 3,413 | -11.46 | 3,022 |
| Ralls, Crosby | | | | | | | | ‡500 | 1,365 | 1,512 | 1,771 | 2,300 | 1,962 | 2,422 | 2,172 | 3.68 | 2,252 |
| Ranger, Eastland | | | | | | | | 16,201 | 6,208 | 4,553 | 3,989 | 3,313 | 3,094 | 3,142 | 2,803 | -7.81 | 2,584 |
| Raymondville, Willacy | | | | | | | | | 2,050 | 4,050 | 9,136 | 9,385 | 7,987 | 9,493 | 8,880 | 9.61 | 9,733 |
| Refugio, Refugio | | | | | | | 773 | 933 | 2,019 | 4,077 | 4,666 | 4,944 | 4,340 | 3,898 | 3,158 | -6.87 | 2,941 |
| Richardson, Dallas | | | | | | | | | 629 | 720 | 1,289 | 16,810 | 48,582 | 72,496 | 74,840 | 22.66 | 91,802 |
| Richland Hills, Tarrant | | | | | | | | | | | | 7,804 | 8,865 | 7,977 | 7,978 | 1.93 | 8,132 |
| Richmond, Fort Bend | | | | | | | 1,371 | 1,273 | 1,432 | 2,026 | 2,030 | 3,668 | 5,777 | 9,692 | 10,042 | 10.35 | 11,081 |
| Richwood, Brazoria | | | | | | | | | | | | 649 | 1,452 | 2,591 | 2,732 | 10.25 | 3,012 |
| Rio Grande City, Starr | | 439 | | | 1,968 | | | ‡582 | 2,283 | | 3,992 | 5,835 | 5,676 | 8,930 | 10,725 | 11.17 | 11,923 |
| River Oaks, Tarrant | | | | | | | | | | | 7,097 | 8,444 | 8,193 | 6,890 | 6,580 | 6.16 | 6,985 |
| Robert Lee, Coke | | | | | | 582 | | | 490 | 662 | 1,070 | 975 | 1,119 | 1,202 | 1,276 | -8.23 | 1,171 |
| Robinson, McLennan | | | | | | | | | | | | 2,110 | 3,807 | 6,074 | 7,111 | 10.32 | 7,845 |
| Robstown, Nueces | | | | | | | | 948 | 4,183 | 6,780 | 7,278 | 10,266 | 11,217 | 12,100 | 12,849 | -0.95 | 12,727 |
| Rockdale, Milam | | | | | 1,505 | 2,515 | 2,073 | 2,323 | 2,204 | 2,136 | 2,321 | 4,481 | 4,655 | 5,611 | 5,235 | 3.90 | 5,439 |
| Rockport, Aransas | | | | | 1,069 | 1,153 | 1,382 | 1,545 | 1,140 | 1,729 | 2,266 | 2,989 | 3,879 | 3,686 | 5,355 | 37.91 | 7,385 |
| Rocksprings, Edwards | | | | | | 389 | | ‡600 | 998 | 1,339 | 1,433 | 1,275 | 1,221 | 1,317 | 1,339 | -4.03 | 1,285 |
| Rockwall, Rockwall | | | | | | 1,245 | 1,136 | 1,388 | 1,071 | 1,318 | 1,501 | 2,166 | 3,121 | 5,939 | 10,486 | 71.43 | 17,976 |
| Roma-Los Saenz, Starr | | | 479 | | | 843 | 1,198 | 1,279 | 1,941 | 1,414 | 1,576 | 1,496 | 2,154 | 3,384 | 8,059 | 19.33 | 9,617 |
| Rosenberg, Fort Bend | | | | | | | 1,126 | 1,000 | 1,632 | 3,457 | 6,210 | 9,698 | 12,098 | 17,995 | 20,183 | 19.13 | 24,043 |
| Rotan, Fisher | | | | | | | | 900 | 1,173 | 2,029 | 3,163 | 2,788 | 2,404 | 2,284 | 1,913 | -15.79 | 1,611 |
| Round Rock, Williamson | | | | | | | | | | 1,240 | 1,438 | 1,878 | 2,811 | 11,812 | 30,923 | 97.70 | 61,136 |
| Rowlett, Dallas | | | | | | | | | | | | 1,015 | 2,579 | 7,522 | 23,260 | 91.33 | 44,503 |
| Rusk, Cherokee | ‡355 | *395 | ‡1,000 | | 1,383 | 846 | 1,558 | 2,348 | 3,859 | 5,699 | 6,598 | 4,900 | 4,914 | 4,681 | 4,366 | 16.47 | 5,085 |
| Saginaw, Tarrant | | | | | | | | | | | 561 | 1,001 | 2,382 | 5,736 | 8,551 | 44.71 | 12,374 |
| San Angelo, Tom Green | | | | | | | 10,321 | 10,050 | 25,308 | 25,802 | 52,093 | 58,815 | 63,884 | 73,240 | 84,462 | 4.71 | 88,439 |
| San Antonio, Bexar | 3,488 | 8,235 | 12,256 | 20,550 | 37,673 | 53,321 | 96,614 | 161,379 | 231,542 | 253,854 | 408,442 | 587,718 | 654,153 | 785,410 | 959,295 | 19.32 | 1,144,646 |
| San Augustine, San Aug. | | | 920 | 503 | 744 | 261 | 1,204 | 1,268 | 1,247 | 1,516 | 2,510 | 2,584 | 2,539 | 2,930 | 2,337 | 5.91 | 2,475 |
| San Benito, Cameron | | | | | | | | 5,070 | 10,753 | 9,501 | 13,271 | 16,422 | 15,176 | 17,988 | 20,125 | 16.49 | 23,444 |
| Sanderson, Terrell | | | | | | 112 | | ‡500 | ‡1,500 | ‡1,875 | ‡2,150 | ‡2,350 | ‡1,229 | 1,500 | 1,128 | -23.67 | 861 |
| San Diego, Duval | | | | | | | | 1,204 | | 2,674 | 4,397 | 4,351 | 4,490 | 5,225 | 4,983 | -4.62 | 4,753 |
| Sanger, Denton | | | | | | | | | 1,119 | 1,000 | 1,170 | 1,190 | 1,603 | 2,574 | 3,514 | 29.03 | 4,534 |
| San Juan, Hidalgo | | | | | | | | 1,203 | 1,615 | 2,264 | 3,413 | 4,371 | 5,070 | 7,608 | 12,561 | 108.81 | 26,229 |
| San Marcos, Hays | | | 741 | 1,232 | 2,335 | 2,292 | 4,071 | 4,527 | 5,134 | 6,006 | 9,980 | 12,713 | 18,860 | 23,420 | 28,738 | 20.86 | 34,733 |
| San Saba, San Saba | | | | | | | | 2,011 | 2,240 | 2,927 | 3,400 | 2,728 | 2,555 | 2,336 | 2,626 | 0.42 | 2,637 |
| Sansom Park, Tarrant | | | | | | | | | | | 1,611 | 4,175 | 4,771 | 3,921 | 3,928 | 6.44 | 4,181 |
| Santa Fe, Galveston | | | | | | | | | | | | | | 5,413 | 8,429 | 13.28 | 9,548 |
| Sarita, Kenedy | | | | | | | | ‡200 | ‡250 | ‡200 | ‡200 | ‡200 | ‡196 | ‡185 | ‡185 | | ‡250 |
| Schertz, Guadalupe | | | | | | | | | | | | 2,281 | 4,061 | 7,262 | 10,597 | 76.41 | 18,694 |
| Seabrook, Harris | | | | | | | | | | | | | 3,811 | 4,670 | 6,685 | 41.26 | 9,443 |
| Seagoville, Dallas | | | | | | | | | 604 | 760 | 1,927 | 3,745 | 4,390 | 7,304 | 8,969 | 20.67 | 10,823 |
| Seagraves, Gaines | | | | | | | | | 505 | 3,225 | 2,101 | 2,307 | 2,440 | 2,596 | 2,398 | -2.67 | 2,334 |

| City, County | 1850 | 1860 | 1870 | 1880 | 1890 | 1900 | 1910 | 1920 | 1930 | 1940 | 1950 | 1960 | 1970 | 1980 | 1990†† | % Change 90-00 | 2000 |
|---|---|---|---|---|---|---|---|---|---|---|---|---|---|---|---|---|---|
| Sealy, Austin | | | | | | | | | | | 1,942 | 2,328 | 2,685 | 3,875 | 4,541 | 15.57 | 5,248 |
| Seguin, Guadalupe | | *792 | †830 | 1,363 | 1,716 | 2,421 | 3,116 | 3,631 | 5,225 | 7,006 | 9,733 | 14,299 | 15,934 | 17,854 | 18,692 | 17.76 | 22,011 |
| Seminole, Gaines | | | | | | | | | 2,626 | 1,761 | 3,479 | 5,737 | 5,007 | 6,080 | 6,342 | -6.81 | 5,910 |
| Seymour, Baylor | | | | | | | 2,029 | 2,121 | 3,780 | 3,328 | 3,779 | 3,789 | 3,469 | 3,657 | 3,185 | -8.70 | 2,908 |
| Shamrock, Wheeler | | | | | | | | 1,227 | ‡450 | 3,123 | 3,322 | 3,113 | 2,644 | 2,834 | 2,286 | -11.24 | 2,029 |
| Shepherd, San Jacinto | | | | | | 278 | | ‡500 | ‡500 | ‡500 | ‡350 | ‡1,300 | 928 | 1,674 | 1,812 | 11.98 | 2,029 |
| Sherman, Grayson | | | 1,439 | 6,093 | 7,335 | 10,243 | 12,412 | 15,031 | 15,713 | 17,156 | 20,150 | 24,988 | 29,061 | 30,413 | 31,584 | 11.08 | 35,082 |
| Sierra Blanca, Hudspeth | | | | | | | | ‡600 | ‡500 | ‡723 | ‡850 | ‡850 | †600 | ‡700 | ‡700 | | 533 |
| Silsbee, Hardin | | | | | | | | | | 2,525 | 3,179 | 6,277 | 7,271 | 7,684 | 6,368 | 0.39 | 6,393 |
| Silverton, Briscoe | | | | | | 241 | | 416 | 873 | 684 | 855 | 1,168 | 1,026 | 918 | 779 | -1.03 | 771 |
| Sinton, San Patricio | | | | | | | | 1,058 | 1,852 | 3,770 | 4,254 | 6,008 | 5,563 | 6,044 | 5,549 | 2.29 | 5,676 |
| Slaton, Lubbock | | | | | | | | 1,525 | 3,876 | 3,587 | 5,036 | 6,568 | 6,583 | 6,804 | 6,078 | 0.51 | 6,109 |
| Smithville, Bastrop | | | | | 616 | 2,577 | 3,167 | 3,204 | 3,296 | 3,100 | 3,379 | 2,933 | 2,959 | 3,470 | 3,196 | 22.06 | 3,901 |
| Snyder, Scurry | | | | | 500 | 612 | 2,514 | 2,179 | 3,008 | 3,815 | 12,012 | 13,050 | 11,171 | 12,705 | 12,195 | -11.58 | 10,783 |
| Sonora, Sutton | | | | | | | | 1,009 | 1,942 | 2,528 | 2,633 | 2,619 | 2,149 | 3,856 | 2,751 | 6.29 | 2,924 |
| South Houston, Harris | | | | | | | | | 612 | 982 | 4,126 | 7,523 | 11,527 | 13,293 | 14,207 | 11.45 | 15,833 |
| Southlake, Denton | | | | | | | | | | | | 1,023 | 2,031 | 2,808 | 7,082 | 203.85 | 21,519 |
| Spearman, Hansford | | | | | | | | | 1,580 | 1,105 | 1,852 | 3,555 | 3,435 | 3,413 | 3,197 | -5.51 | 3,021 |
| Spring Valley, Harris | | | | | | | | | | | | 3,004 | 3,170 | 3,353 | 3,392 | 6.46 | 3,611 |
| Spur, Dickens | | | | | | | | 1,100 | 1,899 | 2,136 | 2,173 | 2,300 | 1,747 | 1,690 | 1,300 | -16.31 | 1,088 |
| Stafford, Fort Bend | | | | | | | | | | | | 1,485 | 2,906 | 4,755 | 8,395 | 86.79 | 15,681 |
| Stamford, Jones | | | | | | | 3,902 | 3,704 | 4,095 | 4,810 | 5,819 | 5,259 | 4,558 | 4,542 | 3,817 | -4.74 | 3,636 |
| Stanton, Martin | | | | | | | | ‡600 | 1,384 | 1,245 | 1,594 | 2,690 | 2,117 | 2,314 | 2,576 | -0.78 | 2,556 |
| Stephenville, Erath | | | | | 909 | 1,902 | 2,561 | 3,891 | 3,994 | 4,768 | 7,155 | 7,359 | 9,277 | 11,881 | 13,502 | 10.51 | 14,921 |
| Sterling City, Sterling | | | | | | 532 | | ‡532 | ‡700 | 886‡ | 800‡ | 875 | 780 | 915 | 1,096 | -1.37 | 1,081 |
| Stinnett, Hutchinson | | | | | | | | | | 635 | 1,170 | 2,695 | 2,014 | 2,222 | 2,166 | -10.62 | 1,936 |
| Stratford, Sherman | | | | | | | 520 | 472 | 873 | 877 | 1,376 | 1,850 | 2,139 | 1,917 | 1,781 | 11.79 | 1,991 |
| Sugar Land, Fort Bend | *441 | ‡2,500 | | 1,854 | | | | | | | 2,285 | 2,802 | 3,318 | 8,826 | 33,712 | 87.85 | 63,328 |
| Sulphur Springs, Hopkins | | | | | 3,033 | 3,635 | 5,151 | 5,558 | 5,417 | 6,742 | 8,991 | 9,160 | 10,642 | 12,804 | 14,062 | 3.48 | 14,551 |
| Sweeny, Brazoria | | | | | | | | | | | 1,393 | 3,087 | 3,191 | 3,538 | 3,297 | 9.92 | 3,624 |
| Sweetwater, Nolan | | | | | 614 | 670 | 4,176 | 4,307 | 10,848 | 10,367 | 13,619 | 13,914 | 12,020 | 12,242 | 11,967 | -4.61 | 11,415 |
| Taft, San Patricio | | | | | | | | | 1,792 | 2,686 | 2,978 | 3,463 | 3,274 | 3,686 | 3,222 | 5.40 | 3,396 |
| Tahoka, Lynn | | | | | | | | 786 | 1,620 | 2,129 | 2,848 | 3,012 | 2,956 | 3,262 | 2,868 | 1.46 | 2,910 |
| Taylor, Williamson | | | | | 2,584 | 4,211 | 5,314 | 5,965 | 7,463 | 7,875 | 9,071 | 9,434 | 9,616 | 10,619 | 11,472 | 18.33 | 13,575 |
| Taylor Lake Village, Harris | | | | | | | | | | | | | 990 | 3,669 | 3,352 | 10.20 | 3,694 |
| Teague, Freestone | | | | | | | 3,288 | 3,306 | 3,509 | 3,157 | 2,925 | 2,728 | 2,867 | 3,390 | 3,268 | 39.44 | 4,557 |
| Temple, Bell | | | | | 4,047 | 7,065 | 10,993 | 11,033 | 15,345 | 15,344 | 25,467 | 30,419 | 33,431 | 42,483 | 46,150 | 18.12 | 54,514 |
| Terrell, Kaufman | | | | 2,003 | 2,988 | 6,330 | 7,050 | 8,349 | 8,795 | 10,481 | 11,544 | 13,803 | 14,182 | 13,225 | 12,490 | 8.94 | 13,606 |
| Terrell Hills, Bexar | | | | | | | | | | 1,236 | 2,708 | 5,572 | 5,225 | 4,644 | 4,592 | 9.30 | 5,019 |
| Texarkana, Bowie | | | | 1,833 | 2,852 | 5,256 | 9,790 | 11,480 | 16,602 | 17,019 | 24,753 | 30,218 | 30,497 | 31,271 | 32,294 | 7.70 | 34,782 |
| Texas City, Galveston | | | | | | | | 2,509 | 3,534 | 5,748 | 16,620 | 32,065 | 38,908 | 41,403 | 40,822 | 1.71 | 41,521 |
| The Colony, Denton | | | | | | | | | | | | | | 11,586 | 22,113 | 19.98 | 26,531 |
| Throckmorton, Throck. | | | | 37 | 240 | 240 | | 686 | 1,135 | 1,133 | 1,319 | 1,260 | 1,105 | 1,174 | 1,036 | -12.64 | 905 |
| Tilden, McMullen | | | | | 506 | 506 | | ‡250 | | ‡500 | ‡380 | ‡380 | †416 | ‡500 | ‡500 | | ‡450 |
| Tomball, Harris | | | | | | | | | | 668 | 1,065 | 1,713 | 2,734 | 3,996 | 6,370 | 42.68 | 9,089 |
| Trinity, Trinity | | | | | | | | 1,363 | 2,036 | 2,217 | 2,054 | 1,787 | 2,512 | 2,452 | 2,648 | 2.76 | 2,721 |

| City, County | 1850 | 1860 | 1870 | 1880 | 1890 | 1900 | 1910 | 1920 | 1930 | 1940 | 1950 | 1960 | 1970 | 1980 | 1990†† | % Change 90-00 | 2000 |
|---|---|---|---|---|---|---|---|---|---|---|---|---|---|---|---|---|---|
| Tulia, Swisher | | | | | | | 1,216 | 1,189 | 2,202 | 2,055 | 3,222 | 4,410 | 5,294 | 5,033 | 4,703 | 8.80 | 5,117 |
| Tyler, Smith | ‡1,024 | | | 2,423 | 6,908 | 8,069 | 10,400 | 12,085 | 17,113 | 28,279 | 38,968 | 51,230 | 57,770 | 70,508 | 75,450 | 10.87 | 83,650 |
| Universal City, Bexar | | | | | | | | | | | | | 7,613 | 10,720 | 13,057 | 13.72 | 14,849 |
| University Park, Dallas | | | | | | | | | 4,200 | 14,458 | 24,275 | 23,202 | 23,498 | 22,254 | 22,259 | 4.78 | 23,324 |
| Uvalde, Uvalde | | | | | 1,265 | 1,889 | 3,998 | 3,885 | 5,286 | 6,679 | 8,674 | 10,293 | 10,764 | 14,178 | 14,729 | 1.36 | 14,929 |
| Van Horn, Culberson | | | | | | | | | | | 1,161 | 1,953 | 2,889 | 2,772 | 2,930 | -16.89 | 2,435 |
| Vega, Oldham | | | | | | | | 200 | 519 | 515 | 619 | 658 | 839 | 900 | 840 | 11.43 | 936 |
| Vernon, Wilbarger | | | | | 2,857 | 1,993 | 3,195 | 5,142 | 9,137 | 9,277 | 12,651 | 12,141 | 11,454 | 12,695 | 12,001 | -2.84 | 11,660 |
| Victoria, Victoria | *1,440 | | 2,500 | | 3,046 | 4,010 | 3,673 | 5,957 | 7,421 | 11,566 | 16,126 | 33,047 | 41,349 | 50,695 | 55,076 | 10.04 | 60,603 |
| Vidor, Orange | | | | | | | | | | | | 4,938 | 9,738 | 12,117 | 10,935 | 4.62 | 11,440 |
| Waco, McLennan | *749 | | 3,008 | 7,295 | 14,445 | 20,686 | 26,425 | 38,500 | 52,848 | 55,982 | 84,706 | 97,808 | 95,326 | 101,261 | 103,590 | 9.78 | 113,726 |
| Wake Village, Bowie | | | | | | | | | | | | 1,140 | 2,408 | 3,865 | 4,761 | 7.73 | 5,129 |
| Watauga, Tarrant | | | | | | | | | | | | | 3,778 | 10,284 | 20,009 | 9.49 | 21,908 |
| Waxahachie, Ellis | | | | 1,354 | 3,076 | 4,215 | 6,205 | 7,958 | 8,042 | 8,655 | 11,204 | 12,749 | 13,452 | 14,624 | 17,984 | 19.14 | 21,426 |
| Weatherford, Parker | | | | 2,046 | 3,369 | 4,786 | 5,074 | 6,203 | 4,912 | 5,924 | 8,093 | 9,759 | 11,750 | 12,049 | 14,804 | 28.34 | 19,000 |
| Wellington, Collingsworth | | | | | | | 576 | 1,968 | 3,570 | 3,308 | 3,676 | 3,137 | 2,884 | 3,043 | 2,456 | -7.37 | 2,275 |
| Weslaco, Hidalgo | | | | | | | | | 4,879 | 6,883 | 7,514 | 15,649 | 15,313 | 19,331 | 22,739 | 18.45 | 26,935 |
| West Columbia, Brazoria | *175 | †1,823 | | | | | | | | 1,573 | 2,100 | 2,947 | 3,335 | 4,610 | 4,372 | -2.68 | 4,255 |
| West Orange, Orange | | | | | | | | | | | 2,539 | 4,848 | 4,820 | 4,109 | 4,187 | -1.82 | 4,111 |
| W. University Place, Harris | | | | | | | | | 1,322 | 9,221 | 17,074 | 14,628 | 13,317 | 12,010 | 12,920 | 9.99 | 14,211 |
| Westworth Village, Tarrant | | | | | | | | | | | 529 | 3,321 | 4,578 | 3,651 | 2,350 | -9.62 | 2,124 |
| Wharton, Wharton | | | | | | | 1,505 | 2,346 | 2,691 | 4,386 | 4,450 | 5,734 | 7,881 | 9,033 | 9,011 | 2.51 | 9,237 |
| White Oak, Gregg | | | | | | | | | | | | 1,250 | 2,300 | 4,415 | 5,136 | 9.50 | 5,624 |
| Whitesboro, Grayson | | | | 773 | 1,170 | 1,243 | 1,219 | 1,810 | 1,535 | 1,560 | 1,854 | 2,485 | 2,927 | 3,197 | 3,209 | 17.17 | 3,760 |
| White Settlement, Tarrant | | | | | | | | | | | 10,827 | 11,513 | 13,449 | 13,508 | 15,472 | -4.14 | 14,831 |
| Wichita Falls, Wichita | | | | | 1,978 | 2,480 | 8,200 | 40,079 | 43,690 | 45,112 | 68,042 | 101,724 | 96,265 | 94,201 | 96,259 | 8.25 | 104,197 |
| Wills Point, Van Zandt | | | | | 1,025 | 1,347 | 1,398 | 1,811 | 2,023 | 1,976 | 2,030 | 2,281 | 2,636 | 2,631 | 2,986 | 17.08 | 3,496 |
| Windcrest, Bexar | | | | | | | | | | | | 441 | 3,371 | 5,332 | 5,331 | -4.24 | 5,105 |
| Wink, Winkler | | | | | | | | | 3,963 | 1,945 | 1,521 | 1,863 | 1,023 | 1,182 | 1,189 | -22.71 | 919 |
| Winnie, Chambers | | | | | | | | ‡200 | ‡370 | ‡200 | 325‡ | ‡1,114 | ‡1,543 | ‡5,512 | 2,238 | 30.21 | 2,914 |
| Winnsboro, Wood | | | | | | 899 | 1,741 | 2,184 | 1,905 | 2,092 | 2,512 | 2,675 | 3,064 | 3,458 | 2,904 | 23.42 | 3,584 |
| Winters, Runnels | | | | | | | 1,347 | 1,509 | 2,423 | 2,335 | 2,676 | 3,266 | 2,907 | 3,061 | 2,905 | -0.86 | 2,880 |
| Woodville, Tyler | | | | | | | | | 969 | 1,521 | 1,863 | 1,920 | 2,662 | 2,821 | 2,636 | -8.38 | 2,415 |
| Woodway, McLennan | | | | | | | | | | | | | 4,819 | 7,091 | 8,695 | 0.44 | 8,733 |
| Wylie, Collin | | | | | 239 | 773 | 620 | 945 | 771 | 914 | 1,295 | 1,804 | 2,675 | 3,152 | 8,716 | 73.61 | 15,132 |
| Yoakum, Lavaca | | | | | 1,745 | 3,499 | 4,657 | 6,184 | 5,656 | 4,733 | 5,231 | 5,761 | 5,755 | 6,148 | 5,611 | 2.14 | 5,731 |
| Yorktown, DeWitt | | | | 430 | 522 | 846 | 1,180 | 1,723 | 1,852 | 2,081 | 2,596 | 2,527 | 2,411 | 2,498 | 2,207 | 2.90 | 2,271 |
| Zapata, Zapata | | | | | | | | ‡300 | ‡450 | ‡500 | ‡850 | ‡2,031 | ‡2,102 | ‡3,500 | 7,119 | -31.79 | 4,856 |

*Census of incorporated towns of Texas taken in 1858 by tax assessors and collectors in each county.

†Federal census of western part of Texas for 1870, as given in Texas Almanac for 1871.

‡An estimate of that date.

**Pelly, Goose Creek and Baytown merged in 1947, and the single community took the name of the latter — Baytown. Baytown was unincorporated prior to this merger and did not show any previous census. However, Pelly and Goose Creek were previously incorporated, hence the census figures for them in 1930 and 1940.

§ Includes Huntsville prison population.

†† After the publication of the original 1990 official Bureau of the Census population count, many places requested an official review of the counts for their areas. The values shown are the revised values provided by the U.S. Bureau of the Census after those reviews. Many of these values are different from the ones published in the 1992-93 Texas Almanac.

## Population History of Texas' Counties From 1850 to 2000

The population of each county for each United States census beginning with 1850, or the first census after date of organization for counties organized after 1850, is given below.

| County | 1850 | 1860 | 1870 | 1880 | 1890 | 1900 | 1910 | 1920 | 1930 | 1940 | 1950 | 1960 | 1970 | 1980 | 1990 | 2000 |
|---|---|---|---|---|---|---|---|---|---|---|---|---|---|---|---|---|
| Anderson | 2,684 | 10,398 | 9,229 | 17,395 | 20,923 | 28,015 | 29,650 | 34,318 | 34,643 | 37,092 | 31,875 | 28,162 | 27,789 | 38,381 | 48,024 | 55,109 |
| Andrews | | | | | 24 | 87 | 975 | 350 | 736 | 1,277 | 5,002 | 13,450 | 10,372 | 13,323 | 14,338 | 13,004 |
| Angelina | 1,165 | 4,271 | 3,985 | 5,239 | 6,306 | 13,481 | 17,705 | 22,287 | 27,803 | 32,201 | 36,032 | 39,814 | 49,349 | 64,172 | 69,884 | 80,130 |
| Aransas | | | | 966 | 1,824 | 1,716 | 2,106 | 2,064 | 2,219 | 3,469 | 4,252 | 7,006 | 8,902 | 14,260 | 17,892 | 22,497 |
| Archer | | | | 596 | 2,101 | 2,508 | 6,525 | 5,254 | 9,684 | 7,599 | 6,816 | 6,110 | 5,759 | 7,266 | 7,973 | 8,854 |
| Armstrong | | | | 31 | 944 | 1,205 | 2,682 | 2,816 | 3,329 | 2,495 | 2,215 | 1,966 | 1,895 | 1,994 | 2,021 | 2,148 |
| Atascosa | | 1,578 | 2,915 | 4,217 | 6,459 | 7,143 | 10,004 | 12,702 | 15,654 | 19,275 | 20,048 | 18,828 | 18,696 | 25,055 | 30,533 | 38,628 |
| Austin | 3,841 | 10,139 | 15,087 | 14,429 | 17,859 | 20,676 | 17,699 | 18,874 | 18,860 | 17,384 | 14,663 | 13,777 | 13,831 | 17,726 | 19,832 | 23,590 |
| Bailey | | | | | | | 312 | 517 | 5,186 | 6,318 | 7,592 | 9,090 | 8,487 | 8,168 | 7,064 | 6,594 |
| Bandera [1] | | 399 | 649 | 2,158 | 3,795 | 5,332 | 4,921 | 4,001 | 3,784 | 4,234 | 4,410 | 3,892 | 4,747 | 7,084 | 10,562 | 17,645 |
| Bastrop | 3,099 | 7,006 | 12,290 | 17,215 | 20,736 | 26,845 | 25,344 | 26,649 | 23,888 | 21,610 | 19,622 | 16,925 | 17,297 | 24,726 | 38,263 | 57,733 |
| Baylor | | | | 715 | 2,595 | 3,052 | 8,411 | 7,027 | 7,418 | 7,755 | 6,875 | 5,893 | 5,221 | 4,919 | 4,385 | 4,093 |
| Bee | | 910 | 1,082 | 2,298 | 3,720 | 7,720 | 12,090 | 12,137 | 15,721 | 16,481 | 18,174 | 23,755 | 22,737 | 26,030 | 25,135 | 32,359 |
| Bell | | 4,799 | 9,771 | 20,518 | 33,377 | 45,535 | 49,186 | 46,412 | 50,030 | 44,863 | 73,824 | 94,097 | 124,483 | 157,889 | 191,088 | 237,974 |
| Bexar | 6,052 | 14,454 | 16,043 | 30,470 | 49,266 | 69,422 | 119,676 | 202,096 | 292,533 | 338,176 | 500,460 | 687,151 | 830,460 | 988,800 | 1,185,394 | 1,392,931 |
| Bexar Dist. [2] | | | 1,077 | | | | | | | | | | | | | |
| Blanco | | 1,281 | 1,187 | 3,583 | 4,649 | 4,703 | 4,311 | 4,063 | 3,842 | 4,264 | 3,780 | 3,657 | 3,567 | 4,681 | 5,972 | 8,418 |
| Borden | | | | 35 | 222 | 776 | 1,386 | 965 | 1,505 | 1,396 | 1,106 | 1,076 | 888 | 859 | 799 | 729 |
| Bosque | | 2,005 | 4,981 | 11,217 | 14,224 | 17,390 | 19,013 | 18,032 | 15,750 | 15,761 | 11,836 | 10,809 | 10,966 | 13,401 | 15,125 | 17,204 |
| Bowie | | 5,052 | 4,684 | 10,965 | 20,267 | 26,676 | 34,827 | 39,472 | 48,563 | 50,208 | 61,966 | 59,971 | 67,813 | 75,301 | 81,665 | 89,306 |
| Brazoria | 4,841 | 7,143 | 7,527 | 9,774 | 11,506 | 14,861 | 13,299 | 20,614 | 23,054 | 27,069 | 46,549 | 76,204 | 108,312 | 169,587 | 191,707 | 241,767 |
| Brazos | 614 | 2,776 | 9,205 | 13,576 | 16,650 | 18,859 | 18,919 | 21,975 | 21,835 | 26,977 | 38,390 | 44,895 | 57,978 | 93,588 | 121,862 | 152,415 |
| Brewster [3] | | | | | 710 | 2,356 | 5,220 | 4,822 | 6,624 | 6,478 | 7,309 | 6,434 | 7,780 | 7,573 | 8,681 | 8,866 |
| Briscoe [5] | | | | 12 | | 1,253 | 2,162 | 2,948 | 5,590 | 4,056 | 3,528 | 3,577 | 2,794 | 2,579 | 1,971 | 1,790 |
| Brooks [49] | | | | | | | | 4,560 | 5,901 | 6,362 | 9,195 | 8,609 | 8,005 | 8,428 | 8,204 | 7,976 |
| Brown [6] | | 244 | 544 | 8,414 | 11,421 | 16,019 | 22,935 | 21,682 | 26,382 | 25,924 | 28,607 | 24,728 | 25,877 | 33,057 | 34,371 | 37,674 |
| Buchanan [8] | | | | | | | | | | | | | | | | |
| Buchel [7] | | | | | 298 | | | | | | | | | | | |
| Burleson | 1,713 | 5,663 | 8,072 | 9,243 | 13,001 | 18,367 | 18,687 | 16,855 | 19,848 | 18,334 | 13,000 | 11,177 | 9,999 | 12,313 | 13,625 | 16,470 |
| Burnet | | 2,487 | 3,688 | 6,855 | 10,747 | 10,528 | 10,755 | 9,499 | 10,355 | 10,771 | 10,356 | 9,265 | 11,420 | 17,803 | 22,677 | 34,147 |
| Caldwell | 1,329 | 4,481 | 6,572 | 11,757 | 15,769 | 21,765 | 24,237 | 25,160 | 31,397 | 24,893 | 19,350 | 17,222 | 21,178 | 23,637 | 26,392 | 32,194 |
| Calhoun | 1,110 | 2,642 | 3,443 | 1,739 | 815 | 2,395 | 3,635 | 4,700 | 5,385 | 5,911 | 9,222 | 16,592 | 17,831 | 19,574 | 19,053 | 20,647 |
| Callahan | | | | 3,453 | 5,457 | 8,768 | 12,973 | 11,844 | 12,785 | 11,568 | 9,087 | 7,929 | 8,205 | 10,992 | 11,859 | 12,905 |
| Cameron [9][50] | 8,541 | 6,028 | 10,999 | 14,959 | 14,424 | 16,095 | 27,158 | 36,662 | 77,540 | 83,202 | 125,170 | 151,098 | 140,368 | 209,680 | 260,120 | 335,227 |
| Camp | | | | 5,951 | 6,624 | 9,146 | 9,551 | 11,103 | 10,063 | 10,285 | 8,740 | 7,849 | 8,005 | 9,275 | 9,904 | 11,549 |
| Carson | | | | | 356 | 469 | 2,127 | 3,078 | 7,745 | 6,624 | 6,852 | 7,781 | 6,358 | 6,672 | 6,576 | 6,516 |
| Cass [10] | 4,991 | 8,411 | 8,875 | 16,724 | 22,554 | 22,841 | 27,587 | 30,041 | 30,030 | 33,496 | 26,732 | 23,496 | 24,133 | 29,430 | 29,982 | 30,438 |
| Castro | | | | | 9 | 400 | 1,850 | 1,948 | 4,720 | 4,631 | 5,417 | 8,923 | 10,394 | 10,556 | 9,070 | 8,285 |
| Chambers | | 1,508 | 1,503 | 2,187 | 2,241 | 3,046 | 4,234 | 4,162 | 5,710 | 7,511 | 7,871 | 10,379 | 12,187 | 18,538 | 20,088 | 26,031 |
| Cherokee | 6,673 | 12,098 | 11,079 | 16,723 | 22,975 | 25,154 | 29,038 | 37,633 | 43,180 | 43,970 | 38,694 | 33,120 | 32,008 | 38,127 | 41,049 | 46,659 |
| Childress [11] | | | | 25 | 1,175 | 2,138 | 9,538 | 10,933 | 16,044 | 12,149 | 12,123 | 8,421 | 6,605 | 6,950 | 5,953 | 7,688 |
| Clay [51] | | 109 | | 5,045 | 7,503 | 9,231 | 17,043 | 16,864 | 14,545 | 12,524 | 9,896 | 8,351 | 8,079 | 9,582 | 10,024 | 11,006 |
| Cochran | | | | | | | 65 | 67 | 1,963 | 3,735 | 5,928 | 6,417 | 5,326 | 4,825 | 4,377 | 3,730 |
| Coke [12] | | | | | 2,059 | 3,430 | 6,412 | 4,557 | 5,253 | 4,590 | 4,045 | 3,589 | 3,087 | 3,196 | 3,424 | 3,864 |
| Coleman | | | 347 | 3,603 | 6,112 | 10,077 | 22,618 | 18,805 | 23,669 | 20,571 | 15,503 | 12,458 | 10,288 | 10,439 | 9,710 | 9,235 |
| Collin | 1,950 | 9,264 | 14,013 | 25,983 | 36,736 | 50,087 | 49,021 | 49,609 | 46,180 | 47,190 | 41,692 | 41,247 | 66,920 | 144,490 | 264,036 | 491,675 |

| County | 1850 | 1860 | 1870 | 1880 | 1890 | 1900 | 1910 | 1920 | 1930 | 1940 | 1950 | 1960 | 1970 | 1980 | 1990 | 2000 |
|---|---|---|---|---|---|---|---|---|---|---|---|---|---|---|---|---|
| Collingsworth [11] | | | | 6 | 357 | 1,233 | 5,224 | 9,154 | 14,461 | 10,331 | 9,139 | 6,276 | 4,755 | 4,648 | 3,573 | 3,206 |
| Colorado | 2,257 | 7,885 | 8,326 | 16,673 | 19,512 | 22,203 | 18,897 | 19,013 | 19,129 | 17,812 | 17,576 | 18,463 | 17,638 | 18,823 | 18,383 | 20,390 |
| Comal | 1,723 | 4,030 | 5,283 | 5,546 | 6,398 | 7,008 | 8,434 | 8,824 | 11,984 | 12,321 | 16,357 | 19,844 | 24,165 | 36,446 | 51,832 | 78,021 |
| Comanche [4] | | 709 | 1,001 | 8,608 | 15,608 | 23,009 | 27,186 | 25,748 | 18,430 | 19,245 | 15,516 | 11,865 | 11,898 | 12,617 | 13,381 | 14,026 |
| Concho | | | | 800 | 1,065 | 1,427 | 6,654 | 5,847 | 7,645 | 6,192 | 5,078 | 3,672 | 2,937 | 2,915 | 3,044 | 3,966 |
| Cooke | 220 | 3,760 | 5,315 | 20,391 | 24,696 | 27,494 | 26,603 | 25,667 | 24,136 | 24,909 | 22,146 | 22,560 | 23,471 | 27,656 | 30,777 | 36,363 |
| Coryell | | 2,666 | 4,124 | 10,924 | 16,873 | 21,308 | 21,703 | 20,601 | 19,999 | 20,226 | 16,284 | 23,961 | 35,311 | 56,767 | 64,213 | 74,978 |
| Cottle | | | | 24 | 240 | 1,002 | 4,396 | 6,901 | 9,395 | 7,079 | 6,099 | 4,207 | 3,204 | 2,947 | 2,247 | 1,904 |
| Crane [14] | | | | | 15 | 51 | 331 | 37 | 2,221 | 2,841 | 3,965 | 4,699 | 4,172 | 4,600 | 4,652 | 3,996 |
| Crockett [13] | | | | 127 | 194 | 1,591 | 1,296 | 1,500 | 2,590 | 2,809 | 3,981 | 4,209 | 3,885 | 4,608 | 4,078 | 4,099 |
| Crosby | | | | 82 | 346 | 788 | 1,765 | 6,084 | 11,023 | 10,046 | 9,582 | 10,347 | 9,085 | 8,859 | 7,304 | 7,072 |
| Culberson [15] | | | | | | | | 912 | 1,228 | 1,653 | 1,825 | 2,794 | 3,429 | 3,315 | 3,407 | 2,975 |
| Dallam | | | | | 112 | 146 | 4,001 | 4,528 | 7,830 | 6,494 | 7,640 | 6,302 | 6,012 | 6,531 | 5,461 | 6,222 |
| Dallas | 2,743 | 8,665 | 13,314 | 33,488 | 67,042 | 82,726 | 135,748 | 210,551 | 325,691 | 398,564 | 614,799 | 951,527 | 1,327,321 | 1,556,549 | 1,852,810 | 2,218,899 |
| Dawson [16] | | | | 24 | 29 | 37 | 2,320 | 4,309 | 13,573 | 15,367 | 19,113 | 19,185 | 16,604 | 16,184 | 14,349 | 14,985 |
| Davis [10] | | | | | | | | | | | | | | | | |
| Deaf Smith | | | | 38 | 179 | 843 | 3,942 | 3,747 | 5,979 | 6,056 | 9,111 | 13,187 | 18,999 | 21,165 | 19,153 | 18,561 |
| Delta | | | | 5,597 | 9,117 | 15,249 | 14,566 | 15,887 | 13,138 | 12,858 | 8,964 | 5,860 | 4,927 | 4,839 | 4,857 | 5,327 |
| Denton | 641 | 5,031 | 7,251 | 18,143 | 21,289 | 28,318 | 31,258 | 35,355 | 32,822 | 33,658 | 41,365 | 47,432 | 75,633 | 143,126 | 273,525 | 432,976 |
| De Witt | 1,716 | 5,108 | 6,443 | 10,082 | 14,307 | 21,311 | 23,501 | 27,971 | 27,441 | 24,935 | 22,973 | 20,683 | 18,660 | 18,903 | 18,840 | 20,013 |
| Dickens | | | | 28 | 295 | 1,151 | 3,092 | 5,876 | 8,601 | 7,847 | 7,177 | 4,963 | 3,737 | 3,539 | 2,571 | 2,762 |
| Dimmit | | | 109 | 665 | 1,049 | 1,106 | 3,460 | 5,296 | 8,828 | 8,542 | 10,654 | 10,095 | 9,039 | 11,367 | 10,433 | 10,248 |
| Donley | | | | 160 | 1,056 | 2,756 | 5,284 | 8,035 | 10,262 | 7,487 | 6,216 | 4,449 | 3,641 | 4,075 | 3,696 | 3,828 |
| Dunn [17] | | | | | | | | | | | | | | | | |
| Duval [17 18] | | 99 | 1,083 | 5,732 | 7,598 | 8,483 | 8,964 | 8,251 | 12,191 | 20,565 | 15,643 | 13,398 | 11,722 | 12,517 | 12,918 | 13,120 |
| Eastland | | | 88 | 4,855 | 10,373 | 17,971 | 23,421 | 58,505 | 34,156 | 30,345 | 23,942 | 19,526 | 18,092 | 19,480 | 18,488 | 18,297 |
| Ector [19] | | | | | 224 | 381 | 1,178 | 760 | 3,958 | 15,051 | 42,102 | 90,995 | 91,805 | 115,374 | 118,934 | 121,123 |
| Edwards [20] | | | | 266 | 1,970 | 3,108 | 3,768 | 2,283 | 2,764 | 2,933 | 2,908 | 2,317 | 2,107 | 2,033 | 2,266 | 2,162 |
| Ellis | 989 | 5,246 | 7,514 | 21,294 | 31,774 | 50,059 | 53,629 | 55,700 | 53,936 | 47,733 | 45,645 | 43,395 | 46,638 | 59,743 | 85,167 | 111,360 |
| El Paso [21] | | 4,051 | 3,671 | 3,845 | 15,678 | 24,886 | 52,599 | 101,877 | 131,597 | 131,067 | 194,968 | 314,070 | 359,291 | 479,899 | 591,610 | 679,622 |
| Encinal [22] | | 43 | 427 | 1,902 | | | | | | | | | | | | |
| Erath | | 2,425 | 1,801 | 11,796 | 21,584 | 29,966 | 32,095 | 28,385 | 20,804 | 20,760 | 18,434 | 16,236 | 18,141 | 22,560 | 27,991 | 33,001 |
| Falls | | 3,614 | 9,851 | 16,240 | 20,706 | 33,342 | 35,649 | 36,217 | 38,771 | 35,984 | 26,724 | 21,263 | 17,300 | 17,946 | 17,712 | 18,576 |
| Fannin | 3,788 | 9,217 | 13,207 | 25,501 | 38,709 | 51,793 | 44,801 | 48,186 | 41,163 | 41,064 | 31,253 | 23,880 | 22,705 | 24,285 | 24,804 | 31,242 |
| Fayette | 3,756 | 11,604 | 16,863 | 27,996 | 31,481 | 36,542 | 29,796 | 29,965 | 30,708 | 29,246 | 24,176 | 20,384 | 17,650 | 18,832 | 20,095 | 21,804 |
| Fisher | | | | 136 | 2,996 | 2,708 | 12,596 | 11,009 | 13,563 | 12,932 | 11,023 | 7,865 | 6,344 | 5,891 | 4,842 | 4,344 |
| Floyd | | | | 3 | 529 | 2,020 | 4,638 | 9,758 | 12,409 | 10,659 | 10,535 | 12,369 | 11,044 | 9,834 | 8,497 | 7,771 |
| Foard [23] | | | | | | 1,568 | 5,726 | 4,747 | 6,315 | 5,237 | 4,216 | 3,125 | 2,211 | 2,158 | 1,794 | 1,622 |
| Foley [24] | | | | | | | | | | | | | | | | |
| Fort Bend | 2,533 | 6,143 | 7,114 | 9,380 | 10,586 | 16,538 | 18,168 | 22,931 | 29,718 | 32,963 | 31,056 | 40,527 | 52,314 | 130,846 | 225,421 | 354,452 |
| Franklin | | | | 5,280 | 6,481 | 8,674 | 9,331 | 9,304 | 8,494 | 8,378 | 6,257 | 5,101 | 5,291 | 6,893 | 7,802 | 9,458 |
| Freestone | | 6,881 | 8,139 | 14,921 | 15,987 | 18,910 | 20,557 | 23,264 | 22,589 | 21,138 | 15,696 | 12,525 | 11,116 | 14,830 | 15,818 | 17,867 |
| Frio | | 42 | 309 | 2,130 | 3,112 | 4,200 | 8,895 | 9,286 | 9,411 | 9,207 | 10,357 | 10,112 | 11,159 | 13,785 | 13,472 | 16,252 |
| Gaines | | | | 8 | 68 | 55 | 1,255 | 1,018 | 2,800 | 8,136 | 8,909 | 12,267 | 11,593 | 13,150 | 14,123 | 14,467 |
| Galveston | 4,529 | 8,229 | 15,290 | 24,121 | 31,476 | 44,116 | 44,479 | 53,150 | 64,401 | 81,173 | 113,066 | 140,364 | 169,812 | 195,940 | 217,399 | 250,158 |
| Garza [24] | | | | 36 | 14 | 185 | 1,995 | 4,253 | 5,586 | 5,678 | 6,281 | 6,611 | 5,289 | 5,336 | 5,143 | 4,872 |
| Gillespie | 1,240 | 2,736 | 3,566 | 5,228 | 7,056 | 8,229 | 9,447 | 10,015 | 11,020 | 10,670 | 10,520 | 10,048 | 10,553 | 13,532 | 17,204 | 20,814 |
| Glasscock [14] | | | | | 208 | 286 | 1,143 | 555 | 1,263 | 1,193 | 1,089 | 1,118 | 1,155 | 1,304 | 1,447 | 1,406 |

| County | 1850 | 1860 | 1870 | 1880 | 1890 | 1900 | 1910 | 1920 | 1930 | 1940 | 1950 | 1960 | 1970 | 1980 | 1990 | 2000 |
|---|---|---|---|---|---|---|---|---|---|---|---|---|---|---|---|---|
| Goliad | 648 | 3,384 | 3,628 | 5,832 | 5,910 | 8,310 | 9,909 | 9,348 | 10,093 | 8,798 | 6,219 | 5,429 | 4,869 | 5,193 | 5,980 | 6,928 |
| Gonzales | 1,492 | 8,059 | 8,951 | 14,840 | 18,016 | 28,882 | 28,055 | 28,438 | 28,337 | 26,075 | 21,164 | 17,845 | 16,375 | 16,883 | 17,205 | 18,628 |
| Gray | | | | 56 | 203 | 480 | 3,405 | 4,663 | 22,090 | 23,911 | 24,728 | 31,535 | 26,949 | 26,386 | 23,967 | 22,744 |
| Grayson | 2,008 | 8,184 | 14,387 | 38,108 | 53,211 | 63,661 | 65,996 | 74,165 | 65,843 | 69,499 | 70,467 | 73,043 | 83,225 | 89,796 | 95,021 | 110,595 |
| Greer[52] | | | | | 5,336 | | | | | | | | | | | |
| Gregg | | | | 8,530 | 9,402 | 12,343 | 14,140 | 16,767 | 15,778 | 58,027 | 61,258 | 69,436 | 75,929 | 99,487 | 104,948 | 111,379 |
| Grimes | 4,008 | 10,307 | 13,218 | 18,603 | 21,312 | 26,106 | 21,205 | 23,101 | 22,642 | 21,960 | 15,135 | 12,709 | 11,855 | 13,580 | 18,828 | 23,552 |
| Guadalupe | 1,511 | 5,444 | 7,282 | 12,202 | 15,217 | 21,385 | 24,913 | 27,719 | 28,925 | 25,596 | 25,392 | 29,017 | 33,554 | 46,708 | 64,873 | 89,023 |
| Hale | | | | | 721 | 1,680 | 7,566 | 10,104 | 20,189 | 18,813 | 28,211 | 36,798 | 34,137 | 37,592 | 34,671 | 36,602 |
| Hall | | | | 36 | 703 | 1,660 | 8,279 | 11,137 | 16,966 | 12,117 | 10,930 | 7,322 | 6,015 | 5,594 | 3,905 | 3,782 |
| Hamilton[6] | | 489 | 733 | 6,365 | 6,313 | 13,520 | 15,315 | 14,676 | 13,523 | 12,303 | 10,660 | 8,488 | 7,198 | 8,297 | 7,733 | 8,229 |
| Hansford | | | | 18 | 133 | 167 | 935 | 1,354 | 3,548 | 2,783 | 4,202 | 6,208 | 6,351 | 6,209 | 5,848 | 5,369 |
| Hardeman[23] | | | | 50 | 3,904 | 3,634 | 11,213 | 12,487 | 14,532 | 11,073 | 10,212 | 8,275 | 6,795 | 6,368 | 5,283 | 4,724 |
| Hardin | | 1,353 | 1,460 | 1,870 | 3,956 | 5,049 | 12,947 | 15,983 | 13,936 | 15,875 | 19,535 | 24,629 | 29,996 | 40,721 | 41,320 | 48,073 |
| Harris | 4,668 | 9,070 | 17,375 | 27,985 | 37,249 | 63,786 | 115,693 | 186,667 | 359,328 | 528,961 | 806,701 | 1,243,158 | 1,741,912 | 2,409,544 | 2,818,199 | 3,400,578 |
| Harrison | 11,822 | 15,001 | 13,241 | 25,177 | 26,721 | 31,878 | 37,243 | 43,565 | 48,937 | 50,900 | 47,745 | 45,594 | 44,841 | 52,265 | 57,483 | 62,110 |
| Hartley | | | | 100 | 252 | 377 | 1,298 | 1,109 | 2,185 | 1,873 | 1,913 | 2,171 | 2,782 | 3,987 | 3,634 | 5,537 |
| Haskell | | | | 48 | 1,665 | 2,637 | 16,249 | 14,193 | 16,669 | 14,905 | 13,736 | 11,174 | 8,512 | 7,725 | 6,820 | 6,093 |
| Hays | 387 | 2,126 | 4,088 | 7,555 | 11,352 | 14,142 | 15,518 | 15,920 | 14,915 | 15,349 | 17,840 | 19,934 | 27,642 | 40,594 | 65,614 | 97,589 |
| Hemphill[11] | | | | 149 | 519 | 815 | 3,170 | 4,280 | 4,637 | 4,170 | 4,123 | 3,185 | 3,084 | 5,304 | 3,720 | 3,351 |
| Henderson | 1,237 | 4,595 | 6,786 | 9,735 | 12,285 | 19,970 | 20,131 | 28,327 | 30,583 | 31,822 | 23,405 | 21,786 | 26,466 | 42,606 | 58,543 | 73,277 |
| Hidalgo[25][49] | | 1,182 | 2,387 | 4,347 | 6,534 | 6,837 | 13,728 | 38,110 | 77,004 | 106,059 | 160,446 | 180,904 | 181,535 | 283,229 | 383,545 | 569,463 |
| Hill | | 3,653 | 7,453 | 16,554 | 27,583 | 41,355 | 46,760 | 43,332 | 43,036 | 38,355 | 31,282 | 23,650 | 22,596 | 25,024 | 27,146 | 32,321 |
| Hockley | | | | | | 44 | 137 | 137 | 9,298 | 12,693 | 20,407 | 22,340 | 20,396 | 23,230 | 24,199 | 22,716 |
| Hood | | | 2,585 | 6,125 | 7,614 | 9,146 | 10,008 | 8,759 | 6,779 | 6,674 | 5,287 | 5,443 | 6,368 | 17,714 | 28,981 | 41,100 |
| Hopkins | 2,623 | 7,745 | 12,651 | 15,461 | 20,572 | 27,950 | 31,038 | 34,791 | 29,410 | 30,264 | 23,490 | 18,594 | 20,710 | 25,247 | 28,833 | 31,960 |
| Houston | 2,721 | 8,058 | 8,147 | 16,702 | 19,360 | 25,452 | 29,564 | 28,601 | 30,017 | 31,137 | 22,825 | 19,276 | 17,855 | 22,299 | 21,375 | 23,185 |
| Howard | | | | 50 | 1,210 | 2,528 | 8,881 | 6,962 | 22,888 | 20,990 | 26,722 | 40,139 | 37,796 | 33,142 | 32,343 | 33,627 |
| Hudspeth[26] | | | | | | | | 962 | 3,728 | 3,149 | 4,298 | 3,343 | 2,392 | 2,728 | 2,915 | 3,344 |
| Hunt | 1,520 | 6,630 | 10,291 | 17,230 | 31,885 | 47,295 | 48,116 | 50,350 | 49,016 | 48,793 | 42,731 | 39,399 | 47,948 | 55,248 | 64,343 | 76,596 |
| Hutchinson | | | | 50 | 58 | 303 | 892 | 721 | 14,848 | 19,069 | 31,580 | 34,419 | 24,443 | 26,304 | 25,689 | 23,857 |
| Irion[12] | | | | | 870 | 848 | 1,283 | 1,610 | 2,049 | 1,963 | 1,590 | 1,183 | 1,070 | 1,386 | 1,629 | 1,771 |
| Jack | | 1,000 | 694 | 6,626 | 9,740 | 10,224 | 11,817 | 9,863 | 9,046 | 10,206 | 7,755 | 7,418 | 6,711 | 7,408 | 6,981 | 8,763 |
| Jackson | 996 | 2,612 | 2,278 | 2,723 | 3,281 | 6,094 | 6,471 | 11,244 | 10,980 | 11,720 | 12,916 | 14,040 | 12,975 | 13,352 | 13,039 | 14,391 |
| Jasper | 1,767 | 4,037 | 4,218 | 5,779 | 5,592 | 7,138 | 14,000 | 15,569 | 17,064 | 17,491 | 20,049 | 22,100 | 24,692 | 30,781 | 31,102 | 35,604 |
| Jeff Davis[27] | | | | | 1,394 | 1,150 | 1,678 | 1,445 | 1,800 | 2,375 | 2,090 | 1,582 | 1,527 | 1,647 | 1,946 | 2,207 |
| Jefferson | 1,836 | 1,995 | 1,906 | 3,489 | 5,857 | 14,239 | 38,182 | 73,120 | 133,391 | 145,329 | 195,083 | 245,659 | 244,773 | 250,938 | 239,397 | 252,051 |
| Jim Hogg[28][49] | | | | | | | | 1,914 | 4,919 | 5,449 | 5,389 | 5,022 | 4,654 | 5,168 | 5,109 | 5,281 |
| Jim Wells[29] | | | | | | | | 6,587 | 13,456 | 20,239 | 27,991 | 34,548 | 33,032 | 36,498 | 37,679 | 39,326 |
| Johnson | | 4,305 | 4,923 | 17,911 | 22,313 | 33,819 | 24,460 | 27,286 | 33,317 | 30,384 | 31,390 | 34,720 | 45,769 | 67,649 | 97,165 | 126,811 |
| Jones | | | | 546 | 3,797 | 7,053 | 24,299 | 22,323 | 24,233 | 23,378 | 22,147 | 19,299 | 16,106 | 17,268 | 16,490 | 20,785 |
| Karnes | | 2,171 | 1,705 | 3,270 | 3,637 | 8,681 | 14,942 | 19,049 | 23,316 | 19,248 | 17,139 | 14,995 | 13,462 | 13,593 | 12,455 | 15,446 |
| Kaufman | 1,047 | 3,936 | 6,895 | 15,448 | 21,598 | 33,376 | 35,323 | 41,276 | 40,905 | 38,308 | 31,170 | 29,931 | 32,392 | 39,015 | 52,220 | 71,313 |
| Kendall[30][50] | | | 1,536 | 2,763 | 3,826 | 4,103 | 4,517 | 4,779 | 4,970 | 5,080 | 5,423 | 5,889 | 6,964 | 10,635 | 14,589 | 23,743 |
| Kenedy[30][50] | | | | | | | | 1,033 | 701 | 700 | 632 | 884 | 678 | 543 | 460 | 414 |
| Kent | | | | 92 | 324 | 899 | 2,655 | 3,335 | 3,851 | 3,413 | 2,249 | 1,727 | 1,434 | 1,145 | 1,010 | 859 |
| Kerr[31] | | 634 | 1,042 | 2,168 | 4,462 | 4,980 | 5,505 | 5,842 | 10,151 | 11,650 | 14,022 | 16,800 | 19,454 | 28,780 | 36,304 | 43,653 |
| Kimble | | | 72 | 1,343 | 2,243 | 2,503 | 3,261 | 3,581 | 4,119 | 5,064 | 4,619 | 3,943 | 3,904 | 4,063 | 4,122 | 4,468 |

| County | 1850 | 1860 | 1870 | 1880 | 1890 | 1900 | 1910 | 1920 | 1930 | 1940 | 1950 | 1960 | 1970 | 1980 | 1990 | 2000 |
|---|---|---|---|---|---|---|---|---|---|---|---|---|---|---|---|---|
| King | | | | 40 | 173 | 490 | 810 | 655 | 1,193 | 1,066 | 870 | 640 | 464 | 425 | 354 | 356 |
| Kinney [32] | | 61 | 1,204 | 4,487 | 3,781 | 2,447 | 3,401 | 3,746 | 3,980 | 4,533 | 2,668 | 2,452 | 2,006 | 2,279 | 3,119 | 3,379 |
| Kleberg [29] | | | | | | | | 7,837 | 12,451 | 13,344 | 21,991 | 30,052 | 33,166 | 33,358 | 30,274 | 31,549 |
| Knox [23] | | | | 77 | 1,134 | 2,322 | 9,625 | 9,240 | 11,368 | 10,090 | 10,082 | 7,857 | 5,972 | 5,329 | 4,837 | 4,253 |
| Lamar | 3,978 | 10,136 | 15,790 | 27,193 | 37,302 | 48,627 | 46,544 | 55,742 | 48,529 | 50,425 | 43,033 | 34,234 | 36,062 | 42,156 | 43,949 | 48,499 |
| Lamb | | | | | 4 | 31 | 540 | 1,175 | 17,452 | 17,606 | 20,015 | 21,896 | 17,770 | 18,669 | 15,072 | 14,709 |
| Lampasas [6] | | 1,028 | 1,344 | 5,421 | 7,584 | 8,625 | 9,532 | 8,800 | 8,677 | 9,167 | 9,929 | 9,418 | 9,323 | 12,005 | 13,521 | 17,762 |
| La Salle | | | 69 | 789 | 2,139 | 2,303 | 4,747 | 4,821 | 8,228 | 8,003 | 7,485 | 5,972 | 5,014 | 5,514 | 5,254 | 5,866 |
| Lavaca | 1,571 | 5,945 | 9,168 | 13,641 | 21,887 | 28,121 | 26,418 | 28,964 | 27,550 | 25,485 | 22,159 | 20,174 | 17,903 | 19,004 | 18,690 | 19,210 |
| Lee | | | | 8,937 | 11,952 | 14,595 | 13,132 | 14,014 | 13,390 | 12,751 | 10,144 | 8,949 | 8,048 | 10,952 | 12,854 | 15,657 |
| Leon | 1,946 | 6,781 | 6,523 | 12,817 | 13,841 | 18,072 | 16,583 | 18,286 | 19,898 | 17,733 | 12,024 | 9,951 | 8,738 | 9,594 | 12,665 | 15,335 |
| Liberty | 2,522 | 3,189 | 4,414 | 4,999 | 4,230 | 8,102 | 10,686 | 14,637 | 19,868 | 24,541 | 26,729 | 31,595 | 33,014 | 47,088 | 52,726 | 70,154 |
| Limestone | 2,608 | 4,537 | 8,591 | 16,246 | 21,678 | 32,573 | 34,621 | 33,283 | 39,497 | 33,781 | 25,251 | 20,413 | 18,100 | 20,224 | 20,946 | 22,051 |
| Lipscomb [11] | | | | 69 | 632 | 790 | 2,634 | 3,684 | 4,512 | 3,764 | 3,658 | 3,406 | 3,486 | 3,766 | 3,143 | 3,057 |
| Live Oak | | 593 | 852 | 1,994 | 2,055 | 2,268 | 3,442 | 4,171 | 8,956 | 9,799 | 9,054 | 7,846 | 6,697 | 9,606 | 9,556 | 12,309 |
| Llano | | 1,101 | 1,379 | 4,962 | 6,772 | 7,301 | 6,520 | 5,360 | 5,538 | 5,996 | 5,377 | 5,240 | 6,979 | 10,144 | 11,631 | 17,044 |
| Loving [14] | | | | | 3 | 33 | 249 | 82 | 195 | 285 | 227 | 226 | 164 | 91 | 107 | 67 |
| Lubbock | | | | | 33 | 293 | 3,624 | 11,096 | 39,104 | 51,782 | 101,048 | 156,271 | 179,295 | 211,651 | 222,636 | 242,628 |
| Lynn | | | | | 24 | 17 | 1,713 | 4,751 | 12,372 | 11,931 | 11,030 | 10,914 | 9,107 | 8,605 | 6,758 | 6,550 |
| Madison | | | 4,061 | 5,395 | 8,512 | 10,432 | 10,318 | 11,956 | 12,227 | 12,029 | 7,996 | 6,749 | 7,693 | 10,649 | 10,931 | 12,940 |
| Marion | | | 8,562 | 10,983 | 10,862 | 10,754 | 10,472 | 10,886 | 10,371 | 11,457 | 10,172 | 8,049 | 8,517 | 10,360 | 9,984 | 10,941 |
| Martin | | | | 12 | 264 | 332 | 1,549 | 1,146 | 5,785 | 5,556 | 5,541 | 5,068 | 4,774 | 4,684 | 4,956 | 4,746 |
| Mason | | 630 | 678 | 2,655 | 5,180 | 5,573 | 5,683 | 4,824 | 5,511 | 5,378 | 4,945 | 3,780 | 3,356 | 3,683 | 3,423 | 3,738 |
| Matagorda | 2,124 | 3,454 | 3,377 | 3,940 | 3,985 | 6,097 | 13,594 | 16,589 | 17,678 | 20,066 | 21,559 | 25,744 | 27,913 | 37,828 | 36,928 | 37,957 |
| Maverick | | 726 | 1,951 | 2,967 | 3,698 | 4,066 | 5,151 | 7,418 | 6,120 | 10,071 | 12,292 | 14,508 | 18,093 | 31,398 | 36,378 | 47,297 |
| McCulloch | | | 173 | 1,533 | 3,217 | 3,960 | 13,405 | 11,020 | 13,883 | 13,208 | 11,701 | 8,815 | 8,571 | 8,735 | 8,778 | 8,205 |
| McLennan | | 6,206 | 13,500 | 26,934 | 39,204 | 59,772 | 73,250 | 82,921 | 98,682 | 101,898 | 130,194 | 150,091 | 147,553 | 170,755 | 189,123 | 213,517 |
| McMullen | | | 230 | 701 | 1,038 | 1,024 | 1,091 | 952 | 1,351 | 1,374 | 1,187 | 1,116 | 1,095 | 789 | 817 | 851 |
| Medina | | 1,838 | 2,078 | 4,492 | 5,730 | 7,783 | 13,415 | 11,679 | 13,989 | 16,106 | 17,013 | 18,904 | 20,249 | 23,164 | 27,312 | 39,304 |
| Menard | | | 667 | 1,239 | 1,215 | 2,011 | 2,707 | 3,162 | 4,447 | 4,521 | 4,175 | 2,964 | 2,646 | 2,346 | 2,252 | 2,360 |
| Midland [33] | | | | | 1,033 | 1,741 | 3,464 | 2,449 | 8,005 | 11,721 | 25,785 | 67,717 | 65,433 | 82,636 | 106,611 | 116,009 |
| Milam | 2,907 | 5,175 | 8,984 | 18,659 | 24,773 | 39,666 | 36,780 | 38,104 | 37,915 | 33,120 | 23,585 | 22,263 | 20,028 | 22,732 | 22,946 | 24,238 |
| Mills [34] | | | | | 5,493 | 7,851 | 9,694 | 9,019 | 8,293 | 7,951 | 5,999 | 4,467 | 4,212 | 4,477 | 4,531 | 5,151 |
| Mitchell | | | | 117 | 2,059 | 2,855 | 8,956 | 7,527 | 14,183 | 12,477 | 14,357 | 11,255 | 9,073 | 9,088 | 8,016 | 9,698 |
| Montague | | 849 | 890 | 11,257 | 18,863 | 24,800 | 25,123 | 22,200 | 19,159 | 20,442 | 17,070 | 14,893 | 15,326 | 17,410 | 17,274 | 19,117 |
| Montgomery | 2,384 | 5,479 | 6,483 | 10,154 | 11,765 | 17,067 | 15,679 | 17,334 | 14,588 | 23,055 | 24,504 | 26,839 | 49,479 | 128,487 | 182,201 | 293,768 |
| Moore | | | | | 15 | 209 | 561 | 571 | 1,555 | 4,461 | 13,349 | 14,773 | 14,060 | 16,575 | 17,865 | 20,121 |
| Morris | | | | 5,032 | 6,580 | 8,220 | 10,439 | 10,289 | 10,028 | 9,810 | 9,433 | 12,576 | 12,310 | 14,629 | 13,200 | 13,048 |
| Motley | | | | 24 | 139 | 1,257 | 2,396 | 4,107 | 6,812 | 4,994 | 3,963 | 2,870 | 2,178 | 1,950 | 1,532 | 1,426 |
| Nacogdoches | 5,193 | 8,292 | 9,614 | 11,590 | 15,984 | 24,663 | 27,406 | 28,457 | 30,290 | 35,392 | 30,326 | 28,046 | 36,362 | 46,786 | 54,753 | 59,203 |
| Navarro | 2,190 | 5,996 | 8,879 | 21,702 | 26,373 | 43,374 | 47,070 | 50,624 | 60,507 | 51,308 | 39,916 | 34,423 | 31,150 | 35,323 | 39,926 | 45,124 |
| Newton | 1,689 | 3,119 | 2,187 | 4,350 | 4,650 | 7,282 | 10,850 | 12,196 | 12,524 | 13,700 | 10,832 | 10,372 | 11,657 | 13,254 | 13,569 | 15,072 |
| Nolan | | | | 640 | 1,573 | 2,611 | 11,999 | 10,868 | 19,323 | 17,309 | 19,808 | 18,963 | 16,220 | 17,359 | 16,594 | 15,802 |
| Nueces [35] | 698 | 2,906 | 3,975 | 7,673 | 8,093 | 10,439 | 21,955 | 22,807 | 51,779 | 92,661 | 165,471 | 221,573 | 237,544 | 268,215 | 291,145 | 313,645 |
| Ochiltree | | | | | 198 | 267 | 1,602 | 2,331 | 5,224 | 4,213 | 6,024 | 9,380 | 9,704 | 9,588 | 9,128 | 9,006 |
| Oldham | | | | 387 | 270 | 349 | 812 | 709 | 1,404 | 1,385 | 1,672 | 1,928 | 2,258 | 2,283 | 2,278 | 2,185 |
| Orange | | 1,916 | 1,255 | 2,938 | 4,770 | 5,905 | 9,528 | 15,379 | 15,149 | 17,382 | 40,567 | 60,357 | 71,170 | 83,838 | 80,509 | 84,966 |
| Palo Pinto | | 1,524 | | 5,885 | 8,320 | 12,291 | 19,506 | 23,431 | 17,576 | 18,456 | 17,154 | 20,516 | 28,962 | 24,062 | 25,055 | 27,026 |

| County | 2000 | 1990 | 1980 | 1970 | 1960 | 1950 | 1940 | 1930 | 1920 | 1910 | 1900 | 1890 | 1880 | 1870 | 1860 | 1850 |
|---|---|---|---|---|---|---|---|---|---|---|---|---|---|---|---|---|
| Panola | 22,756 | 22,035 | 20,724 | 15,894 | 16,870 | 19,250 | 22,513 | 24,063 | 21,755 | 20,424 | 21,404 | 14,328 | 12,219 | 10,119 | 8,475 | 3,871 |
| Parker | 88,495 | 64,785 | 44,609 | 33,888 | 22,880 | 24,528 | 20,482 | 18,759 | 23,382 | 26,331 | 25,823 | 21,682 | 15,870 | 4,186 | 4,213 | |
| Parmer | 10,016 | 9,863 | 11,038 | 10,509 | 9,583 | 5,787 | 5,890 | 5,869 | 1,699 | 1,555 | 34 | 7 | | | | |
| Pecos[36] | 16,809 | 14,675 | 14,618 | 13,748 | 11,957 | 9,939 | 8,185 | 7,812 | 3,857 | 2,071 | 2,360 | 1,326 | 1,807 | | | |
| Polk | 41,133 | 30,687 | 24,407 | 14,457 | 13,861 | 16,194 | 20,635 | 17,555 | 16,710 | 17,459 | 14,447 | 10,332 | 7,189 | 8,707 | 8,300 | 2,348 |
| Potter | 113,546 | 97,874 | 98,637 | 90,511 | 115,580 | 73,366 | 54,265 | 46,080 | 16,710 | 12,424 | 1,820 | 849 | 28 | | | |
| Presidio[37] | 7,304 | 6,637 | 5,188 | 4,842 | 5,460 | 7,354 | 10,925 | 10,154 | 12,202 | 5,218 | 3,673 | 1,698 | 2,873 | 1,636 | 580 | |
| Rains | 9,139 | 6,715 | 4,839 | 3,752 | 2,993 | 4,266 | 7,334 | 7,114 | 8,099 | 6,787 | 6,127 | 3,909 | 3,035 | | | |
| Randall[38] | 104,312 | 89,673 | 75,062 | 53,885 | 33,913 | 13,774 | 7,185 | 7,071 | 3,675 | 3,312 | 963 | 187 | 3 | | | |
| Reagan[39] | 3,326 | 4,514 | 4,135 | 3,239 | 3,782 | 3,127 | 1,997 | 3,028 | 377 | 392 | | | | | | |
| Real | 3,047 | 2,412 | 2,469 | 2,013 | 2,079 | 2,479 | 2,420 | 2,197 | 1,461 | | | | | | | |
| Red River | 14,314 | 14,317 | 16,101 | 14,298 | 15,682 | 21,851 | 29,769 | 30,923 | 35,829 | 28,564 | 29,893 | 21,452 | 17,194 | 10,653 | 8,535 | 3,906 |
| Reeves[40] | 13,137 | 15,852 | 15,801 | 16,526 | 17,644 | 11,745 | 8,006 | 6,407 | 4,457 | 4,392 | 1,847 | 1,247 | | | | |
| Refugio | 7,828 | 7,976 | 9,289 | 9,494 | 10,975 | 10,113 | 10,383 | 7,691 | 4,050 | 2,814 | 1,641 | 1,239 | 1,585 | 2,324 | 1,600 | 288 |
| Roberts | 887 | 1,025 | 1,187 | 967 | 1,075 | 1,031 | 1,289 | 1,457 | 1,469 | 950 | 620 | 326 | 32 | | | |
| Robertson | 16,000 | 15,511 | 14,653 | 14,389 | 16,157 | 19,908 | 25,710 | 27,240 | 27,933 | 27,454 | 31,480 | 26,506 | 22,383 | 9,990 | 4,997 | 934 |
| Rockwall | 43,080 | 25,604 | 14,528 | 7,046 | 5,878 | 6,156 | 7,051 | 7,658 | 8,591 | 8,072 | 8,531 | 5,972 | 2,984 | | | |
| Runnels | 11,495 | 11,294 | 11,872 | 12,108 | 15,016 | 16,771 | 18,903 | 21,821 | 17,074 | 20,858 | 5,379 | 3,193 | 980 | | | |
| Rusk | 47,372 | 43,735 | 41,382 | 34,102 | 36,421 | 42,348 | 51,023 | 32,484 | 31,689 | 26,946 | 26,099 | 18,559 | 18,986 | 16,916 | 15,803 | 8,148 |
| Sabine | 10,469 | 9,586 | 8,702 | 7,187 | 7,302 | 8,568 | 10,896 | 11,998 | 12,299 | 8,582 | 6,394 | 4,969 | 4,161 | 3,256 | 2,750 | 2,498 |
| San Augustine | 8,946 | 7,999 | 8,785 | 7,858 | 7,722 | 8,837 | 12,471 | 11,998 | 13,737 | 11,264 | 8,434 | 6,688 | 5,084 | 4,196 | 4,094 | 3,648 |
| San Jacinto | 22,246 | 16,372 | 11,434 | 6,702 | 6,153 | 7,172 | 9,056 | 9,711 | 9,867 | 9,542 | 10,277 | 7,360 | 6,186 | | | |
| San Patricio | 67,138 | 58,749 | 58,013 | 47,288 | 45,021 | 35,842 | 28,871 | 23,836 | 11,386 | 7,307 | 2,372 | 1,312 | 1,010 | 602 | 620 | 200 |
| San Saba | 6,186 | 5,401 | 5,693 | 5,540 | 6,381 | 8,666 | 11,012 | 10,273 | 10,045 | 11,245 | 7,569 | 6,641 | 5,324 | 1,425 | 913 | |
| Schleicher[41] | 2,935 | 2,990 | 2,820 | 2,277 | 2,791 | 2,852 | 3,083 | 3,166 | 1,851 | 1,893 | 515 | 155 | | | | |
| Scurry | 16,361 | 18,634 | 18,192 | 15,760 | 20,369 | 22,779 | 11,545 | 12,188 | 9,003 | 10,924 | 4,158 | 1,415 | 102 | | | |
| Shackelford | 3,302 | 3,316 | 3,915 | 3,323 | 3,990 | 5,001 | 6,211 | 6,695 | 4,960 | 4,201 | 2,461 | 2,012 | 2,037 | 455 | 44 | |
| Shelby | 25,224 | 22,034 | 23,084 | 19,672 | 20,479 | 23,479 | 29,235 | 28,627 | 27,464 | 26,423 | 20,452 | 14,365 | 9,532 | 5,732 | 5,362 | 4,239 |
| Sherman | 3,186 | 2,858 | 3,174 | 3,657 | 2,605 | 2,443 | 2,026 | 2,314 | 1,473 | 1,476 | 104 | 34 | | | | |
| Smith | 174,706 | 151,309 | 128,366 | 97,096 | 86,350 | 74,701 | 69,090 | 53,123 | 46,769 | 41,746 | 37,370 | 28,324 | 21,863 | 16,532 | 13,392 | 4,292 |
| Somervell | 6,809 | 5,360 | 4,154 | 2,793 | 2,577 | 2,542 | 3,071 | 3,016 | 3,563 | 3,931 | 3,498 | 3,419 | 2,649 | | | |
| Starr[9][49] | 53,597 | 40,518 | 27,266 | 17,707 | 17,137 | 13,948 | 13,312 | 11,409 | 11,089 | 13,151 | 11,469 | 10,749 | 8,304 | 4,154 | 2,406 | |
| Stephens[8] | 9,674 | 9,010 | 9,926 | 8,414 | 8,885 | 10,597 | 12,356 | 16,560 | 15,403 | 7,980 | 6,466 | 4,926 | 4,725 | 330 | 230 | |
| Sterling[42] | 1,393 | 1,438 | 1,206 | 1,056 | 1,177 | 1,282 | 1,404 | 1,431 | 1,053 | 1,493 | 1,127 | | | | | |
| Stonewall | 1,693 | 2,013 | 2,406 | 2,397 | 3,017 | 3,679 | 5589 | 5,667 | 4,086 | 5,320 | 2,183 | 1,024 | 104 | | | |
| Sutton[41] | 4,077 | 4,135 | 5,130 | 3,175 | 3,738 | 3,746 | 3,977 | 2,807 | 1,598 | 1,569 | 1,727 | 658 | | | | |
| Swisher | 8,378 | 8,133 | 9,723 | 10,373 | 10,607 | 8,249 | 6,528 | 7,343 | 4,388 | 4,012 | 1,227 | 100 | 4 | | | |
| Tarrant | 1,446,219 | 1,170,103 | 860,880 | 716,317 | 538,495 | 361,253 | 225,521 | 197,553 | 152,800 | 108,572 | 52,376 | 41,142 | 24,671 | 5,788 | 6,020 | 664 |
| Taylor | 126,555 | 119,655 | 110,932 | 97,853 | 101,078 | 63,370 | 44,147 | 41,023 | 24,081 | 26,293 | 10,499 | 6,957 | 1,736 | | | |
| Terrell[43] | 1,081 | 1,410 | 1,595 | 1,940 | 2,600 | 3,189 | 2,952 | 2,660 | 1,595 | 1,430 | | | | | | |
| Terry | 12,761 | 13,218 | 14,581 | 14,118 | 16,286 | 13,107 | 11,160 | 8,883 | 2,236 | 1,474 | 48 | 21 | | | | |
| Throckmorton[51] | 1,850 | 1,880 | 2,053 | 2,205 | 2,767 | 3,618 | 4,275 | 5,253 | 3,589 | 4,563 | 1,750 | 902 | 711 | | 124 | |
| Titus | 28,118 | 24,009 | 21,442 | 16,702 | 16,785 | 17,302 | 19,228 | 16,003 | 18,128 | 16,422 | 12,292 | 8,190 | 5,959 | 11,339 | 9,648 | 3,636 |
| Tom Green[44] | 104,010 | 98,458 | 84,784 | 71,047 | 64,630 | 58,929 | 39,302 | 36,033 | 15,210 | 17,882 | 6,804 | 5,152 | 3,615 | | | |
| Travis | 812,280 | 576,407 | 419,335 | 295,516 | 212,136 | 160,980 | 111,053 | 77,777 | 57,616 | 55,620 | 47,386 | 36,322 | 27,028 | 13,153 | 8,080 | 3,138 |
| Trinity | 13,779 | 11,445 | 9,450 | 7,628 | 7,539 | 10,040 | 13,705 | 13,637 | 13,623 | 12,768 | 10,976 | 7,648 | 4,915 | 4,141 | 4,392 | |
| Tyler | 20,871 | 16,646 | 16,223 | 12,417 | 10,666 | 11,292 | 11,948 | 11,448 | 10,415 | 10,250 | 11,899 | 10,877 | 5,825 | 5,010 | 4,525 | 1,894 |
| Upshur | 35,291 | 31,370 | 28,595 | 20,976 | 19,793 | 20,822 | 26,178 | 22,297 | 22,472 | 19,960 | 16,266 | 12,695 | 10,266 | 12,039 | 10,645 | 3,394 |

| County | 1850 | 1860 | 1870 | 1880 | 1890 | 1900 | 1910 | 1920 | 1930 | 1940 | 1950 | 1960 | 1970 | 1980 | 1990 | 2000 |
|---|---|---|---|---|---|---|---|---|---|---|---|---|---|---|---|---|
| Upton [14] | | | | | 52 | 48 | 501 | 253 | 5,968 | 4,297 | 5,307 | 6,239 | 4,697 | 4,619 | 4,447 | 3,404 |
| Uvalde | | 506 | 851 | 2,541 | 3,804 | 4,647 | 11,233 | 10,769 | 12,945 | 13,246 | 16,015 | 16,814 | 17,348 | 22,441 | 23,340 | 25,926 |
| Val Verde [45] | | | | | 2,874 | 5,263 | 8,613 | 12,706 | 14,924 | 15,453 | 16,635 | 24,461 | 27,471 | 35,910 | 38,721 | 44,856 |
| Van Zandt | 1,348 | 3,777 | 6,494 | 12,619 | 16,225 | 25,481 | 25,651 | 30,784 | 32,315 | 31,155 | 22,593 | 19,091 | 22,155 | 31,426 | 37,944 | 48,140 |
| Victoria | 2,019 | 4,171 | 4,860 | 6,289 | 8,737 | 13,678 | 14,990 | 18,271 | 20,048 | 23,741 | 31,241 | 46,475 | 53,766 | 68,807 | 74,361 | 84,088 |
| Walker | 3,964 | 8,191 | 9,766 | 12,024 | 12,874 | 15,813 | 16,061 | 18,556 | 18,528 | 19,868 | 20,163 | 21,475 | 27,680 | 41,789 | 50,917 | 61,758 |
| Ward [14] | | | | | 77 | 1,451 | 2,389 | 2,615 | 4,599 | 9,575 | 13,346 | 14,917 | 13,019 | 13,976 | 13,115 | 10,909 |
| Washington | 5,983 | 15,215 | 23,104 | 27,565 | 29,161 | 32,931 | 25,561 | 26,624 | 25,394 | 25,387 | 20,542 | 19,145 | 18,842 | 21,998 | 26,154 | 30,373 |
| Webb [9] [46] | | 1,397 | 2,615 | 5,273 | 14,842 | 21,851 | 22,503 | 29,152 | 42,128 | 45,916 | 56,141 | 64,791 | 72,859 | 99,258 | 133,239 | 193,117 |
| Wharton | 1,752 | 3,380 | 3,426 | 4,459 | 7,584 | 16,942 | 21,123 | 24,288 | 29,681 | 36,158 | 36,077 | 38,152 | 36,729 | 40,242 | 39,955 | 41,188 |
| Wheeler [11] | | | | 512 | 778 | 636 | 5,258 | 7,397 | 15,555 | 12,411 | 10,317 | 7,947 | 6,434 | 7,137 | 5,879 | 5,284 |
| Wichita | | | | 433 | 4,831 | 5,806 | 16,094 | 72,911 | 74,416 | 73,604 | 98,493 | 123,528 | 120,563 | 121,082 | 122,378 | 131,664 |
| Wilbarger | | | | 126 | 7,092 | 5,759 | 12,000 | 15,112 | 24,579 | 20,474 | 20,552 | 17,748 | 15,355 | 15,931 | 15,121 | 14,676 |
| Willacy [47] | | | | | | | | | 10,499 | 13,230 | 20,920 | 20,084 | 15,570 | 17,495 | 17,705 | 20,082 |
| Williamson | 1,568 | 4,529 | 6,368 | 15,155 | 25,909 | 38,072 | 42,228 | 42,934 | 44,146 | 41,698 | 38,853 | 35,044 | 37,305 | 76,521 | 139,551 | 249,967 |
| Wilson | | | 2,556 | 7,118 | 10,655 | 13,961 | 17,066 | 17,289 | 17,606 | 17,066 | 14,672 | 13,267 | 13,041 | 16,756 | 22,650 | 32,408 |
| Winkler [14] | | | | | 18 | 60 | 442 | 81 | 6,784 | 6,141 | 10,064 | 13,652 | 9,640 | 9,944 | 8,626 | 7,173 |
| Wise | | 3,160 | 1,450 | 16,601 | 24,134 | 27,116 | 26,450 | 23,363 | 19,178 | 19,074 | 16,141 | 17,012 | 19,687 | 26,575 | 34,679 | 48,793 |
| Wood | | 4,968 | 6,894 | 11,212 | 13,932 | 21,048 | 23,417 | 27,707 | 24,183 | 24,360 | 21,308 | 17,653 | 18,589 | 24,697 | 29,380 | 36,752 |
| Yoakum | | | | | 4 | 26 | 602 | 504 | 1,263 | 5,354 | 4,339 | 8,032 | 7,344 | 8,299 | 8,786 | 7,322 |
| Young | | 592 | 135 | 4,726 | 5,049 | 6,540 | 13,657 | 13,379 | 20,128 | 19,004 | 16,810 | 17,254 | 15,400 | 19,001 | 18,126 | 17,943 |
| Zapata [48] [49] | | 1,248 | 1,488 | 3,636 | 3,562 | 4,760 | 3,809 | 2,929 | 2,867 | 3,916 | 4,405 | 4,393 | 4,352 | 6,628 | 9,279 | 12,182 |
| Zavala | | 26 | 138 | 410 | 1,097 | 792 | 1,889 | 3,108 | 10,349 | 11,603 | 11,201 | 12,696 | 11,370 | 11,666 | 12,162 | 11,600 |

1. Part of Bandera taken to form Real in 1913.
2. Comprised the greater part of West Texas until 1876, when it was divided into counties. It was usually referred to as a part of Bexar County, but there was a separate organization, and it was listed separately in the United States Census report of 1870, referred to as Bexar Territory and Bexar District.
3. Organized from part of Presidio in 1887; Buchel and Foley annexed in 1897.
4. Part of Comanche taken to form part of Mills in 1887.
5. No population reported for Briscoe County in 1890.
6. Part taken to form Mills in 1887.
7. Created from part of Presidio in 1887; annexed to Brewster in 1897.
8. Name changed from Buchanan to Stephens in 1861.
9. Cameron, Starr and Webb reported together in 1850; population credited to Cameron.
10. Name of Cass County changed to Davis in 1861; changed back to Cass in 1871.
11. Relocation of the 100th meridian (United States Supreme Court decision of March 17, 1930) resulted in the following changes in Texas counties: Part of Harmon County, Okla., acquired by Childress County, Texas; parts of Beckham and Harmon, Okla., acquired by Collingsworth, Texas; parts of Ellis and Roger Mills, Okla., acquired by Hemphill, Texas; parts of Ellis, Okla., by Lipscomb, Texas; parts of Beckham and Roger Mills, Okla., by Wheeler, Texas.
12. Created from part of Tom Green in 1889.
13. Parts of Crockett taken to form Schleicher and Sutton in 1887, and part of Val Verde in 1885.

14. Created from part of Tom Green in 1887.
15. Culberson created from El Paso in 1911.
16. There was an old Dawson County existing in 1860 before the creation of the present Dawson County of the South Plains. The older Dawson was west of present Uvalde County.
17. Formed from part of Duval County in 1913; later disorganized; no census report.
18. Part of Duval taken to form Jim Hogg in 1913.
19. Ector formed from part of Tom Green in 1887.
20. Part of Edwards taken to form part of Real in 1913.
21. Parts of El Paso taken to form Culberson in 1911 and Hudspeth in 1917.
22. Annexed to Webb in 1899.
23. Foard organized from parts of Hardeman and Knox in 1891.
24. Organized from part of Presidio in 1887; annexed to Brewster 1897.
25. Parts of Hidalgo taken to form parts of Willacy and Brooks in 1911, and to form new boundaries of Willacy in 1921.
26. Hudspeth created from El Paso in 1917.
27. Organized from part of Presidio in 1887.
28. Jim Hogg created from parts of Duval and Brooks in 1913.
29. Jim Wells created from part of Nueces in 1911; Kleberg organized from part of Nueces 1913.
30. Kenedy created from part of Willacy in 1921.
31. Part of Kerr taken to form part of Real in 1913.
32. Part taken to form part of Val Verde in 1885.
33. Created from part of Tom Green in 1885.
34. Created from Brown, Comanche, Hamilton, Lampasas 1887.
35. Parts of Nueces taken to form Jim Wells in 1911, Kleberg in 1913.
36. Parts of Pecos taken to form Reeves in 1883, part of Val Verde in 1885 and part of Terrell in 1905.
37. Parts of Presidio taken to form Buchel, Brewster, Foley and Jeff Davis in 1887.
38. Reagan created from part of Tom Green in 1903.
39. Real created from parts of Bandera, Edwards and Kerr in 1913.
40. Created from part of Pecos in 1883.
41. Created from part of Crockett in 1887.
42. Sterling formed from part of Tom Green in 1891.
43. Terrell created from part of Pecos in 1905.
44. Parts taken to form Midland in 1885; Crane, Ector, Glasscock, Loving, Upton, Ward and Winkler in 1887; Coke and Irion in 1889; Sterling in 1891; and Reagan in 1903.
45. Created from parts of Kinney, Crockett and Pecos in 1885.
46. Encinal annexed in 1899.
47. Old Willacy created from parts of Cameron and Hidalgo in 1911; name changed to Kenedy in 1921; new Willacy organized from parts of Cameron and Hidalgo in 1921.
48. Part of Zapata taken to form part of Brooks in 1911.
49. Brooks created from Hidalgo, Starr, Zapata in 1911; part taken for part of Jim Hogg in 1913.
50. Part of Cameron taken to form Willacy in 1911; part was taken again in 1921 to form part of new area of Willacy when Kenedy was created from Willacy.
51. No population for Clay, Palo Pinto or Throckmorton in 1870.
52. Greer County was organized as Texas civil unit and under Texas administration until 1896, when it was transferred to Oklahoma by decision of the United States Supreme Court.

# Republicans Take Total Control of State Government

### By Carolyn Barta

The historic 2002 elections marked the final step in the Republicanization of Texas.

For the first time in 130 years, Republicans took total control of state government by electing the governor and all other officials running statewide and winning a majority in both houses of the Legislature.

Rick Perry moved out of the shadows of former Gov. George W. Bush by keeping his post as governor in a decisive but hard-fought victory over Democrat Tony Sanchez, a millionaire Laredo banker and oilman who set a gubernatorial spending record of $67 million — most of it his own money — in his first campaign for office.

Perry, the former lieutenant governor, automatically moved up to be governor in December 2000 after Bush was elected president. But Sanchez' charge that "we didn't elect him, we don't have to keep him," failed to resonate with voters.

Both U.S. Senate seats remained in Republican hands as John Cornyn, the state's attorney general and a former Texas Supreme Court justice, succeeded retiring senator Phil Gramm. Cornyn defeated Ron Kirk, a dynamic former Dallas mayor and the secretary of state under Gov. Ann Richards.

Election of a new junior senator made Kay Bailey Hutchison the senior senator from Texas.

*Republican Gov. Rick Perry, right, and Democratic challenger Tony Sanchez shake hands at a campaign debate. File photo.*

### Dream Team Hopes

Millionaire David Dewhurst, who was finishing his first term as land commissioner, wiped out the Democrats' best hope for statewide office when he defeated John Sharp for lieutenant governor.

Sharp had an enviable record in state government as a former legislator and comptroller but was unable to buck the Republican landslide led by the tremendous popularity of President Bush.

Democrats longed for a comeback in 2002 after being shut out of every statewide office for three consecutive elections.

They thought chances were good because they fielded a diverse top-of-the-ballot ticket that they said looked like the face of Texas.

Sharp was instrumental in the creation of the Democratic "dream team" — a trio of top candidates who would appeal to changing demographics such as a mushrooming Hispanic population.

The team included Sharp, a moderate white candidate with strong name identification; Sanchez, a wealthy Hispanic willing to spend on behalf of the ticket; and Kirk, who would have been the first black senator from Texas.

Kirk's campaign drew national attention because only three black U.S. senators have been elected since the post–Civil War era, and none from the South.

### Bush Appeal

However, the multiracial coalition lacked the political clout of President Bush, who made repeated campaign trips to his home state. Other members of the Bush family, Vice President Dick Cheney and Cabinet members also campaigned for the Texas GOP.

Bush's final appearance for Cornyn and the Texas Republican ticket came on election eve. Texas GOP candidates played up their closeness to a president whose popularity had grown following the Sept. 11, 2001, terrorist attacks in New York City, Washington, D.C. and Pennsylvania.

Meanwhile, non-Hispanic white voters, who favored Republicans, far outnumbered the turnout of the growing Hispanic voting population.

### Republican House

When the Legislature convened in January 2003, Republicans had a majority in the Texas House for the first time since Reconstruction days. It was the first session since the 1869–1871 period that Republicans held the office of governor and a majority in both houses of the Legislature.

Perry, once a Democrat, switched parties when he was a state representative, and later was elected agriculture commissioner and lieutenant governor as a Republican.

He became only the third Republican governor since E.J. Davis held the post during Reconstruction, following Bill Clements (1978–82, 1986–90) and George W. Bush (1994–2000).

The Texas House of Representatives had remained the last bastion of Democratic power in Austin until 2002. But redistricting following the 2000 census enabled the election of 88 Republicans among 150 House members.

The change in partisan control resulted in the election of the first Republican speaker since the 19th century — Tom Craddick of Midland, an oilfield supplier

who owns real estate and oil and gas investment firms. Elected to the House in 1968 as one of only eight Republicans, Craddick was the longest-serving Republican House member.

He had led the Republican effort to achieve a majority for three decades. Craddick replaced Pete Laney, a cotton farmer and fellow West Texan who was speaker for five terms.

Republicans elected 19 of 31 state senators, building on their previous 16-to-15 majority in the Texas Senate.

Redistricting and the Republican sweep meant more newcomers in Austin than usual.

Almost one-fourth of the Legislature — 42 of 181 members in both houses — were freshmen, including five senators who had previously served in the House of Representatives.

### Yellow Dog Doghouse

One of the top stories of 2002, according to *The Dallas Morning News*, was the decline of the once-dominant Democrats. The *News* reported: "Yellow Dog Texas is in the doghouse."

The top vote-getters on the ballot were two female candidates running for re-election: Carole Keeton Rylander for comptroller and Susan Combs for agriculture commissioner..

Rylander, who campaigned on the slogan that she was "one tough Grandma," garnered 64 percent or 2,878,732 votes — the most votes of any statewide candidate in a midterm election in at least 10 years.

The first woman to serve as comptroller and a former railroad commissioner and Austin mayor, she beat Marty Akins, a lawyer-rancher and former University of Texas All-American quarterback.

Before being sworn into her second term, Rylander married, changing her name to Carole Keeton Strayhorn.

Lawyer-rancher Combs won a second term as agriculture commissioner, amassing 2,636,129 votes or 59.5 percent in her race against Tom Ramsay, a state representative from Mount Vernon.

Perry was the third top vote-getter with 2,632,591 votes in his 57.8 percent win.

He interpreted his win as a mandate for his campaign message of limited government and no new taxes in the face of a $9.9 billion projected budget deficit for the next biennium — a forecast based on a declining economy.

Dewhurst's race for lieutenant governor was the closest of the state races. With 52 percent of the vote, he won the right to preside over the Texas Senate as the Legislature faced such issues as the budget shortfall, an insurance crisis and an ill-funded, controversial school finance system.

### Newcomers elected

Newcomers took over such top jobs as attorney general and land commissioner. Greg Abbott, a Texas Supreme Court justice, became attorney general by defeating former Austin mayor Kirk Watson.

Jerry Patterson, a former state senator from Houston, defeated state Sen. David Bernsen of Beaumont to win the land commission office vacated by Dewhurst.

Other statewide winners included Michael Williams, who retained his seat on the Railroad Commission by stopping challenger Sherry Boyles, an Austin lawyer.

In other 2002 election results:

– Democrats maintained a 2-to-1 ratio among courthouse officials. However, Republicans won 1,443 of 4,500 county-level offices in the 254 counties in their best showing to date, and they won control of the commissioners courts in counties containing more than 75 percent of the state's population.

– Two black Republican justices — Wallace Jefferson and Dale Wainwright — were elected to the historically white Texas Supreme Court.

*Carolyn Barta is a Dallas Morning News staff writer.*

*Republican Attorney General John Cornyn, left, defeated Democratic nominee Ron Kirk, right, former Dallas mayor, in the race for the U..S. Senate. File photo.*

# Transition in Congressional Leadership as Texans Retire

Texas suffered a big loss in leadership on Capitol Hill in 2002 with the retirement of two prominent Republicans: U.S. Sen. Phil Gramm and House Majority Leader Dick Armey.

After 18 years in the Senate, six years in the U.S. House and an unsuccessful run for the 1996 Republican presidential nomination, Gramm gave up the Senate seat held by such giants as Sam Houston, Lyndon Johnson and John Tower to become a Wall Street investment banker.

Armey, the Denton County Republican who was the architect of the 1994 GOP revolution that ended House Democrats' 40-year lock on power, retired after 18 years in Congress to return to private life.

Meanwhile, the nation responded to President George W. Bush's appeal to strengthen his hand with Congress by giving his party the majority in the U.S. Senate while continuing Republican control in the U.S. House of Representatives.

Tom DeLay, R-Sugar Land, was elected House majority leader, replacing Armey as second in power to

*Dick Armey.*      *Phil Gramm.*

the House speaker. Former Texas Attorney General John Cornyn succeeded Gramm, as Sen. Kay Bailey Hutchison became senior senator from Texas.

Four newcomers from Texas assumed office in the U.S. House. They included Republicans Michael Burgess of Highland Village, an obstetrician who succeeded Armey; Jeb Hensarling of Dallas; John Carter of Round Rock; and Democrat Chris Bell of Houston. Burgess made news by defeating Scott Armey, former Denton County judge and the son of Dick Armey, in the Republican primary.

Republicans picked up two new congressional seats — in suburban Dallas and Houston — that Texas gained because of population growth in the 2000 census.

Pete Sessions was elected to his fourth term in Congress but his first in the newly drawn suburban Dallas-area 32nd District. Hensarling, a businessman and former Gramm aide who defeated Democrat Ron Chapman, a former judge, won the 5th District formerly represented by Sessions.

The other new seat, District 31 in Harris and seven other counties, went to Carter, a retired state district court judge.

Democrat Chris Bell, a radio reporter turned lawyer and Houston city council member, succeeded Democrat Ken Bentsen in the 25th District in Harris and Fort Bend counties.

Bentsen, the nephew of former U.S. Sen. Lloyd Bentsen, relinquished his seat when he unsuccessfully sought the Democratic nomination for U.S. Senate.

All other incumbents were re-elected to their U.S. House seats. Before the election, Democrats had a 17-13 edge in the Texas congressional delegation. After the election, Democrats held a 17-15 majority in the 32-member delegation.

Texas' most senior member of Congress was Martin Frost, a Dallas Democrat, who won his 13th term. He made a brief bid to become minority leader when Rep. Dick Gephardt of Missouri announced he would give up the job.

However, Californian Nancy Pelosi amassed enough votes to turn back Frost's effort.

Rep. Ciro Rodriguez of San Antonio followed Rep. Sylvestre Reyes of El Paso as chairman of the Congressional Hispanic Caucus. — *Carolyn Barta*

## Special Elections, 2001-2003

### STATE SENATE
#### District 30
##### Held Nov. 6, 2001

| | | |
|---|---|---|
| Rick Bunch (Independent) | 520 | 1.45% |
| Craig Estes (Rep.) | 16,870 | 47.21% |
| Doug Jeffrey (Rep.) | 1,139 | 3.18% |
| Harry Reynolds (Rep.) | 2,908 | 8.13% |
| Greg L. Underwood (Dem.) | 8,189 | 22.91% |
| Kirk Wilson (Rep.) | 6,105 | 17.08% |
| Total Vote | 35,731 | |

#### District 30 Runoff
##### Held Dec. 4, 2001

| | | |
|---|---|---|
| Craig Estes (Rep.) | 15,332 | 62.70% |
| Greg L. Underwood (Dem.) | 9,120 | 37.29% |
| Total Vote | 24,452 | |

### STATE SENATE
#### District 17
##### Held Nov. 5, 2002

| | | |
|---|---|---|
| Ronnie Ellen Harrison (Dem.) | 47,164 | 32.58% |
| Kyle Janek (Rep.) | 97,588 | 67.41% |
| Total Vote | 144,752 | |

### U.S. HOUSE OF REPRESENTATIVES
#### District 19
##### Held May 3, 2003

| | | |
|---|---|---|
| Richard Bartlett (Rep.) | 1,046 | 1.79% |
| John D. Bell (Rep.) | 1,883 | 3.22% |
| Jamie Berryhill (Rep.) | 1,907 | 3.26% |
| William M. "Bill" Christian (Rep.) | 1,029 | 1.76% |
| Mike Conaway (Rep.) | 12,270 | 21.02% |
| Thomas Flournoy (Con.) | 93 | 0.15% |
| Kaye Gaddy (Dem.) | 1,396 | 2.39% |
| E.L. "Ed" Hicks (Ind.) | 81 | 0.13% |
| Carl I. Isett (Rep.) | 11,015 | 18.87% |
| David R. Langston (Rep.) | 8,053 | 13.79% |
| Donald May (Rep.) | 629 | 1.07% |
| Randy Neugebauer (Rep.) | 13,091 | 22.42% |
| Julia Penelope (Green) | 223 | 0.38% |
| Richard "Chip" Peterson (Lib.) | 159 | 0.27% |
| Jerri Simmons-Asmussen (Dem.) | 898 | 1.53% |
| Vickie Sutton (Rep.) | 1,987 | 3.40% |
| Stace Williams (Rep.) | 2,609 | 4.46% |
| Total Vote | 58,369 | |

#### District 19 Runoff
##### Held June 3, 2003

| | | |
|---|---|---|
| Mike Conaway (Rep.) | 27,959 | 49.48% |
| Randy Neugebauer (Rep.) | 28,546 | 50.51% |
| Total Vote | 56,505 | |

# Legislature 2003: Fiscal Restraint and Partisanship

The 78th session of the Texas Legislature, reflecting the impact of the 2002 elections, left a mark of fiscal restraint.

Lawmakers, in the first session controlled by the GOP this century, did what critics said was impossible: They crafted a two-year budget with no new taxes and reduced the scope of state government by forcing cuts in agencies and programs.

But the untidy session also was characterized by an increase in partisanship, including a four-day quorum-breaking boycott by state house Democrats to kill a congressional redistricting bill that would guarantee the election of more Republicans to the U.S. House.

Fifty-one Democrats fled across the state line to a Holiday Inn in Ardmore, Okla., where they could avoid being retrieved by state troopers, to wait out the deadline for introducing the redistricting legislation pushed by U.S. Rep. Tom DeLay from Washington.

Later, in the summer, 10 Democrats from the Senate escaped to Albuquerque, N.M., after Gov. Rick Perry called a second special session on redistricting.

As for the budget, Republicans hailed it as historic because it reins in spending in Texas for the first time since World War II.

The $117.4 billion budget reduced general state revenues from the previous state

Two legislators talked on the phone while 51 of their colleagues staged a walkout. AP file photo

budget of $61 billion to $58.6 billion. (The rest of the budget is federal and other funds.)

State agencies were required to pare 7 percent from their current budgets, for starters.

Gov. Perry refused to budge from his no-new-taxes pledge, and House members under the leadership of Speaker Tom Craddick were eager to toe the line so they could go home with campaign promises kept to curb state spending.

Comptroller Carole Keeton Strayhorn's pre-session estimate of a $9.9 billion shortfall (because of reduced sales tax revenues) provided justification for creating a leaner budget, but not without pain. Longtime members called the session the most difficult of their political careers.

Democrats objected that hundreds of thousands of Texans – particularly children, pregnant women and the elderly -- would be denied health care and other services because of Medicaid trims and changes to the Children's Health Insurance Program. City and county officials feared costs were being pushed down to the local level.

To produce more revenues, the Legislature allowed Texas to join a multi-state lottery game such as Powerball and authorized colleges and universities to set their own tuition. And savings were expected by the consolidation of Texas' myriad health and human services departments into three agencies under a new commission.

Gov. Perry saw his three priorities accomplished: the budget, insurance reform aimed at reducing rates for homeowners and medical malpractice reform designed to keep more doctors in practice

Insurers who write homeowners policies will be required to file their rates with state regulators, who will have the power to determine whether consumers are being overcharged.

A major tort reform bill set caps on medical-malpractice lawsuit awards for pain and suffering at $250,000 for physicians or hospitals or nursing homes for a maximum of $750,000 per claimant.

Republicans also flexed their political muscle on long-favored social issues.

They won approval for a 24-hour waiting period before women can have abortions, passed a prenatal protection act that defines a fertilized egg as an individual from conception, and banned the recognition of same-sex marriages and civil unions formed in other states. Students will be required to observe a minute of silence each day, the closest thing the courts have allowed to school prayer.

As for redistricting, its fate was unknown at press time. Republicans contended their strength — again as reflected in 2002 elections — merited more members of Congress than the 17-15 Democrat majority in the state's delegation.

They argued that lawmakers should finish the job of redistricting after allowing the courts to draw the lines in 2001 when a partisan split in the Legislature thwarted an agreement.

The spectacle of Democrats in exile reminded Texans of an earlier walkout when a dozen senate Democrats, called the "Killer Bees," hid out in a West Austin garage apartment in 1979 to block a bill to change the date of the Texas presidential primary to benefit Republican candidate John Connally.

This year, with little fanfare, the primary date was moved up a week from the second to the first Tuesday in March in even-numbered years, to increase the state's influence in presidential nominations and avoid conflicts with spring break. – *Carolyn Barta*

# General Election, 2002

Below are the voting returns of the general election held November 5, 2002, for all statewide races, and for contested congressional, state senate, courts of appeals and state board of education races. These are official returns as canvassed by the State Canvassing Board. Abbreviations used are (Dem.) Democrat, (Rep.) Republican, (Lib.) Libertarian, (Ind.) Independent and (W-I) Write-In.

## STATEWIDE RACES

### U.S. Senator
John Cornyn (Rep.) . . . . . . . . . . . . . . . 2,496,243 . . 55.29%
Ron Kirk (Dem.) . . . . . . . . . . . . . . . . . . 1,955,758 . . 43.32%
Scott Lanier Jameson (Lib.) . . . . . . . . . . . 35,538 . . . 0.78%
Roy H. Williams (Green) . . . . . . . . . . . . . 25,051 . . . 0.55%
James W. (Jim) Wright (W-I) . . . . . . . . . . . 1,422 . . . 0.03%
    Total Vote . . . . . . . . . . . . . . . . . 4,514,012

### Governor
Rick Perry (Rep.) . . . . . . . . . . . . . . . . 2,632,591 . . 57.80%
Tony Sanchez (Dem.) . . . . . . . . . . . . . . . 1,819,798 . . 39.96%
Jeff Daiell (Lib.) . . . . . . . . . . . . . . . . . . 66,720 . . . 1.46%
Rahul Mahajan (Green) . . . . . . . . . . . . . 32,187 . . . 0.70%
Elaine Eure Henderson (W-I) . . . . . . . . . . 1,715 . . . 0.03%
Earl W. (Bill) O'Neil (W-I) . . . . . . . . . . . . . 976 . . . 0.02%
    Total Vote . . . . . . . . . . . . . . . . . 4,553,987

### Lieutenant Governor
David Dewhurst (Rep.) . . . . . . . . . . . . . . 2,341,875 . . 51.77%
John Sharp (Dem.) . . . . . . . . . . . . . . . . 2,082,281 . . 46.03%
Mark David Gessner (Lib.) . . . . . . . . . . . 54,885 . . . 1.21%
Nathalie Paravicini (Green) . . . . . . . . . . . 44,386 . . . 0.98%
    Total Vote . . . . . . . . . . . . . . . . . 4,523,427

### Attorney General
Greg Abbott (Rep.) . . . . . . . . . . . . . . . . 2,542,184 . . 56.72%
Kirk Watson (Dem.) . . . . . . . . . . . . . . . . 1,841,359 . . 41.08%
Jon Roland (Lib.) . . . . . . . . . . . . . . . . . . 56,880 . . . 1.26%
David Keith Cobb (Green) . . . . . . . . . . . . 41,560 . . . 0.92%
    Total Vote . . . . . . . . . . . . . . . . . 4,481,983

### Comptroller of Public Accounts
Carole Keeton Rylander (Rep.) . . . . . . . 2,878,732 . . 64.16%
Marty Akins (Dem.) . . . . . . . . . . . . . . . . 1,476,976 . . 32.92%
Bowie Ibarra (Lib.) . . . . . . . . . . . . . . . . 53,614 . . . 1.19%
Ruben L. Reyes (Green) . . . . . . . . . . . . . 77,177 . . . 1.72%
    Total Vote . . . . . . . . . . . . . . . . . 4,486,499

### Commissioner of General Land Office
Jerry Patterson (Rep.) . . . . . . . . . . . . . . 2,331,700 . . 53.16%
David Bernsen (Dem.) . . . . . . . . . . . . . . 1,819,365 . . 41.48%
Barbara A. Hernandez (Lib.) . . . . . . . . . . 180,870 . . . 4.12%
Michael B. McInerney (Green) . . . . . . . . . 54,130 . . . 1.23%
    Total Vote . . . . . . . . . . . . . . . . . 4,386,065

### Commissioner of Agriculture
Susan Combs (Rep.) . . . . . . . . . . . . . . . 2,636,129 . . 59.53%
Tom Ramsay (Dem.) . . . . . . . . . . . . . . . 1,674,372 . . 37.81%
Vincent J. May (Lib.) . . . . . . . . . . . . . . . 52,234 . . . 1.17%
Jane Woodward Elioseff (Green) . . . . . . . 64,818 . . . 1.46%
    Total Vote . . . . . . . . . . . . . . . . . 4,427,553

### Railroad Commissioner
Michael L. Williams (Rep.) . . . . . . . . . . . 2,407,036 . . 54.81%
Sherry Boyles (Dem.) . . . . . . . . . . . . . . 1,821,751 . . 41.48%
Nazirite R. Flores Perez (Lib.) . . . . . . . . . 110,160 . . . 2.50%
Charles L. Mauch (Green) . . . . . . . . . . . . 52,322 . . . 1.19%
    Total Vote . . . . . . . . . . . . . . . . . 4,391,269

## STATEWIDE JUDICIAL RACES

### Chief Justice, Supreme Court
Tom Phillips (Rep.) . . . . . . . . . . . . . . . . 2,525,581 . . 57.66%
Richard G. Baker (Dem.) . . . . . . . . . . . . 1,774,242 . . 40.50%
Eugene J. Flynn (Lib.) . . . . . . . . . . . . . . 80,185 . . . 1.83%
    Total Vote . . . . . . . . . . . . . . . . . 4,380,008

### Justice, Supreme Court, Place 1
Mike Schneider (Rep.) . . . . . . . . . . . . . . 2,451,791 . . 56.10%
Linda Yanez (Dem.) . . . . . . . . . . . . . . . . 1,815,581 . . 41.54%
Quanah Parker (Lib.) . . . . . . . . . . . . . . . 102,926 . . . 2.35%
    Total Vote . . . . . . . . . . . . . . . . . 4,370,298

### Justice, Supreme Court, Place 2
Dale Wainwright (Rep.) . . . . . . . . . . . . . 2,440,799 . . 56.35%

Jim Parsons (Dem.) . . . . . . . . . . . . . . . 1,814,354 . . 41.88%
Brad Rockwell (Green) . . . . . . . . . . . . . . 76,082 . . . 1.75%
    Total Vote . . . . . . . . . . . . . . . . . 4,331,235

### Justice, Supreme Court, Place 3 (Unexpired term)
Wallace B. Jefferson (Rep.) . . . . . . . . . . 2,442,111 . . 56.76%
William E. Moody (Dem.) . . . . . . . . . . . . 1,860,251 . . 43.23%
    Total Vote . . . . . . . . . . . . . . . . . 4,302,362

### Justice, Supreme Court, Place 4 (Unexpired term)
Steven Wayne Smith (Rep.) . . . . . . . . . . 2,331,140 . . 54.09%
Margaret Mirabal (Dem.) . . . . . . . . . . . . 1,978,081 . . 45.90%
    Total Vote . . . . . . . . . . . . . . . . . 4,309,221

### Judge, Court of Criminal Appeals, Place 1
Tom Price (Rep.) . . . . . . . . . . . . . . . . . 2,493,440 . . 57.66%
John W. Bull (Dem.) . . . . . . . . . . . . . . . 1,692,773 . . 39.14%
Stephan Kinsella (Lib.) . . . . . . . . . . . . . . 71,442 . . . 1.65%
Robert C. (Rob) Owen (Green) . . . . . . . . 66,437 . . . 1.53%
    Total Vote . . . . . . . . . . . . . . . . . 4,324,072

### Judge, Court of Criminal Appeals, Place 2
Paul Womack (Rep.) . . . . . . . . . . . . . . . 2,463,069 . . 57.39%
Pat Montgomery (Dem.) . . . . . . . . . . . . . 1,828,431 . . 42.60%
    Total Vote . . . . . . . . . . . . . . . . . 4,291,500

### Judge, Court of Criminal Appeals, Place 3
Cathy Cochran (Rep.) . . . . . . . . . . . . . . 2,511,958 . . 58.25%
J.R. Molina (Dem.) . . . . . . . . . . . . . . . . 1,725,065 . . 40.00%
Ollie Ruth Jefferson (Green) . . . . . . . . . . 74,984 . . . 1.73%
    Total Vote . . . . . . . . . . . . . . . . . 4,312,007

## U.S. HOUSE OF REPRESENTATIVES

### District 1
John Lawrence (Rep.) . . . . . . . . . . . . . . 66,654 . . 43.55%
Max Sandlin (Dem.) . . . . . . . . . . . . . . . 86,384 . . 56.44%
    Total Vote . . . . . . . . . . . . . . . . . 153,038

### District 2
Van Brookshire (Rep.) . . . . . . . . . . . . . . 53,656 . . 38.18%
Jim Turner (Dem.) . . . . . . . . . . . . . . . . . 85,492 . . 60.84%
Peter Beach (Lib.) . . . . . . . . . . . . . . . . . 1,353 . . . 0.96%
    Total Vote . . . . . . . . . . . . . . . . . 140,501

### District 3
Sam Johnson (Rep.) . . . . . . . . . . . . . . . 113,974 . . 73.94%
Manny Molera (Dem.) . . . . . . . . . . . . . . 37,503 . . 24,33%
John Davis (Lib.) . . . . . . . . . . . . . . . . . . 2,656 . . . 1.72%
    Total Vote . . . . . . . . . . . . . . . . . 154,133

### District 4
John Graves (Rep.) . . . . . . . . . . . . . . . . 67,939 . . 40.37%
Ralph M. Hall (Dem.) . . . . . . . . . . . . . . . 97,304 . . 57.82%
Barbara Robinson (Lib.) . . . . . . . . . . . . . 3,042 . . . 1.80%
    Total Vote . . . . . . . . . . . . . . . . . 168,285

### District 5
Jeb Hensarling (Rep.) . . . . . . . . . . . . . . 81,439 . . 58.20%
Ron Chapman (Dem.) . . . . . . . . . . . . . . 56,330 . . 40.26%
Dan Michalski (Lib.) . . . . . . . . . . . . . . . . 1,283 . . . 0.91%
Thomas J. Kemper (Green) . . . . . . . . . . . 856 . . . 0.61%
    Total Vote . . . . . . . . . . . . . . . . . 139,908

### District 6
Joe Barton (Rep.) . . . . . . . . . . . . . . . . . 115,396 . . 70.34%
Felix Alvarado (Dem.) . . . . . . . . . . . . . . 45,404 . . 27.67%
Frank Brady (Lib.) . . . . . . . . . . . . . . . . . 1,992 . . . 1.21%
B.J. Armstrong (Green) . . . . . . . . . . . . . 1,245 . . . 0.75%
    Total Vote . . . . . . . . . . . . . . . . . 164,037

### District 7
John Culberson (Rep.) . . . . . . . . . . . . . . 96,795 . . 89.18%
Drew Parks (Lib.) . . . . . . . . . . . . . . . . . 11,674 . . 10.75%
John R. Skone-Palmer (W-I) . . . . . . . . . . . . 58 . . . 0.05%
    Total Vote . . . . . . . . . . . . . . . . . 108,527

### District 8
Kevin Brady (Rep.) . . . . . . . . . . . . . . . . .140,575 . . 93.14%
Gil Guillory (Lib.) . . . . . . . . . . . . . . . . . . .10,351 . . . 6.85%
   Total Vote . . . . . . . . . . . . . . . . . . 150,926

### District 9
Paul Williams (Rep.) . . . . . . . . . . . . . . . .59,635 . . 40.30%
Nick Lampson (Dem.) . . . . . . . . . . . . . . .86,710 . . 58.60%
Dean L. Tucker (Lib.) . . . . . . . . . . . . . . . .1,613 . . . 1.09%
   Total Vote . . . . . . . . . . . . . . . . . . 147,958

### District 10
Lloyd Doggett (Dem.) . . . . . . . . . . . . . .114,428 . . 84.37%
Michele Messina (Lib.) . . . . . . . . . . . . . .21,196 . . 15.62%
   Total Vote . . . . . . . . . . . . . . . . . . 135,624

### District 11
Ramsey Farley (Rep.) . . . . . . . . . . . . . . .68,236 . . 47.10%
Chet Edwards (Dem.) . . . . . . . . . . . . . . .74,678 . . 51.55%
Andrew Paul Farris (Lib.) . . . . . . . . . . . . .1,943 . . . 1.34%
   Total Vote . . . . . . . . . . . . . . . . . . 144,857

### District 12
Kay Granger (Rep.) . . . . . . . . . . . . . . . .121,208 . . 91.87%
Edward A. Hanson (Lib.) . . . . . . . . . . . . .10,723 . . . 8.12%
   Total Vote . . . . . . . . . . . . . . . . . . 131,931

### District 13
Mac Thornberry (Rep.) . . . . . . . . . . . . .119,401 . . 79.27%
Zane Reese (Dem.) . . . . . . . . . . . . . . . . .31,218 . . 20.72%
   Total Vote . . . . . . . . . . . . . . . . . . 150,619

### District 14
Ron Paul (Rep.) . . . . . . . . . . . . . . . . . . .102,905 . . 68.09%
Corby Windham (Dem.) . . . . . . . . . . . . .48,224 . . 31.90%
   Total Vote . . . . . . . . . . . . . . . . . . 151,129

### District 17
Rob Beckham (Rep.) . . . . . . . . . . . . . . . .77,622 . . 47.38%
Charlie Stenholm (Dem.) . . . . . . . . . . . .84,136 . . 51.36%
Fred Jones (Lib.) . . . . . . . . . . . . . . . . . . . .2,046 . . . 1.24%
   Total Vote . . . . . . . . . . . . . . . . . . 163,804

### District 18
Phillip J. Abbott (Rep.) . . . . . . . . . . . . . .27,980 . . 21.70%
Sheila Jackson Lee (Dem.) . . . . . . . . . . .99,161 . . 76.91%
Brent Sullivan (Lib.) . . . . . . . . . . . . . . . . .1,785 . . . 1.38%
   Total Vote . . . . . . . . . . . . . . . . . . 128,926

### District 19
Larry Combest (Rep.) . . . . . . . . . . . . . .117,092 . . 91.63%
Larry Johnson (Lib.) . . . . . . . . . . . . . . . .10,684 . . . 8.36%
   Total Vote . . . . . . . . . . . . . . . . . . 127,776

### District 21
Lamar Smith (Rep.) . . . . . . . . . . . . . . . .161,836 . . 72.86%
John Courage (Dem.) . . . . . . . . . . . . . . .56,206 . . 25.30%
DG Roberts (Lib.) . . . . . . . . . . . . . . . . . . .4,051 . . . 1.82%
   Total Vote . . . . . . . . . . . . . . . . . . 222,093

### District 22
Tom DeLay (Rep.) . . . . . . . . . . . . . . . . .100,499 . . 63.17%
Tim Riley (Dem.) . . . . . . . . . . . . . . . . . . .55,716 . . 35.02%
Gerald W. (Jerry) LaFleur (Lib.) . . . . . . . .1,612 . . . 1.01%
Joel West (Green) . . . . . . . . . . . . . . . . . .1,257 . . . 0.79%
   Total Vote . . . . . . . . . . . . . . . . . . 159,084

### District 23
Henry Bonilla (Rep.) . . . . . . . . . . . . . . . .77,573 . . 51.52%
Henry Cuellar (Dem.) . . . . . . . . . . . . . . .71,067 . . 47.20%
Jeffrey C. Blunt (Lib.) . . . . . . . . . . . . . . . .1,106 . . . 0.73%
Ed Scharf (Green) . . . . . . . . . . . . . . . . . . . 806 . . . 0.53%
   Total Vote . . . . . . . . . . . . . . . . . . 150,552

### District 24
Mike Rivera Ortega (Rep.) . . . . . . . . . . . .38,332 . . 33.95%
Martin Frost (Dem.) . . . . . . . . . . . . . . . . .73,002 . . 64.66%
Ken Ashby (Lib.) . . . . . . . . . . . . . . . . . . . .1,560 . . . 1.38%
   Total Vote . . . . . . . . . . . . . . . . . . 112,894

### District 25
Tom Reiser (Rep.) . . . . . . . . . . . . . . . . . .50,041 . . 43.09%
Chris Bell (Dem.) . . . . . . . . . . . . . . . . . . .63,590 . . 54.75%
Guy McLendon (Lib.) . . . . . . . . . . . . . . . .1,096 . . . 0.94%
George Reiter (Green) . . . . . . . . . . . . . . .1,399 . . . 1.20%
   Total Vote . . . . . . . . . . . . . . . . . . 116,126

### District 26
Michael C. Burgess (Rep.) . . . . . . . . . . .123,195 . . .74.80%
Paul William LeBon (Dem.) . . . . . . . . . . .37,485 . . .22.76%
David Wallace Croft (Lib.) . . . . . . . . . . . . .2,367 . . . .1.43%
Gary R. Page (Green) . . . . . . . . . . . . . . . .1,631 . . . .0.99%
   Total Vote . . . . . . . . . . . . . . . .164,678

### District 27
Pat Ahumada (Rep.) . . . . . . . . . . . . . . . .41,004 . . .36.54%
Solomon P. Ortiz (Dem.) . . . . . . . . . . . . .68,559 . . .61.09%
Christopher J. Claytor (Lib.) . . . . . . . . . . .2,646 . . . .2.35%
   Total Vote . . . . . . . . . . . . . . . .112,209

### District 28
Gabriel Perales Jr. (Rep.) . . . . . . . . . . . . .26,973 . . .26.86%
Ciro D. Rodriguez (Dem.) . . . . . . . . . . . .71,393 . . .71.09%
Wm. A. (Bill) Stallknecht (Lib.) . . . . . . . . .2,054 . . . .2.04%
   Total Vote . . . . . . . . . . . . . . . .100,420

### District 29
Gene Green (Dem.) . . . . . . . . . . . . . . . . .55,760 . . .95.16%
Paul Hansen (Lib.) . . . . . . . . . . . . . . . . . . .2,833 . . . .4.83%
   Total Vote . . . . . . . . . . . . . . . . .58,593

### District 30
Ron Bush (Rep.) . . . . . . . . . . . . . . . . . . .28,981 . . .24.18%
Eddie Bernice Johnson (Dem.) . . . . . . . .88,980 . . .74.26%
Lance Flores (Lib.) . . . . . . . . . . . . . . . . . . .1,856 . . . .1.54%
   Total Vote . . . . . . . . . . . . . . . .119,817

### District 31
John R. Carter (Rep.) . . . . . . . . . . . . . . .111,556 . . .69.08%
David Bagley (Dem.) . . . . . . . . . . . . . . . .44,183 . . .27.36%
Clark Simmons (Lib.) . . . . . . . . . . . . . . . .2,037 . . . .1.26%
John S. Petersen (Green) . . . . . . . . . . . . .1,992 . . . .1.23%
R.C. Crawford (Ind.) . . . . . . . . . . . . . . . . .1,716 . . . .1.06%
   Total Vote . . . . . . . . . . . . . . . .161,484

### District 32
Pete Sessions (Rep.) . . . . . . . . . . . . . . .100,226 . . .67.76%
Pauline K. Dixon (Dem.) . . . . . . . . . . . . .44,886 . . .30.34%
Steve Martin (Lib.) . . . . . . . . . . . . . . . . . . .1,582 . . . .1.06%
Carla Hubbell (Green) . . . . . . . . . . . . . . . .1,208 . . . .0.81%
   Total Vote . . . . . . . . . . . . . . . .147,902

## STATE SENATE

### District 1
Bill Ratliff (Rep.) . . . . . . . . . . . . . . . . . . .113,939 . . .68.16%
B.D. Blount (Dem.) . . . . . . . . . . . . . . . . . .53,201 . . .31.83%
   Total Vote . . . . . . . . . . . . . . . .167,140

### District 2
Bob Deuell (Rep.) . . . . . . . . . . . . . . . . . . .80,075 . . .53.94%
David Cain (Dem.) . . . . . . . . . . . . . . . . . .66,151 . . .44.56%
Robert Parker (Lib.) . . . . . . . . . . . . . . . . . .2,217 . . . .1.49%
   Total Vote . . . . . . . . . . . . . . . .148,443

### District 3
Todd Staples (Rep.) . . . . . . . . . . . . . . . .119,993 . . .88.23%
Michael Carter (Lib.) . . . . . . . . . . . . . . . .16,001 . . .11.76%
   Total Vote . . . . . . . . . . . . . . . .135,994

### District 4
Tommy Williams (Rep.) . . . . . . . . . . . . . .97,237 . . .63.53%
Mike Smith (Dem.) . . . . . . . . . . . . . . . . .55,808 . . .36.46%
   Total Vote . . . . . . . . . . . . . . . .153,045

### District 5
Steve Ogden (Rep.) . . . . . . . . . . . . . . . .122,119 . . .86.85%
Randall Barfield (Lib.) . . . . . . . . . . . . . . .18,482 . . .13.14%
   Total Vote . . . . . . . . . . . . . . . .140,601

### District 7
Jon Lindsay (Rep.) . . . . . . . . . . . . . . . . .139,827 . . .91.31%
Edgar L. Buchanan (Lib.) . . . . . . . . . . . .13,305 . . .8.68%
   Total Vote . . . . . . . . . . . . . . . .153,132

### District 8
Florence Shapiro (Rep.) . . . . . . . . . . . . .135,927 . . .89.74%
David Spaller (Lib.) . . . . . . . . . . . . . . . . .15,525 . . .10.25%
   Total Vote . . . . . . . . . . . . . . . .151,452

### District 9
Chris Harris (Rep.) . . . . . . . . . . . . . . . . . .81,994 . . .86.56%
David C. Pepperdine (Lib.) . . . . . . . . . . .12,727 . . .13.43%

Total Vote. . . . . . . . . . . . . . . . . . . . . 94,721

### District 10
Kim Brimer (Rep.). . . . . . . . . . . . . . . . 101,511 . . 58.70%
Hal Ray (Dem.). . . . . . . . . . . . . . . . . . . 69,038 . . 39.92%
John Paul Robinson (Lib.). . . . . . . . . . . . . 2,367 . . . 1.36%
Total Vote. . . . . . . . . . . . . . . . . . . 172,916

### District 11
Mike Jackson (Rep.) . . . . . . . . . . . . . . . 103,204 . . 86.29%
Michael Rubin (Lib.) . . . . . . . . . . . . . . . . 16,384 . . 13.70%
Total Vote. . . . . . . . . . . . . . . . . . . 119,588

### District 12
Jane Nelson (Rep.). . . . . . . . . . . . . . . . 121,991 . . 89.82%
Steve Rushton (Lib.) . . . . . . . . . . . . . . . . 13,818 . . 10.17%
Total Vote. . . . . . . . . . . . . . . . . . . 135,809

### District 14
Ben Bentzin (Rep.) . . . . . . . . . . . . . . . . 77,885 . . 43.12%
Gonzalo Barrientos (Dem.). . . . . . . . . . . . 95,182 . . 52.70%
Marianne Robbins (Lib.) . . . . . . . . . . . . . . 7,537 . . . 4.17%
Total Vote. . . . . . . . . . . . . . . . . . . 180,604

### District 15
Michael P. Wolfe (Rep.) . . . . . . . . . . . . . . 41,003 . . 39.63%
John Whitmire (Dem.). . . . . . . . . . . . . . . 62,458 . . 60.36%
Total Vote. . . . . . . . . . . . . . . . . . . 103,461

### District 16
John Carona (Rep.). . . . . . . . . . . . . . . . 95,853 . . 64.07%
Jan Erik Frederiksen (Dem.). . . . . . . . . . . 50,895 . . 34.01%
Jack Thompson (Lib.) . . . . . . . . . . . . . . . . 2,857 . . . 1.90%
Total Vote. . . . . . . . . . . . . . . . . . . 149,605

### District 17
Kyle Janek (Rep.) . . . . . . . . . . . . . . . . . 88,393 . . 61.42%
Ronnie Ellen Harrison (Dem.). . . . . . . . . . 55,502 . . 38.57%
Total Vote. . . . . . . . . . . . . . . . . . . 143,895

### District 18
Lester Phipps (Rep.). . . . . . . . . . . . . . . . 72,296 . . 45.12%
Ken Armbrister (Dem.) . . . . . . . . . . . . . . 85,401 . . 53.30%
Horace Henley (Lib.) . . . . . . . . . . . . . . . . 2,508 . . . 1.56%
Total Vote. . . . . . . . . . . . . . . . . . . 160,205

### District 21
Judith Zaffirini (Dem.) . . . . . . . . . . . . . . 95,644 . . 89.11%
Jeff Carruthers (Lib.). . . . . . . . . . . . . . . . 11,688 . . 10.88%
Total Vote. . . . . . . . . . . . . . . . . . . 107,332

### District 22
Kip Averitt (Rep.). . . . . . . . . . . . . . . . . 106,371 . . 67.37%
Richard (Richie) J. Renschler Jr. (Dem.). . 51,506 . . 32.62%
Total Vote. . . . . . . . . . . . . . . . . . . 157,877

### District 24
Tom Fraser (Rep.). . . . . . . . . . . . . . . . 122,355 . . 90.47%
Steve Kirby (Lib.). . . . . . . . . . . . . . . . . 12,887 . . . 9.52%
Total Vote. . . . . . . . . . . . . . . . . . . 135,242

### District 25
Jeff Wentworth (Rep.) . . . . . . . . . . . . . . 136,802 . . 66.73%
Joseph (Joe) P. Sullivan (Dem.) . . . . . . . . 61,899 . . 30.19%
Rex Black (Lib.). . . . . . . . . . . . . . . . . . . 6,293 . . . 3.06%
Total Vote. . . . . . . . . . . . . . . . . . . 204,994

### District 28
Robert Duncan (Rep.). . . . . . . . . . . . . . . 119,580 . . 91.31%
Jon Ensor (Lib.). . . . . . . . . . . . . . . . . . . 11,372 . . . 8.68%
Total Vote. . . . . . . . . . . . . . . . . . . 130,952

### District 30
Craig Estes (Rep.). . . . . . . . . . . . . . . . 109,167 . . 67.55%
Donald R. Acheson (Dem.). . . . . . . . . . . . 48,110 . . 29.77%
Diane Wilson (Lib.) . . . . . . . . . . . . . . . . 4,321 . . . 2.67%
Total Vote. . . . . . . . . . . . . . . . . . . 161,598

## COURTS OF APPEALS

### Chief Justice, Fourth District
Paul W. Green (Rep.) . . . . . . . . . . . . . . 209,177 . . 47.50%
Alma L. Lopez (Dem.). . . . . . . . . . . . . . 231,103 . . 52.49%
Total Vote. . . . . . . . . . . . . . . . . . . 440,280

### Chief Justice, Sixth District (Unexpired term)
Josh Morriss (Rep.). . . . . . . . . . . . . . . . 90,956 . . 55.46%

Jim Lovett (Dem.). . . . . . . . . . . . . . . . . 73,034 . . 44.53%
Total Vote. . . . . . . . . . . . . . . . . . . 163,990

### Chief Justice, Seventh District
Phil Johnson (Rep.) . . . . . . . . . . . . . . . 120,430 . . 67.54%
Floyd Holder (Dem.). . . . . . . . . . . . . . . . 57,868 . . 32.45%
Total Vote. . . . . . . . . . . . . . . . . . . 178,298

### Chief Justice, Eighth District
Peter S. Peca Jr. (Rep.) . . . . . . . . . . . . . 85,120 . . 49.34%
Richard Barajas (Dem.). . . . . . . . . . . . . . 87,377 . . 50.65%
Total Vote. . . . . . . . . . . . . . . . . . . 172,497

### Chief Justice, Ninth District
Steve McKeithen (Rep.). . . . . . . . . . . . . 114,491 . . 54.00%
Ronald L. Walker (Dem.) . . . . . . . . . . . . . 97,523 . . 45.99%
Total Vote. . . . . . . . . . . . . . . . . . . 212,014

### Justice, First District, Place 4 (Unexpired term)
Elsa Alcala (Rep.) . . . . . . . . . . . . . . . . 488,062 . . 55.65%
Austin M. O'Toole (Dem.) . . . . . . . . . . . . 388,836 . . 44.34%
Total Vote. . . . . . . . . . . . . . . . . . . 876,898

### Justice, First District, Place 5 (Unexpired term)
Evelyn Keyes (Rep.). . . . . . . . . . . . . . . 492,832 . . 56.10%
Mary Thompson (Dem.) . . . . . . . . . . . . . 385,548 . . 43.89%
Total Vote. . . . . . . . . . . . . . . . . . . 878,380

### Justice, Thirteenth District
Bradford M. Condit (Rep.) . . . . . . . . . . . 112,778 . . 42.02%
Dori Contreras Garza (Dem.). . . . . . . . . . 155,586 . . 57.97%
Total Vote. . . . . . . . . . . . . . . . . . . 268,364

### Justice, Fourteenth District
Kem Thompson Frost (Rep.) . . . . . . . . . 475,090 . . 54.06%
Denise Crawford (Dem.) . . . . . . . . . . . . 403,638 . . 45.93%
Total Vote. . . . . . . . . . . . . . . . . . . 878,728

## STATE BOARD OF EDUCATION

### District 1
Trini Munoz (Rep.) . . . . . . . . . . . . . . . . 89,604 . . 37.06%
Rene Nunez (Dem.). . . . . . . . . . . . . . . . 138,088 . . 57.12%
Catherine F. Harrell (Lib.). . . . . . . . . . . . . 14,033 . . . 5.80%
Total Vote . . . . . . . . . . . . . . . . . . . 241,725

### District 4
Alma A. Allen (Dem.) . . . . . . . . . . . . . . 167,419 . . 94.10%
Kurt R. Kessler (Lib.) . . . . . . . . . . . . . . . 10,486 . . . 5.89%
Total Vote . . . . . . . . . . . . . . . . . . . 177,905

### District 5
Dan Montgomery (Rep.) . . . . . . . . . . . . 206,656 . . 58.92%
Donna Howard (Dem.). . . . . . . . . . . . . . 132,740 . . 37.85%
Irene Meyer Scharf (Lib.). . . . . . . . . . . . . 11,292 . . . 3.21%
Total Vote . . . . . . . . . . . . . . . . . . . 350,688

### District 7
David Bradley (Rep.) . . . . . . . . . . . . . . 170,661 . . 57.77%
Richard Hargrove (Dem.). . . . . . . . . . . . 119,680 . . 40.51%
William J. McNicoll (Lib.) . . . . . . . . . . . . . 5,063 . . . 1.71%
Total Vote . . . . . . . . . . . . . . . . . . . 295,404

### District 9
Don McLeroy (Rep.). . . . . . . . . . . . . . . 193,454 . . 61.50%
Dean W. Woodard (Dem.) . . . . . . . . . . . 111,909 . . 35.57%
Nicole Lightner (Lib.) . . . . . . . . . . . . . . . 9,170 . . . 2.91%
Total Vote . . . . . . . . . . . . . . . . . . . 314,533

### District 10
Cynthia A. Thornton (Rep.) . . . . . . . . . . 230,452 . . 78.29%
Lesley Nicole Ramsey (Green) . . . . . . . . . 63,871 . . 21.70%
Total Vote . . . . . . . . . . . . . . . . . . . 294,323

### District 12
Geraldine (Tincy) Miller (Rep.). . . . . . . . . 217,542 . . 86.36%
Mark Wilson (Lib.) . . . . . . . . . . . . . . . . 34,334 . . 13.63%
Total Vote . . . . . . . . . . . . . . . . . . . 251,876

### District 15
Bob Craig (Rep.) . . . . . . . . . . . . . . . . 201,702 . . 66.70%
David Schaeffer (Dem.). . . . . . . . . . . . . . 94,742 . . 31.33%
Brent A. Russenberger (Lib.) . . . . . . . . . . . 5,937 . . . 1.96%
Total Vote . . . . . . . . . . . . . . . . . . . 302,381

# 2002 General Election Results by County

Listed below are the official results by county for the two candidates who received the most votes for governor, lieutenant governor and U.S. senator. The total number of voters who cast ballots, 4,553,987, was 36.24 percent of those registered to vote. The voting age population was 15,514,289. The statewide turnout of registered voters in the 1998 gubernatorial election was 32.40 percent. *Source: Texas Secretary of State.*

| County | Registered Voters Nov. 02 | Governor PERRY (Rep.) | Governor SANCHEZ (Dem.) | Turnout Percent* | Lt. Governor DEWHURST (Rep.) | Lt. Governor SHARP (Dem.) | U.S. Senator CORNYN (Rep.) | U.S. Senator KIRK (Dem.) |
|---|---|---|---|---|---|---|---|---|
| **Statewide** | 12,563,459 | 2,632,591 | 1,819,798 | 36.24 | 2,341,875 | 2,082,281 | 2,496,243 | 1,955,758 |
| Anderson | 28,073 | 6,386 | 3,758 | 36.67 | 5,703 | 4,478 | 6,347 | 3,882 |
| Andrews | 8,252 | 2,018 | 877 | 36.23 | 1,799 | 1,136 | 1,869 | 1,000 |
| Angelina | 48,301 | 10,892 | 7,760 | 39.40 | 8,655 | 10,124 | 10,623 | 7,991 |
| Aransas | 15,420 | 3,966 | 1,798 | 38.55 | 3,378 | 2,433 | 3,597 | 2,298 |
| Archer | 6,399 | 2,115 | 730 | 45.36 | 1,771 | 1,074 | 1,811 | 967 |
| Armstrong | 1,386 | 566 | 157 | 54.32 | 493 | 234 | 554 | 180 |
| Atascosa | 24,618 | 4,446 | 3,649 | 33.52 | 3,717 | 4,278 | 4,261 | 3,693 |
| Austin | 15,479 | 5,285 | 1,582 | 45.06 | 4,508 | 2,336 | 5,006 | 1,836 |
| Bailey | 3,938 | 1,111 | 437 | 39.81 | 927 | 606 | 1,079 | 472 |
| Bandera | 12,476 | 4,363 | 1,053 | 44.85 | 3,904 | 1,515 | 4,246 | 1,171 |
| Bastrop | 34,986 | 8,932 | 5,392 | 43.12 | 6,845 | 7,628 | 7,862 | 6,734 |
| Baylor | 2,909 | 809 | 360 | 40.87 | 556 | 588 | 675 | 455 |
| Bee | 16,517 | 3,107 | 4,272 | 45.49 | 2,655 | 4,478 | 2,918 | 4,168 |
| Bell | 144,805 | 27,451 | 15,307 | 30.10 | 25,104 | 17,194 | 25,728 | 17,013 |
| Bexar | 884,103 | 142,137 | 125,434 | 30.94 | 129,272 | 136,175 | 138,936 | 128,577 |
| Blanco | 6,250 | 2,274 | 678 | 48.81 | 1,801 | 1,164 | 2,106 | 876 |
| Borden | 488 | 228 | 37 | 56.35 | 154 | 118 | 195 | 74 |
| Bosque | 10,595 | 3,840 | 1,490 | 51.41 | 3,197 | 2,146 | 3,456 | 1,880 |
| Bowie | 53,963 | 10,921 | 9,173 | 37.62 | 10,438 | 9,480 | 11,075 | 8,719 |
| Brazoria | 152,721 | 34,645 | 17,063 | 34.74 | 31,259 | 20,201 | 33,645 | 18,329 |
| Brazos | 92,659 | 20,313 | 7,905 | 31.11 | 16,395 | 11,721 | 17,963 | 9,543 |
| Brewster | 5,963 | 1,254 | 1,121 | 41.50 | 945 | 1,357 | 1,173 | 1,157 |
| Briscoe | 1,306 | 488 | 293 | 61.71 | 336 | 417 | 446 | 299 |
| Brooks | 6,780 | 338 | 2,022 | 35.20 | 329 | 1,882 | 291 | 1,865 |
| Brown | 22,927 | 6,629 | 2,233 | 39.53 | 5,453 | 3,489 | · 6,284 | 2,588 |
| Burleson | 10,848 | 2,992 | 1,767 | 44.51 | 2,333 | 2,381 | 2,625 | 2,070 |
| Burnet | 23,361 | 7,834 | 2,834 | 47.19 | 6,464 | 4,304 | 7,221 | 3,525 |
| Caldwell | 20,807 | 4,000 | 3,294 | 36.32 | 3,061 | 4,236 | 3,575 | 3,714 |
| Calhoun | 14,137 | 2,742 | 2,590 | 38.50 | 1,644 | 3,678 | 2,494 | 2,691 |
| Callahan | 8,944 | 2,787 | 859 | 41.84 | 2,276 | 1,378 | 2,571 | 1,042 |
| Cameron | 154,193 | 17,716 | 27,374 | 29.67 | 15,976 | 26,938 | 14,836 | 28,903 |
| Camp | 6,552 | 1,539 | 1,354 | 44.78 | 1,190 | 1,687 | 1,485 | 1,414 |
| Carson | 4,772 | 1,562 | 514 | 44.88 | 1,321 | 781 | 1,559 | 551 |
| Cass | 18,914 | 3,527 | 3,787 | 39.10 | 3,241 | 4,018 | 3,708 | 3,488 |
| Castro | 4,833 | 1,277 | 729 | 42.00 | 912 | 998 | 1,188 | 726 |
| Chambers | 18,628 | 4,716 | 2,171 | 37.76 | 3,931 | 2,837 | 4,401 | 2,420 |
| Cherokee | 28,615 | 6,616 | 3,410 | 35.61 | 5,403 | 4,639 | 6,391 | 3,582 |
| Childress | 3,934 | 1,048 | 497 | 39.95 | 877 | 672 | 1,051 | 484 |
| Clay | 7,220 | 2,244 | 1,014 | 46.46 | 1,779 | 1,467 | 1,932 | 1,317 |
| Cochran | 2,202 | 612 | 461 | 49.90 | 508 | 509 | 588 | 410 |
| Coke | 2,595 | 898 | 227 | 44.43 | 604 | 509 | 770 | 343 |
| Coleman | 6,565 | 1,786 | 727 | 39.17 | 1,325 | 1,203 | 1,613 | 829 |
| Collin | 319,236 | 95,680 | 30,903 | 40.43 | 88,434 | 37,775 | 88,315 | 36,810 |
| Collingsworth | 2,248 | 673 | 435 | 49.86 | 533 | 553 | 662 | 409 |
| Colorado | 12,066 | 4,178 | 1,623 | 48.82 | 3,139 | 2,609 | 3,629 | 1,999 |
| Comal | 60,331 | 18,560 | 5,047 | 40.08 | 16,506 | 7,186 | 18,158 | 5,696 |
| Comanche | 8,782 | 2,428 | 1,269 | 42.78 | 1,940 | 1,743 | 2,273 | 1,415 |
| Concho | 1,777 | 555 | 204 | 44.06 | 395 | 355 | 515 | 242 |
| Cooke | 24,393 | 7,218 | 2,210 | 39.33 | 6,594 | 2,875 | 6,835 | 2,649 |
| Coryell | 38,850 | 6,214 | 3,257 | 25.05 | 5,828 | 3,682 | 5,734 | 3,782 |
| Cottle | 1,401 | 340 | 191 | 38.82 | 226 | 292 | 283 | 240 |
| Crane | 2,770 | 868 | 434 | 48.77 | 704 | 546 | 828 | 412 |
| Crockett | 2,665 | 558 | 387 | 36.13 | 406 | 527 | 531 | 369 |
| Crosby | 4,288 | 939 | 662 | 38.15 | 706 | 875 | 848 | 741 |
| Culberson | 2,075 | 200 | 401 | 29.44 | 154 | 379 | 176 | 367 |

| County | Registered Voters | Governor | | Turnout | Lt. Governor | | U.S. Senator | |
|---|---|---|---|---|---|---|---|---|
| | Nov. 02 | PERRY (Rep.) | SANCHEZ (Dem.) | Percent* | DEWHURST (Rep.) | SHARP (Dem.) | CORNYN (Rep.) | KIRK (Dem.) |
| Dallam | 3,140 | 622 | 260 | 28.78 | 579 | 296 | 666 | 217 |
| Dallas | 1,208,201 | 229,820 | 208,022 | 36.88 | 209,027 | 225,871 | 217,923 | 224,705 |
| Dawson | 8,758 | 2,328 | 1,395 | 43.04 | 1,612 | 1,886 | 2,182 | 1,279 |
| Deaf Smith | 10,124 | 2,387 | 1,189 | 36.03 | 2,012 | 1,514 | 2,418 | 1,063 |
| Delta | 3,076 | 826 | 454 | 42.13 | 639 | 618 | 778 | 513 |
| Denton | 306,174 | 74,431 | 27,682 | 34.13 | 70,001 | 32,061 | 70,684 | 32,931 |
| DeWitt | 12,542 | 3,220 | 1,156 | 35.24 | 2,246 | 2,090 | 3,045 | 1,295 |
| Dickens | 1,508 | 470 | 269 | 50.53 | 314 | 409 | 413 | 307 |
| Dimmit | 7,974 | 671 | 1,896 | 32.48 | 523 | 1,883 | 581 | 1,808 |
| Donley | 2,584 | 1,035 | 343 | 54.41 | 813 | 553 | 962 | 380 |
| Duval | 10,589 | 377 | 2,772 | 29.93 | 409 | 2,657 | 373 | 2,660 |
| Eastland | 10,648 | 3,630 | 1,298 | 47.56 | 2,877 | 2,080 | 3,249 | 1,607 |
| Ector | 69,257 | 15,239 | 7,614 | 33.84 | 14,648 | 8,270 | 15,378 | 7,576 |
| Edwards | 1,487 | 475 | 216 | 46.80 | 358 | 301 | 447 | 199 |
| Ellis | 71,708 | 20,107 | 7,749 | 39.57 | 18,209 | 9,630 | 19,285 | 8,774 |
| El Paso | 355,201 | 35,324 | 64,702 | 28.81 | 37,229 | 60,123 | 28,649 | 69,491 |
| Erath | 18,983 | 5,954 | 1,996 | 42.93 | 5,042 | 2,968 | 5,478 | 2,514 |
| Falls | 10,196 | 2,371 | 1,807 | 41.57 | 2,001 | 2,146 | 2,121 | 2,115 |
| Fannin | 16,908 | 4,109 | 2,760 | 41.39 | 3,492 | 3,402 | 3,810 | 3,120 |
| Fayette | 14,005 | 5,406 | 1,850 | 52.78 | 3,773 | 3,498 | 4,827 | 2,395 |
| Fisher | 2,905 | 704 | 716 | 49.87 | 429 | 907 | 579 | 817 |
| Floyd | 4,475 | 1,403 | 558 | 44.33 | 1,081 | 835 | 1,268 | 627 |
| Foard | 966 | 186 | 182 | 38.50 | 116 | 248 | 136 | 227 |
| Fort Bend | 224,551 | 52,068 | 34,344 | 39.12 | 48,007 | 37,963 | 49,459 | 37,320 |
| Franklin | 5,784 | 2,032 | 942 | 52.23 | 1,584 | 1,364 | 1,903 | 1,056 |
| Freestone | 10,944 | 3,331 | 1,819 | 48.09 | 2,800 | 2,363 | 3,117 | 2,065 |
| Frio | 10,059 | 1,082 | 2,057 | 31.47 | 895 | 2,087 | 1,044 | 1,929 |
| Gaines | 6,952 | 1,704 | 698 | 35.55 | 1,420 | 991 | 1,628 | 754 |
| Galveston | 177,598 | 33,409 | 26,289 | 34.38 | 30,080 | 29,481 | 32,193 | 27,741 |
| Garza | 2,923 | 836 | 307 | 39.99 | 682 | 438 | 801 | 337 |
| Gillespie | 15,518 | 6,502 | 1,262 | 51.02 | 5,696 | 2,077 | 6,268 | 1,461 |
| Glasscock | 763 | 381 | 42 | 55.83 | 276 | 129 | 339 | 71 |
| Goliad | 5,136 | 1,399 | 847 | 44.29 | 972 | 1,243 | 1,281 | 865 |
| Gonzales | 12,673 | 2,850 | 1,281 | 32.95 | 2,104 | 1,980 | 2,536 | 1,478 |
| Gray | 15,528 | 4,572 | 1,328 | 39.00 | 4,191 | 1,794 | 4,634 | 1,303 |
| Grayson | 74,074 | 18,075 | 9,093 | 37.53 | 16,231 | 10,988 | 16,613 | 10,661 |
| Gregg | 76,163 | 17,847 | 8,713 | 35.27 | 15,983 | 10,607 | 18,310 | 8,250 |
| Grimes | 13,245 | 3,293 | 1,879 | 39.95 | 2,802 | 2,320 | 3,053 | 2,076 |
| Guadalupe | 60,420 | 15,457 | 5,812 | 35.92 | 13,667 | 7,570 | 14,993 | 6,376 |
| Hale | 21,253 | 4,802 | 2,695 | 36.09 | 4,140 | 3,392 | 4,719 | 2,727 |
| Hall | 2,307 | 578 | 407 | 43.56 | 434 | 524 | 551 | 425 |
| Hamilton | 5,202 | 1,930 | 863 | 54.99 | 1,680 | 1,130 | 1,774 | 1,024 |
| Hansford | 3,307 | 1,269 | 185 | 44.51 | 1,034 | 409 | 1,264 | 195 |
| Hardeman | 3,000 | 622 | 354 | 33.10 | 477 | 510 | 530 | 437 |
| Hardin | 32,808 | 6,840 | 3,726 | 32.69 | 6,027 | 4,563 | 6,598 | 3,918 |
| Harris | 1,902,561 | 355,293 | 280,077 | 34.06 | 326,681 | 301,540 | 337,774 | 294,673 |
| Harrison | 43,246 | 8,684 | 7,331 | 37.49 | 7,506 | 8,456 | 8,948 | 6,821 |
| Hartley | 3,031 | 1,143 | 323 | 49.75 | 962 | 462 | 1,168 | 336 |
| Haskell | 4,531 | 1,264 | 687 | 43.94 | 693 | 1,258 | 946 | 954 |
| Hays | 70,854 | 15,919 | 10,508 | 39.24 | 12,837 | 13,726 | 14,813 | 12,286 |
| Hemphill | 2,332 | 791 | 295 | 47.59 | 726 | 464 | 913 | 294 |
| Henderson | 47,794 | 12,444 | 6,498 | 40.54 | 11,050 | 8,052 | 12,082 | 6,928 |
| Hidalgo | 257,763 | 22,108 | 48,964 | 27.87 | 20,445 | 45,553 | 18,862 | 48,367 |
| Hill | 20,282 | 5,476 | 2,576 | 40.35 | 4,782 | 3,312 | 5,068 | 3,020 |
| Hockley | 14,113 | 3,426 | 1,275 | 34.23 | 2,932 | 1,829 | 3,365 | 1,334 |
| Hood | 30,312 | 9,571 | 3,507 | 44.21 | 8,871 | 4,291 | 9,462 | 3,779 |
| Hopkins | 19,174 | 4,716 | 2,678 | 39.14 | 3,659 | 3,717 | 4,413 | 2,944 |
| Houston | 15,104 | 3,627 | 2,163 | 38.82 | 2,691 | 3,069 | 3,385 | 2,276 |
| Howard | 19,017 | 4,324 | 2,386 | 36.04 | 3,700 | 3,008 | 4,169 | 2,523 |
| Hudspeth | 1,624 | 310 | 403 | 44.76 | 267 | 349 | 280 | 359 |
| Hunt | 48,981 | 11,547 | 5,174 | 34.81 | 10,337 | 6,356 | 10,835 | 5,948 |
| Hutchinson | 17,286 | 4,410 | 1,311 | 34.09 | 4,330 | 1,538 | 4,507 | 1,379 |
| Irion | 1,247 | 468 | 142 | 50.76 | 337 | 278 | 423 | 189 |
| Jack | 5,117 | 1,551 | 610 | 43.03 | 1,239 | 906 | 1,419 | 730 |

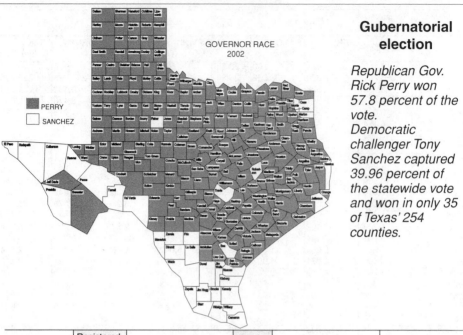

GOVERNOR RACE
2002

PERRY
SANCHEZ

# Gubernatorial election

*Republican Gov. Rick Perry won 57.8 percent of the vote. Democratic challenger Tony Sanchez captured 39.96 percent of the statewide vote and won in only 35 of Texas' 254 counties.*

| County | Registered Voters | Governor | | Turnout | Lt. Governor | | U.S. Senator | |
|---|---|---|---|---|---|---|---|---|
| | Nov. 02 | PERRY (Rep.) | SANCHEZ (Dem.) | Percent* | DEWHURST (Rep.) | SHARP (Dem.) | CORNYN (Rep.) | KIRK (Dem.) |
| Jackson | 9,323 | 2,302 | 1,071 | 36.78 | 1,610 | 1,753 | 2,138 | 1,210 |
| Jasper | 20,963 | 4,178 | 3,062 | 35.09 | 3,356 | 3,888 | 3,954 | 3,202 |
| Jeff Davis | 1,714 | 570 | 379 | 57.17 | 418 | 463 | 513 | 359 |
| Jefferson | 164,006 | 23,991 | 30,751 | 33.81 | 21,197 | 33,042 | 23,217 | 31,272 |
| Jim Hogg | 4,259 | 307 | 1,301 | 37.89 | 225 | 1,330 | 260 | 1,269 |
| Jim Wells | 25,855 | 2,757 | 6,149 | 34.77 | 2,407 | 6,290 | 2,381 | 6,212 |
| Johnson | 74,156 | 18,710 | 7,937 | 36.77 | 17,451 | 9,354 | 18,190 | 8,675 |
| Jones | 10,596 | 2,961 | 1,460 | 43.16 | 2,182 | 2,287 | 2,540 | 1,847 |
| Karnes | 8,426 | 1,933 | 1,342 | 39.36 | 1,448 | 1,764 | 1,796 | 1,387 |
| Kaufman | 44,932 | 12,063 | 5,760 | 40.47 | 10,485 | 7,309 | 11,531 | 6,385 |
| Kendall | 18,743 | 7,074 | 1,367 | 46.04 | 6,281 | 2,156 | 6,883 | 1,596 |
| Kenedy | 376 | 51 | 64 | 30.85 | 38 | 68 | 47 | 63 |
| Kent | 758 | 279 | 134 | 56.59 | 164 | 242 | 200 | 199 |
| Kerr | 32,286 | 11,152 | 2,726 | 43.81 | 10,278 | 3,635 | 10,884 | 2,997 |
| Kimble | 2,962 | 905 | 244 | 39.29 | 603 | 527 | 807 | 294 |
| King | 220 | 100 | 18 | 54.09 | 44 | 55 | 74 | 23 |
| Kinney | 2,539 | 688 | 409 | 43.48 | 557 | 480 | 650 | 371 |
| Kleberg | 18,792 | 2,525 | 3,785 | 34.11 | 2,146 | 4,030 | 2,156 | 4,001 |
| Knox | 2,853 | 830 | 433 | 44.90 | 525 | 705 | 668 | 543 |
| Lamar | 30,165 | 6,454 | 3,914 | 34.85 | 5,227 | 5,186 | 6,205 | 4,246 |
| Lamb | 8,967 | 2,280 | 1,875 | 46.94 | 1,811 | 1,326 | 2,121 | 1,009 |
| Lampasas | 10,906 | 3,366 | 1,324 | 44.15 | 2,975 | 1,756 | 3,137 | 1,568 |
| La Salle | 4,137 | 481 | 1,001 | 36.08 | 381 | 953 | 425 | 902 |
| Lavaca | 13,362 | 4,398 | 1,559 | 45.43 | 2,940 | 3,034 | 3,792 | 2,033 |
| Lee | 8,577 | 3,123 | 1,312 | 52.83 | 2,263 | 2,109 | 2,713 | 1,736 |
| Leon | 11,029 | 3,275 | 1,322 | 42.27 | 2,754 | 1,837 | 3,001 | 1,536 |
| Liberty | 43,616 | 7,766 | 4,750 | 29.42 | 6,559 | 5,921 | 7,308 | 5,145 |
| Limestone | 13,681 | 3,192 | 2,142 | 39.63 | 2,695 | 2,629 | 2,863 | 2,432 |
| Lipscomb | 1,940 | 732 | 222 | 50.00 | 624 | 327 | 706 | 238 |
| Live Oak | 7,349 | 1,864 | 827 | 37.29 | 1,536 | 1,126 | 1,757 | 925 |
| Llano | 13,365 | 5,420 | 1,566 | 53.52 | 4,422 | 2,639 | 5,056 | 1,960 |
| Loving | 152 | 49 | 14 | 41.44 | 36 | 24 | 42 | 16 |
| Lubbock | 152,442 | 38,097 | 15,935 | 36.46 | 34,469 | 20,020 | 38,217 | 16,248 |
| Lynn | 4,477 | 1,113 | 592 | 38.84 | 848 | 820 | 1,038 | 625 |
| Madison | 6,968 | 1,611 | 847 | 35.89 | 1,387 | 1,074 | 1,496 | 944 |
| Marion | 7,526 | 1,125 | 1,404 | 34.20 | 974 | 1,564 | 1,216 | 1,303 |

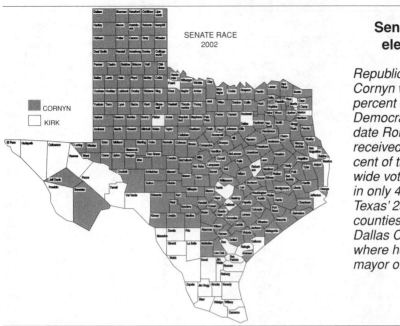

SENATE RACE
2002

CORNYN
KIRK

# Senatorial election

*Republican John Cornyn won 55.3 percent of the vote. Democratic candidate Ron Kirk received 43.3 percent of the state-wide vote and won in only 41 of Texas' 254 counties including Dallas County, where he had been mayor of Dallas.*

| County | Registered Voters | Governor | | Turnout | Lt. Governor | | U.S. Senator | |
|---|---|---|---|---|---|---|---|---|
| | Nov. 02 | PERRY (Rep.) | SANCHEZ (Dem.) | Percent* | DEWHURST (Rep.) | SHARP (Dem.) | CORNYN (Rep.) | KIRK (Dem.) |
| Martin | 3,123 | 917 | 505 | 46.42 | 742 | 553 | 877 | 426 |
| Mason | 2,700 | 1,009 | 276 | 48.88 | 813 | 473 | 917 | 352 |
| Matagorda | 21,810 | 4,945 | 3,309 | 38.63 | 3,942 | 4,289 | 4,722 | 3,427 |
| Maverick | 24,120 | 1,249 | 5,103 | 26.52 | 1,054 | 4,821 | 1,124 | 4,721 |
| McCulloch | 5,525 | 1,476 | 606 | 38.31 | 1,097 | 961 | 1,387 | 670 |
| McLennan | 127,915 | 32,219 | 18,788 | 40.68 | 28,561 | 22,778 | 29,608 | 21,904 |
| McMullen | 662 | 288 | 102 | 59.06 | 202 | 141 | 263 | 89 |
| Medina | 23,460 | 6,578 | 2,967 | 41.61 | 5,480 | 3,991 | 6,268 | 3,151 |
| Menard | 1,834 | 583 | 310 | 50.38 | 402 | 456 | 540 | 301 |
| Midland | 71,027 | 21,866 | 6,634 | 40.97 | 21,140 | 7,537 | 21,761 | 6,815 |
| Milam | 15,069 | 3,689 | 2,341 | 40.85 | 2,763 | 3,288 | 3,172 | 2,879 |
| Mills | 3,166 | 1,157 | 400 | 50.18 | 869 | 703 | 1,048 | 532 |
| Mitchell | 5,468 | 1,271 | 622 | 35.35 | 756 | 1,103 | 1,062 | 767 |
| Montague | 12,565 | 3,212 | 1,478 | 38.18 | 2,768 | 1,980 | 3,005 | 1,715 |
| Montgomery | 196,250 | 57,743 | 15,055 | 37.87 | 54,504 | 18,146 | 56,068 | 16,750 |
| Moore | 10,167 | 3,004 | 1,169 | 42.12 | 2,770 | 1,384 | 3,054 | 1,065 |
| Morris | 8,722 | 1,582 | 1,901 | 40.34 | 1,234 | 2,248 | 1,534 | 1,879 |
| Motley | 922 | 448 | 132 | 64.20 | 324 | 234 | 395 | 159 |
| Nacogdoches | 30,058 | 8,128 | 4,379 | 42.76 | 6,822 | 5,753 | 7,776 | 4,690 |
| Navarro | 27,959 | 6,724 | 3,833 | 38.37 | 5,562 | 5,009 | 6,225 | 4,382 |
| Newton | 9,518 | 1,490 | 1,813 | 35.20 | 1,135 | 2,151 | 1,331 | 1,922 |
| Nolan | 10,363 | 2,318 | 1,209 | 34.92 | 1,659 | 1,883 | 2,038 | 1,480 |
| Nueces | 200,322 | 33,152 | 34,001 | 34.36 | 29,822 | 36,758 | 29,423 | 38,184 |
| Ochiltree | 5,137 | 1,819 | 253 | 41.03 | 1,626 | 451 | 1,837 | 250 |
| Oldham | 1,552 | 489 | 123 | 40.14 | 394 | 215 | 471 | 153 |
| Orange | 55,213 | 10,050 | 7,895 | 33.09 | 8,912 | 9,048 | 9,380 | 8,463 |
| Palo Pinto | 17,414 | 3,944 | 2,260 | 36.39 | 3,458 | 2,752 | 3,796 | 2,418 |
| Panola | 15,322 | 3,505 | 2,465 | 39.39 | 2,791 | 3,132 | 3,580 | 2,291 |
| Parker | 61,165 | 18,352 | 6,629 | 41.72 | 16,753 | 8,302 | 17,803 | 7,283 |
| Parmer | 5,065 | 1,473 | 477 | 39.03 | 1,236 | 692 | 1,454 | 455 |
| Pecos | 8,141 | 1,791 | 2,032 | 47.96 | 1,477 | 2,140 | 1,748 | 1,764 |
| Polk | 38,895 | 6,261 | 4,684 | 28.74 | 5,617 | 5,294 | 5,745 | 5,067 |
| Potter | 57,639 | 11,701 | 6,537 | 32.55 | 11,336 | 7,009 | 11,962 | 6,300 |
| Presidio | 4,536 | 322 | 997 | 29.60 | 252 | 1,023 | 323 | 856 |
| Rains | 5,848 | 1,730 | 966 | 47.33 | 1,426 | 1,225 | 1,647 | 1,077 |
| Randall | 73,862 | 23,770 | 6,627 | 42.15 | 22,422 | 8,416 | 24,360 | 6,452 |

| County | Registered Voters Nov. 02 | Governor PERRY (Rep.) | SANCHEZ (Dem.) | Turnout Percent* | Lt. Governor DEWHURST (Rep.) | SHARP (Dem.) | U.S. Senator CORNYN (Rep.) | KIRK (Dem.) |
|---|---|---|---|---|---|---|---|---|
| Reagan | 1,900 | 526 | 224 | 40.26 | 429 | 285 | 517 | 198 |
| Real | 2,522 | 846 | 235 | 43.45 | 709 | 334 | 865 | 234 |
| Red River | 8,504 | 1,957 | 1,562 | 41.79 | 1,390 | 2,037 | 1,817 | 1,667 |
| Reeves | 7,602 | 782 | 1,716 | 33.18 | 649 | 1,730 | 827 | 1,538 |
| Refugio | 5,566 | 1,065 | 827 | 34.56 | 766 | 1,104 | 897 | 934 |
| Roberts | 782 | 339 | 53 | 51.40 | 268 | 123 | 321 | 68 |
| Robertson | 11,514 | 2,673 | 2,865 | 48.97 | 2,174 | 3,345 | 2,277 | 3,249 |
| Rockwall | 32,431 | 10,999 | 2,833 | 43.43 | 10,001 | 3,817 | 10,566 | 3,390 |
| Runnels | 7,089 | 2,200 | 637 | 41.13 | 1,558 | 1,259 | 1,911 | 879 |
| Rusk | 31,414 | 7,371 | 3,598 | 35.28 | 6,243 | 4,654 | 7,185 | 3,605 |
| Sabine | 7,653 | 1,604 | 1,182 | 37.08 | 1,289 | 1,480 | 1,514 | 1,197 |
| San Augustine | 6,669 | 1,481 | 1,383 | 43.63 | 1,005 | 1,818 | 1,306 | 1,450 |
| San Jacinto | 15,367 | 3,440 | 2,228 | 37.76 | 3,094 | 2,498 | 3,194 | 2,406 |
| San Patricio | 44,663 | 7,123 | 6,199 | 30.45 | 6,003 | 7,183 | 6,228 | 7,050 |
| San Saba | 3,704 | 1,283 | 483 | 48.40 | 1,002 | 751 | 1,172 | 551 |
| Schleicher | 1,842 | 556 | 246 | 44.46 | 383 | 399 | 508 | 269 |
| Scurry | 10,977 | 2,727 | 918 | 33.93 | 1,915 | 1,739 | 2,324 | 1,254 |
| Shackelford | 2,410 | 762 | 147 | 39.00 | 543 | 358 | 689 | 212 |
| Shelby | 15,395 | 3,882 | 2,574 | 42.37 | 2,890 | 3,484 | 3,695 | 2,555 |
| Sherman | 1,628 | 651 | 157 | 51.16 | 522 | 295 | 624 | 182 |
| Smith | 107,976 | 32,763 | 13,609 | 43.49 | 29,823 | 16,450 | 32,537 | 13,984 |
| Somervell | 5,202 | 1,674 | 757 | 47.90 | 1,423 | 955 | 1,593 | 875 |
| Starr | 27,602 | 663 | 5,556 | 22.60 | 671 | 4,770 | 535 | 4,934 |
| Stephens | 5,838 | 1,972 | 787 | 48.93 | 1,474 | 1,295 | 1,767 | 967 |
| Sterling | 1,019 | 352 | 85 | 43.96 | 263 | 166 | 351 | 84 |
| Stonewall | 1,204 | 372 | 210 | 49.83 | 233 | 360 | 288 | 283 |
| Sutton | 2,610 | 699 | 344 | 40.49 | 541 | 483 | 698 | 315 |
| Swisher | 5,033 | 1,163 | 885 | 41.66 | 879 | 1,186 | 1,050 | 1,010 |
| Tarrant | 876,576 | 200,486 | 129,861 | 38.44 | 186,766 | 143,542 | 195,111 | 139,596 |
| Taylor | 80,192 | 21,723 | 7,271 | 36.95 | 18,207 | 10,952 | 20,701 | 8,051 |
| Terrell | 798 | 192 | 207 | 50.62 | 106 | 248 | 149 | 194 |
| Terry | 7,957 | 1,966 | 897 | 36.70 | 1,514 | 1,369 | 1,794 | 1,011 |
| Throckmorton | 1,313 | 497 | 168 | 51.71 | 289 | 361 | 376 | 245 |
| Titus | 15,045 | 3,256 | 2,288 | 37.42 | 2,503 | 3,041 | 3,065 | 2,395 |
| Tom Green | 64,279 | 17,158 | 6,876 | 38.59 | 14,075 | 10,324 | 16,649 | 7,761 |
| Travis | 555,065 | 102,914 | 103,127 | 39.64 | 81,218 | 128,339 | 92,270 | 122,639 |
| Trinity | 10,488 | 2,210 | 1,863 | 39.42 | 1,771 | 2,280 | 2,056 | 1,959 |
| Tyler | 13,127 | 2,436 | 2,123 | 35.27 | 2,032 | 2,523 | 2,249 | 2,235 |
| Upshur | 23,298 | 5,507 | 3,368 | 38.91 | 4,421 | 4,454 | 5,338 | 3,458 |
| Upton | 2,216 | 604 | 241 | 38.76 | 487 | 344 | 575 | 253 |
| Uvalde | 16,411 | 3,159 | 2,965 | 37.84 | 2,611 | 3,398 | 3,057 | 2,887 |
| Val Verde | 25,524 | 3,197 | 4,403 | 30.06 | 2,831 | 4,515 | 3,184 | 4,153 |
| Van Zandt | 32,429 | 9,168 | 3,867 | 41.00 | 7,888 | 5,188 | 8,836 | 4,200 |
| Victoria | 55,061 | 11,385 | 7,494 | 34.92 | 7,310 | 11,573 | 11,171 | 7,121 |
| Walker | 28,239 | 6,448 | 3,807 | 36.98 | 5,818 | 4,428 | 6,448 | 3,807 |
| Waller | 23,130 | 4,765 | 3,071 | 34.43 | 4,233 | 3,509 | 4,498 | 3,282 |
| Ward | 6,999 | 1,697 | 1,399 | 45.87 | 1,414 | 1,627 | 1,621 | 1,375 |
| Washington | 19,794 | 7,020 | 2,270 | 47.69 | 5,706 | 3,560 | 6,639 | 2,568 |
| Webb | 93,451 | 3,958 | 35,101 | 41.99 | 5,969 | 30,350 | 4,922 | 31,714 |
| Wharton | 22,994 | 6,002 | 3,245 | 40.91 | 4,530 | 4,723 | 5,658 | 3,545 |
| Wheeler | 3,846 | 1,122 | 425 | 40.76 | 891 | 635 | 1,094 | 437 |
| Wichita | 79,492 | 16,930 | 8,518 | 32.93 | 15,178 | 10,455 | 16,171 | 9,602 |
| Wilbarger | 8,652 | 2,086 | 857 | 34.59 | 1,627 | 1,324 | 1,841 | 1,088 |
| Willacy | 10,917 | 1,004 | 2,615 | 33.56 | 904 | 2,601 | 865 | 2,681 |
| Williamson | 177,935 | 51,326 | 20,822 | 42.20 | 42,809 | 29,890 | 47,305 | 26,306 |
| Wilson | 22,340 | 5,614 | 3,294 | 40.60 | 4,850 | 3,950 | 5,333 | 3,416 |
| Winkler | 4,345 | 1,036 | 581 | 38.36 | 938 | 647 | 987 | 542 |
| Wise | 31,786 | 8,212 | 3,309 | 37.01 | 7,334 | 4,226 | 7,716 | 3,831 |
| Wood | 21,606 | 7,852 | 3,124 | 51.54 | 6,620 | 4,355 | 7,563 | 3,367 |
| Yoakum | 4,811 | 1,292 | 516 | 38.91 | 1,023 | 788 | 1,215 | 530 |
| Young | 11,900 | 3,804 | 1,422 | 44.64 | 3,035 | 2,181 | 3,490 | 1,747 |
| Zapata | 6,868 | 366 | 2,082 | 35.73 | 388 | 1,864 | 341 | 1,896 |
| Zavala | 8,225 | 430 | 2,195 | 32.25 | 331 | 2,080 | 380 | 2,030 |

*Percent figures for turnout include votes cast statewide for other gubernatorial candidates.

# Texas Primary Elections, 2002

Below are the official returns for the contested races only in the Republican and Democratic Party primaries held March 12, 2002. Included are statewide races and selected district races. The runoffs were held on April 9.

## DEMOCRATIC PRIMARY

### Governor
| | | |
|---|---|---|
| Bill Lyon | 43,011 | 4.28% |
| Dan Morales | 330,873 | 32.97% |
| Tony Sanchez | 609,383 | 60.73% |
| John Worldpeace | 20,121 | 2.00% |
| Total Vote | 1,003,388 | |

### U.S. Senator
| | | |
|---|---|---|
| Ken Bentsen | 255,501 | 26.76% |
| Ed Cunningham | 22,016 | 2.30% |
| Gene Kelly | 44,038 | 4.61% |
| Ron Kirk | 316,052 | 33.10% |
| Victor Morales | 317,048 | 33.21% |
| Total Vote | 954,655 | |

### Commissioner of the General Land Office
| | | |
|---|---|---|
| David Bernsen | 501,383 | 62.32% |
| Ray Madrigal | 303,142 | 37.67% |
| Total Vote | 804,525 | |

### Commissioner of Agriculture
| | | |
|---|---|---|
| Ernesto De Leon | 355,209 | 43.40% |
| Tom Ramsay | 463,190 | 56.59% |
| Total Vote | 818,399 | |

### Railroad Commissioner
| | | |
|---|---|---|
| Sherry Boyles | 492,225 | 63.09% |
| Paul C. Looney | 287,931 | 36.90% |
| Total Vote | 780,156 | |

### Judge, Court of Criminal Appeals, Place 2
| | | |
|---|---|---|
| Pat Montgomery | 500,327 | 68.69% |
| Julius Whittier | 227,956 | 31.30% |
| Total Vote | 728,283 | |

### U.S. HOUSE OF REPRESENTATIVES
#### District 5
| | | |
|---|---|---|
| Bill Bernstein | 5,902 | 22.84% |
| Ron Chapman | 18,298 | 70.82% |
| Wayne Raasch | 1,635 | 6.32% |
| Total Vote | 25,835 | |

#### District 10
| | | |
|---|---|---|
| Lloyd Doggett | 33,083 | 90.29% |
| Jennifer Gale | 3,554 | 9.70% |
| Total Vote | 36,637 | |

#### District 14
| | | |
|---|---|---|
| Sergio Martinez | 16,207 | 43.17% |
| Corby Windham | 21,335 | 56.82% |
| Total Vote | 37,542 | |

#### District 15
| | | |
|---|---|---|
| Mel Hawkins | 7,138 | 13.26% |
| Ruben Hinojosa | 46,688 | 86.73% |
| Total Vote | 53,826 | |

#### District 18
| | | |
|---|---|---|
| Sheila Jackson Lee | 31,563 | 94.40% |
| Lenwood Johnson | 1,871 | 5.59% |
| Total Vote | 33,434 | |

#### District 22
| | | |
|---|---|---|
| Frank (Chip) Briscoe | 4,316 | 48.37% |
| Tim Riley | 4,606 | 51.62% |
| Total Vote | 8,922 | |

#### District 25
| | | |
|---|---|---|
| Chris Bell | 7,443 | 36.09% |
| Paul Colbert | 4,307 | 20.88% |
| Stephen King | 3,274 | 15.87% |
| Carroll G. Robinson | 5,597 | 27.14% |
| Total Vote | 20,621 | |

#### District 32
| | | |
|---|---|---|
| Pauline K. Dixon | 9,384 | 72.42% |
| Walter W. Hofheinz | 3,572 | 27.57% |
| Total Vote | 12,956 | |

### STATE SENATE
#### District 20
| | | |
|---|---|---|
| Barbara Canales-Black | 25,922 | 39.06% |
| Ruben M. Garcia | 4,266 | 6.42% |
| Juan (Chuy) Hinojosa | 28,543 | 43.01% |
| Diana Martinez | 7,624 | 11.48% |
| Total Vote | 66,355 | |

#### District 30
| | | |
|---|---|---|
| Donald R. Acheson | 12,723 | 57.00% |
| Robert H. Fenoglio Sr. | 9,595 | 42.99% |
| Total Vote | 22,318 | |

### COURTS OF APPEALS
#### Justice, Sixth District
| | | |
|---|---|---|
| Charles Lee Attaway | 20,828 | 36.58% |
| Jack Carter | 36,107 | 63.41% |
| Total Vote | 56,935 | |

#### Justice, Thirteenth District
| | | |
|---|---|---|
| Dori Contreras Garza | 70,334 | 57.13% |
| Augustin (Augie) Rivera Jr. | 52,778 | 42.86% |
| Total Vote | 123,112 | |

### STATE BOARD OF EDUCATION
#### District 1
| | | |
|---|---|---|
| Said Abakoui | 8,533 | 7.94% |
| Rene Nunez | 98,809 | 92.05% |
| Total Vote | 107,342 | |

#### District 7
| | | |
|---|---|---|
| Thomas G. (Tom) Butler | 17,931 | 46.23% |
| Richard Hargrove | 20,854 | 53.76% |
| Total Vote | 38,785 | |

#### District 9
| | | |
|---|---|---|
| Robert A. (Bobby) Butler | 26,299 | 43.00% |
| Dean W. Woodard | 34,860 | 56.99% |
| Total Vote | 61,159 | |

### DEMOCRATIC RUNOFF

#### U.S. Senator
| | | |
|---|---|---|
| Ron Kirk | 370,878 | 59.79% |
| Victor Morales | 249,423 | 40.20% |
| Total Vote | 620,301 | |

#### U.S. House, District 25
| | | |
|---|---|---|
| Chris Bell | 9,572 | 54.29% |
| Carroll G. Robinson | 8,056 | 45.70% |
| Total Vote | 17,628 | |

#### State Senate, District 20
| | | |
|---|---|---|
| Barbara Canales-Black | 27,068 | 44.53% |
| Juan (Chuy) Hinojosa | 33,716 | 55.46% |
| Total Vote | 60,784 | |

## REPUBLICAN PRIMARY

### U.S. Senator
| | | |
|---|---|---|
| John Cornyn | 478,825 | 77.31% |
| Lawrence Cranberg | 17,757 | 2.86% |
| Douglas G. Deffenbaugh | 43,611 | 7.04% |
| Bruce Rusty Lang | 46,907 | 7.57% |
| Dudley F. Mooney | 32,202 | 5.19% |
| Total Vote | 619,302 | |

### Lieutenant Governor
| | | |
|---|---|---|
| David Dewhurst | 492,366 | 78.51% |
| Tom Kelly | 134,702 | 21.48% |
| Total Vote | 627,068 | |

### Commissioner of the General Land Office
| | | |
|---|---|---|
| Kenn George | 252,802 | 43.48% |
| Jerry Patterson | 328,523 | 56.51% |
| Total Vote | 581,325 | |

### Justice, Supreme Court, Place 2
| | | |
|---|---|---|
| John Cayce | 150,581 | 26.39% |
| Elizabeth Ray | 244,893 | 42.92% |
| Dale Wainwright | 175,019 | 30.67% |
| Total Vote | 570,493 | |

The Texas
Capitol in Austin
as it faces
Congress Ave.
The University
of Texas tower is
in the back-
ground.
File photo

**Justice, Supreme Court, Place 3** (unexpired)
Wallace B. Jefferson . . . . . . . . . . . . . . . . . 333,369 . .61.79%
Sam Lee . . . . . . . . . . . . . . . . . . . . . . . . . . 206,093 . .38.20%
　　Total Vote . . . . . . . . . . . . . . . . . . . . 539,462

**Justice, Supreme Court, Place 4** (unexpired)
Xavier Rodriguez . . . . . . . . . . . . . . . . . . 266,648 . .46.50%
Steven Wayne Smith . . . . . . . . . . . . . . . . . 306,730 . .53.49%
　　Total Vote . . . . . . . . . . . . . . . . . . . . 573,378

**Judge, Court of Criminal Appeals, Place 1**
Carolyn Denero . . . . . . . . . . . . . . . . . . . . 125,402 . .22.82%
Tom Price . . . . . . . . . . . . . . . . . . . . . . . . . 257,980 . .46.94%
Tim Taft . . . . . . . . . . . . . . . . . . . . . . . . . . . 166,099 . .30.22%
　　Total Vote . . . . . . . . . . . . . . . . . . . . 549,481

**Judge, Court of Criminal Appeals, Place 2**
Steve Mansfield . . . . . . . . . . . . . . . . . . . . 131,773 . .24.99%
David Richards . . . . . . . . . . . . . . . . . . . . . 160,478 . .30.44%
Paul Womack . . . . . . . . . . . . . . . . . . . . . . 234,865 . .44.55%
　　Total Vote . . . . . . . . . . . . . . . . . . . . 527,116

**Judge, Court of Criminal Appeals, Place 3**
Cathy Cochran . . . . . . . . . . . . . . . . . . . . . 228,137 . .42.93%
Blair Davis . . . . . . . . . . . . . . . . . . . . . . . . . 59,971 . .11.28%
Connie J. Kelley . . . . . . . . . . . . . . . . . . . . 97,596 . .18.36%
Guy Williams . . . . . . . . . . . . . . . . . . . . . . . 145,602 . .27.40%
　　Total Vote . . . . . . . . . . . . . . . . . . . . 531,306

**Prop. 1 Protection for public religious speech**
Yes . . . . . . . . . . . . . . . . . . . . . . . . . . . . . . 375,797 . .71.49%
No . . . . . . . . . . . . . . . . . . . . . . . . . . . . . . . 149,807 . .28.50%
　　Total Vote . . . . . . . . . . . . . . . . . . . . 525,604

**U.S. HOUSE OF REPRESENTATIVES**
**District 3**
Thomas (Tom) Caiazzo . . . . . . . . . . . . . . . . 3,184 . .15.65%
Sam Johnson . . . . . . . . . . . . . . . . . . . . . . 17,153 . .84.34%
　　Total Vote . . . . . . . . . . . . . . . . . . . . 20,337

**District 4**
Edward G. Conger . . . . . . . . . . . . . . . . . . . 9,627 . .30.65%
John Graves . . . . . . . . . . . . . . . . . . . . . . . 21,781 . .69.34%
　　Total Vote . . . . . . . . . . . . . . . . . . . . 31,408

**District 5**
Mike Armour . . . . . . . . . . . . . . . . . . . . . . . . 3,247 . .16.60%
Dan Hagood . . . . . . . . . . . . . . . . . . . . . . . . 3,628 . .18.55%
Jeb Hensarling . . . . . . . . . . . . . . . . . . . . . 10,475 . .53.56%
Phil Sudan . . . . . . . . . . . . . . . . . . . . . . . . . 1,632 . .8.34%
Fred A. Wood . . . . . . . . . . . . . . . . . . . . . . . . .574 . .2.93%
　　Total Vote . . . . . . . . . . . . . . . . . . . . 19,556

**District 11**
Rob Curnock . . . . . . . . . . . . . . . . . . . . . . . . 5,792 . .21.27%
Ramsey Farley . . . . . . . . . . . . . . . . . . . . . 17,985 . .66.05%
James (Dub) Maines . . . . . . . . . . . . . . . . . . 3,452 . .12.67%
　　Total Vote . . . . . . . . . . . . . . . . . . . . 27,229

**District 12**
Kay Granger . . . . . . . . . . . . . . . . . . . . . . . 20,769 . .87.13%

Philip Hillery . . . . . . . . . . . . . . . . . . . . . . . 3,067 . . 12.86%
　　Total Vote . . . . . . . . . . . . . . . . . . . . 23,836

**District 22**
Tom DeLay . . . . . . . . . . . . . . . . . . . . . . . . 22,379 . . 79.85%
Mike Fjetland . . . . . . . . . . . . . . . . . . . . . . . . 5,645 . . 20.14%
　　Total Vote . . . . . . . . . . . . . . . . . . . . 28,024

**District 26**
Scott Armey . . . . . . . . . . . . . . . . . . . . . . . 11,493 . . 45.39%
Michael C. Burgess . . . . . . . . . . . . . . . . . . 5,703 . . 22.52%
David Gulling . . . . . . . . . . . . . . . . . . . . . . . . . 204 . . 0.80%
Dave Kovatch . . . . . . . . . . . . . . . . . . . . . . . . . 675 . . 2.66%
Keith A. Self . . . . . . . . . . . . . . . . . . . . . . . . 5,610 . . 22.16%
Roger Sessions . . . . . . . . . . . . . . . . . . . . . 1,630 . . 6.43%
　　Total Vote . . . . . . . . . . . . . . . . . . . . 25,315

**District 30**
Ron Bush . . . . . . . . . . . . . . . . . . . . . . . . . . 3,958 . . 75.33%
Zach Rader . . . . . . . . . . . . . . . . . . . . . . . . 1,296 . . 24.66%
　　Total Vote . . . . . . . . . . . . . . . . . . . . 5,254

**District 31**
Flynn Adcock . . . . . . . . . . . . . . . . . . . . . . . 1,117 . . 3.17%
Brad Barton . . . . . . . . . . . . . . . . . . . . . . . . 5,751 . . 16.35%
John R. Carter . . . . . . . . . . . . . . . . . . . . . . 9,144 . . 26.00%
C. Patrick Meece . . . . . . . . . . . . . . . . . . . . 3,653 . . 10.38%
Roy Streckfuss . . . . . . . . . . . . . . . . . . . . . . . 898 . . 2.55%
Terry S. Ward . . . . . . . . . . . . . . . . . . . . . . . . 600 . . 1.70%
Peter Wareing . . . . . . . . . . . . . . . . . . . . . 12,987 . . 36.93%
Eric Whitfield . . . . . . . . . . . . . . . . . . . . . . . 1,014 . . 2.88%
　　Total Vote . . . . . . . . . . . . . . . . . . . . 35,164

**District 32**
Danny Davis . . . . . . . . . . . . . . . . . . . . . . . . 1,391 . . 6.51%
Pete Sessions . . . . . . . . . . . . . . . . . . . . . 19,973 . . 93.48%
　　Total Vote . . . . . . . . . . . . . . . . . . . . 21,364

**STATE SENATE**
**District 1**
Bill Ratliff . . . . . . . . . . . . . . . . . . . . . . . . . 20,367 . . 69.79%
Jerry Yost . . . . . . . . . . . . . . . . . . . . . . . . . . 8,816 . . 30.20%
　　Total Vote . . . . . . . . . . . . . . . . . . . . 29,183

**District 4**
Martin Basaldua . . . . . . . . . . . . . . . . . . . . . 4,571 . . 20.00%
Michael Galloway . . . . . . . . . . . . . . . . . . . . 7,947 . . 34.78%
Tommy Williams . . . . . . . . . . . . . . . . . . . . 10,327 . . 45.20%
　　Total Vote . . . . . . . . . . . . . . . . . . . . 22,845

**District 10**
Kim Brimer . . . . . . . . . . . . . . . . . . . . . . . . 11,823 . . 62.88%
Karen (Kerry) Lundelius . . . . . . . . . . . . . . . 6,979 . . 37.11%
　　Total Vote . . . . . . . . . . . . . . . . . . . . 18,802

**District 15**
Sam Texas . . . . . . . . . . . . . . . . . . . . . . . . . 1,698 . . 16.95%
Michael P. Wolfe . . . . . . . . . . . . . . . . . . . . . 8,314 . . 83.04%
　　Total Vote . . . . . . . . . . . . . . . . . . . . 10,012

**District 17**
Kyle Janek . . . . . . . . . . . . . . . . . . . . . . . . 16,250 . . 65.80%

Gary Polland . . . . . . . . . . . . . . . . . . . . . . . .8,444 . . 34.19%
   Total Vote . . . . . . . . . . . . . . . . . . . . . . .24,694

### District 18
Lester Phipps . . . . . . . . . . . . . . . . . . . . . .11,774 . . 50.12%
Michael Rozell . . . . . . . . . . . . . . . . . . . . . .11,713 . . 49.87%
   Total Vote . . . . . . . . . . . . . . . . . . . . . . .23,487

### District 22
Kip Averitt . . . . . . . . . . . . . . . . . . . . . . . .20,074 . . 57.63%
Ed Harrison . . . . . . . . . . . . . . . . . . . . . . . .14,758 . . 42.36%
   Total Vote . . . . . . . . . . . . . . . . . . . . . . .34,832

### District 25
John H. Shields . . . . . . . . . . . . . . . . . . . .25,265 . . 48.82%
Jeff Wentworth. . . . . . . . . . . . . . . . . . . . .26,481 . . 51.17%
   Total Vote . . . . . . . . . . . . . . . . . . . . . . .51,746

### District 30
Dave Deison . . . . . . . . . . . . . . . . . . . . . . .11,508 . . 42.29%
Craig Estes . . . . . . . . . . . . . . . . . . . . . . . .15,698 . . 57.70%
   Total Vote . . . . . . . . . . . . . . . . . . . . . . .27,206

## COURTS OF APPEALS

### Chief Justice, Third District
Ken Law. . . . . . . . . . . . . . . . . . . . . . . . . .34,931 . . 56.04%
Lee Yeakel. . . . . . . . . . . . . . . . . . . . . . . .27,394 . . 43.95%
   Total Vote . . . . . . . . . . . . . . . . . . . . . . .62,325

### Chief Justice, Ninth District
Gary A. Hinchman. . . . . . . . . . . . . . . . . .12,104 . . 46.68%
Steve McKeithen. . . . . . . . . . . . . . . . . . .13,821 . . 53.31%
   Total Vote . . . . . . . . . . . . . . . . . . . . . . .25,925

### Justice, Fourth District (unexpired term)
Sandee Bryan Marion . . . . . . . . . . . . . . .36,593 . . 66.07%
Clayton Trotter. . . . . . . . . . . . . . . . . . . . .18,787 . . 33.92%
   Total Vote . . . . . . . . . . . . . . . . . . . . . . .55,380

## STATE BOARD OF EDUCATION

### District 5
Jim Deats. . . . . . . . . . . . . . . . . . . . . . . . .24,874 . . 42.03%
Dan Montgomery. . . . . . . . . . . . . . . . . . .34,304 . . 57.96%
   Total Vote . . . . . . . . . . . . . . . . . . . . . . .59,178

### District 6
Doug Cannon . . . . . . . . . . . . . . . . . . . . . .19,060 . . 44.57%
Terri Leo. . . . . . . . . . . . . . . . . . . . . . . . . .23,703 . . 55.42%
   Total Vote . . . . . . . . . . . . . . . . . . . . . . .42,763

### District 7
David Bradley . . . . . . . . . . . . . . . . . . . . . .26,371 . . 79.98%
Jason W. Ceyanes Sr. . . . . . . . . . . . . . . . .6,597 . . 20.01%
   Total Vote . . . . . . . . . . . . . . . . . . . . . . .32,968

### District 8
Linda Bauer. . . . . . . . . . . . . . . . . . . . . . . .32,569 . . 64.16%
Grace Shore . . . . . . . . . . . . . . . . . . . . . . .18,189 . . 35.83%
   Total Vote . . . . . . . . . . . . . . . . . . . . . . .50,758

### District 9
Patricia (Pat) Harper . . . . . . . . . . . . . . . .19,519. . .48.77%
Don McLeroy . . . . . . . . . . . . . . . . . . . . . .20,503. . .51.22%
   Total Vote . . . . . . . . . . . . . . . . . . . . . . .40,022

### District 11
Blanca A. Castillo. . . . . . . . . . . . . . . . . . . .4,178. . . .9.39%
Patricia (Pat) Hardy . . . . . . . . . . . . . . . . .23,585. . .53.06%
Warren Norred . . . . . . . . . . . . . . . . . . . . .16,684. . .37.53%
   Total Vote . . . . . . . . . . . . . . . . . . . . . . .44,447

### District 14
Lynn Edward Allen . . . . . . . . . . . . . . . . . .17,911. . .39.83%
Gail Lowe . . . . . . . . . . . . . . . . . . . . . . . . .27,050. . .60.16%
   Total Vote . . . . . . . . . . . . . . . . . . . . . . .44,961

### District 15
Bob Craig. . . . . . . . . . . . . . . . . . . . . . . . .36,767. . .57.41%
Joyce Herron . . . . . . . . . . . . . . . . . . . . . .27,265. . .42.58%
   Total Vote . . . . . . . . . . . . . . . . . . . . . . .64,032

## REPUBLICAN RUNOFF

### U.S. House, District 26
Scott Armey . . . . . . . . . . . . . . . . . . . . . . . .8,737. . .45.36%
Michael C. Burgess . . . . . . . . . . . . . . . . .10,522. . .54.63%
   Total Vote . . . . . . . . . . . . . . . . . . . . . . .19,259

### U.S. House, District 31
John R. Carter . . . . . . . . . . . . . . . . . . . . .13,150. . .56.83%
Peter Wareing . . . . . . . . . . . . . . . . . . . . . .9,986. . .43.16%
   Total Vote . . . . . . . . . . . . . . . . . . . . . . .23,136

### State Senate, District 4
Michael Galloway . . . . . . . . . . . . . . . . . . .5,320. . .46.10%
Tommy Williams . . . . . . . . . . . . . . . . . . . .6,218. . .53.89%
   Total Vote . . . . . . . . . . . . . . . . . . . . . . .11,538

### Justice, Supreme Court, Place 2
Elizabeth Ray . . . . . . . . . . . . . . . . . . . . .102,557. . .45.11%
Dale Wainwright . . . . . . . . . . . . . . . . . . .124,785. . .54.88%
   Total Vote . . . . . . . . . . . . . . . . . . . . . .227,342

### Judge, Court of Criminal Appeals, Place 1
Tom Price. . . . . . . . . . . . . . . . . . . . . . . .121,039. . .57.74%
Tim Taft . . . . . . . . . . . . . . . . . . . . . . . . . .88,566. . .42.25%
   Total Vote . . . . . . . . . . . . . . . . . . . . . .209,605

### Judge, Court of Criminal Appeals, Place 2
David Richards. . . . . . . . . . . . . . . . . . . . .88,478. . .43.51%
Paul Womack . . . . . . . . . . . . . . . . . . . . .114,844. . .56.48%
   Total Vote . . . . . . . . . . . . . . . . . . . . . .203,322

### Judge, Court of Criminal Appeals, Place 3
Cathy Cochran . . . . . . . . . . . . . . . . . . . .133,463. . .63.00%
Guy Williams . . . . . . . . . . . . . . . . . . . . . .78,369. . .36.99%
   Total Vote . . . . . . . . . . . . . . . . . . . . . .211,832

# Political Party Organizations

## DEMOCRATIC State Executive Committee
www.txdemocrats.org

**Chair**, Molly Beth Malcolm, 919 Congress, Ste. 600, Austin 78701; **Vice Chair**, Juan Maldonado, Pharr; **Vice Chair for Financial Affairs**, Hilbert Ocañas, San Antonio; **Secretary**, Walter Hinojosa., Austin; **Treasurer**, Jewell McGowen, Houston; **Parliamentarians**, Ed Cogburn, Houston; Corinne Sabo, San Antonio; and Frank Thompson, Houston; **Sergeant-at-Arms**, Bruce Elfant, Austin.

**National Committee members:** Blanche Darley, El Paso; Yvonne Davis, Dallas; Al Edwards, Houston; Jaime Gonzalez, McAllen; David Holmes, Austin; Eddie Bernice Johnson, Dallas; Iris Lawrence, Amarillo; Sue Lovell, Houston; Edward Miller, Texarkana; Carroll Robinson, Houston; Bob Slagle, Sherman; Oscar Soliz, Corpus Christi, and Rosa Walker, Austin.

### District — Member and Hometown
1. Norma Narramore, Winfield; Glenn A. Perry, Longview.

2. Martha Williams, Terrell; Phil Fisher, Seagoville.

3. Kathleen Hawkins, Buna; Dennis Teal, Livingston.

4. Mary Kirkwood, Beaumont; John Baker, Bridge City.

5. Mary Moore, Bryan; Bill Holcomb, Crockett.

6. Rose A. Salas, Houston; James Cumming, Houston.

7. Joy Demark, Houston; Bill Scruggs, Spring.

8. Nancy G. Machen, Plano; David Griggs, Addison.

9. Christine Asberry, Dallas; Marvin Sutton, Arlington.

10. Amber Anderson, Fort Worth; Marc House, Arlington.

11. Eva Hern, Kemah; Daniel Snooks, Houston.

12. Kay Walker, Fort Worth; John Burton, Fort Worth.

13. Mary Ann Seymore, Houston; Rodney Griffin, Houston.

14. Ann McAfee, Austin; Frank Ortega, Austin.

15. Kendra J. Yarbrough, Houston; Michael Harris, Houston.

16. Theresa Daniel, Dallas; Ken Molberg, Dallas.

17. Virgina Stogner, Houston; Gary Horton, Galveston.

18. Dorothy Bottos, Hockley; Phillip Ruiz, Lockhart.

19. Jo Ann McCall, San Antonio; Ben Alexander, San Antonio.

20. Adrian Fernandez, Edinburg; Laura Estrada, Corpus Christi.

21. Maria Luisa Martinez, Laredo; Howard C. Berger, Floresville.

22. JoAnn Jenkins, Ovilla; Danny Trull, Waxahachie.

23. Monica Alonzo, Dallas; Leumuel H. Price, Dallas.

24. T.J. Mabrey, Kempner; Jesse Martin, Buchanan Dam.

25. Barbara Effenberger, Seguin; Don Williamson, Austin.

26. Ann Marie Schroeder, San Antonio; Concepcion Elizondo, San Antonio.

27. Remi Garza, San Benito; Juanita Valdez-Cox, Donna.

28. Mary Hatfield, Lubbock; Ron Michulka, San Angelo.

29. Mary Bowles-Grijalva, El Paso; Frank Lerma, El Paso.

30. Dianne Thueson, Wichita Falls; Boyd Richie, Graham.

31. Roberta Hicks, Amarillo; George Dowlen, Amarillo.

Senate Democratic Caucus: Gonzalo Barrientos, Austin.

House Democratic Caucus: Patricia Gray, Galveston.

Texas Young Democrats: Dennis Speight, Austin; Eva Howe, Houston.

County Chairs Assn.: Philip A. Ruiz, Lockhart; Eddie Pevehouse Sims, Wortham.

Texas Democratic Women: Betty Ritchie, Graham; Mae Jackson, Waco.

Coalition of Black Democrats: Morris Overstreet, Austin; Iris Lawrence, Amarillo.

Non-Urban Caucus: Dennis Teal, Livingston; Anna Marie Hornsby, Texarkana.

Tejano Democrats: Bill Callejo, Dallas; Lonora Sorola-Pohlman, Houston.

Stonewall Democrats: Michael Milliken, Dallas; Nancy Russell, San Antonio.

### Auxiliaries

Texas Democratic Women: Betty Ritchie, Graham; www.tdw.org.

Coalition of Black Democrats: Morris Overstreet, Austin; members.aol.com/tcbdweb.

Non-Urban Caucus: Anna Marie Hornsby, Texarkana.

Tejano Democrats: Juan Maldonado, Pharr; www.tejanodemocrats.com.

Stonewall Democrats: Michael Milliken, Dallas; www.stonewalldemocrats.org.

Young Democrats: Sean Bradley, San Antonio; www.texasyds.org.

### REPUBLICAN State Executive Committee
### www.texasgop.org

Chairman, Susan Weddington, 211 E. 7th, Ste. 620, Austin 78701; Vice Chairman, David Barton; Secretary, Betty Lou Martin; Treasurer, Susan Howard-Chrane; General Counsel, Rene Diaz; Associate General Counsel, Dennis Donley; Parliamentarian, Chris Maska; Finance Chairman, Barry Williamson; Sergeant-at-Arms, Kenneth Clark; Chaplain, Robert Long.

National Committee members: Tim Lambert, Lubbock; Denise McNamara, Dallas.

### District — Member and Hometown

1. Marjorie Chandler, Texarkana; Thomas Whaley, Marshall.

2. Leah Hubbard, Garland; Bob Reese, Canton.

3. Marcia Daughtrey, Tyler; James Wiggins, Conroe.

4. Melina Fredricks, Conroe; David Teuscher, Beaumont.

5. John Gordon, Round Rock; Anne Mazone, Navasota.

6. Larry Bowles, Houston; Amy Jones, Pasadena.

7. Tina Johns Benkiser, Houston; Thomas M. Moon, Houston.

8. Amanda Tschoepe, Plano; Wayne Tucker, Plano.

9. Timothy Hoy, Dallas; Cynthia Jenkins, Irving.

10. William Ford, Fort Worth; Melba McDow, Dallas.

11. Kathy Haigler, Deer Park; Kenneth Clark, League City.

12. Tom Quinones, Haltom City; Shirley Spellerberg, Denton.

13. Vickie Clements, Houston; Eugene Pack, Houston.

14. William Crocker, Austin; Jan Galbraith, Austin.

15. Nelda Eppes, Houston; Louis (Butch) Davis, Houston.

16. Richard Steenson, Richardson; Chris Davis, Richardson.

17. Jim Hotze, Bellaire; Terese Raia, Sugar Land.

18. Emmett Gloyna, Edna; Myrna Patterson McLeroy, Gonzales.

19. Kim Hesley, Pipe Creek; Bob Peden, Hondo.

20. Michael Bergsma, Corpus Christi; Sandra Cararas, McAllen.

21. James Clancy, Portland; Dawn Lothringer, Pleasanton.

22. Helen Quiram, Waco; John Tabor, Waxahachie.

23. Greg Knauer, Duncanville; Marjorie Ford, DeSoto.

24. Belinda Colyer, Brownwood; B.R. Wallace, Lampasas.

25. Roy Casanova, San Antonio; Genevieve Hensz, New Braunfels.

26. Reinette Alecozay, San Antonio; Chris George, San Antonio.

27. Frank Morris, Harlingen; Karen Ballard, Brownsville.

28. Jane Cansino, Lubbock; Tom Mechler, Claude.

29. Connie Roberts, El Paso; David Thackston, El Paso.

30. Katherine Gear, Mineral Wells; Clyde Siebman, Sherman.

31. Chad Weaver, Midland; Sue Hershey, Amarillo.

### Auxiliaries

Texas Federation of College Republicans: Suzanne Tomlin, Austin; www.collegerepublicans.com.

Texas Republican County Chairmen's Association: Hollis Rutledge, McAllen; www.trcca.org.

Republican Veterans of Texas: Jerry Patterson, Austin; jpatterson4@austin.rr.com.

Texas Federation of Republican Women: Gail Suttle, Austin; www.tfrw.org.

Texas Asian Republican Caucus: Sue Chiang, Sugar Land.

Texas Federation of Pachyderm Clubs: A.G. (Pete) Hinojosa, Kingwood; www.pachyderms.org.

Texas Young Republican Federation: Jason Moore, Odessa; www.tyrf.org. ☆

# Texas Vote in Presidential Elections, 1848-2000

Below are the Texas popular vote results for U.S. presidential elections. (Earlier elections listed electors, and often the highest vote recorded by any elector was used as the figure for the presidential candidate.) An asterisk (*) designates the winner of the national election. In the 1860 vote which elected Lincoln president, electors for neither Lincoln nor Stephen Douglas were on the Texas ballot. Texas did not take part in the 1864 and 1868 elections because of the Civil War and Reconstruction.

### Election, 1848
Lewis Cass (Democrat) . . . . . . . . . . . . . . . . . . . 10,668
*Zachary Taylor (Whig) . . . . . . . . . . . . . . . . . . . . 4,509
Total Vote . . . . . . . . . . . . . . . . . . 15,177

### Election, 1852
*Franklin Pierce (Democrat) . . . . . . . . . . . . . 13,552
Winfield Scott (Whig) . . . . . . . . . . . . . . . . . . . 4,995
Total Vote . . . . . . . . . . . . . . . . . . 18,547

### Election, 1856
*James C. Buchanan (Democrat) . . . . . . . . . . . 31,169
Millard Fillmore (Whig) . . . . . . . . . . . . . . . . . 15,639
Total Vote . . . . . . . . . . . . . . . . . . 46,808

### Election, 1860
John C Breckinridge (Democrat) . . . . . . . . . . . . 47,548
John Bell (Constitutional Union) . . . . . . . . . . . . . 15,438
Total Vote . . . . . . . . . . . . . . . . . . 62,986

### CIVIL WAR and RECONSTRUCTION

### Election, 1872
Horace Greeley (Democrat) . . . . . . . . . . . . . 66,546
*Ulysses S. Grant (Republican) . . . . . . . . . . . . 47,468
Charles O'Conor (Labor-Reform) . . . . . . . . . . . . 2,580
Total Vote . . . . . . . . . . . . . . . . . . 116,594

### Election, 1876
Samuel J. Tilden (Democrat) . . . . . . . . . . . . . 104,755
*Rutherford B. Hayes (Republican) . . . . . . . . . . 44,800
Total Vote . . . . . . . . . . . . . . . . . . 149,555

### Election, 1880
Winfield S. Hancock (Democrat) . . . . . . . . . . . . 156,428
*James A. Garfield (Republican) . . . . . . . . . . . . 57,893
Total Vote . . . . . . . . . . . . . . . . . . 214,321

### Election, 1884
*Grover Cleveland (Democrat) . . . . . . . . . . . . . 225,309
James G. Blaine (Republican) . . . . . . . . . . . . . 93,141
John P. St. John (Prohibitionist) . . . . . . . . . . . . 3,534
Benjamin F. Butler (Greenback) . . . . . . . . . . . . . 3,321
Total Vote . . . . . . . . . . . . . . . . . . 325,305

### Election, 1888
Grover Cleveland (Democrat) . . . . . . . . . . . . . 234,883
*Benjamin Harrison (Republican) . . . . . . . . . . . . 88,422
Alson J. Streeter (Union Labor) . . . . . . . . . . . . 29,459
Clinton B. Fisk (Prohibitionist) . . . . . . . . . . . . . 4,749
Total Vote . . . . . . . . . . . . . . . . . . 357,513

### Election, 1892
*Grover Cleveland (Democrat) . . . . . . . . . . . . . 239,148
James B. Weaver (Populist) . . . . . . . . . . . . . . . 99,688
Benjamin Harrison (Republican) . . . . . . . . . . . . 81,144
John Bidwell (Prohibitionist) . . . . . . . . . . . . . . . 2.175
Total Vote . . . . . . . . . . . . . . . . . . 422,155

### Election, 1896
William J. Bryan (Democrat) . . . . . . . . . . . . . 234,298
William J. Bryan (Populist) . . . . . . . . . . . . . . . 78,926
*William McKinley (Republican) . . . . . . . . . . . . 167,520

John McA. Palmer (National Democrat) . . . . . . . . . 5,046
Joshua Levering (Prohibitionist) . . . . . . . . . . . . . 1,786
Total Vote . . . . . . . . . . . . . . . . . . 487,576

### Election, 1900
William J. Bryan (Democrat) . . . . . . . . . . . . . 267,432
*William McKinley (Republican) . . . . . . . . . . . . 130,651
Wharton Barker (Populist) . . . . . . . . . . . . . . . . 20,981
John C. Woolley (Prohibitionist) . . . . . . . . . . . . . 2,644
Eugene V. Debs (Socialist) . . . . . . . . . . . . . . . 1,846
Joseph F. Malloney (Socialist-Labor) . . . . . . . . . . . 162
Total Vote . . . . . . . . . . . . . . . . . . 423,716**

### **POLL TAX instituted as requirement for voting, December 1902

### Election, 1904
Alton B. Parker (Democrat) . . . . . . . . . . . . . 199,799
*Theodore Roosevelt (Republican) . . . . . . . . . . . 65,823
Thomas E. Watson (Populist) . . . . . . . . . . . . . . 8,062
Silas C. Swallow (Prohibitionist) . . . . . . . . . . . . 4,292
Eugene V. Debs (Socialist) . . . . . . . . . . . . . . . 2,791
Charles H. Corregan (Socialist-Labor) . . . . . . . . . . . 421
Total Vote . . . . . . . . . . . . . . . . . . 281,188**

### Election, 1908
William J. Bryan (Democrat) . . . . . . . . . . . . . 224,110
*William H. Taft (Republican) . . . . . . . . . . . . . 70,458
Eugene V. Debs (Socialist) . . . . . . . . . . . . . . . 7,870
Eugene W. Chafin (Prohibitionist) . . . . . . . . . . . . 1,634
Thomas E. Watson (Populist) . . . . . . . . . . . . . . . 994
August Gillhaus (Socialist-Labor) . . . . . . . . . . . . . 176
Thomas L. Hisgen (Independent) . . . . . . . . . . . . . 115
Total Vote . . . . . . . . . . . . . . . . . . 305,357

### Election, 1912
*Woodrow Wilson (Democrat) . . . . . . . . . . . . . 222,589
Theodore Roosevelt (Progressive) . . . . . . . . . . . 28,853
William H. Taft (Republican) . . . . . . . . . . . . . . 26,755
Eugene V. Debs (Socialist) . . . . . . . . . . . . . . . 25,743
Eugene W. Chafin (Prohibitionist) . . . . . . . . . . . . 1,738
Arthur E. Reimer (Socialist-Labor) . . . . . . . . . . . . . 442
Total Vote . . . . . . . . . . . . . . . . . . 306,120

### Election, 1916
*Woodrow Wilson (Democrat) . . . . . . . . . . . . . 286,514
Charles E. Hughes (Republican) . . . . . . . . . . . . 64,999
Allan L. Benson (Socialist) . . . . . . . . . . . . . . . 18,969
J. Frank Hanly (Prohibitionist) . . . . . . . . . . . . . 1,985
Total Vote . . . . . . . . . . . . . . . . . . 372,467

### Election, 1920
James M. Cox (Democrat) . . . . . . . . . . . . . 288,767
*Warren G. Harding (Republican) . . . . . . . . . . . 114,538
James E. Ferguson (American) . . . . . . . . . . . . . 47,968
(Black and Tan Republican) . . . . . . . . . . . . . . . 27,247
Eugene V. Debs (Socialist) . . . . . . . . . . . . . . . 8,121
Total Vote . . . . . . . . . . . . . . . . . . 486,641

### Election, 1924
John W. Davis (Democrat) . . . . . . . . . . . . . 484,605
*Calvin Coolidge (Republican) . . . . . . . . . . . . 130,023
Robert M. LaFollette (Progressive) . . . . . . . . . . 42,881

Total Vote . . . . . . . . . . . . . . . . . . 657,509

### Election, 1928
*Herbert C. Hoover (Republican) . . . . . . . . . . . .367,036
Alfred E. Smith (Democrat) . . . . . . . . . . . . . .341,032
Norman M. Thomas (Socialist) . . . . . . . . . . . . . 722
William Z. Foster (Communist) . . . . . . . . . . . . . . 209
Total Vote . . . . . . . . . . . . . . . . . 708,999

### Election, 1932
*Franklin D. Roosevelt (Democrat) . . . . . . . . . . .760,348
Herbert C. Hoover (Republican) . . . . . . . . . . . . .97,959
Norman M. Thomas (Socialist) . . . . . . . . . . . . .4,450
W.H. Harvey (Liberty) . . . . . . . . . . . . . . . . . 324
William Z. Foster (Communist) . . . . . . . . . . . . . 207
(Jacksonian) . . . . . . . . . . . . . . . . . . . . . . . 104
Total Vote . . . . . . . . . . . . . . . . . 863,392

### Election, 1936
*Franklin D. Roosevelt (Democrat) . . . . . . . . . . .734,485
Alfred M. Landon (Republican) . . . . . . . . . . . . . .103,874
William Lemke (Union) . . . . . . . . . . . . . . . . . .3,281
Norman M. Thomas (Socialist) . . . . . . . . . . . . . .1,075
D. Leigh Colvin (Prohibitionist) . . . . . . . . . . . . . 514
Earl R. Browder (Communist) . . . . . . . . . . . . . . . 253
Total Vote . . . . . . . . . . . . . . . . . 843,482

### Election, 1940
*Franklin D. Roosevelt (Democrat) . . . . . . . . . . . 840,151
Wendell L. Willkie (Republican) . . . . . . . . . . . . . 199,152
Roger W. Babson (Prohibitionist) . . . . . . . . . . . . . 925
Norman M. Thomas (Socialist) . . . . . . . . . . . . . . 728
Earl R. Browder (Communist) . . . . . . . . . . . . . . . 212
Total Vote . . . . . . . . . . . . . . . . . 1,041,168

### Election, 1944
*Franklin D. Roosevelt (Democrat) . . . . . . . . . . 821,605
Thomas E. Dewey (Republican) . . . . . . . . . . . . 191,425
‡(Texas Regulars) . . . . . . . . . . . . . . . . . . 135,439
Claude A. Watson (Prohibitionist) . . . . . . . . . . . . 1,017
Norman M. Thomas (Socialist) . . . . . . . . . . . . . 594
Gerald L.K. Smith (America First) . . . . . . . . . . . . . . 251
Total Vote . . . . . . . . . . . . . . . . . 1,150,331

### Election, 1948
*Harry S Truman (Democrat) . . . . . . . . . . . . . . 750,700
Thomas E. Dewey (Republican) . . . . . . . . . . . . 282,240
J. Strom Thurmond (States Rights) . . . . . . . . . . .106,909
Henry A. Wallace (Progressive) . . . . . . . . . . . . . .3,764
Claude A. Watson (Prohibitionist) . . . . . . . . . . . . .2,758
Norman M. Thomas (Socialist) . . . . . . . . . . . . . . 874
Total Vote . . . . . . . . . . . . . . . . . 1,147,245

### Election, 1952
*Dwight D. Eisenhower (Republican) . . . . . . . . 1,102,878
Adlai E. Stevenson (Democrat) . . . . . . . . . . . 969,228
Stuart Hamblen (Prohibitionist) . . . . . . . . . . . . .1,983
Douglas MacArthur (Christian National) . . . . . . . . . 833
Douglas MacArthur (Constitution) . . . . . . . . . . . . 730
Vincent Hallinan (Progressive) . . . . . . . . . . . . . 294
Total Vote . . . . . . . . . . . . . . . . . 2,075,946

### Election, 1956
*Dwight D. Eisenhower (Republican) . . . . . . . . 1,080,619
Adlai E. Stevenson (Democrat) . . . . . . . . . . . 859,958
T. Coleman Andrews (Constitution) . . . . . . . . . . 14,591
Total Vote . . . . . . . . . . . . . . . . . 1,955,168

### Election, 1960
*John F. Kennedy (Democrat) . . . . . . . . . . . . . 1,167,932
Richard M. Nixon (Republican) . . . . . . . . . . . . 1,121,699
Charles L. Sullivan (Constitution) . . . . . . . . . . . 18,169
Rutherford L. Decker (Prohibitionist) . . . . . . . . . . .3,870
Total Vote . . . . . . . . . . . . . . . . . 2,311,670

### Election, 1964**
*Lyndon B. Johnson (Democrat) . . . . . . . . . . . 1,663,185
Barry Goldwater (Republican) . . . . . . . . . . . . . 958,566
Joseph B. Lightburn (Conservative) . . . . . . . . . . . 5,060
Total Vote . . . . . . . . . . . . . . . . . .2,626,811

### ** First federal election no poll tax required

### Election, 1968
Hubert H. Humphrey (Democrat) . . . . . . . . . . 1,266,804
*Richard M. Nixon (Republican) . . . . . . . . . . . . 1,227,844
George C. Wallace (American) . . . . . . . . . . . . 584,269
Write-in . . . . . . . . . . . . . . . . . . . . . . . . . . . 489
Total Vote . . . . . . . . . . . . . . . . .3,079,406

### Election, 1972
*Richard M. Nixon (Republican) . . . . . . . . . . . 2,298,896
George McGovern (Democrat) . . . . . . . . . . . . 1,154,289
Linda Jenness (Socialist) . . . . . . . . . . . . . . 8,664
John G. Schmitz (American) . . . . . . . . . . . . . . 6,039
Other . . . . . . . . . . . . . . . . . . . . . . . . . . . 3,393
Total Vote . . . . . . . . . . . . . . . . .3,471,281

### Election, 1976
*Jimmy Carter (Democrat) . . . . . . . . . . . . . . 2,082,319
Gerald R. Ford (Republican) . . . . . . . . . . . . 1,953,300
Eugene J. McCarthy (Independent) . . . . . . . . . . 20,118
Thomas J. Anderson (American) . . . . . . . . . . . . 11,442
Peter Camejo (Socialst Worker) . . . . . . . . . . . . 1,723
Write-in Vote . . . . . . . . . . . . . . . . . . . . . . . 2,982
Total Vote . . . . . . . . . . . . . . . . .4,071,884

### Election, 1980
*Ronald Reagan (Republican) . . . . . . . . . . . . . 2,510,705
Jimmy Carter (Democrat) . . . . . . . . . . . . . . 1,881,147
John Anderson (Independent) . . . . . . . . . . . . . 111,613
Ed Clark (Libertarian) . . . . . . . . . . . . . . . . . 37,643
Write-in Vote . . . . . . . . . . . . . . . . . . . . . . . 529
Total Vote . . . . . . . . . . . . . . . . .4,541,637

### Election, 1984
*Ronald Reagan (Republican) . . . . . . . . . . . . . 3,433,428
Walter Mondale (Democrat) . . . . . . . . . . . . . 1,949,276
Lyndon Larouche (Independent) . . . . . . . . . . . . . 14,613
Other . . . . . . . . . . . . . . . . . . . . . . . . . . . .254
Total Vote . . . . . . . . . . . . . . . . .5,397,571

### Election, 1988
*George Bush (Republican) . . . . . . . . . . . . . . 3,036,829
Michael S. Dukakis (Democrat) . . . . . . . . . . . 2,352,748
Ron Paul (Libertarian) . . . . . . . . . . . . . . . . . .30,355
Other . . . . . . . . . . . . . . . . . . . . . . . . . . .7,478
Total Vote . . . . . . . . . . . . . . . . .5,427,410

### Election, 1992
George Bush (Republican) . . . . . . . . . . . . . . . 2,496,071
*Bill Clinton (Democrat) . . . . . . . . . . . . . . . . 2,281,815
Ross Perot (Independent) . . . . . . . . . . . . . . 1,354,781
Andre Marrou (Libertarian) . . . . . . . . . . . . . . . .19,699
Other . . . . . . . . . . . . . . . . . . . . . . . . . . .1,652
Total Vote . . . . . . . . . . . . . . . . .6,154,018

### Election, 1996
Bob Dole (Republican) . . . . . . . . . . . . . . . . . 2,736,167
*Bill Clinton (Democrat) . . . . . . . . . . . . . . . . 2,459,683
Ross Perot (Independent) . . . . . . . . . . . . . . .378,537
Harry Browne (Libertarian) . . . . . . . . . . . . . . . .20,256
Howard Phillips (U.S. Taxpayers) . . . . . . . . . . . .7,472
Ralph Nader (Write-In) . . . . . . . . . . . . . . . . . .4,810
John Hagelin (Natural Law) . . . . . . . . . . . . . . . .4,422
Mary Cal Hollis (Write-In) . . . . . . . . . . . . . . . . . 297
Total Vote . . . . . . . . . . . . . . . . .5,611,644

### Election, 2000
George W. Bush (Republican) . . . . . . . . . . . . . 3,799,639
Al Gore (Democrat) . . . . . . . . . . . . . . . . . . . . . 2,433,746
Ralph Nader (Green) . . . . . . . . . . . . . . . . . . . . . 137,994
Harry Browne (Libertarian) . . . . . . . . . . . . . . . . 23,160
Pat Buchanan (Independent) . . . . . . . . . . . . . . 12,394
Howard Phillips (Write-In) . . . . . . . . . . . . . . . . . . 567
James (Jim) Wright (W-I) . . . . . . . . . . . . . . . . . . . 74
David McReynolds (W-I) . . . . . . . . . . . . . . . . . . . 63
   Total Vote . . . . . . . . . . . . . . . . . 6,407,637

## Presidential primaries in Texas
### May 1976
(This was the first time presidential primaries were held
in the state.)
#### Republican
Ronald Reagan . . . . . . . . . . . . . . . . . . . . . . . 278,300
Gerald Ford . . . . . . . . . . . . . . . . . . . . . . . . . . 139,944
Uncommitted . . . . . . . . . . . . . . . . . . . . . . . . . . 1,162
   Total Vote . . . . . . . . . . . . . . . . . 419,406

#### Democratic
Jimmy Carter . . . . . . . . . . . . . . . . . . . . . . . . . 736,161
Lloyd Bentsen . . . . . . . . . . . . . . . . . . . . . . . . 343,032
George Wallace . . . . . . . . . . . . . . . . . . . . . . . 270,798
Fred Harris . . . . . . . . . . . . . . . . . . . . . . . . . . . 31,379
Sargent Shriver . . . . . . . . . . . . . . . . . . . . . . . . 28,520
Ellen McCormack . . . . . . . . . . . . . . . . . . . . . . . 5,700
Uncommitted . . . . . . . . . . . . . . . . . . . . . . . . 129,478
   Total Vote . . . . . . . . . . . . . . . . 1,545,068

### May 1980
#### Republican
Ronald Reagan . . . . . . . . . . . . . . . . . . . . . . . 268,798
George Bush . . . . . . . . . . . . . . . . . . . . . . . . . 249,819
Uncommitted . . . . . . . . . . . . . . . . . . . . . . . . . . 8,152
   Total Vote . . . . . . . . . . . . . . . . . 526,769

#### Democratic
Jimmy Carter . . . . . . . . . . . . . . . . . . . . . . . . . 770,390
Edward M. Kennedy . . . . . . . . . . . . . . . . . . . . 314,129
Jerry Brown . . . . . . . . . . . . . . . . . . . . . . . . . . 35,585
Uncommitted . . . . . . . . . . . . . . . . . . . . . . . . 257,250
   Total Vote . . . . . . . . . . . . . . . . 1,377,354

### March 1984
#### Republican
Ronald Reagan . . . . . . . . . . . . . . . . . . . . . . . 308,713
Uncommitted . . . . . . . . . . . . . . . . . . . . . . . . . 11,126
   Total Vote . . . . . . . . . . . . . . . . . 319,839

#### Democratic
Democrats held no primary, but voted in precinct caucuses for
169 pledged delegates. With addition of party leaders, the 200-
member delegation to the national convention was divided:
Walter Mondale . . . . . . . . . . . . . . . . . . . . . . . . . . . 119
Gary Hart . . . . . . . . . . . . . . . . . . . . . . . . . . . . . . . . . 41
Jesse L. Jackson . . . . . . . . . . . . . . . . . . . . . . . . . . . 35
Uncommitted . . . . . . . . . . . . . . . . . . . . . . . . . . . . . . . 5

### March 1988
#### Republican
George Bush . . . . . . . . . . . . . . . . . . . . . . . . . 648,178
Pat Robertson . . . . . . . . . . . . . . . . . . . . . . . . 155,449
Bob Dole . . . . . . . . . . . . . . . . . . . . . . . . . . . . 140,795
Jack Kemp . . . . . . . . . . . . . . . . . . . . . . . . . . . 50,586
Pete Du Pont . . . . . . . . . . . . . . . . . . . . . . . . . . 4,245
Alexander M. Haig Jr. . . . . . . . . . . . . . . . . . . . . 3,140
Uncommitted . . . . . . . . . . . . . . . . . . . . . . . . . 12,563
   Total Vote . . . . . . . . . . . . . . . . 1,014,956

#### Democratic
Michael S. Dukakis . . . . . . . . . . . . . . . . . . . . . 579,713
Jesse L. Jackson . . . . . . . . . . . . . . . . . . . . . . 433,335
Al Gore . . . . . . . . . . . . . . . . . . . . . . . . . . . . . 357,764
Dick Gephardt . . . . . . . . . . . . . . . . . . . . . . . . 240,158
Gary Hart . . . . . . . . . . . . . . . . . . . . . . . . . . . . 82,199

Paul Simon . . . . . . . . . . . . . . . . . . . . . . . . . . . 34,499
Bruce Babbitt . . . . . . . . . . . . . . . . . . . . . . . . . . 11,618
Lyndon H. LaRouche Jr. . . . . . . . . . . . . . . . . . . . 9,013
David E. Duke . . . . . . . . . . . . . . . . . . . . . . . . . . 8,808
W.A. Williams . . . . . . . . . . . . . . . . . . . . . . . . . . . 6,238
Norbert G. Dennerll Jr. . . . . . . . . . . . . . . . . . . . . 3,700
   Total Vote . . . . . . . . . . . . . . . . 1,767,045

### March 1992
#### Republican
George Bush . . . . . . . . . . . . . . . . . . . . . . . . . 556,280
Patrick J. Buchanan . . . . . . . . . . . . . . . . . . . . . 190,572
David Duke . . . . . . . . . . . . . . . . . . . . . . . . . . . 20,255
George A. Zimmermann . . . . . . . . . . . . . . . . . . . 1,349
Tennie Rogers . . . . . . . . . . . . . . . . . . . . . . . . . . . 754
Uncommitted . . . . . . . . . . . . . . . . . . . . . . . . . 27,936
   Total Vote . . . . . . . . . . . . . . . . . 797,146

#### Democratic
Bill Clinton . . . . . . . . . . . . . . . . . . . . . . . . . . . 972,235
Paul E. Tsongas . . . . . . . . . . . . . . . . . . . . . . . 285,224
Edmund G. Brown Jr. . . . . . . . . . . . . . . . . . . . . 118,869
Charles Woods . . . . . . . . . . . . . . . . . . . . . . . . . 30,097
Bob Kerrey . . . . . . . . . . . . . . . . . . . . . . . . . . . . 20,298
Tom Harkin . . . . . . . . . . . . . . . . . . . . . . . . . . . 19,618
Lyndon H. LaRouche Jr. . . . . . . . . . . . . . . . . . . 12,220
George W. Benns . . . . . . . . . . . . . . . . . . . . . . . . 7,876
Rufus Higginbotham . . . . . . . . . . . . . . . . . . . . . . 7,677
Tod Howard Hawks . . . . . . . . . . . . . . . . . . . . . . . 4,924
J. Louis McAlpine . . . . . . . . . . . . . . . . . . . . . . . . 4,009
   Total Vote . . . . . . . . . . . . . . . . 1,483,047

### March 1996
#### Republican
Bob Dole . . . . . . . . . . . . . . . . . . . . . . . . . . . . 567,164
Patrick J. (Pat) Buchanan . . . . . . . . . . . . . . . . . 217,974
Steve Forbes . . . . . . . . . . . . . . . . . . . . . . . . . 130,938
Alan Keyes . . . . . . . . . . . . . . . . . . . . . . . . . . . 41,746
Lamar Alexander . . . . . . . . . . . . . . . . . . . . . . . 18,745
Phil Gramm . . . . . . . . . . . . . . . . . . . . . . . . . . 18,629
Richard G. Lugar . . . . . . . . . . . . . . . . . . . . . . . . 2,266
Susan Ducey . . . . . . . . . . . . . . . . . . . . . . . . . . 1,093
Mary (France) LeTulle . . . . . . . . . . . . . . . . . . . . . 650
Charles E. Collins . . . . . . . . . . . . . . . . . . . . . . . . 633
Morry Taylor . . . . . . . . . . . . . . . . . . . . . . . . . . . . 458
Uncommitted . . . . . . . . . . . . . . . . . . . . . . . . . 19,507
   Total Vote . . . . . . . . . . . . . . . . 1,019,803

#### Democratic
Bill Clinton . . . . . . . . . . . . . . . . . . . . . . . . . . . 796,041
Fred Hudson . . . . . . . . . . . . . . . . . . . . . . . . . . 32,232
Heather Harder . . . . . . . . . . . . . . . . . . . . . . . . 28,772
Lyndon H. LaRouche Jr. . . . . . . . . . . . . . . . . . . 28,137
Ted L. Gunderson . . . . . . . . . . . . . . . . . . . . . . 15,550
Elvena E. Lloyd-Duffie . . . . . . . . . . . . . . . . . . . 10,876
Sal Casamassima . . . . . . . . . . . . . . . . . . . . . . . 9,648
   Total Vote . . . . . . . . . . . . . . . . . 921,256

### March 2000
#### Republican
George W. Bush . . . . . . . . . . . . . . . . . . . . . . . 986,416
John McCain . . . . . . . . . . . . . . . . . . . . . . . . . . 80,082
Alan Keyes . . . . . . . . . . . . . . . . . . . . . . . . . . . 43,518
Steve Forbes . . . . . . . . . . . . . . . . . . . . . . . . . . 2,865
Gary Bauer . . . . . . . . . . . . . . . . . . . . . . . . . . . . 2,189
Orrin G. Hatch . . . . . . . . . . . . . . . . . . . . . . . . . 1,324
Charles Bass Urban . . . . . . . . . . . . . . . . . . . . . . . 793
Uncommitted . . . . . . . . . . . . . . . . . . . . . . . . . . 9,570
   Total Vote . . . . . . . . . . . . . . . . 1,126,757

#### Democratic
All Gore . . . . . . . . . . . . . . . . . . . . . . . . . . . . . 631,428
Bill Bradley . . . . . . . . . . . . . . . . . . . . . . . . . . . 128,564
Lyndon H. LaRouche Jr. . . . . . . . . . . . . . . . . . . 26,898
   Total Vote . . . . . . . . . . . . . . . . . 786,890

# Elections of U.S. Senators from Texas

Below is given a compilation of past U.S. senatorial elections in Texas insofar as information is available to the Texas Almanac. Prior to 1916, U.S. senators were appointed by the Legislature.

### 1906
| | |
|---|---|
| J.W. Bailey (unopp.) | 283,315 |

### 1910
**Democratic Primary**
| | |
|---|---|
| C.A. Culberson (unopp.) | 359,939 |

### 1912
**Democratic Primary**
| | |
|---|---|
| Morris Sheppard | 178,281 |
| Jacob F. Wolters | 142,050 |
| Choice B. Randall | 40,349 |
| Matthew Zollner | 3,868 |
| Total vote | 364,548 |

### 1916
**1st Democratic Primary**
| | |
|---|---|
| Carles A. Culberson | 87,421 |
| Robert L. Henry | 37,726 |
| O.B. Colquitt | 119,598 |
| S.P. Brooks | 78,641 |
| T.M. Campbell | 65,721 |
| John Davis | 9,924 |
| *G.W. Riddle | 335 |
| Total vote | 399,366 |
*Had withdrawn

**2nd Democratic Primary**
| | |
|---|---|
| Charles A. Culberson | 163,182 |
| O.B. Colquitt | 94,098 |
| Total Vote | 257,280 |

**\*General Election**
| | |
|---|---|
| Charles A. Culberson (Dem.) | 301,905 |
| Alex W. Atcheson (Rep.) | 48,775 |
| E.H. Conibear (Proh.) | 2,313 |
| T.A. Hickey (Socialist) | 18,616 |
| Total vote | 371,609 |
*First general election for U.S. senator. Prior to 1916, Legislature appointed senators.

### 1918
**Democratic Primary**
| | |
|---|---|
| Morris Sheppard (unopp.) | 649,876 |

**General Election**
| | |
|---|---|
| Morris Sheppard (Dem.) | 155,158 |
| J. Webster Flanagan (Rep.) | 22,183 |
| M.A. Smith (Soc.) | 1,587 |
| Total vote | 178,928 |

### 1922
**1st Democratic Primary**
| | |
|---|---|
| C.A. Culberson | 99,635 |
| Earle B. Mayfield | 153,538 |
| Cullen F. Thomas | 88,026 |
| James E. Ferguson | 127,071 |
| Clarence Ousley | 62,451 |
| R.L. Henry | 41,567 |
| Sterling P. Strong | 1,085 |
| Total vote | 573,373 |

**2nd Democratic Primary**
| | |
|---|---|
| Earle B. Mayfield | 273,308 |
| James E. Ferguson | 228,701 |
| Total vote | 502,009 |

**General Election**
| | |
|---|---|
| Earle B. Mayfield (Dem.) | 264,260 |
| George E.B. Peddy (Rep.) | 130,744 |
| Total vote | 395,004 |

### 1924
**Democratic Primary**
| | |
|---|---|
| Morris Sheppard | 440,511 |
| Fred W. Davis | 159,663 |
| John F. Maddox | 80,070 |
| Total vote | 680,244 |

**General Election**
| | |
|---|---|
| Morris Sheppard (Dem.) | 579,208 |
| T.M. Kennerly (Rep.) | 98,207 |
| Total vote | 677,415 |

### 1928
**1st Democratic Primary**
| | |
|---|---|
| Thomas L. Blanton | 126,758 |
| Tom Connally | 178,091 |
| Minnie Fisher Cunningham | 28,944 |
| Earle B.Mayfield | 200,246 |
| Jeff McLemore | 9,244 |
| Alvin Owsley | 131,755 |
| Total vote | 675,038 |

**2nd Democratic Primary**
| | |
|---|---|
| Tom Connally | 320,071 |
| Earle B. Mayfield | 257,747 |
| Total vote | 577,818 |

**General Election**
| | |
|---|---|
| Tom Connally (Dem.) | 566,139 |
| T.M. Kennerly (Rep.) | 129,910 |
| David Curran (Soc.) | 690 |
| John Rust (Communist) | 114 |
| Total vote | 696,853 |

### 1930
**Democratic Primary**
| | |
|---|---|
| Morris Sheppard | 526,293 |
| C.A. Mitchner | 40,130 |
| Robert L. Henry | 174,260 |
| Total vote | 740,683 |

**Republican Primary**
**(158 counties reporting)**
| | |
|---|---|
| Doran John Haesly | 3,645 |
| *Harve H. Haines | 2,568 |
| *C.O. Harris | 2,784 |
| Total vote | 8,997 |
*No runoff; candidates withdrew.

**General Election**
| | |
|---|---|
| Morris Sheppard (Dem.) | 258,929 |
| D.J. Haesly (Rep.) | 35,357 |
| Guy. L. Smith (Soc.) | 790 |
| W.A. Berry (Com.) | 282 |
| Total vote | 295,358 |

### 1934
**Democratic Primary**
| | |
|---|---|
| Joseph W. Bailey | 355,963 |
| Tom Connally | 567,139 |
| Guy. B. Fisher | 41,421 |
| Total vote | 964,523 |

**General Election**
| | |
|---|---|
| Tom Connally (Dem.) | 439,375 |
| U.S. Goen (Rep.) | 12,895 |
| W.B. Starr (Soc.) | 1,828 |
| L.C. Keel (Com.) | 310 |
| Total vote | 454,408 |

### 1936
**Democratic Primary**
| | |
|---|---|
| Morris Sheppard | 616,293 |
| Guy B. Fisher | 89,215 |
| Richard C. Bush | 37,842 |
| Joseph H. Price | 45,919 |
| Joe H. Eagle | 136,718 |
| J. Edward Glenn | 28,641 |
| Total vote | 954,628 |

**General Election**
| | |
|---|---|
| Morris Sheppard (Dem.) | 774,975 |
| Carlos G. Watson (Rep.) | 59,491 |

| | |
|---|---|
| W.B. Starr (Soc.) | 958 |
| Gertrude Wilson (Union) | 1,836 |
| Total Vote | 837,260 |

### 1940
**Democratic Primary**
| | |
|---|---|
| Tom Connally | 923,219 |
| A.P. Belcher | 66,962 |
| Guy B. Fisher | 98,125 |
| Total vote | 1,088,306 |

**General Election**
| | |
|---|---|
| Tom Connally(Dem.) | 978,095 |
| George Shannon (Rep.) | 59,340 |
| Homer Brooks (Const.) | 408 |
| Total vote | 1,037,843 |

### 1941 Special Election
**June 28, 1941**
**25 Dems., 2 Reps. 1 Ind. and 1 Communist**
| | |
|---|---|
| W. Lee O'Daniel | 175,590 |
| Lyndon B. Johnson | 174,279 |
| Gerald C. Mann | 140,807 |
| Martin Dies | 80,653 |
| *Total vote | 571,329 |
*Above candidates only; votes for others not available.

### 1942
**1st Democratic Primary**
| | |
|---|---|
| James V. Allred | 317,501 |
| Dan Moody | 178,471 |
| W. Lee O'Daniel | 475,541 |
| Floyd E. Ryan | 12,213 |
| Total vote | 983,726 |

**2nd Democratic Primary**
| | |
|---|---|
| James V. Allred | 433,203 |
| W. Lee O'Daniel | 451,359 |
| Total vote | 884,562 |

**General Election**
| | |
|---|---|
| W.Lee O'Daniel (Dem.) | 260,629 |
| Dudley Lawson (Rep.) | 12,064 |
| Charles L. Somerville (P.U.P.) | 1,934 |
| Total vote | 274,627 |

### 1946
**Democratic Primary**
| | |
|---|---|
| Tom Connally | 823,818 |
| Cyclone Davis | 74,252 |
| Floyd E. Ryan | 85,292 |
| Terrell Sledge | 66,947 |
| Laverne Somerville | 42,290 |
| Total vote | 1,092,599 |

**General Election**
| | |
|---|---|
| Tom Connally (Dem.) | 336,931 |
| Murray C. Sells (Rep.) | 43,750 |
| Write-in | 5 |
| Total vote | 380,686 |

### 1948
**1st Democratic Primary**
| | |
|---|---|
| Otis C. Myers | 15,330 |
| F.B. Clark | 7,420 |
| Roscoe H. Collier | 12,327 |
| Coke R. Stevenson | 477,077 |
| Cyclone Davis | 10,871 |
| Frank G. Cortez | 13,344 |
| Jesse C. Saunders | 7,401 |
| George E.B. Peddy | 237,195 |
| Lyndon B. Johnson | 405,617 |
| Terrell Sledge | 6,692 |

James F. Alford. . . . . . . . 9,117
Write-in . . . . . . . . . . . . 1
   Total vote . . . . . . . . . 1,202,392

### 2nd Democratic Primary
Lyndon B. Johnson . . . . . 494,191
Coke R. Stevenson . . . . . 494,104
   Total vote . . . . . . . . . 988,295

### General Election
Lyndon B. Johnson
  (Dem.). . . . . . . . . . . . 702,985
Jack Porter (Rep.) . . . . . 349,665
Sam Morris (Proh.) . . . . . 8,913
   Total vote . . . . . . . . . 1,061,563

### 1952
#### 1st Democratic Primary
Price Daniel . . . . . . . . . . . 940,770
Lindley Beckworth . . . . . . 285,842
E.W. Napier . . . . . . . . . . . 70,132
   Total vote . . . . . . . . . 1,296,744

### General Election
Price Daniel (Dem.) . . . . . 1,425,007
Price Daniel (Rep.) . . . . . . 469,494
Price Daniel (No Party) . . 591
   Total vote . . . . . . . . . 1,895,192

### 1954
#### 1st Democratic Primary
Lyndon B. Johnson . . . . . 883,264
Dudley T. Dougherty. . . . . 354,188
   Total vote . . . . . . . . . 1,237,452

### General Election
Lyndon B. Johnson
  (Dem.). . . . . . . . . . . . 538,417
Carlos G. Watson (Rep.) . 95,033
Fred T. Spangler (Const.). 3,025
   Total vote . . . . . . . . . 636,475

### 1957 Special Election
*On April 2. Price Daniel had resigned to run for governorship.*
Elmer Adams. . . . . . . . . . 2,228
H.J. Antoine Sr. . . . . . . . . 576
M.T. Banks . . . . . . . . . . . 2,153
Jacob Bergolofsky . . . . . . 890
Searcy Bracewell. . . . . . . 33,384
John C. Burns Sr.. . . . . . . 600
*H.Frank Connally Jr.. . . . 514
Frank G. Cortez . . . . . . . . 1,350
*J.Cal Courtney . . . . . . . . 879
*R.W. (Waire) Currin . . . . 646
Martin Dies . . . . . . . . . . . 290,803
C.O.Foerster Jr. . . . . . . . . 776
Curtis Ford. . . . . . . . . . . . 767
Ralph W. Hammonds . . . . 2,372
James P. Hart. . . . . . . . . . 19,739
*Charles W. (Jack) Hill . . . 1,025
Thad Hutcheson . . . . . . . 219,591
Walter Scott McNutt. . . . . 500
Clyde R. Orms . . . . . . . . . 356
John C. White. . . . . . . . . . 11,876
J.Perrin Wills . . . . . . . . . . 817
Hugh Wilson. . . . . . . . . . . 851
Ralph W. Yarborough . . . . 364,605
   Total vote . . . . . . . . . 957,298

*Withdrew, but after ballots printed.*

### 1958
#### 1st Democratic Primary
William A. Blakley . . . . . . 536,073
Ralph W. Yarborough . . . . 760,856
Write-in . . . . . . . . . . . . . 4
   Total vote . . . . . . . . . 1,296,933


### General Election
Ralph W. Yarborough
  (Dem.) . . . . . . . . . . . . 587,030
Roy Whittenburg (Rep.) . . 185,926
Bard A. Logan (Const.). . . 14,172
   Total vote . . . . . . . . . . 787,128

### 1960
#### 1st Democratic Primary
Lyndon B. Johnson. . . . . . 1,407,109
Write-in. . . . . . . . . . . . . . 145
   Total vote . . . . . . . . . . 1,407,254

### General Election
Lyndon B. Johnson
  (Dem.) . . . . . . . . . . . . 1,306,625
John G. Tower (Rep.) . . . . 926,653
Bard A. Logan (Const.). . . 20,506
   Total vote . . . . . . . . . . 2,253,784

### 1961 Special Election
*On April 4. Lyndon B. Johnson resigned to assume office of Vice President.*
John G. Tower. . . . . . . . . 327,308
William A. Blakley. . . . . . . 190,818
Jim Wright . . . . . . . . . . . 171,328
Will Wilson . . . . . . . . . . . 121,961
Maury Maverick Jr.. . . . . . 104,992
Henry B. Gonzalez . . . . . . 97,659

The remaining 71 candidates were: Dr. G.H. Allen, 849; Jim W. Amos, 527; Dale Baker, 612; Dr. Mali Jean Rauch Barraco, 434; Tom E. Barton, 395; R.G. Becker, 462; Jacob Bergolofsky, 377; Dr.Ted Bisland, 831; G.E. Blewett,474, Lawrence S. Bosworth Jr., 410; Joyce J. Bradshaw, 352; Chester D. Brooks, 711; W.L. Burlison, 1,695; Ronald J. Byers, 175; Joseph M. Carter, 185; George A. Davisson, 897, Mrs. Winnie K. Derrick, 327, Harry R. Diehl, 293, Harvill O. Eaton, 178; Rev. Jonnie Mae Eckman, 342; Paul F. Eix, 317; Ben H. Faber, 363; Dr. H.E. Fanning, 293, Charles Otto Foerster Jr., 133; Harold Franklin, 196; George N. Gallagher Jr., 985; Richard J. Gay,939; Van T. George Jr., 307; Arthur Glover, 1,528; Delbert E. Grandstaff, 2,959; Curtis E. Hill, 389; Willard Park Holland, 669; John N. Hopkins, 490; Mary Hazel Houston, 726; Ben M. Johnson, 681;Guy Johnson, 748; Morgan H. Johnson, 334; C.B. Kennedy, 770; H. Springer Knoblauch, 186; Hugh O. Lea, 651; V.C. Logan, 314; Frank A. Matera, 599, Brown McCallum, 323; James E. McKee, 762; Steve Nemecek, 1,017; George E. Noyes, 174; Floyd Payne, 227; Cecil D. Perkins, 773; W.H. Posey, 592; George Red, 99; Wesley Roberts, 386; D.T. Sampson, 417; Eristus Sams, 4,490; A. Dale Savage, 400; Carl A. Schrade, 283; Albert Roy Smith, 341; Homer Hyrim Stalarow, 735; Frank Stanford, 240; John B. Sypert, 252; Mrs. Martha Tredway, 1,227; S.S. Vela, 211, Bill Whitten, 350; Hoyt G. Wilson, 2,165; Hugh Wilson, 2,997; Marcos Zertuche, 442; Write-ins, 42.

   Total vote. . . . . . . . . . 1,058,124

#### *Runoff Election held May 27
William A. Blakley. . . . . . . 437,874
John G. Tower. . . . . . . . . 448,217
   Total vote. . . . . . . . . . 886,091
*Change in state law following 1957 special election required runoff.*

### 1964
#### 1st Democratic Primary
Ralph Yarborough. . . . . . . 905,001
Gordon McLendon . . . . . . 672,573
Write-in. . . . . . . . . . . . . . 23
   Total vote . . . . . . . . . . 1,577,607

#### 1st Republican Primary
George Bush . . . . . . . . . . 62,985
Jack Cox. . . . . . . . . . . . . 45,561


Milton V. Davis. . . . . . . . . 6,067
Robert Morris . . . . . . . . . . 28,279
   Total vote . . . . . . . . . 142,892

### 2nd Republican Primary
George Bush. . . . . . . . . . . 49,751
Jack Cox . . . . . . . . . . . . . 30,333
   Total vote . . . . . . . . . 80,084

### General Election
Ralph Yarborough
  (Dem.) . . . . . . . . . . . . 1,463,958
George Bush (Rep.) . . . . . 1,134,337
Jack Carswell (Const.) . . . 5,542
Write-in . . . . . . . . . . . . . . 19
   Total vote . . . . . . . . . 2,603,856

### 1966
#### 1st Democratic Primary
John R. Willoughby . . . . . . 226,598
Waggoner Carr . . . . . . . . . 899,523
   Total vote . . . . . . . . . 1,126,121

### General Election
Waggoner Carr (Dem.) . . . 643,855
John G. Tower (Rep.) . . . . 842,501
Jas. Barker Holland
  (Const.) . . . . . . . . . . . 6,778
   Total vote . . . . . . . . . 1,493,134

### 1970
#### 1st Democratic Primary
Lloyd Bentsen. . . . . . . . . . 814,316
Ralph Yarborough . . . . . . . 726,447
   Total vote . . . . . . . . . 1,540,763

#### Republican Primary
George Bush. . . . . . . . . . . 96,806
Robert Morris . . . . . . . . . . 13,659
   Total vote . . . . . . . . . 110,465

#### General Election
Lloyd Bentsen (Dem.) . . . . 1,226,568
George Bush (Rep.) . . . . . 1,071,234
Other. . . . . . . . . . . . . . . . 1,808
   Total vote . . . . . . . . . 2,299,610

### 1972
#### 1st Democratic Primary
Thomas M. Cartledge . . . . 66,240
Barefoot Sanders . . . . . . . 787,504
Alfonso Veloz . . . . . . . . . . 53,938
Hugh Wilson . . . . . . . . . . 125,460
Ralph Yarborough . . . . . . . 1,032,606
   Total vote . . . . . . . . . 2,065,748

#### 2nd Democratic Primary
Barefoot Sanders . . . . . . . 1,008,499
Ralph Yarborough . . . . . . . 928,087
   Total vote . . . . . . . . . 1,936,586

#### Republican Primary
John G. Tower (unopp.). . 107,648

#### General Election
Barefoot Sanders (Dem.) . 1,511,985
John G. Tower (Rep.) . . . . 1,822,877
Flores Amaya (Raza) . . . . 63,543
Tom Leonard (Soc.) . . . . . 14,464
Other. . . . . . . . . . . . . . . . 1,034
   Total vote . . . . . . . . . 3,413,903

### 1976
#### 1st Democratic Primary
Lloyd Bentsen . . . . . . . . . 970,983
Leon Dugi . . . . . . . . . . . . 19,870
Phil Gramm. . . . . . . . . . . 427,597
Hugh Wilson . . . . . . . . . . 109,715
Other. . . . . . . . . . . . . . . . 1,003
   Total vote . . . . . . . . . 1,529,168

#### Republican Primary
Louis Leman . . . . . . . . . . 40,651

| | |
|---|---|
| Alan Steelman . . . . . . . . | 251,252 |
| Hugh Sweeney . . . . . . . . | 64,404 |
| Total vote . . . . . . . . . | 356,307 |

### General Election

| | |
|---|---|
| Lloyd Bentsen (Dem.) . . . | 2,199,956 |
| Alan Steelman (Rep.) . . . | 1,636,370 |
| Marjorie P. Gallion (Am.) . | 17,355 |
| Pedro Vasques (Soc. Worker) . . . . . . . | 20,549 |
| Total vote . . . . . . . . . . | 3,874,230 |

## 1978

### 1st Democratic Primary

| | |
|---|---|
| Joe Christie . . . . . . . . . . | 701,892 |
| Robert Krueger . . . . . . . . | 853,485 |
| Total vote . . . . . . . . . . | 1,555,377 |

### Republican Primary

| | |
|---|---|
| John G. Tower . . . . . . . . . | 142,202 |

### General Election

| | |
|---|---|
| Robert Krueger (Dem.) . . | 1,139,149 |
| John G. Tower (Rep.) . . . . | 1,151,376 |
| Luis A. Diaz de Leon (Raza Unida). . . . . . . . | 17,869 |
| Miguel Pendas (Soc. Worker) . . . . . . | 4,018 |
| Other . . . . . . . . . . . . . . . . | 128 |
| Total vote . . . . . . . . . . | 2,312,540 |

## 1982

### 1st Democratic Primary

| | |
|---|---|
| Lloyd Bentsen . . . . . . . . . | 987,985 |
| Joe Sullivan . . . . . . . . . . | 276,453 |
| Total vote . . . . . . . . . . | 1,264,438 |

### Republican Primary

| | |
|---|---|
| Don I. Richardson . . . . . . | 18,616 |
| Jim Collins . . . . . . . . . . . | 152,469 |
| Walter H. Mengden Jr. . . . | 91,780 |
| Total vote . . . . . . . . . . | 262,865 |

### General Election

| | |
|---|---|
| Jim Collins (Rep.) . . . . . . | 1,256,759 |
| Lloyd Bentsen (Dem.) . . . | 1,818,223 |
| John E. Ford (Lib.) . . . . . . | 23,494 |
| Lineaus H. Lorette (Const.) . . . . . . . . . . | 4,564 |
| Darryl Anderson (W-I) . . . | 39 |
| Other . . . . . . . . . . . . . . . | 88 |
| Total vote . . . . . . . . . . | 3,103,167 |

## 1984

### 1st Democratic Primary

| | |
|---|---|
| Lloyd Doggett. . . . . . . . . . | 456,173 |
| Kent Hance . . . . . . . . . . . | 456,446 |
| Robert Krueger . . . . . . . . | 454,886 |
| Harley Schlanger . . . . . . . | 14,149 |
| Robert Sullivan . . . . . . . . | 34,733 |
| David Young . . . . . . . . . . . | 47,062 |
| Total vote . . . . . . . . . . | 1,463,449 |

### 2nd Democratic Primary

| | |
|---|---|
| Lloyd Doggett. . . . . . . . . . | 491,251 |
| Kent Hance . . . . . . . . . . . | 489,906 |
| Total vote . . . . . . . . . . | 981,157 |

### Republican Primary

| | |
|---|---|
| Phil Gramm . . . . . . . . . . . | 246,716 |
| Henry Grover . . . . . . . . . . | 8,388 |
| Robert Mosbacher. . . . . . . | 26,279 |
| Ron Paul . . . . . . . . . . . . . | 55,431 |
| Total vote . . . . . . . . . . | 336,814 |

### General Election

| | |
|---|---|
| Lloyd Doggett (Dem.). . . . | 2,202,557 |
| Phil Gramm (Rep.). . . . . . | 3,111,348 |

| | |
|---|---|
| Other . . . . . . . . . . . . . . . . | 273 |
| Total vote . . . . . . . . . | 5,314,178 |

## 1988

### Democratic Primary

| | |
|---|---|
| Lloyd Bentsen. . . . . . . . . . | 1,365,736 |
| Joe Sullivan . . . . . . . . . . . | 244,805 |
| Total vote . . . . . . . . . . | 1,610,541 |

### 1st Republican Primary

| | |
|---|---|
| Beau Boulter. . . . . . . . . . . | 228,676 |
| Milton E. Fox. . . . . . . . . . . | 138,031 |
| Wes Gilbreath . . . . . . . . . . | 275,080 |
| Ned Snead . . . . . . . . . . . . | 107,560 |
| Total vote . . . . . . . . . . | 749,347 |

### 2nd Republican Primary

| | |
|---|---|
| Beau Boulter. . . . . . . . . . . | 111,134 |
| Wes Gilbreath . . . . . . . . . . | 73,573 |
| Total vote . . . . . . . . . . | 184,707 |

### General Election

| | |
|---|---|
| Lloyd Bentsen (Dem.). . . . | 3,149,806 |
| Beau Boulter (Rep.) . . . . . | 2,129,228 |
| Other . . . . . . . . . . . . . . . . | 44,572 |
| Total vote . . . . . . . . . . | 5,323,606 |

## 1990

### 1st Democratic Primary

| | |
|---|---|
| Hugh Parmer . . . . . . . . . . | 766,284 |
| Harley Schlanger . . . . . . . | 249,445 |
| Total vote . . . . . . . . . . | 1,015,729 |

### 1st Republican Primary

| | |
|---|---|
| Phil Gramm. . . . . . . . . . . . | 687,170 |

### General Election

| | |
|---|---|
| Phil Gram m(Rep.) . . . . . . | 2,302,357 |
| Hugh Parmer (Dem.) . . . . | 1,429,986 |
| Gary Johnson (Lib.) . . . . . | 89,089 |
| Other . . . . . . . . . . . . . . . . | 725 |
| Total vote . . . . . . . . . . | 3,822,157 |

## 1993 Special Election

*Held on May 1. Lloyd Bentsen had resigned to assume post as U.S. Secretary of Treasury.*

| | |
|---|---|
| Kay Bailey Hutchison . . . . | 593,338 |
| Robert Krueger. . . . . . . . . | 593,239 |
| Joe Barton . . . . . . . . . . . . | 284,137 |
| Jack Fields . . . . . . . . . . . . | 277,560 |
| Richard Fisher . . . . . . . . . | 165,560 |

Others: Billy Brown, 2,187; Louis C. Davis, 1,548; Rick Draheim, 5,677; Rose Floyd, 2,301; Jose Angel Gutierrez, 52,103; Lottie Bolling Hancock, 2,242; Rober Henson, 3,092; Stephen Hopkins, 14,753; Charles Ben Howell, 3,866; Gene Kelly, 11,331; C. (Sonny) Payne, 6,782; Don Richardson, 6,209; Chuck Sibley, 2,406; Thomas D. Spink, 2,281; Herbert Spiro, 4,459; Maco Stewart, 1,260; James Vallaster, 2,124; Clymer Wright, 5,111; Lou Zaeske, 2,191.

| | |
|---|---|
| Total vote . . . . . . . . . . | 2,045,757 |

### Runoff Election held June 5

| | |
|---|---|
| Robert Krueger. . . . . . . . . | 574,089 |
| Kay Bailey Hutchison . . . . | 1,183,766 |
| Total vote . . . . . . . . . . | 1,757,855 |

## 1994

### 1st Democratic Primary

| | |
|---|---|
| Michael A. Andrews . . . . . | 159,793 |
| Richard Fisher . . . . . . . . . | 388,090 |
| Evelyn K. Lantz. . . . . . . . . | 63,523 |
| Jim Mattox . . . . . . . . . . . . | 416,503 |
| Total vote . . . . . . . . . . | 1,027,909 |

### 2nd Democratic Primary

| | |
|---|---|
| Richard Fisher. . . . . . . . . | 400,227 |
| Jim Mattox. . . . . . . . . . . . | 346,414 |
| Total vote . . . . . . . . . . | 746,641 |

### 1st Republican Primary

| | |
|---|---|
| James C. Curry . . . . . . . . | 15,625 |
| Roger Henson. . . . . . . . . | 14,021 |
| Stephen Hopkins. . . . . . . | 34,703 |
| Kay Bailey Hutchison . . . | 467,975 |
| M. Troy Mata . . . . . . . . . . | 8,632 |
| Ernest J. Schmidt . . . . . . | 8,690 |
| Tom Spink . . . . . . . . . . . . | 5,692 |
| Total vote . . . . . . . . . . | 555,338 |

### General Election

| | |
|---|---|
| Richard Fisher (Dem.). . . | 1,639,615 |
| Kay Bailey Hutchison (Rep.) | 2,604,218 |
| Pierre Blondeau (Lib.) . . . | 36,107 |
| Total vote . . . . . . . . . . | 4,279,940 |

## 1996

### 1st Democratic Primary

| | |
|---|---|
| John Bryant. . . . . . . . . . . | 267,545 |
| Jim Chapman . . . . . . . . . | 239,427 |
| Victor M. Morales . . . . . . | 322,218 |
| John Will Odam. . . . . . . . | 61,433 |
| Total vote . . . . . . . . . . | 890,623 |

### 2nd Democratic Primary

| | |
|---|---|
| John Bryant. . . . . . . . . . . | 235,281 |
| Victor M. Morales . . . . . . | 246,614 |
| Total vote . . . . . . . . . . | 481,895 |

### 1st Republican Primary

| | |
|---|---|
| Phil Gramm . . . . . . . . . . . | 838,339 |
| Henry C. (Hank) Grover. . | 72,400 |
| David Young . . . . . . . . . . | 75,463 |
| Total vote . . . . . . . . . . | 986,202 |

### General Election

| | |
|---|---|
| Phil Gramm (Rep.) . . . . . | 3,027,680 |
| Victor M. Morales (Dem.) | 2,428,776 |
| Michael Bird (Lib.) . . . . . . | 51,516 |
| John Huff (NLP) . . . . . . . | 19,469 |
| Total vote . . . . . . . . . . | 5,527,441 |

## 2000

### 1st Democratic Primary

| | |
|---|---|
| H. Gerald Bintliff . . . . . . . | 33,979 |
| Don Clark . . . . . . . . . . . . | 139,243 |
| Charles Gandy . . . . . . . . | 140,636 |
| Gene Kelly . . . . . . . . . . . | 220,531 |
| Bobby Wightman. . . . . . . | 83,643 |
| Total vote . . . . . . . . . . | 618,032 |

### 2nd Democratic Primary

| | |
|---|---|
| Charles Gandy . . . . . . . . | 101,983 |
| Gene Kelly. . . . . . . . . . . . | 143,366 |
| Total vote . . . . . . . . . . | 245,349 |

### 1st Republican Primary

| | |
|---|---|
| Kay Bailey Hutchison | 955,033 |
| Total vote . . . . . . . . . . | 955,033 |

### General Election

| | |
|---|---|
| Kay Bailey Hutchison (Rep.) | 4,082,091 |
| Gene Kelly (Dem.). . . . . . | 2,030,315 |
| Mary J. Ruwart (Lib.) . . . . | 72,798 |
| Douglas S. Sandage(Green) | 91,448 |
| Total vote . . . . . . . . . . | 6,276,652 |

## 2002

### 1st Democratic Primary

| | |
|---|---|
| Ken Bentsen . . . . . . . . . . | 255,501 |
| Ed Cunningham . . . . . . . | 22,016 |
| Gene Kelly. . . . . . . . . . . . | 44,038 |
| Ron Kirk . . . . . . . . . . . . . | 316,052 |
| Victor Morales . . . . . . . . . | 317,048 |
| Total vote . . . . . . . . . . | 954,655 |

| 2nd Democratic Primary | |
|---|---|
| Ron Kirk. . . . . . . . . . . . | 370,878 |
| Victor Morales . . . . . . . . | 249,423 |
| Total vote . . . . . . . . . | 620,301 |

| 1st Republican Primary | |
|---|---|
| John Cornyn . . . . . . . . . | 478,825 |
| Lawrence Cranberg. . . . . | 17,757 |
| Douglas G. Deffenbaugh . | 43,711 |
| Bruce Rusty Lang . . . . . | 46,907 |
| Dukdley F. Mooney . . . . . | 32,202 |
| Total vote . . . . . . . . . | 619,302 |

| General Election | |
|---|---|
| John Cornyn (Rep.) . . . . . | 2,497,243 |
| Ron Kirk (Dem.) . . . . . . . | 1,955,758 |
| Scott Lanier Jameson (Lib.) | 35,538 |
| Roy H. Williams (Green). . | 25,051 |
| James W. (Jim) Wright (W-I) | 1,422 |
| Total vote . . . . . . . . . . | 4,515,012 |

Abbreviations used are:
 (Dem.) Democrat,
 (Rep.) Republican,

(Lib.) Libertarian,
(Ind.) Independent,
(Proh.) Prohibitionist,
(NLP) Natural Law,
(P.U.P.) People's Unity,
(Soc.) Socialist,
(Prog.) Progressive,
(Amer.) American,
(Com.) Communist,
(Const.) Constitution,
(Conserv.) Conservative,
(Raza) La Raza Unida.

# Elections of Texas Governors, 1845-1998

Following are the results of elections of governors since Texas became a state in 1845. Party primaries, as well as general elections, are included whenever possible, although Republican totals are not available for some elections. Prior to 1857, most candidates ran independently. Party designations are in parentheses; an explanation of abbreviations is on the last page.

| 1845 | |
|---|---|
| J.P. Henderson . . . . . . | 7,853 |
| J.B. Miller . . . . . . . . . . | 1,673 |
| Scattering . . . . . . . . . . | 52 |
| Total vote . . . . . . . . | 9,578 |

| 1847 | |
|---|---|
| George T. Wood . . . . . . | 7,154 |
| J. B. Miller . . . . . . . . . . | 5,106 |
| N. H. Darnell . . . . . . . . | 1,276 |
| J. J. Robinson . . . . . . . . | 379 |
| Scattering . . . . . . . . . . | 852 |
| Total vote . . . . . . . . | 14,767 |

| 1849 | |
|---|---|
| P. H. Bell . . . . . . . . . . . | 10,319 |
| George T. Wood . . . . . . | 8,764 |
| John T. Mills. . . . . . . . . | 2,632 |
| Total vote . . . . . . . . | 21,715 |

| 1851 | |
|---|---|
| P. H. Bell . . . . . . . . . . . | 13,595 |
| M. T. Johnson . . . . . . . . | 5,262 |
| John A. Greer . . . . . . . . | 4,061 |
| B. H. Epperson . . . . . . . | 2,971 |
| T. J. Chambers . . . . . . . | 2,320 |
| Scattering . . . . . . . . . . | 100 |
| Total vote . . . . . . . . | 28,309 |

| 1853 | |
|---|---|
| E. M. Pease. . . . . . . . . | 13,091 |
| W. B. Ochiltree . . . . . . . | 9,178 |
| George T. Wood . . . . . . | 5,983 |
| L. D. Evans . . . . . . . . . | 4,677 |
| T. J. Chambers . . . . . . . | 2,449 |
| John Dancy . . . . . . . . . | 315 |
| Total vote . . . . . . . . | 35,693 |

| 1855 | |
|---|---|
| E. M. Pease. . . . . . . . . | 26,336 |
| D. C. Dickson. . . . . . . . | 18,968 |
| M. T. Johnson . . . . . . . . | 809 |
| George T. Wood . . . . . . | 226 |
| Total vote . . . . . . . . | 46,339 |

| 1857 | |
|---|---|
| H. R. Runnels (Dem.) . . | 32,552 |
| Sam Houston . . . . . . . . | 28,628 |
| Total vote . . . . . . . . | 61,180 |

| 1859 | |
|---|---|
| *Sam Houston. . . . . . . . | 36,227 |
| H. R. Runnels (Dem.) . . | 27,500 |
| Scattering . . . . . . . . . | 61 |
| Total vote . . . . . . . . | 63,788 |

*Ran as independent but received support of Know-Nothing Party.

Edward Clark succeeded Sam Houston on March 16, 1861, shortly after Texas seceded.

| 1861 | |
|---|---|
| F. R. Lubbock . . . . . . . . | 21,854 |
| Edward Clark . . . . . . . . | 21,730 |
| T. J. Chambers . . . . . . . | 13,759 |
| Total vote. . . . . . . . . | 57,343 |

| 1863 | |
|---|---|
| Pendleton Murrah . . . . . | 17,511 |
| T. J. Chambers . . . . . . . | 12,455 |
| Scattering. . . . . . . . . . | 1,070 |
| Total vote. . . . . . . . . | 31,036 |

A. J. Hamilton was named governor under Reconstruction administration June 17, 1865.

| 1866 | |
|---|---|
| J. W. Throckmorton. . . . . | 49,277 |
| E. M. Pease . . . . . . . . . | 12,168 |
| Total vote . . . . . . . . | 61,445 |

E. M. Pease was appointed governor July 30, 1867.

| 1869 | |
|---|---|
| E. J. Davis . . . . . . . . . . | 39,901 |
| A. J. Hamilton . . . . . . . . | 39,092 |
| Hamilton Stuart . . . . . . . | 380 |
| Total vote . . . . . . . . | 79,373 |

| 1873 | |
|---|---|
| Richard Coke (Dem.) . . . | 85,549 |
| E. J. Davis (Rep.) . . . . . . | 42,633 |
| Total vote. . . . . . . . . | 128,182 |

| 1876 | |
|---|---|
| Richard Coke (Dem.) . . . | 150,581 |
| William Chambers(Rep.) . | 47,719 |
| Total vote. . . . . . . . . | 198,300 |

Lt. Gov. R. B. Hubbard succeeded Dec. 1, 1876, when Coke became U.S. Senator.

| 1878 | |
|---|---|
| O. M. Roberts (Dem.). . . | 158,933 |
| W. H. Hamman (G. B.) . . | 55,002 |
| A. B. Norton (Rep.). . . . . | 23,402 |
| Scattering. . . . . . . . . . | 99 |
| Total vote. . . . . . . . . | 237,436 |

| 1880 | |
|---|---|
| O. M. Roberts (Dem.). . . | 166,101 |
| E. J. Davis (Rep.) . . . . . . | 64,382 |
| W. H. Hamman (G.B.) . . | 33,721 |
| Total vote . . . . . . . . | 264,204 |

| 1882 | |
|---|---|
| John Ireland (Dem.) . . . | 150,809 |
| G. W. Jones (G.B.) . . . . | 102,501 |
| J. B. Robertson (I.Dem.) | 334 |
| Total vote . . . . . . . . | 253,644 |

| 1884 | |
|---|---|
| John Ireland (Dem.) . . . | 212,234 |
| Geo. W. Jones(G.B.) . . . | 88,450 |
| A. B. Norton (Rep.) . . . . | 25,557 |
| Total vote . . . . . . . . | 326,241 |

| 1886 | |
|---|---|
| L. S. Ross (Dem.) . . . . . | 228,776 |
| A. M. Cochran (Rep.) . . . | 65,236 |
| E. L. Dohoney (Prohi.). . | 19,186 |
| Scattering . . . . . . . . . . | 102 |
| Total vote . . . . . . . . | 313,300 |

| 1888 | |
|---|---|
| L. S. Ross (Dem.) . . . . . | 250,338 |
| Marion Martin (Ind.Fus.). | 98,447 |
| Total vote . . . . . . . . | 348,785 |

| 1890 | |
|---|---|
| J. S. Hogg (Dem.) . . . . . | 262,432 |
| W. Flanagan (Rep.). . . . | 77,742 |
| E. C. Heath (Prohi.). . . . | 2,235 |
| Total vote . . . . . . . . | 342,409 |

| 1892 | |
|---|---|
| J. S. Hogg (Dem.) . . . . . | 190,486 |
| George Clark (Dem.) . . | 133,395 |
| T. L. Nugent (Peo.) . . . . | 108,483 |
| A. J. Houston (Ref.Rep.). | 1,322 |
| D. M. Prendergast (Prohi.). . . . . . . . . . | 1,605 |
| Scattering . . . . . . . . . | 176 |
| Total vote . . . . . . . . | 435,467 |

| 1894 | |
|---|---|
| C. A. Culberson (Dem.) . | 207,167 |
| T. L. Nugent (Peo.) . . . . | 152,731 |
| W. K. Makemson (Rep.) . | 54,520 |
| J. B. Schmitz (L.W.Rep.). | 5,036 |
| J. M. Dunn (Prohi.) . . . . | 2,196 |
| Scattering . . . . . . . . . . | 1,076 |
| Total vote . . . . . . . . | 422,726 |

| 1896 | |
|---|---|
| C. A. Culberson (Dem.) | 298,528 |
| J. C. Kearby (Peo.) . . . . . | 238,692 |
| Randolph Clark (Prohi.) | 1,876 |
| Scattering . . . . . . . . . . | 682 |
| Total vote . . . . . . . . | 539,778 |

**1898**

| | |
|---|---|
| J. D. Sayers (Dem.) . . . . | 291,548 |
| Barnett Gibbs (Peo.) . . . | 114,955 |
| R. P. Bailey (Prohi.) . . . | 2,437 |
| G. H. Royall (Soc. Lab.) . | 552 |
| Scattering . . . . . . . . . . | 62 |
| Total vote . . . . . . . . . | 409,554 |

### 1900

| | |
|---|---|
| J. D. Sayers (Dem.) . . . . | 303,586 |
| R. E. Hanney (Rep.). . . . | 112,864 |
| T. J. McMinn (Peo.) . . . . | 26,864 |
| G. H. Royall (Soc. Lab.) . | 155 |
| Scattering . . . . . . . . . . | 6,155 |
| Total vote . . . . . . . . . | 449,624 |

### 1902

| | |
|---|---|
| S. W. T. Lanham (Dem.) . | 219,076 |
| George W. Burkett (Rep.) | 65,706 |
| J. M. Mallett (Peo.) . . . . . | 12,387 |
| G. W. Carroll (Prohi.) . . . | 8,708 |
| Scattering . . . . . . . . . . | 3,273 |
| Total vote . . . . . . . . . | 309,150 |

### 1904

| | |
|---|---|
| S. W. T. Lanham (Dem.) . | 206,160 |
| J. G. Lowden (Rep.). . . . | 56,865 |
| Pat B. Clark (Peo.) . . . . | 9,301 |
| W. D. Jackson (Prohi.) . . | 4,509 |
| Frank Leitner (Soc. Lab.) | 552 |
| W. H. Mills (Soc. Dem.) . | 2,487 |
| Total vote . . . . . . . . . | 279,874 |

### 1906

The popular vote in the state's first primary in the Democratic party was as follows:

| | |
|---|---|
| Thomas M. Campbell. . . | 90,345 |
| M. M. Brooks . . . . . . . . | 70,064 |
| O. B. Colquitt . . . . . . . . | 68,529 |
| Charles K. Bell. . . . . . . | 65,168 |
| Total vote . . . . . . . . . | 294,106 |

#### General Election

| | |
|---|---|
| T. M. Campbell (Dem.). . | 148,264 |
| C. A. Gray (Rep.) . . . . . . | 23,711 |
| J. W. Pearson (Prohi.) . . | 5,252 |
| G. C. Edwards (Soc.). . . | 2,958 |
| A. S. Dowler (Soc. Lab.) . | 260 |
| A. W. Atcheson (Reor. Rep.). . . . . . . . . . . . | 5,395 |
| Total vote . . . . . . . . . | 185,840 |

### 1908
#### Democratic Primary

| | |
|---|---|
| T. M. Campbell. . . . . . . | 202,608 |
| R. R. Williams . . . . . . . . | 117,459 |
| Total vote . . . . . . . . . | 320,067 |

#### General Election

| | |
|---|---|
| T. M. Campbell (Dem.). . | 218,956 |
| J. N. Simpson (Rep.) . . . | 73,305 |
| J. C. Rhodes (Soc.) . . . . | 8,100 |
| W. B. Cook (Soc. Lab.) . | 234 |
| E. C. Heath (Prohi.) . . . . | 148 |
| Total vote . . . . . . . . . | 300,743 |

### 1910
#### Democratic Primary

| | |
|---|---|
| O. B. Colquitt . . . . . . . . | 146,526 |
| William Poindexter. . . . . | 79,711 |
| R. V. Davidson . . . . . . . | 53,187 |
| Cone Johnson . . . . . . . . | 76,050 |
| J. Marion Jones . . . . . . . | 1,906 |
| Total vote . . . . . . . . | 357,380 |

#### General Election

| | |
|---|---|
| O. B. Colquitt (Dem.) . . . | 174,596 |
| J. O. Terrell (Rep.) . . . . . | 26,191 |
| Redding Andrews (Soc.). | 11,538 |

| | |
|---|---|
| A. J. Houston (Prohi.) . . . | 6,052 |
| Carl Schmidt (Soc. Lab.). | 426 |
| Total vote. . . . . . . . | 218,803 |

### 1912
#### Democratic Primary

| | |
|---|---|
| O. B. Colquitt . . . . . . . . | 218,812 |
| William F. Ramsey . . . . | 177,183 |
| Total vote. . . . . . . . . | 395,995 |

#### General Election

| | |
|---|---|
| O. B. Colquitt (Dem.) . . . | 234,352 |
| Ed Lasater (Prog.) . . . . | 15,794 |
| C. W. Johnson (Rep.) . . . | 23,089 |
| A. J. Houston (Prohi.) . . . | 2,356 |
| Redding Andrews (Soc.). | 25,258 |
| K. E. Choate (Soc. Lab.). | 308 |
| Total vote. . . . . . . . . | 301,157 |

### 1914
#### Democratic Primary

| | |
|---|---|
| James E. Ferguson . . . . | 237,062 |
| Thomas H. Ball. . . . . . . | 191,558 |
| Total vote. . . . . . . . . | 428,620 |

#### General Election

| | |
|---|---|
| J. E. Ferguson (Dem.) . . | 176,599 |
| F. M. Etheridge (Prog.) . . | 1,794 |
| John W. Philp (Rep.). . . . | 11,411 |
| E. R. Meitzen (Soc.) . . . . | 24,977 |
| Total vote. . . . . . . . . | 214,781 |

### 1916
#### Democratic Primary

| | |
|---|---|
| James E. Ferguson . . . . | 240,561 |
| Charles H. Morris . . . . . . | 174,611 |
| H. C. Marshall. . . . . . . . | 6,731 |
| Total vote. . . . . . . . . | 421,903 |

#### General Election

| | |
|---|---|
| J. E. Ferguson (Dem.) . . | 296,667 |
| R. B. Creager (Rep.). . . . | 49,118 |
| E. R. Meitzen (Soc.) . . . . | 14,580 |
| H. W. Lewis (Prohi.) . . . . | 3,200 |
| Total vote. . . . . . . . . | 363,565 |

In 1917 Ferguson was removed from office and succeeded by Hobby.

### 1918
#### Democratic Primary

| | |
|---|---|
| W. P. Hobby . . . . . . . . . | 461,479 |
| James E. Ferguson . . . . | 217,012 |
| Total vote. . . . . . . . . | 678,491 |

#### General Election

| | |
|---|---|
| W. P. Hobby (Dem.) . . . . | 148,982 |
| Chas. A. Boynton (Rep.). | 26,713 |
| Wm. D. Simpson (Soc.) . | 1,660 |
| Total vote. . . . . . . . . | 177,355 |

### 1920

In 1918 the primary election law had been amended, requiring a majority for nomination. The **first double primary in the governor's race** was in 1920.

#### 1st Democratic Primary

| | |
|---|---|
| Pat M. Neff . . . . . . . . . . | 149,818 |
| Robert E. Thomason . . . | 99,002 |
| Joseph W. Bailey . . . . . . | 152,340 |
| Ben F. Looney . . . . . . . . | 48,640 |
| Total vote. . . . . . . . . | 449,800 |

#### 2nd Democratic Primary

| | |
|---|---|
| Pat M. Neff . . . . . . . . . . | 264,075 |
| Joseph W. Bailey . . . . . . | 184,702 |
| Total vote. . . . . . . . . | 448,777 |

#### General Election

| | |
|---|---|
| Pat M. Neff (Dem.) . . . . . | 289,188 |
| J. G. Culberson (Rep.) . . | 90,217 |
| H. Capers (B. T. Rep.). . . | 26,091 |

| | |
|---|---|
| T. H. McGregor (Amer.).. | 69,380 |
| L. L. Rhodes (Soc.). . . . . | 6,796 |
| Scattering . . . . . . . . . . . | 59 |
| Total vote . . . . . . . . | 481,731 |

### 1922
#### Democratic Primary

| | |
|---|---|
| Pat M. Neff . . . . . . . . . . | 318,000 |
| W. W. King. . . . . . . . . . . | 18,368 |
| Fred S. Rogers . . . . . . . | 195,941 |
| Harry T. Warner. . . . . . . | 57,671 |
| Total vote . . . . . . . . . | 589,926 |

#### General Election

| | |
|---|---|
| Pat M. Neff (Dem.) . . . . . | 334,199 |
| W. H. Atwell (Rep.) . . . . . | 73,329 |
| Total vote . . . . . . . . . | 407,528 |

### 1924
#### 1st Democratic Primary

| | |
|---|---|
| Felix D. Robertson . . . . . | 193,508 |
| George W. Dixon. . . . . . . | 4,035 |
| W. E. Pope . . . . . . . . . . | 17,136 |
| Joe Burkett . . . . . . . . . . | 21,720 |
| Miriam A. Ferguson . . . . | 146,424 |
| Lynch Davidson . . . . . . . | 141,208 |
| V. A. Collins . . . . . . . . . . | 24,864 |
| T. W. Davidson . . . . . . . . | 125,011 |
| Thomas D. Barton. . . . . | 29,217 |
| Total vote . . . . . . . . . | 703,123 |

#### 2nd Democratic Primary

| | |
|---|---|
| Miriam A. Ferguson . . . . | 413,751 |
| Felix D. Robertson . . . . . | 316,019 |
| Total vote . . . . . . . . . | 729,770 |

#### General Election

| | |
|---|---|
| Miriam A. Ferguson (Dem.) . . . . . . . . . . . | 422,558 |
| George C. Butte (Rep.).. | 294,970 |
| Total vote . . . . . . . . . | 717,528 |

### 1926
#### 1st Democratic Primary

| | |
|---|---|
| Lynch Davidson . . . . . . . | 122,449 |
| Miriam A. Ferguson . . . . | 283,482 |
| Kate M. Johnston . . . . . . | 1,029 |
| Dan Moody . . . . . . . . . . | 409,732 |
| Edith E. Wilmans . . . . . . | 1,580 |
| O. F. Zimmerman . . . . . . | 2,962 |
| Total vote . . . . . . . . . | 821,234 |

#### 2nd Democratic Primary

| | |
|---|---|
| Miriam A. Ferguson . . . . | 270,595 |
| Dan Moody . . . . . . . . . . | 495,723 |
| Total vote . . . . . . . . . | 766,318 |

#### Republican Primary
(Party's first statewide.)

| | |
|---|---|
| H. H. Haines . . . . . . . . . | 11,215 |
| E. P. Scott . . . . . . . . . . . | 4,074 |
| Total vote . . . . . . . . . | 15,289 |

#### General Election

| | |
|---|---|
| Dan Moody (Dem.). . . . . | 233,068 |
| H. H. Haines (Rep.). . . . . | 31,531 |
| M. A. Smith (Soc.). . . . . . | 908 |
| Total vote . . . . . . . . . | 265,507 |

### 1928
#### Democratic Party

| | |
|---|---|
| Wm. E. Hawkins . . . . . . . | 32,076 |
| Dan Moody . . . . . . . . . . . | 442,080 |
| Louis J. Wardlaw. . . . . . . | 245,508 |
| Edith E. Wilmans . . . . . . | 18,237 |
| Total vote . . . . . . . . . | 737,901 |

#### General Election,

| | |
|---|---|
| Dan Moody (Dem.). . . . . | 582,972 |
| W. H. Holmes (Rep.) . . . . | 120,504 |
| T. Stedman (Com.) . . . . . | 109 |

L. L. Rhodes (Soc.) . . . . 738
Scattering. . . . . . . . . . . 2,683
Total vote. . . . . . . . 707,006

### 1930
#### 1st Democratic Primary
Miriam A. Ferguson . . . . 242,959
Thomas B. Love . . . . . . . 87,068
Paul Loven . . . . . . . . . . . 2,724
Earle B. Mayfield . . . . . . 54,459
Barry Miller. . . . . . . . . . . 54,652
C. C. Moody . . . . . . . . . . 4,382
Frank Putnam. . . . . . . . . 2,365
Clint C. Small . . . . . . . . . 138,934
Ross S. Sterling . . . . . . . 170,754
James Young . . . . . . . . . 73,385
C. E. Walker . . . . . . . . . . 1,760
Total vote. . . . . . . . . 833,442

#### 2nd Democratic Primary
Ross S. Sterling . . . . . . . 473,371
Miriam A. Ferguson . . . . 384,402
Total vote. . . . . . . . . 857,773

#### Republican Primary
George C. Butte . . . . . . . 5,001
H. E. Exum . . . . . . . . . . . 2,773
John F. Grant . . . . . . . . . 1,800
John P. Gaines . . . . . . . . 203
Total vote. . . . . . . . . 9,777

#### General Election
Ross S. Sterling (Dem.) . 252,738
Wm. E. Talbot (Rep.) . . . 62,224
Total vote. . . . . . . . . 314,962

### 1932
#### 1st Democratic Primary
Roger Q. Evans . . . . . . . 3,974
Miriam A. Ferguson . . . . 402,238
C. A. Frakes . . . . . . . . . . 2,338
J. Ed Glenn . . . . . . . . . . 2,089
Tom F. Hunter. . . . . . . . . 220,391
Frank Putnam. . . . . . . . . 2,962
Ross S. Sterling . . . . . . . 296,383
M. H. Wolfe. . . . . . . . . . . 32,241
George W. Armstrong. . . . 5,312
Total vote. . . . . . . . . 967,928

#### 2nd Democratic Primary
Ross S. Sterling . . . . . . . 473,846
Miriam A. Ferguson . . . . 477,644
Total Vote . . . . . . . . . 951,490

#### General Election
M.A. Ferguson (Dem.) . . 528,986
Orville Bullington (Rep.) . 317,807
George C. Edwards
(Soc.) . . . . . . . . . . . 1,866
George W. Armstrong
(*Jacksonian Dem.). . 706
Otho L. Heitt (Liberty) . . 101
Philip L. Howe (Com.) . . 72
Total vote. . . . . . . . . 849,538

### 1934
#### 1st Democratic Primary
C. C. McDonald . . . . . . . 206,007
James V. Allred. . . . . . . . 297,656
Clint C. Small . . . . . . . . . 124,206
Tom F. Hunter. . . . . . . . . 241,339
Edgar Witt . . . . . . . . . . . 62,208
Edward K. Russell . . . . . 4,408
Maury Hughes . . . . . . . . 58,187
Total vote. . . . . . . . . 994,011

#### 2nd Democratic Primary
James V. Allred. . . . . . . . 497,808
Tom F. Hunter. . . . . . . . . 457,785
Total vote. . . . . . . . . 995,593

#### Republican Primary

D. E. Waggoner. . . . . . . . 13,043

#### General Election
James V. Allred (Dem.). . 421,422
D. E. Wagonner (Rep.) . . 13,534
George C. Edwards
(Soc.) . . . . . . . . . . . 1,877
Enoch Hardaway (Com.). 244
Total vote . . . . . . . . . 437,077

### 1936
#### Democratic Primary
James V. Allred. . . . . . . . 553,219
P. Pierce Brooks . . . . . . . 33,391
F. W. Fischer . . . . . . . . . . 145,877
Tom F. Hunter . . . . . . . . . 239,460
Roy Sanderford . . . . . . . 81,170
Total vote. . . . . . . . . 1,053,117

#### General Election
James V. Allred(Dem.) . . 782,083
C. O. Harris (Rep.) . . . . . 58,842
Carl Brannin (Soc.). . . . . 962
Homer Brooks (Com.) . . 283
Total vote. . . . . . . . . 842,170

### 1938
#### Democratic Primary
W. Lee O'Daniel . . . . . . . 573,166
Ernest O. Thompson. . . . 231,630
William McCraw . . . . . . . 152,278
Tom F. Hunter . . . . . . . . . 117,634
S. T. Brogdon . . . . . . . . . 892
Joseph King . . . . . . . . . 773
Clarence E. Farmer . . . . 3,869
P. D. Renfro. . . . . . . . . . . 8,127
Karl A. Crowley. . . . . . . . 19,153
Clarence R. Miller. . . . . . 667
James A. Ferguson . . . . 3,800
Thomas Self . . . . . . . . . . 1,405
Marvin P. McCoy. . . . . . . 1,491
Total vote. . . . . . . . . 1,114,885

#### General Election
W. Lee O'Daniel (Dem.) . 473,526
Alexander Boynton
(Rep.) . . . . . . . . . . . 10,940
Earl E. Miller (Soc.) . . . . 398
Homer Brooks (Com.) . . 424
Total vote. . . . . . . . . 485,288

### 1940
#### Democratic Primary
W. Lee O'Daniel . . . . . . . 645,646
Ernest O. Thompson. . . . 256,923
Harry Hines . . . . . . . . . . 119,121
Miriam A. Ferguson . . . . 100,578
Jerry Sadler . . . . . . . . . . 61,396
Arlon B. "Cyclone" Davis
Jr. . . . . . . . . . . . . . . 3,625
R. P. Condron . . . . . . . . . 2,001
Total vote. . . . . . . . . 1,189,290

#### General Election
W. Lee O'Daniel (Dem.) . 1,019,338
George C. Hopkins
(Rep.) . . . . . . . . . . . 59,885
Ben H. Lauderdale
(Com.) . . . . . . . . . . . 202
Scattering. . . . . . . . . . . 113
Total vote. . . . . . . . . 1,079,538

### 1942
#### Democratic Primary
Hal H. Collins . . . . . . . . . 272,469
Alex M. Ferguson . . . . . . 8,370
Gene S. Porter . . . . . . . . 4,933
Charles L. Somerville . . . 4,853
Coke R. Stevenson. . . . . 651,218
Hope Wheeler . . . . . . . . 9,373
Total vote . . . . . . . . . 951,216

#### General Election
Coke R. Stevenson
(Dem.). . . . . . . . . . . 280,735
C. K. McDowell (Rep.). . . 9,204
Total vote . . . . . . . . . 289,939

### 1944
#### Democratic Primary
Coke R. Stevenson . . . . . 696,586
Martin Jones. . . . . . . . . . 21,379
W. J. Minton . . . . . . . . . . 8,537
Alex M. Ferguson . . . . . . 12,649
Minnie F. Cunningham . . 48,039
Gene S. Porter . . . . . . . . 15,243
Edward L. Carey . . . . . . . 4,633
William F. Grimes . . . . . . 9,443
Herbert E. Mills. . . . . . . . 6,640
Write-in votes . . . . . . . . 311
Total vote . . . . . . . . . 823,460

#### General Election
Coke R. Stevenson
(Dem.). . . . . . . . . . . 1,007,826
B. J. Peasley (Rep.). . . . . 100,287
Total vote . . . . . . . . . 1,108,113

### 1946
#### 1st Democratic Primary
Floyd Brinkley . . . . . . . . . 4,249
William V. Brown . . . . . . . 3,902
A. J. Burks. . . . . . . . . . . . 4,881
Chas. B. Hutchison . . . . . 4,616
Beauford Jester . . . . . . . 443,804
Walter Scott McNutt . . . . 4,353
Caso March . . . . . . . . . . 20,529
W. J. Minton . . . . . . . . . . 2,398
Homer P. Rainey . . . . . . . 291,282
Jerry Sadler . . . . . . . . . . 103,120
Grover Sellers. . . . . . . . . 162,431
C. R. Shaw . . . . . . . . . . . 9,764
John Lee Smith. . . . . . . . 102,941
Reese Turner . . . . . . . . . 4,914
Total vote . . . . . . . . . 1,163,184

#### 2nd Democratic Primary
Beauford H. Jester . . . . . 701,018
Homer P. Rainey . . . . . . . 335,654
Total vote . . . . . . . . . 1,056,672

#### General Election
Beauford Jester (Dem.). . 345,513
Eugene Nolte Jr. (Rep.) . 33,231
Total vote . . . . . . . . . 378,744

### 1948
#### Democratic Primary
Beauford H. Jester . . . . . 642,025
Sumpter W. Stockton . . . 21,243
Roger Q. Evans . . . . . . . 279,602
Charles B. Hutchison . . . 24,441
Holmes A. May . . . . . . . . 20,538
Caso March . . . . . . . . . . 187,658
W. J. Minton . . . . . . . . . . 13,659
Denver S. Whiteley . . . . . 16,090
Write-in votes . . . . . . . . 1
Total vote . . . . . . . . . 1,205,257

#### General Election
Beauford H. Jester
(Dem.). . . . . . . . . . . 1,024,160
Alvin H. Lane (Rep.) . . . . 177,399
Gerald Overholt (Prohi.). 3,554
Herman Wright (Prog.) . . 3,747
Total vote . . . . . . . . . 1,208,860

### 1950
#### Democratic Primary
Allan Shivers. . . . . . . . . . 829,730
Caso March . . . . . . . . . . 195,997
Charles B. Hutchison . . . 16,048

| | |
|---|---|
| Gene S. Porter | 14,728 |
| J. M. Wren | 14,138 |
| Benita Louise Marek Lawrence | 9,542 |
| Wellington Abbey | 6,381 |
| Total vote | 1,086,564 |

### General Election

| | |
|---|---|
| Allan Shivers (Dem.) | 355,010 |
| Ralph W. Currie (Rep.) | 39,737 |
| Total vote | 374,747 |

### 1952
#### Democratic Primary

| | |
|---|---|
| Allan Shivers' | 883,861 |
| Ralph W. Yarborough | 488,345 |
| Allene M. Trayler | 34,186 |
| Total vote | 1,356,392 |

#### General Election

| | |
|---|---|
| *Allan Shivers (Dem.) | 1,375,547 |
| *Allan Shivers (Rep.) | 468,319 |
| Total vote | 1,843,866 |
| *Ran on both tickets. | |

### 1954
#### 1st Democratic Primary

| | |
|---|---|
| Allan Shivers | 668,913 |
| Ralph W. Yarborough | 645,994 |
| J. J. Holmes | 19,591 |
| Arlon B. "Cyclone" Davis | 16,254 |
| Total vote | 1,350,752 |

#### 2nd Democratic Primary

| | |
|---|---|
| Allan Shivers | 775,088 |
| Ralph W. Yarborough | 683,132 |
| Total vote | 1,458,220 |

#### General Election

| | |
|---|---|
| Allan Shivers (Dem.) | 569,533 |
| Tod R. Adams (Rep.) | 66,154 |
| Other | 1,205 |
| Total vote | 636,892 |

### 1956
#### 1st Democratic Primary

| | |
|---|---|
| Price Daniel | 628,914 |
| J. Evetts Haley | 88,772 |
| J. J. Holmes | 10,165 |
| W. Lee O'Daniel | 347,757 |
| Reuben Senterfitt | 37,774 |
| Ralph Yarborough | 463,416 |
| Write-in | 72 |
| Total vote | 1,576,870 |

#### 2nd Democratic Primary

| | |
|---|---|
| Price Daniel | 698,001 |
| Ralph Yarborough | 694,830 |
| Total vote | 1,392,831 |

#### General Election

| | |
|---|---|
| Price Daniel (Dem.) | 1,350,736 |
| William R. Bryant (Rep.) | 261,283 |
| W. Lee O'Daniel (Write-in) | 110,234 |
| Other | 1,838 |
| Total vote | 1,724,091 |

### 1958
#### Democratic Primary

| | |
|---|---|
| Price Daniel | 799,107 |
| Henry B. Gonzalez | 246,969 |
| Joe A. Irwin | 33,643 |
| W. Lee O'Daniel | 238,767 |
| Write-in | 6 |
| Total vote | 1,317,492 |

#### General Election

| | |
|---|---|
| Price Daniel (Dem.) | 695,779 |
| Edwin S. Mayer (Rep.) | 94,086 |
| Total vote | 789,865 |

### 1960


#### Democratic Primary

| | |
|---|---|
| Jack Cox | 619,834 |
| Price Daniel | 908,992 |
| Write-in | 8 |
| Total vote | 1,528,834 |

#### General Election

| | |
|---|---|
| Price Daniel (Dem.) | 1,627,698 |
| Wm. M. Steger (Rep.) | 609,808 |
| Total vote | 2,237,506 |

### 1962
#### 1st Democratic Primary

| | |
|---|---|
| John Connally | 431,498 |
| Price Daniel | 248,524 |
| Marshall Formby | 139,094 |
| Edwin A. Walker | 138,387 |
| Will Wilson | 171,617 |
| Don Yarborough | 317,986 |
| Write-in | 9 |
| Total vote | 1,447,115 |

#### 2nd Democratic Primary

| | |
|---|---|
| John Connally | 565,174 |
| Don Yarborough | 538,924 |
| Total vote | 1,104,098 |

#### Republican Primary

| | |
|---|---|
| Jack Cox | 99,170 |
| Roy Whittenburg | 16,136 |
| Total vote | 115,306 |

#### General Election

| | |
|---|---|
| John Connally (Dem.) | 847,038 |
| Jack Cox (Rep.) | 715,025 |
| Jack Carswell (Con.) | 7,135 |
| Total vote | 1,569,198 |

### 1964
#### Democratic Primary

| | |
|---|---|
| John Connally | 1,125,884 |
| Don Yarborough | 471,411 |
| M. T. Banks | 22,047 |
| Johnnie Mae Hackworthe | 10,955 |
| Total vote | 1,630,297 |

#### Republican Primary

| | |
|---|---|
| Jack Crichton | 128,146 |

#### General Election

| | |
|---|---|
| John Connally (Dem.) | 1,877,793 |
| Jack Crichton (Rep.) | 661,675 |
| John C. Williams (Con.) | 5,257 |
| Write-in | 28 |
| Total vote | 2,544,753 |

### 1966
#### Democratic Primary

| | |
|---|---|
| John Connally | 932,641 |
| Stanley C. Woods | 291,651 |
| Johnnie Mae Hackworthe | 31,105 |
| Write-in votes | 3 |
| Total vote | 1,255,400 |

#### Republican Primary

| | |
|---|---|
| T. E. Kennerly | 49,568 |

#### General Election

| | |
|---|---|
| John Connally (Dem.) | 1,037,517 |
| T. E. Kennerly (Rep.) | 368,025 |
| Tommye Gillespie (Con.) | 10,454 |
| Bard Logan (Conserv.) | 9,810 |
| Write-ins | 55 |
| Total vote | 1,425,861 |

### 1968
#### 1st Democratic Primary

| | |
|---|---|
| Preston Smith | 386,875 |
| Pat O'Daniel | 47,912 |
| John Hill | 154,908 |


| | |
|---|---|
| Waggoner Carr | 257,543 |
| Eugene Locke | 218,118 |
| Dolph Briscoe | 225,686 |
| Edward L. Whittenburg | 22,957 |
| Don Yarborough | 421,607 |
| Alfonso Veloz | 9,562 |
| Johnnie Mae Hackworthe | 5,484 |
| Total vote | 1,750,652 |

#### 2nd Democratic Primary

| | |
|---|---|
| Preston Smith | 767,490 |
| Don Yarborough | 621,226 |
| Total vote | 1,388,716 |

#### Republican Primary

| | |
|---|---|
| Paul Eggers | 65,501 |
| John Trice | 28,849 |
| Wallace Sisk | 10,415 |
| Total vote | 104,765 |

#### General Election

| | |
|---|---|
| Preston Smith (Dem.) | 1,662,019 |
| Paul Eggers (Rep.) | 1,254,333 |
| Total vote | 2,916,352 |

### 1970
#### Democratic Primary

| | |
|---|---|
| Preston Smith | 1,011,300 |

#### Republican Primary

| | |
|---|---|
| Paul Eggers | 101,875 |
| Roger Martin | 7,146 |
| Total vote | 109,021 |

#### General Election

| | |
|---|---|
| Preston Smith (Dem.) | 1,232,506 |
| Paul Eggers (Rep.) | 1,073,831 |
| Other | 428 |
| Total vote | 2,306,765 |

### 1972
#### 1st Democratic Primary

| | |
|---|---|
| Ben Barnes | 392,356 |
| Dolph Briscoe | 963,397 |
| Frances Farenthold | 612,051 |
| Robert E. Looney | 10,225 |
| William H. Posey | 13,727 |
| Preston Smith | 190,709 |
| Gordon F. Wills | 10,438 |
| Total vote | 2,192,903 |

#### 2nd Democratic Primary

| | |
|---|---|
| Dolph Briscoe | 1,095,168 |
| Frances Farenthold | 884,594 |
| Total vote | 1,979,762 |

#### 1st Republican Primary

| | |
|---|---|
| Albert Fay | 24,329 |
| Henry C. Grover | 37,118 |
| John A. Hall Sr. | 8,018 |
| J. A. Jenkins | 4,864 |
| Tom McElroy | 19,559 |
| David Reagan | 20,119 |
| Total vote | 114,007 |

#### 2nd Republican Primary

| | |
|---|---|
| Albert Fay | 19,166 |
| Henry C. Grover | 37,842 |
| Total vote | 57,008 |

#### General Election

| | |
|---|---|
| Dolph Briscoe (Dem.) | 1,633,493 |
| Henry C. Grover (Rep.) | 1,533,986 |
| Ramsey Muniz (Raza) | 214,118 |
| Deborah Leonard (Soc.) | 24,103 |
| Other | 3,891 |
| Total vote | 3,409,501 |

### 1974
#### Democratic Primary

| | |
|---|---|
| Dolph Briscoe | 1,025,632 |
| Frances Farenthold | 437,287 |

W. H. Posey . . . . . . . . 31,498
Steve S. Alexander . . . 26,889
Total vote . . . . . . . . 1,521,306

### Republican Primary
Jim Granberry . . . . . . . 53,617
Odell McBrayer . . . . . . 15,484
Total vote . . . . . . . . 69,101

### General Election
Dolph Briscoe (Dem.) . . 1,016,334
Jim Granberry (Rep.). . . 514,725
Ramsey Muniz (Raza). . 93,295
Sherry Smith (Soc.). . . . 8,171
S. W. McDonnell (Am.). . 22,208
Other . . . . . . . . . . . . . . 251
Total vote . . . . . . . . 1,654,984

## 1978
### Democratic Primary
Donald R. Beagle . . . . 14,791
Dolph Briscoe . . . . . . . 753,309
John Hill. . . . . . . . . . . . 932,345
Ray Allen Mayo . . . . . . 20,249
Preston Smith . . . . . . . 92,202
Total vote . . . . . . . . 1,812,896

### Republican Primary
William P. Clements Jr. . 115,345
Ray Hutchison . . . . . . . 38,268
Clarence Thompson . . . 4,790
Total vote . . . . . . . . 158,403

### General Election
John Hill (Dem.). . . . . . 1,166,919
Bill Clements (Rep.}. . . . 1,183,828
Mario C. Compean
 (Raza) . . . . . . . . . . 14,213
Sara Jean Johnston
 (Soc.). . . . . . . . . . . 4,624
Other . 115
Total vote . . . . . . . . 2,369,699

## 1982
### Democratic Primary
David L. Young . . . . . . . 25,386
Bob Armstrong . . . . . . 262,189
Mark White . . . . . . . . . 592,658
Donald R. Beagle . . . . 15,649
Ray Allen Mayo . . . . . . 20,088
*Buddy Temple . . . . . . . 402,693
Total vote . . . . . . . . 1,318,663
*Temple declined to participate in run-
off; White declared winner of race.

### Republican Primary
William P. Clements Jr.. . 246,120
Duke Embs . . . . . . . . . 19,731
Total vote. . . . . . . . . 265,851

### General Election
Mark White (Dem.). . . . . 1,697,870
William P. Clements Jr.
 (Rep.). . . . . . . . . . . 1,465,937
David Hutzelman (Ind.) . 19,143
Bob Poteet (Con.) . 8,065
Other . . . . . . . . . . . . . . 76
Total vote. . . . . . . . . 3,191,091

## 1986
### Democratic Primary
Sheila Bilyeu . . . . . . . . 39,370
Andrew C. Briscoe III . . . 248,850
A. Don Crowder . . . . . . 120,999
Bobby Locke . . . . . . . . 58,936
Ron Slover . . . . . . . . . . 38,861
Mark White . . . . . . . . . . 589,536
Total vote. . . . . . . . . 1,096,552

### Republican Primary
William P. Clements Jr . . 318,808
Kent Hance . . . . . . . . . 108,238
Tom Loeffler . . . . . . . . . 117,673
Total vote. . . . . . . . . 544,719
Following are the **vote totals as can-
vassed by the Republican Party:**
William P. Clements Jr. 318,938
Kent Hance . . . . . . . . . . 108,583
Tom Loeffler . . . . . . . . . 118,224
Total vote. . . . . . . . . 545,745

### General Election
Mark White (Dem.). . . . . 1,584,515
William P. Clements
 Jr.(Rep.). . . . . . . . . . 1,813,779
Theresa Doyle (Lib.). . . 42,496
Other . . . . . . . . . . . . . . 670
Total vote. . . . . . . . . 3,441,460

## 1990
### 1st Democratic Primary
Stanley Adams. . . . . . . . 16,118
Theresa Hearn-Haynes . 31,395
Earl Holmes . . . . . . . . . . 17,904
Jim Mattox . . . . . . . . . . 546,103
Ray Rachal . . . . . . . . . . 9,388
Ann W. Richards. . . . . . . 580,191
Mark White. . . . . . . . . . 288,161
Total vote. . . . . . . . . 1,487,280

### 2nd Democratic Primary
Jim Mattox . . . . . . . . . . . 481,739
Ann W. Richards. . . . . . . 640,995
Total vote . . . . . . . . . 1,122,734

### Republican Primary
Ed Cude . . . . . . . . . . . . 1,077
Kent Hance. . . . . . . . . . 132,142
Tom Luce . . . . . . . . . . . 115,835
W. N. Otwell . . . . . . . . . 2,310
Royce X. Owens. . . . . . . 1,392
Jack Rains . . . . . . . . . . 82,461
Clayton Williams. . . . . . . 520,014
Total vote . . . . . . . . . 855,231

### General Election
Clayton Williams (Rep.) . 1,826,431
Ann W. Richards (Dem.). 1,925,670
Jeff Daiell (Lib.). . . . . . . 129,128
Write-Ins (19) . . . . . . . . 11,517
Total vote . . . . . . . . . 3,892,746

## 1994
### 1st Democratic Primary
Gary Espinosa . . . . . . . 230,337
Ann W. Richards. . . . . . 806,607
Total vote . . . . . . . . . 1,036,944

### 1st Republican Primary
George W. Bush . . . . . . 520,130
Ray Hollis . . . . . . . . . . . 37,210
Total vote . . . . . . . . . 557,340

### General Election
Ann W. Richards (Dem.) 2,016,928
George W. Bush (Rep.). 2,350,994
Keary Ehlers (Lib.) . . . . 28,320
Total vote . . . . . . . . . 4,396,242

## 1998
### 1st Democratic Primary
Garry Mauro . . . . . . . . . 492,419
Total vote . . . . . . . . . 492,419

### 1st Republican Primary
George W. Bush . . . . . . 576,528
R.C. Crawford . . . . . . . . 20,311
Total vote . . . . . . . . . 596,839

### General Election
Garry Mauro (Dem.) . . . 1,165,592
George W. Bush (Rep.). 2,550,831
Lester R. (Les) Turlington
 Jr. (Lib.). . . . . . . . . . . . 20,711
Susan Lee Solar (Write-In) 954
Total vote . . . . . . . . . 4,396,242

*Then Gov. George W. Bush addressed the GOP state convention in 1996.*

*File photo.*

Abbreviations used are:
 (Dem.) Democrat,
 (Rep.) Republican,
 (G.B.) Greenback,
 (Lib.) Libertarian,
 (Ind.) Independent,
 (I. Dem.) Indepdent Democrat,
 (Prohi.) Prohibitionist,
 (Ind. Fus.) Independent Fusion,
 (Peo.) People's (Populist),
 (Ref. Rep.) Reformed Republican,
 (L.W. Rep.) Lily White Republican,
 (Soc. Lab.) Socialist-Labor,
 (Reor. Rep.) Reorganized Republican,
 (Soc.) Socialist,
 (Prog.) Progressive,
 (B.T. Rep.) Black and Tan
  Republican,
 (Amer.) American,
 (Com.) Communist,
 (Con.) Constitution,
 (Conserv.) Conservative,
 (Raz.) La Raza Unida.

# Declaration of Independence of the Republic of Texas

The Declaration of Independence of the Republic of Texas was adopted in general convention at Washington-on-the-Brazos, March 2, 1836.

Richard Ellis, president of the convention, appointed a committee of five to write the declaration for submission to the convention. However, there is much evidence that George C. Childress, one of the members, wrote the document with little or no help from the other members. Childress is therefore generally accepted as the author.

The text of the declaration is followed by the names of the signers of the document. The names are presented here as the signers actually signed the document. Our thanks to the staff of the Texas State Archives for furnishing a photocopy of the signatures.

UNANIMOUS

# DECLARATION OF INDEPENDENCE,

BY THE

## DELEGATES OF THE PEOPLE OF TEXAS,

### IN GENERAL CONVENTION,

AT THE TOWN OF WASHINGTON,

ON THE SECOND DAY OF MARCH, 1836.

When a government has ceased to protect the lives, liberty and property of the people from whom its legitimate powers are derived, and for the advancement of whose happiness it was instituted; and so far from being a guarantee for the enjoyment of those inestimable and inalienable rights, becomes an instrument in the hands of evil rulers for their oppression; when the Federal Republican Constitution of their country, which they have sworn to support, no longer has a substantial existence, and the whole nature of their government has been forcibly changed without their consent, from a restricted federative republic, composed of sovereign states, to a consolidated central military despotism, in which every interest is disregarded but that of the army and the priesthood — both the eternal enemies of civil liberty, and the ever-ready minions of power, and the usual instruments of tyrants; When long after the spirit of the Constitution has departed, moderation is at length, so far lost, by those in power that even the semblance of freedom is removed, and the forms, themselves, of the constitution discontinued; and so far from their petitions and remonstrances being regarded, the agents who bear them are thrown into dungeons; and mercenary armies sent forth to force a new government upon them at the point of the bayonet. When in consequence of such acts of malfeasance and abdication, on the part of the government, anar-

chy prevails, and civil society is dissolved into its original elements: In such a crisis, the first law of nature, the right of self-preservation — the inherent and inalienable right of the people to appeal to first principles and take their political affairs into their own hands in extreme cases — enjoins it as a right towards themselves and a sacred obligation to their posterity, to abolish such government and create another in its stead, calculated to rescue them from impending dangers, and to secure their future welfare and happiness.

Nations, as well as individuals, are amenable for their acts to the public opinion of mankind. A statement of a part of our grievances is, therefore, submitted to an impartial world, in justification of the hazardous but unavoidable step now taken of severing our political connection with the Mexican people, and assuming an independent attitude among the nations of the earth.

The Mexican government, by its colonization laws, invited and induced the Anglo-American population of Texas to colonize its wilderness under the pledged faith of a written constitution, that they should continue to enjoy that constitutional liberty and republican government to which they had been habituated in the land of their birth, the United States of America. In this expectation they have been cruelly disappointed, inasmuch as the Mexican nation has acquiesced

in the late changes made in the government by General Antonio Lopez de Santa Anna, who, having overturned the constitution of his country, now offers us the cruel alternative either to abandon our homes, acquired by so many privations, or submit to the most intolerable of all tyranny, the combined despotism of the sword and the priesthood.

It has sacrificed our welfare to the state of Coahuila, by which our interests have been continually depressed, through a jealous and partial course of legislation carried on at a far distant seat of government, by a hostile majority, in an unknown tongue; and this too, notwithstanding we have petitioned in the humblest terms, for the establishment of a separate state government, and have, in accordance with the provisions of the national constitution, presented the general Congress, a republican constitution which was without just cause contemptuously rejected.

It incarcerated in a dungeon, for a long time, one of our citizens, for no other cause but a zealous endeavor to procure the acceptance of our constitution and the establishment of a state government.

It has failed and refused to secure on a firm basis, the right of trial by jury; that palladium of civil liberty, and only safe guarantee for the life, liberty, and property of the citizen.

It has failed to establish any public system of education, although possessed of almost boundless resources (the public domain) and, although, it is an axiom, in political science, that unless a people are educated and enlightened it is idle to expect the continuance of civil liberty, or the capacity for self-government.

It has suffered the military commandants stationed among us to exercise arbitrary acts of oppression and tyranny; thus trampling upon the most sacred rights of the citizen and rendering the military superior to the civil power.

It has dissolved by force of arms, the state Congress of Coahuila and Texas, and obliged our representatives to fly for their lives from the seat of government; thus depriving us of the fundamental political right of representation.

It has demanded the surrender of a number of our citizens, and ordered military detachments to seize and carry them into the Interior for trial; in contempt of the civil authorities, and in defiance of the laws and constitution.

It has made piratical attacks upon our commerce; by commissioning foreign desperadoes, and authorizing them to seize our vessels, and convey the property of our citizens to far distant ports of confiscation.

It denies us the right of worshipping the Almighty according to the dictates of our own consciences, by the support of a national religion calculated to promote the temporal interests of its human functionaries rather than the glory of the true and living God.

It has demanded us to deliver up our arms; which are essential to our defense, the rightful property of freemen, and formidable only to tyrannical governments.

It has invaded our country, both by sea and by land, with intent to lay waste our territory and drive us from our homes; and has now a large mercenary army advancing to carry on against us a war of extermination.

It has, through its emissaries, incited the merciless savage, with the tomahawk and scalping knife, to massacre the inhabitants of our defenseless frontiers.

It hath been, during the whole time of our connection with it, the contemptible sport and victim of successive military revolutions and hath continually exhibited every characteristic of a weak, corrupt and tyrannical government.

These, and other grievances, were patiently borne by the people of Texas until they reached that point at which forbearance ceases to be a virtue. We then took up arms in defense of the national constitution. We appealed to our Mexican brethren for assistance. Our appeal has been made in vain. Though months have elapsed, no sympathetic response has yet been heard from the Interior. We are, therefore, forced to the melancholy conclusion that the Mexican people have acquiesced in the destruction of their liberty, and the substitution therefor of a military government — that they are unfit to be free and incapable of self-government.

The necessity of self-preservation, therefore, now decrees our eternal political separation.

*We, therefore, the delegates, with plenary powers, of the people of Texas, in solemn convention assembled, appealing to a candid world for the necessities of our condition, do hereby resolve and DECLARE that our political connection with the Mexican nation has forever ended; and that the people of Texas do now constitute a FREE, SOVEREIGN and INDEPENDENT REPUBLIC, and are fully invested with all the rights and attributes which properly belong to the independent nations; and, conscious of the rectitude of our intentions, we fearlessly and confidently commit the issue to the decision of the Supreme Arbiter of the destinies of nations.*

RICHARD ELLIS, president of the convention and Delegate from Red River.

Charles B Stewart

Tho^S Barnett
John S.D. Byrom

Fran^{co} Ruiz
J. Antonio Navarro
Jesse B. Badgett
W^m D. Lacey
William Menefee
Jn^o Fisher
Mathew Caldwell
William Mottley
Lorenzo de Zavala
Stephen H. Everitt
Geo W Smyth

Elijah Stapp
Claiborne West

W^m B Scates
M.B. Menard
A.B. Hardin
J.W. Bunton
Tho^S J. Gasley
R. M. Coleman
Sterling C. Robertson
Benj Briggs Goodrich
G.W. Barnett
James G. Swisher
Jesse Grimes
S. Rhoads Fisher
John W. Moore
John W. Bower
Sam^l A Maverick from Bejar
Sam P. Carson
A. Briscoe
J.B. Woods

Jas Collinsworth
Edwin Waller
Asa Brigham
Geo. C. Childress
Bailey Hardeman
Rob. Potter
Thomas Jefferson Rusk
Chas. S. Taylor
John S. Roberts

Robert Hamilton
Collin McKinney
Albert H Latimer
James Power

Sam Houston
David Thomas

Edw^d Conrad
Martin Parmer
Edwin O. LeGrand
Stephen W. Blount
Ja^s Gaines
W^m Clark, Jr
Sydney O. Penington
W^m Carrol Crawford
Jn^o Turner

Test. H.S. Kimble, Secretary

# Constitution of Texas

The complete official text of the Constitution of Texas, including the original document, which was adopted on Feb. 15, 1876, plus all amendments approved since that time, is available on the State of Texas Web page at this address: **www.capitol.state.tx.us/txconst/toc.html**. An index at that site points you to the Article and Section of the Constitution that deals with a particular subject.

For election information, upcoming elections, amendment or other election votes and voter registration information, go to: **www.sos.state.tx.us/elections/index.shtml**.

According to the **Legislative Reference Library of Texas:** "The Texas Constitution is one of the longest in the nation and is still growing. As of 2001 (77th Legislature), the Texas Legislature has passed a total of 583 amendments. Of these, 409 have been adopted and 174 have been defeated by Texas voters. Thus, **the Texas Constitution has been amended 409 times since its adoption in 1876.**"

Amendment of the Texas Constitution requires a two-thirds favorable vote by both the Texas House of Representatives and the Texas Senate, followed by a majority vote of approval by voters in a statewide election.

Prior to 1973, amendments to the constitution could not be submitted by a special session of the Legislature. But the constitution was amended in 1972 to allow submission of amendments if the special session was opened to the subject by the governor.

Constitutional amendments are not subject to a gubernatorial veto. Once submitted, voters have the final decision on whether to change the constitution as proposed.

The following table lists the total number of amendments submitted to voters by the Texas Legislature and shows the year in which the Legislature approved them for submission to voters; e.g., the 70th Legislature in 1987 approved 28 bills proposing amendments to be submitted to voters — 25 in 1987 and 3 in 1988.

### Constitutional Amendments Submitted to Voters by the Texas Legislature

| Year | No. | Year | No. | Year | No. |
|---|---|---|---|---|---|
| 1879 | 1 | 1925 | 4 | 1969 | 16 |
| 1881 | 2 | 1927 | 8 | 1971 | 18 |
| 1883 | 5 | 1929 | 7 | 1973 | 9 |
| 1887 | 6 | 1931 | 9 | 1975 | 12 |
| 1889 | 2 | 1933 | 12 | 1977 | 15 |
| 1891 | 5 | 1935 | 13 | 1978 | 1 |
| 1893 | 2 | 1937 | 7 | 1979 | 12 |
| 1895 | 2 | 1939 | 4 | 1981 | 10 |
| 1897 | 5 | 1941 | 5 | 1982 | 3 |
| 1899 | 1 | 1943 | 3 | 1983 | 19 |
| 1901 | 1 | 1945 | 8 | 1985 | 17 |
| 1903 | 3 | 1947 | 9 | 1986 | 1 |
| 1905 | 3 | 1949 | 10 | 1987 | 28 |
| 1907 | 9 | 1951 | 7 | 1989 | 21 |
| 1909 | 4 | 1953 | 11 | 1990 | 1 |
| 1911 | 5 | 1955 | 9 | 1991 | 15 |
| 1913 | 7 | 1957 | 12 | 1993 | 18 |
| 1915 | 7 | 1959 | 4 | 1995 | 14 |
| 1917 | 3 | 1961 | 14 | 1997 | 15 |
| 1919 | 13 | 1963 | 7 | 1999 | 17 |
| 1921 | 5 | 1965 | 27 | 2001 | 20 |
| 1923 | 2 | 1967 | 20 | 2003 | 22 |

For more information on bills and constitutional amendments, see the Legislative Reference Library of Texas Web site at: **www.lrl.state.tx.us/legis/lrlhome.cfm**.

## Amendments, 2001

The following 20 amendments were submitted to the voters by the 77th Legislature in an election on **Nov. 6, 2001:**

**HJR 1** — Providing for a four-year term of office for the fire fighters' pension commissioner. **Passed:** 583,552 for; 226,350 against.

**HJR 2** — Authorizing a county commissioners court to declare the office of constable in certain precincts dormant and providing a procedure for reinstating the office. **Passed:** 2,431,757 for; 639,414 against.

**HJR 5** — Prescribing requirements for imposing a lien for work and material used in the construction, repair or renovation of residential homestead property, and including provisions concerning manufactured homes. **Passed:** 453,021 for; 318,517 against.

**HJR 44** — Authorizing the legislature to authorize taxing units other than school districts to exempt certain travel trailers from ad valorem taxation. **Passed:** 408,481 for; 378,557 against.

**HJR 45** — Requiring the governor to call a special session for the appointment of presidential electors under certain circumstances. **Passed:** 507,716 for; 308,643 against.

**HJR 47** — Authorizing the cancellation of an election to fill a vacancy in the legislature when a candidate is running unopposed. **Passed:** 557,707 for; 267,724 against.

**HJR 52** — Clearing certain land titles in Bastrop County by relinquishing and releasing any claim of sovereign ownership or title to the lands. **Passed:** 596,765 for; 205,499 against.

**HJ R 53** — Granting the legislature authority to release the state's interest in land that is held by a person in good faith under color of title. **Passed:** 512,163 for; 284,918 against.

**HJR 75** — To eliminate obsolete, archaic, redundant and unnecessary provisions and to clarify, update and harmonize certain provisions of the Texas Constitution. **Passed:** 619,945 for;189,541 against.

**HJR 81** — Providing for the issuance of additional general obligation bonds by the Texas Water Development Board. **Passed:** 506,077 for; 287,339 against.

**HJR 82** — Authorizing the Veterans' Land Board to issue additional general obligation bonds and to use certain assets in certain funds to provide for veterans' cemeteries. **Passed:** 611,943 for; 207,484 against.

**HJR 85** — To allow current and retired public-school teachers and retired public-school administrators to receive compensation for serving on the governing bodies of local governmental districts. **Passed:** 547,588 for; 275,575 against.

**HJR 97** — Authorizing the issuance of general obligation bonds for construction and repair projects. **Passed:** 509,148 for; 305,265 against.

**SJR 2** — Authorizing the legislature to authorize the board of trustees of an independent school district to donate certain surplus district property of historical significance in order to preserve the property. **Passed:** 658,463 for; 160,048 against.

**SJR 6** — Authorizing the legislature to exempt from ad valorem taxation tangible personal property held at certain locations only temporarily for assembling, manufacturing, processing or other commercial purposes. **Passed:** 499,514 for; 293,764 against.

**SJR 16** — Creating the Texas Mobility Fund and authorizing grants and loans of money and issuance of obligations for financing the construction, reconstruction, acquisition, operation and expansion of state highways, turnpikes, toll roads, toll bridges and other mobility projects. **Passed:** 543,759 for; 259,188 against.

**SJR 32** — Authorizing municipalities to donate outdated and surplus firefighting equipment or supplies to underdeveloped countries. **Passed:** 595,707 for; 239,139 against.

**SJR 37** — Authorizing the issuance of general obligation bonds or notes to provide financial assistance to counties for roadway projects to serve border colonias. **Passed:** 507,357 for; 318,447 against.

**SJR 47** — To authorize the legislature to exempt from ad valorem taxation raw cocoa and green coffee that is held in Harris County. **Passed:** 411,339 for; 386,931 against.

**SJR 49** — To promote uniformity in the collection, deposit, reporting and remitting of civil and criminal fees. **Passed:** 647,439 for; 151,213 against.

## Amendments, 2003

. The following 22 amendments were submitted to the voters by the 78th Legislature in an election on **Sept. 13, 2003:**

**HJR 3** — Concerning civil lawsuits against doctors and health care providers, and other actions, authorizing the legislature to determine limitations on non-economic damages.

**HJR 16** — Authorize a county, a city or town, or a junior college district to establish an ad valorem tax freeze on res-

idence homesteads of the disabled and of the elderly and their spouses.

**HJR 21** — Prohibiting an increase in the total amount of school district ad valorem taxes that may be imposed on the residence homestead of a disabled person.

**HJR 23** — Permitting refinancing of a home equity loan with a reverse mortgage.

**HJR 28** — Authorizing the borrowing of money on a short-term basis by a state transportation agency for transportation-related projects, and the issuance of bonds and other public securities secured by the state highway fund.

**HJR 44** — Permiting a six-person jury in a district court misdemeanor trial.

**HJR 51** — Establishing a two-year period for the redemption of a mineral interest sold for unpaid ad valorem taxes at a tax sale.

**HJR 54** — Providing that certain benefits in certain public retirement systems may not be reduced or impaired.

**HJR 55** — Authorizing the legislature to exempt from ad valorem taxation property owned by a religious organization that is leased for use as a school or that is owned with the intent of expanding or constructing a religious facility.

**HJR 59** — Authorizing the legislature to permit a person to assume an office of a political subdivision without an election if the person is the only candidate to qualify in an election for that office.

**HJR 61** — Authorizing municipalities to donate surplus fire-fighting equipment or supplies for the benefit of rural volunteer fire departments.

**HJR 62** — Authorizing the legislature to permit a person to take office without an election if the person is the only candidate to qualify in an election for that office.

**HJR 68** — Authorizing the Veterans' Land Board to make certain payments on revenue bonds and to use assets in certain funds to provide for veterans homes and a constitutional amendment relating to the use of income and appreciation of the permanent school fund. **Note:** This bill proposes two different ballot propositions: Prop. 1 — Authorizing the Veterans' Land Board to use assets in certain veterans' land and veterans' housing assistance funds to provide veterans homes for the aged or infirm and to make principal, interest, and bond enhancement payments on revenue bonds, and Prop. 9 — Relating to the use of income and appreciation of the permanent school fund.

**HJR 84** — Providing for the filling of a temporary vacancy in a public office created by the activation for military service of a public officer.

**HJR 85** — Allowing the legislature to authorize and govern the operation of wineries in this state.

**SJR 19** — Permitting a current or retired faculty member of a public college or university to receive compensation for service on the governing body of a water district.

**SJR 25** — Authorizing the legislature to exempt certain travel trailers from ad valorem taxation.

**SJR 30** — Relating to the provision of parks and recreational facilities by certain conservation and reclamation districts.

**SJR 42** — Authorizing a home equity line of credit, providing for administrative interpretation of home equity lending law, and otherwise relating to the making, refinancing, repayment, and enforcement of home equity loans.

**SJR 45** — Repealing the authority of the legislature to provide for the creation of rural fire prevention districts.

**SJR 55** — Authorizing the issuance of general obligation bonds or notes to provide loans to defense-related communities for economic development projects, including those that enhance military value of military installations. ☆

---

# Joint Resolution for Annexing Texas
# to the United States

(For an overview of the subject, please see these discussions: The New Handbook of Texas, Texas State Historical Association, Austin, 1996; Vol. 1, pages 192–193. On the Web: **www.tsha.utexas.edu/handbook/online/articles/view/AA/mga2.html**. Also see the Texas State Library and Archives Web site: **www.tsl.state.tx.us/ref/abouttx/annexation/index.html**.)

---

**Resolved**

by the Senate and House of Representatives of the United States of America in Congress assembled, That Congress doth consent that the territory properly included within and rightfully belonging to the Republic of Texas, may be erected into a new State to be called the State of Texas, with a republican form of government adopted by the people of said Republic, by deputies in convention assembled, with the consent of the existing Government in order that the same may by admitted as one of the States of this Union.

2. And be it further resolved, That the foregoing consent of Congress is given upon the following conditions, to wit: First, said state to be formed, subject to the adjustment by this government of all questions of boundary that may arise with other government, --and the Constitution thereof, with the proper evidence of its adoption by the people of said Republic of Texas, shall be transmitted to the President of the United States, to be laid before Congress for its final action on, or before the first day of January, one thousand eight hundred and forty-six. Second, said state when admitted into the Union, after ceding to the United States all public edifices, fortifications, barracks, ports and harbors, navy and navy yards, docks, magazines and armaments, and all other means pertaining to the public defense, belonging to the said Republic of Texas, shall retain funds, debts, taxes and dues of every kind which may belong to, or be due and owing to the said Republic; and shall also retain all the vacant and unappropriated lands lying within its limits, to be applied to the payment of the debts and liabilities of said Republic of Texas, and the residue of said lands, after discharging said debts and liabilities, to be disposed of as said State may direct; but in no event are said debts and liabilities to become a charge upon the Government of the United States. Third -- New States of convenient size not exceeding four in number, in addition to said State of Texas and having sufficient population, may, hereafter by the consent of said State, be formed out of the territory thereof, which shall be entitled to admission under the provisions of the Federal Constitution; and such states as may be formed out of the territory lying south of thirty-six degrees thirty minutes north latitude, commonly known as the Missouri Compromise Line, shall be admitted into the Union, with or without slavery, as the people of each State, asking admission shall desire; and in such State or States as shall be formed out of said territory, north of said Missouri Compromise Line, slavery, or involuntary servitude (except for crime) shall be prohibited.

3. And be it further resolved, That if the President of the United States shall in his judgment and discretion deem it most advisable, instead of proceeding to submit the foregoing resolution of the Republic of Texas, as an overture on the part of the United States for admission, to negotiate with the Republic; then,

Be it resolved, That a State, to be formed out of the present Republic of Texas, with suitable extent and boundaries, and with two representatives in Congress, until the next appointment of representation, shall be admitted into the Union, by virtue of this act, on an equal footing with the existing States, as soon as the terms and conditions of such admission, and the cession of the remaining Texian territory to the United States shall be agreed upon by the governments of Texas and the United States: And that the sum of one hundred thousand dollars be, and the same is hereby, appropriated to defray the expenses of missions and negotiations, to agree upon the terms of said admission and cession, either by treaty to be submitted to the Senate, or by articles to be submitted to the two houses of Congress, as the President may direct.

Approved, March 1, 1845.

*Source: Peters, Richard, ed., The Public Statutes at Large of the United States of America, v.5, pp. 797-798, Boston, Chas. C. Little and Jas. Brown, 1850.*

# Texas' Chief Governmental Officials

On this and following pages are lists of the principal administrative officials who have served the Republic and State of Texas with dates of their tenures of office. In a few instances there are disputes as to the exact dates of tenures. Dates listed here are those that appear the most authentic.

★ ★ ★ ★ ★ ★ ★

## Governors and Presidents
### *Spanish Royal Governors

| | |
|---|---|
| Domingo Terán de los Rios | 1691-1692 |
| Gregorio de Salinas Varona | 1692-1697 |
| Francisco Cuerbo y Valdés | 1698-1702 |
| Mathías de Aguirre | 1703-1705 |
| Martín de Alarcón | 1705-1708 |
| Simón Padilla y Córdova | 1708-1712 |
| Pedro Fermin de Echevers y Subisa | 1712-1714 |
| Juan Valdéz | 1714-1716 |
| Martín de Alarcón | 1716-1719 |
| José de Azlor y Virto de Vera, Marqués de San Miguel de Aguayo | 1719-1722 |
| Fernando Pérez de Almazán | 1722-1727 |
| Melchor de Mediavilla y Azcona | 1727-1731 |
| Juan Antonio Bustillo y Ceballos | 1731-1734 |
| Manuel de Sandoval | 1734-1736 |
| Carlos Benites Franquis de Lugo | 1736-1737 |
| Joseph Fernández de Jáuregui y Urrutia | 1737-1737 |
| Prudencio de Orobio y Basterra | 1737-1741 |
| Tomás Felipe Winthuisen (or Winthuysen) | 1741-1743 |
| Justo Boneo y Morales | 1743-1744 |
| Francisco García Larios | 1744-1748 |
| Pedro del Barrio Junco y Espriella | 1748-1750 |
| Jacinto de Barrios y Jáuregui | 1751-1759 |
| Angel de Martos y Navarrete | 1759-1767 |
| Hugo Oconór | 1767-1770 |
| Juan María Vicencio, Barón de Ripperdá | 1770-1778 |
| Domingo Cabello y Robles | 1778-1786 |
| Rafael Martínez Pacheco | 1787-1790 |
| Manuel Muñoz | 1790-1799 |
| Juan Bautista de Elguezábal | 1799-1805 |
| Antonio Cordero y Bustamante | 1805-1808 |
| Manuel María de Salcedo | 1808-1813 |
| Juan Bautista de las Casas (revolutionary gov.) | 1811-1811 |
| Cristóbal Domínguez, Benito de Armiñan, Mariano Varela, Juan Ignacio Pérez, Manuel Pardo | 1813-1817 |
| Antonio María Martínez | 1817-1821 |

*Some authorities would include Texas under administrations of several earlier Spanish Governors. The late Dr. C. E. Castañeda, Latin-American librarian of The University of Texas and authority on the history of Texas and the Southwest, would include the following four: Francisco de Garay, 1523-26; Pánfilo de Narváez, 1526-28; Nuño de Guzmán, 1528-30; Hernando de Soto, 1538-43.

### Governors Under Mexican Rule

The first two Governors under Mexican rule, Trespalacios and García, were of Texas only as Texas was then constituted. Beginning with Gonzáles, 1824, the Governors were for the joint State of Coahuila y Texas.

| | |
|---|---|
| José Felix Trespalacios | 1822-1823 |
| Luciano García | 1823-1824 |
| Rafael Gonzáles | 1824-1826 |
| Victor Blanco | 1826-1827 |
| José María Viesca | 1827-1830 |
| Ramón Eca y Músquiz | 1830-1831 |
| José María Letona | 1831-1832 |
| Ramón Eca y Músquiz | 1832-1832 |
| Juan Martín de Veramendi | 1832-1833 |
| Juan José de Vidáurri y Villasenor | 1833-1834 |
| Juan José Elguezábal | 1834-1835 |
| José María Cantú | 1835-1835 |
| Agustín M. Viesca | 1835-1835 |
| Marciel Borrego | 1835-1835 |
| Ramón Eca y Músquiz | 1835-1835 |

### Provisional Colonial Governor, Before Independence

Henry Smith (Impeached) .......................................1835

James W. Robinson served as acting Governor just prior to March 2, 1836, after Smith was impeached.

### Presidents of the Republic of Texas

| | |
|---|---|
| David G. Burnet | Mar. 16, 1836-Oct. 22, 1836 |
| (provisional President) | |
| Sam Houston | Oct. 22, 1836-Dec. 10, 1838 |
| Mirabeau B. Lamar | Dec. 10, 1838-Dec. 13, 1841 |
| Sam Houston | Dec. 13, 1841-Dec. 9, 1844 |
| Anson Jones | Dec. 9, 1844-Feb. 19, 1846 |

### Governors Since Annexation

J. Pinckney Henderson ....... Feb. 19, 1846-Dec. 21, 1847

(Albert C. Horton served as acting Governor while Henderson was away in the Mexican War.)

| | |
|---|---|
| George T. Wood | Dec. 21, 1847-Dec. 21, 1849 |
| Peter Hansbrough Bell | Dec. 21, 1849-Nov. 23, 1853 |
| J. W. Henderson | Nov. 23, 1853-Dec. 21, 1853 |
| Elisha M. Pease | Dec. 21, 1853-Dec. 21, 1857 |
| Hardin R. Runnels | Dec. 21, 1857-Dec. 21, 1859 |
| Sam Houston (resigned because of state's secession from the Union) | Dec. 21, 1859-Mar. 16, 1861 |
| Edward Clark | Mar. 16, 1861-Nov. 7, 1861 |
| Francis R. Lubbock (resigned to enter Confederate Army) | Nov. 7, 1861-Nov. 5, 1863 |
| Pendleton Murrah (administration terminated by fall of Confederacy) | Nov. 5, 1863-June 17, 1865 |
| Fletcher S. Stockdale (Lt. Gov. performed some duties of office on Murrah's departure, but is sometimes included in list of Governors. Hamilton's appointment was for immediate succession, as shown by the dates.) | |
| Andrew J. Hamilton (Provisional, appointed by President Johnson) | June 17, 1865-Aug. 9, 1866 |
| James W. Throckmorton | Aug. 9, 1866-Aug. 8, 1867 |
| Elisha M. Pease (appointed July 30, 1867, under martial law) | Aug. 8, 1867-Sept. 30, 1869 |

### Interregnum

Pease resigned and vacated office Sept. 30, 1869; no successor was named until Jan. 8, 1870. Some historians extend Pease's term until Jan. 8, 1870, but in reality Texas was without a head of its civil government from Sept. 30, 1869, until Jan. 8, 1870.

| | |
|---|---|
| Edmund J. Davis (appointed provisional Governor after being elected) | Jan. 8, 1870-Jan. 15, 1874 |
| Richard Coke (resigned to enter United States Senate) | Jan. 15, 1874-Dec. 1, 1876 |
| Richard B. Hubbard | Dec. 1, 1876-Jan. 21, 1879 |
| Oran M. Roberts | Jan. 21, 1879-Jan. 16, 1883 |
| John Ireland | Jan. 16, 1883-Jan. 18, 1887 |
| Lawrence Sullivan Ross | Jan. 18, 1887-Jan. 20, 1891 |
| James Stephen Hogg | Jan. 20, 1891-Jan. 15, 1895 |
| Charles A. Culberson | Jan. 15, 1895-Jan. 17, 1899 |
| Joseph D. Sayers | Jan. 17, 1899-Jan. 20, 1903 |
| S. W. T. Lanham | Jan. 20, 1903-Jan. 15, 1907 |
| Thos. Mitchell Campbell | Jan. 15, 1907-Jan. 17, 1911 |
| Oscar Branch Colquitt | Jan. 17, 1911-Jan. 19, 1915 |
| James E. Ferguson (impeached) | Jan. 19, 1915-Aug. 25, 1917 |
| William Pettus Hobby | Aug. 25, 1917-Jan. 18, 1921 |
| Pat Morris Neff | Jan. 18, 1921-Jan. 20, 1925 |
| Miriam A. Ferguson | Jan. 20, 1925-Jan. 17, 1927 |

Dan Moody ..........................Jan. 17, 1927-Jan. 20, 1931
Ross S. Sterling..................Jan. 20, 1931-Jan. 17, 1933
Miriam A. Ferguson ............Jan. 17, 1933-Jan. 15, 1935
James V. Allred ...................Jan. 15, 1935-Jan. 17, 1939
W. Lee O'Daniel (*resigned to enter United States
  Senate*)............................ Jan. 17, 1939-Aug. 4, 1941
Coke R. Stevenson .............. Aug. 4, 1941-Jan. 21, 1947
Beauford H. Jester.............. Jan. 21, 1947-July 11, 1949
Allan Shivers (*Lt. Governor succeeded on death of
  Governor Jester. Elected in 1950 and re-elected
  in 1952 and 1954*) .......... July 11, 1949-Jan. 15, 1957
Price Daniel ........................Jan. 15, 1957-Jan. 15, 1963
John Connally.....................Jan. 15, 1963-Jan. 21, 1969
Preston Smith .....................Jan. 21, 1969-Jan. 16, 1973
*Dolph Briscoe....................Jan. 16, 1973-Jan. 16, 1979
**William P. Clements ..........Jan. 16, 1979-Jan. 18, 1983
Mark White .........................Jan. 18, 1983-Jan. 20, 1987
**William P. Clements ..........Jan. 20, 1987-Jan. 15, 1991
Ann W. Richards ................. Jan. 15, 1991-Jan. 17, 1995
**George W. Bush................Jan. 17, 1995-Dec. 21, 2000
**Rick Perry (*Lt. Governor succeeded on inauguration
  of Bush as U.S. President*........ Dec. 21, 2000-Present

*Effective in 1975, term of office was raised to 4 years,
according to a constitutional amendment approved by Texas
voters in 1972. See introduction to State Government chapter
in this edition for other state officials whose terms were raised
to four years.
**Republicans.*

★ ★ ★ ★ ★ ★ ★

## Vice Presidents and Lieutenant Governors

### Vice Presidents of Republic

|  | Date Elected |
|---|---|
| Lorenzo de Zavala (*provisional Vice President*) | |
| Mirabeau B. Lamar | Sept. 5, 1836 |
| David G. Burnet | Sept. 3, 1838 |
| Edward Burleson | Sept. 6, 1841 |
| Kenneth L. Anderson | Sept. 2, 1844 |

### Lieutenant Governors

Albert C. Horton...............................................1846-1847
John A. Greer ...................................................1847-1851
J. W. Henderson...............................................Aug. 4, 1851
D. C. Dickson ...................................................1853-1855
H. R. Runnels....................................................Aug. 6, 1855
F. R. Lubbock....................................................Aug. 4, 1857
Edward Clark ....................................................Aug. 1, 1859
John M. Crockett...............................................1861-1863
Fletcher S. Stockdale........................................1863-1866
George W. Jones ..............................................1866
(*Jones was removed by General Sheridan.*)
J. W. Flanagan..................................................1869
(*Flanagan was appointed U.S. Senator and was
never inaugurated as Lt. Gov.*)
R. B. Hubbard ...................................................1873-1876
J. D. Sayers......................................................1878-1880
L. J. Storey .......................................................1880-1882
Marion Martin ...................................................1882-1884
Barnett Gibbs ...................................................1884-1886
T. B. Wheeler....................................................1886-1890
George C. Pendleton ........................................1890-1892
M. M. Crane ................Jan. 17, 1893-Jan. 25, 1895
George T. Jester ...............................................1895-1898
J. N. Browning...................................................1898-1902
George D. Neal .................................................1902-1906
A. B. Davidson ..................................................1906-1912
Will H. Mayes ...................................................1912-1914
William Pettus Hobby........................................1914-1917
W. A. Johnson (*served Hobby's unexpired
term and until*....................................................January 1920)
Lynch Davidson .................................................1920-1922
T. W. Davidson ..................................................1922-1924
Barry Miller .......................................................1924-1931
Edgar E. Witt.....................................................1931-1935
Walter Woodul ..................................................1935-1939

Coke R. Stevenson...........................................1939-1941
John Lee Smith .................................1943-Jan. 21, 1947
Allan Shivers ....................Jan. 21, 1947-July 11, 1949

(*Shivers succeeded to the governorship on death of Governor Beauford H. Jester.*)

Ben Ramsey.....................................1951-Sept. 18, 1961
(*Ben Ramsey resigned to become a member of the State Railroad Commission.*)

Preston Smith....................................................1963-1969
Ben Barnes .......................................................1969-1973
William P. Hobby Jr. ..........................................1973-1991
Robert D. Bullock..............................................1991-1999
Rick Perry..........................................1999-Dec. 21, 2000
*Bill Ratliff.............................Dec. 28, 2000-Jan. 21, 2003
David Dewhurst...............................Jan. 21, 2003-Present

*Elected by Senate when Rick Perry succeeded to governorship on election of George W. Bush as U.S. President.*

★ ★ ★ ★ ★ ★ ★

## Secretaries of State
### Republic of Texas

*Raines Yearbook for Texas, 1901, gives the following record of Secretaries of State during the era of the Republic of Texas:*

**Under David G. Burnet** — Samuel P. Carson, James Collingsworth and W. H. Jack.

**Under Sam Houston** (first term) — Stephen F. Austin, 1836. J. Pinckney Henderson and Dr. Robert A. Irion, 1837-38.

**Under Mirabeau B. Lamar** — Bernard Bee appointed Dec. 16, 1838; James Webb appointed Feb. 6, 1839; D. G. Burnet appointed Acting Secretary of State, May 31, 1839; N. Amory appointed Acting Secretary of State, July 23, 1839; D. G. Burnet appointed Acting Secretary of State, Aug. 5, 1839; Abner S. Lipscomb appointed Secretary of State, Jan. 31, 1840, and resigned Jan. 22, 1841; Joseph Waples appointed Acting Secretary of State, Jan. 23, 1841, and served until Feb. 8, 1841; James S. Mayfield appointed Feb. 8, 1841; Joseph Waples appointed April 30, 1841, and served until May 25, 1841; Samuel A. Roberts appointed May 25, 1841; reappointed Sept. 7, 1841.

**Under Sam Houston** (second term) — E. Lawrence Stickney, Acting Secretary of State until Anson Jones appointed Dec. 13, 1841. Jones served as Secretary of State throughout this term except during the summer and part of this term of 1842, when Joseph Waples filled the position as Acting Secretary of State.

**Under Anson Jones** — Ebenezer Allen served from Dec. 10, 1844, until Feb. 5, 1845, when Ashbel Smith became Secretary of State. Allen was again named Acting Secretary of State, March 31, 1845, and later named Secretary of State.

(*In addition to the above, documents in theTexas State Archives indicate that Joseph C. Eldredge, Chief Clerk of the State Department during much of the Republic's existence, signed a number of documents in the absence of the officeholder in the capacity of "Acting Secretary of State."*)

### State Secretaries of State

Charles Mariner......................Feb. 20, 1846-May 4, 1846
David G. Burnet........................May 4, 1846-Jan. 1, 1848
Washington D. Miller.................Jan. 1, 1848-Jan. 2, 1850
James Webb......................... Jan. 2, 1850-Nov. 14, 1851
Thomas H. Duval..................Nov. 14, 1851-Dec. 22, 1853
Edward Clark.......................... Dec. 22, 1853-Dec., 1857
T. S. Anderson ............................ Dec. 1857-Dec. 27, 1859
E. W. Cave ..........................Dec. 27, 1859-Mar. 16, 1861
Bird Holland........................... Mar. 16, 1861-Nov., 1861
Charles West....................................Nov., 1861-Sept., 1862
Robert J. Townes .................. Sept., 1862-May 2, 1865
Charles R. Pryor...................... May 2, 1865-Aug., 1865
James H. Bell ...............................Aug., 1865-Aug., 1866

John A. Green .............................. Aug., 1866-Aug., 1867
D. W. C. Phillips .............................. Aug., 1867-Jan., 1870
J. P. Newcomb.........................Jan. 1, 1870-Jan. 17, 1874
George Clark .......................Jan. 17, 1874-Jan. 27, 1874
A. W. DeBerry .......................Jan. 27, 1874-Dec. 1, 1876
Isham G. Searcy ...................Dec. 1, 1876-Jan. 23, 1879
J. D. Templeton .......................Jan. 23, 1879-Jan. 22, 1881
T. H. Bowman.......................Jan. 22, 1881-Jan. 18, 1883
J. W. Baines .........................Jan. 18, 1883-Jan. 21, 1887
John M. Moore ......................Jan. 21, 1887-Jan. 22, 1891
George W. Smith..................Jan. 22, 1891-Jan. 17, 1895
Allison Mayfield......................Jan. 17, 1895-Jan. 5, 1897
J. W. Madden .........................Jan. 5, 1897-Jan. 18, 1899
D. H. Hardy ..........................Jan. 18, 1899-Jan. 19, 1901
John G. Tod...............................Jan. 19, 1901-Jan., 1903
J. R. Curl ......................................Jan., 1903-April, 1905
O. K. Shannon ..............................April, 1905-Jan., 1907
L. T. Dashiel ...................................Jan., 1907-Feb., 1908
W. R. Davie ...................................Feb., 1908-Jan., 1909
W. B. Townsend...............................Jan., 1909-Jan., 1911
C. C. McDonald..................................Jan., 1911-Dec., 1912
J. T. Bowman...................................Dec., 1912-Jan., 1913
John L. Wortham .........................Jan., 1913-June, 1913
F. C. Weinert .................................June, 1913-Nov., 1914
D. A. Gregg ..................................... Nov., 1914-Jan., 1915
John G. McKay ...............................Jan., 1915-Dec., 1916
C. J. Bartlett ...................................Dec., 1916-Nov., 1917
George F. Howard ...........................Nov., 1917-Nov., 1920
C. D. Mims ...................................... Nov., 1920-Jan., 1921
S. L. Staples....................................Jan., 1921-Aug., 1924
J. D. Strickland .....................Sept., 1924-Jan. 1, 1925
Henry Hutchings......................Jan. 1, 1925-Jan. 20, 1925
Mrs. Emma G. Meharg.............Jan. 20, 1925-Jan., 1927
Mrs. Jane Y. McCallum....................Jan., 1927-Jan., 1933
W. W. Heath .......................................Jan., 1933-Jan., 1935
Gerald C. Mann .........................Jan., 1935-Aug. 31, 1935
R. B. Stanford .................... Aug. 31, 1935-Aug. 25, 1936
B. P. Matocha ......................Aug. 25, 1936-Jan. 18, 1937
Edward Clark.............................Jan. 18, 1937-Jan., 1939
Tom L. Beauchamp........................Jan., 1939-Oct., 1939
M. O. Flowers......................Oct. 26, 1939-Feb. 25, 1941
William J. Lawson ....................Feb. 25, 1941-Jan., 1943
Sidney Latham..................................Jan., 1943-Feb., 1945
Claude Isbell ................................... Feb., 1945-Jan., 1947
Paul H. Brown .......................Jan., 1947-Jan. 19, 1949
Ben Ramsey ...................... Jan. 19, 1949-Feb. 9, 1950
John Ben Shepperd.............Feb. 9, 1950-April 30, 1952
Jack Ross ......................... April 30, 1952-Jan. 9, 1953
Howard A. Carney ..................Jan. 9, 1953-Apr. 30, 1954
C. E. Fulgham ...................... May 1, 1954-Feb. 15, 1955
Al Muldrow............................Feb. 16, 1955-Nov. 1, 1955
Tom Reavley ......................... Nov. 1, 1955-Jan. 16, 1957
Zollie Steakley .......................Jan. 16, 1957-Jan. 2, 1962
P. Frank Lake .........................Jan. 2, 1962-Jan. 15, 1963
Crawford C. Martin........... Jan. 15, 1963-March 12, 1966
John L. Hill ....................... March 12, 1966-Jan. 22, 1968
Roy Barrera ........................ March 7, 1968-Jan. 23, 1969
Martin Dies Jr. ...................... Jan. 23, 1969-Sept. 1, 1971
Robert D. (Bob) Bullock .......... Sept. 1, 1971-Jan. 2, 1973
V. Larry Teaver Jr. ...................Jan. 2, 1973-Jan. 19, 1973
Mark W. White Jr. ................. Jan. 19, 1973-Oct. 27,1977
Steven C. Oaks......................Oct. 27, 1977-Jan. 16, 1979
George W. Strake Jr...............Jan. 16, 1979-Oct. 6, 1981
David A. Dean.......................Oct. 22, 1981-Jan. 18, 1983
John Fainter.......................... Jan. 18, 1983-July 31, 1984
Myra A. McDaniel ................. Sept. 6, 1984-Jan. 26, 1987
Jack Rains ...........................Jan. 26, 1987-June 15, 1989
George Bayoud Jr.............June 19, 1989-Jan. 15, 1991
John Hannah Jr. .............. Jan. 17, 1991-March 11, 1994
Ronald Kirk....................... April 4, 1994 to Jan. 17, 1995
Antonio O. "Tony" Garza Jr.Jan. 18, 1995 to Nov. 24, 1997
Alberto R. Gonzales ........... Dec. 2, 1997 to Feb. 9, 1999
Elton Bomer......................... Feb. 9, 1999 to Dec. 31, 2000
Henry Cuellar .....................Jan. 2, 2001 to Jan. 7, 2002
*Gwyn Shea ...................... Jan. 7, 2002 -Aug. 4, 2003

*Shea resigned effective Aug. 4, 2003, and a replacement had not been appointed by press time.

★ ★ ★ ★ ★ ★ ★

## Attorneys General

### Of the Republic

David Thomas and
  Peter W. Grayson ..................... Mar. 2-Oct. 22, 1836
J. Pinckney Henderson, Peter W. Grayson,
  John Birdsall, A. S. Thurston ..................... 1836-1838
J. C. Watrous............................Dec., 1838-June 1, 1840
Joseph Webb and F. A. Morris ......................1840-1841
George W. Terrell, Ebenezer Allen ..................1841-1844
Ebenezer Allen ...............................................1844-1846

### *Of the State

Volney E. Howard................... Feb. 21, 1846-May 7, 1846
John W. Harris.....................May 7, 1846-Oct. 31, 1849
Henry P. Brewster .................Oct. 31, 1849-Jan. 15, 1850
A. J. Hamilton.......................Jan. 15, 1850-Aug. 5, 1850
Ebenezer Allen ...................... Aug. 5, 1850-Aug. 2, 1852
Thomas J. Jennings............... Aug. 2, 1852-Aug. 4, 1856
James Willie ...................... Aug. 4, 1856-Aug. 2, 1858
Malcolm D. Graham ............... Aug. 2, 1858-Aug. 6, 1860
George M. Flournoy .............Aug. 6, 1860-Jan. 15, 1862
N. G. Shelley ...........................Feb. 3, 1862-Aug. 1, 1864
B. E. Tarver.........................Aug. 1, 1864-Dec. 11, 1865
Wm. Alexander ..................Dec. 11, 1865-June 25, 1866
W. M. Walton .....................June 25, 1866-Aug. 27, 1867
Wm. Alexander ......................Aug. 27, 1867-Nov. 5, 1867
Ezekiel B. Turner ....................Nov. 5, 1867-July 11, 1870
Wm. Alexander ....................July 11, 1870-Jan. 27, 1874
George Clark ......................Jan. 27, 1874-Apr. 25, 1876
H. H. Boone........................... Apr. 25, 1876-Nov. 5, 1878
George McCormick................. Nov. 5, 1878-Nov. 2, 1880
J. H. McLeary ........................Nov. 2, 1880-Nov. 7, 1882
John D. Templeton .................Nov. 7, 1882-Nov. 2, 1886
James S. Hogg.....................Nov. 2, 1886-Nov. 4, 1890
C. A. Culberson .....................Nov. 4, 1890-Nov. 6, 1894
M. M. Crane ..........................Nov. 6, 1894-Nov. 8, 1898
Thomas S. Smith ...................Nov. 8, 1898-Mar. 15,1901
C. K. Bell ............................ Mar. 20, 1901-Jan., 1904
R. V. Davidson .....................Jan., 1904-Dec. 31, 1909
Jewel P. Lightfoot .................. Jan. 1, 1910-Aug. 31, 1912
James D. Walthall...................Sept. 1, 1912-Jan. 1, 1913
B. F. Looney ........................ Jan. 1, 1913-Jan., 1919
C. M. Cureton ............................Jan., 1919-Dec., 1921
W. A. Keeling ............................Dec., 1921-Jan., 1925
Dan Moody ................................ Jan., 1925-Jan., 1927
Claude Pollard ...........................Jan., 1927-Sept., 1929
R. L. Bobbitt (Apptd.)......................Sept., 1929-Jan., 1931
James V. Allred ...........................Jan., 1931-Jan., 1935
William McCraw ..........................Jan., 1935-Jan., 1939
Gerald C. Mann (resigned)............ Jan., 1939-Jan., 1944
Grover Sellers ...........................Jan., 1944-Jan., 1947
Price Daniel .............................. Jan., 1947-Jan., 1953
John Ben Shepperd ................... Jan., 1953-Jan. 1, 1957
Will Wilson .................. Jan. 1, 1957-Jan. 15, 1963
Waggoner Carr ..................... Jan. 15, 1963-Jan. 1, 1967
Crawford C. Martin ...............Jan. 1, 1967-Dec. 29, 1972
John Hill................................. Jan. 1, 1973-Jan. 16, 1979
Mark White...................... Jan. 16, 1979 to Jan. 18, 1983
Jim Mattox ....................... Jan. 18, 1983 to Jan. 15, 1991
Dan Morales .................... Jan. 15, 1991 to Jan. 13, 1999
John Cornyn ......................... Jan. 13, 1999-Dec. 2, 2002
Greg Abbott ...................................Dec. 2, 2002-Present

*The first few Attorneys General held office by appointment of the Governor. The office was made elective in 1850 by constitutional amendment. Ebenezer Allen was the first elected Attorney General.

★ ★ ★ ★ ★ ★ ★

## Treasurers

### Of the Republic

Asa Brigham ....................................................... 1838-1840
James W. Simmons ............................................ 1840-1841

Asa Brigham.................................................. 1841-1844
Moses Johnson ............................................. 1844-1846

### Of the State

James H. Raymond ............... Feb. 24, 1846-Aug. 2, 1858
*C. H. Randolph..........................Aug. 2, 1858-June, 1865
*Samuel Harris .................... Oct. 2, 1865-June 25, 1866
W. M. Royston........................June 25, 1866-Sept. 1, 1867
John Y. Allen ..............................Sept. 1, 1867-Jan., 1869
**George W. Honey.......................... Jan., 1869-Jan., 1874
**B. Graham (short term) ............beginning May 27, 1872
A. J. Dorn.................................... Jan., 1874-Jan., 1879
F. R. Lubbock ............................. Jan., 1879-Jan., 1891
W. B. Wortham ............................ Jan., 1891-Jan., 1899
John W. Robbins.......................... Jan., 1899-Jan., 1907
Sam Sparks ................................ Jan., 1907-Jan., 1912
J. M. Edwards ............................. Jan., 1912-Jan., 1919
John W. Baker............................. Jan., 1919-Jan., 1921
G. N. Holton ...............................July, 1921-Nov. 21, 1921
C. V. Terrell .......................... Nov. 21, 1921-Aug. 15, 1924
S. L. Staples..........................Aug. 16, 1924-Jan. 15, 1925
W. Gregory Hatcher ......... Jan. 16, 1925-Jan. 1, 1931
Charley Lockhart .................. Jan. 1, 1931-Oct. 25, 1941
Jesse James......................Oct. 25, 1941-Sept. 29, 1977
Warren G. Harding............. Oct. 7, 1977-Jan. 3, 1983
Ann Richards ...................... Jan. 3, 1983- Jan. 2, 1991
Kay Bailey Hutchison.............. Jan. 2, 1991 to June 1993
†Martha Whitehead ...................June 1993 to Aug. 1996

*Randolph fled to Mexico upon collapse of Confederacy. No exact date is available for his departure from office or Harris' succession to the post. It is believed Harris took office Oct. 2, 1865.

**Honey was removed from office for a short period in 1872 and B. Graham served in his place.

† The office of Treasurer was eliminated by Constitutional amendment in an election Nov. 7, 1995, effective the last day of August 1996.

★ ★ ★ ★ ★ ★ ★

## Railroad Commission of Texas

(After the first three names in the following list, each commissioner's name is followed by a surname in parentheses. The name in parentheses is the name of the commissioner whom that commissioner succeeded.)

John H. Reagan ................. June 10, 1891-Jan. 20, 1903
L. L. Foster .......................... June 10, 1891-April 30, 1895
W. P. McLean ...................... June 10, 1891-Nov. 20, 1894
L. J. Storey (McLean) ...... Nov. 21, 1894-Mar. 28,1909
N. A. Stedman (Foster)............May 1, 1895-Jan. 4, 1897
Allison Mayfield (Stedman).....Jan. 5, 1897-Jan. 23, 1923
O. B. Colquitt (Reagan) ........Jan. 21, 1903-Jan. 17, 1911
William D. Williams (Storey)... April 28, 1909-Oct. 1, 1916
John L. Wortham (Colquitt).....Jan. 21, 1911-Jan. 1, 1913
Earle B. Mayfield (Wortham) Jan. 2, 1913-March 1, 1923
Charles Hurdleston (Williams)...... Oct. 10, 1916-Dec. 31, 1918
Clarence Gilmore (Hurdleston).Jan. 1, 1919-Jan. 1, 1929
N. A. Nabors (A. Mayfield) .. March 1, 1923-Jan. 18, 1925
William Splawn (E. Mayfield) March 1, 1923-Aug. 1, 1924
C. V. Terrell (Splawn) .............. Aug. 15, 1924-Jan. 1, 1939
Lon A. Smith ( Nabors) ...........Jan. 29, 1925-Jan. 1, 1941
Pat M. Neff (Gilmore) ................Jan. 1, 1929-Jan. 1, 1933
Ernest O. Thompson (Neff).......Jan. 1, 1933-Jan. 8, 1965
G. A. (Jerry) Sadler (Terrell) .....Jan. 1, 1939-Jan. 1, 1943
Olin Culberson (Smith) .........Jan. 1, 1941-June 22, 1961
Beauford Jester (Sadler) ........Jan. 1, 1943-Jan. 21, 1947
William J. Murray Jr. (Jester) Jan. 21, 1947-Apr. 10, 1963
Ben Ramsey (Culberson) .. Sept. 18, 1961-Dec. 31, 1976
Jim C. Langdon (Murray) ..... May 28, 1963-Dec. 31, 1977
Byron Tunnell (Thompson) . Jan. 11, 1965-Sept. 15, 1973
Mack Wallace (Tunnell)..... Sept. 18, 1973-Sept. 22, 1987
Jon Newton (Ramsey)............Jan. 10, 1977-Jan. 4, 1979
John H. Poerner (Langdon).....Jan. 2, 1978-Jan. 1, 1981
James E. (Jim) Nugent (Newton)Jan. 4, 1979-Jan. 3, 1995
Buddy Temple (Poerner)....... Jan. 2, 1981-March 2, 1986
Clark Jobe (Temple) ............ March 3, 1986-Jan. 5, 1987
John Sharp (Jobe)....................Jan. 6, 1987-Jan. 2, 1991
Kent Hance (Wallace)........... Sept. 23, 1987-Jan. 2, 1991

*Robert Krueger (Hance)........Jan. 3, 1991-Jan. 22, 1993
Lena Guerrero (Sharp) ....... Jan. 23, 1991-Sept. 25, 1992
James Wallace (Guerrero)........Oct. 2, 1992-Jan. 4, 1993
Barry Williamson (Wallace)......Jan. 5, 1993-Jan. 4, 1999
Mary Scott Nabers (Krueger) ..Feb. 9, 1993-Dec. 9, 1994
Carole K. Rylander (Nabers) . Dec. 10, 1994-Jan. 4, 1999
Charles Matthews (Nugent).......... Jan. 3, 1995-Present
Michael L. Williams (Rylander) ........ Jan. 4, 1999-Present
Antonio Garza (Williamson).. Jan. 4, 1999-Nov. 18, 2002
Victor Carrillo (Garza)...................Feb. 19, 2003-Present

* Robert Krueger resigned when Gov. Ann Richards appointed him interim U.S. Senator on the resignation of Sen.Lloyd Bentsen.

★ ★ ★ ★ ★ ★ ★

## Comptroller of Public Accounts

### Of the Republic

John H. Money..................... Dec. 30, 1835-Jan. 17, 1836
H. C. Hudson ........................Jan. 17, 1836-Oct. 22, 1836
E. M. Pease............................... June, 1837-Dec., 1837
F. R. Lubbock ............................... Dec., 1837-Jan., 1839
Jas. W. Simmons................ Jan. 15, 1839-Sept. 30, 1840
Jas. B. Shaw ....................Sept. 30, 1840-Dec. 24, 1841
F. R. Lubbock ........................ Dec. 24, 1841-Jan. 1, 1842
Jas. B. Shaw ...................... Jan. 1, 1842-Jan. 1, 1846

### Of the State

Jas. B. Shaw ...................... Feb. 24, 1846-Aug. 2, 1858
Clement R. Johns ...................Aug. 2, 1858-Aug. 1, 1864
Willis L. Robards.....................Aug. 1, 1864-Oct. 12, 1865
Albert H. Latimer...................Oct. 12, 1865-Mar. 27, 1866
Robert H. Taylor..................Mar. 27, 1866-June 25, 1866
Willis L. Robards................. June 25, 1866-Aug. 27, 1867
Morgan C. Hamilton............... Aug. 27, 1867-Jan. 8, 1870
A. Bledsoe ...........................Jan. 8, 1870-Jan. 20, 1874
Stephen H. Darden.................Jan. 20, 1874-Nov. 2, 1880
W. M. Brown...........................Nov. 2, 1880-Jan. 16, 1883
W. J. Swain .........................Jan. 16, 1883-Jan. 18, 1887
John D. McCall......................Jan. 18, 1887-Jan. 15, 1895
R. W. Finley ..........................Jan. 15, 1895-Jan. 15, 1901
R. M. Love.............................Jan. 15, 1901-Jan., 1903
J. W. Stephen ...........................Jan., 1903-Jan., 1911
W. P. Lane .................................Jan., 1911-Jan., 1915
H. B. Terrell ...............................Jan., 1915-Jan., 1920
M. L. Wiginton ...........................Jan., 1920-Jan., 1921
Lon A. Smith ..............................Jan., 1921-Jan., 1925
S. H. Terrell ...............................Jan., 1925-Jan., 1931
Geo. H. Sheppard ......................Jan., 1931-Jan. 17, 1949
Robert S. Calvert.....................Jan. 17, 1949-Jan., 1975
Robert D. (Bob) Bullock ..............Jan., 1975-Jan. 3, 1991
John Sharp ..........................Jan. 3, 1991 to Jan. 2, 1999
Carole Keeton Strayhorn .............Jan. 2, 1999 to Present

★ ★ ★ ★ ★ ★ ★

## U.S. Senators from Texas

U.S. Senators were selected by the legislatures of the states until the U.S. Constitution was amended in 1913 to require popular elections. In Texas, the first senator chosen by the voters in a general election was Charles A. Culberson in 1916. Because of political pressures, however, the rules of the Democratic Party of Texas were changed in 1904 to require that all candidates for office stand before voters in the primary. Consequently, Texas' senators faced voters in 1906, 1910 and 1912 before the U.S. Constitution was changed.

Following is the succession of Texas representatives in the United States Senate since the annexation of Texas to the Union in 1845:

### Houston Succession

Sam Houston..........................Feb. 21, 1846-Mar. 4, 1859
John Hemphill..........................Mar. 4, 1859-July 11, 1861

Louis T. Wigfall and W. S. Oldham took their seats in the Confederate Senate, Nov. 16, 1861, and served until the Confederacy collapsed. After that event, the State Legislature on Aug. 21, 1866, elected David G. Burnet and Oran M. Roberts to the United States Senate, anticipating immediate readmission to the Union, but they were not allowed to take their seats.

†Morgan C. Hamilton .............Feb. 22, 1870-Mar. 3, 1877
Richard Coke ...........................Mar. 4, 1877-Mar. 3, 1895
Horace Chilton ........................Mar. 3, 1895-Mar. 3, 1901
Joseph W. Bailey ....................Mar. 3, 1901-Jan. 8, 1913
Rienzi Melville Johnston ...........Jan. 8, 1913-Feb. 3, 1913
‡Morris Sheppard (died)......... Feb. 13, 1913-Apr. 9, 1941
Andrew J. Houston ................................June 2-26, 1941
W. Lee O'Daniel ......................Aug. 4, 1941-Jan. 3, 1949
Lyndon B. Johnson ................ Jan. 3, 1949-Jan. 20, 1961
William A. Blakley ............... Jan. 20, 1961-June 15, 1961
†John G. Tower .................... June 15, 1961-Jan. 21, 1985
†Phil Gramm...........................Jan. 21, 1985-Dec. 2, 2002
†John Cornyn .................................. Dec. 2, 2002-Present

## Rusk Succession

Thomas J. Rusk (died)...........Feb 21, 1846-July 29, 1857
J. Pinckney Henderson (*died*). Nov. 9, 1857-June 4, 1858
Matthias Ward (*appointed*
   *interim*) .............................. Sept. 29, 1858-Dec. 5, 1859
Louis T. Wigfall ....................Dec. 5, 1859-March 23, 1861

   *Succession was broken by the expulsion of Texas Senators following secession of Texas from Union. See note above under "Houston Succession" on Louis T. Wigfall, W. S. Oldham, Burnet and Roberts.*

†James W. Flanagan ..............Feb. 22, 1870-Mar. 3, 1875
Samuel B. Maxey....................Mar. 3, 1875-Mar. 3, 1887
John H. Reagan (*resigned*) ...Mar. 3, 1887-June 10, 1891
Horace Chilton (*filled vacancy on
   appointment*) .....................Dec. 7, 1891-Mar. 30,1892
Roger Q. Mills ....................... Mar. 30, 1892-Mar. 3, 1899
‡Charles A. Culberson ............ Mar. 3, 1899-Mar. 4, 1923
Earle B. Mayfield.................... Mar. 4, 1923-Mar. 4, 1929
Tom Connally...........................Mar. 4, 1929-Jan. 3, 1953
Price Daniel ........................Jan. 3, 1953-Jan. 15, 1957
William A. Blakley ................ Jan. 15. 1957-Apr. 27, 1957
Ralph W. Yarborough ........... Apr. 27, 1957-Jan. 12, 1971
§Lloyd Bentsen....................Jan. 12, 1971-Jan. 20, 1993
Robert Krueger....................Jan. 20, 1993-June 14, 1993
†Kay Bailey Hutchison................. June 14, 1993-Present

   † *Republicans*
   ‡ *First election to U.S. Senate held in 1916. Prior to that time, senators were appointed by the Legislature.*
   § *Resigned from Senate when appointed U.S. Secretary of Treasury by Pres. Bill Clinton.*

★ ★ ★ ★ ★ ★ ★

## Commissioners of the General Land Office
### For the Republic

John P. Borden.....................Aug. 23, 1837-Dec. 12, 1840
H. W. Raglin ...........................Dec. 12, 1840-Jan. 4, 1841
*Thomas William Ward .......... Jan. 4, 1841-Mar. 20, 1848

### For the State

George W. Smyth.................. Mar. 20, 1848-Aug. 4, 1851
Stephen Crosby...................... Aug. 4, 1851-Mar. 1, 1858
Francis M. White ....................Mar. 1, 1858-Mar. 1, 1862
Stephen Crosby.................... Mar. 1, 1862-Sept. 1, 1865
Francis M. White .................. Sept. 1, 1865-Aug. 7, 1866
Stephen Crosby.................. Aug. 7, 1866-Aug. 27, 1867
Joseph Spence...................Aug. 27, 1867-Jan. 19, 1870
Jacob Kuechler ................... Jan. 19, 1870-Jan. 20, 1874
J. J. Groos......................... Jan. 20, 1874-June 15, 1878
W. C. Walsh...........................July 30, 1878, Jan. 10, 1887
R. M. Hall .......................... Jan. 10, 1887-Jan. 16, 1891
W. L. McGaughey ............... Jan. 16, 1891-Jan. 26, 1895
A. J. Baker .......................... Jan. 26, 1895-Jan. 16, 1899
George W. Finger.................. Jan. 16, 1899-May 4, 1899
Charles Rogan ................... May 11, 1899-Jan. 10, 1903
John J. Terrell....................... Jan. 10, 1903-Jan. 11, 1909
J. T. Robison ............................Jan, 1909-Sept. 11, 1929
J. H. Walker .........................Sept. 11, 1929-Jan., 1937
William H. McDonald ..................... Jan, 1937-Jan., 1939
Bascom Giles ......................... Jan., 1939-Jan. 5, 1955
J. Earl Rudder.......................Jan. 5, 1955-Feb. 1, 1958
Bill Allcorn............................... Feb. 1, 1958-Jan. 1, 1961
Jerry Sadler........................... Jan. 1, 1961-Jan. 1, 1971

Bob Armstrong...........................Jan. 1, 1971-Jan. 1, 1983
Garry Mauro .............................Jan. 1, 1983-Jan. 7, 1999
David Dewhurst ......................... Jan. 7, 1999-Jan. 3, 2003
Jerry Patterson ............................... Jan. 3, 2003-Present
   *Part of term after annexation.*

★ ★ ★ ★ ★ ★ ★

## Speaker of the Texas House

*The Speaker of the Texas House of Representatives is the presiding officer of the lower chamber of the State Legislature. The official is elected at the beginning of each regular session by a vote of the members of the House.*

| Speaker, Residence | Year Elected | Legislature |
|---|---|---|
| William E. Crump, Bellville | 1846 | 1st |
| William H. Bourland, Paris | 1846 | 1st |
| James W. Henderson, Houston | 1847 | 2nd |
| Charles G. Keenan, Huntsville | 1849 | 3rd |
| David C. Dickson, Anderson | 1851 | 4th |
| Hardin R. Runnels, Boston | 1853 | 5th |
| Hamilton P. Bee, Laredo | 1855 | 6th |
| William S. Taylor, Larissa | 1857 | 7th |
| Matt F. Locke, Lafayette | 1858 | 7th |
| Marion DeKalb Taylor, Jefferson | 1859 | 8th |
| Constantine W. Buckley, Richmond | 1861 | 9th |
| Nicholas H. Darnell, Dallas | 1861 | 9th |
| Constantine W. Buckley, Richmond | 1863 | 9th |
| Marion DeKalb Taylor, Jefferson | 1863 | 10th |
| Nathaniel M. Burford, Dallas | 1866 | 11th |
| Ira H. Evans, Corpus Christi | 1870 | 12th |
| William H. Sinclair, Galveston | 1871 | 12th |
| Marion DeKalb Taylor, Jefferson | 1873 | 13th |
| Guy M. Bryan, Galveston | 1874 | 14th |
| Thomas R. Bonner, Tyler | 1876 | 15th |
| John H. Cochran, Dallas | 1879 | 16th |
| George R. Reeves, Pottsboro | 1881 | 17th |
| Charles R. Gibson, Waxahachie | 1883 | 18th |
| Lafayette L. Foster, Groesbeck | 1885 | 19th |
| George C. Pendleton, Belton | 1887 | 20th |
| Frank P. Alexander, Greenville | 1889 | 21st |
| Robert T. Milner, Henderson | 1891 | 22nd |
| John H. Cochran, Dallas | 1893 | 23rd |
| Thomas Slater Smith, Hillsboro | 1895 | 24th |
| L. Travis Dashiell, Jewett | 1897 | 25th |
| J. S. Sherrill, Greenville | 1899 | 26th |
| Robert E. Prince, Corsicana | 1901 | 27th |
| Pat M. Neff, Waco | 1903 | 28th |
| Francis W. Seabury, Rio Grande City | 1905 | 29th |
| Thomas B. Love, Lancaster | 1907 | 30th |
| Austin M. Kennedy, Waco | 1909 | 31st |
| John W. Marshall, Whitesboro | 1909 | 31st |
| Sam Rayburn, Bonham | 1911 | 32nd |
| Chester H. Terrell, San Antonio | 1913 | 33rd |
| John W. Woods, Rotan | 1915 | 34th |
| Franklin O. Fuller, Coldspring | 1917 | 35th |
| R. Ewing Thomason, El Paso | 1919 | 36th |
| Charles G. Thomas, Lewisville | 1921 | 37th |
| Richard E. Seagler, Palestine | 1923 | 38th |
| Lee Satterwhite, Amarillo | 1925 | 39th |
| Robert L. Bobbitt, Laredo | 1927 | 40th |
| W. S. Barron, Bryan | 1929 | 41st |
| Fred H. Minor, Denton | 1931 | 42nd |
| Coke R. Stevenson, Junction | 1933 | 43rd |
| " | 1935 | 44th |
| Robert W. Calvert, Hillsboro | 1937 | 45th |
| R. Emmett Morse, Houston | 1939 | 46th |
| Homer L. Leonard, McAllen | 1941 | 47th |
| Price Daniel, Liberty | 1943 | 48th |
| Claud H. Gilmer, Rocksprings | 1945 | 49th |
| William O. Reed, Dallas | 1947 | 50th |
| Durwood Manford, Smiley | 1949 | 51st |
| Reuben Senterfitt, San Saba | 1951 | 52nd |
| " | 1953 | 53rd |
| Jim T. Lindsey, Texarkana | 1955 | 54th |
| Waggoner Carr, Lubbock | 1957 | 55th |
| " | 1959 | 56th |
| James A. Turman, Gober | 1961 | 57th |
| Byron M. Tunnell, Tyler | 1963 | 58th |
| Ben Barnes, DeLeon | 1965 | 59th |
| " | 1967 | 60th |
| Gus F. Mutscher, Brenham | 1969 | 61st |
| " | 1971 | 62nd |
| Rayford Price, Palestine | 1972 | 62nd |
| Price Daniel Jr., Liberty | 1973 | 63rd |
| Bill Clayton, Springlake | 1975 | 64th |
| " | 1977 | 65th |
| " | 1979 | 66th |

| | | |
|---|---|---|
| Gibson D. Lewis, Fort Worth | 1981 | 67th |
| " | 1983 | 68th |
| " | 1985 | 69th |
| " | 1987 | 70th |
| " | 1989 | 71st |
| " | 1991 | 72nd |
| James M. (Pete) Laney, Hale Center | 1993 | 73rd |
| " | 1995 | 74th |
| " | 1997 | 75th |
| " | 1999 | 76th |
| Tom Craddick | 2001 | 77th |
| | 2003 | 78th |

★ ★ ★ ★ ★ ★ ★

## Chief Justice of the Supreme Court
### Republic of Texas

James Collinsworth .................. Dec. 16, 1836-July 23, 1838
John Birdsall ..................................... Nov. 19-Dec. 12, 1838
Thomas J. Rusk .................. Dec. 12, 1838-Dec. 5, 1840
John Hemphill .......................... Dec. 5, 1840-Dec. 29, 1845

### Under the Constitutions of 1845 and 1861

John Hemphill ...................... Mar. 2, 1846-Oct. 10, 1858
Royall T. Wheeler .......................... Oct. 11, 1858-April 1864
Oran M. Roberts ...................... Nov. 1, 1864-June 30, 1866

### Under the Constitution of 1866
### (Presidential Reconstruction)

*George F. Moore .................... Aug. 16, 1866-Sept. 10, 1867

*Removed under Congressional Reconstruction by military authorities who appointed members of the next court.

### Under the Constitution of 1866
### (Congressional Reconstruction)

Amos Morrill .............................. Sept. 10, 1867-July 5, 1870

### Under the Constitution of 1869

Lemuel D. Evans ......................... July 5, 1870-Aug. 31, 1873
Wesley Ogden .......................... Aug. 31, 1873-Jan. 29, 1874
Oran M. Roberts ...................... Jan. 29, 1874-Apr. 18, 1876

### Under the Constitution of 1876

Oran M. Roberts .................... Apr. 18, 1876-Oct. 1, 1878
George F. Moore ......................... Nov. 5, 1878-Nov. 1, 1881
Robert S. Gould ...................... Nov. 1, 1881-Dec. 23, 1882
Asa H. Willie ........................ Dec. 23, 1882-Mar. 3, 1888
John W. Stayton ...................... Mar. 3, 1888-July 5, 1894
Reuben R. Gaines .................... July 10, 1894-Jan. 5, 1911
Thomas J. Brown ...................... Jan. 7, 1911-May 26, 1915
Nelson Phillips ...................... June 1, 1915-Nov. 16, 1921
C. M. Cureton ...................... Dec. 2, 1921-Apr. 8, 1940
†Hortense Sparks Ward ............ Jan. 8, 1925-May 23, 1925
W. F. Moore ........................ Apr. 17, 1940-Jan. 1, 1941
James P. Alexander .................. Jan. 1, 1941-Jan. 1, 1948
J. E. Hickman ...................... Jan. 5, 1948-Jan. 3, 1961
Robert W. Calvert ...................... Jan. 3, 1961-Oct. 4, 1972
Joe R. Greenhill .................... Oct. 4, 1972-Oct. 25, 1982
Jack Pope ...................... Nov. 29, 1982-Jan. 5, 1985
John L. Hill Jr. ...................... Jan. 5, 1985-Jan. 4, 1988
Thomas R. Phillips ...................... Jan. 4, 1988-Present

†Mrs. Ward served as Chief Justice of a special Supreme Court to hear one case in 1925.

## Presiding Judges, Court of Appeals (1876-1891)
## and Court of Criminal Appeals (1891-Present)

Mat D. Ector .......................... May 6, 1876-Oct. 29, 1879
John P. White ........................ Nov. 9, 1879-Apr. 26, 1892
James M. Hurt ...................... May 4, 1892-Dec. 31, 1898
W. L. Davidson ...................... Jan. 2, 1899-June 27, 1913
A. C. Prendergast ................. June 27, 1913-Dec. 31, 1916
W. L. Davidson ...................... Jan. 1, 1917-Jan. 25, 1921
Wright C. Morrow ................... Feb. 8, 1921-Oct. 16, 1939
Frank Lee Hawkins ................ Oct. 16, 1939-Jan. 2, 1951
Harry N. Graves ................... Jan. 2, 1951-Dec. 31, 1954
W. A. Morrison ...................... Jan. 1, 1955-Jan. 2, 1961
Kenneth K. Woodley ................ Jan. 3, 1961-Jan. 4, 1965
W. T. McDonald ...................... Jan. 4, 1965-June 25, 1966
W. A. Morrison ................... June 25, 1966-Jan. 1, 1967
Kenneth K. Woodley ................ Jan. 1, 1967-Jan. 1, 1971
John F. Onion Jr. ...................... Jan. 1, 1971-Jan. 1, 1989
Michael J. McCormick ................. Jan. 1, 1989-Jan. 1, 2001
Sharon Keller ........................ Jan. 1, 2001-Present

★ ★ ★ ★ ★ ★ ★

## Administrators of Public Education
### Superintendents of Public Instruction

Pryor Lea ............................ Nov. 10, 1866-Sept. 12, 1867
Edwin M. Wheelock ............ Sept. 12, 1867-May 6, 1871

Jacob C. DeGress ................. May 6, 1871-Jan. 20, 1874
O. H. Hollingsworth ............... Jan. 20, 1874-May 6, 1884
B. M. Baker ...................... May 6, 1884-Jan. 18, 1887
O. H. Cooper ...................... Jan 18, 1887-Sept. 1, 1890
H. C. Pritchett ..................... Sept. 1, 1890-Sept. 15, 1891
J. M. Carlisle ...................... Sept. 15, 1891-Jan. 10, 1899
J. S. Kendall ...................... Jan. 10, 1899-July 2, 1901
Arthur Lefevre ...................... July 2, 1901-Jan. 12, 1905
R. B. Cousins ...................... Jan. 12, 1905-Jan. 1, 1910
F. M. Bralley ...................... Jan. 1, 1910-Sept. 1, 1913
W. F. Doughty ...................... Sept. 1, 1913-Jan. 1, 1919
Annie Webb Blanton .............. Jan. 1, 1919-Jan. 16, 1923
S. M. N. Marrs ............... Jan. 16, 1923-April 28, 1932
C. N. Shaver ...................... April 28, 1932-Oct. 1, 1932
L. W. Rogers ...................... Oct. 1, 1932-Jan. 16, 1933
L. A. Woods ...................... Jan. 16, 1933-*1951

### State Commissioner of Education

J. W. Edgar ...................... May 31, 1951-June 30, 1974
Marlin L. Brockette ................ July 1, 1974-Sept. 1, 1979
Alton O. Bowen ................... Sept. 1, 1979-June 1, 1981
Raymon Bynum ................... June 1, 1981-Oct. 31, 1984
W. N. Kirby ...................... April 13, 1985-July 1, 1991
Lionel R. Meno ................... July 1, 1991-March 1, 1995
Michael A. Moses ............... March 9, 1995-Aug. 18, 1999
Jim Nelson ...................... Aug. 18, 1999-March 25, 2002
**Felipe Alanis ................... March 25, 2002-July 31, 2003

*The office of State Superintendent of Public Instruction was abolished by the Gilmer-Aikin act of 1949 and the office of Commissioner of Education created, appointed by a new State Board of Education elected by the people.

**Alanis resigned effective July 31, 2003, and a replacement had not been appointed by press time.

## First Ladies of Texas

| | |
|---|---|
| Martha Evans Gindratt Wood | 1847-49 |
| †Bell Administration | 1849-53 |
| Lucadia Christiana Niles Pease | 1853-57; 1867-69 |
| ‡Runnels Administration | 1857-59 |
| Margaret Moffette Lea Houston | 1859-61 |
| Martha Evans Clark | 1861 |
| Adele Barron Lubbock | 1861-63 |
| Susie Ellen Taylor Murrah | 1863-65 |
| Mary Jane Bowen Hamilton | 1865-66 |
| Annie Rattan Throckmorton | 1866-67 |
| Ann Elizabeth Britton Davis | 1870-74 |
| Mary Home Coke | 1874-76 |
| Janie Roberts Hubbard | 1876-79 |
| Frances Wickliff Edwards Roberts | 1879-83 |
| Anne Maria Penn Ireland | 1883-87 |
| Elizabeth Dorothy Tinsley Ross | 1887-91 |
| Sarah Stinson Hogg | 1891-95 |
| Sally Harrison Culberson | 1895-99 |
| Orlene Walton Sayers | 1899-1903 |
| Sarah Beona Meng Lanham | 1903-07 |
| Fannie Brunner Campbell | 1907-11 |
| Alice Fuller Murrell Colquitt | 1911-15 |
| §Miriam A. Wallace Ferguson | 1915-17 |
| Willie Cooper Hobby | 1917-21 |
| Myrtle Mainer Neff | 1921-25 |
| Mildred Paxton Moody | 1927-31 |
| Maud Gage Sterling | 1931-33 |
| Jo Betsy Miller Allred | 1935-39 |
| Merle Estella Butcher O'Daniel | 1939-41 |
| **Fay Wright Stevenson | 1941-42 |
| **Edith Will Scott Stevenson | 1942-46 |
| Mabel Buchanan Jester | 1946-49 |
| Marialice Shary Shivers | 1949-57 |
| Jean Houston Baldwin Daniel | 1957-63 |
| Idanell Brill Connally | 1963-69 |
| Ima Mae Smith | 1969-73 |
| Betty Jane Slaughter Briscoe | 1973-79 |
| Rita Crocker Bass Clements | 1979-83 |
| Linda Gale Thompson White | 1983-87 |
| Rita Crocker Bass Clements | 1987-91 |
| Laura Welch Bush | 1995-2000 |
| Anita Thigpen Perry | 2000-Present |

†Gov. Peter Hansbrough Bell was not married while in office.
‡Gov. Hardin R. Runnels never married.
**Mrs. Coke R. (Fay Wright) Stevenson, the governor's wife, died in the Governor's Mansion Jan. 3, 1942. His mother, Edith Stevenson, served as Mistress of the Mansion thereafter. ☆

# State Government

Texas state government is divided into executive, legislative and judicial branches under the Texas Constitution adopted in 1876. The chief executive is the Governor, whose term is for four years. Other elected state officials with executive responsibilities include the Lieutenant Governor, Attorney General, Comptroller of Public Accounts, Commissioner of the General Land Office and Commissioner of Agriculture. The terms of those officials are also four years. The Secretary of State is appointed by the Governor.

Except for making numerous appointments and calling special sessions of the Legislature, the Governor's powers are limited in comparison with those in most states.

Current state executives and their addresses, phone numbers and "not-to-exceed" salaries for the 2004–2005 biennium (maximum possible salaries; actual salaries can be lower):

**Governor: Rick Perry**
P.O. Box 12428, Austin 78711
512-463-2000; www.governor.state.tx.us
$115,345

**Lt. Governor: David Dewhurst**
P.O. Box 12068, Austin 78711
512-463-0001; www.senate.state.tx.us
For salary, see note* below.

**Attorney General: Greg Abbott**
P.O. Box 12548, Austin 78711
512-463-2100; www.oag.state.tx.us
$92,217

**Comptroller of Public Accounts: Carole Keeton Strayhorn**
PO Box 13528, Austin 78774
512-463-4000; www.cpa.state.tx.us
$92,217

**Land Commissioner: Jerry Patterson**
1700 N. Congress, Austin 78701
512-463-5256; www.glo.state.tx.us
$92,217

**Commissioner of Agriculture: Susan Combs**
P.O. Box 12847, Austin 78711
512-463-7664; www.agr.state.tx.us
$92,217

**Secretary of State: Position open at press time**
P.O. Box 12887, Austin 78711
512-463-5770; www.sos.state.tx.us
$117,516

*Salary of Lt. Gov. is same as a Senator when serving as Pres.of the Senate; same as Gov. when serving as Gov.*

**Ombudsman Office** (Citizens' Advocate): Part of the Governor's office, the Ombudsman Office receives citizens's comments and complaints over the toll-free assistance hotline and passes them to government officials and refers citizens to sources of help. **Citizens' Assistance Hotline: 1-800-843-5789.**

## Texas Legislature

The Texas Legislature has **181 members: 31 in the Senate** and **150 in the House of Representatives.** Regular sessions convene on the second Tuesday of January in odd-numbered years, but the governor may call special sessions. Article III of the Texas Constitution deals with the legislative branch. On the Web: **www.capitol.state.tx.us.**

The following lists are of members of the **78th Legislature,** which convened for its Regular Session on Jan. 14, 2003, and adjourned on June 2, 2003. A First Called Special Session convened June 30, 2003, and adjoured July 28, 2003, and a Second Called Special Session convened July 28, 2003, and was still in session at press time. The **79th Legislature** is scheduled to convene on Jan. 11, 2005, and adjourn on May 30, 2005.

### State Senate

**Thirty-one members of the State Senate** are elected to **four-year, overlapping terms. Salary:** The salary of all members of the Legislature, both Senators and Representatives, is $7,200 per year and $124 per diem during legislative sessions; mileage allowance at same rate provided by law for state employees. The per diem payment applies during each regular and special session of the Legislature.

**Senatorial Districts** include one or more whole counties and some counties have more than one Senator.

The **address of Senators** is Texas Senate, P.O. Box 12068, Austin 78711-2068; phone 512-463-0001; Fax: 512-463-0326. On the Web: **www.senate.state.tx.us.**

**President of the Senate** is Lt. Gov. David Dewhurst; **President Pro Tempore** — Eddie Lucio, Jr.; **Secretary of the Senate**, Patsy Spaw; **Sergeant-at-Arms**, Carleton Turner.

### Texas State Senators

District, Member, Party-Hometown, Occupation

1. Bill Ratliff, R-Mount Pleasant; consulting engineer.
2. Bob Deuell, R-Mesquite; family physician.
3. Todd Staples, R-Palestine; businessman/rancher.
4. Tommy Williams, R-Beaumont; businessman.
5. Steve Ogden, R-Bryan;oil and gas producer.
6. Mario Gallegos Jr., D-Houston; retired firefighter.
7. Jon Lindsay, R-Houston; engineer/consultant.
8. Florence Shapiro, R-Plano; company president.
9. Chris Harris, R-Arlington; attorney.
10. Kim Brimer, R-Fort Worth; businessman.
11. Mike Jackson, R-La Porte; businessman.
12. Jane Nelson, R-Lewisville; businesswoman.
13. Rodney G. Ellis, D-Houston; attorney/businessman.
14. Gonzalo Barrientos, D-Austin; advertising/ public relations.
15. John Whitmire, D-Houston; attorney (**Dean of the Senate**).
16. John J. Carona, R-Dallas; company president.
17. Kyle Janek, R-Houston; anesthesiologist.
18. Kenneth L. Armbrister, D-Victoria; businessman.
19. Frank L. Madla, D-San Antonio; real estate, insurance, college instructor.
20. Juan "Chuy" Hinojosa, D-Mission; attorney.
21. Judith Zaffirini, D-Laredo; communications specialist.
22. Kip Averitt, R-McGregor; businessman.
23. Royce West, D-Dallas; attorney.
24. Troy Fraser, R-Horseshoe Bay; businessman.
25. Jeff Wentworth, R-San Antonio; attorney, Realtor.
26. Leticia Van de Putte, D-San Antonio; pharmacist.
27. Eddie Lucio Jr., D-Brownsville; advertising executive.
28. Robert L. Duncan, R-Lubbock; attorney.
29. Eliot Shapleigh, D-El Paso; attorney.
30. Craig Estes, R-Wichita Falls; businessman.
31. Teel Bivins, R-Amarillo; businessman, cattleman.

### House of Representatives

This is a list of the 150 members of the House of Representatives in the 78th Legislature. They were elected for two-year terms from the districts shown below. Representatives and senators receive the same salary (see State Senate). The **address of all Representatives** is House of Representatives, P.O. Box 2910, Austin, 78768-2910; phone: 512-463-3000; Fax: 512-463-5896. On the Web: **www.house.state.tx.us/**

**Speaker:** Tom Craddick (R-Midland). **Speaker Pro Tempore**, Sylvester Turner (D-Houston). **Chief Clerk**, Robert Haney. **Sergeant-at-Arms**, Rod Welsh.

## Members of Texas House of Representatives

**District, Member, Party-Hometown, Occupation**

1. Barry B. Telford, D-DeKalb, businessman.
2. Dan Flynn, R-Austin; businessman, rancher.
3. Mark Homer, D-Paris; restaurant owner.
4. Betty Brown, R-Terrell; rancher.
5. Bryan Hughes, R-Austin; attorney.
6. Leo Berman, R-Tyler; retired military officer.
7. Tommy Merritt, R-Longview; state representative.
8. Byron Cook, R-Corsicana; businessman, rancher.
9. Wayne Christian, R-Center; investment advisor.
10. Jim Pitts, R-Waxahachie; attorney.
11. Chuck Hopson, D-Jacksonville; pharmacist.
12. Jim McReynolds, D-Lufkin; petroleum landman.
13. Lois Kolkhorst, R-Brenham; business owner/investor.
14. Fred Brown, R-Bryan; car dealer.
15. Rob Eissler, R-The Woodlands; executive recruiter.
16. Ruben Hegar Jr., R-Conroe; attorney.
17. Robert "Robby" Cook, D-Eagle Lake; farmer.
18. Dan Ellis, D-Livingston; business administrator.
19. Mike "Tuffy" Hamilton, R-Mauriceville; restaurateur.
20. Ron Gattis, R-Austin; attorney/rancher.
21. Allan Ritter, D-Nederland; lumber-company president.
22. Joe Deshotel, D-Port Arthur; attorney, contractor.
23. Craig Eiland, D-Galveston; attorney.
24. Larry Taylor, R-Austin; businessman.
25. Dennis Bonnen, R-Angleton; insurance.
26. Charlie Howard, R-Sugar Land; real-estate developer.
27. Dora Olivo, D-Missouri City; attorney.
28. Glenn Hegar Jr., R-Austin; farmer.
29. Glenda Dawson, R-Austin; speaker facilitator.
30. Geanie Morrison, R-Victoria; state representative.
31. Ryan Guillen, D-Austin; rancher/businessman.
32. Gene Seaman, R-Corpus Christi; insurance, real estate developer.
33. Vilma Luna, D-Corpus Christi; attorney.
34. Jaime Capelo, D-Corpus Christi; attorney.
35. Gabi Canales, D-Alice; attorney/farmer/rancher.
36. Ismael "Kino" Flores, D-Mission; businessman.
37. Rene Oliveira, D-Brownsville; attorney.
38. Jim Solis, D-Harlingen; attorney.
39. Miguel D. "Mike" Wise, D-Weslaco; attorney.
40. Aaron Pena, D-Edinburg; attorney.
41. Roberto Gutierrez, D-McAllen; petroleum-products distributor.
42. Richard Raymond, D-Laredo; consultant.
43. Juan Escobar, D-Austin; retired.
44. Edmund Kuempel, R-Seguin; salesman.
45. Patrick Rose, D-Dripping Springs; Realtor.
46. Dawnna Dukes, D-Austin; business consultant.
47. Terry Keel, R-Austin; attorney.
48. Todd Baxter, R-Austin; attorney.
49. Elliott Naishtat, D-Austin; attorney.
50. Jack Stick, R-Austin; attorney.
51. Eddie Rodriguez, D-Austin; state representative.
52. Mike Krusee, R-Taylor; education consultant.
53. Harvey Hilderbran, R-Kerrville; businessman.
54. Suzanna Gratia Hupp, R-Lampasas; chiropractor, horse breeder.
55. Dianne White Delisi, R-Temple; self-employed.
56. John Mabry Jr., D-Austin; attorney.
57. Jim Dunnam, D-Waco; attorney.
58. Arlene Wohlgemuth, R-Burleson; flight instructor.
59. Sid Miller, R-Stephenville; farmer/nurseryman.
60. Jim Keffer, R-Eastland; president, iron firm.
61. Phil King, R-Weatherford; attorney.
62. Larry Phillips, R-Sherman, attorney.
63. Mary Denny, R-Flower Mound; businesswoman/rancher.
64. Myra Crownover, R-Lake Dallas; businesswoman/investor.
65. Burt Solomons, R-Carrollton; attorney.
66. Brian McCall, R-Plano; insurance executive.
67. Jerry Madden, R-Plano; insurance executive.
68. Rick Hardcastle, R-Vernon; rancher, businessman.
69. David Farabee, D-Wichita Falls; insurance agent.
70. Ken Paxton, R-Austin; attorney.
71. Bob Hunter, R-Abilene; university administrator.
72. Scott Campbell, R-San Angelo; businessman.
73. Carter Casteel, R-New Braunfels; state representative.
74. Pete Gallego, D-Alpine; attorney.
75. Chente Quintanilla, D-Austin; school administrator.
76. Norma Chavez, D-El Paso; businesswoman.
77. Paul Moreno, D-El Paso; attorney (**Senior House Member**).
78. Pat Haggerty, R-El Paso; real-estate broker.
79. Joseph Pickett, D-El Paso; real-estate broker.
80. Timoteo Garza, D-Eagle Pass; computer consultant.
81. G.E. "Buddy" West, R-Odessa; retired safety engineer.
82. Tom Craddick, R-Midland; sales representative (**Senior House Member**)
83. Delwin Jones, R-Lubbock; businessman/investor.
84. Carl Isett, R-Lubbock; accountant.
85. James E. "Pete" Laney, D-Hale Center; farmer.
86. John Smithee, R-Amarillo; attorney.
87. David Swinford, R-Amarillo; marketing consultant.
88. Warren Chisum, R-Pampa; oil & gas producer.
89. Jodie Laubenberg, R-Austin; state representative.
90. Lon Burnam, D-Fort Worth; consultant.
91. Bob Griggs, R-Austin; consultant.
92. Todd Smith, R-Bedford; attorney.
93. Toby Goodman, R-Arlington; attorney.
94. Kent Grusendorf, R-Arlington; pres., mfg. co.
95. Glenn Lewis, D-Fort Worth; attorney.
96. William Zedler, R-Austin; retired.
97. Anna Mowery, R-Fort Worth; petroleum landman/rancher.
98. Vicki Truitt, R-Southlake; health-care consultant.
99. Charlie Geren, R-River Oaks; restauranteur/real estate broker.
100. Terri Hodge, D-Dallas; retired.
101. Elvira Reyna, R-Mesquite; state representative.
102. Tony Goolsby, R-Dallas; insurance.
103. Steven Wolens, D-Dallas; attorney.
104. Roberto Alonzo, R-Irving; attorney.
105. Linda Harper-Brown D-Dallas; CEO.
106. Ray Allen, R-Grand Prairie; businessman.
107. Bill Keffer, R-Dallas; attorney.
108. Dan Branch, R-Dallas; attorney.
109. Helen Giddings, D-DeSoto; small-business owner.
110. Jesse Jones, D-Dallas; professor.
111. Yvonne Davis, D-Dallas; small-business owner.
112. Fred Hill, R-Richardson; company president.
113. Joe Driver, R-Garland; insurance agent.
114. Will Hartnett, R-Dallas; attorney.
115. Kenny Marchant, R-Carrollton; investor.
116. Trey Martinez Fischer., D-San Antonio; attorney.
117. Ken Mercer, R-San Antonio; systems analyst.
118. Carlos Uresti, D-San Antonio; attorney.
119. Robert Puente, D-San Antonio; attorney.
120. Ruth J. McClendon, D-San Antonio; businesswoman.
121. Elizabeth Ames Jones, R-San Antonio; state representative.
122. Frank Corte Jr., R-San Antonio; property developer/manager.
123. Michael Villarreal, D-San Antonio; businessman.
124. Jose Menendez, D-San Antonio; marketing exec.
125. Joaquin Castro, D-Austin; attorney.
126. Peggy Hamric, R-Houston; small-business owner.
127. Joe Crabb, R-Kingwood; minister, attorney, rancher.
128. Wayne Smith, R-Baytown; civil engineer.
129. John Davis, R-Houston; roofing contractor.
130. Corbin Van Arsdale, R-Houston; attorney.
131. Ron Wilson, D-Houston; attorney.
132. William Callegari, R-Houston; engineer/investor.
133. Joe Nixon, R-Austin; attorney.
134. Martha Wong, R-Houston; business consultant.
135. Gary Elkins, R-Houston; businessman, consultant.
136. Beverly Woolley, R-Houston; small-business owner.
137. Scott Hochberg, D-Houston; software developer.
138. Dwayne Bohac, R-Austin; small-business owner.
139. Sylvester Turner, D-Houston; attorney.
140. Kevin Bailey, D-Houston; political consultant.
141. Senfronia Thompson, D-Houston; attorney.
142. Harold Dutton Jr., D-Houston; attorney.
143. Joe Moreno, D-Jacinto City; state representative.
144. Robert Talton, R-Pasadena; attorney.
145. Rick Noriega, D-Houston; businessman.
146. Al Edwards, D-Houston; real estate.
147. Garnet Coleman, D-Houston; community affairs manager.
148. Jessica Farrar, D-Houston; architect intern.
149. Talmadge Heflin, R-Houston; businessman.
150. Debbie Riddle, R-Houston; horse breeder. ☆

# Texas State Judiciary

The judiciary of the state consists of 9 members of the State Supreme Court; 9 members of the Court of Criminal Appeals; 80 of the Courts of Appeals; 418 of the State District Courts, including 10 Criminal District Courts; 465 County Court judges; 835 Justices of the Peace; and 1,294 Municipal Courts judges.

In addition to its system of formal courts, the State of Texas has established 14 **Alternative Dispute Resolution Centers.** The centers help ease the caseload of Texas courts by using mediation, arbitration, negotiation and moderated settlement conferences to handle disputes without resorting to more costly, time-consuming court actions. Centers are located in Amarillo, Austin, Beaumont, Bryan, Conroe, Corpus Christi, Dallas, El Paso, Fort Worth, Houston, Lubbock, Richmond, San Antonio and Waco. For the fiscal year ending Aug. 31, 2002, the mediation sections of the centers had closed 16,324 cases and had 2,672 cases pending.

(The list of U.S. District Courts in Texas can be found in the Federal Government section of this edition.)

## State Higher Courts

The state's higher courts are listed below and are current as of **August 2003.** Notations in parentheses indicate dates of expiration of terms of office. Judges of the Supreme Court, Court of Criminal Appeals and Courts of Appeals are elected to 6-year, overlapping terms. District Court judges are elected to 4-year terms.

The salaries for judges as of August 2003 were as follows: Chief Justice of the Supreme Court and the Presiding Judge of the Court of Criminal Appeals: each $115,000; Justices, $113,000; Chief Justices of the Courts of Appeals, $107,850; justices, $107,350 from the state. A supplemental amount may be paid by counties, not to exceed $15,000 per year, and total salary must be at least $1,000 less than that received by Supreme Court justices. District Court judges receive $101,700 from the state, plus supplemental pay from various subdivisions. Their total salary must be $1,000 less than that received by justices of the Court of Appeals in which the district court is located.

Below is given information on only the Supreme Court, Court of Criminal Appeals and Courts of Appeals. The information was furnished by each court as of May 2003. Elsewhere in this section can be found names of county court judges by counties, names of District Court judges by district number, and the district numbers of the District Court(s) in each county.

## Supreme Court

**Chief Justice,** Thomas R. Phillips (12-31-08). **Associate Justices:** Nathan L. Hecht (12-31-06); Craig T. Enoch (12-31-04); Priscilla R. Owen (12-31-06); Harriet O'Neill (12-31-04); Wallace B. Jefferson (12-31-06); Michael H. Schneider (12-31-08); Steven W. Smith (12-31-04); and J. Dale Wainwright (12-31-08). **Clerk of Court,** Andrew Weber. Location of court, Austin. Web: **www.supreme.courts.state.tx.us.**

## Court of Criminal Appeals

**Presiding Judge,** Sharon Keller (12-31-06). **Judges:** Lawrence E. Meyers (12-31-05); Tom Price (12-31-08); Paul Womack (12-31-08); Cheryl Johnson (12-31-05); Mike Keasler (12-31-05); Barbara P. Hervey (12-31-06); Charles R. Holcomb (12-31-06); and Cathy Cochran (12-31-08).. **State's Attorney,** Matthew Paul. **Clerk of Court,** Troy C. Bennett Jr. Location of court, Austin. Web: **www.cca.courts.state.tx.us.**

## Courts of Appeals

These courts have jurisdiction within their respective supreme judicial districts. A constitutional amendment approved in 1978 raised the number of associate justices for Courts of Appeals where needed. Judges are elected from the district for 6-year terms. An amendment adopted in 1980 changed the name of the old Courts of Civil Appeals to the Courts of Appeals and changed the jurisdiction of the courts. Web: **www.courts.state.tx.us/appcourt.asp**

**First District — \*Houston. Chief Justice,** Sherry Radack (12-31-04). **Justices:** Elsa Alcala (12-31-08); George C. Hanks Jr. (12-31-04); Adele Hedges (12-31-06); Laura Carter Higley (12-31-08); Terry Jennings (12-31-06); Evelyn Keyes (12-31-08); Sam Nuchia (12-31-06); and Tim G. Taft (12-31-06). **Clerk of Court,** Margie Thompson. Counties in the First District: Austin, Brazoria, Brazos, Burleson, Chambers, Colorado, Fort Bend, Galveston, Grimes, Harris, Trinity, Walker, Waller, Washington.

**Second District — Fort Worth: Chief Justice,** John H. Cayce (12-31-06). **Justices:** Dixon W. Holman (12-31-08); Sam J. Day (12-31-06); Terrie Livingston (12-31-08); Lee Ann Dauphinot (12-31-06); Anne L. Gardner (12-31-04); and Sue Walker (12/31/06). **Clerk of Court,** Stephanie Lavake. Counties in Second District: Archer, Clay, Cooke, Denton, Hood, Jack, Montague, Parker, Tarrant, Wichita, Wise, Young.

**Third District — Austin: Chief Justice,** W. Kenneth Law (12-31-08). **Justices:** Mack Kidd (12-31-06); Bea Ann Smith (12-31-06); Lee Yeakel (12-31-06); Jan P. Patterson (12-31-04); and David Puryear (12-31-06). **Clerk of Court,** Diane O'Neal. Counties in the Third District: Bastrop, Bell, Blanco, Burnet, Caldwell, Coke, Comal, Concho, Fayette, Hays, Irion, Lampasas, Lee, Llano, McCulloch, Milam, Mills, Runnels, San Saba, Schleicher, Sterling, Tom Green, Travis, Williamson.

**Fourth District — San Antonio: Chief Justice,** Alma L. Lopez (12-31-06). **Justices:** Karen Anne Angelini (12-31-06); Sarah B. Duncan (12-31-06); Paul W. Green (12-31-06); Sandee Bryan Marion (12-31-08); Phylis J. Speedlin (12-31-08); and Catherine M. Stone (12-31-06). **Clerk of Court,** Herb Schaefer. Counties in the Fourth District: Atascosa, Bandera, Bexar, Brooks, Dimmit, Duval, Edwards, Frio, Gillespie, Guadalupe, Jim Hogg, Jim Wells, Karnes, Kendall, Kerr, Kimble, Kinney, La Salle, Mason, Maverick, McMullen, Medina, Menard, Real, Starr, Sutton, Uvalde, Val Verde, Webb, Wilson, Zapata, Zavala.

**Fifth District — Dallas: Chief Justice,** Linda Thomas (12-31-06). **Justices:** David L. Bridges (12-31-06); Kerry P. FitzGerald, (12-31-08); Thomas L. James (12-31-06); Michael J. O'Neill (12-31-04); Molly Meredith Francis (12-31-04); Douglas S. Lang (11-4-03); Joseph B. Morris (12-31-06); Jim A. Moseley (12-31-06); Martin E. Richter (12-31-06); Carolyn I. Wright (12-31-04); and Mark Whittington (12-31-08); one position vacant at press time. **Clerk of Court,** Lisa Matz. Counties in the Fifth District: Collin, Dallas, Grayson, Hunt, Kaufman, Rockwall, Van Zandt.

**Sixth District — Texarkana: Chief Justice,** Josh R. Morris III (12-31-04). **Justices:** Donald R. Ross (12-31-06) and Jack Carter (12-31-08). **Clerk of Court,** Linda Rogers. Counties in the Sixth District: Bowie, Camp, Cass, Delta, Fannin, Franklin, Gregg, Harrison, Hopkins, Hunt, Lamar, Marion, Morris, Panola, Red River, Rusk, Titus, Upshur, Wood.

**Seventh District — Amarillo: Chief Justice,** Phil Johnson (12-31-04). **Justices:** Brian P. Quinn (12-31-06); Don H. Reavis (12-31-08); and James T. Campbell (12-31-04). **Clerk of Court,** Peggy Culp. Counties in the Seventh District: Armstrong, Bailey, Briscoe, Carson, Castro, Childress, Cochran, Collingsworth, Cottle, Crosby, Dallam, Deaf Smith, Dickens, Donley, Floyd, Foard, Garza, Gray, Hale, Hall, Hansford, Hardeman, Hartley, Hemphill, Hockley, Hutchinson, Kent, King, Lamb, Lipscomb, Lubbock,

Lynn, Moore, Motley, Ochiltree, Oldham, Parmer, Potter, Randall, Roberts, Sherman, Swisher, Terry, Wheeler, Wilbarger, Yoakum.

**Eighth District — El Paso: Chief Justice,** Richard Barajas (12-31-08). **Justices:** Susan Larsen (12-31-04); Ann Crawford McClure (12-31-06); and David Wellington Chew (12-31-06). **Clerk of Court,** Denise Pacheco. Counties in the Eighth District: Andrews, Brewster, Crane, Crockett, Culberson, Ector, El Paso, Gaines, Glasscock, Hudspeth, Jeff Davis, Loving, Martin, Midland, Pecos, Presidio, Reagan, Reeves, Terrell, Upton, Ward, Winkler.

**Ninth District — Beaumont: Chief Justice,** Steve McKeithen (12-31-08). **Justices:** Don R. Burgess (12-31-04); and David B. Gaultney (12-31-06). **Clerk of Court,** Carol Anne Flores. Counties in the Ninth District: Angelina, Hardin, Jasper, Jefferson, Liberty, Montgomery, Newton, Orange, Polk, San Jacinto, Tyler.

**Tenth District — Waco: Chief Justice,** Rex D. Davis (12-31-06). **Justices:** Thomas W. Gray (12-31-04) and Bill Vance (12-31-08). **Clerk of Court,** Sharri Roessler. Counties in the Tenth District: Bosque, Brazos, Coryell, Ellis, Falls, Freestone, Hamilton, Hill, Johnson, Leon, Limestone, McLennan, Madison, Navarro, Robertson, Somervell.

**Eleventh District — Eastland: Chief Justice,** William G. Arnot III (12-31-06). **Justices:** Terry McCall (12-31-04) and Jim R. Wright (12-31-08). **Clerk of Court,** Sherry Williamson. Counties in the Eleventh District: Baylor, Borden, Brown, Callahan, Coleman, Comanche, Dawson, Eastland, Erath, Fisher, Haskell, Howard, Jones, Knox, Mitchell, Nolan, Palo Pinto, Scurry, Shackelford, Stephens, Stonewall, Taylor, Throckmorton.

**Twelfth District—Tyler: Chief Justice,** Jim Worthen (12-31-04). **Justices:** Sam Griffith (12-31-06) and one position vacant at press time. **Clerk of Court,** Cathy S. Lusk. Counties in the Twelfth District: Anderson, Cherokee, Gregg, Henderson, Hopkins, Houston, Kaufman, Nacogdoches, Panola, Rains, Rusk, Sabine, San Augustine, Shelby, Smith, Upshur, Van Zandt, Wood.

**Thirteenth District—Corpus Christi: Chief Justice,** Rogelio Valdez (12-31-06). **Justices:** Errlinda Castillo (12-31-06); Dori Contreras Garza (12-31-08); Federico G. Hinojosa Jr. (12-31-06); Nelda V. Rodriguez (12-31-06); and Linda Reyna Yañez (12-31-04). **Clerk of court,** Cathy Wilborn. Counties in the Thirteenth District: Aransas, Bee, Calhoun, Cameron, DeWitt, Goliad, Gonzales, Hidalgo, Jackson, Kenedy, Kleberg, Lavaca, Live Oak, Matagorda, Nueces, Refugio, San Patricio, Victoria, Wharton, Willacy.

**Fourteenth District—Houston†: Chief Justice,** Scott A. Brister (12-31-04). **Justices:** John S. Anderson (12-31-06); Richard H. Edelman (12-31-06); Wanda McKee Fowler (12-31-06); Kem Thompson Frost (12-31-82); Eva M. Guzman (12-31-04); J. Harvey Hudson (12-31-06); Charles W. Seymore (12-31-06); and Leslie Brock Yates (12-31-04). **Clerk of court,** Ed Wells. Counties in the Fourteenth District: Austin, Brazoria, Brazos, Burleson, Chambers, Colorado, Fort Bend, Galveston, Grimes, Harris, Trinity, Walker, Waller, Washington.

*The location of the First Court of Appeals was changed from Galveston to Houston by the 55th Legislature, with the provision that all cases originated in Galveston County be tried in that city and with the further provision that any case may, at the discretion of the court, be tried in either city.

†Because of the heavy workload of the Houston area Court of Appeals, the 60th Legislature, in 1967, provided for the establishment of a Fourteenth Appeals Court at Houston.

## Administrative Judicial Districts of Texas

There are nine administrative judicial districts in the state for administrative purposes. An active or retired district judge or an active or retired appellate judge with judicial experience in a district court serves as the Presiding Judge upon appointment by the Governor. They receive extra compensation of $5,000 paid by counties in the respective administrative districts.

The Presiding Judge convenes an annual conference of the judges in the administrative district to consult on the state of business in the courts. This conference is empowered to adopt rules for the administration of cases in the district. The Presiding Judge may assign active or retired district judges residing within the administrative district to any of the district courts within the administrative district. The Presiding Judge of one administrative district may request the Presiding Judge of another administrative district to assign a judge from that district to sit in a district court located in the administrative district of the Presiding Judge making the request.

The Chief Justice of the Supreme Court of Texas convenes an annual conference of the nine Presiding Judges to determine the need for assignment of judges and to promote the uniform administration of the assignment of judges. The Chief Justice is empowered to assign judges of one administrative district for service in another whenever such assignments are necessary for the prompt and efficient administration of justice.

**First District** — John Ovard, Dallas: Anderson, Bowie, Camp, Cass, Cherokee, Collin, Dallas, Delta, Ellis, Fannin, Franklin, Grayson, Gregg, Harrison, Henderson, Hopkins, Houston, Hunt, Kaufman, Lamar, Marion, Morris, Nacogdoches, Panola, Rains, Red River, Rockwall, Rusk, Shelby, Smith, Titus, Upshur, Van Zandt and Wood.

**Second District** — Olen Underwood, Conroe: Angelina, Bastrop, Brazoria, Brazos, Burleson, Chambers, Fort Bend, Freestone, Galveston, Grimes, Hardin, Harris, Jasper, Jefferson, Lee, Leon, Liberty, Limestone, Madison, Matagorda, Montgomery, Newton, Orange, Polk, Robertson, Sabine, San Augustine, San Jacinto, Trinity, Tyler, Walker, Waller, Washington and Wharton.

**Third District** — B. B. Schraub, Seguin: Austin, Bell, Blanco, Bosque, Burnet, Caldwell, Colorado, Comal, Comanche, Coryell, Falls, Fayette, Gonzales, Guadalupe, Hamilton, Hays, Hill, Johnson, Lampasas, Lavaca, Llano, McLennan, Mason, Milam, Navarro, San Saba, Travis and Williamson.

**Fourth District** — David Peeples, San Antonio: Aransas, Atascosa, Bee, Bexar, Calhoun, DeWitt, Dimmit, Frio, Goliad, Jackson, Karnes, LaSalle, Live Oak, Maverick, McMullen, Refugio, San Patricio, Victoria, Webb, Wilson, Zapata and Zavala.

**Fifth District** — Darrell Hester, Brownsville: Brooks, Cameron, Duval, Hidalgo, Jim Hogg, Jim Wells, Kenedy, Kleberg, Nueces, Starr and Willacy.

**Sixth District** — Stephen B. Ables, Kerrville: Bandera, Brewster, Crockett, Culberson, Edwards, El Paso, Gillespie, Hudspeth, Jeff Davis, Kendall, Kerr, Kimble, Kinney, Mason, Medina, Pecos, Presidio, Reagan, Real, Sutton, Terrell, Upton, Uvalde and Val Verde.

**Seventh District** — Dean Rucker, Midland: Andrews, Borden, Brown, Callahan, Coke, Coleman, Concho, Crane, Dawson, Ector, Fisher, Gaines, Garza, Glasscock, Haskell, Howard, Irion, Jones, Kent, Loving, Lynn, Martin, McCulloch, Menard, Midland, Mills, Mitchell, Nolan, Reeves, Runnels, Schleicher, Scurry, Shackelford, Sterling, Stonewall, Taylor, Throckmorton, Tom Green, Ward and Winkler.

**Eighth District** — Jeff Walker, Fort Worth: Archer, Clay, Cooke, Denton, Eastland, Erath, Hood, Jack, Johnson, Montague, Palo Pinto, Parker, Somervell, Stephens, Tarrant, Wichita, Wise and Young.

**Ninth District** — Kelly G. Moore, Brownfield: Armstrong, Bailey, Baylor, Briscoe, Carson, Castro, Childress, Cochran, Collingsworth, Cottle, Crosby, Dallam, Deaf Smith, Dickens, Donley, Floyd, Foard, Gray, Hale, Hall, Hansford, Hardeman, Hartley, Hemphill, Hockley, Hutchinson, King, Knox, Lamb, Lipscomb, Lubbock, Moore, Motley, Ochiltree, Oldham, Parmer, Potter, Randall, Roberts, Sherman, Swisher, Terry, Wheeler, Wilbarger and Yoakum. ☆

# Texas Courts by County

Below are listed the state district court or courts, court of appeals district, administrative judicial district and U.S. judicial district for each county in Texas as of August 2003. For the names of the district court judges, see table by district number on pages 439–440. For the names of other judges in the Texas court system, see listing on pages 435–436.

| County | State Dist. Court(s) | Ct. of App'ls Dist. | Adm. Jud. Dist. | U.S. Jud. Dist. |
|---|---|---|---|---|
| Anderson | 3, 87, 349, 369 | 12 | 1 | E-Tyler |
| Andrews | 109 | 8 | 7 | W-Midland |
| Angelina | 159, 217 | 9 | 2 | E-Lufkin |
| Aransas | 36, 156, 343 | 13 | 4 | S-C.Christi |
| Archer | 97 | 2 | 8 | N-W. Falls |
| Armstrong | 47 | 7 | 9 | N-Amarilllo |
| Atascosa | 81, 218 | 4 | 4 | W-San Ant. |
| Austin | 155 | 1, 14 | 3 | S-Houston |
| Bailey | 287 | 7 | 9 | N-Lubbock |
| Bandera | 216 | 4 | 6 | W-San Ant. |
| Bastrop | 21, 335 | 3 | 2 | W-Austin |
| Baylor | 50 | 11 | 9 | N-W. Falls |
| Bee | 36, 156, 343 | 13 | 4 | S-C.Christi |
| Bell | 27, 146, 169, 264 | 3 | 3 | W-Waco |
| Bexar | 37, 45, 57, 73, 131, 144, 150, 166, 175, 186, 187, 224, 225, 226, 227, 285, 288, 289, 290, 379, 386, 399, 407,408 | 4 | 4 | W-San Ant. |
| Blanco | 33 | 3 | 3 | W-Austin |
| Borden | 132 | 11 | 7 | N-Lubbock |
| Bosque | 220 | 10 | 3 | W-Waco |
| Bowie | 5, 102, 202 | 6 | 1 | E-Texark. |
| Brazoria | 23, 149, 239, 300 | 1, 14 | 2 | S-Galves. |
| Brazos | 85, 272, 361 | 1, 10, 14 | 2 | S-Houston |
| Brewster | 394 | 8 | 6 | W-Pecos |
| Briscoe | 110 | 7 | 9 | N-Amarilllo |
| Brooks | 79 | 4 | 5 | S-C.Christi |
| Brown | 35 | 11 | 7 | N-S. Ang. |
| Burleson | 21, 335 | 1, 14 | 2 | W-Austin |
| Burnet | 33 | 3 | 3 | W-Austin |
| Caldwell | 22, 207, 274 | 3 | 3 | W-Austin |
| Calhoun | 24, 135, 267 | 13 | 4 | S-Victoria |
| Callahan | 42 | 11 | 7 | N-Abilene |
| Cameron | 103, 107, 138, 197, 357, 404 | 13 | 5 | S-Brownsville |
| Camp | 76, 276 | 6 | 1 | E-Marshall |
| Carson | 100 | 7 | 9 | N-Amarilllo |
| Cass | 5 | 6 | 1 | E-Marshall |
| Castro | 64, 242 | 7 | 9 | N-Amarilllo |
| Chambers | 253, 344 | 1, 14 | 2 | S-Galves. |
| Cherokee | 2, 369 | 12 | 1 | E-Tyler |
| Childress | 100 | 7 | 9 | N-Amarilllo |
| Clay | 97 | 2 | 8 | N-W. Falls |
| Cochran | 286 | 7 | 9 | N-Lubbock |
| Coke | 51 | 3 | 7 | N-S. Ang. |
| Coleman | 42 | 11 | 7 | N-S. Ang. |
| Collin | 199, 219, 296, 366, 380, 401 | 5 | 1 | E-Sherman |
| Collingsworth | 100 | 7 | 9 | N-Amarilllo |
| Colorado | 25, 2nd 25 | 1, 14 | 3 | S-Houston |
| Comal | 22, 207, 274 | 3 | 3 | W-San Ant. |
| Comanche | 220 | 11 | 3 | N-Ft. Worth |
| Concho | 119 | 3 | 7 | N-S. Ang. |
| Cooke | 235 | 2 | 8 | E-Sherman |
| Coryell | 52 | 10 | 3 | W-Waco |
| Cottle | 50 | 7 | 9 | N-W. Falls |
| Crane | 109 | 8 | 7 | W-Midland |
| Crockett | 112 | 8 | 6 | N-S. Ang. |
| Crosby | 72 | 7 | 9 | N-Lubbock |
| Culberson | 205, 394 | 8 | 6 | W-Pecos |
| Dallam | 69 | 7 | 9 | N-Amarilllo |
| Dallas | 14, 44, 68, 95, 101, 116, 134, 160, 162, 191, 192, 193, 194,195, 203, 204, 254, 255, 256, 265, 282, 283, 291, 292, 298, 301, 302, 303, 304, 305, 330, 363, Cr.1, Cr2, Cr.3, Cr.4, Cr.5 | 5 | 1 | N-Dallas |
| Dawson | 106 | 11 | 7 | N-Lubbock |
| Deaf Smith | 222 | 7 | 9 | N-Amarilllo |
| Delta | 8, 62 | 6 | 1 | E-Paris |
| Denton | 16, 158, 211, 362, 367, 393 | 2 | 8 | E-Sherman |
| DeWitt | 24, 135, 267 | 13 | 4 | S-Victoria |
| Dickens | 110 | 7 | 9 | N-Lubbock |
| Dimmit | 293, 365 | 4 | 4 | W-San Ant. |
| Donley | 100 | 7 | 9 | N-Amarilllo |
| Duval | 229 | 4 | 5 | S-C.Christi |
| Eastland | 91 | 11 | 8 | N-Abilene |
| Ector | 70, 161, 244, 358 | 8 | 7 | W-Midland |
| Edwards | 63 | 4 | 6 | W-Del Rio |
| Ellis | 40, 378 | 10 | 1 | N-Dallas |
| El Paso | 34, 41, 65, 120, 168, 171, 205, 210, 243, 327, 346, 383, 384, 388, 409 | 8 | 6 | W-El Paso |
| Erath | 266 | 11 | 8 | N-Ft. Worth |
| Falls | 82 | 10 | 3 | W-Waco |
| Fannin | 6, 336 | 6 | 1 | E-Paris |
| Fayette | 155 | 3 | 3 | S-Houston |
| Fisher | 32 | 11 | 7 | N-Abilene |
| Floyd | 110 | 7 | 9 | N-Lubbock |
| Foard | 46 | 7 | 9 | N-W. Falls |
| Fort Bend | 240, 268, 328, 387, 400 | 1, 14 | 2 | S-Houston |
| Franklin | 8, 62 | 6 | 1 | E-Texark. |
| Freestone | 77, 87 | 10 | 2 | W-Waco |
| Frio | 81, 218 | 4 | 4 | W-San Ant. |
| Gaines | 106 | 8 | 7 | N-Lubbock |
| Galveston | 10, 56, 122, 212, 306, 405 | 1, 14 | 2 | S-Galves. |
| Garza | 106 | 7 | 7 | N-Lubbock |
| Gillespie | 216 | 4 | 6 | W-Austin |
| Glasscock | 118 | 8 | 7 | N-S. Ang. |
| Goliad | 24, 135, 267 | 13 | 4 | S-Victoria |
| Gonzales | 25, 2nd 25 | 13 | 3 | W-San Ant. |
| Gray | 31, 223 | 7 | 9 | N-Amarilllo |
| Grayson | 15, 59, 336 | 5 | 1 | E-Sherman |
| Gregg | 124, 188, 307 | 6, 12 | 1 | E-Tyler |
| Grimes | 12, 278 | 1, 14 | 2 | S-Houston |
| Guadalupe | 25, 2nd 25, 274 | 4 | 3 | W-San Ant. |
| Hale | 64, 242 | 7 | 9 | N-Lubbock |
| Hall | 100 | 7 | 9 | N-Amarilllo |
| Hamilton | 220 | 10 | 3 | W-Waco |
| Hansford | 84 | 7 | 9 | N-Amarilllo |
| Hardeman | 46 | 7 | 9 | N-W. Falls |
| Hardin | 88, 356 | 9 | 2 | E-B'mont. |
| Harris | 11, 55, 61, 80, 113, 125, 127, 129, 133, 151, 152, 157, 164, 165, 174, 176, 177, 178, 179, 180, 182, 183, 184, 185, 189, 190, 208, 209, 215, 228, 230, 232, 234, 245, 246, 247, 248, 257, 262, 263, 269, 270, 280, 281, 295, 308, 309, 310, 311, 312, 313, 314, 315, 333, 334, 337, 338, 339, 351 | 1, 14 | 2 | S-Houston |
| Harrison | 71 | 6 | 1 | E-Marshall |
| Hartley | 69 | 7 | 9 | N-Amarilllo |
| Haskell | 39 | 11 | 7 | N-Abilene |
| Hays | 22, 207, 274 | 3 | 3 | W-Austin |
| Hemphill | 31 | 7 | 9 | N-Amarilllo |
| Henderson | 3, 173, 392 | 12 | 1 | E-Tyler |
| Hidalgo | 92, 93, 139, 206, 275, 332, 370, 389, 398 | 13 | 5 | S-McAllen |
| Hill | 66 | 10 | 3 | W-Waco |
| Hockley | 286 | 7 | 9 | N-Lubbock |
| Hood | 355 | 2 | 8 | N-Ft. Worth |
| Hopkins | 8, 62 | 6, 12 | 1 | E-Paris |
| Houston | 3, 349 | 12 | 1 | E-Lufkin |

| County | State Dist. Court(s) | Ct. of App'ls Dist. | Adm. Jud. Dist. | U.S. Jud. Dist. |
|---|---|---|---|---|
| Howard | 118 | 11 | 7 | N-Abilene |
| Hudspeth | 205, 394 | 8 | 6 | W-Pecos |
| Hunt | 196, 354 | 5, 6 | 1 | N-Dallas |
| Hutchinson | 84, 316 | 7 | 9 | N-Amarilllo |
| Irion | 51 | 3 | 7 | N-S. Ang. |
| Jack | 271 | 2 | 8 | N-Ft. Worth |
| Jackson | 24, 135, 267 | 13 | 4 | S-Victoria |
| Jasper | 1, 1A | 9 | 2 | E-B'mont. |
| Jeff Davis | 394 | 8 | 6 | W-Pecos |
| Jefferson | 58, 60, 136, 172, 252, 279, 317, Cr. | 9 | 2 | E-B'mont. |
| Jim Hogg | 229 | 4 | 5 | S-Laredo |
| Jim Wells | 79 | 4 | 5 | S-C.Christi |
| Johnson | 18, 249 | 10 | 3 | N-Dallas |
| Jones | 259 | 11 | 7 | N-Abilene |
| Karnes | 81, 218 | 4 | 4 | W-San Ant. |
| Kaufman | 86 | 5, 12 | 1 | N-Dallas |
| Kendall | 216 | 4 | 6 | W-San Ant. |
| Kenedy | 105 | 13 | 5 | S-C.Christi |
| Kent | 39 | 7 | 7 | N-Lubbock |
| Kerr | 198, 216 | 4 | 6 | W-San Ant. |
| Kimble | 198 | 4 | 6 | W-Austin |
| King | 50 | 7 | 9 | N-W. Falls |
| Kinney | 63 | 4 | 6 | W-Del Rio |
| Kleberg | 105 | 13 | 5 | S-C.Christi |
| Knox | 50 | 11 | 9 | N-W. Falls |
| Lamar | 6, 62 | 6 | 1 | E-Paris |
| Lamb | 154 | 7 | 9 | N-Lubbock |
| Lampasas | 27 | 3 | 3 | W-Austin |
| La Salle | 81, 218 | 4 | 4 | S-Laredo |
| Lavaca | 25, 2nd 25 | 13 | 3 | S-Victoria |
| Lee | 21, 335 | 3 | 2 | W-Austin |
| Leon | 12, 87, 278 | 10 | 2 | W-Waco |
| Liberty | 75, 253 | 9 | 2 | E-B'mont. |
| Limestone | 77, 87 | 10 | 2 | W-Waco |
| Lipscomb | 31 | 7 | 9 | N-Amarilllo |
| Live Oak | 36, 156, 343 | 13 | 4 | S-C.Christi |
| Llano | 33 | 3 | 3 | W-Austin |
| Loving | 143 | 8 | 7 | W-Pecos |
| Lubbock | 72, 99, 137, 140, 237, 364 | 7 | 9 | N-Lubbock |
| Lynn | 106 | 7 | 7 | N-Lubbock |
| Madison | 12, 278 | 10 | 2 | S-Houston |
| Marion | 115, 276 | 6 | 1 | E-Marshall |
| Martin | 118 | 8 | 7 | W-Midland |
| Mason | 198 | 4 | 6 | W-Austin |
| Matagorda | 23, 130 | 13 | 2 | S-Galves. |
| Maverick | 293, 365 | 4 | 4 | W-Del Rio |
| McCulloch | 198 | 3 | 7 | W-Austin |
| McLennan | 19, 54, 74, 170 | 10 | 3 | W-Waco |
| McMullen | 36, 156, 343 | 4 | 4 | S-Laredo |
| Medina | 38 | 4 | 6 | W-San Ant. |
| Menard | 198 | 4 | 7 | N-S. Ang. |
| Midland | 142, 238, 318, 385 | 8 | 7 | W-Midland |
| Milam | 20 | 3 | 3 | W-Waco |
| Mills | 35 | 3 | 7 | N-S. Ang. |
| Mitchell | 32 | 11 | 7 | N-Abilene |
| Montague | 97 | 2 | 8 | N-W. Falls |
| Montgomery | 9, 221, 284, 359, 410 | 9 | 2 | S-Houston |
| Moore | 69 | 7 | 9 | N-Amarilllo |
| Morris | 76, 276 | 6 | 1 | E-Marshall |
| Motley | 110 | 7 | 9 | N-Lubbock |
| Nacogdoches | 145 | 12 | 1 | E-Lufkin |
| Navarro | 13 | 10 | 3 | N-Dallas |
| Newton | 1, 1A | 9 | 2 | E-B'mont. |
| Nolan | 32 | 11 | 7 | N-Abilene |
| Nueces | 28, 94, 105, 117, 148, 214, 319, 347 | 13 | 5 | S-C.Christi |
| Ochiltree | 84 | 7 | 9 | N-Amarilllo |
| Oldham | 222 | 7 | 9 | N-Amarilllo |
| Orange | 128, 163, 260 | 9 | 2 | E-B'mont. |
| Palo Pinto | 29 | 11 | 8 | N-Ft. Worth |
| Panola | 123 | 6, 12 | 1 | E-Tyler |
| Parker | 43 | 2 | 8 | N-Ft. Worth |
| Parmer | 287 | 7 | 9 | N-Amarilllo |
| Pecos | 83, 112 | 8 | 6 | W-Pecos |
| Polk | 258, 411 | 9 | 2 | E-Lufkin |
| Potter | 47, 108, 181, 251, 320 | 7 | 9 | N-Amarilllo |
| Presidio | 394 | 8 | 6 | W-Pecos |
| Rains | 8, 354 | 12 | 1 | E-Tyler |
| Randall | 47, 181, 251 | 7 | 9 | N-Amarilllo |
| Reagan | 83, 112 | 8 | 6 | N-S. Ang. |
| Real | 38 | 4 | 6 | W-San Ant. |
| Red River | 6, 102 | 6 | 1 | E-Paris |
| Reeves | 143 | 8 | 7 | W-Pecos |
| Refugio | 24, 135, 267 | 13 | 4 | S-Victoria |
| Roberts | 31 | 7 | 9 | N-Amarilllo |
| Robertson | 82 | 10 | 2 | W-Waco |
| Rockwall | 382 | 5 | 1 | N-Dallas |
| Runnels | 119 | 3 | 7 | N-S. Ang. |
| Rusk | 4 | 6, 12 | 1 | E-Tyler |
| Sabine | 1, 273 | 12 | 2 | E-Lufkin |
| San Augustine | 1, 273 | 12 | 2 | E-Lufkin |
| San Jacinto | 258, 411 | 9 | 2 | S-Houston |
| San Patricio | 36, 156, 343 | 13 | 4 | S-C.Christi |
| San Saba | 33 | 3 | 3 | W-Austin |
| Schleicher | 51 | 3 | 7 | N-S. Ang. |
| Scurry | 132 | 11 | 7 | N-Lubbock |
| Shackelford | 259 | 11 | 7 | N-Abilene |
| Shelby | 123, 273 | 12 | 1 | E-Lufkin |
| Sherman | 69 | 7 | 9 | N-Amarilllo |
| Smith | 7, 114, 241, 321 | 12 | 1 | E-Tyler |
| Somervell | 18, 249 | 10 | 3 | W-Waco |
| Starr | 229, 381 | 4 | 5 | S-McAllen |
| Stephens | 90 | 11 | 8 | N-Abilene |
| Sterling | 51 | 3 | 7 | N-S. Ang. |
| Stonewall | 39 | 11 | 7 | N-Abilene |
| Sutton | 112 | 4 | 6 | N-S. Ang. |
| Swisher | 64, 242 | 7 | 9 | N-Amarilllo |
| Tarrant | 17, 48, 67, 96, 141, 153, 213, 231, 233, 236, 297, 322, 323, 324, 325, 342, 348, 352, 360, 371, 372, 396, Cr.1, Cr.2, Cr.3, Cr.4 | 2 | 8 | N-Ft. Worth |
| Taylor | 42, 104, 326, 350 | 11 | 7 | N-Abilene |
| Terrell | 63, 83 | 8 | 6 | W-Del Rio |
| Terry | 121 | 7 | 9 | N-Lubbock |
| Throckmorton | 39 | 11 | 7 | N-Abilene |
| Titus | 76, 276 | 6 | 1 | E-Texark. |
| Tom Green | 51, 119, 340, 391 | 3 | 7 | N-S. Ang. |
| Travis | 53, 98, 126, 147, 167, 200, 201, 250, 261, 299, 331, 345, 353, 390, 403 | 3 | 3 | W-Austin |
| Trinity | 258, 411 | 1, 14 | 2 | E-Lufkin |
| Tyler | 1A, 88 | 9 | 2 | E-Lufkin |
| Upshur | 115 | 6, 12 | 1 | E-Marshall |
| Upton | 83, 112 | 8 | 6 | W-Midland |
| Uvalde | 38 | 4 | 6 | W-Del Rio |
| Val Verde | 63, 83 | 4 | 6 | W-Del Rio |
| Van Zandt | 294 | 5, 12 | 1 | E-Tyler |
| Victoria | 24, 135, 267, 377 | 13 | 4 | S-Victoria |
| Walker | 12, 278 | 1, 14 | 2 | S-Houston |
| Waller | 9, 155 | 1, 14 | 2 | S-Houston |
| Ward | 143 | 8 | 7 | W-Pecos |
| Washington | 21, 335 | 1, 14 | 2 | W-Austin |
| Webb | 49, 111, 341, 406 | 4 | 4 | S-Laredo |
| Wharton | 23, 329 | 13 | 2 | S-Houston |
| Wheeler | 31 | 7 | 9 | N-Amarilllo |
| Wichita | 30, 78, 89 | 2 | 8 | N-W. Falls |
| Wilbarger | 46 | 7 | 9 | N-W. Falls |
| Willacy | 103, 107, 138, 197, 357 | 13 | 5 | S-Brownsville |
| Williamson | 26, 277, 368, 395 | 3 | 3 | W-Austin |
| Wilson | 81, 218 | 4 | 4 | W-San Ant. |
| Winkler | 109 | 8 | 7 | W-Pecos |
| Wise | 271 | 2 | 8 | N-Ft. Worth |
| Wood | 402 | 6, 12 | 1 | E-Tyler |
| Yoakum | 121 | 7 | 9 | N-Lubbock |
| Young | 90 | 2 | 8 | N-W. Falls |
| Zapata | 49 | 4 | 4 | S-Laredo |
| Zavala | 293, 365 | 4 | 4 | W-Del Rio |

# District Judges in Texas

Below are the names of all district judges, as of August 2003, in Texas listed in district court order. To determine which judges have jurisdiction in specific counties, refer to the table on pages 437–438.

*Source: Texas Judicial System Directory 2003, Office of Court Administration.*

| Court | Judge | Court | Judge | Court | Judge |
|---|---|---|---|---|---|
| 1 | Joe Bob Golden | 67 | Donald Cosby | 136 | Milton Gunn Shuffield |
| 1A | Monte D. Lawlis | 68 | Charles Stokes | 137 | Cecil G. Puryear |
| 2 | Dwight L. Phifer | 69 | Ronald E. Enns | 138 | Robert Garza |
| 3 | James N. Parsons III | 70 | Jay Gibson | 139 | Leticia Hinojosa |
| 4 | J. Clay Gossett | 71 | Bonnie Leggat | 140 | Jim Bob Darnell |
| 5 | Ralph K. Burgess | 72 | J. Blair Cherry Jr. | 141 | Len Wade |
| 6 | Jim D. Lovett | 73 | Andy Mireles | 142 | George David Gilles |
| 7 | Kerry L. Russell | 74 | Alan M. Mayfield | 143 | Bob Parks |
| 8 | Robert Newsom | 75 | C.T. Hight | 144 | Mark Randal Luitjen |
| 9 | Frederick E. Edwards | 76 | Jimmy L. White | 145 | Campbell Cox II |
| 10 | David Edward Garner | 77 | Horace Dickson Black Jr. | 146 | Jack Richard Morris |
| 11 | Mark Davidson | 78 | Roy T. Sparkman | 147 | Wilford Flowers |
| 12 | William Lee McAdams | 79 | Terry A. Canales | 148 | Rose Vela |
| 13 | John Howard Jackson | 80 | Kent C. Sullivan | 149 | Robert E. May |
| 14 | Mary L. Murphy | 81 | Donna Rayes | 150 | Janet P. Littlejohn |
| 15 | James Fry | 82 | Robert Miller Stem | 151 | Caroline E. Baker |
| 16 | Carmen Rivera-Worley | 83 | Carl Pendergrass | 152 | Kenneth Price Wise |
| 17 | Fred Wallis Davis | 84 | William D. Smith | 153 | Kenneth Charles Curry |
| 18 | John Edward Neill | 85 | J.D. Langley | 154 | Felix Klein |
| 19 | Ralph T. Strother | 86 | Howard Tygrett | 155 | Dan Raymond Beck |
| 20 | Ed Magre | 87 | Deborah Oakes Evans | 156 | Joel B. Johnson |
| 21 | Terry Flenniken | 88 | Earl Stover III | 157 | Randall W. Wilson |
| 22 | Charles R. Ramsay | 89 | Juanita Pavlick | 158 | Jake Collier |
| 23 | Ben Hardin | 90 | Stephen O'Neal Crawford | 159 | Paul E. White |
| 24 | Joseph Patrick Kelly | 91 | Steven R. Herod | 160 | Joseph M. Cox |
| 25 | Dwight E. Peschel | 92 | Edward G. Aparicio | 161 | Tryon D. Lewis |
| 2nd 25 | Gus J. Strauss | 93 | Rodolfo Delgado | 162 | Bill Rhea |
| 26 | Billy Ray Stubblefield | 94 | Jack E. Hunter | 163 | Dennis Powell |
| 27 | Joe Carroll | 95 | Karen Johnson | 164 | Martha Hill Jamison |
| 28 | Nanette Hasette | 96 | Jeff Walker | 165 | Elizabeth Ray |
| 29 | Jerry D. Ray | 97 | Roger E. Towery | 166 | Martha B. Tanner |
| 30 | Robert P. Brotherton | 98 | W. Jeanne Meurer | 167 | Mike F. Lynch |
| 31 | Steven R. Emmert | 99 | Mackey K. Hancock | 168 | Guadalupe Rivera |
| 32 | Glen N. Harrison | 100 | David M. McCoy | 169 | Gordon G. Adams |
| 33 | Guilford L. "Gil" Jones | 101 | Jay Patterson | 170 | Jim Meyer |
| 34 | William E. Moody | 102 | John F. Miller Jr. | 171 | Bonnie Rangel |
| 35 | William Stephen Ellis | 103 | Menton Murray Jr. | 172 | Donald J. Floyd |
| 36 | Mike Welborn | 104 | Lee Hamilton | 173 | Jack H. Holland |
| 37 | David A. Berchelmann Jr. | 105 | J. Manuel Banales | 174 | George H. Godwin |
| 38 | Mickey Ray Pennington | 106 | Carter Tinsley Schildknecht | 175 | Mary D. Roman |
| 39 | Charles Lewis Chapman | 107 | Benjamin Euresti Jr. | 176 | James Brian Rains |
| 40 | Gene Knize | 108 | Abe Lopez | 177 | Carol G. Davies |
| 41 | Mary Anne Bramblett | 109 | James L. Rex | 178 | William T. Harmon |
| 42 | John Wilson Weeks | 110 | John R. Hollums | 179 | J. Michael Wilkinson |
| 43 | Don Chrestman | 111 | Raul Vasquez | 180 | Debbie Mantooth-Stricklin |
| 44 | David D. Kelton | 112 | Brock Jones Jr. | 181 | John B. Board |
| 45 | Barbara Hanson Nellermoe | 113 | Patricia Hancock | 182 | Jeannie S. Barr |
| 46 | Tom A. Neely | 114 | Cynthia Stevens Kent | 183 | Joan Huffman |
| 47 | Hal Miner | 115 | Lauren L. Parish | 184 | Jan Krocker |
| 48 | John Robert "Bob" McCoy | 116 | Robert Henry Frost | 185 | Susan Brown |
| 49 | Manuel R. Flores | 117 | Sandra Watts | 186 | Maria Teresa "Tessa" Herr |
| 50 | David Wayne Hajek | 118 | Robert H. Moore III | 187 | Raymond C. Angelini |
| 51 | Barbara Lane Walther | 119 | Garland Benton Woodward | 188 | David Brabham |
| 52 | Phillip H. Zeigler | 120 | Luis Aguilar | 189 | Jeff Work |
| 53 | Scott H. Jenkins | 121 | Kelly Glen Moore | 190 | Jennifer Walker Elrod |
| 54 | George H. Allen | 122 | John Ellisor | 191 | Catharina Haynes |
| 55 | Jeffrey V. Brown | 123 | Guy William Griffin | 192 | Merrill L. Hartman |
| 56 | Norma Venso | 124 | Alvin G. Khoury | 193 | David W. Evans |
| 57 | Patrick J. Boone | 125 | John A. Coselli | 194 | Mary E. Miller |
| 58 | James William Mehaffy Jr. | 126 | Darlene Byrne | 195 | John Runnels Nelms |
| 59 | Rayburn M. "Rim" Nall Jr. | 127 | Sharolyn P. Wood | 196 | Joe M. Leonard |
| 60 | James Gary Sanderson | 128 | Patrick A. Clark | 197 | Migdalia Lopez |
| 61 | John Donovan | 129 | S. Grant Dorfman | 198 | Emil Karl Prohl |
| 62 | Robert Scott McDowell | 130 | Craig Estlinbaum | 199 | Robert T. Dry Jr. |
| 63 | Thomas F. Lee | 131 | John D. Gabriel Jr. | 200 | Paul R. Davis Jr. |
| 64 | Robert W. Kinkaid Jr. | 132 | Ernie B. Armstrong | 201 | Suzanne Covington |
| 65 | Alfredo Chavez | 133 | Lamar McCorkle | 202 | Bill Peek |
| 66 | F.B. "Bob" McGregor Jr. | 134 | Anne Ashby | 203 | Lana Rolf McDaniel |
| | | 135 | Kemper Stephen Williams | | |

| Court | Judge |
|---|---|
| 204 | Mark Nancarrow |
| 205 | Kathleen H. Olivares |
| 206 | Rose Guerra Reyna |
| 207 | Jack Hollis Robison |
| 208 | Denise Collins |
| 209 | Michael Thomas McSpadden |
| 210 | Gonzalo Garcia |
| 211 | Lawrence Dee Shipman |
| 212 | Susan Criss |
| 213 | Robert Keith Gill |
| 214 | Jose Longoria |
| 215 | Levi James Benton |
| 216 | Stephen B. Ables |
| 217 | David V. Wilson |
| 218 | Stella H. Saxon |
| 219 | Curt B. Henderson |
| 220 | James Edward Morgan |
| 221 | Suzanne Stovall |
| 222 | Roland Saul |
| 223 | Leland W. Waters |
| 224 | David Peeples |
| 225 | John J. Specia Jr. |
| 226 | Sid L. Harle |
| 227 | Philip A. Kazen Jr. |
| 228 | Ted Poe |
| 229 | Alex W. Gabert |
| 230 | Belinda Hill |
| 231 | Randy Catterton |
| 232 | Mary Lou Keel |
| 233 | Mary Lou Keel |
| 234 | Bruce Oakley |
| 235 | Jerry W. Woodlock |
| 236 | Thomas Wilson Lowe III |
| 237 | Sam Medina |
| 238 | John Gary Hyde |
| 239 | Patrick "Pat" Sebesta |
| 240 | Thomas R. Culver III |
| 241 | Diane Vinson DeVasto |
| 242 | Edward L. Self |
| 243 | David C. Guaderrama |
| 244 | Gary L. Watkins |
| 245 | Annette Galik |
| 246 | Jim York |
| 247 | Bonnie Crane Hellums |
| 248 | Joan Campbell |
| 249 | D. Wayne Bridewell |
| 250 | John K. Dietz |
| 251 | Pat Pirtle |
| 252 | Layne Walker |
| 253 | Chap Cain III |
| 254 | Jeffrey V. Coen |
| 255 | Craig Fowler |
| 256 | Brenda Garrett Green |
| 257 | Linda Motheral |
| 258 | Elizabeth E. Coker |
| 259 | Brooks H. Hagler |
| 260 | Buddie J. Hahn |
| 261 | Lora J. Livingston |
| 262 | Mike Anderson |
| 263 | Jim Wallace |
| 264 | Martha Jane Trudo |
| 265 | Keith Dean |
| 266 | Donald Richard Jones |
| 267 | Juergen "Skipper" Koetter |
| 268 | Brady Gifford Elliott |
| 269 | John T. Wooldridge |
| 270 | Brent Gamble |
| 271 | John H. Fostel |
| 272 | Richard Davis |
| 273 | Charles R. Mitchell |
| 274 | Gary L. Steel |
| 275 | Juan R. Partida |
| 276 | William R. "Bill" Porter |

| Court | Judge |
|---|---|
| 277 | Ken Anderson |
| 278 | Kenneth H. Keeling |
| 279 | Thomas Francis Mulvaney |
| 280 | Tony Lindsay |
| 281 | Jane Nenninger Bland |
| 282 | Karen Jane Greene |
| 283 | Vickers L. Cunningham Jr. |
| 284 | Olen Underwood |
| 285 | Michael Peden |
| 286 | Harold Phelan |
| 287 | Gordon Houston Green |
| 288 | Frank Montalvo |
| 289 | Carmen Kelsey |
| 290 | Sharon MacRae |
| 291 | Susan Hawk |
| 292 | Henry Wade Jr. |
| 293 | Cynthia L. Muniz |
| 294 | Teresa Drum |
| 295 | Tracy E. Christopher |
| 296 | Betty Ann Caton |
| 297 | Everett Young |
| 298 | Adolph Canales |
| 299 | Jon Neil Wisser |
| 300 | K. Randall Hufstetler |
| 301 | Susan Amanda Rankin |
| 302 | Frances A. Harris |
| 303 | Richard Johnson |
| 304 | John Sholden |
| 305 | Cheryl Lee Shannon |
| 306 | Steven Baker |
| 307 | Robin D. Sage |
| 308 | Georgia Dempster |
| 309 | Frank Rynd |
| 310 | Lisa Millard |
| 311 | Doug Warne |
| 312 | James D. Squier |
| 313 | Pat Shelton |
| 314 | John F. Phillips |
| 315 | Kent Ellis |
| 316 | John La Grone |
| 317 | Larry Thorne |
| 318 | Dean Rucker |
| 319 | Thomas F. Greenwell |
| 320 | Don Emerson |
| 321 | Carole W. Clark |
| 322 | Frank W. Sullivan |
| 323 | Jean Hudson Boyd |
| 324 | Brian A. Carper |
| 325 | Judith G. Wells |
| 326 | Aleta Hacker |
| 327 | Linda Chew |
| 328 | Ronald R. Pope |
| 329 | Daniel Richard Sklar |
| 330 | Marilea Whatley Lewis |
| 331 | Robert A. Perkins |
| 332 | Mario E. Ramirez Jr. |
| 333 | Joseph James Halbach Jr. |
| 334 | position vacant |
| 335 | Harold Robert Towslee |
| 336 | Ray Felty Grisham |
| 337 | Don R. Stricklin |
| 338 | Tommy Brock Thomas Jr. |
| 339 | Caprice Cosper |
| 340 | Rae Leifeste |
| 341 | Elma Teresa Salinas Ender |
| 342 | Bob McGrath |
| 343 | Janna K. Whatley |
| 344 | Carroll E. Wilborn Jr. |
| 345 | Patrick O. Keel |
| 346 | Richard Abram Roman |
| 347 | Nelva Gonzales-Ramos |
| 348 | Dana M. Womack |
| 349 | Jerry L. Calhoon |

| Court | Judge |
|---|---|
| 350 | Jesse Aaron Holloway |
| 351 | Mark Kent Ellis |
| 352 | Bonnie Sudderth |
| 353 | Margaret A. Cooper |
| 354 | Richard "Rick" Beacom |
| 355 | Ralph H. Walton Jr. |
| 356 | Britton Edward Plunk |
| 357 | Leonel Alejandro |
| 358 | Bill McCoy |
| 359 | Kathleen A. Hamilton |
| 360 | Debra Lehrmann |
| 361 | Steve Lee Smith |
| 362 | Bruce McFarling |
| 363 | Faith Johnson |
| 364 | Bradley S. Underwood |
| 365 | Amado Abascal III |
| 366 | Nathan E. White Jr. |
| 367 | E. Lee Gabriel |
| 368 | Alfred Burton "Burt" Carnes |
| 369 | Bascom W. Bentley III |
| 370 | Noe Gonzalez |
| 371 | James R. Wilson |
| 372 | Scott Wisch |
| 377 | Robert C. Cheshire |
| 378 | Roy A. Scoggins Jr. |
| 379 | Robert C. "Bert" Richardson |
| 380 | Charles F. Sandoval |
| 381 | John A. Pope III |
| 382 | Brett Hall |
| 383 | Mike Herrera |
| 384 | Patrick Michael Garcia |
| 385 | Willie Bryan DuBose |
| 386 | Laura Lee Parker |
| 387 | Robert J. Kern |
| 388 | Patricia A. Macias |
| 389 | Leticia Lopez |
| 390 | Julie Harris Kocurek |
| 391 | Thomas J. Gossett |
| 392 | Carter William Tarrance |
| 393 | Vicki B. Isaacks |
| 394 | Kenneth Daly DeHart |
| 395 | Michael P. Jergins |
| 396 | George W. Gallagher |
| 398 | Aida Salinas Flores |
| 399 | Juanita A. Vasquez-Gardner |
| 400 | Bradley Smith |
| 401 | Mark Joseph Rusch |
| 402 | George Timothy Boswell |
| 403 | Brenda P. Kennedy |
| 404 | Abel C. Limas |
| 405 | Wayne Mallia |
| 406 | Andres Reyes |
| 407 | Karen Pozza |
| 408 | Phylis J. Speedlin |
| 409 | Sam Medrano |
| 410 | K. Michael Mayes |
| 411 | Robert Hill Trapp |

### Criminal District Courts

| Court | Judge |
|---|---|
| Dallas 1 | Janice Lough Warder |
| Dallas 2 | Cliff Stricklin |
| Dallas 3 | Robert Francis |
| Dallas 4 | John Coleman Creuzot |
| Dallas 5 | Manny D. Alvarez |
| Jefferson | Charles Dana Carver |
| Tarrant 1 | Sharen Wilson |
| Tarrant 2 | Wayne Francis Salvant |
| Tarrant 3 | Elizabeth Berry |
| Tarrant 4 | Mike Thomas |
| El Paso | James T. Carter |

# State Agencies

On the following pages is information about several of the many state agencies. The agencies themselves supplied this information to the *Texas Almanac*. The Web address for more information about state agencies, boards and commissions is: **www2.tsl.state.tx.us/trail/**.

## Texas Commission on Environmental Quality

Source: Texas Commission on Environmental Quality; www.tceq.state.tx.us

The Texas Commission on Environmental Quality (TCEQ) is the state's leading environmental agency. Known as the Texas Natural Resource Conservation Commission until September 2002, this agency strives to protect Texas' human and natural resources in a manner consistent with sustainable economic development. The goals are clean air, clean water and the safe management of waste, with an emphasis on pollution prevention.

The TCEQ had approximately 3,000 employees, 16 regional offices and a $395.5 million annual appropriated budget for the 2003 fiscal year. Most of the budget is funded by program fees ($323 million or 81.7 percent). Federal funds provide $38.8 million, or 9.8 percent; state general revenue, including earned federal funds, provides $29.7 million, or 7.5 percent; and other sources provide the remaining $4.1 million, or 1 percent.

Mailing address: PO Box 13087, Austin 78711; phone, 512-239-1000; **www.tceq.state.tx.us**. ☆

## Department of Human Services

Source: Texas Department of Human Services; www.dhs.state.tx.us

The **Texas Department of Human Services (DHS)**, administers state and federal programs that provide financial, health and social services to three main categories of clients: low-income families with children, the elderly or disabled, and victims of family violence. The department's headquarters are in Austin, but its services are provided through 10 administrative regions and more than 400 local offices serving all 254 Texas counties. Determining client eligibility for programs and services is a primary agency function; most direct client services are provided by local service providers that contract with the agency.

### Texas Works

Texas Works is the agency's welfare-to-work program, emphasizing personal responsibility in helping clients identify resources that can assist them in achieving economic self-sufficiency.

• The **Temporary Assistance for Needy Families** (TANF) program provides basic financial assistance for needy children and the parents or caretakers with whom they live. As a condition of eligibility, caretakers must sign and abide by a personal-responsibility agreement. Time limits for benefits have been set by both state and federal welfare-reform legislation. A typical TANF family of three (caretaker and two children) can receive a maximum monthly grant of $213. In fiscal year 2003, an average 358,751 children and caretakers received TANF assistance each month, compared to 349,803 per month in 2001.

• The **Food Stamp program** is an entirely federally funded program that assists low-income families, the elderly and single adults to obtain a nutritionally adequate diet. Those eligible for food stamps include households receiving TANF or federal Supplemental Security Income benefits and non-public assistance households having incomes below 130 percent of the poverty level.

Food stamp and TANF benefits are delivered through the Electronic Benefit Transfer system, through which clients access benefits at about 12,000 retail locations statewide with Lone Star debit cards. In fiscal year 2002, an average of almost 1.58 million Texans per month received food-stamp benefits totaling $1.49 billion for the year.

• DHS determines eligibility for **Medicaid**, which provides access to vital health-care services. An average of 1,388,046 individuals were enrolled in Texas Works Medicaid each month during fiscal year 2002. The TANF-related Medicaid program provides medical coverage to TANF recipients and other income-eligible families, women and children who do not receive TANF cash assistance. Transitional Medicaid is available for four months for recipients who lose TANF cash assistance because of job earnings or state time limits.

### Long-Term Care Services

DHS determines **Medicaid eligibility** for aged and disabled individuals and provides assistance to Medicaid recipients in nursing facilities or community-based programs. In fiscal year 2002, an average of 64,982 individuals per month were enrolled in Medicaid nursing-facility care services and about 137,859 individuals per month in community-based programs. The **Nursing Facility** program pays for nursing-home care for Medicaid recipients who have a documented medical condition requiring the skills of a licensed nurse on a regular basis. **Community Care** programs are designed to avoid prematurely placing elderly or disabled individuals in nursing homes or other facilities by providing services, including assistance with personal care, home-delivered meals, emergency re-sponse, client-managed attendant services, grants for architectural modifications or major-equipment purchases, adult day-activity and health services, supervised residential-care services, adult foster care and respite care.

The **Long-Term Care Regulatory** (LTC-R) program licenses and regulates nursing facilities, intermediate-care facilities for persons with mental retardation, adult day-care facilities, assisted-living facilities, home-health agencies, hospice agencies and personal-assistance services. LTC-R also certifies certain types of facilities for the Medicaid program and investigates complaints and allegations of abuse, neglect and noncompliance.

### Other Programs

The **Family Violence program** educates the public about domestic violence and offers emergency shelter and support services to victims and their children. The program is administered through contracts with family-violence service providers.

The **Disaster Assistance program** processes grant applications for victims of presidentially declared disasters, such as tornados, floods and hurricanes. Victims are eligible for assistance from this state-administered federal program if they do not have insurance and cannot qualify for low-interest loans from the Small Business Administration.

The entirely federally funded **Refugee Resettlement program** provides cash, health care and social services to eligible refugees to help them become self-sufficient as soon as possible after arriving in the United States.

Eight **Special Nutrition** programs, completely funded by the U.S. Dept. of Agriculture, provide meals to eligible recipients, including elderly or functionally impaired adults and to children and low-income individuals and families. ☆

---

### Costs of Services

Costs of most services are shared by the state and federal governments. Expenditures for fiscal year 2002 are as follows (does not include the value of food stamps ($1.49 billion) and food distributed by DHS ($103.4 million):

' **Family self-sufficiency services** . $1,032,681,053
**Family violence services** . . . . . . . .21,669,740
**Long-term care services** . . . . . . 3,590,548,639
**Support services (includes admin-**
    **istrative costs)**. . . . . . . . . . 104,120,505

**Total** . . . . . . . . . . . . . . . **$4,749,019,937**

# The General Land Office

Source: General Land Office of Texas. On the Web: www.glo.state.tx.us

## History of the General Land Office

The Texas General Land Office (GLO) is one of the oldest governmental entities in the state, dating back to the Republic of Texas. The first General Land Office was established in 1836 in the Republic's constitution, and the first Texas Congress enacted the provision into law in 1837. The GLO was established to oversee distribution of public lands, register titles, issue patents on land and maintain records of land granted.

In the early years of statehood, Texas established the precedent of using its vast public domain for public benefit. The first use was to sell or trade off land to eliminate the huge debt remaining from Texas' War for Independence and early years of the Republic.

Texas also gave away land to settlers as homesteads; to veterans as compensation for service; for internal improvements, including building railroads, shipbuilding and improvement of rivers for navigation; and to build the state Capitol.

The public domain was closed in 1898 when the Texas Supreme Court declared that there was no more vacant and unappropriated land in Texas. Only some small tracts were left, and in 1900, all remaining unappropriated land was set aside by the Texas Legislature to benefit public schools.

Today, **21.8 million acres of land and minerals,** owned by the Permanent School Fund, the Permanent University Fund, various other state agencies or the Veterans Land Board, are managed by the General Land Office and the Commissioner of the Texas General Land Office. This includes almost 4 million acres of submerged coastal lands, which consist of bays, inlets and the area from the Texas shoreline to the three-marine-league line (10.36 miles) in the Gulf of Mexico. It is estimated that more than 1 million acres make up the public domain of the state's riverbeds and another 1.7 million acres are excess land dedicated to the Permanent School Fund.

The **Permanent University Fund** holds title to 2,109,000 fee acres, and other state agencies or special schools hold title to another 2 million acres. The **Permanent School Fund** (PSF) owns mineral rights alone in about 7.5 million acres covered under the Relinquishment Act, the Free Royalty Act and the various sales acts, and has outright ownership to approximately 723,896 upland acres, mostly west of the Pecos River. The **Veterans Land Board** has liens on more than 633,000 acres of land in active veterans accounts.

The General Land Office handles leases and revenue accounting on all lands dedicated to the Permanent School Fund and on land owned by various state agencies. The Commissioner of the Texas General Land Office is Jerry Patterson.

## Veterans Programs

### Veterans Land Program

In 1946, the Texas Legislature created a bond program to aid veterans in purchasing farmland. Up to $1.5 billion in bonding authority has been authorized over the years in a series of constitutional amendments; as of May 2003, more than $1.38 billion of the bonds had been sold to fund loans.

Loans cannot exceed $40,000, and tracts purchased through the program must be at least five acres in size. To date, about 119,000 veterans have purchased more than 4.9 million acres of land under the program.

### Veterans Housing Assistance Program

The 68th Legislature created the Veterans Housing Assistance Program, which also is funded through bond proceeds. Over the years, the people of Texas have passed constitutional amendments authorizing the selling of $2.5 billion in bonds to finance this program. To date, more than $2 billion in bonds have been sold to fund housing loans.

Eligible veterans may borrow up to $200,000 toward the purchase of a home. The low-interest loans result in reduced monthly payments for veterans. Since the program began operation in January 1984, more than 51,000 Texas veterans have received housing loans worth about $2.6 billion.

### Veterans Home Improvement Program

In 1986, the Veterans Land Board implemented the Veterans Home Improvement Program, which is funded through the Veterans Housing Assistance Program. This program allows Texas veterans to borrow up to $25,000 to make substantial home repairs and improvements. Since the program's inception, more than 3,200 veterans have received home improvement loans worth more than $47 million.

All three programs are administered by the Texas Veterans Land Board, which is chaired by the GLO commissioner. The bonded debt for the programs and all administrative costs are financed by the veterans who use the programs; there is no cost to Texas taxpayers. Eligible veterans may participate simultaneously in the three loan programs and may apply for additional loans once preceding loans are paid in full.

### Texas State Veterans Homes

In 1997, the 75th Legislature approved legislation authorizing the Texas Veterans Land Board to construct and operate Texas State Veterans Homes under a cost-sharing program with the U.S. Department of Veterans Affairs (USDVA) and to issue revenue bonds to obtain the state's necessary share. The homes provide affordable, quality, long-term care for Texas' aging veteran population. The state provides the land and 35 percent of construction costs, and the USDVA provides 65 percent of construction costs. After an intensive search for host communities, construction began on state veterans homes in Temple and Floresville in 1998, and the first residents were admitted in December 2000. Construction began on the Big Spring and Bonham homes in fall 1999.

In January 2003, the Texas Veterans Land Board selected El Paso and McAllen to host two more state veterans homes, which are expected to open in early 2005.

Because the USDVA subsidizes over half of a veteran's cost to stay in a Texas State Veterans Home, the daily rates are well below market average. A veteran pays about $23,000 per year for a semi-private room, while the average cost to stay in a Texas nursing home is about $40,000. Spouses of Texas veterans and Gold Star parents are also eligible for care in Texas State Veterans Homes.

Each home has 160 beds and provides a broad spectrum of health care services, a comprehensive rehabilitation program, special diets, recreational activities, social services, a library, a gift shop, and certified, safe Alzheimer's wings with secure outdoor courtyards..

### Texas State Veterans Cemeteries

In May 2002, Killeen and Mission were chosen as sites for the first two Texas State Veterans Cemeteries. Burials are expected to begin in 2005.

The Veterans Land Board will own and operate the cemeteries under USDVA guidelines. The USDVA will fund the design and construction of the cemeteries, but the land must be donated.

These cemeteries will complement the four USDVA national cemeteries in Texas, located in San Antonio, Houston, Dallas-Fort Worth and El Paso. There are no known plans for additional national cemeteries in Texas, and approximately 580,000 of Texas' 1.7 million veterans are 65 or older.

For more information on state home, land and home improvement loans for Texas veterans, as well as Texas State Veterans Homes and Texas State Veterans Cemeteries, call (800) 252-VETS, or visit the Texas Veterans Land Board Web site at **www.texasveterans.com.**

| Distribution of the Public Lands of Texas | |
|---|---|
| **Purpose** | **Acres** |
| **Settlers** | **68,027,108** |
|    Spain and Mexico | 24,583,923 |
|    Spanish and Mexican Grants south of the Nueces River, recognized by Act of Feb. 10, 1852 | 3,741,241 |
|    Headrights | 30,360,002 |
|    Republic colonies | 4,494,806 |
|    Preemption land | 4,847,136 |
| **Military** | **9,874,262** |
|    Bounty | 5,354,250 |
|    Battle donations | 1,162,240 |
|    Veterans donations | 1,377,920 |
|    Confederate | 1,979,852 |
| **Improvements** | **37,155,714** |
|    Road | 27,716 |
|    Navigation | 4,261,760 |
|    Irrigation | 584,000 |
|    Ships | 17,000 |
|    Manufacturing | 111,360 |
|    Railroads | 32,153,878 |
| **Education** | **52,329,168** |
|    University, public school and eleemosynary institutions | 52,329,168 |
| **Total of distributed lands** | **167,386,252** |

### Energy Resources

The GLO helps fund public education in Texas by maximizing the natural resources from state lands, including oil and gas. Millions of acres of Permanent School Fund land are leased through the GLO to energy firms for oil and gas exploration and production. Royalties and other fees from this production are paid to the GLO, which dedicates the money to the PSF for use in schools around the state.

In the 1990s the General Land Office also began to accept oil and gas in-kind in lieu of cash royalty payments. Through the In-Kind Gas Program, the GLO sells gas at discounted prices to public entities such as schools and cities. Also, through the GLO's State Power Program, the agency works with private enterprise to convert in-kind oil and gas into electricity. This electricity is sold at below-market rates to public entities, providing a further cost savings to the state.

The GLO has expanded into construction of sustainable energy projects, especially wind energy facilities, on PSF lands. The GLO pioneered wind power in Texas in the 1990s by leasing PSF land in West Texas for a wind energy facility.

### Coastal Stewardship

The General Land Office is the steward of the Texas Gulf Coast, serving as the premier state agency for protect and renourish the coast, and fighting coastal erosion. The GLO manages about $3.6 million a year for beach renourishment and marsh restoration projects along the coast through the Coastal Erosion Planning and Response Act. The GLO has maintained, protected or restored more than 45 miles of Texas coastal shoreline since becoming the lead state agency for coastal erosion in 1999. In 1991, the GLO also was granted the authority to prevent and respond to oil spills on the Texas coast.

In 1986, the General Land Office began its Adopt-A-Beach cleanups, held every spring and fall along the Texas coast. Since the program began, more than 300,000 volunteers have removed more than 5,600 tons of trash from Texas beaches. For more information, call the Adopt-A-Beach toll-free number: 1-877-TX COAST (1-877-892-6278). ☆

# Texas Department of Criminal Justice

*On the Web: www.tdcj.state.tx.us*

The **Texas Board of Criminal Justice** (TBCJ) is composed of nine non-salaried members who are appointed by the Governor for staggered six-year terms. Charged with governing the **Texas Department of Criminal Justice** (TDCJ), the board develops and implements policies that guide agency operations. The TBCJ also serves as the school board for the Windham School District. For a list of members, see the Boards and Commissions list following this article. Christina Melton Crain was appointed board chairman February 2003.

The TDCJ executive director is appointed by the board and is responsible for the day-to-day administration and operation of the agency. Gary L. Johnson was appointed TDCJ executive director on Aug. 1, 2001.

**The department is composed of these divisions:** Administrative Review and Risk Management Division, Office of the General Counsel, Community Justice Assistance Division, State Jail Division, Institutional Division, Parole Division, Programs and Services Division, Health Services Division, Victim Services, Facilities Division, Human Resources Division, Operations Division and the Private Facilities Division.

The chief financial officer oversees the Manufacturing and Logistics Division, the Information Technology Division and Business and Finance for the agency.

The Office of the Inspector General, coordinating with the executive director and the deputy executive director, reports to the TBCJ and oversees the Investigations Division and the Internal Audit Division.

The state counsel for offenders also coordinates with the directors and reports directly to the TBCJ. Correctional Managed Health Care (CMHC) and the Texas Council on Offenders with Mental Impairments (TCOMI) work with the TDCJ directors and report to a board/committee comprised of appointed members from various agencies and the Governor's office.

Among the agency's divisions, the Community Justice Assistance Division, the State Jail Division, the Institutional Division, the Private Facilities Division and the Parole Division are most involved in the everyday confinement/supervision of convicted felons. However, the supervision of probationers is the responsibility of local community supervision and corrections departments.

The **Institutional Division** manages the TDCJ's prisons. As of April 30, 2003, the **total number of prisoners** on-hand was over 128,500.

The **Parole Division** processes offenders for release on parole or mandatory supervision and oversees the supervision and rehabilitative services for reintegration into the community. As of May 1, 2003, more than 76,600 adult offenders were under parole or mandatory supervision.

The **State Jail Division** was started in 1993 to provide

| Inmate Profile | |
| --- | --- |
| **Age/Sex/Ethnicity** | |
| 94 % are male | 44.2 % are black |
| Average age: 35.4 | 30.1 % are white |
| | 25.2 % are Hispanic |
| **Sentences/Length of Time Served** | |
| Average sentence: 20.8 years | |
| Average part of sentence served: 25% | |
| More than 50% of inmates have been in prison before. | |
| **Education** | |
| Average IQ: 91.1 | |
| More than 70 percent lack a high school diploma. | |
| Average education achievement score: 7th grade | |

community-oriented **rehabilitation** for property and drug offenders. In April 30, 2003, there were approximately 15,690 state jail confinees. In February 1996, the State Jail Division assumed administrative management of **Substance Abuse Felony Punishment** (SAFP) facilities. In April 30, 2003, more than 3,800 offenders were participating in a SAFP program.

The **Community Justice Assistance Division** oversees the community supervision and corrections departments that work directly with **probationers**. As of December 2002, approximately 434,000 felony, misdemeanor and pre-trial probationers were under community supervision.

The **Private Facilities Division** was created in October 2000 by the TDCJ executive director to oversee and monitor privately contracted, secure facilities housing state offenders. In July 2001, the division expanded with the addition of non-secure privately operated facilities, such as halfway houses, transitional treatment centers (TTC) and the outpatient TTC substance abuse contracts.

The **Programs and Services Division** and the **Operations Division** administer and manage offender programs and services across division lines. **Victim Services** coordinates a central mechanism for victims and the public to participate in the criminal justice process. The remaining divisions support the overall operation of the agency.

## TDCJ Facilities

The town listed is the nearest one to the facility, although the unit may actually be in another county. For instance, the Middleton Transfer Unit is in Jones County, but the nearest city is Abilene, which is in Taylor County. Units marked by an asterisk (*) are operated by private companies.

### Institutional Division

**Allred,** Iowa Park, Wichita Co.; **Beto,** Tennessee Colony, Anderson Co.; **Boyd,** Teague, Freestone Co.; *__Bridgeport,__ Bridgeport, Wise Co.; **Briscoe,** Dilley, Frio Co.; **Byrd** (diagnostic intake), Huntsville, Walker Co.; **Central,** Sugar Land, Fort Bend Co.; **Clem-

**ens,** Brazoria, Brazoria Co.; **Clements,** Amarillo, Potter Co.; \*Cleveland, Cleveland, Liberty Co.; **Coffield,** Tennessee Colony, Anderson Co.; **Connally,** Kenedy, Karnes Co.; **Dalhart,** Dalhart, Hartley Co.; **Daniel, Snyder,** Scurry Co.; **Darrington,** Rosharon, Brazoria Co.; \***Diboll,** Diboll, Angelina Co.; **Eastham,** Lovelady, Houston Co.; **Ellis,** Huntsville, Walker Co.; **Estelle,** Huntsville, Walker Co.; \***Estes,** Venus, Johnson Co.; **Ferguson,** Midway, Madison Co.; **Gatesville,** Gatesville, Coryell Co. (Women's Unit); **Goree,** Huntsville, Walker Co.; **Hightower,** Dayton, Liberty Co.; **Hilltop,** Gatesville, Coryell Co.; **Hobby,** Marlin, Falls Co.; **Hodge,** Rusk, Cherokee Co.; **Hospital** Galveston, Galveston Co.; **Hughes,** Gatesville, Coryell Co.; **Huntsville,** Huntsville, Walker Co.; **Jester III** and **IV,** Richmond, Fort Bend Co.; **Jordan,** Pampa, Gray Co.; \***Kyle,** Kyle, Hays Co.; **LeBlanc,** Beaumont, Jefferson Co.; **Lewis,** Woodville, Tyler Co.; \***Lockhart,** Lockhart, Caldwell Co.; **Luther,** Navasota, Grimes Co.; **Lynaugh,** Fort Stockton, Pecos Co.; **McConnell,** Beeville, Bee Co.; **Michael,** Tennessee Colony, Anderson Co.; **Montford,** Lubbock, Lubbock Co.; \***B. Moore,** Overton, Rusk Co.; **Mountain View,** Gatesville, Coryell Co.; **Murray,** Gatesville, Coryell Co.; **Neal,** Amarillo, Potter Co.; **Pack,** Navasota, Grimes Co.; **Polunsky,** Livingston, Polk Co.; **Powledge,** Palestine, Anderson Co.; **Ramsey I** and **II,** Rosharon, Brazoria Co.; **Roach,** Childress, Childress Co.; **Robertson,** Abilene, Jones Co.; **Scott,** Angleton, Brazoria Co.; **Segovia,** Edinburg, Hidalgo Co.; **Skyview,** at Rusk State Hospital, Cherokee Co.; **Smith,** Lamesa, Dawson Co.; **Stevenson,** Cuero, DeWitt Co.; **Stiles,** Beaumont, Jefferson Co.; **Telford,** New Boston, Bowie Co.; **C.T. Terrell,** Rosharon, Brazoria Co.; **Torres,** Hondo, Medina Co.; **Vance,** Richmond, Fort Bend Co.; **Wallace,**

Colorado City, Mitchell Co; **Wynne,** Huntsville, Walker Co.; **C. Young,** Dickinson, Galveston Co.

### Transfer Units

**Cotulla,** Cotulla, LaSalle Co.; **Duncan,** Diboll, Angelina Co.; **Fort Stockton,** Fort Stockton, Pecos Co.; **Garza East & West,** Beeville, Bee Co.; **Goodman,** Jasper, Jasper Co.; **Gurney,** Tennessee Colony, Anderson Co.; **Holliday,** Huntsville, Walker Co.; **Middleton,** Abilene, Jones Co.; **C. Moore,** Bonham, Fannin Co.; **Rudd,** Brownfield, Terry Co.; **Tulia,** Tulia, Swisher Co.; **Ware,** Colorado City, Mitchell Co.

### State Jail Division

\***Barlett,** Barlett, Williamson Co.; \***Bradshaw,** Henderson, Rusk Co.; **Cole,** Bonham, Fannin Co.; \***Dawson,** Dallas, Dallas Co.; **Dominguez,** San Antonio, Bexar Co.; **Formby,** Plainview, Hale Co.; **Gist,** Beaumont, Jefferson Co.; **Hutchins,** Dallas, Dallas Co.; **Kegans,** Houston, Harris Co.; \***Lindsey,** Jacksboro, Jack Co.; **Lopez,** Edinburg, Hidalgo Co.; **Lychner,** Humble, Harris Co.; **Plane,** Dayton, Liberty Co.; **Sanchez,** El Paso, El Paso Co.; **Travis County,** Austin, Travis Co.; \***Williacy County,** Raymondville, Williacy Co.; and **Woodman,** Gatesville, Coryell Co.

### SAFP Facilities

**Glossbrenner,** San Diego, Duval Co.; **Halbert,** Burnet, Burnet Co.; **Havins,** Brownwood, Brown Co.; **Henley,** Dayton, Liberty Co.; **Jester I,** Richmond, Fort Bend Co.; **Johnston,** Winnsboro, Wood Co.; **Ney,** Hondo, Medina Co.; **Sayle,** Breckenridge, Stephens Co.; **Wheeler,** Plainview, Hale Co. ☆

### Texas Department of Economic Development

The Texas Department of Economic Development markets Texas. TxED assists communities with economic development in a global economy. The agency offers incentives and information to enhance a community's ability to participate in and benefit from the economic property of Texas. The agency's four core functions are: Market Texas Tourism, Market Texas Business, Market Texas Clearinghouse and Market Texas Finance Incentives. Mailing address: PO Box 12728, Austin 78711; phone: 512-936-0101; TDD: 512-936-0555. On the Web: **www.tded.state.tx.us/;** travel information: **www.traveltex.com.**

### Texas Food and Fibers Commission

The Texas Food and Fibers Commission was originally created in 1941 by the 47th Texas Legislature to increase the marketability and uses of cottonseed and cotton fiber and to set up cotton research facilities in Texas. TFFC's research focuses on short-term results — those that have the potential of impacting industry within two to three years.

TFFC programs over the past 20 years have invested about $29 million and attracted about $42 million in additional supporting funds. TFFC supports more than 50 projects. Recent projects included the introduction of new lines of cotton specific to the different growing regions in Texas; evaluation of a more environmentally friendly dry-cleaning solvent; and promotion of the use of Texas natural fibers through an annual competition among fashion-design students at 17 of the state's universities. Mailing address: PO Box 12046, Austin 78711-2046; phone: 512-936-2450; **www.tffc.state.tx.us.**

### Texas Historical Commission

The Texas Historical Commission protects and preserves the state's historic and prehistoric resources. The Texas State Legislature established the Texas State Historical Survey Committee in 1953 to identify important historic sites across the state. The Texas Legislature changed the agency's name to the Texas Historical Commission in 1973 and increased its mission and its protective powers. Today the agency's concerns include archaeology, architecture, history, economic development, heritage tourism, public administration and urban planning.

Among its many tasks, the commission:

• Provides leadership and training to county historical commissions, heritage organizations and museums in Texas' 254 counties;

• Works with communities to help protect Texas' diverse architectural heritage, including historic county courthouses and other public buildings;

• Administers the state's historical marker program. There are over 11,000 historical markers across Texas;

• Assists Texas cities in the revitalization of their historic downtowns through the Texas Main Street Program;

• Works with property owners to save archaeological sites on private land;

• Assists citizens to obtain historical designations for buildings, cemeteries, sites and other properties important to the state's historic and prehistoric past;

• Ensures that archaeological sites are protected when land is developed for highways and other public projects.

Mailing address: PO Box 12276, Austin 78711-2276; phone:     512-463-6100;     fax:     512-475-4872; **www.thc.state.tx.us.**

### Railroad Commission of Texas

The Railroad Commission of Texas was established in 1891 to prevent discrimination in railroad charges and establish reasonable tariffs. It is the oldest regulatory agency in the state and one of the oldest of its kind in the nation. On Feb. 20, 1917, the Texas Legislature declared oil pipelines to be common carriers and, therefore, under the jurisdiction of the commission. Today the commission's work primarily concerns the petroleum industry and surface-mined coal and uranium. It is also concerned with railroad safety. Mailing address: PO Box 12967, Austin 78711-2967; phone: 512-463-7288; **www.rrc.state.tx.us.**

### Texas Workforce Commission

The Texas Workforce Commission, successor to the Texas Employment Commission, oversees and provides work-force development services to employers and job seekers. TWC offers recruiting, retention, training, retraining and outplacement services. For job seekers, TWC offers career-development information, job search resources, training programs and, where warranted, unemployment benefits. Services are generally free and available through a network of 28 regional work-force boards. Mailing address: 101 E. 15th Street, Rm. 230, Austin 78778; 512-463-2236; **www.twc.state.tx.us.**

### Texas Youth Commission

The Texas Youth Commission administers the juvenile corrections system of the state. **Institutions (15)** are located in Beaumont, Brownwood (2 units), Bryan, Corsicana, Crockett, Edinburg, Gainesville, Giddings, Marlin, Mart, Pyote, San Saba, Sheffield and Vernon. **Half-way houses (9)** are located in Austin, Corpus Christi, Dallas, El Paso, Fort Worth, Harlingen, McAllen, Roanoke and San Antonio. Mailing address: PO Box 4260, Austin 78765; phone: 512-424-6130; **www.tyc.state.tx.us.** ☆

# Texas State Boards and Commissions

Following is a list of appointees to state boards and commissions, as well as names of other state officials, revised to **August 12, 2003.** Information includes, where available, (1) date of creation of agency; (2) whether the position is elective or appointive; (3) length of term; (4) compensation, if any; (5) number of members; (6) names of appointees, their hometowns and the dates of the terminations of their terms. In some instances the dates of expiration of terms have already passed; in such cases, no new appointment had been made by press time, and the official is continuing to fill the position until a successor can be named. Most positions marked "apptv." are appointed by the Governor. Where otherwise, appointing authority is given. Most advisory boards are not listed. Salaries for commissioners and administrators are those that were authorized by the appropriations bill passed by the 78th Legislature for the 2004–2005 biennium. They are "not-to-exceed" salaries; i.e., they are the maximum authorized salaries for the positions. The actual salaries may be less than the ones stated here.

**Acupuncture Examiners, Texas State Board of** – (1993); apptv.; 6 yrs.; per diem; 9 members: Sheng Ting Chen, Austin (2/1/07); Pedro (Pete) V. Garcia Jr., Lubbock (1/31/03); Everett G. Heinze Jr., Austin (1/31/03); Hoang Ziong Ho, San Antonio (2/1/07); Meng-Sheng Lin, Plano (1/31/01); Dee Ann Newbold, Austin (1/31/05); Terry Glenn Rascoe, Temple (2/1/07); Claire H. Smith, Dallas (1/31/05); Marshall D. Voris, Corpus Christi (1/31/05).

**Ad Valorem Tax Rate, Board to Calculate the** – (1907); ex officio; term in other office; 3 members: Governor, State Comptroller of Public Accounts and State Treasurer.

**Adjutant General** – (1836 by Republic of Texas; present office established 1905); apptv.: Gen. Wayne D. Marty (2/1/03) ($94,832, plus house and utilities), PO Box 5218, Austin 78763.

**Adjutant General, Assistant for Air** – Col. Michael B. Smith, PO Box 5218, Austin 78763.

**Adjutant General, Assistant for Army** – Brig. Gen. Wayne D. Marty, PO Box 5218, Austin 78763.

**Administrative Judicial Districts of Texas, Presiding Judges** – (Apptv. by Governor); serve terms concurrent with term as District Judge, subject to reappointment if re-elected to bench. No additional compensation. For names of judges, see Administrative Judicial Districts in index.

**Aerospace Commission, Texas** – (1987; re-established in 1989); apptv.; 6-yr.; 9 members: Richard N. Azar, El Paso (2/1/07); Gale E. Burkett, League City (2/1/05); J. Jan Collmer, Dallas (2/1/05); R. Walter Cunningham, Houston (2/1/03); Arthur R. Emerson, San Antonio (2/1/05); Richard L. "Larry" Griffin, Hunt (2/1/07); Bryon D. Sehlke, Austin (2/1/03); Holly Steger Stevens, Georgetown (2/1/07); Norma H. Webb, Midland (2/1/03). Exec. Dir., Bill Looke ($75,000), PO Box 12088, Austin 78711-2088.

**Aging, Texas Board on** – (1965 as Governor's Committee on Aging; name changed in 1981 to present form); apptv.; 6-yr.; expenses; 9 apptv. members: Ronald A. Brandon, Georgetown (2/1/03); Richard A. Braun, Midland (2/1/07); Frances Ann Brown, Carrollton (2/1/05); Miriam Ann Burton, Montgomery (2/1/03); Mi Yun "Maryann" Choi, Georgetown (2/1/07); Deborah Ann Hoffpauir, Allen (2/1/05); Nancy L. Lund, Texarkana (2/1/07); Thomas E. Oliver, Baytown (2/1/05); Richard E. Tankerson, San Antonio (2/1/05). Exec. Dir., Mary Sapp ($70,000), PO Box 12786, Austin 78711.

**Agricultural Finance Authority, Texas** – (1987); expenses; 2-yr.; 6 members: Darwin D. DeWees, San Angelo (1/1/05); Ruben O. Bosquez, McAllen (1/1/05); Mike Golden, Lake Jackson (1/1/02); Robert Hensley Henry, Vernon (1/1/01); Susan Kennedy, Nacogdoches (1/1/05); Albert Todd Lowry, Laredo (1/1/05); Renato Ramirez, Zapata (1/1/01); Victoria Salin, College Station (1/1/02); Jane Anne Stinnett, Lubbock (1/1/02).

**Agricultural Resources Protection Authority** – (1989 with 9 members; changed to 15 members, 1995); 2-yr.; expenses; 15 members: 9 ex officio: Dir., Texas Agricultural Experiment Station; Dean, College of Agricultural Sciences of Texas Tech University; Dean, University of Texas School of Public Health, Houston; Dir. of Environmental Epidemiology at Texas Department of Health; Chief of Groundwater Conservation section, Texas Commission on Environmental Quality; Dir. of Institute for International Agribusiness Studies, Prairie View A&M; Commissioner of Agriculture; Exec. Dir., Texas Structural Pest Control Board; Exec. Dir., State Soil and Water Conservation Board; 6 apptd. by Gov. (all members' terms expire 2/1/01): Craig Estes, Wichita Falls; L.C. Harrison, Wichita Falls; Gary Johnson, Dalhart; David K. Langford, San Antonio; David M. Nix, Lamesa; Julian H. Treviño, San Antonio.

**Aircraft Pooling Board, State** – (1979); apptv.; 6-yr.; 5 members — 2 ex officio: representative of State Auditor's Office and representative of General Services Commission; 3 apptv. — one by Gov., one by Speaker and one by Lt. Gov. Gov.'s appointee: Scott E. Rozzell, Houston (1/31/01). Exec. Dir., Jerald A. Daniels ($70,000), 4900 Old Manor Road, Austin 78723.

**Alcohol and Drug Abuse, Texas Commission on** – (1953 as Texas Commission on Alcoholism; name changed and membership increased to 9 in 1986; members reduced to 6 and term reduced to 2-yr. in 1995); apptv.; 2-yr.; per diem and expenses; 6 members: Rolland C. Allen, Corpus Christi (2/1/03); Beverly Barron, Odessa (2/1/07); Lisa F. Dickson, Dallas (2/1/05); John F. Longoria, Corpus Christi (2/1/07); Dorothy C. Pettigrew, League City (2/1/03); Robert A. Valadez, San Antonio (2/1/05). Exec. Dir., Jay Kimbrough ($100,000), PO Box 80529, Austin 78708-0529.

**Alcoholic Beverage Commission, Texas** – (1935 as Liquor Control Board; name changed 1970); apptv.; 6-yr; per diem and expenses; administrator apptd. by commission; 3 members: Gail Madden, Dallas (11/15/05); Allan Shivers Jr., Austin (11/15/01); John T. Steen Jr., San Antonio (11/15/03). Admin., Doyne Bailey ($91,000), 5806 Mesa Dr., Austin 78731.

**Alzheimer's Disease and Related Disorders, Texas Council on** – (1987); 2-yr.; expenses; 17 members: 5 agency heads or their designees: Depts. of Aging, Health, Human Services, Mental Health and Mental Retardation and the Long-Term Care Coordinating Council for the Elderly; plus four apptd. by Lt. Gov.; 4 apptd. by Speaker; 4 apptd. by Gov. as follows: Nancy J. Armour, Dallas (8/31/03); Charlene Evans, Harlingen (8/31/07); Davie Lee Wright Johnson, El Paso (8/31/07); Ellen A. MacDonald, Houston (8/31/03).

**Angelina and Neches River Authority, Board of Directors** – (1935 as Sabine-Neches Conservation Dist.; reorganized 1950 and name changed to Neches River Conservation Dist.; changed to present name in 1977); apptv.; expenses; 9 members: Karen Elizabeth Barber, Jasper (9/5/03); Dominick B. (Nick) Bruno, Jacksonville (9/5/03); Julie Dowell, Bullard, (9/5/05); Stewart M. Kenderdine, Palestine (9/5/01); Kimberly R. (Kim) Luna, Nacogdoches (9/5/05); Carl Ray Polk Jr., Lufkin (9/5/05); Roy L. Stark, Palestine (9/5/03); Jack C. Sweeny, Diboll (9/5/01). Gen. Mgr., Kenneth Reneau, PO Box 387, Lufkin 75902-0387.

**Animal Health Commission, Texas** – (1893 as Texas Livestock Sanitary Commission; name changed in 1959, membership increased to 9 in 1973; raised to 12 in 1983); apptv.; per diem and expenses; 6-yr.; 12 members: Quincy Barnes, San Antonio (9/6/03); Tommy Bozka, Shiner (9/6/03); Rob Brown, Throckmorton (9/6/01); Ron Davenport, Friona (9/6/05); Reta K. Dyess, Jacksonville (9/6/05); Tevis Herd, Midland (9/6/01); Romulo Rangel, Harlingen (9/6/05); Dick Sherron, Beaumont (9/6/03); Joe W. Templeton, College Station (9/6/01); Richard Traylor, Carrizo Springs (9/6/03). Exec. Dir., Linda L. Logan, DVM ($87,500), PO Box 12966, Austin 78711-2966.

**Appraiser Licensing and Certification Board, Texas** – (1991); 2-yr.; apptd.; per diem on duty; 9 members: Exec. Sec. of Veterans' Land Board and 8 apptees: Ben E. Barnett, Dallas (1/31/02); Elroy Carson, Ransom Canyon (1/31/02); Malcolm J. Deason, Lufkin (1/31/05); William A. Faulk Jr., Brownsville (1/31/05); Larry D. Kokel, Walburg (1/31/05); Wayne Mayo, Richardson (1/31/05); Debra S. Runyan, San Antonio (1/31/02); Donna Scurry, El Paso (2/31/02); Angelina White, El Paso (1/31/00). Commissioner, Renil C. Linér, PO Box 12188, Austin 78711-2188.

**Architectural Examiners, Texas Board of** – (1937 as 3-member board; raised to 6 members in 1951 and to 9 in 1977); apptv.; 6-yr.; per diem and expenses; 9 members: Steven T. Ellinger, Abilene (1/31/03); Gordon E. Landreth,

Corpus Christi (1/31/07); Alan R. Lauck, Dallas (1/31/05); Chao-Chiung Lee, Houston (1/31/03); Janet Forgey Parnell, Canadian (1/31/07); D. Virginia Roberts, Austin (1/31/03); Linda Diande Steinbrueck, Driftwood (1/31/07); Anthony Trevino Jr., Laredo (1/31/05); R. Nolen Willis, Bellaire (1/31/05). Exec. Dir., Cathy L. Hendricks, ($65,000), PO Box 12337, Austin 78711-2337.

**Arts, Texas Commission on the** – (1965 as Texas Fine Arts Commission; name changed to Texas Commission on the Arts and Humanities and membership increased to 18 in 1971; name changed to present form in 1979); apptv.; 6-yr.; expenses; 18 members: Malouf Abraham Jr., Canadian (8/31/01); Doris Alexander, Amarillo (8/31/01); Sue S. Bancroft, Argyle (8/31/03); Tony L. Chauveaux, Beaumont (8/31/03); Bobbe O. Crawford, Lubbock (8/31/05); Celso Gonzalez-Falla, Corpus Christi (8/31/03); Anne L. Kinder, Houston (8/31/01); Claudia Ladensohn, San Antonio (8/31/05); Mary Anne McCloud, Eastland (8/31/01); Alyn B. Morton, El Paso (8/31/01); Rodolfo N. Perez Jr., Weslaco (8/31/05); Idell G. Rabin, Dallas (8/31/05); C.A. "Tony" Sherman, Missouri City (8/31/03); Kathleen B. Stevens, Fort Worth (8/31/03); Catherine B. Taylor, Midland (8/31/03); Mary H. Teeple, Austin (8/31/05); Constance M. Ware, Marshall (8/31/01); William P. Wright Jr., Abilene (8/31/05). Exec. Dir., John Paul Batiste ($70,000), PO Box 13406, Austin 78711-3406.

**Athletic Trainers, Advisory Board of** – (1971 as Texas Board of Athletic Trainers; name changed and membership increased to 6 in 1975); expenses; 6-yr.; 6 members: T. Ross Bailey, Fort Worth (1/31/05); D. Leilani Cronin, Austin (1/31/07); Lawrence M. Sampleton Jr., Austin (1/31/09); Natalie Steadman, Lubbock (1/31/03); Michael Alan Waters, Diboll (1/31/07); Lawrence M. Sampleton Jr., Austin (1/31/09). Program Dir., Kathy Craft, Texas Dept. of Health, 1100 W. 49th, Austin 78756-3183.

**Attorney, State Prosecuting** – apptv.: Matthew Paul ($101,700), PO Box 12405, Austin 78711.

**Auditor, State** – (1929); apptv. by Legislative Audit Committee, a joint Senate-House committee; 2-yr.: Lawrence F. Alwin, PO Box 12067, Austin 78711-2067.

**Banking Commissioner, State** – (1923); apptv. by State Finance Commission; 2-yr.: Randall S. James ($118,427), 2601 N. Lamar Blvd., Austin 78705 (See also Finance Commission of Texas).

**Bar of Texas, State** – (1939 as administrative arm of Supreme Court); 30 members elected by membership; 3-yr. terms; expenses paid from dues collected from membership. President, president-elect, vice president and immediate past president serve as ex officio members. Exec. Dir., Antonio Alvarado, PO Box 12487, Austin 78711.

**Barber Examiners, State Board of** – (1929 as 3-member board; membership increased in 1975); apptv.; 6-yr.; per diem and expenses; 6 members: Victoria A. Buchanan, Houston (1/31/05); William "Kirk" Kuykendall, Austin (1/31/05); H. Wayne Moore, Garland (1/31/03); Ernest W. Pack Sr., Waco (1/31/01); Janice E. Wiggins, Kingsland (1/31/03); Charles Williams, San Antonio (1/31/01). Exec. Dir., Will K. Brown ($45,816), 333 Guadalupe, Ste. 2-110, Austin 78701.

**Blind and Severely Disabled Persons, Committee on Purchases of Products of** – (See **Disabilities, Texas Council on Purchasing from People with**)

**Blind and Visually Impaired, Governing Board of Texas School for the** – (1979); apptv.; 6-yr.; expenses; 9 members: Gene Iran Brooks, Austin (1/31/09); Donna Florence Vaden Clopton, Mt. Pleasant (1/31/09); Roseanna Davidson, Lubbock (1/31/99); Kerry L. Goodwin, Dallas (1/31/99); Fidel Menchaca, McAllen (1/31/01); Frankie D. Swift, Nacogdoches (1/31/01); Mary Sue Welch, Dallas (1/31/99); Jamie Lou Wheeler, Watauga (1/31/09). Superintendent, Dr. Phil Hatlen ($84,000), 1100 W. 45th, Austin 78756.

**Blind, Texas Commission for the** – (1931 as 6-member State Commission for the Blind; raised to 9 members in 1979; name changed in 1985); apptv.; 6-yr.; expenses; 9 members: James L. Caldwell, Austin (2/1/01); Robert Gene Griffith, Round Rock (2/1/09); C. Robert Keeney Jr., Houston (2/1/01); Frank Mullican, Lubbock (2/1/01); Joseph Muniz, Harlingen (2/1/05); Mary K. Norman, Lubbock (2/1/05); Robert K. Peters, Tyler (2/1/05); Brenda Gail Saxon, Austin (2/1/09); Beverly A. Stiles, Freer (2/1/09). Exec. Dir., Terrell I. Murphy ($80,000), PO Box 12866, Austin 78711.

**Board of** (Note: In most instances, state boards are alphabetized under key word, as **Accountancy, Texas**

**State Board of Public**.)

**Brazos River Authority, Board of Directors** – (1929 as Brazos River Conservation and Reclamation Dist.; name changed to present form in 1953); apptv.; 6-yr; expenses; 21 members: Mary E. Ainslie, Rosenberg (2/1/03); Robert B. Arnot, Breckenridge (2/1/03); Deborah H. Bell, Abilene (2/1/01); Lynn Elliott, Millican (2/1/01); Jack Farrar, Hico (2/1/01); Ramiro A. Galindo, Bryan (2/1/01); Rudy Garcia, Alvin (2/1/03); Shirley Herring, Brenham (2/1/03); Joe B. Hinton, Crawford (2/1/05); Andrew Jackson, Missouri City (2/1/05); Celeste L. Kotter, Marlin (2/1/05); Ernest M. Koy, Bellville (2/1/03); Robert B. Lane, Clifton (2/1/05); Linda Kay Lyle, Plainview (2/1/01); Steve D. Peña, Round Rock (2/1/05); M. Lance Phillips, Mexia (2/1/05); Nancy Rabb, Round Rock (2/1/03); Beverly W. Sawyer, Temple (2/1/03); Ruth C. Schiermeyer, Lubbock (2/1/01); Janet Kay Sparks, Cleburne (2/1/05); Judith Vernon, Evant (2/1/01). Gen. Mgr., Phil Ford, P. O. Box 7555, Waco 76714-7555.

**Canadian River Compact Commissioner** – (1951); apptv.; salary and expenses; (function is to negotiate with other states respecting waters of the Canadian): Roger S. Cox ($10,767), Amarillo (12/31/03).

**Cancer Council, Texas** – (1985); 6-yr.; expenses; 16 members: Chmn., Board of Health (ex-officio, non-voting); 15 apptd.: five each by Gov., Lt. Gov. and Speaker of House: Karen Bonner, Corpus Christi (2/1/04); Patricia T. Castiglia, El Paso (2/1/06); Audreyjane Castro, San Antonio (2/1/04); Clare Buie Chaney, Dallas (2/1/02); James D. Dannenbaum, Houston (2/1/02); Carolyn D. Harvey, Tyler (2/1/06); Rubye H. Henderson, Plainview (2/1/02); Karen B. Heusinkveld, Arlington (2/1/02); Larry Herrera, Temple (2/1/06); William C. Levin, Galveston (2/1/02); John F. Sandbach, Austin (2/1/06); Donald C. Spencer, Austin (2/1/00); Courtney Townsend Jr., Galveston (2/1/04); J. Taylor Wharton, Houston (2/1/04). Exec. Dir., Mickey L. Jacobs ($57,691), PO Box 12097, Austin 78711.

**Central Colorado River Authority** (See **Colorado River Authority, Central**.)

**Chemist, Office of State** – (1911); ex officio, indefinite term: State Chemist, George W. Latimer Jr., P. O. Box 3160, College Station 77841-3160.

**Childhood Intervention, Interagency Council on Early** – (1981); apptv.; 2-yr.; expenses; 9 members: one apptd. by exec. dir. of Texas Education Agency, 8 apptd. by Gov.: Timothy James Flannery, Seabrook (2/1/07); Michael Fuhrman, Carrollton (2/1/05); Maria Dolores Garcia, Hereford (2/1/05); Tanya Huerta, San Antonio (2/1/99); Connie L. Hughes, Idalou (2/1/07); Susan C. Mengden-Ellis, San Antonio (2/1/03); Patrick J. Oliver III, Webster (2/1/07); Dimas Vasquez Jr., El Paso (2/1/03). Exec. Dir., Mary O. Elder ($68,000), 4900 N. Lamar, Austin 78758.

**Children's Trust Fund of Texas Council** – (1985; became independent agency in 1991); apptv., 6-yr; 9 members: Patricia Aguayo, El Paso (9/1/01); Joe Cordova, Fort Worth (9/1/05); Anne C. Crews, Dallas (9/1/01); GiGi Edwards, Austin (9/1/01); Kathleen R. Ehlinger, Raymondville (9/1/03); James Louis Lukefahr, League City (9/1/05); Judy Wilson Semlinger, Lufkin (9/1/03); Katherine Sosa, San Antonio (9/1/05); Sederick E. Susberry, Houston (9/1/03). Exec. Dir., John Chacon ($53,914), 8100 Cameron Rd., Austin 78754-3833.

**Chiropractic Examiners, Texas Board of** – (1949); apptv.; 6-yr.; expenses; 9 members: Cheryl Belinda Barber, Houston (2/1/03); Robert L. Coburn, Sweeny (2/1/05); Cynthia S. Diaz, San Antonio (2/1/05); Serge P. Francois, Irving (2/1/05); Scott Edward Isdale, Killeen (2/1/05); Steve Minors, Austin (2/1/07); Oliver R. Smith Jr., El Paso (2/1/01); Dora Innes Valverde, Mission (2/1/01); Cynthia Sue Vaughn, Austin (2/1/03); John C. Weddle, Rockwall (2/1/01). Exec. Dir., Gary K. Cain ($52,000), 333 Guadalupe, Ste. 3-825, Austin 78701.

**Coastal Water Authority, Board of Directors** – (1967 as Coastal Industrial Water Authority, Board of Directors of; name changed in 1985); 7 members — 4 apptd. by mayor of Houston with advice and consent of governing body of Houston; 3 apptd. by Gov.; per diem and expenses; 2-yr.; Gov's. apptees: Buster French, Dayton (4/1/00); Darryl L. King, Houston (4/1/01); Gary R. Nelson, Baytown (4/1/01). Exec. Dir., Ralph T. Rundle, 1200 Smith St., Ste. 2260, Houston 77002.

**College Opportunity Act Committee** – (1989); 6-yr.; 9 members: 6 ex officio: Commissioner, General Land Office; Exec. Admin., Texas Water Development Board; Comptrol-

ler; State Treasurer; Exec. Dir., Bond Review Board; Commissioner of Higher Education. 3 apptd.: Laura Haley Bley, Fort Worth (2/1/03); Joe Munoz, San Angelo (2/1/01); Michelle Marie Tobias, Austin (2/1/05).

**Colorado River Authority, Central, Board of Directors** – (1935); apptv.; 6-yr.; per diem on duty; 9 members: Ann M. Hargett, Coleman (2/1/01); Alice Hemphill, Coleman (2/1/05); John Hensley, Santa Anna (2/1/05); Jack Horne, Coleman (2/1/03); William Laws, Coleman (2/1/03); Nan K. Markland, Burkett (2/1/01); Ronald W. Owens, Coleman (2/1/01); Ben Scott, Coleman (2/1/05); Barbara Simmons, Santa Anna (2/1/03). Operations Mgr., Laneal Maedgen, PO Box 964, Coleman 76834.

**Colorado River Authority, Lower, Board of Directors** – (1934 as 9-member board; membership increased in 1951 and 1975); apptv.; 6-yr.; per diem on duty; 15 members: Pamela R. Akins, Marble Falls (2/1/03); Ann E. Jones, Brownwood (2/1/03); Patricia Kirk, San Saba (2/1/03); David L. Kithil, Marble Falls (2/1/05); Hilda C. Kroll, Johnson City (2/1/01); F. Scott LaGrone, Georgetown (2/1/05); Robert W. Lambert, Horseshoe Bay (2/1/05); Gale Lincke, La Grange (2/1/03); John H. Matthews, Eagle Lake (2/1/05); Arthur J. Milberger, Bay City (2/1/03); Charles Patrick Oles Jr., Austin (2/1/01); E. Peter Pincoffs, Austin (2/1/99); Steve D. Rivers, Bastrop (2/1/99); Louis Romero Jr., Kerrville (2/1/01); Rosemary Ann Rust, Wharton (2/1/05). Gen. Mgr., Joseph J. Beal, P. O. Box 220, Austin 78767-0220.

**Colorado River Authority, Upper, Board of Directors** – (1935 as 9-member board; reorganized in 1965); apptv.; 6-yr.; per diem and expenses; indefinite number of members: Ray Alderman, Winters (2/1/01); Jack Brewer, Robert Lee (2/1/03); Fred R. Campbell, Paint Rock (2/1/03); Ralph E. Hoelscher, Miles (2/1/01); Hope W. Huffman, San Angelo (2/1/03); Raymond Meza, San Angelo (2/1/05); Jeffie H. Roberts, Robert Lee (2/1/05); Hyman Sauer, Eldorado (2/1/05); Dorris Sonnenberg, Bronte (2/1/01). Ellen Groth, Admin. Asst., PO Box 1482, San Angelo 76902-1482.

**Commissioner of** (See keyword, as **Agriculture, Commissioner of.**)

**Concho River Water and Soil Conservation Authority, Lower** – (1939); 6-yr.; 9 members: Leroy Paul Beach, Millersview (2/1/93); Howard E. Loveless, Eden (2/1/99); Billy J. Mikeska, Eola (2/1/99); Eugene R. Rogers, Eden (2/1/97); Benjamin O. Sims, Paint Rock (2/1/97); Edwin T. Tickle, Eden (2/1/01); T.E. Wells, Paint Rock (2/1/01); Harvey P. Williams, Eola (2/1/01). Office Address: Rt. 1, PO Box 4, Paint Rock 76866.

**Conservatorship Board, State** – (1979); apptv.; expenses; 6-yr.; 3 members: Carolyn Gallagher Austin (2/1/01); Byron Tunnell, Bullard (2/1/97); J. Michael Weiss, Lubbock (2/1/99).

**Consumer Credit Commissioner** – Leslie L. Pettijohn ($90, 000), 2601 N. Lamar, Austin 78705-4207.

**Cosmetology Commission, Texas** – (1935 as 3-member State Board of Hairdressers and Cosmetologists; name changed and membership increased to 6 apptv. and one ex officio in 1971); apptv.; per diem and expenses; 6-yr.; apptv. members: Leif Christiansen, Spring (12/31/03); Comer J. Cottrell Jr., Dallas (12/31/01); Heliana L. Kiessling, Friendswood (12/31/03); Helen R. Quiram, Waco (12/31/05); Lucinda L. Shearer, Edinburg (12/31/07); Elida Zapata, Lubbock (12/31/05). Exec. Dir., Henry Holifield ($46,338), PO Box 26700, Austin 78755-0700.

**Counselors, Texas State Board of Examiners of Professional** – (1981); apptv.; 6-yr.; expenses; 9 members: Ana C. Bergh, Edinburg (2/1/05); Judy Broussard, Levelland (2/1/01); Joseph D. Dameron, Denton (2/1/01); J. Lee Jagers, Richardson (2/1/03); Gay T. McAlister, Longview (2/1/03); Suzanne Moore, San Antonio (2/1/03); Anthony P. Picchioni, Grapevine (2/1/99); Judy Powell, The Woodlands (2/1/05); Gene Ryder, San Antonio (2/1/01). Exec. Sec., John L. Luther, 1100 W. 49th, Austin 78756-3183.

**Court Reporters Certification Board** – (1977 as 9-member Texas Reporters Committee; name changed to present form and membership increased to 12 in 1983); apptv. by State Supreme Court; 6-yr.; expenses Exec. Dir. Michele L. Henricks ($52,000), 205 W. 14th St., Ste. 101, Austin 78701.

**Credit Union Commission** – (1949 as 3-member Credit Union Advisory Commission; name changed and membership increased to 6 in 1969; increased to 9 in 1981); apptv.; 6-yr.; expenses; 9 members: Garold R. Base, Plano (2/15/

01); Floyd W. Burnside Jr., San Antonio (2/15/05); Cynthia Cabaza, McAllen (2/15/03); Richard A. Glasco Jr., Austin (2/15/03); Fran V. Hawkins, Corpus Christi (2/15/05); Robert S. Hayes, Amarillo (2/15/01); Karen A. Jacks, Longview (2/15/01); Carlos Puente, Arlington (2/15/05); J. Howell (Hal) Thomas, Baytown (2/15/03). Exec. Dir., Harold E. Feeney ($95,000), 914 E. Anderson Ln., Austin 78752-1699.

**Crime Stoppers Advisory Council** – (1981); apptv.; 4-yr.; per diem and expenses; 5 members: Janice C. Gillen, Rosenberg (9/1/04); Juan F. Jorge, Tomball (9/1/04); Tina Alexander Sellers, Lufkin (9/1/04); Dorothy Spinks, Marble Falls (9/1/05); Brian Thomas, Amarillo (9/1/05).

**Criminal Justice, Texas Board of** – (1989: assumed duties of former Texas Board of Corrections and Adult Probation Commission; also oversees Board of Pardons and Paroles Division); apptd.; 6-yr.; expenses; 9 members: Adrian A. Arriaga, McAllen (2/1/07); Mary Bacon, Houston (2/1/05); Christina Melton Crain, Dallas (2/1/07); Patricia A. Day, Dallas (2/1/03); Don Jones, Midland (2/1/05); Pierce Miller, San Angelo (2/1/07); Willian "Hank" Moody, Washington (2/1/05); Alfred C. Moran, Arlington (2/1/03); Alfred M. "Mac" Stringfellow, San Antonio (2/1/03. Exec. Dir, Dept. of Criminal Justice: Gary Johnson ($150,000), PO Box 13084, Austin 78711. (512) 463-9988.

**Criminal Justice Policy Council** – (1983); all terms at pleasure of appointor; 11 members: 3 ex officio — Gov., Lt. Gov., Speaker; 2 apptd. by Lt. Gov.; 2 apptd. by Speaker; 4 apptd. by Gov.: Col. James B. Adams, Austin; John Holmes, Houston; D.L. "Sonny" Keesee, Lubbock; Susan D. Reed, San Antonio. Exec. Dir., Tony Fabelo ($98,000), 205 W. 14th St., Ste. 701, Austin 78701.

**Deaf and Hearing Impaired, Governing Board of the Texas School for the** – (1979); 6-yr.; expenses; 9 members: Beatrice M. Burke, Austin (1/31/01); Charles Estes, Plano (1/31/03); Aulby "Larry" Gillett, San Angelo (1/31/01); Theresa Johnson, Spring (1/31/03); Kenneth D. Kesterson, Big Spring (1/31/07); Nancy Munger, San Marcos (1/31/95); Robert Parrish, Carrollton (1/31/99); Lesa Thomas, Corpus Christi (1/31/03); Mary VanManen, Stafford (1/31/97). Superintendent, Claire Bugen ($84,000), P. O. Box 3538, Austin 78764.

**Deaf and Hard of Hearing, Texas Commission for the** – (1971 as 6-member board; membership raised to 9 in 1979); apptv.; 6-yr.; expenses; 9 members: Douglas L. Bush, Houston (1/31/03); Beverly Sue Hill, Arlington (1/31/05); Jeffrey W. Jordan, Midland (1/31/05); Paul A. Locus, Austin (1/31/05); Jean Hale Matney, Fort Worth (1/31/01); Myfe White Moore, Helotes (1/31/01); Robin E. Riccardi, Shallowater (1/31/03); Benna Timperlake, Corpus Christi (1/31/03); Eva Williams, El Lago (1/31/01). Exec. Dir., David W. Myers ($70,000), P. O. Box 12904, Austin 78711.

**Dental Examiners, State Board of** – (1919 as 6-member board; increased to 9 members in 1971; increased to 12 in 1981; increased to 15 in 1991; sunsetted in 1994; reconstituted with 18 members in 1995); appt.; 6-yr.; per diem while on duty; 18 members: Patricia Blackwell, Midland (2/1/01); Tammy R. Fisher, Bedford (2/1/01); Karen F. Hembry, Dallas (2/1/05); J. Kevin Irons, Austin (2/1/05); Amy Landess Juba, Amarillo (2/1/05); James W. Kenedy, Sugar Land (2/1/03); Martha Manley Malik, Victoria (2/1/05); Norman Lewis Mason, Austin (2/1/09); Helen Hayes McKibben, Lubbock (2/1/09); Michael Nogueira, Rancho Viejo (2/1/01); David O. Olson, Bridge City (2/1/01); Ronald G. Smith, Lubbock (2/1/01); Kent T. Starr, Waco (2/1/05); George Strunk, Tyler (2/1/09); Nathaniel George Tippit Jr., Houston (2/1/05); Marcia Waugh, El Paso (2/1/03); Gail Wilks, Longview (2/1/05); Joe D. Zayas, Rancho Viejo (2/1/01); Charles Field Wetherbee, Jourdanton (2/1/09); . Exec. Dir., Jeffry R. Hill ($63,000), 333 Guadalupe, Ste. 3-800, Austin 78701.

**Depository Board, State** – (Abolished May 1997).

**Developmental Disabilities, Texas Planning Council for** – (1971); apptv.; 6-yr.; 27 members — 8 ex officio: Representatives from Dept. of Mental Health and Mental Retardation, Rehabilitation Commission, Dept. of Health, Dept. of Human Services, Texas Dept. on Aging, Texas Education Agency, Texas Commission for the Blind, Texas Commission for the Deaf; 19 apptv. members: Raul Acosta, Lubbock (2/1/05); Kristine Bissmeyer, San Antonio (2/1/05); Oscar Bobbitt, Austin (2/1/93); Joe Colunga III, Brownsville (2/1/05); Mary M. Durheim, McAllen (2/1/05); Marcia Jeanne Dwyer, Plano (2/1/05); J. Robert Hester Jr., Arlington (2/1/01); Jerijean Houchins, Austin (2/1/01); Theda N.

Hoyt, Cypress (2/1/01); Gary D. Kay, Austin (2/1/01); Amy Ley, Euless (2/1/03); Vickie Mitchell, Conroe (2/1/03); John C. Morris, El Paso (2/1/07); Jan R. Newsom, Dallas (2/1/01); Linda Parrish, College Sation (2/1/99); Johnny Sauseda, Victoria (2/1/03); Richard A. Tisch, Spring (2/1/03); Raul Trevino Jr., McAllen (2/1/03); Linda Vancil, Ballinger (2/1/01). Exec. Dir., Roger A. Webb, 4900 N. Lamar, Austin 78751.

**Diabetes Council, Texas** – (1983; with 5 ex officio and 6 public members serving 2-yr. terms; changed in 1987 to 3 ex officio and 8 public members; changed to present configuration in 1991; term length changed from 4 to 6 years eff. 1997); 6-yr.; 17 members — 5 ex officio; 12 apptv. public members as follows: Belinda Bazan-Lara, San Antonio (2/1/05); Gene Bell, Lubbock (2/1/03); Mary-Ann Galley, Houston (2/1/03); Victor Hugo González, McAllen (2/1/03); Judith L. Haley, Houston (2/1/05); Jan B. Hamilton, Plainview (2/1/03); Lawrence B. Harkless, San Antonio (2/1/07); Richard S. Hayley, Corpus Christi (2/1/05); Lenore Frances Katz, Dallas (2/1/07); Margaret G. Pacillas, El Paso (2/1/07); Jeffrey A. Ross, Bellaire (2/1/07); Mike Thompson Jr., Austin (2/1/05). Address: Texas Dept. of Health, 1100 W. 49th, Austin 78756.

**Dietitians, Texas State Board of Examiners of** – (1983); apptv.; 6-yr.; per diem and expenses: 9 members: Elizabeth B. Blakely, San Angelo (9/1/03); Carol Barnett Davis, Dallas (9/1/05); Lucinda M. Flores, Brownsville (9/1/03); Ethelind S. Gibson, Nacogdoches (9/1/01); Ralph McGahagin, Austin (9/1/05); Amy Nicholson McLeod, Lufkin (9/1/07); Amy W. Scott, Spring (9/1/03); Dorothy M. Shafer, Fredericksburg (9/1/01); Eugene E. Wisakowsky, Waxahachie (9/1/05). Texas Dept. of Health, 1100 W. 49th, Austin 78756.

**Disabilities, Governor's Committee on People with** – (1991); 16 members: 4 ex officio: Chmn., TEC; Commissioner, Texas Rehabilitation Comm.; Dir., Texas Commission for the Blind; member, Texas Comm. for the Deaf; 12 members apptd. by Governor serve 2-year terms: Kara Wilson Anglin, Caldwell (2/1/05); Mary Ann Board, Houston (2/1/99); Douglas F. Grady Jr., Fort Worth (2/1/04); Peter Grojean, San Antonio (2/1/04); Roland Guzman, Corpus Christi (2/1/05); Thomas P. Justis, Fort Worth (2/1/05); Kym I. King, Houston (2/1/00); Laura Gerken Redd, Pasadena (2/1/04); Judy Castle Scott, Dallas (2/1/04); Brian D. Shannon, Lubbock (2/1/05); Nancy Kay Shugart, Austin (2/1/04); Kathy S. Strong, Garrison (2/1/04); Shane Whitehurst, Austin (2/1/05). Exec. Dir., Pat Pound, 4900 N. Lamar, Austin 78751-2613.

**Disabilities, Texas Council on Purchasing from People with** – (1979 as 10-member Committee on Purchases of Products and Services of Blind and Severely Disabled Persons; name changed and members reduced to 9 in 1995); apptd.; expenses; 6-yr.; 9 members: Byron E. Johnson, El Paso (1/31/01); John W. Luna, Euless (1/31/03); Eugene F. Matthews, Denton (1/31/99); Gwendolyn C. Morrison, Fort Worth (1/31/99); Margaret Pfluger, San Angelo (1/31/99); Robert A. Swerdlow, Beaumont (1/31/01); Bobbie F. Templeton, Driftwood (1/31/03); Arnold Thorner, Houston (1/31/01); Pat Wilson, Longview (1/31/03).

**Economic Development, Governing Board of the Texas Department of** – (1987 as Texas Dept. of Commerce Policy Bd.; present name 1997); apptv.;6-yr.; exp.; 9 members: Tucker S. Bridwell, Abilene (2/1/01); Javier Garza, Laredo (2/1/01); Patricia Z. Holland-Branch, El Paso (2/1/01); Limas Jefferson, Seabrook (2/1/05); Mark Langdale, Dallas (2/1/03); George T. Richardson Jr., Littlefield (2/1/03); Rance G. Sweeten, McAllen (2/1/03); Marion Szurek, San Angelo (2/1/05); Martha J. Wong, Houston (2/1/05). Exec. Dir., Jeff Moseley ($112,352), PO Box 12728, Austin 78711-2728.

**Education, Board of Control for Southern Regional** – (1969); apptv.; 4-yr.; 5 members: Gov. ex officio, 4 apptd.: Teel Bivins, Austin (6/30/01); Kent Grusendorf, Austin (6/30/04); Roderick R. Paige, Houston (6/30/02); Carol J. Spencer, Dallas (6/30/03). Mark E. Musick, Pres., Southern Regional Education Board, 592 10th St. N.W., Atlanta, GA 30318-5790.

**Education, Commissioner of** – (1866 as Superintendent of Public Instruction; 1949 changed to present name by Gilmer-Aiken Law); apptv. by State Board of Education; 4-yr.: James E. Nelson ($164,748) (See also Education, State Board of).

**Education, State Board of** – (1866; re-created 1928 and re-formed by Gilmer-Aikin Act in 1949 to consist of 21 elective members from districts co-extensive with 21 congressional districts at that time; membership increased to 24 with congressional redistricting in 1971, effective 1973; membership increased to 27 with congressional redistricting in 1981, effective 1983; reorganized by special legislative session as 15-member apptv. board in 1984 to become elective board again in 1988; expenses; 4-yr.; 15 members (numerals before names indicate district numbers): (1) Rene Nuñez, El Paso (1/1/03); (2) Mary Helen Berlanga, Corpus Christi (1/1/03); (3) Joe J. Bernal, San Antonio (1/1/05); (4) Dr. Alma A. Allen, Houston (1/1/05); (5) Dan Montgomery, Fredericksburg (1/1/05); (6) Chase Untermeyer, Houston (1/1/05); (7) David Bradley, Beaumont (1/1/05); (8) Grace Shore, Longview (1/1/03); (9) Don McLeroy, Bryan (1/1/03); (10) Cynthia A. Thornton, Round Top (1/1/05); (11) Richard Neill, Fort Worth (1/1/05); (12) Geraldine "Tincy" Miller, Dallas (1/1/05); (13) Rosie Collins Sorrells, Dallas (1/1/03); (14) Richard Watson, Gorman (1/1/03); (15) Judy Strickland, Plainview (1/1/03). Commissioner of Education, James E. Nelson ($164,748), Texas Education Agency, 1701 N. Congress Ave., Austin 78701-1494 (see also Education, Commissioner of).

**Educator Certification, State Board for** – (1995); apptv.; 6-yr.; expenses; 15 members; 3 non-voting: rep. of Comm. of Education; rep of Comm. of Higher Education; 1 dean of a college of education apptd. by Gov.; 12 voting members apptd. by Gov.: John J. Beck Jr., San Marcos (2/1/05); Carmel Borders, Austin (2/1/01); Annette T. Griffin, Carrollton (2/1/05); James D. Harris, Lubbock (2/1/03); Arthur Lacy, McKinney (2/1/03); James E. Nelson, Odessa (2/1/01); Ed Patton Jr., Abilene (2/1/01); Cynthia Tassos Phillips, Austin (2/1/01); James B. (Jim) Price, Cooper (2/1/03); Mary E. Resendez, San Antonio (2/1/01); Xavier Rodriguez, San Antonio (2/1/05); Antonio Sanchez, Mission (2/1/05); Mary Margaret Rucker, Nassau Bay (2/1/03); Keith Sockwell, Plano (2/1/03). Exec. Dir., Pamela B. Tackett ($78,000), 1001 Trinity, Austin 78701-2603.

**Edwards Aquifer Authority** – (1993); elected from single-member districts; 4-yr.; expenses; 15 apptv. members: Michael D. Beldon. Gen. Mgr., Gregory M. Ellis, 1615 N. St. Mary's St., San Antonio 78215-1415.

**Egg Marketing Advisory Board** – (Abolished May 1997).

**Election Commission, State** – (1973); 9 members, ex officio and apptv. as indicated: Chmn. of Democratic State Executive Committee; Chmn. of Republican State Executive Committee; Chief Justice of Supreme Court; Presiding Judge, Court of Criminal Appeals; 2 persons to be named, one a justice of the Court of Appeals apptd. by Chief Justice of Supreme Court, one a District Judge apptd. by presiding judge of Court of Criminal Appeals; 2 county chairmen, one each from Democratic and Republican parties, named by the parties; Secretary of State.

**Emancipation Juneteenth Cultural and Historical Commission, Texas** – (1997); expenses; 6 yr.; 11 members; 5 ex officio, nonvoting: 2 apptd. by Lt. Gov., 2 apptd. by Speaker of House, and exec. dir. of Texas Historical Comm.; 6 apptd by Gov.: Maceo Crenshaw Dailey Jr., El Paso (2/1/03); Byron E. Miller, San Antonio (2/1/03); Eddie Price Richardson, Lubbock (2/1/05); Stella Roland, Austin (2/1/05); Willard Stimpson, Dallas (2/1/01); Lynda J. Tarr, Houston (2/1/01).

**Emergency Communications, Commission on State** – (1985 as 17-member Advisory Commission on State Emergency Communications; name changed and membership reduced to 12, 2000); expenses; 12 members: 3 ex offico: exec. directors of Dept. of Health, Public Utilities Comm. and General Services Admin.; 9 public members (6 yr.): 2 apptd. by Lt. Gov.; 2 apptd. by Speaker; 5 apptd. by Gov. Gov's apptees: Jose A. Aranda Jr., Eagle Pass (9/1/01); John L. deNoyelles, Tyler (9/1/03); Heberto Gutierrez, San Antonio (9/1/01); Karen B. Hibbitt, Denison (9/1/01); Dorothy Morgan, Brenham (9/1/05). Exec. Dir., James D. Goerke ($75,000), 333 Guadalupe St., Ste. 2-212, Austin 78701.

**Emergency Services Personnel Retirement Fund, Texas Statewide** – (1977; formerly the Fire Fighters' Relief and Retirement Fund); apptv.; expenses; 6-yr.; 9 members: Timothy Bogisch, Seguin (9/1/03); Kyle Donaldson, Sonora (9/1/03); Paul V. Loeffler, Alpine (9/1/01); Landon McLain, El Campo (9/1/03); Maxie Patterson, Spring (9/1/01); Robert Rice, Canyon (9/1/01); Allen Scopel, Rosenberg (9/1/05); Francisco Torres, Raymondville (9/1/05); Robert Weiss, Brenham (9/1/05). Commissioner, Helen L. Camp-

bell, PO Box 12577, Austin 78711.

**Employment Commission, Texas** – (See **Workforce Commission, Texas**)

**Engineers, State Board of Registration for Professional** – (1937 as 6-member board; membership increased to 9 in 1981); apptv.; per diem and expenses; 6-yr.; 9 members: Brenda A. Bradley, Houston (9/26/03); C. Roland Haden, College Station (9/26/07); William Lawrence, Highland Village (9/26/07); Shannon K. McClendon, Dripping Springs (9/26/03); Govind Nadkarni, Corpus Christi (9/26/05); James R. Nichols, Fort Worth (9/26/03); Gerry E. Pate, Magnolia (9/26/07); Vicki T. Ravenburg, San Antonio (9/26/05); Robert M. Sweazy, Lubbock (9/26/05). Exec. Dir., Victoria J.L. Hsu ($75,000), 1917 S. IH-35, Austin 78741.

**Environmental Quality, Texas Commission on** – (1913 as State Board of Water Engineers; name changed in 1962 to Texas Water Commission; reorganized and name again changed in 1965 to Water Rights Commission; reorganized and name changed back to Texas Water Commission in 1977 to perform judicial function for the Texas Dept. of Water Resources; name changed to Texas Natural Resource Conservation Commission in 1993; changed to present form Sept. 1, 2002); apptv.; 6-yr.; 3 members full-time at $107,500–$111,792: John M. Baker Jr., Temple (8/31/01); Robert J. Huston (8/31/03); R.B. (Ralph) Marquez, Texas City (8/31/05). Exec. Dir., Margaret Hoffman ($132,000), PO Box 13087, Austin 78711.

**Ethics Commission, Texas** – (1991); apptd.; 4-yr.; 8 members: 2 apptd. by Speaker, 2 apptd. by Lt. Gov, 4 apptd. by Gov.: Ernestine Glossbrenner, Alice (11/19/01); Jerome W. Johnson, Amarillo (11/19/03); Mickey Jo Lawrence, Houston (11/19/03); Louis E. Sturns, Fort Worth (11/19/01). Exec. Dir., Tom Harrison ($97,000), 201 E. 14th St., 10th Fl., Austin 78701.

**Evergreen Underground Water Conservation District** – (1965); 2-yr.; 5 members — 4 elected: 2 each from Wilson and Atascosa counties; one apptd. by Gov.: Amond Douglas Brownlow, Floresville (2/1/03).

**Family Practice Residency Advisory Committee** – (1977); 3-yr.; expenses; 12 members apptv. as follows: one practicing physician apptd. by Texas Osteopathic Medical Assn.; 2 apptd. by Assn. of Directors of Family Practice Training Programs; one apptd. by Texas Medical Assn.; 2 administrators of hospitals apptd. by Texas Hospital Assn.; president, Texas Academy of Family Physicians; and 3 public members apptd. by the Gov., as follows: Loretta Banowsky, San Antonio (8/29/99); Lourdes Cuellar, Houston (8/29/01); Maria Poradek, Lubbock (8/29/03).

**Finance Commission of Texas** – (1923 as Banking Commission; reorganized as Finance Commission in 1943 with 9 members; membership increased to 12 in 1983; changed back to 9 members in 1989); apptv.; 6-yr.; per diem and traveling expenses; 9 members: Gary D. Akright, Dallas (2/1/08); Jeff Austin Jr., Jacksonville (2/1/00); Kenneth H. Harris, Austin (2/1/04); Steven C. Hastings, Southlake (2/1/00); Wilburn D. Hilton Jr., Greenville (2/1/02); Deborah H. Kovacevich, Jewett (2/1/04); Allan B. Polunsky, San Antonio (2/1/08); Victor (Buddy) Puente Jr., Pantego (2/1/04); John Snider, Center (2/1/00). Banking Commissioner, Randall S. James ($97,072), 2601 N. Lamar, Austin 78705, appointee of Finance Commission. (See also Banking Commissioner, State.)

**Fire Fighters' Pension Commissioner** – (1937); apptv.; 2-yr.: Morris E. Sandefer, Lumberton (7/1/01) ($57,000), PO Box 12577, Austin 78711.

**Fire Protection, Texas Commission on** – (1991; formed by consolidation of Fire Dept. Emergency Board and Commission on Fire Protection Personnel Standards and Education); apptv.; 6-yrs.; expenses; 12 members: David Abernathy Pittsburg (2/1/01); Juan J. Adame, Corpus Christi (2/1/01); Pat Barrett, Bryan (2/1/03); Marvin Dawson, Brownfield (2/1/01); Michael D. Jolly, Georgetown (2/1/05); Alonzo Lopez Jr., Kingsville (2/1/05); Robert H. Price, Grapevine (2/1/01); Gilbert Robinson, Galveston (2/1/03); Ricardo Saldaña, Mission (2/1/05); Kelley Stalder, Parker (2/1/03); Peggy Trahan, South Padre Island (2/1/03); Carl D. Wren, Manchaca (2/1/05). Exec. Dir., Gary L. Warren Sr. ($78,000), PO Box 2286, Austin 78768.

**Food and Fibers Commission, Texas** – (1941 as Cotton Research Committee; name changed in 1971 to Natural Fibers and Food Protein Committee; changed to commission in 1975; changed to present name 1989); 4 members are presidents and chancellor of four major universities (Pres., Texas Woman's University, Denton; Pres., Texas Tech University, Lubbock; Chancellor, Texas A&M University System, College Station; Pres., University of Texas at Austin) serving indefinite terms; and one ex officio member who is director of administrative office in Dallas, apptd. to 2-year term: Exec. Dir., Robert V. Avant Jr., 17360 Coit Rd., Dallas 75252.

**Funeral Service Commission, Texas** – (1903 as State Board of Embalming; 1935 as State Board of Funeral Directors and Embalmers; 1953 as 6-member board; membership increased to 9 in 1979; name changed to present form in 1987; membership reduced to 6 in 1999); apptv.; per diem and expenses; 6-yr.; 6 members: Dorothy L. Grasty, Arlington (2/1/05); John Q. Taylor King, Austin (1/31/03); Frank W. Maresh, Hunt (2/1/01); Martha "Marty" Rhymes, White Oak (1/31/03); Harry Whittington, Austin (2/1/01); Jim Wright, Wheeler (1/31/05). Exec. Dir., O.C. "Chet" Robbins ($45,816), 510 S. Congress, Ste. 206, Austin 78704-1716.

**General Services Commission** – (1919 as Board of Control; name changed to State Purchasing and General Services Commission in 1979; changed to present form and increased to 6 commissioners in 1991); apptv.; 6-yr.; expenses; 6 members: Tomás Cárdenas Jr., El Paso (1/31/05); James A. Cox Jr., Austin (1/31/05); Gilbert A. Herrera, Houston (1/31/07); Barbara Rusling, Waco (1/31/03); Gene Shull, Tyler (1/31/03). Acting Exec. Dir., Ann Dillon ($115,000), PO Box 13047, Austin 78711-3047.

**Geoscientists, Texas Board of Professional** – (2001); apptv.; expenses; 6-yr.; 9 members (6 professional geoscientists, 3 public members): William K. Coleman, Cedar Hill (2/1/05); Kelly K. Doe, Friendswood (2/1/09); Shiela B. Hall, Lubbock (2/1/07); Murray H. Milford, Bryan (2/1/07); Edward G. Miller, San Antonio (2/1/05); Rene D. Pena, El Paso (2/1/09); Danny R. Perkins, Houston (2/1/07); Kimberly R. Phillips, Houston (2/1/05); Gordon D. Ware, Corpus Christi (2/1/09). Exec. Dir., William H. Kuntz Jr., P.O. Box 12157, Austin, TX 78711.

**Growth Fund Board of Trustees, Texas** – (1988); apptv.; 6-yr.; 9 members — one member from and elected by membership of each of the following: Board of Regents, University of Texas System; Board of Regents, Texas A&M University System; Board of Trustees, Teacher Retirement System; Board of Trustees, Employees Retirement System; State Board of Education; 4 public members apptd. by Gov.: J. Michael Bell Sr., Fredericksburg (2/1/99); Patsy W. Nichols, Austin (2/1/03); Alan W. Steelman, Dallas (2/1/05); Catherine S. Woodruff, Houston (2/1/03).

**Guadalupe River Authority, Upper** – (1939); apptv.; 6-yr.; 9 members: Jerry Ahrens, Kerrville (2/1/05); Joseph David Armistead Sr., Center Point (2/1/03); T. Beck Gipson, Kerrville (2/1/01); Peggy J. Henderson, Kerrville (2/1/03); George G. MacDonald Jr., Kerrville (2/1/01); Mollie Maresh, Hunt (2/1/01); Thomas M. Myers, Kerrville (2/1/03); Janet F. Robinson, Kerrville (2/1/05); Calvin Ray Weinheimer, Kerrville (2/1/05). Gen. Mgr., Jim T. Brown, 125 Lehman Dr., Ste. 100, Kerrville 78028.

**Guadalupe-Blanco River Authority** – (1935); apptv.; per diem and expenses on duty; 6-yr.; 9 members: William A. Blackwell, Cuero (2/1/01); Anne Cooper, San Marcos (2/1/01); Kathleen A. Devine, New Braunfels (2/1/05); Pamela M. Hodges, Boerne (2/1/03); Catherine R. McHaney, Victoria (2/1/97); Frederick S. Schlather, Cibolo (2/1/03); John P. Schneider Jr., Lockhart (2/1/05); Ashley H. Turberville, Nixon (2/1/01); Stephen F. Wilson, Port Lavaca (1/2/05). Gen. Mgr., William E. West, 933 E. Court St., Seguin 78155.

**Gulf Coast Waste Disposal Authority** – (1969); apptv.; 2-yr.; per diem and expenses on duty; 9 members: 3 apptv. by Gov., 3 by County Commissioners Courts of counties in district, 3 by Municipalities Waste Disposal Councils of counties in district. Gov's. apptees: Louis S. Dell'Olio Jr., Galveston (8/31/02); Rafael Ortega, Houston (8/31/01); Shirley U. Seale, Anahuac (8/31/02). Gen. Mgr., Dick Brown, 910 Bay Area Blvd., Houston 77058.

**Gulf States Marine Fisheries Commission** – (1949); apptv.; 3-yr.; 3 members — 2 ex officio: exec. dir., Texas Parks & Wildlife Dept.; one member of House; one apptd. by Gov.: L. Don Perkins, Houston (3/17/02). Exec. Dir., Larry B. Simpson, PO Box 726, Ocean Springs, MS 30564.

**Health, Commissioner of** – (1879 as State Health Officer; 1955 changed to Commissioner of Health; 1975 changed to Director, Texas Department of Health Resources; 1977 changed to Commissioner, Texas Depart-

ment of Health; apptv.; 2-yr.: (Vacancy at press time)($155,000), 1100 W. 49th, Austin 78756.

**Health, Texas Board of** – (1903 as State Board of Health; superseded similar department created in 1891; name changed in 1975 to Texas Board of Health Resources and membership increased to 18; name changed in 1977 to present form; membership decreased to 6); apptv.; per diem and expenses on duty; 6-yr.; 6 members: Mario R. Anzaldua, Mission (2/1/03); Mary E. Ceverha, Dallas (2/1/05); Raymond Hannigan, Austin (2/1/07); Amanullah Khan, Dallas (2/1/07); George H. McCleskey, Lubbock (2/1/09); Margo Sneller Scholin, Houston (2/1/05). Acting Commissioner of Health, Charles Bell ($155,000), 1100 W. 49th, Austin 78756.

**Health and Human Services, Texas Commission of** – (1991); apptd.; 2-yr.; Commissioner, Albert Hawkins III ($189,000), (2/1/05). 4900 N. Lamar Blvd., Austin 78751.

**Health Care Information Council, Texas** – (1995); expenses; 18 members: 3 nonvoting ex officio state agency members (commissioner of public health, commissioner of health and human services, commissioner of insurance); 15 apptd. to 6-yr. terms: Candus Ater, Temple (9/1/05); Steven Michael Berkowitz, Austin (9/1/05); Jack Blaz, Dallas (9/1/01); Billy E. Davis, Houston (9/1/03); Bobby S. De Rossett, Flint (9/1/03); Lewis E. Foxhall, Houston (9/1/05); Jean Freeman, Galveston (9/1/01); Woody F. Gilliland, Abilene (9/1/03); Robert W. Gracy, Fort Worth (9/1/03); Jacinto Pablo Juarez, Laredo (9/1/05); Amanullah Khan, Dallas (9/1/01); Verna Melton, Garland (9/1/05); Susan M. Nelson, Plano (9/1/01); Imogen S. Papadopoulos, Houston (9/1/01); Karl W. Swann, San Antonio (9/1/03).

**Healthcare System Board of Directors, Statewide Rural** – (1997); 18 members (6 representatives of care providers; 12 apptd. by Gov.); 6 yr.; Gov's apptees.: Dana W. Cooley, Snyder (2/1/01); Harold R. High, Cuero (2/1/03); Ralph H. Meriwether, Alpine (2/1/03); Thomas E. Mueller, La Grange (2/1/03); Pervaiz Rahman, Gainesville (2/1/99); Doris L. Reding, Littlefield (2/1/03); Joyce A. Roberts, Mount Vernon (2/1/01); Lucille H. Rochs, Fredericksburg (2/1/99); Joe Tom Terrell, Jacksonville (2/1/99); Pablo C. Teveni, Stanton (2/1/01); B.R. (Skipper) Wallace, Lampasas (2/1/01); Hugh H. Wilson Jr., Hale Center (2/1/99).

**Health Coordinating Council, Statewide** – (1975); apptv.; 2-yr.; membership decreased from 21 to 15 in 1993; number increased to 17 in 1997; apptv., as follows: Joan W. Biggerstaff, Plano (8/31/05); James Endicott, Harker Heights (8/1/05); Joe Frush, Abilene (8/1/05); Susan Galindo, Bryan (8/1/05); Laura Gordon, El Paso (8/1/03); Charles Ku, Flower Mound (8/1/03); Elva Concha LeBlanc, Galveston (8/1/07); Ben Raimer, Galveston (8/1/03); Russell K. Tolman, Fort Worth (8/1/05); Rebecca Uribe-Garza, Laredo (8/1/03); David A. Valdez, San Antonio (8/1/01); Judy Wolf, San Antonio (8/1/01); P.J. Wright, Fair Oaks Ranch (8/1/01). Exec. Dir., A. Spires, Texas Dept. of Health, 1100 W. 49th, Austin 78756-3199.

**Healthy Kids Corporation, Texas, Board of Directors** – (1997); all terms expire 9/1/01: J. Coalter Baker, Austin; Rene Daniel Pena, El Paso; Dorothy Nelson Snyder, Waco; Kenneth D. Wells, Houston.

**Hearing Instruments, State Committee of Examiners in the Fitting and Dispensing of** – (1969); apptv.; 6-yr.; expenses; 9 members: Gordon Bisel, Houston (12/31/05); Kenneth W. Earl, Orange (12/31/07); Susan Lee Hargrave, Cedar Hill (12/31/05); Jerome Kosoy, Houston (12/31/07); James McCrae, Fredericksburg (12/31/05); Cherri Ann Robbins, San Antonio (12/31/07); Michael L. Shobe, Lubbock (12/31/03); Eve-Anne Wall, Granbury (12/31/03); John Westmoreland, Waco (12/31/03). Exec. Dir., Bobby Schmidt, 4800 N. Lamar, Ste. 150, Austin 78756.

**Higher Education Coordinating Board, Texas** – (1953 as temporary board; 1955 as permanent 15-member Texas Commission on Higher Education; increased to 18 members in 1965; name changed to present form in 1987); apptv.; 6-yr.; expenses; 18 members: William C. Atkinson, Bryan (8/31/01); Martin Basaldúa, Kingwood (8/31/03); Dolores Hutto Carruth, Irving (8/31/01); Ricardo G. Cigarroa, Laredo (8/31/05); Kevin P. Eltife, Tyler (8/31/03); Raul B. Fernandez, San Antonio (8/31/03); Robert I. Fernandez, Fort Worth (8/31/01); Cathy Obriotti Green, San Antonio (8/31/05); Gerry Griffin, Hunt (8/31/05); Carey Hobbs, Waco (8/31/05); Jodie L. Jiles, Houston (8/31/01); Steve Late, Odessa (8/31/03); Adair Margo, El Paso (8/31/03); Leonard Rauch, Houston (8/31/01); Hector de J. Ruiz, Austin (8/31/05); Robert W. Shepard, Harlingen (8/31/03); Terdema L.

Ussery II, Dallas (8/31/05); Pamela P. Willeford, Austin (8/31/03). Commissioner of Higher Education, Dr. Don W. Brown, PO Box 12788, Austin 78711.

**Higher Education Tuition Board, Prepaid** – (1995); apptv.; expenses; 6-yr.; 7 members: State Comptroller, 2 apptd. by Lt. Gov., 2 apptd. by Gov. Gov's apptees: Michael D. Gollob, Tyler (2/1/03); Beth Miller Weakley, San Antonio (2/1/05).

**Historical Commission, Texas** – (1953); apptv.; expenses; 6-yr.; 18 members: Jean Ann Ables-Flatt, Terrell (2/1/05); Bruce T. Aiken, Brownsville (2/1/01); Jane Cook Barnhill, Brenham (2/1/01); Gail Loving Barnes, Odessa (2/1/05); J.P. Bryan, Houston (2/1/03); Diane D. Bumpas, Dallas (2/1/05); Shirley W. Caldwell, Albany (2/1/01); Chris Carson, San Antonio (2/1/03); T.R. Fehrenbach, San Antonio (2/1/01); Frank W. Gorman, El Paso (2/1/01); Eileen Johnson, Lubbock (2/1/03); Mamie McKnight, Dallas (2/1/05); Carl McQueary, Austin (2/1/03); Susan Mead, Dallas (2/1/01); John Liston Nau III, Houston (2/1/05); Juan F. Sandoval, El Paso (2/1/05); Linda Valdez, San Antonio (2/1/03); Clinton P. White, Wharton (2/1/03). Exec. Dir., F. Lawerence Oaks ($85,000), PO Box 12276, Austin 78711.

**Historical Records Advisory Board, Texas** – (1976); apptv.; 3-yr.; 9 members: State Archivist, 6 apptd. by by director and librarian of Texas State Library and Archives Comm.; two members apptd. by Gov. Public members: Martha Doty Freeman, Austin (2/1/02); Richard L. Hooverson, Belton (2/1/06). State Historical Records Coordinator, Chris LaPlante (2/1/01), State Library, PO Box 12927, Austin 78711.

**Housing and Community Affairs, Board of Texas Dept. of** – (1979 as Texas Housing Agency; merged with Department of Community Affairs and name changed in 1991); apptv.; expenses; 6-yr.; 9 members: Margie Bingham, Houston (1/31/01); Shadrick Bogany, Missouri City (1/31/07); Robert Brewer, San Angelo (1/31/03); C. Kent Conine, Frisco (1/31/03); James A. Daross, El Paso (1/31/03); Vidal González, Del Rio (1/31/07); Michael E. Jones, Tyler (1/31/05); Lydia Saenz, Carrizo Springs (1/31/05); Marsha L. Williams, Dallas (1/31/05). Exec. Dir., Daisy A. Stiner ($112,352), 507 Sabine, Austin 78701.

**Housing Corporation Board of Directors, Texas State Affordable** – (1997); expenses; 5 members: apptd. by Gov., term at Gov's pleasure: Jeffrey S. Baloutine, Houston; Donald S. Currie, Rancho Viejo; Karen S. Lugar, San Antonio; Dawn Enoch Moore, Dallas; Jerry Romero, El Paso.

**Human Rights, State Commission on** – (1983); apptv.; 6-yr.; expenses; 6 members: Mary E. Banks, Houston (9/24/05); Anna Farias, Crystal City (9/24/03); Laura Ayoub Keith, El Paso (9/24/01); Carroll Maclin, Lufkin (9/24/05); David J. Manning, Fort Worth (9/24/03); Charles W. Taylor Jr., Houston (9/24/01). Exec. Dir., William M. Hale ($62,000), P. O. Box 13493, Austin 78711.

**Human Services, Texas Board of** – (1941 as State Board of Public Welfare; name changed to present form in 1985); apptv.; 6-yr.; per diem and expenses; 6 members: Jon M. Bradley, Dallas (1/20/03); John Cuellar, Dallas (1/20/05); David Herndon, Austin (1/20/01); Manson B. Johnson, Houston (1/20/07); Elizabeth Darling Seale, San Antonio (1/20/03); Teresa (Terry) D. Wilkinson, Midland (1/20/05). Commissioner, Eric M. Bost ($150,000), PO Box 149030, Austin 78714-9030.

**Humanities, Texas Council for the** – Kathleen Ford Bay, Austin (12/31/01); Cynthia J. Comparin, Dallas (12/31/04); Maceo C. Dailey Jr., El Paso (12/31/04); Randolph D. Hurt Jr., Fort Stockton, (12/31/01); Wright L. Lassiter Jr., Dallas (12/31/01). Exec. Dir., Monte K. Youngs, 3809 S. 2nd St., Ste. A100, Austin 78704-7058.

**Incentive and Productivity Commission, Texas** – (1987 as Productivity and Bonus Commission and Employee Incentive Commission; commissions merged and name changed to present form in 1989); 9 members — 6 state officials (term on commission is term in other office): Gov.; Lt. Gov.; Comptroller; State Treasurer; Administrator, Texas Workforce Comm.; Chmn., Texas Higher Education Coordinating Bd.; 3 apptd. by Gov.: Janice E. Collins, San Antonio (2/1/01); John Mitchell Moore, Stephenville (2/1/01); Sherry L. Phelps, Bartonville (2/1/02). Exec. Dir., Ed Bloom ($49,500), PO Box 12482, Austin 78711.

**Information Resources, Department of** – (1981 as Automated Information and Telecommunications Council; name changed in 1990); 6-yr.; expenses; 3 members rec-

ommended by Speaker of House, 3 by Lt. Gov.; 3 by Gov.: 9 members: Jennifer Anderson, Mesquite (2/1/01); Walter A. Bradley III, Dallas (2/1/01); Don Gilbert, Austin (2/1/01); Rolf R. Haberecht, Dallas (2/1/03); Charles W. Heald, Austin (2/1/01); Cliff Mountain, Austin (2/1/09); Harry H. Richardson, San Antonio (2/1/01); Leonard W. Riley Jr., Austin (2/1/01); William L. Transier, Houston (2/1/09). Exec. Dir., Carolyn Purcell ($120,000), PO Box 13564, Austin 78711.

**Insurance, Commissioner of** – José O. Montemayor (1/31/05); ($163,800), PO Box 149104, Austin 78714.

**Insurance Purchasing Alliance, Texas** – (1993; formerly the Health Benefits Purchasing Cooperative); 6-yr., apptd.; expenses; 6 members: Esperanza Andrade, San Antonio (2/1/03); Mary Flores, Flower Mound (9/1/01); Larry Forehand, Pasadena (9/1/01); J. McLochlin, Dallas (2/1/99); Jeffrey Lawlor, Austin (9/1/03); Joseph F. Phillips, Mission (2/1/99).

**Interstate Mining Compact Commission** – Melvin Hodgkiss, Austin. Exec. Dir.: Gregory Conrad, 459B Carlisle Drv., Herndon, VA 22070.

**Interstate Oil and Gas Compact Commission, Texas Rep.** – (1935); ex officio or apptv., according to Gov's. choice; per diem and expenses. (Approximately 150 other appointees serve on various committees.) Official representatives for Texas: Antonio O. Garza Jr., Charles R. Matthews, Benjamin E. Streusand, Michael L. Williams. Exec. Dir., Christine Hansen, PO Box 53127, Oklahoma City, OK 73152.

**Interstate Parole Compact Administrator** – (1951); apptv.: Knox Fitzpatrick, Dallas.

**Jail Standards, Texas Commission on** – (1975); apptv.; 6-yr.; expenses; 9 members: Marvalette C. Fentress, Houston (1/31/05); Gonzalo R. Gallegos, San Antonio (2/1/09); David Gutierrez, Lubbock (2/1/09); Jimmy L. Jackson, Carrollton (1/31/05); Evelyn (Kelly) McVay, Nacogdoches (1/31/07); Horace "Ted" Montgomery, Dumas (2/1/09); William C. Morrow, Midland (1/31/07); Michael M. Seale, Houston (1/31/05); Charles J. Sebesta Jr., Caldwell (1/31/07). Exec. Dir., Terry Julian ($61,000), PO Box 12985, Austin 78711.

**Judicial Conduct, State Commission on** – (1965 as 9-member Judicial Qualifications Commission; name changed in 1977 to present form and membership raised to 11); expenses; 6-yr.; 11 members: 5 apptd. by Supreme Court; 2 apptd. by State Bar; 4 apptd. by Gov. as follows: Faye W. Barksdale, Arlington (11/19/07); Rolland Craten Allen III, Corpus Christi (11/19/03); Elizabeth (Dee) Coats, Houston (11/19/03); Gilbert M. Martinez, Austin (11/19/03). Exec. Dir., Margaret J. Reaves ($100,000), PO Box 12265, Austin 78711.

**Judicial Council, Texas** – (1929 as Texas Civil Judicial Council; name changed in 1975); ex officio terms vary; apptv.; 6-yr. terms; expenses; 19 members, increased to 22 in 1997: 16 ex officio and 6 apptd. from general public. Public members: Jean Birmingham, Marshall (6/30/03); Lance Richard Byrd, Dallas (6/30/07); Joseph Alan Callier, Kingwood (6/30/03); Delia Martínez-Carian, San Antonio (6/30/07); José Luis López, Crystal City (6/30/05); Ann Manning, Lubbock (6/10/05). Exec. Dir., Jerry L. Benedict, PO Box 12066, Austin 78711.

**Judicial Districts Board** – (1985); 12 ex officio members (term in other office); one apptv. (4 yrs.); ex officio: Chief Justice of Texas Supreme Court; Presiding Judge, Court of Criminal Appeals; Presiding Judge of each of 9 Administrative Judicial Districts; pres. of Texas Judicial Council; apptee: Joseph W. Wolfe, Sherman (12/12/02).

**Judicial Districts of Texas, Admin., Presiding Judges of** – (See Administrative Judicial Districts, Presiding Judges).

**Juvenile Probation Commission, Texas** – (1981); apptv.; 6-yr.; expenses; 9 members — 3 judges of District Courts and 6 private citizens: Robert P. Brotherton, Wichita Falls (8/31/07); Michael E. Cantrell, Garland (6/30/04); Judge Mary Craft, Houston (6/30/04); Keith H. Kuttler, College Station (8/31/07); Betsy Lake, Houston (8/31/05); Lyle T. Larson, San Antonio (8/31/05); William E. "Bill" Miller, Lubbock (6/30/04); Barbara J. Punch, Missouri City (8/31/07); Carlos Villa, El Paso (8/31/05). Exec. Dir., Vicki Spriggs ($90,000), PO Box 13547, Austin 78711.

**Land Board, School** – (1939); one ex officio (term in other office); 2 apptd. — one by Atty. Gen. and one by Gov. for 2-yr. term; per diem and expenses; ex officio member: Comm. of General Land Office; Gov's. apptee: C. Louis Renaud, Midland (8/29/01).

**Land Surveying, Texas Board of Professional** – (1979); formed from consolidation of membership of Board of Examiners of Licensed Land Surveyors, est. 1977, and State Board of Registration for Public Surveyors, est. 1955); apptv.; 6-yr.; 10 members — Commissioner of General Land Office serving by statute; 3 members of general public, 2 licensed land surveyors, 4 registered public surveyors, as follows: Jerry M. Goodson, Lampasas (1/31/01); Steven C. Hofer, Midland (1/31/05); Daniel E. Martinez, Lubbock (1/31/05); Kelley Neumann, San Antonio (1/31/03); A.W. (Art) Osborn, Tyler (1/31/01); Robert L. Pounds, El Paso (1/31/03); Douglas W. Turner, Houston (1/31/05); Joan White, Brownsville (1/31/03); Raul Wong Jr., Dallas (1/31/01). Exec. Dir., Sandy Smith ($47,000), 7701 N. Lamar, Ste. 400, Austin 78752.

**Lands, Board for Lease of University** – (1929 as 3-member board; membership increased to 4 in 1985); ex officio; term in other office; 4 members: Commissioner of General Land Office, 2 members of Board of Regents of University of Texas, 1 member Board of Regents of Texas A&M University.

**Lavaca-Navidad River Authority, Board of Directors** – (1954 as 7-member Jackson County Flood Control District; reorganized as 9-member board in 1959; name changed to present form in 1969); apptv.; per diem and expenses; 9 members: Gerald M. Boyd, Edna (5/1/03); Mark Cayce, Edna (5/1/01); Charles M. Hasdorff, Ganado (5/1/01); Robert C. Martin, Edna (5/1/03); Mitzi M. Mauritz, Ganado (5/1/03); Michael W. Menefee, Edna (5/1/01); Robert Michael (Mike) Myers, Edna (5/1/05); Sharla Vee Strauss, La Ward (5/1/05); Willard E. Ulbricht, Edna (5/1/05). Gen. Mgr., Jack C. Nelson, PO Box 429, Edna 77957.

**Law Enforcement Officer Standards & Education, Comm. on** – (1965); expenses; 14 members; 5 ex officio: Atty. Gen., Directory of Public Safety, Commissioner of Education, Exec. Dir. of Governor's Office Criminal Justice Division, and Commissioner of Higher Education; 9 apptv. members: Claudia A. Bretz, Odessa (8/30/01); Steven M. Byrd, Dallas (8/30/07); Lilia B. Escajeda, Amarillo (8/30/03); Raymond M. Hunt, Houston (8/30/03); William B. Jackson, Arlington (8/30/05); David N. James, Carrollton (8/30/03); Benigno G. Reyna, Brownsville (8/30/03); Daniel J. Smith, Belton (8/31/07); Joe A. Stivers, Huntsville (8/30/07). Exec. Dir., D.C. Jim Dozier ($76,000), 6330 E. Hwy. 290, Ste. 200, Austin 78723.

**Law Examiners, Board of** – Nine attorneys apptd. by Supreme Court biennially for 2-year terms expiring September 30 of odd-numbered years. Compensation set by Supreme Court not to exceed $20,000 per annum. Exec. Dir., Julia Vaughan, PO Box 13486, Austin 78711.

**Law Library Board, State** – (1971); ex officio; expenses; 3 members: Chief Justice State Supreme Court, Presiding Judge Court of Criminal Appeals and Atty. General. Dir., Kay Schlueter ($58,000), PO Box 12367, Austin 78711.

**Legislative Budget Board** – (1949); 10 members; 6 ex officio members: Lt. Gov.; Speaker of House; Chmn., Senate Finance Comm.; Chmn., Senate State Affairs Comm.; Chmn., House Appropriations Comm.; Chmn., House Ways and Means Comm.; plus 4 other members of Legislature. Director, John Keel, PO Box 12666, Austin 78711-2666.

**Legislative Council, Texas** – (1949); 17 ex officio members — 4 senators named by Lt. Gov.; 9 representatives named by Speaker; Chmn., House Administration Committee; Chmn., Senate Administration Committee; Lt. Gov.; and Speaker. Exec. Dir., Steven R. Collins, PO Box 12128, Austin 78711.

**Legislative Redistricting Board** – (1948); 5 ex officio members; term in other office: Lt. Gov., Speaker of House, Atty. Gen., Comptroller and Commissioner of General Land Office.

**Librarian, State** – (Originally est. in 1839; present office est. 1909); apptv., indefinite term: Robert S. Martin ($65,000), PO Box 12927, Austin 78711.

**Library and Archives Commission, Texas State** – (1909 as 5-member Library and State Historical Commission; number of members increased to 6 in 1953; name changed to present form in 1979); apptv.; per diem and expenses on duty; 6-yr.; 6 members: Carolyn P. Armstrong, San Antonio (9/28/01); Chris A. Brisack, Edinburg (9/28/05); Kenneth R. Carr, El Paso (9/28/03); Sandy Melton, Dallas (9/28/01); Sandra J. Pickett, Liberty (9/28/03); Elizabeth Ann Sanders, Arlington (9/28/05). Dir. and Librarian

Peggy D. Rudd ($85,000), PO Box 12927, Austin 78711.

**Library, State Legislative Reference** – (1909); indefinite term; Director: Dale W. Propp, Box 12488, Austin 78711.

**Licensing and Regulation, Texas Commission on** – (1989); apptv.; 6-yr.; expenses; 6 members: Frank S. Denton, Conroe (2/1/09); Fred N. Moses, Plano (2/1/09); Gina Parker, Waco (2/1/07); Bill C. Pittman, Austin (2/1/07); Patricia P. Stout, San Antonio (2/1/05); Leo R. Vasquez III, Houston (2/1/05). Exec. Dir., Willliam H. Kuntz Jr. ($76,000), PO Box 12157, Austin 78711.

**Lottery Commission, Texas** – (1993); 6-yrs.; apptv.; expenses; 3 members: C. Thomas Clowe Jr., Waco (2/1/05); James A. Cox Jr., Austin (2/1/09); Betsy Whitaker, Dallas (2/1/07). Exec. Dir, Reagan E. Greer ($110,000), PO Box 16630, Austin 78761-6630.

**Lower Colorado River Authority** – (See **Colorado River Authority, Lower**).

**Marriage & Family Therapists, Texas State Board of Examiners of** – (1991); apptd.; 6 yrs.; per diem and transportation expenses; 9 members: Joe Ann Clack, Missouri City (2/1/03); Ellen Harrison, El Paso (2/1/01); Waymon Ray Hinson, Abilene (2/1/01); Marvarene Oliver, Corpus Christi (2/1/03); George P. Pulliam, Dickinson (2/1/01); Carl S. Strain, San Angelo (2/1/03); Brenda B. VanAmburgh, Fort Worth (2/1/05); William H. Watson, Lubbock (2/1/05); Jackie M. Weimer, Plano (2/1/05). Exec. Dir., Bobby D. Schmidt, Dept. of Health, 1100 W. 49th St., Austin 78756-3183.

**Medical Examiners District Review Committee: Dist. 1** – (1977); apptv.; 6-hr.; expenses; 20 members — five from each of 4 districts: Robert J. Bacon Sr., Houston (1/15/98); Sharon J. Barnes, Lake Jackson (1/15/06); Herman L. Koester, Dickinson (1/15/02); Richard Strax, Houston (1/15/06); Frank R. Wellborne, Houston (1/15/06). **Dist. 2:** David Baucom, Sulphur Springs (1/15/06); H. Jane Chihal, Carrollton (1/15/02); Allan N. Shulkin, Dallas (1/15/06); B.R. Sienbenlist, Jonesville (1/15/98); Rodney M. Wiseman, Tyler (1/15/06). **Dist. 3:** Robert C. Henderson, Amarillo (1/15/02); David W. Miller, Abilene (1/15/06); Nalin H. Tolia, Odessa (1/15/98) Lonnie L. Vickers, Brady (1/15/06); Irvin E. Zeitler Jr., San Angelo (1/15/06). **Dist. 4:** Manuel G. Guajardo, Brownsville (1/15/02); Bobby Howard, Corpus Christi (1/15/06); Gladys C. Keene, Laredo (1/15/98); Peter D. Scholl, Austin (1/15/06); Phyllis Strother, Waco (1/15/06).

**Medical Examiners, Texas State Board of** – (1907 as 12-member board, membership raised to 15 in 1981, raised to 18 in 1993); apptv.; 6-yr.; per diem on duty; 18 members: Lee S. Anderson, Fort Worth (4/13/03); Penny Angelo, Midland (4/13/01); Jose Manuel Benavides, San Antonio (4/13/05); Peter Chang, Houston (4/13/03); William H. Fleming III, Houston (4/13/01); David E. Garza, Laredo (4/13/05); Edward S. Hicks Sr., Corpus Christi (4/13/03); Thomas D. Kirksey, Austin (4/13/07); Eddie J. Miles Jr., San Antonio (4/13/07); Elvira Pascua-Lim, Lubbock (4/13/01); Larry Price, Temple (4/13/03); Joyce A. Roberts, Mount Vernon (4/13/05); Vernon L. Ryan, San Angelo (4/13/01); Nancy M. Seliger, Amarillo (4/13/05); Paulette B. Southard, Alice (4/13/05); R. Russell Thomas Jr., Eagle Lake (4/13/99); Janet Tornelli-Mitchell, Dallas (4/13/03); Jenat T. Turner, Austin (4/13/03). Exec. Dir., Donald Patrick ($85,000), PO Box 149134, Austin 78714-9134.

**Medical Physicists, Texas Board of Licensure for Professional** – (1991); apptv.; 6-yrs.; 9 members: Ralph Blumhardt, San Antonio (2/1/01); Phillip D. Bourland, Temple (2/1/05); Shannon Cox, Austin (2/1/03); Kumar Krishen, Seabrook (2/1/05); Adrian Le-Blanc, Houston (2/1/01); Louis Levy, San Antonio (2/1/03); Isabel Menendez, Portland (2/1/03); Rebecca C. Middleton, DeSoto (2/1/05); Paul Murphy, Houston (2/1/01).

**Mental Health and Mental Retardation, Texas Board of** – (1965, superseded Board of Texas State Hospitals and Special Schools); apptv.; 6-yr.; per diem and expenses; 9 members: Kenneth Z. Altshuler, Dallas (1/31/05); Rodolfo Arredondo Jr., Lubbock (1/31/07); Spencer Bayles, Houston (1/31/03); Sharon S. Butterworth, El Paso (1/31/05); Karen Mitchell Frank, Port Aransas (1/31/07); Andrew Hardin, McKinney (1/31/03); Harriet M. Helmle, San Antonio (1/31/03); Richard (Dick) O'Connor, Dallas (1/31/07); Lynda K. Scott-Everett, The Woodlands (1/31/05). Commissioner of MHMR, Karen F. Hale ($140,000), PO Box 12668, Austin 78711-2668.

**Midwestern State University, Board of Regents** –

(1959); apptv.; 6-yr.; 9 members: John C. Bridgman, Wichita Falls (2/25/06); Mac Cannedy Jr., Wichita Falls (2/25/06); Jaime A. Davidson, Dallas (2/25/04); Barbara Jean Dorman, Plainview (2/25/02); Elizabeth A. Gifford, Amarillo (2/25/02); Arnold W. Oliver, Wichita Falls (2/25/02); Carolyn Park, Euless (2/25/04); David L. Stephens, Plano (2/25/06); Chaunce O. Thompson Jr., Breckenridge (2/25/04). Pres., Dr. Henry Moon, 3400 Taft, Wichita Falls 76308.

**Military Facilities Commission, Texas** – (1935 as 3-member National Guard Armory Board; reorganized as 6-member board in 1981; name changed 1997); 6-yr.; 6 members: M.G. (ret.) Darrel Baker, Austin (4/30/05); C. Tammy Linbeck, Houston (4/30/03); R. Gary McClure, San Angelo (4/30/03); Sandra Paret, Dallas (4/30/05); Jorge Perez, McAllen (4/30/05); Michael White, El Paso (4/30/01). Exec. Dir., Jerry D. Malcolm ($57,000), PO Box 5426, Austin 78763.

**Military Planning Commission, Texas Strategic** – (1997); 3 yrs.; exp.; 11 members: 2 ex officio (chairs of House and Senate committees having to do with military matters) and 9 apptv. Apptd. members: Chino Chapa, Dallas (2/1/01); Lewis E. Curtis III, Fair Oaks Ranch (2/1/00); Charles de Wetter, El Paso (2/1/02); Tom Gann, Lufkin (2/1/00); Charles Hines, Prairie View (2/1/01); Fred Hughes, Abilene (2/1/01); S. Loyd Neal Jr., Corpus Christi (2/1/06); Horace G. Taylor, Belton (2/1/02); Robert E. Tokerud, Irving (2/1/02).

**Motor Vehicle Board, Texas Department of Transportation** – (1971 as 6-member board; membership increased to 9 in 1979; reduced to 6 in 1987; made division of Texas Dept. of Transportation, name changed to present form and membership increased to 9 in 1992; decreased to 6); apptv.; 6-yr.; per diem and expenses; members: Robert C. Barnes, Odessa (1/31/03); Frank Breazeale, Gilmer (1/31/07); D. Diane Dillard, Houston (1/31/03); Stuart J. Hamilton, San Antonio (1/31/05); Patricia F. Harless, Spring (1/31/07); Robena E. Jackson, Austin (1/31/05); James R. Leonard, Abilene (1/31/07); Kevin D. Pagan, McAllen (1/31/05); Jimmy C. Payton, Euless (1/31/03). Division Dir. Brett Bray, PO Box 2293, Austin 78768.

**Municipal Retirement System** (See Retirement System, Municipal, Board of Trustees).

**National Guard Armory Board, Texas** – (see Military Facilities Commission, Texas).

**Natural Resource Conservation Commission, Texas** (See Environmental Quality, Texas Commission on).

**Neches River Municipal Water Authority, Upper** – (Est. 1953 as 9-member board; membership changed to 3 in 1959); apptv.; 6-yr.; 3 members: Joe Crutcher, Palestine (2/1/07); Jesse D. Hickman, Palestine (2/1/03); Robert E. McKelvey, Palestine (2/1/05). Gen. Mgr., T.G. Mallory, PO Box 1965, Palestine 75802.

**Neches Valley Authority, Lower** – (1933); apptv.; per diem and expenses on duty; 6-yr.; 9 members: R.C. Aldrich, Nome (7/28/01); Lonnie Arrington, Beaumont (7/28/01); Brian Babin, Woodville (7/28/01); Bill L. Clark, Beaumont (7/28/05); Lois Henderson, Warren (7/28/03); Patricia M. Neild, Beaumont (7/28/03); Cheryl D. Olesen, Beaumont (7/28/05); John W. Robinson, Silsbee (7/28/03). Gen. Mgr. Robert Stroder, PO Box 5117, Beaumont 77726-5117.

**North Texas Tollway Authority Board of Directors** – (1997); apptv.; per diem and expenses; 2-yr.; 7 members: commissioners courts of Collin, Dallas, Denton and Tarrant counties each appt. one member; Gov. appts 3. Gov's. apptees.: Donald D. Dillard, Dallas (9/1/01); Jere W. Thompson Jr., Dallas (9/1/00); Marilyn Kay Walls, Cleburne (8/31/03).

**Nueces River Authority Board of Directors** – (1953 as Nueces River Conservation and Reclamation District; name changed in 1971); apptv.; 6-yr.; per diem and expenses; 21 members: Steve G. Beever, Pearsall (2/1/05); W. Scott Bledsoe III, Oakville (2/1/03); Joe M. Cantu, Pipe Creek (2/1/07); William I. "Bill" Dillard, Uvalde (2/1/07); Robert M. Dullnig, San Antonio (2/1/07); Eduardo L. Garcia, Corpus Christi, (2/1/07); Ernest R. Garza, Robstown (2/1/05); John William Howell, Portland (2/1/03); Leslie W. Kinsel, Cotulla (2/1/03); Beth Reavis Knolle, Sandia (2/1/05); Dan S. Leyendecker, Corpus Christi (2/1/07); August "Bo" Linnartz Jr., Carrizo Springs (2/1/03); Patty Puig Mueller, Corpus Christi (2/1/07); Scott James Petty, Hondo (2/1/07); Thomas M. Reding Jr., Portland (2/1/03); H. Jaime Saenz, Carrizo Springs (2/1/05); J.R. "Bob" Schneider, George West (2/1/05); Patricia Sutton, Camp Wood (2/1/

03); Roxana Proctor Tom, Campbellton (2/1/05); L.B. "Pete" Vaden, Uvalde (2/1/05); Lawrence H. Warburton Jr., Alice (2/1/03). Exec. Dir., Con Mims, PO Box 349, Uvalde 78802-0349.

**Nurse Examiners, State Board of** – (1909 as 6-member board; reorganized and membership increased to 9 in 1981); apptv.; per diem and expenses; 6-yr.; 9 members: Thomas L. Barton, Pampa (1/31/09); Deborah Hughes Bell, Abilene (1/31/09); Virginia Milam Campbell, Mesquite (1/31/07); Lawrence J. Canfield, Temple (1/31/07); Blanca Rosa Garcia, Corpus Christi (1/31/05); Brenda S. Jackson, San Antonio (1/31/09); Marcelo Laijas Jr., Floresville (1/31/99); Phyllis Caves Rawley, El Paso (1/31/07); Linda R. Rounds, Galveston (1/31/05). Exec. Dir., Katherine A. Thomas ($62,000), 333 Guadalupe, Suite 3-460, Austin 78701.

**Nurse Examiners, State Board of Vocational** – (1951 as 9-member board; membership increased to 12 in 1981; later increased to 15); apptv.; 6-yr.; 15 members: Joyce M. Adams, Houston (9/6/01); Janette L. Bowers, Alpine (9/6/03); Ginger M. Brenner, Sugar Land (9/6/01); Lillian K. Brown, San Angelo (9/6/01); Rachel Gomez, Harlingen (9/6/05); Melody Hart, Andrews (9/6/05); Geneva Harvey, Clifton (9/6/03); Rex H. Howard, Richardson (9/6/03); Beverly Jean Nutall, Bryan (9/6/05); Anita Smith Palmer, Megargel (9/6/05); Cathy Parrott, Gatesville (9/6/03); Kathleen Gleeson Powell, North Richland Hills (9/6/01); Wendy L. Prater, Houston (9/6/05); William H. Rice, Austin (9/6/03); Frank D. Sandoval Jr., San Antonio (9/6/01). Exec. Dir., Mary M. Strange ($58,000), PO Box 430, Austin 78767.

**Nursing Facility Administrators, Texas Board of** – (Abolished effective Sept. 1997; responsibilities transferred to the Texas Department of Human Services.)

**Occupational Therapy Examiners, Texas Board of** – (1983 as 6-member board; increased to 9 in 1999); apptv.; 6-yr.; per diem and expenses; 9 members: Gail Blom, Dallas (2/1/01); Judith E. Bowen, Edinburg (2/1/05); Lonnie Cole, San Antonio (2/1/03); Joseph A. Messmer, Corpus Christi (2/1/01); Windi Morris-Fuller, Colorado City (2/1/03); Jean E. Polichino, Houston (2/1/05); Charles Paul R. Turco Sr., Beaumont (2/1/01); Linda Veale, Lubbock (2/1/03); Jo Ann Wofford, Fort Worth (2/1/05). Exec. Dir. of Physical Therapy and Occupational Therapy Examiners, John Maline ($51,198), 333 Guadalupe St., Ste. 2-510, Austin 78701.

**Offenders with Mental Impairments, Texas Council on** – (1987); apptv.; expenses; 6-yr.; 27 members: 18 heads of agencies or their designees: Texas Dept. of Criminal Justice, Texas Dept. of MHMR, Board of Pardons and Paroles, Texas Adult Probation Commission, Texas Juvenile Probation Commission, Texas Youth Commission, Texas Rehabilitation Commission, Texas Education Agency, Criminal Justice Policy Council, Mental Health Assn. in Texas, Texas Commission on Alcohol and Drug Abuse, Commission on Law Enforcement Officer Standards and Education, Texas Council of Community MHMR Centers, Commission on Jail Standards, Texas Planning Council for Developmental Disabilities, Texas Assn. for Retarded Citizens, Texas Alliance for the Mentally Ill, and Parent Assn. for the Retarded of Texas; 9 apptd. by Gov. as follows: James H. Cromwell, Rusk (2/1/01); David Gutierrez, Lubbock (2/1/05); Carl Hays, Dallas (2/1/01); Corinne Ann Mason, Richardson (2/1/01); Melissa L. Mojica, Laredo (2/1/03); Dennis R. Myers, McGregor (2/1/05); Robert C. Strayhan, San Antonio (2/1/03); George A. Urias, San Antonio (2/1/05); Sharon Wilson, Fort Worth (2/1/03). Exec. Dir., Dee Kifowit, 8610 Shoal Creek Blvd., Austin 78757.

**Old San Antonio Road Preservation Commission** – (1989); term at pleasure of governor; 9 members: 4 representatives of state agencies: Texas Dept. of Transportation, Texas Historical Commission, Parks and Wildlife, Texas Dept. of Commerce (Tourism Div.); 5 at large recommended by Texas Historical Commission and apptd. by Gov.: Dr. Archie P. McDonald, Nacogdoches; Gen. John R. McGiffert, San Antonio; Ingrid B. Morris, Hemphill; Nan Olsen, Bastrop; Rose T. Treviño, Laredo.

**Optometry Board, Texas** – (1921 as 6-member State Board of Examiners in Optometry; name changed to present form in 1981 and membership increased to 9); apptv.; per diem; 6-yr.; 9 members: Ann A. Bradford, Midland (1/31/05); Carolyn R. Carman-Merrifield, Arlington (1/31/01); Joe W. DeLoach, Garland (1/31/05); Kevin D. DeWolfe, Austin (1/31/01); Judy E. Eidson, San Antonio (1/31/01); B.J. Garner, Houston (1/31/03); Katherine M. Gear,

Mineral Wells (1/31/03); Donald R. Glenz, Houston (1/31/03); Mark A. Latta, Amarillo (1/31/05); Donnya Elle Stephens, Nacogdoches (1/31/99). Exec. Dir., Lois Ewald ($60,000), 333 Guadalupe St., Ste. 2-420, Austin 78701.

**Orthotics and Prosthetics, Texas Board of** – (1998); apptv.; compensation and travel expenses; 6-yr.; 6 members: Scott Atha, Pflugerville (2/1/03); Wanda Furgason, Brownwood (2/1/05); Kenneth Hart, Kilgore (2/1/01); Thomas Lunsford, The Woodlands (2/1/01); Stanley Thomas, San Antonio (2/1/03); Lupe M. Young, San Antonio (2/1/05).

**Pardons and Paroles, Texas Board of** – (1893 as Board of Pardon Advisers; changed in 1936 to Board of Pardons and Paroles with 3 members; membership increased to 6 in 1983; made a division of the Texas Department of Criminal Justice and membership increased to 18 in 1990); apptv.; 6-yr.; (chairman, $85,500; members, $83,200 each); 18 members: Paddy Lann Burwell, Westhoff (2/1/05); James E. Bush, Huntsville (2/1/03); Lafayette Collins, Round Rock (2/1/05); Linda Garcia, La Porte (2/1/05); Roy Anthony Garcia, Tennessee Colony (2/1/07); Gerald L. Garrett, Gatesville (2/1/07); Juanita Maria Gonzalez, Round Rock (2/1/03); James Paul Kiel Jr., Tyler (2/1/05); Daniel Ray Lang, Houston (2/1/01); Billy Wayne Linson, Cedar Hill (2/1/07); Thomas W. Moss, Amarillo (2/1/01); Rissie L. Owens, Huntsville (2/1/03); Filiberto (Bert) Reyna, Waco (2/1/05); Victor Rodriguez, San Antonio (2/1/01); Brendolyn Rogers-Gardner, Duncanville (2/1/01); Stephen Rosales, Austin (2/1/09); Alvin A. Shaw, San Antonio (2/1/03); Charles A. Shipman, Wichita Falls (2/1/03); Lucinda "Cindy" Simons, Hereford (2/1/05).; Charles C. Speier, San Antonio (2/1/07).

**Pardons and Paroles Policy Board** – (1997); apptv.; 6 members, apptd. from membership of Board of Pardons and Paroles; 6-yr. term concurrent with term on Board of Pardons and Paroles. 6 members: James E. (Jim) Bush, Huntsville (2/1/01); Linda Garcia, La Porte (2/1/05); Roy Anthony Garcia Tennessee Colony (2/1/07); Gerald L. Garrett, Gatesville (2/1/01); James Paul Kiel Jr., Tyler (2/1/05); Rissie Owens, Huntsville (2/1/03); Alvin A. Shaw, San Antonio (2/1/03).

**Parks and Wildlife Commission, Texas** – (1963 as 3-member board; membership increased to 6 in 1971; increased to 9 in 1983); apptv.; expenses; 6-yr.; 9 members: Ernest Angelo Jr., Midland (2/1/03); Lee M. Bass, Fort Worth (2/1/01); Carol E. Dinkins, Houston (2/1/03); Joseph B.C. Fitzsimons, San Antonio (2/1/07); Ned Holmes, Houston (2/1/09); Al Henry, Houston (2/1/05); Katharine Armstrong Idsal, San Antonio (2/1/05); Philip O'B. Montgomery III, Dallas (2/1/07); Mark E. Watson Jr., San Antonio (2/1/05). Exec. Dir., Andrew Sansom ($115,000), 4200 Smith School Rd., Austin 78744.

**Pecos River Compact Commissioner** – (1942); apptv.; 6-yr.; expenses: Julian W. Thrasher Jr., Monahans (1/23/05). ($32,247).

**Pension Boards** – For old age, blind and dependent children's assistance, see Human Services, State Board of. For retirement pay to state and municipal employees and teachers, see proper category under Retirement.

**Pension Review Board, State** – (1979); apptv.; 6-yr.; 9 members — one senator apptd. by Lt. Gov., one representative apptd. by Speaker, 7 apptd. by Gov. as follows: Rafael A. Cantu, Mission (1/31/05); Craig S. Goralski Sr., Houston (1/31/03); Ronald L. Haneberg, Rockwall (1/31/01); William Mahomes Jr., Dallas (1/31/03); Frederick E. Rowe Jr., Dallas (1/31/03); Shari Ovalline Shivers, Austin (1/31/03); Jeanie Rabke Wyatt, San Antonio (1/31/01). Exec. Dir., Rita Horwitz ($52,000), PO Box 13498, Austin 78711.

**Perfusionists, Texas State Board of Examiners of** – (1993); apptv.; per diem; 6-yr.; 9 members: Vincent Conti, Galveston (2/1/01); H.B. Bell, Dallas (2/1/01); Debra Sue Douglass, Grapevine (2/1/03); Gaye Jackson, Houston (2/1/05); M. Adam Mahmood, El Paso (2/1/03); Steve A. Raskin, Richmond (2/1/03); Thomas A. Rawles, Plano (2/1/05); Thomas Kurt Wilkes, Lubbock (2/1/05); Jose Ybarra, San Antonio (2/1/01).

**Pest Control Board, Texas Structural** – (1971 as 7-member board, membership raised to 9 in 1979); apptv.; 6-yr.; expenses; 9 members — 3 ex officio: Commissioner of Agriculture; Commissioner of Health; and head of Entomology Dept., Texas A&M University; 6 apptv. members: Jo-Christy Brown, Austin (2/1/01); Tomas Cantu, McAllen (2/1/05); Madeline Kirvin-Gamble, Dallas (2/1/05); Brenda Hill,

Nacogdoches (2/1/09); John Lee Morrison, San Antonio (2/1/07); Jay D. Stone, Lubbock (2/1/03). Exec. Dir., Benny M. Mathis ($92,000), 1106 Clayton Ln., Ste. 100 LW, Austin 78723-1066.

**Pharmacy, Texas State Board of** – (1907 as 6-member board; membership increased to 9 in 1981); apptv.; 6-yr.; 9 members: Roger W. Anderson, Houston (8/31/05); Juluette F. Bartlett-Pack, Houston (8/31/07); W. Michael Brimberry, Austin (8/31/07); Kim A. Caldwell, Plano (8/31/03); Rosemary F. Combs, El Paso (8/31/05); Wiki Erickson, Waco (8/31/03); Doyle E. High, Haskell (8/31/07); Oren M. Peacock Jr., Sachse (8/31/05); Donna Burkett Rogers, San Antonio (8/31/03). Exec. Dir., Gay Dodson ($70,000), 333 Guadalupe St., Ste. 3-600, Austin 78701.

**Physical Therapy Examiners, Texas State Board of** – (1971); apptv.; 6-yr.; expenses; 9 members: Harvey D. Aikman, Mission (1/31/03); Mark G. Cowart, Odessa (1/31/03); Mary R. Daulong, Houston (1/31/01); Sylvia A. DAvila, San Antonio (1/31/05); Cynthia Fisher, El Paso (1/31/03); Holly R. Hall, Sherman (1/31/05); Michael Grady Hines, Tyler (1/31/05); Mary Thompson, Celina (1/31/05); Susan K. Tripplehorn, Pampa (1/31/01). Exec. Dir. of Occupational Therapy and Physical Therapy Examiners, John Maline ($51,198), 333 Guadalupe St., Ste. 2-510, Austin 78701.

**Physician Assistant Examiners, Texas State Board of** – (1995); apptv.; 6-yr.; per diem; 9 members: Pamela W. Baker, Corpus Christi (2/1/05); Abigail Barrera, San Antonio (2/1/03); Michael Belgard, Center (2/1/03); G. Al Bendeck, Lubbock (2/1/05); Stephen D. Benold, Georgetown (2/1/05); Margaret K. Bentley, DeSoto (2/1/03); Dwight M. Deter, El Paso (2/1/01); Tony Gene Hedges, Littlefield (2/1/01); Timothy Webb, Houston (2/1/01).

**Plumbing Examiners, State Board of** – (1947 as 6-member board; membership increased to 9 in 1981); apptv.; expenses; 6-yr.; 9 members: Walter L. Borgfeld Jr., Lufkin (9/5/03); José L. Cárdenas, Euless (9/5/01); Min Chu, Houston (9/5/05); Lawrence Lemon Jr., Slaton (9/5/03); Nelda Martínez, Corpus Christi (9/5/01); Carol McLemore, La Marque (9/5/05); Terry Wayne Moore, Sachse (9/5/03); Joe Rocha Jr., Blanco (9/5/01); Michael D. Thamm, Cuero (9/5/05). Admin., Robert L. Maxwell ($62,000), 929 E. 41st, Austin 78751.

**Podiatric Medical Examiners, State Board of** – (1923 as 6-member State Board of Chiropody Examiners; name changed to State Board of Podiatry Examiners in 1967; made 9-member board in 1981; name changed to present form in 1997); apptv.; 6-yr.; expenses; 9 members: Teresa Barrios-Ogden, San Antonio (7/10/01); Katherine M. Boyd, Georgetown (7/10/99); C. Stanley Churchill Jr., Carrollton (7/10/01); Donald Wayne Falknor, Sugar Land (7/10/03); Alex L. Garcia Jr., Corpus Christi (7/10/01); Preston Goforth, Temple (7/10/99); Jim D. Lummus, San Angelo (7/10/03); Paul H. Schwarzentraub, Lubbock (7/10/99); Barbara G. Young, Bellaire (7/10/03). Exec. Dir., Allen M. Hymans ($52,000), 333 Guadalupe St., Ste. 2-320, Austin 78701.

**Polygraph Examiners Board** – (1965); apptv.; 6-yr.; 6 members: Elizabeth Perez Bellegarde, El Paso (6/18/01); Michael C. Gougler, Austin (6/18/05); Edward L. Hendrickson, Houston (6/18/05); Robert J. Kruckemeyer, Spring (6/18/03); Horacio Ortiz, Corpus Christi (6/18/01); William K. Teigen, Dallas (6/18/03). Exec. Officer, Frank Di Tucci ($40,000), PO Box 4087, Austin 78773.

**Preservation Board, State** – (1983); 2-yr.; 7 members — 4 ex officio: Gov., Lt. Gov., Speaker and Architect of Capitol; 3 apptv.: one apptd. by Gov., one senator apptd. by Lt. Gov. and one representative apptd. by Speaker. Gov's. apptee: Dealey D. Herndon, Austin (2/1/01). Exec. Dir., Richard L. Crawford ($115,000), PO Box 13286, Austin 78711.

**Prison Board, Texas** – (See Criminal Justice, Texas Dept. of)

**Prison Industry Oversight Authority, Private Sector** – (1997); 6-yr.; expenses; apptd; 9 members: George Fedo, Wichita Falls (2/1/99); Kathy C. Flanagan, Houston (2/1/01); Albert Gonzalez, Dallas (2/1/01); Charles D. "Mickey" Harr, Brownwood (2/1/99); Raymond G. Henderson, Austin (2/1/01); Thomas Ann Hines, Plano (2/1/03); Kelley Renee Siegler, Houston (2/1/03); Carl Casey Spencer, Huntsville (2/1/99); Steven L. Varga, San Antonio (2/1/03).

**Private Security, Texas Commission on** – (1969 as Board of Private Investigators and Private Security Agencies; name and makeup of board changed, 1999); apptv.; expenses; 6-yr.; 10 members — 1 ex officio: Dir., Dept. of

Public Safety; 9 apptd. members: Jim G. Bray Jr., Plano (1/31/03); George Craig, Corpus Christi (1/31/03); Jacob M. Monty, Houston (1/31/05); Joan T. Neuhaus, Houston (1/31/07); Ben C. Nix, Arlington (1/31/05); Cephus S. "Dusty" Rhodes, El Paso (1/31/07); Charlene Ritchey, Valley View (1/31/03); Linda J. Sadler, Lubbock (1/31/07); Michael Samulin, San Antonio (1/31/05). Exec. Dir., Jerry L. McGlasson ($75,000), PO Box 13509, Austin 78711.

**Produce Recovery Fund Board** – (1977 as 3-member board; membership increased to 6 in 1981); apptv.; expenses; 6-yr.; 6 members — 2 each from commission merchants, general public and producer representatives. Ralph Diaz, Corpus Christi (1/31/05); Steven Dexter Jones, Lubbock (1/31/01); Ly H. Nguyen, Lake Jackson (1/31/03); Joyce Cook Obst, Alamo (1/31/03); Jay Pack, Dallas (1/31/05); Byron Edward White, Arlington (1/31/01). Admin., Margaret Alvarez, PO Box 12847, Austin 78711.

**Protective and Regulatory Services, Board of** – (1992); apptv.; 6-yr.; 6 members: Jon M. Bradley, Dallas (2/1/01); Maurine Dickey, Dallas (2/1/01); Richard S. Hoffman, Brownsville (2/1/03); Naomi W. Ledé, Huntsville (2/1/05); Catherine C. Mosbacher, Houston (2/1/05); Cristina "Ommy" Strauch, San Antonio (2/1/05). Exec. Dir., James R. Hine ($125,000), PO Box 149030, Austin 78714-9030.

**Psychologists, Texas Board of Examiners of** – (1969 as 6-member board; membership increased to 9 in 1981); apptv.; 6-yr.; per diem and expenses; 9 members: Barry E. Dewlen, San Antonio (10/31/01); Karla L. Hayes, Amarillo (10/31/05); Betty Holmes Ray, Abilene (10/31/03); Ruben Rendon Jr., Dallas (10/31/05); M. David Rudd, Belton (10/31/03); Nelda Smith, Longview (10/31/01); Stephanie Sokolosky, Wichita Falls (10/31/05); Brian H. Stagner, College Station (10/31/03); Emily G. Sutter, Friendswood (10/31/01). Exec. Dir., Sherry L. Lee ($52,000), 333 Guadalupe St., Ste. 2-450, Austin 78701.

**Public Accountancy, Texas State Board of** – (1945 with 2-year terms; reorganized 1959 as 9-member board with 6-yr. overlapping terms; number of members increased to 12 in 1979; increased to 15 in 1989); per diem and expenses; 15 members: Billy M. Atkinson Jr., Houston (1/31/05); J. Coalter Baker, Austin (1/31/07); Jerry A. Davis, Houston (1/31/01); Kimberly Dryden, Amarillo (1/31/05); David duree, Midland (1/31/09); April L. Eyeington, College Station (1/31/05); Robert C. Mann, Fort Worth (1/31/05); Jimmie L. Mason, Lubbock (1/31/01); Lou Miller, San Antonio (1/31/01); Orville W. Mills Jr., Sugar Land (1/31/09); Paula Martina Mendoza, Houston (1/31/05); Janet Parnell, Canadian (1/31/01); Joseph W. Richardson, Houston (1/31/09); John W. Steinberg, Converse (1/31/07); Edward L. Summers, Austin (1/31/03); John A. Walton, Dallas (1/31/09). Exec. Dir., William Treacy ($70,000), 333 Guadalupe, Suite 3-900, Austin 78701-3900.

**Public Finance Authority, Texas** – (1984, assumed duties of Texas Building Authority); apptv.; per diem and expenses; 6-yr.; membership increased from 3 to 6 in 1991: Daniel H. Branch, Dallas (2/1/01); Helen Huey, Houston (2/1/05); Cynthia L. Meyer, San Antonio (2/1/03); H.L. Bert Mijares Jr., El Paso (2/1/05); Daniel T. Serna, Arlington (2/1/03); Barry Thomas Smitherman, Houston 2/1/07); . Exec. Dir., Kimberly K. Edwards ($95,000), 300 W. 15th St., Ste. 411, Austin 78711.

**Public Safety Commission** – (1935); apptv.; expenses; 6-yr.; 3 members: James B. Francis Jr., Dallas (12/31/05); Robert B. Holt, Midland (12/31/01); M. Colleen McHugh, Corpus Christi (12/31/03). Dir. of Texas Dept. of Public Safety, Col. Thomas A. Davis ($102,000), PO Box 4087, Austin 78773-0001.

**Public Utility Commission** – (1975); apptv.; 6-yr., 3 members at $105,000-$107,500: Rebecca Armendariz Klein, Austin (2/1/01); Julie Caruthers Parsley, Austin (9/1/05); Brett A. Perlman, Houston (9/1/03). Exec. Dir., W. Lane Lanford ($92,000), PO Box 13326, Austin 78711-3326.

**Racing Commission, Texas** – (1986); 6-yr.; per diem and expenses; 8 members — 2 ex officio: Chmn. of Public Safety Commission and Comptroller; 6 apptv.: Jesse R. Adams, Helotes (2/1/09); Treva Boyd, San Angelo (2/1/05); David C. Garza, Brownsville (2/1/03); R. Dyke Rogers, Dalhart (2/1/05); Michael Giles Rutherford, Houston (2/1/07); James L. Schulze, Conroe (2/1/01). Exec. Secretary, Paula C. Flowerday ($77,760), PO Box 12080, Austin 78711.

**Radiation Advisory Board** – (1961 as 9-member board, membership increased to 18 in 1981); apptv.; 6-yr.; expenses; 18 members: Jimmy L. Barker, Granbury (4/16/

01); Susan E. Best, Dallas (4/16/03); Thomas M. Burnette, Plano (4/16/01); Donald S. Butler, Colleyville (4/16/01); Earl P. Erdmann, Midland (4/16/01); Michael S. Ford, Amarillo (4/16/03); David N. Henkes, San Antonio (4/16/99); Walter Kim Howard, Longview (4/16/03); Glen Keith King, Houston (4/16/99); Dale Edward Klein, Austin (4/16/03); Jack S. Krohmer, Georgetown (4/16/99); Justin P. LeVasseur, Wichita Falls (4/16/01); Odis R. Mack, Katy (4/16/01); Troy Marceleno, Dauncanville (4/16/03); Bruce A. Matson, Houston (4/16/03); Connie Rogers, Driftwood (4/16/99); William R. Underdown Jr., George West (4/16/99); Philip M. Wentworth, Plano (4/16/99).

**Railroad Commission of Texas** – (1891); elective; 6-yr.; 3 members, $92,217 each: Tony Garza (1/1/04); Michael L. Williams (1/1/02); Charles R. Matthews (1/1/06). Dir., Kathy Pyka, PO Box 12967, Austin 78711.

**Real Estate Commission, Texas** – (1949 as 6-member board; membership increased to 9 in 1979); apptv.; per diem and expenses; 6-yr.; 9 members: James N. Austin Jr., Fort Worth (1/31/05); Charles Michael Brodie, Plano (1/31/03); Ramon M. Cantu, Houston (1/31/05); Maria Gonzalez-Gil, San Antonio (1/31/03); Louise E. Hull, Victoria (1/31/07); Lawrence D. Jokl, Brownsville (1/31/05); Paul H. Jordan, Georgetown (1/31/07); Kay Sutton, Midland (1/31/03); John Walton, Lubbock (1/31/07). Admin., Wayne Thorburn ($70,000), PO Box 12188, Austin 78711.

**Real Estate Research Advisory Committee** – (1971); apptv.; 6-yr.; 10 members — one ex officio: representative of Texas Real Estate Commission; 9 apptv. members: Joe Adame, Corpus Christi (1/31/03); Carlos Madrid Jr., San Antonio (1/31/01); Catherine Miller, Arlington (1/31/03); Celia Ross Goode-Haddock, College Station (1/31/99); Angela S. Myres, Houston (1/31/01); Nick Nicholas, Dallas (1/31/05); Jerry L. Schaffner, Lubbock (1/31/03); Douglas A. Schwartz, El Paso (1/31/05); Gloria Van Zandt, Arlington (1/31/01). Dir., James Christian, Texas A&M, College Station 77843-2115.

**Red River Authority, Board of Directors** – (1959); apptv.; 6-yr.; per diem and expenses; 9 members: George W. Arrington, Canadian (8/11/01); Carol Carlson, Lakeside City (8/11/03); William K. Daniel, Wichita Falls (8/11/03); Paul F. Engler, Amarillo (8/11/99); James P. Fallon, Sherman (8/11/99); Betty P. Peveto, Gainesville (8/11/01); Edna M. Shepherd, Texarkana (8/11/99); Cliff A. Skiles Jr., Hereford (8/11/03); W.F. Smith Jr., Quanah (8/11/01). Gen. Mgr., Ronald J. Glenn, 900 8th St., Ste. 520, Wichita Falls 76301-6894.

**Red River Compact Commissioner** – (1949); apptv.; 4-yr.; (Function of commissioner is to negotiate with other states respecting waters of the Red.): Joe G. Hanson ($24,225), El Paso (2/1/03).

**Redistricting Board, Legislative** – (See Legislative Redistricting Board).

**Rehabilitation Commission, Texas** – (1969); apptv.; expenses; 6-yr.; 6 members: Matthew T. Doyle, Texas City (8/31/99); Lance L. Goetz, Dallas (8/31/05); Diane M. Novy, Sugar Land (8/31/99); Beverly Stribling, San Angelo (8/31/03); A. Kent Waldrep Jr., Plano (8/31/01); Ray A. Wilkerson, Austin (8/31/01). Commissioner, Vernon "Max" Arrell ($104,000), 4900 N. Lamar Blvd., Austin 78751-2316.

**Retirement System, Municipal, Board of Trustees** – (1947); apptv.; 6-yr.; expenses; 6 members: Connie J. Green, Killeen (2/1/05); Patricia Hernandez, Plainview (2/1/05); Carolyn Linér, San Marcos (2/1/07); Rick Menchaca, Midland (2/1/07); H. Frank Simpson, Webster (2/1/09); Kathryn M. Usrey, Carrollton (2/1/09); Exec. Dir., Gary W. Anderson, PO Box 149153, Austin 78714-9153.

**Retirement System of Texas, Employees** – (1949); apptv.; 6-yr.; 6 members — one apptd. by Gov., one by Chief Justice of State Supreme Court and one by Speaker; 3 are employee members of the system serving 6-yr. overlapping terms: Bill Barton, Austin (8/31/02); Pamela A. Carley, Austin (8/31/03); Carolyn L. Gallagher, Austin (8/31/06); Milton Hixson, Austin (8/31/04); Owen Whitworth, Austin (8/31/05); Janice R. Zitelman, Austin (8/31/01). Exec. Dir., Sheila W. Beckett ($180,000), PO Box 13207, Austin 78711-3207.

**Retirement System, Texas County and District** – (1967); apptv.; 6-yr.; 9 members: Charlotte A. Carey, Fort Stockton (12/31/03); Bridget McDowell, Baird (12/31/07); Robert A. Eckels, Houston (12/31/07); Martha Gustavsen, Conroe (12/31/03); Mitch Liles, Garland (12/31/03); John Marshall, Colleyville (12/31/01); Bill Melton, Dallas (12/31/

01); Kathy Reeves, Midland (12/31/03); Amador E. Reyna, Kountze (12/31/05); John Willy, Angleton (12/31/03). Dir., Joseph Cannon Froh, PO Box 2034, Austin 78768-2034.

**Rio Grande Compact Commissioner of Texas** – (1929); apptv.; 6-yr.: Joe G. Hanson, El Paso (6/9/07). Box 1917, El Paso 79950-1917 ($41,195).

**Rural Healthcare System Board of Directors, Statewide** – (see **Healthcare**)

**Sabine River Authority, Board of Directors** – (1949); apptv.; per diem and expenses; 6-yr.; 9 members: Claudia J. Abney, Marshall (7/6/05); Don O. Covington, Orange (7/6/05); Sammy D. Dance (7/6/01); Calvin E. Ebner, Newton (7/6/05); Karen C. Hampton, Tyler (7/6/01); Joyce P. Hugman, Gladewater (7/6/03); Margin S. Latham, Sulphur Springs (7/6/01); Richard A. Linkenauger, Greenville (7/6/03); Ruben S. Martin III, Longview (7/6/03). Gen. Mgr., Jerry Clark, PO Box 579, Orange 77630.

**Sabine River Compact Commission** – (1953); apptv.; 6-yr.; $8,487 each; 5 members — one member and chmn. apptd. by President of United States without a vote; 2 from Texas and 2 from Louisiana. Texas members: Frank Edward Parker, Center (7/12/01); Thomas Wayne Reeh, Orange (7/12/04). Box 579, Orange 77630.

**San Antonio River Authority** – apptv., 6 yr., 12 members: Sara M. (Sally) Buchanan, San Antonio (1/31/07); Leo J. Gleinser, Goliad (1/31/03); Jim Johnson, San Antonio (1/31/07); Gaylon J. Oehlke, Kenedy (2/1/05); A.D. Kollodziej Jr., Poth (1/16/01); Roberto G. Rodriguez, San Antonio (1/31/03); Louis E. Rowe, San Antonio (1/31/03); H.B. Ruckman III, Karnes City (1/31/03); Nancy Steves, San Antonio (1/31/05); Adair R. Sutherland, Goliad (1/31/01); J.C. Turner, Floresville (1/31/03); Thomas G. Weaver, Universal City (1/31/03). Gen. Mgr., Gregory E. Rothe, PO Box 839980, San Antonio 78283-9980.

**San Jacinto Historical Advisory Board** – (1907 as San Jacinto State Park Commission; changed to San Jacinto Battleground Commission and changed again in 1965 to present name; apptv.; 6-yr.; 5 members — 2 ex officio: Dir., Parks Div., Parks and Wildlife Dept. and pres. of San Jacinto Museum of History Assn.; 3 apptd. by Gov.: Janet Ann DeVault, Houston (9/1/05); Jeffrey Dunn, Bellaire (9/1/01); Nina J. Hendee, Houston (9/1/03). Parks Section, Parks and Wildlife Dept., 4200 Smith School Rd., Austin 78744.

**San Jacinto River Authority, Board of Directors** – (1937); apptv.; expenses while on duty; 6-yr.; 6 members: Linda Koenig, Houston (10/16/05); R. Gary Montgomery, The Woodlands (10/16/01); Richard Ramirez, Houston (10/16/05); Lloyd Tisdale, Conroe (10/16/01); Joseph Turner, The Woodlands (10/16/05). Gen. Mgr., James R. Adams, PO Box 329, Conroe 77305.

**Savings and Loan Commissioner** – Apptv. by State Finance Commission: James L. Pledger ($92,676), PO Box 1089, Austin 78767.

**School Land Board** – (See Land Board, School).

**School Safety Center Board, Texas** – (2001); 2-yr.; expenses; 15 members: 5 ex officio: Attorney General; State Commissioner of Education; Exec. Dir., Texas Juvenile Probation Commission; Exec. Dir., Texas Youth Commission; Commissioner, Department of Mental Health and Mental Retardation; 10 members apptd. by Gov.: James M. Boyle, Temple (2/1/04); Charles A. Brawner, Katy (2/1/04); Garry Edward Eoff, Brownwood (2/1/04); James Richard Pendell, Clint (2/1/05); Janace Ponder, Amarillo (2/1/05); Lucy Rubio, Corpus Christi (2/1/05); Severita Sanchez, Laredo (2/1/05); Cheryl Lee Shannon, Dallas (2/1/05); Jane A. Wetzel, Dallas (2/1/04).

**Securities Board, State** – (Est. 1957, the outgrowth of several amendments to the Texas Securities Act, originally passed 1913); act is administered by the Securities Commissioner, who is appointed by the board members; expenses; 6-yr.; 3 members: Kenneth W. Anderson Jr., Dallas (1/20/05); James J. Simms, Amarillo (1/20/07); José Adan Treviño, Bellaire (1/21/03). Securities Commissioner, Denise Voigt Crawford ($90,000), PO Box 13167, Austin 78711-3167.

**Seed and Plant Board, State** – (1959); apptv.; 2-yr.; 6 members: James Allison, Buchanan Dam (10/6/01); Dick Auld, Lubbock (10/6/01); Joe M. Crane, Bay City (10/6/00); Mark A. Hussey, Bryan (10/6/01); Katherine Cave Patrick, Bishop (10/6/00). Secy., Kelly Book, (member) Seed Quality Branch Chief, Texas Dept. of Agriculture, PO Box 12847, Austin 78711.

**Sex Offender Treatment, Council on** – (1997); apptv.;

6-yr.; expenses; 6 members: Liles Arnold, Plano (2/1/03); Kristy M. Carr, Austin (2/1/05); Patricia Rae Lykos, Houston (2/1/07); Richard N. Mack, Lubbock (2/1/05); Walter J. Meyer III, Galveston (2/1/07). Exec. Dir., Eliza May, PO Box 12546, Austin 78711.

**Skill Standards Board, Texas** – (1995); 11 members serving terms at pleasure of Gov.; expenses; members: Bruce F. Aumack, Round Rock; Gary Forrest Blagg, Grapevine; Les T. Csorba, Houston; Jeanne I. Hatfield, Dallas; Denise Laman, Plano; Dale Miller, Silsbee; Wayne J. Oswald, Freeport; Billie Conley Pickard, Raymondville; Fernando Reyes Jr., San Antonio; Beth Ann Rogers, Austin; Linda M. Stegall, The Woodlands.

**Social Worker Examiners, Texas State Board of** – (1993); apptd.; 6-yr.; per diem and travel expenses; 9 members: Holly L. Anawaty, Houston (2/1/07); Joan Culver, Austin (9/1/03); Jeannie M. Heller, College Station (2/1/03); Willie McGee Jr., Plainview (2/1/05); John Steven Roberts, Midland (2/1/05); Dorothy Stewart, Arlington (2/1/03); Julia Ann Stokes, Fort Worth (2/1/07); Jamie B. Ward, Boerne (2/1/05); Gerrianne Waring, El Paso (2/1/01).

**Soil and Water Conservation Board, Texas State** – (1939); elected by members of individual districts; 2 yrs.; 5 members. Exec. Dir., Robert G. Buckley ($65,000), PO Box 658, Temple 76503.

**Speech-Language Pathology and Audiology, State Board of Examiners for** – (1983); apptv.; 6-yr.; per diem and expenses; 9 members: Rosario Rodriguez Brusniak, Plano (8/31/07); Bertha "Bert" Campbell, Houston (8/31/05); Deborah Carlson, Houston (8/31/05); Judy A. Chambers, Crosby (8/31/03); Matthew "Matt" Lyon, El Paso (8/31/07); Lee Reeves, Plano (8/31/03); R. Eric Reynolds, Arlington (8/31/03); Cheryl "Sherry" Sancibrian, Lubbock (8/31/05); Minnette Son, San Antonio (8/31/07). Exec. Secy., Dorothy Cawthon, 1100 W. 49th, Austin 78756-3183.

**Stephen F. Austin State University, Board of Regents** – (1969); apptv.; expenses; 6-yr.; 9 members: Penny H. Butler, Houston (1/31/03); Margarita de la Garza-Grahm, Tyler (1/31/07); Michael W. Enoch, Mont Belvieu (1/31/03); Kenneth James, Kingwood (1/31/07); Gary Lopez, Dallas (1/31/05); Susan Roberds, Dallas (1/31/03); Lyn Stevens, Beaumont (1/31/05); Mike Wilhite, Henderson (1/31/05); Frederick A. Wulf, Center (1/31/07). Pres., Dr. Dan Angel, PO Box 6078, SFA Sta., Nacogdoches 75962.

**Student Loan Corporation, Texas Guaranteed** – (1979); 6-yr.; 11-members — one ex officio; Comptroller of Public Accounts; one apptd. by Commissioner of Higher Education and one apptd. by Chmn. of Coordinating Board; 8 apptd. by Gov. as follows: Tommy J. Brooks, Sugarland (1/31/09); Ruben E. Esquivel, DeSoto (1/31/09); Albon Head, Aledo (1/31/07); Morgan W. Howard, College Station (1/31/05); Jorja L. Kimball, College Station (1/31/05); James R. Langabeer, Edinburg (1/31/07); Jerry Don Miller, Canyon (1/31/07); Jane Phipps, San Antonio (1/31/05); Grace A. Shore, Longview (1/31/09). Pres., Milton G. Wright, PO Box 201725, Austin 78720.

**Sulphur River Basin Authority, Board of Directors** – (1985); apptd.; 6-yr.; per diem and expenses; 6 members: James Richard (Dick) Goodman, Clarksville (2/1/05); Mike Huddleston, Wake Village (2/1/03); Judy Wicker Lee, Mt. Pleasant (2/1/05); Charles L. Lowry, Mt. Vernon (2/1/05); Patsy R. McClain, Sulphur Springs (2/1/01); Robert L. Parker, Paris (2/1/01).

**Sunset Advisory Commission** – (1977); 10 members: 4 members of House of Representatives, 4 members of Senate, one public member apptd. by Speaker, one public member apptd. by Lt. Gov.; 4-yr.; expenses. Public members: William Jeter III, Bryan (9/1/01); Tim Roth, El Paso (9/1/01). Dir., Joey Longley, PO Box 13066, Austin 78711.

**Tax Board, State** – (1905); ex officio; term in other office; no compensation; 3 members: Comptroller, Secretary of State and State Treasurer.

**Tax Professional Examiners, Board of** – (1977 as Board of Tax Assessor Examiners; name changed to present form 1983); apptv.; expenses; 6-yr.; 6 members: Michael A. Amezquita, Harlingen (3/1/05); Stanton Brown, Benjamin (3/1/07); Deborah M. Hunt, Austin (3/1/05); Linda D. Jaynes, Plainview (3/1/03); Foy Mitchell Jr., Plano (3/1/03); Dorye Kristeen Roe, Robert Lee (3/1/07). Exec. Dir., David E. Montoya ($52,000), 333 Guadalupe, Ste. 2-520 Austin 78701-3942.

**Teacher Retirement System** – (1937 as 6-member board; membership increased to 9 in 1973); expenses; 6-yr.; 9 members — 2 apptd. by State Board of Education, 3

apptd. by Gov. and 4 TRS members apptd. by Gov. after being nominated by popular ballot of members of the retirement system: Mary Alice Baker, Beaumont (8/31/05); Terence S. Ellis, New Ulm (8/31/05); James W. Fonteno Jr., Houston (8/31/07); H. Barham Fulmer II, Lindale (8/31/03); Jarvis Vincent Hollingsworth, Missouri City (8/31/07); Brenda L. Jackson, Dallas (8/31/03); Cecilia M. Moreno, Laredo (8/31/03); Greg Poole, Conroe (8/31/07); Linus Wright, Dallas (8/31/05). Exec. Dir., Charles L. Dunlap, 1000 Red River, Austin 78701.

**Telecommunications Infrastructure Fund Board** – (1995); 6-yr.; expenses; 9 members (3 apptd. by Gov., 3 apptd. by Lt. Gov., 3 apptd. by Gov. from list submitted by Speaker): John Collins, Dallas (8/31/03); Patrick Cordero, Midland (8/31/05); Blair Calvert Fitzsimons, Carrizo Springs (8/31/01); Kay Karr, El Paso (8/31/03); Mart D. Nelson, Richardson (8/31/05); Bill O. Simmons, Sunrise Beach (2/1/07); Edward Torres, San Antonio (8/31/03); Thomas U. Wilkins, Richardson (8/31/05). Exec. Dir., Sam Tessen ($104,000), 1000 Red River, Rm E208, Austin, TX 78701.

**Texas A&M University System Board of Regents** – (1875); apptv.; 6-yr.; expenses; 9 members: Phillip David Adams, College Station, (2/1/07); Anne L. Armstrong, Armstrong (2/1/03); Wendy Lee Gramm, College Station (2/1/07); Lester Lowry Mays, San Antonio (2/1/07); Erle Allen Nye, Dallas (2/1/09); Lionel Sosa, San Antonio (2/1/05); R.H. (Steve) Stevens Jr., Houston (2/1/05); John David White, Houston (2/1/09); Susan Rudd Wynn, Benbrook (2/1/05). Chancellor, Dr. Howard D. Graves, College Station 77843-1123.

**Texas Southern University, Board of Regents** – (1947); expenses; 6-yr.; 9 members: Albert C. Black Jr., Rowlett (2/1/01); Enos M. Cabell Jr., Missouri City (2/1/01); Thomas H. Friedberg, Sugar Land (2/1/03); Regina Giovannini, Houston (2/1/05); Willard L. Jackson Jr., Houston (2/1/05); Lori H. Moon, Cedar Hill (2/1/05); Gene A. Moore Sr., Houston (2/1/01); Carroll W. Phillips, Houston (2/1/95); A. Martin Wickliff Jr., Houston (2/1/03); Fred S. Zeidman, Houston (2/1/03). Pres., Dr. Priscilla Slade, 3100 Cleburne, Houston 77004.

**Texas State Technical College, Board of Regents** – (1960 as Board of the Texas State Technical Institute; changed to present name, 1991); apptv.; expenses; 6-yr.; 9 members: C. "Connie" de la Garza, Harlingen (8/31/01); Peterson (Pete) Foster, Houston (8/31/05); Bernie Francis, Dallas (8/31/03); Jere M. Lawrence, Sweetwater (8/31/03); Jerilyn K. Pfeifer, Abilene (8/31/01); Terry W. Preuninger, Waco (8/31/05); Linda Routh, Corpus Christi (8/31/05); Barbara N. Rusling, China Spring (8/31/03); Thomas L. Whaley Sr., Marshall (8/31/01). Chancellor, Dr. Bill Segura, TSTC System, Waco 76705.

**Texas State University System, Board of Regents** – (1911 as Board of Regents of State Teachers Colleges; name changed in 1965 to Board of Regents of State Senior Colleges; changed to present form in 1975); apptv.; per diem and expenses; 6-yr.; 9 members: Patricia Diaz Dennis, San Antonio (2/1/05); Dionicio (Don) Flores, El Paso (2/1/05); John Philip Hageman, Round Rock (2/1/03); Dan S. Hallmark, Beaumont (2/1/01); James A. "Jimmy" Hayley, Texas City (2/1/05); Nancy R. Neal, Lubbock (2/1/03); Floyd Nickerson, Abilene (2/1/01); Pollyanna A. Stephens, San Angelo (2/1/01); Macedonio Villarreal, Sugar Land (2/1/01). Chancellor, Dr. Lamar G. Urbanovsky, 505 Sam Houston Bldg., Austin 78701.

**Texas Tech University, Board of Regents** – (1923); apptv.; expenses; 6-yr.; 9 members: Carin Marcy Barth, Houston (1/31/05); C. Robert Black, Horseshoe Bay (2/1/07); E.R. (Dick) Brooks, Dallas (1/31/05); J. Robert Brown, El Paso (1/31/07); John W. Jones, Brady (2/1/03); Nancy E. Jones, Abilene (2/1/03); David R. Lopez, Austin (2/1/07); Brian C. Newby, Austin (1/31/05); J. Michael Weiss, Lubbock (2/1/03). Interim Chancellor, Dr. David R. Smith, PO Box 4039, Lubbock 79409.

**Texas Woman's University Board of Regents** – (1901); apptv.; expenses; 6-yr.; 9 members: Therese Bartholomew Bevers, Houston (2/1/07); Jerry L. Brownlee, Cleburne (2/1/05); Harry L. Crumpacker II, Plano (2/1/09); Linda R. Hughes, Dallas (2/1/05); Kenneth L. Ingram, Denton (2/1/07); Sharon Warfield Wilkes, Austin (2/1/03); Cynthia Shepard Perry, Houston (2/1/03); Tegwin Ann Pulley, Dallas (2/1/09); Delia M. Reyes, Dallas (2/1/05); Annie F. Williams, Dallas (2/1/07). Chancellor and Pres., Dr. Ann Stuart, PO Box 23925, TWU Sta., Denton 76204-1925.

**Transportation Commission, Texas** – (1917 as State

Highway Commission; merged with Mass Transportation Commission and name changed to State Board of Highways and Public Transportation in 1975; merged with Texas Dept. of Aviation and Texas Motor Vehicle Commission and name changed to present form in 1991); apptv.; 6-yr.; ($15,914); 3 members: John W. Johnson, Houston (2/1/05); Robert Lee Nichols, Jacksonville (2/1/09); Ric Williamson, Weatherford (2/1/07). Exec. Dir., Charles Heald ($155,000), 125 E. 11th St., Austin 78701-2483.

**Trinity River Authority, Board of Directors** – (1955); apptv.; per diem and expenses; 6-yr.; 24 directors — 3 from Tarrant County, 4 from Dallas County, 2 from area-at-large and one each from 15 other districts: Russell B. Arnold, Trinity (3/15/05); Harold L. Barnard, Waxahachie (3/15/05); Leslie C. Browne, Arlington (3/15/03); Karl R. Butler, Dallas (3/15/05); Patricia T. Clapp, Dallas (3/15/01); Michael Cronin, Terrell (3/15/05); Vincent Cruz Jr., Fort Worth (3/15/05); Hector Escamilla Jr., Carrollton (3/15/03); Benny L. Fogleman, Livingston (3/15/03); Jane M. Fouty, Corsicana (3/15/03); Valerie Freeman, Dallas (3/15/01); Sylvia P. Greene, Arlington (3/15/03); Edward Hargett, Crockett (3/15/03); William H. Hodges, Huntsville (3/15/01); Jerry F. House Sr., Leona (3/15/05); John W. Jenkins, Hankamer (3/15/03); William M. Key, Athens (3/15/01); Maurice L. Locke, Liberty (3/15/01); Lynn Neely, Madisonville (3/15/05); H. Gene Reynolds Jr., Fairfield (3/15/01); Billy V. Richardson, Point Blank (3/15/05); Wanda W. Stovall, Fort Worth (3/15/01); Douglas L. Sumrall, Palestine (3/15/01); Jack C. Vaughn Jr., Dallas (3/15/03). Gen. Mgr., Danny F. Vance, PO Box 60, Arlington 76004-0060.

**Tuition Board, Prepaid Higher Education** – (1996); 6-yr.; 7 members: Comptroller; 4 apptd. by Lt. Gov.; 2 apptd. by Gov.

**Tuition Scholarship Foundation Board, Texas Prepaid** – (1996); indeterminate terms; 5 members: Comptroller; one apptd. by gov.; 3 apptd. jointly by Comptroller and gov's apptee. Gov's apptee: George H. McShan, Harlingen.

**Turnpike Authority, Texas** – (1953 as 9-member board; increased to 12 members in 1971; reorganized as part of Texas Dept. of Transportation 1997, and membership decreased to 7: one ex officio and 6 apptd.); 6 members: Samuel "Sam" Barshop, San Antonio (2/15/05); Robert Glenn Jarvis, McAllen (2/15/03); Alan L. Johnson, Harlingen (2/15/05); Mary Q. Kelly, San Antonio (2/15/01); Pete Winstead, Austin (2/15/03); Manuel Zuniga, Kyle (2/15/01) Dir., Phillip E. Russell, P.E., 125 E. 11th St., Austin 78701.

**Underground Facility Notification Corporation, Texas** – (1997); apptv.; no compensation; 3-yr.; 12 members: Ralph Edward Alonzo, San Antonio (8/31/00); Tony Boyd, DeSoto (8/31/01); Sheila Wilkes Brown, Austin (8/31/01); E. Leon Carter, Plano (8/31/99); Janet W. Holland, Mineral Wells (8/31/01); David Hooper, Portland (8/31/01); Lois W. Kolkhorst, Brenham (8/31/00); Steve F. Landon, Bedford (8/31/99); Howard T. Pebley Jr., McAllen (8/31/00); E. Ashley Smith, Houston (8/31/00); Nancy Lou Sullivan, Colorado City (8/31/99); José L. Valenciano, Lubbock (8/31/99).

**Uniform State Laws, Commission on** – (1941 as 5-member Commissioners to the National Conference on Uniform State Laws; name changed to present form, membership increased to 6 and term of office raised to 6 years in 1977; membership raised to 9 in 2001); apptv.; 6-yr.; 9 members: Marianne Marsh Auld, Waco (9/30/04); Levi J. Benton, Houston (9/30/04); David C. Godbey, Dallas (9/30/04); Peter K. Munson, Pottsboro (9/30/08); Marilyn Phelan, Lubbock (9/30/06); Rodney W. Satterwhite, Midland (9/30/08); Harry L. Tindall, Houston (9/30/06); Karen Roberts Washington, Dallas (9/30/08); Earl L. Yeakel III, Austin (9/30/06).

**University of Houston, Board of Regents** – (1963); apptv.; expenses; 6-yr.; 9 members: Morrie K. Abramson, Houston (8/31/05); Eduardo Aguirre Jr., Houston (8/31/01); Suzette T. Caldwell, Houston (8/31/03); Theresa W. Chang, Houston (8/31/03); George Eugene "Gene" McDavid, Houston (8/31/03); Charles E. McMahen, Houston (8/31/01); Morgan Dunn O'Connor, Victoria (8/31/05); Gary L. Rosenthal, Houston (8/31/01); Thad "Bo" Smith, Sugar Land (8/31/05). Chancellor, Dr. Arthur K. Smith, 4800 Calhoun, Houston 77004.

**University of North Texas Board of Regents** – (1949); apptv.; 6-yr.; expenses; 9 members: Marjorie B. Craft, DeSoto (5/22/01); Roy Gene Evans, Dallas (5/22/05); Richard Knight Jr., Dallas (5/22/05); Tom Lazo Sr., Dallas (5/22/05);

Robert A. Nickell, Irving (5/22/03); George W. Pepper, Fort Worth (5/22/03); Burle Pettit, Lubbock (5/22/01); John Robert "Bobby" Ray, Plano (5/22/01); Gayle W. Strange, Aubrey (5/22/03). Chancellor, Dr. Alfred F. Hurley, PO Box 13737, Denton 76203-3737.

**University of Texas System, Board of Regents** – (1881); apptv.; expenses; 6-yr.; 9 members: Hubbard Scott Caven Jr., Houston (2/1/09); Linnet F. Deily, Houston (2/1/01); Donald L. Evans, Midland (2/1/01); James Huffines, Austin (2/1/09); Woody L. Hunt, El Paso (2/1/05); Thomas G. Loeffler, San Antonio (2/1/01); Charles Miller, Houston (2/1/05); A.W. Riter Jr., Tyler (2/1/03); Raul R. Romero, Houston (2/1/05); Chancellor, Mark G. Yudof, PO Box N, University Sta., Austin 78713-7328.

**Veterans Commission, Texas** – (1927 as Veterans State Service Office; reorganized as Veterans Affairs Commission in 1947 with 5 members; membership increased to 6 in 1981; name changed to present form in 1985); apptv.; 6-yr.; per diem while on duty and expenses; 6 members: Lt. Col. James Russell Adams, Dallas (12/31/05); Leonardo Barraza, El Paso (12/31/05); John A. Brieden III, Brenham (12/31/03); James Stewart Duncan, Houston (12/31/03); Hector Farias, Weslaco (12/31/07); Brig. Gen. Sue Ilen Turner (Ret.), San Antonio (12/31/01). Exec. Dir., James E. Nier ($74,000), PO Box 12277, Austin 78711.

**Veterans Land Board** – (Est. 1949 as 3-member ex officio board; reorganized 1956); 4-yr.; per diem and expenses; 3 members: one ex officio: Comm. of General Land Office; 2 apptd.: Col. D. Ladd Pattillo, USAR (ret.), Austin (12/29/02); M.S. Mike Ussery, Amarillo (12/29/04). Exec. Sec., Douglas Edward Oldmixon, 1700 N. Congress Ave., Ste. 836, Austin 78701-1496.

**Veterinary Medical Examiners, Texas State Board of** – (1911; revised 1953; made 9-member board in 1981); apptv.; expenses on duty; 6-yr.; 9 members: Gary C. Brantley, Richardson (8/26/05); Martin E. Garcia II, Raymondville (8/26/03); Howard Head, Littlefield (8/26/01); D. Carter King, Roanoke (8/26/01); J. Lynn Lawhon, Abilene (8/26/03); Sharon O. Matthews, Albany (8/26/99); Jean McFaddin, Beaumont (8/26/01); Dee Ann Pederson, Austin (8/26/05); Mary Rebecca Terry (Becky), Alpine (8/26/03). Exec. Dir., Ron Allen ($60,000), 333 Guadalupe St., Ste. 2-330, Austin 78701-3998.

**Water Development Board, Texas** – (1957; legislative function for the Texas Dept. of Water Resources, 1977); apptv.; per diem and expenses; 6-yr.; 6 members: Noe Fernandez, McAllen (12/31/01); Jack Hunt, Houston (12/31/03); Wales H. Madden Jr., Amarillo (12/31/03); William B. Madden, Dallas (12/31/01); William W. Meadows, Fort Worth (12/31/05); Kathleen H. White, Valentine (12/31/05). Exec. Admin., Craig D. Pedersen ($108,000), PO Box 13231, Austin 78711.

**Workers' Compensation Commission, Texas** – (1991); 6-yr.; apptv; expenses; 6 members: Jack Abla, Kilgore (2/1/01); Mike Hachtman, Houston (2/1/09); Kenneth Lee Moore, Houston (2/1/05); Rebecca F. Olivares, San Antonio (2/1/03); Richard F. Reynolds, Austin (2/1/01); Lonnie Watson, Cleburne (2/1/05). Exec. Dir., Leonard W. Riley Jr. ($112,000), 4000 S. IH-35, Austin 78704-1287.

**Workers' Compensation Insurance Fund Board, Texas** – (1991); expenses; 6-yr.; 9 members: Ernesto Ancira Jr., San Antonio (2/1/99); Patricia A. (Pat) Crawford, El Paso (2/1/99); Pat O'Neal, Dallas (2/1/01); Brenda Pejovich, Dallas (2/1/03); James D. Ross, Midland (2/1/03); Tommy G. Salome, Crawford (2/1/01); George Wesch Jr., Lake Hills (2/1/99); Charles Hugh Whiteside, Kilgore (2/1/03); Martin H. Young Jr., The Woodlands (2/1/01).

**Workforce Commission, Texas** – (1936 as Texas Employment Commission; name changed 1995); apptv.; $97,000-$99,500; 6-yr.; 3 members: Ron Lehman, Round Rock (2/1/03); T. P. O'Mahoney, Dallas (2/1/05); Diane D. Rath, San Antonio (2/1/07). Exec. Dir., Cassie Carlson Reed ($125,000), 101 E. 15th St., Ste. 618, Austin 78778-0001.

**Youth Commission, Texas** – (1949 as 9-member board; reorganized 1957 and again in 1975); 6-yr.; per diem on duty; 6 apptv. members: Pete C. Alfaro, Baytown (8/31/01); Charles Henry, Pampa (8/31/03); Cahleen C. Herasimchuk, Houston (8/31/05); Leonard E. Lawrence, San Antonio (8/31/03); Nicholas T. Serafy Jr., Brownsville (8/31/05); Lisa Saemann Teschner, Dallas (8/31/01). Exec. Dir., Steve Robinson ($118,000), PO Box 4260, Austin 78765. ☆

# State Government Income and Expenditures

Taxes are the state government's primary source of income. On this and the following pages are summaries of state income and expenditures, tax collections, tax revenue by type of tax, a summary of the state budget for the 2004–2005 biennium, Texas Lottery income and expenditures and the amount of federal payments to state agencies.

## State Revenues by Source and Expenditures by Function

### Amounts (in Millions) and Percent of Total

| Revenues by Source | 2002 | | 2001 | | 2000 | % | 1999 | % | 1998 | % |
|---|---|---|---|---|---|---|---|---|---|---|
| Tax Collections | $26,279 | 47.6 | $27,230 | 50.6 | $25,284 | 50.7 | $23,615 | 49.2 | $22,634 | 50.9 |
| Federal Income | 18,171 | 32.9 | 16,018 | 29.8 | 14,799 | 29.7 | 13,926 | 29.0 | 12,632 | 28.4 |
| Licenses, Fees, Permits, Fines, Penalties | 4,366 | 7.9 | 4,265 | 7.9 | 4,245 | 8.5 | 4,182 | 8.7 | 4,113 | 9.2 |
| Interest & Other Investment Income | 1,696 | 3.1 | 2,060 | 3.8 | 1,883 | 3.8 | 1,576 | 3.3 | 1,565 | 3.5 |
| Net Lottery Proceeds | 1,392 | 2.5 | 1,393 | 2.6 | 1,304 | 2.6 | 1,421 | 3.0 | 1,650 | 3.7 |
| Sales of Goods & Services | 547 | 1.0 | 407 | 0.8 | 359 | 0.7 | 329 | 0.7 | 256 | 0.6 |
| Settlements of Claims | 504 | 0.9 | 392 | 0.7 | 318 | 0.6 | 1,117 | 2.3 | 10 | 0.0 |
| Land Income | 325 | 0.6 | 423 | 0.8 | 270 | 0.5 | 226 | 0.5 | 340 | 0.8 |
| Contributions to Employee Benefits | 142 | 0.3 | 127 | 0.2 | 117 | 0.2 | 100 | 0.2 | 93 | 0.2 |
| Other Revenues | 1,798 | 3.3 | 1,508 | 2.8 | 1,267 | 2.5 | 1,477 | 3.1 | 1,205 | 2.7 |
| **Total Net Revenues** | **$55,221** | **100** | **$53,824** | **100** | **$49,846** | **100** | **$47,970** | **100** | **$44,497** | **100** |
| **Expenditures by Function** | | | | | | | | | | |
| General Government – Total | $1,867 | 3.3 | 2,014 | 3.8 | $1,751 | 3.5 | $1,665 | 3.6 | $1,587 | 3.7 |
| Executive | 1,585 | 2.8 | 1,752 | 3.3 | 1,505 | 3.0 | 1,433 | 3.1 | 1,371 | 3.2 |
| Legislative | 113 | 0.2 | 109 | 0.2 | 97 | 0.2 | 100 | 0.2 | 91 | 0.2 |
| Judicial | 168 | 0.3 | 152 | 0.3 | 149 | 0.3 | 132 | 0.3 | 124 | 0.3 |
| Education | 20,260 | 36.3 | 20,091 | 38.1 | 19,105 | 38.4 | 17,215 | 37.7 | 16,607 | 38.4 |
| Employee Benefits | 2,389 | 4.3 | 2,001 | 3.8 | 1,962 | 3.9 | 1,789 | 3.9 | 1,767 | 4.1 |
| Health and Human Services | 20,123 | 36.1 | 18,023 | 34.2 | 16,332 | 32.9 | 16,043 | 35.1 | 14,700 | 34.0 |
| Public Safety and Corrections | 3,332 | 6.0 | 3,162 | 6.0 | 3,012 | 6.1 | 2,879 | 6.3 | 2,671 | 6.2 |
| Transportation | 5,030 | 9.0 | 4,522 | 8.6 | 4,459 | 9.0 | 3,718 | 8.1 | 3,292 | 7.6 |
| Natural Resources/Recreational Services | 1,073 | 1.9 | 1,075 | 2.0 | 1,349 | 2.7 | 740 | 1.6 | 733 | 1.7 |
| Regulatory Agencies | 212 | 0.4 | 208 | 0.4 | 196 | 0.4 | 188 | 0.4 | 184 | 0.4 |
| Lottery Winnings Paid | 423 | 0.8 | 366 | 0.7 | 250 | 0.5 | 332 | 0.7 | 388 | 0.9 |
| Debt Service – Interest | 564 | 1.0 | 637 | 1.2 | 598 | 1.2 | 479 | 1.0 | 529 | 1.2 |
| Capital Outlay | 464 | 0.8 | 570 | 1.1 | 693 | 1.4 | 648 | 1.4 | 767 | 1.8 |
| **Total Net Expenditures** | **$55,739** | **100** | **$52,699** | **100** | **$49,708** | **100** | **45,687** | **100** | **$43,224** | **100** |

Amounts rounded. Expenditures exclude trust funds. Fiscal years end August 31.
Source: State of Texas 2002 Annual Cash Report, Vol. One, Summary of Financial Information for the year ended August 31, 2002, Comptroller of Public Accounts' Office.

## State Tax Collections, 1990–2002

| Fiscal Year‡ | State Tax Collections | Resident Population* | Per Capita Tax Collections | Taxes as % of Personal Income |
|---|---|---|---|---|
| 1990 | 13,632,640,459 | 17,020,689 | 800.95 | 4.7 |
| 1991 | 14,922,113,980 | 17,319,166 | 861.60 | 4.8 |
| 1992 | 15,848,915,148 | 17,641,580 | 898.38 | 4.8 |
| 1993 | 17,010,737,258 | 17,989,926 | 945.57 | 4.9 |
| 1994 | 18,105,950,592 | 18,340,852 | 987.19 | 4.9 |
| 1995 | 18,858,790,042 | 18,693,032 | 1,008.87 | 4.8 |
| 1996 | 19,762,504,350 | 18,966,000 | 1,042.00 | 4.7 |
| 1997 | 21,187,868,237 | 19,312,000 | 1,097.13 | 4.7 |
| 1998 | 22,634,019,740 | 20,104,000 | 1,126.00 | 4.4 |
| 1999 | 23,614,611,235 | 20,507,000 | 1,152.00 | 4.4 |
| 2000 | 25,283,768,842 | 20,898,000 | 1,210.00 | 4.3 |
| 2001 | 27,230,212,416 | 21,278,000 | 1,280.00 | 4.5 |
| 2002 | 26,279,146,493 | 21,660,000 | 1,213.00 | 4.2 |

‡ Fiscal years end August 31.
* Revised fiscal year estimates

Sources: Texas Comptroller of Public Accounts, Annual Financial Reports of various years. Population and personal income figures, 1990 to 2002: U.S. Dept. of Commerce (U.S. Census Bureau and Bureau of Economic Analysis), adjusted to Texas fiscal years by Comptroller of Public Accounts. Data for 2001 and 2002 include partial estimates by the Texas Comptroller of Public Accounts.

## Tax Revenues, 2001, 2002

Below are listed the major taxes and the amounts each contributed to the state in fiscal years 2001 and 2002.

| Type of Tax | FY 2002 | FY 2001 |
|---|---|---|
| Sales | $14,516,341,226 | $14,663,067,887 |
| Motor Veh. Sales/Rnt* | 2,949,540,192 | 2,905,538,398 |
| Motor Fuels | 2,833,607,460 | 2,765,510,548 |
| Franchise | 1,935,709,140 | 1,960,365,032 |
| Insurance Occupation | 1,045,754,105 | 820,045,596 |
| Natural Gas Production | 628,496,630 | 1,596,885,766 |
| Cigarette/Tobacco | 540,038,314 | 584,586,277 |
| Alcoholic Beverages | 560,197,124 | 541,305,988 |
| Oil Production | 338,661,102 | 442,580,206 |
| Inheritance | 334,190,915 | 322,354,926 |
| Utility | 311,051,398 | 339,403,570 |
| Hotel/Motel | 230,909,206 | 246,813,166 |
| Other Taxes** | 54,649,681 | 41,755,055 |
| **Totals** | **$26,279,146,493** | **$27,230,212,416** |

*Includes tax on manufactured housing sales and taxes on interstate motor carriers.

Source: State of Texas 2002 Annual Cash Report, Vol. One, Summary of Financial Information for the year ended August 31, 2002, Texas Comptroller of Public Accounts.

# State Government Budget Summary, 2004–2005 Biennium

Source: Legislative Budget Board

| Article (Govt. Division) | 2004-05 Budget (all funds) (in millions) |
|---|---|
| Art. I, General Government | $ 2,660.9 |
| Art. II, Health and Human Services | 41,335.5 |
| Art. III, Education | 53,140.8 |
| Art. IV, The Judiciary | 442.5 |
| Art. V, Public Safety & Criminal Justice | 8,316.3 |
| Art. VI, Natural Resources | 2,022.6 |
| Art. VII, Business & Economic Dev. | 14,321.0 |
| Art. VIII, Regulatory | 842.2 |
| Art. IX, General Provisions | (77.6) |
| Art. X, The Legislature | 309.8 |
| Art. XII, Tobacco Settlement Receipts | 1,249.7 |
| Total | $ 124,561.6 |

House Bill 1 passed by the 78th Legislature totals $124.6 billion from all fund sources for state government operations for the 2004–2005 biennium. These numbers do not include adjustments from Governor's vetoes or supplementary appropriations in other legislation. The appropriations represent an $7.4 billion, or 6.3 percent, increase from the 2002–2003 biennium.

General Revenue funding totals $69.7 billion for the 2004–2005 biennium, an increase of $3.0 bilion, or 4.5 percent, over the 2002–2003 biennial spending level. General Revenue funding, including funds dedicated within the General Revenue Fund, totals $64.6 billion.

The text of House Bill 1 may be obtained on the Legislative Budget Board's Web site: **www.lbb.state.tx.us.** ☆

# Texas Lottery

Source: Texas Lottery Commission

The State Lottery Act was passed by the Texas Legislature in July 1991. The constitutional amendment necessary to approve the lottery was passed in an election on Nov. 5, 1991, by a vote of 1,326,154 to 728,994. Total sales since the first ticket was sold on May 29, 1992, through fiscal year 2002 are more than $29.5 billion.

In December 2002, the 10 billionth dollar generated by the Texas Lottery was transferred to the State of Texas. Until Sept. 1, 1997, lottery revenues were deposited in the General Revenue Fund. Since that date, revenues are dedicated to the Foundation School Fund, which supports public education in Texas. In addition, unclaimed prize money is transferred to the Multicategorical Teaching Hospital Account and Tertiary Care Facility Account on a formula set by the Texas Legislature.

Texas Lottery transfers to the state from May 1992 through June 2003 are: General Revenue Fund, $ 4,956,410,731; Foundation School Fund, $5,379,033,871; Multicategorical Teaching Hospital Account, $80,000,000; and Tertiary Care Facility Account, $120,067,884.

Executive Director of the Texas Lottery is Reagan E. Greer.

**Who Plays the Lottery?**

*The executive director of the Texas Lottery Commission is required to conduct a biennial demographic survey of lottery players to determine the income, age, sex, race, education and frequency of participation of players. The information, below, is from the survey conducted for the Texas Lottery Commission by the Office of Survey Research in the College of Communication of The University of Texas at Austin from September through November 2002. A total of 1,715 interviews were completed with Texans 18 and older. The margin of error is approximately plus or minus 2.4 percent.*

The percentage of Texans who report purchasing at least one Texas Lottery ticket in the 12 months preceding the survey was 56 percent. Eighty-six percent of those reported playing Lotto Texas; 66 percent played "scratch off" or instant games; 20 percent reported playing Pick 3 day draw, 17 percent reported playing Pick 3 night draw; 29 percent reported playing Cash Five; 17 percent reported playing Texas Two Step.

**Age:** Sixty-four percent of lottery players were between 26 and 55; 11 percent were 18 to 25; 11 percent were over 65. The most common age range is 35 to 55 (45 percent).

**Educational Level:** College graduates and those with

## Texas Lottery Financial Data

Start-up to August 31, 2002

| Period | Value of Prizes Won (millions) | Cost of Product (millions) | Retailer Comm- issions (millions) | Admin- istration (millions) | To State of Texas (millions) |
|---|---|---|---|---|---|
| Start-up through FY 1993 | $1,250 | $151 | $122 | $23 | $907 |
| FY 1994 | 1,529 | 152 | 138 | 21 | 928 |
| FY 1995 | 1,689 | 169 | 152 | 27 | 1,015 |
| FY 1996 | 1,951 | 195 | 172 | 28 | 1,098 |
| FY 1997 | 2,152 | 206 | 187 | 36 | 1,183 |
| FY 1998 | 1,648 | 167 | 155 | 37 | 1,098 |
| FY 1999 | 1,329 | 141 | 129 | 32 | 953 |
| FY 2000 | 1,509 | 145 | 133 | 32 | 863 |
| FY 2001 | 1,643 | 144 | 141 | 34 | 864 |
| FY 2002 | 1,715 | 135 | 148 | 36 | 929 |

All figures accrued.

some college education (35 and 32 percent, respectively) were the most likely to play lottery games. Only 8 percent of the lottery-playing population has less than a high school education. This segment is by far the least likely to play lottery games.

**Income Level:** Texans most likely to play lottery games have family incomes greater than $50,000 (44 percent); 25 percent make $30,000 to $49,000; 15 percent make $20,000 to $29,000; 10 percent make $10,000 to $19,000; and 6 percent earn less than $10,000.

**Ethnic Background:** More than half of lottery players are Caucasians (62 percent); 28 percent are Hispanics; 8 percent are blacks; and 2 percent are "other."

**Sex:** The number of women playing lottery games is slightly greater than men: 54 percent to 46 percent. ☆

## Federal Revenue by State Agency

Source: Texas Comptroller of Public Accounts, Annual Cash Report for the Year Ended August 31, 2002, Vol. One.

| State Agency | 2002 | 2001 | 2000 | 1999 |
|---|---|---|---|---|
| Texas Health and Human Services Commission | $8,799,561,287 | $7,756,099,712 | $6,967,628,608 | $6,807,116,368 |
| Texas Department of Health | 580,185,493 | 529,240,689 | 518,878,336 | 489,932,013 |
| Department of Human Services | 1,136,811,291 | 1,161,389,164 | 1,046,098,889 | 856,606,856 |
| Texas Education Agency | 2,585,993,100 | 2,283,712,720 | 2,147,842,294 | 1,963,000,811 |
| Texas Department of Transportation | 2,320,038,178 | 1,808,791,584 | 1,849,825,384 | 1,564,430,136 |
| Texas Workforce Commission* | 927,275,459 | 782,423,573 | 702,323,258 | 722,542,908 |
| Department of Protective and Regulatory Services | 267,426,078 | 209,266,976 | 175,646,332 | 185,338,342 |
| Texas Rehabilitation Commission | 267,754,770 | 234,917,087 | 229,152,375 | 236,715,011 |
| Texas Department of Housing and Community Affairs | 195,173,838 | 248,344,165 | 213,966,409 | 225,878,232 |
| All Other Agencies | 1,090,726,480 | 1,003,578,840 | 947,342,201 | 874,440,051 |
| Total All Agencies | $18,170,945,974 | $16,017,764,510 | $14,798,704,086 | $13,926,000,728 |

# Local Governments

Texas has **254 counties**, a number which has not changed since 1931 when Loving County was organized. Loving had a population of 64 according to the 2002 estimate by the State Data Center, compared with 164 in 1970 and a peak of 285 in 1940. It is the **least-populous county** in Texas. In contrast, Harris County has **the most residents** in Texas, with a 2002 population estimate of 3,557,055

Counties range in area from Rockwall's 148.7 square miles to the 6,192.78 square miles in Brewster, which is equal to the combined area of the states of Connecticut and Rhode Island.

The Texas Constitution makes a county a legal subdivision of the state. Each county has a **commissioners court**. It consists of four commissioners, each elected from a commissioner's precinct, and a county judge elected from the entire county. In smaller counties, the county judge retains judicial responsibilities in probate and insanity cases. For names of county and district officials, see tables on pages 474–484.

Twelve hundred and one **incorporated Texas municipalities** range in size from 32 residents to Houston's 1,980,950, according to the State Data Center's 2002 estimate. More than 80 percent of the state's population lives in cities and towns meeting the U.S. Census Bureau definition of urban areas.

Texas had **311 municipalities with more than 5,000 population**, according to State Data Center estimates. Under law, these cities may adopt their own charters by a majority vote. Cities of less than 5,000 may be chartered only under the general law. Some of these cities now show fewer than 5,000 residents, because population has declined since they adopted their home-rule charters. **Home-rule cities are marked in this list by a single-dagger symbol (†) before the name.** ☆

# Mayors and City Managers of Texas Cities

The list below was compiled from questionnaires sent out immediately after the municipal elections in May 2003. Included is the name of each city's mayor, as well as the name of the city manager, city administrator, city coordinator or other managing executive of munipalities having that form of government. If a town's mail goes to a post office with a different name, the mailing address is included.

An asterisk (*) before the city name indicates that the Almanac received no response to the questionnaire and that the information on city officials is from the Texas State Directory 2002, 46th edition.

*Abbott ...................... Robert L. Tufts
Abernathy .................. Bobby Burnett
 City Mgr., Frank Russell
†Abilene.......................... Grady Barr
 City Mgr., Roy L. McDaniel
*Ackerly............. Jimmie L. Schuelke
†Addison............. R. Scott Wheeler
 City Mgr., Ron Whitehead
Adrian ............................ Finis Brown
*Agua Dulce.................. Carl Vajdos
†Alamo ......Rodolfo "Rudy" Villarreal
 City Mgr., Luciano Ozuna Jr.
†Alamo Heights (6116 Broadway, San
 Antonio 78209-4599) Bob Biechlin
 City Admin., Susan Rash
Alba ...................... Owen Reynolds
*Albany ........................Harold Cox
 City Mgr., Bobby R. Russell
Aledo ...................... Robert A. Lewis
 City Admin., Daphne Richardson
†Alice............................Rito Silva Jr.
 City Mgr., Pete Anaya
†Allen....................... Stephen Terrell
 City Mgr., Peter H. Vargas
Alma (140 Alma Dr., Ennis
 75119) ...................... Don Keilers
†Alpine....................Paul R. Weyerts
 City Mgr., (Vacancy)
Alto ...............................Chris Lewis
 City Admin., Terri Grogan
Alton (PO Box 9004, Mission 78572-
 9004) ......................Salvador Vela
 City Mgr., Israel Sagredo
Alvarado......................Tom Durington
 City Mgr., Mary Daly
†Alvin............................. Andy Reyes
 City Mgr., Paul Horn
Alvord........................ Edwin Strange
 City Admin., Richard Tow Jr.
†Amarillo................. Trent Sisemore
 City Mgr., John Q. Ward
*Ames ............................John White
Amherst .............George Thompson
*Anahuac ...............Bruce E. Corner
Anderson ...................Gail M. Sowell
†Andrews ...................... Robert Zap
 City Mgr., Glen E. Hackler
†Angleton .... L.M. "Matt" Sebesta Jr.
 City Admin., Michael Stoldt
*Angus (6008 S. I-45 West, Corsi-
 cana 75110)...... Eben Dale Stover

*Anna ................... Ronald Ferguson
*Annetta (1200 Old Annetta Rd.,
 Aledo 76008)............Olan Usher
Annetta North (PO Box 262,
 Aledo 76008)..... Daniel Wilkerson
Annetta South (PO Box 61, Aledo
 76008) ....... Gerhard Kleinschmidt
*Annona ........ George H. English Sr.
*†Anson ........................Tom Isbell
Anthony ......................... Art Franco
Anton ..........................Greg Hodges
 City Mgr., Larry G. Conkin
*Appleby (RR 10, Box 5186, Nacog-
 doches 75961-9810) ......N. F. Burt
*Aquilla ..........................Lee Mills
†Aransas Pass ............ Karen Gayle
 City Mgr., Rick Ewaniszyk
Archer City ............ Max C. Wood Sr.
*Arcola.........................Roy Jackson
Argyle .................. Richard S. Tucker
 City Admin., (Vacancy at press time)
†Arlington ...................... Elzie Odom
 City Mgr., Chuck Kiefer
Arp................... Vernon L. Bedair
Asherton................. Sam Galvan Jr.
Aspermont......................P. C. Carr
 City Admin., Roger Parker
*†Athens......................Jerry G. King
 City Mgr., Pam J. Burton
†Atlanta ......................... Kay Phillips
 City Mgr., Mike Ahrens
Aubrey ..................... Jason L. Pierce
*Aurora (PO Box 558, Rhome
 76078-0558)........... Steve Derting
†Austin ..........................Kirk Watson
 City Mgr., Jesus Garza
*†Austwell..................Carl Anderson
Avery ...........................Erby Stinson
*Avinger ............... Leif Lowrimore
*†Azle ........................R. Leck Heflin
 City Mgr., Jerry Guillory

*Bailey .........................Don A. Rhine
*Bailey's Prairie (PO Box 71,
 Angleton 77516).......... (vacancy)
Baird...........................Jon Hardwick
*†Balch Springs...........Brenda Haas
 City Mgr., K.M Hubert
*Balcones Heights (123 Altgelt Ave.,
 San Antonio 78201) ..Jim Craven
†Ballinger ............. Robert Moore Sr.

 City Mgr., Tommy New
*Balmorhea .........Ruben M. Fuentez
Bandera .................... Linda C. Stein
 City Mgr., Theresa Helbert
Bangs...................... C.B. Alexander
†Bardwell ..................... Patsy Honza
Barry .............................. John Braly
*Barstow .............Benny Hernandez
Bartlett ..............Janice C. Atchison
Bartonville ..................... John Mayall
Bastrop ............................ Tom Scott
 City Mgr., Jeff Holberg
†Bay City ......... Charles Martinez Jr.
*Bayou Vista (2929 Highway 6, Ste
 100, Hitchcock 77563-2723)
 ........................Kenyon Courtney
Bayside .......................Billy P. Fricks
†Baytown .................... Pete C. Alfaro
 City Mgr., Monte Mercer
Bayview (RR 3 Box 19A, Los Fres-
 nos
 78566-9713) .................. Robert E.
 Middleton Jr.
*Beach City (12723 Tri City Beach
 Rd., Baytown 77520) . A.R. Senac
Bear Creek, Village of (6705 W.
 Hwy 290, #502-244, Austin
 78735)......................... Mark Bohm
Beasley ..................... Frances Smith
†Beaumont ............. David W. Moore
 City Mgr., Stephen J. Bonczek
Beckville................ Thomas Adams
†Bedford .............. R.D. "Rick" Hurt
 City Mgr., Charles P. Barnett
Bee Cave (13333 W. Highway 71,
 Austin 78738-3104) ..... Caroline L.
 Murphy
 City Admin., James Fisher
*†Beeville ...........Kenneth Chesshir
 City Mgr., Ford Patton
*†Bellaire ............. Mary Ann Goode
 City Mgr., Bernard M. Satterwhite Jr.
*Bellevue............. James Broussard
*†Bellmead ....................... Al Lopez
 City Mgr., Scooter Radcliffe
*Bells............................Bob Essary
*Bellville ...............Philip B. Harrison
†Belton........................ Bill Holmes
 City Mgr., Sam A. Listi
*Benavides.............Cynthia Canales
†Benbrook (PO Box 26569, Fort
 Worth 76126-6569)...... F.T. Hebert

City Mgr., Cary K. Conklin
Benjamin......................Mike Sheedy
  City Mgr., Ronnie White
*Berryville (PO Box 908, Frankston 75763-0908) ....... James F. Colvin
  City Mgr., Sharyn Harrison
Bertram................Robert Ricketson
*Bethel (Rt. 2, Box 109K, Whitewright 75491-9712).. Larry Schone
Beverly Hills (3418 Memorial Dr., Waco 76711) ...............Douglas E. Woodward
Bevil Oaks (7390 Sweetgum Rd., Beaumont 77713) ... Erin Galloway
Big Lake......................J.R. Dunn
  City Mgr., Evelyn Ammons
Big Sandy ................Lynda Childress
  City Admin., Everett McWilliams
*†Big Spring...............Russ McEwen
  City Admin., Gary Fuqua
*Big Wells................Gloria V. Flores
*Bishop .................Geraldine Rypple
Bishop Hills (#5 Sheffield Rd., Amarillo 79124) Larry J. "Skip" Johnson
Blackwell....................Ronald Harris
Blanco......................Louann Hayes
Blanket......................John H. Jones
Bloomburg .................Jerrell Ritchie
*Blooming Grove..........Ralph Dozier
Blossom........................Ed Hudson
  City Mgr., Tony Chance
*Blue Mound (301 Blue Mound Rd., Fort Worth 76131-1030) .......Jace Preston
Blue Ridge ...........Frances M. Slater
*Blum ....................Elaine Edwards
†Boerne ......................Patrick Heath
  City Mgr., Ronald C. Bowman
Bogata ....................Randy Kennedy
*†Bonham ...............Carl McEachern
  City Mgr., Blaine R. Hinds
*Bonney (19025 FM 521, Rosharon 77583) ..............Elmer Cannon Jr.
Booker ....................James Roberts
  City Mgr., Darcy D. Long
*†Borger ....................Judy Flanders
Bovina......................Galen Hromas
  City Mgr., Colby Waters
†Bowie .............Benjamin J. Lovette
  City Mgr., James Cantwell
*Boyd ........................Allen Dickey
*Brackettville ... Carmen M. Berlanga
  City Mgr., David G. Luna
†Brady ......................Clarence Friar
  City Mgr., Merle Taylor
Brazoria ....................Harold Burrell
  City Mgr., (Vacancy)
Brazos Country (104 Winding Creek Ln., Sealy 77474) ........Charles A. Kalkomey Sr.
†Breckenridge...... Virgil E. Moore Jr.
  City Mgr., Gary G. Ernest
Bremond ......................Ricky Swick
†Brenham ..........Walter C. Schwartz
  City Mgr., Terry Roberts
Briarcliff ..............James R. Hamnett
*Briaroaks (PO Box 816, Burleson 76097) .....................James Dunn
†Bridge City ...........Bobbie Burgess
  City Mgr., Don Fields
*Bridgeport .........Wm. Ray Cook Jr.
  City Admin., Jeffrey Howell
Broaddus .....................Marion Neill
*Bronte..........................Martin Lee
*Brookshire ............Keith A. Woods
Brookside Village .. George D. Carter
*Browndell (PO Box 430, Brookeland 75931) .....................Alvin Mattox
†Brownfield .................Nancy Wade
  City Mgr., Eldon Jobe
Brownsboro.................Jeff Fulgham
*†Brownsville ...........Blanca S. Vela
  City Mgr., Lanny Lambert

†Brownwood.........Bert V. Massey II
  City Mgr., Gary Butts
Bruceville-Eddy (143 Wilcox Dr., #A, Eddy 76524).....Halbert Wilcox
†Bryan ....................Jay Don Watson
  Acting City Mgr., Hugh Walker
*Bryson.................Kennith Boland
*Buckholts ...............Mary Krwawicz
Buda ............................Billy Gray
  City Admin., W. Grey White
Buffalo .........................Byron Ryder
Buffalo Gap...............David L. Perry
*Buffalo Springs (RR 10, Box 500, Lubbock 79404).........Rick Lujan
Bullard ......................B.J. Langford
*Bulverde .......................Bev Lemes
  City Admin., Bob Hieronymus
Bunker Hill Village (11977 Memorial Dr., Houston 77024) .....William H. Marshall
  City Admin., Ruthie P. Sager
*†Burkburnett ................. Bill Vincent
  City Mgr., Mike Slye
*Burke (RR 3, Box 315, Diboll 75941-9714) ....................J.L. Bell
†Burleson .....................Byron Black
  City Mgr., Kay Godbey
Burnet................ Howard R. Benton
  City Mgr., Johnny Sartain
Burton ........................Steve Miller
Byers ........................W.A. Landrum
*Bynum ......................Jerry Hooker

*Cactus ......................Ray Gutierrez
  City Mgr., Darrel Read
*Caddo Mills ....................Ed Locker
Caldwell..............Bernard E. Rychlik
  City Admin., William L. Broaddus
Callisburg (59 Campbell St., Whitesboro 76273-4700). Larry C. Morrison
*Calvert......................Briscoe Cain
†Cameron............James E. Lafferty
  City Mgr., Janet Sheguit
Campbell ......................Nick Jordan
Camp Wood .....................Ben Cox
Canadian .....................Patti Fulcher
  City Mgr., Dean Looper
*Caney City (15241 Barron Rd., Malakoff 75148-4337) Joe Barron
*Canton ............. William F. Hilliard
  City Mgr., Johnny M. Mallory
*†Canyon...........................Lois Rice
  City Mgr., Glen R. Metcalf
Carbon.........................Dale Walker
Carl's Corner (RR 3, Box 500, Hillsboro 76645) ..........Carl Cornelius
Carmine.............Johnny B. Yarborough
*†Carrizo Springs .. Ralph E. Salinas
  City Mgr., Mario Martinez
*†Carrollton ....................Mark Stokes
  Interim City Mgr., Bob Scott
†Carthage ...........Carson C. Joines
  City Mgr., Charles Thomas
Cashion (412 Cashion Rd., Wichita Falls 76305). Thomas J. Lowry Sr.
Castle Hills (209 Lemonwood Dr., San Antonio 78213) Marcy Harper
  City Mgr., Mike Shands
*Castroville ....... Robert N. Hancock
  City Admin., Ronnie Rand
*†Cedar Hill ..................Rob Franke
  City Mgr., Alan Sims
†Cedar Park ....................Bob Young
  City Mgr., Robert Powers
Celeste ............................Pat Jones
Celina .................Mark D. Peterman
  City Admin., Larry Bartlett
†Center..................John D. Windham
  Interim City Mgr., Melinda Brittain
Centerville ....................Billy Walters
  City Admin., Nancy C. Kiker
Chandler..........................Joye Rains
*Channing..................Leslie Kistner

Charlotte ..................Mark T. Wilson
Chester......................C.E. Lawrence
Chico.....................James Robinson
†Childress .....................Pat Y. Steed
  City Mgr., Jerry Cummins
*Chillicothe ................. Wallace Clay
China....................Robert W. Murff
China Grove (2456 FM 1516, San Antonio 78263......... Dennis Dunk
Chireno....................John A. Ragland
  City Mgr., Joanna Johnson
*Christine ...........Walter W. Stevens
Cibolo ...................Charles Ruppert
  City Admin., Charles Balcar
*†Cisco....................John W. Clinton
  City Mgr., Michael Moore
Clarendon............Leonard Selvidge
  City Admin., Janice Barbee
Clark (10109 Clark Air Field Rd., Justin 76247)................L.E. Clark
Clarksville....................Ann Rushing
  City Mgr., Kenneth V. Martin
Clarksville City (PO Box 1209, Gladewater 75647).. Larry G. Allen
  City Mgr., Billy F. Silvertooth Jr.
Claude............................Rick Jones
Clear Lake Shores Ted K. Guthrie Jr.
†Cleburne.....Thomas C. Hazlewood
  City Mgr., Chester Nolen
*†Cleveland ..............Richard Boyett
  City Mgr., Philip Cook
Clifton ......................W. Leon Smith
  City Admin., Jerry Golden
Clint.....................Charles Gonzales
†Clute...........................Jerry Adkins
  City Mgr., Barbara Hester
Clyde ........................Steve Livingston
  City Admin., Lee Roy George
Coahoma.........................Bill Read
*Cockrell Hill (4125 W. Clarendon Dr.,Dallas 75211) .......Charles P. Slayton
  City Admin., Rosa A. Rios
*Coffee City (PO Box 716, Frankston 75763).....................Ruthie Seward
Coldspring.............Ned V. Alexander
†Coleman ..............Nick Poldrack
  City Mgr., Randy Whiteman
†College Station......Lynn McIlhaney
  City Mgr., Tom Brymer
*†Colleyville.....................Donna Arp
  City Mgr., Bill Lindley
Collinsville ............Wayne McCorkle
Colmesneil ...................Doug Wood
†Colorado City .................Bob Reily
  City Mgr., Stephen K. Shutt
Columbus .....................Paula Frnka
  City Mgr., David Stall
*Comanche ...............Brent Hagood
Combes..................Silvestre Garcia
*Combine (123 Davis Road, Seagoville 75159-0231) Charles Stringer
†Commerce ...............John R. Sands
  City Mgr., Roger McKinney
Como .......................James A. Beach
†Conroe .....................Carter Moore
  City Admin., Craig Lonon
*†Converse ................Craig Martin
  City Mgr., Sam Hughes
Cool (150 So. FM 113, Millsap 76066-2100) Marsha A. McDonald
Coolidge....................Bobby Jacobs
Cooper .........Thomas Scotty Stegall
†Coppell .............Douglas N. Stover
  City Mgr., Jim Witt
†Copperas Cove . Rodney G. Nauert
  City Mgr., Richard Torres
Copper Canyon (400 Woodland Dr., Lewisville 75077) Chuck Wainscott
†Corinth (2003 S. Corinth St., Denton 76210).........J.B. "Babs" Troutman
  Interim City Mgr., Ken Seale

†Corpus Christi................ Loyd Neal
    City Mgr., David Garcia
Corral City (14007 Corral City Dr.,
    Argyle 76226) ....James E. Draper
Corrigan................Franz S. Bladwin
    City Mgr., B.K. Johnson
†Corsicana ...................... April Sikes
    City Mgr., Truitt Gilbreath
*Cottonwood (PO Box 293,
    Scurry 75158)........... E.J. Williams
Cottonwood Shores .....Dale Pickens
*Cotulla ................... Pablo Gonzales
    City Admin., Higinio Martinez Jr.
*Cove (PO Box 2251, Mont Belvieu
    77580)......................Lee Wiley
Covington................Shirley Erickson
Crandall ........................ Joe Baker
    City Mgr., Judy Bell
Crane .................... Terry L. Schul
    City Admin., Dru Gravens
Cranfills Gap ................... Wade Lee
Crawford .......... Robert L. Campbell
*Creedmoor (12108 FM 1625, Austin
    78747)....................Robert Wilhite
†Crockett .................... Wayne Mask
    City Mgr., Billy W. Horn
Crosbyton .........Joseph E. Johnston
    City Mgr., Jared Miller
Cross Plains .................. Ray Purvis
    City Mgr., Debbie Gosnell
Cross Roads (11700 Hwy. 380 E.,
    Aubrey 76227-8246) Doug Daffron
*Cross Timber (PO Box 2042,
    Burleson 76097)Wava McCullough
Crowell......................Robert Kincaid
*†Crowley ...................... Billy Davis
    City Admin., John Daniel
*†Crystal City.......José Angel "Jody"
    Cerda
    City Mgr.,Eleazar Salina Jr.
*†Cuero ............... W.L. "Buzz" Edge
    City Mgr., Corlis Riedesel
*Cumby.......................... Gary Cline
*Cuney ....................... Billy Roberts
*Cushing .................Ben G. Baldwin
    City Mgr., Jarry L. Bowers
Cut and Shoot (PO Box 7364,
    Conroe 77306).....Lang Thompson

†Daingerfield ..... Lou Irvin Slaughter
    City Mgr., Marty Byers
Daisetta ............. Edward Lynn Wells
†Dalhart......................... Gene Rahll
    City Mgr., Greg Duggan
†Dallas..........................Laura Miller
    City Mgr., Teodoro J. Benavides
Dalworthington Gardens (2600
    Roosevelt Dr., Arlington 76016-
    5809) .....................Albert A. Taub
    City Admin., Greg Shugart
Danbury ............................Jeff Lege
*Darrouzett.............Mike Lamberson
    City Mgr., Terry Howard
Dawson................... Yvonne Woods
*†Dayton.........Guy L. "Larry" Harris
    City Mgr., Robert Ewart
*Dayton Lakes (PO Box 1476,
    Dayton 77535) ............ (vacancy)
*Dean (6913 State Hwy. 79N, Wichita
    Falls 76035-9597) Steve L. Sicking
†Decatur...............Joe A. Lambert
    City Mgr., Brett Shannon
De Cordova (4612 Cimmaron Trail,
    Granbury 76049) .......... Dick Pruitt
†Deer Park................. Wayne Riddle
    City Mgr., Ron Crabtree
De Kalb............... Paul G. Meadows
    City Admin., Belinda Peek
†De Leon ................ John R. Adcock
*Dell City ........................Pam Dean
*†Del Rio .............. Dora G. Alcalá
    City Mgr., Rafael Castillo
†Denison ...................... Bill Lindsay

    City Mgr., Larry Cruise
†Denton......................Euline Brock
    City Mgr., Mike Conduff
†Denver City........Sidney C. Reinert
    City Mgr., Stan David
Deport .................... Charles Foster
†DeSoto ................... Michael Hurtt
    City Mgr., Jim Baugh
*Detroit ...................Travis Bronner
*Devers......... (vacent at press time)
*Devine...................Steve A. Lopez
    City Admin., Georgia Vines
Diboll .................... James P. Simms
    City Mgr., Lanny Parish
*Dickens ...............R.L. "Bob" Porter
†Dickinson ................. Ken Hufstetler
    City Admin., Ivan Langford
Dilley.............. Mary Ann Obregon
    Interim City Admin., Irma Rodriguez
†Dimmitt ................... Wayne Collins
    City Mgr., Don Sheffy
*Dodd City .................Jackie Lackey
*Dodson................... Ray Hightower
*Domino....................Marvin Campbell
*†Donna .................Ricardo Morales
Dorchester............... Alice F. Stewart
Double Oak ............... Richard Cook
*Douglassville......... Douglass Heath
Dripping Springs..... Wayne E. Smith
    City Mgr., Michelle Fischer
*Driscoll ...................Rolando Padilla
    City Admin., Rachel Saenz
Dublin ............. James "Red" Seigars
    City Mgr., Brian D. Boudreaux
*†Dumas.................. Rowdy Rhoades
    City Mgr., Vince DiPiazza
†Duncanville............. Glenn A. Repp
    City Mgr., Kent Cagle

*Eagle Lake ....... René Cooper Scott
    City Mgr., Ronald W. Holland
†Eagle Pass ....... José A. Aranda Jr.
    City Mgr., Felix M. Cerna
Early .......................... James Lewis
    City Admin., Ken Thomas
*Earth .......................... Doug Parish
†Eastland ................ Jerry Mathews
    City Mgr., David S. Geeslin
*East Mountain (RR 1, Box 500,
    Gilmer 75644)............. Ronnie Hill
Easton ..................... Willis Sammons
East Tawakoni (288 Briggs Blvd.,
    Point 75472) ..... Bobbie J. Harman
Ector ................ Mary Dean Norris
Edcouch ..................... Ramiro Silva
    City Admin., Belen Montelongo
Eden ................... Thomas F. Kelso
*Edgecliff Village (1605 Edgecliff Rd.,
    Edgecliff 76134-1198) ....Ed Lucas
*Edgewood ...............Charles Prater
†Edinburg ...................... Joe Ochoa
*Edmonson................. Don Ketchum
    City Mgr., Franklin Bain
†Edna......................Joe D. Hermes
    City Mgr., Kenneth W. Pryor
Edom (150 PR 8279, Ben Wheeler
    75754) ....................Barbara Crow
*†El Campo .............Randy Collins
    City Mgr., John Steelman
El Cenizo ................Oralia C. Reyes
Eldorado ................ John Nikolauk
*†Electra............ R.W. "Ron" Pittman
    City Admin., (vacancy)
*†Elgin ................... Eric W. Carlson
    City Mgr., Jim D. Dunaway
*Elkhart....................Diane Parker
El Lago ......................... Brad Emel
*Elmendorf.......George R. Mabry Sr.
*†El Paso ................. Ray Caballero
    City Admin., Charles McNabb
*Elsa ............. Gregorio M. Madrigal
    City Mgr., Leonardo Camarillo
*Emhouse (3825 Joe Johnson Dr.,

    Corsicana 75110).Johnny Pattison
Emory........................... Cay House
Enchanted Oaks (PO Box 5019,
    Gun
    Barrel City 75147) .....Olena Boner
Encinal ......................Javier Mancha
*†Ennis...............Russell R. Thomas
    City Mgr., Steve Howerton
*Estelline .................... David Walker
†Euless ................... Mary Lib Saleh
    City Mgr., Joe Hennig
Eureka (1305 FM 2859, Corsicana
    75110-0754).........Barney Thomas
Eustace .....................Sue January
    City Admin., Drucilla Haynes
Evant ...................Alma "Fritz" Green
†Everman......James A. Stephenson
    City Mgr., Donna R. Anderson

Fairchilds (8713 Fairchilds Rd.,
    Richmond 77469)....Robert Myska
Fairfield...... Steve Spradlin (pro tem)
    City Mgr., Michael R. Gokey
Fair Oaks Ranch ........ E.L. Gaubatz
Fairview (500 S. Highway 5,
    McKinney 75069)Donald T. Phillips
    City Mgr., Ron Clary
Falfurrias ............. Raudel Gonzalez
Falls City......................... Vi Malone
†Farmers Branch ..........Bob Phelps
    Interim City Mgr., John Burke
*Farmersville ....... George G. Crump
    City Mgr., Alan Hein
Farwell..........................Jimmie Mace
Fate ..................................David Hill
    City Mgr., Gerry Boren
*Fayetteville ....Ronald R. Pflughaupt
    City Mgr., Sylvester Schmitt Jr.
Ferris ..................... Jimmie Birdwell
*Flatonia ...................... Lori Berger
    City Mgr., Robert Wood
Florence .............. Thomas R. Estes
Floresville ...... Raymond M. Ramirez
    City Mgr., Gary Pelech
†Flower Mound .........Lori L. DeLuca
    City Mgr., Van James
*Floydada ................. Bobby Gilliland
    City Mgr., Gary Brown
*Follett........................... Lynn Blau
    City Mgr., Robert Williamson
*†Forest Hill (6800 Forest Hill Dr.,
    Fort Worth 76140) ...Malinda Miller
    City Mgr., David Vestal
*†Forney..............Weldon L. Bowen
    City Mgr., Jim McConnell
Forsan.............................Jim Buske
*Fort Stockton ....Howard McKissack
    City Mgr., Jesse Garcia
†Fort Worth ................. Kenneth Barr
    City Mgr., Gary Jackson
Franklin....................Charles Ellison
*Frankston ............... James Gouger
    City Admin., Jean Jennings
†Fredericksburg .......Tim Crenwelge
    City Mgr., Gary Neffendorf
*†Freeport.......James A. Barnett Jr.
    City Mgr., Ron Bottoms
*Freer ....................... Arnoldo Cantu
†Friendswood ..... Harold L. Whitaker
    City Mgr., Ron Cox
Friona ...................... John C. Taylor
    City Mgr., Terri Johnson
†Frisco .....................Mike Simpson
    City Mgr., George Purefoy
*Fritch.........................Kevin Keener
    City Mgr., Richard L. Walton
Frost ............................ Ken Reed
Fruitvale.....................Danny Gilliam
    City Coor., Bea Whisenhunt
*Fulshear.............J. Michael Dinges
*Fulton.....................Leslie Cole Sr.

†Gainesville ................... Glenn Loch
   City Mgr., Mike Land
†Galena Park.............Robert Barrett
   City Admin., John Cooper
Gallatin .................. Bobby Wellborn
†Galveston........ Roger "Bo" Quiroga
   City Mgr., Steve J. LeBlanc
Ganado................. Fred Rickaway
Garden Ridge ........Jay F. Feibelman
   City Admin., (Vacancy at press time)
†Garland....................Jim Spence
   City Mgr., Jeffrey B. Muzzy
*Garrett (208 N. Ferris St., Ennis
   75119-8338) ............. Jami Rogers
Garrison............. Darrell Lunsford Jr.
Gary..................... Jean L. Heaton
*†Gatesville ............. Daren Moore
   City Mgr., Brandon Emmons
†Georgetown ................ Gary Nelon
   City Mgr., Paul Brandenburg
†George West........August Caron Jr.
   City Mgr., Terri Garza
*Gholson (1277 Wesley Chapel Rd.,
   Waco 76705) .... Howard T. Sexton
†Giddings ................... James Arndt
   City Mgr., Paul R. Kipp
†Gilmer ......................Everett Dean
   City Mgr., Thomas B. Smyser
*†Gladewater ....... John Paul Tallent
   City Mgr., Sharon G. Johnson
*†Glenn Heights ......Jesus Humprey
   City Mgr., Dena Daniel
*Glen Rose ...................Connie Kirk
Godley ................. Larry A. Richeson
Goldsmith ..............William Edwards
Goldthwaite...........Danny Hammond
   City Mgr., Bobby Rountree
*Goliad...............William J. Schaefer
Golinda (7021 Golinda Drive, Lorena
   76685) ................ Anthony Wagner
†Gonzales ............. Bobby G. O'Neil
   City Mgr., Buddy Drake
*Goodlow (PO Box 248, Kerens
   75144) ......... Willie Washington Jr.
Goodrich ............... David Armitage
Gordon......................Pat M. Sublett
Goree.............. Darrell Patterson Sr.
†Gorman.................... Robert Ervin
*Graford ..................Carl S. Walston
*†Graham ................George Rogers
   City Mgr., Larry M. Fields
†Granbury................David Southern
   City Mgr., Harold Sandel
Grandfalls ................Leo Bookmiller
   City Admin., Joy Chew
†Grand Prairie Charles Van England
   City Mgr., Tom Hart
*Grand Saline .................. Terry Tolar
*Grandview ............ Michael Schmidt
Granger...........................Jerry Lalla
*Granite Shoals................(vacancy)
*Granjeno (6603 S. FM 494, Mission
   78572-1501) ........... Rafael Garza
   City Admin., Georgia Vines
Grapeland ................... Dick Bridges
†Grapevine ..............William D. Tate
   City Mgr., Roger Nelson
*Grayburg (17572 Grayburg Rd.,
   Sour Lake 77659) ........J.W. Floyd
Grays Prairie (PO Box 116, Scurry
   75158) ......Dean Endres (pro tem)
Greenville ............... Byron W. Chitwood
   City Mgr., Edward Thatcher
Gregory............Fernando P. Gomez
Grey Forest (18502 Scenic Loop Rd.,
   Helotes 78023) ........... Ann Mabry
Groesbeck ...........Mike McLelland
   City Admin., Martha Stanton
Groom...........................Joe Homer
†Groves ................... Brad P. Bailey
   City Mgr., Davis B. Brinson
Groveton ...................Billy Clemons
*Gruver ...................... Mark K. Irwin

   City Mgr., Linda Weller
†Gun Barrel City .......... Tye Thomas
   City Mgr., Bud Henry
Gunter ...............James H. Donohoe
Gustine ............................ Ken Huey

Hackberry (119 Maxwell Rd. , Ste.
   B-7, Frisco 75034).......Jerry Davis
Hale Center ............ Gordon Russell
Hallettsville ........ Warren Grindeland
   City Admin., Tom Donnelly
Hallsburg (1115 Wilbanks Dr.,
   Waco 76705) ......... Mike Glockzin
Hallsville ...............T. Bynum Hatley
*†Haltom City ...............Calvin White
   City Mgr., Richard Torres
Hamilton ...................... Roy Rumsey
   City Admin., Paul Catoe
*Hamlin....................... Melvin Scott
Happy .............................. Sara Tirey
Hardin..................William E. Haynie
†Harker Heights ............Mary Gauer
   City Mgr., Steve Carpenter
†Harlingen.... C. Connie de la Garza
   City Mgr., Roel Rodriguez
Hart ................... Marguerite McLain
Haskell............................. Ken Lane
   City Admin., Sam Watson
Haslet..................Gary D. Hulsey
Hawk Cove (PO Box 670, Quinlan
   75474-3949) ...............Ava Havens
Hawkins.......... Wayne Kirkpatrick Jr.
Hawley...................Ronnie Woodard
*Hays (PO Box 1285, Buda
   78610) ................Joleen B. Brown
   City Admin., Pat Ford
*†Hearne ...................Ruben Gomez
   City Mgr., Kenneth Pryor
Heath.............................Chris Cuny
   City Admin., Dennis Watson
Hebron (4222 Charles St., Carrollton
   75010) .........................Kelly Clem
Hedley .............................Janie Hil
   City Man., Randy Shaw
Hedwig Village (955 Piney Point Rd.,
   Houston 77024).... Dee Srinivasan
Helotes ................Steven F. Hodges
*Hemphill ...............Robert Hamilton
   City Mgr., Donald P. Iles
Hempstead ................Hayden Barry
   City Admin., James R. Vines
*†Henderson ..................Foy Brown
   City Mgr., Kenneth Taylor
Henrietta....................Rick Langford
   City Admin., Joe Pence
†Hereford.........Robert D. Josserand
   City Mgr., (Vacancy at press time)
†Hewitt ............................ Mike Kemp
   City Mgr., Dennis H. Woodard
*Hickory Creek (PO Box 453,
   Lake Dallas 75065) ......Jim Clarke
Hico .............................. Stan Bundy
*†Hidalgo.............John David Franz
   City Mgr., Joe Vera III
Higgins .................. Linda Nicholson
   City Mgr., Randy Immel
Highland Haven ....... Jake Kalisvaart
†Highland Park (4700 Drexel Dr.,
   Dallas 75205) ..Gifford Touchstone
   City Admin., L.A. Patterson
†Highland Village........ Bill Lawrence
   City Mgr., Betty Webb
Hill Country Village (116 Aspen Ln.,
   San Antonio 78232).......T.J. Ralph
   City Admin., David J. Harris
Hillcrest Village (PO Box 1172,
   Alvin 77512) .............Claron Salter
*†Hillsboro ............... Will Lowrance
   City Mgr., Kevin Carruth
Hilshire Village (1003 Wirt Rd., #103,
   Houston 77055) Ershel C. Redd Jr.
*†Hitchcock............Kyle Campbell
*Holiday Lakes (RR 4, Box 747,

Angleton 77515)..Charles Schulze
Holland........................ Frank Horak
*Holliday ........................Allen Moore
Hollywood Park .......... Harold Burris
Hondo.............................Jim Barden
   Acting City Mgr., Beatrice Cervantez
Honey Grove ......... Fred Siebenthall
   City Admin., Don Morrison
Hooks.......................... Steven Foltz
*†Horizon .............Patricia Randleel
†Houston...................Lee P. Brown
Howardwick (HC 2 Box 2230,
   Clarendon 79226) ..Margaret Pettit
Howe ........................Jimmy Haynes
   City Admin., Steven McKay
Hubbard .................Steve Weatherby
   City Mgr., John Moran
Hudson (201 Mount Carmel Rd.,
   Lufkin 75904) ...... Curtis R. Burton
   City Admin., John T. Long
Hudson Oaks (150 N. Oakridge Dr.,
   Weatherford 76087)Gene L. Voyles
   City Admin., Kelly Carta
*Hughes Springs ...... Reba Simpson
   City Mgr., George K. Fite
†Humble.....................Wilson Archer
   City Mgr., James P. Baker
Hunters Creek Village (1 Hunters
   Creek Pl., Houston 77024)
   ..........................Stephen Reichek
Huntington.................Lamar Tinsley
   City Admin., Robert Walker
†Huntsville............. William B. Green
   City Mgr., Bob Hart
†Hurst...............................Bill Souder
   City Mgr., W. Allan Weegar
*Hutchins.....................Artis Johnson
Hutto...........................Mike Fowler
   City Admin., Mel Yantis
Huxley (RR 1, Box 1410, Shelbyville
   75973-9735).............Larry Vaughn

Idalou ........................... Linda Turner
   City Admin., Russell Hamilton
*Impact (PO Box 3116, Abilene
   79604-3116)........... Dallas Perkins
Indian Lake (62 S. Aztec Cove Dr.,
   Los Fresnos 78566) Irene Romero
Industry .........................Alan Kuehn
†Ingleside.......William "Willie" Vaden
   City Mgr., Mike Rhea
*Ingleside on the Bay (PO Box B,
   Ingleside 78362) ... Alfred Robbins
Ingram ............... Monroe Schlabach
*Iowa Colony (12003 County Rd. 65,
   Rosharon 77583) ........ Robert Wall
*Iowa Park............Timothy W. Hunter
   City Admin., Michael C. Price
Iraan ...................... Randy Peterson
Iredell .....................A. D. Woody Jr.
†Irving ...........................Joe Putnam
   City Mgr., Stephen McCullough
Italy.............................Frank Jackson
   City Admin., Lyall Kirton
Itasca...........................Mark Gropp
   City Mgr., Mel Coker

*†Jacinto City ............ Mike Jackson
   City Mgr., Jack Maner
Jacksboro.......................Jerry Craft
   City Mgr., Michael Webb
*†Jacksonville..........Kenneth Durrett
   City Mgr., Ernest Clark
Jamaica Beach (PO Box 5264,
   Galveston 77554)....Victor Pierson
   City Admin., John Brick
†Jasper ................. David G. Barber
   City Mgr., David Douglas
Jayton......................... Albert Brown
*Jefferson ............... Ned Fratangelo
   City Admin., James J. Stokes
†Jersey Village (16501 Jersey Dr.,
   Houston 77040) .......... Stephen C.

Schneider
    City Mgr., R. Dale Brown
Jewett ..................... Judi Kirkpatrick
*Joaquin ................... Steve Hughes
*Johnson City ............Gary Hopkins
*Jolly (194 Milton St., Wichita Falls
    76301) ................. Danny Murphy
Jones Creek (7207 Stephen F. Austin
    Rd., Freeport 77541) ........ George
    Mitchell
    City Admin., Linda Shepard
Jonestown............... Sam G. Billings
    City Admin., Earl C. Hambrick
*Josephine .............. Richard Murray
*†Joshua.....................Randall Luck
    City Mgr., Earl Keaton
Jourdanton............. Tammy K. Clark
    City Mgr., Daniel G. Nick
Junction ............. Jamie Roy Jacoby
Justin ...................... Dale Roberson

Karnes City ........ Edmund R. Prasek
    City Admin., David Carrothers
†Katy ................ Doyle G. Callender
    City Admin., Johnny Nelson
†Kaufman.....................Dennis Berry
    City Mgr., James Blystone
†Keene ....................... Gary Heinrich
    City Admin., James Minor
†Keller................... David C. Phillips
    City Mgr., Lyle H. Dresher
Kemah .................. Richard A. Diehl
Kemp .............. Roy Wayne Friemel
    City Admin., Melinda Oliver
Kempner .................Roger Fancher
Kendleton................. Carolyn Jones
Kenedy............. Minnie S. Robinson
Kenefick (RR 5, Box 525A, Dayton
    77535) ..............Barry D. Bowling
Kennard .........................Bill Thomas
    City Admin., Glenn Westbrook
†Kennedale...............Mark S. Wright
    City Mgr., David Miller
Kerens .........................Gail Christie
    City Admin., Cindy Scott
†Kermit .............. Ted Westmoreland
    City Mgr., Wayne Reynolds
†Kerrville................. Stephen P. Fine
    City Mgr., Ronald K. Patterson Jr.
*†Kilgore.....................Joe T. Parker
    City Mgr., Ronald H. Stephens
*†Killeen ..............Maureen J. Jouett
    City Mgr., David A. Blackburn
†KingsvilleFilemon "Phil" Esquivel Jr.
    City Mgr., Hector M. Hinojosa
†Kirby...................Johnny Duffek Jr.
    City Mgr., Cindy Fox
Kirbyville ................... Dixon Conn Jr.
*Kirvin ............... J.W. "Billy" Walthall
*Knollwood Village (100 Collins Dr.,
    Sherman 75090)... Richard Roelke
*Knox City .........Charles R. Lankford
*Kosse .....................Robert O'Neal
*Kountze .................Fred E. Williams
    City Mgr., Sam M. Barrington
Kress .........................Louise Kirk
    City Admin., Kenny Hughes
Krugerville.................. Shelby Moore
Krum .........................David Polley
*Kurten (1888 N. FM 2038, Bryan
    77808...................Bobby L. Kurten
†Kyle ................. James L. Adkins
    City Man., Thomas Mattis

La Coste ...................... Andy Keller
    City Admin., Ken Roberts
*†Lacy-Lakeview (PO Box 154549,
    Waco 76715) ........ Dennis Cogliati
    City Mgr., Michael Nicoletti
Ladonia.........................Leon Hurse
†La Feria ..................... Carlos Cantu
    City Mgr., Sunny K. Philip
Lago Vista ..................Dennis Jones

    City Mgr., Bob Miller
*†La Grange ...............Janet Moerbe
    City Mgr., Shawn Raborn
*La Grulla (PO Box 197, Grulla
    78548-0197)............Diana Cortez
Laguna Vista (122 Fernandez St.,
    Port Isabel 78578) .... David Privett
*La Joya...........William R. "Billy" Leo
    City Mgr., Mike Alaniz
Lake Bridgeport (301 S. Main St.,
    Bridgeport 76426) .Dwayne Slaten
Lake City (PO Box 177, Mathis
    78368) ............Harold B. McCown
†Lake Dallas................. Steve Wohr
    City Mgr., (Vacancy at press time)
†Lake Jackson......... Shane W. Pirtle
    City Mgr., William P. Yenne
Lakeport (PO Box 7728, Longview
    75607-7728).......Ricky L. Shelton
*Lakeside (129 Lakewood Dr.,
    Mathis 78368).. James M. Thomas
*Lakeside (9830 Confederate Park
    Rd.,Fort Worth 76108). Ed Gentry
    City Admin., Bill Mohr
Lakeside City (PO Box 4287,
    Wichita Falls 76308) ............Steve
    Halloway
    City Admin., Don Sheppard
*Lake Tanglewood (RR 8, Box 35-15,
    Amarillo 79118-9430)...........John
    Langford
Lakeview..........................Kelly Clark
†Lakeway............ Gerald P. Astorino
    City Mgr., Dave Benson
*Lakewood Village . Vincent R. Webb
*†Lake Worth ................Walter Bowen
*†La Marque ......... Larry E. Crow Sr.
    City Mgr., Carol L. McLemore
†Lamesa..................... Mike C. Tyler
    City Mgr., Paul Feazelle
†Lampasas ..................Jack Calvert
    City Mgr., Mike Talbot
†Lancaster....................Joe Tillotson
    City Mgr., Scott Wall
†La Porte........... Norman L. Malone
    City Mgr., Robert T. Herrera
†Laredo ............. Elizabeth G. Flores
    City Mgr., Larry Dovalina
*Latexo .................... David Goolsby
La Vernia ..............Adeline Pierdolla
*La Villa ......................Carlos Perez
    Interim City Mgr., Jaime Gutierrez
*Lavon ...........................Jim Albright
La Ward ................... Hunter Karl
Lawn ................... Johnny B. Hudson
*†League City ......... A. Jeff Harrison
    City Admin., Nicholas J. Finan
*Leakey.....................Jesse Pendley
*†Leander...................Larry Barnett
    City Mgr., Shannon Mattingly
*Leary (RR 5, Box 435, Texarkana
    75501-9434) ...... Randal Mansfield
Lefors.................... Melinda Forsyth
*Leona ..................... Travis J. Oden
*Leonard ................ William J. Yoss
    City Admin., George Henderson
*Leon Valley...............Marcy Meffert
    City Mgr., Walter Geraghty
*Leroy ..................... David Williams
†Levelland ......... Hugh Lynn Bradley
    City Mgr., Greg Ingham
†Lewisville ................... Gene Carey
    City Mgr., Claude King
Lexington ......Robert Lee Willrich Sr.
    City Mgr., Louis Gonzales
†Liberty .................. Bruce Halstead
    City Mgr., Kerry Lacy
Liberty Hill ............. Bob McEachern
*Lincoln Park (110 Parker Pkwy.,
    Aubrey 76227) ............ Loretta Ray
    City Mgr., Nat Parker III
*Lindale .................Bobby McClenny
    City Admin., Owen Scott

Linden ................Wilford S. Penny
Lindsay .....................Norbert Mages
Lipan ................... Alford E. Spencer
†Little Elm ................. Doug Cravey
    City Mgr., J.C. Hughes
†Littlefield.................. Bruce A. Peel
    City Mgr., Brian Carleton
*Little River-Academy (PO Box 521,
    Little River 76554)Ronnie W. White
†Live Oak .......Henry O. Edwards Jr.
    City Mgr., Joseph W. Painter
*Liverpool ................. Allan F. Moore
Livingston .......... Ben R. Ogletree Jr.
    City Mgr., Sam Gordon
Llano ............................. Terry Hutto
†Lockhart ................. Ray Sanders
    City Mgr., Clovia English
Lockney..........................Gary Marr
*Log Cabin ..................Joy Springer
Lometa ...................... Troy Duncan
    City Mgr., Darwin Odom
Lone Oak........... Harold Slemmons
Lone Star.... John Paul Carpenter Jr.
†Longview ....................Earl Roberts
    City Mgr., Rickey Childers
Loraine ...........................Bill Scarber
Lorena.................... Stacy L. Garvin
    City Admin.(vacancy)
*Lorenzo ..............Lester C. Bownds
    City Admin., Mike Cypert
Los Fresnos ............Manuel Abrego
Los Indios ...... Diamantina Bennett
    City Admin., Eluid Garcia
Los Ybañez (1919 CR M, Box 52A,
    Lamesa 79331) ....... Mary Ybañez
*Lott..................... Malcolm Wilkes
Lovelady...........Michael R. Broxson
*Lowry Crossing (1405 S. Bridge-
    farmer Rd., McKinney 75069)
    .....................Jon "Chris" Schroeder
†Lubbock.................Marc McDougal
    City Mgr., Tommy Gonzalez
Lucas (151 Country Club Rd., Allen
    75002-7641)........... Andrea Calve
    City Admin., Linda Shoup
Lueders ................... Russell Mullins
†Lufkin................ Louis A. Bronaugh
    City Mgr., C.G. Maclin
†Luling.....................Mike Hendricks
    City Mgr., Pee Wee Drake
†Lumberton ................... Bill Nelson
    City Admin., Norman P. Reynolds
Lyford ................Rodolfo s. Saldaña
*Lytle ..................... Horace Fincher

Mabank ...................... Larry Teague
    City Admin., Louann Confer
Madisonville ............Scott Singletary
    City Mgr., James K. White
*Magnolia ................Frank Parker III
*Malakoff .................... Pat Isaacson
    City Admin., Jack Caffall
*Malone .............................(vacancy)

Manor ...............................Jeff Turner
†Mansfield..................... David Harry
    City Mgr., Clayton W. Chandler
Manvel............. Delores M. Martin
†Marble Falls........ Scott A. Giddings
    City Mgr., Michael Stoldt
Marfa ................ Oscar Rice Martinez
    City Admin., Curtis A. Schrader
*Marietta..................Glynn Wellborn
Marion .................... Glenn A. Hild
†Marlin .............. Karen Little Meyer
    City Mgr., Arthur Douglas
Marquez .................... Kenneth Clary
*†Marshall ...................... Ed Smith
    City Mgr., Frank Johnson
Marshall Creek (PO Box 1070,
    Roanoke 76262)....Robert Sullivan
    City Admin., Karen Seitzinger
Mart.................... Wanda G. Cornell
Martindale ............. Maebeth Bagley

*Mason ............. Connie Stockbridge
   City Admin., Mark A. Hahn
Matador ................. Rodney Williams
†Mathis ..................... Leonard Cantu
   City Admin., Manuel Lara
Maud ................... Edward M. Holley
*Maypearl ................. Robert Holmes
*†McAllen .................. Leo Montalvo
   City Mgr., Mike R. Perez
McCamey ................. Sherry Phillips
†McGregor ............ James S. Hering
   City Mgr., Dennis McDuffie
†McKinney ..................... Don Dozier
   City Mgr., Lawrence "Larry" W. Rob-
   inson
McLean ............. Charles McClendon
*McLendon-Chisholm (1248 S. St.
   Hwy. 205 Rockwall 75032) ..........
   ....................... Michael D. Donegan
Meadow ................. Brenda Cypert
Meadowlakes ...... Carolyn Richmond

*Meadows Place ....... Mark McGrath
Megargel ...................... Danny Fails
Melissa ................ David E. Dorman
   City Admin., Susan Y. Bradley
Melvin ..................... Bobby David
*Memphis ....................... Joe Davis
Menard ................... Max E. Hooten
   City Admin., Sharon Key
†Mercedes .............. Joel Quintanilla
   City Mgr., Ricardo Garcia
Meridian ............... Jess W. Taylor Jr.
Merkel ................. Jackie Cannon
   City Mgr., Cloy A. Richards
Mertens ..................... Linda Maples
Mertzon ...................... Patsy Kahlig
†Mesquite ............... Mike Anderson
   City Mgr., Ted Barron
†Mexia ...................... Steve Brewer
   City Mgr., Lambert Little
*Miami ..................... Gene Hodges
†Midland ............. Michael J. Canon
   City Mgr., Rick Menchaca
†Midlothian .............. David K. Setzer
   City Mgr., Joseph D. LaBeau
Midway ............ Patrick H. Wakefield
*Milano ........................ Billy Barnett
*Mildred (5417 FM 637, Corsicana
   75110) ................. Nancy Johnson
Miles ...................... Everett Dodson
Milford ................. Othel D. Smith Jr.
*Miller's Cove (RR 3, Box 491, Mt.
   Pleasant 75455)Courtney Marshall
*Millican ......................... (Vacancy)
Millsap ........................... Dick Hess
Mineola .................. Gordon E. Tiner
   City Admin., Dion O. Miller
*†Mineral Wells ... Clarence Holliman
   City Mgr., Lance Howerton
*Mingus ........................... Milo Moffit
*†Mission .............. Norberto Salinas
   Interim City Mgr., Isauro Treviño
†Missouri City .............. Allen Owen
   City Mgr., James Thurmond
Mobeetie ............... Gordon E. Estes
Mobile City (824 Lilac Ln.,
   Rockwall 75087) ... Wanda Cooper
†Monahans ........... David B. Cutbirth
   City Mgr., David Mills
Mont Belvieu ................. Nick Dixon
   City Admin., Bryan Easum
Montgomery ... William B. Cummings

*Moody ...................... Mike Alton
   City Admin., Charleen Dowell
*Moore Station (4818 FM 314S,
   Larue 75770-4552) ...... Arthur Earl
Moran ............................ Marie Smith
Morgan ................ Glenda L. Guidry
*Morgan's Point (PO Box 839,
   La Porte 77572) .. Russell Applebe
   City Admin., Lance Avant
*Morgan's Point Resort ......... Donna

Hartman
   City Mgr., Stacy Hitchman
Morton ........................... Ray Lewis
   City Mgr., Brenda Shaw
Moulton ..................... Harry E. Meyer
Mountain City (PO Box 1494, Buda
   78610-1494) ......... Philip E. Wilbur
   City Man., Jim Herrmann
*Mount Calm .............. Jimmy Tucker
*Mount Enterprise ...... Mark Jackson
†Mount Pleasant ......... Jerry Boatner
   City Mgr., Paul L. Parker
Mount Vernon ............ Darwin McGill
   City Admin., Jim Blanchard
Muenster .............. Henry Weinzapfel
   City Mgr., (Vacancy at press time)
*†Muleshoe ............... Victor E. Leal
   City Mgr., David Brunson
*Mullin ................... A. R. Whisenhunt
*Munday ................. Gary Tidwell
   City Mgr., Jerry Perkins
Murchison ................. Gayle Haynes
Murphy ................. David C. Trudeau
   City Admin., Roger Carlisle
*Mustang (PO Box 325, Corsicana
   75151-0325) ............ Iris Mesker
*Mustang Ridge (12800 Hwy. 183 S.,
   Buda 78610-9407). Alfred Vallejo II

†Nacogdoches ............ Roy Blake Jr.
   City Mgr., J.C. Hughes Jr.
Naples .................. Willie J. Palmore
*Nash ........................... Henry Slaton
   City Admin., Elizabeth Lea
†Nassau Bay (1800 NASA Rd. 1,
   Houston 77058) .. Donald C. Matter
   City Mgr., John D. Kennedy
*Natalia .............. Ruberta C. Vera
Navarro (222 S. Harvard Ave., Corsi-
   cana 75110) ......... Yvonne Capehart
†Navasota .................. Don Otto
   Interim City Mgr., Latham Boone
*Nazareth ............. Ralph Brockman
†Nederland ............ Homer E. Nagel
   City Mgr., André Wimer
*Needville ............. Kermit Blezinger
*Nesbitt (RR 5, Box 88, Marshall
   75670) .............. James R. Watson
Nevada ............. Richard A. Caldwell
Newark ..................... Bill Malone
New Berlin (9180 FM 775, La
   Vernia 78121) ... Freddie Friederick
New Boston ............ Johnny Branson
*†New Braunfels ........ Adam E. Cork
   Interim City Mgr., Charles W. Pinto
Newcastle .................. Wayne Davis
*New Chapel Hill (14039 County Rd.
   220, Tyler 75707) ... J. T. Pinkerton
New Deal .................... Harry Ford
New Fairview (PO Box 855, Rhome
   76078) .................. John Christian
New Home .............. Steve Lisemby
New Hope (PO Box 562, McKinney
   75070) ................. Johnny Hamm
New London ............ Mollie Ward
New Summerfield .... Dan L. Stallings
   City Mgr., B.J. Potts
Newton ..................... David Hines
   City Admin., Donald H. Meek
New Waverly .......... Dan Underwood

*Neylandville (2469 County Road
   4311, Greenville 75401) ...... Kathy
   L. Wilson
Niederwald ................ Rickie Adkins
Nixon ..................... Collie L. Murray
   City Mgr., John D. Byrd
Nocona ...................... Paul S. Gibbs
   City Mgr., Joe Gambill
*Nolanville .......... C.W. "Mike" Carter
*Nome ..................... David Studdert
*Noonday (PO Box 6425, Tyler
   75711) ................. Bennie H. Smith
*Nordheim ............. Vance L. Frosch

*Normangee ................... Larry Huet
*North Cleveland (PO Box 1266,
   Cleveland 77327) ... Robert Bartlett
*Northlake (PO Box 729, Justin
   76247) ............. Michael J. Savoie
†North Richland Hills . Oscar Trevino
   City Mgr., Larry J. Cunningham
*Novice ............................. Don Poe

Oak Grove (PO Box 309, Kaufman
   75142) ............ Kirby McClanahan
*Oakhurst ......... Frank G. AuBuchon
*Oak Leaf ................... Walter Adams
Oak Point.................... Duane Olson
   City Admin., Julie M. Johnston
Oak Ridge (129 Oak Ridge Dr.,
   Gainesville 76240) ...... Karen Paul
Oak Ridge (PO Box 539, Kaufman
   75142) ................. Roy W. Perkins
Oak Ridge North (27424 Robinson
   Rd., Conroe 77385) ... Joe Michels
   City Admin., Paul Mendes
Oak Valley (2211 Oak Valley Ln.,
   Corsicana 75110) ......... Bob O'Dell
*Oakwood .................... Dorothy Bell
*O'Brien ............. Charlene Brothers
*Odem ............. Jessie Rodriguez Sr.
†Odessa ...................... Larry Melton
   City Mgr., Jerry S. McGuire
O'Donnell ............ James E. Williams
Oglesby ................. Kenneth Goodwin
*Old River-Winfree (PO Box 1169,
   Mont Belvieu 77580) ... Joe Landry
Olmos Park (119 W. El Prado Dr.,
   San Antonio 78212) ....... Gerald Z.
   Dubinski Sr.
   City Mgr., Ron Young
†Olney ..................... Phil B. Jeske II
   City Admin., Joe Gambill
Olton ........................ Johnny Adams
   City Mgr., Marvin Tillman
Omaha ................. John Whitecotton
Onalaska ............. Jeanne Ann Byrd
Opdyke West (PO Box 1179,
   Levelland 79336) ... Wayne Riggins
*†Orange ...... William Brown Claybar
   Interim City Mgr., Sam Kittrell
Orange Grove ......... Truett Thomas
   City Admin., Perry R. Young
*Orchard ............. Eugene L. Demny
Ore City ............... Glenn Breazeale
*Overton ................. Wade H. Silvey
   City Mgr., Greg Smith
Ovilla ........................... Bill Turner
   City Admin., Scott Campbell
Oyster Creek ... Richard D. Merriman

*Paducah ...................... Kevin Wood
*Paint Rock ................... Milton Peek
Palacios .................... Bob McMahan
   City Admin., Charles Winfield
*†Palestine .............. George J. Foss
   City Mgr., Curtis Snow
Palisades (115 Brentwood Rd.,
   Amarillo 79118) ............ Pat Knight
*Palmer ............... Michael Greenlee
   City Mgr., (vacancy)
*Palmhurst (4417 N. Shary Rd., Mis-
   sion 78572)Ramiro J. Rodriguez Jr.
   City Mgr., Gary Toothaker
Palm Valley (1313 Stuart Place Rd.,
   Harlingen 78552) . Charles E. Burd
*Palmview(RR11,Box1000, Edinburg
   78539) .................. Jorge G. García
   Interim City Mgr., Ruben
   Gonzales
†Pampa ................... Lonny Robbins
   City Mgr., Mitch Grant
*Panhandle .................. Les McNeill
   City Mgr., Chris Coffman
Panorama (98 Hiwon Dr., Conroe
   77304-1123) ..... Howard L. Kravetz
Pantego .................... Pat Richardson

City Mgr., Larry W. Smith
Paradise................Gerald Cleveland
*†Paris ...............Michael J. Pfiester
City Mgr., Michael E. Malone
Parker (5700 E. Parker Rd., Allen
75002) .....................David Hammel
City Admin., Betty McMenamy
*†Pasadena ..............John Manlove
Pattison...............Linda A. Anderson
Patton Village (16940 Main St.,
Splendora 77372) ...... Cecil White
*Payne Springs (PO Box 2, Mabank
75147) ......J.D. Meredith (pro tem)
†Pearland .......................Tom Reid
City Mgr., Bill Eisen
†Pearsall...............Rolando Segovia
City Mgr., José G. Trevino
*Pecan Gap ........... Warner Cheney
Pecan Hill (PO Box 443, Red Oak
75154) ........... Clinton A. Bittick Jr.
†Pecos ................... Raymond Ortega
City Mgr., Carlos Yerena
Pelican Bay (1300 Pelican Cir.,
Azle 76020) .......... Billy W. Heaton
City Admin., Robert de Saglio
*Penelope .................George Myers
Peñitas ........... Servando Ramírez
City Admin., Alfonso Chapa Jr.
*Pernitas Point (HC 1, Box 1440,
Sandia 78383) .............Joyce Gold
*Perryton........................David Hale
City Mgr., David A. Landis
*Petersburg.........................Jim Fox
City Mgr., Cullen J. Davis
Petrolia...........................G.W. Linton
*Petronila (RR 3, Box 42, Robstown
78380-9677) ...... William J. Ordner
†Pflugerville ................. Scott Winton
City Mgr., T. Steven Jones
†Pharr..................... Ricardo Medina
City Mgr., Benito Lopez
Pilot Point.......Toby Wayland Osburn
City Admin., Carolyn Boerner
*Pine Forest (PO Box 1004, Vidor
77670-1004) ............. Jody Crump
Pinehurst (3640 Mockingbird St.,
Orange 77630) ..........J.L. Runnels
City Admin., C.R. Nash
*Pine Island (RR 3, Box 70AF,
Hempstead 77445) ....Debra Ferris
*Pineland ....................John O. Booker
Piney Point Village (7721 San Felipe,
#100 Houston 77063) .. C. Barrett
Monday II
Pittsburg.................. D. H. Abernathy
City Mgr., Ned C. Muse
Plains...................... Shane McKinzie
City Man., Edward Hansen
†Plainview.............. Lloyd C. Woods
City Mgr., James P. Jeffers
*†Plano .......................... Pat Evans
City Mgr., Thomas H. Muehlenbeck
*Pleak Village (6621 FM 2218 Rd.,
Richmond 77469-9075) .............
............................ Margie M. Krenek
*Pleasant Valley (4006 Highway 287
E, Iowa Park 76367) ...... Raymond
Haynes
City Mgr., Jeff Watts
†Pleasanton.................... Bill Carroll
City Mgr., William O. Lamb
*Plum Grove (PO Box 1358,
Splendora 77372) ...... T.W. Garrett
Point......................Raymond Clifton
Point Blank.....................Lillian Bratton
*Point Comfort .Pamela H. Lambden
Point Venture (549 Venture Blvd. S.
Leander 78645-8547) .......... Terry
Hickman
Ponder .................. Vivian Cockburn
†Port Aransas ................Glenn Martin
City Mgr., Tommy M. Brooks
†Port Arthur ............. Oscar G. Ortiz

City Mgr., Steve Fitzgibbons
†Port Isabel ....... Patrick H. Marchan
City Mgr., Robert H. García
†Portland ........................ Joe Burke
City Mgr., Mike Tanner
†Port Lavaca.....................Alex Davila
City Mgr., Gary Broz
†Port Neches............. Glenn Johnson
City Mgr., A.R. "Randy" Kimler
Post..................................Archie Gill
City Mgr., Fred Stephens
*Post Oak Bend (PO Box 758, Kauf-
man 75142) ......... Wayne Rebholz
*Poteet............... Diana M. Martinez
Poth ..................... LaNell Matthews
Pottsboro ....................Steve Atkins
City Admin., Manuel Leal
Powell ..................... Dennis Bancroft
Poynor ...................... Dannie Smith
*Prairie View ......... Frank D. Jackson
Premont....................Norma Tullos
Presidio................. Alcee M. Tavarez
City Admin., Barry L. Sullivan
*Primera................John D. Osbourne
Princeton ..................... Bill Caldwell
City Admin., Steve Goram
*Progreso .................. Arturo Valdez
City Admin., Fred Espinosa
*Progreso Lakes (PO Box 760,
Progreso 78579)..... Alec G. Young
*Prosper...................... Jim Dunmire
City Admin., Jennifer Finley
*Putnam........................... Roy Petty
*Pyote ........................ Glen Garland

*†Quanah .................Ann Sparkman
City Admin., Dena Daniel
Queen City..............Bobby Bowman
*Quinlan...........................Lois Cagle
Quintana ..................... James Nevil
*Quitaque.............. Roland Hamilton
City Mgr., Maria Cruz
Quitman .............Larry W. Robertson

*Ralls...................Sandra Moore
City Admin., Donald R. Kerns
Rancho Viejo ................ Ray Downs
City Admin., Cheryl J. Kretz
*†Ranger ...................... Todd Mayes
†Rangerville (31850 Rangerville Rd.,
San Benito 78586). Wayne Halbert
Rankin ..... Cora Gaynelle McFadden
Ransom Canyon.Robert G. Englund
City Admin., Melissa Verett
*Ravenna................ Andy H. Walker
*†Raymondville..........Joe Alexandre
City Mgr., Eleazar García Jr.
Red Lick (PO Box 870, Nash
75569) ..................... Michael Peek
†Red Oak ................Todd B. Little
City Mgr., Ken Pfeifer
Redwater ................. Beverly Phares
Refugio .............................Ray Jaso
Reklaw................... Gilbert Stafford
Reno (Lamar Co.).......W.M. "Bubba"
Coston
City Admin., Shannon Barrentine
*Reno (195 W. Reno Rd., Azle
76020) .................. Loyd L. Bailey
*Retreat (125 Ingham Rd., Corsicana
75110) ............. Janice Barfknecht
Rhome ..................... Nell Fernandez
Rice ................................Larry Bailey
†Richardson .................Gary Slagel
City Mgr., Bill Keffler
Richland.................Dolores Baldwin
†Richland Hills ...... Nelda S. Stroder
City Mgr., Jim Quin
Richland Springs Dale McKinnerney
Richmond ............. Hilmar G. Moore
City Mgr., R. Glen Gilmore
Richwood................ Peggy Gartman
Riesel........................ Keith Koester

Rio Bravo (1402 Centeno Lane,
Laredo 78046).. Juan G. Gonzalez
City Admin., Jorge Luis Benavides
*Rio Grande City ....Baldemar Garza
City Admin., Leonardo Olivares
Rio Hondo ......... Marcello Benavidez
City Admin., José L. Lopez
Rio Vista .................Sam C. Bigham
Rising Star................Mike McGinn
City Admin., Jan Clark
†River Oaks (4900 River Oaks Blvd,
Fort Worth 76114) ....Jack Adkison
City Admin., Bonnie Gibbs
Riverside ...........................Frank Rich
Roanoke .....................Randy W. Corn
City Mgr., Jimmy Stathatos
*Roaring Springs ......Corky Marshall
City Mgr., Robert Osborn
*Robert Lee .............. Garland Davis
Robinson ................. Bryan Ferguson
City Mgr., Richard Fletcher
*†Robstown .............Rodrigo Ramon
Roby ............................Lance Green
City Mgr., Claude A. Day
Rochester........Marvin Stegemoeller
City Mgr., Gregg Hearn
†Rockdale .................Wallace Jones
City Mgr., Sue Foster
†Rockport.............Todd W. Pearson
City Mgr., Thomas J. Blazek
Rocksprings....Charles W. Carson III
†Rockwall ......................Ken Jones
City Mgr., Julie Couch
*Rocky Mound (PO Box 795,
Pittsburg 75686) .....Noble T. Smith
City Mgr., Mary L. Smith
Rogers........Thomas Carter-Maddux
Rollingwood.................Thom Farrell
Roma.....................Fernando Pena
*Roman Forest .... Floyd O. Jackson
*Ropesville ...........Hortensia Ochoa
Roscoe ................... Christopher Stice
City Man., Jack Brown
*Rosebud.....................Kenny Hensel
City Mgr., Miles Shaunfield
Rose City (370 S. Rose City Dr.,
Vidor 77662)........... David E. Bush
*Rose Hill Acres (PO Box 8285,
Lumberton 77657)... Steve Barnett
†Rosenberg.............Joe M. Gurecky
City Mgr., Jeff Braun
Ross .................James L. Jaska Sr.
*Rosser........................ Albert Davis
Rotan.....................Jerry A. Marshall
City Admin., Harold Sanders
Round Mountain ....... Alvin Gutierrez
†Round Rock...............Nyle Maxwell
City Mgr., James Nuse
Round Top .................Carole Nagel
†Rowlett ............ C. Shane Johnson
City Mgr., Susan K. Thorpe
*Roxton.......................... Bill Colwell
Royse City ...................Jim Mellody
City Admin., Connie F. Goodwin
Rule ............. Malcolm Herttenberger
Runaway Bay ............. Walt Warner
City Coord., Joe White
Runge......................Jack Roberson
†Rusk ................. Charles A. Horton
City Mgr., Kevin Bowden

Sabinal ................... Henry Alvarado
*†Sachse ......................Hugh Cairns
City Mgr., Bill Atkinson
Sadler .........................Thomas Filip
†Saginaw......................Frankie Robbins
City Mgr., Nan Stanford
St. Hedwig ................Mary Jo Dylla
*Saint Jo ............... Jimmy Dennis Jr.
St. Paul (2505 Butscher's Block,
Wylie 75098) ....... Steve Hufstetler
†San Angelo.............Joseph W. Lown
City Mgr., Thomas L. Adams

†San Antonio ........ Edward D. Garza
City Mgr., Terry M. Brechtel
San Augustine ......Patrick H. Fussell
City Mgr., James Duke Lyons
†San Benito ............Cesar Gonzalez
City Mgr., Victor Trevino
*Sanctuary (PO Box 125, Azle
76098) .................. Floyd Galloway
San Diego .......Zenaida Montemayor
City Admin., Ruben Maldonado
*San Elizario ..................... Raul Diaz
*San Felipe ................. Bobby Byars
Sanford ........................ Gary Moore
*†Sanger .................. Tommy Kincaid
City Mgr., Jack Smith
†San Juan............Roberto F. Loredo
City Mgr., Jorge A. Arcaute
San Leanna (PO Box 1107,
Manchaca 78652)James E. Payne
*†San Marcos . Robert Habingreither
City Mgr., Dan O'Leary
San Patricio (5617 Main St., Mathis
78368) ........ Lonnie Glasscock III
*San Perlita.............Oscar de Luna
*San Saba .................. David Parker
City Admin., Joe Ragsdale
*Sansom Park (5500 Buchanan St.,
Fort Worth 76114) .... Mike Wasser
City Admin., Deana McMullen
Santa Anna ....Jean Robinett Findley
*Santa Clara (PO Box 429, Marion
78124) .......... David D. Mueller
†Santa Fe ................. Robert Cheek
City Mgr., Joe Dickson
Santa Rosa ...... Ruben Ochoa Jr.
City Admin., Javier Mendez
*Savoy........................ Cheryl Halter
†Schertz ..................Hal Baldwin
City Mgr., Mark Marquez
*Schulenburg ..............Leo Kopecky
City Admin., Ronald Brossman
*Scotland ............. Grady Schenk Sr.
*Scottsville ..............Walter Johnson
†Seabrook .............. Robin C. Riley
City Mgr., Robert T. "Bo" McDaniel
Seadrift ........................Billy F. Ezell
*†Seagoville............. David Maroney
City Mgr., Don Gray
Seagraves...... Patrick L. McAdoo Sr.
†Sealy..................... Betty Reinbeck
City Mgr., John Maresh
†Seguin .......... Mark Stautzenberger
City Mgr., Jack Hamlett
Selma ........................ James Parma
City Admin., Ken Roberts
*†Seminole ..................... Bill Prince
City Admin., Tommy Phillips
*Seven Oaks (PO Box 540, Leggett
77350) ..............Gloria K. English
*Seven Points ........ Gerald E. Taylor
Seymour ................. Dan Craighead
City Admin., Joe Shephard
Shady Shores (PO Box 362, Lake
Dallas 75065) ....... Olive Stephens
Shallowater.................. Moe Dozier
*Shamrock ............. Glen Switzer
City Mgr., Johnny Rhodes
*Shavano Park (99 Saddletree Rd.,
San Antonio 78231).........Thomas
Peyton
City Mgr., Matt Smith
*Shenandoah (29811 Interstate 45,
Spring 77381) ....David J. Vetter Jr.
City Admin., Paul Frederiksen
Shepherd ..................... Jerry Wade
City Admin., O.L. Davenport
*†Sherman ................. Tom Osburn
City Mgr., L. Scott Wall
Shiner ..................Laura Watzlavick
Shoreacres .......... Nancy Edmonson
City Man., Shari Tait
†Silsbee..................Regina Lindsey
City Mgr., Ricky Jorgensen

Silverton ..................Lane B. Garvin
City Admin., Jerry Patton
Simonton ................... Dub Sabrsula
†Sinton ................... Pete Gonzales
City Mgr., "Jackie" Knox Jr.
Skellytown .................. Mike Chaney
*†Slaton ..................... Don Kendrick
City Admin., Mitch Grant
*Smiley ...............Donald R. Janicek
Smithville .......... Renee D. Blaschke
City Mgr., Tex Middlebrook
Smyer .................. Mary Beth Sims
*Snook......................John W. See III
*†Snyder.........Francene Allen-Noah
City Mgr., John W. Gayle
*Socorro ............... Irma S. Sanchez
Somerset ............. Richard S. Padilla
City Admin., Linda Wertz
Somerville........ Barbara J. Pederson
Sonora ............... James B. Stephen
City Mgr., R.B. "Brent" Gesch
*Sour Lake.............. Bruce Robinson
City Mgr., Larry Saurage
South Houston .......... Eloise Smith
†Southlake......... Andy Wambsganss
City Mgr., Billy Campbell
Southmayd ...................... Billy Kerr
*South Mountain (107 Barton Ln.,
Gatesville 76528) .....Billy Mayhew
*South Padre Island... Bob Pinkerton
City Mgr., Raymond H. Kendall
Southside Place (6309 Edloe St.,
Houston 77005)Richard Rothfelder
City Mgr., David Moss
Spearman.................. Steve Benton
City Mgr., Robert Patrick
Splendora ......... Carol Wayne Carley
*Spofford....................J. B. Herndon
*Springlake ......... Harlon Watson
Springtown .....................Barry Bobo
City Admin., Bill Herrington
Spring Valley (1025 Campbell Rd.,
Houston 77055)......Tammy Canon
City Admin., Richard R. Rocken-
baugh
Spur........................Jackie Reagan
Stafford .........Leonard Scarcella
Stagecoach (PO Box 364, Tomball
77377) .............. Roger W. Daigger
*†Stamford........... Louis E. Johnson
City Mgr., Ken Roberson
*Stanton...................... Lester Baker
City Mgr., Danny Fryar
*Star Harbor (PO Box 949, Malakoff
75148-0949) ........ Walter Bingham
*†Stephenville...............John Moser
City Admin., Mike Castro
*Sterling City................Terry Wojtek
*Stinnett ............... Tommy Batson
City Admin., James Stroud
*Stockdale .......................Tony Malik
City Mgr., Carl Lambeck
*Stratford ................... David Brown
City Admin., Don Nicholson
*Strawn ............... Paul L. Stephen II
*Streetman ................. Billy R. Butler
Sudan ...............Freddie Maxwell
†Sugar Land.......... David G. Wallace
City Mgr., Allen Bogard
*Sullivan City ...........Gumaro Flores
City Mgr., Robert Montes
*†Sulphur Springs .......Garry Jordan
City Mgr., Marc Maxwell
Sundown........................Jim Winn
City Admin., Brad Stafford
Sunnyvale.......................Jim Phaup
City Admin., Larry Graves
*Sunray ....................Mike Raymond
City Mgr., Greg Smith
Sunrise Beach Village ..... Patricia E.
Frain
Sunset .....................Danny Russell
Sunset Valley ...............Terry Cowan

*Sun Valley (RR 2, Box 800, Paris
75462) ...............Maria Z. Wagnon
Surfside Beach (1304 Monument Dr.,
Freeport 77541) ......Larry Davison
†Sweeny.................. Larry G. Piper
City Mgr., H.T. "Tim" Moss
*†Sweetwater ............Jay Lawrence
City Mgr., David Maddox

Taft................................Jerry L. King
City Mgr., Florencio P. Sauceda
Tahoka ........................Mike Mensch
City Admin., Jerry W. Webster
*Talco.......................K.M. "Mike" Sloan
Talty (PO Box 565, Forney 75126
................................ Allison Weaver
Tatum..........................Bob Harris
*†Taylor ................ Jeffrey M. Berger
City Mgr., Frank L. Salvato
Taylor Lake Village Natalie S. O'Neill
Teague...................Earnest G. Pack
City Admin., Jeff Looney
Tehuacana Herman Douglas East Jr.
†Temple ............... William A. Jones III
City Mgr., Mark S. Watson
Tenaha..................... George N. Bowers
*†Terrell ................Frances Anderson
City Mgr., Gordon C. Pierce
†Terrell Hills .........J. Bradford Camp
City Mgr., Cal D. Johnson
†Texarkana.............James Bramlett
City Mgr., George T. Shackelford
†Texas City.................Carlos Garza
*Texhoma ...................Garland Dahl
*Texline ................... Larry Smith
City Mgr., Clark Teague
†The Colony .................... (vacancy)
City Mgr., Lanny S. Lambert
Thompsons ..... Freddie Newsome Jr.
Thorndale ........... Gerald Niemtschk
City Mgr., Keith Kiesling
Thornton.........James W. Jackson Jr.
Thorntonville (PO Box 740, Mona-
hans 79756) ...........David Mitchell
Thrall .........................James Dvorak
*Three Rivers ........ Jerry D. Wheeler
City Admin., Marian R. Forehand
*Throckmorton............. Will Carroll
*Tiki Island, Village of Charles Everts
Timbercreek Canyon (101 S. Timber-
creek Dr., Amarillo 79118)...Elaine
Dollar
*Timpson ........... Douglas McDonald
Tioga.....................Stanley Kemp
Tira (RR 7, Box 220, Sulphur
Springs 75482)..........John Hadley
*Toco (2103 Chestnut Dr., Brookston
75421)..............John Jason Waller
*Todd Mission (390 N. Millcreek Dr.,
Plantersville 77363)..........George
Coulam
Tolar..............................Tom Brown
†Tomball .................H.G. Harrington
City Mgr., Ben Griffin
Tom Bean ................ Tom Wilthers
*Tool (RR 6, Box 843, Kemp
75143) ......................Scott Confer
Toyah ........................ Ann Marsh
Trent ............................James Wallis
Trenton .....................David Hamrick
Trinidad...................William S. Lundy
City Admin., Nelda Cartlidge
*Trinity ......................... Lyle Stubbs
Trophy Club ............. Scott A. Smith
City Mgr., Donna Welsh
*Troup .........................John Whitsell
City Admin., Russ Obar
*Troy ....................Ernest Thompson
†Tulia .........................Boyd Vaughn
City Mgr., Paula Wilson
*Turkey .................Pat Carson (Mr.)
City Mgr., Jerry Landry
Tuscola ................ Marvin Whiteaker

Tye ...................... Gayland Childers
*†Tyler.......................... Joey Seeber
  City Mgr., Pinkney Butler
Uhland ..................... Dan T. Sorrells
*Uncertain..................... Betty Holder
*Union Grove (RR 2, Box 196FF,
  Gladewater 75647) Randy Simcox
†Universal City.....Wesley D. Becken
  City Mgr., Kenneth A. Taylor
†University Park (3800 University
Blvd.,
  Dallas 75205-1711) Harold F. Peek
  City Mgr., Bob Livingston
†Uvalde....Josue "George" Garza Jr.
  City Man., John H. Harrell
Valentine................ Jesús Calderon
Valley Mills ................. Bill Lancaster
*Valley View ............... Frank Hacker
*Van ............................ E.L. Raulston
Van Alstyne..................Willie Boddie
  City Man., Jerry White
Van Horn.................. Okey D. Lucas
  City Admin., Rebecca L. Brewster
Vega..................... Mark J. Groneman
Venus..................... Carolyn Welcher
  City Admin., Jim Cooper
†Vernon ...................... Kelly Couch
  City Mgr., Jim Murray
*†Victoria ................ Gary Middleton
  City Mgr., Denny L. Arnold
†Vidor ...........................Joe Hopkins
  City Mgr., Brian D. Smith
Village of the Hills (102 Trophy Dr.,
  Austin 78738) .... Virginia W. Jones
Vinton (436 Vinton Rd., Anthony
  79821) ............. Antonio Castro St.

*†Waco ................... Linda Ethridge
  City Mgr., Kathy S. Rice
Waelder ...........................Roy Tovar
Wake Village ........Mike Huddleston
  City Admin., Bob Long
Waller....................Danny Marburger
Wallis ................... Tony I. Salazar Jr.
Walnut Springs ......... David L. Keller
Warren City (3004 George Richey
  Rd., Gladewater 75647).. Ricky J.
  Wallace
Waskom.......................Jesse Moore
*†Watauga ............. Henry J. Jeffries
  Interim City Mgr., Kerry Lacy
†Waxahachie ................ Joe Jenkins
  City Mgr., Robert W. Sokoll
*†Weatherford.............Joe M. Tison
  City Mgr., Larry Patterson

†Webster ............... Donna Rogers
  City Mgr., H. Frank Simpson
*Weimar.................... Bennie Kosler
  City Mgr., Randal W. Jones
*Weinert..................... Julian Estrada
Weir .......................... Mervin Walker
Wellington................... Gary Brewer
  City Mgr., Jon Sessions
*Wellman ................. Marty Lindsey
Wells..................... Jerry D. Ellerbee
†Weslaco................ Joe V. Sanchez
  City Mgr., Francisco Castellanos
West .................. Russell D. Willsey
  City Mgr., Kenneth Kubala
*Westbrook.......................J. L. Rees
*West Columbia....... David E. Foster
  City Mgr., Roger L. Mumby
Westlake ..................... Scott Bradley
  City Mgr., Trent Petty
*West Lake Hills ..Dwight Thompson
  City Admin., Daniel E. "Stump"
  Sowada
*Westminster ................ Phil Gophin
  City Mgr., Peter J. Collumb
Weston ....................Patti Harrington
†West Orange .......... Roy McDonald
*Westover Hills (5824 Merrymount,
  Fort Worth 76107) ............Earle A.
  Shields Jr.
  City Mgr., B.J. Tuttleton
*West Tawakoni (1533 E. Highway
  276, Quinlan 75474)..Don Tanoos
  City Admin., Dick Gillespie
†West University Place (3800
Univer-
  sity Blvd., Houston 77005) .... Burt
  Ballanfant
  City Mgr., Michael Ross
*Westworth Village (311 Burton Hill
  Rd., Fort Worth 76114)
  ............................... Andy Fontenot
†Wharton......... Garland S. Novosad
  City Mgr., Andres Garza Jr.
Wheeler ........................Wanda Herd
White Deer ..................... Bart Wyatt
Whiteface............... Harold Harrison
*†Whitehouse ...................Mike Gray
  City Mgr., Ronny Fite
*White Oak ................... Tim Vaughn
  City Mgr., Ralph J. Weaver
*Whitesboro.................. W.D. Welch
  City Admin., Michael Marter
†White Settlement .. James O. Ouzts
  City Mgr., Peter Nuckolls
Whitewright.................. Bill Goodson

Whitney ........................Gwen Evans
†Wichita Falls .......William K. Altman
  City Mgr., James P. Berzina
Wickett.................. Harold Ferguson
Willis ............................. Leonard Reed
  City Coord., Michael C. Arthur
*Willow Park ....James H. Poythress
  City Admin., Claud Arnold
Wills Point.................... Roy Caldwell
  City Mgr.,C.C. "Butch" Girdley
*Wilmer.......................... Linda Root
  City Admin.,Betty Kay Schlesinger
*Wilson ......................Jackie Bishop
Wimberley ............... Stephen Klepfer
  City Mgr., Stephen Harrison
Windcrest ............... Jack Leonhardt
  City Admin., Ronnie Cain
Windom ................Billy Joe Roberts
*Windthorst............. Sue Steinberger
  City Mgr., Donald Frerich
*Winfield ...................... Mark Rigney
Wink ....................... Betty Lou Dodd
Winnsboro ............Carolyn S. Jones
  City Admin., Ronny Knight
*Winona...........................Pat Schlau
Winters ...............Dawson McGuffin
  City Mgr., Aref Hassan
Wixon Valley (PO Box 105, Kurten
  77862) ...................Ruby Andrews
Wolfe City ...........Richard C. Owens
Wolfforth ..................L.C. Chambers
  City Admin., Frankie Pittman
*Woodbranch Village (PO Box 804,
  New Caney 77357).. Jim Beaird Jr.
Woodcreek ..................... Henry Neil
  City Admin., Peg Tharp
*Woodloch (PO Box 1379, Conroe
  77305) ...............Oran Chappell Jr.
  City Admin., Diane L. Lincoln
Woodsboro .... Joseph A. Hernández
*Woodson ..............Bobby Mathiews
Woodville...............Jimmie R. Cooley
  City Admin., Don Shaw
†Woodway (924 Estates Dr., Waco
  76712) ............... Donald J. Baker
  City Mgr., Yousry "Yost" Zakhary
Wortham..................... Judy Edwards
†Wylie.......................... John Mondy
  City Mgr., Anthony "Biff" Johnson
Yantis..........................Jerry E. Miller
†Yoakum............... Anita Rodriguez
  City Mgr., Calvin Cook
Yorktown......... Wilson Leon Strahan
  City Admin., Milton Ledwig
Zavalla ............. Author Bridges Jr. ☆

# Galveston and Amarillo Were
# Municipal Government Pioneers
### by Mary G. Ramos

The ferment of political change that pervaded turn-of-the-20th-century Texas included agitation for municipal-government reform. The Progressive-era broom was eager to sweep old forms of city government out the door and replace them with new ones. Galveston and Amarillo were the stages on which the two types of city government that would predominate in 20th-century and early 21st century Texas first appeared.

## Galveston's New Government

Galveston invented the commission form of city government in the aftermath of the devastating hurricane of Sept. 8, 1900, which took the lives of 6,000 people in the city of Galveston alone and destroyed at least $17 million worth of property.

The perceived need for a stronger, more centralized, more efficient form of government to direct recovery efforts was the proximate cause of the move to change the form of Galveston's government. But dissatisfaction with Galveston's previous government had been building during the previous decade, especially within the ranks of financial and commercial leaders.

Galveston had operated under a mayor-council charter prior to 1890, with 12 aldermen elected by wards. A charter amendment in 1890 added four aldermen elected at large. The charter was again amended in the mid-

1890s to provide to 12 councilmen who were elected at large, but were required to live in the wards they represented.

Businessmen and commercial interests with substantial financial investments in the city were becoming impatient with a council composed largely of the working class: In 1895, it included two longshoremen, a bartender and a journeyman printer. Many fiscal irregularities were uncovered, probably exacerbated by the fact that the official accountant did not know how to keep books.

Lively competition in the next two municipal elections produced a council dominated by small businessmen. No one faction was in firm control, however, and there was no clear direction for the city. The financial situation was bleak before the storm danced its deadly way across the island. Afterward, it was disastrous.

Two weeks after the storm —while the smoke from the funeral pyres was still rising — the council began discussing the need for a city government that could lead Galveston through the recovery period. At this point, the Deep Water Committee assumed leadership.

The Deep Water Committee had been formed in 1882 to promote harbor improvements that would enable the port of Galveston to handle large ships. The DWC could be described as the power elite of the island city: Members of the committee and their business associates dominated the boards of six of the eight local banks, controlled 62 percent of corporate capital and 75 percent of the most valuable real estate in the city.

In political dry dock during the 1890s, the committee came forward after the storm with a plan for a new form of government. The DWC proposed a commission appointed by the governor and composed of a mayor-president and four commissioners. Each commissioner would administer a division of city government: finance and revenue, police and fire, waterworks and sewerage, and streets and public improvements. The committee further suggested that the state exempt Galveston from paying state and county taxes for two years, that the bonded debt be refinanced at a lower rate, and that a local tax be passed to raise the grade level of the island.

In 1900, any change in city charters had to be approved by the legislature. Rather than try to gain popular support at home, the DWC appealed directly to the state legislature for enabling legislation for their groundbreaking charter. The original plan called for all five commission members to be appointed, which prompted one politician to complain that the plan "disfranchises free citizens of Texas . . . [and] tramples underfoot the fundamental principles of a free republic."

The legislature approved an amended version providing for the election of two commissioners and the appointment of three. In 1903, under the threat of court challenges to the constitutionality of the charter, the legislature required all commissioners to be elected. There were still objections from some quarters that an at-large commission would be unrepresentative. However, Galveston hung onto the commission form of city government, with modifications, until 1960.

Swept up in the fever of municipal reform, many Texas cities followed Galveston's lead. Houston received legislative approval of a commission charter in 1905, soon followed by Dallas, Fort Worth, El Paso, Denison and Greenville. In 1907, Des Moines, Iowa,

became the first of hundreds of cities in other states to embrace the commission form of government. Forty Texas cities had followed Galveston's lead by 1915, and the total reached about 200 by 1950.

Eventually, cities discovered that the commission form of government was as subject to abuse as any other, and the council-manager plan gained favor, particularly among the larger cities.

## Council-Manager Introduced by Amarillo

For several years after Amarillo first incorporated as a city in 1892, it had virtually no municipal government. The Panhandle city's first governing body was a mayor and aldermen. From the first there were fights over how much unpopulated land the city was trying to claim — and tax. The nationwide financial crisis of 1893 added to the confusion, and court injunctions rendered the city council ineffective. From 1894 to 1899, Potter County and the Texas Rangers ran Amarillo's city government.

In 1899, voters approved new articles of incorporation with more realistic city limits. Then the population mushroomed. Amarillo's 1892 population of fewer than 500 residents almost tripled by the turn of the century, and reached almost 10,000 by 1910. The old ward system of government couldn't cope with the population explosion. Years of deficit financing reached a crisis, and Amarillo called upon the 33rd Texas Legislature for help.

The Legislature responded by granting home-rule status to cities of at least 5,000 that wanted it; i.e., they could choose their own form of government within certain limits. Amarillo was the first city in Texas to adopt the council-manager plan, which is the most popular form of government for home-rule cities in Texas today.

Amarillo's' original plan provided that the voters elect a mayor and four commissioners at large every two years. The policies decided upon by the governing body were then carried out by the city manager, an administrator hired by the commissioners.

Terrell adopted the council-manager plan in 1913, followed in 1914 by Taylor and Denton.

Today, most councils or commissions under the council-manager form of government have between five and nine members, many of whom serve without pay or for a token fee. The commission makes policies on issues such as taxation, police protection and zoning ordinances. The manager, a professional municipal administrator, implements those policies.

Of the largest Texas cities, only Houston has chosen not to adopt this form of government. Houston has a strong-mayor government, in which the mayor assumes the responsibilities of both leader of the council and professional administrator.

*Mary G. Ramos* is editor emerita of the Texas Almanac.

## For further reading

Jones, Eugene W. and Joe W. Ericson, Lyle C. Brown and Robert S. Trotter Jr., *"Practicing Texas Politics,"* 2nd edition; Houghton Mifflin Company, Boston, 1974.

McComb, David G., *"Galveston: A History"*; University of Texas Press, Austin 1986.

Miller, Char, and Heywood T. Sanders, eds., *"Urban Texas: Politics and Development"*; Texas A&M University Press, College Station, 1990. ☆

# Regional Councils of Government

The concept of regional planning and cooperation, fostered by enabling legislation in 1965, has spread across Texas since organization of the **North Central Texas Council of Governments** in 1966.

Regional councils are voluntary associations of local governments that deal with problems and planning needs that cross the boundaries of individual local governments or that require regional attention. These concerns may include criminal justice, emergency communications, job-training programs, solid-waste management, transportation needs, and water-quality management. The councils make recommendations to member governments and may assist in implementing the plans.

The **Texas Association of Regional Councils** is at 1305 San Antonio St., Austin 78701; 512-478-4715; fax: 512-478-1049. Financing is provided by the local governments, the state and the federal government.

At right is a **map** showing the locations of the **24 regional councils**, along with a list of the regional councils, the **counties served** and the **executive director**.

**1. Panhandle Regional Planning Commission:** Armstrong, Briscoe, Carson, Castro, Childress, Collingsworth, Dallam, Deaf Smith, Donley, Gray, Hall, Hansford, Hartley, Hemphill, Hutchinson, Lipscomb, Moore, Ochiltree, Oldham, Parmer, Potter, Randall, Roberts, Sherman, Swisher and Wheeler. Gary Pitner, PO Box 9257, Amarillo 79105-9257; 806-372-3381.

**2. South Plains Association of Governments:** Bailey, Cochran, Crosby, Dickens, Floyd, Garza, Hale, Hockley, King, Lamb, Lubbock, Lynn, Motley, Terry and Yoakum. Jerry D. Casstevens, PO Box 3730, Lubbock 79452-3730; 806-762-8721.

**3. Nortex Regional Planning Commission:** Archer, Baylor, Clay, Cottle, Foard, Hardeman, Jack, Montague, Wichita, Wilbarger and Young. Dennis Wilde, PO Box 5144, Wichita Falls 76307-5144; 940-322-5281.

**4. North Central Texas Council of Governments:** Collin, Dallas, Denton, Ellis, Erath, Hood, Hunt, Johnson, Kaufman, Navarro, Palo Pinto, Parker, Rockwall, Somervell, Tarrant and Wise. R. Michael Eastland, PO Box 5888, Arlington 76005-5888; 817-640-3300.

**5. Ark-Tex Council of Governments:** Bowie, Cass, Delta, Franklin, Hopkins, Lamar, Morris, Red River, Titus and Miller County, Ark. L.D. Williamson, PO Box 5307, Texarkana, Texas 75505-5307; 903-832-8636.

**6. East Texas Council of Governments:** Anderson, Camp, Cherokee, Gregg, Harrison, Henderson, Marion, Panola, Rains, Rusk, Smith, Upshur, Van Zandt and Wood. Glynn Knight, 3800 Stone Rd., Kilgore 75662-6937; 903-984-8641.

**7. West Central Texas Council of Governments:** Brown, Callahan, Coleman, Comanche, Eastland, Fisher, Haskell, Jones, Kent, Knox, Mitchell, Nolan, Runnels, Scurry, Shackelford, Stephens, Stonewall, Taylor and Throckmorton. Brad Helbert, PO Box 3195, Abilene 79601-3195; 325-672-8544.

**8. Rio Grande Council of Governments:** Brewster, Culberson, El Paso, Hudspeth, Jeff Davis, Presidio and Doña Ana Co., New Mexico. Jake Brisbin Jr., 1100 N. Stanton, Ste. 610, El Paso 79902-4155; 915-533-0998.

**9. Permian Basin Regional Planning Commission:** Andrews, Borden, Crane, Dawson, Ector, Gaines, Glasscock, Howard, Loving, Martin, Midland, Pecos, Reeves, Terrell, Upton, Ward and Winkler. Gary Gaston, PO Box 60660, Midland 79711-0660; 432-563-1061.

**10. Concho Valley Council of Governments:** Coke, Concho, Crockett, Irion, Kimble, Mason, McCulloch, Menard, Reagan, Schleicher, Sterling, Sutton and Tom Green. Jeffrey Sutton, Box 60050, San Angelo 76906-0050; 915-944-9666.

**11. Heart of Texas Council of Governments:** Bosque, Falls, Freestone, Hill, Limestone and McLennan. Kenneth Simons, 300 Franklin Ave., Waco 76701-2244; 254-756-7822.

**12. Capital Area Planning Council:** Bastrop, Blanco, Burnet, Caldwell, Fayette, Hays, Lee, Llano, Travis and Williamson. Betty Voights, 2512 S. IH 35, Ste. 204, Austin 78704; 512-443-7653.

**13. Brazos Valley Council of Governments:** Brazos, Burleson, Grimes, Leon, Madison, Robertson and Washington. Tom Wilkinson Jr., PO Box 4128, Bryan 77805-4128; 979-775-4244.

**14. Deep East Texas Council of Governments:** Angelina, Houston, Jasper, Nacogdoches, Newton, Polk, Sabine, San Augustine, San Jacinto, Shelby, Trinity and Tyler. Walter G. Diggles, 274 E. Lamar St., Jasper 75951-4108; 409-384-5704.

**15. South East Texas Regional Planning Commission:** Hardin, Jefferson and Orange. Chester Jourdan, 2210 Eastex Freeway, Beaumont 77703; 409-899-8444.

**16. Houston-Galveston Area Council:** Austin, Brazoria, Chambers, Colorado, Fort Bend, Galveston, Harris, Liberty, Matagorda, Montgomery, Walker, Waller and Wharton. Jack Steele, PO Box 22777, Houston 77227-2777; 713-627-3200.

**17. Golden Crescent Regional Planning Commission:** Calhoun, DeWitt, Goliad, Gonzales, Jackson, Lavaca and Victoria. Patrick J. Kennedy, PO Box 2028, Victoria 77902-2028; 361-578-1587.

**18. Alamo Area Council of Governments:** Atascosa, Bandera, Bexar, Comal, Frio, Gillespie, Guadalupe, Karnes, Kendall, Kerr, Medina and Wilson. Al J. Notzon III, 8700 Tesoro Dr., Ste. 700, San Antonio 78217-6228 210-362-5200.

**19. South Texas Development Council:** Jim Hogg, Starr, Webb and Zapata. Amando Garza Jr., 4812 N. Bartlett Ave., Laredo 78044-2187; 956-722-3995.

**20. Coastal Bend Council of Governments:** Aransas, Bee, Brooks, Duval, Jim Wells, Kenedy, Kleberg, Live Oak, McMullen, Nueces, Refugio and San Patricio. John P. Buckner, PO Box 9909, Corpus Christi 78469-9909; 361-883-5743.

**21. Lower Rio Grande Valley Development Council:** Cameron, Hidalgo and Willacy. Kenneth N. Jones Jr., 311 N. 15th, McAllen 78501-4705; 956-682-3481.

**22. Texoma Council of Governments:** Cooke, Fannin and Grayson. Frances Pelley, 1117 Gallagher Dr., Ste. 100, Sherman 75090; 903-813-3512.

**23. Central Texas Council of Governments:** Bell, Coryell, Hamilton, Lampasas, Milam, Mills and San Saba. James Reed, PO Box 729, Belton 76513-0729; 254-933-6036.

**24. Middle Rio Grande Development Council:** Dimmit, Edwards, Kinney, La Salle, Maverick, Real, Uvalde, Val Verde and Zavala. Leodoro Martinez Jr., PO Box 1199, Carrizo Springs 78834-1199; 830-876-3533. ☆

# County Tax Appraisers

*The following list of Chief Appraisers for Texas counties was furnished by the State Property Tax Division of the State Comptroller's office. It includes the mailing address for each appraiser and is current to August 2003.*

**Anderson**—Carson Wages, PO Box 279, Palestine 75802
**Andrews**—Ron Huckabay, 600 N. Main, Andrews 79714
**Angelina**—Keith Kraemer, PO Box 2357, Lufkin 75902
**Aransas**—Jad Smith, 601 S. Church, Rockport 78382
**Archer**—Kimbra York, PO Box 1141, Archer City 76351
**Armstrong**—Deborah J. Sherman, Drawer 835, Claude 79019
**Atascosa**—Domingo Palomo Jr., PO Box 139, Poteet 78065
**Austin**—Phyllis Crawford, 906 E. Amelia St., Bellville 77418
**Bailey**—Kaye Elliott, 302 Main St., Muleshoe 79347
**Bandera**—Elaine Chaney, PO Box 1119, Bandera 78003
**Bastrop**—Mark Boehnke, Drawer 578, Bastrop 78602
**Baylor**—Ronnie Hargrove, 211 N. Washington, Seymour 76380
**Bee**—Bruce Martin, PO Box 1262, Beeville 78104
**Bell**—Roger Chesser, PO Box 390, Belton 76513
**Bexar**—Michael Amezquita, PO Box 830248, San Antonio 78283
**Blanco**—Ms. Hollis Boatright, PO Box 338, Johnson City 78636
**Borden**—Jeanette Koehler, PO Box 298, Gail 79738
**Bosque**—F. Janice Henry, PO Box 393, Meridian 76665
**Bowie**—Wayne Hawkins, PO Box 6527, Texarkana 75505
**Brazoria**—Cheryl Evans, 500 N. Chenango, Angleton 77515
**Brazos**—Gerald L. Winn, 1673 Briarcrest Dr., A-101, Bryan 77802
**Brewster**—Betty Jo Rooney, 107 W. Avenue E, #2, Alpine 79831
**Briscoe**—Carlye Fleming, PO Box 728, Silverton 79257
**Brooks**—Humberto Rivera, Drawer A, Falfurrias 78355
**Brown**—Doran E. Lemke, 403 Fisk Ave., Brownwood 76801
**Burleson**—Curtis Doss, PO Box 1000, Caldwell 77836
**Burnet**—Stan Hemphill, PO Box 908, Burnet 78611
**Caldwell**—Russell Sanders, PO Box 59, Lockhart 78644
**Calhoun**—Andrew J. Hahn, PO Box 49, Port Lavaca 77979
**Callahan**—Bun Barry, 132 W. 4th St., Baird 79504
**Cameron**—Frutoso Gomez Jr., PO Box 1010, San Benito 78586
**Camp**—Geraldine Hull, 143 Quitman St., Pittsburg 75686
**Carson**—Donita Davis, PO Box 970, Panhandle 79068
**Cass**—Ann Lummus, 502 N. Main St., Linden 75563
**Castro**—Jerry Heller, 204 S.E. 3rd (Rear), Dimmitt 79027
**Chambers**—Michael Fregia, PO Box 1520, Anahuac 77514
**Cherokee**—Lee Flowers, PO Box 494, Rusk 75785
**Childress**—Anita Manley, Courthouse Box 13, Childress 79201
**Clay**—A. G. Reis, 101 E. Omega, Henrietta 76365
**Cochran**—H. Loy Kern, 109 S.E. 1st, Morton 79346
**Coke**—Patsy N. Dunn, PO Box 2, Robert Lee 76945
**Coleman**—Bill W. Jones, PO Box 914, Coleman 76834
**Collin**—Jimmie Honea, 2404 Ave. K, Plano 75074
**Collingsworth**—Ann Wauer, 800 W. Ave., Rm. 104, Wellington 79095
**Colorado**—William T. Youens Jr., PO Box 10, Columbus 78934
**Comal**—Lynn E. Rodgers, PO Box 311222, New Braunfels 78131
**Comanche**—Rhonda Woods, PO Box 6, Comanche 76442
**Concho**—Terry Farris, PO Box 68, Paint Rock 76866
**Cooke**—Doug Smithson, 201 N. Dixon St., Gainesville 76240
**Coryell**—Darrell Lisenbe, PO Box 142, Gatesville 76528
**Cottle**—Rue Young, PO Box 459, Paducah 79248
**Crane**—Janet Wilson, 511 W. 8th, Crane 79731
**Crockett**—W. Tom Stokes, Drawer H, Ozona 76943
**Crosby**—Eletia Gowens, PO Box 505, Crosbyton 79322
**Culberson**—Sally Carrasco, PO Box 550, Van Horn 79855
**Dallam**—Huie V. Stanley, PO Box 579, Dalhart 79022
**Dallas**—Foy Mitchell , 2949 N. Stemmons Fwy., Dallas 75247
**Dawson**—Tom Anderson, PO Box 797, Lamesa 79331
**Deaf Smith**—Danny Jones, PO Box 2298, Hereford 79045
**Delta**—Sara Pruit, PO Box 47, Cooper 75432
**Denton**—Joe Rogers, PO Box 2816, Denton 76202
**DeWitt**—John Haliburton, PO Box 4, Cuero 77954
**Dickens**—Dexter Clay, PO Box 119, Dickens 79229
**Dimmit**—Elida Sanchez (interim), 402 N. 7th, Carrizo Springs 78834
**Donley**—Paula Lowrie, PO Box 1220, Clarendon 79226
**Duval**—Ernesto Molina, PO Box 809, San Diego 78384
**Eastland**—Steve Thomas, PO Box 914, Eastland 76448
**Ector**—Karen McCord, 1301 E. 8th, Odessa 79761
**Edwards**—Jodie Greene, PO Box 858, Rocksprings 78880
**Ellis**—Kathy Rodrigue, PO Box 878, Waxahachie 75165
**El Paso**—Cora Viescas, 5801 Trowbridge, El Paso 79925
**Erath**—Jerry Lee, PO Box 94, Stephenville 76401
**Falls**—Sharon Scott, Drawer 430, Marlin 76661
**Fannin**—Mary Woodlee, RR 5, Box 366, Bonham 75418
**Fayette**—Karen Schubert, PO Box 836, La Grange 78945
**Fisher**—Betty Mize, PO Box 516, Roby 79543
**Floyd**—Shelia Faulkenberry, PO Box 249, Floydada 79235
**Foard**—Jo Ann Vecera, PO Box 419, Crowell 79227
**Fort Bend**—Glen Whitehead, 2801 B.F. Terry Blvd., Rosenberg 77471
**Franklin**—John Kirkland, PO Box 720, Mount Vernon 75457
**Freestone**—Bud Black, 218 N. Mount, Fairfield 75840
**Frio**—Irma Gonzalez, PO Box 1129, Pearsall 78061
**Gaines**—Betty Caudle, PO Box 490, Seminole 79360
**Galveston**—Ken Wright, PO Box 3647, Texas City 77592
**Garza**—Shirley A. Smith, Drawer F, Post 79356
**Gillespie**—David Oehler, 101 W. Main St., Unit #11, Fredericksburg 78624
**Glasscock**—Royce Pruit, PO Box 89, Garden City 79739
**Goliad**—E. J. Bammert, PO Box 34, Goliad 77963

**Gonzales**—Glenda Strackbein, PO Box 867, Gonzales 78629
**Gray**—W. Pat Bagley, PO Box 836, Pampa 79066
**Grayson**—Larry Ward, 205 N. Travis, Sherman 75090
**Gregg**—Thomas Hays, 1333 E. Harrison Rd., Longview 75604
**Grimes**—Bill Sullivan, PO Box 489, Anderson 77830
**Guadalupe**—Ed Barnes, 3000 N. Austin, Seguin 78155
**Hale**—Nikki Branscum, PO Box 29, Plainview 79073
**Hall**—Marlin D. Felts, 512 W. Main St., Memphis 79245
**Hamilton**—Doyle Roberts, 119 E. Henry St., Hamilton 76531
**Hansford**—Alice Peddy, PO Box 519, Spearman 79081
**Hardeman**—Twila Butler, PO Box 388, Quanah 79252
**Hardin**—Amador Reyna, PO Box 670, Kountze 77625
**Harris**—Jim Robinson, PO Box 920975, Houston 77292
**Harrison**—David Whitmire, PO Box 818, Marshall 75671
**Hartley**—Mary M. Thompson, PO Box 405, Hartley 79044
**Haskell**—Kenny Watson, PO Box 467, Haskell 79521
**Hays**—Pete Islas, 21001 N. IH-35, Kyle 78640
**Hemphill**—Duane Cox, PO Box 65, Canadian 79014
**Henderson**—Bill Jackson, PO Box 430, Athens 75751
**Hidalgo**—Alonzo Vega, PO Box 632, Pharr 78577
**Hill**—Mike McKibben, PO Box 416, Hillsboro 76645
**Hockley**—Nick Williams, PO Box 1090, Levelland 79336
**Hood**—Jeff Law, PO Box 819, Granbury 76048
**Hopkins**—William Sherman, 109 College, Sulphur Springs 75482
**Houston**—Kathryn Keith, PO Box 112, Crockett 75835
**Howard**—Keith Toomire, PO Box 1151, Big Spring 79721
**Hudspeth**—Zedoch L. Pridgeon, Box 429, Sierra Blanca 79851
**Hunt**—Mildred Compton, PO Box 1339, Greenville 75403
**Hutchinson**—Bill Swink, PO Box 5065, Borger 79008
**Irion**—Frances Grice, PO Box 980, Mertzon 76941
**Jack**—Kathy Conner, PO Box 958, Jacksboro 76458
**Jackson**—Damon D. Moore, 411 N. Wells, Rm. 109, Edna 77957
**Jasper**—David Luther, PO Box 1300, Jasper 75951
**Jeff Davis**—Zedoch L. Pridgeon, PO Box 373, Fort Davis 79734
**Jefferson**—Roland Bieber, PO Box 21337, Beaumont 77720
**Jim Hogg**—Arnoldo Gonzalez, PO Box 459, Hebbronville 78361
**Jim Wells**—Sidney Vela, PO Box 607, Alice 78333
**Johnson**—Jim Hudspeth, 109 N. Main, Cleburne 76031
**Jones**—Susan Holloway, PO Box 348, Anson 79501
**Karnes**—Oscar Caballero, 915 S. Panna Maria, Karnes City 78118
**Kaufman**—Jackie Self, PO Box 819, Kaufman 75142
**Kendall**—Leta Schlinke, PO Box 788, Boerne 78006
**Kenedy**—Clyde Hamilton, PO Box 705, Bastrop 78602
**Kent**—Garth Gregory, PO Box 68, Jayton 79528
**Kerr**—P.H. "Fourth" Coates IV, PO Box 294387, Kerrville 78029
**Kimble**—John Dennis, PO Box 307, Junction 76849
**King**—Sandy Burkett, PO Box 117, Guthrie 79236
**Kinney**—William F. Haenn, PO Box 1377, Brackettville 78832
**Kleberg**—Tina Flores, PO Box 1027, Kingsville 78364
**Knox**—Stanton Brown, PO Box 47, Benjamin 79505
**Lamar**—Cathy Jackson, PO Box 400, Paris 75461
**Lamb**—Lesa Kloiber, PO Box 950, Littlefield 79339
**Lampasas**—Glenda January, Box 175, Lampasas 76550
**La Salle**—Joe R. Lozano, Drawer O, Cotulla 78014
**Lavaca**—Diane Munson, PO Box 386, Hallettsville 77964
**Lee**—Amelia Stayron, 218 E. Richmond, Giddings 78942
**Leon**—Jeff Beshears, PO Box 536, Centerville 75833
**Liberty**—Alan Conner, PO Box 10016, Liberty 77575
**Limestone**—Karen Wietzikoski, Drawer 831, Groesbeck 76642
**Lipscomb**—Jerry Reynolds, PO Box 128, Darrouzett 79024
**Live Oak**—Bob Johanson, PO Box 2370, George West 78022
**Llano**—Gary Eldridge, 103 E. Sandstone, Llano 78643
**Loving**—Sherlene Burrows, PO Box 352, Mentone 79754
**Lubbock**—Dave Kimbrough, PO Box 10542, Lubbock 79408
**Lynn**—Marquita Scott, PO Box 789, Tahoka 79373
**Madison**—Larry Krumnow, PO Box 1328, Madisonville 77864
**Marion**—David Sutton, PO Box 690, Jefferson 75657
**Martin**—Delbert Dickinson, PO Box 1349, Stanton 79782
**Mason**—Ted Smith, PO Box 1119, Mason 76856
**Matagorda**—Vince Maloney, PO Box 179, Bay City 77404
**Maverick**—Victor Perry, PO Box 2628, Eagle Pass 78853
**McCulloch**—Orlando Rubio, 104 N. College St., Brady 76825
**McLennan**—Robert L. Waldrop, PO Box 2297, Waco 76703
**McMullen**—Jesse Bryan, PO Box 38, Tilden 78072
**Medina**—James Garcia, 1410 Ave. K, Hondo 78861
**Menard**—Judy Cavnar, PO Box 1058, Menard 76859
**Midland**—Ron Stegall, PO Box 908002, Midland 79708
**Milam**—Patricia Moraw, PO Box 769, Cameron 76520
**Mills**—Doug Stewart, PO Box 565, Goldthwaite 76844
**Mitchell**—Kaye Cornutt, PO Box 358, Colorado City 79512
**Montague**—June Deaton, PO Box 121, Montague 76251
**Montgomery**—Mark Castleschouldt, PO Box 2233, Conroe 77305
**Moore**—Joyce Cearley, PO Box 717, Dumas 79029
**Morris**—Rhonda Hall, PO Box 563, Daingerfield 75638
**Motley**—Brenda Osborn, PO Box 779, Matador 79244
**Nacogdoches**—Gary Woods, 216 W. Hospital, Nacogdoches 75961
**Navarro**—Bill Worthen, PO Box 3118, Corsicana 75151
**Newton**—Margie Herrin, Drawer X, Newton 75966
**Nolan**—Patricia Davis, PO Box 1256, Sweetwater 79556
**Nueces**—Ollie Grant, 201 N. Chaparral, Corpus Christi 78401

**Ochiltree**—Terry Symons, 825 S. Main, #100, Perryton 79070
**Oldham**—Jen Carter, PO Box 310, Vega 79092
**Orange**—Ms. Pat Sanderson, PO Box 457, Orange 77630
**Palo Pinto**—Donna Rhodes, PO Box 250, Palo Pinto 76484
**Panola**—Louis Wall, 2 Ball Park Rd., Carthage 75633
**Parker**—Larry Hammonds, 118 W. Columbia, Weatherford 76086
**Parmer**—Ron Procter, PO Box 56, Bovina 79009
**Pecos**—Ann Stapp, PO Box 237, Fort Stockton 79735
**Polk**—Carolyn Allen, 114 W. Matthews, Livingston 77351
**Potter**—Jim Childers, PO Box 7190, Amarillo 79114
**Presidio**—Irma Salgado, PO Box 879, Marfa 79843
**Rains**—Carrol Houllis, PO Box 70, Emory 75440
**Randall**—Jim Childers, PO Box 7190, Amarillo 79114
**Reagan**—Byron Bitner, PO Box 8, Big Lake 76932
**Real**—LeAnn Rubio, PO Box 158, Leakey 78873
**Red River**—Jan Raulston, PO Box 461, Clarksville 75426
**Reeves**—Carol King Markham, PO Box 1229, Pecos 79772
**Refugio**—Bettye Kret, PO Box 156, Refugio 78377
**Roberts**—Carol Johnson, PO Box 458, Miami 79059
**Robertson**—Dan Brewer, PO Box 998, Franklin 77856
**Rockwall**—Ray Helm, 841 Justin Rd., Rockwall 75087
**Runnels**—Tylene Gamble, PO Box 524, Ballinger 76821
**Rusk**—Terry Decker, PO Box 7, Henderson 75653
**Sabine**—Jim Nethery, PO Box 137, Hemphill 75948
**San Augustine**—Jamie Doherty, 122 N. Harrison, San
   Augustine 75972
**San Jacinto**—Linda Lewis, PO Box 1170, Coldspring 77331
**San Patricio**—Kathryn Vermillion, PO Box 938, Sinton 78387
**San Saba**—Henry J. Warren, 423 E. Wallace, San Saba 76877
**Schleicher**—Scott Sutton, PO Box 936, Eldorado 76936
**Scurry**—Larry Crooks, 2612 College Ave., Snyder 79549
**Shackelford**—Teresa Peacock, PO Box 565, Albany 76430
**Shelby**—Robert Pigg, 724 Shelbyville St., Center 75935
**Sherman**—Teresa Edmond, PO Box 239, Stratford 79084
**Smith**—Michael Barnett, 245 South S.E. Loop 323, Tyler 75702
**Somervell**—Ronnie Babcock, 112 Allen Dr., Glen Rose 76043
**Starr**—Humberto Saenz Jr., PO Box 137, Rio Grande City 78582
**Stephens**—Troy Sloan, PO Box 351, Breckenridge 76424
**Sterling**—Linda Low, PO Box 28, Sterling City 76951

**Stonewall**—Ozella E. Warner, PO Box 308, Aspermont 79502
**Sutton**—Rex Ann Friess, 300 E. Oak St., Sonora 76950
**Swisher**—Rose Lee Powell, PO Box 8, Tulia 79088
**Tarrant**—John Marshall, 2500 Handley-Ederville Rd., Fort Worth
   76118
**Taylor**—Richard Petree, PO Box 1800, Abilene 79604
**Terrell**—Blain Chriesman, PO Box 747, Sanderson 79848
**Terry**—Ronny Burran, PO Box 426, Brownfield 79316
**Throckmorton**—Linda Carrington, PO Box 788, Throckmorton 76483
**Titus**—Katrina Perry, PO Box 528, Mount Pleasant 75456
**Tom Green**—Bill Benson, PO Box 3307, San Angelo 76902
**Travis**—Art Cory, PO Box 149012, Austin 78714
**Trinity**—Allen McKinley, PO Box 950, Groveton 75845
**Tyler**—Travis Chalmers, Drawer 9, Woodville 75979
**Upshur**—Louise Stracener, 105 Diamond Loch, Gilmer 75644
**Upton**—Sheri Stephens, PO Box 1110, McCamey 79752
**Uvalde**—Rufino H. Lozano, 209 N. High, Uvalde 78801
**Val Verde**—Ricardo Martinez, PO Box 1059, Del Rio 78841
**Van Zandt**—Chris Becker, PO Box 926, Canton 75103
**Victoria**—Terry Turner, 2805 N. Navarro, Ste. 300, Victoria 77901
**Walker**—Grover Cook, PO Box 1798, Huntsville 77342
**Waller**—David Piwonka, PO Box 159, Katy 77492
**Ward**—Arlice Wittie, PO Box 905, Monahans 79756
**Washington**—Willy Dilworth, PO Box 681, Brenham 77834
**Webb**—Sergio Delgado, 3302 Clark Blvd., Laredo 78043
**Wharton**—Larry Holub, PO Box 1068, Wharton 77488
**Wheeler**—Jeanine Hawkins, PO Box 1200, Wheeler 79096
**Wichita**—Eddie Trigg, PO Box 5172, Wichita Falls 76307
**Wilbarger**—Doyle Graham, PO Box 1519, Vernon 76384
**Willacy**—Augustin Colchado, Rt. 2, Box 256, Raymondville 78580
**Williamson**—Bill Carroll, PO Box 1120, Georgetown 78627
**Wilson**—Carlton R. Pape, Box 849, Floresville 78114
**Winkler**—Connie Carpenter, PO Box 1219, Kermit 79745
**Wise**—Mickey Hand, 206 S. State, Decatur 76234
**Wood**—Tracy Nichols, PO Box 518, Quitman 75783
**Yoakum**—Saundra Stephens, PO Box 748, Plains 79355
**Young**—Jerry Patton, 724 Oak St., Graham 76450
**Zapata**—Rosalva Guerra, PO Box 2315, Zapata 78076
**Zavala**—Alberto Mireles, 323 W. Zavala, Crystal City 78839 ☆

# Wet-Dry Counties

When approved in local-option elections in "wet" precincts of counties, sale of **liquor by the drink** is permitted in Texas. This resulted from adoption of an amendment to the Texas Constitution in 1970 and subsequent legislation, followed by local-option elections. This amendment marked the first time in 50 years that the sale of liquor by the drink was legal in Texas.

The list below shows the wet-or-dry status of counties in Texas as of August 31, 2003. A dagger (†) indicates counties in which the sale of mixed beverages is legal in all or part of the county (97). An asterisk (*) indicates counties wholly wet (37). All others are dry in part (80).

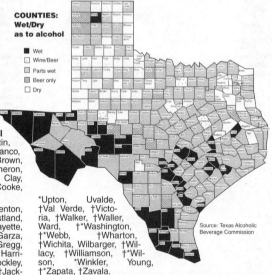

**COUNTIES:
Wet/Dry
as to alcohol**

■ Wet
☐ Wine/Beer
☐ Parts wet
▨ Beer only
☐ Dry

**Counties in Which Distilled Spirits Are Legal (186):** Anderson, †*Aransas, Archer, Atascosa, †*Austin, †Bandera, †*Bastrop, †*Bee, †Bell, †*Bexar, †Blanco, Bosque, †Brazoria, †*Brazos, †*Brewster, Brooks, Brown, Burleson, †Burnet, †Calhoun, Callahan, †*Cameron, †Camp, Carson, Cass, Castro, Chambers, Childress, Clay, Coleman, Collin, †*Colorado, †*Comal, Comanche, Cooke, Coryell, Crane, *Crockett, *Culberson.

Also, Dallam, †Dallas, †Dawson, Deaf Smith, †Denton, †DeWitt, Dickens, †Dimmit, †Donley, †*Duval, Eastland, †Ector, Edwards, Ellis, †*El Paso, †Falls, Fannin, Fayette, †*Fort Bend, Freestone, †Frio, †Galveston, †Garza, †Gillespie, †Goliad, Gonzales, Gray, Grayson, Gregg, †Grimes, †Guadalupe, Hall, Hamilton, Hardin, †Harris, Harrison, †Hays, †Henderson, †*Hidalgo, †Hill, †Hockley, Hood, †Howard, †*Hudspeth, Hunt, Hutchinson, Jack, †Jackson, †Jasper, Jeff Davis.

Also †Jefferson, †*Jim Hogg, †Jim Wells, *Karnes, Kaufman, †*Kendall, Kenedy, †Kerr, Kimble, King, †*Kinney, †Kleberg, †Lamar, Lampasas, †La Salle, †Lavaca, †Lee, Leon, Liberty, Lipscomb, Live Oak, †Llano, †*Loving, †Lubbock, Marion, †Matagorda, †Maverick, †McCulloch, †McLennan, †Medina, Menard, †Midland, Milam, Mills, Mitchell, Montague, †Montgomery, †*Moore, Nacogdoches, †Navarro, Newton, Nolan, †Nueces.

Also, †Orange, Palo Pinto, Parker, Pecos, †Polk, †Potter, †*Presidio, Rains, †Randall, *Reagan, Red River, †Reeves, Refugio, Robertson, †Rockwall, Runnels, San Augustine, San Jacinto, †San Patricio, San Saba, †Schleicher, Shackelford, Shelby, †*Starr, Stonewall, †*Sutton, †Tarrant, †Taylor, *Terrell, †Titus, †Tom Green, †*Travis, *Trinity, Upshur, *Upton, Uvalde, †Val Verde, †Victoria, †Walker, †Waller, Ward, †*Washington, †*Webb, †Wharton, †Wichita, Wilbarger, †Willacy, †Williamson, †*Wilson, *Winkler, Young, †*Zapata, †Zavala.

**Counties in Which Only 4 Percent Beer Is Legal (11):** Baylor, Caldwell, Cherokee, Concho, Hartley, Irion, Mason, McMullen, Oldham, Sabine, Stephens.

**Counties in Which 14 Percent or Less** (or up to 17 percent, depending on local-option election held) **Alcoholic Beverages Are Legal (5):** Glasscock, Johnson, Limestone, Somervell, Wise.

**Counties Wholly Dry (52):** Andrews, Angelina, Armstrong, Bailey, Borden, Bowie, Briscoe, Cochran, Coke, Collingsworth, Cottle, Crosby, Delta, Erath, Fisher, Floyd, Foard, Franklin, Gaines, Hale, Hansford, Hardeman, Hemphill, Hopkins, Houston, Jones, Kent, Knox, Lamb, Lynn, Madison, Martin, Morris, Motley, Ochiltree, Panola, Parmer, Real, Roberts, Rusk, Scurry, Sherman, Smith, Sterling, Swisher, Terry, Throckmorton, Tyler, Van Zandt, Wheeler, Wood, Yoakum. ☆

Source: Texas Alcoholic Beverage Commission

# County Courts

*Below are listed county courts, including county courts at law, probate courts, juvenile/domestic relations courts, criminal courts and criminal courts of appeals as reported by the county clerks as of May 2003. Other courts with jurisdiction in each county can be found in the list on pages 437–438. Other county and district officials can be found on pages 474–484.*

**Anderson County Court at Law:** Jeff Doran. **Probate Courts:** No. 1, Carey G. McKinney; No. 2, Jeff Doran. **Criminal Court at Law, Domestic Relations & Juvenile Courts:** Jeff Doran.

**Angelina County Courts at Law:** No. 1, Lisa Burkhalter; No. 2, Barry Bryan. **Domestic Relations:** David Wilson, Paul White.

**Aransas County Court at Law:** William Adams.

**Austin County Court at Law:** Gladys M. Oakley.

**Bailey County Juvenile Court:** Marilyn Cox.

**Bandera County Probate & Juvenile Courts:** Richard Evans

**Bastrop County Court at Law:** Benton Eskew.

**Baylor County Probate Court:** James D. Coltharp.

**Bee County Criminal Court at Law, Probate & Juvenile Courts:** Jimmy Martinez.

**Bell County Courts at Law:** No. 1, Edward S. Johnson; No. 2, John Barina; No. 3, Gerald Brown.

**Bexar County Courts at Law:** No. 1, Al Alonso; No. 2, H. Paul Canales; No. 3, David J. Rodriguez; No. 4, Sarah E. Garrahan; No. 5, Timothy F. Johnson; No. 6, Phil Meyer; No. 7, Monica E. Gurrero; No. 8, Karen Crouch; No. 9, Oscar Kazen; No. 10, Irene Rios; No. 11, Jo Ann De Hoyos; No. 12, Michael Mery. **Probate Courts:** No. 1, Polly Jackson Spencer; No. 2, Tom Rickhoff.

**Bowie County Court at Law:** Leon Pesek Jr. **Probate Court:** James M. Carlow.

**Brazoria County Courts at Law:** No. 1, Jerri Lee Mills; No. 2, Marc Holder; No. 3, James Blackstock.

**Brazos County Courts at Law:** No. 1, Randy Michel; No. 2, Jim Locke. **Juvenile Court:** Reva Corbet.

**Brooks County Court at Law:** Joe B. Garcia.

**Brown County Court at Law:** Frank Griffin.

**Burleson County Probate & Juvenile Courts:** Mike Sutherland.

**Burnet County Court at Law:** Randy Savage.

**Caldwell County Court at Law:** Edward L. Jarrett.

**Calhoun County Court at Law:** Alex R. Hernandez.

**Cameron County Courts at Law:** No. 1, Janet Leal; No. 2, Elia Cornejo-Lopez.; No. 3, Daniel Robles.

**Camp County Probate Court:** Preston Combest.

**Carson County Probate Court:** Lewis Powers.

**Cass County Probate Court:** Charles L. McMichael.

**Castro County Probate & Juvenile Courts:** William F. Sava.

**Chambers County Probate & Juvenile Courts:** Jimmy Sylvia; **Domestic Relations Court:** Chap Cain III & Carroll E. Wilborn Jr.

**Cherokee County Court at Law:** Daniel B. Childs.

**Cochran County Probate & Juvenile Courts:** James St. Clair.

**Coke County Probate Court:** Roy Blair.

**Collin County Courts at Law:** No. 1, Corine Mason; No. 2, Jerry Lewis; No. 3, John O'Keefe Barry; No. 4, Raymond Wheless; No. 5, Chris Oldner. **Probate Court:** Weldon Copeland.

**Collingsworth County Probate & Juvenile Courts:** Jim Forrester.

**Colorado County Probate & Juvenile Courts:** Al Jamison.

**Comal County Court at Law:** Brenda Chapman.

**Concho County Probate Court:** Allen Amos; **Juvenile Court:** Ben Woodward.

**Cooke County Court at Law:** John Morris.

**Coryell County Court at Law:** Susan Stephens.

**Dallam County Probate Court:** David D. Field. **Domestic Relations:** Ron Enns. **Juvenile:** David D. Field.

**Dallas County Courts at Law:** No. 1, Russell Roden; No. 2, John B. Peyton; No. 3, Sally Montgomery; No. 4, Bruce Woody; No. 5, Mark Greenberg. **County Criminal Courts:** No. 1, Daniel Clancy; No. 2, Neil Pask; No. 3, Daniel Wyde; No. 4, Ralph Taite; No. 5, Tom Fuller; No. 6, Phil Barker; No. 7, Elizabeth Crowder; No. 8, Jane Roden; No. 9, Keith Anderson; No. 10, Lisa Fox; No. 11, Dianne Jones. **Probate Courts:** No. 1, Nikki DeShazo; No. 2, Robert E. Price; No. 3, Joe Loving Jr. **County Criminal Courts of Appeals:** No. 1, Kristin Wade; No. 2, Lynn Burson.

**Deaf Smith County Juvenile Court:** Tim Simons.

**Delta County Probate & Criminal Courts:** Hugh Charles Whitney.

**Denton County Courts at Law:** No. 1, Darlene Whitten; No. 2, Margaret Barnes. **Domestic Relations:** Jim Crouch. **Probate Court:** Don Windle.

**DeWitt County Probate Court:** Ben E. Prause.

**Donley County Probate Court:** Jack Hall.

**Eastland County Probate & Criminal Courts:** Brad Stephenson. **Domestic Relations & Juvenile:** Steven R. Herod.

**Ector County Courts at Law:** No. 1, J.A. "Jim" Bobo; No. 2, Mark Owens. **Juvenile Court:** J.A. "Jim" Bobo.

**Edwards County Probate Court:** Nick Gallegos. **Probate Court:** Thomas F. Lee.

**Ellis County Court at Law:** No. 1, Bob Carroll; No. 2, A. Gene Calvert Jr. **Probate:** Bob Carroll. **Juvenile:** A. Gene Calvert Jr.

**El Paso County Courts at Law:** No. 1, Ricardo Herrera; No. 2, Julie Gonzalez; No. 3, Javier Alvarez; No. 4, Alex Gonzalez; No. 5, Carlos Villa; No. 6, M. Sue Kurita; No. 7, Jose Baca. **Probate Court:** Max D. Higgs.

**Erath County Court at Law:** Bart McDougal.

**Fort Bend County Courts at Law:** No. 1, Larry Wagenbach; No. 2, Walter McMeans; No. 3, Susan Lowery; No. 4, Wandy Bielstein.

**Galveston County Courts at Law:** No. 1, Mary Nell Crapitto; No. 2, C.G. Dibrell III; **Probate Court:** Gladys Burwell.

**Grayson County Courts at Law:** No. 1, James C. Henderson; No.

2, Carol Siebman.

**Gregg County Court at Law:** No. 1, Rebecca Simpson; No. 2, Alfonso Charles.

**Guadalupe County Court at Law:** No. 1, Linda Z. Jones; No. 2, Frank Follis.

**Harris County Courts at Law:** No. 1, R. Jack Cagle; No. 2, Gary Michael Block; No. 3, Lynn Bradshaw-Hull; No. 4, Cynthia Crowe. **County Criminal Courts at Law:** No. 1, Reagan Cartright Helm; No. 2, Michael Peters; No. 3, Don Jackson; No. 4, James E. Anderson; No. 5, Margaret Stewart Harris; No. 6, Larry Standley; No. 7, (vacant); No. 8, Jay Karahan; No. 9, Analia Wilkerson; No. 10, Sherman A. Ross; No. 11, Diane Bull; No. 12, Robin Brown; No. 13, Mark Atkinson; No. 14, Mike Fields; No. 15, Jean Spradling Hughes. **Probate Courts:** No. 1, Russell Austin; No. 2, Mike Wood; No. 3, Rory Robert Olsen; No. 4, William C. McCulloch.

**Harrison County Court at Law:** Jim Ammerman II.

**Hays County Courts at Law:** No. 1, Howard S. Warner II; No. 2, Linda A. Rodriguez.

**Henderson County Court at Law:** D. Matt Livingston.

**Hidalgo County Courts at Law:** No. 1, Rodolfo Gonzalez; No. 2, Jaime Gonzalez. **Probate Court:** Homero Garza.

**Hopkins County Court at Law:** Amy M. Smith.

**Houston County Court at Law:** Sarah Tunnell Clark.

**Hunt County Court at Law:** Steve Shipp.

**Jefferson County Courts at Law:** No. 1, Alfred S. Gerson; No. 2, G.R. Lupe Flores; No. 3, John Paul Davis.

**Johnson County Courts at Law:** No. 1, Robert Mayfield; No. 2, William R. Anderson Jr.

**Kaufman County Court at Law:** Joe Parnell.

**Kerr County Court at Law:** Spencer Brown.

**Kleberg County Court at Law:** Martin J. Chiuminatto Jr.

**Lamar County Court at Law:** Dean Loughmiller.

**Liberty County Court at Law:** Don Taylor.

**Lubbock County Courts at Law:** No. 1, Rusty Ladd; No. 2, Drue Farmer; No. 3, Paula Lanehart.

**McLennan County Courts at Law:** No. 1, Tom Ragland; No. 2, Michael B. Gassaway

**Medina County Court at Law:** Vivian Torres.

**Midland County Courts at Law:** No. 1, Al Walvoord; No. 2, Marvin Moore.

**Montgomery County Courts at Law:** No. 1, Dennis Watson; No. 2, Jerry Winfree.

**Moore County Court at Law:** Delwin McGee.

**Nacogdoches County Court at Law:** Jack Sinz.

**Nolan County Court at Law:** Gary Harger.

**Nueces County Courts at Law:** No. 1, Robert Vargas; No. 2, Lisa Gonzales; No. 3, Marisela Saldaña; No. 4, James E. Klager; No. 5: Carl E. Lewis.

**Orange County Court at Law:** Michael W. Shuff.

**Panola County Court at Law:** Terry D. Bailey.

**Parker County Court at Law:** Graham Quisenberry.

**Polk County Court at Law:** Stephen Phillips.

**Potter County Courts at Law:** No. 1, W.F. "Corky" Roberts; No. 2, Pamela Cook Sirmon.

**Randall County Court at Law:** James Anderson.

**Reeves County Court at Law:** Walter M. Holcombe.

**Rusk County Court at Law:** Darrell Hyatt.

**San Patricio County Court at Law:** Richard D. Hatch III.

**Smith County Courts at Law:** No. 1, Thomas A. Dunn; No. 2, Randall L. Rogers; No. 3: Floyd Getz.

**Starr County Court at Law:** Romero Molina.

**Tarrant County Courts at Law:** No. 1, R. Brent Keis; No. 2, Jennifer Rymell; No. 3, Vince Sprinkle. **County Criminal Courts at Law:** No. 1, Sherry Hill; No. 2, Mike Mitchell; No. 3, Billy D. Mills; No. 4, Deborah Nekhom Harris; No. 5, Jamie Cummings; No. 6, Molly Jones; No. 7, Cheril S. Hardy; No. 8, Daryl Coffee; No. 9, Brent A. Carr; No. 10, Phil Sorrels. **Probate Courts:** No. 1, Steve M. King; No. 2, Pat Ferchill.

**Taylor County Courts at Law:** No. 1, Robert Harper; No. 2, Barbara B. Rollins.

**Tom Green County Court at Law:** No. 1, Ben Nolan; No. 2, Penny Roberts.

**Travis County Courts at Law:** No. 1, J. David Phillips; No. 2, Orlinda Naranjo; No. 3, David Crain; No. 4, Mike Denton; No. 5, Gisela Triana; No. 6, Jan Breland; No. 7, Elizabeth Earle. **Probate Court:** Guy Herman.

**Val Verde County Court at Law:** Sergio J. Gonzalez.

**Victoria County Courts at Law:** No. 1, Laura A. Weiser; No. 2, Juan Velasquez III.

**Walker County Court at Law:** Barbara W. Hale.

**Waller County Court at Law:** June Jackson.

**Washington County Court at Law:** Matthew Reue.

**Webb County Courts at Law:** No. 1, Alvino "Ben" Morales; No. 2, Jesús "Chuy" Garza.

**Wichita County Courts at Law:** No. 1, Jim Hogan; No. 2, Tom Bacus.

**Williamson County Courts at Law:** No. 1, Suzanne Brooks; No. 2, Jim Wright; No. 3, Don Higginbothom.

**Wise County Court at Law:** Melton D. Cude. ✩

# Texas County and District Officials — Table No. 1

Country Seats, County Judges, County Clerks, County Attorneys, County Commissioners, County Treasurers, Tax Assessors-Collectors and Sheriffs.

See Table No. 2 on pages following this table for District Clerks, District Attorneys and County Commissioners. Judges in county courts at law, as well as probate courts, juvenile/domestic relations courts, county criminal courts and county criminal courts of appeal, can be found on page 478. The officials listed here are elected by popular vote. An asterisk (*) before a county name marks a county whose county clerk failed to return our questionnaire; the names of officials for those counties are taken from most recent unofficial sources available to us.

| County | County Seat | County Judge | County Clerk | County Attorney | County Treasurer | Assessor-Collector | Sheriff |
|---|---|---|---|---|---|---|---|
| Anderson | Palestine | Carey G. McKinney | Lena Smith | Douglas E. Lowe | Sharon Peterson | Lynn Palmer | John E. Hobson |
| Andrews | Andrews | Richard H. Dolgener | F. Wm. Hoermann | John L. Pool | Office abolished 11-5-1985. | Royce Underwood | Sam H. Jones |
| Angelina | Lufkin | Joe Berry | JoAnn Chastain | Ed Jones | Lois Warner | Bill Shanklin | Kent Henson |
| Aransas | Rockport | Glenn D. Guillory | Peggy L. Friebele | James L. Anderson Jr. | Marvine D. Wix | Jeri D. Cox | Mark Gilliam |
| Archer | Archer City | Paul O. Wylie Jr. | Karren Winter | R.B. Morris | Victoria Lear | Teresa K. Martin | Ed Daniels |
| Armstrong | Claude | Hugh Reed | Joe Reck | | Margie Ready | Deborah Sherman | J.R. Walker |
| Atascosa | Jourdanton | Diana J. Bautista | Laquita Hayden | R. Thomas Franklin | Lisa Royal | Barbara Schorsch | Tommy Williams |
| Austin | Bellville | Carolyn Bilski | Carrie Gregor | | Betty Krueger | Janice Kokemor | R. DeWayne Burger |
| Bailey | Muleshoe | Marilyn Cox | Sherri Harrison | Carrissa A. Cleavinger | Donna M. Kirk | Berta Combs | Richard Willis |
| Bandera | Bandera | Richard A. Evans | Bernice Bates | Kerry K. Schneider | Kay Welch | Mae Vion Meyer | James MacMillan |
| Bastrop | Bastrop | Ronnie McDonald | Rose Pietsch | | Patsy Holmes | Linda Harmon | Richard M. Hernandez |
| Baylor | Seymour | James D. Coltharp | Clara "Carrie" Coker | Paul Scott | Kevin Hostas | Jeanette Holub | Bob Elliott |
| Bee | Beeville | Jimmy Martinez | Mirella Escamilla Davis | Michael J. Knight | Office abolished 11-2-1982. | Andrea W. Gibbud | Robert L. Horn |
| Bell | Belton | Jon H. Burrows | Vada Sutton | Rick Miller | Charles Jones | Sharon Long | Dan Smith |
| Bexar | San Antonio | Nelson W. Wolf | Gerry Rickhoff | | Office abolished 11-6-1984. | Sylvia S. Romo | Ralph Lopez |
| Blanco | Johnson City | Bill Guthrie | Karen Newman | Dean C. Myane | Camille Swift | Hollis Boatright | Bill Elsbury |
| Borden | Gail | Van L. York | Joyce Herridge | | Kenneth F. Bennett | Billy J. Gannaway | Billy J. Gannaway |
| Bosque | Meridian | Cole Word | Betty Spitzer Outlaw | Patricia Ferguson | Randy Outlaw Pullin | Denise Wallace | Charles E. Jones |
| Bowie | Boston | James M. Carlow | Velma Moore | Carol Dalby | Pansy Baird | Toni Barron | James Prince |
| Brazoria | Angleton | John Willy | Joyce Hudman | | Sharon Reynolds | Ro'vin Garrett | E.J. "Joe" King |
| Brazos | Bryan | Randy Sims | Karen McQueen | Jim Kuboviak | Kay Hamilton | Gerald L. "Buddy" Winn | Chris Kirk |
| Brewster | Alpine | Val C. Beard | Berta Rios Martinez | Steve Houston | Hortencia Ramos | Jerry Ratcliff | Ronny Dodson |
| Briscoe | Silverton | Wayne Nance | Bena Hester | William P. Smith | Mary Jo Brannon | Betty Ann Stephens | Jeff Fuston |
| Brooks | Falfurrias | Joe B. Garcia | Frutoso "Pepe" Garza | David T. Garcia | Gilbert Vela | Baldemar Lozano | Baldemar Lozano |
| Brown | Brownwood | E. Ray West III | Margaret Wood | Shane Britton | Judy Stirman | Linda Lewis Parker | Glen Smith |
| Burleson | Caldwell | Mike Sutherland | Anna L. Schielack | Joseph J. Skrivanek | Beth Andrews Bills | Curtis Doss | Thomas E. Barber |
| Burnet | Burnet | David L. "Dave" Kithil | Janet Parker | Robert Klaeger | Donna Klaeger | Sherri Frazier | Joe Pollock |
| Caldwell | Lockhart | H.T. Wright | Nina S. Sells | | Lori Rangel-Pompa | Mary Vicky Gonzales | Daniel Law |
| Calhoun | Port Lavaca | Michael Pfeifer | Anita Fricke | | Rhonda McMahan | Gloria Ochoa | B.B. Browning |
| Callahan | Baird | Roger Corn | Jeanie Bohannon | Allen Wright | Dianne Alexander | Tammy Walker | Eddie Curtis |
| Cameron | Brownsville | Gilberto Hinojosa | Joe G. Rivera | Yolanda De Leon | Eddie Gonzalez | Antonio Yzaguirre Jr. | Conrado Cantu |
| Camp | Pittsburg | Preston Combest | Elaine Young | James W. Wallace | Pam Nelson | Gale Burns | Alan D. McCandless |
| Carson | Panhandle | Lewis Powers | Celeste Bichsel | Scott Sherwood | Jeannie Cunningham | Barbara Cosper | Gary Robertson |
| Cass | Linden | Charles L. McMichael | Jannis Mitchell | | Martha Sheridan | Becky Watson | James "Troop" Estes |
| Castro | Dimmitt | William F. Sava | Joyce M. Thomas | James R. Horton | Janice Shelton | Billy Hackleman | C.D. Fitzgearold |
| Chambers | Anahuac | Jimmy Sylvia | Susan E. Rosuto | Cheryl S. Lieck | Carren Sparks | Margie Henry | Monroe Kruezer Sr. |
| Cherokee | Rusk | Chris Davis | Laverne Lusk | Craig D. Caldwell | Patsy J. Lassiter | Linda Beard | James E. Campbell |
| Childress | Childress | Jay Mayden | Zona Prince | Greg Buckley | Jeanie Thomas | Juanell Halford | Darrin Smith |
| Clay | Henrietta | Kenneth Liggett | Kay Hutchison | Eddy Atkins | Debra Alexander | Linda J. Sellers | David Hanes |
| Cochran | Morton | James St. Clair | Rita Tyson | J.C. Adams Jr. | Doris Sealy | Linda Huckabee | R.W. Stalcup |
| Coke | Robert Lee | Roy Blair | Mary Grim | Nancy Arthur | Phelan Wrinkle | Gayle Sisemore | Rick Styles |
| Coleman | Coleman | Jimmie Hobbs | JoAnn Hale | Joe D. LeMay | Kay LeMay | Donna Seymore | Wade Turner |
| Collin | McKinney | Ron Harris | Brenda F. Taylor | John Roach | Brenda F. Taylor | Kenneth Maun | Terry Box |
| Collingsworth | Wellington | Jim Forrester | Jackie Johnson | G. Keith Davis | Yvonne Brewer | RoseMary Throne | Russell Lee |
| Colorado | Columbus | Al Jamison | Darlene Hayek | Ken Sparks | Diane Matus | Mary Jane Poenitzsch | R.H. "Curley" Wied |
| Comal | New Braunfels | Danny Scheel | Joy Streater | | Susan Patterson | Sherman Krause | Bob Holder |
| Comanche | Comanche | James R. Arthur | Ruby Lesley | Charles B. Williams | Billy Ruth Rust | Gay Horton Green | John R. Boyd |

| County | County Seat | County Judge | County Clerk | County Attorney | County Treasurer | Assessor-Collector | Sheriff |
|---|---|---|---|---|---|---|---|
| Concho | Paint Rock | Allen Amos | Barbara K. Hoffman | Bill Campbell | Lisa J. Jost | William J. Fiveash | William J. Fiveash |
| Cooke | Gainesville | Bill Freeman | Rebecca Lawson | Tanya Davis | Judy Hunter | Billie Jean Knight | Michael E. "Mike" Compton |
| Coryell | Gatesville | John Hull | Barbara Simpson | Edwin Powell Jr. | Chad Smith | Barbara Thompson | Roger Faught |
| Cottle | Paducah | John D. Shavor | Beckey J. Tucker | John H. Richards | Kathy Biddy | Rue Young | Kenneth A. Burns |
| Crane | Crane | Donnie Henderson | Judy Crawford | James McDonald | Cristy Tarin | Rebecca Gonzales | Danny Simmons |
| Crockett | Ozona | John R. Jones | Debbi Puckett-Moore | William S. Mason | Burl J. Myers | Tom Stokes | Shane Fenton |
| Crosby | Crosbyton | Joe Heflin | Betty J. Pierce | C. Michael Ward | Debra Riley | Anna R. Rodriguez | Lavoice "Red" Riley |
| Culberson | Van Horn | John Conoly | Linda McDonald | Stephen L. Mitchell | Norma Hernandez | Amalia Y. Hernandez | Oscar Carrillo |
| Dallam | Dalhart | David D. Field | LuAnn Taylor | Greg Oelke | Wes Ritchey | Kay Howell | Bruce Scott |
| Dallas | Dallas | Margaret Keliher | Cynthia Figueroa Calhoun | | Lisa Hembry | David Childs | Jim Bowles |
| Dawson | Lamesa | Sam Saleh | Gloria Vera | Steve Payson | Gene DeFee | Tom Anderson | Johnny Garcia |
| Deaf Smith | Hereford | Tom Simons | David Ruland | James Michael English | Paula B. Price | Jeannine Zimmerman | Brent Harrison |
| Delta | Cooper | Hugh Charles Whitney | Barbara Vaughn | Michael Bartley | Glynana Herin | Brenda "Dawn" Curtis | Mark Bassham |
| Denton | Denton | Mary Horn | Cynthia Mitchell | Bruce Isaacks | Cindy BYeatts rown | Steve Mossman | Weldon Lucas |
| DeWitt | Cuero | Ben E. Prause | Elva Petersen | Raymond H. Reese | Peggy Ledbetter | Susie Dreyer | Cliff Foulds Jr. |
| Dickens | Dickens | Woodie McArthur Jr. | Winona Humphreys | David M. Gonzalez (pro tem) | Sandy Vickrey | Dexter Clay | Kenneth Brendle |
| Dimmit | Carrizo Springs | Francisco G. Ponce | Mario Zuvia Garcia | Daniel M. Gonzalez | Elisa G. Duran | Esther Zuvia Perez | Jesus Leal |
| Donley | Clarendon | Jack Hall | Fay Vargas | Kaye Messer (pro tem) | Rebecca Jackson | Wilma Lindley | Butch Blackburn |
| Duval | San Diego | Edmundo B. Garcia Jr. | Oscar Garcia Jr. | Ricardo O. "Rocky" Carrillo | Daniel S. Lopez Jr. | Carlos J. Montemayor Jr. | Santiago Barrera Jr. |
| Eastland | Eastland | Brad Stephenson | Cathy Jentho | | Marti Heyser | Sandra Cagle | Wayne Bradford |
| Ector | Odessa | Jerry D. Caddel | Barbara Bedford | Tracey Bright | Carolyn Sue Bowen | Lea Taylor | Mark Donaldson |
| Edwards | Rocksprings | Nick Gallegos | Sarah McNealy | Allen Ray Moody | Lupe Sifuentes-Enriquez | Jodie S. Greene | Don G. Letsinger |
| Ellis | Waxahachie | Chad Adams | Cindy Polley | Joe F. Grubbs | Ron Langenheder | John Bridges | Ray Stewart |
| El Paso | El Paso | Dolores Briones | Waldo Alarcon | José R. Rodriguez | Edward Dion | Victor A. Flores | Leo Samaniego |
| Erath | Stephenville | Tab Thompson | Gwinda Jones | Carey Fraser | Donna Kelley | Jennifer Schlicke-Carey | Tommy Bryant |
| Falls | Marlin | Thomas Sehon | Frances Braswell | Kathryn J. Gilliam | Sue Ryan | Kate Vande Veegaete | Ben Kirk |
| Fannin | Bonham | Derrell Hall | Margaret Gilbert | Myles Porter | Mike Towery | Pam Richardson | Talmage Moore |
| Fayette | La Grange | Edward F. Janecka | Carolyn Kubos Roberts | John W. Wied | Office abolished 11-3-87. | Carol Johnson | Rick Vandel |
| Fisher | Roby | Marshal Bennett | Melody Appleton | Rudy V. Hamric | Marty Williamson | Betty Mize | Mickey A. Counts |
| Floyd | Floydada | William D. Hardin | Marilyn Holcomb | Lex Herrington | Elva Martinez | Penny Golightly | Billy Royce Gilmore |
| Foard | Crowell | Charlie Bell | Sherry Weatherred | Daryl Halencak | Esther Kajs | Bobby Bond | Bobby Bond |
| Fort Bend | Richmond | Robert E. Hebert | Dianne Wilson | Ben W. "Bud" Childers | Jeanne Parr | Marsha P. Gaines | Milton Wright |
| Franklin | Mount Vernon | Gerald W. Hubbell | Betty Crane | Cecil Solomon | Marla Carrell | Margie Jaggers | Charles L. "Chuck" White |
| Freestone | Fairfield | Linda K. Grant | Mary Lynn White | Robert W. Gage | Kay Taylor Barger | Carolyn Varley | Ralph Billings |
| Frio | Pearsall | Carlos A. Garcia | Angie Tullis | Hector Lozano | Anna L. Hernández | Hector Cantú | Lionel Treviño |
| Gaines | Seminole | Judy House | Vicki Phillips | Sterling Harmon | Lesha Aten | Susan Jones | Jon Key |
| Galveston | Galveston | James D. Yarbrough | Mary Ann Daigle | Harvey Bazzman | Kevin C. Walsh | Trish Gibbins | Gene Leonard |
| Garza | Post | Giles W. Dalby | Jerry Hays | Leslie Acker | Ruth Ann Young | Jeanette Hodges | Kenneth Ratke |
| Gillespie | Fredericksburg | Mark Stroeher | Mary Lynn Rusche | Tamara Y.S. Keener | Laura Lundquist | Leola Brodbeck | Milton E. Jung |
| Glasscock | Garden City | Wilburn Bednar | Rebecca Batla | Hardy Wilkerson | Alan Dierschke | Royce Pruit | Royce Pruit |
| Goliad | Goliad | Harold F. Gleinser | Gail M. Turley | Rob Balamonte | June Bethke | Anna M. López | Robert de la Garza |
| Gonzales | Gonzales | David Bird | Lee Riedel | Robert B. Scheske | Sheryl Barborak | Norma Jean DuBose | Glen A. Sachtleben |
| Gray | Pampa | Richard Peet | Susan Winborne | Todd L. Alvey | Lee Cornelison | Sammie Morris | Don Copeland |
| Grayson | Sherman | Tim McGraw | Wilma Blackshear Bush | Joseph D. Brown | Virginia Hughes | John Ramsey | J. Keith Gary |
| Gregg | Longview | Bill Stoudt | Laurie Woloszyn | Janie Johnson | Office abolished 1-1-88. | William Kirk Shields | Maxey Cerliana |
| Grimes | Anderson | James Dixon | David Pasket | Joe Falco | Phillis Allen | Connie Perry | Don Sowell |
| Guadalupe | Seguin | Donald L. Schraub | Teresa Kiel | Elizabeth Murray-Kolb | Linda Douglass | Tavie Murphy | Arnold S. Zwicke |
| Hale | Plainview | Bill Hollars | Diane Williams | Chris Prentice | Ida A. Tyler | Kemp Hinch | David B. Mull |
| Hall | Memphis | Jack Martin | Raye Bailey | John M. Deaver II | Janet Bridges | Pat Floyd | Robert McGuire |
| Hamilton | Hamilton | Fred Cox | Debbie Rudolph | Thomas E. White | Debbie Eoff | Cynthia Roberts | W.R. "Randy" Murphree |
| Hansford | Spearman | Jim D. Brown | Kim V. Vera | John L. Hutchison | Wanda Wagner | Helen Dry | R.L. McFarlin Jr. |
| Hardeman | Quanah | K. D. McNabb | Judy Cokendolpher | Stanley R. Watson | Mary Ann Naylor | Darlene Gamble | Randy L. Akers |
| Hardin | Kountze | Billy Caraway | Glenda Alston | David Sheffield | Sharon Overstreet | Shirley Stephens | Ed J. Cain |

| County | County Seat | County Judge | County Clerk | County Attorney | County Treasurer | Assessor-Collector | Sheriff |
|---|---|---|---|---|---|---|---|
| Harris | Houston | Robert A. Eckels | Beverly B. Kaufman | Michael Stafford | Jack Cato | Paul Bettencourt | Tommy B. Thomas |
| Harrison | Marshall | Wayne McWhorter | Patsy Cox | | Jamie Marie Noland | Betty R. Wright | Tom McCool |
| Hartley | Channing | Ronnie Gordon | Diane Thompson | William A. Cunningham | Dinkie Parman | Franky Scott | Franky Scott |
| Haskell | Haskell | David C. Davis | Rhonda Moeller | Shane Hadaway | Willie Faye Tidrow | Bobbye Collins | David Halliburton |
| Hays | San Marcos | James L. Powers | Lee Carlisle | Mike Wenk | Michele Tuttle | Luanne Caraway | Don Montague |
| Hemphill | Canadian | Bob W. Gober | Charles M. Cole | Ty M. Sparks | Cindy M. Bowen | Debra L. Ford | A. Dean Butcher |
| Henderson | Athens | David Holstein | Gwen Moffeit | James Owen | Karin Smith | Milburn Chaney | J.R. "Ronny" Brownlow |
| Hidalgo | Edinburg | Ramon Garcia | Juan D. Salinas III | | Norma Garcia | Armando Barrera Jr. | Enrique "Henry" Escalon |
| Hill | Hillsboro | Kenneth Davis | Ruth Pelham | Mark F. Pratt | Linda Polley | Thomas F. Davis | Brent Button |
| Hockley | Levelland | Larry D. Sprowls | Mary K. Walker | J. M. "Pat" Phelan | Denise Bohannon | Christy Clevenger | Donald Caddell |
| Hood | Granbury | Andy Rash | Sally Oubre | R. Kelton Conner | Rebecca Orlowski | Sandy Tidwell | Allen Hardin |
| Hopkins | Sulphur Springs | Cletis Millsap | Debbie Shirley | Dustanna Rabe | Betty Bassham | Debbie Jenkins | Butch Adams |
| Houston | Crockett | R.C. "Chris" Von Doenhoff | Bridget Lamb | Donna Gordon | Dianne Rhone | Joan Lucas | Darrell E. Bobbitt |
| Howard | Big Spring | Ben Lockhart | Donna Wright | Clyde E. "Mike" Thomas | Teresa S. Thomas | Kathy A. Sayles | Dale L. Walker |
| Hudspeth | Sierra Blanca | Becky Dean Walker | Patricia Bramblett | C.R. Kit Bramblett | Rosalinda Gonzales | L. Kay Scarbrough | Arvin West |
| Hunt | Greenville | Joe A. Bobbitt | Linda Brooks | Keith Willeford | Delores Shelton | Joyce J. Barrow | Don Anderson |
| Hutchinson | Stinnett | Jack L. Worsham | Beverly Turner | Michael Milner | Kathy Sargent | Mary Lou Henderson | Guy Rowh |
| Irion | Mertzon | Leon Standard | Reba Criner | James Ridge Jr. | Linda Pierce | Joyce Gray | Jimmy Martin |
| Jack | Jacksboro | Mitchell G. Davenport | Shelly Clayton | Michael G. Mask | Roger Sharp | Gay Low | Danny R. Nash |
| Jackson | Edna | Harrison Stafford II | Kenneth W. McElveen | | Mary Horton | Donna Atzenhoffer | Kelly Janica |
| Jasper | Jasper | Joe Folk | Debbie Newman | | Mary Jane Hancock | Robert Pace | Billy Rowles |
| Jeff Davis | Fort Davis | George Grubb | Sue Blackley | Sandy Stewart | Geen Parrott | Steve Bailey | Steve Bailey |
| Jefferson | Beaumont | Carl R. Griffith Jr. | Sandy Walker | Tom Maness | Linda Robinson | Miriam Johnson | Mitch Woods |
| Jim Hogg | Hebbronville | Agapito Molina Jr. | Noemi G. Salinas | Richard R. Gonzales | Linda Jo G. Soliz | Marina Vasquez | Erasmo Alarcon |
| Jim Wells | Alice | L. Arnoldo Saenz | Ruben Sandoval | Jesusa Sánchez-Vera | Becky Dominguez | Lucila Reynolds | Oscar Lopez |
| Johnson | Cleburne | Roger Harmon | Curtis H. Douglas | Bill Moore | Barbara Robinson | Scott Porter | Bob L. Alford |
| Jones | Anson | Dale Spurgin | Julia McCray | Chad Cowan | Irene Hudson | Mary Ann Lovelady | Larry A. Moore |
| Karnes | Karnes City | Alger H. Kendall Jr. | Alva Jonas | Robert L. Busselman | Nancy L. Duckett | Phillis Ender | Bobby Mutz |
| Kaufman | Kaufman | Wayne Gent | Laura A. Hughes | | Johnny Countryman | Donna Sprague | David Byrnes |
| Kendall | Boerne | Eddie John Vogt | Darlene Herrin | Ross Fischer | Medana Crow | James A. Hudson Jr. | Henry B. Hodge |
| Kenedy | Sarita | J.A. Garcia Jr. | Veronica Vela | Jaime E. Tijerina | Cynthia M. Salinas | Eleuteria S. Gonzalez | Ramiro Medellin Jr. |
| Kent | Jayton | Jim C. White | Rena Jones | Howard Freemyer | Margaret L. McCurry | Matthew K. Moorhead | Matthew K. Moorhead |
| Kerr | Kerrville | Pat Tinley | Jannett Pieper | David Motley | Barbara Nemec | Paula Rector | W.R. Hierholzer |
| Kimble | Junction | Delbert R. Roberts | Haydee Torres | Max Fischer | Sheila D'Spain | Mike Chapman | Mike Chapman |
| King | Guthrie | Duane Daniel | Linda Lewis | Marshall Capps (pro tem) | Kay Miller | Sadie Mote | R.C. Daniel Jr. |
| Kinney | Brackettville | Herbert Senne | Dora Elia Sandoval | Tully Shahan | Janis J. Floyd | Martha P. Padron | Leland Burgess |
| Kleberg | Kingsville | Pete de la Garza | Sam D. Deanda | Delma Rios-Salazar | Rachel S. Alaniz | Melissa T. de la Garza | Antonio Gonzalez |
| Knox | Benjamin | Greg Clonts | Ronnie Verhalen | Bobby D. Burnett | Penny Goodwin | Stanton Brown | Dean Homstad |
| Lamar | Paris | Maurice Superville | Kathy Marlowe | Mark Burtner | Shirley Fults | Peggy Noble | B.J. McCoy |
| Lamb | Littlefield | William A. Thopmsion Jr. | Bill Johnson | Mark Yarbrough | Janice B. Wells | Linda Charlton | Gary Maddox |
| Lampasas | Lampasas | Virgil E. Lilley | Connie Hartmann | Larry W. Allison | Nelda DeRiso | Linda Crawford | Gordon Morris |
| La Salle | Cotulla | Joel Rodriguez Jr. | Peggy Murray | Elizabeth Martinez | Marissa Mancha | Elida A. Linares | Jerry P. Patterson |
| Lavaca | Hallettsville | Ronald L. Leck | Elizabeth A. Kouba | James W. Carr | Lois Henry | Margaret M. Kallus | Robert E. Wurm |
| Lee | Giddings | Evan Gonzales | Carol Dismukes | Ted Weems | Melinda Krause | Virginia Jackson | Joe Goodson |
| Leon | Centerville | Byron Ryder | Carla McEachern | James R. Witt Jr. | Audrey Grimes | Louise Wilson | Michael Price |
| Liberty | Liberty | Lloyd Kirkham | Delia Sellers | A.J. Hartel III | Linda Leonard | Mark McClelland | Greg Arthur |
| Limestone | Groesbeck | Elenor F. Holmes | Sue Lown | Roy DeFriend | Angela Roach | Barbara Rader | Dennis D. Wilson |
| Lipscomb | Lipscomb | Willis V. Smith | Terri Parker | Randy M. Phillips | Pat Wyatt | Ann Word | James Robertson |
| Live Oak | George West | Jim Huff | Karen Irving | J.R. "Rob" Schneider Jr. | Violet Person | Virginia Horton | Larry Busby |
| Llano | Llano | R.G. Floyd | Bette Sue Hoy | Cheryll Mabray | Diana Cummings | Dexter Sagebiel | Nathan Garrett |
| Loving | Mentone | Donald C. Creager | Beverly Hanson | | Ann Blair | Richard Putnam | Richard Putnam |
| Lubbock | Lubbock | Thomas V. Head | Doris Ruff | Benni Hemmeline | Sharon Gossett | Barbara Brooks | David Gutierrez |
| Lynn | Tahoka | H.G. Frankline | Susan Tipton | James Napper | Janet Porterfield | Sherry Pearce | Dennis "Jake" Diggs |

| County | County Seat | County Judge | County Clerk | County Attorney | County Treasurer | Assessor-Collector | Sheriff |
|---|---|---|---|---|---|---|---|
| Madison | Madisonville | Cecil N. Neely | Charlotte Barrett | William M. "Bill" Bennett | Judy Weathers | Lee Ann Williams | Dan Douget |
| Marion | Jefferson | Gene S. Terry | Betty G. Smith | James P. Finstrom | Dorothy Whatley | Mary Alice Biggs | Bill McCay |
| Martin | Stanton | Charles "Corky" Blocker | Susie Hull | James L. McGilvray | H.D. Howard | Kathy Hull | Randy Cozart |
| Mason | Mason | Jerry Bearden | Beatrice Langehennig | Shain V.H. Chapman | Polly McMillan | M.J. Metzger | M.J. Metzger |
| Matagorda | Bay City | Greg B. Westmoreland | Gail Denn | Jill Cornelius | Suzanne Kucera | Cristyn Hallmark | James D. Mitchell |
| Maverick | Eagle Pass | Jose Aranda | Sara Montemayor | Ernest G. Mireles | Manuel Reyes Jr. | Esteban A. Luna | Salvador Rios |
| McCulloch | Brady | Randy Young | Tina A. Smith | Virginia Treadwell | Donna Robinett | Deena G. Moore | Earl Howell |
| McLennan | Waco | Jim Lewis | J.A. "Andy" Harwell | | Bill Helton | A. F. "Buddy" Skeen | Larry Lynch |
| McMullen | Tilden | Linda Lee Henry | Dorairene Garza | René Barrientoes | Donald Haynes Jr. | Mary K. Edwards | Bruce Thomas |
| Medina | Hondo | Jim Barden | Elva Miranda | Ralph Bernsen | Rita Moos | Loraine Neuman | Vivian Torres |
| Menard | Menard | Richard Cordes | Elsie Maserang | Ben Neel | Robert Bean | Brent Bratton | Bruce Hough |
| Midland | Midland | William C. Morrow | Shauna Brown | Russell Malm | JoAnn Carr | Kathy Reeves | Gary Painter |
| Milam | Cameron | Frank Summers | La Verne Soefje | Kerry M. Spears | Danica D. Lara | Doug R. Bryan | Charles L. "Charlie" West |
| Mills | Goldthwaite | Randy L. "Rob" Wright | Beulah L. "Patty" Roberts | Tommy M. Adams | Patsy E. Miller | Doug Storey | Doug Storey |
| Mitchell | Colorado City | Ray Mayo | Debby Carlock | T.L. Rees Sr. | Ann Hallmark | Faye Lee | Patrick Toombs |
| Montague | Montague | James O. Kittrell | Valorie Stout | Jeb McNew | Patty Fenoglio | Sydney Nowell | Chris Hamilton |
| Montgomery | Conroe | Alan B. Sadler | Mark Turnbull | David Walker | Martha Gustavsen | J. R. Moore | Guy Williams |
| Moore | Dumas | Kari Campbell | Brenda McKanna | Rayford A. Ratliff | Pam Cox | Joy Robertson | H.T. "Ted" Montgomery |
| Morris | Daingerfield | J.C. Jennings | Vicki Camp | O.G. Stanley | Nita Beth Traylor | Thelma Awtry | C.R. "Ricky" Blackburn |
| Motley | Matador | Ed. D. Smith | Kate Hurt | Tempie T. Hutton | Eva Barkley | Jo Elaine Hart | James Meador |
| Nacogdoches | Nacogdoches | Sue Kennedy | Carol Wilson | Jefferson Davis | Kay Watkins | Janie Weatherly | Thomas Kerss |
| Navarro | Corsicana | Alan Bristol | Sherry Dowd | | Joe Graves | Peggy Blackwell Moore | Leslie Cotten Sr. |
| Newton | Newton | Truman Dougherty | Mary Cobb | | Bettie Hall Cobb | Bea Westbrook | Wayne Powell |
| Nolan | Sweetwater | Tim Fambrough | Patricia "Pat" McGowan | Lisa Peterson | Gayle Biggerstaff | Fonda Holman | Donnie Rannefeld |
| Nueces | Corpus Christi | Terry Shamsie | Ernest M. Briones | Laura Garza Jimenez | Office abolished 11-3-87. | Ramiro "Ronnie" Canales | Larry Olivarez Sr. |
| Ochiltree | Perryton | Kenneth R. Donahue | Jane Hammerbeck | Bruce Roberson | Ginger Hays | Helen Bates | Joe Hataway |
| Oldham | Vega | Don R. Allred | Becky Groneman | Donald Davis | Charlotte Cook | Cynthia Artho | David T. Medlin |
| Orange | Orange | Carol Thibodeaux | Karen Jo Vance | John D. Kimbrough | Vergie Moreland | Lynda Gunstream | Mike White |
| Palo Pinto | Palo Pinto | Mickey D. West | Bobbie Smith | Phil Garrett | Mary M. Motley | Sandra R. Long | Larry L. Watson |
| Panola | Carthage | David L. Anderson | Mickey Dorman | | Gloria Portman | Jean Whiteside | Jack Ellett |
| Parker | Weatherford | Mark Riley | Jeane Brunson | John Forrest Jr. | Jim Thorp | Larry Lippincott | Jay Brown |
| Parmer | Farwell | Bonnie J. Clayton-Heald | Colleen Stover | Charles F. Aycock | Altha K. Herington | Bobbie Pierson | Randy Geries |
| Pecos | Fort Stockton | Joe Shuster | Judy Deerfield | Jesús Gonzáles Jr. | Barry McCallister | Santa S. Acosta | Cliff Harris |
| Polk | Livingston | John P. Thompson | Barbara Middleton | | Nola Reneau | Marion A. "Bid" Smith | Billy Ray Nelson |
| Potter | Amarillo | Arthur Ware | Sue Daniel | Sonya Letson | (vacant) | Robert Miller | Mike Shumate |
| Presidio | Marfa | Jerry C. Agan | Brenda M. Silva | Teresa Todd | Mario S. Rivera | Norma Arroyo | Danny Dominguez |
| Rains | Emory | Joe Ray Dougherty | Linda Wallace | Robert Vititow | Teresa Northcutt | Richard Wilson | Richard Wilson |
| Randall | Canyon | Ernie Houdashell | Sue Wicker Bartolino | | Glenna Canada | Carol Autry | Joel Richardson |
| Reagan | Big Lake | Larry Isom | Terri Pullig | J. Russell Ash | Nancy Ratliff | Sue Turner | Kirk Pullig |
| Real | Leakey | W.B. Sansom Jr. | Bella A. Rubio | Garry Merritt | Kathy Brooks | Donna Brice | James Earl Brice |
| Red River | Clarksville | Powell W. "P.J." Peek | Lorie Moose | Val Varley | Glenda Garrison | Leslie Nix | Jerry Conway |
| Reeves | Pecos | Jimmy B. Galindo | Dianne O. Florez | Luis U. Carrasco | Linda L. Clark | Elfida Zuniga | Arnulfo "Andy" Gomez |
| Refugio | Refugio | Roger Fagan | Ruby Garcia | Robert P. McGuill | Louise Null Aduddel | Veronica Rocha | Jim Hodges |
| Roberts | Miami | Vernon H. Cook | Donna L. Goodman | Leslie Breeding | Billie J. Lunsford | Carol Johnson | Dana Miller |
| Robertson | Franklin | Fred Elliott | Kathryn N. Brimhall | John C. Paschall | Jacqueline Vann | Carol D. Bielamowicz | Gerald Yezak |
| Rockwall | Rockwall | Bill Bell | Paulette Burks | | Sheréé Jones | Kathryn Feldpausch | Harold Eavenson |
| Runnels | Ballinger | Marilyn Egan | Elesa Ocker | Stuart Holden | Margarette Smith | Robin Burgess | William A. "Bill" Baird |
| Rusk | Henderson | Sandra Hodges | Frank Hudson | Kyle Freeman | Nora Rousseau | Matt Johnson | James Stroud |
| Sabine | Hemphill | Jack H. Leath | Janice McDaniel | Robert G. Neal Jr. | Tricia Woods Jacks | Tammy Reeves | Thomas Maddox |
| San Augustine | San Augustine | Wayne Holt | Diana Kovar | Heather Land Watts | Carol W. Vaughn | Regina A. Barthol | John M. Cartwright |
| San Jacinto | Coldspring | W.H. "Bill" Law | Charlene Vann | | Charlene Everitt | Barbara A. Shelly | Lacy Rogers |
| San Patricio | Sinton | Terry Simpson | Gracie Alaniz-Gonzales | David Aken Jr. | Courtenay Dugat | Thelma Kelley | Leroy Moody |
| San Saba | San Saba | Byron Theodosis | Kim Wells | David M. Williams | Gayla Hawkins | John L. Wells | John L. Wells |

| County | County Seat | County Judge | County Clerk | County Attorney | County Treasurer | Assessor-Collector | Sheriff |
|---|---|---|---|---|---|---|---|
| Schleicher | Eldorado | Johnny F. Griffin | Peggy Williams | Marian B. Overstreet | Karen Henderson | Lou Ann Turner | David Doran |
| Scurry | Snyder | Rod Waller | Joan Bunch | Michael Hartman | Nelda Colvin | Diana Williamson | Darren Jackson |
| Shackelford | Albany | Ross Montgomery | Cheri Hawkins | Colton P. Johnson | Sherry Enloe | Richard Wagman | Richard Wagman |
| Shelby | Center | Floyd A. Watson | Allison Harbison | Gary W. Rholes | Carolyn Bush Golden | Janie Graves | James Moore |
| Sherman | Stratford | Kim Crippen | Mary Lou Albert | Kimberly Allen | Doris Parson | Valerie McAlister | Jack Haile |
| Smith | Tyler | Becky Dempsey | Judy Carnes | | Joyce Woodward Smith | Kay M. Smith | J.B. Smith |
| Somervell | Glen Rose | Walter Maynard | Candace Garrett | Ronald Hankins | Barbara Hudson | Dorothy Keller | Roger D. Hill |
| Starr | Rio Grande City | Eloy Vera | Omar J. Garza | David L. Garza | David Porras | Carmen A. Peña | Reymundo Guerra |
| Stephens | Breckenridge | Gary L. Fuller | Helen Haddock | Gary D. Trammel | Nancy Clary | Terry Simmons Sullivan | James D. "Jim" Reeves |
| Sterling | Sterling City | Robert L. Browne | Diane A. Browne | William J. Stroman | Wanda Foster | Joy Manning | Don Howard |
| Stonewall | Aspermont | Bobby F. McGough | Belinda Page | Norman Arnett | Linda Messick | Jim B. Ward | Bill Mullen |
| Sutton | Sonora | Carla Garner | Veronica E. Hernandez | David W. Wallace | Joyce Chalk | Maura Weingart | Joe M. Fincher |
| Swisher | Tulia | Harold Keeter | Brenda Hudson | Mike Criswell | Tricia Speed | Brenda Gunnels | Larry P. Stewart |
| Tarrant | Fort Worth | Tom Vandergriff | Suzanne Henderson | | Office abolished 4-2-83. | Betsy Price | Dee Anderson |
| Taylor | Abilene | George Newman | Janice Lyons | | Lesa Crosswhite | Lavena Cheek | Jack Dieken |
| Terrell | Sanderson | Leo Smith | Martha Allen | Marsha Monroe | Lynda Helmers | Y.E. "Chel" Duarte | Y.E. "Chel" Duarte |
| Terry | Brownfield | Douglas Ryburn | Ann Willis | G. Dwayne Pruitt | Bobbye Jo Floyd | Redelle Martin | Jerry L. Johnson |
| Throckmorton | Throckmorton | Trey Carrington | Mary "Susie" Walraven | Cheryl M. Taylor | Brenda Rankin | Linda Carrington | John Riley |
| Titus | Mt. Pleasant | Danny Pat Crooks | Sherry Jo Mars | Tim R. Taylor | Debby Rhea | Judy Cook | Arvel Shepard |
| Tom Green | San Angelo | Michael D. Brown | Elizabeth McGill | Chris Taylor | Dianna Spieker | Cindy Jetton | Joe Hunt |
| Travis | Austin | Samuel T. Biscoe | Dana DeBeauvoir | Ken Oden | Dolores Ortega Carter | Nelda Wells Spears | Margo Frasier |
| Trinity | Groveton | Mark Evans | Diane McCrory | Joe Warner Bell | Jo Bitner Bartee | Kathy McCarty | D. Brent Phillips |
| Tyler | Woodville | Jerome P. Owens Jr. | Donece Gregory | | Joyce Moore | Lynette Cruse | Gary Hennigan |
| Upshur | Gilmer | Dean Fowler | Robin Rodenberg | | Myra Harris | Micheal Smith | Anthony Betterton |
| Upton | Rankin | Vikki Bradley | Phyllis Stephens | Melanie Spratt-Anderson | Nancy Poage | Dan W. Brown | Dan W. Brown |
| Uvalde | Uvalde | William R. Mitchell | Lucille C. Hutcherson | John P. Deor | Joni Deorsam | Margarita "Maggie" Del Toro | Terry L. Crawford |
| Val Verde | Del Rio | Manuel "Mike" L. Fernandez | Maria Elena Cardenas | Ana Markowski Smith | Morris L. Taylor | Wayne H. Hyde | A. D'Wayne Jernigan |
| Van Zandt | Canton | Jeff E. Fisher | Elizabeth Everitt | | Judy Peoples | Vicki Looney | R.P. "Pat" Burnett Jr. |
| Victoria | Victoria | Donald R. Pozzi | Val D. Huvar | | Cathy Bailey | Rena Scherer | Michael Ratcliff |
| Walker | Huntsville | Robert D. Pierce | James D. Patton | | Barbara McGilberry | Tom Cauthen | Victor K. Graham |
| Waller | Hempstead | Owen Ralston | Cheryl Peters | Kevin D. Acker | Susan Winfree | Ellen C. Shelburne | Randy Smith |
| Ward | Monahans | Sam G. Massey | Natrell Cain | Julie L. Renken | Teresa Perry | Dolores H. Fine | Mikel Strickland |
| Washington | Brenham | Dorothy Morgan | Beth A. Rothermel | Homero Ramirez | Norman Draehn | Candy Arth | J. W. Jankowski |
| Webb | Laredo | Louis H. Bruni | Margie Ramirez Ibarra | | Delia Perales | Patricia A. Barrera | Juan Garza |
| Wharton | Wharton | John Wesley Murrile | Sandra K. Sanders | G.A. "Trey" Maffett | Donna Schoenfield Kocurek | Patrick Kubala | Jess Howell |
| Wheeler | Wheeler | Jerry Dan Hefley | Margaret Dorman | Bobbye Hill | Jauna Benefield | Lewis Scott Porter | Jimmy Wales Adams |
| Wichita | Wichita Falls | Woodrow W. Gossom Jr. | Lloyd M. Lueck | | Mike Bruckner | Lou H. Murdock | Thomas J. Callahan |
| Wilbarger | Vernon | Gary Streit | Frances McGee | Mike Baskerville | Joann Carter | JoAnn Bourland | David Quisenberry |
| Willacy | Raymondville | Simon Salinas | Terry Flores | Juan Angel Guerra | Arturo "Tuttie" Gomez | LaQuita Garza | Larry G. Spence |
| Williamson | Georgetown | John Doerfler | Nancy E. Rister | Eugene D. Taylor | Vivian Wood | Deborah M. Hunt | John A. Maspero |
| Wilson | Floresville | Marvin Quinney | Eva S. Martinez | Russell H. Wilson | Carolyn Orth | Anna D. Gonzales | Joe D. Tackitt Jr. |
| Winkler | Kermit | Bonnie Leck | Shethelia Reed | Thomas Cameron | Tabby Curtis | Patti Franks | Robert L. Roberts Jr. |
| Wise | Decatur | Richard R. Chase | Sherry Parker | Greg Lowery | Katherine Canova | Pat Younger | Phil Ryan |
| Wood | Quitman | Royce McCoy | Brenda Taylor | | Bryan Jeanes | Tommie Bradshaw | Bill Skinner |
| Yoakum | Plains | Dallas Brewer | Deborah L. Rushing | Richard Clark | Barbara Wright | Betty Rivas | Don Corzine |
| Young | Graham | Stan Peavy III | Shirley Choate | Boyd L. Richie | Charlotte Farmer | Sonja Gray | Carey W. Pettus |
| Zapata | Zapata | David Morales | Consuelo R. Villarreal | José Antonio López | Romeo Salinas | Rosalva D. Guerra | Sigifredo Gonzalez Jr. |
| Zavala | Crystal City | Joe Luna | Oralia G. Treviño | Joe W. Taylor | Susie Perez | Florinda Perez | Eusevio Salinas Jr. |

# Texas County and District Officials — Table No. 2

## District Clerks, District Attorneys and County Commissioners

See Table No. 1 on preceding pages for County Seats, County Judges, County Clerks, County Attorneys, County Treasurers, Tax Assessors-Collectors and Sheriffs. An asterisk (*) before a county name marks a county whose county clerk failed to return our questionnaire; the names of officials for those counties are taken from most recent unofficial sources available to us.
† If more than one District Attorney is listed for a county, the district court number is noted in parentheses after each attorney's name. If no District Attorney is listed, the Country Attorney, whose name can be found in Table No. 1, assumes the duties of that office.

| County | District Clerk | District Attorney† | Comm. Precinct 1 | Comm. Precinct 2 | Comm. Precinct 3 | Comm. Precinct 4 |
|---|---|---|---|---|---|---|
| Anderson | Janice Staples | Douglas E. Lowe | Joe W. Chaffin | Darrell Emanuel | Tim Milliken | Randy Watkins |
| Andrews | Cynthia Jones | John L. Pool | Barney Fowler | Brad Young | Jerry McPherson | Paul Williams |
| Angelina | Reba Squyres | Clyde Herrington | Rick Harrison | Kenneth Timmons | Allen Sumners | Lynn George |
| Aransas | Pam Heard | Patrick Flanigan | Oscar Piña | Floyd Clark | Danny Adams | Howard Murph |
| Archer | Jane Ham | Tim Cole | Richard Shelley | Darin Wolf | Ben Buerger | Darryl Lightfoot |
| Armstrong | Joe Reck | Rebecca King | Dee Aduddell | Mike Baker | Foster Parker | C. M. Bryant |
| Atascosa | Jerome T. Brite | Lynn Ellison | David Caballero | Leslie Mikolajczyk Sr. | Freddie Ogden | Weldon P. Cude |
| Austin | Marie Myers | Travis Koehn | Harlan Schrader | Wilbert Frank Jr. | James "Bubba" Duke | David Hubenak |
| Bailey | Elaine Parker | Johnny Actkinson | Jack Dunham | C. E. Grant Jr. | Joey Kindle | Ginger Damron |
| Bandera | Tammy Kneuper | E. Bruce Curry | Rex Cox | Ronald Basinger | Richard Keese | Doug King |
| Bastrop | Cathy Smith | Bryan Goertz | Johnny Sanders | Clara Beckett | Don Loucks | Lee Dildy |
| Baylor | Clara "Carrie" Coker | Bill Neal | Don Matus | Jack Brown | Jerry Pruitt | Eric Hostas |
| Bee | Sandra Clark | George P. Morrill II | Carlos Salazar Jr. | Susan C. Stasny | Norberto Garcia | Ronnie Olivares |
| Bell | Sheila Norman | Henry L. Garza | Richard Cortese | Tim Brown | Leroy Schiller | John Fisher |
| Bexar | Margaret G. Montemayor | Susan D. Reed | Robert Tejeda | Paul Elizondo | Lyle Larson | Tommy Adkisson |
| Blanco | Debby Elsbury | Sam Oatman | Floyd Cooley | James Sultemeier | Robert Mauck | Paul Granberg |
| Borden | Joyce Herridge | Dana W. Cooley | Doug Isaacs | Randy L. Adcock | Ernest Reyes | Joe T. Belew |
| Bosque | Sandra L. Woosley | B.J. Shepherd | Kenneth Ray Worley | Durwood Koonsman | Jerry Smith | Joe V. Guinn |
| Bowie | Billie Fox | Bobby Lockhart | Jack Stone | John Addington | Dale Barrett | Carl Teel |
| Brazoria | Jerry Deere | Jeri Yenne | Donald "Dude" Payne | James D. Clawson | Jack Harris | Larry L. Stanley |
| Brazos | Marc Hamlin | Bill Turner | Tony Jones | Duane Peters | Kenny Mallard Jr. | Carey Cauley Jr. |
| Brewster | Jo Ann Salgado | Frank Brown | Asa "Cookie" Stone | J.W. "Red" Pattillo | Emilio Salmon | Matilde "Wacky" Pallanez |
| Briscoe | Bena Hester | Becky McPherson | Terry Grimland | Danny Maynard | Larry Comer | Gary Weaks |
| Brooks | Noe E. Guerra Jr. | Joe Frank Garza | Gloria Garza | Ramon Navarro Jr. | Raul Ramirez | Mae Saenz |
| Brown | Jan Brown | Skylar B. Sudderth | Steve Adams | Adron Beck | Richard Gist | David Carroll |
| Burleson | Doris H. Brewer | Renee Mueller | Frank L. Kristof | Donnie Hejl | W.J. Stracener | John B. Landolt Jr. |
| Burnet | Dana DeBerry | Sam Oatman | Billie Neve | Russell Graeter | Ronny Hibler | James Oakley |
| Caldwell | Emma Jean Schulle | Charles Schneider | Herb Schulze | Charles Bullock | Ronnie Duesterheft | Joe Ivan Roland |
| Calhoun | Pamela Martin-Hartgrove | Dan W. Heard | Roger C. Galvan | Michael Balajka | W. H. Floyd | Kenneth W. Finster |
| Callahan | Sharon Owens | | Harold Hicks | Bryan Farmer | Tommy Holland | Charlie Grider |
| Cameron | Aurora de la Garza | Yolanda de Leon | Pedro "Pete" Benavides | John Wood | David Garza | Edna Tamayo |
| Camp | Marianne Groves | Charles C. Bailey | Jack Efurd | Charles A. "Buddy" Jones | Hervey H. Hiner Sr. | Bobby Barrett |
| Carson | Celeste Bichsel | Stuart Messer | Mike Britten | Kenneth Ware | Jerry Strawn | Randy Elliott |
| Cass | Becky Wilbanks | Randall Lee | Kenneth Pate | Danny Joe Shaddix | Paul Cothren | Max Bain |
| Castro | Joyce M. Thomas | James R. Horton | Newlon Rowland | Larry Gonzales | W.A. "Bay" Baldridge | Dan Schmucker |
| Chambers | R. B. "Bobby" Scherer Jr. | Michael R. Little | Mark Huddleston | Judy Edmonds | W.E. "Buddy" Irby | W.O. "Bill" Wallace Jr. |
| Cherokee | Marlys Mason | Elmer C. Beckworth Jr. | R.L. "Bob" Johnson | Kevin Pierce | Moody Glass Jr. | Billy McCutcheon |
| Childress | Zona Prince | Stuart Messer | Denzil Ray | Dan Imhof | Lyall Foster | Don Ray Crook |
| Clay | Dan Slagle | Tim Cole | R.L. "Lindy" Choate | Johnny Ray Gee | Wilson Scaling | Brice Jackson |

| County | District Clerk | District Attorney† | Comm. Precinct 1 | Comm. Precinct 2 | Comm. Precinct 3 | Comm. Precinct 4 |
|---|---|---|---|---|---|---|
| Cochran | Rita Tyson | Gary Goff | Gerald Ramsey | J.B. Allen | Stacey Dunn | Jimmy Mullinax |
| Coke | Mary Grim | Stephen Lupton | Paul Burns | Bill Wheat | Gaylon Pitcock | George Snapp |
| Coleman | Jo Dean Chapman | Joe Lee Rose | Jim Porter | Billy Don McCrary | Mike Barker | Alan Davis |
| Collin | Hannah Kunkle | John Roach | Phyllis Cole | Jerry Hoagland | Joe Jaynes | Jack Hatchell |
| Collingsworth | Jackie Johnson | Stuart Messer | Dan Langford | Zeb Roberson | Eddie Orr | Pat Glenn |
| Colorado | Harvey Vornsand | Ken Sparks | Doug Wessels | Herbert Helmcamp | Tommy Hahn | Darryl Gertson |
| Comal | Katherine "Kathy" Faulkner | Dib Waldrip | Jack Dawson | Jay Millikin | Christina Zamora | Jan Kennady |
| Comanche | LaNell Williams | B.J. Shepherd | Garry Steele | Chris Biggs | Bobby Schuman | Clyde Brinson |
| Concho | Barbara K. Hoffman | Stephen H. Smith | R.M. Kingston | Ralph H. Wilberg | Frankie Wojtek | Aaron B. Browning Jr. |
| Cooke | Patricia Payne | Janelle Haverkamp | Phil Young | Bill Cox | Jerry Lewis | Virgil Hess |
| Coryell | Janice Gray | Riley Simpson | Jack Wall | Cliff Price | Don Jones | Kyle Pruitt |
| Cottle | Beckey J. Tucker | Bill Neal | Willie Rushin | Hazel Biddy | Manuel Cruz Jr. | Gus Timmons |
| Crane | Judy Crawford | Michael Fostel | Jack Damron | Lewis Overton | Domingo Escobedo | Mickey Hurst |
| Crockett | Debbi Puckett-Moore | Ori T. White | Frank Tambunga | Pleas Childress III | Freddie Nicks | Rudy Martinez |
| Crosby | Karla Isbell | C. Michael Ward | Gary Jordan | Frank Mullins | Larry Wampler | Billy Bob Wright |
| Culberson | Linda McDonald | Jaime Esparza | Cornelio Garibay | Manuel Molinar | John Jones | Israel "Rale" Navarrette |
| Dallam | LuAnn Taylor | David Green | Glenn Reagan | Oscar Przilas | Don Bowers | Carl French |
| Dallas | Jim Hamlin | Bill Hill | Jim Jackson | Mike Cantrell | John Wiley Price | Kenneth A. Mayfield |
| Dawson | Carolyn Turner | Ricky B. Smith | Jerry Beaty | Tino Morales | Troy Howard | Foy O'Brien |
| Deaf Smith | Jean Schumacher | James Michael English | Armando Gonzalez | Jerry Roberts | Troy Don Moore | Jerry O'Connor |
| Delta | Barbara Vaughn | Frank Long | C. D. "Mickey" Goforth | David Max Moody | James Campbell | Ted Carrington |
| Denton | Sheri Adelstein | Bruce Isaacks | Cynthia White | Sandy Jacobs | Bobbie J. Mitchell | Jim Carter |
| DeWitt | Tabeth Ruschhaupt | Michael A. Sheppard | Wallace W. Beck | Joe L. Machalec | Gilbert Pargmann | Alfred Rangnow |
| Dickens | Winona Humphreys | Becky McPherson | Don Condron | Billy George Drennan | Doc Edwards | Duane Durham |
| Dimmit | Alicia L. Martinez | Roberto Serna | Larry Speer | Johnny Gloria | Jose P. Martinez | Rodrigo Jaime |
| Donley | Fay Vargas | Stuart Messer | Ernest Johnston | Donnie Hall | Buster Shields | Bob Trout |
| Duval | Richard M. Barton | Heriberto Silva | Alejo C. Garcia | Rene M. Perez | Nestor Garza Jr. | Gilberto Uribe Jr. |
| Eastland | Loretta Key | Russ Thomason | Wayne Honea | Norman Christian | Bill Underwood | Reggie Pittman |
| Ector | Janis Morgan | John Smith | Freddie Gardner | Greg Simmons | Barbara Graff | Bob Bryant |
| Edwards | Sarah McNealy | Fred Hernandez | Robert Pena | F.O. "Tike" Burleson | James E. Epperson Jr. | Chisholm Erwin Parks |
| Ellis | Billie Ann Fuller | Joe F. Grubbs | Hallie Joe Robinson | Larry Jones | Jackie Miller Sr. | Ron Brown |
| El Paso | Gilbert Sanchez | Jaime E. Esparza | Charles Scruggs | Betti Flores | Miguel A. Teran | Daniel R. Haggerty |
| Erath | Wanda Pringle | John Terrill | Jerry Martin | Lynn Tidwell | Doug Eberhart | Randy Lowe |
| Falls | Larry Hoelscher | Kathryn J. Gilliam | Tom Zander | Robert Paul. Sr. | Nelson Coker | Bernhard Neumann |
| Fannin | Rochelle Turner | | Ronnie Rhudy | Stan Barker | Dewayne Strickland | Pat Hilliard |
| Fayette | Virginia Wied | | David R. Noak | Gary Weishuhn | Wilbert L. Gross | Tom Muras |
| Fisher | Tammy Haley | Mark Edwards | Scott Ely | Rodney Tankersley | Earnest Ragan | Gene Terry |
| Floyd | Barbara Edwards | Becky McPherson | Ray Nell Bearden | Lennie Gilroy | Craig Gilly | Jon Jones |
| Foard | Sherry Weatherred | Dan Mike Bird | Rick Hammonds | Jesse Moore | Larry Wright | Edward Crosby |
| Fort Bend | Glory Hopkins | John Healey | Tom D. Stavinoha | James Grady Prestage | Andy Meyers | James Patterson |
| Franklin | Barbara Keith Campbell | Frank Long | Jearl Cooper | Bobby Elbert | Deryl Carr | Sam Young |
| Freestone | Janet Haydon Chappell | | Luke Ward | Craig Oakes | Stanley Gregory | Clyde Ridge Jr. |
| Frio | Ramona Rodriguez | Lynn Allison | Jesus Salinas | Richard Muzquiz | Ruben Maldonado | Jose G. "Pepe" Flores |
| Gaines | Virginia Stewart | Ricky Smith | Robert Wood | Craig Belt | Ray Garrett | Charlie Lopez |
| Galveston | Evelyn Wells Robison | Kurt Sistrunk | Eddie Barr | Eddie Janek | Stephen D. Holmes | Kenneth Clark |

| County | District Clerk | District Attorney† | Comm. Precinct 1 | Comm. Precinct 2 | Comm. Precinct 3 | Comm. Precinct 4 |
|---|---|---|---|---|---|---|
| Garza | Jerry Hays | Ricky B. Smith | Lee Norman | Mason McClellan | John Valdez | Mike Sanchez |
| Gillespie | Barbara Meyer | E. Bruce Curry | Dayton E. Weidenfeller | William A. Roeder | Calvin Ransleben | John E. Thompson |
| Glasscock | Rebecca Batla | Hardy Wilkerson | Jimmy Strube | Mark Halfmann | Hugh Schafer | Michael Hoch |
| Goliad | Gail M. Turley | Michael Sheppard | Arturo Rojas | Jerry Rodriguez | Jim Kreneck | Ted Long |
| Gonzales | Sandra Baker | W.C. Kirkendall | Kenneth O. "Dell" Whiddon | James "Jim" Kelso | David Kuntschik | Otis "Bud" Wuest |
| Gray | Gaye Honderich | Richard J. Roach | Joe Wheeley | Gary Willoughby | Gerald L. Wright | James L. Hefley |
| Grayson | Cyndi Mathis Spencer | Joseph D. Brown | Johnny Waldrip | David Whitlock | Carol Shea | Gene Short |
| Gregg | Barbara Duncan | William M. Jennings | Charles Davis | Darryl Primo | Bob Barbee | Dan Craig |
| Grimes | Wayne Rucker | Tuck McLain | Larry Snook | Bill Pendley | Zac H. Falkenbury | Pam Finke |
| Guadalupe | James D. Behrendt | W. C. Kirkendall | Roger Baenziger | Cesareo Guadarrama III | Roy Richard Jr. | Judy Cope |
| Hale | Carla Cannon | Terry McEachern | Neal Burnett | Mario Martinez | Roy Borchardt | Benny Cantwell |
| Hall | Raye Bailey | Stuart Messer | Milton Beasley | Terry Lindsey | Buddy C. Logsdon | James Fuston |
| Hamilton | Leoma Larance | B.J. Shepherd | Jim Boatwright | Mike Lewis | Jon C. Bonner | Dickie Clary |
| Hansford | Kim V. Vera | Clay L. Ballman | Ira G. "Butch" Reed | Joe T. Venneman | Kent Guthrie | Danny Henson |
| Hardeman | Judy Cokendolpher | Dan Mike Bird | Charles McSpadden | Rodger Tabor | Charles Taylor | Rodney Foster |
| Hardin | Vicki Johnson | Charles Roach | Bob Burgess | Patricia McGallion | Ken Pelt | Bobby Franklin |
| Harris | Charles Bacarisse | Chuck Rosenthal | El Franco Lee | Sylvia Garcia | Steve Radack | Jerry Eversole |
| Harrison | Sherry Griffis | Joe Black | Jerry Lomax | Emma Bennett | James Greer | Jeffrey R. Thompson |
| Hartley | Diane Thompson | David Green | David Vincent | Andy Michael | Jim Yoder | Robert "Butch" Owens |
| Haskell | Penny Anderson | Mike Fouts | Johnny Scoggins | Tiffen Mayfield | Kenny Thompson | Bobby D. Smith |
| Hays | Cecelia Adair | Michael Wenk | Debbie Gonzales-Ingalsbe | H.S. "Susie" Carter | William "Bill" Burnett | Russ G. Molenaar |
| Hemphill | Charles M. Cole | Richard J. "Rick" Roach | Joe Schaef | Ed Culver | John D. Ramp | Lynard G. Schafer |
| Henderson | Becky Hanks | Donna Bennett | Joe D. Hall | Wade McKinney | Ronny Lawrence | Jerry West |
| Hidalgo | Omar Guerrero | Rene A. Guerra | Sylvia Handy | Hector "Tito" Palacios | Joe M. Flores | Oscar L. Garza Jr. |
| Hill | Charlotte Barr | Dan V. Dent | J.K. Lane | James W. Buzbee | Mildred Brustrom | John W. Erwin |
| Hockley | Dennis Price | Gary A. Goff | Jack Ayers | Larry Carter | J. R. Stanley | Billy W. Thetford |
| Hood | Tonna Trumble | Richard Hattox | Robert Anderson | James Ducato | Matt Mills | Al Bulloch |
| Hopkins | Patricia Domer | J. Frank Long | Beth Wisenbaker | Burke Bullock | Don Patterson | Danny Evans |
| Houston | Pam Pugh | Cindy Maria Garner | Jerry McLeod | Willie Kitchen | Pat Perry | Kennon Kellum |
| Howard | Colleen Barton | Hardy Wilkerson | Emma Puga Brown | Jerry Kilgore | W. B. "Bill" Crooker | Gary Simer |
| Hudspeth | Patricia Bramblett | Scott Foster (assistant) | Pilar Ortega | Curtis Carr | Jim Ed Miller | James Kiehne |
| Hunt | Ann Prince | F. Duncan Thomas | Kenneth D. Thornton | Ralph Green | Phillip A. Martin | Jim Latham |
| Hutchinson | Joan Carder | Clay Ballman | R. D. Cornelison | Jerry D. Hefner | S.T. "Red" Isbell | Eddie Whittington |
| Irion | Reba Criner | Stephen Lupton | E. Wayne Smith | Jeff McCutchen | John Nanny | Barbara Searcy |
| Jack | Tracie Pippin | Jana Jones | Joe Paul Nichols | Jerry M. Adams | James L. Cozart | Milton R. Pruitt |
| Jackson | Sharon Whittley | Robert E. Bell | Miller Rutledge | Wayne Bubela | Johnny Belicek | Larry Deyton |
| Jasper | Linda Ryall | Ted E. Walker | Charles "J.R." Shofner | Rod Barger | Willie Stark | Mack Rose |
| Jeff Davis | Sue Blackley | Frank Brown | Bill Cotton | Diane Lacy | Curtis Evans | Bill Gearhart |
| Jefferson | Lolita Ramos | Tom Maness | Jimmie Cokinos | Mark Domingue | Waymon D. Hallmark | Everette "Bo" Alfred |
| Jim Hogg | Noemi G. Salinas | Rodolfo Gutierrez | Antonio Flores | Joe R. Stacy | Ricardo Alaniz | Juan Lino Ramirez |
| Jim Wells | R. David Guerrero | Joe Frank Garza | Pam Canales-Perez | Lawrence Cornelius | Oswald "Wally" Alanis | Javier N. Garcia |
| Johnson | David Lloyd | Dale Hanna | R.C. McFall | John Mathews | Mark C. Carpenter | Troy Thompson |
| Jones | Nona Carter | Britt Thurman | James Clawson | Mike Polk | Buz Wylie | Steve Lollar |
| Karnes | Patricia Brysch | Lynn Ellison | Darrel Blaschke | Jeffrey Wiatrek | James Rosales | Isidro Jr. "Stormy" Rossett Jr. |
| Kaufman | Sandra Featherston | Ed Walton | Rhea Fox | Ken Leonard | Ivan Johnson | Jim Deller |

| County | District Clerk | District Attorney† | Comm. Precinct 1 | Comm. Precinct 2 | Comm. Precinct 3 | Comm. Precinct 4 |
|---|---|---|---|---|---|---|
| Kendall | Shirley R. Stehling | E. Bruce Curry | John C. Kight | Gene Miertschin | Darrel L. Lux | Russell C. Busby |
| Kenedy | Veronica Vela | Carlos Valdez | Leonard May | Roberto Salazar Jr. | Tobin Armstrong | Gus A. Puente |
| Kent | Rena Jones | Michael E. Fouts | Roy W. Chisum | Don Long | Roy H. Parker | Robert Graham |
| Kerr | Linda Uecker | Bruce Curry | H.A. Baldwin | William H. Williams | Jonathan Letz | David E. Nicholson |
| Kimble | Haydee Torres | Ronald L. Sutton | Vicente Menchaca | Charles McGuire | Russell Fleming | Tooter Schulze |
| King | Linda Lewis | Bill Neal | Stephen Brady | Larry Rush | Bobby Tidmore | Darwood Marshall |
| Kinney | Dora Elia Sandoval | Tom F. Lee | Francis Wylis | Joe Montalvo | Natividad Terrazas III | Pat Melancon |
| Kleberg | Martha I. Soliz | Carlos Valdez | David Rosse | Joe Hinojosa | Dewey Hubert | Romeo L. Lomas |
| Knox | Ronnie Verhalen | Bill Neal | Weldon Skiles | Jerry Parker | Jimmy Urbanczyk | Johnny Birkenfeld |
| Lamar | Marvin Ann Patterson | Mark Burtner | Mike Blackburn | Carl Steffey | Rodney Pollard | Jackie Wheeler |
| Lamb | Celia Kuykendall | Mark Yarbrough | Willie Gene Green | T.H. Lewis | Emil Macha | Jimmy Young |
| Lampasas | Terri Cox | | Robert L. Vincent Jr. | Alex Wittenburg | David R. Smith | Jack B. Cox |
| La Salle | Peggy Murray | Lynn Ellison | Raymond A. Landrum Jr. | Roberto F. Aldaco | Albert Aguero | Domingo B. Martinez |
| Lavaca | Calvin J. Albrecht | W.C. "Bud" Kirkendall | Charles A. Netardus | Mark H. Zimmerman | Daniel Peters | Glen Blundell |
| Lee | Adeline Melcher | Ted Weems | Maurice Pitts Jr. | Douglas Hartfield | O.B. "Butch" Johnson | Thomas Kovar |
| Leon | Diane Davis | Ray Montgomery | Joey Sullivan | David Ferguson | Ray Gaskin | Burel Biddle |
| Liberty | Melody Gilmore | Michael Little | Todd Fontenot | Lee Groce | Melvin Hunt | Norman Brown |
| Limestone | Peggy M. Hill | Roy DeFriend | Keith Eaves | Billy G. Waldrop | G. Z. Stone | Don C. Ford |
| Lipscomb | Terri Parker | Rick Roach | Juan Cantu | Stanley Born | Marvin Born | Gene Ashpaugh |
| Live Oak | Lois Shannon | George P. Morrill II | Richard Lee | Barbara Kopplin | Jimmy Strause | Emilio Garza |
| Llano | Debbie Honig | Sam Oatman | W.R. "Bill" Kinney | Henry Parker | Duane Stueven | Leon Tucker |
| Loving | Beverly Hanson | Randy Reynolds | Harlan Hopper | Joe R. Renteria | Skeet Jones | Royce Creager |
| Lubbock | Barbara Sucsy | William C. "Bill" Sowder | Kenny Maines | James Kitten | Gilbert Flores | Patti Jones |
| Lynn | Sandra Laws | Ricky Smith | Don Morton | Michael Braddock | Don Blair | J. T. Miller |
| Madison | Joyce C. Batson | William M. "Bill" Bennett | Reed Reynolds | Don Farris | David Callaham | J.R. "Jim" Andrus |
| Marion | Janie McCay | James P. Finstrom | Bob Higgins | T.W. "Sam" Smith | Eugene Robinson | Charlie Treadwell |
| Martin | Susie Hull | Hardy L. Wilkerson | Sonny Garza | Valentino Sotelo | Bobby Kelly | David Pribyla |
| Mason | Beatrice Langehennig | Ronald "Ron" Sutton | Wayne Hofmann | John D. Fleming | Stanley Toeppich | Eldon Kothmann |
| Matagorda | Becky Denn | Steven E. Reis | Michael Pruett | George Deshotels | Leonard L. Lamar | Percy Carroll |
| Maverick | Irene Rodriguez | Roberto Serna | Johnny Martinez | Edwardo Bebe Sandoval | David Saucedo | Cesar Flores |
| McCulloch | Mackye Johnson | Ronald Sutton | Joe Johnson | Jerry Bratton | Nelson Solsberry | Brent Deeds |
| McLennan | Joe R. Johnson | John W. Segrest | Wendall Crunk | Lester Gibson | Joe Mashek | Ray Meadows |
| McMullen | Dorairene Garza | George Morrill II | Tim Teal | Rodney Swaim Jr. | Paul Koonce | Maximo Quintanilla Jr. |
| Medina | Eva Soto | Anton "Tony" Hackebeil | Royce Hartmann | Beverly Keller | Enrique "Henry" Santos | Kelly Carroll |
| Menard | Elsie Maserang | Ronald Sutton | Boyd Murchison | Sam Brownlee | Bart Wilkinson | Bill Royal |
| Midland | Vivian Wood | Al Schorre | Jimmy Smith | Mike Bradford | Josie D. Ramirez | Randy Prude |
| Milam | Betty R. Robertson | Kerry Spears | Clifford Whiteley | Kenneth Hollas | C. Dale Jaecks | Burke Bauerschlag |
| Mills | Beulah L. "Patty" Roberts | Skylar Sudderth | John Mann | Carroll Bunting | Lee Roy Schwartz | Farrel Thorne |
| Mitchell | Sharon Hammond | Mark Edwards | Edward B. Roach | Carl Guelker | Wyndell B. Inman | Billy H. Preston |
| Montague | Lesia Darden | Tim Cole | Jon A. Kernek | Jerry Clement | Tommy Sparks | Tommie Sappington |
| Montgomery | Barbara Adamick | Mike McDougal | Mike Meador | Craig Meador | Ed Chance | Ed Rinehart |
| Moore | Diane Hoefling | David Green | A. Gordon Clark | Bobby Barker | Milton Pax | Lynn Cartrite |
| Morris | Gwendolyn A. Oney | O.G. Stanley | (vacant) | Dearl Quarles | J.P. Cobb | Gary Camp |
| Motley | Kate Hurt | Beckey McPherson | Ronald L. Davis | Donnie L. Turner | Franklin Jameson | Russell Alexander |
| Nacogdoches | Donna Phillips | Edwin Klein | Tom Bush | Norman Henderson | Charles Simmons | Tom Strickland |

| County | District Clerk | District Attorney† | Comm. Precinct 1 | Comm. Precinct 2 | Comm. Precinct 3 | Comm. Precinct 4 |
|---|---|---|---|---|---|---|
| Navarro | Marilyn Greer | Steve Keathley | Kit Herrington | Olin Nickelberry | William Baldwin | John Paul Ross |
| Newton | Bree Allen | Atmar W. Davis Jr. | William L. "Bill" Fuller | Thomas Gill | Prentiss Hopson | Charles A. Brinson |
| Nolan | Vera Holloman | Mark Edwards | Randall Smith | Leslie Bond | Tommy White | Tony Lara |
| Nueces | Patsy Perez | Carlos Valdez | Frank Schwing | Betty Jean Longoria | Oscar O. Ortiz | Charles Cazalas |
| Ochiltree | Shawn Bogard | | Duane Pshigoda | Doug Barnes | James W. Clark | Larry Hardy |
| Oldham | Becky Groneman | Donald Davis | Quincy Taylor | Donnie Knox | Roger Morris | Billy Don Brown |
| Orange | Vickie Edgerly | John D. Kimbrough | James Stringer | Sue Bearden | John DuBose | Beamon Minton |
| Palo Pinto | Helen Slemmons | Tim Ford | David Lee | Robert Murray | George Nowak | Raymond Procter |
| Panola | Sandra King | Danny Buck Davidson | Ronny LaGrone | Douglas M. Cotton | Hermon Reed Jr. | Dale LaGrone |
| Parker | Elvera Johnson | Don Schnebly | Danny Choate | Joe Brinkley | Charles Akin | Jim Webster |
| Parmer | Sandra Warren | Johnny Actkinson | Kirk Frye | Tom Ware | Ed Corn | Elvis Powell |
| Pecos | Lisa Villarreal | Frank Brown (83rd) Ori White (112th) | George Riggs | Oscar G. Gonzalez | J.H. "Jay" Kent | Paul Valenzuela |
| Polk | Kathy E. Clifton | John S. Holleman | Robert C. "Bob" Willis | Bobby Smith | James J. "Buddy" Purvis | C.T. "Tommy" Overstreet |
| Potter | Caroline Woodburn | Rebecca King | Bill Thomas | Manuel "Perez" Villasenor | Joe Kirkwood | Iris Sanders Lawrence |
| Presidio | Brenda M. Silva | Frank Brown | Felipe Cordero | Eloy Aranda | Jaime Ramirez | Danny Watts |
| Rains | Deborah Traylor | Robert Vittow | Virgil McEnturff | Evelyn Malone | Gary Bishop | Rodney Smith |
| Randall | Jo Carter | James Farren | Robert "Bob" Karrh | Gene Parker | George "Skip" Huskey | Buddy Deford |
| Reagan | Terri Pullig | Ori White (112th) | Jim O'Bryan | Ron Galloway | Mikel Jones | Thomas Strube |
| Real | Bella A. Rubio | Anton E. Hackebeil | Allen Moffett | Clayton Crider | Castulo San Miguel | Joe Connell |
| Red River | Janice Gentry | Val Varley | Rufus Ward Jr. | M.D. Whittle Jr. | Elmer Caton | Mark Megason |
| Reeves | Pat Tarin | Randall "Randy" Reynolds | Felipe Arredondo | Norman Hill | Herman Tarin | Gilberto "Hivi" M. Rayos |
| Refugio | Ruby Garcia | Michael A. Sheppard | Rindle Wilson | Janis Gillespie | Gary Bourland | John Reyna |
| Roberts | Donna L. Goodman | Richard J. Roach | William H. Clark | Ken Gill | Kelly Flowers | James Duvall Jr. |
| Robertson | Cornelia A. Starkey | John C. Paschall | John Anderson | Jim Davis | Michael Byer | Marie Abraham |
| Rockwall | Kay McDaniel | Galen Ray Sumrow | Jerry Wimpee | Scott Self | Bruce Beaty | David Magness |
| Runnels | Loretta Michalewicz | Stephen Smith | Skipper Wheeless | Freddie Groham | James T. Self | Richard W. "Ricky" Strube |
| Rusk | Jean Hodges | Kyle Freeman | W.D. "Bill" Hale | Jerry Weaver | Freddy Swann | Kimble Harris |
| Sabine | Tanya Walker | John Fisher | Keith Clark | Lynn Smith | Doyle Dickerson | Fayne Warner |
| San Augustine | Jean Steptoe | John Fisher | Tommy Hunter | Edward Wilson | Jimmy Craig | B.R. Bryan |
| San Jacinto | Marilyn Nettles | Mark Price | James Hill | Bruce Thomas | Thomas L. Bonds | Joe Johnson |
| San Patricio | Carmen A. Garza | Patrick Flanigan | Enedina "Nina" Treviño | Fred P. Nardini | Pedro G. Rodriguez | Jim Price Jr. |
| San Saba | Kim Wells | Sam Oatman | Roger Crockett | Rickey Lusty | Wayland Perry | Roger McGehee |
| Schleicher | Peggy Williams | Stephen Lupton | Johnny Mayo Jr. | William G. Clark | Kirk Griffin | Matt Brown |
| Scurry | Trina Rodgers | Dana Cooley | Ralph W. Trevey | Jerry House | Howard Limmer | Chloanne Lindsey |
| Shackelford | Cheri Hawkins | Britt Thurman | Danny Peacock | Greg Simpson | Jimmy T. Brooks | Stan West |
| Shelby | Marsha Singletary | Linda K. Russell | Billy Adridge | Jimmy Lout | Travis Rodgers | Kevin Foster |
| Sherman | Mary Lou Albert | David Green | Sandy Tillery | Randy Williams | David Hass | Tommy Asher |
| Smith | Lois Rogers | Jack Skeen Jr. | Sharon Emmert | Donald Ray Pinkerton | F.E. "Frank" Sawyer | Jo Ann Hampton |
| Somervell | Candace Garrett | Dale Hanna | Zach Cummings | Dennis Ramsay | Lloyd Wirt | James Barnard |
| Starr | Juan Erasmo Saenz | Heriberto Silva | Jaime Alvarez | Raul Pena Jr. | Elroy Garza | Abel N. Gonzalez |
| Stephens | Shirley Parker | Stephen Bristow | Jerry Toland | D.C. "Button" Sikes | Joe F. High | Rickie Ray Carr |
| Sterling | Diane A. Browne | Stephen Lupton | Billy Joe Blair | Russell Noletubby | Patsy Bynum | Skeete Foster |
| Stonewall | Belinda Page | Mike Fouts | W.D. Ellison | Kenny Spitzer | Billy Kirk Meador | Gary Myers |
| Sutton | Veronica E. Hernandez | Ori White | Mike Villanueva | John Wade | Milton Cavaness | Belia Castaneda |

| County | District Clerk | District Attorney† | Comm. Precinct 1 | Comm. Precinct 2 | Comm. Precinct 3 | Comm. Precinct 4 |
|---|---|---|---|---|---|---|
| Swisher | Brenda Hudson | Terry McEachern | Lloyd Rahifs | Joe Bob Thompson | Billy Settle | Tim Reed |
| Tarrant | Tom Wilder | Tim Curry | Dionne Bagsby | Marti VanRavenswaay | B. Glen Whitley | J.D. Johnson |
| Taylor | Patricia Henderson | James Eidson | Jack Turner | Nowlin Cox | Stan Egger | Chuck Statler |
| Terrell | Martha Allen | Fred Hernandez | Thelma Calzada | Santiago "Chago" Flores Jr. | Charles Stegall | Kenn Norris |
| Terry | Paige Lindsey | G. Dwayne Pruitt | Earl J. Brown Jr. | Dale Andrews | Don Robertson | Jesse Hartman |
| Throckmorton | Mary "Susie" Walraven | Mike Fouts | Doyle Wells | Jimmy Glenn | Carlton Sullivan | Wilton Cantrell |
| Titus | Debra Bowen | Charles Bailey | R.J. "Bob" Fitch | Mike Fields | Billy Jack Thompson | Thomas Hockaday |
| Tom Green | Sheri Woodfin | Stephen R. Lupton (51st) / Stephen Smith (119th) | Clayton Friend | Karl Booker | Jodie Weeks | Richard S. Easingwood Jr. |
| Travis | Amalia Rodriguez-Mendoza | Ronnie Earle | Ron Davis | Karen Sonleitner | Gerald Daugherty | Margaret Gomez |
| Trinity | Cheryl Cartwright | Joe L. Price | Grover "Tiger" Worsham | Bill Burton | Cecil Webb | Travis Forrest |
| Tyler | Melissie Evans | Joe R. Smith | C.D. Woodrome | James T. "Rusty" Hughes | Joe Marshall | Jack Walston |
| Upshur | Carolyn Bullock | Mike Fetter | Joe "Joey" Orms | Joe F. Ferguson | Rick Jackson | Gary Drennan |
| Upton | Phyllis Stephens | Frank Brown (83rd) / Ori White (112th) | Brent Wrinkle | Tommy Owens | W.M. "Willie" Martinez | Leon Patrick |
| Uvalde | Lydia Steele | Anton E. "Tony" Hackebeil | Randy Scheide | Mariano Pargas Jr. | Rodney Reagan | Jesse R. Moreno |
| Val Verde | Martha Mitchell | Fred Hernandez | Ramiro V. Ramon | Rogelio "Roy" H. Musquiz | Laura Loftin | Jesus E."Cheo" Ortiz |
| Van Zandt | Karen Wilson | Leslie Poynter-Dixon | Ricky LaPrade | David Risner | Jimmy Don Wilson | Ron Carroll |
| Victoria | Cathy Stuart | M.P. "Dexter" Eaves | Chris Rivera | Jerry Nobles | John J. Hammack | Wayne D. Dierlam |
| Walker | Barbara W. Hale | David P. Weeks | B.J. Gaines Jr. | Robert Earl Autery | James C. "Buddy" Reynolds | Tim Paulsel |
| Waller | Patricia Spadachene | Oliver S. Kitzman | Leroy Singleton | Frank Pokluda | Milton G. Whiting | Louis Canales |
| Ward | Patricia Oyerbides | Randy Reynolds | Julian Florez | Kathy Fausett | Ron Widdess | Eddie Nelms |
| Washington | Vicki Lehmann | Renee Ann Mueller | David Simpson | Robert Mikeska | Joyce Boeker | Joy Fuchs |
| Webb | Manuel Gutierrez | Jose M. Rubio Jr. | Jerry Vasquez | Judith Gutierrez | Felix Velasquez | David Cortez |
| Wharton | Denice Malota | Josh McCown | Mickey Reynolds | D.C. "Chris" King | Philip Miller | James "Jimmy" Kainer |
| Wheeler | Sherri Jones | Richard "Rick" Roach | Daryl G. Snelgrooes | Thomas G. Puryear | Hubert Moore | Robbie Robinson |
| Wichita | Dorsey R. Trapp | Barry L. Macha | Joe Miller | Lavada "Pat" Norris | Gordon Griffith | William C. Presson |
| Wilbarger | Brenda Peterson | Dan Mike Byrd | Richard Jacobs | Freddie Streit | Rodney Johnston | Lenville Morris |
| Willacy | Gilbert Lozano | Juan Angel Guerra | Israel Tamez | Noe T. Loya | Alfredo S. Serrato | Jose I. Jimenez |
| Williamson | Bonnie Wolbrueck | John Bradley | Michael Heiligenstein | Greg Boatright | David Hays | Frankie Limmer |
| Wilson | Shirley D. Polasek | Lynn Ellison | Albert Gamez | Leonard Rotter | Robert "Bobby" H. Lynn | Wayne H. Stroud |
| Winkler | Sherry Terry | Michael L. Fostel | Tommy R. Smith | Robbie Wolf | Randy Neal | Jose G. Dominguez |
| Wise | Cristy Fuqua | Jana A. Jones | Kyle E. Stephens | Kevin Burns | Mikel Richardson | Terry Ross |
| Wood | Novis Widsom | Marcus D. Taylor | Roy Don Shipp | Jerry Gaskill | Roger Pace | Jerry Galloway |
| Yoakum | Vicki Blundell | Richard Clark | Woody Lindsey | Ben Caston | Ty Earl Powell | Jack Cobb |
| Young | Carolyn Collins | Stephen Bristow | Duane Downey | John Charles Bullock | R.L. Spivey | David Yoder |
| Zapata | Consuelo R. Villarreal | Joe Rubio Jr. | Jose Luis Flores | Angel Garza | Adolfo Gonzalez Jr. | Norberto Garza |
| Zavala | Rachel P. Ramirez | Roberto Serna | Jesús Vasquez | Miguel "Mike" Acosta | David López | Matthew McHazlett Jr. |

# Texans in Congress

Besides the two members of the U.S. Senate allocated to each state, Texas is allocated 32 members in the U.S. House of Representatives. The term of office for members of the House is two years; the terms of all members will expire on Jan. 1, 2005. Senators serve six-year terms. Sen. Kay Bailey Hutchison's term will end in 2007. Sen. John Cornyn's term will end in 2009.

Addresses and phone numbers of the lawmakers' Washington and district offices are below, as well as the committees on which they serve. Washington **zip codes** are **20515** for members of the House and **20510** for senators. The telephone **area code** for Washington is **202**. On the Internet, House members can be reached through **www.house.gov/writerep**. Members of Congress receive a salary of $154,700.

## U.S. Senate

**CORNYN, John. Republican (Home: Austin); Washington Office:** 370 RSOB, Washington, D.C. 20510-4302; (202) 224-2934, Fax. Website, www.senate.gov/~cornyn; e-mail, cornyn.senate.gov/contact/contact.cfm.

**Committees:** Armed Services, Budget, Environment and Public Works, Judiciary.

**HUTCHISON, Kay Bailey. Republican (Home: Dallas); Washington Office:** 284 RSOB, Washington, D.C. 20510-4304; (202) 224-5922, Fax 224-0776. Website, www.senate.gov/~hutchison; e-mail, hutchison.senate.gov/e-mail.htm.

**Texas Offices:** 961 Federal Bldg., 300 E. 8th St., **Austin** 78701, (512) 916-5834; 500 Chestnut Ste. 1570, **Abilene** 79602, (915) 676-2839; 10440 N. Central Expy. Ste. 1160, **Dallas** 75231, (214) 361-3500; 222 E. Van Buren Ste. 404, **Harlingen**, (956) 425-2253; 1919 Smith St. Ste 800, **Houston** 77002, (713) 653-3456; 8023 Vantage Dr. Ste. 460, **San Antonio** 78230, (210) 340-2885.

**Committees:** Appropriations; Commerce, Science and Transportation; Rules and Administration; Veterans Affairs. Also, Commission on Security and Cooperation in Europe.

## U.S. House of Representatives

**BARTON, Joe, R-Ennis, District 6; Washington Office:** 2109 RHOB; (202) 225-2002. Fax 225-3052; **District Offices:** 6001 West I-20 Ste. 200, Arlington 76017, (817) 543-1000; 303 West Knox Ste. 201, Ennis 75119-3942, (817) 543-1000. **Committees:** Energy and Commerce, Science.

**BELL, Chris, D-Houston, District 25; Washington Office:** 216 CHOB; (202) 225-7508; **District Offices:** 7707 Fannin Ste. 203, Houston 77054, (713) 383-3600; 1300 Rollingbrook Ste. 517, Baytown 77521, (281) 837-8225; 6307 Fairmont Parkway, Pasadena 77505, (281) 991-1300. **Committees:** Government Reform, International Relations, Science.

**BONILLA, Henry, R-San Antonio, District 23; Washington Office:** 2458 RHOB; (202) 225-4511, Fax 225-2237; **District Offices:** 11120 Wurzbach Ste. 300, San Antonio 78230, (210) 697-9055; 1300 Matamoros Ste. 113B, Laredo 78040, (956) 726-4682; 111 E. Broadway Ste. 101, Del Rio 78840, (830) 774-6547; 107 W. Ave. E, Alpine 79830, (432) 837-1313. **Committee:** Appropriations.

**BRADY, Kevin, R-The Woodlands, District 8; Washington Office:** 428 CHOB; (202) 225-4901. **District Offices:** 616 FM 1960 West Ste. 220, Houston 77090 (281) 895-8892; 200 River Pointe Ste. 304, Conroe 77304, (936) 441-5700. **Committee:** Ways and Means. Also, **Deputy Whip**.

**BURGESS, Michael, R-Highland Village, Dis-**trict 26; **Washington Office:** 1721 LHOB; (202) 225-7772. **District Office:** 1660 S. Stemmons Fwy. Ste. 230, Lewisville 75067, (972) 434-9700. **Committees:** Science, Transportation and Infrastructure.

**CARTER, John R. R-Round Rock, District 31; Washington Office:** 408 CHOB; (202) 225-3864. **District Offices:** One Financial Center, 1717 N. I-35 Ste. 303, Round Rock 78664 (512) 246-1600; 1111 University Dr. East Ste. 216, College Station 77840, (979) 846-6068. **Committees:** Education and the Workforce, Government Reform, Judiciary.

**CULBERSON, John Abney, R-Houston, District 7; Washington Office:** 1728 LHOB; (202) 225-2571, Fax 225-4381; **District Office:** 10000 Memorial Dr. Ste. 620, Houston 77024-3490, (713) 682-8828. **Committee:** Appropriations.

**DeLAY, Tom, R-Sugar Land, District 22; Washington Office:** 242 CHOB; (202) 225-5951, Fax 225-5241; **District Office:** 10701 Corporate Dr. Ste. 118, Stafford 77477, (281) 240-3700. **House Majority Leader**.

**DOGGETT, Lloyd, D-Austin, District 10; Washington Office:** 201 CHOB; (202) 225-4865, Fax 225-3073; **District Office:** 300 E. 8th Ste. 763, Austin 78701, (512) 916-5921. **Committee:** Ways and Means.

**EDWARDS, Chet, D-Waco, District 11; Washington Office:** 2459 RHOB; (202) 225-6105, Fax 225-0350; **District Offices:** 116 South East, Belton 76513, (254) 933-2904; 701 Clay Ave. Ste. 200, Waco 76706, (254) 752-9600, Fax 752-7769. **Committees:** Appropriations, Budget.

**FROST, Martin, D-Dallas, District 24; Washington Office:** 2256 RHOB; (202) 225-3605; **District Offices:** 400 South Zang Ste. 506, Dallas 75208, (214) 948-3401; 3020 S.E. Loop 820, Fort Worth 76140, (817) 293-9231; 101 East Randol Mill Rd. Ste 108, Arlington, (817) 303-1530. **Committee:** Rules.

**GONZALEZ, Charlie A., D-San Antonio, District 20; Washington Office:** 327 CHOB; (202) 225-3236, Fax 225-1915; **District Office:** 124-B Federal Building, 727 East Durango, San Antonio 78206, (210) 472-6195. **Committees:** Financial Services, Homeland Security, Small Business.

**GRANGER, Kay, R-Fort Worth, District 12; Washington Office:** 435 CHOB; (202) 225-5071; **District Office:** 1701 River Run Rd. Ste. 407, Fort Worth 76107, (817) 338-0909, Fax 335-5852. **Committees:** Appropriations, Homeland Security.

**GREEN, Gene, D-Houston, District 29; Washington Office:** 2335 RHOB; (202) 225-1688, Fax 225-9903; **District Offices:** 256 N. Sam Houston Pkwy. E. Ste. 29, Houston 77060, (281) 999-5879; 11811 I-10 East Ste. 430, Houston 77029, (713) 330-0761. **Committees:** Energy and Commerce, Standards of Official Conduct.

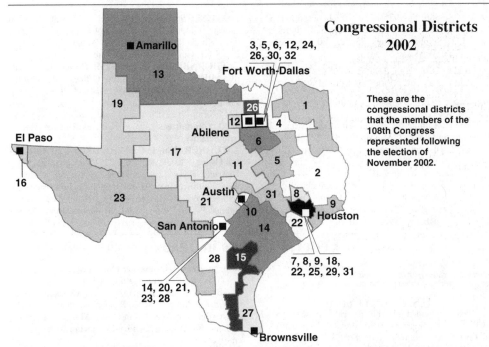

**Congressional Districts 2002**

These are the congressional districts that the members of the 108th Congress represented following the election of November 2002.

**HALL, Ralph M., D-Rockwall, District 4;** Washington Office: 2221 RHOB; (202) 225-6673, Fax (202) 225-3332; **District Offices:** 104 N. San Jacinto, Rockwall 75087, (972) 771-9118; 101 E. Pecan, Sherman 75090, (903) 892-1112; 211 W. Ferguson Ste. 211, Tyler 75702, (903) 597-3729. **Committees:** Energy and Commerce, Science.

**HENSARLING, Jeb, R-Dallas, District 5;** Washington Office: 423 CHOB; (202) 225-3484. **District Offices:** 10675 E. Northwest Hwy. Ste. 1685, Dallas 75238, (214) 349-9996; 100 E. Corsicana Ste. 208, Athens 77571, (903) 675-8288. **Committees:** Budget, Financial Services.

**HINOJOSA, Rubén, D-Mercedes, District 15;** Washington Office: 1535 LHOB; (202) 225-2531, Fax 225-5688; **District Offices:** 311 N. 15th St., McAllen 78501, (956) 682-5545; 107 S. St. Mary's St., Beeville 78102, (361) 358-8400. **Committees:** Education and the Workforce, Financial Services, Resources.

**JACKSON LEE, Sheila, D-Houston, District 18;** Washington Office: 403 CHOB; (202) 225-3816, Fax 225-3317; **District Offices:** 1919 Smith Ste. 1180, Houston 77002, (713) 655-0050; 420 W. 19th St., Houston 77008, (713) 861-4070; 6719 W. Montgomery Ste. 204, Houston 77091. **Committees:** Judiciary, Homeland Security, Science.

**JOHNSON, Eddie Bernice, D-Dallas, District 30;** Washington Office: 1511 LHOB; (202) 225-8885, Fax 225-1477; **District Office:** 2501 Cedar Springs Ste. 550, Dallas 75201, (214) 922-8885; 1634B W. Irving Blvd., Irving 75061, (972) 253-8885. **Committees:** Science, Transportation and Infrastructure.

**JOHNSON, Sam, R-Plano, District 3;** Washington Office: 1211 LHOB; (202) 225-4201, Fax 225-1485; **District Office:** 2929 N. Central Expressway, Ste. 240, Richardson 75080, (972) 470-0892. **Committees:** Education and the Workforce, Ways and Means.

**LAMPSON, Nick, D-Beaumont, District 9;** Washington Office: 405 CHOB; (202) 225-6565. **District Offices:** 300 Willow Ste. 322, Beaumont 77701, (409) 838-0061; 601 Rosenberg Ste. 216, Galveston 77550, (409) 762-5877; 1350 Nasa Rd. 1 Ste 224, Houston 77058, (281) 333-4884. **Committees:** Science, Transportation and Infrastructure.

**NEUGEBAUER, Randy, R-Lubbock, District 19;** Washington Office: 1026 LHOB; (202) 225-4005. **Committees:** Agriculture, Resources, Science.

**ORTIZ, Solomon P., D-Corpus Christi, District 27; Washington Office:** 2470 RHOB; (202) 225-7742, Fax 226-1134; **District Offices:** 3649 Leopard Ste. 510, Corpus Christi 78408, (361) 883-5868; 3505 Boca Chica Blvd. Ste. 200, Brownsville 78521, (956) 541-1242. **Committees:** Armed Services, Resources.

**PAUL, Ron, R-Surfside, District 14, Washington Office:** 203 CHOB; (202) 225-2831; **District Offices:** 200 W. Second Ste. 210, Freeport 77541, (979) 230-0000; 312 S. Main Ste. 228, Victoria 77901, (361) 576-1231. **Committees:** Financial Services, International Relations, Joint Economic.

**REYES, Silvestre, D-El Paso, District 16; Washington Office:** 1527 LHOB; (202) 225-4831, Fax 225-2016; **District Office:** 310 N. Mesa Ste. 400, El Paso 79901, (915) 534-4400. **Committees:** Armed Services, Intelligence, Veterans' Affairs.

**RODRIGUEZ, Ciro D., D-San Antonio, District 28; Washington Office:** 323 CHOB; (202) 225-1640, Fax 225-1641; **District Offices:** 1313 SE Military Dr. Ste. 115, San Antonio 78214, (210) 924-7383; 400 E. Gravis, San Diego 78384, (361) 279-3907; 301 Lincoln, Roma 78584, (956) 847-1111. **Committees:** Armed Services, Resources, Veterans' Affairs.

**SANDLIN, Max, D-Marshall, District 1; Washington Office:** 324 CHOB; (202) 225-3035; **District Offices:** 1300 E. Pinecrest Ste. 30, Marshall 75670,

(903) 938-8386, Fax 935-5772; 700 James Bowie Dr. New Boston 75570, (903) 628-5594; 320 Church St. Rm. 132, Sulphur Springs 75482, (903) 885-8682. **Committee**: Ways and Means.

**SESSIONS, Pete, R-Dallas, District 32; Washington Office**: 1318 LHOB; (202) 225-2231, Fax 225-5878; **District Office**: 12750 Merit Dr. Ste. 1434, Dallas 75251, (972) 392-0505. **Committees**: Homeland Security, Rules.

**SMITH, Lamar S., R-San Antonio, District 21; Washington Office**: 2231 RHOB; (202) 225-4236, Fax 225-8628; **District Offices**: 1100 NE Loop 410 Ste. 640, San Antonio 78209, (210) 821-5024; 1006 Junction Highway, Kerrville 78028, (830) 895-1414. **Committees**: Science, Homeland Security, Judiciary.

**STENHOLM, Charles W., D-Abilene, District 17, Washington Office**: 1211 LHOB; (202) 225-6605, Fax 225-2234; **District Offices**: 1501-A Columbia, P. O.

Box 1237, Stamford 79553, (325) 773-3623; 1500 Industrial Ste. 101, Abilene 79604, (325) 673-7221; 2121 Knickerbocker Ste. A, San Angelo 76903, (325) 942-8881. **Committee**: Agriculture.

**THORNBERRY, William M. (Mac), R-Clarendon, District 13; Washington Office**: 2457 RHOB; (202) 225-3706, Fax 225-3486; **District Offices**: 905 S. Fillmore Ste. 520, Amarillo 79101, (806) 371-8844; 4245 Kemp Ste. 315, Wichita Falls 76308, (940) 692-1700. **Committees**: Armed Services, Budget, Homeland Security.

**TURNER, Jim, D-Crockett, District 2; Washington Office**: 330 CHOB; (202) 225-2401, Fax 225-5955; **District Offices**: 1202 Sam Houston Ave. Ste. 5, Huntsville 77340, (936) 291-3097; 701 N. First Ste. 201, Lufkin 75901, (936) 637-1770; 420 W. Green Ave., Orange 77630, (409) 883-4990. **Committees**: Armed Services, Homeland Security. ☆

# Federal Courts in Texas

*Source: The following list of U.S. district courts was compiled from r*
*Source: The following list of U.S. district courts was compiled from reports of the clerks of the individual courts.*

## U.S. District Courts

Texas is divided into four federal judicial districts, each of which comprises several divisions. Appeal from all Texas federal courts is to the **Fifth Circuit Court of Appeals,** New Orleans. U.S. district judges are appointed for life and receive a salary of $154,700 annually.

### Northern Texas District

**District Judges** — Chief Judge, A. Joe Fish, Dallas. **Senior Judges:** Barefoot Sanders, Dallas; Eldon B. Mahon, Fort Worth; Robert B. Maloney, Dallas. **Judges:** Mary Lou Robinson, Amarillo; Jerry Buchmeyer, Sidney A. Fitzwater, Jorge A. Solis, Sam A. Lindsay, David C. Godbey, Ed Kinkeade, Dallas; John H. McBryde, Terry R. Means, Fort Worth; Sam R. Cummings, Lubbock. **Clerk of District Court:** Karen Mitchell, Dallas. **U.S. Attorney:** Jane J. Boyle, Dallas. **U.S. Marshal:** Randy Ely, Dallas. Court is in continuous session in each division of the Northern Texas District.

Following are the different divisions of the Northern District and the counties in each division:

#### Dallas Division

Dallas, Ellis, Hunt, Johnson, Kaufman, Navarro and Rockwall. **Magistrates:** William F. Sanderson Jr., Jeff Kaplan, Paul Stickney and Irma C. Ramirez, Dallas.

#### Fort Worth Division

Comanche, Erath, Hood, Jack, Palo Pinto, Parker, Tarrant and Wise. **Magistrate:** Charles Bleil, Fort Worth. **Deputy-in-charge:** Pam Murphy.

#### Amarillo Division

Armstrong, Briscoe, Carson, Castro, Childress, Collingsworth, Dallam, Deaf Smith, Donley, Gray, Hall, Hansford, Hartley, Hemphill, Hutchinson, Lipscomb, Moore, Ochiltree, Oldham, Parmer, Potter, Randall, Roberts, Sherman, Swisher and Wheeler. **Magistrate:** Clinton E. Averitte, Amarillo. **Deputy-in-charge:** Lynn Sherman.

#### Abilene Division

Callahan, Eastland, Fisher, Haskell, Howard, Jones, Mitchell, Nolan, Shackelford, Stephens, Stonewall, Taylor and Throckmorton. **Magistrate:** Billy W. Boone,

Abilene. **Deputy-in-charge:** Marsha Elliott.

#### San Angelo Division

Brown, Coke, Coleman, Concho, Crockett, Glasscock, Irion, Menard, Mills, Reagan, Runnels, Schleicher, Sterling, Sutton and Tom Green. **Magistrate:** Philip R. Lane, San Angelo. **Deputy-in-charge:** Beverly Roper.

#### Wichita Falls Division

Archer, Baylor, Clay, Cottle, Foard, Hardeman, King, Knox, Montague, Wichita, Wilbarger and Young. **Magistrate:** R. Kerry Roach, Wichita Falls. **Deputy-in-Charge:** Allison Terry.

#### Lubbock Division

Bailey, Borden, Cochran, Crosby, Dawson, Dickens, Floyd, Gaines, Garza, Hale, Hockley, Kent, Lamb, Lubbock, Lynn, Motley, Scurry, Terry and Yoakum. **U.S. District Judge:** Sam R. Cummings, Lubbock. **Magistrate:** Nancy M. Koenig, Lubbock. **Deputy-in-charge:** Kristy Weinheimer.

### Western Texas District

**District Judges** — Chief Judge, Walter S. Smith Jr., Waco. **Senior Judges:** William Wayne Justice and James R. Nowlin, Austin. **Judges:** Edward C. Prado, Orlando Garcia, Fred Biery and W. Royal Furgeson Jr., San Antonio; Philip R. Martinez and David Briones, El Paso; Sam Sparks, Austin; Alia M. Ludlum, Del Rio; Robert A. Junell, Midland. **Clerk of District Court:** William G. Putnicki, San Antonio. **Chief Deputy Clerk:** Michael J. Simon. **U.S. Attorney:** Johnny Sutton, San Antonio. **U.S. Marshal:** Jack Dean, San Antonio.

Following are the different divisions of the Western District, and the counties in each division.

#### San Antonio Division

Atascosa, Bandera, Bexar, Comal, Dimmit, Frio, Gonzales, Guadalupe, Karnes, Kendall, Kerr, Medina, Real and Wilson. **Magistrates:** Pamela A. Mathy, John W. Primomo and Nancy Stein Nowak, San Antonio. **Bankruptcy Judges:** Leif M. Clark and Ronald B. King, San Antonio. **Clerk of Bankruptcy Court:** Larry Bick, San Antonio. **Divisional Office Manager**: Michael F. Oakes.

#### Austin Division

Bastrop, Blanco, Burleson, Burnet, Caldwell,

Gillespie, Hays, Kimble, Lampasas, Lee, Llano, Mason, McCulloch, San Saba, Travis, Washington and Williamson. **Magistrates:** Andrew W. Austin and Stephen H. Capelle, Austin. **Bankruptcy Judges:** Chief, Larry E. Kelly, and Frank P. Monroe. **Divisional Office Manager:** Paula Allen. **Bankruptcy Court Deputy-in-charge:** Cynthia Gutierrez.

### El Paso Division

El Paso County only. **Magistrates:** Norbert J. Garney, Michael S. McDonald and Richard P. Mesa, El Paso. **Bankruptcy Judge:** Leif M. Clark, San Antonio. **Divisional Office Manager:** Richard Delgado. **Bankruptcy Court Deputy-in-charge:** Mark Vargas.

### Waco Division

Bell, Bosque, Coryell, Falls, Freestone, Hamilton, Hill, Leon, Limestone, McLennan, Milam, Robertson and Somervell. **Magistrate:** Jeffrey C. Manske Jr., Waco. **Bankruptcy Judge:** Larry E. Kelly, Austin. **Divisional Office Manager:** Mark G. Borchardt. **Bankruptcy Court Deputy-in-charge:** Bridget Hardage.

### Del Rio Division

Edwards, Kinney, Maverick, Terrell, Uvalde, Val Verde and Zavala. **Magistrate:** Dennis Green, Del Rio. **Bankruptcy Judge:** Ronald B. King, San Antonio. **Divisional Office Manager:** Vacant.

### Pecos Division

Brewster, Culberson, Hudspeth, Jeff Davis, Loving, Pecos, Presidio, Reeves, Ward and Winkler. **Magistrate:** Durwood Edwards, Pecos/Alpine. **Bankruptcy Judge:** Ronald B. King, San Antonio. **Divisional Office Manager:** Karen J. White.

### Midland-Odessa Division

Andrews, Crane, Ector, Martin, Midland and Upton. Court for the Midland-Odessa Division is held at Midland, but may, at the discretion of the court, be held in Odessa. **Magistrate:** L. Stuart Platt, Midland. **Bankruptcy Judge:** Ronald B. King, San Antonio. **District Court Divisional Office Manager:** Laura Gonzales, Midland. **Bankruptcy Court Deputy-in-charge:** Christy L. Carouth.

## Eastern Texas District

**District Judges — Chief Judge,** John Hannah Jr., Tyler. **Judges:** Thad Heartfield, Howell Cobb and Ron Clark, Beaumont; William M. Steger and Leonard Davis, Tyler; T. John Ward, Marshall; Paul N. Brown, Sherman; David J. Folsom, Texarkana. **Clerk of District Court:** David J. Maland, Tyler. **U.S. Attorney:** Matt Orwig, Beaumont. **U.S. Marshal:** John Moore, Tyler. **Chief U.S. Probation Officer:** Kenneth LaBorde, Beaumont. **Judges in Bankruptcy:** William Parker, Tyler, and Donald R. Sharp, Beaumont. **Federal Public Defender:** G. Patrtick Black, Tyler.

Following are the divisions of the Eastern District and the counties in each division:

### Tyler Division

Anderson, Cherokee, Gregg, Henderson, Panola, Rains, Rusk, Smith, Van Zandt and Wood. **Magistrates:** Henry W. McKee, Tyler, and Judith Guthrie, Tyler. **Chief Deputy:** Jeanne Henderson.

### Beaumont Division

Hardin, Jasper, Jefferson, Liberty, Newton, Orange. **Magistrates:** Earl Hines and Wendell Radford, Beaumont. **Chief Deputy:** Johnette Cartwright.

### Marshall Division

Camp, Cass, Harrison, Marion, Morris, Upshur. **Deputy-in-charge:** Peggy Anderson.

### Sherman Division

Collin, Cooke, Denton and Grayson. **Magistrate:** Don Bush. **Deputy-in-charge:** Sandra Southerland.

### Texarkana Division

Bowie, Franklin and Titus. **Magistrate:** Caroline M. Craven. **Deputy-in-charge:** Rhonda Lafitte.

### Paris Division

Delta, Fannin, Hopkins, Lamar and Red River.

### Lufkin Division

Angelina, Houston, Nacogdoches, Polk, Sabine, San Augustine, Shelby, Trinity, Tyler. **Deputy-in-charge:** Kathy Riley.

## Southern Texas District

**District Judges — Chief Judge,** George P. Kazen, Laredo. **Judges:** Nancy F. Atlas, Kenneth M. Hoyt, Sim Lake, Lynn N. Hughes, David Hittner, John D. Rainey, Melinda Harmon, Vanessa D. Gilmore, Ewing Werlein Jr. and Lee H. Rosenthal, Houston; Hayden W. Head Jr. and Janis Graham Jack, Corpus Christi; Samuel B. Kent, Galveston; Filemon B. Vela, Hilda G. Tagle and Andrew S. Hanen, Brownsville; Ricardo H. Hinojosa and Randy Crane, McAllen; Keith P. Ellison, Laredo. **Clerk of Court:** Michael N. Milby, Houston. **U. S. Attorney:** Michael T. Shelby, Houston. **U.S. Marshal:** Ruben Montzon, Houston. **Bankruptcy Judges:** Chief, William R. Greendyke, Houston; Manuel D. Leal, Letitia Z. Clark, Karen K. Brown and Wesley W. Steen, Houston; Richard S. Schmidt, Corpus Christi.

Following are the different divisions of the Southern District and the counties in each division:

### Houston Division

Austin, Brazos, Colorado, Fayette, Fort Bend, Grimes, Harris, Madison, Montgomery, San Jacinto, Walker, Waller and Wharton. **Magistrates:** Calvin Botley, Frances H. Stacy, Nancy Johnson, Marcia A. Crone and Mary Milloy. **Clerk:** Michael N. Milby.

### Brownsville Division

Cameron and Willacy. **Magistrates:** John Wm. Black, Felix Recio. **Deputy-in-charge:** Juan Barbosa.

### Corpus Christi Division

Aransas, Bee, Brooks, Duval, Jim Wells, Kenedy, Kleberg, Live Oak, Nueces and San Patricio. **Magistrate:** B. Janice Ellington and Jane Cooper-Hill. **Deputy-in-charge:** Monica Seaman.

### Galveston Division

Brazoria, Chambers, Galveston and Matagorda. **Magistrate:** John R. Froeschner. **Deputy-in-charge:** Marrianne Gore.

### Laredo Division

Jim Hogg, La Salle, McMullen, Webb and Zapata. **Magistrates:** Adriana Arce-Flores, Marcel C. Notzon. **Deputy-in-charge:** Rosie Rodriguez.

### Victoria Division

Calhoun, DeWitt, Goliad, Jackson, Lavaca, Refugio and Victoria. **Deputy-in-charge:** Joyce Richards.

### McAllen Division

Hidalgo and Starr. **Magistrates:** Dorina Ramos and Tracy K. Caperton. **Deputy-in-charge:** Eddie Leandro.

☆

*Members of the 401st Military Police Company board a plane at Fort Hood. File photo.*

# Major Military Installations

Below are listed the major military installations in Texas in 2003. Data are taken from the U.S. Department of Defense and other sources. "Civilian" refers to Department of Defense personnel, "other" refers to employees such as contractor personnel.

## U.S. ARMY

### Fort Bliss

**Location**: Northeast El Paso (est. 1849).
**Address**: Fort Bliss, Texas 79916-0058
**Main phone number**: (915) 568-2121
**Personnel**: 9,413 active-duty plus trainees; 2,952 civilians; 3,376 other.
**Major units**: Army Air Defense Artillery School; 32nd Air and Missile Defense Command; 6th, 11th, 31st, 35th and 108th Air Defense Artillery Brigades; 204th Military Intelligence Battalion, 76th Military Police Battalion; Biggs Army Airfield (est. 1916, originally called Bliss Field).

### Fort Hood

**Location**: In Killeen (est. 1942).
**Address**: Fort Hood, Texas 76544-5066
**Main phone number**: (254) 287-1110
**Personnel**: 41,866 active-duty; 3,362 civilians; 2,559 other.
**Major units**: 1st Cavalry Div.; 4th Infantry Div.; Headquarters Command III Corps; 3rd Armored Cavalry Reg.; 13th Corps Support Group; 13th Finance Group; 3rd Personnel Group; 3rd Signal Brigade; 89th Military Police Brigade; 504th Military Intelligence Brigade; 21st Cavalry Brigade (Air Combat); Dental Activity and Medical Support Activity; Army Operational Test Command.

### Fort Sam Houston

**Location**: In San Antonio (est. 1878).
**Address**: Fort Sam Houston, Texas 78234-5000
**Main phone number**: (210) 221-1211
**Personnel**: 4,891 active-duty; 4,660 civilians; 2,187 other.
**Major units**: U.S. 5th Army; 5th Recruiting Brigade; Brooke Army Medical Center; Institute of Surgical Research; Army Medical Command; Army Medical Dept. Center and School; Camp Bullis (est. 1917), training area.

### Red River Army Depot

**Location:** 18 miles west of Texarkana (est. 1941).
**Address:** Red River Army Depot, Texarkana 75507
**Main phone number:** (903) 334-2141
**Personnel:** 60 active-duty; 2,407 civilians; 351 other.
**Major unit:** Defense Distribution Center; U.S. Army Tank-automotive and Armaments Command.

## U.S. AIR FORCE

### Brooks City-Base

**Location**: In San Antonio (est. 1917).
**Address**: Brooks City-Base, San Antonio 78235
**Main phone number**: (210) 536-1110
**Personnel**: 1,395 active-duty; 1,245 civilians.
**Major units**: 311th Human Systems Wing; School of Aerospace Medicine; Armstrong Laboratory; Air Force Institute for Environmental, Safety and Occupational Health Risk Analysis.

### Dyess AFB

**Location**: On west side of Abilene (est. 1942 as Tye Army Airfield, closed at end of

World War II, re-established in 1956).
**Address**: Dyess AFB, Texas 79607-1960
**Main phone number**: (915) 696-0212
**Personnel**: 4,956 active-duty; 359 civilians.
**Major units**: 7th Bomb Wing (Air Combat Command); 317th Airlift Group.

## Goodfellow AFB
**Location**: On south side of San Angelo (est. 1940).
**Address**: Goodfellow AFB, San Angelo, Texas 76908-5000
**Main phone number**: (915) 654-3231
**Personnel**: 1,500 active-duty, approximately 1,200 trainees; 507 civilians.
**Major units**: 17th Training Wing; 344th Military Intelligence Battalion.

## Lackland AFB
**Location**: Eight miles southwest of San Antonio (est. 1942 when separated from Kelly Field).
**Address**: Lackland AFB, Texas 78236-5110
**Main phone number**: (210) 671-1110
**Personnel**: 7,230 active-duty, approximately 9,600 active duty-students; 2,936 civilians.
**Major units**: 37th Training Wing; Defense Language Institute English Language Center, Inter-American Air Forces Academy; 59th Medical Wing-Wilford Hall Medical Center; Kelly Field Annex (was Kelly AFB, est. 1916, closed 2001).

## Laughlin AFB
**Location**: Six miles east of Del Rio (est. 1942).
**Address**: Laughlin AFB, Texas 78843-5000
**Main phone number**: (830) 298-3511
**Personnel**: 1,075 active-duty; 904 civilians.
**Major units**: 47th Flying Training Wing.

## Randolph AFB
**Location**: In San Antonio (est. 1930).
**Address**: Randolph AFB, Texas 78150-4562
**Main phone number**: (210) 652-1110
**Personnel**: 4,256 active-duty; 4,389 civilians.
**Major units**: Air Education and Training Command; Air Force Personnel Center; Air Force Recruiting Service; 19th Air Force; 12th Flying Training Wing.

## Sheppard AFB
**Location**: Four miles north of Wichita Falls (est. 1941).
**Address**: Sheppard AFB, Texas 76311-2943
**Main phone number**: (940) 676-2511
**Personnel**: 3,596 active-duty; 1,325 civilians.
**Major units**: 82nd Training Wing; 80th Flying Training Wing.

## U.S. NAVY

### Naval Air Station Corpus Christi
**Location**: 10 miles southeast of Corpus Christi in the Flour Bluff area (est. 1941).
**Address**: NAS Corpus Christi, 11001 D St., Corpus Christi 78419-5021
**Main phone number**: (361) 961-2811
**Personnel**: 1,880 active-duty; 538 civilians.
**Major units**: Headquarters, Naval Air Training Command; Training Air Wing Four; Commander of Mine Warfare Command; Coast Guard Air Group; Corpus Christi Army Depot (est. 1961).

### Naval Air Station-Joint Reserve Base (Carswell Field)
**Location**: westside Fort Worth (est. 1994) [Carswell, est. 1942 as Fort Worth Army Air Field, closed 1993].
**Address**: NAS-JRB, 1215 Depot Ave., Fort Worth 76127-5000.
**Main phone number**: (817) 782-5000
**Personnel**: 2,352 active-duty; 793 civilians.
**Major units**: Fighter Squadron 201, Marine Air Group 41; 14th Marines; Fleet Support Squadron 59; Army Reserve; Coast Guard Reserve; and Texas Air Guard; 301st Fighter Wing.

### Naval Station Ingleside
**Location**: In Ingleside (est. 1990).
**Address**: 1455 Ticonderoga Rd., #W123, Ingleside 78362-5001
**Main phone number**: (361) 776-4200
**Personnel**: 3,002 active-duty; 181 civilians.
**Major units**: Mine Warfare Force; 14 mine countermeasure-class vessels; 10 hunter-class vessels.

### Naval Air Station Kingsville
**Location**: In Kingsville (est. 1942).
**Address**: NAS Kingsville, Texas 78363-5000
**Main phone number**: (361) 595-6136
**Personnel**: 423 active-duty; 238 civilians.
**Major units**: Naval Auxiliary Landing Field Orange Grove; Squadrons: VT-21, VT-22; Training Air Wing II; and McMullen Target Range, Escondido Ranch.

## TEXAS GUARD
### Camp Mabry
**Location**: 2210 W. 35th St. in Austin. Just west of MoPac.
**Address**: Box 5218, Austin, Texas 78763
**Main phone number**: (512) 465-5101
**Web site**: www.agd.state.tx.us
**Personnel**: Various offices employ 800.
**State Adjutant General's office**: Major General Wayne D. Marty.
**Major units**: Texas National Guard Academy; the U.S. Property and Fiscal Office; the Texas National Guard Armory Board; Headquarters, Armory of the 49th Armored Division. **Texas Military Forces Museum**, open Wednesday-Sunday, 10 a.m. - 4 p.m.

Tracing its history to early frontier days, the Texas Guard is organized into three separate entities: The Texas Army National Guard, the Texas Air National Guard and the Texas State Guard.

When not in active federal service, Camp Mabry, in northwest Austin, is the main storage maintenance and administrative headquarters for the Texas Guard.

Camp Mabry was established in the early 1890s as a summer encampment of the Texas Volunteer Guard, a forerunner of the Texas National Guard. The name, Camp Mabry, honors Woodford Haywood Mabry, adjutant general of Texas from 1891-98.

The Texas State Guard, an all-volunteer backup

force, was originally created by the Texas Legislature in 1941. It became an active element of the state military forces in 1965 with a mission of reinforcing the National Guard in state emergencies, and of replacing National Guard units called into federal service. The Texas State Guard, which has a membership of approximately 1,450 personnel, also participates in local emergencies.

When the Guard was reorganized following World War II, the Texas Air National Guard was added. Texas Air National Guard units serve as augmentation units to major Air Force commands, including the Air Defense Command, the tactical Air Command and the Strategic Air Command. Approximately 3,600 men and women make up the Air Guard in 50 units.

The Army National Guard is available for either national or state emergencies and has been used extensively during hurricanes, tornadoes and floods. There are more than 189 units located in 99 cities in Texas, with a total Army Guard membership of 17,245.

The governor of Texas is commander-in-chief of the Texas National and State Guards. This command function is exercised through an adjutant general appointed by the governor and approved by both federal and state legislative authority.

The adjutant general is the active administrative head of the Texas National Guard, and head of the Adjutant General's Department, a state agency, working in conjunction with the National Guard Bureau, a federal agency.

When called into active federal service, National Guard units come within the chain of command of the Army and Air Force units. ☆

# Federal Funds to Texas by County, 2002

Texas received **$123,431,163,871** in 2002 from the federal government. Below, the distribution of funds is shown by county. The first figure after the county name represents total **direct expenditures to the county** for fiscal year 2002. The second and third figures are that part of the total that went directly for individuals, either in **retirement** payments, such as Social Security, or **other** direct payments, principally Medicare. In the last column are direct payments **other than to individuals**, principally agricultural programs such as crop insurance. *For a more complete explanation, see end of chart.

*Source: Consolidated Federal Funds Report 2002, U.S. Commerce Dept.*

| COUNTY | TOTAL | For INDIVIDUALS | | other direct (ag., etc.) |
|---|---|---|---|---|
| | | retirement | other | |
| | | (Thousand dollars) | | |
| Anderson | $ 265,268 | $ 113,260 | $ 61,539 | $ 772 |
| Andrews | 53,896 | 25,809 | 12,855 | 7,064 |
| Angelina | 337,877 | 179,206 | 97,604 | 1,102 |
| Aransas | 116,339 | 65,824 | 24,835 | 401 |
| Archer | 56,604 | 27,689 | 6,884 | 3,971 |
| Armstrong | 30,504 | 5,072 | 2,410 | 7,713 |
| Atascosa | 151,575 | 75,993 | 31,393 | 1,573 |
| Austin | 561,620 | 52,896 | 27,311 | 6,008 |
| Bailey | 59,173 | 12,589 | 8,697 | 29,387 |
| Bandera | 81,324 | 56,111 | 11,588 | 3,313 |
| Bastrop | 229,338 | 115,144 | 38,549 | 1,502 |
| Baylor | 44,867 | 13,619 | 8,073 | 14,184 |
| Bee | 141,670 | 54,031 | 38,288 | 8,163 |
| Bell | 3,072,987 | 610,194 | 155,418 | 8,979 |
| Bexar | 11,266,539 | 3,650,563 | 1,358,846 | 30,490 |
| Blanco | 69,790 | 44,111 | 15,156 | 163 |
| Borden | 8,707 | 578 | 515 | 4,134 |
| Bosque | 91,816 | 51,560 | 21,704 | 1,116 |
| Bowie | 695,414 | 264,244 | 112,036 | 8,824 |
| Brazoria | 732,993 | 379,352 | 160,470 | 37,348 |
| Brazos | 669,452 | 186,520 | 96,257 | 5,479 |
| Brewster | 54,486 | 20,543 | 11,187 | 744 |
| Briscoe | 29,959 | 4,861 | 3,721 | 13,045 |
| Brooks | 64,106 | 16,179 | 11,939 | 975 |
| Brown | 208,105 | 96,593 | 57,187 | 4,676 |
| Burleson | 88,552 | 40,506 | 16,931 | 5,605 |
| Burnet | 154,554 | 97,727 | 28,185 | 509 |
| Caldwell | 138,087 | 62,320 | 31,589 | 2,920 |
| Calhoun | 102,748 | 42,184 | 17,538 | 16,067 |
| Callahan | 74,937 | 35,806 | 14,029 | 1,691 |
| Cameron | 1,585,252 | 469,013 | 314,507 | 38,629 |
| Camp | 70,755 | 33,851 | 17,868 | 237 |
| Carson | 65,324 | 14,439 | 7,429 | 15,821 |

| COUNTY | TOTAL | For INDIVIDUALS | | other direct (ag., etc.) |
|---|---|---|---|---|
| | | retirement | other | |
| | | (Thousand dollars) | | |
| Cass | $ 193,048 | $ 93,338 | $ 43,064 | $ 602 |
| Castro | 101,781 | 12,274 | 9,248 | 70,941 |
| Chambers | 135,656 | 32,210 | 22,126 | 21,238 |
| Cherokee | 217,726 | 93,258 | 56,472 | 475 |
| Childress | 49,728 | 15,653 | 8,617 | 11,731 |
| Clay | 52,012 | 23,361 | 10,784 | 6,284 |
| Cochran | 45,089 | 7,920 | 5,423 | 26,753 |
| Coke | 22,305 | 9,825 | 4,683 | 1,416 |
| Coleman | 76,867 | 29,395 | 21,201 | 4,541 |
| Collin | 1,451,412 | 512,931 | 145,733 | 12,465 |
| Collingsworth | 49,810 | 8,314 | 6,420 | 26,999 |
| Colorado | 158,491 | 47,764 | 24,980 | 51,780 |
| Comal | 362,388 | 226,339 | 60,427 | 16,531 |
| Comanche | 87,495 | 36,217 | 23,750 | 2,463 |
| Concho | 33,043 | 7,050 | 4,791 | 9,514 |
| Cooke | 158,676 | 78,823 | 39,976 | 2,544 |
| Coryell | 239,213 | 157,375 | 30,944 | 2,201 |
| Cottle | 24,651 | 5,466 | 3,229 | 9,274 |
| Crane | 14,468 | 7,077 | 4,757 | 15 |
| Crockett | 20,888 | 7,322 | 2,907 | 1,051 |
| Crosby | 71,219 | 14,024 | 14,027 | 33,732 |
| Culberson | 15,990 | 4,052 | 3,380 | 1,265 |
| Dallam | 77,802 | 16,981 | 9,671 | 40,862 |
| Dallas | 10,901,498 | 3,137,730 | 1,667,714 | 43,471 |
| Dawson | 133,957 | 27,756 | 27,209 | 53,829 |
| Deaf Smith | 119,705 | 29,488 | 18,293 | 48,075 |
| Delta | 36,506 | 14,170 | 8,466 | 3,086 |
| Denton | 843,390 | 412,481 | 162,803 | 5,950 |
| DeWitt | 109,255 | 41,792 | 27,559 | 1,628 |
| Dickens | 28,134 | 6,813 | 7,881 | 7,210 |
| Dimmit | 71,229 | 16,050 | 12,784 | 772 |
| Donley | 30,066 | 10,954 | 6,528 | 4,830 |
| Duval | 98,982 | 26,035 | 23,989 | 3,637 |
| Eastland | 119,239 | 55,605 | 35,478 | 2,018 |
| Ector | 452,876 | 218,475 | 128,675 | 624 |

| COUNTY | TOTAL | For INDIVIDUALS | | other direct (ag., etc.) | COUNTY | TOTAL | For INDIVIDUALS | | other direct (ag., etc.) |
|---|---|---|---|---|---|---|---|---|---|
| | | retirement | other | | | | retirement | other | |
| | | (Thousand dollars) | | | | | (Thousand dollars) | | |
| Edwards | $ 23,047 | $ 5,120 | $ 6,774 | $ 708 | Kenedy | $ 1,441 | $ 545 | $ 317 | $ 7 |
| Ellis | 365,431 | 190,223 | 89,564 | 13,212 | Kent | 11,477 | 2,650 | 1,284 | 3,292 |
| El Paso | 3,856,066 | 1,254,985 | 608,677 | 16,988 | Kerr | 294,942 | 183,410 | 57,435 | 1,068 |
| Erath | 139,662 | 68,853 | 39,145 | 906 | Kimble | 23,304 | 11,873 | 5,354 | 525 |
| Falls | 141,922 | 44,273 | 22,770 | 8,774 | King | 4,993 | 325 | 173 | 2,585 |
| Fannin | 189,934 | 80,724 | 36,532 | 8,799 | Kinney | 27,819 | 12,255 | 4,578 | 784 |
| Fayette | 136,102 | 62,787 | 31,526 | 1,355 | Kleberg | 319,445 | 58,682 | 41,253 | 11,184 |
| Fisher | 45,920 | 11,528 | 7,255 | 17,894 | Knox | 42,871 | 11,114 | 7,996 | 13,609 |
| Floyd | 91,912 | 15,344 | 10,725 | 51,753 | Lamar | 277,621 | 119,840 | 58,953 | 11,463 |
| Foard | 21,503 | 5,042 | 2,932 | 6,913 | Lamb | 118,704 | 31,777 | 22,541 | 43,008 |
| Fort Bend | 707,531 | 344,930 | 100,821 | 109,591 | Lampasas | 106,269 | 65,842 | 22,847 | 469 |
| Franklin | 45,535 | 22,010 | 10,862 | 418 | La Salle | 62,496 | 10,243 | 6,803 | 1,594 |
| Freestone | 84,886 | 40,864 | 16,487 | 280 | Lavaca | 134,258 | 59,607 | 32,321 | 6,640 |
| Frio | 83,563 | 22,977 | 16,264 | 7,709 | Lee | 59,684 | 30,261 | 12,275 | 452 |
| Gaines | 142,571 | 19,978 | 15,304 | 97,315 | Leon | 109,110 | 52,277 | 23,334 | 230 |
| Galveston | 1,203,884 | 495,732 | 260,350 | 15,521 | Liberty | 333,236 | 139,850 | 90,037 | 27,541 |
| Garza | 29,836 | 9,347 | 8,089 | 5,714 | Limestone | 124,170 | 54,835 | 26,668 | 3,938 |
| Gillespie | 117,122 | 75,602 | 24,927 | 1,293 | Lipscomb | 19,090 | 6,605 | 3,571 | 4,757 |
| Glasscock | 24,356 | 1,714 | 1,180 | 16,010 | Live Oak | 82,569 | 19,909 | 12,115 | 3,402 |
| Goliad | 35,737 | 15,691 | 8,707 | 1,756 | Llano | 100,196 | 67,998 | 23,628 | 162 |
| Gonzales | 126,087 | 46,318 | 22,000 | 1,821 | Loving | 1,181 | 242 | 11 | 7 |
| Gray | 122,940 | 58,000 | 39,453 | 6,531 | Lubbock | 1,119,274 | 452,079 | 296,471 | 42,087 |
| Grayson | 557,993 | 298,224 | 128,227 | 9,104 | Lynn | 70,229 | 13,396 | 9,282 | 37,402 |
| Gregg | 566,416 | 286,318 | 137,195 | 973 | Madison | 48,813 | 23,291 | 10,603 | 147 |
| Grimes | 101,024 | 44,306 | 22,500 | 225 | Marion | 76,992 | 28,703 | 11,879 | 241 |
| Guadalupe | 402,094 | 248,161 | 58,839 | 19,842 | Martin | 60,184 | 8,278 | 5,252 | 38,733 |
| Hale | 282,337 | 66,962 | 46,649 | 101,693 | Mason | 22,662 | 11,203 | 5,339 | 286 |
| Hall | 69,248 | 10,236 | 7,203 | 35,613 | Matagorda | 230,069 | 75,358 | 35,225 | 58,742 |
| Hamilton | 49,745 | 21,658 | 15,199 | 1,026 | Maverick | 226,972 | 63,531 | 48,510 | 1,018 |
| Hansford | 53,569 | 11,018 | 5,258 | 32,898 | McCulloch | 61,335 | 22,623 | 13,752 | 4,436 |
| Hardeman | 48,638 | 13,141 | 7,755 | 9,573 | McLennan | 1,154,720 | 502,981 | 220,875 | 16,810 |
| Hardin | 200,194 | 106,337 | 54,264 | 1,605 | McMullen | 3,789 | 1,647 | 572 | 433 |
| Harris | 16,414,878 | 4,420,068 | 2,546,816 | 85,918 | Medina | 162,605 | 85,199 | 31,539 | 7,459 |
| Harrison | 297,615 | 121,249 | 62,322 | 574 | Menard | 19,424 | 6,549 | 4,260 | 1,218 |
| Hartley | 26,123 | 2,361 | 2,452 | 20,082 | Midland | 408,901 | 205,498 | 98,258 | 9,016 |
| Haskell | 62,139 | 18,227 | 10,891 | 21,596 | Milam | 143,786 | 59,997 | 24,655 | 9,476 |
| Hays | 388,706 | 157,456 | 60,287 | 2,720 | Mills | 30,071 | 14,022 | 8,231 | 725 |
| Hemphill | 14,850 | 6,242 | 3,784 | 2,777 | Mitchell | 54,530 | 19,002 | 11,915 | 10,527 |
| Henderson | 283,937 | 150,662 | 73,708 | 612 | Montague | 111,710 | 59,840 | 28,238 | 1,399 |
| Hidalgo | 2,353,227 | 665,268 | 508,690 | 74,095 | Montgomery | 868,645 | 490,233 | 204,041 | 2,645 |
| Hill | 192,001 | 89,129 | 42,372 | 15,462 | Moore | 72,586 | 30,125 | 11,662 | 22,070 |
| Hockley | 146,154 | 42,027 | 34,146 | 36,701 | Morris | 81,009 | 41,352 | 19,636 | 425 |
| Hood | 212,143 | 138,295 | 38,216 | 417 | Motley | 18,415 | 4,081 | 2,734 | 7,573 |
| Hopkins | 148,950 | 70,840 | 37,481 | 1,127 | Nacogdoches | 290,618 | 116,573 | 72,928 | 9,798 |
| Houston | 209,569 | 60,816 | 32,925 | 2,538 | Navarro | 234,686 | 102,812 | 52,258 | 7,117 |
| Howard | 298,544 | 82,645 | 50,372 | 29,583 | Newton | 70,140 | 30,093 | 16,897 | 159 |
| Hudspeth | 56,909 | 4,417 | 3,301 | 4,335 | Nolan | 107,107 | 40,210 | 25,593 | 8,708 |
| Hunt | 1,087,653 | 169,933 | 86,514 | 5,211 | Nueces | 1,936,297 | 656,965 | 333,325 | 44,658 |
| Hutchinson | 107,623 | 56,680 | 26,937 | 8,210 | Ochiltree | 53,464 | 14,726 | 6,396 | 22,386 |
| Irion | 9,708 | 3,597 | 1,940 | 508 | Oldham | 19,574 | 4,761 | 2,073 | 5,507 |
| Jack | 32,279 | 16,376 | 8,951 | 396 | Orange | 420,179 | 196,062 | 112,042 | 2,706 |
| Jackson | 117,002 | 28,623 | 19,361 | 45,246 | Palo Pinto | 135,153 | 66,707 | 32,640 | 483 |
| Jasper | 192,655 | 82,637 | 51,250 | 393 | Panola | 131,466 | 51,682 | 29,761 | 232 |
| Jeff Davis | 20,061 | 5,408 | 1,825 | 397 | Parker | 285,227 | 180,158 | 57,050 | 549 |
| Jefferson | 1,549,507 | 551,647 | 384,879 | 45,241 | Parmer | 94,936 | 16,174 | 9,595 | 60,056 |
| Jim Hogg | 57,976 | 9,673 | 8,932 | 409 | Pecos | 67,039 | 23,314 | 12,171 | 3,913 |
| Jim Wells | 229,421 | 76,997 | 56,099 | 12,945 | Polk | 320,764 | 210,483 | 65,607 | 1,173 |
| Johnson | 433,617 | 254,310 | 101,126 | 2,412 | Potter | 1,277,497 | 370,980 | 138,970 | 3,518 |
| Jones | 119,179 | 42,302 | 22,855 | 29,287 | Presidio | 50,282 | 13,198 | 7,367 | 155 |
| Karnes | 90,452 | 29,992 | 19,644 | 2,702 | Rains | 39,683 | 23,084 | 8,215 | 251 |
| Kaufman | 357,035 | 190,789 | 91,375 | 3,051 | Randall | 164,754 | 60,295 | 47,787 | 14,135 |
| Kendall | 132,534 | 89,269 | 19,423 | 1,131 | Reagan | 21,944 | 4,936 | 2,750 | 7,692 |

| COUNTY | TOTAL | For INDIVIDUALS | | other direct (ag., etc.) |
|---|---|---|---|---|
| | | retirement | other | |
| | | (Thousand dollars) | | |
| Real | $ 20,369 | $ 11,041 | $ 4,099 | $ 167 |
| Red River | 118,760 | 40,616 | 22,999 | 7,883 |
| Reeves | 69,024 | 22,442 | 13,841 | 5,214 |
| Refugio | 59,725 | 19,930 | 11,514 | 10,765 |
| Roberts | 5,375 | 1,676 | 966 | 2,047 |
| Robertson | 112,796 | 38,944 | 19,314 | 14,679 |
| Rockwall | 169,131 | 69,772 | 20,161 | 783 |
| Runnels | 94,279 | 29,538 | 15,794 | 19,037 |
| Rusk | 197,955 | 91,560 | 48,194 | 663 |
| Sabine | 86,988 | 46,094 | 21,952 | 329 |
| S. Augustine | 61,723 | 25,598 | 14,134 | 204 |
| San Jacinto | 92,458 | 43,681 | 22,182 | 74 |
| San Patricio | 450,813 | 136,250 | 69,936 | 27,429 |
| San Saba | 46,736 | 14,290 | 9,798 | 670 |
| Schleicher | 21,382 | 5,949 | 3,305 | 4,692 |
| Scurry | 85,905 | 34,597 | 20,810 | 10,511 |
| Shackelford | 30,801 | 9,584 | 4,044 | 1,404 |
| Shelby | 165,687 | 63,133 | 36,759 | 350 |
| Sherman | 46,594 | 5,474 | 2,988 | 25,014 |
| Smith | 855,615 | 410,519 | 188,248 | 1,798 |
| Somervell | 35,546 | 13,050 | 6,004 | 44 |
| Starr | 228,347 | 54,903 | 46,995 | 11,278 |
| Stephens | 49,421 | 22,070 | 14,509 | 660 |
| Sterling | 19,601 | 2,136 | 1,372 | 788 |
| Stonewall | 16,180 | 4,684 | 2,753 | 3,809 |
| Sutton | 16,823 | 6,482 | 3,240 | 565 |
| Swisher | 94,040 | 18,105 | 10,118 | 53,428 |
| Tarrant | 8,858,504 | 2,328,865 | 1,009,321 | 33,474 |
| Taylor | 871,032 | 309,012 | 126,390 | 11,169 |
| Terrell | 10,452 | 3,322 | 1,309 | 277 |
| Terry | 105,495 | 26,112 | 19,056 | 41,757 |

| COUNTY | TOTAL | For INDIVIDUALS | | other direct (ag., etc.) |
|---|---|---|---|---|
| | | retirement | other | |
| | | (Thousand dollars) | | |
| Throckmorton | $ 18,345 | $ 5,072 | $ 2,767 | $ 6,682 |
| Titus | 125,053 | 52,653 | 33,177 | 325 |
| Tom Green | 634,698 | 250,861 | 97,177 | 27,968 |
| Travis | 6,925,185 | 1,399,408 | 434,670 | 46,386 |
| Trinity | 90,819 | 45,310 | 24,842 | 122 |
| Tyler | 153,030 | 54,986 | 29,052 | 245 |
| Upshur | 170,007 | 92,837 | 40,948 | 531 |
| Upton | 19,321 | 6,871 | 4,453 | 2,582 |
| Uvalde | 144,404 | 48,530 | 31,291 | 10,024 |
| Val Verde | 345,519 | 87,949 | 30,530 | 2,654 |
| Van Zandt | 212,447 | 115,011 | 59,225 | 1,130 |
| Victoria | 362,899 | 164,970 | 84,261 | 11,855 |
| Walker | 203,663 | 88,792 | 47,979 | 639 |
| Waller | 144,660 | 44,745 | 37,259 | 12,384 |
| Ward | 53,583 | 24,133 | 11,938 | 513 |
| Washington | 157,573 | 71,510 | 34,248 | 713 |
| Webb | 835,761 | 215,873 | 154,271 | 2,292 |
| Wharton | 317,716 | 85,999 | 51,249 | 124,516 |
| Wheeler | 79,403 | 14,862 | 11,458 | 7,801 |
| Wichita | 1,146,369 | 359,861 | 128,977 | 9,773 |
| Wilbarger | 91,072 | 33,857 | 23,913 | 15,893 |
| Willacy | 146,752 | 29,463 | 21,856 | 34,306 |
| Williamson | 1,616,969 | 361,439 | 86,723 | 20,590 |
| Wilson | 125,703 | 67,838 | 20,488 | 4,357 |
| Winkler | 31,769 | 15,152 | 10,533 | 103 |
| Wise | 144,536 | 85,178 | 32,380 | 749 |
| Wood | 203,143 | 116,887 | 50,203 | 461 |
| Yoakum | 57,119 | 13,185 | 7,151 | 27,586 |
| Young | 118,113 | 49,568 | 27,058 | 5,309 |
| Zapata | 53,083 | 16,375 | 16,128 | 127 |
| Zavala | 64,861 | 16,703 | 13,422 | 5,072 |

*Total federal government expenditures include: grants, salaries and wages (Postal Service, Dept. of Defense, etc.), procurement contract awards, direct payments for individuals, and other direct payments other than for individuals, such as some agriculture programs.

Retirement and disability programs include federal employee retirement and disability benefits, Social Security payments of all types, and veterans benefit payments.

Other direct payments for individuals include Medicare, excess earned income tax credits, food stamps, unemployment compensation benefit payments and lower income housing assistance.

Other direct payments other than for individuals include crop insurance, wool and mohair loss assistance program, conservation reserve program, production flexibility payments for contract commodities and postal service funds other than salaries and procurements.

Source: Consolidated Federal Funds Report, Fiscal Year 2002, U.S. Department of Commerce, Bureau of the Census.

# U.S. Tax Collections in Texas

(1,000 of dollars)

This information was furnished by the Internal Revenue Service.

| *Fiscal Year | Individual Income and Employment Taxes | Corporation Income Taxes | Estate Taxes | Gift Taxes | Excise Taxes | Total U.S. Taxes Collected in Texas |
|---|---|---|---|---|---|---|
| 2001 | $127,738,858 | $17,598,181 | $1,242,130 | $248,892 | $14,350,268 | $161,178,329 |
| 2000 | 116,094,820 | 20,310,672 | 1,176,278 | 269,109 | 14,732,513 | 152,583,349 |
| 1999 | 104,408,504 | 13,098,033 | 968,736 | 446,168 | 16,729,589 | 135,651,029 |
| 1998 | 94,404,751 | 14,526,238 | 1,300,104 | 247,989 | 11,877,230 | 122,356,312 |
| 1997 | 90,222,786 | 13,875,653 | 933,616 | 159,111 | 12,185,271 | 117,376,440 |
| 1996 | 76,863,689 | 12,393,992 | 733,282 | 158,237 | 10,418,847 | 101,079,028 |
| 1995 | 69,706,333 | 10,677,881 | 869,528 | 152,683 | 11,135,857 | 92,342,282 |
| 1994 | 63,916,496 | 9,698,069 | 624,354 | 347,900 | 9,528,449 | 84,086,676 |
| 1993 | 59,962,756 | 7,211,968 | 618,469 | 111,896 | 7,552,247 | 75,457,335 |
| 1992 | 57,367,765 | 6,338,621 | 598,918 | 121,164 | 7,558,642 | 71,985,109 |
| 1991 | 55,520,001 | 8,761,621 | 588,298 | 87,739 | 6,647,312 | 71,604,791 |
| 1990 | 52,795,489 | 6,983,762 | 521,811 | 196,003 | 5,694,006 | 66,191,071 |

| *Fiscal Year | Individual Income and Employment Taxes | Corporation Income Taxes | Estate Taxes | Gift Taxes | Excise Taxes | Total U.S. Taxes Collected in Texas |
|---|---|---|---|---|---|---|
| 1989 | 50,855,904 | 8,675,006 | 458,106 | 96,699 | 5,766,594 | 66,052,309 |
| 1988 | 45,080,428 | 6,058,172 | 444,349 | 39,137 | 5,957,085 | 57,579,171 |
| 1987 | 43,165,241 | 4,124,164 | 443,947 | 27,342 | 3,908,826 | 51,669,519 |
| 1986 | 44,090,929 | 4,808,703 | 493,405 | 35,355 | 4,169,857 | 53,598,248 |
| 1985 | 41,497,114 | 5,637,148 | 528,106 | 41,560 | 6,058,110 | 53,762,038 |
| 1984 | 37,416,203 | 4,750,079 | 494,431 | 19,844 | 5,553,491 | 48,234,047 |
| 1983 | 35,856,192 | 4,496,084 | 506,680 | 39,936 | 5,610,894 | 46,511,726 |
| 1982 | 36,072,975 | 6,574,940 | 624,559 | 6,789 | 6,880,102 | 50,159,365 |
| 1981 | 31,692,219 | 7,526,687 | 526,420 | 31,473 | 8,623,799 | 48,400,598 |
| 1980 | 25,707,514 | 7,232,486 | 453,830 | 23,722 | 4,122,538 | 37,540,089 |
| 1979 | 22,754,959 | 5,011,334 | 397,810 | 18,267 | 1,680,118 | 29,862,488 |
| 1978 | 17,876,628 | 5,128,609 | 337,883 | 19,189 | 1,757,045 | 25,119,354 |
| 1977 | 16,318,652 | 4,135,046 | 422,984 | 182,623 | 1,324,989 | 22,384,294 |
| 1976 | 11,908,546 | 2,736,374 | 350,326 | 48,804 | 1,320,496 | 16,364,546 |
| 1975 | 11,512,883 | 2,882,776 | 269,185 | 44,425 | 1,338,713 | 16,047,982 |
| 1974 | 9,884,442 | 1,989,710 | 259,306 | 43,109 | 1,338,656 | 13,515,223 |
| 1973 | 8,353,841 | 1,614,204 | 240,470 | 53,329 | 1,511,754 | 11,773,598 |
| 1972 | 7,125,930 | 1,485,559 | 288,674 | 24,792 | 1,478,340 | 10,403,295 |
| 1971 | 6,277,877 | 1,229,479 | 179,694 | 31,817 | 1,056,540 | 8,775,407 |
| 1970 | 6,096,961 | 1,184,342 | 135,694 | 20,667 | 843,724 | 8,281,389 |
| 1969 | 5,444,372 | 1,180,047 | 158,028 | 23,024 | 810,061 | 7,615,532 |
| 1968 | 4,721,316 | 935,302 | 138,102 | 24,878 | 821,576 | 6,707,952 |
| 1967 | 3,616,869 | 1,133,126 | 124,052 | 20,764 | 691,156 | 5,651,336 |
| 1966 | 3,063,000 | 847,000 | 130,000 | 17,000 | 717,000 | 4,774,000 |
| 1965 | 2,705,318 | 786,916 | 115,733 | 15,771 | 710,940 | 4,334,678 |
| 1964 | 2,745,342 | 716,288 | 93,497 | 14,773 | 670,309 | 4,240,209 |
| 1963 | 2,582,821 | 654,888 | 83,013 | 12,840 | 638,525 | 3,972,087 |
| 1962 | 2,361,614 | 675,035 | 101,263 | 13,095 | 444,279 | 3,595,287 |
| 1961 | 2,131,707 | 622,076 | 80,001 | 9,550 | 266,714 | 3,110,047 |
| 1960 | 2,059,075 | 622,822 | 70,578 | 10,583 | 209,653 | 2,972,712 |
| 1959 | 1,868,515 | 545,334 | 63,138 | 7,205 | 198,285 | 2,682,478 |
| 1958 | 1,786,686 | 625,267 | 68,379 | 10,672 | 206,307 | 2,697,309 |
| 1957 | 1,696,288 | 615,527 | 55,592 | 7,918 | 192,413 | 2,567,739 |

Beginning in 1976, the fiscal year ending date was changed to Sept. 30, from June 30.

# Medal of Freedom honors Van Cliburn

Van Cliburn. File photo.

The nation's highest civilian honor was awarded to Van Cliburn in 2003.

The internationally known pianist received the Presidential Medal of Freedom from President George W. Bush at the White House on July 23, 2003.

Raised in Kilgore, Cliburn rose to world prominence at age 23 when he won the prestigious Tchaikovsky International Piano competition in 1958 in Moscow.

The White House statement about his new honor said the Fort Worth resident "has entertained audiences around the world with his talents and continues to inspire young artists to achieve excellence."

Cliburn is the founder of the Van Cliburn International Piano Competition which began in 1962 and is held in Fort Worth every four years.

Among the ten other leaders in the arts, science and business that were honored by the president in 2003 were master chef Julia Child, actor Charlton Heston and physicist Edward Teller who worked on the Manhattan Project developing the atomic bomb.

President Harry Truman established the Medal of Freedom in 1945 to recognize civilians who had contributed to the efforts in World War II.

In 1963, President John F. Kennedy reintroduced the medal as an honor for distinguished civilian service in peacetime.

Other Texans who received the honor in the past include Barbara Jordan, Lloyd Bentsen, Lady Bird Johnson, J. Frank Dobie, James Farmer, Dr. Michael DeBakey and Willie Velásquez

Also, several astronauts serving in Houston have been honored, as well as national figures who spent part of their lives in Texas, including author James Michener and artist Georgia O'Keeffe. ☆

# Film and Television Work in Texas

*Source: Texas Film Commission*

Film production in Texas is a long-standing and vital part of Texas' economy, bringing thousands of jobs and hundreds of millions of dollars into the state.

It is one of the nation's top filmmaking states, after California and New York.

Texas' attractions to filmmakers are its diverse locations, abundant sunshine and moderate winter weather, and a variety of support services experienced at dealing with the special needs of filmmaking.

The economic benefits of hosting on-location filming are clear. Over the past decade, more than $1.2 billion has been spent in Texas.

Besides salaries paid to locally hired technicians and actors, as well as fees paid to location owners, the production companies do business with hotels, car rental agencies, lumberyards, restaurants, fabric stores, grocery stores, utilities, office furniture suppliers, gas stations, dry cleaners, security services, florists and more.

And it is not just feature films that use Texas. All types of projects come to Texas, such as television specials, commercials, corporate films and videos.

Many projects made in Texas originate in California studios, but

The set near Dripping Springs of the Disney movie about the Alamo. File photo.

Texas is also the home of many independent filmmakers who make films outside the studio system.

### Major projects in Texas by year

| Year | Number | Total Budgets |
|------|--------|---------------|
| 1985 | 27 | $ 56,700,000 |
| 1986 | 27 | 102,100,000 |
| 1987 | 24 | 66,300,000 |
| 1988 | 24 | 93,900,000 |
| 1989 | 32 | 117,100,000 |
| 1990 | 31 | 42,100,000 |
| 1991 | 48 | 133,000,000 |
| 1992 | 30 | 143,500,000 |
| 1993 | 49 | 180,700,000 |
| 1994 | 45 | 205,000,000 |
| 1995 | 51 | 330,300,000 |
| 1996 | 54 | 254,700,000 |
| 1997 | 47 | 233,300,000 |
| 1998 | 47 | 266,900,000 |
| 1999 | 32 | 200,600,000 |
| 2000 | 45 | 294.500,000 |
| 2001 | 45 | 277,300,000 |
| 2002 | 44 | $ 134,500,000 |

*Source: Texas Film Commission*

Some films and television shows made in Texas have become icons. **Giant**, John Wayne's **The Alamo**, and the long-running TV series **Dallas** all made their mark on the world's perception of Texas and continue to draw tourists to their film locations.

The Texas Film Commission, a division of the Office of the Governor, markets to Hollywood Texas' locations, support services and workforce. The commission's free services include location research, employment referrals, red-tape-cutting, and information on laws, weather, travel and other topics affecting filmmakers.

The on-line *Texas Production Manual* includes more than 1,200 individuals and businesses serving every facet of the film industry. ☆

---

# Film Commissions

In addition to the offices listed below, many other Texas cities have employees who specialize in assisting filmmakers. The **Texas Film Commission** (**www.governor.state.tx.us/film**) can provide information on local contacts for most Texas cities and counties:

**Amarillo Film Office**
1000 S, Polk, Amarillo 79101
(806) 374-1497
(800) 692-1338
www.amarillofilm.org
jutta@amarillo-cvb.org

**Austin Film Office**
201 E. 2nd St., Austin 78701
(800) 926-2282
(512) 583-7229
gbond@austintexas.org

www.austintexas.org

**Dallas Film Commission**
325 N. St. Paul Ste. 700
Dallas 75201
(214) 571-1050
film@dallascvb.com
www.dallasfilmcommision.com

**El Paso Film Commission**
1 Civic Center Plaza
El Paso 79901
(915) 534-0698
(800) 351-6024
sgaines@elpasocvb.com
www.elpasocvb.com

**Houston Film Commission**
901 Bagby Ste. 100
Houston 77002
(713) 437-5248
(800) 365-7575
rferguson@ghcvb.org
www.houston-guide.com

**Lubbock-Top of Texas Film Commission**
1301 Broadway Ste. 200
Lubbock 79401
(806) 749-4500
linda.whitman@marketlubbock.org
www.marketlubbock.org

**San Antonio Film Commission**
203 S. St. Mary's, 2nd Floor
San Antonio 78205
(800) 447-3372
(210) 207-6730
leighton@filmsanantonio.com
www.filmsanantonio.com

**South Padre Island Film Commission**
7355 Padre Blvd
South Padre Island 78597
(800) 657-2373
(956) 761-3005
erica@sopadre.com
www.sopadre.com

# State Cultural Agencies Assist the Arts

*Source: Principally, the Texas Commission on the Arts, along with other state cultural agencies.*

Culture in Texas, as in any market, is a mixture of activity generated by both the commercial and the non-profit sectors.

The commercial sector encompasses Texas-based profit-making businesses including commercial recording artists (such as the legendary Willie Nelson), nightclubs, record companies, private galleries, assorted boutiques that carry fine art collectibles and private dance and music halls. In addition, Texas is becoming an important media center, with Texas-based publications, television and film companies gaining national recognition.

Texas also has extensive cultural resources offered by nonprofit organizations that are engaged in charitable, educational and/or humanitarian activities.

The Texas Legislature has authorized five state agencies to administer cultural services and funds for the public good. The agencies are:

**Texas Commission on the Arts**, Box 13406, Austin (78711); **Texas Film Commission**, Box 13246, Austin (78711); **Texas Historical Commission**, Box 12276, Austin (78711); **Texas State Library and Archives Commission**, Box 12927, Austin (78711); and the **State Preservation Board**, Box 13286, Austin (78711).

Although not a state agency, another organization that provides cultural services to the citizens of Texas is the **Texas Council for the Humanities**, 3809 South 2nd, Austin 78704.

The **Texas Commission on the Arts** was established in 1965 to develop a receptive climate for the arts in Texas and to serve as a source of arts information to state government and Texas at large. The commission achieves these objectives by providing financial, informational and technical assistance.

The commission's assistance programs serve as a financial catalyst to assist individuals and organizations in opening doors to local resources. Its clientele includes theaters (professional, civic, children's, ethnic), media (radio, television, film, publications), festivals, music (folk, symphonic, chamber, choral, jazz, opera, and new music), visual arts (sculpture, crafts, photography, painting, environmental), dance (modern, ballet, folkloric), schools, presenters of cultural events, and service organizations.

In 1993, the Texas Legislature created the Texas Cultural Endowment Fund as a public/private funding source to enhance the performing, visual and literary arts and education.

Goals of the Texas Cultural Endowment Fund are to: 1) create financial self-sufficiency for the Texas Commission on the Arts by providing a stable and predictable base of funding no longer dependent on tax-based legislative support; 2) enhance arts education, encourage economic development, and cultivate a higher quality of life in communities throughout Texas; 3) demonstrate leadership by encouraging public and private partnerships, ensuring public access to the arts for all communities statewide; and 4) diversify revenue sources, and increase the state's capacity to introduce the arts to future generations, to build audiences, and to create supporters.

The Texas Commission on the Arts seeks support for the Texas Cultural Endowment Fund and is responsible for the management of the fund. The commission is also ultimately responsible for the distribution of the fund to artists, arts, cultural and educational projects and organizations throughout Texas.

For more information about the services of the commission, call toll-free (800) 252-9415.

---

# Texas Performing Arts Organizations

*Below are the Web addresses of Texas performing arts organizations, including theatre, dance and music.*

### Abilene
Paramount Theatre
www.paramount-abilene.org/
### Addison
Water Tower Theatre
www.watertowertheatre.org/
### Amarillo
Amarillo Symphony
www.amarillosymphony.org/
Lone Star Ballet
www.lonestarballet.org
### Arlington
Theatre Arlington
www.theatrearlington.org/
### Austin
Austin Shakespeare Festival
www.austinshakespeare.org/
Austin Symphony
www.austinsymphony.org/
Ballet Austin
www.balletaustin.org/

Gilbert & Sullivan Society of Austin
www.gilbertsullivan.org
Austin Theatre Alliance (Paramount Theatre and State Theatre)
www.asutintheatrealliance.org
Sharir+Bustamante Danceworks
www.danceworks.org/
Zachary Scott Theatre
www.zachscott.com/
### Canyon
Texas Legacies, Musical Drama
www.epictexas.com/
### Conroe
Crighton Players
www.crightonplayers.org/
main.htm
### Corpus Christi
Corpus Christi Ballet
www.tamu.edu/ccballet/
about.html
Harbor Playhouse
www.harborplayhouse.com/
### Dallas
Dallas Opera
www.dallasopera.org/

Dallas Puppet Theater
www.puppetry.org/
Dallas Summer Musicals
www.dallassummermusicals.org/
Dallas Symphony
www.dallassymphony.com/
Dallas Theater Center
www.dallastheatercenter.org/
Dallas Wind Symphony
www.dws.org/
Junior Players
www.juniorplayers.org/
Pegasus Theatre
www.pegasustheatre.org/
Pocket Sandwich Theatre
www.dallas.net/~pst/
Shakespeare Festival of Dallas
www.shakespearedallas.org/
Teatro Dallas
web2.airmail.net/teatro/
Theatre Three
www.theatre3dallas.com
TITAS (Texas International Theatrical Arts Society)
www.titas.org/

Turtle Creek Chorale
www.turtlecreek.org/
Undermain Theatre
www.undermain.com/
**Del Rio**
The Upstagers
www.upstagers.org
**Denton**
Campus Theatre
campustheatre.com/
**El Paso**
El Paso Playhouse
www.elpasoplayhouse.org/
El Paso Symphony Orchestra
www.epso.org
**Fort Worth**
Casa Manana
www.casamanana.org/
Circle Theatre
www.circletheatre.com/
Contemporary Dance/Fort Worth
www.cdfw.org/
Fort Worth Classic Guitar Society
www.guitarsociety.org/
Fort Worth Dallas Ballet
www.fwdballet.com/
Fort Worth Symphony
www.fwsymphony.org
Shakespeare in the Park
www.alliedtheatre.org
Texas Boys Choir
www.texasboyschoir.org/
**Fredericksburg**
Fredericksburg Theater Company
www.fredericksburgtheater.org/
**Frisco**
Frisco Community Theatre
www.FriscoCommunityTheatre.com
**Galveston**
Galveston Symphony Orchestra
www.galvestonsymphony.org
**Granbury**
Granbury Opera House
www.granburyoperahouse.org/

index.html
**Houston**
Alley Theatre
www.alleytheatre.com/
Clear Lake Symphony
www.nassaubay.com/clsymphony.htm
Gilbert and Sullivan Society of Houston
www.gilbertandsullivan.net/
Houston Ballet
www.houstonballet.org/
Houston Grand Opera
www.houstongrandopera.com/
Houston Symphony
www.houstonsymphony.org/
Masquerade Theatre
masqueradetheatre.com/
Stages Repertory Theatre
www.stagestheatre.com/
Stages Theatre Company (children's)
www.stagestheatre.org/
Theatre Under the Stars
www.TUTS.com/
**Ingram**
Point Theater (Hill Country Arts Foundation)
www.hcaf.com/
**Irving**
Irving Community Theater
www.irvingtheatre.org/
New Philharmonic Orchestra of Irving
home.earthlink.net/~youngj1/npoi.htm
**Kilgore**
Texas Shakespeare Festival
www.texasshakespeare.com/
**Mesquite**
Mesquite Symphony Orchestra
members.aol.com/TchrfromOz/mso.html
**Midland**
Midland-Odessa Symphony

& Chorale
www.mosc.org
**Odessa**
Globe of the Great Southwest
www.GlobeSW.org/
**Orange**
Frances Ann Lutcher Theatre for the Performing Arts
www.lutcher.org/
**Pasadena**
Pasadena Little Theatre
web.wt.net/~plth/
**Round Rock**
Sam Bass Community Theatre
www.SamBassTheatre.com
**Round Top**
Festival-Institute at Round Top (James Dick Foundation)
festivalhill.org/
**San Antonio**
¡Arts San Antonio!
www.ArtsSanAntonio.com
Carver Cultural Center
www.thecarver.org
Guadalupe Cultural Arts Center
www.guadalupeculturalarts.org/
Majestic Theatre
www.themajestic.com/theatre.htm
San Antonio Symphony
www.sasymphony.org/
San Pedro Playhouse
members.tripod.com/~San_Pedro_Playhouse/index.html
Southwest School of Art & Craft
www.swschool.org
**Tyler**
East Texas Symphony Orchestra
www.etso.org/
Tyler Civic Ballet
www.tylercivicballet.com
**Texas**
Texas Nonprofit Theatres
geocities.com/texastheatres/

# Texas Museums

Listed below are the Web addresses of Texas museums. Where required some have indication of the area of emphasis of the exhibits.

**Abilene**
Grace Museum (Art, History)
www.thegracemuseum.org
National Center for Children's Illustrated Literature
www.nccil.org/home.html
**Addison**
Cavanaugh Flight Museum
www.cavanaughflightmuseum.com/
**Albany**
Old Jail Art Center
www.oldjailartcenter.org
**Alpine**
Museum of the Big Bend (History)
www.sulross.edu/~museum/

**Amarillo**
American Quarter Horse Heritage Center & Museum
www.imh.org/imh/qhm/qhmhome.html
Don Harrington Discovery Center (Science, Children's)
www.dhdc.org/
**Angleton**
Brazoria County Historical Museum
www.bchm.org/
**Arlington**
Legends of the Game Baseball Museum
www.rangers.mlb.com/NASApp/mlb/tex/ballpark/tex_ballpark_museum.jsp
**Austin**
Austin Children's Museum
www.austinkids.org/
Austin Museum of Art
www.amoa.org/
Capitol Visitors Center (Historical)

www.tspb.state.tx.us/CVC/home/home.html
Elisabet Ney Museum (Art)
www.ci.austin.tx.us/elisabetney/
French Legation Museum (History)
www.welkin.org/french-legation/
Harry Ransom Humanities Research Center (History, Literature)
www.hrc.utexas.edu/
Jack S. Blanton Museum of Art
www.blantonmuseum.org/
Jourdan-Bachman Pioneer Farm
www.pioneerfarm.org/
Lyndon B. Johnson Library
www.lbjlib.utexas.edu/
Mexic-Arte Museum (Art)
www.mexic-artemuseum.org/
O. Henry Museum (History)
www.ci.austin.tx.us/parks/ohenry.htm
Texas Memorial Museum (History, Natural History)
www.tmm.utexas.edu/

Texas Music Museum
www.texasmusicmuseum.org
Umlauf Sculpture Garden & Museum
www.umlaufsculpture.org
Wild Basin Wilderness Preserve
www.wildbasin.org/
**Beaumont**
Art Museum of Southeast Texas
www.amset.org/
McFaddin-Ward House (History)
www.mcfaddin-ward.org/
Spindletop/Gladys City Boomtown
Museum (History)
hal.lamar.edu/~psce/gladys.html
Texas Energy Museum (History)
www.texasenergymuseum.org
**Bonham**
Sam Rayburn Library/Museum
www.cah.utexas.edu/divisions/
Rayburn.html
**Bryan**
Brazos Valley Museum of Natural
History
bvmuseum.myriad.net/
**Buffalo Gap**
Buffalo Gap Historic Village
www.mcwhiney.org/buffgap/
bghome.html
**Burton**
Burton Cotton Gin and Museum
(Historical)
www.cottonginmuseum.org/
**Canyon**
Panhandle-Plains Historical Museum
www.panhandleplains.org
**Carthage**
Texas Country Music Hall of Fame
www.panola.cc.tx.us/
Carthage%2DPanolaCounty/
Tx_web/index.html
**Clarendon**
Saints' Roost Museum (Historical)
www.saintsroose.org
**College Station**
George Bush Presidential Library
bushlibrary.tamu.edu/
J. Wayne Stark University Center
Galleries
stark.tamu.edu/
Virtual Museum of Nautical
Archaeology
ina.tamu.edu/vm.htm
**Corpus Christi**
Art Museum of South Texas
www.stia.org/
Asian Cultures Museum
www.geocities.com/asiancm/
Corpus Christi Museum of Science
and History
cctexas.com/?fuseaction
=main.view&page=200
U.S.S. Lexington Museum
www.usslexington.com/
**Cotulla**
Brush Country Historical Museum
historicdistrict.com/museum/
**Dalhart**
XIT Museum (Historical)
www.dallam.org/community/
museum.shtml
**Dallas**
Age of Steam Railroad Museum
www.dallasrailwaymuseum.com

American Museum of Miniature Arts
(Doll Houses)
minimuseum.org/
Biblical Arts Center
www.biblicalarts.org/
Dallas Historical Society (Fair Park)
www.dallashistory.org/
Dallas Museum of Art
www.dm-art.org/
Dallas Museum of Natural History
www.dallasdino.org/
Frontiers of Flight Museum
flightmuseum.com/
International Museum of Cultures
www.sil.org/imc/
Meadows Museum (Art)
meadows.smu.edu/
default.asp?page=Museum
Old City Park(History)
www.oldcitypark.org/
The Science Place
www.scienceplace.org/
The Sixth Floor Museum (History)
www.jfk.org/
**Del Rio**
Whitehead Memorial Museum
(History)
whitehead-museum.com
**Denison**
Red River Railroad Museum
www.denisontx.com/railroad/
museum.htm
**Denton**
Courthouse-on-the-Square Museum
(Historical)
www.co.denton.tx.us/dept/
hcm.htm
University of North Texas
Art Galleries
www.art.unt.edu/gallery/
**Edgewood**
Edgewood Heritage Park and
Historical Village
www.vzinet.com/heritage/
index.htm
**Edinburg**
Hidalgo County Historical Museum
www.hiline.net/hchm/
**El Campo**
El Campo Museum of
Natural History
www.elcampomuseum.com/
**El Paso**
El Paso Museum of Art
www.elpasoartmuseum.org/
**Emory**
A.C. McMillan African American
Museum
geocities.com/acmmuseum/
**Fort Davis**
Chihuahuan Desert Research
Institute and Visitor Center
www.cdri.org/
**Fort Worth**
Amon Carter Museum (Art)
www.cartermuseum.org/
Fort Worth Museum of Science
and History
www.fwmuseum.org/
Kimbell Art Museum
www.kimbellart.org/
Log Cabin Village (Historical)
www.logcabinvillage.org

Modern Art Museum of Fort Worth
www.themodern.org
National Cowgirl Museum
and Hall of Fame
www.cowgirl.net/
Sid Richardson Collection
of Western Art
www.sidrmuseum.org/
**Fredericksburg**
Gillespie County Historical Society
www.pioneermuseum.com/
**Galveston**
Lone Star Flight Museum
www.lsfm.org
Texas Seaport Museum and Tallship
"Elissa"
www.tsm-elissa.org/
**Gilmer**
Flight of the Phoenix Aviation
Museum
www.flightofthephoenix.org/
**Greenville**
American Cotton Museum
www.cottonmuseum.com/
**Harlingen**
Rio Grande Valley Museum
(Historical)
www.hiline.net/rgvmuse/
**Henderson**
The Depot Museum (Historical)
www.depotmuseum.com/
**Houston**
Blaffer Gallery, University of Houston
www.hfac.uh.edu/blaffer/
Children's Museum of Houston
www.cmhouston.org/
Contemporary Arts Museum
www.camh.org/
Houston Center for Photography
www.hcponline.org/
Houston Fire Museum (History)
www.houstonfiremuseum.org/
Houston Museum of Natural Science
www.hmns.org/
Lawndale Art Center
www.lawndaleartcenter.org/
The Menil Collection (Art)
www.menil.org/
Museum of Fine Arts
mfah.org/
Museum of Health and
Medical Science
www.mhms.org/
Museum of Printing History
www.printingmuseum.org/
Offshore Energy Center/Ocean Star
(Science, Industry)
www.oceanstaroec.com/
Rice University Art Gallery
www.ruf.rice.edu/~ruag/
San Jacinto Museum of History
www.tpwd.state.tx.us/park/
sanjac/monu.htm
Sarah Campbell Blaffer Foundation
(Art)
www.rice.edu/projects/Blaffer/
Space Center Houston
www.spacecenter.org/
**Huntsville**
Sam Houston Memorial Museum
www.shsu.edu/~smm_www/
**Kerrville**
Cowboy Artists of America Museum

www.caamuseum.com/

**Kilgore**
East Texas Oil Museum
www.kilgore.cc.tx.us/attr/etom/
etom.html

**Lake Jackson**
Lake Jackson Historical Museum
www.lakejacksonmuseum.org/

**La Porte**
San Jacinto Monument and Museum
www.sanjacinto-museum.org/

**League City**
West Bay Common School
Children's Museum (Historical)
www.oneroomschoolhouse.org/

**Llano**
Hill Country Wildlife Museum
pages.tstar.net/~wlm/

**Longview**
Longview Museum of Fine Arts
www.lmfa.org/

**Lubbock**
Buddy Holly Center (Historical)
culturalarts.ci.lubbock.tx.us/
Museum of Texas Tech University
(Art, Humanities, Science)
www.ttu.edu/~museum/
index.html
Ranching Heritage Center
www.ttu.edu/RanchingHeritage
Center/home.htm
Science Spectrum
www.sciencespectrum.com/

**Lufkin**
Texas Forestry Museum
www.texasforestry.org/
museum.htm

**Marfa**
The Chinati Foundation (Art)
www.chinati.org/

**Marshall**
Harrison County Historical Museum
www.cets.sfasu.edu/harrison/

**McAllen**
McAllen International Museum
(Art, Science)
www.mcallenmuseum.org

**McKinney**
Heard Natural Science Museum
www.heardmuseum.org/

**Midland**

American Airpower Heritage
Museum and Commerative
Air Force
www.airpowermuseum.org/
Museum of the Southwest
(Art, Science, Children's)
www.museumsw.org/
Petroleum Museum
www.petroleummuseum.org/

**Mobeetie**
Old Mobeetie Texas Association
www.mobeetie.com/

**New Braunfels**
New Braunfels Sophienburg
Museum (History)
www.nbtx.com/sophienburg/
Children's Museum of New Braunfels
www.nbchildren.org/

**Plano**
Heritage Farmstead Museum
www.heritagefarmstead.org/

**Port Arthur**
Museum of the Gulf Coast
(Historical)
museum.lamarpa.edu/

**Richmond**
George Ranch Historical Park
www.georgeranch.org/

**Rockport**
Texas Maritime Museum
www.texasmaritimemuseum.org/

**Round Top**
Henkel Square (History)
www.rtis.com/reg/roundtop/
henkel.htm
Winedale Historical Center
www.cah.utexas.edu/divisions/
Winedale.html

**San Angelo**
San Angelo Museum of Fine Arts
and Children's Art Museum
web2.airmail.net/samfa/

**San Antonio**
The Alamo
www.drtl.org/
Hertzberg Circus Collection/Museum
www.sat.lib.tx.us/Hertzberg/
hzmain.html
Institute of Texan Cultures
www.texancultures.utsa.edu/
main/

Magic Lantern Castle
Museum (History)
www.magiclanterns.org/
The McNay Art Museum
www.mcnayart.org/
San Antonio Art League Museum
www.saalm.org/
San Antonio Museum of Art
www.sa-museum.org/
Witte Museum (Science, Historical)
www.wittemuseum.org/
Wooden Nickel Historical Museum
www.wooden-nickel.net/

**San Marcos**
Southwestern Writers Collection and
Wittliff Gallery of Southwestern
& Mexican Photography
www.library.swt.edu/swwc/wg/
index.html

**Sherman**
Red River Historical Museum
www.texoma.net/rrhms/

**Sulphur Springs**
Southwest Dairy Center/Museum
www.geocities.com/Heartland/
Ranch/3541/

**Teague**
The B-RI Railroad Museum
www.therailroadmuseum.com/

**Temple**
Railroad and Heritage Museum
www.rrdepot.org/
railroadmuseum.htm

**The Woodlands**
Woodlands Science and Art Center
www.woodsac.org/

**Tyler**
Discovery Science Place
discovery.tyler.com/
Smith County Historical Museum
www.smithcountyhistory.org/
Museum.htm
Tyler Museum of Art
www.tylermuseum.org

**Vernon**
Red River Valley Museum
(History, Art)
www.rrvm.org/

**Waco**
Dr Pepper Museum (History)
www.drpeppermuseum.com/
Mayborn Museum Complex
(including Strecker Museum)
(History, Science)
www3.baylor.edu/Museum_
Studies/strecker.htm
Texas Ranger Hall of Fame/ Museum
www.texasranger.org/
Texas Sports Hall of Fame
www.tshof.org/

**Washington**
Star of the Republic Museum
(Historical)
www.starmuseum.org/

**White Settlement**
White Settlement Historical Museum
wsmuseum.tripod.com/

**Wichita Falls**
Kell House Museum (History)
www.wichitaheritage.org/
kellhouse.html
Wichita Falls Museum & Art Center
www.wfmuseum.org/ ☆

*A reproduction of the 1965 Porsche originally owned by Janis Joplin on display at the Museum of the Gulf Coast in Port Arthur. File photo.*

# Poets Laureate of Texas

| | |
|---|---|
| 1932-34 | Judd Mortimer Lewis, Houston* |
| 1934-36 | Aline T. Michaelis, Austin |
| 1936-39 | Grace Noll Crowell, Dallas |
| 1939-41 | Lexie Dean Robertson, Rising Star |
| 1941-43 | Nancy Richey Ranson, Dallas |
| 1943-45 | Dollilee Davis Smith, Cleburne |
| 1945-47 | DavidRiley Russell, Dallas |
| 1947-49 | Aline B. Carter, San Antonio |
| 1949-51 | Carlos Ashley, Llano |
| 1951-53 | Arthur M. Sampley, Denton |
| 1953-55 | Mildred Lindsey Raiborn, San Angelo<br>Dee Walker, Texas City, alternate |
| 1955-57 | Pierre Bernard Hill, Hunt |
| 1957-59 | Margaret Royalty Edwards, Waco |
| 1959-61 | J.V. Chandler, Kingsville<br>Edna Coe Majors, Colorado City, alternate |
| 1961 | Lorena Simon, Port Arthur |
| 1962 | Marvin Davis Winsett, Dallas |
| 1963 | Gwendolyn Bennett Pappas, Houston<br>Vassar Miller, Houston, alternate |
| 1964-65 | Jenny Lind Porter, Austin<br>Edith Rayzor Canant, Texas City, alternate |
| 1966 | Bessie Maas Rowe, Port Arthur<br>Grace Marie Scott, Abilene, alternate |
| 1967 | William E. Bard, Dallas<br>Bessie Maas Rowe, Port Arthur, alternate |
| 1968 | Kathryn Henry Harris, Waco<br>Sybil Leonard Armes, El Paso, alternate |
| 1969-70 | Anne B. Marely, Austin<br>Rose Davidson Speer, Brady, alternate |
| 1970-71 | Mrs. Robby K. Mitchell, McKinney<br>Faye Carr Adams, Dallas, alternate |
| 1971-72 | Terry Fontenot, Port Arthur<br>Faye Carr Adams, Dallas, alternate |
| 1972-73 | Mrs. Clark Gresham, Burkburnett<br>Marion McDaniel, Sidney, alternate |
| 1973-74 | Violette Newton, Beaumont<br>Stella Woodall, San Antonio, alternate |
| 1974-75 | Lila Todd O'Neil, Port Arthur<br>C.W. Miller, San Antonio, alternate |
| 1975-76 | Ethel Osborn Hill, Port Arthur<br>Gene Shuford, Denton, alternate |
| 1976-77 | Florice Stripling Jeffers, Burkburnett<br>Vera L. Eckert, San Angelo, alternate |
| 1977-78 | Ruth Carruth, Vernon<br>Joy Gresham Hagstrom, Burburnett, alternate |
| 1978-79 | Patsy Stodghill, Dallas<br>Dorothy B. Elfstroman, Galveston, alternate |
| 1979-80 | Dorothy B. Elfstroman, Galveston<br>Ruth Carruth, Vernon, alternate |
| 1980-81 | Weems S. Dykes, McCamey<br>Mildred Crabree Speer, Amarillo, alternate |
| *1981-82* | *none designated* |
| 1982-83 | William D. Barney, Fort Worth<br>Vassar Miller, Houston, alternate |
| *1983-87* | *none designated* |
| 1987-88 | Ruth E. Reuther, Wichita Falls |
| 1988-89 | Vassar Miller, Houston |
| *1989-93* | *none designated* |
| 1993-94 | Mildred Baass, Victoria |
| *1994-99* | *none designated* |
| 2000 | James Hoggard, Wichita Falls |
| 2001 | Walter McDonald, Lubbock |
| *2002* | *none designated* |
| 2003 | Jack Myers, Mesquite |
| 2004 | Cleatus Rattan, Cisco |

# State Artists of Texas

| | |
|---|---|
| 1971-72 | Joe Ruiz Grandee, Arlington* |
| 1972-73 | Melvin C. Warren, Clifton |
| 1973-74 | Ronald Thomason, Weatherford<br>A.C. Gentry Jr., Tyler, alternate |
| 1974-75 | Joe Rader Roberts, Dripping Springs<br>Bette Lou Voorhis, Austin, alternate |
| 1975-76 | Jack White, New Braunfels |
| July 4, 1975<br>-July 4, 1976 | Robert Summers, Glen Rose<br>Bicentennial Artist |
| 1976-77 | James Boren, Clifton<br>Kenneth Wyatt, Lubbock, alternate |
| 1977-78 | Edward "Buck" Schiwetz, DeWitt County<br>Renne Hughes, Tarrant County, alternate |
| 1978-79 | Jack Cowan, Rockport<br>Gary Henry, Palo Pinto County, alternate<br>Joyce Tally, Caldwell County, alternate |
| 1979-80 | Dalhart Windberg, Travis County<br>Grant Lathe, Canyon Lake, alternate |
| 1980-81 | Harry Ahysen, Huntsville<br>Jim Reno, Simonton, alternate |
| 1981-82 | Jerry Newman, Beaumont<br>Raul Guiterrez, San Antonio, alternate |
| 1982-83 | Dr. James H. Johnson, Bryan<br>Armando Hinojosa, Laredo, alternate |
| 1983-84 | Raul Gutierrez, San Antonio<br>James Eddleman, Lubbock, alternate |
| 1984-85 | Covelle Jones, Lubbock<br>Ragan Gennusa, Austin, alternate |
| 1986-87 | Chuck DeHaan, Graford |
| 1987-88 | Neil Caldwell, Angleton<br>Rey Gaytan, Austin, alternate |
| 1988-89 | George Hallmark, Walnut Springs<br>Tony Eubanks, Grapevine, alternate |

| | Two-dimensional | Three-dimensional |
|---|---|---|
| 1990-91 | Mondel Rogers, Sweetwater | Ron Wells, Cleveland |
| 1991-92 | Woodrow Foster, Center | Kent Ullberg, Corpus Christi |
| | Harold Phenix, Houston, alternate | Mark Clapham, Conroe, alternate |
| 1993-94 | Roy Lee Ward | James Eddleman, Lubbock |
| 1994-95 | Frederick Carter, El Paso | Garland A. Weeks, Wichita Falls |
| 1998-99 | Carl Rice Embrey, San Antonio | Edd Hayes, Humble |
| *2000-02* | *none designated* | |
| 2003 | Ralph White, Austin | Dixie Friend Gay, Houston |
| 2004 | Sam Caldwell, Houston | David Hickman, Dallas |

# State Musicians of Texas

| | |
|---|---|
| 2003 | James Dick, Round Top |
| 2004 | Ray Benson, Austin |

*Since 2001, a committee of seven members appointed by the governor, lt. governor, and speaker of the House selects the poet laureate, state artists and state musicians based on recommendations from the Texas Commission on the Arts.*

*Earlier, the Legislature made the nominations.*

*Sources: Texas State Library and Archives; Texas Commission on the Arts; Dallas Morning News.*

# Texas Medal of the Arts Awards

Source: Texas Commission on the Arts

The second Texas Medals of the Arts were presented to artists and arts patrons in March 2003.

The awards are administered by the Texas Cultural Trust Council.

The council was established to raise money and awareness for the Texas Cultural Trust Fund, which was created by the Legislature in 1993 to support cultural arts in Texas (www.txculturaltrust.org).

The first medals were presented in 2001.

Charley Pride, above, and Tommy Tune, right, were among the Texans honored March 2003. File photo.

A concurrent proclamation by the state Senate and House of Representatives honors the recepients, and the governor presents the awards in Austin every two years.

A **Lifetime Achievement Award** was presented to writer John Graves of Glen Rose, author of *Goodbye to A River*.

Other winners were:

**Media-film/television acting**: Fess Parker of Fort Worth, star of *Davy Crockett* and *Daniel Boone*.

**Music**: country singer Charley Pride of Dallas.

**Dance**: choreographer, singer, director, dancer Tommy Tune of Wichita Falls and Houston.

**Theater**: Enid Holm of Odessa, actress and former executive director of Texas Nonprofit Theatres.

**Literary arts**: novelist Sandra Cisneros of San Antonio.

**Visual arts**: sculptor Glenna Goodacre of Dallas.

**Folk arts**: Tejano singer Lydia Mendoza of San Antonio.

**Architecture**: State Capitol Preservation Project of Austin, headed by Dealey Herndon.

**Arts education**: theater teacher Marca Lee Bircher of Dallas.

**Individual arts patron**: philanthropist Nancy B. Hamon of Dallas.

**Corporate arts patron**: Exxon/Mobil based in Irving.

**Foundation arts patron**: Houston Endownment Inc.

The first group of artists and patrons to receive the award in 2001 were:

**Lifetime Achievement**: Van Cliburn of Fort Worth, cited as "acclaimed concert pianist and mentor."

**Film**: actor Tommy Lee Jones of San Saba.

**Music**: singer-songwriter Willie Nelson of Austin.

**Dance**: Debbie Allen of Houston, choreographer, director, actress and composer.

**Theater**: *Texas* musical-drama producer Neil Hess of Amarillo.

**Literary arts**: playwright Horton Foote of Wharton.

**Visual arts**: muralist John Biggers of Houston.

**Folk arts**: musician brothers Santiago Jimenez Jr. and Flaco Jimenez of San Antonio.

**Architecture**: restoration architect Wayne Bell of Austin.

**Arts education**: theater arts director Gilberto Zepeda Jr. of Pharr.

**Individual arts patron**: philanthropist Jack Blanton of Houston.

**Corporate arts patron**: SBC Communications Inc. of San Antonio.

**Foundation arts patron**: Meadows Foundation of Dallas. ☆

---

# National Humanities Medal honors El Paso illustrator

Source: Office of Press Secretary, White House

Jose Cisneros, the artist from El Paso, was among the 2001 recepients of the National Humanities Medal.

Cisneros, 93, is renowned for depicting the people and culture of the old Southwest through his illustrations for magazines, books and newspapers. Born in Mexico, he came to El Paso at the age of 15.

His *Borderlands: The Heritage of the Lower Rio Grande through the Art of Jose Cisneros* (1998) chronicles events in the history of the border between Texas and Mexico.

He has been knighted by Pope John Paul II and the King of Spain, Juan Carlos I, for his contribution to understanding history through his arts.

He previously was honored for his contribution to historical art in the Southest by then Gov. George W. Bush.

In addition to Cisneros, the group of 2001 honorees included William Manchester, historian and writer; Tom Wolfe, author, and Robert Coles, child psychologist.

President Bush presented the awards in April 2002 in Washington.

The humanities medal was inaugurated in 1997 to replace the Charles Frankel Prize, orginated by the National Endowment for the Humanities in 1989. It honors individuals who have made outstanding contributions to the public's understanding of history, literature, philosophy and other humanities disciplies.

Other Texans previously honored include journalists Jim Lehrer and Bill Moyers, Latino scholar Arturo Madrid, who is on the board of directors of the Belo corporation, and Don Henley, former member of the Eagles rock group. ☆

# Texas Institute of Letters Awards

Each year since 1939, the **Texas Institute of Letters** has chosen outstanding literature and journalism that are either by Texans or about Texas subjects. Awards have been made for fiction, nonfiction, Southwest history, general information, magazine and newspaper journalism, children's books, translation, poetry and book design. The awards for recent years are listed below:

**Writer/Designer: Title**

### 2002
Kathi Appelt: *Where, Where Is Swamp Bear?*
Carolee Dean: *Comfort*
Juan Rulfo: *Pedro Paramo*
Ben Fountain III: "Near-Extinct Birds of the Central Cordillera"
Mark Lisheron and Bill Bishop: "Cities of Ideas" in the *Austin American-Statesman*
Lawrence Wright: "The Man Behind Bin Laden" in the *New Yorker*
Dan Rifenburgh: *Advent*
Reginald Gibbons: *It's Time*
Kinky Friedman: *Meanwhile Back at the Ranch*
Michael Gagarin: *Antiphon the Athenian: Oratory, Law, and Justice in the Age of the Sophists*
Ray Gonzalez: *The Underground Heart: A Return to a Hidden Landscape*
Lisa Schamess: *Borrowed Light*
Rick Bass: *Hermit's Story*
Lon Tinkle Award (for career): Shelby Hearon

### 2001
Carmen Bredeson: *Animals that Migrate*
Lori Aurelia Williams: *When Kambia Elaine Flew from Neptune*
Vicki Trego Hill: *Folktales of the Zapatista Revolution*
Tom McNeely: "Tickle Torture"
Mike Tolson, James Kimberly, Steve Brewer, Allan Turner: "A Deadly Distinction" in the *Houston Chronicle*
Larry L. King: "The Book on Willie Morris" in *Texas Monthly*
Ted Genoways: *Bullroarer*
Susan Wood: *Asunder*
Wendy Barker and Saranindranath Tagore: *Final Poems* by Rabindranath Tagore
Marco Perela: *Adventures of a No Name Actor*
Betje Klier: *Pavie in the Borderlands*
Larry McMurtry: *Sacagawea's Nickname: Essays on the American West*
Katherine Tannery: *Carousel of Progress*
Sarah Bird: *The Yokota Officers Club*
Lon Tinkle Award: William H. Goetzmann

### 2000
Rosa Shand: *The Gravity of Sunlight*
Laura Wilson: *Hutterites of Montana*
Richard V. Francaviglia: *The Cast Iron Forest*
Corey Marks: *Renunciation*
Edward Snow: *The Duino Elegies* by Rainer Maria Rilke
Glen Pourciau: "Deep Wilderness"
Pamela Colloff: *"Sins of the Father"*
Joe Holley: "The Hill Country: Loving It to Death"
Anne Coyle: *Crookwood*
Molly Ivins and Lou DuBose: *Shrub*
Bradley Hutchinson: *Willard Clark: Printer and Printmaker*
D.J. Stout and Julie Savasky: *John Graves and the Making of Goodbye to a River*
Lon Tinkle Award: Leon Hale

### 1999
Rick DeMarinis: *New and Selected Stories*
Robert Draper: *Hadrian's Walls*
Ann Rowe Seaman: *Swaggart: The Unauthorized Biography of an American Evangelist*
J.Gilberto Quezada: *Border Boss: Manuel B. Bravo and Zapata County*
Walt McDonald: "Whatever the Wind Delivers"
Jenny Lind Porter: *Verses on Death by Helinand of Froidmont*
Tracy Daugherty: *"Comfort Me With Apples"*
Steven and Rick Barthelme: "Good Losers"
James Hoggard: "Greetings from Cuba"
Benjamin Alire Saenz: *Grandma Fina and Her Wonderful Umbrellas/La Abuelita Fina y Sus Sombrillas Maravillosas*

Neil Barrett Jr.: *Interstate Dreams*
Margerie Adkins West: *Angels on High: Marton Varo's Limestone Angels on Bass Performance Hall*
Peter Brown: *On the Plains*
Lon Tinkle Award: Walt McDonald

### 1998
C.W. Smith: *Understanding Women*
Susan Choi: *The Foreign Student*
William C. Davis: *Three Roads to the Alamo: The Lives and Fortunes of David Crockett, James Bowie, and William Barret Travis*
Don Carleton: *A Breed So Rare: The Life of J.R. Parten, Liberal Texas Oil Man, 1896-1992*
B.H. Fairchild: "The Art of the Lathe"
Marian Schwartz: *The Ladies from St. Petersburg: Three Novellas*
James Hoggard: *Poems from Cuba: Alone Against the Sea*
Jane Roberts Wood: "My Mother Had a Maid"
Rick Bass: "Into the Fire"
Patrick Beach: "The Struggle for the Soul of Kreuz Market"
Bryan Woolley: "A Legend Runs Through It"
Pat Mora: *The Big Sky*
Lon Tinkle Award: Robert Flynn

### 1997
Lisa Sandlin: *A Message to the Nurse of Dreams*
Joseph Skibell: *A Blessing on the Moon*
Tara Holley with Joe Holley: *My Mother's Keeper: A Daughter's Memoir of Growing up in the Shadow of Schizophrenia*
John Miller Morris: *El Llano Estacado*
Bruce Bond: "Radiography"
Debbie Nathan and Willavaldo Delgadillo: *The Moon Will Forever Be a Distant Love*
Clifford Hudder: "Misplacement"
Skip Hollandsworth: "The Curse of Romeo and Juliet"
Michael Leahy: "Oswald: A Brother's Burden"
Jerry Herring: *Charles Schorre*
David Timmons: *The Wild and Vivid Land*
Naomi Shihab Nye: *Habibi*
Lon Tinkle Award: Rolando Hinojosa-Smith

### 1996
Sandra Scofield: *A Chance to See Egypt*
Nolan Porterfield: *Last Cavalier: The Life and Times of John A Lomax*
Kathleen Cambor: *The Book of Mercy*
Rick Bass: *The Book of Yaak*
Isabel Nathaniel: "The Dominion of Light'"
Daniel Stern: "The Passion According to St. John by J.S. Bach"
Debbie Nathan: "The Death of Jane Roe"
Mike Tolson: "When Hope Dies"
D.J. Stout: *Heaven of Animals*
Thomas Taylor and Barbara Whitehead: *Trading in Santa Fe*
J.A. Benner: *Uncle Comanche*
Lon Tinkle Award: Cormac McCarthy

### 1995
Paul Scott Malone: *In an Arid Land: Thirteen Stories of Texas*
Mary Karr: *The Liars' Club: A Memoir*
Jewel Mogan: *Beyond Telling*
Ben Huseman: *Wild River, Timeless Canyon*
Paul Christensen: "Water"
Rick Bass: "The Fires Next Time'
Mike Tolson: "Race to the Future"
Dick Gerdes: *The Fourth World* (trans.)
Ellen McKie: *Codex Telleriano-Remensis*
Diane Stevens: *Liza's Blue Moon*
Lon Tinkle Award: William Humphrey

### 1994
Reginald Gibbons: *Sweetbitter*
Lawrence Wright: *Remembering Satan*
Ron Tyler: *Prints of the West*
Pattiann Rogers: *Firekeeper*
Donley Watt: *Can You Get THere From Here?*
William J. Cobb: " White Circles"
Mimi Swartz: "Promised Land"
Dr. Bertie Acker: *Iphigenia* (trans.)
Florence George Graves: "The Other Woman"
W. Thomas Taylor: *The War Between the United States and Mexico*
Barbara Elmore: *Breathing Room*
Lon Tinkle Award: Américo Paredes ☆

# Public Libraries of Texas

*The following information was furnished by Wendy Clark of the Library Development Division of the Texas State Library, Austin.*

Texas public libraries continue to strive to meet the education and information needs of Texans by providing library services of high quality with oftentimes-limited resources. Each year, services provided by public libraries to the citizens of Texas increase, with more visits to public libraries and higher attendance in library programs.

The challenges facing the public libraries in Texas are many and varied. The costs for providing electronic and on-line sources, in addition to traditional library services, are growing faster than library budgets.

Urban libraries are trying to serve growing populations, while libraries in rural areas are trying to serve remote populations and provide distance learning, most at inadequate levels of support.

When comparing Texas statistics to those nationally, Texas continues to rank below most of the other states. In salary expenditures per capita, Texas ranks 43rd down from 42nd last year, and in total operating expenditures per capita, Texas ranks 43rd up from 46th last year.

The only two measures that Texas ranks above 40th are reference transactions (Texas ranks 20th up from 23rd) and interlibrary loan transactions per capita (Texas ranks 20th up from 38th).

Complete statistical information on public libraries is available on the Texas State Library's web page at: tsl.state.tx.us/ld/pubs/pls/index.html.

The following table lists, by city, Texas public libraries and branches with addresses and phone numbers. Many of these have established homepages on the Internet.

To visit your local libraries web page, call the library for the web address or find a list of libraries with addresses at tsl.state.tx.us/texshare/pl/texlibs.html.

| CITY | LIBRARY | ADDRESS | ZIP | PHONE |
|------|---------|---------|-----|-------|
| Abernathy | Abernathy Public | PO Box 686 | 79311 -0686 | 806 298-4138 |
| Abilene | Abilene Public | 202 Cedar St | 79601 -5793 | 325 676-6328 |
| Alamo | Lalo Arcaute Public | 502 E Duranta St | 78516 -2317 | 956 787-6160 |
| Albany | Shackelford County | PO Box 445 | 76430 -0445 | 325 762-2672 |
| Aledo | East Parker County | PO Box 275 | 76008 -0275 | 817 441-6545 |
| Alice | Alice Public | 401 E 3rd St | 78332 -4798 | 361 664-9506 |
| Allen | Allen Public | 2 Allen Civic Plaza | 75013 -2559 | 972 727-0190 |
| Alpine | Alpine Public | 203 N 7th St | 79830 -4615 | 432 837-2621 |
| Alto | Stella Hill Memorial | Rt 1 Box 724 | 75925 -9791 | 936 858-4343 |
| Alvarado | Alvarado Public | 101 E Patton Ave | 76009 -3873 | 817 783-7323 |
| Alvord | Alvord Public | PO Box 323 | 76225 -0323 | 940 427-2842 |
| Amarillo | Amarillo Public | PO Box 2171 | 79105 -2171 | 806 378-3050 |
| Anahuac | Chambers County | PO Box 520 | 77514 -0520 | 409 267-8263 |
| Andrews | Andrews County | 109 NW 1st St | 79714 -6301 | 432 523-9819 |
| Angleton | Brazoria County | 131 E Live Oak | 77515 -4641 | 979 864-1505 |
| Anson | Anson Public | 1137 12th St | 79501 -4306 | 325 823-2711 |
| Aransas Pass | Ed & Hazel Richmond Public | 110 N Lamont St | 78336 -3698 | 361 758-2350 |
| Archer City | Archer Public | PO Box 957 | 76351 -0957 | 940 574-4954 |
| Arlington | Arlington Public | 101 E Abram St | 76010 -1183 | 817 459-6900 |
| Aspermont | Stonewall County | PO Box H | 79502 -0907 | 940 989-2730 |
| Athens | Henderson County Murchison | 121 S Prairieville St | 75751 -2595 | 903 677-7295 |
| Atlanta | Atlanta Public | 101 W Hiram St | 75551 -2509 | 903 796-2112 |
| Aubrey | Aubrey Area | 109 S Main St | 76227 -9164 | 940 365-9162 |
| Austin | Austin Public | PO Box 2287 | 78768 -2287 | 512 974-7300 |
| Austin/Wells Branch | Wells Branch Community | 14735 Bratton Ln #210 | 78728 -4306 | 512 989-3188 |
| Azle | Azle Public | 609 SE Parkway St | 76020 -3695 | 817 444-7114 |
| Baird | Callahan County | 100 W 4th B1 | 79504 -5305 | 325 854-1718 |
| Balch Springs | Balch Springs Public | 4301 Pioneer Rd | 75180 -4001 | 972 557-6096 |
| Ballinger | Carnegie of Ballinger | 204 N 8th St | 76821 -4706 | 325 365-3616 |
| Bandera | Bandera County | PO Box 1568 | 78003 -1568 | 830 796-4213 |
| Barksdale | Nueces Canyon Public | PO Box 58 | 78828 -0058 | 830 234-3173 |
| Bartlett | Teinert Memorial Public | PO Box 12 | 76511 -0012 | 254 527-3208 |
| Bastrop | Bastrop Public | PO Box 670 | 78602 -0670 | 512 321-5441 |
| Bay City | Bay City Public | 1100 7th St | 77414 -4915 | 979 245-6931 |
| Baytown | Sterling Municipal | Wilbanks Ave | 77520 -4258 | 281 427-7331 |
| Beaumont | Beaumont Public | PO Box 3827 | 77704 -3827 | 409 838-6606 |
| Beaumont | Jefferson County | 7933 Viterbo Rd Ste 7 | 77705 -9295 | 409 727-2735 |
| Bedford | Bedford Public | 1805 L Don Dodson Dr | 76021 -1897 | 817 952-2330 |
| Beeville | Joe Barnhart Bee County | PO Box 760 | 78104 -0760 | 361 362-4901 |
| Bellaire | Bellaire City | 5111 Jessamine St | 77401 -4498 | 713 662-8160 |
| Bellville | Bellville Public | 12 W Palm St | 77418 -1446 | 979 865-3731 |
| Belton | Lena Armstrong Public | 301 E 1st Ave | 76513 -3168 | 254 933-5832 |
| Benbrook | Benbrook Public | 1065 Mercedes St | 76126 -2742 | 817 249-6632 |
| Big Lake | Reagan County | 300 Court House Sq | 76932 -4515 | 325 884-2854 |
| Big Sandy | Holly Community | Rt 1 Box 799 | 75755 -9600 | 903 769-5142 |
| Big Spring | Howard County | 500 S Main St | 79720 -2729 | 432 264-2260 |
| Blanco | Blanco County South | 1118 Main St Ste A | 78606 -4838 | 830 833-4280 |
| Blue Mound/Fort Worth | Blue Mound Community | 1600 Bell Ave | 76131 -1002 | 817 232-4095 |

| CITY | LIBRARY | ADDRESS | ZIP | PHONE |
|---|---|---|---|---|
| Boerne | Boerne Public | 210 N Main St | 78006 -2036 | 830 249-3053 |
| Bonham | Bonham Public | 305 E 5th St | 75418 -4002 | 903 583-3128 |
| Booker | Booker School/Public | PO Box 288 | 79005 -0288 | 806 658-9323 |
| Borger | Hutchinson County | 625 N Weatherly St | 79007 -3621 | 806 273-0126 |
| Bowie | Bowie Public | 301 W Walnut St | 76230 -4828 | 940 872-2681 |
| Boyd | Boyd Public | PO Box 1238 | 76023 -1238 | 940 433-5580 |
| Brackettville | Kinney County Public | PO Box 975 | 78832 -0975 | 830 563-2884 |
| Brady | F.M. (Buck) Richards Memorial | 1106 S Blackburn St | 76825 -6222 | 325 597-2617 |
| Breckenridge | Breckenridge Public | 209 N Breckenridge Ave | 76424 -3503 | 254 559-5505 |
| Bremond | Bremond Public | PO Box 132 | 76629 -0132 | 254 746-7752 |
| Brenham | Nancy Carol Roberts Memorial | 100 W Academy St | 77833 -3107 | 979 277-1271 |
| Bridge City | Bridge City Public | 101 Parkside Dr | 77611 -2442 | 409 735-4242 |
| Bridgeport | Bridgeport Public | 2159 10th St | 76426 -2071 | 940 683-4412 |
| Brownfield | Kendrick Memorial | 301 W Tate St | 79316 -4329 | 806 637-3848 |
| Brownsville | Brownsville Public | 2600 Central Blvd | 78520 -8824 | 956 548-1055 |
| Brownwood | Brownwood Public | 600 Carnegie St | 76801 -7097 | 325 646-0155 |
| Bryan | Bryan/College Station System | 201 E 26th St | 77803 -5356 | 979 209-5600 |
| Buda | Buda Public | PO Box 608 | 78610 -0608 | 512 295-5899 |
| Buffalo | Buffalo Public | PO Drawer 1290 | 75831 -1290 | 903 322-4146 |
| Bullard | Bullard Community | PO Box 368 | 75757 -0368 | 903 894-6125 |
| Buna | Buna Public | PO Box 1571 | 77612 -1571 | 409 994-5501 |
| Burkburnett | Burkburnett | 215 E 4th St | 76354 -3446 | 940 569-2991 |
| Burleson | Burleson Public | 248 SW Johnson Ave | 76028 -4765 | 817 295-6131 |
| Burnet | Burnet County | 100 E Washington St | 78611 -3114 | 512 756-2328 |
| Caldwell | Harrie P. Woodson Memorial | 704 W Highway 21 | 77836 -1198 | 979 567-4111 |
| Cameron | Cameron Public | 304 E 3rd St | 76520 -3350 | 254 697-2401 |
| Camp Wood | Camp Wood Public | PO Box 138 | 78833 -0138 | 830 597-3208 |
| Canadian | Hemphill County | 500 Main St | 79014 -2702 | 806 323-5282 |
| Canton | Van Zandt County | 317 1st Monday Ln | 75103 -1052 | 903 567-4276 |
| Canyon | Canyon Area | 1501 3rd Ave | 79015 -2828 | 806 655-5015 |
| Canyon Lake | Tye Preston Memorial | 1321 Highway 2673 | 78133 -4565 | 830 964-3744 |
| Carrizo Springs | Dimmit County Public | 200 N 9th St | 78834 -3741 | 830 876-5788 |
| Carrollton | Carrollton Public | 4220 N Josey Ln | 75010 -4600 | 972 466-3360 |
| Carthage | Sammy Brown | 522 W College St | 75633 -1408 | 903 693-6741 |
| Castroville | Castroville Public | 802 London St | 78009 -4032 | 830 931-4095 |
| Cedar Hill | Zula Bryant Wylie | 225 Cedar St | 75104 -2655 | 972 291-7323 |
| Cedar Park | Cedar Park Public | 550 Discovery Blvd | 78613 -2200 | 512 259-5353 |
| Celina | Celina Community | 710 E Pecan St | 75009 -6170 | 972 382-3750 |
| Center | Fannie Brown Booth Memorial | 619 Tenaha St | 75935 -3553 | 936 598-5522 |
| Centerville | Elmer P. & Jewel Ward Memorial | PO Box 567 | 75833 -0567 | 903 536-7261 |
| Charlotte | Charlotte Public | PO Box 757 | 78011 -0757 | 830 277-1212 |
| Chico | Chico Public | PO Box 707 | 76431 -0707 | 940 644-2330 |
| Childress | Childress Public | 117 Avenue B NE | 79201 -4509 | 940 937-8421 |
| Cisco | Cisco Public | 600 Avenue G | 76437 -3039 | 254 442-1020 |
| Clarendon | Burton Memorial | PO Box 783 | 79226 -0783 | 806 874-3685 |
| Clarksville | Red River County Public | PO Box 508 | 75426 -0508 | 903 427-3991 |
| Claude | Claude Public | PO Box 109 | 79019 -0109 | 806 226-7881 |
| Cleburne | Cleburne Public | PO Box 657 | 76033 -0657 | 817 645-0936 |
| Cleveland | Austin Memorial | 220 S Bonham Ave | 77327 -4591 | 281 592-3920 |
| Clifton | Nellie Pederson Civic | PO Box 231 | 76634 -0231 | 254 675-6495 |
| Clint | Clint ISD Public | PO Box 779 | 79836 -0779 | 915 851-2302 |
| Clyde | Clyde Public | PO Box 1779 | 79510 -1779 | 325 893-5315 |
| Cockrell Hill/Dallas | Cockrell Hill Public | 4125 W Clarendon | 75211 -4919 | 214 330-9935 |
| Coldspring | Coldspring Area Public | PO Box 1756 | 77331 -1756 | 936 653-3104 |
| Coleman | Coleman Public | 402 Commercial Ave | 76834 -4202 | 325 625-3043 |
| Collinsville | Collinsville Community | PO Box 292 | 76233 -0292 | |
| Colorado City | Mitchell County Public | 340 Oak St | 79512 -6213 | 325 728-3968 |
| Columbus | Nesbitt Memorial | 529 Washington St | 78934 -2326 | 979 732-3392 |
| Comanche | Comanche Public | PO Box 777 | 76442 -0777 | 325 356-2122 |
| Comfort | Comfort Public | PO Box 536 | 78013 -0536 | 830 995-2398 |
| Commerce | Commerce Public | PO Box 308 | 75429 -0308 | 903 886-6858 |
| Conroe | Montgomery County | 104 I 45 N | 77301 -2720 | 936 788-8377 |
| Converse | Converse Area Public | PO Box 36 | 78109 -0036 | 210 659-4160 |
| Cooper | Delta County Public | 300 W Dallas Ave | 75432 -1632 | 903 395-4575 |
| Coppell | William T. Cozby Public | 177 N Heartz Rd | 75019 -2121 | 972 304-3661 |
| Copperas Cove | Copperas Cove Public | 501 S Main St | 76522 -2241 | 254 547-3826 |
| Corpus Christi | Corpus Christi Public | 805 Comanche St | 78401 -2798 | 361 880-7070 |
| Corrigan | Mickey Reily Public | 604 S Mathews St | 75939 -2645 | 936 398-4156 |
| Corsicana | Corsicana Public | 100 N 12th St | 75110 -5205 | 903 654-4810 |
| Cotulla | Alexander Memorial | 201 S Center St | 78014 -2255 | 830 879-2601 |
| Crandall | Crandall-Combine Community | PO Box 128 | 75114 -0128 | 972 427-8170 |
| Crane | Crane County | 701 S Alford St | 79731 -2521 | 432 558-1142 |

| CITY | LIBRARY | ADDRESS | ZIP | PHONE |
|------|---------|---------|-----|-------|
| Crockett | J.H. Wootters Crockett Public | PO Box 1226 | 75835 -1226 | 936 544-3089 |
| Crosbyton | Crosby County | 114 W Aspen St | 79322 -2502 | 806 675-2673 |
| Cross Plains | Cross Plains Public | PO Box 333 | 76443 -0333 | 254 725-7722 |
| Crowell | Foard County | PO Box 317 | 79227 -0317 | 940 684-1250 |
| Crowley | Crowley Public | PO Box 747 | 76036 -0747 | 817 297-6707 |
| Crystal City | Crystal City Memorial | 101 E Dimmit St | 78839 -3505 | 830 374-3477 |
| Cuero | Cuero Public | 207 E Main St | 77954 -3098 | 361 275-2864 |
| Daingerfield | Daingerfield Public | 207 Jefferson St | 75638 -1713 | 903 645-2823 |
| Dalhart | Dallam-Hartley County | 420 Denrock Ave | 79022 -2628 | 806 244-2761 |
| Dallas | Dallas Public | 1515 Young St | 75201 -5499 | 214 670-1400 |
| Dayton | Jones Public | 307 W Houston St | 77535 -2537 | 936 258-7060 |
| De Leon | DeLeon City County | 125 E Reynosa Ave | 76444 -1965 | 254 893-2417 |
| De Soto | DeSoto Public | 211 E Pleasant Run Ste C | 75115 -3939 | 972 230-9658 |
| Decatur | Decatur Public | 1700 Highway 51 S | 76234 -3613 | 940 627-5512 |
| Deer Park | Deer Park Public | 3009 Center St | 77536 -5099 | 281 478-7208 |
| Del Rio | Val Verde County | 300 Spring St | 78840 -5199 | 830 774-7595 |
| Dell City | Grace Grebing Public/School | PO Box 37 | 79837 -0037 | 915 964-2468 |
| Denison | Denison Public | 300 W Gandy St | 75020 -3153 | 903 465-1797 |
| Denton | Denton Public | 502 Oakland St | 76201 -3102 | 940 349-8566 |
| Denver City | Yoakum County/Cecil Bickley | 205 W 4th St | 79323 -3113 | 806 592-2754 |
| Devine | Driscoll Public | 202 E Hondo Ave | 78016 -3342 | 830 663-2993 |
| Diboll | T.L.L. Temple Memorial | 300 Park St | 75941 -1633 | 936 829-5497 |
| Dickinson | Mares Memorial | 4324 Highway 3 | 77539 -6801 | 281 534-3812 |
| Dilley | Dilley Public | PO Box 230 | 78017 -0230 | 830 965-1951 |
| Dimmitt | Rhoads Memorial | 103 SW 2nd St | 79027 -2501 | 806 647-3532 |
| Donna | Donna Public | 301 S Main St | 78537 -3288 | 956 464-2221 |
| Dripping Springs | Dripping Springs Community | PO Box 279 | 78620 -0279 | 512 858-7825 |
| Dublin | Dublin Public | 206 W Blackjack St | 76446 -2204 | 254 445-4141 |
| Dumas | Killgore Memorial | 124 S Bliss Ave | 79029 -3804 | 806 935-4941 |
| Duncanville | Duncanville Public | 201 James Collins Blvd | 75116 -4818 | 972 780-5050 |
| Eagle Lake | Eula & David Wintermann | 101 N Walnut Ave | 77434 -2326 | 979 234-5411 |
| Eagle Pass | Eagle Pass Public | 589 E Main St | 78852 -4518 | 830 773-2516 |
| Earth | Springlake-Earth Community | PO Box 259 | 79031 -0259 | 806 257-3357 |
| Eastland | Centennial Memorial | 210 S Lamar St | 76448 -2794 | 254 629-2281 |
| Eden | Eden Public | PO Box 896 | 76837 -0896 | 325 869-7761 |
| Edinburg | Edinburg Public | 401 E Cano St | 78539 -4596 | 956 383-6246 |
| Edna | Jackson County Memorial | 411 N Wells St | 77957 -2734 | 361 782-2162 |
| El Paso | El Paso Public | 501 N Oregon St | 79901 -1193 | 915 543-5433 |
| Eldorado | Schleicher County Public | PO Box 611 | 76936 -0611 | 325 853-3767 |
| Electra | Electra Public | 401 N Waggoner St | 76360 -2134 | 940 495-2208 |
| Elgin | Elgin Public | 1002 N Avenue C | 78621 -2124 | 512 281-5678 |
| Elsa | Elsa Public | PO Box 1447 | 78543 -1447 | 956 262-3061 |
| Emory | Rains County Public | PO Box 189 | 75440 -0189 | 903 473-2221 |
| Ennis | Ennis Public | 501 W Ennis Ave | 75119 -3803 | 972 875-5360 |
| Euless | Euless Public | 201 N Ector Dr | 76039 -3595 | 817 685-1679 |
| Everman | Everman Public | 212 N Race St | 76140 -3297 | 817 551-0726 |
| Fabens | El Paso County | PO Box 788 | 79838 -0788 | 915 764-3635 |
| Fairfield | Fairfield | 350 W Main St | 75840 -3028 | 903 389-3574 |
| Falfurrias | Ed Rachal Memorial | 203 S Calixto Mora Ave | 78355 -4321 | 361 325-2144 |
| Falls City | Falls City Public | PO Box 220 | 78113 0220 | 830 254-3361 |
| Farmers Branch | Farmers Branch Manske Public | PO Box 819010 | 75381 -9010 | 972 247-2511 |
| Farmersville | Charles J. Rike Memorial | PO Box 352 | 75442 -0352 | 972 782-6681 |
| Ferris | Ferris Public | 514 S Mabel St | 75125 -3028 | 972 544-3696 |
| Flatonia | Flatonia Public | PO Box 656 | 78941 -0656 | 361 865-9244 |
| Florence | Florence Public | PO Box 430 | 76527 -0430 | 254 793-2672 |
| Floresville | Wilson County Public | 1 Library Ln | 78114 -2239 | 830 393-7361 |
| Flower Mound | Flower Mound Public | 3030 Broadmoor Ln | 75022 -2703 | 972 874-6200 |
| Floydada | Floyd County | 111 S Wall St | 79235 -2811 | 806 983-4922 |
| Forney | West Memorial | 800 FM 741 S | 75126 -3913 | 972 564-7027 |
| Fort Davis | Jeff Davis County | PO Box 1054 | 79734 -1054 | 432 426-3802 |
| Fort Hancock | Fort Hancock ISD/Public | PO Box 98 | 79839 -0098 | 915 769-3811 |
| Fort Stockton | Fort Stockton Public | 500 North Water St | 79735 -5634 | 432 336-3374 |
| Fort Worth | Fort Worth Public | 500 W 3rd St | 76102 -7333 | 817 871-7706 |
| Frankston | Frankston Depot | PO Box 639 | 75763 -0639 | 903 876-4463 |
| Fredericksburg | Pioneer Memorial | 115 W Main St | 78624 -3751 | 830 997-6513 |
| Friendswood | Friendswood Public | 416 S Friendswood Dr | 77546 -3906 | 281 482-7135 |
| Friona | Friona Public | 109 W 7th St | 79035 -2548 | 806 250-3200 |
| Frisco | Frisco Public | 8750 McKinney Rd Ste 200 | 75034 -3000 | 972 335-5510 |
| Gainesville | Cooke County | 200 S Weaver St | 76240 -4790 | 940 665-2401 |
| Galveston | Rosenberg | 2310 Sealy Ave | 77550 -2296 | 409 763-8854 |
| Garland | Nicholson Memorial | 625 Austin St | 75040 -6365 | 972 205-2543 |
| Gatesville | Gatesville Public | 811 E Main St | 76528 -1432 | 254 865-5367 |

| CITY | LIBRARY | ADDRESS | ZIP | PHONE |
|---|---|---|---|---|
| George West | Live Oak County | PO Box 698 | 78022 -0698 | 361 449-1124 |
| Georgetown | Georgetown Public | 808 Martin Luther King Jr St | 78626 -5527 | 512 930-3551 |
| Giddings | Giddings Public | 276 N Orange St | 78942 -2830 | 979 542-2716 |
| Gilmer | Upshur County | 702 W Tyler St | 75644 -2198 | 903 843-5001 |
| Gladewater | Lee Public | PO Box 1753 | 75647 -1753 | 903 845-2640 |
| Glen Rose | Somervell County | 108 Allen Dr | 76043 -4526 | 254 897-4582 |
| Goldthwaite | Jennie Trent Dew | PO Box 101 | 76844 -0101 | 325 648-2447 |
| Goliad | Goliad County | PO Box 1025 | 77963 -1025 | 361 645-2291 |
| Gorman | Charlie Garrett Memorial | PO Box 219 | 76454 -0219 | 254 734-3301 |
| Graham | Graham | 910 Cherry St | 76450 -3547 | 940 549-0600 |
| Granbury | Hood County Public | 222 N Travis St | 76048 -2164 | 817 573-3569 |
| Grand Prairie | Grand Prairie Memorial | 901 Conover Dr | 75051 -1590 | 972 237-5700 |
| Grand Saline | Grand Saline Public | 201 E Pacific St | 75140 -1934 | 903 962-5516 |
| Grandview | Grandview Public | PO Box 694 | 76050 -0694 | 817 866-3965 |
| Grapeland | Grapeland Public | PO Box 879 | 75844 -0879 | 936 687-3425 |
| Grapevine | Grapevine Public | 1201 Municipal Way | 76051 -7657 | 817 410-3400 |
| Greenville | W. Walworth Harrison Public | 1 Lou Finney Blvd | 75401 -5988 | 903 457-2992 |
| Groesbeck | Maffett Memorial | 601 W Yeagua St | 76642 -1658 | 254 729-3667 |
| Groves | Groves Public | 5600 W Washington St | 77619 -3629 | 409 962-6281 |
| Groveton | Groveton Public | PO Box 399 | 75845 -0399 | 936 642-2483 |
| Gruver | Gruver City | PO Box 701 | 79040 -0701 | 806 733-2191 |
| Guthrie | Guthrie CSD/King County | PO Box 70 | 79236 -0070 | 806 596-4414 |
| Hale Center | Hale Center Public | PO Box 214 | 79041 -0214 | 806 839-2055 |
| Hallettsville | Friench Simpson Memorial | 705 E 4th St | 77964 -2828 | 361 798-3243 |
| Haltom City | Haltom City Public | PO Box 14277 | 76117 -0277 | 817 222-7790 |
| Hamilton | Hamilton Public | 201 N Pecan St | 76531 -1926 | 254 386-3474 |
| Harker Heights | Harker Heights Public | 100 E Beeline Ln | 76548 -1285 | 254 699-5008 |
| Harlingen | Harlingen Public | 410 76 Dr | 78550 -5072 | 956 430-6650 |
| Haskell | Haskell County | 412 N 1st St | 79521 -5706 | 940 864-2747 |
| Hawkins | Allen Memorial Public | PO Box 329 | 75765 -0329 | 903 769-2241 |
| Hearne | Smith-Welch Memorial | 114 W 4th St | 77859 -2506 | 979 279-5191 |
| Hebbronville | Jim Hogg County Public | 210 N Smith Ave | 78361 -2899 | 361 527-3421 |
| Hemphill | J.R. Huffman Public | Rt 5  Box 2140 | 75948 -9695 | 409 787-4829 |
| Hempstead | Waller County | 2331 11th St | 77445 -6799 | 979 826-7658 |
| Henderson | Rusk County  System | 106 E Main St | 75652 -3117 | 903 657-8557 |
| Henrietta | Edwards Public | 210 W Gilbert St | 76365 -2816 | 940 538-4791 |
| Hereford | Deaf Smith County | 211 E 4th St | 79045 -5521 | 806 364-1206 |
| Hewitt | Hewitt Community | 100 Zuni Dr | 76643 -3008 | 254 666-2442 |
| Hidalgo | Hidalgo Public | 710 E Texano Dr | 78557 -4104 | 956 843-2093 |
| Higgins | Higgins Public | PO Box 250 | 79046 -0250 | 806 852-2214 |
| Highland Park | Highland Park | 4700 Drexel Dr | 75205 -3198 | 214 559-9400 |
| Hillsboro | Hillsboro City | 118 S Waco St | 76645 -7708 | 254 582-7385 |
| Hitchcock | Genevieve Miller Hitchcock Pub. | 8005 Barry Ave | 77563 -3238 | 409 986-7814 |
| Holland | B.J. Hill | PO Box 217 | 76534 -0217 | 254 657-2884 |
| Hondo | Hondo Public | 1011 19th St | 78861 -2431 | 830 426-5333 |
| Honey Grove | Bertha Voyer Memorial | PO Box 47 | 75446 -0047 | 903 378-2206 |
| Hooks | Hooks Public | PO Box 1540 | 75561 -1540 | 903 547-3365 |
| Houston | Houston Public | 500 McKinney St | 77002 -2534 | 832 393-1300 |
| Houston | Harris County Public | 8080 El Rio St | 77054 -4195 | 713 749-9000 |
| Howe | Howe Community | 315 S Collins Fwy | 75459 -4592 | 903 532-5519 |
| Huntington | McMullen Memorial | PO Box 849 | 75949 -0849 | 936 876-4516 |
| Huntsville | Huntsville Public | 1216 14th St | 77340 -4507 | 936 291-5470 |
| Hurst | Hurst Public | 901 Precinct Line Rd | 76053 -4997 | 817 788-7300 |
| Hutchins | Hutchins-Atwell Public | PO Box 888 | 75141 -0888 | 972 225-4711 |
| Idalou | Idalou Public | PO Box 1277 | 79329 -1277 | 806 892-2114 |
| Imperial | Imperial Public | PO Box 307 | 79743 -0307 | 432 536-2236 |
| Ingleside | Ingleside Public | PO Drawer 400 | 78362 -0400 | 361 776-5355 |
| Iowa Park | Tom Burnett Memorial | 400 W Alameda St | 76367 -1616 | 940 592-4981 |
| Iraan | Iraan Public | PO Box 638 | 79744 -0638 | 432 639-2235 |
| Irving | Irving Public | PO Box 152288 | 75015 -2288 | 972 721-2628 |
| Jacksboro | Gladys Johnson Ritchie Public | 626 W College St | 76458 -1655 | 940 567-2240 |
| Jacksonville | Jacksonville Public | 502 S Jackson St | 75766 -2415 | 903 586-7664 |
| Jasper | Jasper Public | 175 E Water St | 75951 -4438 | 409 384-3791 |
| Jayton | Kent County | PO Box 28 | 79528 -0028 | 806 237-3287 |
| Jefferson | Jefferson Carnegie | 301 W Lafayette St | 75657 -2209 | 903 665-8911 |
| Johnson City | Johnson City | PO Box 332 | 78636 -0332 | 830 868-4469 |
| Jonestown | Jonestown Community | 18649 FM 1431 Ste 10A | 78645 -3413 | 512 267-7511 |
| Joshua | Joshua School & Public | 907 S Broadway St | 76058 -3155 | 817 202-8324 |
| Jourdanton | Jourdanton Community | 1101 Campbell Ave | 78026 -3507 | 830 769-3087 |
| Junction | Kimble County | 208 N 10th St | 76849 -4604 | 325 446-2342 |
| Justin | Justin Community | PO Box 877 | 76247 -0877 | 940 648-3649 |
| Karnes City | Karnes City Public | 302 S Panna Maria Ave | 78118 -3240 | 830 780-2539 |

| CITY | LIBRARY | ADDRESS | ZIP | PHONE |
|---|---|---|---|---|
| Kaufman | Kaufman County | 3790 S Houston St | 75142 -3714 | 972 932-6222 |
| Keller | Keller Public | 640 Johnson Rd | 76248 -4136 | 817 431-9011 |
| Kendalia | Kendalia Public | PO Box 399 | 78027 -0399 | 830 336-2002 |
| Kenedy | Kenedy Public | 303 W Main St | 78119 -2795 | 830 583-3313 |
| Kennedale | The Kennedale | PO Box 430 | 76060 -0430 | 817 478-7876 |
| Kermit | Winkler County | 307 S Poplar St | 79745 -4315 | 432 586-3841 |
| Kerrville | Butt-Holdsworth Memorial | 505 Water St | 78028 -5316 | 830 257-8422 |
| Kilgore | Kilgore Public | 301 N Henderson Blvd | 75662 -2799 | 903 984-1529 |
| Killeen | Killeen Public | 205 E Church St | 76541 -4898 | 254 501-8994 |
| Kingsville | Robert J. Kleberg Public | 220 N 4th St | 78363 -4410 | 361 592-6381 |
| Kirbyville | Kirbyville Public | PO Box 567 | 75956 -0567 | 409 423-4653 |
| Kountze | Kountze Public | 800 S Redwood St | 77625 -8965 | 409 246-2826 |
| Krum | Krum Public | PO Box 780 | 76249 -0780 | 940 482-3455 |
| Kyle | Kyle Community | PO Box 366 | 78640 -0366 | 512 268-7411 |
| La Feria | Bailey H. Dunlap Memorial | PO Box 5804 | 78559 -2580 | 956 797-1242 |
| La Grange | Fayette Public | 855 S Jefferson St | 78945 -3230 | 979 968-3765 |
| La Joya | La Joya Municipal | 925 S Leo Ave | 78560 -4008 | 956 581-4533 |
| La Marque | La Marque Public | 1011 Bayou Rd | 77568 -4195 | 409 938-9270 |
| Lago Vista | Lago Vista | 5803 Thunderbird Ste 40 | 78645 -5851 | 512 267-3868 |
| Laguna Vista | Laguna Vista Public | 1300 Palm Blvd | 78578 -2796 | 956 943-7155 |
| Lake Dallas | Lake Cities | PO Box 775 | 75065 -0775 | 940 497-3566 |
| Lake Travis/Austin | Lake Travis Community | 3322 Ranch Road 620 S | 78738 -6804 | 512 533-6131 |
| Lake Worth | Mary Lou Reddick Public | 3801 Adam Grubb Dr | 76135 -3509 | 817 237-9681 |
| Lakehills | Lakehills Area | PO Box 976 | 78063 -0976 | 830 612-2777 |
| Lamesa | Dawson County Public | PO Box 1264 | 79331 -1264 | 806 872-6502 |
| Lampasas | Lampasas Public | PO Box 308 | 76550 -0308 | 512 556-3251 |
| Lancaster | Lancaster Veterans Memorial | 1600 Veterans Memorial Pkwy | 75134 -3270 | 972 227-1080 |
| Laredo | Laredo Public | 1120 E Calton Rd | 78041 -7328 | 956 795-2400 |
| League City | Helen Hall | 100 W Walker St | 77573 -3899 | 281 338-4860 |
| Leakey | Real County Public | PO Box 488 | 78873 -0488 | 830 232-5199 |
| Leander | Leander Public | PO Box 410 | 78646 -0410 | 512 259-5259 |
| Leon Valley | Leon Valley Public | 6425 Evers Rd | 78238 -1453 | 210 684-0720 |
| Leonard | Leonard Public | PO Box 1188 | 75452 -1188 | 903 587-2391 |
| Levelland | Hockley County Memorial | 802 Houston St Ste 108 | 79336 -3705 | 806 894-6750 |
| Lewisville | Lewisville Public | PO Box 299002 | 75029 -9002 | 972 219-3566 |
| Liberty | Liberty Municipal | 1710 Sam Houston Ave | 77575 -4796 | 936 336-8901 |
| Liberty Hill | Liberty Hill Public | PO Box 1072 | 78642 -1072 | |
| Lindale | Lindale | PO Box 1535 | 75771 -1535 | 903 882-1900 |
| Little Elm | Little Elm Community | 400 Lobo Ln | 75068 -5220 | 972 294-5801 |
| Littlefield | Lamb County | 232 Phelps Ave | 79339 -3428 | 806 385-5223 |
| Livingston | Murphy Memorial | 601 W Church St | 77351 -3199 | 936 327-4252 |
| Llano | Llano County | 102 E Haynie St | 78643 -2072 | 325 247-5248 |
| Lockhart | Dr. Eugene Clark | PO Box 209 | 78644 -0209 | 512 398-3223 |
| Lone Oak | Lone Oak Area Public | PO Box 501 | 75453 -0501 | 903 662-4565 |
| Longview | Longview Public | 222 W Cotton St | 75601 -6348 | 903 237-1350 |
| Los Fresnos | Ethel L. Whipple Memorial | 402 W Ocean Blvd | 78566 -3650 | 956 233-5330 |
| Lubbock | Lubbock Public | 1306 9th St | 79401 -2798 | 806 775-2822 |
| Lufkin | Kurth Memorial | 706 S Raguet St | 75904 -3922 | 936 630-0561 |
| Luling | Luling Public | 215 S Pecan Ave | 78648 -2607 | 830 875-2813 |
| Lumberton | Lumberton Public | 130 E Chance Rd | 77657 -7763 | 409 755-7400 |
| Lytle | Lytle Public | PO Box 831 | 78052 -0831 | 830 772-3142 |
| Mabank | Tri-County | PO Box 1770 | 75147 -1770 | 903 887-9622 |
| Madisonville | Madison County | 605 S May St | 77864 -2561 | 936 348-6118 |
| Malakoff | Red Waller Community | PO Box 1177 | 75148 -1177 | 903 489-1818 |
| Mansfield | Mansfield Public | 104 S Wisteria St | 76063 -2424 | 817 473-4391 |
| Marfa | Marfa Public | PO Box U | 79843 -0609 | 432 729-4631 |
| Marion | Marion Community | PO Box 619 | 78124 -0619 | 830 914-4268 |
| Marlin | Marlin Public | 301 Winter St | 76661 -2865 | 254 883-6602 |
| Marshall | Marshall Public | 300 S Alamo Blvd | 75670 -4273 | 903 935-4465 |
| Mason | Mason County/Eckert Memorial | PO Box 1785 | 76856 -1785 | 325 347-5446 |
| Matador | Motley County | PO Box 557 | 79244 -0557 | 806 347-2717 |
| Mathis | Mathis Public | 103 Lamar St | 78368 -2441 | 361 547-6201 |
| Maud | Maud Public | PO Box 100 | 75567 -0100 | 903 585-5255 |
| McAllen | McAllen Memorial | 601 N Main St | 78501 -4666 | 956 682-4531 |
| McCamey | Upton County Public | PO Box 1377 | 79752 -1112 | 432 652-8718 |
| McGregor | McGinley Memorial Public | 317 S Main St | 76657 -1608 | 254 840-3732 |
| McKinney | McKinney Memorial Public | 101 E Hunt St | 75069 -3807 | 972 547-7323 |
| McLean | Lovett Memorial McLean | PO Box 8 | 79057 -0008 | 806 779-2851 |
| Medina | Medina Community | PO Box 300 | 78055 -0300 | 830 589-2825 |
| Melissa | Melissa Public | 1713 Cooper St | 75454 -9542 | 972 837-4540 |
| Memphis | Memphis Public | 303 S 8th St | 79245 -3211 | 806 259-2062 |
| Menard | Menard Public | PO Box 404 | 76859 -0404 | 325 396-2717 |

| CITY | LIBRARY | ADDRESS | ZIP | PHONE |
|---|---|---|---|---|
| Mercedes | Mercedes Memorial | 434 S Ohio St | 78570 -3196 | 956 565-2371 |
| Meridian | Meridian Public | PO Box 679 | 76665 -0679 | 254 435-9100 |
| Merkel | Merkel Public | 100 Kent St | 79536 -3612 | 325 928-5054 |
| Mertzon | Irion County | PO Box 766 | 76941 -0766 | 325 835-2704 |
| Mesquite | Mesquite Public | 300 W Grubb Dr | 75149 -3492 | 972 216-6220 |
| Mexia | Gibbs Memorial | 305 E Rusk St | 76667 -2398 | 254 562-3231 |
| Midland | Midland County Public | 301 W Missouri Ave | 79701 -5108 | 432 688-8991 |
| Midlothian | A.H. Meadows | 921 S 9th St | 76065 -3636 | 972 775-3417 |
| Mineola | Mineola Memorial | 301 N Pacific St | 75773 -1799 | 903 569-2767 |
| Mineral Wells | Boyce Ditto Public | 2300 SE 7th St | 76067 -5763 | 940 328-7880 |
| Mission | Speer Memorial | 801 E 12th St | 78572 -4493 | 956 580-8750 |
| Mission | Hidalgo County | 801 E 12th St | 78572 -4493 | 956 580-8750 |
| Monahans | Ward County | 409 S Dwight St | 79756 -4609 | 432 943-3332 |
| Moody | Moody Community | PO Box 57 | 76557 -0057 | 254 853-2004 |
| Morton | Cochran County Love Memorial | 318 S Main St | 79346 -3006 | 806 266-5051 |
| Mount Calm | Mount Calm Public | PO Box 84 | 76673 -0084 | 254 993-2761 |
| Mt Pleasant | Mt. Pleasant Public | 213 N Madison Ave | 75455 -3944 | 903 575-4180 |
| Mt Vernon | Franklin County | PO Box 579 | 75457 -0579 | 903 537-4916 |
| Muenster | Muenster Public | PO Box 707 | 76252 -0707 | 940 759-4291 |
| Muleshoe | Muleshoe Area Public | 322 W 2nd St | 79347 -3633 | 806 272-4707 |
| Munday | Munday City-County | PO Box 268 | 76371 -0268 | 940 422-4877 |
| Nacogdoches | Nacogdoches Public | 1112 North St | 75961 -4482 | 936 559-2970 |
| Naples | Naples Public | PO Box 705 | 75568 -0705 | 903 897-2964 |
| Navasota | Navasota Public | 1411 E Washington Ave | 77868 -3240 | 936 825-6744 |
| Nederland | Marion & Ed Hughes Public | 2712 Nederland Ave | 77627 -7015 | 409 722-1255 |
| New Boston | New Boston Public | 127 N Ellis St | 75570 -2905 | 903 628-5414 |
| New Braunfels | New Braunfels Public | 700 E Common St | 78130 -4273 | 830 608-2150 |
| New Waverly | New Waverly Public | 200 Gibbs St Ste 1 | 77358 -9743 | 936 344-2198 |
| Newark | Newark Public | PO Box 1219 | 76071 -1219 | 817 489-2224 |
| Newton | Newton County Public | 212 High St | 75966 -3216 | 409 379-8300 |
| Nixon | Aphne Pattillo Nixon Public | 401 N Nixon Ave | 78140 -2709 | 830 582-1913 |
| Nocona | Nocona Public | 10 Cooke St | 76255 -2148 | 940 825-6373 |
| Noonday/Tyler | Noonday Community | 16662 CR 196 | 75703 -7112 | 903 939-0540 |
| North Richland Hills | North Richland Hills Public | 6720 NE Loop 820 | 76180 -7901 | 817 427-6800 |
| Odem | Odem Public | PO Box 636 | 78370 -0636 | 361 368-7388 |
| Odessa | Ector County | 321 W 5th St | 79761 -5066 | 432 332-0633 |
| Olney | Olney Community | PO Box 67 | 76374 -0067 | 940 564-5513 |
| Orange | Orange Public | 220 N 5th St | 77630 -5705 | 409 883-1086 |
| Ozona | Crockett County Public | PO Box 3030 | 76943 -3030 | 325 392-3565 |
| Paducah | Bicentennial City-County | PO Box AD | 79248 -1197 | 806 492-2006 |
| Paint Rock | Harry Benge Crozier Memorial | PO Box 173 | 76866 -0173 | 325 732-4320 |
| Palacios | Palacios | 326 Main St | 77465 -5499 | 361 972-3234 |
| Palestine | Palestine Public | 1101 N Cedar St | 75801 -7607 | 903 729-4121 |
| Pampa | Lovett Memorial | PO Box 342 | 79066 -0342 | 806 669-5780 |
| Panhandle | Carson County Public | PO Box 339 | 79068 -0339 | 806 537-3742 |
| Paris | Paris Public | 326 S Main St | 75460 -5825 | 903 785-8531 |
| Pasadena | Pasadena Public | 1201 Jeff Ginn Memorial Dr | 77506 -4895 | 713 477-0276 |
| Pearsall | Pearsall Public | 200 E Trinity St | 78061 -3351 | 830 334-2496 |
| Pecos | Reeves County | 505 S Park St | 79772 -3735 | 432 445-5340 |
| Perryton | Perry Memorial | 22 SE 5th Ave | 79070 -3112 | 806 435-5801 |
| Petersburg | Petersburg Public | PO Box 65 | 79250 -0065 | 806 667-3657 |
| Pflugerville | Pflugerville Community | 102 10th St | 78660 -3968 | 512 251-9185 |
| Pharr | Pharr Memorial | 200 S Athol St | 78577 -4892 | 956 787-3966 |
| Pilot Point | Pilot Point Community | PO Box 969 | 76258 -0969 | 940 686-5004 |
| Pineland | Arthur Temple Sr. Memorial | PO Box 847 | 75968 -0847 | 409 584-2546 |
| Pittsburg | Pittsburg-Camp County Public | 613 Quitman St | 75686 -1035 | 903 856-3302 |
| Plains | Yoakum County | PO Box 419 | 79355 -0419 | 806 456-8725 |
| Plainview | Unger Memorial | 825 Austin St | 79072 -7235 | 806 296-1148 |
| Plano | Plano Public  System | 2501 Coit Rd | 75075 -3712 | 972 769-4208 |
| Pleasanton | Pleasanton Public | 321 N Main St | 78064 -3554 | 830 569-3622 |
| Ponder | Betty Foster Public | PO Box 582 | 76259 -0582 | 940 479-2683 |
| Port Aransas | William R. Ellis Memorial | 700 W Avenue A | 78373 -4128 | 361 749-4116 |
| Port Arthur | Port Arthur Public | 4615 9th Ave | 77642 -5799 | 409 985-8838 |
| Port Isabel | Port Isabel Public | 213 N Yturria St | 78578 -4602 | 956 943-1822 |
| Port Lavaca | Calhoun County Public | 200 W Mahan St | 77979 -3368 | 361 552-7323 |
| Port Neches | Effie & Wilton Hebert Public | 2025 Merriman St | 77651 -3797 | 409 722-4554 |
| Portland | Bell/Whittington Public | 2400 Memorial Pkwy | 78374 -3208 | 361 777-0921 |
| Post | Post Public | 105 E Main St | 79356 -3229 | 806 495-2149 |
| Poteet | Poteet Public | PO Box 380 | 78065 -0380 | 830 742-8917 |
| Pottsboro | Pottsboro Area Public | PO Box 477 | 75076 -0477 | 903 786-8274 |
| Presidio | City of Presidio | PO Box 2440 | 79845 -2440 | 432 229-3317 |
| Princeton | Princeton Community | 321 Panther Pkwy | 75407 -9099 | 972 736-3741 |

| CITY | LIBRARY | ADDRESS | ZIP | PHONE |
|------|---------|---------|-----|-------|
| Prosper | Prosper Community | PO Box 490 | 75078 -0490 | 972 346-2455 |
| Quanah | Thompson Sawyer Public | 403 W 3rd St | 79252 -3825 | 940 663-2654 |
| Quemado | Quemado Public | PO Box 210 | 78877 -0210 | 830 757-1313 |
| Quitaque | Caprock Public | PO Box 487 | 79255 -0487 | 806 455-1225 |
| Quitman | Quitman Public | PO Box 1677 | 75783 -1677 | 903 763-4191 |
| Ranger | Ranger City | 400 W Main St | 76470 -1295 | 254 647-1880 |
| Rankin | Rankin Public | PO Box 6 | 79778 -0006 | 432 693-2881 |
| Raymondville | Reber Memorial | 193 N 4th St | 78580 -1994 | 956 689-2930 |
| Refugio | Dennis M. O'Connor Public | 815 Commerce St | 78377 -3107 | 361 526-2608 |
| Rhome | Rhome Public | PO Box 427 | 76078 -0427 | 817 636-2767 |
| Richardson | Richardson Public | 900 Civic Center Dr | 75080 -5298 | 972 744-4350 |
| Richland Hills | Richland Hills Public | 6724 Rena Dr | 76118 -6273 | 817 299-1860 |
| Richmond | Fort Bend County Libraries | 1001 Golfview Dr | 77469 -5199 | 281 342-4455 |
| Rio Hondo | Rio Hondo Public | PO Box 389 | 78583 -0389 | 956 748-3322 |
| River Oaks | River Oaks Public | 4900 River Oaks Blvd | 76114 -3007 | 817 624-7344 |
| Roanoke | Roanoke Public | 308 S Walnut St | 76262 -6626 | 817 491-2691 |
| Robert Lee | Coke County | PO Box 637 | 76945 -0637 | 325 453-2495 |
| Robstown | Nueces County | 710 E Main Ave Ste 2 | 78380 -3198 | 361 767-5228 |
| Rockdale | Lucy Hill Patterson Memorial | 201 Ackerman St | 76567 -2901 | 512 446-3410 |
| Rockport | Aransas County Public | 701 E Mimosa St | 78382 -4150 | 361 790-0153 |
| Rocksprings | Claud H. Gilmer Memorial | PO Box 157 | 78880 -0157 | 830 683-8130 |
| Rockwall | Rockwall County | 105 S 1st St | 75087 -3649 | 972 882-0340 |
| Rosebud | D. Brown Memorial | PO Box 657 | 76570 -0657 | 254 583-2328 |
| Rotan | Rotan Public | 404 E Sammy Baugh Ave | 79546 -3820 | 325 735-3362 |
| Round Rock | Round Rock Public | 216 E Main Ave | 78664 -5245 | 512 218-7010 |
| Round Top | Round Top | PO Box 245 | 78954 -0245 | 979 249-2700 |
| Rowlett | Rowlett Public | PO Box 1017 | 75030 -1017 | 972 412-6161 |
| Runge | Runge Public | PO Box 37 | 78151 -0037 | 830 239-4192 |
| Rusk | Singletary Memorial | 207 E 6th St | 75785 -1103 | 903 683-5916 |
| Sabinal | Sabinal Public | PO Box 245 | 78881 -0245 | 830 988-2911 |
| Sachse | Sachse Public | 5560 S Hwy 78 | 75048 -3763 | 972 530-8966 |
| Saginaw | John Ed Keeter Public | PO Box 79070 | 76179 -0070 | 817 232-2100 |
| Salado | Salado Public | PO Box 706 | 76571 -0706 | 254 947-9191 |
| San Angelo | Tom Green County | 113 W Beauregard Ave | 76903 -5834 | 325 655-7321 |
| San Antonio | San Antonio Public | 600 Soledad St | 78205 -1200 | 210 207-2500 |
| San Augustine | San Augustine Public | 413 E Columbia St | 75972 -2111 | 936 275-5367 |
| San Benito | San Benito Public | 101 W Rose St | 78586 -5169 | 956 361-3860 |
| San Diego | Duval County/San Diego Public | 404 S Mier St | 78384 -3108 | 361 279-8201 |
| San Juan | San Juan Public | 1010 S Standard Ave | 78589 -2511 | 956 702-0926 |
| San Marcos | San Marcos Public | 625 E Hopkins St | 78666 -6313 | 512 393-8200 |
| San Saba | Rylander Memorial | 103 S Live Oak St | 76877 -4799 | 325 372-3079 |
| Sanderson | Terrell County Public | PO Box 250 | 79848 -0250 | 432 345-2294 |
| Sanger | Sanger Public | PO Box 1729 | 76266 -1729 | 940 458-3257 |
| Santa Anna | Santa Anna | 606 Wallis Ave | 76878 -2031 | 325 348-3395 |
| Santa Fe | Mae S. Bruce | PO Box 950 | 77510 -0950 | 409 925-5540 |
| Schertz | Schertz Public | 608 Schertz Pkwy | 78154 -1911 | 210 658-6011 |
| Schulenburg | Schulenburg Public | 700 Bohlmann Ave | 78956 -1316 | 979 743-3345 |
| Seagoville | Seagoville Public | 702 N Highway 175 | 75159 -1774 | 972 287-7720 |
| Sealy | Virgil & Josephine Gordon | 917 N Circle Dr | 77474 -3333 | 979 885-7469 |
| Seguin | Seguin Guadalupe County Public | 707 E College St | 78155 -3299 | 830 401-2422 |
| Seminole | Gaines County | 704 Hobbs Hwy | 79360 -3402 | 432 758-4007 |
| Seven Points | Cedar Creek Lake | PO Box 43711 | 75143 -0711 | 903 432-4185 |
| Seymour | Baylor County | 101 S Washington St | 76380 -2558 | 940 889-2007 |
| Shamrock | Shamrock Public | 712 N Main St | 79079 -2038 | 806 256-3921 |
| Shepherd | Shepherd Public | 30 N Liberty St | 77371 -2460 | 936 628-3515 |
| Sheridan | Sheridan Memorial | PO Box 274 | 77475 -0274 | 979 234-5154 |
| Sherman | Sherman Public | 421 N Travis St | 75090 -5975 | 903 892-7240 |
| Shiner | Shiner Public | PO Box 1602 | 77984 -1602 | 361 594-3044 |
| Silsbee | Silsbee Public | Santa Fe Park | 77656 -4000 | 409 385-4831 |
| Silverton | Silverton Public | PO Box 69 | 79257 -0069 | 806 823-2339 |
| Sinton | Sinton Public | 212 E Sinton St | 78387 -2655 | 361 364-4545 |
| Slaton | Slaton City | 200 W Lynn St | 79364 -4136 | 806 828-2008 |
| Smiley | Stella Ellis Hart Public | PO Box 88 | 78159 -0088 | 830 587-6101 |
| Smithville | Smithville Public | 507 Main St | 78957 -1430 | 512 237-2707 |
| Snyder | Scurry County | 1916 23rd St | 79549 -1910 | 325 573-5572 |
| Sonora | Sutton County | 306 E Mulberry St | 76950 -2603 | 325 387-2111 |
| Sour Lake | Alma M. Carpenter Public | PO Box 536 | 77659 -0536 | 409 287-3592 |
| Southlake | Southlake Public | 1400 Main St Ste 130 | 76092 -7628 | 817 481-5718 |
| Spearman | Hansford County | 122 Main St | 79081 -2064 | 806 659-2231 |
| Spring Branch | Bulverde/Spring Branch | 20475 Highway 46 W Ste 340 | 78070 -6147 | 830 438-3666 |
| Springtown | Springtown Public | PO Box 428 | 76082 -0428 | 817 523-5862 |
| Spur | Dickens County Spur Public | PO Box 282 | 79370 -0282 | 806 271-3714 |

| CITY | LIBRARY | ADDRESS | ZIP | PHONE |
|---|---|---|---|---|
| Stamford | Stamford Carnegie | 600 E McHarg St | 79553 -4310 | 325 773-2532 |
| Stanton | Martin County | PO Box 1187 | 79782 -1187 | 432 756-2472 |
| Stephenville | Stephenville Public | 174 N Columbia St | 76401 -3421 | 254 918-1240 |
| Sterling City | Sterling County Public | PO Box 1130 | 76951 -1130 | 325 378-2212 |
| Stratford | Sherman County Public | PO Box 46 | 79084 -0046 | 806 366-2200 |
| Sulphur Springs | Sulphur Springs Public | 611 Davis St N | 75482 -2621 | 903 885-4926 |
| Sunnyvale | Sunnyvale Public | 402 Tower Pl | 75182 -9278 | 972 226-4491 |
| Sweetwater | County-City | 206 Elm St | 79556 -4524 | 325 235-4978 |
| Taft | Taft Public | PO Box 416 | 78390 -0416 | 361 528-3512 |
| Tahoka | City County | PO Box 1018 | 79373 -1018 | 806 561-4050 |
| Taylor | Taylor Public | 400 Porter St | 76574 -3600 | 512 352-3434 |
| Teague | Teague Public | 400 Main St | 75860 -1641 | 254 739-3311 |
| Temple | Temple Public | 100 W Adams Ave | 76501 -7658 | 254 298-5556 |
| Terrell | Terrell Public | 301 N Rockwall St | 75160 -2618 | 972 551-6663 |
| Texarkana | Texarkana Public | 600 W 3rd St | 75501 -5054 | 903 794-2149 |
| Texas City | Moore Memorial Public | 1701 9th Ave N | 77590 -5496 | 409 643-5979 |
| Texline | Texline Public | PO Box 356 | 79087 -0356 | 806 362-4849 |
| The Colony | The Colony Public | 6800 Main St | 75056 -1133 | 972 625-1900 |
| Throckmorton | The Depot Public | PO Box 6 | 76483 -0006 | 940 849-3076 |
| Tornillo | Tornillo Media Center | PO Box 170 | 79853 -0170 | 915 764-2040 |
| Trinity | Blanche K. Werner Public | PO Box 1168 | 75862 -1168 | 936 594-2087 |
| Troup | Cameron-Troup Municipal | PO Box 721 | 75789 -0721 | 903 842-3101 |
| Tulia | Swisher County | 127 SW 2nd St | 79088 -2747 | 806 995-3447 |
| Turkey | Turkey Public | PO Box 415 | 79261 -0415 | 806 423-1033 |
| Tyler | Tyler Public | 201 S College Ave | 75702 -7381 | 903 593-7323 |
| Universal City | Universal City Public | 100 Northview Dr | 78148 -4150 | 210 659-7048 |
| University Park/Dallas | University Park Public | 6517 Hillcrest Ste 110 | 75205 -1857 | 214 363-9095 |
| Utopia | Utopia Memorial | PO Box 677 | 77884 -0677 | 830 966-3448 |
| Uvalde | El Progreso Memorial | 129 W Nopal St | 78801 -5284 | 830 278-2017 |
| Valley Mills | Valley Mills Public | PO Box 25 | 76689 -0025 | 254 932-6370 |
| Van Alstyne | Van Alstyne Public | PO Box 629 | 75495 -0629 | 903 482-5991 |
| Van Horn | Van Horn City County | PO Box 129 | 79855 -0129 | 432 283-2855 |
| Vega | Oldham County Public | PO Box 640 | 79092 -0640 | 806 267-2635 |
| Venus | Hall High School and Community | PO Box 364 | 76084 -0364 | 972 366-8353 |
| Vernon | Carnegie City-County | 2810 Wilbarger St | 76384 -4597 | 940 552-2462 |
| Victoria | Victoria Public | 302 N Main St | 77901 -6592 | 361 572-2704 |
| Vidor | Vidor Public | 440 E Bolivar St | 77662 -5098 | 409 769-7148 |
| Village Mills | Wildwood Civic | PO Box 774 | 77663 -0774 | 409 834-2924 |
| Waco | Waco-McLennan County | 1717 Austin Ave | 76701 -1794 | 254 750-5941 |
| Waelder | Waelder Public | PO Box 428 | 78959 -0428 | 830 788-7167 |
| Wallis | Austin County | PO Box 519 | 77485 -0519 | 979 478-6813 |
| Watauga | Watauga Public | 7109 Whitley Rd | 76148 -2024 | 817 514-5855 |
| Waxahachie | Nicholas P. Sims | 515 W Main St | 75165 -3235 | 972 937-2671 |
| Weatherford | Weatherford Public | 1014 Charles St | 76086 -5098 | 817 598-4150 |
| Weimar | Weimar Public | 1 Jackson Sq | 78962 -2019 | 979 725-6608 |
| Wellington | Collingsworth Public | 711 15th St | 79095 -3600 | 806 447-2116 |
| Wells | Rube Sessions Memorial | PO Box 120 | 75976 -0120 | 903 867-4757 |
| Weslaco | Weslaco Public | 525 S Kansas Ave | 78596 -6215 | 956 968-4533 |
| West | West Public | PO Box 513 | 76691 -0513 | 254 826-3070 |
| West Lake Hills/Austin | Westbank Community | 1309 Westbank Dr | 78746 -6565 | 512 327-3045 |
| West Tawakoni | Tawakoni Area Public | 340 W Highway 276 | 75474 -2644 | 903 447-3445 |
| Wharton | Wharton County | 1920 N Fulton St | 77488 -2845 | 979 532-8080 |
| Wheeler | Wheeler Public | PO Box 676 | 79096 -0676 | 806 826-5977 |
| White Oak | White Oak School Community | 200 S White Oak Rd | 75693 -1520 | 903 291-2052 |
| White Settlement | White Settlement Public | 8215 White Settlement Rd | 76108 -1604 | 817 367-0166 |
| Whitehouse | Whitehouse Community | 107 Bascom Rd | 75791 -3230 | 903 839-2949 |
| Whitesboro | Whitesboro Public | 308 W Main St | 76273 -1639 | 903 564-5432 |
| Whitewright | Whitewright Public | PO Box 984 | 75491 -0984 | 903 364-2955 |
| Whitney | Lake Whitney Public | PO Box 2050 | 76692 -2050 | 254 694-4639 |
| Wichita Falls | Wichita Falls Public | 600 11th St | 76301 -4604 | 940 767-0868 |
| Wills Point | Wills Point School/Wingo Public | 1800 W South Commerce St | 75169 -2378 | 903 873-2371 |
| Wilmer | Gilliam Memorial Public | 205 E Belt Line Rd | 75172 -1127 | 972 441-3713 |
| Wimberley | Wimberley Village | PO Box 1240 | 78676 -1240 | 512 847-2188 |
| Winnsboro | Gilbreath Memorial | 916 N Main St | 75494 -2120 | 903 342-6866 |
| Winters | Winters Public | 120 N Main St | 79567 -5108 | 325 754-4251 |
| Wolfe City | Wolfe City Public | PO Box 109 | 75496 -0109 | 903 496-7311 |
| Wolfforth | Wolfforth | PO Box 36 | 79382 -0036 | 806 866-9280 |
| Woodville | Allan Shivers | 302 N Charlton St | 75979 -4806 | 409 283-3709 |
| Wylie | Rita & Truett Smith Public | 800 Thomas St | 75098 -3872 | 972 442-7566 |
| Yoakum | Carl & Mary Welhausen | 810 Front St | 77995 -3058 | 361 293-5001 |
| Yorktown | Yorktown Public | PO Box 308 | 78164 -0308 | 316 564-3232 |
| Zapata | Zapata County Public | 2806 STOP 28-A | 78076 -2836 | 956 765-5351 |

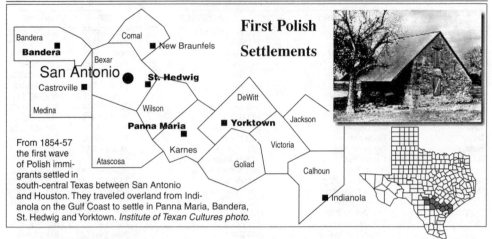

### First Polish Settlements

Bandera
**Bandera** ■
Comal
■ New Braunfels
Bexar
San Antonio ●
Castroville ■
St. Hedwig ■
Medina
Wilson
**Panna Maria** ■
DeWitt
■ **Yorktown**
Jackson
Karnes
Atascosa
Goliad
Victoria
Calhoun
■ Indianola

From 1854-57 the first wave of Polish immigrants settled in south-central Texas between San Antonio and Houston. They traveled overland from Indianola on the Gulf Coast to settle in Panna Maria, Bandera, St. Hedwig and Yorktown. *Institute of Texan Cultures photo.*

# Polish-Texans: From Frontier Settlements to Urbanization

In December 1854, one hundred Polish families arrived in Galveston on the *Weser*. Traveling by wagon down the coast to Indianola and then inland, the group reached a spot on the coastal prairie about 55 miles southeast of San Antonio. With the celebration of a Christmas Mass, they founded Panna Maria, the first Polish settlement in North America.

Today there are at least 228,309 Texans of Polish ancestry, according to the 2000 U.S. census, making them the seventh largest ethnic group in the state. But, the history of Polish Texans goes back before Panna Maria.

### Earlier Arrivals

A few Poles arrived in Texas as early as 1818. These were members of the predominately French group that sought refuge near present-day Liberty. General Charles Lallemand, a close lieutenant of Napoleon, led several hundred veterans and families into exile at a place they called Champ d'Alise (Field of Asylum).

The upheavals in Europe amidst the French Revolution and Napoleon's reign influenced the alliance of the Poles. The nations of Prussia, Austria and Russia had partitioned Poland in the 1790s, leaving a small Kingdom of Poland around Warsaw. However, this "kingdom" was subject to the Russian czar and had limited independence.

So, many Poles had joined the French forces against the occupying powers and at least four of these veterans were members of the short-lived colony in Texas: their last names were recorded as Malczewski, Skierdo, Salanav and Boril. In less than a year after the settlement was founded, the Champ d'Alise colonists fled to New Orleans as supplies ran out and the Spanish military was moving up from Mexico to disperse them.

In Poland in 1830 an uprising against the Russian rulers failed and the limited independence ended. All segments of society, military and civilian, were assimilated into Russian institutions. The same pressures were also occurring in the Prussian sector of Poland, where

the government was encouraging ethnic Germans to move into the Polish territories and, related to that, was not opposed to the Polish moving out.

The effect of these government policies left the Polish people with only their language and the Polish Catholic church structure to distinguish them from the Orthodox Russians and Lutheran Prussians.

This situation pushed other individuals to leave for Texas. These Poles soon found themselves caught up in the simmering Texas Revolution. Michael Debicki, an engineer, served at Goliad. Others serving with Colonel James Fannin were Francis and Adolph Petrussewicz, John Kornicky and Joseph Schrusnecki. All died at Goliad. Felix Wardzinski served at the Battle of San Jacinto.

### Panna Maria

But it was a series of disasters in the 1850s in Poland that created the real impetus for significant immigration to Texas. Severe weather, a poor economy, floods, lack of food, epidemics of typhoid and cholera; all these spurred interest in a better life elsewhere.

How that came to be Texas was through the efforts of a Polish priest who had been serving the German parishes in New Braunfels and Castroville, Rev. Leopold Moczygemba. The Franciscan had arrived in 1852, and it was his correspondence home to the province called Silesia that served as the catalyst for emigration (see map on page 514).

The 1854 group, some 300 people in all, was made up of farmers and artisans, including Father Moczygemba's father and several brothers. The Polish immigrants were not destitute but from a propertied class with the resources to finance the long journey by rail, ship, boat and wagon to their eventual settlements in Texas.

Father Moczygemba had picked the location in Karnes County near the convergence of the San Antonio River and Cibolo Creek and had helped arrange the purchase of land. But soon, many on the party were unhappy with the primitive conditions of the locale and blamed the priest. As a way of reconciliation, a banquet was arranged to hear the complaints of the settlers. The pastor assured them that the wilderness hardships were behind them. Then, as they all began their meal, a rattlesnake fell to the table from the rafters.

In 1856, whether because of the continued ill-feeling or merely because of needed service elsewhere, the Franciscans moved Father Moczygemba to the Midwest where other Poles were moving into cities.

Today their legacy is seen in the large Polish communities from Illinois to Pennsylvania. Father Moczygemba died in Michigan in 1891 and was buried in Detroit, but in 1974 his remains were brought to Panna Maria (Virgin Mary in Polish) and reinterred at the spot where he had celebrated the inaugural Mass in 1854.

Rev. Leopold Moczygemba.
Institute of Texan Cultures photo.

Other groups of Poles quickly followed their relatives to Texas but many stayed in settled towns such as Yorktown and San Antonio rather than enduring the more rugged conditions of new settlement.

But some new towns were started. One of the first after Panna Maria was St. Hedwig in Bexar County. In 1855, another group of Polish immigrants moved out of the frontier west of San Antonio, settling in Bandera.

In their everyday life, there was significant contact with the Mexican-Texans living close to the Polish colonies and who worshiped in the same Catholic parishes. Sources say that often the Polish immigrants learned Spanish before they were proficient in English.

### Blue and Gray

By 1861, there were some 1,500 Poles in the state, and they were quickly faced with the choice of participation in the Civil War. Most, for as long as possible, tried to stay out of the struggle, but they eventually were involved. In all, some 70,000 Texans served in the Confederate forces, and this included the unit called the Panna Maria Grays, made up of Anglos and Poles.

The Confederate fortifications at Galveston, Sabine Pass and other coastal sites were planned by Col. Valerian Salkowski, and several Silesians from Panna Maria served in Wilke's Battalion of Light Artillery.

### Polish guide for La Réunion

When La Réunion settlers started their cooperative colony near Dallas in 1855, they were guided by Kalikst Wolski, a Polish writer.

Wolski, born in Lublin, Poland, in 1816, studied in France and became involved in socialist causes there before coming to New York in 1852.

He was employed as guide by the utopian group's leader, Victor Prosper Considérant, because of his knowledge of the English language. Wolski led the French-speaking group, made up of Belgians, Swiss and French, from Houston to the Dallas-area in February. He left the colony in November after becoming convinced it would fail.

Wolski returned to Krakow around 1860 and wrote extensively about Texas. He died in 1885.

But, there were also more than 2,000 Texans who served in the Union Army. Many of these Unionists were recent immigrants who found slavery morally repugnant and whose allegiance was to their new homeland, "America."

There are accounts of Poles who, after being captured as Confederates, accepted offers of release from prisoner-of-war camps in return for joining units of the Union Army. One Union officer wrote that most of the Confederates who chose to do this were "foreigners, Germans, Polanders, etc."

One such soldier from Karnes County, Peter Kiolbassa, started as a bugler in the Panna Maria Grays but ended the war as captain in command of a company of the Sixth U.S. Colored Cavalry.

After the war he settled in Chicago and became the first Polish-born state legislator in America and a leading figure in Chicago politics.

Another Polish soldier from Texas was Joseph Cotulla who enlisted in the First Texas Cavalry in the Union Army. The county seat in La Salle County, where he settled after the war, is named for him.

### Second Wave in 1870s

Back in Poland, another insurrection was put down in 1863, resulting in increased restrictions from the ruling powers. In the Prussian partition, Bismarck's Kulturkampf, a program enforcing German culture onto the Polish people, caused about 152,000 Poles to leave the provinces of Pozan, Bydgoszcz and Silesia.

This new wave of immigration in the 1870s brought Poles to the Texas towns of Anderson, Stoneham, Brenham, Bremond, Chappell Hill, New Waverly and others. Many of them started as sharecroppers on what used to be large plantations and eventually acquired their own land.

Later, Polish settlement branched out from south-central Texas to start farming communities at White Deer in the Panhandle in 1909 and McCook in the Rio Grande Valley in 1927.

Thurber, an important mining town west of Fort Worth, was populated in the late 19th century mainly by European immigrants, including a large segment of Poles. When the mining ended in the 1920s, many of the Polish laborers went to mining areas in other states or moved into Texas cities.

### Into the 20th Century

The 20th century phenomenon of urbanization included Texas Poles. The Polish community in San Antonio grew as young people left the farms for life in the city. Houston attracted other young Poles. By 1900 there were some 200 Polish families in the port city. A century later there is said to be 55,000 people of Polish descent in Houston.

Unlike the reticence at the start of the Civil War, the young Polish-Texans were quick to enlist for service in World War I. The isolation that had been a result of their language and other differences had given way through assimilation to closer ties to the rest of Texas society.

It was through this war effort that their ancestral homeland would again be an independent nation. Ironically, when they returned from the service to their Texas homes, they were faced with a resurgent nativism during the 1920s. Ku Klux Klan harassment and anti-Polish and anti-Catholic discrimination were evident at this time.

## Texans from Silesia

Present-day Poland is outlined at right. In the 19th century, the white area around Warsaw belonged to Russia, the light-gray area around Krakow belonged to Austria-Hungary, and the dark-gray area belonged to Prussia. Most Polish-Texans' ancestors emigrated from the Prussian province of Silesia.

Another group of Polish immigrants arrived in Texas in the 1980s when the faltering Communist regime was cracking down on the Solidarity movement. Most of this group were professional people who made their homes in Texas' urban areas.

About the same time, the shift of population from the Rust Belt to the Sun Belt brought more Polish-Americans from the northern and midwestern states to become Texans.

### Important Polish Figures

Polish contributors to Texas culture include Carl von Iwonski. The paintings by this German-Polish artist portrayed the pioneers in Texas from the 1850s into the 1870s. In the later part of this period, he also became known for his photography. Brought to New Braunfels as a child, he worked in San Antonio and was a leader there during Reconstruction of the Radical Republicans. He returned to Breslau (now Wroclaw, Poland) and died there in 1912.

Another figure in the arts was Pola Negri, who spent the last decades of her life in San Antonio after being a Hollywood star in the silent era.

A more recent film star is Nina Kaczorowski, who grew up in Houston, the daughter of immigrants. Her films include *Pearl Harbor* and *The Minority Report*.

### Religion

The importance of Catholicism as the overwhelming factor in maintaining Polish identity can be seen right from that first Mass at Panna Maria. Almost immediately, as each new location was settled, a church would be started with the priest serving as principal leader and advocate to the civil society around them.

Important figures among them were Rev. Vincent Barzynski (1838-1899), pastor in St. Hedwig and San Antonio and who later led the largest Polish parish in Chicago; Rev. Thomas Moczygemba (Leopold's nephew, 1863-1950) who was the acknowledged leader of the Polish community in San Antonio; and Rev. Edward Dworaczyk (1906-1965) who wrote *The First Polish Colonies of America in Texas*.

Through the church the Polish community has maintained contact with leaders of their ancestral home. In the last decades, Lech Walesa, who lead the Solidarity movement and served as president of Poland, has visited in Texas, as have Polish cardinals and bishops who participate in Polish Catholic feasts.

In 1982, amid the last wave of immigration, the Catholic bishop in Houston established Our Lady of Czestochowa Church as a Polish parish. It now has about 250 Polish families and a school teaching the Polish language.

### Language, Music and Food

A few people in the older rural communities still speak an antiquated Silesian dialect that is difficult for modern Polish speakers to understand. Of course, many of the Poles who arrived in the 1980s speak the modern language. Today, two universities in the state, the University of Texas at Austin and Rice University, offer studies of the language and culture.

The Mexican-Polish connection that began in 1854 also brought the blending of music, mixing sounds from the polka groups and adding the use of the accordion to Mexican bands in South Texas.

However, even though the accordion is a part of Polish polka, the fiddle is the centerpiece and is what distinguishes Polish from Czech and German polka bands. One popular band today, Brian Marshall and the Tex-Slavik Playboys, continues this legacy. Marshall is from the Houston area but with Bremond roots.

Polka music is still heard on more than 20 radio stations statewide, including Austin, Dallas and Houston and Polish dance groups are active in those cities and in the San Antonio area, home of the Polish Eagle Dance Group and the South Texas Polish Dancers.

Classical music from Poland is the focus of two groups in the state, the Fryderyk Chopin Society of Texas, in Corpus Christi and the Rio Grande Valley, and the Chopin Society of Houston. The Houston group annually stages the Polish Music Festival in that city. The performances include not only Chopin but also Paderewski and others.

Also in Houston, the Polish Institute of Arts and Sciences publishes a scholarly journal, *The Sarmatian Review,* and holds a Polish Film Festival annually.

Festivals also abound in the smaller cities with servings of Polish food. Preeminent is the kielbasa, the Polish sausage with lots of garlic.

Other foods include the pierogi, a dumpling often stuffed with various fillings; bigos, a kind of stew; babka, a cake served at Easter; rosol, chicken soup, and golbaki, cabbage rolls.

But, the Texas cultural mix shows up prominently in the annual homecoming turkey dinner in Panna Maria, where the menu includes tamales. — *Robert Plocheck.*

**Festivals**
Panna Maria Homecoming Dinner, October
Polish Film Festival, Houston, November
Parish festivals,
    St. Stanislaus, Anderson, October
    St. Stanislaus, Bandera, May
    St. Mary, Bremond, October
    St. Stanislaus, Chappell Hill, September
    St. Ann, Kosciusko, August
    St. Joseph, New Waverly, September
    St. Mary, Stockdale, October
    Holy Cross, Yorktown, September
Polish Heritage Festival, Brenham, October
Polski Dzien Festival, Bremond,
    (including the Polish Pickle 5K run), June
Slavic Heritage Day, Houston, October
Various music festivals and competitions, annually,
    Chopin Society of Houston

**Groups**
Polish Institute of Arts and Sciences, *The Sarma-
    tian Review,* Houston
Polish Genealogical Society of Texas
Polish National Alliance, various chapters
Polish American Congress, Texas division
Polish-American Club of Rio Grande Valley
Kosciuszko Foundation, Houston Chapter, encourages
    cultural exchanges with Poland.
Polish Education and Cultural Center - Ognisko
    Polski, Houston.
Polish Roman Catholic Union of America, Texas
    division, a fraternal and benevolent society.
Polish Home (Dom Polski), founded in Houston in
    1891 to assist less fortunate of Polish community.

**Sources**:
    *The First Polish Americans: Silesian Settlements in*

*Texas,* by T. Lindsay Baker, Texas A&M University Press, 1979.
    *The Polish Texans*, staff, University of Texas Institute of Texan Cultures, 1972.
    *New Handbook of Texas*, 1996, various: "Poles," by Jan L. Perkowski and Jan Maria Wozniak. Others, "Leopold Moczygemba," by T. Lindsay Baker; "Carl G. von Iwonski," by James Patrick McGuire; "Barbara Apollonia Chalupec [Pola Negri]," by Christopher Long; "Vincent Barzynski," by Joseph W. Schmitz; "Thurber," by James C. Maroney; "Grimes County," by Charles Christopher Jackson; "Karnes County," by Christopher Long; "First Texas Cavalry USA," by Eugene M. Ott Jr. and Glen E. Lich.
    *The Medallion*, Texas Historical Commission, 1990: "Historic Karnes County" and "Panna Maria, Texas."
    *Chronology of Central European Colonization in Texas*, by Lera Patrick Tyler, online.
    *Polish Genealogical Society of Texas*, "Polish Texans" and "First Polish Catholic Settlements in Texas," compiled by Virgina Felchak Hill, online.
    *Polish American Journal*, June 1997, "Preserving 'Polonia's Plymouth Rock': Panna Maria, Texas."
    *The Reaction of Former Peasants to American Slavery: A Case Study of the First Silesian Settlement in North America, Panna Maria, Texas*, by Eric Opiela, online.
    *A History of La Salle and McMullen Counties*, online.
    *Texas Art Teaches Texas History*, online.
    *Polish Roots*, "What 19th Century Provinces Now Belong to Poland?" and "The Poles of Pittsburgh and Western Pennsylvania," online.
    *Polonia Today*, "A Brief History of Poland," online.
    *Polonia: United States of America*, "Panna Maria, Texas: The First Polish Settlement in America," by Richard Lysiak Jr., online. ☆

*Texas' Brian Marshall performs Polish polkas at Centrum's 2002 Festival of American Fiddle Tunes. Photo Centrum/Keven Elliff.*

# Holidays, Anniversaries and Festivals, 2004 and 2005

Below are listed the principal federal and state government holidays; Christian, Jewish and Islamic holidays and festivals; and special recognition days for 2004 and 2005. Technically, the United States does not observe national holidays. Each state has jurisdiction over its holidays, which are usually designated by its legislature. This list was compiled partially from *Astronomical Phenomena 2004* and *2005*, published by the U.S. Naval Observatory, and from the Texas Government Code. See the footnotes for explanations of the symbols.

## 2004

| | |
|---|---|
| †§New Year's Day | Thurs., Jan. 1 |
| Epiphany | Tues., Jan. 6 |
| ‡Sam Rayburn Day | Tues., Jan. 6 |
| †*Confederate Heroes Day | Mon., Jan. 19 |
| †§Martin Luther King, Jr., Day | Mon., Jan. 19 |
| †§**Presidents' Day | Mon., Feb. 16 |
| §§Islamic New Year | Sun., Feb. 22 |
| Ash Wednesday | Wed., Feb. 25 |
| †Texas Independence Day | Tues., March 2 |
| ‡Sam Houston Day | Tues., March 2 |
| ‡Texas Flag Day | Tues., March 2 |
| Primary Election Day | Tues., March 2 |
| †César Chávez Day | Wed., March 31 |
| Palm Sunday | Sun., April 4 |
| ¶Passover (Pesach), first day of | Tues., April 6 |
| †§Good Friday | Fri., April 9 |
| ‡Former Prisoners of War Recognition Day | Fri., April 9 |
| Easter Day | Sun., April 11 |
| †San Jacinto Day | Wed., April 21 |
| Mother's Day | Sun., May 9 |
| Armed Forces Day | Sat., May 15 |
| Ascension Day | Thurs., May 20 |
| ¶Shavuot (Feast of Weeks) | Wed., May 26 |
| Whit Sunday — Pentecost | Sun., May 30 |
| †§Memorial Day | Mon., May 31 |
| Trinity Sunday | Sun., June 6 |
| Flag Day (U.S.) | Mon., June 14 |
| †Emancipation Day in Texas (Juneteenth) | Sat., June 19 |
| Father's Day | Sun., June 20 |
| †§Independence Day | Sun., July 4 |
| †Lyndon Baines Johnson Day | Fri., Aug. 27 |
| †§Labor Day | Mon., Sept. 6 |
| Grandparents Day | Sun., Sept. 12 |
| ¶Rosh Hashanah (Jewish New Year) | Thurs., Sept. 16 |
| ¶Yom Kippur (Day of Atonement) | Sat., Sept. 25 |
| ¶Sukkot (Tabernacles), first day of | Thurs., Sept. 30 |
| §‡Columbus Day | Mon., Oct. 11 |
| §§Ramadan, first day of | Fri., Oct. 15 |
| Halloween | Sun., Oct. 31 |
| †General Election Day | Tues., Nov. 2 |
| ‡Father of Texas (Stephen F. Austin) Day | Wed., Nov. 3 |
| †§Veterans Day | Thurs., Nov. 11 |
| †§††Thanksgiving Day | Thurs., Nov. 25 |
| First Sunday in Advent | Sun., Nov. 28 |
| ¶Hanukkah, first day of | Wed., Dec. 8 |
| †§Christmas Day | Sat., Dec. 25 |

## 2005

| | |
|---|---|
| †§New Year's Day | Sat., Jan. 1 |
| Epiphany | Thurs., Jan. 6 |
| ‡Sam Rayburn Day | Thurs., Jan. 6 |
| †§Martin Luther King, Jr., Day | Mon., Jan. 17 |
| †*Confederate Heroes Day | Wed., Jan. 19 |
| Inauguration Day | Thurs., Jan. 20 |
| Ash Wednesday | Wed., Feb. 9 |
| §§Islamic New Year | Thurs., Feb. 10 |
| †§**Presidents' Day | Mon., Feb. 21 |
| †Texas Independence Day | Wed., March 2 |
| ‡Sam Houston Day | Wed., March 2 |
| ‡Texas Flag Day | Wed., March 2 |
| Palm Sunday | Sun., March 20 |
| †§Good Friday | Fri., March 25 |
| Easter Day | Sun., March 27 |
| †César Chávez Day | Thurs., March 31 |
| ‡Former Prisoners of War Recognition Day | Sat., April 9 |
| †San Jacinto Day | Thurs., April 21 |
| ¶Passover (Pesach), first day of | Sun., April 24 |
| Ascension Day | Thurs., May 5 |
| Mother's Day | Sun., May 8 |
| Whit Sunday — Pentecost | Sun., May 15 |
| Trinity Sunday | Sun., May 22 |
| Armed Forces Day | Sat., May 21 |
| †§Memorial Day | Mon., May 30 |
| ¶Shavuot (Feast of Weeks) | Mon., June 13 |
| Flag Day (U.S.) | Tues., June 14 |
| †Emancipation Day in Texas (Juneteenth) | Sun., June 19 |
| Father's Day | Sun., June 19 |
| †§Independence Day | Mon., July 4 |
| †Lyndon Baines Johnson Day | Sat., Aug. 27 |
| †§Labor Day | Mon., Sept. 5 |
| Grandparents Day | Sun., Sept. 11 |
| §§Ramadan, first day of | Tues., Oct. 4 |
| ¶Rosh Hashanah (Jewish New Year) | Tues., Oct. 4 |
| §‡Columbus Day | Mon., Oct. 10 |
| ¶Yom Kippur (Day of Atonement) | Thurs., Oct. 13 |
| ¶Sukkot (Tabernacles), first day of | Tues., Oct. 18 |
| Halloween | Mon., Oct. 31 |
| ‡Father of Texas (Stephen F. Austin) Day | Thurs., Nov. 3 |
| †§Veterans Day | Fri., Nov. 11 |
| †§††Thanksgiving Day | Thurs., Nov. 24 |
| First Sunday in Advent | Sun., Nov. 27 |
| †§Christmas Day | Sun., Dec. 25 |
| ¶Hanukkah, first day of | Mon., Dec. 26 |

¶ §§ In these tables, the Jewish (¶) and Islamic (§§) holidays are tabular, which means they begin at sunset on the previous evening.

† State holiday in Texas. For state employees, the Friday after Thanksgiving Day, Dec. 24, and Dec. 26 are also holidays. Optional holidays are César Chávez Day, Good Friday, Rosh Hashanah, and Yom Kippur. Partial-staffing holidays are Confederate Heroes Day, Texas Independence Day, San Jacinto Day, Emancipation Day in Texas, and Lyndon Baines Johnson Day. State offices will be open on optional holidays and partial-staffing holidays.

‡ State Recognition Days, designated by the Texas Legislature. In addition, the legislature has designated the week of May 22–26 International Trade Awareness Week.

§ Federal legal public holiday.

*Confederate Heroes Day combines the birthdays of Robert E. Lee (Jan. 19) and Jefferson Davis (June 3).

**Presidents' Day combines the birthdays of George Washington (Feb. 15) and Abraham Lincoln (Feb. 12).

†† Between 1939 and 1957, Texas observed Thanksgiving Day on the last Thursday in November. As a result, in all Novembers having five Thursdays, Texas celebrated national Thanksgiving on the fourth Thursday and Texas Thanksgiving on the fifth Thursday. In 1957, Texas changed the state observance to coincide in all years with the national holiday. ☆

*"Ascension Thursday," watercolor by Stefan Kramar of Amarillo. Fray Juan de Padilla, a Franciscan accompanying the Coronado Expedition, celebrated a Eucharistic liturgy in 1541 in a canyon of the Texas Panhandle.*

# Franciscan Missionaries in Texas before 1690

The first Christian missionaries came to Texas by way of New Mexico.

This odd historical fact was the result of three influences: the goals of the earliest Spanish explorers, the geography of New Spain and the Spanish sense of responsibility for spreading the faith. That the religion was introduced from the west is odd because other development of Texas — social, economic and cultural — came from the east and south.

## Explorers' Goals

Spain's early goals in the Southwest were primarily materialistic, and the search for wealth resulted first in the Coronado expedition of 1540-42. Considering the context of the times, it was not far-fetched to believe that immense wealth was over the horizon. The Inca Empire of Peru had been conquered a mere seven years earlier. The Incas ruled the second grand system of civilization the Spanish had encountered in the New World. The first, the Aztecs, was conquered in 1519-22.

Then came bits of evidence of a possible third indigenous "empire" north of Texas. The reports included mention of people who lived in houses. The physical evidence included samples of fine woven cloth, as well as a few gemstones and metal objects. Of course, the Pueblo people of northern New Mexico, as it turned out, did not possess the kind of wealth Spanish explorers sought. But, there Spain was.

## Crusading Mission

Abandonment of the area was not conceivable. This was because of Spain's sense of Christian mission that came out of their own peculiar history. It is beyond our

purposes to go into that history in this article, except to say the Spanish were a crusading society, and they had acquired a keen sense of responsibility for all peoples to receive the *Santa Fe* (Holy Faith).

Unlike the English and French colonizers who wanted the Indians just to get out of the way, the Spanish were continuously wrestling with dual and conflicting impulses toward the Indians — greed and charity. The greed for new wealth was witnessed mostly in the soldiers and civilian explorers, who often exploited the Indians as labor. The protective missionaries, some say overly protective, bore evangelistic charity toward the native people, wishing to instruct them in the new faith but also to teach them crafts and agricultural techniques through the elaborate mission system.

With the pursuit of wealth a dashed hope, the Spanish religious mission became the primary catalyst for policy in the Southwest for the following two centuries.

The Franciscan order was given the job of teaching the Indians, and before 1690, when the Spanish turned their interest to East Texas, there was much activity in West Texas in spreading the Christian faith.

## Geographical Avenues

The geography, especially the layout of the river systems, was the third element that influenced where and when different tribes received the missionaries' message. New Spain's northern frontier by the 1570s had reached mining areas around Santa Bárbara at the headwaters of the Río Conchos (see map following).

From there, movement along the Conchos to its junction (*La Junta*) with the Rio Grande provided an

avenue for travel northward. La Junta de los Ríos became an important stopover on most excursions. It had been a settled farming area since 1500 B.C. and in the late 1500s A.D. it was the home to several different Indian groups. Nancy Parrot Hickerson, in her study of the Jumano Indians in the region, says there were eight villages at La Junta on both sides of the Rio Grande, some of them with more than 2,000 people.

In 1598, Juan de Oñate led the *entrada* through El Paso del Norte that began the colonizing of New Mexico. The Spanish founded the first settlement and mission near present Española. In 1610, the capital of New Mexico was moved to Santa Fe. As the New Mexico base became established with the arrival of more Franciscans at the Isleta monastery (at least 53 between 1612-1629), there was a burst of missionary activity in all directions.

### Concho-Colorado

In 1629, the deepest missionary activity into West Texas occurred at the confluence of the Colorado (then called the San Clemente) and the Concho (then called the Nueces) rivers, most sources say. (Anthropologist Hickerson says it was at a Jumano base [*ranchería*] north of there, possibly at the headwaters of the Red River in Palo Duro Canyon.)

This mission came on the pleadings of the Jumanos who showed some familiarity with Christianity, all sources agree. Believers hold that the Indians encountered a mysterious "Woman in Blue" who spoke to them in their languages and told them to seek further religious instruction (see **Spanish Nun**, following). Skeptics say it was the weaker tribes' fear of the encroaching Apaches that spurred their interest in Spanish protection.

A second mission to the Plains Jumanos occurred in 1632. Sources disagree on whether Fray Juan de Salas participated or merely directed it, but all agree the second mission was to the Colorado-Concho area near present-day San Angelo.

In 1630, there was a brief attempt for a mission in the El Paso area to serve the primitive Mansos Indians. Around 1656 there was a second attempt there, and finally a successful and permanent mission in 1659.

In 1674-1675, there were brief forays from Monclova in Mexico. These occurred near Del Rio and Eagle Pass and were efforts to reach tribes who had crossed the Rio Grande from missions in Coahuila.

### Santa Fe Uprising

On Aug. 10, 1680, the Pueblo Uprising began in New Mexico, and within weeks the 2,000 Spanish colonists were forced to flee to El Paso. After decades of enduring inept and sometimes malicious governors, the Indians established an alliance strong enough to successfully revolt. There had also been overzealous missionaries who prohibited Indian customs and ceremonies they deemed pagan and diabolical.

When the Spanish refugees arrived at El Paso del Norte, they camped in what were thought to be short-lived settlements.

Instead, it would be twelve years before they were to return to Santa Fe. In the meantime, the Spanish established a government-in-exile in San Lorenzo a short distance down river from the El Paso mission. And, for the Indian allies who had fled with them, settlements and missions were established that still exist today at Ysleta and Socorro.

In 1683, some of the missionaries from El Paso moved down river to establish other missions for La Junta. Also in that year, Juan Domínguez de Mendoza led an expedition that returned to the area near present San Angelo, first reached in 1629-32 by Salas.

In all, some 32 Franciscans worked to advance the Christian faith into West Texas before the emphasis switched to East Texas and later still to the area around San Antonio. — *Robert Plocheck*

**Following are listed the Franciscans connected to ministry in Texas before 1690, grouped by expedition. The letters following in parenthesis indicate locations on the accompanying map where they worked. Sources are also named (NHB, [New Handbook of Texas], etc). A complete list of sources follows.**

### CORONADO 1540

**PADILLA, Fray Juan de**. Came to the New World from his native Andalucia in Spain, where he had been a soldier before joining the Franciscan order. The exact date of his arrival is not known, but his signature did appear on a letter from the New World dated Oct. 19, 1529. ... Padilla was among the party that journeyed in **1541** with Francisco Vázquez de **Coronado** to Quivira, the Wichita village in present-day Kansas. He reportedly conducted a service of thanksgiving [**Eucharist**] in Palo Duro Canyon [or Blanco Canyon]. When the disillusioned Coronado declared his intention to return to New Spain in the spring of 1542, Padilla chose to remain and continue missionary efforts among the Plains tribes. He and two lay brothers worked in the New Mexico pueblos and reportedly were martyred. ...

Padilla and his companions set out for the buffalo plains. Some accounts claim that they followed the **Canadian River** as far as the area of present **Hutchinson** and **Roberts** counties before turning north to Quivira, where they were warmly received by the natives. After working in the area about two years, Padilla, with companions, wanted to expand their ministry to neighboring tribes in unexplored territory.

About Nov. 30, **1544**, at a little more than a day's journey from their home base, they were suddenly set upon by a war party of enemy tribesmen. Urging his companions to flee, the account goes, the friar knelt and deliberately sacrificed himself to the arrows of the Indians, who "threw him into a pit, covering his body with innumerable stones." The actual location of Padilla's death is disputed, as are certain details surrounding the episode, such as who was really with him. However, he has been revered by Texans as the first Christian martyr of Texas. In 1936 a monument commemorating the martyrdom was erected jointly by the State of Texas and the Knights of Columbus in Amarillo's Ellwood Park. — Anderson, NHB. (A,B)

**DANIEL, Fray.** One of three lay Franciscans on **Coronado** expedition **1541-44**. No last name given. — Castañeda. (A,B)

**DE LA CRUZ, Fray Juan.** One of two lay Franciscan brothers who remained after **Coronado** returned to Mexico. Worked with **Padilla** in the New Mexico pueblos and reportedly was martyred Nov. 25, **1542**. Aged missionary. Had labored for many years among Indians of Jalisco. Little is known except he remained alone among Tiguex. Died pierced by arrows. "He was so highly regarded for his saintly life by Coronado himself, that the latter gave orders to his soldiers that each should touch his hat or helmet whenever the name of this holy man was mentioned." — Castañeda. (A,B)

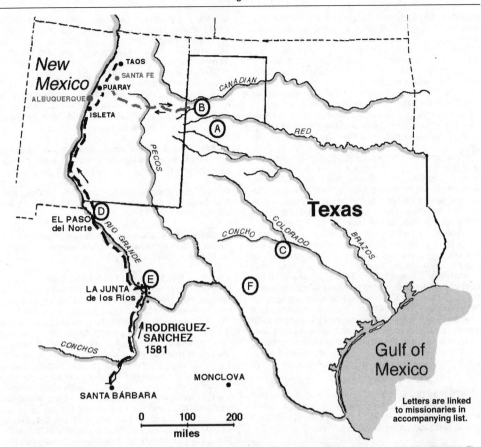

*The Rodriquez-Sánchez expedition, one of the earliest, took a route northward followed by most later travelers (dashed line). The northern frontier of New Spain had reached the mining areas of Santa Bárbara by the 1570s, and the Río Conchos provided a connecting path. The Rodriquez-Sánchez side-trip eastward to the Plains Indians was also followed by many later excursions.*

**ESCALONA, Fray Luis de (or Descalona/Ubeda).** One of two lay Franciscan brothers who remained after Coronado returned to Mexico. Worked with **Padilla** (who was youngest of three) in the New Mexico pueblos and reportedly martyred circa **1544.** (A)

**NIZA, Fray Marcos de.** Had served in Central America and Peru. Controversial Franciscan explorer, led the 1539 expedition into the American Southwest. ...It was based on his reports — some say exaggerations — that the Coronado expedition was initiated. Niza traveled in **1540** to Cíbola with **Coronado.** Niza (from Niče) returned to Mexico City where he died in 1558.— Weber, NHB. (A,B)

**RODRIGUEZ and ESPEJO 1581-83**
**RODRÍGUEZ, Fray Agustín** (d.1582). Lay brother on upper Río Conchos in 1570s when he read Cabeza de Vaca's account of adventures and heard reports from **La Junta** about Indians in cotton clothes who lived in houses. Secured permission (**1581**) to explore Pueblo areas, went from Santa Bárbara up to Taos. Martyred at Puaray, N.M., after the soldier escorts (including leader Sanchez) returned to Mexico. (B,D,E)

**BELTRÁN, Franciscan Fray Bernardino.** Resident in monastery in Durango, Mexico. Accompanied Antonio de **Espejo** on mission of **1582-83** in attempt to rescue Fray Rodriguez and companions. At Pauray, urged returning to

Mexico once martyrdom of friars determined. (D,E)

**LÓPEZ, Fray Francisco.** As priest, was designated superior when he accompanied Fray **Rodriguez** on **1581** entrada. Martyred at Puaray with Rodriguez. (D,E)

**SANTA MARÍA, Fray Juan de.** Accompanied Fray **Rodriguez** on **1581** entrada along Rio Grande. Turning back to Mexico alone, he was killed by Indian war party. (D,E)

**OÑATE 1598**
**VELASCO, Fray Francisco de.** In company of **Oñate** in **1598-1601** at El Paso and in Texas **Panhandle.** (D,B)

**VERGARA, Fray Pedro de.** Lay brother with **Oñate** in **1598-1601** at El Paso and in Texas **Panhandle.** (D,B)

**SALAS 1629**
**SALAS, Fray Juan de.** Franciscan, came to New Mexico in 1613 or 1622 and founded **Isleta** mission, near present Albuquerque. Benavides says Indians had special fondness for Salas. In **1629** Jumano Indians went to the monastery and asked for religious instruction, stating that they came at the request of the **"Woman in Blue,"** María de Ágreda.

It was while they were living on a stream which the Spaniards called Noeces or Nueces that they were visited by María de Ágreda. This river, erroneously thought to be the Arkansas, has definitely been identified with the

present middle Concho, in Texas...Salas and Father Fray Diego López [set out] with a guard of three soldiers...guided on this occasion by the friendly delegation that had come to seek for them ... going approximately 300 miles east-southeast from old Isleta.— Castañeda.

[Salas and companions reached] **southwest Texas** where they were welcomed by a large band of Indians, who claimed they had been advised of approaching Christian missionaries by the Woman in Blue. Although no permanent mission was set up among the Jumanos, in 1632 Fray Ascencio de Zarate and Fray Pedro de Ortega lead a follow-up expedition to the same locale. — Chipman.

A senior and much respected priest must have been in attendance at [1629] meeting ... [where] **Jumanos** requested missionaries because, says Benavides, they were influenced by the virtuous reputation of the Franciscans, and they acted out of a special fondness for Fray Salas. ... [who] would have understood (the Jumanos) situation. Salas had worked among the Tompiros and Jumanos in the Salinas (in New Mexico) for many years ... He had a reputation for skill with native languages and had become acquainted with Jumano leaders such as Captain Tuerto. Benavides indicated ... Salas was eager to undertake the mission. ... [Plains Jumanos] optimal location near **Canadian, Red** and **Brazos** suggests possibly a protected site in a canyon or barranca such as **Palo Duro Canyon**. ... After an indefinite period of time — a month at most — during which they worked at catechizing, erected a large cross, conducted healing sessions, and met with the ambassadors from neighboring tribes, the priest departed....it was evidently their intention to return. — N. Hickerson. (C) *[or A,B, according to Hickerson].*

**LÓPEZ, Fray Diego.** Young ... perhaps one of the [**1629**] arrivals in New Mexico. Accompanied Fray **Salas** on first mission to Jumanos in Texas. — N.Hickerson. Some (Blake, NHB) say surname was LEON. (C)

**ORTEGA, Fray Pedro (or Juan) de.** Priest-missionary to Jumanos in **1632**. Worked six months at confluence of **Concho-Colorado** in West Texas. ..."Died among the Jumanos," Benavides, *Memorial of 1634*, "... worn out by the long and severe hardships of the march, the evangelical preaching, and the catechizing of the Indians in the Christian doctrine." Some sources say he was poisoned by Indians. Unlike **Salas**, he had difficulties with Indians. In Taos, Indians "gave him tortillas of corn made with urine and mice meat." — N.Hickerson. (C)

**ZÁRATE, Fray Asencíon de.** Priest-missionary to Jumanos in **1632**. Accompanied **Ortega** to confluence of **Concho-Colorado** in West Texas. ... Posada, *Report of 1686*: "two hundred leagues southeast of Santa Fe, on a stream called the Nueces (Concho)." — N.Hickerson. (C)

### EL PASO 1630-59

**SAN FRANCISCO y ZÚÑIGA, Fray García.** In 1659, founded Nuestra Señora de Guadalupe Mission at **El Paso** del Norte, coming from Senecú in New Mexico. Mission still stands in downtown Juárez, the oldest structure in the El Paso area. Some sources say he started a branch mission also called Senecú in Texas before 1662. It is said that he refused [to receive Holy] Orders until he set out for New Mexico, when he was ordained under oath of obedience. Founded New Mexico's Socorro mission. At El Paso until 1671 when he returned to New Mexico. He died in 1673. — Castañeda. (D)

**ARTEAGA, Fray Antonio de** (b. 1589). Native of Mexico, son of distinguished family from Canary Islands. Attended University of Mexico. Joined Franciscans 1612 at age of 23. Attained distinction as a sacred orator. One of 30 missionaries arriving in New Mexico in 1628. At Senecú (N. M.) where he was a colleague of **San Francisco y Zúñiga**: "By his tender care and ardent zeal he succeeded in winning the heart of this heretofore unconquered nation [Mansos]." (Baltzar Medina in his 1682 *Chrónica*.) ... In **1630**, he made first attempt at mission in El Paso; obliged to abandon his work among the El Paso Mansos shortly after his arrival. Just how long he stayed is not known. — Castañeda. (D)

**CABAL, Fray Juan.** Franciscan priest and colleague of **San Francisco y Zúñiga** in second **El Paso** mission attempt **1656**. (D)

**PÉREZ, Fray Francisco.** Franciscan priest colleague of **San Francisco y Zúñiga** in second **El Paso** mission attempt **1656**. (D)

**SALAZAR, Fray Juan de.** Franciscan priest and colleague of **San Francisco y Zúñiga** in third and permanent **El Paso** mission **1659**. (D)

### DEL RIO and EAGLE PASS 1675

**LARIOS, Fray Juan.** On April 30, **1675**, Fernando del Bosque, Fray Larios, and company set out from the mission of Nuestra Señora de Guadalupe, at present Monclova, Coahuila. ... On May 11 they reached the Rio Grande, probably below present **Eagle Pass**. Bosque took formal possession of the river, erected a wooden cross, and renamed the river the San Buenaventura del Norte. On May 15, the expedition was met by several Indian chiefs, who asked the missionaries to come to teach and baptize their followers. The oath of allegiance to the king was administered to all the Indians, a portable altar was set up, and Mass was celebrated.

In all, the Spaniards traveled 40 leagues past the Rio Grande and made six halts in south central Texas. On May 25 they reached a site in **Edwards County** that they called San Pablo Hermitano. They returned by a northerly route to Guadalupe, where they arrived on June 12; there Bosque made a formal report to Antonio de Balcárcel. The latter recommended that three mission districts be established, including land and Indians north of the Rio Grande.

Indian hostilities and disputes with Nuevo León about the jurisdiction of the area, however, delayed implementation of the plan for more than a decade, and by that time the focus of efforts had shifted to East Texas to counteract French incursions. — Walker, NHB. (F)

**DE LA CRUZ, Fray Manuel.** A lay brother sent by **Larios** into Texas in **1674** ... crossed between present Eagle Pass and Del Rio. He came to a "mountain range which the Indians called Dacate" — probably the hills along Devil's River in Val Verde County. Spent three weeks among Indians of **Maverick, Kinney** and **Val Verde** counties. — Castañeda. (F)

**PEÑASCO de LOZANO, Fray Francisco.** Crossed Rio Grande near **Del Rio** in **1674** after return of Brother **Manuel de la Cruz**. Brought Indians back to mission at Santa Rosa, Coahuila. Colleague of **Larios**. (F)

**SAN BUENAVENTURA, Fray Dionisio de.** With **Larios** at Eagle Pass and Edwards County in **1675**. (F)

### YSLETA and SOCORRO 1680

**AYETA, Fray Francisco de** (b.1640). Born in Pamplona. He entered the Franciscan order at the age of 19, was ordained a priest the next year, and was assigned to the

province of New Mexico. He provided vital assistance to refugees at **El Paso** del Norte when they arrived after the Pueblo Revolt of **1680**. Father Ayeta, in ill health and physically impaired, left the frontier and returned to Spain in 1683. There he took up his pen in defense of the missionary (regular) clergy, who were increasingly challenged by bishops and the secular clergy. Ayeta died in Spain during the decade of the 1690s. — NHB. (D)

**GUERRA, Fray Antonio.** First missionary stationed at **Socorro**, Texas, **1680-82**. (D)

**YNOJOSA, Fray Joaquin (or de Hinojosa).** First missionary stationed at **Ysleta**, Texas **1680-82**. Assisted Fray Colina at **La Junta** missions in **1687**. (D,E)

**ZAVALETA, Fray Juan de**. Celebrated first Mass at **Ysleta**, Texas **1680**. Missionary to **La Junta** in **1683**. Went on with Mendoza-Lopez to **San Clemente** at junction of Colorado-Concho 1683. — Castañeda. (D,E,C)

### PRESIDIO and SAN CLEMENTE 1683

**LÓPEZ, Fray Nicolas.** Was custodian of the missions in New Mexico in 1680 when the Indian revolt drove the Spanish back to El Paso. ... with Fray Juan de Zavaleta and Fray Antonio Acevedo established two missions at **La Junta**, La Navidad en las Cruces and Apostol Santiago, in December of **1683**.

López and Zavaleta joined Juan Domínguez de **Mendoza** at Apostol Santiago and accompanied his expedition to Concho-Colorado (**San Clemente**). Interpretations of Mendoza's route have placed the mission variously on the Colorado River west of Ballinger (Bolton), near the confluence of the Concho and Colorado rivers (Castañeda), and on the South Llano River (Williams). ... Seymour V. Connor, locates the mission on the San Saba River west of Menard. ... During [Mendoza-López] six-week stay at San Clemente, the Spaniards were joined by 2,000 to 3,000 Indians, most of whom were baptized by the two priests ... After several attacks by the Apaches from the north and the Salineros from Nueva Vizcaya, the Spaniards abandoned the mission.— Standifer NHB (E,C)

**ACEVEDO, Fray Antonio.** Missionary with Fray Nicolas **Lopez** to **La Junta** in **1683-84**. (E)

**COLINA, Fray Agustín de**. As priest, was stationed in **1687** at the struggling missions of **La Junta** de los Ríos, at the site of present Presidio, Texas, and Ojinaga, Chihuahua. There in the fall of that same year, widely traveled Cíbolo and Jumano Indians approached Colina and asked him for a letter that they could take to "the Spaniards (French)" who were coming and going among the Tejas" in East Texas. ... It is possible, but by no means certain, that Colina continued to labor as a missionary in the La Junta region. (E)

### CHRONICLER

**BENAVIDES, Franciscan Fray Alonso de** (ca. 1578-1635). Custodian of the Franciscan missions in the Southwest from **1626 to 1629** and interviewer of María de Agreda in Spain. Son of Pedro Alonso Nieto and Antonia Murato de Benavides, was born on the island of San Miguel in the Azores about 1578. He is noted for his **memorials** (reports) which comprise one of the basic sources for history of the West Texas missions. He arrived in New Spain in 1598 and took vows with the Franciscans some three years later in Mexico City. Benavides filled the office of novice master at Puebla for a time and was later associated with the Inquisition, while residing at the friary of Cuernavaca. — Weddle, NHB. (D,E) ☆

## Sources

Ashford, Gerald. *Spanish Texas: Yesterday and Today,* Jenkins Publishing Co., Austin and New York, 1971.

Bannon, John Francis. *The Spanish Borderlands Frontier 1513-1821*, University of New Mexico Press, Albuquerque, 1974.

Boxer, C.R. *The Church Militant and Iberian Expansion 1440-1700*, Johns Hopkins University Press, Baltimore and London, 1978.

Castañeda, Carlos E. *Our Catholic Heritage in Texas 1519-1936*, Von Boeckmann-Jones Company, Austin, 1936.

Chipman, Donald E. *Spanish Texas 1519-1821*, University of Texas Press, Austin, 1992.

Habig, Marion A. O.F.M. *Spanish Texas Pilgrimage: The Old Franciscan Missions and Other Spanish Settlements of Texas 1632-1821*, Franciscan Herald Press, Chicago, 1990.

Hickerson, Nancy Parrott. *The Jumanos: Hunters and Traders of the South Plains*, University of Texas Press, Austin, 1994.

Simons, Helen and Cathryn A. Hoyt, eds. *Hispanic Texas: A Historical Guide*, University of Texas Press, 1992. "The Spanish Missions in Texas" by Robert S. Weddle.

Sonnichsen, C.L. *Pass of the North I-II*, Texas Western Press, El Paso, 1968.

Syers, William Edward. *Texas: The Beginning 1519-1834*, Texian Press, Waco, 1978.

Weber, David J., ed. *New Spain's Far Northern Frontier: Essays on Spain in the American West 1540-1821*, University of New Mexico Press, Albuquerque, 1979.

*New Handbook of Texas*, Texas State Historical Association, 1996, various: "Marcos de Niza" by David J. Weber. "Agustín Rodríguez" by Christopher Long. "Alonso de Benavides," "Juan Domínguez de Mendoza" and "Rodríguez-Sánchez Expedition" by Robert S. Weddle. "La Junta de los Ríos" by María Eva Flores C.D.P. and Julia Cauble Smith. "Espejo-Beltrán Expedition," "Oñate Expedition," "La Isla," "Antonio de Otermín," and "El Paso Del Norte," by W.H. Timmons. "Diego Pérez de Luxán," "Agustín de Colina," "Juan de Zaldívar," and "María de Jesús de Agreda" by Donald E. Chipman. "Juan de Padilla" by H. Allen Anderson. "Coronado Expedition" by David Donoghue. "Catholic Church" and "Spanish Missions" by Robert E. Wright O.M.I. "Antonio de Espejo," "Juan de Salas" and "Diego de Guadalajara," by Robert Bruce Blake. "Hiabu Indians," "Posalime Indians" and "Topacolme Indians" by Thomas N. Campell. "San Francisco de la Junta Pueblo" by Rosalind Z. Rock. "Nicolás López." "Fort Leaton State Historic Site," by Julia Cauble Smith. "San Clemente Mission," by Mary M. Standifer. "Hernán Martín," by Frank Goodwyn. "Diego Del Castillo." "San Antonio de Senecú," by John H. McNeely. "Catholic Diocese of El Paso," by Okla A. McKee. "San Lorenzo, Texas," by Martin Donell Kohout. "Corpus Christi de la Isleta Mission," by Rick Hendricks. "Nuestra Señora de la Limpia Concepción de Socorro Mission," by Ernest J. Burrus S.J. "Socorro, Texas."

*Journal of Texas Catholic History and Culture*, Texas Catholic Historical Society, 1992. "The Legacy of Columbus: Spanish Mission Policy in Texas" by Félix D. Almaráz Jr. "Before They Crossed the Great River: Cultural Background of the Spanish Franciscans in Texas" by Kieran McCarty O.F.M.

*Encyclopaedia Britannica*, "María de Ágreda," "Conceptionists," and "Philip IV."

*Catholic Encyclopedia*, "María de Ágreda."

Archdiocese of San Antonio, 75th Anniversary.

National Park Service, Washington, D.C.

Texas Historial Commission, Austin. ☆

# Spanish Nun Part of Religious History of Texas

Sister María de Ágreda was born María Fernández Coronel on April 2, 1602. Her birthplace, Ágreda, Spain, is located north of Madrid between the capital city and Pamplona.

On Feb. 2, 1620, taking the name María de Jesús, she became a Conceptionist nun. The religious order is based mostly in Spain and Belgium. It began in the late 1400s as a cloistered community of 12 women following the Cistercian rule, but through the influence of Ximnenes de Cisneros, Archbishop of Toledo, the Conceptionists were subordinated to the Franciscans.

The Conceptionists adopted the rules of the Order of St. Clare in 1501. Their distinctive habit is white with a blue cloak.

### Lady in Blue

The mysterious "Lady in Blue" has been associated in Texas religious history with María de Ágreda since 1629 when Jumano Indians went to the Friary of San Antonio in Isleta (New Mexico, south of present-day Albuquerque) to seek out Christian missionaries.

The Jumanos said a woman dressed in blue had appeared in their midst and, speaking in their own language, had taught them about the Christian faith and told them to ask for further instruction and baptism from the Franciscan missionaries.

*María de Ágreda. Institute of Texan Cultures.*

Fray Alonso de Benavides, custodian of the Franciscans in New Mexico from 1626-29, returned to Spain immediately after this incident and composed his *memorial* (report) of 1630 for the Spanish court which included this story.

He also visited the abbess in Ágreda in 1631 and interviewed her.

Fray Benavides wrote about her story of bilocation to the tribes of the Southwest:

"The first time she went was in the year 1620. She had continued ever since … She gave me all their signs and [declared] she had been with them. She knows Captain Tuerto (the one-eye captain) very well, having given me his personal characteristics and that of all the others. She herself sent the messengers from Quivira [the Jumano village on the Plains] to call the missionaries."

### Figure of the Southwest

Carlos E. Castañeda quotes this report in his *Our Catholic Heritage of Texas* (1936) and goes on to say, "These and many other details, the modest and saintly abbess communicated to Father Benavides, constrained by the request of Father General [of the Franciscans] who commanded her under oath of obedience to tell the former *custodio* all she knew of those lands and their people whom she had visited."

Other historians of the Southwest have had to deal with this Spanish mystic as a central character in the unfolding of the religious history.

The *New Handbook of Texas* includes reference in the article on Fray Juan de Salas by Robert Bruce Blake that the Jumanos asked for religious instruction "at the request of the 'Woman in Blue,' María de Jesús de Ágreda."

And, Donald E. Chipman gives a more extensive account in the *Handbook's* article on the nun herself: "Her alleged miraculous bilocations took her to eastern New Mexico and western Texas, where she contacted several Indian cultures."

### Skeptic's View

Nancy Parrott Hickerson, in her book, *The Jumanos* (1994), gives a skeptic's account of the miracle story. She questions the Indians' motives, suggesting they may have wanted Spanish protection from other tribes.

She says also that their elementary foreknowledge of Christianity could have been acquired over decades of contacts with the Spanish. And, she sees leading questions and a flawed investigation.

But, whether believer or skeptic, all agree on certain points, beginning with the fact that the Indians requested instruction, and that the same tale was told on both sides of the Atlantic.

### International Prominence

María de Jesús was not only a character on the stage of Texas history. She became well-known in Spain in her own time and, from 1643 until her death, she was a frequent correspondent with King Philip IV.

The Encyclopaedia Britannica notes that her best-known work is *The Mystical City of God* (1670), "a life of the Virgin Mary ostensibly based on divine revelations granted to Maria."

The Spanish Inquisition approved the book after 14 years of study, but the work got her into trouble with the Roman Inquisition and was prohibited from circulation by the Vatican. The ban was lifted in 1747.

There have been at least two instances when she was considered for canonization as a saint.

Her body— exhumed in 1909 and found incorrupt — remains on display in a glass-lidded coffin in Ágreda, in the convent where she served as abbess until her death in 1665.—*RP.*

# Timeline of Events: 1500s-1600s

| TEXAS/Southwest | ELSEWHERE |
|---|---|
| 1535 – Cabeza de Vaca, from Galveston to El Paso. | 1533 – Pizarro conquers Incas in Peru. |
| 1541 – Coronado crosses Texas Panhandle. Company of 1,000 plus; men, women, children, livestock, and two priests, **Fray Marcos de Niza** and **Fray Juan de Padilla.** Father Padilla said Mass on Ascension Thursday (May 26) in a canyon below the Llano Estacado. Also in party were three lay Franciscans **Fray Luis de Escalona** and **Fray Juan de la Cruz** and a **Fray Daniel.** | 1541 – Francis Xavier is missionary to India. |
| 1542-44 – Martyrdoms of **Padilla, Escalona** and **De la Cruz,** who stayed behind when Coronado returned to Mexico. | 1542 – Dominican Bartholome de las Casas instrumental in attaining from the Spanish court "New Laws" protecting rights of Indians. |
| | 1545 – Council of Trent opens. |
| | 1549-51 – Francis Xavier brings Christianity to Japan. |
| | 1556 – Abdication of Charles V.<br>Philip II succeeds as King of Spain (to 1598). |
| | 1558 – Elizabeth I reigns in England (to 1603). |
| | 1563 – Council of Trent ends. Rite of Tridentine Mass detailed. |
| | 1571 – Battle of Lepanto. |
| 1579 – Don Luis de Carvajal y de la Cueva receives large grant from Phillip II. Includes in its northeastern corner San Antonio area. | |
| 1581 – **Fray Agustín Rodríguez, Fray Francisco López** and **Fray Juan de Santa Maria** and eight soldiers under command of Francisco Sánchez travel to Rio Conchos-Rio Grande, then up to New Mexico. | |
| 1582-83 – Antonio de Espejo-**Fray Bernardino Beltrán**, attempt to rescue Rodríguez, returned down Pecos to Balmorhea to Limpia Canyon, Conchos-Rio Grande, into Mexico. | 1582 – Gregorian calendar introduced. |
| | 1588 – Defeat of Spanish Armada. |
| 1590 – Luis de Carvajal dies in prison in Mexico. Family accused of being secretly faithful to Judaism. | |
| 1590-92 – Carvajal lieutenant Gaspar Castaño de Sosa leads unauthorized expedition from Monclova (Almadén) up Pecos. Company of almost 200. | |
| 1598 – Juan de Oñate leads settlement of northern New Mexico. | 1598 – Philip III of Spain (to 1621). |
| 1601 – Oñate explores through Texas Panhandle to Kansas with Father **Fray Francisco de Velasco** and **Fray Pedro de Vergara**, a lay brother. | |
| | 1602 – Dutch East India Company formed. |
| | 1607 – Virginia founded. |
| | 1612 – Japan rulers drive out Christian missionaries. |
| | 1620 – **Sor María de Agreda** (1602-1665) takes religious vows in Old Castile. |
| | 1621 – Philip IV of Spain (to 1665). |
| 1629 – **Fray Juan de Salas** leads brief missionary journey from New Mexico to Jumano Indians, [most sources say] at Concho-Colorado confluence, along with **Fray Diego Lopez** (or **León**).<br>**Sor María de Agreda**, Lady in Blue, said to have preceded them (bilocation). | |
| 1630 — **Fray Antonio de Arteaga** attempts mission to Mansos in El Paso area. | |

*The Rio Grande, right, was the way of passage for the early Spanish Franciscan missionaries as they made their way through the dry, rugged terrain of West Texas. The junction of the Rio Grande and the Rio Conchos (called La Junta) at Presidio allowed the expeditions to travel from north-central Mexico to Santa Fe in New Mexico. File photo.*

1632 – Return of two Franciscans to Jumanos. [Some sources say] Fray Salas, who leaves **Fray Pedro de Ortega** at Concho-Colorado. Hickerson and Morris say two were Ortega with **Fray Asencíon de Zárate**. Ortega dies there six months later.

1638 – Japanese Christians slaughtered.

1642 – French found Montreal.
1645 – Franciscan Capuchin missionaries in Congo.

1650 – Captains Hernán Martín and Diego del Castillo from New Mexico to Concho-Colorado area. Stayed six months.

1652 – Capetown founded by Dutch.

1654 – Captain Diego de Guadalajara from Santa Fe to Concho-Colorado, briefly.

1656 — **Fray García de San Francisco y Zúñiga** makes second attempt at mission in El Paso area. With **Fray Juan Cabal** and **Fray Francisco Perez**.

1659 – **San Francisco y Zúñiga** in third attempt permanently founds Mission Nuestra Señora de Guadalupe. Site now in Ciudad Juarez. With **Fray Juan de Salazar.**

1661 – Louis XIV absolute monarch in France. English acquire Bombay.

1665 – Charles II (at age 4) ascends Spanish throne (to 1700, said to be insane). No heir; War of Spanish Succession until 1713.

1675 – Don Fernando del Bosque-**Fray Juan Laríos** (into Edwards County). High Mass, May 16, near Eagle Pass.

1680 – **Fray Francisco de Ayeta** helps settle refugees from Pueblo Uprising around El Paso, including Spaniards at site named San Lorenzo.
Gov. Antonio de Otermín establishes residence at San Lorenzo in October. (Later absorbed into El Paso, [some sources say]).
Corpus Christi de Ysleta del Sur mission, also called Santísimo Sacramento.
**Fray Juan de Zavaleta** celebrated first Mass.
La Purísima del Socorro, briefly named San Pedro de Alcántara.

1683-84 – **Fray Nicolas López**-Don Domínguez de Mendoza. Missions La Navídad en las Cruces and El Apóstol Santiago founded at Conchos-Rio Grande. On to Concho-Colorado and San Clemente mission.

1681 – Frenchman La Salle explores Mississippi.

1685 – La Salle establishes Fort St. Louis on Gulf coast.
1690 – Spanish missionary effort shifts to East Texas.

# Church Affiliation Change: 1990 to 2000

Texas remains one of the nation's more "churched" states, even though a smaller portion of Texans is affiliated with a church than ten years ago.

Texas ranks 18th among the states in percentage of the population belonging to a denomination. According to *Churches and Church Membership in the United States 2000*, at least 55.5 percent of Texans are adherents to a religion.

The survey, from the Glenmary Research Center in Nashville, is the only U.S. survey to report church membership at the state and county level. It relies on reports from the different denominations for membership numbers.

But in 2000, the African-American churches did not participate in the study. This probably leaves out more than one million church-going Texans.

In 1990, when the survey was last done, it was estimated that there were 815,000 black Baptists in Texas. A conservative estimate of the membership in black Pentecostal churches in 2000 would be about 300,000. And, an estimate for black Methodists in Texas would be approximately 200,000.

Adjusting for those additions, then the percentage of Texans that are members of a religion would be closer to 61.7 percent. Although that is higher than the 55.5 percent figure compiled from the reporting churches, still, it would be down from 67.1 percent ten years ago, indicating a move away from church membership.

This decrease occurred while many indicators have been showing that Americans are more interested in their spiritual lives than any time in recent decades. Churches reported an increase of 1.5 million members while the total population of Texas increased by 4 million from 1990 to 2000. During the same period, the number of Texans not attached to a religion rose by 2.5 million.

Thus, according to the *Texas Almanac* analysis from a variety of sources, there are 7.9 million persons in the state who are not claimed by a church and about 13 million who are church members. (The U.S. census counted 20,851,820 persons in Texas in 2000.)

From the 2000 church survey, diversity among religious believers can be seen in the congregations of Muslims, Hindus, Buddhists and other non-Christian faiths. In 1990, these groups were not surveyed, so increases cannot be determined.

The estimate of Jewish Texans, 128,000, is from the congregations in the state. The number increased by 20,000 from 1990.

During the decade, the number of Catholics increased by almost 800,000, the greatest numerical gain among the churches. However, the percentage of Texans who are Catholic remained at 21 percent.

The largest faith group, the Baptists, increased by 314,761 members, a rate less than the statewide population increase. Thus in 2000, Baptists made up 21.8 percent of the population, down from 24.9 percent in 1990.

The trend in the state's two largest denominations,

## Texas' ranking among states

According to *Churches and Church Membership in the United States 2000*, Texas ranks:
● First in number of Evangelical Protestants, with 5,083,087. California, ranked second, has less than half as many with 2,432,285.
● Second, behind Pennsylvania, in number of Mainline Protestants at 1,705,394.
● Third in number of Catholics, behind California and New York.
● Third in number of Buddhist congregations.
● Fifth in number of Muslims.
● Fifth in number of Hindu congregations.
● Sixth in number of Mormons.
● Tenth in number of Jews.

Roman Catholic and Southern Baptist, which together make up over 40 percent of the population, was especially noticeable in the four largest metropolitan areas. More than half of all Texans live in these areas.

In the eight-county Houston metro area, the percentage of Catholics rose from 17.3 percent to 18.2 percent, while the percentage of Southern Baptists went down slightly from 14.9 percent to 14.8.

In the five-county Austin metro area, the percentage of Catholics increased from 13.6 percent to 18.4 percent. The percentage of Southern Baptists decreased from 13.5 percent to 10.2 percent.

In the four-county San Antonio metro area, the percentage of Catholics increased from 36.0 to 38.8, while the percentage of Southern Baptists decreased from 10.4 to 8.8.

The 12-county Dallas-Forth Worth metro area is the only one of the four where the number of Southern Baptists, 855,680, is higher than Catholics, 808,167. But, here also, the percentage of Southern Baptists declined from 19.0 to 16.4, while the percentage of Catholics rose from 9.0 in 1990 to 15.5 in 2000.

As noted, while these shifts in religious make-up were occurring, the number of persons not affiliated with a religious group was increasing.

In Houston in 1990, the percentage of the population not counted as church members was 43.1. In 2000, that had risen to 50.1 percent.

In Austin, the figure increased from 52.4 percent to 55.3 percent.

In San Antonio, the percentage of non-adherents to a religion was 36.2 in 1990. In 2000, it had risen slightly to 37.0 percent.

In the Dallas-Fort Worth area, it increased from 43.6

percent in 1990, to 47.7 percent in 2000.

These trends reflect what was happening in the nation at large, where the percentage of the population not affiliated with a church rose from 44.9 to 55.1.

The Southern Baptists and Catholics also were the largest religious groups in the nation. And, the percentage of Catholics remained about the same, 21.5 in 1990 and 22.0 in 2000, while the percent of the total population that was Southern Baptist declined from 13.8 to 7.1.

The Glenmary study is a combined effort of the Catholic research center and the Church of the Nazarene, a Protestant denomination with headquarters in Kansas City, Mo..

The study distinguishes between members, which includes adult members only, and adherents, which includes adults and children. **All figures used by the *Texas Almanac* refer to adherents**.

## Sources

*Churches and Church Membership in the United States 2000*, Glenmary Research Center, Nashville, Tenn., 2002.

National Council of Churches of Christ in the USA, New York, *Yearbook of American and Canadian Churches*, annual.

*New Handbook of Texas*, 1996, various: "Christian Methodist Episcopal Church," by Charles E. Tatum; "African-American Churches," "African Methodist Episcopal Church," and "African Methodist Episcopal Zion Church," by William E. Montgomery; "Religion," by John W. Storey.

| Religious Groups in Texas | 1990 | Change | 2000 |
|---|---|---|---|
| Baha'i | | | 10,777 |
| **Baptist** | 4,223,157 | + 314,761 | 4,537,918 |
| American Baptist Association | | | 61,272 |
| American Baptist Churches in the USA | 12,905 | - 5,848 | 7,057 |
| Baptist General Conference | 278 | + 62 | 340 |
| Baptist Missionary Association of America | 125,323 | - 2,125 | 123,198 |
| Conservative Baptist Association of America (1 congregation) | | | |
| Free Will Baptist, National Association of, Inc. | 4,936 | - 2,114 | 2,822 |
| Interstate & Foreign Landmark Missionary Baptists Association | 76 | + 17 | 93 |
| Landmark Baptist, Indep. Assns. & Unaffil. Churches | | | 964 |
| National Primitive Baptist Convention, USA | | | 4,463 |
| North American Baptist Conference | 1,634 | - 65 | 1,569 |
| Primitive Baptists Associations | 2,544 | | |
| Primitive Baptist Church — Old Line (118 congregations) | | | NR |
| Progressive Primitive Baptists | | | 197 |
| Reformed Baptist Churches (10 congregations) | | | |
| Regular Baptist Churches, General Association of | | | 684 |
| Seventh Day Baptist General Conference | 242 | | |
| Southern Baptist Convention | 3,259,395 | + 260,064 | 3,519,459 |
| Southwide Baptist Fellowship (13 congregations) | | | |
| Two-Seed-in-the-Spirit Predestinarian Baptists | 53 | - 24 | 29 |
| *(Black Baptists Estimate)** | *(815,771)** | — | *(815,771)** |
| **Buddhism** (88 congregations) | | | NR |
| **Catholic Church** | 3,574,728 | + 794,241 | 4,368,969 |
| **(Independent) Christian Churches & Churches of Christ** | 33,766 | + 9,836 | 43,602 |
| **Churches of Christ** | 380,948 | - 3,684 | 377,264 |
| **(Disciples of Christ)** Christian Church | 105,495 | + 5,793 | 111,288 |
| **Episcopal** | 169,227 | + 8,683 | 177,910 |
| Episcopal Church, The | 169,112 | + 8,798 | 177,910 |
| Reformed Episcopal Church | 115 | | |
| **Hindu** (34 congregations) | | | NR |
| **Holiness** | 61,487 | + 25,052 | 86,539 |
| Christian & Missionary Alliance, The | 3,082 | + 776 | 3,858 |
| Church of God (Anderson, Ind.) | 5,854 | - 1,185 | 4,669 |
| Free Methodist Church of North America | 886 | - 12 | 874 |
| Nazarene, Church of the | 45,097 | + 5,431 | 50,528 |
| Salvation Army | 5,676 | + 19,394 | 25,070 |
| Wesleyan Church, The | 892 | +648 | 1,540 |
| **Independent Non-Charismatic** Churches | 132,292 | + 12,957 | 145,249 |
| **Jain** (6 congregations) | | | NR |
| **Jewish**, estimate | 107,980 | + 20,020 | 128,000 |
| **Lutheran** | 294,524 | + 6,994 | 301,518 |
| Church of the Lutheran Brethren of America | 71 | | |
| Church of the Lutheran Confession | 144 | | |
| Evangelical Lutheran Church in America | 155,276 | - 257 | 155,019 |
| Evangelical Lutheran Synod | 146 | | |
| Free Lutheran Congregations, The Association of | 144 | + 224 | 368 |
| Lutheran Church—Missouri Synod, The | 134,280 | + 5,826 | 140,106 |
| Wisconsin Evangelical Lutheran Synod | 4,463 | + 1,562 | 6,025 |

| Religious Groups in Texas | 1990 | Change | 2000 |
|---|---|---|---|
| **Mennonite/Amish** | 2,608 | + 2,011 | 4,619 |
| Amish, Old Order | 400 | - 376 | 24 |
| Amish, other | | | 68 |
| Beachy Amish Mennonite Churches | 70 | + 57 | 127 |
| Church of God in Christ (Mennonite) | 522 | + 327 | 849 |
| Conservative Mennonite Conference | | | 191 |
| Evangelical Bible Churches, Fellowship of (was Ev. Menn. Bre.) | 20 | | |
| Eastern Pennsylvania Mennonite Church | 39 | + 26 | 65 |
| Mennonite Brethren Churches, U.S. Conference of | 329 | + 96 | 425 |
| Mennonite, other | | | 1,655 |
| Mennonite Church USA | 1,228 | - 13 | 1,215 |
| **Methodist** | 1,202,991 | + 16,542 | 1,219,533 |
| African Methodist Episcopal Zion | 2,191 | — | (2,191)* |
| *(African Methodist Episcopal estimate)\*(300 congregations)* | *(150,000)\** | — | *(150,000)\** |
| *(Christian Methodist Episcopal estimate)\** | *(45,000)\** | — | *(45,000)\** |
| Evangelical Methodist Church | 1,482 | | |
| United Methodist Church, The | 1,004,318 | + 18,024 | 1,022,342 |
| **(Mormons)** Church of Jesus Christ of Latter-day Saints | 111,276 | + 44,175 | 155,451 |
| **Muslim**, estimate | | | 114,999 |
| **Orthodox** | 2,082 | + 20,673 | 22,755 |
| Antiochian Orthodox of North America | | | 4,642 |
| Armenian Apostolic Church/Cilicia | | | 80 |
| Armenian Apostolic Church/Etchmiadzin | | | 1,275 |
| Assyrian Apostolic Church | 282 | | |
| Coptic Orthodox Church (8 congregations) | | | NR |
| Greek Orthodox Archdiocese of America | | | 9,444 |
| Greek Orthodox Archdiocese of Vasiloupulis | | | 135 |
| Malankara Archdiocese/Syrian Orthodox Church in North Amer. | | | 825 |
| Malankara Orthodox Syrian Church, American Diocese of the | | | 2,675 |
| Orthodox Church in America (Romanian Diocese) | | | 413 |
| Orthodox Church in America (Territorial Dioceses) | | | 2,096 |
| Russian Orthodox Church Outside of Russia (4 congregations) | | | NR |
| Serbian Orthodox Church in the USA | | | 1,110 |
| Serbian Orthodox Ch./New Gracanica Metropolitanate (1 cong) | | | NR |
| Syrian Orthodox Church of Antioch | 1,800 | - 1,740 | 60 |
| **Pentecostal/Charismatic** | 682,769 | + 80,301 | 763,070 |
| Assemblies of God | 202,082 | + 26,016 | 228,098 |
| Pentecostal Church of God | 12,296 | - 704 | 11,592 |
| Pentecostal Holiness Church, International | 5,517 | + 4,748 | 10,265 |
| Church of God (Cleveland, Tenn.) | 27,828 | + 10,431 | 38,259 |
| Church of God of Prophecy | 2,918 | - 12 | 2,906 |
| *(Church of God in Christ estimate)\*(268 congregations)* | *(300,000)\** | — | *(300,000)\** |
| International Church of the Foursquare Gospel | 4,278 | + 8,223 | 12,501 |
| Independent Charismatic Churches | 127,850 | + 31,599 | 159,449 |
| **Presbyterian** | 217,277 | - 12,473 | 204,804 |
| Associate Reformed Presbyterian Church | | | 28 |
| Cumberland Presbyterian Church | 10,373 | - 1,951 | 8,422 |
| Evangelical Presbyterian Church | 490 | + 959 | 1,449 |
| Orthodox Presbyterian Church, The | | | 644 |
| Presbyterian Church (USA) | 200,969 | - 20,654 | 180,315 |
| Presbyterian Church in America | 5,445 | + 8,501 | 13,946 |
| **(Quakers)** Friends | 2,548 | - 1,474 | 1,074 |
| **Seventh-day Adventists** | 41,470 | + 4,798 | 46,268 |
| **Sikh** (13 congregations) | | | NR |
| **Tao** (1 congregation) | | | NR |
| **United Church of Christ** | 20,950 | - 4,363 | 16,587 |
| **Zoroastrian** (3 congregations) | | | NR |
| **OTHERS** (less than 12,000 reported) | | | |
| Advent Christian Church | 221 | | |
| Apostolic Christian Churches of America | 13 | + 14 | 27 |
| Brethren In Christ Church | 73 | | |
| Calvary Chapel Fellowship Church (19 congregations) | | | NR |
| Christ Catholic Church | 3 | | |
| Christian (Plymouth) Brethren | 6,766 | | |
| Christian Reformed Church | 866 | + 1,070 | 1,936 |
| Church of Christ, Scientist (93 congregations) | | | NR |
| Church of God General Conference, Abrahamic Faith | 93 | - 38 | 55 |

| Religious Groups in Texas | 1990 | Change | 2000 |
|---|---|---|---|
| Church of God (Seventh Day) Denver, Col., The | 1,743 | | |
| Church of the Brethren | 302 | - 18 | 284 |
| Community of Christ | | | 2,817 |
| Congregational Christian Churches, National Association of | 721 | | |
| Congregational Christian Churches (Not part of CCC body) | 23 | | |
| Conservative Congregational Christian Conference | 104 | - 79 | 25 |
| Evangelical Covenant Church, The | | | 1,022 |
| Evangelical Free Church of America, The | 5,463 | + 4,257 | 9,720 |
| Independent Fundamental Churches of America (4 cong.) | | | NR |
| International Churches of Christ | | | 4,041 |
| International Council of Community Churches | | | 1,152 |
| Metropolitan Community Churches, Universal Fellowship of | | | 5,570 |
| Missionary Church USA | | | 403 |
| Open Bible Standard Churches, Inc. (2 congregations) | | | NR |
| Reformed Church in America | 1,592 | + 448 | 2,040 |
| Unitarian Universalist Association | 5,843 | + 1,029 | 6,872 |
| Vineyard USA | | | 11,637 |
| **Statewide Totals** | **11,391,401** | **+ 1,483,617** | **12,875,018** |
| Unclaimed (not counted as adherent to religion) | 5,460,358 | + 2,516,444 | 7,976,802 |

*Compiled principally from Glenmary Research Center, also other sources. NR, not reported. *Almanac estimates.*

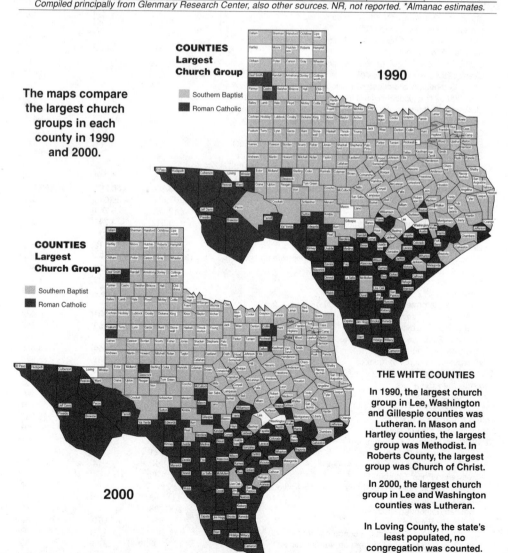

The maps compare the largest church groups in each county in 1990 and 2000.

**COUNTIES**
**Largest Church Group**

Southern Baptist
Roman Catholic

1990

**COUNTIES**
**Largest Church Group**

Southern Baptist
Roman Catholic

2000

**THE WHITE COUNTIES**

In 1990, the largest church group in Lee, Washington and Gillespie counties was Lutheran. In Mason and Hartley counties, the largest group was Methodist. In Roberts County, the largest group was Church of Christ.

In 2000, the largest church group in Lee and Washington counties was Lutheran.

In Loving County, the state's least populated, no congregation was counted.

# Smaller portion of Texans are church members

The percentage of Texans affiliated with a church decreased during the 1990s. According to *Churches and Church Membership in the United States 2000*, some 55.5 percent of the population were church members. In all, 195 Texas counties (unshaded in this list) showed a reduction in church membership as a percentage of the total population. The counties that went against the trend are shaded in gray.

| County | 1990 | 2000 |
|---|---|---|
| TEXAS | 64.2 | 55.5 |
| Anderson | 54.8 | 54.9 |
| Andrews | 76.6 | 84.4 |
| Angelina | 68.3 | 68.1 |
| Aransas | 43.7 | 35.7 |
| Archer | 78.0 | 71.6 |
| Armstrong | 78.0 | 72.4 |
| Atascosa | 65.3 | 62.7 |
| Austin | 71.8 | 51.8 |
| Bailey | 74.7 | 85.6 |
| Bandera | 49.2 | 42.1 |
| Bastrop | 46.1 | 42.2 |
| Baylor | 106.0 | 101.7 |
| Bee | 64.3 | 42.6 |
| Bell | 49.7 | 47.9 |
| Bexar | 64.9 | 65.1 |
| Blanco | 59.2 | 50.2 |
| Borden | 26.9 | 35.4 |
| Bosque | 74.0 | 69.3 |
| Bowie | 68.3 | 61.6 |
| Brazoria | 62.0 | 53.2 |
| Brazos | 49.6 | 50.6 |
| Brewster | 91.4 | 57.0 |
| Briscoe | 82.0 | 105.0 |
| Brooks | 76.7 | 55.8 |
| Brown | 73.0 | 72.7 |
| Burleson | 60.2 | 46.1 |
| Burnet | 57.2 | 52.6 |
| Caldwell | 52.1 | 51.0 |
| Calhoun | 98.7 | 55.6 |
| Callahan | 67.6 | 57.8 |
| Cameron | 95.5 | 52.8 |
| Camp | 82.1 | 82.0 |
| Carson | 93.8 | 88.9 |
| Cass | 71.0 | 66.7 |
| Castro | 112.5 | 79.2 |
| Chambers | 59.4 | 55.5 |
| Cherokee | 64.7 | 58.3 |
| Childress | 96.0 | 64.7 |
| Clay | 76.9 | 72.2 |
| Cochran | 109.7 | 97.8 |
| Coke | 84.0 | 73.2 |
| Coleman | 67.7 | 64.8 |
| Collin | 45.0 | 53.7 |
| Collingsworth | 81.4 | 90.2 |
| Colorado | 103.7 | 63.8 |
| Comal | 58.6 | 54.7 |
| Comanche | 63.8 | 64.8 |
| Concho | 58.5 | 43.0 |
| Cooke | 68.1 | 60.7 |
| Coryell | 46.9 | 39.0 |

| County | 1990 | 2000 |
|---|---|---|
| Cottle | 125.1 | 109.8 |
| Crane | 70.1 | 59.7 |
| Crockett | 82.7 | 84.6 |
| Crosby | 75.4 | 85.0 |
| Culberson | 101.1 | 95.9 |
| Dallam | 118.7 | 64.4 |
| Dallas | 60.3 | 55.1 |
| Dawson | 100.3 | 79.7 |
| Deaf Smith | 84.4 | 82.2 |
| Delta | 76.1 | 56.5 |
| Denton | 37.7 | 34.5 |
| DeWitt | 80.9 | 56.3 |
| Dickens | 110.0 | 87.2 |
| Dimmit | 81.0 | 111.4 |
| Donley | 77.0 | 70.7 |
| Duval | 75.3 | 71.2 |
| Eastland | 81.2 | 76.5 |
| Ector | 64.2 | 54.3 |
| Edwards | 97.5 | 79.3 |
| Ellis | 67.3 | 58.0 |
| El Paso | 82.3 | 63.4 |
| Erath | 68.0 | 57.4 |
| Falls | 73.8 | 56.5 |
| Fannin | 75.7 | 74.7 |
| Fayette | 91.5 | 80.3 |
| Fisher | 90.3 | 105.4 |
| Floyd | 124.3 | 82.3 |
| Foard | 102.4 | 90.1 |
| Fort Bend | 44.5 | 45.8 |
| Franklin | 78.1 | 72.8 |
| Freestone | 68.1 | 56.5 |
| Frio | 84.9 | 82.7 |
| Gaines | 87.2 | 81.2 |
| Galveston | 51.1 | 45.0 |
| Garza | 65.7 | 85.6 |
| Gillespie | 66.9 | 75.5 |
| Glasscock | 61.5 | 59.4 |
| Goliad | 72.2 | 68.0 |
| Gonzales | 71.4 | 58.4 |
| Gray | 86.9 | 82.5 |
| Grayson | 72.3 | 60.8 |
| Gregg | 83.4 | 73.1 |
| Grimes | 63.0 | 47.4 |
| Guadalupe | 48.0 | 37.8 |
| Hale | 94.4 | 88.0 |
| Hall | 112.3 | 84.2 |
| Hamilton | 72.5 | 67.3 |
| Hansford | 88.0 | 94.1 |
| Hardeman | 89.3 | 122.3 |
| Hardin | 69.4 | 58.6 |
| Harris | 58.3 | 50.4 |
| Harrison | 61.6 | 56.2 |
| Hartley | 44.6 | 59.0 |
| Haskell | 109.5 | 107.8 |
| Hays | 42.7 | 43.5 |
| Hemphill | 78.5 | 87.2 |
| Henderson | 48.0 | 49.3 |
| Hidalgo | 94.1 | 50.4 |
| Hill | 65.6 | 51.1 |
| Hockley | 75.6 | 87.1 |
| Hood | 50.5 | 52.9 |
| Hopkins | 74.8 | 71.3 |
| Houston | 68.9 | 52.5 |
| Howard | 82.3 | 67.3 |
| Hudspeth | 84.6 | 56.5 |
| Hunt | 62.6 | 53.9 |

| County | 1990 | 2000 |
|---|---|---|
| Hutchinson | 83.0 | 84.6 |
| Irion | 74.4 | 73.2 |
| Jack | 87.2 | 54.6 |
| Jackson | 72.1 | 72.4 |
| Jasper | 71.9 | 61.0 |
| Jeff Davis | 109.0 | 54.9 |
| Jefferson | 78.5 | 65.0 |
| Jim Hogg | 90.8 | 101.2 |
| Jim Wells | 84.5 | 59.6 |
| Johnson | 57.9 | 49.5 |
| Jones | 78.9 | 62.7 |
| Karnes | 91.3 | 72.7 |
| Kaufman | 63.4 | 52.1 |
| Kendall | 65.6 | 64.4 |
| Kenedy | 95.7 | 41.1 |
| Kent | 95.7 | 86.1 |
| Kerr | 49.3 | 53.1 |
| Kimble | 65.5 | 55.9 |
| King | 68.4 | 50.6 |
| Kinney | 69.6 | 74.8 |
| Kleberg | 82.2 | 36.1 |
| Knox | 110.8 | 119.7 |
| Lamar | 69.1 | 65.4 |
| Lamb | 88.0 | 91.2 |
| Lampasas | 76.6 | 46.9 |
| La Salle | 110.7 | 103.4 |
| Lavaca | 85.5 | 98.3 |
| Lee | 69.3 | 58.6 |
| Leon | 70.3 | 62.1 |
| Liberty | 70.9 | 57.7 |
| Limestone | 62.1 | 56.7 |
| Lipscomb | 98.4 | 83.8 |
| Live Oak | 81.9 | 51.5 |
| Llano | 62.3 | 45.0 |
| Loving | NR | NR |
| Lubbock | 65.8 | 59.7 |
| Lynn | 93.3 | 84.8 |
| Madison | 62.5 | 49.0 |
| Marion | 61.3 | 44.1 |
| Martin | 71.5 | 67.3 |
| Mason | 70.8 | 77.5 |
| Matagorda | 74.7 | 62.0 |
| Maverick | 84.5 | 34.7 |
| McCulloch | 70.0 | 65.7 |
| McLennan | 73.6 | 60.5 |
| McMullen | 47.0 | 56.9 |
| Medina | 75.2 | 59.0 |
| Menard | 94.3 | 58.5 |
| Midland | 70.0 | 61.5 |
| Milam | 66.6 | 67.1 |
| Mills | 82.7 | 81.8 |
| Mitchell | 78.9 | 56.2 |
| Montague | 66.8 | 63.0 |
| Montgomery | 47.9 | 50.2 |
| Moore | 65.4 | 53.8 |
| Morris | 69.4 | 78.0 |
| Motley | 94.3 | 82.0 |
| Nacogdoches | 52.6 | 56.7 |
| Navarro | 68.5 | 64.4 |
| Newton | 47.9 | 41.4 |
| Nolan | 90.0 | 74.6 |
| Nueces | 74.6 | 55.7 |
| Ochiltree | 69.1 | 66.3 |
| Oldham | 71.6 | 65.9 |
| Orange | 75.2 | 65.6 |
| Palo Pinto | 69.3 | 58.2 |

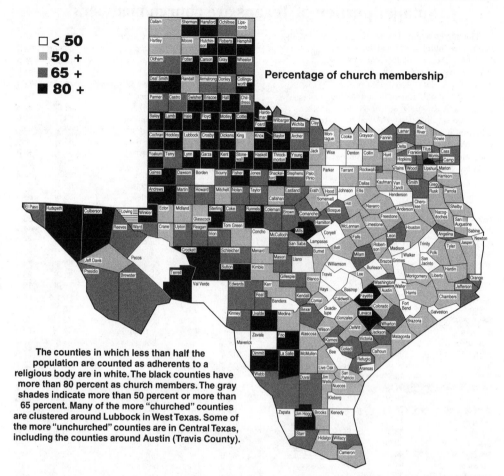

□ < **50**

▨ **50 +**

▤ **65 +**

■ **80 +**

**Percentage of church membership**

The counties in which less than half the population are counted as adherents to a religious body are in white. The black counties have more than 80 percent as church members. The gray shades indicate more than 50 percent or more than 65 percent. Many of the more "churched" counties are clustered around Lubbock in West Texas. Some of the more "unchurched" counties are in Central Texas, including the counties around Austin (Travis County).

| County | 1990 | 2000 |
|---|---|---|
| Panola | 56.4 | 56.1 |
| Parker | 54.9 | 49.5 |
| Parmer | 65.6 | 77.7 |
| Pecos | 55.1 | 45.3 |
| Polk | 60.7 | 50.5 |
| Potter | 100.6 | 86.4 |
| Presidio | 80.0 | 65.1 |
| Rains | 59.8 | 29.0 |
| Randall | 40.8 | 50.1 |
| Reagan | 70.6 | 75.4 |
| Real | 78.6 | 77.0 |
| Red River | 57.4 | 59.6 |
| Reeves | 127.5 | 75.6 |
| Refugio | 100.2 | 65.5 |
| Roberts | 141.6 | 86.1 |
| Robertson | 68.6 | 51.5 |
| Rockwall | 67.7 | 69.6 |
| Runnels | 86.1 | 88.7 |
| Rusk | 61.0 | 55.7 |
| Sabine | 49.0 | 39.1 |
| San Augustine | 58.6 | 57.9 |
| San Jacinto | 31.7 | 31.9 |
| San Patricio | 80.7 | 56.5 |
| San Saba | 81.1 | 64.8 |
| Schleicher | 75.4 | 61.9 |

| County | 1990 | 2000 |
|---|---|---|
| Scurry | 73.5 | 79.8 |
| Shackelford | 85.0 | 96.1 |
| Shelby | 59.2 | 59.3 |
| Sherman | 80.8 | 104.4 |
| Smith | 70.2 | 65.3 |
| Somervell | 57.1 | 48.7 |
| Starr | 85.6 | 78.8 |
| Stephens | 77.3 | 70.5 |
| Sterling | 80.9 | 86.6 |
| Stonewall | 79.6 | 97.6 |
| Sutton | 75.0 | 84.7 |
| Swisher | 99.7 | 89.2 |
| Tarrant | 56.1 | 52.4 |
| Taylor | 72.5 | 67.1 |
| Terrell | 80.3 | 100.6 |
| Terry | 70.3 | 71.8 |
| Throckmorton | 128.0 | 102.8 |
| Titus | 69.8 | 71.0 |
| Tom Green | 63.2 | 60.0 |
| Travis | 48.4 | 46.2 |
| Trinity | 57.7 | 46.8 |
| Tyler | 74.0 | 61.4 |
| Upshur | 64.7 | 56.5 |
| Upton | 108.9 | 66.5 |
| Uvalde | 72.5 | 89.4 |

| County | 1990 | 2000 |
|---|---|---|
| Val Verde | 35.2 | 49.5 |
| Van Zandt | 66.8 | 57.3 |
| Victoria | 83.0 | 70.6 |
| Walker | 49.5 | 33.1 |
| Waller | 51.2 | 33.2 |
| Ward | 133.5 | 78.2 |
| Washington | 68.7 | 71.6 |
| Webb | 80.6 | 73.6 |
| Wharton | 79.3 | 76.9 |
| Wheeler | 90.3 | 75.2 |
| Wichita | 75.8 | 62.3 |
| Wilbarger | 87.6 | 75.1 |
| Willacy | 104.7 | 77.4 |
| Williamson | 46.9 | 40.0 |
| Wilson | 61.3 | 59.6 |
| Winkler | 139.6 | 117.9 |
| Wise | 52.3 | 41.2 |
| Wood | 73.4 | 62.2 |
| Yoakum | 86.6 | 103.6 |
| Young | 85.0 | 90.4 |
| Zapata | 38.5 | 34.9 |
| Zavala | 83.6 | 47.9 |

Source: *Churches and Church Membership in the United States 2000*, Glenmary Research Center, Nashville, Tenn., 2002.

# Death, Birth Rates Continue Trends in Texas Statistics

Heart disease and cancer remained the major causes of death in 2001, the latest year for which statistics are available from the Bureau of Vital Statistics, Texas Department of Health.

Heart disease accounted for 28.3 percent of the 152,526 deaths. Cancer accounted for 21.9 percent of the deaths during the year. These two diseases have been the leading causes of death in Texas and the nation since 1950.

Cerebrovascular diseases (strokes), accidents and pulmonary (chronic lower respiratory) diseases ranked third, fourth and fifth, respectively.

Together, these five leading causes of death represented 67.3 percent of all deaths in 2001.

The leading cause of death for Texas residents ages 1-44 was accidents.

While the number of babies born to Texas mothers continued to increase in 2001 (365,092), the state's birth rate was at an all-time low of 17.2 per 1,000 population. In 1961, that figure was 24.8. *(See accompanying chart comparing other state and world birth rates.)*

The proportion of C-section deliveries increased from 24.1 percent in 1999 to 25.3 in 2000 to 26.7 in 2001.

Although there has been a general decrease since 1990 in the number of abortions, there was a slight increase in 2001 as well as 1995 and 1996.

Abortions were induced in an estimated 15.5 percent of the state's pregnancies in 2000, down from 20 percent in 1995.

## Health Care and Deaths in Texas Counties

| County | Patient Care, 2003 | | Total Deaths | | | Leading Causes of Death by County, 2001 | | | | | | | | | | Misc., 2001 | |
|---|---|---|---|---|---|---|---|---|---|---|---|---|---|---|---|---|---|
| | Physicians | Hospital Beds* | 1999 | 2000 | 2001 | Heart Disease | Cancer | Cerebrovascular | Accidents | Pulmonary | Diabetes | Pneumonia | Alzheimer's | Kidney Disease | Suicides | Pregnancy Rate* | Abortions |
| Statewide Total | 37,188 | 72,994 | 146,649 | 149,763 | 152,526 | 43,100 | 33,437 | 10,596 | 7,854 | 7,735 | 5,445 | 3,597 | 3,436 | 2,268 | 2,214 | 91.9 | 74,101* |
| Anderson | 83 | 249 | 601 | 626 | 573 | 127 | 175 | 29 | 30 | 23 | 14 | 9 | 18 | 10 | 9 | 86.3 | 73 |
| Andrews | 11 | 85 | 119 | 94 | 99 | 29 | 27 | 10 | 3 | 11 | 4 | 2 | 2 | 0 | 1 | 77.4 | 16 |
| Angelina | 149 | 406 | 779 | 823 | 806 | 221 | 166 | 89 | 49 | 48 | 15 | 25 | 24 | 11 | 11 | 80.0 | 95 |
| Aransas | 17 | 0 | 287 | 299 | 262 | 58 | 76 | 23 | 11 | 8 | 7 | 7 | 9 | 4 | 8 | 70.5 | 43 |
| Archer | 1 | 0 | 75 | 71 | 66 | 14 | 9 | 7 | 12 | 3 | 5 | 0 | 0 | 2 | 0 | 66.5 | 16 |
| Armstrong | 0 | 0 | 31 | 24 | 19 | 2 | 4 | 1 | 1 | 0 | 0 | 2 | 0 | 0 | 0 | 74.9 | 7 |
| Atascosa | 26 | 67 | 303 | 306 | 314 | 83 | 83 | 32 | 13 | 13 | 17 | 3 | 5 | 5 | 4 | 89.8 | 83 |
| Austin | 10 | 32 | 244 | 272 | 285 | 109 | 61 | 17 | 6 | 11 | 5 | 8 | 7 | 5 | 2 | 77.6 | 50 |
| Bailey | 6 | 31 | 60 | 55 | 56 | 16 | 10 | 1 | 6 | 5 | 1 | 5 | 1 | 4 | 0 | 317.9 | 281 |
| Bandera | 4 | 0 | 146 | 143 | 160 | 47 | 42 | 9 | 9 | 9 | 4 | 3 | 3 | 1 | 2 | 63.8 | 24 |
| Bastrop | 21 | 36 | 371 | 446 | 451 | 129 | 109 | 27 | 25 | 31 | 6 | 12 | 3 | 7 | 10 | 92.8 | 185 |
| Baylor | 3 | 49 | 67 | 64 | 79 | 28 | 19 | 7 | 0 | 4 | 2 | 5 | 0 | 0 | 0 | 72.4 | 4 |
| Bee | 19 | 69 | 204 | 227 | 246 | 71 | 42 | 15 | 9 | 13 | 14 | 7 | 6 | 7 | 5 | 83.5 | 57 |
| Bell | 676 | 961 | 1,463 | 1,554 | 1,540 | 442 | 355 | 86 | 70 | 70 | 68 | 29 | 39 | 26 | 24 | 112.2 | 1,109 |
| Bexar | 3,441 | 6,309 | 10,108 | 10,184 | 9,995 | 2,817 | 2,094 | 722 | 412 | 449 | 500 | 167 | 245 | 144 | 147 | 97.9 | 7,969 |
| Blanco | 3 | 0 | 79 | 104 | 111 | 30 | 22 | 19 | 8 | 5 | 4 | 2 | 2 | 1 | 0 | 71.9 | 12 |
| Borden | 0 | 0 | 6 | 3 | 4 | 1 | 2 | 1 | 0 | 0 | 0 | 0 | 0 | 0 | 0 | 27.6 | 2 |
| Bosque | 9 | 40 | 255 | 278 | 276 | 114 | 53 | 22 | 14 | 11 | 6 | 11 | 5 | 4 | 3 | 76.2 | 15 |
| Bowie | 237 | 954 | 910 | 987 | 984 | 286 | 215 | 77 | 45 | 58 | 30 | 24 | 21 | 15 | 12 | 64.6 | 34 |
| Brazoria | 168 | 249 | 1,540 | 1,607 | 1,692 | 471 | 410 | 93 | 95 | 93 | 59 | 26 | 38 | 20 | 38 | 85.0 | 350 |
| Brazos | 330 | 427 | 678 | 739 | 748 | 223 | 161 | 56 | 42 | 40 | 31 | 18 | 17 | 10 | 10 | 59.8 | 536 |
| Brewster | 10 | 40 | 69 | 79 | 81 | 18 | 16 | 2 | 7 | 5 | 0 | 6 | 3 | 2 | 3 | 68.3 | 18 |
| Briscoe | 0 | 0 | 23 | 19 | 21 | 8 | 5 | 2 | 2 | 1 | 0 | 0 | 0 | 0 | 0 | 132.3 | 21 |
| Brooks | 3 | 0 | 101 | 69 | 71 | 29 | 13 | 4 | 4 | 3 | 5 | 1 | 0 | 1 | 0 | 96.6 | 20 |
| Brown | 65 | 218 | 464 | 466 | 451 | 121 | 109 | 54 | 18 | 31 | 20 | 10 | 1 | 5 | 4 | 67.1 | 25 |
| Burleson | 3 | 25 | 141 | 162 | 144 | 33 | 42 | 9 | 15 | 4 | 2 | 3 | 8 | 2 | 2 | 71.2 | 27 |
| Burnet | 37 | 42 | 350 | 376 | 411 | 101 | 105 | 30 | 27 | 28 | 17 | 11 | 15 | 4 | 3 | 87.8 | 85 |
| Caldwell | 12 | 30 | 279 | 269 | 283 | 65 | 62 | 18 | 17 | 19 | 14 | 2 | 11 | 4 | 6 | 84.9 | 78 |
| Calhoun | 22 | 49 | 176 | 152 | 169 | 43 | 40 | 13 | 12 | 14 | 6 | 2 | 4 | 3 | 0 | 85.1 | 44 |
| Callahan | 3 | 0 | 147 | 150 | 143 | 44 | 42 | 10 | 12 | 4 | 3 | 3 | 0 | 1 | 0 | 56.1 | 6 |
| Cameron | 442 | 1,207 | 1,747 | 1,808 | 1,996 | 573 | 438 | 123 | 87 | 63 | 112 | 56 | 19 | 42 | 20 | 121.2 | 878 |
| Camp | 9 | 43 | 145 | 171 | 132 | 41 | 30 | 8 | 4 | 14 | 3 | 4 | 2 | 2 | 3 | 83.4 | 15 |
| Carson | 0 | 0 | 67 | 62 | 62 | 16 | 15 | 2 | 4 | 7 | 1 | 1 | 1 | 0 | 1 | 66.1 | 3 |
| Cass | 15 | 90 | 382 | 392 | 380 | 99 | 98 | 40 | 24 | 18 | 10 | 15 | 8 | 3 | 1 | 58.8 | 8 |
| Castro | 7 | 41 | 63 | 59 | 71 | 18 | 13 | 6 | 5 | 8 | 5 | 1 | 3 | 1 | 0 | 83.0 | 7 |
| Chambers | 3 | 39 | 176 | 192 | 192 | 58 | 43 | 11 | 14 | 14 | 12 | 3 | 3 | 2 | 2 | 61.7 | 33 |
| Cherokee | 74 | 104 | 557 | 500 | 542 | 180 | 117 | 58 | 24 | 26 | 13 | 10 | 6 | 6 | 8 | 86.7 | 43 |
| Childress | 7 | 49 | 87 | 92 | 88 | 23 | 22 | 8 | 3 | 7 | 6 | 4 | 3 | 0 | 1 | 96.3 | 5 |
| Clay | 4 | 32 | 108 | 110 | 91 | 26 | 21 | 11 | 1 | 4 | 3 | 4 | 0 | 1 | 2 | 44.5 | 11 |
| Cochran | 1 | 18 | 41 | 42 | 45 | 9 | 9 | 3 | 2 | 2 | 3 | 1 | 1 | 0 | 1 | 88.7 | 1 |

| County | Patient Care, 2003 | | Total Deaths | | | Leading Causes of Death by County, 2001 | | | | | | | | | | Misc., 2001 | |
|---|---|---|---|---|---|---|---|---|---|---|---|---|---|---|---|---|---|
| | Physicians | Hospital Beds* | 1999 | 2000 | 2001 | Heart Disease | Cancer | Cerebrovascular | Accidents | Pulmonary | Diabetes | Pneumonia | Alzheimer's | Kidney Disease | Suicides | Pregnancy Rate* | Abortions |
| Coke | 3 | 0 | 64 | 42 | 63 | 24 | 12 | 2 | 1 | 7 | 2 | 0 | 1 | 0 | 1 | 63.3 | 15 |
| Coleman | 4 | 46 | 163 | 157 | 145 | 43 | 32 | 9 | 5 | 11 | 5 | 8 | 6 | 7 | 1 | 68.7 | 7 |
| Collin | 749 | 1,016 | 1,654 | 1,812 | 1,945 | 492 | 481 | 131 | 116 | 90 | 52 | 58 | 41 | 30 | 37 | 87.2 | 1,289 |
| Collingswth | 4 | 16 | 49 | 47 | 53 | 19 | 12 | 2 | 2 | 2 | 0 | 0 | 3 | 0 | 3 | 60.3 | 6 |
| Colorado | 27 | 103 | 277 | 266 | 290 | 98 | 57 | 16 | 12 | 9 | 13 | 10 | 4 | 2 | 2 | 74.6 | 25 |
| Comal | 120 | 132 | 653 | 639 | 668 | 160 | 147 | 57 | 43 | 30 | 28 | 9 | 28 | 5 | 7 | 81.9 | 169 |
| Comanche | 14 | 50 | 212 | 209 | 203 | 51 | 33 | 15 | 13 | 5 | 5 | 8 | 3 | 13 | 1 | 69.3 | 9 |
| Concho | 2 | 16 | 32 | 36 | 39 | 9 | 7 | 7 | 1 | 1 | 2 | 2 | 2 | 0 | 0 | 41.3 | 2 |
| Cooke | 23 | 99 | 380 | 380 | 383 | 120 | 86 | 40 | 16 | 14 | 11 | 8 | 12 | 9 | 1 | 78.7 | 46 |
| Coryell | 21 | 55 | 326 | 354 | 329 | 103 | 70 | 15 | 13 | 15 | 14 | 9 | 9 | 6 | 6 | 56.8 | 184 |
| Cottle | 0 | 0 | 29 | 38 | 25 | 8 | 9 | 2 | 1 | 1 | 0 | 0 | 0 | 2 | 0 | 59.6 | 3 |
| Crane | 4 | 28 | 38 | 36 | 28 | 3 | 3 | 3 | 1 | 2 | 5 | 2 | 4 | 2 | 1 | 56.1 | 14 |
| Crockett | 1 | 0 | 50 | 40 | 33 | 3 | 8 | 1 | 6 | 3 | 2 | 2 | 0 | 0 | 0 | 77.7 | 6 |
| Crosby | 3 | 49 | 85 | 84 | 75 | 21 | 11 | 7 | 8 | 5 | 4 | 1 | 2 | 0 | 0 | 83.2 | 16 |
| Culberson | 3 | 25 | 22 | 23 | 21 | 10 | 3 | 0 | 1 | 3 | 0 | 0 | 0 | 0 | 0 | 78.9 | 6 |
| Dallam | 8 | 0 | 63 | 48 | 40 | 10 | 8 | 3 | 2 | 3 | 2 | 0 | 0 | 3 | 0 | 66.8 | 7 |
| Dallas | 5,515 | 7,910 | 13,518 | 13,966 | 14,063 | 3,932 | 3,177 | 943 | 716 | 652 | 357 | 316 | 325 | 199 | 224 | 100.8 | 10,739 |
| Dawson | 10 | 44 | 146 | 147 | 157 | 36 | 37 | 9 | 5 | 4 | 12 | 6 | 3 | 4 | 0 | 79.9 | 10 |
| Deaf Smith | 11 | 40 | 164 | 153 | 158 | 40 | 24 | 12 | 7 | 12 | 6 | 10 | 8 | 4 | 3 | 97.1 | 18 |
| Delta | 1 | 0 | 83 | 78 | 59 | 15 | 14 | 2 | 1 | 2 | 3 | 4 | 2 | 1 | 0 | 58.0 | 2 |
| Denton | 521 | 565 | 1,662 | 1,751 | 1,805 | 448 | 410 | 103 | 116 | 126 | 69 | 37 | 45 | 13 | 28 | 77.4 | 1,194 |
| DeWitt | 12 | 60 | 259 | 280 | 253 | 101 | 47 | 10 | 8 | 8 | 5 | 4 | 8 | 1 | 2 | 71.4 | 27 |
| Dickens | 1 | 0 | 37 | 41 | 44 | 17 | 8 | 1 | 2 | 2 | 3 | 1 | 2 | 1 | 1 | 94.3 | 9 |
| Dimmit | 11 | 48 | 98 | 104 | 92 | 27 | 17 | 8 | 3 | 6 | 5 | 7 | 0 | 0 | 0 | 102.9 | 22 |
| Donley | 1 | 0 | 66 | 53 | 55 | 21 | 6 | 3 | 3 | 7 | 3 | 2 | 2 | 0 | 0 | 49.0 | 2 |
| Duval | 3 | 0 | 79 | 133 | 137 | 42 | 29 | 6 | 13 | 3 | 12 | 2 | 2 | 4 | 0 | 84.9 | 26 |
| Eastland | 12 | 83 | 319 | 291 | 312 | 85 | 64 | 30 | 12 | 30 | 8 | 15 | 4 | 6 | 2 | 65.2 | 15 |
| Ector | 188 | 503 | 954 | 1,015 | 965 | 263 | 218 | 53 | 44 | 113 | 23 | 27 | 16 | 5 | 13 | 92.0 | 306 |
| Edwards | 1 | 0 | 16 | 14 | 15 | 3 | 2 | 1 | 4 | 0 | 0 | 0 | 0 | 1 | 1 | 76.3 | 5 |
| Ellis | 76 | 122 | 860 | 859 | 936 | 273 | 215 | 72 | 30 | 51 | 33 | 20 | 35 | 11 | 15 | 81.7 | 240 |
| El Paso | 880 | 2,123 | 3,930 | 3,947 | 4,035 | 1,017 | 943 | 202 | 224 | 166 | 202 | 91 | 97 | 53 | 41 | 101.7 | 1,899 |
| Erath | 39 | 98 | 310 | 320 | 338 | 81 | 70 | 26 | 28 | 17 | 6 | 10 | 14 | 5 | 7 | 64.4 | 46 |
| Falls | 11 | 44 | 247 | 226 | 242 | 77 | 61 | 14 | 14 | 9 | 6 | 12 | 2 | 2 | 3 | 51.2 | 37 |
| Fannin | 26 | 75 | 411 | 449 | 411 | 149 | 67 | 30 | 21 | 22 | 8 | 26 | 6 | 7 | 9 | 70.3 | 38 |
| Fayette | 22 | 50 | 299 | 316 | 317 | 122 | 54 | 18 | 10 | 20 | 4 | 18 | 4 | 6 | 2 | 76.4 | 17 |
| Fisher | 2 | 14 | 52 | 67 | 59 | 26 | 10 | 3 | 2 | 3 | 2 | 0 | 1 | 1 | 1 | 35.4 | 1 |
| Floyd | 4 | 27 | 88 | 94 | 95 | 33 | 24 | 6 | 4 | 4 | 3 | 2 | 5 | 1 | 0 | 77.1 | 6 |
| Foard | 0 | 0 | 24 | 22 | 15 | 5 | 3 | 3 | 1 | 0 | 0 | 0 | 0 | 1 | 0 | 59.5 | 2 |
| Fort Bend | 341 | 427 | 1,380 | 1,375 | 1,533 | 415 | 373 | 120 | 88 | 42 | 55 | 24 | 33 | 31 | 3 | 74.3 | 865 |
| Franklin | 9 | 49 | 108 | 90 | 110 | 28 | 29 | 15 | 5 | 5 | 2 | 0 | 1 | 3 | 2 | 80.3 | 21 |
| Freestone | 8 | 48 | 179 | 215 | 209 | 60 | 32 | 15 | 12 | 21 | 7 | 5 | 4 | 5 | 6 | 82.2 | 27 |
| Frio | 11 | 40 | 123 | 124 | 128 | 41 | 24 | 12 | 6 | 2 | 13 | 0 | 1 | 2 | 0 | 95.2 | 28 |
| Gaines | 7 | 49 | 87 | 103 | 81 | 20 | 15 | 3 | 4 | 12 | 3 | 1 | 3 | 2 | 1 | 79.7 | 15 |
| Galveston | 678 | 1,030 | 2,087 | 2,152 | 2,183 | 589 | 469 | 143 | 91 | 115 | 94 | 39 | 52 | 43 | 41 | 79.0 | 633 |
| Garza | 2 | 0 | 51 | 62 | 57 | 21 | 13 | 4 | 4 | 8 | 1 | 0 | 1 | 0 | 2 | 90.4 | 10 |
| Gillespie | 59 | 77 | 276 | 319 | 266 | 68 | 60 | 31 | 13 | 11 | 8 | 9 | 7 | 2 | 4 | 79.8 | 22 |
| Glasscock | 0 | 0 | 5 | 4 | 4 | 0 | 1 | 0 | 0 | 0 | 2 | 0 | 0 | 0 | 0 | 68.5 | 1 |
| Goliad | 2 | 0 | 57 | 87 | 62 | 11 | 12 | 6 | 8 | 1 | 4 | 3 | 1 | 4 | 0 | 73.5 | 9 |
| Gonzales | 12 | 110 | 221 | 233 | 213 | 53 | 44 | 17 | 12 | 10 | 12 | 8 | 9 | 1 | 2 | 98.1 | 44 |
| Gray | 23 | 115 | 282 | 294 | 283 | 79 | 52 | 24 | 13 | 18 | 9 | 6 | 6 | 3 | 7 | 69.9 | 21 |
| Grayson | 216 | 664 | 1,257 | 1,301 | 1,280 | 419 | 267 | 63 | 62 | 90 | 30 | 55 | 42 | 10 | 26 | 78.3 | 170 |
| Gregg | 264 | 676 | 1,162 | 1,209 | 1,213 | 343 | 234 | 99 | 51 | 71 | 43 | 33 | 20 | 13 | 21 | 79.1 | 119 |
| Grimes | 13 | 25 | 240 | 255 | 254 | 91 | 59 | 6 | 11 | 8 | 16 | 1 | 6 | 6 | 5 | 83.9 | 52 |
| Guadalupe | 59 | 113 | 609 | 603 | 616 | 172 | 133 | 29 | 33 | 48 | 26 | 11 | 15 | 8 | 11 | 66.8 | 160 |
| Hale | 43 | 100 | 287 | 316 | 310 | 79 | 59 | 23 | 20 | 21 | 10 | 7 | 9 | 5 | 3 | 92.0 | 50 |
| Hall | 2 | 0 | 69 | 59 | 58 | 15 | 13 | 3 | 4 | 4 | 4 | 3 | 1 | 1 | 0 | 109.5 | 4 |
| Hamilton | 8 | 49 | 145 | 150 | 143 | 47 | 29 | 10 | 8 | 3 | 3 | 3 | 2 | 7 | 1 | 77.6 | 11 |
| Hansford | 3 | 28 | 57 | 63 | 56 | 14 | 9 | 4 | 7 | 2 | 1 | 3 | 3 | 2 | 0 | 73.8 | 4 |
| Hardeman | 6 | 50 | 81 | 65 | 61 | 18 | 10 | 7 | 1 | 4 | 2 | 0 | 1 | 3 | 0 | 53.1 | 1 |
| Hardin | 17 | 0 | 484 | 488 | 465 | 140 | 115 | 31 | 28 | 23 | 15 | 10 | 9 | 8 | 6 | 73.2 | 97 |
| Harris | 8,021 | 14,815 | 19,204 | 19,615 | 20,652 | 5,679 | 4,543 | 1,479 | 1,169 | 815 | 658 | 434 | 411 | 347 | 334 | 100.6 | 18,656 |
| Harrison | 52 | 149 | 611 | 613 | 641 | 165 | 145 | 62 | 32 | 53 | 27 | 12 | 15 | 4 | 10 | 61.6 | 23 |
| Hartley | 0 | 21 | 44 | 26 | 35 | 7 | 11 | 5 | 0 | 3 | 0 | 2 | 0 | 0 | 0 | 92.9 | 5 |
| Haskell | 2 | 30 | 80 | 109 | 85 | 39 | 14 | 2 | 1 | 2 | 2 | 1 | 2 | 3 | 2 | 80.9 | 4 |
| Hays | 132 | 113 | 490 | 504 | 542 | 121 | 112 | 48 | 41 | 22 | 18 | 12 | 15 | 6 | 15 | 74.7 | 412 |

| County | Patient Care, 2003 | | Total Deaths | | | Leading Causes of Death by County, 2001 | | | | | | | | | | Misc., 2001 | |
|---|---|---|---|---|---|---|---|---|---|---|---|---|---|---|---|---|---|
| | Physicians | Hospital Beds* | 1999 | 2000 | 2001 | Heart Disease | Cancer | Cerebrovascular | Accidents | Pulmonary | Diabetes | Pneumonia | Alzheimer's | Kidney Disease | Suicides | Pregnancy Rate* | Abortions |
| Hemphill | 4 | 26 | 46 | 26 | 36 | 7 | 9 | 2 | 7 | 1 | 2 | 0 | 2 | 1 | 0 | 72.9 | 4 |
| Henderson | 60 | 117 | 861 | 912 | 932 | 310 | 231 | 63 | 35 | 64 | 16 | 22 | 22 | 9 | 13 | 76.9 | 116 |
| Hidalgo | 647 | 1,475 | 2,675 | 2,724 | 2,985 | 931 | 610 | 148 | 168 | 112 | 160 | 93 | 41 | 51 | 22 | 124.7 | 1,524 |
| Hill | 27 | 141 | 438 | 362 | 430 | 135 | 85 | 39 | 26 | 23 | 9 | 7 | 12 | 3 | 3 | 91.9 | 52 |
| Hockley | 16 | 48 | 215 | 178 | 202 | 59 | 31 | 17 | 12 | 18 | 8 | 8 | 5 | 2 | 1 | 74.4 | 40 |
| Hood | 40 | 56 | 456 | 482 | 496 | 129 | 148 | 30 | 19 | 34 | 11 | 9 | 23 | 8 | 3 | 67.6 | 50 |
| Hopkins | 30 | 90 | 368 | 373 | 357 | 106 | 100 | 30 | 8 | 23 | 8 | 8 | 12 | 6 | 1 | 82.2 | 37 |
| Houston | 17 | 80 | 308 | 338 | 321 | 91 | 66 | 18 | 8 | 19 | 12 | 11 | 8 | 5 | 3 | 81.7 | 66 |
| Howard | 55 | 150 | 356 | 397 | 383 | 106 | 70 | 12 | 23 | 31 | 9 | 8 | 11 | 1 | 6 | 81.5 | 48 |
| Hudspeth | 0 | 0 | 18 | 16 | 16 | 2 | 6 | 2 | 0 | 0 | 1 | 1 | 0 | 0 | 0 | 59.6 | 3 |
| Hunt | 73 | 172 | 764 | 704 | 716 | 230 | 165 | 60 | 46 | 22 | 30 | 10 | 13 | 10 | 14 | 76.9 | 143 |
| Hutchinson | 22 | 99 | 259 | 268 | 283 | 82 | 58 | 10 | 11 | 24 | 8 | 6 | 6 | 4 | 3 | 74.0 | 9 |
| Irion | 1 | 0 | 8 | 12 | 11 | 1 | 4 | 0 | 1 | 1 | 2 | 0 | 0 | 0 | 0 | 33.2 | 1 |
| Jack | 5 | 41 | 87 | 90 | 95 | 32 | 21 | 7 | 4 | 3 | 1 | 5 | 2 | 0 | 2 | 69.0 | 6 |
| Jackson | 9 | 35 | 164 | 171 | 138 | 53 | 30 | 7 | 7 | 7 | 4 | 2 | 0 | 2 | 1 | 73.0 | 31 |
| Jasper | 35 | 86 | 395 | 422 | 353 | 123 | 70 | 26 | 22 | 16 | 16 | 8 | 11 | 2 | 7 | 73.1 | 60 |
| Jeff Davis | 1 | 0 | 24 | 23 | 24 | 12 | 2 | 1 | 3 | 1 | 2 | 0 | 0 | 1 | 0 | 61.4 | 6 |
| Jefferson | 533 | 1,953 | 2,505 | 2,616 | 2,571 | 860 | 540 | 167 | 99 | 114 | 87 | 71 | 36 | 50 | 31 | 75.1 | 562 |
| Jim Hogg | 2 | 0 | 37 | 42 | 61 | 21 | 16 | 4 | 2 | 0 | 2 | 1 | 0 | 1 | 1 | 87.0 | 9 |
| Jim Wells | 38 | 211 | 330 | 335 | 353 | 107 | 75 | 23 | 14 | 9 | 32 | 7 | 0 | 13 | 4 | 83.9 | 95 |
| Johnson | 100 | 137 | 987 | 1,042 | 1,042 | 295 | 256 | 79 | 51 | 70 | 32 | 13 | 26 | 15 | 16 | 75.5 | 200 |
| Jones | 6 | 95 | 214 | 235 | 250 | 84 | 52 | 13 | 10 | 19 | 8 | 11 | 10 | 0 | 3 | 70.2 | 17 |
| Karnes | 5 | 43 | 159 | 159 | 175 | 46 | 32 | 13 | 5 | 8 | 12 | 1 | 2 | 3 | 3 | 78.9 | 29 |
| Kaufman | 80 | 221 | 625 | 673 | 711 | 201 | 149 | 35 | 28 | 54 | 22 | 15 | 28 | 6 | 12 | 79.2 | 132 |
| Kendall | 32 | 0 | 210 | 239 | 243 | 62 | 53 | 22 | 12 | 12 | 6 | 4 | 5 | 4 | 4 | 70.2 | 31 |
| Kenedy | 0 | 0 | 3 | 5 | 19 | 0 | 3 | 2 | 1 | 0 | 0 | 0 | 0 | 0 | 0 | 98.8 | 0 |
| Kent | 0 | 0 | 12 | 17 | 17 | 7 | 3 | 0 | 12 | 2 | 2 | 1 | 0 | 0 | 4 | 106.9 | 7 |
| Kerr | 132 | 152 | 598 | 612 | 629 | 147 | 139 | 43 | 30 | 35 | 20 | 8 | 26 | 8 | 10 | 80.6 | 74 |
| Kimble | 3 | 15 | 55 | 59 | 76 | 31 | 17 | 4 | 4 | 6 | 2 | 4 | 0 | 0 | 0 | 91.3 | 5 |
| King | 0 | 0 | 1 | 2 | 3 | 0 | 1 | 0 | 0 | 0 | 0 | 0 | 0 | 0 | 0 | 42.3 | 1 |
| Kinney | 1 | 0 | 35 | 40 | 42 | 15 | 9 | 2 | 3 | 0 | 3 | 1 | 1 | 1 | 0 | 75.1 | 1 |
| Kleberg | 21 | 100 | 216 | 236 | 273 | 95 | 61 | 16 | 7 | 16 | 16 | 6 | 1 | 3 | 2 | 81.4 | 88 |
| Knox | 3 | 28 | 70 | 65 | 73 | 22 | 11 | 9 | 2 | 1 | 1 | 5 | 1 | 1 | 0 | 60.5 | 2 |
| Lamar | 100 | 435 | 601 | 582 | 572 | 197 | 126 | 41 | 20 | 23 | 10 | 25 | 9 | 10 | 3 | 70.2 | 76 |
| Lamb | 6 | 75 | 177 | 197 | 169 | 52 | 30 | 10 | 10 | 10 | 8 | 5 | 3 | 2 | 0 | 81.4 | 12 |
| Lampasas | 8 | 25 | 150 | 182 | 193 | 54 | 48 | 12 | 14 | 11 | 6 | 3 | 9 | 4 | 7 | 76.8 | 30 |
| La Salle | 3 | 0 | 54 | 48 | 50 | 16 | 8 | 4 | 3 | 1 | 0 | 2 | 0 | 2 | 0 | 98.9 | 11 |
| Lavaca | 21 | 71 | 249 | 279 | 273 | 92 | 52 | 26 | 13 | 14 | 4 | 9 | 10 | 3 | 4 | 78.2 | 11 |
| Lee | 3 | 0 | 177 | 148 | 132 | 54 | 22 | 10 | 11 | 1 | 7 | 3 | 5 | 3 | 0 | 78.7 | 33 |
| Leon | 5 | 0 | 211 | 175 | 212 | 66 | 52 | 9 | 19 | 12 | 3 | 2 | 1 | 3 | 5 | 73.5 | 18 |
| Liberty | 48 | 142 | 651 | 622 | 702 | 184 | 175 | 40 | 53 | 53 | 19 | 2 | 10 | 12 | 10 | 69.2 | 105 |
| Limestone | 21 | 79 | 320 | 295 | 291 | 77 | 56 | 27 | 15 | 16 | 10 | 19 | 5 | 4 | 2 | 89.6 | 48 |
| Lipscomb | 0 | 0 | 31 | 43 | 30 | 15 | 4 | 2 | 2 | 0 | 0 | 1 | 0 | 2 | 0 | 70.8 | 2 |
| Live Oak | 4 | 0 | 116 | 120 | 96 | 36 | 18 | 7 | 2 | 8 | 4 | 2 | 4 | 0 | 0 | 74.9 | 18 |
| Llano | 14 | 30 | 249 | 265 | 259 | 56 | 70 | 15 | 14 | 22 | 4 | 19 | 5 | 2 | 4 | 81.0 | 17 |
| Loving | 0 | 0 | 1 | 0 | 0 | 0 | 0 | 0 | 0 | 0 | 0 | 0 | 0 | 0 | 0 | * | 1 |
| Lubbock | 709 | 1,859 | 1,985 | 1,925 | 1,961 | 549 | 383 | 134 | 122 | 144 | 9 | 52 | 30 | 24 | 36 | 75.9 | 638 |
| Lynn | 2 | 24 | 72 | 72 | 55 | 16 | 15 | 5 | 0 | 2 | 2 | 1 | 0 | 0 | 0 | 60.2 | 4 |
| Madison | 7 | 25 | 127 | 159 | 142 | 51 | 35 | 10 | 8 | 8 | 4 | 1 | 6 | 2 | 2 | 98.9 | 25 |
| Marion | 5 | 0 | 135 | 152 | 152 | 41 | 36 | 9 | 5 | 10 | 7 | 3 | 7 | 3 | 2 | 62.9 | 3 |
| Martin | 3 | 25 | 43 | 64 | 52 | 21 | 9 | 2 | 0 | 8 | 2 | 2 | 0 | 1 | 1 | 80.1 | 7 |
| Mason | 1 | 0 | 59 | 47 | 57 | 17 | 11 | 5 | 2 | 1 | 3 | 0 | 5 | 0 | 1 | 71.4 | 6 |
| Matagorda | 39 | 117 | 357 | 384 | 367 | 112 | 75 | 27 | 22 | 27 | 11 | 8 | 9 | 6 | 5 | 77.3 | 36 |
| Maverick | 38 | 77 | 275 | 263 | 266 | 78 | 62 | 19 | 15 | 11 | 24 | 7 | 1 | 4 | 0 | 112.0 | 74 |
| McCulloch | 6 | 49 | 145 | 130 | 119 | 40 | 26 | 8 | 1 | 8 | 6 | 6 | 2 | 4 | 1 | 67.5 | 7 |
| McLennan | 393 | 566 | 2,023 | 1,990 | 1,951 | 499 | 439 | 170 | 64 | 86 | 81 | 46 | 68 | 34 | 22 | 78.3 | 633 |
| McMullen | 0 | 0 | 7 | 9 | 3 | 0 | 1 | 0 | 0 | 0 | 0 | 0 | 0 | 1 | 0 | 54.1 | 3 |
| Medina | 14 | 25 | 275 | 346 | 313 | 93 | 71 | 23 | 11 | 17 | 16 | 10 | 1 | 5 | 6 | 81.1 | 68 |
| Menard | 1 | 0 | 42 | 35 | 32 | 13 | 6 | 2 | 1 | 0 | 0 | 1 | 0 | 0 | 0 | 75.2 | 3 |
| Midland | 178 | 520 | 839 | 893 | 922 | 268 | 214 | 53 | 40 | 55 | 23 | 77 | 19 | 8 | 14 | 80.8 | 268 |
| Milam | 10 | 69 | 301 | 306 | 306 | 73 | 72 | 24 | 20 | 15 | 12 | 5 | 20 | 2 | 1 | 90.2 | 53 |
| Mills | 2 | 0 | 72 | 65 | 95 | 24 | 27 | 9 | 1 | 6 | 4 | 1 | 4 | 1 | 0 | 58.1 | 3 |
| Mitchell | 5 | 39 | 106 | 134 | 100 | 38 | 11 | 12 | 7 | 10 | 1 | 3 | 0 | 1 | 0 | 70.0 | 9 |
| Montague | 13 | 87 | 326 | 290 | 278 | 78 | 47 | 23 | 8 | 19 | 13 | 10 | 5 | 4 | 3 | 71.7 | 16 |
| Montgomery | 349 | 643 | 1,946 | 2,038 | 2,104 | 595 | 515 | 102 | 137 | 121 | 57 | 33 | 52 | 31 | 41 | 81.3 | 502 |
| Moore | 16 | 60 | 121 | 141 | 132 | 34 | 30 | 5 | 15 | 4 | 7 | 3 | 2 | 3 | 2 | 93.4 | 16 |

| County | Patient Care, 2003 | | Total Deaths | | | Leading Causes of Death by County, 2001 | | | | | | | | | | Misc., 2001 | |
|---|---|---|---|---|---|---|---|---|---|---|---|---|---|---|---|---|---|
| | Physicians | Hospital Beds* | 1999 | 2000 | 2001 | Heart Disease | Cancer | Cerebrovascular | Accidents | Pulmonary | Diabetes | Pneumonia | Alzheimer's | Kidney Disease | Suicides | Pregnancy Rate* | Abortions |
| Morris | 3 | 0 | 155 | 205 | 190 | 56 | 50 | 15 | 12 | 8 | 10 | 4 | 1 | 4 | 6 | 69.0 | 20 |
| Motley | 2 | 0 | 23 | 21 | 19 | 5 | 6 | 3 | 0 | 0 | 0 | 0 | 2 | 0 | 0 | 80.6 | 3 |
| Nacdoches | 124 | 346 | 517 | 581 | 515 | 172 | 110 | 43 | 21 | 23 | 17 | 10 | 10 | 7 | 3 | 60.2 | 95 |
| Navarro | 45 | 162 | 536 | 554 | 539 | 142 | 116 | 48 | 29 | 23 | 18 | 16 | 25 | 5 | 6 | 87.5 | 92 |
| Newton | 7 | 0 | 150 | 136 | 142 | 51 | 29 | 6 | 6 | 13 | 4 | 3 | 3 | 3 | 1 | 57.5 | 16 |
| Nolan | 16 | 85 | 204 | 207 | 179 | 55 | 36 | 13 | 7 | 11 | 8 | 11 | 3 | 1 | 1 | 69.5 | 10 |
| Nueces | 740 | 1,808 | 2,428 | 2,535 | 2,524 | 665 | 538 | 166 | 86 | 154 | 136 | 70 | 47 | 40 | 28 | 88.4 | 1,018 |
| Ochiltree | 6 | 49 | 78 | 73 | 70 | 20 | 12 | 3 | 4 | 10 | 3 | 0 | 2 | 1 | 3 | 83.6 | 2 |
| Oldham | 0 | 0 | 23 | 14 | 22 | 8 | 4 | 1 | 0 | 4 | 0 | 1 | 1 | 0 | 0 | 43.4 | 3 |
| Orange | 46 | 239 | 832 | 831 | 911 | 298 | 216 | 69 | 55 | 61 | 31 | 21 | 13 | 9 | 5 | 66.5 | 127 |
| Palo Pinto | 26 | 99 | 314 | 340 | 399 | 114 | 79 | 33 | 20 | 37 | 12 | 8 | 4 | 4 | 10 | 73.9 | 10 |
| Panola | 13 | 49 | 255 | 236 | 251 | 75 | 48 | 17 | 18 | 15 | 14 | 4 | 14 | 2 | 4 | 61.9 | 6 |
| Parker | 58 | 99 | 739 | 719 | 741 | 212 | 171 | 53 | 36 | 42 | 25 | 12 | 22 | 11 | 10 | 64.9 | 74 |
| Parmer | 3 | 25 | 79 | 88 | 85 | 30 | 13 | 7 | 3 | 7 | 0 | 7 | 2 | 1 | 1 | 75.9 | 7 |
| Pecos | 11 | 40 | 120 | 97 | 128 | 30 | 33 | 7 | 8 | 2 | 5 | 3 | 5 | 2 | 0 | 74.1 | 12 |
| Polk | 25 | 35 | 486 | 559 | 530 | 161 | 129 | 22 | 26 | 18 | 17 | 7 | 12 | 7 | 7 | 76.9 | 33 |
| Potter | 421 | 903 | 1,201 | 1,146 | 1,199 | 321 | 242 | 77 | 59 | 90 | 36 | 23 | 35 | 14 | 19 | 96.4 | 190 |
| Presidio | 1 | 0 | 53 | 48 | 27 | 6 | 9 | 0 | 0 | 1 | 2 | 3 | 0 | 1 | 0 | 99.2 | 4 |
| Rains | 1 | 0 | 118 | 100 | 112 | 30 | 28 | 9 | 10 | 4 | 2 | 2 | 4 | 1 | 3 | 64.2 | 9 |
| Randall | 72 | 4 | 692 | 712 | 716 | 177 | 174 | 40 | 42 | 71 | 13 | 7 | 20 | 8 | 19 | 61.2 | 181 |
| Reagan | 2 | 14 | 26 | 29 | 21 | 8 | 3 | 0 | 0 | 1 | 3 | 1 | 0 | 0 | 0 | 53.4 | 2 |
| Real | 3 | 0 | 49 | 28 | 40 | 13 | 9 | 0 | 3 | 4 | 1 | 2 | 1 | 0 | 0 | 59.4 | 5 |
| Red River | 9 | 49 | 210 | 237 | 224 | 85 | 49 | 11 | 14 | 11 | 7 | 5 | 3 | 5 | 2 | 66.3 | 16 |
| Reeves | 10 | 49 | 115 | 105 | 100 | 26 | 24 | 6 | 8 | 5 | 5 | 5 | 1 | 4 | 1 | 87.3 | 9 |
| Refugio | 2 | 20 | 95 | 93 | 90 | 23 | 25 | 4 | 4 | 8 | 6 | 0 | 0 | 2 | 1 | 81.1 | 17 |
| Roberts | 0 | 0 | 8 | 9 | 2 | 1 | 0 | 0 | 0 | 0 | 0 | 0 | 1 | 0 | 0 | 31.4 | 0 |
| Robertson | 4 | 0 | 220 | 213 | 209 | 74 | 43 | 11 | 12 | 7 | 4 | 5 | 3 | 8 | 3 | 80.5 | 31 |
| Rockwall | 51 | 97 | 249 | 307 | 302 | 98 | 63 | 19 | 17 | 20 | 3 | 8 | 7 | 6 | 6 | 84.2 | 87 |
| Runnels | 6 | 50 | 134 | 157 | 137 | 43 | 35 | 8 | 6 | 2 | 6 | 4 | 6 | 4 | 0 | 75.0 | 10 |
| Rusk | 28 | 158 | 550 | 530 | 542 | 188 | 115 | 31 | 31 | 20 | 8 | 21 | 7 | 5 | 4 | 69.0 | 36 |
| Sabine | 4 | 36 | 180 | 169 | 178 | 57 | 45 | 14 | 7 | 7 | 17 | 2 | 3 | 1 | 0 | 65.7 | 10 |
| S. Augustine | 3 | 25 | 145 | 121 | 109 | 36 | 21 | 8 | 7 | 11 | 2 | 2 | 1 | 1 | 0 | 73.1 | 5 |
| San Jacinto | 3 | 0 | 214 | 196 | 213 | 53 | 59 | 9 | 17 | 13 | 4 | 4 | 2 | 4 | 1 | 73.9 | 19 |
| SanPatricio | 32 | 75 | 558 | 523 | 533 | 141 | 121 | 45 | 28 | 24 | 30 | 13 | 13 | 10 | 3 | 91.6 | 147 |
| San Saba | 3 | 0 | 63 | 73 | 97 | 39 | 17 | 9 | 4 | 4 | 3 | 2 | 0 | 3 | 0 | 80.9 | 10 |
| Schleicher | 1 | 14 | 31 | 30 | 30 | 8 | 8 | 0 | 0 | 2 | 4 | 0 | 0 | 0 | 0 | 87.8 | 1 |
| Scurry | 13 | 99 | 192 | 170 | 178 | 38 | 39 | 11 | 9 | 11 | 4 | 5 | 4 | 3 | 3 | 82.7 | 20 |
| Shackelford | 2 | 0 | 41 | 41 | 34 | 10 | 10 | 0 | 3 | 1 | 1 | 2 | 0 | 0 | 2 | 72.7 | 1 |
| Shelby | 12 | 54 | 332 | 317 | 295 | 87 | 55 | 28 | 20 | 16 | 16 | 8 | 2 | 1 | 1 | 81.8 | 4 |
| Sherman | 1 | 0 | 20 | 24 | 30 | 5 | 7 | 2 | 4 | 2 | 1 | 1 | 1 | 2 | 0 | 86.6 | 13 |
| Smith | 598 | 1,112 | 1,638 | 1,700 | 1,819 | 537 | 383 | 138 | 96 | 91 | 52 | 60 | 42 | 37 | 22 | 80.0 | 306 |
| Somervell | 9 | 16 | 66 | 72 | 81 | 18 | 8 | 9 | 5 | 7 | 3 | 3 | 8 | 1 | 1 | 73.7 | 4 |
| Starr | 17 | 49 | 229 | 249 | 272 | 100 | 44 | 11 | 14 | 13 | 10 | 5 | 2 | 5 | 3 | 121.1 | 66 |
| Stephens | 7 | 40 | 118 | 105 | 112 | 33 | 22 | 4 | 11 | 10 | 3 | 6 | 0 | 2 | 1 | 89.5 | 5 |
| Sterling | 0 | 0 | 12 | 5 | 12 | 6 | 1 | 0 | 1 | 0 | 0 | 1 | 0 | 0 | 0 | 65.6 | 3 |
| Stonewall | 0 | 20 | 34 | 21 | 30 | 11 | 5 | 2 | 1 | 3 | 0 | 3 | 1 | 0 | 0 | 131.2 | 14 |
| Sutton | 2 | 12 | 41 | 40 | 25 | 9 | 5 | 2 | 0 | 0 | 1 | 2 | 0 | 0 | 1 | 96.4 | 6 |
| Swisher | 3 | 30 | 80 | 81 | 76 | 21 | 12 | 9 | 4 | 8 | 3 | 2 | 3 | 1 | 2 | 104.8 | 5 |
| Tarrant | 2,568 | 4,478 | 9,282 | 9,351 | 9,679 | 2,682 | 2,067 | 775 | 446 | 504 | 300 | 180 | 261 | 129 | 143 | 91.1 | 4,868 |
| Taylor | 265 | 710 | 1,213 | 1,142 | 1,176 | 311 | 232 | 89 | 54 | 72 | 49 | 40 | 40 | 15 | 11 | 73.4 | 133 |
| Terrell | 0 | 0 | 20 | 12 | 4 | 1 | 0 | 0 | 0 | 2 | 0 | 0 | 0 | 0 | 0 | 133.7 | 20 |
| Terry | 9 | 45 | 136 | 117 | 120 | 45 | 23 | 7 | 10 | 3 | 4 | 2 | 3 | 2 | 0 | 87.2 | 19 |
| Throckmortn | 1 | 30 | 25 | 22 | 25 | 7 | 3 | 1 | 0 | 4 | 1 | 1 | 0 | 0 | 1 | 65.8 | 1 |
| Titus | 49 | 165 | 280 | 266 | 287 | 72 | 71 | 24 | 18 | 23 | 10 | 6 | 2 | 8 | 2 | 95.6 | 50 |
| Tom Green | 211 | 608 | 992 | 1,024 | 1,014 | 290 | 206 | 79 | 37 | 62 | 35 | 26 | 10 | 13 | 14 | 74.2 | 211 |
| Travis | 2,035 | 2,207 | 3,871 | 3,998 | 4,002 | 972 | 872 | 248 | 274 | 185 | 130 | 71 | 96 | 74 | 102 | 92.2 | 4,910 |
| Trinity | 6 | 30 | 215 | 195 | 195 | 58 | 47 | 11 | 12 | 8 | 6 | 4 | 5 | 4 | 3 | 74.4 | 15 |
| Tyler | 12 | 49 | 236 | 238 | 253 | 106 | 60 | 11 | 9 | 11 | 6 | 1 | 5 | 7 | 3 | 88.1 | 99 |
| Upshur | 12 | 0 | 370 | 467 | 413 | 112 | 112 | 47 | 16 | 17 | 10 | 8 | 4 | 3 | 6 | 74.4 | 27 |
| Upton | 2 | 29 | 30 | 33 | 45 | 25 | 7 | 2 | 1 | 2 | 0 | 2 | 0 | 0 | 0 | 57.7 | 0 |
| Uvalde | 22 | 66 | 203 | 223 | 256 | 61 | 58 | 17 | 20 | 17 | 14 | 9 | 3 | 3 | 1 | 105.4 | 63 |
| Val Verde | 36 | 93 | 326 | 311 | 315 | 99 | 66 | 12 | 7 | 14 | 2 | 9 | 2 | 9 | 6 | 99.2 | 98 |
| Van Zandt | 15 | 52 | 594 | 576 | 589 | 198 | 119 | 43 | 23 | 35 | 14 | 28 | 15 | 5 | 10 | 72.5 | 64 |
| Victoria | 196 | 772 | 680 | 661 | 698 | 228 | 130 | 40 | 33 | 33 | 27 | 8 | 18 | 6 | 12 | 83.8 | 128 |
| Walker | 62 | 127 | 444 | 435 | 419 | 117 | 86 | 35 | 23 | 18 | 13 | 7 | 8 | 7 | 11 | 59.3 | 138 |

| County | Patient Care, 2003 | | Total Deaths | | | Leading Causes of Death by County, 2001 | | | | | | | | | | Misc., 2001 | |
|---|---|---|---|---|---|---|---|---|---|---|---|---|---|---|---|---|---|
| | Physicians | Hospital Beds* | 1999 | 2000 | 2001 | Heart Disease | Cancer | Cerebrovascular | Accidents | Pulmonary | Diabetes | Pneumonia | Alzheimer's | Kidney Disease | Suicides | Pregnancy Rate* | Abortions |
| Waller | 6 | 0 | 218 | 225 | 239 | 71 | 47 | 23 | 17 | 11 | 7 | 7 | 7 | 9 | 3 | 69.4 | 86 |
| Ward | 7 | 49 | 114 | 115 | 83 | 17 | 17 | 8 | 5 | 7 | 4 | 3 | 3 | 2 | 2 | 74.3 | 8 |
| Washington | 31 | 60 | 320 | 355 | 340 | 101 | 70 | 26 | 13 | 24 | 8 | 21 | 10 | 2 | 3 | 72.9 | 56 |
| Webb | 188 | 621 | 856 | 904 | 1,016 | 268 | 188 | 73 | 71 | 16 | 67 | 27 | 8 | 9 | 12 | 143.8 | 865 |
| Wharton | 60 | 210 | 410 | 345 | 424 | 131 | 95 | 34 | 19 | 20 | 17 | 10 | 6 | 9 | 3 | 74.7 | 40 |
| Wheeler | 7 | 59 | 87 | 66 | 99 | 35 | 15 | 7 | 4 | 9 | 3 | 1 | 1 | 0 | 2 | 52.2 | 6 |
| Wichita | 271 | 746 | 1,300 | 1,261 | 1,298 | 313 | 275 | 117 | 65 | 61 | 70 | 32 | 42 | 10 | 14 | 75.5 | 213 |
| Wilbarger | 23 | 47 | 171 | 186 | 178 | 65 | 36 | 16 | 8 | 7 | 6 | 2 | 4 | 0 | 0 | 79.3 | 18 |
| Willacy | 10 | 0 | 116 | 101 | 102 | 23 | 26 | 8 | 8 | 1 | 9 | 5 | 0 | 2 | 0 | 107.3 | 44 |
| Williamson | 261 | 291 | 1,134 | 1,186 | 1,159 | 259 | 297 | 78 | 92 | 46 | 33 | 43 | 37 | 18 | 20 | 89.7 | 711 |
| Wilson | 12 | 44 | 254 | 249 | 242 | 68 | 54 | 13 | 9 | 17 | 8 | 4 | 8 | 2 | 2 | 72.1 | 47 |
| Winkler | 5 | 25 | 87 | 82 | 77 | 30 | 13 | 7 | 6 | 4 | 2 | 2 | 0 | 0 | 5 | 76.2 | 6 |
| Wise | 29 | 85 | 411 | 437 | 395 | 128 | 91 | 23 | 28 | 30 | 12 | 3 | 7 | 4 | 8 | 71.2 | 55 |
| Wood | 29 | 80 | 493 | 492 | 525 | 161 | 96 | 38 | 23 | 29 | 11 | 16 | 6 | 8 | 7 | 75.9 | 32 |
| Yoakum | 5 | 24 | 60 | 54 | 51 | 16 | 8 | 2 | 5 | 4 | 4 | 1 | 1 | 4 | 0 | 73.7 | 8 |
| Young | 14 | 86 | 269 | 280 | 257 | 83 | 48 | 19 | 20 | 23 | 6 | 10 | 5 | 2 | 1 | 72.6 | 10 |
| Zapata | 3 | 0 | 94 | 79 | 89 | 35 | 17 | 5 | 4 | 2 | 3 | 2 | 0 | 2 | 0 | 118.1 | 31 |
| Zavala | 5 | 0 | 99 | 107 | 102 | 31 | 17 | 5 | 9 | 2 | 4 | 4 | 0 | 4 | 0 | 90.5 | 9 |

Sources: **Texas Department of Health: Vital Statistics, 2001**(by county of residence) and **Center for Health Statistics,** February 2003. **Texas State Board of Medical Examiners**, February 2003.
Physicians - All practicing licensed M.D.s and D.O.s.
*Hospital Beds - Acute Care Hospital Beds Licensed (2003), not including U.S. military and veteran's hospitals.
Definition of categories of death: Cerebrovascular - pertaining to the blood vessels of the brain; Pulmonary - bronchitis, emphysema, asthma; Kidney Disease - nephritis, nephrosis.
*Pregnancy Rate figured per 1,000 women age 15-44.
*Abortion total statewide includes abortions performed in Texas plus abortions obtained outside the state by Texas residents.

# Comparison of Birth Rates, 2001

| Country, State | Birth Rate |
|---|---|
| **Birth Rates*** | |
| *Selected states: those bordering Texas, other large states, and lowest (Vermont) and highest (Utah) states.* | |
| **TEXAS.** | **17.2** |
| Arkansas | 14.4 |
| California | 15.6 |
| Florida | 13.0 |
| Georgia | 16.3 |
| Illinois | 15.0 |
| Louisiana | 15.4 |
| Massachusetts | 13.1 |
| Michigan | 13.5 |
| New Mexico | 15.6 |
| New York | 14.0 |
| Ohio | 13.6 |
| Oklahoma | 14.6 |
| Utah | 21.7 |
| Vermont | 11.1 |
| **United States** | **14.5** |
| | |
| Afghanistan | 41.4 |
| Albania | 19.0 |
| Algeria | 22.8 |
| Angola | 46.5 |
| Argentina | 18.4 |
| Armenia | 11.5 |
| Australia | 12.9 |
| Austria | 9.7 |
| Bangladesh | 25.3 |
| Belarus | 9.6 |
| Belguim | 10.7 |
| Brazil | 18.5 |
| Canada | 11.2 |
| Chile | 16.8 |
| China | 16.0 |

| Country | Birth Rate |
|---|---|
| Colombia | 22.4 |
| Congo (Kinshasa) | 46.0 |
| Cuba | 12.4 |
| Czech Republic | 9.1 |
| Denmark | 12.0 |
| Egypt | 24.9 |
| El Salvador | 28.7 |
| Eritrea | 45.5 |
| Estonia | 8.7 |
| Ethiopia | 44.7 |
| Finland | 10.7 |
| France | 12.1 |
| Gaza Strip | 42.5 |
| Germany | 9.2 |
| Ghana | 29.0 |
| Greece | 9.8 |
| Guatemala | 34.6 |
| Iceland | 14.6 |
| India | 24.3 |
| Indonesia | 22.3 |
| Iran | 17.1 |
| Iraq | 34.6 |
| Ireland | 14.6 |
| Israel | 19.1 |
| Italy | 9.1 |
| Jamaica | 18.1 |
| Japan | 10.0 |
| Jordan | 25.4 |
| Lebanon | 20.2 |
| Mexico | 22.8 |
| Morocco | 24.2 |
| Netherlands | 11.9 |
| New Zealand | 14.3 |
| Nicaragua | 27.6 |
| Nigeria | 39.7 |
| Norway | 12.6 |

| Country | Birth Rate |
|---|---|
| Pakistan | 31.2 |
| Philippines | 27.4 |
| Poland | 10.2 |
| Portugal | 11.5 |
| Russia | 9.4 |
| Saudi Arabia | 37.3 |
| Senegal | 37.5 |
| Singapore | 12.8 |
| Slovakia | 10.1 |
| Slovenia | 9.3 |
| Somalia | 47.2 |
| South Africa | 21.1 |
| Spain | 9.3 |
| Sri Lanka | 16.6 |
| Sudan | 37.9 |
| Sweden | 9.9 |
| Switzerland | 10.1 |
| Syria | 30.6 |
| Taiwan | 14.3 |
| Tanzania | 39.7 |
| Trinidad/Tobago | 13.7 |
| Tunisia | 17.1 |
| Turkey | 18.3 |
| Uganda | 47.5 |
| Ukraine | 9.3 |
| United Arab Emirates | 18.1 |
| United Kingdom | 11.5 |
| Uruguay | 17.4 |
| Venezuela | 20.7 |
| Vietnam | 21.2 |
| West Bank | 35.8 |
| Yemen | 43.4 |
| Zambia | 41.5 |
| Zimbabwe | 24.7 |
| **World** | **21.4** |

*Births per 1,000 population. The data for other states are from the Statistical Abstract of the United States: 2001. The world figures are 2001 estimates from the World Factbook, Central Intelligence Agency.*

# State Institutions for Mental Health Services

*Source: Texas Department of Mental Health and Mental Retardation.*

The Texas Department of Mental Health and Mental Retardation provides services and assistance to more than 218,000 Texans each year. The agency employs about 20,000 people, and operates on an annual appropriation of $2.4 billion.

The agency's core focus is improving service quality and efficiency so that individuals with mental illness or mental retardation can lead dignified and independent lives.

The department was created in 1965 to assume the duties of what was then the Board of Texas State Hospitals and Special Schools. In that era, individuals were served predominantly in large, state-run facilities.

Today, as one of 11 agencies under the umbrella of the Texas Health and Human Services Commission, the department's role has become dual-pronged: primary service provider, and coordination, oversight and policy development.

The agency, which is overseen by a board appointed by the governor, provides services at 11 state school campuses, two state centers and eight state hospitals.

Individuals access these services through 42 community-level MHMR centers across the state, which link people with appropriate service providers.

TXMHMR delegates duties to the local authorities that serve as the "front door" for obtaining all services. These local entities implement state policy and community input to administer community-based service delivery through various providers.

Each of these quasi-governmental authorities is governed by a board of directors, manages its own budget and employs its own staff.

TXMHMR is headquartered in Austin. The mailing address is P.O. Box 12668, Austin, Texas 78711. The toll-free number for Consumer Services and Rights Protection is 1-800-252-8154.

For more information about the agency and its services, go to www.mhmr.state.tx.us.

Information in the following list includes the city where the facility is located, facility name, the executive in charge, the year it was established and the number of clients served. (MH) for mental health, (MR) for mental retardation.

## Hospitals for Persons With Mental Illness

**Austin State Hospital** — Austin; 1857; Carl Schock, superintendent; 3,323 patients.

**Big Spring State Hospital** — Big Spring; 1937; Ed Moughon, superintendent; 1,250 patients.

**Kerrville State Hospital** — Kerrville; 1950; Gloria P. Olsen, Ph.D., superintendent; 681 patients.

**Rusk State Hospital** — Rusk; 1919; Ted Debbs, superintendent; 2,034 patients.

**San Antonio State Hospital** — San Antonio; 1892; Robert C. Arizpe, superintendent; 2,703 patients.

**Terrell State Hospital** — Terrell; 1885; Fred Hale, superintendent; 2,327 patients.

**North Texas State Hospital at Vernon** — 1969; James E. Smith, superintendent; 2,933 patients*.

**North Texas State Hospital at Wichita Falls** — 1922; James E. Smith, superintendent; *combined census.

**Waco Center for Youth** — Waco; 1979; Steve Anfinson, superintendent; 217 patients.

## Schools for Persons with Mental Retardation

**Abilene State School** — Abilene; 1901; Bill Waddill, superintendent; 566 individuals.

**Austin State School** — Austin; 1917; Ray Wells; 454 individuals.

**Brenham State School** — Brenham; 1974; Richard Browder, superintendent; 461 individuals.

**Corpus Christi State School** — Corpus Christi; 1970; Gail Sharp, superintendent; 400 individuals.

**Denton State School** — Denton; 1960; Jim Sibley; 677 individuals.

**Lubbock State School** — Lubbock; 1969; Jackie Porch, superintendent; 399 individuals.

**Lufkin State School** — Lufkin; 1962; Randy Spence, superintendent; 458 individuals.

**Mexia State School** — Mexia; 1946; William H. Lowry, Ph. D., superintendent; 597 individuals.

**Richmond State School** — Richmond; 1968; Adalberto Barrera, superintendent; 570 individuals.

**San Angelo State School** — Carlsbad; 1969; Philip Baugh, superintendent; 322 individuals.

**San Antonio State School** — San Antonio; 1978; Ric Savage, superintendent; 310 individuals.

## State Centers

**El Paso State Center** — El Paso; 1974; John Mark Friedmann, director; 164 customers.

**Rio Grande State Center** — Harlingen; 1962; Sonia Hernandez-Keeble, M.S.W., director; 1,086 customers.

## Community Mental Health and Mental Retardation Centers

*(The persons whose names appear in the list below are the executive directors of the centers, unless otherwise specified.)*

**Abilene** — Betty Hardwick MHMR Center; 1971; Bill Dillard; 1,515 (MH); 273 (MR).

**Amarillo** — Texas Panhandle MHMR; 1968; Bud Schertler; 3,217 (MH); 558 (MR).

**Austin** — Austin-Travis County MHMR Center; 1967; David L. Evans; 7,046 (MH); 691 (MR).

**Beaumont** — Spindletop MHMR Services; 1967; N. Charles Harris, Ph.D.; 5,072 (MH); 818 (MR).

**Big Spring** — West Texas Centers for MHMR; 1997; Shelley Smith; 3,043 (MH); 305 (MR).

**Brownwood** — Center for Life Resources; 1969; Ghasem Nahvipour; 840 (MH); 143 (MR).

**Bryan-College Station** — MHMR Authority of Brazos Valley; 1972; Jack Leon Bawcom; 1,845 (MH); 222 (MR).

**Cleburne** — Johnson-Ellis-Navarro County MHMR Center; 1985; Joseph P. Mirisciotti; 1,195 (MH); 417 (MR).

**Conroe** — Tri-County MHMR Services; 1983; Cynthia Sill; 2,708 (MH); 403 (MR).

**Corpus Christi** — Nueces County MHMR Community Center; 1970; Wallace E. Whitworth; 3,264 (MH); 407 (MR).

**Dallas** — Dallas MetroCare; 1967; James G. Baker, M.D.; (MH included in Dallas NorthSTAR); 2,042 (MR).

**Dallas** — NorthSTAR; 1999; John Theiss, Ph.D., project director; 31,537 (MH).

**Denison** — MHMR Services of Texoma; 1974; Anthony Mattox; 1,110 (MH); 179 (MR).

**Denton** — Denton County MHMR Center; 1987; Bill Drybread; 2,392 (MH); 331 (MR).

**Edinburg** — Tropical Texas Center for MHMR; 1967; Ernesto Santos (interum); 5,420 (MH); 777 (MR).

**El Paso** — Community Center; 1968; Gary Larcenaire; 6,521 (MH); 406 (MR).

**Fort Worth** — MHMR of Tarrant County; 1969; Jim McDermott, Ph.D.; 9,607 (MH); 1,728 (MR).

**Galveston** — Gulf Coast Center; 1969; G. Michael Winburn; 3,080 (MH); 618 (MR).

**Greenville** — Hunt County MHMR; 1971; John Gill, Ph.D.

(interum); (MH included in Dallas NorthSTAR); (MR) 204.

**Houston — MHMR Authority of Harris County;** 1965; Steven Schnee, Ph.D.; 21,197 (MH); 2,868 (MR).

**Jacksonville — Anderson-Cherokee Community Enrichment Services;** 1995; Alan Lang; 1,691 (MH); 211 (MR).

**Kerrville — Hill Country Community MHMR;** 1997; Linda Parker; 3,539 (MH); 704 (MR).

**Laredo — Border Region MHMR Community Center;** 1969; Juan Sanchez; 2,458 (MH); 321 (MR).

**Longview — Sabine Valley Center;** 1970; Inman White; 2,877 (MH); 264 (MR).

**Lubbock — Lubbock Regional MHMR Center;** 1969; Danette Castle; 3,244 (MH); 701 (MR).

**Lufkin — Burke Center;** 1975; Susan L. Rushing; 2,251 (MH); 332 (MR).

**Lytle — Camino Real Community MHMR Center;** 1996; Emma Garcia; 1,783 (MH); 241 (MR).

**McKinney — LifePath Systems;** 1986; Randy Routon, Ph.D.; (MH with Dallas NorthSTAR); 271 (MR).

**Midland/Odessa — Permian Basin Community Centers for MHMR;** 1969; Larry Carroll; 2,556 (MH); 307 (MR).

**Plainview — Central Plains Center for MHMR;** 1969; Ron Trusler; 899 (MH); 155 (MR).

**Portland — Coastal Plains Community MHMR;** 1996; Charles Sportsman; 3,098 (MH); 418 (MR).

**Rosenberg — Texana MHMR Center;** 1996; George Patterson; 3,268 (MH); 740 (MR).

**Round Rock — Bluebonnet Trails Community MHMR Center;** 1997; Nancy Gettelfinger; 6,175 (MH); 875 (MR).

**San Angelo — MHMR Services for the Concho Valley;** 1969; Lynn Rutland; 891 (MH); 267 (MR).

**San Antonio — The Center for Health Care Services;** 1966; Leon Evans; 9,052 (MH); 1,796 (MR).

**San Marcos — Hill Country Community MHMR;** (see Kerrville).

**Stephenville — Pecan Valley MHMR Region;** 1977; Theresa Mulloy, Ed.D.; 1,816 (MH); 127 (MR).

**Temple — Central Counties Center for MHMR Services;** 1967; Eldon Tietje; 2,559 (MH); 408 (MR).

**Terrell — Lakes Regional MHMR Center;** 1996; Robert Evans; 1,858 (MH); 400 (MR).

**Texarkana — Northeast Texas MHMR Center;** 1974; Joe Bob Hall; 906 (MH); 167 (MR).

**Tyler — Andrews Center;** 1970; Richard J. DeSanto; 2,255 (MH); 508 (MR).

**Victoria — Gulf Bend MHMR Center;** 1970; Don Polzin; 1,304 (MH); 118 (MR).

**Waco — Heart of Texas Region MHMR Center;** 1969; Dean Maberry; 2,588 (MH); 536 (MR).

**Wichita Falls — Helen Farabee Regional Centers;** 1969; Raymond Atkins; 4,230 (MH); 307 (MR). ☆

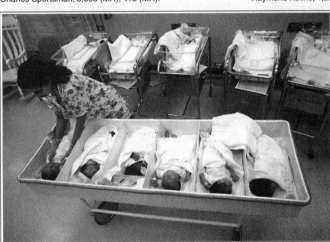

### Texas hospital

*A nurse at Parkland Hospital in Dallas with babies in the nursery. Because of the large number of babies at the hospital, they use custom-designed 'six-packs' (carts that hold six babies) to transport newborns to and from their mothers.*

*File photo.*

# Hospital Care in Texas

*Source: The Texas Hospital Association*

As the population increases and technological advances continue, this field of essential services is greatly expanding in Texas. Houston, Dallas and other Texas cities are internationally known for their medical centers.

However, many small communities in the state have no hospital or access to professional medical care. As the population ages, access to health care becomes a greater concern for many Texans, as evidenced by coverage of health-care issues in the Texas media.

Of the 467 reporting hospitals in Texas in 2001, 411 were considered community hospitals. A community hospital is defined as either a nonfederal, short-term general hospital or a special hospital whose facilities and services are available to the public. A hospital may include a nursing home-type unit and still be classified as short-term, provided that the majority of its patients are admitted to units where the average length-of-stay is less than 30 days.

These 411 hospitals employed 259,573 full-time equivalent people (FTEs) with a payroll, including benefits, of more than $12.4 billion.

These community hospitals contained approximately 56,250 beds. One of every 12 community hospitals in the country is located in Texas.

The average length-of-stay was 5.1 days in 2001, compared to 6.8 days in 1975. This was more than half a day less than the U.S. average of 5.7 days.

The average cost per adjusted admission in Texas was $6,717 or $1,338 per day. This was 3.75 percent less than the U.S. average of $6,979.

There were 2,461,016 admissions in Texas, which accounted for 12,650,063 inpatient days.

There were 31,453,948 out-patient visits in 2001, of which 7,806,334 were emergency room visits.

Of the 3,873,295 births in U.S. hospitals in 2001, 366,373 were in Texas community hospitals.

Of the FTEs working in community hospitals within Texas, there were 64,359 registered nurses, 13,650 licensed vocational nurses and 4,867 trainees. ☆

# Texans in National Academy of the Sciences

*Source: National Academy of Sciences*

*Thomas Südhof.*

The National Academy of Sciences is a private organization of scientists and engineers dedicated to the furtherance of science and its use for the general welfare.

Established by congressional acts of incorporation, which were signed by Abraham Lincoln in 1863, the academy acts as official adviser to the federal government in matters of science or technology.

Selected to the academy in 2003, were **Stephen J. Elledge**, professor of biochemistry and molecular genetics at Baylor College of Medicine in Houston, and **Masashi Yanagisawa**, professor of molecular genetics at the University of Texas Southwestern Medical Center, Dallas. Both are also investigators in the Howard Hughes Medical Institute, a research organization.

Among other recent honorees was **Thomas Südhof**, professor of neuroscience at the University of Texas Southwestern Medical Center, Dallas, selected to the academy in 2002. Added in 2001 were **Lewis R. Binford**, professor of anthropology at Southern Methodist University, and **Marlan O. Scully**, professor of physics at Texas A&M University.

Election to the academy is one of the highest honors that can be accorded a U.S. scientist.

As of May 1, 2003, the number of active members was 1,922. Fifty-six scientists who have been affiliated with Texas institutions are full, voting members.

In addition, 341 scientists with citizenship outside the United States are nonvoting foreign associates. In 1970, D.H.R. Barton from Texas A&M University, and, in 1997, Johann Deisenhofer of the University of Texas Southwestern Medical Center at Dallas, were elected as foreign associates.

In 1948, Karl Folkers of the University of Texas at Austin became the first Texan elected to the academy. Folkers, de Vaucouleurs, Knobil, Pike, and Starr are deceased. ☆

---

\* A&M - Texas A&M University
UT-Austin - The University of Texas at Austin
U of H - University of Houston
UT-Dallas - The University of Texas at Dallas
UTSWMC - The University of Texas Southwestern Medical Center at Dallas
Baylor Med. - Baylor College of Medicine
Rice - Rice University
Welch - Robert A. Welch Foundation
UTHSC - Houston - The University of Texas Health Science Center at Houston
SIL - Summer Institute of Linguistics
SMU - Southern Methodist University

| Academy Member | Affiliation* | Yr. Elected |
| --- | --- | --- |
| Perry L. Adkisson | A&M | 1979 |
| Abram Amsel | UT-Austin | 1992 |
| Neal R. Amundson | U of H | 1992 |
| Charles J. Arntzen | A&M | 1983 |
| David H. Auston | Rice | 1991 |
| Allen J. Bard | UT-Austin | 1982 |
| Brian J.L. Berry | UT-Dallas | 1975 |
| Lewis R. Binford | SMU | 2001 |
| Norman E. Borlaug | A&M | 1968 |
| Michael S. Brown | UTSWMC | 1980 |
| Karl W. Butzer | UT-Austin | 1996 |
| Luis A. Caffarelli | UT-Austin | 1991 |
| C. Thomas Caskey | Baylor Med. | 1993 |
| Joseph W. Chamberlain | Rice | 1965 |
| C.W. Chu | U of H | 1989 |
| F. Albert Cotton | A&M | 1967 |
| Robert F. Curl | Rice | 1997 |
| Gerard H. de Vaucouleurs | UT-Austin | 1986 |
| Bryce DeWitt | UT-Austin | 1990 |
| Stephen J. Elledge | Baylor Med. | 2003 |
| Ronald W. Estabrook | UTSWMC | 1979 |
| Karl Folkers | UT-Austin | 1948 |
| Marye Anne Fox | UT-Austin | 1994 |
| David L. Garbers | UTSWMC | 1993 |
| Quentin H. Gibson | Rice | 1982 |
| Alfred G. Gilman | UTSWMC | 1985 |
| Joseph L. Goldstein | UTSWMC | 1980 |
| William E. Gordon | Rice | 1968 |
| Verne E. Grant | UT-Austin | 1968 |
| Norman Hackerman | Welch | 1971 |
| A. James Hudspeth | UTSWMC | 1991 |
| James L. Kinsey | Rice | 1991 |
| Ernst Knobil | UTHSC-Houston | 1986 |
| Jay K. Kochi | U of H | 1982 |
| John L. Margrave | Rice | 1974 |
| S.M. McCann | UTSWMC | 1983 |
| Steven L. McKnight | UTSWMC | 1992 |
| Ferid Murad | UTHSC-Houston | 1997 |
| Jack Myers | UT-Austin | 1975 |
| Eric N. Olson | UTSWMC | 2000 |
| Bert W. O'Malley | Baylor Med. | 1992 |
| Kenneth L. Pike | SIL | 1985 |
| Lester J. Reed | UT-Austin | 1973 |
| Marlan O. Scully | A&M | 2001 |
| Richard E. Smalley | Rice | 1990 |
| Esmond E. Snell | UT-Austin | 1955 |
| Richard C. Starr | UT-Austin | 1976 |
| Max D. Summers | A&M | 1989 |
| Thomas Südhof | UTSWMC | 2002 |
| Harry L. Swinney | UT-Austin | 1992 |
| John T. Tate | UT-Austin | 1969 |
| Karen K. Uhlenbeck | UT-Austin | 1986 |
| Jonathan W. Uhr | UTSWMC | 1984 |
| Roger H. Unger | UTSWMC | 1986 |
| Ellen S. Vitetta | UTSWMC | 1994 |
| Salih J. Wakil | Baylor Med. | 1990 |
| Steven Weinberg | UT-Austin | 1972 |
| D. Fred Wendorf | SMU | 1987 |
| Jean D. Wilson | UTSWMC | 1983 |
| James E. Womack | A&M | 1999 |
| Masahi Yanagisawa | UTSWMC | 2003 |

*Source: National Academy of Sciences*

# Crime in Texas — 2002

Source: Texas Department of Public Safety, Austin

The **total number of major crimes** committed in Texas in 2002 increased by 3 percent compared to 2001. In addition, the **2002 crime rate** — the number of crimes per 100,000 population — increased 0.9 percent over 2001.

The **violent crime rate** increased 1.2 percent from 2001 to 2002: from 572.4 to 579.2 offenses per 100,000 population. The **nonviolent, or property, crime rate** increased 0.8 percent from 2001 to 2002: from 4,579.9 to 4,617.4 offenses per 100,000 population. The **value of property stolen** during the commission of index crimes in 2002 was more than $1.8 billion. The **value of stolen property recovered** by Texas law-enforcement agencies in 2002 was more than $726 million.

The crime rate is tabulated on seven major offenses designated Index Crimes by the Federal Bureau of Investigation's **Uniform Crime Reporting program**. These seven categories include four violent offenses (murder, rape, robbery and aggra-

vated assault) and three nonviolent crimes (burglary, larceny-theft and motor-vehicle theft). In Texas, these figures are collected by the Texas Department of Public Safety for the national UCR program. In 2002, 989 Texas law enforcement agencies participated in the Texas UCR program, representing 99.6 percent of the population. Data are estimated for non-reporting agencies.

## Arson

In 2002, reported arson offenses totaled 8,243, down 2.2 percent from the 8,432 offenses reported in 2001. Property damage from arson was more than $111 million in 2002. Although arson is an index crime in that data on offenses are collected, arson is not part of the UCR Crime Index. ☆

## Texas Crime History 1981–2002

| Year | Murder | Rape | Robbery | Aggra-vated Assault | Burglary | Larceny-Theft | Motor Vehicle Theft | Rate Per 100,000 Population |
|------|--------|------|---------|---------------------|----------|---------------|---------------------|------------------------------|
| 1981 | 2,438 | 6,816 | 28,516 | 40,673 | 275,652 | 454,210 | 83,244 | 6,042.4 |
| 1982 | 2,463 | 6,814 | 33,603 | 45,221 | 285,757 | 501,312 | 87,090 | 6,297.5 |
| 1983 | 2,238 | 6,334 | 29,769 | 42,195 | 262,214 | 503,555 | 82,522 | 5,907.1 |
| 1984 | 2,091 | 7,340 | 28,537 | 42,764 | 266,032 | 529,469 | 87,781 | 6,029.2 |
| 1985 | 2,124 | 8,367 | 31,693 | 47,868 | 289,913 | 596,130 | 99,561 | 6,570.9 |
| 1986 | 2,255 | 8,605 | 40,018 | 59,002 | 341,560 | 664,832 | 119,095 | 7,408.2 |
| 1987 | 1,960 | 8,068 | 38,049 | 57,903 | 355,732 | 711,739 | 123,378 | 7,724.3 |
| 1988 | 2,021 | 8,122 | 39,307 | 60,084 | 362,099 | 739,784 | 134,271 | 8,019.6 |
| 1989 | 2,029 | 7,953 | 37,910 | 63,978 | 342,360 | 741,642 | 150,974 | 7,926.8 |
| 1990 | 2,388 | 8,746 | 44,316 | 73,860 | 314,346 | 730,926 | 154,387 | 7,823.7 |
| 1991 | 2,651 | 9,265 | 49,698 | 84,104 | 312,719 | 734,177 | 163,837 | 7,818.6 |
| 1992 | 2,240 | 9,368 | 44,582 | 86,067 | 268,864 | 689,515 | 145,039 | 7,055.1 |
| 1993 | 2,149 | 9,923 | 40,464 | 84,892 | 233,944 | 664,738 | 124,822 | 6,438.5 |
| 1994 | 2,023 | 9,101 | 37,639 | 81,079 | 214,698 | 624,048 | 110,772 | 5,873.1 |
| 1995 | 1,694 | 8,526 | 33,666 | 80,377 | 202,637 | 632,523 | 104,939 | 5,684.5 |
| 1996 | 1,476 | 8,374 | 32,796 | 80,572 | 204,335 | 659,397 | 104,928 | 5,708.3 |
| 1997 | 1,328 | 8,007 | 30,513 | 77,239 | 200,966 | 645,174 | 101,687 | 5,478.2 |
| 1998 | 1,343 | 7,914 | 28,672 | 73,648 | 194,872 | 606,805 | 96,614 | 5,110.7 |
| 1999 | 1,218 | 7,629 | 29,424 | 74,165 | 190,347 | 614,478 | 91,992 | 5,035.2 |
| 2000 | 1,236 | 7,821 | 30,186 | 73,987 | 188,205 | 634,575 | 92,878 | 4,952.4 |
| 2001 | 1,331 | 8,191 | 35,330 | 77,221 | 204,240 | 669,587 | 102,838 | 5,152.3 |
| 2002 | 1,305 | 8,541 | 37,599 | 78,713 | 212,702 | 690,028 | 102,943 | 5,196.7 |

Source: Texas Department of Public Safety, Austin, and the Federal Bureau of Investigation, Washington. Population figures used to determine crime rate per 100,000 population based on U.S. Bureau of Census. The population figure used in determining the crime rate for 2002 in Texas was 21,779,893.

### Family Violence in Texas in 2002

Family violence increased 1.7 percent in 2002 over 2001. In 2002, there were 183,440 reported incidents of family violence committed against 198,538 victims by 194,211 offenders. In 2001, there were 180,385 incidents of family violence reported committed against 194,112 victims by 190,059 offenders.

In 53.1 percent of the 2002 incidents, the relationship of victim to offender was marital. Of the total number of these victims, 24 percent were wives and 16.8 percent were common-law wives.

Of the remaining offenses, 15.4 percent involved parents against children or children against parents; and 31.5 involved other family/household relationships, such as grandparents or grandchildren, siblings, step-siblings, roommates or in-laws.

There are six general categories of family violence: assault, homicide, kidnapping/abduction, robbery, forcible sex offenses and nonforcible sex offenses. Assaults (including aggravated, simple and intimidation) accounted for 97.6 percent of all family violence in 2002.

Family violence is defined in the Texas Family Code as an act by a member of a family or household against another member that is intended to result in physical harm, bodily injury, assault or a threat that reasonably places the member in fear of imminent physical harm.

By definition, "family" includes individuals related by blood or affinity, marriage or former marriage, biological parents of the same child, foster children, foster parents and members or former members of the same household, including roommates. The 77th Legislature amended the Texas Family Code to also

include violence that occurs in a "dating relationship."

Investigation of reports of domestic violence can be hazardous to police officers. During 2002, 600 Texas law officers were assaulted while investigating such reports.

### Hate Crimes in Texas in 2002

Hate crimes in Texas decreased by 19.8 percent from 2001 to 2002. The total number of reported Texas hate crimes in 2002 was 344, down from 429 in 2001. The offenses involved 429 victims and 470 offenders.

Motivation of 44.7 percent of hate crimes in 2002 was race; 30.7 percent was ethnicity or national origin; 12.5 percent was sexual orientation; and 12.1 percent was religious; There were no reported incidents of physical or mental disability as motivation for hate crimes in 2002.

Hate crimes, as defined by the Texas Hate Crimes Act, are crimes motivated by prejudice and hatred. Federal law defines hate crimes as those that manifest evidence of prejudice based on race, religion, sexual orientation, ethnicity or disability. The Texas Hate Crimes Act directs all law enforcement agencies in Texas to report bias offenses to the DPS.

### Law Enforcement Deaths, Injuries

In 2002, five Texas law enforcement officers were killed in the line of duty because of criminal activity, and nine officers were killed in duty-related accidents.

There were 5,075 officers assaulted during 2002 compared to 4,936 in 2001. This represents an increase of 2.8 percent. ☆

# Crime Profile of Texas Counties for 2002

| County | Agencies | Commissioned Personnel † | Murder | Rape | Robbery | Assault | Burglary | Larceny-Theft | Auto Theft | Total Index Crimes (see page 539 for definition) | Crime Rate Per 100,000 |
|---|---|---|---|---|---|---|---|---|---|---|---|
| Anderson | 3 | 66 | 4 | 20 | 20 | 100 | 508 | 986 | 71 | 1,709 | 2,969.0 |
| Andrews | 2 | 26 | 0 | 2 | 0 | 32 | 84 | 226 | 13 | 357 | 2,628.3 |
| Angelina | 5 | 143 | 5 | 37 | 40 | 428 | 838 | 1,723 | 173 | 3,244 | 3,875.9 |
| Aransas | 2 | 59 | 1 | 5 | 9 | 50 | 405 | 979 | 53 | 1,502 | 6,648.4 |
| Archer | 2 | 9 | 0 | 1 | 3 | 12 | 46 | 56 | 14 | 132 | 1,427.3 |
| Armstrong | 1 | 3 | 0 | 1 | 0 | 3 | 6 | 22 | 2 | 34 | 1,515.8 |
| Atascosa | 5 | 59 | 2 | 5 | 6 | 49 | 203 | 553 | 42 | 859 | 2,110.6 |
| Austin | 4 | 53 | 0 | 4 | 3 | 37 | 127 | 274 | 33 | 478 | 1,939.9 |
| Bailey | 2 | 11 | 0 | 6 | 0 | 11 | 38 | 87 | 8 | 150 | 2,178.0 |
| Bandera | 1 | 21 | 1 | 6 | 2 | 23 | 140 | 343 | 27 | 542 | 2,940.9 |
| Bastrop | 4 | 85 | 6 | 19 | 25 | 129 | 641 | 1,157 | 113 | 2,090 | 3,463.9 |
| Baylor | 2 | 10 | 1 | 0 | 0 | 15 | 14 | 32 | 7 | 69 | 1,614.0 |
| Bee | 2 | 37 | 1 | 13 | 6 | 44 | 149 | 406 | 23 | 642 | 1,899.4 |
| Bell ‡ | 12 | 449 | 6 | 124 | 261 | 763 | 3,025 | 7,496 | 703 | 12,378 | 4,979.8 |
| Bexar | 28 | 2,918 | 114 | 547 | 2,261 | 7,656 | 15,436 | 72,922 | 6,372 | 105,308 | 7,238.5 |
| Blanco | 3 | 17 | 0 | 1 | 0 | 3 | 34 | 61 | 5 | 104 | 1,182.8 |
| Borden | 1 | 2 | 0 | 0 | 0 | 1 | 4 | 8 | 0 | 13 | 1,708.3 |
| Bosque | 4 | 18 | 1 | 1 | 2 | 10 | 88 | 59 | 10 | 171 | 951.5 |
| Bowie | 7 | 168 | 6 | 39 | 113 | 330 | 867 | 2,605 | 251 | 4,211 | 4,514.3 |
| Brazoria | 20 | 440 | 11 | 111 | 124 | 435 | 1,575 | 4,882 | 512 | 7,650 | 3,005.2 |
| Brazos | 4 | 328 | 6 | 106 | 98 | 490 | 1,402 | 6,093 | 344 | 8,539 | 5,363.7 |
| Brewster | 3 | 23 | 0 | 1 | 0 | 17 | 74 | 103 | 5 | 200 | 2,159.6 |
| Briscoe | 1 | 2 | 1 | 0 | 0 | 2 | 3 | 12 | 0 | 18 | 926.6 |
| Brooks | 2 | 12 | 0 | 1 | 3 | 35 | 62 | 226 | 12 | 339 | 4,069.1 |
| Brown | 4 | 63 | 1 | 15 | 18 | 222 | 445 | 1,217 | 171 | 2,089 | 5,308.6 |
| Burleson | 3 | 29 | 1 | 6 | 3 | 46 | 69 | 109 | 20 | 254 | 1,476.5 |
| Burnet | 7 | 85 | 0 | 7 | 7 | 78 | 213 | 531 | 55 | 891 | 2,318.4 |
| Caldwell | 4 | 73 | 0 | 21 | 8 | 104 | 274 | 527 | 25 | 959 | 2,885.5 |
| Calhoun | 4 | 44 | 0 | 15 | 5 | 48 | 198 | 418 | 41 | 725 | 3,361.8 |
| Callahan | 3 | 14 | 0 | 0 | 0 | 8 | 30 | 53 | 14 | 105 | 779.0 |
| Cameron | 15 | 572 | 11 | 108 | 279 | 1,110 | 3,159 | 17,005 | 955 | 22,627 | 6,462.1 |
| Camp | 2 | 18 | 2 | 0 | 3 | 40 | 108 | 189 | 27 | 369 | 3,058.9 |
| Carson | 2 | 9 | 0 | 4 | 1 | 7 | 8 | 22 | 1 | 43 | 631.8 |
| Cass | 5 | 39 | 0 | 10 | 9 | 69 | 182 | 424 | 69 | 763 | 2,399.9 |
| Castro | 3 | 14 | 0 | 1 | 1 | 17 | 42 | 98 | 10 | 169 | 1,953.1 |
| Chambers | 2 | 41 | 0 | 6 | 16 | 53 | 215 | 499 | 38 | 827 | 3,450.0 |
| Cherokee ‡ | 6 | 63 | 4 | 45 | 22 | 174 | 519 | 726 | 87 | 1,577 | 3,242.3 |
| Childress | 2 | 13 | 0 | 0 | 2 | 17 | 32 | 131 | 2 | 184 | 2,291.4 |
| Clay | 1 | 11 | 0 | 2 | 2 | 10 | 50 | 108 | 16 | 188 | 1,635.4 |
| Cochran | 1 | 8 | 0 | 0 | 1 | 6 | 30 | 46 | 4 | 87 | 2,233.1 |
| Coke | 1 | 5 | 0 | 0 | 0 | 5 | 23 | 36 | 2 | 66 | 1,635.3 |
| Coleman | 3 | 16 | 0 | 0 | 0 | 5 | 97 | 90 | 7 | 199 | 2,063.0 |
| Collin | 12 | 729 | 13 | 171 | 231 | 746 | 3,108 | 11,001 | 874 | 16,144 | 3,595.0 |
| Collingsworth | 1 | 5 | 0 | 2 | 1 | 7 | 33 | 58 | 5 | 106 | 3,165.1 |
| Colorado | 4 | 43 | 0 | 1 | 5 | 39 | 157 | 290 | 24 | 516 | 2,422.8 |
| Comal | 2 | 154 | 3 | 38 | 29 | 323 | 593 | 2,608 | 158 | 3,752 | 4,569.5 |
| Comanche | 3 | 21 | 0 | 1 | 1 | 27 | 80 | 123 | 12 | 244 | 1,665.5 |
| Concho | 2 | 7 | 0 | 0 | 0 | 4 | 18 | 12 | 1 | 35 | 844.8 |
| Cooke | 3 | 63 | 3 | 2 | 13 | 126 | 296 | 772 | 102 | 1,314 | 3,459.6 |
| Coryell | 3 | 82 | 1 | 11 | 15 | 183 | 381 | 1,027 | 67 | 1,685 | 2,147.6 |
| Cottle | 2 | 2 | 0 | 0 | 0 | 2 | 3 | 1 | 0 | 6 | 301.8 |
| Crane | 2 | 15 | 0 | 2 | 0 | 1 | 20 | 50 | 4 | 77 | 1,845.2 |
| Crockett | 1 | 13 | 0 | 0 | 0 | 4 | 15 | 64 | 2 | 85 | 1,985.5 |
| Crosby | 2 | 8 | 0 | 2 | 0 | 1 | 18 | 10 | 3 | 34 | 460.3 |
| Culberson | 1 | 7 | 0 | 1 | 0 | 4 | 0 | 3 | 2 | 10 | 321.9 |
| Dallam | 2 | 19 | 1 | 0 | 1 | 49 | 157 | 181 | 19 | 408 | 4,433.3 |
| Dallas | 35 | 5,411 | 241 | 960 | 9,421 | 10,671 | 30,958 | 95,375 | 25,044 | 172,670 | 6,864.9 |
| Dawson | 2 | 23 | 0 | 5 | 2 | 43 | 85 | 198 | 13 | 346 | 2,227.1 |
| Deaf Smith | 2 | 34 | 4 | 3 | 79 | 199 | 430 | 20 | 735 | 3,791.2 | 2,996.2 |
| Delta | 1 | 10 | 0 | 0 | 0 | 9 | 43 | 79 | 9 | 140 | 2,516.2 |
| Denton ‡ | 19 | 671 | 12 | 152 | 181 | 544 | 2,168 | 8,333 | 868 | 12,258 | 3,404.6 |
| DeWitt | 3 | 26 | 0 | 4 | 8 | 35 | 132 | 286 | 14 | 479 | 2,565.5 |
| Dickens | 2 | 4 | 0 | 1 | 0 | 4 | 5 | 11 | 2 | 23 | 797.2 |
| Dimmit | 1 | 10 | 3 | 2 | 0 | 31 | 107 | 193 | 6 | 342 | 3,195.1 |
| Donley | 1 | 5 | 0 | 0 | 0 | 3 | 23 | 26 | 7 | 59 | 1,475.7 |
| Duval | 3 | 30 | 0 | 1 | 1 | 66 | 144 | 157 | 25 | 394 | 2,704.9 |
| Eastland | 6 | 35 | 0 | 4 | 2 | 43 | 88 | 369 | 28 | 534 | 2,794.1 |
| Ector | 4 | 271 | 3 | 41 | 95 | 533 | 1,294 | 5,265 | 330 | 7,561 | 5,925.5 |
| Edwards | 1 | 4 | 0 | 0 | 0 | 12 | 25 | 11 | 4 | 52 | 2,302.9 |

| County | Agencies | Commissioned Personnel † | Murder | Rape | Robbery | Assault | Burglary | Larceny-Theft | Auto Theft | Total Index Crimes (see page 539 for definition) | Crime Rate Per 100,000 |
|---|---|---|---|---|---|---|---|---|---|---|---|
| Ellis | 8 | 197 | 5 | 41 | 43 | 240 | 1,002 | 2,747 | 236 | 4,314 | 3,882.6 |
| El Paso | 10 | 1,517 | 17 | 272 | 601 | 3,410 | 2,711 | 20,754 | 2,247 | 30,012 | 4,227.8 |
| Erath | 4 | 68 | 0 | 10 | 5 | 34 | 153 | 693 | 33 | 928 | 2,692.2 |
| Falls | 3 | 9 | 1 | 4 | 5 | 48 | 108 | 204 | 13 | 383 | 1,974.1 |
| Fannin | 2 | 36 | 0 | 13 | 3 | 76 | 212 | 492 | 58 | 854 | 2,617.0 |
| Fayette | 3 | 30 | 0 | 5 | 0 | 5 | 68 | 219 | 7 | 304 | 1,334.8 |
| Fisher | 1 | 5 | 0 | 1 | 1 | 2 | 26 | 30 | 1 | 61 | 1,344.5 |
| Floyd | 3 | 11 | 0 | 0 | 1 | 5 | 34 | 78 | 8 | 126 | 1,552.5 |
| Foard | 2 | 4 | 0 | 0 | 0 | 1 | 2 | 14 | 4 | 21 | 1,239.7 |
| Fort Bend ‡ | 11 | 626 | 8 | 97 | 275 | 721 | 2,089 | 6,267 | 624 | 10,081 | 2,960.7 |
| Franklin | 1 | 9 | 1 | 3 | 2 | 15 | 43 | 82 | 8 | 154 | 1,689.0 |
| Freestone | 4 | 33 | 1 | 2 | 1 | 22 | 82 | 129 | 17 | 254 | 1,361.1 |
| Frio | 3 | 25 | 2 | 5 | 4 | 28 | 240 | 266 | 23 | 568 | 3,345.9 |
| Gaines | 3 | 22 | 0 | 2 | 1 | 16 | 54 | 129 | 12 | 214 | 1,416.2 |
| Galveston | 15 | 738 | 15 | 97 | 212 | 754 | 1,967 | 5,701 | 741 | 9,497 | 3,519.1 |
| Garza | 1 | 8 | 0 | 0 | 1 | 2 | 30 | 23 | 3 | 59 | 1,159.4 |
| Gillespie | 2 | 47 | 0 | 1 | 1 | 5 | 76 | 286 | 10 | 379 | 1,743.3 |
| Glasscock | 1 | 3 | 0 | 0 | 0 | 0 | 0 | 1 | 0 | 1 | 68.1 |
| Goliad | 1 | 12 | 0 | 1 | 0 | 8 | 32 | 14 | 0 | 55 | 760.1 |
| Gonzales | 3 | 34 | 4 | 8 | 8 | 57 | 83 | 127 | 8 | 295 | 1,516.2 |
| Gray | 2 | 34 | 0 | 10 | 26 | 95 | 461 | 1,024 | 40 | 1,656 | 6,970.9 |
| Grayson | 11 | 202 | 3 | 22 | 81 | 212 | 943 | 3,357 | 271 | 4,889 | 4,232.2 |
| Gregg | 5 | 270 | 9 | 163 | 192 | 349 | 1,448 | 5,336 | 628 | 8,125 | 6,591.6 |
| Grimes | 2 | 37 | 5 | 4 | 3 | 39 | 192 | 398 | 33 | 674 | 2,739.8 |
| Guadalupe | 3 | 76 | 4 | 25 | 29 | 187 | 667 | 2,192 | 109 | 3,213 | 3,449.8 |
| Hale | 4 | 89 | 0 | 12 | 19 | 88 | 339 | 1,046 | 37 | 1,541 | 3,954.2 |
| Hall | 2 | 7 | 0 | 0 | 0 | 5 | 35 | 34 | 5 | 79 | 2,000.0 |
| Hamilton | 2 | 13 | 0 | 0 | 0 | 10 | 35 | 25 | 3 | 73 | 849.3 |
| Hansford | 3 | 9 | 0 | 0 | 0 | 7 | 10 | 30 | 4 | 51 | 909.4 |
| Hardeman | 2 | 8 | 0 | 5 | 0 | 6 | 25 | 49 | 2 | 87 | 1,762.9 |
| Hardin | 5 | 75 | 1 | 7 | 6 | 115 | 312 | 702 | 96 | 1,239 | 2,467.5 |
| Harris ‡ | 38 | 9,372 | 340 | 1,372 | 13,442 | 17,637 | 39,683 | 110,619 | 31,168 | 214,261 | 5,992.5 |
| Harrison | 2 | 90 | 1 | 19 | 39 | 160 | 765 | 1,419 | 136 | 2,539 | 4,017.1 |
| Hartley | 1 | 4 | 0 | 0 | 0 | 1 | 16 | 13 | 2 | 32 | 1,039.0 |
| Haskell | 2 | 5 | 0 | 1 | 0 | 6 | 7 | 62 | 1 | 77 | 1,218.5 |
| Hays | 4 | 215 | 1 | 42 | 55 | 145 | 665 | 2,158 | 205 | 3,271 | 3,209.0 |
| Hemphill | 1 | 7 | 0 | 1 | 1 | 3 | 11 | 13 | 0 | 29 | 828.6 |
| Henderson | 9 | 127 | 3 | 14 | 24 | 408 | 929 | 1,329 | 263 | 2,970 | 3,880.4 |
| Hidalgo ‡ | 20 | 971 | 46 | 176 | 611 | 2,060 | 6,484 | 22,517 | 2,270 | 34,164 | 5,743.7 |
| Hill | 5 | 53 | 1 | 10 | 9 | 47 | 221 | 677 | 68 | 1,033 | 3,059.8 |
| Hockley | 4 | 37 | 0 | 6 | 5 | 47 | 122 | 316 | 17 | 513 | 2,162.1 |
| Hood | 3 | 50 | 0 | 1 | 7 | 50 | 318 | 930 | 92 | 1,398 | 3,256.5 |
| Hopkins | 2 | 55 | 1 | 10 | 7 | 54 | 240 | 459 | 36 | 807 | 2,417.4 |
| Houston | 3 | 30 | 2 | 7 | 4 | 25 | 117 | 266 | 16 | 437 | 1,804.5 |
| Howard | 2 | 58 | 2 | 19 | 10 | 53 | 364 | 729 | 58 | 1,235 | 3,516.2 |
| Hudspeth | 1 | 12 | 0 | 0 | 1 | 11 | 6 | 16 | 1 | 35 | 1,002.0 |
| Hunt | 8 | 121 | 0 | 18 | 83 | 366 | 1,245 | 2,658 | 224 | 4,594 | 5,742.1 |
| Hutchinson ‡ | 3 | 37 | 1 | 14 | 7 | 28 | 205 | 677 | 30 | 962 | 3,860.5 |
| Irion | 1 | 4 | 0 | 2 | 1 | 4 | 4 | 17 | 0 | 28 | 1,513.5 |
| Jack | 2 | 17 | 0 | 1 | 1 | 10 | 32 | 75 | 5 | 124 | 1,354.7 |
| Jackson | 3 | 24 | 0 | 2 | 6 | 19 | 60 | 184 | 16 | 287 | 1,909.4 |
| Jasper | 3 | 38 | 0 | 6 | 21 | 77 | 329 | 648 | 40 | 1,121 | 3,014.4 |
| Jeff Davis | 1 | 3 | 1 | 0 | 0 | 1 | 11 | 4 | 2 | 19 | 824.3 |
| Jefferson | 7 | 535 | 14 | 217 | 633 | 811 | 3,181 | 10,304 | 1,063 | 16,223 | 6,162.1 |
| Jim Hogg | 1 | 22 | 0 | 3 | 0 | 21 | 14 | 30 | 1 | 69 | 1,250.9 |
| Jim Wells | 4 | 82 | 1 | 12 | 7 | 258 | 501 | 1,297 | 73 | 2,149 | 5,343.9 |
| Johnson | 7 | 189 | 3 | 42 | 32 | 275 | 1,078 | 3,219 | 318 | 4,967 | 3,667.8 |
| Jones | 5 | 24 | 0 | 5 | 3 | 22 | 92 | 117 | 8 | 247 | 1,541.6 |
| Karnes ‡ | 3 | 21 | 0 | 1 | 1 | 29 | 59 | 84 | 14 | 188 | 1,165.2 |
| Kaufman | 5 | 106 | 11 | 22 | 62 | 411 | 780 | 1,950 | 291 | 3,527 | 4,735.6 |
| Kendall | 2 | 51 | 0 | 4 | 5 | 21 | 75 | 320 | 21 | 446 | 1,849.0 |
| Kenedy | 1 | 10 | 0 | 1 | 0 | 3 | 5 | 2 | 1 | 12 | 2,777.8 |
| Kent | 1 | 2 | 0 | 0 | 0 | 1 | 6 | 4 | 1 | 12 | 1,337.8 |
| Kerr | 3 | 97 | 1 | 14 | 5 | 28 | 258 | 787 | 50 | 1,143 | 2,506.8 |
| Kimble | 2 | 12 | 0 | 1 | 0 | 9 | 25 | 82 | 4 | 121 | *2,592.7 |
| King | 1 | 1 | 0 | 0 | 0 | 0 | 0 | 0 | 0 | 0 | 0.0 |
| Kinney | 1 | 7 | 0 | 0 | 0 | 0 | 0 | 0 | 2 | 2 | 56.7 |
| Kleberg | 3 | 70 | 3 | 24 | 18 | 248 | 338 | 1,467 | 74 | 2,172 | 6,591.2 |
| Knox | 3 | 8 | 0 | 2 | 0 | 3 | 23 | 49 | 7 | 84 | 1,891.0 |
| Lamar | 4 | 94 | 6 | 63 | 46 | 394 | 761 | 2,479 | 144 | 3,893 | 7,684.9 |
| Lamb ‡ | 4 | 30 | 1 | 3 | 3 | 27 | 46 | 85 | 8 | 173 | 1,126.1 |

| County | Agencies | Commissioned Personnel † | Murder | Rape | Robbery | Assault | Burglary | Larceny-Theft | Auto Theft | Total Index Crimes (see page 539 for definition) | Crime Rate Per 100,000 |
|---|---|---|---|---|---|---|---|---|---|---|---|
| Lampasas | 2 | 36 | 1 | 14 | 0 | 18 | 99 | 308 | 17 | 457 | 2,482.5 |
| La Salle | 1 | 15 | 0 | 0 | 1 | 14 | 37 | 71 | 4 | 127 | 2,072.8 |
| Lavaca | 3 | 25 | 0 | 1 | 3 | 8 | 65 | 196 | 5 | 278 | 1,246.8 |
| Lee | 3 | 26 | 0 | 4 | 4 | 41 | 86 | 170 | 17 | 322 | 1,968.9 |
| Leon | 1 | 15 | 2 | 4 | 1 | 39 | 109 | 83 | 19 | 259 | 1,616.9 |
| Liberty | 4 | 83 | 1 | 25 | 33 | 198 | 848 | 1,326 | 186 | 2,617 | 3,571.4 |
| Limestone | 4 | 45 | 1 | 6 | 8 | 75 | 239 | 583 | 41 | 953 | 4,137.7 |
| Lipscomb | 1 | 5 | 0 | 0 | 0 | 1 | 4 | 3 | 0 | 8 | 250.5 |
| Live Oak | 2 | 18 | 0 | 0 | 0 | 7 | 29 | 40 | 5 | 81 | 630.1 |
| Llano ‡ | 3 | 28 | 0 | 9 | 0 | 19 | 108 | 306 | 19 | 461 | 3,065.8 |
| Loving | 1 | 2 | 0 | 0 | 0 | 0 | 0 | 0 | 0 | 0 | 0.0 |
| Lubbock | 9 | 503 | 11 | 152 | 306 | 2,197 | 3,279 | 9,378 | 667 | 15,990 | 6,328.0 |
| Lynn | 3 | 12 | 0 | 0 | 0 | 5 | 28 | 84 | 7 | 124 | 1,782.4 |
| Madison | 2 | 17 | 1 | 2 | 3 | 35 | 67 | 173 | 22 | 303 | 2,241.8 |
| Marion | 2 | 18 | 0 | 6 | 8 | 41 | 156 | 127 | 22 | 360 | 3,150.2 |
| Martin | 2 | 8 | 1 | 2 | 1 | 5 | 14 | 24 | 6 | 53 | 1,069.2 |
| Mason | 1 | 5 | 0 | 1 | 0 | 2 | 10 | 43 | 2 | 58 | 1,485.7 |
| Matagorda | 4 | 86 | 1 | 9 | 39 | 119 | 418 | 1,172 | 80 | 1,838 | 4,636.0 |
| Maverick | 2 | 99 | 2 | 0 | 6 | 98 | 271 | 976 | 107 | 1,460 | 2,955.3 |
| McCulloch | 2 | 13 | 0 | 5 | 0 | 39 | 53 | 91 | 9 | 197 | 2,298.7 |
| McLennan | 17 | 492 | 15 | 99 | 311 | 865 | 3,042 | 9,660 | 876 | 14,868 | 6,666.7 |
| McMullen | 1 | 3 | 0 | 0 | 0 | 0 | 3 | 4 | 2 | 9 | 1,012.4 |
| Medina | 3 | 42 | 1 | 24 | 8 | 75 | 300 | 494 | 53 | 955 | 2,345.5 |
| Menard | 1 | 5 | 0 | 0 | 0 | 1 | 10 | 4 | 0 | 15 | 608.5 |
| Midland | 3 | 237 | 4 | 69 | 76 | 445 | 1,002 | 2,832 | 239 | 4,667 | 3,886.4 |
| Milam | 4 | 32 | 0 | 17 | 8 | 38 | 214 | 464 | 38 | 779 | 3,077.1 |
| Mills | 1 | 5 | 0 | 0 | 0 | 2 | 15 | 13 | 3 | 33 | 613.4 |
| Mitchell | 2 | 12 | 0 | 1 | 0 | 10 | 42 | 123 | 8 | 184 | 1,816.6 |
| Montague ‡ | 4 | 26 | 5 | 6 | 5 | 31 | 248 | 388 | 36 | 719 | 3,600.8 |
| Montgomery | 8 | 464 | 14 | 75 | 260 | 842 | 2,306 | 6,994 | 681 | 11,172 | 3,646.6 |
| Moore | 2 | 37 | 0 | 9 | 9 | 46 | 88 | 462 | 26 | 640 | 3,045.2 |
| Morris ‡ | 4 | 21 | 0 | 4 | 3 | 32 | 109 | 169 | 24 | 341 | 2,502.0 |
| Motley | 1 | 2 | 2 | 0 | 0 | 1 | 2 | 0 | 1 | 6 | 402.7 |
| Nacogdoches | 3 | 76 | 2 | 31 | 19 | 238 | 417 | 1,159 | 56 | 1,922 | 3,108.1 |
| Navarro | 2 | 107 | 0 | 22 | 34 | 55 | 524 | 1,384 | 112 | 2,131 | 4,521.3 |
| Newton | 1 | 10 | 2 | 0 | 1 | 26 | 71 | 71 | 6 | 177 | 1,124.3 |
| Nolan | 3 | 33 | 1 | 8 | 3 | 37 | 169 | 225 | 28 | 471 | 2,853.7 |
| Nueces | 7 | 631 | 20 | 277 | 540 | 1,457 | 3,978 | 15,447 | 1,536 | 23,255 | 7,100.0 |
| Ochiltree | 2 | 15 | 0 | 1 | 0 | 32 | 55 | 169 | 8 | 265 | 2,817.1 |
| Oldham | 1 | 5 | 0 | 0 | 1 | 1 | 9 | 11 | 4 | 26 | 1,139.4 |
| Orange | 7 | 149 | 4 | 87 | 62 | 358 | 848 | 2,330 | 280 | 3,969 | 4,472.3 |
| Palo Pinto | 2 | 46 | 1 | 16 | 10 | 29 | 234 | 619 | 64 | 973 | 3,190.0 |
| Panola | 2 | 33 | 1 | 0 | 10 | 71 | 172 | 351 | 54 | 659 | 2,798.9 |
| Parker | 5 | 127 | 5 | 12 | 16 | 94 | 619 | 1,441 | 133 | 2,320 | 2,620.7 |
| Parmer | 4 | 14 | 0 | 2 | 0 | 8 | 56 | 54 | 5 | 125 | 1,194.9 |
| Pecos | 2 | 32 | 1 | 3 | 2 | 23 | 100 | 238 | 17 | 384 | 2,187.0 |
| Polk | 4 | 69 | 2 | 7 | 20 | 93 | 295 | 663 | 66 | 1,146 | 2,667.3 |
| Potter | 4 | 412 | 7 | 110 | 331 | 1,046 | 2,544 | 8,797 | 982 | 13,817 | 7,061.1 |
| Presidio | 2 | 9 | 0 | 0 | 0 | 10 | 23 | 22 | 3 | 58 | 760.3 |
| Rains | 1 | 8 | 1 | 0 | 0 | 6 | 81 | 93 | 17 | 198 | 2,074.2 |
| Randall | 3 | 90 | 0 | 6 | 3 | 56 | 214 | 434 | 50 | 763 | 2,393.6 |
| Reagan | 1 | 9 | 0 | 1 | 0 | 1 | 6 | 23 | 1 | 32 | 921.1 |
| Real | 1 | 3 | 0 | 0 | 0 | 0 | 7 | 6 | 1 | 14 | 439.8 |
| Red River | 3 | 22 | 1 | 3 | 6 | 27 | 118 | 154 | 13 | 322 | 2,153.7 |
| Reeves | 2 | 31 | 0 | 0 | 5 | 31 | 130 | 270 | 13 | 449 | 3,272.1 |
| Refugio | 2 | 19 | 0 | 0 | 0 | 12 | 54 | 76 | 9 | 151 | 1,846.6 |
| Roberts | 1 | 4 | 0 | 0 | 0 | 1 | 3 | 13 | 1 | 18 | 1,943.8 |
| Robertson | 2 | 19 | 0 | 3 | 5 | 72 | 84 | 182 | 8 | 354 | 2,118.2 |
| Rockwall | 4 | 43 | 1 | 13 | 16 | 69 | 243 | 652 | 100 | 1,094 | 2,916.4 |
| Runnels | 3 | 17 | 0 | 2 | 1 | 31 | 80 | 131 | 12 | 257 | 2,140.6 |
| Rusk | 4 | 82 | 2 | 34 | 11 | 244 | 387 | 951 | 53 | 1,682 | 3,567.3 |
| Sabine | 2 | 11 | 1 | 0 | 0 | 14 | 77 | 164 | 5 | 261 | 2,386.8 |
| San Augustine | 2 | 6 | 0 | 4 | 5 | 48 | 126 | 130 | 11 | 324 | 3,467.5 |
| San Jacinto | 1 | 13 | 3 | 1 | 8 | 37 | 170 | 250 | 39 | 508 | 2,186.3 |
| San Patricio | 9 | 104 | 3 | 11 | 20 | 120 | 520 | 1,435 | 93 | 2,202 | 3,097.0 |
| San Saba | 2 | 7 | 1 | 0 | 0 | 6 | 23 | 42 | 6 | 78 | 1,207.2 |
| Schleicher | 1 | 5 | 0 | 0 | 0 | 1 | 11 | 7 | 1 | 20 | 652.3 |
| Scurry | 2 | 27 | 0 | 3 | 3 | 15 | 107 | 198 | 21 | 347 | 2,030.5 |
| Shackelford | 1 | 3 | 0 | 0 | 0 | 1 | 6 | 9 | 1 | 17 | 492.9 |
| Shelby | 2 | 29 | 1 | 6 | 10 | 67 | 231 | 414 | 41 | 770 | 2,922.5 |
| Sherman | 2 | 4 | 0 | 0 | 1 | 5 | 28 | 26 | 3 | 63 | 1,893.6 |

| County | Agencies | Commissioned Personnel † | Murder | Rape | Robbery | Assault | Burglary | Larceny-Theft | Auto Theft | Total Index Crimes (see page 539 for definition) | Crime Rate Per 100,000 |
|---|---|---|---|---|---|---|---|---|---|---|---|
| Smith ‡ | 11 | 343 | 8 | 127 | 179 | 600 | 1,862 | 5,683 | 602 | 9,061 | 4,966.6 |
| Somervell | 1 | 20 | 0 | 1 | 1 | 13 | 55 | 91 | 9 | 170 | 2,390.0 |
| Starr | 3 | 72 | 6 | 11 | 12 | 138 | 356 | 442 | 146 | 1,111 | 1,984.9 |
| Stephens | 2 | 17 | 0 | 3 | 0 | 5 | 59 | 73 | 4 | 144 | 1,425.0 |
| Sterling | 1 | 3 | 0 | 0 | 0 | 2 | 2 | 2 | 0 | 6 | 412.4 |
| Stonewall | 1 | 3 | 0 | 0 | 0 | 0 | 4 | 7 | 0 | 1 | 622.2 |
| Sutton | 2 | 9 | 0 | 0 | 1 | 4 | 14 | 51 | 1 | 71 | 1,667.1 |
| Swisher | 3 | 14 | 0 | 2 | 3 | 18 | 44 | 135 | 15 | 217 | 2,479.7 |
| Tarrant | 38 | 3,659 | 80 | 640 | 2,761 | 4,470 | 17,495 | 59,061 | 7,467 | 91,974 | 6,210.1 |
| Taylor | 5 | 255 | 5 | 65 | 114 | 289 | 1,423 | 3,579 | 250 | 5,725 | 4,150.9 |
| Terrell | 1 | 3 | 0 | 0 | 0 | 0 | 0 | 0 | 0 | 0 | 0.0 |
| Terry | 2 | 24 | 1 | 2 | 2 | 36 | 50 | 174 | 16 | 281 | 2,108.2 |
| Throckmorton | 1 | 3 | 3 | 2 | 0 | 3 | 1 | 0 | 1 | 10 | 517.6 |
| Titus | 2 | 49 | 0 | 2 | 6 | 107 | 194 | 679 | 62 | 1,050 | 3,575.2 |
| Tom Green | 3 | 196 | 0 | 65 | 50 | 296 | 1,152 | 4,314 | 245 | 6,122 | 5,635.1 |
| Travis | 13 | 2,118 | 29 | 340 | 1,244 | 2,076 | 8,290 | 34,354 | 3,499 | 49,832 | 5,798.2 |
| Trinity | 2 | 18 | 2 | 3 | 2 | 40 | 106 | 166 | 23 | 342 | 2,376.3 |
| Tyler | 2 | 27 | 0 | 0 | 1 | 34 | 129 | 131 | 14 | 309 | 1,417.4 |
| Upshur ‡ | 5 | 56 | 2 | 2 | 7 | 36 | 302 | 506 | 53 | 908 | 2,647.3 |
| Upton | 1 | 9 | 0 | 0 | 0 | 4 | 9 | 28 | 4 | 45 | 1,265.5 |
| Uvalde | 3 | 45 | 2 | 6 | 7 | 110 | 340 | 718 | 62 | 1,245 | 4,597.7 |
| Val Verde | 2 | 99 | 2 | 2 | 11 | 55 | 228 | 989 | 92 | 1,379 | 2,943.2 |
| Van Zandt ‡ | 6 | 63 | 2 | 3 | 8 | 111 | 446 | 737 | 159 | 1,465 | 2,913.5 |
| Victoria | 2 | 192 | 15 | 60 | 115 | 399 | 824 | 2,986 | 186 | 4,585 | 5220.3 |
| Walker | 2 | 72 | 1 | 20 | 38 | 178 | 344 | 929 | 107 | 1,617 | 2,506.7 |
| Waller | 6 | 65 | 2 | 9 | 20 | 65 | 282 | 529 | 95 | 1,002 | 2,974.8 |
| Ward | 2 | 22 | 0 | 4 | 1 | 11 | 29 | 93 | 4 | 142 | 1,246.2 |
| Washington | 2 | 61 | 1 | 19 | 16 | 117 | 267 | 638 | 76 | 1,134 | 3,574.5 |
| Webb | 5 | 528 | 8 | 59 | 203 | 916 | 2,074 | 9,288 | 920 | 13,468 | 6,676.8 |
| Wharton | 3 | 81 | 2 | 16 | 41 | 184 | 578 | 947 | 90 | 1,858 | 4,318.8 |
| Wheeler | 2 | 9 | 0 | 3 | 1 | 7 | 25 | 29 | 7 | 72 | 1,304.3 |
| Wichita | 6 | 262 | 11 | 41 | 253 | 759 | 1,916 | 5,745 | 539 | 9,264 | 6,736.3 |
| Wilbarger | 2 | 29 | 0 | 13 | 5 | 28 | 172 | 549 | 25 | 792 | 5,166.7 |
| Willacy | 3 | 35 | 2 | 1 | 12 | 79 | 266 | 358 | 31 | 749 | 3,570.7 |
| Williamson | 11 | 442 | 3 | 82 | 71 | 442 | 1,100 | 4,016 | 256 | 5,970 | 2,383.7 |
| Wilson | 3 | 41 | 0 | 0 | 4 | 39 | 100 | 250 | 19 | 412 | 1,217.1 |
| Winkler | 3 | 19 | 0 | 1 | 0 | 23 | 26 | 63 | 4 | 117 | 1,561.5 |
| Wise | 4 | 73 | 0 | 16 | 4 | 125 | 303 | 580 | 101 | 1,129 | 2,215.2 |
| Wood | 5 | 58 | 5 | 10 | 3 | 46 | 298 | 457 | 16 | 835 | 2,132.9 |
| Yoakum | 2 | 17 | 0 | 0 | 2 | 12 | 34 | 87 | 8 | 143 | 1,869.8 |
| Young | 3 | 37 | 3 | 11 | 1 | 33 | 113 | 339 | 15 | 515 | 2,747.8 |
| Zapata | 1 | 32 | 2 | 1 | 4 | 53 | 196 | 168 | 31 | 455 | 3,575.9 |
| Zavala | 2 | 10 | 1 | 0 | 4 | 19 | 77 | 112 | 12 | 225 | 1,857.0 |

* County population figures used for calculation of crime rate are the U.S. Census Bureau revised figures for 2002.
† The commissioned officers listed here are those employed by sheriffs' offices and police departments of municipalities; universities, colleges and public-school districts; transit systems; park departments; and medical facilities. The Texas Department of Public Safety also has 3,031 commissioned personnel stationed statewide.
‡ County in which one or more law-enforcement agencies did not report data for 2002 to the DPS. The number of commissioned officers listed for this county does not include those employed by nonreporting agencies. The numbers of index crimes for the county includes estimates for nonreporting agencies to enable the DPS to provide comparable data for 2002.

## Crime Rates by States, 2000

(Index Crimes per 100,000 population*)

| | | |
|---|---|---|
| 1. | Washington, D.C. | 7,277 |
| 2. | Arizona | 5,830 |
| 3. | Florida | 5,695 |
| 4. | New Mexico | 5,519 |
| 5. | Louisiana | 5,423 |
| 6. | South Carolina | 5,221 |
| 7. | Hawaii | 5,199 |
| 8. | Washington | 5,106 |
| 9. | **Texas** | **4,956** |
| 10. | North Carolina | 4,919 |
| 11. | Tennessee | 4,890 |
| 12. | Oregon | 4,845 |
| 13. | Maryland | 4,816 |
| 14. | Georgia | 4,751 |
| 15. | Oklahoma | 4,559 |
| 16. | Alabama | 4,546 |
| | **United States** | **4,124** |

Source: Statistical Abstract of the United States, 2002.
*Based on Census Bureau estimated resident population as of July 1, 2000.

# Texas Public Schools

Source: Texas Education Agency; www.tea.state.tx.us

Public school enrollment in Texas reached a peak of 4,146,653 in 2001–2002, according to the **Texas Education Agency**. In 2000–2001, school enrollment was 4,059,619.

The **seven largest districts** (listed in descending order by average daily attendance), are Houston, Dallas, Austin, Fort Worth, Northside (Bexar Co.), Cypress-Fairbanks and El Paso.

In Texas, there are 1,040 independent and common school districts and 180 charter districts. Independent school districts are administered by an elected, district-wide board of trustees and deal directly with the Texas Education Agency. Common districts are supervised by elected county school superintendents and county trustees. Charter schools are discussed later in this article..

Paul Lopez and Anna Montes join other children during a fiesta at Pilot Point High School to celebrate the success of a summer bilingual education program for migrant families in the Denton County area. File photo.

## Brief History of Public Education

Public education was one of the primary goals of the early settlers of Texas, who listed the failure to provide education as one of their grievances in the **Texas Declaration of Independence** from Mexico.

As early as 1838, **President Mirabeau B. Lamar's** message to the Republic of Texas Congress advocated setting aside public domain for public schools. His interest caused him to be called the **"Father of Education in Texas."** In 1839 Congress designated three leagues of land to support public schools for each Texas county and 50 leagues for a state university. In 1840 each county was allocated one more league of land.

The Republic, however, did not establish a public school system or a university. The 1845 State Constitution advocated public education, instructing the Legislature to designate at least 10 percent of the tax revenue for schools. Further delay occurred until **Gov. Elisha M. Pease**, on Jan. 31, 1854, signed the bill setting up the **Texas public school system.**

The public school system was made possible by setting aside $2 million out of $10 million Texas received for relinquishing its claim to land to the north and west of its present boundaries in the Compromise of 1850.

During 1854, legislation provided for state apportionment of funds based upon an annual census. Also, railroads receiving grants were required to survey alternate sections to be set aside for public-school financing. The **first school census** that year showed 65,463 students; state fund apportionment was 62 cents per student.

When adopted in 1876, the present Texas Constitution provided: "All funds, lands and other property heretofore set apart and appropriated for the support of public schools; all the alternate sections of land reserved by the state of grants heretofore made or that may hereafter be made to railroads, or other corporations, of any nature whatsoever; one half of the public domain of the state, and all sums of money that may come to the state from the

## Enrollment and Expenditures per Student

| School Year | Enrollment | Spending per student |
|---|---|---|
| 2001-2002 | 4,146,653 | $6,913 |
| 2000-2001 | 4,059,619 | 6,638 |
| 1999-2000 | 3,991,783 | 6,354 |
| 1998-1999 | 3,945,367 | 5,853 |
| 1997-1998 | 3,900,488 | 5,597 |
| 1996-1997 | 3,628,975 | 5,282 |
| 1995-1996 | 3,740,260 | 5,358 |
| 1994-1995 | 3,670,196 | 5,057 |
| 1993-1994 | 3,601,839 | 4,898 |

## Graduates and Dropouts

| School Year | Graduates | Dropouts |
|---|---|---|
| 2000-2001 | 215,316 | 17,563 |
| 1999-2000 | 212,925 | 23,457 |
| 1998-1999 | 203,393 | 27,592 |
| 1997-1998 | 197,186 | 27,550 |
| 1996-1997 | 181,794 | 26,901 |
| 1995-1996 | 171,844 | 29,207 |
| 1994-1995 | 169,085 | 29,518 |
| 1993-1994 | 163,191 | 40,211 |
| 1992-1993 | 161-399 | 43,,402 |

## Texas School Personnel & Salaries

| Year/ Personnel Type | Personnel (Full-Time Equivalent)* | Average Total Salaries† |
|---|---|---|
| **2001-2002 Personnel** | **560,063** | **$32,427** |
| Teachers | 282,583 | 40,049 |
| Campus Administrators | 15,234 | 58,898 |
| Central Administrators | 5,756 | 70,305 |
| Support Staff* | 49,904 | 42,270 |
| Total Professionals | 353,477 | 41,668 |
| Educational Aides | 57,941 | 14,569 |
| Auxiliary Staff | 148,645 | 17,415 |
| **2000-2001 Personnel** | **541,342** | **$31,745** |
| Teachers | 274,817 | 39,122 |
| Campus Administrators | 13,916 | 58,367 |
| Central Administrators | 4,491 | 70,369 |
| Support Staff* | 42,092 | 45,900 |
| Total Professionals | 335,317 | 41,190 |
| Educational Aides | 55,467 | 14,154 |
| Auxiliary Staff | 150,559 | 17,191 |

*Support staff includes supervisors, counselors, educational diagnosticians, librarians, nurses/physicians, therapists and psychologists.

†Supplements for non-teaching duties and career-ladder supplements are not included in this figure.

## Permanent School Fund

The Texas public school system was established and the permanent fund set up by the Fifth Legislature, Jan. 31, 1854.

| Year | Total Investment Fund* | Total Income Earned by P.S.F. |
|---|---|---|
| 1854 | $ 2,000,000.00 | ... |
| 1880 | 3,542,126.00 | ... |
| 1900 | 9,102,872.75 | $ 783,142.08 |
| 1910 | 16,752,406.93 | 1,970,526.52 |
| 1920 | 25,698,281.74 | 2,888,555.44 |
| 1930 | 38,718,106.35 | 2,769,547.05 |
| 1940 | 68,299,081.91 | 3,331,874.12 |
| 1950 | 161,179,979.24 | 3,985,973.60 |
| 1960 | 425,821,600.53 | 12,594,000.28 |
| 1970 | 842,217,721.05 | 34,762,955.32 |
| 1980 | 2,464,579,397.00 | 163,000,000.00 |
| 1985 | 5,095,802,979.00 | 417,080,383.00 |
| 1988 | 6,493,070,622.00 | 572,665,253.00 |
| 1989 | 6,873,610,771.00 | 614,786,823.00 |
| 1990 | 7,328,172,096.00 | 674,634,994.00 |
| 1991 | 10,227,777,535.00 | 661,744,804.00 |
| 1992 | 10,944,944,872.00 | 704,993,826.00 |
| 1993 | 11,822,465,497.00 | 714,021,754.00 |
| 1994 | 11,330,590,652.00 | 716,972,115.00 |
| 1995 | 12,273,168,900.00 | 737,008,244.00 |
| 1996 | 12,995,820,070.00 | 739,996,574.00 |
| 1997 | 15,496,646,496.00 | 692,678,412.00 |
| 1998 | 16,296,199,389.00 | 690,802,024.00 |
| 1999 | 19,615,730,341.00 | 661,892,466.00 |
| 2000 | 22,275,586,452.00 | 698,487,305.00 |
| 2001 | 19,021,750,040.00 | 794,284,231.00 |
| 2002 | 17,047,245,212.00 | 764,554,567.00 |

*For years before 1991, includes cash, bonds at par and stocks at book value. For years beginning with 1991, includes cash, bonds and stocks at fair value.

## PSF Apportionment, 1854–2001

The first apportionment by Texas to public schools was for school year 1854-1855

| Years | Amount of P.S.F. Distributed to Schools |
|---|---|
| 1854-55 | $ 40,587 |
| 1880-81 | 679,317 |
| 1900-01 | 3,002,820 |
| 1910-11 | 5,931,287 |
| 1920-21 | 18,431,716 |
| 1930-31 | 27,342,473 |
| 1940-41 | 34,580,475 |
| 1950-51 | 93,996,600 |
| 1960-61 | 164,188,461 |
| 1970-71 | 287,159,758 |
| 1980-81 | 3,042,476 |
| 1985-86 | 807,680,617 |
| 1988-89 | 882,999,623 |
| 1989-90 | 917,608,395 |
| 1990-91 | 700,276,846 |
| 1991-92 | 739,200,044 |
| 1992-93 | 739,494,967 |
| 1993-94 | 737,677,545 |
| 1994-95 | 737,008,244 |
| 1995-96 | 739,996,574 |
| 1996-97 | 692,678,412 |
| 1997-98 | 690,802,024 |
| 1998-99 | 661,892,466 |
| 1999-00 | 698,487,305 |
| 2000-01 | 794,284,231 |
| 2001-02 | 764,554,567 |

Source: Texas Education Agency.

sale of any portion of the same shall constitute a **perpetual public school fund**."

Over 52 million acres of the Texas **public domain** were allotted for school purposes. (See table, **Distribution of the Public Lands of Texas** on page 442.)

The Constitution also provided for one-fourth of occupation taxes and a poll tax of one dollar for school support and made provisions for local taxation. No provision was made for direct ad valorem taxation for maintenance of an **available school fund**, but a maximum 20-cent state ad valorem school tax was adopted in 1883, and raised to 35 cents in connection with provision of **free textbooks** in the amendment of 1918.

In 1949, the **Gilmer-Aikin Laws** reorganized the state system of public schools by making sweeping changes in administration and financing. The Texas Education Agency, headed by the governor-appointed Commissioner of Education, administers the public-school system. The policy-making body for public education is the 15-member State Board of Education, which is elected from separate districts for overlapping four-year terms. Current membership of the board may be found in the State Government section of this Almanac.

### Recent Changes in Public Education

Members of the 68th Legislature passed a historic education-reform bill in the summer of 1984. House Bill 72 came in response to growing concern over deteriorating literacy among Texas' schoolchildren over two decades, reflected in students' scores on standardized tests.

Provisions of HB 72 raised teachers' salaries, but tied those raises to teacher performance. It also introduced more stringent teacher certification and initiated competency testing for teachers.

Academic achievement was set as a priority in public education with stricter attendance rules; adoption of a no-pass, no-play rule prohibiting students who were failing courses from participating in sports and other extracurricular activities for a six-week period; and national norm-referenced testing throughout all grades to assure parents of individual schools' performance through a common frame of reference. No-pass, no-play now requires only a three-week suspension for a failing course grade, during which time the student can continue to practice, but not participate in competition.

The 74th Legislature passed the Public Schools Reform Act of 1995, which increased local control of public schools by limiting the Texas Education Agency to recommending and reporting on educational goals; overseeing charter schools; managing the permanent, foundation and available school funds; administering an accountability system; creating and implementing the student

testing program; recommending educator appraisal and counselor evaluation instruments; and developing plans for special, bilingual, compensatory, gifted and talented, vocational and technology education.

Texas students, beginning with the Class of 1987, have been required to pass an exit-level exam, along with their courses, in order to receive a diploma from a Texas public high school.

Beginning with the Class of 2005, Texas students must pass the exit-level Texas Assessment of Knowledge and Skills (TAKS) to meet this graduation requirement. TAKS, which is the most rigorous graduation test ever given to Texas students, covers English language arts, mathematics, science and social studies.

The United States flag briefly hides the hot summer sun as the Coppell High School band practices for a Fourth of July parade. File photo.

To give citizens a sense of how schools are performing, Texas has issued ratings for its public school districts and campuses since 1993. The school accountability system is being renovated in 2003–2004. The new system is expected to be based on TAKS scores and high school completion rates.

A teacher also may remove a disruptive student from class and, subject to review by a campus committee, veto the student's return to class. The district must provide alternative education for students removed from class. A student must be placed in alternative education for assault, selling drugs or alcohol, substance abuse or public lewdness. A student must be expelled and referred to the appropriate court for serious offenses, such as murder or aggravated assault.

## Actions of the 78th Texas Legislature

### Affecting Public Schools

The 78th Texas Legislature passed about 135 education bills during the 2003 regular session. The legislation ranged from one requiring the national motto "In God We Trust" to be posted in classrooms to one sunsetting the state's current school finance system.

One of the most far-reaching bills approved is HB3459, which includes provisions that repeal the current school finance system as of Sept. 1, 2004, contingent on the passage of a comprehensive replacement system; substantially decrease the level of state monitoring of public schools; and require the content of the state's student tests to be made public every other year instead of every year.

In response to concerns about the state's high school dropout rate and increased graduation requirements, the legislature passed the High School Completion and Success Initiative, which will dedicate more than $100 million to high school reform efforts and programs designed to keep students in schools.

Another bill, SB618, requires the commissioner of education to "reconstitute" a campus that has been rated low-performing for two years in a row under the state's school accountability system. Reconstituting a campus means replacing all or most of a school's staff. Displaced staff members are moved to other positions in the district. This new law replaces an older law that made reconstitution permissible, rather than mandatory.

The rise in patriotism seen around the country after the Sept. 11 terrorist attack seems to have helped spur the passage of some legislation. Beginning in fall 2003, schools must set aside a minute each day for silent prayer or meditation, followed by the recitation of the pledges of allegiance to the United States and Texas flags. It has been a voluntary but common-place occurrence for the U.S. Pledge of Allegiance to be said in Texas public schools. Another new law requires public schools to display the national motto "In God We Trust" in each classroom, auditorium and cafeteria.

## Charter Schools

Charter-school legislation in Texas provides for three types of charter schools: the home-rule school district charter, the campus or campus-program charter and the open-enrollment charter.

As of July 2003, no district has expressed official interest in home-rule charter status, because of its complex developmental procedures. Houston, Dallas, Nacogdoches, San Antonio and Spring Branch school districts have created campus charter schools, which are overseen by each school district's board of trustees.

Open-enrollment charter schools are public schools released from some Texas education laws and regulations. These schools are granted by the State Board of Education (SBOE). This charter contract is typically granted for 5 to 10 years and can be revoked if the school violates its charter.

As of July 15, 2003, a total of 225 open-enrollment charter schools have been chartered. As of the summer of 2003, 184 charters are open and educating about 49,000 students. Many charter schools have focused their efforts on educating young people who are at risk of dropping out of school or who have dropped out and then returned to school. ☆

# Brief History of Higher Education in Texas

While there were earlier efforts toward higher education, the first permanent institutions established were church-supported schools:

• **Rutersville University**, established in 1840 by Methodist minister Martin Ruter in Fayette County, predecessor of **Southwestern University**, Georgetown, established in 1843;

• **Baylor University,** now at Waco, but established in 1845 at Independence, Washington County, by the Texas Union Baptist Association; and

• **Austin College**, now at Sherman, but founded in 1849 at Huntsville by the Brazos Presbytery of the Old School Presbyterian Church.

Students pass through the main quadrangle on the campus of Texas State University –San Marcos in Hays County. In 2003, the school's name was changed from Southwest Texas State University, which it had been called since 1969. In the school's 100-year history, its name has changed six times. File photo.

Other historic Texas schools of collegiate rank included: **Larissa College**, 1848, at Larissa, Cherokee County; **McKenzie College**, 1841, Clarksville; **Chappell Hill Male and Female Institute**, 1850, Chappell Hill; **Soule University**, 1855, Chappell Hill; **Johnson Institute**, 1852, Driftwood, Hays County; **Nacogdoches University**, 1845, Nacogdoches; **Salado College**, 1859, Salado, Bell County. **Add-Ran College**, established at Thorp Spring, Hood County, in 1873, was the predecessor of present **Texas Christian University**, Fort Worth.

## Texas A&M and University of Texas

The **Agricultural and Mechanical College of Texas** (now **Texas A&M University**), authorized by the Legislature in 1871, opened its doors in 1876 to become the first publicly supported institution of higher education. In 1881, Texans established the **University of Texas** in Austin, with a medical branch in Galveston. The Austin institution opened Sept. 15, 1883, the Galveston school in 1891.

## First College for Women

In 1901, the 27th Legislature established the **Girls Industrial College**, which began classes at its campus in Denton in 1903. A campaign to establish a state industrial college for women was led by the State Grange and Patrons of Husbandry.

A bill was signed into law on April 6, 1901, creating the college. It was charged with a dual mission, which continues to guide the university today — to provide a liberal education and to prepare young women with a specialized education "for the practical industries of the age." In 1905 the name of the college was changed to the **College of Industrial Arts**; in 1934, it was changed to **Texas State College for Women**. Since 1957 the name of the institution, which is now the largest university principally for women in the United States, has been the **Texas Woman's University.**

## Historic, Primarily Black Colleges

A number of Texas schools were established primarily for blacks, although collegiate racial integration is now complete in the state. The black-oriented institutions include state-supported **Prairie View A&M University** (originally established as **Alta Vista Agricultural College** in 1876), Prairie View; **Texas Southern University**, Houston; and privately supported **Huston-Tillotson College**, Austin; **Jarvis Christian College**, Hawkins; **Wiley College**, Marshall; **Paul Quinn College**, originally located in Waco, now in Dallas; and **Texas College**, Tyler.

Predominantly black colleges that are important in the history of higher education in Texas, but which have ceased operations, include **Bishop College**, established in Marshall in 1881, then moved to Dallas; **Mary Allen College**, established in Crockett in 1886; and **Butler College**, originally named the **Texas Baptist Academy,** in 1905 in Tyler. ☆

---

# Recent Developments in Texas Higher Education

Source: Texas Higher Education Coordinating Board; www.thecb.state.tx.us/

## State Appropriations

For the 2004–2005 biennium, beginning Sept. 1, 2003, and ending Aug. 31, 2005, general revenue appropriations to higher education will be $10,060,200,000, which represents a 1.7 percent ($173,300,000) decrease from the $10,233,400,000 appropriated for the previous biennium (Sept. 1, 2001, through Aug. 31, 2003).

## Enrollment

Enrollment in Texas' public and independent, or private, colleges and universities in fall 2002 totaled 1,102,502 students, an increase of 67,184, or 6.5 percent, from fall 2001.

Enrollment in the 35 public universities increased by 24,948 students (5.8 percent) to 455,718 students. Thirty-two universities reported enrollment increases, while three reported decreases.

The state's public community college districts and Lamar state colleges, which award two-year degrees, reported fall 2002 enrollments totaling 505,211 students, an increase of 37,010 students, or 7.9 percent, over the previous fall. All but one of the state's 50 community college districts reported enrollment increases, while two two-year state colleges and one technical institute reported decreases.

The public Texas State Technical College System reported fall 2002 enrollments totaling 10,559 students, an increase of 447 students, or 4.4 percent, over fall 2001.

Enrollments for fall 2002 at the 37 independent senior colleges and universities in Texas increased to 115,279 students, up 4,020 students, or 3.6 percent, from fall 2001. The state's two independent junior colleges reported 678 students in fall 2002, an increase of eight students over

2001.

Public medical, dental, nursing and allied-health institutions of higher education reported enrollments totaling 13,795 students in fall 2002, up 695 students, or 5.3 percent, from fall 2001.

Enrollment at independent health-related institutions totaled 1,262 students, up 56 students from the previous fall.

## "Closing the Gaps by 2015"

Closing the Gaps by 2015, the state's higher education plan, was adopted in 2000. It establishes four goals to "close the gaps" — both within Texas and in comparison with other states — in student participation, student success, quality academic programs and research efforts by 2015.

The plan's first goal calls for enrolling in Texas higher education by 2015 an additional 300,000 academically prepared students — beyond the 200,000 students already expected based on past trends.

The second goal calls for the state to increase by 50 percent the number of degrees and other higher education academic credentials awarded by 2015.

The third goal challenges the state to substantially increase the number of nationally recognized programs and services at colleges and universities in our state.

The fourth goal aims at increasing federal science and research funding to Texas higher education institutions by 50 percent.

To support the plan, the Legislature in recent years has increased funding for financial aid programs to help students pay college costs, strengthened the curriculum for public school students, and established a statewide higher education awareness and motivational campaign (see College for Texans campaign Web site: http://www.thecb.state.tx.us/SAMC/index.cfm). These and other legislative efforts support the state's higher education institutions as they work to close the gaps in other ways, based on their strengths and using their creativity.

For more information about Closing the Gaps by 2015, including progress reports, see the Texas Higher Education Coordinating Board's Web site at www.thecb.state.tx.us.

## Academics

The 78th Legislature repealed the Texas Academic Skills Program and replaced it with a new program, called the Success Initiative, which gives public colleges and universities more flexibility in helping students succeed in college. The Success Initiative requires public higher education institutions to assess students' basic academic skills, work with students to improve those skills when nec-

essary, and determine when students have achieved the appropriate skill level.

The higher education and public education communities continue to work closely to ensure that students are prepared to succeed as they advance through the state's educational system. Through the state's P-16 Council, for example, representatives of the Texas Higher Education Coordinating Board, the Texas Education Agency, the State Board for Educator Certification, other public and higher education organizations, and legislative and other political leaders to meet regularly to improve and coordinate education at every level throughout Texas.

## Tuition, Fees and Financial Aid

Tuition rates were deregulated by the 78th Legislature, which allowed Texas public universities to charge tuition rates that its governing board considers necessary for the effective operation of the institution. This legislation also allows a university's governing board to set a different tuition rate for each degree program, for different course levels, or as otherwise considered appropriate by the governing board to increase graduation rates, encourage efficient use of facilities, or enhance employee performance. Institutions will be required to set aside some of any additional revenues they raise to provide financial aid for undergraduate students.

To help students pay for college, the 78th Texas Legislature established the Texas B-On-Time Student Loan Program. This program offers zero-interest educational loans to recent high school graduates who have completed the Recommended High School Program (college-preparatory curriculum) and who enroll full-time at a Texas public higher education institution. If the student graduates with a "B" average and on time, the student isn't required to repay the loan, For example, the student must complete a four-year degree within four years, or receive credit for no more than six semester credit hours of college work beyond the number of hours required for the student's degree.

The 78th Legislature also increased funding for the TEXAS Grant program to $324 million for the 2004-05 biennium. This program provides grants to students who take the Recommended High School Program (college-preparatory curriculum) in high school and have financial need. In addition, funding for work-study financial aid was increased, and other financial aid programs were maintained.

The Doctoral Incentive Loan Repayment Program was also established by the legislature to increase the number of people from underrepresented groups in faculty and administrative positions at public and independent institutions of higher education in Texas. ☆

---

# Multi-Institution Teaching Centers

*A number of higher-education institutions have opened multi-institution cooperative teaching centers off their main campuses. Below are listed the ones open as of August 2003.*

**Austin: North Austin/Williamson County MITC:** 12515 Mellow Meadow Lane, 78750; Texas State University–San Marcos, Austin Community College, Temple College at Taylor.

**Dallas: The University Center of Dallas**, 1901 Main St., 75201; University of Texas at Dallas, University of Texas at Arlington, Texas A&M University-Commerce, Midwestern State University, University of North Texas, Texas Woman's University.

**Denton: University of North Texas System Center at Dallas**, P.O Box 311306, 76203-1306; University of North Texas system institutions.

**Killeen: Tarleton State University at Central Texas,** 1901 S. Clear Creek Road, 76540-1416; Tarleton State University system institutions.

**San Antonio: Texas A&M University–Kingsville System Center at Palo Alto,** 1400 West Villaret, 78224; Texas A&M University–Kingsville and Palo Alto College.

**Sugar Land: University of Houston System–Sugar Land**, 5500 Julie Rivers Dr., Ste. 330, 77478; the University of Houston System colleges.

**The Woodlands: The University Center**, 3232 College Park Dr., 77384; North Harris Montgomery Community College District, Prairie View A&M University, Texas A&M University, University of Houston, Sam Houston State University, Texas Southern University, University of Houston–Downtown. ☆

# Universities and Colleges

*Source: Texas Higher Education Coordinating Board and institutions. In some cases, dates of establishment differ from those given in the preceding discussion because schools use the date when authorization was given, rather than actual date of first classwork. For explanation of type of institution and other symbols, see notes at end of table.* **www.thecb.state.tx.us**

| Name of Institution; Location; (Type* - Ownership, if private sectarian institution); Date of Founding; President (unless otherwise noted) | Number of Faculty† | Enrollment | | |
|---|---|---|---|---|
| | | Fall Term 2002 | Summer Session 2002 | Extension or Continuing Ed. |
| ‡Abilene Christian University—Abilene; (3 - Church of Christ); 1906 (as Childers Classical Institute; became **Abilene Christian College** by 1914; became university in 1976); Dr. Royce Money | 310 | 4,761 | 2,103 | 233 |
| **ALAMO COMMUNITY COLLEGE DISTRICT (9) — Dr. J. Parker Chesson, Chancellor** | | | | |
| Northwest Vista College — San Antonio; (7); 1995; Dr. Jacqueline Claunch | 298 | 5,987 | 2,817 | 285 |
| Palo Alto College—San Antonio; (7); 1985; Dr. Ana M. "Cha" Guzmán | 433 | 7,061 | 4,157 | 597 |
| ‡ St. Philip's College—San Antonio; (7); 1898; Dr. Angie S. Runnels | 200 | 9,336 | 3,758 | 8,323 |
| San Antonio College—San Antonio; (7); 1925; Dr. Robert E. Zeigler | 1,042 | 21,537 | 14,697 | 1,818 |
| Alvin Community College—Alvin; (7); 1949; Dr. A. Rodney Allbright | 92 | 4,166 | 4,043 | 2,387 |
| Amarillo College—Amarillo; (7); 1929; Dr. William H. Lindemann Jr. | 250 | 9,229 | 3,705 | 15,091 |
| Amberton University—Garland; (3); 1971 (as **Amber University**; name changed in spring 2001); Dr. Douglas W. Warner | 65 | 1,625 | 1,500 | NA |
| Angelina College—Lufkin; (7); 1968; Dr. Larry Phillips | 110 | 4,968 | 2,613 | 2,574 |
| Angelo State University—San Angelo (See **Texas State University System**) | | | | |
| ‡Arlington Baptist College—Arlington; (3 - Baptist); 1939 (as **Bible Baptist Seminary**; changed to present name in 1965); Dr. David Bryant | 26 | 224 | 70 | 6 |
| Austin College—Sherman; (3 - Presbyterian USA); 1849; Dr. Oscar C. Page | 90 | 1,323 | ** | ** |
| ‡Austin Community College—Austin; (7); 1972; Dr. Richard Fonte | 1,389 | 25,420 | 19,099 | 6,666 |
| Austin Presbyterian Theological Seminary—Austin; Presbyterian; 3-yr; 1902 (successor to **Austin School of Theology**, est. 1884); Theodore J. Wardlaw | 23 | 260 | 62 | 14 |
| Baptist Missionary Association Theological Seminary—Jacksonville; Baptist Missionary, 3-yr.; 1955; Dr. Charley Holmes | 8 | 100 | 104 | 0 |
| ‡ Baylor College of Medicine—Houston; (5 - Baptist until 1969); 1903 (Dallas; moved to Houston, 1943); Ralph D. Feigin, M.D. | ** | 1,199 | ** | ** |
| Baylor University—Waco; (3 - So. Baptist); 1845 (at Independence; merged with Waco University in 1887 and moved to Waco); Dr. Robert B. Sloan Jr. | 777 | 14,159 | 5,851 | ** |
| Bee County College—Beeville (see **Coastal Bend College**) | | | | |
| Blinn College—Brenham; (7); 1883 (as academy; jr. college, 1927); Dr. Donald E. Voelter | 589 | 13,806 | 8,556 | 967 |
| Brazosport College—Lake Jackson; (7); 1967; Dr. Millicent M. Valek | 205 | 4,140 | 2,656 | 6,892 |
| Brookhaven College—Farmers Branch (See **Dallas County Community College District**) | | | | |
| Cedar Valley College—Lancaster (See **Dallas County Community College District**) | | | | |
| Central Texas College District—Killeen; (7); 1965; Dr. James R. Anderson, Chancellor | 424 | 11,270 | 11,949 | 708 |
| Cisco Junior College—Cisco; (7); 1909 (as private institution; became state school in 1939); Dr. John Muller | 149 | 2,967 | 1,973§ | 553 |
| ‡Clarendon College—Clarendon; (7); 1898 (as church school; became state school in 1927); Dr. W. Myles Shelton | 29 | 1,000 | NA | NA |
| Coastal Bend College—Beeville; (7); (1966 as **Bee Co. College**, name changed in 1999); Dr. John Brockman | 99 | 3,694 | 2,266 | 588 |
| College of the Mainland—Texas City; (7); 1967; Dr. Homer M. Hayes | 89¶ | 3,628 | 2,949 | ** |
| College of St. Thomas More—Fort Worth; (3-Roman Catholic); 1981 (as **St. Thomas More Inst.**; became college 1989; accredited as 2-year college 1994); Dr. Dean M. Cassella, Provost | 14 | 76 | 4 | NA |
| Collin County Community College—McKinney; (7); 1985; Dr. Cary A. Israel | 975 | 15,970 | 8,351 | 2,003 |
| Concordia University—Austin; (3 - Mo. Lutheran); 1926 (as **Concordia Lutheran College**; name changed in 1995); Dr. Tom Cedel | 200 | 1,075 | 300 | 300 |
| Cooke County College—Gainesville (See **North Central Texas College**) | | | | |
| Corpus Christi State University—(See **Texas A&M University–Corpus Christi** listing under **Texas A&M University System**) | | | | |
| Dallas Baptist University—Dallas; (3 - Southern Baptist).; 1891 (as **Northwest Texas Bible College**; name changed to **Decatur Baptist College** in 1897; moved to Dallas and name changed to **Dallas Baptist College** in 1965; became university in 1985); Dr. Gary Cook | 344 | 4,417 | 2,305 | NA |
| Dallas Christian College—Dallas; (3 - Christian); 1950; Dr. John Derry | 10 | 250 | NA | NA |
| **DALLAS COUNTY COMMUNITY COLLEGE DISTRICT (9) — Dr. Jesus "Jess" Carreon, Chancellor** | | | | |
| Brookhaven College—Farmers Branch; (7); 1978; Dr. Alice W. Villadsen | 533 | 10,123 | 6,813 | 4,366 |
| Cedar Valley College—Lancaster; (7); 1977; Dr. Jennifer Wimbish | 182 | 4,345 | 2,652 | 1,858 |
| Eastfield College—Mesquite; (7); 1970; Dr. Rodger A. Pool | 509 | 10,504 | 7,006§ | 3,386 |
| El Centro College—Dallas; (7); 1966; Dr. Wright Lassiter | 372 | 6,015 | 1,937 | 5,127 |
| Mountain View College—Dallas; (7); 1970; Dr. Monique Amerman | 382 | 6,598 | 3,786 | 2,631 |
| North Lake College—Irving; (7); 1977; Dr. David England | 550 | 8,322 | 3,844 | 4,148 |
| Richland College—Dallas; (7); 1972; Dr. Stephen K. Mittelstet | 903 | 14,128 | 16,946§ | 8,200 |

| Name of Institution; Location; (Type* - Ownership, if private sectarian institution); Date of Founding; President (unless otherwise noted) | Number of Faculty† | Enrollment | | |
|---|---|---|---|---|
| | | Fall Term 2002 | Summer Session 2002 | Extension or Continuing Ed. |
| Dallas Theological Seminary—Dallas; private, graduate; 1924 (as **Evangelical Theological College**; name changed in 1936); Dr. Mark L. Bailey . . . . . . . . . . . . . . . . . | 88 | 1,617 | 837 | 335 |
| Del Mar College—Corpus Christi; (7); 1935; Dr. Gustavo R. Valadez Ortiz . . . . . . . . . . . . | 250 | 10,000 | NA | ** |
| Eastfield College—Mesquite (See **Dallas County Community College District**) | | | | |
| East Texas Baptist University—Marshall; (3 - Baptist); 1913 (as **College of Marshall**; became **East Texas Baptist Coll.**, 1944; became university in 1984); Dr. Bob E. Riley . . | 76 | 1,496 | ** | NA |
| East Texas State University (see **Texas A&M University-Commerce** in **Texas A&M System** listing) | | | | |
| East Texas State University at Texarkana (see **Texas A&M University-Texarkana** in **Texas A&M System** listing) | | | | |
| El Centro College—Dallas (See **Dallas County Community College District**) | | | | |
| # El Paso Community College District—El Paso; (7); 1969; three campuses: **Rio Grande, TransMountain** and **Valle Verde**; Dr. Richard Rhodes . . . . . . . . . . . . . . . . . . . . . . . . . . | 1,200 | 20,000 | ** | ** |
| Episcopal Theological Seminary of the Southwest—Austin; Episcopal; Graduate-level; 1952; Very Rev. Dr. Titus L. Presler . . . . . . . . . . . . . . . . . . . . . . . . . . . . . . . . . . . . . . | 29 | 127 | NA | NA |
| Frank Phillips College—Borger; (7); 1948; Dr. Herbert J. Swender. . . . . . . . . . . . . . . . . . | 111 | 1,333 | 563§ | NA |
| Galveston College—Galveston; (7); 1967; Dr. Elva Concha LeBlanc . . . . . . . . . . . . . . . . . | 59 | 2,369 | ** | 5,000 |
| Grayson County College—Denison; (7); 1963; Dr. Alan Scheibmeir . . . . . . . . . . . . . . . . | 125 | 3,512 | 2,700 | 3,600†† |
| Hardin-Simmons University—Abilene; (3 - So. Baptist); 1891 (as **Simmons College**; became **Simmons University**, 1925; present name since, 1934); Dr. W. Craig Turner . . . | 196 | 2,291 | 1,219 | 78 |
| Hill College—Hillsboro; (7); 1923 (as **Hillsboro Junior College**; name changed, 1962); Dr. William R. Auvenshine . . . . . . . . . . . . . . . . . . . . . . . . . . . . . . . . . . . . . . . . . | 66 | 2,933 | 724 | 404 |
| Houston Baptist University—Houston; (3 - Baptist); 1960; Dr. Doug Hodo . . . . . . . . . . . . | 250 | 2,900 | 990 | 800 |
| **HOUSTON COMMUNITY COLLEGE SYSTEM**—Houston; (9); 1971; **Bruce H. Leslie, Chancellor**. System consists of following colleges (president): <br>    **Central College** (Dr. Patricia Williamson) <br>    **Northeast College** (Dr. Margaret Forde) <br>    **Northwest College** (Dr. Zachary Hodges) <br>    **Southeast College** (Dr. Diane Castillo) <br>    **Southwest College** (Dr. Sue Cox) | 3,010 | 54,758 | 39,875 | 1,366 |
| # Howard College—Big Spring; (7); 1945; (includes **SouthWest Collegiate Institute for the Deaf**, Ron Brasel, Provost); Dr. Cheryl T. Sparks . . . . . . . . . . . . . . . . . . . . . . . | 170 | 2,854 | 1,348 | 3,462 |
| Howard Payne University—Brownwood; (3 - Baptist); 1889; Dr. Lanny Hall . . . . . . . . . . . . | 130 | 1,410 | 521 | 148 |
| Huston-Tillotson College—Austin; (3 - Methodist/Church of Christ); 1875 (**Tillotson College**, 1875, **Samuel Huston College**, 1876; merged 1952); Dr. Larry L. Earvin . . . . . | 36 | 642 | 107 | NA |
| International Bible College—San Antonio; (3); 1944; Rev. David W. Cook . . . . . . . . . . . . . | 20 | 117 | NA | NA |
| Jacksonville College—Jacksonville; (8 - Missionary Baptist); 1899; Dr. Edwin Crank . . . . . | 25 | 220 | 100 | NA |
| ‡ Jarvis Christian College—Hawkins; (3); 1912; Dr. Sebetha Jenkins . . . . . . . . . . . . . . . . | ** | 537 | ** | ** |
| Kilgore College—Kilgore; (7); 1935; Dr. William M. Holda . . . . . . . . . . . . . . . . . . . . . . . | 263 | 4,578 | 3,045§ | 4,167 |
| Kingwood College—Kingwood (See **North Harris Montgomery Community College Dist.**) | | | | |
| Lamar University and all branches (see **Texas State University System**) | | | | |
| ‡ Laredo Community College—Laredo; (7); 1946; Dr. Ramon H. Dovalina . . . . . . . . . . . . . | 337 | 7,259 | 4,480 | 3,545 |
| Lee College—Baytown; (7); 1934; Dr. Martha Ellis . . . . . . . . . . . . . . . . . . . . . . . . . . . . . | 364 | 6,406 | 4,615 | 2,616 |
| LeTourneau University—Longview; (3); 1946 (as **LeTourneau Technical Institute**; became 4-yr. college in 1961); Dr. Alvin O. Austin . . . . . . . . . . . . . . . . . . . . . . . . . . . | 62 | 3,338 | 2,174 | 25 |
| Lon Morris College—Jacksonville; (8 - Methodist); 1854 (as **Danville Academy**; changed in 1873 to **Alexander Inst.**; present name, 1923); Dr. Clifford M. Lee . . . . . . . . . . . . . | ** | 462 | NA | NA |
| Lubbock Christian University—Lubbock; (3 - Church of Christ); 1957; Dr. L. Ken Jones . . | 135 | 1,851 | 816 | 0 |
| ‡ McLennan Community College—Waco; (7); 1965; Dr. Dennis Michaelis . . . . . . . . . . . . . | ** | 5,721 | ** | ** |
| ‡ McMurry University—Abilene; (3 - Methodist); 1923; Dr. Robert E. Shimp . . . . . . . . . . . . | 104 | 1,344 | 612 | NA |
| ‡ Midland College—Midland; (7); 1972; Dr. David E. Daniel . . . . . . . . . . . . . . . . . . . . . . . | ** | 4,841 | ** | ** |
| Midwestern State University—Wichita Falls; (2); 1922; Dr. Jesse W. Rogers . . . . . . . . . . . | 1,346 | 6,035 | 2,587 | 2,073 |
| Montgomery College—Conroe (See **North Harris Montgomery Community College Dist.**) | | | | |
| Mountain View College—Dallas (See **Dallas County Community College District**) | | | | |
| ‡ Navarro College—Corsicana; (7); 1946; Dr. Richard Sanchez . . . . . . . . . . . . . . . . . . . . | 325 | 4,050 | 1,562 | 1,488 |
| North Central Texas College—Gainesville; (7); 1924 (as **Gainesville Jr. College**; **Cooke County College**, 1960; present name, 1994); Dr. Ronnie Glasscock . . | 256 | 6,181 | 2,609 | 1,316 |
| Northeast Texas Community College—Mount Pleasant; (7); 1984; Dr. Charles B. Florio . | 50 | 2,423 | 1,454 | 722 |
| # NORTH HARRIS MONTGOMERY COMMUNITY COLLEGE DISTRICT (9)— Dr. John E. Pickelman, Chancellor. Includes these colleges, location (president) . . . . | 485 | 35,320 | 18,721 | 10,846 |
| :‡ Cy-Fair College (Dr. Diane Troyer) | | | | |
| : :Kingwood College, Kingwood (Dr. Linda Stegall) | 350 | 6,100 | 3,082 | 1,953 |
| : :Montgomery College, Conroe (Dr. Thomas Butler) | 300 | 6,500 | 3,300 | 5,000 |
| :‡ North Harris College, Houston (Dr. David Sam) | | | | |
| : :Tomball College, Tomball (Dr. Ray H. Hawkins) | ** | 8,232 | 4,637 | ** |
| North Lake College—Irving (See **Dallas County Community College District**) | | | | |

| Name of Institution; Location; (Type* - Ownership, if private sectarian institution); Date of Founding; President (unless otherwise noted) | Number of Faculty† | Enrollment | | |
|---|---|---|---|---|
| | | Fall Term 2002 | Summer Session 2002 | Extension or Continuing Ed. |
| Northwest Vista College (see Alamo Community College District) | | | | |
| ‡ Northwood University—Cedar Hill; private; 1966; Dr. William C. Oliver, Provost ....... | 50 | 1,200 | 250 | 300 |
| Oblate School of Theology—San Antonio; Rom. Catholic, 4-yr.; 1903 (formerly DeMazenod Scholasticate); Rev. J. William Morell, O.M.I. ......................... | ** | 205 | 30 | 45 |
| Odessa College—Odessa; (7); 1946; Dr. Vance Gipson ....................... | 287 | 4,953 | 2,503§ | 3,915 |
| Our Lady of the Lake University of San Antonio—San Antonio; (3 - Catholic); 1895 (as acad. for girls; sr. college, 1911; university, in 1975); Sally Mahoney .................. | 281 | 3,395 | 458 | NA |
| Palo Alto College—San Antonio (See Alamo Community College District) | | | | |
| Panola College—Carthage; (7); 1947 (as Panola Junior College; name changed, 1988); Dr. Gregory Powell ................................................ | 63 | 1,694 | 735 | 157 |
| Paris Junior College—Paris; (7); 1924; Dr. Bobby R. Walters ....................... | 205 | 3,653 | 2,786 | 1,554 |
| Paul Quinn College—Dallas; (3-AME Church); 1872 (Waco; Dallas, 1990); Dr. Dwight Fennell | 146 | 860 | 170 | 472 |
| Prairie View A&M University—Prairie View (See Texas A&M University System) | | | | |
| Ranger College—Ranger; (7); 1926; Dr. Joe Mills ..................................... | 65 | 894 | 617 | 125 |
| Rice University (William Marsh)—Houston; (3); chartered 1891, opened 1912 (as Rice Institute; name changed in 1960); Dr. Malcolm Gillis ............................ | 688 | 4,633 | NA | 2,492 |
| Richland College—Dallas (See Dallas County Community College District) | | | | |
| St. Edward's University—Austin; (3 - Roman Catholic); 1885; Dr. George E. Martin ...... | 388 | 4,267 | 2,051 | 447 |
| St. Mary's University—San Antonio; (3 - Catholic); 1852; Dr. Charles Cotrell ........... | 324 | 4,242 | 1,786§ | 52 |
| St. Philip's College—San Antonio (See Alamo Community College District) | | | | |
| Sam Houston State University—Huntsville (See Texas State University System) | | | | |
| San Antonio College—San Antonio (See Alamo Community College District) | | | | |
| SAN JACINTO COLLEGE DISTRICT (9) — Dr. Bill Lindemann Includes these campuses, location (president):............................. | 1,152 | 23,9932 | 12,660 | 22,615 |
| Central, Pasadena ( Dr. Monte Blue); North, Houston (Dr. Charles Grant) South, Houston (Dr. Linda Watkins) | | | | |
| Schreiner University—Kerrville; (3 - Presbyterian); 1923; Dr. Charles Timothy Summerlin . | 73 | 780 | 120 | 0 |
| Southern Methodist University—Dallas; (3 - Methodist); 1911; Dr. R. Gerald Turner ..... | 528 | 10,000 | 4,029 | NA |
| South Plains College—Levelland; (7); 1957; Dr. Gary D. McDaniel ................... | 289 | 9,032 | 2,500 | ** |
| South Texas College of Law—Houston; private, 3-yr.; 1923; Frank T. Read, Dean and Pres. | 90 | 1,200 | 547 | NA |
| South Texas Community College—McAllen; (7); NA; Dr. Shirley A. Reed .............. | 296 | 13,691 | 5,479 | 1,000†† |
| Southwest Collegiate Institute for the Deaf — Big Spring (See Howard College) | | | | |
| ‡ Southwest Texas Junior College—Uvalde; (7); 1946; Dr. Ismael Sosa .............. | ** | 3,716 | ** | ** |
| Southwest Texas State University—San Marcos (see Texas State University–San Marcos under Texas State University System) | | | | |
| Southwestern Adventist University—Keene; (3 - Seventh-Day Adventist); 1893 (as Keene Industrial Acad.; named Southwestern Jr. College in 1916; changed to Southwestern Union College in 1963, then to Southwestern Adventist College in 1980; became university in 1996); Dr. Don Sahly ............................. | 75 | 1,103 | 260 | 289 |
| Southwestern Assemblies of God University—Waxahachie; (3 - Assemblies of God); 1927 (in Enid, Okla., as Southwestern Bible School; moved to Fort Worth and merged with South Central Bible Institute in 1941; moved to Waxahachie as Southwestern Bible Institute in 1943; changed to Southwestern Assemblies of God College,1963; university since 1996); Dr. Kermit S. Bridges ................................ | 96 | 1,676 | ** | NA |
| Southwestern Baptist Theological Seminary—Fort Worth; Southern Baptist, 4-yr.; 1908; Dr. Kenneth Hemphill ....................................................... | 162 | 3,156 | NA | 2,236 |
| Southwestern Christian College—Terrell; (3 - Church of Christ); 1948 (as Southern Bible Inst. in Fort Worth; moved to Terrell, changed name to present, 1950); Dr. Jack Evans Sr. | 18 | 213 | NA | NA |
| Southwestern University—Georgetown; (3 - Methodist); 1840 (Southwestern University was a merger of Rutersville (1840), Wesleyan (1846) and McKenzie (1841) colleges and Soule University (1855). First named Texas University; chartered under present name in 1875); Dr. Jake B. Schrum .......................................... | 150 | 1,266 | NA | NA |
| Stephen F. Austin State University—Nacogdoches; (2); 1921; Dr. Roland Smith ........ | 685 | 11,356 | 5,960 | 800 |
| Sul Ross State University—Alpine (See Texas State University System) | | | | |
| Sul Ross State University-Rio Grande College —Uvalde (See Texas State University System) | | | | |
| Tarleton State University—Stephenville (See Texas A&M University System) | | | | |
| Tarrant County College District—Fort Worth; (7); 1965 (as Tarrant County Junior College; name changed 1999); Dr. Leonardo de la Garza, Chancellor; four campuses (location, campus president): ........................................... | 1,320 | 31,169 | 21,889 | 20,981 |
| Northeast (Hurst, Dr. Larry Darlage), | 412 | 10,975 | 7,130 | 5,553 |
| Northwest (Fort Worth, Dr. Michael Saenz) | 261 | 5,259 | 2,987 | 8,597 |
| South (Fort Worth, Dr. Ernest Thomas) | | | | |
| Southeast (Arlington, Dr. Judith Carrier) | | | | |
| Temple College—Temple; (7); 1926; Dr. Marc A. Nigliazzo ...................... | 82 | 3,664 | 2,376 | 1,349 |
| Texarkana College—Texarkana; (7); 1927; Dr. Frank Coleman ..................... | 110 | 4,129 | 1,841 | 10,300 |

| Name of Institution; Location; (Type* - Ownership, if private sectarian institution); Date of Founding; President (unless otherwise noted) | Number of Faculty† | Enrollment | | |
|---|---|---|---|---|
| | | Fall Term 2002 | Summer Session 2002 | Extension or Continuing Ed. |
| Texas A&I University—Kingsville (See **Texas A&M University-Kingsville** listing under **Texas A&M University System**) | | | | |
| **TEXAS A&M UNIVERSITY SYSTEM (1)** —Dr. Howard D. Graves, Chancellor | | | | |
| Prairie View A&M University—Prairie View; (2); 1876 (as **Alta Vista Agricultural College**; changed to **Prairie View State Normal Institute** in 1879; later **Prairie View Normal and Industrial College**; in 1947 changed to **Prairie View A&M College** as branch of **Texas A&M University System**; present name since 1973); Dr. Charles A. Hines . . . . . . . . . . | 385 | 6,609 | 2,657 | NA |
| Tarleton State University—Stephenville; (2); 1899 (as **John Tarleton College**; taken over by state in 1917 as **John Tarleton Agricultural College**; changed 1949 to **Tarleton State College**; present name since 1973; includes campus in Killeen); Dr. Dennis McCabe . . . . . . . . . . . . . . . . . . . . . . . . . | 453 | 8,320 | 4,865 | NA |
| Texas A&M International University-Laredo; (2); 1970 (as **Laredo State University**; name changed to present form 1993); Dr. Ray M Keck | 135 | 3,726 | 3,861§ | 88 |
| Texas A&M University—College Station; (2); 1876 (as **Agricultural and Mechanical College of Texas**; present name since 1963; includes **College of Veterinary Medicine** and **College of Medicine** at College Station); Robert Gates. . . . . . . . . . . . . . . | 2,158 | 44,026 | 18,228 | NA |
| Texas A&M University - Commerce—Commerce; (2); 1889 (as **East Texas Normal College**; renamed **East Texas State Teachers College** in 1923; "Teachers" dropped, 1957; university status conferred and named changed to **East Texas State University**, 1965; transferred to Texas A&M system 1995; includes **ETSU Metroplex Commuter Facility**, Mesquite); Dr. Keith D. McFarland . . . . . . . . . . . . . . | 545 | 8,483 | 4,900 | 3,775 |
| Texas A&M University-Corpus Christi —Corpus Christi; (2); 1973 (as upper-level **Corpus Christi State Univ.**; present name since 1993; 4-year in 1994); Dr. Robert R. Furgason . | 513 | 7,607 | 4,387 | NA |
| Texas A&M University at Galveston—Galveston; (2); 1962 (as **Texas Maritime Academy**; changed to **Moody College of Marine Sciences and Maritime Resources** and became 4-yr. college in 1971); Dr. W. Michael Kemp | 135 | 1,363 | 521 | 1,210 |
| Texas A&M University-Kingsville—Kingsville; (2); 1925 (as **South Texas Teachers College**; name changed to **Texas College of Arts and Industries** in 1929; to **Texas A&I University**, 1967; made part of **Univ. of South Texas System** in 1977; entered A&M system in 1993); Dr. Rumaldo Z. Juárez . . . . . . . . . . . . . . . . . . . . . . . | 325 | 6,560 | 6,292§ | 206 |
| Texas A&M University System Health Science Center —(Includes **Baylor College of Dentistry, College of Medicine, Graduate School of Biomedical Sciences, Institute of Biosciences and Technology, School of Rural Public Health**, and **HSC Statellite** locations) | | | | |
| Texas A&M University - Texarkana—Texarkana; (2 - upper-level); 1971 (as **East Texas State University at Texarkana**, transferred to Texas A&M system and name changed, 1995); Dr. Stephen R. Hensley . . . . . . . . . . . . . . . . . . . . . . | 43 | 1,362 | 781 | NA |
| West Texas A&M University—Canyon; (2); 1910 (as **West Texas State Normal College**; became **West Texas State Teachers College** in 1923; **West Texas State College**, 1949; changed to **West Texas State Univ.**, 1949; present name, 1993); Dr. Russell C. Long . . . | 293 | 6,780 | 4,212 | 2,220 |
| Texas Baptist Institute-Seminary—Henderson; (3 - Calvary Baptist); 1948; Dr. Ray O. Brooks . . . . . . . . . . . . . . . . . . . . . . . . . | 13 | 127 | NA | NA |
| Texas Christian University—Fort Worth; (3 - Disciples of Christ); 1873 (as **Add- Ran College** at Thorp Spring; name changed to **Add-Ran Christian Univ.** 1890; moved to Waco 1895; present name, 1902; moved to Fort Worth 1910); Dr. Michael R. Ferrari, Chancellor | 415 | 8,074 | 2,768 | NA |
| Texas College—Tyler; (3 - C.M.E.); 1894; Dr. Billy C. Hawkins . . . . . . . . . . . . . . . . . . . . . . | 42 | 617 | 109 | 0 |
| Texas College of Osteopathic Medicine—Fort Worth (See **University of North Texas Health Science Center at Fort Worth**) | 152 | 416 | NA | NA |
| Texas Lutheran University—Seguin; (3 - Lutheran); 1891 (in Brenham as **Evangelical Lutheran College**; moved to Seguin, 1912 and renamed **Lutheran College of Seguin**; renamed **Texas Lutheran College**, 1932; changed to university, 1996); Dr. Jon N. Moline | 125 | 1,368 | 230 | 142 |
| Texas Southern University—Houston; (2); 1926 (as **Houston Colored Junior Coll.**; upper level added, name changed to **Houston College for Negroes** in mid-1930s; became **Texas State University for Negroes**, 1947; present name, 1951); Dr. Priscilla D. Slade . | ** | (,739 | 2,674 | 500 |
| Texas Southmost College—Brownsville (see **The University of Texas at Brownsville** under **University of Texas System** listing) | | | | |
| ‡TEXAS STATE TECHNICAL COLLEGE SYSTEM (6) — Dr. r. Bill Segura, Chancellor Includes extension centers in Abilene, Breckenridge and Brownwood, and the colleges listed below (location, president): | ** | ** | ** | ** |
|    Texas State Technical College-Harlingen (Dr. J. Gilbert Leal) | ** | ** | ** | ** |
|    Texas State Technical College-Marshall (Dr. J. Gary Hendricks) | 46 | 605 | 393 | 246 |
|    Texas State Technical College-West Texas—Sweetwater (Homer K. Taylor) | ** | 1,663 | 1,211 | 1,353 |
|    Texas State Technical College- Waco (established as James Connally Technical Institute; name changed in 1969), (Dr. Elton E. Stuckly). | 280 | 4,203 | 2,602 | 88 |
| **TEXAS STATE UNIVERSITY SYSTEM (1)—Dr. Lamar G. Urbanovsky, Chancellor** | | | | |
| Angelo State University—San Angelo; (2); 1928; Dr. E. James Hindman . . . . . . . . . . . . . | 316 | 6,268 | 4,304 | 686 |
| Lamar University—Beaumont; (2); 1923 (as **South Park Junior Coll.**; name changed to **Lamar Coll.**, 1932; name changed to **Lamar State Coll. of Technology**, 1951; present name, 1971; transferred from **Lamar Univ. System**, 1995); Dr. James M. Simmons . . . . | 314 | 9,802 | 4,984 | 1,366 |

| Name of Institution; Location; (Type* - Ownership, if private sectarian institution); Date of Founding; President (unless otherwise noted) | Number of Faculty† | Enrollment | | |
|---|---|---|---|---|
| | | Fall Term 2002 | Summer Session 2002 | Extension or Continuing Ed. |
| Lamar State College - Orange—Orange; (10); 1969 (transferred from Lamar University System, Sept. 1995; name changed to State College, 2000); Dr. J. Michael Shahan .... | 93 | 1,985 | 813§ | 117 |
| Lamar State College - Port Arthur—Port Arthur; (10); 1909 (as Port Arthur College; became part of Lamar Univ. in 1975; part of TSU system, 1995; name changed to State College, 2000); Dr. W. Sam Monroe ......... | 140 | 2,765 | 2,596 | 574 |
| Lamar Institute of Technology—Beaumont; (10); (part of TSU system, 1995); Dr. Robert D. Krienke ......... | 200 | 2,500 | 500 | 500 |
| Sam Houston State University—Huntsville; (2); 1879; Dr. James F. Gaertner ......... | 551 | 13,091 | 9,973 | 1,414 |
| Sul Ross State University—Alpine; (2); 1917 (as Sul Ross State Normal Coll.; changed to Sul Ross State Teachers Coll., 1923; to Sul Ross State Coll., 1949; present name since 1969) Dr. R. Vic Morgan ......... | 103 | 1,954 | 884 | 0 |
| Sul Ross State University-Rio Grande College—Uvalde, Eagle Pass and Del Rio (2 - upper level); 1973 (name changed from Sul Ross State University, Uvalde Center 1995) Dr. Joel Vela, vice president; Dr. Frank Abbott, dean. | 48 | 907 | 700 | 0 |
| Texas State University–San Marcos—San Marcos; (2); 1903 (as Southwest Texas Normal School; changed1918 to Southwest Texas State Normal College, in 1923 to Southwest Texas State Teachers College, in 1959 to Southwest Texas State College, in 1969 to Southwest Texas State University, and to present form in 2003); Dr. Denise M. Trauth ......... | 1,142 | 25,065 | 9,911 | 146 |
| **TEXAS TECH UNIVERSITY (1) —David R. Smith, Interim Chancellor** | | | | |
| Texas Tech University—Lubbock; (2); 1923 (as Texas Technological College; present name since 1969); Dr. Donald R. Haragan, interim president ......... | 1,437 | 27,500 | 9,156 | 2,137 |
| Texas Tech University Health Sciences Center—Lubbock; (4); 1972; Roy Wilson, M.D. ... | 750 | 1,972 | 931 | NA |
| Texas Wesleyan University—Fort Worth; (3 - United Methodist); 1891 (as college; present name since 1989); Dr. Harold G. Jeffcoat ......... | 138 | 2,834 | 1,702 | 0 |
| Texas Woman's University—Denton; (2); 1901 (as Coll. of Industrial Arts; name changed to Texas State Coll. for Women, 1934; present name, 1957); Dr. Ann Stuart, Chancellor and President......... | 729 | 8,736 | 4,761 | 6,947 |
| Tomball College—Tomball (See North Harris Montgomery Community College Dist.) | | | | |
| Trinity University—San Antonio; (3 - Presbyterian); 1869 (at Tehuacana; moved to Waxahachie, 1902; to San Antonio, 1942); Dr. John R. Brazil ......... | 223 | 2,700 | 360 | NA |
| Trinity Valley Community College—Athens; also campus at Terrell; (7); 1946 (originally Henderson County Junior College); Dr. Ronald C. Baugh ......... | 120 | 5,847 | 2,200 | 1,280 |
| Tyler Junior College—Tyler; (7); 1926; Dr. William R. Crowe ......... | 410 | 9,060 | 4,300 | 10,700 |
| University of Central Texas—Killeen (see Texas A&M University System, Tarleton State University Systems Center/Central Texas) | | | | |
| University of Dallas—Irving; (3 - Catholic); 1956; Msgr. Milam J. Joseph ......... | 130 | 3,170 | 1,500 | 300 |
| **UNIVERSITY OF HOUSTON SYSTEM (1) — Dr. Arthur K. Smith, Chancellor** | | | | |
| ‡ University of Houston—Houston; (2); 1927; Arthur K. Smith——————————— | ** | 34,400 | ** | ** |
| University of Houston-Clear Lake—Houston; (2 - upper level and grad.); 1974; Dr. William A. Staples......... | 486 | 7,753 | 4,492 | NA |
| University of Houston-Downtown—Houston; (2); 1948 (as South Texas College; became part of University of Houston in 1974) ; Dr. Max Castillo ......... | 493 | 10,528 | 7,114 | 6,212 |
| University of Houston-Victoria—Victoria; (2 - upper-level); 1973; Dr. Karen S. Haynes ... | 108 | 2,183 | 1,955 | NA |
| University of the Incarnate Word—San Antonio; (3 - Catholic); 1881 (as Incarnate Word College; name changed 1996); Dr. Louis J. Agnese Jr. ......... | 341 | 4,264 | 1,701 | NA' |
| University of Mary Hardin-Baylor—Belton; (3 - So. Baptist); 1845; Dr. Jerry G. Bawcom .. | 200 | 2,656 | 982 | 24 |
| University of North Texas—Denton; (2); 1890 (as North Texas Normal College; name changed 1923 to North Texas State Teachers Coll.; in 1949 to North Texas State Coll.; became university, 1961; present name since 1988); Dr. Norval F. Pohl ......... | 2,017 | 30,183 | 26,248 | NA |
| University of North Texas Health Science Center at Fort Worth—Fort Worth; (4);1966 (as private college; came under direction of North Texas State University in 1975; present name since 1993); Dr. Ronald R. Blanck, D.O. | 198 | 969 | 768 | 6,431 |
| University of St. Thomas—Houston; (3); 1947; Rev. J. Michael Miller, CSB ......... | 190 | 5,550 | ** | NA |
| **UNIVERSITY OF TEXAS SYSTEM (1) — Mark G. Yudof, Chancellor** | | | | |
| University of Texas at Arlington, The—Arlington; (2); 1895 (as Arlington Coll.; became state inst. in 1917 and renamed Grubbs Vocational Coll.; 1923 became North Texas Agricultural and Mechanical Coll.; became Arlington State Coll., 1949; present name since 1967); Dr. Robert E. Witt ......... | 990 | 23,821 | 11,205 | 3,257 |
| University of Texas at Austin, The—Austin; (2); 1883; Dr. Larry R. Faulkner ......... | 2,027 | 49,996 | 17,871 | NA |
| University of Texas at Brownsville, The (2 - upper-level); 1973 (as branch of Pan American Coll.; changed to Univ. of Texas-Pan American - Brownsville; present name, 1991) and Texas Southmost College (7); 1926 (as Brownsville Jr. Coll.; name changed, 1949) — Brownsville; Dr. Juliet V. Garcia ......... | 506 | 9,974 | 5,396 | 1,395 |
| University of Texas at Dallas, The—Richardson; (2); 1961 (as Graduate Research Center of the Southwest; changed to Southwest Center for Advanced Studies in 1967; joined U.T. System and present name, 1969; full undergraduate program, 1975); Dr. Franklyn G. Jenifer ......... | ** | 10,945 | ** | NA |
| University of Texas at El Paso, The—El Paso; (2); 1913 (as Texas Coll. of Mines and Metallurgy; changed to Texas Western Coll. of U.T., 1949; present name, 1967); Dr. Diana S. Natalicio ......... | 945 | 17,232 | 8,000 | 2,857 |

| Name of Institution; Location; (Type* - Ownership, if private sectarian institution); Date of Founding; President (unless otherwise noted) | Number of Faculty† | Enrollment | | |
|---|---|---|---|---|
| | | Fall Term 2002 | Summer Session 2002 | Extension or Continuing Ed. |
| **University of Texas-Pan American, The**—Edinburg; (2); 1927 (as **Edinburg Junior Coll.**; changed to **Pan American College** and made 4-yr., 1952; became **Pan American University** in 1971; present name since 1991); Dr. Miguel A. Nevárez . . . . . . . . . . . . . . . . . | 570 | 14,392 | 9,243 | 732 |
| ‡ **University of Texas of the Permian Basin, The**—Odessa; (2); 1969 (as 2-yr. upper- level institution; expanded to 4-yr., Sept. 1991); Dr. W. David Watts . . . . . . . . . . . . . . . . . . | 158 | 2,695 | 1,185 | NA |
| **University of Texas at San Antonio**—San Antonio; (2); 1969; Dr. Ricardo Romo . . . . . . . | ** | 22,016 | 10,530 | 512 |
| **University of Texas at Tyler**—Tyler; (2 - upper-level); 1971 (as **Tyler State Coll.**; became **Texas Eastern University**, 1975; joined U.T. System, 1979); Dr. Rodney H. Mabry . . . . . | 302 | 4,254 | 2,854 | ** |
| **University of Texas Health Science Center at Tyler (4) — Dr. Kirk A. Calhoun, M.D.** Established 1949 as East Texas Tuberculosis Sanatorium; renamed Easts Texas Chest Hospital, 1971; joined UT system and gained present name in 1977). Primary emphasis is on pulmonary and heart disease | 125 | 75 | NA | NA |
| **University of Texas Health Science Center at Houston (4) — Dr. James T. Willerson** Established 1972; consists of following divisions (year of founding): **Dental Branch** (1905); **Graduate School of Biomedical Sciences** (1963); **Medical School** (1970); **School of Allied Health Sciences** (1973); **School of Nursing** (1972); **School of Public Health** (1967); **Division of Continuing Education** (1958). | 1,198 | 3,335 | NA | NA |
| **University of Texas Health Science Center at San Antonio (4) — Dr. Francisco G. Cigarroa, M.D.** Established 1968; consists of following divisions (year of founding): **Dental School** (1970); **Graduate School of Biomedical Sciences** (1970); **Health Science Center** (1972); **Medical School** (1959 as **South Texas Medical School** of UT; present name, 1966); **School of Allied Health Sciences** (1976); **School of Nursing** (1969). | 1,400 | 2,700 | NA | NA |
| **University of Texas M.D. Anderson Cancer Center — Dr. John Mendelsohn, M.D.** | 1,050 | 101 | NA | 2,252 |
| **University of Texas Medical Branch at Galveston (4) — Dr. John D. Stobo** Established 1891; consists of following divisions (year of founding): **Graduate School of Biomedical Sciences** (1952); **Medical School** (1891); **School of Allied Health Sciences** (1968); **School of Nursing** (1890). | 1,984 | 2,005 | 1,481 | NA |
| **University of Texas Southwestern Medical Center at Dallas (4) — Dr. Kern Wildenthal, M.D.** Established 1943 (as private institution; became **Southwestern Medical Coll.** of UT 1948; became **UT Southwestern Medical School at Dallas**, 1967; made part of **UT Health Science Center at Dallas**, 1972); consists of following divisions (year of founding): **Graduate School of Biomedical Sciences** (1947); **School of Allied Health Sciences** (1968); **Southwestern Medical School** (1943). | 1,573 | 1,640 | NA | NA |
| **Vernon Regional Junior College**—Vernon; (7); 1970; Dr. Steve Thomas . . . . . . . . . . . . . | 71 | 2,526 | 1,224 | 2,245 |
| **Victoria College, The** —Victoria; (7); 1925; Dr. Jimmy Goodson . . . . . . . . . . . . . . . . . . . | ** | 4,022 | 1,837 | ** |
| **Wayland Baptist University**—Plainview; (3 -Southern Baptist); 1910; Dr. Wallace Davis Jr., Chancellor; Dr. Paul W. Ames, President . . . . . . . . . . . . . . . . . . . . . . . . . . . . . . . . . . . . | 110 | 5,778 | ** | NA |
| **Weatherford College**—Weatherford; (7); 1869 (as branch of **Southwestern Univ.**; 1922, became denominational junior college; became muni. jr. college, 1949); Dr. Don Huff . . . | 173 | 3,166 | 1,904 | 1,834 |
| **Western Texas College**—Snyder; (7); 1969; Dr. Gregory Williams . . . . . . . . . . . . . . . . . . | 72 | 1,652 | 1,099 | 876 |
| **Wharton County Junior College**—Wharton; (7); 1946; Betty A. McCrohan . . . . . . . . . . . . | 413 | 5,800 | 2,612 | 740 |
| **Wiley College**—Marshall; (3 - Methodist); 1873; Dr. Haywood L. Strickland . . . . . . . . . . . . | 62 | NA | ** | 100 |

## Key to Table Symbols

**\*Type:** (1) Public University System
(2) Public University
(3) Independent Senior College or University
(4) Public Medical School or Health Science Center
(5) Independent Medical or Dental School

(6) Public Technical College System
(7) Public Community College
(8) Independent Junior College
(9) Public Community College System
(10) Public Lower-Level Institution

NA - Not applicable

† Unless otherwise noted, faculty count includes professors, associate professors, adjunct professors, instructors and tutors, both full and part-time, but does not include voluntary instructors.

‡ No reply received to questionnaire. Name of president and number of students enrolled in fall 2000 was obtained from the institutions Web site or the Texas Higher Education Coordinating Board Web site: www.thecb.state.tx.us/DataAndStatistics/institutions.htm.

# Includes faculty and enrollment at all branches or divisions.

§ Includes all students in two summer sessions.

¶ Full-time faculty only.

** Information not supplied by institution.

†† Approximate count.

§§ Latest figures available from institution's Web page were for 2002–2003 school year.

§§§ Enrollment in online courses only.

¶¶ Number of students in extension courses or continuing education for all of fiscal year 2002.

# Belo Covers the Nation

Belo, a Dallas-based media company, has been a part of Texas history since the days of the Republic. The oldest continuously operating business in Texas, Belo had its origins in the one-page Galveston *Daily News,* which began publication in April 1842. Today Belo is one of the nation's largest media companies with a diversified group of market-leading broadcasting, publishing, cable and interactive media assets. A Fortune 1000 company with approximately 7,800 employees and $1.4 billion in annual revenues, Belo operates news and information franchises in some of the most desirable markets in the country.

The company owns 19 television stations reaching 13.7 percent of U. S. television households, manages one television station under a local marketing agreement, owns or operates nine cable news channels, and publishes four daily newspapers, including *The Dallas Morning News,* which publishes the *Texas Almanac.* Belo Interactive, the company's Internet subsidiary, operates 34 Web sites associated with Belo's newspapers and television stations and other businesses, which include several interactive alliances and a broad range of Internet-based products.

## The Early Days

*The Daily News* in Galveston was established in 1842, three years before the Republic of Texas achieved statehood. The newspaper was printed on equipment owned by Massachusetts native Samuel Bangs together with his brother-in-law and *Daily News* publisher, George H. French. In June 1843, Bangs leased the printing equipment to Wilbur F. Cherry and Michael Cronican; Cherry soon acquired sole ownership of *The News.*

Another Massachusetts émigré, Willard Richardson, became editor of the paper in 1844 and its sole owner in 1845. He campaigned editorially for annexation, fiscal responsibility and railroads. In 1857, Richardson conceived and founded the *Texas Almanac,* which he hoped would help attract settlers to the new state. Eight years later, he hired Alfred Horatio Belo, a former Confederate colonel from North Carolina, as bookkeeper. Belo was made a full partner in the growing company after only three months. The company eventually was named for him.

In 1874, George Bannerman Dealey, a 15-year-old English emigrant, was hired as an office boy. Working tirelessly, he made his way from office boy to business manager and then to publisher of *The Dallas Morning News.* It was Dealey who chose the then-small settlement of Dallas as the site for a sister publication. Dealey and several other members of the Galveston newspaper's staff relocated to Dallas, and the company prospered and grew.

## Belo Was a Radio Broadcasting Pioneer

On June 26, 1922, Belo began operating a 50-watt radio station, WFAA-AM, which was the first network station in the state. The company sold its radio properties in 1987.

## The Newspaper Group

*The Dallas Morning News* began publication on Oct. 1, 1885, with a circulation of 5,000 subscribers. After being in operation only two months, *The Dallas Morning News* acquired its first competitor, the *Dallas Herald* (not to be confused with the *Dallas Times Herald* that closed in December 1991). Rather than compete with each other for subscribers, the two newspapers combined, keeping the name of *The Dallas Morning News.*

In 1906, on the 21st anniversary of *The Dallas Morning News,* Dealey gave a speech that became the motto for the company: "Build the news upon the rock of truth and righ-

teousness. Conduct it always upon the lines of fairness and integrity. Acknowledge the right of the people to get from the newspaper both sides of every important question." Today these words are carved in a three-story-high space above the entrance to *The Dallas Morning News.* The *News* building, a long-standing dream of Dealey's, was completed in 1949, three years after his death.

While Belo has become one of the nation's largest media companies, *The Dallas Morning News* remains the flagship newspaper of the company's publishing business.

In 1997, Belo purchased *The Press-Enterprise,* a daily newspaper serving Riverside County and the inland Southern California area. Also in 1997, through the acquisition of The Providence Journal Company, Belo acquired *The Providence Journal,* the leading newspaper in Rhode Island and southeastern Massachusetts. Founded in 1829, *The Providence Journal* is America's oldest major daily newspaper of general circulation in continuous publication.

In 1999, Belo acquired the Denton Publishing Company, whose assets included the *Denton Record-Chronicle,* a daily newspaper serving Denton County and surrounding areas in North Texas.

## The Television Group

Belo entered the television broadcasting business in 1950 with the acquisition of its flagship station, ABC affiliate WFAA-TV in Dallas/Fort Worth. In 1983, in the nation's largest broadcast acquisition to date, Belo acquired KHOU-TV (CBS) in Houston; KXTV (ABC), Sacramento/Stockton/Modesto, Calif.; WVEC-TV (ABC), Hampton/Norfolk, Va.; and KOTV (CBS), Tulsa, Okla. In June 1994, Belo acquired WWL-TV (CBS) in New Orleans, La., and in Sept. 1994, the company acquired KIRO-TV, Seattle/Tacoma, Wash.

Belo's acquisition of The Providence Journal Company in 1997 is the largest transaction to date in the Company's history. The acquisition included five NBC affiliates (KING-TV in Seattle/Tacoma, Wash.; KGW-TV, Portland, Ore.; WCNC-TV, Charlotte, N.C.; KHNL-TV, Honolulu, Hawaii; and KTVB-TV, Boise, Idaho); one ABC affiliate (WHAS-TV, Louisville, Ky.); one CBS affiliate (KREM-TV, Spokane, Wash.); two FOX affiliates (KASA-TV, Albuquerque/Santa Fe, and KMSB-TV, Tucson); and NorthWest Cable News (NWCN), Seattle/Tacoma. Belo also assumed the management of four television stations through local marketing agreements and became the managing general partner of The Television Food Network, a cable channel in New York, N.Y.

In connection with the acquisition of The Providence Journal Company, Belo agreed to exchange KIRO-TV for a station in another market to comply with Federal Communications Commission regulations, which prohibited a company from owning multiple television stations in a single market. The agreement resulted in Belo's June 2, 1997, acquisition of KMOV-TV (CBS) in St. Louis, Mo.

In early 1997, the company opened its Capital Bureau in Washington, D.C., which houses Washington-based journalists representing the company's 17 network-affiliated television stations as well as *The Dallas Morning News* and *The Providence Journal.*

On Dec. 4, 1997, Belo exchanged its interest in Television Food Network for KENS-TV (CBS) and KENS-AM in San Antonio.

On Feb. 27, 1998, Belo's WFAA made television history by becoming the first VHF station in the country to transmit a digital signal on a permanent basis.

On Jan. 1, 1999, Belo launched Texas Cable News (TXCN), the first 24-hour regional cable news channel in Texas. On June 1, 1999, Belo exchanged KXTV (ABC) in Sacramento/Stockton/Modesto for KVUE-TV (ABC) in Austin. By the end of 1999, the combined reach of Belo's

Texas television stations reached 67 percent of all television households in Texas.

In November 1999, Belo acquired KTVK-TV (Ind.) in Phoenix along with the rights to operate KASW-TV, the Phoenix WB affiliate; a 50 percent interest in the Arizona News Channel; and azfamily.com, Arizona's leading Web publishing and design services firm. Also in November 1999, Belo divested KHNL and KASA.

In March 2000, Belo acquired two television stations that it had previously operated under local marketing agreements, KONG-TV (Ind.) in Seattle/Tacoma and KASW-TV in Phoenix. Belo began operation of KBEJ-TV (UPN) in San Antonio under a local marketing agreement in August 2000. Together with Cox Communications, Belo launched ¡Mas! Arizona, the Southwest's first Spanish-language cable news, information and sports channel in Phoenix, in October 2000.

With Belo's divestiture of Tulsa station KOTV in December 2000, the company's Television Group reaches 13.7 percent of all U.S. television households.

## Belo Interactive, Inc.

Belo Interactive, Inc., established in 1999, manages 34 Web sites that are affiliated with Belo's television stations, cable news operations and newspapers. As of May 2003, these sites had an audience of over 110 million page views per month and nearly 4 million registered users.

## Belo Officers

Officers of Belo are Robert W. Decherd, chairman of the board, president and chief executive officer; John L. (Jack) Sander, executive vice president/media operations and president/television group; Dunia A. Shive, executive vice president/chief financial officer; James M. Moroney III, publisher and chief executive officer of *The Dallas Morning News;* Guy H. Kerr, senior vice president/law and government and secretary; Colleen B. Brown, senior vice president; Marian Spitzberg, senior vice president/human resources; Dennis A. Williamson, senior corporate vice president;

David S. Boone, senior vice president/finance; Lee Salzberger, senior vice president/administration; Donald F. (Skip) Cass Jr., senior vice president; Richard Keilty, senior vice president/television group; Glenn C. Wright, senior vice president/television group;

Scott L. Baradell, vice president/corporate communications; Robert W. Barner, vice president/management development; Daniel J. Blizzard, vice president/operations; Janice E. Bryant, vice president/controller; Kathleen A. Cholette, vice president/tax; Russell F. Coleman, vice president/general counsel; Carey P. Hendrickson, vice president/investor relations; Ric D. Lutz, vice president/technology programs; Brenda C. Maddox, vice president/treasurer and assistant secretary; J. William Mosley, vice president/operational analysis; Jon E. Roe, vice president/chief technology officer; and Stephen E. Shelton, vice president/internal audit. Judith Garrett Segura is president of The Belo Foundation.

### The Dallas Morning News

Officers of *The Dallas Morning News* are James M. Moroney III, publisher and chief executive officer; Robert W. Mong Jr., president and editor; Barry T. Peckham, executive vice president; Evelyn Miller, executive vice president; Steven Weaver, senior vice president/advertising; Gilbert Bailon, vice president and executive editor; Lee Qualls, senior vice president/marketing and research; Keven Ann Willey, vice president/editorial page editor; Stuart Wilk, vice president and managing editor;

Paul Webb, vice president/production; Scott Messer, vice president/finance; Nancy Barry, vice president/community services; Lorie Schrader, vice president/information technology; Frank Leto, vice president/classified advertising; Harold Gaar, vice president/retail display advertising; Dave Smith, vice president/deputy managing editor/executive sports editor; Jason Kays, vice president/advertising marketing; Genevieve Poirier-Richards, vice president/marketing.

### The Providence Journal

Officers of *The Providence Journal* are Howard G. Sutton, chairman of the board, publisher, president and chief executive officer; Sandra J. Radliffe, senior vice president/finance; Joel P. Rawson, senior vice president and executive editor; Mark T. Ryan, executive vice president/general manager; Robert A. Shadrick, senior vice president/operations; Michael J. Dooley, vice president/circulation; Donald J. Ross, vice president/advertising; and Robert B. Whitcomb, vice president and editorial pages editor.

### The Press-Enterprise

Officers of *The Press-Enterprise* include David Cornwall, publisher and chief executive officer; Maria De Varenne, vice president/news and editor; Susan Marquez, vice president/administration; Sue Barry, vice president/advertising; Kathy Michalak, vice president/circulation; Ed Lasak, vice president/finance and operations; and Joe Frederickson, vice president/marketing and public affairs.

### The Denton Record-Chronicle

Officers of the *Denton Record-Chronicle* include Bill Patterson, publisher and chief executive officer and Barry Boesch, executive editor.

### The Television Group

Officers of Belo's Television Group include John L. (Jack) Sander, executive vice president/media operations and president/television group; Richard J. Keilty, senior vice president/television group; and Glenn C. Wright, senior vice president/television group. Officers of Belo's television stations are Kathy Clements-Hill, president and general manager, WFAA-TV; David F. Muscari, vice president/strategic alliances; Lawrence D. (Nick) Nicholson, vice president/marketing, WFAA-TV; Peter Diaz, president and general manager, KHOU-TV;

Mike Devlin, vice president/news, KHOU-TV; David Lougee, vice president and general manager, KING-TV and KONG-TV; Jay Cascio, vice president/programming and creative services, KING-TV; Deborah (DJ) Wilson, vice president/assistant general manager, KING-TV; Donald (Skip) Cass, president and general manager, KTVK-TV and president of KASW-TV; Mark Higgins, vice president and general manager, KASW-TV; Allan R. Cohen, president and general manager, KMOV-TV; R. Paul Fry, president and general manager,

KGW-TV; Stuart B. Powell, vice president and general manager, WCNC-TV; Robert G. McGann, vice president and general manager, KENS-TV; Mario A. Hewitt, vice president and general manager, WVEC-TV; Jimmie Phillips, vice president and general manager, WWL-TV; Robert A. Klingle, vice president and general manager, WHAS-TV;

Patti C. Smith, vice president and general manager, KVUE-TV; Diane E. Frisch, vice president and general manager, KMSB-TV; Albert (Bud) Brown, vice president and general manager, KREM-TV; and Douglas Armstrong, president and general manager, KTVB-TV.

### The Capital Bureau

George Rodrigue is vice president of Belo's Capital Bureau; David Lougee is president and general manager of NorthWest Cable News; and James T. Aitken is president and general manager of Texas Cable News.

### Belo Interactive, Inc.

Officers of Belo Interactive, Inc. include Eric A. Christensen, vice president/general manager; Christopher J. Feola, vice president/technology; Linda M. Fisk, vice president/audience development and management; John Granatino, vice president/news and operations; Wesley A. Jackson, vice president/sales; and Guy Boyle, director of finance/controller. ✩

# Belo Corp. Directors

## Robert W. Decherd

Robert W. Decherd has served as a director of Belo since March 1976. He has been chairman of the board and chief executive officer of Belo since January 1987. Decherd became president of Belo in January 1994, and previously served as president from January 1985 through December 1986. From January 1984 through December 1986, he served as chief operating officer.

Decherd is a member of the board of directors of Kimberly-Clark Corporation. He also serves on the Advisory Council for Harvard University's Center for Ethics and the Professions, and is a member of the Media Security and Reliability Council, which is part of President Bush's Homeland Security initiative.

## Henry P. Becton Jr.

Henry P. Becton Jr. has served as a director of Belo since May 1997. He served as a director of The Providence Journal Company from 1992 to 1997. Becton has been president of WGBH Educational Foundation since 1984 and served as its general manager from 1978 until 1999. He is a member of the board of directors of Becton Dickinson and Company, and is a trustee or director of 18 Scudder Fund investment companies or trusts advised by Deutsche Asset Management. Becton served as a director of The Providence Journal Company from 1992 to 1997. He served as a director of Public Broadcasting Service from June 1987 until June 1993 and from June 1995 until October 2001.

## Louis E. Caldera

Louis E. Caldera has served as a director of Belo since July 2001. In August 2003, Caldera assumed his duties as president of the University of New Mexico. He has served as vice chancellor for university advancement at The California State University from June 2001 until June 2003. Caldera was secretary of the Army in the Clinton Administration from July 1998 until January 2001.

Caldera previously served as managing director and chief operating officer for the Corporation for National and Community Service, a federal grantmaking agency, from September 1997 to June 1998. He served in the California Legislature from 1992 to 1997 representing the 46th Assembly District (Los Angeles). He is a member of the boards of directors of Southwest Airlines Co., IndyMac Bancorp, Inc. and Iomega Corporation.

## France A. Córdova, Ph.D.

France Córdova has served as a director of Belo since May 2003. She has served as chancellor of University of California Riverside since July 2002. From August 1996 to July 2002, she was vice chancellor for research and professor of physics at University of California Santa Barbara.

She served as chief scientist of National Aeronautics and Space Administration (NASA) from 1993 to 1996. Córdova was professor of astronomy and astrophysics at Pennsylvania State University from 1989 until 1996 and served as department head from 1989 to 1993. Córdova currently serves on advisory committees for the National Academy of Sciences' Policy and Global Affairs Division.

## Judith L. Craven, M.D., M.P.H.

Judith L. Craven, M.D., M.P.H. has served as a director of Belo since December 1992. From July 1992 until her retirement in October 1998, she served as president of the United Way of the Texas Gulf Coast. From 1983 to 1992, Craven served as dean of the School of Allied Health Sciences of the University of Texas Health Science Center at Houston, and from 1987 to 1992 as vice president of Multicultural Affairs for the University of Texas Health Science Center.

Craven is a member of the board of regents of The University of Texas System and serves on the boards of directors of SYSCO Corporation, Luby's, Inc., SunAmerica Mutual Funds, and Variable Annuity Life Insurance Company of America.

## Roger A. Enrico

Roger A. Enrico has been a director of Belo since July 1995. He is the former chairman and chief executive officer of PepsiCo, Inc. He was chief executive officer of PepsiCo from April 1996 until May 2001, chairman of the board from November 1996 to May 2001, and vice chairman from May 2001 until April 2002.

Enrico joined PepsiCo in 1971 and held numerous other senior positions, including chairman and chief executive officer of PepsiCo Worldwide Restaurants from 1994 to 1997.

Enrico is a member of the boards of directors of PepsiCo, Inc., Target Corporation, Electronic Data Systems Corporation, The National Geographic Society, The Dallas Center for the Performing Arts, The Eisenhower Fellowships and The National Center for Public Policy and Higher Education.

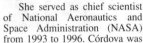

## Stephen Hamblett

Stephen Hamblett has served as a director of Belo since May 1997. Hamblett served as chairman of the board of The Providence Journal Company from February 1997, when The Providence Journal Company became a wholly-owned subsidiary of Belo, through December 2000. From February 1997 until April 1999, Hamblett also served as chief executive officer and publisher of The Providence Journal Company. From 1987 to 1997,  he was chairman, chief executive officer and publisher of the pre-merger Providence Journal Company.

Hamblett is currently a member of the boards of directors of the Inter-American Press Association, the Smithsonian National Board, the Rhode Island School of Design and the Rhode Island Heritage Harbor Museum.

## Arturo Madrid, Ph.D.

Arturo Madrid, Ph.D., has served as a director of Belo since January 1994. He is the Norine R. and T. Frank Murchison Distinguished Professor of the Humanities at Trinity University in San Antonio, Texas. From 1984 to 1993, he served as the founding president of the Tomás Rivera Center, a national institute for policy studies on Latino issues. In addition, he has held academic and administrative  positions at Dartmouth College, the University of California, San Diego, the University of Minnesota and the U.S. Department of Education.

Dr. Madrid is a member of the Council for Foreign Relations and a fellow of the National Academy for Public Administration. In 1996, he was awarded the Charles Frankel Prize by the National Endowment for the Humanities.

## Dealey D. Herndon

Dealey D. Herndon has served as a director of Belo since May 1986. She has been president of Herndon, Stauch & Associates, a project and construction management firm, since September 1995. From January 2001 to October 2001, she also served as director of appointments for Texas Governor Rick Perry. From 1991 to September 1995, she was the executive director of the State Preservation Board of the State of Texas and managed the Texas Capitol Restoration in that capacity.

Herndon is a trustee of the National Trust for Historic Preservation in Washington, D.C., and serves as president of the Texas State History Museum Foundation.

## Wayne R. Sanders

Wayne Sanders has served as a director of Belo since May 2003. He is the former chairman and chief executive officer of Kimberly-Clark Corporation. He served as president and chief executive officer of Kimberly-Clark from 1991 until September 2002 and as chairman of the board from 1992 until February 2003.

From 1987 to 1991, Sanders held numerous senior positions with Kimberly-Clark. He also serves on the boards of directors of Texas Instruments Incorporated and Adolph Coors Company and its principal subsidiary, Coors Brewing Company. Sanders is the chairman of the board of Marquette University and serves as national trustee and governor of the Boys and Girls Clubs of America.

## Laurence E. Hirsch

Laurence E. Hirsch has served as a director of Belo since August 1999. Hirsch has been chief executive officer of Centex Corporation since July 1988. He has served as a director of Centex Corporation since 1985 and has been its chairman of the board since July 1991. He has also served as a director of its affiliate, Centex Construction Products, Inc., since January 1994 and was named chairman of the board in July 1999.

Hirsch is a member of the board of directors of Luminex Corporation and is an advisory director of Heidelberger Zement AG. Hirsch also serves as a trustee of the University of Pennsylvania.

## William T. Solomon

William T. Solomon has served as a director of Belo since April 1983. He is chairman of the board of Austin Industries, Inc., a general construction company, a position he has held since 1987.

Solomon was chairman and chief executive officer from 1987 to March 2001 and, prior to 1987, was president and chief executive officer of Austin Industries, Inc. He also serves on the boards of the Hoblitzelle  Foundation and the Southwestern Medical Foundation.

## Lloyd D. Ward

Lloyd D. Ward has served as a director of Belo since July 2001. Ward is the former chief executive officer and secretary general of the United States Olympic Committee, positions he held from October 2001 until March 2003.

Ward was chairman and chief executive officer of iMotors from January 2001 until May 2001. Ward was chairman and chief executive officer of Maytag Corporation from August 1999 to November 2000, president and chief operating officer of Maytag from 1998 to August 1999, and executive vice president of Maytag from 1996 to 1998. Ward served in various senior management positions with PepsiCo, Inc. from 1988 through 1996. He is a member of the board of directors of General Motors Corp.

## J. McDonald Williams

J. McDonald Williams has served as a director of Belo since April 1985. Williams served as chairman of Trammell Crow Company, a real estate services firm, from August 1994 until May 2002, when he was named chairman emeritus.

From 1991 until July 1994, Williams was president and chief executive officer of Trammell Crow, and from 1977 to December 1990, he was managing partner of Trammell Crow.

Williams also serves on the boards of Children's Medical Center of Dallas, Children's Medical Center Foundation, The Enterprise Foundation, Urban League of Greater Dallas, Abilene Christian University, Blanks Color Imaging, the Hoblitzelle Foundation, Southern Methodist University Perkins School of Theology and the Dallas Foundation. ☆

# History of the Texas Almanac

### First Published in 1857

The first edition of the *Texas Almanac* was issued by the Galveston *Daily News* in January 1857, 21 years after Texas won its independence from Mexico and only 12 years after it became a state. Willard Richardson, who served as both *Daily News* and Almanac editor, focused the earliest editions of the *Texas Almanac* on history and the workings of the state government. An edition was published each year through 1873, except for 1866, totaling 16 annual editions.

The editions for the years 1862–65, during the Civil War, were of pamphlet size, ranging from 48 to 64 pages. Because Galveston was one of the Gulf Coast ports blockaded by the Union Navy and there was constant threat of armed conflict during the war, production of the 1862 edition was moved to Houston, and the next three editions were published in Austin.

Post–Civil War publication was resumed in Galveston in 1867. With the 1869 edition, the name was changed to *The Texas Almanac and Emigrant's Guide to Texas,* reflecting the state's need to attract settlers. The 1873 *Texas Almanac* was the last 19th century edition; Willard Richardson died in 1875, and no one at the Galveston paper took on the challenge.

### The Move from Galveston to Dallas

In 1885, *The Daily News* spun off *The Dallas Morning News* as a sort of North Texas branch newspaper. George Bannerman Dealey was sent from Galveston to Dallas to establish the Dallas paper. Dealey thought that the Almanac would be a way to encourage the economic development of the state. In 1904, *The Dallas Morning News* resumed publication of the *Texas Almanac*. Just three years earlier, the Spindletop Oil Field had been discovered near Beaumont, boosting Texas into the petroleum and industrial age. To reflect this change in economic focus of the state, the

George B. Dealey

name again was changed, this time to *Texas Almanac and State Industrial Guide*.

Following another hiatus, the Almanac resumed publication with editions in 1910, 1911, 1912 and 1914. Another gap in the series ensued with the outbreak of World War I but was resumed by *The Dallas Morning News* in 1925. Annual editions were published through 1929, when the effects of the Great Depression caused a change to a biennial cycle. This schedule since has been maintained, with only a couple of exceptions.

### Biennial Cycle

Beginning with the 1941–42 edition, all *Texas Almanacs* have carried a two-year designation. There have been four special editions: the 100th anniversary of the Almanac (1956–57); the George Bannerman Dealey memorial edition (1958–59); the 125th anniversary of the founding of Belo Corp. (1966–67); and the Texas Sesquicentennial edition (1986–87), celebrating the 150th anniversary of the founding of the Republic of Texas.

By 1950, the *Texas Almanac* had become a reference book on resources, industries, commerce, history, government, population, and other subjects relating to the political, civic and economic development of Texas.

### Almanac Editors

Stuart Malcolm McGregor, who had edited the *Texas Almanac* since 1925, retired in 1961 after publication of the 1961–62 edition, which was dedicated to him by the publishers. The editorial policies and format that he established were continued in later editions. In 1961, Walter B. Moore became editor of the publication.

Fred R. Pass succeeded Moore in June 1973. Upon Pass's resignation in 1981, Michael T. Kingston became editor. Kingston served as editor until his death in 1994, at which time Mary G. Ramos was named editor. Ramos had worked for the *Texas Almanac* since 1995, when she was named assistant and then associate editor, replacing Ruth Harris, who had worked for *The Dallas Morning News* for 49 years. Ramos retired as editor in 2003. The Almanac is now edited by Elizabeth Cruce Alvarez and Robert Plocheck. ☆

# Texas Newspapers, Radio and Television Stations

*In the list of print and broadcast media below, frequency of publication of newspapers is indicated after the names by the following codes: (D), daily; (S), semiweekly; (TW), triweekly; (BW), biweekly; (SM), semimonthly; (M), monthly; all others are weeklies. "DT" following the call letters of a TV station indicates digital transmission. The radio and television stations are those with valid operating licenses as of July 25, 2003. Not included are those with only construction permits or with applications pending. Sources: Newspapers: 2003 Texas Newspaper Directory, Texas Press Association, Austin; Broadcast Media: Federal Communications Commission Web site: http://svartifoss2.fcc.gov/prod/cdbs/pubacc/prod/cdbs_pa.htm.*

**Abernathy - Newspaper:** Abernathy Weekly Review.

**Abilene - Newspaper:** Abilene Reporter-News (D). **Radio-AM:** KSLI,1280 kHz; KWKC, 1340; KEAN, 1470; KZQQ, 1560. **Radio-FM:** KGNZ, 88.1 MHz; KACU, 89.7; KAGT, 90.5; KAQD, 91.3; KULL, 92.5; KHYS, 100.7; KEAN, 105.1; KKHR, 106.3; KEYJ, 107.9. **TV:** KRBC-Ch. 9; KXVA-Ch. 15; KTAB-Ch. 32.

**Alamo - Radio-FM:** KJAV, 104.9 MHz.

**Alamo Heights - Radio-AM:** KDRY, 1100 kHz.

**Albany - Newspaper:** Albany News.

**Aledo - Newspaper:** The Community News.

**Alice - Newspaper:** Alice Echo-News-Journal (D). **Radio-AM:** KOPY, 1070 kHz. **Radio-FM:** KOPY, 92.1 MHz; KNDA, 102.9.

**Allen - Newspaper:** Allen American (S). **Radio-FM:** KESN, 103.3 MHz.

**Alpine - Newspaper:** Alpine Avalanche. **Radio-AM:** KVLF, 1240 kHz. **Radio-FM:** KALP, 92.7 MHz.

**Alvarado - Newspapers:** Alvarado Post; Alvarado Star.

**Alvin - Newspaper:** Alvin Sun. **Radio-AM:** KTEK, 1110 kHz. **Radio-FM:** KACC, 89.7 MHz. **TV:** KFTH-Ch. 67.

**Alvord - Newspaper:** Alvord Gazette.

**Amarillo - Newspapers:** Globe-News (D). **Radio-AM:** KGNC, 710 kHz; KIXZ, 940; KTNZ, 1010; KZIP, 1310; KDJW, 1360; KPUR, 1440. **Radio-FM:** KJRT, 88.3 MHz; KXLV, 89.1; KACV, 89.9; KXRI, 91.9;; KQIZ, 93.1; KMXJ, 94.1; KMML, 96.9; KGNC, 97.9; KPRF, 98.7; KBZD, 99.7; KPQZ, 100.9; KATP, 101.9; KRGN, 103.1; KAEZ, 105.7. **TV:** KACV-Ch. 2; KAMR-Ch. 4; KVII-Ch. 7; KFDA-DT-Ch. 9; KFDA-Ch. 10; KCIT-Ch. 14.

**Amherst - Newspaper:** The Amherst Press (SM).

**Anahuac - Newspaper:** The Progress.

**Andrews - Newspaper:** Andrews County News (S). **Radio-AM:** KACT, 1360 kHz. **Radio-FM:** KACT, 105.5 MHz.

**Angleton - Newspaper:** Angleton Times (S).

**Anson - Newspapers:** Jones County Journal; Western Observer. **Radio-FM:** KFQX, 98.1 MHz.

**Aransas Pass - Newspaper:** Aransas Pass Progress; The Coastal Bend Herald.

**Archer City - Newspaper:** Archer County News.

**Arlington - Radio-FM:** KLTY, 94.9 MHz. **TV:** KPXD-DT-Ch. 42; KPXD-Ch. 68.

**Aspermont - Newspaper:** Stonewall County Courier.

**Athens - Newspaper:** Athens Daily Review (D). **Radio-AM:** KLVQ, 1410 kHz.

**Atlanta - Newspaper:** Atlanta Citizens Journal (S). **Radio-AM:** KPYN, 900 kHz; KALT, 1610. **Radio-FM:** KNRB, 100.1 MHz.

**Aubrey - Newspaper:** The Town Charter.

**Austin - Newspapers:** Austin American-Statesman (D); Austin Business Journal; Austin Chronicle; Austin Monthly (M); Daily Texas (D); Lake Travis View; Texas Observer (BW); Texas Weekly; Westlake Picayune. **Radio-AM:** KLBJ, 590 kHz; KVET, 1300; KFON, 1490. **Radio-FM:** KAZI, 88.7 MHz; KMFA, 89.5; KUT, 90.5; KVRX, 91.7; KLBJ, 93.7; KKMJ, 95.5; KVET, 98.1; KASE, 100.7; KPEZ, 102.3. **TV:** KTBC-Ch. 7; KLRU-Ch. 18; KVUE-Ch. 24; KXAN-Ch. 36; KEYE-Ch. 42; KNVA-Ch. 54.

**Azle - Newspaper:** Azle News. **Radio-FM:** KZMP,101.7 MHz.

**Baird - Newspapers:** Baird Banner; Callahan Co. Star. **Radio-FM:** KNCE, 95.1 MHz.

**Balch Springs - Radio-AM:** KSKY, 660 kHz.

**Ballinger - Newspaper:** Ballinger Ledger. **Radio-AM:** KRUN, 1400 kHz. **Radio-FM:** KKCN, 103.1 MHz.

**Bandera - Newspapers:** The Bandera Bulletin; Bandera Review. **Radio-FM:** KEEP, 103.1 MHz.

**Bartlett - Newspaper:** Tribune-Progress.

**Bastrop - Newspaper:** Bastrop Advertiser (S) **Radio-FM:** KMHF, 88.5 MHz; KGSR, 107.1.

**Bay City - Newspaper:** The Bay City Tribune (S). **Radio-FM:** KXGJ, 101.7 MHz; KMKS, 102.5.

**Baytown - Newspaper:** Baytown Sun (D). **Radio-AM:** KWWJ, 1360 kHz. **TV:** KAZH-Ch. 57.

**Beaumont - Newspaper:** Beaumont Enterprise (D). **Radio-AM:** KLVI, 560 kHz; KZZB, 990; KRCM, 1380; KIKR, 1450. **Radio-FM:** KTXB, 89.7 MHz; KVLU, 91.3; KQXY, 94.1; KYKR, 95.1; KRWP, 97.5; KTCX, 102.5; KQQK, 107.9. **TV:** KFDM-Ch. 6; KBMT-Ch. 12; KFDM-DT-Ch. 21; KITU-Ch. 34.

**Beeville - Newspaper:** Beeville Bee-Picayune (S). **Radio-AM:** KIBL, 1490 kHz. **Radio-FM:** KVFM, 91.3 MHz; KTKO, 105.7; KRXB, 107.1.

**Bellaire - Radio-AM:** KILE, 1560 kHz.

**Bells - Radio - FM:** KMKT, 93.1 MHz.

**Bellville - Newspaper:** Bellville Times. **Radio-FM:** KNUZ, 1090 kHz.

**Belton - Newspaper:** The Belton Journal. **Radio-AM:** KTON, 940 kHz. **Radio-FM:** KOOC, 106.3 MHz. **TV:** KNCT-Ch. 46.

**Benbrook - Newspaper:** Benbrook Star. **Radio-FM:** KDXX, 107.1 MHz.

**Big Lake - Newspaper:** Big Lake Wildcat. **Radio-FM:** KDPB, 98.3 MHz; KWTR, 104.1

**Big Sandy - Newspaper:** Big Sandy-Hawkins Journal. **Radio-FM:** KTAA, 90.7 MHz.

**Big Spring - Newspaper:** Big Spring Herald (D). **Radio-AM:** KBYG, 1400; KBST, 1490. **Radio-FM:** KBCX, 91.5 MHz; KBTS, 94.3 MHz; KBST, 95.7. **TV:** KWAB-Ch. 4.

**Bishop - Radio-FM:** KFLZ, 106.9 MHz.

**Blanco - Newspaper:** Blanco County News.

**Bloomington - Radio-FM:** KLUB, 106.9 MHz.

**Blossom - Newspaper:** Blossom Times.

**Boerne - Newspapers:** Boerne Star (S); Hill Country Recorder. **Radio-AM:** KBRN, 1500 kHz.

**Bogata - Newspaper:** Bogata News.

**Bonham - Newspaper:** Bonham Journal. **Radio-AM:** KFYN, 1420 kHz. **Radio-FM:** KFYZ, 98.3 MHz.

**Booker - Newspaper:** Booker News.

**Borger - Newspaper:** Borger News-Herald (D). **Radio-AM:** KQTY, 1490 kHz. **Radio-FM:** KASV, 88.7 MHz; KAVO, 91.5; KQFX, 104.3; KQTY, 106.7.

**Bovina - Newspaper:** Bovina Blade.

**Bowie - Newspaper:** Bowie News (S). **Radio-AM:** KNTX, 1410 kHz.

**Brackettville - Newspaper:** The Brackett News.

**Brady - Newspaper:** Brady Standard-Herald (S). **Radio-AM:** KNEL, 1490 kHz. **Radio-FM:** KNEL, 95.3 MHz.

**Breckenridge - Newspaper:** Breckenridge American (S). **Radio-AM:** KROO, 1430 kHz. **Radio-FM:** KLXK, 93.5 MHz.

**Bremond - Newspaper:** Bremond Press.

**Brenham - Newspaper:** Brenham Banner-Press (D). **Radio-AM:** KWHI, 1280 kHz. **Radio-FM:** KULF, 94.1 MHz; KTTX, 106.1.

**Bridgeport - Newspaper:** Bridgeport Index. **Radio-FM:** KBOC, 98.3 MHz.

**Brookshire - Newspaper:** The Times Tribune. **Radio-AM:** KCHN, 1050 kHz.

**Brownfield - Newspaper:** Brownfield News (S). **Radio-AM:** KKUB, 1300 kHz. **Radio-FM:** KPBB, 88.5 MHz; KLZK, 104.3.

**Brownsboro - Newspaper:** Brownsboro and Chandler Statesman.

**Brownsville - Newspaper:** The Brownsville Herald (D). **Radio-AM:** KBOR, 1600 kHz, KQXX, 1700. **Radio-FM:** KBNR, 88.3 MHz; KKPS, 99.5; KTEX, 100.3. **TV:** KVEO-Ch. 23.

**Brownwood - Newspaper:** Brownwood Bulletin (D). **Radio-AM:** KXYL, 1240 kHz; KBWD, 1380. **Radio-FM:** KPBE, 89.3 MHz; KBUB, 90.3; KHPU, 99.7; KXYL, 96.9; KPSM, 99.3; KOXE, 101.3.

**Bryan - Newspaper:** Bryan-College Station Eagle (D). **Radio-AM:** KTAM, 1240 kHz; KAGC, 1510. **Radio-FM:** KORA, 98.3 MHz; KNFX, 99.5; KKYS, 104.7. **TV:** KBTX-Ch. 3; KYLE-Ch. 28.

**Buda - Newspaper:** The Free Press. **Radio-FM:** KROX, 101.5 MHz.

**Buffalo - Newspapers:** Buffalo Express; Buffalo Press.

**Bullard - Newspaper:** Bullard Weekly News.

**Buna - Newspaper:** The Buna Beacon.

**Burkburnett - Newspaper:** Burkburnett Informer Star. **Radio-FM:** KYYI, 104.7 MHz.

**Burleson - Newspaper:** Burleson Star (S).

**Burnet - Newspapers:** Burnet Bulletin; Citizens Gazette. **Radio-AM:** KHLB, 1340 kHz. **Radio-FM:** KBEY, 92.5 MHz; KHLB, 106.9.

**Caldwell - Newspaper:** Burleson Co. Citizen-Tribune. **Radio-FM:** KLTR, 107.3 MHz.

**Callisburg - Radio-FM:** KPFC, 91.9 MHz.

**Calvert - Newspaper:** Calvert Tribune.

**Cameron - Newspaper:** The Cameron Herald. **Radio-AM:** KMIL, 1330 kHz. **Radio-FM:** KHTZ, 94.3 MHz; KXCS, 103.9 MHz.
**Campbell - Radio-FM:** KRVA, 107.1 MHz.
**Camp Wood - Radio-FM:** KAYG, 99.1 MHz.
**Canadian - Newspaper:** Canadian Record.
**Canton - Newspapers:** Canton Herald; Van Zandt News. **Radio-AM:** KVCI, 1510 kHz.
**Canyon - Newspaper:** The Canyon News (S). **Radio-AM:** KZRK, 1550 kHz. **Radio-FM:** KWTS, 91.1 MHz; KPUR, 107.1; KZRK, 107.9.
**Canyon Lake - Newspaper:** Times Guardian.
**Carrizo Springs - Newspaper:** Carrizo Springs Javelin. **Radio-AM:** KBEN, 1450 kHz. **Radio-FM:** KCZO, 92.1 MHz.
**Carthage - Newspaper:** Panola Watchman (S). **Radio-AM:** KGAS, 1590 kHz. **Radio-FM:** KTUX, 98.9 MHz; KGAS, 104.3.
**Castroville - Newspaper:** Castroville News Bulletin.
**Cedar Hill - Newspapers:** Cedar Hill Sentinel; Cedar Hill Today.
**Cedar Park - Newspapers:** Hill Country News Weekender. **Radio-FM:** KXMG, 93.3 MHz.
**Celina - Newspaper:** Celina Record.
**Center - Newspaper:** The Light & Champion (S). **Radio-AM:** KDET, 930 kHz. **Radio-FM:** KQBB, 100.5 MHz.
**Centerville - Newspaper:** Centerville News. **Radio-FM:** KTCJ, 105.9 MHz.
**Chico - Newspaper:** Chico Texan.
**Childress - Newspaper:** The Childress Index (TW). **Radio-AM:** KCTX, 1510 kHz. **Radio-FM:** KCTX, 96.1 MHz.
**Cisco - Newspaper:** Cisco Press (S).
**Clarendon - Newspaper:** Clarendon Enterprise. **Radio-FM:** KEFH, 99.3 MHz.
**Clarksville - Newspaper:** Clarksville Times. **Radio-AM:** KCAR, 1350 kHz. **Radio-FM:** KGAP, 98.5 MHz.
**Claude - Newspaper:** The Claude News. **Radio-FM:** KARX, 95.7 MHz.
**Clear Lake - Newspaper:** The Citizen.
**Cleburne - Newspaper:** Cleburne Times-Review (D). **Radio-AM:** KCLE, 1140 kHz.
**Cleveland - Newspaper:** Cleveland Advocate. **Radio-FM:** KTHT, 97.1 MHz.
**Clifton - Newspaper:** Clifton Record (S). **Radio-FM:** KWOW, 104.1 MHz.
**Clute - Newspaper:** The Facts (D).
**Clyde - Newspaper:** Clyde Journal.
**Cockrell Hill - Radio-AM:** KRVA, 1600 kHz.
**Coleman - Newspaper:** Chronicle & Democrat-Voice (S). **Radio-AM:** KSTA, 1000 kHz. **Radio-FM:** KXCT, 102.3 MHz.
**College Station - Newspaper:** The Battalion (D). **Radio-AM:** KZNE, 1150 kHz, WTAW, 1620. **Radio-FM:** KEOS, 89.1 MHz; KAMU, 90.9; KNDE, 95.1. **TV:** KAMU-DT-Ch. 12; KAMU-Ch. 15.
**Colorado City - Newspaper:** Colorado City Record. **Radio-AM:** KVMC, 1320 kHz. **Radio-FM:** KAUM, 107.1 MHz.
**Columbus - Newspapers:** Banner Press Newspaper; Colorado County Citizen. **Radio-FM:** KULM, 98.3 MHz.
**Comanche - Newspaper:** Comanche Chief. **Radio-AM:** KCOM, 1550 kHz. **Radio-FM:** KYOX, 94.3 MHz.
**Comfort - Newspaper:** The Comfort News. **Radio-FM:** KCOR, 95.1 MHz.
**Commerce - Newspaper:** Commerce Journal. **Radio-FM:** KETR, 88.9 MHz.
**Conroe - Newspaper:** The Courier (D). **Radio-AM:** KJOJ, 880 kHz; KYOK, 1140. **Radio-FM:** KAXF, 88.3 MHz; KHPT, 106.9. **TV:** KPXB-Ch. 49; KTBU-CH. 55.
**Cooper - Newspaper:** Cooper Review.
**Coppell - Newspaper:** Coppell Citizens' Advocate.
**Copperas Cove - Newspaper:** Copperas Cove Leader-Press. **Radio-FM:** KSSM, 103.1 MHz.
**Corpus Christi - Newspapers:** Caller-Times (D); Coastal Bend Legal & Business News (D); Flour Bluff Sun; South Texas Catholic (BW). **Radio-AM:** KCTA, 1030 kHz; KCCT, 1150; KSIX, 1230; KRYS, 1360; KUNO, 1400; KEYS, 1440. **Radio-FM:** KKLM, 88.7 MHz; KEDT, 90.3; KBNJ, 91.7; KMXR, 93.9; KBSO, 94.7; KZFM, 95.5; KLTG, 96.5; KRYS, 99.1. **TV:** KIII-Ch. 3; KRIS-Ch. 6; KZTV-Ch. 10; KEDT-Ch. 16; KORO-CH. 28.
**Corrigan - Newspaper:** Corrigan Times.
**Corsicana - Newspaper:** Corsicana Daily Sun (D). **Radio-AM:** KAND, 1340 kHz.
**Crane - Newspaper:** Crane News. **Radio-AM:** KXOI, 810 kHz. **Radio FM:** KKKK, 101.3 MHz.
**Creedmoor - Radio AM:** KQQA, 1530 kHz.
**Crockett - Newspaper:** Houston Co. Courier (S). **Radio-AM:** KIVY, 1290 kHz. **Radio-FM:** KCKT, 88.5 MHz; KIVY, 92.7; KBHT, 93.5.
**Crosbyton - Newspaper:** Crosby Co. News & Chronicle.
**Cross Plains - Newspaper:** Cross Plains Review.

**Crowell - Newspaper:** Foard Co. News.
**Crowley - Newspaper:** Crowley Star.
**Crystal Beach - Radio FM:** KSTB, 101.5 MHz; KLTO, 105.3.
**Crystal City - Newspaper:** Zavala County Sentinel. **Radio-FM:** KHER, 94.3 MHz.
**Cuero - Newspaper:** Cuero Record. **Radio-FM:** KNGT, 97.7 MHz.
**Cypress - Radio-AM:** KYND, 1520 kHz.
**Daingerfield - Newspaper:** The Bee. **Radio-AM:** KEGG, 1560 kHz.
**Dalhart - Newspaper:** Dalhart Daily Texan (D). **Radio-AM:** KXIT, 1240 kHz. **Radio-FM:** KXIT, 95.9 MHz.
**Dallas - Newspapers:** The Dallas Morning News (D); Dallas Business Journal; Daily Commercial Record (D); Oak Cliff Tribune; Park Cities News; Park Cities People; Texas Jewish Post; The White Rocker. **Radio-AM:** KLIF, 570 kHz; KGGR, 1040; KRLD, 1080; KFXR, 1190; KTCK, 1310; KHCK, 1480. **Radio-FM:** KNON, 89.3 HMz; KERA, 90.1; KCBI, 90.9; KVTT, 91.7; KZPS, 92.5; KBFB, 97.9; KLUV, 98.7; KRBV, 100.3; WRR, 101.1; KDMX, 102.9; KKDA, 104.5; KLLI, 105.3. **TV:** KDFW-Ch. 4; WFAA-Ch. 8; WFAA-DT-Ch. 9; KERA-Ch. 13; KDFI-Ch. 27; KDAF-Ch. 33; KDFW-DT-Ch. 35; KXTX-Ch. 39; KXTX-DT-Ch. 40; KDTX-Ch. 58.
**Decatur - Newspaper:** Wise County Messenger (S). **Radio-FM:** KDKR, 91.3 MHz. **TV:** KMPX-Ch. 29.
**Deer Park - Newspaper:** Deer Park Progress.
**De Kalb - Newspaper:** De Kalb News (S).
**De Leon - Newspapers:** De Leon Free Press.
**Dell City - Newspaper:** Hudspeth County Herald.
**Del Mar Hills - Radio-AM:** KVOZ, 890 kHz.
**Del Rio - Newspaper:** Del Rio News-Herald (D). **Radio-AM:** KTJK, 1230 kHz; KWMC, 1490. **Radio-FM:** KDLK, 94.3 MHz; KTDR, 96.3. **TV:** KTRG-Ch. 10.
**Del Valle - Radio-AM:** KIXL, 970 kHz.
**Denison - Newspapers:** The Denison Daily Post (D); Herald Democrat (D). **Radio-AM:** KYNG, 950 kHz. **Radio-FM:** KZMP, 101.7 MHz.
**Denton - Newspaper:** Denton Record-Chronicle (D). **Radio-AM:** KTNO, 1440 kHz. **Radio-FM:** KNTU, 88.1 MHz; KHCK, 99.1; KHKS, 106.1. **TV:** KDTN-Ch. 2.
**Denver City - Newspaper:** Denver City Press (S).
**Deport - Newspaper:** Deport Times.
**DeSoto - Newspapers:** Focus Daily News (D); DeSoto Today.
**Detroit - Newspaper:** Detroit Weekly.
**Devine - Newspaper:** Devine News. **Radio-FM:** KSJL, 92.5 MHz.
**Diboll - Newspaper:** The Free Press. **Radio-AM:** KSML, 1260 kHz. **Radio-FM:** KAFX, 95.5 MHz.
**Dilley - Radio-FM:** KLMO, 98.9 MHz.
**Dimmitt - Newspaper:** Castro County News. **Radio-AM:** KDHN, 1470 kHz. **Radio-FM:** KNNK, 100.5 MHz.
**Dripping Springs - NewspaperS:** Dripping Springs Century News (S); The News-Dispatch.
**Dublin - Newspaper:** Dublin Citizen.
**Dumas - Newspaper:** Moore County News-Press (S). **Radio-AM:** KDDD, 800 kHz. **Radio-FM:** KDDD, 95.3 MHz.
**Duncanville - Newspaper:** Duncanville Today.
**Eagle Lake - Newspaper:** Eagle Lake Headlight.
**Eagle Pass - Newspapers:** The News Gram; Eagle Pass News-Guide (S). **Radio-AM:** KEPS, 1270 kHz. **Radio-FM:** KEPI, 88.7 MHz; KEPX, 89.5; KINL, 92.7. **TV:** KVAW-Ch. 16.
**East Bernard - Newspaper:** East Bernard Tribune.
**Eastland - Newspaper:** Eastland Telegram (S). **Radio-AM:** KEAS, 1590 kHz. **Radio-FM:** KATX, 97.7 MHz.
**Eden - Newspaper:** The Eden Echo.
**Edgewood - Newspaper:** Edgewood Enterprise.
**Edinburg - Newspaper:** Edinburg Daily Review (D). **Radio-AM:** KURV, 710 kHz. **Radio-FM:** KOIR, 88.5 MHz; KBFM, 104.1; KVLY, 107.9.
**Edna - Newspaper:** Jackson Co. Herald-Tribune. **Radio-AM:** KTMR, 1130 kHz. **Radio-FM:** KGUL, 96.1 MHz.
**El Campo - Newspaper:** El Campo Leader-News (S). **Radio-AM:** KULP, 1390 kHz. **Radio-FM:** KIOX, 96.9 MHz.
**Eldorado - Newspaper:** Eldorado Success.
**Electra - Newspaper:** Electra Star-News. **Radio-FM:** KOLI, 94.9 MHz.
**Elgin - Newspaper:** Elgin Courier. **Radio-FM:** KKLB, 92.5 MHz.
**El Paso - Newspapers:** El Paso Times (D). **Radio-AM:** KROD, 600 kHz; KTSM, 690; KAMA, 750; KBNA, 920; KXPL, 1060; KSVE, 1150; KVIV, 1340; KHEY, 1380; KELP, 1590; KBIV, 1650. **Radio-FM:** KTEP, 88.5 MHz; KXCR; 89.5; KVER, 91.1; KOFX, 92.3; KSII, 93.1; KINT, 93.9; KHRO, 94.7; KLAQ, 95.5; KHEY, 96.3; KBNA, 97.5; KTSM, 99.9; KPRR, 102.1. **TV:** KDBC-Ch. 4; KVIA-Ch. 7; KTSM-Ch. 9; KCOS-Ch. 13; KFOX-Ch. 14; KINT-Ch. 26; KSCE-Ch. 38; KTFN-Ch. 65.
**Emory - Newspaper:** Rains Co. Leader.

**Ennis - Newspaper:** Ennis Daily News (D).
**Fabens - Radio-FM:** KPAS, 103.1 MHz.
**Fairfield - NewspaperS:** Freestone County Times; The Fairfield Recorder. **Radio-FM:** KNES, 99.1 MHz.
**Falfurrias - Newspaper:** Falfurrias Facts. **Radio-AM**: KLDS, 1260 kHz. **Radio-FM:** KDFM, 103.3 MHz; KPSO, 106.3.
**Farmersville - Newspaper:** Farmersville Times. **Radio-AM:** KXXL, 990 kHz. **Radio-FM:** KXEZ, 92.1 MHz.
**Farwell - Newspaper:** State Line Tribune. **Radio-AM:** KIJN, 1060 kHz. **Radio-FM:** KIJN, 92.3 MHz; KICA, 98.3. **TV:** KPTF-Ch. 18.
**Ferris - Newspaper:** Ellis County Press. **Radio-AM:** KDFT, 540 kHz.
**Flatonia - Newspaper:** The Flatonia Argus.
**Floresville - Newspapers:** Floresville Chronicle-Journal; Wilson County News. **Radio-FM:** KWCB, 89.7 MHz; KLEY, 94.1.
**Flower Mound - Radio-FM:** KMEO, 96.7 MHz.
**Floydada - Newspaper:** Floyd Co. Hesperian-Beacon. **Radio-AM:** KFLP, 900 kHz. **Radio-FM:** KFLP, 95.3 MHz.
**Follett - Newspaper:** The Golden Spread.
**Forney - Newspaper:** Forney Messenger.
**Fort Davis - Newspaper:** Jeff Davis Co. Mt. Dispatch.
**Fort Stockton - Newspaper:** Fort Stockton Pioneer. **Radio-AM:** KFST, 860 kHz. **Radio-FM:** KFST, 94.3 MHz.
**Fort Worth - Newspapers:** Fort Worth Business Press; Commercial Recorder (D); Fort Worth Star-Telegram (D); NW Tarrant Co. Times-Record; Weekly Livestock Reporter. **Radio-AM:** WBAP, 820 kHz; KFJZ, 870; KHVN, 970; KESS, 1270; KNAX, 1630. **Radio-FM:** KTCU, 88.7 MHz; KLNO, 94.1; KSCS, 96.3; KEGL, 97.1; KPLX, 99.5; KDGE, 102.1; KOAI, 107.5. **TV:** KXAS-Ch. 5; KTVT-Ch. 11; KTXA-DT-Ch. 18; KTVT-DT-Ch. 19; KTXA-Ch. 21; KXAS-DT-Ch. 41; KFWD-DT-Ch. 51; KFWD-Ch. 52.
**Franklin - Newspapers:** Franklin Advocate; Franklin News Weekly. **Radio FM:** KZTR, 101.9 MHz.
**Frankston - Newspaper:** The Frankston Citizen. **Radio-FM:** KOYE, 96.7 MHz.
**Fredericksburg - Newspaper:** Standard/Radio Post. **Radio-AM:** KNAF, 910 kHz. **TV:** KBEJ-Ch. 2.
**Freeport - Radio-AM:** KBRZ, 1460 kHz. **Radio-FM:** KJOJ, 103.3 MHz.
**Freer - Newspaper:** Freer Press. **Radio-FM:** KBRA, 95.9 MHz.
**Friendswood - Newspapers:** Friendswood Journal; Friendswood Reporter News.
**Friona - Newspaper:** Friona Star. **Radio FM:** KGRW, 94.7 MHz.
**Frisco - Newspaper:** Frisco Enterprise (S).
**Fritch - Newspaper:** The Eagle Press.
**Gail - Newspaper:** Borden Star.
**Gainesville - Newspaper:** Gainesville Daily Register (D). **Radio-AM:** KGAF, 1580 kHz. **Radio-FM:** KSOC, 94.5 MHz.
**Galveston - Newspaper:** Galveston Co. Daily News (D). **Radio-AM:** KHCB, 1400 kHz; KGBC, 1540. **Radio-FM:** KOVE, 106.5 MHz. **TV:** KLTJ-Ch. 22; KTMD-Ch. 48.
**Ganado - Radio-FM:** KZAM, 104.7 MHz.
**Gardendale - Radio-FM:** KFZX, 102.1 MHz.
**Garland - Radio-AM:** KAAM, 770 kHz. **TV:** KUVN-Ch. 23; KUVN-DT-Ch. 24.
**Garrison - Newspaper:** Garrison In The News.
**Gatesville - Newspaper:** Gatesville Messenger and Star Forum (S). **Radio-FM:** KVLZ, 98.3 MHz.
**Georgetown - Newspapers:** Sunday Sun; Williamson Co. Sun. **Radio-FM:** KHFI, 96.7 MHz; KINV, 107.7.
**Giddings - Newspaper:** Giddings Times & News. **Radio-FM:** KANJ, 91.5 MHz.
**Gilmer - Newspaper:** Gilmer Mirror (S). **Radio-AM:** KOFY, 1060 kHz. **Radio-FM:** KFRO, 95.3 MHz.
**Gladewater - Newspaper:** Gladewater Mirror. **Radio-AM:** KEES, 1430 kHz.
**Glen Rose - Newspaper:** Glen Rose Reporter. **Radio-FM:** KTFW, 92.1 MHz.
**Goldthwaite - Newspaper:** Goldthwaite Eagle.
**Goliad - Newspaper:** The Texan Express. **Radio FM:** KHMC, 95.9 MHz.
**Gonzales - Newspaper:** Gonzales Inquirer (S). **Radio-AM:** KCTI, 1450 kHz. **Radio-FM:** KOOT, 106.3 MHz.
**Gorman - Newspaper:** Gorman Progress.
**Graford - Newspaper:** Lake Country Sun.
**Graham - Newspaper:** The Graham Leader (S). **Radio-AM:** KSWA, 1330 kHz. **Radio-FM:** KWKQ, 94.7 MHz.
**Granbury - Newspaper:** Hood County News (TW). **Radio-AM:** KPIR, 1420 kHz. **Radio-FM:** KDXT, 106.7 MHz.
**Grand Prairie - Radio-AM:** KKDA, 730 kHz.
**Grand Saline - Newspaper:** Grand Saline Sun.
**Grandview - Newspaper:** Grandview Tribune.
**Granger - Newspaper:** Granger News.
**Grapeland - Newspaper:** Grapeland Messenger.

**Greenville - Newspaper:** Greenville Herald-Banner (D). **Radio-AM:** KGVL,1400 kHz. **Radio-FM:** KIKT, 93.5 MHz. **TV:** KTAQ-Ch. 47.
**Greenwood - Newspaper:** Greenwood Ranger.
**Gregory - Radio-FM:** KPUS, 104.5 MHz.
**Groesbeck - Newspaper:** Groesbeck Journal.
**Groom - Newspaper:** Groom/McLean News.
**Groves - Radio-FM:** KTFA, 92.5 MHz.
**Groveton - Newspaper:** Groveton News.
**Gun Barrel City - Newspaper:** Cedar Creek Pilot.
**Hale Center - Newspaper:** Hale Center American.
**Hallettsville - Newspaper:** Hallettsville Tribune-Herald. **Radio-AM:** KHLT, 1520 kHz. **Radio-FM:** KTXM, 99.9 MHz.
**Haltom City - Radio FM:** KDBN, 93.3 MHz.
**Hamilton - Newspaper:** Hamilton Herald-News. **Radio-AM:** KCLW, 900 kHz.
**Hamlin - Newspaper:** Hamlin Herald. **Radio-FM:** KCDD, 103.7 MHz.
**Harker Heights - Radio-FM:** KUSJ, 105.5 MHz.
**Harlingen - Newspaper:** Valley Morning Star (D). **Radio-AM:** KGBT, 1530 kHz. **Radio-FM:** KMBH, 88.9 MHz; KFRQ, 94.5; KBTQ, 96.1. **TV:** KGBT-Ch. 4; KLUJ-Ch. 44; KMBH-Ch. 60.
**Hart - Newspaper:** Hart Beat.
**Haskell - Newspaper:** Haskell Free Press. **Radio-FM:** KVRP, 97.1 MHz.
**Hearne - Newspaper:** Hearne Democrat. **Radio-FM:** KVJM, 103.1 MHz.
**Hebbronville - Newspapers:** Hebbronville View; Jim Hogg Co. Enterprise. **Radio-FM:** KAZF, 91.9 MHz; KEKO, 101.7.
**Helotes - Radio-FM:** KONO, 101.1 MHz.
**Hemphill - Newspaper:** The Sabine Co. Reporter. **Radio-AM:** KPBL, 1240 kHz. **Radio-FM:** KTHP, 103.9 Mhz.
**Hempstead - Newspaper:** Waller County News-Citizen. **Radio-FM:** KEZB, 105.3 MHz.
**Henderson - Newspaper:** Henderson Daily News (D). **Radio-AM:** KWRD, 1470 kHz.
**Henrietta - Newspaper:** Clay County Leader.
**Hereford - Newspaper:** Hereford Brand (D). **Radio-AM:** KPAN, 860 kHz. **Radio-FM:** KJNZ, 103.5 MHz; KPAN, 106.3.
**Hico - Newspaper:** Hico News Review.
**Highland Park - Radio-AM:** KBIS, 1150 kHz. **Radio-FM:** KVIL, 103.7 MHz.
**Highlands - Newspaper:** Highlands Star/Crosby Courier.
**Highland Village - Radio-FM:** KWRD, 100.7 Mhz.
**Hillsboro - Newspaper:** Hillsboro Reporter (S). **Radio-AM:** KHBR, 1560 kHz. **Radio-FM:** KBRQ, 102.5 MHz.
**Hondo - Newspaper:** Hondo Anvil Herald. **Radio-AM:** KCWM, 1460 kHz. **Radio-FM:** KRIO, 105.9 MHz.
**Honey Grove - Newspaper:** Weekly Gazette.
**Hooks - Radio-FM:** KPWW, 95.9 MHz.
**Hornsby - Radio FM:** KOOP, 91.7 MHz.
**Houston - Newspapers:** Houston Business Journal; Houston Chronicle (D); Daily Court Review (D); Houston Forward Times; Houston Informer and Texas Freeman; Jewish Herald-Voice; Texas Catholic Herald (SM). **Radio-AM:** KILT, 610 kHz; KTRH, 740; KBME, 790; KEYH, 850; KPRC, 950; KLAT, 1010; KKHT, 1070; KQUE, 1230; KXYZ, 1320; KCOH, 1430; KMIC, 1590. **Radio-FM:** KUHF, 88.7 MHz; KPFT, 90.1; KTSU, 90.9; KTRU, 91.7; KKRW, 93.7; KTBZ, 94.5; KHJZ, 95.7; KHMX, 96.5; KBXX, 97.9; KODA, 99.1; KILT, 100.3; KLOL, 101.1; KMJQ, 102.1; KLTN, 102.9; KRBE, 104.1; KHCB, 105.7. **TV:** KPRC-Ch. 2; KUHT-Ch. 8; KUHT-DT-Ch. 9; KHOU-Ch. 11; KTRK-Ch. 13; KETH-Ch. 14; KTXH-DT-Ch. 19; KTXH-Ch. 20; KRIV-Ch. 26; KHOU-DT-Ch 31; KTRK-DT-Ch. 32; KPRC-DT-Ch. 35; KHWB-DT-Ch. 38; KHWB-Ch. 39; KZJL-Ch. 61.
**Howe - Newspaper:** Texoma Enterprise. **Radio-FM:** KHYI, 95.3 MHz.
**Hubbard - Newspaper:** Hubbard City News.
**Hudson - Radio-FM:** KLSN, 96.3 MHz.
**Humble - Radio-AM:** KGOL, 1180 kHz. **Radio-FM:** KSBJ, 89.3 MHz.
**Huntington - Radio-FM:** KYBI, 101.9 MHz.
**Huntsville - Newspaper:** Huntsville Item (D). **Radio-AM:** KHCH, 1400 kHz; KHVL, 1490. **Radio-FM:** KSHU, 90.5 MHz; KUST, 99.7; KSAM, 101.7.
**Hurst - Radio-AM:** KAHZ, 1360 kHz.
**Hutto - Newspaper:** Hutto Herald. **Radio-FM:** KQJZ, 92.1 MHz.
**Idalou - Newspaper:** Idalou Beacon. **Radio-FM:** KRBL, 105.7 MHz.
**Ingleside - Newspaper:** Ingleside Index. **Radio FM:** KCCG, 107.3 MHz.
**Ingram - Radio-FM:** KTXI, 90.1 MHz.
**Iowa Park - Newspaper:** Iowa Park Leader.
**Iraan - Newspaper:** Iraan News.
**Irving - TV:** KSTR-DT-Ch. 48; KSTR-Ch. 49.
**Italy - Newspaper:** Italy News-Herald.

**Jacksboro - Newspapers:** Jacksboro Gazette-News; Jack County Herald.
**Jacksonville - Newspaper:** Jacksonville Daily Progress (D). **Radio-AM:** KEBE, 1400 kHz. **Radio-FM:** KBJS, 90.3 MHz; KLJT, 102.3; KOOI, 106.5. **TV:** KETK-Ch. 56.
**Jasper - Newspaper:** The Jasper NewsBoy. **Radio-AM:** KTXJ, 1350 kHz. **Radio-FM:** KWYX, 102.7 MHz; KJAS, 107.3.
**Jefferson - Newspaper:** Jefferson Jimplecute. **Radio-FM:** KJTX, 104.5 MHz.
**Jewett - Newspaper:** Jewett Messenger.
**Johnson City - Newspaper:** Johnson City Record-Courier. **Radio-FM:** KFAN, 107.9 MHz.
**Joshua - Newspaper:** Joshua Star.
**Jourdanton - Radio-FM:** KBUC, 95.7 Mhz.
**Junction - Newspaper:** Junction Eagle. **Radio-AM:** KMBL, 1450 kHz. **Radio-FM:** KOOK, 93.5 MHz.
**Karnes City - Newspaper:** The Countywide. **Radio-AM:** KAML, 990 kHz.
**Katy - Newspaper:** Katy Times (S). **TV:** KNWS-Ch. 51.
**Kaufman - Newspaper:** Kaufman Herald.
**Keene - Newspaper:** Keene Star. **Radio-FM:** KJCR; 88.3 MHz.
**Kenedy - Radio-AM:** KAML, 990 kHz. **Radio-FM:** KTNR, 92.1 MHz.
**Kerens - Newspaper:** Kerens Tribune. **Radio-FM:** KRVF, 106.9 MHz.
**Kermit - Newspaper:** Winkler Co. News. **Radio-AM:** KERB, 600 kHz. **Radio-FM:** KERB, 106.3 MHz.
**Kerrville - Newspapers:** Kerrville Daily Times (D); The Mountain Sun. **Radio-AM:** KERV, 1230 kHz. **Radio-FM:** KKER, 88.7 MHz; KHKV, 91.1; KRNH, 92.3; KRVL, 94.3. **TV:** KRRT-Ch. 35.
**Kilgore - Newspaper:** Kilgore News Herald (D). **Radio-AM:** KBGE, 1240 kHz. **Radio-FM:** KTPB, 88.7 Mhz; KKTX, 96.1.
**Killeen - Newspaper:** Killeen Daily Herald (D). **Radio-AM:** KRMY, 1050 kHz. **Radio-FM:** KNCT, 91.3 MHz; KIIZ, 92.3. **TV:** KAKW-Ch. 62.
**Kingsville - Newspaper:** Kingsville Record and Bishop News (S). **Radio-AM:** KINE, 1330 kHz. **Radio-FM:** KTAI, 91.1 MHz; KKBA, 92.7; KFTX, 97.5.
**Kirbyville - Newspaper:** East Texas Banner.
**Knox City - Newspaper:** Knox Co. News.
**Kress - Newspaper:** Kress Chronicle.
**La Feria - Newspapers:** La Feria News.
**La Grange - Newspaper:** Fayette County Record (S). **Radio-AM:** KVLG, 1570 kHz. **Radio-FM:** KBUK, 104.9 MHz.
**Lake Dallas - Newspaper:** Lake Cities Sun. **TV:** KLDT-Ch. 55.
**Lake Jackson - Radio-FM:** KYBJ, 91.1 MHz; KLDE, 107.5.
**Lamesa - Newspaper:** Lamesa Press Reporter (S). **Radio-AM:** KPET, 690 kHz. **Radio-FM:** KBKN, 91.3 MHz.
**Lampasas - Newspaper:** Lampasas Dispatch Record (S). **Radio-AM:** KCYL, 1450 kHz.
**Lancaster - Newspaper:** Lancaster Today.
**La Porte - Newspaper:** Bayshore Sun (S).
**Laredo - Newspaper:** Laredo Morning Times (D). **Radio-AM:** KLAR, 1300 kHz; KLNT, 1490. **Radio-FM:** KHOY, 88.1 MHz; KBNL, 89.9; KJBZ, 92.7; KQUR, 94.9; KRRG, 98.1; KNEX, 106.1. **TV:** KGNS-Ch. 8; KVTV-Ch. 13; KLDO-Ch. 27.
**La Vernia - Newspaper:** La Vernia News.
**Leakey - Newspaper:** Real American Newspape **Radio-FM:** KBLT, 104.9 MHz.
**Leander - Radio-FM:** KHHL, 98.9 MHz.
**Leonard - Newspaper:** Leonard Graphic.
**Levelland - Newspaper:** Levelland and Hockley Co. News-Press (S). **Radio-AM:** KLVT, 1230 kHz. **Radio-FM:** KLVT, 105.5 MHz.
**Lewisville: Radio-FM:** KESS, 107.9 MHz.
**Lexington - Newspaper:** Lexington Leader.
**Liberty - Newspaper:** Liberty Vindicator (S). **Radio-FM:** KSHN, 99.9 MHz.
**Liberty Hill - Newspapers:** The Liberty Hill Independent.
**Lindale - Newspapers:** Lindale News and Times.
**Linden - Newspaper:** Cass County Sun.
**Little Elm - Newspaper:** The Little Elm Journal.
**Littlefield - Newspaper:** Lamb Co. Leader-News (S). **Radio-AM:** KZZN, 1490 kHz. **Radio-FM:** KAIQ, 95.5 MHz.
**Livingston - Newspaper:** Polk Co. Enterprise (S). **Radio-AM:** KETX, 1440 kHz. **Radio-FM:** KETX, 92.3 MHz.
**Llano - Newspaper:** Llano News. **Radio-FM:** KBAE, 96.3 MHz. **TV:** KXAM-Ch. 14.
**Lockhart - Newspaper:** Lockhart Post-Register. **Radio-AM:** KFIT, 1060 kHz.
**Lometa - Radio-FM:** KACQ, 101.9 MHz.
**Longview - Newspaper:** Longview News-Journal (D). **Radio-AM:** KFRO, 1370 kHz. **Radio-FM:** KYKX, 105.7 MHz. **TV:** KFXK-Ch. 51.
**Lorenzo - Radio-FM:** KKCL, 98.1 MHz.

**Los Ybañez - Radio-FM:** KYMI, 98.5 MHz.
**Lubbock - Newspaper:** Lubbock Avalanche-Journal (D). **Radio-AM:** KRFE, 580 kHz; KFYO, 790; KJTV, 950; KKAM, 1340; KLFB, 1420; KBZO, 1460; KDAV, 1590. **Radio-FM:** KTXT, 88.1 MHz; KOHM, 89.1; KAMY, 90.1; KYFT, 90.9; KXTQ, 93.7; KFMX, 94.5; KLLL, 96.3; KQBR, 99.5; KONE, 101.1; KZII, 102.5; KEJS, 106.5. **TV:** KTXT-Ch. 5; KCBD-DT-Ch. 9; KCBD-Ch. 11; KLBK-Ch. 13; KPTB-Ch. 16; KAMC-Ch. 28; KJTV- Ch. 34.
**Lufkin - Newspaper:** Lufkin Daily News (D). **Radio-AM:** KRBA, 1340 kHz. **Radio-FM:** KLDN, 88.9 Mhz; KSWP, 90.9; KAVX, 91.9. KUEZ, 100.1; KYKS, 105.1. **TV:** KTRE-Ch. 9.
**Luling - Newspaper:** Luling Newsboy and Signal. **Radio-FM:** KAMX, 94.7 MHz.
**Lytle - Newspapers:** Leader News; Medina Valley Times. **Radio-FM:** KZLV, 91.3 MHz.
**Mabank - Newspaper:** The Monitor (S).
**Madisonville - Newspaper:** Madisonville Meteor. **Radio-AM:** KMVL, 1220 kHz. **Radio-FM:** KAGG, 96.1 MHz; KMVL, 100.5.
**Malakoff - Newspaper:** Malakoff News. **Radio-FM:** KCKL, 95.9 MHz.
**Manor - Radio-AM:** KELG, 1140 kHz.
**Mansfield - Newspaper:** Mansfield News-Mirror (S).
**Marble Falls - Newspapers:** Marble Falls Highlander (S); The River Cities Tribune. **Radio-FM:** KBMD, 88.5 MHz; KXXS, 104.9 MHz.
**Marfa - Newspaper:** The Big Bend Sentinel.
**Marion - Radio-AM:** KBIB, 1000 kHz.
**Markham - Radio-FM:** KZRC, 92.5 Mhz.
**Marlin - Newspaper:** The Marlin Democrat. **Radio-FM:** KLRK, 92.9 MHz.
**Marshall - Newspaper:** Marshall News Messenger (D). **Radio-AM:** KCUL, 1410 kHz; KMHT, 1450. **Radio-FM:** KBWC, 91.1 MHz; KCUL, 92.3; KMHT, 103.9.
**Mart - Newspaper:** Mart Texan.
**Mason - Newspaper:** Mason County News.
**Matador - Newspaper:** Motley Co. Tribune.
**Mathis - Newspaper:** Mathis News.
**McAllen - Newspaper:** The Monitor (D). **Radio-AM:** KRIO, 910 kHz. **Radio-FM:** KHID, 88.1 MHz; KVMV, 96.9; KGBT, 98.5. **TV:** KNVO-Ch. 48.
**McCamey - Newspaper:** McCamey News. **Radio-FM:** KPBM, 95.3 MHz.
**McCook - Radio-FM:** KCAS, 91.5 Mhz.
**McGregor - Newspaper:** McGregor Mirror and Crawford Sun.
**McKinney - Newspaper:** McKinney Courier-Gazette (D). **Radio-FM:** KNTU, 88.1 MHz.
**Memphis - Newspaper:** Memphis Democrat. **Radio-FM:** KLSR, 105.3 MHz.
**Menard - Newspaper:** Menard News and Messenger.
**Mercedes - Newspaper:** Mercedes Enterprise. **Radio-FM:** KMAZ, 106.3 MHz.
**Meridian - Newspaper:** Bosque Co. News.
**Merkel - Newspaper:** Merkel Mail. **Radio-AM:** KMXO, 1500 kHz. **Radio-FM:** KHXS, 102.7 MHz.
**Mesquite - Radio-FM:** KEOM, 88.5 MHz.
**Mexia - Newspaper:** Mexia Daily News (D). **Radio-AM:** KRQX, 1590 kHz. **Radio-FM:** KYCX, 104.9 MHz.
**Miami - Newspaper:** Miami Chief.
**Midland - Newspaper:** Midland Reporter-Telegram (D). **Radio-AM:** KCRS, 550 kHz; KWEL, 1070; KJBC, 1150; KMND, 1510. **Radio-FM:** KNFM, 92.3 MHz; KBAT, 93.3; KQRX, 95.1; KCRS, 103.3; KCHX, 106.7. **TV:** KMID-Ch. 2; KUPB-Ch. 18.
**Midlothian - Newspapers:** Midlothian Mirror; Midlothian Today.
**Miles - Newspaper:** Miles Messenger.
**Mineola - Newspaper:** Mineola Monitor. **Radio-FM:** KMOO, 99.9 MHz.
**Mineral Wells - Newspaper:** Mineral Wells Index (D). **Radio-AM:** KJSA, 1120 kHz. **Radio-FM:** KFWR, 95.9 MHz.
**Mirando City - Radio-FM:** KBDR, 100.5 MHz.
**Mission - Newspaper:** Progress-Times. **Radio-AM:** KIRT, 1580 kHz. **Radio-FM:** KBOR, 105.5 MHz.
**Missouri City - Radio-FM:** KPTY, 104.9 MHz.
**Monahans - Newspaper:** Monahans News. **Radio-AM:** KLBO, 1330 kHz. **Radio-FM:** KGEE, 99.9 MHz.
**Moody - Newspaper:** Moody Courier.
**Morton - Newspaper:** Morton Tribune.
**Moulton - Newspaper:** Moulton Eagle.
**Mount Pleasant - Newspaper:** Daily Tribune (D). **Radio-AM:** KIMP, 960 kHz.
**Mount Vernon - Newspaper:** Mount Vernon Optic-Herald.
**Muenster - Newspaper:** Muenster Enterprise. **Radio-FM:** KKDL, 106.7 MHz.
**Muleshoe - Newspaper:** Muleshoe Journal. **Radio-AM:** KMUL, 1380 kHz. **Radio-FM:** KMUL, 103.1 MHz.
**Munday - Newspaper:** The Munday Courier.

**Nacogdoches - Newspaper:** Nacogdoches Daily Sentinel (D). **Radio-AM:** KSFA, 860 kHz; KEEE, 1230. **Radio-FM:** KSAU, 90.1 MHz; KJCS, 103.3; KTBQ, 107.7. **TV:** KLSB-Ch. 19.

**Naples - Newspaper:** The Monitor.

**Navasota - Newspaper:** The Navasota Examiner. **Radio-AM:** KWBC, 1550 kHz. **Radio-FM:** KMBV, 92.5 MHz.

**Nederland - Radio-AM:** KQHN, 1510 kHz.

**Needville - Newspaper:** The Gulf Coast Tribune.

**New Boston - Newspaper:** Bowie County Citizen Tribune (S). **Radio-AM:** KNBO, 1530 kHz. **Radio-FM:** KEWL, 95.1 MHz; KZRB, 103.5.

**New Braunfels - Newspaper:** Herald-Zeitung (D). **Radio-AM:** KGNB, 1420 kHz. **Radio-FM:** KNBT, 92.1 MHz.

**Newton - Newspaper:** Newton Co. News.

**New Ulm - Newspaper:** New Ulm Enterprise. **Radio-FM:** KNRG, 92.3 MHz.

**Nixon - Newspaper:** Cow Country Courier.

**Nocona - Newspaper:** Nocona News.

**Nolanville - Radio FM:** KLFX, 107.3 MHz.

**Normangee - Newspaper:** Normangee Star.

**Odem - Newspaper:** Odem-Edroy Times. **Radio-FM:** KLHB, 98.3 MHz.

**Odessa - Newspaper:** Odessa American (D). **Radio-AM:** KFLB, 920 kHz; KRIL, 1410. **Radio-FM:** KBMM, 89.5 MHz; KFLB, 90.5 MHz; KOCV, 91.3; KMRK, 96.1; KMCM, 96.9; KODM, 97.9; KHKX, 99.1; KQLM, 107.9. **TV:** KOSA-Ch. 7; KWES-Ch. 9; KPEJ-Ch. 24; KPXK-Ch. 30; KOCV-Ch. 36; KMLM-Ch. 42.

**O'Donnell - Newspaper:** O'Donnell Index-Press.

**Olney - Newspaper:** Olney Enterprise.

**Olton - Newspaper:** Olton Enterprise.

**Orange - Newspaper:** Orange Leader (D). **Radio-AM:** KOGT, 1600 kHz. **Radio-FM:** KKMY, 104.5 MHz; KIOC, 106.1.

**Ore City - Radio-FM:** KAZE, 106.9 Mhz.

**Overton - Newspaper:** Overton Press. **Radio-FM:** KPXI, 100.7 Mhz.

**Ozona - Newspaper:** Ozona Stockman. **Radio-FM:** KYXX, 94.3 Mhz.

**Paducah - Newspaper:** Paducah Post.

**Paint Rock - Newspaper:** Concho Herald.

**Palacios - Newspaper:** Palacios Beacon. Radio-FM: KROY, 99.7 MHz.

**Palestine - Newspaper:** Palestine Herald Press (D). **Radio-AM:** KNET, 1450 kHz. **Radio-FM:** KYFP, 89.1 MHz; KYYK, 98.3.

**Pampa - Newspaper:** Pampa News (D). **Radio-AM:** KGRO, 1230 kHz. **Radio-FM:** KAXH, 90.9 MHz; KOMX, 100.3.

**Panhandle - Newspaper:** Panhandle Herald.

**Paris - Newspaper:** Paris News (D). **Radio-AM:** KPJC, 1250 kHz. **Radio-FM:** KHCP, 89.3 MHz; KOYN, 93.9; KBUS, 101.9; KPLT, 107.7.

**Pasadena - Newspaper:** Pasadena Citizen (D). **Radio-AM:** KIKK, 650 kHz; KLVL, 1480. **Radio-FM:** KFTG, 88.1 MHz; KKBQ, 92.9.

**Pearland - Newspapers:** Pearland Journal; Pearland Reporter News.

**Pearsall - Newspaper:** Frio-Nueces Current. **Radio-AM:** KVWG, 1280 kHz. **Radio-FM:** KVWG, 95.3 MHz; KMFR, 104.1.

**Pecan Grove - Radio-AM:** KREH, 900 kHz.

**Pecos - Newspaper:** Pecos Enterprise (D). **Radio-AM:** KIUN, 1400 kHz. **Radio-FM:** KKLY, 97.3 MHz; KPTX, 98.3.

**Perryton - Newspaper:** Perryton Herald (S). **Radio-AM:** KEYE, 1400 kHz. **Radio-FM:** KEYE, 96.1 MHz.

**Petersburg - Newspaper:** Petersburg Post.

**Pflugerville - Newspaper:** Pflugerville Pflag. **Radio-AM:** KOKE, 1600 kHz.

**Pharr - Newspaper:** Advance News Journal. **Radio-AM:** KVJY, 840 kHz.

**Pilot Point - Newspaper:** Pilot Point Post-Signal. **Radio-FM:** KTCY, 104.9 MHz.

**Pittsburg - Newspaper:** Pittsburg Gazette. **Radio-FM:** KSCN, 96.9 MHz; KDVE, 103.9.

**Plains - Newspaper:** Cowboy Country News. **Radio-FM:** KPHS, 90.3 MHz.

**Plainview - Newspaper:** Plainview Daily Herald (D). **Radio-AM:** KKYN, 1090 kHz; KREW, 1400. **Radio-FM:** KPMB, 88.5 Mhz; KBAH, 90.5; KWLD, 91.5; KHDY, 97.3; KRIA, 103.9; KKYN, 106.9.

**Plano - Newspaper:** Plano Star Courier (D). **Radio AM:** KMKI, 620 kHz.

**Pleasanton - Newspaper:** Pleasanton Express. **Radio-AM:** KFNI, 1380 kHz.

**Point Comfort - Radio-FM:** KAJI, 94.1 MHz.

**Port Aransas - Newspaper:** Port Aransas South Jetty.

**Port Arthur - Newspaper:** Port Arthur News (D). **Radio-AM:** KDEI, 1250 kHz; KOLE, 1340. **Radio-FM:** KQBU, 93.3 MHz; KTJM, 98.5. **TV:** KBTV-Ch. 4.

**Port Isabel - Newspaper:** Port Isabel/South Padre Press (S). **Radio-FM:** KNVO, 101.1 MHz.

**Portland - Newspaper:** Portland News. **Radio-FM:** KSGR, 91.1 MHz; KMJR, 105.5.

**Port Lavaca - Newspaper:** Port Lavaca Wave (S). **Radio-FM:** KITE, 93.3 MHz.

**Port Neches - Radio-AM:** KUHD, 1150 kHz.

**Post - Newspaper:** Post Dispatch. **Radio-FM:** KOFR, 107.3 MHz.

**Pottsboro - Newspaper:** Texoma Press.

**Prairie View - Radio-FM:** KPVU, 91.3 MHz.

**Premont - Radio-FM:** KMFM, 100.7 MHz.

**Presidio - Newspaper:** The International Presidio Paper.

**Princeton - Newspaper:** Princeton Herald.

**Quanah - Newspaper:** Quanah Tribune-Chief (S). **Radio-AM:** KVDL, 1150 kHz. **Radio-FM:** KIXC, 100.9 MHz.

**Quinlan - Newspaper:** The Tawakoni News.

**Quitaque - Newspaper:** Valley Tribune.

**Quitman - Newspaper:** Wood Co. Democrat.

**Ralls - Newspaper:** Crosby Co. Reporter-Examiner. **Radio-AM:** KCLR, 1530 kHz.

**Ranger - Newspaper:** Ranger Times (S).

**Rankin - Newspaper:** Rankin News.

**Raymondville - Newspaper:** Chronicle/Willacy Co. News. **Radio-AM:** KSOX, 1240 kHz. **Radio-FM:** KILM, 102.1 MHz; KBIC, 105.7.

**Red Oak - Newspapers:** Ellis Co. Chronicle (S).

**Refugio - Newspaper:** Refugio Co. Press. **Radio-FM:** KTKY, 106.1 MHz.

**Richmond - Newspaper (see Rosenberg).**

**Riesel - Newspaper:** Riesel Rustler.

**Rio Grande City - Newspaper:** Rio Grande Herald. **Radio-FM:** Kqbo, 103.1 MHz. **TV:** KTLM-Ch. 40.

**Rising Star - Newspaper:** Rising Star Star.

**Robert Lee - Newspaper:** Observer/Enterprise.

**Robinson- Radio-FM:** KDOS, 107.9 MHz.

**Robstown - Newspaper:** Nueces Co. Record-Star. **Radio-AM:** KROB, 1510 kHz. **Radio-FM:** KLUX, 89.5 MHz; KSAB, 99.9; KMIQ, 104.9.

**Rochester - Newspaper:** Twin Cities News.

**Rockdale - Newspaper:** Rockdale Reporter and Messenger. **Radio-FM:** KRXT, 98.5 MHz.

**Rockport - Newspapers:** Rockport Pilot (S); The Herald. **Radio-FM:** KKPN, 102.3 MHz.

**Rocksprings - Newspaper:** Texas Mohair Weekly.

**Rockwall - Newspaper:** Rockwall County News.

**Rollingwood - Radio-AM:** KJCE, 1370 kHz.

**Roma - Newspaper:** South Texas Reporter. **Radio-FM:** KBMI, 97.7 MHz.

**Rosebud - Newspaper:** Rosebud News.

**Rosenberg - Newspaper:** Rosenberg Herald-Coaster (D). **Radio-AM:** KRTX, 980 kHz. **TV:** KXLN-Ch. 45.

**Rotan - Newspaper:** Rotan Advance-Star-Record.

**Round Rock - Newspaper:** Round Rock Leader (S). **Radio-FM:** KNLE, 88.1 MHz; KFMK, 105.9.

**Rowena - Newspaper:** Rowena Press.

**Rowlett - Newspaper:** The Rowlett Lakeshore Times.

**Rudolph - Radio-FM:** KTER, 90.7 MHz.

**Rusk - Newspaper:** Cherokeean/Herald. **Radio-AM:** KTLU, 1580 kHz. **Radio-FM:** KWRW, 97.7 Mhz.

**Saint Jo - Newspaper:** Saint Jo Tribune.

**San Angelo - Newspaper:** San Angelo Standard-Times (D). **Radio-AM:** KGKL, 960 kHz; KKSA, 1260; KCRN, 1340. **Radio-FM:** KUTX, 90.1 MHz; KDCD, 92.9; KCRN, 93.9; KIXY, 94.7; KGKL, 97.5; KELI, 98.7; KYZZ, 100.1; KWFR, 101.9; KMDX, 106.1; KSJT, 107.5. **TV:** KACB-Ch. 3; KIDY-Ch. 6; KLST-Ch. 8.

**San Antonio - Newspapers:** San Antonio Business Journal; Commercial Recorder (D); Express-News (D); North San Antonio Times; Today's Catholic (BW). **Radio-AM:** KTSA, 550 kHz; KSLR, 630; KKYX, 680; KTKR, 760; KONO, 860; KENS, 1160; WOAI, 1200; KZDC, 1250; KXTN, 1310; KCOR, 1350; KCHL, 1480; KEDA, 1540. **Radio-FM:** KPAC, 88.3 MHz; KSTX, 89.1; KSYM, 90.1; KYFS, 90.9; KRTU, 91.7; KROM, 92.9; KXXM, 96.1; KAJA, 97.3; KISS, 99.5; KCYY, 100.3; KQXT, 101.9; KTFM, 102.7; KZEP, 104.5; KXTN, 107.5. **TV:** WOAI-Ch. 4; KENS-Ch. 5; KLRN-Ch. 9; KSAT-Ch. 12; KHCE-Ch. 23; KABB-Ch. 29; KVDA-DT-Ch. 38; KWEX-Ch. 41; KSAT-DT-Ch. 48; WOAI-DT-Ch. 58; KVDA-Ch. 60.

**San Augustine - Newspaper:** San Augustine Tribune. **Radio-FM:** KQSI, 92.5 MHz.

**San Benito - Newspaper:** San Benito News (S).

**San Diego - Newspaper:** Duval County Picture (S). **Radio-FM:** KUKA, 105.9 MHz.

**Sanger - Newspaper:** Sanger Courier. **Radio-FM:** KTPW, 89.7 MHz; KTDK, 104.1.

**San Juan - Radio-AM:** KUBR, 1210 kHz.

**San Marcos - Newspaper:** San Marcos Daily Record (D).

**Radio-AM:** KUOL, 1470 kHz. **Radio-FM:** KTSW, 89.9 MHz; KEYI, 103.5.
**San Saba - Newspaper:** San Saba News & Star. **Radio-AM:** KBAL, 1410 kHz. **Radio-FM:** KBAL, 106.1 MHz.
**Santa Fe - Radio-FM:** KJIC, 90.5 MHz.
**Schertz - Radio-FM:** KBBT, 98.5 MHz.
**Schulenburg - Newspaper:** Schulenburg Sticker.
**Seabrook - Radio-FM:** KRTS, 92.1 MHz.
**Seadrift - Radio-FM:** KMAT, 105.1 MHz.
**Seagoville - Newspaper:** Suburbia News.
**Sealy - Newspaper:** The Sealy News (S).
**Seguin - Newspaper:** Seguin Gazette-Enterprise (D). **Radio-AM:** KWED, 1580 kHz. **Radio-FM:** KSMG, 105.3 MHz.
**Seminole - Newspaper:** Seminole Sentinel (S). **Radio-AM:** KIKZ, 1250 kHz. **Radio-FM:** KSEM, 106.3 MHz.
**Seymour - Newspaper:** Baylor Co. Banner. **Radio-AM:** KSEY, 1230 kHz. **Radio-FM:** KSEY, 94.3 MHz.
**Shamrock - Newspaper:** County Star-News. **Radio-FM:** KBKH, 92.9 MHz.
**Shepherd - Newspaper:** San Jacinto News-Times.
**Sherman - Newspaper:** Herald Democrat (D). **Radio-AM:** KXEB, 910 kHz; KJIM, 1500; KTBK, 1700. **TV:** KXII-Ch. 12; KXII-DT-Ch. 20.
**Shiner - Newspaper:** The Shiner Gazette.
**Silsbee - Newspaper:** Silsbee Bee. **Radio-AM:** KSET, 1300 kHz. **Radio-FM:** KAYD, 101.7 MHz.
**Silverton - Newspaper:** Briscoe Co. News.
**Sinton - Newspaper:** San Patricio Co. News. **Radio-AM:** KDAE, 1590 kHz. **Radio-FM:** KNCN, 101.3 MHz; KOUL, 103.7.
**Slaton - Newspaper:** Slaton Slatonite. **Radio-FM:** KJAK, 92.7 MHz.
**Smithville - Newspaper:** Smithville Times.
**Snyder - Newspaper:** Snyder Daily News (D). **Radio-AM:** KSNY, 1450 kHz. **Radio-FM:** KLYD, 98.9 MHz; KSNY, 101.5. **TV:** KPCB-Ch. 17.
**Somerset - Radio-AM:** KSJL, 810 kHz.
**Sonora - Newspaper:** Devil's River News. **Radio-AM:** KHOS, 980 kHz. **Radio-FM:** KHOS, 92.1 MHz.
**South Padre Island - Radio-FM:** KESO, 92.7 MHz; KZSP, 95.3.
**Spearman - Newspaper:** Hansford Co. Reporter-Statesman. **Radio-FM:** KRDF, 98.3.
**Springtown - Newspaper:** Springtown Epigraph. **Radio-FM:** KSQX, 89.1 MHz.
**Spur - Newspaper:** Texas Spur.
**Stamford - Newspaper:** Stamford American. **Radio-AM:** KVRP, 1400 kHz. **Radio-FM:** KOES, 106.9 Mhz.
**Stanton - Newspaper:** Martin Co. Messenger. **Radio-FM:** KKJW, 105.9 MHz.
**Stephenville - Newspaper:** Stephenville Empire-Tribune (D). **Radio-AM:** KSTV, 1510 kHz. **Radio-FM:** KCUB, 98.3 MHz.
**Sterling City - Newspaper:** Sterling City News-Record. **Radio-FM:** KCSE, 96.5 MHz.
**Stratford - Newspaper:** Stratford Star.
**Sudan - Newspaper:** Sudan Beacon-News.
**Sugar Land - Newspaper:** The Fort Bend Mirror.
**Sulphur Springs - Newspaper:** News-Telegram (D). **Radio-AM:** KSST, 1230 kHz. **Radio-FM:** KSCH, 95.9 MHz.
**Sweetwater - Newspaper:** Sweetwater Reporter (D). **Radio-AM:** KXOX, 1240 kHz. **Radio-FM:** KXOX, 96.7 MHz. **TV:** KTXS-Ch. 12.
**Taft - Newspaper:** Taft Tribune.
**Tahoka - Newspaper:** Lynn Co. News. **Radio-FM:** KXAL, 100.3 MHz; KAMZ, 103.5.
**Talco - Newspaper:** Talco Times.
**Tatum - Newspaper:** Trammel Trace Tribune. **Radio-FM:** KDVE, 100.3 MHz.
**Taylor - Newspaper:** Taylor Daily Press (D). **Radio-AM:** KWNX, 1260 kHz. **Radio FM:** KQBT, 104.3 MHz.
**Teague - Newspaper:** Teague Chronicle.
**Temple - Newspaper:** Temple Daily Telegram (D). **Radio-AM:** KTEM, 1400 kHz. **Radio-FM:** KVLT, 88.5 MHz; KBDE, 89.9; KLTD, 101.7 MHz. **TV:** KCEN-Ch. 6.
**Terrell - Newspaper:** Terrell Tribune (D). **Radio-AM:** KPYK, 1570 kHz.
**Terrell Hills - Radio-AM:** KLUP, 930 kHz. **Radio-FM:** KCJZ, 106.7 MHz.
**Texarkana - Newspaper:** Texarkana Gazette (D). **Radio-AM:** KCMC, 740 kHz; KTFS, 940; KKTK, 1400. **Radio-FM:** KTAL, 98.1 MHz; KKYR, 102.5. **TV:** KTAL-Ch. 6.
**Texas City - Newspaper:** Texas City Sun (D). **Radio-AM:** KYST, 920 kHz.
**Thorndale - Newspaper:** Thorndale Champion.
**Three Rivers - Newspaper:** The Progress. **Radio-FM:** KEMA, 94.5 MHz.
**Throckmorton - Newspaper:** Throckmorton Tribune.
**Timpson - Newspaper:** Timpson & Tenaha News.

**Tomball - Radio-AM:** KSEV, 700 kHz.
**Trenton - Newspaper:** Trenton Tribune.
**Trinity - Newspaper:** Trinity Standard.
**Tulia - Newspaper:** Tulia Herald. **Radio-AM:** KTUE, 1260 kHz. **Radio-FM:** KBTE, 104.9 Mhz.
**Tye - Radio-FM:** KBCY, 99.7 MHz.
**Tyler - Newspapers:** Tyler Morning Telegraph (D); Catholic East Texas (SM). **Radio-AM:** KTBB, 600 kHz; KZEY, 690; KGLD, 1330; KYZS, 1490. **Radio-FM:** KVNE, 89.5 MHz; KGLY, 91.3; KDOK, 92.1; KTYL, 93.1; KNUE, 101.5; KKUS, 104.1. **TV:** KLTV-Ch. 7.
**Universal City - Radio-AM:** KSAH, 720 kHz.
**University Park - Radio-AM:** KZMP, 1540 kHz.
**Uvalde - Newspaper:** Uvalde Leader-News (S). **Radio-AM:** KVOU, 1400 kHz. **Radio-FM:** KBNU, 93.9 MHz; KUVA, 102.3; KVOU, 104.9. **TV:** KPXL-Ch. 26.
**Valley Mills - Newspaper:** Valley Mills Progress.
**Van - Newspapers:** The Area Dispatch; Van Banner.
**Van Alstyne - Newspaper:** Van Alstyne Leader.
**Van Horn - Newspaper:** Van Horn Advocate.
**Vega - Newspaper:** Vega Enterprise.
**Vernon - Newspaper:** Vernon Daily Record (D). **Radio-AM:** KVWC, 1490 kHz. **Radio-FM:** KVWC, 103.1 MHz.
**Victoria - Newspaper:** Victoria Advocate (D). **Radio-AM:** KRNX, 1340 kHz; KNAL, 1410. **Radio-FM:** KAYK, 88.5 MHz; KXBJ, 89.3; KVRT, 90.7; KQVT, 92.3; KVIC, 95.1; KTXN, 98.7; KEPG, 100.9; KIXS, 107.9. **TV:** KVCT-Ch. 19; KAVU-Ch. 25.
**Vidor - Newspaper:** Vidor Vidorian.
**Waco - Newspapers:** The Waco Citizen (S); Waco Tribune-Herald (D). **Radio-AM:** KBBW, 1010; KWTX, 1230 kHz; KTFW, 1460; KRZI, 1580; KRZX, 1660. **Radio-FM:** KBCT, 94.5 MHz; KBGO, 95.7; KWTX, 97.5; WACO, 99.9; KWBU, 103.3. **TV:** KWTX-Ch. 10; KXXV-Ch. 25; KWBU-Ch. 34; KWKT-Ch. 44.
**Wake Village - Radio-FM:** KHTA, 92.5 Mhz.
**Wallis - Newspaper:** Wallis News-Review.
**Waxahachie - Newspaper:** Waxahachie Daily Light (D). **Radio-AM:** KBEC, 1390 kHz.
**Weatherford - Newspaper:** Weatherford Democrat (D). **Radio-AM:** KZEE, 1220 kHz. **Radio-FM:** KYQX, 89.5 MHz.
**Weimar - Newspaper:** Weimar Mercury.
**Wells - Radio-FM:** KVLL, 94.7 MHz.
**Wellington - Newspaper:** Wellington Leader.
**Weslaco - Radio-AM:** KRGE, 1290 kHz. **TV:** KRGV-Ch. 5; KRGV-DT-Ch. 13.
**West - Newspaper:** West News.
**West Lake Hills - Radio-AM:** KTXZ, 1560 kHz.
**West Odessa - Radio-FM:** KLVW, 88.7 MHz.
**Wharton - Newspaper:** Wharton Journal-Spectator (S). **Radio-AM:** KANI, 1500 kHz.
**Wheeler - Newspaper:** The Wheeler Times. **Radio-FM:** KPDR, 90.5 MHz.
**Whitehouse - Newspaper:** Tri Co. Leader. **Radio-FM:** KISX, 107.3 MHz.
**White Oak - Newspaper:** White Oak Independent. **Radio-FM:** KIXK, 99.3 MHz.
**Whitesboro - Newspaper:** Whitesboro News-Record. **Radio-FM:** KMAD, 102.5 MHz.
**Whitewright - Newspaper:** Whitewright Sun.
**Whitney - Newspaper:** Lake Whitney Views (M).
**Wichita Falls - Newspaper:** Wichita Falls Times-Record-News (D). **Radio-AM:** KCAF, 990 kHz; KWFS, 1290. **Radio-FM:** KMCU, 88.7 MHz; KMOC, 89.5; KTEO, 90.5; KNIN, 92.9; KLUR, 99.9; KWFS, 102.3; KQXC, 103.9; KBZS, 106.3. **TV:** KFDX-Ch. 3; KAUZ-Ch. 6; KJTL-Ch. 18.
**Willis - Radio FM:** KVST, 103.7 MHz.
**Wills Point - Newspaper:** Wills Point Chronicle.
**Wimberley - Newspaper:** Wimberley View (S).
**Winfield - Radio-FM:** KALK, 97.7 MHz.
**Winnie - Newspaper:** The Hometown Press. **Radio FM:** KOBT, 100.7 MHz.
**Winnsboro - Newspapers:** Winnsboro News. **Radio-FM:** KWNS, 104.7 MHz.
**Winona - Radio-FM:** KBLZ, 102.7 MHz.
**Winters - Newspaper:** Winters Enterprise. **Radio-FM:** KORQ, 96.1 Mhz.
**Wolfe City - Newspaper:** Wolfe City Mirror.
**Wolfforth - TV:** KUPT-Ch. 22.
**Woodville - Newspaper:** Tyler Co. Booster. **Radio-AM:** KWUD, 1490 kHz.
**Wylie - Newspaper:** The Wylie News.
**Yoakum - Newspaper:** Yoakum Herald-Times. **Radio-FM:** KYKM, 92.5 MHz.
**Yorktown - Newspaper:** Yorktown News-View.
**Zapata - Newspaper:** Zapata Co. News. **Radio-FM:** KBAW, 93.5 MHz. ☆

# Texas Economy: Productivity amid National Recession

*Source: The State of Texas Annual Cash Report 2002, Comptroller of Public Accounts.*

The Texas economy was affected by the national recession. From August 2001 to August 2002, statewide nonfarm employment fell by 87,600, declining 0.9 percent, compared to a 0.4 percent gain during the same period of fiscal 2001 and an average annual growth rate of 4 percent during the economic boom of 1997 and 1998. Since the productivity of Texas workers has increased at a faster rate than the loss of jobs, however, Texas avoided joining the nation in recession.

## Manufacturing and High-Tech

Like 2001, fiscal 2002 was a year that most Texas manufacturers will not want to remember. Faced with weighty inventories and faltering personal computer sales worldwide, Dell Computer Corporation and Compaq Computer Corporation both announced job layoffs during this period.

Largely because of the personal computer market, the state's semiconductor and electronic component producers also felt the effects.

Outside of high-tech, the news was not much happier. Apparel manufacturers, largely concentrated along the Texas-Mexico border, continued to be affected by international competition, and they reduced their work forces in response.

In fiscal 2002, statewide manufacturing employment declined by 4.3 percent, or 45,400 jobs, or slightly better than the 4.8 percent loss in manufacturing employment nationwide.

## Oil and Gas

Through much of 2001, the resurgence of the state's oil and gas sector, owing to relatively high energy prices in the winter of 2000-01, partially countered losses by the state's manufacturers. Because of a slowing economy and excess supplies, oil prices, however, subsequently declined until November 2001, when they began to turn upward again.

Largely because of fears of an Iraqi conflict, prices mostly have been rising since then, from $17 to $25 a barrel in the summer of 2002. But because of the lag between energy prices, drilling

*Construction workers in Grapevine. File photo.*

activity and new hiring, and the generally weak near-term outlook, year-over-year mining employment has continued to decline.

By August 2002, the rig count of 334 was down 33 percent from its August 2001 level. And by fiscal 2002 year-end, sector jobs were down by 6,900, or 4.2 percent, from the fiscal 2001 level.

## Construction

With a slow economy and overbuilt nonresidential markets, Texas construction job growth buckled from an eye-popping 9.2 percent at the end of 1998 to a 1.8 percent annual loss in March 2002 before the picture began to improve.

In fiscal 2002, Texas construction saw a job loss of 0.5 percent, or 3,000 jobs. These losses could have been worse without the unusually robust single-family housing construction.

But even with the revival of residential construction, the state's economic cycle and higher office vacancy rates point to a further deceleration in statewide construction employment growth over the short term, thereby dampening the demand for new construction projects.

## Transportation, Communication, Utilities

The transportation, communications and public utilities sector was the most affected by the attacks on September 11. After the terrorist attacks, U.S. air traffic abated and layoffs were announced at most major U.S. air carriers, including Texas-based American and Continental Airlines.

Although Southwest Airlines avoided mass layoffs, year-over-year job growth in the state's once-vibrant air transportation industry fell from a gain of 4,100 in August 2001 to a loss of 8,300 by August 2002. Combined with other job loses, including trucking and warehousing and communications, the sector lost a total of 21,800 jobs, down 3.7 percent during this period.

In recent years, Texas' trucking, warehousing, and a number of other transportation services have benefited from the expanding national and state economies, as well as from increasing trade with Mexico. Through much of

2001, while the U.S. and Texas economies were retrenching, trade with Mexico remained fairly resilient. But the U.S. recession eventually affected this industry as well, such that trucking and warehousing employment lost 2,400 jobs in fiscal 2002.

With the rapidly growing popularity of the Internet and cellular communication, Texas communication employment boomed at a 7 percent average annual rate from 1999 to 2001. The national downturn took hold and intensified here as well, so that by August 2002, employment in the sector had fallen by 7,600 jobs statewide, mostly because of job reductions at the state's major telecommunications providers.

Finally, utilities employment — until the folding of Enron — had enjoyed a trend-bucking year, growing by 4,000 jobs, or 5.4 percent, from October 2000 to October 2001, largely because of the deregulation of the state's electric utility sector.

The construction of gas-fired electricity generation facilities in Texas has boomed in recent years, as the prospect of selling power at a reasonable return to the state's rapidly growing residential, industrial and commercial sectors emerged.

However, with Enron's bankruptcy and ensuing layoffs, the utilities sector quickly gave back the 4,000 jobs it had gained the previous year. By August 2002 the utilities sector overall had 2,900 fewer employees than in August 2001, a loss of 3.7 percent.

*The Texas service sector lost jobs during fiscal 2002 for the first time in more than 30 years*

### Finance, Insurance, Real Estate

Finance, insurance and real estate turned in a relatively weak twelve months, with a 0.9 percent loss of 4,600 jobs from August 2001 to August 2002. During this period, all sectors of the industry lost jobs.

Employment in banks and other financial institutions suffered only mild losses (down 0.5 percent), being supported by the state's growing population and healthy demand for new financing.

Likewise, jobs among the state's insurance providers also fell slightly, down 1.0 percent. However, real estate, holding companies, and securities and investment industries accounted for over 80 percent of this

sector's net employment decline during this period (down 3,700 jobs, or 2.1 percent).

### Trade

Consumer confidence and spending faltered as job layoffs mounted in fiscal 2001. Confidence generally fell further in fiscal 2002 following the September 11 attacks, the bad publicity about corporate accounting practices and the faltering stock market.

During fiscal 2002, state sales tax receipts — of which just more than 50 percent come from household expenditures — fell by 1.0 percent, compared with a gain of almost 5 percent in all of fiscal 2001. Partially spurred by dealer incentives at the beginning of the fiscal year, motor vehicle sales tax collections increased 1.5 percent during the same period.

By August 2002, the Conference Board's West South Central consumer confidence index stood nearly 19 percent below its August 2001 pre-attack level. Consequently, flagging consumer expenditures have reduced the wholesale and retail trade job count by 1.5 percent during this period, compared with annual average gains of more than three percent in fiscal 1999 through 2001.

About one-third of this loss was in wholesale trade, which was hurt by a decreased demand for manufactured products. Net job losses in wholesale trade totaled 9,400 over the past year, a 1.8 percent loss.

Retail trade — including building materials, restaurants, automobile dealers and service stations, food, furniture, clothing, general merchandise stores, and other miscellaneous retailers — cut back 25,400 jobs, a 1.5 percent decline.

Bucking the trend, a few sectors — sellers of building materials, automobile dealers/service stations, and eating and drinking places — added jobs.

### Services

Because of the breadth of the national downturn, the Texas service sector lost jobs during fiscal 2002 for the first time in more than 30 years. As of August 2002, total services employment remains down another 6,200 jobs, for a relatively small 0.4 percent drop from its August 2001 level.

Within this sector, employment in health services is up by 18,800 jobs, or 2.6 percent, due to the aging of the population, the availability and use of new medical procedures, and rapidly increasing spending on pre-

*Jets at Austin Bergstrom Airport. The transportation sector lost 21,800 jobs in fiscal year 2002. File photo*

scription drugs and other medical services. Jobs at establishments providing social and rehabilitation services increased 2.9 percent and accounted for 5,800 new jobs.

Private educational services added 5,500 jobs, a 4.4 percent increase, and agricultural services took advantage of a particularly strong demand for veterinary and landscape/horticultural services to add 2,000 jobs, a 3.2 percent increase.

Most of the state's service industries, in fact, added or lost a relatively small portion of their employment over the past year — with two notable exceptions.

First, motion pictures lost 2,500 jobs, nearly an 8.0 percent decrease, as terrorism concerns and economic weakness cut into discretionary consumer expenditures.

Second, and much more significantly, business services, owing mostly to adjustments in the once-booming temporary help and personnel supply sector, lost 32,800 jobs over the year, a 4.7 percent decline and more than one-third of all the jobs lost statewide in fiscal 2002.

The silver lining in this otherwise troubling statistic is that these were largely temporary, part-time jobs, so

*Government employment growth continued with nearly half of gains coming in public schools and other local governments*

the state's loss of full-time jobs was a smaller share of the losses than the bottom-line number might indicate.

### Government

Federal, state and local government employment growth continued at a moderate and steady rate. Overall, in fiscal 2002, public sector employment was up 2.2 percent, or 35,100 jobs, with nearly half of these gains coming from increased hiring at public schools and other local governments.

Texas' civilian federal government employment rose 0.6 percent, or by 1,100, during this period. The number of jobs in state government increased by 1.7 percent, or by 5,500 jobs.

Local government employment, almost two-thirds of which is fueled by public schools, increased by 28,500 jobs, or 2.7 percent, over the past year. The remaining local government job gains were in various other programs at the city, county and special district level.

A relatively high birthrate and the influx of new students from the other states and countries continue to keep the state's school-age population growing. ☆

## Texas Gross State Product, 1993-2002, By Industry (in millions)

| Industry | 1993 | 1994 | 1995 | 1996 | 1997 | 1998 | 1999 | 2000 | 2001 | 2002* |
|---|---|---|---|---|---|---|---|---|---|---|
| Agriculture | $ 7,836 | $ 7,740 | $ 7,347 | $ 7,175 | $ 8,331 | $ 8,197 | $ 9,309 | $ 9,639 | $ 10,152 | $ 9,967 |
| %change | 10.2 | (1.2) | (4.7) | (2.7) | 16.1 | (1.6) | 13.6 | 3.5 | 5.3 | (1.8) |
| | | | | | | | | | | |
| Mining | 34,157 | 31,848 | 33,470 | 41,543 | 44,289 | 35,601 | 35,921 | 46,247 | 45,324 | 45,429 |
| %change | 4.0 | (6.8) | 5.1 | 24.1 | 6.6 | (19.6) | 0.9 | 28.7 | (2.0) | 0.2 |
| | | | | | | | | | | |
| Construction | 18,378 | 20,346 | 21,945 | 24,433 | 25,498 | 29,262 | 32,841 | 36,066 | 37,779 | 38,976 |
| %change | 5.8 | 10.7 | 7.9 | 11.3 | 4.4 | 14.8 | 12.2 | 9.8 | 4.7 | 3.2 |
| | | | | | | | | | | |
| Manufacturing | 63,736 | 73,435 | 78,902 | 81,215 | 90,363 | 94,198 | 96,049 | 101,105 | 101,545 | 96,497 |
| %change | 7.6 | 15.2 | 7.4 | 2.9 | 11.3 | 4.2 | 2.0 | 5.3 | 0.4 | (5.0) |
| Transportation and Utilities | 50,452 | 53,815 | 56,945 | 61,452 | 65,662 | 70,595 | 75,984 | 82,927 | 87,504 | 89,222 |
| %change | 8.9 | 6.7 | 5.8 | 7.9 | 6.9 | 7.5 | 7.6 | 9.1 | 5.5 | 2.0 |
| Wholesale and Retail Trade | 73,861 | 80,313 | 85,130 | 91,281 | 100,803 | 110,401 | 118,945 | 127,095 | 130,416 | 136,109 |
| %change | 6.0 | 8.7 | 6.0 | 7.2 | 10.4 | 9.5 | 7.7 | 6.9 | 2.6 | 4.4 |
| Finance, Insurance and Real Estate | 65,229 | 68,013 | 72,892 | 77,744 | 89,235 | 95,857 | 103,475 | 109,676 | 120,075 | 127,036 |
| %change | 6.0 | 4.3 | 7.2 | 6.7 | 14.8 | 7.4 | 7.9 | 6.0 | 9.5 | 5.8 |
| | | | | | | | | | | |
| Services | 81,922 | 87,377 | 94,537 | 103,160 | 115,542 | 125,615 | 136,548 | 148,674 | 158,377 | 168,918 |
| %change | 6.2 | 6.7 | 8.2 | 9.1 | 12.0 | 8.7 | 8.7 | 8.9 | 6.5 | 6.7 |
| Local, State and Federal Government | 57,079 | 59,819 | 62,687 | 65,178 | 68,898 | 71,679 | 75,864 | 80,845 | 84,899 | 95,250 |
| %change | 6.6 | 4.8 | 4.8 | 4.0 | 5.7 | 4.0 | 5.8 | 6.6 | 5.0 | 12.2 |
| | | | | | | | | | | |
| TOTAL** | $ 452,650 | $ 482,706 | $ 513,882 | $ 553,181 | $ 608,621 | $ 641,405 | $ 684,936 | $ 742,274 | $ 776,071 | $ 807,404 |
| %change | 6.6 | 6.6 | 6.5 | 7.6 | 10.0 | 5.4 | 6.8 | 8.4 | 4.6 | 4.0 |
| Total (in 1996 $) | $ 482,498 | $ 505,461 | $ 528,264 | $ 553,181 | $ 598,103 | $ 631,688 | $ 665,047 | $ 684,260 | $ 703,391 | $ 720,829 |
| % change | 3.9 | 4.8 | 4.5 | 4.7 | 8.1 | 5.6 | 5.3 | 2.9 | 2.8 | 2.5 |

*2002 numbers are estimated from incomplete data. **Totals may not add due to rounding.*
*Source: U.S. Bureau of Economic Analysis and Texas Comptroller of Public Accounts. The Bureau revised historical data contained in this table due to changes in methodology, inflation factors, price indicators and revisions to interim census figures. Texas 2002 Comprehensive Annual Financial Report.*

# Economies in Largest Metropolitan Areas

Source: Annual Cash Report 2002, Comptroller of Public Accounts.

The **AUSTIN-San Marcos** metropolitan area (which includes Bastrop, Caldwell, Hays, Travis and Williamson counties) grew at a frantic pace during the 1990s. Of the five counties, Williamson County has been responsible for much of the population expansion, experiencing a 79.1 percent increase in population from 1990 to 2000. Overall, the Austin area was the third-fastest growing metro area in Texas from 1990 to 2000, following Laredo and the McAllen-Edinburg-Mission areas.

Over the last decade, the Austin-San Marcos area economy was also one of the fastest growing in the nation, posting steady gains in employment and consistently low unemployment rates. However, in fiscal 2002, the rapid economic expansion slowed considerably. In August 2000, the metro area's unemployment rate was at 2.0 percent, but by August 2001 the rate had climbed to 4.5 percent. In August 2002, the rate reached 5.4 percent. Despite this climb, the area's unemployment rate remains the second lowest, behind San Antonio, of the six largest metropolitan areas in the state.

In another sign of a cooling economy, the Austin-San Marcos metro area lost 1,200 jobs in fiscal 2002, compared to 12,000 jobs added the previous year. Employment contracted by 0.2 percent, compared to the 1.8 percent job growth-rate in the year ending August 2001.

Job losses in the construction, manufacturing, transportation and retail sectors were slightly above modest job gains in mining; financial, insurance and real estate; services; and government sectors.

For the past three years, the largest job gains were seen in the services sector. However, in fiscal 2002 the largest number of jobs, 7,200, were added in the government sector. Government sector employment accounts for 22.3 percent of overall employment in the metro area.

Manufacturing, representing 10.3 percent of the economy, posted the largest job losses, finishing the year with 7,600 fewer jobs.

*In Austin, the University of Texas now outranks Dell as the top employer*

This job loss represents a drop of 10 percent in manufacturing employment since 2001. These statistics show the impact on the local economy of the slowing in the high-tech sector, particularly in semiconductor manufacturing.

During 2001, nearly 23,100 total business layoffs occurred, of which approximately 19,100 were in the high-tech sector. Layoffs were reported at large Central Texas high-tech employers including Dell and Motorola, while a number of local Internet start-ups closed their doors.

During the first eight months of 2002, 22 additional business closures were reported. Also during the first eight months of 2002, more than 5,700 layoffs were reported. Of those layoffs, 4,100, or 71.5 percent, are attributed to the high-tech sector.

In keeping with job losses in the high-tech sector,

research and development activities slowed. From January to August 2002, 1,261 patents were issued in the Austin-San Marcos metro area, a decrease of 10.2 percent compared to the same period last year.

Losses in other sectors were not as significant. The transportation sector lost almost 800 jobs, construction nearly 300 and the wholesale and retail trade sector dropped approximately 140 jobs. While construction employment has dropped, the City of Austin reports an increase of 3.3 percent in the number of commercial construction permits being issued from August 2001 through August 2002.

Sales subject to tax in the Austin area climbed from $15.6 billion in 2000 to $15.7 billion in 2001, an increase of 0.5 percent. During the first quarter of 2002, sales subject to tax in the Austin metro area was $3.6 billion, a decrease of 5.4 percent over the same period in 2001.

While Austin's five top employers remained the same from 2001 to 2002, government-sector employers replaced high-tech employers in the first and third place rankings by employment. The University of Texas at Austin (20,200 employees) now outranks Dell Computer Corporation (16,000 employees), and Austin Independent School District (10,408 employees) and the City of Austin (10,000 employees) now lead Motorola (7,500 employees).

Total employment in the **DALLAS** metropolitan area (which includes the counties of Collin, Dallas, Denton, Ellis, Henderson, Hunt, Kaufman, and Rockwall) decreased by 0.7 percent, or 13,000 from August 2001 to August 2002, to 1,988,900.

The jobless rate rose from 5.4 percent a year before to 6.9 percent in 2002. Of Texas' large metro areas, this unemployment rate is second highest after El Paso.

The only sectors that experienced employment growth were mining and government. Mining employment increased 2.3 percent, reaching 9,200. Government employment experienced the largest growth, up 4.4 percent, employing 229,500.

Other sectors experienced decreases in employment of less than two percent with the exception of construction (-2.4 percent), manufacturing (-2.7 percent) and transportation (-2.2 percent).

As in other cities, the most jobs are in the service sector, which includes 31.3 percent of non-farm workers. Employment in the sector decreased 0.4 percent during fiscal 2002, dropping to a total of 619,900.

The next largest sector, wholesale and retail trade, which accounts for 24.5 percent of jobs, decreased employment by 1.5 percent, for a total of 487,400 jobs. Jobs in manufacturing dropped to 231,400 from 237,300.

Finance, insurance and real estate sector employment dropped to 156,800, a decrease of 0.4 percent during the year. Transportation employment decreased by 2.2 percent, reaching 137,300, or 6.9 percent of the working population. Construction jobs, accounting for 5.4 percent of total Dallas area employment, decreased 2.4 percent.

Defense and electronic manufacturing is a big part of the Dallas manufacturing sector. Raytheon employs

*The Buffalo Bayou Waterfront near downtown Houston. File photo.*

9,000 in McKinney, where they produce defense, government and commercial electronics and business aviation and special mission aircraft. Texas Instruments manufactures a wide range of electronic goods, with a total of 10,000 employees in the Dallas area.

In addition to the manufacturing jobs in defense and other electronics, telecommunications research, development and production form an important part of the local economy. SBC, formerly Southwestern Bell, has over 18,000 people in the area providing local calling, long distance calling, and DSL (Digital Subscriber Line).

Dallas serves as a hub of transportation and trade. Southwest Airlines and Delta combine to employ almost 11,000 in Dallas. United Parcel Service employs more than 7,000 locally.

Additionally, both Neiman Marcus and JC Penney keep their headquarters in Dallas and Plano respectively. Healthcare and educational institutions also provide a large number of jobs in Dallas, as they do in many large, regional centers.

In recent years, however, the city and its suburbs have grown in importance as a base of operations for big corporations. In 2001, Dallas served as headquarters for 17 of the Fortune 500 companies.

In 2001, Dallas development included adding 32.6 million square feet of business expansions and/or start-ups. These developments were reported to have created about 37,000 new jobs in the area.

Single-family building permits increased on an annual basis in the area between 1995 and 2000. In 2001 they dropped slightly, less than 1 percent. The average value of the dwellings dropped as well, falling from $165,700 to $163,100.

Sales subject to the sales tax in the Dallas area totaled about $53 billion, a decrease of 3.2 percent from the previous year. In the first quarter of 2002, taxable sales in Dallas totaled $11.5 billion, a decrease of almost $1.2 million from the same period in 2001.

**EL PASO** is the fifth most populated city in Texas. In addition, Ciudad Juárez — El Paso's sister city across the U.S.-Mexico border — is among the largest cities in Mexico.

El Paso is at the approximate geographical center of the U.S.-Mexico border, a strategic location providing access to an extensive transportation system for business and international trade, including two international airports, three major highways, four ports of entry, and three rail service providers.

Economic growth has slowed in the El Paso metro area (which includes El Paso County) as the unemployment rate flattened after decreasing for six consecutive years. The unemployment rate in El Paso stabilized at 8.3 percent in August 2002, the same rate seen in August 2001.

Although El Paso's unemployment rate remains the highest of Texas' big six metropolitan areas, El Paso was the only one of the state's major metropolitan areas whose unemployment rate did not increase.

The El Paso economy lost 900 jobs in fiscal 2002, a 0.4 percent decrease. The sectors experiencing a decrease in employment were manufacturing (-7.6 percent); transportation (-5.3 percent); and to a lesser degree the wholesale/retail trade sector (-0.8 percent).

Construction, services, government, and financial sectors all experienced employment growth. The largest percentage increase in jobs occurred in the construction sector, where employment grew by 4.3 percent between August 2001 and August 2002, adding almost 500 jobs.

Employment in the services and government sectors increased about 2.0 percent each, with both adding 1,200 jobs.

One of the largest contributors to the local economy is Fort Bliss — the home for the Army's Air Defense Artillery Training Center. The base supports 118,900 combined military and civilian personnel (active and retired, and family members). The economic impact on increased sales volume is $1.7 billion annually.

Service sector employment in El Paso is driven by the area's role as a regional health-care provider and by its location on the border defining its role as an international trade center along with the presence of the maquiladoras (assembly plants) and their need for professional and business services.

With a total of 61,000 jobs in 2002, wholesale and retail trade employment accounted for 24 percent of the employment.

Sales subject to the sales tax from all industries increased 0.3 percent, growing from $4.22 billion to $4.23 billion.

Single-family building permits increased 15 percent between 2000 and 2001. In 2001, permits totaled more than 3,300 and new homes had an average value of $54,800.

The top three private employers in El Paso are in the apparel, health services and retail sectors. Many companies have taken advantage of El Paso's vital labor market to manufacture everything from basic plastic molding to high-tech products.

According to economic development officials, historically, El Paso's economic development progressed from focusing on the military, maquiladoras, and manufacturing. Now, in the last few years, the emphasis has changed to include technology and transportation.

El Paso economic development efforts through September 2002 have been projected to create more than 4,000 new jobs for the area. Additionally, about 1.5 million square feet in new facilities will be created or put into use, representing a total capital investment of almost $81 million in the metro area.

Economic growth has slowed in the **FORT WORTH**-Arlington metro area (which includes Hood, Johnson, Parker and Tarrant counties) with unemployment increasing the previous year. The unemployment rate in Fort Worth-Arlington rose from 4.3 percent in August 2001 to 5.9 percent in August 2002.

Contributing to the slowdown was the loss of jobs in almost every employment sector in the metro area. Total employment dropped by 9,300 jobs, a decrease of 1.2 percent overall.

The employment sectors experiencing increases were construction, which increased 0.2 percent, or 100 jobs; mining which saw the largest percentage increase — 4.7 percent, or 200 jobs; government, which increased 0.3 percent, or by 300 jobs; and finance, insurance and real estate, which saw very slight gains.

All other employment sectors saw employment decreases, with the largest being in manufacturing, which lost 3,200 jobs, or a decline of 3 percent. The transportation sector lost 1,800 jobs, or a decrease of 2.2 percent; wholesale and retail trade lost 3,300 jobs, or a decrease of 1.7 percent; and the services sector lost 1,600 jobs, or a decline of only 0.7 percent.

Single-family building permits have increased annually in the Fort Worth-Arlington area since 1995. In 2001 they totaled more than 12,100 units, a 16 percent increase from the previous year. However, the average value of new dwellings in the area dropped to $123,400, a decrease of 2 percent.

The decrease in manufacturing employment continued a trend established between August 1999 and August 2000 when the sector lost just over 700 jobs (0.7 percent) and continued between August 2000 and August 2001, when employment decreased by 1,500 jobs (1.4 percent).

Even so, manufacturing remains the third-largest sector in the economy and accounted for 104,900 jobs in 2002, ranking behind only services (216,400 jobs) and wholesale and retail trade (195,600 jobs). Government is the fourth-largest sector, with 103,000 jobs.

Taxable sales totaled $17.4 billion in 2000 and grew to $17.5 billion in 2001, a slight increase of 0.5 percent.

The top private employers in the area include American Airlines (28,500 employees); Lockheed Martin Tactical Aircraft Systems (11,400 employees); Delta Airlines (6,800 employees); Sabre (5,400 employees, and Radio Shack (4,300 employees).

The **HOUSTON** metropolitan area (which includes the counties of Chambers, Fort Bend, Harris, Liberty, Montgomery, and Waller) had an unemployment rate of 5.8 percent in August 2002, higher than the 4.5 percent unemployment rate seen in August 2001. Houston's unemployment rate is the third-highest of the state's six major metropolitan areas, behind El Paso and Dallas.

Employment decreased by 700 jobs from August 2001 through August 2002, a loss of less than 1 percent, compared to the annual job growth rate of 2.8 percent posted in August 2001.

*The largest sector of Houston's economy remains services*

In a year in which the metro area experienced a major flood and was home to one of the largest business bankruptcies in history (Enron), Houston's slowed growth would be expected.

Like the other large metro areas in Texas, Houston's unemployment gains and losses varied by sector. The most significant losses, 8,500 jobs, were in the transportation sector, representing 6.8 percent of total employment. Airline passenger volume in 2001 was well ahead of the 2000 pace until the terrorist attacks of September 11.

Volume over the final four months of 2001 dropped 14 percent from the same period in 2000. Passenger volume in the first six months of 2002 trailed the same period in 2001 by 6.3 percent. Air freight has also stagnated. The Port of Houston foreign shipments from January through May of 2002 lagged behind the same period in 2001 by 9.9 percent.

The manufacturing sector, 10 percent of the local economy, posted job losses of 3,700, and the mining sector (3.2 percent of total metro employment) lost 1,700 jobs.

The largest sector of Houston's economy remains services, which accounted for nearly one-third of all

metro jobs (662,200) in 2002, followed by wholesale/retail trade (479,800), and government (274,292).

The three largest sectors gained jobs between August 2001 and August 2002. Of the three, the highest percentage increase in jobs (3,200) occurred in the government sector with a 1.2 percent increase in employment. Employment in the services sector increased by 5,500, representing an increase of just over 0.8 percent, while employment in the wholesale/retail trade sector grew by only 400 jobs.

Construction employment increased by 2.7 percent with 4,300 jobs added in a sector that represents 7.7 percent of metro area employment.

According to the City of Houston, new residential building permits in Houston continued to increase as they have for more than a decade. New residential building permits were up 16.7 percent, while new non-residential building permits were down 12.0 percent from January 2002 to August 2002 as compared to the same period a year earlier.

Sales subject to tax jumped from $46.6 billion in 2000 to nearly $50 billion in 2001. The first quarter of 2002 showed growth in sales subject to tax for the Houston metro area with an increase of 1.8 percent over the same quarter in 2001.

Metro Houston touts the largest population in Texas and is continuing to grow.

Houston is home to the Texas Medical Center, the largest medical center in the world with more than 61,000 employees working in its facilities, serving 5.4 million patients in 2000, and delivering an economic punch of $11.5 billion to the area.

The Houston area also hosts over 400 chemical plants with more than 38,000 employees. The Houston-Gulf Coast region has nearly 49 percent of the nation's base petrochemical capacity — more than quadruple that of any state excluding Texas.

The Port of Houston ranked first among U.S. ports in volume of foreign tonnage in 2001. The port ranks as the world's sixth-largest port, and its top trading partners by value in 2001 were Mexico, Germany, Brazil, Venezuela and Saudi Arabia. The top five commodities traded through the port were petroleum and petroleum products, machinery, organic chemicals, iron and steel and electric machinery.

Houston is a major corporate center, ranking fifth among U.S. metro areas in number of corporate headquarters of Fortune 500 companies. Houston is universally acknowledged as the nation's energy capital with more than 5,000 energy-related firms, is a focal point for international trade and banking, a major health care center, and one of the nation's largest consumer markets.

Houston's five largest private employers, were Wal-Mart Stores (20,000), Continental Airlines (19,455), Administaff (17,671), Exxon Mobil (17,220) and Halliburton (15,804).

Unemployment in the **SAN ANTONIO** metro area (which includes Bexar, Comal, Guadalupe, and Wilson counties) rose from 4.1 percent in August 2001 to 5.1 in August 2002. During the same period, San Antonio lost just over 2,000 jobs, a decrease of 0.3 percent.

San Antonio's largest number of job losses (2,500)

*The San Antonio skyline with the Tower of the Americas and the Alamodome in the foreground. File photo.*

occurred in the wholesale/retail sector, which represents 24.1 percent of overall employment in the metro area. Other sectors posting losses in fiscal 2002 were transportation (2,100), finance, insurance and real estate (1,000) and manufacturing (700).

The largest increase in jobs occurred in the government sector, which added 2,700 jobs and represents 18.4 percent of metro area employment. Construction employment increased by 1,300. The services and mining sectors both added just under 100 jobs each. The services sector represents nearly one-third of the San Antonio metro area employment base.

Single-family home construction is continuing at a strong pace, with the City of San Antonio reporting an increase of building permits of 17.2 percent from the second quarter of 2001 compared to the second quarter of 2002.

Non-residential permits are also up by 16.6 percent when comparing the second quarter of 2001 with the second quarter of 2002. However, the valuation of those permits is down by 36.4 percent.

Sales subject to tax in the San Antonio metro area reached $15.7 billion in 2001, an increase of nearly 2.0 percent since 2000. However, in the first quarter of 2002, sales subject to tax fell 2.8 percent, compared to the same quarter in 2001.

San Antonio is the state's fourth most populated metro area, and is drawing businesses due to its advantageous strategic south-central location, coupled with the presence of many bilingual workers.

A major focal point for trade under the North American Free Trade Agreement (NAFTA), San Antonio benefits from its location at the confluence of several interstate highways which span the nation from coast to coast and from Mexico to Canada.

A growing component of the San Antonio economy, the medical and bio-medical industry is considered to be one of the metro area's major economic generators with an $8.1 billion direct annual impact.

Over 96,000 medical industry employees work in hospitals, medical suppliers, insurance organizations, pharmaceuticals, bio-science research, and military medical institutions.

Research and development activities are increasingly bringing capital investment into the San Antonio metro area, including $128.8 million in funding in 2001 from the National Institutes of Health.

Often referred to as "Military City, USA," the city boasts a strong military presence with facilities employing over 65,000 civilian and military personnel. The Air Force maintains two bases — Lackland and Randolph. They have operational functions including flight training, air transport maintenance, and aerospace medicine. Lackland provides basic military training for all enlisted and reserve members.

The former Kelly Air Force Base was officially turned over to the Greater Kelly Development Corporation during July 2001 for development as a business and industrial park. Now operating as KellyUSA, the site has more than 60 commercial occupants. In July 2002, Brooks Air Force Base was conveyed to the City of San Antonio and became Brooks City-Base, where some military units remain. The city, along with local educational and community organizations, is transforming Brooks City-Base into a technology business park.

In 2002, the Pentagon decided to relocate the U.S. Army's Southern Command from Puerto Rico to San Antonio's Fort Sam Houston. The command oversees all Army operations in the Caribbean, and Central and South America, including National Guard and construction activities. In late 2003, the Army will move into renovated space in the Brooke Army Medical Center complex. The relocation means about 500 new jobs to the San Antonio area and an estimated $25 million in federal payroll.

San Antonio's top five private employers are United Services Automobile Association, H.E.B. Grocery Company, H.B. Zachry Company, SBC Communications, and Baptist Health System. ☆

# Personal Income, Per Capita Income by County, 2001

Source: Bureau of Economic Analysis, U.S. Department of Commerce.

| County | Total Income ($ mil) | % change 00/01 | Per capita income | Rank |
|---|---|---|---|---|
| United States | $8,677,490 | 3.3 | $30,413 | - |
| Metropolitan | 7,428,050 | 3.4 | 32,336 | - |
| Nonmetro | 1,249,440 | 2.9 | 22,472 | - |
| Texas | 608,466 | 3.7 | 28,472 | - |
| Metropolitan | 542,213 | 3.9 | 29,794 | - |
| Nonmetro | 66,253 | 2.4 | 20,886 | - |
| Anderson | 1,018 | 6.1 | 18,797 | 194 |
| Andrews | 268 | 0.7 | 20,942 | 144 |
| Angelina | 1,892 | 4.0 | 23,543 | 79 |
| Aransas | 593 | 4.6 | 26,339 | 38 |
| Archer | 209 | 1.8 | 23,475 | 83 |
| Armstrong | 41 | 2.7 | 18,912 | 191 |
| Atascosa | 772 | 6.4 | 19,310 | 181 |

| County | Total Income ($ mil) | % change 00/01 | Per capita income | Rank |
|---|---|---|---|---|
| Austin | 638 | 2.8 | 26,343 | 37 |
| Bailey | 154 | 0.7 | 23,544 | 78 |
| Bandera | 459 | 6.1 | 24,994 | 58 |
| Bastrop | 1,287 | 5.6 | 20,939 | 145 |
| Baylor | 82 | 4.0 | 20,669 | 153 |
| Bee | 489 | 1.6 | 15,141 | 240 |
| Bell | 6,133 | 3.8 | 25,396 | 49 |
| Bexar | 38,518 | 3.5 | 27,138 | 32 |
| Blanco | 208 | 5.8 | 23,968 | 68 |
| Borden | 10 | -4.1 | 14,790 | 244 |
| Bosque | 371 | 2.0 | 21,210 | 131 |
| Bowie | 2,057 | 0.7 | 22,969 | 91 |
| Brazoria | 6,409 | 3.6 | 25,695 | 46 |
| Brazos | 3,233 | 3.6 | 21,028 | 140 |
| Brewster | 208 | 6.0 | 23,314 | 86 |
| Briscoe | 34 | -6.9 | 19,657 | 176 |

| County | Total Income ($ mil) | % change 00/01 | Per capita income | Rank | County | Total Income ($ mil) | % change 00/01 | Per capita income | Rank |
|---|---|---|---|---|---|---|---|---|---|
| Brooks | $ 142 | 5.5 | $ 18,396 | 199 | Frio | $ 244 | 3.2 | $ 15,033 | 241 |
| Brown | 779 | 1.7 | 20,632 | 156 | Gaines | 261 | -4.3 | 18,137 | 205 |
| Burleson | 319 | 4.3 | 18,998 | 190 | Galveston | 7,088 | 3.6 | 27,786 | 29 |
| Burnet | 845 | 7.5 | 23,533 | 82 | Garza | 100 | 4.4 | 19,757 | 173 |
| Caldwell | 657 | 2.1 | 19,386 | 178 | Gillespie | 553 | 4.4 | 26,132 | 40 |
| Calhoun | 436 | -4.9 | 20,976 | 142 | Glasscock | 25 | -1.2 | 18,310 | 203 |
| Callahan | 272 | 3.1 | 21,326 | 126 | Goliad | 136 | 3.9 | 19,348 | 179 |
| Cameron | 5,283 | 4.9 | 15,334 | 238 | Gonzales | 433 | 6.3 | 23,166 | 88 |
| Camp | 301 | 3.6 | 26,305 | 39 | Gray | 586 | 3.5 | 26,399 | 36 |
| Carson | 171 | -2.2 | 26,668 | 34 | Grayson | 2,633 | 1.0 | 23,366 | 84 |
| Cass | 686 | -0.3 | 22,713 | 95 | Gregg | 3,306 | 7.4 | 29,503 | 18 |
| Castro | 215 | -9.6 | 26,491 | 35 | Grimes | 427 | 4.5 | 17,628 | 212 |
| Chambers | 692 | 3.9 | 25,908 | 43 | Guadalupe | 2,063 | 4.0 | 22,399 | 103 |
| Cherokee | 1,048 | 2.5 | 22,236 | 109 | Hale | 790 | -0.3 | 21,881 | 113 |
| Childress | 127 | 0.5 | 16,620 | 227 | Hall | 63 | 1.2 | 16,633 | 226 |
| Clay | 242 | 6.2 | 21,716 | 116 | Hamilton | 184 | 0.7 | 22,641 | 98 |
| Cochran | 80 | -1.3 | 21,894 | 112 | Hansford | 189 | -4.9 | 35,571 | 6 |
| Coke | 71 | 1.1 | 18,219 | 204 | Hardeman | 97 | 1.6 | 21,054 | 138 |
| Coleman | 180 | -1.8 | 19,832 | 172 | Hardin | 1,120 | 3.9 | 23,050 | 89 |
| Collin | 21,379 | 2.1 | 39,823 | 2 | Harris | 130,257 | 6.3 | 37,389 | 3 |
| Collingsworth | 71 | 3.1 | 22,782 | 92 | Harrison | 1,308 | 2.2 | 20,952 | 143 |
| Colorado | 461 | -1.4 | 22,754 | 93 | Hartley | 155 | -6.0 | 28,139 | 27 |
| Comal | 2,417 | 7.0 | 29,491 | 19 | Haskell | 132 | 11.3 | 22,061 | 111 |
| Comanche | 308 | 7.7 | 22,461 | 100 | Hays | 2,440 | 7.6 | 23,351 | 85 |
| Concho | 57 | 15.1 | 14,797 | 243 | Hemphill | 112 | 0.3 | 33,584 | 8 |
| Cooke | 900 | 4.3 | 24,296 | 65 | Henderson | 1,593 | 1.3 | 21,355 | 125 |
| Coryell | 1,273 | 1.6 | 17,021 | 224 | Hidalgo | 8,170 | 7.5 | 13,788 | 249 |
| Cottle | 45 | 5.0 | 24,677 | 61 | Hill | 667 | 3.0 | 20,193 | 166 |
| Crane | 72 | -3.6 | 18,420 | 198 | Hockley | 477 | 3.4 | 21,014 | 141 |
| Crockett | 68 | -0.4 | 17,751 | 210 | Hood | 1,290 | 6.9 | 30,062 | 17 |
| Crosby | 129 | -5.9 | 18,565 | 195 | Hopkins | 700 | 2.8 | 21,754 | 115 |
| Culberson | 44 | 0.1 | 15,359 | 237 | Houston | 544 | 3.1 | 23,554 | 77 |
| Dallam | 197 | -6.1 | 31,746 | 11 | Howard | 704 | 4.4 | 21,212 | 130 |
| Dallas | 81,658 | 0.1 | 36,035 | 4 | Hudspeth | 50 | -2.9 | 14,827 | 242 |
| Dawson | 321 | 1.1 | 21,457 | 123 | Hunt | 1,625 | 1.6 | 20,812 | 147 |
| Deaf Smith | 449 | -4.6 | 24,503 | 63 | Hutchinson | 551 | 0.3 | 23,700 | 74 |
| Delta | 110 | -1.0 | 20,448 | 162 | Irion | 35 | 3.0 | 20,333 | 163 |
| Denton | 14,399 | 5.2 | 31,037 | 15 | Jack | 160 | 1.7 | 18,349 | 201 |
| DeWitt | 430 | 2.1 | 21,386 | 124 | Jackson | 323 | -4.7 | 22,559 | 99 |
| Dickens | 43 | -2.5 | 15,940 | 233 | Jasper | 775 | 1.3 | 21,668 | 118 |
| Dimmit | 148 | 3.6 | 14,597 | 246 | Jeff Davis | 39 | 5.1 | 17,300 | 220 |
| Donley | 74 | 0.8 | 19,124 | 188 | Jefferson | 6,245 | 2.1 | 24,985 | 59 |
| Duval | 202 | 7.5 | 15,611 | 235 | Jim Hogg | 91 | 3.8 | 17,692 | 211 |
| Eastland | 396 | 1.9 | 21,872 | 114 | Jim Wells | 791 | 5.5 | 19,865 | 170 |
| Ector | 2,742 | 6.1 | 22,671 | 97 | Johnson | 2,966 | 0.9 | 22,435 | 101 |
| Edwards | 36 | 11.2 | 17,080 | 223 | Jones | 328 | 2.9 | 16,084 | 232 |
| Ellis | 2,937 | 2.7 | 25,307 | 50 | Karnes | 250 | 3.3 | 16,169 | 231 |
| El Paso | 13,230 | 5.4 | 19,186 | 185 | Kaufman | 1,797 | 3.3 | 23,838 | 71 |
| Erath | 746 | 3.5 | 22,691 | 96 | Kendall | 705 | 6.5 | 28,665 | 23 |
| Falls | 317 | -1.0 | 17,316 | 217 | Kenedy | 11 | 7.9 | 27,576 | 30 |
| Fannin | 620 | 0.3 | 19,749 | 174 | Kent | 18 | 0.2 | 22,268 | 107 |
| Fayette | 557 | 3.1 | 25,165 | 53 | Kerr | 1,265 | 7.2 | 28,522 | 25 |
| Fisher | 89 | 12.0 | 21,054 | 138 | Kimble | 77 | 3.6 | 17,176 | 222 |
| Floyd | 163 | -13.8 | 21,497 | 122 | King | 8 | -0.4 | 23,539 | 80 |
| Foard | 36 | 4.2 | 22,224 | 110 | Kinney | 57 | 6.6 | 16,530 | 228 |
| Fort Bend | 11,774 | 8.7 | 31,232 | 13 | Kleberg | 596 | 3.3 | 19,164 | 186 |
| Franklin | 232 | 8.3 | 24,105 | 67 | Knox | 86 | -1.6 | 21,145 | 136 |
| Freestone | 362 | 9.8 | 19,945 | 169 | Lamar | 1,093 | -1.1 | 22,423 | 102 |

| County | Total Income ($ mil) | % change 00/01 | Per capita income | Rank |
|---|---|---|---|---|
| Lamb | $ 308 | -5.4 | $ 21,073 | 137 |
| Lampasas | 346 | 3.5 | 18,901 | 192 |
| La Salle | 102 | 14.2 | 17,479 | 213 |
| Lavaca | 447 | 2.7 | 23,622 | 76 |
| Lee | 312 | 1.3 | 19,321 | 180 |
| Leon | 329 | 3.9 | 21,206 | 132 |
| Liberty | 1,463 | 6.3 | 20,317 | 165 |
| Limestone | 468 | 7.4 | 21,160 | 135 |
| Lipscomb | 77 | 3.0 | 25,517 | 48 |
| Live Oak | 209 | 4.0 | 17,231 | 221 |
| Llano | 365 | -0.8 | 20,914 | 146 |
| Loving | 4 | 10.5 | 64,636 | 1 |
| Lubbock | 6,090 | 0.8 | 24,788 | 60 |
| Lynn | 114 | -9.1 | 17,867 | 209 |
| Madison | 255 | 4.2 | 19,740 | 175 |
| Marion | 183 | 2.1 | 16,523 | 229 |
| Martin | 82 | 4.2 | 17,409 | 215 |
| Mason | 71 | 4.7 | 18,836 | 193 |
| Matagorda | 785 | 0.9 | 20,656 | 155 |
| Maverick | 588 | 3.3 | 12,258 | 252 |
| McCulloch | 188 | 7.0 | 23,537 | 81 |
| McLennan | 5,029 | 2.9 | 23,302 | 87 |
| McMullen | 25 | 8.6 | 29,489 | 20 |
| Medina | 783 | 4.8 | 19,535 | 177 |
| Menard | 36 | 0.0 | 15,258 | 239 |
| Midland | 3,877 | -0.2 | 33,384 | 9 |
| Milam | 522 | -0.5 | 21,322 | 127 |
| Mills | 108 | 1.3 | 21,161 | 134 |
| Mitchell | 150 | 2.2 | 15,868 | 234 |
| Montague | 396 | 1.9 | 20,659 | 154 |
| Montgomery | 9,580 | 7.2 | 30,621 | 16 |
| Moore | 441 | -2.6 | 21,716 | 116 |
| Morris | 286 | 1.7 | 21,653 | 119 |
| Motley | 24 | 7.8 | 17,963 | 208 |
| Nacogdoches | 1,232 | 2.3 | 20,727 | 151 |
| Navarro | 954 | 1.4 | 20,703 | 152 |
| Newton | 222 | -0.7 | 14,684 | 245 |
| Nolan | 321 | 0.1 | 20,795 | 149 |
| Nueces | 7,848 | 2.4 | 25,091 | 55 |
| Ochiltree | 260 | 1.4 | 28,536 | 24 |
| Oldham | 53 | -9.1 | 24,268 | 66 |
| Orange | 1,942 | 1.2 | 22,974 | 90 |
| Palo Pinto | 580 | 2.2 | 21,306 | 128 |
| Panola | 489 | 3.6 | 21,585 | 121 |
| Parker | 2,324 | 2.2 | 25,275 | 51 |
| Parmer | 251 | -5.4 | 25,722 | 45 |
| Pecos | 232 | 0.9 | 14,105 | 248 |
| Polk | 1,077 | 4.0 | 25,058 | 56 |
| Potter | 2,721 | 0.1 | 23,733 | 73 |
| Presidio | 107 | 4.7 | 14,302 | 247 |
| Rains | 171 | 5.2 | 17,356 | 216 |
| Randall | 2,646 | 0.8 | 25,052 | 57 |
| Reagan | 59 | 4.0 | 18,428 | 197 |
| Real | 55 | 0.3 | 18,457 | 196 |
| Red River | 260 | 0.6 | 18,363 | 200 |
| Reeves | 210 | 0.3 | 16,463 | 230 |
| Refugio | 203 | -0.5 | 26,111 | 41 |
| Roberts | 17 | -3.1 | 19,267 | 182 |

| County | Total Income ($ mil) | % change 00/01 | Per capita income | Rank |
|---|---|---|---|---|
| Robertson | 291 | 4.4 | 18,100 | 207 |
| Rockwall | 1,539 | 6.4 | 32,651 | 10 |
| Runnels | 224 | 3.4 | 20,075 | 167 |
| Rusk | 1,002 | 1.7 | 21,196 | 133 |
| Sabine | 237 | 1.4 | 22,722 | 94 |
| San Augustine | 171 | 1.9 | 19,219 | 183 |
| San Jacinto | 464 | 3.5 | 20,319 | 164 |
| San Patricio | 1,373 | 2.9 | 20,495 | 160 |
| San Saba | 118 | 0.4 | 19,066 | 189 |
| Schleicher | 50 | 8.5 | 16,754 | 225 |
| Scurry | 355 | 3.5 | 22,397 | 104 |
| Shackelford | 81 | 7.6 | 24,557 | 62 |
| Shelby | 538 | -0.2 | 21,251 | 129 |
| Sherman | 113 | -9.6 | 35,656 | 5 |
| Smith | 5,131 | 4.7 | 28,824 | 22 |
| Somervell | 196 | 3.5 | 28,125 | 28 |
| Starr | 537 | 4.6 | 9,769 | 254 |
| Stephens | 212 | 4.1 | 22,298 | 106 |
| Sterling | 23 | 14.9 | 17,305 | 219 |
| Stonewall | 41 | 14.4 | 25,680 | 47 |
| Sutton | 83 | 8.9 | 20,517 | 159 |
| Swisher | 196 | -8.8 | 23,859 | 70 |
| Tarrant | 46,566 | 6.2 | 31,232 | 13 |
| Taylor | 3,051 | -4.2 | 24,304 | 64 |
| Terrell | 29 | 5.6 | 28,195 | 26 |
| Terry | 280 | -1.7 | 22,330 | 105 |
| Throckmorton | 46 | 12.3 | 26,040 | 42 |
| Titus | 607 | 2.5 | 21,608 | 120 |
| Tom Green | 2,592 | 2.9 | 25,104 | 54 |
| Travis | 29,835 | 2.9 | 35,267 | 7 |
| Trinity | 252 | 1.2 | 18,132 | 206 |
| Tyler | 377 | 2.5 | 18,322 | 202 |
| Upshur | 732 | 2.0 | 20,525 | 158 |
| Upton | 65 | 1.2 | 19,839 | 171 |
| Uvalde | 499 | 1.2 | 19,129 | 187 |
| Val Verde | 791 | 4.6 | 17,466 | 214 |
| Van Zandt | 1,022 | 1.2 | 20,804 | 148 |
| Victoria | 2,300 | 3.7 | 27,158 | 31 |
| Walker | 1,074 | 1.7 | 17,310 | 218 |
| Waller | 691 | 4.6 | 20,746 | 150 |
| Ward | 211 | 2.2 | 20,052 | 168 |
| Washington | 879 | 2.5 | 28,828 | 21 |
| Webb | 3,125 | 6.9 | 15,508 | 236 |
| Wharton | 980 | 3.0 | 23,781 | 72 |
| Wheeler | 161 | 0.9 | 31,396 | 12 |
| Wichita | 3,375 | 1.4 | 25,869 | 44 |
| Wilbarger | 337 | 2.7 | 23,888 | 69 |
| Willacy | 253 | -4.3 | 12,760 | 251 |
| Williamson | 7,454 | -1.8 | 26,940 | 33 |
| Wilson | 745 | 5.2 | 22,240 | 108 |
| Winkler | 144 | 5.3 | 20,493 | 161 |
| Wise | 1,215 | 3.4 | 23,633 | 75 |
| Wood | 722 | 1.9 | 19,214 | 184 |
| Yoakum | 151 | 5.4 | 20,566 | 157 |
| Young | 447 | -0.2 | 25,188 | 52 |
| Zapata | 164 | 6.3 | 13,120 | 250 |
| Zavala | 139 | 3.9 | 12,004 | 253 |

# Employment in Texas by Industry

*Source: Texas Workforce Commission. Additional information available at Web site: www.twc.state.tx.us.*

Employment in Texas increased to 9,440,900 in April 2003, up from 9,431,300 in April 2002.

The following table shows Texas Workforce Commission estimates of the nonagricultural labor force by industry for April 2002 and 2003. The final column shows the percent change in the number employed.

**(in thousands)**

| Industry | 2003 | 2002 | Chng. |
|---|---|---|---|
| **GOODS PRODUCING** | 1,638.6 | 1,670.7 | -1.9 |
| **Mining** | 139.3 | 142.4 | -2.2 |
| Oil & Gas Extraction | 63.5 | 63.8 | -0.5 |
| Support Activities | 67.7 | 68.8 | -1.6 |
| **Construction** | 575.2 | 570.0 | 0.9 |
| **Manufacturing** | 921.8 | 956.2 | -3.6 |
| Durable Goods | 570.2 | 597.7 | -4.6 |
| Wood Products | 28.4 | 30.0 | -5.3 |
| Furniture/Fixtures | 32.0 | 32.1 | -0.3 |
| Cement/Concrete | 23.1 | 23.6 | -2.1 |
| Primary Metals | 24.9 | 26.3 | -5.3 |
| Fabricated Metal Industries | 107.2 | 115.5 | -7.2 |
| Architectual/Structural Metal. | 43.2 | 47.0 | -8.1 |
| Machinery | 79.9 | 82.7 | -3.4 |
| Agriculture/Constru./Mining | 33.2 | 35.7 | -7.0 |
| Computers/Electronics | 120.2 | 132.8 | -9.5 |
| Semiconductors | 54.9 | 59.4 | -7.6 |
| Transportation Equipment | 80.0 | 78.5 | 1.9 |
| Aerospace/Parts | 41.5 | 40.1 | 3.5 |
| Misc. Manufacturing Industries | 34.8 | 35.5 | -2.0 |
| Non-Durable Goods | 351.6 | 358.5 | -1.9 |
| Food | 93.9 | 92.7 | 1.3 |
| Meat Products | 38.5 | 38.3 | 0.5 |
| Fruit/Vegetables | 8.0 | 7.9 | 1.3 |
| Beverage/Tobacco | 11.0 | 11.0 | 0.0 |
| Apparel Manufacturing | 16.4 | 21.8 | -24.8 |
| Paper | 24.3 | 25.2 | -3.6 |
| Printing | 39.9 | 40.9 | -2.4 |
| Petroleum/Coal Products | 24.3 | 24.3 | 0.0 |
| Chemicals | 78.5 | 79.3 | -1.0 |
| Rubber/Plastics | 47.2 | 47.3 | -0.2 |
| **SERVICE PROVIDING** | 7,802.3 | 7,760.6 | 0.5 |
| **Trade/Transportation/Utilities** | 1,929.9 | 1,952.4 | -1.2 |
| Wholesale Trade | 458.5 | 460.9 | -0.5 |
| Merchants/Durable Goods | 262.6 | 267.7 | -1.9 |
| Merchants/Non-Durable Goods | 152.2 | 151.2 | 0.7 |
| Retail Trade | 1,094.5 | 1,102.7 | -0.7 |
| Building/Garden Supplies | 86.1 | 84.5 | 1.9 |
| General Merchandise | 226.4 | 234.3 | -3.4 |
| Food/Beverage Stores | 198.4 | 202.0 | -1.8 |
| Motor Vehicle/Parts Dealers | 154.9 | 151.8 | 2.0 |
| Clothing/Accessories Stores | 94.5 | 93.1 | 1.5 |
| Furniture | 41.3 | 41.2 | 0.2 |
| Electronics/Appliances | 42.4 | 42.9 | -1.2 |
| Gasoline Stations | 69.0 | 69.9 | -1.3 |
| Office Supplies | 27.8 | 27.6 | 0.7 |
| Transportation/Utilities | 376.9 | 388.8 | -3.1 |
| Utilities | 51.9 | 51.6 | 0.6 |
| Electric Services | 37.0 | 36.9 | 0.3 |
| Natural Gas | 9.6 | 9.8 | -2.0 |
| Transportation | 325.0 | 337.2 | -3.6 |
| Air | 68.4 | 71.8 | -4.7 |
| Rail | 14.8 | 14.7 | 0.7 |
| Trucking | 100.6 | 102.3 | -1.7 |
| Pipeline | 14.7 | 15.4 | -4.5 |
| Information | 235.6 | 251.5 | -6.3 |
| Newspapers/Books | 32.5 | 33.7 | -3.6 |
| Broadcasting | 25.4 | 24.8 | 2.4 |
| Telecommunications | 101.7 | 113.8 | -10.6 |
| Internet Providers/Data | 38.5 | 39.9 | -3.5 |
| **Financial Activities** | 582.5 | 576.6 | 1.0 |
| Depository Institutions | 123.5 | 122.7 | 0.7 |
| Insurance Carriers | 161.6 | 159.5 | 1.3 |
| Real Estate | 108.7 | 108.8 | -0.1 |
| Securities/Investments | 40.0 | 39.2 | 2.0 |
| **Professional Services** | 1,047.2 | 1,055.5 | -0.8 |
| Legal Services | 80.4 | 77.5 | 3.7 |
| Accounting/Tax Preparation | 55.3 | 61.1 | -9.5 |
| Architectual/Engineering | 113.8 | 114.2 | -0.4 |
| Computer Systems Design | 68.4 | 74.7 | -8.4 |
| Employment Services | 214.4 | 204.0 | 5.1 |
| Services to Buildings/Homes | 119.9 | 117.6 | 2.0 |
| **Education/Health** | 1,121.5 | 1,075.5 | 4.3 |
| Health Care | 979.1 | 939.6 | 4.2 |
| Child Day Care | 109.4 | 109.0 | 0.4 |
| **Leisure/Hospitality** | 852.6 | 848.4 | 0.5 |
| Accommodations | 89.3 | 90.8 | -1.7 |
| Dining/Drinking Places | 666.5 | 661.9 | 0.7 |
| Amusements/Recreation | 68.3 | 67.7 | 0.9 |
| **Other Services** | 358.2 | 356.5 | 0.5 |
| Repair/Maintenance | 105.8 | 105.8 | 0.0 |
| Religious/Civic | 162.3 | 157.1 | 3.3 |
| **Total Government** | 1,674.8 | 1,644.2 | 1.9 |
| Federal | 178.4 | 177.9 | 0.3 |
| State | 350.9 | 346.5 | 1.3 |
| Local | 1,145.5 | 1,119.8 | 2.3 |

# Average Hours and Earnings

The following table shows the average weekly earnings, weekly hours worked and hourly wage in Texas for selected industries in 2003. Figures are provided by the Texas Workforce Commission and the U. S. Bureau of Labor Statistics.

| Industry | Earnings | Hours | Wage |
|---|---|---|---|
| **NATURAL RESOURCES** | $676.91 | 43.7 | $15.49 |
| Oil/Gas Extraction | 832.32 | 40.8 | 20.40 |
| Support Activities | 714.38 | 46.6 | 15.33 |
| **MANUFACTURING** | 580.05 | 41.7 | 13.91 |
| **Durable Goods** | 551.45 | 41.4 | 13.32 |
| Lumber/Wood Products | 423.33 | 41.3 | 10.25 |
| Fabricated Metal Products | 545.28 | 42.6 | 12.80 |
| Machinery | 534.49 | 40.8 | 13.11 |
| Agriculture/Mining | 619.70 | 45.3 | 13.68 |
| Semiconductor/Electronic | 559.93 | 34.8 | 16.09 |
| Transportation Equipment | 676.50 | 41.0 | 16.50 |
| Furniture | 356.66 | 38.6 | 9.24 |
| **Non-Durable Goods** | 621.61 | 42.2 | 14.73 |
| Food Manufacturing | 536.64 | 43.7 | 12.28 |
| Chemicals | 897.49 | 45.1 | 19.90 |
| Plastics/Rubber | 568.67 | 41.6 | 13.67 |
| **TRADE, TRANSPORT., UTILITIES** | 455.18 | 34.8 | 13.08 |
| **Wholesale** | 585.86 | 37.7 | 15.54 |
| Electronic/Electical Goods | 599.73 | 45.4 | 13.21 |
| Motor Vehicle/Parts | 711.84 | 40.7 | 17.49 |
| Grocery | 588.31 | 42.6 | 13.81 |
| **Retail** | 346.65 | 31.6 | 10.97 |
| Automotive Dealers | 528.28 | 28.1 | 18.80 |
| Building/Garden Supply | 400.29 | 35.9 | 11.15 |
| Clothing Stores | 260.52 | 26.0 | 10.02 |
| Food/Beverage | 288.30 | 31.1 | 9.27 |
| Grocery Stores | 273.86 | 29.8 | 9.19 |
| Furniture | 389.62 | 30.8 | 12.65 |
| Electronics/Appliances | 569.22 | 34.9 | 16.31 |
| Gasoline Stations | 267.93 | 35.3 | 7.59 |
| Sporting Goods | 162.79 | 22.3 | 7.30 |
| Office Supplies | 327.00 | 32.7 | 10.00 |
| Newpapers/Periodicals | 482.11 | 37.2 | 12.96 |
| Telecommunications | 633.35 | 41.1 | 15.41 |
| Internet Service Providers | 465.37 | 37.2 | 12.51 |
| **Finance, Depository Insts.** | 465.92 | 40.2 | 11.59 |

**Selected Metro Areas**

| | Earnings | Hours | Wage |
|---|---|---|---|
| **DALLAS** | | | |
| Manufacturing | $ 543.91 | 40.2 | $ 13.53 |
| Durable Goods | 557.80 | 39.9 | 13.98 |
| Non-Durable Goods | 520.96 | 40.7 | 12.80 |
| **FORT WORTH-ARLINGTON** | | | |
| Manufacturing | 686.41 | 39.7 | 17.29 |
| Durable Goods | 813.66 | 42.4 | 19.19 |
| Non-Durable | 454.22 | 34.7 | 13.09 |
| **HOUSTON** | | | |
| Manufacturing | 737.40 | 43.3 | 17.03 |
| Durable Goods | 609.55 | 43.2 | 14.11 |
| Non-Durable | 953.52 | 43.5 | 21.92 |
| **SAN ANTONIO** | | | |
| Manufacturing | 418.35 | 38.7 | 10.81 |
| Durable Goods | 429.07 | 38.9 | 11.03 |
| Non-Durable Goods | 408.87 | 38.5 | 10.62 |

# Leading Commercial Banks Ranked by Deposits

*Source: Federal Reserve Bank of Dallas, Dec. 31, 2002*
Abbreviations: Bk-Bank; St-State; NB-National Bank; B&Tc-Bank and Trust; NA-National Association; Cmrc-Commerce

**In thousands of dollars (000)**

| Rank | Name, Location | Deposits |
|---|---|---|
| 1 | Wells Fargo Bk Tx NA, San Antonio | $ 20,751,109 |
| 2 | Frost NB, San Antonio | 7,713,377 |
| 3 | Southwest Bk Of Tx NA, Houston | 3,723,805 |
| 4 | International Bk Of Cmrc, Laredo | 3,338,522 |
| 5 | Comerica Bk-Tx, Dallas | 3,243,000 |
| 6 | Texas St Bk, McAllen | 3,158,505 |
| 7 | Sterling Bk, Houston | 2,678,795 |
| 8 | Laredo NB, Laredo | 2,178,962 |
| 9 | Bank Tx NA, Dallas | 1,894,903 |
| 10 | Prosperity Bk, El Campo | 1,481,671 |
| 11 | Pnb Fncl Bk, Lubbock | 1,366,296 |
| 12 | American St Bk, Lubbock | 1,245,130 |
| 13 | Amarillo NB, Amarillo | 1,238,444 |
| 14 | Texas Cap Bk NA, Dallas | 1,209,867 |
| 15 | First NB, Edinburg | 1,197,814 |
| 16 | Woodforest NB, Houston | 1,137,240 |
| 17 | Broadway NB, San Antonio | 1,104,691 |
| 18 | Texas Bk, Weatherford | 1,015,712 |
| 19 | American NB Tx, Terrell | 943,969 |
| 20 | Southside Bk, Tyler | 819,783 |
| 21 | North Dallas B&Tc, Dallas | 718,460 |
| 22 | Legacy Bk of Tx, Plano | 696,694 |
| 23 | Metrobank NA, Houston | 695,960 |
| 24 | Extraco Bks NA, Temple | 675,941 |
| 25 | Northern Tr Bk of Tx NA, Dallas | 673,848 |
| 26 | American Bk of Tx, Sherman | 654,970 |
| 27 | First NB, Abilene | 624,262 |
| 28 | Inwood NB, Dallas | 623,652 |
| 29 | Summit Bk NA, Fort Worth | 582,617 |
| 30 | First Victoria NB, Victoria | 570,605 |
| 31 | Lone Star NB, Pharr | 534,548 |
| 32 | Southern NB of Tx, Sugar Land | 526,349 |
| 33 | Inter NB, McAllen | 524,962 |
| 34 | Moody NB, Galveston | 510,488 |
| 35 | Austin Bk Tx NA, Jacksonville | 509,981 |
| 36 | Citizens NB, Henderson | 495,546 |
| 37 | State NB, El Paso | 487,098 |
| 38 | State NB, Lubbock | 482,726 |
| 39 | Klein Bk, Klein | 475,848 |
| 40 | City Bk, Lubbock | 457,996 |
| 41 | Longview B&Tc, Longview | 456,452 |
| 42 | State Bk, La Grange | 454,631 |
| 43 | American Bk NA, Corpus Christi | 451,615 |
| 44 | First B&Tc East Tx, Diboll | 449,557 |
| 45 | South Tx NB, Laredo | 446,198 |
| 46 | Bank of the West, El Paso | 439,080 |
| 47 | First St Bk, Temple | 436,904 |
| 48 | Tib Independent Bankersbank, Irving | 431,211 |
| 49 | Guaranty Bond Bk, Mount Pleasant | 427,194 |
| 50 | Jefferson St Bk, San Antonio | 406,186 |
| 51 | International Bk of Cmrc, Brownsville | 405,516 |
| 52 | Security St B&Tc, Fredericksburg | 383,416 |
| 53 | First NB Tx, Killeen | 363,848 |
| 54 | Republic NB, Houston | 349,955 |
| 55 | First Bk Sw NA, Amarillo | 349,722 |
| 56 | American Bk Cmrc, Wolfforth | 347,782 |
| 57 | Century Bk NA, New Boston | 339,760 |
| 58 | Central NB, Waco | 336,740 |
| 59 | Alliance Bk, Sulphur Springs | 334,155 |
| 60 | Commerce Bk, Laredo | 329,670 |

| Rank | Name, Location | Deposits |
|---|---|---|
| 61 | Western NB, Odessa | $ 325,449 |
| 62 | Lubbock NB, Lubbock | 321,225 |
| 63 | First St Bk, Uvalde | 302,336 |
| 64 | Citizens NB, Waxahachie | 302,082 |
| 65 | Texas First NB, Houston | 297,186 |
| 66 | Citizens 1st Bk, Tyler | 293,467 |
| 67 | Community Bk, Granbury | 292,549 |
| 68 | First NB, Bryan | 288,311 |
| 69 | Herring NB, Vernon | 276,167 |
| 70 | First Cmnty Bk NA, Houston | 265,426 |
| 71 | United Central Bk, Garland | 263,812 |
| 72 | West Tx NB, Midland | 263,275 |
| 73 | National Bk, Gatesville | 260,165 |
| 74 | Commercial Bk, Nacogdoches | 252,029 |
| 75 | San Angelo NB, San Angelo | 251,931 |
| 76 | Community NB, Midland | 251,535 |
| 77 | Omnibank NA, Houston | 247,824 |
| 78 | Maximbank, Dickinson | 245,217 |
| 79 | Central Bk, Houston | 244,569 |
| 80 | First United Bk, Dimmitt | 241,571 |
| 81 | Horizon Cap Bk, Webster | 239,522 |
| 82 | Legend Bk NA, Bowie | 235,188 |
| 83 | First NB, Waco | 231,968 |
| 84 | First NB, Granbury | 227,943 |
| 85 | First St Bk, Athens | 227,089 |
| 86 | Falcon Intl Bk, Laredo | 226,163 |
| 87 | First St B&Tc, Carthage | 225,126 |
| 88 | Community B&T, Waco | 221,614 |
| 89 | Southwest Bk, Fort Worth | 216,465 |
| 90 | American NB, Wichita Falls | 211,223 |
| 91 | First NB, Bastrop | 209,335 |
| 92 | North Houston Bk, Houston | 205,032 |
| 93 | American Bk NA, Waco | 204,913 |
| 94 | Union St Bk, Florence | 204,502 |
| 95 | First Tx Bk, Georgetown | 203,765 |
| 96 | Alamo Bk of Tx, Alamo | 200,268 |
| 97 | First NB, Huntsville | 198,754 |
| 98 | Citizens Bk, Kilgore | 197,744 |
| 99 | Independent Bk, McKinney | 196,996 |
| 100 | Worth NB, Lake Worth | 196,790 |
| 101 | First NB, Athens | 195,575 |
| 102 | State B&T, Seguin | 195,247 |
| 103 | Town North Bk NA, Farmers Branch | 192,987 |
| 104 | Citizens NB, Cameron | 191,705 |
| 105 | Lone Star Bk, Dallas | 190,063 |
| 106 | Weatherford NB, Weatherford | 189,630 |
| 107 | Liberty NB, Paris | 189,478 |
| 108 | International Bk of Cmrc, Zapata | 188,940 |
| 109 | First St Bk, Gainesville | 188,856 |
| 110 | Pilgrim Bk, Pittsburg | 188,458 |
| 111 | Northstar Bank of Texas, Denton | 187,460 |
| 112 | First Fncl Bk NA, Cleburne | 182,715 |
| 113 | Texas Gulf Bk NA, Freeport | 182,029 |
| 114 | First St Bk, Livingston | 179,811 |
| 115 | Heritage NB, Granbury | 177,925 |
| 116 | Main Bk NA, Dallas | 177,424 |
| 117 | Bank of The West, Irving | 174,653 |
| 118 | American Fnb, Houston | 169,592 |
| 119 | Hcsb St Bkg Assn, Plainview | 169,367 |
| 120 | Mercantile Bk Tx, Fort Worth | 167,979 |

# Deposits and Assets of Insured Commercial Banks by County

Source: Federal Reserve Bank of Dallas as of Dec. 31, 2002.
in thousands of dollars (000)

| COUNTY | Banks | Deposits | Assets |
|---|---|---|---|
| Anderson | 3 | $ 227,724 | $ 255,936 |
| Andrews | 2 | 125,219 | 137,778 |
| Angelina | 2 | 556,317 | 627,178 |
| Armstrong | 1 | 25,509 | 28,352 |
| Atascosa | 3 | 158,011 | 188,038 |
| Austin | 4 | 444,675 | 507,678 |
| Bailey | 2 | 127,558 | 146,012 |
| Bandera | 1 | 22,439 | 25,380 |
| Bastrop | 3 | 318,275 | 365,640 |
| Baylor | 2 | 68,700 | 76,769 |
| Bee | 2 | 163,974 | 179,456 |
| Bell | 8 | 1,816,971 | 2,111,027 |
| Bexar | 11 | 30,352,247 | 37,279,267 |
| Blanco | 3 | 201,838 | 221,027 |
| Bosque | 3 | 157,010 | 173,799 |
| Bowie | 3 | 564,867 | 629,239 |
| Brazoria | 7 | 628,336 | 745,198 |
| Brazos | 1 | 288,311 | 327,061 |
| Briscoe | 1 | 29,841 | 34,269 |
| Brooks | 2 | 71,291 | 80,893 |
| Brown | 2 | 248,717 | 292,089 |
| Burleson | 2 | 191,713 | 215,445 |
| Burnet | 3 | 241,110 | 291,284 |
| Caldwell | 2 | 138,649 | 156,110 |
| Calhoun | 2 | 124,681 | 151,127 |
| Callahan | 3 | 210,798 | 234,737 |
| Cameron | 4 | 547,921 | 753,160 |
| Camp | 1 | 188,458 | 234,695 |
| Carson | 1 | 12,728 | 14,370 |
| Cass | 4 | 188,404 | 217,151 |
| Castro | 1 | 241,571 | 270,349 |
| Chambers | 3 | 145,307 | 166,549 |
| Cherokee | 2 | 561,080 | 635,166 |
| Childress | 1 | 50,932 | 55,658 |
| Clay | 1 | 47,721 | 54,534 |
| Coke | 2 | 51,704 | 61,949 |
| Coleman | 3 | 107,223 | 122,258 |
| Collin | 10 | 1,419,864 | 1,655,192 |
| Collingsworth | 2 | 124,817 | 138,067 |
| Colorado | 4 | 258,312 | 312,000 |
| Comal | 1 | 113,131 | 129,286 |
| Comanche | 2 | 148,798 | 173,902 |
| Concho | 2 | 63,960 | 73,211 |
| Cooke | 3 | 392,512 | 459,558 |
| Coryell | 3 | 285,766 | 319,403 |
| Cottle | 1 | 38,871 | 44,291 |
| Crockett | 2 | 244,062 | 280,236 |
| Crosby | 3 | 204,624 | 233,497 |
| Culberson | 1 | 20,224 | 25,754 |
| Dallam | 2 | 52,825 | 59,340 |
| Dallas | 40 | 12,301,914 | 16,334,783 |
| Dawson | 2 | 249,149 | 286,491 |
| Deaf Smith | 2 | 114,610 | 132,456 |
| Delta | 3 | 48,574 | 55,904 |
| Denton | 8 | 776,388 | 861,586 |
| DeWitt | 2 | 174,329 | 202,409 |
| Dickens | 1 | 26,445 | 28,818 |
| Dimmit | 1 | 27,241 | 29,624 |

| COUNTY | Banks | Deposits | Assets |
|---|---|---|---|
| Donley | 1 | $ 27,751 | $ 35,162 |
| Duval | 2 | 73,177 | 81,185 |
| Eastland | 2 | 81,055 | 97,260 |
| Ector | 4 | 632,375 | 746,762 |
| Edwards | 1 | 34,324 | 39,501 |
| Ellis | 6 | 486,662 | 546,298 |
| El Paso | 4 | 1,111,803 | 1,284,402 |
| Erath | 4 | 283,448 | 312,817 |
| Falls | 1 | 22,636 | 39,382 |
| Fannin | 5 | 233,507 | 288,810 |
| Fayette | 6 | 733,947 | 898,470 |
| Fisher | 1 | 35,848 | 43,594 |
| Floyd | 1 | 64,876 | 76,619 |
| Foard | 1 | 20,989 | 23,553 |
| Fort Bend | 2 | 563,094 | 617,804 |
| Franklin | 2 | 129,832 | 159,117 |
| Freestone | 2 | 126,172 | 143,111 |
| Frio | 2 | 186,601 | 304,653 |
| Galveston | 7 | 1,365,438 | 1,595,456 |
| Gillespie | 2 | 448,868 | 540,955 |
| Goliad | 1 | 40,807 | 44,562 |
| Gonzales | 2 | 175,019 | 193,751 |
| Gray | 1 | 9,774 | 11,092 |
| Grayson | 7 | 992,122 | 1,107,234 |
| Gregg | 7 | 918,830 | 1,084,527 |
| Grimes | 3 | 162,173 | 185,353 |
| Guadalupe | 4 | 403,386 | 493,492 |
| Hale | 2 | 208,309 | 253,754 |
| Hall | 2 | 56,393 | 66,464 |
| Hamilton | 2 | 50,789 | 56,671 |
| Hansford | 3 | 145,132 | 168,550 |
| Hardeman | 3 | 76,595 | 88,265 |
| Harris | 32 | 12,036,383 | 15,235,046 |
| Harrison | 2 | 65,987 | 79,424 |
| Haskell | 1 | 54,041 | 60,223 |
| Hemphill | 2 | 117,489 | 131,331 |
| Henderson | 5 | 672,138 | 772,164 |
| Hidalgo | 10 | 5,971,806 | 7,164,610 |
| Hill | 4 | 161,416 | 191,667 |
| Hockley | 2 | 81,765 | 88,136 |
| Hood | 5 | 768,811 | 845,473 |
| Hopkins | 2 | 490,350 | 615,442 |
| Houston | 5 | 257,213 | 300,330 |
| Howard | 2 | 213,880 | 246,412 |
| Hunt | 1 | 32,429 | 35,668 |
| Hutchinson | 1 | 37,962 | 42,372 |
| Irion | 1 | 101,752 | 116,741 |
| Jack | 2 | 166,777 | 183,951 |
| Jackson | 1 | 38,661 | 41,782 |
| Jasper | 1 | 162,714 | 183,440 |
| Jeff Davis | 1 | 38,989 | 42,421 |
| Jefferson | 1 | 97,755 | 109,062 |
| Jim Hogg | 2 | 93,200 | 113,538 |
| Jim Wells | 1 | 107,963 | 133,898 |
| Johnson | 3 | 335,848 | 384,325 |
| Jones | 2 | 101,416 | 119,478 |
| Karnes | 3 | 165,563 | 187,145 |
| Kaufman | 2 | 987,069 | 1,092,681 |
| Kent | 1 | 17,943 | 21,837 |
| Kerr | 1 | 153,182 | 165,011 |

# COUNTIES
## Total
## Bank Assets

■ $10 bil +
■ $1 bil +
▨ $500 mil +

### Leading counties 2002

Total bank assets in Dallas County were $16.3 billion, down from $44.1 billion in 2000. In Bexar County (San Antonio), assets were $37.2 billion, up from $31.1 billion in 2000, and, in Harris County (Houston), assets were $15.2 billion, up from $13.6 billion in 2000. Among the top counties are three on the Rio Grande: Webb County (Laredo) with $8.9 billion, El Paso with $1.3 billion and Hidalgo (McAllen) with $7.2 billion.

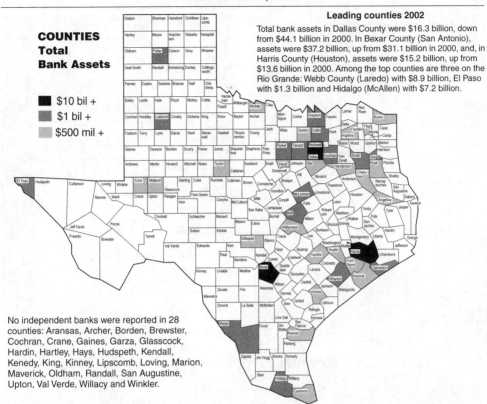

No independent banks were reported in 28 counties: Aransas, Archer, Borden, Brewster, Cochran, Crane, Gaines, Garza, Glasscock, Hardin, Hartley, Hays, Hudspeth, Kendall, Kenedy, King, Kinney, Lipscomb, Loving, Marion, Maverick, Oldham, Randall, San Augustine, Upton, Val Verde, Willacy and Winkler.

| COUNTY | Banks | Deposits | Assets |
|---|---|---|---|
| Kimble | 2 | $ 63,327 | $ 73,931 |
| Kleberg | 2 | 183,604 | 209,644 |
| Knox | 1 | 58,817 | 62,507 |
| Lamar | 4 | 368,494 | 451,154 |
| Lamb | 3 | 87,752 | 105,644 |
| Lampasas | 1 | 75,522 | 90,461 |
| La Salle | 1 | 32,145 | 36,049 |
| Lavaca | 3 | 287,856 | 336,361 |
| Lee | 1 | 71,819 | 81,888 |
| Leon | 4 | 163,029 | 189,353 |
| Liberty | 3 | 224,609 | 259,715 |
| Limestone | 4 | 233,116 | 255,991 |
| Live Oak | 2 | 148,471 | 172,552 |
| Llano | 3 | 215,389 | 243,556 |
| Lubbock | 11 | 4,618,967 | 5,591,070 |
| Lynn | 3 | 119,521 | 135,911 |
| Madison | 2 | 167,778 | 189,857 |
| Martin | 1 | 46,542 | 55,460 |
| Mason | 2 | 58,228 | 76,003 |
| Matagorda | 1 | 41,929 | 46,632 |
| McCulloch | 2 | 128,729 | 147,078 |
| McLennan | 10 | 1,341,571 | 1,520,485 |
| McMullen | 1 | 35,701 | 38,130 |
| Medina | 7 | 324,079 | 367,186 |
| Menard | 2 | 36,578 | 42,034 |
| Midland | 3 | 592,341 | 680,479 |
| Milam | 3 | 354,687 | 408,970 |
| Mills | 1 | 125,164 | 139,717 |
| Mitchell | 2 | 71,756 | 83,504 |
| Montague | 2 | 261,317 | 291,888 |

| COUNTY | Banks | Deposits | Assets |
|---|---|---|---|
| Montgomery | 2 | $ 162,898 | $ 186,366 |
| Moore | 1 | 92,445 | 113,255 |
| Morris | 3 | 143,296 | 166,264 |
| Motley | 1 | 11,034 | 12,278 |
| Nacogdoches | 1 | 252,029 | 287,261 |
| Navarro | 5 | 215,854 | 260,307 |
| Newton | 1 | 92,377 | 109,553 |
| Nolan | 3 | 203,759 | 230,184 |
| Nueces | 6 | 866,757 | 968,805 |
| Ochiltree | 1 | 55,127 | 63,279 |
| Orange | 2 | 106,638 | 116,354 |
| Palo Pinto | 4 | 213,445 | 245,297 |
| Panola | 2 | 288,655 | 362,983 |
| Parker | 3 | 1,297,415 | 1,467,566 |
| Parmer | 2 | 178,366 | 204,570 |
| Pecos | 3 | 126,223 | 147,163 |
| Polk | 3 | 378,927 | 447,090 |
| Potter | 3 | 1,619,382 | 1,972,008 |
| Presidio | 2 | 46,970 | 54,231 |
| Rains | 1 | 61,839 | 70,807 |
| Reagan | 1 | 31,200 | 34,740 |
| Real | 1 | 23,956 | 27,373 |
| Red River | 1 | 18,140 | 20,264 |
| Reeves | 1 | 78,497 | 89,917 |
| Refugio | 2 | 69,979 | 87,487 |
| Roberts | 1 | 31,416 | 33,745 |
| Roberston | 2 | 212,240 | 239,977 |
| Rockwall | 1 | 34,212 | 37,896 |
| Runnels | 4 | 121,824 | 140,068 |
| Rusk | 3 | 633,888 | 710,595 |

| COUNTY | Banks | Deposits | Assets |
|---|---|---|---|
| Sabine | 1 | $ 48,359 | $ 55,044 |
| San Jacinto | 2 | 75,588 | 82,820 |
| San Patricio | 2 | 103,843 | 116,163 |
| San Saba | 1 | 38,809 | 45,462 |
| Schleicher | 1 | 34,415 | 41,604 |
| Scurry | 2 | 164,364 | 185,582 |
| Shackelford | 1 | 162,530 | 191,520 |
| Shelby | 3 | 230,596 | 266,130 |
| Sherman | 1 | 128,114 | 144,427 |
| Smith | 6 | 1,353,391 | 2,229,826 |
| Somervell | 1 | 35,347 | 39,798 |
| Starr | 1 | 47,525 | 57,179 |
| Stephens | 1 | 55,759 | 62,192 |
| Sterling | 1 | 29,993 | 37,208 |
| Stonewall | 1 | 21,548 | 32,505 |
| Sutton | 1 | 106,671 | 116,569 |
| Swisher | 2 | 134,731 | 163,801 |
| Tarrant | 24 | 2,357,811 | 2,696,092 |
| Taylor | 3 | 679,983 | 769,079 |
| Terrell | 1 | 15,450 | 17,810 |
| Terry | 1 | 97,433 | 115,405 |
| Throckmorton | 1 | 18,828 | 21,092 |
| Titus | 2 | 490,230 | 589,503 |
| Tom Green | 2 | 382,990 | 463,987 |
| Travis | 2 | 83,578 | 98,585 |

| COUNTY | Banks | Deposits | Assets |
|---|---|---|---|
| Trinity | 3 | $ 81,241 | $ 92,290 |
| Tyler | 1 | 91,229 | 121,100 |
| Upshur | 3 | 339,696 | 384,368 |
| Uvalde | 2 | 349,897 | 428,531 |
| Van Zandt | 5 | 210,779 | 236,202 |
| Victoria | 1 | 570,605 | 683,453 |
| Walker | 2 | 300,876 | 343,331 |
| Waller | 1 | 57,251 | 64,443 |
| Ward | 1 | 69,009 | 84,069 |
| Washington | 4 | 196,873 | 229,799 |
| Webb | 5 | 6,519,515 | 8,941,984 |
| Wharton | 5 | 1,861,193 | 2,149,629 |
| Wheeler | 1 | 26,684 | 28,975 |
| Wichita | 4 | 572,758 | 638,915 |
| Wilbarger | 3 | 428,991 | 499,155 |
| Williamson | 9 | 815,140 | 928,578 |
| Wilson | 1 | 24,097 | 28,752 |
| Wise | 2 | 180,617 | 200,673 |
| Wood | 5 | 344,147 | 394,535 |
| Yoakum | 1 | 16,983 | 19,450 |
| Young | 5 | 275,946 | 315,563 |
| Zapata | 2 | 242,697 | 364,655 |
| Zavala | 1 | 50,488 | 58,083 |
| | | | |
| Total 2002 | 669 | $128,898,604 | $157,401,479 |

## Texas Bank Resources and Deposits—1905-2002

On Dec. 31, 2002, Texas had a total of 669 national and state banks, the lowest number since 1906. In 1986, the number of independent banks in the state peaked at 1,972. In 2002, the total assets were $157.4 billion. The peak for total assets was in 1997 with $235 billion.

*Source: Federal Reserve Bank of Dallas.*

| Date | National Banks | | | State Banks | | | Combined Total | | |
|---|---|---|---|---|---|---|---|---|---|
| | No. Banks | Assets (add 000) | Deposits (add 000) | No. Banks | Assets (add 000) | Deposits (add 000) | No. Banks | Assets (add 000) | Deposits (add 000) |
| Sept. 30, 1905 | 440 | $ 189,484 | $ 101,285 | 29 | $ 4,341 | $ 2,213 | 469 | $ 193,825 | $ 103,498 |
| Oct. 31, 1906 | 483 | 221,574 | 116,331 | 136 | 19,322 | 13,585 | 619 | 240,896 | 129,916 |
| Dec. 3, 1907 | 521 | 261,724 | 141,803 | 309 | 34,734 | 20,478 | 830 | 296,458 | 162,281 |
| Nov. 27, 1908 | 535 | 243,240 | 115,843 | 340 | 40,981 | 27,014 | 875 | 284,221 | 142,857 |
| Dec. 31, 1909 | 523 | 273,473 | 139,024 | 515 | 72,947 | 51,472 | 1,038 | 346,420 | 190,496 |
| Nov. 10, 1910 | 516 | 293,245 | 145,249 | 621 | 88,103 | 59,766 | 1,137 | 381,348 | 205,015 |
| Dec. 5, 1911 | 513 | 313,685 | 156,083 | 688 | 98,814 | 63,708 | 1,201 | 412,499 | 219,791 |
| Nov. 26, 1912 | 515 | 352,796 | 179,736 | 744 | 138,856 | 101,258 | 1,259 | 491,652 | 280,994 |
| Oct. 21, 1913 | 517 | 359,732 | 183,623 | 832 | 151,620 | 101,081 | 1,349 | 511,352 | 284,704 |
| Dec. 31, 1914 | 533 | 377,516 | 216,953 | 849 | 129,053 | 73,965 | 1,382 | 506,569 | 290,648 |
| Dec. 31, 1915 | 534 | 418,094 | 273,509 | 831 | 149,773 | 101,483 | 1,365 | 567,867 | 374,992 |
| Dec. 27, 1916 | 530 | 567,809 | 430,302 | 836 | 206,396 | 160,416 | 1,366 | 774,205 | 590,718 |
| Dec. 31, 1917 | 539 | 679,316 | 531,066 | 874 | 268,382 | 215,906 | 1,413 | 947,698 | 746,972 |
| Dec. 31, 1918 | 543 | 631,978 | 431,612 | 884 | 259,881 | 191,500 | 1,427 | 891,859 | 623,112 |
| Dec. 31, 1919 | 552 | 965,855 | 777,942 | 948 | 405,130 | 336,018 | 1,500 | 1,370,985 | 1,113,960 |
| Dec. 29, 1920 | 556 | 780,246 | 564,135 | 1,031 | 391,127 | 280,429 | 1,587 | 1,171,373 | 844,564 |
| Dec. 31, 1921 | 551 | 691,087 | 501,493 | 1,004 | 334,907 | 237,848 | 1,555 | 1,025,994 | 739,341 |
| Dec. 29, 1922 | 557 | 823,254 | 634,408 | 970 | 338,693 | 262,478 | 1,527 | 1,161,947 | 896,886 |
| Sept. 14, 1923 | 569 | 860,173 | 648,954 | 950 | 376,775 | 306,372 | 1,519 | 1,236,948 | 955,326 |
| Dec. 31, 1924 | 572 | 999,981 | 820,676 | 933 | 391,040 | 322,392 | 1,505 | 1,391,021 | 1,143,068 |
| Dec. 31, 1925 | 656 | 1,020,124 | 832,425 | 834 | 336,966 | 268,586 | 1,490 | 1,357,090 | 1,101,011 |
| Dec. 31, 1926 | 656 | 1,020,113 | 820,778 | 782 | 290,554 | 228,741 | 1,438 | 1,310,667 | 1,049,519 |
| Dec. 31, 1927 | 643 | 1,134,595 | 938,129 | 748 | 328,574 | 267,559 | 1,391 | 1,463,168 | 1,205,688 |
| Dec. 31, 1928 | 632 | 1,230,469 | 1,017,168 | 713 | 334,870 | 276,875 | 1,345 | 1,565,339 | 1,294,043 |
| Dec. 31, 1929 | 609 | 1,124,369 | 897,538 | 699 | 332,534 | 264,013 | 1,308 | 1,456,903 | 1,161,551 |
| Dec. 31, 1930 | 560 | 1,028,420 | 826,723 | 655 | 299,012 | 231,909 | 1,215 | 1,327,432 | 1,058,632 |
| Dec. 31, 1931 | 508 | 865,910 | 677,307 | 594 | 235,681 | 172,806 | 1,102 | 1,101,591 | 850,113 |
| Dec. 31, 1932 | 483 | 822,857 | 625,586 | 540 | 208,142 | 148,070 | 1,023 | 1,030,999 | 773,653 |
| Dec. 30, 1933 | 445 | 900,810 | 733,810 | 489 | 185,476 | 132,389 | 934 | 1,086,286 | 866,199 |
| Dec. 31, 1934 | 456 | 1,063,453 | 892,264 | 460 | 197,969 | 148,333 | 916 | 1,261,422 | 1,040,597 |
| Dec. 31, 1935 | 454 | 1,145,488 | 1,099,172 | 442 | 205,729 | 162,926 | 896 | 1,351,217 | 1,172,098 |

| Date | National Banks | | | State Banks | | | Combined Total | | |
|---|---|---|---|---|---|---|---|---|---|
| | No. Banks | Assets (add 000) | Deposits (add 000) | No. Banks | Assets (add 000) | Deposits (add 000) | No. Banks | Assets (add 000) | Deposits (add 000) |
| June 30, 1936 | 456 | 1,192,845 | 1,054,284 | 426 | 228,877 | 169,652 | 882 | 1,421,722 | 1,223,936 |
| Dec. 31, 1937 | 453 | 1,343,076 | 1,194,463 | 415 | 217,355 | 177,514 | 868 | 1,560,431 | 1,371,977 |
| Sept. 28, 1938 | 449 | 1,359,719 | 1,206,882 | 406 | 217,944 | 170,286 | 855 | 1,577,663 | 1,377,168 |
| Dec. 31, 1939 | 445 | 1,565,108 | 1,409,821 | 395 | 235,467 | 201,620 | 840 | 1,800,575 | 1,611,441 |
| Dec. 31, 1940 | 446 | 1,695,662 | 1,534,702 | 393 | 227,866 | 179,027 | 839 | 1,923,528 | 1,713,729 |
| Dec. 31, 1941 | 444 | 1,975,022 | 1,805,773 | 391 | 312,861 | 269,505 | 835 | 2,287,883 | 2,075,278 |
| Dec. 31, 1942 | 439 | 2,696,768 | 2,525,299 | 391 | 417,058 | 353,109 | 830 | 3,113,826 | 2,878,408 |
| Dec. 31, 1943 | 439 | 3,281,853 | 3,099,964 | 391 | 574,463 | 536,327 | 830 | 3,856,316 | 3,636,291 |
| Dec. 31, 1944 | 436 | 4,092,473 | 3,891,999 | 398 | 780,910 | 738,779 | 834 | 4,873,383 | 4,630,778 |
| Dec. 31, 1945 | 434 | 5,166,434 | 4,934,773 | 409 | 998,355 | 952,258 | 843 | 6,164,789 | 5,887,031 |
| Dec. 31, 1946 | 434 | 4,883,558 | 4,609,538 | 418 | 1,019,369 | 964,938 | 852 | 5,902,927 | 5,574,476 |
| Dec. 31, 1947 | 437 | 5,334,309 | 5,039,963 | 436 | 1,149,887 | 1,087,347 | 873 | 6,484,196 | 6,127,310 |
| Dec. 31, 1948 | 437 | 5,507,823 | 5,191,334 | 444 | 1,208,884 | 1,137,259 | 881 | 6,716,707 | 6,328,593 |
| Dec. 31, 1949 | 440 | 5,797,407 | 5,454,118 | 446 | 1,283,139 | 1,203,244 | 886 | 7,080,546 | 6,657,362 |
| Dec. 31, 1950 | 442 | 6,467,275 | 6,076,006 | 449 | 1,427,680 | 1,338,540 | 891 | 7,894,955 | 7,414,546 |
| Dec. 31, 1951 | 443 | 6,951,836 | 6,501,307 | 453 | 1,571,623 | 1,473,569 | 896 | 8,523,659 | 7,974,876 |
| Dec. 31, 1952 | 444 | 7,388,030 | 6,882,623 | 457 | 1,742,270 | 1,631,757 | 901 | 9,130,300 | 8,514,380 |
| Dec. 31, 1953 | 443 | 7,751,667 | 7,211,162 | 460 | 1,813,034 | 1,696,297 | 903 | 9,564,701 | 8,907,459 |
| Dec. 31, 1954 | 441 | 8,295,686 | 7,698,690 | 465 | 1,981,483 | 1,851,724 | 906 | 10,277,169 | 9,550,414 |
| Dec. 31, 1955 | 446 | 8,640,239 | 7,983,681 | 472 | 2,087,066 | 1,941,706 | 918 | 10,727,305 | 9,925,387 |
| Dec. 31, 1956 | 452 | 8,986,456 | 8,241,159 | 480 | 2,231,497 | 2,067,927 | 932 | 11,217,953 | 10,309,086 |
| Dec. 31, 1957 | 457 | 8,975,321 | 8,170,271 | 486 | 2,349,935 | 2,169,898 | 943 | 11,325,256 | 10,340,169 |
| Dec. 31, 1958 | 458 | 9,887,737 | 9,049,580 | 499 | 2,662,270 | 2,449,474 | 957 | 12,550,007 | 11,499,054 |
| Dec. 31, 1959 | 466 | 10,011,949 | 9,033,495 | 511 | 2,813,006 | 2,581,404 | 977 | 12,824,955 | 11,614,899 |
| Dec. 31, 1960 | 468 | 10,520,690 | 9,560,668 | 532 | 2,997,600 | 2,735,726 | 1,000 | 13,518,290 | 12,296,394 |
| Dec. 30, 1961 | 473 | 11,466,767 | 10,426,812 | 538 | 3,297,588 | 3,009,499 | 1,011 | 14,764,355 | 13,436,311 |
| Dec. 28, 1962 | 486 | 12,070,803 | 10,712,253 | 551 | 3,646,404 | 3,307,714 | 1,037 | 15,717,207 | 14,019,967 |
| Dec. 30, 1963 | 519 | 12,682,674 | 11,193,194 | 570 | 4,021,033 | 3,637,559 | 1,089 | 16,703,707 | 14,830,753 |
| Dec. 31, 1964 | 539 | 14,015,957 | 12,539,142 | 581 | 4,495,074 | 4,099,543 | 1,120 | 18,511,031 | 16,638,685 |
| Dec. 31, 1965 | 545 | 14,944,319 | 13,315,367 | 585 | 4,966,947 | 4,530,675 | 1,130 | 19,911,266 | 17,846,042 |
| Dec. 31, 1966 | 546 | 15,647,346 | 13,864,727 | 591 | 5,332,385 | 4,859,906 | 1,137 | 20,979,731 | 18,724,633 |
| Dec. 31, 1967 | 542 | 17,201,752 | 15,253,496 | 597 | 6,112,900 | 5,574,735 | 1,139 | 23,314,652 | 20,828,231 |
| Dec. 31, 1968 | 535 | 19,395,045 | 16,963,003 | 609 | 7,107,310 | 6,489,357 | 1,144 | 26,502,355 | 23,452,360 |
| Dec. 31, 1969 | 529 | 19,937,396 | 16,687,720 | 637 | 7,931,966 | 7,069,822 | 1,166 | 27,869,362 | 23,757,542 |
| Dec. 31, 1970 | 530 | 22,087,890 | 18,384,922 | 653 | 8,907,039 | 7,958,133 | 1,183 | 30,994,929 | 26,343,055 |
| Dec. 31, 1971 | 530 | 25,137,269 | 20,820,519 | 677 | 10,273,200 | 9,179,451 | 1,207 | 35,410,469 | 29,999,970 |
| Dec. 31, 1972 | 538 | 29,106,654 | 23,892,660 | 700 | 12,101,749 | 10,804,827 | 1,238 | 41,208,403 | 34,697,487 |
| Dec. 31, 1973 | 550 | 32,791,219 | 26,156,659 | 716 | 14,092,134 | 12,417,693 | 1,266 | 46,883,353 | 38,574,352 |
| Dec. 31, 1974 | 569 | 35,079,218 | 28,772,284 | 744 | 15,654,983 | 13,758,147 | 1,313 | 50,734,201 | 42,530,431 |
| Dec. 31, 1975 | 584 | 39,138,322 | 31,631,199 | 752 | 17,740,669 | 15,650,933 | 1,336 | 56,878,991 | 47,282,132 |
| Dec. 31, 1976 | 596 | 43,534,570 | 35,164,285 | 761 | 19,846,695 | 17,835,078 | 1,357 | 63,381,265 | 52,999,363 |
| Dec. 31, 1977 | 604 | 49,091,503 | 39,828,475 | 773 | 22,668,498 | 20,447,012 | 1,377 | 71,760,001 | 60,275,487 |
| Dec. 31,1978 | 609 | 56,489,274 | 44,749,491 | 786 | 25,987,616 | 23,190,869 | 1,395 | 82,476,890 | 67,940,360 |
| Dec. 31, 1979 | 615 | 65,190,891 | 50,754,782 | 807 | 30,408,232 | 26,975,854 | 1,422 | 95,599,123 | 77,730,636 |
| Dec. 31,1980 | 641 | 75,540,334 | 58,378,669 | 825 | 35,186,113 | 31,055,648 | 1,466 | 110,726,447 | 89,434,317 |
| Dec. 31, 1981 | 694 | 91,811,510 | 68,750,678 | 829 | 42,071,043 | 36,611,555 | 1,523 | 133,882,553 | 105,362,233 |
| Dec. 31, 1982 | 758 | 104,580,333 | 78,424,478 | 841 | 48,336,463 | 41,940,277 | 1,599 | 152,916,796 | 120,364,755 |
| Dec. 31, 1983 | 880 | 126,914,841 | 98,104,893 | 848 | 55,008,329 | 47,653,797 | 1,728 | 181,923,170 | 145,758,690 |
| Dec. 31, 1984 | 999 | 137,565,365 | 105,862,656 | 855 | 60,361,504 | 52,855,584 | 1,854 | 197,926,869 | 158,718,240 |
| Dec. 31, 1985 | 1,058 | 144,674,908 | 111,903,178 | 878 | 64,349,869 | 56,392,634 | 1,936 | 209,024,777 | 168,295,812 |
| Dec. 31, 1986 | 1,077 | 141,397,037 | 106,973,189 | 895 | 65,989,944 | 57,739,091 | 1,972 | 207,386,981 | 164,712,280 |
| Dec. 31, 1987 | 953 | 135,690,678 | 103,930,262 | 812 | 54,361,514 | 47,283,855 | 1,765 | 190,052,192 | 151,214,117 |
| Dec. 31, 1988 | 802 | 130,310,243 | 106,740,461 | 690 | 40,791,310 | 36,655,253 | 1,492 | 171,101,553 | 143,395,714 |
| Dec. 31, 1989 | 687 | 133,163,016 | 104,091,836 | 626 | 40,893,848 | 36,652,675 | 1,313 | 174,056,864 | 140,744,511 |
| Dec. 31, 1990 | 605 | 125,808,263 | 103,573,445 | 578 | 45,021,304 | 40,116,662 | 1,183 | 170,829,567 | 143,690,107 |
| Dec. 31, 1991 | 579 | 123,022,314 | 106,153,441 | 546 | 46,279,752 | 41,315,420 | 1,125 | 169,302,066 | 147,468,861 |
| Dec. 31, 1992 | 562 | 135,507,244 | 112,468,203 | 529 | 40,088,963 | 35,767,858 | 1,091 | 175,596,207 | 148,236,061 |
| Dec. 31, 1993 | 502 | 139,409,250 | 111,993,205 | 510 | 44,566,815 | 39,190,373 | 1,012 | 183,976,065 | 151,183,578 |
| Dec. 31, 1994 | 481 | 140,374,540 | 111,881,041 | 502 | 47,769,694 | 41,522,943 | 983 | 188,144,234 | 153,403,984 |
| Dec. 31, 1995 | 456 | 152,750,093 | 112,557,468 | 479 | 49,967,946 | 42,728,454 | 935 | 202,718,039 | 155,285,922 |
| Dec. 31, 1996 | 432 | 152,299,695 | 122,242,990 | 445 | 52,868,263 | 45,970,674 | 877 | 205,167,958 | 168,213,664 |
| Dec. 31, 1997 | 417 | 180,252,942 | 145,588,677 | 421 | 54,845,186 | 46,202,808 | 838 | 235,098,128 | 191,791485 |
| Dec. 31, 1998 | 402 | 128,609,813 | 106,704,893 | 395 | 50,966,996 | 42,277,367 | 797 | 179,576,809 | 148,982,260 |
| Dec. 31, 1999 | 380 | 128,878,607 | 99,383,776 | 373 | 52,266,148 | 42,579,986 | 753 | 181,144,755 | 141,963,762 |
| Dec. 31, 2000 | 358 | 112,793,856 | 88,591,657 | 351 | 53,561,550 | 43,835,525 | 709 | 166,355,406 | 132,427,182 |
| Dec. 31, 2001 | 342 | 85,625,768 | 72,812,548 | 344 | 59,047,520 | 47,843,799 | 686 | 144,673,288 | 120,656,347 |
| Dec. 31, 2002 | 332 | $ 95,308,420 | $ 79,183,418 | 337 | $ 62,093,220 | $ 49,715,186 | 669 | $157,401,640 | $128,898,604 |

# Texas State Banks

Consolidated Statement, Foreign and Domestic
Offices, as of Dec. 31, 2002
*Source: Federal Reserve Bank of Dallas*

| Number of Banks | 337 |
|---|---|
| In thousands of dollars (000) | |
| **Assets** | |
| Cash and balances due from banks: | |
| Non-interest-bearing balances and currency and coin | $ 2,756,338 |
| Interest-bearing balances | 595,514 |
| Held-to-maturity securities | 4,265,026 |
| Available-for sale securities | 13,721,573 |
| Federal funds sold in domestic offices | 2,036,721 |
| Securities purchases under agreements to resell | 5,682 |
| Loans and lease financing receivables: | |
| Loans and leases held for sale | 1,335,756 |
| Loans and leases, net of unearned income | 33,995,712 |
| Less: allowance for loan and lease losses | 448,075 |
| Loans and leases, net | 33,547,637 |
| Trading Assets | 175,992 |
| Premises and fixed assets | 1,282,039 |
| Other real estate owned | 87,418 |
| Investments in unconsolidated subsidiaries and associated companies | 9,851 |
| Customers liability on acceptances outstanding | 1,537 |
| Intangible assets: | |
| Goodwill | 372,154 |
| Other intangible assets | 136,005 |
| Other assets | 1,763,976 |
| **Total Assets** | **$ 62,093,220** |
| **Liabilities** | |
| Deposits: | |
| In domestic offices | $ 49,715,186 |
| Non-interest-bearing | 10,766,733 |
| Interest-bearing | 38,948,449 |
| In foreign offices, edge & agreement subsidiaries and IBF's | 0 |
| Non-interest-bearing | 0 |
| Interest-bearing | 0 |
| Federal funds purchased and securities sold under agreements to repurchase: | |
| in domestic offices | 1,315,649 |
| securities sold under agreement to repurchase | 801,304 |
| Trading Liabilities | 0 |
| Other borrowed money (mortgages/leases) | 3,546,365 |
| Banks' liability on acceptances executed and outstanding | 1,537 |
| Subordinated notes and debentures | 102,065 |
| Other liabilities | 519,435 |
| **Total Liabilities** | **$ 56,001,542** |
| Minority interest in consolidated subsidiaries | 6,001 |
| **Equity Capital** | |
| Perpetual preferred stock | 1,963 |
| Common stock | 428,428 |
| Surplus (exclude surplus related to preferred stock) | 2,996,471 |
| Retained earnings | 2,412,814 |
| Accumulated other comprehensive income | 246,341 |
| Other equity capital components | -66 |
| **Total Equity Capital** | **$ 6,085,679** |
| **Total liabilities, minority interest and equity capital** | **$ 62,093,220** |

# Texas National Banks

Consolidated Statement, Foreign and Domestic
Offices, as of Dec. 31, 2002
*Source: Federal Reserve Bank of Dallas*

| Number of Banks | 332 |
|---|---|
| In thousands of dollars (000) | |
| **Assets** | |
| Cash and balances due from banks: | |
| Non-interest-bearing balances and currency and coin | $ 6,061,928 |
| Interest-bearing balances | 3,502,119 |
| Held-to-maturity securities | 2,163,549 |
| Available-for sale securities | 19,666,117 |
| Federal funds sold in domestic offices | 7,894,692 |
| Securities purchases under agreements to resell | 58,425 |
| Loans and lease financing receivables: | |
| Loans and leases held for sale | 1,370,603 |
| Loans and leases, net of unearned income | 48,759,531 |
| Less: allowance for loan and lease losses | 792,929 |
| Loans and leases, net | 47,966,602 |
| Trading Assets | 1,089,444 |
| Premises and fixed assets | 1,797,504 |
| Other real estate owned | 98,562 |
| Investments in unconsolidated subsidiaries and associated companies | 5,689 |
| Customers liability on acceptances outstanding | 15,345 |
| Intangible assets: | |
| Goodwill | 1,247,522 |
| Other intangible assets | 244,989 |
| Other assets | 2,125,330 |
| **Total Assets** | **$ 95,308,420** |
| **Liabilities** | |
| Deposits: | |
| In domestic offices | $ 79,183,418 |
| Non-interest-bearing | 19,240,110 |
| Interest-bearing | 59,943,313 |
| In foreign offices, edge & agreement subsidiaries and IBF's | 188,517 |
| Non-interest-bearing | 0 |
| Interest-bearing | 188,517 |
| Federal funds purchased and securities sold under agreements to repurchase: | |
| in domestic offices | 444,406 |
| securities sold under agreement to repurchase | 2,307,752 |
| Trading Liabilities | 68,402 |
| Other borrowed money (mortgages/leases) | 2,878,921 |
| Banks' liability on acceptances executed and outstanding | 15,345 |
| Subordinated notes and debentures | 148,838 |
| Other liabilities | 744,363 |
| **Total Liabilities** | **$85,979,962** |
| Minority interest in consolidated subsidiaries | 4,050 |
| **Equity Capital** | |
| Perpetual preferred stock | 3,069 |
| Common stock | 471,636 |
| Surplus (exclude surplus related to preferred stock) | 4,902,378 |
| Retained earnings | 3,557,209 |
| Accumulated other comprehensive income | 393,030 |
| Other equity capital components | -2,913 |
| **Total Equity Capital** | **$ 9,324,409** |
| **Total liabilities, minority interest and equity capital** | **$ 95,308,420** |

# Texas Credit Unions

*Source: Texas Credit Union League and the National Credit Union Administration.*

There are **679** credit unions in Texas, and 6,798,828 credit union members. At the end of **2002**, share (savings) accounts stood at $36.6 billion, and loans amounted to $26.3 billion.

Nationally, there are more than 10,000 credit unions with $480 billion in assets. They serve some 79 million people.

Credit unions are chartered at federal and state lev-els. The **National Credit Union Administration** (NCUA) is the regulatory agency for the federal char-tered credit unions in Texas. The **Texas Credit Union Department**, Austin, is the regulatory agency for the state-chartered credit unions.

The **Texas Credit Union League** has been the state association for federal and state chartered credit unions since October 1934. The league's address is 4455 LBJ Freeway Ste. 909, Farmers Branch 75244-5998.

They also can be reached at (469) 385-6400, Fax 385-6505 or (800) 442-5762. Their Web site address is www.tcul.org. ☆

# Savings and Loan Associations in Texas

For the purpose of this table, this section includes all thrifts that are not also classified as banks under federal law: that is, it includes federal savings and loan associations, federal savings banks and state-chartered savings and loan associations. *Source: Texas Savings and Loan Department.*

| Year ending | Number of Institutions | Total Assets | *Mortgage Loans | †Cash | †Investment Securities | Deposits | FHLB/ Borrowed Money | ‡Net Worth |
|---|---|---|---|---|---|---|---|---|
| | | | | | in thousands of dollars (000) | | | |
| Dec. 31, 2002 | 24 | $ 43,940,058 | $ 31,604,285 | $ 4,900,880 | ... | $ 23,264,510 | $ 11,662,118 | $ 3,189,629 |
| Dec. 31, 2001 | 24 | 42,716,060 | 35,823,258 | 9,542,688 | ... | 22,182,152 | 15,532,159 | 3,608,222 |
| Dec. 31, 2000 | 25 | 55,709,391 | 43,515,610 | 1,512,444 | ... | 28,914,234 | 17,093,369 | 4,449,097 |
| Dec. 31, 1999 | 25 | 45,508,256 | 40,283,186 | 2,615,072 | ... | 26,369,005 | 14,790,241 | 3,802,977 |
| Dec. 31, 1998 | 30 | 40,021,239 | 35,419,110 | 5,236,596 | ... | 21,693,469 | 15,224,654 | 3,101,795 |
| Dec. 31, 1997 | 32 | 40,284,148 | 33,451,365 | 4,556,626 | ... | 21,854,620 | 15,190,014 | 3,089,458 |
| Dec. 31, 1996 | 37 | 54,427,896 | 27,514,639 | 5,112,995 | ... | 28,053,292 | 20,210,616 | 4,345,257 |
| Dec. 31, 1995 | 45 | 52,292,519 | 27,509,933 | 5,971,364 | ... | 28,635,799 | 15,837,632 | 3,827,249 |
| Dec. 31, 1994 | 50 | 50,014,102 | 24,148,760 | 6,790,416 | ... | 29,394,433 | 15,973,056 | 3,447,110 |
| Dec. 31, 1993 | 62 | 42,983,595 | 14,784,215 | 10,769,889 | ... | 25,503,656 | 13,356,018 | 2,968,840 |
| Dec. 31, 1992 | 64 | 47,565,516 | 14,137,191 | 14,527,573 | ... | 33,299,278 | 10,490,144 | 2,917,881 |
| Dec. 31, 1991 | 80 | 53,500,091 | 15,417,895 | 11,422,071 | ... | 41,985,117 | 8,189,800 | 2,257,329 |
| Dec. 31, 1990§ | 131 | 72,041,456 | 27,475,664 | 20,569,770 | ... | 56,994,387 | 17,738,041 | -4,566,656 |
| Conservatorship | 51 | 14,952,402 | 6,397,466 | 2,188,820 | ... | 16,581,525 | 4,304,033 | -6,637,882 |
| Privately Owned | 80 | 57,089,054 | 21,078,198 | 18,380,950 | ... | 40,412,862 | 13,434,008 | 2,071,226 |
| Dec. 31, 1989§ | 196 | 90,606,100 | 37,793,043 | 21,218,130 | ... | 70,823,464 | 27,158,238 | -9,356,209 |
| Conservatorship | 81 | 22,159,752 | 11,793,445 | 2,605,080 | ... | 25,381,494 | 7,103,657 | -10,866,213 |
| Privately Owned | 115 | 68,446,348 | 25,999,598 | 18,613,050 | ... | 45,441,970 | 20,054,581 | 1,510,004 |
| Dec. 31, 1988 | 204 | 110,499,276 | 50,920,006 | 26,181,917 | ... | 83,950,314 | 28,381,573 | -4,088,355 |
| Dec. 31, 1987 | 279 | 99,613,666 | 56,884,564 | 12,559,154 | ... | 85,324,796 | 19,235,506 | -6,677,338 |
| Dec. 31, 1986 | 281 | 96,919,775 | 61,489,463 | 9,989,918 | ... | 80,429,758 | 14,528,311 | 109,807 |
| Dec. 31, 1985 | 273 | 91,798,890 | 60,866,666 | 10,426,464 | ... | 72,806,067 | 13,194,147 | 3,903,611 |
| Dec. 31, 1984 | 273 | 77,544,202 | 45,859,408 | 10,424,113 | ... | 61,943,815 | 10,984,467 | 2,938,044 |
| Dec. 31, 1983 | 273 | 56,684,508 | 36,243,290 | 6,678,808 | ... | 46,224,429 | 6,317,947 | 2,386,551 |
| Dec. 31, 1982 | 288 | 42,505,924 | 28,539,378 | 4,713,742 | ... | 34,526,483 | 5,168,343 | 1,631,139 |
| Dec. 31, 1981 | 311 | 38,343,703 | 30,013,805 | 3,294,327 | ... | 30,075,258 | 4,846,153 | 1,493,795 |
| Dec. 31, 1980 | 318 | 34,954,129 | 27,717,383 | 3,066,791 | ... | 28,439,210 | 3,187,638 | 1,711,201 |
| Dec. 31, 1975 | 303 | 16,540,181 | 13,367,569 | 167,385 | $ 1,000,095 | 13,876,780 | 919,404 | 914,502 |
| Dec. 31, 1970 | 271 | 7,706,639 | 6,450,730 | 122,420 | 509,482 | 6,335,582 | 559,953 | 531,733 |
| Dec. 31, 1965 | 267 | 5,351,064 | 4,534,073 | 228,994 | 230,628 | 4,631,999 | 286,497 | 333,948 |
| Dec. 31, 1960 | 233 | $ 2,508,872 | $ 2,083,066 | $ 110,028 | $ 157,154 | $ 2,238,080 | $ 48,834 | $ 166,927 |

# Texas Savings Banks

The savings bank charter was approved by the Legislature in 1993 and the first savings bank was chartered in 1994. Savings banks operate similarly to savings and loans associations in that they are housing-oriented lenders. Under federal law a savings bank is categorized as a commercial bank and not a thrift. Therefore savings-bank information is also reported with state and national-bank information. *Source: Texas Savings and Loan Department.*

| Year ending | Number of Institutions | Total Assets | *Mortgage Loans | †Cash | †Investment Securities | Deposits | FHLB/ Borrowed Money | ‡Net Worth |
|---|---|---|---|---|---|---|---|---|
| | | | | | in thousands of dollars (000) | | | |
| Dec. 31, 2002 | 24 | $ 15,445,211 | $ 7,028,139 | $ 3,147,381 | ... | $ 10,009,861 | $ 3,422,600 | $ 1,910,660 |
| Dec. 31, 2001 | 25 | 11,956,074 | 5,845,605 | 1,305,731 | ... | 8,742,372 | 1,850,076 | 1,270,273 |
| Dec. 31, 2000 | 25 | 11,315,961 | 9,613,164 | 514,818 | ... | 8,644,826 | 1,455,497 | 1,059,638 |
| Dec. 31, 1999 | 28 | 13,474,299 | 8,870,291 | 4,101,480 | ... | 7,330,776 | 4,822,372 | 1,188,852 |
| Dec. 31, 1998 | 23 | 12,843,828 | 7,806,738 | 193,992 | ... | 7,299,636 | 4,477,546 | 1,067,977 |
| Dec. 31, 1997 | 17 | 7,952,703 | 6,125,467 | 892,556 | ... | 5,608,429 | 1,615,311 | 745,515 |
| Dec. 31, 1996 | 15 | 7,872,238 | 6,227,811 | 856,970 | ... | 5,329,919 | 1,930,378 | 611,941 |
| Dec. 31, 1995 | 13 | 7,348,647 | 5,644,591 | 1,106,557 | ... | 4,603,026 | 2,225,793 | 519,827 |
| Dec. 31, 1994 | 8 | $ 6,347,505 | $ 2,825,012 | $ 3,139,573 | ... | $ 3,227,886 | $ 2,628,847 | $ 352,363 |

* Beginning in 1982, net of loans in process.
† Beginning in 1979, cash and investment securities data combined.
‡ Net worth includes permanent stock and paid-in surplus general reserves, surplus and undivided profits.
§ In 1989 and 1990, the Office of Thrift Supervision, U.S. Department of the Treasury, separated data on savings and loans (thrifts) into two categories: those under the supervision of the Office of Thrift Supervision (Conservatorship Thrifts) and those still under private management (Privately Owned).

# Insurance in Texas

Source: 2002 Annual Report, Texas Department of Insurance

The **Texas Department of Insurance** reported that on Aug. 31, 2002, there were **2,780** firms licensed to handle insurance business in Texas, including **824** Texas firms and **1,956** out-of-state companies.

Annual premium volume of firms operating in Texas, $70 billion, ranked third among all states, behind California and New York.

The former **Robertson Law**, enacted in 1907 and repealed in 1963, encouraged the establishment of many Texas insurance firms.

It required life insurance companies operating in the state to invest in Texas three-fourths of all reserves held for payment of policies written in the state.

Many out-of-state firms withdrew from Texas. Later many companies re-entered Texas and the law was liberalized and then repealed.

Until 1993, the State Board of Insurance administered legislation relating to the insurance business. This agency was established in 1957, following discovery of irregularities in some firms.

It succeeded two previous regulatory groups, established in 1913 and changed in 1927.

Under terms of sunset legislation passed by the 73rd Legislature in the spring of 1993, most of the board's authority transferred on Sept. 1, 1993, to the **Commissioner of Insurance** appointed by the governor for a two-year term in each odd-numbered year and confirmed by the Texas Senate.

The new law permitted the board to continue its authority over the area of rates, policy forms and related matters until Aug. 31, 1994. On Nov. 18, 1993, however, the board voted unanimously to turn over full authority to the commissioner as of Dec. 16, 1993.

## Companies in Texas

The following table shows the number and kinds of insurance companies licensed in Texas on Aug. 31, 2002:

| Type of Insurance | Texas | Out-of-State | Total |
|---|---|---|---|
| Stock Life . . . . . . . . . . . . . . . . . . . . | 132 | 535 | 667 |
| Mutual Life . . . . . . . . . . . . . . . . . . . | 3 | 43 | 46 |
| Stipulated Premium Life. . . . . . . . . | 40 | 0 | 40 |
| Non-profit Life. . . . . . . . . . . . . . . . . | 0 | 1 | 1 |
| Stock Fire. . . . . . . . . . . . . . . . . . . | 1 | 6 | 7 |
| Stock Fire and Casualty. . . . . . . . . | 100 | 680 | 780 |
| Mutual Fire and Casualty . . . . . . . . | 7 | 56 | 63 |
| Stock Casualty . . . . . . . . . . . . . . . . | 7 | 120 | 127 |
| Mexican Casualty. . . . . . . . . . . . . . | 0 | 9 | 9 |
| Lloyds. . . . . . . . . . . . . . . . . . . . . . . | 71 | 0 | 71 |
| Reciprocal Exchanges . . . . . . . . . . | 11 | 15 | 26 |
| Fraternal Benefit Societies. . . . . . . | 10 | 25 | 35 |
| Titles. . . . . . . . . . . . . . . . . . . . . . . . | 4 | 24 | 28 |
| Non-profit Legal Services. . . . . . . . | 2 | 0 | 2 |
| Health Maintenance . . . . . . . . . . . . | 54 | 3 | 57 |
| Risk Retention Groups. . . . . . . . . . | 1 | 0 | 1 |
| Multiple Employers Welfare Arrang. | 6 | 3 | 9 |
| Joint Underwriting Associations . . . | 0 | 3 | 3 |
| Third Party Administrators . . . . . . . | 293 | 431 | 724 |
| Continuing Care Retirement Communities. . . . . . . . . . . . . . . . | 19 | 2 | 21 |
| **Total** | **761** | **1,956** | **2,717** |
| Statewide Mutual Assessment. . . . | 1 | 0 | 1 |
| Local Mutual Aid Associations . . . . | 4 | 0 | 4 |
| Burial Associations. . . . . . . . . . . . . | 2 | 0 | 2 |
| Exempt Associations . . . . . . . . . . . | 10 | 0 | 10 |
| Non-profit Hospital Service . . . . . . | 5 | 0 | 5 |
| County Mutual Fire. . . . . . . . . . . . . | 24 | 0 | 24 |
| Farm Mutual Fire . . . . . . . . . . . . . . | 17 | 0 | 17 |
| **Total** | **63** | **0** | **63** |
| **Grand Total** | **824** | **1,956** | **2,780** |

| Top Homeowner Insurers, 2001 | |
|---|---|
| Company | % of market |
| 1. State Farm Lloyds | 30.25 |
| 2. Allstate Texas Lloyds | 15.63 |
| 3. Farmers Insurance Exchange | 11.55 |
| 4. Fire Insurance Exchange | 4.52 |
| 5. United Services Automobile Assoc. | 4.14 |
| 6. Travelers Lloyds of Texas | 4.03 |
| 7. Nationwide Lloyds | 2.76 |

## Premium Income and Losses Paid, 2001

| (Texas business only) | Texas Companies | Out-of-State Companies |
|---|---|---|
| **Legal Reserve Life Insurance Companies** | | |
| Life premiums | $ 762,425,014 | $ 6,423,945,449 |
| Claims & benefits paid | 1,245,514,273 | 14,128,953,265 |
| Accident & health premiums | 3,806,052,215 | 8,934,233,828 |
| Accident & health loss paid | 3,554,314,045 | 6,511,889,573 |
| **Mutual Fire & Casualty Companies** | | |
| Premiums | $ 557,104,726 | $ 3,450,377,654 |
| Losses | 253,035,576 | 2,783,941,013 |
| **Lloyds Insurance** | | |
| Premiums | $ 3,301,944,092 | . . . |
| Losses | 2,726,473,755 | . . . |
| **Reciprocal Insurance Companies** | | |
| Premiums | $ 644,708,621 | $ 766,868,242 |
| Losses | 467,638,925 | 639,432,349 |
| **Fraternal Benefit Societies** | | |
| No. Life Certificates issued | 10,858 | 24,453 |
| Amount issued 2001 | $ 188,834,886 | $ 1,608,821,468 |
| Considerations from members: | | |
| Life | 62,292,355 | 183,192,314 |
| Accident & Health | 0 | 18,538,329 |
| Benefits paid to members: | | |
| Life | 35,153,852 | 105,119,820 |
| Accident & Health | 0 | 11,106,050 |
| Amount of insurance in force | 2,466,035,006 | 14,016,897,440 |
| **Title Guaranty Companies** | | |
| Premiums | $ 404,339,320 | $ 656,616,296 |
| Paid Losses | 5,668,511 | 13,840,535 |
| **Stock Fire, Stock Casualty, and Stock Fire & Casualty Companies** | | |
| Premiums | $ 2,101,558,399 | $ 9,489,431,889 |
| Losses | 1,783,402,825 | 7,264,487,872 |

# Construction Industry

Contract awards for construction in 2002 totaled $7,297,909,363. Although the number of contracts stayed near 3,000, dollar value surpassed the volume of 1993 after several years below that mark, as shown in the Comparision of Years table below. Another table shows the approved Texas construction for 2003. These data were compiled by editors of *Texas Contractor* from official sources.

## Comparison of Construction Awards by Years, 1953-2002

Source: Texas Contractor

| Year | Total Awards | Year | Total Awards | Year | Total Awards |
|---|---|---|---|---|---|
| 2002 | $ 7,297,909,363 | 1986 | $ 4,636,310,266 | 1969 | $ 1,477,125,397 |
| 2001 | 6,067,377,351 | 1985 | 4,806,998,065 | 1968 | 1,363,629,304 |
| 2000 | 5,232,788,835 | 1984 | 3,424,721,025 | 1967 | 1,316,872,998 |
| 1999 | 4,941,352,362 | 1983 | 4,074,910,947 | 1966 | 1,421,312,029 |
| 1998 | 4,951,275,224 | 1982 | 3,453,784,388 | 1965 | 1,254,638,051 |
| 1997 | 5,088,017,435 | 1981 | 3,700,112,809 | 1964 | 1,351,656,302 |
| 1996 | 4,383,336,574 | 1980 | 3,543,117,615 | 1963 | 1,154,624,634 |
| 1995 | 4,771,332,413 | 1979 | 3,353,243,234 | 1962 | 1,132,607,006 |
| 1994 | 4,396,199,988 | 1978 | 2,684,743,190 | 1961 | 988,848,239 |
| 1993 | 5,394,342,718 | 1977 | 2,270,788,842 | 1960 | 1,047,943,630 |
| 1992 | 4,747,666,912 | 1976 | 1,966,553,804 | 1959 | 1,122,290,957 |
| 1991 | 3,926,799,801 | 1975 | 1,737,036,682 | 1958 | 1,142,138,674 |
| 1990 | 3,922,781,630 | 1974 | 2,396,488,520 | 1957 | 1,164,240,546 |
| 1989 | 4,176,355,929 | 1973 | 1,926,778,365 | 1956 | 1,220,831,984 |
| 1988 | 3,562,336,666 | 1972 | 1,650,897,233 | 1955 | 949,213,349 |
| 1987 | 4,607,051,270 | 1971 | 1,751,331,262 | 1954 | 861,623,224 |
|  |  | 1970 | 1,458,708,492 | 1953 | 1,180,320,174 |

## Approved Texas Construction, 2003

**Federal:**

| | |
|---|---|
| General Services Administration | $ 8,000,000 |
| Federal Aviation Administration | 95,000,000 |
| Department of Veterans Affairs | 17,500,000 |
| NASA | 3,000,000 |
| Department of Defense | 280,000,000 |
| Rural Utilities Service | 120,000,000 |
| U.S. Department of Agriculture | 120,000,000 |
| Department of Energy | 3,000,000 |
| Natural Res. Conserv. Service | 6,000,000 |
| Department of Justice | 1,750,000 |
| Department of the Interior | 1,850,000 |
| Federal Highway Administration | 2,298,993,029 |
| **Total Federal** | **$ 2,955,093,029** |

**State:**

| | |
|---|---|
| Texas Dept. of Transportation | $ 2,107,036,179 |
| State Agencies | 209,424,125 |
| State Colleges and Universities | 1,115,000,000 |
| **Total State** | **$ 3,431,460,304** |

**Water Projects:**

| | |
|---|---|
| Corps of Engineers | $ 94,500,000 |
| Bureau of Reclamation | 500,000 |
| River Authorities | 618,000,000 |
| Clean Water (SRF) | 430,400,000 |
| Drinking Water (SRF) | 90,000,000 |
| **Total Water Projects** | **$ 1,233,400,000** |

**Cities:**

| | |
|---|---|
| Schools | $ 252,000,000 |
| New Streets, Bridges | 902,267,000 |
| Street Maintenance | 308,888,000 |
| Waterworks, Sewers | 295,746,250 |
| Apartments, Residences | 755,360,000 |
| Commercial | 114,000,000 |
| City Buildings | 460,441,800 |
| **Total Cities** | **$3,088,703,050** |

**Counties:**

| | |
|---|---|
| New Roads | $ 408,000,000 |
| Road Maintenance | 524,300,000 |
| Machinery Purchases | 57,130,000 |
| County Buildings | 112,680,000 |
| **Total Counties** | **$ 1,102,110,000** |
| **Grand Total** | **$11,810,766,383** |

## Analysis of Awards

The following table analyzes and classifies awards in Texas for the year 2002, as compared with 2001, as reported by **Texas Contractor**.

| Category | 2002 | | 2001 | |
|---|---|---|---|---|
| | No. | Amount | No. | Amount |
| Civil Engineering Awards | 2,212 | $ 5,259,497,254 | 2,186 | $ 4,442,076,065 |
| Non-Residential Awards | 821 | 2,038,412,109 | 808 | 1,625,301,286 |
| **Total** | **3,033** | **$ 7,297,909,363** | **2,994** | **$ 6,067,377,351** |

### CIVIL ENGINEERING AWARDS

| Type of Project | 2002 | | 2001 | |
|---|---|---|---|---|
| | No. | Amount | No. | Amount |
| Highways, Streets, Airports | 1,637 | $ 3,967,842,000 | 1,648 | $ 3,346,925,040 |
| Waterworks, Sewers, etc. | 473 | 1,256,030,054 | 440 | 1,058,170,925 |
| Irrigation, Drainage, etc. | 102 | 35,625,200 | 98 | 36,980,100 |
| Misc. | 0 | 0 | 0 | 0 |
| **Total** | **2,212** | **$ 5,259,497,254** | **2,186** | **$ 4,442,076,065** |

### NON-RESIDENTIAL CONSTRUCTION AWARDS

| Type of Project | 2002 | | 2001 | |
|---|---|---|---|---|
| | No. | Amount | No. | Amount |
| Educational Bldgs | 288 | $ 1,044,150,145 | 223 | $ 462,050,350 |
| Churches, Theaters, etc. | 27 | 26,114,000 | 30 | 27,210,000 |
| Hospitals, Hotels, Motels | 26 | 76,381,950 | 28 | 77,538,500 |
| Public Bldgs | 218 | 601,427,914 | 223 | 673,400,036 |
| Commercial/ Industrial | 262 | 290,338,100 | 304 | 385,102,400 |
| Misc. | 0 | 0 | 0 | 0 |
| **Total** | **821** | **$2,038,412,109** | **808** | **$ 1,625,301,286** |

# Foreign Trade Zones in Texas

Source: The International Trade Reporter, copyright 1979 by the Bureau of National Affairs, Inc., Washington, D.C.

Foreign-trade-zone status endows a domestic site with certain customs privileges, causing it to be considered outside customs territory and therefore available for activities that might otherwise be carried on overseas.

Operated as public utilities for qualified corporations, the zones are established under grants of authority from the Foreign-Trade Zones board, which is chaired by the U.S. Secretary of Commerce.

Zone facilities are available for operations involving storage, repacking, inspection, exhibition, assembly, manufacturing and other processing.

A foreign-trade zone is especially suitable for export processing or manufacturing operations when foreign components or materials with a high U.S. duty are needed to make the end product competitive in markets abroad.

Additional information on the zones is available from each zone manager; from U.S. customs offices; from the executive secretary of the Foreign-Trade Zones Board, Dept. of Commerce, Washington, D.C., or from the nearest Dept. of Commerce district office.

Source: U.S. Department of Commerce

There are 31 Foreign-Trade Zones in Texas as of January 2003.

**Addison,** FTZ 223
Foreign Trade Zone Operating Co.
P.O. Box 613307
Dallas 75261

**Amarillo,** FTZ 252
City of Amarillo
600 S. Tyler Ste. 1503
Amarillo 79101

**Austin,** FTZ 183
FTZ of Central Texas Inc.
101 E. Old Settlement Rd., Ste. 200
Round Rock 78664

**Beaumont,** FTZ 115,
**Port Arthur,** FTZ 116
**Orange,** FTZ 117
FTZ of Southeast Texas Inc.
P.O. Drawer 2297
Beaumont 77704

**Brownsville,** FTZ 62
Brownsville Navigation District
1000 Foust Road
Brownsville 78521

**Calhoun/Victoria** Counties FTZ 155
Calhoun-Victoria Foreign-Trade
    Zone Inc.
P.O. Drawer 397
Point Comfort 77978

**Corpus Christi,** FTZ 122
Port of Corpus Christi Authority
P.O. Box 1541
Corpus Christi 78403

**Dallas/Ft.Worth,** FTZ 39
D/FW International Airport Board
P.O. Drawer 619428
D/FW Airport 75261

**Dallas/Fort Worth,** FTZ 168
FTZ Operating Company of Texas
P.O. Box 742916
Dallas 75374

**Del Rio,** FTZ 97
City of Del Rio
114 West Martin St.
Del Rio 78841

**Eagle Pass,** FTZ 96
Maverick County Development Corp.
P.O. Box 3693
Eagle Pass 78853

**Edinburg,** FTZ 251
City of Edinburg
P.O. Box 1079
Edinburg 78540

**Ellis County,** FTZ 113
Trade Zone Operations Inc.
1500 N. Service Road, Highway 67
P.O. Box 788
Midlothian 76065

**El Paso,** FTZ 68
City of El Paso
5B Butterfield Trail Blvd.
El Paso 79906

**El Paso,** FTZ 150
Westport Economic Dev. Corp.
4401 N. Mesa, Ste. 201
El Paso 79982

**Fort Worth,** FTZ 196
Alliance Corridor Inc.
13600 Heritage Pkwy., Ste. 200
Fort Worth 76177

**Freeport,** FTZ 149
Brazos River Harbor Navigation Dist.
Box 615
Freeport 77541

**Galveston,** FTZ 36
Port of Galveston
P.O. Box 328
Galveston 77553

**Gregg County,** FTZ 234
Gregg County
101 E. Methvin, Ste. 300
Longview 75601

**Harris County,** FTZ 84
Port of Houston Authority
111 East Loop North
Houston 77029

**Laredo,** FTZ 94
Laredo International Airport
5210 Bob Bullock Loop
Laredo 78041

**Liberty County,** FTZ 171
Liberty Co. Economic Development
    Corp.
P.O. Box 857
Liberty 77575

**McAllen,** FTZ 12
McAllen Economic Development
    Corp.
6401 South 33rd Street
McAllen 78501

**Midland,** FTZ 165
City of Midland
c/o Midland International Airport
P.O. Box 60305
Midland 79711

**Port Arthur** (see Beaumont)

**Orange** (see Beaumont)

**San Antonio,** FTZ 80
City of San Antonio
P.O. Box 839966
San Antonio 78283-3966

**Starr County,** FTZ 95
Starr County Industrial Foundation
P.O. Box 502
Rio Grande City 78582

**Texas City,** FTZ 199
Texas City Harbor FTZ Corp.
P.O. Box 2608
Texas City 77592

**Waco,** FTZ 246
City of Waco
P.O. Box 1220
Waco 76703

**Weslaco,** FTZ 156
City of Weslaco
500 South Kansas
Weslaco 78596

# Foreign Consulates in Texas

In the list below, these abbreviations appear after of the city: (CG) Consulate General; (C) Consulate; (VC) Vice Consulate. The letter "H" before the designation indicates honorary status. Compiled from "Foreign Consular Offices in the United States," U.S. Dept. of State, Spring/Summer 2002, and recent Internet sources. Note: Possible changes in telephone area codes.

**Albania: Houston (HC)**; 20682 Sweetglen Dr., Porter, 77365. (281) 354-9599.
**Argentina: Houston (CG)**; 3050 Post Oak Blvd., Ste. 1625, 77056. (713) 871-8935.
**Australia: Houston (HC)**; 5757 Woodway, Ste. 175, 77057. (713) 782-7502.
**Austria: Houston (HCG)**; 1717 Bissonet St., Ste 306, 77005. (713) 526-0127.
**Bangladesh: Houston (HCG)**; 35 N. Wynden Dr., 77056. (713) 621-8462.
**Barbados: Houston (HC)**; 25226 Sandi Lane, Katy, 77494. (281) 392-9794.
**Belgium: Houston (HCG)**; 2009 Lubbock St., 77019. (713) 426-3933.
　**Dallas (HC)**; 8350 N. Central Expy., Ste. 2000, 75206. (214) 987-4391.
　**San Antonio (HC)**; 105 S. St. Mary's St., 78205. (210) 271-8820.
**Belize: Dallas (HC)**; 1315 19th St., Ste. 2A, Plano, 75074. (972) 579-0070.
　**Houston (HC)**; 7101 Breen, 77086. (713) 999-4484.
**Bolivia: Houston (HCG)**; 1880 Dairy Ashford, Ste. 691, 77077. (713) 497-4068.
　**Dallas (HC)**; 611 Singleton,75212. (214) 571-6131.
**Botswana: Houston (HC)**; 4615 Post Oak Pl. Ste.104, 77077. (713) 622-1900.
**Brazil: Houston (CG)**; 1700 W. Loop S., Ste. 1450, 77027. (713) 961-3063.
**Cameroon: Houston (HC)**; 2711 Weslayan, 77027. (713) 499-3502.
**Canada: Dallas (CG)**; 750 N. Saint Paul, Ste. 1700, 75201. (214) 922-9806.
**Chile: Houston (CG)**;1360 Post Oak Blvd., Ste. 1330, 77056; (713) 963-9066.
　**Dallas (HC)**; 3500 Oak Lawn, Apt. 200, 75219. (214) 528-2731.
**China: Houston (CG)**; 3400 Montrose, Ste. 700, 77006. (713) 524-0780.
**Colombia: Houston (CG)**; 5851 San Felipe, Ste. 300, 77057; (713) 527-8919.
**Costa Rica: Houston (CG)**; 3000 Wilcrest, Ste. 112, 77042. (713) 266-0484.
　**Austin (C)**; 1730 E. Oltorf, Unit 320, 78741. (512) 445-0023.
　**Dallas (C)**; 7777 Forrest Lane, Ste. B-445, 75230. (972) 566-7020.
　**San Antonio (CG)**; 6836 San Pedro, Ste. 206-B, 78216. (210) 824-8474.
**Cyprus: Houston (HCG)**; 320 S. 66th St., 77011. (713) 928-2264.
**Czech Republic: Dallas (HC)**; 7979 Inwood Rd., 75209. (214) 350-9611.
　**Houston (HC)**; 4544 Post Oak Pl., Ste. 378, 77027. (713) 629-6963.
**Denmark: Dallas (HC)**; 2100 McKinney Ave., Ste. 700, 75201. (214) 661-8399.
　**Houston (HC)**; 4545 Post Oak Place, Ste. 347, 77027. (713) 622-9018.
**Dominican Republic: Houston (C)**; 3300 S. Gessner, Ste. 113, 77024. (713) 266-0165.
**Ecuador: Houston (CG)**; 4200 Westheimer, Ste. 218, 77027. (713) 622-1787.
　**Dallas (HC)**; 7510 Acorn Lane, Frisco, 75034. (972) 712-9107.
**Egypt: Houston (CG)**; 3 Post Oak Central, 1990 Post Oak Blvd., Ste. 2180, 77056. (713) 961-4915.
**El Salvador: Dallas (CG)**; 1555 W. Mockingbird Lane, Ste. 216, 75235.
　**Houston (CG)**; 6420 Hillcroft, Ste. 100, 77081. (713) 270-6239.
**Ethiopia: Houston (HC)**; 9301 Southwest Freeway,

Ste. 250, 77074. (713) 271-7567.
**Finland: Dallas (HC)**; 1445 Ross Ave., Ste. 3200, 75202. (214) 855-4715.
　**Houston (HC)**; 31 Pinewold Circle, 77056. (713) 552-1722.
**France: Houston (CG)**; 777 N. Post Oak Blvd. Ste. 600, 77056. (713) 572-2799.
　**Austin (HC)**; 515 Congress Ave, 78701. (512) 480-5605.
　**Dallas (HC)**; 6370 LBJ Freeway, Ste. 272, 75240. (972) 789-9305.
　**San Antonio (HC)**; Route 1, 78109. Box 229, 78109. (210) 659-3101.
**Georgia: Houston (HC)**; 3040 Post Oak Blvd., Ste. 700, 77056. (281) 633-3500.
**Germany: Houston (CG)**; 1330 Post Oak Blvd., Ste. 1850, 77056. (713) 627-7770.
　**Corpus Christi (HC)**; 5440 Old Brownsville Rd., 78469. (512) 289-2416.
　**Dallas (HC)**; 5580 Peterson Lane, Ste. 160, 75240. (214) 239-0707.
　**San Antonio (HC)**; 1500 Alamo Bldg., 105 S. St. Mary's St., 78205. (210) 224-4455.
**Ghana: Houston (HC)**; 3434 Locke Lane, 77027. (713) 960-8806.
**Greece: Houston (HC)**; 520 Post Oak Blvd., Ste. 310, 77027. (713) 840-7522.
**Guatemala: Houston (CG)**; 3013 Fountain View, Ste 230, 77057. (713) 953-9531.
　**San Antonio (HC)**; 4840 Whirlwind, 78217.
**Guyana: Houston (HC)**; 1810 Woodland Park Dr., 77077. (713) 497-4466.
**Haiti: Houston (HC)**; 3535 Sage Rd., 77027.
**Honduras: Houston (CG)**; 4151 Southwest Fwy., Ste. 700, 77027. (713) 622-4572.
**Hungary: Houston (HC)**; 2800 Post Oak Blvd., Ste. 5230, 77056. (713) 529-2727.
**Iceland: Dallas (HC)**; 1301 Commerce Dr., Plano, 75093. (972) 699-5417.
　**Houston (HC)**; 2348 W. Settler's Way, The Woodlands, 77380. (713) 367-2777.
**India: Houston (CG)**; 1990 Post Oak Blvd., Ste 600, 77056. (713) 626-2148.
**Indonesia: Houston (CG)**; 10900 Richmond Ave., 77042.
**Ireland: Houston (HC)**; 1331 Lamar St., Ste. 600, 77010, (713) 654-8115.
**Israel: Houston (CG)**; 24 Greenway Plz., Ste. 1500, 77046. (713) 627-3780.
**Italy: Houston (CG)**; 1300 Post Oak Blvd., Ste. 660, 77056. (713) 850-7520.
　**Dallas (HC)**; 6255 W. Northwest Hwy., Apt. 304, 75225. (214) 368-4113.
**Jamaica: Houston (HC)**; 7737 Southwest Fwy., Suite 580, 77074. (713) 541-3333.
　**Dallas (HC)**; 3068 Forrest, 75234. (972)396-7969.
**Japan: Houston (CG)**;1000 Louisiana, Ste. 2300, 77002. (713) 652-2977.
**Jordan: Houston (HC)**; 723 Main St., Ste. 408, 77002. (713) 224-2911.
**Korea: Houston (CG)**; 1990 Post Oak Blvd., Ste. 1250, 77056. (713) 961-0186.
　**Dallas (HC)**; 13111 N. Central Expy., 75243. (214) 454-1112.
**Kyrgyzstan: Houston (HCG)**; 2302 Greens Ct., Richmond, 77469. (281) 341-5309.
**Latvia: Houston (HC)**; 5847 San Felipe, Ste. 3400, 77057. (713) 785-0807.
**Lebanon: Houston (HC)**; 1701 Hermann Dr., Ste. 1305, (713) 526-1141.
**Lesotho: Austin (HC)**; 7400 Valburn Dr., 78731.
**Luxembourg: Fort Worth (HC)**; 48 Valley Ridge Rd,

76107. (817) 738-8600.
**Madagascar: Houston (HC)**; 18010 Widcombe Dr., 77084. (713) 550-2559.
**Malta: Houston (HCG)**; 1221 Lamar, Ste. 620, 77060. (713) 654-7900.
   **Dallas (HC)**; 500 N. Akard St., Ste. 4170, 75201. (214) 777-5210.
**Mexico: Austin (CG)**; 200 E. 6th St., Ste. 200, 78701. (512) 478-2866.
   **Brownsville (C);** 724 E. Elizabeth, 78520. (956) 542-4431.
   **Corpus Christi (C)**; 800 N. Shoreline, Ste. 410, 78401.
   **Dallas (CG)**; 8855 N. Stemmons Fwy, 75247. (214) 522-9740.
   **Del Rio (C)**; 2398 Spur 239, 78840. (830) 774-5031.
   **Eagle Pass (C)**; 140 Adams St., 78852. (830) 773-9255.
   **El Paso (CG)**; 910 E. San Antonio St., 79901. (915) 533-3644.
   **Fort Worth (HC)**; 813 W. Magnolia Ave., 76104, 76104. (817) 870-2270.
   **Houston (CG)**; 4507 San Jacinto St., 77004. (713) 271-6800. **Tourism Office:** 2707 N. Loop, Ste. 450, 77008.
   **Laredo (CG)**; 1612 Farragut St., 78040. (956) 723-6369.
   **McAllen (C)**; 600 S. Broadway, 78501. (956) 686-0243.
   **Midland (C)**; 511 W. Ohio St., Ste. 121, 79701.
   **Presidio (C)**; 6717 Kelley Addition 1 Hwy, 79845. (915) 229-2788.
   **San Antonio (CG)**; 127 Navarro St., 78205. (210) 227-9145. **Commercial Affairs Office**: 203 S. Saint Mary's St., 78213.
**Monaco: Dallas (HC)**; 4700 St. Johns Dr., 75205. (214) 521-1058.
**Mongolia: Houston (HCAgent)**; 1221 Lamar, Ste. 1201, 77010. (713) 759-1922.
**Netherlands: Houston (CG)**; 2200 Post Oak Blvd., Ste. 610, 77056. (713) 622-8000.
**New Zealand: Houston (HC)**; 246 Warrenton Dr., 77024. (713) 973-8680.
**Nicaragua: Houston (CG)**; 8989 Westheimer, Ste. 103, 77063. (713) 789-2762.
**Norway: Houston (CG)**; 2777 Allen Parkway, Ste. 1185, 77019. (713) 521-2900.
   **Dallas (HC)**; 4605 Live Oak St., 75204. (214) 826-5231.
**Panama: Houston (CG)**; 24 Greenway Plaza, Ste. 1307, 77046. (713) 622-4451.
**Peru: Houston (CG)**; 5177 Richmond Ave., Ste. 695, 77056. (713) 355-9571.
   **Dallas (HC)**; 306 N. Loop 288, Ste. 183, Denton, 76201. (940) 565-8569.

**Philippines: Houston (HCG)**; 8 Greenway Plaza, Ste. 930, 77046. (713) 764-1330.
**Poland: Houston (HC)**; 2718 St. Annes Dr., Sugar Land, 77479. (281) 565-6277.
**Portugal: Houston (HC)**; 600 Travis, Ste. 6700, 77002. (713) 759-1188.
**Qatar: Houston (CG)**; 1990 Post Oak Blvd, Ste. 810, 77056. (713) 355-8221.
**Romania: Dallas (HC)**; 220 Ross Ave., Ste. 2200, 75201. (214) 740-8608.
**Saint Kitts/Nevis: Dallas (HC)**; 6336 Greenville Ave., 75206.
**Saudi Arabia: Houston (CG)**; 5718 Westheimer, Ste. 1500, 77057. (713) 785-5577.
**Slovenia: Houston (HC)**; 2925 Briarpark, 7 Floor, 77042. (713) 430-7350.
**Spain: Houston (CG)**; 1800 Bering Dr., Ste. 660, 77057. (713) 783-6200.
   **Corpus Christi (HC)**; 7517 Yorkshire Blvd., 78413 (361) 994-7517.
   **Dallas (HC)**; 5499 Glen Lakes Dr., Ste. 209, 75231. (214) 373-1200.
   **El Paso (HC)**; 420 Golden Springs Dr., 79912. (915) 534-0677.
   **San Antonio (HC)**; 8350 Delphian, 78148.
**Sweden: Houston (HC)**; 2909 Hillcroft, Ste. 515, 77057. (713) 953-1417.
   **Dallas: (HC)**; 1341 W. Mockingbird Lane, Ste. 500, 75247; (214) 630-9112.
**Switzerland: Houston (CG)**; 1000 Louisiana, Ste. 5670, 77002. (713) 650-0000.
   **Dallas (HC)**; 2651 N. Harwood, Ste. 455, 75201. (214) 965-1025.
**Syria: Houston (HCG)**; 5433 Westheimer Rd., Ste. 1020, 77056. (713) 622-8860.
**Thailand: Houston (HCG)**; 600 Travis St., Ste. 2800, 77002. (713) 229-8733.
   **Dallas (HCG);** 1717 Main St., Ste. 4100, 75201.
   **El Paso (HCG)**; 4401 N. Mesa, Ste. 204, 79902. (915) 533-5757.
**Trinidad/Tobago: Houston (HC)**; 1330 Post Oak Blvd., 77056. (713) 840-1100.
**Tunisia: Dallas (HC)**; 4227 N. Capistrano Dr., 75287. (972) 267-4191.
**Turkey: Houston (CG);** 1990 Post Oak Central, Ste.1300, 77056. (713) 622-5849.
**Ukraine: Houston (HC)**; 2934 Fairway Dr., Sugar Land, 77478. (281) 242-2842.
**United Kingdom: Houston (CG)**; 1000 Louisiana St., Ste. 1900, 77002. (713) 659-6270.
   **Dallas (C)**; 2911 Turtle Creek, Ste. 940, 75219. (214) 637-3600.
**Venezuela : Houston (CG)**; 2925 Briarpark Dr., Ste. 900, 77027. (713) 961-5141. ☆

*The Houston Ship Channel, an international avenue of trade, winds through refineries and oil and chemical storage facilities.*

*File photo.*

# Tonnage Handled by Texas Ports, 1992-2001

Table below gives consolidated tonnage (**x1000**) handled by Texas ports. All figures are in short tons (2,000 lbs.). Note that " - " indicates no commerce was reported, "0" means tonnage reported was less than 500 tons. *Source: Corps of Engineers, U.S. Army*

| Port | 2001* | 2000 | 1999 | 1998 | 1997 | 1996 | 1995 | 1994 | 1993 | 1992 |
|---|---|---|---|---|---|---|---|---|---|---|
| Beaumont | 79,131 | 76,894 | 69,406 | 60,052 | 48,665 | 35,705 | 20,937 | 21,201 | 25,410 | 22,702 |
| Brownsville | 4,100 | 3,268 | 2,487 | 2,799 | 2,284 | 2,401 | 2,656 | 3,396 | 1,735 | 1,594 |
| Corpus Christi | 77,576 | 81,164 | 78,003 | 86,140 | 86,806 | 80,436 | 70,218 | 76,060 | 58,409 | 58,679 |
| Freeport | 30,143 | 28,966 | 28,076 | 29,014 | 26,281 | 24,571 | 19,662 | 17,450 | 14,025 | 14,953 |
| Galveston | 9,038 | 10,402 | 10,336 | 11,049 | 10,126 | 11,641 | 10,465 | 10,257 | 9,755 | 12,318 |
| Houston | 185,050 | 186,567 | 158,828 | 169,070 | 165,456 | 148,183 | 135,231 | 143,663 | 141,477 | 137,664 |
| Matagorda Chl. (Port Lavaca) | 9,086 | 10,552 | 9,078 | 8,040 | 9,429 | 9,151 | 9,237 | 7,380 | 5,893 | 5,391 |
| Port Arthur | 22,802 | 20,524 | 18,308 | 29,557 | 37,318 | 37,158 | 49,800 | 45,586 | 38,327 | 33,526 |
| Sabine Pass | 1,203 | 910 | 949 | 1,200 | 725 | 135 | 231 | 296 | 394 | 419 |
| Texas City | 62,270 | 58,109 | 49,503 | 49,477 | 56,646 | 56,394 | 50,403 | 44,351 | 53,653 | 43,104 |
| Victoria Chl. | 4,733 | 5,104 | 5,522 | 5,298 | 5,000 | 4,351 | 4,624 | 4,567 | 3,937 | 4,265 |
| Anahuac | - | - | - | - | - | 0 | - | 0 | 0 | 0 |
| Aransas Pass | | 6 | 169 | 48 | 91 | 39 | 181 | 45 | 25 | 13 |
| Arroyo Colorado (Harlingen) | | 837 | 940 | 992 | 928 | 964 | 994 | 1,016 | 898 | 787 |
| Port Isabel | 5 | 7 | 30 | 88 | 114 | 130 | 206 | 231 | 235 |  |
| Cedar Bayou | | 1,002 | 955 | 666 | 435 | 404 | 473 | 321 | 350 | 303 |
| Chocolate Byu. | | 3,488 | 3,329 | 4,048 | 3,983 | 3,845 | 3,480 | 3,757 | 3,715 | 3,343 |
| Clear Creek | - | 11 | - | - | 0 | - | 5 | 0 | 0 |  |
| Colorado River | | 445 | 388 | 503 | 570 | 622 | 576 | 639 | 537 | 505 |
| Dickinson | | 904 | 954 | 1,073 | 669 | 625 | 657 | 556 | 423 | 449 |
| Double Bayou | 0 | - | 0 | 0 | 0 | 0 | - | 0 | 0 | 0 |
| Harbor Island (Port Aransas) | | 151 | 143 | 40 | 38 | 44 | 209 | 64 | 1,227 | 2,154 |
| Liberty Chl. | - | - | 18 | - | 39 | - | - | 0 | 3 |  |
| Orange | | 681 | 873 | 756 | 691 | 616 | 693 | 686 | 579 | 553 |
| Palacios | - | 0 | - | - | 0 | - | - | 0 | 0 |  |
| Port Mansfield | - | 1 | 3 | 8 | 8 | 20 | 10 | 4 | 3 |  |
| Rockport | - | 2 | - | - | 1 | - | 3 | 0 | 0 |  |
| San Bernard Rr. | | 633 | 666 | 565 | 578 | 565 | 653 | 724 | 718 | 684 |
| Other Ports | 0 | 0 | 0 | 0 | 0 | 0 | 0 | 0 | 0 | 0 |
| TOTAL** | 454,765 | 452,991 | 406,166 | 427,296 | 422,592 | 385,585 | 371,021 | 373,668 | 361,01 | 390,567 |

*2001 figures available for principal ports only. **Totals exclude duplication.*

## Foreign/Domestic Commerce: Breakdown for 2000

Data below represent inbound and outbound tonnage for major Texas ports in **2000**. Note that "-" means no tonnage was reported. *Source: U.S. Army Corps of Engineers*

**(All figures in short tons x1000)**

| Port | Foreign | | Domestic | | | | Local |
|---|---|---|---|---|---|---|---|
|  |  |  | Coastwise | | Internal | |  |
|  | Imports | Exports | Receipts | Shipments | Receipts | Shipments |  |
| Beaumont | 55,570 | 5,901 | 351 | 2,695 | 5,185 | 7,132 | 680 |
| Brownsville | 1,357 | 41 | 63 | 8 | 1,258 | 72 | - |
| Corpus Christi | 48,414 | 8,912 | 704 | 7,909 | 3,510 | 9,198 | 2,516 |
| Freeport | 20,628 | 2,739 | 130 | 634 | 2,780 | 1,969 | 86 |
| Galveston | 3,241 | 3,551 | 15 | 1,460 | 1,692 | 436 | 8 |
| Houston | 87,031 | 36,918 | 2,987 | 8,352 | 21,744 | 16,247 | 13,287 |
| Matagorda Chl. (Port Lavaca) | 5,556 | 1,618 | 701 | 242 | 423 | 2,012 | - |
| Port Arthur | 10,103 | 1,939 | 84 | 733 | 2,796 | 4,747 | 114 |
| Sabine Pass | 1 | 1 | 12 | - | 69 | 828 | - |
| Texas City | 33,317 | 4,461 | 238 | 6,303 | 7,004 | 6,375 | 410 |
| Victoria | - | - | - | - | 1,552 | 3,552 | - |

## Gulf Intracoastal Waterway by Commodity (Texas portion)

**(All figures in short tons** x1000) *Source: U.S. Army Corps of Engineers*

| | 2000 | 1999 | 1998 | 1997 | 1996 | 1995 |
|---|---|---|---|---|---|---|
| Total | 66,440 | 61,563 | 63,105 | 65,112 | 76,080 | 78,386 |
| Coal | 121 | 136 | 71 | 126 | 224 | 162 |
| Petroleum products | 34,816 | 30,886 | 32,763 | 33,816 | 38,412 | 40,496 |
| Chemicals | 21,382 | 20,540 | 20,723 | 21,958 | 26,238 | 26,818 |
| Raw materials | 5,822 | 5,535 | 4,979 | 4,860 | 6,397 | 6,544 |
| Manufactured goods | 2,301 | 1,872 | 1,826 | 2,171 | 2,393 | 2,056 |
| Food, farm products | 960 | 789 | 736 | 759 | 1,370 | 1,216 |

## U.S. ports ranked by tonnage 2001
(x1000)

1. S. Louisiana . . . 212,565
2. **Houston** . . . . . 185,050
3. New York . . . . . 137,484
4. New Orleans . . . 85,628
5. **Beaumont** . . . . . 79,131
6. **Corpus Christi** . 77,576
7. Huntington, WV . 76,670
8. Long Beach . . . 67,644
9. **Texas City** . . . . . 62,270
10. Baton Rouge . . 61,415

## States ranked by tonnage 2000
(x1000)

1. Louisiana . . . . . 507,259
2. **Texas** . . . . . . . . 452,991
3. California . . . . . 185,083
4. Ohio . . . . . . . . . 130,915
5. Florida . . . . . . . 125,305
6. Pennsylvania . . 121,552
7. Illinois . . . . . . . . 118,382
8. Washington . . . 113,732
9. New York . . . . . 103,280
10. New Jersey . . . 99,418

# Texas Transportation System

Texas is a leader among the states in a number of transportation indicators, including total road and street mileage, total railroad mileage and total number of airports. Texas ranks second behind California in motor-vehicle registrations. The Texas transportation system includes 300,000 miles of streets, highways and Interstate roads, more than 10,000 miles of railroad line, and approximately 1,600 airports and landing strips. Texans operate more than 18 million motor vehicles, and the state has more than 47,000 pilots.

The transportation industry is a major employer in Texas. Texas Workforce Commission indicates that transportation employs some 379,000 Texans. The largest group, 120,000, is employed in trucking and warehousing. Air transportation involves 70,000 workers.

The largest state agency involved, the **Texas Department of Transportation**, is responsible for highway construction and maintenance, motor vehicle titles and registration, general aviation, public transportation, commercial trucking, automobile dealer licensing and the state's official Tourist Welcome Centers. The **Railroad Commission** has intrastate authority over railroad safety, truck lines, buses and pipelines.

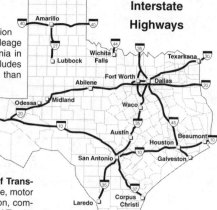

### Interstate Highways

## Vehicles, Highway Miles, Construction, Maintenance, 2002

*The following mileage, maintenance and construction figures refer only to roads that are maintained by the state: Interstates, U.S. highways, state highways, farm-to-market roads and some loops around urban areas. Not included are city- or county-maintained streets and roads. A lane mile is one lane for one mile; i.e., one mile of four-lane highway equals four lane miles. Source: Texas Dept. of Transportation.*

| COUNTY | Vehicles Registered | Lane Miles of Highways | Vehicle Miles Driven Daily | State Maintenance Expenditures | State Construction Expenditures | Vehicle Registration Fees | County Net Receipts | State Net Receipts |
|---|---|---|---|---|---|---|---|---|
| Anderson | 43,257 | 962 | 1,160,102 | $ 3,725,613 | $ 5,086,526 | $ 2,534,263 | $ 1,042,092 | $ 1,492,171 |
| Andrews | 12,638 | 540 | 405,437 | 1,337,109 | 1,215,339 | 765,256 | 437,160 | 328,096 |
| Angelina | 76,244 | 919 | 2,087,572 | 8,516,132 | 14,251,740 | 5,100,559 | 1,729,896 | 3,370,662 |
| Aransas | 19,706 | 184 | 407,757 | 2,518,087 | 8,818,549 | 1,127,246 | 509,850 | 617,396 |
| Archer | 10,076 | 530 | 357,994 | 2,941,062 | 468,499 | 595,473 | 444,146 | 151,328 |
| Armstrong | 2,669 | 378 | 311,840 | 1,592,406 | 6,558,616 | 154,536 | 152,818 | 1,718 |
| Atascosa | 31,216 | 1,011 | 1,254,944 | 4,108,952 | 7,303,227 | 1,828,707 | 819,415 | 1,009,292 |
| Austin | 28,495 | 607 | 1,231,125 | 2,332,771 | 1,618,172 | 1,750,594 | 776,064 | 974,530 |
| Bailey | 6,190 | 490 | 205,934 | 1,617,496 | 564,060 | 426,842 | 377,796 | 49,046 |
| Bandera | 20,137 | 393 | 357,489 | 2,726,869 | 420,221 | 1,110,311 | 660,670 | 449,641 |
| Bastrop | 57,749 | 788 | 1,800,218 | 2,848,296 | 12,680,276 | 3,422,187 | 1,615,561 | 1,806,626 |
| Baylor | 4,415 | 437 | 187,467 | 2,311,135 | 592,643 | 274,596 | 251,798 | 22,798 |
| Bee | 20,016 | 639 | 598,828 | 8,873,648 | 893,333 | 1,189,913 | 661,702 | 528,211 |
| Bell | 212,915 | 1,469 | 5,381,235 | 11,678,032 | 19,046,104 | 13,432,052 | 5,039,061 | 8,392,991 |
| Bexar | 1,138,183 | 3,031 | 23,076,999 | 32,609,677 | 216,107,001 | 74,715,112 | 24,674,530 | 50,040,582 |
| Blanco | 10,590 | 462 | 513,649 | 2,257,630 | 1,569,435 | 681,703 | 398,704 | 283,000 |
| Borden | 967 | 344 | 50,166 | 1,747,096 | 4,111,541 | 44,100 | 43,646 | 454 |
| Bosque | 18,096 | 695 | 537,537 | 3,313,675 | 140,583 | 1,006,822 | 594,589 | 412,233 |
| Bowie | 83,821 | 1,182 | 2,603,946 | 5,901,276 | 25,192,575 | 5,014,376 | 1,837,786 | 3,176,590 |
| Brazoria | 234,533 | 1,254 | 4,128,655 | 13,866,525 | 30,110,962 | 13,200,360 | 3,482,742 | 9,717,618 |
| Brazos | 118,791 | 828 | 2,820,897 | 5,450,194 | 20,432,347 | 7,665,074 | 2,705,541 | 4,959,534 |
| Brewster | 8,037 | 591 | 212,844 | 5,725,158 | 565,521 | 477,188 | 346,670 | 130,519 |
| Briscoe | 2,017 | 326 | 51,527 | 1,162,705 | 327,969 | 120,373 | 118,430 | 1,944 |
| Brooks | 5,474 | 310 | 501,964 | 1,975,850 | 449,713 | 308,564 | 232,003 | 76,561 |
| Brown | 38,652 | 756 | 737,324 | 3,484,761 | 7,551,944 | 2,289,203 | 1,051,723 | 1,237,480 |
| Burleson | 17,508 | 504 | 682,285 | 1,867,319 | 5,957,295 | 1,035,016 | 619,235 | 415,780 |
| Burnet | 41,522 | 794 | 1,187,572 | 2,420,620 | 11,919,527 | 2,479,760 | 1,075,790 | 1,403,970 |
| Caldwell | 27,130 | 604 | 858,300 | 2,429,448 | 3,183,441 | 1,571,746 | 739,382 | 832,363 |
| Calhoun | 19,325 | 382 | 453,804 | 1,568,382 | 1,676,618 | 1,041,330 | 491,027 | 550,303 |
| Callahan | 15,839 | 750 | 824,968 | 2,726,008 | 11,629,973 | 936,791 | 654,149 | 282,642 |
| Cameron | 202,162 | 1,599 | 5,006,717 | 14,941,536 | 59,822,829 | 12,829,608 | 3,931,072 | 8,898,536 |
| Camp | 12,841 | 272 | 265,753 | 1,061,080 | 3,038,273 | 958,616 | 488,815 | 469,801 |
| Carson | 6,652 | 775 | 673,444 | 3,044,620 | 15,056,484 | 378,102 | 331,346 | 46,756 |
| Cass | 30,175 | 986 | 1,006,872 | 4,653,212 | 13,650,885 | 1,744,490 | 818,261 | 926,230 |
| Castro | 7,300 | 533 | 255,656 | 2,185,397 | 160,290 | 550,410 | 438,147 | 112,264 |
| Chambers | 29,994 | 747 | 1,965,251 | 2,070,156 | 4,080,674 | 1,856,930 | 753,615 | 1,103,316 |
| Cherokee | 39,194 | 1,133 | 1,194,466 | 6,907,133 | 7,743,614 | 2,306,870 | 1,017,570 | 1,289,300 |
| Childress | 6,147 | 477 | 330,537 | 1,986,520 | 9,353,582 | 349,444 | 322,273 | 27,172 |
| Clay | 12,683 | 792 | 795,408 | 4,455,215 | 6,516,555 | 711,519 | 570,821 | 140,698 |
| Cochran | 3,109 | 470 | 91,364 | 1,485,615 | 2,186,378 | 201,696 | 198,844 | 2,852 |
| Coke | 4,528 | 357 | 166,216 | 2,091,569 | 2,589,498 | 248,206 | 239,559 | 8,647 |
| Coleman | 9,896 | 755 | 338,676 | 2,991,331 | 691,120 | 546,795 | 451,624 | 95,172 |

| COUNTY | Vehicles Registered | Lane Miles of Highways | Vehicle Miles Driven Daily | State Maintenance Expenditures | State Construction Expenditures | Vehicle Registration Fees | County Net Receipts | State Net Receipts |
|---|---|---|---|---|---|---|---|---|
| Collin | 485,855 | 1,325 | 6,626,558 | 13,048,552 | 64,179,440 | 30,261,923 | 10,503,903 | 19,758,020 |
| Collingsworth | 3,213 | 445 | 89,150 | 1,362,706 | 615,292 | 186,545 | 183,445 | 3,101 |
| Colorado | 22,990 | 757 | 1,545,784 | 4,278,191 | 2,877,011 | 1,455,542 | 720,581 | 734,961 |
| Comal | 89,325 | 614 | 2,711,039 | 3,796,342 | 20,692,977 | 5,918,459 | 2,188,732 | 3,729,727 |
| Comanche | 15,175 | 734 | 449,112 | 2,089,371 | 3,082,166 | 920,454 | 607,775 | 312,679 |
| Concho | 3,190 | 440 | 242,562 | 2,233,622 | 3,008,615 | 163,018 | 160,378 | 2,640 |
| Cooke | 37,543 | 849 | 1,348,372 | 5,852,921 | 5,436,891 | 2,259,443 | 979,954 | 1,279,489 |
| Coryell | 42,307 | 684 | 980,811 | 3,700,663 | 4,009,428 | 2,412,173 | 1,025,503 | 1,386,670 |
| Cottle | 1,897 | 391 | 81,215 | 2,196,514 | 4,973,038 | 102,893 | 101,080 | 1,813 |
| Crane | 4,855 | 319 | 170,250 | 535,241 | 1,009,334 | 305,506 | 211,609 | 93,896 |
| Crockett | 4,045 | 790 | 455,824 | 2,381,837 | 5,091,360 | 219,810 | 216,929 | 2,881 |
| Crosby | 5,835 | 569 | 180,489 | 1,952,554 | 130,889 | 342,155 | 325,205 | 16,949 |
| Culberson | 2,004 | 749 | 575,686 | 3,818,827 | 342,104 | 127,654 | 125,814 | 1,840 |
| Dallam | 5,769 | 606 | 310,163 | 1,553,761 | 4,488,761 | 428,595 | 366,137 | 62,458 |
| Dallas | 1,850,499 | 3,200 | 34,263,783 | 36,667,687 | 277,756,763 | 121,927,634 | 40,649,910 | 81,277,725 |
| Dawson | 11,231 | 713 | 358,363 | 5,557,186 | 3,886,939 | 729,008 | 549,411 | 179,597 |
| Deaf Smith | 16,839 | 603 | 357,376 | 2,781,882 | 9,675,242 | 1,286,705 | 665,798 | 620,907 |
| Delta | 5,733 | 342 | 179,871 | 3,733,692 | 543,390 | 332,576 | 271,438 | 61,138 |
| Denton | 389,433 | 1,352 | 7,791,807 | 9,533,801 | 51,341,114 | 24,127,504 | 7,418,043 | 16,709,460 |
| DeWitt | 17,984 | 641 | 442,959 | 7,340,831 | 8,007,998 | 1,033,717 | 620,346 | 413,371 |
| Dickens | 2,718 | 460 | 95,528 | 1,534,775 | 344,124 | 124,836 | 123,277 | 1,559 |
| Dimmit | 7,250 | 507 | 307,265 | 2,865,740 | 9,617,284 | 454,488 | 341,345 | 113,143 |
| Donley | 3,579 | 455 | 405,309 | 6,360,237 | 1,072,260 | 202,426 | 198,871 | 3,555 |
| Duval | 10,112 | 630 | 429,729 | 4,251,378 | 1,730,671 | 779,483 | 461,026 | 318,457 |
| Eastland | 20,558 | 1,023 | 1,041,988 | 3,438,470 | 5,091,263 | 1,329,322 | 673,478 | 655,845 |
| Ector | 113,399 | 957 | 1,531,690 | 4,021,435 | 14,193,155 | 7,794,820 | 2,595,606 | 5,199,214 |
| Edwards | 2,385 | 499 | 98,304 | 2,119,244 | 1,760,437 | 128,809 | 126,780 | 2,029 |
| Ellis | 124,615 | 1,525 | 3,810,083 | 7,821,726 | 24,216,744 | 7,961,593 | 2,213,968 | 5,747,625 |
| El Paso | 483,799 | 1,556 | 8,729,456 | 13,098,226 | 87,852,691 | 29,916,827 | 8,993,554 | 20,923,273 |
| Erath | 31,499 | 820 | 1,012,196 | 2,871,007 | 4,984,740 | 1,900,455 | 883,342 | 1,017,114 |
| Falls | 14,273 | 706 | 677,847 | 4,056,269 | 15,009,420 | 807,533 | 554,083 | 253,449 |
| Fannin | 33,783 | 991 | 747,144 | 6,125,246 | 6,707,158 | 1,917,835 | 982,324 | 935,511 |
| Fayette | 27,422 | 1,034 | 1,453,737 | 3,871,589 | 9,667,524 | 1,611,445 | 807,191 | 804,255 |
| Fisher | 4,368 | 555 | 140,438 | 1,952,088 | 292,065 | 235,716 | 232,067 | 3,648 |
| Floyd | 7,371 | 670 | 180,373 | 2,066,522 | 4,391,264 | 447,978 | 404,448 | 43,530 |
| Foard | 1,582 | 299 | 66,238 | 828,012 | 435,966 | 89,287 | 87,898 | 1,390 |
| Fort Bend | 296,846 | 1,073 | 4,985,679 | 8,389,393 | 78,674,081 | 19,232,559 | 5,737,761 | 13,494,798 |
| Franklin | 9,310 | 336 | 435,475 | 2,154,400 | 2,175,119 | 517,727 | 388,907 | 128,820 |
| Freestone | 19,427 | 800 | 1,429,244 | 2,695,813 | 8,036,776 | 1,107,901 | 730,556 | 377,345 |
| Frio | 10,530 | 758 | 761,447 | 2,282,057 | 2,182,719 | 691,411 | 509,089 | 182,323 |
| Gaines | 12,940 | 668 | 439,113 | 2,607,510 | 161,492 | 781,753 | 419,674 | 362,079 |
| Galveston | 218,951 | 1,039 | 4,456,534 | 11,137,275 | 24,144,466 | 13,026,933 | 4,103,366 | 8,923,567 |
| Garza | 4,367 | 460 | 410,787 | 3,766,458 | 287,255 | 257,062 | 216,428 | 40,634 |
| Gillespie | 23,940 | 689 | 627,841 | 2,543,667 | 4,079,237 | 1,386,645 | 729,019 | 657,627 |
| Glasscock | 2,232 | 274 | 158,698 | 921,807 | 860,629 | 172,770 | 155,252 | 17,517 |
| Goliad | 6,763 | 500 | 324,757 | 3,419,953 | 2,500,018 | 344,199 | 302,693 | 41,507 |
| Gonzales | 18,180 | 878 | 1,023,728 | 2,949,819 | 7,784,065 | 1,091,231 | 598,750 | 492,481 |
| Gray | 23,882 | 770 | 560,700 | 2,865,160 | 13,920,327 | 1,261,787 | 544,673 | 717,114 |
| Grayson | 115,828 | 1,173 | 2,996,339 | 5,959,629 | 25,584,239 | 7,028,801 | 2,418,015 | 4,610,786 |
| Gregg | 119,503 | 773 | 2,464,389 | 4,270,381 | 20,322,158 | 8,057,076 | 2,850,398 | 5,206,678 |
| Grimes | 22,465 | 611 | 763,319 | 2,365,666 | 1,657,953 | 1,275,900 | 709,279 | 566,621 |
| Guadalupe | 86,833 | 901 | 2,430,930 | 4,176,461 | 14,553,704 | 5,326,560 | 1,876,010 | 3,450,550 |
| Hale | 29,690 | 1,052 | 755,762 | 3,482,312 | 18,343,066 | 1,860,102 | 845,090 | 1,015,013 |
| Hall | 3,235 | 458 | 190,185 | 1,912,786 | 5,047,129 | 203,724 | 200,940 | 2,785 |
| Hamilton | 8,929 | 580 | 338,619 | 2,845,472 | 2,816,360 | 515,199 | 427,674 | 87,524 |
| Hansford | 6,169 | 526 | 126,517 | 2,697,904 | 4,480,350 | 391,346 | 352,277 | 39,068 |
| Hardeman | 4,382 | 466 | 315,564 | 3,475,414 | 8,913,978 | 255,247 | 251,095 | 4,152 |
| Hardin | 51,146 | 568 | 1,234,983 | 2,782,708 | 7,608,562 | 2,994,093 | 1,310,234 | 1,683,859 |
| Harris | 2,823,438 | 4,564 | 53,733,807 | 50,067,031 | 357,194,779 | 189,014,637 | 66,022,219 | 122,992,418 |
| Harrison | 58,148 | 1,185 | 2,423,262 | 7,103,981 | 12,079,777 | 3,446,756 | 1,291,786 | 2,154,970 |
| Hartley | 5,324 | 535 | 352,613 | 1,288,439 | 3,331,998 | 395,551 | 303,419 | 92,132 |
| Haskell | 7,084 | 646 | 202,302 | 1,974,850 | 3,963,158 | 409,586 | 387,319 | 22,267 |
| Hays | 89,082 | 664 | 3,323,054 | 4,015,051 | 22,945,787 | 5,541,897 | 2,040,316 | 3,501,581 |
| Hemphill | 4,613 | 386 | 127,710 | 1,329,372 | 167,946 | 269,430 | 236,050 | 33,380 |
| Henderson | 75,091 | 968 | 1,622,892 | 3,805,590 | 9,809,387 | 4,394,021 | 1,435,046 | 2,958,975 |
| Hidalgo | 342,583 | 2,013 | 8,517,526 | 12,126,068 | 104,751,948 | 23,068,391 | 6,980,168 | 16,088,223 |
| Hill | 33,919 | 1,073 | 2,067,114 | 4,841,859 | 9,327,017 | 2,027,940 | 936,426 | 1,091,514 |
| Hockley | 20,297 | 751 | 543,362 | 2,877,043 | 1,784,383 | 1,363,888 | 669,855 | 694,033 |
| Hood | 49,176 | 376 | 927,067 | 2,022,658 | 16,779,044 | 2,917,556 | 1,233,572 | 1,683,984 |
| Hopkins | 33,913 | 1,000 | 1,354,725 | 7,537,223 | 11,647,992 | 2,100,436 | 1,018,961 | 1,081,475 |
| Houston | 20,752 | 843 | 598,996 | 5,180,646 | 12,497,432 | 1,197,935 | 665,212 | 532,723 |
| Howard | 27,992 | 856 | 847,941 | 2,816,947 | 8,310,755 | 1,732,693 | 845,980 | 886,713 |

| COUNTY | Vehicles Registered | Lane Miles of Highways | Vehicle Miles Driven Daily | State Maintenance Expenditures | State Construction Expenditures | Vehicle Registration Fees | County Net Receipts | State Net Receipts |
|---|---|---|---|---|---|---|---|---|
| Hudspeth | 2,675 | 824 | 1,030,223 | 6,031,215 | 46,610,055 | 127,853 | 126,265 | 1,589 |
| Hunt | 77,279 | 1,285 | 2,393,907 | 10,123,306 | 20,567,432 | 4,475,825 | 1,611,079 | 2,864,746 |
| Hutchinson | 26,878 | 478 | 319,974 | 1,461,737 | 772,357 | 1,568,284 | 583,975 | 984,309 |
| Irion | 2,851 | 247 | 101,575 | 1,160,609 | 71,898 | 186,138 | 154,209 | 31,929 |
| Jack | 8,967 | 574 | 329,192 | 3,155,734 | 6,058,713 | 570,741 | 439,819 | 130,922 |
| Jackson | 14,085 | 635 | 825,134 | 3,819,087 | 4,975,543 | 834,715 | 559,395 | 275,320 |
| Jasper | 36,923 | 738 | 1,153,907 | 3,259,341 | 15,435,959 | 2,050,570 | 797,854 | 1,252,715 |
| Jeff Davis | 2,651 | 469 | 177,286 | 1,775,261 | 6,619,537 | 190,502 | 147,588 | 42,914 |
| Jefferson | 210,299 | 1,123 | 4,547,540 | 8,183,941 | 26,674,197 | 13,380,645 | 4,386,012 | 8,994,633 |
| Jim Hogg | 4,571 | 288 | 180,290 | 560,665 | 12,910,086 | 303,023 | 247,938 | 55,086 |
| Jim Wells | 32,098 | 715 | 1,142,448 | 2,842,111 | 4,199,902 | 2,213,123 | 964,922 | 1,248,202 |
| Johnson | 125,648 | 918 | 2,745,873 | 4,834,775 | 23,209,376 | 7,633,553 | 2,330,905 | 5,302,648 |
| Jones | 16,406 | 1,010 | 475,778 | 3,114,027 | 8,850,953 | 1,010,877 | 691,091 | 319,787 |
| Karnes | 10,736 | 693 | 354,271 | 3,334,161 | 507,903 | 617,920 | 492,126 | 125,795 |
| Kaufman | 82,016 | 1,194 | 3,476,849 | 7,688,357 | 15,140,167 | 4,817,528 | 2,002,784 | 2,814,744 |
| Kendall | 40,075 | 444 | 844,051 | 2,336,945 | 152,137 | 2,424,156 | 1,514,409 | 909,746 |
| Kenedy | 655 | 188 | 461,921 | 458,947 | 636,410 | 29,432 | 28,981 | 451 |
| Kent | 1,710 | 325 | 51,167 | 1,340,586 | 72,531 | 80,060 | 78,052 | 2,008 |
| Kerr | 47,408 | 702 | 987,149 | 3,387,978 | 1,320,817 | 2,768,849 | 1,130,105 | 1,638,744 |
| Kimble | 5,508 | 687 | 465,493 | 1,815,538 | 923,108 | 299,911 | 267,412 | 32,499 |
| King | 429 | 199 | 70,456 | 979,759 | 69,866 | 47,225 | 46,979 | 245 |
| Kinney | 2,920 | 407 | 179,171 | 1,128,020 | 484,061 | 166,742 | 140,130 | 26,612 |
| Kleberg | 23,952 | 369 | 684,096 | 1,588,891 | 1,344,324 | 1,444,029 | 707,063 | 736,965 |
| Knox | 3,881 | 434 | 130,519 | 2,646,816 | 7,702,571 | 244,696 | 241,528 | 3,168 |
| Lamar | 48,434 | 983 | 1,157,776 | 5,251,925 | 12,594,233 | 3,019,907 | 1,191,738 | 1,828,169 |
| Lamb | 13,112 | 805 | 442,334 | 4,735,453 | 10,885,667 | 831,158 | 578,096 | 253,062 |
| Lampasas | 20,725 | 475 | 459,261 | 1,600,055 | 3,165,138 | 1,211,069 | 816,025 | 395,044 |
| La Salle | 3,946 | 649 | 557,932 | 2,965,169 | 19,885,979 | 244,468 | 214,188 | 30,280 |
| Lavaca | 22,286 | 641 | 514,508 | 2,270,438 | 2,341,795 | 1,289,062 | 681,507 | 607,554 |
| Lee | 19,087 | 531 | 625,314 | 1,783,031 | 7,966,818 | 1,208,152 | 680,193 | 527,959 |
| Leon | 16,789 | 834 | 1,203,173 | 3,634,659 | 6,053,920 | 1,005,185 | 554,563 | 450,622 |
| Liberty | 64,638 | 816 | 1,854,310 | 4,396,765 | 4,688,753 | 4,219,802 | 1,441,066 | 2,778,736 |
| Limestone | 21,689 | 770 | 705,154 | 3,461,951 | 2,334,430 | 1,277,520 | 702,058 | 575,462 |
| Lipscomb | 3,232 | 411 | 74,011 | 1,668,889 | 12,656 | 244,898 | 233,862 | 11,036 |
| Live Oak | 11,181 | 995 | 1,168,442 | 5,136,527 | 14,736,077 | 674,107 | 544,245 | 129,863 |
| Llano | 20,257 | 500 | 433,457 | 1,278,075 | 2,040,521 | 1,153,649 | 642,754 | 510,895 |
| Loving | 266 | 67 | 12,684 | 149,705 | 0 | 15,244 | 15,132 | 112 |
| Lubbock | 210,820 | 1,677 | 3,244,161 | 15,450,203 | 91,169,080 | 13,704,751 | 4,787,019 | 8,917,732 |
| Lynn | 5,743 | 7112 | 331,075 | 5,230,429 | 7,003,098 | 332,212 | 316,068 | 16,143 |
| Madison | 14,287 | 570 | 802,692 | 3,592,675 | 3,908,067 | 842,969 | 670,518 | 172,451 |
| Marion | 9,711 | 323 | 313,327 | 1,934,369 | 1,744,403 | 522,289 | 402,904 | 119,385 |
| Martin | 5,383 | 571 | 350,052 | 2,336,776 | 467,199 | 307,721 | 304,639 | 3,083 |
| Mason | 4,233 | 423 | 161,642 | 1,377,674 | 0 | 224,260 | 213,766 | 10,493 |
| Matagorda | 33,404 | 680 | 717,344 | 4,514,099 | 9,486,544 | 1,996,184 | 896,575 | 1,099,609 |
| Maverick | 27,352 | 488 | 674,759 | 2,326,320 | 11,294,816 | 1,761,258 | 705,809 | 1,055,449 |
| McCulloch | 9,238 | 608 | 272,636 | 2,169,517 | 4,535,839 | 524,964 | 435,582 | 89,382 |
| McLennan | 182,732 | 1,625 | 5,320,837 | 8,359,005 | 29,869,750 | 12,260,438 | 3,736,235 | 8,524,202 |
| McMullen | 2,202 | 317 | 112,170 | 1,033,136 | 1,922,086 | 209,511 | 170,795 | 38,715 |
| Medina | 38,693 | 745 | 1,031,813 | 4,002,563 | 2,010,990 | 2,232,551 | 1,103,133 | 1,129,418 |
| Menard | 2,638 | 346 | 130,152 | 3,829,730 | 713,604 | 129,967 | 127,950 | 2,018 |
| Midland | 117,049 | 957 | 1,661,894 | 3,993,905 | 12,465,149 | 8,078,194 | 2,540,260 | 5,537,933 |
| Milam | 24,597 | 689 | 774,589 | 5,755,075 | 14,521,188 | 1,422,042 | 711,734 | 710,308 |
| Mills | 6,226 | 432 | 232,542 | 1,588,594 | 10,459 | 333,922 | 322,777 | 11,145 |
| Mitchell | 6,531 | 661 | 504,069 | 2,879,152 | 337,985 | 349,206 | 313,033 | 36,173 |
| Montague | 21,918 | 861 | 702,651 | 4,247,654 | 2,520,547 | 1,338,938 | 690,442 | 648,496 |
| Montgomery | 288,071 | 1,166 | 6,543,051 | 12,302,941 | 46,680,964 | 17,909,708 | 5,501,280 | 12,408,428 |
| Moore | 18,628 | 467 | 463,872 | 1,833,195 | 693,040 | 1,308,818 | 607,306 | 701,512 |
| Morris | 13,429 | 356 | 449,291 | 1,899,849 | 2,347,651 | 785,274 | 469,921 | 315,354 |
| Morley | 1,614 | 331 | 61,736 | 1,207,474 | 192,455 | 92,330 | 90,916 | 1,414 |
| Nacogdoches | 49,347 | 946 | 1,680,261 | 7,612,285 | 11,474,645 | 2,921,197 | 1,242,464 | 1,678,733 |
| Navarro | 41,996 | 1,163 | 1,826,465 | 4,781,667 | 18,480,758 | 2,512,332 | 1,063,972 | 1,448,360 |
| Newton | 12,955 | 547 | 457,252 | 3,312,537 | 1,490,498 | 661,725 | 469,356 | 192,369 |
| Nolan | 14,431 | 695 | 776,040 | 4,251,043 | 3,738,578 | 917,912 | 582,613 | 335,299 |
| Nueces | 254,038 | 1,416 | 5,223,986 | 10,583,160 | 60,839,190 | 16,259,204 | 5,394,179 | 10,865,025 |
| Ochiltree | 10,591 | 428 | 206,284 | 897,839 | 7,173,503 | 726,647 | 538,996 | 187,651 |
| Oldham | 2,365 | 473 | 821,639 | 2,834,034 | 13,072,240 | 162,605 | 155,600 | 7,005 |
| Orange | 77,607 | 594 | 2,384,609 | 8,490,664 | 30,191,726 | 4,527,475 | 1,454,846 | 3,072,629 |
| Palo Pinto | 29,598 | 830 | 896,374 | 4,172,869 | 3,743,984 | 1,784,356 | 780,848 | 1,003,507 |
| Panola | 24,045 | 768 | 980,824 | 4,343,675 | 22,552,695 | 1,225,571 | 514,101 | 711,470 |
| Parker | 105,442 | 872 | 2,616,908 | 4,702,694 | 7,719,522 | 6,349,055 | 2,385,961 | 3,963,094 |
| Parmer | 9,521 | 611 | 369,368 | 2,256,482 | 283,898 | 661,992 | 508,863 | 153,130 |
| Pecos | 12,881 | 1,662 | 766,288 | 5,116,177 | 4,688,906 | 734,102 | 485,446 | 248,656 |
| Polk | 54,781 | 835 | 1,712,068 | 6,251,415 | 8,290,433 | 3,990,575 | 1,421,674 | 2,568,900 |

| COUNTY | Vehicles Registered | Lane Miles of Highways | Vehicle Miles Driven Daily | State Maintenance Expenditures | State Construction Expenditures | Vehicle Registration Fees | County Net Receipts | State Net Receipts |
|---|---|---|---|---|---|---|---|---|
| Potter | 100,167 | 8911 | 2,540,611 | 14,449,207 | 25,516,385 | 6,565,246 | 2,281,000 | 4,284,246 |
| Presidio | 6,209 | 546 | 184,228 | 1,672,125 | 6,021,180 | 380,483 | 290,080 | 90,403 |
| Rains | 12,240 | 268 | 287,534 | 1,590,252 | 1,743,479 | 603,691 | 411,398 | 192,292 |
| Randall | 107,095 | 893 | 1,207,995 | 4,269,152 | 16,750,080 | 6,767,860 | 2,460,239 | 4,307,621 |
| Reagan | 3,496 | 320 | 94,134 | 1,770,964 | 120,111 | 233,309 | 207,794 | 25,516 |
| Real | 3,466 | 297 | 83,767 | 1,212,460 | 455,839 | 204,077 | 186,229 | 17,848 |
| Red River | 13,809 | 748 | 412,971 | 2,797,754 | 4,159,398 | 741,272 | 532,735 | 208,537 |
| Reeves | 8,735 | 1,179 | 639,331 | 3,438,215 | 2,083,574 | 485,473 | 403,933 | 81,540 |
| Refugio | 7,246 | 464 | 725,596 | 4,407,443 | 7,085,234 | 445,008 | 335,348 | 109,661 |
| Roberts | 1,067 | 241 | 62,500 | 535,799 | 2,429,228 | 53,699 | 53,041 | 658 |
| Robertson | 15,021 | 625 | 717,080 | 2,244,901 | 9,484,871 | 877,688 | 575,397 | 302,291 |
| Rockwall | 47,862 | 327 | 1,348,732 | 2,121,143 | 23,573,112 | 3,177,498 | 1,010,052 | 2,167,447 |
| Runnels | 12,238 | 741 | 343,046 | 4,018,317 | 1,138,273 | 783,935 | 551,866 | 232,069 |
| Rusk | 43,886 | 1,167 | 1,242,559 | 5,041,961 | 23,850,527 | 2,645,648 | 1,029,183 | 1,616,465 |
| Sabine | 10,665 | 474 | 304,053 | 3,547,914 | 2,365,219 | 624,662 | 446,381 | 178,282 |
| San Augustine | 8,458 | 532 | 286,622 | 4,496,572 | 3,212,672 | 497,671 | 392,894 | 104,777 |
| San Jacinto | 19,597 | 510 | 711,797 | 4,448,820 | 7,368,740 | 1,227,400 | 607,959 | 619,441 |
| San Patricio | 55,879 | 922 | 1,830,973 | 2,959,274 | 5,908,336 | 3,480,322 | 1,321,966 | 2,158,356 |
| San Saba | 7,303 | 437 | 151,008 | 2,409,897 | 5,507,340 | 420,016 | 400,377 | 19,639 |
| Schleicher | 3,483 | 362 | 128,786 | 1,211,791 | 784,010 | 201,217 | 188,838 | 12,379 |
| Scurry | 17,737 | 674 | 557,110 | 2,383,739 | 5,612,529 | 1,331,989 | 668,327 | 663,662 |
| Shackelford | 3,746 | 353 | 156,394 | 3,221,593 | 4,220,886 | 234,927 | 213,063 | 21,864 |
| Shelby | 23,413 | 858 | 813,575 | 6,874,537 | 21,906,856 | 1,589,007 | 758,951 | 830,056 |
| Sherman | 2,905 | 429 | 263,412 | 1,726,499 | 8,892,029 | 183,015 | 180,620 | 2,395 |
| Smith | 181,607 | 1,570 | 4,589,682 | 9,193,517 | 14,327,726 | 11,044,253 | 3,914,559 | 7,129,694 |
| Somervell | 7,537 | 184 | 243,107 | 841,359 | 6,596,444 | 358,590 | 247,000 | 111,590 |
| Starr | 28,886 | 477 | 886,725 | 2,358,376 | 2,594,819 | 1,816,313 | 801,058 | 1,015,255 |
| Stephens | 9,799 | 561 | 230,290 | 1,983,053 | 1,228,374 | 585,408 | 443,516 | 141,892 |
| Sterling | 1,716 | 265 | 153,933 | 662,345 | 5,318,015 | 73,952 | 72,817 | 1,134 |
| Stonewall | 1,917 | 329 | 90,066 | 1,610,490 | 3,197,155 | 121,370 | 119,940 | 1,430 |
| Sutton | 5,699 | 592 | 473,884 | 2,068,959 | 4,303,380 | 414,303 | 304,880 | 109,422 |
| Swisher | 6,302 | 806 | 354,775 | 2,162,041 | 433,216 | 387,962 | 350,981 | 36,981 |
| Tarrant | 1,316,357 | 3,083 | 26,868,091 | 23,925,186 | 166,279,669 | 85,465,669 | 26,928,130 | 58,537,539 |
| Taylor | 116,553 | 1,189 | 2,051,826 | 5,302,721 | 18,328,633 | 7,445,305 | 2,671,645 | 4,773,660 |
| Terrell | 1,153 | 353 | 90,531 | 1,916,095 | 58,456 | 56,396 | 55,652 | 744 |
| Terry | 11,652 | 630 | 402,516 | 3,186,496 | 35,575 | 770,072 | 557,520 | 212,552 |
| Throckmorton | 1,964 | 341 | 77,421 | 1,537,492 | 758,599 | 103,458 | 102,122 | 1,335 |
| Titus | 29,234 | 541 | 979,245 | 4,574,615 | 8,310,189 | 1,720,997 | 874,236 | 846,761 |
| Tom Green | 97,760 | 968 | 1,368,414 | 5,570,826 | 26,173,750 | 6,040,918 | 2,175,194 | 3,865,723 |
| Travis | 700,570 | 1,712 | 15,863,981 | 16,044,704 | 110,419,238 | 45,099,386 | 16,022,998 | 29,076,388 |
| Trinity | 12,684 | 429 | 352,584 | 3,062,810 | 11,393,578 | 750,597 | 491,758 | 258,839 |
| Tyler | 18,344 | 518 | 542,475 | 2,579,295 | 1,019,415 | 1,018,176 | 573,226 | 444,950 |
| Upshur | 35,989 | 759 | 914,453 | 7,889,040 | 17,818,902 | 2,018,575 | 893,880 | 1,124,696 |
| Upton | 3,397 | 388 | 149,013 | 1,111,318 | 127,417 | 198,436 | 165,434 | 33,001 |
| Uvalde | 21,701 | 729 | 695,683 | 2,316,960 | 5,828,349 | 1,527,947 | 633,510 | 894,437 |
| Val Verde | 36,375 | 712 | 470,114 | 3,148,172 | 4,179,122 | 2,297,648 | 946,138 | 1,351,510 |
| Van Zandt | 53,891 | 1,163 | 2,024,483 | 5,853,043 | 9,063,912 | 3,046,900 | 1,169,757 | 1,877,144 |
| Victoria | 82,472 | 758 | 1,828,540 | 3,715,093 | 37,083,006 | 5,079,744 | 1,805,354 | 3,274,390 |
| Walker | 40,329 | 792 | 1,927,488 | 5,461,911 | 11,471,291 | 2,382,043 | 1,086,675 | 1,295,368 |
| Waller | 38,835 | 584 | 1,671,023 | 6,775,683 | 4,964,300 | 2,340,899 | 1,313,476 | 1,027,423 |
| Ward | 10,451 | 670 | 466,644 | 2,870,063 | 4,759,374 | 611,188 | 327,478 | 283,710 |
| Washington | 33,952 | 657 | 1,121,266 | 2,270,994 | 14,675,287 | 2,226,106 | 945,312 | 1,280,795 |
| Webb | 113,753 | 1,006 | 2,346,431 | 4,743,059 | 39,373,336 | 8,595,616 | 2,673,146 | 5,922,470 |
| Wharton | 40,504 | 882 | 1,431,883 | 5,664,310 | 5,256,458 | 2,799,810 | 1,018,526 | 1,781,284 |
| Wheeler | 5,923 | 672 | 499,055 | 1,368,954 | 24,318,764 | 324,063 | 311,032 | 13,031 |
| Wichita | 115,120 | 1,087 | 1,880,862 | 6,697,684 | 24,240,988 | 7,008,284 | 2,499,742 | 4,508,542 |
| Wilbarger | 13,407 | 736 | 612,161 | 3,656,923 | 8,270,070 | 780,501 | 566,049 | 214,452 |
| Willacy | 12,346 | 479 | 444,914 | 2,630,269 | 11,984,905 | 797,965 | 571,611 | 226,355 |
| Williamson | 245,033 | 1,440 | 5,701,792 | 9,054,464 | 97,313,192 | 15,725,398 | 5,196,339 | 10,529,059 |
| Wilson | 31,298 | 745 | 708,895 | 2,871,922 | 8,632,855 | 1,764,097 | 792,625 | 971,472 |
| Winkler | 6,588 | 295 | 137,710 | 913,631 | 586,371 | 415,924 | 297,560 | 118,364 |
| Wise | 61,357 | 852 | 2,310,278 | 7,295,039 | 6,810,594 | 4,135,486 | 1,503,770 | 2,631,717 |
| Wood | 43,690 | 896 | 806,394 | 4,723,299 | 1,092,542 | 2,491,843 | 1,013,754 | 1,478,090 |
| Yoakum | 8,300 | 427 | 225,911 | 1,858,863 | 124,901 | 564,239 | 438,074 | 126,166 |
| Young | 20,729 | 707 | 355,443 | 2,854,063 | 2,470,342 | 1,320,637 | 669,765 | 650,872 |
| Zapata | 7,684 | 250 | 377,078 | 1,650,309 | 567,695 | 476,489 | 315,007 | 161,482 |
| Zavala | 6,793 | 542 | 293,699 | 1,493,734 | 2,522,854 | 411,081 | 303,883 | 107,198 |
| **Total** | 18,248,018 | 188,388 | 428,868,139 | 1,109,045,155 | 3,676,728,816 | 1,165,239,674 | 430,237,097 | 735,002,577 |
| State collect. | | | | | | 57,682,709 | | 57,682,709 |
| Exempt reg. | 397,740 | | | | | | | |
| Special veh. | 61,728 | | | | | | | |
| **Grand Total** | 18,707,486 | 188,388 | 428,868,139 | $1,109,045,155 | $3,676,728,816 | $1,222,922,384 | $430,237,097 | $792,685,287 |

# Motor Vehicle Accidents, Losses

| Year | Number Killed | †Number Injured | Accidents by Kinds | | | | ‡ Vehicle Miles Traveled | | | |
|------|------|------|------|------|------|------|------|------|------|------|
| | | | Fatal | ÷ Injury | ÷ Non-Injury | ÷ Total | *Number (000,000) | Deaths per 100 mil miles | Economic Loss (000,000) |
| 1960 | 2,254 | 127,980 | 1,842 | 71,100 | 239,300 | 312,242 | 46,353 | 4.9 | $ 350 |
| 1961 | 2,314 | 132,570 | 1,899 | 73,650 | 248,600 | 324,149 | 47,937 | 4.8 | 356 |
| 1962 | 2,421 | 144,943 | 2,002 | 80,524 | 277,680 | 360,206 | 49,883 | 4.9 | 388 |
| 1963 | 2,729 | 161,543 | 2,251 | 89,746 | 307,920 | 399,917 | 52,325 | 5.2 | 433 |
| 1964 | 3,006 | 182,081 | 2,486 | 101,156 | 351,120 | 454,762 | 55,677 | 5.4 | 487 |
| 1965 | 3,028 | 186,062 | 2,460 | 103,368 | 365,160 | 470,988 | *52,163 | 5.8 | 498 |
| 1966 | 3,406 | 208,310 | 2,784 | 115,728 | 406,460 | 524,972 | 55,261 | 6.2 | 557 |
| 1967 | 3,367 | 205,308 | 2,778 | 114,060 | 768,430 | 885,268 | 58,124 | 5.8 | 793 |
| 1968 | 3,481 | 216,972 | 2,902 | 120,540 | 816,830 | 940,272 | 62,794 | 5.5 | 837 |
| 1969 | 3,551 | 223,000 | 2,913 | 124,000 | 850,000 | 976,913 | 67,742 | 5.2 | 955 |
| 1970 | 3,560 | 223,000 | 2,965 | 124,000 | 886,000 | 1,012,965 | ‡ 68,031 | 5.2 | 1,042 |
| 1971 | 3,594 | 224,000 | 2,993 | 124,000 | 890,000 | 1,016,993 | 70,709 | 5.1 | 1,045 |
| 1972 | 3,688 | 128,158 | 3,099 | 83,607 | 346,292 | 432,998 | 76,690 | 4.8 | 1,035 |
| 1973 | 3,692 | 132,635 | 3,074 | 87,631 | 373,521 | 464,226 | 80,615 | 4.6 | 1,035 |
| 1974 | 3,046 | 123,611 | 2,626 | 83,341 | 348,227 | 434,194 | 78,290 | 3.9 | 1,095 |
| 1975 | 3,429 | 138,962 | 2,945 | 92,510 | 373,141 | 468,596 | 84,575 | 4.1 | 1,440 |
| 1976 | 3,230 | 145,282 | 2,780 | 96,348 | 380,075 | 479,203 | 91,279 | 3.5 | 1,485 |
| 1977 | 3,698 | 161,635 | 3,230 | 106,923 | 393,848 | 504,001 | 96,998 | 3.8 | 1,960 |
| 1978 | ¶ 3,980 | 178,228 | 3,468 | 117,998 | **304,830 | **426,296 | 102,624 | 3.9 | 2,430 |
| 1979 | 4,229 | 184,550 | 3,685 | 122,793 | 322,336 | 448,814 | 101,909 | 4.1 | 2,580 |
| 1980 | 4,424 | 185,964 | 3,863 | 123,577 | 305,500 | 432,940 | 103,255 | 4.3 | 3,010 |
| 1981 | 4,701 | 206,196 | 4,137 | 136,396 | 317,484 | 458,017 | 111,036 | 4.2 | 3,430 |
| 1982 | 4,271 | 204,666 | 3,752 | 135,859 | 312,159 | 451,770 | ††124,910 | 3.4 | 3,375 |
| 1983 | 3,823 | 208,157 | ¶ 3,328 | 137,695 | 302,876 | 443,899 | 129,309 | 3.0 | 3,440 |
| 1984 | 3,913 | 220,720 | 3,466 | 145,543 | 293,285 | 442,294 | 137,280 | 2.9 | §3,795 |
| 1985 | 3,682 | 231,009 | 3,270 | 151,657 | 300,531 | 452,188 | 143,500 | 2.6 | 3,755 |
| 1986 | 3,568 | 234,120 | 3,121 | 154,514 | 298,079 | 452,593 | 150,474 | 2.4 | 3,782 |
| 1987 | 3,261 | 226,895 | 2,881 | 146,913 | 246,175 | 395,969 | 151,221 | 2.2 | 3,913 |
| 1988 | 3,395 | 238,845 | 3,004 | 152,004 | 237,703 | 392,711 | 152,819 | 2.2 | 4,515 |
| 1989 | 3,361 | 243,030 | 2,926 | 153,356 | 233,967 | 390,249 | 159,679 | 2.1 | 4,873 |
| 1990 | 3,243 | 262,576 | 2,882 | 162,424 | 216,140 | 381,446 | 163,103 | 2.0 | 4,994 |
| 1991 | 3,079 | 263,430 | 2,690 | 161,470 | 207,288 | 371,448 | 162,780 | 1.9 | 5,604 |
| 1992 | 3,057 | 282,025 | 2,690 | 170,513 | 209,152 | 382,355 | 162,769 | 1.9 | 6,725 |
| 1993 | 3,037 | 298,891 | 2,690 | 178,194 | 209,533 | 390,417 | 167,988 | 1.8 | §11,784 |
| 1994 | 3,142 | 326,837 | 2,710 | 192,014 | 219,890 | 414,614 | 172,976 | 1.8 | 12,505 |
| 1995 | 3,172 | 334,259 | 2,790 | 196,093 | 152,190 | 351,073 | 183,103 | 1.7 | § 13,005 |
| 1996 | 3,738 | 350,397 | 3,247 | 204,635 | 90,261 | 298,143 | 187,064 | 2.0 | 7,766 |
| 1997 | 3,508 | 347,881 | 3,079 | 205,595 | 97,315 | 305,989 | 194,665 | 1.8 | 7,662 |
| 1998 | 3,576 | 338,661 | 3,160 | 202,223 | 102,732 | 308,115 | 201,989 | 1.8 | 8,780 |
| 1999 | 3,519 | 339,448 | 3,106 | 203,220 | 105,375 | 311,701 | 213,847 | 1.6 | 8,729 |
| 2000 | 3,775 | 341,097 | 3,247 | 205,569 | 110,174 | 318,990 | 210,340 | 1.8 | $ 9,163 |

*Vehicle miles traveled since 1964 were estimated on the basis of new data furnished by U.S. Bureau of Public Roads through National Safety Council.

† In August 1967, amended estimating formula received from National Safety Council. Starting 1972, actual reported injuries are listed rather than estimates.

‡ Vehicle miles traveled estimated by Texas Highway Department starting with 1970. Method of calculation varies from that used for prior years.

§ Economic loss formula changed. Last changed in July 1995, when only property damage accidents having at least one vehicle towed due to damages is tabulated.

¶ Change in counting fatalities. In 1978, counted when injury results in death within 90 days of accident. In 1983,counted when injury results in death within 30 days.

**Total accidents and non-injury accidents for 1978 and after cannot be compared with years prior to 1978 due to changes in reporting laws.

†† Method of calculating vehicle miles traveled revised 1982 by Texas Department of Transportation. The 1981 mileage adjusted for comparison purposes.

Source: Analysis Section, Accident Records Bureau of the **Texas Department of Public Safety**, Austin.

## Accidents by road class

| 2000 | Miles of road | Accidents |
|------|------|------|
| City/Town | 78,686 | 124,698 |
| Interstate | 3,233 | 47,561 |
| U.S./State | 28,263 | 93,022 |
| Farm-Market | 40,984 | 33,892 |
| County | 142,170 | 19,817 |
| Total | 301,081* | 318,990 |

*Total includes park and toll roads and interstate frontage.

Texas Department of Public Safety and Texas Department of Transportation.

# Drivers' Licenses

In 2002, the Texas Department of Public Safety issued 5,200,446 driver's licenses and identification cards, including renewals.

The following list shows the number of licensed drivers by year for Texas and for all the states. Sources are the Texas Department of Public Safety and the Federal Highway Administration.

| Year | Texas licensed drivers | Total U.S. licensed drivers |
|------|------|------|
| 2002 | **14,639,132** | NA |
| 2001 | 14,303,799 | 191,275,719 |
| 2000 | 14,024,305 | 190,625,023 |
| 1999 | 13,718,319 | 187,170,420 |
| 1998 | 13,419,288 | 184,980,177 |
| 1997 | 12,833,603 | 182,709,204 |
| 1996 | 12,568,265 | 179,539,340 |
| 1995 | 12,369,243 | 176,628,482 |
| 1994 | 12,109,960 | 175,403,465 |
| 1993 | 11,876,268 | 173,149,313 |
| 1992 | 11,437,571 | 173,125,396 |
| 1991 | 11,293,184 | 168,995,076 |
| 1990 | 11,136,694 | 167,015,250 |
| 1989 | 11,103,511 | 165,555,295 |
| 1988 | 11,080,702 | 162,853,255 |
| 1987 | 11,153,472 | 161,818,461 |
| 1986 | 11,129,193 | 159,487,000 |
| 1985 | 10,809,078 | 156,868,277 |
| 1984 | 10,855,549 | 155,423,709 |
| 1983 | 11,406,433 | 154,389,178 |
| 1982 | 10,154,386 | 150,233,659 |
| 1981 | 9,673,885 | 147,075,169 |
| 1980 | 9,287,286 | 145,295,036 |
| 1979 | 8,945,853 | 143,283,995 |
| 1978 | 8,568,930 | 140,843,907 |
| 1975 | 7,509,497 | 129,790,666 |
| 1970 | 6,380,057 | 111,542,787 |
| 1965 | 5,413,887 | 98,502,152 |
| 1960 | 4,352,168 | 87,252,563 |
| 1955 | 3,874,834 | 74,685,949 |
| 1950 | 2,687,349 | 59,322,278 |

— The driving age in Texas changed in 1967 from 14 to 16 years of age with driver's education.
— The first photos appeared on Texas driver's licenses in 1967.
Texas Department of Public Safety.

# Railroads in Texas

All data in the charts below are for the year **2000**, the latest statistics available. Included are reports for tons of freight transported by rail, the number of carloads moved within the state and comparisons with other states. A complete list of railroads operating in Texas is at the beginning of the counties section on page 139.

| Texas Freight Railroads | Miles Operated |
|---|---|
| Union Pacific Railroad Co. | 6,190 |
| Burlington Northern/Santa Fe Rwy. Co. | 4,806 |
| Kansas City Southern Railway Co. | 381 |
| Class I (total of three above) | 11,377 |
| Regional | 924 |
| Local | 678 |
| Switching & Terminal | 1,027 |
| Total | 14,006 |
| TOTAL exluding trackage rights* | 10,749 |

*Trackage rights – track provided by another railroad.
Source: Association of American Railroads.

| Rank | Miles of rail | Rank | Car-loads |
|---|---|---|---|
| Texas | 10,749 | Illinois | 10,255,429 |
| Illinois | 7,368 | Texas | 7,418,716 |
| California | 6,405 | Missouri | 6,549,956 |
| Ohio | 5,383 | Ohio | 6,294,306 |
| Kansas | 5,167 | Indiana | 6,204,777 |
| Pennsylvania | 5,103 | California | 5,356,141 |
| Georgia | 4,734 | Wyoming | 4,997,131 |
| Minnesota | 4,417 | Nebraska | 4,901,032 |
| Indiana | 4,178 | Iowa | 4,782,916 |
| Iowa | 4,162 | Kansas | 4,702,594 |

Source: Association of American Railroads.

## Freight Traffic in Texas

| Tons originated | | Tons terminated | |
|---|---|---|---|
| Chemicals | 40,681,860 | Coal | 53,817,611 |
| Nonmetallic Minerals | 22,292,999 | Nonmetallic Minerals | 28,453,140 |
| Petroleum | 7,848,888 | Farm Products | 27,096,649 |
| Mixed Freight | 6,847,440 | Chemicals | 21,346,584 |
| Stone/Glass Products | 4,884,136 | Food Products | 10,354,589 |
| All other | 27,923,008 | All other | 48,368,995 |
| Total | 110,478,331 | Total | 189,437,568 |

Source: Association of American Railroads.
Total rail tons orginated in the United States in 2000 was 1,855,852,229. Total rail tons terminated in the United States in 2000 was 1,918,580,562.

| State Rank | Freight tons carried |
|---|---|
| Illinois | 454,446,412 |
| Wyoming | 417,136,246 |
| Nebraska | 396,710,156 |
| Missouri | 336,768,880 |
| Texas | 327,464,869 |
| Ohio | 307,282,526 |
| Kentucky | 303,720,347 |
| Indiana | 279,497,149 |
| Kansas | 262,816,126 |
| Iowa | 260,631,701 |

A Union Pacific freight train heads east over a railroad bridge just west of Loraine in Mitchell County. File photo.

# Amtrak in Texas: Finances Limit Expansion

**By Suzanne Marta**

Amtrak passenger rail service is grappling with financial and travel industry woes, both nationally and in Texas.

Expansion projects, including several in the Lone Star state, have been put on hold as the company gets its finances in order.

Amtrak is seeking nearly $9 billion in funding aid over the next five years to stabilize itself and reduce a backlog of equipment maintenance at a national level. The company asked Congress for $1.8 billion during 2004 – part of which would go to support three passenger routes in Texas.

Like many transportation modes, Amtrak ridership levels stagnated immediately after the Sept. 11, 2001, terrorist attacks in New York and Washington D.C. But ridership began growing again in the first part of 2003, at rates that exceeded 30 percent on some Texas routes.

Amtrak serves 20 Texas cities, though riders primarily board in Fort Worth, San Antonio, Dallas, Houston, Longview and Austin. During the 2002 fiscal year, which ended Sept. 30, Amtrak employed 245, with wages exceeding $8.1 million.

Amtrak recently spent $12.9 million on goods and services for station upgrades and other goods and services in Fort Worth, Houston and Plano.

Ridership has been growing steadily on Amtrak's daily Texas Eagle route, which runs from Chicago to San Antonio, with stops in Dallas, Fort Worth, and Austin.

The Texas Eagle is one of Amtrak's 18 national network trains, and offers coach and sleeping car service, a dining car and a "sightseer" lounge for the more than 1,300 mile route.

Three times a week, the route offers connecting service to the Sunset Limited running west to Los Angeles.

Ticket sales for sleeping accommodations on the Texas Eagle made steady and significant gains in the first part of 2003. The Texas Eagle drew 129,208 passengers during the 2002 fiscal year.

The growth is considered positive news. The Texas Eagle route was nearly eliminated in the mid-1990s, before the state of Texas came up with a loan that kept the trains running three times a week. Amtrak paid off the loan ahead of schedule and the three-days per week service was expanded to daily in 2000.

The Texas Eagle is supported by a volunteer marketing group called TEMPO, or the Texas Eagle Marketing & Performance Organization. Members of the group, which was formed in 1987, include elected officials from cities along the route, citizens involved in transportation or tourism issues, and union and management Amtrak employees. TEMPO posts information about the trains, tourist events, hotels and car rental agencies in each of the Texas cities served on the route. For information, go to www.texaseagle.com.

The Sunset Limited runs between Los Angeles and Orlando, Fla., with stops in El Paso, San Antonio and Houston.

Proposals had been under discussion to change the Texas portion of the trip to run from Houston and up to Dallas-Fort Worth before heading west to El Paso, but are now on hold.

Ridership on the Sunset Limited grew to 97,366 during the 2002 fiscal year.

The Heartland Flyer has operated daily since 1999. The route goes from Fort Worth to Oklahoma City through Gainesville, and drew more than 52,500 passengers during the 2002 fiscal year.

The Heartland Flyer also provides connections to Amtrak's Texas Eagle and Sunset Limited routes.

*Suzanne Marta is a staff reporter with* The Dallas Morning News.

## Amtrak Passengers On/Off at Texas Stations, 1993-2002

| City | 2002 | 2001 | 2000 | 1999 | 1998 | 1997 | 1996 | 1995 | 1994 | 1993 |
|---|---|---|---|---|---|---|---|---|---|---|
| Alpine | 1,474 | 2,141 | 2,380 | 2,281 | 1,884 | 1,934 | 2,373 | 2,417 | 2,668 | 2,767 |
| Austin | 14,801 | 18,374 | 17,276 | 11,516 | 11,173 | 8,185 | 10,783 | 10,440 | 12,116 | 18,954 |
| Beaumont | 1,543 | 2,233 | 2,375 | 2,529 | 2,008 | 2,237 | 2,495 | 2,572 | 2,330 | 2,772 |
| Cleburne | 1,359 | 1,494 | 1,429 | 814 | 618 | 519 | 699 | 655 | 758 | 1,649 |
| College Station-Bryan | — | — | — | — | — | — | — | 2,346 | 3,300 | 9,447 |
| Corsicana | — | — | — | — | — | — | — | 507 | 783 | 1,766 |
| Dallas | 26,580 | 33,287 | 32,649 | 24,197 | 24,526 | 19,815 | 25,851 | 34,197 | 40,991 | 69,823 |
| Del Rio | 931 | 1,123 | 1,639 | 1,624 | 1,103 | 1,134 | 1,213 | 1,369 | 1,532 | 1,221 |
| El Paso | 8,253 | 11,657 | 12,858 | 13,591 | 13,054 | 10,918 | 14,027 | 17,580 | 20,528 | 22,860 |
| Fort Worth | 57,554 | 66,654 | 70,796 | 46,166 | 10,278 | 8,878 | 11,005 | 9,972 | 11,424 | 20,156 |
| Gainesville | 10,844 | 14,096 | 15,764 | 9,574 | — | — | — | — | — | — |
| Houston | 13,776 | 16,544 | 17,336 | 16,038 | 15,391 | 16,663 | 16,005 | 29,158 | 32,314 | 48,638 |
| Longview | 16,039 | 16,610 | 13,305 | 13,585 | 12,666 | 11,525 | 12,439 | 8,459 | 7,142 | 10,679 |
| Marshall | 2,982 | 3,594 | 2,709 | 2,897 | 2,233 | 2,448 | 3,100 | 3,989 | 4,656 | 7,052 |
| McGregor | 1,967 | 2,010 | 2,220 | 1,366 | 1,349 | 1,324 | 1,469 | 1,243 | 1,435 | 3,134 |
| Mineola | 2,212 | 2,455 | 2,981 | 1,855 | 1,527 | 1,500 | 1,836 | — | — | — |
| San Antonio | 34,880 | 42,955 | 45,254 | 35,234 | 42,384 | 47,289 | 34,144 | 33,584 | 35,544 | 50,525 |
| Sanderson | 145 | 212 | 274 | 417 | 163 | 205 | 274 | 326 | 366 | 317 |
| San Marcos | 1,984 | 2,123 | 1,654 | 892 | 828 | 684 | 835 | 860 | 1,152 | 1,933 |
| Taylor | 1,633 | 2,155 | 1,597 | 820 | 958 | 815 | 1,727 | 1,406 | 1,495 | 3,009 |
| Temple | 6,273 | 7,115 | 6,482 | 3,982 | 3,730 | 2,846 | 3,038 | 2,972 | 3,371 | 7,684 |
| Texarkana | 4,326 | 5,466 | 5,732 | 4,507 | 4,555 | 4,536 | 4,173 | 4,914 | 5,689 | 7,821 |
| Totals | 209,556 | 253,666 | 262,709 | 193,885 | 150,428 | 143,455 | 147,486 | 168,966 | 189,594 | 292,207 |

*Source: Amtrak (National Railroad Passenger Corporation) 2003.*

# Aviation in Texas

Source: Texas Transportation Institute

Air transportation is a vital and vigorous part of the Texas economy, and Texans are major users of air transportation. The state's airport system ranks as one of the busiest and largest in the nation.

The state's 47,533 active pilots represent 7.8 percent of the nation's pilots.

The State of Texas has long been committed to providing air transportation to the public. In 1945, the Texas Aeronautics Commission (TAC) was created and directed by the legislature to encourage, foster, and assist in the development of aeronautics within the state, and to encourage the establishment of airports and air navigational facilities.

The Commission's first annual report of December 31, 1946, stated that Texas had 592 designated airports and 7,756 civilian aircraft.

The commitment to providing air transportation was strengthened on October 18, 1989, when the TAC became the Texas Department of Aviation (TDA). This commitment was further strengthened on September 1, 1991, when the Texas Department of Transportation (TxDOT) was created and the TDA became the Aviation Division within the Department.

In 2001, Texas' commercial service airports with scheduled passenger service enplaned more than 69.1 million passengers; scheduled carriers served 27 Texas airports in 24 Texas cities, and more than 91 percent of the state's population lived within 50 miles of an airport with scheduled air passenger service.

Dallas/Fort Worth International, Dallas Love Field, Houston George Bush Intercontinental, and Houston's William P. Hobby together accounted for 76 percent of these enplanements.

Texas leads the nation in the number of landing facilities with more than 1,600, followed by California with approximately 1,000.

One of TxDOT's goals is to develop a statewide system of airports that will provide adequate air access to the population and economic centers of the state.

In the Texas Aeronautical System Plan, TxDOT has identified 300 airports that are needed to meet the forecast aviation demand and to maximize access by aircraft to the state's population, business, and agricultural and mineral resource centers. Of these 300 airports, 27 are commercial service airports, 23 are reliever airports, and 250 are general aviation airports.

Commercial service airports provide scheduled passenger service. The reliever airports provide alternative landing facilities in the metropolitan areas separate

## Texas Air History

Source: FAA
Airline passenger traffic enplaned in Texas by scheduled certificated carriers.

| Fiscal Year | Passengers |
|---|---|
| 1957 | 2,808,558 |
| 1967 | 7,983,634 |
| 1977 | 15,871,147 |
| 1980 | 25,303,214 |
| 1981 | 27,449,480 |
| 1982 | 29,541,788 |
| 1983 | 30,853,297 |
| 1984 | 35,130,762 |
| 1985 | 38,913,027 |
| 1986 | 39,957,392 |
| 1987 | 41,493,225 |
| 1988 | 42,655,971 |
| 1989 | 45,348,326 |
| 1990 | 46,435,641 |
| 1991 | 45,825,027 |
| 1992 | 48,869,034 |
| 1993 | 50,594,658 |
| 1994 | 55,633,180 |
| 1995 | 57,751,285 |
| 1996 | 60,344,460 |
| 1997 | 60,329,687 |
| 1998 | 61,712,217 |
| 1999 | 62,522,075 |
| 2000 | 65,109,179 |

## Passenger Enplanements by Airport

Source: Quarterly Aviation Activity Report, Texas Department of Transportation, Division of Aviation.
*By calendar year.

| City | 1995 | 1997 | 1999* | Percent change | 2001* |
|---|---|---|---|---|---|
| Abilene | 69,555 | 52,864 | 52,714 | 19 | 62,628 |
| Amarillo | 454,536 | 450,432 | 434,110 | -2 | 423,297 |
| Austin | 2,658,039 | 2,948,701 | 3,298,729 | 118 | 7,199,322 |
| Beaumont | 108,520 | 112,456 | 99,343 | -26 | 73,989 |
| Brownsville | — | 81,439 | 70,866 | 0 | 70,854 |
| Brownwood | 2,015 | — | 1,717 | 22 | 2,090 |
| College Station | 85,331 | 93,331 | 94,414 | -9 | 86,115 |
| Corpus Christi | 511,841 | 471,914 | 474,027 | 73 | 821,752 |
| D/FW Intl. | 27,013,761 | 28,152,220 | 29,965,777 | -7 | 27,741,848 |
| Dallas/Love | 3,355,238 | 3,413,519 | 3,409,920 | -2 | 3,350,234 |
| El Paso | 1,835,162 | 1,634,578 | 1,664,890 | 17 | 1,942,543 |
| Harlingen | 489,082 | 461,619 | 469,214 | -7 | 438,565 |
| Houston/Bush | 10,165,671 | 13,212,686 | 16,447,012 | 6 | 17,361,526 |
| Houston/Hobby | 4,111,175 | 3,949,236 | 4,422,032 | -2 | 4,318,209 |
| Houston/Ellington | NA | 50,503 | 49,776 | -36 | 32,064 |
| Killeen | 59,126 | 84,963 | 89,131 | 8 | 96,572 |
| Laredo | 59,948 | 67,664 | 89,524 | -16 | 74,911 |
| Longview | 33,761 | 26,779 | 30,092 | -1 | 29,738 |
| Lubbock | 602,680 | 592,101 | 570,452 | -6 | 535,366 |
| McAllen | 313,082 | 313,506 | 325,861 | -8 | 298,298 |
| Midland | 566,904 | 527,760 | 487,533 | -8 | 450,127 |
| San Angelo | 52,674 | 41,404 | 41,639 | 15 | 47,682 |
| San Antonio | 3,058,274 | 3,343,818 | 3,522,946 | -2 | 3,448,484 |
| Texarkana | 45,242 | 36,367 | 43,527 | -24 | 33,034 |
| Tyler | 78,524 | 69,639 | 77,795 | -18 | 63,834 |
| Victoria | 19,517 | 21,656 | 20,962 | -22 | 16,356 |
| Waco | 55,824 | 58,742 | 56,147 | 7 | 60,135 |
| Wichita Falls | 59,275 | 53,942 | 55,754 | -15 | 47,533 |
| **Total** | **57,751,285** | **60,329,687** | **66,365,904** | **4** | **69,127,106** |

from the commercial service airports, and, together with the transport airports, provide access for business and executive turbine-powered aircraft.

The general and basic utility airports provide access for single- and multi-engine piston-powered aircraft to smaller communities throughout the state.

TxDOT is charged by the legislature with planning, programming, and implementing improvement projects at the general aviation airports. In carrying out these responsibilities, TxDOT channels the Airport Improvement Program (AIP) funds provided by the Federal Aviation Administration (FAA) for all general aviation airports in Texas.

Since 1993, TxDOT has participated in the FAA's state block grant demonstration program. Under this program, TxDOT assumes most of the FAA's responsibility for the administration of the AIP funds for general aviation airports.

The Aviation Facilities Development Program (AFDP) oversees planning and research, assists with engineering and technical services, and provides financial assistance through state grants and loans to public bodies operating airports for the purpose of establishing, enlarging, or repairing airports.

The 77th Legislature appropriated funds to TxDOT which subsequently allocated a portion of those funds to the Aviation Division. TxDOT allocated approximately $15 million annually for the 2002-2003 biennium to the Aviation Division in order to help implement and administer the AFDP.

The Aeronautical Services and Informational Section provides specialized training programs, aeronautical publications, and safety information to individuals and groups throughout the state who are involved or interested in aviation.

Scheduled passenger traffic (air carrier and commuters) continued to grow from 1999 to 2001 but at a slower pace than in the previous period. Scheduled passenger enplanements in Texas increased by more than 2.76 million or 4 percent over the period.

The largest growth occurred at Austin (118 percent)

where a new airport was opened. Other airports experiencing growth since 1999 include Abilene, Corpus Christi, El Paso, Houston Intercontinental, Killeen, San Angelo, and Waco. All of the other airports showed declines in passenger enplanements. This is widely believed to be a result of the September 11, 2001 terrorist events.

According to aviation industry officials, the state of general aviation is strong. For the sixth consecutive year, the industry has set new records for billings. In 2001, total billings reached $8.64 billion, which was up slightly (one percent) from 2000.

However, for the first time since 1994, total aircraft shipments decreased in 2001 by 184 units or 6.5 percent from 2000. The decreases were in single-engine piston aircraft (12.7 percent) and turboprop aircraft (2.9 percent). Increases were seen in multi-engine piston aircraft (42.7 percent) and turbojet aircraft (1.7 percent).

Overall, there were declines in piston-engine aircraft while turbine-engine aircraft stayed about the same. In 2001, piston-engine shipments decreased 9.7 percent and turbine-engine aircraft shipments increased 0.11 percent in 2001 over 2000.

General aviation remains a dominant force in aviation and it is expected that it will continue to play a very large role. The average general aviation aircraft fleet is expected to increase by 0.5 percent per year over the next decade. Increases are expected in nearly all categories including single-engine piston, turbine-powered, and rotorcraft aircraft.

Continued demand in both the new and used markets, an array of new product developments, and heavy backlogs in the supply chain all point to a positive outlook for general aviation. Business aviation continues to lead the way as fractional ownership programs continue to stimulate demand.

Additionally, a recent study of general aviation in Texas showed that it plays a large role in the state's economy. The economic impact of general aviation in Texas includes a total payroll of $1,872,675,700 and total economic output of $5,896,626,900. ☆

## Leading U.S. Routes, 2001

| Rank, Route | Passengers |
|---|---|
| 1. New York to-from Fort Lauderdale | 3.18 million |
| 2. New York to-from Orlando | 2.81 million |
| 3. New York to-from Los Angeles | 2.65 million |
| 4. New York to-from Chicago | 2.47 million |
| 5. New York to-from Atlanta | 2.29 million |
| 8. **Dallas/Fort Worth to-from Houston** | 1.79 million |
| 23. New York to-from **Dallas/Fort Worth** | 1.18 million |

## Leading U.S. Airlines, 2001

| Rank | Airline | Passengers (000) | Planes |
|---|---|---|---|
| 1 | **American*** | 98,742 | 881 |
| 2 | Delta | 94,045 | 588 |
| 3 | United | 75,138 | 543 |
| 4 | **Southwest** | 73,629 | 355 |
| 5 | US Airways | 56,105 | 342 |
| 6 | Northwest | 52,271 | 440 |
| 7 | **Continental** | 42,357 | 352 |
| 8 | America West | 19,578 | 146 |

Air Transport Assoc. of America. *Includes TWA.(Texas-based in boldface.)

## Top U.S. Airports

Ranked by passengers arriving and departing, 2001

| Rank | Airport | (000) |
|---|---|---|
| 1 | Atlanta | 75,849 |
| 2 | Chicago (O'Hare) | 66,805 |
| 3 | Los Angeles (LAX) | 61,025 |
| 4 | **Dallas-Fort Worth** | **55,151** |
| 5 | Denver | 36,087 |
| 6 | Phoenix | 35,482 |
| 7 | Las Vegas | 35,196 |
| 8 | Minneapolis-St. Paul | 35,171 |
| 9 | **Houston (Bush)** | **34,795** |
| 10 | San Francisco | 34,627 |
| 11 | Detroit | 32,294 |
| 12 | Miami | 31,668 |
| 13 | Newark | 30,500 |
| 14 | JFK (New York) | 29,400 |
| 21 | La Guardia | 21,900 |

Source: Airports Council International

# History of Oil Discoveries in Texas

**Oil and natural gas** are the most valuable minerals produced in Texas, contributing 18 percent of the oil production in the United States in 2001, and 30 percent of the gas production in the nation in 2001, the latest figures available.

Oil and gas have been produced from most areas of Texas and from rocks of all geologic eras except the Precambrian.

All of the major sedimentary basins of Texas have produced some oil or gas.

The well-known Permian Basin of West Texas has yielded large quantities of oil since the Big Lake discovery in 1923, although there was a smaller discovery in the Westbrook field in Mitchell County three years earlier. The 1923 discovery, **Santa Rita No. 1** in Reagan County, was on University of Texas land, and it and Texas A&M University both have benefitted from the royalties.

Although large quantities of petroleum have been produced from rocks of Permian age, production in the area also occurs from older Paleozoic rocks.

Production from rocks of Paleozoic age occurs primarily from North Central Texas westward to New Mexico and southwestward to the Rio Grande, but there is also significant Paleozoic production in North Texas.

Mesozoic rocks are the primary hydrocarbon reservoirs of the East Texas Basin and the area south and east of the Balcones Fault Zone. Cenozoic sandstones are the main reservoirs along the Gulf Coast and offshore state waters.

## Earliest Oil

Indians found oil seeping from the soils of Texas long before the first Europeans arrived. They told explorers that the fluid had medicinal values. The first record of Europeans using crude oil, however, was the caulking of boats in 1543 by survivors of the DeSoto expedition near Sabine Pass.

**Melrose,** in Nacogdoches County, was the site in 1866 of the first drilled well to produce oil in Texas. The driller was Lyne T. Barret. Barret used an auger, fastened to a pipe and rotated by a cogwheel driven by a steam engine — a basic principle of rotary drilling that has been used since, although with much improvement.

In 1867 Amory (Emory) Starr and Peyton F. Edwards brought in a well at Oil Springs, in the same area.

Other wells followed and **Nacogdoches County** was the site of Texas' first commercial oil field, pipeline and effort to refine crude. Several thousand barrels of oil were produced there during these years.

Other oil was found in crudely dug wells in Bexar County in 1889 and in Hardin County in 1893. The three small wells in Hardin County led to the creation of a small refinery.

Some of the oilfields and the dates of discovery are indicated on the map. The earliest commercial production was at Melrose in Nacogodoches County and at Corsicana, but significant production really began with the discovery at Spindletop in 1901.

Panhandle, 1921
Levelland, 1945
Electra, 1911
Burkburnett, 1918
Lubbock
Slaughter, 1936
Hawkins, 1940
Kelly-Snyder, 1948
Dallas
East Texas, 1930
Westbrook, 1920
Ranger, 1917
Van, 1929
Hendrick, 1926
Midland
Odessa
Corsicana, 1894
Penwell, 1929
Mexia, 1920
Melrose, 1866
Big Lake, 1923
Santa Rita No. 1
Yates, 1926
Thrall, 1915
Spindletop, 1901
Austin
Luling, 1922
Houston
Goose Creek, 1908
San Antonio
Somerset, 1913
Darst Creek, 1929
Damon Mound, 1915
Pettus, 1929
Greta, 1926
Piedras Pintas, 1907
Seeligson, 1937
Kelsey, 1938

Oilfields are in most regions of the state, but the Permian Basin around Midland-Odessa is one of the most productive areas.

But it was not until June 9, 1894, that Texas had a major discovery. This occurred in the drilling of a water well for the city of **Corsicana**. Oil caused that well to be abandoned, but a company formed in 1895 drilled several producing oil wells.

The first well-equipped refinery in Texas was built, and this plant usually is called the state's **first refinery**, despite the earlier efforts. Discovery of the Powell Field, also near Corsicana, followed in 1900.

## Spindletop, 1901

**Jan. 10, 1901,** is the most famous date in Texas petroleum history. This is the date that the great gusher erupted in the oil well being drilled at Spindletop, near Beaumont, by a mining engineer, Capt. A. F. Lucas. Thousands of barrels of oil flowed before the well could be capped. This was the first salt dome oil discovery.

Spindletop created a sensation throughout the world, and encouraged exploration and drilling in Texas that has continued since.

Texas oil production increased from 836,039 barrels in 1900 to 4,393,658 in 1901; and in 1902 Spindletop alone produced 17,421,000 barrels, or 94 percent of the state's production. Prices dropped to 3 cents a barrel, an all-time low.

The first offshore drilling was in shallow northern Galveston Bay, where the **Goose Creek** Field was discovered in 1908. Several dry holes followed and the field was abandoned. But a gusher in 1916 created the real boom there.

A water-well drilling outfit on the W. T. Waggoner Ranch in Wichita County hit oil, bringing in the **Electra** Field in 1911.

Salt dome oilfields followed at Damon Mound in

1915, Barbers Hill in 1916, and Blue Ridge in 1919.

In 1917, came the discovery of the **Ranger** Field in Eastland County. The **Burkburnett** Field in Wichita County was discovered in 1919.

About this time, oil discoveries brought a short era of swindling, with oil stock promotion and selling on a nationwide scale. It ended after a series of trials in federal courts.

The **Mexia** Field in Limestone County was discovered in 1920, and the second Powell Field in Navarro County in 1924.

Another great area really developed in 1921 in the **Panhandle,** a field with sensational oil and gas discoveries in Hutchinson and contiguous counties and the booming of Borger.

The **Luling** Field was opened in 1922 and 1925 saw the comeback of Spindletop with a production larger than that of the original field.

In 1925 **Howard County** was opened for production. **Hendricks** in Winkler County opened in 1926 and **Raccoon Bend**, Austin County, opened in 1927. **Sugar Land** was the most important Texas oil development in 1928.

The **Darst Creek** Field was opened in 1929. In the same year, new records of productive sand thickness were set for the industry at **Van,** Van Zandt County. **Pettus** was another contribution of 1929 in Bee County.

### East Texas Field

The **East Texas** field, biggest of them all, was discovered near Turnertown and Joinerville, Rusk County, by veteran wildcatter C. M. (Dad) Joiner, in October 1930. The success of this well — drilled on land condemned many times by geologists of the major companies — was followed by the biggest leasing campaign in history. The field soon was extended to Kilgore, Longview and northward. The East Texas field brought overproduction and a rapid sinking of the price. Private attempts were made to prorate production, but without much success.

On Aug. 17, 1931, Gov. Ross S. Sterling ordered the National Guard into the field, which he placed under martial law. This drastic action was taken after the Texas Railroad Commission had been enjoined from enforcing production restrictions.

After the complete shutdown, the Texas Legislature enacted legal **proration,** the system of regulation still utilized.

### West Texas

The most significant subsequent oil discoveries in Texas were those in West Texas. In 1936, oil was discovered west of Lubbock in the Duggan Field in Cochran County. Originally it was thought to be one of two fields, it and the adjacent **Slaughter** Field, but in 1940 the Railroad Commission ruled that the two produced from one reservoir, called Slaughter. The prolific **Levelland** Field, in Cochran and Hockley counties, was discovered in 1945. A discovery well in **Scurry** County on Nov. 21, 1948 was the first of several major developments in that region. Many of the leading Texas counties in minerals value are in that section.

### Austin Chalk

The **Giddings** Field on the Austin Chalk in Lee, Fayette, and Burleson counties had significant drilling in the 1970s that continued into the 1980s. ☆

# Coal Production Resumed in Texas in the 1970s

Coal and lignite occur in rocks of Pennsylvanian, Cretaceous and Tertiary ages. Coal was produced in Texas from about 1850 to the 1940s, when petroleum became the common fuel.

Significant production of coal did not resume until the mid-1970s. Most of the pre-1940 production was **bituminous coal** from North Central Texas, an area near Eagle Pass, and an area near Laredo.

North Central Texas production was from Pennsylvanian rocks. Thurber, Newcastle and Bridgeport all had viable coal industries in the early 1900s.

As early as 1850, soldiers from Fort Duncan near Eagle Pass are reported to have mined coal from the Cretaceous rocks.

Commercial mining of coal from Eocene rocks near Laredo began in 1881. In addition to the commercial mining, small amounts of coal occurring in the Trans-Pecos were used to roast the ore in mercury mining districts in the Big Bend.

Small amounts of "brown coal" or **lignite** have been produced throughout the history of the state. It was mined by many early settlers for family and small industry use. It was also used to generate "coal gas" or "producer gas" for Texas cities around 1900. Today, **Texas ranks fifth** nationally in coal production, and lignite accounts for most of this. Coal mine operators in Texas produced 45.2 million short tons in the year 2002. Almost all of the lignite is consumed by mine-mouth electrical generating plants. Approximately 25 percent of the electricity generated in the state annually is from plants fired by Texas lignite.

**Uranium** occurs in several widely separated Texas localities, but production in the past was limited to the Cenozoic sandstones along the coastal plains of south-central Texas, roughly from Karnes County southwest to Webb County.

The surface mines, active from 1959 to the late-1980s, have largely been abandoned and reclaimed, and production, until recently, was from in-situ leaching. This process requires the injection of a leaching fluid into the uranium-bearing strata, reaction of the fluid with the uranium ore and return of the fluid to the surface for stripping of the uranium.

**As of the year 2000**, however, there was no uranium production in Texas due to decreased prices and demand.

# Chronological Listing of Oil Discoveries

## Major Fields

*The following list gives the name of the field, county and discovery date. Sources include Texas Mid-Continent Oil and Gas Association from records of the U.S. Bureau of Mines; the Oil and Gas Journal; previous Texas Almanacs, the New Handbook of Texas, and the Energy Information Administration of the U.S. Department of Energy.*

**Corsicana**, Navarro, 1894;
**Powell**, Navarro, 1900;
**Spindletop**, Jefferson, 1901;
**Sour Lake**, Hardin, 1902;
**Batson-Old**, Hardin, 1903;
**Humble**, Harris, 1905;
**Mission**, Bexar, 1907;
**Piedras Pintas**, Duval, 1907;
**Goose Creek**, Harris, 1908;
**Panhandle Osborne**, Wheeler, 1910;
**Archer County**, 1911;
**Electra**, Wichita, 1911;
**Burk**, Wichita, 1912;
**Iowa Park**, Wichita, 1913;
**Orange**, Orange, 1913;
**Somerset**, Bexar, 1913
**Damon Mound**, Brazoria, 1915;
**Thrall**, Williamson, 1915;
**Wilbarger County**, 1915;
**Barbers Hill**, Chambers, 1916;
**Stephens County Regular**, 1916;
**Ranger**, Eastland, 1917;
**Young County**, 1917;
**Burkburnett Townsite**, Wichita, 1918;
**Desdemona**, Eastland, 1918;
**Hull**, Liberty, 1918;
**West Columbia**, Brazoria, 1918;
**Blue Ridge**, Fort Bend, 1919;
**KMA** (Kemp-Munger-Allen), Wichita, 1919;
**Mexia**, Limestone-Freestone, 1920;
**Refugio**, Refugio, 1920;
**Westbrook**, Mitchell, 1920;
**Panhandle**, Carson-Collingsworth-Gray-Hutchinson-Moore-Potter-Wheeler, 1921;
**Currie**, Navarro, 1921;
**Mirando City**, Webb, 1921;
**Pierce Junction**, Harris, 1921;
**Thompsons**, Fort Bend, 1921;
**Aviators**, Webb, 1922;
**High Island**, Galveston-Chambers, 1922;
**Luling-Branyon**, Caldwell-Guadalupe, 1922;
**Big Lake**, Reagan, 1923;
**Cooke County**, 1924;
**Richland**, Navarro, 1924;
**Wortham**, Freestone, 1924;
**Boling**, Wharton, 1925;
**Howard-Glasscock**, Howard, 1925;
**Lytton Springs**, Caldwell, 1925;

**McCamey**, Upton, 1925;
**Hendrick**, Winkler, 1926;
**Iatan East**, Howard, 1926;
**McElroy**, Crane, 1926;
**Yates**, Pecos, 1926;
**Raccoon Bend**, Austin, 1927;
**Waddell**, Crane, 1927;
**Agua Dulce-Stratton**, Nueces, 1928;
**Greta**, Refugio, 1928;
**Kermit**, Winkler, 1928;
**Salt Flat**, Caldwell, 1928;
**Sugarland**, Fort Bend, 1928;
**Darst Creek**, Guadalupe, 1929;
**Penwell**, Ector, 1929;
**Pettus**, Bee, 1929;
**Van**, Van Zandt, 1929;
**Cowden North**, Ector, 1930;
**East Texas**, Cherokee-Gregg-Rusk-Smith-Upshur, 1930;
**Fuhrman-Mascho**, Andrews, 1930;
**Sand Hills**, Crane, 1930;
**Conroe**, Montgomery, 1931;
**Manvel**, Brazoria, 1931;
**Tomball**, Harris, 1933;
**Dickinson**, Galveston, 1934;
**Hastings East**, Brazoria, 1934;
**Means**, Andrews, 1934;
**Old Ocean**, Brazoria, 1934;
**Tom O'Connor**, Refugio, 1934;
**Anahuac**, Chambers, 1935;
**Goldsmith**, Ector, 1935;
**Keystone**, Winkler, 1935;
**Plymouth**, San Patricio, 1935;
**Withers**, Wharton, 1936;
**Pearsall**, Frio, 1936;
**Seminole**, Gaines, 1936;
**Slaughter**, Cochran-Hockley, 1936;
**Talco**, Titus-Franklin, 1936;
**Wasson**, Gaines, 1936;
**Webster**, Harris, 1936;

**Jordan**, Crane-Ector, 1937;
**Seeligson**, Jim Wells-Kleberg, 1937;
**Dune**, Crane, 1938;
**Kelsey**, Brooks-Jim Hogg-Starr, 1938;
**Walnut Bend**, Cooke, 1938;
**West Ranch**, Jackson, 1938;
**Diamond M**, Scurry, 1940;
**Hawkins**, Wood, 1940;
**Fullerton**, Andrews, 1941;
**Oyster Bayou**, Chambers, 1941;
**Tijerina-Canales-Blucher**, Jim Wells-Kleberg, 1941;
**Quitman**, Wood, 1942;
**Welch**, Dawson, 1942;
**Russell**, Gaines, 1943;
**Anton-Irish**, Hale-Lamb-Lubbock, 1944;
**Mabee**, Andrews-Martin, 1944;
**Midland Farms**, Andrews, 1944;
**TXL Devonian**, Ector, 1944;
**Block 31**, Crane, 1945;
**Borregos**, Kleberg, 1945;
**Dollarhide**, Andrews, 1945;
**Levelland**, Cochran-Hockley, 1945;
**Andector**, Ector, 1946;
**Kelly-Snyder**, Scurry, 1948;
**Cogdell Area**, Scurry, 1949;
**Pegasus**, Upton-Midland, 1949;
**Spraberry Trend**, Glasscock-Midland, 1949;
**Prentice**, Yoakum, 1950;
**Salt Creek**, Kent, 1950;
**Neches**, Anderson-Cherokee, 1953;
**Dora Roberts**, Midland, 1954;
**Alazan North**, Kleberg, 1958;
**Fairway**, Anderson-Henderson, 1960;
**Giddings**, Lee-Fayette-Burleson, 1960. ☆

*'The Glory Days' in downtown Kilgore in the 1930s. File photo.*

## Petroleum Production and Income in Texas

| Year | Crude Oil & Condensate | | | Natural Gas | | |
|---|---|---|---|---|---|---|
| | Production (thousand barrels) | Value (add 000) | Average Price Per Barrel | Production (million cubic feet) | Value (add 000) | Average Price (Cents Per MCF) |
| 1915 | 24,943 | $ 13,027 | $ 0 .52 | 13,324 | $ 2,594 | 19.5 |
| 1925 | 144,648 | 262,270 | 1.81 | 134,872 | 7,040 | 5.2 |
| 1935 | 392,666 | 367,820 | 0.94 | 642,366 | 13,233 | 2.1 |
| 1945 | 754,710 | 914,410 | 1.21 | 1,711,401 | 44,839 | 2.6 |
| 1955 | 1,053,297 | 2,989,330 | 2.84 | 4,730,798 | 378,464 | 8.0 |
| 1965 | 1,000,749 | 2,962,119 | 2.96 | 6,636,555 | 858,396 | 12.9 |
| 1966 | 1,057,706 | 3,141,387 | 2.97 | 6,953,790 | 903,993 | 13.0 |
| 1967 | 1,119,962 | 3,375,565 | 3.01 | 7,188,900 | 948,935 | 13.2 |
| 1968 | 1,133,380 | 3,450,707 | 3.04 | 7,495,414 | 1,011,881 | 13.5 |
| 1969 | 1,151,775 | 3,696,328 | 3.21 | 7,853,199 | 1,075,888 | 13.7 |
| 1970 | 1,249,697 | 4,104,005 | 3.28 | 8,357,716 | 1,203,511 | 14.4 |
| 1971 | 1,222,926 | 4,261,775 | 3.48 | 8,550,705 | 1,376,664 | 16.1 |
| 1972 | 1,301,685 | 4,536,077 | 3.48 | 8,657,840 | 1,419,886 | 16.4 |
| 1973 | 1,294,671 | 5,157,623 | 3.98 | 8,513,850 | 1,735,221 | 20.4 |
| 1974 | 1,262,126 | 8,773,003 | 6.95 | 8,170,798 | 2,541,118 | 31.1 |
| 1975 | 1,221,929 | 9,336,570 | 7.64 | 7,485,764 | 3,885,112 | 51.9 |
| 1976 | 1,189,523 | 10,217,702 | 8.59 | 7,191,859 | 5,163,755 | 71.8 |
| 1977 | 1,137,880 | 9,986,002 | 8.78 | 7,051,027 | 6,367,077 | 90.3 |
| 1978 | 1,074,050 | 9,980,333 | 9.29 | 6,548,184 | 6,515,443 | 99.5 |
| 1979 | 1,018,094 | 12,715,994 | 12.49 | 7,174,623 | 8,509,103 | 118.6 |
| 1980 | 977,436 | 21,259,233 | 21.75 | 7,115,889 | 10,673,834 | 150.0 |
| 1981 | 945,132 | 32,692,116 | 34.59 | 7,050,207 | 12,598,712 | 178.7 |
| 1982 | 923,868 | 29,074,126 | 31.47 | 6,497,678 | 13,567,151 | 208.8 |
| 1983 | 876,205 | 22,947,814 | 26.19 | 5,643,183 | 14,672,275 | 260.0 |
| 1984 | 874,079 | 25,138,520 | 28.76 | 5,864,224 | 13,487,715 | 230.0 |
| 1985 | 860,300 | 23,159,286 | 26.92 | 5,805,098 | 12,665,114 | 218.0 |
| 1986 | 813,620 | 11,976,488 | 14.72 | 5,663,491 | 8,778,410 | 155.0 |
| 1987 | 754,213 | 13,221,345 | 17.53 | 5,516,224 | 7,612,389 | 138.0 |
| 1988 | 727,928 | 10,729,660 | 14.74 | 5,702,643 | 7,983,700 | 140.0 |
| 1989 | 679,575 | 12,123,624 | 17.84 | 5,595,190 | 8,113,026 | 145.0 |
| 1990 | 672,081 | 15,047,902 | 22.39 | 5,520,915 | 8,281,372 | 150.0 |
| 1991 | 672,810 | 12,836,080 | 19.05 | 5,509,990 | 7,713,986 | 140.0 |
| 1992 | 642,059 | 11,820,306 | 18.41 | 5,436,408 | 8,643,888 | 159.0 |
| 1993 | 572,600 | 9,288,800 | 16.22 | 4,062,500 | 7,365,800 | 181.0 |
| 1994 | 533,900 | 7,977,500 | 14.94 | 3,842,500 | 6,220,300 | 162.0 |
| 1995 | 503,200 | 8,177,700 | 16.25 | 3,690,000 | 5,305,200 | 143.0 |
| 1996 | 478,100 | 9,560,800 | 20.00 | 3,458,100 | 6,945,000 | 200.0 |
| 1997 | 464,900 | 8,516,800 | 18.32 | 3,672,300 | 8,134,200 | 221.5 |
| 1998 | 440,600 | 5,472,400 | 12.42 | 3,557,900 | 6,362,900 | 178.8 |
| 1999 | 337,100 | 5,855,800 | 17.37 | 3,321,600 | 6,789,700 | 204.4 |
| 2000 | 348,900 | 10,037,300 | 28.77 | 3,552,000 | 12,837,600 | 361.4 |
| 2001 | 325,500 | 7,770,500 | 23.87 | 3,732,700 | 13,708,700 | 367.3 |
| 2002 | 329,800 | $ 8,022,000 | $ 24.32 | 3,875,500 | $ 10,920,400 | 281.8 |

*Sources: Data since 1993 are from the state comptroller. Previously from the Texas Railroad Commission, Texas Mid-Continent Oil & Gas Association and, beginning in 1979, data are from Department of Energy. DOE figures do not include gas that is vented or flared or used for pressure maintenance and repressuring, but do include non-hydrocarbon gases. MCF (thousand cubic feet).*

*A pumping unit pumping oil west of Sweetwater. File photo.*

# Drilling Counts
# 1982-2002

**Activity in recent years was higher than it had been in the mid-1990s, but still much lower than the boom years in the early 1980s.**

*Source: Texas Railroad Commission*

| Year | Rotary rigs active* | | Permits† | Texas wells completed | | Wells drilled** |
|---|---|---|---|---|---|---|
| | Texas | U.S. | Texas | Oil | Gas | Texas |
| 1982 | 994 | 3,117 | 41,224 | 16,296 | 6,273 | 27,648 |
| 1983 | 796 | 2,232 | 45,550 | 15,941 | 5,027 | 26,882 |
| 1984 | 850 | 2,428 | 37,507 | 18,716 | 5,489 | 30,898 |
| 1985 | 680 | 1,980 | 30,878 | 16,543 | 4,605 | 27,124 |
| 1986 | 313 | 964 | 15,894 | 10,373 | 3,304 | 18,707 |
| 1987 | 293 | 1,090 | 15,297 | 7,327 | 2,542 | 13,121 |
| 1988 | 280 | 936 | 13,493 | 6,441 | 2,665 | 12,261 |
| 1989 | 264 | 871 | 12,756 | 4,914 | 2,760 | 10,054 |
| 1990 | 348 | 1,009 | 14,033 | 5,593 | 2,894 | 11,231 |
| 1991 | 315 | 860 | 12,494 | 6,025 | 2,755 | 11,295 |
| 1992 | 251 | 721 | 12,089 | 5,031 | 2,537 | 9,498 |
| 1993 | 264 | 754 | 11,612 | 4,646 | 3,295 | 9,969 |
| 1994 | 274 | 775 | 11,030 | 3,962 | 3,553 | 9,299 |
| 1995 | 251 | 723 | 11,244 | 4,334 | 3,778 | 9,785 |
| 1996 | 283 | 779 | 12,669 | 4,061 | 4,060 | 9,747 |
| 1997 | 358 | 945 | 13,933 | 4,482 | 4,594 | 10,778 |
| 1998 | 303 | 827 | 9,385 | 4,509 | 4,907 | 11,057 |
| 1999 | 226 | 622 | 8,430 | 2,049 | 3,566 | 6,658 |
| 2000 | 343 | 918 | 12,021 | 3,111 | 4,580 | 8,854 |
| 2001 | 462 | 1,156 | 12,227 | 3,082 | 5,787 | 10,005 |
| 2002 | 338 | 830 | 9,716 | 3,268 | 5,474 | 9,877 |

*Source: Baker Hughes Inc. This is an annual average from monthly reports.
†Totals shown for 1988 and after are number of drilling permits issued; data for previous years were total drilling applications received.
**Wells drilled are oil and gas well completions and dry holes drilled.

# Receipts by Texas from Tidelands

The Republic of Texas had proclaimed its Gulf boundaries as three marine leagues, recognized by international law as traditional national boundaries. These boundaries were never seriously questioned when Texas joined the Union in 1845. But, in 1930 a congressional resolution authorized the U.S. Attorney General to file suit to establish offshore lands as proper-

ties of the federal government. Congress returned the disputed lands to Texas in 1953, and the U.S. Supreme Court confirmed Texas' ownership in 1960. In 1978, the federal government also granted states a "fair and equitable" share of the revenues from offshore leases within three miles of the states' outermost boundary. The states did not receive any such revenue until April 1986.

The following table shows receipts from tidelands in the Gulf of Mexico by the Texas General Land Office to Aug. 31, 2002. It does not include revenue from bays and other submerged area owned by Texas. *Source: General Land Office*

| From | To | Total | Bonus | Rental | Royalty | Lease |
|---|---|---|---|---|---|---|
| 6-09-1922 | 9-28-1945 | $ 924,363.81 | $ 814,055.70 | $ 61,973.75 | $ 48,334.36 | ... |
| 9-29-1945 | 6-23-1947 | 296,400.30 | 272,700.00 | 7,680.00 | 16,020.30 | ... |
| 6-24-1947 | 6-05-1950 | 7,695,552.22 | 7,231,755.48 | 377,355.00 | 86,441.74 | ... |
| 6-06-1950 | 5-22-1953 | 55,095.04 | — | 9,176.00 | 45,919.04 | ... |
| 5-23-1953 | 6-30-1958 | 54,264,553.11 | 49,788,639.03 | 3,852,726.98 | 623,187.10 | ... |
| 7-01-1958 | 8-31-1959 | 771,064.75 | — | 143,857.00 | 627,207.75 | ... |
| 9-01-1959 | 8-31-1960 | 983,335.32 | 257,900.00 | 98,226.00 | 627,209.32 | ... |
| 9-01-1960 | 8-31-1961 | 3,890,800.15 | 3,228,639.51 | 68,578.00 | 593,582.64 | ... |
| 9-01-1961 | 8-31-1962 | 1,121,925.09 | 297,129.88 | 127,105.00 | 697,690.21 | ... |
| 9-01-1962 | 8-31-1963 | 3,575,888.64 | 2,617,057.14 | 177,174.91 | 781,656.59 | ... |
| 9-01-1963 | 8-31-1964 | 3,656,236.75 | 2,435,244.36 | 525,315.00 | 695,677.39 | ... |
| 9-01-1964 | 8-31-1965 | 54,654,576.96 | 53,114,943.63 | 755,050.12 | 784,583.21 | ... |
| 9-01-1965 | 8-31-1966 | 22,148,825.44 | 18,223,357.84 | 3,163,475.00 | 761,992.60 | ... |
| 9-01-1966 | 8-31-1967 | 8,469,680.86 | 3,641,414.96 | 3,711,092.65 | 1,117,173.25 | ... |
| 9-01-1967 | 8-31-1968 | 6,305,851.00 | 1,251,852.50 | 2,683,732.50 | 2,370,266.00 | ... |
| 9-01-1968 | 8-31-1969 | 6,372,268.28 | 1,838,118.33 | 1,491,592.50 | 3,042,557.45 | ... |
| 9-01-1969 | 8-31-1970 | 10,311,030.48 | 5,994,666.32 | 618,362.50 | 3,698,001.66 | ... |
| 9-01-1970 | 8-31-1971 | 9,969,629.17 | 4,326,120.11 | 726,294.15 | 4,917,214.91 | ... |
| 9-01-1971 | 8-31-1972 | 7,558,327.21 | 1,360,212.64 | 963,367.60 | 5,234,746.97 | ... |
| 9-01-1972 | 8-31-1973 | 9,267,975.68 | 3,701,737.30 | 920,121.60 | 4,646,116.78 | ... |
| 9-01-1973 | 8-31-1974 | 41,717,670.04 | 32,981,619.28 | 1,065,516.60 | 7,670,534.16 | ... |
| 9-01-1974 | 8-31-1975 | 27,321,536.62 | 5,319,762.85 | 2,935,295.60 | 19,066,478.17 | ... |
| 9-01-1975 | 8-31-1976 | 38,747,074.09 | 6,197,853.00 | 3,222,535.84 | 29,326,685.25 | ... |
| 9-01-1976 | 8-31-1977 | 84,196,228.27 | 41,343,114.81 | 2,404,988.80 | 40,448,124.66 | ... |
| 9-01-1977 | 8-31-1978 | 118,266,812.05 | 49,807,750.45 | 4,775,509.92 | 63,683,551.68 | ... |
| 9-01-1978 | 8-31-1979 | 100,410,268.68 | 34,578,340.94 | 7,318,748.40 | 58,513,179.34 | ... |
| 9-01-1979 | 8-31-1980 | 200,263,803.03 | 34,733,270.02 | 10,293,153.80 | 155,237,379.21 | ... |
| 9-01-1980 | 8-31-1981 | 219,126,876.54 | 37,467,196.97 | 13,100,484.25 | 168,559,195.32 | ... |
| 9-01-1981 | 8-31-1982 | 250,824,581.69 | 27,529,516.33 | 14,214,478.97 | 209,080,586.39 | ... |
| 9-01-1982 | 8-31-1983 | 165,197,734.83 | 10,180,696.40 | 12,007,476.70 | 143,009,561.73 | ... |
| 9-01-1983 | 8-31-1984 | 152,755,934.29 | 32,864,122.19 | 8,573,996.87 | 111,317,815.23 | ... |
| 9-01-1984 | 8-31-1985 | 140,568,090.79 | 32,650,127.75 | 6,837,603.70 | 101,073,959.34 | ... |
| 9-01-1985 | 8-31-1986 | 516,503,771.05 | 6,365,426.23 | 4,241,892.75 | 78,289,592.27 | $ 427,606,859.83 |
| 9-01-1986 | 8-31-1987 | 60,066,571.05 | 4,186,561.63 | 1,933,752.50 | 44,691,907.22 | 9,254,349.70 |
| 9-01-1987 | 8-31-1988 | 56,875,069.22 | 14,195,274.28 | 1,817,058.90 | 28,068,202.53 | 12,794,533.51 |
| 9-01-1988 | 8-31-1989 | 61,793,380.04 | 12,995,892.74 | 1,290,984.37 | 35,160,568.40 | 12,345,934.53 |
| 9-01-1989 | 8-31-1990 | 68,701,751.51 | 7,708,449.54 | 1,289,849.87 | 40,331,537.06 | 19,371,915.04 |
| 9-01-1990 | 8-31-1991 | 90,885,856.99 | 3,791,832.77 | 1,345,711.07 | 70,023,601.01 | 15,724,712.14 |
| 9-01-1991 | 8-31-1992 | 51,154,511.34 | 4,450,850.00 | 1,123,585.54 | 26,776,191.35 | 18,803,884.45 |
| 9-01-1992 | 8-31-1993 | 60,287,712.60 | 3,394,230.00 | 904,359.58 | 34,853,679.68 | 21,135,443.34 |
| 9-01-1993 | 8-31-1994 | 57,825,043.59 | 3,570,657.60 | 694,029.30 | 32,244,987.95 | 21,315,368.74 |
| 9-01-1994 | 8-31-1995 | 62,143,227.78 | 8,824,722.93 | 674,479.79 | 34,691,023.35 | 17,951,001.71 |
| 9-01-1995 | 8-31-1996 | 68,166,645.51 | 13,919,246.80 | 1,102,591.39 | 32,681,315.73 | 20,463,491.59 |
| 9-01-1996 | 8-31-1997 | 90,614,935.93 | 22,007,378.46 | 1,319,614.78 | 41,605,792.50 | 25,682,150.19 |
| 9-01-1997 | 8-31-1998 | 104,016,006.75 | 36,946,312.49 | 2,070,802.90 | 38,760,320.91 | 26,238,570.45 |
| 9-01-1998 | 8-31-1999 | 53,565,810.30 | 5,402,171.00 | 2,471,128.47 | 23,346,515.93 | 22,345,994.90 |
| 9-01-1999 | 8-31-2000 | 55,465,763.99 | 3,487,564.80 | 2,171,636.35 | 24,314,241.99 | 25,492,320.85 |
| 9-01-2000 | 8-31-2001 | 68,226,347.58 | 9,963,608.68 | 1,830,378.11 | 23,244,034.74 | 33,188,326.05 |
| 9-01-2001 | 8-31-2002 | 30,910,283.91 | 9,286,015.20 | 1,545,583.01 | 13,369,771.56 | 6,708,914.14 |
| **Total** | | $ 3,308,886,280.35 | $ 676,545,110.87 | $ 135,061,484.39 | $ 1,760,855,913.93 | $ 736,423,771.16 |
| Inside three-mile line | | $ 457,093,797.16 | $ 160,475,816.93 | $ 36,271,205.26 | $ 260,346,774.97 | 0 |
| Between three-mile line and three marine-league line | | $ 2,112,543,346.45 | $ 513,417,209.55 | $ 98,616,997.94 | $ 1,500,509,138.96 | 0 |
| Outside three marine-league line | | $ 739,249,136.74 | $ 2,652,084.39 | $ 173,281.19 | 0 | $ 736,423,771.16 |

# Oil and Gas Offshore Texas

In 2002 in Texas, the offshore natural gas production was 57,333,419 thousand cubic feet (MCF) out of the state's total gas production of 5,694,881,697 MCF. The offshore oil production was 1,549,439 barrels out of the state's total oil production of 405,051,557 barrrels.

BBL refers to barrels and **MCF** to thousand cubic feet.

| Offshore Area | Crude Oil BBL | Casing-head MCF | Gas Well Gas MCF | Conden-sate BBL |
|---|---|---|---|---|
| Matagrda-LB | 139,350 | 0 | 0 | 0 |
| Matagrda-SB | 0 | 0 | 650,191 | 0 |
| **DISTRICT 2** | **139,350** | **0** | **650,191** | **0** |
| | | | | |
| Brazos-LB | 0 | 0 | 5,168,288 | 7,328 |
| Brazos-S | - | - | - | - |
| Brazos-SB | 0 | 0 | 3,099,841 | 4,511 |
| Galveston-LB | 0 | 0 | 4,044,852 | 42,184 |
| Galveston-S | - | - | - | - |
| Galveston-SB | 0 | 0 | 717,151 | 3,773 |
| High Island-E | - | - | - | - |
| High Is.-E,S | - | - | - | - |
| High Is.-LB | 358,924 | 484,261 | 2,766,210 | 14,720 |
| High Is.-S | - | - | - | - |
| High Is.-SB | 111,735 | 42,804 | 33,964 | 0 |
| Matagrda-LB | 0 | 0 | 18,998,780 | 30,498 |
| Matagrda-SB | 0 | 0 | 916,115 | 1,421 |
| **DISTRICT 3** | **470,659** | **527,065** | **35,745,201** | **104,435** |
| | | | | |
| Matagrda-LB | 0 | 0 | 203,770 | 3,438 |
| Matagrda-SB | 0 | 0 | 148,580 | 1,729 |
| Mustang Is.-E | - | - | - | - |
| Mustngls.-LB | 0 | 0 | 7,899,887 | 23,582 |
| Mustngls.-SB | 534,157 | 1,878,603 | 4,754,456 | 121,587 |
| N.Padrels.-E | - | - | - | - |
| N.Padre-LB | 0 | 0 | 5,525,666 | 150,502 |
| N.Padre-SB | - | - | - | - |
| S.Padrels.-E | - | - | - | - |
| S.Padre-LB | 0 | 0 | 0 | 0 |
| S.Padre-SB | - | - | - | - |
| Sabine Pass | 0 | 0 | 0 | 0 |
| **DISTRICT 4** | **534,157** | **1,878,603** | **18,532,359** | **300,838** |
| | | | | |
| **All Offshore (Dist. 2,3,4)** | **1,144,166** | **2,405,668** | **54,927,751** | **405,273** |

*Source: Texas Railroad Commission.*
*"-" No production reported.*

# 2002 Production by Area

*An oil drilling platform positioned in the Gulf of Mexico. File photo.*

# Offshore Production History — Oil and Gas

| Offshore Area | OIL (barrels) | | | | GAS (thousand cubic feet) | | | |
|---|---|---|---|---|---|---|---|---|
| | 1995 | 2000 | 2002 | Total to Jan. 1, 2003 | 1995 | 2000 | 2002 | Total to Jan. 1, 2003 |
| District 2 | 275,059 | 88,237 | 139,350 | **5,369,133** | 1,277,704 | 739,789 | 650,191 | **130,294,300** |
| District 3 | 799,247 | 526,946 | 575,094 | **21,968,671** | 54,168,189 | 34,930,212 | 36,272,266 | **2,745,473,506** |
| District 4 | 196,691 | 158,696 | 834,995 | **9,254,495** | 9,619,480 | 8,801,983 | 20,410,962 | **921,984,793** |
| All Offshore | 1,270,997 | 773,879 | 1,549,439 | **36,592,299** | 65,065,373 | 44,471,984 | 57,333,419 | **3,797,752,599** |

*Source: Texas Railroad Commission.*

# Texas Oil Production History

The table shows the year of oil or gas discovery in each county, oil production in 2001 and 2002 and total oil production from date of discovery to Jan. 1, 2003. The 21 counties omitted have not produced oil.

The table has been compiled by the Texas Almanac from information provided in past years by the Texas Mid-Continent Oil & Gas Assoc. Since 1970, production figures have been compiled from records of the Railroad Commission of Texas. In prior years, U.S. Bureau of Mines and State Comptroller reports were the basis of these compilations. The figures in the final column are cumulative of all previously published figures. The change in sources, due to different techniques, may create some discrepancies in year-to-year comparisons among counties.

| County | Year of Discovery | Production in Barrels* 2001 | Production in Barrels* 2002 | Total Production to Jan. 1, 2003 |
|---|---|---|---|---|
| Anderson | 1928 | 888,801 | 967,731 | 297,761,072 |
| Andrews | 1929 | 26,214,728 | 26,870,636 | 2,736,398,691 |
| Angelina | 1936 | 5,782 | 11,481 | 852,733 |
| Aransas | 1936 | 335,939 | 302,435 | 84,517,685 |
| Archer | 1911 | 1,353,647 | 1,285,800 | 491,705,552 |
| Atascosa | 1917 | 702,417 | 611,426 | 148,309,802 |
| Austin | 1915 | 349,699 | 390,291 | 114,126,189 |
| Bandera | 1995 | 1,940 | 1,804 | 18,160 |
| Bastrop | 1913 | 139,841 | 141,821 | 16,296,916 |
| Baylor | 1924 | 146,751 | 134,533 | 57,735,817 |
| Bee | 1929 | 654,447 | 619,939 | 106,496,437 |
| Bell | 1980 | 0 | 0 | 446 |
| Bexar | 1889 | 148,319 | 127,888 | 35,581,198 |
| Borden | 1949 | 4,591,152 | 4,692,587 | 396,505,116 |
| Bowie | 1944 | 175,843 | 169,296 | 6,166,912 |
| Brazoria | 1902 | 2,430,481 | 2,401,406 | 1,265,522,209 |
| Brazos | 1942 | 2,529,575 | 2,464,261 | 132,418,690 |
| Brewster | 1969 | 0 | 0 | 56 |
| Briscoe | 1982 | 0 | 0 | 3,554 |
| Brooks | 1935 | 1,343,593 | 2,313,444 | 166,310,958 |
| Brown | 1917 | 114,038 | 110,780 | 53,033,860 |
| Burleson | 1938 | 3,815,671 | 3,327,916 | 186,958,124 |
| Caldwell | 1922 | 957,032 | 862,976 | 279,487,312 |
| Calhoun | 1935 | 516,364 | 464,433 | 102,682,547 |
| Callahan | 1923 | 265,570 | 237,234 | 85,528,900 |
| Cameron | 1944 | 2,077 | 720 | 463,906 |
| Camp | 1940 | 420,381 | 381,247 | 28,394,443 |
| Carson | 1921 | 383,859 | 367,998 | 179,150,762 |
| Cass | 1936 | 474,793 | 366,483 | 113,441,668 |
| Chambers | 1916 | 1,502,764 | 1,570,059 | 904,345,681 |
| Cherokee | 1926 | 282,059 | 285,901 | 70,131,591 |
| Childress | 1961 | 35,434 | 24,864 | 1,508,412 |
| Clay | 1917 | 892,949 | 835,757 | 202,551,818 |
| Cochran | 1936 | 4,410,097 | 4,135,086 | 495,155,309 |
| Coke | 1942 | 668,110 | 527,821 | 222,287,462 |
| Coleman | 1902 | 306,776 | 315,726 | 94,055,736 |
| Collin | 1963 | 0 | 0 | 53,000 |
| Collingsworth | 1936 | 2,705 | 3,213 | 1,232,856 |
| Colorado | 1932 | 539,710 | 472,996 | 40,356,380 |
| Comanche | 1918 | 7,962 | 9,790 | 5,928,343 |
| Concho | 1940 | 944,756 | 849,110 | 24,816,621 |
| Cooke | 1924 | 1,699,579 | 1,691,016 | 385,285,310 |
| Coryell | 1964 | 0 | 0 | 1,100 |
| Cottle | 1955 | 76,324 | 83,184 | 4,341,311 |
| Crane | 1926 | 11,126,513 | 10,557,643 | 1,722,593,569 |
| Crockett | 1925 | 3,519,734 | 3,709,869 | 354,253,925 |
| Crosby | 1955 | 755,734 | 687,385 | 23,324,141 |
| Culberson | 1953 | 126,587 | 128,101 | 24,488,652 |
| Dallas | 1986 | 0 | 0 | 231 |
| Dawson | 1934 | 6,022,753 | 5,580,967 | 369,666,375 |
| Delta | 1984 | 576 | 455 | 65,089 |
| Denton | 1937 | 222,151 | 536,541 | 4,282,384 |
| DeWitt | 1930 | 339,217 | 218,369 | 65,947,931 |

| County | Year of Discovery | Production in Barrels* 2001 | Production in Barrels* 2002 | Total Production to Jan. 1, 2003 |
|---|---|---|---|---|
| Dickens | 1953 | 870,409 | 1,375,926 | 13,899,347 |
| Dimmit | 1943 | 590,047 | 536,505 | 104,029,470 |
| Duval | 1905 | 1,654,178 | 1,461,419 | 583,075,876 |
| Eastland | 1917 | 326,497 | 305,506 | 155,811,578 |
| Ector | 1926 | 21,791,013 | 19,565,797 | 3,049,411,320 |
| Edwards | 1946 | 8,847 | 4,877 | 520,613 |
| Ellis | 1953 | 1,810 | 145 | 839,527 |
| Erath | 1917 | 2,443 | 5,342 | 2,075,802 |
| Falls | 1937 | 4,987 | 2,999 | 838,069 |
| Fannin | 1980 | 0 | 0 | 13,281 |
| Fayette | 1943 | 2,913,625 | 2,557,485 | 146,246,954 |
| Fisher | 1928 | 950,086 | 846,039 | 246,991,541 |
| Floyd | 1952 | 1,511 | 1,050 | 152,361 |
| Foard | 1929 | 164,649 | 142,830 | 23,792,961 |
| Fort Bend | 1919 | 2,759,155 | 3,035,419 | 683,126,067 |
| Franklin | 1936 | 451,123 | 465,855 | 175,904,551 |
| Freestone | 1916 | 226,107 | 268,571 | 44,279,703 |
| Frio | 1934 | 658,571 | 656,266 | 144,615,562 |
| Gaines | 1935 | 33,275,897 | 31,750,618 | 2,113,796,610 |
| Galveston | 1922 | 1,778,919 | 2,400,335 | 449,124,842 |
| Garza | 1926 | 5,438,224 | 5,088,240 | 325,683,897 |
| Glasscock | 1925 | 4,853,324 | 4,608,510 | 257,612,004 |
| Goliad | 1930 | 738,824 | 694,536 | 81,204,015 |
| Gonzales | 1902 | 390,904 | 318,883 | 43,101,779 |
| Gray | 1925 | 1,802,196 | 1,645,351 | 669,443,082 |
| Grayson | 1930 | 1,430,520 | 1,380,222 | 252,787,623 |
| Gregg | 1931 | 4,432,488 | 3,663,257 | 3,279,292,197 |
| Grimes | 1952 | 312,648 | 236,786 | 17,766,183 |
| Guadalupe | 1922 | 919,300 | 894,315 | 201,536,712 |
| Hale | 1946 | 3,323,504 | 4,272,137 | 170,100,685 |
| Hamilton | 1938 | 678 | 811 | 147,729 |
| Hansford | 1937 | 183,809 | 187,318 | 38,650,596 |
| Hardeman | 1944 | 2,089,962 | 2,144,731 | 77,725,512 |
| Hardin | 1893 | 1,979,610 | 2,257,550 | 434,016,121 |
| Harris | 1905 | 2,337,769 | 2,127,907 | 1,369,959,069 |
| Harrison | 1928 | 875,379 | 900,299 | 87,223,427 |
| Hartley | 1937 | 350,294 | 314,247 | 6,848,366 |
| Haskell | 1929 | 524,803 | 480,514 | 115,758,134 |
| Hays | 1956 | 0 | 0 | 296 |
| Hemphill | 1955 | 618,070 | 697,998 | 35,188,618 |
| Henderson | 1934 | 1,088,319 | 969,020 | 175,693,238 |
| Hidalgo | 1934 | 3,997,242 | 3,891,564 | 103,709,433 |
| Hill | 1929 | 1,205 | 1,161 | 75,085 |
| Hockley | 1937 | 22,444,786 | 22,164,421 | 1,589,945,012 |
| Hood | 1958 | 560 | 647 | 112,682 |
| Hopkins | 1936 | 309,486 | 290,060 | 88,630,396 |
| Houston | 1934 | 823,416 | 755,114 | 55,168,515 |
| Howard | 1925 | 7,464,270 | 7,139,081 | 798,489,042 |
| Hunt | 1942 | 0 | 0 | 2,024,645 |
| Hutchinson | 1923 | 1,076,479 | 970,007 | 528,716,593 |
| Irion | 1928 | 1,651,359 | 1,601,325 | 97,646,768 |
| Jack | 1923 | 883,408 | 779,998 | 202,355,508 |
| Jackson | 1934 | 1,344,592 | 1,145,786 | 679,000,078 |
| Jasper | 1928 | 630,866 | 634,075 | 33,470,410 |

Leading counties through a century of oil production have been in the Permian Basin of West Texas, the East Texas Field and on the Coastal Plains near Houston (Harris County). Counties not shaded have produced less that 250 million barrels. Of Texas' 254 counties, 21 have not produced oil and are omitted from the list below.

BARRELS

- 1 billion +
- 500 million +
- 250 million +

**OIL PRODUCTION HISTORY**

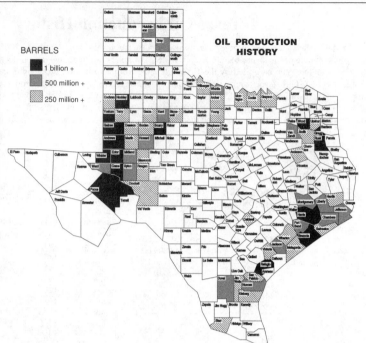

| County | Year of Discovery | Production in Barrels* 2001 | 2002 | Total Production to Jan. 1, 2003 |
|---|---|---|---|---|
| Jeff Davis | 1980 | 0 | 0 | 20,866 |
| Jefferson | 1901 | 2,419,514 | 1,563,162 | 530,992,559 |
| Jim Hogg | 1921 | 725,685 | 606,218 | 111,451,983 |
| Jim Wells | 1931 | 216,172 | 247,966 | 462,144,274 |
| Johnson | 1962 | 0 | 0 | 194,000 |
| Jones | 1926 | 805,150 | 763,810 | 218,875,405 |
| Karnes | 1930 | 315,346 | 306,817 | 107,485,486 |
| Kaufman | 1948 | 77,278 | 64,284 | 24,480,176 |
| Kenedy | 1947 | 353,952 | 453,874 | 38,181,442 |
| Kent | 1946 | 6,263,187 | 6,477,361 | 556,601,044 |
| Kerr | 1982 | 0 | 0 | 77,155 |
| Kimble | 1939 | 585 | 203 | 96,200 |
| King | 1943 | 2,894,848 | 2,783,745 | 171,543,274 |
| Kinney | 1960 | 0 | 0 | 402 |
| Kleberg | 1919 | 509,526 | 1,345,211 | 333,805,515 |
| Knox | 1946 | 314,461 | 283,677 | 61,540,378 |
| Lamb | 1945 | 513,215 | 1,119,341 | 34,476,864 |
| Lampasas | 1985 | 0 | 0 | 111 |
| La Salle | 1940 | 266,747 | 260,525 | 26,983,630 |
| Lavaca | 1941 | 605,122 | 672,682 | 29,493,252 |
| Lee | 1939 | 2,010,303 | 1,840,769 | 130,637,429 |
| Leon | 1936 | 1,063,335 | 872,318 | 60,836,142 |
| Liberty | 1904 | 1,917,900 | 2,431,007 | 522,438,523 |
| Limestone | 1920 | 196,499 | 162,849 | 119,078,028 |
| Lipscomb | 1956 | 484,918 | 459,934 | 58,776,485 |
| Live Oak | 1930 | 654,820 | 655,615 | 82,507,675 |
| Llano | 1978 | 0 | 0 | 647 |
| Loving | 1921 | 1,306,207 | 1,193,292 | 108,222,886 |
| Lubbock | 1941 | 1,598,027 | 1,589,202 | 64,867,289 |
| Lynn | 1950 | 258,469 | 217,656 | 18,772,921 |
| Madison | 1946 | 500,516 | 441,205 | 32,180,702 |
| Marion | 1910 | 211,025 | 183,749 | 55,229,112 |
| Martin | 1945 | 4,957,159 | 4,762,247 | 299,090,362 |
| Matagorda | 1901 | 1,591,816 | 2,028,698 | 276,783,373 |
| Maverick | 1929 | 725,537 | 1,266,135 | 48,830,463 |

| County | Year of Discovery | Production in Barrels* 2001 | 2002 | Total Production to Jan. 1, 2003 |
|---|---|---|---|---|
| McCulloch | 1938 | 117,502 | 138,446 | 1,542,293 |
| McLennan | 1902 | 997 | 1,556 | 332,447 |
| McMullen | 1922 | 1,367,540 | 1,154,677 | 101,410,766 |
| Medina | 1901 | 85,668 | 80,164 | 10,579,086 |
| Menard | 1946 | 118,418 | 123,953 | 7,010,819 |
| Midland | 1945 | 12,087,448 | 11,173,875 | 596,092,336 |
| Milam | 1921 | 765,719 | 686,410 | 19,480,790 |
| Mills | 1982 | 0 | 0 | 28,122 |
| Mitchell | 1920 | 2,919,157 | 2,759,767 | 218,795,766 |
| Montague | 1919 | 1,478,989 | 1,488,465 | 287,373,734 |
| Montgomery | 1931 | 1,231,724 | 1,090,747 | 772,964,976 |
| Moore | 1926 | 264,331 | 226,871 | 29,321,455 |
| Motley | 1957 | 55,552 | 47,701 | 10,858,060 |
| Nacogdoches | 1866 | 61,478 | 84,979 | 3,503,206 |
| Navarro | 1894 | 317,473 | 378,726 | 217,663,000 |
| Newton | 1937 | 919,712 | 679,272 | 61,730,333 |
| Nolan | 1939 | 1,896,132 | 1,588,007 | 195,015,735 |
| Nueces | 1930 | 1,593,724 | 1,535,045 | 558,607,036 |
| Ochiltree | 1951 | 915,252 | 912,865 | 158,216,773 |
| Oldham | 1957 | 76,817 | 108,335 | 13,605,525 |
| Orange | 1913 | 1,119,946 | 1,021,942 | 155,545,427 |
| Palo Pinto | 1902 | 439,608 | 352,682 | 22,910,763 |
| Panola | 1917 | 2,124,837 | 1,860,942 | 88,479,608 |
| Parker | 1942 | 13,437 | 11,294 | 2,856,145 |
| Parmer | 1963 | 0 | 0 | 144,000 |
| Pecos | 1926 | 10,543,671 | 9,421,586 | 1,734,757,910 |
| Polk | 1930 | 1,756,536 | 1,387,984 | 121,722,421 |
| Potter | 1925 | 199,179 | 158,943 | 9,518,441 |
| Presidio | 1980 | 11 | 0 | 4,377 |
| Rains | 1955 | 8 | 2 | 148,896 |
| Reagan | 1923 | 5,031,158 | 4,903,781 | 492,938,399 |
| Red River | 1951 | 329,257 | 289,434 | 7,310,308 |
| Reeves | 1939 | 789,749 | 763,966 | 76,306,618 |
| Refugio | 1920 | 3,980,748 | 4,281,355 | 1,309,332,307 |
| Roberts | 1945 | 462,847 | 418,820 | 45,819,235 |

| County | Year of Discovery | Production in Barrels* 2001 | Production in Barrels* 2002 | Total Production to Jan. 1, 2003 |
|---|---|---|---|---|
| Robertson | 1944 | 1,943,053 | 1,470,362 | 23,359,210 |
| Runnels | 1927 | 599,296 | 582,167 | 146,106,818 |
| Rusk | 1930 | 3,348,655 | 3,108,775 | 1,822,778,000 |
| Sabine | 1981 | 26,410 | 19,506 | 4,881,109 |
| San Augustine | 1947 | 19,210 | 10,770 | 2,446,513 |
| San Jacinto | 1940 | 233,496 | 212,174 | 25,455,691 |
| San Patricio | 1930 | 811,434 | 770,559 | 482,396,276 |
| San Saba | 1982 | 0 | 0 | 32,362 |
| Schleicher | 1934 | 532,430 | 537,557 | 86,826,025 |
| Scurry | 1923 | 7,473,417 | 9,025,877 | 2,006,853,566 |
| Shackelford | 1910 | 971,024 | 876,888 | 180,515,977 |
| Shelby | 1917 | 107,993 | 136,767 | 2,576,688 |
| Sherman | 1938 | 201,698 | 155,057 | 9,042,505 |
| Smith | 1931 | 1,213,356 | 1,252,757 | 261,304,496 |
| Somervell | 1978 | 0 | 0 | 141 |
| Starr | 1929 | 2,414,253 | 3,097,448 | 289,197,134 |
| Stephens | 1916 | 2,823,745 | 2,440,957 | 333,828,950 |
| Sterling | 1947 | 1,115,502 | 1,059,395 | 85,895,726 |
| Stonewall | 1938 | 1,592,594 | 1,432,285 | 259,744,838 |
| Sutton | 1948 | 89,510 | 93,112 | 7,583,873 |
| Swisher | 1981 | 0 | 0 | 6 |
| Tarrant | 1969 | 58 | 465 | 716 |
| Taylor | 1929 | 649,833 | 605,340 | 143,211,139 |
| Terrell | 1952 | 332,674 | 369,578 | 8,238,918 |
| Terry | 1940 | 4,975,637 | 4,767,863 | 429,230,705 |
| Throckmorton | 1925 | 1,184,792 | 1,120,953 | 218,904,133 |
| Titus | 1936 | 524,232 | 517,156 | 210,233,164 |
| Tom Green | 1940 | 513,488 | 483,559 | 91,334,717 |
| Travis | 1934 | 2,468 | 1,673 | 750,237 |
| Trinity | 1946 | 27,515 | 30,676 | 715,350 |

| County | Year of Discovery | Production in Barrels* 2001 | Production in Barrels* 2002 | Total Production to Jan. 1, 2003 |
|---|---|---|---|---|
| Tyler | 1937 | 458,723 | 722,315 | 39,750,183 |
| Upshur | 1931 | 718,481 | 706,554 | 285,951,485 |
| Upton | 1925 | 10,544,486 | 8,752,940 | 810,328,595 |
| Uvalde | 1950 | 0 | 0 | 1,814 |
| Val Verde | 1935 | 2,832 | 2,516 | 136,545 |
| Van Zandt | 1929 | 1,748,289 | 1,349,309 | 548,460,160 |
| Victoria | 1931 | 1,050,733 | 854,179 | 251,203,527 |
| Walker | 1934 | 10,720 | 8,458 | 506,263 |
| Waller | 1934 | 1,094,646 | 1,045,575 | 24,745,716 |
| Ward | 1928 | 5,572,460 | 5,174,026 | 747,538,817 |
| Washington | 1915 | 687,675 | 766,107 | 29,531,271 |
| Webb | 1921 | 1,809,373 | 1,792,028 | 157,272,601 |
| Wharton | 1925 | 3,467,134 | 2,396,969 | 338,388,757 |
| Wheeler | 1910 | 586,578 | 524,707 | 99,443,522 |
| Wichita | 1910 | 2,154,933 | 2,149,212 | 823,346,262 |
| Wilbarger | 1915 | 639,830 | 609,212 | 262,198,713 |
| Willacy | 1936 | 541,506 | 586,574 | 111,987,697 |
| Williamson | 1915 | 10,221 | 7,275 | 9,527,737 |
| Wilson | 1941 | 370,890 | 332,072 | 48,211,095 |
| Winkler | 1926 | 4,220,837 | 4,392,592 | 1,065,701,154 |
| Wise | 1942 | 695,196 | 879,034 | 98,688,929 |
| Wood | 1940 | 6,444,489 | 5,845,781 | 1,189,904,145 |
| Yoakum | 1936 | 25,215,160 | 24,655,826 | 2,013,442,186 |
| Young | 1917 | 1,628,380 | 1,524,451 | 305,940,887 |
| Zapata | 1919 | 299,991 | 266,289 | 46,978,911 |
| Zavala | 1937 | 379,628 | 302,176 | 45,370,467 |

*Total includes condensate production.

**State totals:** (2001) 416,100,026, (2002) 405,051,557.
Source: Railroad Commission, 2001-02 production reports.

# Oil and Gas Production by County 2002

In 2002 in Texas, the total natural gas production was 4,860,455,361 thousand cubic feet (MCF) and total crude oil production was 365,711,328 barrels (BBL). Total condensate was 39,340,129 BBL. Total casinghead was 834,426,336 MCF. Counties not listed in the chart below had no production in 2002.

Source: Texas Railroad Commission.
BBL refers to barrels and MCF to thousand cubic feet.

| County | Crude Oil BBL | Casinghead MCF | Gas Well Gas MCF | Condensate BBL |
|---|---|---|---|---|
| Anderson | 882,574 | 5,190,615 | 9,197,696 | 85,157 |
| Andrews | 26,867,554 | 37,432,349 | 1,906,772 | 3,082 |
| Angelina | 10,337 | 36,991 | 518,755 | 1,144 |
| Aransas | 76,960 | 556,453 | 6,451,672 | 225,475 |
| Archer | 1,285,800 | 734,048 | 0 | 0 |
| Atascosa | 593,673 | 263,364 | 7,722,259 | 17,753 |
| Austin | 329,871 | 58,999 | 9,668,107 | 60,420 |
| Bandera | 1,804 | 0 | 0 | 0 |
| Bastrop | 129,049 | 276,242 | 280,530 | 12,772 |
| Baylor | 134,533 | 80 | 0 | 0 |
| Bee | 419,090 | 356,746 | 37,519,009 | 200,849 |
| Bexar | 127,888 | 622 | 240 | 0 |
| Borden | 4,692,587 | 2,769,882 | 0 | 0 |
| Bowie | 156,645 | 83,368 | 195,067 | 12,651 |
| Brazoria | 1,765,355 | 1,819,807 | 35,553,717 | 636,051 |
| Brazos | 2,333,211 | 7,512,055 | 9,399,808 | 131,050 |
| Brooks | 142,406 | 355,280 | 130,820,786 | 2,171,038 |
| Brown | 109,221 | 341,826 | 1,210,687 | 1,559 |
| Burleson | 3,214,382 | 14,879,118 | 5,135,450 | 113,534 |
| Caldwell | 862,644 | 457,082 | 21,230 | 332 |
| Calhoun | 366,956 | 602,091 | 7,087,673 | 97,477 |

| County | Crude Oil BBL | Casinghead MCF | Gas Well Gas MCF | Condensate BBL |
|---|---|---|---|---|
| Callahan | 234,193 | 356,656 | 717,459 | 3,041 |
| Cameron | 0 | 0 | 1,110,044 | 720 |
| Camp | 381,243 | 46,909 | 808,295 | 4 |
| Carson | 367,998 | 2,579,545 | 24,523,307 | 0 |
| Cass | 347,162 | 444,227 | 5,714,543 | 19,321 |
| Chambers | 1,213,608 | 2,357,669 | 26,464,474 | 356,451 |
| Cherokee | 222,595 | 387,027 | 13,576,160 | 63,306 |
| Childress | 24,864 | 240 | 0 | 0 |
| Clay | 824,808 | 638,021 | 259,117 | 10,949 |
| Cochran | 4,133,524 | 3,839,950 | 304,185 | 1,562 |
| Coke | 524,994 | 2,444,637 | 786,982 | 2,827 |
| Coleman | 313,093 | 708,780 | 1,187,982 | 2,633 |
| Collingswth | 3,213 | 31,889 | 1,485,786 | 0 |
| Colorado | 228,437 | 739,812 | 26,732,056 | 244,559 |
| Comanche | 8,631 | 122,521 | 674,832 | 1,159 |
| Concho | 847,119 | 1,795,511 | 580,841 | 1,991 |
| Cooke | 1,690,421 | 493,859 | 120,906 | 595 |
| Cottle | 44,036 | 56,610 | 5,175,759 | 39,148 |
| Crane | 10,488,838 | 55,106,403 | 11,732,745 | 68,805 |
| Crockett | 3,436,239 | 6,092,956 | 112,111,511 | 273,630 |
| Crosby | 687,385 | 91,551 | 0 | 0 |
| Culberson | 115,070 | 177,886 | 1,278,119 | 13,031 |

| County | Crude Oil BBL | Casinghead MCF | Gas Well Gas MCF | Condensate BBL | County | Crude Oil BBL | Casinghead MCF | Gas Well Gas MCF | Condensate BBL |
|---|---|---|---|---|---|---|---|---|---|
| Dallas | 0 | 0 | 1,457 | 0 | Jefferson | 944,824 | 1,403,920 | 28,502,994 | 618,338 |
| Dawson | 5,580,967 | 6,891,031 | 0 | 0 | Jim Hogg | 92,205 | 183,954 | 46,277,101 | 514,013 |
| Delta | 455 | 0 | 0 | 0 | Jim Wells | 175,899 | 517,407 | 11,531,917 | 72,067 |
| Denton | 12,302 | 66,487 | 104,021,599 | 524,239 | Johnson | 0 | 0 | 27,881 | 0 |
| DeWitt | 87,801 | 87,662 | 13,298,892 | 130,568 | Jones | 762,703 | 462,734 | 42,994 | 1,107 |
| Dickens | 1,375,926 | 124,728 | 0 | 0 | Karnes | 204,297 | 332,002 | 8,258,603 | 102,520 |
| Dimmit | 531,390 | 907,931 | 774,952 | 5,115 | Kaufman | 64,284 | 21,977 | 0 | 0 |
| Donley | 0 | 0 | 19,585 | 0 | Kenedy | 173,140 | 173,920 | 60,063,009 | 280,734 |
| Duval | 1,234,058 | 626,828 | 62,214,640 | 227,361 | Kent | 6,477,361 | 8,78,198 | 0 | 0 |
| Eastland | 288,089 | 1,114,879 | 3,977,665 | 17,417 | Kimble | 198 | 0 | 423,231 | 5 |
| Ector | 19,550,928 | 29,380,937 | 17,597,880 | 14,869 | King | 2,767,393 | 204,274 | 2,403,112 | 16,352 |
| Edwards | 2,408 | 24 | 19,324,632 | 2,469 | Kleberg | 80,849 | 265,319 | 41,300,615 | 1,264,362 |
| Ellis | 145 | 0 | 0 | 0 | Knox | 283,677 | 5,708 | 0 | 0 |
| Erath | 1,814 | 19,194 | 2,663,476 | 3,528 | Lamb | 1,119,341 | 59,363 | 0 | 0 |
| Falls | 2,999 | 12 | 0 | 0 | La Salle | 136,752 | 182,063 | 10,707,480 | 123,773 |
| Fayette | 2,079,859 | 15,074,770 | 19,418,101 | 477,626 | Lavaca | 198,273 | 767,634 | 91,733,849 | 474,409 |
| Fisher | 845,912 | 1,218,827 | 60,131 | 127 | Lee | 1,759,357 | 12,629,647 | 4,722,269 | 81,412 |
| Floyd | 1,050 | 0 | 0 | 0 | Leon | 795,701 | 1,661,699 | 21,593,655 | 76,617 |
| Foard | 142,830 | 2,073 | 1,033,391 | 0 | Liberty | 1,387,201 | 1,170,620 | 32,670,859 | 1,043,806 |
| Fort Bend | 1,648,088 | 1,120,412 | 45,584,903 | 1,387,331 | Limestone | 105,855 | 1,863 | 42,594,415 | 56,994 |
| Franklin | 400,216 | 191,513 | 5,084,404 | 65,639 | Lipscomb | 355,082 | 3,322,717 | 28,558,115 | 104,852 |
| Freestone | 76,017 | 49,037 | 216,980,143 | 192,554 | Live Oak | 338,878 | 373,513 | 28,120,153 | 316,737 |
| Frio | 655,277 | 560,592 | 731,050 | 989 | Loving | 1,189,385 | 2,856,359 | 18,274,740 | 3,907 |
| Gaines | 31,746,447 | 49,458,261 | 10,826,076 | 4,171 | Lubbock | 1,589,202 | 67,195 | 0 | 0 |
| Galveston | 634,260 | 910,188 | 26,286,268 | 1,766,075 | Lynn | 217,656 | 58,361 | 0 | 0 |
| Garza | 5,088,240 | 1,157,310 | 0 | 0 | Madison | 372,941 | 606,017 | 5,489,792 | 68,264 |
| Glasscock | 4,587,839 | 15,039,919 | 1,449,330 | 20,671 | Marion | 119,842 | 75,828 | 5,109,727 | 63,907 |
| Goliad | 340,013 | 830,559 | 37,699,988 | 354,523 | Martin | 4,761,267 | 11,443,983 | 58,125 | 980 |
| Gonzales | 304,757 | 221,517 | 1,503,461 | 14,126 | Matagorda | 1,223,631 | 2,150,522 | 34,194,378 | 805,067 |
| Gray | 1,640,899 | 4,025,276 | 11,707,734 | 4,452 | Maverick | 1,226,959 | 204,713 | 6,037,502 | 39,176 |
| Grayson | 1,353,831 | 3,777,295 | 3,128,798 | 26,391 | McCulloch | 138,446 | 66,148 | 60,428 | 0 |
| Gregg | 3,495,217 | 3,174,139 | 55,069,330 | 168,040 | McLennan | 1,556 | 50 | 0 | 0 |
| Grimes | 134,469 | 603,673 | 21,250,733 | 102,317 | McMullen | 974,444 | 3,570,420 | 20,559,181 | 180,233 |
| Guadalupe | 893,980 | 106,484 | 14,288 | 335 | Medina | 80,164 | 399 | 0 | 0 |
| Hale | 4,272,137 | 173,984 | 0 | 0 | Menard | 123,953 | 24,630 | 118,085 | 0 |
| Hamilton | 811 | 0 | 34,943 | 0 | Midland | 10,624,561 | 39,360,112 | 24,748,459 | 549,314 |
| Hansford | 159,505 | 741,286 | 28,596,530 | 27,813 | Milam | 686,143 | 395,425 | 31,028 | 267 |
| Hardeman | 2,144,731 | 804,600 | 0 | 0 | Mills | 0 | 0 | 15,766 | 0 |
| Hardin | 1,061,392 | 679,797 | 17,778,337 | 1,196,158 | Mitchell | 2,759,767 | 398,163 | 0 | 0 |
| Harris | 1,786,442 | 2,807,695 | 32,058,594 | 341,465 | Montague | 1,484,748 | 1,523,661 | 371,135 | 3,717 |
| Harrison | 475,649 | 2,201,015 | 56,140,590 | 424,650 | Montgomery | 840,127 | 1,038,269 | 21,147,800 | 250,620 |
| Hartley | 314,247 | 180 | 2,287,597 | 0 | Moore | 225,079 | 2,876,208 | 50,464,591 | 1,792 |
| Haskell | 480,514 | 93,014 | 992 | 0 | Motley | 47,701 | 2,060 | 0 | 0 |
| Hemphill | 297,849 | 3,214,737 | 70,710,779 | 400,149 | Nacogdches | 4,716 | 88,624 | 28,858,928 | 80,263 |
| Henderson | 927,986 | 18,381,272 | 23,422,158 | 41,034 | Navarro | 371,121 | 66,071 | 447,752 | 7,605 |
| Hidalgo | 78,024 | 197,721 | 309,349,459 | 3,813,540 | Newton | 562,504 | 2,798,772 | 2,078,125 | 116,768 |
| Hill | 1,161 | 0 | 0 | 0 | Nolan | 1,586,748 | 1,926,710 | 446,598 | 1,259 |
| Hockley | 22,162,603 | 41,215,008 | 153,240 | 1,818 | Nueces | 643,929 | 1,926,710 | 57,202,945 | 891,116 |
| Hood | 0 | 0 | 1,056,377 | 674 | Ochiltree | 828,980 | 3,032,091 | 25,885,279 | 83,885 |
| Hopkins | 277,919 | 149,546 | 1,135,541 | 12,141 | Oldham | 108,335 | 730 | 245,729 | 0 |
| Houston | 724,444 | 334,071 | 2,524,368 | 30,670 | Orange | 368,833 | 411,901 | 13,510,077 | 653,109 |
| Howard | 7,127,913 | 8,766,447 | 1,718,017 | 11,168 | Palo Pinto | 316,242 | 1,756,633 | 12,421,523 | 36,440 |
| Hutchinson | 960,408 | 6,201,597 | 11,723,102 | 9,599 | Panola | 493,980 | 4,353,719 | 237,167,942 | 1,366,962 |
| Irion | 1,573,731 | 8,309,648 | 3,533,708 | 27,594 | Parker | 4,229 | 48,871 | 6,693,911 | 7,065 |
| Jack | 694,323 | 3,941,149 | 13,042,124 | 85,675 | Pecos | 9,183,438 | 40,374,582 | 174,028,122 | 238,148 |
| Jackson | 1,012,642 | 1,732,058 | 16,112,799 | 133,144 | Polk | 388,329 | 246,064 | 31,512,569 | 999,655 |
| Jasper | 187,034 | 1,126,179 | 9,601,414 | 447,041 | Potter | 158,943 | 490,095 | 19,371,520 | 0 |

| County | Crude Oil BBL | Casinghead MCF | Gas Well Gas MCF | Condensate BBL | County | Crude Oil BBL | Casinghead MCF | Gas Well Gas MCF | Condensate BBL |
|---|---|---|---|---|---|---|---|---|---|
| Rains | 0 | 0 | 7,899,271 | 2 | Titus | 517,156 | 2,676 | 201 | 0 |
| Reagan | 4,852,365 | 24,022,656 | 2,421,283 | 51,416 | Tom Green | 480,046 | 2,367,687 | 573,280 | 3,513 |
| Red River | 289,434 | 43,437 | 0 | 0 | Travis | 1,673 | 12 | 0 | 0 |
| Reeves | 714,672 | 2,323,877 | 32,878,947 | 49,294 | Trinity | 30,151 | 223,755 | 46,215 | 525 |
| Refugio | 4,223,831 | 17,068,289 | 21,010,285 | 57,524 | Tyler | 600,555 | 1,694,702 | 2,192,110 | 121,760 |
| Roberts | 296,410 | 3,927,522 | 22,658,926 | 122,410 | Upshur | 143,325 | 22,239 | 63,007,107 | 563,229 |
| Robertson | 1,463,198 | 743,089 | 48,954,191 | 7,164 | Upton | 8,157,873 | 29,920,831 | 32,358,353 | 595,067 |
| Runnels | 579,190 | 1,550,724 | 317,281 | 2,977 | Uvalde | 0 | 0 | 28,498 | 0 |
| Rusk | 2,840,736 | 1,721,616 | 77,098,931 | 268,039 | Val Verde | 1,663 | 4,389 | 26,100,975 | 853 |
| Sabine | 19,193 | 117,917 | 24,416 | 313 | Van Zandt | 1,331,549 | 2,123,348 | 7,000,611 | 17,760 |
| S.Augustine | 10,770 | 58,025 | 122,616 | 0 | Victoria | 642,800 | 716,519 | 22,974,693 | 211,379 |
| San Jacinto | 37,212 | 58,359 | 5,499,122 | 174,962 | Walker | 3,276 | 47,922 | 2,584,081 | 5,182 |
| San Patricio | 485,273 | 1,123,765 | 12,554,304 | 285,286 | Waller | 997,607 | 117,072 | 7,099,240 | 47,968 |
| Schleicher | 477,622 | 1,435,884 | 10,651,868 | 59,935 | Ward | 4,976,863 | 12,693,152 | 59,898,171 | 197,163 |
| Scurry | 9,025,877 | 32,121,398 | 0 | 0 | Washington | 534,916 | 3,833,310 | 41,547,254 | 231,191 |
| Shackelford | 866,347 | 1,190,949 | 2,538,420 | 10,541 | Webb | 164,746 | 89,655 | 279,501,749 | 1,627,282 |
| Shelby | 35,322 | 146,151 | 25,569,003 | 101,445 | Wharton | 1,200,433 | 783,467 | 61,949,557 | 1,196,536 |
| Sherman | 150,412 | 236,503 | 25,446,321 | 4,645 | Wheeler | 343,768 | 835,104 | 30,517,611 | 180,939 |
| Smith | 1,142,553 | 1,852,891 | 13,483,550 | 110,204 | Wichita | 2,149,212 | 122,856 | 0 | 0 |
| Somervell | 0 | 0 | 17,578 | 0 | Wilbarger | 609,212 | 43,320 | 7,092 | 0 |
| Starr | 887,612 | 1,528,186 | 175,713,080 | 2,209,836 | Willacy | 542,632 | 675,017 | 19,214,751 | 43,942 |
| Stephens | 2,393,428 | 2,933,691 | 14,732,437 | 47,529 | Williamson | 7,275 | 72 | 13,093 | 0 |
| Sterling | 973,097 | 11,109,414 | 9,350,105 | 86,298 | Wilson | 331,984 | 46,193 | 11,525 | 88 |
| Stonewall | 1,432,285 | 537,504 | 362 | 0 | Winkler | 4,306,920 | 15,003,901 | 30,394,893 | 85,672 |
| Sutton | 18,398 | 62,922 | 67,941,386 | 74,714 | Wise | 376,191 | 5,945,776 | 128,841,023 | 502,843 |
| Tarrant | 0 | 0 | 17,747,578 | 465 | Wood | 5,812,746 | 3,095,237 | 9,892,071 | 33,035 |
| Taylor | 604,502 | 281,344 | 74,868 | 838 | Yoakum | 24,655,826 | 91,131,684 | 138,095 | 0 |
| Terrell | 50,651 | 1,481,580 | 63,377,950 | 318,927 | Young | 1,511,442 | 2,343,795 | 1,661,453 | 13,009 |
| Terry | 4,767,862 | 1,778,122 | 428,462 | 1 | Zapata | 43,712 | 39,111 | 280,411,946 | 222,577 |
| Throckmrton | 1,120,628 | 1,640,854 | 280,206 | 325 | Zavala | 300,882 | 113,885 | 1,942,059 | 1,294 |

*An employee repairs the fence at a Texas City refinery. File Photo.*

# Nonfuel Mineral Production and Value, 1999, 2000 and 2001

Source: U.S. Geological Survey and the Texas Bureau of Economic Geology.
*(Production measured by mine shipments, sales or marketable production, including consumption by producer. Production and value data given in **thousand metric tons and thousand dollars**, unless otherwise specified.)*

| Mineral | 1999 | | 2000 | | 2001* | |
|---|---|---|---|---|---|---|
| | Production | Value | Production | Value | Production | Value |
| **Cement:** | | | | | | |
| Masonry . . . . . . . . . . . . . . . . . . . . . . | 261 | $ 29,400* | 268 | $28,800* | 250* | $ 27,200* |
| Portland. . . . . . . . . . . . . . . . . . . . . . . | 8,680 | 659,000* | 9,270 | 683,000* | 10,700* | 788,000* |
| **Clays,Common**. . . . . . . . . . . . . . . . | 2,100 | 9,890 | 2,210 | 9,460 | 2,210 | 9,460 |
| **Gemstones** . . . . . . . . . . . . . . . . . . . | NA | 11 | NA | 11 | NA | 12 |
| **Gypsum, crude**. . . . . . . . . . . . . . . . | 2,230 | 15,700 | 1,760 | 8,980 | 1,560 | 8,100 |
| **Lime**. . . . . . . . . . . . . . . . . . . . . . . . . | 1,670 | 111,000 | 1,600 | 105,000 | 1,550 | 94,300 |
| **Salt**. . . . . . . . . . . . . . . . . . . . . . . . . . | 10,200 | 97,500 | 10,800 | 104,000 | 10,800 | 104,000 |
| **Sand and gravel:** | | | | | | |
| Construction . . . . . . . . . . . . . . . . . | 77,100 | 373,000 | 80,800 | 408,000 | 89,000 | 456,000 |
| Industrial . . . . . . . . . . . . . . . . . . . . . | 1,620 | 37,100 | 1,750 | 45,200 | 1,750 | 45,200 |
| **Stone:** | | | | | | |
| Crushed. . . . . . . . . . . . . . . . . . . . . . | 108,000 | 447,000 | 121,000 | 496,000 | 145,000 | 612,000 |
| Dimension (metric tons) . . . . . . . . . . | 82,500 | 24,200 | 84,700 | 11,500 | 84,700 | 11,500 |
| **Talc and pyrophyllite** (metric tons) . . . . | 220,000 | 5,000 | 212,000 | 3,580 | 259,000 | 5,860 |
| **Zeolites** (metric tons). . . . . . . . . . . . . . . | ** | NA | ** | NA | ** | NA |
| **‡Combined value** . . . . . . . . . . . . . . . . | § | 58,400 | § | 44,900 | § | 35,900 |
| **††Total Texas Values** . . . . . . . . . . . . . | § | $1,870,000 | § | $1,950,000 | § | $2,210,000 |

* Estimated . † Preliminary. NA - Not available. W - Data withheld to avoid disclosing proprietary data; value included with "Combined value." ** Withheld to avoid disclosing company proprietary data. § Not applicable.
‡ Includes value of clays [ball, bentonite, fuller's earth, kaolin], helium, magnesium compounds, magnesium metal, sulfur (Frasch), and values indicated by symbol W.
†† Data do not add to total shown because of independent rounding.

# Nonpetroleum Minerals

The nonpetroleum minerals that occur in Texas constitute a long list. Some are currently mined; some may have a potential for future development; some are minor occurrences only. Although overshadowed by the petroleum, natural gas and natural gas liquids that are produced in the state, many of the non-petroleum minerals are, nonetheless, important to the economy. In 1999, they were valued at an estimated $2.05 billion. Texas is annually **among the nation's leading states in value of nonpetroleum mineral production**. In 2000, **Texas ranked fifth nationally** in total mineral output.

The **Bureau of Economic Geology**, which functions as the state geological survey of Texas, revised the following information about nonpetroleum minerals for this edition of the Texas Almanac. Publications of the Bureau, on file in many libraries, contain more detailed information. Among the items available is the Bureau map, "Mineral Resources of Texas," showing locations of resource access of many nonpetroleum minerals.

A catalog of Bureau publications is also available free on request from the Bureau Publications Sales, University Station, Box X, Austin, TX 78713-7508; 512-471-1534. On the Web: www.beg.utexas.edu/.

Texas' nonpetroleum minerals are as follows:

**ALUMINUM** — No aluminum ores are mined in Texas, but three Texas plants process aluminum materials in one or more ways. Plants in San Patricio and Calhoun counties produce **aluminum oxide (alumina)** from imported raw ore **(bauxite)**, and a plant in Milam County reduces the oxide to aluminum.

**ASBESTOS** — Small occurrences of amphibole-type asbestos have been found in the state. In West Texas, **richterite**, a white, long-fibered amphibole, is associated with some of the **talc deposits** northwest of **Allamoore** in Hudspeth County. Another type, **tremolite**, has been found in the **Llano Uplift** of Central Texas where it is associated with **serpentinite** in eastern Gillespie and western Blanco County. No asbestos is mined in Texas.

**ASPHALT (Native)** — Asphalt-bearing Cretaceous limestones crop out in Burnet, Kinney, Pecos, Reeves, Uvalde and other counties. The most significant deposit is in southwestern Uvalde County where asphalt occurs naturally in the pore spaces of the Anacacho Limestone. The material is quarried and used extensively as **road-paving material**. Asphalt-bearing sandstones occur in Anderson, Angelina, Cooke, Jasper, Maverick, Montague, Nacogdoches, Uvalde, Zavala and other counties.

**BARITE** — Deposits of a heavy, nonmetallic mineral, barite (barium sulphate), have been found in many localities, including Baylor, Brown, Brewster, Culberson, Gillespie, Howard, Hudspeth, Jeff Davis, Kinney, Llano, Live Oak, Taylor, Val Verde and Webb counties. During the 1960s, there was small, intermittent production in the **Seven Heart Gap** area of the **Apache Mountains** in Culberson County, where barite was mined from open pits. Most of the deposits are known to be relatively small, but the Webb County deposit has not been evaluated. Grinding plants, which prepare barite mined outside of Texas for use chiefly as a **weighting agent** in well-drilling muds and as a **filler**, are located in Brownsville, Corpus Christi, El Paso, Galena Park, Galveston, and Houston.

**BASALT (TRAP ROCK)** — Masses of basalt — a

hard, dark-colored, fine-grained igneous rock — crop out in Kinney, Travis, Uvalde and several other counties along the **Balcones Fault Zone,** and also in the Trans-Pecos area of West Texas. Basalt is quarried near Knippa in Uvalde County for use as **road-building material, railroad ballast and other aggregate.**

**BENTONITE** (see **CLAYS**).

**BERYLLIUM** — Occurrences of beryllium minerals at several Trans-Pecos localities have been recognized for several years.

**BRINE** (see also **SALT, SODIUM SULPHATE**) — Many wells in Texas produce brine by solution mining of subsurface salt deposits, mostly in West Texas counties such as Andrews, Crane, Ector, Loving, Midland, Pecos, Reeves, Ward and others. These wells in the Permian Basin dissolve salt from the **Salado Formation,** an enormous salt deposit that extends in the subsurface from north of the Big Bend northward to Kansas, has an east-west width of 150 to 200 miles, and may have several hundred feet of net salt thickness. The majority of the brine is used in the **petroleum industry,** but it also is used in **water softening, the chemical industry** and other uses. Three Gulf Coast counties, Fort Bend, Duval and Jefferson, have brine stations that produce from **salt domes.**

**BUILDING STONE (DIMENSION STONE)** — **Granite** and **limestone** currently are quarried for use as dimension stone. The granite quarries are located in Burnet, Gillespie, Llano and Mason counties; the limestone quarries are in Shackelford and Williamson counties. Past production of limestone for use as dimension stone has been reported in Burnet, Gillespie, Jones, Tarrant, Travis and several other counties. There has also been production of **sandstone** in various counties for use as dimension stone.

**CEMENT MATERIALS** — Cement is currently manufactured in Bexar, Comal, Dallas, Ector, Ellis, Hays, McLennan, Nolan and Potter counties. Many of these plants utilize Cretaceous limestones and shales or clays as raw materials for the cement. On the Texas High Plains, a cement plant near Amarillo uses impure **caliche** as the chief raw material. **Iron oxide,** also a constituent of cement, is available from the iron ore deposits of East Texas and from smelter slag. **Gypsum,** added to the cement as a retarder, is found chiefly in North Central Texas, Central Texas and the Trans-Pecos area.

**CHROMIUM** — Chromite-bearing rock has been found in several small deposits around the margin of the Coal Creek **serpentinite** mass in northeastern Gillespie County and northwestern Blanco County. Exploration has not revealed significant deposits.

**CLAYS** — Texas has an abundance and variety of ceramic and non-ceramic clays and is one of the country's leading producers of clay products.

Almost any kind of clay, ranging from common clay used to make ordinary brick and tile to clays suitable for manufacture of specialty whitewares, can be used for ceramic purposes. **Fire clay** suitable for use as **refractories** occurs chiefly in East and North Central Texas; **ball clay,** a high-quality plastic ceramic clay, is found locally in East Texas.

Ceramic clay suitable for quality structural clay products such as **structural building brick, paving brick and drain tile** is especially abundant in East and North Central Texas. Common clay suitable for use in the manufacture of cement and ordinary brick is found in most counties of the state. Many of the Texas clays will expand or bloat upon rapid firing and are suitable for the manufacture of lightweight aggregate, which is used mainly in concrete blocks and highway surfacing.

Nonceramic clays are utilized without firing. They are used primarily as **bleaching and absorbent clays, fillers, coaters, additives, bonding clays, drilling muds, catalysts** and potentially as sources of alumina. Most of the nonceramic clays in Texas are **bentonites and fuller's earth**. These occur extensively in the Coastal Plain and locally in the High Plains and Big Bend areas. **Kaolin clays** in parts of East Texas are potential sources of such nonceramic products as **paper coaters and fillers, rubber fillers and drilling agents**. Relatively high in alumina, these clays also are a potential source of metallic aluminum.

**COAL** (see also LIGNITE) — **Bituminous coal,** which occurs in North Central, South and West Texas, was a significant energy source in Texas prior to the large-scale development of oil and gas. During the period from 1895 to 1943, Texas mines produced more than 25 million tons of coal. The mines were inactive for many years, but the renewed interest in coal as a major energy source prompted a revaluation of Texas' coal deposits. In the late 1970s, bituminous coal production resumed in the state on a limited scale when mines were opened in Coleman, Erath and Webb counties.

Much of the state's bituminous coal occurs in North Central Texas. Deposits are found there in Pennsylvanian rocks within a large area that includes Coleman, Eastland, Erath, Jack, McCulloch, Montague, Palo Pinto, Parker, Throckmorton, Wise, Young and other counties. Before the general availability of oil and gas, underground coal mines near **Thurber, Bridgeport, Newcastle, Strawn** and other points annually produced significant coal tonnages. Preliminary evaluations indicate substantial amounts of coal may remain in the North Central Texas area. The coal seams there are generally no more than 30 inches thick and are commonly covered by well-consolidated overburden. Ash and sulphur content are high. Beginning in 1979, two bituminous coal mine operations in North Central Texas — one in southern Coleman County and one in northwestern Erath County — produced coal to be used as fuel by the cement industry. Neither mine is currently operating.

In South Texas, bituminous coal occurs in the Eagle Pass district of Maverick County, and bituminous **cannel coal** is present in the **Santo Tomas district** of Webb County. The Eagle Pass area was a leading coal-producing district in Texas during the late 1800s and early 1900s. The bituminous coal in that area, which occurs in the Upper Cretaceous Olmos Formation, has a high ash content and a moderate moisture and sulfur content. According to reports, Maverick County coal beds range from four to seven feet thick.

The **cannel coals** of western Webb County occur near the Rio Grande in middle Eocene strata. They were mined

for more than 50 years and used primarily as a boiler fuel. Mining ceased from 1939 until 1978, when a surface mine was opened 30 miles northwest of Laredo to produce cannel coal for use as fuel in the cement industry and for export. An additional mine has since been opened in that county. Tests show that the coals of the Webb County Santo Tomas district have a high hydrogen content and yield significant amounts of gas and oil when distilled. They also have a high sulfur content. A potential use might be as a source of various petrochemical products.

Coal deposits in the Trans-Pecos country of West Texas include those in the Cretaceous rocks of the Terlingua area of Brewster County, the Eagle Spring area of Hudspeth County and the **San Carlos** area of Presidio County. The coal deposits in these areas are believed to have relatively little potential for development as a fuel. They have been sold in the past as a soil amendment (see **LEONARDITE**).

**COPPER** — Copper minerals have been found in the **Trans-Pecos** area of West Texas, in the **Llano Uplift** area of Central Texas and in redbed deposits of North Texas. No copper has been mined in Texas during recent years, and the total copper produced in the state has been relatively small. Past attempts to mine the North Texas and Llano Uplift copper deposits resulted in small shipments, but practically all the copper production in the state has been from the **Van Horn-Allamoore** district of Culberson and Hudspeth Counties in the Trans-Pecos area. Chief output was from the **Hazel copper-silver mine** of Culberson County that yielded over 1 million pounds of copper during 1891-1947. Copper ores and concentrates from outside of Texas are processed at **smelters** in El Paso and Amarillo.

**CRUSHED STONE** — Texas is among the leading states in the production of crushed stone. Most production consists of **limestone**; other kinds of crushed stone produced in the state include **basalt (trap rock), dolomite, granite, marble, rhyolite, sandstone and serpentinite.** Large tonnages of crushed stone are used as **aggregate** in concrete, as **road material** and in the manufacture of cement and lime. Some is used as **riprap, terrazzo, roofing chips, filter material, fillers** and for other purposes.

**DIATOMITE (DIATOMACEOUS EARTH)** — Diatomite is a very lightweight siliceous material consisting of the remains of microscopic aquatic plants (diatoms). It is used chiefly as a **filter and filler**; other uses are for **thermal insulation**, as an **abrasive**, as an **insecticide carrier** and as a **lightweight aggregate**, and for other purposes. The diatomite was deposited in shallow fresh-water lakes that were present in the High Plains during portions of the Pliocene and Pleistocene epochs. Deposits have been found in Armstrong, Crosby, Dickens, Ector, Hartley and Lamb counties. No diatomite is mined in Texas.

**DOLOMITE ROCK** — Dolomite rock, which consists largely of the mineral dolomite (calcium-magnesium carbonate), commonly is associated with limestone in Texas. Areas in which dolomite rock occurs include Central Texas, the Callahan Divide and parts of the Edwards Plateau, High Plains and West Texas. Some of the principal deposits of dolomite rock are found in Bell, Brown, Burnet, Comanche, Edwards, El Paso, Gillespie, Lampasas, Mills, Nolan, Taylor and Williamson counties. Dolomite rock can be used as crushed stone (although much of Texas

dolomite is soft and not a good aggregate material), in the manufacture of lime and as a source of **magnesium**.

**FELDSPAR** — Large crystals and crystal fragments of feldspar minerals occur in the Precambrian pegmatite rocks that crop out in the **Llano Uplift** area of Central Texas — including Blanco, Burnet, Gillespie, Llano and Mason counties — and in the **Van Horn area** of Culberson and Hudspeth Counties in West Texas. Feldspar has been mined in Llano County for use as **roofing granules** and as a **ceramic material**. Feldspar is currently mined in Burnet County for use as an aggregate.

**FLUORSPAR** — The mineral fluorite (calcium fluoride), which is known commercially as fluorspar, occurs in both Central and West Texas. In Central Texas, the deposits that have been found in Burnet, Gillespie and Mason counties are not considered adequate to sustain mining operations. In West Texas, deposits have been found in Brewster, El Paso, Hudspeth, Jeff Davis and Presidio counties. Fluorspar has been mined in the **Christmas Mountains** of Brewster County and processed at Marathon. Former West Texas mining activity in the **Eagle Mountains** district of Hudspeth County resulted in the production of approximately 15,000 short tons of fluorspar during the peak years of 1942-1950. No production has been reported in Hudspeth County since that period. Imported fluorspar is processed in Brownsville, Eagle Pass, El Paso and Houston. Fluorspar is used in the **steel, chemical, aluminum, magnesium, ceramics and glass industries** and for various other purposes.

**FULLER'S EARTH** (see **CLAY**).

**GOLD** — No major deposits of gold are known in Texas. Small amounts have been found in the **Llano Uplift** region of Central Texas and in West Texas; minor occurrences have been reported on the **Edwards Plateau** and the **Gulf Coastal Plain** of Texas. Nearly all of the gold produced in the state came as a by-product of silver and lead mining at **Presidio mine**, near **Shafter**, in Presidio County. Additional small quantities were produced as a by-product of copper mining in Culberson County and from residual soils developed from gold-bearing quartz stringers in metamorphic rocks in Llano County. No gold mining has been reported in Texas since 1952. Total **gold production** in the state, 1889-1952, amounted to more than 8,419 troy ounces according to U.S. Bureau of Mines figures. Most of the production — at least 73 percent and probably more — came from the Presidio mine.

**GRANITE** — Granites in shades of red and gray and related intrusive igneous rocks occur in the **Llano Uplift** of Central Texas and in the **Trans-Pecos** country of West Texas. Deposits are found in Blanco, Brewster, Burnet, El Paso, Gillespie, Hudspeth, Llano, McCulloch, Mason, Presidio and other counties. Quarries in Burnet, Gillespie, Llano and Mason counties produce Precambrian granite for a variety of uses as **dimension stone and crushed stone.**

**GRAPHITE** — Graphite, a soft, dark-gray mineral, is a form of very high-grade carbon. It occurs in Precambrian schist rocks of the **Llano Uplift** of Central Texas, notably in Burnet and Llano counties. Crystalline-flake graphite ore formerly was mined from open pits in the **Clear Creek area** of western Burnet County and processed at a plant

near the mine. The mill now occasionally grinds imported material. Uses of natural crystalline graphite are **refractories, steel production, pencil leads, lubricants, foundry facings and crucibles** and for other purposes.

**GRINDING PEBBLES (ABRASIVE STONES)** — Flint pebbles, suitable for use in **tube-mill grinding**, are found in the **Gulf Coastal Plain** where they occur in gravel deposits along rivers and in upland areas. Grinding pebbles are produced from **Frio River terrace** deposits near the McMullen-Live Oak county line, but the area is now part of the Choke Canyon Reservoir area.

**GYPSUM** — Gypsum is widely distributed in Texas. Chief deposits are bedded gypsum in the area east of the **High Plains**, in the **Trans-Pecos** country and in **Central Texas**. It also occurs in **salt-dome caprocks** of the Gulf Coast. The massive, granular variety known as rock gypsum is the kind most commonly used by industry. Other varieties include **alabaster, satin spar and selenite.**

Gypsum is one of the important industrial minerals in Texas. Bedded gypsum is produced from surface mines in Culberson, Fisher, Gillespie, Hardeman, Hudspeth, Kimble, Nolan and Stonewall counties. Gypsum was formerly mined at **Gyp Hill salt dome** in Brooks County and at **Hockley salt dome** in Harris County. Most of the gypsum is calcined and used in the manufacture of **gypsum wallboard, plaster, joint compounds** and other construction products. Crude gypsum is used chiefly as a **retarder in portland cement** and as a **soil conditioner.**

**HELIUM** — Helium is a very light, nonflammable, chemically inert gas. The **U.S. Interior Department has ended its helium operation** near Masterson in the Panhandle. The storage facility at **Cliffside gas field** near Amarillo and the 425-mile pipeline system will remain in operation until the government sells its remaining unrefined, crude helium. Helium is used in **cryogenics, welding, pressurizing and purging, leak detection, synthetic breathing mixtures** and for other purposes.

**IRON** — Iron oxide **(limonite, goethite and hematite)** and **iron carbonate (siderite)** deposits occur widely in East Texas, notably in Cass, Cherokee, Marion and Morris counties, and also in Anderson, Camp, Harrison, Henderson, Nacogdoches, Smith, Upshur and other counties. **Magnetite (magnetic, black iron oxide)** occurs in Central Texas, including a deposit at **Iron Mountain** in Llano County. Hematite occurs in the **Trans-Pecos** area and in the **Llano Uplift** of Central Texas. The extensive deposits of **glauconite** (a complex silicate containing iron) that occur in East Texas and the hematitic and goethitic Cambrian sandstone that crops out in the northwestern Llano Uplift region are potential sources of low-grade iron ore.

Limonite and other East Texas iron ores are mined from open pits in Cherokee and Henderson counties for use in the preparation of **portland cement**, as a **weighting agent in well-drilling fluids**, as an **animal feed supplement** and for other purposes. East Texas iron ores also were mined in the past for use in the iron-steel industry.

**KAOLIN** (see **CLAY**).

**LEAD AND ZINC** — The lead mineral **galena (lead sulfide)** commonly is associated with zinc and silver. It formerly was produced as a by-product of West Texas silver mining, chiefly from the **Presidio mine at Shafter** in Presidio County, although lesser amounts were obtained at several other mines and prospects. Deposits of galena also are known to occur in Blanco, Brewster, Burnet, Gillespie and Hudspeth counties.

Zinc, primarily from the mineral **sphalerite (zinc sulphide)**, was produced chiefly from the **Bonanza** and **Alice Ray mines** in the **Quitman Mountains** of Hudspeth County. In addition, small production was reported from several other areas, including the **Chinati** and **Montezuma mines** of Presidio County and the **Buck Prospect** in the **Apache Mountains** of Culberson County. Zinc mineralization also occurs in association with the lead deposits in Cambrian rocks of Central Texas.

**LEONARDITE** — Deposits of weathered (oxidized) low-Btu value bituminous coals, generally referred to as "leonardite," occur in Brewster County. The name leonardite is used for a mixture of chemical compounds that is high in humic acids. In the past, material from these deposits was sold as **soil conditioner**. Other uses of leonardite include **modification of viscosity of drill fluids and as sorbants in water-treatment.**

**LIGHTWEIGHT AGGREGATE** (see **CLAY, DIATOMITE, PERLITE, VERMICULITE**).

**LIGNITE** — Lignite, a low-rank coal, is found in belts of Tertiary Eocene strata that extend across the Texas Gulf Coastal Plain from the Rio Grande in South Texas to the Arkansas and Louisiana borders in East Texas. The largest resources and best grades (approximately 6,500 BTU/pound) of lignite occur in the Wilcox Group of strata north of the Colorado River in East and Central Texas.

The near-surface lignite resources, occurring at depths of less than 200 feet in seams of three feet or thicker, are estimated at 23 billion short tons. **Recoverable reserves of strippable lignite** — those that can be economically mined under current conditions of price and technology — are estimated to be 9 billion to 11 billion short tons.

Additional lignite resources of the Texas Gulf Coastal Plain occur as deep-basin deposits. Deep-basin resources, those that occur at depths of 200 to 2,000 feet in seams of five feet or thicker, are comparable in magnitude to near-surface resources. The deep-basin lignites are a potential energy resource that conceivably could be utilized by *in situ* (in place) recovery methods such as underground gasification.

As with bituminous coal, lignite production was significant prior to the general availability of oil and gas. Remnants of old underground mines are common throughout the area of lignite occurrence. Large reserves of strippable lignite have again attracted the attention of energy suppliers, and Texas is now the nation's **5th leading producer of coal**, 99 percent of it lignite. Eleven large strip mines are now producing lignite that is burned for **mine-mouth electric-power generation**, and additional mines are planned. One of the currently operating mines is located in Milam and Lee counties, where part of the electric power is used for **alumina reduction**. Other mines are in Atascosa, Bastrop, Franklin, Freestone, Grimes, Harrison, Hopkins, Leon, McMullen, Panola, Robertson, Rusk and Titus counties. New permit applications have been submitted to the Railroad Commission of Texas for Freestone, Lee, Leon and Robertson counties.

**LIME MATERIAL** — **Limestones**, which are abundant in some areas of Texas, are heated to produce lime

(calcium oxide) at a number of plants in the state. High-magnesium limestone and dolomite are used to prepare lime at a plant in Burnet County. Other lime plants are located in Bexar, Bosque, Comal, Hill, Johnson and Travis counties. Lime production captive to the kiln's operator occurs in several Texas counties. Lime is used in **soil stabilization, water purification, paper and pulp manufacture, metallurgy, sugar refining, agriculture, construction, removal of sulfur from stack gases** and for many other purposes.

**LIMESTONE** (see also **BUILDING STONE**) — Texas is one of the nation's leading producers of limestone, which is quarried in more than 60 counties. Limestone occurs in nearly all areas of the state with the exception of most of the Gulf Coastal Plain and High Plains. Although some of the limestone is quarried for use as **dimension stone**, most of the output is crushed for uses such as **bulk building materials (crushed stone, road base, concrete aggregate), chemical raw materials, fillers or extenders, lime and portland cement raw materials, agricultural limestone and removal of sulfur from stack gases.**

**MAGNESITE** — Small deposits of magnesite (natural magnesium carbonate) have been found in Precambrian rocks in Llano and Mason counties of Central Texas. At one time there was small-scale mining of magnesite in the area; some of the material was used as **agricultural stone** and as **terrazzo chips**. Magnesite also can be calcined to form **magnesia**, which is used in **metallurgical furnace refractories** and other products.

**MAGNESIUM** — On the Texas Gulf Coast in Brazoria County, magnesium chloride is **extracted from sea water** at a plant in Freeport and used to produce **magnesium compounds and magnesium metal**. During World War II, high-magnesium Ellenburger dolomite rock from Burnet County was used as magnesium ore at a plant near Austin.

**MANGANESE** — Deposits of manganese minerals, such as **braunite, hollandite and pyrolusite**, have been found in several areas, including Jeff Davis, Llano, Mason, Presidio and Val Verde counties. Known deposits are not large. Small shipments have been made from Jeff Davis, Mason and Val Verde counties, but no manganese mining has been reported in Texas since 1954.

**MARBLE** — Metamorphic and sedimentary marbles suitable for **monument and building stone** are found in the **Llano Uplift** and nearby areas of Central Texas and the **Trans-Pecos** area of West Texas. Gray, white, black, greenish black, light green, brown and cream-colored marbles occur in Central Texas in Burnet, Gillespie, Llano and Mason counties. West Texas metamorphic marbles include the bluish-white and the black marbles found southwest of Alpine in Brewster County and the white marble from **Marble Canyon** north of Van Horn in Culberson County. Marble can be used as **dimension stone, terrazzo and roofing aggregate** and for other purposes.

**MERCURY (QUICKSILVER)** — Mercury minerals, chiefly **cinnabar**, occur in the **Terlingua district** and nearby districts of southern Brewster and southeastern Presidio counties. Mining began there about 1894, and from 1905 to 1935, Texas was one of the nation's leading producers of quicksilver. Following World War II, a sharp drop

in demand and price, along with depletion of developed ore reserves, caused abandonment of all the Texas mercury mines.

With a rise in the price, sporadic mining took place between 1951-1960. In 1965, when the price of mercury moved to a record high, renewed interest in the Texas mercury districts resulted in the reopening of several mines and the discovery of new ore reserves. By April 1972, however, the price had declined and the mines have reported no production since 1973.

**MICA** — Large crystals of flexible, transparent mica minerals in igneous pegmatite rocks and mica flakes in metamorphic schist rocks are found in the **Llano area** of Central Texas and the **Van Horn area** of West Texas. Most Central Texas deposits do not meet specifications for sheet mica, and although several attempts have been made to produce West Texas sheet mica in Culberson and Hudspeth counties, sustained production has not been achieved. A mica quarry operated for a short time in the early 1980s in the Van Horn Mountains of Culberson and Hudspeth counties to mine mica schist for use as an **additive in rotary drilling fluids**.

**MOLYBDENUM** — Small occurrences of molybdenite have been found in Burnet and Llano counties, and **wulfenite**, another molybdenum mineral, has been noted in rocks in the **Quitman Mountains** of Hudspeth County. Molybdenum minerals also occur at **Cave Peak** north of Van Horn in Culberson County, in the **Altuda Mountain area** of northwestern Brewster County and in association with uranium ores of the Gulf Coastal Plain.

**PEAT** — This spongy organic substance forms in bogs from plant remains. It has been found in the **Gulf Coastal Plain** in several localities including Gonzales, Guadalupe, Lee, Milam, Polk and San Jacinto counties. There has been intermittent, small-scale production of some of the peat for use as a **soil conditioner**.

**PERLITE** — Perlite, a glassy igneous rock, expands to a lightweight, porous mass when heated. It can be used as a **lightweight aggregate, filter aid, horticultural aggregate** and for other purposes. Perlite occurs in Presidio County, where it has been mined in the **Pinto Canyon area** north of the **Chinati Mountains**. No perlite is currently mined in Texas, but perlite mined outside of Texas is expanded at plants in Bexar, Dallas, El Paso, Guadalupe, Harris and Nolan counties.

**PHOSPHATE** — Rock phosphate is present in Paleozoic rocks in several areas of Brewster and Presidio counties in West Texas and in Central Texas, but the known deposits are not large. In Northeast Texas, sedimentary rock phosphate occurs in thin conglomeratic lenses in Upper Cretaceous and Tertiary rock units; possibly some of these low-grade phosphorites could be processed on a small scale for local use as a **fertilizer**. Imported phosphate rock is processed at a plant in Brownsville.

**POTASH** — The potassium mineral **polyhalite** is widely distributed in the subsurface Permian Basin of West Texas and has been found in many wells in that area. During 1927-1931, the federal government drilled a series of potash-test wells in Crane, Crockett, Ector, Glasscock, Loving, Reagan, Upton and Winkler counties. In addition to polyhalite, which was found in all of the counties, these

wells revealed the presence of the potassium minerals **carnallite and sylvite** in Loving County and carnallite in Winkler County. The known Texas potash deposits are not as rich as those in the New Mexico portion of the Permian Basin and have not been developed.

**PUMICITE (VOLCANIC ASH)** — Deposits of volcanic ash occur in Brazos, Fayette, Gonzales, Karnes, Polk, Starr and other counties of the Texas Coastal Plain. Deposits also have been found in the Trans-Pecos area, High Plains and in several counties east of the High Plains. Volcanic ash is used to prepare **pozzolan cement, cleansing and scouring compounds and soaps and sweeping compounds**; as a **carrier for insecticides**, and for other purposes. It has been mined in Dickens, Lynn, Scurry, Starr and other counties.

**QUICKSILVER** (see **MERCURY**).

**RARE-EARTH ELEMENTS AND METALS** — The term, "rare-earth elements," is commonly applied to elements of the **lanthanide** group (atomic numbers 57 through 71) plus **yttrium**. Yttrium, atomic number 39 and not a member of the lanthanide group, is included as a rare-earth element because it has similar properties to members of that group and usually occurs in nature with them. The metals **thorium and scandium** are sometimes termed "rare metals" because their occurence is often associated with the rare-earth elements.

The majority of rare-earth elements are consumed as **catalysts** in petroleum cracking and other chemical industries. Rare earths are widely used in the **glass industry for tableware, specialty glasses, optics and fiber optics.** Cerium oxide has growing use as a **polishing compound** for glass, gem stones, cathode-ray tube faceplates, and other polishing. Rare earths are alloyed with various metals to produce materials used in the **aeronautic, space and electronics** industries. Addition of rare-earth elements may improve resistance to metal fatigue at high temperatures, reduce potential for corrosion, and selectively increase conductivity and magnetism of the metal.

Various members of this group, including **thorium,** have anomalous concentrations in the **rhyolitic and related igneous rocks** of the **Quitman Mountains** and the **Sierra Blanca area** of Trans-Pecos.

**SALT (SODIUM CHLORIDE)** (see also **BRINES**) — Salt resources of Texas are virtually inexhaustible. Enormous deposits occur in the subsurface **Permian Basin** of West Texas and in the **salt domes of the Gulf Coastal Plain.** Salt also is found in the alkali **playa lakes** of the High Plains, the **alkali flats or salt lakes in the Salt Basin** of Culberson and Hudspeth counties and along some of the bays and lagoons of the South Texas **Gulf Coast.**

Texas is one of the leading salt-producing states. **Rock salt** is obtained from underground mines in **salt domes at Grand Saline** in Van Zandt County. Approximately one-third of the salt produced in the state is from rock salt; most of the salt is produced by solution mining as brines from wells drilled into the underground salt deposits.

**SAND, INDUSTRIAL** — Sands used for special purposes, due to **high silica content** or to unique physical properties, command higher prices than common sand. Industrial sands in Texas occur mainly in the **Central Gulf Coastal Plain** and in **North Central Texas.** They include **abrasive, blast, chemical, engine, filtration, foundry,** **glass, hydraulic-fracturing (propant), molding and pottery sands.** Recent production of industrial sands has been from Atascosa, Colorado, Hardin, Harris, Liberty, Limestone, McCulloch, Newton, Smith, Somervell and Upshur counties.

**SAND AND GRAVEL (CONSTRUCTION)** — Sand and gravel are among the most extensively utilized resources in Texas. Principal occurrence is along the major streams and in stream terraces. Sand and gravel are important **bulk construction materials, used as railroad ballast, base materials** and for other purposes.

**SANDSTONE** — Sandstones of a variety of colors and textures are widely distributed in a number of geologic formations in Texas. Some of the sandstones have been quarried for use as **dimension stone** in El Paso, Parker, Terrell, Ward and other counties. **Crushed sandstone** is produced in Freestone, Gaines, Jasper, McMullen, Motley and other counties for use as **road-building material, terrazzo stone and aggregate.**

**SERPENTINITE** — Several masses of serpentinite, which formed from the alteration of basic igneous rocks, are associated with other Precambrian metamorphic rocks of the Llano Uplift. The largest deposit is the **Coal Creek serpentinite mass** in northern Blanco and Gillespie counties from which **terrazzo chips** have been produced. Other deposits are present in Gillespie and Llano counties. (The features that are associated with surface and subsurface Cretaceous rocks in several counties in or near the **Balcones Fault Zone** and that are commonly known as **"serpentine plugs"** are not serpentine at all, but are altered igneous volcanic necks and pipes and mounds of altered volcanic ash — **palagonite** — that accumulated around the former **submarine volcanic pipes.**)

**SHELL** — Oyster shells and other shells in shallow coastal waters and in deposits along the **Texas Gulf Coast** have been produced in the past chiefly by dredging. They were used to a limited extent as raw material in the **manufacture of cement, as concrete aggregate and road base**, and for other purposes. No shell has been produced in Texas since 1981.

**SILVER** — During the period 1885-1952, the production of silver in Texas, as reported by the U.S. Bureau of Mines, totaled about **33 million troy ounces.** For about 70 years, silver was the most consistently produced metal in Texas, although always in moderate quantities. All of the production came from the **Trans-Pecos country** of West Texas, where the silver was mined in Brewster County (**Altuda Mountain**), Culberson and Hudspeth counties (**Van Horn Mountains and Van Horn-Allamoore district**), Hudspeth County (**Quitman Mountains and Eagle Mountains**) and Presidio County (**Chinati Mountains area, Loma Plata mine and Shafter district**).

Chief producer was the **Presidio mine in the Shafter district**, which began operations in the late 1800s, and, through September 1942, produced more than 30 million ounces of silver — more than 92 percent of Texas' total silver production. Water in the lower mine levels, lean ores and low price of silver resulted in the closing of the mine in 1942. Another important silver producer was the **Hazel copper-silver mine** in the **Van Horn-Allamoore district** in Culberson County, which accounted for more than 2 million ounces.

An increase in the price of silver in the late 1970s stimulated prospecting for new reserves, and exploration began near the old **Presidio mine**, near the old **Plata Verde mine** in the Van Horn Mountains district, at the **Bonanza mine** in the **Quitman Mountains** district and at the old **Hazel mine**. A decline in the price of silver in the early 1980s, however, resulted in reduction of exploration and mine development in the region. There is no current exploration in these areas.

**SOAPSTONE** (see **TALC AND SOAPSTONE**).

**SODIUM SULFATE (SALT CAKE)** — Sodium sulfate minerals occur in salt beds and brines of the alkali **playa lakes** of the High Plains in West Texas. In some lakes, the sodium sulfate minerals are present in deposits a few feet beneath the lakebeds. Sodium sulfate also is found in underground brines in the Permian Basin. Current production is from brines and dry salt beds at alkali lakes in Gaines and Terry counties. Past production was reported in Lynn and Ward counties. Sodium sulfate is used chiefly by the **detergent and paper and pulp industries**. Other uses are in the **preparation of glass and other products**.

**STONE** (see **BUILDING STONE** and **CRUSHED STONE**).

**STRONTIUM** — Deposits of the mineral **celestite (strontium sulfate)** have been found in a number of places, including localities in Brown, Coke, Comanche, Fisher, Lampasas, Mills, Nolan, Real, Taylor, Travis and Williamson counties. Most of the occurrences are very minor, and no strontium is currently produced in the state.

**SULFUR** — Texas is **one of the world's principal sulfur-producing areas**. The sulfur is mined from deposits of native sulfur, and it is extracted from sour (sulfur-bearing) natural gas and petroleum. **Recovered sulfur** is a growing industry and accounted for approximately 60 percent of all 1987 sulfur production in the United States, but only approximately 40 percent of Texas production. Native sulfur is found in large deposits in the caprock of some of the **salt domes** along the Texas Gulf Coast and in some of the surface and subsurface Permian strata of West Texas, notably in Culberson and Pecos counties.

Native sulfur obtained from the underground deposits is known as **Frasch sulfur**, so-called because of Herman Frasch, the chemist who devised the method of drilling wells into the deposits, melting the sulfur with superheated water and forcing the molten sulfur to the surface. Most of the production now goes to the users in molten form.

Frasch sulfur is produced from only one Gulf Coast salt dome in Wharton County and from West Texas underground Permian strata in Culberson County. Operations at several Gulf Coast domes have been closed in recent years. During the 1940s, acidic sulfur earth was produced in the **Rustler Springs district** in Culberson County for use as a **fertilizer and soil conditioner.** Sulfur is recovered from sour natural gas and petroleum at plants in numerous Texas counties.

Sulfur is used in the preparation of **fertilizers and organic and inorganic chemicals, in petroleum refining** and for many other purposes.

**TALC AND SOAPSTONE** — Deposits of talc are found in the Precambrian metamorphic rocks of the **Allamoore area** of eastern Hudspeth and western Culberson counties. Soapstone, containing talc, occurs in the Precambrian metamorphic rocks of the **Llano Uplift** area, notably in Blanco, Gillespie and Llano counties. Current production is from surface mines in the **Allamoore area.**

Talc is used in **ceramic, roofing, paint, paper, plastic, synthetic rubber** and other products.

**TIN** — Tin minerals have been found in El Paso and Mason counties. Small quantities were produced during the early 1900s in the Franklin Mountains north of El Paso. **Cassiterite (tin dioxide)** occurrences in Mason County are believed to be very minor. The **only tin smelter in the United States**, built at **Texas City** by the federal government during World War II and later sold to a private company, processes tin concentrates from ores mined outside of Texas, tin residues and secondary tin-bearing materials.

**TITANIUM** — The titanium mineral **rutile** has been found in small amounts at the **Mueller prospect** in Jeff Davis County. Another titanium mineral, **ilmenite**, occurs in sandstones in Burleson, Fayette, Lee, Starr and several other counties. Deposits that would be considered commercial under present conditions have not been found.

**TRAP ROCK** (see **BASALT**).

**TUNGSTEN** — The tungsten mineral **scheelite** has been found in small deposits in Gillespie and Llano counties and in the **Quitman Mountains** in Hudspeth County. Small deposits of other tungsten minerals have been prospected in the **Cave Peak area** north of Van Horn in Culberson County.

**URANIUM** — Uranium deposits were discovered in the **Texas Coastal Plain** in 1954 when abnormal radioactivity was detected in the Karnes County area. A number of uranium deposits have since been discovered within a belt of strata extending more than 250 miles from the middle Coastal Plain southwestward to the Rio Grande.

Various uranium minerals also have been found in other areas of Texas, including the **Trans-Pecos**, the **Llano Uplift** and the **High Plains**. With the exception of small shipments from the High Plains during the 1950s, all the uranium production in Texas has been from the Coastal Plain. Uranium has been obtained from surface mines extending from northern Live Oak County, southeastern Atascosa County, across northern Karnes County and into southern Gonzales County.

All mines are now reclaimed. Until recently, uranium was produced by in-situ leaching, brought to the surface through wells, and stripped from the solution at several Coastal Plain recovery operations. There has been no uranium production in Texas since 2000 because of decreased prices and demand.

**VERMICULITE** — Vermiculite, a mica-like mineral that expands when heated, occurs in Burnet, Gillespie, Llano, Mason and other counties in the **Llano region**. It has been produced at a surface mine in Llano County. Vermiculite, mined outside of Texas, is exfoliated (expanded) at plants in Dallas, Houston and San Antonio. Exfoliated vermiculite is used for **lightweight concrete aggregate, horticulture, insulation** and other purposes.

**VOLCANIC ASH** (see **PUMICITE**).

**ZEOLITES** — The zeolite minerals **clinoptilolite** and **analcime** occur in Tertiary lavas and tuffs in Brewster, Jeff Davis and Presidio counties, in West Texas. Clinoptilolite also is found associated with Tertiary tuffs in the southern Texas Coastal Plain, including deposits in Karnes, McMullen and Webb counties, and currently is produced in McMullen County. Zeolites, sometimes called **"molecular sieves,"** can be used in **ion-exchange processes to reduce pollution**, as a catalyst in **oil cracking**, in obtaining **high-purity oxygen and nitrogen** from air, in **water purification** and for many other purposes.

**ZINC** (see **LEAD AND ZINC**). ☆

# Electric Utilities Switch to Full Competition

### By Sudeep Reddy

By the middle of 2003, the state's largest electric utilities were halfway through their transition to full competition, as consumers faced some of their highest electricity bills ever.

Texas was closely watched by other states as it tried to bring lower electricity rates through deregulation and avoid California's disastrous results. But the state faced several challenges to those efforts, such as persistently high natural gas prices and concerns about a heavy dependence on gas-fired power plants for its electricity.

The changes in Texas came amid the worst downturn ever for investor-owned utilities, thanks to the backlash from the late-1990s economic boom and the Enron downfall. Some electric companies were still struggling with the credit crisis and loss of investor confidence as they tried to expand across the state.

Electric competition took effect on Jan. 1, 2002, bringing consumer choice to most Texans. Five of the state's 10 investor-owned utilities face competition from other providers, with as many as 11 companies competing in each of the incumbents' original areas. Only two of the state's 75 cooperatives and none of the 85 municipally owned utilities have elected to participate in competition, generally due to their lower rates.

**The investor-owned utilities** involved in deregulation were required to split their companies into three separate divisions — for transmission and distribution over power lines, generating electricity at power plants and service to retail customers.

On the retail side, Texas' two largest utilities served half the state's consumers. Dallas-based TXU Energy had 2.7 million customers, compared to 1.7 million for Houston-based Reliant Energy. The other former monopolies now acting as competitive providers are First Choice Power, CPL Retail Energy (formerly Central Power & Light), and WTU Retail Energy (formerly West Texas Utilities). Their rates are locked in their original areas until 2005, but they can compete for customers in other parts of the state.

Switching rates were slowly inching upward across all competitive areas. Through early June 2003, switching by residential consumers from incumbents to competitive providers ranged between about 7 percent and 11 percent, according to the Public Utility Commission of Texas. Between 9 percent and 17 percent of small businesses had changed electric retailers.

Larger commercial and industrial users looked for other providers in greater numbers, with more than 80 percent either switching or renegotiating their existing contracts during the first year of competition. By early 2003, competing providers had served almost a third of the state's overall electricity load.

**Two start-up providers** faced trouble in the first 18 months of competition. New Power, a spin-off of Enron and one of the lowest-cost competitors, filed for Chapter 11 bankruptcy protection and stopped serving customers in June 2002. Its 80,000 customers in North Texas and the Houston area were transferred to Reliant and TXU.

Texas Commercial Energy, which served 1,500 commercial and industrial customers, filed for bankruptcy protection in March 2003. The company depended heavily on the spot market for wholesale electricity, and it succumbed to price spikes that hit the state during an ice storm in late February 2003. The provider was forced to drop 80 percent of its business to meet credit requirements, but it continues to serve smaller customers.

**Widespread data glitches** throughout 2002 stymied the transition to competition, leading to delayed bills and problems completing switching requests. In the first year of deregulation, the PUC faced a four-fold increase in complaints from consumers about service.

Consumer-advocacy groups say that the rates of incumbent utilities were set too high to force more switching to competing providers. The incumbents' rate — which most consumers pay unless they switch — is locked until Jan. 1, 2005, except for adjustments based on the market price of natural gas, a key fuel for power generation. The PUC was criticized for not taking other fuels into account in the rate formula, and for allowing changes based on short-term spikes in natural gas prices. (More than half the state's electricity is generated from natural gas-fired power plants. About a third comes from coal-fired plants, while nuclear reactors generated 10 percent and the rest was from hydroelectric facilities or other renewable-energy sources.)

Texas also had allegations of market manipulation and unfair practices similar to those in California. But officials said Texas' excess capacity for electricity generation limits the ability to manipulate the wholesale market. The Electric Reliability Council of Texas, which operates the electricity grid, said it would have 78,715 megawatts of generation capacity available by the end of summer 2003. That would give it a cushion of 38 percent more power than the grid needs at peak demand during the summer.

**PUC officials and industry** leaders maintain that Texas is in good shape on all key aspects of deregulation. Most state legislators agreed, making only minor changes to the Texas Electric Choice Act in the 2003 session and agreeing to wait until 2005 to consider significant adjustments.

*Sudeep Reddy is a staff writer of The Dallas Morning News.*

---

# Electric Cooperatives

Source: The Texas Electric Cooperatives

Electric cooperatives are nonprofit, consumer-owned utilities providing electric service primarily in rural areas. Rates and services are regulated by the Public Utility Commission of Texas.

Texas was home to **64** electric-distribution cooperatives and **11** generation and transmission cooperatives (G&Ts) — which are owned by local distribution cooperatives — serving nearly **3** million member-customers in **231** of the 254 counties.

Three of the G&Ts generate power while the others represent their member distribution systems in wholesale power supply arrangements. The systems operate more than **260,000** miles of line.

As of 2003, only two cooperatives, Nueces and San Patricio, had opted for the competitive market. ☆

# Telecommunications: Changes in the Air

**By Vikas Bajaj**

After a two-year free fall, the telecommunications industry began to find its footing on a tenuous plateau in 2003. The waves of corporate layoffs and bankruptcies that marked the beginning of the millennium finally gave way to relative calm.

There was little to cheer for as

| Texas telecommunications statistics | | | | |
|---|---|---|---|---|
| Service | 2002 | 2001 | 2000 | 1999 |
| **Local phone lines** | 12,949,056 | 13,531,474 | 13,657,444 | 13,188,047 |
| former monopolies | 10,766,127 | 11,365,441 | 11,892,768 | 12,601,936 |
| competitors | 2,182,929 | 2,166,033 | 1,764,676 | 586,111 |
| **Wireless subscribers** | 9,943,429 | 9,062,064 | 7,548,537 | 5,792,453 |
| **Broadband lines** | 1,349,628 | 840,665 | 552,538 | 152,518 |

*Source: Federal Communications Commission.*

the number of basic local-phone lines dropped for two years in a row and threatened to fall for a third. Growth in high-speed, or broadband, Internet connections and wireless-phone service was promising, but even they couldn't make up for the carnage elsewhere in the industry.

Both federal and state policy makers made noteworthy changes to the rules that govern local-phone deregulation, wireless service and broadband. The Federal Communications Commission led the way in substantially deregulating local-phone and cable companies' high-speed Internet services. In Texas, legislators tackled, but ended up leaving alone, broadband rules.

The biggest single development in the industry was arguably the fall of WorldCom Inc., the nation's second-biggest long-distance company and its biggest carrier of Internet traffic.

The Clinton, Miss.-based company revealed in the summer of 2002 that its executives had undertaken a series of accounting improprieties totaling $11 billion. In July 2002, WorldCom declared bankruptcy, the largest in American corporate history.

Ramifications of the scandal reverberated throughout the country as 17,000 workers were dismissed. The impact in Texas was significant because of the company's long ties to Richardson, where it once employed more than 5,000 people. MCI, which was bought by WorldCom in 1998, was one of the main catalysts for the creation of the Richardson Telecom Corridor when it opened an engineering operation there in 1972. At the time, both MCI and the Telecom Corridor were fledgling dreams. (In 2003, WorldCom changed its corporate brand and name to MCI.)

Many of the world's biggest telecommunications equipment makers set up U.S. headquarters in North Texas in the last several decades to serve MCI and other phone companies. As American phone companies severely scaled back spending on telephone gear in the last few years, vendors such as Nortel Networks Corp. and Alcatel were forced to cut their Texas operations by as much as one-half to two-thirds.

Another bankruptcy that hurt Texas was that of Dallas-based Allegiance Telecom Inc. The company, which employed more than 3,000 people, filed for protection from its lenders in May 2003. It had been one of the fastest growing telecommunications firms in the state.

Even the more stable local-phone giant, San Antonio-based SBC Communications Inc., cut tens of thousands of jobs. Beginning in 2002, the company cut 21,000 jobs. It had about 176,000 employees in mid-2003. But SBC and Baby Bell sisters such as Verizon Communications Inc. and BellSouth Corp. remained the strongest and most viable industry players.

They began exercising some of that strength in 2003 when they jointly solicited bids for new high-speed fiber-optic systems that would let them sell broadband, phone and video services to consumers and businesses. Their plans called for initial deployments of the networks in new subdivisions in early 2004 and more widespread installations later that year.

The initiative was meant to counter the dominance of cable companies' high-speed Internet service, which had two-thirds of all broadband subscribers to the phone companies' one-third. (Nationally, there were about 30 million high-speed Internet users, or 16 percent of the population, in 2003.)

An FCC ruling issued in early 2003 emboldened the Baby Bells to earnestly consider the fiber-optic investment, which could cost hundreds of millions or even billions of dollars over time. Such a large investment to replace the nation's copper phone lines with much more capacious fiber had long been anticipated and hoped for by policy makers, technology futurists and consumers.

The FCC ruled in February that any new fiber systems deployed by the Bells would not have to be shared with rivals such as AT&T Corp. SBC and Verizon had long complained that they couldn't be expected to invest in the systems if regulators would later force them to lease them to competitors at discounted rates.

But in that same FCC decision, the Bells lost a similar argument on the sharing of their existing telephone networks. SBC and Verizon wanted the FCC to end a policy that allowed AT&T and MCI to lease their telephone switches at discounted rates.

State regulators and consumer advocates joined AT&T to persuade the FCC that sharing of telephone switches had to be preserved so competitors could offer consumers and small businesses multiple local-phone service choices. The commission voted 3-2 to continue the sharing rules and give states latitude in determining when they were no longer needed.

In other policy news, a U.S. Court of Appeals upheld FCC rules that would let consumers keep their wireless-phone numbers when they change service providers beginning Nov. 24, 2003. The rules were challenged by cellular-phone companies who said "number portability" was unnecessary and costly to implement.

Meanwhile, the Texas Legislature also took up several important telecommunications issues.

Measures that passed included:

• An extension of the Telecommunications Infrastructure Fund tax on telephone companies. The levy – 1.25 percent of phone companies' revenues – was to have ended after it collected $1.5 billion. But legislators, at the last minute, extended it to collect another $250 million and sent the new money to the general

fund, not to a program for technology improvements at schools, libraries and hospitals, as was the case with the previous collections.

• A bill that allowed the local-phone giants SBC and Verizon the flexibility to court customers who had switched to competitors. The law scuttled a Public Utility Commission proposed rule that would have required the companies to wait 30 days before they could solicit former customers again.

The Legislature also commenced a sunset review of the Public Utility Commission. The industry expected many critical issues to be addressed in the processes, including but not limited to rural phone rates, the access charges long-distance companies pay local companies and the subsidization of rural and residential rates by urban and business rates.

But perhaps, legislators' most important policy action on telecommunications was not to vote on House and Senate measures that would have given SBC and Verizon significant freedom from Public Utility Commission oversight.

The bills, sponsored in the House by Rep. Toby Goodman, R-Arlington, and in the Senate by Sen. Ken Armbrister, D-Victoria, would have freed the company's new broadband, high-speed Internet networks from proposed PUC rules that would let rivals rent them at regulated rates as is done with existing phone networks. The measures faltered when the chairman of the new House Regulated Industries committee, Rep. Phil King, R-Weatherford, said the panel wouldn't have enough time to address the issue. In explaining his decision, King said the committee would wait to study the

new FCC broadband rules and the need for state legislation before the 2005 session.

Aside from public policy and corporate troubles, the big telecommunications story was the changing communication patterns. By the end of 2002, almost half of the population, or 141 million people, had cell phones and were using them more than ever.

As more conversations transpired on cell phones, fewer took place on home and business phones. In 2002, for instance FCC data show the average American spent 90 minutes making long-distance calls from home down from 143 minutes in 1995. In the same period, the average wireless user went from making 117 minutes of calls in 1995 to 320 minutes.

In Texas, there were only 2 million fewer wireless phones than local-phone lines, which fell in both 2001 and 2002 and looked set to fall again in 2003.

Many lines being disconnected were second home phone lines previously used to connect to the Internet. But as more people turned to broadband Internet connections, many consumers canceled their second and third phone lines. Texas broadband connections jumped to 1.3 million in 2002 from 152,518 in 1999.

Many experts predicted that both broadband and wireless would continue to take business away from traditional phone lines as Americans become more mobile and dependant on broadband. That forecast carried with it both a boon and a warning for the industry, because as it presaged growth in one area it also signaled losses in others.

*Vikas Bajaj is a staff writer of The Dallas Morning News.*

---

### Top 5 Gas Distribution Utilities 2002

| UTILITY | Customers | Sales (MMcf)* |
|---|---|---|
| TXU Gas Company | 1,386,000 | 119,011 |
| Reliant Energy Entex | 1,206,000 | 107,764 |
| San Antonio Public Service | 304,000 | 75,696 |
| Southern Union Gas Co. | 514,000 | 31,846 |
| Energas Co. | 294,000 | 28,304 |

Note: These utilities represent 91 percent of all distribution sales in Texas. *MMcf: Million cubic feet. Source: Texas Railroad Comm.

### Top 5 Gas Transmission Utilities 2002

| UTILITY | Volume (MMcf) | Average Rate ($/Mcf)* |
|---|---|---|
| Houston Pipe Line Co. | 925,487 | 0.017 |
| PG&E Texas Pipeline, L.P. | 828,707 | 0.113 |
| Tejas Gas Pipeline, L.P. | 498,595 | 0.049 |
| TXU Lone Star Pipeline | 424,720 | 0.176 |
| Oasis Pipe Line Company | 288,727 | 0.079 |

Note: These utilities transport 43 percent of all gas in Texas. *$/Mcf: Dollars per thousand cubic feet. Railroad Commission.

## Gas Utilities

Source: Gas Services Division, Texas Railroad Commission

Approximately **179** investor-owned gas companies in Texas are classified as gas utilities and come under the regulatory jurisdiction of the Texas Railroad Commission. Approximately **120** of these companies reported gas operating revenue of **$9.6** billion in 2001, with operating expenses of **$9.4** billion.

In 2001, fixed investment for distribution facilities in Texas was **$3.3** billion and for transmission facilities, **$4.2** billion. Investment in Texas plants in service totaled **$9.3** billion. There were **33** investor-owned and **84** municipally owned distribution systems in operation in 2001 serving **1,050** Texas cities.

The **eight** largest distribution systems — six private and two municipal — served **97** percent of all residential customers. In 2001, there were approximately **3.6** million residential customers, **289,232** small commercial and industrial users, **4,836** large industrial custom-

ers and **14,276** other gas-utility customers. The breakdown of distribution sales to these customers was: **55** Mcf (thousand cubic feet) per residential customer, **442** Mcf per commercial customer, **7,044** Mcf per industrial customer and **1,133** Mcf for customers in the "other" category. Distribution sales amounted to **232.0** billion cubic feet in 2001. In addition to industrial sales made by distribution companies, transmission companies reported pipeline-to-industry sales of **1.6** trillion cubic feet and revenue from these sales of **$6.1** billion.

In 2000, the average annual residential gas bill in the United States was **$634**. The average annual bill in Texas for the same year was **$413**, down **$28** from the previous year. The State of Texas collected **$4.9** million in gas-utility taxes from gas utilities in fiscal year 2002.

Texas had a total of **126,095** miles of natural-gas pipelines in operation in 2000, including **11,023** miles of field and gathering lines, **35,318** miles of transmission lines and **79,754** miles of distribution lines. ☆

# Agriculture in Texas

*Information was provided by Agricultural Extension Service specialists, Texas Agricultural Statistics Service, U.S. Department of Agriculture, and U.S. Department of Commerce. It was coordinated by Carl G. Anderson, Extension Marketing Economist, Texas A&M University. All references are to Texas unless otherwise specified.*

Agriculture is a mainstay industry of Texas. Many businesses, financial institutions and individuals are involved in providing supplies, credit and services to farmers and ranchers, and in processing and marketing agricultural commodities. Although agribusiness encompasses the many phases of food and fiber production, processing, transporting and marketing, most of the following discussion is devoted to the production phase, which takes place on farms and ranches.

Including all its agribusiness phases, agriculture

*Hannah Hale takes time to hand feed a sheep on her family's farm, Windy Meadow, in Greenville, Hunt County. File photo.*

added about $28 billion in 2002 to the economic activity of the state. The estimated value of farm assets in Texas — the land, buildings, livestock, machinery, crops, inventory on farms, household goods and farm financial assets — totaled approximately $103 billion at the beginning of 2001.

Texas agriculture is a strong industry. Receipts from farm and ranch marketings in 2002 were estimated at $12.6 billion, compared with $13.8 billion in 2001.

The potential for further growth is favorable. With the increasing demand for food and fiber throughout the world, and because of the importance of agricultural exports to this nation's trade balance, agriculture in Texas is destined to play an even greater role in the future.

Major efforts of research and educational programs by the Texas A&M University System are directed toward developing the state's agricultural industry to its fullest potential. The goal is to capitalize on natural advantages that agriculture has in Texas because of the relatively warm climate, productive soils, and availability of excellent export and transportation facilities.

## Texas Farms

The number and nature of farms have changed over time. The number of farms in Texas has decreased from 420,000 in 1940 to 227,000 in 2001 with an average size of 573 acres. Average value per farm of all farm assets, including land and buildings, has increased from $20,100 in 1950 to $366,720 in 2001. The number of small farms is

## Balance Sheet of Texas Farms and Ranches
## Jan. 1, 1992–2001

*Table below shows the financial status of Texas farms and ranches as of Jan. 1 of the years 1992–2001.*

**(All amounts are given in millions of dollars.)**

| Item | 1992 | 1993 | 1994 | 1995 | 1996 | 1997 | 1998 | 1999 | 2000 | 2001 |
|---|---|---|---|---|---|---|---|---|---|---|
| **ASSETS:** | | | | | | | | | | |
| **Physical Assets:** | | | | | | | | | | |
| Real estate . . . . . . . . . . | $59,853 | $61,103 | $60,931 | $62,927 | $64,314 | $68,842 | $70,277 | $72,608 | $78,371 | $103,182 |
| Non-real estate: | | | | | | | | | | |
| *Livestock and poultry . . . . | 8,983 | 8,986 | 8,703 | 6,417 | 6,403 | 8,060 | 7,242 | 8,003 | 8,562 | 8,003 |
| †Machinery and motor vehicles | 5,454 | 5,837 | 5,997 | 6,114 | 6,217 | 6,383 | 6,490 | 6,532 | 6,588 | 6,703 |
| ‡Crops stored on and off farms | 623 | 548 | 641 | 741 | 839 | 1,028 | 1,146 | 1,100 | 795 | 951 |
| Purchased Inputs . . . . . . | 159 | 133 | 170 | 110 | 142 | 159 | 164 | 131 | 159 | 137 |
| **Financial assets:** | 3,514 | 3,950 | 3,958 | 4,056 | 4,014 | 3,966 | 4,097 | 4,226 | 4,391 | 4,708 |
| **Total Assets. . . . . . . . .** | **78,586** | **80,557** | **80,400** | **80,364** | **81,929** | **88,438** | **89,415** | **92,600** | **98,866** | **103,182** |
| **LIABILITIES:** | | | | | | | | | | |
| ††Real estate debt . . . . . . | 4,538 | 4,495 | 4,523 | 4,679 | 4,870 | 5,256 | 5,414 | 5,786 | 5,985 | 6,368 |
| ‡‡Non-real estate debt: | | | | | | | | | | |
| Excluding CCC loans . . . . | 4,828 | 5,210 | 5,386 | 5,469 | 5,601 | 5,884 | 6,004 | 5,956 | 6,368 | 6,475 |
| **Total Liabilities . . . . . . . .** | **9,366** | **9,705** | **9,909** | **10,149** | **10,471** | **11,140** | **11,417** | **11,743** | **12,353** | **12,844** |
| Owners' equities . . . . . . . . . | 69,220 | 70,853 | 70,492 | 70,216 | 71,458 | 77,298 | 77,998 | 80,856 | 86,513 | 90,339 |
| **TOTAL CLAIMS** | **$78,586** | **$80,557** | **$80,400** | **$80,364** | **$81,929** | **$88,438** | **$89,415** | **$92,600** | **$98,866** | **$103,182** |

*Excludes horses, mules and broilers.
†Includes only farm share value for trucks and autos.
‡All non-CCC crops held on farms plus value above loan rate for crops held under CCC.
** Excludes debt for nonfarm purposes.
†† Includes Farm Credit System, Farm Service Agency, commercial banks, life insurance companies, individuals and others, and CCC storage and drying loans.
‡‡ Includes Farm Credit System, Farm Service Agency, commercial banks and individual and others.
*** Nonrecourse CCC loans secured by crops owned by farmers. These crops are included as assets in this balance sheet.
††† As of 1987, investments in Co-ops and Other Financial reported as Financial.
Source: **"Farm Business EconomicReport,"** Farm Business Balance Sheet, USDA/ERS, as of Nov. 7, 2002.*

increasing — but part-time farmers operate them.

Mechanization of farming continues as new and larger machines replace manpower. Even though machinery price tags are high relative to times past, machines are technologically advanced and efficient. Tractors, mechanical harvesters and numerous cropping machines have virtually eliminated menial tasks that for many years were traditional to farming.

Revolutionary agricultural chemicals have been developed along with improved plants and animals and methods of handling them. Many of the natural hazards of farming and ranching have been reduced by better use of weather information, machinery and other improvements; but increased production costs, labor availability and high-energy costs have added to the concerns of farmers and ranchers.

Changes in Texas agriculture in the last 50 years include:

• Record keeping that assists in management and marketing decisions is more detailed

• There are more restrictions on choice or inputs/practices

• Precision agriculture is taking on new dimensions through the use of satellites, computers and other high-tech tools to help producers manage inputs such as seed, fertilizers, pesticides and water.

• Farms have become fewer, larger, specialized and much more expensive to own and operate, but far more productive. The number of small farms operated by part-time farmers is increasing.

• Land ownership is becoming more of a lifestyle, and the use of land for recreation and ecotourism is growing.

• Irrigation has become an important factor in crop production.

• Crops and livestock have made major changes in production areas, as in the concentration of cotton on the High Plains and livestock increases in Central and Eastern Texas.

• Pest and disease control methods have greatly improved. Herbicides are relied upon for weed control.

• Ranchers and farmers are better educated and informed, more science- and business-oriented. Today, agriculture operates in a global, high-tech, consumer-driven environment.

• Feedlot finishing, commercial broiler production, artificial insemination, improved pastures and brush control, reduced feed requirements and other changes have greatly increased livestock and poultry efficiency.

• Biotechnology and genetic engineering promise new breakthroughs in reaching even higher levels of productivity. Horticultural plant and nursery businesses have expanded. Improved wildlife management has increased deer, turkey and other wildlife populations.

• Cooperation among farmers in marketing, promotion and other fields has increased.

• Agricultural producers have become increasingly dependent on off-the-farm services to supply production inputs such as feeds, chemicals, credit and other essentials.

## Agribusiness

Texas farmers and ranchers have developed considerable dependence upon agribusiness. With many producers specializing in the production of certain crops and livestock, they look beyond the farm and ranch for supplies and services. On the input side, they rely on suppliers of production needs and services, and, on the output side, they need assemblers, processors and distributors. The impact of production agriculture and

related businesses on the Texas economy is about $28 billion annually.

Since 1940, the proportion of Texans whose livelihood is linked to agriculture has changed greatly. In 1940, about 23 percent were producers on farms and ranches, and about 17 percent were suppliers or were engaged in assembly, processing, and distribution of agricultural products. The agribusiness alignment in 2002 was less than 2 percent on farms and ranches, and about 15 percent of the labor force providing production or marketing supplies and services, and retailing food and fiber products.

### Cash Receipts

Farm and ranch cash receipts in 2001 totaled $13.8 billion. With estimates of $1.703 million for government payments, $860,000 of non-cash income, and $1.131 billion of other farm-related income included, the realized gross farm income totaled $17.492 billion. Farm production expenses were $13.201 billion, so net farm income totaled $4.291 billion. The value of inventory adjustment was –$206.4 million.

### Farm and Ranch Assets

Farm and ranch assets totaled $103.2 billion in 2001. This was up from the 2000 level of $98.9 billion. Value of real estate increased almost 4.3 percent to $103.2 billion in 2001. Liabilities totaled $12.8 billion, up slightly from $12.4 billion in 2000.

### Percent of Income From Products

Livestock and livestock products accounted for 68 percent of the $13.8 billion cash receipts from farm marketings in 2001 with the remaining 32 percent from crops. Receipts from livestock have trended up largely because of increased feeding operations and reduced crop acreage associated with farm programs and low prices. However, these relationships change because of variations in commodity prices and volume of marketings.

Meat animals (cattle, hogs and sheep) accounted for

## Texas Crop Production, 2002

| Crop | Harvested Acres (000) | Yield Per Acre | Unit | Total Production (000) | Value (000) |
|---|---|---|---|---|---|
| Beans, dry edible | 32.5 | 970 | lb. | 315 | $ 6,300 |
| Corn, grain | 1,820 | 113 | bu. | 205,660 | 534,716 |
| Corn, silage | 120 | 18 | ton | 2,160 | — |
| Cotton, American-Pima | 18.3 | 1,023 | lb. | 39 | 14,920 |
| Cotton, upland | 4,500 | 533 | lb. | 5,000 | 919,200 |
| Cottonseed | — | — | ton | 1,984 | 204,352 |
| Grapefruit * | — | — | box | 5,900 | 23,040 |
| Hay | 5,630 | 2.46 | ton | 13,850 | 930,400 |
| Oats | 160 | 44 | bu. | 7,040 | 11,968 |
| Oranges† | — | — | box | 1,740 | 8,068 |
| Peaches | — | — | lb. | 11,400 | 6,840 |
| Peanuts | 280 | 3,100 | lb. | 868,000 | 157,976 |
| Pecans | — | — | lb. | 40,000 | 37,300 |
| Potatoes | 20.3 | 264 | cwt. | 5,360 | 57,156 |
| Rice | 206 | 7,100 | lb. | 14,616 | 61,387 |
| Sorghum, grain | 2,550 | 2,856 | lb. | 72,828 | 305,878 |
| Sorghum, silage | 90 | 12 | ton | 1,080 | — |
| Soybeans | 215 | 28 | bu. | 6,020 | 31,304 |
| Sugar cane | 45 | 37.5 | ton | 1,687 | — |
| Sunflowers | 34 | 935 | lb. | 31,800 | 4,594 |
| Sweet potatoes | 3.3 | 170 | cwt. | 561 | 10,042 |
| Vegetables, commercial: | | | | | |
|   Fresh market ‡ | 97.3 | — | cwt. | 20,555 | 390,477 |
|   Processing § | 31.3 | — | cwt. | 3,887 | 38,367 |
| Wheat, winter | 2,700 | 29 | bu. | 78,300 | 234,900 |
| **Total of Listed Crops** | **18,549.4** | **—** | **—** | **—** | **$3,993,057** |

*Grapefruit, 80-lb. box reflects 2001–2002 crop year. † Oranges, 85-lb. box, reflects 2001-2002 crop year. ‡ Includes processing total for dual-usage crops (asparagus, broccoli and cauliflower). Total Texas fresh-market vegetables include bell peppers, cabbage, cantaloupes, carrots, cauliflower, celery, cucumbers, honeydew melons, onions, spinach, sweet corn, tomatoes and watermelons. § Total Texas processing vegetables include carrots, cucumbers, snap beans, spinach and tomatoes.
Source: "Texas Ag Facts Annual Summary," TASS/USDA, 2/20/03.

50.4 percent of total cash receipts received by Texas farmers and ranchers in 2001. Most of these receipts were from cattle and calf sales. Dairy products made up 5.8 percent of receipts; poultry and eggs, 9.0 percent; and miscellaneous livestock, 1.8 percent.

Cotton accounted for 7.3 percent of total receipts; feed crops, 7.0 percent; food grains, 2.4 percent; vegetables, 3.7 percent; greenhouse/nursery products, 8.9 percent; oil crops, 1.7 percent; fruits and nuts, 1 percent; and other crops, 1 percent.

## Texas' Rank Among States

Measured by cash receipts for farm and ranch marketings, Texas ranked second in 2001. California ranked first and Iowa third.

Texas normally leads all other states in numbers of farms and ranches, amount of farm and ranch land, cattle slaughtered, cattle on feed, calf births, sheep and lambs, goats, cash receipts from livestock marketings, cattle and calves, beef cows, sheep and lambs, wool production, mohair production, and exports of fats, oils and greases. The state also usually leads in production of cotton.

## Texas' Agricultural Exports

The value of Texas' share of agricultural exports in fiscal year 2001 was $3.333 billion. Cotton accounted for

## *Realized Gross Income and Net Income from Farming, Texas, 1980-2001

| Year | **Realized Gross Farm Income | Farm Production Expenses | Net Change In Farm Inventories | ***Total Net Farm Income | ***Total Net Income Per Farm |
|------|------|------|------|------|------|
| | — Million Dollars — | | | | Dollars |
| 1980 | 9,611.4 | 9,154.6 | − 542.5 | 456.8 | 2,330.6 |
| 1981 | 11,545.7 | 9,643.1 | 699.9 | 1,902.6 | 9,756.9 |
| 1982 | 11,404.5 | 10,016.2 | − 127.8 | 1,388.3 | 7,156.2 |
| 1983 | 11,318.1 | 9,796.5 | − 590.7 | 1,521.6 | 7,843.3 |
| 1984 | 11,692.6 | 10,285.7 | 186.1 | 1,406.9 | 7,252.1 |
| 1985 | 11,375.3 | 9,882.4 | − 9.0 | 1,492.9 | 7,775.5 |
| 1986 | 10,450.1 | 9,341.3 | − 349.0 | 1,108.8 | 5,835.8 |
| 1987 | 12,296.6 | 10,185.0 | 563.2 | 2,111.5 | 11,231.4 |
| 1988 | 12,842.8 | 10,816.8 | − 128.4 | 2,026.0 | 10,552.1 |
| 1989 | 12,843.1 | 10,703.7 | − 798.6 | 2,139.4 | 11,027.8 |
| 1990 | 14,463.2 | 11,412.4 | 361.7 | 3,050.8 | 15,565.3 |
| 1991 | 14,393.4 | 11,551.4 | 150.0 | 2,842.0 | 14,426.4 |
| 1992 | 14,392.5 | 10,994.9 | 464.1 | 3,397.6 | 17,159.6 |
| 1993 | 15,758.5 | 11,612.1 | 197.0 | 4,146.4 | 20,732.0 |
| 1994 | 15,450.5 | 11,593.4 | 107.7 | 3,857.1 | 17,532.0 |
| 1995 | 15,709.7 | 12,984.4 | 243.7 | 2,725.3 | 12,276.0 |
| 1996 | 15,076.8 | 12,552.9 | − 290.1 | 2,524.0 | 11,268.0 |
| 1997 | 16,515.8 | 13,240.5 | 709.2 | 3,275.3 | 14,557.0 |
| 1998 | 15,552.3 | 12,556.1 | − 817.0 | 2,996.2 | 13,258.0 |
| 1999 | 17,522.5 | 12,489.3 | 194.4 | 5,033.2 | 22,173.0 |
| 2000 | 16,679.2 | 12,655.9 | − 327.4 | 4,023.3 | 17,803.0 |
| 2001 | 17,491.5 | 13,200.5 | − 206.4 | 4,291.0 | 18,903.0 |

*Details for items may not add to totals because of rounding. Series revised, September, 1981.

**Cash receipts from farm marketings, government payments, value of home consumption and gross rental value of farm dwellings.

***Farm income of farm operators.

†A positive value of inventory change represents current-year production not sold by Dec. 31. A negative value is an offset to production from prior years included in current-year sales.

§Starting in 1977, farms with production of $1,000 or more used to figure income.

Source: "Economic Indicators of the Farm Sector, State Financial Summary, 1985," 1987," 1989," 1993," USDA/ERS; "Farm Business Economics Report", Aug. 1996; "Texas Agricultural Statistics Service, 2001."

$464.7 million of the exports; feed grains and products, $310.4 million; wheat and products, $106.1 million; rice, $59.0 million; fats, oil and greases, $48.5 million; cottonseed and products, $21.5 million; hides and skins, $304.6 million; live animals and meat, excluding chickens, $721.0 million; fruits, $41.4 million; peanuts and products, $34.3 million; soybeans and products, $17.4 million; vegetables, $56.4 million; poultry and products, $137.7 million; dairy products, $28.8 million; and miscellaneous and other products, $972.6 million.

In 2000, Texas exported $3.407 billion in farm and ranch products; this total was $2.791 billion in 1999 and $3.376 billion in 1998.

## Hunting

The management of wildlife as an economic enterprise through hunting leases makes a significant contribution to the economy of many counties. Leasing the right of ingress on a farm or ranch for the purpose of hunting is the service marketed. After the leasing, the consumer — the hunter— goes onto the land to seek the harvest of the wildlife commodity. Hunting lease income to farmers and ranchers in 2002 was estimated at $361 million.

The demand for hunting opportunities is growing while the land capable of producing huntable wildlife is decreasing. As a result, farmers and ranchers are placing more emphasis on wildlife management practices to help meet requests for hunting leases.

## Irrigation

Irrigation is an important factor in the productivity of Texas agriculture. The value of crop production from irrigated acreage is 50 to 60 percent of the total value of all crop production, although only about 30 percent of the state's total harvested cropland acreage is irrigated.

Irrigation in Texas peaked in 1974 at 8.6 million acres. Over the next 20 years, irrigation declined due to many factors including poor farm economics, falling water tables and conversion to more efficient technologies. In the 1990s, irrigation stabilized at 6.4 million acres. This puts Texas third in the nation, behind California and Nebraska.

Although some irrigation is practiced in nearly every county of the state, about 50 percent of the total irrigated acreage in Texas is on the High Plains. Other concentrated areas of irrigation are the Gulf Coast rice producing area, the Lower Rio Grande Valley, the Winter Garden area of South Texas, the Trans-Pecos area of West Texas, and the peanut producing area in North-Central Texas, especially Erath, Eastland and Comanche counties. The largest growth in irrigation is occurring in the Coastal Bend area.

Sprinkler irrigation is used on about 63 percent of the total irrigated acreage, with surface irrigation methods, primarily furrow and surge methods, being used on the remaining irrigated area. Texas farmers lead the nation in the adoption of efficient irrigation technologies, particularly LEPA (low energy precision application) and LESA (low elevation spray application) center pivot systems, both of which were developed by Texas A&M.

The use of drip irrigation is increasing, with present acreage estimated at 150,000 acres. Drip irrigation is routinely used on tree crops such as citrus, pecans and peaches. Some drip irrigation of cotton and forages is practiced in West Texas. Farmers continue to experiment with drip irrigation, and recent advances in drip tape technology have improved the economics of drip.

Irrigation uses about 64 percent of all fresh water in the state. To meet future water demand for our rapidly growing cities and industries, several regions of the state are looking at water transfers from agriculture. Water utilities in San Antonio are developing water transfer programs with irrigators in the Edwards Aquifer region. The effects of such transfers on farm and rural economies are uncertain at this time. In about 20 percent of the irrigated

area, water is delivered to farms by irrigation and water districts through canals and pipelines. Many of these delivery networks are aging, are in poor condition and have high seepage losses. Efforts are under way to secure federal, state and local funding to help cover the costs of rehabilitation.

Approximately 80 percent of the state's irrigated acreage is supplied with water pumped from wells. Surface water sources supply the remaining area. Declining groundwater levels in several of the major aquifers is a serious problem, particularly in the Ogallala Aquifer beneath the Texas High Plains and in the southern portion of the Carrizo-Wilcox formation beneath the South Texas Plains. As the water level declines, well yields decrease and pumping costs increase.

## I. Principal Crops

In most recent years, the value of crop production in Texas is less than 40 percent of the total value of the state's agricultural output. Cash receipts from farm sales of crops are reduced somewhat because some grain and roughage is fed to livestock on farms where produced. Drought and low prices have reduced receipts in recent years.

Receipts from all Texas crops totaled $4.5 billion in 2001, $4.2 billion in 2000 and $4.5 billion in 1999.

Cotton, corn and grain sorghum account for a large part of the total crop receipts. In 2001, cotton contributed about 19.3 percent of the crop total; corn, 8.5 percent; wheat, 6.2 percent; and grain sorghum, 6.1 percent. Hay, vegetables, rice, cottonseed, peanuts and soybeans are other important cash crops.

### Cotton

Cotton has been a major crop in Texas for more than a century. It ranks first in dollar value among crops and second only to beef cattle among all agricultural commodities. Since 1880, Texas has led all states in cotton production in most years, and today the annual Texas cotton harvest amounts to approximately a fourth of total production in the United States. The annual cotton crop has averaged 4.52 million bales since 1990.

Total value of upland and American-Pima lint cotton produced in Texas in 2002 was $934,120,000. Cottonseed value in 2002 was $204,352,000, making the total value of the Texas crop around $1.138 billion.

Upland cotton was harvested from 4.5 million acres in 2002 and pima from 18,300 acres, for a total of 4.518 million acres. Yield for upland cotton in 2002 was 533 pounds per harvested acre, with pima yielding 1,023 pounds per acre. Cotton acreage harvested in 2001 totaled 6 million, with a yield of 481 pounds per acre for upland cotton and 1,059 pounds per acre for pima. Total cotton production amounted to 4.183 million bales in 2001 and 3.971 million in 2000. Counties leading in production of upland cotton in 2001 included Hale, Lamb, Gaines, Floyd, San Patricio and Castro.

Cotton is the raw material for processing operations at gins, oil mills, compresses and a small number of textile mills in Texas. Less than 10 percent of the raw cotton produced is processed within the state.

Cotton in Texas is machine harvested. Field storage of harvested seed cotton is gaining in popularity as gins decline in number. Much of the Texas cotton crop is exported. Japan, South Korea and Mexico are major buyers. With the continuing development of fiber spinning technology and the improved quality of Texas cotton, more utilization of cotton by mills within the state may develop in the future. Spinning techniques can efficiently produce high-quality yarn from relatively strong, short or longer staple upland cotton with fine mature fiber.

The state's major cotton-producing areas are tied together by an electronic marketing system. The network provides farmers with a centralized market that allows

## Export Shares of Commodities

| Commodity* | 1998 | 1999 | 2000 | 2001 | 2001 % of U.S. Total |
|---|---|---|---|---|---|
| | (Figures in Millions of Dollars) | | | | |
| Rice ........... | 89.6 | 83.9 | 67.8 | 59.0 | 7.54 |
| Cotton.......... | 690.5 | 337.8 | 521.2 | 464.7 | 22.18 |
| Fats, oils & greases | 102.4 | 90.4 | 64.6 | 48.5 | 15.17 |
| Hides & skins ..... | 207.8 | 176.6 | 227.0 | 304.6 | 15.67 |
| Meats other than poultry ..... | 618.7 | 665.2 | 794.7 | 721.0 | 11.87 |
| Feed grains ...... | 317.5 | 218.4 | 319.4 | 310.4 | 4.89 |
| Poultry products | 135.0 | 103.0 | 115.6 | 137.7 | 5.46 |
| Fruits ........... | 39.9 | 52.5 | 54.3 | 41.1 | 1.17 |
| Vegetables ....... | 43.9 | 42.2 | 59.5 | 56.4 | 1.24 |
| Wheat & flour ..... | 151.8 | 195.2 | 182.4 | 106.1 | 3.07 |
| Soybeans & prod... | 37.6 | 14.2 | 25.7 | 17.4 | 0.25 |
| Cottonseed & prod. | 29.3 | 17.8 | 28.4 | 21.5 | 24.74 |
| Peanuts ........ | 55.4 | 53.8 | 58.6 | 34.3 | 20.15 |
| Tree nuts ........ | 15.5 | 11.5 | 13.8 | 8.8 | 0.77 |
| Dairy products .... | 21.0 | 18.4 | 24.0 | 28.8 | 2.57 |
| †All other ........ | 820.8 | 710.5 | 850.4 | 972.6 | 9.09 |
| Total........... | 3,375.9 | 2,791.3 | 3,407.4 | 3,332.9 | 6.32 |

*Totals may not add because of rounding.*
*Commodity and related preparations.*
*† Mainly confectionary, nursery and greenhouse, essential oils, sunflower-seed oil, beverages, and other miscellaneous animal and vegetable products.*
*Source: Foreign Agricultural Trade of the United States, various issues, March/April, 1994, 1995, and April/May/June, 1998; www.ers.usda.gov for 2001 data. USDA/ERS.*

## Value of Cotton and Cottonseed

| Crop Year | Upland Cotton | | Cottonseed | |
|---|---|---|---|---|
| | Production (Bales) | Value | Production (Tons) | Value |
| | (All Figures in Thousands) | | | |
| 1900 | 3,438 | $157,306 | 1,531 | $20,898 |
| 1910 | 3,047 | 210,260 | 1,356 | 31,050 |
| 1920 | 4,345 | 376,080 | 1,934 | 41,350 |
| 1930 | 4,037 | 194,080 | 1,798 | 40,820 |
| 1940 | 3,234 | 162,140 | 1,318 | 31,852 |
| 1950 | 2,946 | 574,689 | 1,232 | 111,989 |
| 1960 | 4,346 | 612,224 | 1,821 | 75,207 |
| 1970 | 3,191 | 314,913 | 1,242 | 68,310 |
| *1980 | 3,320 | 1,091,616 | 1,361 | 161,959 |
| 1981 | 5,645 | 1,259,964 | 2,438 | 207,230 |
| 1982 | 2,700 | 664,848 | 1,122 | 90,882 |
| 1983 | 2,380 | 677,443 | 1,002 | 162,324 |
| 1984 | 3,680 | 927,360 | 1,563 | 157,863 |
| 1985 | 3,910 | 968,429 | 1,634 | 102,156 |
| 1986 | 2,535 | 560,945 | 1,053 | 82,118 |
| 1987 | 4,635 | 1,325,981 | 1,915 | 157,971 |
| 1988 | 5,215 | 1,291,651 | 2,131 | 238,672 |
| 1989 | 2,870 | 812,784 | 1,189 | 141,491 |
| 1990 | 4,965 | 1,506,182 | 1,943 | 225,388 |
| 1991 | 4,710 | 1,211,789 | 1,903 | 134,162 |
| 1992 | 3,265 | 769,495 | 1,346 | 145,368 |
| 1993 | 5,095 | 1,308,396 | 2,147 | 255,493 |
| 1994 | 4,915 | 1,642,003 | 2,111 | 215,322 |
| 1995 | 4,460 | 1,597,037 | 1,828 | 201,080 |
| 1996 | 4,345 | 1,368,154 | 1,784 | 230,136 |
| 1997 | 5,140 | 1,482,787 | 1,983 | 226,062 |
| 1998 | 3,600 | 969,408 | 1,558 | 204,098 |
| 1999 | 5,050 | 993,840 | 1,987 | 160,947 |
| 2000 | 3,940 | 868,061 | 1,589 | 162,078 |
| 2001 | 4,260 | 580,723 | 1,724 | 159,470 |
| 2002 | 5,000 | 919,200 | 1,984 | 204,352 |

*Beginning in 1971, the basis for cotton prices was changed from 500-pound gross weight to 480-pound net weight bale. To compute comparable prices for previous years, multiply price times 1.04167.*
*Source: "Texas Agricultural Facts," Annual Summary, Feb., 2003, and "Texas Ag Statistics," Texas Agricultural Statistics Service, Austin, various years.*

many sellers and buyers to trade with each other on a regular basis. The first high-volume instrument cotton-classing office in the nation was opened at Lamesa in 1980.

## Grain Sorghum

Grain sorghum ranked sixth in dollar value among Texas crops in 2002. Much of the grain is exported, as well as being used in livestock and poultry feed throughout the state.

Total production of grain sorghum in 2002 was 72,828,000 hundredweight (cwt.), with a 2,856 pound per acre yield. With an average price of $4.20 per cwt., the total value reached $305,878,000. In 2001, 2.60 million acres of grain sorghum were harvested, yielding an average of 2,800 pounds per acre for a total production of 72,800,000 cwt. It was valued at $3.64 per cwt., for a total value of $264,992,000. In 2000, 2.35 million acres were harvested with an average of 3,416 pounds per acre, or 80,276,000 cwt. The season's price was $3.29 per cwt. for a total value of $263,764,000.

Although grown to some extent in all counties where crops are important, the largest concentrations are in the High Plains, Rolling Plains, Blackland Prairie, Coastal Bend and Lower Rio Grande Valley areas. Counties leading in production in 2001 were Hidalgo, Wharton, Nueces, San Patricio, Hill and Cameron. Research to develop high-yielding hybrids resistant to diseases and insect damage continues.

## Rice

Rice, which is grown in about 20 counties on the Coast Prairie of Texas, ranked third in value among Texas crops for a number of years. However, in recent years, cotton, grain sorghum, wheat, corn, peanuts and hay have outranked rice.

Farms are highly mechanized, producing rice through irrigation and using airplanes for much of the planting, fertilizing, and application of insecticides and herbicides.

Texas farmers grow long- and medium-grain rice only. The Texas rice industry, which has grown from 110 acres in 1850 to a high of 642,000 acres in 1954, has been marked by significant yield increases and improved varieties. Record production was in 1981, with 27,239,000 cwt. harvested. Highest yield was 7,100 pounds per acre in 2002.

Several different types of rice milling procedures are in use today. The simplest and oldest method produces a product known as regular milled white rice, the most prevalent on the market today.

During this process, rice grains are subjected to additional cleaning to remove chaff, dust and foreign seed, and then husks are removed from the grains. This results in a product that is the whole unpolished grain of rice with only the outer hull and a small amount of bran removed. This product is called brown rice and is sometimes sold without further treatment other than grading. It has a delightful nutlike flavor and a slightly chewy texture.

When additional layers of the bran are removed, the rice becomes white in color and begins to appear as it is normally recognized at retail level. The removal of the bran layer from the grain is performed in a number of steps using two or three types of machines. After the bran is removed, the product is ready for classification as to size. Rice is more valuable if the grains are not broken. In many cases, additional vitamins are added to the grains to produce what is called "enriched rice."

Another process may be used in rice milling to produce a product called parboiled rice. In this process, the rice is subjected to a combination of steam and pressure prior to the time it is milled. This process gelatinizes the starch in the grain and helps retain the natural vitamin and mineral content. After cooking, parboiled rice tends to be fluffy, more separate and plump.

Still another type of rice is precooked rice, which is actually milled rice that, after milling, has been cooked. Then the moisture is removed through a dehydration process. Precooked rice requires a minimum of preparation time since it needs merely to have the moisture restored to it.

The United States produces only a small part of the world's total rice production, but it is one of the leading exporters. American rice is popular abroad and is exported to more than 100 foreign countries.

Rice production in 2002 totaled 14,616,000 cwt. from 206,000 harvested acres, with a yield of 7,100 pounds per acre. The crop value totaled $61,387,000. Rice production was 14,790,000 in 2001 on 216,000 harvested acres, yielding 6,850 pounds per acre. Total value in 2001 was $68,182,000. Rice production was 14,342,000 cwt. in 2000 on 214,000 harvested acres. Production in 2000 was valued at $83,470,000, with a yield of 6,700 pounds per acre. Counties leading in production in 2001 included Wharton, Colorado, Matagorda, Brazoria, Jackson and Jefferson.

## Wheat

Wheat for grain is one of the state's most valuable cash crops. In 2002, wheat was exceeded in value by cotton, hay, corn and sorghum. Wheat pastures also provide considerable winter forage for cattle that is reflected in the value of livestock produced.

Texas wheat production totaled 78,300,000 bushels in 2002 as yield averaged only 29.0 bushels per acre. Planted acreage totaled 6,400,000 acres and 2,700,000 acres were harvested. With an average price of $3.00 per bushel, the 2002 wheat value totaled $234,900,000. In 2001, Texas wheat growers planted 5,600,000 acres and harvested 3,200,000 acres. The yield was 34.0 bushels per acre for 2001 with total production of 108,800,000 bushels at $2.78 per bushel valued at $302,464,000.

Texas wheat growers planted 6,000,000 acres in 2000 and harvested grain from 2,200,000 acres. The yield was 30 bushels per acre for a total production of 66,000,000 bushels valued at $166,320,000.

Leading wheat-producing counties, based on production in 2001, were Hansford, Sherman, Ochiltree, Deaf Smith, Dallam and Parmer. The leading counties, based on acreage planted in 2001, were Hansford, Knox, Castro, Ochiltree, Deaf Smith and Haskell.

Wheat was first grown commercially in Texas near Sherman around 1833. The acreage expanded greatly in North-Central Texas after 1850 because of rapid settlement of the state and introduction of the well-adapted Mediterranean strain of wheat. A major family flour industry was developed in the area around Fort Worth, Dallas and Sherman between 1875 and 1900. Now, around half of the state's acreage is planted on the High Plains and about a third of this is irrigated. Most of the Texas wheat acreage is of the hard red winter class. Because of the development of varieties with improved disease resistance and the use of wheat for winter pasture, there has been a sizable expansion of acreage in Central and South Texas.

Most all wheat harvested for grain is used in some phase of the milling industry. The better-quality hard red winter wheat is used in the production of commercial bakery flour. Lower grades and varieties of soft red winter wheat are used in family flours. By-products of milled wheat are used for feed.

## Corn

Interest in corn production throughout the state has increased since the 1970s as yields improved with new varieties. Once the principal grain crop, corn acreage declined as plantings of grain sorghum increased. Only 500,000 acres were harvested annually until the mid-1970s when development of new hybrids occurred.

Harvested acreage was 1,820,000 in 2002, 1,420,000 in 2001 and 1,900,000 in 2000. Yield was 113 bushels per acre in 2002, 118 in 2001 and 124 in 2000.

Most of the acreage and yield increase has occurred in Central and South Texas. In 2002, corn ranked fourth in value among the state's crops. It was valued at $534,716,000 in 2002, $383,712,000 in 2001, and $513,608,000 in 2000. The grain is largely used for livestock feed, but other important uses are in food products. The leading counties in production for 2001 were Dallam, Hartley, Moore, Sherman and Castro.

## Rye

Rye is grown mainly on the northern and southern High Plains, the northern Low Plains, Cross Timbers, Blacklands and East Texas areas. Minor acreages are seeded in South-Central Texas, the Edwards Plateau and the Upper Coast. Rye is grown primarily as a cover crop and for grazing during the fall, winter and early spring. Estimated production data was discontinued in 1999.

## Oats

Oats are grown extensively in Texas for winter pasture, hay, silage and greenchop feeding, and some acreage is harvested for grain.

Of the 750,000 acres planted in oats in 2002, 160,000 acres were harvested. The average yield was 44 bushels per acre. Production totaled 7,040,000 bushels with a value of $11,968,000. In 2001, 725,000 acres were planted. From the plantings, 160,000 acres were harvested, with an average yield of 45 bushels per acre for a total production of 7,200,000 bushels. Average price per bushel was $2.20, and total production value was $15,840,000. In 2000, Texas farmers planted 600,000 acres of oats. They harvested 100,000 acres that averaged 43 bushels per acre for a total production of 4,300,000 bushels. The average price of $1.60 per bushel adds up to an estimated value of $6,880,000.

Most of the acreage was used for grazing. Almost all oat grain produced in Texas is utilized as feed for livestock within the state. A small acreage is grown exclusively for planting seed. Leading oat grain-producing counties in 2001 were Hamilton, Medina, McLennan, Coryell and Uvalde.

## Barley

Texas barley acreage and production falls far below that of wheat and oats. Barley is usually harvested from 10,000 of the 15,000 acres planted, with total production value of less than $500,000. Estimated production data was discontinued in 2000.

## Sugar Cane

Sugarcane is grown from seed cane planted in late summer or fall. It is harvested 12 months later and milled to produce raw sugar and molasses. Raw sugar requires additional refining before it can be offered to consumers.

The sugarcane grinding mill operated at Santa Rosa in Cameron County is considered one of the most modern mills in the United States. Texas sugarcane-producing counties are Hidalgo, Cameron and Willacy.

At a yield of 37.5 tons per acre, sugarcane production in 2002 totaled 1,687,000 tons from 45,000 harvested acres. In 2001, 47,000 acres were harvested for total production of 1,962,000 tons valued at $56,702,000, or $28.90 per ton. The yield was 41.7 tons per acre. In 2000, 46,300 acres were harvested, from which 1,789,000 tons of sugarcane were milled. The yield averaged 38.6 tons per acre. The price averaged $29.80 per ton for a total value of $53,312,000.

## Hay, Silage, and Other Forage Crops

A large proportion of Texas' agricultural land is devoted to forage crop production. This acreage produces forage needs and provides essentially the total feed requirements for most of the state's large domestic livestock population, as well as game animals.

Approximately 86.1 million acres of native rangeland, which are primarily in the western half of Texas, provide grazing for beef cattle, sheep, goats, horses and game animals. An additional 20 million acres are devoted to introducing forage species. Of this total, approximately 16 million acres are used for improved perennial grasses and legumes and are harvested by grazing animals. The average annual acreage of crops grown for hay, silage and other forms of machine-harvested forage is increasing, with the estimated value in excess of $700 million.

Hay accounts for a large amount of this production, with some corn and sorghum silage being produced. The most important hay crops are annual and perennial grasses and alfalfa. Production in 2002 totaled 13,850,000 tons of hay from 5,630,000 harvested acres at a yield of 2.46 tons per acre. Value of hay was $930,400,000, or $79.50 per ton. In 2001, 10,837,000 tons of hay was produced from 5,230,000 harvested acres at a yield of 2.07 tons per acre. The value in 2001 was $743,591,000, or $75.00 per ton. In 2000, the production of hay was 8,880,000 tons from 4,120,000 harvested acres with a value of $607,080,000, or $76.00 per ton, at a yield of 2.16 tons per acre.

Alfalfa hay production in 2002 totaled 650,000 tons, with 130,000 acres harvested and a yield of 5.0 tons per acre. At a value of $152 per ton, total value was $98,800,000. In 2001, 637,000 tons of alfalfa hay was harvested from 130,000 acres at a yield of 4.9 tons per acre. Value was $91,091,000, or $143 per ton. Alfalfa hay was harvested from 120,000 acres in 2000, producing an average of 4 tons per acre for total production of 480,000 tons valued at $65,280,000.

An additional sizable acreage of annual forage crops is grazed, as well as much of the small grain acreage. Alfalfa, sweet corn, vetch, arrowleaf clover, grasses and other forage plants also provide income as seed crops.

## Peanuts

Peanuts are grown on more than 300,000 acres in Texas. Well over three-fourths of the crop annually produced is on acreage that is irrigated. Texas ranked second nationally in production of peanuts in 2002. Among Texas crops, peanuts rank about seventh in value.

Until 1973, essentially all of the Texas acreage was planted to the Spanish type, which was favored because of its earlier maturity and better drought tolerance than other types. The Spanish variety is also preferred for some uses due to its distinctive flavor. The Florunner variety, a runner market type, is now planted on a sizable proportion of the acreage where soil moisture is favorable. The variety is later maturing but better yielding than Spanish varieties under good-growing conditions. Florunner peanuts have acceptable quality to compete with the Spanish variety in most products.

In 2002, peanut production totaled 868,000,000 pounds from 280,000 harvested acres, yielding 3,100 pounds per acre. At 18.2 cents per pound, value of the crop was estimated at $157,976,000. In 2001, peanut production amounted to 895,900,000 pounds from 425,000 acres planted and 310,000 harvested. Average yield of 2,890 pounds per acre and average price of 22.6 cents per pound combined for a 2001 value of $202,473,000. Production in 2000 amounted to 698,500,000 pounds of peanuts from 425,000 acres planted and 275,000 acres harvested, or an average of 2,540 pounds per harvested acre valued at 24.6 cents per pound for a total value of $171,831,000.

Leading counties in peanut production in 2001 included Gaines, Terry, Yoakum, Collingsworth, Dawson and Frio.

## Soybeans

Production is largely in the areas of the Upper Coast, irri-

gated High Plains and Red River Valley of Northeast Texas. Soybeans are adapted to the same general soil climate conditions as corn, cotton or grain sorghum, provided moisture, disease and insects are not limiting factors. The major counties in soybean production in 2001 were Lamar, Wharton, Victoria, Matagorda, Jackson and Ochiltree.

In low-rainfall areas, yields have been too low or inconsistent for profitable production under dryland conditions. Soybeans' need for moisture in late summer minimizes economic crop possibilities in the Blacklands and Rolling Plains. In the Blacklands, cotton root rot seriously hinders soybean production. Limited moisture at critical growth stages may occasionally prevent economical yields, even in high-rainfall areas of Northeast Texas and the Coast Prairie.

Because of day length sensitivity, soybeans should be planted in Texas during the long days of May and June to obtain sufficient vegetative growth for optimum yields. Varieties planted during this period usually cease vegetative development and initiate reproductive processes during the hot, usually dry months of July and August. When moisture is insufficient during the blooming and fruiting period, yields are drastically reduced. In most areas of the state, July and August rainfall is insufficient to permit economical dryland production. The risk of dryland soybean production in the Coast Prairie and Northeast Texas is considerably less when compared to other dryland areas because moisture is available more often during the critical fruiting period.

The 2002 soybean crop totaled 6,020,000 bushels and was valued at $31,304,000, or $5.20 per bushel. Of the 230,000 acres planted, 215,000 were harvested with an average yield of 28 bushels per acre. In 2001, the Texas soybean crop averaged 26 bushels per acre from 225,000 acres harvested. Total production of 5,850,000 bushels was valued at $26,910,000, or $4.60 per bushel. In 2000, the Texas soybean crop averaged 27 bushels per acre from 260,000 acres harvested. Total production of 7,020,000 bushels was valued at $30,888,000, or $4.40 per bushel. Soybeans were planted on acreage that had been planted to cotton but was lost to adverse weather.

## Sunflowers

Sunflowers constitute one of the most important annual oilseed crops in the world. The cultivated types, which are thought to be descendants of the common wild sunflower native to Texas, have been successfully grown in several countries including Russia, Argentina, Romania, Bulgaria, Uruguay, Western Canada and portions of the northern United States. Extensive trial plantings conducted in the Cotton Belt states since 1968 showed sunflowers have considerable potential as an oilseed crop in much of this area including Texas. This crop exhibits good cold and drought tolerance, is adapted to a wide range of soil and climate conditions, and tolerates higher levels of hail, wind and sand abrasion than other crops normally grown in the state.

In 2002, sunflower production totaled 31,800,000 pounds and was harvested from 34,000 acres at a yield of 935 pounds per acre. With an average price of $14.50 per cwt., the crop was valued at $4,594,000. In 2001, 103,000 of the 108,000 acres planted to sunflowers were harvested with an average yield of 1,168 pounds per acre. Total production of 120,300,000 pounds was valued at $12,326,000, or $10.30 per pound.

In 2000, of 60,000 acres planted to sunflowers, 45,000 acres were harvested, yielding 778 pounds per acre for a total yield of 35,000,000 pounds valued at $3,616,000, or $10.30 per pound. The leading counties in production in 2001 were Moore, Hartley, Sherman, Lamb and Ochiltree.

Reasons for growing sunflowers include the need for an additional cash crop with low water and plant nutrient

requirements, the development of sunflower hybrids, and interest by food processors in Texas sunflower oil, which has a high oleic acid content. Commercial users have found many advantages in this high-oleic oil, including excellent cooking stability particularly for use as a deep-frying medium for potato chips, corn chips and similar products.

Sunflower meal is a high-quality protein source free of nutritional toxins that can be included in rations for swine, poultry and ruminants. The hulls constitute a source of roughage, which can also be included in livestock rations.

## Flaxseed

Earliest flax planting was at Victoria in 1900. Since the first planting, Texas flax acreage has fluctuated depending on market, winterkill, and drought. Flax acreage has dropped in recent years and estimates were discontinued in 1980.

## Forest Products

For information on the Texas forest resource, refer to the section titled "Texas Forest Resources."

## Horticultural Specialty Crops

The trend to increase production of horticulture specialty crops continues to rise as transportation costs on long-distance hauling increases. This has resulted in a marked increase in the production of container-grown plants within the state. This increase is noted especially in the production of bedding plants, foliage plants, sod and the woody landscape plants.

Plant rental services have become a multi-million dollar business. This relatively new service provides the plants and maintains them in office buildings, shopping malls, public buildings and even in some homes for a fee. The response has been good as evidenced by the growth of companies providing these services.

Texans are creating colorful and green surroundings by improving their landscape plantings. The interest in plants for interior landscapes is also on the rise and is not confined to specific age group, as both retail nurseries and florist shops report that people of all ages are buying their plants — from the elderly in retirement homes to high

## Texas Vegetable Production, 2002

| Crop | Harvested Acres (000) | Yield Per Acre, Cwt. | Production (000) Cwt. | Value (000) |
|---|---|---|---|---|
| Bell Peppers | 800 | 200 | 160 | 7,520 |
| Cabbage | 8,700 | 320 | 2,784 | 45,101 |
| Cantaloupes | 9,500 | 270 | 2,565 | 80,798 |
| Carrots | 2,900 | 200 | 580 | 12,760 |
| Chiles | 5,500 | 50 | 275 | 11,000 |
| Cucumbers | 1,800 | 250 | 450 | 11,070 |
| Honeydew Melons | 1,700 | 300 | 510 | 14,433 |
| Onions, Spring | 15,000 | 315 | 4,725 | 101,115 |
| Onions, Summer | 2,800 | 350 | 980 | 21,756 |
| Spinach | 2,200 | 110 | 242 | 11,132 |
| Squash | 1,300 | 120 | 156 | 5,460 |
| Sweet Corn | 3,600 | 80 | 288 | 5,962 |
| Tomatoes | 900 | 200 | 180 | 5,760 |
| Watermelons | 37,000 | 180 | 6,600 | 56,610 |
| **Total Fresh Market\*** | **93,700** | - | **20,555** | **390,477** |
| Processed† | 31,300 | - | 3,887 | 38,367 |
| **Total Vegetables** | **125,000** | **24,442** | **428,844** | **345,548** |

*Numbers may not add due to rounding.*
*\* Includes some quantities of processed vegetables.*
*†Carrots, cucumbers and spinach. Excludes celery, mustard greens, okra and turnip greens; estimates discontinued in 2002.*
*Source: "Texas Ag Facts," Texas Agri. Statistics Svc./USDA, 2003.*

school and college students in dormitory rooms and apartments.

Texas Cooperative Extension specialists estimated cash receipts from horticultural specialty crops in Texas to be around $1.3 billion in 2002. Leading counties in specialty crops are Harris, Dallas, Rusk, Fort Bend, Cherokee and Smith.

cwt. from 17,800 harvested acres and was valued at $122,871,000, at a yield of 333 cwt. per acre. In 2001, 5,655,000 cwt. of onions were harvested from 16,800 acres and valued at $106,386,000, at a yield of 363 cwt. per acre. A total of 5,235,000 cwt. of onions were produced from 17,000 harvested acres and valued at

## II. Truck Crops

Some market vegetables are produced in almost all Texas counties, but most of the commercial crop comes from about 200 counties. Hidalgo County is the leading Texas county in vegetable acres harvested, followed by Presidio and Frio counties. Other leading producing counties are Uvalde, Jeff Davis, Zavala, Pecos and Gaines.

Texas is one of the five leading states in the production of fresh market vegetables. Nationally, in 2002, Texas ranked fifth in harvested acreage, exceeded by California, Florida, Arizona and Georgia; fifth in production, exceeded by California, Florida, Arizona and Georgia; and fourth in value of fresh-market vegetables. Texas had 4.8 percent of the harvested acreage, 4.5 percent of the production and 4.2 percent of the value of fresh-market vegetables produced. Texas ranked second behind California in the production of spinach for processing. Onions were the number-one cash crop, and cantaloupes were second. Other vegetables leading in value of production are watermelons, cabbage, honeydew melons, carrots and cucumbers.

In 2002, total vegetable production of 24,442,000 cwt. was valued at $428,844,000 from 125,000 acres harvested. In 2001, Texas growers harvested total commercial vegetable crops valued at $423,151,000 from 136,600 acres with a production of 27,060,000 cwt. Texas growers harvested 23,461,000 cwt. of commercial vegetable crops from 127,700 acres, valued at $336,458,000 in 2000.

### Onions

Onion production in 2002 totaled 5,705,000

## Cash Receipts for Commodities, 1997–2001

| Commodity * | 1997 | 1998 | 1999 | 2000 | 2001 | % of 2001 |
|---|---|---|---|---|---|---|
| | (All values in thousands of dollars) | | | | | |
| **All Commodities:** | $13,210,220 | $13,154,341 | $13,032,108 | $13,370,108 | $13,795,570 | 100.00 |
| Livestock and products . . . | 8,147,414 | 8,150,732 | 8,483,751 | 9,159,332 | 9,339,465 | 67.70 |
| Crops, Fruits and others | 5,062,806 | 5,003,609 | 4,548,709 | 4,210,776 | 4,456,105 | 32.30 |
| **Livestock and products:** | | | | | | |
| Cattle and calves . . . . . . | 5,885,151 | 5,775,190 | 6,124,290 | 6,815,081 | 6,812,228 | 49.38 |
| Broilers . . . . . . . . . . . . . | 774,595 | 842,400 | 883,227 | 880,498 | 1,058,616 | 7.67 |
| Milk . . . . . . . . . . . . . . . | 787,339 | 876,531 | 839,400 | 766,078 | 802,008 | 5.81 |
| Eggs . . . . . . . . . . . . . . . | 267,904 | 253,646 | 240,509 | 256,903 | 267,077 | 1.94 |
| Hogs . . . . . . . . . . . . . . . | 101,139 | 85,073 | 70,456 | 113,497 | 102,455 | 0.74 |
| Sheep and lambs. . . . . . | 60,902 | 61,759 | 56,488 | 38,274 | 40,175 | 0.29 |
| Mohair . . . . . . . . . . . . . . | 14,556 | 12,044 | 9,384 | 10,088 | 3,775 | 0.03 |
| Wool . . . . . . . . . . . . . . . | 11,607 | 5,815 | 3,898 | 3,678 | 3,122 | 0.02 |
| Horses and mules . . . . . | 86,000 | 90,000 | NA | NA | NA | 0.00 |
| † Other livestock . . . . . . | 158,221 | 148,274 | 256,099 | 275,235 | 250,009 | 1.81 |
| **Crops:** | | | | | | |
| Cotton lint . . . . . . . . . . | 1,252,357 | 1,469,246 | 1,205,274 | 720,002 | 859,954 | 6.23 |
| Corn. . . . . . . . . . . . . . . . | 577,034 | 436,281 | 414,197 | 460,349 | 376,653 | 2.73 |
| Hay . . . . . . . . . . . . . . . | 201,719 | 152,656 | 178,364 | 280,671 | 318,248 | 2.31 |
| Wheat . . . . . . . . . . . . . | 357,582 | 343,328 | 241,528 | 185,775 | 276,012 | 2.00 |
| Sorghum grain . . . . . . . | 472,950 | 214,263 | 254,206 | 295,151 | 271,290 | 1.97 |
| Peanuts . . . . . . . . . . . . | 199,782 | 225,803 | 190,921 | 171,831 | 202,473 | 1.47 |
| Cottonseed . . . . . . . . . . | 197,609 | 180,390 | 149,999 | 145,536 | 140,547 | 1.02 |
| Onions . . . . . . . . . . . . . | 50,168 | 90,226 | 93,788 | 96,342 | 106,386 | 0.77 |
| Cantaloupes . . . . . . . . . | 27,160 | 66,990 | 56,743 | 42,412 | 69,720 | 0.51 |
| Cabbage . . . . . . . . . . . | 33,813 | 69,360 | 41,290 | 52,480 | 66,011 | 0.48 |
| Rice . . . . . . . . . . . . . . . | 168,967 | 148,783 | 115,404 | 81,397 | 51,733 | 0.37 |
| Potatoes. . . . . . . . . . . . | 46,344 | 44,103 | 44,423 | 50,985 | 45,410 | 0.33 |
| Sugar cane for sugar . . . | 23,091 | 26,494 | 26,962 | 53,312 | 44,908 | 0.33 |
| Carrots . . . . . . . . . . . . . | 11,687 | 21,994 | 32,259 | 15,684 | 34,704 | 0.25 |
| Soybeans. . . . . . . . . . . . | 58,323 | 49,864 | 31,058 | 39,253 | 30,212 | 0.22 |
| Watermelons . . . . . . . . . | 58,434 | 35,643 | 29,611 | 21,840 | 28,800 | 0.21 |
| Cucumbers . . . . . . . . . . | 15,952 | 22,350 | 22,396 | 19,688 | 21,258 | 0.15 |
| Peppers, Chile . . . . . . . | NA | NA | NA | 11,963 | 16,965 | 0.12 |
| Honeydew melons . . . . . | 9,492 | 16,650 | 17,111 | 14,131 | 13,608 | 0.10 |
| Peppers, Green . . . . . . . | 9,688 | 5,308 | 6,224 | 9,048 | 11,083 | 0.08 |
| Spinach . . . . . . . . . . . . | 9,697 | 12,903 | 11,344 | 12,239 | 10,493 | 0.08 |
| Sunflowers . . . . . . . . . . | 7,848 | 6,922 | 5,670 | 5,866 | 7,849 | 0.06 |
| Corn, sweet . . . . . . . . . | 3,700 | 8,424 | 7,785 | 8,011 | 7,020 | 0.05 |
| Tomatoes, fresh . . . . . . . | 8,840 | 5,292 | 6,086 | 5,879 | 6,480 | 0.05 |
| Beans, Dry. . . . . . . . . . . | 1,958 | 2,145 | 6,812 | 5,473 | 5,127 | 0.04 |
| Greens | NA | NA | NA | 8,983 | 4,955 | 0.04 |
| Oats. . . . . . . . . . . . . . . . | 2,023 | 2,099 | 1,305 | 1,375 | 4,458 | 0.03 |
| Celery . . . . . . . . . . . . . | 4,496 | 4,170 | 3,757 | 3,120 | 3,900 | 0.03 |
| Sweet potatoes . . . . . . . | 14,015 | 5,614 | 5,512 | 4,680 | 3,650 | 0.03 |
| Okra. . . . . . . . . . . . . . . . | NA | NA | NA | 2,222 | 959 | 0.01 |
| Broccoli . . . . . . . . . . . . | 1,758 | 2,238 | 1,940 | NA | NA | 0.00 |
| Rye . . . . . . . . . . . . . . . | 933 | 1,135 | 908 | NA | NA | 0.00 |
| Barley . . . . . . . . . . . . . | 285 | 222 | 322 | 15 | NA | 0.00 |
| Sugarbeets . . . . . . . . . . | 9,523 | NA | NA | NA | NA | 0.00 |
| ‡ Other crops. . . . . . . . . | 75,633 | 80,820 | 98,574 | 101,156 | 95909 | 0.70 |
| **Fruits and Nuts** | | | | | | |
| Pecans. . . . . . . . . . . . . . | 58,370 | 34,500 | 68,000 | 34,600 | 50,000 | 0.36 |
| Peaches. . . . . . . . . . . . . | 5,600 | 9,880 | 6,820 | 10,034 | 14,820 | 0.11 |
| Grapefruit . . . . . . . . . . . | 20,909 | 29,631 | 39,472 | 29,636 | 10,564 | 0.08 |
| Grapes | NA | NA | NA | NA | 8,370 | 0.06 |
| Oranges. . . . . . . . . . . . . | 5,484 | 7,106 | 2,625 | 6,090 | 6,154 | 0.04 |
| §Other fruits and nuts . | 5,928 | 4,593 | 7,930 | 13,215 | 4,178 | 0.03 |
| **Other Farm Income:** | | | | | | |
| Greenhouse/nursery . . . | 1,052,226 | 1,166,183 | 1,122,089 | 1,190,332 | 1,225,244 | 8.88 |

*Commodities are listed in order of importance for 2001 by crop items and by livestock items.
†For 1999–2001, includes milkfat, turkey eggs, equine, goats, goat milk and other poultry and livestock. For 1998, includes milkfat, turkey eggs, goats, goat milk, catfish and other poultry and livestock. ‡For 1997–1999, includes peppers, chile, grapes, greens, okra, miscellaneousvegetables, field crops, fruit and nuts. For 2000, includes grapes, miscellaneous vegetables, field crops, fruits and nuts. For 2001, includes miscellaneous vegetables, field crops, fruit and nuts.
Source: Texas Agricultural Statistics, USDA/Texas Agricultural Statistics Service, Sept. 2002; various issues of Texas Agricultural Statistics and Texas Agricultural Cash Reciptrs and Price Statistics, USDA/TASS.

$96,342,000 in 2000, yielding 343 cwt. per acre.

### Carrots

Carrot production in 2002 totaled 580,000 cwt. from 2,900 harvested acres at a yield of 200 cwt. per acre. Production was valued at $12,760,000. In 2001, carrots were harvested from 3,200 acres with a value of $24,864,000. At a yield of 300 cwt. per acre, 2001 production was 960,000 cwt. Carrot production was valued at $14,071,000 in 2000 from 4,600 acres harvested. Production was 874,000 cwt. at a yield of 190 cwt. per acre.

The winter carrot production from South Texas accounts for about three-fourths of total production during the winter season.

### All Potatoes

In 2002, all potatoes were harvested from 20,300 acres with production of 5,360,000 cwt. valued at $57,156,000 at a yield of 264 cwt. per acre. All potatoes were harvested from 17,000 acres with production of 5,190,000 cwt. valued at $53,681,000 in 2001, yielding 305 cwt. per acre. This compares with 17,100 acres harvested in 2000 and valued at $52,277,000, with production of 5,196,000 cwt. and a yield of 304 cwt. per acre.

### Cantaloupes - Honeydews

Cantaloupe production in 2002 totaled 2,565,000 cwt. from 9,500 harvested acres and was valued at $80,798,000 at a yield of 270 cwt. per acre. In 2001, cantaloupes were harvested from 11,200 acres for total production of 2,800,000 cwt. valued at $69,720,000, yielding 250 cwt. per acre. Of the 10,800 harvested acres in 2000, 1,836,000 cwt. cantaloupes were produced at a yield of 170 cwt. per acre and were valued at $42,412,000.

Honeydew production totaled 510,000 cwt. and was valued at $14,433,000 at a yield of 300 cwt. per acre in 2002. In 2001, 360,000 cwt. of honeydew melons were harvested from 1,800 acres for total value of $13,608,000, yielding 200 cwt. per acre. Honeydew melons valued at $14,131,000 were harvested on 2,400 acres, producing a yield of 230 cwt. per acre for a total production of 552,000 cwt. in 2000.

### Cabbage

In 2002, 8,700 acres were harvested and yielded total production of 2,784,000 cwt. that was valued at $45,101,000. Yield was 320 cwt. per acre. In 2001, 9,300 acres of cabbage were harvested yielding total production of 3,627,000 cwt., or 390 cwt. per acre, valued at $66,011,000. The 10,000 acres of cabbage harvested in Texas in 2000 brought a value of $52,480,000. At a yield of 410 cwt. per acre, total production was 4,100,000 cwt.

### Broccoli

Broccoli is primarily a South Texas crop. It is produced on 800 to 900 harvested acres. Estimated production data was discontinued in 2000.

### Watermelons

Watermelon production in 2002 was 6,600,000 cwt. from 37,000 acres with a value of $56,610,000, yielding 180 cwt. per acre. In 2000, at a yield of 160 cwt. per acre, 7,200,000 cwt. watermelons were harvested from 45,000 acres and valued at $32,400,000. Watermelon production was 5,600,000 cwt. from 40,000 acres in 2000, with a value of $21,840,000 at a yield of 140 cwt. per acre.

### Tomatoes

Commercial tomatoes are marketed throughout the year from Texas partly as a result of recent increases in greenhouse production during the winter.

In 2002, 900 harvested acres of tomatoes at a yield of 200 cwt. per acre produced 180,000 cwt. of tomatoes with a value of $5,760,000. In 2000, 1,200 acres of tomatoes were harvested, producing 180,000 cwt. at a yield of 150 cwt. per acre for a value of $6,480,000. The tomato crop in 2000 was valued at $5,879,000 from 1,400 harvested acres. Tomato production was 182,000 cwt. at a yield of

130 cwt. per acre.

### Bell Peppers

Bell pepper production in 2002 of 160,000 cwt. from 800 harvested acres was valued at $7,520,000 with a yield of 200 cwt. per acre. In 2001, bell peppers were harvested from 1,100 acres valued at $11,083,000. At a yield of 250 cwt. per acre, 275,000 cwt. were produced. Bell peppers in 2000 were harvested from 1,300 acres valued at $9,048,000. Production of bell peppers was 260,000 cwt. with a yield of 200 cwt. per acre.

### Sweet Potatoes

In 2002, 561,000 cwt. sweet potatoes were harvested from 3,300 acres for a value of $10,042,000 at a yield of 170 cwt. per acre. Sweet potatoes in 2001 produced 380,000 cwt. from 3,800 harvested acres with a value of $7,106,000. Yield was 100 cwt. per acre. This compared with 230,000 cwt. produced at a yield of 45 cwt. from 5,500 harvested acres valued at $3,795,000 in 2000.

### Spinach

Spinach production is primarily concentrated in the Winter Garden area of South Texas.

The 2002 production value of spinach was estimated at $11,132,000. Production of 242,000 cwt. was harvested from 2,200 acres with a yield of 110 cwt. per acre. In 2001, 2,500 acres were harvested with a value of $8,145,000. At a yield of 90 cwt. per acre, production was 225,000 cwt. The 2,600 acres, harvested in 2000, produced 221,000 cwt. at a yield of 85 cwt. per acre and valued at $8,332,000.

### Cucumbers

In 2002, 1,800 acres of cucumbers were harvested. Production totaled 450,000 cwt. and was valued at $11,070,000. The 2002 yield was 250 cwt. per acre. In 2001, 1,800 acres of cucumbers were harvested with a value of $9,148,000. Production was 378,000 cwt. with a yield of 210 cwt. per acre. At a yield of 200 cwt. per acre, the 360,000 cwt. cucumber crop in Texas during 2000 was harvested from 1,800 acres and valued at $8,676,000.

### Sweet Corn

In 2002, 288,000 cwt. of sweet corn was harvested from 3,600 acres. Value of production was estimated at $5,962,000 with a yield of 80 cwt. per acre. In 2001, 390,000 cwt. of sweet corn was produced from 3,900 harvested acres at a yield of 100 cwt. per acre and valued at $7,020,000. Sweet corn was harvested in Texas from 4,800 acres valued at $8,011,000 in 2000. Production was 387,000 cwt. at a yield of 90 cwt. per acre.

### Vegetables for Processing

In 2002, 3,887,000 cwt. of cucumbers, carrots, and spinach for processing were harvested from 31,300 acres and valued at $38,367,000. In 2001, 28,500 acres were harvested and valued at $32,248,000 with a production of 3,835,000 cwt. In 2000, 21,900 acres were harvested and valued at $21,536,000, producing 2,759,000 cwt.

## III. Fruits and Nuts

Texas is noted for producing a wide variety of fruits. The pecan is the only commercial nut crop in the state. The pecan is native to most of the state's river valleys and is the Texas state tree. Citrus is produced in the three southernmost counties in the Lower Rio Grande Valley. Production has continued to increase since the severe freeze several years ago. Some new orchards have been planted. Peaches represent the next most important Texas fruit crop, yet there is a considerable amount of interest in growing apples.

### Citrus

Prior to the 1989 freeze, Texas ranked with Florida, California and Arizona as leading states in the production of citrus. Most of the Texas production is in Cameron,

Hidalgo and Willacy counties of the Lower Rio Grande Valley. In 2001–2002, grapefruit production was estimated at 5,900,000 boxes. At $3.91 per box, value of production was $23,040,000. Grapefruit production in 2000–2001 was 7,200,000 boxes at $2.68 per box for a total value of $19,324,000. Production in 1999–2000 was 5,930,000 boxes at $6.30 per box with a value of $37,342,000.

Production of oranges in 2001–2002 was 1,740,000 boxes. At $4.64 per box, total value was $8,068,000. In 2000–2001, production was 2,235,000 boxes at $2.48 per box for a total value of $5,539,000. Production was 1,660,000 boxes in 1999–2000 at $6.13 per box for a value of $10,173,000.

### Peaches

Primary production areas are East Texas, the Hill Country and the West Cross Timbers. Production varies substantially due to adverse weather conditions. Recently, peach production has spread to South and West Texas. Low-chilling varieties for early marketings are being grown in Atascosa, Frio, Webb, Karnes and Duval counties.

The Texas peach crop totaled 11,400,000 pounds in 2002 for a value of $6,840,000 or 60 cents per pound. In 2001, production was 26,000,000 pounds. Value of production was $14,820,000 or 57 cents per pound. In 2000, production was 17,300,000 pounds that was valued at $10,034,000 or 58 cents per pound.

The demand for high-quality Texas peaches greatly exceeds the supply. Texas ranked 11th nationally in peach production in 2002. Leading Texas counties in production are Gillespie, Parker, Montague, Comanche, Limestone and Eastland.

### Apples

Small acreages of apples, usually marketed in the state, are grown in a number of counties. The leading counties in production are Montague and Gillespie. Other counties which have apples include Callahan, Collingsworth, Clay, Cass, Donley, Eastland, Hudspeth, Jeff Davis, Lampasas, Parker, San Saba and Young. The crop is harvested and marketed from July to October.

A considerable number of apple trees have been planted in the Hill Country. Most of the trees are new varieties of Red and Golden Delicious types on semi-dwarfing rootstocks. Trees are established in high-density plantings of 100 to 200 trees per acre. Most of the apples are sold at roadside stands or go to nearby markets.

### Pears

Well adapted for home and small orchard production, the pear is not commercially significant in Texas. Comanche, Parker, Lampasas, Cooke, McCulloch and Eastland counties lead in trees. Usually the fruit goes for home consumption or to nearby markets..

### Apricots

Not a commercial crop, apricots are grown chiefly in Comanche, Denton, Wilbarger, Parker and Collingsworth counties. Other reporting apricots include Martin, Clay, Young, Lampasas, Gillespie, Anderson, Erath, Wichita and Eastland counties.

### Plums

Plum production is scattered over a wide area of the state with the heaviest production in East and Central

Texas ranked 11th nationally in peach production in 2002. Leading counties are Gillespie, Parker, Montague, Comanche, Limestone and Eastland.

Texas. The leading counties in production are Smith, Gillespie and Knox. Most of the production goes to nearby markets or to processors.

### Blackberries

Smith County is a blackberry center with the Tyler-Lindale area having processed the crop since 1890. Other counties with blackberry acreage include Wood, Van Zandt and Henderson. The Brazos blackberry is grown as a local market or "pick-your-own" fruit in many sections of the state. Dewberries grow wild in Central and East Texas and are gathered for home use and local sale in May and June.

### Strawberries

Atascosa County is the leading commercial area, although strawberries are grown for local markets in Wood, Van Zandt and Smith counties in East Texas. The most concentrated production occurs in the Poteet area south of San Antonio.

## Texas Cattle Marketed, 1965–2002 by Size of Feedlot

| Year | Feedlot Capacity (head) | | | | | | Total |
|---|---|---|---|---|---|---|---|
| | Under 1,000 | 1,000-1,999 | 2,000-3,999 | 4,000-7,999 | 8,000-15,999 | 16,000 & Over | |
| | Cattle Marketed — 1,000 head — | | | | | | |
| 1965 | 104 | 108 | 205 | 324 | 107 | 246 | 1,094 |
| 1970 | 98 | 53 | 112 | 281 | 727 | 1,867 | 3,138 |
| 1975 | 50 | 22 | 51 | 134 | 485 | 2,325 | 3,067 |
| 1976 | 60 | 33 | 62 | 170 | 583 | 3,039 | 3,947 |
| 1977 | 146 | 22 | 38 | 206 | 604 | 3,211 | 4,277 |
| 1978 | 80 | 20 | 50 | 242 | 697 | 3,826 | 4,915 |
| 1979 | 54 | 19 | 46 | 227 | 556 | 3,543 | 4,445 |
| 1980 | 51 | 18 | 47 | 226 | 533 | 3,285 | 4,160 |
| 1981 | 50 | 20 | 50 | 220 | 510 | 3,110 | 3,960 |
| 1982 | 55 | 20 | 60 | 210 | 540 | 3,190 | 4,075 |
| 1983 | 100 | 20 | 80 | 130 | 490 | 3,580 | 4,400 |
| 1984 | 60 | 20 | 180 | 150 | 540 | 4,140 | 5,090 |
| 1985 | 70 | 10 | 20 | 170 | 620 | 4,140 | 5,030 |
| 1986 | 90 | 10 | 40 | 180 | 550 | 4,390 | 5,260 |
| 1987 | 90 | 20 | 35 | 170 | 625 | 4,375 | 5,255 |
| 1988 | 30 | 15 | 35 | 185 | 650 | 4,120 | 5,035 |
| 1989 | 40 | 15 | 40 | 165 | 675 | 3,810 | 4,745 |
| 1990 | 35 | 24 | 56 | 180 | 605 | 3,940 | 4,840 |
| 1991 | 35 | 25 | 45 | 225 | 500 | 4,250 | 5,080 |
| 1992 | 50 | 10 | 25 | 140 | 505 | 4,065 | 4,795 |
| 1993 | 30 | 20 | 70 | 160 | 640 | 4,370 | 5,290 |
| 1994 | 14 | 13 | 55 | 173 | 725 | 4,680 | 5,660 |
| 1995 | 12 | 24 | 43 | 166 | 630 | 4,665 | 5,540 |
| 1996 | NA | 17 | 43 | 180 | 460 | 4,800 | 5,500 |
| 1997 | NA | 17 | 48 | 250 | 485 | 5,000 | 5,800 |
| 1998 | NA | 10 | 20 | 140 | 420 | 5,470 | 6,060 |
| 1999 | NA | 10 | 20 | 140 | 385 | 5,510 | 6,065 |
| 2000 | NA | 8 | 17 | 125 | 470 | 5,570 | 6,190 |
| 2001 | NA | 8 | 22 | 90 | 450 | 5,460 | 6,030 |
| 2002 | NA | 10 | 15 | 85 | 390 | 5,480 | 5,980 |

Number of feedlots with 1,000 head or more capacity is number of lots operating any time during the year. Number under 1,000 head capacity and total number of all feedlots is number at end of year.
Source: "Texas Agricultural Facts, 1997," Texas Agricultural Statistics Service, Sept. 1998. Numbers for 1986-1992, "1993 Texas Livestock Statistics," Bulletin 252, August 1994. "Cattle on Feed" annual summary, USDA/NASS, Feb. 2003.

## Avocados

Avocados grow on a small acreage in the Lower Rio Grande Valley. Interest in this crop is increasing and production is expected to expand. Lulu is the principal variety.

## Pecans

The pecan, the state tree, is one of the most widely distributed trees in Texas. It is native to over 150 counties and is grown commercially in some 30 additional counties. The pecan is also widely used as a dual-purpose yard tree. The commercial plantings of pecans have accelerated in Central and West Texas with many of the new orchards being irrigated. Many new pecan plantings are being established under trickle-irrigation systems. The development and use of the new USDA pecan varieties have helped to increase quality and yields.

In 2002, pecan production totaled only 40,000,000 pounds because of drought and was valued at $37,300,000 or 93 cents per pound. In 2001, 75,000,000 pounds were produced. Total value was estimated at $50,000,000 as price averaged 66.7 cents per pound. The 2000 crop totaled 30,000,000 pounds valued at $34,600,000 or $1.15 per pound. In 1999, the crop totaled 90,000,000 pounds valued at $68,000,000 or 75.6 cents per pound.

Nationally, Texas ranked second behind Georgia in pecan production in 2002. Leading Texas counties in pecan production are Hood, El Paso, Pecos, San Saba, Mills, Comanche, Wharton and Gonzales.

## IV. Livestock and Their Products

Livestock and their products accounted for about 67.7

percent of the agricultural cash receipts in Texas in 2001. The state ranks first nationally in all cattle, beef cattle, cattle on feed, sheep and lambs, wool, goats and mohair.

Meat animals normally account for around 50.4 percent of total cash receipts from marketings of livestock and their products. Sales of livestock and products in 2001 totaled $9.34 billion, up from $9.16 billion in 2000.

Cattle dominate livestock production in Texas, contributing more than 65 percent of cash receipts from livestock and products each year. The Jan. 1, 2003, inventory of all cattle and calves in Texas totaled 14,000,000 head, valued at $8.4 billion, compared to 13,600,000 as of Jan. 1, 2002, valued at $8.296 billion.

On Jan. 1, 2003, the sheep and lamb inventory stood at 1,050,000 head, valued at $82,950,000, compared with 1,130,000 head as of Jan. 1, 2002, valued at $88,140,000. Sheep and lambs numbered 3,214,000 on Jan. 1, 1973, down from a high of 10,829,000 in 1943. Sheep and lamb production fell from 148,295,000 pounds in 1973 to 48,860,000 pounds on Jan. 1, 2003. Wool production decreased from 26,352,000 pounds valued at $23,190,000 in 1973 to 5,530,000 pounds valued at $3,760,000 in 2002. Production was 6,003,000 pounds in 2001 valued at $3,122,000. The price of wool per pound was 88 cents in 1973, 52 cents in 2001, and 68 cents in 2002.

## Hog Production, 1960–2002

| Year | Production (1,000 Pounds) | Avg. Market Wt. (Pounds) | Avg. Price Per Cwt. (Dollars) | Gross Income (1,000 Dollars) |
|---|---|---|---|---|
| 1960 | 288,844 | 228 | $14.70 | $44,634 |
| 1970 | 385,502 | 241 | 22.50 | 75,288 |
| 1980 | 315,827 | 259 | 35.90 | 111,700 |
| 1981 | 264,693 | 256 | 41.70 | 121,054 |
| 1982 | 205,656 | 256 | 49.60 | 112,726 |
| 1983 | 209,621 | 256 | 45.20 | 95,343 |
| 1984 | 189,620 | 262 | 45.50 | 95,657 |
| 1985 | 168,950 | 266 | 43.40 | 72,512 |
| 1986 | 176,660 | 269 | 47.30 | 82,885 |
| 1987 | 216,834 | NA | 50.60 | 103,983 |
| 1988 | 236,658 | NA | 41.30 | 100,029 |
| 1989 | 224,229 | NA | 39.90 | 93,178 |
| 1990 | 196,225 | NA | 48.20 | 92,222 |
| 1991 | 207,023 | NA | 45.10 | 97,398 |
| 1992 | 217,554 | NA | 36.40 | 79,436 |
| 1993 | 221,130 | NA | 39.90 | 90,561 |
| 1994 | 224,397 | NA | 35.10 | 78,394 |
| 1995 | 221,323 | NA | 35.50 | 81,509 |
| 1996 | 203,761 | NA | 45.90 | 93,526 |
| 1997 | 224,131 | NA | 47.40 | 106,238 |
| 1998 | 270,977 | NA | 30.70 | 83,190 |
| 1999 | 274,572 | NA | 27.50 | 71,604 |
| 2000 | 328,732 | NA | 36.60 | 115,105 |
| 2001 | 260,875 | NA | 38.98 | 105,217 |
| 2002 | 224,641 | NA | 29.42 | 67,255 |

Source: "1985 Texas Livestock, Dairy and Poultry Statistics," USDA, Bulletin 235, June 1986, pp. 32, 46; 1991 "Texas Livestock Statistics"; USDA, "Meat Animals - Prod., Dips., & Income," April 1996–2003; "1993 Texas Livestock Statistics," Bulletin 252, Texas Agricultural Statistics Service, Aug. 1994; "Texas Agricultural Facts, 2001," Sept. 2002; "Texas Ag Facts," various years.

## Goats and Mohair, 1900–2003

| Year | Goats *Number | Goats Farm Value | Mohair Production (lbs) | Mohair Value |
|---|---|---|---|---|
| 1900 | 627,000 | $924,000 | 961,000 | $268,000 |
| 1910 | 1,135,000 | 2,514,000 | 1,998,000 | 468,000 |
| 1920 | 1,753,000 | 9,967,000 | 6,786,000 | 1,816,000 |
| 1930 | 2,965,000 | 14,528,000 | 14,800,000 | 4,995,000 |
| 1940 | 3,300,000 | 10,560,000 | 18,250,000 | 9,308,000 |
| 1950 | 2,295,000 | 13,082,000 | 12,643,000 | 9,735,000 |
| 1960 | 3,339,000 | 29,383,000 | 23,750,000 | 21,375,000 |
| 1970 | 2,572,000 | 19,033,000 | 17,985,000 | 7,032,000 |
| 1980 | 1,400,000 | 64,400,000 | 8,800,000 | 30,800,000 |
| 1981 | 1,380,000 | 53,130,000 | 10,100,000 | 35,350,000 |
| 1982 | 1,410,000 | 57,810,000 | 10,000,000 | 25,500,000 |
| 1983 | 1,420,000 | 53,250,000 | 10,600,000 | 42,930,000 |
| 1984 | 1,450,000 | 82,215,000 | 10,600,000 | 48,160,000 |
| 1985 | 1,590,000 | 76,797,000 | 13,300,000 | 45,885,000 |
| 1986 | 1,770,000 | 70,977,000 | 16,000,000 | 40,160,000 |
| 1987 | 1,780,000 | 82,592,000 | 16,200,000 | 42,606,000 |
| 1988 | 1,800,000 | 108,180,000 | 15,400,000 | 29,876,000 |
| 1989 | 1,850,000 | 100,270,000 | 15,400,000 | 24,794,000 |
| 1990 | 1,900,000 | 93,100,000 | 14,500,000 | 13,775,000 |
| 1991 | 1,830,000 | 73,200,000 | 14,800,000 | 19,388,000 |
| 1992 | 2,000,000 | 84,000,000 | 14,200,000 | 12,354,000 |
| 1993 | 1,960,000 | 84,280,000 | 13,490,000 | 11,197,000 |
| 1994 | 1,960,000 | 74,480,000 | 11,680,000 | 30,602,000 |
| 1995 | 1,850,000 | 81,400,000 | 11,319,000 | 20,940,000 |
| 1996 | 1,900,000 | 89,300,000 | 7,490,000 | 14,606,000 |
| 1997 | 1,650,000 | 70,950,000 | 6,384,000 | 14,556,000 |
| 1998 | 1,400,000 | 71,400,000 | 4,650,000 | 12,044,000 |
| 1999 | 1,350,000 | 71,550,000 | 2,550,000 | 9,384,000 |
| 2000 | 1,300,000 | 74,100,000 | 2,346,000 | 10,088,000 |
| 2001 | 1,400,000 | 105,000,000 | NA | NA |
| 2002 | 1,250,000 | 106,250,000 | 1,896,000 | 3,034,000 |
| 2003 | 1,200,000 | 109,200,000 | NA | NA |

*Goat number includes all goats, not just Angora goats.
NA = not available.
Source: "1985 Texas Livestock, Dairy and Poultry Statistics," USDA Bulletin 235, June 1986, p. 25. "Texas Agricultural Facts," Crop and Livestock Reporting Service, various years; "1993 Texas Livestock Statistics," Texas Agricultural Statistics Service, Bulletin 252, August 1994. "Texas Agricultural Statistics, 2001," Sept. 2002.

Lamb prices averaged $75.90 per cwt. as of Jan. 1, 2003, $74.80 per cwt. in 2002, and $81.20 per cwt. in 2001. The average price of sheep was $35.30 per cwt. as of Jan. 1, 2003, $42.70 in 2002, and $41.10 in 2001.

Mohair production in Texas has dropped from a 1965 high of 31,584,000 pounds to 1,896,000 pounds in 2002. Production was valued at $3,034,000 or $1.60 per pound. In 2001, production was 1,716,000 pounds valued at $3,775,000 or $2.20 per pound. Mohair production in 2000 was 2,346,000 pounds valued at $10,088,000 or $4.30 per pound.

## Beef Cattle

Raising beef cattle is the most extensive agricultural operation in Texas. In 2001, 49.4 percent of total cash receipts from farm and ranch marketings — $6,812,228 of $13,795,507 — came from cattle and calves, compared with $6,815,081 of $13,370,108 in 2000 (51 percent) and $6,124,290 of $13,032,460 in 1999 (47 percent). The next leading commodity is cotton.

Nearly all of the 254 counties in Texas derive more revenue from cattle than from any other agricultural commodity, and those that don't usually rank cattle second in importance.

Within the boundaries of Texas is 15 percent of all U.S. cattle, as are 17 percent of the beef breeding cows, and 13 percent of the calf crop as of Jan. 1, 2003, inventory. The number of all cattle in Texas as of that date totaled 14,000,000, compared with 13,600,000 on Jan. 1, 2002, and 13,700,000 in 2001. Calves born on Texas farms and ranches in 2002 totaled 5,000,000, compared with 5,050,000 in 2001, and 5,100,000 in 2000.

Sale of cattle and calves at approximately 162 livestock auctions inspected by the Texas Animal Health Commission totaled 4,837,894 head in 2002; 5,059,000 head in 2001; and 5,612,000 in 2000. The number of cattle and calves shipped into Texas totaled 2,430,058 head in Jan. 1, 2003; 3,350,000 head in Jan. 1, 2002; and 3,373,000 head in Jan. 1, 2001.

## Livestock Industries

A large portion of Texas livestock is sold through local auction markets. In 2002, the Texas Animal Health Commission reported 162 livestock auctions. Auctions sold 4,837,894 head of cattle and calves, 67,761 hogs, and 1,537,448 sheep and goats in 2002. This compared with 5,059,000 cattle and calves, 64,000 hogs, and 1,323,000 sheep and goats in 2001. Figures for 2000 were 5,612,000 cattle and calves, 81,000 hogs, 1,565,000 sheep and goats.

The Commission reported that in 2002 there were 1,116,070 cattle and calves shipped from Texas to other states and 3,298,943 shipped in, compared with 1,372,913 shipped out and 3,373,361 shipped in during 2001, and 1,345,419 shipped out and 3,637,844 shipped in during 2000. (Figures exclude cattle shipped direct to slaughter where no health certificates are required.)

Also during 2002, Texas shipped out 472,815 sheep and lambs and shipped in 127,300, compared with 429,753 shipped out and 76,591 shipped in during 2001, and 423,775 shipped out and 65,934 shipped in during 2000.

Feedlot production of livestock, mainly cattle, is a major industry in Texas. Annual fed cattle marketings totaled 5,980,000 for 1,000 and over feedlot capacity (head) in 2002. Texas lots marketed a total of 6,030,000 head of grain-fed cattle in 2001, compared with 6,190,000 in 2000; and 6,065,000 in 1999. In recent years, more cattle have been fed in Texas than any other state in the United States.

During 2002, there were 136 feedlots in Texas with capacity of 1,000 animals or more. This compared with 138 in 2001, 137 in 2000, and 142 in 1999.

Federally inspected slaughter plants in Texas numbered 43 in 2002. This compared with 44 in 2001 and 42 in 2000. In 2002, the number of cattle slaughtered in Texas totaled 6,435,800 cattle, 338,300 hogs and 17,200

calves. This compared with 6,427,200 cattle, 286,800 hogs and 17,900 calves in 2001, and 6,566,000 cattle, 247,000 hogs and 23,000 calves in 2000.

Feeding of cattle in commercial feedlots is a major economic development that has stimulated the establishment and expansion of beef slaughtering plants. Most of this development is in the Panhandle-Plains area of Northwest Texas. This area alone accounts for around 81 percent of the cattle fed in the state in 2001.

Feedlots with capacities of 1,000 head or more accounted for more than 99 percent of the cattle fed in Texas in 2001. Total feedlot marketings represented about 25 percent of total U.S. fed cattle marketings in 2002. Large amounts of capital are required for feedlot operations. This has forced many lots to become custom feeding facilities.

Feedlots are concentrated on the High Plains largely because of extensive supplies of corn, sorghum and other feed. Beef breeding herds have increased most in East Texas, where grazing is abundant.

## Dairying

Most of the state's dairy industry is located east of the line from Wichita Falls to Brownwood to San Antonio to Corpus Christi. As of Jan. 1, 2002, inventory, leading counties in milk production are Erath, Hopkins, Comanche, El Paso, Archer and Hamilton, which combined, produce 58 percent of the milk in the state, with Erath producing over 26 percent of the total.

All the milk sold by Texas dairy farmers is marketed under the terms of Federal Marketing Orders. Most Texas dairymen are members of one of four marketing coopera-

## Texas Sheep and Wool Production, 1850–2003

| Year | Sheep | | Wool | |
|---|---|---|---|---|
| | *Number | Value | Production (lbs) | Value |
| 1850 | 100,530 | N A | 131,917 | N A |
| 1860 | 753,363 | N A | 1,493,363 | N A |
| 1870 | 1,223,000 | $2,079,000 | N A | N A |
| 1880 | 6,024,000 | 12,048,000 | N A | N A |
| 1890 | 4,752,000 | 7,128,000 | N A | N A |
| 1900 | 2,416,000 | 4,590,000 | 9,630,000 | N A |
| 1910 | 1,909,000 | 5,536,000 | 8,943,000 | $1,699,170 |
| 1920 | 3,360,000 | 33,600,000 | 22,813,000 | 5,019,000 |
| 1930 | 6,304,000 | 44,758,000 | 48,262,000 | 10,135,000 |
| 1940 | 10,069,000 | 49,413,000 | 79,900,000 | 23,171,000 |
| 1950 | 6,756,000 | 103,877,000 | 51,480,000 | 32,947,000 |
| 1960 | 5,938,000 | 85,801,000 | 51,980,000 | 21,832,000 |
| 1970 | 3,708,000 | 73,602,000 | 30,784,000 | 11,082,000 |
| 1980 | 2,400,000 | 138,000,000 | 18,300,000 | 17,751,000 |
| 1981 | 2,360,000 | 116,820,000 | 20,500,000 | 24,600,000 |
| 1982 | 2,400,000 | 100,800,000 | 19,300,000 | 16,212,000 |
| 1983 | 2,225,000 | 86,775,000 | 18,600,000 | 15,438,000 |
| 1984 | 1,970,000 | 76,830,000 | 17,500,000 | 16,100,000 |
| 1985 | 1,930,000 | 110,975,000 | 16,200,000 | 13,284,000 |
| 1986 | 1,850,000 | 107,300,000 | 16,400,000 | 13,284,000 |
| 1987 | 2,050,000 | 133,250,000 | 16,400,000 | 19,844,000 |
| 1988 | 2,040,000 | 155,040,000 | 18,200,000 | 35,854,000 |
| 1989 | 1,870,000 | 133,445,000 | 18,000,000 | 27,180,000 |
| 1990 | 2,090,000 | 133,760,000 | 17,400,000 | 19,662,000 |
| 1991 | 2,000,000 | 108,000,000 | 16,700,000 | 13,861,000 |
| 1992 | 2,140,000 | 111,280,000 | 17,600,000 | 16,896,000 |
| 1993 | 2,040,000 | 118,320,000 | 17,000,000 | 11,050,000 |
| 1994 | 1,895,000 | 106,120,000 | 14,840,000 | 15,582,000 |
| 1995 | 1,700,000 | 100,300,000 | 13,468,000 | 15,488,000 |
| 1996 | 1,650,000 | 108,900,000 | 9,900,000 | 8,316,000 |
| 1997 | 1,400,000 | 100,800,000 | 10,950,000 | 11,607,000 |
| 1998 | 1,530,000 | 122,400,000 | 9,230,000 | 5,815,000 |
| 1999 | 1,350,000 | 95,850,000 | 7,956,000 | 3,898,000 |
| 2000 | 1,200,000 | 94,800,000 | 7,506,000 | 3,678,000 |
| 2001 | 1,100,000 | 88,000,000 | NA | NA |
| 2002 | 1,130,000 | 88,140,000 | 5,530,000 | 3,760,000 |
| 2003 | 1,050,000 | 82,950,000 | NA | NA |

NA = not available.
Source: "1985 Texas Livestock, Dairy and Poultry Statistics," USDA Bulletin 235, June 1986, p. 25. "Texas Agricultural Facts," Crop and Livestock Reporting Service, various years; "1993 Texas Livestock Statistics," Texas Agricultural Statistics Service, Bulletin 252, August 1994. "Texas Agricultural Statistics, 2001," Sept. 2002.

tives. Associate Milk Producers, Inc., is the largest, representing the majority of the state's producers.

Texas dairy farmers received an average price for milk of $12.90 per hundred pounds in 2002, $15.80 in 2001, and $13.40 in 2000. A total of 5.276 billion pounds of milk was sold to plants and dealers in 2002, bringing in cash receipts from milk to dairy farmers of $680,604,000. This compared with 5.083 billion pounds sold in 2001 that brought in $803,114,000 in cash receipts. In 2000, Texas dairymen sold 5.717 billion pounds of milk, which brought in cash receipts of $766,078,000.

The annual average number of milk cows in Texas was 311,000 head as of Jan. 1, 2003, inventory. This compared with 310,000 head as of Jan. 1, 2002, and 345,000 as of Jan. 1, 2001. Average production per cow in the state has increased steadily over the past several decades. The average production per cow in 2002 was 17,152 pounds. Milk per cow in 2001 was 15,711 pounds. In 2000, milk per cow was 16,483 pounds. Total milk production in Texas was 5.300 billion pounds in 2002, compared with 5.106 billion pounds in 2001 and 5.736 billion pounds in 2000.

There were 1,900 operations reporting milk cows in Texas in 2002, compared with 2,100 operations in 2001 and in 2,500 operations in 2000.

### Dairy Manufacturing

The major dairy products manufactured in Texas include condensed, evaporated and dry milk; creamery butter; and cheese. However, this data are not available because of the small number of manufacturing plants producing these products.

### Frozen Desserts

Production of frozen desserts in Texas totaled 102,425,000 gallons in 2002. The 2001 production amounted to 114,496,000 gallons and the 2002 total was 119,893,000 gallons. Ice cream production in Texas in 2002 amounted to 53,098,000 gallons, compared to 61,740,000 gallons in 2001 and 63,542,000 gallons in 2000. Ice cream mix produced in Texas in 2002 totaled 30,848,000 gallons, compared with 32,787,000 gallons in 2001 and 33,983,000 gallons in 2000. Milk sherbet mix in Texas totaled 1,107,000 gallons in 2002, compared with 1,197,000 gallons in 2001 and 1,290,000 gallons in 2000. Milk sherbet production in 2002 totaled 1,752,000 gallons. This compared with 2001 milk sherbet production of 1,897,000 gallons.

### Swine

Texas had 930,000 head of swine on hand, Dec. 1, 2002 — only 1.5 percent of the U.S. swine herd. Swine producers in the state usually produce about one-fifth of the pork consumed by the state's population, or about 1,358,000 head marketed annually.

Although the number of farms producing hogs has steadily decreased, the size of production units has increased substantially. There is favorable potential for increased production.

In 2002, 1,358,000 head of hogs were marketed in Texas, producing 224,641,000 pounds of pork valued at $28.70 per 100 pounds, or $64,472,000. In 2001, 1,219,000 head of hogs were marketed, producing 260,875,000 pounds of pork valued at $102,002,000, or $39.10 per 100 pounds. Comparable figures for 2000 were 1,314,000 head marketed, and 328,732,000 pounds of pork produced with a value of $120,316,000, or $36.60 per 100 pounds.

### Goats and Mohair

Goats in Texas numbered 1,200,000 on Jan. 1, 2003. This compares with 1,250,000 on Jan. 1, 2002, and 1,400,000 on Jan. 1, 2001. They had a value of $109,200,000 or $91 per head in 2003; $106,250,000 or $85.00 per head in 2002; and $105,000,000 or $75.00 per head in 2001.

The goat herd largely consists of Angora goats for mohair production. Angora goats totaled 260,000 as of 2003; 250,000 as of 2002; and 300,000 as of 2001. Spanish goats and others numbered 940,000 as of 2003; 1,000,000 as of 2002; and 1,100,000 as of 2001.

Mohair production during 2002 totaled 1,896,000 pounds. This compares with 1,716,000 in 2001 and 2,346,000 in 2000. Average price per pound in

2002 was $1.60 from 240,000 goats clipped for a total value of $3,034,000. In 2001, producers received $2.20 per pound from 260,000 goats clipped for a total value of $3,775,000. In 2000, producers received $4.30 per pound from 345,000 goats clipped for a total value of $10,088,000.

Nearly half of the world's mohair and 89 percent of the U.S. clip are produced in Texas. The leading Texas counties in Angora goats are Edwards, Val Verde, Sutton, Kinney, Uvalde, Crockett, Gillespie, Kimble, Mills and Concho.

### Sheep and Wool

The sheep herd continues to decline. Sheep and lambs in Texas numbered 1,050,000 head on Jan. 1, 2003, down from 1,130,000 as of 2002; and 1,150,000 as of 2001. All sheep were valued at $82,950,000 or $79.00 per head on Jan. 1, 2003, compared with $88,140,000 or $78.00 per head as of 2002 and $92,000,000 or $80.00 per head as of 2001.

Breeding ewes 1 year old and over numbered 680,000 as of 2003; 720,000 as of 2002; and 710,000 as of 2001. Replacement lambs less than 1 year old totaled 130,000 head as of 2003; 130,000 as of 2002; and 95,000 as of 2001. Sheep operations in Texas were estimated to be 6,800 as of 2003; 6,800 as of 2002; and 6,800 as of 2001.

Texas wool production in 2002 was 5,530,000 pounds from 790,000 sheep. Value totaled $3,760,000 or 68 cents per pound. This compared with 6,003,000 pounds of wool from 870,000 sheep valued at $3,112,000 or 52 cents per pound in 2001; and 7,506,000 pounds from 1,130,000 sheep valued at $3,678,000 or 49 cents per pound in 2000.

Most sheep and lambs in Texas are concentrated in the Edwards Plateau area of West-Central Texas and nearby counties. As of Jan. 1, 2002, the 10 leading counties are Crockett, Val Verde, Tom Green, Pecos, Schleicher, Concho, Gillespie, Menard, Sterling and Sutton. Sheep production is largely dual purpose, for both wool and lamb production.

San Angelo long has been the largest sheep and wool market in the United States and the center for wool and mohair warehouses, scouring plants and slaughterhouses.

### Horses

Nationally, Texas ranks as one of the leading states in horse numbers and is the headquarters for many national horse organizations. The largest single breed registry in America, the American Quarter Horse Association, has its headquarters in Amarillo. The National Cutting Horse Association and the American Paint Horse Association are both located in Fort Worth. In addition to these national associations, Texas also has active state associations that include Palominos, Arabians, Thoroughbreds, Appaloosa and Ponies.

Horses are still used to support the state's giant beef cattle and sheep industries. However, the largest horse numbers within the state are near urban and suburban areas where they are mostly used for recreation activities. State participation activities consist of horse shows, trail rides, play days, rodeos, polo and horse racing. Residential subdivisions have been developed within the state to provide facilities for urban and suburban horse owners.

### Poultry and Eggs

Poultry and eggs annually contribute about 9 percent to the average yearly cash receipts of Texas farmers. In 2002, Texas ranked sixth among the states in broilers produced, seventh in eggs produced and seventh in hens.

In 2002, cash receipts to Texas producers from the production of poultry and eggs totaled $1.169 billion. This compares with $1.328 billion in 2001 and $1.140 in 2000.

Gross income from eggs was $273,312,000 in 2002. This compares with $267,077,000 in 2001 and $267,077,000 in 2000. Eggs produced in 2002 totaled 4.77 billion, compared with 4.73 billion in 2001 and 4.423 billion in 2000. The average price received per dozen in 2002 was 68.7 cents, compared with 67.7cents in 2001, and 69.7cents in 2000.

Broiler production in 2002 totaled 588,100,000 birds, compared with 565,500,000 in 2001 and 551,000,000 in 2000. Value of production from broilers totaled $893,327,000 in 2002; $1.059 billion in 2001; and $880,498,000 in 2000. Price per pound averaged 31 cents in 2002, 39 cents in 2001, and 34 cents in 2000. ☆

# Texas Pronunciation Guide

Texas' rich cultural diversity is reflected nowhere better than in the names of places. Standard pronunciation is used in many cases, but purely colloquial pronunciation often is used, too.

In the late 1940s, George Mitchel Stokes, a graduate student at Baylor University, developed a list of pronunciations of 2,300 place names across the state.

Stokes earned his doctorate and eventually served as director of the speech division in the Communications Studies Department at Baylor University. He retired in 1983.

In the following list based on Stokes' longer list, pronunciation is by respelling and diacritical marking. Respelling is employed as follows: "ah" as in the exclamation, ah, or the "o" in tot; "ee" as in meet; "oo" as in moot; "yoo" as in use; "ow" as in cow; "oi" as in oil; "uh" as in mud.

Note that ah, uh and the apostrophe(') are used for varying degrees of neutral vowel sounds, the apostrophe being used where the vowel is barely sounded. Diacritical markings are used as follows: bāle, băd, lĕt, rīse, rĭll, ōak, brōōd, fŏŏt.

The stressed syllable is capitalized. Secondary stress is indicated by an underline as in Atascosa—ăt uhs KŌ suh.

## A

Agua Dulce—ah wuh DŌŌL sĭ
Agua Nueva—ah wuh nyōō Ā vuh
Algoa—ăl GŌ uh
Alief—Ā leef
Altair—awl TĂR
Alta Loma—ăl tuh LŌ muh
Alto—ĂL tō
Altoga—ăl TŌ guh
Alvarado—ăl vuh RĂ dō
Alvord—ĂL vord
Amarillo—ăm uh RĬL ŏ
Anahuac—ĂN uh wăk
Andice—ĂN dĭs
Angelina—ăn juh LEE nuh
Anna—ĂN uh
Annona—ă NŌ nuh
Anton—ĂNT n
Aquilla—uh KWĬL uh
Aransas—uh RĂN zuhs
Aransas Pass—uh răn zuhs PĂS
Arbala—ahr BĀ luh
Arcadia—ahr KĀ dĭ uh
Arcola—ahr KŌ luh
Argo—AHR gō
Arneckeville—AHR nĭ kĭ vĭl
Arp—ahrp
Artesia Wells—ahr tee zh' WĔLZ
Aspermont—ĂS per mahnt
Atascosa—ăt uhs KŌ suh
Attoyac—AT uh yăk
Austin—AWS t'n
Austonio—aws TŌ nĭ ŏ
Austwell—AWS wĕl
Avalon—ĂV uhl n
Avinger—Ā vĭn jer
Avoca—uh VŌ kuh
Axtell—ĂKS t'l
Azle—Ā z'l

## B

Ballinger—BĂL ĭn jer
Balmorhea—băl muh RĂ
Bandera—băn DĔR uh
Banquete—băn KĔ tĭ
Bastrop—BĂS trahp
Beasley—BEEZ lĭ
Beaukiss—bō KĬS
Beaumont—BŌ mahnt

Bebe—bee bee
Bedias—BEE dĭs
Belcherville—BĔL cher vĭl
Bellevue—BĔL vyōō
Benavides—bĕn uh VEE d's
Ben Hur—bĕn HER
Berclair—ber KLĂR
Bessmay—bĕs MĂ
Bettie—BĔT ĭ
Bexar—BA är
Biardstown—BĂRDZ t'n
Birome—bī RŌM
Blanco—BLĂNG kō
Boerne—BER nĭ
Bogata—buh GŌ duh
Bolivar—BAH lĭ ver
Bomarton—BŌ mer t'n
Bonham—BAH n'm
Bonita—bō NEE tuh
Bonney—BAH nĭ
Bon Wier—bahn WEER
Borger—BŌR ger
Bosque—BAHS kĭ
Boston—BAWS t'n
Bovina—bō VEE nuh
Bowie—BŌŌ Ĭ
Boyce—bawis
Brashear—bruh SHĬR
Brazoria—bruh ZŌ rĭ uh
Brazos—BRĂZ uhs
Breckenridge—BRĔK uhn rĭj
Bremond—bree MAHND
Brenham—BRĔ n'm
Brewster—BRŌŌ ster
Briscoe—BRĬS kō
Britton—BRĬT n
Broaddus—BRAW d's
Bronte—brahnt
Brundage—BRUHN dĭj
Bruni—BRŌŌ nĭ
Buchanan Dam—buhk hăn uhn DĂM
Buda—BYŌŌ duh
Buena Vista—bwă nuh VEES tuh
Buffalo—BUHF uh lō
Bula—BYŌŌ luh
Bullard—BŌŌL erd
Bulverde—bōōl VER dĭ
Buna—BYŌŌ nuh
Burkburnett—berk ber NET

Burkett—BER kĭt
Burleson—BER luh s'n
Burnet—BER nĕt
Bustamante—buhs tuh MAHN tĭ

## C

Caddo Mills—kă dō MĬLZ
Calallen—kăl ĂL ĭn
Calaveras—kăl uh VĔR's
Camilla—kuh MEEL yuh
Candelaria—kăn duh LĔ rĭ uh
Canton—KĂNT n
Caradan—KĂR uh dăn
Carlisle—KAHR lĭl
Carlsbad—KAHR uhlz bad
Carmine—kahr MEEN
Carmona—kahr MŌ nuh
Caro—KAH rō
Carrizo Springs—kuh ree zuh SPRĬNGZ
Carrollton—KĂR 'l t'n
Carthage—KAHR thĭj
Cason—KĀ s'n
Castell—kăs TĔL
Castroville—KĂS tro vĭl
Catarina—kăt uh REE nuh
Cayuga—kă YŌŌ guh
Cedar Bayou—see der BĪ ō
Cee Vee—see VEE
Celeste—suh LĔST
Celina—suh LĪ nuh
Centralia—sĕn TRĂL yuh
Charco—CHAHR kō
Cherokee—CHĔR uh kee
Chico—CHEE kō
Chicota—chĭ KŌ tuh
Childress—CHĬL drĕs
Chillicothe—chĭl ĭ KAH thĭ
Chireno—sh' REE nō
Chisholm—CHĬZ uhm
Chita—CHEE tuh
Chocolate Bayou—chah kuh lĭt BĪ ō
Chriesman—KRĬS m'n
Christoval—krĭs TŌ v'l
Cibolo—SEE bō lō
Cisco—SĬS kō
Clarendon—KLĂR ĭn d'n
Cleburne—KLEE bern
Clodine—klaw DEEN

Clute—klōōt
Coahoma—kuh HŌ muh
Cockrell Hill—kahk ruhl HĬL
Colfax—KAHL făks
College Station—<u>kah</u> līj STĀ sh'n
Colmesneil—KŌL m's neel
Colorado—<u>kahl</u> uh RAH dō
Colorado City—kah luh <u>rā</u> duh SĬT ĭ
Columbus—kuh LUHM b's
Comal—KŌ măl
Comanche—kuh MĂN chĭ
Combes—kōmz
Comfort—KUHM fert
Como—KŌ mō
Concan—KAHN kăn
Concepcion—kuhn sep sĭ ŌN
Concho—KAHN chō
Concrete—kahn KREET
Cone—kōn
Conlen—KAHN lĭn
Conroe—KAHN rō
Cooper—KŌŌ per
Coppell—kuhp PĔL or kuh PĔL
Copperas Cove—kahp ruhs KŌV
Corbett—KAWR bĭt
Cordele—kawr DĔL
Corinth—KAH rĭnth
Corpus Christi—<u>kawr</u> p's KRĬS tĭ
Corrigan—KAWR uh g'n
Corsicana—<u>kawr</u> sĭ KĂN uh
Coryell—kō rĭ ĔL
Cottle—KAH t'l
Cotulla—kuh TŌŌ luh
Coupland—KŌP l'n
Cresson—KRĔ s'n
Crockett—KRAH kĭt
Crowell—KRŌ uhl
Crowley—KROW li
Cuero—KWĔR o
Culberson—KUHL ber s'n
Cumby—KUHM bĭ
Cuney—KYŌŌ nĭ
Currie—KER rĭ
Cuthand—KUHT hănd

**D**

Dacosta—duh KAHS tuh
Dacus—DĂ k's
Daingerfield—DĀN jer feeld
Daisetta—dā ZĔT uh
Danciger—DĂN sĭ ger
Danevang—DĂN uh văng
Darrouzett—dăr uh ZĔT
Davilla—duh VĬL uh
Deaf Smith—dĕf SMĬTH
De Berry—duh BĔ rĭ
Decatur—<u>dee</u> KĀT er
De Kalb—dĭ KĂB
De Leon—da lee AHN
Del Rio—dĕl REE o
Delvalle—dĕl VĂ lĭ
Denhawken—DĬN haw kĭn
Denton—DĔNT n
Deport—dĭ PŌRT
Derby—DER bĭ
Desdemona—<u>dĕz</u> dĭ MŌ nuh
DeSoto—dĭ SŌ tuh
Detroit—dee TROIT
Devers—DĔ vers

Devine—duh VĬN
DeWitt—dĭ WĬT
D'Hanis—duh HĂ nĭs
Dialville—DĬ uhl vil
Diboll—DĬ bawl
Dilley—DĬL i
Dimmit—DĬM ĭt
Dinero—dĭ NĔ rō
Direct—duh RĔKT
Dobrowolski—<u>dah</u> bruh WAHL skĭ
Donie—DŌ nĭ
Dorchester—dawr CHĔS ter
Doucette—DŌŌ sĕt
Dougherty—DAHR tĭ
Dozier—DŌ zher
Dryden—DRĬD n
Duffau—DUHF ō
Dumas—DŌŌ m's
Dumont—DYŌŌ mahnt
Durango—duh RĂNG go
Duval—DŌŌ vawl

**E**

East Bernard—<u>eest</u> ber NAHRD
Edcouch—ĕd KOWCH
Eddy—E di
El Campo—ĕl KĂM pō
Eldorado—<u>ĕl</u> duh RĀ duh
Electra—ĭ LĔK truh
Elgin—ĔL gĭn
El Indio—ĕl ĬN dĭ ō
Ellinger—ĔL ĭn jer
Elmendorf—ĔLM 'n dawrf
Elm Mott—ĕl MAHT
Elmo—ĔL mō
Eloise—ĔL o <u>eez</u>
El Paso—ĕl PĂS ō
Encinal—ĕn suh NAHL
Encino—ĕn SEE nō
Engle—ĔN g'l
Enloe—ĔN lō
Ennis—ĔN ĭs
Enochs—EE nuhks
Eola—ee Ō luh
Era—EE ruh
Erath—EE răth
Esperanza—<u>ĕs</u> per RĂN zuh
Estelline—ĔS tuh leen
Etoile—ĭ TOIL
Etter—ĔT er
Eula—YŌŌ luh
Euless—YŌŌ lis
Eureka—yōō REE kuh
Eustace—YŌŌS t's
Evant—EE vănt
Everman—Ĕ ver m'n

**F**

Fabens—FĀ b'nz
Falfurrias—făl FYŌŌ rĭ uhs
Fannett—fă NĔT
Fannin—FĂN ĭn
Fargo—FAHR gō
Farrar—FĂR uh
Farwell—FAHR w'l
Fashing—FĂ shĭng
Fayette—fă ĔT
Fayetteville—FĀ uht vĭl
Flatonia—flă TŌN yuh

Flomot—FLŌ maht
Florence—FLAH ruhns
Floresville—FLŌRZ vil
Florey—FLŌ ri
Floydada—floi DĀ duh
Fluvanna—<u>flōō</u> VĂN uh
Fodice—FŌ dĭs
Follett—fah LĔT
Fordtran—förd TRĂN
Forney—FAWR nĭ
Forsan—FŌR săn
Fort Chadbourne—<u>fört</u> CHĂD bern
Fort Worth—fört WERTH
Fowlerton—FOW ler t'n
Francitas—frăn SEE t's
Fredericksburg—FRĔD er rĭks berg
Fredonia—<u>free</u> DŌN yuh
Freer—FREE er
Frelsburg—FRĔLZ berg
Frio—FREE ō
Friona—free O nuh
Frisco—FRĬS ko
Frydek—FRĬ dĕk
Fulshear—FUHL sher

**G**

Gallatin—GĂL uh t'n
Galveston—GĂL vĕs t'n
Ganado—guh NĀ dō
Garceno—gahr SĀ nō
Garciasville—gahr SEE uhs vĭl
Garza—GAHR zuh
Gause—gawz
Geneva—juh NEE vuh
Geronimo—<u>juh</u> RAH nĭ mō
Giddings—GĬD ĭngz
Gillespie—guh LĔS pĭ
Gillett—juh LĔT
Gilliland—GĬL ĭ l'nd
Gilmer—GĬL mer
Ginger—JĬN jer
Girard—juh RAHRD
Girvin—GER vĭn
Glazier—GLĀ zher
Glidden—GLĬD n
Gober—GŌ ber
Godley—GAHD lĭ
Goldthwaite—GŌLTH wāt
Goliad—GŌ lĭ ăd
Golindo—gō LĬN duh
Gonzales—<u>guhn</u> ZAH l's
Goree—GŌ ree
Gouldbusk—GŌŌLD buhsk
Grand Saline—grăn suh LEEN
Granger—GRĂN jer
Greenville—GREEN v'l
Groesbeck—GRŌZ bĕk
Gruene—green
Grulla—GRŌŌL yuh
Gruver—GRŌŌ ver
Guadalupe—<u>gwah</u> duh LŌŌ pĭ
Guerra—GWĔ ruh
Gustine—GUHS <u>teen</u>
Guthrie—GUHTH rĭ

**H**

Hallettsville—HĂL ĕts vĭl
Hamshire—HĂM sher
Hankamer—HĂN kăm er

Hardeman—HAHR duh m'n
Harleton—HAHR <u>uhl</u> t'n
Harlingen—HAHR lĭn juhn
Haskell—HĂS k'l
Haslam—HĂZ l'm
Haslet—HĂS lĕt
Hasse—HĂ sĭ
Hatchell—HĂ ch'l
Hearne—hern
Heath—heeth
Hebbronville—HĔB r'n vĭl
Heidenheimer—HĪD n hīmer
Helena—HĔL uh nuh
Helotes—hĕl Ō tĭs
Hempstead—HĔM stĕd
Hermleigh—HER muh lee
Hico—HĪ kō
Hidalgo—hĭ DĂL gō
Hillister—HĬL ĭs ter
Hindes—hīndz
Hochheim—HŌ hīm
Hondo—HAHN dō
Houston—HYŌŌS t'n or YŌŌS t'n
Hubbard—HUH berd
Huckabay—HUHK uh bĭ
Hudspeth—HUHD sp'th
Humble—HUHM b'l
Hungerford—HUHNG ger ferd
Hutto—HUH tō
Hye—hī
Hylton—HĬL t'n

**I**

Iago—ī Ă gō
Idalou—Ī duh lōō
Inadale—Ī nuh dāl
Iola—ī Ō luh
Iraan—ī ruh ĂN
Iredell—Ī ruh dĕl
Irion—ĪR i uhn
Italy—ĪT uh lĭ
Itasca—ī TĂS kuh
Ivan—Ī v'n
Ivanhoe—Ī v'n hō

**J**

Jardin—JAHRD n
Jarrell—JĂR uhl
Jeddo—JĔ dō
Jermyn—JER m'n
Jewett—JŌŌ ĭt
Jiba—HEE buh
Joaquin—waw KEEN
Jolly—JAH lĭ
Jollyville—JAH lĭ vĭl
Jonah—JŌ nuh
Joshua—JAH sh' wa
Jourdanton—JERD n t'n
Juliff—JŌŌ lĭf
Juno—JŌŌ nō

**K**

Kalgary—KĂL gĕ rĭ
Kamay—KĂ ĭm ā
Kanawha—KAHN uh wah
Karnack—KAHR năk
Katemcy—kuh TĔM sĭ
Kaufman—KAWF m'n
Keechi—KEE chĭ

Keene—keen
Kemah—KEE muh
Kendalia—kĔn DĀL yuh
Kennard—kuh NAHRD
Kerens—KER 'nz
Kerr—ker
Kerrville—KER vĭl
Kilgore—KĬL gōr
Killeen—kuh LEEN
Kleberg—KLĀ berg
Knickerbocker—NĬK uh <u>bah</u> ker
Knippa—kuh NĬP uh
Kosciusko—kuh SHŌŌS kō
Kosse—KAH sĭ
Kountze—kōōntz
Kress—kres
Krum—kruhm
Kurten—KER t'n
Kyle—kīl

**L**

La Blanca—lah BLAHN kuh
La Coste—luh KAWST
Ladonia—luh DŌN yuh
LaFayette—lah fĭ ĔT
Laferia—luh FĔ rĭ uh
Lagarto—luh GAHR tō
La Gloria—lah GLŌ rĭ uh
La Grange—luh GRĀNJ
Laguna—luh GŌŌ nuh
Laird Hill—lārd HĬL
La Joya—luh HŌ yuh
Lamarque—luh MAHRK
Lamasco—luh MĂS kō
Lamesa—luh MEE suh
Lamkin—LĂM kĭn
Lampasas—lăm PĂ s's
Lancaster—LĂNG k's ter
Langtry—LĂNG trĭ
Lanier—luh NĬR
La Paloma—<u>lah</u> puh LŌ muh
La Porte—luh PŌRT
La Pryor—luh PRĪ er
Laredo—luh RĂ dō
Lariat—LĂ ri uht
La Rue—luh RŌŌ
La Salle—luh SĂL
Lasara—luh SĔ ruh
Lassater—LĂ sĭ ter
Latexo—luh TĔKS ō
Lavaca—luh VĂ kuh
La Vernia—luh VER nĭ uh
La Villa—lah VĬL uh
Lavon—luh VAHN
La Ward—luh WAWRD
Lazbuddie—LĂZ buh dĭ
Leakey—LĂ kĭ
Leander—lee ĂN der
Leary—LĬ er ĭ
Lefors—lĭ FŌRZ
Leggett—LĔ gĭt
Leigh—lee
Lela—LEE luh
Lelia Lake—<u>leel</u> yuh LĀK
Leming—LĔ mĭng
Lenorah—lĕ NŌ ruh
Leon—lee AHN
Leona—<u>lee</u> Ō nuh
Leroy—LEE roi

Levelland—LĔ v'l lănd
Levita—luh VĪ tuh
Lewisville—LŌŌ ĭs vĭl
Lindenau—lĭn duh NOW
Lipan—lĭ PĂN
Lipscomb—LĬPS k'm
Lissie—LĬ sĭ
Llano—LĂ nō
Lockney—LAHK nĭ
Lodi—LŌ dĭ
Lohn—lahn
Lolita—lō LEE tuh
Loma Alto—<u>lō</u> muh ĂL tō
Lometa—lō MEE tuh
London—LUHN d'n
Long Mott—lawng MAHT
Lopeno—lō PEE nō
Loraine—lō RĂN
Lorena—lō REE nuh
Los Angeles—laws AN juh l's
Los Ebanos—lōs ĔB uh nōs
Los Fresnos—lōs FRĔZ nōs
Los Indios—lōs ĬN dĭ ōs
Losoya—luh SAW yuh
Lubbock—LUH buhk
Lueders—LŌŌ derz
Luella—lōō ĔL uh
Lufkin—LUHF kĭn
Luling—LŌŌ lĭng
Lund—luhnd
Lutie—LŌŌ tĭ

**M**

McAdoo—MĂK uh dōō
McCamey—muh KĂ mĭ
McCaulley—muh KAW lĭ
McCulloch—muh KUH luhk
McLean—muh KLĂN
McLennan—muhk LĔN uhn
McLeod—măk LOWD
McQueeney—muh KWEE nĭ
Mabank—MĂ băngk
Macune—muh KŌŌN
Magnolia—măg NŌL yuh
Malakoff—MĂL uh kawf
Malone—muh LŌN
Malta—MAWL tuh
Manchaca—MĂN shăk
Manheim—MĂN hīm
Manor—MĂ ner
Manvel—MĂN v'l
Marathon—MĂR uh th'n
Marfa—MAHR fuh
Marquez—mahr KĂ
Maryneal—mă rĭ NEEL
Matador—MĂT uh dōr
Matagorda—măt uh GAWR duh
Mathis—MĂ thĭs
Maud—mawd
Mauriceville—maw REES vĭl
Maverick—MĂV rĭk
Maydell—MĂ dĕl
Maypearl—<u>mă</u> PERL
Medill—mĕ DĬL
Medina—muh DEE nuh
Megargel—muh GAHR g'l
Menard—muh NAHRD
Mendoza—mĕn DŌ zuh
Mentone—mĕn TON

Mercedes—<u>mer</u> SĂ deez
Mereta—muh RĔT uh
Meridian—muh RĬ dĭ uhn
Merkel—MER k'l
Mertens—<u>mer</u> TĔNZ
Mertzon—MERTS n
Mesquite—muhs KEET
Mexia—muh HĂ uh
Miami—mĭ ĂM ĭ
Mico—MEE kō
Midland—MĬD l'nd
Midlothian—<u>mĭd</u> LŌ thĭ n
Milam—MĬ l'm
Milano—mĭ LĂ nō
Millett—MĬL ĭt
Millheim—MĬL hĭm
Millican—MĬL uh kuhn
Millsap—MĬL săp
Minden—MĬN d'n
Mineola—mĭn ĭ Ō luh
Minerva—mĭ NER vuh
Mingus—MĬNG guhs
Minter—MĬNT er
Mirando City—mĭ răn duh SĬT ĭ
Missouri City—muh zŏŏr uh SĬT ĭ
Mitchell—MĬ ch'l
Mobeetie—mō BEE tĭ
Moline—mō LEEN
Monahans—MAH nuh hănz
Montague—mahn TĂG
Montalba—mahnt ĂL buh
Mont Belvieu—mahnt BĔL vyōō
Montell—mahn TĔL
Montgomery—<u>mahnt</u> GUHM er ĭ
Monthalia—mahn THĂL yuh
Moody—MŌŌ dĭ
Moore—mor
Morales—muh RAH lĕs
Moran—mō RĂN
Moscow—MAHS kow
Mosheim—MŌ shĭm
Moss Bluff—maws BLUHF
Motley—MAHT lĭ
Moulton—MŌL t'n
Muenster—MYŌŌNS ter
Muldoon—muhl DŌŌN
Muleshoe—MYŌŌL shōō
Munday—MUHN dĭ
Murchison—MER kuh s'n
Mykawa—mĭ KAH wuh
Myra—MĬ ruh

### N

Nacogdoches—<u>năk</u> uh DŌ chĭs
Nada—NĂ duh
Natalia—nuh TĂL yuh
Navarro—nuh VĂ rō
Navasota—năv uh SŌ tuh
Neches—NĂ chĭs
Nederland—NEE der l'nd
Neuville—NYŌŌ v'l
Nevada—nuh VĂ duh
Newark—NŌŌ erk
New Baden—nyōō BĂD n
New Braunfels—nyōō BROWN fĕlz
New Caney—nyōō KĂ nĭ
New Ulm—nyōō UHLM
New Waverly—nyōō WĂ ver lĭ
New Willard—nyōō WĬL erd

Nimrod—NĬM rahd
Nineveh—NĬN uh vuh
Nocona—nō KŌ nuh
Nopal—NŌ păl
Nordheim—NAWRD hĭm
Normangee—NAWR m'n <u>jee</u>
Normanna—nawr MĂN uh
North Zulch—nawrth ZŌŌLCH
Nueces—nyōō Ă sĭs

### O

Oakalla—ō KĂL uh
Ochiltree—AH k'l tree
Odell—ō DĔL
Odem—Ō d'm
Odessa—ō DĔS uh
Oenaville—ō EEN uh v'l
Oglesby—Ō g'lz bĭ
Oilton—OIL t'n
Oklaunion—<u>ōk</u> luh YŌŌN y'n
Olivia—<u>ō</u> LĬV ĭ uh
Olmito—awl MEE tuh
Olmos Park—ahl m's PAHRK
Olney—AHL nĭ
Olton—ŌL t'n
Omaha—Ō muh haw
Omen—Ō mĭn
Onalaska—<u>uhn</u> uh LĂS kuh
Oplin—AHP lĭn
Osceola—ō sĭ Ō luh
Otey—Ō tĭ
Ottine—ah TEEN
Ovalo—ō VĂL uh
Ozona—ō ZŌ nuh

### P

Paducah—puh DYŌŌ kuh
Palacios—puh LĂ sh's
Palestine—PAL uhs <u>teen</u>
Palito Blanco—p' <u>lee</u> to BLAHNG kō
Palo Pinto—<u>pă</u> lō PĬN tō
Paluxy—puh LUHK sĭ
Panna Maria—<u>păn</u> uh muh REE uh
Papalote—pah puh LŌ tĭ
Paris—PĂ rĭs
Pasadena—<u>păs</u> uh DEE nuh
Patroon—puh TRŌŌN
Pawnee—paw NEE
Pearland—PĂR lănd
Pearsall—PEER sawl
Peaster—PEES ter
Pecos—PĂ k's
Penelope—puh NĔL uh pĭ
Penitas—puh NEE t's
Peoria—<u>pee</u> Ō rĭ uh
Percilla—per SĬL uh
Petrolia—puh TRŌL yuh
Petteway—PĔT uh wā
Pettit—PĔT ĭt
Pettus—PĔT uhs
Pflugerville—FLŌŌ ger vĭl
Pharr—fahr
Phelps—fĕlps
Pidcoke—PĬD kŏk
Placedo—PLĂS ĭ dō
Plano—PLĂ nō
Plaska—PLĂS kuh
Plateau—plă TŌ
Pledger—PLĔ jer

Plum—pluhm
Ponta—pahn TĂ
Pontotoc—PAHNT uh tahk
Port Aransas—pōrt uh RĂN zuhs
Port Bolivar—<u>pōrt</u> BAH lĭ ver
Port Isabel—pōrt ĬZ uh bĕl
Port Lavaca—<u>pōrt</u> luh VĂ kuh
Port Neches—pōrt NĂ chĭs
Posey—PŌ zĭ
Poteet—pō TEET
Poth—pŏth
Potosi—puh TŌ sĭ
Poynor—POI ner
Prairie Lea—prĕr ĭ LEE
Premont—PREE mahnt
Presidio—pruh SĬ dĭ ō
Priddy—PRĬ dĭ
Primera—<u>pree</u> MĔ ruh
Pritchett—PRĬ chĭt
Progreso—prō GRĔ sō
Purdon—PERD n
Purley—PER lĭ
Purmela—per MEE luh
Pyote—PĬ ŏt

### Q

Quanah—KWAH nuh
Quemado—kuh MAH dō
Quihi—KWEE <u>hee</u>
Quintana—kwĭn TAH nuh
Quitaque—KĬT uh kwa
Quitman—KWĬT m'n

### R

Ratcliff—RĂT klĭf
Ravenna—rĭ VĔN uh
Reagan—RĂ g'n
Real—REE awl
Realitos—<u>ree</u> uh LEE t's
Refugio—rĕ FYŌŌ rĭ ō
Reklaw—RĔK law
Reno—REE nō
Ricardo—rĭ KAHR dō
Riesel—REE s'l
Ringgold—RĬNG gōld
Rio Frio—<u>ree</u> ō FREE ō
Rio Grande City—ree ō grahn dĭ SĬT ĭ
Rio Hondo—<u>ree</u> ō HAHN dō
Riomedina—<u>ree</u> ō muh DEE nuh
Rios—REE ōs
Rio Vista—<u>ree</u> ō VĬS tuh
Riviera—ruh VĬR uh
Roane—rōn
Roanoke—RŌN ōk
Roans Prairie—rōnz PRĔR ĭ
Roby—RŌ bĭ
Rochelle—rō SHĔL
Roganville—RŌ g'n vĭl
Roma—RŌ muh
Romayor—rō MĂ er
Roosevelt—RŌŌ suh v'lt
Rosanky—rō ZĂNG kĭ
Rosenberg—RŌZ n berg
Rosenthal—RŌZ uhn thawl
Rosharon—rō SHĔ r'n
Rosita—rō SEE tuh
Rosser—RAW ser
Roswell—RAHZ w'l
Rotan—rō TĂN

Rowena—rō EE nuh
Rowlett—ROW lĭt
Royse City—roi SĪT ĭ
Rugby—RUHG bĭ
Ruidosa—<u>ree</u> uh DŌ suh
Runge—RUHNG ĭ
Rutersville—RŌŌ ter vĭl
Rye—rī

### S

Sabinal—SĂB uh năl
Sabine—suh BEEN
Sachse—SĂK sĭ
Sacul—SĂ k'l
Salado—suh LĂ dō
Salesville—SĂLZ vĭl
Salineno—suh LEEN yō
Salmon—SĂL m'n
Saltillo—săl TĬL ō
Samfordyce—săm FOR dis
Samnorwood—săm NAWR wŏŏd
San Angelo—<u>săn</u> ĂN juh lō
San Antonio—<u>săn</u> ăn TŌ nĭ ō
San Augustine—<u>săn</u> AW g's teen
San Benito—săn buh NEE tuh
Sandia—săn DEE uh
San Diego—<u>săn</u> dĭ Ā gō
San Felipe—<u>săn</u> fuh LEEP
San Gabriel—săn GĂ brĭ uhl
San Jacinto—<u>săn</u> juh SĬN tuh
San Juan—săn WAHN
San Marcos—<u>săn</u> MAHR k's
San Patricio—<u>săn</u> puh TRĬSH ĭ ō
San Perlita—<u>săn</u> per LEE tuh
San Saba—<u>săn</u> SĂ buh
Santa Anna—săn tuh ĂN uh
Santa Elena—săn tuh LEE nuh
Santa Maria—<u>săn</u> tuh muh REE uh
Santa Rosa—<u>săn</u> tuh RŌ suh
Santo—SĂN tō
San Ygnacio—<u>săn</u> ĭg NAH sĭ ō
Saragosa—<u>sĕ</u> ruh GŌ suh
Saratoga—<u>sĕ</u> ruh TŌ guh
Sargent—SAHR juhnt
Sarita—suh REE tuh
Saspamco—suh SPĂM kō
Savoy—suh VOI
Schattel—SHĂT uhl
Schertz—sherts
Schleicher—SHLĪ ker
Schroeder—SHRĂ der
Schulenburg—SHŌŌ lĭn berg
Schwertner—SWERT ner
Scyene—sī EEN
Segno—SĔG nō
Segovia—<u>sĭ</u> GŌ vĭ uh
Seguin—sĭ GEEN
Seminole—SĔM uh nōl
Shafter—SHĂF ter
Shiro—SHĪ rō
Shive—shĭv
Sierra Blanca—sĭer ruh BLĂNG kuh
Siloam—suh LŌM
Silsbee—SĬLZ bĭ
Simonton—SĪ m'n t'n
Sinton—SĬNT n
Sipe Springs—SEEP sprĭngz
Sivells Bend—<u>sĭ</u> v'lz BĔND
Slaton—SLĂT n

Slidell—slĭ DĔL
Slocum—SLŌ k'm
Smyer—SMĪ er
Somervell—SUH mer vĕl
Somerville—SUH mer vĭl
Sonora—suh NŌ ruh
South Bosque—sowth BAHS kĭ
Southmayd—sowth MĀD
Splendora—splĕn DŌ ruh
Spofford—SPAH ferd
Spurger—SPER ger
Sterley—STER lĭ
Stiles—stīlz
Stinnett—stĭ NĔT
Stoneham—STŌN uhm
Stout—stowt
Stowell—STO w'l
Study Butte—styŏŏ dĭ BYŌŌT
Sublime—s'b LĪM
Sudan—SŌŌ dăn
Sunray—SUHN rā
Swan—swahn
Sweeny—SWEE nĭ

### T

Tahoka—tuh HŌ kuh
Talco—TĂL kō
Talpa—TĂL puh
Tankersley—TĂNG kers lĭ
Tarzan—TAHR z'n
Tascosa—tăs KŌ suh
Tatum—TĂ t'm
Tavener—TĂV uh ner
Tehuacana—<u>tuh</u> WAW kuh nuh
Telferner—TĔLF ner
Tenaha—TĔN uh haw
Terlingua—TER lĭng guh
Texarkana—tĕks ahr KĂN uh
Texhoma—tĕks Ō muh
Texline—TĔKS līn
Texon—tĕks AHN
Thalia—THĂL yuh
Tioga—tī Ō guh
Tivoli—tĭ VŌ luh
Tokio—TŌ kĭ ō
Tolosa—tuh LŌ suh
Tornillo—tawr NEE yō
Tow—tow
Toyah—TOI yuh
Toyahvale—TOI yuh văl
Trinidad—TRĬN uh dăd
Troup—trŏŏp
Truby—TRŌŌ bĭ
Trumbull—TRUHM b'l
Truscott—TRUHS k't
Tuleta—tŏŏ LEE tuh
Tulia—TŌŌL yuh
Tulsita—tuhl SEE tuh
Tundra—TUHN druh
Tunis—TŌŌ nĭs
Tuscola—tuhs KŌ luh
Tuxedo—TUHKS ĭ dō

### U

Uhland—YŌŌ l'nd
Umbarger—UHM bahr ger
Urbana—<u>er</u> BĂ nuh
Utley—YŌŌT lĭ
Utopia—yŏŏ TŌ pĭ uh

Uvalde—yŏŏ VĂL dĭ

### V

Valdasta—văl DĂS tuh
Valera—vuh LĬ ruh
Van Alstyne—văn AWLZ <u>teen</u>
Vashti—VĂSH tī
Vega—VĂ guh
Velasco—vuh LĂS kō
Veribest—VĔR ĭ bĕst
Victoria—vĭk TŌ rĭ uh
Vidor—VĪ der
Vienna—<u>vee</u> ĔN uh
Vinegarone—<u>vĭn</u> er guh RŌN
Voca—VŌ kuh
Von Ormy—vahn AHR mĭ
Votaw—VŌ taw

### W

Waco—WĂ kō
Waelder—WĔL der
Waka—WAH kuh
Waldeck—WAWL dĕk
Waller—WAW ler
Wallis—WAH lĭs
Warda—WAWR duh
Waskom—WAHS k'm
Wastella—wahs TĔL uh
Watauga—wuh TAW guh
Waxahachie—<u>wawks</u> uh HĂ chĭ
Weches—WEE chĭz
Weesatche—WEE săch
Weimar—WĪ mer
Weinert—WĪ nert
Weir—weer
Weser—WEE zer
Weslaco—WĔS luh kō
Westhoff—WĔS tawf
Westphalia—<u>wĕst</u> FĂL yuh
Whitharral—HWĬT hăr uhl
Whitsett—HWĬT sĭt
Whitson—HWĬT s'n
Whitt—hwĭt
Whon—hwahn
Wichita—WĬCH ĭ taw
Wiergate—WEER găt
Wilbarger—WĬL bahr ger
Wildorado—wĭl duh RĂ dō
Willacy—WĬL uh sĭ
Wimberley—WĬM ber lĭ
Windthorst—WĬN thr'st
Wingate—WĬN găt
Winona—wĭ NŌ nuh
Woden—WŌD n
Wolfforth—WŎŎL forth
Woodbine—WŎŎD bĭn
Wylie—WĪ lĭ

### Y

Yancey—YĂN sĭ
Yantis—YĂN tĭs
Yoakum—YŌ k'm
Ysleta—ĭs LĔT uh

### Z

Zapata—zuh PAH tuh
Zavalla—zuh VĂL uh
Zephyr—ZĔF er
Zuehl—ZEE uhl ☆

# Obituaries: July 2001-July 2003

**Adams, John G.**, 91; served as general counsel for the Army in the 1950s when he was nemesis to Sen. Joe McCarthy during televised hearings; in Dallas, June 26, 2003.

**Ahn, Suzanne**, 51; neurologist and Dallas community leader, Korean native raised in Tyler, served on the Texas Air Quality Control Board and the State Board of Medical Examiners; from cancer, in Dallas, June 22, 2003.

**Allison, Joe**, 77; McKinney native co-wrote Jim Reeves hit "He'll Have to Go," and other songs; helped form the Country Music Disc Jockey Assoc., which later became the Country Music Assoc.; in Nashville, Aug. 2, 2002.

**Armstrong, John B.**, 83; former King Ranch CEO and third generation rancher; ran unsuccessfully for agriculture commissioner in 1964 and served on the Texas Animal Commission; in San Antonio, Feb. 20, 2003.

**Ash, Mary Kay**, 83; her cosmetics company (known for its signature color pink) grew from 11 employees in 1963 to a multimillion-dollar global empire at her death; in Dallas, November 22, 2001.

**Astronauts of Columbia**; all had spent training in Texas and were seen as Texas' own; two had strong Texas ties, Rick Husband to Amarillo and William McCool to Lubbock; others were Michael Anderson, David Brown, Kalpana Chawla, Laurel Clark and Ilan Ramon; shuttle broke apart over Texas, Feb. 1, 2003.

**Attlesey, Sam**, 56; distinguished reporter of Texas politics for 28 years for *The Dallas Morning News*, serving as deputy director of the Austin bureau at his death from cancer; in Sulphur Springs, April 2, 2003.

**Bittle, Jerry**, 53; Dallas-area cartoonist of the nationally syndicated *Geech* and *Shirley & Son* comic strips; of a heart attack while scuba diving in Honduras, April 7, 2003.

**Bonham, Donald L.**, 74; co-founder in 1972 of Fiesta Mart supermarkets specializing in international foods, one store grew to chain of 49 across Texas; in Houston, April 5, 2003.

**Bowers, Elliot**, 83; associated for 52 years with Sam Houston State University where he was president from 1970 until 1989, its greatest period of growth; in Huntsville, May 30, 2003.

**Brinkley, David**, 82; famed television newsman with NBC's *Huntley-Brinkley Report* and later with ABC; in Houston where he had retired, June 11, 2003.

**Brown, Caro**, 93; reporter for the *Alice Daily Echo* whose coverage of Duval County political boss George Parr earned her a Pulitzer Prize in 1955; in Boerne, Aug. 5, 2001.

**Burnett, Warren**, 75; legendary Odessa trial lawyer who fought for school integration, the United Farm Workers Union, defended La Raza Unida activists; in Fort Davis, Sept. 23, 2002.

**Carr, Billie**, 74; leading Democratic party figure and activist over four decades, nicknamed "godmother of liberal politics in Texas;" in Houston, Sept. 9, 2002.

**Christian, George**, 75; former press secretary to President Lyndon B. Johnson and adviser to many other Texas political leaders; in Austin, Nov. 27, 2002.

**Clements, W.W. "Foots,"** 88; soft-drink delivery-truck driver starting in 1935 who eventually became CEO of Dr Pepper Co., chairman emeritus at his death; in Dallas, Oct. 3, 2002.

**Connally, Merrill L. Sr.**, 80; younger brother of Gov. John Connally; rancher, Wilson County judge, and movie and television actor; in Floresville, Sept. 4, 2001.

**Cox, John L.**, 78; Burkburnett native was oilman known as "King of the Spraberry" for making the Permian Basin field productive, served as trustee for Rice University; in Midland, July 11, 2003.

**Criswell, Rev. W.A.**, 92; national evangelical leader who was pastor of Dallas' First Baptist Church from 1944, becoming pastor emeritus in 1994; headed the Southern Baptist Convention for two terms; in Dallas, Jan. 10, 2002.

**Daniel, Jean Houston Baldwin**, 86; descendant of Sam Houston and widow of former U.S. Senator and Gov. Price Daniel; in Liberty, Dec. 14, 2002.

**Dedman, Robert H. Sr.**, 76; philanthropist who built a multibillion-dollar empire of golf clubs and resorts; former chairman of Texas State Highway Commission; in Dallas, Aug. 20, 2002.

**DeHartog, Jan**, 88; Dutch-born author who in the 1960s exposed deplorable conditions at Houston's Jeff Davis Hospital; wrote Tony-Award winning hit "Fourposter"; in Houston, Sept. 22, 2002.

**De La O, Jesús "Chuy,"** 74; a fixture in El Paso politics, champion of poor and elderly; ran unsuccessfully for mayor in 1981; in El Paso, April 8, 2002.

**Eakin, Ed**, 74; Chilton native founded the state's largest non-academic press in 1979; credited with preserving Texas lore through the Austin-based Eakin Press; in Austin, Feb. 20, 2002.

**Eckhardt, Bob**, 88; liberal Democrat spent 1967-81 in Congress representing Houston's 8th District; previously in the Legislature from 1958; in Austin, Nov. 13, 2001.

**Flournoy, Lucien**, 83; Alice oilman and philanthropist; former mayor; served on Texas Aeronautics Commission and Texas Economic Development Commission; in Corpus Christi, March 27, 2003.

**Formby, Margaret**, 73; rancher's daughter who was impetus behind the creation of the National Cowgirl Hall of Fame in 1975, first in Hereford and now in Fort Worth; in Hereford, April 10, 2003.

**Freeman, Charles E. III**, 54; one of two blacks to desegregate Rice University in 1965, later student activist at Texas Southern University; defense lawyer, devout Muslim; from cancer, in Houston, May 12, 2003.

**Freeman, Dovie Frances**, 83; from 1954-89 served up sizzling steaks as a waitress at Austin's Hoffbrau, known for her wit and signature jumpsuit; in Austin, Oct. 1, 2002.

**Furr, Donald**, 74; CEO from 1959-85 of the family cafeteria business headquartered in Lubbock; he served on Texas Tech University President's Council; in Maryland, July 30, 2002.

**Galloway, Harry M.**, 86; chief chemist at Pearl Brewery where he worked from 1954-81; distinguished Navy pilot in World War II; in San Antonio, Aug. 4, 2002.

**Garcés, Ramon**, 76; Laredo native was influential journalist and advocate for migrant farm workers; headed Spanish branch of the Voice of America 1979-81; in Austin, Sept. 14, 2002.

**Garcia, Clotilde P.**, 86; known as "Dr. Cleo", delivered 10,000 babies, civic leader and sister of civil rights leaders Hector and Xico Garcia, 75, who died April 28; in Corpus Christi, May 27, 2003.

**Garcia, Irene Martinez**, 86; oldest child of founders of El Fenix restaurants where she served as chairman of the board; in Dallas, March 31, 2003.

**Garibay, Randy**, 62; guitarist and singer known as the "Godfather of San Antonio Blues" and the "Chicano Bluesman"; began with doo-wop groups from the city's West Side in the 1950s; in San Antonio, May 23, 2002.

**Gjemre, Ken**, 81; corporate dropout became business icon after co-founding Half Price Books in Dallas in 1972, grew to 73 stores located in 11 states; in California, May 27, 2002.

**Gladden, Don**, 71; Fort Worth civil-

Cosmetics entrepreneur Mary Kay Ash.

Olympic, NFL champion Bob Hayes.

Country music's Waylon Jennings.

Sarah McClendon at the White House.

rights lawyer, activist for integration and against the poll tax, legislator from 1959-68; in Fort Worth, Feb. 14, 2002.

**Gonzales, Raymond B. Jr.,** 90; co-founded with his wife Carmen in 1948 the popular Austin restaurant La Tapatia which operated until 1993; in Austin, Oct. 24, 2001.

**Gordon, Harry Bernard Sr.,** 92; Houston philanthropist who turned a family store into jewelry empire by pioneering the practice of offering credit to customers; in Houston, Jan. 22, 2002.

**Green, Cecil Howard,** 102; international philanthropist; one of the founders in 1941 of what became Texas Instruments, which helped make Dallas, Houston and Austin technology centers; in La Jolla, Calif., April 12, 2003.

**Greene, A.C.** 78; Abilene native was noted historian, author and newspaper columnist; director emeritus of the University of North Texas' Center for Texas Studies; in Salado, April 5, 2002.

**Guerrero, Eberardo "Larry,"** 75; owner of landmark Mexican restaurant, "Larry's," in Richmond for more than 40 years; was a construction foreman building NASA; in Richmond, March 27, 2003.

**Gump, Richard A.,** 85; founded in 1945 along with political adviser Robert Strauss Texas' largest law firm, Akin, Gump, Strauss, Hauer & Feld LLP; in Dallas, June 21, 2003.

**Gunby, David,** 58; engineer who was a student Aug. 1, 1966, when shot by Charles Whitman from the University of Texas tower; spent the rest of his life in kidney dialysis, death ruled the 15th homicide from the incident; in Fort Worth, Nov. 12, 2001.

**Gunn, Warren,** 84; Fredericksburg rancher who was one of the organizers of the first rodeo performers association in 1936, named to the

Cowboy Hall of Fame in 2000; in San Antonio, May 29, 2002.

**Hayes, Bob,** 59; Olympic gold-medal sprinter in 1964 and Dallas Cowboy receiver for 10 years, earning a Super Bowl ring in 1972; of kidney failure, in Florida, Sept. 18, 2002.

**Henderson, Luther A.,** 82; bought Pier 1 Imports in 1966 and transformed it into a nationwide retail force; was founder-chairman of the company until 1993; in Fort Worth, Sept. 28, 2002.

**Hinckley, Margaret A. "Marty" Jenkins;** 74; Clarendon native married into Dallas family with ice cream business, came up with the idea for chocolate nut bar for vendors at the State Fair of Texas, evolved into the "Drumstick"; in Mabank, March 3, 2003

**Hill, Bobby Joe,** 59; leader of the all-black Texas Western team that won the 1966 NCAA championship against the all-white Kentucky team, a landmark in college basketball; apparent heart attack in El Paso, Dec. 8, 2002.

**Hofner, Emil "Bash,"** 83; played steel guitar in brother Adolph Hofner's band that blended Western swing with Czech polkas; in San Antonio, Jan. 16, 2002.

**Hubenak, Joe,** 64; member of the Texas House of Representatives from 1968-79 and a leader in agricultural legislation; ran unsuccessfully for agricultural commissioner in 1978; in Richmond, Nov. 14, 2001.

**Hurd, John Gavin,** 87; Republican leader, was president of the Texas independent oilmen's association and former U.S. ambassador to South Africa; in San Antonio, Sept. 6, 2001.

**Jackson, Maynard Jr.,** 65; Dallas native who became the first black mayor of Atlanta, Ga., in 1973; in Washington, D.C., June 23, 2003.

**Jacobsen, Jake,** 83; legal assistant

to President Lyndon B. Johnson, former Department of Public Safety commissioner, accused John Connally of taking bribe as Treasury secretary; in Giddings, June 30, 2003.

**Jennings, Waylon,** 64; Littlefield native was part of country music's outlaw movement, had 16 No. 1 hits, songwriter and guitarist had played in Buddy Holly's band; in Arizona, Feb. 13, 2002.

**Johnson, J. Lee III,** 84; business and civic leader was part of team in 1960s that negotiated agreement between Fort Worth and Dallas to build D-FW International Airport; in Fort Worth, Aug. 18, 2002.

**Johnson, Lee Otis,** 62; student leader in the 1960s at Texas Southern University, arrested on a marijuana charge; "Free Lee Otis" became chant across Texas; in Houston, June 12, 2002.

**Jones, Luther,** 85; leader in Corpus Christi over four decades, first as commander of the Army Depot and then as mayor for eight years, granted title of mayor emeritus; in Corpus Christi, March 3, 2002.

**Josey, Jack Symth,** 86; Houston oilman who with others (see Sawtelle, below) developed Lakeway community on Lake Travis; on boards of University of Texas, Rice University and Hermann Hospital; in California, Feb. 27, 2003.

**Katz, Sol,** 88; Corsicana native started throwing *The Dallas Morning News* in high school and went on the serve on the board of directors of Belo, the parent company; in Plano, May 9, 2002.

**Kazen, Jimmy,** 90; one of four sons of Lebanese immigrants who achieved pominence in South Texas politics; former prosecutor and judge; in Laredo, Feb. 25,

2003.

**Kitchens, C.T. "Jack,"** 85; with McBrayer (see below) developed the first offset newspaper press; in Fort Worth, Dec. 15, 2002.

**Kozmetsky, George,** 85; benefactor of the University of Texas where he headed the College of Business Adminstration from 1966-82; laid groundwork for Austin's emergence as a technology center; in Austin, April 30, 2003.

**Lampman, Hugh W.,** 69; 50-year broadcast veteran; hosted for nine years "Music til Dawn" at KRLD in Dallas; won Peabody Award; in Dallas, July 15, 2002.

**Lane, Dick "Night Train,"** 73; Austin high school athlete whose football career with the Los Angeles Rams and Detroit Lions earned him a place in the NFL Hall of Fame; in Austin, Jan. 29, 2002.

**LaSelle, Dorothy Antoinette "Toni,"** 100; painter who during her 44-year tenure at Texas Woman's University inspired generations of young artists; in Denton, July 26, 2002.

**Lemons, Abe,** 79; one of college basketball's winningest and wittiest coaches, at the University of Texas from 1977-82, also coached at Pan American; in Oklahoma, Sept. 2, 2002.

**Lewis, Sam,** 80; West Texas public relations figure who promoted jalapeños and armadillo racing; one of the original supporters of the Terlingua Chili Cook-off; in San Angelo, Jan. 10, 2003.

**Liedtke, J. Hugh,** 81; oilman founded Zapata Petroleum Corp. in 1953 in Midland with former President George H.W. Bush, firm became Pennzoil Co. where he was CEO; in Houston, March 28, 2003.

**Logan, Horace Lee,** 86; began country music's radio program *Louisiana Hayride* in 1948 where artist such as Elvis Presley and Hank Williams got their breaks; in Victoria, Oct. 13, 2002.

**Manente, Rev. Vladimiro,** 81; Italian-born priest in Laredo credited with starting the cursillo retreat movement in the United States in 1958; in Laredo, April 28, 2002.

**Marcus, Stanley,** 96; internationlly known retailer heading Neiman Marcus from 1950-77; civic leader and commentator, wrote books on merchandising and fashion; in Dallas, Jan. 22, 2002.

**Matocha, Lee Roy,** 70; bandleader who for four decades entertained Texans with broadcasts of Czech music, raised in Plum; in Fayette County, July 12, 2003.

**Matthews, Gordon,** 65; Austin inventor who created the first voice mail system in the late 1970s and patented it in 1982; in Dallas, Feb. 23, 2002.

*Rev. W.A. Criswell.*

*Historian, writer A.C. Greene.*

**Maverick, Maury Jr.,** 82; liberal lawyer, legislator and newspaper columnist, civil rights advocate for 50 years; son of New Deal congressman and San Antonio mayor; in San Antonio, Jan. 28, 2003.

**McBrayer, Staley Thomas,** 92; credited with bringing offset printing to small newspapers in the 1950s when he and a team of engineers developed the offset newspaper press; in Fort Worth, April 14, 2002.

**McClendon, Sarah,** 92; Tyler native known as the colorful and agressive White House reporter from the administration of Franklin D. Roosevelt to that of George W. Bush; served in the Army in World War II, champion of veterans' causes; in Washington, D.C., Jan. 8, 2003.

**McGrew, Jack,** 88; Denton native was a pioneer in Texas broadcasting beginning in 1930; was program director at KPRC in Houston during coverage of the Texas City explosions in 1947; in Las Cruces, N.M., Nov. 25, 2001.

**McKool, Mike,** 84; Dallas lawyer

was longtime Democratic leader, state senator from 1968-72; son of immigrant Lebanese parents; in Dallas, Feb. 22, 2003.

**Michels, Doug,** 59; Houston artist who created the Panhandle landmark of 10 Cadillacs planted nose down; in Australia in a climbing accident, June 12, 2003.

**Milkovisch, Mary,** 85; with husband, John, created the famed Beer Can House which has become a Houston folk art landmark; in Houston, March 18, 2002.

**Moody, Chip,** 54; television anchorman during a 30-year career in Dallas-Fort Worth, Houston, El Paso and Waco; in Dallas, Dec. 26, 2001, after a series of health problems.

**Morehead, Richard M. Sr.,** 89; former Austin bureau chief of *The Dallas Morning News* where he worked for 36 years, retiring in 1978; served on the Texas Judicial Council for 31 years; in Austin, Jan. 31, 2003.

**Moursund, A.W.,** 82; Central Texas lawyer who with friend Lyndon B. Johnson worked to bring electricity to the region; served in Texas House from 1948-52; in Round Mountain, April 22, 2002.

**Newbury, Mickey,** 62; Houstonian was among the Texas songwriters of the 1960s, first hit was "Funny, Familiar, Forgotten Feelings"; his "An American Trilogy" was a Elvis Presley standard; in Oregon, Sept. 29, 2002.

**Nixon, Joan Lowery,** 76; award-winning author of more than 140 books, including murder mysteries and historical novels for children and for young adults; in Houston, June 28, 2003.

**Olson, Barbara Bracher,** 45; Houston native and national conservative political commentator, wife of U.S. solicitor general; killed at the Pentagon in the Sept. 11, 2001, terrorist attacks.

**Pate, James Leonard,** 67; former CEO of Pennzoil-Quaker State Co., assistant secretary of commerce and economic spokesman for President Gerald Ford; in Houston, Jan. 18, 2003.

**Patterson, Earl,** 99; the oldest former drum major at Texas A&M University, in the 1920s helped start the Elephant Walk tradition; in Tomball, Aug. 4, 2002.

**Pequeno, Reymunda Trevino,** 93; Dallas native, wife of Methodist minister, was mother of 16 sons and four daughters, left 700 descendants; in Abilene, April 21, 2003.

**Perry, Oma Bell,** 90; Bay City native was a descendant of the sister of Stephen F. Austin, gave 7,500-acre ranch in Real County for an orphans' home and retirement village; May 29, 2003.

**Phillips, Jimmy,** 88; populist in the Legislature 1945-1959 and later mentor to some of the state's leading politicians; played key role in exposing 1950s veterans' land scandal; at Bailey's Prairie, Jan. 14, 2002.

**Prigogine, Ilya,** 86; winner of the Nobel Prize for chemistry in 1977 and for 35 years a professor at the University of Texas at Austin; in Brussels, Belgium, May 28, 2003.

**Pulido, Dionicia,** 92; founded with her husband their first restaurant in 1966 which grew into a chain of 13 across North Texas; in Benbrook, June 23, 2003.

**Raillard, Raymond,** 85; helped found the outdoor drama *Texas* staged each year in Palo Duro Canyon; in Canyon, Jan. 1, 2002.

**Rangel, Irma,** 71; Kingsville Democrat was first Hispanic woman elected to the Legislature where she served for 26 years; advocate of higher education; in Austin, March 18, 2003.

**Riley, John E. "Jack,"** 78; served 33 years with NASA, broadcast voice of the Apollo program, providing commentary for the first moon walk; in La Porte, April 17, 2003.

**Rogers, Sol J.,** 87; Houston-area philanthropist who in 1937 founded Texas State Optical in Beaumont, firm spread into Louisiana and New Mexico; in Houston, Jan. 18, 2002.

**Rostow, Walt,** 86; economist, University of Texas professor for 33 years and adviser to John F. Kennedy and Lyndon B. Johnson; was an advocate of military intervention in Vietnam; in Austin, Feb. 13, 2003.

**Rote, Kyle,** 73; San Antonio high school athlete, former SMU All-American and NFL star of the 1950s, playing with the New York Giants; sports broadcaster in the 1960s and 1970s; in Baltimore, Aug. 15, 2002.

**Sawtelle, G. Flint,** 82; oilman who with others developed land around Lake Travis in 1962 into resort and retirement center known as Lakeway Inn and Marina; in Fort Worth, Aug. 24, 2001.

**Schramm, Texas E. "Tex,"** 83; president and general manager for 29 years of the Dallas Cowboys, making them into "America's Team," University of Texas journalism graduate; in Dallas, July 15, 2003.

**Schwartz, Walter,** 81; mayor of Brenham, chancellor and former president of Blinn College when it grew from 3,500 in 1984 to 9,000, also served two terms as state legislator; in Houston, July 7, 2003.

**Scurlock, Elizabeth,** 99; philanthropist who with her husband, oilman Eddy Scurlock, benefited the Texas Medical Center and the Institute of Religion in Houston;

*Irma Rangel, first Hispanic woman legislator.*

*Stanley Marcus, mercantile giant.*

Edna native died in Houston, June 9, 2003.

**Speir, Col. Wilson E. "Pat,"** 84; director of the Texas Department of Public Safety from 1968 to 1980; began 36-year service in the department as a highway patrolman; in Austin, April 22, 2002.

**Steinbeck, Elaine,** 88; Austin native and former actress was widow of author John Steinbeck and supporter of his legacy; in New York, April 27, 2003.

**Sutton, A.C. Sr.,** 83; godchild of George Washington Carver and former president of the Texas NAACP; former member of the Texas Youth Commission; in San Antonio, March 30, 2002.

**Taylor, J.W. "Bill,"** 90; starting in 1939, Anson native helped build Taylor Publishing into one of the nation's largest sellers of school yearbooks; in Dallas, June 10, 2002.

**Thompson, John P.,** 77; Dallas philanthropist and civic leader who for decades held top positions at the Southland Corp., now 7-Eleven Inc.; former chairman of the chancellor's council at the University of Texas; in Dallas, Jan. 28, 2003.

**Tijerina, Pete,** 80; Laredo native and attorney who created the Mexican American Legal Defense and Education Fund in 1968, a national civil-rights organization; in San Antonio, May 14, 2003.

**Tolar, Charlie,** 65; running back for the AFL Houston Oilers, because of his height (5 ft.-6 in.) known as the "Human Bowling Ball"; in Houston, April 28, 2003.

**Topfer, Angela,** 55; Austin civic leader, wife of Dell Computer executive, benefactor gave millions of dollars to social causes; complications from cancer, in Austin, June 3, 2003.

**Trejo, Frank,** 95; Elmendorf native known as dean of Hispanic journalists in Texas; wrote "Frank Talk" and "Around the Plaza" columns in the *San Antonio Light*; in San

Antonio, Sept. 29, 2002.

**Tupa, Julius Victor;** 71; editor of the *Texas Polka News*, director of the Texas Polka Music Assoc., called Houston's polka king; in Houston, Oct. 5, 2002.

**Wallace, Mack,** 73; former Railroad Commission chairman, Athens native was legal counsel to Gov. Dolph Briscoe; in Dallas, June 28, 2003.

**Ware, Rev. Browning,** 73; for 20 years, beginning in 1976, pastor of First Bapist Church in Austin, community and ecumenical leader; in Austin, Oct. 29, 2002.

**West, James T.,** 86; Corsicana native was former co-owner and president of Wolf Brand Chili and son of the founder; in Dallas, Aug. 14, 2002.

**Wilson, Mary Robert,** 87; the first woman to be awarded the Silver Star for her heroics as a nurse in World War II; Tom Brokaw wrote a chapter on her in his book *The Greatest Generation*; in Duncanville, Nov. 19, 2001.

**Wisch, Jessard "Jimmy,"** 85; publisher and co-founder of the *Texas Jewish Post*, and a fixture in the Jewish community in North Texas; former president of the American Jewish Press Association; in Fort Worth, Jan. 26, 2002.

**Wisenbaker, Royce E.,** 84; East Texas businessman and benefactor to Texas A&M University and the University of Texas at Tyler; in Tyler, Sept. 11, 2001.

**Young, John A.,** 85; Democratic congressman from Corpus Christi for 22 years until 1978, and former Nueces County judge and prosecutor; in Virginia, Jan. 22, 2002.

**Youngblood, Guadalupe "Lupe" Jr.,** 55; South Texas political activist in the 1960s and 70s, former state chairman of La Raza Unida Party; lecturer in Mexican-American studies at several colleges; in Robstown, Feb. 4, 2002. ☆

# Advertisers' Index

Haverty's ........................................................ 2
CC Carpet ..................................................... 3
Ebby Halliday ............................................... 5
Irving Auto Dealers...................................... 8
Heritage Ranch ............................................ 9

TXCN, Texas Cable News ............................................. 15
Belo Interactive ............................................................. 30
Richardson Regional Medical Center............................ 33
Texas A&M University Press.......................................... 56
Richardson Bike Mart................................................... 120

# General Index

Page numbers in italics refer to photographs, illustrations and maps. Bold face page numbers indicate major discussions of the topic. For cities and towns not listed in the index, see lists of towns on pp. 300–377 and pp. 460–468. Also see the "Cities and Towns" tabbed section.

**A**
Abbott, Greg, 396, 433
Abilene
  airline passengers, 597
  mayor and city manager, 460
  mental health services, 536
  military installation in, 490-91
  museums, 498
  newspaper, 560
  performing arts organization, 497
  population, 299, 300, 378
  prisons in, 444
  profile and map location, **276**
  public library, 504
  television and radio stations, 560
Abilene Christian University, 549
Abilene, Lake, 73
Abilene State Park, 119, 122
Abilene State School, 536
Abortions, 531-35
Accidents
  as cause of death, 531-35, 594
  motor vehicle accidents, 594
Acevedo, Fray Antonio, 521
Acton State Historic Sites, 119, 122
Acupuncture Examiners, State Board of, 445
Adams, John G., 638
Addicks Reservoir, 73, 133
Addison
  Foreign Trade Zone, 586
  mayor and city manager, 460
  museum, 498
  performing arts organization, 497
  population (2000 and 2002), 300
  profile and map location, **174**
Add-Ran College, 547
Adjutant General, 445
Administrative Judicial Districts, 436-38, 445
Admiral Nimitz Museum State Historic Site, 123, 128
Ad Valorem Tax Rate, Board to Calculate, 445
Aerial cable-car tramway, 130
Aerospace Commission, 445
Affordable Housing Corporation Board of
  Directors, 450
Age of majority, 55
Aggravated assault, 539-43
Aging, Board on, 445
Agricultural Finance Authority, 445
Agricultural Resources Protection Authority, 445
Agriculture. *See also* Ranching; and specific crops
  agribusiness, 621
  assets and liabilities of farms and ranches
    (1992-2001), 620, 621
  cash receipts of farms and ranches, 621
  comparative ranking with other states, 11, 622
  by county, 139-295
  crop production statistics (2002), 621
  drought and, 92
  exports of agricultural products, 622, 623
  fruits and nuts, 628-30
  gross state product (1993-2002), 568
  growing season by county, 104-9
  history of, 37, 42, 43, 46, 48, 51
  hunting lease income and, 622
  irrigation for, 69, 71, 132, 622-23
  livestock and their products, 629, 630-32
  number and nature of farms, 620-21
  percent of income from products, 621-22
  principal crops, 10, 623-27
  in soil subdivisions, 64-66
  statistics, 10
  truck crops, 627-28
Agriculture Commissioner, 396, 399, 407
Agua Adentro Mountains, *152*
Agustín de Iturbide, Emperor, 36
Ahn, Suzanne, 638
Aircraft Pooling Board, 445
Air Force, U.S., 490-91
Airlines, 566, 598
Airports, 597, 598
Akins, Marty, 396
Alabama Creek Wildlife Management Area, 91
Alamo (city)
  map location, *207*
  mayor and city manager, 460
  population, 207, 300, 378
  public library, 504
  television and radio stations, 560
Alamo Area Council of Governments, 470
Alamo, battle of, 38

Alamo Community College District, 549
Alamo (mission), 34
Alan Henry Reservoir, 73
Albania, consular office, 587
Albany
  fairs/festivals in, 136
  mayor and city manager, 460
  museum, 498
  newspaper, 560
  population, 300-301, 378
  profile and map location, **268**
  public library, 504
Alcoa Lake, 73
Alcohol
  liquor-by-the-drink, 55, 472, *472*
  local-option clause for, 48, 52
  prohibition movement and, 48, 49, 52
  and repeal of prohibition, 52
  rum distillery, 130
  wet-or-dry status of counties, 472, *472*
Alcohol and Drug Abuse, Commission on, 445
Alcoholic Beverage Commission, 445
Alger, Bruce, 54
Alibates Flint Quarries National Monument, 131
Alice
  mayor and city manager, 460
  newspaper, 560
  population, 301, 378
  profile and map location, **217**
  public library, 504
  radio stations, 560
Allen, Debbie, 502
Allen
  map location, *165*
  mayor and city manager, 460
  newspaper, 560
  population, 165, 301, 378
  public library, 504
Alligators, 89
Allison, Joe, 638
Allred, James V., 52, 419
Alluvial fans, 63
Alpine
  Amtrak passengers on/off at, 596
  mayor and city manager, 460
  museum, 498
  newspaper, 560
  population, 301, 378
  profile and map location, **153**
  public library, 504
  radio stations, 560
Alsatian immigrants, 127
Alternative Dispute Resolution Centers, 435
Altitude, of counties, 139
Aluminum, 610
Alvarez, Elizabeth Cruce, 559
Alvin
  mayor and city manager, 460
  newspaper, 560
  population, 301, 378
  profile and map location, **151**
  television and radio stations, 560
Alzheimer's disease, 531-35
Alzheimer's Disease and Related Disorders,
  Council on, 445
Amarillo
  airline passengers, 597
  council-manager form of government in, 47, 469
  Dust Bowl and, 52
  fairs/festivals in, 136
  Film Office, 496
  Foreign Trade Zone, 586
  mayor and city manager, 460
  mental health services, 536
  museums, 498
  newspapers, 560
  performing arts organizations, 497
  population, 299, 301, 378
  prisons in, 443, 444
  profile and map location, **256**
  public library, 504
  television and radio stations, 560
Amarillo College, 549
Amberton University, 549
American Indians. *See* Native Americans
Amistad Dam, 69
Amistad National Recreation Area, 131
Amistad Reservoir, 73
Amon G. Carter, Lake, 73
Amphibians, 85, 86

Amtrak, 596
Anahuac
  mayor, 460
  newspaper, 560
  population, 302, 378
  profile and map location, **161**
  public library, 504
  tonnage handled by port, 589
Anahuac, Lake, 73
Anahuac National Wildlife Refuge, 89
Analcime, 616
Anderson, Michael, 638
Anderson (town), 136, 198, 302, 460
Anderson County
  alcohol sales (wet-or-dry status), 472
  banks and bank assets, 578
  church membership, 529
  county and district officials, 474, 479
  courts, 437, 473
  crime and law enforcement, 540
  deaths, 531
  federal funds to, 492
  general election results (2002), 402
  health care, 531
  income, 573
  map of, *139*
  oil and gas production, 605, 607
  population, 139, 389
  profile of, **139**
  tax appraiser, 471
  timber production and value in, 82
  vehicles and highways, 590
  weather data, 104
Andrews (city)
  mayor and city manager, 460
  newspaper, 560
  population, 302, 378
  profile and map location, **140**
  public library, 504
  radio stations, 560
Andrews County
  alcohol sales (wet-or-dry status), 472
  banks and bank assets, 578
  church membership, 529
  county and district officials, 474, 479
  courts, 437, 473
  crime and law enforcement, 540
  deaths, 531
  federal funds to, 492
  general election results (2002), 402
  health care, 531
  income, 573
  map of, *140*
  oil and gas production, 605, 607
  population, 140, 389
  profile of, **140**
  tax appraiser, 471
  vehicles and highways, 590
  weather data, 104
Angelina and Neches River Authority, 445
Angelina College, 549
Angelina County
  alcohol sales (wet-or-dry status), 472
  banks and bank assets, 578
  church membership, 529
  county and district officials, 474, 479
  courts, 437, 473
  crime and law enforcement, 540
  deaths, 531
  federal funds to, 492
  general election results (2002), 402
  health care, 531
  income, 573
  map of, *140*
  oil and gas production, 605, 607
  population, 140, 389
  profile of, **140**
  tax appraiser, 471
  timber production and value in, 82
  vehicles and highways, 590
  weather data, 104
Angelina National Forest, 83, 133
Angelina-Neches Wildlife Management Area, 91
Angelina River, 71
Angelo State University, 552
Angleton
  fairs/festivals in, 136
  mayor and city administrator, 460
  museum, 498
  newspaper, 560

population, 302, 378
prison in, 444
profile and map location, **151**
public library, 504
Anglos
educational attainment, 298
as immigrants to Texas in early 1800s, 35-37
income statistics, 297
poverty statistics, 298
state population statistics, 10
Animal Health Commission, 445
Animals. *See also* specific animals
of Cenozoic Era, 63
at frontier forts, 23
livestock industries, 629, 630-32
of Mesozoic Era, 62-63
number of species, 86
state mammals, 14
wildlife, **86-89**
Annexation of Texas by U.S., 41, 426
Anson
mayor and city manager, 460
newspapers, 560
population, 302, 378
profile and map location, **219**
public library, 504
radio stations, 560
Antitrust laws, 48
Anzalduas Channel Dam, 73
Appomattox, surrender at, 44
Appraiser Licensing and Certification Board, 445
Aquifers, 67-68, *67*
Aquilla Lake, 73, 133
Aquilla Wildlife Management Area, 91
Aransas County
alcohol sales (wet-or-dry status), 472
church membership, 529
county and district officials, 474, 479
courts, 437, 473
crime and law enforcement, 540
deaths, 531
federal funds to, 492
general election results (2002), 402
income, 573
map of, *141*
oil and gas production, 605, 607
population, 141, 389
profile of, **141**
tax appraiser, 471
vehicles and highways, 590
weather data, 104
Aransas National Wildlife Refuge, 89
Archaeological sites, 27, *27*, 29, 29, 120, 121
Archer City
mayor and city manager, 460
newspaper, 560
population, 302, 378
profile and map location, **141**
public library, 504
Archer County
alcohol sales (wet-or-dry status), 472
church membership, 529
county and district officials, 474, 479
courts, 437
crime and law enforcement, 540
deaths, 531
federal funds to, 492
general election results (2002), 402
health care, 531
highway through, *289*
income, 573
map of, *141*
oil and gas production, 605, 607
population, 141, 389
profile of, **141**
tax appraiser, 471
vehicles and highways, 590
weather data, 104
Architectural Examiners, Board of, 445-46
Area
of counties, 139-295, 460
of state, 10, 56
Argentina, consular office, 587
Arista, Mariano, 132
Ark-Tex Council of Governments, 470
Arlington
fairs/festivals in, 136
mayor and city manager, 460
museum, 498
performing arts organizations, 497
population, 10, 299, 302, 378
profile and map location, **274-75**
public library, 504
radio stations, 560
Arlington Baptist College, 549
Arlington, Lake, 73
Armadillos, 14, 86
Armbrister, Ken, 619
Armey, Dick, 397, *397*
Armey, Scott, 397
Armstrong, John B., 638
Armstrong County
alcohol sales (wet-or-dry status), 472
banks and bank assets, 578
church membership, 529
county and district officials, 474, 479
courts, 437
crime and law enforcement, 540
deaths, 531
federal funds to, 492
general election results (2002), 402
health care, 531
income, 573
map of, *142*
population, 142, 389

profile of, **142**
tax appraiser, 471
vehicles and highways, 590
weather data, 104
Army Corps of Engineers, 73, 133
Army, U.S., 490
Arnold, Hendrick, 39
Arredondo, Joaquín, 36
Arrowhead, Lake, 73, 126
Arson, 539
Arteaga, Fray Antonio de, 520, 523
Artists, 501, 502, 514
Arts and culture, **496-516**
artists, 501, 502
film and television, 496
holidays, anniversaries, and festivals, 516
Medal of the Arts Awards, 502
museums, 498-500
musicians, 501, 502
National Humanities Medal, 502
performing arts organizations, 497-98
poets laureate, 501
Polish-Texans, 512-15
public libraries, 504-11
state agencies, 497
Texas Institute of Letters Awards, 503
writers, 503
Arts, Commission on, 446, 497
Asbestos, 610
Ash, Mary Kay, 638, *639*
Aspermont
mayor and city administrator, 460
newspaper, 560
population, 303, 378
profile and map location, **272**
public library, 504
Asphalt, 610
Assassination of Kennedy, 54, *54*
Assault, 539-43
Assessor-collectors, county, 474-78
Astronauts of Columbia, 638
Astronomical calendar, 110-17
Atascosa County
alcohol sales (wet-or-dry status), 472
banks and bank assets, 578
church membership, 529
county and district officials, 474, 479
courts, 437
crime and law enforcement, 540
deaths, 531
federal funds to, 492
general election results (2002), 402
health care, 531
income, 573
map of, *142*
oil and gas production, 605, 607
population, 142, 389
profile of, **142**
tax appraiser, 471
vehicles and highways, 590
weather data, 104
Atascosa River, 70
Atchafalaya, 72
Athens
fairs/festivals in, 136
Freshwater Fisheries Center in, 134
mayor and city manager, 460
newspaper, 560
population, 303, 378
profile and map location, **206**
public library, 504
radio station, 560
Athens, Lake, 73
Athletic Trainers, Advisory Board of, 446
Atkinson Island Wildlife Management Area, 91
Atlanta State Park, 119, 122
Attlesey, Sam, 638
Attorneys
county attorneys, 474-78
district attorneys, 479-84
Attorneys General, 396, 399, 429, 433
Attwater Prairie Chicken Preserve, 85, 89
Auditor, State, 446
Austin, Moses, 35
Austin, Stephen F., 28, 35-36, *36*, 37, 39, 127-28, 129, 130
Austin (city)
airline passengers, 597
Amtrak passengers on/off at, 596
church membership, 525
economy of, 569
fairs/festivals in, 136
Film Office, 496
foreign consulates in, 587-88
Foreign Trade Zone, 586
history of, 44
mayor and city manager, 460
mental health services, 536
military installation in, 491-92
museums, 498-99
newspapers, 560
performing arts organizations, 497
population, 10, 303, 378
profile and map location, **280**
public library, 504
selection of site of, 70
television and radio stations, 560
"Austin Chalk," 63, 600
Austin College, 547, 549
Austin Community College, 549
Austin County
alcohol sales (wet-or-dry status), 472
banks and bank assets, 578
church membership, 529
county and district officials, 474, 479

courts, 437, 473
crime and law enforcement, 540
deaths, 531
federal funds to, 492
general election results (2002), 402
health care, 531
income, 573
map of, *143*
oil and gas production, 605, 607
population, 143, 389
profile of, **143**
tax appraiser, 471
vehicles and highways, 590
weather data, 104
Austin, Lake, 60, 70, 73
Austin State Hospital, 536
Austin State School, 536
Australia, consular office, 587
Austria, consular office, 587
Authors, 503
Automobiles. *See* Motor vehicles
Aviation industry, 566, 597-98
Ayeta, Fray Francisco de, 520-21, 524

**B**

Badgers, 86
Baha'i religion, 526
Bailey, Joseph W., 49
Bailey County
alcohol sales (wet-or-dry status), 472
banks and bank assets, 578
church membership, 529
county and district officials, 474, 479
courts, 437, 473
crime and law enforcement, 540
deaths, 531
federal funds to, 492
general election results (2002), 402
health care, 531
income, 573
map of, *143*
population, 143, 389
profile of, **143**
tax appraiser, 471
vehicles and highways, 590
weather data, 104
Baird
mayor, 460
newspapers, 560
population, 303
profile and map location, **157**
public library, 504
radio station, 560
Balch Springs
map location, *174*
mayor and city manager, 460
population, 174, 303, 378
public library, 504
radio station, 560
Balcones Canyonlands National Wildlife Refuge, 89, *90*
Balcones Fault and Escarpment, 58, *59*, 60, 63, 69, 70
Bald eagles, 121, 127
Ballet, 497-98
Ballinger
mayor and city manager, 460
newspaper, 560
population, 303, 378
profile and map location, **263**
public library, 504
radio stations, 560
Ballinger, Lake, 73
Balmorhea, Lake, 73
Balmorhea State Park, 119, 122
Bandera
mayor and city manager, 460
newspapers, 560
Polish immigrants in, 513
population, 303, 378
profile and map location, **144**
public library, 504
Bandera Bat Cave, 87
Bandera County
alcohol sales (wet-or-dry status), 472
banks and bank assets, 578
church membership, 529
county and district officials, 474, 479
courts, 437, 473
crime and law enforcement, 540
deaths, 531
federal funds to, 492
general election results (2002), 402
health care, 531
income, 573
map of, *144*
oil and gas production, 605, 607
population, 144, 389
profile of, **144**
tax appraiser, 471
vehicles and highways, 590
weather data, 104
Bandera Pass, 126
Bangladesh, consular office, 587
Bangs, Samuel, 555
Banking Commissioner, State, 446
Banks and banking
commercial banks ranked by deposits, 577
by county, 578-80, *579*
credit unions, 582
deposits, assets of banks by county, 578-80, *579*
in early twentieth century, 48
employment in, 576
in Great Depression, 52
national banks, 580-82

number of banks, 10
resources and deposits (1905-2002), 10, 580-82
savings and loan associations, 10, 583
savings banks, 10, 583
Sharpstown scandal, 54
state banks, 580-82
wages in, 576
Bannister Wildlife Management Area, 91
Baptist Church, 525-26, 526, 528
Baradell, Scott L., 556
Barbados, consular office, 587
Barber Examiners, State Board of, 446
Bardwell Lake, 73, 133
Barite, 610
Barker Reservoir, 73, 133
Barley, 625
Barner, Robert W., 556
Barnes, Ben, 54
Barney M. Davis Cooling Reservoir, 73
Bar of Texas, State, 446
Barret, Lyne T., 599
Bartlett Peak, 57
Barton, D. H. R., 538
Barton, Joe, 486
Barton Springs, 60
Barton Warnock Environmental Education Center, 119, 122
Barzynski, Rev. Vincent, 514
Basalt, 610-11
Basin and Range Province, 59, 60-61, 64, 78, 79
Bass, Sam, 127
Bastrop, Baron de, 35
Bastrop (town)
  mayor and city manager, 460
  newspaper, 560
  population, 304, 378
  profile and map location, 144
  public library, 504
  radio stations, 560
Bastrop County
  alcohol sales (wet-or-dry status), 472
  banks and bank assets, 578
  church membership, 529
  county and district officials, 474, 479
  courts, 437, 473
  deaths, 531
  federal funds to, 492
  general election results (2002), 402
  health care, 531
  income, 573
  map of, 144
  oil and gas production, 605, 607
  population, 144, 296, 389
  profile of, 144
  tax appraiser, 471
  vehicles and highways, 590
  weather data, 104
Bastrop, Lake, 74
Bastrop State Park, 119, 122
Bats, 14, 86-87, 126
Battleship Texas State Historic Site, 123, 129
Bay City
  fairs/festivals in, 136
  mayor, 460
  newspaper, 560
  population, 304, 378
  profile and map location, 237
  public library, 504
  radio stations, 560
Baylor, John R., 20
Baylor County
  alcohol sales (wet-or-dry status), 472
  banks and bank assets, 578
  church membership, 529
  county and district officials, 474, 479
  courts, 437, 473
  crime and law enforcement, 540
  deaths, 531
  federal funds to, 492
  general election results (2002), 402
  health care, 531
  income, 573
  map of, 145
  oil and gas production, 605, 607
  population, 145, 389
  profile of, 145
  tax appraiser, 471
  vehicles and highways, 590
  weather data, 104
Baylor Creek Lake, 74
Baylor University, 547, 549
Bayside Resaca Area, 85
Baytown
  mayor and city manager, 460
  newspaper, 560
  population, 304, 378
  profile and map location, 203
  public library, 504
  television and radio stations, 560
Bears, 87
Beaumont
  airline passengers, 597
  fairs/festivals in, 136
  foreign/domestic commerce, 589
  Foreign Trade Zone, 586
  MA, 596
  mayor and city manager, 460
  mental health services, 536
  museums, 499
  newspaper, 560
  population, 304, 378
  prisons in, 444
  profile and map location, 216
  public library, 504
  television and radio stations, 560

tonnage handled by port, 589
Beaver Creek Cavern, 87
Beavers, 87
Becton, Henry P. Jr., 557, 557
Bedford
  mayor and city manager, 460
  population, 304, 378
  profile and map location, 275
  public library, 504
Bee County
  alcohol sales (wet-or-dry status), 472
  banks and bank assets, 578
  church membership, 529
  county and district officials, 474, 479
  courts, 437, 479
  crime and law enforcement, 540
  deaths, 531
  federal funds to, 492
  general election results (2002), 402
  health care, 531
  income, 573
  map of, 145
  oil and gas production, 605, 607
  population, 145, 389
  profile of, 145
  tax appraiser, 471
  vehicles and highways, 590
  weather data, 104
Bee County College, 549
Beeville
  mayor and city manager, 460
  newspaper, 560
  population, 304, 378
  prisons in, 444
  profile and map location, 145
  public library, 504
  radio stations, 560
Belgium, consular office, 587
Belize, consular office, 587
Bell, Chris, 397, 486
Bell, Wayne, 502
Bellaire
  mayor and city manager, 460
  population, 304, 378
  profile and map location, 203
  public library, 504
  radio stations, 560
Bell County
  alcohol sales (wet-or-dry status), 472
  banks and bank assets, 578
  church membership, 529
  county and district officials, 474, 479
  courts, 437, 473
  crime and law enforcement, 540
  deaths, 531
  federal funds to, 492
  general election results (2002), 402
  health care, 531
  income, 573
  map of, 146
  oil and gas production, 605
  population, 146, 223, 389
  profile of, 146
  tax appraiser, 471
  vehicles and highways, 590
  weather data, 104
Bellville
  fairs/festivals in, 136
  mayor, 460
  newspaper, 560
  population, 305, 379
  profile and map location, 143
  public library, 504
Belo, Alfred Horatio, 555
Belo Corporation, 555-59
Belton
  mayor and city manager, 460-61
  newspaper, 560
  population, 305, 379
  profile and map location, 146
  public library, 504
  television and radio stations, 560
Belton Lake, 71, 74, 133
Beltrán, Fray Bernardino, 519, 523
Benavides, Fray Alonso de, 521, 522
Benbrook
  mayor and city manager, 461
  newspaper, 560
  population, 305, 379
  profile and map location, 275
  public library, 504
Benbrook Lake, 71, 74, 133
Benjamin (town), 225, 305, 379, 461
Bentsen, Ken, 397
Bentsen, Lloyd, 53, 413, 495
Bentsen-Rio Grande Valley State Park, 120, 122
Bernsen, David, 396
Beryllium, 611
Bexar County
  alcohol sales (wet-or-dry status), 472
  banks and bank assets, 578
  church membership, 529
  county and district officials, 474, 479
  courts, 437, 473
  crime and law enforcement, 540
  deaths, 531
  federal funds to, 492
  general election results (2002), 402
  health care, 531
  income, 573
  map of, 147
  oil and gas production, 599, 605, 607
  population, 147, 223, 389
  profile of, 146-47
  tax appraiser, 471

vehicles and highways, 590
  weather data, 104
Big Bend, 59, 61, 69
Big Bend National Park, 61, 62, 69, 131
Big Bend Ranch State Park, 120, 122
Big Bend State Park, 152
Big Boggy National Wildlife Refuge, 89
Big Creek Reservoir, 74
Biggers, John, 502
Biggs Field, 183
Big Lake
  mayor and city manager, 461
  newspaper, 560
  population, 305, 379
  profile and map location, 258
  public library, 504
Big Lake Bottom Wildlife Management Area, 91
Big Spring
  fairs/festivals in, 136
  mayor and city administrator, 461
  mental health services, 536
  newspaper, 560
  population, 305, 379
  profile and map location, 210
  public library, 504
  television and radio stations, 560
Big Spring State Hospital, 536
Big Spring State Park, 120, 122
Big Thicket National Preserve, 131
Binford, Lewis R., 538
Bircher, Marca Lee, 502
Birds and birding, 10, 14, 85, 86, 130
Births
  comparative rankings with other states, 11, 535
  by county, 139-295
  international statistics on, 535
  state statistics, 10, 531, 535
Bishop College, 547
Bison, 87, 119, 127
Bittle, Jerry, 638
Bituminous coal, 600
Bivins Lake, 74
Black bean lottery, 41, 128
Black-capped vireos, 121, 127
Black colleges, 547
Black Creek Lake, 133
Black Gap Wildlife Management Area, 91
Black Kettle National Grassland, 83, 133
Blackland Belt, 58, 59, 65, 78-79, 78
Blacks
  as Buffalo Soldiers, 21, 24, 131
  discrimination against and segregation of, 46, 49
  education of, 44, 45, 298
  higher education for, 547
  income statistics, 297
  organizations for, 50
  as politicians, 47, 54
  poverty statistics, 298
  prejudice against black soldiers on frontier, 21-22
  during Reconstruction, 44-45
  religion and, 525
  Republican Party and, 47
  state population statistics, 10
  in Texas Legislature, 54
  Texas Revolution and, 39
  on Texas Supreme Court, 396
  violence against, 45
  voting rights for, 50, 53
  voting statistics, 45, 47
Blake, Robert Bruce, 522
Blanco County
  alcohol sales (wet-or-dry status), 472
  banks and bank assets, 578
  church membership, 529
  county and district officials, 474, 479
  courts, 437
  crime and law enforcement, 540
  deaths, 531
  federal funds to, 492
  general election results (2002), 402
  health care, 531
  income, 573
  map of, 148
  population, 148, 389
  profile of, 148
  tax appraiser, 471
  vehicles and highways, 590
  weather data, 104
Blanco State Park, 120, 122
Blanton, Jack, 502
Blind and Visually Impaired, School for, 446
Blind, Commission for, 446
Blinn College, 549
Blizzard, Daniel J., 556
Blizzards. See Snowfall
Blowout Cave, 87
Bluebonnet (state flower), 10, 14
Blue topaz (state gem), 14
Board of Education. See Education, State Board of
Board of Insurance. See Insurance, State Board of
Boards and commissions, 445-57
Bobcats, 87
Bob Sandlin, Lake, 74, 126
Boca Chica State Park, 120, 122
Boerne
  fairs/festivals in, 136
  mayor and city manager, 461
  newspapers, 560
  population, 307, 379
  profile and map location, 221
  public library, 505
  radio stations, 560
Bolivar Peninsula, 192, 307
Bolivia, consular office, 587
Bonham, Donald L., 638

Bonham
  mayor and city manager, 461
  museum, 499
  newspaper, 560
  population, 307, 379
  prison in, 444
  profile and map location, **185**
  public library, 505
  radio stations, 560
Bonham, Lake, 74
Bonham State Park, 120, 122
Bonilla, Henry, 486
Boone, David S., 556
Boquillas canyon, 61, 69
Borden County
  alcohol sales (wet-or-dry status), 472
  county and district officials, 474, 479
  courts, 437
  crime and law enforcement, 540
  deaths, 531
  federal funds to, 492
  general election results (2002), 402
  health care, 531
  income, 531
  map of, *148*
  oil and gas production, 605, 607
  population, 148, 389
  profile of, **148**
  tax appraiser, 471
  vehicles and highways, 590
  weather data, 104
Borger
  mayor and city manager, 461
  newspaper, 560
  population, 307, 379
  profile and map location, **212**
  public library, 505
  radio stations, 560
Bosque County
  alcohol sales (wet-or-dry status), 472
  banks and bank assets, 578
  county and district officials, 474, 479
  courts, 437
  crime and law enforcement, 540
  deaths, 531
  federal funds to, 492
  general election results (2002), 402
  health care, 531
  income, 573
  map of, *149*
  population, 149, 389
  profile of, **149**
  tax appraiser, 471
  vehicles and highways, 590
  weather data, 104
Boston, 150, 307
Botswana, consular office, 587
Boundary lines of Texas, 57, 69, 70, 71-72
Bouton Lake, 133
Bowers, Elliot, 638
Bowie, James, 38
Bowie County
  alcohol sales (wet-or-dry status), 472
  banks and bank assets, 578
  church membership, 529
  county and district officials, 474, 479
  courts, 437, 473
  crime and law enforcement, 540
  deaths, 531
  federal funds to, 492
  general election results (2002), 402
  health care, 531
  income, 573
  map of, *150*
  oil and gas production, 605, 607
  population, 150, 389
  profile of, **150**
  tax appraiser, 471
  timber production and value in, 82
  vehicles and highways, 590
  weather data, 104
Boykin Springs, 133
Boyles, Sherry, 396
Bracken Cave, 87
Brackettville
  fairs/festivals in, 136
  mayor and city manager, 461
  newspaper, 560
  population, 307, 379
  profile and map location, **224**
  public library, 505
Bradburn, Davis, 27-28
Brady, Kevin, 486
Brady
  mayor and city manager, 461
  newspaper, 560
  population, 307, 379
  profile and map location, **238**
  public library, 505
  radio stations, 560
Brady Creek Reservoir, 74
Brandy Branch Reservoir, 74
Brazil, consular office, 587
Brazilian freetail bats, 126
Brazoria County
  alcohol sales (wet-or-dry status), 472
  banks and bank assets, 578
  church membership, 529
  county and district officials, 474, 479
  courts, 437, 473
  crime and law enforcement, 540
  deaths, 531
  federal funds to, 492
  general election results (2002), 402
  health care, 531

income, 573
map of, *151*
oil and gas production, 605, 607
population, 151, 223, 389
profile of, **151**
tax appraiser, 471
vehicles and highways, 590
weather data, 104
Brazoria National Wildlife Refuge, 89-90
Brazoria Reservoir, 74
Brazos Bend State Park, 120, 122
Brazos County
  alcohol sales (wet-or-dry status), 472
  banks and bank assets, 578
  church membership, 529
  county and district officials, 474, 479
  courts, 437, 473
  crime and law enforcement, 540
  deaths, 531
  educational attainment, 298
  federal funds to, 492
  general election results (2002), 402
  health care, 531
  income, 573
  map of, *152*
  oil and gas production, 605, 607
  population, 152, 223, 389
  profile of, **152**
  tax appraiser, 471
  vehicles and highways, 590
  weather data, 104
Brazos Indian Reservation, 26, *26*
Brazosport, 151, 308
Brazosport College, 549
Brazos River, *69*, 70-71, 97
Brazos River Authority, 71, 446
Brazos Santiago, 44
Brazos Valley Council of Governments, 470
Breadth and length of Texas, 57
Breckenridge
  mayor and city manager, 461
  newspaper, 560
  population, 308, 379
  prison in, 444
  profile and map location, **271**
  public library, 505
  radio station, 560
Brenham
  fairs/festivals in, 136
  mayor and city manager, 461
  mental health services, 536
  newspaper, 560
  population, 308, 379
  profile and map location, **287**
  public library, 505
  radio stations, 560
Brenham State School, 536
Breweries, 128
Brewster County
  alcohol sales (wet-or-dry status), 472
  area of, 153, 460
  church membership, 529
  county and district officials, 474, 479
  courts, 437
  crime and law enforcement, 540
  deaths, 531
  federal funds to, 492
  general election results (2002), 402
  health care, 531
  income, 573
  map of, *153*
  oil and gas production, 605
  population, 153, 389
  profile of, **153**
  tax appraiser, 471
  vehicles and highways, 590
  weather data, 104
Bridgeport, Lake, 74
Bridgeport Reservoir, 71
Brine, 611
Brinkley, David, 638
Briscoe, Dolph, 54, 420-21
Briscoe County
  alcohol sales (wet-or-dry status), 472
  banks and bank assets, 578
  church membership, 529
  county and district officials, 474, 479
  courts, 437
  crime and law enforcement, 540
  deaths, 531
  federal funds to, 492
  general election results (2002), 402
  health care, 531
  income, 573
  map of, *154*
  oil and gas production, 605
  population, 154, 389
  profile of, **154**
  tax appraiser, 471
  vehicles and highways, 590
  weather data, 104
Brooke, George M., 16
Brooks City-Base, *147*, 490
Brooks County
  alcohol sales (wet-or-dry status), 472
  banks and bank assets, 578
  church membership, 529
  county and district officials, 474, 479
  courts, 437, 473
  crime and law enforcement, 540
  deaths, 531
  educational attainment, 298
  federal funds to, 492
  general election results (2002), 402
  health care, 531

income, 574
income statistics, 297
map of, *154*
oil and gas production, 605, 607
population, 154, 389
poverty rates, 298
profile of, **154**
tax appraiser, 471
vehicles and highways, 590
weather data, 104
Brown, Caro, 638
Brown, Colleen B., 556
Brown, David, 638
Brown County
  alcohol sales (wet-or-dry status), 472
  banks and bank assets, 578
  church membership, 529
  county and district officials, 474, 479
  courts, 437, 473
  crime and law enforcement, 540
  deaths, 531
  federal funds to, 492
  general election results (2002), 402
  health care, 531
  income, 574
  map of, *155*
  oil and gas production, 605, 607
  population, 155, 389
  profile of, **155**
  tax appraiser, 471
  vehicles and highways, 590
  weather data, 104
Brownfield
  mayor and city manager, 461
  newspaper, 560
  population, 308, 379
  prison in, 444
  profile and map location, **277**
  public library, 505
Brownsville
  airline passengers, 597
  birding center, 130
  fairs/festivals in, 136
  foreign/domestic commerce, 589
  Foreign Trade Zone, 586
  mayor and city manager, 461
  Mexican consulate in, 588
  newspaper, 560
  in nineteenth century, 23
  population, 308, 379
  profile and map location, **158**
  public library, 505
  television and radio stations, 560
  tonnage handled by port, 589
Brownwood
  airline passengers, 597
  mayor and city manager, 461
  mental health services, 536
  newspaper, 560
  population, 308, 379
  prison in, 443
  profile and map location, **155**
  public library, 505
  television and radio stations, 560
Brownwood, Lake, 74, 126
Bruseth, James, 29
Brush Country, 59
Bryan, William Jennings, 47, 411
Bryan
  Amtrak passengers on/off at, 596
  mayor and city manager, 461
  mental health services, 536
  museum, 499
  newspaper, 560
  population, 308, 379
  profile and map location, **152**
  public library, 505
  television and radio stations, 560
Bryant, Janice E., 556
Bryan Utilities Lake, 74
Buchanan, James P., 52
Buchanan Dam, **233**
Buchanan, Lake, 60, 70, 74
Buchel County, 389
Buddhism, 526
Buescher State Park, 120, 122
Buffalo, 21
Buffalo Bayou, 71
Buffalo Lake, 74
Buffalo Lake National Wildlife Refuge, 90
Buffalo Soldiers, 21, 24, 131
Buffalo Springs Lake, 74
Building stone, 611
Burgess, Michael, 397, 486
Burglary, 539-43
Burleson (city)
  mayor and city manager, 461
  newspaper, 560
  population, 308, 379
  profile and map location, **218**
  public library, 505
Burleson County
  alcohol sales (wet-or-dry status), 472
  banks and bank assets, 578
  church membership, 529
  county and district officials, 474, 479
  courts, 437, 473
  crime and law enforcement, 540
  deaths, 531
  federal funds to, 492
  general election results (2002), 402
  health care, 531
  income, 574
  map of, *155*
  oil and gas production, 605, 607

**For CITIES and TOWNS not listed in the index, see complete list of towns on pages 300–377.**

population, 155, 389
profile of, **155**
tax appraiser, 471
vehicles and highways, 590
weather data, 104
Burnet, David, 39
Burnet (city)
  mayor and city manager, 461
  newspapers, 560
  population, 309, 379
  prison in, 443
  profile and map location, **156**
  public library, 505
  radio stations, 560
Burnet County
  alcohol sales (wet-or-dry status), 472
  banks and bank assets, 578
  church membership, 529
  county and district officials, 474, 479
  courts, 437, 473
  crime and law enforcement, 540
  deaths, 531
  federal funds to, 492
  general election results (2002), 402
  health care, 531
  income, 574
  map of, *156*
  population, 156, 389
  profile of, **156**
  tax appraiser, 471
  vehicles and highways, 590
  weather data, 104
Burnett, Warren, 638
Bush, George, 412, 413
Bush, George W., 395, 397, 413, 421, *421*, 495, 502
Bush Mountain, 72
Business. *See also* Economy
  comparative rankings with other states, 11
  Dun & Bradstreet ratings for, 300-377
  frontier posts and, 25
  retail sales by county, 139-295
  state data, 10
Bustamante, Anastasio, 28, 36
Butler College, 547
Butterfly (state insect), 14

**C**
Cabal, Fray Juan, 520, 524
Cabeza de Vaca, Alvar Núñez, 31, 69-70
Caddoan Mounds State Historic Site, 120, 122
Caddo Confederacy, 32, 34
Caddo Lake, 72, 74, 77
Caddo Lake State Park, 91, 120, 122
Caddo National Grasslands, 83, 91
Calaveras Lake, 74
Caldera, Louis E., 557, *557*
Caldwell (city)
  mayor and city administrator, 461
  newspaper, 560
  population, 310, 379
  profile and map location, **155**
  public library, 505
Caldwell County
  alcohol sales (wet-or-dry status), 472
  banks and bank assets, 578
  church membership, 529
  county and district officials, 474, 479
  courts, 437, 473
  crime and law enforcement, 540
  deaths, 531
  federal funds to, 492
  general election results (2002), 402
  health care, 531
  income, 574
  map of, *156*
  oil and gas production, 605, 607
  population, 156, 389
  profile of, **156**
  tax appraiser, 471
  vehicles and highways, 590
  weather data, 104
Calendar (1894-2094), 118
Calhoun County
  alcohol sales (wet-or-dry status), 472
  banks and bank assets, 578
  church membership, 529
  county and district officials, 474, 479
  courts, 437, 473
  crime and law enforcement, 540
  deaths, 531
  federal funds to, 492
  Foreign Trade Zone, 586
  general election results (2002), 402
  health care, 531
  income, 574
  map of, *157*
  oil and gas production, 605, 607
  population, 157, 389
  profile of, **157**
  tax appraiser, 471
  vehicles and highways, 590
  weather data, 104
Callahan County
  alcohol sales (wet-or-dry status), 472
  banks and bank assets, 578
  church membership, 529
  county and district officials, 474, 479
  courts, 437
  crime and law enforcement, 540
  deaths, 531
  federal funds to, 492
  general election results (2002), 402
  health care, 531
  income, 574
  map of, *157*

oil and gas production, 605, 607
population, 157, 389
profile of, **157**
tax appraiser, 471
vehicles and highways, 590
weather data, 104
Cameron (town)
  mayor and city manager, 461
  newspaper, 560
  population, 310, 379
  profile and map location, **242**
  public library, 505
  radio stations, 560
Cameron County
  alcohol sales (wet-or-dry status), 472
  banks and bank assets, 578
  church membership, 529
  county and district officials, 474, 479
  courts, 437, 473
  crime and law enforcement, 540
  deaths, 531
  federal funds to, 492
  general election results (2002), 402
  health care, 531
  income, 574
  map of, *158*
  oil and gas production, 605, 607
  population, 158, 223, 389
  profile of, **158**
  tax appraiser, 471
  vehicles and highways, 590
  weather data, 104
Cameroon, consular office, 587
Campbell, Thomas M., 48, 418
Camp Cooper, 26, *26*
Camp County
  alcohol sales (wet-or-dry status), 472
  banks and bank assets, 578
  church membership, 529
  county and district officials, 474, 479
  courts, 437, 473
  crime and law enforcement, 540
  deaths, 531
  federal funds to, 492
  general election results (2002), 402
  health care, 531
  income, 574
  map of, *159*
  oil and gas production, 605, 607
  population, 159, 389
  profile of, **159**
  tax appraiser, 471
  timber production and value in, 82
  vehicles and highways, 590
  weather data, 104
Camp Creek Lake, 74
Camp Ford, 44
Camp Mabry, 491-92
Camp Rice, 20
Canada, consular office, 587
Canadian
  mayor and city manager, 461
  newspaper, 560
  population, 310, 379
  profile and map location, **206**
  public library, 505
Canadian River, *69*, 72, *72*
Canadian River Compact Commissioner, 446
Canales, J. T., 49
Canary Islanders, 34
Cancer, 531-35
Cancer Council, 446
Candy Abshier Wildlife Management Area, 91
Caney Creek, 133
Canton
  mayor and city manager, 461
  newspapers, 560
  population, 310, 379
  profile and map location, **284**
  public library, 505
  radio stations, 560
Canyon
  fairs/festivals in, 136
  mayor and city manager, 461
  museum, 499
  newspaper, 560
  performing arts organization, 497
  population, 310, 379
  profile and map location, **258**
  public library, 505
  radio stations, 560-61
Canyon Lake, 70, 74, 133
Capital Area Planning Council, 470
Caprock Escarpment, 59, *59*, 60, 63, 72
Carpenter, Stephen, 19
Carranza, Venustiano, 48
Carr, Billie, 638
Carrizo Springs
  mayor and city manager, 461
  newspaper, 561
  population, 311, 379
  profile and map location, **179**
  public library, 505
  radio stations, 561
Carrizo-Wilcox aquifer, *67*, 68
Carrollton, 174, 311, 379, 461, 505
Carson County
  alcohol sales (wet-or-dry status), 472
  banks and bank assets, 578
  church membership, 529
  county and district officials, 474, 479
  courts, 437, 473
  crime and law enforcement, 540
  deaths, 531
  federal funds to, 492

general election results (2002), 402
health care, 531
income, 574
map of, *159*
oil and gas production, 605, 607
population, 159, 389
profile of, **159**
tax appraiser, 471
vehicles and highways, 590
weather data, 104
Carswell Field, 491
Carter, Jimmy, 55, 412, 413
Carter, John, 397
Carter, John R., 486
Carter, Robert G., 23
Carthage
  mayor and city manager, 461
  museum, 499
  newspaper, 561
  population, 311, 379
  profile and map location, **253**
  public library, 505
  radio stations, 561
"Cart war," 42
Casa Blanca Lake, 74
Casa Blanca, Lake, 126
Casa Navarro State Historic Site, 120, 122
Cass County
  alcohol sales (wet-or-dry status), 472
  banks and bank assets, 578
  church membership, 529
  county and district officials, 474, 479
  courts, 437, 473
  crime and law enforcement, 540
  deaths, 531
  federal funds to, 492
  general election results (2002), 402
  health care, 531
  income, 574
  map of, *160*
  oil and gas production, 605, 607
  population, 160, 389
  profile of, **160**
  tax appraiser, 471
  timber production and value in, 82
  vehicles and highways, 590
  weather data, 104
Cass, Donald F. (Skip) Jr., 556
Castañeda, Carlos E., 522
Castro County
  alcohol sales (wet-or-dry status), 472
  banks and bank assets, 578
  church membership, 529
  county and district officials, 474, 479
  courts, 437, 473
  crime and law enforcement, 540
  deaths, 531
  federal funds to, 492
  general election results (2002), 402
  health care, 531
  income, 574
  map of, *160*
  population, 160, 389
  profile of, **160**
  tax appraiser, 471
  vehicles and highways, 590
  weather data, 104
Cat family, 87
Catfish Creek, 85
Catholicism, 514, 517-24, 525-26, *528*
Cattle
  beef cattle production, 629, 631
  dairy industry, 631-32
  grazing of, in national forests, 84
  longhorn cattle, 14, 119, 121, 124, 126, 128
  on Matagorda Island, *250*
  statistics, 35
Caverns of Sonora, 85
Caves, 85, 86-87
Cedar Bayou Coiling Reservoir, 74
Cedar Creek Islands Wildlife Management Area, 91
Cedar Creek Reservoir, 71, 74
Cedar Hill
  mayor and city manager, 461
  newspapers, 561
  population, 311, 379
  profile and map location, **174-75**
  public library, 505
Cedar Hill State Park, 120-21, 122
Cedar Park, 291, 311, 379, 461, 505
Cement, 610, 611
Cenozoic Era, 63
Cenozoic Pecos Alluvium aquifer, *67*, 68
Center
  mayor and city manager, 461
  newspapers, 561
  population, 312, 379
  profile and map location, **268**
  public library, 505
  radio stations, 561
Centerville
  mayor and city administrator, 461
  newspaper, 561
  population, 312, 379
  profile and map location, **229**
  public library, 505
  radio station, 561
Central Basin soils, 64
Central Colorado River Authority, 70, 447
Central Mineral Region, 60
Central Rio Grande Plain soils, 65
Central Texas Council of Governments, 470
Cerebrovascular disease, 531-35
Chambers County
  alcohol sales (wet-or-dry status), 472

banks and bank assets, 578
church membership, 529
county and district officials, 474, 479
courts, 437, 473
crime and law enforcement, 540
deaths, 531
federal funds to, 492
Fort Anahuac in, 27-29, *27*, 29
general election results (2002), 402
health care, 531
income, 574
map of, *161*
oil and gas production, 605, 607
population, 161, 389
profile of, **161**
tax appraiser, 471
timber production and value in, 82
vehicles and highways, 590
weather data, 104
Chamizal National Memorial, 131, *131*
Champion Creek Reservoir, 74
Chamuscado, Francisco Sánchez, 32
Channing, 204, 312, 379, 461
Chaparral Wildlife Management Area, 91
Chapman, Helen, 23, 24
Chapman, Ron, 397
Chappell Hill Male and Female Institute, 547
Charles III, King of Spain, 34-35
Charles IV, King of Spain, 35
Charter schools, 546
Chawla, Kalpana, 638
Chemist, Office of State, 446
Cheney, Dick, 395
Cherokee County
  alcohol sales (wet-or-dry status), 472
  banks and bank assets, 578
  church membership, 529
  county and district officials, 474, 479
  courts, 437, 473
  crime and law enforcement, 540
  deaths, 531
  federal funds to, 492
  general election results (2002), 402
  health care, 531
  income, 574
  map of, *162*
  oil and gas production, 605, 607
  population, 162, 389
  profile of, **162**
  tax appraiser, 471
  timber production and value in, 82
  vehicles and highways, 590
  weather data, 105
Cherokee, Lake, 74
Cherokees, 35, 40
Cherry, Wilbur F., 555
Chicot aquifer, 67
Chihuahuan Desert, 125, 132, *133*
Childhood Intervention, Interagency Council on
  Early, 446
Child, Julia, 495
Child labor, 47
Children's Trust Fund of Texas Council, 446
Childress (city)
  mayor and city manager, 461
  newspaper, 561
  population, 312, 379
  prison in, 444
  profile and map location, **162**
  public library, 505
  radio station, 561
Childress County
  alcohol sales (wet-or-dry status), 472
  banks and bank assets, 578
  church membership, 529
  county and district officials, 474, 479
  courts, 437
  crime and law enforcement, 540
  deaths, 531
  federal funds to, 492
  general election results (2002), 402
  health care, 531
  income, 574
  map of, *162*
  oil and gas production, 605, 607
  population, 162, 389
  profile of, **162**
  tax appraiser, 471
  vehicles and highways, 590
  weather data, 105
Chile, consular offices, 587
Chili (state dish), 14
Chiltepin (state pepper), 14
China
  consular office, 587
  immigrants from, 10
Chipman, Donald E., 522
Chipmunks, 87
Chiropractic Examiners, Board of, 446
Chisos Mountains, 61, 69
Choke Canyon Reservoir, 70, 74
Choke Canyon State Park, 121, 122
Cholette, Kathleen A., 556
Christian, George, 638
Christianity. *See* Religion; and specific churches
Chromium, 611
Chronological eras and cycles, 111
Chuckwagons, *49*
Churches. *See* Religion; and specific religions and
  churches
Churches of Christ (Disciples of Christ), 526
Cibolo Creek, 70
Cisco, Lake, 74
Cisneros, Jose, 502
Cisneros, Sandra, 502

Cities and towns
  Consolidated Metropolitan Statistical Areas
    (CMSAs), 399
  by county, 139-295
  economy of large metropolitan areas, 569-73, 576
  highest town, 57
  home-rule cities, 460-68
  largest cities, 10
  map of Metropolitan Statistical Areas (MSAs), *299*
  mayors and city managers, 460-68
  newspapers, 560-65
  number of, 10, 460
  population (1850-2000), 378-88
  population (2000 and 2002), 299-377
  population in urban areas generally, 49, 52, 55
  post offices in, 300-377
  Primary Metropolitan Statistical Areas (PMSAs),
    299
  prisons in, 443-44
  public libraries, 504-11
  television and radio stations, 560-65
City governments. *See* Local governments
City managers, 460-68
Civil War, 20, 26, 43-44, 513
Clarendon
  mayor and city administrator, 461
  museum, 499
  newspaper, 561
  population, 313, 380
  profile and map location, **179**
  public library, 505
Clarendon College, 549
Clark, Edward, 43, 417
Clark, George, 47
Clark, Laurel, 638
Clarksville
  mayor and city manager, 461
  newspaper, 561
  population, 313, 380
  profile and map location, 259
  public library, 505
  radio stations, 561
Claude
  mayor, 461
  newspaper, 561
  population, 313, 380
  profile and map location, **142**
  public library, 505
  radio station, 561
Clay County
  alcohol sales (wet-or-dry status), 472
  banks and bank assets, 578
  church membership, 529
  county and district officials, 474, 479
  courts, 437
  crime and law enforcement, 540
  deaths, 531
  federal funds to, 492
  general election results (2002), 402
  health care, 531
  income, 574
  map of, *163*
  oil and gas production, 605, 607
  population, 163, 389
  profile of, **163**
  tax appraiser, 471
  vehicles and highways, 590
  weather data, 105
Claypan Area soils, 65
Clays, 610, 611
Clear Fork, 70
Clear Lake Area, profile and map location, **203**
Cleburne
  Amtrak passengers on/off at, 596
  mayor and city manager, 461
  mental health services, 536
  newspaper, 561
  population, 313, 380
  profile and map location, **218**
  public library, 505
  radio station, 561
Cleburne, Lake Pat, 74
Cleburne State Park, 121, 122
Clements, William P., 55, 395, 421
Clements, W. W. "Foots," 638
Cliburn, Van, 495, *495*, 502
Climate. *See* Precipitation; Temperature; Weather
Clinoptilolite, 616
Clinton, Bill, 22, 412, 413
Clyde, Lake, 74
Coahuila y Texas legislature, 37
Coal production, 600, 611-12
Coastal Bend College, 549
Coastal Bend Council of Governments, 470
Coastal Birding Trail, 130, *130*
Coastal Plains, 58, *59*, 66
Coastal Water Authority, Board of Directors, 446
Coast Prairie soils, 66
Coast Saline Prairies soils, 66
Coatis, 87
Cochran County
  alcohol sales (wet-or-dry status), 472
  church membership, 529
  county and district officials, 474, 480
  courts, 437, 473
  crime and law enforcement, 540
  deaths, 531
  federal funds to, 492
  general election results (2002), 402
  health care, 531
  income, 574
  map of, *163*
  oil and gas production, 605, 607
  population, 163, 296, 389
  profile of, **163**

tax appraiser, 471
vehicles and highways, 590
weather data, 105
Coffee Mill Lake, 74
Coffee Mill Lake Recreation Area, 133
Coke, Richard, 45, 46, 417
Coke County
  alcohol sales (wet-or-dry status), 472
  banks and bank assets, 578
  church membership, 529
  county and district officials, 474, 480
  courts, 437, 473
  crime and law enforcement, 540
  deaths, 532
  federal funds to, 492
  general election results (2002), 402
  health care, 532
  income, 574
  map of, *164*
  oil and gas production, 605, 607
  population, 164, 389
  profile of, **164**
  tax appraiser, 471
  vehicles and highways, 590
  weather data, 105
Cold. *See* Ice storms; Snowfall; Temperature
Coldspring, 265, 314, 380, 461, 505
Coleman (city)
  mayor and city manager, 461
  newspaper, 561
  population, 314, 380
  profile and map location, **164**
  public library, 505
  radio stations, 561
Coleman County
  alcohol sales (wet-or-dry status), 472
  banks and bank assets, 578
  church membership, 529
  county and district officials, 474, 480
  courts, 437
  crime and law enforcement, 540
  deaths, 532
  federal funds to, 492
  general election results (2002), 402
  health care, 532
  income, 574
  map of, *164*
  oil and gas production, 605, 607
  population, 164, 389
  profile of, **164**
  tax appraiser, 471
  vehicles and highways, 590
  weather data, 105
Coleman, Lake, 74
Coles, Robert, 502
Coleto Creek Reservoir, 74
Colina, Fray Agustín de, 521
College of St. Thomas More, 549
College Opportunity Act Committee, 446-47
Colleges. *See* Higher education; specific colleges
College Station
  airline passengers, 597
  Amtrak passengers on/off at, 596
  mayor and city manager, 461
  mental health services, 536
  museums, 499
  newspaper, 561
  population, 314, 380
  profile and map location, **152**
  television and radio stations, 561
Colleyville, 275, 314, 380, 461
Collin County
  alcohol sales (wet-or-dry status), 472
  banks and bank assets, 578
  church membership, 529
  county and district officials, 474, 480
  courts, 437, 473
  crime and law enforcement, 540
  deaths, 532
  educational attainment, 298
  federal funds to, 492
  general election results (2002), 402
  health care, 532
  income, 574
  income statistics, 297
  map of, *165*
  oil and gas production, 605
  population, 165, 223, 296, 389
  poverty rates, 298
  profile of, **165**
  tax appraiser, 471
  vehicles and highways, 591
  weather data, 105
Collingsworth County
  alcohol sales (wet-or-dry status), 472
  banks and bank assets, 578
  church membership, 529
  county and district officials, 474, 480
  courts, 437, 473
  crime and law enforcement, 540
  deaths, 532
  federal funds to, 492
  general election results (2002), 402
  health care, 532
  income, 574
  map of, *166*
  oil and gas production, 605, 607
  population, 166, 390
  profile of, **166**
  tax appraiser, 471
  vehicles and highways, 591
  weather data, 105
Colombia, consular office, 587
Colorado Bend State Park, 121, 122
Colorado City

mayor and city manager, 461
newspaper, 561
population, 314, 380
prisons in, 444
profile and map location, **243**
public library, 505
radio stations, 561
Colorado City, Lake, 74, 126
Colorado County
  alcohol sales (wet-or-dry status), 472
  banks and bank assets, 578
  church membership, 529
  county and district officials, 474, 480
  courts, 437, 473
  crime and law enforcement, 540
  deaths, 532
  federal funds to, 492
  general election results (2002), 402
  health care, 532
  income, 574
  map of, *166*
  oil and gas production, 605, 607
  population, 166, 390
  profile of, **166**
  tax appraiser, 471
  vehicles and highways, 591
  weather data, 105
Colorado River, *69*, 70, 518, 589
Colorado River Authority, 70, 447
Colquitt, Oscar B., 48, 51, 418
Columbia Astronauts, 638
Columbus, Christopher, 31
Columbus
  fairs/festivals in, 136
  mayor and city manager, 461
  newspapers, 561
  population, 314, 380
  profile and map location, **166**
  public library, 505
  radio station, 561
Comal County
  alcohol sales (wet-or-dry status), 472
  banks and bank assets, 578
  church membership, 529
  county and district officials, 474, 480
  courts, 437, 473
  crime and law enforcement, 540
  deaths, 532
  federal funds to, 492
  general election results (2002), 402
  health care, 532
  income, 574
  map of, *167*
  population, 167, 390
  profile of, **167**
  tax appraiser, 471
  vehicles and highways, 591
  weather data, 105
Comal River, 70
Comal Springs, 60
Comanche (city)
  mayor, 461
  newspaper, 561
  population, 314, 380
  profile and map location, **168**
  public library, 505
  radio stations, 561
Comanche County
  alcohol sales (wet-or-dry status), 472
  banks and bank assets, 578
  church membership, 529
  county and district officials, 474, 480
  courts, 437
  crime and law enforcement, 540
  deaths, 532
  federal funds to, 492
  general election results (2002), 402
  health care, 532
  income, 574
  map of, *168*
  oil and gas production, 605, 607
  population, 168, 390
  profile of, **168**
  tax appraiser, 471
  vehicles and highways, 591
  weather data, 105
Comanche Indian Reservation, 26, *26*
Combs, Susan, 396
Commissioners courts, 460
Commission form of local government, 47, 468-69
Commissions and boards, 445-57
Community colleges, 55, 549-54
Community mental health and mental retardation
  centers, 536-37
Compaq Computer Corporation, 566
Compromise of 1850, 42, *42*
Comptroller of Public Accounts, 396, 399, 430, 433
Computer industry, 566, 576
Concho County
  alcohol sales (wet-or-dry status), 472
  banks and bank assets, 578
  church membership, 529
  county and district officials, 475, 480
  courts, 437, 473
  crime and law enforcement, 540
  deaths, 532
  federal funds to, 492
  general election results (2002), 402
  health care, 532
  income, 574
  map of, *168*
  oil and gas production, 605, 607
  population, 168, 297, 390
  profile of, **168**
  tax appraiser, 471

vehicles and highways, 591
  weather data, 105
Concho River, 70, 518
Concho River Water and Soil Conservation
  Authority, 447
Concho Valley Council of Governments, 470
Concordia University, 549
Confederacy. See Civil War
Confederate Air Force, 14
Confederate flag, *12*
Confederate Reunion Grounds State Historic Site,
  121, 122
Congressional districts map, *487*
Congress, U.S.
  contact information for current lawmakers, 486-88
  current members of House of Representatives,
    486-88
  current members of Senate, 486
  elections of U.S. Senators from Texas (1906-
    2002), 399, 402-7, 414-17
  list of U.S. Senators from Texas (1846-2003),
    430-31
  map of congressional districts, *487*
  number of Texas members in, 486
  retirements from, 397
  2002 elections, 397, 399-400, 402-409
Connally, John B., 53, 54, 398, 420
Connally, Merrill L. Sr., 638
Connally, Tom, 51
Conroe
  fairs/festivals in, 136
  mayor and city administrator, 461
  mental health services, 536
  newspaper, 561
  performing arts organization, 497
  population, 314, 380
  profile and map location, **244**
  public library, 505
  radio stations, 561
Conroe, Lake, 71, 74
Conservation Passport for state parks, 119
Conservation. See Environment; soil conservation
Conservatorship Board, 447
Consolidated Metropolitan Statistical Areas
  (CMSAs), 399
Constitution of Texas, 10, 41, 45-46, 55, **425-26**,
  544-45
Construction industry, 566, 568, 576, 585
Consulates, 587-88
Consumer Credit Commissioner, 447
Cooke County
  alcohol sales (wet-or-dry status), 472
  banks and bank assets, 578
  church membership, 529
  county and district officials, 475, 480
  courts, 437, 473
  crime and law enforcement, 540
  deaths, 532
  federal funds to, 492
  general election results (2002), 402
  health care, 532
  income, 574
  map of, *169*
  oil and gas production, 605, 607
  population, 169, 390
  profile of, **169**
  tax appraiser, 471
  vehicles and highways, 591
  weather data, 105
Cooper
  mayor, 461
  newspaper, 561
  population, 315, 380
  profile and map location, **176**
  public library, 505
Cooper, Lake, 74, 133
Cooper Wildlife Management Area, 91
Copano Bay State Fishing Pier, 121, 122
Coppell, 175, 315, 380, 461-62, 505
Copper, 612
Copperas Cove
  mayor and city manager, 462
  newspaper, 561
  population, 315, 380
  profile and map location, **169**
  public library, 505
  radio station, 561
Copper Breaks State Park, 121, 122
Copperhead snakes, 89
Copper Lake State Park, 121, 122
Coral snakes, 89
Córdoba, France A., 557, *557*
Corn, 621, 624-25
Cornyn, John, 395, *396*, 397, 399, 402-7, 405, 486
Coronado, Francisco Vázquez de, 32, 70, 518-19,
  523
Corps of Engineers, 73, 133
Corpus Christi
  airline passengers, 597
  fairs/festivals in, 136
  foreign consulates in, 587, 588
  foreign/domestic commerce, 589
  Foreign Trade Zone, 586
  mayor and city manager, 462
  mental health services, 536
  military installation near, 491
  museums, 499
  newspapers, 561
  performing arts organizations, 497
  population, 10, 299, 315, 380
  profile and map location, **250**
  public library, 505
  surfing near, *227*
  television and radio stations, 561
  tonnage handled by port, 589

Corpus Christi, Lake, 70, 74, 126
Corpus Christi State School, 536
Correctional facilities, 443-44
Corsicana
  Amtrak passengers on/off at, 596
  mayor and city manager, 462
  newspaper, 561
  oil and gas production, 599
  population, 315, 380
  profile and map location, **248**
  public library, 505
  radio stations, 561
Cortina, Juan, 28
Coryell County
  alcohol sales (wet-or-dry status), 472
  banks and bank assets, 578
  church membership, 529
  county and district officials, 475, 480
  courts, 437, 473
  crime and law enforcement, 540
  deaths, 532
  federal funds to, 492
  general election results (2002), 402
  health care, 532
  income, 574
  map of, *169*
  oil and gas production, 605
  population, 169, 390
  profile of, **169**
  tax appraiser, 471
  vehicles and highways, 591
  weather data, 105
Cos, Martín Perfecto de, 37, 38, 39
Cosmetology Commission, 447
Costa Rica, consular offices, 587
Cottle County
  alcohol sales (wet-or-dry status), 472
  banks and bank assets, 578
  church membership, 529
  county and district officials, 475, 480
  courts, 437
  crime and law enforcement, 540
  deaths, 532
  federal funds to, 492
  general election results (2002), 402
  health care, 532
  income, 574
  map of, *170*
  oil and gas production, 605, 607
  population, 170, 296, 390
  profile of, **170**
  tax appraiser, 471
  vehicles and highways, 591
  weather data, 105
Cotton
  acreage limitation, 51
  exports, 622, 623
  nineteenth-century production of, 37, 42, 43, 46
  production (2002), 621, **623-24**
  as state fiber and fabric, 14
  twentieth-century production of, 51
  value of cotton and cottonseed (1900-2002), 623
Cottonmouth snakes, 89
Cottonwood Lake, 133
Cotulla, Joseph, 513
Cotulla
  mayor and city administrator, 462
  museum, 499
  population, 315, 380
  prison in, 444
  profile and map location, **228**
  public library, 505
Cougars, 87
Council-manager form of local government, 47, 469
Counselors, Board of Examiners of Professional,
  447
Counties, **139-295**. *See also* specific counties
  abortions, 531-35
  agriculture, 139-295
  alcohol sales (wet-or-dry status), 472, *472*
  altitude of, 139
  area of, 139-295, 460
  banks and bank assets, 578-80, *579*
  births, 139-295
  centers of population (1850-2000), *377*
  churches, church membership, *528*, 529-30, *530*
  cities and towns by, 139-295
  commissioners courts, 460
  county and district officials, 474-84
  county courts, 473
  county seats, 474-78
  courts, 437-38, 473
  crimes, 540-43
  deaths and causes of death, 139-295, 531-35
  economy, 139-295
  employment and unemployment, 139-295
  federal funds to, 492-94
  freeze dates by, 104-9
  growing season by, 104-9
  highways, 590-93
  history, 138-295
  hospital beds, 531-35
  income, 573-75
  largest/smallest counties by population, 223, 460
  law enforcement, 540-43
  maps of, *139-295*
  marriages and divorces, 139-295
  minerals, 139-295
  motor vehicles registered, 590-93
  number of, 10, 460
  oil and gas production, 605-9, *606*
  physical features, 139-295
  physicians, 531-35
  population (1850-2000), *377*, 389-94
  population change rate, 296-297

**For CITIES and TOWNS not listed in the index, see complete list of towns on pages 300–377.**

population in 2002, 139-295
population, fastest growing/declining counties, 296
precipitation by, 104-9, 139-295
pregnancy rate, 531-35
prisons in, 443-44
property value, 139-295
race/ethnicity statistics, 138-295
recreation, 139-295
regional councils of government in, 470
retail sales, 139-295
tax appraisers, 471-72
temperature by, 104-9
timber production and value by, 82
2002 elections, 396
2002 general election results by, 402-6, *404, 405*
vehicle registration fees, 590-93
wages, 139-295
weather data by, 104-9, 139-295
County and District officials, 474-84
County and District Retiremen System, 455
County assessor-collectors, 474-78
County attorneys, 474-78
County clerks, 474-78
County commissioners, 479-84
County commissioners courts, 460
County courts, 473
County governments. *See* Local governments
County judges, 474-78
County seats, 474-78
County tax appraisers, 471-72
County treasurers, 474-78
Court of Criminal Appeals, 399, 407, 408, 409, 432, 435
Court Reporters Certification Board, 447
Courts of Appeals, 401, 407, 409, 435-38
Courts. *See* Judiciary; Supreme Court, Texas
Covered wagons, *50*
Cox, John L., 638
Cox Creek Reservoir, 74
Coyotes, 87
Crabs, 134
Craddick, Tom, 395-96, 398
Crane (town)
    mayor and city administrator, 462
    newspaper, 561
    population, 316, 380
    profile and map location, **170**
    public library, 505
    radio stations, 561
Crane County
    alcohol sales (wet-or-dry status), 472
    church membership, 529
    county and district officials, 475, 480
    courts, 437
    crime and law enforcement, 540
    deaths, 532
    federal funds to, 492
    general election results (2002), 402
    health care, 532
    income, 574
    map of, *170*
    oil and gas production, 605, 607
    population, 170, 390
    profile of, **170**
    tax appraiser, 471
    vehicles and highways, 591
    weather data, 105
Crape myrtle (state shrub), 14
Craven, Judith L., 557, *557*
Credit Union Administration, National, 582
Credit Union Commission, 447
Credit Union Department, 582
Credit Union League, 582
Credit unions, 582
Cretaceous rocks, 62
Crime, **539-43**
    comparative ranking with other states, 543
    by counties, 540-43
    types of (1981-2002), 539
Crime Stopper Advisory Council, 447
Criminal district court judges, 440
Criminal Justice, Board of, 443, 447
Criminal Justice, Department of, 443-44
Criminal Justice Policy Council, 447
Criswell, Rev. W. A., 638, *640*
Crock Canyons State Park, 120, 122
Crockett, David, 38, 119
Crockett, Elizabeth, 119
Crockett (town), 210, 316, 380, 462, 506
Crockett County
    alcohol sales (wet-or-dry status), 472
    banks and bank assets, 578
    church membership, 529
    county and district officials, 475, 480
    courts, 437
    crime and law enforcement, 540
    deaths, 532
    federal funds to, 492
    general election results (2002), 402
    health care, 532
    income, 574
    map of, *171*
    oil and gas production, 605, 607
    population, 171, 296, 390
    profile of, **171**
    tax appraiser, 471
    vehicles and highways, 591
    weather data, 105
Cronican, Michael, 555
Crook, Lake, 74
Crosby County
    alcohol sales (wet-or-dry status), 472
    banks and bank assets, 578
    church membership, 529
    county and district officials, 475, 480

courts, 437
crime and law enforcement, 540
deaths, 532
federal funds to, 492
general election results (2002), 402
health care, 532
income, 574
map of, *171*
oil and gas production, 605, 607
population, 171, 390
profile of, **171**
tax appraiser, 471
vehicles and highways, 591
weather data, 105
Crosbyton
    mayor and city manager, 462
    newspaper, 561
    population, 316, 380
    profile and map location, **171**
    public library, 506
Cross Timbers region. *See* Eastern and Western
    Cross Timbers
Crowell, 187, 316, 380, 462, 506, 561
Crowed stone, 610, 612
Crustaceans, endangered, 85
Crystal City
    mayor, 462
    newspaper, 561
    population, 316, 380
    profile and map location, **295**
    public library, 506
    radio station, 561
Cuero
    mayor and city manager, 462
    newspaper, 561
    population, 316, 380
    prison in, 444
    profile and map location, **178**
    public library, 506
    radio station, 561
Culberson, John Abney, 486
Culberson County
    alcohol sales (wet-or-dry status), 472
    banks and bank assets, 578
    church membership, 529
    county and district officials, 475, 480
    courts, 437
    crime and law enforcement, 540
    deaths, 532
    federal funds to, 492
    general election results (2002), 402
    health care, 532
    income, 574
    map of, *172*
    oil and gas production, 605, 607
    population, 172, 390
    profile of, **172**
    tax appraiser, 471
    vehicles and highways, 591
    weather data, 105
Cultural Trust Council, 502
Culture. *See* Arts and culture
Cuney, Norris Wright, 47, *47*
Custer, George Armstrong, 21
Cypress Creek, 72
Cypress Springs, Lake, 74
Cyprus, consular office, 587
Czech Republic, consular offices, 587

**D**

Daingerfield
    mayor and city manager, 462
    newspaper, 561
    population, 317, 380
    profile and map location, **245**
    public library, 506
    radio station, 561
Daingerfield State Park, 121, 122
Dairy industry, 631-32
Dalhart
    mayor and city manager, 462
    museum, 499
    newspaper, 561
    population, 317, 380
    prison in, 443
    profile and map location, **173, 204**
    public library, 506
    radio stations, 561
Dallam County
    alcohol sales (wet-or-dry status), 472
    banks and bank assets, 578
    church membership, 529
    county and district officials, 475, 480
    courts, 437
    crime and law enforcement, 540
    deaths, 532
    federal funds to, 492
    general election results (2002), 403
    health care, 532
    income, 574
    map of, *173*
    population, 173, 390
    profile of, **173**
    tax appraiser, 471
    vehicles and highways, 591
    weather data, 105
Dallas (city)
    airline passengers, 597
    Amtrak passengers on/off at, 596
    church membership, 525-26
    comparative ranking with U.S. metro areas, 202
    economy of, 567
    employment and wages in, 569-70, 576
    fairs/festivals in, 136
    Film Commission, 496

foreign consulates in, 587-88
Foreign Trade Zone, 586
mental health services, 536
museums, 499
newspapers, 555, 559, 561
population, 10, 55, 299, 317, 380
profile and map location, **174**
public library, 506
television and radio stations, 561
Dallas, performing arts organizations, 497-98
Dallas Baptist University, 549
Dallas Christian College, 549
Dallas County
    alcohol sales (wet-or-dry status), 472
    banks and bank assets, 578
    church membership, 529
    county and district officials, 475, 480
    courts, 437, 473
    crime and law enforcement, 540
    deaths, 532
    federal funds to, 492
    general election results (2002), 403
    health care, 532
    income, 574
    map of, *174*
    oil and gas production, 605, 608
    population, 175, 223, 390
    profile of, **174-75**
    tax appraiser, 471
    vehicles and highways, 591
    weather data, 105
Dallas County Community College District, 549
Dallas-Fort Worth CMSA, 299
Dallas, Lake, 71
Dallas PMSA, 299
Dance
    organizations, 497-98
    polka, 514
    state folk dance, 14
Daniel, Fray, 518, 523
Daniel, Jean Houston Baldwin, 638
Daniel, Lake, 74
Daniel, Price, 53, 420
Daniel, Price Jr., 55
Davis, E. J., 44, *44, 45*, 47, 395, 417
Davis, Helen Fuller, *23*
Davis, Jefferson, 19
Davis, Lake, 74
Davis Mountains, *59*, 61, 131, 215
Davis Mountains State Park, 121, 122
Davy Crockett, Lake, 133
Davy Crockett National Forest, 83, 133
Dawson, Nicholas, 128
Dawson County
    alcohol sales (wet-or-dry status), 472
    banks and bank assets, 578
    church membership, 529
    county and district officials, 475, 480
    courts, 437
    crime and law enforcement, 540
    deaths, 532
    federal funds to, 492
    general election results (2002), 403
    health care, 532
    map of, *175*
    oil and gas production, 605, 608
    population, 175, 390
    profile of, **175**
    tax appraiser, 471
    vehicles and highways, 591
    weather data, 105
Deaf and Hard of Hearing, Commission for, 447
Deaf and Hearing Impaired, School for, 447
Deaf Smith County
    alcohol sales (wet-or-dry status), 472
    banks and bank assets, 578
    church membership, 529
    county and district officials, 475, 480
    courts, 437
    crime and law enforcement, 540
    deaths, 532
    federal funds to, 492
    general election results (2002), 403
    health care, 532
    income, 574
    map of, *176*
    population, 176, 390
    profile of, **176**
    tax appraiser, 471
    vehicles and highways, 591
    weather data, 105
Dealey, George B., 555, 559, *559*
Dealey, Sam, 52
Deaths
    causes of, 531-35
    by county, 139-295, 531-35
    from destructive weather, 97-102
    of law enforcement officers, 539
    from motor vehicle accidents, 594
    statistics, 10
DeBakey, Michael, 495
Decatur
    mayor and city manager, 462
    newspaper, 561
    population, 318, 380
    profile and map location, **293**
    public library, 506
    television and radio stations, 561
Dechard, Robert W., 556, 557, *557*
Declaration of Independence, Republic of Texas,
    130, 422-24, 544
Dedman, Robert H. Sr., 638
Deep East Texas Council of Governments, 470
Deer, 87
Deer Park, 203, 318, 380, 462, 506, 561

DeHartog, Jan, 638
Deisenhofer, Johann, 538
De la Cruz, Fray Juan, 518, 523
De la Cruz, Fray Manuel, 520
De La O, Jesús "Chuy," 638
De las Piedras, Jose, 28
DeLay, Tom, 397, 398, 486
Dell Computer Corporation, 566
Del Mar College, 95, 550
Del Rio
  Amtrak passengers on/off at, 596
  Foreign Trade Zone, 586
  mayor and city manager, 462
  Mexican consulate in, 588
  military installation near, 491
  museum, 499
  newspaper, 561
  performing arts organization, 498
  population, 318, 380
  profile and map location, **283**
  public library, 506
  Spanish missionaries and, 520
  television and radio stations, 561
Delta County
  alcohol sales (wet-or-dry status), 472
  banks and bank assets, 578
  church membership, 529
  county and district officials, 475, 480
  courts, 437
  crime and law enforcement, 540
  deaths, 532
  federal funds to, 492
  general election results (2002), 403
  health care, 532
  income, 574
  map of, *176*
  oil and gas production, 605, 608
  population, 176, 390
  profile of, **176**
  tax appraiser, 471
  vehicles and highways, 591
  weather data, 105
Delta Lake Reservoir, 74
Democratic Party
  in early- to mid-twentieth century, 47, 50-53
  in gubernatorial elections (1845-1998), 417-21
  national committee members, 409
  in nineteenth century, 43, 45
  in presidential elections (1842-2000), 411-13
  state executive committee, district members, and
    auxiliaries, 409-10
  Texas Legislature (2003), 395-97, 398-409, 433-34
  in U.S. Senatorial elections (1906-2002), 402-7,
    414-17
Demographics. See Population
Denison
  mayor and city manager, 462
  mental health services, 536
  museum, 499
  population, 318, 380
  profile and map location, **196**
  public library, 506
  radio stations, 561
Denmark, consular offices, 587
Dental Examiners, Board of, 447
Denton (city)
  fairs/festivals in, 136
  mayor and city manager, 462
  mental health services, 536
  museums, 499
  newspaper, 561
  performing arts organization, 498
  population, 318, 380
  profile and map location, **177**
  public library, 506
  television and radio stations, 561
Denton County
  alcohol sales (wet-or-dry status), 472
  banks and bank assets, 578
  church membership, 529
  county and district officials, 475, 480
  courts, 437, 473
  crime and law enforcement, 540
  deaths, 532
  educational attainment, 298
  federal funds to, 492
  general election results (2002), 403
  health care, 532
  income, 574
  income statistics, 297
  map of, *177*
  oil and gas production, 605, 608
  population, 177, 223, 296, 390
  profile of, **177**
  tax appraiser, 471
  vehicles and highways, 591
  weather data, 105
Denton State School, 536
Depository Board, 447
Depression. See Great Depression
De Soto, Hernando, 32
DeSoto, 175, 318, 380, 462, 506, 561
Developmental Disabilities, Planning Council for,
  447-48
Devils River, 69
Devil's River State Natural Area, 121, 122
Devil's Sink Hole, 85, 87
Devil's Sinkhole State Natural Area, 121, 122
Dewhurst, David, 395, 396, 399, 402-7, 433
DeWitt, Green, 36, 37
DeWitt County
  alcohol sales (wet-or-dry status), 472
  banks and bank assets, 578
  church membership, 529
  county and district officials, 475, 480

courts, 437
crime and law enforcement, 540
deaths, 532
federal funds to, 492
general election results (2002), 403
health care, 532
income, 574
map of, *178*
oil and gas production, 605, 608
population, 178, 390
profile of, **178**
tax appraiser, 471
vehicles and highways, 591
weather data, 105
DHS. See Human Services, Department of
Diabetes, 531-35
Diabetes Council, 448
Diablo Plateau, 60
Diatomite (diatomaceous earth), 612
Dickens (town), 178, 318, 380, 462
Dickens County
  alcohol sales (wet-or-dry status), 472
  banks and bank assets, 578
  church membership, 529
  county and district officials, 475, 480
  courts, 437
  crime and law enforcement, 540
  deaths, 532
  federal funds to, 492
  general election results (2002), 403
  health care, 532
  income, 574
  map of, *178*
  oil and gas production, 605, 608
  population, 178, 390
  profile of, **178**
  tax appraiser, 471
  vehicles and highways, 591
  weather data, 105
Dickinson, Susanna, 38
Dickinson, 192, 318, 381, 444, 462, 506, 589
Dietitians, Board of Examiners, 448
Dimmit County
  alcohol sales (wet-or-dry status), 472
  banks and bank assets, 578
  church membership, 529
  county and district officials, 475, 480
  courts, 437
  crime and law enforcement, 540
  deaths, 532
  federal funds to, 492
  general election results (2002), 403
  health care, 532
  income, 574
  income statistics, 297
  map of, *179*
  oil and gas production, 605, 608
  population, 179, 390
  profile of, **179**
  tax appraiser, 471
  vehicles and highways, 591
  weather data, 105
Dimmitt (city)
  mayor and city manager, 462
  newspaper, 561
  population, 318, 381
  profile and map location, **160**
  public library, 506
  radio stations, 561
Dinosaurs, 14, 63, 121
Dinosaur Valley, 85
Dinosaur Valley State Park, 121, 122, 124
Disabilities, Council on Purchasing from People with,
  448
Disabilities, Governor's Committee on People with,
  448
Disaster Assistance program, 441
Diseases
  as causes of death, 531-53
  at frontier forts, 24
  influenza pandemic in early twentieth century, 49
District attorneys, 479-84
District clerks, 479-84
District courts
  federal courts, 488-89
  state courts, 437-38
District judges, 439-40, 488-89
Diversion, Lake, 74
Divorce
  by county, 139-295
  statewide statistics, 10
Dobie, J. Frank, 495
Doctors, 531-35
Doggett, Lloyd, 486
Dolan Falls, 121
Dolomite rock, 612
Domestic violence, 539
Dominican Republic, consular office, 587
Donley County
  alcohol sales (wet-or-dry status), 472
  banks and bank assets, 578
  church membership, 529
  county and district officials, 475, 480
  courts, 437
  crime and law enforcement, 540
  deaths, 532
  federal funds to, 492
  general election results (2002), 403
  health care, 532
  income, 574
  map of, *179*
  population, 179, 390
  profile of, **179**
  tax appraiser, 471
  vehicles and highways, 591

weather data, 105
Donna, 207, 319, 381, 462, 506
Double Lake, 133
Double Mountain Fork, 70
Dowling, Richard W., 44, 129
Drivers' licenses, 594
Drivers. See Motor vehicles and drivers
Droughts, 92, 94, 98, 102
Drug abuse. See Substance abuse
D.R. Wintermann Wildlife Management Area, 91
Dumas
  mayor and city manager, 462
  newspaper, 561
  population, 319, 381
  profile and map location, **245**
  public library, 506
  radio stations, 561
Dun & Bradstreet ratings for businesses, 300-377
Dunbar, Chaplain, 25
Duncanville, 175, 319, 381, 462, 506, 561
Dunlap, Lake, 74
Dust Bowl, 52
Dust storms, 52, 100
Duval County
  alcohol sales (wet-or-dry status), 472
  banks and bank assets, 578
  church membership, 529
  county and district officials, 475, 480
  courts, 437
  crime and law enforcement, 540
  deaths, 532
  federal funds to, 492
  general election results (2002), 403
  health care, 532
  income, 574
  income statistics, 297
  map of, *180*
  oil and gas production, 605, 608
  population, 180, 390
  profile of, **180**
  tax appraiser, 471
  vehicles and highways, 591
  weather data, 105
Dyess Air Force Base, 490-91

**E**

Eagle Lake, 74
Eagle Mountain Lake, 74
Eagle Mountain Reservoir, 71
Eagle Nest Lake, 74
Eagle Pass
  Foreign Trade Zone, 586
  mayor and city manager, 462
  newspapers, 561
  population, 320, 381
  profile and map location, **238**
  public library, 506
  Spanish missionaries nd, 520
  television and radio stations, 561
Eagles, 121, 125, 127
Eakin, Ed, 638
Early Childhood Intervention, Interagency Council
  on, 446
Eastern and Western Cross Timbers, 58, 59-60, *59*,
  65, *78*, 79
East Fork, 71
Eastland (town)
  mayor and city manager, 462
  newspaper, 561
  population, 320, 381
  profile and map location, **180**
  public library, 506
  radio stations, 561
Eastland County
  alcohol sales (wet-or-dry status), 472
  banks and bank assets, 578
  church membership, 529
  county and district officials, 475, 480
  courts, 437
  crime and law enforcement, 540
  deaths, 532
  federal funds to, 492
  general election results (2002), 403
  health care, 532
  income, 574
  map of, *180*
  oil and gas production, 605, 608
  population, 180, 390
  profile of, **180**
  tax appraiser, 471
  vehicles and highways, 591
  weather data, 105
Eastman Lakes, 74
East Texas Baptist University, 550
East Texas Council of Governments, 470
East Texas Timberland soils, 66
Eckhardt, Bob, 638
Eclipses, 111
Economic Development, Department of, 444
Economic Development, Governing Board of
  Department of, 448
Economic Geology, Bureau of, 610
Economy, **566-619.** See also Agriculture; Business;
  Employment; Finance; Income
comparative ranking with other states, 11
construction, 566, 568, 576, 585
by county, 139-295
earnings and hours by industry, 576
employment by industry, 576
film and television production, 496
finance, insurance, real estate, 567, 568, 576,
  577-84
gross state product (1993-2002) by industry, 568
in large metropolitan areas, 569-73, 576
manufacturing and high-tech, 566, 568, 576

**For CITIES and TOWNS not listed in the index, see complete list of towns on pages 300–377.**

mining, 568, 576
oil and gas industry, 566, 568, 576, 599-609
overview of state economy, 10, 566-68
services, 567-68, 576
transportation, 566-67, 568, 576, 589-98
utilities, 567, 568, 576, 617-19
wholesale and retail trade, 567, 568, 576
Ector County
 alcohol sales (wet-or-dry status), 472
 banks and bank assets, 578
 church membership, 529
 county and district officials, 475, 480
 courts, 437, 473
 crime and law enforcement, 540
 deaths, 532
 federal funds to, 492
 general election results (2002), 403
 health care, 532
 income, 574
 map of, 181
 oil and gas production, 605, 608
 population, 181, 223, 390
 profile of, 181
 tax appraiser, 471
 vehicles and highways, 591
 weather data, 105
Ecuador
 consular office, 587
 consular offices, 587
Edinburg
 birding center, 130
 Foreign Trade Zone, 586
 mayor, 462
 mental health services, 536
 museum, 499
 newspaper, 561
 population, 320, 381
 prison in, 444
 profile and map location, 207
 public library, 506
 radio stations, 561
Edinburg Lake. See Retama Reservoir
Edna
 fairs/festivals in, 136
 mayor and city manager, 462
 newspaper, 561
 population, 320, 381
 profile and map location, 214
 public library, 506
 radio stations, 561
Education, 544-54
 of blacks, 44, 45, 298
 budget for, in 1970s, 55
 charter schools, 546
 college graduates, 298
 community colleges, 55
 J.B. Connally and, 53
 enrollment in public schools, 544
 expenditures on public schools, 544
 at frontier forts, 25
 Gilmer-Aiken Laws, 545
 higher education, 547-54
 high school graduates and dropouts, 298, 544
 history of, 40, 45, 46, 544-45
 integration of schools, 53
 kindergarten, 54
 legislation (2003) on, 546, 548
 number of school districts, 544
 of prisoners, 443
 public schools, 544-46
 recent changes in public education, 545-46
 salaries of teachers and other public school
   personnel, 545
 segregation of schools, 46
 teachers and other personnel in public schools, 545
 Texas Assessment of Knowledge and Skills
   (TAKS), 546
Education Agency, Texas, 544, 545
Education, Board of Control for Southern Regional,
   448
Education Commissioners, 432, 448, 545
Education, State Board of, 401, 407, 409, 448, 546
Educator Certification, Board for, 448
Edwards, Chet, 486
Edwards, Peyton F., 599
Edwards Aquifer Authority, 448
Edwards (Balcones Fault Zone) aquifer, 67-68, 67
Edwards County
 alcohol sales (wet-or-dry status), 472
 banks and bank assets, 578
 church membership, 529
 county and district officials, 475, 480
 courts, 437
 crime and law enforcement, 540
 deaths, 532
 federal funds to, 493
 general election results (2002), 403
 health care, 532
 income, 574
 map of, 181
 oil and gas production, 605, 608
 population, 181, 390
 profile of, 181
 tax appraiser, 471
 vehicles and highways, 591
 weather data, 105
Edwards Plateau, 59, 59, 60, 64, 68, 70, 78, 79
Edwards-Trinity (Plateau) aquifer, 67, 68
Egg Marketing Advisory Board, 448
Egg production, 632
Egypt, consular office, 587
Eisenhower, Dwight, 53, 412
Eisenhower Birthplace State Historic Site, 122, 124
Eisenhower State Park, 122, 124
El Capitan, 57, 60, 172

Eldorado, 266, 321, 381, 462, 506, 561
Election Commission, 448
Elections, 395-421
 blacks and, 45, 47, 50
 Congressional (2002), 397, 399-400, 402-409
 county elections, 396
 election-reform law (1903), 47
 governors (1845-1998), 417-21
 poll tax and, 47, 54, 411
 presidential elections (1848-2000), 411-13
 primary elections (2002), 407-9
 primary system, 47, 50
 registered voters (2002), 402-6
 special elections (2001-2003), 397
 2002 elections, 395-97, 399-409
 2002 general election results by county, 402-6,
   404, 405
 U.S. Senators from Texas (1906-2002), 399,
   402-7, 414-17
 voter turnout (2002), 402-6
 voting-age population, 10
 woman suffrage and, 49
Electra, Lake, 74
Electric cooperatives, 617
Electric utilities, 617
Elephant Mountain Wildlife Management Area, 91
Elk, 87
Elledge, Stephen J., 538
Ellis County
 alcohol sales (wet-or-dry status), 472
 banks and bank assets, 578
 church membership, 529
 county and district officials, 475, 480
 courts, 437, 473
 crime and law enforcement, 541
 deaths, 532
 federal funds to, 493
 Foreign Trade Zone, 586
 general election results (2002), 403
 health care, 532
 income, 574
 income statistics, 297
 map of, 182
 oil and gas production, 605, 608
 population, 182, 223, 390
 profile of, 182
 tax appraiser, 471
 vehicles and highways, 591
 weather data, 105
Ellison Creek Reservoir, 74
El Paso (city)
 airline passengers, 597
 alcohol sales (wet-or-dry status), 472
 Amtrak passengers on/off at, 596
 church near, 182
 county and district officials, 475, 480
 economy of, 570-71
 Film Commission, 496
 first permanent settlement in Texas in, 32
 foreign consulates in, 588
 Foreign Trade Zone, 586
 mayor, 462
 mental health services, 536
 Mexican Revolution and, 48
 military installation in, 490
 missions, 520
 museum, 499
 newspapers, 561
 performing arts organizations, 498
 population, 10, 299, 321, 381
 profile and map location, 183
 public library, 506
 tax appraiser, 471
 television and radio stations, 561
El Paso Community College District, 550
El Paso County
 banks and bank assets, 578
 church membership, 529
 courts, 437, 473
 crime and law enforcement, 541
 deaths, 532
 federal funds to, 493
 general election results (2002), 403
 health care, 532
 income, 574
 map of, 183
 population, 183, 223, 390
 profile of, 183
 vehicles and highways, 591
 weather data, 105
El Paso State Center, 536
El Salvador
 consular offices, 587
 immigrants from, 10
Emancipation Juneteenth Cultural and Historical
   Commission, 448
Emergency Communications, Commission on, 448
Emergency Services Personnel Retirement Fund,
   Statewide, 448
Emory
 mayor, 462
 museum, 499
 newspaper, 561
 population, 321, 381
 profile and map location, 257
 public library, 506
Employees Retirement System of Texas, 455
Employment. See also Wages
 child labor, 47
 civilian labor force statistics, 10
 comparative ranking with other states, 11
 by county, 139-295
 hearings and hours, 11, 576
 by industry, 566-68, 567
 in large metropolitan areas, 569-73, 576

minimum-wage law, 54
 right-to-work law, 53
Employment Commission. See Workforce
   Commission
Enchanted Rock, 85, 232
Enchanted Rock State Natural Area, 122, 124
Encinal County, 390
Endangered and threatened species, 85-86
Engineers, State Board of Registration for
   Professional, 449
Ennis
 fairs/festivals in, 136
 mayor and city manager, 462
 newspaper, 561
 population, 321, 381
 profile and map location, 182
 public library, 506
Enrico, Roger A., 557, 557
Enron, 567
Environment, 57-109
 area of Texas, 10, 57
 boundary lines of Texas, 57, 69, 70, 71-72
 forests, 80-84
 geographic center of Texas, 10, 377
 geology, 61-63, 62
 highest points of Texas, 10, 57, 61
 lakes and reservoirs, 73-77
 land area of Texas, 10, 57
 latitude and longitude of Texas, 57
 length and breadth of Texas, 57
 lowest point of Texas, 10, 57
 natural landmarks, 85
 physical regions, 58-61, 59
 plants, 78-79
 soils, 63-66
 threatened and endangered species, 85-86
 water area of Texas, 10, 57
 water resources, 66-72
 weather, 10, 92-109
 wildlife, 86-91
Environmental Quality, Commission on, 66, 449
E.O. Siecke State Forest, 84
Episcopal Church, 526
Erath County
 alcohol sales (wet-or-dry status), 472
 banks and bank assets, 578
 church membership, 529
 county and district officials, 475, 480
 courts, 437, 473
 crime and law enforcement, 541
 deaths, 532
 federal funds to, 493
 general election results (2002), 403
 health care, 532
 income, 574
 map of, 184
 oil and gas production, 605, 608
 population, 184, 390
 profile of, 184
 tax appraiser, 471
 vehicles and highways, 591
 weather data, 105
Escalona, Fray Luis de, 519, 623
Escandón, José de, 34
Espejo, Antonio de, 68-69, 121
Estevanico, 31
Ethics Commission, 449
Ethiopia, consular office, 587
Ethnicity. See Anglos; Blacks; Hispanics;
   Race/ethnicity
Euless, 274, 275, 322, 381, 462, 506
Evangeline aquifer, 67
Evans, Hiram Wesley, 50
Evening stars, 111
Evergreen Underground Water Conservation
   District, 449
Explorers. See French exploration; Spanish
   exploration
Exports, 589, 622, 623
Ezell's Cave, 85

                        F

Fairfield
 fairs/festivals in, 136
 mayor and city manager, 462
 newspaper, 561
 population, 322, 381
 profile and map location, 190
 public library, 506
 radio station, 561
Fairfield Lake, 74
Fairfield Lake State Park, 122, 124
Fairs, festivals, and special events, 136-37
Falcon Reservoir, 69, 75
Falcon State Park, 122, 124
Falfurrias
 mayor, 462
 newspaper, 561
 population, 322, 381
 profile and map location, 154
 public library, 506
 radio stations, 561
Falls County
 alcohol sales (wet-or-dry status), 472
 banks and bank assets, 578
 church membership, 529
 county and district officials, 475, 480
 courts, 437
 crime and law enforcement, 541
 deaths, 532
 federal funds to, 493
 general election results (2002), 403
 health care, 532
 income, 574
 map of, 184

**For CITIES and TOWNS not listed in the index, see complete list of towns on pages 300–377.**

oil and gas production, 605, 608
population, 184, 390
profile of, **184**
tax appraiser, 471
vehicles and highways, 591
weather data, 105
Family Practice Residency Advisory Committee, 449
Family violence, 539
Family Violence program, 441
Fannin, James, 38, 512
Fannin Battleground State Historic Site, 122, 124
Fannin County
alcohol sales (wet-or-dry status), 472
banks and bank assets, 578
church membership, 529
county and district officials, 475, 480
courts, 437
crime and law enforcement, 541
deaths, 532
federal funds to, 493
general election results (2002), 403
health care, 532
income, 574
map of, 185
oil and gas production, 605
population, 185, 390
profile of, **185**
tax appraiser, 471
vehicles and highways, 591
weather data, 105
Fanthorp Inn State Historic Site, 122, 124
Farmer, James, 495
Farmers Branch, 175, 323, 381, 462, 506
Farmers Creek Reservoir, 75
Farming. See Agriculture
Farwell, 255, 323, 462, 561
Fayette County
alcohol sales (wet-or-dry status), 472
banks and bank assets, 578
church membership, 529
county and district officials, 475, 480
courts, 437
crime and law enforcement, 541
deaths, 532
federal funds to, 493
general election results (2002), 403
health care, 532
income, 574
map of, 186
oil and gas production, 605, 608
population, 186, 390
profile of, **186**
tax appraiser, 471
vehicles and highways, 591
weather data, 105
Federal courts, 488-89
Federal government. See also Congress, U.S.;
  Military installations
employment in, 568, 576
funds to counties, 492-94
gross state product (1993-2003), 568
tax collections, 494-95
Feit, Rachel, 29
Feldspar, 612
Feral pigs, 88
Ferdinand VII, King of Spain, 35
Ferguson, James E. "Farmer Jim," 48, 48, 50, 418
Ferguson, Miriam A. "Ma," 50, 51-52, 418, 419
Ferrets, 87
Festivals, fairs, and special events, 136-37, 515
Film Commission (state), 496, 497
Film Commissions (city), 496
Films, 496, 502, 514
Finance. See also Banks and banking; Insurance
employment in, 576
gross state product (1993-2002), 568
overview in 2002, 10, 567
wages in, 576
Finance Commission, 449
Finland, consular offices, 587
Fire Fighters' Pension Commissioner, 449
Fire Protection, Commission on, 449
Fires
arson, 539
forest fires, 83
First Ladies of Texas, 432
Fish and fishing
commercial fisheries, 134
endangered and threatened species, 85, 86
fisheries, 134
freshwater fish and fishing, 134
Freshwater Fisheries Center, 134
license for fishing, 135
in national forests, 84
saltwater fish and fishing, 134
Sea Center Texas, 135
state fish, 14
Fisher County
alcohol sales (wet-or-dry status), 472
banks and bank assets, 578
church membership, 529
county and district officials, 475, 480
courts, 437
crime and law enforcement, 541
deaths, 532
federal funds to, 493
general election results (2002), 403
health care, 532
income, 574
map of, 186
oil and gas production, 605, 608
population, 186, 390
profile of, **186**
tax appraiser, 471
vehicles and highways, 591

weather data, 105
Fisheries, 134
Fisher, William S., 40-41
Flag
Lone Star Flag, 12-13, 12
pledge to Texas flag, 13, 546
pledge to U.S. flag, 546
rules for display of, 13
six flags of Texas, 12, 12
Flash floods. See Flooding
Flatwoods soils, 66
Flaxseed, 626
Flipper, Henry Ossian, 21-22, 21, 133
Flooding, 92, 95, 97, 99-102
Floresville, 292, 323, 381, 462, 506
Flournoy, Lucien, 638
Flower Mound, 177, 324, 381, 462, 506
Flower of Texas, 10, 14
Floydada
mayor and city manager, 462
newspaper, 562
population, 324, 381
profile and map location, **187**
public library, 506
radio stations, 562
Floyd County
alcohol sales (wet-or-dry status), 472
banks and bank assets, 578
church membership, 529
county and district officials, 475, 480
courts, 437
crime and law enforcement, 541
deaths, 532
federal funds to, 493
general election results (2002), 403
health care, 532
income, 574
map of, 187
oil and gas production, 605, 608
population, 187, 390
profile of, **187**
tax appraiser, 471
vehicles and highways, 591
weather data, 105
Fluorspar, 612
Foard County
alcohol sales (wet-or-dry status), 472
banks and bank assets, 578
church membership, 529
county and district officials, 475, 480
courts, 437
crime and law enforcement, 541
deaths, 532
federal funds to, 493
general election results (2002), 403
health care, 532
income, 574
map of, 187
oil and gas production, 605, 608
population, 187, 390
profile of, **187**
tax appraiser, 471
vehicles and highways, 591
weather data, 105
Foley County, 390
Folk dance, 14, 514
Folkers, Karl, 538
Food. See also Agriculture
at frontier forts, 23-24
frozen desserts, 632
of Polish immigrants, 514
poultry and eggs, 632
Food and Fibers Commission, 444, 449
Food Stamp program, 441
Foote, Horton, 502
Ford, Gerald, 55
Ford, John S. "Rip," 44
Foreign consulates, 587-88
Foreign Trade Zones (FTZ), 586
Foreman, Ed, 54
Forest Grove Reservoir, 75
Forests. See also Trees
acreage and ownership of, 80
cattle grazing in national forests, 84
economic impact of, 81
fires in, 83
national forests and grasslands, 83-84, 133
pests in, 83
recreation on national forests, 133
reforestation, 83
state forests, 84, 84
timber growth and removal, 81, 83
timber harvest of 2001, 81-83
timber production in 2001, 82, 84
timber volume and number of trees, 80-81
types of, 80
urban forests, 83
Forest Service, Texas, 83
Formby, Margaret, 638
Fort Anahuac, 27-29, 27, 29
Fort Belknap, 18, 19, 20, 25, 26, 26
Fort Bend County
alcohol sales (wet-or-dry status), 472
banks and bank assets, 578
church membership, 529
county and district officials, 475, 480
courts, 437, 473
crime and law enforcement, 541
deaths, 532
educational attainment, 298
federal funds to, 493
general election results (2002), 403
health care, 532
income, 574
income statistics, 297

map of, 188
oil and gas production, 605, 608
population, 188, 223, 296, 390
profile of, **188**
tax appraiser, 471
vehicles and highways, 591
weather data, 105
Fort Bliss, 19, 20, 22, 23, 48, 183, 490
Fort Boggy State Park, 122, 124
Fort Brown, 16, 19, 20, 22, 23, 24
Fort Chadbourne, 18, 18, 19, 20, 22
Fort Clark, 17, 19, 20, 22, 24
Fort Concho, 19-23, 25
Fort Croghan, 18, 19, 23
Fort Davis, 19-24, 20
Fort Davis National Historic Site, 121, 131
Fort Duncan, 17, 19, 22-24, 48
Fort Elliott, 21
Fort Ewell, 16, 18, 19
Fort Gates, 16, 19
Fort Graham, 18, 19, 23
Fort Griffin, 19-23, 25
Fort Griffin State Historic Site, 122, 124
Fort Hancock, 19, 20, 22
Fort Hood, 490, 490
Fort Inge, 17, 19
Fort Lancaster, 19, 20, 22, 23
Fort Lancaster State Historic Site, 122, 124
Fort Leaton State Historic Site, 122, 124
Fort Lincoln, 16, 19
Fort Martin Scott, 17, 19, 23
Fort Mason, 17, 19
Fort McIntosh, 17, 19, 22, 23
Fort McKavett, 16, 17-19, 22-24
Fort McKavett State Historic Site, 122, 124
Fort Merrill, 16, 19
Fort Parker State Park, 122, 124
Fort Phantom Hill, 18-20, 18, 22
Fort Phantom Hill, Lake, 75
Fort Quitman, 19-22
Fort Richardson, 19, 20, 20, 22-25, 24
Fort Richardson State Historic Site, 122, 124-25
Fort Saint Louis, 32
Fort Sam Houston, 147, 490
Fort Sill, 20-21
Forts. See Frontier forts and specific forts.
Fort Stockton (city)
mayor and city manager, 462
newspaper, 562
population, 324, 381
prisons in, 444
profile and map location, **255**
public library, 506
radio stations, 562
Fort Stockton (frontier fort), 19-22
Fort Terrett, 18, 19
Fort Worth
airline passengers, 597
Amtrak passengers on/off at, 596
church membership, 525-26
comparative ranking with U.S. metro areas, 202
economy of, 571
employment and wages in, 571, 576
fairs/festivals in, 136
foreign consulate in, 587-88
Foreign Trade Zone, 586
mayor and city manager, 462
mental health services, 536
military installation near, 491
museums, 499
newspaper, 562
performing arts organizations, 498
population, 10, 299, 324, 381
profile and map location, **274**
public library, 506
runners along Trinity River in, 275
television and radio stations, 562
Fort Worth-Arlington PMSA, 299
Fort Worth (frontier fort), 18, 19
Fort Worth Nature Center and Refuge, 85
Fossil palmwood, 14, 63
Foxes, 87
France, consular offices, 587
Franciscan missionaries, 517-24
Franklin (city)
mayor, 462
newspaper, 562
population, 324
profile and map location, **262**
radio stations, 562
Franklin County
alcohol sales (wet-or-dry status), 472
banks and bank assets, 578
church membership, 529
county and district officials, 475, 480
courts, 437
crime and law enforcement, 541
deaths, 532
federal funds to, 493
general election results (2002), 403
health care, 532
income, 574
map of, 189
oil and gas production, 605, 608
population, 189, 390
profile of, **189**
tax appraiser, 471
timber production and value in, 82
vehicles and highways, 591
weather data, 105
Franklin Mountains State Park, 121, 122, 125, 130
Frank Phillips College, 550
Fredericksburg
fairs/festivals in, 136
history of, 42

---

**For CITIES and TOWNS not listed in the index, see complete list of towns on pages 300–377.**

mayor and city manager, 462
museum, 499
newspaper, 562
performing arts organization, 498
population, 324, 381
profile and map location, **193**
public library, 506
television and radio stations, 562
Freedman's Bureau, 44, 45
Freeman, Charles E. III, 638
Freeman, Dovie Frances, 638
Freeman, William Grigsby, 16-18
Freeport
  foreign/domestic commerce, 589
  Foreign Trade Zone, 586
  map location, *151*
  mayor and city manager, 462
  population, 151, 325
  tonnage handled by port, 589
Freestone County
  alcohol sales (wet-or-dry status), 472
  banks and bank assets, 578
  church membership, 529
  county and district officials, 475, 480
  courts, 437
  crime and law enforcement, 541
  deaths, 532
  federal funds to, 493
  general election results (2002), 403
  health care, 532
  income, 574
  map of, *190*
  oil and gas production, 605, 608
  population, 190, 390
  profile of, **190**
  tax appraiser, 471
  vehicles and highways, 591
  weather data, 105
Freeze dates, by county, 104-9
French, George H., 555
French exploration, 32, 72
Freshwater Fisheries Center, 134
Friendswood
  map location, *192*
  mayor and city manager, 462
  newspapers, 562
  population, 192, 325, 381
  public library, 506
Frio County
  alcohol sales (wet-or-dry status), 472
  banks and bank assets, 578
  church membership, 529
  county and district officials, 475, 480
  courts, 437
  crime and law enforcement, 541
  deaths, 532
  federal funds to, 493
  general election results (2002), 403
  health care, 532
  income, 574
  map of, *190*
  oil and gas production, 605, 608
  population, 190, 390
  profile of, **190**
  tax appraiser, 471
  vehicles and highways, 591
  weather data, 105
Frio River, 70
Frisco
  map location, *165*
  mayor and city manager, 462
  newspaper, 562
  performing arts organization, 498
  population, 165, 325, 381
  public library, 506
Frontier forts
  Civil War and, 20, 26
  closing of, 22, 44
  entertainment for, 25
  food at, 23-24
  Freeman's inspection of, 16-18
  health and hospitals at, 24, *24*
  housing at, 23
  Indian reservations and, 26, 26
  list of, 19
  map of, *17*
  Native Americans and, 16-22, 26
  officers' wives at, 24
  and prejudice against black soldiers, 21-22
  schools at, 25
  settlements near, 25
  Trans-Pecos posts, 18-19
  U.S. Army's return to, after Civil War, 20
  Victorio campaign and, 21
  and West Texas wars, 20-21
  westward expansion and, 16
  women at, 22-25
Frost, Martin, 397, 486
Fruits, 14, 621, 623, 628-30
FTZ. *See* Foreign Trade Zones (FTZ)
Fuller, F.O., 48
Fulton Mansion State Historic Site, 122, 125
Funeral Service Commission, 449
Furr, Donald, 638

**G**

Gail, 148, 325, 381, 562
Gaines County
  alcohol sales (wet-or-dry status), 472
  church membership, 529
  county and district officials, 475, 480
  courts, 437
  crime and law enforcement, 541
  deaths, 532
  federal funds to, 493

general election results (2002), 403
health care, 532
income, 574
map of, *191*
oil and gas production, 605, 608
population, 191, 390
profile of, **191**
tax appraiser, 471
vehicles and highways, 591
weather data, 106
Gainesville
  Amtrak passengers on/off at, 596
  mayor and city manager, 462
  newspaper, 562
  population, 325, 381
  profile and map location, **169**
  public library, 506
  radio stations, 562
Galloway, Harry M., 638
Galveston (city)
  commission form of government in, 47, 468-69
  fairs/festivals in, 136
  foreign/domestic commerce, 589
  Foreign Trade Zone, 586
  history of, 43, 44
  hurricane (1900) in, 47, 98
  mayor and city manager, 463
  mental health services, 536
  museums, 499
  newspaper, 555, 559, 562
  performing arts organization, 498
  population, 325, 382
  prison in, 443
  profile and map location, **192**
  public library, 506
  railroads in, 46
  television and radio stations, 555, 559, 562
  tonnage handled by port, 589
Galveston County
  alcohol sales (wet-or-dry status), 472
  banks and bank assets, 578
  church membership, 529
  county and district officials, 475, 480
  courts, 437, 473
  crime and law enforcement, 541
  deaths, 532
  federal funds to, 493
  general election results (2002), 403
  health care, 532
  income, 574
  map of, *192*
  oil and gas production, 605, 608
  population, 192, 223, 390
  profile of, **192**
  tax appraiser, 471
  vehicles and highways, 591
  weather data, 106
Galveston County Industrial Water Reservoir, 75
Galveston Island State Park, 122, 125
Galveston-Texas City PMSA, 299
Gálvez, Bernardo, 34
Gálvez, José de, 34
Garcés, Ramon, 638
Garcia, Clotilde P., 638
Garcia, Irene Martinez, 638
Garden City, 194, 325, 382
Garibay, Randy, 638
Garland
  mayor and city manager, 463
  population, 10, 326, 382
  profile and map location, **174**
  public library, 506
  television and radio stations, 562
Garner, John Nance, 51, 52
Garner State Park, 122, 125
Garza County
  alcohol sales (wet-or-dry status), 472
  church membership, 529
  county and district officials, 475, 481
  courts, 437
  crime and law enforcement, 541
  deaths, 532
  federal funds to, 493
  general election results (2002), 403
  health care, 532
  income, 574
  map of, *193*
  oil and gas production, 605, 608
  population, 193, 390
  profile of, **193**
  tax appraiser, 471
  vehicles and highways, 591
  weather data, 106
Garza-Little Elm, 71
Gas industry. *See* Oil and gas industry
Gasoline tax, 49, 458
Gas utilities, 619
Gatesville
  mayor and city manager, 463
  newspaper, 562
  population, 326, 382
  prisons in, 443, 444
  profile and map location, **169**
  public library, 506
  radio station, 562
Gemstones, 14, 610
Gene Howe Wildlife Management Area, 91
General Land Office, 53, 442
General Land Office Commissioners, 396, 399, 407, 431, 433
General Services Commission, 449
Geographic center of Texas, 10, *377*
Geology, 61-63, *62*
Georgetown
  mayor and city manager, 463

newspapers, 562
population, 326, 382
profile and map location, **291**
public library, 507
radio stations, 562
Georgetown, Lake, 75, 133
George West, 232, 326, 382, 463, 507
Georgia, consular office, 587
Geoscientists, Board of Professional, 449
Gephardt, Dick, 397
German immigrants/German Americans, 42, 49
Germany, consular offices, 587
Ghana, consular office, 587
Gibbons Creek Reservoir, 75
Giddings
  mayor and city manager, 463
  newspaper, 562
  population, 326, 382
  profile and map location, **229**
  public library, 507
  radio station, 562
Giles, Bascom, 53
Gillespie County
  alcohol sales (wet-or-dry status), 472
  banks and bank assets, 578
  church membership, 529
  county and district officials, 475, 481
  courts, 437
  crime and law enforcement, 541
  deaths, 532
  federal funds to, 493
  general election results (2002), 403
  health care, 532
  income, 574
  map of, *193*
  population, 193, 390
  profile of, **193**
  tax appraiser, 471
  vehicles and highways, 591
  weather data, 106
Gilmer
  fairs/festivals in, 136
  mayor and city manager, 463
  museum, 499
  newspaper, 562
  population, 326, 382
  profile and map location, **282**
  public library, 507
  radio stations, 562
Gilmer-Aikin Act, 53, 545
Gilmer Reservoir, 75
Gjemre, Ken, 638
Gladden, Don, 638-39
Gladewater, Lake, 75
Glasscock County
  alcohol sales (wet-or-dry status), 472
  church membership, 529
  county and district officials, 475, 481
  courts, 437
  crime and law enforcement, 541
  deaths, 532
  federal funds to, 493
  general election results (2002), 403
  health care, 532
  income, 574
  map of, *194*
  oil and gas production, 605, 608
  population, 194, 390
  profile of, **194**
  tax appraiser, 471
  vehicles and highways, 591
  weather data, 106
Glen Rose
  mayor and city administrator, 463
  newspaper, 562
  population, 327, 382
  profile and map location, **270**
  public library, 507
  radio station, 562
Glorieta Pass, Battle of, 20
Goats and mohair, 60, 630, 632
Gold, 612
Golden-cheeked warblers, 121, 125, 127, 128
Golden Crescent Regional Planning Commission, 470
Goldthwaite, 242, 327, 463, 507, 562
Goliad (town)
  mayor, 463
  newspaper, 562
  population, 327, 382
  profile and map location, **194**
  public library, 507
  radio station, 562
Goliad County
  alcohol sales (wet-or-dry status), 472
  banks and bank assets, 578
  church membership, 529
  county and district officials, 475, 481
  courts, 437
  crime and law enforcement, 541
  deaths, 532
  federal funds to, 493
  general election results (2002), 403
  health care, 532
  income, 574
  map of, *194*
  oil and gas production, 605, 608
  population, 194, 391
  profile of, **194**
  tax appraiser, 471
  vehicles and highways, 591
  weather data, 106
Goliad, massacre of, 38, 512
Goliad State Historic Site, 122, 125
Gómez Pedraza, Manuel, 36

Gonzales, Raymond B. Jr., 639
Gonzales (city), 195, 327, 382, 463, 562
Gonzales, Battle of, 37-38
Gonzales County
  alcohol sales (wet-or-dry status), 472
  banks and bank assets, 578
  church membership, 529
  county and district officials, 475, 481
  courts, 437
  crime and law enforcement, 541
  deaths, 532
  federal funds to, 493
  general election results (2002), 403
  health care, 532
  income, 574
  map of, *195*
  oil and gas production, 605, 608
  population, 195, 391
  profile of, **195**
  tax appraiser, 471
  vehicles and highways, 591
  weather data, 106
Gonzales, Lake, 75
Gonzalez, Charlie A., 486
Goodacre, Glenna, 502
Goodfellow Air Force Base, 491
Goodman, Toby, 619
Goodnight, Charles, 87, 128
Goose Creek, 382
Goose Island State Park, 122, 125
Gophers, 87-88
Gordon, Harry Bernard Sr., 639
Gould, Jay, 46
Government. *See* Federal government; Local governments; Republic of Texas; State government
Governors. *See also* specific governors
  contact information, 433
  election (2002), 395, 396, 399, 402-7, *404*
  elections (1845-1998), 417-21
  First Ladies, 432
  list of (1847-2003), 427-28
  under Mexican rule, 427
  Spanish royal governors, 427
Gov. Hogg Shrine State Historic Site, 122, 125
Graham
  fairs/festivals in, 136
  mayor and city manager, 463
  newspaper, 562
  population, 327, 382
  profile and map location, **294**
  public library, 507
  radio stations, 562
Graham, Lake, 75
Grain sorghum, 621, 624
Gramm, Phil, 395, 397, *397*
Granbury
  mayor and city manager, 463
  newspaper, 562
  performing arts organization, 498
  population, 327, 382
  profile and map location, **209**
  public library, 507
  radio station, 562
Granbury, Lake, 75
*SS Grandcamp* explosion, 53
Grand Prairie (city)
  fairs/festivals in, 136
  mayor and city manager, 463
  population, 327, 382
  profile and map location, **175**
  public library, 507
  radio station, 562
Grand Prairie (region), 59, *59,* 65
Granger, Gordon, 44
Granger, Kay, 486
Granger Lake, 33, 75
Granger Wildlife Management Area, 91
Granite, 611, 612
Granite Shoals (Lyndon B. Johnson Lake), 60, 70, 75
Grant, Ulysses S., 124, 132, 411
Grapefruit (state fruit), 14
Grapevine, 275, 327, 382, 463, 507
Grapevine Lake, 75, 133
Graphite, 612-13
Grasses and grasslands, 14, 78, 83-84
Graves, Curtis, 54
Graves, John, 502
Gray County
  alcohol sales (wet-or-dry status), 472
  banks and bank assets, 578
  church membership, 529
  county and district officials, 475, 481
  courts, 437
  crime and law enforcement, 541
  deaths, 532
  federal funds to, 493
  general election results (2002), 403
  health care, 532
  income, 574
  map of, *195*
  oil and gas production, 605, 608
  population, 195, 391
  profile of, **195**
  tax appraiser, 471
  vehicles and highways, 591
  weather data, 106
Grayson County
  alcohol sales (wet-or-dry status), 472
  banks and bank assets, 578
  church membership, 529
  county and district officials, 475, 481
  courts, 437, 473
  crime and law enforcement, 541
  deaths, 532
  federal funds to, 493

general election results (2002), 403
health care, 532
income, 574
map of, *196*
oil and gas production, 605, 608
population, 196, 391
profile of, **196**
tax appraiser, 471
vehicles and highways, 591
weather data, 106
Grayson County College, 550
Great Depression, 51-52
Great Plains, *59,* 60
Greece, consular office, 587
Green, Cecil Howard, 639
Green, Gene, 486
Greenbelt Lake, 75
Green Cave, 126
Greene, A.C., 639, *640*
Greenville
  fairs/festivals in, 136
  mayor and city manager, 463
  mental health services, 536-37
  museum, 499
  newspaper, 562
  population, 328, 382
  profile and map location, **212**
  public library, 507
  television and radio stations, 562
Greenville City Lakes, 75
Greenwood Canyon, 85
Greer County, 391
Gregg County
  alcohol sales (wet-or-dry status), 472
  banks and bank assets, 578
  church membership, 529
  county and district officials, 475, 481
  courts, 437, 473
  crime and law enforcement, 541
  deaths, 532
  federal funds to, 493
  Foreign Trade Zone, 586
  general election results (2002), 403
  health care, 532
  income, 574
  map of, *197*
  oil and gas production, 605, 608
  population, 197, 391
  profile of, **197**
  tax appraiser, 471
  timber production and value in, 82
  vehicles and highways, 591
  weather data, 106
Gregory, E.M., 44
Grierson, Alice K., 23, *23,* 24, 25
Grierson, Benjamin H., 21, *21,* 23
Grierson, Edith, 24
Grimes County
  alcohol sales (wet-or-dry status), 472
  banks and bank assets, 578
  church membership, 529
  county and district officials, 475, 481
  courts, 437
  crime and law enforcement, 541
  deaths, 532
  federal funds to, 493
  general election results (2002), 403
  health care, 532
  income, 574
  map of, *198*
  oil and gas production, 605, 608
  population, 198, 391
  profile of, **198**
  tax appraiser, 471
  timber production and value in, 82
  vehicles and highways, 591
  weather data, 106
Grinding pebbles (abrasive stones), 613
Groesbeck, 230, 328, 382, 463, 507, 562
Ground squirrels, 88
Groves, 216, 328, 382, 463, 507
Groveton, 281, 328, 463, 507, 562
Growing season, by county, 104-9
Growth Fund Board of Trustees, 449
Gruene, 167
Guadalupe bass fish (state fish), 14
Guadalupe-Blanco River Authority, 449
Guadalupe County
  alcohol sales (wet-or-dry status), 472
  banks and bank assets, 578
  church membership, 529
  county and district officials, 475, 481
  courts, 437, 473
  crime and law enforcement, 541
  deaths, 532
  federal funds to, 493
  general election results (2002), 403
  health care, 532
  income, 574
  map of, *198*
  oil and gas production, 605, 608
  population, 198, 391
  profile of, **198**
  tax appraiser, 471
  vehicles and highways, 591
  weather data, 106
Guadalupe Delta Wildlife Management Area, 91
Guadalupe Mountains National Park, 57, 131-32, 133, *172*
Guadalupe Mountain voles, 88
Guadalupe Peak, 10, 57, 60, 131-32, *172*
Guadalupe Range, 60
Guadalupe River, *69,* 70, *167*
Guadalupe River Authority, 449
Guadalupe River State Park, 122, 125

Guano, 86-87
Guaranteed Student Loan Corporation, 456
Guatemala, consular offices, 587
Guerra, Fray Antonio, 521
Guerrero, Eberardo "Larry," 639
Guerrero, Vicente, 36
Guitar (state musical instrument), 14
Gulf Coastal Plains, 58, *59,* 66, 78, 78
Gulf Coast aquifer, 67, *67*
Gulf Coast Marsh soils, 66
Gulf Coast Waste Disposal Authority, 449
Gulf Intracoastal Waterway, 71, 589
Gulf of Mexico, 10, 53, *227,* 603
Gulf States Marine Fisheries Commission, 449
Gump, Richard A., 639
Gunby, David, 639
Gunn, Warren, 639
Gus Engling Wildlife Management Area, 91
Guthrie, 224, 328, 382
Gutiérrez de Lara, José Bernardo, 36
Guyana, consular office, 587
Gypsum, 610, 611, 613

**H**

Hagerman National Wildlife Refuge, 90
Hailstorms, 92, 95, 96, 101, 102
Haiti, consular office, 587
Halbert, Lake, 75
Hale County
  alcohol sales (wet-or-dry status), 472
  banks and bank assets, 578
  church membership, 529
  county and district officials, 475, 481
  courts, 437
  crime and law enforcement, 541
  deaths, 532
  federal funds to, 493
  general election results (2002), 403
  health care, 532
  income, 574
  map of, *199*
  oil and gas production, 605, 608
  population, 199, 391
  profile of, **199**
  tax appraiser, 471
  vehicles and highways, 591
  weather data, 106
Half-way houses for youth, 444
Hall, Ralph M., 487
Hall County
  alcohol sales (wet-or-dry status), 472
  banks and bank assets, 578
  church membership, 529
  county and district officials, 475, 481
  courts, 437
  crime and law enforcement, 541
  deaths, 532
  federal funds to, 493
  general election results (2002), 403
  health care, 532
  income, 574
  map of, *199*
  population, 199, 391
  profile of, **199**
  tax appraiser, 471
  vehicles and highways, 591
  weather data, 106
Hallettsville
  fairs/festivals in, 136
  mayor and city administrator, 463
  newspaper, 562
  population, 329, 382
  profile and map location, **228**
  public library, 507
  radio stations, 562
Haltom City, 275, 329, 382, 463, 507
Hamblett, Stephen, 558, *558*
Hamilton, A.J., 43, 44, 45, 417
Hamilton (town)
  mayor and city administrator, 463
  newspaper, 562
  population, 329, 382
  profile and map location, **200**
  public library, 507
  radio station, 562
Hamilton County
  alcohol sales (wet-or-dry status), 472
  banks and bank assets, 578
  church membership, 529
  county and district officials, 475, 481
  courts, 437
  crime and law enforcement, 541
  deaths, 532
  federal funds to, 493
  general election results (2002), 403
  health care, 532
  income, 574
  map of, *200*
  oil and gas production, 605, 608
  population, 200, 391
  profile of, 200
  tax appraiser, 471
  vehicles and highways, 591
  weather data, 106
Hamilton Poll Preserve, *90*
Hamon, Nancy B., 502
Hancock, Winfield S., 45
Hansford County
  alcohol sales (wet-or-dry status), 472
  banks and bank assets, 578
  church membership, 529
  county and district officials, 475, 481
  courts, 437
  crime and law enforcement, 541
  deaths, 532

federal funds to, 493
general election results (2002), 403
health care, 532
income, 574
map of, *200*
oil and gas production, 605, 608
population, 200, 391
profile of, **200**
tax appraiser, 471
vehicles and highways, 591
weather data, 106
Hardeman County
alcohol sales (wet-or-dry status), 472
banks and bank assets, 578
church membership, 529
county and district officials, 475, 481
courts, 437
crime and law enforcement, 541
deaths, 532
federal funds to, 493
general election results (2002), 403
health care, 532
income, 574
map of, *201*
oil and gas production, 605, 608
population, 201, 391
profile of, **201**
tax appraiser, 471
vehicles and highways, 591
weather data, 106
Hardin County
alcohol sales (wet-or-dry status), 472
church membership, 529
county and district officials, 475, 481
courts, 437
crime and law enforcement, 541
deaths, 532
federal funds to, 493
general election results (2002), 403
health care, 532
income, 574
map of, *201*
oil and gas production, 599, 605, 608
population, 201, 391
profile of, **201**
tax appraiser, 471
timber production and value in, 82
vehicles and highways, 591
weather data, 106
Hardin-Simmons University, 550
Harker Heights
map location, *146*
mayor and city manager, 463
population, 146, 329, 382
public library, 507
radio station, 562
Harlingen
airline passengers, 597
birding center, 130
mayor and city manager, 463
mental health services, 536
museum, 499
newspaper, 562
population, 329, 382
profile and map location, **158**
public library, 507
television and radio stations, 562
tonnage handled by port, 589
Harris, Ruth, 559
Harris County
alcohol sales (wet-or-dry status), 472
banks and bank assets, 578
church membership, 529
county and district officials, 476, 481
courts, 437, 473
crime and law enforcement, 541
deaths, 532
federal funds to, 493
Foreign Trade Zone, 586
general election results (2002), 403
health care, 532
income, 574
map of, *202*
oil and gas production, 605, 608
population, 202, 223, 391, 460
profile of, **202-3**
tax appraiser, 471
timber production and value in, 82
vehicles and highways, 591
weather data, 106
Harris (William) Reservoir, 75
Hartley County
alcohol sales (wet-or-dry status), 472
church membership, 529
county and district officials, 476, 481

courts, 437
crime and law enforcement, 541
deaths, 532
federal funds to, 493
general election results (2002), 403
health care, 532
income, 574
map of, *204*
oil and gas production, 605, 608
population, 204, 297, 391
profile of, **204**
tax appraiser, 471
vehicles and highways, 591
weather data, 106
Haskell (town)
mayor and city administrator, 463
newspaper, 562
population, 330, 382
profile and map location, **205**
public library, 507
radio station, 562
Haskell County
alcohol sales (wet-or-dry status), 472
banks and bank assets, 578
church membership, 529
county and district officials, 476, 481
courts, 437
crime and law enforcement, 541
deaths, 532
federal funds to, 493
general election results (2002), 403
health care, 532
income, 574
map of, *205*
oil and gas production, 605, 608
population, 205, 391
profile of, **205**
tax appraiser, 471
vehicles and highways, 591
weather data, 106
Hate crimes, 539
Hawkins, Lake, 75
Hayes, Bob, 639, *639*
Hays, Jack, 40
Hays County
alcohol sales (wet-or-dry status), 472
church membership, 529
county and district officials, 476, 481
courts, 437, 473
crime and law enforcement, 541
deaths, 532
federal funds to, 493
general election results (2002), 403
health care, 532
income, 574
map of, *205*
oil and gas production, 605
population, 205, 296, 391
profile of, **205**
tax appraiser, 471
vehicles and highways, 591
weather data, 106
Hay, silage, and forage crops, 621, 625
Health
abortions, 531-35
birth rates, 531, 535
causes of deaths, 531-35
employment in health services, 567-68, 576
at frontier forts, 24
hospital beds, 531-35
mental health services, 536-37
physicians, 531-35
pregnancy rate, 531-35
Health and Human Services, Commission of, 450
Health, Board of, 450
Health Care Information Council, 450
Healthcare System Board of Directors, Statewide
  Rural, 450
Health, Commissioner of, 449
Health Coordinating Council, Statewide, 450
Healthy Kids Corporation, Board of Directors, 450
Hearing Instruments, State Committee of Examiners
  in the Fitting and Dispensing of, 450
Heart disease, 531-35
Heart of Texas Council of Governments, 470
Heat discomfort chart, 103
Heat stress index, 103
Hebbronville, 217, 330, 382, 507, 562
Hebert, Paul O., 43-44
Helium, 613
Hemphill (town)
mayor and city manager, 463
newspaper, 562
population, 330, 382
profile and map location, **264**
public library, 507
radio station, 562
Hemphill County
alcohol sales (wet-or-dry status), 472
banks and bank assets, 578
church membership, 529
county and district officials, 476, 481
courts, 437
crime and law enforcement, 541
deaths, 533
federal funds to, 493
general election results (2002), 403
income, 574
map of, *206*
oil and gas production, 605, 608
population, 206, 391
profile of, **206**
tax appraiser, 471
vehicles and highways, 591
weather data, 106

Hempstead
fairs/festivals in, 136
mayor and city administrator, 463
newspaper, 562
population, 330, 382
profile and map location, **285**
public library, 507
radio station, 562
Henderson, J. Pinckney, 40, 417
Henderson, Luther A., 639
Henderson (city)
mayor and city manager, 463
museum, 499
newspaper, 562
population, 330, 382
profile and map location, **263**
public library, 507
radio stations, 562
Henderson County
alcohol sales (wet-or-dry status), 472
banks and bank assets, 578
church membership, 529
county and district officials, 476, 481
courts, 437, 473
crime and law enforcement, 541
deaths, 533
federal funds to, 493
general election results (2002), 403
health care, 533
income, 574
map of, *206*
oil and gas production, 605, 608
population, 206, 391
profile of, **206**
tax appraiser, 471
timber production and value in, 82
vehicles and highways, 591
weather data, 106
Hendrickson, Carey P., 556
Henley, Don, 502
Henrietta, 163, 330, 382, 463, 507, 562
Hensarling, Jeb, 397, 487
Hereford
mayor and city manager, 463
newspaper, 562
population, 331, 382
profile and map location, **176**
public library, 507
radio stations, 562
Herndon, Dealey, 502, 558, *558*
Hess, Neil, 502
Heston, Charlton, 495
Hickerson, Nancy Parrot, 518, 522
Hidalgo, Father Francisco, 34
Hidalgo County
alcohol sales (wet-or-dry status), 472
banks and bank assets, 578
church membership, 529
county and district officials, 476, 481
courts, 437, 473
crime and law enforcement, 541
deaths, 533
federal funds to, 493
general election results (2002), 403
health care, 533
income, 574
map of, *207*
oil and gas production, 605, 608
population, 207, 223, 391
poverty rates, 298
profile of, **207**
tax appraiser, 471
vehicles and highways, 591
weather data, 106
Higher education. *See also* Education
academics, 548
black colleges, 547
Closing the Gaps program, 548
college graduates, 298
enrollment, 547-54
faculty, 549-54
history of, 547
list of universities and colleges, 549-54
multi-institution teaching centers, 548
recent developments, 547-48
state appropriations, 547
tuition, fees and financial aid, 548
for women, 547
Higher Education Coordinating Board, 450, 548
Higher Education Tuition Board, Prepaid, 450, 457
Highland Lakes Country, 60, 70
High Plains, 60, 64, 78, 79
High Plains Natural Area, 85
high school graduates, 298
High-tech industry, 566, 576
Highway map of Texas, 124
Highway system, 49, 590-93, *590*
Hill, Bobby Joe, 639
Hill College, 550
Hill Country, *59*, 60, 70
Hill Country State Natural Area, 122, 125
Hill County
alcohol sales (wet-or-dry status), 472
banks and bank assets, 578
church membership, 529
county and district officials, 476, 481
courts, 437
crime and law enforcement, 541
deaths, 533
federal funds to, 493
general election results (2002), 403
health care, 533
income, 574
map of, *208*
oil and gas production, 605, 608

**For CITIES and TOWNS not listed in the index, see complete list of towns on pages 300–377.**

population, 208, 391
profile of, **208**
tax appraiser, 471
vehicles and highways, 591
weather data, 106
Hillsboro
  mayor and city manager, 463
  newspaper, 562
  population, 331, 382
  profile and map location, **208**
  public library, 507
  radio stations, 562
Hinckley, Margaret A. "Marty" Jenkins, 639
Hinduism, 526
Hinojosa, Rubén, 487
Hirsch, Laurence E., 558, *558*
Hispanics
  educational attainment, 298
  income statistics, 297
  in nineteenth century, 36
  organizations for, 50
  poverty statistics, 298
  state population statistics, 10
  in U.S. Congress, 397
  voting rights for, 53
Historical Commission, 27, 29, 444, 450, 497
Historical Records Advisory Board, 450
History of Texas, **16-55**
  American immigrants in early 1800s, 35-37
  annexation by U.S., 41, 426
  capital and labor in late nineteenth century, 45-46
  Civil War, 20, 26, 43-44, 513
  conservatives vs. liberals in 1940s-1960s, 52-53
  by county, 138-295
  Declaration of Independence, 130, 422-24, 544
  in early twentieth century, 47-49
  French exploration, 32, 72
  frontier forts, 16-29
  Great Depression, 51-52
  KKK and minorities, 49-51
  maps of, *17, 26, 37, 42, 519*
  Mexican Revolution, 48
  Mexican rule, 36-38, 427
  Mexican War, 42
  Mexico's land policy in early nineteenth century, 36
  New Deal, 52
  oil and gas industry, 47, *47,* 51, 599-601
  prehistoric Texas, 31, 61-63
  prosperity in 1970s, 55
  Reconstruction, 44-45
  Republic of Texas, 39-41
  secession, 42-43
  Sharpstown scandal, 54
  slavery, 28, 36, 37, 41, 42-43, 44
  Spanish exploration, 31-32, *32,* 68-72, 517-24
  Spanish missionaries, 517-24
  Spanish rule, 32, 34-35, 427
  statehood, 10, 41
  technological growth, 53
  Texas Revolution, 27-29, 37-39, 512
  World War I, 48-49
  World War II, 52
Hobby, William P., 49, 418
Hockley County
  alcohol sales (wet-or-dry status), 472
  banks and bank assets, 578
  church membership, 529
  county and district officials, 476, 481
  courts, 437
  crime and law enforcement, 541
  deaths, 533
  federal funds to, 493
  general election results (2002), 403
  health care, 533
  income, 574
  map of, *208*
  oil and gas production, 605, 608
  population, 208, 391
  profile of, **208**
  tax appraiser, 471
  vehicles and highways, 591
  weather data, 106
Hofner, Emil "Bash," 639
Hogg, James Stephen, 46, *46,* 47, 125, 126, 417
Hog production, 630, 632
Holbrook, Lake, 75
Holidays, 516
Holiness churches, 526
Holm, Enid, 502
Home-rule cities, 460-68
Homestead exemption, 52
Hondo
  fairs/festivals in, 136
  mayor and city manager, 463
  newspaper, 562
  population, 332, 382
  prisons in, 444
  profile and map location, **240**
  public library, 507
  radio stations, 562
Honduras, consular office, 587
Honey Creek State Natural Area, 122, 125
Hood County
  alcohol sales (wet-or-dry status), 472
  banks and bank assets, 578
  church membership, 529
  county and district officials, 476, 481
  courts, 437
  crime and law enforcement, 541
  deaths, 533
  federal funds to, 493
  general election results (2002), 403
  health care, 533
  income, 574
  map of, *209*

oil and gas production, 605, 608
population, 209, 391
profile of, **209**
tax appraiser, 471
vehicles and highways, 591
weather data, 106
Hoover, Herbert, 51, 412
Hopkins County
  banks and bank assets, 578
  church membership, 529
  courts, 437, 473
  crime and law enforcement, 541
  deaths, 533
  federal funds to, 493
  general election results (2002), 403
  health care, 533
  income, 574
  map of, *209*
  oil and gas production, 605, 608
  population, 209, 391
  profile of, **209**
  vehicles and highways, 591
  weather data, 106
Hords Creek Lake, 75, 133
Horned lizards, 89
Horned toads, 89
Horse racing, 52
Horses, *273,* 632
Horticultural specialty crops, 626-27
Hospitals. *See also* Health
  at frontier forts, 24, *24*
  infant nursery, *537*
  number of hospital beds by county, 531-35
  for persons with mental illness, 536
  statistics on, 537
House of Representatives, Texas. *See* Legislature
House of Representatives, U.S. *See* Congress, U.S.
Housing and Community Affairs, Department of, 450
Housing Corporation Board of Directors, Affordable, 450
Houston, Andrew Jackson, 47, 52
Houston, Sam, 12, 38-41, *40,* 42, 43, 124, 126, 417
Houston (city)
  airline passengers, 597
  Amtrak passengers on/off at, 596
  church membership, 525
  comparative ranking with U.S. metro areas, 202
  economy of, 571-72
  employment and wages in, 571-72, 576
  fairs/festivals in, 136-37
  Film Commission, 496
  foreign consulates in, 587-88
  foreign/domestic commerce, 589
  history of, 44
  mayor, 463
  mental health services, 537
  museums, 499
  newspaper, 562
  performing arts organizations, 498
  Polish immigrants in, 513, 514
  population, 10, 55, 299, 332-33, 383
  profile and map location, **202-3**
  public library, 507
  railroads in, 46
  television and radio stations, 562
  tonnage handled by port, 589
Houston Baptist University, 550
Houston CMSA, 299
Houston Community College System, 550
Houston County
  alcohol sales (wet-or-dry status), 472
  banks and bank assets, 578
  church membership, 529
  county and district officials, 476, 481
  courts, 437, 473
  crime and law enforcement, 541
  deaths, 533
  federal funds to, 493
  general election results (2002), 403
  health care, 533
  income, 574
  map of, *210*
  oil and gas production, 605, 608
  population, 210, 391
  profile of, **210**
  tax appraiser, 471
  timber production and value in, 82
  vehicles and highways, 591
  weather data, 106
Houston County Lake, 75
Houston-Galveston Area Council, 470
Houston, Lake, 71, 75, 126
Houston PMSA, 299
Houston Ship Channel, 47, 71, *203, 588*
Howard College, 550
Howard County
  alcohol sales (wet-or-dry status), 472
  banks and bank assets, 578
  church membership, 529
  county and district officials, 476, 481
  courts, 438
  crime and law enforcement, 541
  deaths, 533
  federal funds to, 493
  general election results (2002), 403
  health care, 533
  income, 574
  map of, *210*
  oil and gas production, 605, 608
  population, 210, 391
  profile of, **210**
  tax appraiser, 471
  vehicles and highways, 591
  weather data, 106
Howard Payne University, 550

Hubbard Creek Reservoir, 75
Hubenak, Joe, 639
Hudspeth County
  alcohol sales (wet-or-dry status), 472
  church membership, 529
  county and district officials, 476, 481
  courts, 438
  crime and law enforcement, 541
  deaths, 533
  educational attainment, 298
  federal funds to, 493
  general election results (2002), 403
  health care, 533
  income, 574
  income statistics, 297
  map of, *211*
  population, 211, 391
  poverty rates, 298
  profile of, **211**
  tax appraiser, 471
  vehicles and highways, 592
  weather data, 106
Hueco-Mesilla Bolson aquifers, *67,* 68
Hueco Mountains, 60
Hueco Tanks State Historic Site, *31,* 122, 125
Hughes, Sarah T., 54
Humanities, Council for, 450, 497
Humanities Medal, 502
Human Rights, Commission on, 450
Human Services, Board of, 450
Human Services, Department of, 441
Humble, 203, 333, 383, 463, 562
Humidity, in heat discomfort chart, 103
Hungary, consular office, 587
Hunt County
  alcohol sales (wet-or-dry status), 472
  banks and bank assets, 578
  church membership, 529
  county and district officials, 476, 481
  courts, 438, 473
  crime and law enforcement, 541
  deaths, 533
  federal funds to, 493
  general election results (2002), 403
  health care, 533
  income, 574
  map of, *212*
  oil and gas production, 605
  population, 212, 391
  profile of, **212**
  tax appraiser, 471
  vehicles and highways, 592
  weather data, 106
Hunter Peak, 57
Hunting
  farmers' hunting lease income, 622
  license for, 135
  in national forests, 84
  statistics on, 135
Huntington, Collis P., 46
Huntsville
  mayor and city manager, 463
  museum, 499
  newspaper, 562
  population, 333, 383
  prisons in, 443, 444
  profile and map location, **285**
  public library, 507
  radio stations, 562
Huntsville State Park, 122, 125-26
Hurd, John Gavin, 639
Hurricanes, 47, 97-101
Hurst, 274, 275, 333, 383, 463, 507
Husband, Rick, 638
Huston, Felix, 40
Huston-Tillotson College, 547, 550
Hutchinson County
  alcohol sales (wet-or-dry status), 472
  banks and bank assets, 578
  church membership, 529
  county and district officials, 476, 481
  courts, 438
  crime and law enforcement, 541
  deaths, 533
  federal funds to, 493
  general election results (2002), 403
  health care, 533
  income, 574
  map of, *212*
  oil and gas production, 605, 608
  population, 212, 391
  profile of, **212**
  tax appraiser, 471
  vehicles and highways, 592
  weather data, 106
Hutchison, Kay Bailey, 395, 397, 486

**I**

Ice Age, 63
Iceland, consular offices, 587
Ice storms, 101, 102
I.D. Fairchild State Forest, 84, *84*
Illnesses. *See* Diseases; Health
Immigrants, 10, 512-15
Impeachment of governor, 48, 50
Imperial Reservoir, 75
Imports, 589
Incentive and Productivity Commission, 450
Income. *See also* Wages
  by county, 573-75
  geographical differences, 297
  median household income, 297
  in metropolitan versus nonmetropolitan areas, 573
  per capita income, 10, 297, 573-75
  racial/ethnic differences, 297

---

**For CITIES and TOWNS not listed in the index, see complete list of towns on pages 300–377.**

state data, 10, 573
taxes as percent of, 458
U.S. statistics, 573
India
  consular office, 587
  immigrants from, 10
Indian Mounds Recreation Area, 133
Indians
  frontier forts and, 16-22, 26
  at La Junta de los Ríos, 518
  and missionaries and missions, 32, 34, 517-24
  in Neo-American period of prehistory, 31
  Paleo-Indians in prehistoric period, 31
  pictographs by, 31, 125, 129, 131
  Pueblo Uprising by, 518
  Republic of Texas and, 40
  reservations for, 26, 26
  as settlers in Texas in early 1800s, 35
  and Spanish rule, 32, 34
  Victorio campaign and, 21
  West Texas wars against, 20-21
Indian Territory, 26
Indonesia, consular office, 587
Industry. See Manufacturing; Oil and gas industry;
  Timber industry
Influenza pandemic, 49
Information Resources, Department of, 450-51
Inks Lake, 60, 70, 75
Inks Lake State Park, 122, 126
Insects, 14, 23, 83
Insurance, Commissioner of, 451, 584
Insurance, Department of, 584
Insurance industry, 567, 568, 576, 584
Insurance Purchasing Alliance, 451
Insurance, State Board of, 53, 584
Integration of schools, 53
Interior Lowlands, 59-60, 59
Interstate Mining Compact Commission, 451
Interstate Oil and Gas Compact Commission, 451
Interstate Parole Compact Administrator, 451
Ireland, consular office, 587
Irion County
  alcohol sales (wet-or-dry status), 472
  banks and bank assets, 578
  church membership, 529
  county and district officials, 476, 481
  courts, 438
  crime and law enforcement, 541
  deaths, 533
  federal funds to, 493
  general election results (2002), 403
  health care, 533
  income, 574
  map of, 213
  oil and gas production, 605, 608
  population, 213, 391
  profile of, 213
  tax appraiser, 471
  vehicles and highways, 592
  weather data, 106
Iron, 613
Iron oxide, 611
Iron works, 129
Irrigation, 69, 71, 132, 622-23
Irving
  mayor and city manager, 463
  newspaper, 562
  performing arts organizations, 498
  population, 334, 383
  profile and map location, 174
  public library, 507
  television station, 562
Israel, consular office, 587
Italy, consular offices, 587
Iwonski, Carl von, 514

**J**

Jack, Patrick, 28
Jack County
  alcohol sales (wet-or-dry status), 472
  banks and bank assets, 578
  church membership, 529
  county and district officials, 476, 481
  courts, 438
  crime and law enforcement, 541
  deaths, 533
  federal funds to, 493
  general election results (2002), 403
  health care, 533
  income, 574
  map of, 213
  oil and gas production, 605, 608
  population, 213, 391
  profile of, 213
  tax appraiser, 471
  vehicles and highways, 592
  weather data, 106
Jacksboro
  mayor and city manager, 463
  newspaper, 562
  population, 334, 383
  profile and map location, 213
  public library, 507
  radio stations, 562
Jackson, Andrew, 40, 41
Jackson, Maynard Jr., 639
Jackson, Stonewall, 124
Jackson County
  alcohol sales (wet-or-dry status), 472
  banks and bank assets, 578
  church membership, 529
  county and district officials, 476, 481
  courts, 438
  crime and law enforcement, 541
  deaths, 533

federal funds to, 493
general election results (2002), 404
health care, 533
income, 574
map of, 214
oil and gas production, 605, 608
population, 214, 391
profile of, 214
tax appraiser, 471
vehicles and highways, 592
weather data, 106
Jackson Lee, Sheila, 487
Jacksonville College, 550
Jacksonville, Lake, 75
Jacksonville mental health services, 537
Jacobsen, Jake, 639
Jaguars, 87
Jaguarundis, 87
Jails, 443
Jail Standards, Commission on, 451
Jain, 526
Jalapeño pepper (state pepper), 14
Jamaica, consular offices, 587
James E. Daughtrey Wildlife Management Area, 91
James River Bat Cave, 86-87
Japan, consular office, 587
Japanese Garden of Peace, 128
Jarvis Christian College, 547, 550
Jasper (city)
  mayor and city manager, 463
  newspaper, 562
  population, 334, 383
  prison in, 444
  profile and map location, 214
  public library, 507
  radio stations, 562
Jasper aquifer, 67
Jasper County
  alcohol sales (wet-or-dry status), 472
  banks and bank assets, 578
  church membership, 529
  county and district officials, 476, 481
  courts, 438
  crime and law enforcement, 541
  deaths, 533
  federal funds to, 493
  general election results (2002), 404
  health care, 533
  income, 574
  map of, 214
  oil and gas production, 605, 608
  population, 214, 391
  profile of, 214
  tax appraiser, 471
  timber production and value in, 82
  vehicles and highways, 592
  weather data, 106
Javelinas, 88
Jayton, 222, 334, 383, 463, 507
J.B. Thomas, Lake, 75
J.D. Murphree Wildlife Management Area, 75, 91
Jeff Davis County
  alcohol sales (wet-or-dry status), 472
  banks and bank assets, 578
  church membership, 529
  county and district officials, 476, 481
  courts, 438
  crime and law enforcement, 541
  deaths, 533
  educational attainment, 298
  federal funds to, 493
  general election results (2002), 404
  health care, 533
  highest points of, 57, 61
  income, 574
  map of, 215
  oil and gas production, 606
  population, 215, 391
  profile of, 215
  tax appraiser, 471
  vehicles and highways, 592
  weather data, 106
Jefferson, Wallace, 396
Jefferson (town)
  fairs/festivals in, 137
  mayor and city administrator, 463
  newspaper, 562
  population, 334, 383
  profile and map location, 236
  public library, 507
  radio station, 562-63
Jefferson County
  alcohol sales (wet-or-dry status), 472
  banks and bank assets, 578
  church membership, 529
  county and district officials, 476, 481
  courts, 438, 473
  crime and law enforcement, 541
  deaths, 533
  federal funds to, 493
  general election results (2002), 404
  health care, 533
  income, 574
  map of, 216
  oil and gas production, 606, 608
  population, 216, 223, 391
  profile of, 216
  tax appraiser, 471
  timber production and value in, 82
  vehicles and highways, 592
  weather data, 106
Jennings, Waylon, 639, 639
Jester, Beauford H., 53, 419
Jim Chapman Lake, 75
Jim Crow laws. See Segregation

Jimenez, Flaco, 502
Jimenez, Santiago Jr., 502
Jim Hogg County
  alcohol sales (wet-or-dry status), 472
  banks and bank assets, 578
  church membership, 529
  county and district officials, 476, 481
  courts, 438
  crime and law enforcement, 541
  deaths, 533
  federal funds to, 493
  general election results (2002), 404
  health care, 533
  income, 574
  map of, 217
  oil and gas production, 606, 608
  population, 217, 391
  profile of, 217
  tax appraiser, 471
  vehicles and highways, 592
  weather data, 106
Jim Hogg Historic Site, 122, 126
Jim Wells County
  alcohol sales (wet-or-dry status), 472
  banks and bank assets, 578
  church membership, 529
  county and district officials, 476, 481
  courts, 438
  crime and law enforcement, 541
  deaths, 533
  federal funds to, 493
  general election results (2002), 404
  health care, 533
  income, 574
  map of, 217
  oil and gas production, 606, 608
  population, 217, 391
  profile of, 217
  tax appraiser, 471
  vehicles and highways, 592
  weather data, 106
Joe Pool Reservoir, 75, 133
John Henry Kirby State Forest, 84, 84
Johnson, Andrew, 45
Johnson, Eddie Bernice, 487
Johnson, J. Lee III, 639
Johnson, Lady Bird, 127, 495
Johnson, Lee Otis, 639
Johnson, Lyndon B., 52, 53, 54, 54, 127, 132, 412
Johnson, Sam, 487
Johnson City
  fairs/festivals in, 137
  mayor, 464
  newspaper, 563
  population, 335, 383
  profile and map location, 148
  public library, 507
  radio station, 563
Johnson County
  alcohol sales (wet-or-dry status), 472
  banks and bank assets, 578
  church membership, 529
  county and district officials, 476, 481
  courts, 438, 473
  crime and law enforcement, 541
  deaths, 533
  federal funds to, 493
  general election results (2002), 404
  health care, 533
  income, 574
  map of, 218
  oil and gas production, 606, 608
  population, 218, 223, 391
  profile of, 218
  tax appraiser, 471
  vehicles and highways, 592
  weather data, 106
Johnson Creek Reservoir, 75
Johnson Institute, 547
Johnston, Albert Sidney, 26, 40
Joiner, C. M. "Dad," 51, 600
Jones, Anson, 41, 124, 130
Jones, Jesse, 52
Jones, Luther, 639
Jones, Tommy Lee, 502
Jones County
  alcohol sales (wet-or-dry status), 472
  banks and bank assets, 578
  church membership, 529
  county and district officials, 476, 481
  courts, 438
  crime and law enforcement, 541
  deaths, 533
  federal funds to, 493
  general election results (2002), 404
  health care, 533
  income, 574
  map of, 219
  oil and gas production, 606, 608
  population, 219, 297, 391
  profile of, 219
  tax appraiser, 471
  vehicles and highways, 592
  weather data, 106
Jones Creek, 151, 335, 383, 464
Jordan, Barbara, 54, 495
Joseph Bonparte, 35
Josey, Jack Smyth, 639
Jourdanton
  map location, 142
  mayor and city manager, 464
  population, 142, 335, 383
  public library, 507
  radio station, 563
Journalists, 503. See also Newspapers

Judaism, 526
Judges. See Judiciary
Judicial Conduct, Commission on, 451
Judicial Council, 451
Judicial Districts Board, 451
Judiciary, **435-40.** See also Supreme Court, Texas
  Administrative Judicial Districts, 436-38, 445
  Chief Justices of Supreme Court of Texas (1836-
    2003), 432
  by county, 437-38
  county commissioners courts, 460
  county courts, 473
  county judges, 474-78
  Court of Criminal Appeals, 399, 407, 408, 409, 432,
    435
  Courts of Appeals, 401, 407, 409, 435-38
  criminal district court judges, 440
  federal courts, 488-89
  Judges of Appeals Courts (1876-2003), 432
  state district courts, 437-38
  state district judges, 439-40
  2002 elections, 399, 401, 407-8, 409
  U.S. district courts and judges, 488-89
Junction
  mayor, 464
  newspaper, 563
  population, 335, 383
  profile and map location, **223**
  public library, 507
  radio stations, 563
Jurassic rocks, 62
Juvenile Probation Commission, 451

**K**

Karnes City
  mayor and city administrator, 464
  newspaper, 563
  population, 335, 383
  profile and map location, **219**
  public library, 507
  radio station, 563
Karnes County
  alcohol sales (wet-or-dry status), 472
  banks and bank assets, 578
  church membership, 529
  county and district officials, 476, 481
  courts, 438
  crime and law enforcement, 541
  deaths, 533
  federal funds to, 493
  general election results (2002), 404
  health care, 533
  income, 574
  map of, 219
  oil and gas production, 606, 608
  Polish immigrants in, 512-13
  population, 219, 391
  profile of, **219**
  tax appraiser, 471
  vehicles and highways, 592
  weather data, 106
Katz, Sol, 639
Kaufman (city), 220, 335, 383, 464, 508, 563
Kaufman County
  alcohol sales (wet-or-dry status), 472
  banks and bank assets, 578
  church membership, 529
  county and district officials, 476, 481
  courts, 438, 473
  crime and law enforcement, 541
  deaths, 533
  federal funds to, 493
  general election results (2002), 404
  health care, 533
  income, 574
  map of, 220
  oil and gas production, 606, 608
  population, 220, 296, 391
  profile of, **220**
  tax appraiser, 471
  vehicles and highways, 592
  weather data, 107
Kazen, Jimmy, 639-40
Keechi Creek Wildlife Management Area, 91
Keilty, Richard, 556
Keller, 275, 336, 383, 464, 508
Kelly base site, 147
Kemp, Lake, 75
Kendall County
  alcohol sales (wet-or-dry status), 472
  church membership, 529
  county and district officials, 476, 482
  courts, 438
  crime and law enforcement, 541
  deaths, 533
  educational attainment, 298
  federal funds to, 493
  general election results (2002), 404
  health care, 533
  income, 574
  map of, 221
  population, 221, 391
  profile of, **221**
  tax appraiser, 471
  vehicles and highways, 592
  weather data, 107
Kenedy, Mifflin, 42
Kenedy County
  alcohol sales (wet-or-dry status), 472
  church membership, 529
  county and district officials, 476, 482
  courts, 438
  deaths, 533
  federal funds to, 493
  general election results (2002), 404

health care, 533
income, 574
map of, 221
oil and gas production, 606, 608
population, 221, 391
profile of, **221**
tax appraiser, 471
vehicles and highways, 592
weather data, 107
Kennedy, John F., 53, 54, 54, 412, 495
Kent County
  alcohol sales (wet-or-dry status), 472
  banks and bank assets, 578
  church membership, 529
  county and district officials, 476, 482
  courts, 438
  crime and law enforcement, 541
  deaths, 533
  federal funds to, 493
  general election results (2002), 404
  health care, 533
  income, 574
  map of, 222
  oil and gas production, 606, 608
  population, 222, 296, 391
  profile of, 222
  tax appraiser, 471
  vehicles and highways, 592
  weather data, 107
Kermit
  mayor and city manager, 464
  newspaper, 563
  population, 336, 383
  profile and map location, **292**
  public library, 508
  radio stations, 563
Kerr County
  alcohol sales (wet-or-dry status), 472
  banks and bank assets, 578
  church membership, 529
  county and district officials, 476, 482
  courts, 438, 473
  crime and law enforcement, 541
  deaths, 533
  federal funds to, 493
  general election results (2002), 404
  health care, 533
  income, 574
  map of, 222
  oil and gas production, 606
  population, 222, 391
  profile of, **222**
  tax appraiser, 471
  vehicles and highways, 592
  weather data, 107
Kerrville
  fairs/festivals in, 137
  mayor and city manager, 464
  mental health services, 536, 537
  museum, 499-500
  newspapers, 563
  population, 336, 383
  profile and map location, **222**
  public library, 508
  television and radio stations, 563
Kerrville-Shreiner State Park, 122, 126
Kerrville State Hospital, 536
Kerr Wildlife Management Area, 91
Kickapoo Cavern State Park, 122, 126
Kickapoo, Lake, 75
Kidney disease, 531-35
Kilby, Jack, 53
Kilgore College, 550
Killeen
  airline passengers, 597
  mayor and city manager, 464
  military installation in, 490
  newspaper, 563
  population, 336, 383
  profile and map location, **146**
  public library, 508
  television and radio stations, 563
Kimble County
  alcohol sales (wet-or-dry status), 472
  banks and bank assets, 579
  church membership, 529
  county and district officials, 476, 482
  courts, 438
  crime and law enforcement, 541
  deaths, 533
  federal funds to, 493
  general election results (2002), 404
  health care, 533
  income, 574
  map of, 223
  oil and gas production, 606, 608
  population, 223, 391
  profile of, 223
  tax appraiser, 471
  vehicles and highways, 592
  weather data, 107
King, Phil, 619
King, Richard, 42
King County
  alcohol sales (wet-or-dry status), 472
  church membership, 529
  county and district officials, 476, 482
  courts, 438
  crime and law enforcement, 541
  deaths, 533
  federal funds to, 493
  general election results (2002), 404
  health care, 533
  income, 574
  map of, 224

oil and gas production, 606, 608
population, 224, 296, 392
profile of, **224**
tax appraiser, 471
vehicles and highways, 592
weather data, 107
Kingston, Michael T., 559
Kingsville
  mayor and city manager, 464
  military installation in, 491
  newspaper, 563
  population, 336, 383
  profile and map location, 225
  public library, 508
  radio stations, 563
Kinney County
  alcohol sales (wet-or-dry status), 472
  church membership, 529
  county and district officials, 476, 482
  courts, 438
  crime and law enforcement, 541
  deaths, 533
  federal funds to, 493
  general election results (2002), 404
  health care, 533
  income, 574
  map of, 224
  oil and gas production, 606
  population, 224, 392
  profile of, **224**
  tax appraiser, 471
  vehicles and highways, 592
  weather data, 107
Kiolbassa, Peter, 513
Kiowa, Lake, 75
Kirby, Lake, 75
Kirk, Ron, 395, 396, 399, 402-7, 405
Kitchens, C.T. "Jack," 640
Kleberg County
  alcohol sales (wet-or-dry status), 472
  banks and bank assets, 579
  church membership, 529
  county and district officials, 476, 482
  courts, 438, 473
  crime and law enforcement, 541
  deaths, 533
  federal funds to, 493
  general election results (2002), 404
  health care, 533
  income, 574
  map of, 225
  oil and gas production, 606, 608
  population, 225, 392
  profile of, **225**
  tax appraiser, 471
  vehicles and highways, 592
  weather data, 107
Know-Nothing Party, 43
Knox, Frank, 52
Knox County
  alcohol sales (wet-or-dry status), 472
  banks and bank assets, 579
  church membership, 529
  county and district officials, 476, 482
  courts, 438
  crime and law enforcement, 541
  deaths, 533
  federal funds to, 493
  general election results (2002), 404
  health care, 533
  income, 574
  map of, 225
  oil and gas production, 606, 608
  population, 225, 392
  profile of, **225**
  tax appraiser, 471
  vehicles and highways, 592
  weather data, 107
Korea, consular offices, 587
Kountze, 201, 337, 383, 464, 508
Kozmetsky, George, 640
Kriesche Brewery State Historic Site, 123, 128
Ku Klux Klan (KKK), 49-50, 514
Kurth, Lake, 75
Kyrgyzstan, consular office, 587

**L**

La Bahia, 38, 125
Labor. See Employment
Labor unions, 11
Lackland Air Force Base, 147, 491
La Grange, 186, 337, 383, 464, 508, 563
Laguna National Atascosa Wildlife Refuge, 90
Lake Arrowhead State Park, 123, 126
Lake Bob Sandlin State Park, 123, 126
Lake Brownwood State Park, 123, 126
Lake Casa Blanca International State Park, 123, 126
Lake Colorado City State Park, 123, 126
Lake Corpus Christi State Park, 123, 126
Lake Creek Lake, 75
Lake Davy Crockett Recreation Area, 133
Lake Fork Reservoir, 75
Lake Houston State Park, 123, 126
Lake Jackson
  map location, 151
  mayor and city manager, 464
  museum, 500
  newspaper, 563
  population, 151, 337, 383
  radio stations, 563
Lake Livingston State Park, 123, 126
Lake Meredith National Recreation Area, 132
Lake Mineral Wells State Park, 61, 123, 126-27
Lake O' the Pines, 72, 75, 133
Lakes and reservoirs. See also specific lakes and

reservoirs
Corps of Engineers lakes, 133
list of, **73-77**
recreational facilities at Corps of Engineers lakes, 133
statistics on, 73
Lake Somerville State Park, 123, 127
Lake Tawakoni State Park, 123, *125*, 127
Lake Texana State Park, 123, 127
Lake Whitney State Park, *88*, 123, 126, 127
Lamar, Mirabeau B., 12, 40, *40*, 41, 544
Lamar County
alcohol sales (wet-or-dry status), 472
banks and bank assets, 579
church membership, 529
county and district officials, 476, 482
courts, 438, 473
crime and law enforcement, 541
deaths, 533
federal funds to, 493
general election results (2002), 404
health care, 533
income, 574
map of, *226*
population, 226, 392
profile of, **226**
tax appraiser, 471
vehicles and highways, 592
weather data, 107
Lamar State College, 553
Lamar University, 552
Lamb County
alcohol sales (wet-or-dry status), 472
banks and bank assets, 579
church membership, 529
county and district officials, 476, 482
courts, 438
crime and law enforcement, 541
deaths, 533
federal funds to, 493
general election results (2002), 404
income, 575
map of, *226*
oil and gas production, 606, 608
population, 226, 392
profile of, **226**
tax appraiser, 471
vehicles and highways, 592
weather data, 107
Lamesa
fairs/festivals in, 137
mayor and city manager, 464
newspaper, 563
population, 336, 383
prison in, 444
profile and map location, **175**
public library, 508
radio stations, 563
Lampasas (town)
mayor and city manager, 464
newspaper, 563
population, 338, 383
profile and map location, **227**
public library, 508
radio station, 563
Lampasas County
alcohol sales (wet-or-dry status), 472
banks and bank assets, 579
church membership, 529
county and district officials, 476, 482
courts, 438
crime and law enforcement, 542
deaths, 533
federal funds to, 493
general election results (2002), 404
health care, 533
income, 575
map of, *227*
oil and gas production, 606
population, 227, 392
profile of, **227**
tax appraiser, 471
vehicles and highways, 592
weather data, 107
Lampman, Hugh W., 640
Lampson, Nick, 487
Land area of Texas, 10, 57
Land Board, School, 451
Landmark Inn State Historic Site, 123, 127
Land Office. *See* General Land Office
Lands, Board for Lease of University, 451
Land Surveying, Board of Professional, 451
Land use, 63-64, 78, 442
Lane, Dick "Night Train," 640
Laney, Pete, 396
Lanham, Fritz G., 52
La Porte, 203, 337, 383, 464, 500, 563
Larceny-theft, 539-43
Laredo
airline passengers, 597
fairs/festivals in, 137
Foreign Trade Zone, 586
history of, 34
mayor and city manager, 464
mental health services, 537
Mexican consulate in, 588
newspaper, 563
population, 299, 338, 383
profile and map location, **287**
public library, 508
television and radio stations, 563
Larios, Fray Juan, 520, 524
Larissa College, 547
La Salle, René Robert Cavelier, Sieur de, 32, 127
La Salle County

alcohol sales (wet-or-dry status), 472
banks and bank assets, 579
church membership, 529
county and district officials, 476, 482
courts, 438
crime and law enforcement, 542
deaths, 533
educational attainment, 298
federal funds to, 493
general election results (2002), 404
health care, 533
income, 575
income statistics, 297
map of, *228*
oil and gas production, 606, 608
population, 228, 392
profile of, **228**
tax appraiser, 471
vehicles and highways, 592
weather data, 107
LaSelle, Dorothy Antoinette "Toni," 640
Las Palomas Wildlife Management Area, 91
Latitude and longitude of Texas, 57
Latvia, consular office, 587
Laughlin Air Force Base, 283, 491
Laundresses, at frontier forts, 24
Lava, 63
Lavaca County
alcohol sales (wet-or-dry status), 472
banks and bank assets, 579
church membership, 529
county and district officials, 476, 482
courts, 438
crime and law enforcement, 542
deaths, 533
federal funds to, 493
general election results (2002), 404
health care, 533
income, 575
map of, *228*
oil and gas production, 606, 608
population, 228, 392
profile of, **228**
tax appraiser, 471
vehicles and highways, 592
weather data, 107
Lavaca-Navidad River Authority, 451
Lavaca River, *69*, 70
Lavon Lake, 71, 75, 133
Law enforcement
by county, 540-43
deaths and injuries of law enforcement officers, 539
sheriffs and sheriffs' offices, 474-78, 540-43
Law Enforcement Officer Standards & Education, Commission on, 451
Law Examiners, Board of, 451
Law Library Board, 451
Lead and zinc, 613
League City, 192, 338, 384, 464, 500, 508
League of United Latin American Citizens (LULAC), 50
Leakey, 259, 339, 384, 464, 508, 563
Lebanon, consular office, 587
Lee, Arthur T., 19
Lee, Robert E., 26, 44, 124
Lee College, 550
Lee County
alcohol sales (wet-or-dry status), 472
banks and bank assets, 579
church membership, 529
county and district officials, 476, 482
courts, 438
crime and law enforcement, 542
deaths, 533
federal funds to, 493
general election results (2002), 404
health care, 533
income, 575
map of, *229*
oil and gas production, 606, 608
population, 229, 392
profile of, **229**
tax appraiser, 471
vehicles and highways, 592
weather data, 107
Legislative Budget Board, 451
Legislative Council, 451
Legislative Redistricting Board, 451
Legislative Reference Library, 452
Legislature, Texas
blacks in, 54
contact information for members, 433
list of members (2003), 433-34
number of members, 433
President of Senate (2003), 433
redistricting and, 398
Speaker of House (2003), 433
Speakers of Texas House (1846-2003), 431-32
telecommunications and, 618-19
2002 elections, 395-97, 400-401, 407-9
2003 (78th) session, 395-96, 398, 433-34, 546, 548
Lehrer, Jim, 502
Lemons, Abe, 640
Length and breadth of Texas, 57
León, Alonso de, 32, 69, 70, 71
León, Casimira de, 37
León, Martin de, 36
Leonardite, 613
Leon County
alcohol sales (wet-or-dry status), 472
banks and bank assets, 579
church membership, 529
county and district officials, 476, 482
courts, 438
crime and law enforcement, 542

deaths, 533
federal funds to, 493
general election results (2002), 404
health care, 533
income, 575
map of, *229*
oil and gas production, 606, 608
population, 229, 392
profile of, **229**
tax appraiser, 471
timber production and value in, 82
vehicles and highways, 592
weather data, 107
Leon, Lake, 75
Leopard cats, 87
Lesotho, consular office, 587
LeTourneau University, 550
Levelland
mayor and city manager, 464
newspaper, 563
population, 339, 384
profile and map location, **208**
public library, 508
radio stations, 563
Lewis, Sam, 640
Lewis Creek Reservoir, 75
Lewisville, 177, 339, 384, 464, 508
Lewisville Lake, 71, 75, 133
Liberty (city)
mayor and city manager, 464
newspaper, 563
population, 339, 384
profile and map location, **230**
public library, 508
radio station, 563
Liberty County
alcohol sales (wet-or-dry status), 472
banks and bank assets, 579
church membership, 529
county and district officials, 476, 482
courts, 438, 473
crime and law enforcement, 542
deaths, 533
federal funds to, 493
Foreign Trade Zone, 586
general election results (2002), 404
health care, 533
income, 575
map of, *230*
oil and gas production, 606, 608
population, 230, 392
profile of, **230**
tax appraiser, 471
timber production and value in, 82
vehicles and highways, 592
weather data, 107
Librarian, State, 451
Libraries
at frontier forts, 25
public libraries, 504-11
state library, 451, 497
Library and Archives Commission, 451, 497
Library, Legislative Reference, 452
Licensed drivers. *See* Motor vehicles and drivers
Licenses
drivers' licenses, 594
fishing license, 135
hunting license, 135
Licensing and Regulation, Commission on, 452
Liedtke, J. Hugh, 640
Lieutenant Governors, 395, 396, 399, 402-7, 428, 433
Lighthouses, 127, 128
Lightning strikes, 102
Lightning whelk (state seashell), 14
Lignite, 600, 613
Lime material, 610, 613-14
Limestone, 611, 614
Limestone County
alcohol sales (wet-or-dry status), 472
banks and bank assets, 579
church membership, 529
county and district officials, 476, 482
courts, 438
crime and law enforcement, 542
deaths, 533
federal funds to, 493
general election results (2002), 404
health care, 533
income, 575
map of, *231*
oil and gas production, 606, 608
population, 231, 392
profile of, **230-31**
tax appraiser, 471
vehicles and highways, 592
weather data, 107
Limestone, Lake, 75
Lincoln, Abraham, 43
Linden, 160, 340, 464, 563
Lipantitlan State Historic Site, 123, 127
Lipscomb (town), 231, 340
Lipscomb County
alcohol sales (wet-or-dry status), 472
church membership, 529
county and district officials, 476, 482
courts, 438
crime and law enforcement, 542
deaths, 533
federal funds to, 493
general election results (2002), 404
health care, 533
income, 575
map of, *231*
oil and gas production, 606, 608

**For CITIES and TOWNS not listed in the index, see complete list of towns on pages 300–377.**

population, 231, 392
profile of, **231**
tax appraiser, 471
vehicles and highways, 592
weather data, 107
Liquor. *See* Alcohol
Literature, 503
Little Blanco River Bluff, 85
Littlefield
  mayor and city manager, 464
  newspaper, 563
  population, 340, 384
  profile and map location, **226**
  public library, 508
  radio stations, 563
Little River, 71
Live Oak County
  alcohol sales (wet-or-dry status), 472
  banks and bank assets, 579
  church membership, 529
  county and district officials, 476, 482
  courts, 438
  crime and law enforcement, 542
  deaths, 533
  federal funds to, 493
  general election results (2002), 404
  health care, 533
  income, 575
  map of, *232*
  oil and gas production, 606, 608
  population, 232, 297, 392
  profile of, **232**
  tax appraiser, 471
  vehicles and highways, 592
  weather data, 107
Livestock industries, 629, 630-32
Livingston
  mayor and city manager, 464
  newspaper, 563
  population, 340, 384
  prison in, 444
  profile and map location, **256**
  public library, 508
  radio stations, 563
Livingston, Lake, 71, 75, 126
Lizards, 14
Llano
  mayor, 464
  museum, 500
  newspaper, 563
  population, 340, 384
  profile and map location, **233**
  public library, 508
  television and radio stations, 563
Llano Basin, *59*, 60, 64
Llano County
  alcohol sales (wet-or-dry status), 472
  banks and bank assets, 579
  church membership, 529
  county and district officials, 476, 482
  courts, 438
  crime and law enforcement, 542
  deaths, 533
  federal funds to, 493
  general election results (2002), 404
  health care, 533
  income, 575
  map of, *233*
  oil and gas production, 606
  population, 233, 392
  profile of, **233**
  tax appraiser, 471
  vehicles and highways, 592
  weather data, 107
Llano Estacado, *59*, 60, 70
Llano River, 70
Llano Uplift, 61, 63, 610, 612, 614, 615, 616
Local governments, **460-84**
  commision form of, in Galveston, 47, 468-69
  council-manager form of, in Amarillo, 47, 469
  employment in, 568, 576
  gross state product (1993-2003), 568
  mayors and city managers, 460-68
Lockhart
  mayor and city manager, 464
  newspaper, 563
  population, 340, 384
  profile and map location, **156**
  public library, 508
  radio station, 563
Lockhart State Park, 123, 127
Lockridge, Joe, 54
Logan, Horace Lee, 640
Loma Alta Lake, 75
Lone Star Flag, 12-13, *12*
Longhorn cattle, 14, 119, 121, 124, 126, 128
Longhorn Cavern, 85
Longhorn Cavern State Park, 123, 127
Long, Huey, 51
Longitude and latitude of Texas, 57
Long-Term Care Regulatory (LTC-R) program, 441
Long-term care services, 441
Longview
  airline passengers, 597
  Amtrak passengers on/off at, 596
  fairs/festivals in, 137
  mayor and city manager, 464
  mental health services, 537
  museum, 500
  newspaper, 563
  population, 341, 384
  profile and map location, **197**
  public library, 508
  television and radio stations, 563
Lon Morris College, 550

López, Fray Diego, 32, 520, 523
López, Fray Francisco, 519, 523
López, Fray Nicolas, 521, 524
Lord, Walter, 38
Lost Creek Reservoir, 75
Lost Maples State Natural Area, 85, 123, 127
Lost Pines, 58, 119
Lottery, 459
Lottery Commission, 452
Louisiana Territory, 34
Loving County
  alcohol sales (wet-or-dry status), 472
  church membership, 529
  county and district officials, 476, 482
  courts, 438
  crime and law enforcement, 542
  deaths, 533
  educational attainment, 298
  federal funds to, 493
  general election results (2002), 404
  health care, 533
  income, 575
  map of, *233*
  oil and gas production, 606, 608
  population, 233, 392, 460
  poverty rates, 298
  profile of, **233**
  tax appraiser, 471
  vehicles and highways, 592
  weather data, 107
Lower Colorado River Authority, 70, 447
Lower Neches Wildlife Management Area, 91
Lower Rio Grande Plain soils, 65
Lower Rio Grande Valley, 58, *59*, 65, 69
Lower Rio Grande Valley Development Council, 470
Lower Rio Grande Valley National Wildlife Refuge,
  90
Lubbock Christian University, 550
Lubbock (city)
  airline passengers, 597
  fairs/festivals in, 137
  Film Commission, 496
  mayor and city manager, 464
  mental health services, 536, 537
  museums, 500
  newspaper, 563
  population, 299, 341, 384
  prisons in, 444
  profile and map location, **234**
  public library, 508
  television and radio stations, 563
Lubbock County
  alcohol sales (wet-or-dry status), 472
  banks and bank assets, 579
  church membership, 529
  county and district officials, 476, 482
  courts, 438, 473
  crime and law enforcement, 542
  deaths, 533
  federal funds to, 493
  general election results (2002), 404
  health care, 533
  income, 575
  map of, *234*
  oil and gas production, 606, 608
  population, 223, 234, 392
  profile of, **234**
  tax appraiser, 471
  vehicles and highways, 592
  weather data, 107
Lubbock State School, 536
Lucas, A. F., 599
Lufkin
  fairs/festivals in, 137
  mayor and city manager, 464
  mental health services, 536, 537
  museum, 500
  newspaper, 563
  population, 341, 384
  profile and map location, **140**
  public library, 508
  television and radio stations, 563
Lufkin State School, 536
LULAC (League of United Latin American Citizens),
  50
Lumber production. *See* Timber industry
Lutheran Church, 526
Lutz, Ric D., 556
Luxembourg, consular office, 587-88
Lynchburg Reservoir, 75
Lyndon B. Johnson Lake (Granite Shoals), 60, 70, 75
Lyndon B. Johnson National Grassland, 83
Lyndon B. Johnson National Historic Site, 132
Lyndon B. Johnson State Historic Site, 123, 127
Lynn County
  alcohol sales (wet-or-dry status), 472
  banks and bank assets, 579
  church membership, 529
  county and district officials, 476, 482
  courts, 438
  crime and law enforcement, 542
  deaths, 533
  federal funds to, 493
  general election results (2002), 404
  health care, 533
  income, 575
  map of, *235*
  oil and gas production, 606, 608
  population, 235, 392
  profile of, **235**
  tax appraiser, 471
  vehicles and highways, 592
  weather data, 107

**M**

Mackenzie, Ranald Slidell, 20, 128

Mackenzie Reservoir, 75
Madagascar, consular office, 588
Maddox, Brenda C., 556
Mad Island Wildlife Management Area, 91
Madison County
  alcohol sales (wet-or-dry status), 472
  banks and bank assets, 579
  church membership, 529
  county and district officials, 477, 482
  courts, 438
  crime and law enforcement, 542
  deaths, 533
  federal funds to, 493
  general election results (2002), 404
  health care, 533
  income, 575
  map of, *235*
  oil and gas production, 606, 608
  population, 235, 392
  profile of, **235**
  tax appraiser, 471
  timber production and value in, 82
  vehicles and highways, 592
  weather data, 107
Madisonville
  mayor and city manager, 464
  newspaper, 563
  population, 342, 384
  profile and map location, **235**
  public library, 508
  radio stations, 563
Madrid, Arturo, 502, 558, *558*
Magee, Augustus W., 36
Magnesite, 614
Magnesium, 614
Magoffin, Joseph, 127
Magoffin Home State Historic Site, 123, 127
Magruder, John B., 44
Malta, consular offices, 588
Mammals. *See also* Animals
  endangered and threatened species, 85
  list and description of, **86-89**
  state mammals, 14
Manchester, William, 502
Manente, Rev. Vladimiro, 640
Manganese, 614
Manor Lake. *See* Eagle Nest Lake
Mansfield, J. J., 52
Mansfield, 275, 342, 384, 464, 508, 563
Manufacturing
  in early twentieth century, 51
  employment in, 566, 576
  gross state product (1993-2002), 568
  in nineteenth century, 42, 46
  overview in 2002, 566
  principal products, 10
  wages in, 576
  in World War II, 52
Maplecroft (mansion), 129
Marble, 614
Marble Falls, Lake, 75
Marble Falls Reservoir, 60, 70
Marcus, Stanley, 640, *641*
Marcy, R.B., 128
Marfa
  mayor and city manager, 464
  museum, 500
  newspaper, 563
  population, 342, 384
  profile and map location, **257**
  public library, 508
Margays, 87
Margil de Jesús, Father Antonio, 34
María de Ágreda, Sor, 518, 519, 522, 522, 523
Marion County
  alcohol sales (wet-or-dry status), 472
  church membership, 529
  county and district officials, 477, 482
  courts, 438
  crime and law enforcement, 542
  deaths, 533
  federal funds to, 493
  general election results (2002), 404
  health care, 533
  income, 575
  map of, *236*
  oil and gas production, 606, 608
  population, 236, 392
  profile of, **236**
  tax appraiser, 471
  timber production and value in, 82
  vehicles and highways, 592
  weather data, 107
Mariscal canyon, 61, 69
Marlin
  mayor and city manager, 464
  newspaper, 563
  population, 343, 384
  profile and map location, **184**
  public library, 508
  radio station, 563
Marriage
  by county, 139-295
  statewide statistics, 10
Marriage and Family Therapists, Board of
  Examiners, 452
Marsh, William J., 13
Marshall, Brian, 514
Marshall
  Amtrak passengers on/off at, 596
  mayor and city manager, 464
  museum, 500
  newspaper, 563
  population, 343, 384
  profile and map location, **204**

**For CITIES and TOWNS not listed in the index, see complete list of towns on pages 300–377.**

public library, 508
radio stations, 563
Martin County
alcohol sales (wet-or-dry status), 472
banks and bank assets, 579
church membership, 529
county and district officials, 477, 482
courts, 438
crime and law enforcement, 542
deaths, 533
federal funds to, 493
general election results (2002), 405
health care, 533
income, 575
map of, 236
oil and gas production, 606, 608
population, 236, 392
profile of, 236
tax appraiser, 471
vehicles and highways, 592
weather data, 107
Martin Creek Lake State Park, 123, 127
Martin Dies Jr. State Park, 123, 127
Martin Lake, 75
Marvin, Lake, 133
Mary Allen College, 547
Mason (town), 237, 343, 384, 464, 508, 563
Mason County
alcohol sales (wet-or-dry status), 472
banks and bank assets, 579
church membership, 529
county and district officials, 477, 482
courts, 438
crime and law enforcement, 542
deaths, 533
federal funds to, 493
general election results (2002), 405
health care, 533
income, 575
map of, 237
population, 237, 392
profile of, 237
tax appraiser, 471
vehicles and highways, 592
weather data, 107
Mason Mountain Wildlife Management Area, 91
Massanet, Father Damián, 32, 34
Matador, 246, 343, 384, 464, 508, 563
Matador Wildlife Management Area, 91
Matagorda County
alcohol sales (wet-or-dry status), 472
banks and bank assets, 579
church membership, 529
county and district officials, 477, 482
courts, 438
crime and law enforcement, 542
deaths, 533
federal funds to, 493
general election results (2002), 405
health care, 533
income, 575
map of, 237
oil and gas production, 606, 608
population, 237, 392
profile of, 237
tax appraiser, 471
vehicles and highways, 592
weather data, 107
Matagorda Island, 250
Matagorda Island National Wildlife Refuge, 90
Matagorda Island State Park and Wildlife
Management Area, 123, 127
Matagorda Island Wildlife Management Area, 91
Matocha, Lee Roy, 640
Matthews, Gordon, 640
Maverick, Maury Jr., 640
Maverick County
alcohol sales (wet-or-dry status), 472
church membership, 529
county and district officials, 477, 482
courts, 438
crime and law enforcement, 542
deaths, 533
educational attainment, 298
federal funds to, 493
general election results (2002), 405
health care, 533
income, 575
income statistics, 297
map of, 238
oil and gas production, 606, 608
population, 238, 392
poverty rates, 298
profile of, 238
tax appraiser, 471
vehicles and highways, 592
weather data, 107
Mayfield, Earle, 50
Mayors, 460-68
Mays, Reuben, 20
McAllen
airline passengers, 597
birding center, 130
Foreign Trade Zone, 586
mayor and city manager, 465
Mexican consulate in, 588
museum, 500
newspapers, 563
population, 343, 384
profile and map location, 207
public library, 508
television and radio stations, 563
McBrayer, Staley Thomas, 640
McClellan Creek National Grassland, 83
McClellan, Lake, 133

McClendon, Sarah, 639, 640
McCool, William, 638
McCulloch County
alcohol sales (wet-or-dry status), 472
banks and bank assets, 579
church membership, 529
county and district officials, 477, 482
courts, 438
crime and law enforcement, 542
deaths, 533
federal funds to, 493
general election results (2002), 405
as geographic center of state, 10, 377
health care, 533
income, 575
map of, 238
oil and gas production, 606, 608
population, 238, 392
profile of, 238
tax appraiser, 471
vehicles and highways, 592
weather data, 107
McDonald Observatory, 57, 215
McFaddin National Wildlife Refuge, 90
McGovern, George, 54
McGregor, Stuart Malcolm, 559
McGrew, Jack, 640
McKenzie College, 547
McKinney
mayor and city manager, 465
mental health services, 537
museum, 500
newspaper, 563
population, 344, 384
profile and map location, 165
public library, 508
radio stations, 563
McKinney Falls State Park, 123, 127-28
McKittrick Canyon, 57, 131
McKool, Mike, 640
McLendon-Chisholm, 262
McLennan County
alcohol sales (wet-or-dry status), 472
banks and bank assets, 579
church membership, 529
county and district officials, 477, 482
courts, 438, 473
crime and law enforcement, 542
deaths, 533
federal funds to, 493
general election results (2002), 405
health care, 533
income, 575
map of, 239
oil and gas production, 606, 608
population, 223, 239, 392
profile of, 239
tax appraiser, 471
vehicles and highways, 592
weather data, 107
McMullen County
alcohol sales (wet-or-dry status), 472
banks and bank assets, 579
church membership, 529
county and district officials, 477, 482
courts, 438
crime and law enforcement, 542
deaths, 533
federal funds to, 493
general election results (2002), 405
health care, 533
income, 575
map of, 240
oil and gas production, 606, 608
population, 240, 392
profile of, 240
tax appraiser, 471
vehicles and highways, 592
weather data, 107
McMurry University, 550
McQueeney, Lake, 76
Medal of Freedom, 495
Medal of the Arts Awards, 502
Media, 555-65
Belo Corporation, 555-59
history of Texas Almanac, 559
newspapers, radio and television stations, 560-65
Medicaid, 441
Medical Examiners, Board of, 452
Medical Examiners District Review Committee, 452
Medical Physicists, Board of Licensure for
Professional, 452
Medina County
alcohol sales (wet-or-dry status), 472
banks and bank assets, 579
church membership, 529
county and district officials, 477, 482
courts, 438, 473
crime and law enforcement, 542
deaths, 533
federal funds to, 493
general election results (2002), 405
health care, 533
income, 575
map of, 240
oil and gas production, 606, 608
population, 240, 392
profile of, 240
tax appraiser, 471
vehicles and highways, 592
weather data, 107
Medina Lake, 76
Medina River, 70
Medina River, Battle of, 36
Meharg, Emma Grigsby, 50

Memorial Day, display of flag on, 13
Memphis
mayor, 465
newspaper, 563
population, 344, 384
profile and map location, 199
public library, 508
radio station, 563
Menard (town), 241, 344, 384, 465, 508, 563
Menard County
alcohol sales (wet-or-dry status), 472
banks and bank assets, 579
church membership, 529
county and district officials, 477, 482
courts, 438
crime and law enforcement, 542
deaths, 533
federal funds to, 493
general election results (2002), 405
health care, 533
income, 575
map of, 241
oil and gas production, 606, 608
population, 241, 392
profile of, 241
tax appraiser, 471
vehicles and highways, 592
weather data, 107
Mendoza, Lydia, 502
Mennonite/Amish church, 527
Mental Health and Mental Retardation, Board of, 452
Mental Health and Mental Retardation, Department
of, 536-37
Mental illness, 536-37
Mental retardation, 536-37
Mentone, 233, 344, 384
Mercedes
fairs/festivals in, 137
mayor and city manager, 465
newspaper, 563
population, 344, 384
profile and map location, 207
public library, 509
radio station, 563
Mercury (quicksilver), 614
Meredith, Lake, 72, 76, 132
Meridian, 149, 344, 465, 509, 563
Meridian State Park, 123, 128
Mertzon, 213, 344, 384, 465, 508
Mesozoic Era, 62-63
Mesquite
fairs/festivals in, 137
mayor and city manager, 465
performing arts organization, 498
population, 344, 384
profile and map location, 175
public library, 508
radio station, 563
Meteor Crater, 85
Meteor showers, 111
Methodist Church, 525, 527
Metropolitan Statistical Areas (MSAs), 299
Meusebach, John O., 42
Mexia, mental health services, 536
Mexia, Lake, 76
Mexia State School, 536
Mexican free-tailed bat, 14, 86
Mexican Revolution, 48
Mexican-Texans. See Hispanics
Mexican voles, 88
Mexican War, 16, 26, 42, 132
Mexico
and Anglo immigrants to Texas, 36-38
border problems with, 48, 49
consular offices, 588
Fort Anahuac and, 27-28
frontier forts and, 16
governments of, in nineteenth century, 36
governors of Texas under Mexican rule, 427
immigrants from, 10
Mexican Revolution, 48
raids on Republic of Texas by, 40-41
Texas Revolution and, 27-29, 37-39
war for independence from Spain (1810-1821), 36
MHMR. See Mental Health and Mental Retardation,
Department of
Miami, 261, 344, 384, 465, 563
Mica, 614
Mice, 88
Michels, Doug, 640
Michener, James, 495
Middle Rio Grande Development Council, 470
Midland (city)
airline passengers, 597
Foreign Trade Zone, 586
mayor and city manager, 465
mental health services, 537
Mexican consulate in, 588
museums, 500
newspaper, 563
performing arts organization, 498
population, 344, 384
profile and map location, 241
public library, 508
television and radio stations, 563
Midland College, 550
Midland County
alcohol sales (wet-or-dry status), 472
banks and bank assets, 579
church membership, 529
county and district officials, 477, 482
courts, 438, 473
crime and law enforcement, 542
deaths, 533
federal funds to, 493

general election results (2002), 405
health care, 533
income, 575
map of, 241
oil and gas production, 606, 608
population, 223, 241, 392
profile of, 241
tax appraiser, 471
vehicles and highways, 592
weather data, 107
Midwestern State University, 550
Midwestern State University, Board of Regents, 452
Mier, battle of, 41
Mier y Terán, Manuel, 36-37
Milam County
  alcohol sales (wet-or-dry status), 472
  banks and bank assets, 579
  church membership, 529
  county and district officials, 477, 482
  courts, 438
  crime and law enforcement, 542
  deaths, 533
  federal funds to, 493
  general election results (2002), 405
  health care, 533
  income, 575
  map of, 242
  oil and gas production, 606, 608
  population, 242, 392
  profile of, 242
  tax appraiser, 471
  vehicles and highways, 592
  weather data, 107
Military Facilities Commission, 452
Military installations, 490-92
Military Planning Commission, Strategic, 452
Milkovich, Mary, 640
Miller, Evelyn, 556
Millers Creek Reservoir, 76
Mills County
  alcohol sales (wet-or-dry status), 472
  banks and bank assets, 579
  church membership, 529
  county and district officials, 477, 482
  courts, 438
  crime and law enforcement, 542
  deaths, 533
  general election results (2002), 405
  health care, 533
  income, 575
  map of, 242
  oil and gas production, 606, 608
  population, 242, 392
  profile of, 242
  tax appraiser, 471
  vehicles and highways, 592
  weather data, 107
Minerals
  comparative ranking with other states, 610
  by county, 139-295
  principal products, 10, 610-16
  production and value (1999-2001), 610
Mineral Wells
  mayor and city manager, 465
  newspaper, 563
  population, 345, 384
  profile and map location, 252
  public library, 509
  radio stations, 563
Mineral Wells, Lake, 76, 126-27
Mining, 568, 576, 600, 611-12, 615-16
Minks, 88
Mission (city)
  birding center, 130
  mayor and city manager, 465
  newspaper, 563
  population, 345, 384
  profile and map location, 207
  public library, 508
  radio stations, 563
Missions and missionaries, 32, 34, 125, 128, 132, 517-24
Mission Tejas State Historic Site, 123, 128
Mississippi drainage basin, 72
Missouri City, 188, 345, 384, 465
Mitchell County
  alcohol sales (wet-or-dry status), 472
  banks and bank assets, 579
  church membership, 529
  county and district officials, 477, 482
  courts, 438
  crime and law enforcement, 542
  deaths, 533
  federal funds to, 493
  general election results (2002), 405
  health care, 533
  income, 575
  map of, 243
  oil and gas production, 606, 608
  population, 243, 297, 392
  profile of, 243
  tax appraiser, 471
  vehicles and highways, 592
  weather data, 107
Mitchell County Reservoir, 76
Mockingbird (state bird), 10, 14
Moczygemba, Rev. Leopold, 512-13, 513
Moczygemba, Rev. Thomas, 514
Mohair production, 60, 630, 632
Moles, 88
Mollusks, endangered, 85
Molybdenum, 614
Monaco, consular office, 588
Monahans
  fairs/festivals in, 136, 137

mayor and city manager, 465
newspaper, 563
population, 345, 384
profile and map location, 286
public library, 508
radio stations, 563
Monahans Sandhills State Park, 123, 128
Monarch butterfly (state insect), 14
M.O. Neasloney Wildlife Management Area, 91
Mongolia, consular office, 588
Monod, Cesar, 127
Montague (town), 107, 243, 346
Montague County
  alcohol sales (wet-or-dry status), 472
  banks and bank assets, 579
  church membership, 529
  county and district officials, 477, 482
  courts, 438
  crime and law enforcement, 542
  deaths, 533
  federal funds to, 493
  general election results (2002), 405
  health care, 533
  income, 575
  map of, 243
  oil and gas production, 606, 608
  population, 243, 392
  profile of, 243
  tax appraiser, 471
  vehicles and highways, 592
Montgomery County
  alcohol sales (wet-or-dry status), 472
  banks and bank assets, 579
  church membership, 529
  county and district officials, 477, 482
  courts, 438, 473
  crime and law enforcement, 542
  deaths, 533
  federal funds to, 493
  general election results (2002), 405
  health care, 533
  income statistics, 297
  map of, 244
  oil and gas production, 606, 608
  population, 223, 244, 296, 297, 392
  profile of, 244
  tax appraiser, 471
  timber production and value in, 82
  vehicles and highways, 592
  weather data, 107
Monticello Reservoir, 76
Monument Hill State Historic Site, 123, 128
Moody, Chip, 640
Moody, Dan, 50, 418
Moon phases, 112-17
Moonrise and moonset, 110, 111-17
Moore, Walter B., 559
Moore County
  alcohol sales (wet-or-dry status), 472
  banks and bank assets, 579
  church membership, 529
  county and district officials, 477, 482
  courts, 438, 473
  crime and law enforcement, 542
  deaths, 533
  federal funds to, 493
  general election results (2002), 405
  health care, 533
  income, 575
  map of, 245
  oil and gas production, 606, 608
  population, 245, 392
  profile of, 245
  tax appraiser, 471
  vehicles and highways, 592
  weather data, 107
Moore Plantation Wildlife Management Area, 91
Morehead, Richard M. Sr., 640
Morfit, Henry, 40
Mormons, 527
Morning stars, 111
Moroney, James M. III, 556
Morris County
  alcohol sales (wet-or-dry status), 472
  banks and bank assets, 579
  church membership, 529
  county and district officials, 477, 482
  courts, 438
  crime and law enforcement, 542
  deaths, 534
  federal funds to, 493
  general election results (2002), 405
  health care, 534
  income, 575
  map of, 245
  population, 245, 392
  profile of, 245
  tax appraiser, 471
  timber production and value in, 82
  vehicles and highways, 592
  weather data, 107
Morton, 163, 346, 385, 465, 509, 563
Moscoso Alvarado, Luis de, 32
Mosley, J. William, 556
Moss (Hubert H.) Lake, 76
Mother Neff State Park, 123, 128
Motley County
  alcohol sales (wet-or-dry status), 472
  banks and bank assets, 579
  church membership, 529
  county and district officials, 477, 482
  courts, 438
  crime and law enforcement, 542
  deaths, 534
  federal funds to, 493

general election results (2002), 405
health care, 534
income, 575
map of, 246
oil and gas production, 606, 608
population, 246, 296, 392
profile of, 246
tax appraiser, 471
vehicles and highways, 592
weather data, 107
Motor Vehicle Board, 452
Motor vehicles and drivers
  accidents, 594
  comparative data with other states, 11
  by county, 590-93
  deaths from motor vehicle accidents, 594
  drivers' licenses (1950-2002), 594
  miles driven daily, 590-93
  number registered by county, 590-93
  registration fees for, 590-93
  theft of vehicles, 539-43
Motto of Texas, 10, 13
Mountain Creek Lake, 76
Mountain lions, 87
Mountains, 57, 59, 60-61
Mount Emory, 61
Mount Livermore (Baldy Peak), 57, 61
Mount Locke, 57
Mount Pleasant
  fairs/festivals in, 137
  mayor and city manager, 465
  newspaper, 563
  population, 347, 385
  profile and map location, 279
  public library, 509
  radio station, 563
Mount Vernon, 189, 347, 385, 465, 563
Moursund, A.W., 640
Movies, 496, 502, 514
Moyers, Bill, 502
Muleshoe
  mayor and city manager, 465
  newspapers, 563
  population, 347, 385
  profile and map location, 143
  public library, 509
  radio stations, 563
Muleshoe National Wildlife Refuge, 85, 90
Municipal governments. See Local governments
Municipal Retirement System, 455
Murder, 45, 539-43
Murphy, Audie, 52
Murvaul Lake, 76
Museums, 498-500
Musical instruments, 14, 514, 515
Musicians, 501, 502, 514, 515
Music organizations, 497-98, 514
Muskrats, 88
Muslims, 527
Mustang Island State Park, 123, 128
Mustang Lake, 76
Mutscher, Gus, 54

N
NAACP (National Association for the Advancement of Colored People), 50
Nacogdoches (city)
  fairs/festivals in, 137
  founding of, 34
  mayor and city manager, 465
  newspaper, 563
  population, 347, 385
  profile and map location, 247
  public library, 509
  television and radio stations, 563
Nacogdoches County
  alcohol sales (wet-or-dry status), 472
  banks and bank assets, 579
  church membership, 529
  county and district officials, 477, 482
  courts, 438, 473
  crime and law enforcement, 542
  deaths, 534
  federal funds to, 493
  general election results (2002), 405
  health care, 534
  income, 575
  map of, 247
  oil and gas production, 599, 606, 608
  population, 247, 392
  profile of, 247
  tax appraiser, 471
  timber production and value in, 82
  vehicles and highways, 592
  weather data, 107
Nacogdoches, Lake, 76
Nacogdoches University, 547
Napoleon Bonaparte, 35
Narváez, Panfilo de, 31
NASA, 53
Nasworthy, Lake, 76
National Academy of the Sciences, 538
National Aeronautics and Space Administration. See NASA
National Credit Union Administration, 582
National Guard, Texas, 491-92
National Humanities Medal, 502
National Museum of the Pacific War, 123, 128
National parks. See Parks
Native Americans. See Indians
Natural Bridge Caverns National Natural Landmark, 85, 85
Natural Dam Lake, 76
Natural gas. See Oil and gas industry
Natural landmarks, 85

Salt (sodium chloride), 610, 615
Salt domes, 62, 616
Salt Fork, 70
Salt springs, 72
Salzberger, Lee, 556
Sam Bell Maxey House State Historic Site, 123, 129
Sam Houston National Forest, 83, 133
Sam Houston National Forest Wildlife Management Area, 91
Sam Houston State University, 553
Sam Rayburn Reservoir, 76, 133, *246*
San Angelo
  airline passengers, 597
  fairs/festivals in, 137
  mayor and city manager, 466
  mental health services, 536, 537
  military installation in, 491
  museum, 500
  newspaper, 564
  population, 299, 361, 386
  profile and map location, **279**
  public library, 510
  television and radio stations, 564
San Angelo State Park, 123, 129
San Angelo State School, 536
San Antonio
  airline passengers, 597
  Amtrak passengers on/off at, 596
  battle of the Alamo, 34
  church membership, 525
  economy of, 572-73
  employment and wages in, 572-73, 576
  fairs/festivals in, 137
  Fiesta in, *146*
  Film Commission, 496
  foreign consulates in, 587
  Foreign Trade Zone, 586
  founding of, 34
  history of, 34, 35, 36, 38, 40, 43
  mayor and city manager, 466
  mental health services, 536, 537
  military installations in, *147*, 490, 491
  missions in, 34, 132
  museums, 500
  newspapers, 564
  performing arts organizations, 498
  Polish immigrants in, 513
  population, 10, 55, 299, 361, 386
  profile and map location, **147**
  public library, 510
  skyline, *572*
  television and radio stations, 564
San Antonio Missions National Historic Site, 132
San Antonio River, *69*, 70
San Antonio River Authority, 455
San Antonio State Hospital, 536
San Antonio State School, 536
San Augustine (town)
  mayor and city manager, 467
  newspaper, 564
  population, 361, 386
  profile and map location, **264**
  public library, 510
  radio station, 564
San Augustine County
  alcohol sales (wet-or-dry status), 472
  church membership, 530
  county and district officials, 477, 483
  courts, 438
  crime and law enforcement, 542
  deaths, 534
  federal funds to, 494
  general election results (2002), 406
  health care, 534
  income, 575
  map of, *264*
  oil and gas production, 607, 609
  population, 264, 393
  profile of, **264**
  tax appraiser, 472
  timber production and value in, 82
  vehicles and highways, 593
  weather data, 108
San Benito
  mayor and city manager, 467
  newspaper, 564
  population, 361, 386
  profile and map location, **158**
  public library, 510
San Bernard National Wildlife Refuge, 90
San Bernard Reservoirs, 76
San Buenaventura, Fray Dionisio de, 520
Sánchez, Tomás, 34
Sanchez, Tony, 395, 395, 399, 402-7, *404*
Sand and gravel, 610, 615
Sander, John L. (Jack), 556
Sanders, Wayne R., 558, *558*
Sanderson, 137, 277, 361, 386, 510, 596
San Diego
  mayor and city manager, 467
  newspaper, 564
  population, 362, 386
  prison in, 443
  profile and map location, **180**
  public library, 510
  radio station, 564
Sand, industrial, 615
Sandlin, Max, 487-88
Sandstone, 615
Sandy Creek, 133
Sandy Creek Reservoir. *See* Pinkston Reservoir
San Elizario, 61, 69
San Felipe de Austin, 71, 129
San Francisco y Zúñiga, Fray García, 520, 524
San Jacinto Battleground State Historic Site,

123, 129
San Jacinto, Battle of, 27, 39, 71, 512
San Jacinto College District, 551
San Jacinto County
  alcohol sales (wet-or-dry status), 472
  banks and bank assets, 580
  church membership, 530
  county and district officials, 477, 483
  courts, 438
  crime and law enforcement, 542
  deaths, 534
  federal funds to, 494
  general election results (2002), 406
  health care, 534
  income, 575
  map of, *265*
  oil and gas production, 607, 609
  population, 265, 393
  profile of, **265**
  tax appraiser, 472
  timber production and value in, 82
  vehicles and highways, 593
  weather data, 108
San Jacinto Historical Advisory Board, 455
San Jacinto River, *69*, 71
San Jacinto River Authority, 455
San Jacinto State Park and monument, 71
San Juan
  map location, *207*
  mayor and city manager, 467
  population, 207, 362, 386
  public library, 510
  radio station, 564
San Marcos
  Amtrak passengers on/off at, 596
  economy of, 569
  mayor and city manager, 467
  mental health services, 537
  museum, 500
  newspaper, 564
  population, 362, 386
  profile and map location, **205**
  public library, 510
  radio stations, 564
San Marcos River, 70
San Marcos Springs, 60
San Patricio County
  alcohol sales (wet-or-dry status), 472
  banks and bank assets, 580
  church membership, 530
  county and district officials, 477, 483
  courts, 438, 473
  crime and law enforcement, 542
  deaths, 534
  federal funds to, 494
  general election results (2002), 406
  health care, 534
  income, 575
  map of, *265*
  oil and gas production, 607, 609
  population, 265
  profile of, **265**
  tax appraiser, 472
  vehicles and highways, 593
  weather data, 108
San Saba (town)
  mayor and city administrator, 467
  newspaper, 565
  population, 362, 386
  profile and map location, **266**
  public library, 510
  radio stations, 565
San Saba County
  alcohol sales (wet-or-dry status), 472
  banks and bank assets, 580
  church membership, 530
  county and district officials, 477, 483
  courts, 438
  crime and law enforcement, 542
  deaths, 534
  federal funds to, 494
  general election results (2002), 406
  health care, 534
  income, 575
  map of, *266*
  oil and gas production, 607
  population, 266, 393
  profile of, **266**
  tax appraiser, 472
  vehicles and highways, 593
  weather data, 108
San Saba River, 70
San Solomon Springs, 61
Santa Ana National Wildlife Refuge, 85, 90
Santa Anna, Antonio López de, 28, 36, 37-41, 129
Santa Elena canyon, 61, 69
Santa María, Fray Juan de, 519, 523
Santa Rita 1 oil well, *47*, 599
Santa Rosa Lake, 76
Sarita, **221**, 362, 386
Saudi Arabia, consular office, 588
Savings and loan associations, 10, 583
Savings and Loan Commissioner, 455
Savings banks, 10, 583
Saw milling, 42, 81-82
Sawtelle, G. Flint, 641
Scandium, 615
Schertz
  map location, *198*
  mayor and city manager, 467
  population, 198, 363, 386
  public library, 510
  radio station, 565
Schleicher County
  alcohol sales (wet-or-dry status), 472

banks and bank assets, 580
church membership, 530
county and district officials, 478, 483
courts, 438
crime and law enforcement, 542
deaths, 534
federal funds to, 494
general election results (2002), 406
health care, 534
income, 575
map of, *266*
oil and gas production, 607, 609
population, 266, 393
profile of, **266**
tax appraiser, 472
vehicles and highways, 593
weather data, 108
School Land Board, 451
School Safety Center Board, 455
Schools. *See* Education; and specific colleges and universities
Schramm, Texas E. "Tex," 641
Schreiner University, 551
Schwartz, Walter, 641
Sciences, National Academy of, 538
Scott, Winfield, 42, 411
Scully, Marlan O., 538
Scurlock, Elizabeth, 641
Scurry County
  alcohol sales (wet-or-dry status), 472
  banks and bank assets, 580
  church membership, 530
  county and district officials, 478, 483
  courts, 438
  crime and law enforcement, 542
  deaths, 534
  federal funds to, 494
  general election results (2002), 406
  health care, 534
  income, 575
  map of, *267*
  oil and gas production, 607, 609
  population, 267, 393
  profile of, **267**
  tax appraiser, 472
  vehicles and highways, 593
  weather data, 108
Sea Center Texas, 135, *135*
Seal of Texas, 13-14, *14*
Sea Rim State Park, 123, 129
Seashells, 14
Seasons, 111
Seawell, Washington, 19
Sebastopol State Historic Site, 123, 129
Secession, 42-43
Secretaries of State, 428-429, 433
Securities Board, 455
Seed and Plant Board, 455
Segregation, 46
Seguin, Juan, 39
Seguin
  fairs/festivals in, 137
  mayor and city manager, 467
  newspaper, 565
  population, 363, 387
  profile and map location, **198**
  public library, 510
  radio stations, 565
Segura, Judith Garrett, 556
Seminole
  mayor and city administrator, 467
  newspaper, 565
  population, 363, 387
  profile and map location, **191**
  public library, 510
  radio stations, 565
Seminole Canyon State Historic Site, 123, 129
Senate, Texas. *See* Legislature, Texas
Senate, U.S. *See* Congress, U.S.
Serpentinite, 611, 615
Service industries, 567-68, 576
Sessions, Pete, 397, 488
Seventh-day Adventists, 527
Sex Offender Treatment, Council on, 455-56
Seymour
  mayor and city administrator, 467
  newspaper, 565
  population, 363, 387
  profile and map location, **145**
  public library, 510
  radio stations, 565
Seymour aquifer, *67*, 68
Shackelford County
  alcohol sales (wet-or-dry status), 472
  banks and bank assets, 580
  church membership, 530
  county and district officials, 478, 483
  courts, 438
  crime and law enforcement, 542
  deaths, 534
  federal funds to, 494
  general election results (2002), 406
  health care, 534
  income, 575
  map of, *268*
  oil and gas production, 607, 609
  population, 268, 393
  profile of, **268**
  tax appraiser, 472
  vehicles and highways, 593
  weather data, 108
Shafter, William Rufus "Pecos Bill," 21
Shannon, Tommy, 94
Sharp, Frank, 54
Sharp, John, 395, 399, 402-7

Sharpstown scandal, 54
Sheep, 89, *620*, 631, 632
Shelby County
  alcohol sales (wet-or-dry status), 472
  banks and bank assets, 580
  church membership, 530
  county and district officials, 478, 483
  courts, 438
  crime and law enforcement, 542
  deaths, 534
  federal funds to, 494
  general election results (2002), 406
  health care, 534
  income, 575
  map of, *268*
  oil and gas production, 607, 609
  population, 268, 393
  profile of, **268**
  tax appraiser, 472
  timber production and value in, 82
  vehicles and highways, 593
  weather data, 108
Sheldon Lake State Park and Wildlife Management
  Area, 123, 129
Sheldon Reservoir, 76
Shell, 615
Shellfish, 134
Shelton, Stephen E., 556
Sheppard Air Force Base, 289, 491
Sheppard, Morris, 49, 52
Sheridan, Philip M., 44, 45
Sheriffs and sheriffs' offices, 474-78, 540-43
Sherman (city)
  mayor and city manager, 467
  museum, 500
  newspaper, 565
  population, 364, 387
  profile and map location, **196**
  public library, 510
  television and radio stations, 565
Sherman County
  alcohol sales (wet-or-dry status), 472
  banks and bank assets, 580
  church membership, 530
  county and district officials, 478, 483
  courts, 438
  crime and law enforcement, 542
  deaths, 534
  federal funds to, 494
  general election results (2002), 406
  health care, 534
  income, 575
  map of, *269*
  oil and gas production, 607, 609
  population, 268, 393
  profile of, **268**
  tax appraiser, 472
  vehicles and highways, 593
  weather data, 108
Ship (state), 14
Shipping, 589
Shive, Dunia A., 556
Shivers, Allan, 53, 419-20
Shrews, 89
Shrub (state), 14
Shumard Peak, 57
Sibley, Henry Hopkins, 20
Sideoats grama, 14, 78
Sierra Blanca, 211, 364, 387
Sierra Diablo Wildlife Management Area, 91
Sikh religion, 527
Silver, 615-16
Silverton, **154**, 364, 387, 467, 565
Sinton
  mayor and city manager, 467
  newspaper, 565
  population, 365, 387
  profile and map location, **265**
  public library, 510
  radio stations, 565
Skill Standards Board, 456
Skunks, 89
Slavery, 28, 36, 37, 41, 42-43, 44
Slovenia, consular office, 588
Smith, Al, 50-51
Smith, Erastus "Deaf," 39
Smith, Henry, 38, 39
Smith, Lamar S., 488
Smith, Preston, 54, 420
Smith County
  alcohol sales (wet-or-dry status), 472
  banks and bank assets, 580
  church membership, 530
  county and district officials, 478, 483
  courts, 438, 473
  crime and law enforcement, 543
  deaths, 534
  federal funds to, 494
  general election results (2002), 406
  health care, 534
  income, 575
  map of, *269*
  oil and gas production, 607, 609
  population, 223, 269, 393
  profile of, **269**
  tax appraiser, 472
  timber production and value in, 82
  vehicles and highways, 593
  weather data, 108
Smithers Lake, 76
Snowfall, 99, 101, 102
Snyder
  mayor and city manager, 467
  newspaper, 565
  population, 365, 387

prison in, 443
profile and map location, **267**
public library, 510
television and radio stations, 565
Soapstone, 616
Social Worker Examiners, Board of, 456
Socorro, 61, 69, 521
Sodium sulfate (salt cake), 616
Soil and Water Conservation Board, 63, 456
Soil conservation, 63-64
Soils, 63-66
Solomon, William T., 558, *558*
Somervell, Alexander, 40
Somervell County
  alcohol sales (wet-or-dry status), 472
  banks and bank assets, 580
  church membership, 530
  county and district officials, 478, 483
  courts, 438
  crime and law enforcement, 543
  deaths, 534
  federal funds to, 494
  general election results (2002), 406
  health care, 534
  income, 575
  map of, *270*
  oil and gas production, 607, 609
  population, 270, 393
  profile of, **270**
  tax appraiser, 472
  vehicles and highways, 593
  weather data, 108
Somerville Lake, 76, 127, 133
Somerville Wildlife Management Area, 91
Song of Texas, 10, 13
Sonora
  mayor and city manager, 467
  newspaper, 565
  population, 365, 387
  profile and map location, **272**
  public library, 510
  radio stations, 565
Sorghum, 621, 624
Soule University, 547
South East Texas Regional Planning Commission,
  470
Southern Baptists. See Baptist Church
Southern Methodist University, 551
South Houston, 202, 203, 365, 387, 467
Southlake, 275, 365, 387, 467, 510
South Llano River State Park, 123, 129
South Padre Island, 130, 496, 565
South Plains Association of Governments, 470
South Plains College, 551
South Texas Development Council, 470
South Texas Plains, plants of, *78*, 79
South Texas Project Reservoir, 77
Southwest Airlines, 566
Southwestern Adventist University, 551
Southwestern Assemblies of God University, 551
Southwestern Christian College, 551
Southwestern University, 547, 551
Southwest Texas State University, *547*, 553
Soybeans, 621, 622, 623, 625-26
Spain, consular offices, 588
Spanish exploration, 31-32, 32, 68-72, 517-24
Spanish missionaries, 517-24
Spanish Nun, 518, 519, 522, 522, 523
Spanish rule of Texas, 32, 34-35, 427
Spearman
  mayor and city manager, 467
  newspaper, 565
  population, 366, 387
  profile and map location, **200**
  public library, 510
  radio station, 565
Speech-Language Pathology and Audiology, Board
  of Examiners for, 456
Speir, Wilson E. "Pat," 641
Spence (E.V.) Reservoir, 74, 77
Spindletop, 47, 599-600
Spitzberg, Marian, 556
Sports, rodeo as state sport, 14
Square dance (state dance), 14
Squaw Creek Reservoir, 77
Squirrels, 88, 89
Stacy Reservoir. See O.H. Ivie Reservoir
Stafford, 188, 366, 387, 467
Staked Plains (Llano Estacado), *59*, 60
Stamford, Lake, 77
Stanton
  mayor and city manager, 467
  newspaper, 565
  population, 366, 387
  profile and map location, **236**
  public library, 511
  radio station, 565
Starr, Amory (Emory), 599
Starr County
  alcohol sales (wet-or-dry status), 472
  banks and bank assets, 580
  church membership, 530
  county and district officials, 478, 483
  courts, 438, 473
  crime and law enforcement, 543
  deaths, 534
  educational attainment, 298
  federal funds to, 494
  Foreign Trade Zone, 586
  general election results (2002), 406
  health care, 534
  income, 575
  income statistics, 297
  map of, *270*
  oil and gas production, 607, 609

population, 270, 393
poverty rates, 298
profile of, **270**
tax appraiser, 472
vehicles and highways, 593
weather data, 108
Starr Family State Historic Site, 129
State Boards. See specific state boards, such as
  Education, State Board of
State Capitol Preservation Project, 502
State government, **433-59**. See also Legislature,
  Texas; Supreme Court, Texas
  budget (2002-2003), 398, 459
  contact information for executives, 433
  employment in, 568, 576
  four-year terms for state officials, 55
  gross state product (1993-2003), 568
  highway construction and maintenance
    expenditures, 590-93
  income, expenditures (1996-2000), 441, 458, 459
  judiciary, 435-40
  lottery, 459
  officials, (1846-2003), 427-32
  state agencies, 441-57
  state boards and commissions, 445-57
  state cultural agencies, 457
  state tax collections and revenues, 458
  2002 elections, 395-409
Statehood for Texas, 10, 41
State hospitals for mentally ill, 536
State motto and symbols, 10, 13, 14
State parks. See Parks
State schools for mentally retarded, 536
State seal, 13-14, *14*
State song, 10, 13
St. Edward's University, 551
Steinbeck, Elaine, 641
Steinhagen (B. A.) Lake, 71, 77
Stenholm, Charles W., 488
Stephen F. Austin State Historic Site, 123, 129
Stephen F. Austin State University, 551
Stephen F. Austin State University Board of
  Regents, 456
Stephens County
  alcohol sales (wet-or-dry status), 472
  banks and bank assets, 580
  church membership, 530
  county and district officials, 478, 483
  courts, 438
  crime and law enforcement, 543
  deaths, 534
  federal funds to, 494
  general election results (2002), 406
  health care, 534
  income, 575
  map of, *271*
  oil and gas production, 607, 609
  population, 271, 393
  profile of, **271**
  tax appraiser, 472
  vehicles and highways, 593
  weather data, 108
Stephenville
  mayor and city administrator, 467
  mental health services, 537
  newspaper, 565
  population, 367, 387
  profile and map location, **184**
  public library, 511
  radio stations, 565
Sterling, Ross S., 51-52, 419, 600
Sterling City
  mayor, 467
  newspaper, 565
  population, 367, 387
  profile and map location, **271**
  public library, 511
  radio station, 565
Sterling County
  alcohol sales (wet-or-dry status), 472
  banks and bank assets, 580
  church membership, 530
  county and district officials, 478, 483
  courts, 438
  crime and law enforcement, 543
  deaths, 534
  federal funds to, 494
  general election results (2002), 406
  health care, 534
  income, 575
  map of, *271*
  oil and gas production, 607, 609
  population, 271, 393
  profile of, **271**
  tax appraiser, 472
  vehicles and highways, 593
  weather data, 108
Stevenson, Adlai, 53
Stevenson, Coke, 53, 419
Stillhouse Hollow Lake, 77, 133
Stinnett, 212, 367, 387, 467, 565
St. Mary's University, 551
Stockton Plateau, 60
Stokes, George Mitchel, 633
Stones. See Rocks
Stonewall County
  alcohol sales (wet-or-dry status), 472
  banks and bank assets, 580
  church membership, 530
  county and district officials, 478, 483
  courts, 438
  crime and law enforcement, 543
  deaths, 534
  federal funds to, 494
  general election results (2002), 406

---

**For CITIES and TOWNS not listed in the index, see complete list of towns on pages 300–377.**

health care, 534
income, 575
map of, *272*
oil and gas production, 607, 609
population, 272, 296, 393
profile of, **272**
tax appraiser, 472
vehicles and highways, 593
weather data, 108
Strategic Military Planning Commission, 452
Stratford, 268, 367, 387, 467, 511, 565
Stratigraphy, 61
Strayhorn, Carole Keeton, 396, 398, 433
Striker Creek Reservoir, 77
Strontium, 616
Structural panel products, 82
Stubblefield Lake, 133
Student Loan Corporation, Texas Guaranteed, 456
Substance abuse felony punishment facilities, 443-44
Südhof, Thomas, 538, *538*
Sugar cane, 621, 625
Sugar Land, 188, 367, 387, 467, 565
Suicides, 531-35
Sulfur, 616
Sulphur River, 72
Sulphur River Basin Authority, 456
Sulphur Springs
 fairs/festivals in, 137
 mayor and city manager, 467
 museum, 500
 newspaper, 565
 population, 368, 387
 profile and map location, **209**
 public library, 511
 radio stations, 565
Sulphur Springs, Lake, 77
Sul Ross State University, 553
Sumners, Hatton W., 52
Sunflowers, 621, 626
Sunnyvale, **175**
Sunrise and sunset, 110, 111-17
Sunset Advisory Commission, 456
Supreme Court, Texas
 black justices of, 396
 Chief Justices (1836-2003), 432
 election results (2002), 396, 399, 407-8, 409
 Justices (2003), 435
Sutton, A.C. Sr., 641
Sutton County
 alcohol sales (wet-or-dry status), 472
 banks and bank assets, 580
 church membership, 530
 county and district officials, 478, 484
 courts, 438
 crime and law enforcement, 543
 deaths, 534
 federal funds to, 494
 general election results (2002), 406
 health care, 534
 income, 575
 map of, *272*
 oil and gas production, 607, 609
 population, 272, 393
 profile of, **272**
 tax appraiser, 472
 vehicles and highways, 593
 weather data, 108
Sweden, consular offices, 588
Sweet onion (state vegetable), 14
Sweetwater
 fairs/festivals in, 137
 mayor and city manager, 467
 newspaper, 565
 population, 368, 387
 )profile and map location, **249**
 public library, 511
 television and radio stations, 565
Sweetwater, Lake, 77
Swine, 630, 632
Swisher County
 alcohol sales (wet-or-dry status), 472
 banks and bank assets, 580
 church membership, 530
 county and district officials, 478, 484
 courts, 438
 crime and law enforcement, 543
 deaths, 534
 federal funds to, 494
 general election results (2002), 406
 health care, 534
 income, 575
 map of, *273*
 oil and gas production, 607
 population, 273, 393
 profile of, **273**
 tax appraiser, 472
 vehicles and highways, 593
 weather data, 109
Switzerland, consular offices, 588
Symphonies, 497-98
Syria, consular office, 588

**T**

Tahoka
 mayor and city administrator, 467
 newspaper, 565
 population, 368, 387
 profile and map location, **235**
 public library, 511
 radio stations, 565
TAKS (Texas Assessment of Knowledge and Skills), 546
Talc and soapstone, 610, 616
Tao, 527

Tarantulas, 89
Tarleton State University, 552
Tarrant County
 alcohol sales (wet-or-dry status), 472
 banks and bank assets, 580
 church membership, 530
 county and district officials, 478, 484
 courts, 438, 473
 crime and law enforcement, 543
 deaths, 534
 federal funds to, 494
 general election results (2002), 406
 health care, 534
 income, 575
 map of, *274*
 oil and gas production, 607, 609
 population, 223, 275, 393
 profile of, **274-75**
 tax appraiser, 472
 vehicles and highways, 593
 weather data, 109
Tarrant County College District, 551
Tartan (state), 14
Tawakoni, Lake, 77, 127
Tawakoni Wildlife Management Area, 91
Tax appraisers in counties, 471-72
Taxation
 gasoline tax, 49, 458
 revenues from taxes (1999 and 2000), 458
 sales tax, 53, 458, 567, 569-73
 state tax collections (1988-2000), 458
 types of taxes, 458
 U.S. tax collections, 494-95
Tax Board, 456
Tax Professional Examiners, Board of, 456
Taylor, J. W. "Bill," 641
Taylor, Zachary, 42, 132, 411
Taylor (city)
 Amtrak passengers on/off at, 596
 mayor and city manager, 467
 newspaper, 565
 population, 368, 387
 profile and map location, **291**
 public library, 511
 radio stations, 565
Taylor County
 alcohol sales (wet-or-dry status), 472
 banks and bank assets, 580
 church membership, 530
 county and district officials, 478, 484
 courts, 438, 473
 crime and law enforcement, 543
 deaths, 534
 federal funds to, 494
 general election results (2002), 406
 health care, 534
 income, 575
 map of, *276*
 oil and gas production, 607, 609
 population, 223, 276, 393
 profile of, **276**
 tax appraiser, 472
 vehicles and highways, 593
 weather data, 109
Teacher Retirement System, 456
Teachers. See Education
Tejas Indians, 32, 34
Telecommunications, 567, 618-19
Telecommunications Infrastructure Fund Board, 456
Telephone companies, 68-19
Television programs, 496
Television stations, 555-56, 560-65
Teller, Edward, 495
Temperature
 average temperatures in 2001-2002, 92, 93
 by county, 104-9, 139-295
 extremes, 10, 93, 95, 96, 99, 101, 102
 heat discomfort chart, 103
 heat stress index, 103
 wind chill, 103
Temple
 Amtrak passengers on/off at, 596
 mayor and city manager, 467
 mental health services, 537
 museum, 500
 newspaper, 565
 population, 369, 387
 profile and map location, **146**
 public library, 511
 television and radio stations, 565
Temple College, 551
Temporary Assistance for Needy Families, 441
Terrell, A.W., 47
Terrell City Lake, 77
Terrell County
 alcohol sales (wet-or-dry status), 472
 banks and bank assets, 580
 church membership, 530
 county and district officials, 478, 484
 courts, 438
 crime and law enforcement, 543
 deaths, 534
 federal funds to, 494
 general election results (2002), 406
 health care, 534
 income, 575
 map of, *277*
 oil and gas production, 607, 609
 population, 277, 296, 393
 profile of, **277**
 tax appraiser, 472
 vehicles and highways, 593
 weather data, 109
Terrell State Hospital, 536
Terry County

alcohol sales (wet-or-dry status), 472
banks and bank assets, 580
church membership, 530
county and district officials, 478, 484
courts, 438
crime and law enforcement, 543
deaths, 534
farm in, *191*
federal funds to, 494
general election results (2002), 406
health care, 534
income, 575
map of, *277*
oil and gas production, 607, 609
population, 277, 393
profile of, **277**
tax appraiser, 472
vehicles and highways, 593
weather data, 109
Texana, Lake, 70, 77, 127
Texans, Texians, 13
Texarkana
 airline passengers, 597
 Amtrak passengers on/off at, 596
 fairs/festivals in, 137
 mayor and city manager, 467
 mental health services, 537
 military installation near, 490
 newspaper, 565
 population, 299, 369, 387
 profile and map location, **150**
 public library, 511
 television and radio stations, 565
Texarkana College, 551
Texas. *See also* Cities and towns; Counties; History of Texas; State government
 area of, 10
 comparative rankings with other states, 11, 57
 geographic center, 10, *377*
 nickname of, 10
 origin of name, 10
 statehood for, 10, 41
 state motto and symbols, 10, 14
Texas A&M University System, 547, 548, 552, 620
Texas A&M University System Board of Regents, 456
*Texas Almanac*, 559
Texas Assessment of Knowledge and Skills (TAKS), 546
*Texas* battleship, 14
U.S.S. *Texas* battleship, 129
Texas Christian University, 547, 552
Texas City
 explosion of *SS Grandcamp* at, 53
 foreign/domestic commerce, 589
 Foreign Trade Zone, 586
 mayor, 467
 newspaper, 565
 population, 369, 387
 profile and map location, **192**
 public library, 511
 radio station, 565
 tonnage handled by port, 589
Texas College, 547, 552
Texas Guard, 491-92
Texas history. *See* History of Texas
Texas Institute of Letters Awards, 503
Texas Instruments, 53
Texas Lutheran University, 552
"Texas" musical drama, 128, 502
"Texas, Our Texas," 10, 13
Texas Point National Wildlife Refuge, 90
Texas Rangers, 46, 48, 49
Texas Republic. *See* Republic of Texas
Texas Revolution, 27-29, 37-39, 512
Texas Southern University, 547
Texas Southern University Board of Regents, 456
Texas State Railroad State Historic Site, 123, 129
Texas State Technical College Board of Regents, 456
Texas State Technical College System, 552
Texas State University System, 552-53
Texas State University System Board of Regents, 456
Texas State University–San Marcos, *547*, 553
Texas Tech University, 49, 553
Texas Tech University Board of Regents, 456
Texas Wesleyan University, 553
Texas Woman's University, 547
Texas Woman's University Board of Regents, 456-57
Texas Works, 441
Texoma Council of Governments, 470
Texoma, Lake, 72, 77, 133
Thailand, consular offices, 588
Theatre arts, 497-98, 502
The Colony, 177, 314, 387, 467, 511
Theft, 539-43
Thompson, Ernest O., 51
Thompson, John P., 641
Thorium, 615
Thornberry, William M., 488
Threatened and endangered species, 85-86
Throckmorton, J.W., 45, 417
Throckmorton (town), **278**, 369, 387, 467, 511, 565
Throckmorton County
 alcohol sales (wet-or-dry status), 472
 banks and bank assets, 580
 church membership, 530
 county and district officials, 478, 484
 courts, 438
 crime and law enforcement, 543
 deaths, 534
 federal funds to, 494
 general election results (2002), 406

health care, 534
income, 575
map of, *278*
oil and gas production, 607, 609
population, 278, 296, 393
profile of, **278**
tax appraiser, 472
vehicles and highways, 593
weather data, 109
Thunderstorms, 92, 95, 96, 101, 102
Tidelands issue, 53, 603
Tierra Blanca Creek, 72
Tijerina, Pete, 641
Tilden, 240, 370, 387
Timber industry, 80-83. *See also* Forests
Tin, 616
Titanium, 616
Titus County
  alcohol sales (wet-or-dry status), 472
  banks and bank assets, 580
  church membership, 530
  county and district officials, 478, 484
  courts, 438
  crime and law enforcement, 543
  deaths, 534
  federal funds to, 494
  general election results (2002), 406
  health care, 534
  income, 575
  map of, *278*
  oil and gas production, 607, 609
  population, 278, 393
  profile of, **278-79**
  tax appraiser, 472
  timber production and value in, 82
  vehicles and highways, 593
  weather data, 109
Tolar, Charlie, 641
Toledo Bend Reservoir, 77, 133
Tollway Authority, North Texas, 452
Tom Green County
  alcohol sales (wet-or-dry status), 472
  banks and bank assets, 580
  church membership, 530
  county and district officials, 478, 484
  courts, 438, 473
  crime and law enforcement, 543
  deaths, 534
  federal funds to, 494
  general election results (2002), 406
  health care, 534
  income, 575
  map of, *279*
  oil and gas production, 607, 609
  population, 279, 393
  profile of, **279**
  tax appraiser, 472
  vehicles and highways, 593
  weather data, 109
Tonnage handled by ports, 589
Tony Houseman Wildlife Management Area, 91
Topaz (state gem), 14
Topfer, Angela, 641
Tornadoes, 92, 95-102
Towash Village, 127
Tower, John, 53
Town Bluff Lake, 133
Town Lake, 60, 70, 77
Towns. *See* Cities and towns
Toyah Basin, 59, 60
TPW. *See* Parks and Wildlife Department
Tradinghouse Creek Reservoir, 77
Tramway in Franklin Mountains, 130
Trans-Pecos region, *59*, 60-61, 64, 78, 79
Transportation
  aviation industry, 566, 597-98
  drivers' licenses (1950-2002), 594
  employment in, 566-67, 576, 590
  gross state product (1993-2002), 568
  map of interstate highways, 590
  motor vehicle accidents, 594
  railroads, 595-96
  tonnage handled by ports, 589
  trucking and warehousing, 566-67
  vehicles and highways by county, 590-93
Transportation Commission, 457
Transportation, Department of, 124, 590, 597-98
Travel Guide, 124
Travis, William Barret, 27, 28, *28*, 37, 38
Travis County
  alcohol sales (wet-or-dry status), 472
  banks and bank assets, 580
  church membership, 530
  county and district officials, 478, 484
  courts, 438, 473
  crime and law enforcement, 543
  deaths, 534
  educational attainment, 298
  federal funds to, 494
  general election results (2002), 406
  health care, 534
  income, 575
  map of, *280*
  oil and gas production, 607, 609
  population, 223, 280, 297, 393
  profile of, **280**
  tax appraiser, 472
  vehicles and highways, 593
  weather data, 109
Travis, Lake, 60, 70, 77
Treasurers
  county treasurers, 474-78
  Republic of Texas, 429-30
  state treasurers (1846-1996), 430
Treaty of Guadalupe Hidalgo, 16, 26, 42, 70

Trees. *See also* Forests
  forest resources, 80-84
  pecan tree as state tree, 10, 14
  in physical regions of Texas, 58-61, 78-79
Trejo, Frank, 641
Tremolite, 610
Tres Castillos, Battle of, 21
Trinidad Lake, 77
Trinidad/Tobago, consular office, 588
Trinity aquifer, *67*, 68
Trinity County
  alcohol sales (wet-or-dry status), 472
  banks and bank assets, 580
  church membership, 530
  county and district officials, 478, 484
  courts, 438
  crime and law enforcement, 543
  deaths, 534
  federal funds to, 494
  general election results (2002), 406
  health care, 534
  income, 575
  map of, *281*
  oil and gas production, 607, 609
  population, 281, 393
  profile of, **281**
  tax appraiser, 472
  timber production and value in, 82
  vehicles and highways, 593
  weather data, 109
Trinity Improvement Association, 71
Trinity River, *69*, 71, *275*
Trinity River Authority, 71, 457
Trinity River National Wildlife Refuge, 90
Trinity University, 553
Tropical storms, 92, 94, 95, 99, 101, 102
Troup, George, 40
Trucking and warehousing, 566-67
Truman, Harry S., 53, 412, 495
Truscott Brine Lake, 77
Tuition Board, Prepaid Higher Education, 450, 457
Tuition Scholarship Foundation Board, Prepaid, 457
Tulia
  mayor and city manager, 467
  newspaper, 565
  population, 371, 388
  prison in, 444
  profile and map location, **273**
  public library, 511
  radio stations, 565
Tune, Tommy, 502, *502*
Tungsten, 616
Tunisia, consular office, 588
Tupa, Julius Victor, 641
Turkey, consular office, 588
Turkeys, 129
Turner, Jim, 488
Turnley, Parmenas Taylor, 23
Turnpike Authority, 457
Turtles, 127
Twiggs, David E., 20
Twin Buttes Reservoir, 77
Twin Oaks Reservoir, 77
Tyler, John, 41
Tyler (city)
  airline passengers, 597
  fairs/festivals in, 137
  mayor and city manager, 468
  mental health services, 537
  museums, 502
  newspapers, 565
  performing arts organizations, 498
  population, 299, 371, 388
  profile and map location, **269**
  public library, 511
  television and radio stations, 565
Tyler County
  alcohol sales (wet-or-dry status), 472
  banks and bank assets, 580
  church membership, 530
  county and district officials, 478, 484
  courts, 438
  crime and law enforcement, 543
  deaths, 534
  federal funds to, 494
  general election results (2002), 406
  health care, 534
  income, 575
  map of, *281*
  oil and gas production, 607, 609
  population, 281, 393
  profile of, 281
  tax appraiser, 472
  timber production and value in, 82
  vehicles and highways, 593
  weather data, 109
Tyler, Lake, 77
Tyler State Park, 123, 129-30

**U**
Ugartechea, Domingo de, 37
Ukraine, consular office, 588
Underground Facility Notification Corporation, 457
Unemployment, by county, 139-295
Uniform State Laws, Commission on, 457
Unions. *See* Labor unions
United Church of Christ, 527
United Kingdom, consular offices, 588
U.S. government. *See* Congress, U.S.; Federal
  government; Military installations
Universal City
  map location, *147*
  mayor and city manager, 468
  population, 147, 371, 388
  public library, 511

radio station, 565
Universities. *See* Higher education; and specific
  universities
Universities Center at Dallas, 548
University Lands, Board for Lease of, 451
University of Dallas, 553
University of Houston Board of Regents, 457
University of Houston System, 548, 553
University of Mary Hardin-Baylor, 553
University of North Texas Board of Regents, 457
University of North Texas System, 548, 553
University of St. Thomas, 553
University of Texas System, 48, 49, 547, 553-54
University of Texas System Board of Regents, 457
University of the Incarnate Word, 553
University Park, 174, 175, 371, 388, 468, 511
Upper Colorado River Authority, 70, 447
Upper Nueces Lake, 77
Upper Pecos, Canadian Valleys and Plains soils, 64
Upper Rio Grande Valley, *59*, 61
Upshur County
  alcohol sales (wet-or-dry status), 472
  banks and bank assets, 580
  church membership, 530
  county and district officials, 478, 484
  courts, 438
  crime and law enforcement, 543
  deaths, 534
  federal funds to, 494
  general election results (2002), 406
  health care, 534
  income, 575
  map of, *282*
  oil and gas production, 607, 609
  population, 282, 393
  profile of, **282**
  tax appraiser, 472
  timber production and value in, 82
  vehicles and highways, 593
  weather data, 109
Upton County
  alcohol sales (wet-or-dry status), 472
  church membership, 530
  county and district officials, 478, 484
  courts, 438
  crime and law enforcement, 543
  deaths, 534
  federal funds to, 494
  general election results (2002), 406
  health care, 534
  income, 575
  map of, *282*
  oil and gas production, 607, 609
  population, 282, 394
  profile of, **282**
  tax appraiser, 472
  vehicles and highways, 593
  weather data, 109
Uranium, 600, 616
Urrea, José de, 38
Utilities industry, 567, 568, 576, 617-19
Uvalde (city)
  mayor, 468
  newspaper, 565
  population, 372, 388
  profile and map location, **283**
  public library, 511
  television and radio stations, 565
Uvalde County
  alcohol sales (wet-or-dry status), 472
  banks and bank assets, 580
  church membership, 530
  county and district officials, 478, 484
  courts, 438
  crime and law enforcement, 543
  deaths, 534
  federal funds to, 494
  general election results (2002), 406
  health care, 534
  income, 575
  map of, *283*
  oil and gas production, 607, 609
  population, 283, 394
  profile of, **283**
  tax appraiser, 472
  vehicles and highways, 593
  weather data, 109

**V**
Valley Acres Reservoir, 77
Valley Lake, 77
Val Verde County
  alcohol sales (wet-or-dry status), 472
  church membership, 530
  county and district officials, 478, 484
  courts, 438, 473
  crime and law enforcement, 543
  deaths, 534
  federal funds to, 494
  general election results (2002), 406
  health care, 534
  income, 575
  map of, *283*
  oil and gas production, 607, 609
  population, 283, 394
  profile of, **283**
  tax appraiser, 472
  vehicles and highways, 593
  weather data, 109
Van Horn, 172, 372, 388, 468, 511, 565
Van Horne, Jefferson, 19
Van Zandt, Isaac, 41
Van Zandt County
  alcohol sales (wet-or-dry status), 472
  banks and bank assets, 580